INSURANCE LAW

A GUIDE TO FUNDAMENTAL PRINCIPLES, LEGAL DOCTRINES, and COMMERCIAL PRACTICES

Student Edition

By

Robert E. Keeton
Langdell Professor Emeritus
Harvard University

and

Alan I. Widiss
Josephine R. Witte Professor of Law
University of Iowa

This book is an abridgement of Keeton & Widiss' "Insurance Law, A Guide to Fundamental Principles, Legal Doctrines, and Commercial Practices, Practitioner's Edition"

WEST PUBLISHING CO.
ST. PAUL, MINN., 1988

This is an abridgement of Keeton and Widiss' "*Insurance Law, A Guide to Fundamental Principles, Legal Doctrines, and Commercial Practices, Practitioner's Edition*", West Publishing Co., 1988.

Library of Congress Cataloging-in-Publication Data

Keeton, Robert E.
  Insurance law.

  Includes index.
  1. Insurance law—United States. I. Widiss, Alan I., 1938– .
II. Title.
KF1164.K376 1988   346.73'086   88–5490
ISBN 0–314–39187–8   347.30686

*TEXT IS PRINTED ON 10% POST
CONSUMER RECYCLED PAPER*

Keeton & Widiss—Ins.Law HBSE
2nd Reprint–1997

Preface

Insurance is one of the pervasive institutions of the twentieth century. The billions of dollars of insurance coverage and the very substantial number of different types of insurance currently in use in the United States mirror both the dimensions of the American economy and the diverse activities engaged in by individuals, corporate entities, the states, and the federal government.

The insurance law of this country encompasses literally hundreds of thousands of judicial decisions, legislative provisions, and administrative regulations. Moreover, the cumulative volume of these legal materials is increasing by a significant amount each year. The scope and variety of the matters encompassed within the field of insurance law require that the authors of any text on this subject make choices among the possible goals for the undertaking.

The objectives which guided the preparation of this text are very similar to those selected for the predecessor to this volume, *Basic Text on Insurance Law* by Professor Keeton. The primary goal continues to be a book that explicates the fundamental principles and legal doctrines that comprise the law of insurance. Each of the chapters has been designed with a view to facilitating an understanding and an appreciation of the significance of general principles and doctrines.

Although the objective is to provide a broad perspective on the topics which are being considered, in several instances a substantial portion of a chapter is devoted to the applications of the general principles or doctrines to specific types of insurance. Organizing the materials in this way facilitates an analysis of the reasons why general principles or doctrines are sometimes treated rather differently depending on the type of insurance which is involved. Furthermore, to attain a complete understanding, often it is also necessary to be aware of the commercial practices employed by insurers and the reasons for those practices.

The secondary objective which guided the development of this text was to include discussions of significant issues or problems which are repeatedly the subject of disputes, with a view both to examining the general principles that are relevant to these questions and to suggesting lines of analysis that should be considered when such matters must be addressed. The footnotes to the text in these sections include references to many judicial decisions and secondary sources. Although no attempt has been made to provide a comprehensive body of references, the items cited in footnotes will almost always lead the reader to the larger body of relevant materials.

iii

Insurance disputes frequently involve concepts that have been developed in other areas of the law. Principles, doctrines, rules, and public policy concerns from contracts, procedure, property, and torts are often employed in the analysis of insurance law questions. Doctrines from constitutional law, corporations, and criminal law are also involved, though somewhat less frequently. Furthermore, the law student or lawyer who has studied administrative law, estate planning, or regulated industries will find that topics analyzed in each of those fields are relevant to issues that will be discussed in this text. However, one cautionary note should be stated: even though many concepts from other areas of the law are relevant to and have been incorporated into the body of insurance law, it is essential that these principles, doctrines, rules, and public policy interests be carefully reviewed and reconsidered when they are to be applied to questions that arise as a consequence of an insurance transaction.

ROBERT E. KEETON
ALAN I. WIDISS

August, 1988

Acknowledgments

The preparation of this text has spanned several years. We are especially appreciative of the support provided during this period by the University of Iowa College of Law, and N. William Hines who has been the College's Dean throughout this period. We are also grateful for the secretarial services of Ms. Melinda Phelps, Ms. Sandy Carman, and Ms. Lillian DiBlasi, whose contributions have been essential to the completion of this text.

Students who have provided assistance both to the research and to ensuring the accuracy of the citations have included:

Joe Adam	Michael Lanford	Sharon Sorholtz
Joanne Baumbrind	Robert Lieske	Vicki Stratman
Lori Beam	Paul Luiki	John Tavana
Bruce Braley	Mary Murphy	Dale Vlasek
Tom Currie	Robert Murphy	Brian Wallman
Denis Faber	Elizabeth Oxley	David Whitlock
Don Houghton	William Rector	Greg Williams, and
Susanne Kruse	Jackson Schmidt	Deborah Widiss.

ROBERT E. KEETON
Boston, Massachusetts

ALAN I. WIDISS
Iowa City, Iowa

August, 1988

＊

WESTLAW Introduction

Keeton and Widiss' *Insurance Law, A Guide to Fundamental Principles, Legal Doctrines, and Commercial Practices* offers a detailed and comprehensive treatment of basic rules, principles, and issues in insurance law. However, readers occasionally need to find additional authority. In an effort to assist with comprehensive research of insurance law, preformulated WESTLAW references are included after each chapter in this edition. The WESTLAW references are designed for use with the WESTLAW computer-assisted legal research service. By joining this publication with the extensive WESTLAW databases in this way, the reader is able to move straight from the text into WESTLAW with great speed and convenience.

Some readers may desire to use only the information supplied within the printed pages of this text. Others, however, will encounter issues in insurance law that require further information. Accordingly, those who opt for additional material can rapidly and easily gain access to WESTLAW, an electronic law library that possesses extraordinary currency and magnitude.

The preformulated WESTLAW references in this text provide illustrative searches for readers who wish to do additional research on WESTLAW. The WESTLAW references are approximately as general as the material in the text to which they correspond. Readers should be cautioned against placing undue emphasis upon these references as final solutions to all possible issues treated in the text. In most instances, it is necessary to make refinements to the search references, such as the addition of other search terms or the substitution of different proximity connectors, to adequately fit the particular needs of an individual reader's research problem. The freedom, and also the responsibility, remains with the reader to "fine tune" the WESTLAW references in accordance with his or her own research requirements. The primary usefulness of the preformulated references is in providing a basic framework upon which further query construction can be built. Appendix VI gives concise, step-by-step instruction on how to coordinate WESTLAW research with this book.

THE PUBLISHER

*

Summary of Contents

CHAPTER FIVE. THE RISKS TRANSFERRED

CHAPTER SIX. RIGHTS AT VARIANCE WITH INSURANCE POLICY PROVISIONS

CHAPTER SEVEN. CLAIMS: PROCESSES AND SETTLEMENTS

CHAPTER EIGHT. INSURANCE REGULATION AND GOVERNMENT SPONSORSHIP OF INSURANCE

CHAPTER NINE. RESOLVING DISPUTED CLAIMS INVOLVING INSURANCE

Appendices

*

Table of Contents

xiii

CHAPTER FOUR. PERSONS AND INTERESTS PROTECTED

CHAPTER FIVE. THE RISKS TRANSFERRED

CHAPTER SIX. RIGHTS AT VARIANCE WITH INSURANCE POLICY PROVISIONS

CHAPTER SEVEN. CLAIMS: PROCESSES AND SETTLEMENTS

CHAPTER EIGHT. INSURANCE REGULATION AND GOVERNMENT SPONSORSHIP OF INSURANCE

CHAPTER NINE. RESOLVING DISPUTED CLAIMS INVOLVING INSURANCE

APPENDICES

INSURANCE LAW

A GUIDE TO
FUNDAMENTAL PRINCIPLES,
LEGAL DOCTRINES, and
COMMERCIAL PRACTICES

Student Edition

*

Chapter One

INSURANCE: CONCEPTUALIZATION AND CLASSIFICATION

Table of Sections

§ 1.1 Insurance, Insurance Transactions, and Insurance Law

§ 1.1(a) Introduction

Insurance is an important, and perhaps essential, aspect of the business and personal lives of the vast majority of individuals living in the United States. For example, insurance is acquired by most businesses to transfer at least some portion of the risks associated with the fabrication, distribution, and use of manufactured or processed products. Similarly, billions of dollars of liability insurance coverage are purchased by enterprises and individuals to cover the risks incident to the use or ownership of property, operation of motor vehicles, and the pursuit of various business or professional activities.

Health insurance (including the federal and state Medicare and Medicaid programs, Blue Cross/Blue Shield plans, and coverages available from private insurance companies) provides benefits for literally millions of individuals and is now one of the institutional systems that facilitates the delivery of health care in the United States. Disability insurance, both as an important facet of the federal government's social security system and as coverage that is purchased from insurers, is increasingly significant for almost all Americans as protection against incapacitating accidents or illnesses. Life insurance is a trillion dollar business in the United States, and the ramifications of the investments generated by the life insurance premiums paid to insurers are of monumental significance to the nation's economy.

Insurance may well be an essential system for risk distribution in any industrialized society comprised of independently owned and operated businesses. However, whether or not it is indispensable, insurance is a pervasive institution in twentieth century America. Individuals and businesses in the United States are repeatedly confronted with important decisions about when to buy insurance, what risks to insure, what kinds of insurance to purchase, and how much coverage to acquire. Each of these determinations can prove to be of critical significance in the event a loss occurs. As a result, insurance counseling by a lawyer requires the same care as tax planning for clients. It is extremely important for an attorney not only to be aware of the role of insurance and insurance institutions, but also to be sensitive to the situations in which the acquisition of insurance should be considered.

The court decisions, legislation, and administrative actions that comprise the corpus of insurance law discussed in this text have been evolving as an identifiable body of doctrines and rules for over three hundred years, first in England and then in the United States. The considerable economic significance of insurance transactions for both individual insureds and insurers in many situations has produced a continuous and unabated flow of insurance litigation. Indeed, judicial decisions in cases involving insurance have repeatedly contributed to the development of fundamental legal doctrines. This point is well illustrated by the fact that many of the common law contract rules resulted from the judicial resolution of insurance disputes. Furthermore, during the first half of the twentieth century, principles that established the foundations for consumer law often developed in the context of insurance litigation because it was economically feasible, given the amounts at issue, for attorneys to accept contingency fees in exchange for representing individuals whose claims had been rejected by insurers.

Insurance litigation has frequently been a forum in which issues of significant public concern have been considered by the courts. For example, the quest during most of this century for an adequate and appropriate approach to providing indemnification for persons injured in automobile accidents has been an almost classic case study in the interactions of (1) the public interest in providing compensation for accident victims, (2) the needs and capacities of the insurance industry, and (3) various attempts by state legislatures to develop better approaches to using insurance to provide compensation. Similarly, for the past two decades, the increasing concern over assuring that persons shall not be treated differently on the basis of sex, race, or physical handicaps has repeatedly been at the center of litigation over the appropriate use of actuarial data in setting premiums and benefits for annuities, life insurance, property coverages, and various types of liability insurance. Thus, the law reports abound with many fascinating insurance disputes that reflect some of the most important public questions and social issues being confronted by the nation.

§ 1.1(b) The Problem of Definition

The concept of sharing risks has long been generally understood and employed in societies throughout the world, and agreements to share risk continue to be among the most important types of consensual arrangements. Insurance is generally understood to be an arrangement for transferring and distributing risks. Unfortunately, this characterization is neither very precise nor universally applicable as a definition of insurance because it describes many other arrangements and relationships which almost uniformly are not regarded or treated as insurance transactions.[1]

The articulation of a generally applicable definition of insurance has proven to be a very difficult task. The crafting of a definition of insurance that is both precise enough to be of use in distinguishing among various transactions and broad enough to be viewed as generally applicable has been an elusive goal in major part because the basic concept of sharing risks has been employed for a vast array of purposes in many different types of cultures and economic contexts.

Authors of treatises and text books on insurance have devoted considerable attention to the development of a comprehensive definition,[2] but none of the formulations has been widely accepted as definitive. Moreover, attempts in the United States to formulate a general definition of insurance in regulatory statutes, with a view to prescribing the appropriate reach for the regulatory authority of administrative agencies and courts, have had only limited success because such statutes typically need to respond to a variety of matters and situations with very different characteristics.[3]

---

§ 1.1(b)

1. See the text and accompanying notes in both § 1.2 and § 1.3, below, and the authorities cited therein.

2. See, e.g., James L. Athearn, RISK AND INSURANCE (1977), at pp. 23–25; Herbert Denenberg, Robert D. Eilers, Joseph J. Melone, and Robert A. Zelten, RISK AND INSURANCE (Second edition, 1974), in Chapter 10; Mark Greene and James Trieschmann, RISK AND INSURANCE (Fifth edition, 1981), in Chapters 1 and 2; C.A. Kulp, CASUALTY INSURANCE (Third edition, 1956), at p. 9; Robert I. Mehr and Emerson Cammach, PRINCIPLES OF INSURANCE (Sixth edition, 1976), at p. 31; Robert I. Mehr and Bob A. Hedges, RISK MANAGEMENT IN THE BUSINESS ENTERPRISE (1963), at p. 144; Robert Riegel and Jerome S. Miller, INSURANCE PRINCIPLES AND PRACTICES (Fifth edition, 1966), at p. 28; Allan H. Willett, THE ECONOMIC THEORY OF RISK AND INSURANCE (1951), at p. 72.

For an English perspective on the definitional problem, see MACGILLIVRAY & PARKINGTON ON INSURANCE LAW (Seventh edition, Michael Parkington, General Editor, 1981), at p. 3.

3. See the discussion of insurance regulation in Chapter 8, below.

An insurance contract generally involves an agreement by which one party (usually identified as an insurer) is committed to do something which is of value for another party (usually identified as an insured or a beneficiary) upon the occurrence of some specified contingency. In most litigation involving this type of contractual arrangement, attorneys do not need to address issues that involve the definition of what constitutes insurance either (1) because there is a generally shared assumption that the transaction in question is insurance, or (2) because it makes no difference to the resolution of the dispute whether the contractual commitments involved in the litigation constitute an insurance transaction since the issue will be resolved in accordance with general principles of contracts, property, torts, or restitution. Occasionally, however, legal consequences either are determined or are influenced by whether a particular contractual relationship is an insurance transaction.

When it is essential to decide whether a transaction involves insurance, neither the characterizations of the parties in the contract (that is, whether the parties are explicitly identified as insurer and insured, by some other comparable nomenclature, or by terms that bear no relationship to such designations) nor the fact that one party is committed to do something upon the occurrence of a specified contingency for the other party, will necessarily dictate the resolution of a dispute about the nature of the arrangement at issue. Similarly, recognition that a particular contractual arrangement involves the transfer and distribution of risk generally is not sufficient to answer the question.[4] Although risk transference and risk distribution are among the basic characteristics of almost all insurance transactions, the resolution of a dispute about what constitutes insurance usually is predicated on additional factors or considerations.

It is, perhaps, quite natural to anticipate that a definition of insurance would be provided at the beginning of a text on insurance law. There are several reasons, in addition to the problems described in the preceding paragraphs, for not setting forth a definition in this section. First, the question "What is insurance?" arises in many different contexts. Not only are the purposes for which definitions of insurance are sought diverse, but the socio-economic and other factors that influence the definition often differ substantially from one situation to the next. Consequently, the appropriateness of a particular characterization usually depends on the reason why a definition is needed. For example, the definition of insurance that is either explicit or implicit for purposes of the statutes regulating entities engaged in an insurance business may be quite different from the definition of insur-

---

Also see, Herbert Denenberg, *The Legal Definition of Insurance*, 30 Journal of Insurance 319–343 (1963).

4. However, examining these characteristics does provide some insight into the fundamental nature of insurance transactions. See the discussion in § 1.3, below.

ance used in an estate tax law concerned with determining whether it is appropriate to tax payments made to a beneficiary.

There is no single conception of insurance that is universally applicable for use in disputes involving questions of law. Furthermore, in a particular jurisdiction the applicable definition of insurance may also be significantly influenced by legislative actions and, in some instances, prior judicial decisions. Accordingly, in the process of selecting or framing an appropriate response to a definitional question, an essential first step for a lawyer is to ascertain both the reasons why the issue arises and the legislative provisions or judicial precedents which may be relevant to the resolution of the question.

Another reason for not attempting to provide a definition of insurance at the beginning of this text is that in order to understand fully the meaning of insurance in any particular context, it is very useful — and perhaps necessary — both to be aware of several fundamental insurance principles and to appreciate the basic nature of the business of insurance. In other words, mastery of a certain amount of insurance law and familiarity with some insurance business practices is essential to a comprehension of the problems entailed in perceiving both the characteristics of and limitations on what may constitute appropriate definitions of either insurance or an insurance transaction for purposes of a matter being considered in connection with a question of law.

It should also be recognized that the definitions of insurance employed to resolve disputes in various contexts may change as human ingenuity produces innovations which in turn may create a need to revise or modify then existing legal doctrines or definitions. Furthermore, such new concepts may then be applied to older types of transactions as well. In a complex commercial society, it is both appropriate and desirable that insurance concepts, including definitions of insurance, remain flexible enough to be adapted to changing and differing circumstances rather than being so rigid that they become shackles to thought, expression, or innovation.

Accordingly, it is important to appreciate (1) that the concept of insurance for purposes of legal analysis is neither fixed nor universal, (2) that a definition of insurance often needs to be formulated for or adapted to the specific circumstances, (3) that a comprehensive understanding of the circumstances in which an issue arises is essential when addressing a definitional question, and (4) that an appreciation of the socio-economic significance of a particular transaction is often critical to determining what will constitute an appropriate definition of insurance. In other words, a complete answer to the question "What is insurance?" would be, in Learned Hand's phrase, "mythically prolix, and fantastically impractical." [5]

5. Sinram v. Pennsylvania R.R., 61 F.2d 767 at p. 771 (2d Cir.1932).

§ 1.2 Disputes About What Constitutes Insurance

Controversies about what is insurance arise most frequently as a consequence of disputes over the applicability of regulatory measures promulgated in statutory provisions or administrative rulings.[1] Although it is generally agreed that two of the principal characteristics of insurance are transferring and distributing risk, demonstrating that a contractual arrangement has these characteristics usually has not been sufficient to resolve a dispute about the nature of a particular transaction. For example, a warranty that guarantees the quality of merchandise [2] or an agreement to maintain a truck in good repair [3] are both transactions that involve risk transference and risk distribution. Similarly, if a lawyer is retained for a fixed fee at a time when neither the attorney nor the client knows precisely what legal services will be required,[4] the agreement also involves the transfer of a risk. Although

§ 1.2

1. Concerning the scope of regulatory measures generally, see § 8.3, below.

2. See, e.g., Guaranteed Warranty Corp., Inc. v. State ex rel. Humphrey, 23 Ariz.App. 327, 533 P.2d 87 (1st Div., Dept. A, 1975) (a "Warranty Agreement" whereby a corporation, which is neither the manufacturer nor the seller of television sets or picture tubes, is committed to replace a picture tube which failed as a result of manufacturing defects after a manufacturer's warranty period expired constituted an "insurance contract" and therefore could not be sold without a license to sell insurance); State ex rel. Herbert v. Standard Oil Company, 138 Ohio St. 376, 35 N.E.2d 437 (1941) (new tire guarantee applicable if used "under usual conditions" for a specified period of time; held not insurance although there was evidence that the company's agents orally represented that the guarantee protected "against such hazards as cuts, bruises, wheels out of alignment and blowouts" and that tires purposely mutilated had been replaced under the guarantee).

But see, e.g., State ex rel. Duffy v. Western Auto Supply Company, 134 Ohio St. 163, 16 N.E.2d 256, 119 A.L.R. 1236 (1939) (guarantee issued with new automobile tires found to be an illegal contract of insurance because the form of agreement constituted "an undertaking to indemnify against failure from any cause except fire or theft and therefore covers loss or damage resulting from any and every hazard of travel, not excepting negligence of the automobile driver or another"). In later years Western Auto described its guarantee only a little more cautiously by including in its advertisements a footnote as fol-

lows: "In Ohio, complete tire service guaranteed under proper and normal operating conditions." Time Magazine, May, 1957, p. 23. Also see Little v. Woodall, 244 Md. 620, 224 A.2d 852 (1966).

See generally § 8.3(c), below.

3. See, e.g., Transportation Guarantee Company, Ltd. v. Jellins, 29 Cal.2d 242, 174 P.2d 625 (1946) ("guaranteed maintenance contract" to maintain truck in mechanical repair, to garage and fuel it, and to cause it to be insured; held not void as an insurance contract contrary to public policy since the "controlling object" of the contract was service, not insurance).

See generally § 8.3(c), below.

4. See Transportation Guarantee Company, Ltd. v. Jellins, 29 Cal.2d 242 at p. 248, 174 P.2d 625 at p. 629 (1946) (dictum that "the lawyer who contracts to prosecute a case to final judgment for a fixed or contingent fee assumes the risk of long litigation, of repeated trials and reversals * * *" but is not engaged in the business of insurance).

A contract providing for prepaid legal services may present similar problems. See, e.g., Feinstein v. Attorney-General, 36 N.Y.2d 199, 326 N.E.2d 288, 366 N.Y.S.2d 613, 326 N.E.2d 288 (1975) (under a literal reading, New York Insurance Law 40, subd. 1, would take into insurance regulation some prepaid or reimbursable fees for legal services that would not be required until a "fortuitous event" occurred; under a reading of the statute for its sense and purpose, however, two proposed plans under review, one a union proposed "closed panel" plan and the other for a Bar Association proposed "open panel" plan, are "not

questions about the character of such contractual arrangements have sometimes been raised, these commitments almost uniformly are not treated as insurance transactions, and they are not subject to laws that regulate insurance contracts.

Disagreements about what constitutes insurance have frequently arisen in relation to taxation questions. For example, estate tax laws have commonly provided for special treatment of amounts receivable "as insurance under policies on the life of the decedent" when a decedent possessed none of the incidents of ownership at the time of death.[5] A tax loophole would exist if dovetailed annuity and life insurance contracts, which provide both for payment of an annuity to the purchaser for life and payment of death proceeds to designated beneficiaries, could be used to pass funds at death as life insurance proceeds that were entitled not to be included in the estate of the decedent. For this reason, even though aspects of a transaction are in the form of traditional life insurance — and therefore subject to the regulatory authority of the relevant insurance commission or agency — payments made pursuant to a death benefit provision may be determined not to be proceeds of "life insurance" for purposes of a tax law.[6]

Annuity investment arrangements, even when they are not characterized as insurance plans and are not combined with a life insurance program, have frequently presented definitional problems in regard to both insurance law and tax law. For example, whenever an annuity contract provides for a payment if death occurs under certain circumstances, the annuity may be viewed as being in some respects an insurance contract. Even if the death payment is characterized in the agreement as a repayment of part of the annuity premiums — that is, as an investment providing for a minimum return if death occurs early[7] — this characterization usually is not accepted as conclusive on the question of how payments made before death should be treated for income tax purposes or how payments made after death should be treated for purposes of the estate tax exclusions that apply to insurance proceeds. In such cases, the tax issues will be resolved in the light of considerations relevant to the objectives of the statutes involved.[8]

insurance businesses or insurance contracts * * * ").

See generally § 8.3(c), below.

5. See 26 U.S.C.A. § 2042 (1967); Annotation, *Estate tax: Constitutionality and construction of § 2042 of the Internal Revenue Code of 1954 dealing with proceeds of life insurance,* 14 L.Ed.2d 817–875 (1966).

Cf. Fidelity-Philadelphia Trust Company v. Smith, 356 U.S. 274, 78 S.Ct. 730, 2 L.Ed. 2d 765 (1958).

Also see Douglas A. Kahn and Lawrence W. Waggoner, *Federal Taxation of the Assignment of Life Insurance,* 5 Duke Law Journal 941–982 (1977).

6. See, e.g., Fidelity-Philadelphia Trust Company v. Smith, 356 U.S. 274, 78 S.Ct. 730, 2 L.Ed.2d 765 (1958), in which, however, the majority of the court treated the particular contracts in question as life insurance for purposes of the estate tax computation, the purchaser having divested herself, before death, of all interests in them.

7. Concerning the nature of annuities generally, see § 1.5(c)(4), below.

8. See, e.g., In re Barr's Estate, 104 Cal. App.2d 506, 231 P.2d 876 (2d Dist., Div. 2, 1951) (refund annuity contract issued by an insurance company was not an insur-

Annuity contracts have produced at least one other interesting definitional controversy. The development of variable annuities [9] presented the issue of whether state regulation of these annuity contracts as insurance transactions thereby exempted such contracts from regulation as security transactions. The determination about whether these financial arrangements were within the jurisdictional authority of the Federal Securities and Exchange Commission could not be satisfactorily resolved by resorting to definitions of insurance.[10]

§ 1.3 Concepts Underlying Insurance

The concepts of "risk" and "risk management" are recognized as underlying all insurance transactions, and an awareness of these concepts is fundamental to understanding what is meant by an insurance transaction.

§ 1.3(a) Risk

(1) The Concept

Risk is an abstract concept. To observe that an individual or a corporation is subject to a risk of loss of a specified type during a designated period of time is to state essentially no more than that it is impossible to know whether a particular type of loss will occur. If all the facts about a given venture could be known and fully understood, including the effects of all outside forces, it would be possible to know whether a loss would or would not occur. However, since only some portion of the relevant facts that affect any endeavor can ever be known, predictions about the occurrence of a potential loss inevitably are based partly on estimates or guesswork. This speculative aspect is generally understood as the "element of risk" in an insurance transaction.[1] Recognition of the risk element is essential to developing tech-

---

ance risk and was not exempt from inheritance tax).

Also see Central Hanover Bank & Trust Company v. Kelly, 319 U.S. 94, 63 S.Ct. 945, 87 L.Ed. 1282 (1943), affirming the decisions of the New Jersey courts.

Cf. In re Fligman's Estate, 113 Mont. 505, 129 P.2d 627 (1942) (annuity contracts constituted insurance within the meaning of the *inheritance tax* laws of Montana and therefore are exempt from imposition of inheritance tax).

Also *cf.* In re Howerton, 21 B.R. 621 (Bkrtcy., N.D.Tex., Fort Worth, 1982) (individual retirement annuity contracts were not life insurance and therefore the Texas exemption statute, which provides for an exemption for the cash surrender values of insurance policies, was inapplicable).

9. Concerning the nature of variable annuities generally, see § 1.5(c)(4), below.

10. See Securities and Exchange Commission v. Variable Annuity Life Insurance Company of America, 359 U.S. 65, 79 S.Ct. 618, 3 L.Ed. 640 (1959).

§ 1.3(a)

1. A prediction concerning potential loss, partly reasoned from things known and partly predicated on guesswork, is generally understood as the "risk" that is the basis of the computation of a premium that an insured pays to the insurer to acquire insurance.

Risk is also regarded as "a psychological phenomenon that is meaningful only in terms of human reactions and experiences." Denenberg, Eilers, Hoffman, Kline, Melone & Snider, RISK AND INSURANCE (1964), at p. 4 [hereinafter cited as Denenberg *et al.*].

niques for managing the unknown and the unknowable, and the transfer of the element of risk in regard to the unknown is the characteristic that is almost invariably associated with any conceptualization of insurance.

A good illustration of the range of risks that may be involved in an activity is provided by considering the possible consequences of an automobile accident from several vantage points. For example, suppose a pedestrian is in danger of being struck by a speeding car. From the standpoint of the pedestrian in such a hypothetical situation, there is a risk of bodily harm resulting in injuries that may cause pain, temporary or permanent disability, disfigurement, and medical expenses. If the pedestrian has a policy of accident or health insurance, some portion of the medical costs which may result from such an accident constitute a risk that has been transferred to the insurer. If the pedestrian is employed, there is also a risk of income loss which may be covered by disability insurance, some type of wage replacement insurance plan, or "sick leave" provided by an employer. If the injured person is married, the injured person's spouse is also subject to a variety of risks, such as possible responsibility to pay medical expenses incurred by the injured spouse and the loss of companionship. The driver of the car in such a hypothetical accident is subject to a risk of legal liability for negligence in speeding.

A driver who carries motor vehicle liability insurance transfers some portion of the risks that may result from either a tort claim by a person injured in an accident or a tort claim for consequential damages by someone such as a spouse of the injured person who seeks indemnification for loss of companionship. Even if the accident occurs in a jurisdiction in which there is a judicial precedent that limits or precludes any liability to the spouse of an injured person, there is still the possibility that this precedent will be overturned. This uncertainty is also within the bundle of risks that is transferred to the insurer by the driver's liability insurance policy.

The risks identified in this brief discussion of a hypothetical accident situation actually represent only a portion of those that could be involved in such an occurrence. Obviously, when considered from several points of view, even a simple traffic accident typically involves a large array of risks which in many instances are quite complicated. Some consequences of human activity, such as the general risk of bodily injury, are harmful to a person without reference to any legal significance of anyone's conduct. Other consequences of a venture, such as economic losses that result from tort liability claims which are determined in accordance with rules of law, occur only in the context of a legal system. For example, when an insurer has issued an accident, health, or liability insurance policy, the insurer's obligation to provide reimbursement or indemnification as a consequence of certain events will be determined by contractual terms that are applied and interpreted in accordance with rules of law. In the event of a dispute between the insured and the insurer, the insured's rights, if any, will be enforced by the prevailing legal system. Moreover, the conditions and the extent of liability for an insurer (which has issued a liability policy that covers the risk arising from negligent conduct) depend not only on the contractual relationship between the company and the insured, but also on the rules of law that govern tort liability.

(2) Terminology: Risk, Hazard, and Peril

Some insurance literature suggests distinctive meanings for the terms "risk," "hazard," and "peril." [2] However, there is no commonly accepted standard usage which establishes or recognizes separate and distinct definitions for these terms.[3] "Hazard" and "risk" are used interchangeably by many writers and judges. "Peril," although it is frequently used to connote a potential physical cause of loss, is sometimes employed as a term that is essentially synonymous with "risk" or "hazard".

Any human activity involves a variety of risks, which are often referred to as a "bundle of risks." Some persons prefer to consider the composite risk associated with any activity as a unit, using the unqualified term "risk" (rather than "bundle of risks") to refer to that composite, and the term "aspect of risk" to refer to a part of the composite.

§ 1.3(b) Risk Management

The recognition and identification of risks is an important step in dealing with the unknown.[1] In any given venture, some uncertainty invariably exists. Nevertheless, in most circumstances the greater the awareness and understanding of the relevant facts, the smaller is the role played by guesswork in estimating the risks because it is possible to make more reliable predictions. Although the total elimination of uncertainty is not possible, management of risk is an attainable goal.

---

2. See Denenberg *et al.,* note 1, above, at p. 8; James L. Athearn, RISK AND INSURANCE (1977), Chapter One; Mark R. Greene and James S. Trieschmann, RISK AND INSURANCE (1981), at pp. 1–10.

See also § 6.5(c)(2), below.

3. *Cf.* Brainard, *Book Review,* 33 Journal of Risk and Insurance 344 at p. 348 (1966) (review of Denenberg *et al.,* note 1, above).

§ 1.3(b)

1. Like other concepts based on probability, the concept of risk is a rational device for managing ignorance. Ignorance can be too profound for use of this device, however. In customary usage the concept of risk does not extend to a sequence of events, even though it is ineluctably leading to loss, if human observers do not know enough to recognize the possibility that

loss of that type will occur. Pressing this point further (and using what is perhaps an unusual sense of the term "created"), some commentators speak of risk as being "created" by a change in human knowledge:

"For example, the discovery of the relation between smoking and lung cancer created a risk where none has previously existed. Losses may have occurred in the past as a result of excess smoking, but smoking involved no risk at that time because the relationship was not recognized; today we recognize the relationship, and risk does exist."

Herbert Denenberg, Eilers, Hoffman, Kline, Melone & Snider, RISK AND INSURANCE (1964), at p. 4 [hereinafter cited as Denenberg *et al.*].

There are several approaches to risk management, including (1) risk control, (2) risk transference and risk distribution, and (3) risk retention.

(1) Risk Control

One form of risk management is risk control. Risk control is accomplished by conducting a venture so that risk is minimized.[2] Brakes, train whistles, fire escapes, and safety campaigns are common instruments of such risk management. Risk control may be effected either through risk avoidance (as, for example, by effective enforcement of regulations against accumulations of flammable waste[3]) or through risk reduction (such as the removal of accumulated waste materials to reduce the risk of fire). Risk control activities by an insurance company may even extend to participation in the design of a business operation (such as the specifications for the asphalt surfaces of loading platforms in amusement parks to assure firm footing under all weather conditions[4]).

(2) Risk Transference, Risk Distribution, and Reinsurance

Risk Transference

Risk management may be facilitated by using insurance for risk transference.[5] For a price, usually referred to as a premium, an insured transfers to an insurer the risk of loss or the responsibility for certain costs that may arise. In addition, even though the main objective of the insurance contract is to transfer a specified loss, one incident of shifting such a risk will be that an insured will be able to avoid sustaining further losses which might result in the absence of insurance if the loss caused a forced sale of assets to meet the exigency arising from the specified loss. In other words, an insurance company is often more likely than an insured to be able to absorb the specified loss without the necessity of an uneconomical forced sale of assets.

The policyholder purchasing insurance for a venture pays an insurer a premium which is calculated by estimating a number of factors, including (1) the proportionate part of the total predicted cost of

---

2. See, e.g., Denenberg *et al.*, note 1, above at p. 9, and at pp. 87–120; Robert I. Mehr and Robert A. Hedges, RISK MANAGEMENT IN THE BUSINESS ENTERPRISE (1963), at pp. 41–59 and pp. 64–69.

Also see C. Arthur Williams & Richard M. Heins, RISK MANAGEMENT AND INSURANCE (1964), at p. 42 [hereinafter cited as Williams & Heins]; Bobbitt, *Risk Management,* 14 Annals Society Chartered & Casualty Underwriters (1961), at pp. 148–149 [hereinafter cited as Bobbitt].

3. Professors Williams and Heins offer another concept of risk avoidance as a tool of risk management: "Risk may be avoided by refusing to assume it even momentarily. For example, a firm that wishes to avoid the risks associated with a particular operation or business may refuse to engage in that activity." Williams & Heins, at p. 40.

4. See news story, "Modern boom in amusement parks has insurer spinning special covers," Business Insurance, June 14, 1976, at p. 76.

5. See, e.g., Denenberg *et al.,* note 1, above, at p. 9; Robert I. Mehr and Robert A. Hedges, RISK MANAGEMENT IN THE BUSINESS ENTERPRISE (1963), at pp. 64–87; Williams & Heins, note 2, above, at p. 42; Bobbitt, note 2, above, at p. 150.

meeting specified types of losses in the ventures that have been grouped by the insurer into a "pool of risks," (2) appropriate amounts for a reserve fund in the event the total risk was underestimated, (3) the administrative costs of the insurer, (4) other expenses of doing business (including fees for sales representatives such as agents and brokers), and (5) profits for companies engaging in insurance as a business enterprise. In exchange for the premium, the insured receives a measure of certainty. If a loss of a specified type occurs, payment from the insurer provides an indemnification for the loss. If no loss of the specified type occurs, the insured has secured a right to indemnification that, in hindsight, turned out not to have been needed. Even in the absence of a loss, however, the insured has still enjoyed the certainty that if the insured event had occurred, insurance benefits would have been available as an offset.

All insurance contracts concern risk transference, but not all contracts involving risk transference are insurance.[6] Even in those states that have the broadest statutory or decisional definitions of insurance,[7] which if literally applied would include all or nearly all contracts transferring risk, many arrangements encompassed within the scope of such definitions still are not treated as insurance transactions in legal contexts.[8]

Risk transference may also be accomplished by other measures. For example, when the lighted bomb of Scott v. Shepherd [9] was tossed into the crowd, each person who picked it up and tossed it again was changing the risk of bodily harm from one pattern to another, and, in at least some degree, transferring the risk of bodily injury. The degrees of risk to each of the persons in the group changed as the lighted bomb moved about the crowd.

Risk Distribution

When insurance is considered from the viewpoint of an insurer or of society, it is appropriately viewed as a system for risk distribution, as well as risk transference. Insurers deal with the uncertainty of whether a given insured will sustain a loss by combining the risks of loss for many ventures of a given type into a "pool."[10] As the number of ventures included in a group or "pool" is increased, there is a greater

---

6. See § 1.2, above.

The complex bundle of risks from a venture gives rise to a variety of kinds of risk transference, some of which are not regarded as insurance for any purpose, and some of which are regarded as insurance for one purpose but not for another.

7. See § 8.3(a), below.

8. See § 8.3, below.

9. 2 B.W. 892, 96 Eng.Rep. 525 (1775).

10. See Williams & Heins, note 2, above, at p. 43, characterizing this tool of risk management as "combination." "Insurers are the major users of this device for its own sake; they insure a large number of persons in order to improve their ability to predict their losses. In other words, the purchase of insurance, from the point of view of the insured, is a transfer; from the viewpoint of the insurer, it is a combination." *Ibid.*

See also Denenberg *et al.*, note 1, above, at p. 9, and at pp. 143–144; Bobbitt, note 2, above, at p. 150.

likelihood that the favorable and the harmful experiences will tend to be balanced — that is, grouping a large number of ventures in a pool increases the probability that the losses suffered by all the ventures will be spread over time.[11] Through risk distribution, the possibility that the loss experience of one venture will be substantial may be successfully managed by insurance companies.

The grouping of a large number of similar ventures in an insurance pool does not improve the ability to predict whether harm will come to any given venture in the group. But, if the number of ventures included in the insurance pool is great and if the information accumulated about the experience of comparable ventures in the past is both substantial and accurate, an actuary usually can project the average incidence and the average cost of the harmful experiences with sufficient precision for an insurer to establish an appropriate premium to charge for undertaking to insure the risk. In other words, when these conditions exist, the total costs of bearing the risk of loss for a great number of similar activities or enterprises can be reliably estimated for purposes of risk distribution.

Reinsurance

Insurers seek to include enough ventures in a risk pool so that the theory of risk distribution operates satisfactorily. If an insurer does not sell enough policies to pool a sufficient number of insureds, the insurer may still attain the requisite risk distribution by arranging with another insurer to reinsure part or all of the risk undertaken.[12] Reinsurance allows an insurer to secure adequate risk distribution by transferring part of the risk to another insurer or group of insurers.

(3) Risk Retention ("Self-Insuring")

Risk transference or risk distribution may be accomplished without using insurance. If one entity, such as a corporation or a governmental agency, engages in a sufficient volume of ventures of a given type, the risks of all the ventures in the group can be spread by the enterprise acting on its own. For example, entities that provide goods or services to many individuals (such as a municipally owned utility with hundreds of customers, or a bus or an airline company with thousands of passengers) could choose to handle the risk of personal injury claims by "setting aside" assets — either by accounting entries or by actually establishing a special fund — from which it will pay such claims, rather than by purchasing insurance. An arrangement of this type might be funded by allocating a part of the revenue from each venture — that is,

---

11. You can usually observe this phenomenon by flipping a coin: the percentages of heads and tails in the flipping of a coin tend to stay more nearly in balance as the number of tosses of the coin increases.

12. See generally, R.L. Carter, REINSURANCE (1981); Barry R. Ostrager and

Thomas R. Newman, Insurance, EXCESS, AND REINSURANCE COVERAGE DISPUTES (1984); REINSURANCE (edited by Robert W. Strain, 1980).

by taking a small portion of the fare each passenger pays and depositing it in an accident claims account or fund. Although an entity that handles the risk of tort claims in this manner is sometimes referred to as a "self-insurer," [13] this approach involves no insurance as the term is ordinarily used in regulatory statutes or in other legal contexts.[14] Risk management by the technique of setting aside assets to meet foreseeable future losses is more appropriately characterized as "risk retention." [15]

§ 1.3(c) Adverse Selection

Adverse selection occurs whenever potential insureds are treated alike irrespective of some factor that differentiates them as insurance risks. When an insurer does not distinguish among potential insureds, a disproportionately high percentage of applications for insurance will usually come from the less desirable applicants because they get a better bargain.[1]

Renewable term insurance,[2] which grants a policyholder the privilege of renewing the insurance for another term without regard to the insured's health at the time when a renewal is due, provides an illustration of how and why adverse selection may occur. The renewal

13. Traditional thought is that "if a funded reserve is not used, one does not have self-insurance but instead has a system of non-insurance." Bobbitt, note 2, above, at p. 150. Another view has been urged by some commentators:

"More recently, however, a different concept has been developed. Self-insurance is considered to be any plan of risk retention in which a program or procedure has been established to meet the adverse results of a financial loss. Although this does not exclude either the practice of pooling or the establishment of an inviolate reserve, it includes many other practices that the business world has considered self-insurance but insurance scholars have not. * * * This newer concept recognizes that the traditional requisites of self-insurance are seldom, if ever, achieved in practice but that a planned program of risk retention differs significantly from simple risk retention."

Denenberg et al., note 1, above, at pp. 79–80.

Also see Lenz, Self-Insurance, Semantics, and Other Hang-Ups, Chartered Property and Casualty Underwriters Annals XXVIII (June, 1975).

14. "Self-insurance as a technique for treating risk has long been surrounded with confusion and controversy. * * * For those who believe that transfer of risk is a requisite for insurance, the term self-insurance is a misnomer since it permits no transfer. For those who define insurance in terms of pooling, the term self-insurance is not a misnomer but an accurate description of a process by which uncertainty is reduced or eliminated." Denenberg et al., note 1, above, at p. 79. See also Williams & Heins, note 2, above, at p. 41.

15. The development of "claims made" coverage under which an insured (such as a physician) does not pay in the current year a premium to cover the "long tail" of future claims arising from alleged malpractice in the current year illustrates the problem. Tax officials may be more skeptical of the insured's estimate than of the insurer's premium as a legitimate expense of the current year.

Also, as physicians and other professionals have learned to their dismay, such a "set aside" may not be recognized as an expense for income tax purposes as readily as insurance premiums are so recognized.

Concerning "claims made" coverage, see generally § 5.10(d)(3), below.

§ 1.3(c)

1. See, e.g., James L. Athearn, RISK AND INSURANCE (1977); Denenberg, Eilers, Hoffman, Kline, Melone & Snider, RISK AND INSURANCE (1964), at pp. 191–92.

2. See the discussion of term life insurance in § 1.5(c)(1), below.

feature, which precludes an insurer from selectively withdrawing an insured's privilege to continue the coverage, is a way of insuring one's insurability. Experience demonstrates that persons who are in good health when the time for renewal is reached are somewhat less likely to take advantage of the right to renew such life insurance policies than persons who are in bad health when the renewal point is reached. Moreover, the probability that such adverse selection will occur among persons who purchase renewable term insurance is even greater when the premium rate for the new term is higher than the rate for the earlier term, which is often the case because the premium for term life insurance is frequently fixed in accordance with attained age rather than age at the inception of the contract.[3] In this type of situation, if adverse selection does occur, the death rate among those who renew their policies is likely to be in excess of what would otherwise be the normal mortality rate for the entire group of insureds who initially purchased the renewable term life insurance policies.

There are numerous circumstances in which adverse selection may occur,[4] and this possibility should always be taken into account by insurers. In most situations, insurers employ techniques to avoid or minimize the occurrence of adverse selection. However, in some situations adverse selection is unavoidable.

When adverse selection occurs among those eligible for any type of insurance, it will usually result in claims that are somewhat higher than they would be in the absence of such an influence. If an insurance plan cannot include adequate protections against adverse selection, an appropriate allowance for this phenomenon should be made in setting the premiums. In the case of renewable term insurance, the effects of adverse selection generally account for only a small percentage of the overall risk transferred to insurers. Insurers can usually provide an adequate allowance for the problem by setting the premiums charged, either during the coverage period prior to renewal or for the coverage that is purchased as a result of renewals, slightly higher than would be necessary in the absence of the occurrence of adverse selection among the individuals opting to renew the coverage.

3. *Cf.* Joseph B. Maclean, LIFE INSURANCE (Ninth edition, 1962), at p. 33.

4. See § 2.3(c)(3) (life insurance binding receipts), § 2.6(b) (group insurance), and § 8.6(c)(8) (life insurance for war risks, insurance for nuclear energy risks, and flood insurance), below.

Consider also the closely related concept of adverse financial selection, arising from the substantial investment element in many life insurance contracts.

"A substantial proportion of the assets of life insurance companies [is] invested in long-term investments. As a result the average rate of investment return earned by life insurers at any given time seldom coincides with the going rate of interest on similar investments. Also, the rates of return earned by insurers often vary from the rate available on alternative investments. Thus, when the investment earnings rate of insurers is low relative to alternative investments, policyholders may be encouraged to withdraw their funds from the insurance company. The reverse is true when insurers are earning a higher return on investments than is available from other investment media."

Denenberg, Eilers, Hoffman, Kline, Melone & Snider, RISK AND INSURANCE (1964), at p. 192.

§ 1.4 The Role of Classification in Insurance Law

Classification is essential to the common law system which treats each judicial decision as a precedent, but with decreasing authoritative import as the significance of factual distinctions from a new situation increases. In this way, it tends to develop distinctive rules for various types of fact situations. Furthermore, classification is a particularly useful way of identifying either similarities that warrant the same treatment or differences that justify contrasting treatment — that is, it is important in helping to identify significant factors that should be evaluated in the application of legal doctrines. Also, it helps to keep the number of particularized rules within administratively manageable bounds. In the context of insurance law, as elsewhere, classification involves not only striking an appropriate balance among interests at stake in a specific case, but also between generalization and particularization in the entire body of applicable legal principles.

Classification is often an important step in the process of searching for organizing principles. Moreover, in the analysis of a particular problem, classification can also serve the creative function of suggesting ideas that may be useful to the analysis or the resolution of a problem. Unfortunately, classification can also be constricting because it often serves to impose limits on the perspectives from which a problem is examined.

Wise generalizations or classifications advance the quest for a system of predictable and evenhanded adjudication — that is, for the "rule of law", in contrast with a system, however well-intentioned it may be, that is open to the possibilities of whim or bias. Moreover, in the absence of constant testing of particularized rules by standards of generalization, inconsistencies of principle are almost certain to develop.[1]

In some instances the classifications that are used in insurance law, as elsewhere in the legal system, require that the person applying the criteria to a particular case make an interpretive judgment rather than merely a finding of fact — that is, the analytical process entails evaluative determinations.[2] An application of an evaluative criterion

---

§ 1.4

1. Insurance law contains striking illustrations of sets of rules reflecting inconsistencies of principle. For example, see the discussion of insurable interest rules, Chapter 3, below, and the discussion of limited interest problems in property insurance, § 4.6, below.

2. The treatment of highly expectable losses is an example in point. Ordinarily insurance contracts do not cover instances of economic detriment of a type occurring so regularly that they are regarded as part of the cost of an activity or enterprise rather than the materialization of risks

associated with it. A preclusion of coverage for highly expectable losses is sometimes predicated on an implied exception based on the general nature of insurance and at other times is specified in the express terms of a policy. See § 5.4(c), below. In either event, the criterion for classifying particular incidents as within or outside the preclusion is evaluative rather than merely factual in character.

It often happens, also, that the evaluative criterion cannot be applied to an individual case without resolving disputed issues of underlying fact. For example, applying the criterion of "permission" un-

to a particular situation often involves the exercise of a considerable measure of discretion. As a practical matter, opportunities to exercise discretion assure flexibility by affording a decision maker the freedom to weigh factors that affect equities in an individual case. Flexibility, however, usually imposes costs as well as permitting benefits. For example, there is less assurance of consistency and impartiality when flexible criteria are used. In addition, administrative expenses tend to rise with increases in the degree of discretion conferred on those responsible for making such decisions.[3] In practice, it is almost always necessary to strike an accommodation between the competing demands for flexibility and certainty in any system of classification.[4]

The classifications used in insurance law are numerous. Although many decisions in disputes involving insurance appear to employ doctrines or rules which encompass a relatively high degree of flexibility that is inherent in the evaluative criteria of classification, this is not an invariable characteristic of insurance law. Nevertheless, it is appropriate to observe that many rules and doctrines of insurance law have developed in ways that frequently require considerable sensitivity to the facts of the case. The resolution of coverage questions frequently involves classifications which are very "fact sensitive."[5]

der the omnibus clause of an automobile insurance policy typically involves disputed issues of both fact (e.g., what was said or otherwise communicated by the named insured to the driver about the use of the car, and what was the use that was going on when the accident occurred?) and evaluation (e.g., was the use within the scope of the permission, express or implied, given in the communication between the named insured and the driver?). This interrelation between fact issues and evaluative issues commonly leads courts to submit the entire mix to a jury rather than treating the evaluative issue as one for the court. As is well illustrated by the issue of permission under the omnibus clause of automobile policies, the interrelation between fact issues and evaluative issues also tends to breed litigation. See § 4.7(a), § 4.7(b)(1), § 4.7(b)(2), and § 4.7(c), below.

Though less notable as a source of litigation, the meaning of "use" in automobile policies also illustrates the case-by-case difficulties of applying standards that involve an element of evaluation as well as an element of fact finding. See § 5.2(b), below.

Concerning evaluative standards generally, see Robert E. Keeton, VENTURING TO DO JUSTICE (1969), at pp. 65–74.

3. John Frank, AMERICAN LAW—THE CASE FOR RADICAL REFORM (1969), at pp. 85–

110 calls attention to the costs, in a broad sense, of multiplication of decision points in a legal system. The lawmaker's choice of an evaluative criterion confronts the law administrator with a type of decision point that is especially costly both because such a criterion has a capacity for generating numerous sub-points as factors to be taken into account and because its generality and imprecision reduce predictability and thereby impede the settlement process by which the necessity for formal decisions can often be avoided.

4. See the observations about the competing demands for flexibility and certainty in relation to the requirement of "delivery" of a life insurance policy in § 2.1(c), below.

5. See, e.g., § 4.7 (coverage for permitted users of motor vehicles under omnibus clauses); § 4.11(d)(1) (assignment of life policy by means not complying with formalities); § 4.11(e)(2) ("substantial compliance" with requisites for changing beneficiary of life policy); § 5.2(b) ("arising" out of "use" of automobile); § 7.2(a) and § 7.2(b) ("reasonable time" for notice or proof of loss); § 8.2 (objectives of regulated "insurance" transactions); § 8.4 (rates shall be "adequate" and neither "excessive" nor "unfairly discriminatory").

In this text, classification is usually discussed in relation to a particular principle or doctrine of insurance law to which it is relevant. However, classification of insurance by the type of risk involved is widely recognized and used for a variety of different purposes, and therefore this system of classification is discussed and described in the next section of this introductory chapter.

§ 1.5   Classification by the Nature of the Risks

§ 1.5(a)   Introduction

(1) Influences on Classification By Risk

Insurance transactions are frequently classified by the nature of the risk that is being transferred. In the United States, the combined influence of voluntary specialization by insurers and statutory regulations which were adopted in many states led to the widespread recognition of three principal classes of insurance. These three main classes of insurance are commonly referred to as "fire and marine," "life and accident," and "casualty" insurance. Regulatory statutes in many states formerly limited insurers to writing only those types of coverages that were considered to be within one of the three classes — that is, an insurer was only permitted to sell the types of insurance that were recognized as being included in a single class. Some insurance companies opted to be even more specialized, and limited their underwriting to only one type or line of insurance within a class.

By the middle of the twentieth century, the regulatory significance of these three classifications was substantially reduced in the United States. During the first half of the twentieth century, most states moved to allow "multiple-line" underwriting which authorized marine and fire insurers to sell casualty insurance, and vice-versa, so that these insurers could sell all types of coverage other than life insurance.[1] Even in those states which did not allow a single company to engage in multiple-line underwriting, many insurers developed an equivalent to multiple-line underwriting by arranging for the affiliation of several insurance companies whose common agents could provide an insured with a single policy that included several different classes of coverages, each of which was written by one of the affiliated companies. Generally, this marketing arrangement involved a parent company and a group of subsidiaries. Occasionally, the arrangement was among a group of otherwise independent insurers. In both cases, the group of insurers came to be referred to as a "fleet." Furthermore, in most states multiple-line underwriting evolved into an even broader marketing approach that is referred to as "all-line" underwriting because it

§ 1.5(a)

1. G.F. Michelbacher & Nestor R. Roos, Multiple-Line Insurers: Their Nature and Operation (Second edition, 1970), at pp. 4–9.

Also see Denenberg, Eilers, Hoffman, Kline, Melone & Snider, Risk and Insurance (1964), at pp. 335–346.

encompasses all of the three main classes: life insurance, casualty insurance, fire and marine insurance.

Despite the development of statutes that provide for multiple-line and all-line underwriting, the classification of insurance by the type of risk is of more than historical significance. For example, some insurers continue to limit their underwriting to one class of insurance. Furthermore, in many states legislation has not abolished the classes of insurance, but has merely authorized insurance companies to operate in the entire field of insurance. And in some situations, all-line underwriting is still achieved by fleet marketing.[2] Most important, however, is the fact that despite the growth of all-line underwriting by insurers, some distinctive regulations, doctrines, and practices continue to exist with respect to these three classes of insurance.

(2) All-Risk and All-Lines Insurance

The term "all-risk" insurance is generally used to refer to a method of defining insured events as all fortuitous losses. So long as insurers were precluded from selling all types of insurance, there were legal obstacles in the way of providing "all-risk" insurance in many commercial fields.

The term "all-risk insurance" does not have a single, consistent meaning in usage. In some contexts it refers to a broad combination of underwriting that includes life insurance as well as casualty and fire and marine. This combination may also be referred to as "all-lines" insurance. In most instances, so-called "all-risk" coverages include some limitations that are specified in the insurance policy terms.

The development of multiple-line and all-line underwriting has not in itself produced such "all-risk" insurance,[3] though in the long run it could facilitate such coverages. However, so long as multiple-line and all-line insurers continue to use basically the same policy forms and offer the same types of coverages as other insurers, "all-risk" insurance in many areas will continue to remain a theoretical possibility rather than an available choice in the market place.

§ 1.5(b)   Marine, Inland Marine, and Fire Insurance

(1) Marine Insurance

In the 1600s, persons who sought to arrange contracts of insurance against perils of the sea gathered at Lloyd's Coffee House in London.[1]

---

2. Woodson, *All-Lines Underwriting: New Fashion or New Era?*, 12 Journal American Society Chartered Life Underwriters 69 at pp. 75–76 (1957). With regard to authorization for all-line underwriting by a single company, but with special provision for life insurance reserves, see Wisconsin Statutes § 201.05(2) (1967).

Also see Connecticut General Life Insurance Company v. Superintendent of Insurance, 10 N.Y.2d 42, 176 N.E.2d 63, 217

N.Y.S.2d 39 (1961) (licensed foreign life insurance company not barred, by New York Insurance Law § 42(3) and § 193(2) then in force, from purchasing 80 per cent or more of the common stock of a fire and casualty insurance company).

3. "All-risk" insurance is discussed in § 5.1(b), below.

§ 1.5(b)

1. Also see the discussion of Lloyd's insurers in § 2.1(a)(1), below.

A person interested in obtaining insurance on a vessel or cargo would pass around a slip containing relevant information, including an indication of the total amount of insurance desired. Each individual who was willing to become an insurer for the voyage would initial the slip and indicate the portion of the requested coverage for which the "underwriter" was willing to be responsible. The slip would continue to be passed until the full amount was subscribed, and each of the underwriters became an insurer for the subscribed amount — that is, the "underwritten" amount. In 1769, the underwriters who transacted business at Lloyd's formed a society, and ten years later this society adopted the "Lloyd's policy" as a standard form for marine insurance. Little change was made in this insurance policy form for almost two centuries, and until very recently contemporary marine insurance forms bore a striking resemblance to the original Lloyd's marine insurance policy.[2]

As insurance companies developed in the 19th and 20th centuries, an increasingly significant portion of the marine insurance bought by ship owners and merchants was written by insurance companies rather than by individual underwriters. The role of these insurers in marine insurance was important to the development of insurance in other fields. When companies writing marine insurance extended operations into other areas of property insurance, particularly those involving transportation of goods over inland waterways, the insurance contracts were modeled on the terms used for marine insurance. These coverages came to be referred to as "inland marine" insurance.

(2) Inland Marine Insurance

Inland marine insurance is used to provide coverage for many risks that one who was not familiar with the historical development would never expect to be included in this classification. Inland marine insurance now includes three main branches: domestic shipments; bridges, tunnels, and other instrumentalities of transportation and communication; and personal property coverage. Thus, inland marine coverage is used not only to insure transportation risks generally, but may also be used to insure any type of goods or property that might be affected by movement.[3] The policies insuring moveable goods irrespective of location are often referred to as personal property "floater" policies.

---

2. A modern marine insurance form is included in Appendix C.

See also Russell Mining Company v. Northwestern Fire & Marine Insurance Company, 207 F.Supp. 162 (1962), *reversed* 322 F.2d 440 (6th Cir.1963), for an example of the problems of applying antiquated terminology to current transactions. The disputed insurance was coverage for a barge moored permanently on an inland waterway, and the case concerned application of the Inchmaree clause, devised in the late 1800's to apply to the insurance of ocean-going vessels.

Also see the discussion of marine insurance as an "all-risk" insurance policy in § 5.1(b)(1), below.

3. See, e.g., Denenberg, Eilers, Hoffman, Kline, Melone & Snider, RISK AND INSURANCE (1964), at pp. 337–339.

(3) Fire Insurance

Fire insurance is customarily understood to include coverage of loss caused by what are termed hostile fires [4] or by lightning. Fire insurance companies are usually also authorized to write several "allied lines" which provide coverage for damages to property from wind, rain, collision, riot and civil commotion, explosion, water damage, and earthquake.

§ 1.5(c)　Life and Accident Insurance

Life insurance, as one of the three main classes of insurance, includes personal accident insurance, health insurance, and annuity contracts, as well as contracts providing for payment of specified benefits upon the death of a person whose life is insured.

(1) Life Insurance

Life insurance, in the narrow or literal sense, includes many different types of coverages. Some of the terms used to describe and distinguish different plans or types of life insurance [1] are set forth in the following paragraphs.

Whole–Life Insurance

Whole-life insurance, which matures for payment at the death of the person insured, has both an insurance and a savings feature. There are several distinct types of whole-life insurance, including:

> *Ordinary life insurance.*[2] Premiums are paid either throughout the lifetime of the person insured or until the person reaches a predetermined specified age (such as 50, 65 or 70 years) at which point the coverage continues without the payment of additional premiums. This type of coverage, which is also known as straight life insurance, combines insurance with a savings feature that usually provides the insured with a relatively conservative rate of return on the investment.

> *Limited-payment life insurance.* Premiums are paid only during a specified number of years or until a specified event occurs.

> *Single-premium life insurance.* The coverage is acquired by the payment of a single premium.

---

4. The distinction between "friendly" and "hostile" fires is discussed in § 5.3(d), below.

§ 1.5(c)

1. *Cf.* Joseph B. Maclean, LIFE INSURANCE (Ninth edition, 1962), at pp. 21–34.

2. The term "ordinary life insurance" is sometimes used to signify the marketing arrangement in which a policy is sold by individual solicitation, as distinguished from group marketing. For example, see Fuller, *Foreword to The Wage-Earner's Life Insurance,* 2 Law & Contemporary Problems 1–2 (1935).

Cf. Maclean, LIFE INSURANCE (Ninth edition, 1962), at pp. 406–412, using the phrase "ordinary life insurance" in this sense.

Several types of life insurance are marketed through individual solicitations.

Joint-life insurance. Coverage is payable upon the first death among two or more insureds. Although this type of insurance may cover any number of persons, it is usually purchased by business partners or spouses. Upon the death of one of the insureds, the insurance is paid to the survivor(s).

Universal life insurance. This coverage emphasizes the separation of the portion of the premium that is used to cover the insurance protection from the portion of the premium allocated to an investment that is used to build the policy's cash value. Investments are usually selected with a view to maximizing the rate of return. Many companies offer policies that allow the insured to vary both the amount and the allocation of the premiums between the insurance and the investment options.

Variable-life insurance. Some amount of death benefit provided by a variable life insurance policy is guaranteed by the insurer, but the total death benefit and the cash-value of the insurance before death depend on the investment performance of that portion of the premium which is allocated to a separate fund. Some variable-life insurance policies allow the insured to decide how the separate account is to be invested. Variable life policies are sold with a prospectus, like a security, and the sales representative must be registered with the National Association of Securities Dealers.

Endowment life insurance. Endowment life insurance provides for the payment of a specified amount in the event of death before the end of the endowment period, commonly twenty years. In addition, this coverage also provides that if the insured survives to a specified maturity date, the insured will be paid a specified endowment.

Term Life Insurance

Term life insurance provides for the payment of a specified amount if death occurs within the time period designated in the policy. Term policies typically are written for periods of one to five years. Term life insurance contracts may allow the policy owner to renew the coverage or to convert the coverage to another type of life insurance such as a whole life policy. The terms used to describe these options are:

Convertible term insurance, which confers the right, without regard to health at the time the option is exercised, to change to a permanent plan of whole life or endowment insurance.

Renewable term insurance, which confers the right to renew for an additional term without regard to health at the time of exercising the option. Renewable term policies usually provide for repeated renewals until the insured has attained a specified age.

Modified Life Insurance

Modified life insurance is generally understood to describe a policy that combines term and whole life insurance in a single insurance policy.[3] The objective is to provide a coverage in which the premiums paid by the insured during the first few years are substantially less than the cost of a whole life policy. During the remaining policy term, the premiums increase, and the total cost is usually greater than the purchaser would have paid for a comparable policy if a whole life insurance policy had been purchased at the outset. However, the total cost is less than the amount an insured would pay to acquire a new whole life policy at the attained age.

(2) Industrial Life Insurance

The phrase "industrial life insurance" is used to refer to a type of life insurance that is typically written with small coverages, often in amounts that are barely adequate for burial expenses, and with premiums that are paid in frequent installments. For example, weekly collection of insurance premiums for industrial insurance is common. The term "industrial life insurance" derives from the fact that industrial workers were among those to whom this type of insurance was first marketed, and industrial workers still purchase most of these policies.[4] The shorter phrase "industrial insurance" usually also refers to such life insurance, but sometimes this term is used to refer to health and accident policies that are sold to industrial workers.

The frequency of premium installments for industrial life insurance is what principally distinguishes this coverage from other types of life insurance.[5] In this respect, industrial life insurance is similar to group insurance for employees whose contributions to the cost of the insurance are made weekly, bi-weekly, or monthly through payroll deductions.[6] But in contrast with employee group insur-

---

3. See Albert H. Mowbray, Ralph H. Blanchard & C. Arthur Williams, INSURANCE (Sixth edition, 1969), at p. 306.

Most "plans" of life insurance involve, to a significant extent, features of savings and investment as well as purely insurance features. See, e.g., H. Denenberg, Eilers, Hoffman, Kline, Melone & Snider, RISK AND INSURANCE (1964), at p. 192 and pp. 243–249. Indeed, these features are so familiar that the particular form in which they exist in a contract may affect whether it is classified as insurance.

Also see, e.g., Securities & Exchange Commission v. Variable Annuity Life Insurance Company, 359 U.S. 65, 79 S.Ct. 618, 3 L.Ed.2d 640 (1959), discussed in § 8.3(d), below.

4. See Joseph B. Maclean, LIFE INSURANCE (Ninth edition, 1962), at p. 406.

5. Industrial life insurance is written on various plans (endowment, limited-payment life, etc.). Joseph B. Maclean, LIFE INSURANCE (Ninth edition, 1962), at pp. 408–409. An industrial policy on the ordinary (straight life) plan is sometimes referred to as an "ordinary" industrial policy.

6. The extent of the contrast between the methods of marketing "ordinary" and industrial insurance was reduced by rapid development during the late 1950's of monthly payment plans for "ordinary" life insurance under which the insured authorizes drafts on the insured's bank account in the amount of the monthly premium signed by a representative of the insurer (called by various names, such as "check-o-matic" and "premiumatic"). See Eastern Underwriter, August 22, 1958, p. 10.

ance,[7] industrial life insurance is marketed through direct solicitation by an agent, who usually also collects the premiums personally.

The relatively high cost of solicitation and premium collection, together with the minimal use of medical examination or evaluation in determining whether to issue coverage [8] and a somewhat higher death rate for individuals comprising the low-income groups usually insured under such policies,[9] almost invariably result in notably higher premium rates for industrial life than for other forms of life insurance. Nevertheless, as Professor Patterson observed in 1935, industrial life insurance had nearly blanketed its field.[10] This observation remained true for several more decades. In 1955, approximately 112 million industrial life policies were in force, representing more than 39 billion dollars of insurance and more than ten per cent of the total amount of life insurance in force in the United States.[11] The convenience of small installment payments combined with effective solicitation to make industrial life insurance a very significant part of the total life insurance market.

The number of industrial life insurance policies has declined steadily since 1955. By 1969, the number of policies had dropped to approximately 79 million, and represented somewhat less than three per cent of the total amount of life insurance in force in the United States.[12] In 1982 — when over 4 trillion dollars worth of life insurance was in force — the amount of industrial life insurance had fallen to less than 34 billion dollars, a market share of less than one percent.[13]

The development and marketing of industrial life insurance is something more than a mere historical curiosity because of several innovations that were developed by insurers for this coverage. For example, a purchaser is usually allowed to return a policy at any time during the first two or three weeks from the date of issue and receive a complete refund of the premium payment.[14] Furthermore, industrial life insurance policies usually provide coverage for several risks. A typical policy will pay the face amount of the insurance if an insured loses both hands or both feet or the entire sight of both eyes, and under such circumstances industrial life insurance policies often provide that the company will also continue the policy in force without the payment

7. See the discussion of group insurance in § 2.6, below.

8. Joseph B. Maclean, LIFE INSURANCE (Ninth edition, 1962), at p. 408.

9. *Ibid.*

10. Patterson, *The Distribution of Wage-Earner's Life Insurance*, 2 Law & Contemporary Problems 3–9 at p. 6 (1935).

11. Institute of Life Insurance, LIFE INSURANCE FACT BOOK (1982), at p. 15.

12. Institute of Life Insurance, LIFE INSURANCE FACT BOOK (1970), at p. 32 and p.

103. This compares to 118 million ordinary policies in 1969, representing over 678 billion dollars of insurance, a bit more than half of the total life insurance in force in the United States. *Id.,* at p. 26 and p. 103.

13. Institute of Life Insurance, LIFE INSURANCE FACT BOOK (1982), at p. 15.

14. Malvin E. Davis, INDUSTRIAL LIFE INSURANCE (1944), at p. 36 and p. 46; Joseph B. Maclean, LIFE INSURANCE (Ninth edition, 1962), at p. 413.

of additional premiums.[15] In addition, most industrial life policies do not contain any suicide limitation.[16]

Industrial life insurance policies usually prohibit any assignment of either the policy or the benefits thereunder. However, most industrial life insurance policies provide the insurer some discretion over disposition of the death benefit. The latter provision, known as the "facility of payment clause," authorizes payment to a person appearing to the insurer to be equitably entitled to the insurance proceeds by reason of having incurred expenses on behalf of the insured for medical treatment, burial, or any other purpose. This provision was designed to avoid necessitating the appointment of an administrator, executor, or guardian to collect and use the insurance proceeds, and to facilitate settlement of disputes among rival claimants without the delay and expense of litigation. Although the possibility of abuse of the discretion given to the insurer by the facility of payment clause is apparent, the clause has nevertheless been defended as a wise provision,[17] and some group life insurance contracts include a similar "facility of payment clause."[18]

(3) Trip Insurance

Trip insurance is a limited form of accident insurance coverage that is commonly available at airports, often through vending machines. Motoring trip insurance has similar characteristics, though it is less readily available and not as widely used.[19]

(4) Annuities

An annuity contract ordinarily provides for the payment of a fixed-dollar annual benefit commencing at a specified date and continuing as long as the annuitant lives. The traditional annuity contract is in essence and in principal purpose a risk transferring and a risk distributing contract, and this type of contract is frequently treated as a form of insurance. The uncertainty in this context is the risk of long life, in which case the annuity contract will pay the annuitant substantially more than the company received (as a result of both premium payments and investment earnings) on behalf of that annuitant to create the annuity benefit.

Many annuity contracts provide that if an annuitant dies before annuity payments begin or within some specified period after annuity payments begin, the company will pay a specified sum as a "refund" of a part of the premium or premiums paid to purchase the contract. The

---

15. Joseph B. Maclean, LIFE INSURANCE (Ninth edition, 1962), at p. 416.

16. Malvin E. Davis, INDUSTRIAL LIFE INSURANCE (1944), at p. 46.

17. L. Fuller, *The Special Nature of the Wage-Earner's Life Insurance Problem,* 2 Law & Contemporary Problems 10–48, at pp. 28–29 (1935), expressing the opinion

that "the companies have been guided by a sound instinct in preferring the dangers of paternalism to those of legalism."

18. David W. Gregg, GROUP LIFE INSURANCE (Third edition, 1962), at p. 99.

19. Also see the discussion in § 2.7, below.

refund aspect of such an annuity contract is properly regarded as a device for making an annuity contract something more than purely insurance against the risk of long life. This feature in an annuity contract is analogous to hedging; that is, an annuity with a refund feature is partly an insurance arrangement against the economic contingencies of long life and partly an investment providing for a minimum return even though death occurs early.

Variable annuities are a relatively recent invention. Pioneered by the College Retirement Equities Fund (CREF) and its parent, Teachers Insurance and Annuity Association (TIAA), the variable annuity was first introduced in 1952. The CREF annuity was designed to provide retirement income based on common stock investments and to complement other investments or savings programs an annuitant could make to provide a fixed-dollar retirement income.[20]

The variable annuity contracts now available from numerous companies differ in many details.[21] In general, however, during the pay-in period the purchaser of a variable annuity buys units of ownership in a portfolio of common stocks. The cost of units purchased at different times and the value of the purchaser's accumulated holdings vary with the changing value of the common stocks in the portfolio. During the pay-out period, the annuitant receives payments that are usually based on the number of units acquired by the annuitant during the pay-in period. Under a common form of annuity contract, the payments are actuarially calculated and depend on factors affecting life expectancy at the date the pay-out period commences. Though the number of units owned by the annuitant remains constant throughout the pay-out period (subject to agreed exceptions such as providing for more units while both the annuitant and the annuitant's spouse are living than when only one is surviving), the payments provided by a variable annuity increase or decrease as the value of a unit continues to change with the value of the common stocks in the portfolio.[22]

§ 1.5(d) Casualty Insurance

The word "casualty" is generally used in legal contexts to mean either an "accident" or an event that results from a "sudden, unexpected, or unusual cause."[1] Thus, in a sense almost all types of insurance could be regarded as casualty insurance.

20. William C. Greenough & Francis P. King, BENEFIT PLANS IN AMERICAN COLLEGES (1969), at pp. 43–99.

21. See generally George E. Johnson & Donald S. Grubbs, THE VARIABLE ANNUITY (Second edition, 1970).

22. See § 8.3(d), below.

§ 1.5(d)

1. See Graham v. Chicago, Rock Island and Pacific Railroad Company, 431 F.Supp. 444 at p. 447 (W.D.Okl.1976); Tank v. Commissioner of Internal Revenue, 270 F.2d 477 at p. 482 (6th Cir.1959).

Also see BALLENTINE'S LAW DICTIONARY (Third edition, 1969), at p. 180; BLACK'S LAW DICTIONARY (Fifth edition, 1979), at p. 198.

Casualty insurance as a class encompasses a tremendous variety of coverages including: liability, workers' compensation, accident and health, glass, burglary, theft, boiler and machinery, property damage, collision, and credit insurance, as well as fidelity and surety bonds.[2] The past century has seen a proliferation of different types of insurance coverages that clearly are neither "fire insurance" nor "life insurance." The combined effect of multi-line underwriting and this proliferation of coverages has tended to blur the meaning of the term "casualty insurance" to such an extent that the term is no longer used by some authorities.

§ 1.5(e)   Title Insurance

Title insurance has been regarded as a distinct type of coverage that does not fall within any of the three basic classes of insurance. The risks insured against typically result from incomplete information about legal rights already existing at the time the contract is written,[1] rather than being the result of fortuitous subsequent events, as are the risks covered by most other kinds of insurance. The subsequent assertion of a claim can be viewed as a fortuitous loss-producing event against which the title insurance is being provided. The formulation of limitations on the scope of coverage under title insurance has produced distinctive problems of interpretation and application.[2]

---

2. See the samples of casualty insurance policies included in the volumes of FIRE CASUALTY AND SURETY BULLETINS (The National Underwriter Co., 1987).

§ 1.5(e)

1. In the nineteenth century, legal opinions of title validity were insured. See Brown, *Insured Legal Opinions,* 36 Journal of The State Bar of California 411 (1961), reprinted in 1961 Insurance Law Journal 712. Brown suggests the possibility of devising insurance to cover the risk of depending on the legal advice of counsel. *Ibid.* Such insurance would probably be subsumed under the "casualty" classification. In many states, most of the risks associated with the validity of a title to property can be covered by title insurance.

2. See, e.g., Hansen v. Western Title Insurance Company, 220 Cal.App.2d 531, 33 Cal.Rptr. 668 (1st Dist.1963) 98 A.L.R.2d 520 (1964) (a claim arising out of a poorly drafted option agreement between the insured and the claimant was settled by the insured, who then sought recovery from his title insurer; held, the defect was not "created by" the insured within the meaning of a coverage restriction).

Also see Demopoulos v. Title Insurance Company, 61 N.M. 254, 298 P.2d 938 (1956), 60 A.L.R.2d 969 (1958) (mortgagee insured to the limit of its $8,500 interest in a mortgage for that amount procured by a mortgagor who misrepresented the value and identification of the property involved, recorded a fraudulent deed to show his title to the property, and forged his wife's name to the mortgage contract; held, the mortgagee could recover only $1,200, the actual value of the land, since that was all the mortgagee could have recovered had the mortgage been valid and foreclosed).

In Shaver v. National Title & Abstract Company, 361 S.W.2d 867 (Tex.1962), 98 A.L.R.2d 531 (1964), unknown to the insured, a large gas main was buried under his land pursuant to a recorded easement that was not discovered when the insured bought the land. The court held that the defect in the title created by the easement was not within the coverage restriction concerning rights of persons in possession of the land.

WESTLAW REFERENCES

§ 1.1 Insurance, Insurance Transactions, and Insurance Law
> **(b) The Problem of Definition**
>> insurance /s share* sharing distribut! transfer! /2 risk

§ 1.3 Concepts Underlying Insurance
> **(a) Risk**
>> **(1) The Concept**
>>> element /3 risk /s insurance
>>
>> **(2) Terminology: Risk, Hazard, and Peril**
>>> di risk
>>> di hazard
>>> di peril
>
> **(b) Risk Management**
>> **(2) Risk Transference, Risk Distribution, and Reinsurance**
>>> *Risk Transference*
>>> sy,di(risk /2 transfer! shift!)
>>>
>>> *Risk Distribution*
>>> risk /2 distribut!
>>>
>>> *Reinsurance*
>>> di(reinsurance /s risk)
>>
>> **(3) Risk Retention ("Self-Insuring")**
>>> sy,di(self-insur**** /s risk)

§ 1.4 The Role of Classification in Insurance Law
> di(classif! /3 insurance)

§ 1.5 Classification by the Nature of the Risks
> **(a) Introduction**
>> **(1) Influences on Classification by Risk**
>>> sy,di(insurance /s classif! /5 risk)
>
> **(b) Marine, Inland Marine, and Fire Insurance**
>> **(1) Marine Insurance**
>>> di lloyd's of london
>>
>> **(2) Inland Marine Insurance**
>>> "inland marine" /2 insurance
>>> "floater policy" /s inusrance
>>
>> **(3) Fire Insurance**
>>> "fire insurance" /s cover! inclu! /s "hostile fire" lightning
>
> **(c) Life and Accident Insurance**
>> **(2) Industrial Life Insurance**
>>> "industrial life insurance" /s defin! mean***
>>
>> **(3) Trip Insurance**
>>> "trip insurance"
>>
>> **(4) Annuities**
>>> "annuity contract" /7 purpose defin! mean***
>
> **(e) Title Insurance**
>> "title insurance" /3 purpose defin! mean***

Chapter Two

THE MARKETING OF INSURANCE

Table of Sections

---

§ 2.1   Organization of Marketing

§ 2.1(a)   Organizations That Sell Insurance

Insurance in the United States is provided by many different types of entities, including:

(1) Lloyd's insurers,

(2) stock companies,

(3) mutual insurers, and

(4) governmental units.[1]

Although all insurers share many common characteristics,[2] each type of insurer has several distinctive features, some of which are particularly significant in regard to marketing practices.[3]

§ 2.1(a)

1. The insurance programs of the federal government include (1) the Pension Benefit Guaranty Corporation which insures employee benefit plan participants, (2) the Federal Crop Insurance Corporation, (3) Federal Flood Insurance, (4) Nuclear Power Plan Liability Insurance, (5) War Risk Insurance, (6) Federal Deposit Insurance Corporation and the Federal Savings and Loan Insurance Corporation which provide coverage for depositors, (7) the Securities Investor Protection Corporation, (8) Postal Service Insurance Coverages, (9) Mortgage Loan Insurance, (10) Federal Crime Insurance, (11) Small Business Administration Surety Guaranty Programs, and (12) the Social Security system. See Wolcott Dunham, Jr., *Federal Regulation of Insurance: A Survey of Selected Federal Statutes,* 16 Forum 180–224 at pp. 218–224 (1980); Emmett Vaughan, FUNDAMENTALS OF RISK AND INSURANCE (Third Edition, 1982), Chapter 9—The Government as an Insurer.

State governments also operate insurance programs such as unemployment compensation, workers' compensation funds, and disability insurance plans. See Emmett Vaughan, FUNDAMENTALS OF RISK AND INSURANCE (Third Edition, 1982), at pp. 123–125 and pp. 132–133.

Also see the discussion of governmental sponsorship of insurance or insurance programs in § 8.6, below.

2. A few insurers are structured in such a way that they cannot be exclusively classed in any one of these categories.

3. See generally Edwin Patterson, ESSENTIALS OF INSURANCE LAW (Second edition, 1957), at § 9; Vance, LAW OF INSURANCE (Third edition, Anderson 1951), at pp. 17–18 and at pp. 122–125.

(1) Lloyd's Insurers

For three hundred years, insurance transactions have been conducted at Lloyd's Coffee House in London, England.[4] In fact, many contemporary insurance practices, especially in regard to marketing, are derived from customs that developed in the latter part of the 17th century among the individuals who gathered at Lloyd's to buy and sell insurance for ships and cargo. For example, it was customary for a ship owner or merchant who sought insurance to retain a broker who would represent the prospective purchaser in working out the arrangement with the insurers. Although there have been many significant changes in the ways insurance is marketed since this practice was established, brokers continue to participate as intermediaries between insurers and insureds for a significant portion of the insurance sold throughout the world.[5]

The insurance for which brokers made arrangements at Lloyd's was provided either by an individual or a group of individuals who were, and still are, generally referred to as a syndicate. When insurance was acquired from several members of a Lloyd's syndicate, they were individually responsible for their respective shares. Each member of a syndicate who agreed to accept responsibility for some portion of a risk would in effect enter into a separate contract with the insured so that an individual underwriter was only liable for the specified fraction of the total coverage and there was no joint liability among two or more individual insurers comprising a syndicate.[6]

Lloyd's syndicates continue to sell insurance both in England and in other nations.[7] In the United States, insurance is often provided by Lloyd's underwriters, especially for risks that would not be covered by insurance policies that are generally available from American companies[8] (that is, when the risk that the purchaser seeks to insure is in

---

4. See the discussion of the Lloyd's Coffee House insurers in § 1.5(b), above.

Also see Anthony Brown, HAZARD UNLIMITED: THE STORY OF LLOYD'S OF LONDON (Peter Davies, London, 1973).

5. See generally, Curtis M. Elliott, FUNDAMENTALS OF RISK AND INSURANCE (1974), at p. 79; Denenberg, Eilers, Hoffman, Kline, Melone & Snider, RISK AND INSURANCE (1964), at pp. 170–172, reprinted in Herbert Denenberg, Robert D. Eilers, Joseph J. Melone & Robert A. Zelten, RISK AND INSURANCE (Second Edition, 1974), at pp. 194–96 [hereinafter cited as Denenberg *et al*, 2d].

6. See 1 Arnould, LAW OF MARINE INSURANCE AND AVERAGE (Sixteenth Edition, 1981), at § 45 and § 125; Harold E. Raynes, INSURANCE (1960), at pp. 13–14; Emmett Vaughn, FUNDAMENTALS OF RISK AND INSURANCE (Third Edition, 1982), at pp. 70–71; C. Arthur Williams and Richard M.

Heins, RISK MANAGEMENT AND INSURANCE (Third Edition, 1976), at p. 441.

7. For examples of the types of services provided by such associations, see e.g., Denenberg, Eilers, Hoffman, Kline, Melone & Snider, RISK AND INSURANCE (1964) at p. 171, reprinted in Herbert Denenberg, Robert D. Eilers, Joseph J. Melone & Robert A. Zelten, RISK AND INSURANCE (Second Edition, 1974) at p. 195. DeWolf, *The Proposed Surplus Line Law: Constructive or Destructive,* 1961 Insurance Law Journal 259–264.

Also see generally articles in Business Insurance, which is a weekly publication of interest to corporate buyers of property-liability insurance, employee benefits, safety-security systems, and financial services, published by Crain Communications, Inc., Chicago.

8. See Mark R. Greene, RISK AND INSURANCE (Third Edition, 1973), at p. 118.

some way unusual so that it does not conform to a type of risk for which insurance coverage is marketed in the United States).[9] The insurance written by English Lloyd's syndicates to cover risks in the United States is usually placed through brokers.

In 1871, the Corporation of Lloyd's was organized in England. The Corporation, which does no underwriting, regulates the operations of the underwriters and provides various services to insurers, including the gathering and publication of data useful to the underwriters.

Lloyd's syndicates are sometimes referred to as Lloyd's Associations. Several business organizations that are also called "Lloyds Associations," which are patterned after the English syndicates, have been formed in the United States.[10] Legislation has been enacted in many states that specifically regulates both the English Lloyd's syndicates and the American Lloyds Associations.[11] These statutes typically provide that the legislative provisions apply to any aggregation of individuals who engage in the business of insurance under a common name through an attorney-in-fact who has authority to obligate the underwriters.[12] Some of these statutes also specify that a "Domestic Lloyds" means a group having its home office in that state, that a "Foreign Lloyds" means a group having its home office in any other state of the United States, and that an "Alien Lloyds" means a group having its home office or principal place of business in any country other than the United States.[13]

There are approximately thirty American Lloyds Associations, and most of them have their home offices in Texas.[14] In a few states, legislative provisions either prohibit or impose very restrictive regulations on such associations. For example, the New York insurance statute long provided, "No Lloyds underwriters shall hereafter be organized in this state and no foreign or alien Lloyds underwriters shall be licensed to do an insurance business in this state." [15] In 1978, however, New York adopted legislation authorizing an "insurance

---

Also see DeWolf, *The Proposed Surplus Line Law: Constructive or Destructive,* 1961 Insurance Law Journal 259–264 at p. 259.

In 1978, for example, it was estimated that "more than $4 billion in insurance premiums went [from the United States] to foreign insurance companies, often because no one in this country would underwrite the risk." *Lloyd's American Cousins,* 55–56 Journal of American Insurance (Fall, 1979) 7–9 at p. 7.

9. *Cf.* Klos v. Mobile Oil Company, 55 N.J. 117, 259 A.2d 889 (1969). Also see the discussion of standardized coverages in § 2.8, below.

10. See, e.g., Robert I. Mehr & Emerson Cammach, PRINCIPLES OF INSURANCE (Sixth edition, 1976), at pp. 94–95; C. Arthur Wil-

liams & Richard M. Heins, RISK MANAGEMENT AND INSURANCE (Third edition, 1976), at pp. 441–443.

11. See, e.g., Arizona Insurance Statutes, Chapter 4, Article 8, Lloyd's Associations (1975); Illinois Insurance Code, Article V, Lloyds (1965); and Pennsylvania Insurance Laws, Article IX, Lloyds Associations (1971).

12. *Ibid.*

13. See, e.g., Illinois Insurance Code 73 § 698(2) (1965).

14. See the annual edition of BEST INSURANCE REPORTS.

15. New York—McKinney's Insurance Law, Article XII, § 425.4 (1980). Also see Alabama Insurance Code 1977, § 27–3–16.

exchange" patterned after Lloyd's of London.[16] By 1983, the New York Insurance Exchange had approved its 38th syndicate.[17] The New York Exchange "provides a facility for underwriting all kinds of domestic and international reinsurance, direct insurance on all kinds of risks located entirely outside the U.S., and direct insurance for some New York risks *   *   *." [18] In 1979, Illinois and Florida enacted legislation authorizing the establishment of insurance exchanges in those states.[19]

(2) Stock Companies

A stock insurance company is a private corporation that engages in the insurance business. As is generally true of private corporations, an insurer which is organized in this way is owned by investors (usually described as shareholders) who receive the profits, if any, through dividends. The shareholders of a corporation engaged in the insurance business are not personally liable to creditors of the corporation. In addition, the stockholders are also not liable to insureds in the event the company's reserves for the payment of claims are depleted.

The purchaser of an insurance policy from a stock company pays a predetermined price (generally referred to as a "premium"), and usually receives what is characterized as a "non-participating" policy. In some instances, however, stock companies issue "participating" policies which provide for the return of a portion of the profits to policyholders when the insurer's loss experience is better than that which was anticipated at the time the premium rates were set. When insurance is purchased from a stock company, neither participating nor non-participating policyholders are subject to assessments in the event an insurer does not have sufficient resources to pay claims. In contrast, purchasers of insurance policies from mutual insurers, discussed in the next sub-section, may in some circumstances be subject to such assessments.

(3) Mutual Insurers

There are several types of insurance organizations that are appropriately characterized as mutual insurers. Most mutual insurers are incorporated under state laws that establish special provisions for such entities. In general, mutual insurers are nonprofit associations or corporations in which each insured becomes a part owner of the entity and therefore is in effect both an insured and an insurer. When first arranging to acquire insurance from a mutual insurer, a person frequently pays a membership fee in addition to the premium which is charged for the coverage.

Historically mutual insurers often issued "assessable policies," under which policy holders were subject to being assessed in the event the

---

16. New York—McKinney's Insurance Law § 425(a) (1978).

17. *U.S. Exchanges Compared; New York Seen Becoming Significant Competitor of Lloyd's,* 94 Insurance Advocate (June 25, 1983) 21–22 at p. 21.

18. *Ibid.*

19. *Ibid.*

Also see *Lloyd's American Cousins,* 55–56 Journal of American Insurance (Fall, 1979), pp. 7–9.

insurers did not have sufficient funds to pay claims.[20]   When such policies are issued, the assessment provisions usually limit the amount a member may be required to contribute if the insurer's reserves are insufficient.   Although some policies with assessment provisions are still issued in the United States, most mutual insurers have accumulated adequate reserves so that the provisions are no longer essential, and policies currently sold by mutuals usually are non-assessable.[21]

In the early part of the twentieth century, many stock insurance companies were converted to mutuals.[22]   This trend was especially prevalent among companies providing life insurance, and a very substantial portion of the life insurance coverage sold in the United States is now written by mutual insurers.[23]

A *mutual benefit society,* often referred to as a *fraternal society,* is an insurer that is organized to provide insurance for members of an existing group such as a fraternity, sorority, or lodge.   In several states, such societies, which are probably the most ancient form of an insurance organization, have received favored treatment under state regulatory and tax laws.   During the first half of the twentieth century, however, a disturbing number of mutual benefit society financial failures led to a tightening of the regulations applicable to such insurers, especially with respect to the maintenance of reserves.[24]

20.   Some mutuals have generally operated by levying an assessment after losses have been determined.   For example, a system of assessments was used in the arrangement that was involved in Commissioner of Internal Revenue v. Treganowan, 183 F.2d 288 (2d Cir.1950), *cert. denied* 340 U.S. 853, 71 S.Ct. 82, 95 L.Ed. 625 (1950).

21.   "The bulk of insurance coverage currently written by mutual insurance companies is nonassessable * * *.   The nonassessable arrangement is made possible by the fact that, before nonassessable insurers are licensed to operate in a particular state, they must meet, in general, the same financial requirements stipulated for stock insurers.   Instead of having capital, however, the minimum surplus of nonassessable mutuals must equal the combined capital and surplus requirements of stock companies."   Denenberg, Eilers, Hoffman, Kline, Melone & Snider, RISK AND INSURANCE (1964), at p. 173, reprinted in Herbert Denenberg, Robert D. Eilers, Joseph J. Melone & Robert A. Zelten, RISK AND INSURANCE (Second Edition, 1974), at p. 197.

22.   Stock companies still write more insurance than mutuals in the fields of fire and casualty insurance.   See, e.g., Herbert Denenberg, Robert D. Eilers, Joseph J. Melone & Robert A. Zelten, RISK AND INSURANCE (Second Edition, 1974), at p. 205.

23.   According to the Institute of Life Insurance, LIFE INSURANCE FACT BOOK (1982), at p. 89:

"Of the companies in business at midyear 1981, a total of 1,842, or 93%, were owned by stockholders.   The remaining 136 were mutual companies.   Mutual companies, which are generally older and larger than the stockholder-owned companies, had 58% of the assets of all U.S. life companies and accounted for 44% of life insurance in force.   In the past 15 years, five companies have converted from the status of a mutual company to a stock company and two stock companies have converted to a mutual."

"At the year-end 1980, there were 189 life insurance companies that had been in business more than 50 years. * * *"

"The older companies, those over 100 years old, held the majority of assets and life insurance in force at the end of 1980, 63.7% and 48.5%, respectively. * * *"

24.   James L. Athearn, RISK AND INSURANCE (Second Edition, 1969), at p. 483; Albert H. Mowbray, Ralph H. Blanchard & C. Arthur Williams Jr., Insurance (Sixth Edition, 1969), at pp. 382–383.

Also see, New York—McKinney's Consolidated Laws Service, Insurance Law, Art. XIV, §§ 470–471 (1980).

Another type of mutual insurer is a *reciprocal association,* which is also referred to as an *inter-insurance exchange.* The members of such an association or aggregation [25] may be either individuals or entities, and they are usually referred to as "subscribers." The association members agree to share the losses for designated risks. Reciprocal associations operate through an attorney-in-fact, which is usually a corporation that has been established to manage and administer the contractual arrangements necessary for a reciprocal insurance arrangement.[26] The activities of an attorney-in-fact for a reciprocal association are often subject to regulation.[27] For example, the statutes in several states provide that the attorney-in-fact shall periodically file — with the commissioner of insurance — financial statements [28] and declarations of the kinds of insurance to be offered.[29] Originally, most reciprocal associations were created to provide either fire or automobile insurance.[30] More recently, such associations have been organized by hospitals and doctors for medical malpractice liability coverage.[31]

§ 2.1(b) Control Over Underwriting

(1) Centralization of the Power to Contract

One of the most fundamental and important aspects of any insurance company's operation is the process by which the decision is made about whether to underwrite a risk or a group of risks. Essentially, this is a question of who is authorized to make contracts on behalf of an

25. United States v. Weber Paper Company, 320 F.2d 199 (8th Cir.1963).

Also see Hoopeston Canning Company v. Cullen, 318 U.S. 313 at pp. 314–315, 63 S.Ct. 602 at p. 604, 87 L.Ed. 777, 145 A.L.R. 1113 (1943).

26. See the discussion in COUCH ON INSURANCE (Second Edition, 1984), at § 18:11.

27. Many states have recognized the peculiar character of reciprocal insurers and have enacted statutes which apply solely to reciprocals. For example, see West's Ann. California Insurance Code §§ 1280–1560 (1572 and 1983 Supp.); Iowa Code Ann. §§ 520.1–520.23 (West Supp.1983); Illinois—S.H.A. ch. 73, §§ 673–697; Massachusetts Gen. Laws Ann. c. 175, §§ 94A–94M; and New York McKinney's Insurance Law §§ 410–425–a (1980).

Wisconsin has adopted a somewhat different approach. In Wisconsin there is no specific statutory regulation of reciprocal insurers, but there is an expression of intent to subject reciprocals to the same accumulation of surplus requirements as those applicable to mutual corporations. See Wisconsin Legislative Service § 618.23 and the comment following that section.

28. West's Ann. California Insurance Code § 1430 (1972 & Supp.1983); Iowa Code Ann. § 520.4(8) (West Supp.1983).

29. West's Ann. California Insurance Code § 1320(b) (1972 & Supp.1983); Iowa Code Ann. § 520.4(3) (West Supp.1983).

30. However, reciprocal associations have been used for other types of insurance, as well. For example, the dispute in United States v. Weber Paper Company, 320 F.2d 199 (8th Cir.1963) involved the tax treatment of payments to the National Flood Underwriters, an inter-insurance exchange for flood insurance.

31. West's Ann. California Insurance Code § 1280.7 provides an exemption from reserve fund requirements when a reciprocal association or inter-insurance exchange consists of physicians and surgeons licensed in California, and contracts to indemnify solely in respect to medical malpractice claims against such members. However, such a reciprocal association of physicians and surgeons is required to create an initial medical liability trust fund in an amount not less than ten million dollars, and there are specific regulations that govern the investment of the trust fund. See West's Ann. California Insurance Code § 1280.7(a)(1) and (4) (Supp. 1983).

insurer. Insurers have developed many different approaches to exerting control over the underwriting decision. In some contexts, insurance companies seek to severely limit the number of persons who have the authority to contract with insurance purchasers. In its most extreme form, this is achieved through centralization of the authority so that the responsibility for deciding whether to issue insurance policies is restricted to a few persons. For example, companies marketing life insurance almost uniformly do not authorize their sales representatives (that is, agents, brokers or employees who deal with purchasers in the field) to decide whether to accept applications for insurance. The responsibility for deciding whether to issue "regular" contracts of life insurance, as distinguished from agreements for temporary or interim contracts,[1] is vested almost exclusively in persons who work in the home offices of life insurance companies.

(2) Decentralization of the Power to Contract

There are many marketing situations in which insurance companies have chosen to decentralize the authority to contract, so that numerous and widely scattered sales representatives of the insurer are expressly empowered to make commitments on behalf of a company.[2] Fire insurers and casualty insurers, for example, customarily grant sales representatives the authority to countersign, issue and deliver policies.[3] However, these insurers typically retain an element of centralized control over underwriting by including provisions, especially in fire [4] and other casualty [5] insurance policy forms, which give the insurer a right to cancel the coverage after the sales representative provides the company with a report of the transaction.[6] In some states, howev-

---

§ 2.1(b)

1. The power to make temporary or informal life insurance contracts is now explicitly given to many sales representatives, and in some circumstances may be created by a judicially imposed implied-in-law contract. See generally the discussion of temporary insurance contracts in § 2.3, below.

2. See generally, Emmett Vaughan & Curtis M. Elliott, FUNDAMENTALS OF RISK AND INSURANCE (1972), at pp. 78–79; G.F. Michelbacher & Nestor R. Roos, MULTIPLE-LINE INSURERS: THEIR NATURE AND OPERATION (Second edition, 1970), at pp. 4–9.

3. Granting sales representatives the power to bind on temporary insurance contracts constitutes a significant departure from centralized decisions on underwriting, and granting the power to issue long-term contracts is an even more substantial departure.

4. For example, see the provisions involved in National Security Fire & Casualty Company v. Mid-State Homes, Inc., 370 So.2d 1351 (Miss.1979), which provided in

part that the company reserved the right to cancel the policy "at any time."

5. For example, the following provision used in some casualty policies allows the insurer to cancel the policy for any reason, including for the company's convenience:

"＊ ＊ ＊ This policy *may be cancelled at any time* by this company by giving the insured five days written notice of cancellation ＊ ＊ ＊."

See Holder v. Hartford Fire Insurance Company, 257 So.2d 862 at p. 864 and p. 865 (Miss.1972) (emphasis added).

6. In many situations, a notice of cancellation is only effective when it is actually communicated to the insured. See, e.g., National Investors Fire & Casualty Insurance Company v. Chandler, 4 Ark.App. 116, 628 S.W.2d 593 (1982).

The exercise of the right to cancel can produce some interesting disputes, especially when the guidelines for cancellation included in the policy are not strictly adhered to by the insurer. For example, see Bradshaw v. Motors Insurance Corp., 263 Ark. 516, 566 S.W.2d 134 (1978).

er, cancellations by an insurance company are now subject to statutory regulations which limit the use of this approach to centralization.[7]

(3) Factors Bearing on Centralization

There are numerous factors which influence the degree to which insurers choose to centralize the authority to contract. Although some of these factors are common to all types of insurance, others are a function of the particular type of coverage being marketed. For this reason, insurers issuing policies covering similar risks or combinations of risks often adopt the same approaches to controlling the authority to contract. In addition, similar marketing patterns for some types of insurance may result from pressures for uniformity exerted by public regulatory authorities. Yet, it is also clear that variations in the degree of centralization occur not only in regard to different types of insurance, but also, though to a lesser extent, among insurers writing a single type of insurance.

The success of some types of insurance underwriting depends heavily on the experience and expertise of persons entrusted with the responsibility to decide whether to accept or reject an individual application for insurance. Accordingly, one of the most important of the factors which influence the allocation of underwriting authority is the extent to which there is or there should be an element of judgment exercised by the insurer. When it is desirable or essential that a substantial degree of discretion be employed, insurers tend to limit the power to contract to only a few persons situated in a home office. Centralized control over such underwriting is achieved by denying sales representatives the authority to bind an insurer, even temporarily, without home office approval. Life insurance companies that employ this approach regard the determination to underwrite a given risk as a highly judgmental matter.

To the extent that it is possible or desirable to dispense with the exercise of discretion in regard to underwriting, centralization of the authority to contract is not essential. If an insurance company decides that coverage will be sold to anyone who is willing to pay the premium, the need for centralization can be eliminated. The issuance of such an insurance contract can even be entrusted to a vending machine, which

In some states, the right of an insurer to cancel is now regulated by statutes. See note 7, below.

7. See, e.g., West's Ann. California Insurance Code (1984 Supplement), Chapter 9, Rescission; Chapter 10, Cancellation or Failure to Renew; Chapter 11, Cancellation and Failure to Renew Certain Property Insurance; Massachusetts General Laws Annotation §§ 187B–187D; New York C.L.S. Annotated Statutes 167–b (1980); Wisconsin Insurance Statutes Ann. §§ 631.36–631.37 (West Annotated Edition and 1984 Supplement).

Also see Terry v. Mongin Insurance Agency, 105 Wis.2d 575, 314 N.W.2d 349 (1982) (statute required insurance company to give its insured ten days notice of any midterm cancellation including coverage provided by a binder); State Automobile Mutual Insurance Company v. Babcock, 54 Mich.App. 194, 220 N.W.2d 717 (Div. 2, 1974) (coverage provided by a binder subject to the statute requiring ten days' notice for cancellation).

is exactly what is done in the case of life and accident insurance for air travel that is sold in many airports.[8] Similarly, when the entire membership of a large group or class will be covered, centralized control over underwriting decisions in regard to each individual in the group is usually not deemed essential. For example, when everyone in a large employee group is to be included as an insured for some type of coverage such as life, health, or disability insurance, an insurer usually does not review the insurability of individuals in the group. However, the underwriting decision in regard to the entire group would almost certainly be made by the executives of the insurer and would be influenced by factors that were characteristic of the particular group, such as hazardous activities involved in the employees' jobs.[9]

The length of time for which insurance policies are written usually is viewed as a factor that is relevant to centralization of the underwriting decision. Other considerations being equal, the longer the term of an insurance contract, the greater is a company's exposure and concomitantly the greater is the desire to exercise discretion in underwriting. Executives of most insurance companies believe that long-term risks should be considered by personnel in a home office before a commitment to provide coverage is made. It is possible, however, for an insurer to authorize field representatives to make long-term contracts and still maintain substantial centralized control by including a provision in those contracts for a right of cancellation that may be exercised at the discretion of underwriters in the home office. This is commonly done in the marketing of fire insurance and some allied lines,[10] and — in the absence of legislatively imposed restrictions — such provisions are undoubtedly enforceable so long as the purchaser is aware of the provision and the insurer gives the insured adequate notice of the decision to cancel the coverage. On the other hand, centralization is generally not practical for short term insurance contracts such as life and accident insurance for persons traveling by commercial airlines (often referred to as air travel trip insurance).[11]

A third factor bearing on centralization is the likelihood that prospective insureds will need or want coverage immediately upon making an application.[12] When delay in effecting coverage will be a substantial problem for purchasers, decentralization obviously has marketing advantages for an insurer.

A fourth factor bearing on centralization is the risk of liability that may result from commitments by sales representatives for insurance transactions that an insurer desires to avoid. Generally, sales repre-

---

8. See the discussion in § 2.7, below.

9. See Denenberg, Eilers, Hoffman, Kline, Melone & Snider, RISK AND INSUR-ANCE (1964), at p. 299 and p. 305, reprinted in Herbert Denenberg, Robert D. Eilers, Joseph J. Melone, and Robert A. Zelten, RISK AND INSURANCE (Second edition, 1974), at p. 157 and at p. 164.

10. See the discussion accompanying note 6, above.

11. See the discussion of trip insurance in § 2.7, below.

12. See the discussion in § 2.2(a), below.

sentatives in the field are less easily controlled by an insurer than are persons who work in a home office — that is, more mistakes and misfeasances in underwriting are likely to occur under a decentralized system. Accordingly, concern about this factor favors centralization on the rationale that proximity usually facilitates control over the performance of employees.

§ 2.1(c) Structuring the Marketing Transaction

(1) Offer, Acceptance, and Counteroffer

Insurance companies typically exercise considerable care in structuring their marketing arrangements, employing concepts or approaches that are fundamental to the formation of all contractual relationships.

A marketing transaction with an insurance purchaser is often initiated by an insurance company's sales representative, and the initiative frequently is structured as an invitation to the purchaser to make an offer.[1] In such a sales transaction, the sales representative[2] typically provides an application form for the purchaser to use in making known his or her interest in acquiring insurance, and a person who decides to purchase insurance is usually referred to as an applicant. The completed application is forwarded by the sales representative to the insurer for evaluation of the risk. By employing this type of marketing arrangement, an insurance company preserves its freedom to consider whether to undertake the risks entailed in providing insurance for the applicant. When this pattern is followed, the insurance company is placed in a position to form a contract by accepting the applicant's offer, thereby facilitating the centralization sought by many insurers.

Insurers frequently desire that an insurance contract will not be formed until some time after the insurer decides to issue the policy. For example, the application forms used by many insurers provide that the insurer's acceptance will not occur until and unless the insurer issues an insurance policy. And in some instances, insurance companies have even specified in the application forms that acceptance of an applicant's offer will not occur until the insurance policy is literally delivered to the applicant — that is, the insurer chooses to structure

---

§ 2.1(c)

1. See e.g., Simses v. North American Company for Life and Health Insurance, 175 Conn. 77, 394 A.2d 710 (1978); Barnes v. Atlantic & Pacific Life Insurance Company of America, 295 Ala. 149, 325 So.2d 143 (1975); United Insurance Company v. Headrick, 275 Ala. 594, 157 So.2d 19 (1963).

Also see Atkinson v. American Agency Life Insurance Company, 165 Ga.App. 102, 299 S.E.2d 600 (1983); Batiste v. Security

Insurance Group, 416 So.2d 279 at p. 282 (La.App., 3d Cir., 1982) (application for fire insurance); Reynolds v. Guarantee Reserve Life Insurance Company, 44 Ill.App.3d 764, 3 Ill.Dec. 397, 358 N.E.2d 940 (5th Dist., 1976).

See generally, 12 Appleman, INSURANCE LAW (1981), at § 7121 and § 7151.

2. See the discussion of sales representatives in § 2.5, below.

the arrangement so that acceptance is to be manifested by the physical delivery of the insurance policy to the applicant.[3]

Contract formation, or in some instances the effective date for coverage under a new insurance policy, may even be delayed to some time after an insurance policy is delivered to an applicant. For example, when a premium is not tendered with an application, a company may condition the initiation of coverage on receipt by the insurer of the first premium payment.[4]

In some marketing situations, insurers do intend to make offers that the potential purchaser may accept.[5] Life and accident insurance for travellers (often referred to as "trip insurance"), for example, is frequently sold through vending machines at airports.[6] In these circumstances, the communications from the company in the notices posted on or near the vending machines, as well as the terms stated in the forms dispensed by the machines, indicate that the insurer intends to make an offer to the purchaser. The purchaser's payment of the premium together with the completion of the forms constitutes an acceptance. The clear intent in such a marketing arrangement is that the transaction is concluded before the applicant departs on the trip by the insertion of the completed form and premium payment into the machine.

An insurance company sometimes responds to an application by proffering a coverage which differs from that which an applicant has sought. When a company tenders such a policy, its response is almost uniformly treated as a counteroffer, so that a contract is formed only if the applicant accepts the tendered policy.[7]

---

3. See, e.g., Reynolds v. Guarantee Reserve Life Insurance Company, 44 Ill.App. 3d 764, 3 Ill.Dec. 397, 358 N.E.2d 940 (5th Dist.1976); Hartford Accident & Indemnity Company v. McCullough, 235 Cal.App.2d 195, 44 Cal.Rptr. 915 (5th Dist.1965).

Also see Barnes v. Atlantic & Pacific Life Insurance Company of America, 295 Ala. 149, 325 So.2d 143 (1975).

The importance of delivery in some transactions is discussed in the following sub-sections.

4. For example, see the insurance clauses involved in Saunders v. National Old Line Insurance Company, 266 Ark. 247, 583 S.W.2d 58 (Div. 2, 1979); Shipley v. Ohio National Life Insurance Company, 199 F.Supp. 782 (W.D.Pa.1961), *affirmed* 296 F.2d 728 (3d Cir.1961).

Also see 1 COUCH ON INSURANCE (Second Edition, 1984), § 7:16 and § 7:18.

5. *Cf.* Riordan v. Auto Club of New York, Inc., 100 Misc.2d 638, 422 N.Y.S.2d 811 (New York County, 1979); Klos v. Mobile Oil Company, 55 N.J. 117, 259 A.2d 889 (1969).

6. Concerning trip insurance generally, see § 2.7, below.

7. See, e.g., Liberty National Life Insurance Company v. Smith, 356 So.2d 646 (Ala.1978); Dunford v. United of Omaha, 95 Idaho 282 at p. 285, 506 P.2d 1355 at p. 1358 (1973).

Also see United States Fire Insurance Company v. Western, 586 S.W.2d 153 (Tex. Civ.App., Fort Worth, 1979) (fire insurance policy).

Cf. Long v. New York Life Insurance Company, 106 Wash. 458, 180 P. 479 (1919).

See generally 12 Appleman, INSURANCE LAW (1981), § 7151; 1 COUCH ON INSURANCE (Second edition, 1959), § 7:17 and § 7:20; Annotation, *Temporary, life, accident, or health insurance pending approval of application or issuance of policy,* 2 A.L.R.2d 943–1022 at p. 982 (1948).

But cf. Wanshura v. State Farm Life Insurance Company, 275 N.W.2d 559 (Minn.1978), in which the court upheld a constructive delivery of a life insurance policy with a monthly premium that was

An insurer's carefully planned structuring of the marketing transaction may be overridden by legal constraints imposed by statute, administrative regulation, or judicial precedent. The responses of the courts in numerous cases involving the marketing strategies employed by many insurers for life insurance provide a clear example of such judicial intervention, and these decisions are discussed in the next subsection and in Section 2.3, below.

(2) Interim Coverage

When an individual submits an application for life insurance together with the payment of the first premium, insurers sometimes provide interim coverage.[8] In addition, in many jurisdictions interim coverage arises as a matter of law when an application for life insurance is accompanied by the payment of the first premium.[9]

The existence of interim or temporary coverage leads to questions about when such coverage terminates. In instances when an insurer decides not to underwrite the insurance the applicant sought, the insurer will either reject the application or offer the applicant coverage terms which differ from those sought in the application. The communication from the insurer — which either proposes coverage that differs in some respect from the insurance plan that was applied for or rejects the application — is generally an important and sometimes a critical factor in determining when the temporary coverage ceases to exist.

Delivery of an insurer's counteroffer to or rejection of an application for insurance has been held by courts in many jurisdictions to be an essential step in terminating the interim coverage [10] — that is, many judicial decisions hold that insurance applicants are entitled to have the interim coverage continued until the applicant is actually informed of the insurer's actions on the application by receipt of the communication from the insurer.[11] In these decisions, the courts employ principles that serve to protect the reasonable expectations of an applicant.[12]

more than 2 times the amount the agent indicated the premium would be and that did not contain a waiver of premium disability clause requested by the applicant.

8. See the discussion of temporary coverage in § 2.3, below.

9. *Ibid.*

10. See, e.g., Quindlen v. Prudential Insurance Company of America, 482 F.2d 876 (5th Cir.1973); National Investors Fire and Casualty Insurance Company, 4 Ark.App. 116, 628 S.W.2d 593 (1982).

Also see State Automobile Mutual Insurance Company v. Babcock, 54 Mich.App. 194, 220 N.W.2d 717 (Div. 2, 1974) (binder for automobile insurance while application for automobile insurance was pending).

In Collister v. Nationwide Life Insurance Company, 479 Pa. 579 at p. 583, 388 A.2d 1346 at p. 1348 (1978), *cert. denied* 439 U.S.

1089, 99 S.Ct. 871, 59 L.Ed.2d 55 (1979), the court observed the temporary insurance contract extended "from acceptance of the premium deposit until Nationwide either rejected the application * * * or accepted the application and issued the policy applied for."

11. See, e.g., Smith v. Westland Life Insurance Company, 15 Cal.3d 111, 123 Cal.Rptr. 649, 539 P.2d 433 (1975); Dunford v. United of Omaha, 95 Idaho 282 at p. 285, 506 P.2d 1355 at p. 1358 (1973).

See generally, Annotation, *Temporary life, accident, or health insurance pending approval of application or issuance of policy,* 14 A.L.R.3d 943–1022 (1948).

Also see the discussion in § 2.3, below.

12. See, e.g., Smith v. Westland Life Insurance Company, 15 Cal.3d 111, 123 Cal.Rptr. 649, 539 P.2d 433 (1975).

The appropriateness of applying the contract rules that govern offer, acceptance, and counteroffer depends on several factors. When a coverage dispute arises, in many situations an examination of the communications may provide a clear rationale for determining the rights of the parties on the basis of an application of traditional concepts and doctrines of contract law.[13] In some instances, however, disputes are and should be resolved on the basis of other legal constraints or public policy interests.[14]

(3) Delivery of an Insurance Policy

Attaching importance to the delivery of an insurance policy as an essential step in the formation of a contractual relationship has largely been restricted to the marketing of life insurance. Delivery of a life insurance policy has been viewed as significant in several respects.[15] *First,* delivery of the policy is frequently designated as the means by which the insurer communicates acceptance of the applicant's offer so that a contract is formed.[16] *Second,* when an insurer tenders a policy that differs from the coverage requested in an application, delivery of such a policy serves as a counteroffer.[17] *Third,* in situations when acceptance of an application may be effective without delivery, delivery of the policy to an insured may still be established by the insurer as a condition precedent to commencement of responsibility for the risk that is the subject of insurance — as, for example, when coverage is conditioned on delivery to an applicant who is alive and in good health.[18] *Fourth,* especially if delivery has been used to determine when coverage begins, the date of delivery may be used to ascertain the date that coverage terminates in the absence of a renewal of the

Also see Hornaday v. Sun Life Insurance Company of America, 597 F.2d 90 (7th Cir. 1979) (applying Indiana law that notification and a return of the consideration paid is required for termination, but that coverage did not extend beyond the expiration of the 60 day period specified in the conditional receipt).

See generally the discussion in § 6.3, below.

13. See e.g., Klos v. Mobile Oil Company, 55 N.J. 117, 259 A.2d 889 (1969) (under special arrangement for marketing to credit card holders, the company's communications constituted an offer and the completed "application" was an acceptance); Scott Transfer, Inc. v. Excalibur Insurance Company, Inc., 149 Ga.App. 46, 253 S.E.2d 438 (1979) (acceptance may be inferred from acts and conduct of an insured).

14. See especially the discussion of judicial restructuring of life insurance marketing transactions in 2.3(c), below.

Cf. Hemenway v. MFA Life Insurance Company, 211 Neb. 193, 318 N.W.2d 70 (1982), in which the court held that a policy of health insurance was effective on the date of the application, rather than on the delivery of the policy to the applicant, when the application was accompanied by the payment of the initial premium and the condition that the applicant was insurable for the plan applied for was satisfied by the insurer's decision to provide such a policy.

15. See generally Edwin Patterson, *Delivery of a Life Insurance Policy,* 33 Harvard Law Review 198–222 (1919); 1 Appleman, INSURANCE LAW (1981), at § 131–133; 12 Appleman, INSURANCE LAW (1981), at § 7156.

16. See the discussion of "delivery" in § 2.1(c)(1), above.

17. *Ibid.*

18. United Travelers Insurance Company v. Perkins, 611 S.W.2d 152 (Tex.Civ. App., Waco, 1981); Saunders v. National Old Line Insurance Company, 266 Ark. 247, 583 S.W.2d 58 (Div. 2, 1979).

Also see the cases discussed in § 2.3(c), above.

insurance policy.[19] *Fifth,* delivery of a policy to an individual has frequently been viewed by courts as evidence of the existence of coverage.[20] Although possession of an insurance policy by an individual is not a conclusive demonstration that an insurance contract is in effect, courts have concluded that possession justifies that inference in the absence of another explanation or the presentation of some defense by an insurer. *Sixth,* delivery of the insurance policy is an act that often marks the end of the temporary coverage.[21] *Finally,* delivery of a policy serves to terminate the insurer's opportunity to decide to decline the coverage sought by an applicant.[22]

Life insurers often include clauses in both insurance applications and insurance policy forms which provide that the coverage shall not take effect until the policy is delivered.[23] These terms may result in a relatively rigid or formalistic approach to claims that result from occurrences that precede the physical delivery of an insurance policy. Insurance marketing is highly standardized and systematized so that it is usually possible to determine from written records what action has been taken on any particular application without reference to whether an insurance policy was physically delivered to an applicant.[24] Courts have sometimes rendered such a delivery requirement ineffectual by finding constructive delivery,[25] or by recognizing some barrier to en-

19. See the discussion of the duration of coverage and anniversary dates for insurance coverages in § 5.10(b), below.

20. *Cf.* Scott Transfer, Inc. v. Excalibur Insurance Company, Inc., 149 Ga.App. 46, 253 S.E.2d 438 (1979).

21. See, e.g., the binding receipt language for clause "C" on the "Termination of Temporary Insurance Under This Receipt," used by Liberty National Insurance Company, and reproduced in Blanton v. Liberty National Life Insurance Company, 434 So.2d 773 at p. 774–75 (Ala.1983), *appeal after remand* 476 So.2d 67 (Ala.1985).

Also see Collister v. Nationwide Life Insurance Company, 479 Pa. 579 at p. 583, 388 A.2d 1346 at p. 1348 (1978) (temporary coverage extends until the insurer "either rejected the application * * * or accepted the application and issued the policy applied for").

22. Also consider the discussion in § 2.3(c), below.

23. See the cases and commentaries cited in § 2.1(c)(1), above.

A variation on this theme is a clause in an application form declaring that if the premium is not paid at the time when the application is made, the insurance applied for "shall become effective on the date of issue stated in the policy PROVIDED the Company has approved this application at its Home Office, the premium has been paid, and the policy delivered to me while I am in good health."

Concerning the requirement of delivery during "good health" of the applicant, see generally § 6.6(e)(4), below.

24. Other forms of communication of the insurer's acceptance or counter-offer may be used instead of delivery, and other evidence of the consummation of an agreement may be available.

25. See, e.g., Kramer v. Metropolitan Life Insurance Company, 494 F.Supp. 1026 at p. 1031 (D.N.J.1980). The court concluded that "even though the sales representative of the insurer's had no authority to deliver the policy to the Kramers without first determining their state of health * * * constructive delivery may still be found if the failure to actually deliver the policy to the insured was caused by the negligence of the agent who had possession of the policy."

Also see Wanshura v. State Farm Life Insurance Company, 275 N.W.2d 559 (Minn.1978) (constructive delivery of a life insurance policy occurred when the insurer delivered the policy to its agent and the only remaining acts for the agent were ministerial).

Cf. Powell v. Republic National Life Insurance Company, 337 So.2d 1291 (Ala. 1976) (delivery of a disability insurance

forcement of terms in an application or an insurance policy stipulating delivery to be essential.[26] Professor Patterson aptly described the judicial responses to the development of such delivery terms and to other provisions used by life insurance companies to delay the effective date for life insurance coverage, as "flanking movements" by the courts to prevent injustices that would otherwise result from adherence to the terms prescribed by insurers.[27]

§ 2.2 Oral Contracts of Insurance

§ 2.2(a) Usefulness and Disadvantages of Oral Agreements

Applicants for insurance often desire that coverage start immediately. For example, an insurance purchaser may request that the commencement of coverage coincide with the imminent transfer of some property interest.[1] Requests for immediate coverage often can be facilitated through the use of an oral agreement. In general it seems desirable to allow insurers to meet the need or desire for immediate coverage through the use of oral agreements if this can be done without an undue sacrifice of other public interests.

policy complete when the policy was mailed by the company to the agent).

Also see discussion of constructive delivery in New York Life Insurance Company v. Ollich, 42 F.2d 399 (6th Cir.1930) and Kramer v. Metropolitan Life Insurance Company, 494 F.Supp. 1026 (D.N.J.1980).

But cf. Pruitt v. Great So. Life Insurance Company, 202 La. 527, 12 So.2d 261 (1942), 145 A.L.R. 1427 (1943). In *Pruitt,* the court held that when the policy clause specified *actual* delivery to and acceptance by the applicant of the policy while he was in good health, there was no coverage in effect when the applicant died after the policy had been issued and sent to the insurance agent but before the agent acted to deliver the policy.

See generally Annotation, *Transmission of insurance policy to as satisfying provisions requiring delivery to insured,* 19 A.L.R.3d 953–1002 (1968).

26. Prudence Mutual Casualty Company v. Switzer, 253 Miss. 143, 175 So.2d 476 (1965), 19 A.L.R.3d 946 (1968) (under entire contract statute, requirement of delivery to the applicant during the applicant's lifetime ineffective when not incorporated into policy); Pierce v. New York Life Insurance Company, 174 Mo.App. 383, 160 S.W. 40 (1913) (finding a waiver of the requirement of delivery).

27. Edwin Patterson, *Delivery of a Life Insurance Policy,* 33 Harvard Law Review 198–222 (1919).

Concerning accommodation between demands for flexibility and certainty, and related problems of use of evaluative standards of judgment, see § 1.4, above.

§ 2.2(a)

1. Insurance coverage for motor vehicles often is the subject of oral exchanges between a sales representative and an insurance purchaser who desires immediate coverage. For example, see Hartford Accident & Indemnity Company v. Oglesby, 293 Ala. 620, 308 So.2d 695 (1975), in which the court held the agent had authority to make a preliminary oral contract.

Hail insurance. One who thinks of the social need as affected by the human tendency to postpone the buying of insurance until exposure to the risk reaches some high point in the curve of fluctuations (specifically, the tendency to wait until the hail season to buy hail insurance) and also considers it desirable to encourage large numbers of people to carry the insurance so as to spread the risk widely, may conclude that there is even more reason for upholding an arrangement for immediate insurance in the case of the hail risk than in the case of fire and collision. *Cf.* Gulbrandson v. Empire Mutual Insurance Company, 251 Minn. 387, 87 N.W.2d 850 (1958).

That oral transactions are disadvantageous in some ways cannot be denied. Among the principal disadvantages are the difficulties of ascertaining both the existence of an agreement and the terms in the event a coverage dispute arises.[2] Oral transactions also increase the risk that a sales representative may fail to raise with an applicant matters that should be considered and decided in selecting the types of coverage or in settling some important terms of an insurance contract, with the consequence that a claimant either has no coverage when a loss occurs or coverage is afforded under conditions that the insured would not have chosen or approved. In addition, uncertainties of proof also enhance the possibilities for some types of misfeasance in regard to such transactions. For example, an insurance agent or broker may be tempted to help out a friend after an uninsured loss has occurred by falsely testifying that an oral agreement for an insurance coverage had been made before the event occurred. Although the imposition of a prompt reporting requirement for coverage commitments made by sales representatives may reduce such risks for insurers, that procedure will not eliminate all the possibilities for various types of misfeasance and mistakes by sales representatives.[3]

The disadvantages that could result from oral transactions for insurance have not been viewed as sufficiently compelling to warrant general statutory prohibitions that restrict or limit the enforceability of insurance commitments that have not been reduced to writing. Furthermore, despite some early dicta [4] and occasional subsequent assumptions to the contrary,[5] it is well established that there is no prohibition of decisional origin against oral contracts of insurance or oral binders.[6]

2. See, e.g., Special Jet Services, Inc. v. Federal Insurance Company, 643 F.2d 977 (3d Cir.1981).

Cf. Hilt Truck Lines, Inc. v. Riggins, 756 F.2d 676 (8th Cir.1985).

3. When an insurer operates under a marketing arrangement that allows oral contracts to be made in the field, it usually will exercise closer supervision over its field personnel than if contracts are made only in the home office. The costs to insurers of allowing such contracts is more than the expense of such supervision, however, because the creation of insurance contracts in the field often proves to be a fertile ground in which to find evidence that supports a claim of rights at variance with policy provisions. See the discussion of variance claims in Chapter 6, below.

4. See, e.g., Cockerill v. Cincinnati Mutual Insurance Company, 16 Ohio 148 (1847). The decision in *Cockerill* was discredited by later Ohio decisions, including Newark Mach. Company v. Kenton Insurance Company, 50 Ohio St. 549, 555, 35 N.E. 1060, 1062 (1893).

5. See, e.g., Gulbrandson v. Empire Mutual Insurance Company, 251 Minn. 387, 87 N.W.2d 850 (1958), treating the question of validity of a partly oral contract of hail insurance as a debatable issue and resolving the issue in favor of validity after observing that previous cases in the same jurisdiction had upheld oral contracts of fire, collision, and workers' compensation insurance.

6. For example, in State Farm Mutual Automobile Insurance Company v. Newell, 270 Ala. 550, 120 So.2d 390 at p. 390 (1960) (involving motor vehicle insurance), the court observed: "Our cases follow the general rule that, unless prohibited by statute, an oral contract of insurance is valid * * *."

In Brandywine Shoppe, Inc. v. State Farm Fire & Casualty Company, 307 A.2d 806 at p. 808 (Del.Sup.1973), the court observed: "It is well recognized that oral contracts of insurance, or binders, are valid and this is so even in jurisdictions which require that insurance contracts be in writing."

Though it is a common practice to use oral agreements for temporary commitments (that is, to arrange for the immediate extension of insurance for various types of fire, marine, and casualty insurance), both insurers and insureds ordinarily find it desirable to reduce such oral exchanges to some type of written record relatively soon after the transaction occurs. Especially when it is anticipated that an appreciable time is likely to pass before the insurance policy will be issued by the insurer, sales representatives — agents or brokers — often will use a written binder. When a written binder is used, uncertainty about either the existence of or the terms of the contract is substantially reduced.

§ 2.2(b) Requisites for Oral Contracts

The elements that are required for an enforceable oral agreement for insurance are derived from basic contract law rules that require a manifestation of agreement on all essential terms. In an insurance transaction, the essential terms include (1) the subject matter to be covered by the insurance, (2) the risk insured against, (3) the premium, (4) the duration of the contract, (5) the amount of the coverage, and (6) the identity of the parties.[1] However, not all of these matters must be specifically referred to in the communications between the parties. In some situations, the requisite elements may be proved by evidence that

Also see Gulf Insurance Company v. Grisham, 126 Ariz. 123, 613 P.2d 283 (1980) (In Division) (liability and hull insurance for a small plane); Rabb v. Public National Insurance Company, 243 F.2d 940 (6th Cir. 1957) (Kentucky law).

Cf. Service v. Pyramid Life Insurance Company, 201 Kan. 196, 440 P.2d 944 (1968) (life insurance); Harden v. St. Paul Fire & Marine Insurance Company, 51 N.M. 55, 178 P.2d 578 (1947); Elliott v. Standard Accident Insurance Company, 92 N.H. 505, 33 A.2d 562 (1943) (motor vehicle insurance); Milwaukee Bedding Company v. Graebner, 182 Wis. 171, 196 N.W. 533 (1923).

See generally, 12 Appleman, INSURANCE LAW AND PRACTICE (1943), § 7191; 1 COUCH ON INSURANCE (1959), at pp. 573–81, § 14.5; Annotation, *Oral contracts of insurance,* 92 A.L.R. 232–240 (1934); and Annotation, *Temporary fire, wind, or hail insurance pending issuance of policy,* 14 A.L.R.3d 568–623 (1967).

Legislation in Wisconsin specifically authorized oral contracts of insurance. See Wisconsin Statutes Annotated § 631.05, (Stats.1979–80.)

Also see cases cited in § 2.2(c), below.

§ 2.2(b)

1. See Gulf Insurance Company v. Grisham, 126 Ariz. 123, 613 P.2d 283 (1980) (In Division) (involving liability insurance for a small plane); Cormack v. American Underwriters Corp., 94 Mich.App. 379, 288 N.W.2d 634 (1979) (automobile insurance); Saggau v. State Farm Mutual Insurance Company, 16 Ariz.App. 361, 493 P.2d 528 (Div. 1, Dept. B., 1972) (automobile insurance).

Also see National Surety Corporation v. Brunswick Corporation, 391 F.2d 26 (5th Cir.1968) (fire insurance).

But see, e.g., Rabb v. Public National Insurance Company, 243 F.2d 940 at p. 942 and p. 944 (6th Cir.1957) (applying Kentucky law), sustaining a lower court finding against the claim of an oral contract of automobile insurance for a soldier applicant who experienced difficulty in finding a company interested in writing insurance for his class of risk.

Also see Annotation, *What constitutes "Direct Loss" under windstorm insurance coverage,* 65 A.L.R.3d 1128–1173 (1975); Annotation, *Temporary fire, wind, or hail insurance pending issuance of policy,* 14 A.L.R.3d 568–623 (1967), and Annotation, *Temporary automobile insurance pending issuance of policy,* 12 A.L.R.3d 1304–1340 (1967).

shows an understanding, express or implied, that customary terms for the policy ordinarily used by the insurer are to apply.[2]

In practice, a transaction between an applicant and an insurer is hardly ever completely oral. Yet the phrase "oral contract" is commonly used to refer to any transaction in which a major aspect is oral, including instances when an oral understanding adopts the terms of the insurer's standard form by either an express or an implied reference.[3]

§ 2.2(c) Oral Insurance Contracts and the Statutes of Frauds

In general, oral insurance contracts have not been held to be unenforceable as a result of the application of the provisions which have typically been included in statutes of frauds. Although insurance contracts usually have not been treated as subject to statutes of frauds, occasionally attempts have been made to subject certain types of insurance transactions to the statutes' requirements.

(1) Oral Agreements to Arrange for Renewals

Most of the cases in which the courts have considered a defense based on the statute of frauds have arisen as a result of commitments by sales representatives to keep insurance in force by arranging for insurance policies to be renewed. These cases involve the provision, commonly included in statutes of frauds, that a writing is a prerequisite to enforceability of a contract that is not to be performed within one year. This provision potentially applies to any agreement by which an intermediary makes a commitment to ensure the continuance of insurance coverage by arranging for renewals.

There are some appellate decisions which hold that in the absence of a writing, the statute of frauds provision precluding enforcement of contracts not to be performed within one year applies to an oral agreement by which an insurance agent or broker promises to keep an insurance policy in force by taking care of periodic renewals. In regard to the applicability of this statute of frauds provision to such arrangements, it has been suggested that a distinction should be drawn be-

---

2. See, e.g., Terry v. Mongin Insurance Agency, 105 Wis.2d 575, 314 N.W.2d 349 (1982); Cormack v. American Underwriters Corp., 94 Mich.App. 379, 288 N.W.2d 634 (1979) (court will infer an implied promise to pay the ordinary amount charged by an insurer for added coverage).

Also see Humenik v. Siwek, 266 Minn. 491, 124 N.W.2d 191 (1963) (oral contract of automobile liability insurance based only on uncontradicted testimony that the agent had assured the defendant that the driver of car would be "covered"; terms of coverage apparently assumed by the court to be those of an earlier written policy issued by the company or of a written policy on the car that did not provide coverage for driver); Elliott v. Standard Acci-

dent Insurance Company, 92 N.H. 505, 33 A.2d 562 (1943).

Cf. Milwaukee Bedding Company v. Graebner, 182 Wis. 171, 196 N.W. 533 (1923) (statutory prescription).

The representations or statements made by a sales representative may bind the insurer. General Insurance Company of America v. Truly Nolen of America, Inc., 136 Ariz. 142, 664 P.2d 686 (App., Div. 1, Dept. D, 1983).

Also see the discussion of the authority of a sales representative to bind an insurer in § 2.5(b), below.

3. In any event, the evidence of customary terms will ordinarily be based on documentary evidence.

tween two types of such agreements. One class would include both agreements to issue policies from year to year for a specified period of years [1] and agreements to arrange for a renewal at the end of a specified period (such as three years).[2] The other class would be agreements that, though they are similar in nature and purpose in that there is a commitment by a sales representative to arrange for the renewal of policies in subsequent years, are expressly subject to being terminated in the event the insured so notifies the sales representative.[3] The suggestion is that the statute of frauds only applies to the first class of cases. Distinguishing between the two types of cases on the basis of the insured's express right to terminate the agreement seems to be a distinction of dubious merit.[4]

There appears to be little justification for any differentiation in regard to whether such agreements are or should be subject to the statute of frauds limitation. Any insured almost surely has an option to terminate an arrangement in the first type of situation as well as the second.[5] Moreover, even if the option to terminate does not exist in both types of transactions, such an option should not be a decisive difference in these cases because the possibility of premature termination within a year, as distinguished from complete performance within that period, is not generally regarded as exempting an agreement from the statute of frauds.[6]

§ 2.2(c)

1. See, e.g., Harrower v. Insurance Company of North America, 144 Ark. 279, 222 S.W. 39 (1920).

2. See, e.g., Green v. Hartford Fire Insurance Company, 157 Miss. 316, 128 So. 107, 69 A.L.R. 554 (1930).

3. See, e.g., First Baptist Church v. Brooklyn Fire Insurance Company, 19 N.Y. 305 (1859).

Contra. See, e.g., Klein v. Liverpool & London & Globe Insurance Company, 22 Ky.L.Rep. 301, 57 S.W. 250 (Court of Appeals, 1900).

Professor Patterson and Professor Vance, in criticism of the *Klein* decision, argue that the latter agreement is outside the statute of frauds because it might be wholly performed within one year. See Patterson, ESSENTIALS OF INSURANCE LAW (Second edition, 1957), at p. 83 and Vance, LAW OF INSURANCE (Third edition, Anderson, 1951), at p. 222, n. 42.

Also see the discussion in Frontier Insurance Agency, Inc. v. Hartford Fire Insurance Company, 262 Or. 470, 499 P.2d 1302 (1972). The Oregon Supreme Court concluded that where the fire insurance policy itself could be cancelled either at the request of the insured or by the insurer giving the insured five days' written notice, neither party was bound for more than one year, and thus an oral contract for additional coverage under such policy was not unenforceable under the statute of frauds.

4. There may, of course, be an express right to terminate an insurance agreement, as well as the agreement to renew the coverage.

5. In Frontier Insurance Agency, Inc. v. Hartford Fire Insurance Company, 262 Ore. 470, 499 P.2d 1302 (1972), the court noted that the fire insurance policy itself could be cancelled at any time by the insured or the insurer, and then held that "if a contract, otherwise to continue for more than a year, is by its own terms subject to termination within a year, it is not within the Statute of Frauds." *Id.*, 499 P.2d at p. 1308.

Professor Corbin takes the view that the words "agreement that is not to be performed" indicate that the statute of frauds will not operate if the slightest possibility exists that the contract can be fully performed within one year. See 2 Corbin, CONTRACTS (1950), § 444, at p. 535.

6. See Lon L. Fuller & Robert Braucher, BASIC CONTRACT LAW (1964), at p. 806; 3 Williston, CONTRACTS (Third edition, 1960), at § 498 and § 596.

Any attempt to enforce an alleged oral agreement for periodic renewal of an insurance policy presents a conflict between the principle underlying the statute of frauds and the principle underlying redress for detrimental reliance. Even if the application of a statute of frauds would defeat a claim based merely on breach of an oral contract for periodic renewals, a claim grounded on estoppel and supported by proof of detrimental reliance should be sustained.[7] And this contention is significantly strengthened in those instances in which transactions were arranged for several years before the occasion when a renewal was overlooked, thereby precipitating a claim.[8]

(2) Guaranty Insurance

The limited judicial precedents in point support the proposition that guaranty insurance is not affected by the provision in many statutes of frauds which requires that a promise to answer for the debt of another be in writing.[9] This result is sound. It is realistic to view guaranty insurance as coverage against the risk that the debtor will default. The more difficult question is whether distinguishing between such oral insurance contracts and oral promises to answer for the debts of another erodes the public policy underlying the statute of frauds. It probably does not, at least in the case of insurance contracts made by a professional insurer whose business is in any event regulated extensively under other and more specialized statutes.

(3) Reinsurance Agreements

A reinsurance arrangement is an independent contract between an original insurer and another insurer, providing that the latter shall pay the former. Reinsurance is not a contract by which the reinsurer

---

7. Estoppel has been repeatedly recognized as a basis for avoidance of the statute of frauds generally. See Annotation, *Promissory estoppel as basis for avoidance of statute of frauds,* 56 A.L.R.3d 1037–1077 (1974). Also see 3 Williston, CONTRACTS (Third edition, 1960), § 533A, and 2 Corbin, CONTRACTS (Supps.1971 and 1980), § 422A.

The view in the Restatement of Contracts, Second, is that an oral contract, otherwise unenforceable by operation of the statute of frauds, is enforceable if the promisor should reasonably have expected reliance on the part of the promisee and if injustice can be avoided only by enforcement of the contract. See, Restatement of Contracts, Second, § 139.

8. See, e.g., Sanborn v. Maryland Casualty Company, 255 Iowa 1319, 125 N.W.2d 758 (1964).

Concerning detrimental reliance generally see § 6.3, below; concerning this and other theories of rights at variance with policy provisions in marketing contexts, see § 6.8, below.

Keeton & Widess, Ins.Law—3

9. See, e.g., Quinn-Shepherdson v. United States Fidelity & Guaranty Company, 142 Minn. 428, 172 N.W. 693 (1919).

Contra. See, e.g., Commonwealth v. Hinson, 143 Ky. 428, 136 S.W. 912 (1911); Wainwright Trust Company v. United States Fidelity & Guaranty Company, 63 Ind.App. 309, 114 N.E. 470 (1916).

Only a few cases have confronted this issue. *Quinn-Shepherdson* appears to be the only case which explicitly supports the proposition in the text, and the court recognized the logical force of the arguments made in *Commonwealth v. Henson* and *Wainwright v. U.S. Fidelity.* In a 1941 Montana case, Austin v. New Brunswick Fire Insurance Company, 111 Mont. 192, 108 P.2d 1036 (1940), which involved an automobile liability policy, the court held that the primary intent was to protect the insured rather than the third party, and therefore the purpose was indemnity rather than guaranty.

promises to pay the original insurer's obligation to the original insured. It is the "debtor" who is being insured, not the "creditor." This is not an agreement with a creditor to answer for a default of a debtor,[10] and it seems clear that contracts of reinsurance should not be affected by a statutory provision requiring that a promise to answer for the debt of another be in writing.[11]

§ 2.2(d)   Oral Contracts and the Potential Impact of Sanctions

A court or legislature attempting to evaluate the full range of problems associated with oral commitments for insurance should consider what would be the effect of sanctions if the statute of frauds were to be recognized as a defense to the enforcement of an oral agreement for insurance. It might be argued that consistently imposing the loss on the insurance purchaser whenever the requisites for a valid oral contract were not met would lead, especially in the business community, to a general awareness of the effect of such restrictive rules and of the consequences of violating them.[1] However, it seems doubtful that even a uniform denial of recovery would accomplish this objective. In fact, because insurers are the parties who are in the better position to affect the nature of the marketing transactions, imposing sanctions on the insurer would seem to offer a superior prospect for influencing conduct in the market place.

Unfortunately, there is no obvious way to enforce either the outright restrictions against oral contracts — or even the less rigorous restrictions implicit in requiring the particular requisites for oral contracts — without causing the losses to fall generally on insurance purchasers rather than on insurance companies. Recognition of this fact — even though it is rarely, if ever, articulated — almost certainly contributes to the reluctance of the courts to allow the statute of frauds provisions to be raised as a defense to claims that arise from oral commitments by the sales representatives of insurers.

§ 2.2(e)   Specific Provisions That Require Written Contracts or Written Documents

To the extent that oral agreements for insurance are unenforceable, this is almost always a result of statutory provisions directed at specific types of insurance transactions. State legislatures, of course, have the power to require that insurance contracts be in writing. For

---

10. *Cf.* the transactions involved in Weingart v. Allen & O'Hara, Inc., 654 F.2d 1096 (5th Cir.1981), and Barclays Bank of New York v. Goldman, 517 F.Supp. 403 (S.D.N.Y.1981).

11. See, e.g., Commercial Mutual Marine Insurance Company v. Union Mutual Insurance Company, 60 U.S. (19 How.) 318, 15 L.Ed. 636 (1856).

Also see 3 Williston, CONTRACTS (Third edition, 1960), 482 n. 19.

But see Egan v. Firemen's Insurance Company, 27 La.Ann. 368 (1875).

§ 2.2(d)

1. The argument might be further extended to suggest that this would result in fewer situations in which persons think they are insured and only discover that is not the case after suffering a loss.

example, before the development of statutes of general application which regulated the formation of insurance companies, a prohibition against oral transactions was occasionally included in a charter for an insurance company that was granted by a special act of legislation.[1] In addition, some jurisdictions have adopted statutes which limit the duration of oral binders.[2]

In some states, statutory provisions — such as those requiring certain standard provisions[3] in specific types of insurance coverages or regulating the manner in which a policy is to be executed[4] — have on rare occasions been interpreted as implicitly forbidding oral agreements for insurance.[5]

In a few states, prohibitions against oral contracts, which are imposed only rarely in relation to property insurance, have been applied somewhat more frequently in relation to life, health, and accident insurance.[6]

§ 2.2(e)

1. See, e.g., Head & Amory v. Providence Insurance Company, 6 U.S. (2 Cranch) 127, 167, 1 L.Ed. 229, 242 (1804).

Concerning the effect of charter provisions on oral contracts, see, e.g., Franklin Fire Insurance Company v. Colt, 87 U.S. (20 Wall.) 560, 22 L.Ed. 423 (1874); Sanborn v. Fireman's Insurance Company, 82 Mass. (16 Gray) 448, 77 Am.Dec. 419 (1860).

See also Annotation, *Oral contracts of insurance,* 15 A.L.R. 995–1021 at pp. 1001–1004 (1921).

2. Such a statute was considered in National Liberty Insurance Company v. Jones, 165 Va. 606, 183 S.E. 443 (1936).

Similar statutes include New Jersey Statutes Ann. § 17:36–5:16 (Supp.1982) (effectiveness of oral binders for temporary insurance shall not exceed 10 days). *But see,* Restaurant Enterprises, Inc. v. Sussex Mutual Insurance Company, 243 A.2d 808 (New Jersey, 1968), for an illustration of the New Jersey Court's reluctance to apply this statute against an insured. The court reasoned that a statutory provision that fixed a maximum duration of 60 days for binders was not meant to void an action by an insurance purchaser.

3. Georgia Code §§ 56–2402, 56–2413 (1960). Although the Code language is somewhat ambiguous, case law strongly suggests that § 56–2402 in particular (formerly § 56–213) makes oral contracts of insurance invalid. See, e.g., Home Insurance Company v. Tanner, 220 F.2d 41 (5th Cir.1955) and Hawkins Iron & Metal Company, Inc. v. Continental Insurance Co., 128 Ga.App. 462, 196 S.E.2d 903 (1973).

Also *cf.* Mississippi Code 1968, § 5719.

4. E.g., Munhall v. Travelers' Insurance Company, 300 Pa. 327, 150 A. 645 (1930) (life insurance).

Contra. See, e.g., Sanford v. Orient Insurance Company, 174 Mass. 416, 54 N.E. 883 (1899).

Also see Rossi v. Firemen's Insurance Company, 310 Pa. 242, 165 A. 16 (1932) (reaching a result contrary to Munhall in a case involving a temporary and preliminary contract of fire insurance).

5. See, e.g., Pralle v. Metropolitan Life Insurance Company, 346 Ill. 58, 178 N.E. 371 (1931).

Contra. See, e.g., National Liberty Insurance Company v. Milligan, 10 F.2d 483 (9th Cir.1926); Lea v. Atlantic Insurance Company, 168 N.C. 478, 84 S.E. 813 (1915); Milwaukee Bedding Company v. Graebner, 182 Wis. 171, 196 N.W. 533 (1923).

See generally the cases cited in 12A Appleman, INSURANCE LAW AND PRACTICE (1981), at § 7195 (Effect of Statute, Charter, or By-Laws); Annotation, *Oral contracts of insurance,* 92 A.L.R. 232–240 at p. 235 (1934).

6. See Shipley v. Ohio National Life Insurance Company, 199 F.Supp. 782 at p. 783 (W.D.Pa.1961), *affirmed* 296 F.2d 728 (3d Cir.1961), for an illustration of judicial reluctance to allow an insurer's agent to bind the insurer to an oral contract of life insurance, when the terms stated in the application for insurance clearly "negated the existence of oral contract" by indicating any "contract was to be in writing."

For an illustration of the contrasting treatment of the issue in these different

§ 2.3 Temporary Contracts of Insurance

§ 2.3(a) The Need for Temporary Contracts of Insurance

A substantial period of time may pass between the moment insurance is applied for and the date when an insurance policy is issued. Sometimes this occurs because an applicant is dealing with a sales representative who does not have the authority to issue a policy. In other instances, an agent or a broker empowered to issue an insurance contract may be required by an insurer to initiate some investigation or await a report before deciding whether to accept the application for a policy. Delays may also result from the clerical work involved or from administrative errors in the processing of insurance applications.

A lack of coverage before the issuance of an insurance policy, especially when the period extends for weeks or months, is disadvantageous to an applicant. During such an interval, there is both the risk that a loss will occur and the risk that a change of circumstances during the interval may make the risk "uninsurable" (as for example when a serious illness develops during the period while a life insurance application is pending).

Not surprisingly, upon deciding to acquire insurance purchasers often desire immediate coverage. To accommodate the needs or desires of purchasers during periods while applications for insurance are pending, many insurers have developed the practice of employing temporary arrangements designed to provide applicants with some measure of protection while an insurance application is being processed. Typically the forms used for such temporary or interim insurance are little more than a relatively simple written memorandum which specifies only a few terms of the agreement. If a claim dispute subsequently develops, other terms of the insurance agreement are usually determined by reference to the standard policy forms and customary practices applicable to the type of coverage involved.[1]

During the period while an insurer considers an application, an applicant may change his or her mind and either buy insurance from a competitor or decide not to buy any insurance. When either event occurs, an insurer processing an application may already have incurred expenses in the course of investigating and processing the application.[2] As is the marketing practice in other types of consumer transactions in which the seller encourages a buyer to make a down payment or a

contexts, see Milwaukee Bedding Company v. Graebner, 182 Wis. 171, 196 N.W. 533 (1923), holding that a fire insurance statute prescribing a standard form of coverage did not prohibit oral contracts, even though a previous decision had construed similar language in another statute as prohibiting oral contracts of health and accident insurance.

§ 2.3(a)

1. For example, see Terry v. Mongin Insurance Agency, 105 Wis.2d 575, 314 N.W.2d 349 (1982) (citing Professor Keeton's original insurance text); Turner v. Worth Insurance Company, 106 Ariz. 132, 472 P.2d 1 (1970).

2. *Cf.* Comment, *Operation of Binding Receipts in Life Insurance,* 44 Yale Law Journal 1223–1232 (1935).

deposit, many insurers prefer that a buyer manifest an additional commitment to the transaction (beyond the submission of the application) by paying at least some portion of the premium. In order to encourage applicants to make a deposit, many insurers offer applicants the inducement of temporary (interim) coverage. Thus, temporary insurance is frequently used to facilitate the marketing interests of insurers, as well as the interests of applicants in gaining immediate coverage.

Conditional versus Temporary or Interim Coverage

Instead of temporary coverage, many insurers offer applicants who include deposits the commitment that if an application is accepted, the effective date for the coverage will precede the actual delivery of the policy to the applicant — that is, the company states that the coverage will be made retroactive to some point in time such as when the application was made or the medical examination was completed.

Life Insurance Coverage: Temporary, Interim, or Conditional?

Temporary, interim, or conditional life insurance coverage is offered by some insurers when an application for insurance is accompanied by payment of the first premium installment in cash or by check. The memoranda used in such life insurance transactions are characterized in a variety of ways, including "conditional receipt," "conditional premium receipt," "binding receipt," or "conditional binding receipt." [3]

Fire Insurance, Casualty Insurance, and Liability Insurance: Temporary Coverage

The practices in regard to fire insurance, casualty insurance, and liability insurance differ from the marketing approach used for life insurance in that temporary coverage is often, though not invariably, issued in situations in which there is no advance payment of any premium. A memorandum issued for such coverage is usually called a "binder." [4] The term "binder," however, is sometimes used more broadly to refer to a document that is technically a "binding receipt." An oral agreement for temporary insurance is usually called an "oral binder," [5] but references are often abbreviated so that such a transaction is often also referred to as a "binder."

3. See discussion of binding receipts and life insurance coverage in § 2.3(b) and § 2.3(c), below, and the clauses involved in the cases cited in those subsections.

Conditional Coverage Receipts are also used for health insurance. For example, see Hemenway v. MFA Insurance Company, 211 Neb. 193, 318 N.W.2d 70 (1982).

4. See, e.g., Terry v. Mongin Insurance Agency, 105 Wis.2d 575, 314 N.W.2d 349 (1982); Ginsberg v. North River Insurance Company, 56 N.Y.2d 719, 451 N.Y.S.2d 736, 436 N.E.2d 1339 (1982), affirming the decision reported at 67 A.D.2d 694, 412 N.Y. Supp.2d 637 (1979); State Automobile Mutual Insurance Company v. Babcock, 54 Mich.App. 717, 220 N.W.2d 717 (Div. 2, 1974).

5. The terms for temporary coverage afforded under a binder are usually determined in accordance with the provisions of the insurance policy ordinarily used by the

The conditions and limitations set forth in the memoranda employed by insurers for temporary or interim insurance contracts may be subject to statutory restrictions, administrative regulation, and judicial rulings. The impact of judicial "regulatory" actions on such arrangements is illustrated in the following discussion of conditional binding receipts that have been used in marketing life insurance.

§ 2.3(b) The Use of Conditional Receipts in Life Insurance Marketing

At the beginning of the twentieth century, centralized control of underwriting was the "watchword" in the marketing of life insurance. Although some intrusions upon centralization were introduced by the use of conditional receipts, the desire of many insurers to preserve centralized control produced coverage limitations which were so restrictive that an applicant was actually provided little more than an elusive hope for generosity in a company's exercise of unfettered discretion.[1] Conditional receipts often did no more than authorize an insurer to back-date an insurance policy after deciding to issue a life insurance contract. Insurers retained the option not to back-date, and the discretion to back-date a policy typically would only be exercised by insurers when it provided no advantage for an applicant or intended beneficiaries — that is, the conditional binding receipt did not require an insurer to provide the coverage retroactively and a policy would seldom be back-dated by an insurer when it would be detrimental to the company. The misleading quality of such qualified binding receipts produced a considerable body of case law and commentary. In some of the cases, litigation about the coverage provided by such receipts yielded judicial determinations that the drafters of the conditional binding receipts almost certainly never envisioned as possible on the basis of the terms used in these forms.

Disputes over the scope of coverage provided by conditional binding receipts, which are representative of the many battles between the drafters of insurance documents and the nation's courts with which the history of insurance law is replete,[2] ultimately caused significant

company for the policy that would subsequently have been used. *Cf.* State Automobile Mutual Insurance Company v. Babcock, 54 Mich.App. 717, 220 N.W.2d 717 at p. 722 (Div. 2, 1974). However, an insurer may be bound by representations or statements made by an agent or broker even though such representations do not conform to such policy provisions. General Insurance Company of America v. Truly Nolan of America, Inc., 136 Ariz. 142, 664 P.2d 686 (App., Div. 1, Dept. D, 1983).

Also see the discussion of the sales representatives authority to bind an insurer in § 2.5(b), below.

§ 2.3(b)

1. See generally Note, *Life Insurance Policies and "Binding" Receipts: Is the Insurer Bound?* 1968 Utah Law Review 448–452; O'Neill, *Interim Coverage: Conditional Receipts,* 1964 University Illinois Law Forum 571–591; Comment, *"Binding Receipts" in California,* 7 Stanford Law Review 292–300 (1955); Comment, *Life Insurance Receipts: The Mystery of the Non-Binding Binder,* 63 Yale Law Journal 523–537 (1954); Comment, *Operation of Binding Receipts in Life Insurance,* 44 Yale Law Journal 1223–1232 (1935); *Recent cases,* 60 Harvard Law Review 1164–1166 (1947).

2. See generally the discussion in § 6.5, below.

changes in the scope and extent of coverage provided when such marketing techniques are employed by insurers. The following selection of coverage terms from conditional binding receipt forms illustrates the metamorphosis these forms have undergone over the last 75 years. In general the more rigorously restrictive forms set out below are those of more ancient vintage. Less restrictive forms have increasingly been used in the past few decades. The six examples are identified by letter designations to facilitate the discussion that follows.

Form A: The insurance hereby applied for shall not take effect unless the first premium is paid and the policy is delivered to and received by me during my lifetime and good health, and unless otherwise agreed in writing the policy shall then relate back to and take effect as of the date of this application.[3]

Form B: If the application is approved at the home office of the company, in New York, the policy will be delivered if the insured is alive on its date of issue; and subject to the same conditions, should the death of the person upon whose life the policy is applied for occur prior to the date of issue of the policy and within eight weeks from the date of such application, the company will, upon surrender of this receipt, pay such amount as would have been due under the terms of the policy had it been issued on the date of such deposit.[4]

Form C: If the amount of such premium is paid to the said company's agent at the time of making this application the insurance (subject to the provisions of the said company's regular form of policy for the plan applied for) shall be effective from the date of my medical examination therefor and such a policy shall be issued and delivered to me or my legal representatives, provided the said company in its judgment shall be satisfied as to my insurability, on

3. *Cf.* Long v. New York Life Insurance Company, 106 Wash. 458, 180 P. 479 (1919) (recovery denied because policy issued by company, but not delivered to applicant before his death, substituted a date for taking effect different from the date stated in the application and was, therefore, a rejection of the applicant's offer by way of counteroffer).

4. *Cf.* Gaunt v. John Hancock Mutual Life Insurance Company, 160 F.2d 599 (2d Cir.1947), *cert. denied* 331 U.S. 849, 67 S.Ct. 1736, 91 L.Ed. 1858 (1947) (Form B type provision found ambiguous when combined with a "satisfaction of insurability" type provision like Form C; receipt construed to provide coverage though application not approved before applicant's death by homicide).

Also see Allen v. Metropolitan Life Insurance Company, 44 N.J. 294, 208 A.2d 638 (1965) (coverage without regard to insurability subject only to termination on

company's approval or rejection of permanent coverage applied for); Leube v. Prudential Insurance Company, 147 Ohio St. 450, 72 N.E.2d 76 (1947), 2 A.L.R.2d 936 (1948) (application was rejected before injury resulting in death occurred; coverage denied though actual notice of rejection was not given until after injury); DeCesare v. Metropolitan Life Insurance Company, 278 Mass. 401, 180 N.E. 154, 81 A.L.R. 327 (1932) (receipt dated March 7, policy delivered March 25 dated to take effect April 1, and applicant died March 31; held, coverage under the receipt).

Also consider Morgan v. State Farm Life Insurance Company, 240 Or. 113, 400 P.2d 223 (1965) (combined Form B, "approval", and Form C, "satisfaction of insurability", provisions; held, coverage subject to insurability of applicant on date of application under objective test similar to that of Form D).

the plan applied for, on the date of such medical examination; and if said company shall not be so satisfied the amount of the premium paid shall be returned.[5]

Form D: If the first full premium is paid at the time of making this application, and if at that time the applicant is insurable under the company's rules and practices, for the amount and upon the plan applied for without modification, then the insurance (subject to the provisions of the company's "regular form" of policy for the plan applied for) shall be effective from the time of making application. If the underwriting rules of the company prevent issuance of a policy exactly as applied for but permit issuance on another basis, and the insured dies within sixty days and the issuable policy has neither become effective nor been refused, the insurance shall be in force for such lesser amount as the premium would have purchased when applied as the first premium on the issuable policy.

Form E: If the first premium is paid at the time of application, the company will be liable from and after said payment to the same extent as if the policy, as applied for, had been issued and delivered at that time; provided, however, that (1) the company reserves the absolute right to reject said application and if said application is rejected (and without notice thereof) all liability on the part of the company shall thereupon terminate except as to claims maturing before such rejection; and (2) if said application is neither approved nor rejected by the company at its home office

---

5. *Cf.* Taylor v. New York Life Insurance Company, 324 F.2d 768 (10th Cir. 1963) (applying Colorado law) (denial of coverage under binder valid though application was rejected after applicant's death, because he failed to meet the insurer's requirements in not satisfactorily explaining weight loss before application; insurability in fact irrelevant); New England Mutual Life Insurance Company v. Hinkle, 248 F.2d 879 (8th Cir. 1957), *cert. dismissed* 358 U.S. 65, 79 S.Ct. 116, 3 L.Ed.2d 106 (1958) (applying Iowa law) (sustaining a denial coverage for an applicant who customarily engaged in aviation activities, when the company showed it did not customarily insure such persons at the rate the applicant applied for; coverage denied); Johnson v. Equitable Life Assurance Soc'y, 275 F.2d 315 (7th Cir.1960) (applying Illinois law) (provision inapplicable to contemporaneous temporary term life insurance for which a separate premium was stated and paid); Brunt v. Occidental Life Insurance Company, 223 Cal.App.2d 179, 35 Cal.Rptr. 492 (2d Dist.1963) (health and accident insurance; "satisfaction of insurability" held to be a condition subsequent to coverage).

Also see Reynolds v. Northwestern Mutual Life Insurance Co., 189 Iowa 76, 176 N.W. 207 (1920) (unclear whether subjective test of insurability or Form D type, objective test applied); Simpson v. Prudential Insurance Co., 227 Md. 393, 177 A.2d 417 (1962) (construed to require an objective test of insurability "according to the general standards of the industry"); Morgan v. State Farm Life Ins. Co., 240 Or. 113, 400 P.2d 223 (1965) (combined Form B and Form C provisions; held, coverage subject to Form D type objective test of insurability; Fanning v. Guardian Life Insurance Company, 59 Wash.2d 101, 366 P.2d 207 (1961) (accident occurred between dates of application for permanent policy of health and accident insurance and rejection and cancellation of the receipt by the company. In coverage based on the agent's oral representation of immediate effectiveness, the agent had the apparent authority to bind the company).

In United Founders Life Insurance Company v. Carey, 363 S.W.2d 236 (Tex.1962), the court concluded that the plaintiff was required to prove that a prudent, authorized officer acting in good faith would have found applicant insurable.

within 45 days from the date thereof it shall be deemed to have been rejected as of the last day of such 45 day period, without notice to that effect.[6]

Form F: If the first premium is paid at the time of making application, the company will make payment in accordance with the terms of the policy applied for, in the event applicant dies on the day of application or within 21 days thereafter.[7]

From an insurer's point of view, discretion in the acceptance of risks, which is clearly allowed under Form A, potentially affords a significant advantage in regard to underwriting by allowing the insurer to avoid some losses. However, this approach may produce a competitive disadvantage for the insurer in the market place, because purchasers may prefer to seek coverage from insurers who provide more extensive protection while an application is pending. Form C, which may also provide an underwriting advantage, has the additional disadvantage of not being clear in its meaning. As a result, judicial interpretation of the coverage provided by this form can not be predicted with assurance. Consequently, this type of form has tended to induce litigation.[8]

From the perspective of an applicant, Forms D, E, and F are preferable to Forms A, B, and C. The choice among Forms D, E, and F depends on whether an applicant is more interested in long-term coverage or short-term coverage. Form D is arguably the best in regard to disputes that may arise in regard to long-term coverage, because it may more readily be construed by a court as a commitment for the long term.[9] If a purchaser is more interested in immediate short-term coverage, Form F is probably the best since it plainly offers that commitment. Forms C, B, and A are decreasingly desirable, in that order.

From the perspective of public officials — such as commissioners of insurance, legislators, or judges — with some responsibility for approval or disapproval, or enforcement of the provisions used in binding receipts, terms such as those in Form A could be disapproved as inequitable. The benefits received by an applicant in exchange for a premium paid at the time of an application are minimal under provisions such as those used in Form A. In reply to this observation, insurers might urge that an approach that charges for less than a full

---

6. *Cf.* Western & Southern Life Insurance Company v. Lottes, 116 Ind.App. 559, 64 N.E.2d 405 (1946), *rehearing denied* 116 Ind.App. 559, 64 N.E.2d 805 (1946) (only question at issue was whether applicant had paid first premium in full).

7. *Cf.* Ranellucci v. John Hancock Mutual Life Insurance Company, 200 Misc. 1111, 112 N.Y.S.2d 94 (City Court of Albany, 1951) (receipt constitutes a binding contract between applicant and company; materiality of misrepresentation in application a question of fact, not law, under New York Laws 1939, ch. 882).

8. See the cases cited in n. 4 and n. 5, above.

Also see Duesenberg, *Recent Developments in Insurance Law,* 1965 Insurance Law Journal 465–474 at pp. 468–469.

9. See the discussion of the possible obligation to issue long term coverage in § 2.3(c)(3), below.

year of coverage during the first year is warranted because of the additional administrative costs that are incurred by an insurer during the initial year of coverage. However, if the terms of such a receipt are rigorously enforced, the length of coverage during the first year is determined by the length of the delay between the date of application and the date of completion of all other requisites. Accordingly, those persons whose applications are acted upon with less dispatch pay a higher per day cost for coverage. This seems an arbitrary way of allocating either the full costs or a portion of the costs of administering applications. It wholly lacks a foundation in any principle that appeals to a sense of fairness.

Arguably Form B is also inequitable.[10] And perhaps forms like C should be disapproved as misleading.[11]

§ 2.3(c) Judicial Restructuring of the Life Insurance Marketing Transaction

Generalizations about the effect of conditional binding receipts are at best difficult because the terms used for these forms clearly are not all of a kind. Accordingly, the comments in the following discussion should be understood to be subject to limitations that inevitably exist whenever generalizations are made about a large body of transactions some of which may involve contract forms containing many different terms and unusual provisions.

It was quite common when conditional binding receipts were first developed by insurers for companies to use forms that stated both a condition of "approval" (see Form B) and a condition of "satisfaction" as to insurability (see Form C). Describing such a form, Professor Patterson stated: "When issued by an agent having authority, this receipt makes a temporary contract of insurance, subject to a condition, rejection by the insurance company — *which terminates the coverage.*" [1] Patterson further observed that the company probably "need not prove that the rejection was reasonable or justifiable, but it could not reject, for instance, merely because a healthy applicant was accidentally killed before the policy was issued." [2] Professor Patterson's observation about

---

10. *Cf.* Allen v. Metropolitan Life Insurance Company, 44 N.J. 294, 208 A.2d 638 (1965) ("approval" provision construed as providing temporary coverage until the application had been rejected by the insurer, without regard to insurability).

11. *Cf.* Clark, J. concurring in Gaunt v. John Hancock Mutual Life Insurance Company, 160 F.2d 599 at p. 603 (2d Cir.1947), *cert. denied* 331 U.S. 849, 67 S.Ct. 1736, 91 L.Ed. 1858 (1947); O'Connell, J., dissenting in Morgan v. State Farm Life Insurance Company, 240 Or. 113 at p. 118, 400 P.2d 223 at p. 225 (1965).

§ 2.3(c)

1. Patterson, ESSENTIALS OF INSURANCE LAW (Second edition, 1957) (Emphasis added), at p. 100, citing Gaunt v. John Hancock Mutual Life Insurance Company, 160 F.2d 599 (2d Cir.1947), *cert. denied* 331 U.S. 849, 67 S.Ct. 1736, 91 L.Ed. 1858 (1947), and Reck v. Prudential Insurance Company, 116 N.J.L. 444, 184 A. 777 (Court of Errors & Appeals, 1936).

2. Patterson, ESSENTIALS OF INSURANCE LAW (Second edition, 1957), at pp. 100–101.

Also see Reynolds v. Northwestern Mutual Life Insurance Company, 189 Iowa 76, 176 N.W. 207 (1920) (involving a binding receipt like Form C); Gaunt v. John Han-

the termination of coverage seems clearly to assume that temporary coverage exists for some period of time — that is, the comment suggests that a conditional binding receipt normally provides more than an unresolved possibility of temporary coverage.

Professor Patterson's comment is not in accord with the specific language that was typically being used by insurers for binding receipts in provisions such as Form B, and, to a lesser degree, the language of Form C and Form D. However, the accuracy of Professor Patterson's comment did not depend on the meaning, or even on the most reasonable interpretation, of the terms that are used for such receipts;[3] rather, it almost certainly rested on the results of judicial regulation of these transactions. And because of increasing judicial regulation during the past two or three decades, precedents undoubtedly now provide substantially greater support for Patterson's position than when he wrote.

There are many judicial decisions which boldly restructure the terms under which temporary life insurance coverage is provided while an application is pending. In essence, these decisions hold that when an insurer's rejection occurs after a death, the company is liable for the life insurance benefits even though specific conditions in the conditional binding receipt have not been satisfied.[4] Courts have imposed liability even in instances in which the insurer provided evidence that

cock Mutual Life Insurance Company, 160 F.2d 599 (2d Cir.1947), *cert. denied* 331 U.S. 849, 67 S.Ct. 1736, 91 L.Ed. 1858 (1947) (involving a combination of Form B and Form C type provisions).

3. In 1948, an ALR annotator advanced the following description of the case law:

"The general rule adhered to by most of the courts, at least in their earlier decisions, is to the effect that where a binding receipt is issued to the applicant making the obligation of the insurance company conditional upon acceptance and approval by the company, the company is not bound until it approves and accepts the application, on the ground that the expressed condition of acceptance has not occurred." Annotation, *Temporary life, accident, or health insurance pending approval of application of issuance of policy*, 2 A.L.R.2d 943–1022 at p. 964 (1948).

Although this statement may have been an accurate characterization of the results in those "earlier decisions," it no longer represents the prevailing trend of recent cases.

4. See, e.g., Puritan Life Insurance Company v. Guess, 598 P.2d 900, (Alaska 1979); Simses v. North American Company for Life & Health Insurance, 175 Conn. 77, 394 A.2d 710 (1978); Collister v. Nationwide Life Insurance Company, 479 Pa. 579,

388 A.2d 1346 (1978), *cert. denied* 439 U.S. 1089, 99 S.Ct. 871, 59 L.Ed.2d 55 (1979).

Also see Smith v. Westland Life Insurance Company, 15 Cal.3d 111, 123 Cal. Rptr. 649, 539 P.2d 433 (1975); Long v. United Beneficial Life Insurance Company, Inc., 29 Utah 2d 204, 507 P.2d 375 (1973); Dunford v. United of Omaha, 95 Idaho 282, 506 P.2d 1355 (1973); Tripp v. Reliable Life Insurance Company, 210 Kan. 33, 499 P.2d 1155 (1972).

Cf. Meding v. Prudential Insurance Company of America, 444 F.Supp. 634 (N.D.Ind. 1978); Damm v. National Insurance Company of America, 200 N.W.2d 616 (N.D.1972); Toevs v. Western Farm Bureau Life Insurance Company, 94 Idaho 151, 483 P.2d 682 (1971); Turner v. Worth Insurance Company, 106 Ariz. 132, 472 P.2d 1 (1970) (automobile insurance); and Service v. Pyramid Life Insurance Company, 201 Kan. 196, 440 P.2d 944 (1968).

Contra. Grandpre v. Northwestern National Life Insurance Company, 261 N.W.2d 804 (S.D.1977); Atkinson v. American Agency Life Insurance Company, 165 Ga.App. 102, 299 S.E.2d 600 (1983); Reynolds v. Guarantee Insurance Company, 44 Ill.App.3d 764, 3 Ill.Dec. 397, 358 N.E.2d 940 (1976).

Also see the discussion in § 2.3(c)(2) and § 2.3(d), below.

the applicant was uninsurable by the company's customary standards.[5] Some of the opinions predicate the results on the resolution of ambiguities.[6] Other decisions justify such liability on the basis of honoring the

5. See, e.g., Metropolitan Life Insurance Company v. Wood, 302 F.2d 802 (9th Cir. 1962) (construing Ransom v. Penn Mutual Life Insurance Company, which is discussed in the next paragraph), as establishing that under California law rejection of an application only terminates temporary coverage and does not affect an applicant's insured status before that action; the fact that an applicant may not have been insurable does not negate the insurer's liability); Prudential Insurance Company v. Lamme, 83 Nev. 146, 425 P.2d 346 (1967) (Form C type receipt held to provide temporary coverage subject to rejection, even though applicant never took medical examination to establish insurability and died of a heart attack about seven weeks after application; candid imposition of liability inconsistent with terms of the receipt).

Though less candid and clear about adopting measures of judicial regulation, each of the following opinions is subject to being interpreted as disallowing a defense of honest rejection after death based on evidence of uninsurability at the time of application: Slobojan v. Western Travelers Life Insurance Company, 70 Cal.2d 432, 450 P.2d 271, 74 Cal.Rptr. 895 (1969) (Form C type receipt held to provide temporary life insurance subject to termination only by rejection of the application for permanent coverage; tendering a policy at a slightly higher rate was not a rejection; no showing of uninsurability); Ransom v. Penn Mutual Life Insurance Company, 43 Cal.2d 420, 274 P.2d 633 (1954) (Form C type receipt held to provide temporary life insurance subject to termination; defense argument that applicant was uninsurable under company rules rejected, the court stating that a request for further medical examination indicated the company had not yet decided whether applicant was an acceptable risk and that a court need not decide whether temporary contract can be terminated only by actual rejection and return of premium); Dunford v. United of Omaha, 95 Idaho 282, 506 P.2d 1355 (1973) (Form C type receipt held to provide temporary life insurance subject to termination only by rejection of the application for permanent coverage; preparation and mailing to agent of modified policy with rated-up premium, a counteroffer, did not constitute a rejection because it had not been communicated to the applicant before his death; dissent on the ground that the form was not ambiguous, the applicant did

not meet its conditions, and the counteroffer had not been accepted).

Cf. Allen v. Metropolitan Life Insurance Company, 44 N.J. 294, 208 A.2d 638 (1965) (Form B type receipt construed to provide temporary coverage without regard to insurability subject only to termination by the company's rejecting permanent coverage for which application was made).

Decisions involving binding receipts do not always hold that insurability should be disregarded. Rather, the courts often convert conditions of subjective "approval" or "acceptance" into objective criteria of insurability under existing company standards and practices.

6. See, e.g., Gaunt v. John Hancock Mutual Life Insurance Company, 160 F.2d 599 (2d Cir.1947), *cert. denied* 331 U.S. 849, 67 S.Ct. 1736, 91 L.Ed. 1858 (1947).

Accord. Puritan Life Insurance Company v. Guess, 598 P.2d 900 at p. 904 (Alaska 1979); Collister v. Nationwide Life Insurance Company, 479 Pa. 579, 388 A.2d 1346 at pp. 1348–1349 (1978); Simses v. North American Company for Life and Health Insurance, 175 Conn. 77, 394 A.2d 710 (1978); Smith v. Westland Life Insurance Company, 15 Cal.3d 111 at p. 120–121, 123 Cal.Rptr. 649 at p. 655, 539 P.2d 433 at p. 439 (1975).

Also see Toevs v. Western Farm Bureau Life Insurance Company, 94 Idaho 151, 683 P.2d 682 (1971), discussed in Richard K. Smith, *The Conditional Receipt as a Temporary Contract of Life Insurance in Idaho,* 9 Idaho Law Review 15–27 (1972).

But see Grandpre v. Northwestern National Life Insurance Company, 261 N.W.2d 804 at p. 807 (S.D.1977).

But cf. Machinery Center, Inc. v. Anchor National Life Insurance Company, 434 F.2d 1 (10th Cir.1970) (applying Utah law) (president of Machinery Center applied for $60,000 declining term life insurance; on same day Machinery Center, owner and contingent beneficiary of policy, paid first premium and obtained conditional premium receipt, which declared no insurance was effective "until the application is approved and accepted by the company at its Home Office and the policy manually delivered to and accepted by the Proposed Insured (or the Owner, if other than the Proposed Insured) during the lifetime and continued insurability" of the Proposed Insured; applicant died before defendant de-

applicant's reasonable expectations.[7] Courts have protected such expectations in many different situations, including instances when a careful analysis of the terms would have revealed to the applicant that the insurer did not intend to provide coverage.[8] In an increasingly significant portion of the appellate decisions, judges have specifically declared that conditions which limit the coverage provided by binding receipts are not enforceable on grounds of public policy.[9] In addition to

cided to accept or reject risk; although insurer's doctor had classified applicant as a good risk a month earlier, underwriting investigation was still incomplete because requested information had not been received; summary judgment for insurer affirmed; applying Utah law, the court distinguished earlier cases, including those in Note, *Life Insurance Policies and "Binding" Receipts: Is the Insurer Bound?,* 1968 Utah Law Review 448–452 at p. 449, by noting that receipt was explicitly "conditional" and not "binding," that a "fair, understandable condition precedent or prerequisite to liability is not objectionable," and that, therefore, there was no detrimental reliance).

7. Miller v. Republic National Life Insurance Company, 714 F.2d 958 at p. 961 (9th Cir.1983), *appeal after remand* 789 F.2d 1336 (9th Cir.1986) (applying California law); Puritan Life Insurance Company v. Guess, 598 P.2d 900 at pp. 904–905 (Alaska 1979); Collister v. Nationwide Insurance Company, 479 Pa. 579, 388 A.2d 1346 at pp. 1353–1355 (1978).

Also see Smith v. Westland Life Insurance Company, 15 Cal.3d 111, 123 Cal. Rptr. 649, 539 P.2d 433 (1975) (en banc); Allen v. Metropolitan Insurance Company, 44 N.J. 294, 208 A.2d 638 (1965).

Cf. Quindlen v. Prudential Insurance Company of America, 342 F.Supp. 9 (W.D. La.1971) (court's interpretation of the Louisiana Insurance Code required that actual notice of rejection be received even though the decedent's wife was aware that it was essential that the decedent's military medical records had to be submitted to the insurer and that the medical records had not been furnished to the company; the company's decision to reject the application took place before the applicant's death, but notice of the rejection was mailed on the day following the applicant's death).

Cf. Anderson v. Metropolitan Life Insurance Company, 69 Misc.2d 205, 329 N.Y.S.2d 197 (New York County, Trial Term, Pt. 44, 1972), discussed in Note, *Conditional Receipts: New York Precedent and the Potential for Change,* 43 Albany Law Review 645–660 (1979).

Cf. Hemenway v. MFA Life Insurance Company, 211 Neb. 193, 318 N.W.2d 70 (1982) (application for health insurance).

Also see the discussion of the reasonable expectations theory in regard to a medical doctor who was aware of his heart condition in Blair v. Manhattan Life Insurance Company, 692 F.2d 296 (3d Cir.1982) (applying Pennsylvania law developed in Collister, supra).

See also Anderson, *Life Insurance Conditional Receipts and Judicial Intervention,* 63 Marquette Law Review 591–609 at pp. 598–602 (1980).

8. See, e.g., Collister v. Nationwide Life Insurance Company, 479 Pa. 579, 388 A.2d 1346 (1978).

Cf. Kaiser v. National Farmers Union Life Insurance Company, 167 Ind.App. 619, 339 N.E.2d 599 (1st Dist.1976), in which the court concluded that "any conditions contained in the receipt are to be treated as conditions subsequent thereby compelling an insurer to act affirmatively or negatively on the application * * *[and] an insurer cannot terminate the risk so assumed unless the applicant is so notified in his lifetime." Also see Note, *Life Insurance Conditional Receipts in Indiana,* 12 Indiana Law Review 777–796 (1979).

Also see the cases cited in notes 4 through 6, above, the terms set out in the text of § 2.3(b), above, and the discussion in § 6.3(b), below.

9. E.g., Prudential Insurance Company v. Lamme, 83 Nev. 146, 425 P.2d 346 (1967) (Form C type receipt held to provide temporary coverage subject to rejection, regardless of insurability).

See also Morgan v. State Farm Life Insurance Company, 240 Or. 113, 400 P.2d 223 (1965) (rejecting the "fiction" of "constructive ambiguity" as inapplicable, yet finding temporary coverage under Form B and C type provisions subject to an objective, Form D type, test of insurability; O'Connell, J., dissenting, would have allowed temporary coverage without regard to insurability subject only to termination by the company's rejection of the permanent coverage for which application was made).

protecting reasonable expectations,[10] the public policy involved in these cases — although not always articulated in the decisions — is to preclude insurers from taking an unconscionable advantage in such transactions.[11]

There are several additional considerations, not often discussed in the judicial decisions resolving these coverage disputes, which deserve attention.

(1) Conditional Binding Receipts as Contracts of Adhesion

Conditional binding receipts are often regarded as contracts of adhesion by both judges and commentators. Although such receipts are undoubtedly form contracts, they often do not involve the type of transaction that the contract of adhesion concept was originally envisoned as describing.[12]

Cf. Hemenway v. MFA Life Insurance Company, 211 Neb. 193, 318 N.W.2d 70 (1982) (holding application for a health insurance contract accompanied by premium payment was effective on date of application since conditions in receipt were satisfied).

10. See, e.g., Collister v. Nationwide Life Insurance Company, 479 Pa. 579, 388 A.2d 1346 (1978) in which the court observed that the insurer "failed to establish by clear and convincing evidence that the appellant's husband could not have entertained a reasonable expectation" that the insurer was obligating itself to provide insurance coverage beginning with the first premium payment.

But cf. Jacobson v. Kansas City Life Insurance Company, 652 P.2d 909 (Utah 1982), upholding a clause in the receipt that temporary coverage was not to commence until "any and all medical examinations required by the Company" were completed.

Several opinions have included comments that insurers could avoid such temporary insurance coverage. For example, the Alaska Supreme Court observed that an "insurer may avoid such temporary insurance coverage only by including clear and *unequivocal language* in the conditional receipt indicating its intent to condition its liability upon prior approval of the application and the finding of insurability." Puritan Life Insurance Company v. Guess, 598 P.2d 900 at p. 906 (Alaska 1979) (emphasis added). The court then added: "Furthermore, we require that the insurer's agent, who negotiates the application, personally draw to the attention of the applicant any limiting conditions." *Ibid.*

In Grandpre v. Northwestern Life Insurance Company, 261 N.W.2d 804 at p. 807 (S.D.1977), the court concluded that when the front of the receipt stated in "boldface letters":

IMPORTANT: THIS RECEIPT DOES NOT PROVIDE INSURANCE UNTIL AFTER ITS CONDITIONS ARE MET

the "ordinary meaning of the words * * * would alert any ordinary person to understand what had to be completed before the temporary or interim insurance would be effective."

See also § 6.3(b), below, concerning application of the principle of honoring reasonable expectations.

11. See, e.g., Smith v. Westland Life Insurance Company, 15 Cal.3d 111, 123 Cal.Rptr. 649, 539 P.2d 433 (1975) (en banc) discussed in Note, *Termination of Temporary Insurance Coverage, Allen v. Metropolitan Life Insurance Co., 44 N.J. 294, 208 A.2d 638 (1965);* 64 Georgetown Law Journal 1199–1212 (1976).

Also see Meding v. Prudential Insurance Company of America, 444 F.Supp. 634 at pp. 636–637 (N.D.Ind.1978).

Also consider the discussion of "unconscionability" in § 6.2, below.

12. See especially the discussion in Collister v. Nationwide Life Insurance Company, 479 Pa. 579, 388 A.2d 1346 (1978).

Also see 2 COUCH ON INSURANCE (Second Edition, 1984), § 14:35 (" * * * there is little uniformity in the forms of binding receipts employed").

It is, of course, true that binding receipts are typically used in situations in which there is a tremendous disparity in the bargaining positions of the parties — that is, an individual consumer is dealing with an insurance company, and the company is often a very large national or international corporate entity. Yet, it is equally true that most insurers offer an insurance purchaser more than one choice in such transactions. At a minimum, an applicant for life insurance almost always has the option of not making any payment with the application. Although this may not be a preferred choice for an applicant who desires immediate coverage, the possibility does clearly indicate that the consumer is not faced with a total absence of options in regard to purchasing insurance. Moreover, even if a particular insurer chooses to market life insurance only to consumers who will make a deposit and does not extend interim coverage in exchange for such deposit, other marketing choices are available to life insurance purchasers. There are numerous life insurance companies that will sell interim coverage, especially for the risk of death from accidental causes.

The consumer who seeks to purchase life insurance in the United States has literally hundreds of insurance companies from which to choose. Unlike those marketing situations in which an entire industry offers the same contract terms or identical products, the life insurance industry affords consumers many choices. The life insurance applicant is not confronted with a marketing situation in which the only choice is to accept a product that is essentially the same regardless of the individual company with which a consumer deals. There are over one thousand companies selling life insurance in the United States, and these insurers offer many highly differentiated products. The examples of binding receipt forms set out above are not only illustrative of the evolution of such forms over the span of this century, they also exemplify the variety of approaches now available to consumers in the market place. Thus, although it is certainly true that many insurance transactions do involve contracts of adhesion, considerable care should be exercised before concluding that a transaction involving a conditional receipt for a payment made by an applicant for life insurance is a contract of adhesion situation.

(2) Unconscionability in Binding Receipt Transactions

Standardized contracts are used throughout the United States for many types of transactions. Indeed, it is difficult to envision a highly industrialized, commercial society with a population that exceeds two hundred million persons which would not rely heavily on the use of such contracts. Consequently, even when an adhesion situation prevails, the courts frequently enforce the terms in standard form contracts. Courts generally uphold the enforceability of the terms in such contracts unless it can also be demonstrated that some aspect of the transaction at issue was unconscionable.[13] Unconscionability is, at best, an elusive standard.[14] Accordingly, though applications for life insurance may involve contracts of adhesion, that fact does not in and of itself warrant the conclusion that the provisions of a conditional binding receipt should always be disregarded.

The judicial imposition of liability in many of the coverage disputes involving conditional binding receipts used by insurance companies often seems to rest on the conclusion that insurers reap an economic windfall either (1) as a result of the insurer's beneficial use of applicants' deposits (which frequently is the first premium payment) while life insurance applications are being processed and evaluated, or (2) by fixing the anniversary date so that the actual period of time that coverage is provided is fewer days than that which would be purchased by the premium payment if the payment were deferred until after the insurer decided to accept the application.[15] Furthermore, there is an additional assumption in regard to deposits, not always explicitly articulated, that the economic value of these actions to a particular insurer or to all insurers substantially exceeds the losses that result or would result if interim coverage were provided for all life insurance applicants. Whether this conclusion is actuarially correct has rarely, if ever, been established in such coverage disputes.

A question that should be posed and answered — in regard to whether insurers are reaping a financial windfall — is how the time value of deposits paid by applicants for life insurance compares with the coverage losses resulting from the deaths of applicants that occur while applications are pending. The answer to this question is certainly obtainable. Yet, thus far, at least on the basis of the reasoning presented in the appellate court decisions, it has played at best an insignificant role in the analysis of this problem. The answer might either provide clear support for the assumption of unjust enrichment and the associated sense of unconscionability, or it might refute that supposition. In either case, the answer certainly seems worth determining so long as judicial analysis of the problem continues to be predicated, explicitly or implicitly, on the basis that insurers are deriving undeserved substantial net economic benefits.

The imposition of interim coverage by the courts in cases involving the newer forms of conditional binding receipt terms used by many life

---

13. See the discussion in § 6.2, below. Also see discussion in § 2.8, below.

14. *Ibid.*

15. See, e.g., Meding v. Prudential Insurance Company of America, 444 F.Supp. 634 at pp. 636–637 (N.D.Ind.1978):

"* * * an insurer cannot accept a premium from an applicant, who has completed the insurer's own application and received a complicated and legalistically phrased receipt, giving the applicant reason to believe he is insured, and then disclaim insurance liability for the interim period because it is not satisfied that the applicant was an insurable risk."

Also see Collister v. Nationwide Life Insurance Company, 479 Pa. 579 at p. 598, 388 A.2d 1346 at p. 1355 (1978) ("If * * * the insurer wishes to enjoy the substantial benefits it receives by securing the customer's cash at the time of taking the application * * *.").

insurance companies may also mean that insurers will in effect be compelled to provide more than a year's coverage for an annual premium. Many insurers now have binding receipts that provide for a full term of insurance coverage once the conditions specified in the receipts are satisfied — that is, even though coverage may be delayed for some period of time after the application is submitted, once the coverage goes into effect the insurer provides coverage for a full term of weeks, months or years. Insurers will undoubtedly be held to the coverage period specified in these forms. When an insurer's binding receipt terms together with the insurance policy that is subsequently issued provide coverage for a period that is in accord with the amount of premium paid, the judicial imposition of interim coverage that antedates the point when coverage begins under such terms obviously increases the scope of the insurer's liability. In other words, just as many of the early binding receipt practices of insurers shortchanged the insureds,[16] the imposition of interim coverage by judicial action may now serve to shortchange insurers who use modern binding receipt forms and anniversary dates for the insurance policy that provide a full period (such as a year) of coverage for applicants. If this occurs, insurers ultimately will have to pass the burden along to other insureds by an adjustment of their general rate structure. Thus, a full assessment of the impact of decisions invoking unconscionability should take account of effects on rates and any differential effects of those rates among applicants.

(3) Adverse Selection Problems

Construing binding receipts so as to extend coverage beyond that intended by insurers allows the process of adverse selection to operate in some situations.[17] For example, consider the effect of disregarding a condition in a binding receipt that an applicant must be "now insurable for the amount, plan and rating applied for" in the case of an applicant whose aviation activities would disqualify that person for the insurance plan or the premium rate applied for.[18] A rule imposing liability on an insurer while an application was pending might not be applied in favor of individuals who are aware from prior experiences that they are clearly uninsurable for the type of coverage applied for.[19] However, for those persons whose insurability may be in doubt, the effect of disregarding an insurability condition in a binding receipt could be quite significant.

16. See the discussion in § 2.3(b), above.

17. Concerning the problem of adverse selection, also see the discussion § 1.3(c), above.

18. This is the position urged in the dissent of Woodrough, J., in New England Mutual Life Insurance Company v. Hinkle, 248 F.2d 879 (8th Cir.1957), *cert. dismissed* 358 U.S. 65, 79 S.Ct. 116, 3 L.Ed.2d 106 (1958).

19. Similarly, it is possible that the rule would have little import for an applicant who was so plainly uninsurable that his or her application could not even be submitted to a sales representative for subsequent consideration by an insurer without making a material misrepresentation.

The provision of temporary insurance coverage for border-line applicants who may prove to be uninsurable upon examination and investigation creates an inducement for some applicants to pay premiums in advance. Some adverse selection almost certainly occurs — that is, a disproportionately higher percentage of the applicants who make advance premium payments will come from the group who comprise the border-line risks. Moreover, the losses paid would tend to be higher in proportion to the premiums collected for the temporary coverage than for permanent coverage, at least in the absence of appropriate adjustments of the premiums to take account of the adverse selection.

(4) Free Temporary Insurance for "Uninsurables"?

Binding receipts almost uniformly provide for repayment of the full premium (which was submitted as a deposit) upon rejection of an application. Construing conditional binding receipts so as to extend coverage for all applicants in some sense provides an individual whose application is rejected with almost cost-free temporary insurance. The only "out-of-pocket" cost for an applicant who receives a refund is the loss of the discretionary use of the amount of the deposit while the application is pending.

Even though almost all binding receipts provide for a full refund of an applicant's deposit, the temporary coverage is not absolutely free. From the standpoint of a technical analysis of whether a contract exists, the transaction certainly involves sufficient "consideration" to satisfy the requirement for a contract that provides temporary insurance coverage: on the one hand, for the applicant the consideration is the benefit of having the application considered by the insurer and the detriment of having lost the use of the premium amount during the period the insurer considers the application; and, on the other hand, for the insurer the consideration is the benefit of the value of the premium deposited during the period while the application is pending, and the detriment of incurring the costs of processing the application.

(5) Funding Judicially Imposed Temporary Coverage

The "uninsurables," [20] who live through the application period and have their premiums returned when their applications for insurance are rejected, receive temporary protection without contributing any premiums to the insurance fund. The insurer may benefit from interest which is earned if the deposits of applicants are invested while applications are pending. However, such interest — if earned on the premiums held while applications are pending — when combined with the premiums paid by those applicants who die while an application is pending, may not provide insurers with an adequate insurance pool to pay the claims.

---

20. See the discussion of equity and discrimination in § 8.4(b), below.

The only premiums an insurer collects and retains are those which are paid by the insurable applicants and by the uninsurable applicants who die during the period while applications are pending. If the interest income and retained premiums from applicants who die while an application is pending provide funds that are not sufficient to pay claims resulting from the deaths that occur while applications are pending, an insurer ultimately has to cover such losses by setting the premiums paid by the "insurables" high enough to provide funds for the payment of the claims that arise under the temporary insurance coverage. In the event this occurs, the insurable applicants — the consumers whose applications mature into insurance contracts — make up for the relative underpayment by applicants who die while applications are pending. Thus, some portion of the costs of providing temporary coverage to those whose applications are rejected may actually be borne by the individuals whose applications are accepted — that is, the funds for paying claims that result from temporary coverage extended to applicants, irrespective of the ultimate determination as to insurability under the plan and rate applied for, may ultimately come from premiums paid by all persons who are insured by life insurance companies.

Comment

The inequity incident to providing some persons with almost free insurance, as well as the possibility of adverse selection discussed above, have not been considered sufficiently significant factors to overcome the inclination of courts to extend temporary coverage beyond the bounds purportedly established by the terms of the binding receipts. In part, this probably results from recognition of the fact that insurance premium rates are never perfectly adjusted to the infinite variations in risks.[21] Moreover, the effects of "free" insurance and "adverse selection" in this context are probably relatively small. Thus, when the courts are essentially asked to weigh these disadvantages against the advantages of avoiding a marketing system which has been viewed as likely to mislead a substantial percentage of applicants for life insurance, many judges have clearly been disposed to favor the interests of persons who have been induced to make an initial premium payment when the application is submitted to the insurer.

(6) Temporary Coverage and the Question of the Obligation to Issue Long Term Coverage

The question whether a binding receipt imposes an obligation to issue a life insurance policy if the conditions of insurability specified in the binding receipt are met has received little direct attention. The primary area of concern about whether such an obligation exists arises

---

21. The losses paid, at least theoretically, would tend to be higher in proportion to the premiums collected for the temporary coverage than for permanent coverage, be-cause of the lack of any adjustment of the premiums to take account of the adverse selection.

in situations in which the language of the binding receipt, standing alone, might be interpreted to mean that an insurer agrees to issue an insurance policy if the conditions specified in regard to the initiation of coverage are satisfied.[22] In this situation, the question is whether a company is always free to terminate all potential liability by returning the premium and delivering to the applicant a notice rejecting the application. In 1957, Professor Patterson observed, in a discussion of binding receipts: "Apparently, the company must prove an honest rejection of the risk as it stood at the time of the application."[23] Professor Patterson's analysis suggests that as a result of terms used in a binding receipt, an insurer might be under an obligation to issue the life insurance policy an applicant seeks (as well as an obligation to provide temporary coverage).

Imposing an obligation to issue a life insurance policy would make considerably deeper inroads on underwriting control than the judicial decisions which hold that insurers are required to provide temporary coverage when an applicant pays some portion of the first premium and the insurer issues a binding receipt. Such a result would obviously be inconsistent with the objectives sought to be attained by insurers through centralized control over underwriting in the marketing of life insurance.[24] In some instances, it may be possible for an applicant to establish a claim of having been misled on the issue of the right to a permanent policy. In most marketing situations, however, neither the statements by sales representatives of an insurer nor the terms used in binding receipts are likely to cause an applicant to believe that the company committed itself to issue an insurance policy following submission of an application. This is true even when the binding receipt declares that the insurance is to be "effective from the time of making application," rather than more explicitly declaring, for example, that insurance is to be "effective from the time of making application until the company accepts or rejects the application."

The dearth of direct authority on this question is not surprising. When an insurer notifies the applicant of its refusal to issue a policy and encloses a draft refunding the premium, the applicant usually cashes the draft and thus, by accord and satisfaction, virtually precludes a successful contention at a later time that the company was obliged to issue a permanent policy.

§ 2.3(d) Avoiding the Binding Receipt Coverage Controversy

It has long been evident that it is within the power of the insurance companies selling life insurance to reduce sharply further controversies arising from the use of binding receipts. One approach would be to

22. See the examples of binding receipt terms set out in § 2.3(b), above.

23. Patterson, ESSENTIALS OF INSURANCE LAW 100–101 (Second edition, 1957), citing Reynolds v. Northwestern Mutual Life Insurance Company, 189 Iowa 76, 176 N.W.

207 (1920) (involving a binding receipt similar to form C, set out in § 2.3(b), above).

24. See the discussion of centralized control over underwriting in § 2.1(b), above.

eliminate the advance payments of premiums by applicants. However, insurers adopting this approach would also forfeit the marketing advantages sought to be attained by encouraging applicants to make deposits.

A second approach would be to extend full interim coverage to all applicants who make a payment from the time of the application until either the coverage is issued or the application is rejected and the premium is returned. This approach, which appears at least implicitly to be the preferred resolution of many courts when such coverage controversies are litigated, potentially entails the prospect for insurers of unacceptable levels of adverse selection, and perhaps a substantial incidence of fraud as well.

A third approach would be for insurers to adopt procedures that ensure that each applicant is explicitly and clearly informed of exactly when and under what conditions either interim coverage will be provided, or, in the absence of providing interim coverage, when the coverage applied for will begin as a result of paying an initial premium at the time the application is made. It is possible to develop both forms and marketing techniques that fully inform insurance applicants. Almost anyone who has rented an automobile has experienced the explanations that accompany the decision to either accept or reject the insurance for the rented vehicle that is offered as an optional part of the rental agreement. Although this particular transaction may not be a perfect model for life insurance applications and conditional binding receipts, it surely points a possible way.

The California Supreme Court, in several of the landmark decisions on the binding receipt controversy, has repeatedly remarked:

> "* * * that if the insurer wishes to avoid its obligation of providing such [temporary] protection it must not only use clear and unequivocal language evidencing its intent to limit temporary coverage pending its approval of the policy, but [it] must also call such limiting condition to the attention of the applicant."[1]

Some insurers have designed simple, easily understood application forms with prominently displayed explanations of both the limitations as to when coverage will commence and the advantage to the insured of paying the initial premium at the time the application is made so as to secure an effective date for the coverage that is sooner than that which would apply in the absence of such a payment (but one that nevertheless begins some time after the submission of the application). In essence, insurers employing this approach have adopted specific measures designed to assure either that the applicant has the same actual expectations as the insurer in regard to the effect of making a deposit, or that no reasonable person submitting an application for insurance to that insurer could have expectations that temporary insurance cover-

---

§ 2.3(d)

1. Smith v. Westland Life Insurance Company, 15 Cal.3d 111 at p. 122, 123 Cal. Rptr. 649 at p. 657, 539 P.2d 433 at p. 441 (1975).

age would result from the payment of a deposit when the application was submitted. The enforceability of such terms has been upheld.[2]

§ 2.4 Delay in Acting on an Application for Insurance

§ 2.4(a) The Duty to Act Promptly

There is a clear split of judicial authority on the question whether an insurance company has an obligation to respond to an application for insurance, and if so, how quickly a response must be made. The views set forth in a substantial number of opinions are either that an insurer does not have any duty to act on an application for insurance or that an insurer does not have a duty to act promptly on an application.[1]

2. Hildebrandt v. Washington National Insurance Company, 181 Mont. 231, 593 P.2d 37 (1979); Hildebrand v. Franklin Life Insurance Company, 118 Ill.App.3d 861, 74 Ill.Dec. 280, 455 N.E.2d 553 (4th Dist.1983); Fields v. Franklin Life Insurance Company, 115 Ill.App.3d 954, 71 Ill. Dec. 776, 451 N.E.2d 930 (5th Dist.1983).

In Reynolds v. Guarantee Reserve Life Insurance Company, 44 Ill.App.3d 764 at p. 769, 3 Ill.Dec. 397, 358 N.E.2d 940 at p. 944 (5th Dist.1976), the court distinguished cases such as *Gaunt v. John Hancock Mutual Life Insurance Company* on the basis that in Reynolds "the language is clear that no coverage exists until either issuance or delivery and there is no language inducing the belief of immediate or nearly immediate coverage * * *."

Cf. Rhode v. Massachusetts Mutual Life Insurance Company, 632 F.2d 667 at p. 669 6th Cir., (applying the law of Ohio) (concluding that the binding receipt at issue was "unambiguous and cannot be construed to provide applicant with coverage prior to the defendant's [the insurer] determination that the applicant is insurable," but also holding that the insurer was liable because the determination was made in "bad faith."); Grandpre v. Northwestern National Life Insurance Company, 261 N.W.2d 804 (S.D.1977), discussed in Note, *Grandpre v. Northwestern National Life Insurance Co.: South Dakota Takes the Technical Approach to Conditional Receipts for Life Insurance,* 24 South Dakota Law Review 200–216 (1979); Brown v. Equitable Life Insurance Company, 60 Wis.2d 620, 211 N.W.2d 431 (1973); Hancock Mutual Life Insurance Company v. McNeill, 27 Ariz.App. 502, 556 P.2d 803 (Div. 1, Dept. B, 1976).

Furthermore, courts have sustained the time limitations on coverage in binding receipts which clearly specify that tempo-rary coverage will be provided for a period such as sixty days. See, e.g., Hornaday v. Sun Life Insurance Company of America, 597 F.2d 90 (7th Cir.1979) (applying Indiana law to a sixty day period).

Also see Spangler v. State Farm Fire & Casualty Company, 221 Tenn. 37, 424 S.W.2d 191 (1968) (30 day binder while application for automobile insurance was pending).

But cf. Miney v. Baum, 170 N.J.Super. 282, 406 A.2d 234 (Law Division, 1979) (coverage was extended even though binder for automobile policy had been in effect for more than 60 days at time of accident; coverage was controlled by statute which states the circumstances under which an insurance policy may be cancelled, and thus where there had been no formal notice of cancellation at time of accident, coverage was provided even though no premium had been paid).

§ 2.4(a)

1. In Cameron v. First National Bank in Bozeman, 186 Mont. 345, 607 P.2d 1113 at p. 1117 (1980), the court observed that "the insurer's delay in accepting or rejecting an application does not create a contract of insurance."

In Megee v. United States Fidelity & Guaranty Company, 391 A.2d 189 at p. 192 (Delaware 1978) (application for disability insurance) the court observed, "Because no premium had been paid by the plaintiff under the explicit terms of the application, neither USF & G nor Vertex had a duty to act within a time certain."

In Usher v. Allstate Insurance Company, 300 Minn. 52, 218 N.W.2d 201 (1974), the court observed, since 1934 "there is no duty on the part of an insurer to accept or reject an application for insurance" and therefore "mere delay on the part of the company in passing on an application will

The cases which adopt either of these views are probably appropriately characterized as applying a minority rule.

A majority of the appellate courts that have considered this issue have rendered decisions which support the general proposition that an insurer is subject to liability when there is an unreasonable delay in acting on an application for insurance.[2] Within this general view, however, there is considerable diversity about both the grounds of liability and the scope of the insurer's obligation. Four principal theories of liability have been advanced in these judicial decisions:

Estoppel: The combination of the marketing actions by representatives of the insurer and the failure of the insurer to act on an application for insurance estops the insurer from denying that the application has been accepted.[3]

Implied agreement to act promptly: The solicitation of an application for insurance constitutes an implied agreement that the insurer will act upon the application either without unreasonable delay or within a reasonable period of time [4] — especially when the applicant pays some portion of the premium — and an insurer's

not support either an action for breach of contract or one sounding in tort." *Id.*, 300 Minn. at p. 55, 218 N.W.2d at p. 204. However, in *Usher*, the Supreme Court reversed a directed verdict for the insurer on the basis that the record would have supported jury findings that would have warranted recognition that an interim contract arose by implication.

In Watkins v. Coastal States Life Insurance Company, 118 Ga.App. 145, 162 S.E.2d 788 (Div. 2, 1968), the court concluded that mere filing of an application did not impose a duty to act reasonably or promptly or even to act.

Also see, United Insurance Company v. Headrick, 275 Ala. 594, 157 So.2d 19 (1963); LeVasseur v. Knights of Columbus, 96 R.I. 34, 188 A.2d 469 (1963).

Cf. Patten v. Continental Casualty Company, 162 Ohio St. 18, 120 N.E.2d 441 (1954); Zayc v. John Hancock Mutual Life Insurance Company, 338 Pa. 426, 13 A.2d 34 (1940).

Any theory of liability based on unjust enrichment is also arguably weak as a basis for imposing liability in the amount that would have been payable had a policy been issued promptly, since the "enrichment" of the insurer is almost always insubstantial in comparison with the amount of coverage that the applicant sought. But see the comments of the Minnesota Supreme Court in Usher v. Allstate Insur-

ance Company, 300 Minn. 52, 218 N.W.2d 201 at pp. 205–206 (1974).

See generally, Annotation, *Liability of insurer for damages resulting in delay in passing upon application for health insurance*, 18 A.L.R.4th 1115–1143 (1982), and Annotation, *Liability of insurer for damages resulting from delay in passing upon an application for life insurance*, 1 A.L.R. 4th 1202–1243 (1980); Annotation, *Rights and remedies arising out of delay in passing upon application for insurance*, 32 A.L.R.2d 487–539 (1953).

2. Of course, not all delays are unreasonable. For example, in Cartwright v. Maccabees Mutual Life Insurance Company, 398 Mich. 238, 247 N.W.2d 298 (1976), the court observed the delay was solely attributable to the avoidance by the applicant's attending physician of repeated requests for medical information.

3. See the discussion of estoppel and detrimental reliance in § 6.5, below.

4. See, e.g., Ryan v. Security Industrial Insurance Co., 386 So.2d 939 (La.App., 3d Cir., 1980) (burial insurance policy); Combined American Insurance Company v. Parker, 377 S.W.2d 213 (Tex.Civ.App., Austin, 1964, writ refused, no reversible error) (hospitalization insurance policy).

But cf. Franklin Life Insurance Company v. Hamilton, 335 So.2d 119 (Miss.1976).

failure to respond for an extended period of time constitutes a breach of that implied agreement.[5]

Formation of a contract of insurance: An application for insurance is an offer which is regarded as having been accepted (that is, acceptance is inferred or implied) when an insurer remains silent after receiving the application, especially when such silence is accompanied by the retention of a premium payment.[6]

Tort: An insurer has a duty to act on an application for insurance either without unreasonable delay or within a reasonable period of time, and violation of this duty subjects the insurer to liability.[7] This duty arises from the relationship between the applicant and the insurer, and is supported by those tort principles which justify duties of affirmative action[8] and by the special nature of the insurance business, which is affected by a public interest[9] — especially when the application was accompanied by the payment of a premium.[10]

Among these theories, the implied agreement to act promptly and the tort duty have most frequently been recognized by appellate courts as grounds for imposing liability on insurers.[11] However, the application of any of these theories to a coverage dispute often presents certain

---

5. See, e.g., Travelers Insurance Company v. Anderson, 210 F.Supp. 735 (W.D.S.C. 1962) (automobile trip insurance; applying South Carolina law, court recognizes both implied agreement from nature of coverage and tort theories); Gorham v. Peerless Life Insurance Company, 368 Mich. 335, 118 N.W.2d 306 (1962) (health and accident insurance; agreement to act without delay implied from advertising and application form).

6. *Cf.* Brand v. International Investors Insurance Company, 521 P.2d 423 (Okl. App., Div. 2, 1974) (agreement to act without delay inferred from insurer's solicitation of life insurance application and insured's payment of first premium).

7. See, e.g., Snyder v. Redding Motors, 131 Cal.App.2d 416, 280 P.2d 811 (3d Dist. 1955).

But see Cameron v. First National Bank in Bozeman, 186 Mont. 345, 607 P.2d 1113 at p. 1117 (1980).

8. See, e.g., Demarlor v. Foley Carter Insurance Company, 386 So.2d 22 (Fla. App., 2d Dist., 1980).

Also see Travelers Insurance Company v. Anderson, 210 F.Supp. 735 (W.D.S.C.1962) (automobile trip insurance; applying South Carolina law, court recognizes both implied agreement from nature of coverage and tort theories); Hinds v. United Insurance Company, 248 S.C. 285, 149 S.E.2d 771 (1966).

Cf. Republic National Life Insurance Company v. Chilcoat, 368 P.2d 821 (Okl. 1961); Duffie v. Bankers' Life Association, 160 Iowa 19 at p. 27, 139 N.W. 1087 at p. 1090 (1913).

9. See, e.g., Continental Life and Accident Co. v. Songer, 124 Ariz. 294, 603 P.2d 921 (App.1979).

Also see the discussion of tort liability in § 2.4(b)(4), below.

10. See, e.g., Duffie v. Bankers' Life Association, 160 Iowa 19 at p. 27, 139 N.W. 1087 at p. 1090 (1913).

Also see Republic National Life Insurance Company v. Chilcoat, 368 P.2d 821, 824 (Okl.1961); Talbot v. Country Life Insurance Company, 8 Ill.App.3d 1062, 291 N.E.2d 830 (3d Dist.1973).

But see, e.g., Zayc v. John Hancock Mutual Life Insurance Company, 338 Pa. 426 at p. 434, 13 A.2d 34 at p. 38 (1940) (legal relevancy of operation under a state franchise rejected).

See generally, Annotation, *Liability of insurer for damages resulting from delay in passing upon an application for life insurance,* 1 A.L.R.4th 1202–1243 (1980).

Also see the discussion in § 2.4(c), below.

11. See, e.g., Continental Life & Accident Company v. Songer, 124 Ariz. 294, 603 P.2d 921, 18 A.L.R.4th 1099 (App., Div. 1, Dept. A, 1979) (application for health insurance).

theoretical problems, as well as involving a number of pragmatic considerations. As a result, even though each theory justifies an outcome that provides some benefits to the claimant(s), the facts of a given transaction often influence the theoretical basis on which a claimant's suit will be predicated.[12]

§ 2.4(b) Comparisons of Judicially Recognized Grounds for Liability

(1) Estoppel

A claim of estoppel typically entails proof of facts that also would support many of the essential elements of a tort claim. In some situations, however, predicating a claim on the estoppel theory may be advantageous for a claimant because the tort claim also requires proof of negligence. Moreover, an estoppel theory may also be preferred by a claimant because a tort claim would be subject to the defense of contributory negligence.[1]

Estoppel, as an equitable doctrine, applies to situations in which a party is precluded from taking a given position in litigation as a consequence of some action or conduct. Insurers have sometimes been denied the right to deny that an application for insurance had been accepted on the basis of an estoppel. The justification for concluding that an insurer is estopped from rejecting an insurance application is undoubtedly strongest when the claimant (in most instances, either the applicant or an individual named as a beneficiary) can also show that the applicant justifiably relied to his or her detriment. For example, such reliance might be demonstrated by proof that some action or statement by the insurer or a sales representative of the insurer caused the applicant not to seek insurance from another insurer who would have provided the coverage that the insured sought in the application. Alternatively, there might be proof that the applicant relied on statements that the insurer would act on the application.

Some courts hold that the estoppel doctrine should only be applied when a claimant can show that an applicant detrimentally relied on some action or statement of the insurer or its representative, that such reliance was reasonably foreseeable by the insurer, that the applicant's

But cf. Duke v. Valley Forge Life Insurance Company, 341 So.2d 1366, 1 A.L.R. 4th 1193 (La.App., 4th Cir., 1977) (rehearing denied 1977) (group life insurance application).

12. See Annotation, *Liability of insurer for damages resulting from delay in passing upon an application for life insurance,* 1 A.L.R.4th 1202–1243 (1980).

Also *cf.* Funk, *The Duty of an Insurer to Act Promptly on Application,* 75 University Pennsylvania Law Review 207–226 (1927); Prosser, *Delay in Acting on an Application for Insurance,* 3 University Chicago Law Review 39–60 (1935); 12 Appleman, INSURANCE LAW §§ 7226 and 4267; Annotation, *Rights and remedies arising out of delay in passing upon application for insurance,* 32 A.L.R.2d 487 (1953).

§ 2.4(b)

1. See, e.g., Duffie v. Bankers' Life Association, 160 Iowa 19, 139 N.W. 1087 (1913).

Also see the discussion of possible contributory negligence in Mann v. Policyholders' National Life Insurance Company, 78 N.D. 724, 51 N.W.2d 853 (1952).

reliance (either action or forebearance) was of a definite and substantial nature, and, at least in some situations, that the applicant's reliance was reasonable.[2] However, the estoppel doctrine has sometimes been applied even though it is not possible for the claimant to show that the applicant would have sought coverage from another insurer or that another insurer from which such coverage was sought would have agreed to insure the applicant, or that any representation was made that the insurer would act on the application. A court that approves an estoppel claim in the absence of such proof is, of course, applying the doctrine to a situation in which there is no proof of detrimental reliance.[3] The soundness of such decisions has been questioned. Consequently, a potential problem for a claimant who predicates an action on the estoppel theory on the basis of a factual similarity to such cases, especially when those precedents are from other jurisdictions, is the possibility that a court may decline to apply the estoppel doctrine in the absence of proof of all the elements that comprise a prima facie case for detrimental reliance.[4]

Even though it may not be possible for a claimant to show that an applicant would have taken the initiative to obtain insurance elsewhere, reasonable latitude for claimants could be provided by adopting the position that so long as an applicant does not attempt to obtain insurance from another insurer recovery in these situations is warranted because it is appropriate to find that the applicant is relying upon the insurer to respond within a reasonable time after an application for coverage is submitted. One rationale in support of this approach is that if the price to be paid for insurance is not an issue, almost all risks are insurable. For example, there are insurers who specialize in underwriting for persons suffering from medical conditions that would lead to the rejection of life insurance applications by most companies, and therefore there is considerable foundation for finding justifiable reliance in this context. In essence, this approach would hold that all that is required in order to justify an application of estoppel in favor of an applicant (and the intended beneficiaries) is proof that an application was submitted and that the loss occurred while the applicant had a reasonable expectation of a response to the application from the insurer.[5]

2. When reviewing the cases which base liability on the theory that an insurer is estopped from denying acceptance of an application, one finds no explanation for the extension of estoppel beyond the classic formulation. Developing a clear statement of grounds for imposing liability seems preferable to such unexplained extensions of estoppel theory. See generally § 6.5, below.

3. The estoppel theory also may be less advantageous than tort theory in this type of situation in those jurisdictions which adopt the view that the duty in tort arises upon commencement of performance without regard to whether the applicant can show a detriment.

4. Concerning standards of detrimental reliance in insurance law, see generally § 6.5(f), below.

5. See the discussion in WILLISTON ON CONTRACTS, (Third Edition, edited by Walter H.E. Jaeger, 1963), § 904.

(2) Implied Agreement to Act Promptly

Predicating liability on an implied-in-fact agreement to act promptly necessitates a judicial determination that the facts warrant such an inference.[6] In many situations such an inference conflicts with explicit language in the application form used by the insurer.[7] For example, application forms commonly state that the company shall incur no liability until it acts on the application. When this type of statement is clearly made in large print on the front of the application form, in most situations there is little justification for the fact findings essential to sustain a determination that an implied-in-fact agreement is warranted. The determination that an implied-in-fact agreement exists in such cases would almost always be an obvious fiction.[8] Consequently, a claimant would not prevail unless such an agreement is implied as a matter of law.

(3) Silence as Acceptance

The theory that silence is a manifestation of consent to a contract often presents difficult questions for a court. In general, there is considerable reluctance to treat any form of inaction, including silence, as a manifestation of assent unless it is so intended. Furthermore, insurers typically include provisions in application forms and conditional receipts that explicitly state the insurer does not intend inaction or silence to be taken as an acceptance. For example, one provision that is commonly used in application forms expressly states that a company will not incur liability before it acts on the application. Consequently, in most situations sustaining a claim based on treating silence as acceptance is only possible when a court will resort to an obvious legal fiction.

(4) Tort Liability

Judicial recognition of a tort action when an insurer fails to act on an application almost always poses at least one significant theoretical

---

6. See, e.g., the discussion in United Travelers Insurance Company v. Perkins, 611 S.W.2d 152 at p. 156 (Tex.Civ.App., Waco, 1981) (life insurance policy provision stated insurance would not take effect until, *inter alia,* policy was delivered to applicant during her lifetime and good health); Adams v. State Capital Life Insurance Company, 11 N.C.App. 678, 182 S.E.2d 250 (1971), *cert. denied* 279 N.C. 393, 183 S.E.2d 244 (1971) (provision stipulating coverage would become effective only upon home office approval).

7. Any theory based on unjust enrichment is also weak as an argument for imposing liability in the amount that would have been payable had a policy been issued promptly, because the "enrichment" of the insurer is almost always insubstan-

tial in comparison with the amount of coverage that the applicant sought.

See the discussion of interim coverage in § 2.3, above.

8. See, e.g., Adams v. State Capital Life Insurance Company, 11 N.C.App. 678, 182 S.E.2d 250 (1971), *cert. denied* 279 N.C. 393, 183 S.E.2d 244 (1971) (silence and inaction do not amount to acceptance of insurance contract).

But cf. National Bank of Commerce v. Royal Exchange Assurance of America, 455 F.2d 892 at p. 898 (6th Cir.1972), in which the court observed that "an implied acceptance can be recognized as a basis for relief when an insurance company fails to accept or reject an application with reasonable promptness * * *."

problem in regard to the basis of the insurer's duty in such a case. Recognition of a possible duty for insurers to act on applications for insurance specifically presents courts with the question, much disputed in the "Good Samaritan" cases, as to when and under what circumstances anyone has a tort duty of affirmative action (as contrasted with the generally recognized duty not to act negligently).[9] For example, in cases in which someone begins to render assistance, there is considerable debate in regard to whether a duty arises from mere commencement of such an act,[10] or whether a duty arises only when an actor has proceeded far enough so that by stopping, the actor's total course of conduct has made the situation worse.[11] When the appellate court opinions imposing tort liability in insurance disputes are analyzed, it is often not clear which of these two approaches to the insurer's duty is being applied in regard to not acting on applications for insurance.[12]

There is considerable support among the American precedents for the proposition that a tort duty of affirmative action only applies when the conditions have been worsened.[13] Under such a standard, strictly applied, in order to prove that the insurer's total course of conduct has worsened the situation of the applicant or the intended beneficiary, it would seem necessary for the claimant to show that the applicant would and could have obtained insurance elsewhere — before the death occurred — had the agent not approached the applicant.

§ 2.4(c)   Recognizing an Additional Justification for Liability

The distinctive nature of insurance transactions supports a basis for the liability of insurers that fail to act on insurance applications

---

9. See, e.g., William L. Prosser & W. Page Keeton, Torts (Fifth edition, 1984), at pp. 339–343.

10. See, e.g., Continental Life & Accident Company v. Songer, 124 Ariz. 294, 603 P.2d 921 at p. 929 (App., Div. 1, Dept. A., 1979).

Also see, Warren Seavey, *Reliance on Gratuitous Promises or Other Conduct,* 64 Harvard Law Review 913–928 (1951).

11. See, e.g., Hinds v. United Insurance Company, 248 S.C. 285, 149 S.E.2d 771 (1966), in which the complaint alleged delay of about two months in issuing health and accident policy. The policy that was issued contained an exclusion clause that restricted liability for conditions arising within the first six months. The insured had a heart attack five days before the policy had been in effect six months. The court held that the complaint stated cause of action for the loss as one for which the applicant would have been covered "but for the negligence of the agent". This decision suggests several questions. Does this mean it would be enough to show that the policy that was in fact issued would have

been issued more than five days sooner but for the agent's negligence? Or would it be necessary to show a worsening in some sense, e.g., that the agent's negligence made the applicant's position worse than it was before the agent took the application because otherwise the applicant would have effected coverage elsewhere?

12. See Prosser & Keeton, Torts (Fifth edition, 1984), at pp. 373–385.

It has been said that liability in such a case is supported by a jury finding that but for the negligence of the company a certificate of insurance would have been issued by the company before the applicant's death. See, e.g., Continental Life and Accident Co. v. Songer, 124 Ariz. 294, 603 P.2d 921 (App., Div. 1, Dept. A, 1979); Duffie v. Bankers' Life Association, 160 Iowa 19, 139 N.W. 1087 (1913). This phrasing of the rule does not require a showing that the claimant's position is worse than it would have been if the agent had not approached the applicant.

13. See Prosser & Keeton, Torts (Fifth edition, 1984), at pp. 378–382.

beyond that which has been explicitly set forth in most of the judicial opinions to date.

An extension of liability in regard to insurance applications to which the insurer has not responded is certainly a matter of public interest. Furthermore the capacity of insurers to bear and spread risk, including the risk of harm from delay in acting on applications, is the very essence of the insurance system.[1] In considering the import of these points in regard to insurance applications, the following views should be compared:

First: Although a statute requiring insurance companies to act upon applications within a reasonable time would be constitutional, courts should not impose a duty upon insurers merely because the legislature might do so.[2] Banking and employment are also matters of great public interest, and there is no duty on enterprises to act without delay on an application for a bank loan or a job. The business of insurance does not call for any different rule.[3] Moreover, the harm complained of in cases of delay in acting on applications for insurance is nonphysical economic loss growing out of negotiations. Comparable liability in other situations of negotiation is very limited, and is much narrower in scope than for physical harms.

Second: The standardized mass contract, developed by a large business firm such as an insurance company and used in substantially every transaction for its product or service, places the individual at a distinct disadvantage in bargaining with such a firm. The doctrines of contract law, which are based upon freedom of contract, developed primarily to govern transactions between individuals or entities of relatively comparable status. Therefore, they are not suited to determining the rights of consumers who wish to purchase insurance and who are obliged both to use the application forms and to accept coverage terms that are embodied in form contracts. The applications and policies used by insurance companies are frequently highly standardized contract forms and the courts should develop different doctrines for such consumer transactions rather than allowing technical doctrines of contract law to

§ 2.4(c)

1. All insurers engage in risk distribution: the risk is distributed either to the premium-payers or to other insurers through the use of reinsurance. Insurers bear risks only temporarily. Also see the discussion of risk distribution in § 1.3, above.

One might question whether the burden falls fairly. One response, at least for losses that do not imperil an insurer's existence, is that it is not important in insurance law to trace the shifting of the burden any farther than to premium-payers.

2. See the discussion in Brown v. Equitable Life Insurance Company, 60 Wis.2d 620, 211 N.W.2d 431 at p. 436 (1973).

Cf. Patten v. Continental Casualty Company, 162 Ohio St. 18, 120 N.E.2d 441 (1954); LeVasseur v. Knights of Columbus, 96 R.I. 34, 188 A.2d 469 (1963).

3. See William Prosser, *Delay in Acting on an Application for Insurance,* 3 University of Chicago Law Review 39–60 at pp. 52–53 (1935).

Cf. Zayc v. John Hancock Mutual Life Insurance Company, 338 Pa. 426, 13 A.2d 34 (1940).

defeat coverage claims when the public interest would be served by imposing liability.[4]

In general, judicial decisions — especially in the last three or four decades — seem to have moved away from the rationales and views set out in the first statement. Increasingly judicial opinions seem to be consistent with the second view, though the decisions are not always expressed in such terms.[5]

Some courts have included comments in opinions which recognize that the special nature of the insurance business means that these transactions are affected by a public interest and that the public interest should be considered by the courts when resolving a coverage dispute resulting from a death that occurs while an application for life insurance is being considered by an insurance company.[6] Public service enterprises, such as railroad companies and airlines, are required to furnish transportation to all qualified passengers and shippers. Thus, one approach to the issue of the delays that inevitably occur in connection with the processing of applications for insurance would be to treat insurance companies as public service companies that are under a legal duty to insure every applicant from the date of application until the insurer notifies the applicant that the application is either accepted or rejected.[7]

All applicants would gain some benefit from the provision of interim coverage while applications are pending. Although the premium-payers whose applications are processed promptly receive a relatively modest benefit in regard to the extent of interim coverage,[8] the economic burden borne by these premium payers in providing funds that are needed to cover claims that arise while applications are pending would be quite small in relation to the total cost of the insurance program that must be paid for out of premium income.[9] The differences among policyholders as to the need for interim or temporary

---

4. *Cf.* Dunford v. United of Omaha, 95 Idaho 282 at p. 284, 506 P.2d 1355 at p. 1357 (1973); Toevs v. Western Farm Bureau Life Insurance Company, 94 Idaho 151, 483 P.2d 682 (1971).

Also see Kessler, *Contracts of Adhesion—Some Thoughts About Freedom of Contract,* 43 Columbia Law Review 629–642 (1943).

5. Concerning principles that may account for these decisions, see the discussion in Chapter 6, below.

6. See, e.g., Continental Life & Accident Company v. Songer, 124 Ariz. 294, 603 P.2d 921 at pp. 929–930 (App., Div. 1, Dept. A, 1979).

This is especially the case when the submission of an application has been accompanied by the payment of some portion of the initial premium. See the discussion of interim coverage in § 2.3, above.

Also see Duffie v. Bankers' Life Association, 160 Iowa 19 at p. 27, 139 N.W. 1087 at p. 1090 (1913); Republic National Life Insurance Co. v. Chilcoat, 368 P.2d 821 at p. 824 (Okl.1961).

But see Watkins v. Coastal States Life Insurance Company, 118 Ga.App. 145, 162 S.E.2d 788 at p. 791 (Div. 2, 1968).

7. *Cf.* Edwin Patterson, *The Delivery of a Life Insurance Policy,* 33 Harvard Law Review 198–222 at pp. 216–217 (1919); Herbert Denenberg, *Meeting the Insurance Crisis of our Cities: An Industry in Revolution,* 1970 Insurance Law Journal 205–220 at pp. 210–212.

8. They do receive some benefit, especially in the sense of the security of the availability of such temporary coverage in case of need.

9. One might think of a small fraction of the premium as a payment for insurance

coverage may be regarded as a permissible degree of variation within a single rate category.[10]

Requiring insurers to provide interim or temporary coverage for all applicants while applications for insurance are pending obviously represents a rule of considerably broader import than imposing liability on insurers when an insurer has not acted with reasonable promptness. Such a rule would also be a substantial extension beyond the liability imposed by the judicial decisions that require insurers who receive applications accompanied by deposits to provide interim coverage without regard to the terms and conditions set out in the conditional receipts.[11]

§ 2.4(d) Whose Cause of Action?

In most instances, the matter of who is entitled to assert a cause of action for delay in acting on an application for insurance is not a question of great significance. The person who is identified as the intended beneficiary of the policy applied for is often the same person who would inherit from the estate of the deceased. In some situations, however, discerning who is entitled to assert a cause of action is a matter of great consequence because of differences in the identity of such claimants, because of tax consequences, or because of claims against the deceased's estate.

If the cause of action is contractual in nature, the intended beneficiary of the insurance policy should be entitled to recover, because the person so designated is the one who would have been entitled to recover under the policy had the insurer acted affirmatively upon the application.[1]

If the remedy for delay in acting on an application is based on a tort theory, the cause of action should also belong to the person or persons who suffer a loss as a result of the insurer's breach of duty — that is, the person(s) designated in the application as beneficiary would be entitled to recover.[2] However, there is authority holding that a tort cause of action belongs to the estate of the insured.[3]

that there will be coverage if undue delay happens to occur.

10. See the discussion equity and discrimination in § 8.4(b), below.

11. Also consider the discussion of life insurance applications in § 2.3, above.

§ 2.4(d)

1. See, e.g., Ryan v. Security Industrial Insurance Company, 386 So.2d 939 (La. App., 3d Cir., 1980) (a contract action in which the beneficiary was entitled to recover, under an estoppel to deny coverage, when the insurer failed to either accept or reject application for a burial policy within reasonable period of time).

Also see Bekken v. Equitable Life Assurance Society, 70 N.D. 122, 293 N.W. 200 (1940).

2. Cf. Travelers Insurance Company v. Anderson, 210 F.Supp. 735 (W.D.S.C.1962) (beneficiary asserted a counter-claim in declaratory judgment action instituted by insurer).

Also cf. § 6.5(b), below.

3. See, e.g., Rosin v. Peninsular Life Insurance Company, 116 So.2d 798 (Fla. App., 2d Dist., 1960); Duffie v. Bankers' Life Association, 160 Iowa 19, 139 N.W. 1087 (1913).

§ 2.5 Intermediaries in Insurance Marketing

§ 2.5(a) The Agents, Brokers, and Employees Who Sell Insurance

Many types of transactions between insurance companies and insureds are conducted through intermediaries. This is particularly true in the merchandising of insurance.[1]

Insurance is marketed in a variety of ways. Many insurers deal with consumers through sales representatives who are employees of the insurance company. Sales representatives may also be employees of separate companies that are wholly or partially owned by insurers. And a very substantial portion of the insurance coverage in the United States is sold by entrepreneurs and their employees who are generally known as independent insurance agents or insurance brokers. Some independent entrepreneurs are sales representatives for only one company, while others represent many insurers.

Terms such as "agent" and "broker" that are used to describe sales representatives are generally familiar to the public. However, they have become increasingly imprecise as descriptions of the status or role of persons who sell insurance. In many situations, these terms are used interchangeably by people in the insurance business, as well as by lawyers and courts. Another problem with terms such as "agent" is that insurers use the terms in different ways depending on the type of insurance being marketed.[2] In recent years, however, the insurance industry and trade press have increasingly used the term "producer" to describe all of the different types of intermediaries who "produce" the sales transactions.

§ 2.5(b) Insurance Terminology and Agency Law

A determination of the rights of an insured and an insurer resulting from a particular insurance transaction sometimes depends upon the extent to which an intermediary, such as an agent or a broker, had the authority to represent one or the other of the parties to the transaction. Coverage disputes resulting from marketing transactions often involve an issue about whether a sales representative had either the actual or the apparent authority to represent an insurer. Courts resolving such problems have often yielded to the temptation to present explanations for decisions exclusively on the basis of concepts developed in legislative provisions and judicial precedents that apply to other agency relationships. There is, however, an almost insuperable difficulty in attempting to conform the applicable body of law — which includes both the statutory provisions that regulate insurance marketing arrangements and the judicial precedents in disputes between

§ 2.5(a)

1. Frequently, it is also a characteristic of other aspects of the insurance business such as claims adjusting.

2. See the discussion of terminology in § 2.5(b), below.

insurance companies and claimants — within the bounds of the concepts that are generally encompassed by the rules and doctrines of agency law. Consequently, this approach has frequently produced confusion and, in some instances, notable distortions of agency law doctrines.[1]

The relationships between insurance companies and sales representatives in regard to the authority to contract on behalf of insurers have been established in a multitude of patterns that often cannot be accurately described or characterized by the terms that are generally used to define relationships in agency law. Thus, a fundamental error can result in some instances when a concept from agency law is applied to a disputed insurance transaction as if it were a universally applicable general proposition. In general, considerable skepticism should be applied to any assertion that a particular result in an insurance dispute is warranted by the law that governs agency relationships.[2] Moreover, as the following discussion illustrates, insurers use terms such as "agents" to refer to or to describe individuals in vastly different situations.

(1) Life Insurance Terminology

The marketing organization used by most insurers for life insurance employs a network of offices which are directed by either *general agents* or *branch managers*.[3] A general agent is usually an independent business person who has agreed to represent a life insurance company within a given geographical area.[4] In return for their efforts, general agents are paid a commission on the insurance they sell or "produce," but usually are not reimbursed for the expense of operating the agency. A branch manager, on the other hand, is almost always a salaried employee of an insurance company whose home office usually pays all of the branch office's overhead expenses.[5] Many life insurance companies, however, offer branch managers compensation systems which reflect the amount of business produced. Additionally, many insurers marketing life insurance through the independent agency system now provide such sales representatives with expense allowances. Conse-

§ 2.5(b)

1. Illustrations of the misuse of agency concepts are discussed in § 2.5(d) and § 7.5(c), below.

2. In many instances, a better explanation for a decision favoring a claimant would be to recognize that the result is predicated on some overriding principle that justifies liability at variance with policy provisions. See Chapter 6, below.

Also see Herbert Denenberg, Eilers, Hoffman, Kline, Melone & Snider, RISK AND INSURANCE (1964), at p. 299 and p. 305.

3. See, e.g., Herbert Denenberg, Robert D. Eilers, Joseph J. Melone & Robert A. Zelten, RISK AND INSURANCE (Second edition, 1974), at pp. 580–81.

4. *Id.*, at p. 580. Also see Joseph B. Maclean, LIFE INSURANCE (Ninth edition, 1962), at pp. 360–361.

5. Herbert Denenberg, Robert D. Eilers, Joseph J. Melone & Robert A. Zelten, RISK AND INSURANCE (Second edition, 1974), at p. 581.

quently, especially in recent years, the distinctions between the two marketing systems have been considerably diminished.[6]

There are many sales representatives who represent more than one insurer. Intermediaries who are in a position to sell the life insurance products of several companies are frequently referred to as brokers.[7] However, this characterization is not invariably used to identify such sales representatives. For example, an examination of the insurance listings in the classified telephone book for any large metropolitan area will almost always serve to identify persons representing several different insurers who denote themselves as insurance agents.

Life insurance companies usually do not extend to branch managers or general agents the broad authority to make contracts that is characteristic of persons who are called general agents in the marketing systems for fire, marine, and casualty insurance.[8] In the life insurance industry, final underwriting authority is customarily retained in the home office of an insurance company.[9] Ordinarily, persons selling life insurance at most are granted authority by a life insurance company to enter into temporary, conditional, life insurance contracts.[10]

In life insurance sales organizations, general agents or branch managers typically delegate their authority to bind an insurer to a conditional, temporary insurance contract to subagents. However, while some subagents are explicitly empowered to extend binders for such temporary coverage, others — who are often referred to as *soliciting agents* — are not authorized to bind the company they represent and, at least theoretically, are only permitted to solicit and forward applications for life insurance.[11] A soliciting agent typically is

6. Emmett Vaughan and Curtis M. Elliott, FUNDAMENTALS OF RISK AND INSURANCE (Second edition, 1978), at p. 70.

7. Whether a broker is acting as the representative of the insurer or the insured may depend on the law of the state in which the transaction occurs. See S.S. Huebner and Kenneth Black, Jr., LIFE INSURANCE (Ninth edition, 1976) at p. 508.

In the terminology of the life insurance industry, anyone who acts as an agent for more than one insurer is often referred to as a broker. See, e.g., Joseph B. Maclean, LIFE INSURANCE (Ninth edition, 1962), p. 362 at n. 3. Individuals who are sales representatives for several companies are sometimes referred to as soliciting agents. See, e.g., Albert H. Mowbray, Blanchard & C. Arthur Williams, Jr., INSURANCE (Sixth edition, 1969), at pp. 401–402.

8. *But cf.* Service v. Pyramid Life Insurance Company, 201 Kan. 944, 440 P.2d 944 (1968).

9. See discussion of control over underwriting in § 2.1(b).

The Alabama Supreme Court has clearly recognized a distinction between a *general agent* and a *soliciting agent* selling life insurance, which assumes that a soliciting agent has no power to issue policies, no power to bind the company by an oral contract, and no power to waive policy or application provisions. McGhee v. Paramount Life Insurance Company, 385 So.2d 969 (Ala.1980).

Also see United Insurance Company v. Headrick, 275 Ala. 594, 157 So.2d 19 (1963) ("soliciting agent" of life insurance company not authorized to bind company to oral contract of insurance).

10. See discussion of temporary life insurance contracts in § 2.3.

11. See, e.g., Watson v. Prudential Insurance Company of America, 399 So.2d 285 (Ala.1981).

Questions regarding the ability of a soliciting agent to bind an insurer, however, are often resolved not by examining an agent's actual authority but, rather, by determining whether the agent possessed

authorized to do nothing more than ministerial acts on behalf of an insurer. Nevertheless, courts have sometimes concluded that the activities of a soliciting agent may bind the insurer.[12]

(2) Fire, Marine, and Casualty Insurance Terminology

Insurance companies selling fire, marine, and casualty insurance generally market coverages through *soliciting agents, special agents,* or *general agents.* In the strictest usage of the term, a *soliciting agent* is one who has authority only to seek and receive applications for transmission to an insurance company. A soliciting agent is not authorized to make any commitment on behalf of a fire, marine, or casualty insurer.

A *general agent* typically has almost unlimited authority to make insurance contracts which are subsequently reported to the insurer's home office.[13] Although the contractual relationship between a general agent and an insurer usually calls for the agent to report sales transactions promptly, the failure of such a sales representative to do so ordinarily will not affect the validity of the insurance contract.

The term *special agent* is generally used by these insurers to refer to a person in a sales organization whose authority to make insurance contracts is subject to explicit limitations. The limitations are usually specified in the contractual arrangement between the special agent and the insurer. Although the term "special agent" is used to designate persons with limited authority to bind an insurer, the term remains indefinite and imprecise because of the multitude of possible variations that exist in the authority which is conferred on such individuals. The meaning of the term "special agent" is also somewhat ambiguous because of its use in other types of insurance activities. For example, the term is sometimes used to designate a person who is an intermediary between the field force and the home office, including a person who may also have responsibilities for the adjustment of claims.

(3) Insurance Brokers

The term "insurance broker" is often used to characterize an individual who is thought to act primarily on behalf of a purchaser in an insurance transaction. This delineation, as well as the presump-

---

"apparent authority". See, e.g., Hartford Accident & Indemnity Company v. Oglesby, 293 Ala. 620, 308 So.2d 695 (1975). See also 3 COUCH ON INSURANCE (Second edition, 1960), § 26:61.

Also see decisions cited in § 2.5(b)(4), below.

12. For example, knowledge obtained by a soliciting agent may be imputed to the insurer so that the company will be estopped from denying coverage on the basis of misinformation in an application for insurance. See, e.g., Jackson v. Prudential Insurance Company of America, 564 F.Supp. 229 at pp. 233–234 (W.D.Ark.1983), *reversed* 736 F.2d 450 (8th Cir.1984), predicated on the trial court's interpretation of the Arkansas precedents. However, as noted in the citation, the trial court decision was reversed on appeal. Jackson v. Prudential Insurance Company of America, 736 F.2d 450 (8th Cir.1984) (Judge Gibson, dissenting).

Also see the discussion of estoppel in § 6.1(c), below.

13. See, e.g., Hartford Accident & Indemnity Company v. Oglesby, 293 Ala. 620, 308 So.2d 695 (Ala.1975).

tions associated with it, is employed by some courts and writers even though almost all insurance brokers are actually compensated for their services through commissions that are paid by the insurers. Because brokers receive compensation from the insurers, it seems evident that a persuasive argument can be made for not treating a broker as an agent of the insurance purchaser. In response to this point, it has sometimes been urged that a "broker" is an agent of the insurer, but only for the limited purpose of collecting premiums on policies transmitted to the broker for delivery.[14] Although such a limited agency relationship may actually exist in a few situations, it almost certainly is the exception rather than the general pattern. The relationships between most brokers and the insurance companies they place coverages with typically involve significantly greater ongoing contacts and interactions than the relationship with any individual applicant for insurance or insured. Accordingly, so long as the general rule prevails that an agent may not serve two principals simultaneously, it seems clear that in most contexts there is more justification for treating a broker as an agent of an insurer than as an agent of the purchaser.

The term "insurance broker" has sometimes been used to encompass all of the individuals who represent insurers in the marketing of insurance, ranging from persons who are soliciting agents in the strictest sense to those who have the most extensive authority to extend coverage on behalf of insurers (who are often characterized as general agents).

(4) Terminology, Contractual Limitations on Authority, and Liability: Herein of Express Authority and Apparent Authority

(i) Express Authority

Insurance companies often enter into express written contracts with the individuals who are authorized to represent them in sales transactions. Occasionally when a dispute arises as a consequence of some aspect of an insurance transaction, the terms of contracts between an insurer and a sales representative — which limit the sales representative's authority — are submitted by an insurer as a defense to an insured's claim. There are several reasons why the provisions of such an agreement are rarely determinative in regard to a claim by a purchaser against either an insurer or a sales representative.

First, the provisions used in contracts between insurers and sales representatives are frequently inconclusive or at least somewhat ambiguous on questions of authority and liability.

14. See, e.g., Patterson, ESSENTIALS OF INSURANCE LAW (Second edition, 1957), at p. 45; Vance, LAW OF INSURANCE (Third edition Anderson, 1951), at pp. 443–445; Albert H. Mowbray. Ralph H. Blanchard & C. Arthur Williams, Jr., INSURANCE (Sixth edition, 1969), at pp. 403–405.

Also see, Hughes v. Equitable Life Assurable Society of United States, 465 F.2d 743 (5th Cir.1972) (life insurance); Jester v. Hill, 161 Ga.App. 778, 288 S.E.2d 870 (1982) (automobile insurance); Duncan v. Michigan Mutual Liability Company, 67 Mich.App. 386, 241 N.W.2d 218 (1976) (fire insurance).

Second, the terms used in such contract provisions are often imprecise and are not consistent with the general conventions that have developed in regard to either marketing arrangements or terminology. For example, some contracts between insurance companies and sales representatives use the term "soliciting agent," but grant the individual — either expressly or by implication — substantial authority to make contracts for the insurer in various circumstances.

Third, even if an agreement of the insurer with a sales representative is precisely phrased so as to avoid any ambiguities and is carefully structured to conform to the general industry conventions, the restrictive terms in this contract should not be determinative in regard to disputes between an insurer and an insured because in almost all instances an insurance purchaser is completely unaware of the provisions in such an agreement, including any limitations on the sales representative's authority. In the absence of actual notice to the consumer, it is unreasonable for provisions in such agreements to be significant factors in resolving claims by insureds, especially when a claim is predicated on the apparent authority of the sales representative.[15]

(ii) Apparent Authority

Claims by an insurance purchaser frequently turn on an intermediary's apparent authority to act on behalf of an insurer.[16] A sales representative in an insurance transaction will be held to have apparent authority whenever an insurer places such an individual in a position that causes a prospective purchaser to reasonably believe that the insurer (the principal) has consented to the exercise of authority the agent or broker purports to possess.[17] Factual elements such as advertisements, business cards, and stationery — as well as statements by the sales representative — have all been considered by courts to be relevant to the determination of apparent authority. Furthermore, although not all courts agree on the proposition, there is substantial judicial precedent for the extensions of coverage beyond the express

15. *Cf.* Weaver v. Metropolitan Life Insurance Company, 545 F.Supp. 74 at p. 77 (E.D.Mo.1982).

16. See, e.g., Fryar v. Employers Insurance of Wausau, 94 N.M. 77, 607 P.2d 615 (1980) (holding that there was substantial evidence of acts by the insurer to support a determination that the broker had apparent authority to modify the insurance contract); Johnson v. United Investors Life Insurance Company, 263 N.W.2d 770 (Iowa 1978), discussed in Note, *Reformation of Policy May be Obtained on Ground of Mutual Mistake Even Where Agents Representations Exceed Principal's Scope of Business—Johnson v. United Investors Life Insurance Co.,* 27 Drake Law Review 749–760 (1978); Cameron Mutual Insurance

Company of Missouri v. Bouse, 635 S.W.2d 488 (Mo.App., Southern District, Div. 3, 1982); Insurance Management of Washington, Inc. v. Eno & Howard Plumbing Corp., 348 A.2d 310 (D.C.App.1975) (security bond for subcontractor).

Also see Baker & Company, Florida v. Preferred Risk Mutual Insurance Company, 569 F.2d 1347 (5th Cir.1978), in which the court discusses both apparent authority and implied actual authority; Hartford Accident and Indemnity Company v. Oglesby, 293 Ala. 620, 308 So.2d 695 (Ala.1975) (corporate automobile policy).

17. See the cases cited in note 16, above.

terms — including limitations and exclusions — of an insurance policy as a consequence of the representations of a sales representative.[18]

If there is a dispute between an intermediary and an insurer in regard to the allocation of the responsibility for a loss when the intermediary has not acted in accordance with the terms of an express contract with the insurer, it is frequently appropriate that the issues be resolved on the basis of the actual authority as determined by either the principles or agency law or the provisions set forth in the contract of the parties.[19]

§ 2.5(c) Liability of Insurers and Intermediaries in Insurance Marketing Transactions

(1) Introductory Note

Insurance marketing produces several distinct types of disputes that involve the possible liability of both insurers and intermediaries such as agents or brokers. For example, claims may arise as a consequence of events that occur even before an insurance policy has ever been issued. In some instances, disputes involving a marketing transaction are a consequence of the alleged failure of an intermediary

18. See, e.g., General Insurance Company of America v. Truly Nolen of America, Inc., 136 Ariz. 142, 664 P.2d 686 at p. 688 (App., Div. 1, Dept. D, 1983) (insurer may be estopped from denying coverage by reason of the oral representations of its agent when the insured did not receive the insurance policy before the loss occurs); Harr v. Allstate Insurance Company, 54 N.J. 287, 255 A.2d 208 at p. 218 (1969) ("equitable estoppel" is available to bar a defense in an action on a policy even where the estopping conduct arose before or at the inception of the contract).

But cf. holdings that oral representations by an agent may not extend coverage beyond the terms of an insurance policy. See, e.g., Henne v. Glens Falls Insurance Company, 245 Mich. 378, 222 N.W. 731 at p. 733 (1929) ("local agent, who is authorized to solicit insurance, sign and issue policies, collect and receipt for premiums, has not the authority to waive express provisions of the policy"); Employers Fire Insurance Company v. Speed, 242 Miss. 341, 133 So.2d 627 at p. 629 (1961) ("Waiver or estoppel cannot operate so as to bring within the coverage of the policy property, or a loss, or a risk, which by the terms of the policy is expressly excepted or otherwise excluded.").

Also see § 6.1(b)(c) below (as to whether estoppel and waiver may affect "coverage provisions.").

19. See, e.g., Manufacturers Casualty Insurance Company v. Martin-Lebreton In-surance Agency, 242 F.2d 951 (5th Cir. 1957), *cert. denied* 355 U.S. 870, 78 S.Ct. 121, 2 L.Ed.2d 76 (1957); Cameron Mutual Insurance Company of Missouri v. Bouse, 635 S.W.2d 488 (Missouri App., Southern District, Div. 3, 1982).

An intermediary may be bound to indemnify an insurance company against the cost of discharging any liability to the applicant sustained by the company because of his deviation from authorized procedure. See, e.g., Manufacturers Casualty Insurance Co. v. Martin-Lebreton Insurance Agency, 242 F.2d 951 (5th Cir.), *cert. denied* 355 U.S. 870, 78 S.Ct. 121, 2 L.Ed.2d 76 (1957). This proposition appears to be an assumption underlying the opinion in Pennsylvania Millers Mutual Insurance Company v. Walton, 236 Ark. 336, 365 S.W.2d 859 (1963). The company was denied recovery on its cross-claim against the agent for indemnification of its liability on a contract of insurance reformed to provide coverage because of mutual mistake of the applicant and the agent. The court held that there was no detriment to the company resulting from the agent's mistake because first, he was authorized to issue the coverage provided by the contract as reformed and, second, the applicant's recovery was reduced by the difference between the premium actually paid and the premium that would have been paid had the contract as reformed been issued originally.

to secure the type or amount of insurance coverage requested by a purchaser. When such claims are asserted, the possible liability of both an intermediary and an insurance company often comes into question, that is, an aggrieved potential purchaser of an insurance policy or a purchaser of a policy (such as an insured who believes the wrong coverage was obtained by an intermediary) may seek indemnification from both the insurance company and the intermediary.[1] The determination of whether an intermediary or an insurer will be individually or jointly liable is a function of several factors.

One consideration that has often been viewed as significant in these cases is whether an intermediary has in some way indicated the specific insurance company with which the coverage has been placed, or will be placed, or to which an application for coverage will be submitted. Therefore, the following discussion includes separate subsections that consider the questions related to liability depending on whether there has been some identification, either explicitly or implicitly, of a particular insurance company.

(2) Liability of Intermediary and Insurer When an Insurance Company Has Been Specified or Otherwise Indicated

In many insurance marketing situations, the intermediary[2] is clearly representing a particular insurance company in the transaction.[3] The identification of the insurance company may result from the

§ 2.5(c)

1. In most instances the intermediary is a sales representative. In some cases, the intermediary is involved in some other way.

The liability of an intermediary who is not an agent or broker is generally based on an explicit contractual undertaking. See, e.g., Mid-America Corp. v. Roach, 412 P.2d 188 (Okl.1966); Walker Bank & Trust Company v. First Security Corp., 9 Utah 2d 215, 341 P.2d 944 (1959). See also Annotation, *Covenant of lessee to insure as running with the land,* 18 A.L.R.2d 1051 (1951).

One who is not an agent or broker may also be held to a noncontractual duty. See, e.g., Wellens v. Perpetual Building Association, 184 A.2d 36 (D.C.Mun.App.1962) (mortgagee subject to liability for failure to act with reasonable care in obtaining fire insurance that did not cover garage detached from main building on mortgaged property).

Also see note 3, in § 2.5(d), below.

2. Intermediaries are often described as agents or brokers. These terms no longer have a precise meaning in the context of insurance marketing (see the discussion in § 2.5(b), above). In the following discus-

sion, such persons will be referred to as sales representatives or intermediaries.

When a dispute arises before a policy has been issued, the claimant is usually referred to as an applicant.

A transaction may involve more than one intermediary. For example, the procurement of credit life insurance often involves two intermediaries—a lending institution and its employee who acts as an insurance agent or broker. In such transactions, questions sometimes arise as to the liability of one intermediary (the employee) to the other (the lending institution) for error in procuring insurance. See, e.g., First Federal Savings & Loan Association v. Continental Equity Life Insurance Company, 124 So.2d 802 (La.App., 2d Cir., 1960).

Usually, however, litigation arising from such transactions is between the lending institution and the estate of the debtor-applicant or a joint debtor, and problems associated with the presence of a second intermediary do not arise. See, e.g., Consumers Financing Corp. v. Lam, 218 Ga. 343, 127 S.E.2d 914 (1962); Mid-America Corp. v. Roach, 412 P.2d 188 (Okl.1966).

3. *Cf.* Larry E. Johnson, *The Captive Insurance Agent—A Last Hurrah For An*

preferences of the purchaser, the representations of the intermediary, the forms used in the transaction, or other comparable factors.

The identification of a particular insurer has been viewed as a significant factor in regard to the liability of a sales representative in the event a loss is not covered when the intermediary in effect breaks an agreement to secure coverage (1) by failing to seek the coverage requested, (2) by failing to inform the purchaser that the coverage sought cannot be purchased, or (3) by arranging coverage that does not conform to that requested by the purchaser. Appleman's treatise provides a succinct statement of a proposition that addresses one aspect of the liability question in this context:

> "An insurance agent is not liable as an insurer where his principal is disclosed."[4]

There is substantial support for this statement in the case law.[5] And, as a general proposition, this is a reasonable rule. It makes pragmatic sense because few insurance agents are authorized to conduct the business of being insurers in addition to acting as sales representatives. Intermediaries have, however, urged a broader proposition that extends well beyond a rule that an intermediary "is *not* liable *as an insurer*." [6]

In response to claims against a sales representative who is an agent of an insurance company arising from marketing transactions, it has been argued that when an agent's principal is disclosed an agent is not liable in either tort or contract,[7] and that therefore an aggrieved purchaser cannot secure compensation for an uninsured loss from a

---

Independent Contractor?, 25 Drake Law Review 845–869 (1976).

4. 16A Appleman, INSURANCE LAW & PRACTICE (1981), at § 8832.

5. An alternate statement of the rule is "an agent for a disclosed principal who actually binds the principal is not personally liable for breach of the insuring agreement by the insurer." Keller Lorenz Company, Inc. v. Insurance Associates Corp., 98 Idaho 678, 570 P.2d 1366 at p. 1369 (1977).

In Milwaukee Bedding Company v. Graebner, 182 Wis. 171, 196 N.W. 533 (1923), the agent called at the applicant's office on February 24 to see about renewal of a fire insurance policy in one company, due to expire on March 1. A renewal was agreed upon, and there was conversation asserted by the applicant to be an agreement for an additional $2,000 coverage, though no specific company was identified in the conversation. Before leaving plaintiff's office (it was assumed), the agent made a memorandum on a card that was construed as identifying a second company as the one with which the additional coverage was to be placed. This card was deposited in a customary place in the agent's office, where it remained until a time after

a fire occurred shortly after noon the following day. A jury verdict in the applicant's action against the agent included a finding that by local custom fire insurance was dated to take effect from the noon preceding the order in the absence of agreement otherwise. The agent was held not liable, on the theory that a contract binding the second insurance company became effective before the fire. With respect to this basis for liability of the company, see § 2.2(c), above.

The rule stated in the text above ordinarily does not apply in actions against the intermediary based on deceit.

6. *Cf.* Pennsylvania Millers Mutual Insurance Company v. Walton, 236 Ark. 336, 365 S.W.2d 859 (1963) (agent was not liable to indemnify insurer for loss required to be paid by insurer as the result of a judgment that reformed the policy to include water escape coverage).

7. See, e.g., Belanger v. Silva, 114 R.I. 266, 331 A.2d 403 (1973).

Cf. Keller Lorenz Company, Inc. v. Insurance Associates Corp., 98 Idaho 678, 570 P.2d 1366 (1977).

sales representative. Although there are some judicial precedents for this proposition,[8] the soundness of such a rule is very suspect.[9]

There is no persuasive theoretical justification for concluding either that there is not or that there should not be any possibility of a claim against an intermediary as a consequence of some aspect of an insurance marketing transaction merely because an insurance company has been identified. Rather, there are several cogent reasons why in some circumstances sales representatives should be jointly liable, or even individually liable when the principal is not.

First, the insurance purchaser usually is not versed in the intricacies of the insurance business. The prospective insured seeks the assistance of a specialist and relies on the sales representative's knowledge of both the insurance business in general and insurance coverages in particular. If a sales representative fails to secure the appropriate insurance — by purporting to make a contract that is in fact beyond his or her authority, or arranging for coverage that turns out to be defective in some way, or fails to make any insurance arrangements — the applicant or purchaser should have a cause of action against the

---

8. Cardente v. Maggiacomo Insurance Agency, Inc., 108 R.I. 71, 272 A.2d 155 at p. 156 (1971) ("It has long been settled that an agent acting on behalf of a disclosed principal is not personally liable to a third party for acts performed within the scope of authority."); Belanger v. Silva, 114 R.I. 266, 331 A.2d 403 (1975).

Cf. Gibbs v. Home Insurance Company of New York, 252 App.Div. 805, 298 N.Y.S. 856 (3d Dept.1937), *appeal dismissed* 277 N.Y. 529, 13 N.E.2d 459 (1938).

Also see Emersons, Ltd. v. Max Wolman Company, 388 F.Supp. 729 at p. 735 (D.D.C.1975), *affirmed* 530 F.2d 1093 (D.C. Cir.1976); American Insurance Company v. Material Transit, Inc., 446 A.2d 1101 at p. 1105 (Sup.Delaware 1982) ("It is established law that an agent for a disclosed principal is not a party to the contract and is not liable for its nonperformance.").

The Restatement of Agency, Second, § 320, which provides that:

"Unless otherwise agreed, a person making or purporting to make a contract with another as agent for a disclosed principal does not become a party to the contract."

and § 328 which provides that:

"An agent, by making a contract only on behalf of a disclosed principal * * * when he has power so to bind, does not become liable for its performance."

Also *cf.* Milwaukee Bedding Company v. Graebner, 182 Wis. 171, 196 N.W. 533 (1923).

9. To the extent the proposition is grounded on the argument "that an agent is not liable as an insurer", few agents or brokers are qualified to be insurers. In cases in which a claimant alleges that an agent had actually assumed the obligation to provide the insurance, such claims posed significant theoretical problems which were circumvented by an application of this rule when the insurer had been disclosed. See, e.g., Shultz v. Commercial Standard Insurance Company, 297 F.Supp. 1154 (W.D.Okl.1969); Fields v. Goldstein, 97 Ga.App. 286, 102 S.E.2d 921 (Div. 1, 1958). In other words, this doctrine has been appropriately applied in response to claims that the intermediary undertook an obligation to actually provide insurance.

Among the precedents cited in support of the broad proposition urged by sales representatives, there are also few instances involving the liability of an agent to an insurer. See, e.g., Pennsylvania Millers Mutual Insurance Company v. Walton, 236 Ark. 336, 365 S.W.2d 859 (1963).

In at least one instance the judicial statement to this effect was made in support of a determination that an insurance company, which previously had been held liable in regard to an insured's claim, was not entitled to reimbursement from a sales representative as a consequence of liability arising from reformation of a policy that was not properly requested by the agent.

sales representative who has committed such a misfeasance without regard to whether the insurance company has explicitly or implicitly been identified.[10] This seems even more justified today than in the past, as agents and brokers have increasingly promoted their professional expertise in serving the public's insurance needs.

Second, a significant portion of the intermediaries who sell insurance, as well as many insurance companies, have widely advertised the importance and desirability of acquiring insurance through the offices of independent insurance agents who possess substantial expertise that can be used to guide the consumer. As a result of such advertising, many purchasers undoubtedly have either an actual awareness or reasonable expectations that sales representatives are independent business entrepreneurs.

Third, it is unreasonable to burden an applicant or an insured with the litigation of questions about whether a sales representative was acting for a particular company or whether an intermediary had the authority to bind the insurer. Although these may be important determinations if the insurer and the sales representative choose to litigate their respective liabilities,[11] it does not serve the ends of justice to require the resolution of such matters in regard to whether the claimant should be indemnified.

Finally, a sales representative often acts on behalf of both the insurer and the applicant, and such an intermediary owes a duty to exercise due care and reasonable diligence in the pursuit of the insured's or the applicant's business.[12]

---

10. Port Clyde Foods, Inc. v. Holiday Syrups, Inc., 563 F.Supp. 893 (S.D.N.Y. 1982) [applying New York law, including Wings & Wheels Express, Inc. v. Sisak, 73 Misc.2d 846, 342 N.Y.S.2d 891 at p. 895 (Special Term, Queens County, 1973)].

In Franklin v. Western Pacific Insurance Company, 243 Or. 448, 414 P.2d 343 (1966) (allegation that insurance agent intermediary promised to procure $10,000 of unconditional fire insurance coverage but delivered a policy conditioned on the maintenance of a pre-existing policy, which resulted in applicant's recovering only $2,000 on the policy issued, states a cause of action against both the intermediary and the insurance company; the opinion does not explicitly consider whether liability of the company would relieve the intermediary of personal liability to the applicant).

Also see the discussion in Keller Lorenz Company, Inc. v. Insurance Associates Corp., 98 Idaho 678, 570 P.2d 1366 at pp. 1369–1371 (1977).

Cf. Cameron Mutual Insurance Company v. Bouse, 635 S.W.2d 488 (Mo.App., Southern Dist., Div. 3, 1982).

11. Cf. Cameron Mutual Insurance Company v. Bouse, 635 S.W.2d 488 at p. 490 (Mo.App., Southern District, Div. 3, 1982); Pennsylvania Millers Mutual Insurance Company v. Walton, 236 Ark. 336, 365 S.W.2d 859 (1963) (agent was not liable to indemnify insurer for loss required to be paid by insurer as the result of a judgment that reformed the policy to include water escape coverage).

However, an intermediary may be bound to indemnify the company against the cost of discharging any liability to the applicant sustained by the company because of the intermediary's departure from authorized procedure. See, e.g., Manufacturers Casualty Insurance Company v. Martin-Libreton Insurance Agency, 242 F.2d 951 (5th Cir.1957), cert. denied 355 U.S. 870, 78 S.Ct. 121, 2 L.Ed.2d 76 (1957).

Cf. Pennsylvania Millers Mutual Insurance Company v. Walton, 236 Ark. 336, 365 S.W.2d 859 (1963).

12. See, e.g., Fli-Back Company, Inc. v. Philadelphia Mfrs. Mutual Insurance Company, 502 F.2d 214 at p. 217 (4th Cir.1974) (applying the law of North Carolina); Dai-

The discussion in the preceding portions of this section is not intended to suggest that insurance companies should be insulated from liability. The proposition set forth here is that a sales representative, especially an individual who is an independent entrepreneur, should not be immune from liability solely because an insurance company has been explicitly or implicitly identified. Rather, when a sales representative has been negligent or has broken an agreement, it is submitted that such an intermediary should be liable as well as the company the intermediary represents.[13]

In the years before errors and omissions liability insurance coverage was generally available to and purchased by sales representatives, the absence of such coverage may have constituted an unarticulated, but nevertheless significant, factor in support of the proposition that the agent for a disclosed principal would not be liable. However, errors and omissions coverage for sales representatives is now widely acquired by agents and brokers, so that effective risk distribution is readily attainable by such sales representatives.[14]

(3) Liability of Intermediaries and Insurers in Marketing Transactions When No Insurance Company Has Been Specified

It sometimes happens that as a result of oral communications and the inferential adoption of the insurance form provision normally used for the coverage sought by an applicant, all of the terms which are essential for the formation of an insurance contract are readily ascertainable except for the specification of the company that is intended to be the insurer. If the sales representative with whom an applicant is dealing represents only one company which issues the kind of insurance applied for, the inference that this company was to be the insurer is clearly warranted. The inference follows even if the applicant does not know the identity of the insurer. When an intermediary represents several companies, however, some evidence of selection of a

ley v. Elicker, 447 F.Supp. 436 at pp. 438–439 (D.Colo.1978).

Cf. Bell v. O'Leary, 744 F.2d 1370 at p. 1372 (8th Cir.1984), holding, "When an insurance broker agrees to obtain insurance for a client, with a view to earning a commission, the broker becomes the client's agent and owes a duty to the client to act with reasonable care, skill, and diligence."

Also see Annotation, *Liability of insurance agent or broker on ground of inadequacy of liability insurance coverage procured,* 72 A.L.R.3d 704–729 at p. 735 and p. 747 (1976).

13. *Cf.* Port Clyde Foods, Inc. v. Holiday Syrups, Inc., 563 F.Supp. 893 (S.D.N.Y. 1982); Bogley v. Middleton Tavern, Inc., 42 Md.App. 314, 400 A.2d 15 (1979); Carter v. Empire Mutual Insurance Company, 6 Mass.App.Ct. 114, 374 N.E.2d 585 at p. 591 (1978).

Contra. Fryar v. Employers Insurance of Wausau, 94 N.W. 77, 607 P.2d 615 at p. 619 (1980), holding that a broker is not liable when the broker "acted within the apparent scope of his authority, though possibly not within the scope of his actual authority" *and* when "[t]here is no evidence the broker manifested any intent to be bound by his representations."

Also see Annotation, *Liability of insurance broker or agent to insured for failure to procure insurance,* 64 A.L.R.3d 398–495 (1975).

14. Concerning the coverage of agents' and brokers' errors and omissions insurance, see, e.g., Otteman v. Interstate Fire & Casualty Company, 172 Neb. 574, 111 N.W.2d 97 (1961), 89 A.L.R.2d 1182 (1963).

particular company is almost always required before a court will hold an insurer liable.[15]

Testimony by a sales representative that there was a mental selection of a company usually is not accepted by courts as a sufficient basis to warrant imposing liability on an insurer.[16] Most courts hold that there must have been some express manifestation of the selection of a particular company. Courts have found that a designation was sufficient when a memorandum had been prepared to guide later preparation of either a written binder or a longer-term contract.[17] A memorandum need not have been completely explicit; it is only necessary that a document show in some way that a selection or designation of a particular company had been made before the loss occurred. For example, in an often cited decision, Milwaukee Bedding Co. v. Graebner,[18] the agent, before leaving the office of the applicant, noted on a card that the fire insurance coverage was to be continued and also that it was to be "$2,000 add'l in L. & A. Co." Although the card with the notation was filed so that in the ordinary course of the agency's business the claimant's application for coverage should have been sent to the insurer (which would have resulted in a policy being issued by the insurer identified by the notation), no policy was ever requested from the company.[19] In a decision that both sustained the claim for coverage and absolved the sales representative of personal liability,[20] the court held that the card which bore the notation "$2,000 add'l in L. & A. Co." was sufficient for purposes of identifying the insurer. Similarly, even if a sales representative's memorandum fails to identify a company, courts have extended liability to insurers so long as it is possible to ascertain by some explicit manifestation that a designation was made.[21]

15. See, e.g., Maryland Casualty Company v. Foster, 76 N.M. 310, 414 P.2d 672 (1966) (workers' compensation insurer not bound by agent's "secret intention" to bind insurer when there was not the "slightest act" to indicate that insurance was being placed with a given company rather than other companies he represented).

In Employers Fire Insurance Company v. Speed, 242 Miss. 341, 133 So.2d 627 (1961), the agent agreed to procure fire and extended coverage insurance on building to be constructed, but failed to do so or to designate in any way which one or ones among the eight companies he represented were to be selected. The court held that there was no contract, even with the six of the eight companies with which the applicant was already insured for other fire insurance coverage.

16. But cf. Elliott v. Standard Accident Insurance Company, 92 N.H. 505 at pp. 511–512, 33 A.2d 562 at p. 568 (1943).

17. See, e.g., Milwaukee Bedding Company v. Graebner, 182 Wis. 171, 196 N.W. 533 (1923).

18. Ibid.

19. Id., 182 Wis. at p. 173, 196 N.W. at p. 534.

20. Also see the discussion of personal liability for agents in the preceding portions of this section.

21. See, e.g., Julien v. Spring Lake Park Agency, Inc., 283 Minn. 101, 166 N.W.2d 355 (1969), in which there was an oral agreement for builder's risk policies on two houses. The agent wrote such coverage with four or five companies, and his memorandum did not name a company. Another person in agent's office arranged a policy on one of the houses, but for some "inexplicable reason" not on the other house. The agent had previously written eight such policies for applicant, all with the defendant company. The agent testified that when making memorandum he did not remember which company, but he

If it were possible to bind an insurer who is not explicitly identified in any way before a loss occurs, there would be a substantial risk that an intermediary would dishonestly select a company after the loss in order to avoid personal liability. Because of this risk, it seems appropriate to adopt a rule that does not allow a sales representative the opportunity to escape responsibility by testifying that there was a mental, though unrecorded, selection of an insurer. The few adjudicated cases in point support the conclusion that an intermediary will not be allowed to impose liability on an insurer on the basis of a mental, but unrecorded, selection of an insurer.[22]

In the absence of an explicit identification of an insurer, an action may be brought against a sales representative. The potential liability of a sales representative, however, is little comfort to an applicant if the agent or broker is financially irresponsible and does not have adequate errors and omissions insurance coverage. In this situation, it should not necessarily follow that a person attempting to purchase insurance has no cause of action on any theory against any of the insurers that might have been bound if the sales representative had made a record of a selection before the loss occurred. Arguably such an applicant should not have to bear the risk which results from the combination of inefficiency and financial irresponsibility of the sales representative.

A better solution, especially when the errors and omissions coverage either does not exist or is inadequate to indemnify the claimant, would be to apply proportionate liability to the several insurers that such an intermediary represents. This approach is somewhat analogous to the joint and several liability of tortfeasors whose separate actions contribute to an indivisible injury. In the insurance marketing context, arguably the acts of the several insurers in authorizing one agent to represent them — though obviously independent acts of each insurer — have collectively contributed to creating a problem that would not have existed had the agent represented only one company, since the identification of the insurer would then have been clear.

consciously intended it be the same company as before. The court held that though "the question is close," the designation was sufficient. The company's claim against agent for indemnity was denied because the agent's failure to advise company caused no damage.

But cf. Nelson v. Glens Falls Insurance Company, 251 Ark. 805, 475 S.W.2d 690 (1972). An agent representing five companies agreed to effect renewals as needed. The agent testified that except for oversight, he would have renewed coverage on a catering van in the same company, Glens Falls, as was his practice. The agent and his errors and omissions carrier paid the claimant and proceeded as subrogees in action against Glens Falls. The court held for Glens Falls, and the decision in *Julien*

was distinguished on the facts and because "it does not deal with renewals."

Concerning builder's risk coverage generally, see Annotation, *Builder's risk insurance policies,* 94 A.L.R.2d 221–266 (1964).

22. See, e.g., Employers Fire Insurance Company v. Speed, 242 Miss. 341, 133 So.2d 627 (1961).

In Gulf Insurance Company v. Grisham, 126 Ariz. 123, 613 P.2d 283 at p. 286 (1980) (In Division), the court observed, "Were we to allow an unauthorized agent to bind an unknown principal to liability such as is present in this case, we would encourage fraud and injustice in the future, as anyone who represented themselves as agents could bind completely innocent principals."

Accordingly, like joint tortfeasors in other contexts, the insurers should be jointly and severally liable to the applicant.[23]

(4) Theories of Liability for Intermediaries

Claims by an applicant or an insured against sales representatives based on both contract and tort theories have been affirmed by the courts. In such cases, the courts have also been called on to consider whether contributory fault constitutes a defense. The various theories and the defense of contributory fault are discussed in the following subsections.

(i) Liability Based on Contract.

Liability sometimes has been founded on a breach of contract theory when there was a failure to procure insurance for an applicant,[24] a failure to seasonably notify an applicant in the event the sales representative is not able to obtain insurance,[25] or a failure to perform

---

23. If this view is adopted, one concern would be the allocation of the risk among the several companies represented by the intermediary. There is no great problem with joint and several liability and contribution in this context.

A counter-argument could be made that liability should be several for proportionate shares. Cf. Loui v. Oakley, 50 Hawaii 260, 438 P.2d 393 (1968). This is discussed in William L. Prosser and W. Page Keeton, Torts (1984), at § 52, on apportioning liability.

24. See, e.g., Keller Lorenz Company, Inc. v. Insurance Associates Corp., 98 Idaho 678, 570 P.2d 1366 (1977) (agent failed to procure fire insurance); Consumers Financing Corp. v. Lamb, 218 Ga. 343, 127 S.E.2d 914 (1962) (assignee finance company failed to procure credit life insurance that assignor of debt, vendor of automobile, orally promised would be obtained); Sroga v. Lund, 259 Minn. 269, 106 N.W.2d 913 (1961) (contract to procure complete insurance coverage on business; failure to procure fire insurance).

Also see Hause v. Schesel, 42 Wis.2d 628, 167 N.W.2d 421 (1969) (policy obtained stated effective date as April 3, rather than April 2 as orally promised; agent held liable; reasoned partly on inconsistency between applicant's proving agent's breach of conduct to procure and applicant's attacking, on appeal, a directed verdict for defendant company; court seems not to recognize agent's standing to attack the directed verdict on the ground that establishing the company's liability would have been a defense for the agent).

Cf. White v. Calley, 67 N.M. 343, 355 P.2d 280 (1960) (contract to procure in-

creased fire insurance coverage effective immediately); Mid-America Corp. v. Roach, 412 P.2d 188 (Okl.1966) (lender failed to procure credit life insurance, $75 having been deducted from loan proceeds to pay first annual premium on insurance); Franklin v. Western Pacific Insurance Company, 243 Or. 448, 414 P.2d 343 (1966) (failure to procure unconditional fire insurance coverage); Hamacher v. Tumy, 222 Or. 341, 352 P.2d 493 (1960) (failure to procure additional fire insurance coverage as promised).

In deMarlor v. Foley Carter Insurance Company, 386 So.2d 22 at p. 23 (Fla.App., 2d Dist., 1980), the court observed that "an agent or broker who agrees * * * to procure certain insurance owes his principal a duty to do so within a reasonable time," and that "even when he is not to blame for the failure to obtain coverage the agent may nevertheless become liable for damages if he fails to inform his principal that the requested insurance has not been procured."

See also 16 Appleman, Insurance Law (1968), at §§ 8831, 8840, 8841; Annotation, Duty and liability of insurance broker or agent to insured with respect to procurement, continuance, terms, and coverage of insurance policies, 29 A.L.R.2d 171–205 (1953).

25. See, e.g., Bell v. O'Leary, 744 F.2d 1370 at p. 1372 (8th Cir.1984), where the court concluded, "Failure to notify a client that insurance is not available will render the agent liable to the client for negligent breach of the agent's duty."

Also see Haeuber v. Can-Do, Inc., II, 666 F.2d 275 at p. 280 (5th Cir.1982); Bulla v.

some function related to the insurance coverage.[26] For example, a promise by a sales representative to arrange "complete insurance protection" for a business has been held to be sufficiently definite [27] to be the basis of a breach of the contract when the agent failed to procure insurance.[28] Similarly, liability existed when an intermediary agreed to study an appraisal of an individual's property to determine its "insurable value" in order to insure a certain percentage of that value, and accordingly it was not necessary that there be an agreement about either a specific dollar amount of insurance or the exact premium to be paid.[29] Liability may also be held to result from an agreement to procure a desired coverage at the lowest obtainable premium rate.[30]

It is occasionally suggested that the liability of an intermediary might also be founded on a breach of a contract *to insure.* [31] In most situations, this approach encounters two difficulties. First, ordinarily the facts, reasonably interpreted, do not warrant the conclusion that an intermediary made a commitment *to insure,* rather than a promise to *procure insurance.* Second, an intermediary is almost never qualified to be an insurer under the state regulatory statutes.

Donahue, 174 Ind.App. 123, 366 N.E.2d 233 (3d Dist.1977).

26. See, e.g., Port Clyde Foods, Inc. v. Holiday Syrups, Inc., 563 F.Supp. 893 (S.D. N.Y.1982) (insurance broker failed to discover that the requested coverage had not been provided); Spiegel v. Metropolitan Insurance Company, 6 N.Y.2d 91, 188 N.Y.S. 2d 486, 160 N.E.2d 40 (1959) (insurance agent failed to pay premiums on life insurance policy as promised to prevent lapse); Walker Bank & Trust Company v. First Security Corp., 9 Utah 2d 215, 341 P.2d 944 (1959) (bank failed to honor monthly drafts drawn by insurance company on insured's account as it had agreed to do).

Cf. deMarlor v. Foley Carter Insurance Company, 386 So.2d 22 (La.App., 2d Dist., 1980) (alleged failure to procure adequate fire insurance on a restaurant).

27. The requisites of a contract to *procure insurance* are not as stringent as those of an oral contract of *insurance.* For example, the clear identification of the insurance company, a requisite of an oral contract binding the company, is not a requisite of an oral contract to procure insurance.

Concerning oral contracts of *insurance,* see § 2.2(c), above.

28. Sroga v. Lund, 259 Minn. 269, 106 N.W.2d 913 (1961).

But cf. Boston Camping Distributor Company v. Lumbermens Mutual Casualty Company, 361 Mass. 769, 282 N.E.2d 374 (1972) (plaintiff told broker "he wanted insurance coverage from A to Z, second to none, to which the [broker] replied that he would definitely comply"; the coverage obtained was subject to an "exclusion" of injury to a building arising out of leakage from an automatic sprinkler system, which exclusion defeated the claim against the insurer in this case for loss occurring when an employee of plaintiff corporation, while moving stock, accidentally struck a sprinkler head, causing water to escape; held, for defendant broker; the oral exchange "looked to the making of a contract" but "cannot be regarded as a part of the contract that was made"; the broker's reply "was expressive of present intention but was not in its effect a contract * * *").

29. Hamacher v. Tumy, 222 Or. 341, 352 P.2d 493 (1960).

30. *Ibid.*

31. In Mid-America Corp. v. Roach, 412 P.2d 188 (Okl.1966), the court speaks of the intermediary's "liability as an insurer," but it is clear that the theory of the action was breach of a contract to procure insurance.

Also see Annotation, *Duty and liability of insurance broker or agent to insured with respect to procurement, continuance, terms, and coverage of insurance policies,* 29 A.L.R.2d 171–205 at pp. 179–180 (1953).

But see, e.g., Bentley v. Fayas, 260 Wis. 177, 50 N.W.2d 404 (1951), 29 A.L.R.2d (1953), specifically rejecting, in an alternative holding, the view that the intermediary can be held liable as an insurer.

(ii) Liability Based on Tort. Liability of sales representatives has frequently been predicated on the theory that the individual acted negligently.[32] In most cases, the duty to an applicant or an insured is based on the intermediary's superior knowledge, on a representation by an intermediary of expertise in insurance matters,[33] or on a professional duty owed to clients.[34]

When the conduct of an intermediary induces an applicant to rely on that person to obtain insurance for the applicant, a legal duty of reasonable care should be and commonly is imposed upon the intermediary.[35] The standard of reasonable care by which such an intermedia-

---

32. See, e.g., Bell v. O'Leary, 744 F.2d 1370 (8th Cir.1984) (affirming the decision of the District Court for the Eastern District of Missouri); Port Clyde Foods, Inc. v. Holiday Syrups, Inc., 563 F.Supp. 893 at p. 897 (S.D.N.Y.1982) ("* * * a broker is under a duty to provide skill, care, and diligence in procuring coverage for the insured"); Clary Insurance Agency v. Doyle, 620 P.2d 194 (Alaska 1980).

Also see Mayo v. American Fire & Casualty Company, 282 N.C. 346, 192 S.E.2d 828 (1972) (an agent has duty to use reasonable diligence to procure requested insurance and is liable for loss proximately caused by negligent failure to do so); Riddle-Duckworth, Inc. v. Sullivan, 253 S.C. 411, 171 S.E.2d 486 (1969) (agent undertook to procure complete business premises liability coverage for home and auto appliance business and represented that a policy he had procured afforded the desired protection; liable for negligent failure to procure coverage for freight elevator occasionally used to transport people).

Also see Hardt v. Brink, 192 F.Supp. 879 (W.D.Wash.1961) (insurance agent through whom insurance had been purchased for years negligent in failing to advise fire insurance coverage on leasehold of which he had been informed); McCall v. Marshall, 398 S.W.2d 106 (Tex.1965) (insurance agent not negligent in failing to procure fire insurance on additional location of customer's business though he had knowledge of that addition, because there is no duty to act unless there is evidence of previous dealings in which the agent customarily procured insurance for customer without consulting him).

In Rider v. Lynch, 42 N.J. 465, 201 A.2d 561 (1964), the insurance broker was negligent in obtaining non-owner motor vehicle liability policy and was charged with the duty of knowing that it would not provide the coverage desired.

Cf. Walker v. Pacific Indemnity Company, 183 Cal.App.2d 513, 6 Cal.Rptr. 924 (1st Dist.1960) (insurance broker negligent in obtaining policy with smaller limits of coverage than had been agreed upon); Minor v. Universal C.I.T. Credit Corp., 27 Ill.App. 2d 330, 170 N.E.2d 5 (1st Dist.1960) (credit company by exercising its option to purchase collision insurance on financed automobile assumed duty to provide insurance during term of loan contract or to notify debtor to procure own insurance and was negligent in failing to renew coverage without notice to debtor).

See, generally, 16 Appleman, INSURANCE LAW (Revised edition, 1968), at § 8831, § 8840, and § 8841.

33. See, e.g., Hardt v. Brink, 192 F.Supp. 879 (W.D.Wash.1961); Riddle-Duckworth, Inc. v. Sullivan, 253 S.C. 411, 171 S.E.2d 486 (1969).

Also see Bulla v. Donahue, 174 Ind.App. 123, 366 N.E.2d 233 (3d Dist.1977).

In some cases, it has appeared that both of these factors were present and influenced the resolution of the dispute. See, e.g., Fiorentino v. Travelers Insurance Company, 448 F.Supp. 1364 (E.D.Pa.1978).

34. Keller Lorenz Company, Inc. v. Insurance Associates Corp., 98 Idaho 678, 570 P.2d 1366 at p. 1369 (1977).

35. See e.g., Hamacher v. Tumy, 222 Or. 341, 352 P.2d 493 (1960); Hardt v. Brink, 192 F.Supp. 879 (W.D.Wash.1961).

Also see Bell v. O'Leary, 744 F.2d 1370 at p. 1373 (8th Cir.1984).

Cf. McCall v. Marshall, 398 S.W.2d 106 (Tex., 1965) (agent not liable because no evidence of previous conduct of agent acting to procure insurance coverage without specific instructions of applicant for him to do so).

ry is judged is usually that of a prudent person possessing the expert knowledge that the intermediary has or represents himself or herself as having, whichever is greater.[36] The courts have held that representations of expertise may be made either to the individual applicant[37] or to the general public.[38] The recognition of such a duty for sales representatives of insurers is consistent with tort rules of general application that enforce obligations of affirmative action when one has worsened another's position by leading that person to reasonably expect action and then failing to fulfill the expectation.[39]

Tort liability for an insurance agent or broker is most often warranted on the basis of an individual's expertise or on representations by the person about his or her expertise.[40] Occasionally, however, the facts involved in claims against a sales representative have sup-

36. Fiorentino v. Travelers Insurance Company, 448 F.Supp. 1364 at pp. 1369–1370 (E.D.Pa.1978) ("The duty owed by an insurance agent to an insured is to obtain the coverage that a reasonable and prudent professional insurance agent would have obtained under the circumstances.").

Cf. Bell v. O'Leary, 744 F.2d 1370 at p. 1373 (8th Cir.1984), where the court stated that a broker "is charged with knowledge of his business, which includes an awareness of what facts render his clients ineligible for insurance coverage."

Also see 2 Restatement of Torts, Second, § 290, Comment f (1965).

In discussing Hardt v. Brink, 192 F.Supp. 879 (W.D.Wash.1961), one writer has warned that "if the *Hardt* * * * approach is accepted * * * [the agent] must review leases, contracts, etc., with a view to determining potential liability. This is a large undertaking. How many agents are aware, for example, of the risks in being a director or an officer of a corporation? * * * These and many other liability and loss exposures indicate that the agent either had better tell his client to see his lawyer and then request specific coverages or take the job of advisor and make sure his own errors and omissions coverage is in order." Hoeveler, *Architects, Engineers & Insurance Agents Professional Liability,* 1966 A.B.A. Section Insurance, Negligence & Compensation Law Proceedings 222–229 at pp. 227–228. It seems unlikely, however, that courts would impose on the agent a duty that would amount to the unauthorized practice of law in the absence of a representation that, in effect, this was what the agent purported to undertake.

Concerning the coverage of agents' and brokers' errors and omissions insurance, see, e.g., Otteman v. Interstate Fire & Casualty Company, 172 Neb. 574, 111 N.W.2d 97 (1961), 89 A.L.R.2d 1182 (1963).

37. See, e.g., Sroga v. Lund, 259 Minn. 269, 106 N.W.2d 913 (1961); Spiegel v. Metropolitan Life Insurance Company, 6 N.Y.2d 91, 188 N.Y.S.2d 486, 160 N.E.2d 40 (1959).

38. See, e.g., Bell v. O'Leary, 744 F.2d 1370 at p. 1373 (8th Cir.1984) where the court observed that the broker "held himself out to the public as one who had superior knowledge of a specific area of business insurance."

Also see Rider v. Lynch, 42 N.J. 465, 201 A.2d 561 (1964).

39. See § 2.4, above, discussing this theory of liability in relation to delay in acting on an application for insurance.

Also see William L. Prosser & W. Page Keeton, TORTS (Fifth edition, 1984), at pp. 373–385.

40. Liability has also been upheld in credit life insurance transactions in which the officers or employees of a lending institution served as the intermediaries. For example, in Keene Investment Corporation v. Martin, 104 N.H. 518 at p. 520, 191 A.2d 521 at p. 522 (1963), the court observed that "the plaintiff [lending institution] undertook to act * * * in a matter * * * where its knowledge and experience far exceeded [that of the defendant debtor] * * *."

Also see Mid-America Corp. v. Roach, 412 P.2d 188 (Okl.1966).

ported a tort theory of deceit,[41] or a blend of tort and contract theories.[42]

(iii) **Contributory Fault.** If an intermediary is held to have a duty (1) to secure coverage, (2) to select the correct coverage, or (3) to arrange for coverage that is to go into effect at a time designated by the applicant, conduct of an intermediary violating the applicable standard of care may support either a tort action based on negligence [43] or an action for breach of contract.[44] The recognition of such causes of action leads to the question whether the insurance purchaser is also required to exercise some care in regard to the transaction, especially in regard to monitoring the application process or reviewing the coverage that the intermediary secures — that is, whether contributory fault on the part of an applicant or an insured is a defense to an action against an intermediary.

In this type of situation, it has been argued that contributory fault should be a defense to an action in contract as well as to one in tort. Although the appropriateness of recognizing the existence of contributory fault as a defense is perhaps most obvious when the claimant initiates a tort suit founded on negligence, consideration of the facts which would support a finding of contributory negligence is usually equally warranted when a liability claim is based on contract. Certainly the character of the relationships and events that lead to such disputes is the same regardless of whether the action is based on a tort theory or a contract theory. And even if contributory negligence is not formally recognized as a defense to an action for breach of contract, contributory fault is in a broader sense relevant to a claimant's rights in regard to a breach of contract. For example, the theory that recovery in contract is disallowed for consequences that would have been avoidable by a claimant's exercise of reasonable care is usually grounded on essentially the same considerations.[45]

41. See, e.g., Anderson v. Knox, 297 F.2d 702 (9th Cir.1961), *cert. denied* 370 U.S. 915, 82 S.Ct. 1555, 8 L.Ed.2d 498 (1962) (insurance agent represented that $150,000 of bank-financed life insurance was a suitable plan for one earning less than $10,000 annually, knowing that it was not suitable or with wilful disregard as to the suitability of the plan); Clark v. Kelly, 217 Ga. 449, 122 S.E.2d 731 (1961), (insurance agent represented that he had issued binder of fire insurance, knowing that he had not and did not intend to do so; company identified but not liable on oral contract because of Georgia statutes forbidding oral contracts of insurance) *on remand,* see 105 Ga.App. 104, 123 S.E.2d 711 (1961).

42. See, e.g., Skyways Aircraft Ferrying Service, Inc. v. Stanton, 242 Cal.App.2d 272, 51 Cal.Rptr. 352 (2d Dist.1966), in which case, however, the intermediary was found to have had "ostensible authority."

43. See § 2.5(c)(4), below.

44. "For the breach of its agreement or for its negligent performance of it the plaintiff would be liable in damages to the defendant." Keene Investment Corporation v. Martin, 104 N.H. 518, 520, 191 A.2d 521, 522 (1963).

See also the cases cited in § 2.5(c)(4), below.

45. *Cf.* Restatement of Contracts, Second, § 350, Avoidability as a Limitation on Damages.

Furthermore, even when the duty is viewed as contractual, in many instances it is based on an implied-in-fact agreement that the intermediary would use reasonable professional efforts, and not on the

Courts do not uniformly recognize that contributory fault by an applicant for insurance will bar a claim, and this is particularly true when a claimant's action is based on a contract theory. For example, in a case in which an intermediary agreed to effect increased fire insurance coverage on the applicant's business premises immediately, but then arranged for a policy which provided that the increased coverage was to take effect at the expiration of the existing coverage, the intermediary was held liable on a contract theory for damage from a fire occurring before the increased coverage took effect.[46] In that case, the appellate court observed that the insured's contributory negligence in not ascertaining that the policy failed to take effect immediately does not bar liability when the action is for breach of contract.[47]

When an intermediary has held himself or herself out as an expert, that fact often bears heavily not only upon the prima facie basis of liability, but also upon the contributory fault question in whatever guise it may be presented.[48] In some instances, of course, the rejection of the contributory fault defense may be justified on the basis that an applicant's reliance upon an expert's assurances was reasonable. This has sometimes been an explicit ground of decision.[49] Moreover, an applicant's reliance may be found reasonable even though the representations in other contexts might arguably be considered nonactionable misrepresentations either of opinion[50] or of law.[51]

premise that the intermediary would guarantee results.

46. White v. Calley, 67 N.M. 343, 355 P.2d 280 (1960).

47. *Id.*, 67 N.W. at p. 345, 355 P.2d at p. 281.

Accord. Sroga v. Lund, 259 Minn. 269 at pp. 271–272, 106 N.W.2d 913 at p. 915 (1961).

Also see Franklin v. Western Pacific Insurance Company, 243 Or. 448 at p. 453, 414 P.2d 343 at p. 346 (1966), reasoning that the intermediary was the agent of the applicant and that a principal is entitled to assume that his agent performed the duty as undertaken.

48. E.g., Rider v. Lynch, 42 N.J. 465, 201 A.2d 561 (1964). The applicant desired liability insurance coverage for herself and her father while driving her fiancee's car, which had been left in her care, and the intermediary, an insurance broker, promised that such coverage would be obtained and stated that a policy subsequently issued provided the coverage desired. The applicant's father having been held liable for injuries to another arising from an accident involving the vehicle, liability was imposed on the intermediary on a theory of negligence, since the policy he procured (a non-owner contract) specifically excluded the coverage desired. The court held as a

matter of law that the applicant was not contributorily negligent in failing to read the policy since she (and her father) were reasonable in relying on the broker's assurance that the policy provided the coverage desired.

Also see Riddle-Duckworth, Inc. v. Sullivan, 253 S.C. 411, 171 S.E.2d 486 (1969) (treating the contributory negligence issue as one of fact, taking into account the knowledge and means of knowledge of the agent and applicant respectively).

49. Rider v. Lynch, 42 N.J. 465, 201 A.2d 561 (1964); Riddle-Duckworth, Inc. v. Sullivan, 253 S.C. 411, 171 S.E.2d 486 (1969).

50. See, e.g., Anderson v. Knox, 297 F.2d 702 (9th Cir.1961), *cert. denied* 370 U.S. 915, 82 S.Ct. 1555, 8 L.Ed.2d 498 (1962) (representation that plan of life insurance was "suitable" held actionable).

51. See, e.g., Clark v. Kelly, 217 Ga. 449, 122 S.E.2d 731 (1961), opinion on remand *sub nom.* Kelly v. Georgia Casualty & Surety Company, 105 Ga.App. 104 at pp. 106–107, 123 S.E.2d 711 at p. 713 (1961) (representation that binder providing immediate fire insurance coverage had been effected held actionable although state law required all contracts of insurance to be in writing).

§ 2.5(d) Misleading and Erroneous Applications of Agency Classifications

The critical question in a determination of an intermediary's liability should be whether the relationship was such that the intermediary was obligated to exercise reasonable care in procuring the insurance coverage sought by the applicant or the purchaser. The resolution of this question should not depend on whether an agency relationship existed.

The analysis of the liability of intermediaries in the preceding portions of this section has been in terms of principles and rules that do not turn on whether the intermediary is either an "agent" (acting as the sales representative of one or more insurers) whose principal is an insurer *or* an "agent/broker" (acting on behalf of a party who desires to procure insurance) whose principal is the applicant.[1] In some cases, however, judicial analysis has focused upon the existence or nonexistence of an agency relationship[2] — that is, liability has been predicated on whether the intermediary was an agent of the applicant for purposes of procuring insurance.[3] And some courts have also characterized the intermediary as an agent of the applicant in cases involving the liability of an insurer.[4] The theory that an intermediary owes a duty to the applicant as his or her agent presents difficulties.

There are several reasons for questioning whether an intermediary who is a sales representative in an insurance marketing transaction is ever appropriately treated as an agent of an insurance purchaser. An agency relationship is fundamentally based upon a principal's right of control over the agent. In most situations, it would be difficult to sustain a finding that the applicant has such a right, especially when there is a pre-existing contractual relationship between the sales representative and the insurance company. And the case against such a principal-agent relationship between an applicant and an intermediary is even stronger when the actions of a sales representative conflict with

Also see Annotation, *Misrepresentation by one other than insurance agent as to coverage, exclusion, or legal effect of insurance policy, as actionable,* 29 A.L.R.2d 213–215 (1953).

§ 2.5(d)

1. See the discussion of these terms in § 2.5(a) and § 2.5(b), above.

2. See, e.g., Bulla v. Donahue, 174 Ind. App. 123, 366 N.E.2d 233 (1977); Beavers Insurance Agency, Inc. v. Roland, 135 Ga. App. 263, 217 S.E.2d 484 (1975).

Also see 16A Appleman, INSURANCE LAW AND PRACTICE (1981), at § 8831.

3. In some instances, courts have observed that even though the intermediary was not an agent, liability could still exist if there is a fiduciary relationship between the intermediary and the applicant. But even in cases in which both of these characterizations of the relationship are dubious, a finding of a duty of reasonable care to procure insurance may nevertheless be well supported either on the basis that a contractual commitment was made or because the conduct of the intermediary created reasonable expectations upon which the applicant detrimentally relied.

4. See, e.g., Franklin v. Western Pacific Insurance Company, 243 Or. 448, 414 P.2d 343 (1966).

Also see Hardt v. Brink, 192 F.Supp. 879 (W.D.Wash.1961); Sroga v. Lund, 259 Minn. 269, 106 N.W.2d 913 (1961); White v. Calley, 67 N.M. 343, 355 P.2d 280 (1960); Spiegel v. Metropolitan Life Insurance Company, 6 N.Y.2d 91, 188 N.Y.S.2d 486, 160 N.E.2d 40 (1959).

provisions that are set forth in a pre-existing written contract between the insurer and the sales representative.

Erroneous characterizations of a relationship as one of agency frequently result when one overlooks the requirement of a right of control over performance that is an essential characteristic of agency.[5] All too often the right of an applicant for insurance to request that an intermediary accomplish a specified result has been treated as the basis of a principal-agent relationship. However, if an agency relationship were held to exist on that single facet in the relationship, all intermediaries would be agents for applicants in every case of an agreement to procure insurance and this is obviously an inappropriate and fallacious conclusion about these transactions.

Another problem with attempting to characterize or treat an intermediary as an agent of the applicant in cases involving the acquisition of insurance is the general principle of agency law that an individual cannot act (and should not be allowed to) as the agent for both parties to a transaction without the informed consent of both.[6] Such a disclosure to the applicant is rarely, if ever, made in insurance transactions. Since the sales representative frequently is an "agent" of the insurer, it seems clear that it is not appropriate to treat the intermediary as an agent of the applicant in the absence of an appropriate disclosure of the nature of the relationship of the intermediary with the insurer.

A contract to procure insurance can sustain an action by an applicant against an intermediary without the fortification provided by treating a sales representative as either an agent, or even as a fiduciary, in relation to the purchaser.[7] Similarly, in an applicant's action against an intermediary for deceit, the existence of an agency relationship between the intermediary and the applicant is not essential to the liability of the intermediary. Furthermore, in such a deceit action, the existence of an agency relationship between the intermediary and the company is not an essential requisite to the applicant's claim and the absence of such a relationship would not affect the intermediary's liability.[8]

The nature of the relationship between an insurer and an intermediary with regard to marketing transactions may be quite important because the liability of the insurer to the applicant[9] may rest on either the actual or the apparent authority of the intermediary to act on behalf of the insurer.[10]

5. See Restatement of Agency, Second (1958), § 14.

6. See Restatement of Agency, Second (1958), § 313, § 391, and § 392.

7. See cases cited in § 2.5(c), above.

8. See, e.g., Anderson v. Knox, 297 F.2d 702 at p. 706 (9th Cir.1961), *cert. denied* 370 U.S. 915, 82 S.Ct. 1555, 8 L.Ed.2d 498 (1962).

Cf. Clark v. Kelly, 217 Ga. 449, 122 S.E. 2d 731 (1961), *opinion on remand sub nom.* Kelly v. Georgia Casualty & Surety Company, 105 Ga.App. 104 at p. 106, 123 S.E.2d 711 at p. 713 (1961).

9. Except as noted above in relation to an action against an intermediary based on deceit.

10. See § 2.5(b)(4), above.

Comment

The doctrinal statements included in some judicial decisions about agency relationships in regard to insurance marketing transactions, usually as dicta, could lead to very erroneous results in subsequent disputes involving similar problems.[11] This would be especially so if such statements were to be applied in circumstances in which an intermediary does not have authority to bind a company [12] or to an intermediary who is only incidentally engaged in an insurance transaction.[13] In such cases, an intermediary is usually not a party to a pre-existing agency relationship with the insurance company, and any attempt to apply the type of doctrinal analysis suggested by such judicial statements could inappropriately complicate the question of both the intermediary's and the insurer's liability to the applicant, as well as the question of the authority of the intermediary to bind the company.[14]

11. Erroneously characterizing the relationship as one in which the sales representative is an agent of the applicant poses an improper obstacle to relief in favor of the applicant against the insurance company. Ordinarily the company is bound only if a sales representative had actual or apparent authority as its agent, a position usually inconsistent with the intermediary's being agent for the applicant in procuring insurance.

12. See, e.g., Walker v. Pacific Indemnity Company, 183 Cal.App.2d 513, 6 Cal. Rptr. 924 (1st Dist.1960).

Cf. Rider v. Lynch, 42 N.J. 465, 201 A.2d 561 (1964); Hamacher v. Tumy, 222 Or. 341, 352 P.2d 493 (1960).

13. See, e.g., Mid-America Corp. v. Roach, 412 P.2d 188 (Okl.1966); Walker Bank & Trust Company v. First Security Corp., 9 Utah 2d 215, 341 P.2d 944 (1959).

14. See, e.g., First Federal Savings & Loan Association v. Continental Equity Life Insurance Company, 124 So.2d 802 (La.App., 2d Cir., 1960). An intermediary was held not to be liable to a lending institution because of an agency relationship held to have existed between the intermediary and the debtor-applicant. The debtor of the plaintiff lending institution applied for credit life insurance in the amount of his loan, placing the application through the assistant secretary of the lending institution. The application and assumed coverage was for $4,800 although the policy expressly limited coverage to $2,000; the mistake was not discovered until after the debtor's death, which occurred less than two weeks after the application was made. Plaintiff brought suit against the insurance company under the policy, against its own employee as an independent insurance broker, and against the employee's errors and omissions liability insurer, recovering in the trial court $2,056, $250, and $2,494, respectively, from the defendants. The employee's liability insurer appealed, and the judgment was reversed as to it. The court characterized the employee intermediary as an independent insurance broker and, as such, the agent of the applicant in the insurance transaction; basing its decision on this characterization, the court held that "plaintiff occupied the status of a stranger or a third party without interest or rights against the agent for acts of negligence or errors which were detrimental to the principal." 124 So.2d at p. 804.

In credit life insurance transactions, the lending institution's employee through whom applications for insurance are made is, in fact, generally functioning on behalf of and under the control of the lending institution, regardless of his legal status as a licensed insurance agent or broker. See, e.g., Mid-America Corp. v. Roach, 412 P.2d 188 (Okl.1966). Moreover, the insurance coverage procured is often under a group contract (see First Federal Savings & Loan Association v. Continental Equity Life Insurance Company, supra), and the master policy or contract is usually issued to the lending institution. Characterizing the employee-intermediary as the agent of the applicant-debtor ignores these practical aspects of the transaction and implies a set of relationships between the parties that produces unacceptable legal consequences. The applicant-debtor's estate may thus be foreclosed from asserting liability of the

§ 2.6   Group Marketing and Coverage Under Group Contracts

§ 2.6(a)   Introduction

In the marketing of any product or service, economy can be achieved through a high volume of transactions. The principal way of doing this in the insurance field is by marketing a single insurance contract that provides coverage for many individuals.[1] Coverage provided in this way is generally referred to as "group insurance."[2] In its original and most common form, group insurance provides life or health insurance coverage for the employees of one employer. The first modern group insurance policies in the United States appear to have been issued by the Equitable Life Assurance Society in 1911.[3] Group marketing has now been employed to provide insurance in many other contexts including creditor-debtor groups,[4] labor union groups,[5] industry groups that include the employees of several employers,[6] trade groups,[7] and professional associations.[8]

lending institution as an intermediary and be left with recourse only against an individual who may be judgment proof. Under these circumstances, an analysis more consistent with the facts is to recognize the actual control of the lending institution and to allow the applicant-debtor recourse against the institution. In the *First Federal Savings & Loan Association* case, this analysis would have called for resolving the question of the employee's liability to the lending institution on the basis of the employment relationship between them, also allowing the debtor's estate the possibility of holding the institution liable for the negligence of its employee in the insurance transaction.

Also see Note, *Regulation of the Sale of Property Insurance by Savings and Loan Associations,* 42 University of Chicago Law Review 182–198 (1974).

§ 2.6(a)

1. See, e.g., Herbert Denenberg, Eilers, Hoffman, Kline, Melone & Snider, Risk and Insurance (1964), at pp. 293–316.

Also see Davis W. Gregg, Group Life Insurance (Third edition, 1962); Davis W. Gregg, Life and Health Insurance Handbook (Second edition, 1964).

2. See Davis W. Gregg, Group Life Insurance (Third edition, 1962); Davis W. Gregg, An Analysis of Group Insurance (1950); Group Insurance Handbook (R. Eilers & R. Crowe, editors, 1965), especially the articles by Eddy, *Development and Significance of Group Life Insurance* and Follman, *Development and Significance of Group Health Insurance.*

3. Davis W. Gregg, Group Life Insurance (Third edition, 1962), at pp. 5–7.

4. See, e.g., Gulf Guaranty Life Insurance Company v. Kelley, 389 So.2d 920 (Miss.1980); Seymore v. Greater Mississippi Life Insurance Company, 362 So.2d 611 (Miss.1978).

Also see Hayes Truck Lines, Inc. v. Investors Insurance Corp., 269 Or. 565, 525 P.2d 1289 (1974) (group credit life insurance).

5. See, e.g., Frost v. Porter Leasing Corp., 386 Mass. 425, 436 N.E.2d 387 (1982) (group insurance policy issued to a union health plan and paid for by the insured's employer); Talley v. Teamsters, Chauffeurs, Etc., Local No. 377, 48 Ohio St.2d 142, 357 N.E.2d 44 (1976) (group life insurance policy, paid for by weekly contributions of the employer to union health and welfare fund, where the coverage dispute resulted from an error by the union fund's clerical staff).

Cf. Dyer v. Occidental Life Insurance Company, 182 F.2d 127 (9th Cir.1950), 17 A.L.R.2d 923 (1951) (members of the Teamsters Union).

6. See, e.g., Vandenberg v. John Hancock Mutual Life Insurance Company, 48 N.J.Super. 1, 136 A.2d 661 (App.Div.1957) (merchant seamen).

7. See, e.g., Washington National Insurance Company v. Burch, 293 F.2d 365 (5th Cir.1961) (members of the American Turpentine Farmers' Association Cooperative);

8. See note 8 on page 104.

The coverage terms for group insurance are usually stated in a master agreement that is issued by the insurer to a representative of the group or to an administrator of the insurance program, such as an employer or executive director of the group. When a group coverage is provided solely at the expense of one party to the master agreement, such as an employer, it is called a non-contributory group plan. If individual certificate holders pay part of the premiums, either directly or by payroll deductions, it is usually referred to as a contributory plan.

Individuals participating in a group insurance plan are frequently described or designated as subscribers. Typically, each subscriber is sent a certificate or a pamphlet which sets out a general statement of the insurance and the principal conditions of the coverage. However, the coverage descriptions sent to subscribers usually do not include all of the provisions specified in the master agreement.[9]

The material used to promote or explain a group insurance plan to the subscribers is often written in a style or a format that is less complicated, and frequently less precise, than the coverage terms used in the master agreement. Statements in the booklets, brochures, certificates, or similar material distributed to the individuals who are insured often can be reasonably interpreted to indicate that the insurance benefits are more extensive than those which are clearly specified by the coverage terms in the master agreement. When this occurs, courts have sometimes concluded that an insurer is barred (usually under a theory of "estoppel" or "waiver") from asserting a denial based on terms included in the master agreement.[10] Courts have also held that differences between the descriptions in such literature and the actual coverage terms create an ambiguity that should be construed in favor of an insured.[11]

Bishop v. J.E. Crofts & Sons, 545 P.2d 520 (Utah 1976) (nonprofit trade association established for purpose of providing group insurance to members of Utah Automobile Dealers Association).

8. See, e.g. Simses v. North American Company for Life & Health Insurance, 175 Conn. 77, 394 A.2d 710 (1978) (life insurance for members of the American Society of Oral Surgeons); Miller v. Insurance Company of North America, 123 Ga.App. 274, 180 S.E.2d 274 (Div. 2, 1971) (life insurance for members of medical profession and their employees).

9. See, e.g., Martin v. Crown Life Insurance Company, 202 Mont. 461, 658 P.2d 1099 (1983).

Also see Annotation, *Group insurance: Binding effects of limitations on or exclusions of coverage contained in master group policy but not in literature given individual insureds,* 6 A.L.R.4th 835–849 (1981); An-

notation, *Group insurance: Waiver or estoppel on basis of statements in promotional or explanatory literature issued to insureds,* 36 A.L.R.3d 541–546 (1971).

10. See, e.g., Providential Life Insurance Company v. Clem, 240 Ark. 922, 403 S.W.2d 68 (1966).

Also see Annotation, *Group insurance: Waiver or estoppel on basis of statements in promotional or explanatory literature issued to insureds,* 36 A.L.R.3d 541–546 (1971).

11. See, e.g., Martin v. Crown Life Insurance Company, 202 Mont. 461, 658 P.2d 1099 (1983).

Cf. Sparks v. Republic National Life Insurance Company, 132 Ariz. 529, 647 P.2d 1127 (1982) (advertising sales brochure describing health insurance coverage did not communicate the limitation of coverage urged by the insurer).

Initially group insurance was used almost exclusively in the areas of life,[12] health, and accident coverage. The nature of the underwriting for these coverages undoubtedly contributed to the rapid and widespread development of group insurance in these areas. The principal variations of life, health, and accident risks among a group of individuals are generally associated with age, occupation, and health. It is, of course, relatively easy to adjust the premiums for a group of insureds—either individually or collectively—according to the age of the persons in the group. And for many employee groups there is a high degree of homogeneity as to occupation, which therefore can be easily accounted for in the computation of a premium. If other characteristics of the group members are deemed important, an actuary can determine an appropriate average premium that reflects the composition of the group. However, as discussed in the next subsection, for many variables that would be important in regard to underwriting insurance for one individual, an insurer typically does not need to individualize the rate structure if the group is large enough.

Another factor that probably accounts for the growth of group life, health, and accident insurance is that marketing these coverages on a group basis affords insurers the opportunity to reduce the relatively high administrative expense involved in the home office review of individual applications for such insurance. Generally, these are costs which either are not incurred or are relatively minor under the decentralized system of marketing that is used for most casualty, fire, liability, and inland marine insurance. Consequently, comparable savings would not be achieved through the group marketing of these coverages. Furthermore, some of the principal variations of risk in relation to casualty, fire, and marine insurance might be less readily dealt with on a group basis. For example, fire insurance on the scattered homes of a group of employees of one enterprise would almost certainly involve some individual underwriting considerations for the different risks that would be associated with specific properties. Even so, some of the economies of mass marketing undoubtedly can be attained in the fields of casualty, fire, and inland marine (property) insurance.[13]

In the late 1960's several insurers began merchandising automobile insurance to groups,[14] and it is reasonable to expect that considerable amounts of casualty and fire insurance will also be written on this basis. In the future, insurers will probably establish group premium rates for such coverages because the lower transactional costs in con-

12. In most instances, the life coverage was provided by term insurance policies. See Webb, *Group and Quasi-Group Property-Liability Insurance,* 24 C.L.U.J., No. 3, at pp. 31–37 (1970).

13. See, e.g., Herbert Denenberg, Eilers, Hoffman, Kline, Melone & Snider, Risk and Insurance (1964), at p. 315.

14. See Spencer L. Kimball & Herbert Denenberg, Mass Marketing of Property and Liability Insurance (U.S. Department

Transportation Automobile Insurance & Compensation Study, 1970); Webb, *Group and Quasi-Group Property-Liability Insurance,* 24 C.L.U.J., No. 3, 31–37 (1970).

Also see the comments in Shavers v. Attorney General, 402 Mich. 554, 267 N.W.2d 72 at p. 101 (1978), in regard to the enhanced feasibility of marketing motor vehicle insurance as a group coverage by shifting to a no-fault insurance system.

nection with the marketing, billing, and collection of premiums will make such group plans financially attractive to consumers.[15]

§ 2.6(b) Group Insurance and Adverse Selection

An insurer providing coverage for a group frequently agrees not to exercise judgment on individual applications. However, when insurance is sold to the individuals who comprise a group as optional coverage which need not be purchased by all of the individuals who comprise the group, the insurer typically reviews each application in order to protect against undue adverse selection which may result if too many of the desirable risks elect not to be covered. Consequently, the design of a sound group insurance system should take into account the possibility that adverse selection may occur, especially if members of a group are allowed to decide not to be covered by the group policy.[1]

Insurers often seek to prevent, or at least limit, adverse selection by requiring that a high percentage of the persons within a group become insureds. For example, an insurer may require that at least a stated portion (such as ninety percent) of the eligible employees in a group of several thousand employees of one employer must be participants in the insurance plan. If the percentage of participants from a large group of individuals is high enough, the problem of adverse selection[2] can usually be avoided or at least reduced to the point that it is not a significant consideration.

Adverse selection may also occur if individuals who are not actually members of the group are allowed to enroll as insureds. Insurers generally seek to minimize the prospects for such adverse selection by establishing eligibility requirements for participation in a group plan, such as requiring that participants be full-time employees.[3] The ratio-

---

15. *Cf.* the comments in Independent Insurance Agents and Brokers of Washington v. Herrmann, 79 Wash.2d 462 at p. 464, 486 P.2d 1068 at p. 1069 (1971).

§ 2.6(b)

1. See the discussion of "adverse selection" in § 1.3(c), above.

2. See the comments on adverse selection in the context of group insurance in Simpson v. Phoenix Mutual Life Insurance Company, 24 N.Y.2d 262 at pp. 268–269, 299 N.Y.S.2d 835 at pp. 840–841, 247 N.E.2d 655 at pp. 658–659 (1969).

For a discussion of adverse selection generally see § 1.3(c), above.

3. See, e.g., comment in Crawford v. Equitable Life Assurance Society of the United States, 56 Ill.2d 41, 305 N.E.2d 144 at p. 150 (1973).

Also see Larson v. Wycoff Company, 624 P.2d 1151 (Utah 1981) (insurer has right to cancel employee's group coverage when employee converts from full-time to part-time employment).

Cf. Jackson v. Continental Casualty Company, 412 So.2d 1364 at p. 1365 (La. 1982); Larson v. Wycoff Company, 624 P.2d 1151 (Utah 1981).

Also see, Annotation, *Group insurance: Construction of provision limiting coverage to active employees or to persons working actively in conduct of business,* 58 A.L.R.3d 993–1018 (1974); Annotation, *Group insurance: Construction of provision limiting coverage to full time employees,* 57 A.L.R.3d 801–820 (1974); Davis W. Gregg, GROUP LIFE INSURANCE (Revised edition, 1957), at pp. 34–36.

But cf. Krauss v. Manhattan Life Insurance Company of New York, 700 F.2d 870 (2d Cir.1983), where the insurer was barred from asserting the limitation specified in the master policy when the insurer failed to inquire about the insured's part time

nales for such a requirement are (1) that part-time employees may be subject to considerably different hazards in connection with other employment and (2) that some part-time individuals may be particularly undesirable risks who might be included in a covered group of employees through the ruse of partial employment. Another means used by insurers to limit adverse selection is to establish constraints on when employees may elect to enroll in a group plan.[4]

By requiring that a high percentage of all eligible employees participate in group plans, by excluding part-time employees, and by limiting the open enrollment periods, insurers generally can offer group coverage without incurring significant levels of adverse selection. And, even if there is some adverse selection, the insurer can maintain a financially sound plan by adjusting premiums to the average level of risk among the large number of participants. Occasionally, some of the members of a participating group may pay more than they would otherwise have to pay for coverage if there were no adverse selection. In most instances, however, the economic advantages of the group coverage are sufficiently great that even the members of the group who are the best risks would pay more if they sought to acquire comparable coverage as individual purchasers. Thus, although the financial benefit — lower premium charges — to the poorer risks in the group is greater, even the better risks among the participants typically derive a net benefit from the group arrangement because of economies in marketing.

§ 2.6(c)   Mistakes by the Group Administrator

Mistakes are sometimes made by the administrator(s) of group insurance programs. Consideration of several of these situations illustrates the range of problems which may arise from errors in the administration of group insurance. For example, an employer acting as an administrator for the group plan sometimes fails to notify the insurer of a new employee, and does not pay the portion of the premiums due from either the employer or the employee.[1] Another type of recurring mistake involves an incorrect report to an insurer that a particular worker's employment has terminated, and a subsequent failure to remit premiums that should have been paid to the insurer. When such mistakes are made and litigation ensues as a consequence of the occurrence of what otherwise would clearly have been an insured event, issues often arise as to who bears the risk of such a loss [2] — that is, whether the group administrator (the person or

status on the application forms or in any other way before the insured's death.

4. See, e.g., Home Life Insurance Company v. Chandler, 402 So.2d 356 (Miss. 1981).

§ 2.6(c)

1. See Annotation, *Termination of employee's individual coverage under group*

policy for nonpayment of premiums, 22 A.L.R.4th 321–355 (1983).

2. See, e.g., Bass v. John Hancock Mutual Life Insurance Company, 10 Cal.3d 792, 112 Cal.Rptr. 195, 518 P.2d 1147 (1974).

entity[3] that selects and pays the administrative staff) or the insurer is liable when such a mistake is made, or, alternatively, that the group member has no coverage.

There are related, but distinguishable, questions that arise if an error by a group administrator is discovered when no insured event has occurred. For example, is the insurer entitled to recover the missed premium payments from the employer? The resolution of this question may be influenced by the rules that apply to the questions that were identified in the preceding paragraph in regard to the allocation of the risk of a loss when a mistake has been made by a group administrator. If the risk of such a mistake in this type of situation is placed on either the employee or the employer, so that the insurer would not be liable, the insurer should not be entitled to recover the omitted premiums.[4] If, on the other hand, the risk of such a mistake is placed on the insurer — that is, a coverage claim for a loss would be successful against the insurer — then it follows that an insurer should be able to recover the premiums mistakenly omitted.

Mistakes by a group administrator may lead an individual to sue the insurer or the administrator (which usually means that a claim or a law suit is against the entity or person for whom the administrator or administrative staff works). When an alleged group member is an employee who in fact satisfies the condition of eligibility for participation, the employee (or the beneficiaries in the case of a group life insurance program) frequently initiates an action, sometimes as a third-party beneficiary of the contract between the insurer and the employer, against the insurer.[5] If such an action is brought against the insurer underwriting a group policy without also suing the employer, a court may hold that the group insurer is not accountable for a mistake made by the group administrator. For example, a persuasive case exists for concluding that an insurer should not be held liable when an employer

---

3. See, e.g., Talley v. Teamsters, Chauffeurs, Etc., Local 377, 48 Ohio St.2d 142, 357 N.E.2d 44 (1976), where weekly contributions were made by an employer to a union fund, and a mistake was made by the union fund's clerical staff.

But see, e.g., Rivers v. State Capital Life Insurance Company, 245 N.C. 461, 96 S.E.2d 431 (1957), 68 A.L.R.2d 205 (1959).

But cf., Henderson v. First Federal Savings and Loan Association, 119 Ariz. 409, 581 P.2d 254 (App., Div. 1, Dept. B, 1978) (under Arizona's statutory regulations for group life insurance, employer has no duty to notify terminated employee of his right to convert from group to individual coverage when employee knew the exact date of termination and had a certificate of insurance that explained the conversion privilege).

See also Annotation, *Termination of coverage under group policy with regard to termination of employment,* 68 A.L.R.2d 8–147 at p. 132 (1959).

4. If a payroll deduction had been made, it would be small comfort to recognize an entitlement in the worker to reimbursement for the amount deducted on the principle of unjust enrichment. The interests of group members would be better served by rules that provided coverage and held that the insurer is entitled to collect the omitted premiums.

5. See comments in Bass v. John Hancock Mutual Life Insurance Company, 10 Cal.3d 792, 112 Cal.Rptr. 195, 518 P.2d 1147 (1974), citing 2 Williston, CONTRACTS (Third edition, 1959), § 369 at pp. 906–907; and 4 Corbin, CONTRACTS (1951), § 807 at p. 213.

(acting in the capacity of the program administrator) fails to enroll an employee and to remit premiums for the employee's coverage.[6]

The decision in a suit by a claimant against an insurer may be rendered by a court without considering whether the employee may have a remedy against the employer. In the event a claim against the insurer has proved to be unsuccessful, an action should be allowed against the employer for the amount of coverage that was lost as a consequence of such a mistake. However, if a court, which denies a claim against the insurer, is not asked to also address the employee's (or a beneficiary's) rights against the employer in the same suit, the resolution of that issue in a subsequent proceeding may not sustain the claim. It does not automatically follow that the employee will prevail in an action which subsequently asserts that the risk of mistakes concerning the payment of premiums is to be borne by the employer.

In a case in which the employer's mistake precipitated a coverage dispute, the California Supreme Court reasoned that "the employer is the agent for the insurer in performing the duties of administering group insurance policies, including payment of premiums" and therefore "the insurer shares responsibility for the employer's mistake."[7] The court noted that this result was especially warranted when the record in the case included an admission by the insurer's representative that "if an * * * employee were not included in the calculation of premium by reason of clerical error or mistake, Hancock [Mutual Insurance Company] would nevertheless honor the claim under the group policy and backcharge Ford [the employer] for the unpaid premium."[8] Although, as noted below in the next subsection, the agency rationale of this decision is open to criticism, the result may nevertheless be justified on other grounds. For example, if the contractual documents fail to specify who would bear the risk of mistakes in administration, it may be a reasonable construction that this risk is to be borne by the insurer. The force of this argument varies with the text of the documents and the relationship among the parties. When the contract between the insurer and the employer clearly specifies that the risk of administrative mistakes is to be borne by the employer, a judicial allocation of liability to the insurer for mistakes made by an

---

6. See, e.g., Magee v. Equitable Life Assurance Society, 62 N.D. 614, 244 N.W. 518 (1932), 85 A.L.R. 1457 (1938).

Accord. Newman v. Home Life Insurance Company, 255 N.C. 722, 122 S.E.2d 701 (1961) (termination of master contract for nonpayment of premium ended employee's rights against insurer even though employer continued to deduct the employee's proportionate part of the premium from employee's pay); Gilford v. Emergency Aid Insurance Company, 252 Ala. 311, 40 So.2d 868 (1949) (company defense of alleged failure of employer to add employee's name to contract precludes liability of company).

Cf. Larson v. Wycoff Company, 624 P.2d 1151 (Utah 1981) (insurer has right to cancel employee's group coverage when employee converts from full-time to part-time employment when employee was on notice from information in the employee handbook that clearly stated insurance benefits were only provided for regular full-time employees).

7. Bass v. John Hancock Mutual Life Insurance Company, 10 Cal.3d 792 at p. 797, 112 Cal.Rptr. 195 at p. 198, 518 P.2d 1147 at p. 1150 (1974).

8. *Id.,* 10 Cal.3d at p. 798, 112 Cal.Rptr. at p. 198, 518 P.2d at p. 1150.

employer in the administration of a group plan would impose a result that clearly was not contemplated by the parties' contractual arrangement, and such a rule would be a significant infringement on freedom of contract. In the absence of specific statutory or administrative provisions, the merits of such a rule are debatable on public policy grounds.[9]

The decision concerning how the risk of mistake should be allocated, that is, whether upon the insurer,[10] the employer, or the employee, is independent of the nature of the group plan as contributory or noncontributory. The argument for an action in favor of the employee against the employer may appear on the surface to be stronger under a contributory plan, but viewed realistically either type of group insurance plan involves a contribution by the employee because the employer's contribution — whether it is the total premium or only part of it — is made as part of the total compensation which is being paid for the services of the employee.

One method of dealing with the risk of the various types of administrative errors in regard to group insurance is a contractual provision of the following type:

> Unintentional neglect on the part of the employer to furnish the name of any employee eligible hereunder shall not invalidate the insurance for such employee.[11]

In many situations, such a provision would be an appropriate way of addressing this problem.[12] Unfortunately, this type of arrangement may also result in the insurer's assuming the risk of dishonesty by an employer as well as the risk of mistakes.[13]

§ 2.6(d) Group Insurance and Agency Concepts

Occasionally, the relationship among the parties to a group insurance plan is described by referring to the group administrator as an agent for one of the parties.[1] When the administrative personnel are also employees of the employer whose employees comprise the group of

---

9. *Cf.* Chapter 6, below. Also see the discussion in § 2.3(c)(1) and § 2.3(c)(2), above.

10. A decision against the insurer would not necessarily preclude a later action by the insurer against the employer.

11. *Cf.* the clause in All States Life Insurance Company v. Tillman, 226 Ala. 245, 248, 146 So. 393 at p. 394 (1933) (coverage allowed although the insurer had not been notified of the re-employment of the worker, and, apparently, had not received premiums covering him under a contributory plan).

Also see Paulson v. Western Life Insurance Company, 292 Or. 38, 636 P.2d 935 (1981) (policy provision declaring that failure of employer to report to insurer the

name of a qualified employee shall not defeat employee's coverage).

12. See Davis W. Gregg, GROUP LIFE INSURANCE (Third edition, 1962), at p. 39.

13. Compare the risk of dishonesty of an agent, considered in relation to liability to oral contracts. See § 2.2(a), above.

§ 2.6(d)

1. The Oregon Supreme Court's opinion in Paulson v. Western Life Insurance Company, 292 Or. 38, 636 P.2d 935 (1981), includes an excellent discussion on this point.

Also see Washington National Insurance Company v. Burch, 293 F.2d 365 (5th Cir. 1961) (Georgia law); Metropolitan Life Insurance Company v. State Board of Equali-

insureds, in most situations neither the insurer nor an individual who is insured has the power of direction and control over the administrator that is characteristic of an agency relationship. The relationship of an employer to the employee insureds with respect to the typical employee group plan is better described as that of a "fiduciary." [2] The argument for regarding a group administrator as an agent of the insurer generally also lacks merit in relation to group credit life insurance plans.[3]

An insurer is, of course, free to establish an agency relationship with an administrator of a group plan. For example, in some instances a credit life insurance group administrator (such as a bank) is designated by an insurer as its agent for the writing of individual certificates of insurance under the group policy.[4]

If there is an agreement that an insurer is to bear the risk of mistakes that may occur in the administration of a group plan, it is not necessary to the enforcement of that agreement that the administrator be characterized as agent of the insurer in receiving the premium contributions from the employees. Rather, such an arrangement should be viewed as a contractual allocation of the risk that a mistake may be made.

§ 2.6(e)   Modification of Group Contracts

One of the more difficult problems that has arisen with some frequency in regard to group insurance involves modifications of the insurance plan, particularly coverage changes that are viewed as reductions in the benefits provided by the insurance. This question is

zation, 32 Cal.3d 649, 186 Cal.Rptr. 578, 652 P.2d 426 (1982); Bass v. John Hancock Mutual Life Insurance Company, 10 Cal.3d 792, 12 Cal.Rptr. 195, 518 P.2d 1147 (1974).

Cf., Home Life Insurance Company v. Chandler, 402 So.2d 356 (Miss.1981) (evidence was insufficient for jury to find that employer was insurer's agent with the power to waive or alter).

See generally, Stephen K. Evgster, *Group Insurance: Agency Characterization of the Master Policy-Holder,* 46 Washington Law Review 377–409 (1971); Richard S. Borst, *Group Policyholder as Agent of Insurer or Group Member,* 14 Federation of Insurance Counsel Quarterly 11–30 (Winter, 1963–64); Note, *Group Insurance Policies: The Employer/Insurer Agency Relationship,* 1968 Duke Law Journal 824–828.

2. See, e.g., Atlantic National Life Insurance Company v. Bank of Sulligent, 271 Ala. 541, 125 So.2d 702 (1960). The vice-president of bank was said to have been designated by the insurer as its agent, though the opinion does not disclose details of the arrangement and designation. The court declined to permit insurer to defend on grounds of agent's misrepresenting cer-

tificate holder's health. The court reasoned that having established dual relation, the insurer cannot assert it as limitation of authority.

Also see Seymore v. Greater Mississippi Life Insurance Company, 362 So.2d 611 (Miss.1978).

3. See Restatement of Agency, Second (1958), § 314F.

Also see § 2.5(b), above, concerning use of agency terminology generally, and § 2.5(d), above, on the misleading applications of agency classifications.

4. See, e.g., South Branch Valley National Bank v. Williams, 151 W.Va. 775, 155 S.E.2d 845 (1967), involving a bank signed group contract with the insurer containing a clause denying coverage on life of any debtor over 65 years of age when executing agreement for loan. The court held that no coverage existed, and that the insurer was not responsible for actions of bank cashier in transaction with two debtors one of whom was over 65.

Also see Seymore v. Greater Mississippi Life Insurance Company, 362 So.2d 611 (Miss.1978).

appropriately viewed in terms of what rights, if any, individual insureds have when the scope or extent of coverage provided by a group insurance plan is changed.

Typically, the certificates sent to individual members of a group do not specify the conditions under which the coverage subsequently may be modified or the procedures for making changes in the insurance coverage provided members of a group.[1] When disputes arise in regard to changes, the issues usually involve the questions whether each insured must be notified of the modifications, and, in a few instances, whether each insured must consent to any alteration in the coverage terms. The determination of whether either notice to, or the consent of, the certificate holders is required for modifications of a group insurance contract may be influenced by several factors.

There are obviously practical obstacles to obtaining the consent of all the certificate holders, in almost any group plan, to every modification in the insurance coverage. Courts generally have not been willing, except when a loss has already occurred or an insured event has commenced before the effective date of the coverage provisions (as in the case of continuing disability),[2] to infer a requirement that certificate holders must consent to a change in the master policy.[3] Further-

§ 2.6(e)

1. The relationships of the master policyholder to the certificate holder and the insurer create unique problems and unique variations on problems that exist in other insurance contexts. See, e.g., Larson v. Union Cent. Life Insurance Company, 272 Minn. 177, 137 N.W.2d 327 (1965) (provision causing forfeiture for nonpayment of premiums by master policyholder held not to apply to noncontribution to premium by individual insured, and, in the absence of a specific forfeiture provision, contributing to premium by individual insured held to be a contractual obligation only, and not a condition precedent to coverage); Layman v. Continental Assur. Company, 416 Pa. 155, 205 A.2d 93 (1964) (statute precluding defenses based on statements in an insurance application unless a copy of the application is attached to the policy held not to apply to defense based on statements in the application of an individual certificate holder under a group policy).

Cf. White v. Blue Cross-Blue Shield of South Carolina, 267 S.C. 543, 229 S.E.2d 854 (1976) (the court concluded that a clause in the contract authorized the state director of personnel to approve changes in a state health insurance plan).

Also see Annotations, *Termination of employee's individual coverage under group policy for nonpayment of premiums,* 22 A.L.R.4th 321–355 (1983); *Initiation and termination of coverage under group credit*

life or disability insurance, 5 A.L.R.3d 962–967 (1966); *Nonpayment of premiums as termination of individual coverage under group policy,* 68 A.L.R.2d 215–239 (1959); *Time of disability or death with regard to termination of coverage under group policy,* 68 A.L.R.2d 150–205 (1959); *Effective date of group life insurance, as to individual policies of employees,* 35 A.L.R.2d 798–799 (1954).

2. Christian v. Metropolitan Life Insurance Company, 566 P.2d 445 at pp. 448–449 (Okl.1977).

3. See, e.g. Metropolitan Life Insurance Company v. Korneghy, 37 Ala.App. 497, 71 So.2d 292 (1954), 68 A.L.R.2d 239 (1959).

Cf. Alvarez v. John Hancock Mutual Insurance Company, 362 So.2d 360 at p. 361 (Fla.App., 3d Dist., 1978), in which the court held "that in the absence of an allegation of fraud or misrepresentation, the contract between the insurance company and the employer for the benefit of the employees may be altered by negotiations between the insurance company and the employer."

But see Schlosser v. Allis-Chalmers Corporation, 86 Wis.2d 226, 271 N.W.2d 879 (1978), where the court held that an employer could not unilaterally invoke its reserved right to amend a group life insurance program to the detriment of its retired employees.

more, a consent requirement might even prevent changes from being introduced which would be improvements in the coverage for the vast majority of the group members.[4]

Providing notice to the individuals who participate in a group insurance plan is substantially less burdensome and plainly more feasible than a requirement that their consent must be obtained for modifications in the insurance plan. Accordingly, in the absence of express provisions in the master insurance agreement or the subscribers' certificate about what needs to be done to alter a group plan, it is undoubtedly more reasonable for a court to infer a requirement of notice than a requirement of consent. By resort to arguments about the sense of the agreement as a whole, courts have usually held that insureds only need to be provided notice of changes in group coverages. In the absence of notice, however, insureds are generally entitled to the benefits described in the pre-existing coverage.[5] Although it is customary to speak of a "requirement of notice" for changes in coverage provided by group insurance plans, this actually means that a coverage continues unchanged in the absence of notice to the persons insured by a group plan.[6]

Providing notice of coverage changes to certificate holders goes as far as is usually feasible toward affording each individual an opportunity to make appropriate modifications in that person's own personal insurance program to compensate for changes in the group plan.

§ 2.6(f) Termination or Cancellation of Coverage

Termination of coverage provided by a group insurance plan may arise either (1) because a person is no longer eligible (as, for example, an employee who leaves a job or an individual who terminates membership in some organization) or (2) because the entire group insurance contract is ended. Most of the case law in this area has involved disputes that arose as a consequence of employment termination. In

---

4. See, e.g., Ogden v. Continental Casualty Company, 208 Kan. 806, 494 P.2d 1169 (1972); Vandenberg v. John Hancock Mutual Life Insurance Company, 48 N.J. Super. 1, 136 A.2d 661 (App.Div.1957).

Also see the discussion in Schlosser v. Allis-Chalmers Corp., 86 Wis.2d 226, 271 N.W.2d 879 (1978).

In Harrison v. Insurance Company of North America, 294 Ala. 387, 318 So.2d 253 (1975), the court concluded that employees were entitled to notices of changes in a group disability plan when the insurer sought to cancel one policy that was replaced with a new policy and that notice of the changes to the employer, T.V.A., was not sufficient.

5. See, e.g., Ogden v. Continental Casualty Company, 208 Kan. 806, 494 P.2d 1169 (1972) (group disability insurance modified

by an endorsement with an effective date of several months after claimant's certificate of insurance was issued, and approximately a year before the employee became disabled).

Cf. Vandenberg v. John Hancock Mutual Life Insurance Company, 48 N.J.Super. 1, 136 A.2d 661 (App.Div.1957) (employee died five and one-half months after employment terminated; held, covered by group contract of life insurance originally providing coverage for approximately six months after employment terminated, though master policy had been amended without notice to provide coverage for only approximately three months after employment terminated).

6. See Christian v. Metropolitan Life Insurance Company, 566 P.2d 445 at p. 449 (Okl.1977).

many instances, courts have concluded that the contractual provisions require that an insured must be provided with notice of the termination or cancellation of the insurance coverage.[1] In other cases, a notice requirement has been held to exist as a matter of fairness in the sense of giving an insured an opportunity to exercise any conversion privilege afforded to members of a group who are no longer eligible to continue the coverage, or, in the absence of such a conversion provision, so that an insured may decide whether to obtain replacement coverage.[2]

When the coverage provided by a group insurance plan terminates (either immediately or after a grace period), the requirement of notice for an effective cancellation of an individual's insurance coverage is particularly justified if the insured is afforded a conversion privilege upon the termination of the group coverage.[3] However, if the coverage is coterminus with some specified affiliation or condition (such as employment or full-time employment) *and* if there is no conversion privilege when that status ends or that condition no longer is satisfied, there is relatively little justification for requiring notice to the individual. Furthermore, this conclusion is especially warranted when the

§ 2.6(f)

1. See, e.g., Parks v. Prudential Insurance Company, 103 F.Supp. 493 (E.D.Tenn. 1951), *affirmed per curiam* 195 F.2d 302 (6th Cir.1952); Poch v. Equitable Life Assurance Society, 343 Pa. 119, 22 A.2d 590 (1941), 142 A.L.R. 1279 (1943).

Also see Harris v. St. Cristopher's Hospital for Children, 291 Pa.Super. 451, 436 A.2d 203 (1981) (statutory extension of conversion privilege for a period of sixty days when an insured is not notified of the conversion privilege).

See generally, Annotation, *Cancellation or modification of master policy as termination of coverage under group policy,* 68 A.L.R.2d 249–284 at p. 254 (1959).

2. See, e.g., Ogden v. Continental Casualty Company, 208 Kan. 806, 494 P.2d 1169 (1972).

3. See, e.g., Neider v. Continental Assurance Company, 213 La. 621, 35 So.2d 237, 2 A.L.R.2d 846 (1948).

Also consider Newman v. Home Life Insurance Company, 255 N.C. 722, 122 S.E.2d 701 (1961) (employee's rights against insurer ended on termination of master contract for nonpayment of premium though employer continued to deduct premium contributions from employee's pay).

In Magee v. Equitable Life Assurance Society, 62 N.D. 614, 244 N.W. 518 (1932), 85 A.L.R. 1457 (1933), the court held that the insurer was under no duty to notify the employee of cancellation of coverage because actual discharge of the employee would have been notice of cancellation

without more, and from the insurer's point of view, the employee had been discharged and, therefore, had been given notice of cancellation. In effect this decision applies a rule that the employee was "conclusively presumed to know" that, under its terms, the group insurance policy ceased to cover him upon termination of his employment and, therefore, that the insurer was under no duty to notify him of its cancellation. In reality, of course, this is a fictional way of saying that the employee need not be notified that termination of his employment also terminates his coverage under the group insurance. This view cannot be reconciled with the rule, noted in the text above, that coverage is not effectively terminated when the employee has not had actual notice of termination of his coverage.

But see, e.g., Rivers v. State Capital Life Insurance Company, 245 N.C. 461, 96 S.E.2d 431 (1957), 68 A.L.R.2d 205 (1959).

But cf., Henderson v. First Federal Savings and Loan Association, 119 Ariz. 409, 581 P.2d 254 (App., Div. 1, Dept. B, 1978) (under Arizona's statutory regulations for group life insurance, employer has no duty to notify terminated employee of his right to convert from group to individual coverage when employee knew the exact date of termination and had a certificate of insurance that explained the conversion privilege).

Also see Annotation, *Termination of coverage under group policy with regard to termination of employment,* 68 A.L.R.2d 8–147 at p. 132 (1959).

record is clear that the individual is aware of the facts both that the group coverage will end and that there is no conversion right.[4]

The marketing of group insurance plans to many different types of associations or affiliations of individuals other than employees, as well as the expansion of the types of insurance which may be marketed as group coverages, have increased both the number and variety of disputes which result from the termination or cancellation of coverage.[5]

§ 2.7 Marketing Insurance Without Sales Representatives: Vending Machines, Advertisements, and Mail Solicitations

Many insurance companies market some types of insurance without depending on sales representatives. These companies communicate with potential purchasers in a variety of ways including advertisements in publications such as magazines or newspapers, advertisements on radio or television, mailings to consumers, and notices posted at vending machines. Insurers that employ these marketing techniques invite a purchaser to enter into an insurance transaction by sending a communication directly to the insurance company. The coverage disputes which have arisen from the marketing of "trip" insurance in airports are instructive in regard to the judicial treatment of marketing transactions that do not involve sales representatives.

Life and accident insurance for individuals using commercial airlines (often referred to as "air travel trip insurance") is commonly made available to travellers at airports through vending machines. The purchaser is directed to deposit cash or insert a credit card into the machine, to complete a form provided by the insurer that is either dispensed by the machine or is available from containers on the machine, and, in the latter case, to deposit part of the completed form in a receptacle in the machine. The directions usually also include the instruction that the insured should mail the remainder of the completed policy form to an appropriate place, such as the purchaser's home or

4. See, e.g., Larson v. Wycoff Company, 624 P.2d 1151 (Utah 1981). The court concluded that the employee handbook clearly stated that insurance benefits were only provided to full-time employees, and that the claimant had discussed his concern about his continuing eligibility for insurance benefits with his supervisor should he change position. After this discussion the claimant decided to quit his full-time job and take a part-time job in a different department rather than waiting for a transfer to the desired position as a full-time employee in the company's diesel shop.

Also see Evans v. Hartford Life Insurance Company, 704 F.2d 1177 (10th Cir.

1983) (parties were bound by a clear and unambiguous rider which limited coverage for laid off employees to 12 months).

5. See, e.g., Gulf Guaranty Life Insurance Company v. Kelley, 389 So.2d 920 (Miss.1980) (cancellation of a credit life insurance policy that named a bank as the beneficiary).

Also see Note, *The Requirement of Notice to Employee of the Termination or Cancellation of His Group Policy,* 42 Notre Dame Lawyer 523–533 (1967); Note, *Cancellation of Group Insurance Policy by Employer Without Consent of Employee,* 49 Yale Law Journal 585–590 (1940).

office.[1] This type of marketing means that typically a passenger does not have time to read the coverage terms before boarding a flight and often does not have a copy of the terms to read after boarding.[2]

Most of the cases involving trip insurance appear to have concerned the enforceability of limitations on the scope or extent of coverage.[3] For example, one decision considered whether recovery should be denied on three of eight $5,000 policies because of a limitation that restricted the total amount of such coverage for an individual to $25,000. The limitation was plainly indicated on the vending machines and on the policies.[4] Several other coverage disputes have considered whether coverage was provided for a trip on a non-scheduled flight.

The coverage limitations in trip insurance, such as a provision restricting coverage to scheduled airline flights, are usually stated both on the vending machine and in the insurance policy. When appellate courts consider the enforceability of such restrictions, they seem to be significantly influenced by the "total" marketing arrangement. For example, even though a "scheduled flight restriction" was stated on a vending machine from which a trip insurance policy was purchased, enforcement of the restriction was denied when the provision in the policy was in fine print and the vending machine was placed in front of an airport counter used by all nonscheduled airlines as a processing point for their passengers.[5]

§ 2.7

1. See, e.g., Roberts v. Fidelity and Casualty Company of New York, 452 F.2d 981 at p. 983 (9th Cir.1971); Travelers Insurance Company v. Anderson, 210 F.Supp. 735 (W.D.S.C.1962).

2. In Daburlos v. Commercial Insurance Company of Newark, New Jersey, 521 F.2d 18 at p. 25 (3d Cir.1975), the court noted, "There would seem to be little time for examination of the [travel insurance] policy by the insured" which was purchased from an employee of the insurer at a sales counter in the Philadelphia airport, and the insured was given no sample policy "for further and more extended consideration" after the copy of the policy provided by the insurer was mailed to the designated beneficiary. In this commercial context, the court observed that a strong case can be made for holding that an insurer has the burden of establishing that the purchasers were aware of the exclusion and that its effect was explained to them. In Daburlos, the court concluded that "the record does not even support the conclusion that insureds are given a reasonable opportunity to comprehend the terms of the policy." Ibid.

Accord. Kronfeld v. Fidelity & Casualty Company of New York, 53 A.D.2d 190, 385

N.Y.S.2d 552 (1st Dept.1976), appeal denied 40 N.Y.2d 807, 391 N.Y.S.2d 1025, 359 N.E.2d 1002 (1976).

3. See, e.g., Fidelity & Casualty Company v. Smith, 189 F.2d 315 (10th Cir. 1951), 25 A.L.R.2d 1025 (1952); Steven v. Fidelity & Casualty Company, 58 Cal.2d 862, 27 Cal.Rptr. 172, 377 P.2d 284 (1962).

Also see Mutual of Omaha Insurance Company v. Russell, 402 F.2d 339 (10th Cir. 1968) 29 A.L.R.3d 753 (1970), cert. denied 394 U.S. 973, 89 S.Ct. 1456, 22 L.Ed.2d 753 (1969) (general accident policy enforced according to its terms despite alleged misunderstanding as to duration of coverage growing out of insured's unsuccessful efforts to purchase airplane passengers' trip insurance of narrower coverage for longer period).

4. Slater v. Fidelity & Casualty Company, 277 App.Div. 79, 98 N.Y.S.2d 28 (1st Dept.1950).

5. Lachs v. Fidelity & Casualty Company, 306 N.Y. 357, 118 N.E.2d 555 (1954).

Cf. Steven v. Fidelity & Casualty Company, 58 Cal.2d 862, 27 Cal.Rptr. 172, 377 P.2d 284 (1962) (fatal accident in crash of "air taxi" substituted by decedent for cancelled scheduled flight; held covered, in spite of limitation of policy to scheduled

When insurance is purchased as a result of advertisements or direct mailings to consumers, the wording of the advertisement or a descriptive brochure often becomes the focus of a coverage dispute.[6] For example, in a case that arose as a result of a direct mailing by the Mobil Oil Company of an advertisement for accident insurance to be provided by American Home Assurance Company, the New Jersey Supreme Court noted "that the techniques used in marketing the insurance * * * are quite different from traditional methods * * *" and that the letter included with the brochure stated that the insurer "takes pride in offering you its policy."[7] The court then reasoned that although "generally an application for insurance constitutes an offer to the insurer which it may accept or reject," the rule is not applicable in this type of marketing situation when "there is nothing * * * to do after the application is made other than the [insurer's] * * * purely mechanical operation of processing the matter."[8] Thus, the material used in marketing the insurance and the insurer's underwriting practices created a situation in which the insurance contract was formed by the sending of the application form to the insurer. Similarly, an Ohio court concluded that when a health and accident insurer solicits business by advertising in newspapers, the company is bound by the statements in the advertisements.[9]

As might be expected, the marketing arrangements for insurance sales through machines or by advertising are not invariably found to warrant a judgment in favor of the claimants. For example, the Ninth Circuit Court of Appeals affirmed the appropriateness of a claims rejection based on a limitation that was stated in the following way:

flights, because of ambiguity in policy terms; clear notice test of the *Lachs* decision, supra, cited and used).

Also see Mark A. Cohen, *Flight Insurance: Conforming to the Reasonable Expectations of the Insured,* 30 Federation of Insurance Counsel Journal 19–28 (1979).

6. See, e.g., Fritz v. Old American Insurance Company, 354 F.Supp. 514 (S.D. Tex.1973) (*Erie* conclusion that under Texas law reasonable expectations of person responding to advertisement for "Traffic & Travel Accident Policy" must be honored).

In Riordan v. Motor Club of New York, Inc., 100 Misc.2d 638, 422 N.Y.Supp.2d 811 (New York County, 1979), the court decided that the insureds could reasonably assume from the "misleading" advertisement that travel accident insurance would be provided if they correctly filled out and mailed the forms they received with a brochure from the insurer — that is, the advertised mail order solicitation was an offer that could be accepted by returning the enrollment form and a check.

Also see Klos v. Mobil Oil Company, 55 N.J. 117, 259 A.2d 889 (1969) (accident insurance).

Cf. Craver v. Union Fidelity Life Insurance Company, 37 Ohio App.2d 100, 307 N.E.2d 265 (Hamilton County, 1973) (hospitalization insurance); Crawford v. Mid-America Insurance Company, 488 S.W.2d 255 (Mo.App., Kansas City, 1972) (student accident policy); Fuller v. Standard Oil Company (Indiana), 1 Ill.App.3d 799, 274 N.E.2d 865 (3d Dist.1971) (travel accident insurance).

See generally § 6.3, below, for a discussion of reasonable expectations.

7. Klos v. Mobil Oil Company, 55 N.J. 117 at p. 122, 259 A.2d 889 at pp. 891–892 (1969).

8. *Id.,* 55 N.J. at p. 123, 259 A.2d at p. 892.

9. Carver v. Union Fidelity Life Insurance Company, 37 Ohio App.2d 100, 307 N.E.2d 265 (1973).

Accord. Riordan v. Auto Club of New York, 100 Misc.2d 638, 422 N.Y.S.2d 811 (New York County, 1979).

"THIS POLICY IS NON–RENEWABLE AND COVERS ONE WAY FLIGHT ONLY UNLESS TICKETING FOR RETURN FLIGHT IS OBTAINED BEFORE LEAVING POINT OF DEPARTURE" * * *.[10]

The court noted that the limitation (1) was displayed in large letters on the vending machine, (2) was printed in bold-face type on the bottom of the specimen policy, and (3) was "not unusual" nor "patently designed to defeat the normal expectations of the average traveler." [11]

When insurance is marketed without the benefit of sales representatives, the courts often conclude that possibilities for a misunderstanding about the coverage are substantial. Several of the competing considerations that influence the scope of coverage which may be imposed by courts when insurance is marketed without the use of sales representatives are well summarized in the statement of a federal district judge who observed that "when the potential insurance purchaser cannot consult with an agent to ascertain the parameters of the proposed policy the concept of an informed meeting of the minds is a myth unless the insurance company clearly and explicitly explains the policy in its literature" and "the reasonable expectations which such literature raises or does not rebut must govern the interpretations of such policies." [12] He added, "In this situation more than any other, the company must be held accountable for misstatements and ambiguities in its literature." [13]

§ 2.8 The Development and Marketing of Standard Insurance Contracts

§ 2.8(a) The Role of Standardization

When purchasing an item such as an automobile or a refrigerator, buyers typically select what is regarded as a suitable model and give moderate attention to the choice of some special features. Similarly, insurance purchasers usually indicate the type of insurance that is desired, the coverage limits, and may even select some endorsements for the insurance policy that either increase or decrease the scope of coverage.[1] The average buyer, having only a general knowledge of insurance and the needs to be served by insurance policies, lacks information that would be essential to a reasoned choice about details of the transaction.

---

10. Roberts v. Fidelity & Casualty Company of New York, 452 F.2d 981 at p. 984 (9th Cir.1971).

11. Roberts v. Fidelity & Casualty Company of New York, 452 F.2d 981 at p. 984 (9th Cir.1971).

Also see Fuller v. Standard Oil Company (Indiana), 1 Ill.App.3d 799, 274 N.E.2d 865 (3d Dist.1971).

12. Fritz v. Old American Insurance Company, 354 F.Supp. 514 at p. 518 (S.D. Tex.1973).

13. *Ibid.*

§ 2.8(a)

1. See discussion in § 2.8(c), below.

The insurance policies most individuals acquire are comprised of standard terms that the insurer uses for all similar transactions. The use of standard insurance provisions imposes substantial constraints on the choices the typical purchaser can exercise in buying insurance, just as an automobile purchaser's range of selections is far less extensive than it would be if cars were custom crafted. This disadvantage is balanced by the benefits that result from the use of standard forms in insurance marketing, just as substantial advantages are derived from mass production in the manufacture and distribution of products such as automobiles and home appliances.

One of the major benefits of standardization for the consumer is lower costs: in insurance, as in other areas, customization invariably costs more than standardization. By using standard policy forms, insurers are able to avoid incurring many expenses that would inevitably result from individualizing millions of transactions.

Standardization of insurance coverages is also important to insurers because it is a very significant factor in the basic process of transferring risks from an insured to an insurer. In fact, risk distribution on the scale that exists in a complex commercial society may only be feasible if insurance transactions employ standardized insurance policy terms. To visualize the importance of standardization for insurance, consider the problem from the point of view of ten businesses contemplating the formation of a mutual insurance group. If the risks each owner wants to transfer to the insurance pool are substantially different from those of any other owner in the group, the problems in establishing an appropriate premium contribution for each of the prospective insureds are significantly increased. Furthermore, even if it is possible to determine an appropriate premium for each of the businesses, it seems evident that the costs entailed in such an undertaking will be substantially greater than would be the case if each individual is only allowed to transfer the same risk or an essentially comparable risk. Multiplying such considerations by a factor of several thousand provides some sense of the problems underwriters would need to surmount if standard forms were not used for most insurance transactions.

Another advantage of standardized insurance policies is that they make it possible to buy appropriate insurance even though an individual is not able to describe or define precisely the scope of coverage needed. A well-conceived standard policy reflects the typical insurance needs of purchasers on the basis of the industry's previous experiences with other insureds who were similarly situated — that is, standard policies generally should be, and often have been, designed by insurers to meet the needs of typical consumers. Such insurance policies are formulated so that appropriate coverage is provided for individual purchasers who are not aware of the specific characteristics of their needs. In general, the less someone understands about risks and insurance, the greater is the potential value of a standard insurance product.

The public interest in the regulation of insurance relates to many facets of the business, and in regard to some types of insurance it has resulted in mandates for standard coverage provisions — that is, standardization has been required by state legislation as a means of implementing public policy. Both legislation and administrative rulings have imposed standardization for some entire coverages and for particular aspects of other types of insurance policies.

The advantages of standardization enumerated in the preceding paragraphs have been important factors in the development of policy forms in the United States. That the use of standard insurance forms generally serves the interests of individual policyholders, the public, and insurance companies in having efficient and economical insurance operations appears to be a proposition beyond effective challenge.[2] The techniques and processes which have produced standard policy forms, described in the next subsection, clearly reflect these interests.

There remains, however, the problem of maintaining an appropriate balance between standardization, on the one hand, and sufficient flexibility to meet the individual needs of insureds, on the other. It is very important that insurers retain the freedom and flexibility to provide insurance coverages for the individualized needs of innovative and unique ventures. The range of adaptability of standard coverages, as well as the availability of insurance contracts that are specifically

---

2. For discussions of other advantages of standardization of insurance policies see, e.g., Thomas Wenck, *The Historical Development of Standard Policies,* 35 Journal of Risk & Insurance 537–550 (1968); Grissom, *The Scope of Windstorm Coverage,* New York Law Journal, Oct. 3, 1960, p. 4; Robert G. Ward, *Policy Simplification,* 1959 Insurance Law Journal 535–542.

For comments on standardization and contracts of adhesion generally, and for references to other writings on this subject, see Restatement of Contracts, Second (1979), § 211, Comment a; Lewis A. Kornhauser, *Unconscionability in Standard Forms,* 64 California Law Review 1151–1183 (1976); W. David Slawson, *Mass Contracts: Lawful Fraud in California,* 48 Southern California Law Review 1–54 (1974); Karl Nickerson Llewellyn, The Common Law Tradition: Deciding Appeals (1960), at pp. 362–371; Arthur Allen Leff, *Contract as Thing,* 19 American University Law Review 131–157 (1970); Friedrich Kessler, *Contracts of Adhesion—Some Thoughts About Freedom of Contract,* 43 Columbia Law Review 629–642 (1943).

Also see Alan Siegel, *Plain English in the Real World,* Best's Review: Life/Health Edition (February, 1980), p. 28.

The term "contract of adhesion" is used to describe transactions in which an economic entity, such as an insurer or group of insurers, markets goods or services to purchasers under marketing conditions such that buyers have no choice but to acquiesce ("adhere") to the form contract employed by the seller. In many instances, courts, as well as commentators, have considered insurance policies to be the prototypical contract of adhesion. See, e.g., Steven v. Fidelity Insurance Company, 58 Cal.2d 862, 27 Cal.Rptr. 172, 377 P.2d 284 (1962); Gray v. Zurich Insurance Company, 65 Cal.2d 263, 54 Cal.Rptr. 104, 419 P.2d 168 (1966).

However, it is evident that even though insurance companies typically do employ standard policy forms, a very significant portion of the transactions afford the potential purchaser many reasonable choices in the marketplace, including the option of acquiring more extensive protection by the payment of an additional premium. Furthermore, a vast number of insurance transactions are between parties where the purchaser has substantial, and often superior, bargaining power which could be employed to influence the coverage terms. See the discussion in § 2.8(c), below.

designed for individual insurance purchasers, is considered in the final subsection of this chapter.

§ 2.8(b)   The Processes That Produce Standardization

Factors That Affect the Process of Standardization

Several factors have affected the systems, processes, and techniques that have produced the standard forms used by insurers in the United States. Some of these factors have also been significant influences on the extent or degree of standardization that insurers have chosen to employ for particular types of insurance.

First, the insurance industry has accorded great importance to standardizing some types of insurance. In regard to these coverages, insurers have cooperated extensively in the development of coverage terms. Thus, standard forms and standard coverage terms have been developed by insurers in the absence of any statutory prescription.

Second, standardization is often very important for smaller companies who do not have sufficient volume to produce their own actuarial data on risks. The use of standard coverage terms facilitates the sharing of information on loss experience that is essential to setting appropriate premiums. Similarly, when the incidence of losses nationwide or worldwide is not great, standard coverage terms enable insurers, large and small, to share loss data.

Third, the governmental regulatory measures and actions that apply to coverage terms have been almost exclusively the province of the legislatures and administrative agencies in each of the fifty states. And among the state governments, there have been notably different attitudes and practices in regard to the degree of regulation of coverage terms that is viewed as either necessary or desirable. Consequently, there is considerable diversity among the states both as to the regulatory statutes and the pattern of overall regulatory activity in regard to the standardization of coverage terms. In some states, statutes prescribe standard terms either for some types of insurance [1] or for particular coverage provisions, although there are no comparable legislative mandates in other states. However, when coverage terms are prescribed by one state, insurers often choose to use the same policy terms in other jurisdictions.

Fourth, competition among insurers is a factor that may be a significant influence in regard to uniformity, if not standardization, among the coverage terms employed by insurers. An unusual policy form or coverage provision that proves attractive to purchasers, espe-

---

§ 2.8(b)

1. For some types of coverage statutes prescribe whether standardization is to be required, and if so to what degree and by what method.

New York is among the states whose insurance regulatory statutes have been most carefully developed. For their bearing on standardization of policies, see New York—McKinney's Insurance Law § 21, § 141, § 154, § 164, §§ 167–169, and § 183 (1966) and New York—McKinney's Vehicle & Traffic Law § 311(4) (1960).

cially one that provides a competitive advantage to an insurer using it, is likely to be imitated by other insurers. In this respect, competition works as an influence toward standardization. Competition can also work against standardization, because sometimes it encourages individual insurers to exercise ingenuity in the development of new features in the hope that they will be more attractive to purchasers.

The combined effect of these factors has led to the development of many different systems and processes which have been employed to formulate insurance policies. In some fields the process that produced the standard forms has been rather complex.

Each of the processes or systems described in the following subsections has played a significant role in the development of at least one type of insurance marketed in the United States today.

(1) Legislative Prescription and Proscription of Policy Terms

Statutory prescription of insurance policy terms, which reflects a public interest in standardization, is generally viewed as the most rigid or inflexible method of imposing standard terms for insurance contracts because legislatures have generally been slow to amend or repeal such legislation. This method is widely used throughout the United States for fire insurance. The 1943 New York Standard Fire Insurance Policy — which, with minor modifications, is now used in nearly every state — is prescribed by statute in New York [2] and in many other states. And in a few states, the form is required by administrative regulation.

In many states, the legislatively prescribed standard coverage form for fire insurance is not always adequate to meet some special problems that are usually covered by such insurance contracts. Endorsements are needed. In most states, the applicable statutes or administrative regulations do not specify terms for the forms that may be used as endorsements to the standard fire insurance policy. However, in a few states, including New York, the statute provides for the administrative prescription of endorsement forms.[3]

Standardization imposed by statute is more common in regard to fire insurance than for any other type of insurance. This may be attributed, in part at least, to the fact that fire insurance for structures has been in wide use since the colonial period, and that the coverage variations which affect the underwriting for fire insurance fit well into patterns to which both rates and standard insurance provisions can be readily adapted.

There are also many statutes that establish specifications for the exact language for some clauses [4] or prescribe the general content of

---

2. New York—McKinney's Insurance Law § 3404 (1985 & 1987 Supp.)

3. See, e.g., New York—McKinney's Insurance Law § 2307(b) (1985).

4. E.g., New York—McKinney's Insurance Law § 3216 (1985 & 1987 Supp.), prescribing "standard provisions" for accident and health insurance policies.

coverage terms [5] for various types of coverage without delineating the terms for the entire insurance form.

Statutes (and in some states, administrative regulations under statutory authorization) also establish proscriptions that apply to certain types of insurance contracts or policy provisions. In every state there are a few statutes that prohibit certain provisions in some types of insurance contracts. Although the most extensive use of such proscriptions has occurred in the field of life insurance, similar regulatory actions have been taken in regard to other types of insurance.[6]

(2) Administrative Prescription of Policy Forms Under Statutory Authorization

The standardization that results from administrative regulation is often not as rigid as that which results from statutes. There are several reasons for this. *First*, a regulatory agency is often more responsive to requests for changes in its rules than a legislature is in regard to amending or repealing laws. *Second*, it is often possible for insurers to convince an insurance commissioner to adopt rules that allow insurers to experiment with new forms, recognizing that approval usually can be easily withdrawn if experience proves such forms to be undesirable. *Third*, administrative regulations often provide at the outset that variations will be permitted in the forms submitted for approval. Although administrative regulations often involve less rigorous standardization than statutory prescriptions, administrative regulation can also prohibit all variations from the prescribed forms.

To observe that a particular insurance policy form is prescribed by administrative regulation (or even by a statute) does not necessarily warrant the conclusion that public officials bear the primary responsibility either for the original design of the form or for modifications in the form. The insurance industry has historically been represented by effective lobbyists before regulatory authorities and in legislatures. For example, with respect to forms prescribed by administrative regulation, it appears clear that proposals for change come more often from insurers than from any other source.[7] Insurers, of course, are likely to be aware of changes in the needs of insureds, of changing business

---

5. E.g., Massachusetts Gen.Laws Ann. ch. 175, § 113A (1958 and Supp.1970), concerning compulsory motor vehicle liability insurance.

Concerning legislative prescription generally, see Spencer Kimball & Werner Pfennigstorf, *Legislative and Judicial Control of the Terms of Insurance Contracts: A Comparative Study of American and European Practice*, 39 Indiana Law Journal 675–731 (1964).

6. See § 6.9 and § 7.2, below.

7. Although changes in statutory provisions are too infrequent to justify firm conclusions as to the usual source of the initia-

tives, there is at least some basis on which to speculate that the stimulus usually comes from the insurance industry.

For articles on the relationship between insurance companies and insurance regulators, see George R. Walker, *Relationship Between Insurance Companies and Insurance Regulators*, 26 Federation of Insurance Counsel Quarterly 99–109 (1976); Clarence E. Galston, *How To Handle Government Relations With The Insurance Department and The Legislature*, 49 New York State Bar Journal 470–473, 508–518 (1977).

circumstances, or of coverage problems that become apparent in the course of the claims process. Administrative agencies frequently do not have comparable contacts with either prospective insurance purchasers or insurance claimants. Insurance commission administrators usually are approached by insurance purchasers or insureds only in cases of acute dissatisfaction. Moreover, insurance commissions rarely have had staffs large enough to allow someone to be assigned to take initiatives in considering whether to require changes in policy forms. Thus, it should not be surprising that proposals for new forms or for changes in existing forms frequently emanate from insurers and are considered by the regulatory agency primarily on the basis of information presented by insurers.

(3) Legislative Requirements for Administrative Approval of Policy Forms

The insurance laws in most states require that insurers file all policy forms for at least some — if not all — types of insurance, and such statutes often provide that the regulatory authority must "approve" the forms which are submitted by insurers. Some statutes require approval before the form is used.[8] In other states, legislation specifies that a form must be filed and may then be used until and unless it is subsequently disapproved by the administrator.[9]

In practice, the regulation of insurance policy forms in most states usually involves little more than a system of perfunctory administrative assent to the forms that have been filed. However, this observation does not apply to every situation, and, particularly in recent years, there are some instances of vigorous regulation of coverage terms by insurance commissions.

There is considerable variation as to the standards that govern the review of insurance forms by the state regulatory authorities. There is even a degree of uncertainty in several states as to the range within which the administrator has discretion to examine proposals to determine whether some statute or common law doctrine has been violated.[10]

---

8. See, e.g., New York—McKinney's Insurance Law § 154 (1966) (life, accident, health, annuity); Pennsylvania Stat. tit. 40, § 751 (1954) (accident and health); Pennsylvania Stat. tit. 40, § 813 (1954) (workers' compensation); Pennsylvania Stat. tit. 40, § 477b (Supp.1970) (general section).

9. See, e.g., West's Ann. California Insurance Code § 10290 (1955) (disability) (if not disapproved in 30 days); New Jersey Stat.Ann. § 17:35B–4 (Supp.1968) (life); New Jersey Stat.Ann. § 17:38–1 (Supp. 1953) (accident and health); Ohio Rev.Code § 3915.14 (Page 1953) (life); Wisconsin Stat.Ann. § 204.–31(3)(g)(2) (1967) (accident and sickness).

10. In a few states, the regulatory statutes specifically provide that the administrator only has the power to disapprove forms proposed by the insurers who operate within the jurisdiction. See, generally, Spencer Kimball & Werner Pfennigstort, *Administrative Control of the Terms of Insurance Contracts: A Comparative Study*, 40 Indiana Law Journal 143–231 at pp. 144–177 (1965).

(4) Cooperation Among Insurers in Developing Policy Forms

The development of the standard forms for the various coverages included in motor vehicle insurance provides an excellent example of how cooperation among insurers produces standardized forms that are used by almost every insurance company. This process and the coverage terms it developed for motor vehicle insurance are considered at some length in Chapter 4.[11]

(5) Standardization of a Single Company's Policy Forms

Even in areas in which standard forms have not been produced through the cooperation of insurers generally, an insurer usually develops and uses its own set of standard coverage terms.[12] An insurer typically offers purchasers a limited number of insurance forms, and only in unusual circumstances are insurance contracts negotiated without primary — and often unvarying — reliance upon the company's existing forms. The fact that a purchaser desiring insurance with a particular company usually must accept one of the insurer's standard coverage forms is one of the principal reasons that insurance contracts are often characterized as contracts of adhesion.[13]

§ 2.8(c) Individualization, Standardization, and Adhesion

Most consumers do not concern themselves with trying to understand the detailed structure and the actual operation of products such as insurance contracts or automobiles. If a defect in an automobile or a refrigerator or an insurance policy produces an operational problem, the individual seeks assistance. The failure of an electrical contact in an appliance or a car generally causes the owner to seek a service department for assistance. An insured who has a problem with an insurance company in regard to coverage provided by an insurance policy usually turns to an insurance consultant or to a lawyer for help.

When the terms in an insurance contract result in rejection of a claim, frequently there is not much that can be done to help a claimant.[1] Insureds often learn, as a result of such an experience with

---

11. Also see discussion of standardization in § 2.8(c), below.

12. For an example of a rather drastic and consciously undertaken standardization of policy forms by one company, John Hancock Mutual Life Insurance Company, see Robert G. Ward, *Policy Simplification,* 1959 Insurance Law Journal 535–542.

Also see the description of Fidelity Union Life Insurance Company's program to simplify the language of its policies in Alan Siegel, *Plain English in the Real World.* Best's Review: Life/Health Edition (February, 1980), at pp. 28–30 and pp. 82–86.

13. Concerning rights at variance with policy provisions, many of which can be traced to recognition that insurance contracts are contracts of adhesion, see Chapter 6, below.

§ 2.8(c)

1. However, there are numerous instances in which courts have concluded the insured's rights were not determined by the terms of the applicable insurance policy. Cases involving such decisions can be found throughout this text. The many illustrations from varied contexts are brought together in Chapter 6, and examined with a view to identifying underlying principles and their implications for future development of insurance law.

an insurance coverage problem, that they had a deplorably inadequate understanding of the insurance product that was purchased. If an individual subsequently sets about to purchase precisely the insurance coverage that is needed or desired, the endeavor may provide considerable insight into the prevalence of standardization in insurance marketing, the extent to which standardized coverages can or will be adapted to individual needs, and the availability of non-standardized coverage which can be specifically structured to meet the needs of an individual purchaser. In the course of such an endeavor, the potential purchaser would begin to discover the answers to several fundamental questions about the characteristics of insurance policies marketed in the United States, including:

> First, to what extent is a buyer presented with a complete set of standard provisions by all insurance companies and given only the choice to accept or reject such an insurance package?

> Second, to what extent is a buyer able to influence the scope of coverage provided by a standard insurance policy used by a particular insurer through the use of endorsements?

> Third, to what extent and under what circumstances is a buyer able to acquire individualized coverage that is more comprehensive or extensive than the coverage available from the insurers who employ standard form contracts?

Standardization in the insurance business has produced some situations in which it is almost impossible for a consumer to acquire insurance with *basic* coverage terms that vary from the policy form used by all insurers. For example, although hundreds of insurers sell insurance to cover the risks incident to the ownership of an automobile, the basic policy forms these companies use for coverages such as motor vehicle liability insurance, uninsured motorist insurance, and automobile comprehensive insurance are virtually identical.

The general desire of insurers for standardization is counterbalanced by competitive forces that also operate in the market place. Accordingly, even in regard to coverages that are the subject of the highest levels of uniformity among insurers, such as motor vehicle insurance, consumers are afforded considerable latitude in selecting or arranging some aspects of the insurance contract and certain types of coverage features in such insurance policies. *First,* a consumer usually has significant choices in regard to several types of insurance that may be included or deleted from even the most standardized policies. For example, coverages such as comprehensive, collision, medical payments, or towing insurance can be omitted from the motor vehicle insurance package. *Second,* a consumer has considerable latitude in selecting the coverage limits and, in some cases the deductible amount as well, for each of the coverages in standardized policies such as the motor vehicle insurance. *Third,* there are almost always numerous endorsements which may be employed to affect the coverage provided by the standard policy forms. For example, there are many endorsements that can be used with the standard coverage forms for motor vehicle insurance to increase or decrease the scope of coverage. However, this does not mean that an insurer will modify the basic coverage terms of a standard form in response to an individual consumer's request to have a particular coverage restriction either struck from a policy form or rewritten.

Few insurers are likely to approve the selective elimination or reworking of coverage terms that establish general restrictions or limitations. Nevertheless, when a purchaser understands the effects of restrictions or limitations in such standard forms, it is often possible either to arrange for endorsements that expand the scope of coverage provided by the insurance policy which is being purchased or to acquire other types of insurance that will provide indemnification for losses that will not be covered by a given standardized policy. For example, in states where liability insurers customarily use the family member exclusion, insurers would almost certainly not eliminate this provision.[2] Nevertheless, other types of insurance that provide indemnification for the medical costs and wage losses sustained in any accident, including one caused by the negligence of a family member, can easily be acquired by a purchaser who seeks such coverage for family members.

In some marketing situations, an insurance purchaser may select from among several different standard coverage forms that are generally offered to consumers by insurance companies. For example, a purchaser considering homeowners' insurance almost always can choose from among at least three or four standard forms that provide a range of coverage choices. Furthermore, the scope of homeowners' coverage can be further influenced by endorsements that significantly broaden or restrict the scope of insurance provided. And for some types of insurance, consumers have numerous insurance policy forms with distinctive coverage features which they may select. The prospective purchaser of life insurance who considers the offerings of several companies, for example, is often confronted by a bewildering array of policies with a vast assortment of different features. When the policy forms used by the hundreds of companies that sell life insurance are analyzed, many of the coverage features are so different that often meaningful comparisons are virtually impossible. Thus, even though an individual insurance company may insist on not varying the coverage terms used for a particular type of insurance, similar coverage with distinctly different features may be obtained by consumers from other insurers.

Coverage that is specifically designed to meet the unusual needs or desires of an insurance purchaser may be available when the premiums to be paid to the insurer are very substantial — that is, insurers may agree either to adapt existing insurance terms or develop new coverage

---

2. This is likely to be especially the case if the state is one that has abolished the intra-family tort immunity.

provisions when a policy will cover large numbers of insureds or risks. For example, when a single group policy covers several thousand insureds, an insurer will often be willing to provide coverage that complies with requirements specified by the purchasers. Similarly, a major corporation seeking insurance to cover a large number of individual risks (such as those associated with the liability that might result from a very substantial number of passengers on an airline) often will have sufficient bargaining power to influence the insurance coverage terms. Individualized coverage terms may also be adapted or specially designed for persons who are interested in purchasing substantial amounts of insurance. For example, the role of life insurance and annuities in estate planning is well recognized, and many insurers attach considerable importance to offering products that can be structured to the specific needs or desires of the individuals who are interested in making such purchases. Thus, in many situations, it is possible for the purchaser to have a substantial influence on the coverage terms, and the desires of purchasers occasionally have been the stimulus for important contributions to the development of new approaches to insurance coverage.[3]

Finally, in some situations, an individual can arrange for customized coverage. There are insurers — most notably, but not exclusively among the underwriters at Lloyd's of London — who continue to specialize in making available insurance coverage that is specifically designed to satisfy the unusual needs of individual insureds. There are even reference books which list American insurers who specialize in underwriting particular types of unusual risks. In general, insurance is almost always available if cost is not a constraint. So long as the requisite elements of uncertainty and an appropriate insurable interest in regard to the risk exist,[4] if the amount of the premium is not a barrier to purchasing insurance, there are almost always insurers who will provide individualized coverage.

The discussion in this subsection is not intended to suggest that insurance is not a standardized product. An individual who seeks to have a particular term or provision either rewritten or eliminated from an insurance policy is not likely to be successful in such an effort. Furthermore, the market choices for purchasers who lack knowledge, who do not seek skilled assistance, and who are unwilling to pay a higher price for more comprehensive protection, certainly will be limited by the coverage terms of the standard forms generally marketed by insurers. However, even a consumer whose choices are limited by both price and ignorance is afforded an opportunity to select insurance products that generally will provide comprehensive coverage.

The preceding discussion also should not be understood as indicating that an insurance purchaser seeking to satisfy specific coverage

---

3. See the insurance provisions developed by the University of Iowa Committee on Funded Retirement and Insurance included in Appendix F, below.

4. See the discussion of insurable interest in Chapter 3, below.

requirements will invariably secure insurance that precisely conforms to those needs. In many instances, however, requests by a purchaser for specific coverage features will reveal that insurance policies, even when the coverage is to be provided by the standard forms, are often highly adaptable if such individual requirements are made known to an insurer at the time the purchase is being considered. Moreover, a prospective insurance purchaser who identifies specific requirements frequently finds that the market place is not entirely comprised of standard coverages. The characteristics of insurance marketed in the United States are in fact quite diverse. Thus, although an individual consumer may not always be able to bargain successfully for customized insurance provisions, purchasers nevertheless are generally afforded considerable latitude in the design of a total insurance plan provided by the various insurance products available in the marketplace.

The fact that the terms of an insurance policy at issue in a particular case may appropriately be viewed as a standard contract which is used by that insurer or a form contract that is employed generally by insurers for a particular type of insurance does not, in and of itself, justify the often expressed view that insurance policies are unconscionable contracts of adhesion. In many instances, when a particular risk is not covered by a claimant's insurance, it is the result of the insured's imperfect knowledge of the coverage needed, an imprecise articulation by the insured of the coverage which is sought, an ineptitude on the part of a sales representative in regard to understanding the purchaser's needs, or an inadequate knowledge on the part of a sales representative in regard to the insurance coverages available to meet the purchaser's needs. In such circumstances, the insured's problem does not stem from unavailability — which often seems to be either an implicit assumption or an unsupported assertion in the analysis of insurance coverage disputes — of insurance appropriate to the claimant's needs. Although it is true that most insurance transactions involve standardized products, this does not warrant an automatic presumption that the insurance policy involved in a particular case is a contract of adhesion. Perceptions of both the degree of standardization in the market generally and the lack of choices afforded to individuals are often unwarranted and are the result of failure of the litigants, the lawyers, and the courts to explore fully the market opportunities that were (and are) actually available to insurance purchasers.[5]

 WESTLAW REFERENCES

§ 2.1 **Organization of Marketing**

   (a) **Organizations that Sell Insurance**

      (3) **Mutual Companies**
          "mutual benefit" fraternal /2 association society organization /5 defin! mean***

---

5. Moreover, even if it is a situation in which the consumer's choices are extremely limited, it does not automatically follow that the contract provisions should be disregarded because they are unconscionable. See the discussion of disallowing an unconscionable advantage in § 6.2, below.

(b) Control Over Underwriting

(2) Decentralization of the Power to Contract
217k228 /p right /3 cancel! terminat!

(c) Structuring the Marketing Transaction

(1) Offer, Acceptance, and Counteroffer
find 394 a2d 710
217k130(1) /p offer
217k130(8) /p counter-offer accept!

(2) Interim Coverage
di(temporar! interim /3 cover! insur*** insurance policy /s
terminat! cancel!)
find 539 p2d 433

(3) Delivery of an Insurance Policy
217k136(4)
actual! physical! /3 deliver! convey! /s "life insurance"

§ 2.2 Oral Contracts of Insurance

(a) Usefulness and Disadvantages of Oral Agreements
217k131 /p oral! /3 agree! contract***

(c) Oral Insurance Contracts and the Statutes of Frauds

(1) Oral Agreements to Arrange for Renewals
oral! /3 agree**** contract*** /7 continu*** continua! renew! /
s coverage insurance policy

(e) Specific Provisions that Require Written Contracts or Written Statements
oral! /3 agree**** contract*** /s health accident /3 coverage
insurance policy

§ 2.3 Temporary Contracts of Insurance

(a) The Need for Temporary Contracts of Insurance

(2) Life Insurance Coverage: Temporary, Interim or Conditional?
217k132 /p temporar! interim /3 cover! insurance policy

(3) Fire Insurance, Casualty Insurance and Liability Insurance: Temporary Coverage
di binder

(b) The Use of Conditional Receipts in Life Insurance Marketing
find 208 a2d 638
objective! /s insurab! uninsurab! non-insurab!
sy(first initial /2 premium payment /5 pay paid paying /5
policy)
temporar! interim /3 cover! insurance policy /s reject! /s
insurer assurer company

(c) Judicial Restructuring of the Life Insurance Marketing Transaction
di(approv! satisf! /7 insurab!)
temporar! interim /3 cover! insurance policy /s application /s
pending
di("reasonable expectation" /s coverage insurance policy /s liab!)

(1) Conditional Binding Receipts as Contracts of Adhesion
collister /s "nationwide life"

(3) Adverse Selection Problems
find 248 f2d 879

217k132　/p　insurab!

(5) Funding Judicially Imposed Temporary Coverage
adverse　/3　selection

§ 2.4　Delay in Acting on an Application for Insurance
　　(a) The Duty to Act Promptly
　　　　duty　/9　act acti**　reject!　accept!　/7　application　/s　coverage
　　　　insurance policy
　　　　217k130(4)
　　　　application　/7　accept!　/s　retain!　retention keep!　kept　/5　premium
　　　　payment

　　(d) Whose Cause of Action?
　　　　agent broker　/5　act acti** misrepresent! fraud! negligen!　/s　recover!　/
　　　　s　beneficiary

§ 2.5　Intermediaries in Insurance Marketing
　　(a) The Agents, Brokers, and Employees Who Sell Insurance
　　　　di agent
　　　　di broker

　　(b) Insurance Terminology and Agency Law
　　　　217k144(2)

　　　　(1) Life Insurance Terminology
　　　　　　217k188 217k129　/p　general special soliciting　/3　agent　/p
　　　　　　authori! power　/p　bind!

　　**(c) Liability of Insurers and Intermediaries in Insurance Marketing
　　　　Transactions**
　　　　**(2) Liability of Intermediary and Insurer When an Insurance
　　　　　　Company Has Been Specified or Otherwise Indicated**
　　　　　　di(agent　/2　liab! non-liab!　/s　principal　/s　disclos!)
　　　　　　agent broker intermediary　/3　"due care" "reasonabl! diligen!"　/s
　　　　　　applicant client insured assured

　　　　**(3) Liabilities of Intermediaries and Insurers in Marketing
　　　　　　Transactions When No Insurance Company Has Been
　　　　　　Specified**
　　　　　　"milwaukee bedding"　/s　graebner

　　　　(4) Theories of Liability for Intermediaries
　　　　　　(i) Liability Based on Contract
　　　　　　　sy(agent broker intermediary　/s　duty fail***　obligation　/s
　　　　　　　obtain! procur! secur!　/s　coverage insurance policy　/s
　　　　　　　contract)

　　　　　　(ii) Liability Based On Tort
　　　　　　　agent broker intermediary　/s　duty　/7　skill care diligen!　/s
　　　　　　　procur! obtain! secur!　/s　coverage insurance policy

　　(d) Misleading and Erroneous Applications of Agency Classifications
　　　　intermediary　/s　broker agent　/s　insured applicant client assured

§ 2.6　Group Marketing and Coverage Under Group Contracts
　　(a) Introduction
　　　　217k151(3)
　　　　sparks　/s　"republic national"
　　　　mass group　/s　market! merchandis!　/s　insurance

(b) Group Insurance and Adverse Selection
> group /s coverage insurance policy plan /s full-time /2 employ****

(c) Mistakes by the Group Administrator
> cancel! terminat! /s group /s coverage insurance policy plan /s premium /5 unpaid (not /2 pay paid) (fail*** discontinu! lack*** /3 pay paying payment)
>
> bass /s "john hancock"

(d) Group Insurance and Agency Concepts
> 217k73.3 /p agen**

(e) Modification of Group Contracts
> di(chang! modif! /7 coverage insurance policy plan /s group /s member employee employe)
>
> 217k144(3)

(f) Termination or Cancellation of Coverage
> 217k178 /p group /s coverage insurance policy plan /s conversion convert! /3 right privilege provision

§ 2.7 Marketing Insurance Without Sales Representatives: Vending Machines, Advertisements, and Mail Solicitations
> misrepresent! mislead! misled decept! deceiv! false! fraud! /7 advertis! brochure flier literature "direct mail" /s coverage insurance policy
>
> "vending machine" /s flight airplane travel trip accident /7 coverage insurance policy
>
> misstat! ambigu! /s literature brochure advertis! flier

§ 2.8 The Development and Marketing of Standard Insurance Contracts

(c) Individualization, Standardization, and Adhesion
> standard! form /5 coverage insurance policy plan contract /s adhesion

Chapter Three

INDEMNITY AND INSURABILITY

------

§ 3.1 Indemnity and Insurability: An Introduction

§ 3.1(a) The Principle of Indemnity

One of the fundamental characteristics of any insurance system is the use of contracts that are in the form of an agreement for the transfer of a loss by obligating an insurer to confer an offsetting benefit to an insured. Conceptualizing insurance in terms of either a "transfer of a *loss*" or the conferring of an "*offsetting* benefit" is implicitly to indicate that the amount of insurance benefits paid when a loss is sustained by an insured is not to exceed the economic measure of the loss.

Almost all types of insurance are designed to provide no more than reimbursement for an insured. Moreover, it is now a generally accepted fundamental tenet of insurance law that opportunities for net gain to an insured through the receipt of insurance proceeds exceeding a loss should be regarded as inimical to the public interest. In other words, insurance arrangements are structured to provide funds to offset a loss either wholly or partly, and the payments made by an insurer generally are limited to an amount that does not exceed what is required to restore the insured to a condition relatively equivalent to that which existed before the loss occurred. The concept that insurance contracts shall confer a benefit no greater in value than the loss suffered by an insured is usually referred to as the "principle of indemnity."

The principle of indemnity does not imply that the amount of an insurance payment must be equal to the loss. Insurance that provides only partial reimbursement does not offend the indemnity principle, and in many situations purchasers acquire insurance contracts that will not provide complete indemnification in the event a loss occurs.

The principle of indemnity, which influences outcomes throughout the body of insurance law, is only one of the factors that affect legal disputes involving questions about the amount of insurance benefits a claimant is entitled to receive. The application of other important principles occasionally produces an insurance payment that exceeds a loss, a result that is not consistent with a rigorous application of the principle of indemnity. One of the primary objectives of this chapter is to analyze both the influences of the indemnity principle on insurance law and the areas in which limitations on the effects of this principle have been imposed by courts and legislatures.[1]

§ 3.1(b) The Doctrine of Insurable Interest

The principle of indemnity is almost inextricably intertwined with the "doctrine of insurable interest." Essentially, the insurable interest doctrine requires that there be some significant relationship between the insured and the person, the object, or the activity that is the subject of an insurance transaction. The specific justifications articulated by courts and commentators for the doctrine of insurability — avoiding one or more of the potential evils which might result from allowing insurance contracts that afford opportunities for net gain as a result of

§ 3.1(a)

1. There are also instances when other principles result in insurance payments that fall short of indemnifying loss, a consequence that is consistent with the principle of indemnity.

the occurrence of an insured event [1] — are the same ones that are almost uniformly associated with the principle of indemnity.[2] The insurable interest requirement, an amalgam that has resulted from both legislative and judicial actions,[3] applies to all types of insurance transactions and it is frequently employed by courts to implement the indemnification principle.[4]

§ 3.1(c) Potential Evils of Net Gains From Insurance

Foremost among the potential evils that were originally regarded as an undesirable consequence of insurance contracts which permitted a net gain by an insured was the prospect that such transactions would be used for gambling — that is, if an insured were allowed to derive a net gain from an insurance policy, it would encourage the use of insurance as a means of wagering. Public opposition to gambling appears to have been a major influence in the development both of the principle of indemnity and the insurable interest doctrine. A number of harmful social consequences have been thought to result from wagering, including the encouragement of idleness, vice, and a socially parasitic way of life that results in the increase of impoverishment, misery, and crime.[1]

There was considerable public hostility to gambling in England during the seventeenth and eighteenth centuries. However, wagering contracts, including those cast in the form of insurance transactions, were usually upheld by the English courts until Parliament established explicit legislative prohibitions in the mid-eighteenth century.[2] The

---

§ 3.1(b)

1. The specific concerns, which are discussed in the next subsection, include avoiding inducements to wagering, preventing inducements to the destruction of life or property, and avoiding economic waste.

2. For example, see Robert Stuart Pinzur, *Insurable Interest: A Search for Consistency*, 46 Insurance Counsel Journal 109–129 (1979); Stanley Fuchs, *The Significance of Insurable Interest*, 47 New York State Bar Journal 365–367 at pp. 388–393 (1975); William T. Vukowich, *Insurable Interest: When It Must Exist in Property and Life Insurance*, 7 Willamette Law Journal 1–42 (1971).

3. In addition to the sources cited in the other footnotes in this subsection, see Lynch v. Dalzell, 4 Bro.P.L. 431, 2 Eng.Rep. 292 (1729); Craufurd v. Hunter, 8 Term R. 13, 101 Eng.Rep. 1239 (1798).

4. See Emeric Fisher, *The Rule of Insurable Interest and the Principle of Indemnity: Are They Measures of Damages in Property Insurance?*, 56 Indiana Law Review 445–471 (1981); Robert S. Pinzur, *Insurable Interest: A Search for Consistency*,

46 Insurance Counsel Journal 109–129 (1979); Telford F. Hollman, *The Doctrine of Insurable Interest*, 662 Insurance Law Journal 160–167 (March, 1978); Bertram Harnett and John V. Thornton, *Insurable Interest in Property: A Socio-Economic Reevaluation of a Legal Concept*, 48 Columbia Law Review 1162–1188 (1948).

Also see Note, *Insurance: Necessity for Pecuniary Interest Held to Provide A Practical Limitation on the Expansive Doctrine of Insurable Interest*, 1971 Duke Law Journal 479–485 (1971), discussing the decision in Royal Insurance Co. v. Sisters of the Presentation, 430 F.2d 759 (Ninth Circuit, 1970); Note, *Insurable Interest in Property: An Expanding Concept*, 44 Iowa Law Review 513–522 (1958).

§ 3.1(c)

1. For example, see the discussion in Edwin Patterson, *Insurable Interest in Life*, 18 Columbia Law Review 381–421 at p. 386 (1918). Wagering has also been thought to discourage useful business activities.

2. See *Id.*, at p. 392; Dalby v. India & London Life Assurance Co., 15 C.B. 365, 139 Eng.Rep. 465 (Ex.Ch.1854).

first legislative provisions enacted by Parliament against the gambling aspects of insurance transactions were specifically directed at some aspects of marine insurance policies which were declared to be unlawful wagering contracts. Subsequently, the English Parliament adopted legislation that made similar prohibitions applicable to other types of insurance transactions. Thereafter, the English courts vigorously enforced these legislative proscriptions.

In the United States, questions comparable to those which were raised in England in regard to certain types of insurance transactions were initially considered by several courts in the New England states. The decisions in these cases adopted prohibitions that were similar to the English rules established by Parliament. These decisions appear to be based on both the English judicial precedents [3] (which applied the legislative proscriptions enacted by Parliament) and on what was then viewed in America as an appropriate public response to the "immorality" of gambling. The American courts that subsequently ruled on such questions in other states usually followed the precedents established by the courts in the New England states. Thus, insurance transactions that appeared to be wagers generally were declared to be illegal in the United States by judicial action, even though there was usually no basis for these decisions in statutory prohibitions.[4]

Cf. Craufurd v. Hunter, 8 Term R. 13, 101 Eng.Rep. 1239 (1798).

Also see Halsbury's Law of England, Volume 22 (Third edition, 1958).

But cf. The Sadlers' Co. v. Badcock, 26 Eng.Rep. 733, 2 Ark. 554 (1743) (insurance claim by a former lessee was denied under a fire insurance policy covering a house that burned after the lease had terminated, but while the insurance policy had not expired, because an insured must have an interest in the house at the time the fire happens). Also see the discussion of the Sadlers' Co. case in Robert Stuart Pinszur, *Insurable Interest: A Search for Consistency,* 46 Insurance Counsel Journal 109–129 (1979); Lynch v. Dalzell, 4 Bro.P.L. 431, 2 Eng.Rep. 292 (1729).

3. E.g., Amory v. Gilman, 2 Mass. 1 at pp. 10–11 (1806).

4. E.g., Ruse v. Mutual Benefit Life Insurance Company, 23 N.Y. 516 at p. 523 (1861) ("A policy obtained by a party who has no interest in the subject is a mere wager. * * * In respect to insurances against fire, the obvious temptation presented by a wagering policy to the commission of the crime of arson has generally led the courts to hold such policies void, even at common law. * * * In this State such policies would fall under the condemnation of our statute avoiding all wagers and gambling contracts of every sort, but they would, no doubt, also be held void, independently of that statute, at common law.").

Also see Connecticut Mutual Life Insurance Co. v. Schaefer, 94 U.S. (4 Otto) 457 at p. 460, 24 L.Ed. 251 (1876); Fowler v. The New York Indemnity Co., 26 N.Y. 422 at pp. 423–424 (1863) (The court observed that in New York insurance "obtained by a party who has no interest in the subject of the insurance" is "a mere wager policy" and in New York "such policies would fall under the condemnation of our statute avoiding all wagers and gambling contracts of every sort; but they would, no doubt, also be held void, independently of the statute, at common law.").

Cf. Horton v. State Farm Fire & Casualty Co., 550 S.W.2d 806 at p. 809 (Mo.App., Div. 4, 1977) (" 'Insurable interest' is a requirement of public policy prerequisite to the enforcement of an insurance contract" that "is intended to foreclose gambling contracts, which are void.")

Contra. Dunman v. Strother, 1 Tex. 39, 46 Am.Dec. 97 (1846) (wager on horse race); Trenton Mutual Life Insurance Co. v. Johnson, 24 N.J.L. 576 (Supreme Court, 1854) (since wagering contracts were not illegal at common law, and no statute is applicable in New Jersey, there is no requirement of insurable interest for life insurance).

In the twentieth century, public opposition to gambling does not seem either as evident or as far reaching as that which prevailed in England and the United States during the seventeenth, eighteenth, or nineteenth centuries.[5] Accordingly, although an important historical justification for the principle of indemnity and the insurable interest doctrine was to prevent insurance contracts from being used either as a means of or an inducement to wagering, the principle of indemnity and the insurable interest doctrine now rest increasingly on other public interests. First, there is a general goal of preventing societal waste.[6] When insurance is acquired by a person who does not have an insurable interest in the subject of the insurance contract, it is viewed as an unproductive transaction. Moreover, and probably even more important, allowing persons who do not have insurable interests to purchase insurance affords the potential for inducing the intentional destruction of insured lives[7] or property[8] — that is, it creates the prospect of a transformation of insurance from indemnification for fortuitous events to payments for planned occurrences. To destroy life or property in order to receive insurance benefits is, to say the least, unproductive for a society. Furthermore, such destruction almost invariably involves conduct that is criminal, as well as being offensive to the principle of indemnity. Thus, even though societal opposition to gambling appears to have moderated substantially in the twentieth century — as reflected by the various forms of gambling which are now not only permitted in, but are actively fostered by many states — indemnity and insurability retain their significance as doctrines of major importance because they

See generally, 1 Richards, LAW OF INSURANCE 329–330 (Fifth edition, Freedman 1952), at § 65. Richards discusses New Jersey developments after *Johnson* decision. Also see Fulda, *Insurable Interest in Life, New Jersey View,* 1 Rutgers University Law Review 29–55 (1947).

5. However, many contemporary judicial decisions continue to observe that the obvious purpose of the insurable interest requirement is to prevent wagering contracts. See, e.g., Peeler v. Doster, 627 S.W.2d 936 at p. 940 (Tenn.1982); Southeastern Fidelity Insurance Co. v. Gann, 340 So.2d 429 at p. 434 (Miss.1976); Mutual Savings Life Insurance Co. v. Noah, 291 Ala. 444, 282 So.2d 271 at p. 274 (1973).

Also see Lopez v. Life Insurance Company of America, 406 So.2d 1155 (Fla.App., Fourth Dist., 1981); Bowman v. Zenith Life Insurance Co., 67 Ill.App.3d 393, 24 Ill.Dec. 82, 384 N.E.2d 949 (1st Dist., Div. 3, 1978).

6. The argument is that allowing the purchase of insurance as a wager for fortuitous profits, rather than as a means of securing protection against fortuitous losses, is unproductive. Such contracts do not, either directly or indirectly, provide any needed service or aid in the making of any product, and in these circumstances the administrative costs of making such contracts available result in a net societal loss.

7. In Ruse v. The Mutual Benefit Life Insurance Company, 23 N.Y. 516 at p. 526 (1861), the court observed that "policies without interest, upon lives, are more pernicious and dangerous than any other class of wager policies because temptations to tamper with life are more mischievous than incitements to mere pecuniary frauds").

8. *Cf.* Fowler v. New York Indemnity Insurance Co., 26 N.Y. 422 at p. 423 (1863) ("In respect to insurance against fire, the obvious temptation presented, by a wagering policy, to the commission of the crime of arson, has generally led the courts to hold such policies void, even at common law."). See also Spencer Kimball, INSURANCE AND PUBLIC POLICY (1960), at p. 33.

Also see the discussion of rules for preventing net gain in § 3.6, below.

reinforce a generally shared goal of protecting against the intentional destruction of insured lives or property.

Vocational Wagering. It has sometimes been suggested that a distinction be drawn between vocational wagering in which the person who is to receive insurance proceeds enters into the transaction as a regular business, and nonvocational wagering in which a person is only involved in isolated transactions.[9] The purpose of proposing such a distinction is to impose more severe legal restrictions against vocational wagering on the ground that it involves more substantial evils.[10] There does not appear to be any persuasive rationale that supports a distinction between vocational and nonvocational wagering, and little support can be found in judicial precedents for such a distinction.[11]

§ 3.1(d) Conflicts Between the Principle of Indemnity and Other Principles or Goals

(1) Introduction

A legal system often produces situations in which accommodations must be made among conflicting doctrines or public interests.[1] This generalization is well illustrated by several significant legal principles that conflict with the desire to limit insurance payments to providing indemnity — that is, there are several important legal principles that clearly are not in accord with a strict adherence to the principle of indemnity. The three principles or goals which probably represent the most severe conflicts are discussed in subsequent portions of this chapter: the principle of freedom of contract and the associated objective of assuring the stability of contractual relationships,[2] the principle

9. See Patterson, ESSENTIALS OF INSURANCE LAW (Second edition, 1957), at pp. 170–172.

10. Some cases have arisen in which it might be argued that vocational wagering involving insurance policies has performed a socially useful function. For example, there was a time when industrial life insurance policies commonly contained no provisions for cash surrender value. In some communities a business developed of purchasing assignments of these policies. See, e.g., Hack v. Metz, 173 S.C. 413, 176 S.E. 314 (1934), 95 A.L.R. 196 (1935) (holding the assignments invalid). Although such transactions certainly represented a form of vocational wagering, the enforcement of such assignments arguably served a socially useful purpose in enabling poverty-stricken holders of industrial life insurance policies to realize something on the potential value of contracts they might otherwise have allowed to lapse.

It is perhaps true that the likelihood that a transaction will operate as an inducement to murder is greater in non-vocational wagering. A vocational wagerer or-

dinarily would be in the business of making money by wagering only, rather than by murdering as well. On the other hand, most non-vocational life insurance wagerers would be related by consanguinity or affinity to the person whose life was insured, and love and affection arguably would tend to counter the influence of the economic inducement to murder.

11. Providing for cash surrender value could be an alternative way of making it possible for an insured to realize some of the value of a life insurance contract in this situation. However, especially if the person whose life is insured has become uninsurable, the value of the contract is much greater than cash surrender value and the insured would have no enforceable way of realizing that higher value during the insured's lifetime if assignments were void.

§ 3.1(d)

1. See Robert E. Keeton, VENTURING TO DO JUSTICE (1969), at pp. 164–166.

2. See § 3.3(e), below.

of equity underlying the doctrine of estoppel,[3] and the principle of repose underlying the doctrine of incontestability.[4]

Safeguarding against violations of the principle of indemnity can add administrative costs for insurance transactions. Although some administrative costs may be increased, the additional expenses are probably more than offset by the savings which are effected by discouraging the overinsurance of property, limiting recoveries to actual losses, and discouraging the intentional destruction of property (and perhaps of lives, as well). Adherence to the indemnification principle may also reduce flexibility in regard to certain types of insurance arrangements. Sacrifices in efficiency and flexibility are sometimes part of the price that is collectively paid by society for the advantages realized from adhering to the principle of indemnity.

(2) Insurance as a "Personal" Contract

The principle of indemnity sometimes comes into conflict with the proposition that "insurance is a personal contract."[5] The statement that "insurance is a personal contract" usually is a euphemism for what are sometimes characterized as the "moral hazards" an insurer may encounter because there is always a potential risk that someone who wants to receive insurance proceeds will arrange for the occurrence of an insured event. Therefore, an insurer has an interest in knowing the identity of every person who will be entitled to receive benefits under an insurance contract. In addition to being entitled to know who is insured, generally insurers are also accorded free choice in regard both to the persons and to the risks that they decide to insure. Both of these concepts are embodied in the characterization of insurance as a personal contract. Furthermore, it is supposed, or at least hoped, that by knowing the individuals who seek to be covered or by being informed of events that may change either the person who is to be covered or the nature of the risks involved, insurers will be able to exclude undesirable persons and risks, thereby reducing the cost of insurance for those risks a company chooses to accept.

Courts sometimes confront a very difficult dilemma when faced with choosing whether (1) to allow an insured to receive a net gain by requiring an insurer to pay the full amount of insurance coverage applicable to a loss, (2) to allow an insurer to reduce its liability by paying less than it would normally pay in the event of such a loss, or (3) to avoid such results by deviating from a rigorous application of the proposition that an insurance transaction is a personal contract.[6]

---

3. See § 3.3(c)(2), below.

4. See § 3.3(c)(3), below.

5. See, e.g., McHugh v. Manhattan Fire and Marine Insurance Co., 363 Mich. 324 at p. 328, 109 N.W.2d 842 at p. 844 (1961) (" * * * the general rule appears to hold that fire insurance contracts are personal and that the identity of the insured is a

matter of importance to the insurance company.").

6. See the discussion of rules for preventing net gain in § 3.6, below.

Also see the discussion of the right to question insurable interest in § 3.3(a), below, and the allocations of losses between

The effect of a broad and inflexible application of the personal contract concept would preclude the use of several of the possible approaches to preventing net gains from insurance which are discussed in Section 3.6.[7]   At least in some cases, judges probably have avoided the use of certain techniques for preventing a net gain from the payment of insurance that they otherwise might have chosen to use were it not for the concept that insurance is regarded as a personal contract.[8]   However, in many instances the proposition that an insurance relationship involves a personal contract yields to other considerations that mitigate against its rigorous implementation.

§ 3.1(e) Characterization of All Insurance Policies as Contracts of Indemnity

Most types of insurance arrangements are viewed as contracts of indemnity.   The appropriateness of invariably characterizing all insurance policies as contracts of indemnity, however, is not always evident. For example, even though property insurance is usually treated so as to conform to the indemnity principle, some deviations from an unvarying adherence to the principle can be identified without much difficulty.[1]

Some writers have concluded that life insurance policies are not contracts of indemnity because life insurers often make no attempt to accurately value a beneficiary's insurable interest.   It has also been argued that life insurance policies are not indemnity contracts because various rules which are applied to life insurance arrangements — including the doctrines which define or determine (1) the requisite duration of an insurable interest,[2] (2) the possible rights of subrogation,[3] and (3) overvaluation — are inconsistent with the indemnity principle.[4] Other writers suggest that it is nevertheless still appropriate to classify

---

vendors and purchasers of property in § 4.3(b), below.

7. One way of avoiding net gain involves provisions that the insurer make part of its payments to someone other than the person it agreed to pay, thus violating the principle that insurance is personal in character.

It happens that in some instances preventing net gain by modified-gross-liability-to-designee rules (discussed in § 3.6), involve impairments of the principle that insurance is personal. For example, subrogation rules remain consistent with the personal character of insurance insofar as they merely allow an insurer to assert in its insured's stead some other claim of its insured against another, but if the other claim of the insured is against an insurer too, then allowing the first insurer to benefit from it is an impairment of the personal character of the insurance provided by the second insurer.

The nonliability rules and liability-for-net-loss rules could still be employed as ways of preventing net gain.

8. For example, courts have often declined to order an insurer to pay insurance benefits directly to someone other than the person it had agreed to pay.

§ 3.1(e)

1. See § 3.1(d), above.

Also see the discussion in Andrew Lindblad, *How Relevant Is the Principle of Indemnity in Property Insurance?*, 1976 Insurance Law Journal 271–276.

2. See § 3.3(c), below.

3. See § 3.10, below.

4. Patterson, ESSENTIALS OF INSURANCE LAW 155 (Second edition, 1957); Edwin Patterson, *Insurable Interest in Life*, 18 Columbia Law Review 381–421 at p. 388 (1918).

Cf. Keckley v. Coshocton Glass Co., 86 Ohio St. 213 at p. 225, 99 N.E. 299 at p. 300 (1912).

life insurance policies as contracts of indemnity because the insurance proceeds are usually provided to a beneficiary who has sustained a loss of some benefits as a consequence of the decedent's death.[5]

Observations

The most accurate conceptualization of insurance arrangements is to observe, first, that neither life insurance nor any other form of insurance is invariably a pure indemnity contract; second, that all forms of insurance are subject to the influence of the principle of indemnity; and third, that the influence of the indemnity principle is less pervasive in some forms of insurance, such as life insurance, than in other forms of insurance, such as property insurance. In other words, although the characterization of insurance as an indemnity contract is useful as a statement of a tendency or as a generalization, it is not always a reliable guide when answers are sought to specific problems of insurance law.

§ 3.2   History of the Insurable Interest Doctrine

The modern doctrine of insurability is the product of several centuries of actions by both courts and legislatures. This section describes the most significant events in the development of the doctrine of insurable interest in Anglo-American law.

§ 3.2(a)   The Statute of George II

In the early eighteenth century, underwriters began to issue marine insurance policies in which they agreed not to demand proof of the insured's interest in the ship or cargo that was the subject of insurance.[1] The origins of the insurable interest doctrine can be traced to the English response to these insurance policies by an Act of Parliament in the year 1746, during the nineteenth year of the reign of George II.[2] The preamble of the Statute of George II declared that such insurance contracts had "been productive of many pernicious practices, whereby great numbers of ships, with their cargoes, have * * * been fraudulently lost and destroyed, * * *" and whereby there was introduced "a mischievous kind of gaming or wagering, under the pretence of assuring the risque on shipping."[3] The Statute of George II, which applied only to marine insurance, declared that "no assurance or assurances shall be made * * * interest or no interest, or without

---

5. E.g., Richards, Law of Insurance (Third edition, 1925), § 24, at pp. 27–28.

   Cf. 1 Couch on Insurance, 2d (1984), § 69.

   But cf. Richards, Law of Insurance (Fifth edition, Freedman 1952), Volume 1, § 89 at p. 370: "To call the contract of life insurance a contract of strict indemnity, on the one hand, or, on the other, to isolate it from the general law of insurance and clas-

sify it as an investment, as many have done, is unwise. It partakes of the nature of both arrangements."

§ 3.2(a)

1. 1 Arnould, Marine Insurance [9 British Shipping Laws] (Fifteenth edition, 1961), at § 364.

2. 19 Geo. 2, c. 37 (1746).

3. Ibid.

further proof of interest than the policy, or by way of gaming or wagering, or without benefit of salvage to the assurer; and that every such assurance shall be null and void to all intents and purposes." [4]

§ 3.2(b)   The Statute of George III

The next major statutory contribution to the development of the insurable interest doctrine in England was enacted in 1774, during the reign of George III.[1] The preamble to this statute addressed "a mischievous kind of gaming" in relation to "the making of insurances on lives, or other events, wherein the assured shall have no interest." [2] Nothing was said of the destruction of the subject matter of insurance, an evil that was specifically adverted to in the preamble of the marine insurance act of 1746.[3] Apparently, the members of Parliament were not inclined to charge that no-interest life insurance had produced pernicious practices that amounted to murder. The 1774 act declared that "no insurance shall be made * * * on the life or lives of any person or persons, or on any other event or events whatsoever, wherein the person or persons for whose use, benefit, or on whose account such policy or policies shall be made, shall have no interest * * *." [4]

§ 3.2(c)   British Marine Insurance Acts of 1906 and 1909

Early in the twentieth century, a movement developed for codification and reform of the British law of marine insurance. The Marine Insurance Acts of 1906 and 1909 resulted.[1] The 1906 legislation reenacted the earlier statutory declaration that contracts of marine insurance "by way of gaming or wagering" were void,[2] and also defined more explicitly than the Acts of 1746 and 1774 what was meant by "gaming or wagering" contracts.[3] Further development of these explicit provisions occurred in the Marine Insurance (Gambling Policies) Act of 1909.[4]

§ 3.2(d)   "Legal" Versus "Factual" Insurable Interests: The Emergence of Competing Theories

Several English judicial precedents contributed significantly to the development of the insurable interest doctrine, especially in regard to the determination of the type of interest that is needed to satisfy the requirement.

4. *Ibid.*

§ 3.2(b)

1. 14 Geo. 3, c. 48 (1774).

2. *Ibid.*

3. See § 3.2(a), above.

4. 14 Geo. 3, c. 48 (1774).

§ 3.2(c)

1. Marine Insurance Act, 1906, 6 Edw. 7, c. 41; Marine Insurance (Gambling Policies) Act, 1909, 9 Edw. 7, c. 12.

2. Marine Insurance Act, 1906, 6 Edw. 7, c. 41, § 4(1).

3. *Id.*, § 4(2).

4. 9 Edw. 7, c. 12, § 1(1).

The decision in LeCras v. Hughes,[1] written by Lord Mansfield, established the foundation upon which almost all contemporary analysis of insurable interests rests. The *LeCras* case involved an action on a policy of insurance obtained on the Spanish ship "St. Domingo" that was captured by British forces in the harbor of St. Fernando de Omoa. The ship and its cargo were subsequently lost during the voyage to a British port. Before the voyage, the officers and crew of the British naval squadron that participated in the capture of the Spanish ship had arranged insurance on the "St. Domingo" and part of its cargo. After the loss occurred, the insurer disputed the insureds' right to recover under the insurance policy on the ground that they lacked a sufficient interest to meet the insurable interest requirements of the Statute of George II. In response to the insurer's contentions, Lord Mansfield observed that although the officers and crew did not own the ship or the cargo, they did have the expectation of benefit growing out of the practice of grants by the Crown following the capture of foreign vessels. Lord Mansfield concluded that the Prize Act and the royal proclamation granting rights to naval personnel participating in capture of an enemy vessel provided the "strongest ground" for upholding the insurance contract.

A second important English precedent was established several years later in the case of Lucena v. Craufurd,[2] which also grew out of the capture of a foreign naval vessel. In *Lucena,* insurance was obtained on several captured vessels by Royal Commissioners, and the claims resulted when the loss occurred while the ships were being sailed to English ports. In this litigation, the first count alleged that the Commissioners' interest in the vessels arose under an Act of Parliament that authorized Commissioners to take possession in wartime of ships and cargoes of inhabitants of the United Provinces that were then neutral, and that such ships could be "detained in or brought into ports of this Kingdom." [3] The second count alleged interest in the Crown, and that the insurance was obtained for the benefit of the Crown. The third count alleged interest in foreigners.[4] The trial court rendered a verdict for the commissioners on the first count, and for the insurer on the second and third counts. On appeal, the House of Lords ordered a new trial because the jury was misdirected on the first count.

§ 3.2(d)

1. 3 Doug. 81, 99 Eng.Rep. 549 (K.B.1782).

2. 2 Bos. & P.N.R. 269, 127 Eng.Rep. 630 (House of Lords 1805); on appeal from second trial, 1 Taunt. 325, 127 Eng.Rep. 858 (House of Lords 1808).

Also see the decision in Craufurd v. Hunter, 8 Term.R. 13 (1798).

3. 35 Geo. 3, c. 80, § 21 (1795).

4. At various times in September, 1795, several of the vessels that were the subject of insurance were lost by perils of the sea during voyages from a foreign port to a port of the Kingdom. There was a declaration of hostilities against the United Provinces on September 15, before the loss at sea of one of the vessels, the "Zeelelye", and after the loss of the others.

Some of the opinions by members of the House of Lords [5] in *Lucena* included comments that no recovery could be permitted under the first count. The opinions also stated that an opportunity ought to be allowed for the development of evidence that would sustain a recovery under the second count averring the interest to be in the King. Although many of the views expressed in the House of Lords opinions in the first *Lucena* appeal were not critical to the final disposition of the case,[6] they are of interest because of their influence on the development of the doctrine of insurable interest. Support can be found in these opinions for at least three distinct and inconsistent theories of insurable interest.

The opinion of Lawrence, J., after noting various definitions of insurance, concludes that a contract of insurance "is applicable to protect men against uncertain events which may in anywise be of disadvantage to them ＊ ＊ ＊." [7] He observed that cases had arisen in which recovery on an insurance contract had been disallowed because the interest was too uncertain to be the subject of insurance, but for the reason of "impossibility of valuing, and not the want of property ＊ ＊ ＊." [8] Lawrence concluded that to confine insurance "to the protection of the interest which arises out of property ＊ ＊ ＊" would be to add "a restriction to the contract which does not arise out of its nature." [9] Thus, Lawrence formulated a view of insurable interest based on a broadly conceived factual expectancy of advantage from nonoccurrence of a peril insured against, or, conversely, factual expectancy of loss from its occurrence.

Lord Eldon, in contrast, declared that the "interest" required under the Statute of George II is an "intermediate thing between a strict right, or a right derived under a contract, and a mere expectation or hope," and that he could find no way of identifying that intermediate thing "unless it be a right in the property, or a right derivable out of some contract about the property, which in either case may be lost upon some contingency affecting the possession or enjoyment of the party?" [10] He added: "If the Omoa case [LeCras v. Hughes] was decided upon the expectation of a grant from the Crown, I never can give my assent to such a doctrine. That expectation, though founded upon the highest probability, was not interest, and it was equally not interest, whatever might have been the chances in favour of the expectation." [11] The conclusion seems inescapable that Lord Eldon's

---

5. Lucena v. Craufurd, 2 Bos. & P.N.R. 269, 127 Eng.Rep. 630 (House of Lords 1805).

6. At the second trial, there was a verdict for plaintiffs on the second count as to all the vessels, and this verdict was sustained on appeal. 1 Taunt. 325, 127 Eng. Rep. 858 (House of Lords, 1808).

7. Lucena v. Craufurd, 2 Bos. & P.N.R. 269, 301, 127 Eng.Rep. 630, 642 (House of Lords, 1805).

8. *Id.*, 2 Bos. & P.N.R. at pp. 301–302, 127 Eng.Rep. at p. 643.

9. *Id.*, 2 Bos. & P.N.R. at p. 302, 127 Eng.Rep. at p. 643.

10. *Id.*, 2 Bos. & P.N.R. at p. 321, 127 Eng.Rep. at p. 650.

11. *Id.*, 2 Bos. & P.N.R. at p. 323, 127 Eng.Rep. at p. 651.

conception of insurable interest included a requirement of some kind of legally enforceable right.[12]

A passage in a third opinion in Lucena v. Craufurd, attributed to seven members of the tribunal (Graham, B., Le Blanc, Rooke, Grose, and Heath, JJ., MacDonald, Ch.B., and Sir James Mansfield, Ch.J.), concluded that "Where there is an expectancy coupled with a present existing title, there is an insurable interest * * *."[13] The opinion appears to proceed on the theory that the commissioners had such an interest. This view seems inconsistent with the Lawrence opinion, because Lawrence did not require that an insurable interest be based on legal right. It also seems inconsistent with the Eldon opinion, both because Eldon did not require an expectation of advantage and because Eldon appeared not to regard the Act of Parliament as a sufficient legal basis for insurable interest. Indeed Lord Eldon said, "If I were bound now to state my opinion judicially upon this first count [alleging interest in the commissioners authorized by the Act of Parliament to take possession of the ships and cargoes], I should be obliged very strongly to say, that the claims of the Plaintiffs could not be supported * * *."[14] In some respects the approach articulated in this opinion is consistent with the position that Professor Vance set forth a century later in his textbook. Professor Vance's position is that an expectation is not an insurable interest unless it "has a basis of legal right" and he urged that the facts in Lucena v. Craufurd well illustrate what is meant by an expectation supported by a legal basis since "this expectation was based on an Act of Parliament, which must operate if the vessels come to port."[15]

The following passage from the third opinion (attributed to seven members of the tribunal) seems to support the Lawrence view that a broadly conceived factual expectancy of advantage from nonoccurrence of a peril insured against is sufficient for an insurable interest under the Statute of George II.

> "The case of *LeCras v. Hughes* was a case of mere expectation and the circumstances were not near so strong in favour of the assured as the circumstances of this case. The doctrine there laid down by that great expositor of marine law Lord Mansfield, twenty-four years ago, has been recognized as law in subsequent cases; and if it were now to be decided that the interest of these commissioners was not insurable, it would render unintelligible that doc-

---

12. Lord Eldon probably would have sustained the existence of an insurable interest if a legally recognized property right existed even when the factual expectation was that the right would be economically worthless. *Id.,* 2 Bos. & P.N.R. at p. 324, 127 Eng.Rep. at p. 652. Lord Eldon observed: "Suppose A. to be possessed of a ship limited to B. in case A. dies without issue; that A. has 20 children, the eldest of whom is 20 years of age; and B. 90 years of age; it is a moral certainty that B. will never come into possession, yet this is a clear interest." *Ibid.*

13. *Id.,* 2 Bos. & P.N.R. at p. 293, 127 Eng.Rep. at p. 639.

14. *Id.,* 2 Bos. & P.N.R. at p. 326, 127 Eng.Rep. at p. 652.

15. Vance, LAW OF INSURANCE (Third edition, Anderson, 1951), at pp. 157–158.

trine upon which merchants and underwriters have acted for years, and paid and received many thousand pounds."[16]

§ 3.2(e) Adoption and Development of the Doctrine in America

In the United States, the insurable interest doctrine appears to have been first recognized in most jurisdictions as a matter of decisional doctrine that was not based on any predicate in applicable state legislation. American courts have often cited the English precedents that required an insurable interest,[1] sometimes without making any explicit reference to the fact that the English decisions were based on applications of Parliamentary actions such as the Statute of George II or the Statute of George III.[2]

Several states have now enacted statutory provisions which establish insurable interest requirements. The New York Insurance Law, for example, contains several sections on insurable interest which were first enacted in 1939, and which were drafted with extreme care.[3] The California Insurance Code also contains numerous sections on insurable interest, although the language leaves considerable leeway for judicial interpretation.[4] A third example of insurable interest legislation is a section of the Texas Insurance Code that establishes an insurable interest requirement for life insurance.[5] The Texas statute was first enacted in 1953 under the prodding of proponents for change in the decidedly distinctive rule that had prevailed in Texas before the statute. Even though relevant legislation now exists in a number of states,

---

16. Lucena v. Craufurd, 2 Bos. & P.N.R. at p. 294, 127 Eng.Rep. at p. 640.

§ 3.2(e)

1. See, e.g., Connecticut Mutual Life Insurance Co. v. Schafer, 94 U.S. (4 Otto) 457 at pp. 460–461, 24 L.Ed. 251 (1876).

Also see Ruse v. The Mutual Benefit Life Insurance Company, 23 N.Y. 516 (1816), which includes an excellent discussion of the evolution of the doctrine in the United States in relation to the development of the rules in England.

In Fowler v. The New York Indemnity Co., 23 Barb. 143 at pp. 146–147, 26 N.Y. 422 at pp. 423–424, 23 Barb. 143 at pp. 146–147 (1856), the court observed that in New York insurance "obtained by a party who has no interest in the subject of the insurance" is "a mere wager policy," and in New York "such policies would fall under the condemnation of our statute avoiding all wagers and gambling contracts of every sort; but they would, no doubt, also be held void, independently of the statute, at common law.").

2. Loomis v. Eagle Life & Health Insurance Co., 72 Mass. (6 Gray) 396 (Massachusetts Supreme Judicial Court, 1856).

3. New York—McKinney's Insurance Law §§ 146–148 (1966). These sections were part of an extensive recodification and revision of the insurance laws of New York enacted as New York Acts 1939, ch. 882. This legislation was the product of a special committee chaired by Professor Patterson. Note, *New York Insurance Code of 1939*, 40 Columbia Law Review 880–897 at p. 880, n. 3 (1940). Sections 146 and 147 have been amended since the 1939 recodification. *Ibid.*

Arkansas legislation, for example, defines an "insurable interest" to mean "any actual, lawful, and substantial economic interest in the safety of * * * [or] preservation of the subject of the insurance free from loss, destruction, or pecuniary damage or impairment." Arkansas Stat. 66–3205, Para. 2 (1947).

4. E.g., West's Ann. California Insurance Code §§ 280–287, and §§ 300–305 (1955).

5. V.A.T.S. Texas Insurance Code, art. 3.49–1 (1963).

the insurable interest requirement generally continues to be treated as an appropriate subject of decisional doctrine.[6]

§ 3.2(f)   The Policy Proof of Interest (P.P.I.) Clause and Honor Policies

Marine insurance policies in which underwriters agreed not to demand proof of an insured's interest in the insured property technically became unenforceable in England as a result of the enactment of the Statute of George II in 1746. However, some insurers continued to issue policies that did not require an insurable interest. Many insurance policies of this type used the term "policy proof of interest," and the insurance provisions that set out such terms are often referred to as "P.P.I. clauses." Other comparable insurance provisions employed phrases such as "interest or no interest," "all interest admitted," "without further proof of interest than the policy itself," and "without benefit of salvage to the insurer."[1] The opportunity for an insured to recover under such policies was dependent on the "honor" of the underwriter, and these insurance contracts came to be called "honor policies."[2]

In many situations, honor policies were used as a commercial convenience for persons who in fact possessed an interest in property covered by the insurance. Sometimes an honor policy was used because the insured's interest was of a type that might not be recognized by a court or because the insured's interest might be very difficult to prove under the then prevailing legal standards.

Honor policies provided wagering opportunities for persons without any interest in the subject of the insurance, and the term "wager policy" has generally been used to characterize all honor policies, including situations in which such insurance contracts were used as a commercial convenience for individuals who actually had some interest in the subject-matter that was insured.[3] The continuing potential for circumventing Parliament's legislative prohibitions through the use of honor policies led to several English judicial decisions which held that any policy containing a P.P.I. clause was unenforceable, even when an insured had an insurable interest.[4] In addition, to further discourage the use of honor policies in England, the Parliamentary Act of 1909 provided that in some circumstances even the making of such an insurance policy was a criminal offense.[5]

6. See § 3.5(d), below.

§ 3.2(f)

1. 1 Arnould, MARINE INSURANCE [9 British Shipping Laws] (Fifteenth edition 1961), at § 363.

2. *Id.,* § 11.

3. Arnould refers to the latter type as the "genuine *honour policy* as opposed to the mere wager." *Id.,* § 11.

4. Cheshire v. Vaughn Brothers Co. [1920] 3 K.B. 240. See Gedge v. Royal Assurance Corp., [1900] 2 Q.B. 214.

5. Marine Insurance (Gambling Policies) Act, 1909, 9 Edw. 7, c. 12, § 1(2). See 1 Arnould, MARINE INSURANCE [9 British Shipping Laws] (Fifteenth edition, 1961), at § 366.

In the United States, insurance provisions that are similar to the P.P.I. clauses are commonly used in marine insurance coverages.[6] The parties to these insurance contracts probably assume that such provisions are enforceable, and undoubtedly presume that the presence of these clauses in an insurance policy does not affect the enforceability of other aspects of the coverage provided by the insurance contract. Although at least the second assumption appears to be sound,[7] it is obviously possible that an American court might decide to follow the English approach.

§ 3.3　Applications of the Insurable Interest Doctrine

§ 3.3(a)　Introduction

The objectives underlying the insurable interest doctrine are usually well served by considerations which are dictated by the self-interest of insurers — that is, insurers ordinarily desire to provide coverage only for the benefit of persons who have an interest in the subject of the insurance.[1] Insurers often include policy provisions which require that the insured have an interest in the preservation of the property that is the subject of insurance. However, not all insurance contracts include such requirements. For example, life insurance policies typically do not state that the purchaser or the designated beneficiaries must have an insurable interest. Nevertheless, information in an application for life insurance almost always provides a basis for the insurer to decide whether an appropriate interest exists when the underwriting decision is made about whether to accept the application. Thus, the objective of requiring such an interest is usually attained even though no express contract provision is included in most life insurance policies. Furthermore, the insurable interest doctrine is of sufficient importance that it

---

6. "Disbursements insurance" is a common example. Originally such coverage applied to money that the master of the vessel spent during the voyage to pay charges incurred in various ways. Though the term is still used in this sense, it is also customary to speak of disbursements insurance as P.P.I. or F.I.A. (full interest admitted) insurance placed by the hull owner on the vessel in an amount over and above the hull valuation. See Winter, MARINE INSURANCE (Third edition, 1952) at pp. 278–279 and at pp. 385–386.

Insurance of "anticipated freight" under an expected contract, not yet made at the time of insuring, is another example of P.P.I. or F.I.A. insurance. See *Id.*, at pp. 320–321.

7. See Cabaud v. Federal Insurance Co., 37 F.2d 23 (2d Cir.1930); Hall & Co. v. Jefferson Insurance Co., 279 Fed. 89 (S.D. N.Y.1921).

§ 3.3(a)

1. Insurers typically seek to limit the benefits so that the amount paid does not exceed the interest of the person or persons who receive the payments. Property insurance contracts, for example, almost always contain several provisions which are designed to limit benefits paid by an insurer to an amount that does not exceed the insurable interest of the insured. See, e.g., Bertram Harnett and John V. Thornton, *Insurable Interest in Property: A Socio Economic Reevaluation of a Legal Concept,* 48 Columbia Law Review 1162–1188 (1948).

Also see Emeric Fischer, *The Rule of Insurable Interest and the Principle of Indemnity: Are They Measures of Damages in Property Insurance?* 56 Indiana Law Review 445–471 (1981); Robert Pinzur, *Insurable Interest: A Search for Consistency,* 46 Insurance Counsel Journal 109–129 (1979).

will generally be enforced by courts even when there is no clause that explicitly sets forth a requirement in any of the documents used by the insurer.

Insurers usually ascertain whether the requisite insurable interest exists before entering into an insurance contract. However, in some contexts — including several types of property insurance — insurers typically will only make a careful examination after a loss occurs (1) of whether the requisite interest exists or (2) of the value of an insured's interest. The question as to when an insurer is free to investigate and to thereafter question whether the requisite insurable interest exists or existed is, of course, a different matter from the question as to when an insured must have an insurable interest.

§ 3.3(b) The Time When an Insurable Interest Must Exist

(1) Life Insurance

It is commonly said in regard to life insurance that it is only necessary for an insurable interest to be in existence at the time of effecting a life insurance contract, and that if an insurable interest existed when the life insurance policy was purchased the contract is enforceable even though no insurable interest exists when the person whose life is insured dies.[1] In support of this proposition, it has been argued that it would be inequitable for an insurer to be entitled to either reduce or to avoid the payment of insurance benefits because the recipient of the life insurance proceeds either did not have an insurable interest in a decedent's life at the time when death occurred or did not

---

§ 3.3(b)

1. See, e.g., Dalby v. India & London Life Assurance Co., 15 C.B. 365, 139 Eng. Rep. 465 (Ex.Ch.1854); Connecticut Mutual Life Insurance Co. v. Shaefer, 94 U.S. (4 Otto) 457, 24 L.Ed. 251 (1876); Speroni v. Speroni, 406 Ill. 28, 92 N.E.2d 63 (1950).

Cf. Mullenax v. National Reserve Life Insurance Co., 485 P.2d 137 (Colo.App., Div. I, 1971); Secor v. Pioneer Foundry Co., 20 Mich.App. 30, 173 N.W.2d 780 (Div. 2, 1969).

Contra. McBride v. Clayton, 140 Tex. 71, 166 S.W.2d 125 (1942); but consider the effect of the 1953 Texas statute on this decision, § 3.5(e), below.

The rule that insurable interest at the time of effecting life insurance supports the contract despite want of insurable interest at the time of death has been applied to validate a ten-year extension of term insurance on the basis of insurable interest at the inception of the original ten-year term. Marquet v. Aetna Life Insurance Co., 128 Tenn. 213, 159 S.W. 733 (1913). See also Butterworth v. Mississippi Valley Trust Co., 362 Mo. 133, 240 S.W.2d 676 (1951), 30 A.L.R.2d 1298 (1953) (insura-ble interest of beneficiary at time of "conversion" of term to ordinary life policy sufficient to validate later assignment of policy to beneficiary and reassignment of it by him to trust not having an insurable interest at insured's death). *Dalby* applied this distinctive life insurance rule to a reinsurance agreement, even though reinsurance of a primary insurer's obligation on a life policy is more like property insurance than life insurance in that it is plainly intended as a contract of indemnity. Even if insurable interest at the time of loss were required in cases of reinsurance of a primary insurer's obligation on a life contract, however, the requirement would be met despite the primary insurer's lack of insurable interest at that time, so long as the primary insurer's obligation was enforceable. But in the peculiar circumstances of *Dalby*, the primary insurer's obligation had been discharged by settlement.

Also see 2 Appleman, INSURANCE LAW 123, 763 n. 32 (Revised edition, 1966); William T. Vukowich, *Insurable Interest: When It Must Exist in Property And Life Insurance,* 7 Willamette Law Journal 1–42 (1971).

have the same insurable interest that existed at the inception of contract. Whether it is unfair for an insurer to pay a variable sum (that would depend on the actual value of the beneficiary's interest at the time of death) when the insurer received premiums calculated on the face amount of the policy,[2] involves considerations that are not necessarily self-evident. Particularly in some circumstances, the merits and persuasiveness of the justifications for what is commonly said to be the insurable interest rule for life insurance are open to question.

Requiring an insurable interest at the time of an insured's death need not be viewed as unfair or unconscionable conduct by the insurer. This point is illustrated by a consideration of property insurance. A property insurance premium purchases coverage for a stated period of time during which the patterns and the extent of the risk for both the insured and the insurer may change. For example, in some situations, an insured's interest in property is variable over time. Even when an insured pays a premium predicated on a given value for the insured property that existed at the outset, the principle of indemnity and the insurable interest doctrine limit an insured's recovery to indemnification for the interests that exist when the loss occurs.[3] Furthermore, if it is deemed essential to establish some form of special rating approach for this type of situation, it can be achieved by taking these changes into account in setting the premium for the fluctuating conditions. Similarly, fair rating for life insurance that would limit a beneficiary's recovery to the insurable interest at death could be achieved by taking the expectation of changing patterns of risk into account when fixing the premiums. Alternatively, the alleged unfairness could also be avoided by distributing any "excess amount" of life insurance to persons with an economic interest in the life of the decedent when the death occurs.[4]

The generally recognized insurable interest rule for life insurance, which focuses exclusively on the existence of the requisite interest at the outset of the insurance arrangement, almost certainly is the result of three factors. First, life insurance is often acquired for the benefit of relatives and spouses. The existence of familial relationships, such as parents to children, does not change with the passage of time. Accordingly, if an insurable interest based on a family relationship existed at the time the life insurance was initially purchased, normally the interest still exists when the death occurs. Consequently, there was no reason for either insurers or the courts to review the matter following an insured's death. Moreover, when this rule evolved marital relationships were also very stable, and therefore it was reasonable to have the same rule for a spouse who was named as a beneficiary in a life insurance contract insuring the other spouse's life.

---

2. See, e.g., Dalby v. India & London Life Assurance Co., 15 C.B. 365, 139 Eng. Rep. 465 (Ex.Ch., 1854).

3. Not only may the value of property change during the period of coverage, but also the loss may be either total or partial.

4. Cf. the Texas rule discussed in § 3.5(e), below.

Second, substantial amounts of life insurance were and are marketed as investments, as well as insurance. A rule that only requires an insurable interest for life insurance at the inception of the contractual arrangement facilitates the liquidity of such investments — that is, requiring an insurable interest when death occurs would limit the transferability of the "asset" and thereby reduce its value.

Third, there apparently was, and perhaps continues to be, a strong sense of protecting the integrity of the life insurance transaction in terms of both preserving the contractual freedom of the parties and assuring the stability of the contractual commitment. As the Supreme Court of the United States commented in 1876, when "a fair and proper insurable interest, of whatever kind" existed "at the time of taking out the policy" and "the policy was taken out in good faith, the object and purpose of the rule which condemns wager policies is sufficiently attained" so that "there is then no good reason why the contract should not be carried out according to its terms."[5] The Court then noted that "it would be very difficult, after the policy had continued for any considerable time, for the courts, without the aid of legislation, to attempt an adjustment of equities arising from a cessation of interest in the insured life."[6]

In the twentieth century, life insurance — especially term life insurance — is employed in many contexts in which neither an investment interest nor a family relationship exists. For example, term life insurance is used by some businesses to provide an economic benefit to offset the consequences that result from the death of a "key" employee. Term insurance is also employed by partnerships to assure sufficient liquidity to allow a withdrawal of the decedent's interest in the event of a partner's death without forcing a sale of the partnership's assets.[7] Sometimes term life insurance on employees or partners is maintained after the business relationship has ended. The appropriateness of continuing to apply the rule that an insurable interest is only required at the inception for life insurance coverages acquired in business situations is particularly open to question when it is evident that the commercial reason for the coverage has ceased and that no other relationship, familial or economic, exists at the time of death.[8]

5. Connecticut Mutual Life Insurance Company v. Schaefer, 94 U.S. (4 Otto) 457 at p. 462, 24 L.Ed. 251 (1876).

6. *Ibid.*

7. See COUCH ON INSURANCE 2d (Revised Edition, 1984), at §§ 24:146–148.

8. *Cf.* Bauer v. Bates Lumber Company, Inc., 84 N.M. 391, 503 P.2d 1169 (1972), *cert. denied* 84 N.M. 390, 503 P.2d 1168 (1972), in which the court found that Bauer was neither an officer nor a key employee, and then concluded that the employer had no insurable interest in the employee's life because naming the employer as the beneficiary was prohibited by New Mexico Statutes Annotated, § 58–8–17 (1953); Manhattan Life Insurance Company v. Lacy J. Miller Machine Company, Inc., 60 N.C. App. 155; 298 S.E.2d 190 (1982) (employee who has been legally barred from employer's premises by a restraining order—issued by a court in response to the employer's claims that they were alarmed by the individual's incompetence—was ineligible for protection under a "key man" policy which was therefore void).

Also see McBride v. Clayton, 140 Tex. 71, 166 S.W.2d 125 (1942).

(2) Property Insurance

A statement by Lord Chancellor Hardwicke, in Sadlers Co. v. Badcock,[9] is often said to have established the insurable interest rule for property insurance which states that it is necessary for the insured to have an interest at the time of insuring *and* at the time of the loss. In *Badcock*, however, the person who obtained the insurance was a "lessee for years" whose lease expired before the property was destroyed by a fire. Thus, the assertion that an insurable interest was necessary at the time of insuring was dictum, and arguably the point was not carefully considered in that case.

The proposition attributed to the *Badcock* decision — that an insurable interest is required for property insurance at the time of loss *and* at the time of effecting the contract — has now been repeated so often, in both judicial opinions [10] and elsewhere, that many writers have been led to suppose that it is a highly esteemed majority rule that should be applied to all property insurance transactions.[11]

There are many situations in which a rigorous application of the *Badcock* rule would produce undesirable results, and the rule has been subject to trenchant criticism.[12] Even if it is the majority rule, it is not the better rule and ultimately it seems likely to be displaced by an

But cf. the discussion in COUCH ON INSURANCE 2d (Revised edition, 1984), at § 24:149.

9. 2 Ark. 554 at p. 555, 26 Eng.Rep. 733, 1 Wils. K.B. 10, 95 Eng.Rep. 463 (1743). It is interesting to note, however, that the Lord Chancellor's statement was phrased in the disjunctive: "If the insured was not to have a property at the time of the insurance *or* loss, anyone might insure upon another's house, which might have a bad tendency to burning houses." (Emphasis added).

10. See, e.g., Kingston v. Great Southwest Fire Insurance Co., 578 P.2d 1278 at p. 1279 (Utah 1978); Armbrust v. Travelers Insurance Co., 232 Or. 617, 376 P.2d 669 (1962); Rube v. Pacific Insurance Co., 131 So.2d 240 (La.App., 1st Cir., 1961) (alternate holding).

11. See, e.g., 4 Appleman, Insurance Law (Revised edition, 1969), § 2122 at p. 31: "Probably the majority of cases hold that such insurable interest must exist both at the time of making the contract and at the time of loss." Appleman also observes, however: "If the insured had such interest during the duration of the risk and at the time of loss, a few well reasoned opinions * * * hold that sufficient." *Id.,* at p. 32.

12. See, e.g., McCluskey v. Providence Washington Insurance Co., 126 Mass. 306 (1879).

But cf. Womble v. Dubuque Fire & Marine Insurance Co., 310 Mass. 142 at p. 144, and at pp. 146–147, 37 N.E.2d 263 at pp. 265–266 (1941):

"If the person insured has no insurable interest in the property covered when the policy by its terms would become operative as to that property, the policy never takes effect as valid insurance on the property. McCluskey v. Providence Washington Insurance Co., 126 Mass. 306, 308 [(1879)]. * * * [T]he insureds [trustees of a church group that had long used the insured church building, but did not have title to it] had an insurable interest in the building when the policy was issued, within the broad definitions of such an interest illustrated by the cases cited above. See also Liverpool & London & Globe Insurance Co., Ltd. v. Bolling, 176 Va. 182, 10 S.E.2d 518 (1940). The requirement of an insurable interest when the risk is assumed arose merely to prevent the use of insurance for illegitimate purposes. It should not be extended beyond the reasons for it by excessively technical construction. * * * The insurable interest which renders a policy valid at the outset need not continue. A new insurable interest existing at the time of the loss will support recovery, the policy remaining in a state of suspension during the interval in which there is no insurable interest."

insurable interest rule for property that only requires that an interest exist when a loss occurs.[13]   To the extent that some additional safeguard is deemed essential, a requirement of good faith on the part of the purchaser in acquiring property insurance would provide a flexible standard that courts could employ in appropriate cases.[14]

(3) Observations

There is some measure of disagreement in regard to when an insurable interest must exist for property and marine insurance. Professor Vance concluded that there were several well settled rules that applied to acquisition and use of property and marine insurance, including (1) that an open marine policy may properly cover a return cargo to be purchased in the future; (2) that a floating policy on a fluctuating stock of goods is enforceable as to after-acquired property; (3) that alienation of insured property does not defeat recovery if the insured reacquires it before loss; (4) that the risk attaches under a builder's risk policy in proportion as the construction progresses and the builder's interest increases; and (5) that reinsurance against risks to be insured by the primary insurer in the future is valid.[15]   Vance endorsed the validity of these rules. In his view, the various types of marine insurance contracts were not wagers and the rules facilitated insurance for valuable business interests that would otherwise go unprotected because it often is impracticable to obtain insurance at the moment an interest is acquired. He concluded that the rule requiring an insurable interest at the inception of the policy has no more import

---

13. See Miller v. New Jersey Insurance Underwriting Association, 82 N.J. 594, 414 A.2d 1322 (1980) (citing the original edition of this text).

Cf. Lititz Mutual Insurance Co. v. Lengacher, 248 F.2d 850 (7th Cir.1957).

Also see William T. Vukowich, *Insurable Interest: When It Must Exist in Property and Life Insurance,* 7 Williamette Law Journal 1–42 at pp. 12–20 (1971).

Also consider Note, *Insurance—Recovery May Be Had on a Property Insurance Policy Antedated to Include Time at Which Loss Occurred. Burch v. Commonwealth County Mutual Insurance Company, 450 S.W.2d 838 (Texas 1970),* 2 Texas Tech Law Review 140–143 (1970).

14. *Cf.* the comment of the Supreme Court in regard to the dual requirements of an insurable interest and "good faith" in Connecticut Mutual Life Insurance Company v. Schaefer, 94 U.S. (4 Otto) 457 at p. 462, 24 L.Ed. 251 (1876):

"The essential thing is that the policy shall be obtained in good faith, and not for the purpose of speculating upon the hazard of a life in which the insured has no interest."

15. Vance, LAW OF INSURANCE (Third edition, Anderson, 1951), at pp. 179–183. An interesting example of one of the situations cited by Vance is found in Osborne v. Pacific Insurance Co., 91 R.I. 469, 165 A.2d 725 (1960). Osborne purchased the insured property subject to an outstanding mortgage and took an assignment of a fire insurance policy with the consent of the insurer; the policy contained a standard mortgage clause (see § 4.2(b), below). Subsequently the mortgage was foreclosed, and the property was sold to a third party with an assignment of the mortgagee's rights under the policy (again with the insurer's consent). The mortgagee's vendee then reconveyed to Osborne and cancelled the insurance, receiving in return some twenty dollars in unearned premiums. Osborne then incurred a loss from fire damage and claimed under the policy; held that Osborne could recover since, first, the intervening lack of insurable interest did not terminate Osborne's rights under the policy and, second, the mortgagee's vendee could effectively cancel only the rights the mortgagee had under the policy as mortgagee.

Also see § 4.2 below.

than that a policy intended as a wager will not be enforceable even if the policyholder subsequently acquires an interest in the property.[16]

Professor Patterson took a sterner view than Professor Vance. Patterson observed:

> "For the purpose of setting a pious example, the courts might well deny * * * [a recovery to one who has taken out a policy while having no interest or expectation of interest and has subsequently acquired an interest], because he started out to wager; but the decision of such a bizarre case would have no effect on wagering generally, and such fanciful dangers ought not to be allowed to interfere with the protection of legitimate interests in a workaday world." [17]

Many of the judicial pronouncements in regard to property and marine insurance are in accord with the dicta in Lord Chancellor Hardwicke's opinion in *Badcock* that an interest must exist both at the time of insuring and at the time of loss. However, attempting to determine a majority view on this point is unproductive because, as Professor Patterson has observed,[18] insurers often choose not to invoke a defense which, if successful, would destroy many lucrative kinds of insurance business.

The contrast between life insurance and property or marine insurance with respect to the time when insurable interest must exist, at the inception of a contract for life insurance and at the time of loss for property coverages, may seem curious. Nevertheless, in most instances the results produced by applications of these rules are rational.

For life insurance, satisfaction of the requirement of insurable interest at inception serves the objectives of the principle of indemnity in most instances. In addition, not requiring an insurable interest at the time of loss avoids the sacrifice of other interests which are regarded as important, including that of making life insurance arrangements with investment features that produce assets which are freely transferable so as to enhance their value to the purchaser.

In general, property insurance doctrines almost uniformly adhere as closely as possible to the principle of indemnity.[19] Under the principle of indemnity, the insurance benefit is limited to offsetting a loss. One can suffer loss from property damage arising out of an event insured against even though no insurable interest existed at the time the contract was made. The only critical question should be whether an insured has an interest in the insured property at the time it is damaged, destroyed or lost. Thus, although strict adherence to the principle of indemnity clearly requires an insurable interest at the time of loss, it does not require one at the time of making the contract.

16. Vance, Law of Insurance (Third edition, Anderson 1951), at pp. 182–183.

17. Patterson, Essentials of Insurance Law (Second edition, 1957), at p. 133.

18. *Id.,* at p. 131.

19. *Cf.* § 3.1(e), above.

§ 3.3(c) The Right to Question Insurable Interest

(1) Generally

There is considerable support in judicial decisions for the rule that only the insurer can raise the question whether a claimant had the requisite insurable interest.[1] A corollary to this rule is that other persons do not have standing to question whether an insured or a beneficiary had the requisite insurable interest. The theory which appears to be the rationale underlying these decisions is that only a party to the contract has a legitimate interest in questioning the absence of an insurable interest in regard to any insurance arrangement.[2] The assertion is also made that this rule applies with equal force to both property insurance [3] and life insurance.[4] Although it appears that the majority rule is that only an insurer can raise the lack of an insurable interest, many of the judicial statements to this effect are either dicta or alternative grounds for a court's decision.

If an insurer is the only party that has standing to question whether an insurable interest exists, the public interest may be poorly served. Once an underwriting decision has been made by an insurer, it is quite likely that for business reasons the insurer will decline to raise a defense of want of an insurable interest — even if there is an opportunity for a net gain under the contract terms — unless there are also other reasons for denying the claim.

The full implementation of the public interest that produced the insurable interest doctrine may be impeded if insurers elect not to question the adequacy or existence of the required interest.[5] Indeed, an examination of cases in which the doctrine has been asserted as a defense by insurers suggests that in many (and perhaps most) instances the motivation for an insurer to raise the lack of insurable interest is to defeat a claim when an insurer either has some evidence or has strong suspicions of fraud, and that the existence of the fraud would be more difficult for the insurer to establish than a defense based on the lack of an insurable interest.[6]

§ 3.3(c)

1. See the cases cited in notes 3 and 4, below. Also see § 3.3(b)(1), above, as to when an insurable interest must exist.

2. *Ibid.*

3. See, e.g., Ezra Wheeler & Co. v. Factors & Traders' Insurance Co., 101 U.S. (11 Otto) 439, 25 L.Ed. 1055 (1879).

4. See, e.g., Ryan v. Tickle, 210 Neb. 630, 316 N.W.2d 580 (1982); Poland v. Fisher's Estate, 329 S.W.2d 768 (Mo.1959); Edgington v. Equitable Life Assurance Society, 236 Iowa 903, 20 N.W.2d 411 (1945).

Also see Secor v. Pioneer Foundry Co., 20 Mich.App. 30, 173 N.W.2d 780 (1969).

See generally, Annotation, *Life insurance: Right to raise question of lack of insurable interest* 175 A.L.R. 1276–1289 (1948); Vance, LAW OF INSURANCE (Third edition, Anderson 1951), at p. 199.

But see 1 Richards, LAW OF INSURANCE (Fifth edition, Freedman, 1952), at p. 372.

5. Insurers may choose to invoke the doctrine for reasons that are at best only tangentially related to the public policies underlying the doctrine.

6. *Cf.* Stebane Nash Co. v. Cambellsport Mutual Insurance Co., 27 Wis.2d 112, 133 N.W.2d 737, 16 A.L.R.3d 760 (1965).

Also see the discussion of *Macaura v. Northern Assurance Co.,* § 3.4(b)(2), below.

There are some decisions that are inconsistent with the foregoing propositions about who may raise the insurable interest

Observations

Judicial decisions restricting the right to question the existence of an insurable interest to the insurer can be justified on several rationales. First, allowing other persons to raise these questions almost certainly would serve to encourage litigation. Second, and perhaps an even more important consideration, allowing individuals who are not parties to the insurance contract to have standing to raise the insurable interest question would increase the prospect for intrusions on the stability of the contractual relationship.[7] Nevertheless, arguably the decisions that deny anyone other than the insurer standing to question whether the requisite insurable interest exists do not represent the most desirable approach on this matter.[8]

The objectives of the insurable interest doctrine would almost certainly be more broadly implemented if persons who suffer a loss as a result of the occurrence of an insured event were permitted to raise the doctrine as a means of recovering the insurance proceeds. In other words, a persuasive case can be made that rather than paying insurance proceeds to someone who does not have an insurable interest because an insurer chooses not to raise the question, it would be preferable to allow other persons both to have standing on this issue (even though such persons were not named as insureds or beneficiaries of the insurance contract) *and* to distribute the insurance to such persons — to the extent of their interests — if they prevail in the resolution of the insurable interest questions.[9] This approach would serve the societal interest in assuring that insurance contracts provide

question. In Virginia, it appears any interested party may raise the insurable interest question. See Smith v. Coleman, 183 Va. 601, 32 S.E.2d 704 (1945). The view that the insurable interest question may be raised by parties other than the insurer is discussed in 3 COUCH ON INSURANCE, 2d (1984), at § 24:7 on the basis of several cases decided in 1930's and 1940's.

7. See, e.g., Butterworth v. Mississippi Valley Trust Co., 362 Mo. 133, 240 S.W.2d 676 (1951), 30 A.L.R.2d 1298 (1953) (action for an accounting brought by insured's legal representatives against a trust to which the policy had been assigned by the insured's creditor, to whom the policy had been assigned by the insured, alleging lack of insurable interest and wagering); Allgood v. Wilmington Savings & Trust Co., 242 N.C. 506, 88 S.E.2d 825 (1955) (permitting an action for money had and received against the trustee of a pension trust, to get at proceeds of an insurance policy on a theory that involved challenging as a wagering arrangement the rules of the pension trust, purporting to make the proceeds payable to the trust).

Also see authorities allowing attacks upon the validity of assignments of life insurance policies, § 3.5(d), below.

Also compare the former Texas rule on insurable interest for life insurance, under which the insurer could not invoke the doctrine as a defense but one to whom proceeds would go upon disqualification of the designated beneficiary was permitted to invoke it, § 3.5(e), below.

8. Allowing persons who are not parties to an insurance arrangement to have standing to question whether an insured or a beneficiary had the required insurable interest is implicitly, if not explicitly, to embrace — even more firmly than does the rule allowing insurers to question whether the requisite insurable interest exists — the precept that the insurable interest doctrine is sufficiently important to warrant an impairment of the insured's and the insurer's freedom of contract on the basis of an overriding public interest.

Also see § 3.1(d), above.

9. *Cf.* Peeler v. Doster, 627 S.W.2d 936 (Tenn.1982).

benefits to those who sustain losses. Given the competing considerations, this approach provides a more defensible accommodation among competing principles than the rule that only an insurer is entitled to invoke the insurable interest doctrine as a defense to a claim.[10]

(2) Estoppel and the Insurable Interest Doctrine

Whether the public policies underlying the insurable interest doctrine (particularly the societal interests in avoiding circumstances that create inducements for the destruction of a life or a property for profit)[11] outweigh the considerations which underlie the doctrine of estoppel is clearly a matter of substantial disagreement that is reflected in the relevant judicial precedents. There is significant support in judicial opinions for the proposition that the insurable interest defense should not be defeated by an application of the estoppel doctrine.[12] There are also decisions which adopt the position that the doctrine of estoppel is fully applicable in this context. And many courts have taken an intermediate position which holds that although an insurer will not be precluded from asserting a complete want of insurable interest, once it is shown that an insured had some insurable interest, thereafter an insurer is estopped from asserting any defense that is based on the rationale that the insured's interest is worth less than the amount of the insurance payment that is due under the policy provisions.[13] Although judicial opinions frequently do not make a clear choice among these three approaches, the intermediate position seems to reflect the results reached in a large portion of the cases.

In regard to life insurance, the intermediate position is consistent with the proposition, discussed below, that if a person has an insurable interest in the subject of a life insurance contract, the interest will support any amount of coverage the insurer is willing to sell to the purchaser.[14] Consequently, it is not surprising that there is little inclination on the part of courts to search beyond the point of ascertaining whether some interest can be established, and then concluding that an insurer is estopped from such a challenge whenever some insurable interest is shown.

Standard forms used for property insurance commonly include clauses providing that in no event is the insurer to be liable for an amount in excess of the interest of the insured in the covered proper-

---

10. See § 3.3(e), below.

11. See § 3.1(c), above.

12. See, e.g., Colver v. Central States Fire Insurance Co., 130 Kan. 556, 287 P. 266 (1930); Price v. Trinity Universal Insurance Company, 8 Kan.App.2d 223, 654 P.2d 485 (1982); Rube v. Pacific Insurance Co., 131 So.2d 240 (La.App., 1st Cir., 1961).

Also see Rubenstein v. Mutual Life Insurance Company of New York, 584 F.Supp. 272 at p. 279 (E.D.La.1984).

See generally, Annotation, *Insurer's Waiver, of, or estoppel to assert, lack of insurable interest in property insured under fire policy,* 91 A.L.R.3d 513–519 (1979).

13. See, e.g., Liverpool & London & Globe Insurance Co., Ltd. v. Bolling, 176 Va. 182, 10 S.E.2d 518 (1940).

Also see 4 Appleman, INSURANCE LAW (Revised edition, 1969), § 2247 at p. 112.

14. See § 3.5(a), below.

ty.[15] Thus, an insurer desiring to defend on the ground that an insured either has no interest or has an interest of less value than the amount claimed, can ordinarily do so under the terms of the insurance policy. It is almost never necessary for property insurers to predicate a defense based on the lack of an insurable interest on the rationale either that the public interest overrides the contract provisions or that the public interest warrants an application of the insurable interest requirement even though there is no provision in the insurance policy.

The insurable interest doctrine is relevant to property insurance claims if a claimant asserts that the conduct of various representatives of the insurer estops the company from predicating a defense on the basis of the restrictive provisions in the insurance policy.[16] When this defense is urged by a claimant, an insurer may argue that the insured's claim — whether under the insurance policy provisions or based on rights that are at variance with the contract terms — is unenforceable because even if the estoppel applies, public policy still requires that a claimant have the requisite insurable interest in the property that was destroyed. Insurers should prevail in such situations unless there is some very compelling reason that bears specifically on the fairness of requiring an insurable interest in the particular circumstances.

(3) Incontestability Clauses

Life insurance contracts generally include, and in many states are by statute required to have,[17] a clause providing that the policy shall be "incontestable" after a specified time period.[18] The time period specified in such clauses is usually either one year or two years. The public policy underlying the statutory requirements for incontestability clauses is a desire both to preclude stale defenses by insurers and to protect the interests (including the expectations) of insurance purchasers and the beneficiaries of such insurance policies.

The need for protection against stale defenses is especially apparent when one surveys the issues involved in cases litigated before the adoption of the statutory provisions which require incontestability clauses to be included in life insurance policies. In many of these cases, the insurer's assertion of a defense based on an allegation of fraud by the insured often seems especially unconscionable when raised by the insurer after death has occurred. Support for incontestability clauses also is provided by recognition of the fact that there is reason for special concern about the stability and reliability of economic arrangements that are made by a decedent, who is no longer in a position to make any additional or substitute arrangements, for the benefit of his or her survivors. However, this justification often does not apply to life

15. For example, see the Fire Insurance Form in Appendix A.

16. Concerning estoppel generally, see § 6.5, below.

17. See, e.g., Michigan Insurance Code of 1956 § 24.14014; New York—McKin-

ney's Insurance Law § 155; Texas Life, Health and Accident Art. 3.44.

18. Also see the discussion of incontestability clauses in § 6.6(d).

insurance when the coverage was not arranged or was not paid for by the decedent.

The public policy goals underlying incontestability clauses sometimes conflict with those generally associated with the insurable interest requirement.[19] In many situations, a persuasive argument can be made that the public policies concerned with wagering and inducements to destruction of life are sufficiently important that the insurable interest requirement should be enforced by courts even when it would conflict with the goal of requiring that disputes in regard to life insurance policies must be instituted within a relatively short period of "contestability" after an insurance policy is written.

It has been suggested that judicial decisions upholding an insurer's defense of want of insurable interest can be distinguished from cases in which courts denied such a defense on the basis of whether the incontestability clause in the insurance policy at issue had been required by a statute.[20] The purported distinction rests on the observation that in the cases in which an insurer's defense was not allowed, there was a statutory requirement for the inclusion of such a clause, while insurers prevailed in instances in which there was no statutory mandate which compelled the inclusion of the incontestability clause at issue in the case. However, in the decisions sustaining the insurer's defense, the court's holding has usually been broadly framed without any qualification — that is, the court has said that an incontestability clause does not bar the defense of want of insurable interest.[21]

§ 3.3(d) Return of Premiums When an Insurable Interest Was Lacking

Insurers sometimes tender a return of premiums when a claim is denied on the basis of lack of an insurable interest. The tender is probably made in the hope either of avoiding a claim by the insured or the beneficiaries, or of enhancing the insurer's image and thereby improving the chances of presenting a successful defense to a claim.[1]

19. *Cf.* Hulme v. Springfield Life Insurance Company, Inc., 565 P.2d 666 (Okl. 1977).

20. See, e.g., Bogacki v. Great-West Life Assurance Co., 253 Mich. 253, 234 N.W. 865 (1931), denying the defense of want of insurable interest. An interesting sequel involving some of the same persons appears in Sun Life Assurance Co. v. Allen, 270 Mich. 272, 259 N.W. 281 (1935).

21. See, e.g., Bromley's Administrator v. Washington Life Insurance Co., 122 Ky. 402, 92 S.W. 17 (1906).

Cf. Wharton v. Home Security Life Insurance Co., 206 N.C. 254, 173 S.E. 338 (1934).

But cf. Hulme v. Springfield Life Insurance Co., 565 P.2d 666 (Okl.1977).

Also see 2 Appleman, INSURANCE LAW (Revised edition, 1966), § 764, n. 46.

Concerning other aspects of the enforcement of incontestability clauses, see generally § 6.5(d), below.

§ 3.3(d)

1. See, e.g., Commonwealth Life Insurance Co. v. Wood's Administratrix, 263 Ky. 361, 92 S.W.2d 351 (1936); Colver v. Central States Fire Insurance Co., 130 Kan. 556, 287 P. 266 (1930).

Also see McHugh v. Manhattan Fire & Marine Insurance Co., 363 Mich. 324, 109 N.W.2d 842 (1961).

There are relatively few judicial decisions on whether an insurer is obligated to return premiums that have been paid by an insured who lacked the required insurable interest — that is, there are not many instances in which courts have addressed the question whether an insurer that successfully avoids paying a claim on the basis of the absence of the requisite insurable interest is obligated to return the premiums that were paid for the insurance policy.[2]

Some courts have been disturbed about the inequity of allowing an insurer to collect premiums and then defend against a claim seeking the insurance benefits on the basis of the lack of insurable interest.[3] Any unjust enrichment incident to collection of the premiums and non-payment of the promised benefits could be redressed — at least in part — by ordering a refund of premiums collected, with interest, when an insurance contract is held to be unenforceable.[4] Some of the decisions in point have held that one may recover premiums paid with a bona fide belief that the insurance was valid.[5] A few decisions, however, have gone to the opposite extreme of denying a recovery of premiums even upon a showing that the purchase was made with a bona fide

---

2. Professor Vance summarized the law concerning return of premiums in two propositions:

"When the risk has once attached the whole premium is deemed to be earned, and no portion thereof is returnable, in the absence of a stipulation to the contrary, even though the risk may terminate before the expiration of the term contracted for, unless, (a) Such termination is due to the wrong of the insurer, or (b) Such return is required by statute."

"When the risk has never attached, the premium paid is always returnable unless — (a) The contract was rendered void ab initio by the fraud of the insured, or (b) The contract is illegal, and the parties in pari delicto."

Vance, LAW OF INSURANCE (Third Edition, Anderson, 1951), § 58 at p. 347.

Professor Vance's conclusions seem to leave little basis for the successful assertion of a right to the recovery of premiums when policy benefits have been denied for want of insurable interest.

If one accepts Professor Vance's statements as authoritative, a claimant could successfully argue for the return of premiums in only the very limited number of situations that are described by the "unless" clause of the first paragraph and by the second of the paragraphs quoted above. Ordinarily, the purchaser of an insurance policy for a risk that has "never attached"

is not in "pari delicto" with the insurer, and such contracts — save for transactions that are actually wagers — are rarely illegal. Consequently, a premium refund would be due to such a claimant either if parties were not in "pari delicto" or if the person seeking the return of premiums could prove that a bona fide belief was induced by some type of representation (innocent, negligent, or fraudulent) of the insurer's agent. See, e.g., Magers v. Western & So. Life Insurance Co., 344 S.W.2d 312 (Mo.App.1961).

3. *Cf.* Dalby v. India & London Life Assurance Co., 15 C.B. 365, 139 Eng.Rep. 465 (Ex.Ch.1854).

4. *But cf.* the comment of the United States Supreme Court in Connecticut Mutual Life Insurance Company v. Schaefer, 94 U.S. (4 Otto) 457 at p. 462, 24 L.Ed. 251 (1876): "A right to receive the equitable value of the policy would probably come as near to a proper adjustment as any that could be devised. But if the parties themselves do not provide for the contingency, the courts cannot do for them."

5. See, e.g., Commonwealth Life Insurance Co. v. George, 248 Ala. 649, 28 So.2d 910, 170 A.L.R. 1032 (1947); Washington v. Atlanta Life Insurance Co., 175 Tenn. 529, 136 S.W.2d 493, 129 A.L.R. 54 (1940).

The courts have justified this result even when there is no proof of fraud on the part of the insurer's sales representative.

belief in the validity of the insurance arrangement that was induced by the fraudulent act of the insurer's agent.[6]

Refunding the premiums paid provides a degree of amelioration that makes it easier to accept the idea that on balance the justifications for not enforcing the insurer's commitment outweigh the disadvantages. As a matter of litigation strategy, however, it appears that many attorneys do not include claims for a return of premiums because they do not want to provide courts with the opportunity to predicate a judgment on such a compromise.

§ 3.3(e) The Insurable Interest Doctrine as an Impairment of Freedom of Contract and Stability of Contract

Insurers ordinarily do not make contracts that are not in accord with the insurable interest doctrine, and in most situations it would not matter if the doctrine did not exist. There are some instances, however, in which insurers apparently are willing to issue insurance policies that provide coverage that would produce a conflict with the implementation of insurable interest doctrine if the insurance benefits were paid as a consequence of the occurrence of the insured event.

Legitimate insurers[1] sometimes market insurance contracts that afford coverage for insureds who do not have an insurable interest that has been clearly recognized as an appropriate basis for an insurance transaction. For example, marine insurance honor policies were marketed and insurers paid claims despite the fact that claimants sometimes lacked an insurable interest.[2] In some instances, such insurance transactions may be defended on the basis that they are designed to serve the commercial convenience of persons having legitimate interests in the property covered by the insurance, but interests that are difficult to prove under legal standards.[3] Even so, it is clear that they can be used for wagering. Furthermore, given the continued existence of the possibilities referred to in the preambles of the Statutes of George II and George III, there is a continuing realistic need for the insurable interest doctrine.[4]

Insurers may decide to underwrite some risks, even when it is clear that there is no insurable interest, because an insurer's reputation for declining coverage requests might cause it to lose lucrative business opportunities in the future. Similarly, insurers may also choose to pay

---

6. See, e.g., American Mutual Life Insurance Co. v. Mead, 39 Ind.App. 215, 79 N.E. 526 (1906) (on demurrer to complaint; the court was influenced by the notion that a representation concerning validity of the contract was a representation of law).

§ 3.3(e)

1. As distinguished from gambling syndicates seeking to use the form of insurance as a cloak. Historically, a significant part of the public concern that produced the insurable interest requirement probably resulted not from concern about legitimate insurers, but rather about others who sought to cloak strictly gambling transactions as insurance contracts.

2. See the discussion in § 3.2(f), above.

3. See § 3.2(f), above.

4. See the discussion in § 3.1 and § 3.2, above.

claims in order to maintain good public relations or to avoid expensive litigation.[5]

The likelihood that insurers will enter into contracts with parties who lack insurable interests almost certainly is increased by rules that allow the lack of an insurable interest to be raised as a defense after a claim is made as a consequence of a loss. The relative equities between an insurer and an insured in this type of situation are not self-evident. When an insurer is allowed to invoke the insurable interest doctrine to avoid making a payment of insurance benefits, a persuasive argument can be made that it may impair either the parties' freedom in regard to the contract terms or the stability of the contractual relationship. In effect, an insurer is allowed to deny its obligation to provide coverage for which it has received premium payments.[6]

If the doctrine of insurable interest justifies withholding an insurance benefit by allowing insurers to predicate a defense on an application of the insurable interest doctrine, it seems almost self evident that this can only be warranted on the ground that the public interests associated with the insurable interest doctrine are overwhelmingly important. To justify such a result, in many instances it would seem essential for a court to decide that the public interest in preventing the evils associated with opportunities for net gain from an insurance payment has an overpowering import.

Another approach to considering the question is to analyze the probable effect of precluding insurers from basing any defense on the lack of an insurable interest. If insurers were foreclosed from raising insurable interest defenses after the occurrence of a loss, it would probably mean that the doctrine would become a matter of little import. Insurers could, of course, put resources into investigating whether the requisite interest exists before issuing a policy. Whether incurring these costs for each transaction would be cost efficient seems problematic. The great majority of insurance transactions do not involve any problems in regard to insurable interest, and it seems likely that some (and perhaps all) insurers would choose not to incur extra costs in the hope of discovering the relatively few instances in which an insurable interest was not present. Furthermore, to require insurers to make such investigations would almost certainly ultimately increase the cost of insurance for all purchasers.

In general, there is no public official who has either the right or the responsibility to assure that the insurable interest doctrine is appropriately applied when insurance is purchased or when claims are

---

5. Other situations in which related questions arise may come about because of lack of foresight or skill in drafting policy provisions to protect adequately against opportunities for net gain or because of a considered decision to use standard policy provisions that lack fully effective restrictions against net gain. For example, insurers often do not include any subrogation clause in health and accident insurance policies. See § 3.10(a), below.

6. See especially the discussion in Chapter 6.

Also see Robert E. Keeton, *Insurance Law Rights at Variance With Policy Provisions*, 83 Harvard Law Review 961–985 (1970).

made. Therefore, the enforcement of the insurable interest doctrine depends almost exclusively on the initiative of insurers, pursuant to a rule that only an insurer may invoke the doctrine and thereby cause it to come to the attention of a court. Insurers generally appear reluctant to present such a defense, perhaps because widespread judicial precedents invalidating claims on this basis might impair the insurers' subsequent freedom of contract. Consequently, the principal impact of the doctrine seems to be as a defensive tool in instances when insurers wish to deny claims for other reasons, such as suspected fraud[7] — that is, the most significant impact of the insurable interest doctrine has been in instances in which the insurer either would not be able to, or anticipates that it would be significantly more difficult to, sustain another defense to the enforcement of the insurance policy.

§ 3.4   Insurable Interests for Property Insurance

§ 3.4(a)   Types of Insurable Interest in Property

(1) Generally

In general, the existence of an insurable interest in property covered by a contract of insurance is determined on the basis of whether the insured's relationship to the property is such that as a consequence of an injury to the property a loss will be sustained by the insured.[1] For the purpose of providing advice in connection with the acquisition of insurance and for the evaluation of coverage disputes after the occurrence of a loss, it is sometimes essential to consider exactly which type or types of property interest exist. The basic types of property interests[2] include:

(1) Property (ownership) rights;

(2) Contract rights;

(3) Legal liabilities;

(4) Representative relationships; and

(5) Factual expectancies.

When an insurable interest question is presented in a coverage dispute, courts sometimes scrutinize the nature of an insured's interest and then treat the claim differently as a consequence of the type of interest which the claimant possessed.

---

7. In other words, sometimes it is easier for an insurer to establish the absence of an insurable interest as a ground for denying a claim than it would be to establish the existence of the suspected fraud.

§ 3.4(a)

1. See, e.g., Gendron v. Pawtucket Mutual Insurance Company, 384 A.2d 694 at p. 696 (Me.1978), *appeal after remand* 409 A.2d 656 (Me.1979).

2. *Cf.* Harnett & Thornton, *Insurable Interest in Property: A Socio-Economic Reevaluation of a Legal Concept,* 48 Columbia Law Review 1162–1188 (1948).

Also see John M. Stockton, *Analysis of Insurable Interest Under Article Two of the Uniform Commercial Code,* 17 Vanderbilt Law Review 815–834 (1964).

Caveat. In many instances, a person or an entity that has some right or duty in regard to a particular property actually has two or more of these types of interests in that property. However, even when only one type of interest is present, it is still very likely that the requisite insurable interest will exist if an appropriate kind of insurance is purchased. Accordingly, an accurate assessment of the insurable interest question may be essential before an insurance policy is acquired.

(2) Property and Contract Rights

Property rights, which are also characterized as ownership interests, are uniformly recognized as sufficient to satisfy the insurable interest requirement.

In many circumstances, contract rights can be "transformed" into property rights — that is, a contract establishes rights or interests which, through judicial action, may mature into an ownership interest in a property.[3] For example, a buyer's executory contract for the purchase of real estate is appropriately treated as a property right because the courts will usually enforce the contract in accordance with the doctrine of equitable conversion if the purchaser seeks specific performance.[4] Similarly, a lien on a property, which often exists as a result of a contractual relationship such as a construction contract,[5] is also recognized as an enforceable property interest. Such contract rights are appropriately accorded the same status as property rights so that they are always sufficient to satisfy the insurable interest requirement.

In some circumstances there is an economic interest in the preservation of a property by virtue of a contract even though there is neither a property interest nor a right which may be transformed into a property right. Although the courts have not uniformly recognized such contractual rights as insurable interests, the requisite interest may be held to exist, especially when there has been a full disclosure to the insurer of the nature of that interest when the insurance was purchased or, if not at that time, at some point sufficiently before the loss occurs to allow the insurer to appraise the situation.

(3) Legal Liabilities as Insurable Interests

There are several types of legal liability that are appropriately treated as sufficient to satisfy both the letter and the spirit of the insurable interest rule.

3. See, e.g., Thurston National Insurance Company v. Hays, 260 Ark. 855, 544 S.W.2d 853 (Div. 2, 1977).

Also see the discussion in § 4.3, below.

4. See the discussion of the doctrine of equitable conversion and its impact on the allocation of risks between a vendor and purchaser in § 4.3(b), below.

5. See the discussion of a contractor's insurable interest in § 3.4(a)(3), below.

For purposes of liability insurance, the existence of an insurable interest should be determined on the basis of whether the insured may be liable, not on whether the insured has a recognized legal or equitable interest in some property or activity.

Legal liability may serve as an insurable interest for property insurance as well as liability insurance. Thus, liability will satisfy the insurable interest requirement when coverage is acquired for damage to property which is owned by other persons. For example, a building contractor who is responsible to the owner for completion of a building has an insurable interest in a building under construction which may be damaged in many different ways.[6] This type of responsibility constitutes an insurable interest that is usually appropriately limited to the value of the property and any liability the insured may have for consequential damages.

A person who makes a legally enforceable agreement to obtain insurance on property for the benefit of another has an insurable interest because such an individual would be liable on a breach of contract claim for the value of loss if the appropriate insurance coverages were not arranged for the property. Furthermore, the interest probably even extends to supporting an insurance contract in his or her own name.[7] For example, an insurance broker who agrees to procure insurance is liable to the full extent of a loss, up to the policy limits of the projected policy, and accordingly such a broker has an insurable interest in the property.[8] Essentially the same analysis has been applied to a mortgagee who had assigned the mortgage to the Federal National Mortgage Association. The mortgagee's commitment to the Association to keep the property insured was held to be an insurable interest in such mortgaged premises.[9]

Another type of liability is that which arises as a consequence of an injury to a third party. In the event a tort claim by a third party produces legal liability, there is no possibility that an insured will derive a net benefit so long as the insurance proceeds are ultimately used either to pay a liability claim or to indemnify an insured who has paid such a claim. Accordingly, the possibility that an insured will be

6. See, e.g., Calvert Fire Insurance Co. v. Environ Development Corp., 601 F.2d 851 at pp. 857–858 (5th Cir.1979); Baker v. Aetna Insurance Co., 274 S.C. 231, 262 S.E.2d 417 at p. 418 (1980).

Also see National Fire Insurance Co. v. Kinney, 224 Ala. 586, 141 So. 350 (1932); E.C. Long, Inc. v. Brennan's of Atlanta, Inc., 148 Ga.App. 796, 252 S.E.2d 642 at p. 645 (1979).

7. See, e.g., Liverpool & London & Globe Insurance Co. v. Crosby, 83 F.2d 647 (6th Cir.1936), *cert. denied,* 299 U.S. 587, 57 S.Ct. 111, 81 L.Ed. 433 (1936); Shaw v. Aetna Insurance Co., 49 Mo. 578, 8 Am. Rep. 150 (1872).

Also see Capital Mortgage Corp. v. Michigan Basic Property Insurance Association, 78 Mich.App. 570, 261 N.W.2d 5 (1977); Isabell v. Aetna Insurance Company, Inc., 495 S.W.2d 821 (Tenn.App. Western Dist. 1971).

8. Prince v. Royal Indemnity Co., 541 F.2d 646 at p. 650 (7th Cir.1976) (applying Illinois law), *cert. denied* 429 U.S. 1094, 97 S.Ct. 1108, 51 L.Ed.2d 540 (1977).

9. See, e.g., Capital Mortgage Corp. v. Michigan Basic Property Insurance Association, 78 Mich.App. 570, 261 N.W.2d 5 (1977).

exposed to legal liability to a third party provides the requisite insurable interest for any amount of liability insurance generally without regard to what is the relationship of the insured to the property that is involved in the tort claim.[10]

(4) Representative Relationship as an Insurable Interest

There are numerous situations in which it is useful, and often very convenient, to have insurance on property taken out by one person for the interest of another. Although in many situations a person or entity having a representative relationship also has one or more of the other types of insurable interests, there are some circumstances in which a person who seeks insurance has no other type of interest in the property. The desirability of allowing someone who in essence represents the interests of the owner to insure extends to some individuals who have no other insurable interest, and insurance arrangements involving such coverage have been quite generally approved.[11] For example, this type of interest has long been recognized as sufficient to support insurance that is acquired by bailees, trustees, receivers, administrators, and executors. The interests that exist in this type of situation are sometimes regarded as a distinct type of insurable interest in property, which can be characterized as a "representative relationship as an insurable interest." In practice, however, this term is only rarely used to describe the status of such persons.

There are a variety of circumstances in which questions involving an application of the theory of a representative insurable interest have been raised, and these issues are considered in conjunction with other matters that relate to the persons and interests protected.[12]

10. See, e.g., James v. Pennsylvania General Insurance Company, 167 Ga.App. 427, 306 S.E.2d 422 (1983).

Also see, Special Jet Services, Inc. v. Federal Insurance Co., 643 F.2d 977 at p. 982 (3d Cir.1981); Western Casualty & Surety Co. v. Herman, 318 F.2d 50, 1 A.L.R.3d 1184 (8th Cir.1963); American Mutual Fire Insurance Co. v. Passmore, 275 S.C. 618, 274 S.E.2d 416 (1981).

Cf. Pennsylvania National Mutual Casualty Insurance Co. v. State Farm Mutual Automobile Insurance Co., 605 S.W.2d 125 (Mo.1980) (holding that even though the possibility of liability is the only interest necessary to the validity of an automobile liability policy, no coverage existed because insurer was not notified of transfer of title by the insureds to their son).

But cf. Bendall v. Home Indemnity Co., 286 Ala. 146, 238 So.2d 177 (1970), in which the court concluded that the named insured's automobile liability policy was void because she was not the owner and had no insurable interest to support liability insurance coverage. It would seem the court errs in reasoning that the named insured would have to be "primarily liable for injury to persons or property that might arise out of the operation" of the described car in order to have an insurable interest to support automobile liability coverage. The insured's liability for her own negligence is operating the described car, or another car under DOC coverage, is plainly an expectancy of loss arising from legal obligations.

11. *Cf.* Patterson, ESSENTIALS OF INSURANCE LAW (Second edition, 1957), at pp. 123–130.

Also see Southeastern Fidelity Insurance Co. v. Gann, 340 So.2d 429 (Miss.1976).

Cf. Grain Processing Corporation v. Continental Insurance Company, 726 F.2d 403 (8th Cir.1984) (holding that an insurance policy which was issued for the "account of whom it may concern" indicated insured shipper's intent to cover consignee with an insurable interest).

12. See § 3.4(c), below.

(5) Factual Expectancies as Insurable Interests

Whether a factual expectancy of economic disadvantage from damage to property is sufficient to satisfy the insurable interest requirement is a question that is still not fully settled. Despite early recognition of this type of interest in English judicial precedents, such as LeCras v. Hughes and in the opinion of Lawrence, J., in Lucena v. Craufurd,[13] this theory has not gained complete acceptance as a basis for satisfying the insurable interest requirement when a loss occurs.[14]

One of the most notable American decisions supporting the view that a factual expectancy is an adequate insurable interest is an opinion by the New York Court of Appeals in 1887. In this case, National Filtering Oil Co. v. Citizens' Insurance Co.,[15] the court carefully considered and approved the factual expectancy theory of insurable interest. The National Filtering Company owned a patent and had licensed Ellis & Co. to use the patented process in the Ellis oil reduction and filtering works. The license granted Ellis exclusive rights to the use of the process as long as Ellis continued the normal operations of its works. The agreement between the companies also provided that the right to use the process was to remain exclusively with Ellis & Co. even if royalties under the licensing contract were diminished because of damage to or destruction of the Ellis plant by fire. The contract further provided that in the event the plant was damaged or destroyed, National Filtering would be entitled only to the minimum royalties that were guaranteed in the agreement. Although National Filtering had no ownership interest in the Ellis' filtering plant, National Filtering procured insurance on the Ellis' plant as protection against diminution of royalties because of fire damage to the plant.

After a fire occurred at the Ellis plant, the insurer challenged National Filtering's claim on the basis that National Filtering lacked an insurable interest in the Ellis property. In response to this argument, the court reasoned that in the event of damage to the plant by a fire the licensing contract placed the risk of loss of royalties above the

---

13. See § 3.2(d), above.

14. In Butler v. Farmers Insurance Company of Arizona, 126 Ariz. 379, 616 P.2d 54 at p. 55 (1980), the court observed, "We believe the better view is that there is an insurable interest whenever the insured would gain economic advantage from the continued existence of the property or suffer economic disadvantage upon damage to or loss of the property."

Accord. Granite State Insurance Co. v. Lowe, 362 So.2d 240 (Ala.Civ.App.1978); Scarola v. Insurance Company of North America, 31 N.Y.2d 411, 340 N.Y.2d 630, 292 N.E.2d 776 (1972); Treit v. Oregon Automobile Insurance Co., 262 Or. 549, 499 P.2d 335 (1972).

Cf. Fenter v. General Accident Fire and Life Insurance Corp., 258 Or. 545, 484 P.2d 310 (1971); Barnett v. London Assurance Corporation, 138 Wash. 673, 245 P. 3 (1926).

Also see Reznick v. Home Insurance Co., 45 Ill.App.3d 1058, 4 Ill.Dec. 525, 360 N.E.2d 461 (1st Dist., Div. 2, 1977).

See generally, Emeric Fischer, *The Rule of Insurable Interest and the Principle of Indemnity: Are They Measures of Damages in Property Insurance?,* 56 Indiana Law Review 445–471 (1981); Emeric Fischer, *Insurable Interest: A Search for Consistency,* 46 Insurance Counsel Journal 109–129 (1979); Bertram Harnett & John V. Thornton, *Insurable Interest in Property: A Socio-Economic Reevaluation of a Legal Concept,* 48 Columbia Law Review 1162–1188 at pp. 1171–1175 (1948).

15. 106 N.Y. 535, 13 N.E. 337 (1887).

guaranteed minimum on National Filtering, and that this risk "had a direct and necessary connection with the safety of the structures burned." [16] The court held that a fire destroying the plant destroyed the royalties *pro tanto,* and that it thereby became "the efficient cause of ＊ ＊ ＊ [National Filtering's] loss, and so established the needed connection between the premises insured and the royalties dependent upon their safety. ＊ ＊ ＊" [17] The court further concluded that an "interest in property connected with its safety and situation as will cause the insured to sustain a direct loss from its destruction is an insurable interest ＊ ＊ ＊." [18] Although the relationship between the companies in the *National Filtering* case probably could have supported a theory of insurable interest in the property based on a contract right, the court clearly did not adopt that approach. Instead, after citing three precedents,[19] the opinion states "that an interest, legal or equitable, in the property burned, is not necessary to support an insurance upon it; that it is enough if the assured is so situated as to be liable to loss if it be destroyed by the peril insured against ＊ ＊ ＊." [20]

In 1939, slightly more than a half century after the *National Filtering* decision, New York enacted insurance legislation with a section on insurable interest [21] which declares that no contract of insurance on property "shall be enforceable except for the benefit of some person having an insurable interest in the property insured ＊ ＊ ＊" and further states that insurable interest "shall be deemed to include *any lawful and substantial economic interest* in the safety or preservation of property from loss, destruction or pecuniary damage." [22] Although it might be argued that the phrase "lawful and substantial economic interest" implies that the expectancy must be coupled with a legal interest, it seems more reasonable to read "lawful ＊ ＊ ＊ interest" as meaning any legitimate interest in the sense that it is not, for example, an interest that exists only because of an expectation of profit from illegal activity (such as an interest in contraband liquor). This interpretation of the legislative provision is supported by and is consistent with the judicial development of the insurable interest doctrine in New York.

16. *Id.,* 106 N.Y. at p. 541, 13 N.E. at p. 339.

17. *Id.,* 106 N.Y. at p. 541, 13 N.E. at p. 339.

18. *Id.,* 106 N.Y. at p. 541, 13 N.E. at p. 339.

19. *Ibid.,* citing Rohrbach v. Germania Fire Insurance Co., 62 N.Y. 47 (1875); Springfield Fire & Marine Insurance Co. v. Allen, 43 N.Y. 389 (1871), and Herkimer v. Rice, 27 N.Y. 163 (1863).

20. *Id.,* 106 N.Y. at p. 541, 13 N.E. at p. 339.

See also Scarola v. Insurance Company of North America, 31 N.Y.2d 411, 340

N.Y.S.2d 630, 292 N.E.2d 776 (1972) (bona fide purchaser of stolen car has insurable interest on factual expectancy theory).

21. New York Acts 1939, ch. 882. Professor Patterson was the chairman of the committee that drafted this legislation. Also see Note, *New York Insurance Code of 1939,* 40 Columbia Law Review 880–897 at p. 892, n. 3 (1940).

22. New York—McKinney's Insurance Law § 148 (1966). The current New York law is essentially unchanged from the older statute. See New York—McKinney's Insurance Law § 3401 (1985).

The New York legislation was first enacted as part of a comprehensive set of statutes on insurance, and it seems likely that it was intended to codify the *National Filtering* doctrine.[23] If the drafters of the New York legislation had sought to change the rule of the *National Filtering* case, it seems reasonable to expect that the statute would have clearly manifested that intent — that is, the legislature would have been considerably more explicit in stating an intent to change the rule of *National Filtering*. Certainly there were explicit provisions in the legislation of other states which the drafters could have used if they had intended to require a legally enforceable interest, rather than employing a phrasing that seems to allow a factual expectancy to satisfy the statutory requirement.[24]

There is an instructive contrast between the approach adopted in the *National Filtering* decision and a Pennsylvania opinion decided in 1888, the year after the New York decision. In the Pennsylvania case, the New Holland Turnpike Company had obtained a policy of property insurance on a county-owned bridge, which was an essential means of access to the privately owned New Holland Turnpike.[25] A claim resulted from the accidental destruction of the bridge. As the court saw the issue, the critical question was "whether the turnpike company had an insurable interest in the bridge." Although the turnpike company had contributed one-third of the total cost of erecting the bridge, the court observed that the contribution was voluntary and that the turnpike company was not obligated to contribute to the reconstruction of the bridge in the event it was damaged or destroyed. The court upheld the insurer's denial of the turnpike company's claim on the ground that the company had no insurable interest in the bridge. The opinion asserted that "all the definitions of an 'insurable interest' import an interest in the property insured which can be enforced at law or in equity."[26]

---

23. New York—McKinney's Insurance Law § 148 (1966). The current New York law is almost unchanged from the older statute. Section 3401 provides:

"No contract or policy of insurance on property made or issued in this state, or made or issued upon any property in this state, shall be enforceable except for the benefit of some person having an insurable interest in the property insured. In this article, 'insurable interest' shall include any lawful and substantial economic interest in the safety or preservation of property from loss, destruction, or pecuniary damage."

24. See, e.g., West's Ann.California Insurance Code § 283 (1955): "Contingent or expectant interests. A mere contingent or expectant interest in anything, not founded on an actual right to the thing, nor upon any valid contract for it, is not insurable."

25. Farmers Mutual Insurance Co. v. New Holland Turnpike Co., 122 Pa. 37, 15 A. 563 (1888).

26. *Id.*, 122 Pa. at p. 46, 15 A. at p. 565.

But cf. Van Cure v. Hartford Fire Insurance Co., 435 Pa. 163, 253 A.2d 663 (1969). In *Van Cure*, the majority opinion seems to favor the "factual expectation" over the "legally enforceable interest" theory, but finds that the condemnee, though still in possession, had no insurable interest after the condemning authority's bond had been filed and approved and title had passed. The concurring opinion disapproves of the "factual expectation" theory. The dissent finds insurable interest under the "factual expectation" theory because the taking was conditional and the condemnor had absolute discretion to return the property to the condemnee.

Concerning valuation of a condemnee's interest, see § 3.9(d), below.

The *National Filtering* and *New Holland Turnpike* cases can be reconciled on the facts. There was a contract right to receive royalties in *National Filtering* and an explicit commitment in the insurance policy in regard to a loss of royalties from specified perils. There was no contract relation of any kind supporting the expectancy in *New Holland,* and the insurance policy apparently purported to insure against damage to the bridge itself, rather than against loss of turnpike tolls because of damage to the bridge. But even though such a rationale for these decisions is conceivable, the opinions are plainly not compatible: *New Holland* is consistent with the view of that an insurable interest requires some legally enforceable right;[27] *National Filtering* is in accord with the view that a factual expectancy is a sufficient insurable interest.

These two cases are also instructive in another way which may have a bearing on the relative merits of these competing views of insurable interest, and which may be helpful in terms of avoiding insurable interest disputes. In the *New Holland* situation, if part or all of the insurance was desired to reimburse the turnpike company for lost tolls, rather than for the cost of contributing to reconstruction of the bridge, an insurable interest question probably could have been avoided by making this goal explicit in the insurance contract, as was done in *National Filtering.*[28] If, on the other hand, a purchaser's objective is to provide funds for the reconstruction of the insured facility, the strict legal-interest requirement could be satisfied by creating some legal arrangement. For example, in the *New Holland* case, it probably would have been possible to arrange for the turnpike company to have had a legal interest in the continued existence of the bridge itself by its entering into an enforceable legal obligation to contribute toward reconstruction of the bridge and designating the insurance coverage as the means to fulfill that obligation.[29]

In most situations when there is a factual expectancy that produces a desire for insurance protection, it is possible for a lawyer to devise a contractual relationship that not only is compatible with the expectancy, but is one that also constitutes a legally enforceable obligation which satisfies at least one of the generally recognized tests for an adequate insurable interest. Accordingly, one of the implicit teachings of the legal precedents in this area is that the imposition of the insurable interest requirement in terms of a legal interest, rather than a factual expectancy, may serve as little more than a trap for the unwary who have entered into insurance arrangements with perfectly legitimate objectives but without adequate counseling from persons who

---

27. See § 3.2(d), above.

28. Such a step would, at a minimum, have called attention to the potential loss in which the policyholder had an interest, and the insurer might have been estopped from subsequently challenging the evaluation of that interest. See § 3.3(c)(2), above.

29. This agreement could include a condition subsequent which would terminate the obligation in the event the insurance proceeds were not paid. In addition, in order to assure that no violation of the principle of indemnity occurred, provision could be made for the insurance benefits to be held in trust for the construction.

understand the intricacies of the insurable interest rule applicable in the jurisdiction.

Insurable Interest in Stolen Vehicles

One of the areas in which the factual expectancy theory has been increasingly applied by courts when insurers have rejected claims is in regard to insurance acquired by a good faith purchaser of a stolen vehicle. Although there is not complete unanimity among the appellate courts that have considered whether a person who purchases a stolen vehicle has an insurable interest, there seems to be a definite trend among the more recent cases. These decisions reach the conclusion — that such a purchaser has an insurable interest[30] — essentially on the rationale that the insured generally stands to benefit from the continued existence of the vehicle even though such an insured could not maintain possession against a claim by the true owner of the property.[31] For example, in a case involving a stolen tractor-trailer rig which was demolished in an accident, the Tennessee Supreme Court ruled that the insured's business suffered a considerable economic detriment by the destruction of the vehicle.[32] In a similar case, which has been cited frequently, the New York Court of Appeals explicitly relied on the general development of the case law in the United States in support of a holding that the owner of a stolen automobile had a

---

30. See, e.g. Castle Cars, Inc. v. United States Fire Insurance Company, 221 Va. 773, 273 S.E.2d 793 (1981) (used car dealer paid $2,600 and received a title certificate which appeared to agree with a vehicle identification number plate which the thief apparently had transferred from a similar vehicle that had been wrecked); Phillips v. Cincinnati Insurance Co., 60 Ohio St.2d 180, 398 N.E.2d 564 (1979) (good faith purchaser for value of a stolen vehicle who possesses an Ohio certificate of title that is valid on its face has an insurable interest in the vehicle), discussed in Note, *Insurable Interest—Good Faith purchaser of a stolen motor vehicle has an insurable interest,* 9 Capital University Law Review 831–834 (1980).

Also see Duncan v. State Farm Fire and Casualty Co., 587 S.W.2d 375 (Tenn.1979) [overruling earlier Tennessee precedents including Insurance Company of North America v. Cliff Pettit Motors, Inc., 513 S.W.2d 785 (Tenn.1974)], discussed in Note, *Insurance—A Bona Fide Purchaser Has an Insurable Interest in a Stolen Vehicle,* 10 Memphis State University Law Review 390–399 (1980); Granite State Insurance Co. v. Lowe, 362 So.2d 240 (Ala.Civ. App.1978).

Also see Scarola v. Insurance Company of North America, 31 N.Y.2d 411, 340

N.Y.S.2d 630, 292 N.E.2d 776 (1972) (affirming the decisions of the lower New York courts), discussed in Note, *Insurable Interest in a Stolen Automobile,* 38 Albany Law Review 524–540 (1974).

Accord. Treit v. Oregon Automobile Insurance Co., 262 Or. 549, 499 P.2d 335 (1972); Butler v. Farmers Insurance Company of Arizona, 126 Ariz. 379, 616 P.2d 54 (App., Div. 2, 1980); Reznick v. Home Insurance Co., 45 Ill.App.3d 1058, 4 Ill.Dec. 525, 360 N.E.2d 461 (1977); Skaff v. United States Fidelity & Guaranty Co., 215 So.2d 35 (Fla.App., 1st Dist., 1968).

Contra. Ernie Miller Pontiac, Inc. v. Home Insurance Co., 534 P.2d 1 (Okl.1975); Horton v. State Farm Fire & Casualty Co., 550 S.W.2d 806 (Mo.App., Div. 4, 1977).

31. The proposition that the good faith purchaser has the right to possession against anyone in the world except the true owner has been affirmed by the courts for over fifty years. See, e.g., Barnett v. London Assurance Corp., 138 Wash. 673, 245 P. 3 (1926). Of course, this is an interest that is enforceable against all but the true owner, as well as being a factual expectancy of loss from destruction of the property.

32. Duncan v. State Farm Fire and Casualty Co., 587 S.W.2d 375 (Tenn.1979).

sufficient insurable interest to warrant recovery under a comprehensive automobile insurance policy.[33]

The judicial decisions which recognize an insurable interest in a stolen vehicle seem in large measure to rest on the good faith of the purchaser in regard to the acquisition of the stolen vehicle. The existence of such good faith on the part of the purchaser of any stolen vehicle would seem to be an increasingly difficult status to achieve as the comprehensive use of computer systems to keep track of motor vehicle title registration in general, and the identity of stolen vehicles in particular, is employed throughout the United States. Thus, as precedents for the proposition that a purchaser will have an insurable interest in stolen vehicles, these decisions seem destined to have a rather limited import in the not too distant future. On the other hand, such decisions may be interpreted as providing support for broader acceptance and application of the factual expectancy theory in other types of situations. The force of such decisions in this respect, however, is somewhat limited by the fact that a good faith purchaser has not only a factual expectancy, but also possesses an interest that is legally enforceable against claims of persons other than the true owner.

§ 3.4(b)   Relationships Between Objectives and Theories of Insurable Interest and Indemnity

(1) Generally

The objectives that underlie the insurable interest doctrine and the principle of indemnity include avoiding inducements to wagering, avoiding inducements to destruction of insured property, and avoiding net gain to an insured through receipt of insurance proceeds that exceed the loss suffered by the claimant.[1] As the case law on the insurable interest doctrine and the principle of indemnity has developed, however, there are judicial decisions which have produced consequences that are beyond those warranted by these underlying objectives, as well as some decisions that apply less rigorous requirements.

(2) Deviations Toward More Rigorous Insurable Interest Requirements Than Those Warranted by the Principle of Indemnity

Some insurance law decisions establish rules that may be viewed as deviations from the principle of indemnity toward more rigorous requirements of insurable interest. These are cases in which, despite the existence of a factual risk of loss from the perils insured against, a

---

33. Scarola v. Insurance Company of North America, 31 N.Y.2d 411, 340 N.Y.S.2d 630, 292 N.E.2d 776 (1972).

§ 3.4(b)

1. See, e.g., Southeastern Fidelity Insurance Co. v. Gann, 340 So.2d 429 at p. 434 (Miss.1976) (property insurance); Bowman v. Zenith Life Insurance Co., 67 Ill. App.3d 393, 24 Ill.Dec. 82, 384 N.E.2d 949

at p. 950 (1st Dist., Div. 3, 1978) (life insurance).

Such inducements usually depend upon factual expectancy as seen by the insured, and therefore the factual expectancy theory of insurable interest is arguably the theory that is truest to the principle of indemnity. Also consider the discussion in § 3.4(a)(5), above.

claim for insurance benefits was rejected for want of any interest that the court viewed as qualifying as an insurable interest. For example, it has been held that one who enters into an oral contract to purchase realty with improvements upon it, has no insurable interest in the property.[2] The result in such cases seems to be based on the fact that an oral contract for the sale of real property is legally unenforceable under a statute of frauds. Courts which adopt this approach apparently choose to disregard the fact that the insured may be expecting to profit from the use of the property. For example, the purchaser who plans to establish and maintain a business ordinarily would have a factual expectancy and would occupy a less advantageous economic position if a fire destroyed the improvements on the property before the conveyance was completed.[3] This type of expectation may, of course, exist even though the purchase contract was oral.

A denial of recovery in situations in which an unenforceable agreement exists might be justified on the basis that the special economic value of the property to the purchaser is so difficult to assess that a risk of overvaluation would be unavoidable, thus leaving open a prospect of gain to the insured through the collection of the insurance proceeds if the property is destroyed. It might also be argued that because such interests are so difficult to evaluate, insurance for these situations would be too expensive to administer. However, the doctrine of insurable interest seems an unduly crude instrument to prevent abuses or to address such valuation problems. Applications of insurable interest doctrine should not lead to the elimination of all such insurance contracts. Continuing to follow precedents that deny liability on property insurance purchased by a buyer of real property on the grounds of want of insurable interest seems unwarranted.[4]

---

2. E.g., Cherokee Foundries, Inc. v. Imperial Assurance Co., 188 Tenn. 349, 219 S.W.2d 203, 9 A.L.R.2d 177 (1949).

Also see 4 Appleman, INSURANCE LAW (Revised Edition, 1969), at § 2185.

3. A defense other than lack of insurable interest may exist, however, if the insurance policy purports to cover only a kind of interest different from the expectancy of the intending purchaser under the unenforceable oral agreement.

The terms of the policy are not quoted in Cherokee Foundries, Inc. v. Imperial Assurance Co., 188 Tenn. 349, 219 S.W.2d 203 (1949), 9 A.L.R.2d 177 (1951). If it was in the most common form, insuring against "direct loss by fire," it would provide no coverage except in so far as the worsening of Cherokee's economic position was due to damage to the physical property itself as distinguished from collateral consequences of such damage. Even as to the physical damage loss, it might be argued that the standard policy does not purport to cover the kind of expectancy the prospective pur-

chaser has under an enforceable oral contract of purchase. It might be argued that this construction is supported by a customary policy clause, "nor in any event for more than the interest of the insured."

Cf. Higgins v. Insurance Co. of North America, 256 Or. 151, 469 P.2d 766 (1970) (purchaser of building has insurable interest above actual cash value because of practical problem created by depreciation; under contractual provisions of "Replacement Cost" coverage, however, he cannot recover repair costs when he does not repair).

4. The development of coverages such as business interruption insurance and contingent business interruption insurance represents a significant departure from the rigorous view of insurable interest implicit in holding that a prospective purchaser of realty under an unenforceable oral contract has absolutely no insurable interest.

"Contingent Business Interruption Insurance is the coverage applicable where the Insured desires to be indemnified for

Another example of a deviation toward a more rigorous insurable interest requirement than the underlying justifications require is the denial of coverage on the basis of the lack of an adequate interest in a mortgagee under a title that was in litigation at the time a fire loss occurred, final judgment against that title having been entered before the action on the insurance policy was decided.[5] However, the result in such cases might also be defended on grounds concerned with the speculative character of the interest.

A well known English case, Macaura v. Northern Assurance Co., provides another example of a denial of insurable interest in the face of a real economic interest.[6] Macaura, who was owner of the Killymoon estate, obtained five policies of fire insurance on timber situated on the estate. Title to the timber was in the Irish Canadian Saw Mills, Ltd., of which Macaura was the sole stockholder. He was also the sole creditor of the corporation except for debts "trifling in amount." The court concluded that Macaura had no insurable interest in the timber. Plainly it would have been simple for counsel, if consulted at the time of insuring, to devise arrangements that would not have run afoul of the doctrine of insurable interest applied in the case. For example, the arrangement involving the least change would have been to name the corporation as an additional insured. An added measure of protection could have been provided if Macaura, as a creditor of the corporation, had been identified as a beneficiary under a loss payable clause in the insurance contract. Alternatively, a transaction could have been arranged between Macaura and the corporation so as to clearly give Macaura an insurable interest in the timber. This could have been done by giving Macaura a lien on the timber to secure payment of the debt, or by having Macaura agree to obtain insurance. The choice among these possibilities would depend on considerations other than the doctrine of insurable interest. Thus, the doctrine as formulated and applied by the court in Macaura illustrates how the insurable interest doctrine sometimes serves to trap the unwary person whose interest truly satisfies the principle of indemnity.

Comment

The Macaura case is not representative of the law generally on the questions of insurable interest of stockholders and creditors.[7] Macaura involved charges of fraud. Though the fraud charges were not proved, they almost certainly influenced the court to accept the insurer's theory in regard to the lack of an insurable interest even though the

the loss he sustains if business premises not owned or operated by him, but upon which his business is dependent in whole or in part, are prevented by property damage from operating." Klein, BUSINESS INTERRUPTION INSURANCE (Third edition, 1957), at p. 140. This type of insurance serves a legitimate need, and insurable interest doctrine should not be a barrier to its develop-

ment. But it might well be a barrier in jurisdictions not recognizing factual expectancy as insurable interest.

5. Colver v. Central States Fire Insurance Co., 130 Kan. 556, 287 P. 266 (1930).

6. Macaura v. Northern Assurance Co., [1925] A.C. 619.

7. See § 3.4(c), below.

precedent that resulted is a theory of insurable interest that is nothing short of pernicious. The sense that fraud was involved probably served both to induce the insurer to contest liability and to persuade the court that the insurer should prevail.[8] *Macaura* is another instance in which the doctrine of insurable interest appears to have been invoked by an insurer as the basis for a denial of recovery when fraud was suspected, but difficult to prove. The risk of undesirable distortion of the doctrine under such influences is great.

(3) Deviations Toward Less Rigorous Insurable Interest Requirements Than Those Warranted by the Principle of Indemnity

Some judicial applications of the insurable interest doctrine have produced results that are not in accord with what a strict adherence to the principle of indemnity would produce. Such a deviation is inherent in the view of the insurable interest doctrine, as articulated in the Eldon opinion, under which someone with a legally enforceable right in property has an insurable interest even though the right has no economic value.[9] For example, the holder of an almost worthless lien was allowed to recover in full on a policy in an amount not exceeding the debt secured by the lien.[10] Similarly, the owner of an equity of redemption has been said to have an insurable interest equal to the value of the insurable property, without regard either to whether the person is personally liable for the mortgage debt or to whether the right has been or will be exercised.[11] Also, a prospective purchaser who is in possession of a property that is under a contract for sale has been found to have an insurable interest which is equal to the full value of the property, even though it had become apparent that a seller could never perfect title and that under the circumstances the prospective purchaser had an option to cancel without ever having paid more than monthly installments which then were to be treated as rent.[12] And, in some circumstances, tenants at will have been allowed to recover as if they held a far more valuable interest [13] such as a fee simple title.[14]

Several justifications have been offered for decisions that plainly deviate from the principle of indemnity and thereby leave open the

---

8. See § 3.3(c), above.

9. See § 3.2(d), above.

10. Royal Insurance Co. v. Stinson, 103 U.S. (13 Otto) 25, 26 L.Ed. 473 (1880).

11. *Id.,* 103 U.S. at p. 29, 26 L.Ed. at p. 477 (dictum).

Accord. First Westchester National Bank of New Rochelle v. New England Insurance Co., 11 A.D.2d 192, 204 N.Y.S.2d 754 (2d Dept.1960) (alternative holding).

12. Hartford Fire Insurance Co. v. Cagle, 249 F.2d 241 (10th Cir.1957).

Accord. Thurston National Insurance Co. v. Hays, 260 Ark. 855, 544 S.W.2d 853 (1977) (purchaser had an insurable interest

even where the purchase agreement provided that until the closing the risk of loss was assumed by the seller).

13. Liverpool & London & Globe Insurance Co., Ltd. v. Bolling, 176 Va. 182, 10 S.E.2d 518 (1940).

Also see Aetna Insurance Co. v. Doheca A & W Family Restaurant, No. 501, Inc., 503 F.Supp. 199 at p. 201 (E.D.Mo.1980); Aetna Insurance Co. v. Emmons, 348 So.2d 1267 (La.App., 4th Cir., 1977).

14. Liverpool & London & Globe Insurance Company v. Bolling, 176 Va. at pp. 197–198, 10 S.E.2d at pp. 524–525 (dissenting opinion so interpreting the majority opinion).

risks of allowing a net gain for an insured from collecting insurance proceeds that are larger than losses. In many of the cases, an insurable interest of some value exists, and frequently it is not worth the administrative costs to enforce a requirement that the insurance proceeds should never exceed, to any appreciable extent, the value of the insurable interest at the time of loss. Also, it has sometimes been thought desirable to allow an insured to be protected not only against the risk of economic loss caused by a hazard such as fire, but also against the risk of an insured's inability to establish the precise amount of that loss when an interest that is less than the full ownership is involved.

On the basis of the rationales used in cases that deviate from the principle of indemnity, it might be thought desirable to generally estop insurers from contesting the value of economic rights of a type that are very difficult to evaluate. This might be done with a view to causing insurers to investigate carefully before underwriting. However, the notion that insurers would actually investigate more carefully or extensively under such a rule — that is, more carefully than is the practice under the existing rule which entitles an insurer to limit a recovery to the insured's loss — probably should be discounted in light of the experience under valued policy laws.[15]

§ 3.4(c) Common Factual Patterns

This subsection briefly describes several types of recurring situations in regard to which questions about insurable interest often are asked and with respect to which some generalizations have been drawn about the existence or nonexistence of insurable interest.

(1) Property Owned by a Spouse

Each spouse ordinarily has at least some insurable interest in the property of the other spouse.[1] The factual-expectancy theory of insurable interest would, of course, almost invariably support a finding that each spouse has an insurable interest in virtually all property of the other spouse. However, even under a rule that the doctrine requires a legally enforceable insurable interest, such an interest would often be supportable by homestead rights, by rights of curtesy or dower, or by community property rights.

---

15. See § 3.12 below.

Cf. Thomas v. Penn Mutual Fire Insurance Co., 244 S.C. 581, 137 S.E.2d 856 (1964).

§ 3.4(c)

1. See, e.g., National Security Fire and Casualty Co. v. Minchew, 372 So.2d 327 (Ala.1979) (common law husband had an insurable interest in a homestead the title to which was held by his wife); Ginsberg v. Goldstein, 404 So.2d 1098 at p. 1100 (Fla.

App., 3d Dist., 981) (as head of the household a husband has an insurable interest in personal property owned by his wife, a result that might be defended as to either spouse, without characterizing one as "head" of the household).

Also see North British & Mercantile Insurance Co. v. Sciandra, 256 Ala. 409, 54 So.2d 764, 27 A.L.R.2d 1047 (1951).

Cf. 4 Appleman, INSURANCE LAW (Revised edition, 1969), at § 2149.

(2) Property Owned by a Corporation

With rare exceptions, American decisions support the view that a stockholder, although having neither legal nor equitable title to the property of a corporation, nevertheless has an insurable interest in property owned by the corporation.[2]

(3) Property Owned by a Creditor

It is usually said by American courts and writers that an unsecured creditor has no insurable interest in a living debtor's property,[3] even though it is generally acknowledged both in legal doctrine and in practice that a creditor may insure a debtor's life. The recognition of a distinction between a creditor's interest in a debtor's life and an interest in the debtor's property is defensible on the ground that ordinarily an unsecured creditor depends less on the debtor's assets than upon the debtor's personal reliability and earning power, both of which are dependent upon the person's continuing to live. In general, there is less of a factual expectancy of loss to the unsecured creditor from destruction of a piece of the debtor's property in which the creditor has no security interest than from death of an obligor who owes an unsecured debt.

After a debtor's death, a strong argument can be made that an unsecured creditor should have an insurable interest in a deceased debtor's property because the creditor can then make a claim against the property in the estate of the deceased debtor.

§ 3.5   Insurable Interests for Life Insurance

§ 3.5(a)   Introduction

Some of the most intriguing insurable interest questions arise in connection with life insurance. In 1881, the United States Supreme Court commented on the type of relationship that must exist in regard to life insurance:

> " * * * in all cases there must be reasonable ground, founded upon the relations of the parties to each other, either pecuniary or of blood or affinity, to expect some benefit or advantage from the

---

2. See, e.g., American Indemnity Co. v. Southern Missionary College, 195 Tenn. 513, 260 S.W.2d 269 (1953), 39 A.L.R.2d 714 (1955).

Also see Nationwide Mutual Fire Insurance Co. v. Rhee, 160 Ga.App. 468, 287 S.E.2d 257 (1981) (individual insured was sole shareholder of corporation); Riggs v. Commercial Mutual Insurance Co., 125 N.Y. 7, 25 N.E. 1058 (1890).

See generally, Annotation, *Insurable interest of stockholder in corporation's property,* 39 A.L.R.2d 723–727 (1955); 4 Appleman, INSURANCE LAW (Revised Edition, 1969), § 2145.

Concerning English authority, see Macaura v. Northern Assurance Co., [1925] A.C. 619, discussed in § 3.4(b)(2), above.

3. See, e.g., Chapman v. England, 231 F.2d 606 at pp. 610–611 (9th Cir.1956); 4 Appleman, INSURANCE LAW (Revised edition, 1969), at § 2138; Patterson & McIntyre, *Unsecured Creditor's Insurance,* 31 Columbia Law Review 212–237 at pp. 218–219 (1931).

Concerning English authority, see the well known case Macaura v. Northern Assurance Co., [1925] A.C. 619, discussed in § 3.4(b)(2), above.

continuance of the life of the assured. Otherwise the contract is a mere wager, by which the party taking the policy is directly interested in the early death of the assured." [1]

This oft quoted statement, which expresses the generally accepted view of the insurable interest doctrine for purposes of life insurance, suggests that there are two classes or types of relationships that are appropriately recognized as insurable interests for a life insurance policy: one class predicated on the existence of a pecuniary interest, the other based on interests that exist as a consequence of a family relationship of either blood or affinity.[2] The common or unifying characteristic of these two types of relationships is that in both there is a reason for the beneficiary of the life insurance to anticipate that some economic benefits either will or may result from the continuation of the assured's life, and that such benefits will be lost in the event of the assured's death — that is, there is a factual expectancy which will be curtailed by the assured's death.

Life insurance transactions can also be divided into two other general groups on the basis of whether (1) the policy is taken out by an insured on his or her own life or (2) the policy is purchased by someone on the life of another person.

Each of the four possible classes of situations identified in the preceding paragraphs has one or more distinctive characteristics that have had a significant influence on the analysis of the insurable interest questions in regard to life insurance which are discussed in the following subsections.

§ 3.5(b) Obtaining Insurance on One's Own Life

(1) Generally

It is often said that every person has an unlimited insurable interest in his or her own life.[1] This statement connotes a meaning for the concept of insurable interest that is not easily reconcilable with the principle of indemnity [2] because indemnification usually implies the existence of a quantifiable pecuniary interest.

§ 3.5(a)

1. Warnock v. Davis, 104 U.S. (14 Otto) 775 at p. 779, 26 L.Ed. 924 at p. 926 (1881).

Cf. Connecticut Mutual Life Insurance Co. v. Schaefer, 94 U.S. (4 Otto) 457, 24 L.Ed. 251 (1876).

Also see Peeler v. Doster, 627 S.W.2d 936 at p. 940 (Tenn.1982); Mutual Savings Life Insurance Co. v. Noah, 291 Ala. 444, 282 So.2d 271 at p. 273 (1973).

Also consider the comments in Edwin Patterson, *Insurable Interest in Life,* 18 Columbia Law Review 381–421 (1918).

2. "Affinity" is generally understood to define the relationship between a wife and her husband's blood relatives or a husband and his wife's blood relatives. See, e.g., Washington State Public Employees' Board v. Cook, 88 Wash.2d 200, 559 P.2d 991 (1977).

§ 3.5(b)

1. See, e.g., Langford v. National Life & Accident Insurance Co., 116 Ark. 527, 173 S.W. 414 (1915), citing Cooley, LAW OF IN-SURANCE (First edition, 1905): "That one has an insurable interest in his own life is an elementary principle as to the existence of which the cases are unanimous."

Also see Peeler v. Doster, 627 S.W. 936 at p. 940 (Tenn.1982).

2. It would seem to be a corollary of the principle of indemnity that the test for

When the question of indemnification is considered from the vantage point of the insured person's estate, an irony emerges. It would be something of an anomaly to think of one's estate, the legal entity that succeeds upon death, as having a pecuniary interest in a decedent's life. One's estate, rather than suffering a loss through death, is thereby and only thereby enabled to come into possession of the decedent's interests.

The statement that every person has an insurable interest in his or her own life is a legal fiction,[3] a way of articulating a proposition which essentially means that even though the insurable interest doctrine generally applies to life insurance contracts, every person — that is, everyone not under some type of legal disability — may validly contract for insurance on his or her own life in any amount an insurer is willing to issue because it is impossible to assess the value of life in economic terms. Although there is some debate over precisely how this rule should be expressed, there is little disagreement about the proposition it sets forth.[4] Furthermore, an individual insuring his or her own life is entitled to designate anyone or any entity as the recipient of the insurance benefits — that is, an insured who acquires insurance on his or her own life is permitted essentially complete freedom in designating the "beneficiary."

(2) Wagering Transactions

Courts will decline to enforce a life insurance policy that was obtained as a cloak for what is in essence a genuine wager.[5] Typically, this kind of situation involves an individual who obtains a policy on his or her own life and then immediately makes an assignment or transfer of the rights to recover in the event of the death.[6] However, this discussion should not be understood as being indicative of a general rule that precludes the assignment of life insurance contracts.[7]

interest adequate to support life insurance should be pecuniary interest in the continued life of the person whose death is the event insured against.

3. This is most clearly seen, perhaps, if pecuniary interest in continued life is examined in its converse form of expectancy of suffering a pecuniary loss in the event of death.

4. See, e.g., American Casualty Co. v. Rose, 340 F.2d 469 (10th Cir.1964); Ducros v. Commissioner, 272 F.2d 49 (6th Cir. 1959); Aetna Life Insurance Co. v. Patton, 176 F.Supp. 368 (S.D.Ill.1959).

Also see Corder v. Prudential Insurance Co., 42 Misc.2d 423, 248 N.Y.S.2d 265 (1964).

See generally, 2 Appleman, INSURANCE LAW (Revised edition, 1966), § 761 at pp. 109–113, n. 12.

5. E.g., Bromley's Administrator v. Washington Life Insurance Co., 122 Ky. 402, 92 S.W. 17 (1906).

6. See § 3.5(d), below.

Similar issues may exist when insurance is taken out and paid for by the beneficiary.

7. See, e.g., Ramey v. Carolina Life Insurance Co., 244 S.C. 16, 135 S.E.2d 362 (1964); Lopez v. Life Insurance Company of America, 406 So.2d 1155 at pp. 1158–1159 (Fla.App., 4th Dist., 1981).

But cf. Dixon v. Western Union Assurance Co., 251 S.C. 511, 164 S.E.2d 214 (1968). The court held that a life insurance policy issued to parents on the life of a son, who was in the military service and was serving in Vietnam, was not void for reasons of public policy on the theory that the insurance would put the son in danger of his life at the hands of his parents. The result seems especially justified on the facts, not only because the son was obviously far removed from the parents, but also because the policy was purchased by the parents as a result of a solicitation

§ 3.5(c)　Relationships Supporting an Insurable Interest in Another's Life

(1) Introduction

To obtain valid insurance on the life of another individual,[1] a purchaser must have an insurable interest in the other's life.[2] One might conclude that the most rigorous application of this doctrine is justified in regard to life insurance because life is more precious than property. On the other hand, arguably there are significant influences other than the doctrine of insurable interest that deter the destruction of a life so that a somewhat less rigorous administration of the insurable interest requirement is needed for life insurance than for property insurance. In any event, the insurable interest requirement for purposes of life insurance is often considered rather differently depending on whether a family relationship is involved.

(2) Family Relationships

The treatment of the insurable interest question in relation to close family relationships of either consanguinity or affinity is predicated on the presumption that "love and affection" normally exist between family members, and that this relationship provides an adequate safeguard against destruction of life. The analysis of the insurable interest requirement in regard to family members almost invariably rests on this presumption about the characteristics of the relationship between family members, rather than on an appraisal of facts which show the particular nature of the relationship which actually exists in each case.

In general, an individual has an insurable interest in all the members of his or her nuclear family, including the life of a spouse[3] and of a minor child.[4] And a minor child has an insurable interest in

they received as parents of a serviceman, from the insurer.

Consent of the person whose life was insured has been held not to be an adequate answer to the defense of lack of an insurable interest. See, e.g., National Life & Accident Insurance Co. v. Middlebrooks, 27 Ala.App. 247, 170 So. 84 (1936); National Life & Accident Insurance Co. v. Ball, 157 Miss. 163, 127 So. 268 (1930).

§ 3.5(c)

1. It is useful to have a phrase other than "the insured" to designate the one whose life is insured (*i.e.*, whose death is the event insured against), when someone else procures the insurance contract or holds incidents of ownership. "*Cestui que vie*" ("CQV") is a phrase sometimes used to designate the person whose life is insured, whether or not that person procures the insurance.

2. See, e.g., Peeler v. Doster, 627 S.W.2d 936 at p. 940 (Tenn.1982).

See generally, Gary I. Salzman, *Insurable Interest in Life Insurance,* 1965 Insurance Law Journal 517–552.

3. E.g., Bowers v. Missouri Mutual Association, 333 Mo. 492, 62 S.W.2d 1058 (1933).

It has also been held that former spouses continue to have an insurable interest in each other's lives after a marriage has been dissolved. See, e.g., Pitts v. Ashcraft, 586 S.W.2d 685 at p. 695 (Tex.Civ.App., Corpus Christi, 1979); Mullenax v. National Reserve Life Insurance Co., 29 Colo.App. 418, 485 P.2d 137 (Div. I, 1971).

Also see the discussion in § 3.3(b)(1), above, on the time when an insurable interest must exist for a life insurance contract.

4. See, e.g., Volunteer State Life Insurance Co. v. Pioneer Bank, 46 Tenn.App. 244, 327 S.W.2d 59 (1959).

the life of a parent.[5] However, the judicial precedents are in conflict as to whether in the absence of a specific pecuniary interest an adult child and a parent have an insurable interest in each other's lives,[6] or whether siblings have an insurable interest in each other's lives.[7]

When a beneficiary of a life insurance policy is a relative but not a member of the insured's nuclear family, a demonstration of some pecuniary interest has been held sufficient to satisfy the insurable interest requirement for a life insurance policy.[8] The family relationships in such cases have included that of uncle, aunt, nephew, niece, step-brother, step-sister, step-child, step-mother, or step-father.[9] For

Also see National Life & Accident Insurance Co. v. Alexander, 226 Ala. 325, 147 So. 173 (1933) (dictum).

Cf. Life & Casualty Insurance Co. v. Womack, 60 Ga.App. 284, 3 S.E.2d 791 (1939).

5. Judicial statements concerning the insurable interest of a minor child in a parent's life are generally dicta [e.g., Rosenberg v. Robbins, 289 Mass. 402, 194 N.E. 291 (1935)], or are found in cases concerned with the interest of the child as beneficiary under rather than as procurer of insurance on the parent's life [e.g., Drane v. Jefferson Standard Life Insurance Co., 139 Tex. 101, 161 S.W.2d 1057 (1942) (policy on life of godmother who was *in loco parentis*)].

This scarcity of direct authority is most likely the result of the relative rarity of the instances in which a minor child procures insurance on the life of the mother or father. Moreover, a minor's insurable interest is hardly open to doubt. In addition to the love-and-affection interest which normally exists, the minor child is owed a legal obligation of support by the parent and ordinarily has a factual expectancy of pecuniary loss, which is even greater than the minimum support required by law, should the parent die.

6. See, e.g., Life Insurance Clearing Co. v. O'Neill, 106 Fed. 800 (3d Cir.1901) (applying Pennsylvania law) (adult child has no insurable interest in father's life merely because of the relationship); Mitchell v. Union Life Insurance Co., 45 Me. 104 (1856) (dictum that parent has no insurable interest in life of adult child merely because of the relationship).

Also see Bowman v. Zenith Life Insurance Company, 67 Ill.App.3d 393, 24 Ill. Dec. 82, 384 N.E.2d 949 (1st Dist., Div. 3, 1978) (father had an insurable interest in the life of a son, who had primarily lived with his mother, especially in regard to a $3,000 policy that was not viewed by the court as grossly disproportionate to the father's interest).

Cf. Golden State Mutual Life Insurance Co. v. White, 374 S.W.2d 901 (Tex.Civ.App., Dallas, 1964), writ refused, no reversible error) (absent fraud, no public policy against adult daughter procuring life insurance policy on her mother's life, naming daughter as beneficiary, on which daughter paid all premiums).

See generally, 1 Richards, LAW OF INSURANCE (Fifth edition, Freedman, 1952), at pp. 389–391.

7. Siblings have been held to have an insurable interest in life of a brother or sister. See, e.g., Mutual Savings Life Insurance Co. v. Noah, 291 Ala. 444, 282 So. 2d 271 at p. 274 (1973); Century Life Insurance Co. v. Custer, 178 Ark. 304, 10 S.W.2d 882, 61 A.L.R. 914 (1928); Rettenmaier v. Rettenmaier, 255 Iowa 952, 124 N.W.2d 453 (1963) (alternative holding).

Also see Penn v. Lighthouse Life Insurance Co., Inc., 392 So.2d 181 (La.App., 2d Cir., 1980).

Cf. Magers v. Western & So. Life Insurance Co., 344 S.W.2d 312 (Mo.App.1961).

Contra. See, e.g., Gulf Life Insurance Co. v. Davis, 52 Ga.App. 464, 183 S.E. 640 (1936); Abernathy v. Springfield Mutual Ass'n, 284 S.W. 198 (Mo.App., St. Louis, 1926).

See generally, Annotation, *Insurable Interest of Brother or Sister in Life of Sibling,* 60 A.L.R.3d 98–122 (1974).

8. See the cases cited in the following notes.

9. See, e.g., National Life & Accident Insurance Co. v. Davis, 179 Ark. 621, 17 S.W.2d 312 (1929).

But cf. Commonwealth Life Insurance Co. v. George, 248 Ala. 649, 28 So.2d 910, 170 A.L.R. 1032 (1947) (aunt has no insurable interest without showing of pecuniary interest); National Life & Accident Insurance Co. v. Alexander, 226 Ala. 325, 147 So. 173 (1933) (cousin has no insurable interest without showing of pecuniary interest); National Life & Accident Insur-

example, a woman who had supported her niece from infancy was held to have an insurable interest in the niece's life on the basis of an expectation of pecuniary benefit incident to what the court viewed as a moral obligation of the niece to the aunt.[10]

The Principle of Indemnity. A rigorous adherence to the principle of indemnity in relation to life insurance procured for the benefit of a family member would still require a showing of a factual expectancy of economic gain from the continued life of the insured person and, conversely, of economic loss from the death. In some instances, the results in these cases only conform with the principle of indemnity if one accepts as conclusive an assumption that pecuniary interests are a normal incident to this type of relationship — in short, only by adopting a legal fiction.[11]

(3) Non-Family Relationships

When an insurable interest issue arises in a situation that does not involve family members, courts almost always focus considerable attention upon the nature of the relationship between the individuals. The presence of the requisite insurable interest in regard to such individuals usually depends on whether there is an actual economic or pecuniary connection or association.[12] An adequate insurable interest may be based on many different types of relationships including that of a creditor in the life of a debtor,[13] of one partner in the life of another,[14] of a business entity in the life of a key employee,[15] and even of business associates who accommodated each other through exchanges of infor-

ance Co. v. Ball, 157 Miss. 163, 127 So. 268 (1930) (son-in-law has no insurable interest without showing of pecuniary interest).

See generally, Gary I. Salzman, *Insurable Interest in Life Insurance,* 1965 Insurance Law Journal 517–552 at p. 532.

10. Cronin v. Vermont Life Insurance Co., 20 R.I. 570, 40 A. 497 (1898).

Cf. Young v. Hipple, 273 Pa. 439, 117 A. 185, 25 A.L.R. 1541 (1922) (in which the court assumed that a step-daughter had no insurable interest in the step-father's life merely by reason of that relationship, but the court held that an insurable interest based on moral obligation was proved).

11. For an excellent discussion of legal fictions see Lon L. Fuller, LEGAL FICTIONS (1967, Stanford University Press, Stanford, California).

12. See, e.g., Hulme v. Springfield Life Insurance Co., Inc., 565 P.2d 666 at p. 670 (Okl.1977); Poland v. Fisher's Estate, 329 S.W.2d 768 (Mo.1959).

13. See, e.g., New York Life Insurance Co. v. Baum, 700 F.2d 928 (5th Cir.1983), *on rehearing* 707 F.2d 870 (5th Cir.1983); Metcalf v. Montgomery, 229 Ala. 156, 155 So. 582 (1934).

Also see 2 Appleman, INSURANCE LAW (Revised edition, 1966), at § 851; 1 Richards, LAW OF INSURANCE (Fifth edition, Freedman, 1952), at pp. 393–398.

14. See, e.g., Gerstel v. Arens, 143 Fla. 20, 196 So. 616 (1940); Rahders, Merritt & Hagler v. People's Bank, 113 Minn. 496, 130 N.W. 16 (1911).

But cf. Lakin v. Postal Life & Casualty Insurance Co., 316 S.W.2d 542 (Mo.1958), 70 A.L.R.2d 564 (1960) (holding that the legal relation of partnership does not in itself create an insurable interest of one partner in the life of the other, and that evidence in the case at hand was insufficient as proof of such interest).

Also see 2 Appleman, INSURANCE LAW (Revised edition, 1966) at § 871; 1 Richards, LAW OF INSURANCE (Fifth edition, Freedman 1952), at pp. 398–399.

15. See, e.g., Murray v. G.F. Higgins Co., 300 Pa. 341, 150 A. 629, 75 A.L.R. 1360 (1930) (corporation officer); Secor v. Pioneer Foundry Co., 20 Mich.App. 30, 173 N.W.2d 780 (Div. 2, 1970) (corporate employee).

Also see 2 Appleman, INSURANCE LAW (Revised edition, 1966), at § 872; Annota-

mation, equipment, and employees.[16] When a beneficiary is not a relative and does not appear to suffer any quantifiable pecuniary loss as a result of an individual's death, the claims of beneficiaries have on occasion presented some rather difficult dilemmas for courts.[17] When there is no reasonable expectation of pecuniary benefits from the continued life of an insured or when the amount of the life insurance is grossly disproportionate to the beneficiary's pecuniary relationship to an insured, the requisite insurable interest has been held not to exist.[18]

Comment

The arguments for applying an expectation theory to life insurance in business situations are considerably less compelling than the substantial justification which exists for the factual-expectancy theory of insurable interest as applied to property insurance.[19] Courts should be at least somewhat reluctant to recognize highly speculative interests incident to business relationships, and especially in regard to former business associations, as sufficient insurable interests for life insurance.

(4) Consent of the Person Whose Life Is Insured

The insurable interest requirement usually provides an adequate safeguard for the person whose life is insured. Nevertheless, there remains an appropriate concern about the creation of an incentive to murder that is inherent in allowing someone to insure another person's life, especially when life insurance can be arranged without securing the insured's consent.[20] For example, the determination of an insurable interest for purposes of life insurance is often based on defined relationships of consanguinity or affinity, which in some situations involve little or no factual expectancy of pecuniary disadvantage from

---

tion, *Insurance on life of officer for benefit of corporation,* 143 A.L.R. 293–297 (1943).

16. Hulme v. Springfield Life Assurance Co., Inc., 565 P.2d 666 (Okl.1977).

Also see Washington State Public Employee's Board v. Cook, 88 Wash.2d 200, 559 P.2d 991 (1977); Moore v. Hansen, 250 Ark. 367, 465 S.W.2d 684 (1971).

Cf. Empire Life Insurance Company of America v. Moody, 584 S.W.2d 855 (Tex. 1979).

17. See, e.g., Peeler v. Doster, 627 S.W.2d 936 (Tenn.1982); United Benefit Life Insurance Company of Omaha v. Boyd, 453 S.W.2d 332 (Tex.Civ.App., 1970) (eighteen year old minor purchased a $5,000 whole life insurance policy upon his own life, naming an older friend with whom he lived for intermittent periods during a preceding three year time span, as the beneficiary).

Also see, Note, *Insurable Interest Requirements Upon Life Insurance Purchased by a Minor,* 23 Baylor Law Review 312–318 (1971), discussing the *Boyd* decision, above.

18. See, e.g. Rubenstein v. Mutual Life Insurance Company of New York, 584 F.Supp. 272 at pp. 278–279 (E.D.La.1984).

Also see Travia v. Metropolitan Life Insurance Company, 186 La. 934, 173 So. 721 (1937).

19. See § 3.4(a)(5), above.

20. See, e.g., Lopez v. Life Insurance Company of America, 406 So.2d 1155 (Fla. App., 4th Dist., 1981), affirmed 443 So.2d 947, (Fla.1981).

This would be true even if a strict factual expectancy theory of insurable interest were enforced in life insurance law.

Also see discussion of potential evils of allowing net gains from insurance payments in § 3.1(c), above.

death of the person whose life is insured. Thus, the risk of inducement to murder clearly exists.

Relatively few cases have dealt with the question whether consent of the person whose life is insured is essential to the validity of an insurance contract obtained by another individual. Especially in situations in which the person who is purchasing the life insurance does not appear to have a significant relationship with the person to be insured, it is plainly evident that it should be necessary to at least have the person's formal consent to the acquisition of coverage [21] *and* probably also his or her active participation in the application for the insurance coverage. Even when the person obtaining insurance is someone with a substantial and generally recognized insurable interest, it still seems desirable to require the consent of the person whose life is being insured.

A modest body of judicial precedent requires the consent of the person whose life is insured.[22] Furthermore, in many states, statutes impose a similar requirement.[23]

§ 3.5(d) Beneficiaries and Assignees Without an Insurable Interest

There is general recognition of the rule that one who obtains insurance on his or her own life is free to designate anyone as a beneficiary.[1] In contrast, there is considerable conflict regarding the

---

21. See, e.g., Ramey v. Carolina Life Insurance Co., 244 S.C. 16, 135 S.E.2d 362 (1964); Lopez v. Life Insurance Company of America, 406 So.2d 1155 at pp. 1158–1159 (Fla.App., 4th Dist., 1981).

But cf. Dixon v. Western Union Assurance Co., 251 S.C. 511, 164 S.E.2d 214 (1968). The court held that a life insurance policy issued to parents on the life of a son, who was in the military service and was serving in Vietnam, was not void for reasons of public policy on the theory that the insurance would put the son in danger of his life at the hands of his parents. The result seems especially justified on the facts, not only because the son was obviously far removed from the parents, but also because the policy was purchased by the parents as a result of a solicitation they received as parents of a serviceman, from the insurer.

Consent of the person whose life was insured has been held not to be an adequate answer to the defense of lack of an insurable interest. See, e.g., National Life & Accident Insurance Co. v. Middlebrooks, 27 Ala.App. 247, 170 So. 84 (1936); National Life & Accident Insurance Co. v. Ball, 157 Miss. 163, 127 So. 268 (1930).

22. See, e.g., Watson v. Massachusetts Mutual Life Insurance Co., 140 F.2d 673 (D.C.Cir.1943), *cert. denied* 322 U.S. 746, 64 S.Ct. 1156, 88 L.Ed. 1578 (1944); Metropolitan Life Insurance Co. v. Monohan, 102 Ky. 13, 42 S.W. 924 (1897); Ramey v. Carolina Life Insurance Co., 244 S.C. 16, 135 S.E.2d 362, 9 A.L.R.3d 1164 (1964).

Cf. Life & Casualty Insurance Co. v. Womack, 60 Ga.App. 284, 3 S.E.2d 791 (1939).

23. See, e.g., Hawaii Rev.Stats. § 431–416 (1968); Maryland Code 1957, Art. 48A, § 371; Massachusetts Gen.Laws Ann. c. 175, § 123 (Supp.1970); New York—McKinney's Insurance Law § 146(3) (1966); Virginia Code 1953, § 38.1–330.

Such statutes generally except from the consent requirement group insurance contracts and insurance procured on the life of a minor who is a dependent of the procurer or in whom the procurer otherwise has an insurable interest; many except insurance procured by one spouse on the life of the other; and Maryland and Massachusetts, for example, except family policies procured by one or more adult members of the family, including a step-parent.

§ 3.5(d)

1. See § 3.5(b), above.

question whether one may validly assign an insurance policy on one's own life to another who has no insurable interest.[2] A clear split of judicial authority has developed over the treatment of situations in which an individual purchased a valid policy on his or her own life, and thereafter the individual "assigned" the policy to some person having no insurable interest in the policyholder's (assignor's) life.

A substantial minority of the courts hold that an assignment of a life insurance policy to one having no insurable interest is void as a matter of law, and that this rule applies without regard to whether an intention to assign existed at the time the insurance policy was issued.[3] Several reasons are urged in support of this rule, including: *first,* that there is no material distinction between assignment of a policy to one without insurable interest and procurement of a policy by such a person; *second,* that such an assignment constitutes a wagering contract; and *third,* that the effect of such an assignment is to afford a temptation to murder.[4]

The majority rule is that an assignment of a life insurance policy to a person who does not have an insurable interest is valid.[5] This result is supported by the fact that usually the objectives of the person who made the assignment could easily have been attained by other actions. For example, in many instances the desired result could have been produced by changing the beneficiary of the insurance policy to the estate of the person whose life is insured, and then including a provision in a will for the insurance proceeds to go to the intended assignee. Even more simply, in many circumstances the insured could have changed the designation of the beneficiary to name the intended assignee.[6] Thus, a rule invalidating assignments to persons who do not have an insurable interest arguably serves to do little more than trap the unwary who do not receive adequate guidance about alternative ways to accomplish the desired result.

The minority rule, which invalidates assignments, is difficult to reconcile with the virtually undisputed proposition that one may valid-

2. See § 3.5(b)(1), above.

Cases involving use of the assignment as part of a cloak for a transaction in which the policy was originally obtained for wagering are to be distinguished; in such a case the entire policy is unenforceable. See § 3.5(b)(2), above.

3. See, e.g., Griffin v. McCoach, 123 F.2d 550 (5th Cir.1941), *cert. denied* 316 U.S. 683, 62 S.Ct. 1270, 86 L.Ed. 1755 (1942) (applying Texas law); Milliken v. Haner, 184 Ky. 694, 212 S.W. 605 (1919).

4. See, e.g., Milliken v. Haner, 184 Ky. 694 at pp. 698–699, 212 S.W. 605 at pp. 606–607.

Also see Annotation, *Validity of assignment of life insurance policy to one who has no insurable interest in insured,* 30 A.L.R.2d 1310–1385 at pp. 1315–1316 (1953).

5. The results in Grigsby v. Russell, 222 U.S. 149, 32 S.Ct. 58, 56 L.Ed. 133 (1911) and in Langford v. National Life & Accident Insurance Company, 116 Ark. 527, 173 S.W. 414 (1915), are consistent with the view that only the insurer can raise the want of insurable interest. The reason given in *Grigsby* is a more satisfactory proposition, because the idea that only the insurer can raise the defense is inconsistent with the notion that it is a defense based on public interest.

Also see the discussion in § 3.3(c), above.

6. Unless the right to change the beneficiary has been limited or lost. See the discussion in § 4.11(e), below.

ly obtain insurance on one's own life and designate any beneficiary one wishes. The arguments against the validity of an assignment to one without insurable interest seem equally applicable to the question of the validity of a life insurance contract if it appears that a beneficiary who paid the premium was the instigator of the insurance contract. That case is analogous to one in which the person whose life is insured obtains the policy as a cloak for what is in essence a genuine wager.[7]

If the person whose life is insured is the instigator of the insurance contract *and* if the beneficiary is designated before any arrangement for the beneficiary's payment of subsequent premiums, the situation can be distinguished from one involving an assignment of the insurance policy on the ground that the original designation of the beneficiary is more likely to have been a choice free of the vices associated with an assignment of life insurance to someone that does not have an insurable interest.[8] In addition, the original arrangement for such an insurance policy is, at least arguably, less likely to be the product of undue pressure on the insured.

Some aspects of the arguments concerning the possible encouragement of wagering or the inducement to murder (which probably account for the minority rule that an assignment to one without insurable interest is invalid) are applicable even to policies obtained and paid for by the person whose life is insured. However, these arguments should not be sufficient, in the face of countervailing considerations, to cause the courts to hold such contracts invalid. Furthermore, in regard to assignments, there is an added countervailing consideration derived from the desirability of allowing an insured to use a life insurance policy, especially coverages that include an investment component, as an asset which can be employed to obtain cash or in other ways. Thus, on balance, it seems doubtful that the minority rule on assignments should be maintained in view of the well established rule that allows an individual to obtain a policy on his or her own life and to designate anyone as the beneficiary.

If an assignment of an insurance policy can be invalidated, it leads to the question whether an insurance company totally escapes liability or must still pay the policy proceeds when death occurs. In general, a persuasive case can be made for limiting the payment to an assignee to the amount of the insurable interest, if any, with any excess above the loss of the assignee to be paid to the previously designated beneficiary or to the estate of the deceased.[9] Applying this approach, if an

---

7. See § 3.5(b)(1), above.

8. E.g., Langford v. National Life & Accident Insurance Co., 116 Ark. 527, 173 S.W. 414 (1915).

9. If the arguments supporting the majority rule, presented in Grigsby v. Russell, 222 U.S. 149, 32 S.Ct. 58, 56 L.Ed. 133 (1911), do not make an adequate case against application of the indemnity principle, that principle could be adhered to with provision for any excess above the loss of the assignee to be paid to the designated beneficiary or to the estate of the deceased.

Also see the discussion in § 3.1(c), above.

assignment is invalidated, the full insurance benefits would be payable to such beneficiaries.

If an assignment is said to be "void," this implies that the beneficiary would be permitted to question the "validity" of an assignment on the ground that the assignee lacked an insurable interest.[10] However, allowing a beneficiary to raise the issue would be inconsistent with the general proposition that only an insurer can raise the lack of insurable interest.

§ 3.5(e)   The Distinctive Texas Rule

Before the enactment of a statute in 1953, Texas decisions had allowed a rival claimant to defeat a designated beneficiary's right to life insurance proceeds by showing that the beneficiary had no insurable interest in the life of the insured at the time of death. The insurer, on the other hand, could not escape liability altogether by raising want of insurable interest because the estate of the deceased would be entitled to the proceeds in the absence of another qualified claimant.[1] This approach adhered more rigorously to the principle of indemnity than did the rules of other states, because it limited a beneficiary's recovery to the beneficiary's insurable interest. Also, it was more consistent with the public policy basis of the insurable interest doctrine because it allowed individuals to raise the doctrine of insurable interest, rather than restricting the right to question this matter to the insurer.[2] The desirability of allowing rights in insurance policies to be assigned as property interests not only worked against the adoption of the Texas rule elsewhere, it ultimately influenced legislative action in Texas.

In 1953 Texas adopted legislation that specifically declared that any person may obtain insurance on his or her own life, and may validly designate any person as a beneficiary.[3] The statute, in its operative effect, also authorized the assignment of a life insurance policy to a person without an insurable interest. The statute accomplished this result by the fictional technique of declaring that any beneficiary or assignee who is properly designated "shall at all times

10. The results in Grigsby v. Russell, 222 U.S. 149, 32 S.Ct. 58, 56 L.Ed. 133 (1911) and in Langford v. National Life & Accident Insurance Company, 116 Ark. 527, 173 S.W. 414 (1915), are consistent with the view that only the insurer can raise the want of insurable interest, but the reason given in *Grigsby* is a more satisfactory one than the proposition in the text would be, since the idea that only the insurer can raise the defense is inconsistent with the notion that it is a defense based on public interest.

Also see the discussion in § 3.3(c), above.

§ 3.5(e)

1. See Swift, *Insurable Interest Changes*, 16 Texas Bar Journal 583–584 and 606–608 (1953), reprinted in 1953 Insurance Law Journal 666–670. See also Note, 32 Texas Law Review 346–348 (1954).

2. On this matter, see § 3.3(c), above.

3. V.A.T.S. Texas Insurance Code, art. 3.49–1, § 1 (1963).

Also see Note, *Insurable Interest Requirements Upon Life Insurance Purchased by a Minor*, 23 Baylor Law Review 312–318 (1971), discussing the impact of the Texas legislative changes on the insurable interest requirement when a minor purchases insurance naming someone who is not a relative as a beneficiary.

thereafter have an insurable interest" subject to certain specific statutory exceptions that are primarily concerned with legal entities engaged in the business of burying the dead.[4]

§ 3.5(f)   The Risk of Inducement to Murder

Sometimes decisions holding that a designation of a beneficiary without an insurable interest or an assignment to a person without an insurable interest is valid when made by the person whose life is insured[1] have given little, if any, recognition to avoidance of inducement to murder as an objective of the insurable interest doctrine. In such cases, it frequently has been observed that the central objective of the insurable interest rule is the avoidance of wagering, and participation in the transaction by the person whose life is insured adequately protects against wagering.[2] However, avoidance of an inducement to murder increasingly has been recognized as an important objective in some judicial decisions.[3]

One of the most striking illustrations of the societal concern in regard to the risks that insurance may provide an inducement to murder has been the recognition of a tort cause of action against insurers that have issued life insurance policies without due care for the creation of a situation that might lead to homicide.[4] For example, the father of a minor child was held to have an action against insurers who had issued life insurance policies to an aunt who did not have any pecuniary interest, on the theory that the violation of the insurable interest doctrine contributed to the minor's death at the hands of the aunt.[5]

When an insurable interest requirement is set forth in a state's insurance legislation, one of the apparent objectives of such a statutory provision is to avoid the issuance of insurance that may provide an inducement to murder. If a death by homicide occurs in circumstances such as those involving the aunt and the niece, arguably this is the type

---

4. V.A.T.S. Texas Insurance Code, art. 3.49–1, §§ 2–3.

In McCain v. Yost, 155 Tex. 174, 284 S.W.2d 898 (1955), it was held that the statute applied when the insured died after its enactment, although the beneficiary (the insured's ex-wife at the time of his death), had been designated before the effective date of the statute, and that the beneficiary "had an insurable interest and was entitled under the law to have the proceeds of the policy paid to her." 155 Tex. at p. 178, 284 S.W.2d at p. 900. The contesting claimant was the insured's estate.

§ 3.5(f)

1. See § 3.5(a) through § 3.5(c), above.

2. See, e.g., Grigsby v. Russell, 222 U.S. 149, 32 Sup.Ct. 58, 56 L.Ed. 133 (1911).

3. See, e.g., Ruse v. The Mutual Benefit Life Insurance Company, 23 N.Y. 516 at pp. 525–527 (1861).

Cf. Rubenstein v. Mutual Life Insurance Company of New York, 584 F.Supp. 272 (E.D.Louisiana, 1984).

Also see discussion in § 4.11(g)(3) on the disposition of insurance benefits when a murder is involved.

4. See, e.g., Ramey v. Carolina Life Insurance Co., 244 S.C. 16, 135 S.E.2d 362 (1964), 9 A.L.R.3d 1164 (1966); Lopez v. Life Insurance Company of America, 406 So.2d 1155 (Florida Court of Appeal, Fourth District, 1981).

5. Liberty National Life Insurance Co. v. Weldon, 267 Ala. 171, 100 So.2d 696, 61 A.L.R.2d 1346 (1958).

of harm that the statute is designed to prevent.[6] In such circumstances, there is a persuasive rationale for the theory that the insurer's conduct — allowing the acquisition of such an insurance policy — constitutes negligence per se.[7]

The doctrine of negligence per se relates to violations of statutes, and in some states to violations of ordinances or administrative regulations as well. Thus, in a state in which insurable interest requirements are of decisional rather than statutory origin, negligence per se does not apply. But the analogy is close, and it seems reasonable to adopt a similar rule for a doctrine of decisional origin — that is, avoidance of inducement to murder should be one of the important objectives of the insurable interest doctrine generally, and therefore application of the negligence per se doctrine in regard to a tort cause of action against the insurer would be appropriate in all cases in which it is shown that the insurer's issuance of a policy in violation of insurable interest doctrine was related to the murder of the person whose life was insured.

A problem that involves issues that are similar to questions considered in regard to the insurable interest doctrine may arise in relation to statutory provisions requiring the person whose life is insured to consent to the insurance arrangement. For example, it has been held that a cause of action against the insurer for negligence was stated by a complaint alleging that the issuance of a policy on the life of the plaintiff to his wife (without his knowledge or consent) provided the motive for her attempt to murder him by arsenic poisoning.[8] This case was predicated on the requirement of securing the consent of the person whose life was insured.[9] The foregoing comments about the applicability of negligence per se theory to an insurer's failure to adequately review the existence of an insurable interest can reasonably be extended to situations in which an insurer fails to comply with the statutory provisions that require the person whose life is insured to consent to the insurance arrangement.

§ 3.5(g) Insurable Interests for Industrial Life Insurance

It has been suggested that the insurable interest doctrine has no application to industrial life insurance.[1] The principal justification advanced in support of this proposition is that applying the doctrine would interfere with free use of the "facility-of-payment" clause commonly included in industrial life insurance policies. This clause autho-

---

6. See RESTATEMENT OF TORTS, SECOND (1965), § 288B(1).

7. On the other hand, if the statute is not aimed at prevention of murders that are in no way related to the freedom of "the whole world of the unscrupulous" to wager, then violation of the statute is not negligence per se. The quoted phrase is that of Holmes, J., in Grigsby v. Russell, 222 U.S. 149, 155, 32 Sup.Ct. 58, 56 L.Ed. 133, 136 (1911).

8. Ramey v. Carolina Life Insurance Co., 244 S.C. 16, 135 S.E.2d 362 (1964), 9 A.L.R.3d 1164 (1966).

9. See § 3.5(c)(4), above.

§ 3.5(g)

1. E.g., Liberty National Life Insurance Co. v. Weldon, 267 Ala. 171, 100 So.2d 696, 61 A.L.R.2d 1346 (1958).

rizes payment of funeral and burial expenses without resort to proceedings for administration of a deceased's estate, which would be very expensive in relation to the small amounts involved.[2] In general, this clause makes possible prompt and informal settlements. Another justification, or perhaps explanation, for the results in those cases is that the small amounts of insurance coverage that typically are provided by such policies are not likely to operate as inducements to murder.[3] On the other hand, with the safeguard of insurable interest doctrine withdrawn, vocational wagering could occur.[4] On balance, however, the rule that the insurable interest doctrine does not apply to industrial life insurance seems justified.

§ 3.6   Rules for Preventing Net Gain

§ 3.6(a)   The Rules

Insurance arrangements that clearly satisfy the insurable interest requirements could still lead to situations in which claimants would be paid amounts in excess of the losses sustained if insurers were always required to pay the benefits provided for in insurance contracts. There are several types of rules that can be used by courts and insurers to prevent payments that would produce a net gain to an insured. The possible rules or techniques, which are characterized in the following discussion according to the nature of the results they would produce, include:

(1) Nonliability

(2) Liability for Net Economic Loss

(3) Liability for Modified Gross Loss

(4) Liability for Distributed Gross Loss.

Each of these rules or techniques is described in the following discussion, and several terms of art that have become associated with them are also explained. Some of the rules or techniques have been widely applied by both insurers and courts.

This section also includes a final subsection which discusses the associated problem of whether there is an "unearned" premium in those instances when an insurer is not required to make a full payment, and, if so, what should be the disposition of such an unearned premium.

2. *Ibid.* As to "facility-of-payment" clauses generally, see § 1.5(f), above.

3. Minimizing or eliminating the insurable interest requirement for industrial life insurance may incidentally serve the useful purpose of enabling policyholders to realize the cash value of policies they would otherwise forfeit for nonpayment of premiums.

4. See, e.g., Hack v. Metz, 173 S.C. 413, 176 S.E. 314 (1934), 95 A.L.R. 196 (1935).

Cf. Magers v. National Life & Accident Insurance Co., 329 S.W.2d 752 (Missouri Supreme Court, 1959).

Also see § 3.1(c), above.

(1) Nonliability

A nonliability rule provides a complete or full defense to an insured's claim: the insurer has no liability for any part of the stated benefits when the insurance payments would produce a net gain for the person designated to receive the proceeds.

The situation that presents the strongest case for nonliability arises when a person designated to receive insurance benefits has suffered *no* economic loss as a result of the occurrence of the event insured against. For example, when a property owner has maintained coverage on property that has been sold and fully paid for by a purchaser who has taken full and complete title to the property, the former owner sustains no economic loss in the event the property is destroyed following the transaction.

The nonliability rule could also be applied if a claimant (or a designee) seeks a recovery from an insurer that is greater than the loss that was suffered. For example, a person who owns a property worth $50,000 and insures it for $75,000 may be seeking a chance at a gain rather than only reimbursement for loss. The rationale for an application of the rule in this context is that the nonliability rule should be imposed as a penalty on such a claimant for seeking a fortuitous gain, and that such a result would be a stronger deterrent than would a denial of benefits in excess of what the loss would be. The imposition of such a penalty would, however, have the disadvantage of denying reimbursement for what is presumed, in the absence of proof to the contrary, to be a fortuitous loss. Accordingly, the desirability of applying this rule when a claimant has sustained some loss undoubtedly depends on an appraisal of the relative merits of these opposing interests.

(2) Liability for Net Economic Loss

Net economic loss rules provide that an insurer will be liable up to the amount of the net loss suffered by a person designated to receive insurance benefits, but no more. A net loss rule can appropriately be applied either when the property is over-insured or when there is more than one source of indemnification. If there are several sources of indemnification, the term "net economic loss" is used to describe the amount of a loss that remains uncompensated after the actual value of other rights of indemnification (including the rights to compensation from other insurers) is taken into account. There are two types of net-economic-loss rules that can be used to limit an insured's recovery in situations involving multiple sources of indemnification:

Insurance as Excess Coverage Rule. An excess coverage rule treats one source of indemnification as primary and other sources, such as insurance, as secondary. A secondary source is only available to an insured to the extent that the insured is not indemnified from other sources. An excess coverage rule could apply not only when there is more than one insurance policy applicable, but also when sources other than insurance (such as a tortfeasor who was responsible for the loss) may be available to provide indemnification.

Proration Rule.[1] A proration rule treats an insured's rights to indemnification from two or more sources as proratable. Each right to recovery is proportionately reduced so that the total compensation received by an insured does not exceed the loss sustained. Although theoretically proration rules might be applied with respect to any group of indemnification sources, in practice such rules are almost invariably applied only to insurance coverages.

(3) Liability for Modified Gross Loss

Modified gross liability rules provide that an insurer will make payments to a claimant up to the amount of the gross economic loss. In order to prevent an insured from receiving a net economic gain, under modified gross loss rules either the insured's rights to indemnification from other sources are subject to subrogation or the other sources of indemnification are treated as excess coverages:

A *subrogation rule*[2] transfers the insured's other rights of indemnification to the insurer. Depending on the situation, an insurer asserting a subrogation right may be entitled to either indemnification or a proratable contribution from the other sources.

An *other-rights-as-excess-coverage rule* reduces or terminates the insured's rights to indemnification from other sources by treating the other sources of indemnification as excess coverage.

(4) Liability for Distributed Gross Loss

A distributed-gross-loss approach imposes liability on an insurer for the full amount of the benefits stated in the insurance contract, and avoids net gains to an insured by specific rules providing that portions of the insurance proceeds are to be paid to other entities who sustained economic losses. The specific rules used to implement this approach include:

All-Excess-to-Another Rule. An all-excess-insurance-benefits-to-another rule provides that an insurer pays to the insured an amount not exceeding the net loss, and pays all of any excess insurance benefits to another person or entity who sustained a loss.

Excess-over-Gross-Loss Rule. Under this approach, an insurer pays to another person or entity the excess above gross loss. To the extent necessary to prevent net gain, the designee's other rights of indemnification are subject to either a subrogation rule or

---

§ 3.6(a)

1. Concerning application of this type of rule, see the discussion of other insurance pro-ration clauses in § 3.11, below.

2. Concerning application of this type of rule, see § 3.10, below.

Keeton & Widess, Ins.Law—6

an other-rights-as-excess-coverage rule. Under a *subrogation* rule the designee's other rights of indemnification pass to the insurer (who may get either indemnity or a proratable contribution). Under an *other-rights-as-excess-coverage* rule, the designee's other rights of indemnification are treated as "excess coverage" which are thereby reduced or terminated.

An illustration may help to clarify these distributed gross rules. Suppose the insured, a life tenant, has a $50,000 policy on a residence. Suppose also that a fire causes $40,000 damage. If the insured has a good tort action against a person who negligently caused the fire, there may be no net loss. Plainly, though there is gross loss. However, since the insured has only a life tenancy, the insured's gross loss is less than $40,000, and for purposes of this discussion it will be assumed to be $35,000. The remaining $5,000 is a gross loss to the owner of the remainder after the life tenancy. If the insurer is held liable for $40,000, this is an illustration of an excess-over-gross-loss rule. If the insurer, (because the gross loss of the insured was only $35,000) having paid, is subrogated to the tort claim, subrogation is thereby combined with the excess-over-gross-loss rule. If the insured had taken out a second policy before the fire but after the value of the house had appreciated, other insurance clauses of the two policies would be relevant. One possible outcome would be that rights under the second policy would be treated as excess coverage, illustrating an *other-rights-as-excess-coverage* rule.

§ 3.6(b) The "Unearned" Premium Question

The application of several of the above methods of preventing an insured from deriving a net gain from insurance benefits raises the question as to whether an insurer thereby acquires an unfair profit when the insurer does not pay as much as was contemplated when the premium rate for the coverage was set.[3] Although there may be disagreement with respect to the scope of the risk contemplated in setting premium rates, at least in some circumstances it seems clear that there is a disparity between the risk contemplated in rating and the risk actually insured. For example, if the insureds covered by liability insurance were never subject to any risk of economic loss from any event insured against by the policy, there would be no possibility of liability and arguably the entire premium would be "unearned."

The possible desirability of denying insurers the benefit of "unearned" premiums is only one among several factors influencing the development of rules of law concerning the disposition of "unearned" premiums in those situations in which the principle of indemnity is invoked to defeat claims for insurance benefits.[4] One approach to the disposition of such "unearned" premiums is to view instances in which

---

3. It might be concluded either that there is no obligation to return any part of the premiums or that the insurer must return "unearned premiums."

4. See § 3.3(d), above.

an insurance company is not liable for a loss are part of the collective industry experience which contributes to the actuarial computations that establish future premiums. Accordingly, the retention of premiums in such situations ultimately will be reflected positively in the ratios of premium income to losses that determine subsequent premiums for the purchasers of such coverage.[5]

§ 3.7 The Measure of Recovery in Marine Insurance

§ 3.7(a) Types of Marine Losses

Marine losses are to some extent distinctive in nature, and the terminology traditionally used to describe them is even more distinctive. An introduction to this terminology is presented here.[1] Although some of these terms are also used in relation to other types of insurance, it is never safe to assume that the same meaning is accorded to such terms in different contexts. The discussion in this section provides brief descriptions of the following terms:

(1) Total Loss: actual or constructive

(2) Average and General Average

(3) Particular Average

(4) the "Memorandum."

One of the interesting aspects of marine insurance is that a total loss may be either "actual" or "constructive." When an insured event — which in marine terminology is a casualty from an insured peril — makes it impossible for the insured property to reach its destination in specie, an actual total loss has been suffered.[2] A constructive total loss exists when it would be possible for the property to be brought to the intended destination in specie, but the cost of doing so would exceed the value of the property.[3] Under both American and English law, unless provisions to the contrary appear in the insurance policy,

---

5. It might be argued that an allocation between unearned and earned premiums could be made on the basis of the ratio between the insurer's enforceable risk of liability and the risk contemplated in setting the premium rates. A weakness in the argument is the difficulty of quantifying the "enforceable risk" and the "contemplated risk."

§ 3.7(a)

1. See generally Winter, MARINE INSURANCE (Third edition, 1952), at pp. 369–371, pp. 392–400, and pp. 405–412; Gilmore & Black, ADMIRALTY (1957), at pp. 72–80.

Also see Leslie J. Buglass, MARINE INSURANCE AND GENERAL AVERAGE IN THE UNITED STATES (Second edition, 1981), at pp. 3–11.

2. E.g., Roux v. Salvador, 3 Bing.N.C. 266–267 at p. 286, 132 Eng.Rep. 413 at pp. 420–421 (Ex.Ch., 1836).

See 2 ARNOULD, MARINE INSURANCE [10 British Shipping Laws] (Fifteenth edition, 1961), at pp. 1023–1026 and at pp. 1046–1049. An actual total loss is also sometimes referred to as an absolute total loss. Id., at p. 1023.

Also see L. Buglass, MARINE INSURANCE AND GENERAL AVERAGE IN THE UNITED STATES (Second edition, 1981), at pp. 88–93; L. Buglass, MARINE INSURANCE CLAIMS (Second edition, 1972), at pp. 14–15.

3. See, e.g., L. Buglass, MARINE INSURANCE AND GENERAL AVERAGE IN THE UNITED STATES (Second edition, 1981), at p. 94; 2 ARNOULD, MARINE INSURANCE (Sixteenth edition, 1981), at p. 1168.

an insured may treat a loss in this situation as total by notifying the underwriter of the election to abandon to the underwriter all of the insured's rights in the property.[4] Under American law, but not English law, this election may also be made when the cost of bringing the insured property to the intended destination would be more than half of the property's value.[5]

The term average is used in admiralty and marine insurance law to mean a partial loss, in contrast with a total loss. A *general average* is a partial loss that, under admiralty law, falls generally on all the interests at risk in a maritime venture and is incurred when some of the property at risk is sacrificed to save the remainder.[6] The typical case for which the legal rule of general average was developed occurred when part of the cargo was cast overboard in a storm to save a ship and its other cargo. In this situation, the effect of the rule is that each of the owners of the property at risk in the venture is required to bear a proportionate share of the loss which results from casting part of the ship's cargo overboard. When this approach is applied, each of the owners of the ship and cargo that is saved is required to make a contribution to the owner of the cargo that was sacrificed, and thereby suffers loss. The owner of the sacrificed cargo, who receives the reimbursement from the other owners, also suffers a partial loss — that is, the owner suffers a loss of the general average type because the reimbursement to that owner is less than full reimbursement, the

4. See Id., at pp. 1085–1086 and at pp. 1097–1099.

Also see Herbert M. Lord, *The Hull Policy: Actual and Constructive Total Loss and Abandonment,* 41 Tulane Law Review 347–380 (1967).

5. E.g., Bradlie v. Maryland Insurance Co., 37 U.S. (12 Pet.) 378 at pp. 398–399, 9 L.Ed. 1123 at p. 1132 (1838).

Also see 2 ARNOULD, MARINE INSURANCE [10 British Shipping Laws] (Fifteenth edition, 1961), at p. 1099.

The American rule is not often applicable to hull losses, however, since hull policies commonly include a clause providing that there shall be no recovery for a constructive total loss "unless the expense of recovery and repairing the vessel shall exceed the insured value." See Winter, Marine Insurance (Third edition, 1952), at pp. 394–395. This stipulation for comparing the expense to insured value also effects a change from the rule, applied in the absence of such stipulation, that expense is to be compared with *actual repaired* value. See Gilmore & Black, ADMIRALTY (1957), at p. 78. See also, L. Buglass, MARINE INSURANCE AND GENERAL AVERAGE IN THE UNITED STATES (Second edition, 1981), at pp. 93–94.

In regard to the measure of recovery for hull losses, see § 3.7(c), below.

6. This proposition states the stricter English rule of general average. The American rule extends "the consequences of the general average act to include certain expenses incurred after safety has been attained. For example, expenses incurred for the mutual benefit of ship and cargo to enable the voyage to be completed, such as temporary repairs at a port of refuge, are made good [under the American rule] as general average." Buglass, GENERAL AVERAGE AND THE YORK/ANTWERP RULE (1959), at p. 12. See *Id.,* at pp. 11–17 for a comparison of the general principles of the American and English rules and their relation to the "York/Antwerp Rules, 1950," a set of model provisions developed for inclusion in marine cargo contracts to facilitate uniformity of application of the law of general average.

In regard to the measure of recovery for hull losses, see § 3.7(c), below.

Also see L. Buglass, MARINE INSURANCE AND GENERAL AVERAGE IN THE UNITED STATES (Second edition, 1981), at p. 115 and pp. 201–230; 2 ARNOULD, MARINE INSURANCE (Sixteenth edition, 1981), at p. 915A; Vaughan and Elliot, FUNDAMENTALS OF RISK AND INSURANCE (Second edition, 1978), at pp. 501–502.

deficiency being in the ratio of the value of the lost goods at risk to the total value of all goods at risk in the venture.

The term *particular average* is used to describe a partial loss that falls on one interest alone because it is not due to the type of sacrifice to which the law of general average applies.[7] Thus, a distinction is made between *particular average* and a total loss of a part of the cargo, as, for example, when a bale of cotton in the cargo is totally destroyed by a small fire that is subsequently extinguished before it damages either other cargo or the ship.

Marine underwriters have also used a special provision known traditionally as the "Memorandum". This provision was designed to exclude coverage of any *particular average* that is normal and expectable in view of the "inherent susceptibility" of certain types of goods to deterioration.[8] The "Memorandum" has also been used to exclude coverage of small *particular average* that, though accidental, is trifling in amount.[9] The "Memorandum" with its long list of products, is not as commonly used today as formerly. A similar result is obtained, however, by use of a "free of particular average" ("F.P.A.") clause, providing either for exclusion of all particular average or for exclusion of low-percentage particular average, depending upon the kind or kinds of goods at risk.[10]

---

7. See, e.g., 2 ARNOULD, MARINE INSURANCE (Sixteenth edition, 1981), at p. 1100; L. Buglass, MARINE INSURANCE AND GENERAL AVERAGE IN THE UNITED STATES (Second edition, 1981), at pp. 115–175; Vaughan and Elliot, FUNDAMENTALS OF RISK AND INSURANCE (Second edition, 1978), at p. 501.

8. The manner of expression in the provision may seem somewhat quaint: "It is also agreed, that * * * [1] tobacco * * * and all other articles that are perishable in their own nature, are warranted by the assured free from average, unless general; [2] * * * tobacco stems * * * free from average under *twenty per cent* unless general; [3] and sugar * * * and bread, are warranted by the assured free from average under *seven per cent* unless general; [4] and coffee in bags or bulk * * * free from average under *ten per cent* unless general." See Winter, MARINE INSURANCE (Third edition, 1952) at p. 212. The omitted phrases include a hodgepodge of other articles.

The meaning of the part of the quoted passage that, for convenience, has been designated "[1]" is that particular average involving tobacco (*i.e.*, partial losses otherwise than by liability for general average contribution, or by sacrifice of the tobacco to save other property in a general average situation) is not covered, though general average and total losses of tobacco are covered.

Clause "[2]" means that particular average involving tobacco stems, if under 20 per cent of the value, is not covered. That is, the insured bears any particular average involving tobacco stems if the loss is less than 20 per cent of the value, but if the loss is 20 per cent or more, the insurer bears the *whole* loss (not just the amount above 20 per cent). Again, of course, general average and total losses are covered.

Clauses "[3]" and "[4]" provide different percentage exclusions for particular average involving other products.

9. See 2 ARNOULD, MARINE INSURANCE (Sixteenth edition, 1981), at pp. 839–840.

10. The fixing of the percentage (called the "franchise") is in the hands of specialists. *Id.*, at p. 201. Also, the F.P.A. clauses, by the addition of an "unless" phrase, allow coverage of most particular average that is plainly due to casualty rather than "inherent susceptibility" to deterioration. The F.P.A., E.C. clause (English conditions) provides: "Free of particular average unless the vessel be stranded, sunk, or burnt, or in collision." The F.P.A., A.C. clause (American conditions) provides: "Free of particular average unless caused by stranding, sinking, burning, or collision with other vessel." Note that under the English conditions the underwriter is liable for particular average if the vessel is "stranded, sunk, or burnt, or in collision," even though casualty to the ves-

§ 3.7(b) The Measure of Recovery for Cargo Losses

The rules that govern the measure of recovery for cargo losses covered by marine insurance are orderly and relatively uncomplicated.[1] The basic principle for the measure of recovery under a marine policy on cargo is that the recovery can be found by determining the fraction of loss and multiplying by the smaller of the underwritten amount and the value (using prime value if the policy is unvalued and stipulated value if the policy is valued).[2] Different and more complex statements of the rule for determining the measure of recovery are sometimes used. In most instances, however, they are merely corollaries or amplifications of this basic principle.[3] In order to understand the principle fully, one must take account of the following three characteristics of marine insurance.

First, marine insurance is customarily coinsurance unless the policy is written in an amount as great as the "value" of the property insured. If the underwritten amount (that is, the stated amount of insurance) is less than the "value" (to be explained in the next paragraph) of the cargo that is the subject of insurance, the owner is a coinsurer. This means that the owner bears a portion of the risk.[4] For example, if the owner takes insurance in an amount that is 75% of the value, the owner bears 25% of the risk and recovers from the underwriter only 75% of the "loss." Thus, if the loss is $16,000, the insured recovers $12,000.[5]

---

sel had no causal connection with the particular average. Burnett v. Kensington, 7 T.R. 210, 101 Eng.Rep. 937 (K.B.1797).

Also see London Assur. v. Companhia De Moagens Do Barreiro, 167 U.S. 149 at pp. 162–168, 17 S.Ct. 785 at pp. 790–792, 42 L.Ed. 113 at pp. 121–123 (1897).

See generally, 2 ARNOULD, MARINE INSURANCE [10 British Shipping Laws] (Fifteenth edition, 1961), at § 882.

Both the American and English F.P.A. clauses, as quoted above, have the same effect as the Memorandum with respect to coverage of total losses and general average. If the phrase "under x per cent" is added, they similarly have the effect of excluding a small percentage loss but covering the whole loss if it is as great as the specified percentage. Sometimes, however, there is added to the clause the phrase "under x per cent, which is deductible." In such case, the insured always bears that part of the loss up to the deductible percentage, and the underwriter pays only the excess.

§ 3.7(b)

1. See generally, 2 ARNOULD, MARINE INSURANCE [10 British Shipping Laws], at §§ 979–983, § 991, §§ 1004–1028. A lucid and less detailed treatment of the subject

appears in Gilmore & Black, ADMIRALTY (1957), at pp. 72–85.

Many of the American cases are discussed in Gulf Refining Co. v. Atlantic Mutual Insurance Co., 279 U.S. 708, 49 S.Ct. 439, 73 L.Ed. 914 (1929).

The obscurity of the traditional statement of rules concerning the measure of recovery in marine insurance tempts those who master it to preserve its labyrinths as an ordeal of initiation for others who dare to intrude. Once the obscurity is penetrated, however, it is possible to understand the rules with relative ease.

2. This statement is in accord with the rules commonly applied by American and British courts. There has been a lack of uniformity among these rules concerning some details.

3. Some of the variations in expression of the principle will be considered below.

4. Section 81 of the British Marine Insurance Act of 1906, stating this rule, is declaratory of the distinctive rule that had been developed for marine insurance in the absence of legislation on the point.

5. Other forms of property insurance are customarily not coinsurance in the absence of a special endorsement. For example, if a householder has insurance of

Second, in marine insurance the term "value"[6] refers to the market value of the insured property at the port and time of departure.[7] This property value is also referred to as the "prime value" of the property insured. The value of the cargo at the time and place of loss at sea may be either more or less than the prime value. If more, the insured who has insurance in the full amount of the stipulated or prime value nevertheless receives less than indemnity. If the value at time and place of loss is less than the stipulated or prime value, such an insured receives more than indemnity. Thus, in theory the marine insurance contract on cargo,[8] even when enough coverage is obtained to avoid operation of the coinsurance principle, is aimed at restoring the insured to the financial position occupied at the commencement of the voyage, rather than either the position the owner occupied just before the loss or the position the owner would have occupied if the voyage had been completed without casualty.

Third, the term "stipulated value" is used to describe the arrangement in which the "value" of the cargo at commencement of the voyage is specified in an insurance policy, rather than being left to determination after loss.[9] The policy in which value is so stipulated is referred to as a "valued" policy. If value of the property is not so stipulated, the policy is referred to as an "open" or "unvalued" policy.[10] Most marine policies are valued. The use of valued policies may result in a further deviation from the principle of indemnity, since a stipulated value which is substituted for a prime value may be either more or less than the prime value.

An awareness of the concepts set out in the preceding paragraphs is essential to understanding how the measure of recovery is deter-

$15,000 on personal property worth $20,000, the householder recovers against the insurer the full amount of any loss, except that in no case is the recovery more than $15,000. Thus, if the loss is $16,000, the recovery is $15,000. A coinsurance endorsement is often added to fire insurance policies on commercial buildings and goods, and will be considered below.

Also see § 3.8, below.

6. The term "value" should not be confused with the term "stipulated value" described in the text below.

7. A deviation from the principle of indemnity is implicit in this meaning of value. See 1 ARNOULD, MARINE INSURANCE [9 British Shipping Laws] (Fifteenth edition, 1961), §§ 391–393 at pp. 360–363. Also see 1 ARNOULD, MARINE INSURANCE (Sixteenth edition, 1981), at p. 445.

8. Note, however, that this statement does not apply to insurance against particular average to hull, at least under the British rule, and perhaps under the American rule as well. See § 3.7(c), below.

Also see 2 ARNOULD, MARINE INSURANCE (Sixteenth edition, 1981), at p. 838; L. Buglass, MARINE INSURANCE AND GENERAL AVERAGE IN THE UNITED STATES (Second edition, 1981), at pp. 167–171.

9. See 1 ARNOULD, MARINE INSURANCE (Sixteenth edition, 1981), at p. 424.

10. The term "open" has been more often used, but "unvalued" is adopted in the British Marine Insurance Act of 1906, since the term "open" is also used in a completely different sense to denote a "floating" policy (or "floater") that does not specify the property insured, but rather covers, for example, a number of cargoes to be shipped in the future during the definite or indefinite term of the policy. See 1 ARNOULD, MARINE INSURANCE [9 British Shipping Laws] (Fifteenth edition, 1961), § 7 and § 8 at p. 242. Also see 1 ARNOULD, MARINE INSURANCE (Sixteenth edition, 1981), at pp. 445–448. *Cf.* Winter, MARINE INSURANCE (Third edition, 1952), at pp. 140 and pp. 149–150.

mined under a marine insurance policy. (One must also always bear in mind, as already noted, that marine insurance is designed to restore the insured to the position that existed at commencement of the voyage.) The simplest way to calculate the recovery under a marine insurance policy is to find the fraction of "loss" and multiply the underwritten amount by this fraction. The value at time of loss is used to determine the fraction of loss. More precisely, the value that the insured property would have had at the port of adjustment (usually the port of destination) in undamaged condition (called "sound value") is compared to the value at the port of adjustment in damaged condition to determine the fraction of loss. This is the form in which the principle is stated at the beginning of this discussion.

The formulae discussed below need not be remembered if one finds it easier to work from the principle itself. The following symbols are used in the formulae:

X—amount of a single underwriter's liability

U—amount underwritten in the policy

P—prime value

V—value stipulated in the policy

S—sound value at port of adjustment

D—damaged value at port of adjustment

L—loss suffered by the insured as measured in monetary units of value at the port of adjustment

%L—fraction of loss (or percentage of loss, expressed in decimal form — that is, 60% being expressed .60)

The following two propositions can be derived from the foregoing definitions of symbols:

$$L = S - D$$

$$\%L = \frac{S - D}{S} = \frac{L}{S}$$

In terms of these symbols, the principle stated above can be expressed for all cases, subject to an exception for a few unusual situations (which typically involve a mistake) of valued policies with U exceeding V and unvalued policies with U exceeding P. For the exceptional cases, the same formulae may be used except that V or P, as the case may be, must be substituted for U. The formula for all but the exceptional cases is:

$$X = (\%L)\ U$$

$$\text{or } X = \frac{L}{S}\ U$$

$$\text{or } X = \frac{(S - D)}{S}\ U$$

Traditionally the method of determining the amount due for partial damage under a valued policy is expressed in a way that is represented by the following formula: [11]

$$X = \frac{V(S - D)}{S}$$

The formula is correct only if the valuation (V) is equal to or less than the underwritten amount (U). Commonly the sum of the amounts underwritten by separate underwriters is equal to the valuation, and this formula can be used to determine the combined total liability of all underwriters. To find the liability of a single underwriter, it is then necessary to multiply by the fraction of the total underwritten amount for which the single underwriter is responsible. In terms of the formula, and this is the result:

$$X = \frac{V(S - D)}{S}\left(\frac{U}{V}\right) = \frac{(S - D)}{S}U = \frac{L}{S}U = (\% L)U$$

The same answer can be derived in a less roundabout way by using the principle stated at the outset.

Looking back to the next to the last step in developing the formula (and from the explanation above), one finds that the principle stated at the outset can be expressed as follows:

$$X = \frac{L}{S}U = L\frac{U}{S}$$

This means that an underwriter's liability can be determined by finding the "loss" of value at port of adjustment and multiplying this by the "fraction of coverage" at the time of loss (determined by comparing the underwritten amount and the *sound value* at port of adjustment).[12] The reason for preferring the other form of stating the principle, used at the outset of this discussion, is that "fraction of coverage" is likely to be misunderstood as the comparison between the underwritten amount and the *stipulated value*. The risk of such confusion is increased by the fact that this latter meaning of "fraction of coverage" is sometimes applicable in hull insurance adjustments.[13]

11. This formula is supported by the opinion of Lord Mansfield in Lewis v. Rucker, 2 Burr. 1167, 97 Eng.Rep. 769 (K.B.1761). This is also the formula for the "measure of indemnity" as defined in the British Marine Insurance Act of 1906. See § 3.7(c), n. 6, below.

12. Compare the formulation in a clause of the American Institute Time (Hulls) form, under which American vessels are usually insured: "When the contributory value of the Vessel [that is, S] is greater than the valuation herein [that is, V], the liability of these Underwriters for General Average contribution ＊ ＊ ＊ shall not exceed that proportion of the total contribution due from the Vessel that the amount insured hereunder bears to the contributory value ＊ ＊ ＊." L. Buglass, General Average and the New York/Antwerp Rules (1959), at p. 81.

13. See § 3.7(c), below.

§ 3.7(c) The Measure of Recovery for Hull Losses

The British rule for the measure of recovery for *general average* (hull losses) can be determined by the formula used for cargo losses.[1]

A different formula applies, however, to *particular average,* which can be computed by multiplying the loss by the "fraction of coverage" at commencement of the voyage, determined through a comparison between the underwritten amount and the stipulated value (if the policy is valued) or prime value (if the policy is unvalued).[2] The loss is commonly the cost of making repairs minus the improvement resulting. Thus for particular average to hull under a valued policy, by the British rule, recovery is determined by:

$$X = L \frac{U}{V}$$

Under an unvalued policy, recovery is determined by:

$$X = L \frac{U}{P}$$

In case of total loss of the hull, the stipulated or prime value would also control the valuation of "L." Thus, the underwriter's liability would be U, the amount underwritten. Of course the underwriter's liability for total loss of cargo is also the underwritten amount; in the third from the last formula above, L and S would be identical, leaving X equal to U. Thus the simplified formula

$$X = U$$

is valid for total loss of either hull or cargo (except that in no event can the recovery under an unvalued policy exceed the prime value).

The American rule with respect to hull losses is in doubt. The opinion of the United States Supreme Court in Gulf Refining Co. v. Atlantic Mutual Insurance Co.[3] contains a statement of the petitioner's contention that in a case concerning loss to cargo by general average contribution, the rule applied "should be the same as that applied to insurance on hulls, where the insured is allowed to recover in full for a partial loss up to the amount of the insurance,"[4] and a dictum that

---

§ 3.7(c)

1. See 2 ARNOULD, MARINE INSURANCE [10 British Shipping Laws] (Fifteenth edition, 1961), §§ 1005–1008, at pp. 923–927 and pp. 976–1008.

2. *Id.,* § 1024, at pp. 997–998; Winter, MARINE INSURANCE (Third edition, 1952), at p. 385. This difference between methods of computing liability for particular average to hull and cargo is customarily explained on the ground that a ship is not intended for sale, and it is presumed that repairs will be made by the owner, whereas cargo is intended for sale and is usually salable even in damaged condition. Perhaps an additional justification exists in the fact that this method of computing

liability for hull loss avoids the difficult problem of determining a sound value of the hull at port of adjustment. Sound value of cargo (which is used in the computation of liability for cargo losses, whether particular or general average) is usually less difficult to determine than sound value of a hull. In case of general average to hull, sound value must be determined for another purpose in any event, since it is used in the computation of the general average contribution for which the hull is liable.

3. 279 U.S. 708, 49 S.Ct. 439, 73 L.Ed. 914 (1929).

4. 279 U.S. at p. 711, 49 S.Ct. at p. 440, 73 L.Ed. at p. 916.

"the insured may recover in full for partial losses under hull insurance."[5] Though rejecting the contention as to cargo loss, the court appears to have acquiesced in petitioner's statement of the rule as to a hull loss. The cases cited in support of the dictum, however, are all cases of valued policies with a total underwritten amount equal to the stipulated value. Of course the British rule stated by Arnould would also produce full recovery, up to the amount of the insurance, in those circumstances.[6] But the dictum has been repeated uncritically.[7]

§ 3.8   Coinsurance Provisions in Property Insurance

§ 3.8(a)   Generally

Many property insurers use coinsurance clauses, especially in connection with coverage for commercial buildings and homes, to encourage insurance purchasers to acquire coverage that approaches or is equal to the full value of the property. Coinsurance clauses provide that unless an insured maintains coverage for an insured property which is at least equal to some specified percentage (typically eighty or ninety per cent) of the full value of the property, the insured bears a portion of the risk for either a partial or a total destruction of the property.[1] Property insurance coverages, other than marine insurance,

---

5. 279 U.S. at p. 713, 49 S.Ct. at p. 440, 73 L.Ed. at p. 917.

6. Some misunderstanding of the British rule may have arisen from the special sense in which "measure of indemnity" is used in the British Marine Insurance Act of 1906. The "measure of indemnity" and measure of recovery are not the same amount unless the underwritten amount is equal to the stipulated (in case of a valued policy) or prime value (in case of an unvalued policy).

The following are relevant provisions of the British Marine Insurance Act of 1906:

"67.—(1) The sum which the assured can recover in respect of a loss on a policy by which he is insured, in the case of an unvalued policy to the full extent of the insurable value, or, in the case of a valued policy to the full extent of the value fixed by the policy, is called the measure of indemnity.

(2) Where there is a loss recoverable under the policy, the insurer, or each insurer if there be more than one, is liable for such proportion of the measure of indemnity as the amount of his subscription bears to the value fixed by the policy in the case of a valued policy, or to the insurable value in the case of an unvalued policy.

"69. Where a ship is damaged, but is not totally lost, the measure of indemni-

ty, subject to any express provision in the policy, is as follows:—

(1) Where the ship has been repaired, the assured is entitled to the reasonable cost of the repairs, less the customary deductions, but not exceeding the sum insured in respect of any one casualty:

(2) Where the ship has been only partially repaired, the assured is entitled to the reasonable cost of such repairs, computed as above, and also to be indemnified for the reasonable depreciation, if any, arising from the unrepaired damage, provided that the aggregate amount shall not exceed the cost of repairing the whole damage, computed as above:

(3) Where the ship has not been repaired and has not been sold in her damaged state during the risk, the assured is entitled to be indemnified for the reasonable depreciation arising from the unrepaired damage, but not exceeding the reasonable cost of repairing such damage, computed as above."

7. E.g., Aetna Insurance Co. v. United Fruit Co., 304 U.S. 430 at p. 435, 58 S.Ct. 959 at p. 961, 82 L.Ed. 1443 at p. 1446 (1938).

§ 3.8(a)

1. See, e.g., Schnitzer v. South Carolina Insurance Company, 62 Or.App. 300, 661 P.2d 550 (1983), review dismissed 295 Or. 259, 705 P.2d 1157 (1983) (insureds having

is not treated as coinsurance unless the insurance policy specifically so provides. Instead an insurer is liable for the full amount of any insured loss up to the underwritten amount.

The importance of applying the coinsurance approach when insurance is being provided for buildings results from the fact that the rates for property insurance for a particular type of risk have commonly been fixed without regard to either the total value of the property or the amount of coverage purchased by an insured.[2] For example, when coverage is purchased for a structure that has a total value of $100,000, the purchaser pays the same premium rate (that is, the same number of dollars of premium) for the first thousand dollars of coverage as for the one hundredth thousand dollars of coverage. Although an insurance purchaser pays the same premium rate for the lowest and the highest thousand dollar segment of the coverage which is acquired, experience has shown that a partial destruction of a structure — either a business or a residence — is considerably more likely to occur than a complete destruction. Thus, because an insurer will more often be required to provide indemnification for partial losses, the cost — as reflected in losses — to the insurer of providing the first thousand dollars of coverage is considerably more than the cost of providing the highest thousand dollars of the coverage for a structure. These factors — the premium rate and the higher incidence of partial destruction of property — cause, especially in the absence of a coinsurance feature in the coverage arrangement, some insurance purchasers to take a chance by acquiring some amount of insurance that is less than the full value of the property.

§ 3.8(b) The New York Standard Coinsurance Clause

To encourage the purchase of property insurance in amounts that approach the full value of an insured property, insurers developed a type of provision that eventually became known as the New York Standard Coinsurance Clause. In some states, legislation now requires that all fire insurance policies issued on commercial real property include a coinsurance provision. The typical clause reads in part as follows:

> "This Company shall not be liable for a greater proportion of any loss or damage to the property described herein than the sum hereby insured bears to the percentage specified on the first page of this policy of the actual cash value of said property at the time such loss shall happen, nor for more than the proportion which this policy bears to the total insurance thereon."

An insurance policy with this type of provision can be priced at a more favorable rate per thousand dollars of insurance than one without such a clause.

---

failed to insure buildings for 90% of the actual cash value as determined at the time of the loss, the co-insurance clause applied to the loss).

2. See Uriel Procaccia and Robert M. Shafton, *Coinsurance Clauses and Rate Equity,* 661 Insurance Law Journal 69–94 at pp. 72–73 (February, 1978).

A better understanding of coinsurance clauses may be facilitated by translating the coinsurance statement into a formula.[1] For example, if the coinsurance "percentage" (usually specified on the first page of a policy) is 80 per cent, which is a commonly used figure,[2] the measure of recovery can then be expressed in the following way:

$$\text{Recovery} = \frac{(\text{Amount of Insurance})}{(80\% \text{ Value of Property})} \text{ Loss}^{[3]}$$

$$X = \frac{(U)}{(80\% \text{ S})} \text{ L}$$

From this presentation of the rule, it is easy to see that a recovery under a New York standard coinsurance clause involves an element of coinsurance only when the total underwritten amount is not as high as the percentage of value designated in the coinsurance clause. If the insured purchases coverage at least up to the level specified as the appropriate percentage, the insured will not be a coinsurer for any loss up to that amount. For example, if the total underwritten amount on a $100,000 property is $80,000 (which is 80 per cent of S) and there is an $8,000 loss, then the coverage is:

$$X = \frac{(\$80,000)}{.80 \times \$100,000} \$8,000 = \$8,000.$$

If, however, the value of the property, at both inception date and time of loss, is $100,000 and the total underwritten amount is $50,000, a loss of $8,000 resulting from damage to the property would be indemnified to the extent of

$$X = \frac{(\$50,000)}{.80 \times \$100,000} \$8,000 = \$5,000$$

If the coinsurance factor is set at 100%, as it sometimes is for property insurance and customarily is for marine insurance, purchasing a $50,000 policy on a $100,000 property would mean that an $8,000 loss would result in $4,000 being paid by the insurer.

$$X = \frac{(\$50,000)}{1.00 \times \$100,000} \$8,000 = \$4,000^{[4]}$$

§ 3.8(b)

1. The formula is framed in terms of the symbols used in the marine insurance formulae. See § 3.7(b), above.

The symbols used in this section are similar to those used in the formulae for marine insurance, except for having "S" here represent sound value in the sense of "actual cash value of the property at the time such loss shall happen" — a sense closely analogous to that of S in the marine formulae.

2. An earlier version of the clause was known as the New York 80% Average Clause.

3. With the qualification that X cannot exceed L or U or L multiplied by the fraction derived by placing U over the total of all insurance on the property.

4. See § 3.7(b), above.

The result is the same as under the marine insurance provisions:

$$X = \frac{(\$8,000)}{(\$100,000)} \$50,000 = \$4,000$$

Algebraically, the formulae in this case are equivalents since the marine formula

$$X = \frac{L}{S} U$$

can also be written

$$X = \frac{U}{S} L$$

which is the same as saying

$$X = \frac{U}{1.00S} \text{ L.}$$

The use of the New York Standard Coinsurance Clause for insurance on commercial properties poses some practical problems for insureds in a period of inflation (that is, rising price levels). In such circumstances, an amount of insurance which was at least 80 per cent of the value of the property at the time of inception of the coverage, might be less than 80 per cent at the time of loss as a result of a rise in the value of the property in the interval. Suppose, for example, the value of the property when the insurance policy was acquired was $100,000 and the total underwritten amount was $80,000 with a specified coinsurance percentage of 80 per cent. And suppose that the value of the property rose so that at the time of a loss of $8,000 the value was $200,000. The resulting recovery would be

$$X = \frac{(\$80,000)}{(.80 \times \$200,000)} \; \$8,000 = \$4,000.$$

In this illustration, the substantial increase in the value of the property means that the recovery is one-half of what it would have been if the property value had remained the same.

Once an increase of value is great enough to cause the face amount of coverage to be no more than the percentage stated in the coinsurance clause, the coverage of a particular loss decreases with any further rise in value of the property. Similarly, if the face amount of coverage is less than the percentage of value stated in the coinsurance clause, but only in that event, a decrease in value causes the coverage for a particular loss to increase (subject to a maximum recovery of 100 per cent of loss).

If "actual cash value" is subject to dispute either because of conflicting evidence or because of doubt about the legal definition of the term, an insured who is making a claim under a policy containing a standard coinsurance clause may establish a higher percentage of coverage by proving a lower "actual cash value" than the insurer alleges.[5]

One way for an insured to avoid, or at least reduce, the risk that a coinsurance clause will be applied to reduce the amount to be paid is to initially acquire coverage in an amount that exceeds the value computed by an application of the stated percentage (which is usually 80 per cent) to the then current value of the property.[6] An insured can also avoid the problem by arranging for a periodic review of an insured property's value with a view to increasing the amount of insurance when warranted by a change in the valuation.

This last formula is the same as the New York formula with a speified percentage of 100 per cent.

5. See, e.g., Jefferson Insurance Co. v. Superior Court of Alameda County, 3 Cal. 3d 398, 90 Cal.Rptr. 608, 475 P.2d 880 (1970) ("actual cash value" of hotel as used in 70% coinsurance clause was equivalent to "fair market value," and not the higher amount of "replacement cost less deprecia-

tion," and because of the difference insured's recovery was for entire loss rather than for pro rata share thereof).

Concerning "actual cash value" generally, see § 3.9, below.

6. Thus, in the foregoing illustration, the insured could originally buy at least $90,000 of coverage, and anything up to $100,000 would be permissible.

There are several other approaches that may, at least theoretically, be used by insureds to avoid such problems. First, it may be possible to get a commitment from the insurer, preferably by an endorsement that is included in the insurance policy, to a stipulated value for the purpose of the coinsurance clause. Second, an insurer may agree that the application of the principle of coinsurance will depend upon value at the time of inception of the contract rather than at the time of loss.[7] If the value thus agreed upon were such that the amount of the insurance in relation to the total value of the property equaled or exceeded the percentage stated in the coinsurance clause, the effect would be the same as if the clause were not in the policy.[8] Third, the insurer and the insured can agree to automatic adjustments in the amount of coverage that reflect increases in value of an insured property produced by inflation.

A trap for the unwary insured has developed as a consequence of clauses in homeowner insurance policies that are similar to coinsurance clauses in commercial insurance policies. A homeowner insurance policy often includes a clause providing for the reimbursement of repair costs, without deduction for depreciation, if the face amount of the insurance is at least a stated percentage (for example, 80%) *of replacement cost.* However, because the replacement cost of an older house may be far higher than *actual cash value* (usually determined by the market value of the property) — the term used in the New York Standard Coinsurance Clause — the amount of insurance required to avoid the adverse effect of this type of clause in a homeowner policy will ordinarily be much higher in relation to market value than would be required to avoid the adverse effect of a New York Standard Coinsurance Clause. For example, an old house in depreciated condition may have a market value of $100,000 even though the replacement cost for the structure would be $150,000. If the homeowner buys $90,000 worth of insurance coverage, this is more than 80% of the *actual cash value,* but far less than 80% of the *replacement cost.* The homeowner therefore loses the benefit of the provision allowing reimbursement of repair costs *without deduction for depreciation.* Thus, the insurance proceeds that will be paid if repairs are necessary as a result of a partial loss will only cover a portion of the repair costs. In this illustration, the amount of coverage required to avoid this adverse effect of the 80% clause would be 80% of $150,000, which is $120,000 and this would be 120% of the *actual cash value.*

---

7. Compare the effort of counsel, albeit quite properly unsuccessful, to have a policy interpreted in this way in American Insurance Co. v. Iaconi, 47 Del. 167, 89 A.2d 141 (1952), 36 A.L.R.2d 604 (1954).

However, also consider the effect of using a valued policy approach. See the discussion in § 3.12.

Also *cf.* the court's analysis in Ehlert v. Graue, 292 Minn. 393, 195 N.W.2d 823 at p. 825 (1972).

8. It is unlikely that an insurer would make such an agreement; rather, it would be more likely either to strike the coinsurance clause by endorsement or else to stand on the requirements implicit in the clause.

§ 3.9 The Measure of Recovery in Property Insurance

§ 3.9(a) Generally

Property insurance policies commonly provide that, subject to certain qualifications, the company insures the designated property to the extent of the "actual cash value."[1] Insurers that use this type of coverage provision usually contemplate that the loss will be determined by the value of the property when the insured event occurs, and some coverages explicitly provide that the valuation is to be made at that time. However, other coverage terms are also used. For example, some property policies provide coverage for the "actual value" as determined at the time coverage commences.

There are several approaches that have been used to establish the "actual cash value" of insured property, including techniques based on determinations of the market value, the replacement or repair cost, and replacement (or repair) cost less an appropriate adjustment for depreciation. In some situations the various valuation approaches may produce essentially the same result, while in other instances they will produce markedly different measures of recovery.

When the market value of a property that has been damaged can be readily determined, this value has usually been regarded as the appropriate measure of "actual cash value."[2] For example, the commonly used measure of recovery for purposes of insurance on buildings is the diminution in the fair market value of the structure as determined by an appraisal of the difference between what a willing buyer would pay a willing seller (that is, when neither is under any compulsion in regard to the sale) for the building before and after the

§ 3.9(a)

1. By the customary phrasing of fire insurance policies on buildings and personal property generally, the insurer "does insure [*name insured*] and legal representatives, to the extent of the actual cash value of the property at the time of loss, but not exceeding the amount which it would cost to repair. * * *" See Appendix A.

The comprehensive coverage clause of most motor vehicle policies, on the other hand, customarily provides that the insurer agrees to pay for "direct and accidental loss of or damage to" the automobile. In these policies, the phrase "actual cash value" is used only in the "limit of liability" provisions. See Appendix H.

2. The measure of recovery commonly applied is the difference between fair market value before and after damage. See, e.g., Forer v. Quincy Mutual Fire Insurance Co., 295 A.2d 247 (Me.1972) (subject to a limit set by the cost of repair for a loss caused by the freezing of the plumbing and heating system); Jefferson Insurance Co. of New York v. Superior Court of Alameda County, 3 Cal.3d 398, 475 P.2d 880, 90 Cal. Rptr. 608 (1970).

Cf. Cassel v. Newark Insurance Co., 274 Wis. 25, 79 N.W.2d 101 (1956) (stock of merchandise); Engh v. Calvert Fire Insurance Co., 266 Wis. 419, 63 N.W.2d 831 (1954) (motor vehicle).

Also see Crandall v. Country Mutual Insurance Co., 81 Ill.App.3d 140, 36 Ill.Dec. 520, 400 N.E.2d 1100 (4th Dist.1980) (motor vehicle damaged to an extent that it was uneconomical to repair);

See generally, Annotation, *Test or criterion of "actual cash value" under insurance policy insuring to extent of cash value at time of loss*, 61 A.L.R.2d 711–743 at pp. 733–736 (1958).

occurrence of the insured event that caused a loss.[3] Although the same approach can, of course, also be applied to personal property,[4] it has not been as widely used in regard to personal property claims.

There are some situations in which it is generally recognized that indemnification based upon the differential in market value before and after the occurrence of an insured event would not be an appropriate measure of compensation for an insured's loss — that is, coverage for the "actual cash value" of property is not invariably treated as synonymous with market value.[5] Insurance for household furniture provides a good illustration of this type of situation. Used home furnishings have a very low market value if an owner wishes to sell. However, an owner who needs to replace destroyed property will find that it is virtually impossible to acquire comparable used furniture, and that replacement of destroyed furniture involves purchasing new items at a significantly greater cost than the market value of the furniture which was destroyed. In such circumstances, courts have held that a recovery under a property insurance policy is appropriately determined by reference to the cost of replacement or, at least in some instances, to the original purchase price paid by the insured.[6] Replacement cost has also been viewed as the appropriate measure of recovery when that cost was shown to be lower than either the original cost of the property or the market value of the property just before the occurrence of an insured event.[7]

Another approach to the determination of "actual cash value" (or "actual value" which is a term that appears in some policy forms) is to assess the loss in terms of the cost to either replace or reproduce the property and then to reduce this amount by an appropriate factor for depreciation.[8] When this approach to valuation is employed, the tech-

---

3. See cases cited in note 2, above.

Also see Gendron v. Pawtucket Mutual Insurance Company, 384 A.2d 694 at p. 697 (Me.1978), appeal after remand 409 A.2d 656 (Me.1979); Elliano v. Assurance Company of America, 45 Cal.App.3d 170, 119 Cal.Rptr. 653 (2d Dist., 4th Div., 1975).

4. See, e.g., Alber v. Wise, 53 Del. (Storey) 126, 166 A.2d 141 (1960).

5. *Cf.* Leslie Salt Co. v. St. Paul Mercury Insurance Co., 637 F.2d 657 at p. 660 (9th Cir.1981); Fedas v. Insurance Co. of Pennsylvania, 300 Pa. 555, 151 A. 285 (1930).

Also see Judge v. Celina Mutual Insurance Co., 303 Pa.Super. 221, 449 A.2d 658 at p. 661 (1981).

See the discussion of approaches to valuation in Stephen A. Cozen, *Measure and Proof of Loss to Buildings and Structures Under Standard Fire Insurance Policies— The Alternatives and Practical Approaches,* 12 Forum 647–665 (1977); Paul J. McGeady, *Fair Market Value Concept in*

Total Loss Adjustments, 8 Forum 627–633 (1973).

See generally, Annotation, *Test or criterion of "actual cash value" under insurance policy insuring to extent of actual cash value at time of loss,* 61 A.L.R.2d 711–743 (1958); McCormick on Damages (1935), at § 45.

6. *Cf.* Thomas v. American Family Mutual Insurance Company, 233 Kan. 775, 666 P.2d 676 at p. 679 (1983) (the term "actual cash value" when applied to damages from a storm that partially destroyed a residence means the cost to repair without any reduction for depreciation).

7. See, e.g., Reliance Insurance Company v. Substation Products Corp., 404 So.2d 598 at p. 609 (Ala.1981).

8. McAnarney v. Newark Fire Insurance Co., 247 N.Y. 176, 159 N.E. 902, 56 A.L.R. 1149 (1928).

Also see Elberon Bathing Co., Inc. v. Ambassador Insurance Co., Inc., 77 N.J. 1, 389 A.2d 439 (1978); Braddock v. Memphis

nique for determining the effect of depreciation can often be a significant factor in ascertaining the amount of recovery under property insurance.[9]

It should be recognized that no particular approach to valuation is necessarily conclusive in regard to the measure of recovery in the event an insured property is destroyed. Each of the techniques described in the preceding paragraphs is based on a valuation theory that is used by appraisers, and each has been held to be relevant for consideration by a judge or jury on the question of measure of recovery in one or more of the types of situations that may arise under property insurance policies.[10] Furthermore, some courts have adopted an approach which either requires or permits a fact-finder to consider all of the evidence an expert would view as relevant; this approach is usually referred to as the "broad evidence rule." [11]

The preceding discussion of the possible "measures of recovery" should not be viewed as having presented a comprehensive list of the rules or principles courts apply when valuation disputes arise. Other approaches or techniques are sometimes employed when the value of an insured property is at issue. For example, insureds have been allowed to recover the costs of repairing a structure without being required to introduce proof of the market value[12] or without any reduction for depreciation.[13]

Fire Insurance Corporation, 493 S.W.2d 453 (Tenn.1973).

Cf. Note, *Valuation and Measure of Recovery Under Fire Insurance Policies*, 49 Columbia Law Review 818–836 at p. 824 (1949).

But cf. Jefferson Insurance Co. of N.Y. v. Supreme Court of Alameda County, 3 Cal. 3d 398, 90 Cal.Rptr. 608, 475 P.2d 880 (1970).

Also see discussion in § 3.9(b), below.

9. See, e.g., Patriotic Order Sons of America Hall Association v. Hartford Fire Insurance Co., 305 Pa. 107, 157 A. 259 (1931), 78 A.L.R. 899 (1932).

10. For example, the Connecticut Supreme Court commented that "under the so-called broad evidence rule, any evidence logically tending to the formation of a correct estimate of the value of the destroyed or damaged property might be considered by the trier of facts in determining 'actual cash value' at the time of the loss." Sullivan v. Liberty Mutual Fire Insurance Co., 174 Conn. 229, 384 A.2d 384 at p. 386 (1978).

Also see Agoos Leather Companies, Inc. v. American & Foreign Insurance Co., 342

Mass. 603, 174 N.E.2d 652 (1961); Pinet v. New Hampshire Fire Insurance Co., 100 N.H. 346, 126 A.2d 262 (1956), 61 A.L.R.2d 706 (1958).

11. See especially the discussion in Elberon Bathing Co., Inc. v. Ambassador Insurance Co., Inc., 77 N.J. 1, 389 A.2d 439 at pp. 442–445 (1978), and the cases cited in note 4 of the opinion.

Also see Strauss Bros. Packing Co., Inc. v. American Insurance Company, 98 Wis. 2d 706, 298 N.W.2d 108 (1980); Braddock v. Memphis Fire Insurance Corporation, 493 S.W.2d 453 (Tenn.1973).

Cf. Ohio Casualty Insurance Company v. Ramsey, 439 N.E.2d 1162 (Ind.App., 2d Dist., 1982).

See generally, Stephen D. Marcus, *Actual Cash Value, Illinois and the Broad Evidence Rule: "A Modest Proposal"*, 59 Illinois Bar Journal 1000–1014 (1971).

12. See, e.g., Imperial Insurance Company v. National Homes Acceptance Corp., 626 S.W.2d 327 (Tex.App., Tyler, 1981).

13. See, e.g., Thomas v. American Family Mutual Insurance Company, 233 Kan. 775, 666 P.2d 676 (1983).

§ 3.9(b)   Depreciation

It is clear that the actual condition of property affects its value. The effects of age and wear on property are frequently conceptualized in terms of depreciation, and the amount of indemnification provided by insurance may be influenced by considerations that involve an appropriate allowance for depreciation.[1] However, the determination of the effects of depreciation for purposes of insurance can prove to be difficult. Furthermore, assessing an insured's recovery with a due allowance for depreciation may leave an insured with a significant out-of-pocket loss.

Depreciation and Motor Vehicle Property Insurance

There is some doubt about the extent to which depreciation is or should be taken into account in the settlement of losses, especially partial losses that can be repaired, covered by motor vehicle insurance which provides indemnification for physical damage to an insured vehicle. In addition, there also seems to be some disagreement about the desirability of making a deduction for depreciation in calculating "actual cash value of motor vehicles."[2] The following discussion provides some perspectives on the problem of making an appropriate allowance for depreciation when coverage claims result from damage to motor vehicles.

Consider, for example, some of the factors that affect the value when a vehicle is damaged as the result of a collision and has to be repaired. On the one hand, it might be argued that neither the "loss" nor the reduction in "actual cash value" is equal to the cost of making the repairs because the repaired vehicle will often be in somewhat better condition than it was in just before it was damaged. On the other hand, a once-wrecked and repaired vehicle ordinarily is not as valuable in the market place as a comparable one that has not been damaged.

Another perspective on the problems of valuation in regard to motor vehicles is provided by considering how an automobile's value is affected by the theft and replacement of a spare tire. It can reasonably be argued that a new tire is clearly worth more than the used tire it replaces. When the value of a car is considered as a unit, however, it is doubtful that whether the fact that a spare tire is new or used would make much of a difference in the market value of the vehicle. However, a new spare tire may be different in one basic respect from a new door that is purchased to replace a door that is destroyed in an accident. The value of the new door can almost never be separately

---

§ 3.9(b)

1. See, e.g., Elberon Bathing Co., Inc. v. Ambassador Insurance Co., Inc., 77 N.J. 1, 389 A.2d 439 (1978); Braddock v. Memphis Fire Insurance Corporation, 493 S.W.2d 453 (Tenn.1973).

2. Cf., e.g., Potomac Insurance Co. v. Wilkinson, 213 Miss. 520, 57 So.2d 158 (1952), 43 A.L.R.2d 321 (1955).

realized because the rest of the car will wear out sooner than the door and the door will have almost no market value independent of the vehicle, whereas it may be possible to sell a tire separately from the rest of the vehicle.

In light of such considerations, courts have adopted various rules for property insurance claims involving motor vehicles. For example, for over forty years the Iowa Supreme Court has applied the following approach:

"1. When the automobile is totally destroyed, the measure of damages is its reasonable market value immediately before its destruction.

"2. Where the injury to the car can be repaired, so that, when repaired, it will be in as good condition as it was before the injury, then the measure of damages is the reasonable cost of repair plus the reasonable value of the use of the car while being repaired, with ordinary diligence, not exceeding the value of the car before the injury.

"3. When the car cannot, by repair, be placed in as good condition as it was in before the injury, then the measure of damages is the difference between its reasonable market value immediately before and immediately after the accident." [3]

When an insurer in Iowa sought to introduce a new method of settling third party claims under the liability coverage for property damages, the Iowa insurance department challenged the approach as not being in accord with Iowa law.[4] In affirming the rulings of the insurance commission and the district court, the Iowa Supreme Court concluded the proposed change "complicates and blurs the clear and well understood rule * * * applied for over half a century." [5]

§ 3.9(c) Replacement Coverage

In some situations, insurers agree to provide coverage that does not reduce an insured's recovery because of depreciation. For example, some insurance policies state that in case of a partial loss, the full repair cost will be paid without any reduction in the measure of recovery on account of depreciation. This type of coverage is often

---

3. Aetna Casualty & Surety Co. v. Insurance Department of Iowa, 299 N.W.2d 484 at p. 485 (Iowa 1980).

4. The insurer sought to modify the second part of the Iowa approach by not requiring an insurer to pay the repair costs unless the repairs were actually made. The court reported that:

"The petitioner argues that there is an increased tendency on the part of automobile owners to pocket the proceeds from insurance claims and to leave dam-age unrepaired. The petitioner also complains that independent body shop owners have interjected themselves into negotiating the price of repairs. In the petitioner's view these two developments have increased the costs incurred by the companies, costs which it says are necessarily being passed on to the consumer in the form of higher insurance premiums."

Ibid.

5. *Ibid.*

referred to as "replacement insurance." [1] Some insurance policies of this type require an insured to repair the structure in order to collect; other insurance policies allow an insured to collect without imposing an obligation to rebuild.[2]

Replacement insurance, which was first developed for commercial properties in the 1950s, is now available to homeowners in some insurance policies under the title "replacement cost coverage." A typical replacement cost coverage clause states:

> If at the time of loss the limit of liability for the dwelling [stated on the face of the policy] is 80 per cent or more of the full replacement cost of the dwelling covered, [the coverage under this policy is] extended to include the full cost of repair or replacement without deduction for depreciation.[3]

If an insurance contract uses this policy language, an additional contractual provision is needed when an insurer wants to preclude the recovery of replacement or repair costs in the event a policyholder does not in fact make repairs or replace the property.[4] For example, an insurer may include a provision that specifies:

> "When the cost to repair or replace the damage is more than $1000 or more than 5% of the amount of insurance in this policy on the building, whichever is less, we will pay no more than the actual cash value of the damage until actual repair or replacement is completed." [5]

§ 3.9(c)

1. Also see Note, *Valuation and Measure of Recovery Under Fire Insurance Policies*, 49 Columbia Law Review 818–836 at p. 832 (1949).

2. For example, the Supreme Court of Washington concluded, "The replacement cost method of payment does not require the rebuilding of the structure as a condition precedent to the payment of the proceeds" under a policy that provided the valuations for insured property "at the full cost to repair or replace the property (without deduction for depreciation) * * * but not to exceed * * * [t]he cost to replace the property covered on the same site in a condition equal to, but not superior to or more extensive than, the condition when new." National Fire Insurance Company of Hartford v. Solomon, 96 Wn.2d 763, 638 P.2d 1259 at p. 1260 and p. 1262 (1982).

3. It should be noted that a rise in value of the property insured carries a potential for a problem, and surprise, for the insured under this homeowner's replacement provision analogous to but in one respect more severe than those under the New York Standard Coinsurance Clause. See § 3.8(b), above.

This type of provision relates to *replacement cost* rather than *actual cash value*. Coverage that is 80 per cent of actual cash value would very likely be well below 80 per cent of replacement cost. And a rise in value that causes 80 per cent of "the full replacement cost of the dwelling covered" to exceed the limit of liability would, in fact, cause a replacement provision of the type quoted in the text to become completely inoperative.

4. See, e.g., Higgins v. Insurance Co. of North America, 256 Or. 151, 469 P.2d 766 (1970).

5. See, e.g., Huggins v. Hanover Insurance Company, 423 So.2d 147 at p. 149 (Ala.1982). The insurance policy also provided:

> " * * * we will pay the cost of repair or replacement, without deduction for depreciation, but not exceeding the smallest of the following amounts:

> (a) the limit of liability under this policy applying to the building;

> (b) the replacement cost of that part of the building damaged for equivalent construction and use on the same premises; or

If an insured elects not to repair or replace the insured structure, this clause means that the insured will only be entitled to the actual cash value.[6]

§ 3.9(d) Obsolescence

The effect of obsolescence in determining the appropriate measure of recovery under a property insurance policy has often proved to be a perplexing problem. The opinion in McAnarney v. Newark Fire Insurance Co.[1] appears to be the first reported opinion that explicitly considered the question whether obsolescence should be a factor in determining "actual cash value."[2] In *McAnarney* the court decided obsolescence should be considered in such a determination, and this view has been applied in many subsequent decisions.[3]

A distinction may be observed between obsolescence and depreciation with respect to the method of calculation.[4] Depreciation is usually computed on some theoretical basis. Moreover, depreciation rules almost uniformly do not take into account obsolescence. Thus, when either "value" or "actual cash value" is determined by computing replacement cost less depreciation, that calculation typically makes no allowance for obsolescence.

Obsolescence is almost always appraised in terms of the market. However, the market place measure of obsolescence can prove to be an imprecise guide to value. For example, an item that is regarded as obsolete by some persons may be valued as an antique by others. Similarly, buildings that some persons have regarded as having reached the end of their useful life increasingly are being converted into viable merchandising and office centers by entrepreneurs with a different vision.

An interesting case study on obsolescence and valuation would be presented by a theatre building designed for the presentation of vaudeville shows. The structure, or at least a significant portion of the

---

(c) the amount actually and necessarily spent to repair or replace the damaged building."

6. Kolls v. Aetna Casualty & Surety Company, 503 F.2d 569 (8th Cir.1974); Huggins v. Hanover Insurance Company, 423 So.2d 147 (Ala.1982).

§ 3.9(d)

1. 247 N.Y. 176 at p. 185, 159 N.E. 902 at p. 905, 56 A.L.R. 1149 (1928).

2. See Note, *Valuation and Measure of Recovery Under Fire Insurance Policies,* 49 Columbia Law Review 818–836 at p. 824 (1949).

3. See, e.g., American States Insurance Co. v. Mo-Lex, Inc., 427 S.W.2d 236 (Ky. 1968); Doelger & Kirsten, Inc. v. National Union Fire Insurance Co. of Pittsburgh, Pa., 42 Wis.2d 518, 167 N.W.2d 198 (1969).

4. The reproduction-cost-less-depreciation rule of valuation could be viewed as suggesting, at least by implication, that a distinction could be drawn between obsolescence and depreciation with respect to "actual cash value" of an insured property. In most respects, the recognition of a distinction between depreciation and obsolescence in regard to the valuation of property for purposes of a recovery under an insurance policy seems untenable. Both factors obviously are relevant to the value of a property in virtually any sense in which that term is used. And both are surely relevant to market value, though ordinarily no separate calculation of either is made when market value is determined by evidence as to what a willing buyer would pay a willing seller for the property.

building, might be viewed as obsolete in the sense that it has excessive space backstage if it is used exclusively as a theater for motion pictures. If such a structure were destroyed by a fire, it could lead to disputes over how the loss should be calculated. The obsolescence of such a facility could be accounted for by deducting the unusable space, and estimating the current reproduction cost of a building equal in size to the usable space.[5] Obviously, this approach is defensible. However, it does not take into account the possibility that such a facility — including the under-utilized backstage space — may, on the one hand, prove to have great value if the building were either restored so that it could be used as a theatre for live performances or if the unused space were converted for other functions. On the other hand, the building's space may ultimately have proved to be so impractical that it would have warranted the razing of the structure.

§ 3.9(e)   Property Subject to a Condemnation Order, an Executory Demolition Contract, or a Right of Redemption

Property Subject to a Condemnation Order

The problem of valuing property that is the subject of condemnation proceedings when a loss occurs presents difficult questions that involve some considerations comparable to those which are relevant to valuing obsolete property.

So long as a condemnation order is not final, the condemnee [1] has a risk of loss from destruction of the property, and therefore it has been held that a condemnee may recover in full under a property insurance policy.[2] Similarly, in jurisdictions where a condemnee is allowed to

---

5. *Cf.* B.F. Keith Columbus Co. v. Board of Revision of Franklin County, 148 Ohio St. 253, 74 N.E.2d 359 (1947).

§ 3.9(e)

1. Assuming that the condemnee is the owner but for the effect of the condemnation proceeding.

2. See, e.g., Edlin v. Security Insurance Co., 269 F.2d 159 (7th Cir.1959), *cert. denied* 361 U.S. 932; 80 S.Ct. 370; 4 L.Ed.2d 354 (1960); Kingston v. Great Southwest Fire Insurance Co., 578 P.2d 1278 (Utah 1978); American National Bank & Trust Co. v. Reserve Insurance Co., 38 Ill.App.2d 315, 187 N.E.2d 343 (1st Dist.1962).

Cf. Redevelopment Agency of City & County of San Francisco v. Maxwell, 193 Cal.App.2d 414, 14 Cal.Rptr. 170 (1st Dist. 1961), 89 A.L.R.2d 1070 (1963); Heidisch v. Globe & Republic Insurance Co., 368 Pa. 602, 84 A.2d 566 (1951), 29 A.L.R.2d 884 (1953).

Also see Fenter v. General Accident Fire & Life Assur. Corp., 258 Or. 545, 484 P.2d 310 (1971) in which the court concluded that since the Oregon statutes provided that "any county court may at any time * * * sell and convey * * * to the record owner or his assigns, any property acquired by the county for delinquent taxes * * *.", the former owner had an insurable interest even though on the date the fire occurred the property had been foreclosed for nonpayment of taxes, and the statutory redemption period of one year had expired. The court concluded, "We think the pleadings disclose a possibly marketable interest of undisclosed value at the time of the fire * * * [and the claimant] should have an opportunity to prove what he stood to lose, and what loss he actually suffered, as a result of the fire." Id., 484 P.2d at p. 314.

But cf. Van Cure v. Hartford Fire Insurance Co., 435 Pa. 163, 253 A.2d 663 (1969), summarized in § 3.4(a)(5), note 26, above, and Western Pennsylvania National Bank v. American Insurance Company of Newark, N.J., 428 F.2d 1220 (3d Cir.1970) (decided on the basis of the *Van Cure* decision).

continue to use a condemned commercial property until an ejectment petition is fully processed, tenants have been held to have a sufficiently definite prospect of doing business so as to have an insurable interest under a business interruption coverage.[3]   The approach employed in such decisions might be reconciled with the approach set forth in the *McAnarney* decision (discussed in the preceding subsection) on the theory that as long as the condemnation proceeding may be abandoned, there is only a prospective obsolescence and not obsolescence in fact. However, if the insurance compensation for the condemnee is measured by the full extent of damage to the property, this approach can produce substantial overcompensation for the condemnee when that amount is combined with the condemnation payments from the condemnor.[4]

If a condemnation resolution is final and not subject to being rescinded, the value of a condemned structure is obviously minimal, and should be so treated when an insurance claim is made.[5]   On the other hand, if effecting certain repairs on such a property would cause the public authority to change the condemnation order, the situation is materially different.   Thus, although a condemnation resolution is obviously relevant in assessing the loss to the owner(s) when a property subject to that order is damaged or destroyed, it is certainly possible to envision situations where the structures could be appropriately assessed as having considerable value before the occurrence of the insured event.

Property Subject to an Executory Contract for Demolition

Several courts have confronted the problem of valuing a building that was subject to an executory contract for demolition, but was destroyed by a fire before the demolition could take place.   In considering the effect of such a contract on the value of a property, the Maine Supreme Court reasoned that the "particular circumstances might render a building utterly worthless by the time fire consumes it * * * if the process of demolition has been commenced, or if the owner has abandoned the building" but that if "the building has not been 'irrevocably committed to demolition or abandoned', the insured retains an insurable interest." [6]

---

3. Dileo v. United States Fidelity and Guaranty Co., 109 Ill.App.2d 28, 248 N.E.2d 669 (1st Dist.1969).

4. Many of these problems were presented by a case that involved the value of a fraternity house that had been declared by a city resolution to be a nuisance and had been ordered demolished. See Bailey v. Gulf Insurance Co., 406 F.2d 47 (10th Cir.1969) (applying Oklahoma law).

5. *Cf.* Chicago Title & Trust Co. v. United States Fidelity & Guaranty Co., 511 F.2d 241 (7th Cir.1975).

Also *cf.* Gendron v. Pawtucket Mutual Insurance Co., 384 A.2d 694 at p. 698 (Me.

1978), *appeal after remand* 409 A.2d 656 (Me.1979), in which the court found that the salvage value of a gasoline service station was valued at approximately $10,000 for materials that could be used to build another garage at a different location.

6. Gendron v. Pawtucket Mutual Insurance Co., 384 A.2d 694 (Me.1978).

Cf. Tublitz v. Glens Falls Insurance Co., 179 N.J.Super. 275, 431 A.2d 201 (Law Div. 1981).

Also see Garcy Corporation v. Home Insurance Co., 496 F.2d 479 (7th Cir.1974), *cert. denied* 419 U.S. 843, 95 S.Ct. 75, 42 L.Ed.2d 71 (1974), in which the court con-

Property Subject to a Right of Redemption

When property that has been subject to a foreclosure or is taken by the state or one of its entities (as for example, to satisfy some tax obligation or judgment), the owner often has a right of redemption. Although the public taking obviously substantially diminishes the value of the property to the owner, the right of redemption continues to provide the owner with an insurable interest.[7] If a fire destroys the property while the owner's right of redemption could still be exercised, it presents a difficult valuation question. If the right is exercised, the loss may be substantial. Thus, the insured's right to the insurance may turn on whether the right of redemption is exercised or would have been exercised but for the casualty to the insured property.

The cases discussed in this section indicate that in unusual situations, valuation should be approached with special care. There are, of course, presumptions underlying the approaches to valuation that should be carefully scrutinized to ensure that they are warranted in the particular circumstances.[8]

§ 3.9(f)   Use and Occupancy Losses

Property insurance policies, as commonly written and interpreted, do not provide coverage for the economic consequences occasioned by the loss of the use of the insured property — that is, property insurance usually provides indemnification only for damage that results directly from injury to the insured property. For example, the 1943 New York

cluded that the owner could recover the actual cash value of a seven-story building that the owner still hoped to sell even though a contract for the demolition of the building had been agreed to. At the time of the fire the building had not yet been stripped of the salvageable material (or otherwise prepared for demolition), and was being used as a warehouse for inventory and equipment. In reaching the decision in this case, the court reviewed and relied on a number of precedents involving condemnation proceedings.

7. See, e.g., Miller v. New Jersey Insurance Underwriting Association, 82 N.J. 594, 414 A.2d 1322 (1980), *on remand* 177 N.J.Super. 175, 427 A.2d 135 (1981).

8. A similar, but distinguishable, problem is presented when a leasehold is prematurely terminated because of fire damage and a court must determine the measure of recovery by a lessee who has purchased improvements and betterments coverage.

In Daeris, Inc. v. Hartford Fire Insurance Co., 105 N.H. 117, 193 A.2d 886 (1963) 97 A.L.R.2d 1238 (1964), a fire policy provided that the measure of damages was the proportion of the original cost of the improvements that the unexpired term of the lease bore to the period from the date of making the improvements to the date of expiration; the insurer resisted a claim under the policy because the lessor had exercised its option to terminate after the fire. The court's decision allowing the lessee to recover is defensible since the lessee probably would not have been deprived of the use of the improvements by premature termination of the lease but for the fire damage; that is, the loss to the lessee was the result of the risk insured against since the premature termination of the lease was a result of the fire damage.

Also see Vendriesco v. Aetna Casualty & Surety Co., 68 A.D.2d 946, 444 N.Y.S.2d 64 (3d Dept.1979), in which the court concluded that when the improvements were not repaired or replaced within a reasonable time after the loss, the lessee-insured's recovery should be limited to the unexpired "use and interest" in the betterments and improvements, and approved a formula based on the original cost for the improvements and the amount of time remaining on the lease.

Standard Fire Insurance Policy provides that the insurer "does insure [a blank space for the name for the insured] and legal representatives, to the extent of the actual cash value of the property at the time of loss, but not exceeding the amount which it would cost to repair * * *, nor in any event for more than the interest of the insured, against all direct loss by fire * * * to the property described hereinafter * * *." [1]

The economic consequences caused by the destruction of an insured property, especially a commercial structure, as a result of losing the use of the structure while the building is repaired or rebuilt may be much greater than the reconstruction costs. Insurance coverages developed to cover these risks are variously referred to as "use and occupancy," "loss of rents or profits," and "business interruption" insurance.[2] "Business interruption" or "loss of rents and profits" endorsements are commonly added to fire insurance policies on commercial buildings. Furthermore, a homeowner's comprehensive policy often includes coverage for living expenses, within specified limits, if the insured dwelling becomes "untenantable" because of one of the risks covered by the insurance policy.

§ 3.9(g) Relation to the Principle of Indemnity

The measure of recovery in property insurance does not always conform precisely to the principle of indemnity. In theory, as well as in practice, neither "actual cash value" nor "reproduction cost less depreciation" invariably produces a measure of recovery that accomplishes exact indemnity of an insured's loss. For example, either approach might produce more than indemnity for an insured who was about to accept an offer to sell at a price that was less than the insurance benefit when the fire occurred. Either measure also might produce less than indemnity for an old building that must be replaced by a new structure following an insured loss.

In some insurance policies coverage is provided for the cost of replacement or reproduction, and no reduction is made for depreciation.[1] This arrangement protects the insured against the risk of having to make a cash outlay beyond what the amount of the insurance proceeds would be if a deduction were made for depreciation. The insurance proceeds that are paid under such coverage are likely to provide an insured more than indemnity as measured by the standards usually applied to assess losses.[2] However, so long as the insurance

---

§ 3.9(f)

1. See Appendix A.

2. The development of such coverages has, as might be expected, created further variations of measure of recovery problems. In Washington Restaurant Corporation v. General Insurance Co., 64 Wn.2d 150, 390 P.2d 970 (1964), for example, the insured was allowed to recover under its business interruption policy even though its continuing expenses after fire damage were less than its operating loss before the fire.

§ 3.9(g)

1. See § 3.9(b), above.

2. See generally, Williams, *The Principle of Indemnity: A Critical Analysis*, 1960 Insurance Law Journal 471–480.

benefits are used to make the repairs or replacement, there—at most—is only a minimal deviation from the indemnity principle.

There are other situations in which the principle of indemnity may not be the only relevant consideration. For example, a valuation based on reproduction cost less depreciation or actual cash value does not take into account any special relationship that an insured bears to the property.[3] Individuals and insurers should remain free to create and employ insurance that provides coverage for such special interests in property.

Decisions that allow compensation for a building destroyed by fire or other casualty after its real value to the insured has been reduced by condemnation proceedings or a demolition order also present results that are sometimes questionable when considered in relation to the indemnity principle.[4]

§ 3.10   Subrogation

§ 3.10(a)   Subrogation Rights by Type of Insurance

(1) Introduction

Subrogation, which developed as an equitable doctrine, facilitates an adjustment of rights to avoid unjust enrichment in many types of situations by substituting one person or entity in place of another in regard to some claim or right the second person or entity has against a third party.[1] In the insurance context, when an insurer indemnifies an insured who is entitled to recover compensation for that loss from another source, in some situations the insurer may be subrogated to the insured's rights. This means the insurer is "substituted" for the insured in regard to either all or some portion of the rights that the insured has to receive compensation from another source. An insurer asserting a subrogation right is usually viewed as "standing in the shoes" of the insured so that the insurer's rights are equal to, but no greater than, those of the insured.[2]

---

3. On grounds of administrability, however, the *McAnarney* concept is nevertheless defensible on the basis that getting into the area of special value to the insured would substantially increase problems of proof. See discussion of *McAnarney* in § 3.9(c), above.

4. See § 3.9(c) and § 3.9(d), above.

§ 3.10(a)

1. See, e.g., Frost v. Porter Leasing Corp., 386 Mass. 425 at pp. 426–428, 436 N.E.2d 387 at pp. 388–391 (1982).

Cf. Liverpool & Great Western Steam Co. v. Phenix Insurance Co., 129 U.S. 397 at p. 462, 9 S.Ct. 469 at p. 479, 32 L.Ed. 788 (1889).

Also see M.L. Marasinghe, *An Historical Introduction to the Doctrine of Subrogation: The Early Story of the Doctrine,* 10 Valparaiso University Law Review 45–65, 275–299 (1976); 11 Appleman, INSURANCE LAW & PRACTICE (1981), § 6501, et seq.; 16 COUCH ON INSURANCE (Second edition, 1983), at § 61.

The doctrine has also been applied for the benefit of sureties who paid the debt of a principal. See H. McClintock, HANDBOOK OF THE PRINCIPLES OF EQUITY (Second edition, 1948), at § 123.

2. See generally, R. Horn, SUBROGATION IN INSURANCE THEORY AND PRACTICE (1964); Spencer L. Kimball and Dan A. Davis, *The*

An insurer's subrogation right may be expressly provided for by a clause that is included either in the applicable insurance policy or in a settlement agreement with an insured. This type of subrogation right is often referred to as "conventional subrogation,"[3] a term that apparently was derived from the fact that the insurer's subrogation interest is established by a convention (that is, an understanding, agreement or contract) of the parties. Furthermore, occasionally a right of subrogation for insurers in regard to a particular type of insurance will be specifically provided for in a state's insurance legislation.[4]

When there is no contractual provision or legislative act that explicitly sets forth a right of subrogation, an insurer may be entitled to seek subrogation on the basis of a judicially created right:[5] a right of subrogation which exists as a consequence of a judicial determination is often referred to as "legal subrogation" (even though such rights originally resulted from the actions of the equity courts).[6] In the absence of an express subrogation provision in an insurance policy, whether an insurer will be entitled to assert a right of subrogation is significantly influenced by the type of insurance coverage and the circumstances.

In considering whether a subrogation right should exist in the absence of an express provision in an insurance policy or a legislative provision, courts are usually concerned about whether an insured will receive compensation that provides more than full indemnification as a result of recoveries from the insurer and other sources.[7] Courts also tend to favor subrogation if it appears that a third party tortfeasor would be likely to escape financial responsibility if the insurer were not accorded a subrogation right. Thus, subrogation often is appropriately viewed as an important technique for serving the ends of justice by placing the economic responsibility for injuries on the party whose fault

---

Extension of Insurance Subrogation, 60 Michigan Law Review 841–872 (1962).

Also see Uriel Procaccia, *The Effect and Validity of Subrogation Clauses in Insurance Policies,* 1973 Insurance Law Journal 573–586.

3. See, e.g., George A. Hoagland & Co. v. Decker, 118 Neb. 194, 224 N.W. 14 (1929); Wyoming Building and Loan Association v. Mills Construction Co., 38 Wyo. 515, 269 P. 45 (1928).

4. This is particularly true in regard to uninsured motorist coverage. See, e.g., West's Ann. California Insurance Code § 11580.2(f); West's Ann. Indiana Code § 27–7–5–6 (1982); and Virginia Code Annotated, § 38.1(f) (1966).

Also see the discussion of the Trust Agreement provision included in uninsured motorist insurance policies in Widiss, UNINSURED AND UNDERINSURED MOTORIST INSURANCE (1987), at § 18.4 and § 19.1 through § 19.7.

5. Frost v. Porter Leasing Corporation, 386 Mass. 425, 436 N.E.2d 387 (1982); Home Owners' Loan Corp. v. Sears, Roebuck & Co., 123 Conn. 232, 193 A. 769 at p. 772 (1937).

See generally, 3 Appleman, INSURANCE LAW (1967), at § 1675.

Also see discussion in § 3.10(a)(2), below.

6. See 5 POMEROY, EQUITY JURISPRUDENCE (Second edition, 1918), at § 2348; Henry R. Sheldon, SUBROGATION (Second edition, 1893), at § 4.

7. See the rules for preventing net gains in § 3.6, above.

Also see Rixmann v. Somerset Public Schools, St. Croix County, 83 Wis.2d 571, 266 N.W.2d 326 (1978), in which the court discusses at some length the operation of subrogation and the collateral source rule in personal injury cases.

caused the loss without also allowing a recovery by the injured person from both an insurer and the tortfeasor that would violate the principle of indemnification.

Subrogation Against an Insured. In most situations, an insurer is not entitled to be subrogated to rights that may exist as a consequence of a liability claim against its own insured[8] — that is, there is no right of subrogation for an insurer against either one who is covered as a named insured in relation to the loss at issue, or any party who is covered as an additional insured in relation to that loss.[9] Thus, an insurer's subrogation interest usually is limited to rights an insured may have against third persons — that is, persons who are not parties to or beneficiaries of the insurance relationship that gives rise to the subrogation claim by an insurer.

Claims for Indemnification by an Insured versus Rights to Subrogation. Courts have often been presented with disputes in regard to the allocation of recoveries when an insurer asserts a subrogation right for reimbursement in a situation in which an injured party has not been fully indemnified. When an insured has not been completely compensated for the loss that gave rise to the insurer's payments, a court must

---

8. See, e.g., New York Board of Fire Underwriters v. Trans Urban Construction Co., Inc., 91 A.D.2d 115, 458 N.Y.S.2d 216 at p. 219 (1st Dept.1983), *affirmed* 60 N.Y.2d 912, 470 N.Y.S.2d 578, 458 N.E.2d 1255 (1983).

9. See, e.g., Westendorf by Westendorf v. Stasson, 330 N.W.2d 699 at p. 703 (Minn. 1983); New York Board of Fire Underwriters v. Trans Urban Construction Co. Inc., 91 A.D.2d 115, 458 N.Y.S.2d 216 (1st Dept. 1983), *affirmed* 60 N.Y.2d 912, 470 N.Y.S. 2d 578, 458 N.E.2d 1255 (1983).

There are many decisions holding that when an insurer has provided compensation to a general contractor, the insurer cannot then seek to recover from a subcontractor who is named either directly or indirectly (that is, in other documents or agreements) as an additional insured. See, e.g., Frank Briscoe Company, Inc. v. Georgia Sprinkler Company, Inc., 713 F.2d 1500 (11th Cir.1983) (applying Georgia law) (the declarations page of the insurance policy named the insureds as "Frank Briscoe Co., Inc. [the general contractor], and all sub and sub-contractors"); Harvey's Wagon Wheel, Inc. v. Macsween, 96 Nev. 215, 606 P.2d 1095 (1980); Baugh-Belarde Construction Company v. College Utilities Corp., 561 P.2d 1211 (Alaska 1977); Truck Insurance Exchange v. Transport Indemnity Company, 180 Mont. 419, 591 P.2d 188 (1979); Chrysler Leasing Corporation v. Public Adm'r, New York County, 85 A.D.2d 410, 448 N.Y.S.2d 181 (1982), and the cases cited therein.

Cf. Transamerica Insurance Company v. Gage Plumbing and Heating Company, 433 F.2d 1051 (10th Cir.1970); Cincinnati Insurance Company v. Vulcan, 587 F.Supp. 466 (N.D.Ala.1984).

But see, Turner Construction Company v. John B. Kelly Co., 442 F.Supp. 551 (E.D.Pa. 1976); Public Service Company of Oklahoma v. Black & Veatch, Consul. Eng., 328 F.Supp. 14 (N.D.Okl.1971).

Also see Note, *Conflicts Regarding the "No Subrogation Against Insured" Rule,* 29 Drake Law Review 811–831 (1980). The author points out that "there has been a minor trend away from this general rule in cases involving builder's risk insurance contracts." *Id.,* at p. 813.

See generally, Patterson, ESSENTIALS OF INSURANCE LAW (1957), at § 33. COUCH ON INSURANCE (Second edition, 1966), at § 61.61; Note, *Extension of the No Subrogation Against Insured Rule,* 56 Nebraska Law Review 765–782 (1977).

Also see the discussion of the possibility that a liability insurer might be entitled to seek reimbursement when it is required to provide compensation to the innocent victim who is injured as the result of an intentional tort by an insured in § 3.10(a) (3), below. *Cf.* Note, *Liability Insurance for Intentional Torts—Subrogation of the Insurer to the Victim's Rights Against the Insured: Ambassador Insurance Co. v. Montes,* 32 Rutgers Law Review 155–172 (1979).

decide how to apportion a recovery from another source such as a tortfeasor: specifically whether an insured who has received insurance benefits, but has not been fully indemnified, should be entitled to take "first" or "last" or proportionally from any sum recovered from another source of indemnification. The judicial approaches to this problem are discussed in Section 3.10(b), below.

Enforcement Issues. When an insurer seeks to enforce a subrogation right against a third party, there are a number of interesting problems which may arise, including the role of an insurer as a real party in interest and the remedies that may be asserted by an insurer in the event that a right of subrogation is lost or impaired by an insured. Several of these questions are discussed in Section 3.10(c), below.

Impediments to Subrogation. Some limitations on an insurer's right to subrogation have been recognized by the courts. Several of these limitations, also referred to as "impediments," are described in Section 3.10(d).

The discussion in the following subsections of Section 3.10(a) considers several specific subrogation rules and doctrines which have been developed by the courts in regard to different types of insurance, and some of the underlying societal objectives which have both influenced the doctrinal development and affected the way these rules are applied.

(2) Property Insurance

A property insurer is almost always entitled to assert a subrogation right in regard to any tort claims or contract claims its insured may have against other persons or entities. In this context, the principal rationale for subrogation is that it prevents violations of the principle of indemnification. Although property insurance policies commonly include a subrogation clause and property insurers often also require a formal assignment to the insurer of an insured's claims against others in connection with the payment of insurance benefits, the public interest in preventing recoveries that provide a property owner with compensation which exceed the value of the insured property is sufficiently compelling that courts will usually enforce a right of subrogation even when no specific provision is included either (1) in the applicable property insurance policy or (2) in an agreement made by the insured and the insurer in the course of settling a claim under a property insurance policy.[10] This public interest only applies when the combined recoveries under the insurance policy and from other sources would add up to an amount that exceeds the insured's loss. The

---

10. See, e.g., Skauge v. Mountain States Telegraph and Telephone Co., 172 Mont. 521, 565 P.2d 628 (1977); New York Board of Fire Underwriters v. Trans Urban Construction Co., Inc., 91 A.D.2d 115, 458 N.Y.S.2d 216 at p. 219 (First Department, 1983), *affirmed* 60 N.Y.2d 912, 470 N.Y.S.2d 578, 458 N.E.2d 1255; Pelzer Manufacturing Co. v. Sun Fire Office of London, 36 S.C. 213 at p. 267, 15 S.E. 562 at p. 582 (1892); 6 APPLEMAN, INSURANCE LAW (1942), § 4052, note 46.

Concerning subrogation to contract claims, see § 4.2(d), note 8, below.

principle of indemnity is not violated when there is underinsurance and the value of other rights of recovery does not exceed the difference between the loss and the partial insurance coverage.

An insurer conceivably could either waive or limit all or part of its subrogation rights by an express provision in a property insurance policy.[11] However, "waiver," since it entails the intentional and voluntary relinquishment of a known right, generally will not result from the omission of a subrogation provision in a property insurance policy. Moreover, a waiver of an insurer's subrogation rights will not result even when the omission of such a clause is followed by the insurer's paying an insurance claim without requiring an assignment of any right the insured may have against a person or persons who may be liable.[12] Although the proposition that a property insurer is entitled to a right of subrogation — even in the absence of an express contract provision — is almost uniformly recognized, litigation about whether a subrogation right exists in regard to property insurance has involved claims that a specific subrogation provision in an insurance policy either is too narrow to include or is ambiguous with respect to the right in issue.[13]

(3) Liability Insurance

Liability insurance policies commonly include a subrogation provision, and validity of such clauses usually is not questioned.[14] Moreover, there is support among the judicial precedents for the recognition of a

11. See, e.g., Aetna Insurance Co. v. United Fruit Co., 92 F.2d 576 (2d Cir.1937), affirmed 304 U.S. 430, 58 S.Ct. 959, 82 L.Ed. 1443 (1938); Skauge v. Mountain States Telephone and Telegraph Co., 172 Mont. 521, 565 P.2d 628 at p. 630 (1977).

Also see Fire Association of Philadelphia v. Schellenger, 84 N.J.Eq. 464, 94 A. 615 (1915).

A bar to recovery, not truly a "waiver", may sometimes arise by other means. See, e.g., Powers v. Calvert Fire Insurance Co., 216 S.C. 309, 57 S.E.2d 638 (1950), 16 A.L.R.2d 1261 (1951); Leonard v. Bottomley, 210 Wis. 411, 245 N.W. 849 (1932).

Also consider the discussion in § 3.10(b), below, and § 6.1, below.

12. See, e.g., Hartford Accident & Indemnity Co. v. Chung, 37 Conn.Sup. 587, 429 A.2d 158 (Appellate Session 1981).

But cf. Lumbermens Mutual Casualty Co. v. Foremost Insurance Co., 425 So.2d 1158 (Fla.App., 3d Dist., 1983).

13. See, e.g., Travelers Indemnity Co. v. United States, 543 F.2d 71 (9th Cir.1976); Home Insurance Co. v. Bishop, 140 Me. 72, 34 A.2d 22 (1943).

Also see Note, Conflicts Regarding the "No Subrogation Against Insured" Rule, 29 Drake Law Review 811–831 (1980).

14. See, e.g., Aetna Casualty & Surety Co. v. Porter, 181 F.Supp. 81 (D.D.C.1960) (liability insurer subrogated to indemnity claim of insured against joint tortfeasor who was primarily liable for the tort); Zeglen v. Minkiewicz, 12 N.Y.2d 497, 240 N.Y.S.2d 965, 191 N.E.2d 450 (1963) (subrogated insurer of tortfeasor on behalf of whom high limits, $50,000, of liability policy were paid out allowed contribution from another tortfeasor, also an insured of the same company under a policy with lower limits, $10,000, with the result that the second tortfeasor-insured was personally liable to the insurer for $20,000).

Also see Aetna Casualty & Surety Co. v. Buckeye Union Casualty Co., 157 Ohio St. 385, 105 N.E.2d 568 (1952), 31 A.L.R.2d 1317 (1953) (driver's own liability insurer, which had provided coverage under a temporary substitute vehicle clause, subrogated to driver's claim as an additional insured for primary coverage under car owner's liability policy).

But see Aetna Insurance Co. v. Gilchrist Brothers, Inc., 85 N.J. 550, 428 A.2d 1254 (1981).

broad subrogation right in regard to liability insurance that may even go beyond the scope of the rights provided for by the typical subrogation terms included in liability insurance policies.[15] For example, an attorney's malpractice insurer, having reached a settlement with claimants who had purchased a property and were injured as a result of a lawyer's negligent title examination, was allowed to assert a subrogation claim against the sellers of the property for breach of a warranty provision contained in the real estate conveyance. The Oklahoma Supreme Court concluded that the subrogation right existed by operation of law under the circumstances, because "as between the two parties * * * natural justice places the burden of bearing the loss where it ought to be, on the sellers, who breached the warranty and were unjustly enriched." [16] Nevertheless, disputes about the scope of a liability insurer's subrogation rights have occasionally produced litigation involving whether the proposition that an insurer may not be subrogated to a claim against its own insured means that claims may not be asserted against individuals who are in some way related to the insured.[17]

(4) Uninsured Motorist Insurance

The uninsured motorist insurance policy provisions include a section, often titled a "Trust Agreement," which provides that in the event a payment is made to any person under the uninsured motorist insurance "the company shall be entitled to the extent of such payment to the proceeds of any settlement or judgment that may result from the exercise of any rights of recovery of such person against any person or organization legally responsible for the bodily injury because of which such payment is made." [18] This provision purports both to entitle the insurer to reimbursement from any sum an insured may secure from *anyone* who is legally responsible for the accident,[19] and to entitle the insurer to be reimbursed by any recovery from a third party until the

15. See, e.g., Hartford Accident & Indemnity Co. v. Pacific Indemnity Co., 249 Cal.App.2d 432, 57 Cal.Rptr. 492 (2d Dist. 1967) (subrogation to effect sharing of malpractice insurers in costs of defense).

16. Lawyers' Title Guaranty Fund v. Sanders, 571 P.2d 454 at p. 456 (Okl.1977).

17. See, e.g., Turner Construction Company v. John B. Kelly Company, 442 F.Supp. 551 (E.D.Pa.1976) (although subcontractor was an insured for purposes of protecting its property interests, nothing relieved the subcontractor for its negligence in causing damage to property owned by the general contractor and therefore the general contractor's insurance carrier could proceed against subcontractor as subrogee of the general contractor); PPG Industries, Inc. v. Continental Heller Corporation, 124 Ariz. 216, 603 P.2d 108 (1st

Div., Dept. A., 1979) (insurance company is entitled to be subrogated to rights of its insured, a contractor, when a subcontractor broke an agreement to procure insurance for the benefit of the contractor and the contractor had taken the precaution of obtaining excess coverage with an insurer that had paid a settlement reached with an injured worker).

18. For example see the 1966 Standard Form, Part V: Additional Terms, G. Trust Agreement set out in Appendix H.

Also see the other forms for the uninsured motorist coverage set out in that Appendix.

19. See the discussion of the Trust Agreement in Widiss, UNINSURED AND UNDERINSURED MOTORIST Insurance (1987), in Chapter 19.

company has been fully repaid (including payment for all costs incurred in connection with securing the recovery).

The enforceability of provisions in the uninsured motorist insurance that set forth the insurer's claim to a priority in regard to a recovery from other sources has been considered in a number of judicial opinions. Some courts have concluded that this type of provision is an enforceable subrogation right.[20] Courts have also decided that it is permissible for an insurer to establish this right as a Trust Agreement, and that the insurer's priority in regard to any recovery will be upheld, without reaching any determination in regard to whether this provision does create a "subrogation" right.[21] However, courts in many states have invalidated this provision on the ground that it violates the state's public policy which precludes the reduction of an insurer's liability in instances when the insured has not been fully indemnified.[22] These decisions are grounded on a public policy similar, if not identical, to that controlling other multiple coverage situations in which the courts have favored indemnification over a literal application of provisions in the uninsured motorist insurance policies.[23] In essence, these courts hold that the state's uninsured motorist insurance legislation should be construed to mean that an uninsured motorist coverage insurer should

20. See, e.g., Senn v. J.S. Weeks & Co., 255 S.C. 585, 180 S.E.2d 336 (1971); Glidden v. Farmers Automobile Insurance Association, 11 Ill.App.3d 81, 296 N.E.2d 84 (2d Dist.1973); Kroeker v. State Farm Mutual Automobile Insurance Co., 466 S.W.2d 105 (Mo.App., Kansas City, 1971).

In several states, including California, the insurer's right of subrogation is provided for in the uninsured motorist statute.

Also see Kirkley v. State Farm Mutual Insurance Co., 17 Cal.App.3d 1078, 95 Cal. Rptr. 427 (4th Dist.1971).

Some state courts have concluded that the Trust Agreement creates a right of subrogation and that subrogation of an insurer to a claim for personal injuries is not permitted. See, e.g., Berlinski v. Ovellette, 164 Conn. 482, 325 A.2d 239 (1973); Gallego v. Strickland, 121 Ariz. 160, 589 P.2d 34 (App.Div. 2, 1978). These decisions are in accord with a common law rule that causes of action for personal injuries were not assignable. See RESTATEMENT OF CONTRACTS (1932), at § 547; Annotation, *Assignability of claim for personal injury or death*, 40 A.L.R.2d 500–519 at p. 562 (1955).

21. See, e.g., Cotton States Mutual Insurance Co. v. Torrance, 110 Ga.App. 4, 137 S.E.2d 551 (1964), *affirmed* 220 Ga. 639, 140 S.E.2d 840 (1965).

Cf. State ex rel. Manchester Insurance & Indemnity Co. v. Moss, 522 S.W.2d 772 at p. 775 (Mo.1975).

22. See, e.g., Perez v. Ford Motor Co., 408 F.Supp. 318 (E.D.La.1975), *affirmed* 527 F.2d 1391 (5th Cir.1976); Milbank Mutual Insurance Co. v. Kluver, 302 Minn. 310, 225 N.W.2d 230 (1974); Shamey v. State Farm Mutual Automobile Insurance Co., 229 Pa.Super. 215, 331 A.2d 498 (1974).

In Berlinski v. Ovelette, 164 Conn. 482, 325 A.2d 239 (1973), the Connecticut Supreme Court held that the trust agreement was an assignment of a personal injury claim that violated the state's public policy against such transfers. [See Rice v. Stone, 83 Mass. (1 Allen) 566 (1861) for an early judicial opinion on the public interest against the assignment of personal injury claims.] Other courts have also employed this justification for reaching similar conclusions about the effect of the Trust Agreement in the uninsured motorist coverage. Also see the discussion in Wesley W. Horton, *Subrogation Suits after Berlinski*, 1973 Insurance Law Journal 516–527.

Also see discussion in Widiss, UNINSURED AND UNDERINSURED MOTORIST INSURANCE (1987), at Chapter 19.

23. See generally, Alan I. Widiss, *Aggregating Uninsured Motorist Coverage: Judicial Construction of "Pyramids" to Provide Indemnification*, 15 Connecticut Law Review 565–616 (1983).

be entitled to be subrogated only when it will avoid a duplicative recovery by an insured.[24]

(5) Casualty Insurance

Casualty insurers are often accorded subrogation rights by the courts in the absence of express contract provisions.[25] However, recognition of subrogation rights (in the absence of a contract provision) is not a universal practice for all forms of casualty insurance. This point is well illustrated by considering the extent to which a casualty insurer will be subrogated to its insured's claims against a third party for losses due to check forgeries. In this context, subrogation is often limited and may depend upon (1) the nature of the third party (that is, whether that party is the original wrongdoer (such as the forger) or an "innocent" intermediary such as the bank upon which the forged check was drawn), (2) the specific type of insurance under which the loss is covered, and (3) the allocation-of-loss rules of negotiable instruments law.[26] If the insured is a drawee-bank (that is, the bank upon which the forged check was drawn) with coverage under a forgery bond, the insurer is generally subrogated to the bank's claim against the "innocent" party who had cashed the check for the forger.[27] But, if the insured is an employer with coverage against forgery by an employee under a general fidelity bond, the insurer is generally not allowed to be subrogated to the employer's claim against an "innocent" intermediary such as the drawee-bank.[28] In either case, if the insurer is only

24. See, e.g., Milbank Mutual Insurance Co. v. Kluver, 302 Minn. 310, 225 N.W.2d 230 at p. 233 (1974).

25. First National Bank of Columbus v. Hansen, 84 Wis.2d 422, 267 N.W.2d 367 (1978) (fidelity insurer that pays loss caused by the wrongful acts of a bonded employee is subrogated to any right of action that the employer may have against the defaulting employee or against third persons).

Also *cf.* Daniel Mungall, Jr., *The Buffeting of the Subrogation Rights of the Construction Contract Bond Surety by United States v. Munsey,* 46 Insurance Counsel Journal 607–628 (1979).

26. See generally, E. Allen Farnsworth, *Insurance Against Check Forgery,* 60 Columbia Law 284–325 (1960).

27. See, e.g., Borserine v. Maryland Casualty Co., 112 F.2d 409 (8th Cir.1940) (applying Missouri law); First & Tri State National Bank & Trust Co. of Fort Wayne v. Massachusetts Bonding & Insurance Co., 102 Ind.App. 361, 200 N.E. 449 (1936); Metropolitan Casualty Insurance Co. v. First National Bank in Detroit, 261 Mich. 450, 246 N.W. 178 (1933).

Also see E. Allen Farnsworth, *Insurance Against Check Forgery,* 60 Columbia Law Review at pp. 319–320.

28. See, e.g., American Surety Co. v. Bank of California, 133 F.2d 160 (9th Cir. 1943) (applying Oregon law); Oxford Prod. Credit Association v. Bank of Oxford, 196 Miss. 50, 16 So.2d 384 (1944); Meyers v. Bank of American National Trust & Savings Association, 11 Cal.2d 92, 77 P.2d 1084 (1938).

Also see Baker v. American Surety Co., 181 Iowa 634, 159 N.W. 1044 (1916).

The rule discussed in the text is subject to considerable criticism. See E. Allen Farnsworth, *Insurance Against Check Forgery,* 60 Columbia Law Review at pp. 316–319. Professor Farnsworth concludes that "as opportunities to spread the risk of forgery increase, and as more states adopt the *Uniform Commercial Code* [which changes much of the former negotiable instruments law underlying the denial-of-subrogation rule], the popularity of the rule * * * can be expected to wane." *Id.,* at p. 325.

subrogated to a claim against a forger, subrogation is generally of little value.[29]

(6) Life and Accident Insurance

Life insurance and accident insurance policies usually have not included subrogation clauses, and courts rarely, if ever, have imposed an implied subrogation right in regard to claims that might exist in connection with events that produced losses that were compensated by such coverages. Thus, for example, ordinarily a life insurer would not have any subrogation right in regard to a legal action for wrongful death. Furthermore, accident insurance policies have usually been treated in the same manner as life insurance contracts,[30] and accordingly it is not suprising that in the absence of subrogation provisions in either life insurance or accident insurance contracts,[31] legal disputes regarding the right of an insurer to be subrogated seldom arise.

There are some basic differences between property insurance, on the one hand, and life and accident insurance on the other, that provide support for the contrasting rules with respect to the subrogation rights in relation to such insurance contracts. Although recognition of these differences does not make an overwhelming case for the distinction that has developed, they at least help to explain why courts generally have not recognized a subrogation right on behalf of a life or accident insurer in the absence of an express provision, and also why courts have been reluctant to adopt expansive interpretations when a subrogation provision is included in a life or accident insurance policy. Three differences, in particular, should be noted.

First, the amount of economic damage is not as readily evaluated in regard to the loss of a life or an accidental injury to a person as it is in property losses. Placing a monetary value on a person's life, the loss of a limb, or a personal injury is, at best, far more of an approximation than determining the market value or replacement cost of a building.

Second, life and accident insurance policies are seldom in amounts that are sufficient to provide full indemnity; property insurance often does so.

Third, many types of life insurance are appropriately viewed as an "investment" as well as an "indemnity" contract.[32] When an insurance arrangement involves an investment component, courts have been inclined to minimize the importance of the indemnity principle. However, although policies such as whole life insurance have an investment feature,[33] the existence of that feature is not inconsistent with the

29. See E. Allen Farnsworth, *Insurance Against Check Forgery*, 60 Columbia Law Review at p. 299, note 71, for "salvage" figures on forgery bonds and fidelity insurance.

30. Also see the discussion of insurance policies as contracts of indemnity in § 3.1(e).

31. See, e.g., Connecticut Mutual Life Insurance Co. v. New York & N.H.R.R., 25 Conn. 265 (1856).

32. See § 1.5(c)(1), above.

33. See the description of whole life insurance policies in § 1.5(c)(1), above.

conclusion that the insurance contract is still one of indemnity as well as investment. Accordingly, the statement that life insurance is an investment does not in and of itself provide a reason for a denial of subrogation.

Insurers have begun to include subrogation provisions in some types of life and accident policies. For example, in a case which involved a life insurance policy that specifically provided the insurer was subrogated to the "insured's right of recovery for loss", an Illinois court of appeal concluded that subrogation by an insurance company against the proceeds of a wrongful death action is contrary to public policy and that subrogation could not be equitably applied because the amount recovered by the widow may be "much less than the actual loss sustained by her." [34]

In most circumstances, there is little reason to question the resolution of issues involving subrogation rights in life and accident insurance policies generally.[35] However, a persuasive case for allowing an insurer to be subrogated exists in a situation in which it is possible to specifically quantify the economic loss sustained by a beneficiary, as, for example, when a life insurance coverage is used in a business context.[36]

(7) Medical and Health Insurance

Medical and hospitalization insurers have generally been denied subrogation rights in the absence of an express provision in the insurance contract.[37] The practices of insurers in regard to the inclusion of subrogation clauses in various types of medical and hospitalization insurance have varied. For example, until 1958 the subrogation clauses that were included in the standard forms for automobile insurance specifically were not applicable to medical payments coverages included in the automobile insurance package. However, some insurers used nonstandard forms that contained subrogation clauses which applied when payments were made under the medical payments coverages.[38] Since 1958, several of the standard forms for automobile and

34. Matter of Schmidt's Estate, 79 Ill. App.3d 456, 34 Ill.Dec. 766, 398 N.E.2d 589 at p. 591 (2d Dist.1979).

Also see National Bank of Bloomington v. Podgorski, 57 Ill.App.3d 265, 14 Ill.Dec. 951, 373 N.E.2d 82 (4th Dist.1978) (an insurer who paid a widow survivor's benefits under an automobile policy was precluded from asserting subrogation rights to a wrongful death award).

35. See George Steven Swan, *Subrogation in Life Insurance: Now is the Time*, 48 Insurance Counsel Journal 634–638 (1981); R. Horn, SUBROGATION IN INSURANCE THEORY AND PRACTICE (1964), at pp. 27–37.

Also see the discussion of Medical and Health Insurance in § 3.10(a)(7), below.

36. See the discussion of an insurable interest in another's life in nonfamily rela-

tionships in § 3.5(c)(3), above. Also see § 3.3(b)(1), above.

37. See, e.g., Frost v. Porter Leasing Corp., 386 Mass. 425, 436 N.E.2d 387 (1982) (group health plan paid for by employer); Rixmann v. Somerset Public Schools, St. Croix County, 83 Wis.2d 571, 266 N.W.2d 326 (1978).

Also see Michigan Hospital Services v. Sharpe, 339 Mich. 357, 63 N.W.2d 638 (1954), 43 A.L.R.2d 1167 (1955) (hospitalization insurance); Hack v. Great American Insurance Co., 175 So.2d 594 (Fla.App. 1965) (medical payments insurance).

Cf. Note, *Insurance Subrogation in Personal Injury Torts*, 39 Ohio State Law Journal 621–638 (1978).

38. See, e.g., Smith v. Motor Club of America Insurance Co., 54 N.J.Super. 37,

motor vehicle insurance have provided for subrogation under medical payments coverages. And, more recently other types of medical, surgical, and hospitalization insurance have included provisions for subrogation. Especially since the advent of no-fault automobile insurance, there has been a movement to include subrogation provisions in such insurance policies or plans, including the coverages provided by the Blue Cross and Blue Shield insurance companies.[39]

At least three distinct judicial views have been developed in the cases that have considered the enforceability of subrogation clauses in medical and health insurance coverages. First, many courts have sustained the enforceability of subrogation clauses.[40] Second, courts in

148 A.2d 37 (1959), *affirmed* 56 N.J.Super. 203, 152 A.2d 369 (1959).

39. See, e.g., Associated Hospital Services, Inc. v. Milwaukee Automobile Mutual Insurance Co., 33 Wis.2d 170, 147 N.W.2d 225 (1967) (action by Blue Cross against tortfeasor's liability insurer; judgment for Blue Cross affirmed). Compare cases sustaining a clause excluding coverage of injuries for which a third person is legally liable unless insured is unable to recover from that person: Smith v. Idaho Hospital Services, Inc., 89 Idaho 499, 406 P.2d 696 (1965).

Also see Michigan Medical Services v. Sharpe, 339 Mich. 574, 64 N.W.2d 713 (1954) (action allowed against subscribers but not against tortfeasor); Barmeier v. Oregon Physicians' Services, 194 Or. 659, 243 P.2d 1053 (1952).

See also Spencer L. Kimball & Don A. Davis, *The Extension of Insurance Subrogation*, 60 Michigan Law Review 841–872 at pp. 860–862 (1962). The authors point out that some hospital and insurance plans began including subrogation provisions in the 1950's.

A clause providing for subrogation generally, however, may not apply to some of the insured's claims against others. See, e.g., Morin v. Massachusetts Blue Cross, Inc., 365 Mass. 379, 311 N.E.2d 914 (1974) (Blue Cross-Blue Shield not subrogated to claim under motor vehicle medical payments coverage).

40. Many of the cases have involved subrogation provisions in medical payment coverage included in motor vehicle policies. See, e.g., Smith v. Travelers Insurance Co., 50 Ohio St.2d 43, 4 Ohio Op.3d 114, 362 N.E.2d 264 (1977), discussed in Note, *Medical Payments Subrogation Agreements: Valid Provisions in Indemnity Insurance Policies* in 7 Capitol University Law Review 255–270 (1977); Travelers Indemnity Co. v. Vaccari, 310 Minn. 97, 245 N.W.2d 844 (1976); Sentry Insurance Co. v. Stuart,

246 Ark. 680, 439 S.W.2d 797 (1969) (insurer, having paid $1,000 under medical payments coverage, sued insured and third parties with whom insured settled tort claim; trial court's action in sustaining demurrer reversed); State Farm Mutual Insurance Co. v. Farmers Insurance Exchange, 22 Utah 2d 183, 450 P.2d 458 (1969).

Motto v. State Farm Mutual Automobile Insurance Co., 81 N.M. 35, 462 P.2d 620 (1969) (suit by insured under medical payments coverage after insured had settled with tortfeasor; held, violation of subrogation rights is a defense); Geertz v. State Farm Fire & Casualty, 253 Or. 307, 451 P.2d 860 (1969) (suit by insured under automobile insurance medical payments coverage after insured had settled with tortfeasor; held, violation of subrogation rights is a defense); State Farm Mutual Insurance Co. v. Farmers Insurance Exchange, 22 Utah 2d 183, 450 P.2d 458 (1969) (summary judgment holding subrogation clause valid; affirmed); Travelers Indemnity Co. v. Rader, 152 W.Va. 699, 166 S.E.2d 157 (1969) (declaratory judgment of validity of subrogation clause).

Also see Decespedes v. Prudence Mutual Casualty Co. of Chicago, Ill., 193 So.2d 224 (Fla.App.3d, Dist., 1966), *affirmed* 202 So. 2d 561 (Fla.1967) (suit by insured under medical payments coverage after insured had settled with tortfeasor; held, violation of subrogation rights is a defense); National Union Fire Insurance Co. v. Grimes, 278 Minn. 45, 153 N.W.2d 152 (1967) (insurer paid insured $970.20 under medical payments coverage; thereafter insured settled with tortfeasor, Stanke; insurer sued insured only for $970.20; declining to pass on issues of assignability since this action was against insured for a share of proceeds of settlement, held, insurer entitled to recover, subject to an offset to the extent of "the reasonable worth and value of the efforts expended and expenses incurred by defendant properly chargeable to that por-

several states have declared such clauses to be unenforceable, usually on the theory that they violate rules against the assignability of causes of action for injury to a person.[41] A few courts have adopted a third position.[42] These courts hold that a traditionally phrased subrogation clause is enforceable against both the insured and a third party tortfeasor, but that a subrogation clause phrased so as to grant rights in the proceeds of any settlement or judgment (a phrasing designed to circumvent the rule against assignments of personal injury claims [43]) is enforceable only as a claim to the proceeds and not as a claim against the tortfeasor for violation of the subrogee's rights by settling with the insured after notice of those rights.[44]

In relation to subrogation, medical and hospitalization coverages occupy something of a middle ground between property insurance, on

tion of the recovery from Stanke attributable to these medical expenses"); Spirek v. State Farm Mutual Automobile Insurance Co., 65 Ill.App.3d 440, 21 Ill.Dec. 817, 382 N.E.2d 111 (1st Dist., 1st Div., 1978).

Kimball & Davis, *The Extension of Insurance Subrogation,* 60 Michigan Law Review 841 at pp. 858 and pp. 866–868 (1962) [hereinafter cited as Kimball & Davis], persuasively distinguishing between subrogation, whether legal or conventional, and assignment.

Also consider the cases collected in Appendix A of Rex Capwell and Thomas E. Greenwald, *Legal and Practical Problems Arising from Subrogation Clauses in Health and Accident Policies,* 22 Federation of Insurance Counsel Journal 23–66 at pp. 65–67 (1972). The authors conclude that "without question the majority of the jurisdictions ＊ ＊ ＊ have held such a clause is valid." *Id.,* at pp. 32–33.

41. See, e.g., State Farm Fire and Casualty Co. v. Knapp, 107 Ariz. 184, 484 P.2d 180 (1971); Peller v. Liberty Mutual Fire Insurance Co., 220 Cal.App.2d 610, 34 Cal. Rptr. 41 (4th Dist.1963) (medical payments subrogation clause was void because contrary to common law and legislative prohibition against assignment of causes of action for personal injury); Travelers Indemnity Co. v. Chumbley, 394 S.W.2d 418 (Mo.App., Springfield, 1965), 19 A.L.R.3d 1043 (1968) (denying subrogation right of medical payments insurer because of prohibition against assignment of cause of action for personal injury).

Even in a jurisdiction denying subrogation for medical loss because of prohibitions against the assignment of a cause of action for personal injury, however, a "trust receipt" or "loan receipt" giving the insurer a share in any *recovery* obtained by the insured may be found valid. E.g.,

Block v. California Physicians' Services, 244 Cal.App.2d 266, 53 Cal.Rptr. 51 (2d Dist.1966) (medical services coverage).

Cf. see Rixmann v. Somerset Public Schools, St. Croix County, 83 Wis.2d 571, 266 N.W.2d 326 (1978), discussed in Note, *Insurance—Subrogation—Accident and Health Insurance Policy Still Characterized as "Investment" Contract,* 62 Marquette Law Review 306–312 (1978).

Also see A. Corbin, Corbin on Contracts (1958), at § 857; Annotation, *Assignability of claim for personal injury or death,* 40 A.L.R.2d 500–519 (1955).

42. Also see § 3.10(c), below.

43. See Note, *Uninsured Motorist Coverage,* Cleveland Marshall Law Review 66–84 at pp. 69–73 (1963); Annotation, *Assignability of claim for personal injury or death,* 40 A.L.R.2d 500–519 (1955).

44. State Farm Mutual Automobile Insurance Co. v. Pohl, 255 Or. 46, 464 P.2d 321 (1970). It may be suggested that the distinction drawn in this case is also supported by decisions that, in a context that might be regarded as a converse of the problem considered here, recognize the validity of a "loan receipt" type of transaction even in a jurisdiction that strikes down a traditionally phrased subrogation clause as an invalid attempt to assign a claim for personal injury. Just as the "loan receipt" sometimes proves to be an effective way around the rule against assignability, might the insurer get around the rule of Pohl by suing the third party tortfeasor, or that person's liability insurer, or both, on the theory that they knowingly participated in an arrangement under which the insured intended to break the insured's contract with the insurer by declining to pay to the insurer its share of the proceeds of the settlement?

the one hand, and life and accident insurance, on the other. Medical and hospitalization policies often provide benefits that are close to, and in some instances equal to, full indemnification for medical expenses. In this respect, these coverages are similar to property insurance. The payments provided by life or accident insurance — typically a predetermined fixed amount either for death (in the case of life insurance) or for specified types of injuries and disabilities (in the case of accident insurance) — in general do not represent total indemnification for the loss sustained by the recipients of such insurance.

Recognition and enforcement of a right of subrogation for health insurers is primarily premised on precluding duplicative recoveries.[45] There is, of course, an indemnity character to medical and hospital insurance — that is, the medical and hospital expenses that result from an accident are specifically reflected in the bills rendered for such services. However, when the consequences of an accident are viewed as a whole, the isolation of such expenses from the other losses sustained — such as an insured person's pain, suffering, physical impairments, or diminished earning capacity — can be viewed as rather artificial.[46] It seems evident that a cogent argument can be made that the indemnification of medical expenses should not be evaluated without reference to whether an injured person has been fully compensated for the other losses that were sustained as a consequence of the insured event. Moreover, this approach is certainly in accord with the expectations held by many persons that recovery under several medical or health insurance policies is possible, expectations which are fostered by the massive television advertising campaigns employed by some insurers who sell these coverages.

Express subrogation provisions in medical and hospitalization policies have sometimes been held to be invalid because of statutory or common law prohibitions against the assignment of causes of action for personal injuries.[47] Moreover, even when the clauses are enforceable, courts usually have been inclined to limit the scope of subrogation rights conferred by express provisions in various forms of health insurance.[48]

In general, judicial decisions have only rarely sustained an insurer's denial of liability under medical payments coverage on the rationale of avoiding a double recovery, and most of these few decisions

---

45. Also see Group Hospital Services, Inc. v. State Farm Insurance Co., 517 S.W.2d 897 (Tex.Civ.App., Eastland, 1974).

See generally, Uriel Procaccia, *Denying Subrogation in Personal Injury Claims: A Needed Change of Direction,* 15 William and Mary Law Review 93–116 (1973).

46. *Cf.* Frost v. Porter Leasing Corp., 386 Mass. 425, 436 N.E.2d 387 at p. 390 (1982).

47. See the decisions cited in note 41, above.

48. *Cf.* Morin v. Massachusetts Blue Cross, Inc., 365 Mass. 379, 311 N.E.2d 914 (1974).

Also see Westendorf by Westendorf v. Stasson, 330 N.W.2d 699 (Minn.1983) (Health Maintenance Organization's reimbursement clause applies only to payments specifically collected by the enrollee for those medical expenses and does not apply unless the enrollee has had a full recovery).

involve specific coverage limitations in the applicable insurance policy.[49]

(8) Workers' Compensation Insurance

Professor Vance observed over a half century ago that there was a split of judicial authority as to whether a workers' compensation insurer, in the absence of an explicit statutory provision, is subrogated to an employee's rights against a third party tortfeasor. Upon assessing these decisions, Professor Vance argued that the jurisdictions which denied subrogation rights were misled by a false analogy to cases involving life and accident insurance: [50]

> "[T]he primary reason for refusing subrogation to the life or accident insurer is that the insurer's liability is fixed by his contract, and not by the principle of indemnity to the insured. But the [workers' compensation] insurance carrier recovers from the tort-feasor, not on the basis of subrogation strictly speaking, but directly on the ground that it has been injured by the negligence of the tort-feasor. The loss suffered by the insurance carrier, being fixed by the terms of a public statute, was clearly foreseeable by the tort-feasor, and therefore may properly be regarded as a proximate consequence of such negligence." [51]

Professor Vance's observation of a contrast between life insurance and workers' compensation insurance with respect to judicial recognition of insurer's rights of recoupment from tortfeasors is well supported because a right of recoupment is hardly ever applied to life insurance.[52] Recoupment is often provided for workers' compensation statutes and insurance contracts.[53]

---

49. In Gunter v. Lord, 242 La. 943, 140 So.2d 11 (1962), for example, it was held that a passenger in the insured's car could not recover twice for the same loss, once under the medical payments coverage of the insured's policy and once under the liability coverage of the same policy, because it was not the intention of the insured and insurer that double recovery under the two provisions be allowed.

Accord. Yarrington v. Thornburg, 58 Del. (8 Storey) 152, 205 A.2d 1, 11 A.L.R.3d 1110 (1964).

But cf. Blocker v. Sterling, 251 Md. 55, 246 A.2d 226 (1968) ("we find nothing in the policy implicitly suggesting an intent that medical expense payments were not to be in addition to liability payments"). When two or more policies are involved, however, double recovery, even from the same insurer, has been allowed, the rationale being that a different result would allow the third-party tortfeasor to benefit from the contributions of another and that the identity of the insurer is irrelevant. E.g., Sonnier v. State Farm Mutual Auto-

mobile Insurance Co., 179 So.2d 467 (La. App.1965). This, of course, is a restatement of the collateral source rule of tort law, a rule not applicable when only one policy is involved (since the insured tortfeasor is the "contributor" of the benefit, whether it be through medical payments or liability coverage). Yarrington v. Thornburg, above. If a valid right of subrogation had been recognized, whether express or not, double recovery could have been avoided in all of these cases in spite of the collateral source rule. Of course this is not to say that recognizing subrogation rights is the best means of denying double recovery.

50. Vance, LAW OF INSURANCE (Third edition, Anderson, 1951), at p. 798.

51. *Id.*, at p. 798, n. 59.

52. See the discussion of life insurance in § 3.10(a)(6), above.

53. See, e.g., Travelers' Insurance Co. v. Brass Goods Manufacturing Co., 239 N.Y. 273, 146 N.E. 377, 37 A.L.R. 826 (1925);

Professor Vance's explanation of a workers' compensation insurer's direct right in tort against the third party whose negligence injured the worker is unpersuasive. The argument for such a direct action, as distinguished from "subrogation strictly speaking," would be as applicable to life insurers as it is to workers' compensation insurers. In one of the few appellate decisions to consider this question, subrogation was sought by an insurer having a life policy on one who allegedly was killed by the negligence of a railroad; the railroad had paid the insured's administratrix damages for causing his death, and the insurer then sued the railroad for the amount it had been required to pay under the terms of its policy. Judgment was rendered for the defendant railroad.[54] As to the theory of a right by direct action, the court based its decision on the ground that the injury to the insurer by the tortfeasor was too remote.[55] Remoteness or proximity seems substantially comparable in relation to the right when asserted by life insurers and workers' compensation insurers. Thus, the contrasting treatment of life insurers and workers' compensation insurers in relation to a direct tort action should be viewed as nothing more than another manifestation of the justifications for the contrasting treatment in relation to subrogation.[56]

§ 3.10(b) Allocation of Recoveries When an Insurer Has a Subrogation Interest

(1) Approaches to Allocation

When an insurer has paid an insured the benefits specified in the insurance contract, there are several possible approaches to determining the priority between the interests of the insurer and the insured in

---

Fort Worth Lloyds v. Haygood, 151 Tex. 149, 246 S.W.2d 865 (1952).

Also see—McKinney's New York Workmen's Comp. Law § 29 (1965) (enacted subsequent to the *Brass Goods* decision, above, and specifying a different result though retaining subrogation).

In Patrick v. South Central Bell Telephone Company, 641 F.2d 1192 (6th Cir. 1980), the court concluded that unless there is a subrogation provision in the workers' compensation policy, an insurer cannot be subrogated to the rights of its insured against a negligent third party.

54. Connecticut Mutual Life Insurance Co. v. New York & N.H.R.R., 25 Conn. 265 (1856).

55. *Id.,* 25 Conn. at pp. 276–277.

56. Kimball and Davis note that there is a two-level subrogation problem in relation to workers' compensation, expressed by two questions: First, is the employer subrogated to its employee's claims against third persons, and second, is the employer's insurer subrogated to the employer's

rights against the third party tortfeasor. They argue that the answer to the second question should clearly be yes by analogy to the liability insurer's generally accepted right to be subrogated to its insured's claims for indemnity and contribution and that the primary question is, therefore, whether the employer is subrogated to its employee's claims. Kimball & Davis, *The Extension of Insurance Subrogation,* 60 Michigan Law Review 841 at pp. 846–847 (1962). In contrast to Vance's analysis, they conclude that the divergent answers given to this question are dependent upon the applicable worker's compensation statutes, that "it would seem that on the authorities there is no subrogation of the employer to the rights of the employee absent a statutory provision to that effect." *Id.,* at p. 848.

Also see Note, *Employer Subrogation: The Effect of Injured Employee Negligence in Workers' Compensation/Third Party Actions,* 18 San Diego Law Review 301–323 (1981).

regard to any recovery that results from the insured's claim against a third party alleged to be responsible for the loss. One of the following three rules or approaches [1] will almost always be applied:

(1) The insurer is to be reimbursed first out of the recovery from the third party for the full amount of the insurance benefits paid to the insured, and the insured is then entitled to any remaining balance.[2]

(2) The recovery from the third person is to be prorated between the insurer and the insured in accordance with the percentage of the total original loss for which the insurer provided indemnification to the insured under the policy.[3]

(3) The insured is to be reimbursed first out of the recovery from the third party for any loss that was not covered by insurance,[4]

§ 3.10(b)

1. A fourth approach is that the insurer is the sole beneficial owner of the claim against the third party and is entitled to the full amount recovered whether or not it exceeds the amount paid by the insured. *Cf.*, Travelers' Insurance Co. v. Brass Goods Manufacturing Co., 239 N.Y. 273, 146 N.E. 377, 37 A.L.R. 826 (1925) (applying this rule under the then-existing workers' compensation law that required an injured employee to make an exclusive election either to receive compensation benefits or to sue in tort).

A fifth approach would be that the insured is the sole owner of the claim against the third party and is entitled to the full amount recovered, whether or not the total thus received from the third party and the insurer exceeds the insured's loss. This rule is a rejection of subrogation. It is, in effect, the result for the types of insurance coverage under which subrogation is customarily disallowed, as is often the case in regard to life insurance or health insurance. See § 3.10(a)(7), above.

Also see Julius Denenberg, *Subrogation Recovery: Who Is Made Whole,* 29 Federation of Insurance Counsel Journal 185–198 (1979); Note, *Profits in Subrogation: An Insurer's Claim to Be More than Indemnified,* 1979 Brigham Young University Law Review 145–160, reprinted in 30 Federation of Insurance Counsel Journal 249–263 (1980); Kimball & Davis, *The Extension of Insurance Subrogation,* 60 Michigan Law Review 841 at pp. 865–866 (1962).

2. Foremost Life Insurance Co. v. Waters, 415 Mich. 303, 329 N.W.2d 688 (1982) (subrogation clause did confer upon group disability insurer the right to be reimbursed out the injured person's recovery from third-party tortfeasor); Ervin v. Garner, 25 Ohio St.2d 231, 267 N.E.2d 769

(1971) (insured assigned to insurer all rights of recovery against the tortfeasor to the extent of the insurance payment occasioned by the destruction of a barn and its contents); Forth Worth Lloyds v. Haygood, 151 Tex. 149, 246 S.W.2d 865 (1952) (so interpreting the state workers' compensation law).

Cf. Repo v. Capitol Elevator Company, Division of International Multifoods Corporation, 312 Minn. 364, 252 N.W.2d 248 (1977) (sickness and accident insurer who pays benefits under a policy which excludes injuries covered by workers' compensation is entitled to reimbursement from the proceeds of a settlement with the workers' compensation insurer).

Also see State ex rel. Manchester Insurance & Indemnity Co. v. Moss, 522 S.W.2d 772 (Mo.1975); Travelers Indemnity Company v. Ingebretsen, 38 Cal.App.3d 858, 113 Cal.Rptr. 679 (2d Dist., 5th Div., 1974).

3. See, e.g., Pontiac Mutual County Fire & Lightning Insurance Co. v. Sheibley, 279 Ill. 118, 116 N.E. 644 (1917); General Exchange Insurance Corp. v. Driscoll, 315 Mass. 360, 52 N.E.2d 970 (1944).

Also see Scales v. Skagit County Medical Bureau, 6 Wn.App. 68, 491 P.2d 1338 (Div. 1, Panel One, 1971), in which the court concluded that when the injured person was only able to recover $10,000 of a $37,500 general verdict against the tortfeasor, the group medical and hospital expenses insurer was only entitled to be subrogated to a prorated amount of $2,000 which was attributable to the hospital and medical services costs that amounted to $7,241.84 of the verdict.

4. See, e.g., Wimberly v. American Casualty Company of Reading, Pennsylvania (CNA) 584 S.W.2d 200 at p. 203 (Tenn.1979) ("resolution of this case must be guided by

the insurer is then entitled to be reimbursed fully, and the insured is entitled to anything that remains from the amount paid by the third party [5] so that any "windfall" goes to the insured [6].

The first rule, reimbursing the insurer first, is employed in many instances as a consequence of an express provision either in the applicable insurance policy or in a document executed by an insured in

general principles of equity, to wit, the insured must be made whole before subrogation rights arise in favor of the insurers" who paid a loss was covered by fire insurance), discussed in Note, *Subrogation—Insured Must Be Paid in Full for Loss Before Insurer Is Entitled to Subrogation Against Tortfeasor,* 10 Memphis State Law Review 161–169 (1979).

Also see Garrity v. Rural Mutual Insurance Company, 77 Wis.2d 537, 253 N.W.2d 512 (1977) (fire insurance paid policy limits of $67,227 on a loss of $110,000); Skauge v. Mountain States Telephone and Telegraph Co., 172 Mont. 521, 565 P.2d 628 at pp. 631–632 (1977).

Cf. Lyon v. Hartford Accident Indemnity Company, 25 Utah 2d 311, 480 P.2d 739 (1971); Newcomb v. Cincinnatti Insurance Company, 22 Ohio St. 382 at p. 388 (1872).

5. See, e.g., Thiringer v. American Motors Insurance Co., 91 Wn.2d 215, 588 P.2d 191 (1978) (personal injury protection insurance).

Cf. Union Insurance Society of Canton v. Consolidated Ice Co., 261 Mich. 35, 245 N.W. 563 (1932).

Kimball and Davis seem to rely implicitly on what is here called the Second Rule as a means of allocation that would protect the rights of the insured yet allow a rational extension of subrogation to life insurance and related coverages. See Kimball & Davis, *The Extension of Insurance Subrogation,* 60 Michigan Law Review 841 at pp. 850–860 (1962).

Also see uninsured motorist cases cited in § 3.10(a), and the discussion in Frost v. Porter Leasing Corporation, 386 Mass. 425, 436 N.E.2d 387 at p. 390–391 (1982).

6. *Cf.* Yorkshire Insurance Co. v. Nisbet Shipping Co., [1962] 2 9.B. 330. The insured had several valued hull policies on one of its ships in a total amount of £ 72,000, each policy stating a value of the amount for the ship. The ship was wrecked and sunk in 1945, the result of a collision with a ship owned by the Canadian government. Nisbet was paid £ 72,000 by the insurers in 1945 and, with the insurers' permission and subject to their sub-

rogation rights commenced suit against the Canadian government in 1946. After a long history of litigation (including one appeal to the Privy Council), Nisbet won. The ship was valued at £ 74,514 as of the date of the collision, and payment was made in Canadian dollars at the 1945 exchange rate. However, the English pound sterling had been devalued in 1949, so Nisbet's recovery in Canadian dollars was worth somewhat over £ 26,971 in 1955.

Nisbet admitted its obligation to reimburse the insurers and paid £ 2,000 to them. But one of the insurers claimed and brought suit to recover its pro tanto share of the excess retained by Nisbet, on the theory that the entire recovery belonged to the insurers. The court held that the insurers were entitled only to what they had paid Nisbet and gave judgment denying recovery beyond the £ 2,000 that Nisbet had voluntarily paid them.

The rule applied by the court seems sound, but the judgment does not. Because of the devaluation in 1949, the £ 2,000 paid Nisbet in 1945 was not equivalent to the £ 2,000 paid the insurers in 1955. If the rule had been correctly applied, both the recovery equal to the full 1945 loss and the £ 2,000 paid by the insurers in that year would have been converted to 1955 pounds sterling; Nisbet would have been allowed to retain the difference between the two as unreimbursed loss, and the insurers would have been allowed the 1955 equivalent of their 1945 payment.

The rule of allocation chosen by the court would have had practical significance, therefore, even if the court had properly revalued the amount paid by the insurers; it had special meaning under the court's method of disposition because Nisbet was allowed to retain the "excess" over the sum of his unreimbursed loss and the amount paid by the insurers. The court speaks of the "windfall" produced by the devaluation of the pound sterling in relation to the last part of the allocation, but Nisbet's windfall was produced by the court's decision concerning the effect of the devaluation, not by the devaluation itself.

the course of settling an insurance claim.[7] However, when subrogation is sought as an equitable right asserted by an insurer in the absence of an express contract provision, it is unclear whether an insurer is or should be entitled to reimbursement in situations where its insured has not been fully indemnified.[8]

The second rule, reimbursing the insurer and the insured under a proration formula, has been applied occasionally in contested cases.[9] Moreover, it is undoubtedly a result that is reached by an insured and an insurer in many instances as a compromise which settles a dispute about the rights to a recovery from a tortfeasor.

The third rule, reimbursing the insured first, has the greatest support of the three among the more recent judicial precedents.[10] The application of this rule maximizes the prospect of "making the insured whole," which is consonant with the equitable origins of the subrogation doctrine. In the absence of any explicit contractual provisions, courts are free to adopt this approach as an equitable allocation of a recovery from a tortfeasor. The justification for applying this approach in the absence of contract provisions is fortified by the fact that ordinarily there is no barrier to the use of explicit subrogation terms that provide either for proration or for a disposition of recoveries from third persons that is even more favorable to the insurer's interests.

There are some instances when insureds have been awarded a priority over the insurer even though that result does not conform to the subrogation right set forth in the insurance policy. When there are applicable contract provisions which state that the insurer is entitled to be reimbursed first, the insured's claim for a priority will rest on a determination of whether a court will recognize rights that vary from such contract provisions. Given the equitable nature of the subrogation concept, the likelihood of prevailing on such a claim is and should be especially propitious in this context.

In a number of respects, precedents concerning subrogation rights are insufficient to support the characterization of any one of these three approaches as a majority or even a prevailing rule. For example, there is no clear answer in the judicial precedents as to whether the

---

7. See, e.g., Peterson v. Ohio Farmers Ins. Co., 175 Ohio St. 34, 191 N.E.2d 157 (1963); Firestone Service Stores, Inc. of Gainsville v. Wynn, for Use and Benefit of Home Ins. Co., New York, 131 Fla. 94, 179 So. 175 (1938).

Also see decisions cited in note 2, above.

8. The lack of certainty in this regard is reflected in a comment of the Ohio Supreme Court, written in 1872, that an "assured will not, in the forum of conscience, be required to account for more than the surplus * * * after satisfying his own * * * loss in full * * * unless the underwriter shall, on notice and opportunity given, have contributed to and made com-

mon cause with him, in the prosecution." 22 Ohio St. 382 at p. 388 (1872). Although this comment suggests a clear rule — that an insurer is not entitled to subrogation — when an insurer does not participate in an action against the tortfeasor, in the event an insurer does participate the measure of the insurer's rights to the proceeds are left to the reader's speculation.

9. See note 3, above.

10. See note 4, above.

Also see Uriel Procaccia, *The Effect and Validity of Subrogation Clauses in Insurance Policies,* 1973 Insurance Law Journal 573–586.

choice a court makes among these rules as a method of allocating rights in the proceeds of a settlement with the tortfeasor is also to be applied to a recovery *in full* upon a judgment against the tortfeasor. One reason for the lack of a clear answer to this question is that a full recovery of a judgment against a tortfeasor occurs in an extremely small percentage of cases.[11]

All of these approaches to allocating the insured's and the insurer's rights in regard to an insured's claim against a third party are based on the assumption that a contract of insurance is personal in nature so that the insurance benefits exist for the benefit of the insured and the existence of the insurance does not affect the third party's liability to the insured. In addition, these rules also assume that the existence of a possible claim against the third party does not affect the liability of the insurer to the insured. Occasionally courts reject these assumptions, and some of the situations in which the validity of these assumptions is questioned are examined in the next chapter.[12]

(2) Settlements

In theory, the judgment recoverable in a valid tort claim against a third person is the amount that is necessary to fully compensate the claimant for the loss, so that the recovery of such an amount would allow for the full reimbursement of an insurer who has previously provided indemnification for an insured. Thus, the insured and the insurer could, at least theoretically, be made whole if the tort claim is valid and collected in full. However, when a tort claim is settled, the amount paid by a tortfeasor rarely is sufficient to both fully indemnify the insured and completely reimburse the insurer, thereby necessitating a choice among approaches described in the preceding section.

If the insured is entitled to be reimbursed first out of any compromise settlement, insurers may tend to reject settlement proposals and insist on trials, unless this rule is supplemented by recognition of the proposition that the insurer has a duty not to oppose a settlement it would have found acceptable had it held the entire interest in the claim against the third party.[13] Moreover, any assessment of the insurer's view of a possible settlement is complicated not only by the uncertainties associated with both litigation and prospects for the collection of any judgment obtained, but also by the adoption of comparative negligence in an increasingly large number of the states.

---

11. Another reason is that even when there is a full recovery of a judgment, usually it is just enough to "fully" reimburse both the insurer and the insured as long as litigation expenses are disregarded.

Also consider the discussion in § 3.10(b)(3) and § 3.10(b)(4), below.

12. See especially §§ 4.1–4.6, below.

13. Compare the rules developed in relation to the duty of a liability insurer with a low policy limit not to decline a claimant's settlement offer within that limit if it would have accepted the offer had no policy limit applied. See § 7.8, below.

(3) Litigation Costs and Attorney Fees

Costs of investigation and litigation of a tort claim pose an additional problem in regard to the allocation of any recovery that is subject to a subrogation right. For example, suppose the payment by the insurer to the insured is $20,000, the total loss suffered by the insured is $40,000, and the judgment collected from the third party on account of the loss is $40,000. Further, assume that the cost of investigation and litigation (exclusive of attorney fees) to effect that recovery is $5,000 and the fee for the attorney is an additional $10,000. Is the allocation to be computed on the basis of the net recovery of $25,000 ($40,000 — $15,000 = $25,000) or on the basis of the gross recovery of $40,000? If the insured is entitled to be indemnified first — that is, if the third rule of allocation is applied — is the recovery a net of $25,000 with $20,000 to the insured and $5,000 to the insurer, or is the recovery $40,000 with $20,000 allocated to each, leaving responsibility for litigation costs and the lawyer's fee to be determined independently? This is a debatable question, and there is very little judicial authority on point.[14]

---

14. The justification for not taking litigation costs and attorney fees into account in the allocation of a recovery from a tortfeasor is strengthened when each of the parties having an interest in the claim against the third party is represented by a separate attorney and the tort claim is tried to judgment rather than being compromised. In pursuing the tort claim against the third person, an insurer and an insured with separate attorneys and separate expenses would each receive a full share of the judgment and bear their own expenses thereby realizing a net recovery somewhat less than full reimbursement. If the insurer and insured were represented by one attorney and incurred other expenses jointly in pressing the tort claim, proration would achieve virtually the same result. Similarly, an argument for proration could also be made when the insured (and the insured's attorney) presses the claim to conclusion without participation of any separate attorney employed by the insurer. There is some support in precedents for such apportionment of the expenses of collection, including attorney fees.

See, e.g., St. Paul Fire and Marine Insurance Co. v. Truesdell Distributing Corp., 207 Neb. 152, 296 N.W.2d 479 (1980) (an insurer that accepts the benefits of an action, without becoming a party, is liable for a proportionate share of the expenses of the litigation, including attorney fees); National Union Fire Insurance Co. v. Grimes, 278 Minn. 45, 153 N.W.2d 152 (1967) (subrogated insurer recovered part of proceeds of insured's settlement with tortfeasor, but

subject to an offset to the extent of "the reasonable worth and value of the efforts expended and expenses incurred" by the insured properly chargeable to that portion of the claim attributable to medical expenses, for which the insurer had paid under medical payments coverage); Lemmer v. Karp, 56 Ill.App.3d 190, 13 Ill.Dec. 720, 371 N.E.2d 655 (2d Dist.1977).

Cf. United Services Automobile Association v. Hills, 172 Neb. 128, 109 N.W.2d 174 (1961), 2 A.L.R.3d 1422 (1965) (when collision insurer abandoned its hostility to inclusion of its subrogation claim in insured's attorney's negotiations with tortfeasor, by seeking to collect a share of the settlement fund secured solely by the efforts of the insured and the insured's attorney, attorney had claim against insurer's share of settlement fund for expenses, including value of the attorney's services).

In Travelers Insurance Company v. Williams, 541 S.W.2d 587 at p. 590 (Tenn. 1976), the attorney who represented the insured sought to recover one-third of the amount of the insurer's subrogation claim of $1,000. The court observed that whether "an attorney is entitled to collect from the insurer a fee with respect to a subrogation claim depends upon whether an express or implied contract or a quasi contract relation exists between them."

Also see O'Connor v. Lee Hy Paving Corp., 480 F.Supp. 716 (E.D.N.Y.1979).

See also the discussion of the right of an attorney to collect fee in Rex Capwell and Thomas E. Greenwald, *Legal and Practical Problems Arising from Subrogation Clauses*

Ordinarily, damages are established on the assumption that the amount due will be paid without litigation, and attorneys' fees are not an element of damages. The law which determines the measure of recovery is fashioned on the theory that obligations will be paid in full, and to the extent that it is necessary to incur expenses because this is not the case, they are left to be borne by the litigants. Thus, in some respects independent treatment of the costs of effecting a recovery from a tortfeasor would be consistent with the usual treatment of attorneys' fees in American law. Nevertheless, that approach does not comport with the generally accepted goal of providing full indemnification for the injured person.

If one subscribes to the goal of providing full indemnification to insureds, the preferable approach to the allocation of a recovery is to allow the insured to assert a priority in the net recovery (that is, the amount which remains after the expenses have been paid) to the extent of losses that have not been indemnified, with the remainder — if any — being paid to the insurer.[15]

(4) Comment

The choice among the rules for allocating rights to a tort recovery from a third person could depend, at least in part, on why a share of the loss was to be borne by the insured in the absence of third party claims. For example, was an insured's share solely an excess of the loss over the amount of the insurance coverage (as when the coverage under a fire insurance policy is $10,000 and the loss is $12,000, leaving the insured a $2,000 share of the loss to bear personally in the absence of a tort cause of action against a third person for negligently starting the fire)? Alternatively, did the insured's loss arise entirely or in part from a policy provision such as a deductible (as when $1,800 of a $2,000 collision loss is paid by an automobile collision insurer under a policy with a $200 deductible) or a coinsurance clause (as when a fire insurance policy on commercial property, with a New York Standard Coinsurance Clause, provides for payment of only a stated percentage of the loss, leaving the insured to bear the remaining percentage)?

The reasons that, absent a tort recovery against a third person, part of the loss would be borne by the insured should be relevant to the interpretation of the insurance policy provisions bearing on the insurer's right to assert a right of subrogation in preference to the insured's right to seek to full indemnification. For example, if the contract provides for coinsurance of the loss, with the insured bearing part of the risk, this implies an agreement that the rule for allocation of

in Health and Accident Policies, 22 Federation of Insurance Counsel Journal 23–67 at pp. 53–62 (1972).

15. There is some support for the proposition that in applying the third rule, reimbursing the insured first, the insured should not be regarded as having been reimbursed fully unless the net recovery above all expenses is at least as much as the amount by which the insured's loss exceeded the benefits paid to the insured by the insurer. See, e.g., Union Insurance Society of Canton v. Consolidated Ice Co., 261 Mich. 35, 245 N.W. 563 (1932).

recovery from a third party should be the second rule: proration. However, in response to this point it can be reasonably pointed out that the coinsurance principle is aimed at creating an inducement to the maintenance of full insurance and not at division of recoupment from other sources.

Similarly, it might be urged that a clause providing that there shall be a "deductible" of $200 is fairly construed as an agreement that the insured shall bear the first $200 of loss and that the subrogation interest should be computed on the basis that, if the total recovery against the third party is just $200 less than the total loss of the insured, the insurer shall have full reimbursement of its insurance payment and the $200 loss remaining shall be borne by the insured. On the other hand, the deductible provision is not an agreement about bearing net loss after recoupment from other sources: deductibles eliminate insurance coverage for losses that are small enough that they are better borne by the insured as costs of the activity because the administrative expenses for an insurer are substantial in relation to the amount of such losses.

The arguments for preferring one over another of the rules of allocation are rather inconclusive in principle, and they are unsettled in the precedents. There is a tendency in the few decisions resolving such an issue to adopt rules that essentially produce something of a "compromise." For example, courts sometimes apply a proration principle to the portion of a collision loss within the deductible, rather than giving preference either to the insurer or to the insured.[16] And no doubt there is a similar tendency for insurers and their insureds to settle these issues on a compromise basis rather than pressing for an adjudication.

§ 3.10(c) Enforcement of Subrogation Rights

(1) Parties to Actions

When an insurer, asserting a right of subrogation, wants to initiate an action against a third party, the insurer usually prefers to present the controversy — especially when a jury may be involved — as one between the insured and the third party. One justification for presenting such an action as the insured's claim is that this approach avoids the possible effect of prejudice on the part of jury members against insurers.[1] Disputes have arisen in regard to the appropriateness of structuring law suits in this way.

---

16. See, e.g., General Exchange Insurance Corp. v. Driscoll, 315 Mass. 360, 52 N.E.2d 970 (1944).

§ 3.10(c)

1. See, e.g., Lines v. Ryan, 272 N.W.2d 896 (Minn.1978); Ellsaesser v. Mid-Continent Casualty Co., 195 Kan. 117, 403 P.2d 185 (1965), 13 A.L.R.3d 133 (1967). The car owner, who was paid by his insurer for all but a small part of damages to his car, sued alleged tortfeasor and others. The trial court ruled that insurer, as a real party in interest, had to be made a party plaintiff or the suit would be dismissed. The appellate court reversed, reasoning that in a case of partial coverage and partial payment for loss, the insurer is not a necessary party and the insured is the proper party plaintiff who will hold in trust that part of a recovery which belongs in equity to the insurer.

The justification for permitting an insurer's subrogation action against a third party to be brought in the name of an insured is most persuasive when the insurer has paid only part of the loss, so that the insured continues to retain a beneficial interest in the claim.[2] However, in some cases it has been held that the insurer is entitled to have the suit presented in this way even when it is clear that the insurer's subrogation rights will entitle it to the full amount of any recovery in the event of a favorable result from trial.[3]

Some courts treat an insurer asserting a subrogation right as a "real party in interest." This means that an insurer not only has the right to bring an action against the tortfeasor,[4] but also that the insurer may be required to bring the action in its own name as the claimant who will derive the benefit of a favorable determination.[5] In an effort to improve the chances that a claim, if carried to trial, can be presented as one between an insured and a third party, many insurers adopt the practice — when making an "advance" payment of the amount due on the insurance contract — of requiring the insured to sign a "loan receipt" in which the insured agrees to repay the insurer out of the recovery from the third party.[6] The question whether a transaction of

2. The arguments for the special treatment of insurance subrogation claims are much like those against disclosure that a defendant has liability insurance. In both situations, the purpose of avoiding disclosure to the jury that an insurer has an interest is directed at minimizing the effect of a presumed substantial bias on the part of jurors against insurers.

See the discussion in White Hall Building Corp. v. Profexray Division of Litton Industries, Inc., 387 F.Supp. 1202 at p. 1206 (E.D.Pa.1974), *affirmed* 578 F.2d 1375 (3d Cir.1978); Northern Assurance Co. of America v. Associated Independent Dealers, 313 F.Supp. 816 at p. 817 (D.Minn. 1970).

Cf. Celanese Corp. of America v. John Clark Industries, Inc., 214 F.2d 551 at p. 557 (5th Cir.1954).

But cf. Pace v. General Electric Co., 55 F.R.D. 215 at pp. 218–219 (W.D.Pennsylvania, 1972).

Also see discussion in § 3.10(e), below.

3. See, e.g., Garcia v. Hall, 624 F.2d 150 at p. 152 (10th Cir.1980) (applying the law of Texas); Warren v. Kirwan, 598 S.W.2d 598 (Mo.App.1980).

Also see Catalfano v. Higgins, 55 Del. (5 Storey) 470, 188 A.2d 357 (1962) (held, "real party in interest" provision of Civil Procedure Act did not change common law rule that an insurer's subrogation suit must be brought in insured's name).

Cf. Myers v. Thomas, 143 Tex. 502, 186 S.W.2d 811 (1945) (pro tanto subrogation claim of workmen's compensation insurer).

In Lines v. Ryan, 272 N.W.2d 896 at p. 903 (Minn.1978), the court's conclusion appeared to rest on the fact that "[t]he release and subrogation trust agreement signed by Jones (the insured) * * * expressly authorized such an action." Accord. Henderson v. Aetna Casualty and Surety Co., 55 N.Y.2d 947, 449 N.Y.S.2d 178, 434 N.E.2d 247 (1982).

4. Smith v. Travelers Insurance Co., 50 Ohio App.2d 349, 363 N.E.2d 750 (1976), *affirmed* 50 Ohio St.2d 43, 362 N.E.2d 264 (1977).

5. See, e.g., Dondlinger & Sons' Construction Company, Inc. v. Emcco, Inc., 227 Kan. 301, 606 P.2d 1026 at p. 1030 (1980); Ellis Canning Co. v. International Harvester Co., 174 Kan. 357, 255 P.2d 658 (1953) (overruling earlier decision to the contrary); Haueter v. Peguillan, 586 P.2d 403 (Utah 1978).

Also see Shambley v. Jobe-Blackley Plumbing & Heating Co., 264 N.C. 456, 142 S.E.2d 18 (1965), 13 A.L.R.3d 224 (1967) (insurer having paid in full for damages to home resulting from explosion of defective heaters, it was real party in interest in tort action; action in name of insured dismissed).

6. See, e.g., Pacific Indemnity Co. v. Thompson-Yaeger, Inc., 258 N.W.2d 762 (Minn.1977); Central National Insurance Company of Omaha v. Dixon, 93 Nev. 86, 559 P.2d 1187 (1977).

Cf. Luckenbach v. W.J. McCahan Sugar Refining Co., 248 U.S. 139, 39 S.Ct. 53, 63 L.Ed. 170 (1918).

this type should allow an insurer to avoid being identified as a party in the action against the third person has been repeatedly contested.[7]

(2) Splitting the Cause of Action

When a subrogation interest exists, a court may be called on to decide whether the insured and the subrogated insurer will each be allowed to proceed independently on their respective shares of the cause of action or, instead, will be required to proceed jointly. Although the judicial decisions are in conflict, a majority hold that a

Also see Comment, *Settling Multiparty Contract Disputes Through the Use of Loan Receipt Agreements,* 76 Northwestern University Law Review 271–299 (1981); Annotation, *Loan-Receipt Agreement With Co-tortfeasor,* 62 A.L.R.3d 1111–1137 (1975); Note, *The Loan Receipt Transaction—Form and Application,* 12 Washburn Law Journal 366–377 (1973).

Loan receipt agreements have been criticized on the grounds that they inappropriately attempt to circumvent the prohibitions against the assignment of certain causes of action. See, e.g., Reese v. Chicago, Burlington & Quincy Railroad Co., 55 Ill.2d 356, 303 N.E.2d 382 at p. 387 (1973) (Schaefer, J., dissenting) (arguing that agreement in question violated prohibition against assigning personal injury and wrongful death claims); John E. McKay, *Loan Agreement: A Settlement Device That Deserves Close Scrutiny,* 10 Val.U.L.Rev. 231–259 at p. 254 (1976). Also see Cullen v. Atchison, T. & S.F. Railway Co., 211 Kan. 368, 507 P.2d 353, 360 (1973) (loan receipt agreement did not constitute unlawful assignment of a tort claim); Biven v. Charlie's Hobby Shop, 500 S.W.2d 597 at p. 599 (Ky.1973).

7. See, e.g., Northern Assurance Company of America v. Associated Independent Dealers, 313 F.Supp. 816 (D.Minn.1970); Crocker v. New England Power Co., 348 Mass. 159, 202 N.E.2d 793 (1964) (*held,* receipt was not shown to be other than the loan arrangement it purported to be, and the insurer's payment to plaintiff under the terms of the receipt did not extinguish plaintiff's rights against defendant).

Also see Waterway Term. Co. v. P.S. Lord Mech. Contractors, 242 Or. 1, 406 P.2d 556 (1965), 13 A.L.R.3d 1 (1967) (action by property owner against contractor and subcontractors for damage from fire caused by defendants' negligence; trial court dismissed pleas in abatement founded on theory property owner was not real party in interest since it had been paid for the loss under fire insurance coverage; jury verdict for defendants; held, reversed for new trial because of errors in rulings on evidence and instructions to jury; pleas

in abatement were properly dismissed since payments were made under loan receipts); American Chain & Cable Company, Inc. v. Brunson, 157 Ga.App. 833, 278 S.E.2d 719 (1981); United States Fire Insurance Co. v. Farris, 146 Ga.App. 177, 245 S.E.2d 868 (1978).

Contra. See, e.g., American Dredging Co. v. Federal Insurance Company, 309 F.Supp. 425 (S.D.N.Y.1970); Kopperud v. Chick, 27 Wis.2d 591, 135 N.W.2d 335 (1965) (held, insured's suit against tortfeasor for indemnity properly dismissed since insurer was real party in interest, the execution of a loan receipt between insurer and insured not having preserved the insured's status as the real party in interest on the claim; dicta, however, that loan receipts are valid and effective in some contexts).

See also New York—McKinney's Civil Practice Laws and Rules § 1004 (1963): "Except where otherwise prescribed by order of the court, an * * * insured person who has executed to his insurer either a loan or subrogation receipt, trust agreement, or other similar agreement * * * may sue or be sued without joining with him the person for or against whose interest the action is brought."

In Todd v. Ratcliffe, 603 S.W.2d 925 at p. 928 (Ky.App.1980), the court observed that loan receipts "are a legal fiction by which insurance companies are permitted to file a subrogation action in the name of their insured" and then concluded that the insurer's "right to silently participate in the action terminated when appellants joined the company as a third-party defendant * * *."

Also see Francis I. Kenney, Jr., *The loan receipt and its use by insurers: considerations and suggestions,* 10 The Forum 920–942 (1975); Comment, *The Loan Receipt and Insurers' Subrogation—How To Become the Real Party in Interest Without Really Lying,* 50 Tulane Law Review 115–134 (1975); Comment, *The Loan Receipt Transaction—Form and Application,* 12 Washburn Law Journal 366–377 (1973).

splitting of a tort cause of action is not allowed.[8] Furthermore, at least some of the decisions that appear to approve splitting the action actually can be explained on a rationale that is consistent with the majority rule.

In some cases, there are several distinct claims between the parties, and the question whether a cause of action may be split arises when there has been a settlement of one claim (or even an agreed or stipulated judgment, as distinguished from a judgment reached in a trial on the merits) followed by the filing of an action in court on the unresolved claim. This type of situation can be distinguished from decisions applying the rule against splitting the cause of action when a second action is filed after a trial on the merits in a first action. Thus, a court in a jurisdiction that generally disallows splitting causes of action might nevertheless permit a separate action in this type of situation. For example, the settlement of a property damage claim asserted by a subrogated insurer would not affect the right to an action on a personal injury claim by the insured.[9]

Courts might allow an insured to settle with the alleged tortfeasor as to the insured's share of the cause of action without affecting the subrogated insurer's share of the cause of action, even if disallowing splitting in other contexts.[10] Circumstances involving two separate claims by a single person, holding all the legal and equitable interests in both claims, can be distinguished from cases in which one of the claims involves an insurer's subrogation interests and the other involves the insured's residual interests.

Even in jurisdictions having precedents against splitting a cause of action, when there are genuinely disparate interests it may be found that the desirability of avoiding the difficulties arising from conflicting interests between insurer and insured if splitting is disallowed — a conflict that is especially troublesome when a personal injury claim as well as property damage claim is involved — outweighs the additional litigation burden that is imposed on the court. If the rule against splitting is applied in this context despite the conflict of interests

---

8. See, e.g., Rush v. Maple Heights, 167 Ohio St. 221, 147 N.E.2d 599 (1958), *cert. denied* 358 U.S. 814, 79 S.Ct. 21, 3 L.Ed.2d 57 (1958), and Spinelli v. Maxwell, 430 Pa. 478, 243 A.2d 425 (1968), both denying recovery for personal injuries sustained in automobile accidents because of previous adjudications of property damage claims.

Cf. Warner v. Hedrick, 147 W.Va. 262, 126 S.E.2d 371 (1962) (judgment for plaintiff on $300 property damage claim precluded subsequent assertion of his cause of action for medical expense and loss of consortium because of injury to his wife).

Contra. See, e.g., Carter v. Hinkle, 189 Va. 1, 52 S.E.2d 135 (1949). Compare Holbert v. Safe Insurance Co., 114 W.Va. 221, 171 S.E. 422 (1933) (allowing insured to recover from insurer after settling with

tortfeasor for amount of loss in excess of part covered by insurance, the release involved preserving for the insured and his insurer the right to proceed against the tortfeasor for the amount of loss equal to the part insured).

Also see Smith v. Travelers Insurance Co., 50 Ohio App.2d 349, 363 N.E.2d 750 (1976); Annotation, *Simultaneous injury to person and property as giving rise to single cause of action.* 62 A.L.R.2d 977–1009 (1958).

But also consider the discussion of reciprocal claims in § 7.5, below.

9. See the discussion of reciprocal claims in § 7.5, below.

10. *Ibid.*

between insurer and insured, then it would seem appropriate to hold the subrogated insurer to a requirement that it give reasonable consideration to the interest of the insured in the claim, rather than being free to assert its subrogation claim without being accountable to the insured for the collateral effect on the insured's interests.[11] The imposition of such an obligation on an insurer, because of the nature of the relationship of the parties, would be a counterpart of the insured's obligation (imposed under equitable doctrines even in the absence of contractual stipulations) to respect the insurer's subrogation interest.

(3) Precluding Interference With Subrogation Rights

Legal protection against interference with an insurer's subrogation interest is granted in some instances (1) in proceedings between an insurer and a third party against whom the insured had a claim subject to subrogation, (2) in proceedings between an insurer and insured, and (3) occasionally in proceedings involving all three parties.

The majority rule allows a subrogated insurer to proceed against a tortfeasor who settled with an insured in violation of the insurer's subrogation rights. Thus, a payment to an insured (or another) by a third party who knew of an insurer's subrogation interest does not discharge the third party's liability to the extent of the insurer's subrogation interest.[12]

(4) Remedies for an Insured's Breach or Impairment of the Insurer's Subrogation Rights

The remedies available to an insurer as a consequence of an insured's action that constitutes a breach or impairment of the insurer's subrogation right in part depend on whether insurance benefits have previously been paid. If the insurer has not yet paid the insurance policy benefits to the insured, the insured's violation of the insurer's subrogation rights serves as a partial or complete defense to a

11. Compare the argument for accountability of the liability insurer for affecting adversely the interests of its insured in the insured's reciprocal claim, § 7.10(a), below.

12. See, e.g., St. Paul Fire and Marine Insurance Co. v. Amerada Hess Corporation, 275 N.W.2d 304 at p. 308 (N.D.1979) (property insurance on a derrick); Homes Insurance Co. v. Hertz Corporation, 7 Ill.2d 210, 16 Ill.Dec. 484, 375 N.E.2d 115 (1978) (automobile insurance) [discussed in Note, *Insurance Subrogation Actions No Longer Barred by General Releases in Illinois,* 28 Depaul Law Review 189–203 (1978)]; Travelers Indemnity Company v. Vaccari, 310 Minn. 97, 245 N.W.2d 844 (1976) (liability insurer willfully disregarded notice of the subrogation claim of an insurer that provided compensation under a medical payments insurance policy).

Also see Sentry Insurance Co. v. Stuart, 246 Ark. 680, 439 S.W.2d 797 (1969) (medi-

cal payments coverage; trial court's action in sustaining demurrer reversed); Great American Insurance Co. v. Watts, 393 P.2d 236 (Okl.1964) (settlement was expressly limited to excess of loss over insurance proceeds).

Also see Calvert Fire Insurance Co. v. James, 236 S.C. 431, 114 S.E.2d 832 (1960), 92 A.L.R.2d 97 (1963); Nationwide Mutual Insurance Co. v. Spivey, 259 N.C. 732, 131 S.E.2d 338 (1963) (held, fact that consent judgment had been entered was irrelevant since consent judgment is a contract and is to be interpreted as such); Cleaveland v. Chesapeake & Potomac Telephone Co., 225 Md. 47, 169 A.2d 446 (1961).

Cf. National Insurance Underwriters v. Piper Aircraft Corporation, 595 F.2d 546 at p. 551 (10th Cir.1979).

subsequent claim by the insured for insurance benefits.[13] When insurance benefits have been paid to the insured, a subrogated insurer may be entitled to enforce one or another among several possible remedies in a separate action against the insured. Causes of action, subject to some qualifications,[14] have been recognized on each of the following theories:

(i) *Breach of Contract.* A settlement with a third party tortfeasor, responsible for the insured loss, constitutes a breach of an express subrogation provision included either in the insurance policy or in a collateral agreement (such as an assignment, "loan receipt," or subrogation agreement executed at the time of payment of the policy claim), and either damages are recovered for the breach or the insurer is entitled to predicate a denial of a claim for insurance benefits on the insured's breach.[15]

(ii) *Quasi-contract.* The insured who receives a settlement from a third person, in equity and good conscience is required to render such funds to the insurer.[16]

13. See, e.g., Benson v. Farmers Insurance Company, Inc., 227 Kan. 833, 610 P.2d 605 (1980) (uninsured motorist coverage); Worobec v. State Farm Mutual Automobile Insurance Company, 200 Neb. 210, 263 N.W.2d 95 (1978) (uninsured motorist coverage); Motto v. State Farm Mutual Automobile Insurance Co., 81 N.M. 35, 462 P.2d 620 (1969) (medical payments coverage).

Also see Decespedes v. Prudence Mutual Casualty Co., 193 So.2d 224 (Fla.App.1966), affirmed 202 So.2d 561 (Fla.1967) (medical payments coverage); Armijo v. Foundation Reserve Insurance Co., 75 N.M. 592, 408 P.2d 750 (1965) (automobile collision insurance); Flanary v. Reserve Insurance Co., 364 Mich. 73, 110 N.W.2d 670 (1961) (automobile collision insurance); Hilley v. Blue Ridge Insurance Co., 235 N.C. 544, 70 S.E. 2d 570 (1952), 38 A.L.R.2d 1090 (1954) (automobile collision insurance).

In Havanich v. Safeco Insurance Company of America, 557 F.2d 948 at p. 950 (2d Cir.1977), the court concluded that although an "unauthorized settlement by an insured with an uninsured motorist normally gives a carrier a defense to an uninsured motorist coverage claim * * * when Safeco improperly denied coverage initially, it breached the terms of its contract and therefore cannot take advantage of the defense provided by the policy."

Also see Geertz v. State Farm Fire & Casualty, 253 Or. 307, 451 P.2d 860 (1969); Gulf Insurance Company v. Texas Casualty Insurance Company, 580 S.W.2d 645 (Tex. Civ.App., Fort Worth, 1979).

14. Under some decisions an insurer has no right of direct action against an insured who has allegedly interfered with the insurer's subrogation rights if the insured's settlement with the tortfeasor does not preclude action by the insurer against the tortfeasor — e.g., Farm Bureau Mutual Insurance Co. v. Anderson, 360 S.W.2d 314 (Mo.App.1962) (tortfeasor having knowledge of insurer's subrogation interest) — or if the insured has, without the insurer's knowledge or consent, prosecuted to an unsuccessful conclusion a tort action against the third party — e.g., Providence Washington Insurance Co. v. Hogges, 67 N.J. Super. 475, 171 A.2d 120 (App.Div.1961) (adverse result in the insured's tort action treated as a determination that the third party was not liable and therefore that the insurer's rights were valueless).

15. See, e.g., Sentry Insurance Co. v. Stuart, 246 Ark. 680, 439 S.W.2d 797 (1969) (subrogation clause in medical payments coverage; trial court's action in sustaining demurrer reversed); National Union Fire Ins. Co. v. Grimes, 278 Minn. 45, 153 N.W.2d 152 (1967) (medical payments coverage; breach of agreement to repay insurer out of settlement proceeds; offset allowed for expenses).

Also see United States Fidelity & Guaranty Co. v. Covert, 242 Miss. 1, 133 So.2d 403 (1961) (action based on "subrogation receipt" rather than insurance policy).

16. E.g., General Exchange Insurance Corp. v. Driscoll, 315 Mass. 360, 52 N.E.2d 970 (1944).

Also see Hartford Accident and Indemnity Co. v. Chung, 37 Conn.Supp. 587, 429 A.2d 158 at p. 162 (App.Session, 1981), in which the court held that fire insurer which had paid homeowners for a fire loss was entitled to assert a subrogation right on the basis of the doctrine of unjust en-

(iii) *Constructive Trust.* The insurer is entitled in equity and good conscience to money received by the insured from the third person, and therefore the insured is regarded as a constructive trustee who receives and holds the money for the benefit of the insurer.[17]

(iv) *Injunction.* When the subrogation interest of the insurer is clear, an insured may be restrained from settling or receiving proceeds of a settlement with a third person in derogation of such interest because remedies at law are inadequate.[18]

The pecuniary value of the remedy to the insurer may be affected by the choice among these different grounds of relief. For example, under the quasi-contract theory of "money had and received" by the insured from a third person, the insurer would recover from the insured the sum that the insured had recovered from the alleged tortfeasor on account of the claim (or that proportion of the claim) to which the insurer was subrogated. And an insurer may be entitled to recover the insurance benefits paid to the insured before violation, or even after the violation if the insurer had no notice of the violation.[19]

Issues concerning the possible loss of an insurer's subrogation rights against a third person sometimes are presented by an insured's actions before any insurance benefits have been paid. Under the theory that violation of subrogation rights is a breach of contract that provides the insurer with a complete defense to any subsequent claim for insurance benefits by the insured, the insurer would thereafter have no obligation to the insured. One line of precedents holds that an insured's violation of the insurer's subrogation rights totally relieves the insurer of liability under the policy if insurance benefits have not yet been paid to the insured.[20] There are also precedents that support an insurer's right to recover from the insured any insurance payment made before the violation occurred.[21]

richment when the homeowners were subsequently compensated by their contractor's insurer for the same loss.

17. See, e.g., Norwich Union Fire Insurance Society v. Stang, 18 Cir.Ct.R. 464, 9 Ohio C.Dec. 576 (1897).

Also see Pavone v. Aetna Casualty and Surety Co., 91 Misc.2d 658, 398 N.Y.2d 630 (Monroe County, 1977) (insurer entitled to enforce a constructive trust when insurer incorrectly paid first party PIP benefits to a claimant who slipped and fell on accumulated ice and snow as she was approaching her automobile in the parking lot of her apartment house in reliance on a misrepresentation, and insurer is also entitled to assert a right of subrogation against any recovery obtained from the owner of an apartment house); Providence Washington Insurance Co. v. Hogges, 67 N.J.Super. 475, 171 A.2d 120 (1961) (dictum).

Cf. Florida Farm Bureau Insurance Co. v. Martin, 377 So.2d 827 (Fla.App., 1st

Dist., 1979), in which the court held that an insurer is entitled to accounting from its insured when the insured is fully compensated by insurance and subsequently obtains satisfaction from a wrongdoer; North River Insurance Co. v. McKenzie, 261 Ala. 353, 74 So.2d 599 (1954), 51 A.L.R.2d 687 (1957).

18. See, e.g., Hartford Insurance Co. v. Pennell, 2 Ill.App. 609 (3d Dist.1878).

If the only matter at issue in such a case is money being paid by the tortfeasor, equitable relief of this type is unlikely to be granted by most courts.

19. See, e.g., Illinois Auto Insurance Exchange v. Braun, 280 Pa. 550, 124 A. 691 (1924), 36 A.L.R. 1262 (1925).

20. See, e.g., Hockelberg v. Farm Bureau Insurance Co., 407 N.E.2d 1160 (Ind. App., 3d Dist., 1980).

21. *Ibid.* See also note 17 above.

If the objective of an insurer's cause of action is damages for breach of contract by the insured, troublesome questions may arise concerning the measure of damages. The insurer's rights depend to a large extent on views regarding the respective interests of the insured and the subrogated insurer in the third party claim.

A conflicting line of precedents, which includes several variants, limits an insurer's relief to an amount that is consistent with the harm done by the breach. For example, in one leading case, the court stated that in order to prove the harm done by violation of its subrogation rights an insurer "must show that in fact it might have recovered against * * *" the third party "as a wrongdoer." [22] The insurer had issued collision coverage for a car and had a subrogation interest in the claim for damage to the car, but no interest in the insured's very substantial claim for personal injury. The use of the word "might" in this opinion is ambiguous. Was it intended to mean that in order to recover the insurer must show both that it would have litigated the tort claim and that it would have recovered judgment against the alleged tortfeasor if the settlement had not been made? Alternatively, is it sufficient for an insurer to show that the prospect of a suit would have been sufficient to have effected some recovery by way of compromise of the disputed liability? [23] The second interpretation of what the insurer should be required to prove seems the fairest, because it is essentially comparable to the position the insurer would have occupied had the subrogation rights not been violated.

If the passage quoted in the preceding paragraph means that the insurer must prove that it would have recovered in the event the claim had been litigated rather than being settled, then the compromise settlement figure is not treated as the true value of the third party claim. If the passage means that the insurer must show only that there is such a possibility of a recovery because the claim had settlement value, then it would be open to the insurer to show damages in an amount equal to the compromise settlement figure allocable to the portion of the claim to which it was subrogated (the property damage claim, but not the personal injury claim). Although an insurer would be free to urge that the reasonable compromise settlement value exceeded the amount the insured accepted in settlement, the insured would have little cause for complaint if the insurer were satisfied to treat the actual settlement figure as the true value.

22. Hamilton Fire Insurance Co. v. Greger, 246 N.Y. 162 at p. 169, 158 N.E. 60 at p. 62 (1927), 55 A.L.R. 921 at p. 926 (1928) (emphasis added).

Also see Twin States Insurance Co. v. Bush, 183 So.2d 891 (Miss.1966). The court held that the insurer must prove that it "could have recovered from the person to whom the release was given * * *," and therefore the insurer must allege and prove, in its claim against the insured, "that the other driver caused or contributed to the accident * * *." 183 So.2d at p. 893.

23. Or only that there was a prospect of effecting some recovery by compromise? This interpretation seems implausible, because any value placed on such a prospect would be more speculative than damages findings are ordinarily allowed to be.

§ 3.10(d) Impediments to Subrogation

(1) Introduction

Allowing an insurer to be subrogated to the rights of its insured in exchange for the payment of insurance proceeds is not uniformly recognized as appropriate in all circumstances. Some limitations have been recognized in several jurisdictions.[1]

(2) The Primary Obligation Rule

It has sometimes been argued that either because of the basic nature of the type of insurance coverage involved or because of the terms of a particular policy clause, an insurer in paying insurance benefits is discharging a primary obligation (rather than a secondary obligation) and that when an insurer makes such a payment it may not enforce a right of subrogation against any payment made by a tortfeasor.[2] In judicial opinions setting forth this proposition, the characterization of an insurer's obligation as primary is typically advanced as a legal conclusion that expresses — often without any statement of supporting reasons — the proposition that subrogation is not allowed.

The premise upon which arguments invoking the primary obligation rule are advanced is patently fallacious in most situations because an insurer's payments are always made in satisfaction, wholly or partially, of the insurer's contractual obligation. Moreover, in almost all such instances, the persons to whom insurance payments were made would be entitled to assert a claim against the tortfeasor, as for example when parents have been indemnified by an insurer for medical costs incurred when injuries were sustained by a minor child in an automobile accident caused by a negligent motorist. Both the parents, who sustain consequential damages, and the injured child could seek indemnification from such a tortfeasor.

In some circumstances the primary obligation rule appears to be applied by courts with a view to maximizing the insured's indemnification. In an Illinois case, for example, the court decided that an insurer that paid the cost of medical treatment ($1,109) for a four-year-old child injured in an automobile accident was not entitled to enforce a right of subrogation against a payment of $5,000, by the tortfeasor's insurer, to

---

§ 3.10(d)

1. Impediments to subrogation also arise from enforcement of rights that are at variance with policy provisions. See § 6.1 and § 6.9(c), below.

2. See, e.g., Michigan Hospital Service v. Sharpe, 339 Mich. 357, 63 N.W.2d 638 (1954), 43 A.L.R.2d 1167 (1955); United States Fidelity & Guaranty Co. v. Valdez, 390 S.W.2d 485 (Tex.Civ.App.1965) (writ refused, no reversible error) (alternate holding; voluntary workers' compensation insurance).

In a companion case to *Michigan Hospital Service,* however, it was held that an express subrogation provision in a contract for medical and surgical services supported a suit for breach of contract by the Sharpes in settling with the tortfeasor. Michigan Medical Services v. Sharpe, 339 Mich. 574, 64 N.W.2d 713 (1954). The court thus impliedly recognized that the "primary" obligation argument for denying rights of subrogation, at most, applies only in the absence of an express subrogation provision.

the minor's estate.[3] Although the Illinois court predicated its analysis on the rule that a minor's medical expenses were necessaries for which her parents were primarily liable and that "the minor's estate * * * received no benefit from the payment of the medical expenses," [4] reading between the lines of the opinion one may infer that the court's greater concern was directed at increasing the recovery for the minor's estate.

(3) Voluntary Payments by Insurers

In some instances, an insurer pays a claim for which it is not liable. When this occurs, occasionally it has been urged that the insurer thereby becomes a volunteer and is not entitled to subrogation because a person who volunteers to pay the debt of another cannot acquire a right of subrogation.[5] This argument, which is sometimes referred to as the "volunteer doctrine," has not been recognized by many courts.[6] Furthermore, few, if any, of the decisions denying subrogation on the ground that the insurer was a volunteer have done so when liability was genuinely in dispute.[7] Rather, when such decisions are carefully analyzed, the cases in which recovery was barred on this theory are consistent with the view that this defense applies only if an insurer has full knowledge of the facts when the claim is paid [8] — that is, the courts applying the volunteer rule to insurers have only done so when the

3. Estate of Woodring v. Liberty Mutual Fire Insurance Co., 71 Ill.App.3d 158, 27 Ill.Dec. 399, 389 N.E.2d 211 (2d Dist.1979).

4. Id., 389 N.E.2d at p. 212.

5. See the discussion in Commercial Union Insurance Co. v. Postin, 610 P.2d 984 at pp. 986–993 (Wyo.1980).

6. See, e.g., North-West Insurance Co. v. Western Pacific Insurance Co., 249 Or. 662, 439 P.2d 1006 (1968) (action by liability insurer of one car against liability insurer of second car, owned by same insured, to recover money paid on property damage claims under mistaken belief plaintiff's coverage was involved).

Also see Charles B. Robison, *Voluntary Payment by the Insurer: Its Effect on the Insurer's Right to Subrogation*, 27 Federation of Insurance Counsel Quarterly 19–32 (1976).

7. Professor Patterson suggested that an insurer is entitled to subrogation although it pays a claim despite a good defense "based upon a breach of condition which an honest insurer would ordinarily be willing to overlook * * *," but not if the loss "is not covered by the policy or falls within an exception." Patterson, ES-SENTIALS OF INSURANCE LAW (Second edition, 1957), at p. 149 citing the *Old Colony* case, n. 8, below, for the latter proposition.

Cf. Continental Insurance Co. v. Federal Insurance Co., 153 Ga.App. 712, 266 S.E.2d 351 (1980), in which the court concluded that an insurer which paid more than its pro rata share did not become a volunteer so as to bar contribution from a co-insurer. The court observed that sound public policy encourages the swift settlement of claims, and therefore it would be against public policy to force litigation prior to settlement to determine the respective liabilities of two or more insurers.

8. See, e.g., Old Colony Insurance Co. v. Kansas Public Serv. Co., 154 Kan. 643, 121 P.2d 193, 138 A.L.R. 1166 (1942) (husband's homestead interest in residence owned by wife was not "unconditional and sole ownership" required by policy naming him as the insured: insurer was a "mere volunteer" in paying husband's claim).

Also see e.g., Grain Dealers Mutual Insurance Co. v. White, 103 Ga.App. 260, 119 S.E.2d 38 (1961) (insurer's statutory cause of action for indemnity against insured defeated by lack of proof that insurer was not a volunteer in paying liability claims against insured); American Reliable Insurance Co. v. St. Paul Fire & Marine Insurance Co., 79 S.D. 226, 110 N.W.2d 344 (1961) (fire insurer could not recover contribution from second fire insurer, both having issued policies on the same property containing "other insurance" clauses, because payment to insured of amount in excess of insurer's pro rata share of loss was voluntary).

circumstances clearly indicated that the insurer was aware of a valid defense and nevertheless elected to pay the policy claim.[9]

The effect of the voluntary payments doctrine probably can be avoided by the insurer's taking an assignment of the claim of the "insured" (at the time of its payment to the claimant) in jurisdictions that do not impose restrictions on assignability,[10] or by resorting to a "loan receipt" transaction (even in the face of a rule against assignability).[11] Both of these actions would provide at least some support to a claim by the insurer that the claim was paid with the expectation of subsequently asserting a right of subrogation and therefore the insurer, in making such a payment, should not be treated as a "volunteer."

In most circumstances, applications of the so-called "volunteer doctrine" are very suspect because a rule denying subrogation to a "volunteer" insurer tends to discourage an insurer from settling with the insured in a case of doubtful coverage, especially when the insurer is not able to obtain an effectual assignment of the insured's claims against third parties as part of the settlement agreement. Such a rule is generally undesirable.

(4) Claims Against Common Carriers

For many years insurers and common carriers (such as truckers and railroads) engaged in an extended struggle with regard to the insurers' assertion of claims against carriers for damage to goods covered by insurance obtained by shippers.[12] The following description of some main events in this struggle indicates the nature of the controversy and its relation to subrogation.[13]

9. In Yeargin v. Farmers Mutual Insurance Association of Walker County, Georgia, 142 Ga.App. 76, 234 S.E.2d 856 at p. 857 (Div. 3, 1977), the court held that a fire insurer that paid benefits was not to be treated as having made a "voluntary payment" when it established "that none of its officers or employees was aware" of a second policy of insurance that was forbidden by a provision forbidding multiple coverage, and therefore the insurer was entitled to demand a return of its payment.

Also see the comments in Commercial Union Insurance Co. v. Postin, 610 P.2d 984 at pp. 988–990 (Wyo.1980).

10. See, e.g., Atlantic Mutual Insurance Co. v. Cooney, 303 F.2d 253 at pp. 262–263 (9th Cir.1962) (fire insurer reimbursed insured for loss in excess of $300,000 although applicable policy limit was $100,000; held, insurer could recover under California law as subrogee to insured's contract claim against bailee of property, rejecting the volunteer argument on the alternate grounds, first, that the insured had given express assignments of its rights to the insurer, and, second, that the *moral* obligation of the insurer to reimburse its insured was sufficient to support equitable

subrogation); Freeport Motor Casualty Co. v. McKenzie Pontiac, Inc., 171 Neb. 681, 107 N.W.2d 542 (1961) (volunteer argument irrelevant when insured's release of automobile comprehensive insurer expressly states that insurer is subrogated to claims of insured).

11. For instances of use of "loan receipts" in other contexts, see § 3.10(b)(2), above, and § 3.10(c)(1), above.

See also the reference to "loan receipts" in the majority opinion and the discussion of the "volunteer" argument in both the majority and dissenting opinions in Employers Casualty Co. v. Transport Insurance Co., 444 S.W.2d 606 (Tex.1969), which concerns conflicting "other insurance" clauses discussed in § 3.11(a)(3), below.

12. This struggle is sometimes referred to as the "battle of the forms." Entitlement to recognition as *the* battle of the forms has also been claimed for other controversies. See, e.g., Apsey, *The Battle of the Forms,* 34 Notre Dame Law Review 556–575 (1959).

13. See generally, VANCE, LAW OF INSURANCE (Third edition, Anderson, 1951), at pp. 794–796; Campbell, *Non-Consensual Sure-*

One of the early events in the conflict was the adoption by carriers of a bill-of-lading clause giving a carrier the benefit of insurance effected by a shipper.[14] Insurers responded to this clause in the bill-of-lading with a policy clause providing for nonliability of an insurer upon shipment under a bill of lading that gave a carrier the benefit of a shipper's insurance.[15] Since carriers then had nothing to gain and shippers had much to lose by retention of the clause previously used in bills of lading, the carriers modified the bill-of-lading clause to give a carrier the benefit of any insurance effected on the goods so far as this did not defeat the insurer's liability.[16] This strategic retreat by the carriers still left the insurers with a problem. If an insurer paid a shipper, would it be a "volunteer"[17] and therefore not entitled to subrogation to the shipper's claim against the carrier? If it did not pay the shipper, how could it maintain good business relations with an insured who wanted prompt payment from somebody and did not like waiting for the carrier and insurer to resolve a dispute as to ultimate responsibility for the loss? To avoid this problem, insurers resorted to loan receipts: an insurer paid a shipper an amount equal to the promised insurance benefits, but the transaction was cast as a loan repayable out of the prospective recovery from the carrier. The effectiveness of a loan receipt in preserving rights against a common carrier has been recognized in a number of judicial decisions.[18] Thus, at least as reflected in such precedents, the insurers prevailed in the struggle with carriers over form provisions concerning responsibility for losses of insured property during shipment.[19] And this result is also fortified by decisions that a "benefit of insurance" clause in a bill of lading is invalid under statutory prohibitions against rate discrimination, since a carrier would be receiving greater compensation from a shipper who had insurance than from one who did not.[20]

tyship, 45 Yale Law Journal 69–104 at pp. 81–85 (1935).

The discussion in the text does not provide a comprehensive or detailed description of the ways in which forms were manipulated by the insurers and common carriers.

14. See, e.g., Phoenix Insurance Co. of Brooklyn v. Erie & W. Transportation Co., 117 U.S. 312, 6 S.Ct. 750, 29 L.Ed. 873 (1886).

15. See, e.g., Fayerweather v. Phenix Insurance Co., 118 N.Y. 324, 23 N.E. 192 (1890); Hartford Fire Insurance Co. v. Payne, 199 Iowa 1008, 203 N.W. 4, 39 A.L.R. 1109 (1925).

16. See, e.g., Adams v. Hartford Fire Insurance Co., 193 Iowa 1027, 188 N.W. 823 (1922), 24 A.L.R. 182 (1923); Richard D. Brew & Co. v. Auclair Transportation, Inc., 106 N.H. 370, 211 A.2d 897 (1965), 27 A.L.R.3d 978 (1969).

Also see Aetna Insurance Co. v. Newton, 456 F.2d 655 (3d Cir.1972).

17. See § 3.10(d)(3), above.

18. E.g., Luckenbach v. W.J. McCahan Sugar Refining Co., 248 U.S. 139, 39 S.Ct. 53, 63 L.Ed. 170, 1 A.L.R. 1522 (1918).

Concerning loan receipts and their validity, see § 3.10(c)(1), above.

19. *But cf.* Grain Processing Corporation v. Continental Insurance Co., 726 F.2d 403 (8th Cir.1984) (sustaining the insurance claim when the insurance policy issued to the shipper provided that it was for the "account of whom it may concern" and the court concluded this indicated that the insured shipper's intent was to cover the consignee).

20. See, e.g., Salon Service, Inc. v. Pacific & Atlantic Shippers, 24 N.Y.2d 15, 298 N.Y.S.2d 700, 246 N.E.2d 509 (1969).

Contra. Home Insurance Co. v. Northern Pacific Railroad Co., 18 Wn.2d 798, 140 P.2d 507, 147 A.L.R. 849 (1943).

§ 3.10(e) Observations

The treatment accorded subrogation rights has varied with the type of insurance involved. In general, the attitude of the courts toward subrogation is appropriately described as one of allowing substantial freedom of contract, which means that generally explicit subrogation provisions — that facilitate the insurer's intention as manifested in the insurance policy — will be enforced even when that result means that an insured will not be fully indemnified.

The judicial attitude toward subrogation often is in marked contrast with that which seems to prevail in relation to the insurable interest doctrine.[1] Courts accord little, if any, significance to either the intention of the parties or the express terms in an insurance policy which purport to provide for rights that are not in accord with the public policies that underlie the insurable interest doctrine. This contrast is all the more intriguing when one takes account of the fact that both the insurable interest and subrogation doctrines are essentially corollaries of the principle of indemnity [2] which are used to prevent an insured from realizing a net gain from insurance proceeds.[3]

Some courts, although acknowledging the importance of contractual freedom, have favored outcomes that clearly are not in accord with specific insurance policy provisions. In these decisions, the courts disregard the policy terms in order to foster more complete indemnification for insureds. The results in these cases accord with the increasingly recognized societal goal of providing full indemnification for accident victims—especially for individuals injured in motor vehicle accidents.

§ 3.10(e)

1. See § 3.1, above, concerning that principle generally.

2. See § 3.6, above, concerning techniques of preventing net gain.

3. *Cf.* Spencer L. Kimball and Don A. Davis, *The Extension of Insurance Subrogation,* 60 Michigan Law Review 841–872 at pp. 868–872 (1962).

But consider the observation of James J. Meyers, who at the time of writing the article was Senior Vice President of Crum & Forster Insurance Companies:

"Effective subrogation practices by insurers can mean the difference between an underwriting profit or a loss. Efficient administration of the insurance industry's subrogation program should result in an accurate distribution of loss experience by line or class of business, *which in turn purifies rate-making statistics, thereby serving the public interest.*"

James J. Meyers, *Subrogation Rights and Recoveries Arising out of First Party Contracts,* 9 The Forum 83–90 at p. 83 (1973).

Julius Denenberg has observed that despite various extensive criticisms "subroga-

tion actions are flourishing" and he concludes that this "appears to be attributable to the increasing size of judgments, paralleling the consumer movement." He also commented, "As long as juries continue to reach multi-million dollar verdicts in cases involving products liability, negligence and other property loss, insurance companies must take advantage of the doctrine of subrogation to recoup their losses." Julius Denenberg, *Subrogation Recovery: Who Is Made Whole,* 29 Federation of Insurance Counsel Quarterly 185–198 at pp. 185–86 (1979).

Also see Jay S. Bybee, *Profits in Subrogation: An Insurer's Claim to Be More than Indemnified,* 1979 Brigham Young Law Review 145–159; Herbert P. Polk, *Attorney's Primer on Some First Steps in Prosecution of a Subrogation Claim,* 10 The Forum 465–476 (1974). Note, *Subrogation and Indemnity Rights Under the Minnesota No-Fault Automobile Act,* 4 William Mitchell Law Review 119–162 (1978) (discussing the retention of subrogation rights for insurers under the Minnesota Act).

§ 3.11　Other Insurance Clauses

§ 3.11(a)　Introduction

(1) Types of Other Insurance Clauses

Several different types of insurance include "Other Insurance" provisions. In general, an Other Insurance clause will provide for one of three consequences when a claimant may be entitled to indemnification from more than one insurance coverage:

First, that the insurer shall have no liability if there is other insurance. This type of provision is usually referred to as an "escape" clause.[1]

Second, that the insurer's liability shall be limited to a proportional share of the loss. This type of clause is usually referred to as a "pro rata" clause.[2]

Third, that "the policy" shall apply only as excess insurance over any other insurance. This type of clause is usually referred to as an "excess" clause.[3]

§ 3.11(a)

1. See, e.g., clauses at issue in Insurance Company of North America v. Continental Casualty Company, 575 F.2d 1070 (3d Cir.1978); Graves v. Traders & General Insurance Company, 252 La. 709 at p. 710, 214 So.2d 116 at p. 117 (1968).

An escape clause typically provides that the insurer "shall not be liable to make any payment in connection with any claim made against an insured * * * which is insured by another valid policy * * *." The effect of this provision was at issue in American Home Assurance Company v. Fish, 122 N.H. 711, 451 A.2d 358 (1982).

2. See, e.g., clauses at issue in Insurance Company of North America v. Continental Casualty Company, 575 F.2d 1070 (3d Cir.1978); Concord General Mutual Insurance Co. v. Patrons-Oxford Mutual Insurance Co., 411 A.2d 1017 (Me.1980).

Also see Travelers Insurance Company v. Chappell, 246 So.2d 498 at pp. 501–02 (Miss.1971); Continental Insurance Co. v. Federal Insurance Co., 153 Ga.App. 712, 266 S.E.2d 351 (1980).

For example, a typical pro rata clause provides "If the insured has other insurance against a loss covered by this policy the Company shall not be liable under this policy for a greater proportion of such loss than the applicable limit of liability stated in the declarations bears to the total applicable limit of liability of all valid and collective insurance against such loss."

Pro rata clauses often provide that when other coverage applies the insurer's liability will not exceed its proportionate share

of the total insurance coverage, so that the insurer's maximum liability may be limited by such a clause to something less than the maximum limit of liability specified in the policy.

Courts in several states have prorated liability among insurers when the applicable other insurance provisions were in conflict. See, e.g., Mission Insurance Co. v. Allendale Mutual Insurance Co., 95 Wn.2d 464, 626 P.2d 505 (1981), in which the court adopted the rule that each company is required to contribute equally until the limit of the smaller policy is exhausted, with any remaining portion of the loss then being paid from the larger policy. This approach is sometimes referred to as the "maximum loss" rule, and differs from the majority rule which prorates the insurance payments on the basis of the maximum coverage limits of each of the insurance policies applicable to the accident. Also see Hardware Dealers Mutual Fire Insurance Co. v. Farmers Insurance Exchange, 444 S.W.2d 583 at p. 589 (Tex.1969).

3. See, e.g., the clauses at issue in St. Ann v. American Insurance Co., 206 So.2d 817 at p. 819 (La.App., 4th Cir., 1968).

Also see Continental Insurance Company v. Weekes, 74 So.2d 367 at pp. 367–368 (Fla.1954).

The following clause appears in a form of Mercantile Open Stock Policy:

"If there is any other valid and collectible insurance which would apply in the absence of this policy, the insurance under this policy shall apply only as excess insurance over such other insurance;

Some Other Insurance provisions combine these features to create provisions such as excess-escape clauses or excess pro-rata clauses.

Other Insurance clauses are often referred to as "exculpatory clauses" in that such clauses are intended to "clear" the insurer from liability (that is, to avoid liability for an insurer) by declaring either that another insurer provides primary coverage or that the insurance contract containing the clause provides no coverage when another insurance coverage applies to the loss.

Other Insurance clauses often produce litigation.[4] For example, many coverage disputes have involved situations in which a conflict occurs because each policy declares that it is excess insurance and that any other insurance which applies to the insured event is primary.[5] Disputes as to the meaning and effect of such provisions have revealed the existence of difficult and frequently irreconcilable conflicts among Other Insurance clauses used in various coverages. As a consequence, insurers have developed policy provisions with refinements that seek to avoid some of the problems or pitfalls that have become most evident,

provided, the insurance shall not apply to property otherwise insured unless such property is owned by the insured."

Compare the following clause, appearing in a form of American marine policy on cargo:

"If an interest insured hereunder is covered by other insurance which attached prior to the coverage provided by this Policy, then this Company shall be liable only for the amount in excess of such prior insurance; the Company to return to the Assured premium equivalent to the cost of the prior insurance at this Company's rates. If an interest insured hereunder is covered by other insurance which attached subsequent to the coverage provided by this Policy, then this Company shall nevertheless be liable for the full amount of the insurance without right to claim contribution from the subsequent Insurers. Other insurance upon the property of same attaching date as the coverage provided by this Policy shall be deemed simultaneous, and this Company will be liable for a ratable contribution to the loss or damage in proportion to the amount for which this Company would otherwise be liable under this Policy, and will return to the Assured an amount of premium proportionate to such reduction of liability."

Cf. Commercial Union Insurance Co. v. Sneed, 541 S.W.2d 943 (Tenn.1976), in which the court held that where there was in force a valued insurance policy and an open policy, under a valued policy statute the pro rata payment provision of the valued policy was unenforceable and invalid, and therefore valued policy insurer had to pay the full amount of coverage so that the

insurer on the open policy was liable only for the excess loss above the valued policy limits.

Also see the clauses discussed in § 3.11(b), below.

4. In 1972, Judge Donald Lay of the Eighth Circuit Court of Appeals commented that the case before the court again presented "the repetitive task of untangling another web of confusion created by the inarticulate language of two automobile liability policies." Miller v. National Farmers Union Property and Casualty Co., 470 F.2d 700 at p. 701 (8th Cir.1972).

Writing a few years earlier, Justice Tobriner observed that there was a "plethora of cases coming to the courts in which insurance carriers engage in an internecine struggle to determine which carrier should discharge a loss under primary and 'excess' coverage provisions." American Automobile Insurance Co. v. Transport Indemnity Co., 200 Cal.App.2d 543 at p. 544, 19 Cal.Rptr. 558 at p. 559 (1962). Justice Tobriner also commented, "In entering this legalistic labyrinth of the provisions of these policies, we are not favored, like Theseus, with any thread of principle. * * *" Ibid.

More recently, in Schoenecker v. Haines, 88 Wis.2d 665 at p. 675, 277 N.W.2d 782 at pp. 786–787 (1979), Justice Heffernan commented that despite "the clear dissatisfaction of the courts with the way insurance companies have handled the other insurance problem, the onerous task of reconciling these disputes continues to be forced on the courts resulting in a waste of policyholder's money and the court's time."

5. See § 3.11(f), below.

and the clauses in some policies have become rather complex. For example, the following terms from a garage liability insurance policy is in marked contrast to the relative simplicity of Other Insurance clauses in older insurance forms:

"(1) If there is other valid and collectible insurance whether primary, excess or contingent, available to the garage customer and the limits of such insurance are sufficient to pay damages up to the amount of the applicable Financial Responsibility limits, no damages are collectible under this policy.

"(2) If there is other valid and collectible insurance available to the garage customer, whether primary, excess or contingent, and the limits of such insurance are insufficient to pay damages up to the amount of the applicable Financial Responsibility limit, then this insurance shall apply to the excess of damages up to such limit.

"(3) If there is no other valid and collectible insurance, whether primary, excess or contingent, available to the garage customer, this insurance shall apply, but the amount of damages payable under this policy shall not exceed the applicable Financial Responsibility limit."[6]

This type of clause is intended to eliminate or at least circumvent some of the problems which courts found particularly objectionable in regard to the absolute nature of the escape clauses. At the same time, this type of clause is designed to limit an insurer's maximum liability to the coverage limits required by the applicable state financial responsibility law.[7]

(2) Purposes of Other Insurance Clauses

The objectives of Other Insurance clauses vary to some extent depending on the type of insurance. In some situations, Other Insurance clauses have been designed to protect insurers against the moral risks incident to overinsurance. Such clauses reduce or eliminate the liability of the insurer in whose policy they appear when an insured has a right to be indemnified by another coverage of a specified type. In effect, the clauses are intended to deter insureds from overinsuring property.

When a property owner obtains insurance policies from two or more insurers in a total amount that exceeds the property's value, the insured may have an inducement to destroy the property for the purpose of collecting the insurance.[8] To the extent property owners are

---

6. See Western States Mutual Insurance Co. v. Continental Casualty Co. and Hardward Mutual Casualty Co., 133 Ill. App.2d 694, 272 N.E.2d 439 (2d Dist.1971).

7. See the discussions in Maryland Casualty Co. v. Horace Mann Insurance Co., 551 F.Supp. 907 (W.D.Pa.1982), *affirmed* 720 F.2d 664 (3d Cir.1983) and in John P. Kurtock, Jr., *Overlapping Liability Coverage—The "Other Insurance" Provision*, 1974 Federation of Insurance Counsel Quarterly 45–72 at pp. 70–72.

8. Compare § 3.1(d)(1).

Concerning moral hazard clauses generally, see § 6.6(e)(3), below.

In addition, when a property is either fully insured or over-insured, the incentive for an insured to take care might operate less forcefully upon such a person than

not deterred from overinsuring property, the Other Insurance clauses in property insurance have been designed to protect the insurance company from the hazards incident to overinsurance by eliminating the insured's right to collect the insurance.[9] In general, however, it seems clear that Other Insurance provisions have not been primarily designed with a view to influencing the conduct of an insured.

Typically, insurers do little, if anything, to make insureds aware of Other Insurance clauses. For example, this is true for motor vehicle liability insurance generally,[10] and uninsured motorist coverage in particular.[11] Undoubtedly, the purpose of the Other Insurance Clauses in these coverages is to reduce or eliminate the insurer's liability for an insured loss. When more than one insurance policy is applicable to an insured event, the Other Insurance provisions in these coverages both prescribe a priority or order for payment in regard to the coverages, and limit the insurer's liability. Moreover, these clauses have often been designed to eliminate the insurer's liability [12] without regard to whether an insured has been fully indemnified.

Many insureds now acquire layers of insurance coverage — that is, an insured purchases one or more insurance policies which are designed to provide coverage only when the amount of an insured loss reaches a predetermined level or plateau. For example, a purchaser who decides to be a self-insurer for losses of up to $250,000, may purchase a policy that provides up to $1,000,000 of coverage for losses that exceed $250,000. Furthermore, such an insured might also decide to purchase a second policy that provides up to $10,000,000 of coverage for losses that exceed $1,250,000. Several characterizations can be used to describe this type of arrangement. These policies are specifically structured as excess coverage. Thus, one way to design such a coverage is by using an "excess other insurance coverage" clause.[13] The second policy is also sometimes described or referred to as a "$10,000,000

upon one who has an interest in a property that is not fully insured.

9. Yeargin v. Farmers Mutual Insurance Association of Walker County, Georgia, 142 Ga.App. 76, 234 S.E.2d 856 (Div. 3, 1977) (in the absence of the property insurer's consent to the insured taking out a second policy of fire insurance, insurer was entitled to a return of its claims payment to the insured made before the insurer became aware of the second policy of insurance).

Also see Note, *Primary Liability Under Excess Insurance Clauses: State Capital Insurance Co. v. Mutual Assurance Society Against Fire on Buildings*, 13 University of Richmond Law Review 165–173 (1978).

10. See the discussion of liability insurance in § 3.11(e), below.

11. See the discussion of the uninsured motorist insurance in § 3.11(f), below.

12. See, e.g., General Accident Fire & Life Assurance Corp. v. Continental Casu-

alty Co., 287 F.2d 464 (9th Cir.1961); St. Paul Fire & Marine Insurance Co. v. Crutchfield, 162 Tex. 586, 350 S.W.2d 534 (1961); American Insurance Co. v. Kelley, 160 Tex. 71, 325 S.W.2d 370 (1959); Continental Casualty Co. v. Weekes, 74 So.2d 367 (Fla.1954), 46 A.L.R.2d 1159 (1956).

One commentator has observed that "the specialty policy escape clause is philosophically oriented to shifting the liability for payment to others, to escape liability when other insurance protection is available to the operator of the vehicle." John P. Kurtock, Jr., *Overlapping Liability Coverage—The "Other Insurance" Provision*, 25 Federation of Insurance Counsel Journal 45–72 at p. 50 (1974).

13. See Thomas B. Alleman, *Resolving the "Other Insurance" Dilemma: Ordering Disputes Among Primary and Excess Policies*, 30 Kansas Law Review 75–95 at pp. 80–90 (1981).

umbrella policy" with a "$1,250,000 deductible." Alternatively, such a $10,000,000 policy could include a clause that is referred to as "coinsurance provisions."[14] "Coinsurance provisions," as the term is used in this context, are policy contract terms which specify that if an insured does not maintain coverage to a specified value the insured bears part of the specified risk.[15]

(3) Enforceability of Other Insurance Clauses

The enforceability and effect of Other Insurance clauses repeatedly have been the subject of judicial consideration, especially when there is a conflict between the provisions of the insurance policies. For example, when two policies both include escape clauses which specify that each insurer is allowed to avoid liability completely if other insurance applies to the insured event, a coverage dispute may result. The array of possible conflicts include the following situations:

      Escape Clause vs. Escape Clause

      Escape Clause vs. Excess Clause

      Escape Clause vs. Pro rata Clause

      Excess Clause vs. Excess Clause

      Excess Clause vs. Pro rata Clause

Insurers often use escape clauses which state that the insurer provides no coverage if the policyholder has other insurance applicable to the loss without regard to whether the other "applicable" insurance is valid and collectible.[16] The enforcement of such Other Insurance provisions in instances where the primary coverage is not available can create a situation in which the insured is precluded from recovering under either insurance coverage. As might be expected, many claimants have sought to avoid the literal enforcement of Other Insurance clauses that either eliminated or reduced an insurer's liability below the applicable limits of liability in circumstances in which the insured was not fully indemnified for the loss. Courts have often been receptive to such claims when insureds were seeking coverage payments that would not violate the principle of indemnification.[17] However, this is

---

14. See Annotation, *Validity, construction, and effect of insurance policy provision requiring insured to maintain coverage to specified value of property (coinsurance clause)*, 43 A.L.R.3d 566–590 (1972).

15. The meaning of the term "coinsurance provision" in this context differs from the meaning of the term "concurrent insurance," which is sometimes used to describe the other insurance situation when two or more insurers provide coverage for the same risk. Also, the term "coinsurance" is used differently in other contexts. See, e.g., § 3.7(b) and § 3.8, above.

An interesting question, rarely presented in disputes considered by appellate courts, concerns what types of additional indemnification from another source constitute "other insurance" for the purpose of a particular insurance coverage. In Gustafson v. Central Iowa Mutual Insurance Ass'n, 277 N.W.2d 609 (Iowa 1979), 7 A.L.R.4th 484 (1979), the court concluded that the repairs provided were a consequence of a builder's warranty and were not "other insurance" within the meaning of the property insurance policy.

16. See, e.g., Wilson Co. v. Hartford Fire Insurance Co., 300 Mo. 1, 254 S.W. 266 (1923).

17. See, e.g., Gustafson v. Central Iowa Mutual Insurance Association, 277 N.W.2d 609 (Iowa 1979), 7 A.L.R.4th 484 (1979) (prohibitions against insured securing "other insurance" did not apply to manufacturer's express warranty to replace steel farm buildings free of charge if directly damaged by snow or wind); Alabama Farm Bureau

not invariably the result in such cases, as the courts have adopted a variety of approaches in resolving coverage questions when there are conflicting clauses.

Many of the disputes which first presented the Other Insurance clause coverage issues involved property insurance, and the solutions adopted by the courts in those cases now seem to be primarily of historical interest (especially in regard to other types of insurance). For example, some courts examined the applicable policies with a view to allocating liability on the basis of which policy predated the other — that is, which policy first provided coverage for the risk that resulted in the insured's loss.[18] When the courts began to consider coverage disputes involving liability insurance, other theories were developed, such as allocating the insurers' liability on the basis (1) of the policy with the more specific coverage in relation to the loss (in preference to the policy with a more general coverage which was either excluded or treated as an excess insurance),[19] (2) of which insurer covered the party who was primarily liable,[20] or (3) of the amount of premiums charged by each company in relation to the total premium paid by the insured.[21] The approaches adopted in those decisions also are now mostly matters of historical interest.

Other Insurance provisions have frequently been determined to be unenforceable as they are written either because the provisions of the clauses are in conflict or because of overriding public policy considera-

---

Insurance Co. v. McCurry, 336 So.2d 1109 (Ala.1976).

Also see St. Paul Fire & Marine Insurance Co. v. Crutchfield, 162 Tex. 586, 350 S.W.2d 534 (1961) (interests of mortgagor and first mortgage under policy obtained by mortgagor not avoided by policy procured by agent of second mortgagee without their knowledge); American Insurance Co. v. Kelley, 160 Tex. 71, 325 S.W.2d 370 (1959) (recovery allowed under policy first obtained; policy obtained subsequently was unenforceable from inception and insured had acted in good faith in obtaining second policy). Decisions of this type may be regarded as illustrations of the principle of honoring reasonable expectations. See § 6.3, below.

Cf. Concord General Mutual Insurance Co. v. Patrons-Oxford Mutual Insurance Company, 411 A.2d 1017 (Me.1980) (provision in the body of the insurance contract did not constitute an endorsement "attached" to the policy as required by the statute which authorized insurers to prohibit or limit the amount of additional insurance on a property).

See the decisions discussed in § 3.11(e) and § 3.11(f), below.

18. See the discussions in Automobile Insurance Company of Hartford, Conn. v. Springfield Dyeing Co., 109 F.2d 533 (3d

Cir.1940). This approach is often referred to as the "prior-in-time" theory.

Also see Kearns Coal Corp. v. United States Fidelity & Guaranty Co., 118 F.2d 33 at p. 35 (2d Cir.1941), *cert. denied* 313 U.S. 579, 61 S.Ct. 1099, 85 L.Ed. 1536 (1941) (automobile liability policy); New Amsterdam Casualty Co. v. Hartford Accident & Indemnity Co., 108 F.2d 653 at p. 656 (6th Cir.1940) (truck insured by liability policy).

19. See, e.g., Hartford Steam Boiler Inspection & Insurance Co. v. Cochran Oil Mill & Ginnery Co., 26 Ga.App. 288, 105 S.E. 856 (Div.2, 1921); Trinity Universal Insurance Company v. General Accident, Fire & Life Assurance Corp., 138 Ohio St. 488, 35 N.E.2d 836 (Ohio 1941) (the specific insurer is primarily liable).

20. See, e.g., American Auto Insurance Company v. Pennsylvania Mutual Indemnity Co., 161 F.2d 62 (3d Cir.1947); Maryland Casualty Company v. Bankers Indemnity Insurance Co., 51 Ohio App. 323, 200 N.E. 849 (1935).

21. See, e.g., Insurance Company of Texas v. Employers Liability Assurance Corp., 163 F.Supp. 143 (S.D.Cal.1958); Nationwide Mutual Insurance Company v. State Farm Mutual Auto Insurance Co., 209 F.Supp. 83 (N.D.W.Va.1962).

tions. When this occurs, it is necessary to decide how the liability of the insurers will be allocated or apportioned. Although the most common approach has been to apportion the total loss on the basis of the coverage limits of each policy and to limit the total insurance payment to the highest coverage limit,[22] the desirability and appropriateness of uniformly applying this approach is open to question in a number of contexts.[23]

(4) Comment

Especially when the case law is considered retrospectively, it appears clear that the approaches developed by courts for one type of insurance coverage frequently are not equally suitable for resolving disputes about the effect of similar or even identically phrased Other Insurance clauses used in different types of insurance coverages.[24] Accordingly, the following subsections consider the rules applied by the courts in relation to several different types of insurance. The discussion in these subsections surveys the judicial treatment accorded to Other Insurance clauses in various types of insurance coverages, together with some of the approaches courts have used to apportion or allocate liability when more than one insurance coverage applies to loss. Liability insurance and uninsured motorist coverage are discussed in greater detail because these are the areas which have most frequently been the focus of recent litigation.

§ 3.11(b)   Property Insurance

Other Insurance clauses in property insurance contracts originally were designed to deal with the problem of individuals who overinsured property — that is, insurers sought to avoid the risk that an insured might be tempted to intentionally destroy the overinsured property in order to collect on each of the insurance policies.[1] The drafters of insurance contracts developed escape clauses with the goal of penalizing the insured by eliminating all liability under the insurance contract when the insured purchased additional protection without the permission of the original insurer. Thus, such clauses not only implemented the principle of indemnification, but also sought to influence the conduct of insureds by discouraging the purchase of insurance that duplicated protection already provided by one policy.

Courts generally agreed with insurers that when additional insurance was purchased for an insured property without securing the permission of the insurer that had already insured the property, it increased the prospect that such property might be intentionally destroyed — especially when the property was over-insured — in order to

22. See the discussion of allocation in § 3.11(e)(3), below.

23. See § 3.11(e) and § 3.11(f), below.

24. *Cf.* John P. Kurtock, Jr., *Overlapping Liability Coverage—The "Other Insurance" Provision,* 25 Federation of Insurance Counsel Quarterly 45–72 at pp. 47 (1974).

§ 3.11(b)

1. See, e.g., Sloviaczek v. Estate of Puckett, 98 Idaho 371 at p. 373, 565 P.2d 564 at p. 566 (1977).

Also see the discussion of moral hazard in § 3.1(d)(1).

recover the insurance. Accordingly, escape clauses in property insurance policies were often upheld.[2] However, when the property was not overinsured, courts and legislators were increasingly troubled by the results such clauses produced.[3] Comparable provisions are still included in some types of property insurance.[4]

The 1943 New York Standard Fire Insurance Policy[5] does not provide for the use of the many moral hazard clauses that had previously been employed by insurers for such insurance contracts, including various types of Other Insurance clauses. Although this insurance policy form does not include any type of Other Insurance provision, an insurer is permitted to attach an endorsement imposing restrictions concerning other insurance[6] which states that the insurer "shall not be liable for a greater proportion of any loss than the amount hereby insured shall bear to the whole insurance covering the property against the peril involved, whether collectible or not."[7]

§ 3.11(c) Life Insurance

Life insurers are often very concerned about the amount of life insurance an applicant already has, and life insurance companies

2. Olbrich v. Mutual Fire Insurance Co. of Marshfield, Fond Du Lac County, 184 Wis. 413, 198 N.W. 607 (1924); O'Leary v. Merchants' & Bankers Mutual Insurance Company, 100 Iowa 173, 66 N.W. 75 (1898), affirmed in a second opinion reported at 69 N.W. 420 (1896).

Also see Northern Assurance Company of London v. Grand View Building Association, 183 U.S. 308 at p. 317, 22 S.Ct. 133, 46 L.Ed. 213 (1902); New Brunswick Fire Insurance Company v. Morris Plan Bank of Portsmouth, 136 Va. 402, 118 S.E. 236 (1923) (property insurance policy for an automobile).

3. See, e.g., St. Paul Fire & Marine Insurance Co. v. Crutchfield, 162 Tex. 586, 350 S.W.2d 534 (1961) (interests of mortgagor and first mortgagee under policy obtained by mortgagor not avoided by policy procured by agent of second mortgagee without their knowledge); American Insurance Co. v. Kelley, 160 Tex. 71, 325 S.W.2d 370 (1959) (recovery allowed under policy first obtained; policy obtained subsequently was unenforceable from inception and insured had acted in good faith in obtaining second policy).

Decisions of this type may be regarded as illustrations of the principle of honoring reasonable expectations. See the discussion of reasonable expectations in § 6.3, below.

In Gustafson v. Central Iowa Mutual Insurance Association, 277 N.W.2d 609 (Iowa 1979), the court concluded that an insured may recover under a property insurance contract when an insured building that was destroyed by a windstorm was repaired or replaced by the manufacturer under a builder's warranty. The court rejected the contentions that the insured sustained no actual loss and that the warranty was "other insurance" such that the clauses precluding recovery for losses to property covered by other insurance were applicable.

Also see, Note, *Insurance—An Insured May Recover Under a Policy of Insurance for Damage to or the Destruction of an Insured Building Even if the Building Is Repaired or Replaced at No Cost to the Insured Under a Builder's Warranty*, 28 Drake Law Review 998–1009 (1979).

4. See, e.g., N.C. Grange Mutual Insurance Company v. Johnson, 51 N.C.App. 447, 276 S.E.2d 469 at p. 470 (1981), sustaining the enforceability of a provision stating that unless or until the insurer was notified that the insured acquired other hail insurance on crops covered by the insurance policy, the coverage provided by the original coverage would be suspended.

5. See New York—McKinney's Insurance Law 168 (1966), reproduced in Appendix A.

6. "Other insurance may be prohibited or the amount of insurance may be limited by endorsement attached hereto." New York—McKinney's Insurance Law § 168 (McKinney, 1966), at lines 25–27. See Appendix A.

7. *Id.*, lines 86–89. Also see Appendix A.

commonly include questions on this subject in application forms. Even though insurers solicit this information, life insurance policies ordinarily do not contain Other Insurance clauses.[1] Arguably, there is less need[2] for Other Insurance provisions in life insurance than in other types of coverages because of the fact that the total life insurance on a single life is rarely as great as the total risk of economic loss to interested persons from early death.

§ 3.11(d) Health and Accident Insurance

Many policies providing health, accident, medical, or hospitalization coverage do not contain any clauses concerning other insurance. In the absence of an Other Insurance provision in these coverages, the courts have almost uniformly held that an insured is entitled to receive the insurance benefits without regard to the amount of total benefits provided by other insurance.[1] This result is consistent with the public policy underlying the collateral source rule — that is, just as courts have generally held that the benefits received by a claimant from a source wholly independent of and collateral to the wrongdoer do not diminish the liability of a wrongdoer,[2] the courts have usually concluded that the liability of a health or accident insurer is not reduced by other possible sources of indemnification or compensation.

Increasingly, health and accident insurance contracts are including Other Insurance clauses. This change is at least in part attributable to the legislatively mandated no-fault compensation for motor vehicle accident victims. The terms of the Other Insurance clauses in these coverages vary widely.[3]

§ 3.11(c)

1. Note, however, that this statement applies to "life insurance" in a narrow sense that excludes health and accident coverage. "Life insurance" as one of the three main classes of insurance is a broader concept that includes health and accident coverage. See § 1.5(c), above.

Other insurance provisions are occasionally used in some forms of life insurance in the narrow sense. For an example of such a policy, containing a clause concerning "other insurance" and limiting coverage to a schedule amount, according to age, less the face amount of the other insurance, see Prudential Insurance Co. v. Fuqua's Administrator, 314 Ky. 166, 234 S.W.2d 666 (1950), 22 A.L.R.2d 803 (1952) (holding, however, that the insurer was precluded by the incontestability clause of the policy from defending on the basis of the other insurance clause).

2. See the discussion in the role of indemnity in regard to life insurance in § 3.5(b), above.

§ 3.11(d)

1. See generally, Annotation, *Collateral Source Rule: Injured person's hospitalization or medical insurance as affecting damages recoverable,* 77 A.L.R.3d 415–435 (1977).

2. *Ibid.*

Also see the discussion of (2) subrogation rights in regard to these coverages in § 3.10(a), above, and the (2) limit of liability provisions in § 5.9(a), below.

3. See, e.g., Moody v. American Fidelity Assurance Co., 252 Ark. 899, 481 S.W.2d 700 (1972) (medical insurance protection provided in accordance with a statutory provision that "hospital and medical expense protection shall be excess insurance coverage or indemnity over and above any other collectible insurance" did not apply to any part of medical expenses covered by other insurance); Laurie v. Holland American Insurance Co., 31 Ill.App.2d 437, 176 N.E.2d 678 (1st Dist.1961) (involving two accident insurance policies with "other insurance" clauses of the "excess" coverage type).

Also see Slater v. Fidelity & Casualty Co., 277 App.Div. 79, 98 N.Y.S.2d 28 (1st Dept.1950) (recovery denied on three of eight $5,000 air travel trip insurance poli-

§ 3.11(e) Liability Insurance

(1) Generally

The significance of Other Insurance provisions increases with each expansion of the scope of coverage of liability insurance policies in general [1] and of motor vehicle liability insurance in particular.[2] For example, more Other Insurance problems have arisen because the coverage afforded by the standard forms used for motor vehicle liability insurance has been expanded by provisions such as omnibus clauses [3] and drive other vehicle coverage clauses.[4]

There are now many situations in which a claim by a person injured in an accident may be covered by more than one liability insurance policy. For example, when an insured driver has borrowed another person's vehicle, in the event an accident occurs both the driver's and the owner's liability insurance policies potentially provide coverage if the accident resulted from the driver's negligence. In order to avoid providing duplicative coverage for such situations, most insurance companies include Other Insurance provisions in liability policies designed to limit, reduce, or eliminate the coverage when other liability insurance is available to provide indemnification for an insured who may be liable as a consequence of motor vehicle accidents.[5]

(2) Enforceability

In many situations, the Other Insurance provisions of two or more liability insurance policies are in conflict.[6] For example, a clear con-

---

cies because of express limitation in policies to $25,000 total insurance).

§ 3.11(e)

1. See, e.g., Thomas B. Alleman, *Resolving the "Other Insurance" Dilemma: Ordering Disputes Among Primary and Excess Policies,* 30 Kansas Law Review 75–95 (1981); John P. Kurtock, Jr. *Overlapping Liability Coverage—The "Other Insurance" Provision,* 25 Federation of Insurance Counsel Journal 45–72 (1974).

2. See, e.g., Note, *Is There a Solution to the Circular Riddle? The Effect of "Other Insurance" Clauses on the Public, the Courts and the Insurance Industry,* 25 South Dakota Law Review 37–54 (1980); Note, *The Dilemma of Concurrent Coverage: Carriers Insurance Co. v. American Policyholders Insurance Co.,* 32 Maine Law Review 471–495 (1980).

Also see Note, *Double Insurance Coverage in Automobile Insurance Policies—The Problem of "Other Insurance" Clauses,* 47 Tulane Law Review 1038–1055 (1973); Comment, *Concurrent Coverage in Automobile Liability Insurance,* 65 Columbia Law Review 319–332 (1965).

See generally 8D BLASHFIELD, AUTOMOBILE LAW & PRACTICE (Third edition, 1966), at § 345.10.

3. See discussion of omnibus clauses in § 4.7, below.

4. See discussion of drive other vehicle coverage in § 4.9, below.

5. See clauses in the liability forms included in Appendix G, Appendix H, and Appendix J.

Also see John P. Kurtock, Jr., *Overlapping Liability Coverage—The "Other Insurance" Provision,* 25 Federation of Insurance Counsel Quarterly 45–72 (1974); Ronald Anderson, *Other Insurance Clauses in Automobile Liability Insurance Policies: An Analysis and Legislative Proposal;* 1976 Insurance Law Journal 222–242.

6. Several commentators have analysed the appellate decisions in terms of the types of other insurance clauses that are in conflict. For example, in John P. Kurtock, Jr., *Overlapping Liability Coverage—The "Other Insurance" Provision,* 25 Federation of Insurance Counsel Journal 45–72 (1974), Mr. Kurtock includes an extensive body of citations of decisions which are analysed state-by-state to determine whether the "Conflicts between 'other insurance' provisions involve either similar, dissimilar clauses."

flict occurs when the applicable Other Insurance clause in each of the policies declares that the policy in which it appears shall be excess insurance. The great weight of judicial authority supports the rule that when this occurs, such clauses are to be disregarded (as mutually repugnant) and each of the coverages is treated as primary insurance [7] (and the liability of the insurers is prorated [8]). Most decisions allow a liability insurer that defends and settles a claim against the insured who is covered by one or more other policies to thereafter recover a proportionate amount from the other insurer.[9] This rule is grounded on the general public interest of encouraging insurance companies to make swift settlements of claims, and recognition of the fact that such settlements might be significantly impeded if one insurer were foreclosed from subsequently seeking a contribution from other insurers whose policies also applied to the loss.

The scope of the judicially imposed rule which transforms two or more liability insurance policies with conflicting Other Insurance

7. See, e.g., Rouse v. Greyhound Rent-A-Car, Inc., 506 F.2d 410 at pp. 415–416 (5th Cir.1975); Carriers Insurance Co. v. American Policyholders' Insurance Co., 404 A.2d 216 (Me.1979).

Also see Pacific Indemnity Co. v. Federation American Insurance Co., 76 Wn.2d 249, 456 P.2d 331 (1969); State Farm Mutual Automobile Insurance Co. v. Union Insurance Co., 181 Neb. 253, 147 N.W.2d 760 (1967); Cosmopolitan Mutual Insurance Co. v. Continental Casualty Co., 28 N.J. 554, 147 A.2d 529 (1959), 69 A.L.R.2d 1115 (1960).

Cf. Farmers Insurance Exchange v. Fidelity & Casualty Co., 374 P.2d 754 (Wyo. 1962).

But cf. Schoenecker v. Haimes, 88 Wis.2d 665 at pp. 674–675, 277 N.W.2d 782 at pp. 786–787 (1979).

8. See, e.g. Carriers Insurance Co. v. American Policyholders' Insurance Co., 404 A.2d 216 (Me.1979). Also see the discussion in § 3.11(f)(2), below.

This approach is often referred to as the *Lamb-Weston* rule. In Lamb-Weston, Inc. v. Oregon Automobile Insurance Co., 219 Or. 110, 341 P.2d 110, *rehearing denied* 219 Or. 110, 346 P.2d 643 (1959), the court decided that proration would apply when two insurers had attempted to limit their respective liabilities by an excess and prorata other insurance provisions. The court concluded that when any other insurance terms come into conflict with the other insurance clause of another insurer, "regardless of the nature of the clause, they are in fact repugnant and each should be rejected in toto." *Id.*, 210 Or. at p. 129, 341 P.2d at p. 119.

9. See, e.g., Canal Insurance Co. v. Ranger Insurance Co., 489 F.Supp. 492 at p. 497 (D.S.C.1980); Truck Insurance Exchange v. Maryland Casualty Co., 167 N.W.2d 163 (Iowa 1969) (recovery allowed on theory of contribution, explicitly not on theory of subrogation to insured's rights); Firemen's Insurance Co. v. St. Paul Fire & Marine Insurance, 243 Or. 10, 411 P.2d 271 (1966); Continental Insurance Co. v. Federal Insurance Co., 153 Ga.App. 712, 266 S.E.2d 351 (1980).

Also see Firemen's Insurance Co. v. St. Paul Fire & Marine Insurance, 243 Or. 10, 411 P.2d 271 (1966).

But cf. Employers Casualty Co. v. Transport Insurance Co., 444 S.W.2d 606 (Tex. 1969) (action by truck lessee's insurer against truck lessor's insurer to recover pro rata contribution of sum paid in settlement and as costs of defense of tort claim against insured; held, since insurers' obligations were independent, payment by plaintiff insurer of more than its pro rata part of loss gave it no right of contribution; its remedy lies in a suit based on "contractual or conventional" subrogation to the right of the insured, which was not within the pleadings; intermediate court's remand for new trial affirmed).

But see the persuasive dissenting opinion, 444 S.W.2d at p. 611, taking the position that the insurer's remedy should not be limited to contractual subrogation and that an independent right of contribution should be recognized in this context, with the consequence that the trial court's summary judgment for five-eights contribution (based on policy limits of $500,000 and $300,000) should be reinstated. Multiple liability insurance coverage also gives rise to special problems concerning the duty to defend; see § 9.1(d), below.

clauses into primary coverages has been expanded by decisions concluding that clauses are in conflict despite the existence of a reasonable theory of reconciliation — that is, the rule which makes two or more coverages both primary has sometimes been applied to insurance policies where the "conflict" in the Other Insurance provisions was not clearly evident. One justification offered for this expansive application of the rule is that the interests of an insured are better served by this approach because otherwise an insured would be prejudiced by a delay in the disposition of claims. Furthermore, given the public interests at stake, arguably courts should decline to legitimate the development of labyrinthian insurance policy provisions, the reconciliation of which requires inordinately complex analysis and occasions wasteful litigation.[10]

In general, escape clauses in liability insurance policies are viewed with disfavor by the courts, and there is considerable support for the rule that when a liability insurance policy includes an escape clause it will be treated as primary coverage in relation to another policy which includes an excess clause.[11] For example, the rule of primary coverage has been applied to cases involving one policy with an "excess" clause and another with a "nonliability" or "escape" clause.[12] However, if one coverage is declared to be excess, the excess coverage is normally applicable only when a loss is proved in an amount that exceeds the limit of the primary coverage.[13]

Many courts will consider the provisions stated in the Other Insurance clauses in each liability insurance policy, and will recognize the priorities established by the insurance policies if these provisions do not conflict. When a careful reading of the language used in two insurance policies serves to reconcile them in regard to which is the

---

10. See discussion and notes in § 3.11(a), above.

11. See, e.g., Insurance Company of North America v. Continental Casualty Co., 575 F.2d 1070 (3d Cir.1978); Maryland Casualty Company v. Horace Mann Insurance Co., 551 F.Supp. 907 (W.D.Pa.1982), *affirmed* 720 F.2d 664 (3d Cir.1983); Tahash v. Flint Dodge Company, 115 Mich. App. 471, 321 N.W.2d 698 (1982) (escape clause in an automobile dealer's liability insurance was void as a matter of public policy because it violated the state financial responsibility act).

Also see Peerless Casualty Co. v. Continental Casualty Co., 144 Cal.App.2d 617, 301 P.2d 602 at p. 607 (1956).

12. See, e.g., Union Insurance Co. (Mut.) v. Iowa Hardware Mutual Insurance Co., 175 N.W.2d 413 (Iowa 1970); Hardware Dealers Mutual Fire Insurance Co. v. Farmers Insurance Exchange, 444 S.W.2d 583 (Tex.1969); State Farm Mutual Automobile Insurance Co. v. Universal Underwriters Insurance Co., 594 S.W.2d 950 at p. 958 (Mo.App., E.D., Div. 4, 1980).

Contra. Federal Insurance Co. v. Prestemon, 278 Minn. 218, 153 N.W.2d 429 (1967).

But see Insurance Company of North America v. Continental Casualty Co., 575 F.2d 1070 (3d Cir.1978), reversing the decision reported at 431 F.Supp. 316 (E.D.Pa. 1977).

13. This approach has been adopted in several cases. For example, in P.L. Kanter Agency, Inc. v. Continental Casualty Co., 541 F.2d 519 at pp. 522–523 (6th Cir.1976), the court concluded in regard to two errors and omissions policies that Michigan had adopted the "majority view that * * * when an excess clause conflicts with * * * a 'pro rata' clause, in a second policy, the excess clause controls and is to be given full effect" so that the insurer with the pro rata other insurance provision is the primary insurer.

Accord. Jones v. Medox, Inc., 430 A.2d 488 (D.C.App.1981) (malpractice coverages for a nurse).

primary coverage, then it seems appropriate to enforce the clauses as written [14] unless enforcement produces adverse and unexpected consequences for the insured or the interlocking provisions are so complex that they are likely to breed an inordinate number of litigated cases. Absent adverse consequences or complexity that produces litigation,[15] the rights of the insured are adequately protected.

(3) Allocation of Liability

When two or more liability insurance policies are treated as primary coverages, a choice must be made among different methods of proration. Several distinct approaches, which have been developed in response to this problem, are currently in use.[16]

(i) Proportional Proration Rule.

The method of proration that is frequently used is that the insurers pay shares of the loss proportional to their respective coverage limits that is, the loss is apportioned on the basis of the maximum coverage limits of each of the policies.[17] This approach is often set forth in liability insurance Other Insurance clauses. For example, a typical pro rata clause provides, "If the insured has other insurance against a loss covered by this policy the Company shall not be liable under this policy

14. Although consistent with decisions of the majority of courts of last resort, the view stated in the text cannot be reconciled with results reached by some courts, especially in regard to such provisions in the uninsured motorist coverage. See, e.g., Werley v. United Services Automobile Ass'n., 498 P.2d 112 (Alaska 1972) (treating other insurance clauses of identical uninsured motorist coverages as conflicting).

See generally the discussion in § 3.11(f), below.

15. But consider the comments in note 4, § 3.11(a), above.

16. There is at least one judicial precedent for a rule that proration should be based on the amount of premium paid for each of the applicable coverages. See e.g., Insurance Company of Texas v. Employers Liability Assurance Corp., 163 F.Supp. 143 (S.D.Cal.1958). See the discussion of this case in Note, *Automobile liability insurance—double coverage and the effect of the "other insurance" clauses,* 1 Willamette Law Journal 485–491 at p. 489 (1961).

Also see Note, *Double Insurance Coverage in Automobile Insurance Policies—The Problem of "Other Insurance" Clauses,* 47 Tulane Law Review 1039–1055 at pp. 1049–1054 (1973).

17. See, e.g., Blue Bird Body Company, Inc. v. Ryder Truck Rental, Inc., 583 F.2d 717 at p. 727 (5th Cir.1978); Lamb-Weston, Inc. v. Oregon Automobile Insurance Co., 219 Or. 110, 341 P.2d 110 (1959), 76 A.L.R.2d 485 (1961).

Also see Pacific Indemnity Co. v. Federation American Insurance Co., 76 Wn.2d 249, 456 P.2d 331 (1969); Liberty Mutual Insurance Co. v. Truck Insurance Exchange, 245 Or. 30, 420 P.2d 66 (1966); United Services Automobile Association v. Hartford Accident & Indemnity Co., 222 Tenn. 168, 433 S.W.2d 850 (1968), *remand from* 220 Tenn. 120, 414 S.W.2d 836 (1967); Farmers Insurance Exchange v. Fidelity & Casualty Co., 374 P.2d 754 (Wyo.1962).

When proration is provided for by the terms of a policy, rather than being ordered by the court because of inconsistency between the provisions of two policies, this rule that the insurers shall pay shares proportional to their limits of coverage is often expressed in both policies. See and the 1966 Standard General Liability-Automobile Policy, Appendix G, *below,* which provides in part:

"6. *Other Insurance* * * *.

"(b) Contribution by Limits. If any of such other insurance does not provide for contribution by equal shares, the company shall not be liable for a greater proportion of such loss than the applicable limit of liability under this policy for such loss bears to the total applicable limit of liability of all valid and collectible insurance against such loss."

Also see the 1943 New York Standard Fire Insurance Policy provision quoted in § 3.11(b), above.

for a greater proportion of such loss than the applicable limit of liability stated in the declarations bears to the total applicable limit of liability of all valid and collective insurance against such loss."

Some insurance policies provide for "contribution for equal shares."[18] When the applicable coverages provide for equal sharing, courts have sustained this approach.[19]

(ii) Maximum Loss Rule. In some jurisdictions, the rule of proration has been that all of the insurers with applicable policies are to pay equal shares of the loss up to the limits of their respective coverages.[20] For example, in Mission Insurance Co. v. Allendale Mutual Insurance Co.[21] the court adopted the rule that each company is required to contribute equally until the limits of the smaller policy is exhausted, with any remaining portion of the loss then being paid from the larger policy. This approach is sometimes referred to as the "maximum loss" rule.

The maximum loss rule differs from the proportional proration rule which allocates liability of the insurers on the basis of the maximum coverage limits of each of the insurance policies applicable to the accident and usually also limits the total liability to the highest limit of liability.

The rule of proration is sometimes applied to a case involving one policy with an "excess" clause and another with a proration clause.[22] The Other Insurance provisions of the 1955 and 1958 automobile

18. For example, such clauses provide: "*Contribution by Equal Shares.* If all of such other valid and collectible insurance provides for contribution by equal shares, the company shall not be liable for a greater proportion of such loss than would be payable if each insurer contributes an equal share until the share of each insurer equals the lowest applicable limit of liability under any one policy or the full amount of the loss is paid, and with respect to any amount of loss not so paid the remaining insurers then continue to contribute equal shares of the remaining amount of the loss until each such insurer has paid its limit in full amount ∗ ∗ ∗."

19. See, e.g., Employers Casualty Company v. Employers Commercial Union Insurance Company, 632 F.2d 1215 (5th Cir. 1980); Liberty Mutual Insurance Company v. Home Insurance Company, 583 F.Supp. 849 (W.D.Pa.1984) (predicting the approach the Pennsylvania courts will adopt).

20. See, e.g., Cosmopolitan Mutual Insurance Co. v. Continental Casualty Co., 28 N.J. 554, 147 A.2d 529 (1959), 69 A.L.R.2d 1115 (1960).

Several courts have observed that this is now emerging as the more equitable rule

for apportionment. *Cf.* Mission Insurance Company v. Allendale Mutual Insurance Company, 95 Wn.2d 464, 626 P.2d 505 (1981) (property insurance); Carriers Insurance Co. v. American Policyholders' Insurance Co., 404 A.2d 216 (Me.1979).

The "other insurance" clause of the 1966 Standard General Liability Automobile Policy provides for equal share proration when the other insurance also so provides. See Appendix G.

21. 95 Wn.2d 464, 626 P.2d 505 (1981).

Also see Carriers Insurance Company v. American Policyholders' Insurance Co., 404 A.2d 216 (Me.1979) (prorate loss equally up to the limits of the lower policy, with any remaining portion being paid from the larger policy up to its limits).

22. See, e.g., Liberty Mutual Insurance Co. v. Truck Insurance Exch., 245 Or. 30, 420 P.2d 66 (1966); Lamb-Weston, Inc. v. Oregon Automobile Insurance Co., 219 Or. 110, 341 P.2d 110 (1959), 76 A.L.R.2d 485 (1961).

Also see Note, *"Other Insurance" Clauses: The Lamb-Weston Doctrine,* 47 Oregon Law Review 430–447 (1968).

liability forms (invoked, for example, when an owner's policy and a borrower's policy both apply) have been construed in this way by most courts, with the result that the owner's policy is primary coverage, and the borrower's is excess.[23] This result is perhaps more clearly directed by the provision in the 1966 revision of the automobile liability forms.[24]

§ 3.11(f) Other Insurance Clauses in Uninsured Motorist Insurance

(1) Introduction

Uninsured motorist coverage was developed by the insurance industry in the mid-1950s in response to the increasingly severe problem created by financially irresponsible motorists,[1] and was first offered to

23. See, e.g., Rouse v. Greyhound Rent-A-Car, Inc., 506 F.2d 410 (5th Cir.1975) (applying Florida law); Commercial Union Insurance Co. v. Insurance Company of North America, 155 Ga.App. 786, 273 S.E.2d 24 (1980); Associated Indemnity Co. v. Insurance Company of North America, 68 Ill.App.3d 807, 25 Ill.Dec. 258, 386 N.E.2d 529 (1st Dist., 4th Div., 1979).

Cf. Continental Casualty Co. v. American Fidelity & Casualty Co., 275 F.2d 381 (7th Cir.1960) (applying Illinois law; result characterized as subrogation of excess insurer to rights of insured against primary insurer); Citizens Mutual Automobile Insurance Co. v. Liberty Mutual Insurance Co., 273 F.2d 189 (6th Cir.1959) (applying Michigan law) with respect to a "hired automobile or a non-owned automobile, this insurance shall be excess insurance over any other valid and collectible insurance available to the insured." See Appendix G.

Primary coverage is provided for the owner's vehicle when other coverages are excess, and proration is called for when two or more policies are either all primary or all excess. See Appendix G.

The 1958 form clause reads as follows:

"If the insured has other insurance against a loss covered by Part I of this policy the company shall not be liable under this policy for a greater proportion of such loss than the applicable limit of liability stated in the declarations bears to the total applicable limit of liability of all valid and collectible insurance against such loss; provided, however, the insurance with respect to a temporary substitute automobile or non-owned automobile shall be excess insurance over any other valid and collectible insurance." Risjord & Austin, Automobile Liability Insurance Cases—Standard Provisions and Appendix 62 (1964).

See generally Annotation, *Apportionment of liability between automobile liability insurers where one of the policies has an "excess insurance" clause and the other a "proportionate" or "prorata" clause,* 76 A.L.R.2d 502–514 (1961).

24. "With respect to a hired automobile or a non-owned automobile, this insurance shall be excess insurance over any other valid and collectible insurance available to the insured."

§ 3.11(f)

1. See generally, Committee to Study Compensation for Automobile Accidents, REPORT TO THE COLUMBIA UNIVERSITY COUNCIL FOR RESEARCH IN THE SOCIAL SCIENCES (1932); Emma Corstvet, *The Uncompensated Accident and Its Consequences,* 3 Law & Contemporary Problems 466–475 (1936); Joseph P. Murphy & Roos D. Netherton, *Public Responsibility and the Uninsured Motorist,* 47 Georgetown Law Journal 700–745 (1959); Norman E. Risjord & June M. Austin, *The Problem of the Financially Irresponsible Motorist,* 24 University of Kansas City Law Review 82–96 (1955).

Also see Raymond N. Caverly, *New Provision for Protection From Injuries Inflicted by an Uninsured Automobile,* 396 Insurance Law Journal 19–24 (1956); REPORT OF THE CALIFORNIA SENATE INTERIM COMMITTEE ON VEHICLES AND AIRCRAFT, THE FINANCIALLY IRRESPONSIBLE MOTORIST (1953–1955).

Portions of this section were adapted from material that was published in Alan I. Widiss, *Aggregating Uninsured Motorist Coverage: Judicial Construction of "Pyramids" to Provide Indemnification,* 15 Connecticut Law Review 565–616 (1983), and Volume I of Professor Widiss's treatise, UNINSURED AND UNDERINSURED MOTORIST COVERAGE (1985).

insurance purchasers in 1956.[2] In 1957, New Hampshire enacted legislation requiring insurance companies to include the coverage in all automobile liability policies issued or delivered in that state.[3] Comparable legislative requirements were subsequently adopted throughout the United States.[4]

Uninsured motorist insurance policies typically include several provisions that are intended by insurance companies to determine how the existence of more than one uninsured motorist coverage will affect the coverage provided by each policy. For example, in the 1966 Standard Uninsured Motorist Insurance Form (1966 Standard Form), the "Other Insurance" section comprises two paragraphs.[5] The first paragraph (hereinafter referred to as Paragraph One), which applies only when an insured is injured while occupying a highway vehicle other than a vehicle owned by a person who is a named insured in the policy under which the uninsured motorist claim is made, provides:

> "With respect to bodily injury to an insured while occupying a highway vehicle not owned by the named insured, this insurance shall apply only as excess insurance over any other similar insurance available to such insured and *applicable to such vehicle as primary insurance,* and this insurance shall then apply only in the amount by which the limit of liability for this coverage exceeds the applicable limit of liability of such other insurance."[6]

The portion of Paragraph One which states that the claimant's own policy applies "only as excess insurance over any other similar insurance available to such insured and applicable to such vehicle as primary insurance"[7] is intended to govern situations in which an insured is covered by more than one uninsured motorist coverage, and one of the insurance policies can be identified as the primary coverage. Uninsured motorist coverages almost uniformly provide that the primary coverage is the uninsured motorist insurance applying to the vehicle

---

2. See Widiss, UNINSURED AND UNDERIN- SURED MOTORIST INSURANCE (1985), at § 1.10.

3. *Id.,* at § 1.11.

4. The statutes in the following states are representative of the provisions that typically are included in such legislation: Illinois Rev.Stat.1981, ch. 73, § 755a; Iowa Code Annotation § 516.A (West Supp. 1981); Minnesota Stat.Annotation § 65B.49(4) (West Supp.1982); Nebraska Rev.Stat. § 60–509.01 (1978).

Uninsured motorist insurance is a first party insurance. The insurance company provides indemnification directly to the insureds. Third-party insurance commits the insurance company to pay to an individual who is not a party to the contract the sums an insured becomes legally obligated to pay when liability arises out of acts of the insured which are included in the definition of coverage.

5. A committee comprised of representatives from the National Bureau of Casualty Underwriters and Mutual Insurance Rating Bureau, respectively, associations of stock and mutual insurance companies, first drafted a group of provisions, called the Standard Coverage Part, for endorsement in 1956. This group of provisions, which is now generally known as "Protection Against Uninsured Motorist Insurance" or "Family Protection Coverage Endorsement Against Uninsured Motorists," was revised several times and culminated in the 1966 Standard Form.

6. 1966 Standard Form: Part VI: Additional Conditions: E. Other Insurance (emphasis added).

7. *Ibid.* (emphasis added).

in which the claimant was riding when the injury occurred. When a claimant also is either a named insured in another motor vehicle policy which includes uninsured motorist insurance or a relative who resides with a named insured, this uninsured motorist insurance is the secondary coverage — that is, the Paragraph One other insurance provision provides that the claimant's own uninsured motorist insurance is a secondary coverage and applies only if its limits of liability coverage are more extensive than those of the primary coverage.

Paragraph One of the 1966 Standard Form also provides that the insurance applies "only in the amount by which the limit of liability for this coverage exceeds the applicable limit of liability of such other insurance." [8] This type of combination provision is generally referred to as an "excess-escape" clause: "escape" because the clause entitles an insurance company to escape liability unless the maximum coverage limit exceeds the other insurance applicable to the accident; "excess" because it limits liability to situations when its coverage exceeds the "primary coverage," and also limits liability to the amount by which the limit of liability exceeds the applicable limit of liability of the other insurance.

The enforceability of this Other Insurance clause has been considered by literally hundreds of courts in instances in which claimants have sought to stack coverages (also referred to as "aggregating" or "pyramiding") to secure complete indemnification. [9] In these cases, insurance companies have repeatedly urged that the coverage terms allow an insurance company to reduce its liability even when the claimant has not been fully indemnified. The appellate court decisions on the enforceability of these Other Insurance provisions have made a significant contribution to the development of judicial trends in regard to the effect and treatment of Other Insurance clauses generally.

(2) Enforcement of the Excess-Escape Provision

In what is now clearly a minority view, courts in some states conclude that the excess-escape Other Insurance clause is enforceable. In these states, the only relevant questions are whether the claimant was occupying a vehicle when the accident occurred, whether the vehicle was owned by someone other than the claimant, and whether there was an uninsured motorist coverage applicable to that vehicle. In a few of these states, this result follows from a specific provision in the uninsured motorist insurance statute. [10] In other states, the courts have accepted the insurance company's position that the excess-escape Other Insurance clause is a clear and unambiguous provision, and therefore have allowed companies to reject claims even when a claimant has not been fully compensated by the primary coverage. In

---

8. *Id.* (emphasis added).

9. See cases collected in Widiss, UNIN- SURED AND UNDERINSURED MOTORIST INSUR- ANCE (1985), Chapter 13.

10. See, e.g., West's Ann.California In- surance Code § 11580.2(c)(2) and § 11580.2(d) (West Supp.1982); Maryland Code 1979, Art. 48A, § 543(a) (1979); Ore- gon Revised Statutes § 743.792(9)(a)(1979).

essence, these decisions hold that when one uninsured motorist coverage is applicable to the accident, the insured is in the same position that would have existed if the tortfeasor had been covered by a liability insurance policy with the minimum limits of liability required by the state financial responsibility law, and that it is irrelevant whether the uninsured motorist insurance is disbursed to other claimants.[11]

(3) Limitations on the Enforceability of the Excess-Escape Other Insurance Provision

The inequity of enforcing the excess-escape Other Insurance provision is illustrated by examining the consequences of its application to a hypothetical accident involving an uninsured motorist in which one person is killed and four persons each sustain damages in excess of the per-person limit of liability such as $10,000. Uninsured motorist coverage is typically written with a $20,000 per accident limit, although some states require only $10,000 and a few states mandate at least $50,000 per accident.[12] In this hypothetical case, the primary coverage could be distributed in several ways. All of the insurance coverage could be paid to one or two of the possible claimants whose damages exceed the amount of insurance provided by the policy. Alternatively, the coverage could be divided among the injured persons, providing only partial indemnification for each of the claimants. The Other Insurance provision included in a secondary uninsured motorist coverage would preclude recovery in this situation even though an injured claimant received either no indemnification or only partial indemnification from the primary coverage. The terms of the Other Insurance provision give no consideration to whether the primary insurance is either completely exhausted by payments to other persons who were injured or prorated among the claimants so that no claimant is fully indemnified.

In this type of situation, passengers have argued that a literal interpretation of the Other Insurance clause creates a paradox because they would have been entitled to recover up to the per-person limit ($10,000 in this illustration) under their own coverage if the driver of the vehicle in which they were riding had not been covered by uninsured motorist insurance. These claimants reason that their companies ought to be liable to the extent that the other insurance did not indemnify them to the limits of liability of their own policies.

---

11. Courts in Arkansas, California, Maryland, Massachusetts, New York, Utah, and perhaps Illinois, Michigan, and South Carolina, uphold the enforceability of this aspect of the other insurance provisions regardless of the amount of indemnification, if any, that the claimant has received from the primary coverage. See, e.g., Yarmuth v. Government Employees Insurance Co., 286 Md. 256, 407 A.2d 315 (1979); Morelock v. Millers Mutual Insurance Association, 49 Ill.2d 234, 274 N.E.2d 1 (1971);

Lyon v. Hartford Accident & Indemnity Co., 25 Utah 2d 311, 480 P.2d 739 (1971); Harris v. Southern Farm Bureau Casualty Insurance Co., 247 Ark. 961, 448 S.W.2d 652 (1970); Whitmire v. Nationwide Mutual Insurance Co., 254 S.C. 184, 174 S.E.2d 391 (1970).

12. However, it should be noted that many insureds now opt to purchase underinsured motorist coverage.

Courts in several jurisdictions have concluded that, notwithstanding the terms of the Other Insurance clause, a claimant should be assured a recovery of the minimum amount mandated by the state financial responsibility legislation — that is, these courts hold that an injured person is entitled to be indemnified to the minimum amount required by the applicable financial responsibility law.[13]

(4) Invalidation of the Excess-Escape Other Insurance Clause Provision

Courts in most states have nullified the excess-escape clause set out in Paragraph One of the Other Insurance provision in the 1966 Standard Form.[14] In general, these decisions conclude that an excess-escape clause is contrary to the objectives underlying the statutory mandate requiring that all insurance policies issued or delivered in the state include uninsured motorist coverage. In more than two-thirds of the states in which the issue has been raised, this portion of the Other Insurance provision has been invalidated when the claimant was not fully indemnified by the primary uninsured motorist coverage.[15] These courts reason that insurance companies violate the public policy embodied in the uninsured motorist insurance legislation by issuing coverage with clauses that permit insurers to reduce or eliminate liability when the claimant has not yet been fully indemnified, even in instances when the claimant has received compensation equal to the minimum amounts specified in the state's financial responsibility law. For example, several courts have commented in decisions invalidating the other insurance clause that "it would be unconscionable to permit insurers to collect a premium for a coverage which they are required by statute to provide, and then to avoid payment of loss because of language of

---

13. Courts in Arizona, Connecticut, Iowa, Tennessee, and Wisconsin have adopted this view. See, e.g., Lemrick v. Grinnell Mutual Reinsurance Co., 263 N.W.2d 714, 719 (Iowa 1978); Nelson v. Employers Mutual Casualty Co., 63 Wis.2d 558, 217 N.W.2d 670 (1974); Fidelity & Casualty Co. v. Darrow, 161 Conn. 169, 286 A.2d 288 (1971); Transportation Insurance Co. v. Wade, 106 Ariz. 269, 475 P.2d 253 (1970).

Also see Scherr v. Drobac, 53 Wis.2d 308, 193 N.W.2d 14 (1972); Leatherman v. American Family Mutual Insurance Co., 52 Wis.2d 644, 190 N.W.2d 904 (1971).

14. See, e.g., Bradbury v. Aetna Casualty & Surety Co., 91 Wn.2d 504, 589 P.2d 785 (1979); State Farm Mutual Automobile Insurance Co. v. Williams, 481 Pa. 130, 392 A.2d 281 (1978); Anderson v. Illinois Farmers Insurance Co., 269 N.W.2d 702 (Minn. 1978).

Also see Woods v. State Farm Mutual Automobile Insurance Co., 234 Ga. 782, 218 S.E.2d 65 (1975); Clayton v. Alliance Mutual Casualty Co., 212 Kan. 640, 512 P.2d 507 (1973), *rehearing denied* 213 Kan. 84, 515 P.2d 1115 (1973).

Cf. Hogan v. Allstate Insurance Co., 287 Ala. 696, 255 So.2d 35 (1971); Harthcock v. State Farm Mutual Automobile Insurance Co., 248 So.2d 456, 461–62 (Miss.1971).

In Landvatter v. Globe Security Insurance Co., 100 Wis.2d 21, 300 N.W.2d 875 (App.1980), the court concluded that the enactment of an amendment to the uninsured motorist insurance statute "provides the legislative mandate which was missing at the time the *Leatherman, Scheer, and Nelson* cases considered the public policy considerations governing reducing clauses." *Id.*, 100 Wis.2d at p. 26, 300 N.W.2d at p. 878. The court then decided that reading the original statute and the amendments together permits "the stacking of uninsured motorist coverages."

15. See Alan I. Widiss, *Aggregating Uninsured Motorist Coverages Judicial Construction of "Pyramids" to Provide Indemnification,* 15 Connecticut Law Review 565–616 at pp. 573–580 (1983).

limitation devised by themselves." [16] This reasoning may be questioned, however, because the premium that is collected will be affected by whether the Other Insurance clause is enforced as written.

In coverage disputes involving uninsured motorist insurance, courts have been disposed to favor the interests of the insureds in securing indemnification to a much greater degree than in litigation involving any other type of insurance. The explanation and justification for this judicial treatment rests in part on a generally recognized societal goal of providing indemnification for innocent accident victims. When this general objective was specifically recognized by uninsured motorist insurance legislation [17] — which established either mandatory offering requirements (specifying that the insurance must be offered to all purchasers of motor vehicle insurance) or mandatory coverage requirements (providing that the insurance must be included as an additional coverage in all motor vehicle policies) — uninsured motorist insurance assumed a unique status. No other insurance coverage has ever been mandated by legislation in states throughout the nation. Thus, it is not surprising that a substantial body of judicial opinions has developed pertaining to coverage disputes involving various terms in the uninsured motorist insurance which provide for reductions in or elimination of coverage when some indemnification is available from another source.[18]

A clear majority of these judicial decisions hold that the rights of insureds are not limited by coverage limitations such as those provided for in the Other Insurance clauses. The volume of appellate court decisions holding the various provisions for reducing coverage to be unenforceable has no counterpart in the entire field of insurance litigation. This volume of litigation has influenced both the standard terms developed for uninsured motorist insurance and judicial interpretations of those terms. This is particularly evident in the most recent standard forms prepared by the Insurance Services Office which provide markedly improved coverage for insureds in multiple coverage situations.

(5) The Other Insurance Provision of the 1977 Insurance Services Office Uninsured Motorist Insurance Form

The simplified approach to coverage terms developed for the 1977 Insurance Services Office Personal Auto Policy is nowhere more apparent than in the Other Insurance provision. The long and rather complex statements of earlier forms have been reduced to three sentences:

---

16. Simpson v. State Farm Mutual Automobile Insurance Co., 318 F.Supp. 1152 at p. 1156 (S.D.Ind.1970).

Also see Protective Fire & Casualty Co. v. Woten, 186 Neb. 212 at p. 217, 181 N.W.2d 835 at pp. 837–38 (1970).

17. See Widiss, UNINSURED AND UNDERINSURED MOTORIST INSURANCE (1985), at § 1.11, § 2.3, and § 15.1.

18. Id., at Chapter 13 and Chapter 14.

"If there is other applicable similar insurance we will pay only our share of the loss. Our share is the proportion that our limit of liability bears to the total of all applicable limits. However, any insurance we provide with respect to a vehicle you do not own shall be excess over any other collectible insurance."[19]

Although this provision has not yet been the subject of many appellate decisions, it undoubtedly will be considered by the courts in the future. In one respect, this provision is comparable to the language of the 1966 Standard Form, which has been repeatedly the subject of judicial review. Both sections provide that in the event a claimant is injured while occupying a vehicle that is not owned by the named insured or the spouse of a named insured who resides in the same household,[20] the coverage shall be excess over any other collectible insurance.[21] The differences, however, are far more significant than the similarities.

First, the new provision uses the phrase "other collectible insurance."[22] This is in marked contrast to the terms of the older policy, which used the phrase "other similar insurance available to such insured."[23] The new language seems to speak in terms of both entitlement and collectibility by using the term "other collectible insurance."[24] Also, the clause does not apply when the compensation paid to the claimant has not reached the level specified by the state's financial responsibility laws.

Second, the provision that the "insurance shall then apply only in the amount by which the limit of liability for this coverage exceeds the applicable limit of liability of such other insurance"[25] has been omitted, so that there is no "escape" feature. Rather, the new provision states that the coverage will be "excess over any other collectible insurance." Accordingly, it appears that this clause adopts the indemnification approach, urged by many courts and commentators, when a named insured or the spouse of a named insured is injured while occupying a non-owned vehicle.

19. 1977 Insurance Services Office Personal Auto Policy: Part C—Uninsured Motorist Coverage: Limit of Liability (revised June 1980).

20. The Insurance Services clause states that "any insurance we provide with respect to a vehicle you do not own shall be excess over any other collective insurance." "You" is defined to mean the "named insured" shown in the "Declaration" and the "spouse if a resident of the same household." *Id.* Definitions, at 1 (emphasis added). The comparable provision in the 1966 Standard Form would also apply to other clause (a) insureds.

21. See text accompanying notes 5–9, above, for a discussion of Paragraph One of the 1966 Standard Form.

22. 1977 Insurance Services Office Personal Auto Policy: Part C—Uninsured Motorist Coverage: Other Insurance (revised June 1980).

23. 1966 Standard Form: Part VI: Additional Conditions: E. Other Insurance.

24. "The 'excess escape' clause was not carried over into the PAP due to adverse case law in many jurisdictions." Letter from Domenick J. Yessi, Jr., Assistant Manager Industry Relations, Insurance Services Office, to Professor Widiss (June 4, 1982).

25. 1966 Standard Form: Part VI: Additional Conditions: E. Other Insurance.

Third, it might be argued that because the new provision uses the term "you" it does not refer to family members; instead, the argument goes, the coverage is intended to apply only to the named insured and the spouse of a named insured who resides in the same household because the term "you" is defined in the policy to mean the named insured and the spouse of any named insured who resides in the same household.[26] But, for purposes of the uninsured motorist coverage, class (a) — or class (1) — insureds are defined in both forms as "you or any family member."[27] Even though the terms of this Other Insurance provision do not refer to family members, the better approach would be to treat all such insureds the same way.

Fourth, because the new provision states that the insurer's "share is the proportion that our limit of liability bears to the total of all applicable limits."[28] it appears to mean that when several coverages exist, they will be aggregated to determine the total amount of coverage. Although this interpretation of the language is not wholly free from doubt, it seems clear when the language of this provision is compared to the terms used in the 1966 Standard Form, which provided that "if the insured has other similar insurance available to him and applicable to the accident, *the damages shall be deemed not to exceed the higher of the applicable limits of liability of this insurance and such other insurance.*"[29] The italicized language was the basis on which insurance companies urged that the other insurance clauses precluded aggregating uninsured motorist coverages. The omission of this language in the Insurance Services Office Standard Form would foreclose a similar defense to aggregating. Thus, when claims are made under two or more policies, the Other Insurance clause no longer addresses the stacking question. When several vehicles are covered under a single policy, however, the limit of liability provision states: "[T]he limit of liability shown in the Declarations for this coverage is our maximum limit of liability for damages resulting from any one accident * * * regardless of the number of * * * [v]ehicles or premiums shown in the Declarations."[30] Accordingly, the focus for future disputes about stacking or pyramiding of coverages when several vehicles are covered by a single policy undoubtedly will be the enforceability of this limit of liability provision.

§ 3.11(g) Observations on Other Insurance Clauses

For over a half century, there has been an almost continuous flow of appellate decisions involving Other Insurance clauses. Although it is somewhat of an oversimplification to view these cases in

26. 1977 Insurance Services Office Personal Auto Policy: Part C—Uninsured Motorist Coverage: Other Insurance (revised June 1980).

27. *Ibid.*

28. *Ibid.*

29. 1966 Standard Form: Part VI: Additional Conditions: E. Other Insurance (emphasis added).

30. 1977 Insurance Services Office Personal Auto Policy: Part C—Uninsured Motorist Coverage: Limit of Liability (revised June 1980).

terms of clearly distinguishable litigation "waves," it is reasonable to observe that initially most of the disputes involved property insurance. This body of litigation was followed by numerous cases involving liability insurance provisions, which have continued into the 1980s. Then, beginning in the 1960s, there was a substantial number of suits involving the clauses included in uninsured motorist insurance. The sheer number of appellate decisions involving the uninsured motorist provisions is unprecedented even in an area of law which has witnessed significant volumes of litigation to resolve coverage disputes.

Courts in a majority of the jurisdictions that have considered the enforceability of the Other Insurance terms in the uninsured motorist coverage (used almost uniformly by all insurance companies from 1956 until the late 1970s) have concluded that the provisions were unenforceable. These judicial decisions are based on a strong public policy in favor of providing indemnification whenever possible for the innocent victims of uninsured tortfeasors, and the judicial recognition of this public interest is predicated on the "foundation" established by the enactment of an uninsured motorist insurance statute in each state. The public policy manifested by this legislation served to reinforce the substantial hostility that the courts had already developed in regard to Other Insurance provisions. Before the advent of the uninsured motorist coverage, however, this hostility manifested itself in decisions which concluded that when the terms of the Other Insurance provisions were in conflict or were ambiguous, the clauses were unenforceable, and it generally resulted in the liability of two or more insurers being prorated. In contrast, the vast majority of courts have concluded in regard to the uninsured motorist coverage that rather than being prorated, the applicable uninsured motorist coverages may be cumulated (that is, they may be stacked or pyramided) so as to maximize the possibility that the injured persons will be fully indemnified.

The appropriateness of stacking coverages to facilitate the indemnification of injured persons was almost certainly brought to the forefront of judicial consideration by the litigation involving the uninsured motorist coverage. Even though that was in some respects a distinctive context, it seems quite likely that the public interest in indemnification of injured persons increasingly will become a compelling concern when judges consider comparable contract provisions in other types of insurance policies. Accordingly, it seems more than possible that courts will adopt a similar approach in regard to other insurance coverage so long as the "stacking" of several insurance coverages does not violate the principle of indemnification.

§ 3.12 Valued Policies

§ 3.12(a) Property Insurance

(1) Real Property Insurance

Many states have adopted valued policy statutes that apply to insurance contracts for real property.[1] Typically, such statutes provide that in the event there is a total destruction of the insured property, the insured will be entitled to recover the full amount of the insurance.[2] In other words, in case of a total loss of an insured property, the measure of recovery under the policy shall be the face amount of the policy regardless of the actual value of the insured property when the insured event occurred.[3] However, in some statutes there is a provision which allows an insurer to reduce the payment by some factor which takes account of depreciation.[4]

Valued policy statutes, which were first enacted in the nineteenth century, were intended to prevent insurance companies from taking "reckless risks in order to obtain large premiums" by compelling insurers to pay the value agreed upon when the policy was issued. The statutes, in essence, precluded an insurer from questioning the valuation stated in the insurance policy after the loss occurred, and therefore

§ 3.12(a)

1. See, e.g., Kansas Statutes Ann. § 40–905 (1964) (fire, tornado and lightning); Kentucky Revised Statutes § 304.907 (1962) (livestock only); Minnesota Statutes Ann. § 65A.08(3) (1979) (insurance on farm buildings or other structures); R.C.M. 1947, § 40–4302; (insurance for any improvements on real property against loss by fire ∗ ∗ ∗); Wisconsin Statutes Ann. § 203.21 (1977).

As may be inferred from the foregoing the statutes generally are applicable to a type of risk or risks. The New Hampshire statute, however, is an example of one the application of which has been limited to a type of risk on a specific type of object—fire insurance on buildings owned by the insured. See, e.g., Daeris, Inc. v. Hartford Fire Insurance Co., 105 N.H. 117, 193 A.2d 886 (1963), 97 A.L.R.2d 1238 (1964) (statute held not to apply to improvements and betterments fire insurance obtained by lessee of premises).

2. See the discussion in Stahlberg v. Travelers Indemnity Co., 568 S.W.2d 79 (Mo.App., Div. 1, 1978). Also see Vernon's Ann.Missouri Statutes § 379.140 (1969).

3. See, e.g. Arkansas Statutes 66–3901 (1966); Minnesota Statutes Ann. § 65A.08 (1969); V.A.T.S. Texas Insurance Code, art. 6.13 (1963).

Also see Ehlert v. Graue, 292 Minn. 393, 195 N.W.2d 823 (Minn.1972).

It has been held that a compromise or settlement between insured and insurer for an amount less than that stated in the policy is contrary to public policy and void. See, e.g., Gimbels Midwest, Inc. v. Northwestern National Insurance Company of Milwaukee, 72 Wis.2d 84, 240 N.W.2d 140 (1976); Coddington v. Safeguard Insurance Co., 237 Ark. 457, 373 S.W.2d 413 (1963).

It has also been held that a clause in the policy giving the insurer an option to repair is void since the statutes state that the insured shall recover the face amount of the policy in the event of a total loss. See, e.g., Tedder v. Hartford Fire Insurance Co., 246 S.C. 163, 143 S.E.2d 122 (1965).

The fact that the insured, as vendor under a contract to sell, has been paid the full purchase price out of proceeds of insurance separately obtained by the vendee does not defeat or reduce the insured's claim. Hensley v. Farm Bureau Mutual Insurance Co., 243 Ark. 408, 420 S.W.2d 76 (1967).

4. See, e.g., Stahlberg v. Travelers Indemnity Company, 568 S.W.2d 79 at p. 83, n. 3 (Mo.App., Div. 1, 1978).

theoretically encouraged insurers to investigate the value of the property when the coverage was purchased.[5]

In some instances valued policy laws apply to partial losses. However, in most states the statutory provision is for recovery of the "actual" (or "full") amount of loss for partial damage,[6] which apparently establishes the same measure of recovery as would be used for a partial loss if the valued policy law did not apply.[7] The language of several statutes [8] provides some support for allowing recovery of a percentage of the valuation equal to the percentage of damage suffered, and there is also support for this result independent of the statutory direction.[9]

One of the theories underlying the legislation providing for the use of valued policies is that the denial of an opportunity to contest the valuation when a claim is filed will cause insurers to investigate more carefully before underwriting, and that accordingly policies in excessive amounts will not be written.[10] In fact, however, insurers often find it

---

5. *Ibid.*

Also see discussion in Daggs v. Orient Insurance Co., 136 Mo. 382, 38 S.W. 85 (1896).

6. See, e.g., West's Florida Statutes Ann. § 627.0801 (1960); Minnesota Statutes Ann. § 65A.08 (1969); South Carolina Code § 37–154 (1962).

Also see Hunt v. General Insurance Co., 227 S.C. 125, 87 S.E.2d 34 (1955), holding, partly because of the Valued Policy Statute, that life tenants could recover for the full amount of a partial fire loss although their interest in the property (as life tenants) had been grossly overvalued. This would seem to be a misapplication of the idea of awarding "full" or "actual" loss, since the court awarded an amount equal to the full loss on the entire property rather than the full loss to the life tenants' interest.

7. See, e.g., American Insurance Co. v. Iaconi, 47 Del. (8 Terry) 167, 89 A.2d 141 (1952), 36 A.L.R.2d 604 (1954).

Also see Note, *Valuation and Measure of Recovery Under Fire Insurance Policies*, 49 Columbia Law Review 818–836 at p. 827 (1949).

8. See, e.g., North Dakota Cent.Code § 26–18–07 (1970).

9. *Cf.* Billmayer v. Farmers Union Property & Casualty Co., 146 Mont. 38, 404 P.2d 322 (1965), 20 A.L.R.3d 916 (1968) (hail-crop policies held to be valued; measure of recovery based on percentage of damage and not limited to actual loss). The policies in *Billmayer* were not subject to the Montana Valued Policy Law, Rev. Codes Montana § 40–4302 (1961), which

applies only to total losses to improvements upon realty. The court found support for its application of a valued-policy rule in Rev.Codes Montana § 40–4301 (1961), prescribing the measure of indemnity that applies when "there is no valuation in the policy."

Also see Williams, *The Valued Policy and Value Determination*, 1961 Insurance Law Journal 71–83 at p. 78, suggesting that under laws providing a special measure of recovery for partial losses, the "criteria are either so broad or so ambiguous that any of the recognized standards of measurement may be applied."

But cf. Division of General Services v. Ulmer, 256 S.C. 523, 183 S.E.2d 315 at pp. 318–319 (1971). The court held, "Insofar as a partial loss is concerned we are of the opinion that the result is the same whether it be considered as coming under the valued policy statute or coming purely under the terms of the contract" because under either method of determining the amount to be paid the rule allows recovery in the actual amount of the loss sustained based upon the cost to repair.

10. Stahlberg v. Travelers Indemnity Co., 568 S.W.2d 79 (Mo.App., St. Louis Dist., Div. 1, 1978).

Cf. Wisconsin Screw Co. v. Detroit Fire & Marine Insurance Co. of Detroit, Mich., 183 F.Supp. 183 at p. 189 (E.D.Wis.1960), holding, however, that the valued policy provision was modified by another statute that limited recovery to actual loss when two or more policies were in effect covering the same property. Although recognizing that, if one policy had been issued in the same amount as the sum of the two poli-

more expensive to investigate fully before underwriting than to accept as an additional risk the increased moral hazards that result when some applicants acquire excessive insurance. Thus, many insurers typically do not investigate and recognize that when the full sum of the insurance is paid in all total losses covered by valued policies in which no other defense can be proved, payments will be made in a few cases in which applicants obtained excessive coverage and then destroyed the insured property to collect the insurance. In several cases, however, courts have clearly indicated that either fraud on the part of the purchaser or arson (that is, the intentional destruction of the property) provides an insurer with a defense,[11] and that these defenses can be proved by an insurer even when coverage is sought under a valued policy.

A distinct problem is presented when a valued policy statute is invoked in relation to the claim of one of two co-owners of property.[12]

(2) Personal Property Insurance

Valued policies are widely used to insure personal property when an insured wants to establish a particular value for an item. Insurers charge a slightly higher premium for comparable levels of coverage for property covered by such valued policies, which are usually referred to as personal property "floaters".[13]

cies before the court, the insured would have been entitled to the full amount stated in the policy, the court reasoned that to allow full recovery on several valued policies would encourage the procurement of excessive coverage by the insured. In a different phase of the same case, this resolution of the interaction between the statutes is adopted by the Court of Appeals for the Seventh Circuit as its own. Ludwig v. Detroit Fire & Marine Insurance Co., 342 F.2d 608 (7th Cir.1965).

If the multiple policies insure different interests, however, the face amount of each is collectible in the event of total loss. E.g., Springfield Fire & Marine Insurance Co. v. Boswell, 167 So.2d 780 (Fla.App. 1964) (vendor and vendee of property subject to contract of sale).

11. Zuraff v. Empire Fire and Marine Insurance Co., 252 N.W.2d 302 (N.D.1977); Ehlert v. Graue, 292 Minn. 393, 195 N.W.2d 823 at p. 825 (1972); Meccage v. Spartan Insurance Company, 156 Mont. 135, 477 P.2d 115 (1970) ("false or misleading representation" by the insured would be a defense); Home Insurance Company v. Hardin, 528 S.W.2d 723 at p. 725 (Ky.1975).

But cf. the comments in Gamel v. Continental Insurance Company, 463 S.W.2d 590 at p. 594 and p. 595 (Mo.App., St. Louis

Dist., 1971). The court observed that "a statement or misrepresentation of value, even if false, where the parties occupy an equal footing, is the mere expression of an opinion on which a charge of fraud cannot be predicated." The court also observed that "where the means of knowledge are at hand and are equally available to both parties and the subject matter is available to both parties and subject matter is alike open to their investigation, if one of them does not avail himself of those means and opportunities he will not be heard to say that he was deceived by the other party's misrepresentation, * * *."

12. See Smith v. Nationwide Mutual Fire Insurance Co., 564 F.Supp. 350 at p. 352 (N.D.Fla.1983), in which the court held that "where there are two persons with an insurable interest but only one who may collect on the policy because of the wrongdoing of the other," the innocent coinsured would be entitled "to recover * * * the face amount of the policy" and the recovery would not be limited to the claimant's insurable interest.

Also see Board of Trustees v. Cream City Mutual Insurance Company, 255 Minn. 347, 96 N.W.2d 690 (1959).

13. See discussion in § 1.5(b)(2), above.

Many of the valued policy statutes do not apply to various types of personal property.[14]

(3) Use and Occupancy-Business Interruption Insurance

Valued policies have also been developed for use and occupancy and business interruption coverages.[15] In such policies, the parties stipulate an amount for a daily or monthly valued payment to be made to the insured in the event an insured event disrupts the business,[16] and valuation disputes are avoided in regard to the losses sustained as the result of an occurrence of an insured event. This type of policy can also provide coverage for partial suspensions of a business.

§ 3.12(b) Marine Insurance

In marine insurance, a valued policy is one stipulating a value for the insured cargo or hull at commencement of the voyage (rather than leaving the value at that time, called prime value, to be determined after a loss occurs whenever relevant to calculating the measure of recovery). Most marine policies are valued, and this represents a potential deviation from the principle of indemnity because both the prime value (for which the stipulated value is substituted [1]) and the sound value at time of loss may in fact be less than the stipulated value.

If no value stipulation appears in a marine insurance policy, it is referred to as an "open" or "unvalued" policy.[2]

 WESTLAW REFERENCES

§ 3.1   **Indemnity and Insurability: An Introduction**

    (a) The Principle of Indemnity
       di indemnity

    (b) The Doctrine of Insurable Interest
       di insurable interest

    (c) Potential Evils of Net Gains from Insurance
       insurance /s wager! gambl! bet betting /2 contract agreement

    (d) Conflicts between the Principle of Indemnity and Other Principles or Goals

      (2) Insurance as a "Personal" Contract
         217k124 /p personal /5 contract

§ 3.2   **History of the Insurable Interest Doctrine**

    (a) The Statute of George II
       "insurable interest" /s gambl! gaming wager! bet betting

14. See, e.g., Hilltop Bowl, Inc. v. United States Fidelity & Guaranty Co., 259 F.Supp. 649 (W.D.La.1966); Home Insurance Company v. Hardin, 528 S.W.2d 723 at p. 725 (Ky.1975).

15. Omaha Paper Stock Company v. Harbor Insurance Company, 596 F.2d 283 (8th Cir.1979) (quoting from the discussion in the original edition of this text).

16. Id., 596 F.2d at p. 288.

§ 3.12(b)

1. See § 3.7(b), above.

2. See § 3.6(b), n. 6, above.

(d) "Legal" Versus "Factual" Insurance Interests: The Emergence of Competing Theories

217k115(2) & sy("insurable interest")

(e) Adoption and Development of the Doctrine in America

no not +5 interest /s insurance /s wager! gambl! gaming bet betting

§ 3.3   Applications of the Insurable Interest Doctrine

(b) The Time When an Insurable Interest Must Exist

(2) Property Insurance

sy,di(property /s insured assured /s interest /s time /2 loss contract issu! policy)

217k115(1) /p insurable /p property

(3) Comment

"property insurance" /s indemni!

(c) The Right to Question Insurable Interest

(2) Estoppel and the Insurable Interest Doctrine

sy,di("insurable interest" /s estop! waiv!)

(3) Incontestability Clauses

sy,di("life insurance" /s incontestab!)

(d) Return of Premiums When an Insurable Interest Was Lacking

tender! return! refund! /s premium /s "insurable interest"

§ 3.4   Insurable Interests for Property Insurance

(a) Types of Insurable Interest in Property

(1) Generally

"insurable interest" /s property /s loss /s injur! /s insured assured claimant

(2) Property and Contract Rights

217k282 /p interest

sy,di("insurable interest" /p economic)

"insurable interest" /s contractor

(3) Legal Liabilities as Insurable Interests

sy("insurable interest" /s mortgage)

(5) Factual Expectancies as Insurable Interests

expect! /s "insurable interest"

(b) Relationships Between Objectives and Theories of Insurable Interest and Indemnity

(2) Deviations Toward More Rigorous Insurable Interest Requirements Than Those Warranted by the Principle of Indemnity

di("insurable interest" /s mortgagee)

217k116(5) /p "insurable interest"

(3) Deviations Toward Less Rigorous Insurable Interest Requirements Than Those Warranted by the Principle of Indemnity

sy("insurable interest" /s vendor seller purchaser buyer)

(c) Common Factual Patterns

(1) Property Owned by a Spouse

property /5 husband wife spouse /s "insurable interest"

(2) Property Owned by a Corporation
s* * * *holder /s "insurable interest"

§ 3.5 Insurable Interests for Life Insurance

(a) Introduction
warnock /s davis
"insurable interest" /s life /s blood affinity consanguinity pecuniary monetar!

(c) Relationships Supporting an Insurable Interest in Another's Life

(2) Family Relationsips
217k114 /p beneficiary

(3) Non–Family Relationships
partner! /s "insurable interest"

(d) Beneficiaries and Assignees Without an Insurable Interest
assign! /s "life insurance" /s "insurable interest"
217k114 /p beneficiary assign!
standing /p lack! want! absen! no not /s "insurable interest"

(e) The Distinctive Texas Rule
find 284 sw2d 898

(f) The Risk of Inducement to Murder
find 100 so2d 696

(g) Insurable Interests for Industrial Life Insurance
217k583(2) /p facility-of-payment

§ 3.6 Rules for Preventing Net Gain

(a) Introduction

(4) Liability for Distributed Gross Loss
di subrogation

(5) The "Unearned" Premium Question
sy(insurer assurer /s "unearned premium") & di("unearned premium")

§ 3.7 The Measure of Recovery in Marine Insurance

(b) The Measure of Recovery for Cargo Losses
marine /3 policy insurance /7 open valued unvalued

§ 3.9 The Measure of Recovery in Property Insurance

(a) Generally
sy("actual cash value" /s property)
sy(valu! /5 property /3 destroyed damaged)
di(recover! /s cost price /3 repair! replac! /s structure property building premises /p insurance)

(b) Depreciation
property /s valu! /s depreciat! /s insurance

(e) Property Subject to a Condemnation Order, an Executory Demolition Contract, or a Right of Redemption

Property Subject to an Executory Contract for Demolition
abandon! demoli! /s "insurable interest"

Property Subject to a Right of Redemption
di(lessee tenant /s "insurable interest")

(f) Use and Occupancy Losses
217k507   %   217k507.1

§ 3.10 Subrogation

(a) Subrogation Rights by Type of Insurance

(1) Introduction
subrogat!   /s   "collateral source"   /2   rule doctrine principle

Subrogation Against an Insured
find 330 nw2d 699

(3) Liability Insurance
di(liability   malpractice   /2   coverage   insurance   policy   /p
subrogat!   /2   right provision clause)   &   sy(subrogat!)
217k606(5)   /p   subrogat!   &   sy(subrogat!)

(4) Uninsured Motorist Insurance
217k601.25   &   he(uninsured)

(6) Life and Accident Insurance
life accident "personal injury"   /3   coverage insurance policy   /s
subrogat!   /2   right clause provision

(7) Medical and Health Insurance
to(217)   /p   medical hospital! health   /5   insurance coverage policy
payment   /s   subrogat!   /2   right clause provision
"traveler indemnity"   /s   chumbley

(8) Worker's Compensation Insurance
sy(worker workman   /2   compensation   /s   subrogat!   /2   right
clause provision)

(b) Allocation of Recoveries When an Insurer Has a Subrogation Interest

(1) Approaches to Allocation
subrogat!   /p   allocat! distribut!   /7   recovery   amount   settlement
payment reimbursement proceeds   /p   insurance

(2) Settlements
217k606(10)   /p   subrogat!

(c) Enforcement of Subrogation Rights

(1) Parties to Actions
insurer assurer   /s   necessary real proper   /2   party   /s   jury
fact-finder

(4) Remedies for an Insured's Breach or Impairment of the Insurer's Subrogation Rights

(i) Breach of Contract
breach!   /2   agreement contract   /s   subrogat!

(ii) Quasi–Contract
sy,di(subrogat!   /s   (unjust!   /2   enrich!) quasi-contract)

(d) Impediments to Subrogation

(3) Voluntary Payments by Insurers
366k26
volunt!   /s   assign! "loan receipt"   /s   insurer assurer

(4) Claims Against Common Carriers
luckenbach   /s   mccahan   /p   carrier shipper

§ 3.11 Other Insurance Clauses

(a) Introduction

(1) Types of Other Insurance Clauses

di escape clause

di pro rata clause

di excess clause

(3) Enforceability of Other Insurance Clauses

apportion! allocat! distribut! /s liab! responsib! /s excess /2 coverage insurance

(d) Health and Accident Insurance

217k532.5(2)

(e) Liability Insurance

(2) Enforceability

sy(vehicle car auto automobile truck /2 coverage insurance policy /s pro-rat★ ★ ★)

(3) Allocation of Liability

(i) Proportional Proration Rule

lamb-weston /s oregon /p pro-rat★ ★ ★

(f) Other Insurance Clauses in Uninsured Motorist Insurance

(1) Introduction

217k532.5(2) /p "uninsured motorist"

217k531 & sy("uninsured motorist" /2 coverage insurance policy claim /s excess)

(2) Enforcement of the Excess–Escape Provision

sy,di(illegal! legal★ ★ ★ invalid! valid! ambiguous! unambiguous! vague! clear ★ ★ enforc! /7 excess escape /3 clause provision)

(3) Limitations on the Enforceability of the Excess–Escape Other Insurance Provision

find 475 p2d 253

217k435.1(2) /p "financial responsibility" /3 act law statut!

(4) Invalidation of the Excess–Escape Other Insurance Clause Provision

find 318 fsupp 1152

§ 3.12 Valued Policies

(a) Property Insurance

(1) Real Property Insurance

di valued policy

217k500 /p home house building structure premises (real +1 property estate)

daggs /s orient

di(mis-represent★ ★ ★ mis-representation mis-lead! misled fraud fraudulent! /5 value★ valuing valuation /p insurance)

(2) Personal Property Insurance

"valued policy" /s "personal property"

(3) Use and Occupancy—Business Interruption Insurance

217k507 % 217k507.1

(b) Marine Insurance

unvalued open /2 policy coverage insurance /s marine

Chapter Four

PERSONS AND INTERESTS PROTECTED

Table of Sections

§ 4.1 Methods of Defining the Persons and the Interests Protected

§ 4.1(a) Introduction

Insurance policies have been notorious for contract provisions that set forth statements of extensive protection in general terms, often in large print, and then limit the protection afforded by the inclusion of numerous restrictive provisions, frequently set forth in relatively small print.[1] Although the most outrageous practices of this type have been curtailed, almost all insurance policies still begin with statements describing a broad scope of protection [2] which is then reduced or limited by various types of restrictive provisions. Even so-called "all risk" insurance policies [3] usually include some provisions which eliminate protection for certain types of losses that would otherwise be within the scope of coverage set out in the general coverage description of the risks that are transferred to the insurer.[4]

Restrictions on the scope of coverage provided by an insurance policy typically are set forth under headings such as *Exclusions, Conditions,* or *Limitations of Liability.* However, in some instances restrictions are incorporated into the basic coverage description as well.

This chapter focuses on the methods and the provisions commonly used by insurers to define and to limit either the persons or the interests [5] covered by an insurance policy. These methods and coverage

§ 4.1(a)

1. Restrictive provisions are more likely to be sources of disputes and litigation than the language of broad grants of coverage.

2. Insurance coverages are commonly identified by the broad grants and are generally classified by types on that basis. The distinctions among major classifications of insurance relate mainly to the portions of the definitions of coverage according to the nature of the risk transferred, a subject treated in the next chapter.

3. See the discussion of all-risk coverages in § 1.5(a), above, and § 5.1(b), below.

4. For example, see Sipowicz v. Wimble, 370 F.Supp. 442 (S.D.N.Y.1974).

Cf. Inland Rivers Service Corp. v. Hartford Fire Insurance Company, 66 Ohio St. 2d 32, 418 N.E.2d 1381 (1981).

Also see John P. Gorman, *All Risks of Loss v. All Loss: An Examination of Broad Form Insurance Coverage,* 34 Notre Dame Law Review 346–357 (1959); Milford L. Landis, *All Risks Insurance,* 1951 Insurance Law Journal 709–716 (September, 1951).

5. In the context of property insurance, many coverage disputes about interests protected are encompassed within the basic question: What property is the subject matter of the contract. For example, a dispute may arise concerning whether a particular item of the insured's personal property is included within coverage under a fire insurance policy that does not identify the property except by reference to the location where it is kept. With respect to the effectiveness of a provision concerning location as a "coverage" provision rather than a "warranty," see § 6.7(c), below.

provisions tend to vary with the type of coverage, and therefore many portions of this chapter include discussions of specific types of insurance. [Insurance contracts typically also include provisions concerning the nature of the risks which are transferred to the insurer. The methods and approaches to defining risks are generally the subject of the next chapter.[6]]

The terminology used by insurers, as well as by judges and commentators, to describe various types of restrictive provisions is something less than uniform. With a view to establishing some standard practices in regard to such policy terms, Professor Patterson advocated a system of terminology that was designed to distinguish between provisions used to define excluded events (which he called "exclusions"[7]) and provisions used to define excepted causes (which he called "exceptions").[8] However, neither Professor Patterson's system nor any other uniform terminology which distinguishes among different types of restrictions has been widely adopted by insurers, and it is quite common to find terms such as "exclusion" used to designate or identify several different types of restrictive provisions.[9]

Note. If you are reading this book as part of your initial study of insurance law, we recommend that you not linger over portions of the text in this chapter that you find difficult. After completing your initial reading of the entire chapter, then return to those sections for another reading. In some instances, following the cross-references provided in the footnotes to other portions of the text, which provide more detailed descriptions and explanations of identified topics, may be helpful.

§ 4.1(b) Ways of Designating Insureds in Various Types of Insurance

(1) Designating Insureds in Property Insurance

Several different approaches are used to designate who is an insured in property insurance policies. Many, and perhaps most, insurance contracts specifically identify the persons or entities (such as corporations) who are the insureds on a schedule (often referred to or characterized as "Declarations") that is usually set out on a separate

Ordinarily whatever interest the insured has in the property that is the subject of the insurance contract is covered. This is not always the case, however. For example, it may happen that a fire insurance contract is unclear as to whether it is intended to protect the insured's interest in the property itself, or instead in the insured's expectations of profit from uses of the property, or both. See § 3.4(a)(5), above. In those contexts, identifying the interest covered involves more than merely identifying property to which the contract relates.

6. One provision that relates to risks is considered in this chapter. See the discussion of exclusions of injuries to described persons and classes in § 4.9(c), below.

7. Professor Patterson also used the term "exclusion" for a provision that was restrictive with respect to persons or interests rather than events. See Patterson, ESSENTIALS OF INSURANCE LAW (Second edition, 1957), at pp. 248–257.

8. See Patterson, ESSENTIALS OF INSURANCE LAW (Second edition, 1957), at pp. 248–257.

Also see § 5.5(a), below.

9. See the exclusion terms in the forms set out in the Appendices.

page attached to a standard policy form.[1] Another approach is to fill in a blank space on the first page of the policy with the name or names of the persons who are insured. The blank space typically follows the words "does insure" or some phrase of similar import.

Property insurance contracts often identify more than one person or entity as insureds, including persons or entities holding significantly different interests in an insured building — such as owner, first mortgagee, second mortgagee, tenant, or holder of a remainder interest — who can all be insureds in a single policy. Sometimes such individuals are listed as insureds in an insurance policy without any indication of their respective interests in the insured property.

It is both possible and appropriate to specify in a property insurance policy the nature of the individual interest of each of the insureds in an insured property. Particularly when insurance is secured by a person who does not have an ownership interest in the insured property, such as someone acting in a fiduciary capacity, it is desirable that the individual's relationship to the property be both described to the insurer and appropriately characterized in the insurance contract in order to reduce the possibility of subsequent disputes about matters such as whether the insurable interest requirement was satisfied.[2]

When several persons are identified as insureds in a property insurance policy, the terms will often include a coverage clause with the phrase "as their interests may appear." The inclusion of this provision means that in the event of a loss the insurance proceeds will be paid to these persons in proportion to the damage to their respective interests in the insured property.[3]

In some circumstances, the original insured may want to arrange to have a property insurance coverage extended to additional persons or entities. When this is done, such persons or entities often will be characterized as "additional insureds." For example, this arrangement can be used when there is a contract for the sale of an insured structure, and the purchaser asks to be designated as an additional insured under the seller's insurance policy until the sales transaction is completed.[4] One or more additional insureds can be designated by adding an endorsement to a property insurance policy. If coverage is to be provided for additional insureds, there will usually also be provisions elsewhere in the policy or in an endorsement which state what interests are insured.

§ 4.1(b)

1. Also see the discussion of ways that are used to designate insureds in casualty insurance in § 4.1(b)(4), below.

2. See the discussion of insurable interest in § 3.1 and § 3.2, above.

3. See the discussion of multi-party insurance arrangements in § 4.1(b)(2), below, and the discussion of distinguishing insureds from others benefiting from property insurance in § 4.1(b)(3), below.

4. See the discussion of insurance for vendors and purchasers of real property in § 4.3, below.

(2) Allocating Insurance Benefits in Multi-Party Property Insurance Arrangements

There are several types of multi-party arrangements, commonly used in connection with property insurance, which may affect the allocation of insurance benefits.

First, as briefly described in the preceding subsection, persons who have varied interests in an "insured property" may be designated, either by name or by a description of their status, as insureds under a single insurance policy. This type of arrangement is commonly referred to as a "designation of insureds" or as coverage for a "named insured and additional insureds." When insurance policies provide coverage for more than one insured, as noted above, insurers often include a clause stating that the insurance shall be payable "as their interests may appear." In the event of an insured loss, this provision is understood to mean that the insureds are to be indemnified in proportion to the harms to their respective interests in the insured property.[5] For example, the clauses used when an additional insured is a mortgagee typically provide that the insurance "shall be payable to the mortgagee * * * as interest may appear under all present or future mortgages."[6] With this type of insurance arrangement, each of the insureds will be entitled to receive part of the insurance proceeds in the event his or her interest in the property is damaged by an occurrence within the scope of one of the risks which is insured.[7]

Second, an insured may arrange with an insurer that in the event of a loss, all or part of the proceeds will be paid to someone who does not have any interest in the insured property. This is the type of arrangement which is normally intended when one person's name appears in the blank following the words "does insure" (or elsewhere as a designation of who is the "insured"), and another name identifies the person (or entity) who will be paid the insurance proceeds. Some policies, for example, include a clause stating, "loss, if any, payable to _____." An arrangement of this type may be used when a property insurance policy is pledged as collateral for an otherwise unsecured debt, and the creditor has no lien on the property. Occasionally, this arrangement is also used when a creditor has a secured interest in the insured property — that is, the creditor is a mortgagee of the insured property. When this type of loss payable arrangement, often referred to as an "open loss payable clause," identifies a mortgagee without also

---

5. See the forms in Appendix A and Appendix I.

6. For example, see the coverage terms in Burritt Mutual Savings Bank of New Britain v. Transamerica Insurance Company, 180 Conn. 71, 428 A.2d 333 (1980).

7. See Christopher & John, Inc. v. Maryland Casualty Company, 484 F.Supp. 609 (S.D.N.Y.1980).

Cf. Third Establishment, Inc. v. 1931 North Park Apartments, 93 Ill.App.3d 234, 48 Ill.Dec. 765, 417 N.E.2d 167 (1st Dist., 4th Div., 1981), in which the court concluded that the lessor was not entitled to any insurance proceeds because the lessor suffered no loss when the contents or trade fixtures of the leased premises were destroyed. The lessor (though one of the named insureds) had no interest or right to the contents or trade fixtures on the day the fire occurred.

arranging for the mortgagee to be specifically identified as an insured or additional insured, it has led to disputes about whether the mortgagee should nevertheless be treated as an additional insured.[8]

When an insurance policy specifically provides insurance for a person or an entity identified as a "creditor" *and* the policy includes the clause that extends coverage "as his/her interest may appear" this arrangement generally is understood to mean that the insurance proceeds are payable to the creditor only up to the amount of the debt. A creditor named in this way will usually receive the insurance proceeds even when there was no security interest in the insured property, and therefore the creditor in fact has no greater interest in the insured property than that of any other unsecured creditor of such a debtor. As a result of the phraseology commonly used in setting up this type of arrangement, the language included in the insurance policy is generally referred to as a "loss payable clause." A party who is designated in this way — as, in essence, a beneficiary of the insurance proceeds — usually is not intended or entitled to be treated as an "additional insured."

Occasionally, the term "loss payable clause" is used to refer to or describe contract provisions employed for transactions in which additional "insureds" are designated by a provision that also uses the "loss payable" phraseology. Even though the use of this provision generally does entitle such persons to be additional insureds, they usually are not specifically identified as insureds in the blank on the face of the insurance policy after the words "does insure". Accordingly, when the "loss payable" language has been used in an insurance policy provision or to refer to an arrangement, the transaction should be carefully examined to ascertain the type of relationship it establishes.

Third, an insured may (even without the consent of the insurer) transfer the right to receive insurance proceeds, and this type of transaction is commonly referred to as an assignment of a chose in action.[9] An assignment of a chose in action transfers the right to receive insurance proceeds without affecting an insured's interests in the insured property and is usually arranged without including any provision in the insurance policy itself that relates to the payment of the insurance benefits. Sometimes such an assignment is also referred to as a "loss payable" insurance transaction, even when the provisions are set forth in some document other than the insurance policy and is not agreed to by the insurer. An insured may make an assignment of the right to receive the insurance payment either before or after a loss occurs. If it is made before a loss, it is usually referred to as an

---

8. For example, see Central National Insurance Company of Omaha v. Manufacturers Acceptance Corporation, 544 S.W.2d 362 (Tenn.1976) (claim by a lender that held a chattel mortgage on a motor cycle); Pearson v. First National Bank of Martinsville, 408 N.E.2d 166 (Ind.App., 4th Dist., 1980).

Also see the discussion of this problem in § 4.1(b)(3), below.

9. Also see the discussion of such assignments in § 4.1(c), below.

"anticipatory assignment of a chose in action." Depending on the circumstances and the type of coverage involved, an anticipatory assignment may not be enforceable if it violates an explicit restriction or a public policy against transfers of interests.[10]

An insurer's obligation to pay the insurance proceeds in the event of an insured loss usually is not affected by the type of transaction or the contractual commitment that an insured employs either (1) to establish an arrangement for more than one person to receive some portion of the insurance proceeds or (2) to transfer a right to receive insurance proceeds — that is, in relation to most insurance claims, the different arrangements described in the preceding paragraphs do not affect either the insurer's obligation to provide coverage for an insured occurrence or the amount of the insurance payment that is due in the event of a loss. Furthermore, in most instances the choice of a particular arrangement will not affect the distribution of the insurance proceeds.[11]

In some situations, however, the nature of the transaction employed for an arrangement that purports to affect the allocation of insurance may be a significant factor in regard to the right to insurance proceeds following a loss, and the results will be radically different depending on the way the transaction was structured. For example, a mortgagor of realty or personal property may obtain an insurance policy with a clause declaring that in the event of a loss, the insurance is payable to the mortgagee. If the mortgagee is not treated as an "additional insured" as the result of such a transaction, then the only interest that is covered by the insurance continues to be that of the mortgagor.[12] Even though the mortgagee is designated to receive the insurance proceeds, when an insurer has a defense against a claim for loss to the mortgagor's interest, it will also be a good defense against an insurance claim by a mortgagee designated to receive the insurance proceeds.[13] In contrast, if the arrangement is treated as coverage for

---

10. An assignment of a chose in action should not be confused with an assignment of an insurance policy. See the discussion of assignments of insurance policies in § 4.1(c), below.

11. These observations are especially likely to be true when each claimant has a recognized interest in the insured property that defines the amount of his or her claim. For example, when a secured creditor is included in the arrangement, the creditor's interest in the insurance proceeds is usually consistent with the lien on the insured property.

12. See, e.g., Calvert Fire Insurance Company v. Environs Development Corp., 601 F.2d 851 at p. 858 (5th Cir.1979).

Also see the cases cited in notes 20 through 22 of § 4.1(b)(3), below, and the accompanying text.

13. See, e.g., Whitney National Bank of New Orleans v. State Farm Fire and Casualty Company, 518 F.Supp. 359 (E.D.La. 1981) (bank, which was the holder of a chattel mortgage on the contents of a building, and was named as a loss payee in an insurance policy pursuant to an "open mortgage" clause, but was not protected by a "union mortgage clause", was not entitled to insurance when fire loss was caused by arson instigated by the President of the insured firm, whose common stock was owned by the President's wife); Central National Insurance Company of Omaha v. Manufacturers Acceptance Corporation, 544 S.W.2d 362 (Tenn.1976).

Similarly, in Grosvenor v. Atlantic Fire Insurance Company of Brooklyn, 17 N.Y. 391 (1858), the insurer's defense was upheld, the mortgagor having committed policy violations, apparently in transferring to

an additional insured, the mortgagee's claim would not necessarily be defeated by what would be a good defense to a claim for insurance by the mortgagor.[14] Therefore, in the latter case, it would be necessary to decide whether a defense to a claim by the mortgagor would also be grounds for a successful defense to a claim by the mortgagee.

If an issue arises as to the precise nature of an insurance arrangement or a provision for the distribution of insurance benefits in the event of a loss, it is always essential to be cautious when interpreting terminology which may seem to establish a particular type of arrangement — especially when terms such as "assign," "assignment" or "loss payable" are used in the documents. However, in some instances, even a careful examination of the documents does not provide a clear indication of what the parties intended, and disputes result from differing views of how the transaction should be treated.[15]

An early New York case, Traders' Insurance Company v. Robert,[16] provides a good illustration of the difficulties that may be presented in regard to assessing the nature of a particular transaction. The insurance policy at issue in *Robert* provided that it would no longer be effective if other insurance was obtained on the property without providing notice to the insurer within a reasonable time. The insured, who was the mortgagor of the insured property, assigned an interest in the insurance to a mortgagee with the consent of the insurer. Thereaf-

another his interest in the realty that was the subject of insurance. Note, however, that there is an inconsistency between terminology used in *Grosvenor* and that described in the text above. The court refers to "an assignment of the policy to a mortgagee to be held by him as collateral security for his debt, with the consent of the insurer," though they are speaking of a transaction in which "the insurance is upon the interest of the mortgagor" and "the money shall be paid, not to the party who has sustained the loss, but to his appointee or assignee for his benefit." 17 N.Y. at p. 395.

Also see Armbrust v. Travelers Insurance Company, 232 Or. 617, 376 P.2d 669 (1962) (recovery denied assignee of loss payee because of failure to prove insurable interest of insured although loss payee had clear interest in her own right because of an outstanding debt from her conditional sale of the insured vehicle to another person).

It has also been held that construction of a loss payable clause as an assignment of the chose in action permits subrogation of the insurer to tort claims of the mortgagor-assignor against the mortgagee-assignee. See, e.g., Insurance Company of North America v. Gulf Oil Corporation, 106 Ga. App. 382, 127 S.E.2d 43 (1962). Gulf had sold products to North America's insured, holding a mortgage on them; the insured also leased from Gulf part of a warehouse where the products were stored. After loss from a fire caused by the negligence of one of Gulf's employees, North America paid the policy proceeds to its insured and Gulf, the payment to the latter being made under an "open" loss payable clause (as opposed to a "union" or "standard" clause, which is discussed in § 4.2(b), below). The insurer was then allowed to recover from Gulf as subrogee to its insured's claim in tort.

14. See, e.g., Old Colony Co-operative Bank v. Nationwide Mutual Fire Insurance Company, 114 R.I. 289, 332 A.2d 434 (1975).

Cf. Calvert Fire Insurance Company v. Environs Development Corporation, 601 F.2d 851 at p. 855 (5th Cir.1979); Alabama Farm Bureau Insurance Company v. McCurry, 336 So.2d 1109 at p. 1112 (Ala.1976).

15. Moreover, sometimes it is even difficult to determine how a court has treated a given transaction or relationship when it has ordered a particular distribution of the insurance. Occasionally, a result that appears to depend on treating a given situation as one type of transaction, could in fact also be explained or justified even if the arrangement were treated as a transaction of another type.

16. 9 Wend. 404 (N.Y.1832).

ter, the mortgagor effected other insurance without giving notice to the insurer. When a loss occurred, the mortgagee brought an action against the first insurer in the name of the assignor (the mortgagor).

The trial court which considered the "mortgagee's" case (brought in the name of the mortgagor) held that the conduct of the mortgagor in obtaining other insurance did not affect the rights to recover. No appeal was taken, and the decision of the trial court in favor of the mortgagor against the insurer became the law of the case. The mortgagee then received payment of the mortgage debt, apparently from the mortgagor. After making the payment to the mortgagee, the mortgagor sought to collect upon the judgment in his name against the insurer. In a second law suit, the trial court stayed proceedings for collection, but its order was reversed by the Court for the Correction of Errors.[17]

The first opinion in the *Robert* case included the statement that "after the assignment of the policy [to Bolton, the mortgagee], Robert [the mortgagor], in whose name it was originally taken, had no interest in it, [and] * * * [t]he rights of the parties are the same as if the policy * * * had been given to * * * Bolton. * * *"[18] This would be an accurate observation only as to a substitution of insureds (a transaction of the first type of the two types discussed at the beginning of this subsection, and an arrangement which is different from the addition of an insured). But if there had been a substitution, then the insurer should have been subrogated to the contract claim of its substituted insured (the mortgagee) against the mortgagor, Robert, who by reason of the substitution would no longer be an insured.

Allowing Robert (the mortgagor) to collect on the judgment against the insurer, as the assignee of that judgment, would ignore the insurer's right of subrogation. Assertion of the subrogation right would cause the casualty loss to fall on the uninsured (as to this policy) mortgagor, the insurance having served its purpose as a guarantee to the mortgagee alone (that is, that the mortgagee would not suffer a casualty loss). Thus, the protection actually afforded under the second opinion to the mortgagor, Robert, against the casualty loss was in effect either treating him as continuing to be an insured or else declining (perhaps on procedural grounds) to give effect to the subrogation right. A holding that Robert continued to be an insured is a result that is possible if there was an addition rather than a substitution of an insured. In either case, this holding would depend on rejection of the insurer's defense based on the alleged violation of the no-other-insurance clause. Since such a rejection is not suggested in the opinions, it seems more likely that the explanation of the case is that the subrogation right was overlooked or denied on procedural grounds. For example, the subrogation right might have been lost by nonassertion.

17. Robert v. Traders' Insurance Company, 17 Wend. 631 (N.Y.1836).

18. Traders' Insurance Company v. Robert, 9 Wend. 404 at pp. 409–410 (N.Y.1832).

(3) Distinguishing "Insureds" From Others Benefiting From Property Insurance

In the context of property insurance (and casualty insurance, as well [19]) the term "insured" ordinarily identifies a person who both (1) has a risk of a designated type that is partially or fully transferred to an insurer by an insurance contract and (2) is the person to whom the insurance benefits are payable. Thus, the occurrence of an insured event which causes a loss is the occasion for the insurer to pay benefits to the insured who actually sustained the economic detriment.

In some situations an insured who actually sustains a loss may have arranged for property insurance benefits to be paid to someone else. For example, as described in the preceding subsection, an insurance arrangement may be structured so that in the event of a loss the insurance will be paid to a mortgagee who has a security interest in the insured property or to an unsecured creditor. Even though such an arrangement is made before the occurrence of a loss, a designee or an assignee of prospective rights against an insurer does not necessarily become an "insured."

The status accorded to a claimant who is someone other than the named insured can prove to be significant — that is, rights under the coverage may differ depending on whether the person designated to receive the insurance proceeds is covered as an "additional insured." If the insurance transaction does not include a commitment by the insurer to treat the designated recipient of the insurance proceeds as an "additional insured," then a defense available against the named insured also will provide a basis for rejecting a claim by the designated assignee.[20] For example, the fact that the mortgagor and the mortgagee may have explicitly agreed before a loss that the insurance benefits would be paid either to the mortgagee or to the mortgagor and mortgagee jointly does not affect the rights of an insurer to assert against both parties any defenses it has against the mortgagor.[21]

---

19. See § 4.1(b)(4), below.

20. In Central National Insurance Company of Omaha v. Manufacturers Acceptance Corporation, 544 S.W.2d 362 at p. 364 (Tenn.1976), the court concluded that even though the owner of a motorcycle that was subject to a chattel mortgage had covenanted that he would keep the motorcycle insured and that the insurance on a loss would be payable to the mortgagee, still since the "insurance contract does not contain any * * * 'standard' or 'union' mortgage clause * * * the invalidating acts or omissions of the insured-mortgagor operate not only to defeat his own rights but those of the mortgagee as well."

Also see Whitney National Bank of New Orleans v. State Farm Fire and Casualty Company, 518 F.Supp. 359 (E.D.La.1981); Miyata v. Peerless Insurance Company, 95

Ill.App.3d 584, 51 Ill.Dec. 79, 420 N.E.2d 493 (1st Dist., 5th Div., 1981); Pearson v. First National Bank of Martinsville, 408 N.E.2d 166 at pp. 169–170 (Ind.App., 4th Dist., 1980).

An insurance policy provision by which the insurer is directed to pay the loss to someone other than the owner of an insured property is often described as an "open" mortgage clause, and such a payee — even when it is a mortgagee of an insured property — has no greater rights than those of the insured.

21. See the discussion in Hartford Fire Insurance Co. v. Associates Capital Corporation, 313 So.2d 404 (Miss.1975), in which the court considered whether different results would be produced by a "simple 'loss payable' clause" and a standard mortgage clause.

An insurance contract may specifically provide coverage for a mortgagee, and the mortgagee can be fully protected through the use of a standard mortgage clause,[22] which is also referred to as a union mortgage clause.[23] This provision sets forth the understanding among the parties (the mortgagor, the mortgagee, and the insurer) that in the event a loss occurs, the mortgagee's rights under the policy are those of an additional "insured"[24] and not merely an interest that is derived from the mortgagor either as the designated recipient of the insurance proceeds or as an assignee of a mortgagor's chose in action against the insurer.

(4) Designating Insureds in Casualty Insurance

The persons (or entities such as corporations) insured by casualty insurance policies[25] are usually identified on a "declarations schedule" that is attached to the standard terms used for the insurance policy, and are generally referred to as the "named insureds."[26]

Casualty insurance frequently provides coverage for some persons in addition to those who are identified as the named insureds. For example, motor vehicle liability insurance ordinarily specifies that any person driving an insured vehicle with the permission of a named insured is an additional insured.[27] Provisions of this type are often referred to or described as "omnibus" clauses, even though they are rarely so identified or characterized in insurance policies. Although insurers have used many different omnibus provisions,[28] the clauses all share the common characteristic of designating the persons who are additional insureds on the basis of some specified relationship, such as (1) a person who has received permission from a named insured to use an insured vehicle or (2) a person who is a relative of and who resides with a named insured. Many claims disputes turn on the scope of coverage provided by such clauses.[29]

---

22. "Standard" mortgage clauses are also referred to as "union" mortgage clauses. The effects of such clauses can be significant. For example, the Tennessee Supreme Court concluded that when the "insurance contract does not contain any provision, sometimes called 'standard' or 'union' mortgage clause, protecting the interest of the mortgagee from acts or omissions of the insured-mortgagor which, under the terms of the policy, may operate to invalidate the coverage ⋆ ⋆ ⋆ invalidating acts or omissions of the insured-mortgagor operate not only to defeat his [the mortgagor's] own rights but those of the mortgagee as well." Central National Insurance Company of Omaha v. Manufacturers Acceptance Corporation, 544 S.W.2d 362 at p. 364 (Tenn.1976).

But cf. Southern Insurance Company v. First National Bank at Orlando, 237 So.2d 302 (Fla.App., 4th Dist., 1970).

23. Such a clause stands in contrast with a so-called "open mortgage" clauses. See the discussion in the following subsections: § 4.1(c) and § 4.2, below.

24. See, e.g., Christopher & John, Inc. v. Maryland Casualty Company, 484 F.Supp. 609 (S.D.N.Y.1980); Burritt Mutual Savings Bank of New Britain v. Transamerica Insurance Company, 180 Conn. 71, 428 A.2d 333 (1980).

25. See the discussion of casualty insurance in § 1.5(d), above.

26. For example, see the insurance forms in Appendix A and Appendix H.

27. See § 4.7(b)(1), below.

28. See § 4.7, below.

29. Similar coverage issues arise in regard to whether the tortfeasor had received permission from a named insured to use such a vehicle. See the discussion of omnibus clauses in § 4.7, below.

The medical payments coverage and uninsured motorist insurance — which are included in most motor vehicle insurance policies — typically contain provisions that, though they are not usually referred to as omnibus clauses, identify additional insureds by defining as "insureds" a class of persons who bear a particular relationship to the named insured. For example, medical payments insurance typically provides coverage for members of a named insured's household.[30] The uninsured motorist insurance terms almost uniformly provide coverage for all relatives who are residents of a named insured's household.[31]

(5) Designating Insureds in Life Insurance

In life insurance agreements, the term "insured" is generally understood to refer to the person whose life is the subject of the insurance contract. In most instances, the insurance proceeds are intended as a means of providing a financial benefit for persons who will suffer an economic detriment when an insured dies.[32] The term "beneficiary" is commonly used to signify the persons who are to receive the proceeds of a life insurance contract. [The term "beneficiary" is not commonly used in relation to property and casualty insurance, even though the rights and status of some persons often could be accurately described as those of a third party beneficiary of an insurance contract between the insurer and the insured.]

When the person who purchases a life insurance policy is the individual whose death is the occasion for an insurer's liability, there is little possibility for confusion about who is the insured under such a policy. However, if someone other than the person whose life is the subject of the insurance contract obtains a life insurance policy, confusion may arise if the term "insured" is also used to describe the purchaser of the policy. Therefore, it seems more sensible not to employ the term "insured" to refer to the purchaser of a life insurance policy — that is, it is preferable to use the term "insured" (or "assured") to refer to the person whose death will occasion the payment of the insurance. To put it another way, the "insured" is the person whose death is the subject of the contract regardless of who buys the life insurance policy, who pays the premiums for the coverage, or who is to receive the insurance benefits upon the insured's death.[33] Of course, terminology is not, or at least ought not to be, decisive. But imprecise usage may produce confusion, uncertainty, and misunderstanding.

---

30. Some medical payments coverages even expand the scope of such insurance to include guests in a named insured's household. This is commonly done in the medical payments coverage of homeowners policy forms, as well as in automobile medical payments forms. But it often happens that the insurance policy itself does not refer to these persons as "insureds." See Appendix H.

31. See the forms in Appendix H.

32. It seems artificial to describe the risk transferred as merely "death," or even as "harm resulting from death."

33. See the discussion of interests in life insurance in § 4.11, below. There are also several other problems concerning interests protected that are distinctive to life insurance.

§ 4.1(c) Assignments

(1) Introduction

Insureds occasionally assign either some portion of the rights created by an insurance contract (as, for example, the right to receive payment from the insurer) or an entire insurance contract. Such transactions may present a variety of legal problems, and resolution of the questions presented by assignments is often significantly influenced by the type of insurance involved.

The right to receive the payment of the insurance proceeds as the result of an assignment, whether created before or after the occurrence of an insured event, is derivative. It is the assignor's right to payment that is transferred, and therefore the assignee's right to receive insurance benefits usually is subject to any defense that could have been asserted against the assignor. This is one of the most important differences between, on the one hand, being identified as an additional "insured" in an insurance contract [1] (or being the assignee of an insurance contract so as to be substituted for the original named insured), and, on the other hand, being an assignee of an insured's chose in action against an insurer [2] or being designated as the recipient of the insurance payments.[3] Thus, when a transaction either involves the transfer of an insurance contract to the assignee or entitles someone (such as a mortgagee) to receive benefits even when the insurer has a good defense against an original insured (such as a mortgagor), such a person or entity should be both regarded and referred to as an "insured." [4]

(2) Assignments of Insurance Policies

The right to assign an insurance policy depends both on the type of insurance involved and on whether the insurance policy includes terms which restrict the right to transfer ownership of the insurance contract.[5] The following discussion of property insurance, life insurance,

§ 4.1(c)

1. See § 4.1(b), above.

2. See § 4.1(c)(3), below.

3. See § 4.1(b)(1), above. Also see the discussion of distinguishing "insureds" from others benefiting from property insurance in § 4.1(b)(3), above.

4. Sometimes the term "insured" appears to be used by property insurers in a much narrower sense than that which is indicated by the preceding descriptions. For example, some property insurance policy forms that confer on a mortgagee independent rights (essentially comparable to those provided to insureds) make no reference to the mortgagee as either a named or an additional insured. In these policies, the implication is that only the mortgagor is an insured.

5. In general, the insurer's express consent is required for a valid assignment of most types of insurance. See, e.g., McHugh v. Manhattan Fire & Marine Insurance Company, 363 Mich. 324, 109 N.W.2d 842 (1961).

Transfers by operation of law, however, are distinguishable. See, e.g., Gulf Insurance Company, Dallas, Texas v. Thieman, 356 P.2d 360 (Okl.1960). A trustee in bankruptcy claimed insurance benefits for a fire loss under policy issued to the insured prior to the filing in bankruptcy. The court held that a transfer of policy to trustee by operation of bankruptcy laws was not an assignment within meaning of policy clause prohibiting assignment of policy without consent of insurer.

In Loomis v. Vernon Mutual Fire Insurance Co., 14 Wis.2d 470, 111 N.W.2d 443

and marine insurance presents representative illustrations of the ways in which the right to assign a policy may be influenced by the type of insurance involved in a particular transaction.

(i) Property Insurance. When the phrase "assignment of the policy" is used in connection with a property insurance contract, it ordinarily is understood to mean an arrangement under which an insured transfers all interests in a property insurance policy to another who is substituted for the assignor as the insured. In other words, such an assignment of a property insurance policy serves to substitute a new insured, rather than to designate an additional insured. This type of transaction can appropriately be used when an original insured transfers all interests in an insured property to the new insured. Indeed, if a complete transfer of the property interests occurred without the insurer approving an assignment of the insurance policy, the policy would no longer provide coverage for anyone. The original insured would lack an insurable interest in the property and the insurer normally would not be obligated to the new owner of the property because a property insurer usually is not required to pay benefits to anyone it has not specifically agreed to insure.[6]

Property insurance contracts generally contain a clause prohibiting an assignment of a policy without the consent of the insurer.[7] Property insurers want the privilege of deciding whether to insure a new owner

(1961), the insured had acquired a three year fire insurance policy in 1954. The insured died intestate later in 1954, and the property passed to insured's heirs. The final probate decree was filed in 1955. The court concluded that the heirs could recover under the insurance policy for a fire loss that occurred in 1956 on alternative grounds that assignment-without-consent provision was inapplicable to transfer by operation of law and that heirs were within meaning of clause naming insured as intestate "and his legal representatives."

6. *Cf.* Eagle Star Insurance Company, Ltd. v. General Accident Fire and Life Assurance Corporation, 315 So.2d 826 at p. 830 (La.App., 3d Cir., 1975).

Caveat. However, if the original owner sold the property subject to a security interest, the seller would continue to have an insurable interest in the property. Furthermore, subject to certain defenses, the insurance policy that provided coverage for the ownership interest would also provide coverage for the seller's security interest.

Also see the discussion of fire insurance in this subsection, and the discussion of coverage in § 4.2 and § 4.3, below.

Also consider the discussion in the "Observations" subsection of Section 4.6.

7. For example, see the forms in Appendix A.

Older insurance policies usually included a provision that voided the policy if any change occurred in regard to the title to the insured property without the insurer's knowledge and consent. However, not all insurance contracts contained these provisions. See, e.g., Wriedt v. Beckenhauer, 183 Neb. 311, 159 N.W.2d 822 (1968). Moreover, such provisions may be unenforceable in particular circumstances. Also see the discussion of the enforceability of moral hazard clauses in § 6.6(e)(3), below.

When a property insurance policy does not include a provision that voids the insurance policy in the absence of the insurer's consent and the property is subsequently sold subject to a mortgage security interest, if no steps are taken to make the purchaser an additional insured, the insurance is usually treated as coverage for the seller's interest in the property as a mortgagee. See the cases cited in § 4.2(b) and § 4.2(c), below.

of the property and compliance with such consent requirements is essential.[8]

Once an insured event has occurred, an insured is free to assign the right to recover from the insurer.[9] A nonassignability clause in a property insurance policy only limits "the assignability of an interest in the policy before the insured-against loss has occurred," [10] and does not preclude assignment of the chose in action to recover for a loss that occurred before the assignment.

Fire Insurance. The risk that a property will be destroyed by a fire is one of a number of risks that may be covered by a property insurance policy. However, because the losses from fires are probably the most significant risks for most property owners, this portion of property insurance policies has often been subject to specific legislative or administrative actions. For example, before 1943, many fire insurance policies included a clause stating that the entire policy would be void in the event an assignment was made without the insurer's consent.[11] Since 1943, as a result of the widespread influence of the New York legislation that prescribes a standard form for fire insurance, fire insurance policies have almost uniformly included a provision that an "assignment of this policy shall not be valid except with the written consent of this Company." [12] The enforceability of this policy provision is supported by the view that a fire insurance contract is by its nature "personal." This means that fire insurance is intended to insure the interests of a particular insured in a property, rather than being a policy that insures the property without regard to who owns it.[13]

(ii) Life Insurance. When the phrase "assignment of the policy" is used in connection with a life insurance contract, it is

---

8. That is, insurers generally want to decide whether the new owner is a desirable insured, and whether the use to which the property will be put involves comparable risks for the insurer. For example, see Eagle Star Insurance Company, Ltd. v. General Accident Fire and Life Assurance Corporation, 315 So.2d 826 at p. 829 (La. App., 3d Cir., 1975), in which the court observed that an insurance policy issued on an aircraft was a personal contract that was not transferred with the aircraft when it was sold.

Also see Porat v. Hanover Insurance Company, 583 F.Supp. 35 (E.D.Pa.1983).

9. See the cases cited in § 4.1(c)(3), below.

10. International Rediscount Corp. v. Hartford Accident and Indemnity Company, 425 F.Supp. 669 at p. 673 (D.Del., 1977).

Also consider the cases cited in § 4.1(c)(3)(ii), below, and the accompanying text.

11. Even in the absence of such a specific policy clause, an attempted assignment of a fire insurance policy may not have been effective without the insurer's consent. Before 1943 there were several cases that, at least theoretically, presented the question of whether valid assignments could be made of the fire insurance policies that did not contain any provision against assignment. *Cf.* Swaine v. Teutonia Fire Insurance Co., 222 Mass. 108, 109 N.E. 825 (1915); Jecko v. St. Louis Fire and Marine Insurance Company, 7 Mo.App. 308 (1879).

Also see Simeral v. The Dubuque Mutual Fire Insurance Company, 18 Iowa 319 at pp. 323–324 (1865), and the decisions cited therein.

12. See the 1943 New York Standard Fire Insurance Policy, in Appendix A.

Similar consent provisions are often included in liability insurance policies.

13. See, e.g., Wilson v. Hill, 44 Mass. (3 Metc.) 66 (1841).

Also consider the discussion in Vance, LAW OF INSURANCE (Third edition, Anderson, 1951), at pp. 757–758, n. 1.

Also see § 3.1(d), above.

commonly understood to describe a transfer of the incidents of ownership.[14] The ownership interests may be few or many depending on the particular life insurance contract. The ownership interests usually include the right to change the designation of beneficiaries. Sometimes an insurance policy will provide a right to convert an existing insurance policy to another form of life insurance or to increase the amount of coverage. When a life insurance policy includes an investment feature as well, the ownership interests typically include both (1) the right to obtain a loan from the insurer (often based on using the insurance policy as collateral) and (2) the right to surrender the insurance policy in return for a cash payment by the insurer.

Life insurance policies ordinarily contain a clause prescribing several "formalities" that must be complied with in order to make a valid assignment, and the consent of the insurer is customarily specified as one of the requirements in such provisions.[15]

Generally, an assignment of a life insurance policy would not be used either to make a change in the designation of the "beneficiaries" or to describe such a change. However, an assignment of a life insurance policy may result in a change of beneficiaries — that is, the assignee of a life insurance policy may acquire the right to change the beneficiaries and thereafter exercise that right.

An assignment of a life insurance policy may have essentially the same effect as a change in the designation of the beneficiaries, even if there is no formal alteration in the designation of the beneficiaries, because an assignee may acquire rights to the insurance proceeds which are superior to those of the named beneficiaries.[16] For example, when an assignment of rights in a life insurance policy is made as part of a transaction in which the policy is pledged as security for a loan to the insured — from the insurer, from some other entity such as a bank, or from an individual — the lender will be entitled to be repaid from the insurance benefits in the event of the insured's death — that is, the lender's claim will prevail over a claim by the beneficiaries who otherwise would have been the recipients of the insurance proceeds.

Control over the incidents of ownership in regard to a life insurance contract usually does not present problems so long as the purchaser is the person whose life is insured, *and* that person continues to retain all of the rights. However, when someone other than the insured is the purchaser or when some transaction serves to create

---

14. One form of "assignment," the delivery of an insurance policy as collateral security for some transaction, occurs with some frequency. See Annotation, *Effectiveness, as pledge, of transfer of non-negotiable instruments which represent obligation,* 53 A.L.R.2d 1396 at pp. 1404–1406 (1957).

15. For further treatment of assignment of life insurance policies, see § 4.11, below.

Whether anyone aside from the insurer has standing to question whether the requirements specified for a valid assignment were complied with is sometimes a matter of considerable import, and it is discussed in § 4.11(e).

16. See § 4.11(e), below.

interests in regard to a life insurance policy in someone other than the insured, difficult problems may ensue.[17]

(iii) Marine Insurance. Marine insurance policies originally did not include policy stipulations that restricted assignments, and the English courts held that such policies were assignable without the consent of the insurer.[18] This common law rule was incorporated into the British Marine Insurance Act of 1906.[19] In American insurance policies today, however, and to a lesser extent in English policies, provisions against assignment of a marine policy without the insurer's consent are widely used.

In non-marine property insurance, the transfer of an insured property (other than by operation of law) generally does not affect the ownership of a property insurance policy and does not entitle the transferee to collect the insurance in the event of an insured loss.[20] This rule also applies in marine insurance.[21]

17. For example, consider the situation in which before marriage a woman had maintained a $250,000 term life insurance policy which named her younger siblings as beneficiaries. Shortly after the marriage, the policy was assigned by the woman to her husband who thereafter continued the policy in effect for a period of twenty years, at which point the spouses were divorced. During the marriage, the husband was designated as the beneficiary. Suppose that after the divorce, the wife were to learn that her former husband has continued to maintain the policy in effect, and has named his second wife as the primary beneficiary. Upon discovering this, the first wife communicates with the insurance company and demands either that the coverage be cancelled or that she be allowed to designate the beneficiary. When a notice of the first wife's wishes is sent to her former husband, he is equally vehement in a response to the insurer that the policy is not to be cancelled and that he is still entitled to designate the beneficiary. Whose wishes should prevail?

Although it seems that the husband is almost certainly the owner of the insurance policy, that conclusion does not appear to provide a sufficient or a satisfactory basis for resolving the controversy this type of a situation would present to an insurance company. Such questions obviously do not arise in regard to most life insurance transactions, but they do occur with sufficient frequency — especially as a consequence of marriage dissolutions and loan transactions — to make disputes about the effect of the transfer or potential transfer of interests in life insurance a significant problem area. See the discussion of life insurance in § 4.11(e), below.

18. See, e.g., Spring and Sons v. South Carolina Insurance Company, 21 U.S. (8 Wheat.) 268, 5 L.Ed. 614 (1823).

Also see 1 ARNOULD, MARINE INSURANCE [9 British Shipping Laws] (Fifteenth edition, 1961), at §§ 231 and 236; Vance, LAW OF INSURANCE (Third edition, Anderson, 1951), at p. 756.

19. 6 Edw. 7, c. 41, § 50(1).

20. See, e.g., Davis v. Oregon Mutual Insurance Company, 71 Wn.2d 579, 429 P.2d 886 (1967) (fire insurance on house; conveyance of house does not transfer insurance; assignment to third person of vendor's interest under policy obtained in part for his benefit by purchaser distinguished).

If the vendor retains an interest in the property, as, for example, a purchase-money mortgagee, his interest will continue to be protected under the policy in the absence of a provision voiding the policy on alienation of the property. See, e.g., American Equitable Assurance Company of New York v. Pioneer Cooperative Fire Insurance Company, 100 R.I. 375, 216 A.2d 139 (1966).

Cf. Imperial Enterprises, Inc. v. Fireman's Fund Insurance Company, 535 F.2d 287 at pp. 292–293 (5th Cir.1976), *rehearing denied* 540 F.2d 1085 (5th Cir.1976), in which the court concluded that in the absence of an increase in the risk or the hazard to the insurer, "the no assignment clause should not be applied ritualistically and mechanically to forfeit coverage" when the transfer of the policy resulted from a statutory merger which transferred

21. See note 21 on page 302.

Automatic Assignments of Marine Insurance Policies

Many courts recognize what is essentially an "automatic" assignment when an insured property is transferred in one type of situation. Marine insurance policies often provide coverage "for the account of whom it may concern" (the phrase used in American policies) or for all persons to whom an interest in the property "doth, may, or shall appertain" (the phrase used in English policies). American judicial decisions appear to adopt the proposition that these phrases imply an expression of the insurer's agreement that a future transfer of the insured property will carry with it the right to protection under the insurance policy in cases in which it can be said that the transferee is among those whom, by name or by present or future status in relation to the property, the person named intended to insure.[22] English courts have applied a somewhat different approach to the effect that if the claimant does not prove a valid assignment of the policy, the claimant must offer extrinsic proof that the named insured had the claimant in contemplation at the time of making the insurance contract.[23]

The explanation for such favorable treatment of assignees in this context, and disfavor toward unnamed beneficiaries of the original agreement, probably is primarily historical. In the middle of the eighteenth century the practice arose in England of effecting policies in blank, without inserting the name either of the party for whom the insurance was obtained or of the party by whom it was obtained. Legislation aimed at prohibiting the use of such blank policies culminated in a provision in the British Marine Insurance Act of 1906 that a marine policy must specify the name of the assured or of some person who effects the insurance on his behalf.[24] Although neither this act nor the earlier legislation specifies that the named insured must have the claimant in contemplation at the time of making the contract, the legislation and the circumstances out of which it arose probably contributed to the development of this rule.[25]

the insurance policy by operation of law. The federal court concluded that "in light of the developing Georgia law in this area," the anti-assignment clause's "application is at least ambiguous in the circumstance of this case." *Id.,* at p. 291.

21. The following provision appears in the British Marine Insurance Act of 1906, 6 Edw. 7, c. 41, 15:

"Where the assured assigns or otherwise parts with his interest in the subject-matter insured, he does not thereby transfer to the assignee his rights under the contract of insurance, unless there be an express or implied agreement with the assignee to that effect.

"But the provisions of this section do not affect a transmission of interest by operation of law."

22. See, e.g., Hagan v. Scottish Union & National Insurance Company, 186 U.S. 423, 22 S.Ct. 862, 46 L.Ed. 1229 (1902).

See generally 5A Appleman, Insurance Law (1970), at § 3336.

23. See, e.g., Boston Fruit Company v. British & Foreign Marine Insurance Company, [1906] A.C. 336.

Also see 1 Arnould, Marine Insurance [9 British Shipping Laws] (Sixteenth edition, 1981), at §§ 242–244.

24. 6 Edw. 7, c. 41, § 41, § 23(1).

25. See generally 1 Arnould, Marine Insurance [9 British Shipping Laws] (Sixteenth edition, 1981), at § 242 and § 243.

(3) Assignments of the Right to Be Paid Insurance

(i) Arrangements That Follow the Occurrence of a Loss.

Following the occurrence of a loss, an insured may want to transfer the right to be paid by the insurer.[26] This type of transaction is usually described or referred to as an assignment of the insured's chose in action against the insurer.[27]

Insurance policies commonly do not contain any provision against an assignment of an insured's chose in action against an insurer. In the absence of a provision to the contrary in the insurance policy, an assignment of a chose in action is generally recognized as a valid transfer of the right to receive the proceeds of the insurance.[28] Moreover, several courts have stated that in general a restriction in an insurance policy against an assignment of an insured's rights after a loss has occurred would be invalid.[29] Thus, it usually is not necessary to have the insurer's consent to an assignment of the chose in action.[30]

In several states, Blue Cross/Blue Shield health insurance contracts provide that the benefits payable to a subscriber (the individual

---

26. It is not uncommon that a person to whom such an assignment of a chose in action in regard to a property insurance claim is made also has an interest in the insured property. But it is not essential that an assignee have such an interest in order for such an assignment of a chose in action against a property insurer to be enforceable. Although this happens frequently, it is a matter of coincidence rather than a requirement for effective assignment of the chose in action. Even when a mortgagee is an assignee of a mortgagor's rights against an insurer, if it is solely a loss to the mortgagor's interest that is the occasion for and the measure of the insurer's liability, the mortgagee is not viewed or treated as an "insured."

27. See, e.g., Gimbels Midwest, Inc. v. Northwestern National Insurance Company of Milwaukee, 72 Wis.2d 84, 240 N.W.2d 140 (1976); St. Paul Fire & Marine Insurance Company v. Allstate Insurance Co., 25 Ariz.App. 309, 543 P.2d 147 (Div. 1, Dept. A., 1975).

Also see Time Finance Corporation v. Johnson Trucking Company, 23 Utah 2d 115, 458 P.2d 873 (1969); Aetna Casualty & Surety Company v. Valley National Bank of Arizona, 15 Ariz.App. 13, 485 P.2d 837 (Div. 1, Dept. B, 1971), and the cases cited therein.

See generally, 6B APPLEMAN, INSURANCE, LAW & PRACTICE (Revised edition, 1979), at § 4269.

Also see § 4.1(b)(2), above.

28. See, e.g., Ocean Accident & Guarantee Corp. v. Southwestern Bell Telephone Company, 100 F.2d 441, 122 A.L.R. 133 (8th Cir.1939), *cert. denied* 306 U.S. 658, 59 S.Ct. 775, 83 L.Ed.2d 1056 (1939) (employer's liability insurance); Windey v. North Star Farmers Mutual Insurance Company, 231 Minn. 279, 43 N.W.2d 99 (1950) (tornado insurance).

Also see 5A APPLEMAN, INSURANCE LAW (Revised edition, 1970), at § 3459.

29. E.g., Max L. Bloom Company v. United States Casualty Company, 191 Wis. 524, 210 N.W. 689 (1926) (burglary insurance).

Contra. See, e.g., Dallas County Hosp. Dist. v. Pioneer Casualty Company, 402 S.W.2d 287 (Tex.Civ.App.1966) (insured assigned her rights under her $1,000 limit medical payments coverage to hospital that had already provided services worth $400; after insured had incurred expenses in excess of $1,000, the hospital gave the insurer notice of the assignment, after which the insurer, not having consented to the assignment, paid its $1,000 limit to the insured, who subsequently disappeared without paying the hospital; held, the hospital could not recover anything from the insurer since the policy prohibited the assignment of "any interest" without the insurer's consent).

Also see Vance, LAW OF INSURANCE (Third edition, Anderson, 1951), at p. 761.

30. *Cf.* Reese v. Chicago, Burlington, Quincy R.R. Co., 55 Ill.2d 356, 303 N.E.2d 382 (1973) (J. Schaefer dissenting).

covered by the insurance) may not be assigned. When the enforceability of such provisions has been litigated, Blue Cross/Blue Shield representatives have justified this provision as a means of helping to "keep down the costs of medical services to subscribers" by encouraging health care providers (that is, individuals or entities, such as physicians, nursing homes, and hospitals) to join the Blue Shield program.[31] Providers who join Blue Cross or Blue Shield agree to accept the amount paid by Blue Cross or Blue Shield as payment in full for the medical services rendered to the patient. However, the only inducement that Blue Cross or Blue Shield can offer in exchange for the provider's commitment to accept such an amount is the prompt payment directly to the provider. In several decisions which have addressed such restraints on a subscriber's right to assign, to a nonmember provider, the right to collect health insurance benefits, the courts have concluded the provisions were not void as a matter of public policy.[32] These decisions were, at least in part, predicated on the uniqueness of Blue Cross or Blue Shield as a non-profit health service corporation that is afforded special status — including exemptions from many or all regulatory provisions that apply to traditional insurers in order to facilitate cost containment — under the respective state insurance laws.

(ii) Arrangements That Precede the Occurrence of a Loss.

In some situations an insured may want to arrange in advance that in the event an insured loss occurs, the insurance proceeds will be paid to an unsecured creditor, a mortgagee, or someone else — that is, the insured wants to structure the arrangement so that a designated recipient will receive either a portion or all of the insurance proceeds in the event of a loss even though that person is not entitled to be treated as an insured under the policy. When an assignment of a prospective right (that is, an assignment made before a loss occurs) to a chose in action is made without an insurer's consent to the transaction, such an assignment *may* be valid.[33] However, this type of transaction is perilously close to transgressing the public policy considerations which support the treatment of insurance transactions as "personal contracts." [34] Accordingly, proceeding with such a transaction without the consent of the insurer is needlessly risky and should be avoided.

31. See Obstetricians-Gynecologists, P.C. v. Blue Cross and Blue Shield of Nebraska, 219 Neb. 199, 361 N.W.2d 550 (1985).

32. See, e.g., Obstetricians-Gynecologists, P.C. v. Blue Cross and Blue Shield of Nebraska, 219 Neb. 199, 361 N.W.2d 550 (1985).

Also see Kent General Hospital, Inc. v. Blue Cross & Blue Shield of Delaware, Inc., 442 A.2d 1368 (Del.1982), and Augusta Medical Complex, Inc. v. Blue Cross, 230 Kan. 361, 634 P.2d 1123 (1981).

33. See, e.g., Hartford Fire Insurance Company v. Mutual Savings & Loan Company, 193 Va. 269, 68 S.E.2d 541 (1952), 31 A.L.R.2d 1191 (1953).

34. See the discussion of insurance as a "personal" contract in § 3.1(d)(2). Also see the discussion of "loss payable" clauses in § 4.1(b)(2).

§ 4.1(d) Observations on Ascertaining the Status of a Claimant

The rights of various persons to the proceeds of insurance policies are primarily questions of contract law, and courts assessing claims for insurance payments almost invariably seek to discern the manifested intent of the parties. For example, the fact that the phrase "loss payable" appears somewhere in an agreement will not prevent a finding, based on other evidence of the parties' manifested intention, that the arrangement is a designation of either substitute or additional insureds. The mere use of phrases such as "loss payable clause" will not invariably lead a court to conclude that the arrangement intended by the parties was the type of transaction that the usage of such a term normally connotes. Thus, even if the parties have used a phraseology commonly associated with one type of transaction, clear indications — especially when it is manifested in a written agreement — that they intended another form of transaction will usually be given effect by courts so long as the result of doing so will not conflict with some regulatory provision or fundamental public policy concern (such as the insurable interest doctrine).

§ 4.2 Interests in Property That Is Mortgaged, Including Subrogation Rights

§ 4.2(a) Questions Underlying Conflicting Claims When Insurance Is Paid to a Mortgagee

When property that is the subject of a mortgage is protected by insurance which is payable to a mortgagee, the destruction of property often produces interesting and complex issues.[1] Several fundamental and inter-related problems are indicated by the following four questions concerning persons and interests protected by an insurance policy on mortgaged property:

First, may a mortgagee collect and retain the proceeds of both an insurance contract and a mortgage debt?

Second, is an insurer that pays a mortgagee entitled to assert a right of subrogation?

Third, does an insurer's payment of insurance benefits due to a mortgagee under the policy discharge the mortgage debt pro tanto (that is, to the extent of the amount paid)?

Fourth, if all parties are solvent and all legal rights are enforced, will the economic loss resulting from the destruction of an insured property ultimately fall on the mortgagor, the mortgagee, or the insurer?

§ 4.2(a)

1. Essentially the same questions may arise when an insured property is the subject of a "conditional sales contract" designed to serve functions similar to those of a mortgage. See § 4.3, below, for a discussion of issues that arise when the contract is a "purchase and sale contract."

The first question is probably the easiest to resolve. To allow a mortgagee to retain the insurance and then also to collect the mortgage debt would violate the principle of indemnity.[2] Thus, if the principle of indemnity is applied in this type of situation, an insured mortgagee[3] will not be allowed to profit by a double recovery. However, even when it is clear that the principle of indemnity will be rigorously applied in determining the rights to the insurance, another basic decision remains in regard to answering these questions: either (1) the mortgage debt is not discharged by the insurance payments, and the insurer is subrogated to the mortgagee's rights, so that the ultimate loss (if all parties are solvent and all rights are enforced) will fall on the mortgagor, or (2) the mortgage debt is discharged to the extent of the payment (often referred to as "pro tanto" discharge), and the ultimate loss will fall on the insurer.

The choices presented by the type of situation outlined above implicitly suggest that certain fundamental assumptions about the effects of insurance, described in an earlier section,[4] may not always be valid. These assumptions include:

(1) That the existence of insurance coverage does not affect the liability of "third persons" to an "insured," and

(2) That the existence of claims of an "insured" against "third persons" does not affect the liability of an insurer.

Indeed, as will be evident from the discussion in the following subsections, one of the critical issues in the resolution of the respective rights of the mortgagor, the mortgagee, and the insurer is whether the mortgagee is also treated as an "insured" in regard to the mortgagor's insurance. This determination is an important step in the process of providing a complete answer to the four questions set forth above.

§ 4.2(b) The Right of Subrogation When Insurance Is Paid to a Mortgagee

Insurance for a property that is subject to a mortgage may be acquired by either the mortgagor or the mortgagee individually, or jointly by the parties. Furthermore, when the insurance is acquired by a mortgagor or a mortgagee, it may be arranged as protection for either the acquirer's individual interest or the joint interests of the two. Thus, when the acquisition of insurance is not undertaken jointly, the insurance policy purchased by a mortgagor or a mortgagee may only identify the purchaser as the insured. For example, especially when the mortgagor's ownership interests include title to the property, the mortgagor's insurance policy frequently does not provide coverage for the mortgagee.

---

2. See the discussion of the indemnity principle in § 3.1, above.

3. Essentially the same analysis applies to a conditional vendor, and usually as well to a financing party who becomes an as-signee of either a mortgagee or a conditional vendor.

4. See the discussion in § 3.10(c)(4), above.

Either a mortgagor or a mortgagee may acquire insurance that covers both the mortgagor's and the mortgagee's interest in the property. And, in many situations the mortgagor arranges the insurance transaction so that the mortgagee is also an "insured". Similarly, lenders, such as banks, sometimes are responsible for acquiring insurance that also provides coverage for the borrower.

In general, an insurer cannot be subrogated to a claim against its own insured.[1] This rule is predicated on the rationale that *if* an insurer could be subrogated to rights against someone to whom insurance benefits have been paid on account of the coverage with respect to which that person was an "insured," it would in effect nullify the benefits of the insurance. However, when mortgaged property is insured, the effect of this rule often depends on a determination of the party or parties who are accorded the status of being an "insured" or "insureds."

When an insurance policy on mortgaged realty is arranged by the mortgagor, the mortgagor's name is usually typed on the form contract in a space within a printed statement that the insurer "does insure _____ and legal representatives * * *" or is listed as a named insured on a declarations page. If the mortgagee is also insured, the mortgagee's name is typically typed in another space within a printed statement, sometimes referred to as a "loss payable clause," stating that a loss "shall be payable to: _____" subject to provisions of the mortgage clause.

When a mortgagor and mortgagee are both identified as insureds in an insurance policy on realty, the policy almost invariably contains a "standard" mortgage clause, which is also referred to as a "union" mortgage clause.[2] This clause has several important elements, includ-

§ 4.2(b)

1. See, e.g., Federal Insurance Company v. Tamiami Trail Tours, Inc., 117 F.2d 794 (5th Cir.1941).

Cf. Mutual Fire Insurance Co. of Harford Cty. v. Dilworth, 167 Md. 232, 173 A. 22 (1934), discussed in 83 University of Pennsylvania Law Review 273–276 (1934). The insurance policy at issue included a standard mortgage clause with loss payable to first mortgagee and second mortgagee as interest may appear. The insurer claimed nonliability as to mortgagor, paid the first mortgagee a sum equal to the full amount of his mortgage, received an assignment, and asserted a lien which the insurer urged was superior to that of the second mortgagee. The insurer's claim of priority over second mortgagee disallowed.

2. The term "loss payable clause" sometimes is used to refer to the "standard" or "union" mortgage clause. It is also used in a narrower sense, [described in § 4.1(b)(2) and § 4.1(b)(3), above], which is often referred to as an "open" mortgage clause to distinguish it from the "standard" or "union" clause. See Insurance Company of North America v. Gulf Oil Corporation, 106 Ga.App. 382, 127 S.E.2d 43 (1962); Conard v. Moreland, 230 Iowa 520, 523, 298 N.W. 628, 629 (1941).

As previously suggested, in § 4.1(b)(2), above, the manifested intentions of the parties, rather than a technical interpretation of the language used, should determine whether the "loss payable" clause is given the narrower effect of an assignment of the chose in action or instead the broader effect of the standard-mortgage clause. In the *Gulf Oil* case, however, the clause involved was characterized as the "open" type, apparently without regard to the parties' intentions, and the insurer was allowed to recover as subrogee to its insured's (the mortgagor's) tort claim against the mortgagee.

In contrast, it was held in Commercial Credit Corporation v. Premier Insurance

ing provisions which specify (1) that the insurance shall be payable to the mortgagee "as its interest may appear," (2) that insurance for the interest of the mortgagee "shall not be invalidated by any act or neglect of the mortgagor * * *," and (3) that whenever the insurer pays the mortgagee and establishes that it has no liability to the mortgagor because of an act or neglect of the mortgagor, the insurer shall be subrogated to the rights of the mortgagee on the mortgage debt subject to the mortgagee's right to recover the full amount of the mortgagee's claim. Similar clauses often appear in motor vehicle insurance policies.[3] When an insurance contract includes such policy provisions, in the absence of any act or neglect in violation of policy terms on the part of a mortgagor, both the mortgagor and the mortgagee are insured and the ultimate economic loss which results from an insured event will normally fall on the insurer.[4]

Company, 12 Utah 2d 321, 366 P.2d 476 (1961), that cancellation of a policy of collision insurance by the named insured without notice to the mortgagee did not defeat the latter's claim under the policy, although the clause involved was practically identical to that in *Gulf Oil.* The broader construction was not based explicitly on the parties' manifested intentions, however, but on the principle of construing against the insurer an ambiguity with respect to whether cancellation without notice to the mortgagee affected the mortgagee's interests. See the discussion of "ambiguity" in § 6.3, below.

Also see Christopher & John, Inc. v. Maryland Casualty Company, 484 F.Supp. 609 (S.D.N.Y.1980); Burritt Mutual Savings Bank of New Britain v. Transamerica Insurance Company, 180 Conn. 71, 428 A.2d 333 (1980); Grady v. Utica Mutual Insurance Company, 69 A.D.2d 668, 419 N.Y. Supp.2d 565 (2d Dept.1979).

3. See, e.g., Bennett Motor Company v. Lyon, 14 Utah 2d 161, 380 P.2d 69 (1963), holding that the insured's intentional burning of the insured vehicle did not preclude recovery by the insured's conditional sale vendor and that as to the latter the loss was accidental.

Also see Southwestern Funding Corporation v. Motors Insurance Corporation, 59 Cal.2d 91, 28 Cal.Rptr. 161, 378 P.2d 361 (1963). The clause provided coverage for mortgagee in spite of insured's violation of "terms or conditions" of policy. The court held that a mortgagee can recover for loss from accident that occurred in Mexico although policy provided, under heading "Conditions," that coverage was applicable only while automobile was within the United States.

But cf. Savings Society Commercial Bank v. Michigan Mutual Liability Company, 118 Ohio App. 297, 25 Ohio Op.2d 143, 194 N.E.2d 435 (1963), 98 A.L.R.2d 1312 (1964) (insurer not required to give notice to mortgagee under standard mortgage clause of exercise of option to repair damaged automobile, since policy did not so require).

Motor vehicle policies also employ the so-called "open" mortgage arrangement, in which case any "invalidating acts or omissions of the insured-mortgagor operate not only to defeat his own rights but those of the mortgagee as well." Central National Insurance Company of Omaha v. Manufacturers Acceptance Corporation, 544 S.W.2d 362 at p. 364 (Tenn.1976).

4. E.g., Palisano v. Bankers & Shippers Insurance Co., 276 App.Div. 523, 95 N.Y.S.2d 543 (4th Dept.1950), *appeal denied* 277 App.Div. 945, 98 N.Y.S.2d 664 (1950).

If the mortgage debt is wholly satisfied, even subsequent to fire damage to the mortgaged property, the mortgagor becomes the only "insured" still entitled to a share of the insurance proceeds and is thus entitled to the full amount. But inequitable results may be produced if a court regards the debt as wholly satisfied when the mortgagee has in fact received less than full payment. Rosenbaum v. Funcannon, 308 F.2d 680 (9th Cir.1962), and Northwestern National Insurance Company v. Mildenberger, 359 S.W.2d 380 (Mo. App., St. Louis, 1962), are interesting illustrations of this point. In both cases the debt was "extinguished" by foreclosure sale at which the mortgagee bid in and bought the property for the amount of the outstanding debt, and the mortgagor was

In the event some act or neglect by a mortgagor limits or excludes the mortgagor's right of recovery against the insurer, a mortgagee who has been identified as an insured will usually still be entitled to receive the insurance proceeds.[5] In such a situation, the mortgagor is not treated as an insured for purposes of that loss, and therefore the insurer who pays the mortgagee may seek to assert a right of subrogation. Allowing an insurer to enforce subrogation rights (which are usually set out in the mortgage clause of the insurance policy) in such circumstances does not violate the rule against allowing an insurer to "have subrogation against its own insured" because the mortgagor ceased to be an insured as a consequence of the act or neglect (which frequently is the failure to pay the insurance premium) — that is, in this type of situation, a provision in the insurance contract which states that the insurer is entitled to be subrogated to the mortgagee's rights against the mortgagor on the mortgage debt does not contravene the

held to be entitled to the full insurance proceeds.

In an extreme case such as *Rosenbaum,* this injudicious action of the mortgagee, together with the court's treating the debt as extinguished, produces a massive windfall for the mortgagor, who retains the insurance proceeds and is relieved of the debt as well as the damaged property. In that case, the original debt of $25,000 had been reduced only to $24,898 when an insured fire loss of $22,500 occurred. The mortgagee subsequently foreclosed, exercising his power to have the property sold, and bid the amount of the outstanding debt for the damaged property. Subsequently the mortgagee-purchaser sued to recover the insurance proceeds from the mortgagor and lost. As a result, the mortgagor, though having lost the property, had a large net gain (perhaps over $22,000, depending on whether the property was worth more than the debt, before the fire) and the mortgagee suffered a loss of approximately the same amount.

Also see Burritt Mutual Savings Bank of New Britain v. Transamerica Insurance Company, 180 Conn. 71, 428 A.2d 333 (1980) (quoting the discussion of this portion of the text from the original edition);

In a similar (though arguably distinguishable) case, Kolehouse v. Connecticut Fire Insurance Company, 267 Wis. 120, 65 N.W.2d 28 (1954), 46 A.L.R.2d 983, (1956) a more equitable result was reached by allowing a conditional vendor to recover collision insurance proceeds equal to the mortgage debt at the time of the accident, although shortly thereafter the vendor had improperly repossessed and resold the vehicle for its salvage value, with the result

that the vendee was released from all obligation under the conditional sale contract. In so deciding, however, the court held that rights in the insurance proceeds were fixed as of the date of loss and subsequent cancellation of the debt was of no effect. Surely such a broad holding would have to be qualified to apply only to a somewhat technical "cancellation" of the debt as distinguished from a discharge by actual payment. Perhaps an analogous qualification is implicit in the court's requiring an allowance to the vendee for the amount realized in sale of the damaged truck at salvage.

In Pearson v. First National Bank of Martinsville, 408 N.E.2d 166 at p. 170 (Ind. App., 4th Dist., 1980), the court concluded that "the mortgagee is entitled to the proceeds of the policy to the extent of his interest in the mortgage debt and may apply the proceeds to the outstanding mortgage debt as it falls due."

Also see § 4.2(c), note 2, below.

5. See, e.g., Old Colony Co-operative Bank v. Nationwide Mutual Fire Insurance Company, 114 R.I. 289, 332 A.2d 434 at p. 436 (1975), in which the court observed that "although there is some authority to the contrary, the large majority of courts read such [standard or union] clauses as effectively creating two separate contracts." The court then stated that "we have no difficulty in reading the clause requiring notice to the mortgagee before cancellation as indicating the creation of two contracts." *Ibid.*

Also see Grady v. Utica Mutual Insurance Company, 69 A.D.2d 668, 419 N.Y.S.2d 565 (2d Dept.1979).

rule forbidding an insurer from asserting a right of subrogation against an insured.[6]

A similar problem may arise when a mortgagor who owns an insured property conveys the property, subject to security interest, to a purchaser who agrees to pay the mortgage debt to the original mortgagee. The mortgagor, who sold the property, continues to have an insurable interest so long as the mortgage debt is not paid. Furthermore, the mortgagor-seller would also have an insurable interest in the property so long as the property continued to be a security for the fulfillment of the buyer's contractual obligations to the seller. If the mortgagor's insurance policy is continued after the sale of the property *and* if that policy contains a standard mortgage clause whereby coverage is provided for the original mortgagee as well as the original mortgagor, a problem may be created in the event the property is subsequently destroyed. For example, suppose that following a fire the insurer pays the original mortgagee in full and takes an assignment of the mortgagee's claims. An application of the general rule that an insurer should not be allowed subrogation against its own insured would result in the insurer's not being allowed to recover on the mortgage debt against such a mortgagor-seller (unless the conveyance to the purchaser violated a policy clause). However, having paid the mortgagor-seller's debt, the insurer should be subrogated to the mortgagor-seller's interest against the uninsured purchaser, and the principle that a fire insurance contract is personal would support a rule that the insurer should be allowed to assert this subrogation claim against a purchaser who is not an insured. To argue against subrogation in regard to such a purchaser would be the functional equivalent of urging that the insurance should run with the property, and that the purchaser should be treated as an insured even without the insurer's consent. The judicial precedents on this issue are inconclusive.[7]

Several of the competing considerations discussed in the preceding paragraphs were involved in an interesting coverage dispute considered by the Ninth Circuit Court of Appeals. The insured, who had purchased fire insurance on her home, sold the property subject to a security interest for the portion of the selling price that was yet to be paid by the purchasers. At the time of the fire, the insured's only interest in the property was as a mortgagee.[8] The court concluded that the policy provided coverage for her as a mortgagee,[9] and that the

6. *Cf.* Burritt Mutual Savings Bank of New Britain v. Transamerica Insurance Company, 180 Conn. 71, 428 A.2d 333 at p. 339 (1980) (when an insurer pays a mortgagee that forecloses without receiving full satisfaction, the insurer will be entitled to recover on a third-party complaint against mortgagor).

7. For an expression of different points of view concerning this problem, see Palisano v. Bankers & Shippers Insurance Co., 193 Misc. 647, 84 N.Y.S.2d 637 (Erie Coun-

ty 1948), *affirmed* 276 App.Div. 523, 95 N.Y.S.2d 543 (4th Dept.1950), and Note, *Subrogation of Insurer to Mortgagee's Rights Against Substituted Mortgage Debtor,* 49 Columbia Law Review 866–868 (1949).

8. A mortgage loan from a local bank to the insured had been paid off before the insured's sale of the house.

9. Mann v. Glens Falls Insurance Company, 541 F.2d 819 (9th Cir.1976) (revers-

insurer was entitled to be subrogated to claims the seller/mortgagee may have had against the mortgagor (the purchaser). The decision seems to be predicated on the appellate court's view of the actual and reasonable expectations of the parties, the seller and the buyer, in regard to the allocation of the risk of loss. The opinion points out that not only were the buyers in possession of the property, but also they were expressly obligated to insure the house against any loss caused by a fire and that the insurance contract the buyers were to have purchased was to name the seller as the loss-payable mortgagee.[10] However, no insurance policy had been purchased by the buyers. The court also explicitly concluded that there was no justification for extending the benefits of the insurance policy to the buyer because the insurance policy was a "personal contract" for the insured's interests only.[11]

§ 4.2(c) Mortgagee-Only Insurance: Subrogation and Premium Rates

Insurance can be acquired to protect only a mortgagee's interest in an insured property. Furthermore, as described in the preceding subsection, sometimes a policy purchased by an owner-mortgagor may be transformed into coverage for such an individual as a mortgagee in the event the property is sold to someone else subject to a mortgage security interest, and no steps are taken to make the purchaser an additional insured or to transfer the seller's insurance coverage to the purchaser.

When an insured property is destroyed, the debt secured by a mortgage on the property usually is not affected by the destruction of the property — that is, the debt is still enforceable.[1] Consequently, if a

---

ing the judgment of the district court for the District of Nevada).

10. *Id.,* 541 F.2d at p. 820. The buyers "agreed orally to insure the house against fire loss and to name Mrs. Mann [the insured seller] as loss-payable mortgagee."

11. The named insured, Mrs. Mann, wanted to use the insurance proceeds to rebuild the house, thereby reestablishing a habitable residence and to then receive her monthly mortgage payments from the buyers. She therefore refused the insurer's settlement offer which was made subject to her signing an agreement containing a "partial, subordinated assignment" that would have confirmed the insurer's right of subrogation. In commenting on her desire to take the insurance proceeds "free of the company's claim as a subrogee" the court stated that "her motive — to confer a benefit upon the Bates family [the uninsured purchasers] at the expense of her insurance carrier — however generous it may have been, was not a motive the insurance company had any duty to share." *Id.,* 541 F.2d at p. 822. Finally, the court also

concluded: "The general subrogation clause * * * clearly authorizes the company to require pro tanto assignments." *Id.,* 541 F.2d at p. 823.

§ 4.2(c)

1. However, following the occurrence of an insured loss to a mortgaged property, if a mortgagee subsequently bids the full amount of a secured debt at a foreclosure sale in order to obtain the mortgaged property (and without any agreement or stipulation as to what happens to the insurance claim), the mortgage may be discharged and the mortgagee may not be entitled to seek indemnification under a mortgagee loss payable clause. See, e.g., Whitestone Savings & Loan Association v. Allstate Insurance Company, 28 N.Y.2d 332, 321 N.Y. S.2d 862, 270 N.E.2d 694 (1971). This decision is subject to criticism for having failed to take account of evidence of the manifested intention of the parties as to whether a right to the insurance proceeds was transferred, along with title to the property, at the foreclosure sale.

mortgagee's insurer is denied a subrogation right against a mortgagor when the mortgagor is not designated as an "insured," the mortgagee who has been indemnified by an insurer would be entitled to also enforce the debt obligation of the mortgagor. In other words, when the mortgagee is fully indemnified by the insurance either the mortgagor would receive a windfall if the debt is held to be discharged, or the mortgagee would receive a windfall if the mortgagee were allowed to collect the insurance and enforce the debt obligation as well. Accordingly, when the mortgage debt is not discharged, it is usually held that the insurer may be subrogated to the mortgagee's claim.[2]

When an insurance payment to a mortgagee does not affect the mortgagor's debt *and* the insurer is entitled to seek reimbursement through an assertion of the right of subrogation, it seems clear that insurance written exclusively for the benefit of a mortgagee entails a somewhat smaller risk for an insurer than that which exists when an insurance policy provides coverage for both the mortgagor and the mortgagee of an insured property.[3] Accordingly, one might expect that property insurance for a mortgagee would be available at somewhat lower rates (per thousand dollars of coverage) than a policy with a standard mortgage clause that is purchased to protect both the mortgagor and the mortgagee. This is not usually the case: the premium rates for property insurance which only covers a mortgagee's interest is almost always the same as for a policy protecting both the mortgagor's and mortgagee's interests.[4] Although the analysis set forth above

Also see Mann v. Glenns Falls Insurance Company, 541 F.2d 819 (9th Cir.1976); Burritt Mutual Savings Bank of New Britain v. Transamerica Insurance Company, 180 Conn. 71, 428 A.2d 333 (1980).

Cf. Powell v. Motors Insurance Corporation, 235 So.2d 593 (La.App., 1st Cir., 1970) (following the loss of an automobile by fire, mortgagee caused the vehicle to be sold).

But cf. Federal National Mortgage Association v. Great American Insurance Company, 157 Ind.App. 347, 300 N.E.2d 117 (3d Dist.1973).

2. See the discussion of Mann v. Glens Falls Insurance Company in § 4.2(b), notes 9–11, above.

3. *But see* King, *Subrogation Under Contracts Insuring Property*, 30 Texas Law Review 62–92 at pp. 72–76 (1951), in which the author argues that the mortgagor should be given the benefit of the insurance in a number of situations in which most courts have concluded that the mortgagor has no beneficial interest in the policy and that the insurer is subrogated to the mortgagee's claims against the mortgagor.

In re Future Manufacturing Cooperative, Inc., 165 F.Supp. 111 (N.D.Cal.1958), discussed in Note, 72 Harvard Law Review 1380–1383 (1959), is a decision that is consistent with the result urged by King. The conditional sales contract in that case provided that the vendee was to assume the risk of casualty loss and was to insure in the vendor's favor. The vendee failed to obtain insurance, and the vendor arranged for a policy naming only the vendor as insured. The court held that insurance proceeds received by the vendor, less an amount equal to the insurance premiums paid by the vendor, were to be credited on the contract price.

But cf. Flint Frozen Foods, Inc. v. Firemen's Insurance Company, 8 N.J. 606, 86 A.2d 673 (1952), denying a claim against the creditor's insurer presented by the debtor, who also held an assignment of the creditor's rights under a policy obtained by the creditor after the debtor failed to comply with the contractual obligation to obtain insurance for the creditor's benefit.

4. See Note, 72 Harvard Law Review 1380–1383 at p. 1382 (1959).

indicates that there is an apparent premium rate inequity among such insureds,[5] there are at least two countervailing considerations.

First, in some situations a request for insurance of the mortgagee's interest alone is a sign of some "trouble" in regard to the mortgagor. For example, the acquisition of insurance by a mortgagee may indicate a higher than normal moral risk or a likelihood that a subrogation interest would be of little or no value because of financial instability of the mortgagor. In such situations, it is possible that the potential advantage to an insurer of providing coverage only for a mortgagee's interest is offset by an increase of risk in other respects so that — if the loss data for these two different types of insurance policies were analyzed separately rather than being combined — the actual net losses of insurers under coverage for mortgagees only are no less than under coverage for mortgagees and mortgagors.[6]

Second, the rate inequity in this situation may be so small that it is a permissible variation within a single rate category.[7] Indeed, if the rate differential is at most slight, the costs of administering differential pricing might actually exceed the projected savings.

§ 4.2(d) Personal Property Insurance: Subrogation to a Mortgagee's Rights

There are several types of circumstances in which personal property is commonly used as the security for a debt.[1] The most common situation in which this occurs is when an individual purchases a motor vehicle by arranging a loan that is secured by a mortgage on the vehicle.[2] When motor vehicle collision insurance is written as part of a transaction involving a loan secured by a mortgage on (or a conditional sales agreement for) a motor vehicle such as an automobile, an endorsement often is attached to the insurance policy with provisions that are substantially the same as those set out in the standard (union) mort-

---

5. It has also been suggested that the same rates are used for mortgagee-only insurance because subrogation in general plays no part, or only a minor part, in rate schedules and that when subrogation leads to a recovery by an insurer it is treated as a "windfall" that is not built into the rate structure. Patterson, ESSENTIALS OF INSURANCE LAW (Second edition, 1957), at pp. 151–152.

There is, of course, no windfall to the insurer if the rates for both types of insurance are adjusted to take account of the subrogation recoveries that are realized.

6. This hypothesis also suggests that there is a compelling argument for allowing an insurer in such a situation subrogation rights in the absence of an understanding, express or implied, that the insurer would not be entitled to subrogation. Many precedents reach this result. See, e.g., Mann v. Glenns Falls Insurance

Company, 541 F.2d 819 (9th Cir.1976); Drewicki v. Fidelity & Guaranty Fire Corporation of Baltimore, Md., 162 Kan. 10, 174 P.2d 75 (1946).

Also see Wriedt v. Beckenhauer, 183 Neb. 311, 159 N.W.2d 822 (1968); Twin City Fire Insurance Company v. Walter B. Hannah, Inc., 444 S.W.2d 131 at p. 135 (Ky. 1969).

7. See § 8.4(b), below.

§ 4.2(d)

1. See, e.g., Miyata v. Peerless Insurance Company, 95 Ill.App.3d 584, 51 Ill. Dec. 79, 420 N.E.2d 493 (1st Dist., 5th Div., 1981).

2. Ordinarily the standard forms used for motor vehicle collision insurance do not contain a clause which provides for payment of insurance solely to a creditor who has loaned the owner the funds used to buy the vehicle.

gage clause used for realty.[3] If such an endorsement is requested by a bank or other creditor, it ordinarily will be added by an insurer without an increase in the premium charged for the insurance.

The endorsement terms used by most insurers include an express provision for subrogation of the insurer to the rights of the mortgagee against the mortgagor. If a mortgagor is not allowed to recover under an insurance policy because of a wrongful act or neglect, the subrogation clause is important because in some states,[4] in the absence of an express subrogation provision, an insurer is not subrogated to the mortgagee's contractual claim (on the debt) against a mortgagor.

In a leading New York decision, Fields v. Western Millers Mutual Fire Insurance Co.,[5] the conditional vendee (referred to hereafter as the mortgagor) failed to pay the insurance premiums, and the insurer proceeded to cancel the policy. Notice of the cancellation was sent to the mortgagor. However, apparently by inadvertence, the insurer failed to give notice to the mortgagee. The insurer acknowledged its liability to the mortgagee, and then sought to be subrogated to the mortgagee's claim against the mortgagor. The majority decision denied the insurer's right to subrogation. The opinion for the majority — which asserted that the mortgagor "was, and remained, the insured under the policy, so long as the policy remained in existence * * *,"[6] — does not address the point that it is quite possible to distinguish the coverage for the mortgagee from that for the mortgagor, and that as a distinct coverage the former was free of some defenses available against the latter. The dissent, on the other hand, took the position that subrogation should be allowed because the mortgagor was not an insured.

In the *Fields* case, the basis for the insurer's liability to the mortgagee was the promise made for the benefit of the mortgagee *and* the insurer's failure to provide the mortgagee with notice of the cancellation of the insurance policy for the nonpayment of a premium by the mortgagor. Treating the insurance for the mortgagor and mortgagee as distinct coverages in circumstances such as that in *Fields* is analogous to the situation in which a mortgagee obtains a separate policy explicitly covering that interest and not that of the mortgagor.

The appropriateness of treating insurance for a mortgagor's and a mortgagee's interests as distinct coverages, even in the absence of any subrogation clause, is strengthened by the terms of a standard clause (used in most insurance policies) which provides for subrogation to "all right of recovery against any party." In regard to the effects of this provision, the majority opinion in *Fields* stated that this clause should be interpreted only to apply to a possible "claim against some third

---

3. See, e.g., Fields v. Western Millers Mutual Fire Insurance Company, 290 N.Y. 209, 48 N.E.2d 489, 146 A.L.R. 434 (1943).

4. The judicial precedents are divided. See the decisions cited in the following notes.

5. 290 N.Y. 209, 48 N.E.2d 489, 146 A.L.R. 434 (1943).

6. Id., 290 N.Y. at p. 212, 48 N.E.2d at p. 490, 146 A.L.R. at p. 437.

party for damaging the vehicle," and not to a claim against the mortgagor.[7] This interpretation of the insurance policy language is certainly open to question. The policy provides for "all right of recovery," which seems to clearly include a contract claim because it is not phrased in terms of a possible *tort* claim.[8] Moreover, once the insurance policy has been cancelled as to the mortgagor, the mortgagor is not a "party" as to the coverage for the mortgagee which continues (despite the cancellation as to the mortgagor) until the mortgagee is actually notified.

One additional matter should be considered in connection with this type of coverage question: should the practice of not charging a higher premium for an endorsement that extends coverage to a mortgagee, even after a mortgagor's default until the mortgagee is notified, be a significant consideration? By affording such protection for a mortgagee, an insurance company incurs somewhat greater risk of liability than would otherwise prevail. This is true regardless of the answer given to the question presented in *Fields*. Furthermore, under the rule urged in the dissenting opinion, an insurance company would be required to indemnify the mortgagee and might not be able to collect on its subrogation claim against the mortgagor because of the mortgagor's financial irresponsibility. And the increase in the risk for insurers is, of course, greater under the doctrine adopted by the majority in *Fields*, which held that the insurer is not entitled to assert a subrogation right after paying a mortgagee's claim.

It might be argued that the practice of not charging an additional premium indicates that the added risk undertaken is minimal,[9] and that one of the reasons it is minimal is that an insurer reasonably expects that in the event an insurer provides indemnification to a mortgagee it will be subrogated to the mortgagee's claim against the mortgagor. However, from the vantage point of the mortgagor, it could be argued that the practice of not charging an added premium supports the conclusion that insurance rates have been set in contemplation of providing coverage for both the mortgagee and the mortgagor. Yet, even if this latter argument is accepted, it still does not necessarily lead to the conclusion that the scope of the coverage of the two separate interests is identical, particularly so when the ground of defense urged is a neglect of one party only.

7. *Id.,* 290 N.Y. at p. 216, 48 N.E.2d at p. 492, 146 A.L.R. at p. 439.

8. For a precedent allowing subrogation to contract claims of the insured in other contexts, see, e.g., Atlantic Mutual Insurance Company v. Cooney, 303 F.2d 253 (9th Cir.1962) (applying California law; bailor's insurer subrogated to contract claim against bailee).

Cf. Employers Mutual Casualty Company v. Shepherd-Vineyard Motors, Inc., 189 Kan. 525, 370 P.2d 388 (1962) (insurer subrogated to contract right of insured under "warranty" of new car destroyed by fire caused by defect in construction).

But cf. Patent Scaffolding Company v. William Simpson Construction Company, 256 Cal.App.2d 506, 64 Cal.Rptr. 187 (2d Dist., 5th Div., 1967); Victor B. Levit, *Court Denies Subrogation to Contractual Rights,* 1968 Insurance Law Journal 105–107 (commenting on *Patent Scaffolding*).

9. See the discussion of differential rating, above, in this subsection.

§ 4.2(e) Assignability of a Mortgagee's Interest

In general, an interest in a property insurance contract cannot be transferred without securing the approval of the insurer. However, in some circumstances applications of this rule are questionable. For example, a mortgagee sometimes assigns an insurance coverage on a mortgaged property, without requesting the consent of the insurer, to a person or entity to whom the mortgagee transferred the mortgage debt and all interests in the security for the debt's payment. When a mortgagee is an insured under a standard mortgage clause, it has been argued the general rule applies and that the insurer's consent is essential because the insurer is always entitled to know precisely who has an interest in an insured property, at least in regard to any assignee whose interests are not merely derivative from the mortgagor.

It appears clear that requiring the approval of an insurer to complete a transaction which involves a transfer of a debt and insurance of the property that provides the security interest for the debt may constitute an impediment to such transactions, thereby reducing the market value of the mortgage to the mortgagee. Although it might be urged that acquiring the consent of the insurer to such an assignment of a mortgagee's interests in the property insurance is not a substantial burden, the significance or importance to the insurer of preserving the right to approve all assignments is not always evident.

To the extent that it actually is very important for an insurer to know who holds an interest as a mortgagee on an insured property, enforcing the insurer's position should — and probably will — be viewed as an essential incident of such transactions. However, in many types of circumstances insurers do not have a substantial interest in the identity of mortgagees, and requests for an insurer's approval of a transfer of the insurance for a mortgagee's interest from one mortgagee to another in connection with an assignment of the mortgage are regularly approved without investigation. Therefore, the importance to an insurer of knowing and approving assignments by a mortgagee of the mortgagee's interest in an insurance policy on a property which is the subject of the mortgage may be outweighed by the societal interest in making insurance on property that is used as security for debts freely assignable, thereby enhancing the transferability of the debt. In this context, if it can be shown that securing an insurer's approval involves essentially no more than a perfunctory action by the insurer, it seems appropriate not to require that the insurer consent in order to allow the interest of a mortgagee provided under a standard mortgage clause in a property insurance contract to be assigned when the mortgagee's interests in the debt and security are also being fully transferred. Such an assignment has been held valid.[1]

§ 4.2(e)

1. Central Union Bank v. New York Underwriters' Insurance Company, 52 F.2d 823 (4th Cir.1931), 78 A.L.R. 494 (1932). In this case, the mortgagee named in the fire policy was a life insurance company that had taken an assignment of the mortgage under an agreement that it would be repurchased by one to whose interests plaintiff succeeded, in the event of default by

Providing an Insurer with Notice of a Mortgagor's Default

Property insurance policies often include a provision which requires a mortgagee to report a default on the debt obligation by a mortgagor to the insurer. A rather difficult question can arise in regard to this requirement when a mortgagee has assigned the debt, the security interest, and the interest in an insurance contract. Knowledge of a default by a mortgagor may occur either before or after such an assignment. When the mortgagee is aware of a breach by the mortgagor *before* the assignment and that awareness would provide the insurer with a defense to the mortgagee's claim for insurance if an insured event occurred, the assignee's rights to collect insurance should be barred by the mortgagee's failure to notify the insurer. Otherwise the change of insureds would have the effect of "curing" a policy defense without the consent of the insurer. This should be the result even though a jurisdiction approves transfers, without requiring the insurer's consent, of a mortgagee's interest in insurance coverage provided by a standard mortgage clause.

When knowledge of a mortgagor's default is acquired by a mortgagee after an assignment has been made — that is, a mortgagee learns of some default by the mortgagor that the mortgagee would have been obligated to report to the insurer in the absence of the assignment — arguably the insurer should still have the benefit of an obligation of reporting by the party who was most interested and most likely to have knowledge of the mortgagor's breach.[2] In the absence of a contractual provision that explicitly sets forth such an obligation, however, the desirability of imposing a continuing requirement on the former mort-

the mortgagor. Pursuant to this agreement to repurchase, plaintiff took an assignment from the life insurance company shortly before the fire loss occurred. On first appeal, the Court of Appeals reversed a judgment on directed verdict for the insurer and remanded for a new trial. On new trial, the insurer contended that the plaintiff was barred from recovering because of failure to give notice of change of ownership in accordance with the requirement of the standard mortgage clause that the mortgagee should notify the insurer of any change of ownership coming to its knowledge. Directed verdict for the plaintiff against the insurer was affirmed on the theory that a reasonable length of time for notification of the insurer had not expired, since, though plaintiff had knowledge of the change of ownership at an earlier time, it was not until the policy was received in the mail, on the day before the fire, that the plaintiff could have had knowledge that the policy as written was not consistent with the ownership after the change. It did not appear that the mortgagee named in the insurance policy (that is, the life insurance company) had notice of the breach.

Cf. New York Underwriters Insurance Company v. Central Union Bank of South Carolina, 65 F.2d 738 (4th Cir.1933); Wriedt v. Beckenhauer, 183 Neb. 311, 159 N.W.2d 822 (1968).

Also see Federal National Mortgage Association v. Ohio Casualty Insurance Company, 46 Mich.App. 587, 208 N.W.2d 573 (1st Div.1973) (mortgagee's purchase of property at sheriff's sale before the fire did not extinguish rights under standard mortgage clause).

Accord. Guardian Savings & Loan Association v. Reserve Insurance Company, 2 Ill.App.3d 77, 276 N.E.2d 109 (1st Dist., 2d Div., 1971).

2. It may be that the assignee is often a distant financial institution, less likely than the original mortgagee to be well informed about the physical property and the mortgagor.

gagee may be outweighed by the general societal goal of maximizing the free assignability of mortgagee interests.

§ 4.2(f) Subrogation to a Mortgagee's Tort Claim Against a Third Person That Caused a Motor Vehicle Accident

A bank or a finance company holding a mortgage interest in a motor vehicle may also have an interest in a property insurance policy against damage to the motor vehicle that is written so as to apply to the interests of both the mortgagor and the mortgagee. [Essentially the same situation may exist for a conditional vendor of a motor vehicle.] In this situation, when there is a legal claim against a third person for tortiously damaging the insured vehicle, an insurer that has paid insurance benefits for the joint interests of the mortgagor and mortgagee is subrogated to the tort claim against the negligent third person. However, when a collision that damages an insured vehicle results from the negligence of both the mortgagor and a third person, the potential right to subrogation involves somewhat different considerations. In such circumstances, the mortgagor's tort claim against the third person either would be barred in jurisdictions applying the contributory negligence doctrine, or the tortfeasor's liability would be reduced in jurisdictions that have adopted comparative negligence.

Under a rule that prevails in many states, however, the mortgagee is still entitled to recover in tort against the third person — that is, the mortgagor's negligence is not imputed to the mortgagee.[1] In jurisdictions that apply this approach, the obvious next question is whether the collision insurer of a mortgaged automobile is subrogated to the mortgagee's claim in tort against the third person.

In Harvard Trust Co. v. Racheotes,[2] the Massachusetts Supreme Judicial Court decided that an insurer was entitled to be subrogated to the mortgagee's claim when a tort action was being pressed in the Trust Company's name and in the interest of the collision insurer. The balance outstanding on the mortgage debt was $318; the cost of repairing the car was $506.11; the insurer issued a check in the amount of $456.11 payable to the Trust Company and the mortgagor, and it was endorsed over to the repairer. Although, the Court reasoned that the insurer should recover $318 as subrogee to the mortgagee's claim, several questions about this recovery were not clearly answered by the decision, including: What was the nature of the mortgagee's

---

§ 4.2(f)

1. See, e.g., Commercial Credit Corp. v. Satterthwaite, 107 N.J.L. 17, 150 A. 235 (1930), *affirmed* per curiam 108 N.J.L. 188, 154 A. 769 (Err. & App., 1931); Lacey v. Great Northern Railway Company, 70 Mont. 346, 225 P. 808 (1924), 38 A.L.R. 1331 (1925).

2. 337 Mass. 73, 147 N.E.2d 817 (1958), 67 A.L.R.2d 596 (1959). The discussion of

this case in the text is adapted from Professor Keeton's discussion in 1958 ANNUAL SURVEY OF MASSACHUSETTS LAW 33–37 (Huber edition, 1959).

A contrary appraisal of the case is presented by Professor Hogan, in the 1958 ANNUAL SURVEY OF MASSACHUSETTS LAW, at pp. 78–80.

claim? What would have been the rights of the various parties, incident to the mortgagee's claim, in the absence of insurance?

Before *Racheotes,* the Massachusetts courts had decided that a mortgagee (or a conditional vendor) could recover against a negligent third party despite contributory negligence of the mortgagor (or conditional vendee).[3] However, the status of the debt after such a recovery was not clear. There appear to be only three possibilities. First, the mortgagee could still enforce the debt, thus enabling the mortgagee to obtain a double payment if the debtor is solvent. Second, the negligent third party's payment to the mortgagee could discharge the debt pro tanto, thus enabling the debtor to obtain indirectly a benefit the debtor could not obtain directly because of the debtor's contributory negligence. Third, the negligent third party could be entitled to receive any sum subsequently collected on the debt.

The first choice unjustly enriches the mortgagee, by giving the mortgagee double payment. The second unjustly enriches the mortgagor.[4] Consequently, the third possibility appears to be the best choice. As between the two negligent drivers, it places the ultimate legal responsibility in the same place, without regard to the mortgage. Furthermore, it gives the non-negligent mortgagee (or a conditional vendor) a claim against the negligent third party to protect itself against the risk of non-payment by the debtor. Thus the mortgagee's claim against the third party shifts to the latter the risk of financial irresponsibility of the mortgagor and does not provide an added benefit to either the mortgagee or the mortgagor.

Whether it is characterized as a security interest in property or a chose in action, the mortgagee's interest which is harmed by the third party's negligence is an interest intended only as security for payment of a debt. Ordinarily the amount remaining due on the debt is a fair measure of the maximum possible harm done to the mortgagee's interest. The actual harm will be less if subsequently the debtor makes some payment or if something is realized from the remaining value of the damaged chattel. Nevertheless, if there is uncertainty about the debtor's payment or about the value of the damaged chattel, it would be unfair to the mortgagee to make the mortgagee's award against the negligent third party less than the sum remaining due on the debt,

3. See, e.g., Bell Finance Company v. Gefter, 337 Mass. 69, 147 N.E.2d 815 (1958), 67 A.L.R.2d 578 (1959) (involving a conditional sale and indicating that mortgages and conditional sales are similarly treated in this context); Morris Plan Company v. Hillcrest Farms Dairy, Inc., 323 Mass. 452, 82 N.E.2d 889 (1948) (involving a conditional sale).

Also see Annotation, *Recovery by conditional seller or buyer, or person standing in his shoes, against third person for damage or destruction of property,* 67 A.L.R.2d 582–596 (1959); Annotation, *Recovery by chattel mortgagee or mortgagor, or person standing in his shoes, against third person for damage or destruction of property,* 67 A.L.R.2d 599–613 (1959).

4. Note that a reason given by the Court in *Racheotes* for disallowing any recovery in excess of the debt was that the mortgagor would then obtain indirectly a recovery he could not obtain directly. 337 Mass. 73 at p. 76, 147 N.E.2d 817 at p. 819, 67 A.L.R.2d 596 at p. 598.

because it may finally turn out that the mortgagee loses the entire amount still owed.

To make certain that the mortgagee is not undercompensated for the loss caused by the negligent third party, it is appropriate to measure the amount of the mortgagee's recovery by the sum outstanding on the debt. To make certain that the negligent third party is not required to pay more than compensation, a necessary corollary is that the third party, upon paying the full sum to the mortgagee, becomes the beneficial owner of whatever value remains in the mortgagee's security interest. Thus, if the mortgagor is financially responsible, the third party will recover on the debt and the mortgagor will be left with the damaged chattel; the ultimate loss will fall on the mortgagor as would have been true if there had been no mortgage. This legal relation may be described as a subrogation right — that is, as an instance in which the third party's payment to the mortgagee entitles the third party to sue on the mortgagee's claim in debt against the mortgagor. Or it may be said that any further recovery by the mortgagee against the mortgagor is held in trust for the third party who has fully compensated the mortgagee.[5]

In the next legislative session after *Racheotes* was decided, a statute was enacted in Massachusetts, providing as follows: "In any action to recover for damage to a motor vehicle brought in the name of a person or persons holding a security interest in said motor vehicle, any defense which would be available as against any registered owner thereof shall be available as against the person or persons holding said security interest."[6] Literal enforcement of this legislation will change not merely the insurance-subrogation rule of *Racheotes,* but, more basically, the tort rule that the mortgagor's negligence is not imputed to the mortgagee. It might be questioned whether the legislative objective was this broad, however. A narrower objective is suggested by the title of the act, "An Act Relative to Subrogated Automobile Property Damage Claims."[7]

§ 4.3 Interests In Real Property That Is Being Sold: Providing Coverage for the Vendor and Purchaser of Realty

§ 4.3(a) Introduction

Buildings that are in the process of being sold, especially when they are the subject of mortgages or conditional sales contracts, are often covered by one or more fire or casualty insurance policies. When a

---

5. The legal relation may be thought of as one of forced purchase, analogous to that imposed by the action of trover upon one whose tortious damage to a chattel is so severe as to amount to conversion; the tortfeasor must pay a sum equal to the full value of the interest in an undamaged condition, but in return the judgment vests in the tortfeasor the title to the interest in its damaged condition.

6. Massachusetts Acts 1959, c. 300; Massachusetts General Laws Ann. c. 231, § 85E (1974).

7. Massachusetts Acts 1959, c. 300.

structure which is insured by one or more policies suffers a partial or complete destruction, the liability of each insurer and the rights of either the buyer or seller to the insurance proceeds depend on several determinations, including:

(1) The allocation, either by rule of law or by an agreement of the parties, of the risk of a casualty loss as between the vendor and the purchaser;

(2) The defenses the insurer(s) may be entitled to assert based on the failure of one or more of the insureds to comply with the terms of the insurance contract(s);[1] and

(3) An interrelated group of factors concerning the principle of indemnity, subrogation rights, approaches to either assigning priorities or prorating coverages when more than one insurance policy provides coverage, and the judicial construction (interpretation) of the policy or policies of insurance — obtained by the vendor, by the purchaser, or by both of them — as protection for their respective interests or for the interests of both.

The material in this section focuses on each of these matters. Several of the possible approaches to allocating the risk of loss and the possible defenses an insurer may raise to insurance claims will be considered before attention is directed to the sharp controversy concerning the interrelationships of the several factors enumerated in subparagraph (3), above.

§ 4.3(b)   Allocation of the Risk of Casualty Loss as Between a Vendor and a Purchaser of Realty

Courts in the United States generally hold that a purchaser under an enforceable contract for sale of realty becomes an equitable owner of the property.[1] The term "equitable conversion" is commonly used to describe the doctrine which is applied by courts in assessing the rights

§ 4.3(a)

1. Property insurance contracts have often specified that any change of the quality or extent of the insured's ownership of a property constitutes a violation of the policy that produces an immediate forfeiture of the insured's right to coverage. For example, see Annotation, *Conditional sale as affecting provision in insurance policy against change of title, interest, or possession,* 133 A.L.R. 785–791 (1941).

The following discussion in this section assumes that the coverage provided by the insurance is not voided by reason of the sales contract.

§ 4.3(b)

1. See e.g., Hauben v. Harmon, 605 F.2d 920 (5th Cir.1979); Patrick & Wilkins Company v. Reliance Insurance Company, 500 Pa. 399, 456 A.2d 1348 (1983).

However, the doctrine of equitable conversion does not apply until there is an executory contract for a sale. Thus, in a case in which the prospective purchaser had not exercised an option on the property, the risk of loss remained with the vendor. Tate v. Wood, 169 W.Va. 584, 289 S.E.2d 432 (1982). Also see Annotation, *Right to proceeds of insurance, as between holder of title to real estate and one having an option to purchase it,* 65 A.L.R.2d 989–994 (1959).

Furthermore, the equitable conversion doctrine applies only when a seller is able to convey title as required by the contract, and the risk would not pass when the title to a property was subject to an encumbrance that could not be eliminated. *Cf.* Phillips v. Bacon, 245 Ga. 814, 267 S.E.2d 249 (1980).

and liabilities of the parties when disputes arise involving such transactions.[2] Although the equitable conversion doctrine is generally recognized, courts have developed at least three distinct views or approaches in regard to the allocation of the risk of a loss for a property that is subject to an executory contract.

A substantial number of American courts follow an English precedent [3] which decided that an equitable owner of property bears the risk of a casualty loss — that is, in the absence of contract provisions to the contrary, the risk of loss passes to the purchaser even though neither possession nor title has been transferred.[4] The consequence of this approach is that the purchaser is obligated to pay the full purchase price without regard to the condition of the property when the transfer of title subsequently takes place.

Somewhat fewer courts, following a doctrine more nearly like that applicable to contracts for sale of personal property, hold that in the absence of contract stipulations to the contrary, the risk of loss remains with the vendor until title to the realty is conveyed to the purchaser — that is, the risk of loss "follows" the title.[5]

Finally, there are a number of appellate court decisions which adopt the theory that as between a vendor and a purchaser, the person

See generally, Note, *Risk of Loss in Executory Contracts for the Sale of Real Property,* 14 Columbia Journal of Law and Social Problems 453–490 (1979); Annotation, *Vendor and purchaser: risk of loss by casualty pending contract for conveyance,* 27 A.L.R.2d 444–471 at p. 446 (1953).

Also see Annotation, *Change of conditions after execution of contract or option for sale of real property as affecting right to specific performance,* 11 A.L.R.2d 390–455 at pp. 395–396 (1950), which points out that "there is considerable authority for the proposition that where subsequent events have worked great and unexpected hardship, equity may refuse to intervene * * *." For example, when all or part of the property is destroyed, the vendor's right to specific performance is ordinarily determined by the allocation of the risk of loss. If the risk of loss is on the vendor, the vendor will not be entitled to secure specific performance because the vendor can no longer deliver the property which was promised in the contract.

2. See, e.g., Coolidge & Sickler, Inc. v. Regn, 7 N.J. 93, 80 A.2d 554 (1951), 27 A.L.R.2d 437 (1953).

3. Paine v. Meller, 6 Ves.Jr. 349, 31 Eng.Rep. 1088 (1801).

Also see Samuel Williston, *The Risk of Loss After an Executory Contract of Sale in the Common Law,* 9 Harvard Law Review 106–130 (1895).

4. E.g., McGinley v. Forrest, 107 Neb. 309, 186 N.W. 74 (1921), 22 A.L.R. 567 (1923).

Also see Fellmer v. Gruber, 261 N.W.2d 173 at p. 174 (Iowa 1978); Hall v. Pioneer Crop Care, Inc., 212 Kan. 554 at p. 558, 512 P.2d 491 at p. 495 (1973).

Cf. Duhon v. Dugas, 407 So.2d 1334 (La. App.1981) (valid verbal agreement for the sale of a house); Northwest Kansas Area Vocational-Technical School v. Wolf, 6 Kan.App.2d 817, 635 P.2d 1268 (1981).

See generally Annotation, *Rights of vendor and purchaser, as between themselves, in insurance proceeds,* 64 A.L.R.2d 1402–1420 at pp. 1406–1412 (1959); Annotation, *Vendor and purchaser: risk of loss by casualty pending contract for conveyance,* 27 A.L.R.2d 444–471 at p. 446 (1953).

5. See, e.g., Libman v. Levenson, 236 Mass. 221, 128 N.E. 13 (1920), 22 A.L.R. 560; Thompson v. Gould, 37 Mass. (20 Pick.) 134 (1838).

Also see Hauben v. Harmon, 605 F.2d 920 at p. 925 (5th Cir.1979), in which the court concluded that under Florida law the "vendor carries the burden of loss before execution of the contract and the vendee carries the burden of loss after execution of the contract."

See generally Annotation, *Vendor and purchaser: risk of loss by casualty pending contract for conveyance,* 27 A.L.R.2d 444–471 at pp. 454–459 (1953).

in possession of the realty pending the conveyance bears the risk of loss in the absence of any specific provisions in the contract of sale.[6] Thus, the risk of loss would only be allocated to a purchaser who had taken possession of the property. Possession of property is, of course, often treated as a very significant factor in the allocation of risks. For example, possession is a crucial factor under the Uniform Vendor and Purchaser Risk Act Section 1, which provides:

"Any contract hereafter made in this State for the purchase and sale of realty shall be interpreted as including an agreement that the parties shall have the following rights and duties, unless the contract expressly provides otherwise:

"(a) If, when neither the legal title nor the possession of the subject matter of the contract has been transferred, all or a material part thereof is destroyed without fault of the purchaser or is taken by eminent domain, the vendor cannot enforce the contract, and the purchaser is entitled to recover any portion of the price that he has paid;

"(b) If, when either the legal title or the possession of the subject matter of the contract has been transferred, all or any part thereof is destroyed without fault of the vendor or is taken by eminent domain, the purchaser is not thereby relieved from a duty to pay the price, nor is he entitled to recover any portion thereof that he has paid."[7]

6. See Anderson v. Yaworski, 120 Conn. 390 at p. 398, 181 A. 205 at p. 208 (1935), 101 A.L.R. 1232 at pp. 1237–1238 (1936): "Now that we are directly confronted with the question whether, under [a contract for sale of land] * * * the risk of loss is upon the vendee, we are not able to accept as authoritative the statement in [Hough v. City Fire Insurance Co., 29 Conn. 10, 76 Am.Dec. 581 (1860)] * * * that it is, at least where possession has not passed, but hold that risk of loss is upon the vendor."

Also see Smith v. Phenix Insurance Co., 91 Cal. 323, 27 P. 738 (1891).

For a more recent discussion of the possession issue, see McGuire v. Wilson, 372 So.2d 1297 (Ala.1979), and Long v. Keller, 104 Cal.App.3d 312, 163 Cal.Rptr. 532 (5th Dist.1980) (applying the Uniform Vendor and Purchaser Risk Act which was adopted as California Civil Code 1662).

7. 9C Uniform Laws Annotated 314 (1957). The remaining sections of the Act concern uniformity of interpretation, short title, repeal, and time of taking effect. The Act has been adopted in a substantial number of states, though a minority, and in some instances with modifications. *Id.,* at p. 194 (Supp.1967).

The Uniform Vendor and Purchaser Risk Act has now been incorporated into the Uniform Land Transactions Act as § 2–406, with several modifications in the language of the original act. As of 1984, no states have adopted the Uniform Land Transactions Act. The new provision states:

Section 2–406. [Risk of Loss, Casualty Loss, Real Estate Other than Leaseholds.]

(a) This section does not apply to transfers of leaseholds.

(b) Risk of loss or of taking by eminent domain and owner's liabilities remain on the seller until the occurrence of the events specified in subsection (c). In case of a casualty loss or taking by eminent domain while the risk is on the seller:

(1) if the loss or taking results in a substantial failure of the real estate to conform to the contract, the buyer may cancel the contract and recover any portion of the price he has paid, or accept the real estate with (i) reduction of the contract price for the loss or taking, or (ii) the benefit of the seller's insurance coverage or the eminent domain payment for the loss or taking, but without further right against the seller; or

Given the clear possibility that the risk of loss may rest with a purchaser before title to realty is transferred, it is not surprising that purchasers often acquire their own insurance coverage for property soon after a contract for the sale is agreed to, before possession is transferred or title is conveyed. Acquisition of insurance by a buyer may create a situation in which either a seller and a buyer both have insurance coverage in effect simultaneously, or one in which only the buyer has insured the property. In addition, of course, there are instances when only a vendor has insured the property. When the distinct approaches to allocating risk (identified above) are considered in relation to the variable patterns of insuring realty that is the subject of an executory contract, there are obviously several permutations. The various combinations of these factors have been the source of a significant number of coverage disputes when the parties' executory sales contract does not explicitly allocate the risk of loss and no provision is included in the contract with respect to insuring the property.

When no provision has been included in an executory contract for the sale of realty in regard to either an allocation of the risk of loss or which of the parties is responsible for insuring the property *and* only the vendor has insured the property, a vendor is usually entitled to collect the insurance payments. However, in jurisdictions where the risk of loss passes to the buyer, in this situation there are judicial precedents for the proposition that the vendor's insurance should ultimately benefit the buyer who actually must bear the loss resulting from the injury to the property.[8] Thus, when insurance is paid to the vendor and the risk is on the buyer, the application of this approach means that the vendor in effect holds the insurance for the benefit of the buyer. In other words, in the event the property is damaged and the vendor is paid the insurance benefits, the buyer essentially receives a credit on the unpaid purchase price so that vendor is only entitled to

(2) if the real estate substantially conforms to the contract after the loss or taking, the buyer must accept the real estate, but is entitled to (i) reduction of the contract price for the loss or taking or (ii) the benefit of the seller's insurance coverage or the eminent domain payment with respect to the loss or taking but without further right against the seller.

(c) Risk of loss or taking and owner's liabilities pass to the buyer;

(1) if sale is not to be consummated by means of an escrow, at the earlier of delivery of the instrument of conveyance or transfer of possession of the real estate to him; or

(2) if sale is to be consummated by means of an escrow, at the earlier of transfer of possession or fulfillment of the conditions of the escrow.

(d) Any loss or taking the real estate after risk of loss or taking has passed to the buyer does not discharge him from his obligations under the contract of purchase.

Also see Long v. Keller, 104 Cal.App.3d 312, 163 Cal.Rptr. 532 (5th Dist.1980); Note, *Risk of Loss in Executory Contracts for the Sale of Real Property,* 14 Columbia Journal of Law and Social Problems 453–490 at p. 464 (1979).

8. See, e.g., Balsam v. Buehner, 278 N.W.2d 425 (N.D.1979); Gilles v. Sprout, 293 Minn. 53, 196 N.W.2d 612 (1972).

Also see cases cited in Annotation, *Rights of vendor and purchaser, as between themselves, in insurance proceeds,* 64 A.L.R.2d 1402–1420 at pp. 1406–1414 (1959); Annotation, *Amount of insurer's liability as affected by insured's executory contract to sell the property,* 8 A.L.R.2d 1408–1426 at p. 1411 (1949).

the unpaid portion of the purchase price.[9] This approach, which is obviously advantageous to the buyer, also produces full protection for the vendor.

When a vendor has fully insured the property, there is no possibility of a loss for the vendor. The vendor will receive either the equivalent of the agreed purchase price (the insurance plus the remainder of the purchase price) if the buyer goes through with the transaction, or the insurance and continued possession of the property if the buyer declines to complete the transaction.[10] The only significant problem with this approach is that it deprives the insurer of the opportunity to decide whether to insure the buyer. The insurer's interest in deciding whether to insure a particular individual, which is often referred to by the characterization that property insurance is "personal," [11] is viewed as a very significant consideration in many contexts — especially when it appears that there may be some increase in the risks covered by the insurance policy.[12]

When a property has been less than fully insured by an owner-vendor, the situation is somewhat more complicated. On the one hand, if the purchaser is entitled to withdraw from the transaction because of the damage to the property, the owner-vendor is entitled to retain the insurance proceeds, and the fact that the insured owner is not fully indemnified is no more than the appropriate result of the owner's decision not to fully insure. Thus, the owner who partially insures sustains the same loss which would have been incurred if the owner had never entered into the sales transaction. If the purchaser is entitled to specific performance with an appropriate reduction in the purchase price,[13] then the risk of loss is on the owner-vendor, and the insurance covers that risk. The owner-vendor who underinsures again bears the portion of the risk that would have existed in the absence of a contract for sale. If, on the other hand, the purchaser is not entitled to withdraw and must pay the full purchase price for the damaged property, then it is equitable for the insurance to be held for the benefit of the purchaser, subject to the considerations regarding the insurer's interest in determining whom it will insure.

When a purchaser acquires insurance, a similar analysis applies. If the purchaser completes the transaction and pays the full purchase

---

9. Furthermore, it has also been held that any "remainder" from the insurance proceeds is held in a constructive trust for the buyer. See, e.g., Partrick & Wilkins Company v. Reliance Insurance Company, 500 Pa. 399, 456 A.2d 1348 at p. 1351 (1983).

Also see Smith v. Prudential Property and Casualty Insurance Company, 508 F.Supp. 452 at p. 454 (W.D.Pa.1980).

10. See the cases discussed in the Annotation, *Amount of insurer's liability as affected by insured's executory contract to sell the property*, 8 A.L.R.2d 1408–1426 (1949).

11. See the discussion of insurance as a "personal" contract in § 3.1(d)(2).

12. In such circumstances, if the risks have been increased, a persuasive case may exist for reconsidering the extent of the insurer's obligation to the vendor.

13. *Cf.* Long v. Keller, 104 Cal.App.3d 312, 163 Cal.Rptr. 532 (5th Dist.1980) (buyer who sought either specific performance of the land contract together with the insurance or rescission, was held to have no right to the insurance and was granted rescission).

price, clearly the insurance provides coverage for the risk and the purchaser is appropriately indemnified. If the purchaser completes the transaction and pays a price that is reduced because of the damage to the property, the purchaser has suffered no loss and would not be entitled to collect the insurance. In a few jurisdictions, however, courts have held that a purchaser who pays a reduced price for a property is a constructive trustee of the insurance proceeds which are held for the benefit of an uninsured vendor.[14] This approach presents the issue that fire insurance is typically treated as a personal contract between the insurer and the insured, and the vendor is not a party to that insurance contract.[15]

If a purchaser who has acquired insurance exercises the right to withdraw from a sales transaction, depending on the facts the purchaser may or may not have sustained a loss. Although a purchaser might urge that the insurance should be treated as covering an expectancy interest, it seems probable that most property insurance policies would not be so interpreted. In order to collect property insurance in this type of situation, a purchaser will have to show more than the loss of an expectancy interest, either by acquiring property the value of which has been diminished by an insured event or as a consequence of a rescission of the purchase agreement that leaves the purchaser in a worsened position because of an insured event. Thus, when the purchaser is not in fact in a worse position than if no insured event had occurred, the purchaser cannot prove a loss and would not be entitled to collect the insurance unless the purchaser is allowed to recover insurance proceeds for the benefit of the seller.[16]

§ 4.3(c) Explicit Contractual Provisions

A contract covering the sale of a property should clearly specify the policy or policies of insurance that will be maintained or obtained, by either the vendor or the purchaser, unless there is some reason not to focus attention upon the problem.[1] In practice, lawyers drafting a

---

14. *Cf.* the following comment: "While a vendee is not ordinarily a trustee of insurance policies procured by him for his own benefit, yet where a contract for the sale of realty has been rescinded at the instance of the vendor because of fraud of the vendee, and in place of his obligation to pay the purchase price, an obligation arises to restore the premises to the vendor, it has been held that the vendee holds any insurance moneys paid to him for a fire loss occurring during his possession, for the benefit of the vendor." Annotation, *Rights of vendor and purchaser, as between themselves, in insurance proceeds,* 64 A.L.R.2d 1402–1420 at pp. 1415–1416 (1959), citing Cetkowski v. Knutson, 163 Minn. 492, 204 N.W. 528 (1925), 40 A.L.R. 599 (1926). The Annotation also points out that the majority rule is that in the absence of a provision in the purchase contract imposing upon the purchaser an obligation to insure for the benefit of the vendor, the purchaser will not be compelled to account for any part of the insurance proceeds collected unless the vendor has a claim based on special equitable rights. *Id.,* 64 A.L.R.2d at p. 1414.

15. See, e.g., Long v. Keller, 104 Cal. App.3d 312 at p. 320, 163 Cal.Rptr. 532 (5th Dist.1980).

Also see the discussion of insurance as a personal contract in § 3.1(d), above, and § 4.6, below.

16. See the discussion in § 4.3(e), below.

§ 4.3(c)

1. For example, there might be concern that if the negotiators focused on the prob-

comprehensive contract for the sale of realty rarely leave the rights of the parties concerning insurance and the risk of casualty loss to be determined by rules of law that are applicable in the absence of specific contract provisions.

One way of arranging insurance for a property that is the subject of an executory contract is to have a single insurance policy endorsed by the insurer so that it covers both the vendor and the purchaser "as their interests may appear". Usually, when requested insurers will add this endorsement to an insurance contract without any additional cost. However, arranging for this type of endorsement does not always serve to cover all the risks that may exist for the parties, nor does it eliminate every coverage problem that may arise in such situations. For example, it does not resolve questions about the risks, rights, and liabilities of a vendor and a purchaser in the event that damage causes a property to be unsuitable for the intended use during an extended period of time while the insurance proceeds are used to repair the property.

When the parties to a sales agreement have provided that a vendor will carry the insurance on a property until some predetermined time or occurrence (such as the transfer of possession), if the property is destroyed some courts conclude that the vendor holds the insurance proceeds as an actual or constructive trustee for the purchaser.[2] The purchaser's right to the insurance proceeds matures when, and if, the purchase is completed. If the purchase is not completed, ordinarily the right to the insurance remains entirely with the vendor.[3]

When the parties agree that the purchaser will maintain insurance, the seller should be entitled either to a judgment for specific performance of the contract at the full contract price or to an equitable lien on the insurance proceeds.[4] However, if the seller cannot convey title as required by the sales contract, the vendor will not be entitled to such equitable relief[5] and may have no claim to the buyer's insurance coverage.[6] Furthermore, when the risk of loss is allocated to the buyer — in accordance with either an explicit contract provision or a statutory provision — the buyer would not be entitled to compel a credit on the purchase price for the amount of the insurance proceeds paid by a seller's insurance and there would be no unjust enrichment to the seller in the event the transaction were rescinded.[7]

lem, the question would be resolved against the interest of the person raising the point. Such calculated nonresolution of the issue always has the disadvantage, however, of risks of expensive dispute resolution if a casualty occurs.

2. Fellmer v. Gruber, 261 N.W.2d 173 at p. 174 (Iowa 1978).

3. See notes 8 through 12, in § 4.3(b), above, and the accompanying text.

4. See, e.g., Nevada Refining Co. v. Newton, 88 Nev. 333, 497 P.2d 887 (1972)

(seller had an equitable lien on insurance proceeds).

Cf. Northwest Kansas Area Vocational-Technical School v. Wolf, 6 Kan.App.2d 817, 635 P.2d 1268 (1981).

5. See authorities cited in note 1, § 4.3(a), above.

6. See, e.g. Phillips v. Bacon, 245 Ga. 814, 267 S.E.2d 249 (1980).

7. *Cf.* Long v. Keller, 104 Cal.App.3d 312, 163 Cal.Rptr. 532 (5th Dist.1980).

To avoid controversy, when the parties to a purchase and sale make an agreement that one will maintain insurance for the benefit of both, they should also obtain the explicit consent of the insurer to the arrangement.

§ 4.3(d) Defenses Based on an Insured's Failure to Comply With Coverage Terms

The term "moral hazard clause" is used to describe or characterize several types of insurance policy provisions that are commonly used by insurers, including (1) provisions that preclude an insured from purchasing other insurance on an insured property, (2) provisions against any change of an ownership interest in an insured property, and (3) provisions which require the interest of the named insured in an insured property to be as an unconditional and sole owner. The term "moral hazard clause" did not and still does not appear in most property insurance policies.

Absent some form of regulation (statutory, administrative, or judicial), violation of a moral hazard clause by an insured generally provides an insurer with a defense to any subsequent claims.[1] Inadvertent violations of such policy terms have been particularly likely when an insured entered into an executory contract for the sale of an insured property. In many of the older appellate court cases, as well as a small number of recent disputes, insurers have contended that a contract of sale for an insured property produced a violation of one or more of the moral hazard clauses.

The 1943 New York Standard Fire Insurance Policy eliminated the various moral hazard clauses, with the exception of provisions concerning other insurance which an insurer is allowed to add by a special endorsement. In general, the widespread adoption of the 1943 form has reduced the danger that all insurance protection will be lost by an inept arrangement of a sales transaction. However, there are still some circumstances that may provide an insurer with the basis for a defense. For example, there is at least a small danger from the operation of other insurance clauses. Coverage may also be lost as a consequence of violating clauses concerning vacancy, lack of occupancy, or increase of hazard.

§ 4.3(e) Solutions to Coverage Claims When Both the Vendor and the Purchaser Have Acquired Property Insurance *and* the Contract Provisions Are Inconclusive

The discussion in this subsection presents a summary of approaches that may be employed when both a vendor and a purchaser of a property have acquired insurance coverage *and* there are no provisions

---

§ 4.3(d)

1. See, e.g., Jones & Pickett, Ltd. v. Michigan Fire & Marine Insurance, 132 La. 847, 61 So. 846 (1913).

Also see Henry Kolbus, *The Moral Hazard and the Increased Risk,* 1948 Insurance Law Journal 731–737; Note, *The Moral Hazard Clauses of the Standard Fire Insurance Policy,* 37 Columbia Law Review 410–428 (1937).

in the sales contract which allocate the risk of loss or specify who shall maintain insurance. Though the following discussion is neither an exhaustive nor an all-inclusive compilation of the possible approaches to the resolution of such disputes, it does identify the most apparent solutions that a court or legislator might consider when both parties are insured.

(1) Liability-for-Insurable-Interest

Under a liability-for-insurable-interest approach each insurer would be fully liable, but only to the extent of its insured's insurable interest at the time of the loss. The rights in the insurance policy proceeds could be allocated in one of three ways.

First, insurance benefits could be paid without any right to subrogation. Each insured would be entitled to receive insurance proceeds and would be required to comply with the obligations to the other party under the contract of sale. No insurer would be subrogated to the rights of its insured against the other party under the contract of sale.

A liability-for-insurable-interest rule with no subrogation will conflict with the principle of indemnity if the sum of the insurable interests which are insured exceeds the market value of the property. For example, if, as between vendor and purchaser, the risk of loss is on the purchaser and both parties have insurance to the full extent of their insurable interests (valued according to loss that would have existed in the absence of the rights created by the executory contract), then each insurer would pay, and the vendor would also be entitled to either specific performance or damages from the purchaser. Thus, the vendor would profit from a fire. This approach therefore has the disadvantage of working against the objectives underlying the principle of indemnity.[1] This disadvantage seems to clearly outweigh the simplicity of the rule in operation and the avoidance of a second round of loss shifting through the operation of subrogation rights (which usually is an uneconomic process from an overall — that is, a societal — point of view).

Second, full insurance benefits could be paid, and the insurers could each be accorded a right of subrogation. Each insured would be entitled to receive insurance proceeds and each insurer would be

---

§ 4.3(e)

1. If one rejects contingent valuation, however, and adopts the rationale that the vendor incurs no legal loss if it later turns out that the executory contract is completed subsequent to the fire loss — e.g., see Paramount Fire Insurance Company v. Aetna Casualty & Surety Company, 163 Tex. 250, 353 S.W.2d 841 (1962) (refusing to allow the vendee's insurer pro rata recovery from the vendor's insurer) — the objectives of the insurable interest doctrine are indirectly affirmed. The dissent in this case, however, makes a strong case for valuing loss as of the time of the fire without regard to subsequent events (i.e., the completion of the sale transaction), a result more consistent with the express terms of most policies. In that event, the vendor's loss might be termed "contingent." Even so, one of various possible arrangements might be adopted to take the contingency into account and yet not allow a profit to the vendor; for example, in this case, the vendee's insurer sought a proration between the insurers to prevent net profit to the vendor. See below in the text of this section.

subrogated to its insured's claim against the other party as established by the contract of sale, and subject to defenses which would be available against each of the insureds. For example, if the risk of loss is determined to be on the purchaser, the vendor's insurer would be able to recover against the purchaser on the agreement to pay the purchase price. The purchaser, if fully insured, would be "made whole" by a recovery against his or her own insurer. Likewise, if the risk of loss is determined to be on the vendor and the sale is completed, either the purchaser would be entitled to a reduction of the purchase price, or the purchaser's insurer would pay the purchaser and would be entitled to recover on the purchaser's claims against the vendor for repair of the damage.

A liability-for-insurable-interest rule with subrogation allowed adheres to the principle of indemnity. This rule is supported by English authorities, particularly Castellain v. Preston [2] and Rayner v. Preston.[3] Under those decisions, a vendor's insurer was subrogated to the vendor's rights incident to the fact that the rules of law applicable to the contract of purchase and sale placed the risk of loss on the purchaser. The results produced by this approach sometimes appear objectionable due to the way the risk of loss is allocated as between vendor and purchaser.[4] The New York Court of Appeals decision in Brownell v. Board of Education [5] might be thought to be inconsistent with the

2. 11 Q.B.D. 380 (1883). Before contracting to sell a house, the owner had procured fire insurance on it; the contract of sale mentioned neither the insurance nor the risk of casualty loss pending completion of the sale. The house was damaged by fire after the date of the contract of sale and before completion of the transaction; the vendor recovered under the insurance without the insurer's knowing of the contract of sale, but the purchase price was not reduced because of the damage to the house.

In *Rayner,* note 3, below, the vendee was denied recovery of the insurance proceeds from the vendor, but in *Castellain* the insurer was allowed to recover out of the purchase money received by the vendor an amount equal to the benefits paid because of its right to be subrogated to the vendor's contract claim against the vendee.

Compare these cases with Paramount Fire Insurance Company v. Aetna Casualty & Surety Company, 163 Tex. 250, 353 S.W.2d 841 (1962) (holding that, when the vendor and the vendee are insured by different insurers, the entire loss must be borne by the vendee's insurer; reserving the question of rights in the proceeds when only the vendor is insured).

3. 18 Ch.D. 1 (1881). The decision in *Rayner* (and, therefore, that in *Castellain*

in regard to vendor-vendee interests) was changed in 1922 by statute. Law of Real Property Act, 1922, 12 & 13 Geo. 5, c. 16, 105.

See also Law of Property Act, 1925, 15 Geo. 5, c. 20, 47; E.R. Hardy Ivamy, GENERAL PRINCIPLES OF INSURANCE LAW (1966), at p. 373. Compare Hepburn v. A. Tomlinson (Hauliers) Ltd., [1966] 1 All E.R. 418 (H.L.), reaching in a bailment situation, without benefit of statute, a result directly contrary to *Rayner* in the sense that the bailee was allowed to recover in full with the understanding that the bailee would hold in trust for the bailor any surplus above the sum necessary to indemnify the bailee.

Also see E.R. Hardy Ivamy, GENERAL PRINCIPLES OF INSURANCE LAW, at pp. 374–375, p. 460 and p. 462, indicating that this result would be reached only if the parties to the insurance contract so intended at the time of effecting it.

4. Objections to this rule also appear to based on the expectation of some lay persons that insurance will run with the property.

5. 239 N.Y. 369, 146 N.E. 630, 37 A.L.R. 1319 (1925).

liability-for-insurable-interest rule. However, in *Brownell,* the determination that the purchaser was not entitled to recover the vendor's insurance proceeds actually is consistent with this rule because the contract of purchase and sale, as construed, gave the purchaser no cause of action against the vendor for more than $3,000 (apparently merely in effect the return of $3,000 deposited by the purchaser and not $3,000 in addition to return of the deposit). The profit to the vendor produced by the decision arose because the value placed on the vendor's insurable interest was unrealistically high in view of the obsolete character of the building.

Third, all insurance benefits could be paid subject to the imposition of a trust-for-the purchaser rule. The vendor would retain the insurance benefits to the extent needed to give the vendor total receipts (from the purchaser and the insurer) equal to the agreed purchase price, and any excess amount would be held in trust for the benefit of the purchaser.

A liability-for-insurable-interest rule with a trust imposed for the benefit of the purchaser is predicated on the proposition that in some situations insurance, at least in a limited sense, is allowed to run with the land.[6] It also potentially allows a deviation from the principle of indemnity because the combination of the purchaser's own insurance and that of the vendor, accruing to the purchaser's benefit in trust, may exceed the purchaser's loss. This problem can be avoided by adding a primary-and-excess-coverage rule, whereby the insurance is treated as running with the land, subject to the limitation that the payments may not exceed the total loss.

The result in a leading New York decision, *Raplee v. Piper,*[7] is consistent with the trust-for-the-purchaser and the primary-and-excess-coverage rules. In *Raplee,* it was not necessary for the court to choose between the two rules. The opinions in *Raplee* make it appear that the result of allowing the purchaser to benefit from the vendor's insurance depended on the fact that the premiums on the vendor's policy were paid by the purchaser, pursuant to terms of the contract of purchase and sale. The terms of the purchase contract and the fact that

---

6. See, e.g., Skelly Oil Co. v. Ashmore, 365 S.W.2d 582 (Mo.1963) (vendee allowed specific performance of contract to purchase property with the purchase price reduced by the amount of insurance proceeds paid vendor because of fire damage that occurred before sale was completed); Dubin Paper Company v. Insurance Company of North America, 361 Pa. 68, 63 A.2d 85, 8 A.L.R.2d 1393 (1949) (contract to sell property entered into before loss and consummated after loss but before payment of insurance proceeds held not to affect insurer's liability, although vendor would hold proceeds in trust for the benefit of the vendee).

Also see Balsam v. Buehner, 278 N.W.2d 425 at p. 428 (N.D.1979).

7. 3 N.Y.2d 179, 164 N.Y.S.2d 732, 143 N.E.2d 919 (1957), 64 A.L.R.2d 1397 (1959).

Also see Matter of Burns' Estate, 227 Kan. 573, 608 P.2d 942 (1980).

In Gard v. Razanskas, 248 Iowa 1333, 85 N.W.2d 612, 65 A.L.R.2d 982 (1957), a lessee-optionee was held to be entitled to credit on purchase price in the amount of insurance proceeds paid to lessor-optioner when a loss occurred after option to purchase was created and before it was exercised.

premiums were paid by the purchaser may have been known to the insurer, though this point is not made clear in the opinion.

(2) Liability-for-Full-Loss

Under a liability-for-full-loss approach, each insurer would be liable for the full loss to the property, subject to the coverage limits in the relevant insurance policy, and one of the several choices in regard to the allocation of the insurance proceeds outlined in subsection (i) would be made as to rights in the insurance policy proceeds. This approach would be inconsistent with the provision in fire insurance policy forms which states that the amount of the insurance shall not be "in any event for more than the interest of the insured." The liability-for-full-loss approach is clearly not supported by decisions.[8]

(3) Primary-and-Excess-Coverage

Under a primary-and-excess-coverage approach, insurance in the name of the party having the risk of loss — as determined by a court or other appropriate authority — under the contract of sale would be treated as primary coverage and insurance in the name of the other party to the contract would be excess coverage in the event of a loss to the property, and the total amount of insurance benefits paid would not be allowed to exceed that loss.

(4) Proration of Coverage

Under a proration of coverage approach, a vendor's insurance and a purchaser's insurance are treated as complementary coverages, with the total recovery limited to the loss to the property. The portion of the loss to be paid by each insurer would be determined by a principle of proration.[9] A prorated-coverage approach is consistent with the principle of indemnity, but is not fully in accord with the principle that the fire insurance contract is personal.

---

8. Perhaps one reason for lack of precedents supporting this rule is that, as stated in the text, policy forms ordinarily declare that in no event shall the insurer's liability be for an amount in excess of the interest of the insured in the property. Thus, the question whether a larger recovery can be obtained is not likely to arise except when a valued policy statute applies (although even then it is subject to the qualification that the statutes proscribe any challenge of the dollar amount of the insured's interest so that, in form at least, an *insurable-interest* and not a *full-loss* rule is applicable).

In Springfield Fire & Marine Insurance Company v. Boswell, 167 So.2d 780 (Fla. App., 1st Dist., 1964), for example, the insured property was to be sold for $12,500, and the vendor and vendee independently obtained valued policies in the amounts of $6,000 and $15,000 respectively. After a fire that totally destroyed the improvements on the property, vendee collected the face amount of the vendee's policy and paid $12,000 of the proceeds (an amount equal to the then unpaid part of the purchase price) to the vendor in return for the conveyance of the property to the vendee. The vendor then claimed and recovered the face amount of the vendor's policy, the court not questioning the amount of the vendor's loss but, rather, speaking of the total loss as having been $21,000 since that was the sum of the two policies on the property.

9. Concerning the choice among principles of proration, compare the discussion of Other Insurance clauses in § 3.11(e)(3), above.

The prorated coverage approach has been applied in many cases by agreement among the insurers after a dispute has arisen. For example, in Insurance Company of North America v. Alberstadt,[10] Rose Alberstadt, while the owner of the property in question, obtained a $3,500 fire insurance policy. Thereafter, the property was sold to Patterson at sheriff's sale for delinquent taxes. The sale price was $2,600. Patterson then obtained a $2,500 fire insurance policy. A few weeks later a fire occurred, damaging the property (the court assumed) to the extent of $3,175.

After the fire Patterson paid the sheriff the amount of his bid and obtained the sheriff's deed. Though the policies reserved to the insurers the right to discharge their obligations by repairing the property, they lost that right by failing to assert it within the time stipulated in the policies.[11] Rose Alberstadt demanded $3,175 (the full loss) from her insurer, and Patterson demanded $2,500 (the policy limit) from his insurer. The lower court entered judgments for both Alberstadt and Patterson. The companies offered to pay $3,175, by proration agreed upon between them.

The Supreme Court of Pennsylvania modified the judgments so as to limit the total recovery to $3,175 [12] and to distribute the loss between the insurers consistently with their proration agreement. The court also concluded that as between Rose Alberstadt and Patterson, she was entitled to retain none of the insurance proceeds because she sustained no loss. This conclusion seems dubious. It was based on a presump-

---

10. 383 Pa. 556, 119 A.2d 83 (1956).

Also see Smith v. Prudential Property and Casualty Insurance Co., 508 F.Supp. 452 (W.D.Pa.1980); Songer v. State Farm Fire and Casualty Co., 91 Ill.App.3d 248, 46 Ill.Dec. 715, 414 N.E.2d 768 (5th Dist.1980), appeal after remand 106 Ill.App.3d 141, 62 Ill.Dec. 150, 435 N.E.2d 948 (1982).

11. If the vendor's insurer were to elect to repair the property in a situation like that in *Alberstadt*, however, it might lose its opportunity to cause the loss to be borne either primarily by the purchaser's insurer, with its own coverage being treated as excess, or else proportionately by the two insurers. The disputed rule denying subrogation to a volunteer might be invoked by the purchaser's insurer. See § 3.10(d)(3), above.

Moreover, if — mindful of the fact that when the option to repair is exercised, the insured cannot compel appraisal of the damage, see, e.g., Michigan Fire Repair Contractors' Association v. Pacific National Fire Insurance Co., 362 Mich. 552, 107 N.W.2d 811 (1961) — the company was considering the repair option because of a belief that the insured's claim might be padded and that the total cost to the insurer

could be reduced by contracting directly for the repairs, it would be unlikely that the insurer could get an assignment from its insured for the purpose of avoiding the rule against volunteers.

12. In reaching this result, the Pennsylvania court acted differently from a federal court's prediction of its action made in Vogel v. Northern Assurance Co., 219 F.2d 409 (3d Cir.1955). Subsequent to agreeing on the terms of a sale of improved property for $15,000, Vogel and his vendor independently obtained fire insurance on the property in amounts of $9,000 and $6,000 respectively. Before conveyance of the property to Vogel, a fire caused $12,000 damage. Vogel completed his part of the transaction and received from the vendor, in addition to the deed to the property, an assignment of the vendor's rights against his insurer. Vogel brought suit against both his insurer and the vendor's and obtained a verdict for the full amount of each policy, a total recovery $3,000 in excess of the loss. The Court of Appeals affirmed, holding that, although there were good arguments against the result, it was supported by Pennsylvania law, which governed the case.

tion, in the absence of averment to the contrary, that the price the property brought at sheriff's sale was the value of the property. This presumption is surely contrary to fact with respect to sheriffs' sales generally and this sale in particular because the amount of loss admittedly exceeded the price at sheriff's sale. Alberstadt should have been allowed to retain proceeds of her own policy equal to the value of her right of redemption. One way, but not necessarily the only way, of arriving at that value would be to determine the excess of the market value of the property over the amount she would have had to pay to redeem it. The fact that the right was not exercised and that it expired before trial, but after the fire, does not establish that it was worthless. The uncertainties arising from the fire and the disputed insurance claims may have made it impractical to exercise the right, even though it had value just before the fire.

The decisions in *Alberstadt* and *Brownell*[13] may seem to be in conflict because *Alberstadt* permits the purchaser to benefit from the vendor's insurance and *Brownell* declines to allow that result. But the cases can be reconciled. Despite the fact that the contract of purchase and sale in *Brownell* placed the risk of loss on the vendor, the contract was held to place a limitation on the purchaser's remedy for breach that was inconsistent with the purchaser's argument that the purchaser was entitled to insurance proceeds; the return of the $3,000 deposit discharged the vendor's obligations to the purchaser. Also, the cases might be distinguished on the ground that in *Alberstadt* the insurers were resisting payment in excess of loss to the property, whereas in *Brownell* the payment had been made by the insurer and the dispute was one between vendor and purchaser over the insurance proceeds.

§ 4.4 Leases and Life Estates in Realty

§ 4.4(a) Rules Applicable When Contractual Provisions in Leases Are Inconclusive

Leaseholds constitute another situation in which divided property interests can produce complex insurance issues. Both a lessor and a tenant have interests in a leased property which are sufficient to satisfy the insurable interest requirement. Recognition that a tenant has an insurable interest does not, however, foreclose difficult coverage issues from arising. For example, there may be problems about the value of the insurable interests of a tenant either when there is damage to the property that has been leased, or when there is damage to improvements of the property that have been made by the tenant and which will revert with the leasehold to the lessor at the end of the lease term. Another example of a difficult question of valuation arises when insurance is arranged for a tenancy at will. Selecting the appropriate

---

13. Discussed in the text accompanying note 5, above.

amount of insurance to cover the risk of injuries to such property interests may prove exceedingly difficult.

Disputes in regard to the right to recover insurance and the amount of the loss sustained by an insured are most likely to occur when a lease contract does not address matters such as the allocation of various risks as between a lessor and a tenant, or whether either party has a responsibility for acquiring insurance coverage for its own or the other party's interests. When the parties to a lease have not reached an accord on these questions, it is not uncommon for both a lessor and a tenant to acquire property insurance. Questions involving the persons and interests protected by insurance in regard to a leasehold may also arise when only a lessor or only a tenant has insurance on the leased property, as well as when both parties have insurance. In the event a leased property is damaged or destroyed, the rights of the parties, including the insurers, may depend on the jurisdiction in which an insurance claim is made — that is, there is conflict among precedents with respect to the rights of the parties in regard to insurance for leased property which has been damaged.

One line of decisions addressing the rights of parties to insurance on a leased property adheres to the principle of indemnity in assessing the liability of insurers of either the lessor or the tenant. The decision in Ramsdell v. Insurance Company of North America[1] provides an example of this approach. In *Ramsdell*, the tenant had a five-year lease that permitted the tenant to repair or remodel the premises at his own expense. The tenant, who had an option to purchase the premises at the expiration of the lease, remodeled the building at an expense of $7,800 and obtained fire insurance of $7,500 on the leased building. The lessors also had obtained insurance in the amount of $3,000 (policies of $1,000 each with three different companies). A fire in the building caused damage in the amount of $4,264. Although neither the tenant nor the lessors were required to repair the building after a fire, the tenant restored the building and then sued its insurer. The lessors, too, sued on their policies, and the suits were consolidated. In the trial court, the lessors recovered the full amount of their coverage ($3,000), and the tenant recovered an amount equal to the total damage caused by the fire ($4,264). Following the judgment, the tenant's claim was paid in full. The lessors' insurers appealed, and the judgment against them was reversed on the ground that since the tenant had repaired the damage, the lessors could not show any loss. The appellate court concluded "in equity and good conscience the insurance companies may

§ 4.4(a)

1. 197 Wis. 136, 221 N.W. 654 (1928). For an interesting judicial discussion of the *Ramsdell* decision, see Gustafson v. Central Iowa Mutual Insurance Association, 277 N.W.2d 609 at p. 613 (Iowa 1979).

Also see 6 APPLEMAN, INSURANCE LAW (1972) at § 3861; Annotation, *Improvements and betterments insurance*, 97 A.L.R.2d 1243–1255 at pp. 1249–1250 (1964).

yet prorate the loss, but we cannot see how it can be held that plaintiffs below had any actual loss." [2]

On its facts, the application of the principle of indemnity in *Ramsdell* is certainly justified. Once the tenant had completed repairs which restored the property, it seems clear that the lessors sustained no loss and accordingly any payment of insurance benefits to the lessors would have provided compensation in violation of the indemnity principle. The same conclusions would not seem warranted if the tenant, not being obligated to repair the property, had chosen to let the fire damage stand unrepaired. In such circumstances, the lessors would have sustained a loss, and it seems evident that the lessors should have been entitled to recover $3,000 under their fire insurance coverages. Moreover, if the lease still had several years to run, it seems equally evident that the fire caused an identifiable loss to the tenant who would not have had the benefits of the improvements that the tenant made in the leasehold.

The value of an improvement, that has become part of the leasehold and therefore will revert with the property at the end of the lease, to a tenant depends at least in part on the duration of the lease. If the lease period has several years remaining after the occurrence of the insured event, the reduced value of the improvements to the tenant will often approach or equal the repair costs (in the *Ramsdell* case, $4,264). Accordingly, if no repairs had been made by either party in *Ramsdell* and the tenant continued to lease the property with the rent unchanged, the tenant would have had a persuasive case for a recovery of an amount, perhaps as much as $4,264, even though this would have meant that the total amount of insurance benefits paid to the lessors and lessee would be $7,564 — that is, $3,000 more than it would have cost to repair the property.

Another line of judicial authority ruling on the rights of a tenant appears to suggest the possibility of a departure from the principle of indemnity. In Citizens Insurance Co. of New Jersey v. Foxbilt, Inc.,[3] an insurance policy was obtained by the tenant, Foxbilt, on improvements to a leased building. The insurance policy in *Foxbilt* provided that the insurer agreed "to accept and consider the insured in the event of loss in the position of sole and unconditional owner of such Improvements and Betterments, any contract or lease the insured may have made to the contrary notwithstanding." [4] The lease provided that the lessor should make repairs with reasonable speed, and provided for termination if damages were not repairable within ninety days. Even though

---

2. *Id.*, 197 Wis. at p. 139, 221 N.W. at p. 655.

3. 226 F.2d 641 (8th Cir.1955), 53 A.L.R.2d 1376 (1957). For an interesting judicial discussion of the *Foxbilt* decision, see Gustafson v. Central Iowa Mutual Insurance Association, 277 N.W.2d 609 at p. 613 (Iowa 1979).

Also see Annotation, *Lessee's or lessor's right to recover on fire insurance policy for destroyed or damaged property which the other has replaced or repaired*, 53 A.L.R.2d 1382–1385 (1957).

4. *Id.*, 226 F.2d at p. 642, 53 A.L.R.2d at p. 1379.

the lessor made the repairs without expense to the insured tenant,[5] the District Court held the insurer liable for damage to the improvements, and the Court of Appeals affirmed.[6]

The possibility of profiting from fire damage to the leased building was inherent in the *Foxbilt* policy clause declaring that the tenant should be regarded as sole and unconditional owner of the improvements irrespective of the terms of the lease. Thus, given the terms used in the insurance policy, the insurer had little basis for complaint because the lessor repaired the damage. The opposite result might have been reached on the basis of a judicially imposed rule aimed at serving the principle of indemnity. In this situation, the proposition that an insurer should not or cannot benefit from an insured's recoupment of a loss from another source arguably conflicts with the principle of indemnity. Although it is conceivable that the insurance benefits could be transferred to the lessor (who made the repairs), this obviously goes beyond both the insurance policy and lease terms. If a similar denial of any transfer of benefit from a lessee to an insurer were applied when a lessee-insured has a legal right to recoupment from another source, it would in effect foreclose a right of subrogation (which is another technique that is employed to implement the principle of indemnity).

The problems and possible solutions to lessor and tenant situations are similar to those outlined elsewhere in this text with respect to contracts of purchase and sale.[7] For example, in *Ramsdell*, it might be argued that the lease was analogous to a contract of purchase and sale

---

5. Also see Alwood v. Commercial Union Assurance Company, 107 Ga.App. 797, 131 S.E.2d 594 (1963) (lessee's "gratuitous" repair of fire damage does not defeat lessor's claim, which arose when damage occurred); Alexandra Restaurant, Inc. v. New Hampshire Insurance Company of Manchester, 272 App.Div. 346, 71 N.Y.S.2d 515 (1st Dept.1947), affirmed 297 N.Y. 858, 79 N.E.2d 268 (1948) (structural improvements to leased property were made and insured by lessee; subsequent to fire damage, repairs were made by lessor, which was his obligation under the lease; held, lessee could recover under his insurance).

6. Citizens Insurance Co. of New Jersey v. Foxbilt, 226 F.2d 641, 53 A.L.R.2d 1376 at p. 1381 (1957) at p. 644 (8th Cir.1955):

"Since the liability of the insurer is for indemnity against loss to property and attaches on the happening of the loss and since the amount of the liability is determinable as of that time, it reasonably can be argued that the subsequent repair or restoration of the insured property by a third party without cost to the insured cannot relieve the insurer of its accrued liability. That is the law in some of the states."

Keeton & Widess, Ins.Law—9

The Court of Appeals, though allowing this result, seems not to adopt the rule as its own but merely to hold that the District Court's adoption of this rule is permissible.

It seems a strange notion that under *Erie*, the District Court's choice of a rule of law should be sustained as a "permissible" one among conflicting views, none of which has been authoritatively adopted by the state courts. In this aspect, Foxbilt treats the issue as if it were a question of fact rather than a question of law.

Also see Annotation, *Improvement and betterments insurance*, 97 A.L.R.2d 1243–1255 (1964).

7. See § 4.3(e), above.

Also see John T. Even, *A Critique of Lease Terms and Their Effect on Insurance Administration*, 7 Forum 130–155 (1972). Mr. Even cautions against assuming that it is always appropriate to name both the lessee and the lessor as insureds. He points out that although "[l]ease conditions of this character appear to be very innocuous" they "may cause many difficulties" in some situations. *Id.* at p. 133.

placing the risk of casualty loss on the purchaser. Neither party was required to restore the building, and apparently the tenant was not excused from the rental obligation because it had been damaged through casualty. But the two situations are only analogous, and are not identical: a lessor may ultimately bear the risk of loss because a tenant may elect not to repair the damage during the lease period, in which event the lessor would ultimately be left with a damaged building at the end of a lease term.

Arguably, any allocation or division of a loss — when both a lessor and a tenant have insured the property — between an insurer of a tenant and an insurer of a lessor ought to be on a basis that is consistent with the division of the risk of loss between a lessor and a tenant. The application of such a proration approach ought not to be impeded by acceptance of either the argument that an insurer who pays the full amount of a loss to its insured is a volunteer to the extent of payment above the prorated share, or the argument that the insured who repairs and then sues its insurer is a volunteer in making the repairs so as to bar that party's insurer from seeking contribution after being held liable for the full cost of repairs.[8] Furthermore, each insurer should be subrogated to its insured's rights. However, the complexity of determining the appropriate allocation on this basis is a cogent argument for a simpler approach which would treat all insurance policies as if they were written for the joint interests of the lessor and the tenant so that the loss would be prorated among the insurers.

Some lessee's "improvements and betterments" policies declare that the measure of recovery will be some fraction of the original cost as determined by a formula that takes account of the proportion of the lease term that has expired at the time a loss occurs. Decisions applying this measure of recovery[9] can easily be reconciled with the *Ramsdell* rule when, as is ordinarily the case, no recovery in excess of the loss results.

Insurers are generally in a position to restrict the total payment of insurance benefits to the cost of repair — that is, two or more insurers could agree to exercise the option to repair and to contribute jointly to a single fund for the repair costs.[10]

---

8. See the discussion of the volunteer doctrine in regard to an insurer's right to reimbursement or subrogation in § 3.10(d)(3).

The closing sentence in the text from the *Ramsdell* opinion offers only a little hope for recognition that the lessee's insurer has an enforceable right of contribution from the lessor's insurer. However, in *Ramsdell,* argument for proration would have been strengthened if the actions had all been prosecuted to final judgment before any repairs were effected because the "volunteer" arguments against this result would not then have been available.

9. See, e.g., Daeris, Inc. v. Hartford Fire Insurance Company, 105 N.H. 117, 193 A.2d 886 (1963), 97 A.L.R.2d 1238 (1964).

10. If insurers elected to apply this approach, no allowance would be made for depreciation, and consequently the total insurance paid might exceed the amount of damages that would be assessed for the damage to the insured property if it were calculated on some basis that allowed for depreciation. Significantly, some policies are now providing for cash recovery to this same extent — that is, without deduction for depreciation. See discussion of depreci-

§ 4.4(b)   Subrogation of the Lessor's Insurer to the Lessor's Claims for Indemnity Against the Tenant

In the absence of specific provisions in a lease, a lessor may be entitled to recover from a tenant when the tenant's tortious conduct causes an injury to the leased premises.[1] The potential liability of tenants in these circumstances was given scant attention before a trial court decision in the late 1940s which imposed a substantial liability ($142,500) upon a tenant of a commercial building.[2] Once a lessor's right to such a recovery is recognized in a jurisdiction, the potential for subrogation claims by a lessor's insurer is evident. Although fire insurers only rarely make claims against tenants on the basis of subrogation to the lessor's rights either in tort or in contract,[3] there is a line of judicial authority which holds that adherence to the principle of indemnity [4] clearly warrants recognizing that a lessor's insurer may be subrogated to the lessor's claims against the tenant for indemnity.[5]

A tenant may request to be named as an insured in the lessor's insurance contract so that the insurer would be precluded from asserting a subrogation claim against the tenant — that is, the subrogation claim would be precluded as a consequence of the rule that an insurer may not assert a claim against one of its own insureds.[6] Alternatively, in the 1950s it became possible to obtain an endorsement on a lessor's fire policy by which the insurer prospectively waives any right of recovery against a tenant for loss to an insured property. Ordinarily, no additional premium is charged for such an endorsement,[7] and a tenant alert to this risk may seek such protection by insisting upon the inclusion of this endorsement in the lessor's insurance. Protection for a tenant can be arranged in other ways as well. For example, a tenant may request a provision in the lease that allocates, as between the

ation and replacement coverage in § 3.9(b), above.

§ 4.4(b)

1. See, e.g., Page v. Scott, 263 Ark. 684, 567 S.W.2d 101 (1978).

See also Annotation, *Liability of tenant for damage to the leased property due to his acts or neglect,* 10 A.L.R.2d 1012–1028 (1950).

2. See General Mills, Inc. v. Goldman, 184 F.2d 359 (8th Cir.1950), *cert. denied* 340 U.S. 947, 71 S.Ct. 532, 95 L.Ed. 683 (1951), reversing the trial court decision on the basis of the higher court's interpretation of the lease and without rejecting the possibility of subrogation of a lessor's insurer to the lessor's claims against the lessee in the absence of inconsistent provisions in the lease.

3. See Milton R. Friedman, *Landlords, Tenants and Fires—Insurer's Right of Subrogation,* 43 Cornell Law Quarterly 225–235 (1957); Brewer, *An Indicative Ap-* *proach to the Liability of the Tenant for Negligence,* 31 Boston University Law Review 47–67 at p. 50 (1951).

4. See the discussion of the indemnity principle in § 3.1 through § 3.5, above. Also see § 4.4(a), above.

5. See, e.g., Wichita City Lines, Inc. v. Puckett, 156 Tex. 456, 295 S.W.2d 894 (1956).

Also see Omni Aviation Managers, Inc. v. Buckley, 97 N.M. 477, 641 P.2d 508 (1982); Page v. Scott, 263 Ark. 684, 567 S.W.2d 101 (1978).

But see Alaska Insurance Company v. RCA Alaska Communications, Inc., 623 P.2d 1216 (Alaska 1981).

6. The same result could also be achieved by the endorsement referred to in the text.

7. See the discussion of subrogation and premium rates for mortgagee-only insurance in § 4.2(c), above.

lessor and the tenant, all the insurable risks to the lessor.[8] Also, a tenant could, of course, obtain separate insurance that would protect against all of the insurable risks assumed under a lease.

Allocating the risk of loss to a lessor in a lease contract is advantageous for a tenant because it eliminates the risk of responsibility for all fortuitous losses to the property, including those caused by the tenant's negligence. A lessor may resist such a comprehensive lease provision, and one reason for such resistance could be because such a provision might be held to be an interference with the insurer's rights of subrogation and, as such, a defense to an insurance claim by the lessor if the lease provision has not been expressly approved by the lessor's insurer.[9] Furthermore, if an inquiry is made of the insurer, there is a distinct possibility that the lessor's insurer will not consent to the provision.

Observations

Even if a tenant is named as an insured in the lessor's insurance or the lease includes provisions designed to protect the tenant, this does not eliminate the possibility that a tenant will sustain an economic loss in the event a fire occurs. For example, a tenant may still need insurance to protect against the consequences of business interruption [10] or, in some situations, losses that result from the destruction of improvements made at the expense of the tenant. Furthermore, whenever a tenant acquires insurance to cover such risks, consideration should also be given to purchasing a policy which covers the tenant's obligations to the lessor for the repair of damage caused by the tenant's negligence.

The possibility that a lessor's insurer may proceed against a lessee almost certainly is not within the expectations of most landlords and tenants unless they have been forewarned by expert counseling. When lease provisions are either silent or ambiguous in this regard — and

---

8. *Cf.* Parsons Manufacturing Corporation, Inc. v. Superior Court (General Accident Fire & Casualty Corporation, Ltd.), 156 Cal.App.3d 1151 at p. 1161, 203 Cal. Rptr.3d 419 at p. 424 (1st Dist., 3d Div., 1984), holding that a lessor's insurer was barred from suing the tenant for a negligently caused fire where the lease "agreement adverts to the possibility of fire and there is no clear language or other admissible evidence showing an agreement to the contrary, a lease agreement should be read to place on the lessor the burden of insuring the premises (as distinguished from the lessee's personal property) against lessor and lessee negligence."

9. See, e.g., Continental Manufacturing Corp. v. Underwriters at Lloyds London, 185 Cal.App.2d 545, 8 Cal.Rptr. 276 (2d Dist.1960), rehearing denied 185 Cal.App.

2d 545, 9 Cal.Rptr. 115 (1960). See also 3.10(c)(2), above.

Moreover, inexplicit attempts at contractual exculpation from responsibility for negligence may be ineffectual. *Cf.*, e.g., Poslosky v. Firestone Tire & Rubber Company, 349 S.W.2d 847 (Missouri, Div. 1, 1961) (lessee held liable for its negligence even in the face of lease provisions obligating the lessor to carry fire insurance, declaring that the insurance proceeds should on demand by the lessee be used to repair, and allowing the lessee to terminate if the premises were untenantable or if the lessor failed to repair on demand; thus, the court concluded the lessor and its subrogated insurer could recover against the lessee).

10. See Alan G. Miller, *Business Interruption Insurance, A Legal Primer*, 24 Drake Law Review 799–808 (1975).

especially when a lessor's insurance policy is also silent or ambiguous — courts should adopt a rule against allowing the lessor's insurer to proceed against the tenant.[11] As the result of the judicial imposition of such a rule in the absence of an express agreement between the parties, statutory provisions, or administrative regulations, the lessor's insurer should not be subrogated to claims against the tenant.

In some instances, the question of risk allocation is addressed in leases. When provisions in a lease clearly express an agreement that the risk of damages to the leased property is allocated to a tenant, a persuasive argument can be made for allowing the insurer to be subrogated to the lessor's claim when a fire is attributable to a tenant's negligence.

§ 4.4(c) Life Estates and Other Limited Interests in Realty

Life estates in real property can present perplexing insurance problems. The rights to the insurance proceeds produce issues in a variety of distinct ways which depend on several factors including how much insurance coverage was acquired, who was designated to receive the insurance benefits, the life expectancy of the life tenant, the desires of the life tenant and the remainder interest holder in regard to rebuilding or repairing the property, and the state of the economy in regard to inflation.

It would, of course, be better to work out solutions to the questions that may arise in advance of an event which causes an injury to a property that is subject to a life estate. For example, the parties could jointly arrange for insurance with an explicit understanding as to how the insurance proceeds would be used, including a provision for financing any costs in excess of the insurance needed to effect complete repairs. However, there are instances when such steps are not taken, and the following discussion of the issues that are involved when there is an insured loss to a property after a life estate has vested[1] is intended to be illustrative of the problems that may arise as the result of damages to property that is held by a life tenant.

11. See, e.g., Alaska Insurance Company v. RCA Alaska Communications, Inc., 623 P.2d 1216 (Alaska 1981), in which the court held "that if the landlord in a commercial lease covenants to maintain fire insurance on the leased premises, and the lease does not otherwise clearly establish the tenant's liability for the fire loss caused by its own negligence, by reserving to the landlord's insurer the right to subrogate against the tenant, the tenant is, for the limited purpose of defeating the insurer's subrogation claim, an implied coinsured of its landlord." Id., 623 P.2d at p. 1220 (Emphasis added).

Cf. Omni Aviation Managers, Inc. v. Buckley, 97 N.M. 477, 641 P.2d 508 (1982) (which involved the interpretation of a standard form rental agreement for an aircraft).

Also see § 6.3, below.

§ 4.4(c)

1. Another context in which a dispute with respect to rights of a life tenant and a remainderman in insurance proceeds arises is when an owner of insured property dies and persons in these two groups are the owner's successors in interest.

Destruction of the Property After a Life Estate Has Vested

In general, when there are no stipulations to the contrary in the documents creating a life tenancy or in an agreement between a life tenant and the person with the remainder interest, the life tenant is not bound to keep the improvements on a property insured for the benefit [2] of the owner of the remainder interest. Furthermore, the life tenant usually is not obligated to repair fortuitous damage to the property that is not attributable to the fault of the life tenant,[3] and a life tenant is also not obligated to arrange insurance for his or her own benefit.

A life tenant does have an insurable interest in property that is held in such a tenancy. If the insurance proceeds collected by a life tenant do not exceed the present estimated value of the life tenant's interest, the arguments for allowing the life tenant to retain the full beneficial interest in the insurance proceeds are very compelling. However, it has been held that the destruction of an insured structure which is the subject of a life tenancy converts the life tenant's interests in the real property to personal property (often referred to as "personalty") and that the life tenant is only entitled to a life estate in the proceeds of the insurance contract.[4] This rule in effect transforms the life tenant's insurance into coverage for the separate interests of both the life tenant and the owner of remainder interests in the property. When this rule is applied, the life tenant does not enjoy the exclusive benefit of the insurance coverage. Furthermore, in practice this approach usually also means that the insurance proceeds cannot be used to repair the loss without the concurrence of both parties.

Upon initial consideration it may appear that a rule that requires insurance proceeds, paid upon a loss sustained by a structure held in a life estate, to be held as a life estate serves the interests of both the life tenant and the owner of the remainder interest. However, it is possible that neither the life tenant nor the owner of the remainder interest is well and completely protected by an application of this approach to the rights to the insurance benefits. The relative merits of adopting this approach depend, at least, in part, on the amount of insurance coverage.

2. See, e.g., Farmers' Mutual Fire & Lightning Insurance Company v. Crowley, 354 Mo. 649, 190 S.W.2d 250 (1945).

3. 1 RESTATEMENT OF PROPERTY (1936), § 146.

4. See, e.g., Citizens & Southern National Bank v. Martin, 246 Ga. 284, 271 S.E.2d 192 (1980).

Also see Millard v. Beaumont, 194 Mo. App. 69, 185 S.W. 547 (1916).

Some judicial decisions do not require the life tenant to hold the proceeds of property insurance as a trustee for the remainder interest owner — that is, the insurance is simply paid to the life tenant. See the cases cited in note 7, below.

Insurance for the Value of the Life Estate

The insurable interest of a life tenant is frequently calculated on the basis of the "present (that is, either at the time the insurance is arranged or when a loss occurs) cash value" of the life estate, which is determined on the basis of the tenant's life expectancy and a reasonable rate of return on the "investment" (that is, on market value of the property which is the subject of the life estate). A life tenant who obtains separate coverage in an amount that is equal to the present cash value of the life estate often has inadequate protection. The insurance proceeds may not be sufficient to repair the damage to the property, and the life tenant might be in a much less advantageous economic position than before the damage occurred if the repairs could not be made because the insurance was inadequate. In such circumstances, the life tenant would face both the problem of obtaining additional funds from sources other than insurance proceeds and the problem of possible disagreement with the holder of the remainder interest over the arrangements for repairs.

If the entire or full value of the expectation of economic loss to the life tenant from a fortuitous destruction of a property is recognized as an appropriate measure of the life tenant's insurable interest, the value of this interest may exceed the present cash value of the life estate. This is true because it may be that no investment the life tenant could arrange for the amount of insurance proceeds (as determined by the present cash value of the life interest) would be as valuable to the life tenant as the life estate in the fully repaired property.

It is debatable whether the risk of economic loss beyond the present cash value of the life estate is within the coverage of a fire insurance policy which ordinarily is an agreement that a company insures "to the extent of the actual cash value of the property at the time of loss, but not exceeding the amount which it would cost to repair * * *, nor in any event for more than the interest of the insured, against all DIRECT LOSS BY FIRE * * *." [5] Even if an insurance policy technically does not provide coverage for this aspect of the risk, an insurer might choose as a matter of business judgment not to seek to limit its liability. In the first place, by contending for such a limitation an insurer would be asserting a position inconsistent with its being entitled to the full amount of premiums if the coverage limit was higher than the maximum value of the interest actually covered under its contention. Second, the amount saved by contending successfully for the limitation might not be worth the cost of the coverage dispute, in terms both of actual litigation costs and of goodwill which could be lost.

---

5. See the Standard Fire Insurance Policy in Appendix A.

Insuring for the Market Value of the Fee Simple

If a life tenant obtains an insurance policy for the full market value of the property as a fee simple *and* does not designate the remainder interest owner as an additional insured, a question may be raised with respect to whether allowing the life tenant to recover in excess of the present cash value of the life estate would violate the indemnity principle.

The insurer's obligation to pay an amount equal to the full value of a building could be upheld on the theory that the life tenant has a representative insurable interest [6] which allows the life tenant to obtain insurance for the benefit of the remainder interest owner. If this approach is accepted, it follows that the life tenant should derive the beneficial interest of the insurance proceeds for the duration of the life estate with the "corpus" being held for the benefit of the remainder interest owner. However, in these circumstances it might be urged that when such a property is fully insured, a life tenant should be required to use the insurance proceeds to repair or replace the structure — a step that protects the remainder interests as well as the life estate, and is therefore consistent with the life tenant's obligations as a "trustee."

Some judicial decisions have allowed a life tenant to collect insurance proceeds equal to the full value of a building, without also imposing an obligation to either rebuild or to hold some portion of the insurance benefits as a constructive trustee, even over the opposition of the remainder interest owner.[7] Usually such results have been predicated, at least in part, on the ground that property insurance is a personal contract.[8] Standing alone, however, this is not an adequate justification for allowing a life tenant to recover — without any limita-

---

6. At least, in the absence of explicit provisions in either the insurance contract or in the documents which established the life estate in the insured property.

Also see § 3.4(a)(3), above.

7. See, e.g., Farmers' Mutual Fire & Lightning Insurance Company v. Crowley, 354 Mo. 649, 190 S.W.2d 250 (1945). The life tenant had an endorsement (added to the insurance policy originally obtained by his grantor) that recognized the demise of the grantor and named life tenant as the owner of the property. After a fire causing damage to the property the insurer interpleaded the life tenant and the remainderman. The court held that the life tenant was entitled to receive and use as his own the entire proceeds of the policy.

Cf. Hunt v. General Insurance Company of America, 227 S.C. 125, 87 S.E.2d 34 (1955). The life tenants procured an $8,000 valued fire policy on their interest and remainderman procured a $3,000 fire

policy on his interest, by coincidence with the same insurer. After a fire caused $1,290.45 damage, the remainderman would not consent to repair. *Held,* though their interest was grossly overvalued, life tenants could recover full amount of loss because of Valued Policy Statute and insurer's retention of full premiums. The majority opinion noted that the court was not here concerned with any judgment rendered in favor of the remainderman. The dissenting opinion pointed out that the remainderman had been awarded a judgment by the trial court on the basis of a percentage of total loss in proportion to the remainderman's interest in the total value of the property, 71.5 per cent, as determined on the basis of a mortality table used by the court.

8. See, e.g., Farmers' Mutual Fire & Lightning Insurance Co. v. Crowley, 354 Mo. 649, 190 S.W.2d 250 (1945).

tion — an amount in excess of his or her interest in the life estate. Consistency and conformity with both the principle of indemnity and the principle that fire insurance is personal could be achieved by limiting recovery to the amount of the life tenant's interest or the imposition of a constructive trust for the benefit of the owner of the remainder interest.[9]

§ 4.4(d) Interest of Personal Representatives; Survivorship

The executor or administrator of a deceased who insured the value of a life tenancy is generally regarded as the proper person to collect under a fire policy for a loss to an insured property, whether occurring before the insured's death [1] or after.[2] However, a personal representative who receives insurance may be obligated to apply the proceeds in a special way rather than as part of the personal assets of the estate. For example, in a case involving a fire loss shortly before an insured's death, it was held that the proceeds of an insurance policy received as a consequence of a barn that was destroyed should be treated as "real estate" in place of the barn, and not as personalty.[3]

§ 4.5 Interests in Personal Property Held in Bailment, "In Trust," "On Commission," or in Analogous Ways

§ 4.5(a) Generally

When personal property is entrusted to a warehouse either for storage or on consignment for sale, a distinct type of insurance problem may arise.[1] Insurance policies for warehouse businesses have commonly included a provision referred to as an "in trust or on commission"

---

9. See the cases cited in note 7, above.

§ 4.4(d)

1. See, e.g., In re Mullin's Estate, 121 Misc. 867, 202 N.Y.S. 758 (Surr.Ct.1921).

2. See, e.g., Oldham's Trustee v. Boston Insurance Co., 189 Ky. 844, 226 S.W. 106 (1920), 16 A.L.R. 305 (1922).

3. In re Mullin's Estate, 121 Misc. 867, 202 N.Y.S. 758 (Surr.Ct.1921).

Accord. Rock County Savings & Trust Company v. London Assurance Company, 17 Wis.2d 618, 117 N.W.2d 676 (1962), 4 A.L.R.3d 422 (1965) (joint tenant died one day after fire loss; *held,* in denying claim of deceased's estate, insurance proceeds to be treated in equity as if they were the insured building, thereby passing entirely to surviving tenant).

But cf. In re Barry's Estate, 208 Okl. 8, 252 P.2d 437 (1952), 35 A.L.R.2d 1052 (1954) (collision insured died shortly after accident that severely damaged insured vehicle; held, legatee of vehicle was entitled

only to salvage value of vehicle after the accident and not to the collision insurance proceeds).

§ 4.5(a)

1. There are, of course, other situations in which coverage is needed for property owned by persons other than the named insured. For example, mercantile forms covering furniture, fixtures, equipment, and supplies have sometimes included coverage of property of others for which the insured is "liable" while located in the described building. See, e.g. Penn v. Commercial Union Fire Insurance Company of New York, 233 Miss. 178, 101 So.2d 535 (1958), 67 A.L.R.2d 1238 (1959) ("liability" referred to general liability of bailee and did not condition coverage on proof of "particular fixed legal liability as a consequence of a fire").

Also see Saul Sorkin, *Allocation of the Risk of Loss in the Transportation of Freight—The Function of Insurance,* 40 Fordham Law Review 67–100 (1971).

clause [or, in some policies an "on consignment" clause]. This clause is designed to extend coverage for damage to property held, but not owned, by an insured. A number of different forms have been used for such clauses, and even though some of the provisions do not contain the words "in trust or on commission," this phrase has come to be the shorthand description for all such coverage clauses.

In general, courts have tended to construe "in trust or on commission" provisions so as to afford more extensive insurance coverage than a literal interpretation of the specific terms would warrant. Often this result has been predicated on the rule of resolving ambiguities against an insurer.[2] However, in some instances the conclusion that an ambiguity existed has been, at best, a strained judgment.[3] The justifications for either straining to find ambiguity or predicating coverage on some other rationale for extending protection beyond the reasonable bounds of the insurance policy terms seem highly questionable in this context because the warehouse insurance contract is generally sold to relatively sophisticated business persons who are in a position to make sound judgments about the scope of their insurance needs.

The fact situation presented in United States v. Globe and Rutgers Insurance Company [4] provides an excellent vehicle for examining various perspectives on the problems that arise when insurance is arranged for property that is entrusted to a warehouse. In that case, the Commodity Credit Corporation had contracted with the McCoy Gin Company for the latter to purchase for the Corporation cotton seed from eligible producers under the federal price support program. A fire at the McCoy premises destroyed 114,130 pounds of seed purchased under that contract and in McCoy's custody at the time. Without claiming that the fire was due to the negligence of McCoy, the government brought suit to recover under six Texas standard-form fire insurance policies obtained by McCoy and in force at the time of the fire, each of which contained the following coverage clause:

> "On cotton, ginned and unginned, baled and unbaled, seed cotton, cotton seed, supplies of sacks and other packaging material containing or to contain cotton seed, and bagging and ties, their own, and *provided the insured is legally liable therefor,* this policy shall also cover such property sold but not delivered, held in trust or on consignment or for storage." (Emphasis added)[5]

The insurer in this case argued that the court's interpretation of the clause in favor of broad coverage rendered sterile the limiting phrase

---

2. See § 6.3, below.

3. See § 6.3, below.

A more candid description of the results in these cases is that for other reasons of public policy, such as honoring reasonable expectations, courts decline to enforce the express coverage limitations.

4. 104 F.Supp. 632 (N.D.Tex.1952), affirmed 202 F.2d 696 (5th Cir.1953).

Also see 4 APPLEMAN, INSURANCE LAW (Revised edition, 1969) at §§ 2345–2346; Annotation, *Fire policy on contents or the like as covering property of insured's customers or bailors,* 67 A.L.R.2d 1241–1262 (1959).

5. United States v. Globe & Rutgers Fire Insurance Company, 104 F.Supp. 632 at pp. 632–633 (N.D.Tex.1952), *affirmed* 202 F.2d 696 (5th Cir.1953).

"provided the insured is legally liable therefor." The trial court stated that this argument overlooks "the frequent tendency of bailees to attempt contractual stipulations against their common law liability."[6] Presumably the suggestion is that to give effect to the statement that this clause grants coverage only if "the insured is legally liable" for the damaged property would be to render the coverage virtually worthless to the bailor because bailees are seldom liable. But the court's answer is unconvincing because the bailee's attempt to contract away its potential liabilities can seldom, if ever, be so fully effective as to render virtually worthless an "in trust or on commission" clause covering only the property for which the insured is legally liable.

Warehouse operators continue to need protection against the risk of legal liability for property damaged by hazards such as fire while property is in their custody. Even though this protection might be obtained in other ways,[7] the "in trust or on commission" clause of a property insurance policy is a suitable approach to arranging for such protection. To further limit the coverage by adding a limiting phrase, such as "provided the insured is legally liable therefor," would be to require that warehouse owners or operators (who seek this protection through property insurance) buy additional coverage against losses for which owners or operators are not legally liable. Plainly a requirement that warehouse owners or operators buy protection applicable to all loss from designated hazards to property in order to get protection to the extent of legal liability cannot be justified unless bailors or others having an interest in the property may be held to be entitled to part or all of the proceeds.[8]

In effect then, the court's refusal to enforce the limiting language forces the warehouse to confer added benefits on others if the warehouse owner or operator wishes to buy the insurance that is clearly needed. And, if rates are appropriately adjusted to loss experience, this also means that warehouse owners must pay higher rates for this coverage than they would if they were allowed to buy the more limited form of coverage the clause was plainly designed to give. The requirement thus imposed on the contracting parties to afford coverage beyond the terms of their agreement does not appear to be justified by any considerations of public policy advanced in cases of this type. In short, judicial insistence on granting coverage which is inconsistent with the limiting phrase seems to be an unwarranted intrusion on freedom of contract in the warehouse insurance transaction. Moreover, even if a concept of representative interest is invoked to avoid inconsistency with

6. *Id.*, 104 F.Supp. at p. 634.

7. Liability insurance might be a viable alternative or a complementary coverage.

8. *Cf.* Hepburn v. A. Tomlinson (Hauliers) Ltd., [1966] 1 All England Reports 418 (H.L.) (a carrier procured an inland marine policy on goods in transit, which was in force when goods were stolen from the carrier's truck without its negligence; held, carrier could recover under the policy the full value of the goods although it was not legally liable to the owner for the loss, but the carrier would then be under a duty to turn over to the owner of the goods any proceeds in excess of its own loss).

the insurable interest doctrine, with the consequence that some other person is entitled to the proceeds from this coverage, it still may reasonably be asserted that the interest of such other persons is not within the terms of the insurance coverage. This is true because the provisions of the basic policy form declare that the coverage is not "in any event for more than the interest of the insured." It is debatable whether an "in trust or on commission" clause modifies this provision of the basic policy form or, instead, merely expands the description of property beyond that owned by the insured.

Another argument advanced in favor of judicial expansion of liability under "in trust or on commission" clauses is that the basic nature of policies in which these clauses appear is *property* insurance and not *liability* insurance. This argument, pressed to its logical conclusion, would preclude any definition of coverage under an "in trust or on commission" clause by standards concerned with the bailee's legal liability for the property in the bailee's possession. Yet, with a curiously logical inconsistency, the argument that the coverage is basically *property* insurance has been invoked only in the interest of construing a particular clause in favor of broader coverage while conceding that judicial precedents giving effect to legal-liability limitations in forms of "in trust or on commission" clauses with only slightly different phrasing remain authoritative.[9]

In summary, reasons advanced for the expansive construction of "in trust or on commission" clauses are unconvincing and a more faithful adherence to the policy language seems appropriate.[10]

§ 4.5(b)   Relation to Coinsurance Provisions

The coinsurance provisions customarily included in commercial property insurance contracts apply the coinsurance principle if the amount of insurance is less than a stated percentage (80 per cent, for example) "of the actual cash value of the property described herein" immediately before loss.[1] When a policy contains both a coinsurance clause and an "in trust or on commission" clause, a claim may present the question whether property of other persons that is held in trust or on commission is included or excluded in calculating the "actual cash value of the property described herein."

---

9. See, e.g., United States v. Globe & Rutgers Fire Insurance Company, 104 F.Supp. 632 (N.D.Tex.1952), *affirmed* 202 F.2d 696 (5th Cir.1953).

10. *Cf.* Aaro Packaging Corp. v. Fire Insurance Exchange, 280 Minn. 159, 158 N.W.2d 586 (1968) (denying a bailor's claim to policy proceeds, by giving effect to the limitation, "provided the insured is legally liable therefor"; distinguishable, however, because the contest was one for priority among creditors of the insured warehouseman after the insurer had made a payment, by settlement, to the receiver).

Also see § 4.5(b), below (relation to coinsurance provisions) for another context in which enforcement of the limiting language seems especially likely.

§ 4.5(b)

1. See § 3.8, above.

There is little in the judicial precedents that is directly relevant to this difficult question.[2] Sometimes the issue has been avoided by a narrow construction of the "in trust or on commission" clause, in sharp contrast with the expansive construction accorded those clauses to increase the insurer's liability.[3] Here, of course, an expansive construc-

2. See Conklin, *Insurance of Warehousing and Other Bailment Risks*, 1957 University of Illinois Forum 560–585 at p. 579, reprinted 1959 Insurance Counsel Journal 76–92 at pp. 88–89:

"There has been little or no litigation which has reached the higher courts with respect to this controversial question. It is obvious that this is of great importance because the value of property of others in the possession of bailees may fluctuate from time to time from a very small quantity to values running into millions, as in * * * [Texas City Terminal Railway Company v. American Equitable Assurance Company, 130 F.Supp. 843 (S.D.Texas, 1955)]."

3. See, e.g., Texas City Terminal Railway Company v. American Equitable Assurance Company, 130 F.Supp. 843, at pp. 853–856 (S.D.Tex.1955). Property of the plaintiff railway with an actual cash value of $4,437,864 was destroyed in the Texas City disaster of April 16, 1947. This property was covered by an explosion insurance policy in the amount of $2,300,000 that contained both coinsurance and "in trust or on commission" clauses which read:

"Coinsurance, Reduced rate contribution or average clauses—In consideration of the reduced rates and/or form under which this policy is written, it is expressly stipulated and made a condition of this contract that in the event of loss this Company shall be liable for no greater proportion thereof than the amount hereby assured bears to Ninety Per Cent of the actual cash value of the property described herein at the time when such loss shall happen, nor for more than the proportion which this policy bears to the total insurance thereon.

* * *

"It is understood and agreed that this insurance also covers the interest of the assured in and/or liability for similar property belonging in whole or in part to others, and held by the assured either sold but not removed on storage or for repairs, or otherwise held."

Id. at p. 853.

American Equitable, the insurer, contended that the policy covered all of the goods of others on plaintiff's property at the time of the explosion (having an actual cash value of $19,632,143) or, in the alternative, that plaintiff was liable for the loss of that property and that the property was thereby covered; that, in either case, the value of the property of others, was includible in applying the coinsurance clause; and, therefore, that it was liable for only 10.617% of plaintiff's own loss. (The owners of the other property had all been impleaded in the case but had either defaulted or disclaimed any interest in the policy proceeds.) Citing the approval in United States v. Globe & Rutgers Fire Insurance Company, 104 F.Supp. 632 (N.D. Tex.1952), *affirmed* 202 F.2d 696 (5th Cir. 1953), of cases in which "in trust or on commission" clauses were held to cover liability only (see § 4.5(a), above), the court in *Texas City* so construed the above clause and held that plaintiff was not legally liable for the loss to the property of others, thereby avoiding the question whether the value of the other's property was includible in the coinsurance computation.

Against the interpretation of the "in trust or on commission" clause in *Texas City* it might be argued that "the interest of the assured in * * * similar property" of others held by the assured includes the assured's representative interest—that the coverage is as broad as the doctrine of insurable interest permits when the phrase "interest of the assured" is used. Also, the phrases "interest of the insured in" and "liability for" appear as alternatives, being connected by "and/or," and to be given any meaning the former phrase must be construed as providing some coverage in situations in which the insured was not liable for damage to the other property.

It has been argued, however, that other differences in phraseology between the clauses in *Texas City* and *Globe & Rutgers* (see § 4.5(a), *above*) justify the different interpretations given by the two courts, despite the points made here. Also, in view of the different purposes for which the broad interpretation of the clause was invoked—being invoked in *Globe & Rutgers* by the owner of the property held by the insured to expand the insurer's liability and being invoked in *Texas City* by the insurer to limit its liability through application of the coinsurance clause—one might argue that the cases are reconcilable on the theory of resolving ambiguity

tion of the "in trust or on commission" clause would reduce the insurer's liability because of the coinsurance provisions.

As used in the coinsurance clause, it might be said that the phrase "the property described herein" refers only to the insured's property and not to the added property that is "described" — if at all — only in the separate "in trust or on commission" clause. Or, it might be said that the amount included in calculating actual cash value, because of property covered by the "in trust or on commission," clause would be limited to the valuation of the insured's interest in such property, rather than its total value. The latter contention is perhaps less readily squared with the policy language than the former, which happens also to be the position more favorable to insureds generally. The probability that the former contention will prevail is fortified by the availability of the argument that the policy is unclear on this point and that the ambiguity should be resolved against insurers.[4] Since the answer to questions about the relationship between these two types of clauses is in doubt, a bailee with a property insurance policy including both provisions should be certain either that coverage is carried in an amount adequate to avoid application of the coinsurance clause even if the property held in trust or on commission is included in the calculation, or that the insurer has made an explicit agreement that property belonging to others will not be taken into account in determining applicability of the coinsurance clause.

§ 4.6 Searching for Generalizations Applicable to "Multiple Interests" Problems in Property Insurance

The relationships of mortgagor-mortgagee, vendor-purchaser, lessor-lessee, life tenant-remainderman, and bailor-bailee — considered in the preceding sections of this chapter — have in common the fact that they involve multiple interests in a single property. When an insurance policy is obtained by one of the persons in such a relationship, it presents what is often referred to either as a "multiple interests" problem (multiple in that two or more persons have interests in the property being covered) or as a "limited-interest" problem (limited in that no single person has all of the elements in the bundle of rights that represent complete ownership of the property).[1] One or more of these relationships frequently exist in relation to a property. Accord-

against the insurer in both instances. See § 6.3, below. The most vulnerable aspect of this last argument is the assumption that the clauses were ambiguous in relation to the point at issue.

4. See § 6.3, below.

§ 4.6

1. There are, of course, other relationships involving multiple interests in one property. See, e.g., Newsome v. St. Paul Mercury Insurance Company, 331 S.W.2d 497 (Tex.Civ.App., Fort Worth, 1960) (a husband and wife were divorced without a division of their community property, and the ex-husband continued to reside in and obtained insurance on their residence, which under Texas law became a tenancy in common; after fire loss, the ex-wife sought a share of the insurance proceeds; held — without discussing whether that amount exceeded the value of the insured's interest or, if it did, what effect that would have — the contract was personal, and the insured could retain the full amount of proceeds received).

ingly, it seems appropriate to consider whether some generalizations can be formulated in regard to the rules that are applicable to insurance coverage claims by such parties — that is, whether there are general insurance law principles which can be applied to resolve questions in these multiple interest cases, or instead a separate body of rules must be employed for each type of relationship.

The formulation of workable generalizations for multiple interests or limited interest situations is complicated by the fact that insurance claims arising in connection with coverage for property that is subject to such interests often become a "battle ground" for several competing principles, including (1) the principle of indemnity, (2) the principle that property insurance is "personal," (3) the principle that an insurer should not be allowed the "unjust enrichment" incident to collection of premiums computed on coverage that exceeds an insured's interest, and (4) the principle that reasonable expectations of an insured should be protected.

Among the judicial precedents that have addressed the issues presented when there are various multiple or limited interests in an insured property, there are three clearly recognizable basic approaches. In many of the cases involving such interests, judges clearly are faced with hard choices in regard to selecting one of these three major approaches.[2] And, in some instances when there is a loss involving property that is subject to divided property interests, courts apply elements of more than one of the basic approaches outlined below.[3]

Also see Rock County Savings & Trust Company v. London Assurance Company, 17 Wis.2d 618, 117 N.W.2d 676 (1962), 4 A.L.R.3d 422 (1965) (joint tenant who had insured property in names of both tenants died one day after fire loss and her estate sought a share of the insurance proceeds; held, insurance proceeds to be treated in equity as if they were the property, passing thereby to the surviving tenant).

See also, John D. Ingram, *Valuing An Insurable Interest in Property Where The Insured is not the Sole Owner,* 17 Idaho Law Review 523–546 (1981).

2. *Cf.* Edward S. Godfrey, *Some Limited-Interest Problems,* 15 Law & Contemporary Problems 415–430 at pp. 419–420 (1950).

Also see Williams F. Young, *Some "Windfall Coverages" in Property and Liability Insurance,* 60 Columbia Law Review 1063–1082 (1960).

3. *Cf.* J. McCoid, *Allocation of Loss and Property Insurance,* 39 Indiana Law Journal 647–674 (1964), adding to the solutions identified in the text above two more: though limiting the insured to indemnity,

let the source of recovery be left to the insured's choosing; let the loss be apportioned between the insurer and the third party. The first of these additional solutions permits the insured to choose between allowing the insurer to escape responsibility (the first of the three solutions in the text above) and imposing the loss entirely on the insurer (the third solution in the text) or perhaps partly on the insurer (a further mixture). The second of these additional solutions (apportionment) involves a mixture, or perhaps one would wish to say a compromise, between the first and third of the text rules. The apportionment might also involve a compromise in still another dimension by allocating part of the loss to the insured, as happens when rights in a tort claim against a third person are apportioned between the insurer and the insured, leaving part of the insured's loss uncompensated from either of the two sources (the insurer and the third party) against whom the injured person has claimed.

Concerning subrogation claims generally, see § 3.10, above.

One approach is to hold that an insurer is only responsible for the actual loss sustained by its named insured, even when the insured's premium payments were based on a higher level of insurance coverage because the amount of insurance purchased exceeded the value of the insured's interest in the property. This approach serves the principle of indemnity and the personal-contract principle, but may disappoint the purchaser's reasonable expectations. This approach also results in what might be regarded as an unjust enrichment of the insurer. To the extent that there is a "windfall" of benefits to an insurer, it could be at least substantially, if not entirely, eliminated by providing for an insured to have a right to a refund of "unearned" premiums.

A second basic approach is to allow persons other than a named insured to recover indemnification from an insurer either directly or indirectly by requiring a named insured who effects a recovery to hold the insurance proceeds in excess of his or her own interest for the benefit of others having interests in the property. Although this approach remains faithful to the principle of indemnity and forecloses the possibility that there will be unjust enrichment for the insurer, it often violates the personal-contract principle by requiring an insurer in effect to provide coverage for someone the insurer has not agreed to insure. Arguably, this approach is also in accord with the principle of protecting reasonable expectations, although that conclusion might not be warranted in all circumstances.

A third basic approach is to allow a named insured to recover the entire amount of insurance, up to the amount of damage to the insured property, for his or her own benefit without regard to the insured's actual interest in the property. While remaining faithful to the principles concerned with treating property insurance as a personal contract and with avoidance of unjust enrichment of the insurer, this approach provides payments that violate the principle of indemnity. In many instances this approach also adheres to the principle of protecting reasonable expectations, even though the justification for such expectations may be challenged.

The approaches outlined in the preceding paragraphs were described without reference to rights of subrogation. Issues in regard to an insurer's right of subrogation often do arise in relation to insurance coverage for property that is subject to multiple or limited interests. Allowing an insurer to be subrogated to its insured's interests generally serves the principle of indemnity. Although subrogation is a useful device for effectuating the principle of indemnity, it is not the only way to avoid a violation of the indemnity principle. Allowing other persons to recover from an insured's insurer, or deciding that an insured holds for the benefit of such other persons any insurance proceeds that are in excess of that required to indemnify, also serve the principle of indemnity, and the loss then falls on the insurer. The choice of a particular approach, including whether it is appropriate to allow a right of subrogation, may be influenced by the other principles and considerations discussed above.

Multiple Interests and Separate Insurance Policies

Another dimension is added to the insurance problem if several persons with limited interests in a single property obtain separate insurance policies. Frequently when there are two or more insurance policies, payment of the full amounts of the applicable coverage would exceed the amount of damage to the property. The prospect of a total disbursement of insurance proceeds that exceeds the loss is enhanced if the second solution outlined above — that is, allowing persons other than the insured to recover either directly or indirectly — is applied. In such a situation, a judge faces a choice of, *first,* allowing such total recovery to exceed the damage to the property, or *second,* classifying the policies as primary and excess coverage, or *third,* utilizing rules that provide for proration or contribution in regard to the insurance coverages.

A judge may be moved toward one or another of the possible approaches by particular provisions in either the insurance contract or in a separate contract concerning the limited-interest relationship. For example, if both contracts specify that the insurance coverage is for the benefit of all owners of limited interests "as their interests may appear," a court will almost always adopt a solution that allows these persons to recover (whether referring to them as additional "named insureds" or instead as persons other than the "named insured"). Furthermore, even though the applicable insurance policy only designates one insured, the provisions in a separate contract between the owners of various interests in the property — as, for example, a provision stating that one party is to obtain insurance for the benefit of the other party — will sometimes be a significant factor in support of allowing persons other than the insured to recover either directly from the insurer or indirectly through the imposition of a constructive trust. However, the import of such contract provisions is notably lessened if the insurer has included provisions in the insurance policy that clearly impose restrictions on the scope of coverage or who is to be insured.

Observations

Ownership by one individual or entity of all interests in a physical unit of real estate increasingly is an exceptional situation. Few properties are held for significant periods of time with all the property interests vested in a single owner. For example, when an individual purchases a property typically there is a temporary period of the vendor-vendee relationship, followed by consummation of the transaction and the simultaneous creation of a mortgagor-mortgagee relationship. In turn, the mortgagor is apt to become a vendor before the mortgage debt is paid. In addition, the mortgagor of commercial property is very likely to be a lessor as well. There are also many forms of joint ownership that are frequently employed for real estate, including joint tenancy, tenancy in common, tenancy by the entirety (especially in regard to property that is owned by a husband and wife or among heirs or devisees), or community property. In resolving conflicts among different fundamental or general principles of insurance law in cases involving insurance for property that is subject to divided interests, the courts are repeatedly being confronted with the question whether they should seek to apply a uniform set of rules for all types of multiple interests or limited-interest cases (subject, of course, to exceptions that result from specific provisions which are included in the relevant documents).

Among the judicial decisions addressing various issues related to insurance that applies to property which is the subject of multiple interests, at least one trend appears to be developing. The shifting patterns of interests in property increasingly militate against treating a property insurance policy as a "personal contract" which cannot be transferred without the express approval of the insurer. Courts have recognized that a pervasive and inflexible application of the "personal contract" principle would produce results which in many cases would be both harsh and contrary to the reasonable expectations of insurance purchasers unfamiliar with either the details or the intricacies of insurance law and theory.[4]

The principle that property insurance is "personal" means that insurance will not be treated as coverage of the property for the benefit of whoever may happen to have interests in it and that it will not "run with the property." In many instances, judicial decisions have departed from this principle in vendor-purchaser situations — when a structure has been destroyed during the pendency of an executory contract for the sale of the property — by allowing the purchaser to benefit from the vendor's insurance.[5] Another departure has occurred in life tenancy cases, in which many decisions allow an owner of a remainder interest to benefit from the life tenant's insurance.[6] And the results in some bailment cases indicate a tendency to favor the construction of the insurance terms so as to provide coverage for multiple interests.[7] On the other hand, the "personal" character of the property insurance still appears to have great vitality in cases involving leased property.

The principle that insurance is personal has usually been justified on the theory that an insurer has an interest in selecting its insureds because of moral hazards. The justifications for the moral hazard doctrine, to whatever extent they existed at the time the doctrine evolved, are subject to increased scrutiny in the modern context. Only

---

4. Concerning the principle of honoring reasonable expectations generally, see § 6.3, below.

5. See cases cited in § 4.3, above.

6. See the discussion of life tenancies in § 4.4(c), above.

7. See the discussion in § 4.5, above.

a very low percentage of the multiple interests cases involve situations in which an insurer would have hesitated to modify the insurance contract to provide coverage for the interests of the parties had such an arrangement been requested before the occurrence of the insured event. Moreover, insurers generally do not treat multiple interests situations as involving greater moral hazard. In fact, insurers typically invest very little effort in considering moral hazards at all. Thus, the actual practices of insurers in regard to moral hazards raise serious doubts about both the justification for and the desirability of adhering to the principle that fire insurance is personal in character.

The differences in the treatment of various types of multiple interests situations represent varying degrees of a general trend away from rigid adherence to the principle that property insurance is personal and toward a principle that property insurance will be treated as coverage for the benefit of whatever persons happen to hold insurable interests.[8] On the whole, this trend seems a desirable one.[9] Moreover, in most instances, such a resolution of these coverage disputes is compatible with the principle of indemnity.

Fidelity to the indemnity principle has been and continues to be a factor of considerable — and in most instances, paramount — importance in the adjudication of coverage claims when there are divided property interests. A decision that allows a departure from indemnity should always be scrutinized with considerable skepticism and usually is only justified under rather extraordinary circumstances in which some overriding element of justice or fairness warrants the result.

§ 4.7   Omnibus Clauses

§ 4.7(a)   Generally

The term "omnibus clause" has frequently been used to refer to or characterize the provisions of liability insurance policies, particularly the clauses in automobile insurance, specifying or extending coverage to persons other than the named insured. The persons thus covered are often referred to as "additional insureds." Similar coverage provisions now commonly appear in other types of liability insurance. For example, comparable clauses are included in various comprehensive personal liability insurance policies such as the forms developed for homeowners insurance.[1]

---

8. Some of the differences can be accounted for on the basis either of differences in types of relationships to the insured property or of differences in insurance policy terms. In addition, to some extent the different decisions probably represent conflicts among jurisdictions rather than different treatment of multiple-interest cases within a single jurisdiction.

9. *But cf.* J. McCoid, *Allocation of Loss and Property Insurance,* 39 Indiana Law Journal 647–674 at pp. 664–674 (1964), generally favoring allocation of loss to the "third party" rather than the insurer, by means of subrogation.

§ 4.7(a)

1. See insurance forms in Appendix I.

Although the term "omnibus clause" is frequently used in discussions of coverage provisions, it rarely appears in insurance policy forms.[2] In most insurance policies, clauses which describe classes of persons who are covered as additional insureds are identified under captions or in sections denoted "persons insured" or "definition of insured."[3]

The typical omnibus clause provides coverage for persons on the basis of some relationship to a named insured. For example, motor vehicle liability insurance commonly includes a clause stating that "covered person" means in addition to the "named insured" shown in the declarations, the "spouse" of a named insured if a resident of the same household and any family member who is a resident of that household.[4]

Relatives who reside in the same household as a named insured are "insureds" for purposes of several other coverages which typically are included in the group of coverages comprising the standard automobile insurance policy. Both medical payments insurance and uninsured motorist insurance usually include a provision which extends coverage to such family members.[5]

Motor vehicle insurance policies almost uniformly provide liability insurance coverage for persons who use an insured car with the permission of a named insured.[6] Omnibus clauses in motor vehicle insurance policies, subject to some qualifications, also provide medical payments and uninsured motorist insurance coverage for any person who sustains injury while "occupying" — that is, while "in or upon or getting on, out, or off" — a designated motor vehicle.[7] The persons thereby covered are "insureds" in the usual sense of that term because they are entitled to collect insurance benefits in their own right for indemnification of losses.[8]

The coverage provided by omnibus clauses serves the interests of the purchaser by extending the insurance benefits to persons who are usually objects of a purchaser's concern.[9] For example, a purchaser of an automobile insurance policy ordinarily has both economic and non-economic reasons for desiring the extension of the various coverages included in the policy to other members of

---

2. Also, when the same type of provision is used in other contexts, it is seldom referred to as an "omnibus clause." For example, clauses in health and accident policies which extend coverage to members of a policyholder's family almost never are referred to as omnibus clauses.

3. For example, see the automobile insurance forms in Appendix H.

4. See the forms in Appendix H.

5. *Ibid.*

6. *Ibid.*

7. See insurance forms in Appendix H.

8. Compare § 4.1(c), above.

9. In the absence of some special relationship beyond that of permission to use the vehicle, a person who comes within the terms of an omnibus clause is ordinarily in the position of a donee beneficiary. See, e.g., Johnson v. Doughty, 236 Or. 78, 385 P.2d 760 (1963) (as a donee beneficiary, driver had a right to be notified that the contract existed and that he had certain duties under it before his rights could be terminated for failure to communicate with insurer).

the purchaser's household such as a spouse and children. Furthermore, this approach also conforms to the desires of many insureds who feel an obligation to those who use their property, akin to the personal (some might say "moral") responsibilities that many persons feel as hosts in regard to a guest visiting in an individual's home. In addition, as a practical matter, several potentially troublesome situations are avoided by making permitted users of motor vehicles "insureds." [10]

The coverage provided by omnibus clauses in liability insurance policies obviously serves the interests of accident victims. Although the desirability of assuring a source of indemnification for accident victims has probably been only a minor influence on the voluntary expansion by insurers of the coverage provided by omnibus clauses, it undoubtedly has been a significant factor in regard to legislation requiring the inclusion of various types of omnibus clauses in liability insurance coverages.[11] For example, legislation in several states is designed to reduce the possibility that an automobile accident victim will be unable to secure indemnification from a driver who is legally responsible for accident injuries by requiring that motor vehicle liability insurance policies include an omnibus clause of a specified scope.[12] Moreover, the public interest in favor of assuring indemnification for accident victims undoubtedly has also affected the judicial treatment of coverage issues arising in relation to such insurance provisions.

The extension of various coverages — including liability insurance, medical payments insurance, uninsured motorist insurance, and underinsured motorist insurance — to permitted users of an insured vehicle makes sense pragmatically from the point of view of the insurance purchaser, and it is fully compatible with the societal concern in assuring a source of indemnification for injuries resulting from motor vehicle accidents. Nevertheless, the scope of protection afforded by such clauses has been the subject of much litigation.

---

10. The purchaser of automobile insurance has an interest in the extension of the liability and collision coverages to others who drive an insured vehicle with the named insured's permission because the owner may face a troublesome situation if the insurer is obligated to protect the owner, but free to press a claim for reimbursement against the person driving the insured car with the owner's permission. This is a course the insurer could take as subrogee to the named insured's interests if the driver were not an additional insured. This could occur under the liability coverage if, for example, the named insured were vicariously liable for negligent operation of the vehicle by the driver. It could occur under the collision coverage if the driver negligently caused the damage to the insured car. See § 3.10 above.

11. See the discussion of automobile insurance in § 4.9, below.

12. For example, Wisconsin Statutes Annotated § 632.32(3)(a) provides:

"Coverage provided to the named insured applies in the same manner and under the same provisions to any person using any motor vehicle described in the policy when the use is for purposes and in the manner described in the policy."

Also see South Carolina Code § 46–750.31–.32 (Supp.1969).

Cf. the discussion in National Indemnity Co. v. Manley, 53 Cal.App.3d 126, 125 Cal. Rptr. 513 (1st Dist., Div. 4, 1975).

§ 4.7(b) Omnibus Liability Insurance Coverage for Operators of Motor Vehicles; Problems of Interpretation and Application

(1) Generally

Many of the disputes about the scope of coverage provided by an omnibus clause have involved issues related to either the extent of an express or an implied permission that was given to a person who was using [1] an insured vehicle when an accident occurred, or whether the named insured had imposed limitations on the time during which or the purpose for which the vehicle could be used. Several distinct lines of judicial precedents have developed among the appellate decisions which have addressed questions involving these issues. The results of such cases can be classified into the following three groups:

First, decisions strictly construing the omnibus clause, and requiring proof that the use was clearly within the scope of the permission given by a named insured (referred to as a "strict" rule).[2]

Second, decisions liberally construing the omnibus clause, and generally concluding that almost any use is within the coverage so long as the vehicle was being operated by a person to whom a named insured entrusted it for some purpose (referred to as a "liberal" rule).[3]

Third, decisions applying a "minor" versus "material" deviation standard under which coverage is only defeated when there

---

§ 4.7(b)

1. As to the meaning of "use," see especially note 4, below and § 5.2(b), below.

When it is clear that the driver had neither express nor implied permission to use an insured vehicle, usually coverage will not be extended. Jernigan v. State Farm Mutual Automobile Insurance Company, 16 N.C.App. 46, 190 S.E.2d 866 (1972) (driver did not ask permission to use the car and did not have a driver's license).

Cf. MFA Insurance Companies v. Mendenhall, 205 Neb. 430, 288 N.W.2d 270 (1980) (no express or implied permission for the insured's sister to use the insured vehicle); DeWorken v. State Farm Mutual Automobile Insurance Company, 151 Ga. App. 248, 259 S.E.2d 490 (1979) (owner did not give his son's friend permission to use the car, and the friend was aware of the family rule that no one outside the family was to drive the vehicle).

Also see Note, *Automobile Liability Insurance—Construing the Omnibus Clause—Round One,* 52 North Carolina Law Review 809–822 (1974).

2. See, e.g., Farmers Alliance Mutual Insurance Company v. Jones, 570 F.2d 1384 (10th Cir.1978) (applying Oklahoma law), *cert. denied* 439 U.S. 826, 99 S.Ct. 97, 58 L.Ed.2d 119 (1978); Eagle Fire Company v. Mullins, 238 S.C. 272, 120 S.E.2d 1 (1961) (implied consent of dealer for employee to use car in transportation to and from work and for employee's son to use it in transportation to and from college did not extend to son's use for pleasure trip to beach; consent limited "to the purpose for which it was given").

3. See, e.g., Johnson v. United States Fidelity & Guaranty Company, 601 P.2d 260 at p. 263 (Alaska 1979); Matits v. Nationwide Mutual Insurance Company, 33 N.J. 488, 166 A.2d 345 (1960) (initial permission of husband of named insured made driver an omnibus insured although she used the car for "bar hopping" after completing the trip for which initial permission was given).

Also see United States Fidelity & Guaranty Company v. Continental Insurance Company, 1 Kan.App.2d 722, 573 P.2d 1106 at p. 1108 (1977).

was a material violation of the scope of permission contemplated by a named insured (referred to as a "minor deviation" rule).[4]

These classifications are imprecise, and there are variations in the approaches employed by courts that occur within the judicial decisions that might be classed as being among the precedents comprising any one of these broadly defined lines of authority.[5] In commenting on these rules, for example, the Texas Supreme Court observed:

4. Applications of the minor deviation rule, which is probably the majority view, mean that omnibus coverage is provided for persons who make only a minor deviation from the use of the vehicle contemplated by the owner when permission was given.

See, e.g., Mid-Continent Casualty Company v. Everett, 340 F.2d 65 (10th Cir.1965) (applying Kansas law; intoxicated driver of empty bus who was off route and two and one-half hours behind schedule when accident occurred was no longer permissive user of bus under omnibus clause); Employers Mutual Casualty Company v. Mosqueda, 317 F.2d 609 (5th Cir.1963) (applying Texas law; use of indirect and unauthorized route by employee was within scope of permission under omnibus clause even though employer was relieved of liability because that use was a deviation from the employee's scope of employment); Fisher v. Firemen's Fund Indemnity Company, 244 F.2d 194 (10th Cir.1957) (applying Kansas law; personal trip of employee in employer's truck to a town fifteen miles away on Christmas day authorized; use for a trip out of state, during which an accident occurred at a point one hundred miles from the place of residence and garaging was a flagrant violation).

Cf. Coronado v. Employers' National Insurance Company, 596 S.W.2d 502 (Tex. 1979) (employee's use of a company vehicle after work for an eight-hour drinking spree was a material deviation); Allied Mutual Casualty Company v. Nelson, 274 Minn. 297, 143 N.W.2d 635 (1966) (date of named insured's daughter was given permission to drive to movie and directly back to insured's home; accident occurred while the couple were "driving around," after they decided not to go to the movie; held, permittee was an omnibus insured).

Also cf. Ryan v. Western Pacific Insurance Company, 242 Or. 84, 408 P.2d 84 (1965) (employee of the named insured had permission to use insured's truck to move furniture but was using it for entertainment when accident occurred; held, employee was an omnibus insured since the general use — i.e., personal use as opposed to business use — was that for which per-

mission had been granted and the deviation from the specific use was not "gross"); Foote v. Grant, 56 Wn.2d 630, 354 P.2d 893 (1960) (driver was furnished car for drive from Chicago to West Coast in return for driving it to specified destination by specified route, and accident occurred while driver was on an unauthorized side trip from a route to the specified destination, which was itself a deviation from the specified route; held, the original deviation would have been permissible since it was on route to the specified destination, but the off-route deviation was not permissible and avoided omnibus clause coverage).

Also see Cimarron Insurance Company, Inc. v. Loftus, 5 Kan.App.2d 90, 612 P.2d 1245 (1980); Merrick v. Pilgrim, 44 Ill.App. 3d 703, 3 Ill.Dec. 388, 358 N.E.2d 931 (3d Dist.1976) (driver's trip on a Saturday afternoon to a city located more than 100 miles away from the territory which the owner had assigned to the driver to cover for business calls was a major deviation).

See also Annotation Automobile liability insurance: permission or consent to employee's use of car within meaning of omnibus coverage clause, 5 A.L.R.2d 600–668 at pp. 621–660 (1949).

5. One issue causing variations is the question whether the individual through whom it is claimed permission was given was in a position to give effective permission. One phase of this issue is the problem of the permittee's permittee, discussed in § 4.7(b)(2), below.

Also see Underwood v. National Grange Mutual Liability Company, 258 N.C. 211, 128 S.E.2d 577 (1962) (insurer not liable on policy after car title had been transferred without endorsement of policy; transferee's driver was not permittee of named insured because he no longer had the legal right to give or withhold consent to the use of the car).

See generally William F. Young Jr., Some "Windfall Coverages" in Property and Liability Insurance, 60 Columbia Law Review 1063–1082 at pp. 1078–1082 (1960); Annotation, Automobile liability insurance: conditional vendee of insured as

"We believe the better rule to be the intermediate rule, known as the "minor deviation" rule, which takes a position between the other two more extreme rules. It avoids the possible injustice of the strict rule and yet reasonably gives effect to the terms of the policy. *It is flexible in that it looks to the factual situation of each case.* * * * Under this rule the relationship of the parties and the scope of the initial permission is very important. Obviously, the same construction could not be applied to the permission given to a regular employee to whom a company vehicle is regularly assigned as to a one-time user of the vehicle. Likewise, the construction of the permission given to a close family friend would be different from the specific permission given to a casual acquaintance.

* * *

"The primary reason the minor deviation rule is increasing in use in other jurisdictions is that *each case is permitted to stand on its own facts.* Some deviations would be so slight as to not raise a fact issue that the permission was revoked; other deviations of more significance would raise a fact issue for the fact-finder; while still other deviations might be so gross as to destroy the initial permission as a matter of law." [6]

It is noteworthy that this opinion explicitly points out that one of the justifications for preferring the "minor deviation" rule is the flexibility it provides in regard to allowing a court to examine "the factual situation of each case" — particularly "the relationship of the parties" and "the scope of the initial permission." Any reading of a group of judicial decisions involving the coverage provided by omnibus clauses will confirm the observation that courts generally find that it is desirable that each coverage claim be "permitted to stand on its own facts." However, the disadvantage of such a flexible rule is the high cost of administration that this approach entails by often necessitating a judicial hearing to decide the merits of each claim.

The factfinder's view of the evidence about what was said or done in a specific case frequently is determinative when the scope of someone's permission to use an insured vehicle is at issue.[7] Considerable variation can occur among disputes that involve the same insurance policy language and identically phrased rules of law because these coverage questions are primarily fact-oriented. Frequently, determining in a particular situation whether liability coverage exists for the person driving an insured vehicle depends not on which legal standard applies, but on the resolution of controversies about — and in some instances, the inference to be drawn from — what was said, how it was said, and to whom it was said.

---

within coverage of omnibus clause, 36 A.L.R.2d 673–679 (1954).

6. Coronado v. Employers' National Insurance Company, 596 S.W.2d 502 at pp. 505–506 (Tex.1979) (emphasis added).

7. For example, is a particular violation of conditions stated by the insured severe enough to defeat coverage under the legal standard regarding severity of deviations?

The nature of the relationship between a named insured and a driver often is an extremely important factor in determining whether the driver's use of a vehicle was within the scope of permission expressly or implicitly granted by a named insured.[8] For example, it has been observed that a comprehensive permission is much more readily to be inferred when "the use of the car is for social or non-business purposes" than when "the relationship of master and servant exists and the usage of the car is for business purposes."[9]

The nature of both the specific restrictions and the violation of instructions can also be significant in these cases. Thus, when an employee either uses an employer's automobile for personal purposes in violation of express instructions or allows a third person to use the vehicle despite an express prohibition, it is generally[10] — but not uniformly[11] — held to be without the employer's permission and therefore beyond the scope of coverage.

Ordinarily a claim of coverage under an omnibus clause is made by or on behalf of a person operating an insured vehicle. Occasionally, however, claims have been asserted successfully on a theory of permitted "use" by a passenger.[12] When an employee allows someone to be a passenger even though it is a violation of an express prohibition against permitting riders, coverage is frequently extended.[13]

---

8. *Cf.* Employers Insurance of Wausau v. Woodruff, 568 S.W.2d 625 (Tenn.App., Western Section, 1978) (Although there was testimony that stated the employee was told not to use the vehicle for personal purposes, there was evidence that other employees used company owned vehicles for personal purposes thereby indicating that the injunction, if given, was not enforced).

9. Jordan v. Shelby Mutual Plate Glass & Casualty Company, 51 F.Supp. 240 at p. 242 (W.D.Va.1943). This idea was approved and further developed by the Court of Appeals in the same case in decision reported at 142 F.2d 52 at p. 56 (4th Cir. 1944).

Cf. Foote v. Grant, 56 Wn.2d 630, 354 P.2d 893 (1960).

Also see William F. Young Jr., *Some "Windfall Coverage" in Property and Liability Insurance*, 60 Columbia Law Review 1063–1082 at p. 1077 (1960).

10. See, e.g., Boyd v. Liberty Mutual Insurance Company, 232 F.2d 364 (D.C.Cir. 1956) (use for personal purposes); Hopson v. Shelby Mutual Casualty Company, 203 F.2d 434 (4th Cir.1953) (use by third person).

Also see Smith v. Insurance Company of Pennsylvania, 161 So.2d 903 (La.App., 1st Cir., 1964), *writ refused* 246 La. 344, 164 So.2d 350 (1964) (use by third person).

See generally, Annotation, *Automobile liability insurance: permission or consent to employee's use of car within meaning of omnibus coverage clause*, 5 A.L.R.2d 600–668 at pp. 651–654 and at pp. 657–660 (1949).

11. *Cf.* United States Fidelity and Guaranty Company v. Billingsley, 376 So. 2d 1369 (Ala.1979); Employers Insurance of Wausau v. Woodruff, 568 S.W.2d 625 (Tenn.App., Western Section, 1978).

12. See, e.g., Hardware Mutual Casualty Company v. Milwaukee Automobile Insurance Company, 229 Wis. 215, 282 N.W. 27 (1938).

But cf. Primeau v. Insurance Company of North America, 46 A.D.2d 459, 363 N.Y.S.2d 124 (3d Dep't. 1975) (no coverage for the driver's son who was a passenger in a business vehicle owned by the father's employer).

Also see Annotation, *Automobile liability insurance: permission or consent to employee's use of car within meaning of omnibus coverage clause*, 5 A.L.R.2d 600–668 at pp. 654–657 (1949).

13. In essence, this situation involves a claim by a "permittee's permittee" — which is the subject of the next subsection. Occasionally coverage has been extended to a person not occupying an insured vehicle. Most cases of this type have involved injuries incurred in the course of loading

The particular language of an omnibus clause may influence the resolution of coverage disputes in some circumstances. In 1966, the phrase "within the scope of such permission" was substituted for the phrase "with the permission" that was used in earlier forms.[14] The change in the policy language at the time of the 1966 revision of the standard motor vehicle insurance forms appears to have been designed to limit further extensions of liability in the jurisdictions that had already adopted the "liberal" rule of construction in regard to omnibus clauses.

(2) Coverage for a Permittee's Permittee

There has been a considerable body of litigation involving claims resulting from accidents in which the driver of a vehicle was given permission to use the vehicle by a person who was originally given permission to drive by an insured — that is, a named insured gave permission to one person, and that person in turn permitted someone else to use the vehicle.[15] The driver of the vehicle in such cases is usually referred to as a "permittee's permittee" or the "second permittee," as opposed to the "original permittee" who is a person who was authorized to use the vehicle by the named insured and with whom the named insured has almost always communicated directly.[16] In cases

---

or unloading an insured vehicle. See Lukaszewicz v. Concrete Research, Inc., 43 Wis.2d 335, 168 N.W.2d 581 (1969) (exclusion as to accidents during loading, attached to trucker's policy, held void as in violation of statutory requirement of omnibus clause; liability coverage of trucker's policy extended to concrete company and its employee who, while moving concrete slabs with a travel-lift vehicle to load truck, injured truck driver; "operating" construed broadly to include participation in loading).

Also see § 5.2(b), below.

14. For example, in Market Insurance Company v. Commercial Union Insurance Company, 357 So.2d 591 (La.App., 1st Cir., 1978), Commercial Union urged that the omission of the language "provided ∗ ∗ ∗ the other actual use thereof is with the permission, or reasonably believed to be with the permission, of the owner ∗ ∗ ∗" from its policy meant that something more than the implied permission envisioned by policies containing such language was essential for omnibus coverage to exist.

15. This litigation has also helped to stimulate redrafting of policy forms in an effort to preclude the extension of coverage to the permittee's permittee. This may have been one of the objectives of the 1966 adoption of the phrasing "provided his actual operation or (if he is not operating) his

actual use thereof is *within the scope of such permission.*" See Appendix H.

The corresponding provision in the 1955 form was "provided the actual use of the automobile is by the named insured or such spouse or *with the permission* of either." Risjord & Austin, AUTOMOBILE LIABILITY INSURANCE CASES—Standard Provisions and Appendix 19 (1964) [hereinafter cited as Risjord & Austin].

The corresponding provision in an earlier form was "provided the actual use of the automobile is by the named insured or with his permission." 1947 Standard Basic Automobile Liability Policy. It seems doubtful, however, that this modest change of phrasing will lead many, if any, courts to adopt a more restrictive interpretation of the omnibus clause in relation to the problem of the permittee's permittee. It may have greater impact in another respect; see § 4.7(b)(1) at note 5, above.

16. Also see William E. Larrabee, *Who's aboard the Omnibus?—The "Additional Permittee" Rule Re-examined,* 60 Illinois Bar Journal 470–477 (1972).

Coverage questions involving third, fourth, and even fifth permittees have also arisen. For example, see Hutchings v. Bourdages, 189 N.W.2d 706 (Minnesota Supreme Court, 1971); American Home Assurance Company v. Czarniecki, 255 La. 251, 230 So.2d 253 (1969), discussed in

involving a permittee's permittee, frequently there has been no direct communication between the insured and the driver.

Issues arising from the use of an insured vehicle by a permittee's permittee are complicated by the fact that all too often there is considerable room for doubt about one or more factual questions relating to the permission. The importance necessarily attached to the particular facts of a case in ascertaining whether someone is a permitted user is a serious shortcoming of omnibus clauses in general, and it has been particularly evident in these cases.

When courts resolve coverage questions on the basis of the language in omnibus clause provisions, judges or juries typically have to face a number of factual questions, such as:

> Whether the original permittee received express permission from a named insured to use the vehicle? [17]

> Whether the original permittee expressly consented to the third person's use of the vehicle? [18]

> Whether the nature of the use of the vehicle (apart from who was using it) was within the scope of the permission granted? [19]

> Whether the named insured implicitly authorized the permittee's permittee's to use the vehicle? [20]

> Whether the named insured, if asked, would have authorized the permittee to use the vehicle?

Note, *Insurance—Automobile Liability Policy—Permission to Drive Within Meaning of Omnibus and Non-Owned Automobile Clauses*, 45 Tulane Law Review 175–180 (1970).

17. See, e.g., Travelers Indemnity Company v. State Farm Mutual Automobile Insurance Company, 330 F.2d 250 (Ninth Circuit, 1964) (applying California law) (named insured's minor, unlicensed son took the car against the express orders of his parents and allowed another minor to drive it; held, no coverage under owner's policy).

Also see Rondina v. Employers' Liability Assurance Corp., 286 Mass. 209, 190 N.E. 35 (1934) (driver against whom judgment was rendered had borrowed the car from its true owner, who had fraudulently registered and insured the car in the name of a third person without that person's knowledge or consent; held, no coverage under the policy naming the third person as insured).

18. See, e.g., American Motorists Insurance Company v. Samson, 596 F.2d 804 (8th Cir.1979); Rosenbloom v. St. Paul Fire & Marine Insurance Company, 214 F.Supp. 301 (S.D.N.Y.1963) (applying Virginia law).

Also see Nationwide Mutual Insurance Company v. Chandler, 151 F.Supp. 365 (M.D.N.C.1957).

19. See, e.g., Riverside Insurance Company of America v. Smith, 628 F.2d 1002 (7th Cir.1980) (owner's permission to an adult daughter to the effect that others could be allowed to use the vehicle in emergency situations, did not include a situation in which a third party was confronted with a need to borrow the vehicle); Johnson v. United States Fidelity & Guaranty Company, 601 P.2d 260 (Alaska, 1979).

Also see Ford Marketing Corporation v. National Grange Mutual Insurance Company, 33 N.C.App. 297, 235 S.E.2d 82 (1977), review denied 293 N.C. 253, 237 S.E. 2d 535 (1977).

Also see § 4.7(b)(1), above.

20. See, e.g., American Motorists Insurance Company v. Samson, 596 F.2d 804 (8th Cir.1979); North River Insurance Company v. Gurney, 603 S.W.2d 280 (Tex. Civ.App., Beaumont, 1980).

The problem areas suggested by these questions have often proved to be quite troublesome. Although the articulation of distinct classifications or rules for these cases is almost certainly unrealistic in light of the influence of the particular factual context in each coverage dispute, some broad principles can be suggested.

When a named insured expressly prohibits the use of a vehicle by third persons, generally it will be held that the permittee's permittee is not covered when using the vehicle for his or her own purposes,[21] especially when the permittee's permittee is aware of the prohibition.[22] However, if the named insured's original permission is broad in scope,[23] and especially if the original permittee is expressly authorized to allow others to use the vehicle, courts generally will hold that the permittee's permittee is covered as an additional insured even when the vehicle is used for personal purposes.[24]

When a named insured grants an original permittee essentially unfettered control of an insured vehicle, courts will generally hold that the named insured implicitly authorizes such a permittee to allow others to use the vehicle.[25] And, even when an owner has made an express general prohibition, courts will often examine situations in which a high degree of control was conferred on a permittee to ascertain whether the named insured gave an implied permission to the permittee's permittee to drive the vehicle.[26] Implied permission is also likely to be found when the named insured is aware that an express

21. See, e.g., Farmers Alliance Mutual Insurance Company v. Jones, 570 F.2d 1384 (10th Cir.1978), cert. denied 439 U.S. 826, 99 S.Ct. 97, 58 L.Ed.2d 119 (1978) (applying the law of Oklahoma); Farmers Insurance Company, Inc. v. Schiller, 226 Kan. 155, 597 P.2d 238 (1979).

Also see DeWorken v. State Farm Mutual Automobile Insurance Company, 151 Ga. App. 248, 259 S.E.2d 490 (1979) (driver, who was a friend of the insured's son, was aware of a family rule that the son was not permitted to lend the vehicle to someone who was not a family member).

22. See, e.g., DeWorken v. State Farm Mutual Automobile Insurance Company, 151 Ga.App. 248, 259 S.E.2d 490 (1979).

23. See, e.g., Johnson v. United States Fidelity & Guaranty Company, 601 P.2d 260 (Alaska 1979); Morgan v. Matlack, Inc., 342 So.2d 167 (La.1977), appeal after remand 366 So.2d 1071 (1979), writ denied 369 So.2d 1352 (1979).

Also see Annotation, *Omnibus clause of automobile liability policy as covering accidents caused by third person who is using car with consent of permittee of name insured,* 4 A.L.R.3d 10–133 (1965).

24. See, e.g., Davis v. St. Paul-Mercury Indemnity Company, 294 F.2d 641 (4th Cir. 1961) (applying Texas law).

But cf. American Motorists Insurance Co. v. Samson, 596 F.2d 804 (8th Cir.1979) (applying North Dakota law).

25. See, e.g., American Mutual Fire Insurance Company v. Reliance Insurance Company, 268 S.C. 310, 233 S.E.2d 114 (1977), and the cases cited at 233 S.E.2d at pp. 117–118; Nordahl v. Peterson, 68 Wis. 2d 538, 229 N.W.2d 682 (1975) (the court concluded that for all practical purposes the first permittee, the named insured's son, was the real owner of the car).

Also see Jones v. Smith, 1 Kan.App.2d 331, 564 P.2d 574 (1977).

This result is especially likely if the vehicle was wholly or substantially paid for with funds from the original permittee.

26. See, e.g., Schevling v. Johnson, 122 F.Supp. 87 (D.Conn.1953), *affirmed per curiam* 213 F.2d 959 (2d Cir.1954); Haspel v. Treece, 150 So.2d 120 (La.App., 4th Cir., 1963), *writ refused* 244 La. 218, 219, 151 So. 2d 692 (1963).

prohibition has been violated, and then continues to allow the original permittee to have possession and use of the insured vehicle.[27]

When a permittee's permittee is using a vehicle in a fashion which is contrary to a named insured's express prohibition, but such use is for the benefit of the original permittee or the named insured, courts are divided as to whether the permittee's permittee is an additional insured.[28] However, coverage is especially likely to be extended when some type of emergency arises necessitating the use of the vehicle by someone else for the benefit of the original permittee.[29]

When an original permittee was neither expressly authorized to allow others to drive a vehicle nor expressly prohibited from doing so, courts have often focused on the use to which the vehicle was being put when the accident occurred. If the second permittee's use of the vehicle was for the benefit of the original permittee,[30] courts generally conclude that coverage should be extended to the second permittee. If the evidence shows that the vehicle was being used only for the personal purposes of the second permittee, courts have usually denied coverage,[31] especially when there is some indication that the original

27. *Cf.* Butler v. Bonner & Barnewall, Inc., 56 N.J. 567, 267 A.2d 527 (1970); Crenshaw v. Harleysville Mutual Casualty Company, 246 S.C. 549, 144 S.E.2d 810 at pp. 812–813 (1965).

Also see Employers Insurance of Wausau v. Woodruff, 568 S.W.2d 625 (Tenn.App., Western Section, 1978).

Cf. Employers Mutual Casualty Company v. Mosqueda, 317 F.2d 609 at pp. 612–614 (5th Cir.1963); American Universal Insurance Company v. Dykhouse, 219 F.Supp. 62 at p. 66 (N.D.Iowa 1963), *affirmed* 326 F.2d 694 (8th Cir.1964).

28. *Allowing coverage:* see, e.g., Metcalf v. Hartford Accident & Indemnity Company, 176 Neb. 468, 126 N.W.2d 471 (1964); United States Fidelity & Guaranty Company v. Continental Insurance Company, 1 Kan.App.2d 722, 573 P.2d 1106 (1977).

Denying coverage: see, e.g., Coco v. State Farm Mutual Automobile Insurance Company, 136 So.2d 288 (La.App., 3d Cir., 1961); State Farm Mutual Automobile Insurance Company v. American Casualty Company of Reading, Pa., 150 W.Va. 435, 146 S.E.2d 842 (1966); Prisuda v. General Casualty Company, 272 Wis. 41, 74 N.W.2d 777 (1956).

Also see Annotation, *Automobile liability insurance: permission or consent to employee's use of car within meaning of omnibus coverage clause,* 5 A.L.R.2d 600–668 at p. 657 (1949).

29. *Cf.* the discussion in Gangel v. Benson, 215 Kan. 118 at pp. 124–125, 523 P.2d 330 at pp. 335–336 (1974).

30. See, e.g., Hughes v. Southeastern Fidelity Insurance Company, 340 So.2d 293 (La.1976) (applying a foreseeability rule in interpreting the scope of coverage the omnibus clause provided coverage to a second permittee); Teague v. Tate, 213 Tenn. 269, 375 S.W.2d 840 (1964); North River Insurance Company v. Gurney, 603 S.W.2d 280 (Tex.Civ.App., Beaumont, 1980).

Cf. United Services Automobile Association v. Stevens, 596 S.W.2d 955 (Tex.Civ. App., Amarillo, 1980).

Also see State Farm Mutual Automobile Insurance Company v. Automobile Underwriters, Inc., 255 F.Supp. 404 (S.D.Ind., 1966), *judgment affirmed* 371 F.2d 999 (7th Cir.1967).

Also consider Small v. Schuncke, 42 N.J. 407, 201 A.2d 56 (1964) (applying the "initial permission" rule, see § 4.7(b)(1) above, to find the use of the car within the scope of the permission given by the named insured).

See generally, Annotation, *Automobile liability insurance: permission or consent to employee's use of car within meaning of omnibus coverage clause,* 5 A.L.R.2d 600– 668 at p. 643 and p. 648 (1949).

31. See, e.g., Insurance Company of North America v. State Farm Mutual Insurance Company, 266 Pa.Super. 197, 403 A.2d 611 (1979); Schultz v. Tennessee Farmers Mutual Insurance Company, 218 Tenn. 465, 404 S.W.2d 480 (1966).

Cf. Ford Marketing Corporation v. National Grange Mutual Insurance Company, 33 N.C.App. 297, 235 S.E.2d 82 (1977), *re-*

permission was intended to be limited in some way.[32] The results in these coverage disputes have sometimes turned on whether in the absence of either express permission or express prohibitions, the named insured has conferred an implied authority on the original permittee to allow other persons to use the car — that is, some appellate court decisions have concluded that coverage should be extended on the basis of an implied authority that was conferred by the original permittee.[33] Other courts have concluded in such circumstances that the original permittee was without either the express or implied power to authorize use by a second permittee.[34]

In some cases courts have in effect circumvented the question whether the insured's permission extended to the permittee's permittee, by deciding (1) that the original permittee was still using an insured vehicle even though another person was driving the vehicle, (2) that the use was still within the scope of the named insured's permission, or (3) that the permittee was vicariously liable to a victim because the driver was acting within the scope of employment.[35]

view denied 293 N.C. 253, 237 S.E.2d 535 (1977).

32. See, e.g., Horn v. Allied Mutual Casualty Company, 272 F.2d 76 (10th Cir.1959) (applying Kansas law) (named insured's stepdaughter who was only allowed to drive the car to and from school lent it to a friend who had an accident while driving by herself on business of her own; held, no coverage); Hays v. Country Mutual Insurance Company, 28 Ill.2d 601, 192 N.E.2d 855 (1963) (named insured's son and stepdaughter, who were permitted to take car into town on a pleasure drive on the condition that they not use it for "driving around" while in town, lent the car to a friend who wrecked it while returning from a trip out of town; held, no coverage).

33. See, e.g., Utica Mutual Insurance Company v. Rollason, 246 F.2d 105 (4th Cir.1957) (applying Virginia law); Krebsbach v. Miller, 22 Wis.2d 171, 125 N.W.2d 408 (1963), 4 A.L.R.3d 1 (1965).

Also see Hardware Mutual Casualty Company v. Shelby Mutual Insurance Company, 213 F.Supp. 669 (N.D.Ohio 1962).

34. See, e.g., Duff v. Alliance Mutual Casualty Company, 296 F.2d 506 (10th Cir. 1961) (applying Oklahoma law); Ewing v. Colorado Farm Mutual Casualty Company, 133 Colo. 447, 296 P.2d 1040 (1956).

35. E.g., Melvin v. American Automobile Insurance Company, 232 Md. 476, 194 A.2d 269 (1963).

Cf. Graphic Arts Mutual Insurance Company v. Bakers Mutual Insurance Company, 45 N.Y.2d 551, 410 N.Y.S.2d 571, 382 N.E.2d 1347 (1978).

This approach was one of the grounds on which Souza v. Corti, 22 Cal.2d 454, 139 P.2d 645, 147 A.L.R. 861 (1943) is explained in the majority opinion in Norris v. Pacific Indemnity Company, 39 Cal.2d 420, 247 P.2d 1 (1952). However, in regard to these decisions, as well as a subsequent line of California decisions, it should be noted that in each case some insurer was somehow held liable. Subsequently, several California cases have invalidated, as contrary to the legislative public policy, specific exclusions from the omnibus coverage. The leading case on this point is Wildman v. Government Employees' Insurance Company, 48 Cal.2d 31, 307 P.2d 359 (1957) (invalidating clause purporting to limit coverage to named insured and specified relatives only, and holding that the omnibus clause required by the financial responsibility law must be included in all automobile liability policies written in California). However, the California legislature has since curtailed in a number of ways the broad requirements of the statute construed in *Wildman*. California Laws of 1970, ch. 300, amending West's Ann. California Insurance Code § 11580.1.

For other decisions striking down provisions less expansive than the then required omnibus clause, see, e.g., Atlantic National Insurance Company v. Armstrong, 65 Cal. 2d 100, 52 Cal.Rptr. 569, 416 P.2d 801 (1966) (exclusion from coverage of all drivers of leased vehicle except lessee and exclusion of coverage of liability to occupants of vehicle); National Indemnity Company v. Manley, 53 Cal.App.3d 126, 125 Cal. Rptr. 513 (1st Dist., Div. 4, 1975).

The difficulties occasioned by attempting to discern significant differences where there is little basis for distinctions has almost certainly been a major factor in the development of the rule, applied by many courts in these cases, that initial permission to one person serves to extend coverage to that person's permittee even when a named insured specifically attempted to limit the scope of his or her consent to the first person only.[36] As the Illinois Supreme Court observed, the rationale for this rule [37] was "to bring simplicity to what had become a complex area of the law necessitating frequent litigation and to further implement a policy long adhered to regarding the benefit received by the public from private insurance contracts."[38] Although this rule is probably still appropriately characterized as a minority view, decisions which explicitly or implicitly employ this approach are increasing. The results produced by applying this rule are consistent with the goal of providing injured persons with a source of indemnification, which is recognized as an important consideration by both legislatures and courts.

A rule that would almost invariably extend coverage to a permittee's permittee may not only contravene the express language of the applicable insurance policy, but also may be in conflict with actual agreements between the insurer and a named insured which have been explicitly made known to both the original permittee and to the permittee's permittee. Thus, it is not surprising to find contemporary decisions which withhold coverage, especially when the driver (a permittee's permittee) was well aware that the original permittee was expressly prohibited from allowing other persons to drive the vehicle.[39]

Also see Interinsurance Exchange of Auto Club of Southern Cal. v. Ohio Casualty Insurance Company, 58 Cal.2d 142, 23 Cal.Rptr. 592, 373 P.2d 640 (1962) (exclusion of prospective buyer of vehicle).

36. See, e.g., United States Fidelity and Guaranty Company v. McManus, 64 Ill.2d 239, 1 Ill.Dec. 78, 356 N.E.2d 78 (1976); Western States Mutual Insurance Company v. Verucchi, 66 Ill.2d 527, 6 Ill.Dec. 879, 363 N.E.2d 826 (1977); Hutchings v. Bourdages, 291 Minn. 211, 189 N.W.2d 706 (1971), discussed in Note, *Delegation Under the Omnibus Clause: Permissive Use or Public Interest,* 17 South Dakota Law Review 415–433 (1972); Odolecki v. Hartford Accident & Indemnity Company, 55 N.J. 542, 264 A.2d 38 (1970) (overruling an earlier case directly in point; son permitted friend to drive in direct violation of parent's attempted limitation of scope of consent; friend held to be covered under omnibus clause).

Cf. Farm Bureau Mutual Insurance Company v. Hmelevsky, 97 Idaho 46, 539 P.2d 598 (1975), discussed in Note, *Implied Consent Under an Omnibus Clause,* 12 Idaho Law Review 251–261 (1976).

Note that even this rule does not avoid all fact-oriented questions.

37. The rule is stated as follows in United States Fidelity and Guaranty Company v. McManus, 64 Ill.2d 239 at p. 242, 1 Ill.Dec. 78 at p. 79, 356 N.E.2d 78 at p. 79 (1976):

"When the owner has given permission to someone else to use his car, the owner's insurance will cover not only the first user, but others whom the first user permits to drive the car, even though the granting of such permission violates the terms on which the owner made the vehicle available."

38. United States Fidelity and Guaranty Co. v. McManus, 64 Ill.2d 239, 1 Ill.Dec. 78 at pp. 79–80, 356 N.E.2d 78 at pp. 79–80 (1976).

Also consider Western States Mutual Insurance Company v. Verucchi, 38 Ill.App. 3d 266, 347 N.E.2d 63 (3d Dist.1976), *affirmed in part, reversed in part* 66 Ill.2d 527, 6 Ill.Dec. 879, 363 N.E.2d 826 (1977).

39. See, e.g., Bond v. Pennsylvania National Mutual Casualty Company, 289 Md. 379, 424 A.2d 765 (1981);

(3) Injury to a Named Insured by an Additional Insured

Sometimes a person who is a named insured in the coverage provided by a liability insurance policy has a tort claim resulting from the negligence of a person who is an additional insured under the named insured's policy. For example, an owner of an insured automobile who lends the vehicle to another person may be injured as a result of the negligent operation of the vehicle by the borrower. MacBey v. Hartford Accident & Indemnity Company,[40] one of the earliest cases dealing with a question of this type, arose in Massachusetts and the liability insurance involved was acquired by the named insured to satisfy the state's compulsory automobile insurance requirement. The statute, pursuant to which the compulsory coverage was issued, required that the policy provide "indemnity for or protection to the insured and any person responsible for the operation of the insured's motor vehicle with his express or implied consent against loss by reason of the liability to pay damages to *others* for *bodily* injuries."[41] The Massachusetts Supreme Judicial Court concluded that the term "others" could not be construed to include the named insured.[42]

The ruling in *MacBey* was subsequently applied as a precedent by the Connecticut Supreme Court in construing the coverage provided by a Massachusetts policy.[43] In this Connecticut case, Chief Justice Maltbie concurred in the result, but indicated that he would have reached a different result if not bound by the Massachusetts precedent. He remarked: "The word 'others' in the clause under which the company agrees to indemnify the named insured or any person operating the car with his consent 'against loss by reason of the liability to pay damages to others' means persons other than the one invoking the protection of the policy, whether it be the named insured or one who is operating the car with his consent."[44]

A majority of the decisions on this point in other jurisdictions support the position urged by Chief Justice Maltbie.[45] Furthermore,

DeWorken v. State Farm Mutual Automobile Insurance Company, 151 Ga.App. 248, 259 S.E.2d 490 (1979).

Cf. Gruger v. Western Casualty & Surety Company, 89 N.M. 562, 555 P.2d 683 (1976) (owner of an insured truck clearly prohibited his son from lending the vehicle to anyone outside the family, and school regulations of the New Mexico Military Institute prohibited one student from lending a vehicle to another student).

40. 292 Mass. 105, 197 N.E. 516 (1935), 106 A.L.R. 1248 (1937).

41. Massachusetts General Laws Annotated c. 90, § 34A (Emphasis added).

42. MacBey v. Hartford Accident & Indemnity Company, 292 Mass. 105 at p. 107, 197 N.E. 516 at p. 517 (1935), 106 A.L.R. 1248 at p. 1250 (1937).

43. Cain v. American Policyholders Insurance Company, 120 Conn. 645, 183 A. 403 (1936).

44. *Id.*, 120 Conn. at p. 655, 183 A. at p. 407.

45. See e.g., Iowa Mutual Insurance Company v. Meckna, 180 Neb. 516, 144 N.W.2d 73 (1966), 15 A.L.R.3d 698 (1967); Bachman v. Independence Indemnity Company, 214 Cal. 529, 6 P.2d 943 (1931).

Also see Commercial Insurance Company v. Papandrea, 121 Vt. 386, 159 A.2d 333 (1960) (dictum).

Cf. Ottinger v. Falkenberg, 11 Wis.2d 506, 105 N.W.2d 560 (1960) (reformation allowed to strike name of wife as named insured, because it was included without her knowledge or consent, after injury to her while her brother was driving the insured car with permission; the court re-

the addition of the severability clause in the 1955 revision of the standard automobile insurance policy forms fortifies this conclusion. In the revised policy forms, the term "the insured" is used severally in relation to each claim,[46] and in that light a named insured is not an insured at all in relation to the named insured's claim in tort against an additional insured.

An equally interesting question is presented in regard to how a claim by a spouse of a person who is named as an insured in a motor vehicle liability insurance policy would fare in a jurisdiction following the rationale of *MacBey*. The court's reasoning in *MacBey* was based on the theory that the word "others" in the Massachusetts statute indicates that "inclusion of the named assured within the class of beneficiaries was not within the legislative intent."[47] It proceeds on the theory that the owner of a motor vehicle is placed in a different position from other members of the public in relation to assurance of financial responsibility for injuries from operation of the vehicle. Since the point is expressed in relation to the "owner" or "named assured" rather than in relation to omnibus insureds, it may be argued that the spouse of the owner is not precluded from recovery if either the owner or someone else with the owner's permission drives the automobile and negligently injures the spouse. This distinction is a debatable one, but the likelihood of its being drawn is perhaps increased by the fact that the *MacBey* interpretation of the Massachusetts statute is itself dubious. The problem is further complicated by the fact that the 1958 standard family automobile form defines "named insured" to include the spouse. Apparently the drafting objective was to do away with differences based on whether a policy was issued to one spouse alone or to the two spouses jointly. Nevertheless, it is possible to distinguish the non-owning spouse from the owner with respect to potential application of the *MacBey* rule, on the theory that *MacBey* was an interpretation of the statutory requirement — rather than of the omnibus clause — and that the term "others" in the statute includes all persons other than the owner, irrespective of the relationship of a claimant to the owner.

Some insurance policies include a clause explicitly declaring that the bodily injury liability coverage does not apply to bodily injury to an insured. Absent statutory provisions precluding the inclusion of such a limitation in the insurance contract, coverage may be denied on the basis of the exclusion.[48]

(4) Comment: An Appraisal of Omnibus Clauses

There has been a general trend toward expanding the scope of coverage provided by liability insurance policies. This trend, which has been particularly evident in regard to motor vehicle liability insurance,

---

served the question whether, had she been a named insured, liability for injury to her could have been excluded).

46. See Appendix G and Appendix H, above.

47. MacBey v. Hartford Accident & Indemnity Company, 292 Mass. 105 at p. 107, 197 N.E. 516 at p. 517 (1935), 106 A.L.R. 1248 at p. 1250 (1937).

48. See § 4.9(a)(2), below.

probably reflects (1) an increased preference on the part of insurance purchasers (incident in part to changing social attitudes) to have the benefits of their policies extend quite broadly to others, (2) an increasing recognition, manifested by both legislation and judicial decisions, of the desirability of assuring indemnification for persons injured in motor vehicle accidents, and (3) a diminished apprehension on the part of insurers concerning the costs of providing more extensive coverage in light of their experience with various omnibus clauses that have been included in liability insurance policies. Although the trend has not been manifested in every revision of standard forms for automobile and other motor vehicle insurance, notable extensions occurred in 1955 [49] and 1958.[50] However, somewhat less expansive coverage resulted from the 1966 revision.[51]

In the development of more extensive protection, insurers still have not addressed one — and perhaps the most significant — deficiency of the omnibus clauses in motor vehicle insurance policies. Omnibus coverage continues to be predicated on the existence of "permission" — that is, in one sense or another, permission to use an insured vehicle continues to be employed as the standard for determining the scope of liability insurance coverage. This approach produces substantial amounts of litigation.[52] Furthermore, coverage disputes which focus on issues which relate to permission typically involve controversies that are essentially fact-oriented, and frequently involve substantial costs to resolve coverage questions on the basis of subtle nuances.[53]

The expenses incident to predicating the existence of coverage on the concept of "permission" — actual, implied, presumed, or even imagined — could be avoided by expanding the group of covered drivers so that only very exceptional cases would spawn any controversy over whether the driver was an insured.[54] For example, coverage could be

---

49. See the forms in Appendix G and Appendix H.

50. *Ibid.*

51. See the forms in Appendix G and Appendix H.

52. The coverage provided by omnibus clauses may also produce litigation in regard to the claims process. For example, in Weaver v. Hartford Accident and Indemnity Company, 570 S.W.2d 367 (Tex. 1978), the court concluded that a permissive driver was required to forward suit papers to the insurer as a condition precedent to the insurer's liability. See the discussion of this case in Note, *Weaver v. Hartford Accident and Indemnity Company: The Relationship Between the Omnibus Insured and the Forwarding Suit Papers Provision,* 31 Baylor Law Review 367–374 (1979).

Also see the discussion in Chapter 7, below.

53. See § 4.7(b)(1) and § 4.7(b)(2), above.

54. Another way of avoiding this waste would be to limit omnibus insureds to a group definable in terms less likely to give rise to fact disputes (for example, limiting the group to members of the household of the named insured). This would be an undesirable revision from another point of view, however, since it would work against the public interest in favor of maximizing the probability that drivers will be financially responsible.

Cf. Jones v. Mid-South Insurance Company, 358 F.2d 887 (5th Cir.1966) (applying Louisiana law; held, omnibus clause limiting coverage to named insured, spouse, and an additional named insured valid in absence of statutory requirement of broader omnibus clause coverage).

provided for all persons using an insured automobile *unless* the operator's use of the vehicle amounts to a conversion or theft of the vehicle.[55] Although the question whether a conversion or theft had occurred may still be fact-oriented, it is an issue that will arise in relatively few circumstances. Accordingly, the volume of litigation would undoubtedly be significantly reduced.

There are several reasons why expanding the scope of liability coverage provided by omnibus clauses would not necessarily produce significant increases in the total costs that are borne by motorists. *First,* the resulting savings in litigation expenses should partially offset the amounts needed to provide insurance benefits for the additional claims that would be covered by the more extensive coverage. *Second,* persons injured in such accidents frequently are at least partially indemnified or receive compensation from some source other than compensation from liability insurance. The costs of these measures are ultimately paid by the entire society, by all motorists, or by individuals. Providing indemnification for a larger proportion of accident victims by broadening the scope of liability insurance should serve to only change the way some accidents costs are allocated.[56] Accordingly, although expansion of omnibus clause coverage would probably produce somewhat higher motor vehicle insurance costs, the net costs might not be substantially higher to the motoring public, and it would certainly serve to reduce friction among liability insurers, their insureds, and accident victims.

§ 4.7(c) "Omnibus" Uninsured Motorist Insurance Coverage for Occupants of Motor Vehicles: Problems of Interpretation and Application [1]

Uninsured motorist insurance is provided for all persons who are injured while occupying an insured highway vehicle [2] by coverage provisions which typically specify that a "covered person" includes "Any * * * person occupying your covered auto" and define "occupying" as meaning *"in or upon or entering into or alighting from."* [3] The

---

55. *Cf.* the comment of the Minnesota Supreme Court in Milbank Mutual Insurance Company v. United States Fidelity and Guaranty Company, 332 N.W.2d 160 at p. 162 (Minn.1983):

"[W]hen permission to use a vehicle is initially given, subsequent use short of actual conversion or theft remains permissive within the meaning of the omnibus clause, even if such use was not within the contemplation of the parties or was outside any limitations placed upon the initial grant of permission."

Also see Robert Keeton & Jeffrey O'Connell, BASIC PROTECTION FOR THE TRAFFIC VICTIM (1965), at p. 391.

56. In particular, persons injured in such motor vehicle accidents may be covered by medical payments coverage and, in almost half of the states, by personal injury protection insurance.

§ 4.7(c)

1. Portions of the following section were adapted from Chapter 5 of Widiss, UNINSURED AND UNDERINSURED MOTORIST INSURANCE (1985).

2. Insurance Services Office Personal Auto Policy, Part C, Uninsured Motorist Coverage: Insurance Agreement (Ed. 6–80), at p. 5.

See, e.g., Florida Insurance Guaranty Association v. Johnson, 392 So.2d 1348 (Fla. App., 5th Dist., 1980).

3. 1966 Standard Form, Part V: Additional Definitions.

current Insurance Services Office Auto Policy uses a slightly different phrase that states "occupying" means *"in, upon, getting in, on, out or off."* [4] This is another type of omnibus coverage, although again that term never appears in the insurance policy forms.

In most cases, there is little room for disagreement about whether a claimant is "in" a vehicle, and there have been few appellate opinions in which this aspect of the definition has been considered.[5] There is, however, more latitude for disagreement regarding whether a person is "upon" a vehicle. A number of coverage disputes have turned on whether the claimant was "upon" an insured vehicle. Even though the coverage terms "entering into or alighting from" seem to provide fairly broad coverage, a considerable number of cases have involved disputes about the scope of protection described by these terms. Based on the experience with these terms, it also seems reasonable to anticipate that comparable coverage disputes will occur in regard to the scope of coverage defined by the terms "getting in, on, out or off" an insured vehicle that are used in the Insurance Services Office uninsured motorist insurance and underinsured motorist insurance forms.

(1) Proximity to an Insured Vehicle

The use of terms in insurance policies such as "upon," "entering into," "alighting from," "getting in," "getting out" or "getting off" provide considerable latitude for differing interpretations. Although coverage disputes about the scope of protection for occupants of an insured vehicle have involved a wide spectrum of factual situations, in most of the cases in which these terms were at issue the claimants were injured either as they approached an insured vehicle or after they had alighted from an insured vehicle. These cases are exemplified by decisions that upheld coverage for a claimant who was injured while he stood beside a taxi to pay the driver,[6] and for a claimant who was

In the current Insurance Services Office Form, the relevant policy language states that a "Covered Person" means "2. Any other person while *occupying your covered auto.*" Insurance Services Office Personal Auto Policy (Ed. 6–80), p. 5.

Also see Annotation, *When is a person "occupying" an automobile within meaning of Medical Payments Provision,* 42 A.L.R.3d 501 (1972), and Annotation, *Scope of clause of insurance policy covering injuries sustained while "in or on" or "in or upon" motor vehicle,* 39 A.L.R.2d 952 (1955).

4. Insurance Services Office Personal Auto Policy: Definitions (Ed. 6–80), at p. 1.

5. *But see* Billups v. Alabama Farm Bureau Mutual Casualty Insurance Company, 352 So.2d 1097 at p. 1101 (Ala.1977). The court held that "restricting uninsured mo-

torist coverage to occupants of an automobile only if the automobile is used with express permission of the named insured is repugnant to the statutory requirements * * *." (Emphasis added). Also see the subsequent decision in Alabama Farm Bureau Mutual Casualty Insurance Co. v. Billups, 366 So.2d 1109 (Ala.1979).

Certified Indemnity Co. v. Thompson, 180 Colo. 341, 505 P.2d 962 (1973) (coverage was upheld for a father using his son's automobile).

6. Allstate Insurance Co. v. Flaumenbaum, 62 Misc.2d 32, 308 N.Y.S.2d 447 (New York County, Part VII, 1970). The opinion includes the observation that a person continues to be an occupant so long as the person continues to be "vehicle-oriented," as opposed to "highway-oriented."

struck by an uninsured motorist while unlocking the door of an insured vehicle.[7]

When the judicial opinions that resolve coverage disputes in these and similar situations are considered as a group, they seem to define the coverage provisions "upon," "entering into" or "alighting from" in terms of a reasonable perimeter around an insured vehicle. So long as drivers or passengers are within an area that is reasonably close to an insured vehicle, they are covered by the uninsured motorist insurance.[8]

Comment

Many claimants have been injured while engaged in an activity associated with the vehicle's use or operation. In some instances, the claimant was actually "upon" the insured vehicle. For example, a claimant who was lying on the fender of an insured vehicle to work on a fuel pump was injured when the parked car was struck by an uninsured motorist.[9] Coverage clearly should exist for a person injured under such circumstances without regard to the reason the claimant was upon the insured vehicle. The fact that the claimant was engaged in an activity related to the use of the vehicle simply buttresses the justification for extending coverage. In other instances, however, coverage of an activity related to the use or operation of the insured vehicle is beyond the scope of protection usually accorded to persons who are "entering into," "alighting from" or are "upon" an insured vehicle. The cases discussed in the following paragraphs justify coverage on a basis which is distinguishable from that articulated by judges in decisions which are based on the claimant's proximity to an insured vehicle.

(2) Activities Related to the Use of an Insured Vehicle

There are many appellate opinions interpreting the term "occupying" in situations in which claimants were injured while either preparing to perform or performing an activity related to the maintenance, use, or operation of an insured vehicle. Some of these decisions could be included with the cases discussed in the preceding paragraphs where

---

7. Box v. Doe, 221 So.2d 666 (La.App., 4th Cir.1969), *cert. denied* 254 La. 457, 223 So.2d 868 (1969).

But cf. Smith v. Girley, 242 So.2d 32 at p. 39 (La.App. 1st Cir.1970).

In Robson v. Lightning Rod Mutual Insurance Co., 59 Ohio App.2d 261, 393 N.E.2d 1053, 13 Ohio Op.3d 268 (Franklin County 1978), affirming the decision reported at 59 Ohio Misc. 61, 393 N.E.2d 1056, 13 Ohio Op.3d 280 (Court of Common Pleas, Franklin County, 1978), coverage was upheld for a passenger who was placing a stereo in an insured automobile's trunk.

8. See the decisions cited in Widiss, UNINSURED AND UNDERINSURED MOTORIST INSURANCE (1985), at § 5.2

9. Hart v. Traders and General Insurance Co., 487 S.W.2d 415 (Tex.Civ.App., Fort Worth, 1972).

In Sayers v. Safeco Insurance Company of America, ___ Mont. ___, 628 P.2d 659 (1981), 25 A.L.R. 4th 1, the claimant was standing between two vehicles and "leaning under the hood ∗ ∗ ∗ for the purpose of priming the carburetor ∗ ∗ ∗ when a car driven by ∗ ∗ ∗ [an uninsured motorist] struck the rear" of one of the vehicles, thereby trapping and severely injuring the claimant.

the claimants were either on the vehicle or were still close to the insured vehicle after having alighted. The claimant who was injured by an uninsured motorist while lying on a fender of a parked car to work on the fuel pump is a good illustration of such a case.[10]

In other situations, the act of alighting was clearly completed, and the claimant was simply standing near an insured vehicle when the accident occurred. For example, a Louisiana decision approved recovery by a deputy sheriff (under an endorsement providing coverage for occupants of the sheriff's vehicle) who was standing between the sheriff's vehicle and a stalled car in order to attach a pair of jumper cables. An uninsured motorist ran into the back of the stalled automobile, and pinned the deputy between the two parked cars.[11] Similarly, a Wisconsin decision upheld coverage for an insured who was pinned between two cars. The claimant was standing between the vehicles holding a spare tire that was intended to separate and protect the bumpers of the cars when the second car was used to push the first car. The claimant was injured when the rear car was struck by an uninsured motorist.[12] In such cases, judges have often focused on the fact that claimants were engaged in activities related to the use of an insured vehicle. A California decision, Cocking v. State Farm Mutual Automobile Insurance Company, clearly illustrates this judicial attitude. In the *Cocking* case the claimant was injured while standing several feet from the insured vehicle, preparing to put on snow chains.[13] The court viewed the preparations for affixing the snow chains as placing the claimant "in the requisite physical relationship to the car" to bring him within the protection afforded to persons who are "upon" an insured vehicle.[14]

In these cases, the courts interpreted the insurance policy terms so as to provide indemnification for persons engaged in a task related to the use, operation or maintenance of an insured vehicle. The courts concluded that coverage was provided for persons even though they were not upon, entering into or alighting from an insured vehicle.

---

10. In Sayers v. Safeco Insurance Company of America, ___ Mont. ___, 628 P.2d 659 (1981), the claimant was standing between two vehicles and "leaning under the hood ∗ ∗ ∗ for the purpose of priming the carburetor ∗ ∗ ∗ when a car driven by ∗ ∗ ∗ [an uninsured motorist] struck the rear" of one of the vehicles, thereby trapping and severely injuring the claimant.

11. Smith v. Girley, 260 La. 223, 255 So. 2d 748 (1971) [reversing the decision reported at 242 So.2d 32 (La.App., 1st Cir., 1970)].

12. Moherek v. Tucker, 69 Wis. 41, 230 N.W.2d 148 (1975). The court observed the insured "certainly had not severed his con-

nection with this vehicle and, to use the words from *Flaumenbaum,* he was still vehicle-oriented and therefore occupying the vehicle in the sense of being upon it as construed in the cases cited." The court also commented that "having found the word 'upon' ambiguous, we must apply the rule of strict construction of insurance policies resolving ambiguities against the insurer." *Id.,* 230 N.W.2d at p. 152.

13. Cocking v. State Farm Mutual Automobile Insurance Co., 6 Cal.App.3d 965, 86 Cal.Rptr. 193 (1st Dist., Div. 1, 1970).

14. Cocking v. State Farm Mutual Automobile Insurance Co., 6 Cal.App.3d 965 at p. 971, 86 Cal.Rptr. 193 at p. 197, (1st Dist., Div. 1, 1970).

(3) Claims Beyond the Scope of Protection

When the claimants are not engaged in an activity directly related to an insured vehicle and are not in proximity to an insured vehicle, denials of coverage have been sustained by the courts.[15] In general, the results in these cases seem reasonable. For example, in a New York case the claimant was held not to be an occupant of the insured vehicle after he had parked the car and had walked back to help an injured man who was lying in the center of a turnpike.[16] The court pointed out that:

> Here, the plaintiff's activities when he was struck were in no way related to the Aetna-insured vehicle. Had he been a pedestrian or a passenger in or operator of another vehicle passing that way, the activities placed him in the path of the "hit and run" driver would, doubtless, have still transpired. The only relation between the Aetna-insured vehicle and the accident was the fortuitous circumstance that he was riding in it when he observed the situation that prompted him to respond as a good samaritan.[17]

15. In Government Employees Insurance Company v. Keystone Insurance Company, 442 F.Supp. 1130 (E.D.Pa.1977), there was no coverage for a passenger who got out of the insured vehicle and walked to the uninsured vehicle to confront the uninsured motorist. The claimant was subsequently injured when he fell off the hood of the uninsured vehicle on which he had jumped in order to avoid being struck by the driver who had begun to accelerate the uninsured automobile.

In Southern Farm Bureau Casualty Insurance Co. v. Fields, 262 Ark. 144, 553 S.W.2d 278 (1977), the court defined "occupying" as "having physical contact with an insured vehicle" while "entering into or alighting from" the vehicle. The claimant, a child who had been a passenger on a school bus, was struck when she was about six feet from the bus in the middle of the opposite traffic lane.

In Menchaca v. Hiatt, 59 Cal.App.3d 117, 130 Cal.Rptr. 607 (2d Dist., Div. 5, 1976), the court concluded no coverage existed for a claimant who intended to cross a street from a movie theater to reach the insured car.

In Fidelity & Casualty Company of New York v. Garcia, 368 So.2d 1313 (Fla.App., 3d Dist., 1979), cert. denied 378 So.2d 344 (1979), the court held the claimant was not "alighting from" the insured vehicle when she had stepped from the passenger door of a truck, and was injured in the street after crossing in front of the truck in order to reach her home on the other side of the street.

In Breard v. Haynes, 394 So.2d 1282 (La. App., 1st Cir., 1981), writ denied 399 So.2d 598 (1981), the court concluded that the claimant was no longer an occupant of a vehicle, covered by a $50,000 uninsured motorist coverage, in which he had been a passenger after the vehicle had been parked following a minor collision. The claimant had walked about sixty to seventy feet away to converse with an off-duty police trainee who was directing traffic around the first accident. The claimant was seriously injured in a second accident caused by a negligent uninsured motorist some ten to fifteen minutes after the first accident. [The claimant did recover $10,000 under his own uninsured motorist coverage.]

16. Fischer v. Aetna Insurance Co., 65 Misc.2d 191, 317 N.Y.S.2d 669 (Special Term, Nassau County, Part III, 1971), affirmed 37 A.D.2d 917, 325 N.Y.S.2d 1012 (1971).

17. Id., 317 N.Y.S.2d at p. 671 (emphasis added).

(4) Observations

Analysis of the existing body of appellate case law involving this portion of the uninsured motorist insurance policy language leads to several general observations. *First,* viewed as a group, the decisions buttress the conclusion that judges are disposed to adopt interpretations of the uninsured motorist coverage terms that assure at least one source of indemnification for all reasonable claims. *Second,* when coverage disputes involve the terms that define "occupying", judges usually examine the facts to determine (1) whether the injury occurred while the claimant was in a zone or area that was within reasonable proximity to the insured vehicle, or (2) whether the claimant was injured while engaged in a task related to the operation, maintenance, or use of the vehicle. If either of these conditions is found to exist, judges usually conclude that claimants are entitled to coverage.

§ 4.8   Liability Insurance

§ 4.8(a)   Generally

Liability insurance was initially developed to provide an insured with indemnification for damages, up to the policy limits, for which the insured was responsible as a result of tort liability to a third person. The first liability insurance policies, for example, were purchased by employers as protection against tort liability to employees resulting from work injuries.

From a very early stage in the development of liability coverages, some of these coverages have been viewed by legislatures, courts, and the public as a means of providing for the protection of third parties — that is, liability insurance has been seen as a means of assuring compensation for persons who are injured in the event tortfeasors are financially irresponsible, as well as a source of indemnification for the liability of tortfeasors who are actually the insureds.[1]

Especially during the past half century, third parties have increasingly been treated as intended beneficiaries of motor vehicle liability insurance coverage.[2] This trend, which began in the 1920s, is clearly

---

§ 4.8(a)

1. The comments of an Illinois Court of Appeal are indicative of the attitudes of many courts. The opinion observes, for example, that "liability insurance abounds with public policy considerations, one of which is that the risk spreading theories of such policies should operate to afford members of the public maximum protection possible consonant with fairness to the insurer." The court goes on to conclude, "In this respect, we adopt the position that injured members of the general public are beneficiaries of liability insurance policies." Reagor v. Travelers Insurance Company, 92 Ill.App.3d 99, 47 Ill.Dec. 507, 415

N.E.2d 512 at p. 514 (First Dist., 3d Div., 1980).

2. For example, the Virginia Supreme Court has observed, "An injured party is a beneficiary under the tort-feasor's liability policy from the moment of injury if the vehicle was being operated with the consent of the owner named in the policy." United Services Automobile Association v. Nationwide Mutual Insurance Company, 218 Va. 681, 241 S.E.2d 784 at p. 788 (1978).

Also see Hughes v. Southeastern Fidelity Insurance Company, 340 So.2d 293 (Louisiana Supreme Court, 1976); Barrera v. State Farm Mutual Automobile Insurance

manifested by the provisions of various types of financial responsibility laws.[3] And, particularly in the 1970s, this public interest was evidenced in many states by the enactment of legislation that not only provided for no-fault automobile insurance, but that also made motor vehicle liability insurance mandatory.[4] Thus, accident victims who are injured by the negligent operation of motor vehicles are now the beneficiaries of legislatively mandated motor vehicle liability insurance in over thirty states.[5]

Other legislation which applies to the scope of coverage provided by liability insurance reflects similar concern with providing protection for accident victims. For example, the effects of an insured's insolvency, the possibility that the conduct of an insured tortfeasor will forfeit a liability insurance coverage, demands for non-derivative liability of vehicle owners, and the various types of tort immunity of insureds are all problems which have elicited specific legislative actions (as well as judicial concern[6]) producing modifications in coverage terms. In regard to each of these problems, legislation has been adopted which is designed to provide compensation for third parties in some instances when the status or conduct of an insured might otherwise afford an insurer an opportunity to avoid paying liability insurance benefits.[7]

§ 4.8(b)   Insolvency of an Insured: Insurance Policy Clauses and Statutory Provisions

In its original form, liability insurance was an agreement by an insurer to indemnify an insured against loss arising as a consequence of an insured's tort liability to a third person. As the relationship of the liability insurer to the insureds and the injured persons was originally structured, even after obtaining a tort judgment against an insured an injured victim was not entitled to proceed against the insurer when the insured either could not pay or did not pay. If the injured person sought payments directly from the insurer, the insurer could defend successfully because its obligation was only to the insured.[1] On the

---

Company, 71 Cal.2d 659 at pp. 676–677, 79 Cal.Rptr. 106 at p. 118, 456 P.2d 674 at p. 686 (1969).

See the discussion of coverage under omnibus clauses in § 4.7, above, and the discussion of automobile liability insurance in § 4.8, below.

3. See the discussion of interests in motor vehicle insurance in § 4.9, below and of financial responsibility legislation in § 4.10(b), below.

4. See the discussion of no-fault motor vehicle insurance in § 4.10.

5. See, e.g., Michigan Insurance Code § 24.13101 (1982 & Supp. 1985–86) (Security for Payment of Benefits); New Jersey Statutes Annotated § 39:6A–3 (1973) (Compulsory Automobile Insurance Coverage).

See generally *Compulsory Auto Insurance: How Well Does It Work?,* Journal of American Insurance Law (Spring, 1982), 20–23 at p. 21.

6. For example, see the discussion in § 4.8(b), below.

7. See § 4.8(b), § 4.8(c) and § 4.8(d), below.

The impact of varied liability insurance interests on claims processes and the distinctive conflicts of interests problems that result are considered in § 7.6, below.

§ 4.8(b)

1. In some states, legislation has been adopted that allows an injured person to proceed directly against the tortfeasor's insurer. See Louisiana—L.S.A. Revised Stat.

theory that the contract was one of "indemnity" in the narrowest possible sense, it was held in numerous cases that even an insured could not recover against the insurer without having previously sustained an actual loss by discharging the liability to the victim, as distinguished from merely being adjudged to be liable.[2] Thus, even though a tort judgment had been rendered against the insured, as a practical matter the victim might be unable to realize anything from either the insured or the insured's insurance company. The obvious inequity of such situations led to legislation in some states requiring that liability insurance contracts include a provision to the effect that the insolvency or bankruptcy of an insured shall not release an insurer from liability.[3] In time, similar legislation almost certainly would have been adopted in every state had not insurers revised the standard policy forms used for liability insurance to provide coverage without regard to an insured's solvency.

Insolvency provisions in liability insurance forms, which are commonly included in clauses entitled "Action Against Company," provide that an insured's bankruptcy or insolvency "shall not relieve the company of any of its obligations hereunder." Typically, these clauses also declare, "No action shall lie against the company * * * until the amount of the insured's obligation to pay shall have been finally determined either by judgment against the insured after actual trial or by written agreement of the insured, the claimant and the company."[4] This means that the right to proceed against an insurer[5] "matures" when the extent of the insured's tort liability is established by either a tort judgment or a settlement agreement.

It is generally recognized that a victim may proceed against an insurer, by garnishment or otherwise, with or without an insured's cooperation.[6] In at least this limited sense, then, a victim may be viewed as a "third party beneficiary" of the liability insurance contract.[7] Furthermore, as described in the following subsections, other

§ 22:655; Wisconsin Statutes Annotated § 803.04(2).

Also see Comment, *Compulsory Motor Vehicle Liability Insurance: Joinder of Insurers as Defendants in Actions Arising Out of Automobile Accidents*, 14 Wake Forest Law Review 200–214 (1978); Comment, *Direct Actions Against Insurance Companies: Should They Join the Party?*, 59 California Law Review 525–547 (1971).

2. See, e.g., Shea v. United States Fidelity Company, 98 Conn. 447, 120 A. 286 (1923); Hebojoff v. Globe Indemnity Company, 35 Cal.App. 390, 169 P. 1048 (2d Dist. 1917).

3. See, e.g., New York—McKinney's Insurance Law § 167.

4. See the forms in Appendix H.

5. Rights against the insurer under the payment provisions should be distin-

guished from the provisions providing for defense.

6. See, e.g., Hall v. Harleysville Mutual Casualty Company, 233 N.C. 339, 64 S.E.2d 160 (1951); Lachenmyer v. Central Mutual Insurance Company, 284 Ill.App. 391, 2 N.E.2d 177 (3d Dist.1936).

Also see Reagor v. Travelers Insurance Company, 92 Ill.App.3d 99, 47 Ill.Dec. 507, 415 N.E.2d 512 (1st Dist., 3d Div., 1980).

7. Other advantages of third party beneficiary status are also sometimes judicially conferred. In State Farm Mutual Automobile Insurance Company v. Kendall, 104 Ga.App. 481, 122 S.E.2d 139 (1961), for example, the court held that an attempted rescission of an automobile liability policy by the named insured and his insurer, after an accident involving an employee of the named insured who was driving with

developments in some, but not all,[8] jurisdictions have given victims additional rights as third party beneficiaries of motor vehicle liability insurance contracts.

§ 4.8(c) Non-derivative Liability Statutes: Legislatively Imposed Limitations on Defenses Available to Liability Insurers

Legislatures throughout the nation have been concerned with situations in which it would be undesirable for liability insurers to escape the obligation to provide indemnification for accident victims injured by negligent insureds.[1] Every state has now adopted legislative provisions designed to protect tort victims either by depriving liability insurers of certain defenses that would be good against the insureds,[2] or by limiting the use of such defenses in some circumstances. However, in several states the scope of the restrictions on insurers imposed by such legislation is limited to only a small percentage of the motor vehicle liability insurance contracts.[3] These laws, which are characterized in this

permission, did not defeat the rights of an injured person under the policy.

In Reagor v. Travelers Insurance Company, 92 Ill.App.3d 99 at p. 103, 47 Ill.Dec. 507, 415 N.E.2d 512 at p. 514 (1st Dist., 3rd Div., 1980), an Illinois Court of Appeal concluded that "an injured person has rights under the [liability] policy which vest at the time of the occurrence giving rise to his injuries" and that "the injured person must be given the opportunity to litigate the question of coverage under the liability insurance policy before his interest in the insurance may be terminated." The court also concluded that "where an insurer brings a declaratory judgment action to determine coverage of a claim made against its insured, the injured person is a necessary party to the suit * * *."

In Travelers Insurance Company v. Perez, 384 So.2d 971 (Fla.App., 3d Dist., 1980), the court concluded that the injured person "is a third party beneficiary of the contract between Travelers and its insured" and therefore "she has the right to bring a direct action against Travelers alleging the insurer's bad faith as grounds for an excess judgment."

Cf. Aetna Casualty and Surety Company v. Beane, 385 So.2d 1087 (Fla.App., 4th Dist., 1980).

Also see § 4.8(d), below concerning agreements, after an accident, between the insured and the insurer to assert an immunity that the policy declared would not be asserted.

8. *Cf.* Mercado v. Mitchell, 83 Wis.2d 17 at pp. 29–30, 264 N.W.2d 532 at p. 538

(1978); Lawreszuk v. Nationwide Insurance Company, 59 Ohio App.2d 111, 392 N.E.2d 1094 (Lorain County 1977).

§ 4.8(c)

1. In addition to the insolvency statutes discussed in § 4.8(b), see the discussion of the implementation of this objective through omnibus clauses and statutes requiring them in § 4.7(a), above.

2. See, e.g., Sobina v. Busby, 62 Ill.App. 2d 1, 210 N.E.2d 769 (1st Dist., 3d Div., 1965) (after notice of a suit in Illinois against its insured, insurer obtained a judgment in Alabama that its policy was *void ab initio* because of misrepresentation by the insured; *held,* the victims of the insured's negligence were unaffected by the Alabama judgment since they were neither parties to nor given notice of that action); Aetna Casualty & Surety Company v. O'Connor, 8 N.Y.2d 359, 170 N.E.2d 681, 207 N.Y.S.2d 679 (1960), 83 A.L.R.2d 1099 (1962) (*held,* policy issued under precompulsory insurance law assigned-risk plan can be cancelled for fraud but cannot be rescinded to the prejudice of innocent third parties).

3. See Annotation, *Cancellation of compulsory or "financial responsibility" automobile insurance,* 34 A.L.R.2d 1297–1306 (1954); Annotation, *Construction and application of provision of statute designed to prevent avoidance of automobile liability policy by reason of violation of its exclusions or conditions, or other terms,* 1 A.L.R. 2d 822–824 (1948).

discussion as "non-derivative liability" statutes, protect accident victims by restricting an insurer's right to avoid liability on the ground that an insured has not complied with some condition specified in the insurance contract. Most of these statutes are directed at insurance policy defenses that an insurer would otherwise be free to assert predicated either on late notice from an insured or on noncooperation by an insured.

The most common type of non-derivative liability legislation is a provision in state financial responsibility laws that apply to motor vehicle liability insurance policies which have been used to show financial responsibility [4] (that is, when an insurance policy has been certified to a public official in order for an insured to comply with the requirements that are imposed because the motorist either has been convicted of a serious driving offense or has failed to provide compensation for a victim of an accident). Motor vehicle liability insurance forms often explicitly provide that the coverage afforded by a motor vehicle insurance policy shall comply with the requirements of such statutes when a liability insurance policy has been certified to a regulatory authority.

A negative implication of non-derivative liability legislation, as well as coverage provisions which set forth the commitment by the insurer required by these statutes, is that the restrictions only apply to insurers when an insurance policy has been so certified. The vast majority of insurance contracts have not been used for such certification. Thus, in most cases, an insurer is only precluded from asserting a defense — based on an insured's failure to comply with a provision relating to conduct required after the occurrence of an insured event — when an insurance policy has been certified.[5]

In a few instances non-derivative coverage requirements in a state financial responsibility statute have been held to apply to all motor vehicle liability insurance policies issued in the state.[6] And in some states with compulsory liability insurance legislation, the statutes ei-

---

4. See, e.g., Nimeth v. Felling, 282 Minn. 460, 165 N.W.2d 237 (1969).

5. See, e.g., Porter v. Farmers Insurance Company of Idaho, 102 Idaho 132, 627 P.2d 311 (1981); State Farm Mutual Automobile Insurance Company v. Fahnstrom, 75 Ill.App.3d 736, 31 Ill.Dec. 605, 394 N.E.2d 807 (3d Dist.1979); Transport Indemnity Company v. Teter, 575 S.W.2d 780 at p. 787 (Mo.App., Kansas City Dist., 1978).

Also see Farmers Alliance Mutual Insurance Company v. Bakke, 619 F.2d 885 (10th Cir.1980) (applying the law of New Mexico), and the cases cited therein at 619 F.2d at p. 890; Annotation, *Policy provision extending coverage to comply with financial responsibility act as applicable to insured's first accident,* 8 A.L.R.3d 388–409 (1966).

Cf. Fidelity & Casualty Company v. McConnaughy, 228 Md. 1, 179 A.2d 117 (1962) (filing of form acknowledging coverage of one for whom proof of financial responsibility was not required does not preclude assertion of noncooperation.

6. See, e.g., Farmers Insurance Exchange v. Rose, 411 F.2d 270 (9th Cir.1969) (forecasting Arizona law; defense of fraud in application for insurance unavailable); Farm Bureau Automobile Insurance Company v. Martin, 97 N.H. 196, 84 A.2d 823 (1951), 29 A.L.R.2d 811 (1953) (defense of failure to give notice of replacement of insured vehicle unavailable).

Cf. Jenkins v. Mayflower Insurance Exchange, 93 Ariz. 287, 380 P.2d 145 (1963); Globe Indemnity Company v. Universal

ther explicitly extend or have been held to extend the non-derivative liability requirements to all motor vehicle liability policies.[7]

The standard clauses used by many insurers in motor vehicle insurance policies also provide that an insured shall reimburse a company for any payment the company must make, but would not otherwise have been obligated to make, as a result of non-derivative liability requirements.[8]

§ 4.8(d) Liability Insurance and the Immunity of Insureds From Tort Liabilities

Many entities, such as charitable institutions or governmental units, have been accorded an immunity from tort liability by common law decisions.[1] During the twentieth century the scope of such immunities has been substantially reduced by both judicial decisions and legislative enactments. Especially in light of the judicial trends in regard to these tort immunities, many institutions that have been accorded immunities (such as charities) have purchased liability insurance. Moreover, having acquired liability insurance, institutions have often adopted the view that it is desirable that the insurance be used to indemnify persons who have been injured even though the institution might be entitled to assert an immunity as a defense to a tort claim. To assure that insurers will not avoid liability by invoking the insured's immunity, some institutions specifically arrange for an endorsement to be added to liability insurance policies declaring either (1) that the insurer will not deny liability on the basis of the immunity and will not assert the insured's immunity as a defense in any litigation,[2] or (2) that the insurer agrees to allow the insured to decide whether the immunity will be asserted in response to a tort claim.

In some instances, the contention has been made that the added premium an insured must pay to obtain an endorsement to liability insurance by which an insurer in effect waives either the institution's

Underwriters Insurance Company, 201 Cal. App.2d 9, 20 Cal.Rptr. 73 (1962).

7. See, e.g., Lane v. Iowa Mutual Insurance Company, 258 N.C. 318, 128 S.E.2d 398 (1962) (failure of insured to give insurer notice of suit did not relieve insurer of liability to insured's victims); Andriakos v. Cavanaugh, 350 So.2d 561 (Fla.App., 2d Dist., 1977).

But see, e.g., National Grange Mutual Liability Company v. Fino, 13 A.D.2d 10, 212 N.Y.S.2d 684 (3d Dept. 1961) (noncooperation of insured allowed as a defense to claims of third parties against company).

Also see Annotation, *Failure to give notice, or other lack of cooperation by insured, as defense to action against compulsory liability insurer by injured member of the public,* 31 A.L.R.2d 645–657 (1953); Annotation, *Liability of insurer, under compul-* *sory statutory vehicle liability policy, to injured third persons, notwithstanding insured's failure to comply with policy conditions, as measured by policy limits or by limits of financial responsibility act,* 29 A.L.R.2d 817–818 (1953).

8. See § 5.4(b), note 2, below.

Also see Annotation, *Validity and construction of liability policy provision requiring insured to reimburse insurer for payments made under policy,* 29 A.L.R.3d 291–320 (1970).

§ 4.8(d)

1. See Prosser & Keeton, TORTS (5th edition, 1984), at § 131 and § 133.

2. See, e.g., Taylor v. Knox County Board of Education, 292 Ky. 767, 167 S.W.2d 700 (1942), 145 A.L.R. 1333 (1943).

tort immunity or the right to invoke the insured's tort immunity is an improper use of the purchaser's "trust" funds. This contention seems to be based on an unduly narrow conception of what is an appropriate concern by the persons responsible for managing a charitable or governmental institution for the victims of tortious conduct. Surely charitable institutions, such as hospitals, ought to be allowed to secure liability insurance that will provide indemnification for the victims of negligent conduct by their employees.

The propriety of a public governing body, such as a county or city government, using funds to acquire liability insurance that in effect "waives" a tort immunity may be subject to state legislative actions regulating what types of expenditures can be made. However, the societal interest in assuring indemnification for accident victims is clearly substantial, and therefore in the absence of a clearly manifested legislative prohibition it should be held that governmental officials who are authorized to purchase liability insurance are not misusing funds in paying the added premium necessary to obtain such an endorsement.[3]

The Right to Invoke a Tort Immunity

When an institution with a partial or complete immunity from tort liability has obtained liability insurance coverage, a question [that may arise is] whether either the liability insurer or the insured retains any discretion in regard to invoking an immunity or making payments equivalent to those that would have been due in the absence of the immunity. This issue may arise (1) when the insurance policy includes terms by which the insurer has agreed to allow the insured to decide whether the immunity will be used, (2) when the insurance policy states that the insurer has waived the right to invoke the tort immunity, or (3) when there are no relevant provisions in the insurance policy.[4]

One type of immunity endorsement provides that the insurer will not assert the insured's immunity except with the written consent of the insured. When an immunity endorsement contains such a consent clause, it indicates that the insured and insurer have agreed[5] that the immunity is to be preserved so that the waiver of the immunity is subject to the insured's discretion. An insurer's premium rate for such an endorsement may, of course, be set in contemplation of the possibility that the insured will not consent to the insurer's using an immunity as a defense. Thus, an insurance coverage with such a clause is likely to be virtually as expensive as one in which the insurer unqualifiedly

---

3. A contrary result was reached in Pohland v. City of Sheboygan, 251 Wis. 20, 27 N.W.2d 736 (1947), later overruled by Marshall v. City of Green Bay, 18 Wis.2d 496, 118 N.W.2d 715 (1963).

4. In Miree v. United States, 242 Ga. 126, 249 S.E.2d 573 at p. 578 (1978), *affirmed* 588 F.2d 453 (5th Cir.1979), the court observed that a "county does not waive this immunity in the purchase of a contract of liability insurance, even though the policy of insurance may include a clause allegedly waiving immunity."

5. The fact that an endorsement is attached increases the likelihood that the purchaser will be aware of it. Even so, it may be doubted that the purchaser always knows and fully understands this type of provisions.

agrees not to assert the immunity. Nevertheless, even though there may be no savings in premium charges, there are several reasons why an insured might prefer this approach. An insured institution might elect to purchase coverage with such a consent clause in order to preserve the immunity defense for use in instances when a claim is asserted that appears to be unjustified, but the third party's claim would be difficult or expensive to defeat on other grounds. Furthermore, the right of an insured to assert the immunity might also prove to be a significant factor in settlement negotiations. This last consideration might prove to be particularly important for an insured institution when the claims resulting from an insured occurrence exceed the coverage limits.

When an insurance contract includes an express provision which allows the insured to decide whether to use its tort immunity, it is debatable whether courts should enforce the terms of the insurance contract that allow the insured to invoke the immunity.[6] A serious objection to the enforceability of such a provision is that it gives an insured an opportunity to exercise essentially an unpoliced choice between favoring an insurer and favoring a victim after an accident, and that such discretion in effect invites fraud and chicanery.

The most cogent argument, in support of enforcing a provision conferring discretion on the insured, is the general public interest in preserving and protecting freedom of contract. However, if the interest in preserving the parties freedom of contract is the reason for allowing an insured to exercise such discretion, the cases involving an express provision are clearly distinguishable from instances in which an institution purchases a liability insurance policy that does not contain any provision which addresses questions about whether the immunity may be asserted on the insured's behalf by the insurer. Thus, while enforcing an explicit agreement which confers discretion on an insured can be defended as an appropriate resolution of a close and debatable issue, the judicial creation of a rule allowing unpoliced discretion in the absence of an explicit provision in the endorsement does not rest on a comparable foundation and generally seems inappropriate.[7]

When an entity that is immune from tort liability purchases a liability insurance policy which is silent with respect to decisions about the assertion of the immunity as a defense, a strong case exists for the proposition that a court should not fill the "gap" with a rule allowing the insured to exercise unpoliced discretion. However, courts often

---

6. In contrast, as discussed below, when the contract expressly waives the immunity, it seems likely that in most instances the immunity is not available as a defense.

7. This is a specific illustration of a principle of general application that it is undesirable to give one person an unpoliced discretion to make a choice decisive of a conflict of interests between two others. For other instances in which this principle might be invoked in insurance law, see § 4.11(e) at note 10, below, and § 7.9(c), below.

Cf. Internal Revenue Service v. Blais, 612 F.Supp. 700 at p. 703 (D.Mass.1985) (Keeton, J.) (applying the principle to a claim of discretion in the Internal Revenue Service to settle with one of two taxpayers in a way that would adversely affect the other's interest).

have held that the insured's immunity continues to be available to both the insured and the insurer.[8] In such decisions, courts typically reason that the agreement of the insurer is to pay on behalf of the insured any liability imposed by law, and no such liability exists when the immunity is invoked. Although courts in several jurisdictions have reached a contrary result,[9] these decisions probably are still appropriately characterized as a minority rule.

When an insurance contract specifies that the insurer will not avail itself of immunity defenses available to the insured, it seems likely that courts will find that the insurer is precluded from asserting the insured's immunity.[10]

If there is a compelling public interest [11] in regard to abolition of the common law rule which formerly afforded the insured a tort immunity,[12] a persuasive argument can also be made that liability insurance should provide coverage even when there is an explicit provision in the insurance policy that excludes liability for circumstances that were previously within the scope of the immunity.[13]

8. See, e.g., McGrath Bldg. Company v. City of Bettendorf, 248 Iowa 1386, 85 N.W.2d 616 (1957), 68 A.L.R.2d 1429 (1959); Mann v. County Board of Arlington County, 199 Va. 169, 98 S.E.2d 515 (1957); Kesman v. School District of Fallowfield Township, 345 Pa. 457, 29 A.2d 17 (1942).

Cf. Snyder v. State Department of Health and Mental Hygiene, 40 Md.App. 364, 391 A.2d 863 at p. 868 (1978) ("In the absence of a statute, a County does not become liable for torts because it carries insurance.")

Also see Espinosa v. Southern Pacific Transportation Company, 291 Or. 853, 635 P.2d 638 (1981) (Oregon Tort Claims Act provides for limited tort liability and applies regardless of the purchase of insurance in excess of the specified limited liability so that a school district's purchase of insurance in excess of the statutory limits of liability did not constitute a waiver of its sovereign immunity to the extent of the excess coverage); Sambs v. Brookfield, 66 Wis.2d 296, 224 N.W.2d 582 (1975) (mere purchase by a municipality of a liability insurance policy providing coverage beyond the statutory limit does not constitute a waiver of that statutory limit by the municipality).

9. See, e.g., Morehouse College v. Russell, 219 Ga. 717, 135 S.E.2d 432 (1964); Geislinger v. Watkins, 269 Minn. 116, 130 N.W.2d 62 (1964); O'Connor v. Boulder Colorado Sanitarium Association, 105 Colo. 259, 96 P.2d 835 (1939), 133 A.L.R. 819 (1941).

Cf. Vendrell v. School District No. 26C Malheur County, 226 Or. 263, 360 P.2d 282 (1961). In regard to the *Vendrell* decision, see the subsequent discussion of the case in light of various legislative actions in Espinosa v. Southern Pacific Transportation Company, 291 Or. 853, 635 P.2d 638 (1981).

Also see Annotation, *Immunity of nongovernmental charity from liability for damages in tort*, 25 A.L.R.2d 29–200 at p. 89 and at pp. 139–142 (1952).

10. See, e.g., Stanhope v. Brown County, 90 Wis.2d 823, 280 N.W.2d 711 (1979); Bollinger v. Schneider, 64 Ill.App.3d 758, 21 Ill.Dec. 522, 381 N.E.2d 849 (3d Dist. 1978).

But cf. Lansing v. County of McLean, 69 Ill.2d 562, 14 Ill.Dec. 543, 372 N.E.2d 822 (1978).

11. Consider the comment in Stanhope v. Brown County, 90 Wis.2d 823, at p. 852, 280 N.W.2d 711 at p. 723 (1979):

"We conclude, in the absence of an expression of legislative intent to the contrary, that the public interest in compensating persons injured by wrongful acts of the government takes precedence over other goals."

12. In Lamb v. Redemptorist Fathers of Georgia, Inc., 111 Ga.App. 491, 142 S.E.2d 278 at p. 285 (1965), one of the concurring opinions observed that: "The General Assembly has authorized political subdivisions of the State to procure liability insurance and *to the extent of any insurance carried has removed governmental immunity as a defense* * * *." (Emphasis added).

13. When an insurance contract is silent in regard to the possible immunity

The trend toward abandonment of tort immunities is soundly supported in the public interest that favors indemnification for accident victims, and it is being applied with increasing vigor by the courts.[14] It may be argued that the public interest in the abandonment of the tort immunity should apply with equal force to determinations about the scope of coverage provided by insurance contracts. However, the imposition of such a result would entail a judicially imposed restructuring of the contractual arrangement. Arguably, such "regulatory" modifications of insurance contracts are appropriately the responsibility of legislatures, rather than judges.[15] And some states have taken this step. For example, in Arkansas legislation now provides that, "notwithstanding the terms of the policy itself * * *," an injured person shall have a cause of action against the liability insurer of "any cooperative nonprofit corporation, association or organization or * * * any other organization or association * * * not subject to suit for tort * * *." [16]

§ 4.9 Automobile Insurance

§ 4.9(a) Generally

Motor vehicles in general, and automobiles in particular, have presented increasingly significant accident risk and compensation problems in the United States. In the 1920s, state legislatures began to seek ways to ensure that the victims of highway accidents would be able to secure compensation when they were injured, especially when injuries resulted from the negligent operation of a motor vehicle. Although attaining this goal has proved to be very difficult, the various legislative acts that states have adopted to improve the prospects for indemnification have had a very significant influence on both the development of coverage afforded by motor vehicle insurance and the

defense, the issue sometimes evolves into a question of whether an implicit agreement existed in the absence of any express provision in the insurance contract. The judicial precedents reflect the conflict already noted. See, e.g., Walton v. Glens Falls Indemnity Co., 192 F.2d 189 (5th Cir. 1951), decided for the insurer, following what were conceived to be the implications of a decision of the Supreme Court of Georgia in the related tort suit. The Georgia law may now be different, however. See note 12, above.

The coverage issue might also be considered in terms of whether a victim has any rights as a third party beneficiary of the insurance contract.

14. Using that justification alone in this context proves too much, however, because it supports denial of the tort immunity irrespective of the existence of an applicable liability insurance policy.

Also see Herbert E. Greenstone, *Abolition of Intrafamilial Immunity,* 7 Forum 82–89 (1972).

15. *Cf.* Vendrell v. School District No. 26C Malheur County, 226 Or. 263, 360 P.2d 282 (1961).

16. Arkansas Statutes §§ 66–3240, 66–3242(2) (1980 and Supp.1983). See Michael v. St. Paul Mercury Indemnity Company, 92 F.Supp. 140 (W.D.Ark.1950). Perhaps the statute was intended to protect victims, being enacted in the hope that if hospitals were deprived of the opportunity to buy coverage against only the limited liability existing under the immunity rule, they would then choose the more expensive coverage that waives the immunity within policy limits rather than choosing not to insure at all.

acquisition of such insurance by the owners of vehicles (both individuals and businesses). Moreover, these statutes, as well as the underlying societal interest represented by such legislation, have affected the judicial treatment of disputes that involve provisions in various coverages — especially the liability insurance, medical payments insurance, uninsured motorist insurance, and underinsured motorist insurance — that are included in automobile insurance policies.

When coverage questions arise in regard to automobile insurance, there are numerous factors that are significant, and it sometimes is relatively difficult to predict with certainty either exactly who will be insureds or under what circumstances persons will be entitled to coverage benefits. The discussion in this section focuses on the persons whose interests are insured by the several types of automobile insurance coverages — including liability insurance, medical payments insurance, uninsured motorist insurance, and underinsured motorist insurance — that provide indemnification for bodily injuries, and considers some of the coverage questions that have arisen in regard to who is insured by these coverages.[1]

Insured Persons

The identity of the principal insured for all of the coverages in the typical automobile insurance policy can easily be determined by examining the policy because the person who purchases the coverage is specifically identified as a "named insured" on a page that is characterized by designations such as the "declarations page," "declarations schedule," or simply the "declarations."[2] In many instances, a purchaser explicitly designates other persons who are to be insured to the same extent as the purchaser, and such individuals are usually identified or characterized in the insurance contract as "named insureds" or "designated insureds." The definitions in newer insurance forms typically provide that throughout the policy the term "you" and "your" are intended to refer to the " 'named insured' shown in the Declarations" and the "spouse if a resident of the same household."[3]

§ 4.9(b) Liability Insurance for the Operators of an "Insured" Vehicle

The liability coverage in automobile insurance policies generally provides that insureds — that is, the covered persons, including the named insured and his or her family members who reside in the same household — are covered "for the ownership, maintenance, or use of *any* auto." This means each of these persons is insured both as an

1. Other problems concerning the scope of protection under motor vehicle insurance are considered elsewhere. See § 4.7 (omnibus clauses), § 4.8 (liability insurance generally), and § 4.10 (no-fault insurance), § 5.2(b) ("ownership, maintenance and use"), and § 7.2 (claims processes under liability insurance).

2. Concerning the nature of the risks transferred, see Chapter 5, below.

3. Insurance Services Office, Personal Auto Policy PP 00 01: Definitions (Ed. 6–80), at p. 1.

operator of the vehicle designated in the insurance policy, and, under specified circumstances, when driving other automobiles. Furthermore, most automobile insurance policies, as discussed in the next subsection, provide coverage for specific vehicles that are identified in the insurance policy, so that individuals who are using such vehicles with the owner's permission are also "insureds." Therefore, in order to determine whether a liability insurance policy provides coverage for an automobile accident, it is often essential to analyze the alleged tortfeasor's relationship not only to the person who obtained the policy, but also to the vehicle involved in an accident.

Identifying Covered Vehicles

Automobile liability insurance in the United States generally provides coverage for particular vehicles which are identified in the "declarations" so that permitted users of those vehicles are insured. Thus, usually the declarations page of the insurance policy specifically identifies one or more vehicles that are to be covered.[1] When an insured vehicle is being used with the permission of the owner, the policy terms extend coverage [2] for the operation of that vehicle under the circumstances specified in the insurance policy, which include nearly all the expected uses of a vehicle.[3] In some situations, a single motor vehicle insurance policy will be used to cover a large number of vehicles, in which case the arrangement is commonly referred to as a "fleet" policy.

(1) Pre–1966 Coverage Terms

In automobile insurance policies based on the pre–1966 standard forms, the basic statement of liability coverage usually declared that the insurance company agreed "to pay on behalf of the insured * * * damages * * * arising out of the ownership, maintenance or use of *the* automobile."[4] The scope of coverage was expanded by the clause

§ 4.9(b)

1. When an insured has more than one vehicle to insure, either a separate policy is issued or else each of the automobiles to be covered is described on the face of the policy or in a schedule that is a part of the policy.

In some cases, liability coverage may turn on the "ownership" of a vehicle without regard to the identification of specific vehicles in the declarations. For example, umbrella insurance policies — which are frequently acquired to provide the purchaser with liability insurance coverage in excess of that which is provided by a primary automobile insurance policy, as well as for other risks — typically afford coverage for any vehicle owned by an insured. In Kelly v. Aetna Casualty & Surety Company, 100 Wn.2d 401, 670 P.2d 267 (1983), the court affirmed that the policy did not provide coverage for accident because the insured was "only listed as the legal owner to secure his interest [having financed his son's acquisition of the vehicle by a personal loan] in the car" and that the insured was "not an 'owner'" because he was not the person "able to give the requisite permission for the vehicle's use" — that is, he did exercise control over the use of the vehicle. *Id.,* 670 P.2d at p. 271.

2. See the discussion of omnibus coverage in § 4.7, above.

3. See the discussion of "use" in § 5.2(b).

4. Emphasis added. See, e.g., the 1955 Standard Basic Automobile Liability Policy, in Norman E. Risjord & June M. Austin, Automobile Liability Insurance Cases,

which defined the term "automobile" to include — under restricted circumstances — a "trailer," a "temporary substitute automobile," and a "newly acquired automobile," [5] as well as the automobile described in the declarations on the face of the policy.

Coverage was further extended — that is, beyond the scope specified by the basic coverage declaration in the pre–1966 forms — through the inclusion in most insurance policies of a provision under the caption "Use of Other Automobiles," which is often referred to as a "Drive Other Cars" or "DOC" coverage clause.[6] Furthermore, both the definition of "automobile" and the DOC clause were applicable to some extent to the medical payments and collision coverages, as well as to liability coverages.[7] The principle of the DOC clause was to extend coverage when other vehicles were used [8] by an insured.[9] These cover-

Standard Provisions and Appendix 16 (1964).

5. See AUTOMOBILE LIABILITY INSURANCE CASES (1964), at pp. 20–22.

6. In the 1958 revision, the DOC coverage was provided along with coverage of the insured's own vehicle in a single coverage clause, and the omnibus clause was revised to include the enumeration of persons insured under the DOC coverage:

"Persons Insured

"The following are insureds under Part I:

"(b) With respect to a non-owned automobile,

"(1) the named insured,

"(2) any relative, but only with respect to a private passenger automobile or trailer, provided the actual use thereof is with the permission of the owner * * *."

See Risjord & Austin, AUTOMOBILE LIABILITY INSURANCE CASES (1964), at p. 56. The "permission of the owner" provision did not appear in the 1955 form (see *Id.*, at pp. 22–24).

There have been holdings that in these circumstances permission is irrelevant to the question whether DOC coverage was applicable. See e.g., Sperling v. Great American Indemnity Company, 7 N.Y.2d 442, 199 N.Y.2d 465, 166 N.E.2d 482 (1960), reargument denied 8 N.Y.2d 785, 201 N.Y.S.2d 1027, 168 N.E.2d 136 (1960) (insurer liable under "family" policy not containing requirement of permission for judgment against sixteen-year-old family member who at the time of the accident was driving a stolen car and fleeing from the police). *Cf.* Home Indemnity Company v. Ware, 285 F.2d 852 (3d Cir.1960) (applying Delaware law) (insured's liability policy provided coverage for liability resulting

from collision caused by insured's step-son while driving a stolen car). The "permission of the owner" provision was added in spite of the volume of litigation produced by the permission requirements of omnibus clauses generally. Also see § 4.7(b), above.

It has been successfully contended, however, that the "permission of the owner" requirement qualifies only sub-part (b) of the quoted clause and not the named insured's coverage under subpart (a), the failing contention of the insurer being that the structure of the clause clearly evidences an intent that the requirement qualify both subparts (a) and (b). See, e.g., McMichael v. American Insurance Company, 351 F.2d 665 (8th Cir.1965) (applying Missouri law); Harleysville Mutual Casualty Company v. Nationwide Mutual Insurance Company, 248 S.C. 398, 150 S.E.2d 233 (1966).

7. See, e.g., Risjord & Austin, AUTOMOBILE LIABILITY INSURANCE CASES (1964), at pp. 20–24.

8. An issue sometimes arises with respect to whether the individual claiming coverage under a DOC clause was actually "using" the vehicle involved in the accident. See, e.g., Potomac Insurance Company v. Ohio Casualty Insurance Company, 188 F.Supp. 218 (N.D.Cal.1960) (male passenger was negligent in distracting female driver, thereby causing an accident; held, he was not using the vehicle so as to qualify for DOC coverage under the policy of which he was the named insured).

But cf. decisions concerning the meaning of "use" of an automobile in other contexts, § 4.7(b)(1), above and § 5.2(b), below.

9. However, exceptions or limitations were imposed on the coverage. For example, clause V(c) of the 1955 form read:

"This insuring agreement does not apply:

age terms were designed to provide insurance for the insured during the occasional use of some vehicle other than the insured's own,[10] but

"(1) to any automobile owned by or furnished for regular use to either the named insured or a member of the same household other than a private chauffeur or domestic servant of such named insured or spouse;

"(2) to any accident arising out of the operation of an automobile sales agency, repair shop, service station, storage garage or public parking place;

"(3) [under coverages A, B or C–1], to any automobile while used in a business or occupation of such named insured or spouse except a private passenger automobile operated or occupied by such named insured, spouse, private chauffeur or domestic servant;

"(4) under coverages E–1, E–2 or E–3, to any loss when there is any other insurance which would apply thereto in the absence of this insuring agreement, whether such other insurance covers the interest of the named insured or spouse, the owner of the automobile or any other person or organization."

10. See, e.g., Alabama Farm Bureau Mutual Insurance Company v. Carswell, 374 So.2d 250 at p. 252 (Ala.1979); Dairyland Insurance Company v. Ward, 83 Wn. 2d 353, 517 P.2d 966 at pp. 969–970 (1974).

Cf. Carr v. Home Indemnity Company, 404 Pa. 27, 170 A.2d 588, 83 A.L.R.2d 922 (1961) (insured is not covered while driving a car owned by brother residing at same address since it is not a car "not owned by * * * any relative").

Cf. Schoenknecht v. Prairie State Farmers Insurance Association, 27 Ill.App.2d 83, 169 N.E.2d 148 (2d Dist., 1st Div., 1960) (car regularly used by insured during his employment was not excluded as a car provided for his regular use when accident occurred while he was using it for personal pleasure outside the scope of his employment).

Also see Palmer v. Glens Falls Insurance Company, 58 Wn.2d 88, 360 P.2d 742 (2d Dep't 1961) (insured regularly used son-in-law's car for business purposes for over two months, but accident occurred when he was using it with owner's consent for trip to a repair shop; *held,* special use interrupted regular use and DOC coverage applied); Texas Casualty Insurance Company v. Wyble, 333 S.W.2d 668 (Tex.Civ.App., San Antonio, 1960, no writ history) (insured claimed medical payments coverage for injury to son incurred in an accident

with an automobile while the son was riding on a motor scooter owned by him; held, scooter was not an "automobile" owned by or furnished for the use of a member of the family).

See generally, Annotation, *Exclusion from "drive other cars" provision of automobile liability insurance policy of other automobile owned, hired, or regularly used by insured or member of the household,* 86 A.L.R.2d 937–961. (1962); Annotation, *Construction of provision excluding automobile used in insured's "business or occupation" from nonowned automobile coverage of automobile liability policy,* 85 A.L.R.2d 502–505 (1962); Annotation, *What is a "non-owned" automobile within the meaning of the coverage clause of an automobile liability policy,* 83 A.L.R.2d 926–930 (1962).

Coverage otherwise excluded under the DOC coverage is under some circumstances afforded by other policy provisions, such as the temporary-substitute automobile provision or the after-acquired-automobile provision. See, e.g., Imperial Casualty & Indemnity Company v. Relder, 308 F.2d 761 (8th Cir.1962) (applying Missouri law; insured purchased a second car and insured it with another company but, after an accident involving the second car, reported the purchase to the insurer of his original car and claimed coverage under the after-acquired-automobile clause of that policy; *held,* for the insured since the policy required notice of the purchase of another automobile only during the policy period, which notice the insured had given, and nothing in the policy indicated that the coverage applied only to after-acquired replacements of the described vehicle); Densmore v. Hartford Accident & Indemnity Company, 221 F.Supp. 652 (W.D.Pa.1963) (applying New York law; after demolishing his own car, insured stole another car with which he had an accident; *held,* coverage under substitute automobile clause of policy on demolished car); McKee v. Exchange Insurance Association, 270 Ala. 518, 120 So.2d 690 (1960) (insured's car was demolished in an accident, after which he was in another accident while driving an automobile owned by his mother, who was a resident of the same household; *held,* coverage under the substitute automobile provision of the insured's policy); Mid-Continent Casualty Company v. West, 351 P.2d 398 (Okl. 1959) (insured had an accident while on a business trip in his father's car, which was

without allowing a purchaser to in effect insure several cars for the price of coverage for one vehicle.

(2) Post–1966 Coverage Terms

In 1966, the standard automobile liability insurance policy forms were thoroughly revised. The 1966 and later forms substitute a phrase such as "*any* automobile" (or "the owned automobile or *any* non-owned automobile") for "*the* automobile" in the basic statement of the liability coverages.[11] The effect of this change was to set forth a more inclusive basic statement of the scope of coverage that serves some of the functions previously accomplished by separate clauses that provide coverage for a temporary-substitute-automobile, newly-acquired-automobile, and DOC coverage. Exceptions to this broad coverage statement are commonly set out at the end of Section II of the form (under the title "Persons Insured") in the following language:

> "This insurance does not apply to bodily injury or property damage arising out of (1) a non-owned automobile used in the conduct of any partnership or joint venture of which the insured is a partner or member and which is not designated in this policy as a named insured, or (2) if the named insured is a partnership, an automobile owned by or registered in the name of a partner thereof."[12]

Essentially the same approach is employed in the current standard forms. The Definitions Section of the Personal Auto Policy, which increasingly is the policy form used by insurers throughout the country, states:

being used because the tires on his car were too dangerous for use on a long trip; *held,* coverage under the substitute automobile provision of his policy, the fact that new tires had been ordered for his car evidencing that the use of the father's car was more than merely for convenience); Baxley v. State Farm Mutual Automobile Liability Insurance Company, 241 S.C. 332, 128 S.E.2d 165 (1962) (insured was driving wife's car when involved in an accident; although "insured" was defined to include spouse, *held,* coverage under substitute automobile provision since the involved vehicle was not owned by the named insured either solely or jointly with his wife).

But see, e.g., Gabrelcik v. National Indemnity Company, 269 Minn. 445, 131 N.W.2d 534 (1964) (while her regular taxi was disabled, insured used for her taxi business a car lent by her husband, which was registered in the name of his sole proprietorship; *held,* no coverage); Fullilove v. United States Casualty Company, 240 La. 859, 125 So.2d 389 (1960) (insured used his son's car on a business trip since the tires on his own car were in poor condition; *held,* no coverage since on the day of the accident in the son's car the insured's car was being used by his wife for in-town driving, which had become the "normal use" of the car).

11. Emphasis added. See the forms in Appendix G and Appendix H.

12. *Ibid.*

For illustrations of situations that produced litigation under earlier forms that appear to be governed by this exclusion, see Mission Insurance Company v. Feldt, 62 Cal.2d 97, 41 Cal.Rptr. 293, 396 P.2d 709 (1964) (insured, under a policy covering him only while driving cars he did not own, covered in an accident that occurred while driving a car owned by a joint venture in which he was a partner); Farley v. American Automobile Insurance Company, 137 W.Va. 455, 72 S.E.2d 520 (1952), 34 A.L.R.2d 933 (1954) (partnership covered by policy on car owned by it for accident involving car owned by one partner, which had been temporarily substituted for partnership car).

" 'Your covered auto' means:

1. Any vehicle shown in the Declarations.

2. Any of the following types of vehicles on the date you become the owner:

     a. a private passenger auto; or

     b. a pickup, panel truck or van, not used in any business or occupation other than farm or ranching.

     This provision applies only if you:

     a. acquire the vehicle during the policy period; and

     b. ask us to insure it within 30 days after you become the owner.

4. Any auto or trailer you do not own while used as a temporary substitute for any other vehicle described in this definition which is out of normal use because of its:

     a. breakdown;

     b. repair;

     c. servicing;

     d. loss; or

     e. destruction."[13]

This coverage definition provides very extensive protection for an insured, but it is subject to several exclusions that are set forth in each of the specific coverage sections of the policy. For example, the liability coverage, which is set forth as a Part A in most policies, includes the following exclusions:

"A. We do not provide Liability Coverage for any person:

* * *

4. For bodily injury to an employee of that person during the course of employment. This exclusion does not apply to bodily injury to a domestic employee unless worker's compensation benefits are required or available for that domestic employee.

5. For that person's liability arising out of the ownership or operation of a vehicle while it is being used to carry persons or property for a fee. This exclusion does not apply to a share-the-expense car pool.

6. While employed or otherwise engaged in the business or occupation of:

a. selling;

b. repairing;

c. servicing;

13. Insurance Services Office, Personal Auto Policy PP 00 01: Definitions (Ed. 6–80).

    d.   storing; or

    e.   parking;

         vehicles designed for use mainly on public highways. This includes road testing and delivery. This exclusion does not apply to the ownership, maintenance or use of your covered auto by:

    a.   you;

    b.   any family member; or

    c.   any partner, agent or employee of you or any family member." [14]

In general, it appears that the interests of policyholders and the public are well served by the coverage afforded by these coverage terms.[15]

§ 4.9(c)   Liability Insurance Exclusions

(1) Specified Persons, Classes of Persons, and Family Members

    Automobile liability insurance policies often include clauses designed to exclude coverage for either specific persons or classes of persons. For example, policies frequently state that the liability insurance does not apply to "bodily injury to any insured or any member of the family of an insured residing in the same household as the insured," or words of similar import.[1] In some instances, an exclusion may be included that applies specifically to the named insureds — that is, the clause states that coverage does not apply to "bodily injury to or death of any person who is a named insured." [2] In the absence of statutory provisions precluding the use of such coverage exclusions (as, for example, legislation that requires specific coverage to be provided),[3] such restrictive provisions have usually been upheld by the courts.

---

14. Insurance Services Office, Personal Auto Policy PP 00 01: Part A, Liability Coverage—Exclusions (Ed. 6–80).

15. See the discussion in § 4.9(d), below, on the evolution of the standard coverage terms for motor vehicle policies.

§ 4.9(c)

1. See, e.g., State Farm Mutual Automobile Insurance Company v. Sivey, 404 Mich. 51, 272 N.W.2d 555 (1978); California Casualty Indemnity Exchange v. Hoskin, 82 Cal.App.3d 789, 147 Cal.Rptr. 348 (5th Dist.1978).

It has been noted that the weight of authority supports coverage of an additional insured's liability for injury to a named insured when the policy contains no exclusion clause regarding such claims. See § 4.7(b)(3), above. Those precedents have little weight, however, for cases involving an exclusion clause when the issue becomes primarily one of construction of that clause.

Also see Annotation, *Validity, construction, and application of provision of automobile liability policy excluding from coverage injury or death of member of family or household of insured*, 46 A.L.R.3d 1024–1056 (1972).

2. See, e.g., Frye v. Theige, 253 Wis. 596, 34 N.W.2d 793 (1948), 50 A.L.R.2d 124 (1954).

3. *Cf.* State Farm Mutual Automobile Insurance Company v. Sivey, 404 Mich. 51, 272 N.W.2d 555 (1978).

In some states, legislation specifically provides for such exclusions. See Farmers Insurance Exchange v. Cocking, 29 Cal.3d 383, 173 Cal.Rptr. 846, 628 P.2d 1 (En banc 1981); California Casualty Indemnity Exchange v. Haskin, 82 Cal.App.3d 789, 147 Cal.Rptr. 348 (5th Dist.1978), and West's Ann. California Insurance Code § 11580.1(c)(5) (1972 and 1985 Supp.).

Insurers have developed coverage terms designed to exclude liability for insurers when tort claims are asserted by either a named insured [4] or by any family member residing in the same household [5] against other named insureds or additional insureds. Provisions which exclude coverage for family members, and in some situations friends as well, were designed with a view to protecting insurers from collusive suits. Insurers believed that the opportunities for fraudulent claims would be significantly reduced if claims between family members could be precluded.[6] Until the mid-twentieth century, in many situations the effect of such exclusions was fully consistent with the public policies underlying the intra-family immunity,[7] the inter-spousal tort immunity,[8] and the guest statutes.[9] However, each of these limitations on tort liability has

4. See, e.g., Hepburn v. Pennsylvania Indemnity Corp., 109 F.2d 833 (D.C.Cir. 1939); Jenkins v. Morano, 74 F.Supp. 234 (E.D.Va.1947); Havlik v. Bittner, 272 Wis. 71, 74 N.W.2d 798 (1956); Gibson v. State Farm Mutual Automobile Insurance Company, 378 So.2d 875 (Florida App., 2d Dist. 1979).

Cf. Employers' Liability Assurance Corporation v. Aresty, 11 A.D.2d 331, 205 N.Y.S.2d 711 (1st Dept., 1960), *affirmed per curiam* 11 N.Y.2d 696, 225 N.Y.S.2d 764, 180 N.E.2d 916 (1962) (held, insured's move to Connecticut and endorsement of policy to change the address of the insured did not expand coverage to include injury to spouse, which was excluded under New York statute applicable to policy as originally issued).

Also see Farmers Exchange v. Cocking, 29 Cal.3d 383, 173 Cal.Rptr. 846, 628 P.2d 1 (En banc, 1981); Florida Farm Bureau Insurance Company v. Government Employees Insurance Company, 387 So.2d 932 (Fla.1980); Frye v. Theige, 253 Wis. 596, 34 N.W.2d 793 (1948), 50 A.L.R.2d 124 (1956).

But cf. State Farm Mutual Automobile Insurance Company v. Sivey, 404 Mich. 59, 272 N.W.2d 555 (1978) (exclusion was against public policy because it eliminated coverage required by the state financial responsibility law).

5. See, e.g., Florida Farm Bureau Insurance Company v. Government Employees Insurance Company, 387 So.2d 932 (Fla., 1980).

Also see Tomlyanovich v. Tomlyanovich, 239 Minn. 250, 58 N.W.2d 855, 50 A.L.R.2d 108 (1953); Paiano v. Home Insurance Company, 353 Pa.Super. 519, 385 A.2d 460 (1978).

Cf. State Farm Mutual Automobile Insurance Company v. Meyer, 647 P.2d 683 (Colo.App., Division II, 1982), *judgment reversed* 689 P.2d 585 (1984).

But see, Transamerica Insurance Company v. Royle, 202 Mont. 173, 656 P.2d 820

(1983); Mutual of Enumclaw Insurance Company v. Wiscomb, 95 Wash.2d 373, 622 P.2d 1234 (1980).

In a few states, there are statutory provisions which authorize such exclusions. For example, in California legislation provides that the coverage afforded by automobile liability insurance may be made inapplicable to liability for bodily injury to an insured. See Farmers Insurance Exchange v. Cocking, 29 Cal.3d 383, 173 Cal. Rptr. 846, 628 P.2d 1 (1981), reversing the Court of Appeal decision reported at 108 Cal.App.3d 572, 166 Cal.Rptr. 647 (1980), concluding that the statute is rationally related to a legitimate state purpose and therefore does not constitute a denial of equal protection.

Also see Annotation, *Validity, construction and application of provision of automobile liability policy excluding from coverage injury or death of a family or household member,* 46 A.L.R.3d 1024–1056 (1972).

6. See comments in Mutual of Enumclaw Insurance Company v. Wiscomb, 95 Wn.2d 373, 622 P.2d 1234 at p. 1236 (1980); Freehe v. Freehe, 81 Wn.2d 183, 500 P.2d 771 (1972).

7. See Harper and James, LAW OF TORTS, Volume 1 (1956), at § 8.11; Prosser & Keeton, TORTS (Fifth edition, 1984), at § 122.

Also see Annotation, *Liability of parent for injury to unemancipated child caused by parent's negligence—modern cases,* 6 A.L.R.4th 1066–1142 (1981).

8. *Cf.* State Farm Mutual Automobile Insurance Company v. Leary, 168 Mont. 482, 544 P.2d 444 (1975). In Miller v. Fallon County, ___ Mont. ___, 721 P.2d 342 (1986), the Montana Supreme Court abolished the doctrine of inter-spousal immunity.

9. See Prosser and Keeton, TORTS (Fifth edition, 1984), at pp. 215–216.

been subject not only to trenchant criticism,[10] but also to judicial abrogation in many jurisdictions on the basis of a different view of the public interests that should prevail when an individual is injured — especially when the injuries were sustained in a motor vehicle accident.[11]

When a judicially formulated limitation on tort actions has been overruled, as in violation of the state's current public policy, a cogent case can be made for the proposition that comparable restrictions in an applicable liability insurance coverage are also contrary to that public interest and therefore should be void or voidable.[12] Whether such an invalidation of provisions in insurance policies should be accomplished by legislative action, rather than by courts, is a matter that is appropriately the subject of debate.[13] Nevertheless, in jurisdictions which have abrogated these limitations on tort liability, arguably the judicial precedents upholding the enforceability of such exclusions should be reconsidered.

Observations

In general, the need to evaluate the enforceability of coverage provisions that exclude liability for family members or passengers in automobiles is evident, especially in jurisdictions in which the courts have concluded that the common law tort immunities should be eliminated. With the ever increasing concern focused on assuring that accident victims are indemnified, it seems likely that exclusions and other coverage limitations — that were designed by insurers to "reinforce" common law tort immunities — in motor vehicle liability insurance policies will receive renewed scrutiny by legislatures, administrators, and courts with respect to whether such provisions are consonant with the objectives of the applicable state financial responsibility legislation.

Furthermore, even in the absence of new legislative enactments, the resolution of various coverage issues may be significantly influenced by the judicial views of the clarity and significance of the public policies underlying the financial responsibility statutes. For example,

---

10. Prosser & Keeton, Torts (Fifth edition, 1984), at § 34 and § 122.

Also see Gerald G. Ashdown, *Intrafamily Immunity, Pure Compensation, and the Family Exclusion Clause*, 60 Iowa Law Review 239–260 (1974); Herbert E. Greenstone, *Abolition of Intrafamilial Immunity*, 7 Forum 82–89 at p. 89 (1972) ("The system of liability insurance is meant to protect the public from harm, whether perpetrated by strangers or relative.").

11. See, e.g., Miller v. Fallon County, ___ Mont. ___, 721 P.2d 342 (1986); Fernandez v. Romo, 132 Ariz. 447, 646 P.2d 878 (1982); Hack v. Hack, 495 Pa. 300, 433 A.2d 859 (1981); Rogers v. Yellowstone Park Company, 97 Idaho 14, 539 P.2d 566 (1974).

12. See, e.g., Mutual of Enumclaw Insurance Company v. Wiscomb, 97 Wn.2d 203, 643 P.2d 441 (1982) (exclusion clauses which deny coverage to children of an insured are violative of the state's public policy).

Also see Miller v. Fallon County, ___ Mont. ___, 721 P.2d 342 (1986); Haines v. Mid-Century Insurance Company, 47 Wis. 2d 442, 177 N.W.2d 328 (1970).

13. *Cf.* Porter v. Farmers Insurance Company of Idaho, 102 Idaho 132, 627 P.2d 311 (1981) (public policy indicated by judicial abrogation of spousal immunity did not prohibit contractual exclusion in automobile liability insurance policy).

in a 1978 case which presented the issue of the enforceability of the family member exclusion, the Michigan Supreme Court in essence adopted the analysis of the question that was set out several years earlier in a 1971 dissenting opinion of a then Court of Appeals Judge.[14] The 1978 per curiam Michigan Supreme Court opinion reasoned that the "expression of one exception [for motor vehicle insurance coverages] and the legislative silence as to any others" supports the conclusion that the legislature did not intend to provide for other exceptions or exclusions, and therefore such an exclusion "is against public policy" because its operation "prevents coverage required by the financial responsibility law."[15] Analogous results may well follow in any state in which the financial responsibility law does not specifically provide for the inclusion of such limitations on the coverage afforded by motor vehicle liability insurance.

Other public policy interests may also affect motor vehicle liability insurance. For example, in a case that also involved a family member exclusion clause, the Montana Supreme Court reasoned that the provision was void and unenforceable not only because of the requirements of the state's Motor Vehicle Safety Responsibility Act, but also that "the household exclusion clause is invalid due to its failure to 'honor the reasonable expectations' of the purchaser of the policy."[16]

(2) Employees of an Insured

Automobile liability insurance policies generally contain clauses excluding coverage for bodily injury to an "employee of the insured."[17] The coverage disputes which arise under such employee exclusions involve considerations that are the same as or that are analogous to those discussed in the preceding subsection.

One type of factual situation which has often given rise to litigation involving the "employee of the insured" exclusion is presented when

14. The 1971 opinion was written by then Judge Levin, who was subsequently appointed to the Michigan Supreme Court and was one of the justices who rendered the per curiam decision in 1978.

15. State Farm Mutual Automobile Insurance Company v. Sivey, 404 Mich. 51, 272 N.W.2d 555 at p. 558 (1978).

Accord. Transamerica Insurance Company v. Royle, 202 Mont. 173, 656 P.2d 820 (1983); Mutual of Enumclaw Insurance Company v. Wiscomb, 97 Wn.2d 203, 643 P.2d 441 (1982).

Contra. Florida Farm Bureau Insurance Company v. Government Employees Insurance Company, 387 So.2d 932 (Fla.1980). However, it seems likely that the most severe test of whether the courts will continue to uphold such exclusions will be presented when there is no other source of compensation for the injured person, rather than in instances — such as this Florida decision — in which the dispute is between two or more insurance companies about whether the liability is to be shared or to determine that one insurer provides primary coverage.

16. Transamerica Insurance Company v. Royle, 202 Mont. 173, 656 P.2d 820 at p. 824 (1983).

17. See the forms in Appendix G and Appendix H. Current forms typically include an Exclusion that states, "We do not provide Liability Coverage for any person * * * 4. For bodily injury to an employee of that person during the course of employment." Insurance Services Office, Personal Auto Policy: Part A—Liability Coverage—Exclusions (Ed. 6–80), at p. 2.

Also see Annotation, *Validity, construction, and application of provision in automobile liability policy excluding from coverage injury or death of employee of insured,* 48 A.L.R.3d 13–144 (1973).

The employee exclusion usually does not apply to a domestic employee, unless a worker compensation law applies.

there is an injury to an employee of the *named* insured that was caused by an individual who would be an *additional* insured under the liability insurance in the absence of such an exclusion. For example, in many instances an employee of the named insured has been injured while the insured vehicle was being loaded or unloaded by employees of another employer.[18] In those cases, the injured employee asserts a tort claim against one or more employees of another company who then seek to be covered as "additional insureds" under the liability coverage acquired by the employer of the injured employee. Insurers may contest such a claim on the ground that no coverage is provided for injuries to any employee of the insured.

The general definition of "insured" which has typically been used in motor vehicle policies covering commercial vehicles states that "insured" means "any person or organization qualifying as an insured in the 'Persons Insured' provision * * *." [19] Standing alone, this definition might seem to imply that the use of the unqualified term "insured" includes the named insured at all times, regardless of who is invoking the protection of the policy. But usually this definition has been followed by the statement that "the insurance afforded applies separately to each insured against whom claim is made or suit is brought * * *." [20] If not completely reversing the implications of the primary definition, this clause at least makes the meaning of "employee of the insured" ambiguous and, therefore, subject to being construed against an insurer.[21] There is a division of authority on this question,[22]

---

18. See, e.g., Maryland Casualty Company v. American Fidelity and Casualty Company, 217 F.Supp. 688 (E.D.Tenn.1963), *judgment affirmed* 330 F.2d 526 (6th Cir. 1964).

Also see discussion of coverage for persons injured while loading or unloading an insured vehicle in the cases cited in § 5.2(b), below, and the accompanying text.

It has been noted that the weight of authority supports coverage of an additional insured's liability for injury to a named insured. See § 4.7(b)(3), above. Those decisions have little weight, however, for cases involving an exclusion clause.

19. See insurance forms Appendix G and Appendix H.

It is argued that this definition negates the theory that when injury to an employee of the named insured is caused by one who would be an additional insured but for an exclusion in the applicable coverage terms, the phrase "employee of the insured" should be read as an "employee" of *that insured who is invoking the protection of the insurance policy to cover this claim* — that is, the "additional insured."

20. *Ibid.* The "severability of interest" clause first appeared in the 1955 form.

21. See § 6.3(a), below.

22. The rule allowing coverage was characterized as the "majority" rule in

Travelers Insurance Company v. Auto-Owners (Mutual) Insurance Company, 1 Ohio App.2d 65, 203 N.E.2d 846 (1964), but coverage was denied in Michigan Mutual Liability Company v. Continental Casualty Company, 297 F.2d 208 (7th Cir.1961), on the basis of the "majority rule", the court having found no decision of the question by the courts of Delaware, the law of which controlled the case. Although a three-year period of time separates these cases, an examination of cases in point decided during that period revealed no perceptible shift in the weight of authority.

After another five years, the Minnesota Supreme Court decided against coverage because of an exclusion of "bodily injury to * * * the insured or any member of the family of the insured residing in the same household as the insured," making no special point of the fact that this was a family exclusion rather than an "employee of the insured" exclusion. The court referred to one of its own 1964 opinions containing a dictum that it might have decided an earlier case differently if there had been a severability clause in the contract, and added: "The decisions handed down since 1964 clearly indicate the view that where an exclusionary clause refers to the word 'insured' it includes the named insured, regardless of a severability clause." Fuchs v. Cheeley, 285 Minn. 356 at p. 365, 173

with a substantial number of precedents for [23] and against [24] coverage.

It might be questioned why an individual should be precluded from being an additional insured under a liability insurance policy containing an "employee of the insured" exclusion simply because the injury is to an employee of the named insured — that is, what is the justification for enforcing a coverage provision which means that an individual unloading the insured vehicle is an additional insured when that individual causes injury to an uninvolved bystander, but not when the injury is to the driver of the vehicle who is an employee of the named insured. The significance of the question obviously is reduced when the tortfeasor's acts are covered by a general liability coverage. And, in fact, many of the litigated cases have arisen from a general liability carrier's attempt to secure indemnification from another insurer [25]

N.W.2d 358 at p. 364 (1969). *Fuchs* was overruled in Utica Mutual Insurance Company v. Emmco Insurance Company, 309 Minn. 21, 243 N.W.2d 134 (1976).

But the inference that the tide may have turned toward non-coverage is countered by the actions of the Florida Supreme Court in 1967, resolving a conflict between lower court decisions by approving the decision favoring coverage, and of the Texas Supreme Court in 1970, overruling its own 1960 decision for non-coverage and commenting that the earlier decision had not given adequate emphasis to the severability clause. See the Florida and Texas cases cited in note 23, below.

See generally Annotation, *Construction and application of provision of liability policy, other than automobile liability, excluding from coverage injury or death of employee of insured,* 34 A.L.R.3d 1397–1422 (1970); Annotation, *Construction and application of provision of automobile liability policy excluding from coverage injury or death of employee of insured,* 50 A.L.R.2d 78–107 (1956).

23. See, e.g., Shelby Mutual Insurance Company v. Schuitema, 183 So.2d 571 (Fla. App., 4th Dist., 1966), *affirmed* 193 So.2d 435 (1967); Greaves v. Public Service Mutual Insurance Company, 5 N.Y.2d 120, 155 N.E.2d 390, 181 N.Y.S.2d 489 (1959).

Also see Cimarron Insurance Company v. Travelers Insurance Co., 224 Or. 57, 355 P.2d 742 (Dep't. No. 1, 1960); Commercial Standard Insurance Company v. American General Insurance Company, 455 S.W.2d 714 (Tex.1970), *overruling* Transport Insurance Company v. Standard Oil Company, 161 Tex. 93, 337 S.W.2d 284 (1960).

Cf. Utica Mutual Insurance Company v. Emmco Insurance Company, 309 Minn. 21, 243 N.W.2d 134 (1976); Marwell Construction, Inc. v. Underwriters at Lloyd's, London, 465 P.2d 298 (Alaska 1970); Liber-

ty Mutual Insurance Company v. Iowa National Mutual Insurance Company, 186 Neb. 115, 181 N.W.2d 247 (1970); Lackey v. Virginia Surety Company, 209 Va. 713, 167 S.E.2d 131 (1969) (action for damage to named insured's automobile sustained in collision with another of named insured's automobiles while driven by employee; coverage).

Also see Caribou Four Corners, Inc. v. Truck Insurance Exchange, 443 F.2d 796 (10th Cir.1971); Western Casualty & Surety Company v. Teel, 391 F.2d 764 (10th Cir. 1968), 34 A.L.R.3d 1387 (1970) (child helping employed mother at laundry was not an employee within meaning of employee-of-insured exclusion of non-automobile liability policy).

24. See, e.g., Michigan Mutual Liability Company v. Continental Casualty Company, 297 F.2d 208 (7th Cir.1961) (applying Illinois law); Kelly v. State Automobile Insurance Association, 288 F.2d 734 (6th Cir.1961) (applying Kentucky law); Keithan v. Massachusetts Bonding and Insurance Company, 159 Conn. 128, 267 A.2d 660 (1970); Pennsylvania Manufacturers' Association Insurance Company v. Aetna Casualty & Surety Insurance Company, 426 Pa. 453, 233 A.2d 548 (1967).

Also see Benton v. Canal Insurance Company, 241 Miss. 493, 130 So.2d 840 (1961).

Also see Chrysler Corporation v. Insurance Company of North America, 328 F.Supp. 445 (E.D.Mich.1971).

25. See § 3.10, above, concerning subrogation generally.

The widespread applicability of workers' compensation laws has little bearing on the significance of this distinction, because ordinarily in this situation the "additional insured's" workers' compensation coverage would not provide benefits for the named insured's employee and the applicability of

(that is, the insurer of the employer whose employee caused the injury), rather than as a consequence of a tortfeasor's or victim's search for some source of indemnification.

Changes in the 1966 Standard Liability Form apparently were designed to eliminate coverage for some of the typical circumstances in which injuries to an employee of the named insured are caused while the insured vehicle is being loaded or unloaded by an individual who otherwise qualifies as an additional insured. In addition to the "employee of the insured" exclusion, the 1966 form included a provision that excluded from being an additional insured any person "with respect to bodily injury or property damage arising out of the loading or unloading * * *" of the insured vehicle except "(1) a lessee or borrower of the automobile, or (2) an employee of the named insured or of such lessee or borrower * * *." [26] This type of provision also eliminated the possibility of coverage for injuries to uninvolved bystanders caused by the negligence of a person not within the two excepted groups. Thus, the questionable distinction between an injury to an employee of the named insured and an injury to an uninvolved bystander was thereby avoided.

§ 4.9(d) Medical Payments Coverage

The early form of medical payments coverage, introduced into the standard automobile insurance form in 1939, provided reimbursement for medical and funeral expenses of occupants of the insured automobile.[1] The 1955 revision afforded extended benefits to the named insured and relatives residing in the same household when injured or killed as pedestrians or as occupants of the insured automobile or of any automobile not owned by any person in the eligible group.[2]

The 1955 extension of coverage met an evident need by reducing the gap between the scope of a common risk and the scope of protection provided by this coverage. From the point of view of public and policyholder interests, this expansion of the medical payments coverage is to be criticized, if at all, only on the ground that further extension would have been even better. And subsequently, specific wording was added to the coverage terms to make it clear that the insurance extended to expenses of preparing and furnishing artificial teeth, limbs, and other prosthetic devices.

---

the named insured's workers' compensation coverage would not preclude a tort claim against the "additional insured" by the injured employee (or by the victim's employer or the employer's workers' compensation insurer as subrogee to the victim's claim).

26. See Appendix G for the complete phrasing of the exclusion.

§ 4.9(d)

1. John P. Faude, *The 1955 Revision of the Standard Automobile Policy—Coverage; Insuring Agreements and Exclusions*, 1955 ABA Section Insurance Law Proceedings 48, reprinted 1955 Insurance Law Journal 647–657.

2. The omission of coverage for injuries to one as an occupant of another automobile owned by a person in the eligible group can be justified on the ground that including such coverage without special upward rate adjustments for insuring one car in a two-car family would in effect allow medical payments coverage for two cars to be purchased for the price of such coverage for one. *Id.*, 1955 Insurance Law Journal at p. 647.

In regard to 1955 revision, consideration was given to modifying the clause declaring that, to be covered, medical and other expenses must be "incurred within one year from the date of accident." But no change was made. One drafter, in discussing the 1955 version, called attention to a decision [3] allowing an insured to recover reimbursement under this coverage when the insured made an advance contract and payment for medical services after the accident and before the expiration of one year, even though the treatment in question (such as surgery) could not be commenced during the year.[4] He added that such decisions might in time create a need for "revising this one-year requirement, lest the premium on foresight should become distorted to a temptation for the claims-conscious."[5] In the newer versions of the Medical Payments Insurance, the terms have been modified to provide coverage for "expenses incurred within 3 years from the date of the accident."[6]

§ 4.9(e)　Uninsured and Underinsured Motorist Insurance

(1) Uninsured Motorist Insurance

Uninsured motorist insurance, which is now included in almost all automobile insurance policies, is a hybrid coverage. It is a first-party accident insurance, which means that insurance benefits are paid by the insurance company to the persons who are identified as insureds in the policy terms. It is a fault-based insurance because the coverage for these insureds only applies when they are legally entitled to recover damages from an uninsured motorist[1] or a hit-and-run driver.[2]

This coverage was developed by the insurance industry in response to pressures for reform of the automobile accident reparations system.[3]

---

3. Drobne v. Aetna Cas. & Surety Co., 66 O.L.A. 1, 115 N.E.2d 589 (Ohio App. 1950).

Also see § 5.10(d), below.

4. John P. Faude, *1955 Revision of the Standard Automobile Policy—Coverage Insuring Agreements and Exclusions,* 1955 Insurance Law Journal 647–651 at p. 648.

5. *Ibid.*

6. Insurance Services Office, Personal Auto Policy: PP 00 01: Part B—Medical Payments Coverage (Ed. 6–80), at p. 4.

§ 4.9(e)

1. See generally, Alan I. Widiss, *Uninsured Motorist Coverage: Observations on Litigating Over When a Claimant is "Legally Entitled to Recover."* 68 Iowa Law Review 397–430 (1983).

Also see § 8.6(e), below.

2. See generally Widiss, Uninsured and Underinsured Motorist Insurance (1985), Chapter 9.

Concerning the physical contact requirement in the coverage terms for hit-and-run accidents, see § 5.2(b), below.

3. As pressure was increasing in 1955 for the adoption of compulsory insurance in New York, insurance industry representatives were actively opposing such legislation. See Robert Keeton & Jeffrey O'Connell, Basic Protection for the Traffic Victim (1965) at pp. 91–102 and p. 111. In this setting, "a group of stock companies offered a liability insurance policy endorsement providing benefits for guests in the policyholder's car, and for the policyholder and members of the policyholder's family in the car or elsewhere, in the event of injuries for which the driver or owner of an uninsured car is legally liable. [New York Times, October 5, 1955, pp. 1, 25].

A number of mutual companies forthwith offered an endorsement providing benefits for the policyholder and members of the policyholder's family injured in an accident with an uninsured car, regardless of legal liability of the uninsured driver or owner. [New York Times, October 6, 1955, pp. 20, 31.] Out of this activity came a new coverage, now generally called uninsured motorist coverage." Page Keeton and Robert Keeton, Compensation Sys-

In the mid-1950s insurers began offering uninsured motorist insurance as an option that a purchaser could add to an automobile insurance policy. States subsequently enacted legislation either requiring that it be included in every automobile liability insurance policy (mandatory coverage statutes) or requiring that the coverage be offered to every policyholder (mandatory offering statutes).[4]

Uninsured motorist insurance provides coverage for three distinct classes of insureds: (1) the named insureds and members of a named insured's household,[5] (2) persons who are injured while occupying an insured vehicle,[6] and (3) persons who sustain consequential damages as a result of personal injuries sustained by persons who are "class (1)" or "class (2)" insureds.[7]

The uninsured motorist coverage has spawned an extraordinary amount of litigation.[8] For example, the provision that spouses, relatives, or family members are covered only if they are residents of the same household as a named insured [9] has been the subject of numerous cases. The phrase "residents of the same household" has no precise meaning. The term "resident" is used in other provisions in the typical automobile insurance policy that set forth both inclusions and exclusions — that is, residency is used both in provisions that describe persons who are insured, and in provisions that define persons who are not covered.[10] When the term is employed to define the extent of the coverage (an inclusion), it is usually broadly interpreted by judges.[11] When residency is used in a provision that limits the scope of coverage

TEMS—THE SEARCH FOR A VIABLE ALTERNATIVE TO NEGLIGENCE LAW at p. 8 (1971), reprinted in Page Keeton & Robert Keeton, Cases and Materials on the Law of Torts (1971), at p. 464 (footnotes accompanying the quoted passage inserted in brackets here).

Also see Widiss, UNINSURED AND UNDERINSURED MOTORIST INSURANCE (1985), at § 1.7 through § 1.10.

4. *Id.*, Widiss, UNINSURED AND UNDERINSURED MOTORIST INSURANCE (1985), Chapter 2.

Also see Notman, *A Decennial Study of Uninsured Motorist Endorsements*, 1968 Insurance Law Journal 22–39.

5. See Widiss, UNINSURED AND UNDERINSURED MOTORIST INSURANCE (1985), at § 4.1 and § 4.2.

6. *Id.*, at § 4.1 and § 5.1.

7. *Id.*, at § 4.1 and § 6.1.

8. See Joseph Laufer, *Embattled Victims of the Uninsured: In Court with New York's MVAIC, 1959–1969*, 19 Buffalo Law Review 471–513 (1970); Joseph Laufer, *Insurance Against Lack of Insurance? A Dissent from the Uninsured Motorist Endorsement*, 1969 Duke Law Journal 227–272.

See generally, Widiss, UNINSURED AND UNDERINSURED MOTORIST INSURANCE (1985), Chapters 4–8. Also see Alan I. Widiss, *Enforceability of Arbitration Terms in Uninsured Motorist Coverages and Other Form Contracts*, 66 Iowa Law Review 241–272 (1981); Alan I. Widiss, *The Slow Evolution of a New Automobile Coverage*, 13 Trial 45–50 (September, 1977).

9. Insurance Services Office: Personal Auto Policy: Definitions at p. 1, and Uninsured Motorist Coverage Insuring Agreement at p. 5 (Ed. 6–80).

This litigation has resulted in a number of reforms in the scope of protection afforded by this coverage.

10. For example, see the household family member exclusions in the liability insurance coverage, the medical payments coverage, and the uninsured motorist coverage in Appendix H.

11. See, e.g., American Universal Insurance Co. v. Thompson 62 Wn.2d 595, 384 P.2d 367 (1963).

Consider the comments in a dissenting opinion by Judge Robert Smith, Jr., of the Florida Court of Appeal. Judge Smith argued that "absent restrictive definitions" in the insurance policy, the court should be

(an exclusion), judges generally interpret the phrase narrowly so as to restrict the scope of the coverage reduction.[12]　As one writer observed in the mid-1960s, "in both situations the courts favor an interpretation in favor of coverage."[13]　In other words, courts generally tend to interpret such insurance provisions so as to provide a source of indemnification for injured persons and to this end have adopted opposing rules of construction for the same term depending on whether it is used in an inclusion or an exclusion.

In determining the scope of the limitation imposed by the residence requirement in the context of the uninsured motorist coverage, courts have almost invariably interpreted the term "resident" so as to extend coverage in all reasonable situations.　It should be noted that the judicial approach in these cases may in part be a consequence of the uninsured motorist insurance legislation.[14]　However, it is also important to remember that disputes involving the residence requirement are usually regarded as questions of fact, and that accordingly appellate courts will generally allow trial courts considerable latitude in deciding whether the residence requirement has been satisfied.[15]

"at liberty to define 'household' with due regard to the cultural characteristics given that term" by the person who bought the policy to protect the "household." Furthermore, Judge Smith observed, "In these days of nuclear families, households extend beyond houses to include children, experimenting with independence, who live mostly apart from their parents; estranged spouses living apart in lives of transition; family members who recently lived continuously within the unit, and who still come and go freely, as persons accorded household identity and subjected to household claims." United States Fidelity and Guaranty Co. v. Williams, 375 So.2d 328 at p. 331 (Fla.App. 1st Dist., 1979) (Dissenting Opinion), *cert. denied* 386 So.2d 642 (1980).

12. See, e.g., Island v. Fireman's Fund Indemnity Co., 30 Cal.2d 541 at p. 548, 184 P.2d 153 at p. 157 (1947), 173 A.L.R. 896 at pp. 900–901 (1948).

13. R. Magãna, MOTOR VEHICLE ACCIDENTS (1967), § 470.02, at p. 783.

14. See discussion of uninsured motorist insurance legislation in Widiss, UNINSURED AND UNDERINSURED MOTORIST INSURANCE (1985), Chapter 1 and Chapter 2, especially in regard to the effects of public policy underlying the statutes. In statutes where the courts have decided that the endorsement provisions should be liberally construed in favor of the claimants in order to achieve the objectives of the uninsured motorist statutes, it is probable that the courts may be less demanding in regard to what is necessary to satisfy the residency requirement.

Also see the discussion in Annotation, *Who is "member" or "resident" of same "family" or "household," within no-fault or uninsured motorist provisions of motor vehicle insurance policy,* 96 A.L.R.3d 804–830 (1980).

15. See, e.g. Sanders v. Wausau Underwriters Insurance Company, 392 So.2d 343 at p. 345 (Fla.App., 5th Dist., 1981); State Farm Mutual Automobile Insurance Co. v. Gazeway, 152 Ga.App. 716, 263 S.E.2d 693 (1979) (holding that issues of material fact concerning residency remained for jury determination so that summary judgment was appropriately denied).

Also see Tencza v. Aetna Casualty and Surety Co., 111 Ariz. 226, 527 P.2d 97 (1974), affirming the decision of the trial court and vacating the opinion of the Arizona Court of Appeals on the basis that the trial court had a sufficient basis for its opinion.

In Davenport v. Aetna Casualty & Surety Co. of Illinois, 144 Ga.App. 474 at p. 475, 241 S.E.2d 593 at p. 594 (Div. No. 1, 1978), the court observed that the determination of residency is "a conclusion based on the aggregate details of the living arrangements of the parties" and "a common roof" is not always the controlling element.

In Rosenberger v. American Family Mutual Insurance Co., 309 N.W.2d 305 at p. 309 (Minn.1981), the court concluded, "Since the testimony was conflicting as to whether this relationship was terminated before the date of the accident, we cannot conclude that the district court's finding that Rosenberger [the claimant] was a resi-

The Residence Requirement and Coverage for Spouses

Coverage disputes about the residence requirement in regard to spouses provides an excellent illustration of how courts respond to questions about who is covered by this type of automobile insurance. Issues about coverage for spouses typically arise as a consequence of differing interpretations of the significance that should be awarded to the fact that the spouses were living apart at the time an accident occurred. In these coverage disputes, judges generally examine the situation to ascertain whether a viable marital community existed when the accident occurred. If the evidence indicates that a separation was permanent, usually the courts have upheld the denials of coverage. Thus, if a divorce or dissolution has become final, the courts almost always affirm denials of recovery predicated on the failure to satisfy the residence requirement.[16] For example, the Supreme Court of Nebraska concluded that when the spouses had separated, were living in different places, and a divorce decree had been entered, the wife was no longer a member of her husband's household.[17] [The opinion also pointed out that the wife had no other basis on which to claim coverage since she "was not a named insured" under her former husband's policy.[18]] In instances when the separation of the spouses appears to be either experimental or temporary, the courts usually extend coverage.[19]

(2) The Origins and Development of Underinsured Motorist Coverage [20]

Motor vehicle accidents often result in consequences that involve many thousands of dollars of losses for persons who are injured. The motor vehicle financial responsibility laws enacted by the states are designed to provide a prescribed level of minimum protection for those

dent of her stepfather's home is clearly erroneous."

16. Allstate Insurance Co. v. Luna, 36 A.D.2d 622, 319 N.Y.2d 139 (2d Dept., 1971).

17. State Farm Mutual Automobile Insurance Co. v. Selders, 187 Neb. 342, 190 N.W.2d 789 (1971), appeal after remand 189 Neb. 334, 202 N.W.2d 625 (1972).

18. *Ibid.*

19. Holloway v. Farmers Insurance Exchange, 252 Ark. 899, 481 S.W.2d 328 (1972).

In State Farm Mutual Automobile Insurance Co. v. Gazaway, 152 Ga.App. 716, 263 S.E.2d 693 (1979), the court held that it was an issue of fact for a jury to decide whether the decedent was a resident of her husband's household when they had been residing in separate trailers for about seven years prior to accident.

In Nationwide Mutual Insurance Company v. Allison, 51 N.C.App. 654, 277 S.E.2d 473 (1981), review denied 303 N.C. 315, 281 S.E.2d 652 (1981), the court concluded that the wife was covered under her husband's policy even though the couple was having marital problems. The automobile accident occurred while the wife was on a trip with another man. The court noted that the wife's absence was not intended to be permanent, that she had professed a desire to return home before the accident, and that she did return home after the accident.

The preceding discussion was adapted from § 4.7 and § 4.8 of Widiss, UNINSURED AND UNDERINSURED MOTORIST INSURANCE (1985).

20. The following subsection is adapted from Chapter 31 of the book UNINSURED AND UNDERINSURED MOTORIST INSURANCE (1987), by Professor Widiss.

who may be injured in highway accidents as a consequence of the negligent operation of an insured vehicle. These laws do not ensure that there will be an adequate source of indemnification for all those who may be injured. The losses which result from motor vehicle accidents are frequently far in excess of the amount of liability insurance mandated by the financial responsibility laws, even in those states with the highest minimum levels for liability insurance. Consequently, in many situations, the liability insurance applicable to a motor vehicle accident is not adequate to provide compensation for persons who are seriously injured.

When the uninsured motorist insurance was conceived by the insurance industry, one of the primary objectives was to develop a new form of coverage that would obviate a growing interest in the enactment of statutes — modeled on the Massachusetts financial responsibility legislation that had been in effect since the mid-1920s — which made automobile insurance mandatory.[21] The industry clearly wanted to avoid the adoption of legislation that would have changed the thrust of the then existing financial responsibility laws — which in essence made liability insurance optional — to statutes that would have required all motorists to purchase motor vehicle liability insurance. Accordingly, uninsured motorist insurance was designed as a first party coverage that would place insureds in the position they would have been had a tortfeasor, whose negligent operation of an uninsured motor vehicle caused an accident, been insured by liability insurance that complied with the minimum requirements specified in the applicable financial responsibility law.

Within just a few years of the announcement by insurers that uninsured motorist insurance would be offered in some states as an additional coverage to purchasers of automobile insurance policies, state legislatures throughout the United States concluded that uninsured motorist insurance — with coverage limits at least equal to the minimum amounts required by the state's financial responsibility laws — either (1) had to be offered to all purchasers of motor vehicle liability insurance or (2) had to be included in all motor vehicle liability insurance policies.[22] However, just as was true of the liability insurance required by state financial responsibility laws, the uninsured motorist insurance mandated by these statutes often does not afford insureds complete indemnification.

Inadequacies of the Uninsured Motorist Insurance

Uninsured motorist insurance was almost always only offered by insurers to purchasers with limits of liability that corresponded to the minimum amounts of coverage required by the applicable state finan-

---

21. See the discussion in Widiss, UNINSURED AND UNDERINSURED MOTORIST INSURANCE (1985 and 1987), Chapter 1.

22. See the discussion in *Id.*, § 1.11 and § 2.5.

cial responsibility laws.[23] There are many circumstances in which either uninsured motorist or liability insurance with minimum coverage amounts required by the applicable financial responsibility law is not sufficient to indemnify persons injured as the result of the negligent operation of a motor vehicle — that is, the economic consequences of motor vehicle accidents may be significantly greater than an insurance coverage that is written so as to comply with the minimum requirements of a state financial responsibility law.

The financial responsibility requirements in some states have not changed in several decades. For example, there are states that continue to require coverage limits of $5,000/$10,000 or $10,000/$20,000. The minimum financial responsibility requirements in these states, set several decades ago, clearly do not reflect the radical increases in the level of losses (such as medical expenses and earnings) which now result from motor vehicle accidents. Moreover, the inadequacy of such coverage is too often vividly demonstrated by accidents in which several persons are seriously injured.

Accidents in which several persons were injured produced a number of coverage disputes involving claims under the uninsured motorist insurance on the theory that the coverage should apply when the insured only received a portion of a tortfeasor's liability insurance because there were several claimants. Such claims were sustained by some courts.[24] However, in many of these cases, the appellate court decisions upheld the rejection of such uninsured motorist insurance claims.[25]

There have also been a number of cases in which insureds, who had received the full amount of the liability coverage, sought additional compensation from an uninsured motorist insurance coverage because even though the insured received the total amount of liability coverage, it was not sufficient to provide full indemnification because the losses exceeded the tortfeasor's liability coverage. The courts almost uniformly sustained the rejection of such claims on the ground that there was no justification for redefining the nature of the uninsured motorist

---

23. From the mid-1950s until the 1970s, the almost uniform practice of insurance companies throughout the United States was to issue the uninsured motorist insurance with coverage limits that complied with the applicable uninsured motorist legislation which specified that the coverage was to be at least in the amount of the limits specified for liability insurance in the applicable state financial responsibility law. Thus, while insurers were free to sell uninsured motorist coverage with higher limits, almost no insurers did so and the amount of uninsured motorist coverage available to a purchaser varied for $5,000/$10,000 to $25,000/$50,000 depending on the state in which the uninsured motorist coverage was issued.

Split Limits: Many insurance companies issue liability, uninsured motorist, and underinsured motorist insurance with split limits. The first figure specifies the limit of the insurer's liability for claims resulting from bodily injury to one person as a consequence of an accident. The second figure is the maximum amount of coverage provided by the insurer for claims when two or more persons sustain bodily injuries in an accident.

24. See the discussion in Widiss, UNINSURED AND UNDERINSURED MOTORIST INSURANCE (1985), § 8.22.

25. *Ibid.*

insurance to provide coverage for accidents that clearly involved insured motorists.[26]

Higher Limit Uninsured Motorist Insurance

In the late 1960s and 1970s, legislatures in several states recognized some of the problems which were not addressed by the original uninsured motorist insurance statutes and adopted legislative provisions that required *higher limit* uninsured motorist insurance to be made available to the purchasers of motor vehicle liability insurance.[27] Typically, insurers were required to offer uninsured motorist insurance with limits that were equal to the limits of liability selected by the purchaser for the liability coverage.[28] Compliance with the new legislative requirements in these states was generally implemented through the use of an endorsement, which was characterized as "Supplementary Uninsured Motorist Insurance" in the standard form prepared by the Insurance Services Office.[29]

The introduction of higher limit uninsured motorist insurance led to a coverage question that was a variant of an issue that had been repeatedly litigated in regard to whether an insured who did not receive any indemnification or who received inadequate indemnification from a negligent motorist's liability coverage was entitled to insurance benefits under the uninsured motorist insurance for such injuries. The comparable question in the context of higher limit uninsured motorist insurance was presented by claims resulting from injuries caused by negligent motorists who were insured in the minimum amount mandated by the applicable state financial responsibility law. In these circumstances, some insurers denied liability under the higher limit uninsured motorist coverage on the theory that the insurance only provided coverage when the tortfeasor was *uninsured*. In these disputes the insurers argued that regardless of the amount of losses that remained uncompensated by a tortfeasor's liability insurance, the higher limit uninsured motorist insurance did not apply if the tortfeasor was insured by coverage that complied with the applicable financial responsibility requirements — that is, even though the liability insurance limits were less than the coverage limits of the higher limit uninsured motorist insurance, the higher limit coverage was not applicable. This position was sustained in several coverage disputes that were taken to appellate courts.[30]

When higher limit uninsured motorist coverage is conditioned on the tortfeasor's being uninsured, it creates situations in which insureds

---

26. See the discussion in Widiss, UNINSURED AND UNDERINSURED MOTORIST INSURANCE (1985), § 8.23.

27. See the discussion of higher limit uninsured motorist insurance in *Id.*, § 8.25.

28. *Id.*, see the Chart reprinted in Appendix B.

29. *Id.*, see the discussion of the standard form for higher limit uninsured motorist insurance in § 3.2.

30. *Id.*, see the decisions cited in notes for § 8.25.

are considerably better off if a tortfeasor carries no insurance than when the tortfeasor is covered by insurance which complies with the minimum financial responsibility requirements. Thus, it was soon very apparent that the higher limit uninsured motorist coverage needed to be redesigned so as to avoid this problem.

(3) Underinsured Motorist Insurance

Underinsured motorist insurance developed in response to the public concern in regard both to (1) the inadequacies of uninsured motorist insurance which was often only available with limits of liability that corresponded to the minimum amounts of coverage required by the applicable state financial responsibility laws, and (2) the shortcomings of higher limit uninsured motorist insurance that only applied to accidents caused by uninsured motorists.[31] Once the question of the adequacy of the uninsured motorist insurance became a matter of legislative concern, it was evident that there were many instances in which serious injuries occur as a consequence of the negligence of motorists who are "financially responsible" under the applicable state financial responsibility law. Consequently, there was increasing interest in the development of a first party coverage that would provide insureds with the right to higher levels of indemnification both (1) for accidents involving the uninsured motorists *and* (2) for accidents involving insured motorists with liability coverages that were not sufficient to provide complete compensation for claimants who were entitled to recover — that is, a coverage that would provide first party insurance benefits whenever a tortfeasor was either underinsured or uninsured.

Underinsured Motorist Insurance Legislation

During the 1970s and 1980s, many state legislatures responded to the patent inadequacies of both the uninsured motorist insurance and higher limit uninsured motorist insurance as developed and marketed by the insurance industry. Legislation in numerous states now requires insurance companies to make available to purchasers insurance that provides protection for the risk that the damages sustained by insureds will not be adequately indemnified by the liability coverage carried by a negligent insured motorist.[32]

Legislatures took the approach of either modifying the existing uninsured motorist insurance statutes or adopting new provisions which established requirements for underinsured motorist insurance. By 1988, over half of the states had enacted some statutory provision establishing requirements that mandate broader coverage than that required by the original uninsured motorist insurance legislation.

---

31. See the discussion in note 23, above.

32. See Chapter 32 of Widiss, UNINSURED AND UNDERINSURED MOTORIST INSURANCE (1987).

Distinguishing Disputes Involving Underinsured Motorist From Uninsured Motorist Insurance Decisions

Numerous appellate court decisions addressing various coverage issues have arisen in connection with underinsured motorist insurance and higher limit uninsured motorist insurance. Although many of these cases involve issues that are essentially the same as those considered by the courts in regard to uninsured motorist insurance, there are several reasons why the questions presented in these cases are sufficiently distinctive — especially in regard to the nature of the interests which are protected by this coverage — to warrant being analyzed as a separate body of insurance law.

First, purchasers of uninsured motorist insurance had no choice about the coverage limits. The purchaser of underinsured motorist insurance generally has some latitude in selecting the coverage limits and makes a conscious decision about how much coverage to acquire. The selection of coverage limits by the purchaser brings into play a different set of considerations in regard to questions such as the appropriateness of allowing an insured claimant to recover under several applicable coverages in order to secure indemnification or the enforceability of coverage terms that provide for setoffs. For example, in a case in which the claimants sought to recover under both the liability and underinsured motorist insurance applicable to the vehicle which was involved in a single car accident, the Minnesota Court of Appeals observed that "it was within the insured's power to purchase sufficient liability coverage to adequately protect himself and his other insureds" and therefore the exclusionary clause which precluded converting the underinsured motorist insurance into liability coverage would be enforced.[33] Similarly, an Arizona Court of Appeal reasoned that "the public policy as expressed in the statute has been satisfied" and "excess-escape clauses applying to superfluous amount of coverage fall in the area of contract law between the insuring parties and not in the realm of public interest."[34]

Second, many insurance companies have voluntarily offered underinsured motorist insurance to purchasers in states that have not adopted statutory requirements for such coverages. When coverage issues arise in these states, it should be remembered that the courts may not view the underinsured motorist insurance as being imbued with the same public policy interest that has been generally recognized and applied by courts in regard to the scope of coverage appropriately accorded to the uninsured motorist coverage.[35] Consequently, because

33. Linder by Linder v. State Farm Mutual Automobile Insurance Company, 364 N.W.2d 481 at p. 483 (Minn.App.1985).

Also consider the comments of the Washington Supreme Court in Millers Casualty Insurance Company of Texas v. Briggs, 100 Wn.2d 1, 665 P.2d 891 at p. 895 (1983).

34. Cole v. State Farm Mutual Automobile Insurance Company, 145 Ariz. 578, 703 P.2d 522 at p. 525 (Ariz.App.Div. 2, Dept. A 1985).

35. This view is well illustrated by the comments of the Idaho Supreme Court in Meckert v. Transamerica Insurance Com-

underinsured motorist insurance is not subject to any statutory mandates in approximately half the states, coverage disputes in these states involve distinctly different public interest considerations from similar issues arising in the context of uninsured motorist insurance.[36]

Third, underinsured motorist insurance presents some questions that are not raised by uninsured motorist insurance. For example, an important difference between the coverages relates to the negotiation and settlement of claims, especially the settlement of claims against the tortfeasor, which involve distinctive problems that do not arise in connection with most uninsured motorist insurance cases.

§ 4.9(f) The Standardization of Automobile Insurance Forms

(1) Development of the Standard Forms

The standard provisions for automobile insurance policies have been prepared by cooperation among insurers through industry committees and national rating organizations. In most states, automobile insurance policy forms drafted by these groups have been subject to only a very limited extent to controls or constraints imposed by statutes and administrative rulings.

The adoption by cooperating stock and mutual casualty insurers of a nationally standardized form for automobile liability insurance policies first occurred in 1935.[1] Medical payments coverage was added in

---

pany, 108 Idaho 597, 701 P.2d 217 at p. 220 (1985):

" * * * the Idaho statutes do not regulate underinsured motorist coverage. There are no requirements that insurance carriers offer such underinsured coverage * * *. Neither the Idaho legislature nor the courts have declared that there exists a public policy applicable to underinsured motorist coverage. While such a policy might be desirable [citations omitted] pointing out the anomalous result from regulating (and requiring uninsured, vis-a-vis, underinsured motorist coverage), that public policy should be enunciated by our legislature and not by this Court. Hence, we hold that there is no public policy basis upon which to rule that the language of the exclusion clause presented here is invalid."

Also see Meckert v. Transamerica Insurance Company, 763 F.2d 1071 (9th Cir. 1985), which affirmed the trial court decision on the cases of the answer to the question which the Court of Appeals had certified to the Idaho Supreme Court.

36. Also see the discussion in Votedian v. General Accident Fire and Life Assurance Company, 330 Pa.Super. 13, 478 A.2d 1324 at pp. 1327–1328 (1984). However, effective October 1, 1984, Pennsylvania legislation requires that future motor vehicle policies contain both uninsured and underinsured motorist coverage.

§ 4.9(f)

1. John P. Faude, *The 1955 Revision of the Standard Automobile Policy—Coverage: Insuring Agreements and Exclusions*, 1955 ABA Section Insurance Law Proceedings 48, reprinted 1955 Insurance Law Journal 647–651; Deroy C. Thomas, *Other Provisions—Declarations and Conditions*, 1955 ABA Section Insurance Law Proceedings 56, reprinted 1955 Insurance Law Journal 652–659.

The Committee on Automobile Insurance Law of the American Bar Association also participated in developing the first standard automobile insurance form. *Ibid.*

Also see Adlai H. Rust, *Automobile Liability Insurance Trends*, 1935–1936 ABA section Insurance Law Proceedings 25–33 at pp. 26–27; *Report of the Committee on Automobile Insurance Law*, 1935 ABA Section Insurance Law Program & Committee Reports 8–9.

Note. Allowances have sometimes been made for modifications of the standard provisions.

1939.[2] The national rating organization for automobile physical damage insurance (the National Automobile Underwriters Association) joined the collaborating group at the time of the 1941 revision, and the standardized provisions were extended to automobile fire, theft, collision, and other physical damage coverages.[3]

The next major revision occurred in 1955. It was preceded by a full review of the policy forms by representatives of the cooperating groups, and changes made at that time are of interest both for their effect on automobile insurance coverage and as an example of the process of voluntary standardization. Very soon thereafter a family automobile policy form was developed, including revisions definitely advantageous to policyholders. In the mid-1970s, the Insurance Services Office developed a new basic form for personal automobile insurance, and designated this form as the "Personal Auto Policy." This form — which is often referred to as the simplified language, "plain talk," or "plain English" automobile policy — was again revised in 1980, and increasingly is being used by insurers throughout the country.

§ 4.9(g) Comments on the Adequacy of Coverage Provided by the Standard Automobile Insurance Forms

The history of standard automobile insurance forms suggests that public and policyholder interests have sometimes been fairly well served. However, some observers have concluded that the terms developed by the insurers for the standard automobile insurance policy forms have only advanced the interests of policyholders and the public when those interests were perceived as consistent with the interests of the insurers.[1] It is, of course, within the enlightened self-interest of the industry to develop forms of coverage that minimize dissatisfactions which might lead to reduced business or to outcries for more restrictive public regulation. Coverage that serves the public's needs and desires generally provides substantial support for arguments against more substantial governmental regulation of the insurance business.

It also seems evident that the evolution of the standard forms has not always been responsive to the interests of the public and policyholders. For example, those interests would almost certainly have been better served by the (1) the earlier discontinuance of the one-year limitation in the medical payments coverage, (2) earlier expansions of coverage for injuries occurring to occupants of insured vehicles, (3) earlier and further expansions of the group of drivers covered under the omnibus clauses, and (4) broader and more extensive uninsured motorist coverage.

Nevertheless, the evolution of automobile insurance forms in the United States has involved a notable expansion in the scope of protec-

2. John P. Faude, note 1, above, 1955 Insurance Law Journal at p. 647.

3. *Ibid.*

§ 4.9(g)

1. See the discussion of standardization in § 2.8, above.

tion afforded by these coverages. In general, expanded coverage reduces the likelihood of costly litigation over fringe questions. Moreover, many — and perhaps most — of the expansions have dealt with gaps of the kind that can be covered at little cost, but cause intense policyholder dissatisfaction on occasions when they preclude indemnification to the considerable surprise of a policyholder. In general, the expansions of coverage in the evolution of automobile insurance forms are consistent with the aim of providing indemnification for injured persons as well as reducing the number of surprises for policyholders.[2]

The present automobile insurance policy provides markedly improved protection in comparison with earlier versions of these coverages. However, the standard coverage terms still fail to meet the insured accident victim's needs in too many situations. Coverage terms which trim corners from the scope of protection provided insureds do not serve the interests of either the industry or the public. The public policy underlying several statutes, in particular the motor vehicle financial responsibility legislation and the uninsured motorist insurance statutes, is not adequately served so long as there are gaps in the reasonable scope of protection.

Courts and commentators have pointed out many ways in which automobile insurance could better serve both the public's needs and those of individual purchasers. Less obviously, but no less true, such gaps also jeopardize the industry's interests because they invite further imposition of requirements by legislation and administrative regulations. To argue that the present gaps in protection represent only a small number of the actual cases is not to justify the failure to alter the situation. In fact, an assertion that the number of instances where protection is not afforded by the standard forms is small would be a most eloquent argument in favor of enlarging the scope of coverage because the cost of providing such additional protection would therefore be minimal. If, on the other hand, the problem cases are more numerous, the insurance industry should recognize its responsibility to a sizable segment of the public to deal with these problems and expand the protection by adopting appropriate modifications of the coverage terms.

§ 4.10 No-Fault Motor Vehicle Insurance [1]

§ 4.10(a) Introductory Note: Fault and No-Fault Coverages For Accident Victims

Insurance policies typically provide for the payment of benefits upon the occurrence of described events and without regard to whether

2. Also see the discussion of reasonable expectations in § 6.3, below.

§ 4.10

1. Portions of this Section have been adapted from Alan I. Widiss et al., No-

Fault Automobile Insurance in Action (1977), and Page Keeton and Robert E. Keeton, Torts (Second Edition, 1977), at pp. 800–807.

those events were caused by the fault of either the insured or another person. Thus, most coverages are appropriately characterized as "no-fault insurance." For example, several of the coverages commonly included in automobile insurance policies provide such protection. The principal coverages [1] of this type — that have been and continue to be selected for inclusion by most vehicle owners — are collision coverage (for damage to the insured vehicle as a result of a "collision" with another object), comprehensive coverage (for damage to an insured vehicle caused by falling objects, fire, theft, explosions, earthquakes and a variety of other risks), and medical payments coverage.[2]

In general, the interests protected by "first party" motor vehicle insurance coverages have been those of the named insureds, persons who are closely associated with named insureds such as family members who live in a named insured's household, and persons who are authorized either to drive or to be passengers in an insured vehicle — that is, insurers are committed to provide benefits designed to indemnify such insureds when losses are sustained either by them or by property owned by them unless coverage is subject to a specific exclusion or other restriction. Each of these coverages is appropriately viewed as a first party, no-fault insurance because the insurance benefits are paid to the insured without regard to any fault determination.

During the first half of the twentieth century, every state enacted some type of legislation that was either designed to encourage or that required motorists to acquire liability insurance which would assure accident victims that the insured would be able to provide at least minimum levels of financial responsibility in regard to injuries resulting from the negligent operation of an automobile. Liability insurance is a third party, fault based insurance — that is, the insurance company agrees to provide indemnification for an insured in the event that the insured is legally obligated to a third party who is injured as a consequence of the insured's negligence.

In the 1960s, every state enacted legislation which required that uninsured motorist insurance (which provides indemnification to an insured who is injured by an uninsured motorist) either be included in all automobile insurance policies or that it be offered to all purchasers of automobile insurance policies. In the 1970s and 1980s, legislation in many states has required insurers to afford purchasers underinsured motorist insurance. Uninsured and underinsured motorist insurance, which are described in the preceding section, are fault based, first party insurance: the insurer is only obligated to an insured when the insured

§ 4.10(a)

1. See generally Robert E. Keeton & Jeffrey O'Connell, BASIC PROTECTION FOR THE TRAFFIC VICTIM (1965), at pp. 121–123.

2. For common policy provisions concerning all these insurance coverages, see Appendix H.

Loss of income and disability coverages exclusively for injuries resulting from motor vehicle accidents have been marketed to a very limited extent.

is legally entitled to recover from the uninsured or underinsured motorist.

In the latter portion of the 1960s, proposals for the substantial expansion of the use of no-fault automobile insurance coverage became the center of an active controversy over reform of the automobile accident reparations system.[3] In August of 1970, Massachusetts enacted the first[4] no-fault automobile insurance law in the United States.[5] Thereafter, approximately half the states adopted legislation which mandated that some form of no-fault coverage be included in automobile or motor vehicle insurance policies. The requirements imposed by these statutes served to broaden the extent of no-fault protection that had been afforded by the medical payments coverages which had been commonly included in automobile insurance policies for many years.[6]

Many first party insurance coverages — such as life insurance, health insurance, disability insurance, sick leave, etc. — provide individuals with protection at all times, and these coverages frequently are sources of indemnification when persons are injured in motor vehicle accidents without regard to a determination of fault. Each of these sources of compensation or indemnification is provided without regard to any fault determination.

Consequently, when an individual is injured in a motor vehicle accident, several sources or types of insurance coverage may apply to the occurrence. In some situations, accident victims may be entitled to secure compensation by some insurance that is fault based. In most circumstances, indemnification will be provided by motor vehicle insurance coverages that are not predicated on any determination of fault, as well as first party insurance coverages that are not limited to injuries that result from motor vehicle accidents. For example, most motor vehicle insurance policies have included medical payments coverage which provides a limited amount of no-fault, first party insurance. And no-fault legislation has increased the amount of first-party, no-

---

3. See, e.g., New York Insurance Department, Report, AUTOMOBILE INSURANCE . . . FOR WHOSE BENEFIT? (1970); Robert E. Keeton & Jeffrey O'Connell, BASIC PROTECTION FOR THE TRAFFIC VICTIM (1965).

Numerous proposals are summarized in Robert E. Keeton, COMPENSATION SYSTEMS— THE SEARCH FOR A VIABLE ALTERNATIVE TO NEGLIGENCE LAW 11–23 (1969), reprinted with additions in Seavey, Keeton & Keeton, CASES AND MATERIALS ON THE LAW OF TORTS (1971), at pp. 457–539.

4. Puerto Rico adopted a state-insurance plan of no-fault coverage, effective January 1, 1970, providing extensive medical benefits and limited no-fault benefits of other types while preserving tort actions for larger claims. Though the level of no-fault coverage is relatively low and tort actions are preserved for larger claims, the Puerto Rican legislation marked the adoption of one of the most radical of the various proposals in another sense; it resorts to state rather than private enterprise to provide the insurance.

5. Retaining the long-standing requirement that Massachusetts motorists carry automobile bodily injury liability insurance with limits not lower than $5,000 per person and $10,000 per accident, the no-fault statute added $2,000 of no-fault insurance to the compulsory coverage.

Cf. Morin v. Massachusetts Blue Cross, Inc., 365 Mass. 379, 311 N.E.2d 914 (1974).

6. See the description of medical payments coverage in § 4.9(d), above.

fault insurance coverage for accident victims in approximately half the states.

§ 4.10(b)   Motor Vehicles, Accidents, and Insurance Legislation: A Brief History

The growing number of motor vehicle accidents has been one of the most significant of the many vast economic and social changes in the United States during the twentieth century. The advent of mass-produced automobiles placed the potential for causing serious personal injuries and deaths literally in the hands of millions of persons. Although providing adequate compensation to or reparation for persons who have been injured and killed in highway accidents is a problem that undoubtedly dates from the earliest use of automobiles and other motor vehicles, the adequacy of the then-existing compensation systems became a major social question in the United States during the 1920s.

(1) Tort Liability and Financial Responsibility Legislation

In the United States, the right of an individual injured in an automobile accident to be compensated by another person for injuries resulting from such an accident has primarily been predicated on an attribution of fault, in accordance with the principle that the economic cost of injuries to persons or property attributable to the fault of someone should be borne by the negligent party or a person responsible for that party's conduct. Under the fault theory, in instances where responsibility cannot be assessed, a claimant is at least in principle foreclosed from successfully pursuing indemnification by way of a tort suit. Moreover, unless the doctrine of comparative negligence is implicitly or explicitly applied, recovery in a tort action usually is precluded when an injured person is in some measure contributorily negligent.

When an innocent accident victim has been injured solely as the result of a motorist's negligence, the injured person is still not assured indemnification. There have always been "financially irresponsible" motorists who do not possess sufficient personal financial resources to enable them to respond to such damage claims and who have not purchased liability insurance which would provide a source of indemnification for injured persons.

From 1925 to 1970, state governments tried to alleviate, if not eliminate, the problem of financial irresponsibility by enacting laws that were designed either to induce or, in a few states, to require motorists to acquire liability insurance.[1] The Connecticut financial

§ 4.10(b)

1. See Joseph P. Murphy and Ross D. Netherton, *Public Responsibility and the Uninsured Motorist,* 47 Georgetown Law Journal 700–745 (1959). For an early discussion of the first financial responsibility laws, see W.J. Heyting, *Automobiles and Compulsory Liability Insurance,* 16 American Bar Association Journal 362–366 (1930).

Also see Norman E. Risjord and June M. Austin, *The Problem of the Financially Irresponsible Motorist,* 24 U.Kansas City Law Review 82–96 (1955–56).

An interesting comparative analysis of various legislative enactments dealing with

responsibility law of 1925 was the first financial responsibility legislation enacted in the United States. Under the Connecticut law, motorists were threatened with suspension of driving privileges in the event they were unable to prove that they could satisfy claims arising out of an automobile accident.[2] The Connecticut legislation authorized the State Commissioner of Motor Vehicles to require the operator and the owner of a vehicle involved in an accident causing death or personal injury, or property damage in excess of one hundred dollars, to prove their "financial responsibility to satisfy any claim for damages, by reason of personal injury to, or death of, any person, of at least ten thousand dollars."[3] The Connecticut financial responsibility legislation was the prototype for statutes adopted in 27 states during the succeeding decade, and served for thirty years as a model upon which virtually all financial responsibility laws enacted in the United States were patterned.[4]

During the same year in which the Connecticut legislation was enacted, in Massachusetts proponents of compulsory insurance secured the passage of legislation that required all motorists to acquire liability insurance as a prerequisite to registration of their motor vehicles.[5] For over thirty years, until New York adopted a similar compulsory insurance law in 1956, Massachusetts remained the only state with such an insurance requirement.[6]

For most motorists, acquisition of liability insurance in advance of an accident is the most practical method of being prepared to comply with the applicable financial responsibility requirement. And in those states where the requirements were vigorously enforced, these laws induced most, but not all, motorists to secure liability insurance coverage in at least the minimum amounts specified by the respective state financial responsibility laws.[7]

the problem of financial irresponsibility is found in Peter Ward, *The Uninsured Motorist: National and International Protection Presently Available and Comparative Problems in Substantial Similarity,* 9 Buffalo Law Review 283–320 (1960).

2. Connecticut Public Acts. Ch. 183 (1925). The statute also authorized the commissioner to invoke the same penalties for persons convicted of certain criminal offenses, including reckless driving and driving while intoxicated.

3. *Id.* In the event that such person was not a resident of the state of Connecticut, the commissioner was empowered to "withdraw from such person the privilege of operation, within this state, of any motor vehicle owned by him, or refuse to register any motor vehicle transferred by him if it shall not appear to such commissioner's satisfaction that such a transfer is a bona fide sale."

4. Joseph P. Murphy and Ross D. Netherton, *Public Responsibility and the Uninsured Motorist,* 47 Georgetown Law Journal 700–745 at p. 702 (1959).

5. Massachusetts Acts 1925. Ch. 346. The compulsory insurance requirement for Massachusetts took effect on January 1, 1927.

6. McKinney's New York Vehicle & Traffic Law §§ 310–321 (1970 and 1984 Supp.).

Also see WIDISS, UNINSURED AND UNDERINSURED MOTORIST INSURANCE (1985), at § 1.10, and the articles cited therein.

7. The National Bureau of Casualty Underwriters has compiled estimates of private passenger cars insured in the United States for the years 1956, 1962 and 1963. Also see Joseph P. Murphy and Ross D. Netherton, *Public Responsibility and the Uninsured Motorist,* 47 Georgetown Law Journal 700–745 at pp. 704–07 (1959).

By the mid-1950s, however, new pressures began to develop in several states for additional legislation that would assure compensation for all persons injured by negligent motorists. Particularly in New York there was substantial support for the enactment of a compulsory insurance law. There was also considerable interest in New York, as well as in several other states, in proposals for the creation of an unsatisfied judgment fund from which accident victims could secure reparation if indemnification was not available from negligent motorists who were uninsured.[8] In addition, some persons in New York sought the adoption of a compensation plan that would indemnify all accident victims without regard to fault, thereby incidentally eliminating, or at least substantially reducing, the problem of financial irresponsibility.[9] The legislators, though not accepting that more sweeping proposal, were persuaded that modifications were necessary, and in 1956 — some thirty years after Massachusetts enacted its compulsory

Also see the discussion of the uninsured motorist problem in the 1980s in Widiss, UNINSURED AND UNDERINSURED MOTORIST INSURANCE (1985), at § 1.12, and the studies cited there.

8. This approach to the problems created by the uninsured motorists was pioneered in the Canadian province of Manitoba, which created a state-sponsored fund to indemnify traffic accident victims injured by financially irresponsible motorists. Similar legislation has been enacted in the provinces of Alberta, British Columbia, Newfoundland, Nova Scotia, Ontario, and Prince Edward Island.

North Dakota was the first state to follow suit by enacting legislation in 1947 requiring each owner of a motor vehicle to pay a fee of one dollar (in addition to the regular registration charge) for each motor vehicle registered, until a special fund of $100,000 was created [North Dakota Cent. Code § 39–17–01 (1972)]. Under the provisions of the North Dakota law, any resident of that state who obtains in any court of the state an uncollectible judgment exceeding $300 for bodily injury or death arising out of a motor vehicle operation within the state, may obtain payments from the fund up to certain specified limits. Although this approach has been widely discussed, only a few American states — including Maryland, Michigan, New Jersey, and New York — have established comparable funds. It should be noted that recourse to the fund in each of several states differs from the pattern established in North Dakota in that the injured claimant is not required to first secure a judgment against the uninsured

motorist. On this subject, see Victor Hallman, UNSATISFIED JUDGMENT FUNDS (S.S. Huebner Foundation, 1968), which includes an extensive bibliography at pp. 315–334. For a shorter explication see Peter Ward, *The Uninsured Motorist: National and International Protection Presently Available and Comparative Problems in Substantial Similarity,* 9 Buffalo Law Review 283–320 (1960).

Also see Annotation, *Requirements as to filing of claim against unsatisfied claim and judgment fund,* 2 A.L.R.3d 760–803 (1965); Annotation, *Type of accident or occurrence which will give rise to liability under unsatisfied claim and judgment fund statute,* 7 A.L.R.3d 822–831 (1966); Annotation, *Who is within protection of statutes creating indemnity funds for losses causes by uninsured or unknown motorists,* 10 A.L.R.3d 1166–1187 (1966).

9. By the mid-1950s a "compensation without fault" plan had been in effect for several years in the Canadian Province of Saskatchewan. [Saskatchewan Stat. Chap. 11 (1946)]. The Saskatchewan approach basically follows the principles suggested in the Columbia Report of 1932. See Columbia University Council for Research in the Social Sciences, REPORT BY THE COMMITTEE TO STUDY COMPENSATION FOR AUTOMOBILE ACCIDENTS (1932).

For an interesting appraisal of the Saskatchewan Plan, see O.E. Lang, *The Nature and Potential of the Saskatchewan Insurance Experiment,* 14 University Florida Law Review 352–363 (1961). Also see Albert Ehrenzweig, "FULL AID" INSURANCE FOR THE TRAFFIC VICTIM, p. 1 (1954).

insurance law — New York became the second state to adopt a compulsory insurance requirement.[10]

In the course of the half century following the enactment of the first financial responsibility laws, many aspects of the compensation system have changed. Notably, most drivers acquire liability insurance that at least complies with the minimum amount of the applicable state financial responsibility law. In addition, in many instances persons injured in automobile accidents are indemnified by various types of first party insurance. These include health or medical insurance, and wage replacement coverages such as disability insurance. However, the adequacy of the reparation payments made to automobile accident victims has continued to be a subject of significant public concern.

Serious consideration of no-fault insurance was rekindled in the mid-1960s as a consequence of unsolved and growing social problems, and spurred by a study and book by Professor Keeton and Professor Jeffrey O'Connell. The Keeton-O'Connell study of automobile accident compensation systems concluded that neither the various first-party insurance systems nor the then-existing types of financial responsibility legislation in fact assured that adequate compensation was provided for persons who were seriously injured in automobile accidents,[11] and proposed a more extensive no-fault coverage for traffic victims.[12] By the late 1960s there was increasingly significant support in many states for no-fault insurance legislation.

The no-fault (or "non-fault," as it has sometimes been characterized) approach to providing compensation for automobile accident victims received widespread support in Massachusetts, and in 1970 the legislature adopted the first no-fault law in the United States. It was soon followed by legislation in other states. First in Florida, and subsequently in approximately a third of the states, laws were enacted that like the Massachusetts Act, to some extent substituted no-fault insurance benefits for tort actions. In a few other states laws were adopted that provided for no-fault benefits, but without the substitution feature. Altogether, laws have been enacted in over half of the states

10. The compulsory insurance requirement went into effect in New York on February 1, 1957. McKinney's New York Vehicle and Traffic Law §§ 310–321 (1970 and 1985 Supp.). For an excellent account of the legislative history of the New York compulsory insurance legislation, see Ross D. Netherton and Frederick N. Nabhan, *The New York Motor Vehicle Financial Security Act of 1956*, 5 American University Intramural Law Review 37–55 (1956).

11. Robert E. Keeton and Jeffrey O'Connell, BASIC PROTECTION FOR THE TRAFFIC VICTIM (Little Brown, 1965).

Another work that was completed at about the same time by a research team at the University of Michigan also provides

an excellent analysis and empirical study of the consequences of automobile accidents. See A. Conard, J. Morgan, R. Pratt, C. Voltz, and R. Bombaught, AUTOMOBILE ACCIDENT COSTS AND PAYMENTS: STUDIES IN THE ECONOMICS OF INJURY REPARATION (University of Michigan Press, 1964).

Also see DOLLARS, DELAY AND THE AUTOMOBILE VICTIM: STUDIES IN REPARATION OF HIGHWAY INJURIES AND RELATED COURT PROBLEMS (Bobbs-Merrill Co., Inc., 1968); and the volumes published as a result of the Department of Transportation Automobile Insurance and Compensation Study.

12. Robert E. Keeton and Jeffrey O'Connell, BASIC PROTECTION FOR THE TRAFFIC VICTIM (Little Brown, 1965).

that require, in varying ways, the inclusion of insurance that assures persons injured in automobile accidents no-fault insurance coverage for the losses which result from personal injuries.[13]

§ 4.10(c) No-Fault Automobile Insurance in Massachusetts

The Massachusetts no-fault legislation, which went into effect on January 1, 1971, requires that persons injured in automobile accidents be provided indemnification for medical expenses, lost wages, and the cost of replacement services.[1] This insurance, which is denoted Personal Injury Protection (and is usually referred to by the acronym PIP) provides first party coverage of up to a specified amount (initially $2,000) for these "out-of-pocket" expenses. The PIP insurance must be included in all automobile insurance policies purchased by Massachusetts motorists.

The PIP coverage is designed to assure compensation for all persons who might be injured in an automobile accident. The legislation requires that each PIP policy cover (a) the named insured, (b) members of the named insured's household, (c) any authorized operator of an insured's vehicle, (d) any authorized passenger in the insured's vehicle including guests, and (e) any pedestrian struck by an insured vehicle.[2] The no-fault coverage required in Massachusetts is designed to provide protection for anyone who is injured by the operation of an insured vehicle unless the person has no right to be in the vehicle. In addition, it should be noted that the PIP coverage is provided to pedestrians, even when the automobile is being used by an unauthorized driver.[3] Thus, the objective of the PIP coverage is to provide indemnification on a no-fault basis for all motorists (drivers and passengers) and all pedestrians injured in any automobile accident (except those disqualified by their own serious misconduct), and the injured party is entitled to receive payments up to the specified limit from the appropriate insurance company regardless of who was responsible for the accident.

---

13. See American Insurance Association, SUMMARY OF SELECTED STATE LAWS AND REGULATIONS RELATING TO AUTOMOBILE INSURANCE (January, 1976).

Also see CCH AUTOMOBILE INSURANCE SERVICE for a current summary of statutes in effect.

§ 4.10(c)

1. See Compulsory Motor Vehicle Liability Insurance, Massachusetts Gen.Laws Ann. c. 90, § 34A (1985 Supp.) (originally enacted August 13, 1970). Massachusetts Acts 1970, ch. 670 (Aug. 1970).

See generally, John G. Ryan, *No-Fault Automobile Insurance* in the 1970 Annual Survey of Massachusetts Law at pp. 530–542 (Little Brown, 1971).

Also see M. Woodroof, John Fonseca and Alphonse M. Squillante, AUTOMOBILE INSUR-

ANCE AND NO-FAULT LAW §§ 11:30–:33, at pp. 329–32 (Lawyers Cooperative Publishing Co., 1974); Willis Rokes, NO-FAULT INSURANCE (Insurer's Press, Inc., 1971); Raymond J. Kenny, Jr. and Clement McCarthy. *"No-Fault" in Massachusetts Chapter 670, Acts of 1970—A Synopsis and Analysis,* 55 Massachusetts Law Quarterly 23–51 (1970); James D. Ghiardi and John J. Kircher, *Automobile Insurance: An Analysis of the Massachusetts Plan,* 21 Syracuse Law Review 1135–1147 (1970); and Note, *The Massachusetts "No-Fault" Automobile Insurance Law: An Analysis and Proposed Revision,* 8 Harvard Journal of Legislation 455–517 (1971).

2. Massachusetts General Laws Ann. c. 90, § 34A (1985 Supp.).

3. Massachusetts General Laws Ann. c. 90, § 34A (1985 Supp.) (by inference).

In Massachusetts, no-fault insurance benefits are provided for: (1) reasonable expenses incurred within two years from the date of the accident for necessary medical and hospital services, without deduction for benefits from other sources; (2) costs of substitute services (that is, payments to persons outside the family for services that would have been performed for the family by the injured person but for the injury); and (3) net loss of wages or equivalent for employed persons, including those who are self-employed, and net loss of earning power for unemployed persons, subject to a limit such that the sum of these no-fault benefits and payments under a wage (or wage-equivalent) continuation program shall not exceed 75 per cent of the injured person's average weekly wage (or equivalent) for the year immediately preceding the accident.

Coverage for Wage Losses

Compensation for loss of wages is limited to 75 percent of the wages that are actually lost by reason of the accident.[4] Thus, if a person injured in an accident had an actual wage loss of $1,000, the maximum recovery provided for under the PIP insurance is 75 percent of the $1,000 or $750. When a claimant has any type of wage continuation plan or sick leave, the no-fault payment is reduced by the amount of such payments. In the preceding illustration, if the claimant received sick leave payments of $500, the PIP payments would be reduced from $750 to $250. When the claimant's wages have been fully paid under some type of wage continuation plan, or sick leave, or are covered by workers' compensation, there can be no recovery under the PIP coverage for lost income.

Coverage for Medical Expenses

The coverage for hospital and medical expenses includes all costs incurred within a two-year period following the accident (subject to the coverage limit — which was initially set at $2,000). The injured party may collect medical expenses from both the automobile insurance company and — absent contrary provisions in the other contracts — from any accident or health insurance company, such as Blue Cross/ Blue Shield.[5] A purchaser of a PIP policy may choose to avoid duplication in payments by opting for PIP coverage with a deductible amount.[6]

---

4. A 1971 enactment amended the no-fault law by allowing an injured person who receives benefits under a wage continuation plan to later reimburse the plan without loss of standing. Through reimbursement of the wage continuation plan, an insured's right to benefits are fully restored in regard to amounts and time previously accumulated under the plan. Massachusetts Acts 1971, ch. 794 (Sept. 1971);

Massachusetts General Laws Ann. ch. 90, § 34A (1985 Supp.).

5. Cf. Morin v. Massachusetts Blue Cross, Inc., 365 Mass. 379, 311 N.E.2d 914 (1974).

6. See The Commonwealth of Massachusetts General Court Joint Committee on Insurance, NO-FAULT: ITS EFFECTIVENESS IN MASSACHUSETTS (January, 1973) at p. 11.

Persons Not Covered by P.I.P.

The Massachusetts legislation (and the PIP endorsement form approved by the Insurance Commissioner) provide that no-fault benefits may be withheld in three situations. First, operators under the influence of alcohol or narcotic drugs are not covered. Second, persons committing a felony or seeking to avoid lawful apprehension or arrest by a police officer are not insured in the event of a motor vehicle accident. Third, the no-fault coverage is excluded for operators of motor vehicles who are injured in a situation where the operators specifically intended to cause injury or damage to themselves or others.[7]

Tort Litigation

The Massachusetts statute establishes a limited tort immunity, that is, the no-fault benefits are provided in lieu of damages that would otherwise be recoverable in tort. However, under the Massachusetts legislation, tort claims against a negligent motorist are still permitted in several situations. First, if the economic costs sustained by an insured exceed the $2,000 coverage provided by a PIP policy, a tort action for indemnification is permissible for all out-of-pocket costs not covered by the no-fault insurance.[8] Second, claims for pain and suffering are preserved if the injuries are beyond a threshold level. The Massachusetts legislation only permits an injured person to recover tort damages for pain and suffering if one of the following conditions is satisfied: (1) the reasonable and necessary expenses for medical and hospital services exceed $500; (2) the injury causes death; (3) the injury consists in whole or in part of loss of a body member, or permanent and serious disfigurement, or loss of sight or hearing as defined in specified sections of the workers' compensation law, or a fracture.[9]

For example, if the injured person's medical costs were $400 and the lost wages were $3,100, there would be a total out-of-pocket loss of $3,500. The injured person would recover $2,000 of the $3,500 of out-of-pocket damages sustained as a result of the accident on a no-fault basis from the insured's own insurance company. The insured could then proceed in a tort action for the remaining $1,500 that was not covered by the PIP insurance. The recovery in a suit on such a tort claim would, of course, depend on a showing of negligence. It should be borne in mind that even though this would be a tort action, the injured person in this illustration might not necessarily be entitled to recover damages for pain and suffering. Claims for pain and suffering are foreclosed

---

7. Massachusetts General Laws Ann. c. 90, § 34A (1985 Supp.).

8. See M. Woodroof, John Fonesca, and Alphonse Squillante, AUTOMOBILE INSURANCE AND NO-FAULT LAW 15:15 at p. 450 (1974). The claimant in such an action, however, would not be entitled to recover

damages for pain and suffering unless one of the specified thresholds was met.

9. See the description of the Massachusetts no-fault coverage in Widiss et al., NO-FAULT AUTOMOBILE INSURANCE IN ACTION (1977), at pp. 8–9.

unless one of the thresholds specified in the no-fault legislation is satisfied. In this example, the medical costs were $400, $100 less than the threshold of $500 established by the Massachusetts law. Therefore, the injured party in this case could recover damages for pain and suffering only if the injury sustained in the accident (1) consisted in whole or part of the loss of a body member, (2) consisted in whole or part of permanent and serious disfigurement, (3) resulted in loss of sight or hearing, or (4) consisted of a fracture.

Amounts of Deductibles

The Massachusetts Act also requires that the insurer offer the policyholder a deductible under which the policyholder would give up all no-fault benefits to the extent of the deductible selected from among the figures $250, $500, $1,000, and $2,000. Thus, a policyholder could elect to give up all no-fault benefits by selecting the $2,000 deductible. If an insured covered by a policy with a deductible is injured in an accident, the amount of the claim that is paid is reduced accordingly. By selecting a PIP policy with a deductible, the purchaser acquires insurance with a lower premium cost than a PIP policy with first dollar coverage. The deductible does not apply to persons other than the purchaser and any other family member making a PIP claim under that coverage.

The purpose of requiring that insurers offer purchasers no-fault coverages with very substantial deductibles was to allow persons with other types of insurance coverages that provided indemnification for the losses that result from motor vehicle accidents (coverages such as health insurance or wage continuation plans) to avoid double coverage and thereby reduce their automobile insurance costs accordingly. The election of a deductible by a purchaser does not affect the possibility for tort actions — that is, any person whose no-fault coverage is subject to a deductible is still governed by the same limitations on tort rights.

Compulsory Liability Insurance and Tort Claims

The long standing statutory mandate which requires liability insurance for all residents of Massachusetts still exists.[10] Under the no-fault law, only the first $2,000 of "out-of-pocket" damages arising from a personal injury is collected on a no-fault basis. Claims that are not precluded by the limitations on tort claims are determined on the basis of fault, so that liability insurance is still necessary in order to assure compensation to innocent victims beyond the PIP coverage.

10. Massachusetts General Laws Ann. c. 90, §§ 1A, 34A (1985 Supp.). Section 1A was originally enacted as Massachusetts Acts 1925, ch. 346, § 1 and became effective in 1927.

PIP Coverage: Out–of–State Cars and Out–of–State Accidents

If a person who is insured under a Massachusetts PIP coverage is injured in an accident by an out-of-state car in Massachusetts, the insured is still entitled to receive benefits under the PIP coverage.[11] If a Massachusetts insured is involved in an automobile accident in another state, the insured has the option of collecting under his or her PIP coverage.[12] Alternatively, a Massachusetts insured may elect to sue the out-of-state driver in tort, in which case payment of the no-fault personal injury protection benefits might be withheld by the insurer pending the resolution of that tort claim.

§ 4.10(d) No-Fault Legislation in Other States

During 1971, Florida became the second state to enact a no-fault law with a partial tort exemption[1] and legislative deliberations commenced in many other jurisdictions.[2]

In 1973, Michigan implemented what is generally viewed as "the most comprehensive no-fault automobile insurance law in the nation."[3] The mandatory coverage for owners of motor vehicles in Michigan consists of three parts: Personal Injury Protection (PIP), Residual Bodily Injury and Property Damage Liability Insurance, and Property Protection Insurance (PPI).[4] The first-party no-fault (PIP) coverage provides the following benefits.

(1) Unlimited medical and rehabilitation benefits.

(2) Work or income loss benefits of up to $1,000 per month (as of October 1, 1974) for a maximum period of three years.[5]

(3) Dependent survivor loss benefits of up to $1,000 a month for a maximum period of three years.

(4) Replacement service benefits of up to $20 per day for a maximum period of three years for disabled victims and dependent survivors of death victims.

(5) Funeral and burial expense benefits of $1,000.[6]

---

11. See Massachusetts General Court Joint Committee on Insurance. No-Fault: Its Effectiveness in Massachusetts (January, 1973), at p. 35.

12. *Ibid.*

§ 4.10(d)

1. Florida Automobile Reparations Reform Act, West's Florida Stat.Ann. §§ 627.730–627.741 (1984).

2. See the chart in Appendix H analyzing the laws with partial tort exemptions.

The chart also includes information on the Uniform Motor Vehicle Accident Reparations Act, proposed by the National Conference of Commissioners on Uniform State Laws, but not enacted in any state.

3. Thomas C. Jones, *No-Fault Automobile Insurance in Michigan: A Preliminary Study,* [hereinafter cited as Jones] which appears as Part IV in Widiss *et al,* No-Fault Automobile Insurance in Action— The Experiences in Massachusetts, Florida, Delaware and Michigan (1977).

4. Michigan   Comp.Laws   Ann. §§ 500.3101–500.3179 (1975 Supp.).

5. The income loss benefits increased annually under the statutory cost-of-living provision. The maximum work loss payment effective through September 30, 1986 was $2,434 per month.

6. Jones, note 3, above. The PIP benefits are required by statute to be coordinat-

Eligibility for no-fault benefits in Michigan is broad. In addition to protecting insured motorists, coverage extends to pedestrians and occupants of motorcycles and other vehicles when accidents involve automobiles. Even the family members of an uninsured owner of an automobile are covered.

Persons from other states injured in an accident in Michigan are eligible for PIP benefits if their insurer is licensed in Michigan or, if unlicensed, has voluntarily certified the coverage. Persons from other states are also covered if they are hurt in a Michigan car, or as a pedestrian in Michigan. Michigan residents also are entitled to receive PIP benefits if they are injured while traveling in any other state or in Canada. Exclusions from PIP coverage apply to the owner of a vehicle who does not purchase the mandatory coverage and who is injured in his own vehicle; a person injured in an automobile that he has stolen; and a non-resident who does not have coverage that has been certified by his insurer.

The third portion of the mandatory coverage in Michigan is Property Protection Insurance (PPI). Property Protection Insurance benefits are payable without regard to fault to third parties for damage to tangible property, including damage to parked vehicles. The statutorily prescribed coverage limit for damage from any one accident is $1 million.

Tort liability for damage to automobiles with respect to accidents in Michigan has been abolished for insured car owners.[7] The result is that the third party property damage liability insurance system for car damages has all but been eliminated. First party collision coverages, which are not mandatory, are offered by all automobile insurers operating in Michigan, and collision options with inverse liability features are available to Michigan automobile owners.[8]

In analyzing the experience of the Michigan no-fault law it is important to note that the plan was not enacted with the expectation of decreasing the cost of automobile insurance. In 1972 Governor Milliken in his State of the State message emphasized the fact that although there might be some savings in premiums, the principal thrusts of the no-fault proposals were to compensate accident victims "more promptly and adequately, and to reduce the expense and delay of the tort liability system." [9]

ed with governmental benefits, e.g., social security benefits.

7. Senate Bill 1266, 1976 Regular Session, Michigan Legislature.

8. "The available coverages fall into three categories. Regular collision insurance is offered, which pays the owner of a damaged vehicle his loss after the subtraction of a stated deductible amount. Limited collision pays the loss only if the driver of the damaged vehicle was not a fault, and again after the subtraction of a stated de-

ductible. Broadened collision pays regardless of which driver is at fault, but no deductible is subtracted if the insured is not at fault." Jones, note 3, above, at p. 380.

9. In testimony to a joint Committee of the Michigan legislature in support of the no-fault proposals, Insurance Commissioner Russel Van Hooser set forth the following priorities and standards against which various legislative no-fault proposals could be tested:

During the 1970s, several states adopted legislation that requires companies to offer (and in some instances requiring that motorists obtain) no-fault coverage that was not accompanied by the adoption of any tort exemption. Legislation of this type, often referred to as "add-on" laws to distinguish them from the "partial tort exemption" laws, add coverage without changing the basic system of negligence law and liability insurance. As indicated in the chart included in Appendix H,[10] laws of this type had been enacted in eight states by 1984. A ninth state, Wisconsin, had enacted a law requiring $1,000 of medical payments coverage, but it is generally omitted from the states identified as having an "add-on" law because it made no provision for coverage of wage losses, as all other "add-on" laws have done.

In May, 1974, the United States Senate passed a bill, S. 354, that would have established national standards for state no-fault motor vehicle insurance legislation and — after allowing a period for state action — would have placed in effect in each state an alternative no-fault plan if the state had not enacted within the specified time a plan which provided for the minimum coverage required by the federal legislation. The bill was not passed in the House of Representatives. Support for such federal legislation has diminished during the past decade and, as this book goes to press in the late-1980s, it seems unlikely that federal legislation will be adopted in the near future.

§ 4.10(e) The Impact of No-Fault Motor Vehicle Insurance

With the enactment of no-fault laws, debates about the need for reform were transformed into disagreements over the general performance of the no-fault systems,[1] and the relative effects on insurance costs in the partial-tort-exemption states and in the add-on states.

"(1) Compensate injured persons adequately, promptly, and without regard to fault for medical expenses, wage loss and rehabilitation expenses.

(2) Reduction or elimination of the nuisance value of small claims.

(3) Reduction of the duplication and overlapping of benefits within the auto-insurance system and other systems. If the duplication is not reduced or eliminated, it should at least be subject to greater control by the consumer so that the consumer will have a corresponding control over his costs.

(4) Reduction or elimination of some of the other frictions and inefficiencies of the present system, such as the adversary relationship between insurer and injured party, court congestion, litigation expenses, and overhead expense."

Id., at p. 381.

10. The chart set out in Appendix H also includes information on the Uniform Motor Vehicle Accident Reparations Act, proposed by the National Conference of Commissioners on Uniform State Laws, but not enacted in any state.

§ 4.10(e)

1. See, e.g., *The Human side of No-Fault Car Insurance,* Money Magazine, Vol. 5, No. 11, p. 75, Nov. 1976 (favorable appraisal); Editorial, *No-Fault Concept Sound, But Might Need Repairs,* Detroit Freepress, Oct. 11, 1976 ("good results * * * in compensating accident victims, reducing the time for settling claims, and eliminating ill-conceived lawsuits"); Remarks of an insurance industry executive, an opponent of no-fault insurance, before a meeting of the Boston Chapter of the Chartered Property & Casualty Underwriters and Risk Insurance Management Society, (December 1976); The Standard, Northeast's Insurance Weekly, Vol. 199, No. 19, p. 16, (Dec. 10, 1976) (no-fault programs have worked to the "public's loss—and to the industry's discredit").

At about the same time as the first partial-tort-exemption statutes went into effect (1971 in Massachusetts and 1972 in Florida), the automobile liability insurance industry was enjoying a period of generally improved performance. The period ended abruptly, however, and by 1975 the automobile insurance industry was in what was subsequently identified by many executives as the worst year of the industry's entire experience. In this context, automobile insurance costs were rising everywhere. Some reporters, comparing insurance rates for a specific year in a partial-tort-exemption state with rates in the same state for a year before the no-fault system became effective, concluded that no-fault had failed, and reports to this effect were in some instances publicized under headlines declaring that no-fault had failed to cut rates, even though the text that followed disclosed that the premium increases were occurring throughout the nation and appeared to be caused primarily by inflation.[2] Reports that focused on cost comparisons among the three different types of states — those having partial-tort-exemption statutes, those with add-on statutes, and those with neither — generally showed, with exceptions in some individual states, that during the first half of the 1970s automobile insurance costs were increasing least in the partial-tort-exemption states, were increasing most in the add-on states, and were increasing at an intermediate level in the states that had not enacted either of these types of statutes.[3]

With respect to Massachusetts, Florida and Delaware, studies of performance were conducted under the auspices of the Council on Law Related Studies.[4] Reports of these studies, together with a brief report

Compare Joseph Little, *A Critique of No-Fault Reparation for Traffic Crash Victims,* 51 Indiana Law Journal 635–681 (1976):

"My own assessment is that no-fault is a much ballyhooed concept of modest attainments. Without doubt the most beneficial result is that almost everybody is entitled to prompt treatment of injuries without regard to fault and without delay."

2. See, e.g., *No-Fault Insurance Failing to Cut Rates,* New York Times, January 24, 1976, p. 1 and p. 22; *Casualty Costs—Problems & Premiums on No-Fault Insurance Outpacing Projections—Fast Payouts Help Motorists but Cut Interest Income; Prospects of Federal Law—Shiny Pot of Litigious Gold,* Wall Street Journal, January 21, 1976, pp. 1, 25; *Auto Insurance Rates to Rise 13%–20% This Year, Mostly Because of Inflation,* Wall Street Journal, January 21, 1976, p. 25.

3. See, e.g., Jeffrey O'Connell, *Operation of No-Fault Auto Laws: A Survey of Surveys,* 56 Nebraska Law Review 23–50, at p. 23 and pp. 36–39 (1977); *The Human*

Side of No-Fault Car Insurance, Money Magazine, Vol. 5, No. 11, p. 75, (November 1976).

4. Roger S. Clark & Gerald E. Waterson, *"No-Fault" in Delaware,* 6 Rutgers-Camden Law Journal 225–264 (1974); Joseph Little, *No-Fault Reparation in Florida: An Empirical Examination of Some of Its Aspects,* 9 University of Michigan Journal of Law Reform 1–61 (1975); Alan I. Widiss, *Massachusetts No-Fault Automobile Insurance: Its Impact on the Legal Profession,* 56 Boston University Law Review 323–355 (1976); Alan I. Widiss, *Accident Victims Under No-Fault Automobile Insurance: A Massachusetts Survey,* 61 Iowa Law Review 1–72 (1975); Alan I. Widiss, *A Survey of the No-Fault Personal Injury Claims Experience in Massachusetts,* in Widiss *et al,* No-Fault Automobile Insurance in Action; Randall Bovbjerg, *Massachusetts No-Fault: A Note on Some Changes in the Law and in Rate Levels,* in Widiss, *et al* NO-FAULT AUTOMOBILE INSURANCE IN ACTION (1977).

Early, partial reports of two of these studies were published in Joseph Little,

on Michigan prepared under the auspices of the Commissioner of Insurance of that state, were brought together in a single volume published in 1977.[5]

§ 4.11   Life Insurance

§ 4.11(a)   Generally

Life insurance policies typically afford the purchaser a number of distinct rights, including the right to originally designate and to subsequently change the beneficiary, the right to elect from among various settlement options the way the insurance proceeds will be paid upon death of the person whose life is insured, and, in many instances, the right to receive dividends. Life insurance policies often are sold with an investment feature. These policies, which are frequently referred to by the generic term "whole life insurance,"[1] usually include a variety of additional rights and interests that are not associated with other types of insurance generally or with term life insurance[2] in particular. For example, whole life insurance contracts will usually provide both a right[3] to borrow from the insurer using the policy as security for the loan[3] and a right to surrender the policy in exchange for a payment of the sum—usually denoted the "cash value" of the insurance policy— from the insurer. Consequently, the nature and extent of the various interests that may exist in life insurance contracts are significantly affected by whether the policy includes an investment component.

When a person obtains a life insurance policy on his or her own life, the purchaser generally designates who will be entitled to receive the proceeds upon death. In most situations, the insured retains or reserves the other ownership rights, including the authority to change who is designated as a beneficiary. However, there are situations in which some or all of the various ownership rights, including the right to alter the designation of the beneficiary or beneficiaries, are not retained by the purchaser. In other words, ownership rights which would normally be accorded the purchaser may be vested in or transferred to someone else either as a consequence of a voluntary action by the buyer or by operation of law. For example, following the acquisition of coverage, a buyer may elect to transfer certain rights because estate tax laws may make it desirable for a purchaser to enter into an agreement with or make an assignment to a named beneficiary which

How No Fault is Working in Florida, 59 American Bar Association Journal 1020–1024 (1973); Alan I. Widiss & Randall Bovbjerg, *No Fault in Massachusetts: Its Impact on Courts and Lawyers*, 59 American Bar Association Journal 487–491 (1973).

5. Widiss, Bovbjerg, Cavers, Little, Clark, Waterson, & Jones, No-Fault Automobile Insurance in Action: The Experiences in Massachusetts, Florida, Delaware and Michigan, (1977) [published by Oceana Publications, Inc., Dobbs Ferry, N.Y.].

§ 4.11(a)

1. See description of whole life insurance in § 1.5(c)(1), above.

2. See the description of term life & insurance in § 1.5(c)(1), above.

3. For example, see the form in Appendix E.

irrevocably grants to the beneficiary a vested interest in the insurance proceeds.[4] In other situations, the right to change the beneficiary may be assigned or transferred in connection with a transaction in which the insurance contract is used to secure a loan. The ownership rights may also be subject to commitments made in the provisions of a divorce or dissolution agreement.[5] And, in community property states, the purchaser's spouse may be entitled to an interest in a life insurance policy by operation of law, independently of the insurance contract's terms or the purchaser's actions or intent.[6]

§ 4.11(b) Community Property and Life Insurance

Community property laws vary considerably among the states which apply this doctrine, and consequently the effect of such laws on rights relating to life insurance contracts may differ depending on the state.[1]

In all community property states each spouse has an interest in any life insurance policy that is purchased with assets of the marital community. Although no attempt is made here to consider the intricacies of the rules applied in such states,[2] the holder of a right in a life insurance policy which is classified as community property is, with respect to its exercise, responsible to a spouse and to persons claiming through such a spouse. It has been observed, for example: "All of the

4. See March A. Bergman, *Fiduciary Responsibility and Group Life Assignments,* 119 Trust and Estates 36–39 (August, 1980); Henry C. Wolf, *The Assignment of Group Term Life Insurance: Shoals Between Scylla and Charybdis,* 6 Journal of Corporate Taxation 301–315 (1980); Alan F. Hilfiker, *Assignments of Group Term Life Insurance to Irrevocable Trusts,* 119 Trust and Estates 57–64 (September, 1980); Norman Shaw, *Beneficiary-Owned Insurance and Simultaneous Death,* 116 Trust and Estates 646–649 (October, 1977).

5. See, e.g., Murphy v. Travelers Insurance Company, 534 F.2d 1155 (5th Cir. 1976); Myers v. Myers, 408 A.2d 279 (Del. 1979) (a separation agreement with an irrevocable commitment to name wife as beneficiary of a fifty percent interest in an existing life insurance contract).

Also see McLeod v. Provident Mutual Life Insurance Company, 186 Colo. 234, 526 P.2d 1318 (1974); Great American Reserve Insurance Company v. Maxwell, 38 Colo.App. 305, 555 P.2d 988 (Div. I, 1976).

6. See § 4.11(b), below.

§ 4.11(b)

1. See Samuel D. Thurman, *Federal Estate and Gift Taxation of Community Property Life Insurance,* 9 Stanford Law Review 239–280 (1957); Annotation, *Application of*

community property system to problems arising in connection with life insurance policies, 168 A.L.R. 342–352 (1947); W.O. Huie, *Community Property Laws as Applied to Life Insurance,* 17 Texas Law Review 121–151 at pp. 123–124 (1939), 18 Texas Law Review 121–150 (1940); George E. Ray, *Life Insurance, Community Property and Death Taxes in Texas,* 26 Texas Bar Journal 835–836, continued on pp. 894–897 (1963).

See also Abel, Barry, Halsted & Marsh, *Rights of a Surviving Spouse in Property Acquired by a Decedent While Domiciled Outside California,* 47 California Law Review 211–237 (1959); William F. Fritz, *Survivorship Agreements Between Spouses,* 24 Texas Bar Journal 395–396, continued on pp. 463–466 (1961).

2. See Douglas Anne Munson, *The forgotten community property asset: An overview of the individual whole life insurance policy at the time of marital dissolution,* 53 California State Bar Journal 310–317 (1978); Ted Allen Schmidt, *Common Law Concepts of Life Insurance in Community Property Jurisdictions: Recommendations for a Practical Approach,* 18 Arizona Law Review 182–206 (1976); Note, *Community and Separate Property Interests in Life Insurance Proceeds: A Fresh Look,* 51 Washington Law Review 351–390 (1976).

decided cases in community property jurisdictions agree that if a husband takes out during the marriage a policy on his own life payable at his death to his estate, or to his executors, administrators, or assigns, and pays the premiums with community funds, when the marriage is dissolved by the death of the husband, the proceeds received by the husband's legal representatives belong to the community."[3] Also, "when the wife is named the beneficiary in a policy taken out by the husband upon his own life and paid for with community funds, the proceeds received by the wife at the husband's death are her separate property * * *. By making the policy payable to the wife, the cases usually reason, the husband has manifested an intent to make a gift to her of the proceeds."[4]

Community property laws ordinarily do not affect either the power of a person who is designated in a life insurance policy as the holder of a certain right to enforce that right in a proceeding against the insurer, or the protection which the insurer receives upon taking a release from that person.[5]

§ 4.11(c) Beneficiary Clauses of Life Insurance Policies

(1) Designation of Beneficiaries

In the nineteenth century and early twentieth century, life insurance policy forms often only provided for the designation of a person or persons to receive the policy proceeds, and did not include any provision for alternative dispositions of the policy proceeds should the designated beneficiary die before the death of the person whose life was insured. Furthermore, in some instances, the insurance contracts did not even address the question whether there were any circumstances under which an insured was entitled to change the beneficiary who was named at the outset of the insurance contract. The absence of such provisions may have reflected some sense that a beneficiary, once named, acquired some type of vested interest in the insurance contract. When a life insurance contract did not reserve to the policyholder the right to change the beneficiary, courts generally held that an insured could not take any action — such as an assignment of the policy or a change in the designation of the beneficiary (even with the acquiesence of the insurer) — without obtaining the beneficiary's consent.[1]

---

3. W.O. Huie, *Community Property Laws as Applied to Life Insurance,* 17 Texas Law Review 121–151 (1939), at p. 121.

4. *Id.,* at pp. 123–124.

5. There may be exceptions to this generalization. See, e.g., James R. Swift, *House Bill 900 and Your Life Insurance Policy,* 20 Texas Bar Journal 691–692, continued on pp. 721–723 at p. 722 (1957), suggesting that in Texas, at the time Swift was writing, if the insurance contract vested in the wife the legal title to rights under a policy that was classified as community,

it might be that only the husband could dispose of those rights since Vernon's Ann. Texas Civil Statutes art. 4619, then in effect, provided that during marriage community property "may be disposed of by the husband only * * *."

4.11(c)

1. See, e.g., Mutual Benefit Life Insurance Company v. Swett, 222 Fed. 200 (6th Cir.1915) (applying Michigan law); Davis v. Modern Industrial Bank, 279 N.Y. 405, 18 N.E.2d 639 (1939).

Contemporary insurance contracts usually include provisions that expressly reserve to the policyholder the right to change the beneficiary. When such a provision is included, anyone who is named as a beneficiary does not have a vested right unless there is a specific commitment (such as a promise to a beneficiary by the person who has the right to change the beneficiary named in the policy) that the designation will not be changed.[2] In addition, life insurance contracts now usually either detail contingent beneficiaries (who may be designated by name or by a clause which identifies persons on the basis of some specific relationship to the person whose life is insured), or provide that in the event no designated beneficiary can receive the insurance benefits the proceeds of the policy will be paid to the estate of the person whose life is insured.

(2) Payment Arrangements

Before the twentieth century, life insurance companies frequently used insurance policy forms which simply provided that upon the insured's death the beneficiaries would be paid the policy proceeds in cash. Most life insurance companies now offer purchasers several choices in regard to how the benefits will be paid, and the clauses which specify how and when payments will be made often can be designed so as to conform to the specific desires of a purchaser or to special features in the purchaser's estate plan. Alternatively, many insurers also afford purchasers the option of allowing the beneficiary to decide how the benefits will be paid.

Life insurance frequently serves an important function in estate planning, often providing a significant part of the assets of the estate, especially in the event that death occurs at an early age. Even when estates include substantial properties of other types, life insurance frequently is used to assure a degree of liquidity by providing a fund of ready cash.[3] Most questions relating to the role of life insurance in an estate plan are comparable to those which should be resolved in drafting a will, that is, they are not peculiarly insurance considerations.

The life insurance contract, which is usually comprised of a combination of standard form provisions and occasionally includes some specially drafted clauses, may set forth a complete plan for the use of the proceeds. Alternatively, one or more separate documents (such as a contract, a will, or a trust instrument) can be used to detail and implement the estate plan. Although specifying the terms for the payment or the use of insurance proceeds in separate documents may have some disadvantages, it allows various aspects of the arrangements

Also see Condon v. New York Life Insurance Company, 183 Iowa 658, 166 N.W. 452 (1918).

Also see Columbia Circle v. Mudra, 298 Ill. 599, 132 N.E. 213 (1921).

2. See, e.g., Brunnenmeyer v. Massachusetts Mutual Life Insurance Company, 66 Ill.App.3d 315, 23 Ill.Dec. 652, 384 N.E.2d 446 (3d Dist.1978).

3. See generally Arthur J. Wojta, *Life Insurance Funding of Stock Purchase Agreements,* 48 Nebraska Law Review 961–984 (1969).

to be altered indirectly — that is, without requiring that the insured retain the right to change the beneficiary specified in the insurance contract or the right to control other matters named in the insurance program — and this may afford a significant advantage in regard to estate tax considerations. In some situations, however, it may be either desirable or essential to assure flexibility by retaining the right to change the arrangements through modifications of the insurance contract (rather than through changing an instrument such as a will or a trust arrangement).

Life insurance is now commonly used to fund agreements for the sale and purchase of business interests in the event of a death among business associates such as partners. The survivors are provided insurance proceeds which can be used to acquire the interest of a deceased associate — that is, the insurance on the life of the deceased provides a cash fund that ultimately goes to the deceased's beneficiaries in return for the transfer of the deceased's interest in the business to the surviving business associates without necessitating the withdrawal of assets from the business and without requiring the liquidation of the business. Not surprisingly, tax considerations may greatly influence the design of such agreements.

When there is a possibility that other persons may assert claims to such life insurance proceeds, an insurer sometimes requires that the beneficiary clause of the policy include a provision protecting it from further liability upon payment to the specified person.[4]

§ 4.11(d)   Formalities for Changing Beneficiaries

Most life insurance policies now reserve to a policyholder (usually the person whose life is insured) the right to change the beneficiary.[1] Typically, several formalities are specified in a change-of-beneficiary clause, including provisions such as (1) that the policyholder must submit a written request to the insurer at its home office for a change of beneficiary, often on a form provided by the company, (2) that the insurer must receive either the original insurance policy or proof that the policy has been lost, and (3) that the insurer's endorsement of the change be noted in the original policy or a substitute policy issued in lieu of a lost policy. When the formalities prescribed for a change of beneficiary are fully satisfied, the change is effective against a person claiming under an earlier designation, even though the change was made without the former beneficiary's consent or knowledge.[2]

---

4. Compare the "facility of payment" clause of industrial policies, § 1.5(c)(2), above.

§ 4.11(d)

1. See Brunnenmeyer v. Massachusetts Mutual Life Insurance Company, 66 Ill. App.3d 315, 23 Ill.Dec. 652, 384 N.E.2d 446 (3d Dist.1978).

When a life insurance contract does not reserve the right to change a beneficiary, the designation of the beneficiary has been held to be irrevocable unless the beneficiary consents to a change. See, e.g., Garner v. Germania Life Insurance Company, 110 N.Y. 266, 18 N.E. 130 (1888).

2. Contractual agreements, however, between the policyholder and the original

(1) Partial Compliance with Formalities

When a policyholder attempts to change the designation of one or more beneficiaries in some fashion that does not conform to the formalities specified in a policy, disputes may arise between rival claimants. These cases often present conflicts between the interests served by insistence upon formalism with its attendant certainty, on the one hand, and the desire to carry out the intention of the policy owner, however manifested, on the other.[3] Recognition and application of rules which would allow a change of a beneficiary without complying with the formalities specified in the beneficiary clause of the life insurance policy can produce both uncertainty and the prospect of wasteful litigation, as well as the risk of mistakes by fact finders in determining what the intention was. Nevertheless, if one could always be confident of the inferences drawn from evidence of intention, particularly the inference that the policyholder made a deliberate choice without undue influence, courts would almost certainly adopt rules giving effect to such intention in preference to rules that do not implement expressions of intention which fail to comply with the formal requirements specified in an insurance contract.[4]

The application of a rule which does not require absolute compliance with all formalities specified in a life insurance policy concerning a change of a beneficiary seems appropriate in some situations. This approach is especially justified when the evidence shows that an insured has taken substantial affirmative action in an attempt to effectuate the change. The majority of the decisions in point adopt rules embracing this approach.[5] Several courts have observed or concluded,

---

beneficiary (or another for the original beneficiary's benefit) have been held to create a vested equitable interest in the insurance proceeds superior to the claim of the subsequently designated beneficiary. See, e.g., Kelly v. Layton, 309 F.2d 611 (8th Cir. 1962) (applying Missouri law). The insured, in order to induce divorced wife not to levy on arrears in support payments, agreed not to change designation of daughter as beneficiary. However, the insured subsequently filed a "lost policy" form with the company and named his second wife as beneficiary. The court held that the daughter was entitled to the insurance proceeds.

In Yates v. Yates, 272 F.2d 52 (5th Cir. 1959) (applying Florida law), the insured, who was obligated by property settlement in divorce from first wife to pay off mortgage on home retained by wife and to have his estate assume the obligation if he died before the debt was retired, promised to have insurance made payable to his estate for that purpose. The court held that the second wife, named as beneficiary in policies and named as executrix in will omitting any reference to mortgage obligation,

took subject to first wife's equitable interest, measured by outstanding debt on home at time of insured's death plus interest.

In Lee v. Preiss, 18 Wis.2d 109, 118 N.W.2d 104 (1962), the insured, in order to prevent action for nonsupport, orally agreed with former wife not to change designation of her and children as beneficiaries. The court held that the agreement gave wife and children a cause of action for equitable relief against subsequently designated beneficiary.

3. Concerning the conflict between formalism and flexibility generally, see § 1.4, above.

4. Consider the discussion in Richard Paroutaud, *Should Implied Revocation Be Applied to a Life Insurance Beneficiary Designation?*, 25 Federation of Insurance Counsel Quarterly 357–382 (1975).

5. See, e.g., Continental Assurance Company v. Platke, 295 F.2d 571 (7th Cir. 1961) (applying Illinois law); Equitable Life Assurance Society of U.S. v. Hitchcock, 270 Mich. 72, 258 N.W. 214 (1935), 106 A.L.R. 591 (1937); Boehne v. Guardian Life Insurance Company of America, 224

"All that is required is that every reasonable effort under the circumstances be made to effect the change."[6] These decisions are sometimes viewed as having adopted a rule of substantial compliance. However, characterizing these decisions in terms of a "substantial compliance" rule may be misleading. There are situations in which insureds take definite and substantial steps that clearly manifest intent, but the actions do not amount to "substantial compliance" with the formalities specified in the insurance contract. It seems likely that courts will give effect to some expressions of intent that do not constitute "substantial compliance."

The predictability of results under either a "substantial compliance" rule or a "definite and substantial act" rule is complicated by the fact that both approaches are fact-oriented, evaluative standards.[7] Various courts using these standards may reach quite inconsistent conclusions in the applications of such rules. Consequently, disagreements resulting in litigation are inherently a predictable consequence of any rule that requires consideration of what courses of conduct are sufficient to amount to "reasonable efforts under the circumstances." To predict the outcome of such cases, it is essential not only to evaluate whether the judicial precedents in a jurisdiction support such a rule, but also to consider what is the meaning that is implicit in those judicial precedents in relation to the facts of a current dispute.

Minn. 57, 28 N.W.2d 54 (1947); Fidelity Union Life Insurance Company v. Methven, 162 Tex. 323, 346 S.W.2d 797 (1961); Kotch v. Kotch, 151 Tex. 471, 251 S.W.2d 520 (1952).

Also see Travelers Insurance Company v. Smith, 106 Ill.App.3d 318, 62 Ill.Dec. 216, 435 N.E.2d 1188 at p. 1190 (1st Dist. 4th Div., 1982). The court commented

> "Requiring the insured to at least substantially comply with the policy provisions ensures that his intent is clearly manifested. But technical compliance with the policy provisions is solely for the benefit of the insurer, to protect it from paying the wrong person and being forced to pay twice."

See generally Annotation, *Change of beneficiary in group life insurance policy as affected by failure to comply with policy requirements as to manner of making change,* 78 A.L.R.3d 466–547 (1977); Annotation, *Change of beneficiary in old line insurance policy as affected by failure to comply with requirements as to manner of making of change,* 19 A.L.R.2d 5–129 (1951).

Cf. Note, *Changing the Beneficiary of a Life Insurance Policy in Texas,* 24 Baylor Law Review 121–131 (1972).

6. Provident Mutual Life Insurance Company v. Ehrlich, 508 F.2d 129 (3d Cir. 1975) (applying Pennsylvania law).

Also see Williams v. Sistare, 36 Conn. Supp. 252, 417 A.2d 369 at p. 370 (New London Dist.1980).

In Franklin Life Insurance Company v. Mast, 290 F.Supp. 671 at p. 676 (D.Ariz. 1968), the court concluded that where the decedent attempted to change the beneficiary of her life insurance policy by executing a holographic codicil to her will, it was appropriate to "employ the powers of a court of equity and treat the change of beneficiaries as having been regularly made * * *." The evidence showed that the decedent was in deathly fear of her husband, who was the primary beneficiary, that she did not want her husband to learn of the change. Also see the discussion of this case by the Ninth Circuit, reported at 435 F.2d 1038 (9th Cir.1970).

But see Allen v. Abrahamson, 12 Wn. App. 103, 529 P.2d 469 (Div. 2, 1974) (delivery of the insurance certificates by the insured to his parents was ineffective to designate them as beneficiaries in place of the decedent's former girl friend when he took no other steps to implement his expressed intention to make such a change).

7. Concerning fact-oriented, evaluative issues generally, see § 1.4, above.

(2) Standing to Raise Compliance With Formalities

Clauses requiring compliance with specified formalities to effect a change of beneficiary are undoubtedly included in insurance policies, at least in part, for the company's protection against rival claimants. When a company elects to waive its right to insist upon the formalities specified,[8] it has been successfully argued that an original beneficiary has no standing to contest the insurer's decision that a change in a beneficiary was effective.

Observations

The formalities required by change-of-beneficiary clauses arguably serve both the interests of the policyholder (in protecting the beneficiary formally named by the policyholder from being replaced by one whose supposed selection is merely inferred from informal evidence), and the interests of the third party beneficiary (in protecting that beneficiary from being superseded on the basis of questionable evidence of a change in the policyholder's intention).[9] This interpretation of the functional significance of the formalities specified in such clauses is analogous to the public interest in requiring that various formalities must be followed when executing a will that designates who are to be the beneficiaries of one's estate.[10] It is also consistent with the doc-

8. See, e.g., Provident Mutual Life Insurance Company of Philadelphia v. Ehrlich, 508 F.2d 129 at p. 134 (3d Cir.1975).

Also see Davis v. Modern Industrial Bank, 279 N.Y. 405, 18 N.E.2d 639 (1939), 135 A.L.R. 1035 (1941). In *Davis,* the insured had effected a valid assignment to a creditor "as his interest may appear." After the insured's death a dispute arose between the named beneficiary (the insured's widow) and the creditor-assignee as to the creditor's rights to the proceeds. The beneficiary contended that the assignment did not entitle the creditor to any of the proceeds because there was no formal designation of the creditor as a beneficiary and because the assignment itself did not carry the effect of entitlement to proceeds. The court held for the creditor-assignee on the grounds that the named beneficiary had no right to question the deficiency in meeting the formal requirements of a change of beneficiary when the insurance company had not done so.

In the context of conflicting claims of prior and subsequently designated beneficiaries, it has often been stated that the policy provisions were primarily (or even solely) for the protection of the company. See, e.g., Continental Assurance Company v. Platke, 295 F.2d 571 (7th Cir.1961) (Illinois law; interpleader action); Sears v. Austin, 292 F.2d 690 (9th Cir.1961), *cert. denied* 368 U.S. 929, 82 S.Ct. 365, 7 L.Ed.2d

192 (1961) (federal law; interpleader action); Fidelity Union Life Insurance Company v. Methven, 162 Tex. 323, 346 S.W.2d 797 (1961).

9. *Cf.* Kotch v. Kotch, 151 Tex. 471 at p. 477, 251 S.W.2d 520 at p. 523 (1952):

"But there is also merit in our existing view, which, while disclaiming to recognize a 'vested' right in the named beneficiary and while not denying that the policy provisions may be waived by the insurer, yet regards the matter as one of contract between insurer and insured for the benefit of a third party—the named beneficiary—and apparently represents a policy to forestall belated, informal treatment of these serious economic affairs, which is generally suspicious in appearance and nearly always confusing and litigious in result."

In Fidelity Union Life Insurance Company v. Methven, 162 Tex. 323, 346 S.W.2d 797 (1961), the court decided against the original beneficiary, holding that the change of beneficiary requirement was for the benefit of the insurer and had been waived by the insurer *during the lifetime* of the insured.

10. *Cf.* Stone v. Stephens, 155 Ohio St. 595, 99 N.E.2d 766 (1951), 25 A.L.R.2d 992 (1952), involving an attempt to change the beneficiary by will, a procedure that might seem formal enough in one sense because

trines and standards which are commonly applied in regard to determining the validity of or the intent manifested by contractual documents. Although protection of the insurance company's interests was certainly the primary — and perhaps originally the only — objective of such provisions, it does not necessarily follow that the waiver of compliance with the formalities should now be the exclusive prerogative of the insurer. To now view the formalities in a change-of-beneficiary clause as solely for the benefit of the insurer would be to disregard the fact that compliance with the terms of such clauses serves other interests as well.

The introduction of interpleader has reduced the relative importance of treating the requirements of change-of-beneficiary clauses as exclusively for the benefit of insurers because the use of this procedure provides an insurer with an effective alternative technique for avoiding liability arising from making an incorrect decision in regard to competing claims for the insurance, at least in those instances when the insurer is aware that more than one person has a claim. Therefore, the availability of interpleader provides another justification for refusing to read the change-of-beneficiary provision as one solely for the insurance company's protection.

The considerations set out in the preceding paragraphs provide substantial support for the proposition that the provisions which detail the formalities for changing the designation of beneficiaries in life insurance contracts should no longer to be treated as being exclusively for the benefit of the insurer, and therefore others (such as beneficiaries) should have standing to question whether there is sufficient evidence of the insured's intent to warrant disregarding the failure to comply.

The primary purpose in allowing persons other than the insurer to have standing to question whether there is adequate evidence of the insured's intent is to ensure that a careful evaluation is made in deciding whether to "validate" an informal indication of an intent that is contrary to the designation that was the formal and, at least presumably, a carefully considered choice of the insured. However, recognition that a beneficiary has standing to contest the effectiveness of an attempt to replace that person as a beneficiary also implies that such a duly designated beneficiary, who may benefit from some qualifi-

---

it complied with the requirements for wills. But it failed to comply with the terms of the change-of-beneficiary clause. The court noted the public interest in having insurers pay the beneficiary of a life insurance policy as soon as possible after the death of the person whose life was insured, and remarked: "There is sound reason both in law and in public policy for holding that a change of an insurance policy beneficiary by last will and testament of the insured is ineffective unless authorized by the terms of the policy." 155 Ohio St.

at p. 600, 99 N.E.2d at p. 769, 25 A.L.R.2d at p. 996.

But cf., Sears v. Austin, 292 F.2d 690 (9th Cir.1961), *cert. denied* 368 U.S. 929, 82 S.Ct. 365, 7 L.Ed.2d 192 (1961) (designation of beneficiary of Federal Employees' Group Life Insurance policy by holographic will held valid under Federal law). Of course a policy designating the insured's estate as the beneficiary enables the insured to provide by will for the disposition of the proceeds of the policy.

cations as to the kinds of attempted changes of beneficiary that will be effective, has something more than a mere expectancy interest in the life insurance contract during the life of the insured. This conclusion is not necessarily inconsistent with the theory that it is primarily the interest of the insured, and not that of the duly designated beneficiary, which courts are seeking to protect.

A rule allowing a formally designated beneficiary to contest a change that is based on evidence which does not satisfy the formality requirements established by the insurer is directed, at least in part, at protecting the beneficiary's interests (as well as those of the insured), rather than merely accomplishing this result coincidentally. Of course, it is also clear that a consequence of such a rule is that the formally named beneficiary is thereby afforded some additional protection.

(3) Insurance for Military Personnel

There is a line of cases concerning National Service Life Insurance, which is provided for military personnel, in which it has been said that noncompliance with specified formalities for a change of beneficiary is of less significance than would be true of similar coverage provided by private insurance contracts. For example, one court commented that they should "brush aside all legal technicalities in order to effectuate the manifest intention of the insured." [11] This proposition is of questionable validity.

The choice courts make between requiring adherence to the pre-scribed formalism and a rule which allows enforcement of the most informally expressed intention should be based on a consideration of the interests of the policyholder and of the potential claimants. It is a disservice to the interests of military personnel to brush aside all formalities as mere "technicalities" without analyzing whether they are useful requirements. Nevertheless, a different approach to assessing the requisite degree of compliance with the formalities specified in National Service Life Insurance cases may be justified, especially during times of war or when an insured is involved in combat, because of the varied circumstances under which the insurance forms are completed, the possibly greater likelihood of changes of circumstances, and the greater difficulties of communicating both rapidly and formally an individual's desire that a beneficiary be changed.[12]

---

11. United States v. Pahmer, 238 F.2d 431 at p. 433 (2d Cir.1956), quoting from Roberts v. United States, 157 F.2d 906 at p. 909 (4th Cir.1946), cert. denied 330 U.S. 829, 67 S.Ct. 870, 91 L.Ed. 1278 (1947).

Also see MacFarlane v. United States, 476 F.Supp. 787 (W.D.La.1979).

See generally, Annotation, *National service life insurance: change of beneficiary,* 2 A.L.R.2d 489–511 (1948).

12. *Cf.* Coomer v. United States, 471 F.2d 1 (5th Cir.1973) (upheld the designa-

tion of the serviceman's parents to receive $10,000 of Servicemen's Group Life Insurance on the basis of a form that was countersigned by personnel director and an officer, but that was never forwarded to the Veterans Administration and was found with the decedent's personal effects in his footlocker which was shipped to his parents).

Without regard to the relevance of such special considerations, the National Service Life Insurance cases — and, specifical-

(4) Double Liability for Insurers

The judicial precedents for the proposition that an original beneficiary has standing to contest the effectiveness of an attempted change of beneficiary which does not conform with requirements set out in an insurance contract also mean that insurers are subject to a risk of double liability if a payment is made to the wrong person. An insurer, for example, might be held liable to an original beneficiary after having previously paid the insurance proceeds to a person whom the insured had later sought to designate and whom the insurer had accepted as the new beneficiary.[13]

The magnitude of the risk to an insurer in such situations could be affected by a court's position with respect to whether the insurer's decision to endorse or to decline to endorse a change in the beneficiary as requested by a policyholder is relevant to the issues relating to compliance with the policy requirements. In most circumstances, it should be the nature of the policyholder's actions, rather than the insurer's response, which bears upon the question of the reliability of evidence of the policyholder's intention — that is, the nature of the policyholder's actions should be decisive of the issue of substantial compliance. If this approach were adopted, it would not mean that the company's response was totally irrelevant, however. In those situations in which a sequence of communications occurred between the policyholder and the insurer, the company's responses would be taken into account in assessing the significance of later communications from the policyholder.

Comment

As a general principle, it is undesirable to have rules of law that permit one party to have the power to allocate burdens or benefits between two other parties with no consequent responsibilities or potential liability. Such an unpoliced power is an open invitation not only to arbitrary action, but also to corruption. Thus, if it is held that an

---

ly, the quotation from *Pahmer* in the text, supra — were relied on in Sears v. Austin, 292 F.2d 690 (9th Cir.1961), *cert. denied* 368 U.S. 929, 82 S.Ct. 365, 7 L.Ed.2d 192 (1961), to validate a beneficiary designation by holographic will made by a former Internal Revenue Service employee under his Federal Employees Group Life Insurance. Before making that will, the insured had not designated any beneficiary; his group certificate stated that, if no specific beneficiary was designated according to the prescribed procedure, the proceeds would pass, in his case, to his children in equal shares. After the insured's death, the children as well as the beneficiary designated in the will (an unrelated woman who had apparently provided the insured with nursing services) claimed the proceeds. In validating the designation by will, the court held that the policy formalities were for the benefit of the insurer only, which in this case had interpleaded the rival claimants rather than rely on the protection of the provisions.

Also see Annotation, *Change, or designation, of beneficiary in group life policy issued under Federal Employees' Group Life Insurance Act,* 2 A.L.R.3d 1141–1143 (1965).

13. The problem could arise not only when an insured failed to comply with the formalities specified in the policy, but also when an insured failed even to measure up to those lesser formalities implicit in a judicially created standard such as "substantial compliance."

insurance company's response to a policyholder's "informal" request to change beneficiaries is decisive of rival claims, it should also be held that the company is at least subject to liability for bad faith in exercising this power and perhaps also for negligence. This combination of rules, however, seems less desirable than a criterion based solely on an assessment of the nature of the policyholder's steps toward making a change of beneficiary, rather than on an evaluation of the insurer's response to those actions of a policyholder.

§ 4.11(e) Assignments of Life Insurance

(1) Beneficiaries versus Assignees

A person who is designated as a beneficiary of a life insurance policy is ordinarily entitled to the insurance proceeds upon the death of the individual whose life is insured. When a life insurance policy has been assigned, however, questions may arise as to whether the assignee has a priority in regard to the insurance benefits, and, if so, the extent of the priority of the assignee's right to the insurance proceeds.

If a life insurance policy does not reserve to the policyholder a right to change the beneficiary (a situation more common in the past than currently), generally it has been held that no assignment of the policy could be made that impaired a beneficiary's rights without the beneficiary's consent.[1] Consequently, when an assignment of a life insurance policy was made without securing the beneficiary's consent, the assignee's rights were not accorded a priority over a beneficiary's claim to the insurance. The application of this rule by the courts led to the development of insurance policy provisions which both reserved the right of the policyholder to change beneficiaries and empowered the insured to make assignments which would provide assignees with a priority over beneficiaries.

Most life insurance contracts now include clauses that explicitly allow a purchaser of a life insurance policy to assign the policy. Unfortunately many of the life insurance forms used by insurance companies did not, and in some instances still do not,[2] specify whether a

---

§ 4.11(e)

1. See, e.g., Davis v. Modern Industrial Bank, 279 N.Y. 405 at p. 409, 18 N.E.2d 639 at p. 640 (1939), 135 A.L.R. 1035 at p. 1037 (1941), characterizing this rule as "the law in every jurisdiction in this country except Wisconsin."

2. Compare the more explicit clauses of Appendix E, with the following clauses, taken from a form still widely used as late as 1960:

"*Assignment.* No assignment of this policy shall be binding on the Company unless a duplicate thereof be filed with the Company at its Home office. The Company assumes no responsibility as to the validity of any assignment. Any as-

signment shall be subject to any indebtedness to the Company on account of or secured by this policy."

"*Change of Beneficiary.* The beneficiary designation may be changed at any time, and from time to time, by written request filed at the Home Office of the Company and accompanied by this policy for endorsement. The new designation shall be subject to any existing assignment and shall take effect only upon endorsement hereon by the Company at its Home Office. If there is no beneficiary surviving at the death of the Insured, then, unless otherwise provided herein, the proceeds of this policy shall be paid to the person or persons who,

claim to the insurance proceeds by the beneficiary is superior to that of the assignee. In the absence of any provision establishing a priority as between an assignee and a beneficiary, the clear majority rule is that the assignee of a policy is entitled to the insurance benefits.[3] Moreover, among these precedents are a number of decisions which conclude that an assignee will receive the entire insurance proceeds unless it is clear that the assignment is only for a share of the policy. Assignments are often made to secure a debt,[4] and several questions which relate to these transactions are considered in § 4.11(f).

(2) Compliance with Formalities

Insurers have specified a variety of different formalities which are to be complied with when assigning a life insurance policy. Sometimes these formalities are similar to the requirements established for changing a beneficiary; sometimes different formalities are prescribed for assignments.

When the interests of the insurance company are not prejudiced by the failure to comply with the requirements specified for an assignment, there are notable differences among the judicial precedents with respect to whether a purported assignment which does not comply with

upon proof by affidavit or other written evidence satisfactory to the Company, appear to be the then living lawful bodily and legally-adopted child or children of the Insured, equally if more than one, or, if none, to the executors or administrators of the estate of the Insured. The words 'child' and 'children' are used herein to refer to only the first generation. The right to revoke and change any beneficiary designation is reserved to the Insured unless otherwise specified herein."

Also see Herbert v. Pace, 351 So.2d 529 (Miss.1977).

3. See, e.g., in Herbert v. Pace, 351 So. 2d 529 at p. 530 (Miss.1977). The court concluded that "the absolute assignment by the insured to his [third] wife vested her with all right, title, and interest in the policy together with the proceeds accruing therefrom upon death of the insured to the exclusion of the named beneficiary [a daughter from his second marriage."

Also see McAllen State Bank v. Texas Bank & Trust Company, 433 S.W.2d 167 (Tex.1968); Davis v. Modern Industrial Bank, 279 N.Y. 405, 18 N.E.2d 639 (1939), 135 A.L.R. 1035 (1941).

The beneficiary, however, may have a claim against the estate of the decedent for an amount equal to the part of the policy proceeds applied in discharge of a debt of the decedent. *Cf.* Roundtree v. Frazee, 282 Ala. 142, 209 So.2d 424 (1968).

But cf. In re Estate of Green, 415 Pa. 161, 202 A.2d 17 (1964); Annotation, *Right of life insurance beneficiary against estate of insured who sued policy as collateral,* 91 A.L.R.2d 496–507 (1963).

See generally, Annotation, *Effectiveness, as pledge, of transfer of non-negotiable instruments which represent obligation,* 53 A.L.R.2d 1396–1413 at pp. 1404–1406 (1957). The author of the annotation concludes that: "The rule that an intangible interest or chose in action may be pledged by *delivery of the instrument embodying the right* has often been applied, at least verbally, in cases involving the delivery of insurance policies as collateral security." (Emphasis added). *Id.,* at p. 1404.

4. For example, in Livingston v. Shelton, 11 Wn.App. 854, 526 P.2d 385 (Div. 3, 1974), *cert. denied* 424 U.S. 958, 96 S.Ct. 1437, 47 L.Ed.2d 365 (1976), the court concluded that the beneficiary made out a prima facie case that the insurance was not intended to be the primary security for the payment of a promissory note executed by the insured which was accompanied by other security. Accordingly, the beneficiary was entitled to an equitable lien (essentially a right of subrogation) against the other property in the insured's estate, that was given as security for the loan, for the amount of the insurance proceeds that were applied against the note by the assignee-creditor.

the formalities may nevertheless be effective to give the assignee a claim to the insurance proceeds superior to that of a beneficiary. The dispute may be characterized as one over whether the formalities described in an assignment clause are intended only for the protection of the insurance company, and may therefore be waived by it, or whether they are intended instead to protect the interests of the beneficiary as well, with the consequence that a beneficiary may successfully challenge a purported assignment which did not comply with those formalities. The terms in insurance policy forms or other documents are usually of little use in resolving this dispute.

Some courts conclude that the assignee should prevail[5] even though the required formalities have not been fully satisfied.[6] This result is consistent with a large body of precedent regarding the formalities required for a change of beneficiary.[7] Moreover, in many situations this rule results in fulfilling a clearly manifested intention on the part of the policyholder, even when that intention was not expressed in a way which fully complied with the formalities specified in the insurance contract. Furthermore, arguably any rule which facilitates the assignability of life insurance contracts also enhances the value of life insurance policies as assets, and therefore is a result that serves the interests of insureds generally.

On the other hand, the types of dangers which have given rise to the statute of frauds weigh against the desirability of favoring rules which facilitate assignability of life insurance policies by wholly informal means.[8] Although the relative importance of such considerations in this context may not be self-evident, it is recognized as a factor of more than minimal importance. The New York legislature, for example, enacted a statute rendering unenforceable any "contract to assign or an assignment * * * of a life * * * insurance policy, or a promise * * * to name a beneficiary of any such policy * * *" unless the agreement or a memorandum of it is in writing.[9]

5. See, e.g., Farmers State Bank v. Kelley, 155 Ga. 733, 118 S.E. 197 (1923).

Cf. Abbruzise v. Sposata, 306 Mass. 151, 27 N.E.2d 722 (1940).

See generally 2A APPLEMAN, INSURANCE LAW (Revised edition, 1966) at § 1193, § 1196, §§ 1219–1221 and §§ 1246–1250.

6. The appropriateness of this approach is fortified by drawing an analogy to the assignability rule which is applied by courts in determining the rights of "third party owners" of interests in life insurance policies, which holds that substantial compliance with formalities (rather than strict compliance) is sufficient. Concerning assignments by "third-party owners" generally, see Dibrell, *Life Insurance Policies— Transfers by Third Party Owners*, 4 Forum

26–39 (ABA Section Insurance, Negligence & Compensation Law, 1968).

Concerning rights of creditors-assignees generally, see § 4.11(f), below.

7. See generally the discussion in § 4.11(d), above.

8. *Cf.* Allen v. Abrahamson, 12 Wn. App. 103, 529 P.2d 469 (Div. 2, 1974) (insured delivered certificates of insurance to his parents, but did not take other steps to effect an expression of his intent to change the designation of beneficiary from a former girlfriend to his parents).

9. New York Laws 1943, c. 104, carried forward as McKinney's—New York General Obligations Law § 5–701(9) (1974 and 1984–85 Supp.).

In a leading New York case involving an application of the New York statute,[10] the court observed that the dispute posed two familiar questions: *first*, whether apparent injustice in particular cases from rigid enforcement of a statute of frauds is too great a price to pay for the prevention of other injustices at which such a statute is aimed; and, *second*, whether the statute can be properly construed as allowing exceptions for oral agreements the genuineness of which is attested to by some independent evidence. In this New York case, the independent evidence included payment of the premiums by the plaintiff (assignee), delivery of the policy to the plaintiff, and continued possession by her until the policy was surreptitiously removed by the deceased's sister and the deceased. The complaint had been dismissed in the trial court, and consequently the claim reached the New York Court of Appeals in a procedural context that was favorable to the plaintiff. Taking her allegations as true for the purpose of deciding the issue presented on appeal, the Court of Appeals sustained her contention that her claim was not barred by the statute. However, three of the seven judges dissented, contending that the arrangement alleged by the plaintiff was precisely the kind that the statute should render void.[11]

§ 4.11(f)   Creditors as Beneficiaries or Assignees

A life insurance policyholder will often designate a creditor as either a beneficiary or an assignee of the policy. When this occurs, questions may arise with respect both to the fact and to the extent of the creditor's rights to the proceeds of the policy at the death of the person whose life is insured. Occasionally, issues also develop in regard to other rights such as the authority of the policyholder to change the beneficiary or to arrange a loan from the insurer.

(1) Insurance Acquired by a Debtor

When the proceeds of the insurance policy do not exceed the amount of the debt to a creditor (including any accumulation or interest and charges), ordinarily no disputes arise as a result of the designation of a creditor as a beneficiary or an assignee. In the event the debt remains unpaid at the insured's death, the insurance is paid to the creditor.

When the debt (including any accumulation of interest and charges) is less than the policy proceeds, however, someone — such as the original beneficiary, a contingent beneficiary, or the insured's estate — may claim to be entitled to the policy proceeds that are in excess of the debt. One argument commonly advanced by such a non-creditor claimant is that the designation of a creditor as beneficiary or assignee was intended as security for payment of the debt and no more. When an intention to so limit the creditor's interest is clearly manifest-

---

10. Katzman v. Aetna Life Insurance Company, 309 N.Y. 197, 128 N.E.2d 307 (1955).

11. *Id.*, 309 N.Y. at p. 205, 128 N.E.2d at p. 311.

ed, a persuasive case can be made against allowing the creditor to receive the full amount of the insurance.[1]

Ordinarily the document designating a creditor as beneficiary or assignee is the principal evidence of the policyholder's intention, and of the creditor's actual or reasonable expectations. If the document explicitly limits the arrangement to security for the payment of the debt, that limitation will be enforced. Often, however, such documents do not include provisions which clearly and explicitly characterize the nature of the transaction.

When a document creating an assignment or designating a beneficiary does not state whether or not a creditor's right to the insurance proceeds is to be limited to the amount of the debt, a creditor's claim to all of the insurance benefits is stronger if the creditor was designated as the primary beneficiary of the policy rather than as an assignee (unless someone else was designated as an assignee[2]). This conclusion is supported by the fact that it is common to make an assignment as security for a debt, but uncommon to change the beneficiary for this limited purpose. Thus, if no other indication of intent appears, a court is likely to infer that the policyholder who designated the creditor as a beneficiary of the policy by a change-of-beneficiary endorsement intended that the creditor's right to proceeds at death would not be limited to the amount of the debt. The creditor's claim is also somewhat more persuasive when an insurance policy is taken out contemporaneously with the loan transaction, and the creditor is the designated beneficiary.[3]

When there are conflicts over who is entitled to the proceeds of life insurance policies, it seems clear that both the specific circumstances and a general sense of justice will always be significant influences on the result. For example, even though a designation of the creditor was made by a change-of-beneficiary endorsement at the time the policyholder obtained a loan from the creditor, if it also appears that the policyholder had no other relationship with the creditor, a compelling argument can be presented that the designation was made in this way only because the creditor insisted upon it to avoid any doubt about the priority of his or her rights over those of the beneficiary, and with the understanding that the creditor would receive no more than full payment of the debt (including interest and charges).[4]

---

§ 4.11(f)

1. In considering a claim by the decedent's brother (who was the original beneficiary) seeking any amount of insurance in excess of the insured's debt from a creditor subsequently named as the beneficiary, the Tenth Circuit Court of Appeals commented "that *absent a clear, convincing and cogent expression on the part of the insured to the contrary,* the designated beneficiary in a policy of insurance is entitled to the entire proceeds on maturity of the contract." Zolintakis v. Orfanos, 119 F.2d 571 at p. 577 (10th Cir.1941) (emphasis added).

2. The reason for the proviso is that ordinarily an assignee's claim is prior in right to that of a beneficiary. See § 4.11(e), above.

3. See the discussion on life insurance acquired by a creditor of the insured in § 4.11(f)(2), below.

4. A better way of accomplishing this assurance — at least from the point of view of the policyholder and the beneficiary —

A forceful argument can be made for the proposition that a creditor's interest in life insurance proceeds should always be limited to the amount of the debt as a matter of public policy. This argument is based on the principle of indemnity — that is, if a creditor is allowed to recover more than the amount of the debt (together with an appropriate allowance for interest on the debt and other charges), the creditor is unjustly enriched.

There are numerous judicial precedents which have allowed a creditor beneficiary to retain the full amount of the life insurance proceeds[5] — that is, many courts do not apply the principle of indemnity to such claims by creditors. These decisions appear to be based on at least two distinct rationales. First, a creditor who is designated as a beneficiary should be allowed to recover without regard to the principle of indemnity because it is generally recognized that the person whose life is insured is free to designate anyone as a beneficiary.[6] Second, life insurance policies should be freely and fully transferable (by assignment or by designation of the beneficiary) in order to maximize the value of such contracts as investments, and the imposition of the principle of indemnity (or the insurable interest requirement) would inevitably diminish the value of the life insurance contracts in some degree.[7]

There is a clear division of authority on the issue among the opinions which bear directly on whether a creditor is entitled to the full amount of the life insurance without regard to the amount of the debt.[8] Many judicial decisions have declined to allow a creditor designated as either a beneficiary or an assignee of a life insurance policy to retain more than a sum equal to the debt, plus interest and charges (including premiums paid to keep the policy in force).[9] In these decisions, courts have frequently decided, either explicitly or implicitly, that an assign-

would be to have the beneficiary join in an assignment that acknowledges the priority of the assignee's rights, *and* to have the assignment specify that it is for security only.

5. See, e.g., American Casualty Company v. Rose, 340 F.2d 469 (10th Cir.1964); Zolintakis v. Orfanos, 119 F.2d 571 (10th Cir.1941); Forster v. Franklin Life Insurance Company, 135 Colo. 383, 311 P.2d 700 (1957).

Cf. Rettenmaier v. Rettenmaier, 255 Iowa 952, 124 N.W.2d 453 (1963).

6. See § 3.5(c), above.

7. *Ibid.*

8. See the decisions cited in note 5, above, and note 9, below.

9. See, e.g., General Motors Acceptance Corporation v. Kendrick, 270 Ala. 25, 115 So.2d 487 (1959); Dunn v. Second National Bank, 131 Tex. 198, 113 S.W.2d 165, 115 A.L.R. 730 (1938).

Cf. Sachs v. United States, 412 F.2d 357 at pp. 364–365 (8th Cir.1969) (applying Missouri law), *cert. denied* 396 U.S. 906, 90 S.Ct. 220, 24 L.Ed.2d 182 (1969); Johnson v. Great Heritage Life Insurance Company, 490 S.W.2d 686 (Mo.App.Div. 2, 1973); Balcer v. Peters, 37 Mich.App. 492, 195 N.W. 2d 83 (Div. 1, 1972); Pioneer Homeowners Life Insurance Company v. Hogan, 110 Ga. App. 887, 140 S.E.2d 212 (Div. 3, 1965).

Also see Poe v. Founders Life Assurance Company of Florida, 145 Ga.App. 757, 245 S.E.2d 166 (Div. 2, 1978) (credit life insurance policy); Johnson v. Great Heritage Life Insurance Company, 490 S.W.2d 686 at p. 691 (Mo.App., Div. 2, 1973).

See generally, Annotation, *Rights in respect of proceeds of life insurance under policy naming creditor as beneficiary,* 115 A.L.R. 741–750 (1938); Vance, LAW OF INSURANCE (Third edition, Anderson 1951), at § 123, who attempts to reconcile most of the conflicting authorities.

ment to a creditor was intended to be limited to the amount of the debt even though the indicia of such an intent often are not very specific. Furthermore, the principle of indemnity still seems to be a factor which often is significant in the resolution of disputes when creditors claim insurance benefits exceeding the amount of an insured's debt.[10] Thus, not only is there substantial support among the appellate decisions for the proposition that creditors are not always entitled to the full insurance proceeds, but also there is not even a clear majority in favor of recognizing a rebuttable presumption in favor of the creditors' right to the entire insurance proceeds.

(2) Insurance Acquired by a Creditor

Disagreements about whether a creditor who has taken out a policy on the life of the debtor may recover and retain the full amount of the policy, even though it exceeds the debt, have also produced litigation.[11] When a creditor obtains a life insurance policy on the life of a debtor, arguably the debtor has no interest in such a policy. However, when a life insurance policy is obtained and issued as an integral part of the loan transaction (rather than being obtained by the creditor at a later time, at the creditor's own instance), the debtor in a sense bears the burden of the cost of the insurance because the interest or repayment terms of the loan agreement will almost certainly be influenced by the amount of the insurance premium the creditor expects to pay for the life insurance.

The fact that a creditor obtains a life insurance policy does not, of course, necessarily prove that the debtor and his or her estate have no legal interest in the insurance. For example, even though the creditor appears to have arranged for the insurance and paid the premium(s), it is quite possible for such a policy to include a beneficiary clause that designates the estate of the debtor (the person whose life is insured) as the contingent beneficiary. In such a case, even though the creditor is designated as primary beneficiary, the debtor is not a stranger to the contract, and equitable principles might be appropriately applied to give the debtor's estate a right to that part of the proceeds in excess of the debt. Even in the absence of such arrangements in regard to the designation of a contingent beneficiary, in general it would seem that a

---

10. See Albrent v. Spencer, 275 Wis. 127, 81 N.W.2d 555 (1957), in which the court concluded that "any purported absolute assignment by a debtor to a creditor of a policy, which has previously been pledged as security to the creditor is only valid between the immediate parties to the extent of enabling the creditor to realize * * *" an amount exceeding the debt. 275 Wis. at 139, 81 N.W.2d at 561. This is, of course, inconsistent with the generally applicable rule of free assignability of a life insurance policy by the person whose life is insured when that person is also the owner of the policy interests relevant to assign-

ment. Also see a second opinion in this case reported at 3 Wis.2d 273, 88 N.W.2d 333 (1958).

11. *Cf.* Urquhart v. Alexander and Alexander, Inc., 218 Md. 405 at pp. 412–414, 147 A.2d 213 at p. 218 (1958).

Also see Forster v. Franklin Life Insurance Company, 135 Colo. 383, 311 P.2d 700 (1957).

See generally, Annotation, *Rights in respect of proceeds of life insurance under policy naming creditor as beneficiary,* 115 A.L.R. 741–750 (1938).

case can be made in many situations that the debtor's estate should be accorded an equitable interest in any life insurance which exceeds the debt, at least whenever there is some evidence of an understanding that the insurance is obtained exclusively to secure the debt.

§ 4.11(g)   Disqualification of Beneficiaries

(1) Generally

A beneficiary otherwise entitled to receive the proceeds of a life insurance policy may be disqualified from doing so if that individual was responsible in some way for bringing about the death of the person whose life was insured.[1] Although the principle underlying such disqualifications is often stated to be that "no one shall be allowed to benefit from his own wrong,"[2] this statement actually sets forth a proposition which is of significantly broader scope than is manifested by the holdings in the decisions that are in point — that is, the rules that have evolved from the judicial decisions which have disqualified beneficiaries are considerably more circumscribed than suggested by such a general proposition.[3]

The disqualification of a life insurance beneficiary is almost always limited to situations in which there was an intentional, unlawful killing.[4] Beneficiaries rarely are disqualified in cases in which death

---

§ 4.11(g)

1. See, e.g., Metropolitan Life Insurance Company v. McDavid, 39 F.Supp. 228 (E.D. Mich.1941), and the authorities cited at 39 F.Supp. at p. 231. In some instances, particularly in policies issued by fraternal associations, the insurance provisions may explicitly void the coverage in the event the beneficiary causes the insured's death.

Also see MacKowiak v. Polish Union of America, 236 App.Div. 44, 258 N.Y.S. 134 (4th Dept.1932); Greer v. Supreme Tribe of Ben Hur, 195 Mo.App. 336, 190 S.W. 72 (1916).

Cf. New England Mutual Life Insurance Company v. Null, 605 F.2d 421 (8th Cir. 1979) (life insurance contract was held to be void ab initio when it was shown that the beneficiary obtained the policy with a present intention to murder the insured).

See generally, Annotation, *Killing of insured by beneficiary as affecting life insurance or its proceeds,* 27 A.L.R.3d 794–839 (1964).

See also § 5.3(b), below.

2. Carter v. Carter, 88 So.2d 153 at p. 157 (Fla.1956).

Also see United Benefit Life Insurance Company v. Brady, 443 F.Supp. 762 (D.Mass.1978); Bounds v. Caudle, 560 S.W.2d 925 at p. 928 (Tex.1977); State

Farm Life Insurance Company v. Smith, 66 Ill.2d 591, 6 Ill.Dec. 838, 363 N.E.2d 785 at p. 786 (1977).

Also consider Metropolitan Life Insurance Company v. Hill, 115 W.Va. 515, 177 S.E. 188 (1934).

Cf. New York Life Insurance Company v. Henriksen, 415 N.E.2d 146 at p. 147 (Ind. App., 3d Dist.1981), *rehearing denied* 421 N.E.2d 1117 (Ind.App.1981).

3. See, e.g., Minasian v. Aetna Life Insurance Company, 295 Mass. 1, 3 N.E.2d 17 (1936).

In Reynolds v. American-Amicable Life Insurance Company, 591 F.2d 343 at p. 345 (5th Cir.1979) (applying South Carolina law), the court concluded that the "common law rule * * * does not prevent recovery by a person * * * [who] acted as an accessory after the fact in helping to conceal the murder." The court observed that the acts "were not undertaken in order to benefit under the insurance policy" because if they had been successful in concealing the murder it would have enabled the murderer to recover under the policy.

4. *Cf.* New York Life Insurance Company v. Jones, 86 Wash.2d 44, 541 P.2d 989 (1975).

See generally the discussion in § 5.3(b) (4), below.

resulted from negligent or reckless conduct.[5] Furthermore, the scope of the rule in regard to whether a killing will be treated as "intentional" is not necessarily co-extensive with the definitions of intentional harm that are generally applied in cases involving criminal law or tort law.[6] The meaning of "intentional" used as a criterion for determining whether one is disqualified as a life insurance beneficiary[7] is not always the same as that used for the purpose of classifying an offense under the criminal law as an intentional homicide (instead of a lesser crime) or for the purpose of classifying an offense under tort law as a battery (instead of a reckless or negligent invasion of interests in bodily security).[8]

Some types of conduct which relate to the death of an individual — and which are classified as intentional crimes or torts — do not involve an intent to bring about death (whether that of the victim or of another individual) or even to bring about an intrusion on bodily security likely to produce serious injury or death. Such offenses probably would not disqualify a life insurance beneficiary.[9] In most jurisdictions, disqualification is confined to circumstances involving an intent either to cause death or to cause the type of intrusion on another's physical security that is likely to cause death.[10]

5. See, e.g., Commercial Travelers Mutual Accident Association v. Witte, 406 S.W.2d 145 (Ky.1966), 27 A.L.R.3d 784 (1969) (applying New York law; wife convicted of involuntary manslaughter in death of husband from stabbing during domestic quarrel not disqualified); Provident Life and Accident Insurance Company v. Carter, 345 So.2d 1245 (La.App., 1st Cir., 1977) (beneficiary who killed insured in lawful self-defense is entitled to claim insurance proceeds).

Also consider the comment of the Washington Supreme Court in New York Life Insurance Company v. Jones, 86 Wash.2d 44 at p. 48, 541 P.2d 989 at p. 991 (1975), that: "Since a charge of second-degree felony murder (assault in the second degree) can be sustained without proof that the killing was intentionally done, it follows that a plea of guilty to such a charge does not admit that the killing was willful."

6. *Cf.* In re Vadlamudi's Estate, 183 N.J.Super. 342, 443 A.2d 1113 (Law Division, Probate Part, Middlesex County, 1982).

7. See, e.g., Davis v. Aetna Life Insurance Company, 279 F.2d 304 (9th Cir.1960) (applying California law; guilty plea of beneficiary to charge of voluntary manslaughter was admissible as an admission against interest in dispute over insurance proceeds but was not conclusive on issue).

Cf. Rose v. Rose, 79 N.M. 435, 444 P.2d 762 (1968) (statute disqualifying convicted murderers held to express a legislative intent not to disqualify wife convicted of voluntary manslaughter).

8. Also, the standard of proof applicable to the resolution of the proof of "intent" in a civil proceeding to decide an insurance claim may be less stringent (e.g. "preponderance of the evidence" rather than "beyond a reasonable doubt").

But cf. In re McGowan's Estate, 35 Cal. App.3d 611, 111 Cal.Rptr. 39 (1st Dist., Div. 2, 1973) (observing that the California law was that the proper standard of proof in probate court as to whether a killing was unlawful and intentional was a finding of guilt beyond reasonable doubt).

9. An example that is sometimes used to illustrate this point is the observation that "if one brother, in a boyish quarrel, should give another a slight blow or push, and death should unexpectedly result, a forfeiture of insurance or of inheritance would be a consequence undesired by the deceased and shocking to the community." Minasian v. Aetna Life Insurance Company, 295 Mass. 1 at p. 6, 3 N.E.2d 17 at p. 19 (1936). Of course, even in the law of crime and tort, an intentional impact may be determined to be privileged and therefore not actionable.

10. *Cf.* Minasian v. Aetna Life Insurance Company, 295 Mass. 1 at p. 6, 3 N.E.2d 17 at p. 19 (1936).

In general, the proposition that one shall not be allowed to benefit from one's own wrong is not very helpful as a premise from which to attempt to engage in a logical deduction of an answer to particular questions about the likelihood of disqualification of a given beneficiary. Nevertheless, it is useful as an enunciation of a societal interest with which courts must be concerned in working out the legal rules for particular cases.[11]

(2) The Effect of Legislative Provisions That Affect a Beneficiary's Right to Receive Life Insurance

In several states, legislation specifically precludes the payment of life insurance to a beneficiary who intentionally kills an insured. These statutes also provide that the insurance benefits must still be paid. For example, in New Jersey the statute states payment will be made "as though the killer had predeceased the decedent."[12] In Texas, "the nearest relative of the insured shall receive" the insurance.[13] And in Washington, the insurance "shall be paid * * * to the estate of the decedent, unless the policy or certificate designate[s] some person other than the slayer or his estate as secondary beneficiary to him, and in which case such proceeds shall be paid to such secondary beneficiary in accordance with the applicable terms of the policy."[14] Although the specific provisions are distinctive, the common goal of such statutes is clear. However, the provisions included in these statutes vary in regard to the questions which are to be considered by a court in determining whether a claimant is subject to the legislative prohibition.

In most states, there are no statutory provisions which address questions that arise in connection with the rights of life insurance beneficiaries.[15] In these states, the doctrines and rules which typically

11. It is not uncommon for two broad principles, based on different public interests, to come into competition with each other so that neither alone can be taken as an accurate expression of the foundation for the resulting legal rules. See Robert E. Keeton, VENTURING TO DO JUSTICE (1969) at pp. 164–166. The task of formulating a strictly accurate and complete expression of the underlying aims of a rule would be virtually as complex as stating the precise rule itself. Still, understanding may be aided by a generalization that identifies a broad objective without specifying the extent to which it is carried out in particular applications.

12. New Jersey Statute Annotated § 3A:2A–83(c), which was encoded as part of a Will and Probate Reform Act in 1977, was adapted from the Uniform Probate Code. The statutory provisions are discussed in In re Vadlamudi's Estate 183 N.J.Super. 342, 443 A.2d 1113 (Law Division, Probate Part, Middlesex County, 1982).

13. See, e.g., Deveroex v. Nelson, 517 S.W.2d 658 at p. 662 (Tex.Civ.App.—Houston, 1974), affirmed 529 S.W.2d 510 (Tex., 1975); Simon v. Dibble, 380 S.W.2d 898 (Tex.Civ.App.—San Antonio, 1964).

14. See, e.g., New York Life Insurance Company v. Jones, 86 Wash.2d 44 at p. 46, 541 P.2d 989 at p. 990 (1975).

15. See the discussion in State ex rel. Miller v. Sencindiver, 166 W.Va. 355, 275 S.E.2d 10 at pp. 12–13 (1980).

This is not uniformly true. For example the Kansas legislation states "No person who shall be convicted of feloniously killing, or procuring the killing of, another person shall inherit or take by will, by intestate succession as a surviving joint tenant, *as a beneficiary under a trust or otherwise* from such other person any portion of the estate or property in which the decedent had an interest * * *" Kansas Statutes Annotated § 59–513 (1978) (Emphasis added). This statute has been interpreted to apply to the beneficiary named in an insurance policy. See, e.g., the deci-

have been applied by courts to prevent the payment of life insurance proceeds to a beneficiary who intentionally caused the death of the person whose life was insured have been exclusively developed as common law doctrines. However, all states do have statutes that govern matters of descent and the distribution of a decedent's property.

It appears that most courts assume that the statutory provisions applicable to descent and distribution impose different constraints on courts in regard to disqualifications in relation to the rights of estate beneficiaries than those which determine the rights of life insurance beneficiaries. In some jurisdictions this has produced significantly different treatment of claims involving the disqualification of the life insurance beneficiaries, on the one hand, from claims regarding disqualification of the beneficiaries of an estate, on the other hand.[16] For example, some courts disqualifying a slayer from recovering as a claimant on the insurance policy have nevertheless allowed the same person (the slayer) to recover the insurance proceeds indirectly as a beneficiary of the estate of the decedent.[17] However, this is not uniformly the result in such situations, as some courts have not countenanced this type of result.[18]

With respect to circumstances in which statutes contain no explicit provisions concerning a slaying beneficiary, Dean Wade commented, in an article published in 1936:

"With the exception of the insurance cases, the courts have taken three different views: (1) that complete ownership of the property will pass to the slayer in spite of his wrongs; (2) that no title will pass to the slayer; and (3) that title will pass to the slayer,

---

sions in Chute v. Old American Insurance Company, reported at 233 Kan. 358, 662 P.2d 1264 (1983), and 6 Kan.App.2d 412, 629 P.2d 734 (1981).

16. In Travelers Insurance Company v. Gray, 37 Ohio Misc. 27, 306 N.E.2d 189 at p. 190 (Hamilton County, 1973), the beneficiary entered a plea of guilty to the charge of manslaughter in the first degree. The court concluded that R.C. 2105.19 "titled 'Murderer Not To Benefit' * * * does not affect insurance contracts but applies only to the distribution of a decedent's estate" and that the insurer failed to come forward with sufficient proof as would show that the beneficiary intentionally or willfully killed the insured.

In State Farm Life Insurance Company v. Smith, 66 Ill.2d 591, 6 Ill.Dec. 838, 363 N.E.2d 785 at p. 786 (1977), the court observed, "The Probate Act * * * does not govern the rights of beneficiaries to the proceeds of life insurance policies" and that there "is no statute which disqualifies the beneficiary who has killed the insured

from receiving the proceeds of the policy." However, the court also decided that the "long established policy that one may not profit by his intentionally committed wrongful act should apply * * *."

17. See, e.g., Moore v. Prudential Insurance Company, 342 Pa. 570, 21 A.2d 42 (1941).

Also see Annotation, *Felonious killing of ancestor as affecting intestate succession,* 39 A.L.R.2d 477–505 at pp. 500–505 (1955).

18. See, e.g., United States v. Foster, 238 F.Supp. 867 (E.D.Mich.1965) (applying Hawaiian law) (widow was not eligible to collect insurance because she had caused the insured's death, and proceeds would be distributed through the decedent's estate as if widow had predeceased the insured); Matter of Byer's Will, 208 Misc. 916, 144 N.Y.S.2d 68 (Nassau County, 1955) (insurance proceeds would be distributed as if the decedent had died intestate with no portion going to the decedent's husband who was responsible for death).

but that equity will hold him a constructive trustee for the heir or next of kin of the decedent.

"The first view was adopted in the first case in which the problem arose, and since that time it has been the majority ruling, especially in cases of intestacy." [19]

Dean Wade concluded that there was a trend toward the second view among the judicial decisions which he analyzed.[20] He also observed that in most of the jurisdictions in which the courts refused to engraft on or extrapolate from a statute an exception to exclude the receipt of benefits by a willful killer, a rectifying statute was passed shortly thereafter.[21] However, there are several reasons why such statutes often turn out to provide something short of a fully satisfactory solution to problems presented by cases of this type. First, the statutes are seldom fully consistent with the judicial development of doctrines applied in insurance cases. Second, these statutes rarely deal explicitly with all the possible situations that may arise. And, third, once such a statute is enacted, courts are often reluctant to extend the scope of the statutory policy of disqualification to cases that do not fall within the situations expressly identified by the terms of the statute.[22]

The disadvantages of the statutory method of meeting this problem are well illustrated by statutes thus far enacted. Some statutes governing the disqualification of estate beneficiaries have been very narrow in their definition of the causes of disqualification. For example, one statute only disqualifies "any person convicted of the murder of a decedent * * *" from inheriting or taking by will.[23] When the statute applicable to estate beneficiaries is narrower in scope than the judicial doctrine applicable to life insurance beneficiaries, it may be urged — with some justification — that the judicial doctrine should conform to the same limits.[24] However, courts have usually treated such statutes as applying only to estate beneficiaries and not to life insurance beneficiaries.[25] Certainly a court is justified in inferring that

19. John W. Wade, *Acquisition of Property by Willfully Killing Another—A Statutory Solution,* 49 Harvard Law Review 715–755 at p. 717 (1936).

20. *Id.,* at pp. 717–718.

21. *Id.,* at p. 716.

22. See, e.g., Rose v. Rose, 79 N.M. 435, 444 P.2d 762 (1968).

23. West's Florida Statutes Annotated § 732.802 (1976).

24. Rosenberger v. Northwestern Mutual Life Insurance Co., 182 F.Supp. 633 (S.D. Kan.1960) (question of beneficiary's intent in killing insured could not be relitigated when beneficiary had been convicted of involuntary manslaughter, and she could therefore receive insurance proceeds because Kansas statute required conviction of "felonious killing," interpreted to mean

intentional killing, for forfeiture; in so holding, court construed the phrase "inherit or take by will or *otherwise* from such other person" as applying to a claim as beneficiary of a life insurance policy, and it found support for applying statute to insurance in another statutory provision stating that insurance proceeds inure to the benefit of beneficiaries free of all claims). But see note 15 above.

25. E.g., Continental Bank & Trust Company v. Maag, 285 F.2d 558 (10th Cir. 1960) (circumstantial evidence that beneficiary had killed his insured wife, then taken his own life; in interpleader action between beneficiary's estate and contingent beneficiaries, *held* that public policy prevented beneficiary's estate from taking and that Utah statute providing for forfeiture of "any property or benefit by succession,

the legislature did not mean to overturn the body of decisional doctrine on disqualification of life insurance beneficiaries when it enacted a statute which speaks only of inheriting or taking by will. Judges nevertheless face a difficult choice when they consider whether the rules for disqualification of estate beneficiaries and life insurance beneficiaries should be different and, second, whether the judicially developed rules for disqualification of life insurance beneficiaries are more suitable and just than statutory rules for disqualification of estate beneficiaries.

Dean Wade proposed a comprehensive statutory solution, which at least one state has adopted,[26] that includes the following section on insurance.[27]

"(a) Insurance proceeds payable to the slayer as the beneficiary or assignee of any policy or certificate of insurance on the life of the decedent or as the survivor of a joint life policy shall be paid to the estate of the decedent, unless the policy or certificate designates some person not claiming through the slayer as alternative beneficiary to him.

"(b) If the decedent is a beneficiary or assignee of any policy or certificate of insurance on the life of the slayer, the proceeds shall be paid to the estate of the decedent upon the death of the slayer, unless the policy names some person other than the slayer or his estate as alternative beneficiary, or unless the slayer, by naming a new beneficiary or assigning the policy, performs an act which would have deprived the decedent of his interest in the policy if he had been living.

"(c) No insurance company shall be subject to liability on any policy on the life of the decedent procured and maintained by the slayer or on which all the premiums were paid by him."

will, or otherwise" in case of conviction — thus arguably implying no forfeiture in the absence of conviction — was inapplicable).

In Davis v. Aetna Life Insurance Company, 279 F.2d 304 (9th Cir.1960), the primary beneficiary pleaded guilty to voluntary manslaughter of his wife, who was insured under two policies with Aetna. In an interpleader action involving primary beneficiary and the contingent beneficiaries under the policies, the court held that a California probate statute barring one convicted of murder or voluntary manslaughter from benefitting from the victim's estate was inapplicable to insurance and that the confession was admissible as an admission against interest — but was not conclusive — on the issue of the beneficiary's rights to the proceeds of the policies.

Also see Carter v. Carter, 88 So.2d 153 (Fla., Special Div. A, 1956), where a summary judgment was held to have been properly denied because the issue whether the wife-beneficiary had feloniously killed her husband-insured was one of fact, despite her previous acquittal in a criminal proceeding. In this case, the statute disqualifying "any person convicted of the murder of the decedent * * *" — and by implication declining to disqualify one acquitted — was construed as applying to estate beneficiaries only and not life insurance beneficiaries.

26. South Dakota Codified Laws § 29–9–13 through § 29–9–16 (1984). [A survey by a research assistant in 1984 did not find any other statutes that have been modeled on Professor Wade's proposal.]

27. John W. Wade, *Acquisition of Property by Willfully Killing Another—A Statutory Solution*, 49 Harvard Law Review 715–755 at p. 741 (1936).

On most of the insurance issues dealt with in this statute, Dean Wade's proposals are admirable. However, the broad rule of non-liability for insurers, under paragraph (c) — when the slayer has procured and maintained the policy or paid all the premiums — should be carefully reconsidered. For example, it seems doubtful that the insurer should escape liability if the policy was procured by the slayer twenty years before the slaying and was maintained by the slayer the entire period, and particularly so in the absence of some clear evidence of connection between the insurance and the slaying.[28]

Comment

The application of different rules for the disqualification of estate beneficiaries and life insurance beneficiaries is very questionable. In particular, unless required to do so by a legislature's mandate, a court should not allow one who is disqualified by judicial doctrine from receiving life insurance proceeds directly to receive them indirectly as beneficiary of the estate of the decedent.

Courts often have been unduly timorous in failing to apply to descent and distribution the same doctrines of disqualification which are applied to life insurance beneficiaries. When the applicable statute of descent and distribution is silent on this question, the court should give its own best answer rather than adhering to the position that the legislature's silence on the issue amounts to a mandate against disqualification.[29] Although a continuing reluctance by courts to develop uniform rules may lead to legislation, the problem is in its nature one that can be appropriately resolved through case-by-case development of judicial doctrine.

(3) Who Is Entitled to Proceeds After a Beneficiary's Disqualification?

When the primary beneficiary of a life insurance policy is disqualified as a result of involvement in the killing of the person whose life was insured and the insurer nevertheless acknowledges or is held to an obligation to pay the insurance benefits, a contest for the insurance proceeds may arise between the contingent beneficiary and the estate of the insured or the heirs of the primary beneficiary. Ordinarily, the provisions in life insurance contracts do not address this situation.

---

28. Furthermore, a statutory declaration that the insurer shall not be "subject to liability on any policy" might also be construed as negating tort liability, which might be imposed, for example, because of the insurer's issuing life insurance to one without insurable interest. See § 3.5(e), above. It seems likely, however, that such liability would be held not affected because in its nature it is tort liability rather than liability "on" the policy.

29. Concerning the role of courts in the interpretation of statutes, and the harmful consequences of contrary-to-fact presumptions from legislative silence on an issue, see Robert E. Keeton, VENTURING TO DO JUSTICE (1969), at pp. 78–82 and pp. 92–95; Robert E. Keeton, *Statutes, Gaps, and Values in Tort Law*, 44 Journal Air Law & Commerce 1–21 (1978).

Materials presenting varied views on this subject appear in R. Aldisert, THE JUDICIAL PROCESS (1976), at pp. 170–235.

Typically, the insurance contract will only state that the contingent beneficiary will take if the primary beneficiary *predeceases* the insured.

Some courts have decided that a "slaying beneficiary" is legally entitled to recover the proceeds and holds them in "constructive trust for the estate of the insured." [30] This approach may produce results that would be contrary to the intention of a deceased insured under such circumstances.

The preferable rule, well supported by precedents,[31] is that the proceeds will be distributed as if the slaying beneficiary had predeceased the insured. A contingent beneficiary named in the insurance contract is obviously someone whom the insured has chosen to receive the insurance in certain circumstances, and whom the insured might well have selected to receive the proceeds if these particular circumstances could have been foreseen.[32] Consequently, there is a clear sense that this approach comes as near as possible to carrying out the insured's intention because it is predicated on applying the result desired by the insured for a somewhat analogous situation.

---

30. *Cf.* RESTATEMENT OF RESTITUTION § 189 (1937). Perhaps the implication of the quoted passage from the black-letter section is that the estate takes as against a contingent beneficiary. But that reading may not be sound in view of Comment a, stating: "In such a case ordinarily the executor or administrator of the insured is entitled to receive the proceeds of the policy from the insurer and to apply them in the same way in which they would have been applicable if the beneficiary had predeceased the insured or was otherwise incapable of taking or disqualified from taking the proceeds." Perhaps the drafters of this section of the Restatement of Restitution were thinking of a type of policy that designated no contingent beneficiary at all or one that designated the estate of the insured as the only contingent beneficiary.

The "constructive trust" rule is more appropriately applied in non-insurance situations, in which there is no conflict with secondary designees. E.g., In re Cox' Estate, 141 Mont. 583, 380 P.2d 584 (1963) (husband murdered wife, then committed suicide; held, husband held wife's share of jointly owned property in trust for wife's heirs, and his estate had no rights in the half of the property so held).

Also see RESTATEMENT OF RESTITUTION, Second (Tentative Draft No. 2) (April, 1984), § 30.

31. See, e.g., Brooks v. Thompson, 521 S.W.2d 563 (Tenn.1975); Metropolitan Life Insurance Company v. Wenckus, 244 A.2d 424 (Me.1968).

Also see Carter v. Carter, 88 So.2d 153 (Fla., Special Div. A, 1956).

Also see Annotation, *Right to proceeds of life insurance, as between estate of murdered insured and alternative beneficiary named in policy, where murderer was made primary beneficiary,* 26 A.L.R.2d 987–989 (1952).

32. *Cf.* Draper's Estate v. Commissioner of Internal Revenue, 536 F.2d 944 at p. 948 (1st Cir.1976), in which the court concluded that when a husband, who was the owner and named as the beneficiary in two policies insuring his wife's life, killed his wife and then killed himself, the proceeds "would be distributed only to those claiming through Elizabeth [the wife]" because "under the circumstances equity treats the contract as for the benefit of the insured's estate and not for the wrongdoer."

Similarly, in Bounds v. Caudle, 560 S.W.2d 925 (Tex.1977), the court concluded that when a husband was convicted of negligent homicide of his wife, it was appropriate to impose a constructive trust for the benefit of the couple's children on all the wife's property (which would have passed to the husband under her will) and that it was also appropriate for the proceeds from insurance policies on the wife's life to go to the children.

(4) Arguments for Not Paying the Life Insurance Proceeds

In most situations, an insurer remains liable on a life insurance policy even when the insured is murdered by a beneficiary.[33] However, there is some support for a rule that an insurer is not liable to anyone on a life insurance policy taken out by a named beneficiary who subsequently murders the person whose life is insured.[34] There is also support for a more limited rule that when *no one except the beneficiary* or someone claiming through him has any interest in the policy, and the beneficiary murders the insured, the insurer is under no liability on the policy.[35] The principal justification for these rules arises when the insurer is able to show that a beneficiary planned to murder an insured *and* procured the insurance with this plan in mind. In such a situation, the insurer has a compelling argument that there was an attempt to perpetrate a fraud on the insurer, and therefore the insurance contract should be found to be either void from the beginning or voidable.[36]

Another rationale for the position that an insurer should not be liable is that if a beneficiary who purchased the insurance policy subsequently murders the insured, both the legal and equitable interests fail.[37] In developing this theory, Professor Vance reasoned:

> "* * * where the murderer has taken out the policy upon the life of the slain man, and has himself paid the premiums

33. For example, the RESTATEMENT OF RESTITUTION (1937), § 189(1) provides that "If the beneficiary of a life insurance policy murders the insured, he holds his interest under the policy under a constructive trust for the estate of the insured."

Also see Neff v. Massachusetts Mutual Life Insurance Company, 158 Ohio St. 45, 107 N.E.2d 100 (1952).

Cf. Annotation, *Killing of insured by beneficiary as affecting life insurance or its proceeds,* 27 A.L.R.3d 794–839 (1969).

34. *Cf.* New England Mutual Life Insurance Company v. Null, 605 F.2d 421 at p. 424 (8th Cir.1979) ("* * * a life insurance policy is void *ab initio* when it is shown that the beneficiary thereof procured the policy with a present intention to murder the insured.").

Also see John W. Wade, *Acquisition of Property by Wilfully Killing Another—A Statutory Solution,* 49 Harvard Law Review 715–755 at p. 741 (1936); James Barr Ames, LECTURES ON LEGAL HISTORY (1913) at p. 320; Annotation, *Killing of Insured By Beneficiary as Affecting Life Insurance or Its Proceeds,* 27 A.L.R.3d 794–839 (1969).

35. See, e.g., New York Life Insurance Company v. Henriksen, 415 N.E.2d 146 (Ind.App., 3d Dist., 1981), *rehearing denied* 421 N.E.2d 1117 (Ind.App.1981) (murder committed by sole beneficiary); Boatwright v. Hartford Insurance Group, 64 A.D.2d 262, 409 N.Y.S.2d 860 (1978), *appeal after remand* 46 N.Y.2d 708, 414 N.Y.S.2d 1025, 386 N.E.2d 1337 (1979).

Also see 5 Scott, THE LAW OF TRUSTS (Third edition, 1967), at § 494.2.

Cf. Restatement of the Law of Restitution, § 189(1), Comment (e)(3).

But see the discussion of this Restatement section in Draper's Estate v. Commissioner of Internal Revenue, 536 F.2d 944 (1st Cir.1976).

36. See, e.g., New England Mutual Life Insurance Company v. Null, 554 F.2d 896 at p. 900 (8th Cir.1977), *on remand* 459 F.Supp. 979 (E.D.Mo.1978).

Also see Colyer's Administrator v. New York Life Insurance Company, 300 Ky. 189, 188 S.W.2d 313 (1945).

See generally 1C APPLEMAN, INSURANCE LAW AND PRACTICE (1981), at § 482; and Couch on Insurance 2d (Rev. ed., 1984), Volume 4 at § 27.159; Annotation, *Killing of Insured by Beneficiary as affecting life insurance or its proceeds,* 27 A.L.R.3d 794–839 (1969).

37. See Vance, LAW OF INSURANCE (Third edition, Anderson 1951), at p. 721.

* * * the murderous beneficiary is party to the contract. He has the legal as well as the equitable title to the policy. The insured was absolutely without interest in it. There is no basis for a resulting trust. The entire right in the policy having been forfeited by the crime of its sole owner, the duty of the insurer to pay is wholly extinguished." [38]

The argument that the beneficiary was "sole owner" may be persuasive [39] if no person other than the murderer is named as an owner of any of the rights in the policy or as a contingent beneficiary. Such life insurance contracts were common at one stage in the development of life insurance in the United States.[40] Under current practices, however, this would be a very unusual situation. Most life insurance policy forms currently in use include standard clauses (rarely stricken out or modified by an endorsement even in policies purchased by the primary beneficiary) making contingent provisions for payment to relatives or to the estate of the person whose life is insured.[41] Under such a life insurance contract, it cannot be said that "no one but the beneficiary or one claiming through him has any interest in the policy." [42]

The cases cited by Professor Vance in support of the "failure of interest" theory [43] involve distinctive situations, and a consideration of those categories suggests that the broad rule he postulated is not generally applicable to these cases. First, in a number of decisions the discussion of the doctrine clearly is dictum, as evidenced by the fact that the court concluded the insurer was liable. Second, in several cases the facts suggest that a cogent defense could have been based on fraud because it appears the policy was obtained as part of a plan to

38. *Id.,* at p. 722.

39. Professor Vance's position is supported by Professor Austin Scott. 5 Scott, TRUSTS (Third edition, 1967), at § 494.2.

The result is also supported by a section of the statute proposed by Dean Wade. See § 4.11(g)(2), above, quoting Dean Wade's proposal and questioning this particular aspect of it though applauding his draft statute in general.

40. In relation to policies in which "no one but the beneficiary or one claiming through him has any interest in the policy," Vance's position that the insurer is relieved of liability is supported also by Professor Scott, and the result is also supported by a section of the statute proposed by Dean Wade.

41. See § 4.11(d), note 2, and Appendix E.

But cf. the comment of the Eighth Circuit Court of Appeals in New England Mutual Life Insurance Company v. Null, 605 F.2d 421 at p. 424 (8th Cir.1979) that: "We have been unable, however, to find a decision in any state, including Missouri, which has permitted the estate of the insured to recover on the policy itself from an insurer which has negligently issued a policy." Also see another opinion in this case reported at 554 F.2d 896 (8th Cir. 1977).

42. In Draper's Estate v. Commissioner of Internal Revenue, 536 F.2d 944 at p. 948 (1st Cir.1976), the court observed that premiums were paid to the insurer over a period of fourteen years with "the apparent purpose" of providing for the couple's children, and that the children "were the likely objects of the insurance trust into which the proceeds would have gone had both mother and father died natural deaths." The court then commented that: "There seems to be no sense in saying that they should receive nothing because their father took their mother's life."

43. As well as those cited by Scott for non-liability of the insurer when no one but the beneficiary or one claiming through him has any interest in the policy.

murder for profit.[44] However, some of the opinions do not appear to limit the rule of "non-liability" to cases in which fraud is or could have been proved.

In New York Mutual Life Insurance Co. v. Armstrong,[45] recognized as one of the leading cases, it appeared that the insurer had on December 8, 1877, issued an endowment policy on the life of Armstrong, payable to him or his assigns on the eighth of December, 1897, or if he should die before that time to his legal representatives. The policy was assigned to Hunter. Armstrong died on January 25, 1878. Hunter was subsequently convicted of the murder of Armstrong, and was hanged for the offense. Armstrong's widow, as administrator of Armstrong's estate, sued the insurer. The insurer contended, inter alia, that the policy had been obtained by Hunter with intent to defraud the insurer by bringing about the death of Armstrong. The Supreme Court of the United States reversed a judgment for plaintiff and remanded for a new trial. After holding that it was error to exclude evidence that Hunter obtained insurance policies in other companies on the life of Armstrong at or near the time the policy at issue was obtained, the opinion of the court continues:

> "But, independently of any proof of the motives of Hunter in obtaining the policy, and even assuming that they were just and proper, he forfeited all rights under it when, to secure its immediate payment, he murdered the assured. It would be a reproach to the jurisprudence of the country, if one could recover insurance money payable on the death of a party whose life he had feloniously taken. As well might he recover insurance money upon a building that he had willfully fired." [46]

The concluding sentence in this quoted passage suggests the theory that murder by the person who procured the policy was an excepted risk.[47] Of course, most policies do not contain any provision on this point. Accordingly, to the extent this decision establishes a precedent for contemporary cases, the rule of the case would have to be transformed into a theory that involves an implied exception, rather than a specific limitation of the insurance contract.[48]

---

44. Another decision that can be explained on the same basis is Travelers Insurance Company v. Thompson, 281 Minn. 547, 163 N.W.2d 289 (1968), *app. dism'd* and *cert. denied* 395 U.S. 161, 89 S.Ct. 1647, 23 L.Ed.2d 175 (1969).

45. 117 U.S. 591, 6 S.Ct. 877, 29 L.Ed. 997 (1886).

46. *Id.,* 117 U.S. at p. 600, 6 S.Ct. at p. 881, 29 L.Ed. at p. 1000.

47. *Cf.* 5 Scott, TRUSTS (Third edition, 1967), § 494.2 at p. 3531.

48. Ordinarily that theory applies to losses that are either so regular as to be regarded as a cost rather than a risk of an activity or enterprise, or else are not fortuitous from the point of view of the person who would be entitled to the proceeds of the insurance contract were it enforceable. See § 5.3, above. That the death was fortuitous from the point of view of the murder victim, in a case in which the victim obtained the policy, is not conclusive against the analogy to the friendly-fire and inherent-vice exceptions of property insurance.

Applying the excepted-risk theory to cases in which an insured was murdered by a beneficiary would allow the insurer to escape liability. In most life insurance transactions, the insurance policy is purchased by the person whose life is insured, and the interests intended to be protected by the policy are those of the individuals who the insured felt would suffer an economic loss as a consequence of the insured's death. Consequently, it is not surprising that the contrary result has been consistently reached when the policy was obtained by the insured and especially when the insured identified contingent beneficiaries. These decisions appear to represent a clear rejection of the implied exception theory.[49]

When an insurer is entitled to deny life insurance coverage as a result of a murder committed by a beneficiary, certainly an insurer should not be required to return any premium collected for the coverage provided before the murder. During this period, the insurer was subject to the risk of death under circumstances that would have given rise to liability. An apt analogy would be the fire insurance policy for a period during which no insured loss occurred, and a loss of the structure as a result of the owner's act of arson. Thus, if an implied exception warrants a denial of life insurance benefits, there is little reason to view the situation as one which produces unjust enrichment for an insurer and thus there is little justification for requiring the return of premiums to avoid a supposed "windfall." But if the ground of non-liability is merely that no one but the beneficiary had an interest in the policy and the beneficiary's interest was forfeited by murder, the sense that the non-liability of the insurer produces an unjust enrichment is stronger.

 WESTLAW REFERENCES

§ 4.1 **Methods of Defining Persons and Interests Protected**

  (b) **Ways of Designating Insureds in Various Types of Insurance**

   (1) **Designating Insureds in Property Insurance**
    "their interest" /3 appear! /s cover! insurance policy

   (2) **Allocating Insurance Benefits in Multi-Party Property Insurance Agreements**
    217k581.1(4)

   (3) **Distinguishing "Insureds" from Others Benefiting from Property Insurance**
    217k435.8 /p insured assured /p defin! mean***
    217k581.1(3)

  (c) **Assignments**

   (3) **Assignments of the Right to Be Paid Insurance**

    (i) **Arrangements That Follow the Occurrence of a Loss**
     insured assured /s assign! transfer! /s chose +2 action

49. Moreover, it is also difficult to see why this theory should be applied when a policy is obtained by the beneficiary. Undoubtedly the practice is to charge the same premium in both cases; yet the insurer's risks would be different if the narrower theory of implied exception were adopted.

§ 4.2   Interests in Property That is Mortgaged, Including Subrogation Rights

    (a) Questions Underlying Conflicting Claims When Insurance Is Paid to a Mortgagee

        to(217) /p satisfy! satisfaction discharg! /s mortgage debt /s payment paying pay* paid claim*** settl!

    (d) Personal Property Insurance: Subrogation to a Mortgagee's Rights

        field /s "western miller"

    (e) Assignability of a Mortgagee's Interest

        di(transfer! assign! /s contract insurance coverage /s property /s approv! consen! /s insurer assurer company)

    (f) Subrogation to a Mortgagee's Tort Claim Against a Third Person That Caused a Motor Vehicle Accident

        sy,di(subrogat! /s tort! negligen! /s third /3 person party /s car vehicle auto auto mobile truck)

§ 4.3   Interests in Real Property That Is Being Sold: Providing Coverage for the Vendor and the Purchaser of Realty

    (a) Introduction

        vendor seller owner /s vendee purchaser buyer /s risk /2 loss

    (e) Solutions to Coverage Claims When Contract Provisions Are Inconclusive

        (1) Liability-for-Insurable-Interest

            400k199

        (4) Proration of Coverage

            pro-rat*** /s vendor seller owner /s vendee purchaser buyer

§ 4.4   Leases and Life Estates in Realty

    (a) Rules Applicable When Contractual Provisions in Leases Are Inconclusive

        di(leas! /s "insurable interest")
        217k115(4) /p interest
        ramsdell /s "north america"

    (b) Subrogation of the Lessor's Insurer to the Lessor's Claims for Indemnity Against the Tenant

        find 184 f2d 359
        233k156
        insurer assurer company /s subrogat! /2 right claim /s lessee tenant
        di(insurer assurer company /s subrogat! /s own +1 insured assured)

    (c) Life Estates and Other Limited Interests in Realty

        Destruction of the Property After a Life Estate Has Vested
        240k19
        life /2 tenant estate /s insurance /s remainder!

§ 4.5   Interests in Personal Property Held in Bailment, "In Trust," "On Commission," or in Analogous Ways

    (a) Generally

        sy(bailment /s coverage insurance policy)
        217k580(4)

    (b) Relation to Coinsurance Provisions

        find 130 fsupp 843

§ 4.6 Searching for Generalizations Applicable to "Multiple Interests" Problems in Property Insurance

> di(insurer assurer company /s "unearned premium" windfall (unjust! /3 enrich!) /s property)
>
> *Observations*
> 400k199
> 217k580(6)
> sy,di("moral hazard" /p coverage insurance policy)

§ 4.7 Omnibus Clauses

(a) Generally

> di omnibus clause
> omnibus /s "uninsured motorist"

(b) Omnibus Liability Insurance Coverage for Operators of Motor Vehicles: Problems of Interpretation and Application

(1) Generally

> 217k435.12 & he(permi! allow! let letting /7 use drive)
> find 166 a2d 345
> "minor deviation" /2 rule doctrine
> 217k435.13
> sy,di(omnibus /p load! unload! /s van truck auto automobile vehicle car)

(2) Coverage for a Permittee's Permittee

> sy,di(initial first /2 permission /5 rule doctrine theory principle concept)
> souza /s corti

§ 4.8 Liability Insurance

(a) Generally

> 217k594.3(1) /p liability

(b) Insolvency of an Insured: Insurance Policy Clauses and Statutory Provisions

> victim injured /s third-party /3 beneficiary /s insurance coverage policy

(c) Non-derivative Liability Statutes: Legislatively Imposed Limitations on Defenses Available to Liability Insurers

> sy("safety responsibility" +1 act law /p vehicle auto automobile) & to(217)

(d) Liability Insurance and Immunity of Insureds from Tort Liabilities

> sy(government! sovereign charit! /7 immun! /s liab! /s tort tortious!)

§ 4.9 Automobile Insurance

(b) Liability Insurance for the Operators of an "Insured" Vehicle

> *Identifying Covered Vehicles*
> di(fleet /1 coverage insurance policy)

(1) Pre–1966 Coverage Terms

> "drive other car" /2 coverage insurance provision

(c) Liability Insurance Exclusions

(1) Specified Persons, Classes of Persons, and Family Members

> 217k435.18(2) /p exclu! & sy(coverage insurance policy liability claim clause /4 exclu!)

intra-famil! inter-famil! famil*** /2 immune immuni!
sy,di(inter-spous! intra-spous! spous! /2 immun!)

Observations
217k435.18(3)

(2) Employees of an Insured
217k435.19(2) 217k435.19(4) /p exclu!

§ 4.10 No-Fault Motor Vehicle Insurance

(c) No–Fault Automobile Insurance in Massachusetts
massachusetts /s no-fault

(d) No–Fault Legislation in Other States
sy,di(michigan /s no-fault)

(e) The Impact of No–Fault Motor Vehicle Insurance
cost /3 coverage insurance policy /s no-fault

§ 4.11 Interests in Life Insurance

(b) Community Property and Life Insurance
sy("community property" /s life /3 coverage insurance policy)
205k249(3) /p "community property" /p life /3 coverage insurance policy

(d) "Formalities" for Changing Beneficiaries
sy(retain! retention reserv! /7 right /s chang! alter*** alteration /5 beneficiary /s life /3 coverage insurance policy)

(1) Partial Compliance with Formalities
217k587.2(2) 217k587.2(3)
to(217) /p chang! alter*** alteration /5 beneficiary /s life / 3 coverage insurance policy /s comply! compli! follow!

(2) Standing to Raise Compliance with Formalities
standing(improper proper /3 person party) /s chang! alter*** alteration /5 beneficiary

(3) Insurance for Military Personnel
to(217) /p military (armed +1 force service) "national guard" "air force" army navy marine /s life /3 coverage insurance policy
to(34) /p chang! alter*** alteration /5 beneficiary

(e) Assignments of Life Insurance

(1) Beneficiaries Versus Assignees
217k593(2)

(f) Creditors as Beneficiaries or Assignees

(2) Insurance Acquired by a Creditor
creditor /5 acquir! acquisition obtain! purchase*** buy! bought /s life /3 coverage insurance policy

(g) Disqualification of Beneficiaries

(1) Generally
beneficiary /s life /3 coverage insurance policy /s disqualif! unqualified (not /3 qualif!)
sy(beneficiary /s murder! kill*** manslaughter slay! (tak*** /3 life) /5 insured assured)

(2) The Effect of Legislative Provisions That Affect a Beneficiary's Right to Receive Life Insurance

sy,di(legislat*** law statut! /s pay* paying payment paid /s coverage insurance policy /s murder*** kill*** /5 insured assured)

217k594.1 124k51 /p statut! law legislat!

(4) Arguments for Not Paying the Life Insurance Proceeds

217k515.7

Chapter Five

THE RISKS TRANSFERRED

---

§ 5.1   Defining and Restricting the "Risks" Transferred

§ 5.1(a)   Introductory Note

The facets of risk transference that are related to the events or circumstances that cause a loss involve questions that are central to the determination of whether coverage will be provided by an insurance policy.[1] Determinations about this aspect of the relationship between

---

§ 5.1(a)

1.   The determination of the risks which are transferred to insurers involves ques-   tions that pervade and encompass the entire body of insurance law.

an insurer and an insured depend primarily, although not exclusively,[2] on the coverage provisions specified in the insurance contract.

The discussion in this chapter both considers the principles which influence the design of coverage provisions and analyzes specific contract clauses which are representative of the methods used to define or to restrict the scope of coverage in various types of insurance. In view of the extraordinary consistency that has prevailed for at least the past century in regard to the methods employed in the design and drafting of insurance policies and specific coverage provisions, it seems probable that insurers will continue to use the same basic principles and approaches to define the risks being transferred despite changes which may be introduced either in the terminology of specific insurance provisions or in the conceptualization of the scope of protection for various types of insurance.

The responses by courts, administrative agencies, and legislatures to different types of policy provisions relating to risk transference have had a considerable influence on the determinations of what risks are covered by insurance contracts. In particular, the judicial decisions cited in this chapter illustrate some of the constraints courts have imposed on the freedom of insurers to limit the risks which are transferred, especially when the transaction is between an insurer and an individual consumer.[3] Judges have also imposed some restrictions on insurance arrangements that favor insurers — that is, courts have limited the scope of coverage through the application of implied exceptions in some situations in which insurers have not included explicit coverage limitations.[4]

Another aspect of risk transference involves the original determination by the insurer about whether to provide coverage. In most circumstances, an insurer's underwriting decision — that is, the decision whether to accept a particular application for insurance coverage — is predicated on certain conditions or facts, and a prospective insured is either asked or required to provide information to the insurer. When an applicant either submits incorrect information or conceals some fact, and especially when the matter would either have influenced the insurer's decision to provide coverage or is a factor that directly relates to the events that are involved in the cause of a loss, an insurer is likely to predicate a defense to a coverage claim on doctrines such as warranty, misrepresentation, mistake, and concealment.[5]

In addition to coverage terms that define the risks covered — that is, the kinds of causes of loss that are within the risks covered —

---

2. See especially the discussion in § 5.2 and § 5.4, below.

3. The questions considered in this chapter which concern the justifications for judicial "restructuring" of the insured's right to coverage are also very relevant to the doctrines that are discussed in Chapter 6.

4. See the discussion of implied exceptions that limit coverage in § 5.3, below.

5. See the discussion of warranty (§ 5.6, below), misrepresentations and mistakes (§ 5.7, below) and concealment (§ 5.8, below).

insurance policies generally include various types of clauses that circumscribe, limit, or reduce liability by provisions that (1) impose specific pecuniary limits of liability or (2) prescribe the duration of coverage.[6]

The final section of the chapter discusses policy provisions that provide for the termination of the insurance contract.

§ 5.1(b) Approaches to Defining the Risks Transferred: All-Risk and Specified-Risk Policies

(1) Generally

Two basic techniques are employed in the drafting of insurance policies. One approach is for the coverage terms to state that the insurance policy covers all risks of loss; this approach produces contracts which are generally described as *all-risk insurance policies*. Despite the nomenclature, some limitations on the scope of coverage are invariably included in all-risk policies. Such limitations are often set out in a qualifying phrase or clause in the basic statement of coverage.[1] In addition, some coverage restrictions usually are separately stated under headings such as "conditions," "exclusions," "exceptions," or "limitations."[2] In all-risk policies, most of the coverage restrictions relate to the designation of the subject matter, the persons, or the interests protected — that is, typically, there are very few provisions which limit the risks that are to be transferred.

The other basic approach to designing an insurance arrangement is to state that coverage is provided only for those risks which are expressly specified in the policy terms. Insurance forms employing this approach are usually referred to as *specified-risk policies*. The restrictions in these forms are generally set forth both in the general descrip-

---

6. See the discussion in § 5.9 and § 5.10, below.

§ 5.1(b)

1. Also see the discussion of "all-risk" coverage in § 1.5(a), above.

2. See generally the forms included Appendix G, Appendix H, and Appendix I. Some policies also include limitations which are characterized as "restrictions."

In Safeco Insurance Company of America v. Guyton, 471 F.Supp. 1126 at p. 1129 (C.D.Cal.1979), *judgment affirmed in part, reversed in part* 692 F.2d 551 (9th Cir. 1982), the court observed: "All policies, including policies labeled all risk, have exclusions" and the only limitation on the enforceability of exclusions "is that they must be clear and explicit and must not be illegal or absurd."

Limiting provisions are illustrated by a policy insuring the policyholder's interests in designated property against "all risks by land and water by any conveyance." See Schloss Brothers v. Stevens, [1906] 2 K.B. 665.

Also illustrative is a currently used personal property floater (inland marine insurance) that describes the property covered as "personal property owned, used for, worn by the person in whose name this policy is issued and members of the Insured's family of the same household, while in all situations, except as hereinafter provided." In the same form, under the heading "exclusions," appear provisions of such different nature as a limitation of the scope of coverage by physical location ("property on exhibition at fairgrounds") and a limitation by cause ("against loss or damaged caused by * * * insurrection, rebellion, revolution, civil war * * *."). See Appendix B.

tion of the coverage and in separately stated provisions under the same types of headings as those used by insurers in all-risk policies.

The actual differences between all-risk and specified-risk policies may not always be apparent. Furthermore, because virtually all insurance contracts include at least several restrictions on the risks that are to be transferred to the insurer, sometimes the differences between the two types of insurance policies seem to a reader to be more a matter of style than of substance. Even though the differences between all-risk and specified-risk policies are not always clearly evident, the approach employed in designing an insurance policy may have considerable practical significance in the event coverage provisions are involved in litigation.

There are several factors which increase the likelihood that insureds will be the beneficiaries of more favorable judicial rulings under all-risk coverages than under specified-risk coverages. *First,* the character of an insurance policy's design frequently appears to significantly influence allocations of the burden of proof.[3] *Second,* it is usually more difficult for an insurer to establish a defense predicated on an implied exception under an all-risk coverage — that is, an implied exception is less likely to be recognized as appropriate when the general design of a coverage is relatively broad than when it is relatively narrow in scope.[4] *Third,* and probably most significant, courts seem especially disposed to favor insureds in interpreting coverage terms so as to avoid coverage gaps when the insurance contract involved in a coverage dispute either is or has the appearance of an all-risk policy.[5]

(2) Common Types of All-Risk Insurance

A number of all-risk insurance contracts are widely used. Marine insurance policies are all-risk in character, and typically provide coverage for losses resulting from any peril of the sea.[6] Various types of

---

3. For example, see the discussion in § 5.1(c), below.

4. See the discussion in § 5.1(d), below.

Nonetheless, all-risk coverages are subject to implied exceptions. See § 5.3(b) and § 5.3(c), below, concerning implied exceptions in life and marine insurance respectively.

5. See § 5.1(d), below.

6. See Sipowicz v. Wimble, 370 F.Supp. 442 at pp. 446–448 (S.D.N.Y.1974), which includes the following comment:

"A loss is occasioned by a peril of the sea when it results from the fortuitous (unforseen and unanticipated) action of the sea. A loss is not occasioned by a peril of the sea when it results from the defective deteriorated or decayed condition of the vessel or from ordinary wear and tear."

Also see Inland Rivers Service Corp. v. Hartford Fire Insurance Company, 66 Ohio St.2d 32, 418 N.E.2d 1381 at p. 1383 (1981).

But also consider the following comments of a Louisiana Court of Appeal in Vining v. Security Insurance Company of New Haven, 252 So.2d 754 at pp. 756 and 758 (La.App., 1st Cir., 1971):

"It is settled maritime law that a Marine Policy of Hull Insurance is not an all-risk policy, and that such coverage extends only to losses resulting directly from a peril enumerated in the policy. * * * circumstances which are ordinarily encountered, such as predictable winds, tides, wave actions and conditions of the water, do not fall within the classification of perils of the sea as the term is used in policies of marine hull insurance. In this instance, waves from passing vessels were to be expected as was the possibility of floating logs due to high water

inland marine insurance, such as coverage for personal property, usually are all-risk policies.[7]

Life insurance, though not commonly referred to as such, is often all-risk in character. Typically, life insurance policies are designed to provide coverage without regard to the cause of an insured's death. However, even though most life insurance policies neither specify all the risks that may cause death which are covered nor the causes that are excluded, life insurance coverages may be subject to express restrictions or implied exceptions establishing limits on the all-risk character.[8]

§ 5.1(c) The Effect of an Insurance Policy's Design on Burdens of Proof

The design of an insurance policy as an all-risk or a specified-risk policy may have a significant bearing on either the extent of proof that a claimant will be required to submit or the allocation of the burden of proof in a coverage dispute. The judicial decision in British & Foreign Marine Insurance Company, Limited, v. Gaunt,[1] a leading English case, provides a good illustration of how the design of a coverage may influence the burden of proof.

In *Gaunt,* the insured acquired coverage for a wool shipment, "including all risk of craft, fire, coasters, hulks, transhipment and inland carriage by land and/or water and/or risks from the sheep's back and/or stations while awaiting shipment and/or forwarding and until safely delivered * * *." [2] Although there was clear evidence that the wool arrived in damaged condition, there was no indication of exactly when or how the damage was done during the period covered by the insurance policies. After recognizing that damage must have been "due to some fortuitous circumstances or casualty * * *," [3] Lord

season" and even assuming "arguendo, that plaintiff had established such circumstances, it would not fall within the peril of the sea coverage of his policy."

Also see the discussion of marine insurance in § I.5(b), above.

7. See, e.g., John Ahern, *Some Generalities on Marine And Inland Marine Covers,* 1963 Insurance Counsel Journal 72–88 at p. 84–85; Myron DuBain, *Marine and Inland Marine Insurance,* The Practical Lawyer, Volume 8, No. 7, 61–85 at p. 68–69 (1962); Cases Noted, *Concealment in Application for an Inland Marine Floater Policy,* 49 Columbia Law Review 125–127 at p. 126 (1949).

8. Formerly it was common that the insurer would have *no liability at all* if death resulted from an excepted cause. For example, if death was the result of an execution by the state because an insured had been convicted of crime, some courts treated this as an excepted cause; the insurer owed no death benefits and on the

theory that the premium collected had been fully earned by affording protection in the event of death by a covered cause, no return of premium was required.

At present, under the combined influence of insurer practices and regulatory compulsion, the policy commonly provides that if death results from an excepted cause the insurer shall pay a *sum less than the face amount of the insurance* (e.g., the cash surrender value or a sum equal to premiums paid).

Also see the discussion of an implied exception when an insured is executed by the state in § 5.3(b), below.

§ 5.1(c)

1. [1921] 2 A.C. 41.

2. *Id.,* 2 A.C. at p. 42.

3. *Id.,* 2 A.C. at pp. 46–47. This proof negates the implied exception commonly referred to as the "exception of loss from inherent vice." See § 5.3(c), below.

Birkenhead observed that "where all risks are covered by the policy and not merely risks of a specified class or classes, the plaintiff discharges his special onus when he has proved that the loss was caused by some event covered by the general expression, and he is not bound to go further and prove the exact nature of the accident or casualty which, in fact, occasioned his loss." [4]

Although there has been relatively little development of the analysis set forth in *Gaunt* in subsequent judicial opinions, there is a very persuasive case for the view that the *Gaunt* decision establishes the appropriate rule for comparable situations.[5] And it seems clear that in some circumstances an insured's prospects for recovery are considerably enhanced if the insured does not have the burden of proving exactly what caused a loss — that is, acquisition of an "all risk" insurance policy can serve to materially improve an insured's prospects for recovery in some types of situations.[6]

---

4. *Id.*, 2 A.C. at p. 47. Lord Birkenhead also noted that the words "all risk" cannot be held to cover "such damage as is inevitable from ordinary wear and tear and inevitable depreciation ＊ ＊ ＊"

Cf. Lord Sumner's statement: "When he avers loss by some risk coming within 'all risks,' as used in this policy, he need only give evidence reasonably showing that the loss was due to a casualty, not to a certainty or to inherent vice or to wear and tear." *Id.*, 2 A.C. at p. 58.

Also see 2 ARNOULD, MARINE INSURANCE [British Shipping Laws] (Sixteenth edition, 1981), § 780 at pp. 638–639.

5. See, e.g., Morrison Grain Company, Inc. v. Utica Mutual Insurance Company, 632 F.2d 424 at p. 430 (5th Cir.1980) ("It would seem to be inconsistent with the broad protective purpose of 'all risks' insurance to impose on the insured ＊ ＊ ＊ the burden of proving the precise cause of the loss or damage."); Jewelers Mutual Insurance Company v. Balogh, 272 F.2d 889 (5th Cir.1959) (jewelry placed in safe on Saturday was missing on Monday with no visible evidence of theft; *held*, coverage under all-risk policy that stated there would be no liability of "unexplained loss," "mysterious disappearance," etc., since insurer had failed to prove the applicability of the restriction).

In Glassner v. Detroit Fire & Marine Insurance Company, 23 Wis.2d 532, 127 N.W.2d 761 (1964), the action was for damage to submersible pump under comprehensive coverage of dwelling "against all risks of physical loss" except as otherwise provided. The court held for the policyholder since, after stipulating loss was fortuitous, insurer has burden of showing an applicable exclusion. In *dictum*, the court

stated that under all-risk coverage, an insured has the burden of proving loss was fortuitous and not the result of "an ordinary and almost certain consequence of the inherent qualities and intended use of the property." The court reserved the question as to where the burden would be, absent stipulation, concerning whether loss was caused by "wear and tear, deterioration, and mechanical breakdown," since arguably the policy form treated these causes "as if they were excluded risks."

Cf. 21 APPLEMAN, INSURANCE LAW (revised edition, 1980) at § 12237.

Contra, e.g., Hardware Dealers Mutual Fire Insurance Company v. Berglund, 393 S.W.2d 309 (Tex.1965) (the insured claimed under all-risk policies containing various water-damaged "exclusions" for loss to several properties caused by hurricane; *held*, reinstating the verdict that awarded only the portion of loss due to wind damage, that the burden of proof was on the insured to show the inapplicability of the "exclusions").

6. *Cf.* Betty v. Liverpool and London and Globe Insurance Company, 310 F.2d 308 at pp. 310–311 (4th Cir.1962) (to escape the broad undertaking of a policy insuring all risks of direct loss, it is the insurer's burden to go forward and prove the loss was within one of the numerous exceptions listed in the policy); Jewelers Mutual Insurance Company v. Balogh, 272 F.2d 889 (5th Cir.1959) (under a standardized all risk jewelers block policy, burden was cast on the insurer to show that a loss was within the unexplained loss, mysterious disappearance exception of the policy).

Also consider Austin v. American Casualty Company, 193 A.2d 741 (D.C.App. 1963), 12 A.L.R.3d 860 (1967) ("extended

§ 5.1(d) Insurance "Packages" and Gaps in Coverage

Many contemporary insurance policies, such as homeowners and motor vehicle insurance, were originally developed by combining various then-existing specified-risk coverages that were available as separate policies into "package" insurance plans. When insurance packages are created by essentially doing little more than combining coverage terms that were developed for specified-risk policies, the new insurance policies — which often are described by insurers as "comprehensive policies," "blanket coverages," or comparable characterizations — almost always leave gaps in the scope of protection afforded insureds.[1]

Under the coverage terms of most homeowners insurance policy provisions, and the prevailing legal doctrine which applies to those insurance policies, a policyholder is not provided all-risk coverage for personal property. Accordingly, there are various risks for personal property which are not covered, such as when an item of jewelry is destroyed as a result of being accidentally tossed into a furnace.[2] However, some homeowners insurance policy forms now use the all-risk terminology for at least portions of the coverage that may be acquired for personal property [3] — that is, coverage may now be included in a homeowners insurance policy which is patterned on the type of protection that is provided by inland marine coverage (often referred to as a personal property floater policy).[4]

theft coverage" under endorsement of homeowners policy, defining theft to include "mysterious disappearance"; insured proved she had bracelet on at luncheon and when entering a store to try on clothes, and did not realize it was gone until 48 hours later; *held*, not an "all loss" policy, and insured's proof was insufficient since circumstances suggested bracelet was lost or mislaid rather than stolen); Brier v. Mutual Insurance Company of Hartford, 3 Conn.Cir. 326, 213 A.2d 736 (1965) ("extended theft coverage" defining theft to include "mysterious disappearance"; insured proved only that the insured property, a watch, had been last seen at a given time, then later could not be found; *held*, not an all-risk form and insured's proof was insufficient since it indicated that theft, even including "mysterious disappearance," was improbable).

Also see Alexandre of London v. Indemnity Insurance Company of North America, 183 F.Supp. 715 (D.D.C.1960) (claiming under a policy requiring "conclusive" proof of loss from a covered risk, insured offered proof that loss resulted from either burglary or employee dishonesty, both covered risks under the policy; held, coverage allowed); Vining v. Security Insurance Company of New Haven, 252 So.

2d 754 (La.App., 1st Cir., 1971), and the decisions cited in the *Vining* opinion.

§ 5.1(d)

1. *Cf.* J. Edward Hedges, *Improving Property and Casualty Insurance Coverage,* 15 Law & Contemporary Problems 353–375 at pp. 374–375 (1950).

There may be limitations on the scope of protection under an all-risk policy, however, that are inapplicable to specified-risk coverage. For example, it has been held that certain conditions of a jewelers' block policy are valid, though they would be invalid under the statute prescribing the fire insurance form if that statute were applicable to the fire coverage that is included in this all-risk policy. Woods Patchogue Corp. v. Franklin National Insurance Company, 5 N.Y.2d 479, 186 N.Y.S.2d 42, 158 N.E.2d 710 (1959).

2. See the discussion of the "hostile fire/friendly fire" rule in § 5.3(d), below.

3. See Appendix I.

4. Of course, such coverage may be limited to the extent that specified exceptions (including special limitations on the amount of liability for precious stones) are not applicable.

The coverage terms for inland marine insurance are derived from the provisions developed for marine insurance.[5] Marine insurance developed as an all-risk coverage, using the phrase "perils of the sea" to encompass the wide and varied range of risks that were covered. The comparable language in the personal property floater states that coverage is provided "against all risks of physical loss" to specified property.

Coverage gaps are less likely to exist when insurance policies employ general terms to define the scope of protection, rather than the specification of individual risks or perils. For example, under the "perils of the sea" terminology, in some instances an insured will be able to recover without having to prove exactly what sea peril caused a loss.[6] Similarly, in some instances an insured is entitled to benefits under an inland marine insurance policy by proving that a property loss occurred even though the insured cannot show exactly what caused the loss.[7]

§ 5.2   Insurance Policy Provisions That Expressly Restrict the Risks Transferred

§ 5.2(a)   Generally

Insurance policies almost uniformly include express restrictions on the risks that are to be transferred, and these limitations may be set forth either in the basic statement of coverage (also referred to as the primary definition of coverage) or in other portions of the contract.[1]

The clauses that set forth the basic statement or description of the insurance typically include one or more limitations which can provide a basis for the denial of a claim,[2] even in coverages which are all-risk in character.[3] Although the basic or primary coverage descriptions usually include a few clauses which serve to restrict the insurance, the more a coverage is oriented toward an all-risk character, the less likely it is

---

5. Also see the description of marine insurance in § 1.5(b), above.

6. *Cf.* Boston Insurance Company v. Dehydrating Process Company, 204 F.2d 441 (1st Cir.1953) (insured's barge sank during calm weather after being loaded at a sheltered berth; subsequent inspection of the barge did not reveal any structural defects that could have caused the sinking, and the trial court found that the insured had rebutted the presumption of unseaworthiness due to overloading or improper loading of the barge; held, affirmed).

The likelihood that the insured can recover without proving exactly what happened is affected also by the burden of proof. See § 5.1(b)(3), above.

Modern cases tend to discuss this problem in terms of burdens of proof. Once an insured proves that a property loss has occurred, the insurer then bears the burden of proving that the cause is excluded. *Cf.* Annotation, *Coverage under "all risks" insurance*, 88 A.L.R.2d 1122–1140 at pp. 1129–31 (1963).

7. See § 5.1(b)(3), above.

§ 5.2

1. Restrictive provisions which concern the persons and interests protected are discussed in Chapter 4, above.

Other provisions that concern the nature of the risks transferred by the contract, together with discussion of basic issues they raise, are considered in the section treating distinctions concerning the nature of causal contributions to a loss. See § 5.5(a) and § 5.5(b), below.

2. See generally the insurance forms in Appendix G, Appendix H, Appendix I, and Appendix J.

3. See § 5.1(b), above.

that the basic coverage statement will include terms that serve such a restrictive function. Conversely, the provisions employed to define the coverage in specified-risk policies frequently serve a restrictive function. For example, the phrase "arising out of the ownership, maintenance or use" — which is used in almost all motor vehicle liability insurance policies — not only specifies the scope of one aspect of the insurance, but also constitutes a significant explicit limitation of the risks transferred to an insurer.[4]

Almost all insurance contracts include several express restrictions which are set out in the provisions that follow the basic description of the coverage. Insurance policies, whether all-risk or specified-risk in character, include a number of provisions — variously characterized as conditions, definitions, exceptions, exclusions, limitations, restrictions, etc. — which limit or restrict the risks that are transferred, or, in some instances, exclude certain risks from the coverage. For example, property insurance policies which provide coverage against "all risks of loss" of the insured property nevertheless commonly include a provision against liability for loss caused by a nuclear accident.[5] Similar provisions which eliminate coverage for losses that result from nuclear accidents also are included in many specified-risk policies, such as liability insurance contracts.[6]

Location of Express Restrictions in Insurance Policy Forms

There appears to be a judicial tendency toward less rigorous adherence to or enforcement of coverage restrictions in an insurance policy when such terms are not integrated into the basic or primary coverage statement, especially when the restrictive provisions are widely separated in the policy form from the general coverage descriptions that they modify or limit. Some of the judicial decisions denying an insurer's right to enforce an express provision set out separately from the basic coverage statement have been justified on the ground of resolving ambiguities against the insurer as the drafter of the contract.[7] In response to such judicial decisions, one of the notable format changes in the 1966 revisions of the standard forms for several types of liability insurance was the placement of some express restrictions on risk either within or in proximity to the primary statements and definitions of coverage.[8] The purpose of these changes was to reduce the likelihood of judicial constructions, predicated on the lack of proximity, that were

---

4. Appellate courts have been required to interpret this language in literally hundreds of coverage disputes. See § 5.2(b), below.

5. See Appendix I.

6. See Appendix G, Appendix H, and Appendix J.

Also see the discussion of rights of an insured which may be predicated on reasonable expectations in § 6.3, below.

7. Yet, this rationale often seems to be invoked by courts in regard to coverage disputes involving insurance provisions which do not involve literal ambiguities. The results in many of these cases are probably better explained as applications of the principle of honoring reasonable expectations. See § 6.3, below.

8. See the Insurance forms Appendix G.

contrary to the drafters' intent.[9] Furthermore, it appears likely that in the future the placement of coverage restrictions — that is, the choice between incorporating restrictive phrases into a primary coverage definition and stating them in separate provisions — may increasingly be influenced by a concern about how the location of such terms will affect the treatment of the provisions by the courts.

§ 5.2(b) Insurance Policy Terms That Both Define and Limit Coverage: Illustrations From Motor Vehicle Insurance

Insurance policies frequently include clauses which both define the risks to be transferred and impose restrictions on the scope of protection. Coverage disputes involving the effects of the word "use" in the phrase "arising out of the ownership, maintenance or use" of the insured vehicle [1] (which appears in most motor vehicle insurance policies) provide an excellent illustration of this point.

A motor vehicle can be employed in many ways, and insurers have repeatedly urged that the term "use" in policy provisions limits the coverage to situations in which a vehicle is being utilized in connection with motoring activities. This interpretation conforms to the idea that a motor vehicle insurance policy is designed to cover motoring risks. Several appellate courts have affirmed this interpretation.[2] Other judicial decisions reject this characterization in favor of an interpreta-

---

9. See Ronald J. Wendorff, *The New Standard Comprehensive General Liability Insurance Policy,* 1966 AMERICAN BAR ASSOCIATION SECTION, INSURANCE, NEGLIGENCE & COMPENSATION LAW PROCEEDINGS 250–264 at pp. 251–252.

§ 5.2(b)

1. See Appendix H. Also see Appendix G.

For example, an issue may arise as to whether the vehicle in question was being "used" or "operated" by the individual claiming coverage for events occurring at a time when that individual was not in the vehicle — that is, the claimant was neither driver nor passenger in the vehicle when the injuries were sustained.

2. *Cf.* Mason v. Celina Mutual Insurance Company, 161 Colo. 442, 423 P.2d 24 (1967) (death of one person in parked car caused by accidental discharge of a pistol in hands of another person in the car does not arise out of the "use" of the insured vehicle; to be covered, "the injury would have to be one originating from the use of the vehicle as such"). In *Mason,* the defendant and the victim were not using the car as a vehicle—neither for transportation nor even for entering or leaving incident to transportation. The result should be the same even if the car was moving at the

time but its movement did not contribute to the accidental discharge of the pistol; the injury would not have been one "arising out of the * * * use" as a vehicle. A more difficult case would be presented if movement of the vehicle contributed to the accidental discharge of the pistol. It might then be said both that the car was being used as a vehicle and that such use was a factor in bringing about the injury.

The mere fact that the vehicle was moving at the time the gun was accidentally discharged is insufficient to establish the causal connection required for coverage. See National Union Fire Insurance Company v. Bruecks, 179 Neb. 642, 139 N.W.2d 821 (1966).

Also see Foss v. Cignarella, 196 N.J. Super. 378, 482 A.2d 954 (Law Div., Somerset County, 1984) (coverage did not extend to an insured who stabbed the driver of a vehicle that had sideswiped the insured's vehicle on the rationale that it was not reasonable that the parties would view this as a natural and reasonable consequence of the use of an automobile).

For other decisions on the meaning of "use," see § 4.7(b) and § 4.9(a)(2), note 10, above.

See generally 6B APPLEMAN, INSURANCE LAW (Buckley edition, 1979), at § 4316(e).

tion of the term "use" that encompasses other activities — that is, so as to provide liability insurance for activities in which an insured vehicle is employed in some way that is not directly related to motoring risks, such as employing some part of a vehicle as a "gun rest." [3] In general, it is essential that there be a substantial relationship between the use of the vehicle and the injury.

Another coverage issue involving the term "use" has arisen in regard to the circumstances under which a passenger is engaged in the "use" of a vehicle within the meaning of the liability insurance coverage. This can be a significant question, as for example in a situation in which a claim is made against a passenger by someone who is injured on the ground that the passenger negligently distracted the driver and thereby caused an accident (which injured another person such as the driver, another passenger, a pedestrian, or an occupant of another vehicle), or that an injury resulted when a passenger negligently threw an object from an insured vehicle. No other commonly acquired liability insurance provides coverage for the potential liability of a passenger in such circumstances. If the term "use" in motor vehicle liability insurance (including in the primary liability coverage for the vehicle, in the coverage provided additional persons under an "omnibus" clause provision,[4] and in the coverage provided by a drive-other-cars provision) is not construed to extend the coverage to the actions of a passenger with respect to such tort claims, a potentially serious coverage gap exists for risks that result from "motoring" activities.

Notwithstanding the potential for a significant coverage gap, insurers have urged that a passenger is not engaged in the "use" of an

---

3. Fidelity & Casualty Company of New York v. Lott, 273 F.2d 500 (5th Cir.1960) (forecasting Texas law; bullet from deer rifle resting on top of the insured car failed to clear the curved top and was deflected downward, killing the hunter's companion sitting in the right front seat; *held*, the death arose out of use of the insured vehicle).

Also see, e.g., Allstate Insurance Company v. Gillespie, 455 So.2d 617 at p. 620 (Fla. App.2d Dist.1984) (coverage applied for an insured, who shot another driver who was enraged by the insured's driving and attempted to engage the insured in a fight, on the rationale that the use of the gun by the insured to defend himself was "inexorably tied to his use of his automobile"); Duvigneaud v. Government Employees Insurance Company, 363 So.2d 1292 (La.App. 4th Cir.1978), writ denied 366 So.2d 560 (1979) (large dog jumped out of an open window of an insured automobile that was parked and into a motor bike causing the operator to lose control).

Cf. Wyoming Farm Bureau Mutual Insurance Company, Inc. v. State Farm Mu-

tual Automobile Insurance Company, 467 F.2d 990 (10th Cir.1972) (driver and passengers were discharging trash from a moving car).

Cf. Carter v. Bergeron, 102 N.H. 464, 160 A.2d 348 (1960), 89 A.L.R.2d 142 (1963) (insured, driving the insured pick-up truck, was allegedly driving ahead of a two-ton truck loaded with horses and signaling its driver, his employee, to drive faster; the larger truck struck a car at an intersection, killing the driver of the car; *held*, the death arose out of use of the insured pick-up truck). Arguably *Carter* may be explained as a case in which operation of the insured pick-up truck, its use as a vehicle, was one of the contributing causes of the accident.

Also see cases collected in Annotation, *Automobile liability insurance: what are accidents or injuries "arising out of ownership, maintenance, or use" of insured vehicle*, 89 A.L.R.2d 150–173 (1963).

4. See the discussion of "omnibus" clauses in § 4.7.

insured vehicle in the type of cases described in the preceding paragraph and therefore that there is no coverage afforded for such a passenger by an automobile or motor vehicle liability insurance policy. There are judicial precedents both favoring coverage for claims against the passenger in such situations [5] and upholding denials of coverage on the basis of the insurance terms.[6] Of course, at least in some instances an injured party might be able to successfully assert a claim against the driver, who clearly would be using the vehicle and therefore would be an insured. For example, the cases in which a passenger distracts the operator, liability might be predicated on the theory that it is negligent for a driver to allow himself or herself to be distracted. Similarly, a court might also conclude that it is negligent for an operator to allow objects to be thrown from the vehicle.

It is predictable that a phrase such as "arising out of the * * * use" of an automobile will produce a body of judicial opinions that consider the nature of the causal relationship between an activity and the consequences of the activity at issue,[7] and that decisions turning on

---

5. See, e.g., Gronquist v. Transit Casualty Company, 105 N.J.Super. 363, 252 A.2d 232 (1969).

Cf. Westchester Fire Insurance Company v. Continental Insurance Companies, 126 N.J.Super. 29, 312 A.2d 664 (App.Div.1973), affirmed 65 N.J. 152, 319 A.2d 732 (1974) (bicyclist struck by a stick thrown by a passenger from a moving vehicle); National Union Fire Insurance Company v. Bruecks, 179 Neb. 642, 139 N.W.2d 821 (1966) (accidental discharge of gun in hands of minor passenger; *held,* passenger was "using" automobile but the injury did not arise out of that use); Coletrain v. Coletrain, 238 S.C. 555, 121 S.E.2d 89 (1961) (woman's hand injured when caught in taxi door slammed shut by her husband, a fellow passenger; *held,* he was "using" the vehicle and was an insured under omnibus clause of coverage on the taxi). See 7 APPLEMAN, INSURANCE LAW (Revised edition, 1962), at § 4316.

Also see United States Fidelity & Guaranty Company v. Hokanson, 2 Kan.App.2d 580, 584 P.2d 1264 (1978) (passenger suddenly pulled on the steering wheel causing driver to lose control).

6. See, e.g., Potomac Insurance company v. Ohio Casualty Insurance Company, 188 F.Supp. 218 (N.D.Cal.1960) (male passenger was negligent in distracting female driver, thereby causing accident; *held,* he was not using the vehicle so as to qualify for drive-other-cars coverage under a policy of which he was the named insured).

Cf. United States Fidelity & Guaranty Company v. Western Fire Insurance Company, 450 S.W.2d 491 (Ky.App.1970) (pas-

senger was shot when a pistol being loaded by another passenger in a moving automobile discharged).

Cf. Dunlap v. Maryland Casualty Company, 242 Ark. 533, 414 S.W.2d 397 (1967) (Dan, teen-age son of named insured was passenger in car driven by his friend, Glenn, and owned by Glenn's father; Glenn collided with another car, injuring a child in that car; *held,* no coverage under Dan's father's insurance for the claim against Dan since Dan, as passenger, was not "using" Glenn's father's car). Although the narrow interpretation these opinions place on "use" is subject to criticism, the result in *Dunlap* probably was justified on other grounds; though the clause there involved is not quoted, references to it support the inference that it was like the "driver-other-cars" or "non-owned automobile" provisions of automobile liability insurance forms in common use. Such a clause extends coverage principally to the named insured and the named insured's relatives. To the extent that it extends coverage to others it does so only for their liability because of acts or omissions of the named insured or one of the relatives, that is, for their vicarious liability. In *Dunlap,* the claim was that the driver was liable because of his own negligence, not that he was vicariously liable for negligence of his passenger.

Concerning drive-other-cars coverage see § 4.9(a)(2), above, generally, and see note 6 thereto with respect to the meaning of "use" under the drive-other-cars coverage.

7. See, e.g., Red Ball Motor Freight, Inc. v. Employers Mutual Liability Insur-

such questions will often be heavily fact-oriented in character.[8]   In general, the meaning accorded by courts to such clauses in an insurance policy, when the scope of coverage is at issue, is substantially affected by the particular circumstances.

When interpreting insurance policy provisions — especially terms such as "use," "operate," [9] "load," and "unload," [10] as well as their

ance Company, 189 F.2d 374 (5th Cir.1951) (applying Texas law) (explosion caused by truck driver's negligently failing to close a valve between underground and overground tanks upon completing fueling of the truck; loading and unloading clause not relied upon by the two-to-one majority; accident resulted from fueling and "fueling the truck for the journey was just as much a 'use' of it * * * [as] making the journey would be"); Carter v. Bergeron, 102 N.H. 464, 160 A.2d 348 (1960), 89 A.L.R.2d 142 (1963); Green Bus Lines, Inc. v. Ocean Accident & Guarantee Corp., 287 N.Y. 309, 39 N.E.2d 251 (1942), 162 A.L.R. 241 (1946) (passenger of common carrier attacked by fellow passenger; coverage under a policy issued to meet the requirements of a special statute applicable to vehicles for hire).

Concerning fact-oriented disputes over casual relation between loading or unloading and loss, see, e.g., Ocean Accident & Guarantee Corp. v. J.B. Pound Hotel Company, 69 Ga.App. 447, 26 S.E.2d 116 (1943) (pedestrian slipped on oil leaked from the load of an oil tank truck; no coverage under policy on the truck); Caron v. American Motorists' Insurance Company, 277 Mass. 156, 178 N.E. 286 (1931) (pedestrian slipped on ice dripped in unloading ice truck; no coverage under a policy issued under the compulsory automobile insurance statute); Schmidt v. Utilities Insurance Co., 353 Mo. 213, 182 S.W.2d 181 (1944), 154 A.L.R. 1088 (1945) (pedestrian tripped over wooden blocks negligently left on sidewalk by coal deliveryman; held, injury arose from "use" of delivery truck).

8. Concerning evaluative, fact-oriented issues generally, see § 1.4, above.

9. Cf. Motor Coils Manufacturing Company v. American Insurance Company, 308 Pa.Super. 568, 454 A.2d 1044 (1982).

Also see Annotation, Meaning of "operate" or "being operated" within clause of automobile liability policy limiting its coverage, 51 A.L.R.2d 924–934 (1957).

10. An issue may arise as to whether the vehicle in question was being "used" or "operated" by the individual claiming coverage for events occurring at a time when he was not in the vehicle at all, neither as a driver nor as a passenger. The prece-

dents are not entirely in harmony. See, e.g., Commercial Standard Insurance Company v. New Amsterdam Casualty Company, 272 Ala. 357, 131 So.2d 182 (1961) (after having loaded shrubbery in car and talking with driver for a few minutes, nursery employee slammed car door on hand of passenger; held, loading had been completed before the accident and employee was not, therefore, an omnibus insured under the policy on the car).

Also see Estes Company of Bettendorf, Iowa v. Employers Mutual Casualty Company, 79 Ill.2d 228, 37 Ill.Dec. 611, 402 N.E.2d 613 (1980) (injuries occurred after concrete had been placed in buckets connected to an overhead crane); Travelers Insurance Company v. Buckeye Union Casualty Company, 172 Ohio St. 507, 178 N.E. 2d 792 (1961), 95 A.L.R.2d 1114 (1964) (named insured's tank-truck driver was knocked off the back of the truck and injured as a spout was being swung into place for the purpose of filling the truck with a cargo of fuel; in a contest between insurance companies, held, the person responsible for operation of the spout was not "using" the truck, since the loading of it had not yet begun, and he therefore was not an omnibus insured under the truck owner's policy); Coletrain v. Coletrain, 238 S.C. 555, 121 S.E.2d 89 (1961).

Cf. Amery Motor Company v. Corey, 46 Wis.2d 291, 174 N.W.2d 540 (1970) (owner-lessees of bulk plant brought third party action against insurers of gasoline transporter, alleging they were additional insurers under liability policies; held, for insurers; furnishing key to unlock pipes to tanks when no employee of plant was present and furnishing defective tanks and storage equipment that led to explosion did not constitute "use of truck during unloading operation"); Lukaszewicz v. Concrete Research, Inc., 43 Wis.2d 335, 168 N.W.2d 581 (1969) (exclusion as to accidents during loading, attached to trucker's policy, held void as in violation of statutory requirement of omnibus clause; liability coverage of trucker's policy extended to concrete company and its employee who, while moving concrete slabs with a travel-lift vehicle to load truck, injured truck driver; "operating," as used in statute requiring omni-

derivatives — courts generally adopt an expansive view or interpretation of the terms that define the scope of coverage,[11] and a narrow construction when the same words are used in clauses defining some type of condition, limitation, restriction, or exclusion.[12] In other words, in each context courts usually apply the meaning that serves to sustain the existence of liability insurance coverage for the insured, which also results in assuring the injured third party a possible source of indemnification if negligence on the part of an insured can be proved.

Terms used in insurance policies may also be interpreted in accordance with the connotations of the words in general usage. For example, a factor that weighs strongly in favor of construing a term such as "operate" in a relatively narrow sense is that the ordinary usage of the word "operate" suggests a limited meaning, akin to the generally understood definition of the word "drive." Accordingly, it is not surprising that there are judicial decisions which approve construc-

bus clause, construed broadly to include participation in loading; though statute did not require coverage for loading or unloading, it required that any such coverage for named insured be extended also to omnibus insurers).

See generally, Annotation, *Automobile liability insurance: what are accidents or injuries "arising out of ownership, maintenance, or use" of insured vehicle,* 15 A.L.R.4th 10–104 at pp. 48–50 (1982); Annotation, *Risks within "loading and unloading" clause of motor vehicle liability insurance policy,* 6 A.L.R. 4th 686–757 (1981); Annotation, *Risks within "loading and unloading" clause of motor vehicle liability insurance policy,* 95 A.L.R.2d 1122–1153 (1964).

11. See, e.g., Trans-Continental Mutual Insurance Company v. Harrison, 262 Ala. 373, 78 So.2d 917 (1955), 51 A.L.R.2d 917 (1957) (coverage only when operated by named insured or member of his immediate family; car driven by third person in company of named insured; insured guilty of separate negligence in exhorting driver to speed; *held,* vehicle was being "operated" by named insured.

Also see Mayflower Insurance Exchange v. Kosteriva, 84 Idaho 25, 367 P.2d 572 (1961) (accident occurred while car was being driven by member of armed services, who had been requested to drive by the named insured, who was also a member of the armed services—because the named insured was intoxicated; *held,* car was being "operated" by wife of named insured, who was also in the car, and, therefore, clause denying coverage for operation by mem-

bers of the armed services other than the named insured was not applicable).

Cf. Hay v. Ham, 364 S.W.2d 118 (Mo. App. Kansas City 1962) (while shifting her position to allow another passenger to enter the car, the defendant accidentally touched the accelerator of a car parked in gear by her husband; *held,* she was "operating" the car within the meaning of a statute requiring the "highest" degree of care of persons operating motor vehicles).

12. See, e.g., Ayres v. Harleysville Mutual Casualty Company, 172 Va. 383, 2 S.E.2d 303 (1939) (clause denying coverage for injury to an employee of the insured while "operating" the vehicle; injury to plaintiff, sitting beside driver, *held* covered even though he was to assist the driver in loading and unloading, and at times in driving).

But cf. Wakefern Food Corporation v. General Accident Group, 188 N.J.Super. 77 at p. 86–87, 455 A.2d 1160 at p. 1166 (1983):

"'Use' provisions and 'loading and unloading' clauses are intended to protect the named insured and others who, in the pick-up or delivery process, are actually using the motor vehicle and its contents during the 'complete operation.' When an accident * * * is occasioned by negligent maintenance of the premises and the only connection to that event is the fact that the motor vehicle and its operator are present because a delivery or pick-up is to be made, no realistic social or public policy is served by straining to shift coverage [from the general liability insurer to the automobile insurance carrier]."

tions or interpretations of words such as "operate" that result in denials of coverage.[13]

The coverage terms used for uninsured motorist insurance provide many illustrations of policy clauses that both define and restrict the scope of coverage, and which have been the subject of a substantial body of litigation.[14] For example, in the clause used to define when insurance is provided for injuries caused by a negligent hit-and-run driver, a "hit-and-run vehicle" is frequently defined as one which causes a bodily injury as a result of "physical contact"[15] with either the insured or a vehicle in which the insured is an occupant at the time of the accident.[16] The definition of coverage for such accidents in terms of "physical contact" has often been invoked by insurers as the basis for rejecting claims when injuries resulted either from (1) an accident in which a vehicle driven by an unidentified hit-and-run driver struck some object (such as another vehicle) which was thereby propelled in such a way that there was an impact with the claimant, or (2) an accident in which there was no contact or impact, although there is clear and convincing evidence that the injuries resulted from the operation of a motor vehicle by an unidentified driver.[17] The rejection of claims on the basis of this definition/limitation has produced a continuing flow of litigation to the nation's appellate courts.[18]

§ 5.3　Implied Exceptions to the Risks Transferred

§ 5.3(a)　Principles Underlying Implied Exceptions

The phrase "implied exception" is used to describe a situation in which an insurer's denial of insurance coverage is not based on any specific language in the contract terms, but rather is said to be warranted by the nature of the insurance agreement or the circumstances. Common examples of implied exceptions that are generally recognized for insurance coverages include the rules which sustain denials of recovery under fire insurance for losses caused by "friendly fires,"[1] under marine insurance for losses caused by ordinary deterioration of goods,[2] and under liability insurance for losses intentionally

---

13. See, e.g., Schaffer v. Mill Owners Mutual Insurance Co., 242 Or. 150, 407 P.2d 614 (1965) (clause denying coverage while automobile "is being operated by any male operator under 25 years of age"; named insured was ill and asleep while 17-year-old son drove; *held,* no coverage; when used in this context "operator" is synonymous with "driver"). It may be noted, however, that the court might have reached the same result even if interpreting "operated" in a broader sense.

14. See § 4.9(c), above.

See generally Widiss, UNINSURED AND UNDERINSURED MOTORIST INSURANCE (1985 and 1987).

15. Or some comparable term such as "striking."

16. Widiss, UNINSURED AND UNDERINSURED MOTORIST INSURANCE (1985), § 9.1 through § 9.9.

17. *Id.,* § 9.6 and § 9.7.

18. *Id.,* § 9.1 through 9.9.

See, e.g., Pim Pim H. Su. v. Kemper Insurance Companies/American Motorists Insurance Company, ＿ R.I. ＿, 431 A.2d 416 (1981).

§ 5.3(a)

1. See § 5.3(d), below.

2. See § 5.3(c), below.

caused by an insured.[3] The implied exceptions that apply to insurance transactions almost always are primarily predicated on an application of one of two concepts.

Regularly Recurring Economic Detriments

One of the concepts is that insurance contracts ordinarily do not cover the type of economic detriments that regularly occur in relation to an enterprise or activity. Repeatedly recurring events are usually regarded as a cost of doing business, rather than as a risk that is appropriately the subject of insurance.[4] Unfortunately, like many general propositions, this one lacks the precision that is essential for deciding marginal cases.

Fortuity

The other concept, which is widely viewed as a fundamental principle of insurance law, is that insurance contracts should not provide coverage when a loss is not fortuitous. Fortuity is generally, though not invariably, considered from the point of view of the person (usually the insured) whose interest is the basis of an insurance claim. A loss is not fortuitous, in this sense, if it is caused intentionally by that person.

Fortuity, or the lack thereof, is primarily a matter of intent. Therefore, it is important to bear in mind that in insurance law, as in tort law, questions about intent focus on the *consequences,* not the *acts.*[5] Thus, the concept of fortuity that is relevant to an application of an implied exception — imposed by the courts as a matter of public policy when there is no express limitation set forth in the applicable insurance policy — almost always involves an analysis of whether an individual intended the consequences which resulted in a claim for insurance coverage.

Whether an event is fortuitous is often a matter of considerable debate in regard to some types of circumstances. This is especially the case when a dispute involves questions about the distinction between consequences that were "foreseen" and consequences that were "foreseeable" — even though they are said to have not been foreseen — by the person from whose perspective the matter is being examined.

The significance of "fortuity" to an insurance coverage is often disputed when the person whose conduct caused the loss is not the insured, and therefore arguably the loss should be considered to have been fortuitous because it is appropriate to evaluate the events that caused the loss from the insured's point of view.[6] When such questions

---

3. See § 5.3(f), below.

4. See § 5.3(c), § 5.3(d), and § 5.4(e), below.

5. See Prosser and Keeton, TORTS (Fifth edition, 1984), § 8 at pp. 34–36.

6. Also consider the discussion of selecting the vantage point for assessing whether a loss is accidental in regard to liability insurance in § 5.4(e), below.

arise, courts have generally concluded that a determination about whether the consequences of an act were fortuitous is to be evaluated from the perspective of the person who will receive the insurance benefits, rather than on the basis of the intentions of the person whose actions caused the injury. However, notable exceptions to this approach sometimes prevail in regard to life insurance.

When an individual whose life is insured dies as a consequence of criminal conduct, either as a result of injuries received in the course of committing a crime or as a result of the imposition of the death penalty for the criminal conduct, courts often examine the question from the insured's point of view, rather than the beneficiary's.

The implications of the fortuity principle are developed throughout this section.

Observations

An appreciation and understanding of the principles described in the preceding portion of this section is essential whenever the applicability of an implied exception is drawn into question.

The import of the first concept, that implicit in the nature of an insurance arrangement is that coverage is not provided for repeatedly recurring events, depends on judicial perceptions of what kinds of risks constitute the routine costs of an activity. Furthermore, it is very important to note that this concept usually has little, if any, force in the face of an explicit provision in an insurance contract. An express term in an insurance policy extending coverage for a particular type of loss will almost always be determinative of whether coverage exists, even when the result is contrary to a common understanding or recognition that a particular type of risk is a repeatedly recurring event in a given context.

The second concept, which expresses the concern that insurance arrangements should be limited to the transfer of economic detriments that are fortuitous, is generally regarded as a principle that is central to the basic determination of what risks may or should be transferred by an insurance arrangement. In most circumstances, it is contrary to public policy to permit the enforcement of an insurance contract if it would provide indemnification for losses that are not fortuitous.[7]

Thus, one of these propositions supports the recognition of implied exceptions as essentially an interstitial rule of interpretation which is appropriately employed to limit coverage in certain types of circumstances when there is no provision in the applicable insurance policy that addresses the question. The other concept embodies a fundamental and significant public policy interest that in some contexts is sufficiently important to preclude coverage claims even when there are

---

7. *But see* the discussion of life insurance coverage for death resulting from a suicide in § 5.3(b)(3), and § 5.4(b)(3), below.

Also see the discussion of professional liability coverage in § 5.4(d)(7), below.

explicit agreements to the contrary, but in any case is a very compelling public interest in regard to coverage questions when there is no applicable provision in the insurance agreement. Court opinions explaining a judgment involving an application of an implied exception sometimes include comments that are variations on both of these somewhat incompatible rationales that provide support for the judicial imposition of coverage exceptions, and occasionally decisions set forth statements which include contradictory ideas.[8]

In most cases, judicial opinions do not examine or discuss the basic nature of a particular implied exception in a given area of insurance law. Furthermore, because the basic nature of the rationales which underlie implied exceptions is different, occasionally disputes arise when an application of one concept favors the recognition of an implied exception in the particular situation, while an application of the other weighs against it.

Implied exceptions sometimes result from the influence of other public interests. For example, implied exceptions for life insurance (discussed in the next subsection) have often been predicated on the rationales of (1) preventing a wrongdoer from profiting from his or her criminal acts, (2) deterring crime, and (3) avoiding, or at least minimizing, the opportunities for frauds against insurers, as well as implementing the principle that insurance should not provide coverage when a loss is not fortuitous. Furthermore, the same concerns are sometimes relevant in regard to other types of insurance claims, and accordingly provide support for either implied exceptions or interpretations of the coverage terms that favor an insurer.

§ 5.3(b) Implied Exceptions Applicable to Life Insurance

Several implied exceptions have been generally recognized as applicable to life insurance contracts. In some contexts, the coverage exception undoubtedly is at least in part grounded on the proposition that a loss was not fortuitous. However, in many instances it is evident that a justification for the result predicated on an application of the fortuity principle provides at best a very strained explanation or justification for the denial of the insurance claim. Most of these cases involve manifestations of the significant public interest in discouraging criminal acts — that is, the application of an implied exception that justifies the rejection of a claim for life insurance benefits is almost invariably a manifestation of the public interest in discouraging various types of criminal activity.

Courts have sometimes appeared to be reluctant about applying implied exceptions to life insurance, and there are several factors which probably contribute to this attitude. First, concern for the third party beneficiaries of life insurance contracts undoubtedly exerts an influence

---

8. See, e.g., Burt v. Union Century Life
Insurance Co., 187 U.S. 362, 23 S.Ct. 139,
47 L.Ed. 216 (1902).

on the courts. However, the force of this concern is notably lessened, if not completely eliminated, when the wrongdoer is the primary beneficiary seeking to receive the insurance benefits.

A second factor — which almost certainly also contributes to the reluctance of courts to impose implied exceptions — is a general perception, common to both judges and the public, that life insurance is intended by the purchaser to cover the insured person's death from any cause — that is, a general presumption that life insurance is appropriately viewed as an "all risk" coverage.[1] Of course, it is part of the human condition that death is a certainty, and that only its timing is uncertain. That fact, however, has only limited significance for life insurance contracts.

The acquisition of life insurance does not guarantee that the beneficiaries will be entitled to claim the insurance benefits upon the death of the insured. This point is perhaps most easily understood in regard to term life insurance because it is obviously possible that an individual's death may not occur during the specific term of years to which the insurance policy applies. The "teaching" embodied in this observation is equally applicable to all types or forms of life insurance. There is almost always a possibility that a life insurance contract will not be maintained in force until an insured's death. Just as it is possible that the beneficiaries will not be entitled to receive insurance because the coverage has been terminated, it is also possible that the factors which cause the insured's death may warrant precluding the payment of life insurance benefits on the basis of important public interests that justify the application by a court of an implied exception.

(1) Public Executions

Numerous appellate decisions have concluded that an implied exception should apply when a person whose life is insured is executed by the state for a crime.[2] The results in these cases are generally based on the conclusion that permitting a recovery on a life insurance contract when an insured has been executed "would be contrary to plain principles of public policy."[3] The implied exception could also be

§ 5.3(b)

1. See § 5.1(b)(1), above.

2. See, e.g., Millen v. John Hancock Mutual Life Insurance Company, 300 Mass. 83, 13 N.E.2d 950 (1938); Scarborough v. American National Life Insurance Co., 171 N.C. 353, 88 S.E. 482 (1916); Smith v. Metropolitan Life Insurance Co., 122 Misc. 136, 203 N.Y.S. 173 (Mun.1923), affirmed at 125 Misc. 670, 211 N.Y.S. 755 (2d Dept.1925);

Also see Burt v. Union Central Life Insurance Company, 187 U.S. 362, 23 S.Ct. 139, 47 L.Ed. 216 (1902); Collins v. Metropolitan Life Insurance Co., 27 Pa.Super. 353 (1905).

The rationale of some cases reaching this conclusion has been based in part on the untenable argument that the denial of recovery is inconsistent with statutory and constitutional provisions against corruption of blood and forfeiture for crime. See, e.g., American National Insurance Co. v. Coates, 112 Tex. 267, 246 S.W. 356 (1923).

See generally, 6 WILLISTON, CONTRACTS (Revised edition, 1938), at § 1750; Annotation, *Liability under policy of life insurance where insured is executed for crime*, 36 A.L.R. 1255–1261 (1925).

3. Millen v. John Hancock Mutual Life Insurance Co., 300 Mass. 83 at p. 84, 13 N.E.2d 950 at p. 951 (1938).

predicated on the rationale that the cause of death is not fortuitous because it is neither from a natural cause (that is, disease or age) nor an accidental cause, but rather death results from a volitional act of the state. On the other hand, a death by execution could rarely be regarded as intentional from the point of view of either the decedent or the beneficiary.[4]

Many of the judicial decisions imposing an implied exception in life insurance cases, when the insured's death occurred as a result of a public execution, have involved situations in which the criminal's estate was designated as the beneficiary. Accordingly, it is possible that a recovery would be allowed in some of these jurisdictions if there were a provision, either in the insurance policy or in the law (statutory or decisional), for the insurance proceeds to go elsewhere than to the criminal's estate.[5]

Some courts have taken the position that life insurance death benefits must be paid when an insured is executed by the state. For example, one court concluded that the benefits are due because "granting recovery * * * in no way benefits the criminal who is now dead and at least benefits * * * named beneficiaries who in most instances will be the persons deprived of support and maintenance by his death."[6] In assessing the possible effect on deterrence of the payment of the insurance benefits, the same court observed, "it may well be asked what sort of crime deterrent the voiding of a man's life insurance may be, when the penalty of death does not halt his criminal act."[7]

Of course, even if no implied exception is applicable, an express coverage limitation may be enforced — that is, life insurance policies may include a specific restriction on the insurer's obligation providing that coverage will not apply in the event death is by public execution.[8]

Also see Simmons v. United States, 120 F.Supp. 641 (M.D.Pa.1954).

4. Consider the discussion of selecting the vantage point from which to analyze whether a loss is "accidental" in § 5.4(c), below.

5. See, e.g., John Hancock Mutual Life Insurance Co. v. Tarrance, 244 F.2d 86 (6th Cir.1957) (2–1 decision that recovery by a beneficiary other than the estate of the criminal is allowed under the law of New York).

In Prudential Insurance Co. of America v. Petril, 43 F.Supp. 768 (E.D.Pa.1942) (applying the law of Pennsylvania) recovery was allowed on the rationale based on grounds that the decisional public policy disallowing recovery is applicable only to cases in which the criminal's estate profits and that a similar public policy is expressed in a Pennsylvania statute, which applies directly to this case, that provides the proceeds of a policy *on the life of a*

slayer designating the slain as beneficiary are to be paid to the estate of the slain, unless the contingent beneficiary is one other than the slayer or the slayer's estate.

6. See, e.g., Weeks v. New York Life Insurance Co., 128 S.C. 223, 122 S.E. 586 (1924), 35 A.L.R. 1482 (1925).

Also see Corey v. Massachusetts Mutual Life Insurance Company, 116 W.Va. 63, 178 S.E. 525 (1935).

7. Tarrance v. John Hancock Mutual Life Insurance Company, 139 F.Supp. 769 at p. 770 (W.D.Ky.1956), quoting from Judge Moscowitz's opinion in Prudential Insurance Company of America v. Goldstein, 43 F.Supp. 765 at p. 767 (E.D.N.Y. 1942). The judgment in *Tarrance* was affirmed by the decision in John Hancock Mutual Life Insurance Co. v. Tarrance, 244 F.2d 86 (6th Cir.1957).

8. *Ibid.*

(2) Criminal Activities

In most American jurisdictions, if a life insurance policy contains no clause excluding coverage in the event an insured dies or is fatally injured either in the course of or as a result of a criminal act, the insurer is liable notwithstanding that the insured died as a result of violating the law.[9] However, there are also decisions which hold that an implied exception should apply when an insured dies or is fatally injured as a result of criminal acts.

The minority rule is predicated on drawing a line between "fortuitous" and "nonfortuitous" occurrences at a point that seems very different from the line between "intended" and "unintended" consequences — that is, there has been, and may still be in some states, a minority rule that denies recovery when an insured dies as the result of criminal activity without regard to whether there is an express limitation in the insurance policy.[10] For example, one court reasoned that when an insured was killed in the course of an armed robbery "it was too natural a consequence * * * to be labeled merely a fortuitous, unusual, or unforeseeable event" and the conclusion that the result "at the moment he sustained the fatal injury * * * was not accidental seems inescapable." [11] Furthermore, the minority decisions sustain an implied exception even when the claim for the insurance is made by a designated beneficiary other than the insured's estate.[12] In this respect, such holdings are a clear departure from the proposition that fortuity is appropriately judged from the point of view of the person whose interest is the subject of the insurance.

9. See, e.g., Davis v. Boston Mutual Life Insurance Company, 370 Mass. 602, 351 N.E.2d 207 (1976); Mohn v. American Casualty Company of Reading, 458 Pa. 576, 326 A.2d 346 (1974); Home State Life Insurance Co. v. Russell, 175 Okl. 492, 53 P.2d 562 (1936).

Also see Zurich General Accident & Liability Insurance Company v. Flickinger, 33 F.2d 853 at pp. 855–856, 68 A.L.R. 161 (4th Cir.1929).

See generally Annotation, *Liability under life or accident policy not containing a "violation of the law" clause, for death or injury resulting from violation of law by insured,* 23 A.L.R.2d 1105–1114 (1952).

Also consider the discussion of liability when death is a consequence of criminal activity in § 5.2(b)(4), below.

10. Molloy v. John Hancock Mutual Life Insurance Company, 327 Mass. 181, 97 N.E.2d 422 (1951), 23 A.L.R.2d 1103 (1952), is an example of the minority view: "Decisions of this court have established the proposition that public policy forbids even an innocent beneficiary of a policy of life insurance to recover on the policy where

the death of the insured is the result of his own criminal conduct." 327 Mass. at p. 182, 97 N.E.2d at p. 423, 23 A.L.R.2d at p. 1104. The Supreme Judicial Court overruled Malloy in Davis v. Boston Mutual Life Insurance Company, 370 Mass. 602, 351 N.E.2d 207 (1976).

A similar question occasionally arises in connection with other kinds of insurance— for example, whether loss caused by a fortuitous collision is covered by collision insurance when the collision occurs because of criminal conduct of the insured. See, e.g., Acme Finance Company v. National Insurance Company, 118 Colo. 445, 195 P.2d 728 (1948), 4 A.L.R.2d 131 (1949) (mortgagee of car totally demolished in collision occurring during "getaway" from robbery and murder denied coverage on grounds of public policy).

11. Carlyle v. Equity Benefit Life Insurance Company, 551 P.2d 663 at p. 667 (Okl. App. 1st Div.1976).

12. Also see the discussion of the consequences of criminal acts in § 5.4(b)(4), below.

When a life insurance policy includes an express provision which eliminates coverage for deaths arising from criminal activities, such a limitation will usually be enforced if the insurer is able to sustain the burden of proof in regard to showing that the death or an injury that resulted in death was caused in the commission of a crime or in an attempt to commit a crime.[13]

(3) Suicides

Suicides have presented troublesome coverage questions in regard to life insurance, stemming (1) in part from the "intentional" quality of the actor's behavior, (2) in part from a sense of unfairness to or fraud upon the insurer in situations when there is a clear indication that the insured already intended to commit suicide at the time the insurance policy was purchased, and (3) in part from early English doctrines, both legal and religious, that were designed to discourage suicides.[14] There are judicial precedents for the proposition that courts will, at least in some instances, recognize an implied exception when a suicide is proved.[15] For example, it has been held "that even if an ordinary

---

13. Annotation, *Construction and effect of provisions in life or accident insurance policies referring to "assault," "felony," "fighting," etc., by insured,* 86 A.L.R.2d 443–469 (1962).

14. In England, it was against public policy to allow a life insurance recovery when the insured's death resulted from suicide (and the insured was sane). For a discussion of the early English legal doctrine designed to discourage suicides, see Burgess-Jackson, *The Legal Status of Suicide in Early America: A Comparison with the English Experience,* 29 Wayne Law Review 57–87 (1982).

The primary vehicle used in English law was the classification of suicide as a felony. The English courts then meted out punishment as follows: "First, the suicide's goods were to be forfeited to the state; second, the suicide was denied a traditional Christian burial; and third, the suicide's bodily remains were mutilated." *Id.,* at pp. 76–77.

See, e.g., Beresford v. Royal Insurance Co., (1938) A.C. 586 (no recovery though there was a clause saying the company would not be liable if the insured committed suicide "whether sane or insane, within one year" and the policy had been in force nearly ten years; it appeared that the insured was financially embarrassed and committed suicide for the purpose of making insurance proceeds of 50,000 pounds available to his creditors).

15. There are also English precedents that should be considered. *Cf.* Moore v. Woolsey, 4 Ell. & Bl. 243 at p. 254 (1854).

This case is frequently cited for the proposition that the English courts will impose an implied exception. However, the insurance contract involved in the case included the following two conditions that were printed on the back of the policy:

"8. Policies effected by persons on their own lives, who shall die by duelling or by their own hands, or by the hands of justice, will become void, so far as regards the executors or administrators of the person so dying, but will remain in force only to the extent of any bona fide interest which may have been acquired by any other person under an actual assignment by deed for a valuable consideration in money, or by way of security or indemnity, or by virtue of any legal or equitable lien as a security for money, upon proof of the extent of such interest being given to the directors to their satisfaction."

"9. If a person, who shall have been assured upon his own life for at least five years, or shall have paid a sum equivalent to at least five years' annual premiums, shall die by his own hands, the directors shall be at liberty, if they think proper so to do, but not otherwise, to pay, for the benefit of his family, any sum not exceeding what the Company would have paid for the purchase of his interest in the policy if it had been surrendered on the day previous to his decease; provided the interest in such assurance shall be in the assured, or in a trustee for him, or for his wife or children, at the time of his decease."

policy of life insurance contains no provision in regard to death by suicide, there is no liability * * * if * * * death is intentionally caused by * * * [the insured] when of sound mind!" [16]

Some judicial decisions have concluded that the right to recover life insurance benefits when an insured's death resulted from suicide — in the absence of an applicable provision in the insurance policy — turns on whether the insurance benefits are payable to the decedent's estate or to a beneficiary. When a life insurance policy names a beneficiary other than the estate of the insured, the weight of authority among American cases has allowed a recovery upon a life insurance contract if there is no express provision in the insurance contract concerning suicide [17] — that is, there are numerous judicial decisions in the United States holding that an implied exception, which precludes coverage for an insured's life when death is the result of a suicide, will not be imposed when an insurance contract designates some beneficiary other than the decedent's estate.[18] The potentially inequitable consequences of this rule in regard to instances when the beneficiaries of the estate could have been, but were not, named in the insurance contract have not been extensively considered because insurers have developed express coverage provisions regarding suicides.[19]

In general, an express limitation or exclusion in an insurance policy which eliminates coverage for death by suicide is not contrary to public policy unless it includes a restriction that is in conflict with statutory provisions that govern the use of such terms.[20] However, some of the suicide limitations included in life insurance policies were viewed as overly favorable to the insurers, and legislative provisions now regulate such coverage terms in most states.

Id., at p. 245. The primary focus of the decision appears to be on whether the inclusion of these terms was against public policy because such terms would offer an encouragement to suicide.

Also see Amicable Society v. Bolland, 4 Bligh's Report (N.S.) 194–211 (House of Lords, 1830), which has been cited for this proposition in regard to a death by suicide even though the insured was executed after having been convicted for committing a forgery on the Bank of England.

This rule was even applied when the terms of the contract purported to allow coverage under some circumstances.

16. Davis v. Supreme Council Royal Arcanum, 195 Mass. 402 at p. 404, 81 N.E. 294 at p. 295 (1907). The court concluded that this view represented "the great weight of authority," citing several precedents including Ritter v. Mutual Life Insurance Co., 169 U.S. 139, 18 S.Ct. 300, 42 L.Ed. 693 (1898).

17. See, e.g., Patterson v. Natural Premium Mutual Life Insurance Co., 100 Wis. 118, 75 N.W. 980 (1898).

Also see 2 RICHARDS, LAW OF INSURANCE (Fifth edition, Freedman 1952) at p. 827.

Cf. 43 AM.JUR.2d 605–606, *Insurance,* § 533 and § 534 (1982).

18. See the discussion of beneficiaries and assignees without an insurable interest in § 3.5(d), above.

19. See the discussion in § 5.4(b)(3), below.

The problem that arose when insurers began to include provisions stating that insurance benefits would be paid even though a death was by suicide is related, but distinguishable, and is discussed below.

20. See, e.g., Bigelow v. Berkshire Life Insurance Company, 93 U.S. (3 Otto) 284 at p. 286, 23 L.Ed. 918 at p. 919 (1876); Kiley v. Pacific Mutual Life Insurance Company, 237 Ala. 253, 186 So. 559 (1939).

(4) Claims for Life Insurance Benefits by Wrongdoers

A substantial body of judicial precedent supports the conclusion that courts generally hold that a person "who intentionally and feloniously takes the life of the insured" is precluded from recovering the proceeds of a life insurance policy. Many of these decisions have not been based on either a legislative provision or a specific term of the insurance policy, and accordingly the limitation on coverage in these cases is appropriately viewed as an implied exception that rests on public policy considerations.[21] This rule has been applied both to beneficiaries named in the applicable life insurance policy and to assignees of an insurance policy who were shown to have intentionally killed an insured.[22] However, when an insured's death was not intended by the person who caused it, courts generally have not sustained an attempt by an insurer to avoid paying such a person the proceeds of a life insurance policy.[23]

When an insured's death has been intentionally caused by a beneficiary or an assignee and the person who was responsible for the insured's death is not allowed to collect the life insurance, in most situations the insurer's obligation in regard to the payment of the insurance benefits is not terminated.[24] One exception to this proposition applies when an insurer proves that the beneficiary or assignee arranged for the policy to be purchased in order to collect the insurance

21. See, e.g., Harper v. Prudential Insurance Company of America, 233 Kan. 358, 662 P.2d 1264 (1983); In re Loud's Estate, 70 Misc.2d 1026, 334 N.Y.S.2d 969 (Surr., Kings County, 1972).

Also see Jackson v. Prudential Insurance Company of America, 106 N.J.Super. 61, 254 A.2d 141 (Law Div.1969).

Cf. Brooks v. Thompson, 521 S.W.2d 563 (Tenn.1975); Beck v. West Coast Life Insurance Company, 38 Cal.2d 643, 241 P.2d 544 (1952).

See generally, Annotation, *Killing of insured by beneficiary as affecting life insurance or its proceeds,* 27 A.L.R.3d 794–839 (1969).

Also see § 4.11(g)(4), above.

22. *Cf.* Mutual Life Insurance Company v. Armstrong, 117 U.S. 591, 6 S.Ct. 877, 29 L.Ed. 997 (1886); Jack v. Mutual Reserve Fund Association, 113 Fed. 49 (5th Cir. 1902).

Also see Houser v. Haven, 32 Tenn.App. 670, 225 S.W.2d 559 (Eastern Section 1949).

23. *Cf.* Turner v. Estate of Turner, 454 N.E.2d 1247 (Ind.App., 1st Dist., 1983) (son previously found not responsible for death of parents in a criminal trial by reason of insanity); Calaway v. Southern Farm Bureau Life Insurance Company, 2 Ark.App. 69, 619 S.W.2d 301 (1981) (evidence sup-

ported finding that wife acted in self-defense).

Cf. Provident Life & Accident Insurance Company v. Carter, 345 So.2d 1245 (La. App., 1st Cir., 1977) (coverage would not be precluded for a beneficiary, the decedent's wife, who shot and killed her husband in an act of self-defense).

Also see Schifanelli v. Wallace, 271 Md. 177, 315 A.2d 513 at p. 520 (1974) (husband named as a beneficiary was not barred from recovering the policy proceeds merely because the death of his wife was the result of gross negligence where that determination was accompanied by an express finding that the death was not caused intentionally).

24. *Cf.* Brooks v. Thompson, 521 S.W.2d 563 (Tenn.1975) (insurance proceeds passed to contingent beneficiary); Beck v. West Coast Life Insurance, 38 Cal.2d 643, 241 P.2d 544, 26 A.L.R.2d 979 (1952) (alternative beneficiary entitled to insurance proceeds).

Cf. Jackson v. Prudential Insurance Company of America, 106 N.J.Super. 61, 254 A.2d 141 (Law Div.1969).

Also see Schmidt v. Northern Life Association, 112 Iowa 41, 83 N.W. 800 (1900) (insurance benefits became part of the assured's estate).

by killing the insured — that is, when an insurer proves an intent to defraud.[25]

The right of a beneficiary to life insurance proceeds is now subject to statutory provisions in several states, and there is considerable variation among the statutory provisions.[26] For example, some state legislative provisions are very detailed and even identify the specific characteristics of the type of act which warrants denying a claim for the life insurance benefits.[27]

Insurers have also been allowed to avoid payment both when a policy provision expressly so provided and when a bylaw provision of a fraternal beneficial association so provided.[28]

(5) Payment of Insurance Benefits to "Innocent" Claimants

The principal reasons given for sustaining a denial of a claim for life insurance benefits in the types of cases discussed in the preceding subsections — suicide, legal execution, death that occurs in the course of committing a criminal act or death caused by a criminal act of the insured, and death at the hands of the beneficiary or assignee — have usually included (1) precluding a "profit" for wrongdoers from criminal acts,[29] (2) deterring crime,[30] and (3) avoiding frauds against insurers.[31] In some instances, courts have also commented that a denial of coverage is consistent with maintaining coverage of a scope that is in accord with the purchaser's reasonable expectations on matters as to which no specific intention or expectation was expressed.[32]

In most circumstances, the first two objectives — avoiding profit for wrongdoers and deterring crime — would be served by a rule which merely disqualified individuals from receiving insurance proceeds, rather than excusing insurers from the obligation to pay the life insurance

---

25. See, e.g., New England Mutual Life Insurance Company v. Null, 605 F.2d 421 (8th Cir.1979); Flood v. Fidelity & Guaranty Life Insurance Company, 394 So.2d 1311 (La.App. 1st Cir.1981), certiorari denied 399 So.2d 608 (1981).

Also see Mutual Life Insurance Company v. Armstrong, 117 U.S. 591, 6 S.Ct. 877 at pp. 880–881, 29 L.Ed. 997 (1886).

26. See, e.g., North Carolina General Statutes § 31A–11 (1961); Oregon Revised Statutes, Intestate Succession and Wills § 112.515 (1983); Vernon's Ann.Texas Statutes Insurance Code, article 21.23 (1981).

Cf. West's Ann. California Probate Code § 258 (1956) ("No person convicted of the murder or voluntary manslaughter of the decedent shall be entitled to succeed to any portion of the estate; * * *."), and In re McGowan's Estate, 35 Cal.App.3d 611, 111 Cal.Rptr. 39 (1st Dist. Div. 2 1973), applying the statutory provision to life insurance proceeds.

27. See, e.g., Vernon's Ann.Texas Statutes Insurance Code, article 21.23 (1981)

(willfully brings about the death of the insured); Official Code of Georgia Annotated § 53–4–6 (1982) (kills another person with malice aforethought).

28. See, e.g., McDade v. Mystic Workers of the World, 196 Iowa 857, 195 N.W. 603 (1923); Greer v. Supreme Tribe of Ben Hur, 195 Mo.App. 336, 190 S.W. 72 (1916).

Also see MacKowiak v. Polish Union of America, 236 App.Div. 44, 258 N.Y.S. 134 (4th Dept.1932).

29. *Cf.* Mutual Life Insurance Co. v. Armstrong, 117 U.S. 591, 6 S.Ct. 877, 29 L.Ed. 997 (1886).

30. *Cf.* Burt v. Union Century Life Insurance Co., 187 U.S. 362 at pp. 365–366, 23 S.Ct. 139 at p. 140, 47 L.Ed. 216 at p. 219 (1902).

31. *Cf.* Mutual Life Insurance Company v. Armstrong, 117 U.S. 591, 6 S.Ct. 877, 29 L.Ed. 997 (1886).

32. *Cf.* Burt v. Union Century Life Insurance Company, 187 U.S. 362 at pp. 363–364, 23 S.Ct. 139–140, 47 L.Ed. 216 at p. 218 (1902).

benefits. These two objectives afford weak support, at best, for granting an insurer a complete defense against liability. Thus, it is not surprising that among the judicial precedents in this area, there are numerous decisions which hold that it is appropriate to deny insurance benefits to the wrongdoer (or to the estate of a wrongdoer), but allow others — claimants who are innocent of any wrongful actions — to recover the insurance proceeds.[33]

Significance of Actuarial Judgments to Claims

Acturial computations regarding life expectancy and the incidence of death among persons in any selected age group usually are not related to particular causes of death. Instead, they are based on data concerning deaths in various age groups from all causes. Thus, it is generally appropriate to reject an argument that liability for a particular cause of death such as execution is inconsistent with actuarial computations on which premiums were based.

An actuarial argument may have legitimate weight when an insurer has in fact taken into account both data concerning deaths from all causes and its estimates of risks of death from excepted causes. Even so, although the determination of appropriate premiums for particular risks may be a legitimate consideration, standing alone — that is, without an explicit limitation in the coverage terms — it generally has not been viewed as sufficiently significant to warrant the recognition and application of an implied exception (beyond that justified by the other public interests) which would eliminate an insurer's obligation to pay life insurance benefits to claimants who were innocent of any wrongdoing.

§ 5.3(c) Marine Insurance and the "Inherent Vice" Exception

Marine insurance, though all-risk in character,[1] is subject to a well established implied exception of "inherent vice."[2] The inherent-vice exception means that deterioration, either of goods or of a vessel, which

---

33. *Cf.* Harper v. Prudential Insurance Company of America, 233 Kan. 358, 662 P.2d 1264 (1983).

Also see Continental Bank & Trust Co. v. Maag, 285 F.2d 558 (10th Cir.1960); Carter v. Carter, 88 So.2d 153 (Florida Supreme Court, Div. A, 1956); Beck v. West Coast Life Insurance Co., 38 Cal.2d 643, 241 P.2d 544, 26 A.L.R.2d 979 (1952).

Also consider the discussion of the disqualification of beneficiaries in § 4.11(g), above.

§ 5.3(c)

1. See § 5.1(b)(1), above. However, marine insurance is not uniformly viewed as all-risk insurance. See, e.g., Sipowicz v. Wimble, 370 F.Supp. 442 at pp. 446–448 (S.D.N.Y.1974).

Also see Vining v. Security Insurance Company of New Haven, 252 So.2d 754 at

p. 756 (La.App., 1st Cir., 1971). In *Vining,* the court observed, "It is settled maritime law that a Marine Policy of Hull Insurance is not an all-risk policy, and that such coverage extends only to losses resulting directly from a peril enumerated in the policy" and cited several decisions in support of this proposition, including: Hazard's Administrator v. New England Marine Insurance Company, 33 U.S. (8 Pet.) 557, 8 L.Ed. 1043 (1834) and Union Marine Insurance Company v. Charles D. Stone & Company, 15 F.2d 937 (7th Cir. 1926).

2. See generally British Marine Insurance Act, 1906, § 55(2)(c); 2 ARNOULD, MARINE INSURANCE [British Shipping Laws] (Sixteenth edition, 1981), at § 780, § 782; 5A APPLEMAN, INSURANCE LAW (Revised edition, 1970), at § 3272.

is due to ordinary wear and tear does not come within the coverage provided by a policy covering loss from "perils of the sea."[3]   However, when the natural decay of goods is caused (or hastened) by a peril of the sea, recovery for the loss is permitted.[4]

§ 5.3(d)   An Implied Exception for Property Insurance: The "Friendly Fire" Rule

Courts have commonly recognized an implied exception in fire insurance policies under which a loss caused by a "friendly" — as distinguished from a "hostile" — fire is not covered.   In general, a friendly fire is one that occurs in an ordinary place for a fire such as a stove, a furnace, or a fireplace.[1]   Hostile fires include both those that occur in a place where fire is ordinarily not maintained, and those that originate as friendly fires but which escape their usual confines.

There is increasing judicial support for classifying a fire as hostile when it becomes excessively hot, even though it remains within an intended place.[2]   Most of these cases have involved damage which

---

3. See, e.g., By's Chartering Service, Inc. v. Interstate Insurance Company, 524 F.2d 1045 (1st Cir.1975); Reisman v. New Hampshire Fire Insurance Co., 312 F.2d 17 (5th Cir.1963); Shaver Transportation Company v. Travelers Indemnity Company, 481 F.Supp. 892 at p. 894 (D.Or.1979) ("The Perils clause, almost identical to ancient perils provisions dating back several hundred years, * * * has been interpreted to include only perils that are similar to the enumerated perils * * *" and did not provide coverage for "the 'forced' disposition of caustic soda" that was contaminated at the time of loading).

Also see Larsen v. A.C. Carpenter, Inc., 620 F.Supp. 1084 (E.D.N.Y.1985), *affirmed* 800 F.2d 1128 (2d Cir.1986); Inland Rivers Service Corporation v. Hartford Fire Insurance Company, 66 Ohio St.2d 32, 418 N.E.2d 1381 at p. 1383 (1981).

As to the burden of proof relating to inherent vice, see § 5.1(b)(3), above.   It would appear that the plaintiff has the burden of showing that deterioration of the goods was not due "to a certainty or to inherent vice or to wear and tear."   This is implied in British & Foreign Marine Insurance Co. v. Gaunt, [1921] 2 A.C. 41, both in Lord Birkenhead's comment that "the plaintiff discharges his special onus when he has proved that the loss was caused by some event covered by the general expression * * *" and in Lord Sumner's comment that "he need only give evidence reasonably showing that the loss was due to a casualty * * *." [1921] 2 A.C. at 47, 58.

The burdens of proof have been modified by federal legislation, however.   See, e.g., Associated Metals & Minerals Corp. v. M/

V Rupert De Larrinaga, 581 F.2d 100, 101 (5th Cir.1978).

4. See Lanasa Fruit Steamship & Importing Co. v. Universal Insurance Company, 302 U.S. 556, 58 S.Ct. 371, 82 L.Ed. 422 (1938); 5A APPLEMAN, INSURANCE LAW (Revised edition, 1970), at § 3269.

§ 5.3(d)

1. See, e.g., Youse v. Employee's Fire Insurance Company, 172 Kan. 111, 238 P.2d 472 (1951).

Also see, Levert-St. John, Inc. v. Birmingham Fire & Casualty Company, 137 So.2d 494 (La.App. 3d Cir.1961), in which the court recognized that the "friendly fire" distinction is not usually made in Louisiana but held that the distinction was relevant to the applicability of a fire insurance clause excluding coverage of loss caused by explosion (holding that an explosion set off by a welder's ignition spark was caused by a friendly fire and, therefore, that the exclusionary clause was applicable).

But see, e.g., Harris v. Poland, [1941] 1 K.B. 462 (apprehensive of theft, the insured hid her jewelry under wood and coal on a grate, which she lighted later, having forgotten about the jewelry; held, coverage under a Lloyds Householders Comprehensive Policy insuring "against loss or damage caused by Fire * * *").

Also see Annotation, *Loss by heat, smoke, or soot without external ignition as within standard fire insurance policy,* 17 A.L.R.3d 1155–1172 (1968).

2. See, e.g., Engel v. Redwood County Farmers Mutual Insurance Company, 281 N.W.2d 331 at p. 334 (Minn.1979) ("fire may be hostile * * * if it burns substan-

resulted when temperatures became excessive as a result of the malfunction of some equipment, such as a thermostat designed to control
the intensity of a fire. In essence, the judicial decisions in these cases
hold that coverage should be provided for two interrelated reasons:
first, it is appropriate to consider the coverage question from the
vantage point of the reasonable expectations of the insured; and,
second, when a fire becomes excessive in terms of heat or smoke,
thereby causing damage, it is reasonable for an insured to expect
coverage under a fire insurance policy for such losses.[3]

The precise line of demarcation between friendly and hostile fires
has been and continues to be a subject of considerable disagreement in
the reported judicial decisions.[4] Professor Patterson suggested that in
developing the friendly fire exception, the courts were seeking a functional distinction "between mere irregularities in the process of manufacture or other use of fire as an instrument [as in the case of a baker
who inadvertently overbakes his bread], which would be charged off to

tially longer or in some fashion other than
expected" so that an insurer was liable for
the loss occasioned by the death of sows
that resulted when a thermostat malfunctioned causing temperatures to rise to 120
degrees); L.L. Freeberg Pie Company v. St.
Paul Mutual Insurance Co., 257 Minn. 244,
100 N.W.2d 753 (1960) (excessive heating of
commercial baking oven caused by a mal-
functioning thermostat resulted in structural damage to the oven and heat damage
to hardwood floor underneath and in front
of the oven; *held*, "hostile" fire covered by
standard fire policy).

Also see, Schulze and Burch Biscuit
Company v. American Protection Insurance Company, 96 Ill.App.3d 350, 51 Ill.
Dec. 823, 421 N.E.2d 331 at p. 333 (1st
Dist., Div. 4, 1981) (holding that "it is improper to allow liability to turn on the
location of the fire causing damage apart
from the damage itself" so that coverage
would exist for an unanticipated loss which
occurred when an oven was inadvertently
left to operate and temperatures rose to
excessive levels necessitating repairs and
replacement of the damaged oven that allegedly cost almost $150,000); Karadontes
v. Continental Insurance Company, 139
N.J.Super. 599, 354 A.2d 696 (Bergen
County 1976) (faulty operation of a low
water cut-off valve allowed a boiler to continue to operate without sufficient water so
that the boiler cracked from excessive
heat).

Cf. Bowes v. North Carolina Farm Bureau Mutual Insurance Company, 26 N.C.
App. 234, 215 S.E.2d 855 (1975), *cert. denied* 288 N.C. 238, 217 S.E.2d 662 (1975)
(fire in a church's cooking units that
caused smoke damage could be regarded as
excessive and thereby covered, even
though it remained spatially confined);

Barcalo Manufacturing Co. v. Fireman's
Mutual Insurance Company, 24 A.D.2d 55,
263 N.Y.S.2d 807 (4th Dept.1965), 17
A.L.R.3d 1150 (1968) (automatic controls
on a furnace failed to operate properly
resulting in the destruction of the furnace
and forging being annealed).

Cf. O'Connor v. Queen Insurance Company, 140 Wis. 388, 122 N.W. 1038 (1909)
(material not intended for use in a home
furnace was used as fuel causing both intense heat and "great volumes of smoke to
escape through the registers leading into
the rooms * * *.").

Also see, William E. Mooney, *Is the
"Friendly" Fire Doctrine Becoming Obsolete?*, 1968 Insurance Law Journal 945–49.

But cf. 5 APPLEMAN, INSURANCE LAW (Revised edition, 1970), at § 3082, n. 27 and n.
25.

3. See, e.g., Bowes v. North Carolina
Farm Bureau Mutual Insurance Company,
26 N.C.App. 234, 215 S.E.2d 855 at p. 857
(1975), *cert. denied* 288 N.C. 238, 217 S.E.2d
662 (1975).

Also see cases cited below in this section,
and the associated discussion in the text.

4. *Cf.* Harris v. Poland [1941] 1 K.B.
462, *with*, e.g., Youse v. Employers Fire
Insurance Co., 172 Kan. 111, 238 P.2d 472
(1951).

Also see Robert I. Reis, *The Friendly
Versus Hostile Fire Dichotomy*, 12 Villanova Law Review 109–134 (1966). See also
the cases cited in note 2, above.

Also *cf.* Garfield Mutual Fire and Storm
Insurance Association v. Calhoun, 532
S.W.2d 663 (Tex.Civ.App., Corpus Christi
1975); Robert M. Morrison, *Concerning
Friendly Fires*, 3 Boston College Industrial
& Commercial Law Review 15–28 (1961).

the cost of doing business, and those extraordinary, accidental fires against which a prudent business man insures. * * *" [5] Professor Patterson also observed that " * * * the functional distinction is rather vague, and it is not surprising to find that the test commonly applied by the courts is a mechanical one, namely, was the 'fire' * * * confined to the receptacle or other *place where* it was intended to be." [6]

Not providing coverage for some fire losses can be justified on the basis of the general proposition that insurance is designed to cover extraordinary risks, rather than losses that are part of the regular costs of an activity.[7] For example this is the explanation and justification which is often articulated in decisions denying liability when damage resulted from soot and smoke caused by a fire larger than a given fireplace was designed for, but not so large that flames escape.[8] Arguably, a reasonable person anticipates that occasionally someone will not tend a fire carefully enough so that smoke or soot will "escape" thereby causing some damages, and that this is a risk that is appropriately viewed, especially in a business setting, as a "cost" of using a fire. On the other hand, coverage for at least some cases of this type might now be held to exist on the basis of extending protection to an insured for damages caused by a fire that becomes excessive.

The friendly fire exception has sometimes been applied to claims resulting from a fire which does not escape the confines intended for it, even though there was a loss which an insured could reasonably view as the destruction of property by a fire. For example, courts almost uniformly have held that damage to or the complete destruction of jewelry destroyed by a fire in a stove, furnace or fireplace is not covered by fire insurance.[9] The explanation for the results in these cases does not rest on a general public policy against coverage for the destruction of property in this way, because it is undisputed that this type of loss is insurable under personal property floater policies.[10] Furthermore, the application of an implied exception in this context does not appear to rest on the rationales that generally are understood to warrant such judicial intervention. Certainly, it does not seem justified to view such losses as regularly recurring economic detriments. Furthermore, the

---

5. Edwin Patterson, *The Apportionment of Business Risks Through Legal Devices,* 24 Columbia Law Review 335–359 at p. 338 (1924).

6. *Ibid.* (emphasis is Patterson's).

Despite Professor Patterson's insightful analysis and critique of the "friendly fire rule," many of the cases decided since Patterson's comments were published have tended to limit the scope of the implied exception so that coverage extends well beyond the reasonable bounds defined by such a mechanical test.

Also see the decisions described in note 2, above.

7. See § 5.3(a), above.

8. It might be argued also that "direct loss by fire" (the phrase customarily appearing in fire insurance policies) refers to flame damage rather than damage from soot, smoke, or heat. But that rationale would involve one in an inconsistency since it is well established that these kinds of damage from a *hostile* fire are included within the losses for which an insurer is liable, even though the requirement that they be regarded as within the phrase "direct loss by fire" applies in this context too.

9. See, e.g., Youse v. Employee's Fire Insurance Co., 172 Kan. 111, 238 P.2d 472 (1951).

10. *Ibid.* Also see the insurance form in Appendix B.

loss in such cases may be fortuitous. The explanation and justification for denying claims for losses in these circumstances must lie elsewhere.

Some judicial opinions have advanced the explanation that in common parlance one has not "had a fire" when the fire has burned only in the place where it was intended to burn, even though property has been destroyed.[11] But to determine the existence of coverage on the basis of deciding whether one has "had a fire" is to consider an issue *not* expressly presented by the terms in the insurance contract — that is, the coverage provisions used in most insurance policies require not that one has "had a fire," but only that there be a "direct loss by fire."[12] Moreover, the question whether, in common parlance, a person who accidentally tossed an item of personal property (such as a diamond ring) into a stove or furnace fire has suffered a direct loss by fire might well be answered by many persons in the affirmative — that is, arguably it is reasonable to conclude either (1) that insureds will expect that when a valuable item of personal property is inadvertently destroyed in such fires, it is covered by fire insurance or (2) that an insured's expectations about the coverage is a question of fact that is appropriately resolved as such by a judge or jury.

Another justification which is sometimes advanced in support of the friendly fire rule is that whatever the original merits of the limitation, its existence is now common knowledge and it is understood by policyholders. The counter-argument to this hypothesis is that the friendly fire rule almost certainly is *not* a matter of common knowledge among insurance purchasers, and that such an implied exception arguably does not conform to the reasonable expectations of policyholders about the scope of coverage provided by fire insurance.[13]

Several courts have specifically considered the question of an insured's expectations in regard to whether the doctrine of "friendly" versus "hostile" fires should function as an implied limitation on coverage. Although the following comments were directed at the appropriateness of applying the friendly fire rule to losses that resulted from fires that became excessive, the views of the courts are instructive on the import of an insured's reasonable expectations in regard to the friendly fire rule. For example, an Illinois Court of Appeal commented:

> "Insurers have more than ample opportunity to limit their liability by way of the contract of insurance. In most instances ＊ ＊ ＊ the terms and conditions of insurance contracts are not negotiable. Without express provision, it is our view that it is improper to

---

11. See, e.g., Youse v. Employee's Insurance Co., 172 Kan. 111, 238 P.2d 472 (1951).

Cf. the discussion in Garfield Mutual Fire and Storm Insurance Association v. Calhoun, 532 S.W.2d 663 (Tex.Civ.App., Corpus Christi, 1975).

But cf. Sadlowski v. Liberty Mutual Insurance Co., 487 A.2d 1146 at p. 1149 (Del.

Super., New Castle County, 1984), in which the court concluded that the scope of fire insurance coverage should be determined "in accordance with the reasonable expectations of the purchaser so far as the language of the contract permits."

12. See the insurance forms in Appendix A.

13. See § 6.3, below.

allow liability on the location of the fire causing damage apart from the damage itself. When one purchases standard fire insurance *he does so with the idea in mind of protecting himself and his property from loss or damage. Our decision conserves that expectation.*" [14]

In addressing the issue of coverage when a fire remained spatially confined, but nevertheless caused damages, the North Carolina Court of Appeal observed that it "would be reasonable on the part of an ordinary insured to expect" that even though "a fire may be spatially confined to its intended place, if it is extraordinary, or excessive, and unsuitable for the purpose intended, and is in a measure uncontrollable, then the fire is 'hostile' as distinguished from 'friendly' and is such a fire as would be covered under standard form policies in this State." [15] The rationale of such decisions appears to be grounded on the sense of what fairly and appropriately constitutes the purchaser's objective in purchasing fire insurance. As the North Carolina Court concluded: "The *broader definition* of a hostile fire, with the concept of excessiveness, *is a more realistic recognition of the multiple characteristics of a fire and of the risks contemplated and intended to be covered in the fire insurance policy.*" [16] This analysis has considerable force, and seems persuasive in regard to what is the appropriate scope of the implied exception.[17] Even if the hostile fire rule is now familiar to some sophisticated insurance purchasers, the vast majority of home owners,

---

14. Schulze and Burch Biscuit Company v. American Protection Insurance Company, 96 Ill.App.3d 350, 51 Ill.Dec. 823, 421 N.E.2d 331 at p. 333 (1st Dist., Div., 1981) (emphasis added).

Similarly, in Karadontes v. Continental Insurance Company, 139 N.J.Super. 599, 354 A.2d 696 at p. 699 (Bergen County 1976) (emphasis added), the court commented that since the court was "construing a contract of adhesion" it "should look to the *reasonable expectations* of the plaintiff as a purchaser of insurance in the light of the contract language." The court then concluded that the plaintiff was entitled "to recover for a direct loss resulting from a fire which accidentally became uncontrolled" as a result of a low water cutoff valve that failed, thereby producing excessive heat that cracked the boiler, because the insurance policy "language reasonably permits such an interpretation" and therefore "the court should favor a construction effectuating" the insured's reasonable expectations.

Cf. Sadlowski v. Liberty Mutual Insurance Company, 487 A.2d 1146 (Del.Super., New Castle County, 1984) (holding that because the insurance policy was ambiguous in regard to damages which resulted

when a furnace thermostat malfunctioned, thereby causing excessive heat, the coverage terms should be interpreted in accordance with the reasonable expectations of the purchaser); Engel v. Redwood County Farmers Mutual Insurance Company, 281 N.W.2d 331 (Minn.1979).

15. Bowes v. North Carolina Farm Bureau Mutual Insurance Company, 26 N.C. App. 234, 215 S.E.2d 855 at pp. 857–858 (1975), *cert. denied* 288 N.C. 238, 217 S.E.2d 662 (1975). The court concluded that "it is our opinion that if the size of the fire in terms of heat becomes greater than would be anticipated by the insured and if by excessive heat, damages are caused, then it would *be reasonable on the part of an ordinary insured to expect he would be covered.*" (Emphasis added). The court added, "The question of whether a fire, though spatially confined, has become excessive within the contemplation of the parties to the insurance policy would be properly left to the jury pursuant to proper instructions in any particular case."

16. *Ibid.*

17. *Cf.,* e.g., Harris v. Poland, [1941] 1 K.B. 462.

apartment dwellers, and even commercial insurance purchasers are not likely either to be aware of such a rule or to understand its effect.

Comment

When the friendly fire/hostile fire rule is applied to justify rejecting a claim for damage to a piece of personal property (such as a ring) that a claimant alleges accidentally fell or inadvertently was tossed into a fire burning in a stove, a furnace, or a fireplace, the result is not supported by any specific language of the fire insurance policy. Moreover, a persuasive case exists for the proposition that the imposition of an implied exception so as to preclude coverage for such a loss is not within the reasonable expectations of a policyholder without experience in this aspect of property insurance.

The application of an implied exception when personal property has been destroyed by a "friendly fire" represents one of the few instances in which courts have resolved what can reasonably be viewed as an ambiguity of insurance policy language in favor of insurers — that is, courts have filled in a gap so as to benefit the insurer rather than the insured.[18] In the absence of a friendly fire rule, however, insurers would almost certainly be placed in the position of providing coverage for some — and perhaps, numerous — property losses that were not fortuitous. For example, a piece of jewelry could easily be tossed into a furnace in order to provide the basis for an insurance claim. Whatever the motivation for such destruction might be, the difficulty — and, in many circumstances, the virtual impossibility — in discerning instances of an intentional destruction from those that involve a fortuitous occurrence almost certainly has been and will probably continue to be a major influence on the breadth that courts accord to the friendly fire rule.

When property is destroyed by a fire that did not "escape" the intended location (that is, damages have occurred to an object as a result of a fire that was spatially confined in an intended location), courts should employ the concept of a hostile fire to limit recoveries by insureds to those circumstances in which evidence provides a clear basis for a determination that the loss was fortuitous.[19] In other words, the friendly fire rule should in essence establish both a presumption against coverage and a requirement that in order to recover for personal property destroyed by a fire that remained confined in the place in which it was intended to burn, an insured must provide sufficient evidence (not alone from the insured, and perhaps even from an impartial witness) to convince the court that the loss was fortuitous.

18. See § 6.10(c), below.

19. See cases cited in the preceding portion of this subsection.

§ 5.3(e)   Fire Insurance Coverage for Grossly Negligent or Reckless Conduct

The question whether fire insurance contracts provide coverage for losses that are a result of grossly negligent or reckless conduct has produced a substantial number of judicial opinions. These cases present the basic issue whether it is against public policy for insurance to provide indemnification when losses result from various types of extraordinarily risky conduct.[1]

Some judicial opinions state that there is a general rule that destruction of property caused by gross negligence or recklessness on the part of an insured "may preclude a recovery" under a fire insurance policy.[2] Most, and perhaps all, of the judicial statements to this effect have been dicta. Moreover, often these statements are made in regard to claims in which there was evidence indicating that the actor probably intended to cause the destruction of the insured property.[3] Consequently, the comments and analysis in these decisions arguably are misleading if they are applied to instances in which the evidence does not indicate, and perhaps would not support, a finding of an intentional destruction of the insured property.

A persuasive argument can be made that an insured reasonably expects that fire insurance coverage generally applies without regard to the type of negligence which causes a fire.[4] Although it is doubtful that in regard to fire insurance gross negligence or recklessness will (or should) constitute a defense in the absence of either a statute[5] or an express insurance policy clause[6] which so provides, the consistent

---

§ 5.3(e)

1. One such group of opinions, discussed in a later section, concerns coverage under liability insurance policies for highly expectable losses. See § 5.4(e), below.

2. See, e.g., Winter v. Aetna Casualty & Surety Company, 96 Misc.2d 497, 409 N.Y. Supp.2d 85 (Nassau County, Part V, 1978).

Also see Fidelity-Phenix Fire Insurance Co. v. Lawler, 38 Ala.App. 245, 81 So.2d 908 (1955), quoting Annotation, *Insurance: what amounts to gross negligence, or recklessness which will relieve fire insurer from liability,* 10 A.L.R. 728–731 (1921).

Cf. 5 Appleman, Insurance Law (Revised edition, 1970) at § 3114.

3. See, e.g., Todd v. Traders & Mechanics' Insurance Co., 230 Mass. 595, 120 N.E. 142 (1918). One of the plaintiffs started a fire in tall grass overhanging a raspberry bed to see if a grass path could be burned over without scorching the berries. Being satisfied with the experiment, he stamped out the flames. Shortly thereafter, a flame flared up 15 to 20 feet on the other side of the raspberry bed and burned a barn before it could be controlled. Plain-

tiff had violated a statute prohibiting the lighting of a fire in the open air without permission of a town official. The insurers denied liability on fire insurance policies, and this action was brought. In holding for the plaintiffs the court declared: "Mere negligence on the part of the insured does not prevent recovery on a policy of insurance. One of the objects of insurance is to protect the insured from loss due to carelessness."

4. See the discussion of reasonable expectations in § 6.3, below.

5. See Georgia Code Annotated § 56–819 (1953) (repealed, Georgia Laws 1960, p. 289): "The insured shall be bound to ordinary diligence in protecting the property from fire, and gross negligence on this part shall relieve the insurer. Simple negligence by a servant or the insured, unaffected by fraud or design in the latter, shall not relieve the insurer." This is not a common type of statute.

6. Concerning policy clauses restricting coverage because of negligence, gross negligence, or recklessness of the insured in

repetition of the proposition that coverage does not apply when grossly negligent conduct causes a loss cannot be completely ignored. One explanation for these repeated comments in judicial opinions is that in effect courts have concluded that some conduct involves such incredibly foolish behavior that an insured simply should not be allowed to shift any consequent loss to an insurance company. This suggests the existence of what could be termed a "damn fool" doctrine whereby risk transference is precluded for incredibly foolish conduct [7] even though the consequences were not intended [8] and do not constitute economic detriments which regularly occur in relation to the enterprise or activity.[9] The import and utility of such a "doctrine" is considered in § 5.4(e)(6), below.

§ 5.3(f)   Liability Insurance Coverage for Intentional Torts

Losses which are intentionally caused by an insured generally are not covered by liability insurance, and this rule applies even when there is no clause in the applicable insurance policy that expressly excludes coverage for injuries intentionally inflicted by an insured [1] —

failing to protect property after an accident, see § 5.4(f), below.

7. See § 5.4(f), below.

Also see the scope-limiting interpretations of statutes prohibiting liability insurance against intentional wrongdoing or relieving liability insurers of liability for "willful" acts of the insured, discussed in § 5.4(e)(6), below.

A similar analysis may have caused some courts to impose analogous coverage limitations to liability insurance.

8. In general, see the discussion of "damn fool" conduct in § 5.4(e)(6), below.

Cf. Aetna Insurance Company v. Sachs, 186 F.Supp. 105 (E.D.Mo.1960); Winter v. Aetna Casualty & Surety Company, 96 Misc.2d 497, 409 N.Y.Supp.2d 85 (Nassau County 1978).

9. Pennsylvania Threshermans & Farmers Mutual Insurance Companies v. McCall, 102 Ga.App. 137, 115 S.E.2d 740 (1960) (insured extinguished tractor fire by throwing sand and dirt on it, then failed to clean the tractor thoroughly before using it; a complete breakdown occurred after the tractor was operated for a short time; held, Georgia Code Ann. § 56–819 (1953) [subsequently repealed] would preclude recovery if the jury should find that insured's use of sand and dirt to extinguish the fire and his subsequent failure to clean the tractor thoroughly were gross negligence, which was equated with failure to exercise even *slight* diligence).

See also the discussion of policy provisions regarding care in protecting damaged

property after a covered loss has occurred, in § 5.4(f), below.

§ 5.3(f)

1. There is a relative dearth of direct authority for an implied exception of this nature, in part because of the fact that liability policies almost uniformly include express requirements (e.g., the provision that coverage is provided for injuries "caused by accident") and in part because the proposition is so clearly sound in principle that it would ordinarily go unchallenged even if there were no insurance policy clause in point. The express limitations are discussed at length in § 5.4, below.

See, e.g., Isenhart v. General Casualty Company of America, 233 Or. 49, 377 P.2d 26 (1962).

Cf. Red & White Airway Cab Company v. Transit Casualty Co., 305 Minn. 353, 234 N.W.2d 580 (1975); Haser v. Maryland Casualty Co., 78 N.D. 893, 53 N.W.2d 508 (1952), 33 A.L.R.2d 1018 (1954) (liability coverage for rapist would be contrary to public policy; coverage denied even though "caused by accident" defined coverage of broader scope than merely for negligence).

But cf. Wolff v. General Casualty Co. of America, 68 N.M. 292, 361 P.2d 330 (1961) (reversing summary judgment for insurer, obtained on theory that insurer was not bound to defend and pay judgment on claim for assault and battery by its insured; "Blanket Liability Policy" did not expressly exclude intentional injury from the coverage and referred to "accident"

that is, no coverage exists when a loss results from an intentional tort which is not fortuitous from the point of view of the person whose interest the liability insurance policy is designed to protect.[2] However, in most instances, there is an express limitation included in insurance policies that is at least as extensive in scope as the coverage restriction that might be applied by a court as an implied exception.[3] The doctrines and approaches developed by the courts when liability coverage for an intentional tort is at issue are therefore considered in § 5.4, below.[4]

§ 5.3(g) Liability Insurance Coverage for Punitive Damages

Claims by an insured for coverage by a liability insurance policy for punitive damages awards frequently involve several conflicting considerations and public interests.

When an insured's tortious conduct supports a denial of coverage on the basis of an implied exception which applies to an intentionally caused loss, obviously coverage for both punitive and compensatory damages is not within the scope of the protection afforded by any liability insurance policy. If, on the other hand, liability coverage for compensatory damages is not precluded by either an implied exception or an explicit policy provision,[1] there is a significant question about whether an otherwise applicable liability insurance policy does or should provide coverage for punitive damages which the insured is adjudged to be obligated to pay — that is, such a case presents the

only in a "per-accident" limit on the amount of coverage; note, however, that insured claimed he discharged a tear-gas pencil at victim because he believed himself in danger; see § 5.4(d)(5) thereto, below).

Also see Annotation, *Liability insurance: assault as an "accident," or injuries therefrom as "accidentally" sustained, with coverage clause,* 72 A.L.R.3d 1090–1155 (1976); Annotation, *Liability insurance as covering accident, damage, or injury due to wanton or wilful misconduct or gross negligence,* 20 A.L.R.3d 320–334 at pp. 331–333 (1968).

2. Concerning the proper point of view for considering whether loss is fortuitous, see § 5.4(c), below.

Note that if a financial responsibility statute is construed as intended to protect victims even in cases of intentional tort, allowing the victim to recover may not offend this principle of implied exception. See § 5.4(d)(3), below.

3. See § 5.4(d), below.

4. For example, an implied exception to liability insurance for intentional torts

should not invariably apply to preclude coverage for all losses claimed by a third party as a consequence of such tortious conduct. Sometimes when damages are awarded against an insured defendant, as a consequence of an intentional tort, under a theory of intentional tort, the events are nevertheless fortuitous from the insured's point of view. When this is the case, the determination of whether coverage should be extended is essentially identical in regard to limiting coverage on the basis of either an implied exception or an express restriction. See § 5.4(c) and § 5.4(d), below.

Cf. Armstrong v. Security Insurance Group, 292 Ala. 27, 288 So.2d 134 (1973) (intentional injury exclusion did not apply to co-owner of a sandwich shop who neither explicitly nor implicitly authorized an assault on a patron by the other owner of the shop).

§ 5.3(g)

1. This point applies whether or not tort law classifies a cause of action as intentional tort.

question whether there is or whether there should be an implied exception which precludes coverage for punitive damages.[2]

The principal argument for not providing insurance coverage for punitive damages is that the primary rationale for such awards is either to punish the wrongdoer or to deter similar conduct in the future by both the wrongdoer and others, and therefore to allow an insured to shift the responsibility for punitive damages to an insurer would serve to thwart the public interests in attaining punishment and deterrence.[3] As one court observed, "a person should not be permitted to insure against harms he may intentionally and unlawfully cause others, and thereby acquire a license to engage in such activity."[4] There is a clear split of authority on this question in the United States.[5]

Many judicial precedents support the proposition that liability insurance does not provide coverage for punitive damages on public policy grounds. The decisions in these cases recognize a judicially imposed implied exception on liability insurance.[6] In some of these states, however, exceptions to the general rule have been recognized (1) when punitive damages are imposed on an insured who is vicariously liable,[7] or (2) when the insured committed reckless or wanton, as contrasted with intentional, acts.[8]

Numerous courts have rejected attempts by insurers to impose an implied exception for punitive damages, holding that it is not contrary to public policy for an insured to acquire insurance which provides

---

2. See the cases and articles cited in notes 3 and 4 below.

3. See, e.g., American Surety Co. v. Gold, 375 F.2d 523 (10th Cir.1965), 20 A.L.R. 335 (1968) (forecasting Kansas law).

It has also been suggested that punitive damages should not be covered because to do so would mean that ultimately the public would bear the burden through the increases in premiums that would subsequently result. *Cf.* Northwestern National Casualty Co. v. McNulty, 307 F.2d 432 at p. 440–441 (5th Cir.1962), where the court observed that "since the added liability would be passed along to the premium payers" ultimately "Society would * * * be punishing itself for the wrong committed by the insured."

Also see Note, *The Exclusion Clause: A Simple and Genuine Solution to the Insurance for Punitive Damages Controversy,* 12 University of San Francisco Law Review 743–769 at p. 748 (1978); Scott Conely & David J. Biship, *Punitive Damages and the General Liability Policy,* 25 Federation of Insurance Counsel Quarterly 309–318 (1976).

4. Home Insurance Company v. Neilsen, 165 Ind.App. 445, 332 N.E.2d 240 at p. 244 (3d Dist.1975), quoted in Norfolk &

Western Railway Co. v. Hartford Accident & Indemnity Company, 420 F.Supp. 92 at p. 95 (N.D.Ind.1976).

5. See generally, Note, *An Overview of the Insurability of Punitive Damages Under General Liability Policies,* 33 Baylor Law Review 203–213 (1981).

6. Also see cases cited in notes 3, 4, and the decisions collected in the Annotation cited in note 5.

7. See, e.g., Sinclair Oil Corporation v. Columbia Casualty Company, 682 P.2d 975 (Wyo.1984); Dayton Hudson Corporation v. American Mutual Liability Insurance Company, 621 P.2d 1155, 16 A.L.R. 4th 1 (Okl. 1980).

Also see United States Concrete Pipe Company v. Bould, 437 So.2d 1061 (Fla. 1983).

8. See, e.g., Hensley v. Erie Insurance Company, 168 W.Va. 172, 283 S.E.2d 227 (1981) (public policy does not preclude insurance coverage for punitive damages arising from gross, reckless, or wanton negligence).

Cf. Sinclair Oil Corporation v. Columbia Casualty Company, 682 P.2d 975 (Wyo. 1984).

indemnification for punitive damages. In these jurisdictions, construing the typical liability insurance policy terms stating that the insurer will pay "on behalf of the insured all sums which the insured shall become legally obligated to pay," the courts hold that such liability insurance covers punitive as well as compensatory damages in the absence of policy provisions to the contrary [9] — that is, punitive damages are regarded as a "sum" which an insured is "legally obligated to pay." Although the breadth of the holdings in these decisions is often rather extensive, and occasionally very extensive, most of these cases have actually involved either vicarious liability or wanton conduct, rather than an intentional tort. Furthermore, increasingly the judgments in these cases are premised, at least in part, on the theory that when an insurance carrier has broadly defined coverage through an "all sums" clause, the insured has reasonable expectations of "complete" coverage — subject to the policy's limit of liability — for both vicarious liability and acts of gross, reckless or wanton negligence.

Comment

The issue as to whether liability insurance provides coverage for punitive damages has been well recognized by insurers for several decades. It is clearly a matter that could be easily addressed in the

---

9. See, e.g, Skyline Harvestore Systems, Inc. v. Centennial Insurance Company, 331 N.W.2d 106 (Iowa 1983); Harrell v. Travelers Indemnity Co., 279 Or. 199, 567 P.2d 1013 (1977) (there was sufficient ambiguity so as to require resolution of reasonable doubts against the insurer on whether punitive damages were within the coverage); Southern Farm Bureau Casualty Insurance Co. v. Daniel, 246 Ark. 849, 440 S.W.2d 582 (1969) (automobile collision).

Cf. American Home Insurance Company v. Fish, 122 N.H. 711, 451 A.2d 358 (1982); Carroway v. Johnson, 245 S.C. 200, 139 S.E.2d 908 (1965) (automobile collision); Lazenby v. Universal Underwriters Insurance Co., 214 Tenn. 639, 383 S.W.2d 1 (1964) (automobile collision).

In Colson v. Lloyd's of London, 435 S.W.2d 42 (Mo.App., Kansas City, 1968), the court considered "whether it would be against public policy to permit an association of law enforcement officers to insure themselves against alleged willful and intentional acts." The court concluded that "it would tend to discourage them from entering into that public service" if "they were told by the courts that they could not enter into a contract which would afford them protection against financial loss arising from claims for punitive damages * * *." *Id.*, 435 S.W.2d at p. 47.

In some jurisdictions a distinction is drawn between liability for punitive damages that is directly imposed and liability that is vicariously imposed. In these jurisdictions, even though generally an insured may not insure against liability for punitive damages, the rule against shifting the impact of a punitive damage award does not apply when such liability is vicariously imposed. See, e.g., Commercial Union Insurance Co. v. Reichard, 404 F.2d 868 (5th Cir.1968) (applying Florida law), affirming the decision reported at 273 F.Supp. 952 (S.D.Fla.1967); Norfolk & Western Railway Company v. Hartford Accident & Indemnity Co., 420 F.Supp. 92 (N.D.Ind.1976) (applying Indiana law); Travelers Insurance Co. v. Wilson, 261 So.2d 545 (Fla.App., 4th Dist., 1972).

It has also been held that it is not "against public policy to allow liability therefor to be insured against when the punitive damages are imposed for a grossly negligent act of the insured rather than an intentional wrong of the insured." Continental Insurance Companies v. Hancock, 507 S.W.2d 146 at pp. 151–152 (Ky.1973) (emphasis added).

See generally, 7 APPLEMAN, INSURANCE LAW (Buckley edition, 1979) at § 4312; 12 *Id.* at § 8879; Note, *Insurance Coverage and the Punitive Award in the Automobile Accident Suit,* 19 University of Pittsburg Law Review 144–173 (1957).

coverage provisions, and has been the subject of express restrictions (often an exclusion) in many insurance policy forms. The failure of insurers to generalize this practice for all liability insurance policies provides considerable support for insureds who argue that the coverage terms are ambiguous and therefore should be construed against the insurer.

The award of compensatory tort judgments may, of course, also serve to deter or to punish, and it has sometimes been argued that liability insurance is not compatible with the attainment of these objectives. However, such arguments have not been regarded by courts as sufficient to justify the judicial imposition of restrictions which limit or preclude the use of liability insurance generally,[10] and accordingly insurance coverage for the compensatory damages will almost always be sustained even though precisely the same conduct might have been or is, at least in some instances, the basis for an award of punitive damages.[11] On the other hand, the argument in regard to punishment and deterrence has greater force in regard to precluding coverage for punitive damages, both because punishment and deterrence of wrongdoers are the primary objectives and because in this context the countervailing public interest — which favors the continued availability and applicability of the tortfeasor's liability insurance so as to assure indemnification for victims — is considerably more limited, if not totally absent.

§ 5.4   Insurance Policy Provisions and Other Requirements Concerning the "Accidental" or "Unintentional" Nature of Losses

§ 5.4(a)   Introduction

Insurance transactions are predicated on the general proposition that coverage is provided for fortuitous losses, and not for intended consequences. The importance accorded to the concept that insurance does not provide indemnification for intended losses is reflected by the fact that even when no coverage limitation is explicitly set out in an insurance policy, there is widespread judicial recognition of various implied exceptions which are predicated on the public's interest in restricting the use of insurance to transfer the risk of (1) certain types of losses or (2) an individual's liability to third parties resulting from

---

10. See, e.g., Breeden v. Frankford Marine, Accident & Plate Glass Insurance Company, 220 Mo. 327 at pp. 423–435, 119 S.W. 576 at pp. 606–610 (1909).

Concerning the validity of liability insurance generally, see 6B APPLEMAN, INSURANCE LAW (Revised edition, 1979), at § 4252; Gardner, *Insurance Against Tort Liability—An Approach to the Cosmology of the Law*, 15 Law & Contemporary Problems 455–469 at pp. 462–463 (1950).

11. See, e.g., Crull v. Gleb, 382 S.W.2d 17 (Mo.App., St. Louis, 1964) (reckless operation of automobile).

Cf. Northwestern National Casualty Company v. McNulty, 307 F.2d 432 (5th Cir.1962) (forecasting Virginia and Florida law; disallowing coverage for punitive damages and distinguishing cases holding insurers bound for compensatory damages awarded on the basis of recklessness or willful and wanton misconduct).

certain types of conduct. Thus, as discussed in the preceding section, courts frequently have held that even in the absence of express provisions, insurance contracts only provide coverage for accidental losses. However, insurers generally choose not to leave this restriction or limitation on the risks which are transferred to be determined on the basis of a judicially formulated implied exception.

Insurance policies typically include express provisions which either require that a loss be "accidental" or preclude coverage for intended results.[1] Furthermore, the terms in insurance policies that are used to define accidental losses or to exclude claims for intended results often prescribe coverage limitations that extend well beyond the scope of the judicially developed implied exceptions which have been applied to comparable circumstances.[2] An insurance policy clause stating the requirement that a loss must be accidental or a clause imposing such a limitation may be specified in the basic coverage statement, in separately stated restrictions,[3] or in both types of provisions.

In many insurance contracts, the coverage terms relating to causation define the risks that are transferred to the insurer by using the term "accidental" or some variation of that term.[4] Liability insurance policies, for example, have often been and (with editorial variations) continue to be phrased in terms of providing coverage for all sums which an insured shall be legally obligated to pay as damages because of injuries *caused by accident.*[5] Uninsured motorist insurance policies have employed essentially the same terms as liability insurance forms stating that coverage is provided for "bodily injury sustained by the insured, *caused by accident.* * * *"[6] Life insurance contracts frequently include clauses that state a larger death benefit will be paid

---

§ 5.4(a)

1. For example, see the 1966 Liability Insurance Form, Appendix G, which provides that the company is obligated to pay on the insured's behalf damages imposed by law because of bodily injury or property damage "caused by an occurrence," and defines "occurrence" to mean "an accident, including injurious exposure to conditions, which results, during the policy period, in bodily injury or property damage neither expected nor intended from the standpoint of the insured * * *."

Some implications illustrating the significance of the requirement that the bodily injury or property damage not be "expected" are discussed in § 5.4(d)(2), below. Also see Annotation, *Liability insurance: specific exclusion of liability for injury intentionally caused by insured,* 2 A.L.R.3d 1238–1253 (1965).

Also see the discussion of the term "occurrence" in § 5.4(g), below and the insurance forms in Appendixes.

2. As to implied exceptions, see § 5.3, above.

3. See, e.g., the "Assault and Battery" clause of some liability insurance forms, described in § 5.4(d)(5), below.

4. See, e.g., New York Life Insurance Co. v. Harrington, 299 F.2d 803 (9th Cir. 1962) ("accidental bodily injury" clause).

Also see the discussion in § 5.4(b), § 5.4(c) and § 5.4(d), below.

5. See the discussion in § 5.4(d), below.

Also see the cases collected in Annotation, *Liability insurance: "accident" or "accidental" as including loss resulting from ordinary negligence or insured or his agent,* 7 A.L.R.3d 1262–1274 (1966).

As stated in note 1, above, current forms use the phrase "caused by an occurrence" and then use the word "accident" in defining "occurrence."

6. See Appendix H.

provided that "an insured's death resulted directly, and independently of all other causes, *from accidental bodily injury.* * * * "[7] And similar language is used in accident insurance policies which provide coverage for death and various injuries such as dismemberment or loss of sight.[8]

In addition to the use of the term "accident" or "accidental" in the general coverage statements, many insurance policies also include either provisions that set forth in more explicit detail restrictions or limitations on the type of loss producing circumstances that will be regarded as accidental,[9] or clauses that specifically exclude coverage for injuries which are intentionally caused.[10] For example, various types of liability insurance policies now state that coverage is not provided when a loss is expected or intended from the standpoint of an insured.[11]

The import of the requirement that for a particular type of insurance to provide coverage a loss must be "fortuitous" or "accidental" has produced a substantial body of appellate decisions. The judicial opinions in these cases are a medley: on the one hand, there are decisions based on explicit provisions in the coverage terms and, on the other, there are decisions that articulate and apply implied exceptions — that is, many appellate court decisions involve contract interpretation, others are based exclusively on implementing public policy. Furthermore, in some decisions there is a melding of the considerations and rationales that relate both to the enforcement of express contract provisions and to the implementation of general public policy interests.[12] As might be expected in view of the significant dual influences of very important public policy interests and express contract provisions, in many cases the courts do not always clearly explain either the analytical approach that has been employed or the rationales that have produced a particular decision.

§ 5.4(b) Accidental "Causes" and Accidental "Results"

(1) Life Insurance Policy Provisions

Life insurance contracts usually provide that benefits will be paid in the event of the insured's death, and there are few, if any, coverage limitations specified in the typical policy terms. In most life insurance policies, the only express restrictions on coverage relate to death that results from a suicide. Occasionally, there is also a restriction that applies to a death that occurs while an insured is engaged in some type of criminal conduct.

7. See Appendix E.

8. See Appendix F.

9. See the discussion § 5.4(b), below.

10. See, e.g., Aetna Casualty & Surety Company v. Freyer, 89 Ill.App.3d 617, 44 Ill.Dec. 791, 411 N.E.2d 1157 (1st Dist., Div. 4, 1980).

11. See the discussion of coverage for "occurrences" and the associated limitations in § 5.4(g), below.

12. *Cf.* Annotation, *Liability insurance as covering accident, damage or injury due to wanton or willful misconduct or gross negligence,* 20 A.L.R.3d 320–334 at p. 322 (1968).

Many life insurance contracts provide that additional insurance benefits will be paid in the event an insured's death is accidental.[1] A typical clause states that the larger amount will be paid if the death of the insured "results solely from bodily injury caused directly, exclusively and independently of all other causes by external, violent, and *accidental means*."[2] Such provisions often state that the amount of life insurance will be "doubled" in the event an insured's death is caused by an accident, and these coverage provisions are commonly referred to as "double indemnity clauses."

(2) Accident Insurance Policy Provisions

Accident insurance policy forms typically limit the scope of protection by providing coverage only for deaths or injuries that are caused by "accidental means." Terms such as "accidental means" are often employed by insurers in clauses that are designed to define coverage limitations that are more restrictive than those which are applied by the courts as a consequence of the general requirement that insurance only applies to losses that are fortuitous. For example, accident insurance policies using the term "accidental means" usually declare that death or injury must result "*directly* and *independently* of all other causes."[3] Such clauses have been the basis for rejecting coverage

---

§ 5.4(b)

1. See, e.g., Wynglass v. Prudential Life Insurance Company of America, 68 Mich. App. 514, 242 N.W.2d 824 (1976) (accidental death benefit in life insurance); National Life and Accident Insurance Company v. Franklin, 506 S.W.2d 765 (Tex.Civ.App., Houston, 1974).

In Oldring v. Metropolitan Life Insurance Company, 492 F.Supp. 994 (D.N.J.1980), the court concluded a death was through "accidental means" and therefore a compensable loss within the meaning of the double indemnity provision when an insured died of a self-inflicted gunshot wound to the head that resulted from leaving a bullet in one of the gun's six chambers.

2. See, e.g., Britt v. Travelers Insurance Company, 556 F.2d 336 at pp. 343–344 (5th Cir.1977), *on rehearing* 566 F.2d 1020 (1978); Britt v. All American Assurance Company of Louisiana, 333 So.2d 629 (Miss.1976) (clause employed slightly different wording: "death resulted directly from bodily injury caused solely by external, violent, and accidental means and independent of all other causes * * *."; National Life and Accident Insurance Company v. Franklin, 506 S.W.2d 765 (Tex.Civ.App., Houston, 1974), Great National Insurance Company v. Legg, 444 S.W.2d 324 (Tex.Civ. App., El Paso, 1969).

In Wynglass v. Prudential Life Insurance Company of America, 68 Mich.App. 514 at p. 516, 242 N.W.2d 824 at p. 826 (1976), the opinion states, "In determining whether a death is accidental, a court must view the death through the eyes of the deceased and must ascertain whether his death was a foreseeable occurrence."

In Reserve Life Insurance Company v. Whittemore, 59 Tenn.App. 495, 442 S.W.2d 266 (Middle Section 1969), the policy provided that coverage was provided for "accidental bodily injury due to violent and external means, * * * directly and independently of all other cause * * *." The court concluded that the claimant "failed to carry the burden of offering some evidence excluding the causal connection of preexisting disease, and thereby failed to carry the burden of proving that death resulted from accident 'independently of all other causes.'" *Id.*, 442 S.W.2d at p. 275.

Also see Annotation, *Accident insurance: death or injury intentionally inflicted by another as due to accident or accidental means,* 49 A.L.R.3d 673–718 (1973).

3. See, e.g., the clauses involved in Commercial Travelers Insurance Company v. Walsh, 228 F.2d 200 (9th Cir.1955), 56 A.L.R.2d 796 (1957) (applying Washington law; insured who had a short history of mild heart trouble died of a heart attack

claims in a number of situations in which death was almost indisputably fortuitous, but was not exclusively the result of what would normally be viewed as an accident.[4] Sometimes insurance policies also specify that "bodily injury by accident" must be evidenced by a visible contusion or wound on the exterior of the body, except in the case of a drowning or internal injury revealed by autopsy * * *."[5]

following accidental overexertion; *held,* coverage, without express consideration of the "sole cause" problem); Silverstein v. Metropolitan Life Insurance Company, 254 N.Y. 81, 171 N.E. 914 (1930) (insured who accidentally dropped a large milk can, which hit him in the stomach, died of peritonitis caused by perforation of the stomach at a point where it was found there had been a pea-sized ulcer; *held,* recovery, since the ulcer was at most a "predisposing tendency" and not a disease or infirmity contributing to the death within the meaning of the policy clause).

Also see Hammer v. Mutual Benefit Health & Accident Association, 158 Ohio St. 394, 109 N.E.2d 649 (1952), 36 A.L.R.2d 1084 (1954) (insured who apparently had no history of heart trouble died of a heart attack brought on by heat exhaustion; *held,* recovery, the court treating the death as resulting from accidental means that were the sole cause of death); Pan American Life Insurance Company v. Andrews, 161 Tex. 391, 340 S.W.2d 787 (1960), 93 A.L.R.2d 560 (1964) (psychic trauma incurred when insured witnessed fire that burned his office; death, 34 days later and after intervening brain operation, *held* not covered under double indemnity provision).

Cf. Britton v. Prudential Insurance Company of America, 205 Tenn. 726, 330 S.W.2d 326 (1959), 82 A.L.R.2d 605 (1962) (insured who had a history of arteriosclerosis died of an acute coronary thrombosis after surgery for a fracture caused by an accident; *held,* action to recover accidental death benefits dismissed).

"Sole cause" provisions are also used in conjunction with "accidental injury" clauses. See, e.g., Adkins v. American Casualty Company, 145 W.Va. 281, 114 S.E.2d 556 (1960), 84 A.L.R.2d 169 (1962), *opinion on second appeal* 146 W.Va. 1045, 124 S.E. 2d 457 (1962) (insured received an accidental blow to his head after which he was continually afflicted with severe shoulder and back pains, which, it was determined, were due to aggravation of a degenerative condition of intervertebral discs not uncommon for one of the insured's age; *held,* no coverage under a policy insuring

against "accidental bodily injury which is the sole cause * * *" of loss).

4. For example, in Hodges v. Valley Forge Life Insurance Company, 486 S.W.2d 544 (Tenn.App., Eastern Section, 1971), the court concluded that the claimant was not entitled to recover hospital confinement benefits for a hospitalization "occurring solely as the consequence of direct bodily injury resulting from any accident and independent of all other causes" when the evidence showed that he had been diagnosed as having arteriosclerotic cerebral vascular disease and signs of Parkinson's Disease. Accordingly, the court decided that the disease was necessarily a contributing cause, if not the sole cause of the hospitalization, and the hospitalization was not exclusively the result of an accidental fall.

Cf. Sekel v. Aetna Life Insurance Company, 704 F.2d 1335 (5th Cir.1983).

Also see, Annotation, *Heart attack following exertion or exercise as within terms of accident provision of insurance policy,* 1 A.L.R.4th 1320–1348 (1980); William Meyer, LIFE AND HEALTH INSURANCE LAW (1972).

5. See, e.g., Body v. United Insurance Company of America, 72 Ill.App.3d 594, 28 Ill.Dec. 820, 391 N.E.2d 19 (1st Dist., Div. 3, 1979).

In an Annotation, *Life or accident insurance: Sufficiency of showing that death from drowning was due to accident or accidental means,* 43 A.L.R.3d 1168–1193 at p. 1172 (1972), the writer observed, "It seems clear that the negative presumption against suicide and the affirmative presumption of death by accidental means are based on the love of life and the instinct of self-preservation, the fact that self-destruction is contrary to the general conduct of mankind, and the presumption of innocence of crime."

Although it is not a widespread practice among insurers, some insurance policies specifically exclude losses caused by disease. See Annotation, *What conditions constitute "disease" within terms of life, accident, disability or hospitalization in-*

Terms such as "accidental death," "accidental means," and "accidental bodily injury" are also used by insurers in some types of accident insurance policies, as well as in life insurance policies, to define limits on the double indemnity features of such insurance policies — that is, so that the double indemnity coverage is not provided for all deaths of insureds.[6] Furthermore, the same terms are used in some accident insurance policies to eliminate all coverage for certain types of deaths or injuries. For example, insurers have urged that such terms should be interpreted to mean that a death by drowning which results in part from a disease or a physical infirmity (such as epilepsy) is not within the risks covered by contract provisions providing insurance for "accidental death." [7]

Observations

The scope of protection afforded by insurance policies with coverage provisions framed in terms of "accidental" or "accidental means" is almost certainly less extensive than that which would be provided by these insurance contracts if such terms were used without further elaboration of the meaning intended by insurers. Moreover, the coverage is undoubtedly more circumscribed than would exist on the basis of the implied exceptions formulated and applied by courts in the absence of explicit restrictive policy provisions. Furthermore, in considering the import of terms such as "accidental death" and "accidental means" in contracts for accident insurance, as well as those for life insurance, courts tend to interpret the coverage provisions and limitations so as to favor the interests of the beneficiaries when the evidence indicates the death or injury at issue was essentially fortuitous.[8]

surance policy, 61 A.L.R.3d 822–879 at p. 825 (1975).

Also see Annotation, *Construction and effect of "visible sign of injury" and similar clauses in accident provision of insurance policy,* 28 A.L.R.3d 413–441 (1969).

6. See Barry Rothman, *The Meaning of the "Accidental Means" Clause in Accident Insurance Policies,* 48 Insurance Counsel Journal 231–243 (1981).

These terms are also used in personal accident policies, which are discussed in the following subsection.

7. See National Life and Accident Insurance Company v. Franklin, 506 S.W.2d 765 (Tex.Civ.App., Houston, 1974).

Cf. Britt v. All American Assurance Co. of Louisiana, 333 So.2d 629 (Miss.1976) (death from exposure).

In Britt v. Travelers Insurance Company, 556 F.2d 336 (5th Cir.1977), *on rehearing* 566 F.2d 1020 (1978), the insurer raised the issue whether the insured's death

"from exposure" was an "accidental bodily injury which was the direct and independent cause of death." The insurance contract required that the insurer be provided with due proof that the death resulted from an accidental injury and that "such injury, except in instance of drowning or internal injury revealed by autopsy, provided a visible wound or contusion on the exterior of the body." *Id.,* 556 F.2d at p. 339.

Also see, Annotation, *Life or accident insurance: sufficiency of showing that death from drowning was due to accident or accidental means,* 43 A.L.R.3d 1168–1193 (1972). The annotator pointed out that "[a] finding of death by accidental drowning has * * * been upheld in several cases where the insurer contended that death from drowning was contributed to by disease or physical infirmity." *Id.,* 43 A.L.R.3d at p. 1172.

8. See, e.g., Gottfried v. Prudential Insurance Company of America, 82 N.J. 478,

(3) "Accidental Means" and "Accidental Results"

Some insurers have employed insurance policy clauses phrased in terms of "accidental means" [9] with a view to specifying a broader restriction on the scope of coverage than would be described by the use of the term "accidental results." In 1934, Judge Cardozo observed, in what has now become a widely cited dissent, "The attempted distinction between accidental results and accidental means will plunge this branch of the law into a Serbonian Bog." [10] However, until 1946 a distinction between causes and results was almost uniformly upheld. Among the states in which courts ruled on the question, a great majority rejected the contention that distinctions between "means" and "results" were too nebulous to be rationally applied, and courts held that the scope of coverage provided by policies using the language of "accidental means" was different from that of policies using coverage phrased in terms of "accidental results." [11]

In 1946, the New York Court of Appeals declared, in what is now one of the leading cases on the question, Burr v. Commercial Travelers

---

414 A.2d 544 (1980); Britt v. All American Assurance Company of Louisiana, 333 So. 2d 629 (Miss.1976).

Also see National Life and Accident Insurance Company v. Franklin, 506 S.W.2d 765 at p. 767 (Tex.Civ.App., Houston 1974). In a case in which there was evidence that the insured was subject to mild epileptic seizures, the court observed that " * * * recovery is not defeated by a pre-existing condition or disorder which is so remote in the chain of causation that it does not materially contribute to a death or injury." The insured was found dead in his apartment lying over the edge of the bathtub with the water running and the drain open. An autopsy showed that death was by drowning.

Cf. Hearn v. Southern Life & Health Insurance Company, 454 So.2d 932 (Ala. 1984) (whether death that resulted from smoke inhalation caused by a fire in a crash which occurred just after an officer abandoned a high speed chase, at speeds of 70 or 80 miles per hour, was an accident was a question for the jury).

The results in these cases are essentially comparable to the more numerous judicial resolutions of coverage disputes involving the same terms in accident insurance policies.

But cf. Body v. United Insurance Company of America, 72 Ill.App.3d 594, 28 Ill. Dec. 820, 391 N.E.2d 19 (1st Dist., Div. 3, 1979) (no coverage when death occurred from medical complications following a kidney transplant); Wynglass v. Pruden-

tial Life Insurance Company of America, 68 Mich.App. 514, 242 N.W.2d 824 (1976) (no coverage for a wife, when her deceased husband, the insured, saw a gun in the wife's hand and was warned that she would use it after he had already assaulted her with a knife); Davis v. Boston Mutual Life Insurance Company, 370 Mass. 602, 351 N.E.2d 207 (Mass.1976) (insured was shot and killed by a police officer while committing a felony).

9. See cases cited in Annotation, *Insurance: "accidental means" as distinguishable from "accident," "accidental result," "accidental death," "accidental injury,"* etc., 166 A.L.R. 469–479 (1947).

10. Landress v. Phoenix Mutual Life Insurance Company, 291 U.S. 491 at p. 499, 54 S.Ct. 461 at p. 463, 78 L.Ed. 934 at p. 938, 90 A.L.R. 1382 (1934).

11. See, e.g., John Hancock Mutual Life Insurance Company v. Plummer, 181 Md. 140, 28 A.2d 856 (1942).

Also see INA Life Insurance Company v. Brundin, 533 P.2d 236 (Alaska 1975), 91 A.L.R.3d 1027 (1979); Prudential Insurance Company of America v. Gutowski, 49 Del. 233, 113 A.2d 579 (1955), 52 A.L.R.2d 1073 (1957).

Cf., Haynes v. American Casualty Company, 228 Md. 394, 179 A.2d 900 (1962).

See generally, Annotation, *Insurance: "accidental means" as distinguishable from "accident," "accidental result," "accidental death," "accidental injury,"* etc., 166 A.L.R. 469–479 (1947).

Mutual Accident Association [12], "In this State there is no longer any distinction made between accidental death and death by accidental means, nor between accidental means and accidental results." [13] Since the *Burr* decision, courts in several other jurisdictions have also decided that there should be no distinctions drawn between accidental means and accidental results. [14] However, the distinction between "accidental means" and "accidental results" is still applied by many courts when death or injury results from an insured's criminal acts — that is, the difference between accidental means and accidental results continues to

---

12. Burr v. Commercial Travelers Mutual Accident Association of America, 295 N.Y. 294, 67 N.E.2d 248 (1946), 166 A.L.R. 462 (1947) (insured died after trying to dig his automobile out of a snow-filled ditch where it had come to rest after a minor collision with another car). The insured had told his wife that, after walking some distance to get a shovel, he had been "knocked out" by the strong winds accompanying the snow storm. His wife stated that she had seen him "hit himself or slip and fall against the shovel and then against the rear wheel or rear fender of the car ＊ ＊ ＊" shortly before his death. The court held that coverage was provided under a policy providing "against loss by accidental means".

13. Burr v. Commercial Travelers Mutual Accident Association of America, 295 N.Y. at p. 302, 67 N.E.2d at p. 252, 166 A.L.R. at p. 466.

The affirmance of the judgment on the jury verdict for the plaintiff in *Burr* cannot be supported as a technically accurate interpretation and application of the policy clause which extended coverage for death only if caused solely and exclusively by external, violent, and accidental means. It seems clear, first, that exertions of the deceased in shoveling snow, after being stalled on a highway in a snowstorm, were not within the phrase "external, violent and accidental means," second, that it was a permissible fact inference from the evidence that these exertions contributed to the death, and third, that the trial court's charge permitted the jury to find for the plaintiff even though taking this view of the evidence.

Also see 1B APPLEMAN, INSURANCE LAW (Revised edition, 1981), at §§ 391–397.

14. See, e.g., Vallejos v. Colonial Life & Accident Insurance Company, 91 N.M. 137, 571 P.2d 404 (1977) (coverage exists when death results from consumption or injection of narcotics without intent to injure oneself or commit suicide); Beckham v. Travelers Insurance Company, 424 Pa. 107,

225 A.2d 532 (1967) (death from overdose of narcotics without suicidal intent; distinction between accidental means and accidental results expressly abandoned); Scott v. New Empire Insurance Company, 75 N.M. 81, 400 P.2d 953 (1965).

Also see Schonberg v. New York Life Insurance Company, 235 La. 461, 104 So.2d 171 (1958) (repudiating the distinction though it had been recognized by an earlier Louisiana Supreme Court decision).

In Gottfriend v. Prudential Insurance Company of America, 173 N.J.Super. 370, 414 A.2d 545 (1977), *judgment affirmed* 173 N.J.Super. 381, 414 A.2d 551 (1979), the court concluded that the reasonable expectations of a policyholder would be that a heart attack following strenuous physical activity would constitute "accidental bodily injury" and that "accidental bodily injury" as used in a life insurance policy provides more extensive coverage then a policy which frames coverage in terms of "accidental means".

In Commercial Travelers Insurance Co. v. Walsh, 228 F.2d 200 (9th Cir.1955), 56 A.L.R.2d 796 (1957) (applying Washington law) the insured died of a heart attack caused by over-exertion in straining to prevent a mishap in unloading heavy grain sacks from a truck. The court held that coverage applied. The decision involved distinguishing between "deliberate" and "unintentional" acts of the insured that caused the fatal heart attack, rather than distinguishing between "accidental means" and "accidental death."

But cf. Chally v. Home Insurance Company, 285 A.2d 810 (Del.Super.1971), *affirmed* 293 A.2d 295 (1972); Perrine v. Prudential Insurance Co. of America, 56 N.J. 120, 265 A.2d 521 (1970).

Also see Annotation, *Insurance: "accidental means" as distinguishable from "accident," "accidental result," "accidental death," "accidental injury," etc.*, 166 A.L.R. 469–479 at p. 473 (1947).

be approved in judicial decisions as a basis for rejecting claims in such cases.[15]

Decisions reaching results similar to *Burr* are supportable, at least in part, on the ground that the literal enforcement of such terms would provide insurance of very narrow scope, and that such minimal coverage often would be patently disproportionate to the premiums paid. Thus, if the construction of the insurance policy language urged by insurers were enforced, in many circumstances the actual scope of the protection afforded would be so limited that the acquisition of such insurance would not even be contemplated by a rational individual who understood the risks the insurer proposed to cover.

Decisions during the 1940s and 1950s that rejected the interpretations urged by insurers of terms such as "accidental means" may appropriately be viewed as forerunners of the proposition that courts will not support the literal enforcement of coverage terms so as to produce results that would be inconsistent with the reasonable expectations of insureds.[16] In some of these decisions, despite the fact that judicial opinions state that the result is based on interpreting the intention manifested by the contracting parties, the courts have actually imposed a very considerable restriction on the freedom of contract.

Observations

It seems likely that both "accidental means" and "accidental results" clauses were designed and adopted by insurers with a view to facilitating the rejection of claims that were regarded by insurers as fraudulent or unjustified. In general, however, insurers almost certainly had little reason to expect that they would be permitted to enforce the broad restrictions on coverage set out in these provisions, especially by the "accidental means" clauses. This is one of the contexts in which courts have generally dealt harshly with contract provisions that afford insurers relatively unfettered discretion over the acceptance or rejection of claims.

The judicial inclination to limit the effects of "accidental means" clauses is fully consistent with the proposition that courts will not enforce insurance policy provisions that impose coverage restrictions that do not conform with the scope of protection that purchasers would reasonably expect to receive from such insurance,[17] at least so long as no special steps are taken by an insurer to make sure the insured knows and understands the effect of such clauses in an insurance policy.

15. Also see discussion in § 5.4(b)(5), below.

Also see the discussion of protecting reasonable expectations in § 6.3, below.

16. *Cf.* Perrine v. Prudential Insurance Co. of America, 56 N.J. 120, 265 A.2d 521 (1970).

17. See generally the discussion of reasonable expectations in § 6.3, below.

Courts generally are not favorably disposed to the enforcement of policy terms to preclude insurance when a particular insurer employs provisions which define coverage that is more limited than that afforded by insurance commonly marketed by other companies. This is especially the case when an insurer uses clauses which are significantly more restrictive than the coverage limitations usually included in such insurance contracts *and* does not take steps to apprise a purchaser of the unusual limitation. Moreover, the justification for precluding enforcement of a limitation is even stronger if the premium charged for such coverage is essentially the same as the insured would have paid for more extensive protection from other insurers.

(4) Fortuity and Suicide

Today, almost all life insurance policies contain explicit provisions which specify whether and under what circumstances coverage is provided in the event that an insured's death is by suicide. Generally, insurance policies include clauses which state that an insurer is not liable for a death by suicide within some specified period of time, typically one or two years, from the commencement of the coverage.[18] The great weight of American authority sustains this type of limitation so that insurers are not required to pay death benefits when a suicide takes place before the prescribed period has passed.[19]

In many states, coverage restrictions for suicide are now subject to statutes that specifically regulate the time period an insurer may specify in such clauses. Thus, when a person whose life is insured commits suicide after the time period that is specified — either in the

---

18. See Appendix E.

The suicide clauses of life and accident insurance policies often include the phrase "sane or insane," thereby disallowing coverage, for the period stated in the clause even for a suicide induced by insanity. In the absence of a statute to the contrary, such clauses are generally held valid. Insanity may, however, be found to have negated suicide. Thus, though it is generally held that the insured need not have comprehended the moral or legal nature and consequences of the act for the clause to apply, the decisions are in conflict as to whether the insured must at least have comprehended the nature and consequences of the act. See, e.g., Aetna Life Insurance Company v. McLaughlin, 380 S.W.2d 101 (Tex.1964), 9 A.L.R.3d 1005 (1966) (insured under an accident policy providing a death benefit but excluding loss or death caused by "suicide, sane or insane," died after falling or lunging in front of a bus while intoxicated; *held,* reversing judgment for the insured's widow because of an error in instructions, no coverage if insured died as the result of an act that would be considered suicide if committed by a sane person, regardless of whether he was conscious of the physical nature and consequences of his act or had an intent to kill himself).

In Poling v. North American Life and Casualty Company, 593 P.2d 568 (Wyo. 1979), the court upheld the provisions of a master policy which provided that in the event of death by suicide within two years, the insurer's liability would be limited to the premiums paid for such insurance.

Also see, 1A APPLEMAN, INSURANCE LAW (Revised edition, 1981), at §§ 360–363.

19. See, e.g., Seattle-First National Bank v. Crown Life Insurance Company, 365 F.2d 280 (9th Cir.1966) (applying the law of Washington); New York Life Insurance Company v. Noonan, 215 F.2d 905 (9th Cir.1954), *cert. denied* 348 U.S. 928, 75 S.Ct. 341, 99 L.Ed. 727 (1955) (applying the law of Oregon); New England Mutual Life Insurance Company v. Mitchell, 118 F.2d 414 (4th Cir.1941), *cert. denied* 314 U.S. 629, 62 S.Ct. 60, 86 L.Ed. 505 (1941).

state's legislation or in the insurance policy provision, whichever is shorter — the death benefits must be paid.[20]

Sanity and Insanity

Another dimension to disputes about an insurer's obligation when a suicide occurs is sometimes presented when a coverage limitation is phrased in terms of "death from suicide, sane or insane" or some comparable policy language. For example, in a case in which an insured apparently jumped from an eighth story window of a hospital while under a delusion that the hospital personnel were attempting to kill him, the Virginia Supreme Court observed:

> "The numerical weight of authority supports the view that in order for an insurer to avoid liability under the exclusion of death from self-destruction, while sane or insane, it is not necessary for the insured to realize the physical nature or consequence of his act or to form a conscious purpose to take his life. If the act of self-destruction would be regarded as suicide in the case of a sane person, it would be so treated as to an insane insured, regardless of whether the insured decedent realized or was capable of realizing that such act would cause his death or whether he was capable of entertaining an intention to kill himself. (Citations omitted)"[21]

The court then applied this analysis in an affirmance of the trial judge's decision that the "death was not caused by accidental means, * * * but resulted from self-destruction or self-inflicted injury within the terms of the policy exclusions."[22]

The decisions described in the preceding paragraphs are indicative of the very real dilemma which courts confront in attempting to deal equitably with coverage disputes arising as a result of death by a self-

---

20. See, e.g., N.Y.—McKinney's Insurance Law § 155 (1966) allows a provision against liability for suicide within two years from the date of the policy but forbids clauses more favorable to the insurer. It has been construed as supporting recovery for suicide while insane, even though within two years of the date of the policy. See the discussion in Franklin v. John Hancock Mutual Life Insurance Company, 298 N.Y. 81, 80 N.E.2d 746 (1948).

Cf. Nabor v. Occidental Life Insurance Company of California, 78 Ill.App.3d 288, 33 Ill.Dec. 543, 396 N.E.2d 1267 (1st Dist., Div. 4, 1979) ($100,000 life insurance policy purchased on September 15, 1975, and insured apparently committed suicide on September 15, 1977).

In some states, "raising the defense of suicide is not contesting the policy within the meaning of the incontestability clause" because the insurer "is not contending that

the policy is void * * *." Nabor v. Occidental Life Insurance Company of California, 78 Ill.App.3d 288, 33 Ill.Dec. 543, 396 N.E.2d 1267 at p. 1269 (1st Dist., Div. 4, 1979). *Accord:* National Producers Life Insurance Company v. Rogers, 8 Ariz.App. 53, 442 P.2d 876 at pp. 879–880 (1968), 37 A.L.R.3d 328 (1971).

21. Atkinson v. Life Insurance Company of Virginia, 217 Va. 208, 228 S.E.2d 117 at p. 120 (1976). The omitted citations included Bigelow v. Berkshire Life Insurance Company, 93 U.S. (3 Otto 284) 284, 23 L.Ed. 918 (1876).

Also see, Annotation, *Insurance: construction of "sane or insane" provision of suicide exclusion,* 9 A.L.R.3d 1015–1041 at pp. 1032–1041 (1966).

22. Atkinson v. Life Insurance Company of Virginia, 217 Va. 208, 228 S.E.2d 117 at p. 118 (1976).

destructive act when the insured was suffering from some type of mental illness.[23] Courts have often taken the position that the addition of the words "sane or insane" to suicide coverage restrictions means that the insurer is not required to show that the decedent had any comprehension of the character (in many decisions characterized as the "moral" or "legal" nature) of the act — that is, the fact that the decedent was not able to appreciate that the act of suicide may be viewed either as "morally wrong" or as an illegal action does not preclude the enforcement of the exception.[24] However, there does not appear to be a consensus among the courts on the question whether the clause "death from suicide, sane or insane" precludes coverage when evidence indicates that the decedent lacked the capacity to appreciate or comprehend the nature of the consequences of the destructive act, including the fact that death would result.[25]

Another aspect of the problems presented by insurance claims when decedent's death was an act of suicide relates to the double indemnity clauses, included in some life insurance policies, which provide increased coverage if an insured's death results from external and accidental causes.[26] Again, it is difficult to discern any consensus on how this coverage issue ought to be resolved.

(5) The Consequences of Criminal Acts as Accidents

Some accident insurance policies include provisions explicitly precluding coverage for losses resulting from specified types of criminal acts by an insured.[27] Even in the absence of an explicit policy provision

23. For example, in Searle v. Allstate Life Insurance Company, 96 Cal.App.3d 614 at p. 616, 158 Cal.Rptr. 5 at p. 6 (4th Dist., Div. 1, 1979), *appeal after remand* 137 Cal.App.3d 382, 187 Cal.Rptr. 85 (1982), the court concluded, "The plain meaning of the word suicide is to intentionally take one's life. * * *" and "[t]he phrase 'suicide, sane or insane' is both ambiguous and illogical and the ambiguity will be construed against Allstate because it drafted the policy * * *." Thereafter, the California Supreme Court addressed the issue in a lengthy opinion, reported at 38 Cal.3d 425, 212 Cal.Rptr. 466, 696 P.2d 1308 (1985), which concluded

"To summarize: the clause excludes all nonaccidental self-destruction regardless of the insured's state of mind; intent is therefore immaterial, and the trier of fact need determine only whether the act of self-destruction, objectively viewed, was accidental. In other words, '[i]f the act of self-destruction would be regarded as suicide in the case of a sane person, it would be so treated as to an insane insured. * * *' (Atkinson v.

Life Ins. Co. of Virginia, supra, 228 S.E.2d 117, 120.)"

24. See the cases collected in Annotation, *Insurance: construction of "sane or insane" provision of suicide exclusion,* 9 A.L.R.3d 1015–1041 at pp. 1032 (1966).

25. Annotation, *Insurance: construction of "sane or insane" provision of suicide exclusion,* 9 A.L.R.3d 1015–1041 at p. 1018 and pp. 1032–1040 (1966).

There are also instances when the cause of death is unclear. For example, death by drowning may result from an intent to commit suicide or from the unintended consequences of an undertow, cramps, etc.

26. See the discussion in § 5.4(b)(1), above.

27. See, e.g., the limitation on the double indemnity, accidental death provision of the life insurance policy involved in Powell v. New York Life Insurance Company, 120 So.2d 33 (Fla.App.2d Dist.1960), 86 A.L.R.2d 437 (1962) excluding payment of the accidental death benefit if the death resulted from the commission by the insured of "an assault or felony." The court

excluding compensation or indemnification for injuries suffered as a result of criminal conduct, claims under a life insurance or an accident insurance policy may be denied on the basis of either an implied exception or an interpretation of the general coverage terms.[28]

The courts almost uniformly support an insurer's position when an injury or death was a "natural" and "reasonably foreseeable" risk or consequence of wrongful conduct such as an assault on another person [29] or the injection of an illegal drug such as heroin.[30] The rationale employed by courts in these cases is usually that when a death or an injury either results from an intentional criminal act or occurs while an individual is engaged in any criminal activity involving a foreseeable risk, such a death or injury did not result from "accidental means" or was not an "accidental bodily injury." Many of the appellate decisions upholding denials of coverage in these cases have involved policy provisions that used the phrase "accidental means." [31] However, it appears likely that similar analytical approaches will also be applied

affirmed summary judgment for the insurer in an action to recover the benefit (the face value of the policy having been paid), since the insured was shot and killed by his son while beating his wife.

28. See the cases collected in Annotation, *Liability under life or accident policy not containing a "violation of the law" clause, for death or injury resulting from violation of law by insured,* 43 A.L.R.3d 1120–1136 (1972).

29. See, e.g., Byrd v. Life Insurance Company of Virginia, 219 Va. 824, 252 S.E.2d 307 (1979) (insureds death resulted from a gunshot wound in the head which resulted from the intentional shooting in the gunman's home to which the decedent went to provoke an encounter despite an awareness of the gunman's reputation for violence and a warning that the gunman would kill the insured "out of jealousy"); Davis v. Boston Mutual Life Insurance Company, 370 Mass. 602, 351 N.E.2d 207 (1976) (police officer shot decedent while he was committing two serious felonies).

Cf. Shields v. Prudential Insurance Co., 6 N.J. 517, 79 A.2d 297 (1951), 26 A.L.R.2d 392 (1952); Bernhard v. Prudential Insurance Company of America, 134 Neb. 402, 278 N.W. 846 (1938) (insured attacked a police officer and was shot).

Also *cf.* Funchess v. Metropolitan Life Insurance Company, 94 Ill.App.3d 871, 50 Ill.Dec. 598, 419 N.E.2d 706 (3d Dist.1981); Logan v. Life Insurance Company of North America, Inc., 46 N.C.App. 629, 265 S.E.2d 447 (1980); Kentucky Central Life Insurance Company v. Willett, 557 S.W.2d 222 (Ky.App.1977) (death resulting from an al-

tercation in a car in which a gun was sitting on the front seat was a natural and probable consequence).

See generally, Annotation, *Accident Insurance: death or injury intentionally inflicted by another as due to accident or accidental means,* 49 A.L.R.3d 673–718 (1973).

30. Gordon v. Metropolitan Life Insurance Company, 256 Md. 320, 260 A.2d 338, 41 A.L.R.3d 648 (1970) (self-administered injection of heroin).

Also see Annotation, *Death or injury from taking illegal drugs or narcotics as accidental or result of accidental means within insurance coverage,* 41 A.L.R.3d 654–659 (1972).

31. See, e.g., Roque v. Nationwide Mutual Insurance Company, 502 Pa. 615, 467 A.2d 1128 (1983) (insured who was shot and killed by police while he was in the act of burglarizing a house, was not killed by "accidental means" for purposes of double indemnity clause of life policy, where the insured (1) repeatedly told police that he had gun, (2) that he intended to shoot to kill, and (3) pointed the gun at police).

Also see Jaudon v. Prudential Insurance Co. of America, 279 F.2d 730 (6th Cir.1960) (applying Tennessee law); Davis v. Boston Mutual Life Insurance Company, 370 Mass. 602, 351 N.E.2d 207 (Worcester 1976) (insured shot and killed by a police officer while committing a felony); Powell v. New York Life Insurance Company, 120 So.2d 33 (Fla.App.2d Dist.1960), 86 A.L.R.2d 437 (1962).

to claims under insurance policies using phrases such as "accidental injury" or "accidental death." [32]

Occasionally, courts have justified an insurer's rejection of a coverage claim on the rationale that the results of criminal acts are not "fortuitous." However, to say that death and injuries that result from or in the course of criminal conduct are not "fortuitous" is to adopt a meaning that is probably even more restrictive than that set forth by insurance policy clauses denying coverage for an "expected" loss.[33] Thus, the results in these cases are among the relatively few instances in which courts employ an interpretation of coverage terms that favors insurers.[34]

Observations

Several considerations almost certainly have been significant influences when insurance claims have resulted from injuries that were incurred as a consequence of an individual's participation in some type of criminal activity. The judicial decisions sustaining the rejection of such claims undoubtedly manifest an aversion to the activities which produced the loss. In addition, these decisions may also represent the conclusion that an insured's criminal conduct substantially increases the risk beyond the realm of the potential causes of death which an insurer undertakes to insure.

§ 5.4(c) Selecting the Vantage Point From Which to Analyze Whether a Loss Is "Accidental"

(1) Introductory Note

Terms such as "accidental," which are used in many insurance policies, have repeatedly led to disputes with respect to the point of view from which a determination should be made as to whether a loss is covered. Some courts state that the question of fortuity is to be examined from the vantage point of the insured; [1] other courts have

---

32. See, e.g., Funchess v. Metropolitan Life Insurance Company, 94 Ill.App.3d 871, 50 Ill.Dec. 598, 419 N.E.2d 706 (3d Dist. 1981).

33. Cf. the discussion in § 5.4(d), below.

34. Moreover, a court may even apply a construction of coverage terms that is somewhat at variance with unambiguous policy provisions. See Chapter 6, below.

§ 5.4(c)

1. See, e.g., Smith v. Equitable Life Insurance Society, 614 F.2d 720 at p. 723 (10th Cir.1980) (life insurance); New York Life Insurance Company v. Harrington, 299 F.2d 803 at p. 806 (9th Cir.1962) (applying California law; insured under a life policy providing double indemnity in the event of death caused by "accidental bodily injury" shot himself by placing a loaded gun to his temple and pulling the trigger, thinking, however, that the safety catch was engaged; held, the insured's widow could collect the accidental death benefits, "[o]nce it is established that * * * [the insured's] belief in the safety was not unreasonable as a matter of law, the death was as to him unexpected * * *" and, therefore, accidental).

Also see, Aetna Casualty & Surety Company v. Freyer, 89 Ill.App.3d 617, 44 Ill. Dec. 791, 411 N.E.2d 1157 at p. 1159 (1st Dist., Div.4, 1980); Great National Insurance Company v. Legg, 444 S.W.2d 324 at p. 326 (Tex.Civ.App., El Paso 1969) (insured died as a result of gunshot wound which occurred when he was attempting to take the gun away from his wife).

stated that it is appropriate to make this determination on the basis of considering the position of the person who is injured by the occurrence of an insured event.[2]   Frequently, of course, it does not make any difference which approach is employed because the person who is the insured is also a person who suffers loss.   However, there are also many situations in which such an identity of interests does not exist.

For most types of insurance coverages, appellate court resolutions of issues about the perspective from which to assess whether a loss is fortuitous (or not intended) are consistent with the proposition that the determination should be made from the point of view of the person whose economic interest is protected by the insurance policy.[3]   In a great many instances, the insured is that person.   For example, in the case of property insurance ordinarily the insured is a person who sustains an economic loss as the result of damage to an insured property — that is, a person who is an owner or a mortgagee has arranged to protect that interest by the insurance policy.[4]   Similarly, in the case of accident or health insurance, the insured is frequently the person who actually sustains the physical injury that causes the economic harms which the insurance is designed to compensate.   Consequently, when this type of situation exists it is the insured whose actions and state of mind should be considered in relation to the requirement that the loss be fortuitous.   In the event such an insured

2.   See, e.g., Jernigan v. Allstate Insurance Company, 269 F.2d 353 (5th Cir.1959), *opinion on denial of rehearing* 272 F.2d 857 (5th Cir.1959) (applying Louisiana law; coverage for injury deliberately inflicted by omnibus insured;   dissent on ground the driver was later determined to be insane and that neither the driver nor the insurer should be liable;   perhaps the result reached by the majority could have been rested solely on the impact of the Louisiana Direct Action Statute, but the opinion is reasoned also on the broader ground); Haser v. Maryland Casualty Company, 78 N.D. 893, 53 N.W.2d 508 (1952), 33 A.L.R.2d 1018 (1954) (liability insurance coverage for rapist denied on grounds of public policy;   dictum approving coverage for vicarious liability of his employer and saying that "accident" in contract provisions is to be interpreted from the point of view of the victim); Fox Wisconsin Corporation v. Century Indemnity Company, 219 Wis. 549, 263 N.W. 567 (1935) (liability insurer held liable for judgment recovered against insured and for cost of defense of suit resulting from an assault by an employee of the insured on a patron of the insured's theater).

Also see Wynglass v. Prudential Life Insurance Company of America, 68 Mich. App. 514, 242 N.W.2d 824 (1976) (whether

death was accidental must be viewed "through the eyes of the deceased").

3.   This is not to say, however, that a contract expressly providing otherwise would be invalid for reasons of public policy.   See, e.g., the accident insurance clause quoted in Butler v. Peninsular Life Insurance Co., 115 So.2d 608 (Fla.App. 1st Dist. 1959) ("agreement as to benefits under this policy * * * shall be null and void if the insured's * * * loss * * * results directly or indirectly from * * * intentional act or acts of any person or persons"), and the life insurance clause quoted in Colonial Life & Accident Insurance Company v. Wagner, 380 S.W.2d 224 at p. 225 (Ky.1964) ("insurance under this [group life] certificate shall not cover death or other loss caused * * * by injuries intentionally inflicted upon the Insured Employee by any other person").

There may be some exceptions.   See, e.g. *Jernigan*, note 2, above, which may be such an exception.

4.   See, e.g., Nuffer v. Insurance Company of North America, 236 Cal.App.2d 349, 45 Cal.Rptr. 918 (4th Dist.1965) (hotel manager intentionally set fire to the structure; *held*, recovery by insured-owner, since the manager acted without authority from or knowledge of the insured).

intentionally causes a loss — as, for example, an insured destroys property by committing arson or intentionally inflicts an injury on his or her body — there is no question in regard to the vantage point from which the issue of fortuity should and will be analyzed.

There are also numerous situations in which the person who will receive the insurance benefits is not the individual whose actions caused the loss — that is, there are several types of insurance arrangements in which it is not the insured's economic interest that is being protected. Life insurance is perhaps the clearest illustration: the insurance is payable as a consequence of the insured's death and therefore it is clear that the insured never receives an actual economic benefit from life insurance.[5]

It is sometimes argued that liability insurance should be viewed as another situation in which the insurance benefits are not received by the individual who caused the loss because the insurance payments in almost all instances go directly to a person who was injured. Nevertheless, the insurance payments are made by an insurer on behalf of the insured, *and* they clearly result in an important economic benefit to the insured by discharging the insured's liability to the injured person. Thus, viewing such losses exclusively from the vantage point of the injured person, rather than the insured, will almost certainly not be justified unless it can be predicated on an extremely important public interest that applies to the liability insurance at issue in a given case. A persuasive case may be made that this approach is warranted in some, if not all, circumstances.[6]

Questions in regard to what or whose vantage point should be used in assessing the issue whether a loss is fortuitous arise in at least two distinguishable situations. First, there are instances in which an insured acted and intended the consequence that another person claims to be an insured event, and the insurance benefits are sought (either directly or indirectly) by someone other than the insured. Second, there are circumstances in which a person other than the insured acted and intended a consequence that resulted in what is claimed to be covered as an insured event, and the insurance benefits are sought by someone other than the individual who caused the occurrence.

Life insurance, uninsured motorist insurance, property insurance, and liability insurance — which are discussed in the following subsections — all provide illustrations of judicial responses to various types of

---

5. Arguably, however, the insured may derive some psychic benefits from knowing that the insurance will be paid to that person's estate or the beneficiary the insured has designated.

6. Statutes often require motor vehicle liability insurance as a means of protecting injured persons. In this context, coverage claims have repeatedly presented the issue whether even though a loss was intentionally caused, it was nevertheless a fortuitous event from the vantage point of the tort claimant and should be considered from that perspective because of the public interest that underlies the financial responsibility law of the state. See the discussion of motor vehicle liability insurance in § 5.4(d)(3), below.

issues that can arise in regard to events that were intended by someone and which thereafter led to coverage disputes in regard to the vantage point to be used in evaluating whether a loss was fortuitous or intentional.

(2) Life Insurance and Death Benefits in Accident Insurance

The economic interest being protected by both life insurance and death benefits in accident insurance is that of one or more beneficiaries, rather than that of the person whose life is covered by the insurance policy. In other words, it is the person or persons who receive the life or accident insurance payments, in the event of an insured's death, from the insurer who derive the economic benefits from the insurance, not the person whose life is insured. Persons who are designated specifically in an insurance contract to receive the insurance proceeds are third party beneficiaries, in their own right, of the insurance contract.[7] And when an insurance policy designates the estate of the person whose life is insured as the beneficiary, it is the individual or individuals or entities who succeed to the benefits through the estate of the insured who are beneficiaries of the insurance proceeds. When a life insurance policy includes an exclusion which specifies that the policy does not cover a loss caused intentionally by a beneficiary, a compelling case can be made for precluding an insurer from restricting the coverage so that no other beneficiary will have any right to the insurance benefits — that is, from denying coverage to any remaining beneficiaries.[8] In such a case, the death would be a fortuitous event when viewed from the vantage point of either the decedent or other beneficiaries.

If an insured dies as a result of a homicide intentionally committed by someone other than a beneficiary, the death is not an "intentional" loss from the point of view of the beneficiaries. Similarly, if an insured commits suicide, the death — though caused intentionally — is not (except in most unusual circumstances in which a beneficiary has induced or encouraged an insured to act) a consequence intentionally caused by a beneficiary. Accordingly, if the events related to the death in such instances are analyzed from the beneficiary's point of view, payment of life insurance proceeds following either a homicide or a suicide generally is not contrary to the public policy — underlying the proposition that insurance is only provided for fortuitous losses — because the claimants

---

7. They are not merely beneficiaries as a practical incident of the protection of some other person, as in the case of the victim who receives a benefit of liability insurance coverage by being able to collect against a tortfeasor who might otherwise have been judgment proof. Moreover, even the incidental beneficiaries of liability insurance have, in some courts, been accorded the status of third party beneficiaries. See generally, § 4.8, above.

8. *Cf.* Wilkens v. Fireman's Fund American Life Insurance Company, 107 Idaho 1006, 695 P.2d 391 (1985) (daughters of insured sought life insurance benefits when the insured's wife, who was the named beneficiary, was convicted of first degree murder and no contingent beneficiary was named).

are not involved in the acts which led to the death.[9] Thus, a persuasive case can be made for providing coverage for such beneficiaries even though the losses are consequences intended by some other person. [Subject to statutory restrictions, however, the terms of life insurance contracts may specifically exclude coverage for suicides and homicides in some circumstances.[10] Also, provisions for double indemnity in case of "accidental" death [11] may define "accidental" so as to exclude suicides and homicides.]

When an insured dies as a result of an altercation, courts often focus on the decedent's perspective in deciding whether accidental death benefits are applicable. In such cases, courts will usually conclude that the death is accidental so long as the insured did not provoke the conflict.[12] Furthermore, even when an insured initiated a conflict, courts have stated that "the critical consideration is the extent to which the fatal character was reasonably foreseeable and avoidable" [13] — that is, death will be viewed as accidental for purposes of an insurance coverage so long as it was not "a natural and probable consequence of the insured's actions." [14] Of course, even if the death was "foreseeable" to the insured decedent or was a "natural and probable consequence" of the decedent's actions, that does not prove that the result was intended. Moreover, the same result may also be supported on the broader rationale that the death is fortuitous from the perspective of a designated beneficiary who was not a participant in the

---

9. The annotator, Ferdinand Tinio, in the Annotation, *Accident insurance: death or injury intentionally inflicted by another as due to accident or accidental means*, 49 A.L.R.3d 673–718 at p. 679 (1973), concluded, "The rule seems to be settled that although an insured is intentionally killed or injured by another person, the death or injury is deemed to have been caused by accident or through accidental means" when it was not foreseen, expected, nor anticipated by the insured.

Also see Annotation, *Insurance: construction of "sane or insane" provision of suicide exclusion*, 9 A.L.R.3d 1015–1041 (1966).

But also consider the English view supporting an implied exception for suicide. See § 5.3(b)(3), above.

10. See § 5.4(b)(3), above.

11. See the discussion in § 5.4(b), above.

Cf. Roque v. Nationwide Mutual Insurance Company, 502 Pa. 615, 467 A.2d 1128 (1983).

12. See Smith v. Equitable Life Assurance Society, 614 F.2d 720 at p. 723 (10th Cir.1980).

Cf. King v. State Farm Life Insurance Company, 448 F.2d 597 (8th Cir.1971).

13. Smith v. Equitable Life Assurance Society, 614 F.2d 720 at p. 723 (10th Cir. 1980).

Also see Wade's Estate v. Continental Insurance Company, 514 F.2d 304 (8th Cir. 1975); Byrd v. Life Insurance Company of Virginia, 219 Va. 824, 252 S.E.2d 307 (1979).

14. Stogsdill v. General American Life Insurance Company, 541 S.W.2d 696 at p. 699 (Mo.App., St. Louis Dist., Div.3, 1976). The court also observed that "where the insured's assault invites deadly retaliation, [it] would preclude accidental death benefit coverage." *Ibid.*

Cf. Ocean Accident and Guarantee Corp. v. Glover, 165 Va. 283 at p. 285, 182 S.E. 221 at p. 222 (1935); Maneval v. Lutheran Brotherhood, 281 A.2d 502 at p. 506 (Del. Super., Kent, 1971).

Also see cases collected in Annotation, *Accident Insurance: death or injury intentionally inflicted by another as due to accident or accidental means*, 49 A.L.R.3d 672–718 at pp. 687–706 (1973).

altercation, regardless of whether the event was fortuitous from the point of view of the decedent.

(3) Uninsured Motorist Insurance

Uninsured motorist insurance policy forms provide that the insurer will pay all sums that an insured is "legally entitled to recover as damages ＊ ＊ ＊ because of bodily injury sustained by the insured *caused by accident ＊ ＊ ＊*." [15] The phrase "caused by accident" is not defined elsewhere in the standard forms used for this coverage.[16] When deciding whether a claimant is entitled to indemnification under an uninsured motorist coverage for injuries that result from the acts of an uninsured motorist who intended to cause a collision which resulted in damages to the insured, there are several reasons why it is appropriate to examine the occurrence from the viewpoint of the injured party.

First, from the perspective of the injured person (and especially so when an assault, using a motor vehicle, was not provoked by that person), the cause of the injuries is no less fortuitous than in the situation in which a person is injured as a result of the negligent operation of an uninsured vehicle.

Second, the uninsured motorist insurance is a first party coverage, and the insurance provides no benefits, directly or indirectly, to the tortfeasor. Indeed, if the tortfeasor is financially responsible, the insurer may seek reimbursement for payments made to an insured.

Third, payments made under the uninsured motorist coverage do not reduce the possibility that either the tort system or the criminal law system will operate either to punish or to influence the conduct either of the tortfeasor who caused the loss which is indemnified by the insurance or of other potential tortfeasors.

Fourth, the enactment of the uninsured motorist insurance statutes throughout the country, which mandate either that the insurance be offered to all motor vehicle insurance purchasers or included in all motor vehicle insurance policies, reflects the importance attached to providing a source of indemnification for innocent traffic victims who are injured by financially irresponsible motorists.

Fifth, providing indemnification to insureds under the uninsured motorist coverage is also warranted because a tort action is likely to yield little, if any, compensation, even though such a tortfeasor, if financially responsible, would be liable for an intentional tort.

Comment

Payments under the uninsured motorist coverage do not affect the public policy goals of the tort system and do not impair or erode the foundations of the insurance law system. At least when the claimant is

---

15. See Appendix H.

16. See Appendix H.

Also see Widiss, UNINSURED AND UNDERIN-SURED MOTORIST INSURANCE (1985), at §§ 10.1 through 10.5.

an innocent victim who did not provoke the tortfeasor, the desirability of providing a source of indemnification justifies examining the causation question from the perspective of the injured person. As an Ohio court observed, "To look through the eyes of the uninsured rather than the insured in this factual situation would require an unconscionable twisting of the obvious purpose of purchasing insurance coverage." [17] The Ohio court also commented, "All reason and logic would require a construction and interpretation that intent of mind should be taken from the viewpoint of the insured." [18] These comments are representative of the judicial attitude which usually prevails when this issue is presented to the courts, and the decisions clearly underscore the importance courts have attached to assuring a source of compensation to innocent and unsuspecting accident victims even though the conduct which produced the loss was intended by an uninsured motorist.[19]

Interpreting the phrase "caused by accident" from the perspective of the injured person may produce greater protection for an insured when the tortfeasor is uninsured than when the tortfeasor is insured. This possibility has not dissuaded courts from reaching decisions favorable to extending coverage in such cases.

(4) Property Insurance

If the owner of a building intentionally burns it down, the loss is not fortuitous and no property insurance will be paid to such an owner.[20] However, it is generally recognized that when a structure is destroyed as the result of arson committed by someone who has no connection with the insured owner, fire insurance coverage will provide indemnification for the owner.[21] Furthermore, the concept underlying such decisions — that the loss is a fortuity from the vantage point of the insured — has been extended to an innocent insured when a fire was intentionally set by a co-owner of a property who was also an insured.[22]

---

17. Celina Mutual Insurance Company v. Saylor, 35 Ohio Misc. 81, 63 Ohio Opin. 2d 76, 301 N.E.2d 721 at p. 723 (Com.Pl., Hamilton County, 1973).

18. *Ibid.*

19. *Cf.* American Protection Insurance Company v. Parker, 150 Ga.App. 732, 258 S.E.2d 540 at p. 542 (1979); Davis v. State Farm Mutual Automobile Insurance Company, 264 Or. 547, 507 P.2d 9 (1973).

Also see Widiss, UNINSURED AND UNDERINSURED MOTORIST INSURANCE (1985), at 10.2; Annotation, *Coverage under uninsured motorist clause of injury inflicted intentionally,* 72 A.L.R.3d 1161–1171 (1976).

20. See generally, 5 APPLEMAN, INSURANCE LAW and PRACTICE (1970), at § 3113; 18 COUCH CYCLOPEDIA OF INSURANCE LAW (Revised edition, 1983), at §§ 74:658–677.

21. See notes 20, above, and 22, below.

22. See, e.g. Hedtcke v. Sentry Insurance Company, 109 Wis.2d 461, 326 N.W.2d 727 (1982) [an innocent insured is not barred from recovering under fire insurance policy by virtue of fact that another insured intentionally caused damage to insured property; overruling Bellman v. Home Insurance Company of New York, 178 Wis. 349, 189 N.W. 1028 (1922), and Klemens v. Badger Mutual Insurance Company, 8 Wis.2d 565, 99 N.W.2d 865 (1959)]; St. Paul Fire and Marine Insurance Company v. Molloy, 291 Md. 139, 433 A.2d 1135 (1981); Hosey v. Seibels Bruce Group, South Carolina Insurance Company, 363 So.2d 751 (Ala.1978); Steigler v. Insurance Company of North America, 384 A.2d 398 (Del.Supr.1978).

Also see Safeco Insurance Company of America v. R. Kartsone, 510 F.Supp. 856 (C.D.Cal.1981); Lovell v. Rowan Mutual

Similarly, a wife's claim was upheld in regard to property insurance, issued to the spouses as coinsureds, for a property that was probably stolen by the husband from the wife's residence after she had filed for divorce and obtained a court order barring the husband from entering the residence.[23] The holdings in such cases provide clear illustrations of the proposition that even though a loss may have been intended by someone, coverage may nevertheless be sustained when the loss was fortuitous — that is, not intended — from the standpoint of the person who will receive the insurance benefits.

(5) Liability Insurance

A liability insurance contract is an arrangement that is designed to provide the insureds protection against economic loss which results from their legal liability. Accordingly, it is generally said that the person whose economic interest is protected is the insured and not the person who sustains harm to his or her person or property. The insured is the person from whose vantage point the question of "fortuity" or "intent" has usually been assessed. However, particularly when there is some statutory requirement that either explicitly or implicitly mandates such coverage, liability insurance is increasingly being viewed as a coverage that is designed for and available to protect innocent victims.[24] Consequently, as some types of liability insurance

---

Fire Insurance Company, 302 N.C. 150, 274 S.E.2d 170 (1981); Hildebrand v. Holyoke Mutual Fire Insurance Company, 386 A.2d 329 (Me.1978).

Decisions in support, as well as those which do not adopt this proposition are discussed in Paul B. Butler, Jr., and Bob G. Freemon, Jr., *The Innocent Coinsured: He Burns It, She Claims—Windfall or Technical Injustice?*, 17 Forum 187–211 (1981).

But cf. the position of the Oklahoma Supreme Court in Short v. Oklahoma Farmers Union Insurance Company, 619 P.2d 588 at p. 590 (Okl.1980):

"In today's increasingly urban environment arson is a continuing threat to adjoining landowners, the public at large and the municipality which must combat such conflagrations. To allow recovery on an insurance contract where the arsonist has been proven to be a joint insured would allow funds to be acquired by the entity of which the arsonist is a member and is flatly against public policy."

23. Simon v. Security Insurance Company, 390 Mich. 72, 210 N.W.2d 322 (1973) (an innocent coinsured recovery was not barred by her co-insured, estranged husband's fraud), discussed in Note, *Insurance—Innocent Coinsured's Recovery Not Barred by Fraud of Husband*, 21 Wayne

Law Review 169–174 (1974); Howell v. Ohio Casualty Insurance Co., 130 N.J. Super. 350, 327 A.2d 240 (App.Div.1974).

Also see Fidelity-Phenix Fire Insurance Company v. Queen City Bus & Transfer Co., 3 F.2d 784 at p. 785 (4th Cir.1925) (corporation allowed to recover on a fire insurance policy when the president of the insured corporation, who owned twenty-five percent of the company's stock and held a mortgage on buses owned by the corporation, set fire to the buses when there was "no evidence that the other stockholders and officers participated in or sanctioned the burning").

But see Bryant v. Allstate Insurance Company, 592 F.Supp. 39 (E.D.Ky.1984).

See generally, Annotation, *Right of Innocent Insured to Recover Under Fire Policy Covering Property Intentionally Burned by Another Insured,* 11 A.L.R.4th 1128–1235 (1982).

24. See, e.g., State Fire & Casualty Company v. Tringali, 686 F.2d 821 (9th Cir. 1982) (applying the law of Hawaii, and holding that insurer was required to provide coverage under a compulsory motor vehicle liability insurance policy despite the fact that the injuries were caused intentionally by the insured); Hartford Accident & Indemnity Company v. Wolbarst, 95 N.H. 40, 57 A.2d 151 (1948) (interpreting

have become the subject of statutory mandates in numerous states, the resolution of questions about the selection of the appropriate vantage point in regard to this type of insurance has become more complex. This question is discussed in the following subsection, which also analyzes several other questions that have arisen in regard to liability insurance coverage for intentional torts.

§ 5.4(d) Liability Insurance for Intentional Torts

(1) Generally

The principle that insurance should only be employed to transfer risks associated with fortuitous occurrences means that generally no coverage will exist for a loss that is caused intentionally. In the context of liability insurance, claims seeking indemnification for intentionally caused harm are usually denied on the basis of specific coverage terms — typically set forth in the basic definition of coverage — which state the insurer will pay damages for which an insured (or, in many of the newer forms, a "covered person") becomes legally responsible *because of an accident*.[1] Furthermore, liability insurance policies have generally included clauses that explicitly preclude coverage for an "injury * * * caused intentionally."[2] For example, contemporary liability insurance policies frequently state that insurance is provided

the effect of the state's Motor Vehicle Financial Responsibility Act on the meaning to be given to the word "accident").

Cf. Wheeler v. O'Connell, 297 Mass. 549, 9 N.E.2d 544, 111 A.L.R. 1038 (1937) (interpreting the effect of the state's compulsory motor vehicle policy).

Also see the discussion of liability for intentional torts in § 5.4(d), below and especially the discussion of motor vehicle liability insurance in § 5.4(d)(3).

§ 5.4(d)

1. See, e.g., Sontag v. Galer, 279 Mass. 309, 181 N.E. 182 (1932) (cooking utensil, thrown by landlady at boys who had come on her premises without leave, struck plaintiff).

In Haser v. Maryland Casualty Company, 78 N.D. 893, 53 N.W.2d 508 (1952), 33 A.L.R.2d 1018 (1954), a passenger in taxi who had been raped by driver and another passenger sought coverage of default judgment against driver under policy making driver an additional insured. The court held for the insurer, on the ground that coverage would be contrary to public policy even though the phrase "caused by accident" defined coverage of broader scope than merely for negligent acts of insured. Such a case might also be decided for the insurer on the ground that the liability did not arise "out of the * * * use" of the

vehicle as a vehicle. Also see § 5.2(b), above.

Also see Annotation, *Liability insurance: assault as an "accident," or injuries therefrom as "accidentally" sustained, within coverage clause,* 12 A.L.R.3d 1090–1155 (1976); Wendorff, *The New Standard Comprehensive General Liability Insurance Policy,* in 1966 ABA Section of Insurance, Negligence & Compensation Law Proceedings 250–264.

2. For many years, some liability policies have included an "intentional injury" exclusion clause. See the cases collected in Annotation, *Liability insurance: specific exclusion of liability for injury intentionally caused by insured,* 2 A.L.R.3d 1238–1253 (1965).

See, e.g., Rankin v. Farmers Elevator Mutual Insurance Company, 393 F.2d 718 (10th Cir.1968) (applying Kansas law; farmer chasing motorcyclists who had trespassed on his land, deliberately swerved his pick-up against a cyclist and ran him into ditch; declaratory summary judgment against coverage affirmed; reasoning, however, included the hoary fiction that one is "presumed to intend the natural and probable consequences" of his acts, as to which see Prosser & Keeton, Torts (Fifth edition, 1984), at § 8.

for damages that are caused by an "occurrence" which is defined as an *"accident"* that "results in bodily injury or property damage *neither expected nor intended* from the standpoint of the insured." [3]

The fact that an intentional tort usually involves one or more acts that also constitute transgressions of the criminal laws provides substantial support for the "general principle that an insurer may not contract to indemnify an insured against the civil consequences of * * * willful criminal conduct." [4] As the New Jersey Supreme Court pointed out, "were a person able to insure himself against the economic consequences of wrongdoing, the deterrence attributable to financial responsibility would be missing." [5]

Courts have clearly and repeatedly affirmed the general proposition that public policy prohibits the use of insurance to provide indemnification for civil tort liability that results from an insured's intentional wrongdoing.[6] Thus, even in the absence of express provisions in the applicable liability insurance coverage terms, courts undoubtedly will recognize implied limitations or exceptions that would restrict coverage for many situations when a loss results from an insured's intentional torts — that is, although liability insurance policies almost uniformly include terms that expressly limit or exclude coverage for intentional torts, courts almost certainly would impose some restrictions in the absence of an express provision. However, in addition to affirming the general public policy, the coverage terms in liability insurance policies serve to provide both insureds and the courts with a somewhat more precise articulation of the restriction. Furthermore, the terms of contemporary liability insurance policies probably impose a more extensive limitation or exclusion than that which would be recognized by the courts in the absence of an explicit policy provision.

(2) Approaches to Assessing Whether Liability Coverage Exists for a Consequence That the Tortfeasor Allegedly Did Not Intend

Judicial decisions, either applying explicit insurance policy provisions or predicated on implied exceptions which are imposed as a

---

3. See, e.g. Millard Warehouse, Inc. v. Hartford Fire Insurance Company, 204 Neb. 518, 283 N.W.2d 56 at p. 61 (1979); Hartford Fire Insurance Company v. Spreen, 343 So.2d 649 (Fla.App., 3rd Dist., 1977).

Also see Donald F. Farbstein and Francis J. Stillman, *Insurance for the Commission of Intentional Torts,* 20 Hastings Law Journal 1219–1254 (1969).

See also the discussion in § 9.1, below, of the obligation to defend a person insured by a liability insurance contract when the plaintiff alleges that an injury resulted from an intentional tort.

4. Ambassador Insurance Company v. Montes, 76 N.J. 477 at p. 483, 388 A.2d 603 at p. 606 (1978).

5. *Ibid.*

6. See, e.g., Ambassador Insurance Company v. Montes, 76 N.J. 477 at p. 482, 388 A.2d 603 at p. 606 (1978).

Cf. Davis v. Boston Mutual Life Insurance Company, 370 Mass. 602, 351 N.E.2d 207 at pp. 209–210 (1976); Haser v. Maryland Casualty Company, 78 N.D. 893, 53 N.W.2d 508 (1952), 33 A.L.R.2d 1018 (1954) (briefly described in note 1, above).

matter of public policy, generally hold that liability insurance does not provide coverage when an insured intentionally causes a loss.[7] It is considerably less clear, however, as to whether coverage is provided by contemporary liability insurance policies when the insured urges that even though an action was intended, the specific consequence was not intended.

There are several factors that make it difficult to identify or describe the judicial views on this question. *First,* the range of factual settings — that may present questions about consequences that result from some intended action or that arguably an insured did not know would result — are quite diverse and undoubtedly involve a variety of issues that are not likely to be fully and completely considered by a court when the reasons for the decision in a particular case are set forth in an opinion. *Second,* there are several judicial views or approaches to deciding whether liability insurance should provide coverage for tort liability in such circumstances, especially when there is substantial evidence that the specific consequences of the insured's actions were not intended. *Third,* courts often fail to take account of both (1) whether the consequences on which the intent focuses are to be defined precisely or generally, *and* (2) whether the definition of the state of mind of intent extends not only to purpose or desire to produce the consequences, but also knowledge that the consequences will follow.

One approach to deciding whether liability insurance provides coverage is to focus on whether there was a purpose to do "some" harm. This approach, which disregards the question whether the tortfeasor wanted to cause the particular harm that resulted — or even had knowledge that it was substantially certain to result — precludes coverage for a tortfeasor who intended any type of harm to any person. The breadth of this limitation on coverage is obviously very extensive. This approach is undoubtedly close to one end of the spectrum of rules applied in these cases, and thus far has achieved only very limited support in judicial opinions.

Another approach predicates the scope of the coverage limitation on a determination about whether an insured intended that an act cause the type of injury (if not the specific injury) that was sustained, that is, no limitation applies if the insured did not intend the type of harm that resulted. Furthermore, several decisions, which appear to have employed this approach,[8] have taken the additional step of con-

7. See, e.g. Snyder v. Nelson, 278 Or. 409 at p. 414, 564 P.2d 681 at p. 684 (1977) ("In any event, under usual circumstances it is against public policy for a tortfeasor to insure against liability for intentionally inflicted injury or damage.").

Also see § 5.4(a) and § 5.4(d), above, and the decisions cited below in this section.

But see the discussion of instances in which motor vehicle liability insurance is extended to intentional torts in § 5.4(d)(2), below.

An insurer may be obligated to defend an insured who allegedly committed an intentional tort. See § 9.1, below.

8. *Cf.* Caspersen v. Webber, 298 Minn. 93, 213 N.W.2d 327 at p. 330 (1973) (coverage existed when the insured intentionally pushed a hat-check attendant who was injured when she fell against a metal rack on

cluding that for a limitation on coverage to be warranted, the insured "must have intended to harm *the* individual who was actually injured"[9] — that is, liability coverage applies to harm caused by the intentional torts of an insured if the insured either (1) did not intend that the act cause the type of injury that occurred or (2) did not intend to harm the person who sustained the injury.[10] One rationale for this approach is that a significant public interest is served by providing indemnification for the injured person, and therefore it is important to maximize the scope of coverage provided by liability insurance by minimizing the extent of the coverage limitation. In essence, this type of approach adopts the view that innocent victims should be entitled to indemnification from a tortfeasor's liability insurer so long as the insured did not intend the specific harms that resulted to the specific persons harmed. When so extended, this approach comes close to the opposite end of the spectrum from the first approach. The extent of support for this approach in court decisions is a matter of dispute, largely because of the ambiguity of many opinions and the lack of sharp focus on the issue.

A third approach is indicated by judicial statements to the effect that liability insurance should not apply whenever an injury is the natural and probable consequence of an insured's acts.[11] This approach

---

the basis that the resulting injury was not intended; where "no bodily injury was intended [when the insured pushed aside an attendant for a checkroom at a restaurant], an assault does not come within the exclusionary clause").

Cf. Eberdt v. St. Paul Fire & Marine Insurance Company, 36 Or.App. 679 at p. 682, 585 P.2d 711 at p. 712 (1978) ("* * * it is not sufficient that the insured's intentional, albeit unlawful, acts have resulted in unintended harm; the acts must have been committed for the purpose of inflicting the injury and harm before either a policy provision excluding intentional harm applies or the public policy against insurability attaches.")

Also see Brown v. State Automobile & Casualty Underwriters, 293 N.W.2d 822 at p. 824 (Minn.1980).

Note: Although it is arguable that this approach may not have been employed by all of these courts, the opinions are at least susceptible of being so interpreted.

9. Indiana Lumbermens Mutual Insurance Company v. Brandum, 419 N.E.2d 246 at p. 248 (Ind.App. 1st Dist.1981) (emphasis added).

Cf. United States Fidelity & Guaranty Company v. Perez, 384 So.2d 904 (Fla.App. 3d Dist.1980) [review denied 392 So.2d 1381 (1980)] (coverage applied to an insured

who recklessly fired a gun to frighten the decedent, but without any intent to harm him).

Also see Home Insurance Company v. Neilsen, 165 Ind.App. 445 at p. 450, 332 N.E.2d 240 at p. 244 (3d Dist.1975) (holding that a policy which excluded "bodily injury or property damage caused intentionally" precluded coverage for an act intended to cause injury and that such intent may be established by "showing an actual intent to injure, or by showing the nature and character of the act to be such that intent to cause harm * * * must be inferred as a matter of law.").

10. See, e.g., Rambin v. Wood, 355 So.2d 561 (La.App.3d Cir.1978) (insured intentionally shoved a person riding on a lawn tractor was found not to have intended the injuries that resulted when the driver fell off the tractor and his foot was caught under one of the tractor's wheels resulting in fractured ribs, and muscle sprains).

Cf. Sabri v. State Farm Fire & Casualty Company, 488 So.2d 362 (La.App.3d Cir. 1986) (insured mistook his daughter, who was married and lived elsewhere, for a prowler and shot her).

11. See, e.g., Steinmetz v. National American Insurance Company, 121 Ariz. 268 at p. 271, 589 P.2d 911 at p. 914 (App., Div. 1, Dept. B 1979).

focuses on what a reasonable person would view as the probable consequences of an act, rather than on a tortfeasor's subjective state of mind. For example, if an insured becomes aware that a particular type of loss may result from a given set of conditions, such as when there is an equipment failure and the insured elects to take a calculated risk by deciding not to repair or replace equipment or to alter the methods of operation, a few courts have concluded that subsequent losses that resulted from the same conditions "were not unexpected and thus were not accidents or occurrences as those terms were used in the insurance policy." [12] For a limitation on coverage to apply under this approach, it is not necessary for an insurer to prove that an injury was intended. This approach produces a rather broad — and, at least in some types of circumstances, the most extensive — coverage limitation.[13] This type of approach is arguably compatible with the coverage terms now used in many types of liability insurance which exclude coverage unless an injury "is neither expected nor intended from the standpoint of the insured." [14] The increasing application of this approach by courts in recent years has almost certainly resulted from the inclusion of this clause in insurance contract forms in the 1960s and thereafter. It should be noted, however, that the term "expected" in such coverage provisions has been given a relatively narrower or strict interpretation by many courts.[15]

Cf. Snyder v. Nelson, 278 Or. 409 at p. 414–415, 564 P.2d 681 at pp. 684–685 (1977).

12. City of Carter Lake v. Aetna Casualty & Surety Company, 604 F.2d 1052 at p. 1059 (8th Cir.1979).

Also see the discussion of Coverage for highly expectable losses in § 5.4(e), below.

13. Of course, fidelity to the principle that loss must be fortuitous does not require a court to go this far. The argument for a limitation this sweeping must be based, instead, on interpretation of contractual provisions. It may also be noted that a victim as to whom loss is fortuitous could be allowed protection without giving coverage to a tortfeasor who intentionally injured him. For example, the insurer could be required to pay the victim and be granted a right of reimbursement from the tortfeasor. *Cf.* Annotation, *Validity and construction of liability policy provision requiring insured to reimburse insurer for payments made under policy,* 29 A.L.R.3d 291–320 (1970).

14. See, e.g., Woida v. North Star Mutual Insurance Company, 306 N.W.2d 570 at p. 573 (Minn.1981); Northwestern National Casualty Company v. Phalen, 182 Mont. 448, 597 P.2d 720 (1979); Safeco Insurance Company of America v. Dotts, 38 Wash.

App. 382, 685 P.2d 632 (Div. 3, Panel 4, 1984).

Cf. Steinmetz v. National American Insurance Company, 121 Ariz. 268, 589 P.2d 911 (App., Div. 1, Dept. B, 1979).

Also see Blue Ridge Insurance Company v. Nicholas, 425 F.Supp. 827 (E.D.Mo.1977) (no coverage when a shotgun with a faulty safety was discharged in the course of a scuffle that ensued after the gun was pointed at the victim); Farmers Automobile Insurance Association v. Medina, 29 Ill.App.3d 224, 329 N.E.2d 430 (1975).

See generally Annotation, *Liability insurance: specific exclusion of liability for injury intentionally caused by insured,* 2 A.L.R.3d 1238–1253 (1965).

15. See, e.g., State & Farm Casualty Company v. Muth, 190 Neb. 248 at p. 252, 190 Neb. 272, 207 N.W.2d 364 at p. 366 (1973), treating "expected" in this setting in a way arguably consistent with the RESTATEMENT OF TORTS definition of intended consequences as including not only those the actor desired (or had the purpose) to produce but also those the actor knew were substantially certain to occur.

Also see Prosser and Keeton, TORTS (Fifth edition, 1984), at § 8.

A fourth approach is to construe "expected" — in the phrase "neither expected nor intended from the standpoint of the insured" — to mean that the result is substantially certain to be a consequence of the insured's action. This approach treats "expected" as a way of making clear that "knowledgeable intent" as well as "purposive intent" is enough to preclude coverage under current policy forms.

A fifth approach — applied thus far by only a few courts and more frequently in regard to motor vehicle liability insurance than for other types of liability insurance — limits to a very narrow scope any preclusion of coverage for an intended harm, even when an injury results from criminal acts.[16] Although courts have not always been explicit in stating that such a rule or doctrine is being formulated and applied with the goal of providing compensation to an innocent victim,[17] it seems that this consideration is a significant influence underlying

16. The rationale underlying these decisions is that state financial responsibility laws manifest a very important public policy that favors providing compensation for innocent persons who have been injured. The New Jersey Supreme Court, for example, has concluded that liability insurance payments "to an innocent injured third person will further the public interest in compensating the victim." Ambassador Insurance Company v. Montes, 76 N.J. 477 at p. 484, 388 A.2d 603 at pp. 606–607 (1978). See the discussion of this case in Note, *Liability Insurance for Intentional Torts—Subrogation of the Insurer to the Victim's Rights Against the Insured: Ambassador Insurance Co. v. Montes,* 32 Rutgers Law Review 155–172 (1979).

Cf. Cloud v. Shelby Mutual Insurance Company, 248 So.2d 217 (Fla.App., 3d Dist., 1971) (coverage provided by an automobile insurance policy when an insured sought to push a car out of the way and drove his car into another vehicle that was blocking a driveway causing a serious injury to an occupant in the other car).

Also see, Comment, *The Expansion of Insurance Coverage to Include the Intentional Tortfeasor,* 23 Loyola Law Review 122–143 (1977); Donald F. Farbstein & Francis J. Stillman, *Insurance for the Commission of Intentional Torts,* 20 Hastings Law Journal 1219–1254 (1969).

Cf. Note, *What About the Victims? Compensation for the Victims of Crime,* 48 North Dakota Law Review 473–494 (1972); Note, *Insurance for the Criminal,* 34 Modern Law Review 176–181 at p. 179 (1971).

See the more extensive discussion of this concept in regard to motor vehicle insurance in § 5.4(d)(5), below.

17. *Cf.* Indiana Lumbermens Mutual Insurance Company v. Brandum, 419 N.E.2d 246 (Ind.App., 1st Dist., 1981). The Insured — who observed his fiancee riding in a car and kissing the driver — used his own auto to catch up and repeatedly ram the other car, causing it to spin off the road and land on top of a third vehicle in which the claimants were seated. The appellate court affirmed that the insured's motor vehicle coverage applied because an intent to harm the third parties could not be inferred, which intent was required to warrant an application of the exclusionary clause limiting the insurer's liability for intentionally caused injuries.

Also see, Grange Mutual Casualty Company v. Thomas, 301 So.2d 158 (Fla.App., 2d Dist., 1974) (insured shot a bystander during a family quarrel).

Employment discrimination cases are increasingly emerging as another area in which courts face this type of dilemma. As one writer has observed, although "[c]ompensation for victims of illegal employment discrimination is one of the twin goals of Title VII remedies, * * * the compensation benefits of insurance coverage are occasionally outweighed by the adverse effect insurance coverage may have on deterrence." Steven L. Willborn, *Insurance, Public Policy, and Employment Discrimination,* 66 Minnesota Law Review 1003–1031 at pp. 1018–1–19 (1982). Professor Willborn points out that the insurance law issue is also interesting "because it focuses on a classic but poorly understood employment discrimination issue — the nature of the discriminatory intent element in employment discrimination cases." *Id.,* at pp. 1004–1005.

some, and perhaps many, of the judicial decisions sustaining coverage claims in liability insurance cases when the tortfeasor's conduct is reasonably viewed as having been accompanied by an intent to cause harm.

The different approaches that have been applied to cases involving these situations make it difficult even to ascertain whether there is a clear weight of authority with respect to when liability coverage applies if there is evidence that an insured did not intend to cause the harm that occurred, but did intend to cause some type of injury or harm.[18]

(3) Wanton or Reckless Acts

Injuries to an individual or property sometimes result from acts which courts characterize as "wanton or reckless conduct."[19] Even though this type of conduct is treated in the same way as an intentional tort for some purposes (such as the assessment of punitive damages), the resulting losses are usually not classed as having been intentionally

18. In Aetna Casualty & Surety Company v. Freyer, 89 Ill.App.3d 617, 44 Ill.Dec. 791, 411 N.E.2d 1157 at p. 1159 (1st Dist., Div. 4, 1980), the court states that "The word intent for purposes of exclusionary clauses in insurance policies denotes that the actor desires to cause the consequences of his act or believes that the consequences are substantially certain to result from it."

In Hartford Fire Insurance Company v. Spreen, 343 So.2d 649 (Fla.App., 3d Dist., 1977), the insured, who struck the face of a guest at a party causing a fracture of the orbital floor of the eye, claimed that although he intended to strike the person in the face he did not intend to injure the individual's face or eye. The court held that an intentional assault and battery was not covered—both because the damages were not caused by an "accident" and the policy excluded coverage for damages which are "expected or intended."

In Pachucki v. Republic Insurance Company, 89 Wis.2d 703 at p. 709, 278 N.W.2d 898 at p. 901 (1979), the court discussed three factors bearing upon the situations in which the majority rule applies:

(1) It is necessary that the insured both intend the act and intend to cause bodily injury in order for the exclusion to apply.

(2) Intent is a fact which the fact finder must find to have existed in fact, but the fact-finder may infer from evidence of circumstances of foreseeability of harm that the actor did in fact foresee and intend harm.

(3) Once it is found that harm was intended, it is immaterial that the actual harm caused is of a different character or magnitude than that intended.

Also see State Farm Fire & Casualty Company v. Muth, 190 Neb. 248, 190 Neb. 272, 207 N.W.2d 364 (1973).

See generally 7A Appleman, Insurance Law & Practice (Berdal ed., 1979) at § 4492.02.

On the distinction between the legal standard to be applied (the legal definition of intent) and the use of circumstantial evidence and argument (including the argument that an ordinarily prudent person would have foreseen the consequence and that the actor who under the evidence was at least that bright, should be found in fact to have foreseen the consequence), see Prosser and Keeton, Torts (Fifth edition, 1984) at § 8. See also Boston Mutual Life Insurance Company v. Fireman's Fund Insurance Co., 613 F.Supp. 1090 (D.Mass. 1985) (Keeton, J.) (discussing the meaning of "discovery" and being "aware" and proof by circumstantial evidence in relation to requirement of notice in a fidelity bond).

19. *Cf.* Travelers Indemnity Company v. Hood, 110 Ga.App. 855, 140 S.E.2d 68 (1964), 20 A.L.R.3d 314 (1968) (racing cars on public highway; coverage allowed, the court observing that the fact that an injury is treated for other purposes as "constructively intentional does not remove it from the category of injury 'caused by accident' in the terms of an insurance contract").

caused for purposes of liability insurance. In most instances,[20] liability insurance will provide coverage for such conduct in the absence of an explicit contractual provision to the contrary.[21]

Observations

When an innocent individual is injured as a result of someone's wanton or reckless action, there is considerable concern with assuring compensation for the individual who sustains injuries. This consideration supports the view that the "intentional tort" restriction should not be extended to these situations. On the other hand, there is also concern about allowing insureds to shift the economic responsibility for the type of conduct that the society would like to discourage and deter. Frequently, it is difficult to either discern or predict the appropriate accommodation between these goals or interests.[22] Accordingly, considerable care should be exercised in evaluating existing precedents, and the course of future decisions in this area is certainly not free from doubt.

(4) Motor Vehicle Liability Insurance as Protection for the Victim's Economic Interest

Many states now require that motorists have motor vehicle liability insurance,[23] and all states have financial responsibility statutes that apply when motorists are involved in accidents.[24] Thus, in every state there is legislation which either requires or clearly encourages the acquisition of at least minimum amounts of liability insurance by motorists. The public policy underlying such statutes is a very substantial concern for the protection of innocent victims who are injured in motor vehicle collisions.

20. Courts are sometimes reticent about requiring insurers to provide indemnification under liability insurance for conduct that is so extreme as to fit the characterization of being "a damn fool thing to do," and thus to cast grave doubt on the assertion that in fact the insured was that foolish rather than having intentionally caused the loss. See the discussion in § 5.4(e)(6).

21. See, e.g., United States Fidelity & Guaranty Company v. Perez, 384 So.2d 904 at p. 905 (Fla.App., 3d Dist., 1980), *review denied* 392 So.2d 1381 (1980) ("There was insurance coverage for the incident sued upon * * * because it is properly inferable from this record that the insured defendant * * * did not intend to harm the plaintiff's decedent * * *, but only to frighten him, when she fired her gun and accidentally, recklessly and through culpable negligence killed him; [citations omitted].")

Also see Annotation, *Liability insurance as covering accident, damage, or injury due to wanton or willful misconduct or gross negligence*, 20 A.L.R.3d 320–334 (1968).

22. Also see the discussion in § 5.4(e) of coverage for highly expectable losses and especially in § 5.4(e)(6) of incredibly foolish conduct.

23. See, e.g., Arizona Revised Statutes § 28–1251 (1984–1985 Supp.); Colorado Revised Statutes § 42–4–1213 (1984); Massachusetts General Laws Annotated, Chapter 90, 34–A (1985 Supplement); Michigan Compiled Laws Annotated, Insurance Code of 1956 § 500.3101(1); McKinney's New York Vehicle and Traffic Law § 312 (1983 Supp.).

24. See, e.g., Illinois Statutes Ann. Ch. 95½, § 7–302 (Smith Hurd, 1984–85 Supp.); Iowa Code Annotated § 321A.5 (1984–1985 Supp.); Nebraska Revised Statutes § 60–507 and § 60–508 (1943).

In several states, the courts have held that the state's financial responsibility legislation warrants evaluating questions relating to the existence of coverage for intentional harms from the vantage point of an injured person, rather than resolving such issues on the basis of whether the insured intended to cause the loss.[25] For example, there are instances in which this approach has been applied by courts when the evidence showed that a motor vehicle was deliberately used to commit a battery.[26]

Comment

Construing a statutory provision requiring motorists to carry liability insurance for the protection of motoring victims to expand the scope

25. See, e.g., Wheeler v. O'Connell, 297 Mass. 549, 9 N.E.2d 544, 111 A.L.R. 1038 (1937) (wilfull, wanton and reckless operation of truck, causing injury to officer who was on running board attempting to halt it; declaration of public policy in compulsory automobile insurance law for protection of victims supersedes any rule of public policy in ordinary insurance law).

Cf. Hartford Accident & Indemnity Company v. Wolbarst, 95 N.H. 40, 57 A.2d 151 (1948) (deliberate bumping of another car, unintentionally causing injury to occupants; in declaratory proceedings, held coverage under liability insurance policy containing customary provision that the insurance afforded "shall comply" with any applicable financial responsibility law; opinion notes statutory and policy provisions for insurer's right of reimbursement from tortfeasor).

Also see Nationwide Mutual Insurance Co. v. Roberts, 261 N.C. 285, 134 S.E.2d 654 (1964) (deliberate driving of car against pedestrian; in declaratory proceedings, held coverage under compulsory liability insurance policy; opinion notes statutory and policy provisions for insurer's right of reimbursement from tortfeasor, as to which see § 4.8(c), above).

But cf. Peerless Casualty Company v. Cole, 121 Vt. 258, 155 A.2d 866 (1959) (insurer's settlement with victims constitutes election; cannot rely on insurance contract for right to settle and at the same time claim it is ineffectual; the facts were, however, that settlements were made before notice to the insured that the insurer denied coverage). See also Jernigan v. Allstate Insurance Company, 269 F.2d 353 (5th Cir.1959), *opinion on denial of rehearing* 272 F.2d 857 (5th Cir.1959) (applying Louisiana law; coverage for deliberate injury inflicted by omnibus insured; majori-

ty note the Louisiana Direct Action Statute, designed to protect victims, but reason also on broader ground that this was an accident from the point of view of the victim; dissent on the ground that the driver had later been determined to be insane and that neither the driver nor the insurer should be liable); New Amsterdam Casualty Company v. Jones, 135 F.2d 191 (6th Cir.1943) (purportedly applying Michigan law although the interpretation of Michigan statutes regulating liability insurance seems unpersuasive) (allowing victim of battery to recover under tortfeasor's liability insurance policy).

26. Among the cases cited in the preceding note, only *Roberts* plainly goes this far, but the opinions in the other cases are susceptible of being read in this way.

Also see State Farm Fire & Casualty Company v. Tringali, 686 F.2d 821 (9th Cir. 1982) (applying Hawaiian law); Indiana Lumbermens Mutual Insurance Company v. Brandum, 419 N.E.2d 246 (Ind.App., 1st Dist., 1981); Nationwide Mutual Insurance Company v. Knight, 34 N.C.App. 96, 237 S.E.2d 341 (1977), *review denied* 293 N.C. 589, 239 S.E.2d 263 (1977).

But see Subscribers at the Automobile Club Inter-Insurance Exchange v. Kennison, 549 S.W.2d 587 (Mo.App., St. Louis Dist., Div. 1, 1977) (exclusion providing the coverage did not apply to "damage caused intentionally" applied to damage which resulted when the insured rammed the left rear fender of an occupied automobile that was blocking the traffic lane in a parking lot).

See generally, Annotation, *Liability insurance: assault as an "accident," or injuries from it as "accidental" within coverage clause,* 33 A.L.R.2d 1027–1049 at p. 1030 (1954).

of such insurance to include coverage for a deliberate battery might be criticized as an unwarranted extrapolation or extension of the public interest manifested by the compulsory insurance or financial responsibility laws. However, such a construction of the liability coverage and the legislative provisions designed to require or encourage the acquisition of liability insurance by motorists — so as to provide indemnification for an innocent victim of an intentional harm — arguably would not be offensive to the principles underlying implied exceptions in insurance law if the insurer were allowed to assert a claim against the insured to recoup the amount paid as insurance benefits to innocent accident victims who are injured by the intended torts of an insured.[27] In essence, this approach would allow the insurer to become "subrogated" to the tort claim that the injured person(s) would otherwise assert against the tortfeasor. Although this would create an exception to the rule that an insurer may not assert a claim for indemnification from its own insured,[28] in this context it would be an appropriate limitation on that doctrine in furtherance of the goal of indemnifying innocent victims.

This approach has the advantage of providing a source of indemnification for the injured persons, and the insured is not significantly prejudiced. The difference to the insured is that it is an insurer rather than the victim that "pursues" the tort claim.

Caveat. Among the instances in which persons are injured by the use of a motor vehicle to commit an intentional tort, cases in which there is a deliberate use of a vehicle as a weapon in response to a provocation by the injured person should be distinguished. When the injured person has provoked an altercation, the goal of protecting an "innocent" victim is obviously lessened if not totally obviated.

(5) Vicarious Liability for Intentional Torts and Negligent Supervision

There are various types of situations in which individuals are held to be vicariously liable for an intentional tort of another person.[29] In such cases, the harm for which an insured is vicariously liable often is

---

27. In Ambassador Insurance Company v. Montes, 76 N.J. 477 at p. 484, 388 A.2d 603 at p. 606 (1978), the court observed that payments under a comprehensive general liability insurance policy should be made to provide compensation to the innocent victim of the insured's criminal behavior "so long as the benefit thereof does not enure to the assured" and in "furtherance of that justifiable end * * * it is equitable and just that the insurer be indemnified by the insured for the payment to the injured party." By taking this approach, the court concluded that "the public policy principle * * * that the assured may not be relieved of financial responsibility arising out his criminal act" is "honored." *Ibid.*

28. See the discussion in § 3.10(a), above.

29. For example, in Commercial Union Assurance Companies v. Derry, 118 N.H. 469, 387 A.2d 1171 (1978), the insurer urged that the court impute the police officer's alleged intent to the town. The court decided that although "an employer could be liable for the acts of its employees * * * such liability results vicariously" and there is no policy that precludes "insuring against the consequences of an unauthorized willful wrong allegedly commit-

appropriately viewed as a fortuitous occurrence from the point of view of the insured, as well as the victim. When this is true, courts generally hold that the scope of coverage afforded by liability insurance extends protection for an insured who is vicariously liable for damages resulting from an intentional tort committed by another person.[30]

In most circumstances, courts hold both (1) that the express provisions commonly used in liability insurance policies do not preclude coverage for damages awarded for an intentional tort when the insured is held to be responsible on a theory of vicarious liability, and (2) that it would not be appropriate to imply a limitation that would restrict the coverage. For example, courts have concluded that the intentional torts of a child, such as a battery upon another person or an act of vandalism, are fortuitous as to a parent who is held liable for negligently failing to supervise the child so as to prevent the child from causing harm to others.[31]

Generally, liability coverage is not precluded for one of several named or additional insureds when the harms were intentionally caused by another individual who is also a named or additional insured of the same policy. The approach adopted by courts in such cases generally is not contrary to the public policy principles underlying implied exceptions for intentional torts, and these decisions certainly are in harmony with the desire to assure innocent victims a source of indemnification.[32] Although the evaluation of competing interests may be somewhat more difficult when there are express insurance policy provisions precluding coverage for intentionally-caused injuries, in most instances it seems clear that such coverage restrictions should not be applicable to insureds whose liability is derivative so long as the

ted by another insured." *Id.*, 118 N.H. at p. 473, 387 A.2d at pp. 1173–1174. Accordingly, the court held that the insurer was obligated to both defend and indemnify the insured town in a suit arising from the allegedly intentionally tortious conduct of one of the town's police officers.

30. *Cf.* Allstate Insurance Company v. Harris, 445 F.Supp. 847 at p. 849 (N.D.Cal. 1978).

Also see other decisions cited in this subsection.

31. *Cf.* Unigard Mutual Insurance Co. v. Argonaut Insurance Company, 20 Wash. App. 261 at p. 265, 579 P.2d 1015 at p. 1019 (Div. 3, Panel 1, 1978).

32. See, e.g., Allstate Insurance Company v. Harris, 445 F.Supp. 847 at p. 849 (N.D.Cal.1978); Pawtucket Mutual Insurance Company v. Lebrecht, 104 N.H. 465, 190 A.2d 420 (1963), 2 A.L.R.3d 1229 (1965) (suit against parents of seventeen-year-old

delinquent boy who attacked plaintiff, a girl).

Cf. Unigard Mutual Insurance Co. v. Argonaut Insurance Company, 20 Wash.App. 261, 579 P.2d 1015 (Div. 3, Panel 1, 1978) (coverage upheld for parents of an eleven year old boy who broke into a school building and set fire to contents of a trash can which then spread causing extensive damage to the building); Walker v. Lumbermens Mutual Casualty Co., 491 S.W.2d 696 at p. 699 (Tex.App., Eastland 1973).

Also see Armstrong v. Security Insurance Group, 292 Ala. 27, 288 So.2d 134 (1973) (where husband and wife who operated a sandwich shop were coinsureds intentional injury exclusion which precluded coverage for a husband who was involved in an altercation that led to a gun being fired did not apply to the wife for a bodily injury which she neither expected nor intended and in regard to which she was not a participant).

intentional torts were not committed under the actual direction or control of the insured.[33]

Some liability insurance policies have included a clause, usually in a provision that is separate from the primary definition of coverage, declaring that an "assault and battery shall be deemed an accident unless it is committed by or at the direction of the insured." [34] Courts generally hold that so long as the tortious acts are not specifically directed by an insured, coverage is provided for vicarious liability resulting from assault and battery.[35]

(6) "Assault and Battery": Special Coverage Problems in Regard to Liability Insurance

Injuries that result from an "assault and battery" normally are subject both to specific exclusions that preclude coverage for intentional or expected losses,[36] and to the generally recognized implied coverage

33. See, e.g., Employers Mutual Liability Insurance Company v. Hendrix, 199 F.2d 53 (4th Cir.1952), 41 A.L.R.2d 424 (1955) (applying South Carolina law; named insured allowed coverage as to claim he was vicariously liable for assault committed by employee); Employers Surplus Lines v. Stone, 388 P.2d 295 (Okl.1963) (partner of claimant's assailant settled assault claim and then sued liability insurer for reimbursement). *Cf.* Arenson v. National Automobile & Casualty Insurance Company, 45 Cal.2d 81, 286 P.2d 816 (1955) (minor son started fire that damaged school property; school district obtained judgment against parent under vicarious liability statute; parent's liability covered by liability policy of which parent was named insured).

Also see Morgan v. Greater N.Y. Taxpayers Mutual Insurance Association, 305 N.Y. 243, 112 N.E.2d 273 (1953) (victim of assault by one member of partnership obtained judgment against that partner individually and against the partnership; proceeding to recover the amount of the judgment from the partnership's public liability insurer; held, for victim on the theory that a second partner, who was individually liable for judgment against partnership was a named insured and that the assault and battery clause did not preclude coverage for his liability since the assault was not by him or at his direction);

See generally, 7A APPLEMAN, INSURANCE LAW (Berdal edition, 1979), at § 4492.

34. See the 1955 Standard Basic Automobile Liability Policy, "Conditions" clause 6.

See the cases collected in Annotation, *Liability insurance: specific exclusion of*

Keeton & Widess, Ins.Law—13

liability for injury intentionally caused by insured, 2 A.L.R.3d 1238–1253 at pp. 1246–1248 (1965).

Also see Norman E. Risjord & June M. Austin, AUTOMOBILE LIABILITY INSURANCE CASES—STANDARD PROVISIONS (1964).

35. See, e.g., Huie v. Phoenix Insurance Company, 413 F.2d 613 (8th Cir.1969) (Arkansas law; defense of insanity unavailable in action against insurer on tort judgment, since that defense could have been raised in tort action; in view of "assault and battery" exclusion, not necessary to consider whether same result would be reached under an "intentional injury" exclusion).

Also see § 9.1, below, concerning the duty to defend when a negligence claim is joined with a claim of intentional tort.

36. *Cf.* Selected Risks Insurance Company v. Bruno, 718 F.2d 67 (3d Cir.1983); Iowa Kemper Insurance Company v. Stone, 269 N.W.2d 885 (Minn.1978); Hins v. Heer, 259 N.W.2d 38 (N.D.1977).

Also see Aetna Casualty & Surety Company v. Freyer, 89 Ill.App.3d 617, 44 Ill. Dec. 791, 411 N.E.2d 1157 (1980).

Cf. Putman v. Zeluff, 372 Mich. 553, 127 N.W.2d 374 (1964) (coverage, despite exclusion clause, for claim against young boy who shot pedigreed coon hound, thinking it was a wild dog and shooting for his own safety; reasoned, however, on the ground that in the confused circumstances it was not clear that he had the intent to destroy the animal).

In Walters v. American Insurance Company, 185 Cal.App.2d 776, 8 Cal.Rptr. 665 (1st Dist., Div. 2, 1960) the insured claimed against his liability insurer for both the

restriction, discussed in the preceding section, which limits liability coverage to fortuitous losses. Coverage questions resulting from assaults and batteries involving either express coverage terms or the implied exception have presented several interesting issues in relation to liability insurance.

Intent to Inflict Only a "Minor" Harm

Insureds have sometimes urged that liability coverage should not be foreclosed when an insured only intended to cause minor harm. In most instances, it will not avail an insured to show that only an impact of relatively little significance was intended or that a severe injury which resulted was not intended.[37] For example, it was held that the exclusion applied to an injury that resulted when an insured approached the insured person from behind, spun him around, and struck him on the cheek, knocking him down, even though the court accepted the explanation that the insured "did not intend to inflict * * * the specific injuries sustained."[38] These cases present questions that were addressed in more detail in the discussion, in § 5.4(d)(2), above, of approaches to assessing whether coverage exists for specific consequences that a tortfeasor did not intend.

Mistaken Belief That Acts of Self–Defense Were Warranted

Coverage issues have arisen in several instances when an insured claimed that the intentional injuries were inflicted in the mistaken belief the insured's acts were essential to the individual's self-defense.

costs of defense and the amount of settlement of an assault and battery claim against him that the insurer had refused to defend. There being no "assault and battery" exclusion clause in the policy, the court held, assuming an implied trial court finding that the insured "acted reasonably and in self-defense," that self-defense took the matter out of the intentional injury exclusion and therefore, that the insurer had wrongfully refused to defend and was liable for the amount of the settlement, which the court found reasonable.

37. Similarly, an insured will rarely prevail on claim for liability coverage for an assault and battery on the basis that the injury to the particular person was not intended. *Cf.* Steinmetz v. National American Insurance Company, 121 Ariz. 268, 589 P.2d 911 (App., Div. 1, Dept. B, 1978) (the appellate court affirmed the appropriateness of the trial court jury instruction that "[y]ou are not to consider whether Mr. Currie intended to injure Mr. Steinmetz, but only whether he intended to strike him.").

Cf. Hartford Fire Insurance Company v. Spreen, 343 So.2d 649 (Fla.App., 3d Dist., 1977) (insured struck the victim's face causing serious injury to the orbital floor of the victim's eye).

Also see Butler v. Behaeghe, 37 Colo. App. 282, 548 P.2d 934 (1976); Clark v. Allstate Insurance Company, 22 Ariz.App. 601, 529 P.2d 1195 (Div. 2, 1975) (insured hit another student with a "short-jab" which crushed the right cheekbone and required surgical repair).

38. Pendergraft v. Commercial Standard Fire & Marine Company, 342 F.2d 427 (10th Cir.1965).

But cf. Smith v. Moran, 61 Ill.App.2d 157, 209 N.E.2d 18 (2d Dist.1965) (insured accidentally shot one waitress in a tavern when shooting at another waitress; *held,* insurer was bound to defend the suit against the insured; decision seems unsound, since the mere fact that the harm fortuitously fell on one other than the person the insured intended to injure seems a poor reason for allowing the insured to escape the preclusion of coverage).

In essence, the theory advanced on behalf of the insured in these cases is that when an insured acts in the mistaken belief that acts of self-defense were warranted, the resulting injuries to another person are not caused "intentionally."[39]   In such situations, the insured almost always does intend to cause a physical impact with sufficient force to deter the incorrectly perceived threat of harm — that is, the insured urges that coverage should apply because the insured was *mistaken* about the right of self-defense, and it is this mistake that should be determinative of the coverage question (rather than intention to commit the physical impact that resulted in the injuries suffered by a victim).

If the analysis in such a case shifts to questions that relate to a "mistake," thereby presenting the coverage issue in terms of whether liability coverage applies if an insured can prove that the purpose of an intended impact upon the victim was self-defense in a situation in which the belief that the insured was being attacked arose from a *negligent* mistake, the focus of the coverage dispute is radically transformed.[40]

39. The comment in the text concerns a type of case in which the plea of self-defense *fails* because the person asserting it was unreasonable in believing it necessary to act in self-defense. A somewhat stronger case for coverage as to the duty to defend is presented when the circumstances *support* the plea of self-defense.

Cf. Putman v. Zeluff, 372 Mich. 553, 127 N.W.2d 374 (1964) (coverage, despite exclusion clause, for claim against young boy who shot pedigreed coon hound, thinking it was a wild dog and shooting for his own safety; reasoned, however, on the ground that in the confused circumstances it was not clear that he had the intent to destroy the animal).

In Walters v. American Insurance Company, 185 Cal.App.2d 776, 8 Cal.Rptr. 665 (1st Dist., Div. 2, 1960), the insured claimed against his liability insurer for both the costs of defense and the amount of settlement of an assault and battery claim against him that the insurer had refused to defend. There being no "assault and battery" exclusion clause in the policy, the court held, assuming an implied trial court finding that the insured "acted reasonably and in self-defense," that self-defense took the matter out of the intentional injury exclusion and, therefore, that the insurer had wrongfully refused to defend and was liable for the amount of the settlement, which the court found reasonable.

In Maxon v. Security Insurance Company, 214 Cal.App.2d 603, 29 Cal.Rptr. 586 (1st Dist., Div. 1, 1963), the court held that a liability insurer was not liable for the cost of the insured's successful defense of a malicious prosecution action, distinguishing *Walters* on the tenuous, if not untenable, ground that a pleading was available by which the insurer's duty to defend could be measured (whereas in *Walters* the insurer had refused to defend and the insured had settled before suit was filed by the claimant).

Also see Sabri v. State Farm Fire & Casualty Insurance Company, 488 So.2d 362 (La.App., 3d Cir., 1986) (insured mistakenly shot his daughter who he feared was a burglar attempting to gain entry into his home).

Concerning the ambiguity arising from lack of a pleading, see § 9.1, below. The successful plea of probable cause in *Maxon* was not a negation of intent, but rather an assertion of privilege, as was the plea of self-defense in *Walters;* it would seem that the cases cannot be satisfactorily distinguished.

40. The focus is less on what consequence was intended and more upon why an action known to involve that consequence, or one like it, was taken. *Cf.* Brasseaux v. Girouard, 269 So.2d 590 (La.App., 3d Cir., 1972); Putnam v. Zeloff, 372 Mich. 553, 127 N.W.2d 374 (1964);

Also see Comment, *The Expansion of Insurance Coverage to Include the Intentional Tortfeasor,* 23 Loyola Law Review 122–143 at pp. 133–136 (1977); Annotation, *Insurance: applicability of provisions as to*

A cogent argument in support of providing insurance coverage for intentional harm that results from a negligent mistake can be made on the basis that regardless of whether the insured intended the impact on the victim, both the nature of the insured's behavior and the loss from liability for damages were fortuitous because they resulted from a mistake that is no worse in nature (from the perspective of public interests underlying insurance) than any other type of ordinary negligence. This argument is especially compelling if there is no clause in the insurance policy that precludes coverage of an intentional injury, and a court is therefore confronted only with determining the scope of the implied exception against coverage of nonfortuitous losses.

Extending coverage in this type of situation arguably is also consistent with a requirement of fortuity from the perspective of the insured. Even though the insured person was an "aggressor," an incorrectly perceived need to act in self-defense does not involve, in any sense, premeditated conduct. Thus, such a sequence of events can be viewed as fortuitous from the perspective of the person whose economic interest is protected.

(7) The Capacity to Act and Coverage for Intentional Torts

A clause excluding "injury * * * caused intentionally" may not preclude coverage when an insured is incapable of forming an "intent" within the meaning of that term as used in the liability insurance provision, even though a recovery against the insured is based on an intentional tort.[41] For example, in one case it was held that when a

injuries intentionally inflicted, where insured is injured because of mistake of identity, 8 A.L.R. 322–325 (1920), and Supplemented at 26 A.L.R. 129 (1923).

41. See, e.g., Rosa v. Liberty Mutual Insurance Company, 243 F.Supp. 407 (D.Conn.1965) (sixteen-year-old schizophrenic beat and shot a young girl; held recovery under personal liability coverage of homeowners policy of which the assailant was an additional insured); Ruvolo v. American Cas. Co., 39 N.J. 490, 189 A.2d 204 (1963) (insured shot and killed third person; held, if he did so while derangement deprived him of capacity to govern his conduct, acting on an irrational impulse, his act could not be treated as "intentional" as that term is used in policy exclusion).

But cf. Wagner v. Colonial Life & Accident Insurance Company, 380 S.W.2d 224 (Ky.1964), opinion on second appeal, 408 S.W.2d 612 (Ky.1966) (held, whether or not the killer of the insured had the mental capacity to form an intent to kill, the homicide was intentional within the meaning of a group life insurance policy exclusion of death caused by "injuries intention-

ally inflicted upon the Insured Employee by any other person"); State Farm Mutual Auto Insurance Co. v. Treas, 254 Md. 615, 255 A.2d 296 (1969) (insured denied intent to strike woman who stood in front of vehicle to stop it, with her hands on it, backing up, as insured drove it out driveway; insured accelerated and she fell under car and was dragged and killed; insured testified he blacked out and went berserk; held, trial court finding death was "caused by accident" was clearly erroneous; injuries could not be said to be "unforeseen, unusual or unexpected").

But cf. Aetna Life Insurance Company v. McLaughlin, 380 S.W.2d 101 (Tex.1964), 9 A.L.R.3d 1005 (1966) (held, if insured of accident policy committed the act of throwing himself in front of bus on highway his beneficiary could not recover, in face of clause precluding liability for "suicide, sane or insane," even on proof that he did not appreciate the physical consequences of his act). Wagner and McLaughlin can be distinguished from cases of liability insurance since they involved life or accident insurance and policy language different

six-year-old boy pushed a four-year-old girl, the boy knew that the contact would be offensive and thereby committed a battery which resulted in a broken arm. Nevertheless, the court still reasoned that for purposes of insurance coverage the injury "was not caused intentionally," but was an unintended result of the boy's conduct.[42]

(8) Professional and Business Liability Coverage for Intended Consequences

The principal reasons for disallowing insurance coverage for losses that result from intentional torts frequently are not applicable to liability coverage that is acquired by professionals (such as doctors or dentists) and businesses. This point is illustrated by a type of coverage question that could arise under a psychiatrist's medical malpractice insurance if a patient's claim were predicated on the theory that the doctor's actions involved an intentional tort. For example, if a psychiatrist has a patient committed to an institution because the doctor views the patient as dangerously psychotic, and as a result of such an involuntary commitment the psychiatrist subsequently is held liable on a theory of a false imprisonment, the patient's claim might be asserted as an intentional tort. If a defense on behalf of the psychiatrist based on privilege fails because of a negligent mistake, the insurer might deny liability for the psychiatrist's "intentional" actions. However, if the decision by the psychiatrist — which caused the patient to be confined — was taken in good faith, the loss should surely be treated as

from that of the clauses under discussion here.

See generally 1A APPLEMAN, INSURANCE LAW (Revised edition, 1965), at § 482.

42. Baldinger v. Consolidated Mutual Insurance Company, 15 A.D.2d 526, 222 N.Y.S.2d 736 (2d Dept.1961), *affirmed* mem. decision 11 N.Y.2d 1026, 230 N.Y.S.2d 25, 183 N.E.2d 908 (1962) (comprehensive personal liability coverage within a homeowners policy, including a provision against coverage for "injury * * * caused intentionally by or at the direction of the insured").

Cf. Haynes v. American Casualty Company, 228 Md. 394, 179 A.2d 900 (1962) (insured's employees, being mistaken about location of boundary line, cut trees on land adjoining that on which they were supposed to be working; loss held to be "caused by accident" within meaning of liability policy); J. D'Amico Inc. v. Boston, 345 Mass. 218, 186 N.E.2d 716 (1962) (insurer required to defend action against insured in which the claimant's declaration was broad enough to state a claim for trespass by mistake).

Cf. York Industrial Center, Inc. v. Michigan Mutual Liability Company, 271 N.C.

158, 155 S.E.2d 501 (1967) (surveying mistake and damage to trees on 20-foot strip mistakenly believed to be insured's own land; coverage); City of Burns v. Northwestern Mutual Insurance Company, 248 Or. 364, 434 P.2d 465 (1967) (judgment sustaining insurer's demurrer and dismissing complaint reversed; intent to disinter and move body does not establish intent to cause resulting harm; tort complaint on which judgment was entered stated claim within coverage, even though there was no duty to defend against original complaint alleging the insured's act was done with malice).

Also see Eisenman v. Hornberger, 438 Pa. 46, 264 A.2d 673 (1970) (teenagers, including son of named insured of homeowners policy, broke into another person's house to steal liquor; one of the matches they used to find their way lodged in overstuffed chair and started fire; *held*, loss not intentionally caused within the meaning of exclusion clause; coverage for the teenage son).

Concerning duty of defense, see § 9.1, below).

fortuitous for purposes of a professional liability insurance policy. This argument for coverage is undoubtedly most persuasive as a response to an insurer's contention that a court should recognize an implied exception to an insured's coverage, but it also has considerable force with respect to the interpretation of any provisions in an insurance policy that are urged as a basis for limiting coverage in comparable situations.[43] In this type of circumstance, courts should treat such consequences as fortuitous.

There are various situations in which business enterprises may seek coverage for claims that, though they may be classified as suits based on harms intentionally caused by officers or employees, nevertheless involve losses in regard to which a persuasive argument can be made that they should be treated as fortuitous on the basis of an analysis that is similar to that set forth in the preceding paragraph.[44]

§ 5.4(e) Insurance Coverage for "Highly Expectable" Losses

There are many circumstances in which losses, especially when viewed retrospectively, seem to be appropriately considered as "highly expectable" events. Coverage for such losses is sometimes the subject of disagreements between insureds and insurers, and several of the concepts considered in the preceding portions of this chapter are frequently involved in assessing these coverage questions. First, ordinarily insurance does not provide indemnification for the type of economic detriments that occur so regularly that they are commonly regarded as a cost, rather than as an insurable risk, of an enterprise or activity.[1] Closely associated with this basic principle is the view that it

43. *Cf.* Sommer v. New Amsterdam Casualty Company, 171 F.Supp. 84 (E.D. Mo.1959), denying summary judgment for either plaintiff-insured or defendant insurer. The insured, a psychiatrist, settled a suit for assault brought by a patient wrongfully committed to a mental institution, then sought recovery against his malpractice insurer for the cost of his defense and the amount of the settlement. The insurer defended on the basis of a clause excluding from coverage "injury arising out of the performance of a criminal act * * *."

But cf. Transit Casualty Company v. Snow, 584 F.2d 97 (5th Cir.1978), *rehearing denied* 588 F.2d 828 (5th Cir.1978) (under Alabama law death that resulted when an ambulance attendant intentionally strapped a patient on his back despite the fact that the patient was regurgitating was not "caused by accident"); State v. Glens Falls Insurance Company, 137 Vt. 313, 404 A.2d 101 (1979) (general liability insurer did not provide coverage for damages which resulted from a sheriff's sale of a

mobile home owned by a corporation with a name similar to that of the corporation against which the sheriff was authorized to proceed).

44. See generally Allen, *Coverage Problems in Libel, Slander and Assault and Battery Cases*, 1968 ABA SECTION INSURANCE, NEGLIGENCE & COMPENSATION LAW PROCEEDINGS 531; Dane, *Insurance of Liability for Business Torts*, 2 Forum 85 (1967).

Cf. Brant v. Citizens Mutual Automobile Insurance Company, 4 Mich.App. 596, 145 N.W.2d 410 (Div. 1, 1966) (Comprehensive General Liability Insurance Policy provided coverage when a business sold the wrong type of heater).

§ 5.4(e)

1. The proposition set out in the text should not be understood to suggest that coverage is precluded for losses that result from an insured's own negligence. Most insurance contracts clearly do provide such coverage. For example, see the cases collected in Annotation, *Liability insurance:*

is fundamentally inconsistent with the legitimate purpose of an insurance arrangement for one to seek to use it as protection against calculated risks that one would have chosen not to take had no insurance been available.[2]

In addressing losses which appear to be "highly expectable," courts have often, and sometimes misleadingly, described particular types of losses as "foreseeable" rather than referring to them as "calculated risks," "highly expectable" losses, or some similar characterization that would distinguish them from the type of foreseeable losses that are routinely treated as a risk that is appropriately covered by liability insurance coverage.[3]

The discussion in the following subsections illustrates the range of coverage questions presented by various types of situations in which — at least arguably — there are highly expectable losses, and some of the judicial responses to various types of situations. Although most of the cases cited and the questions considered in the discussion involve liability insurance, the concepts developed in these subsections may also apply to various first party insurance coverages such as property insurance and, at least in some instances, life and accident insurance.

(1) Business Costs

Ordinarily, insurance does not provide indemnification for the type of economic detriments that occur so regularly that they are commonly regarded as a "cost of doing business," rather than as an insurable risk of an enterprise or activity. This proposition underlies some broad preclusions of liability that are specified in insurance policy clauses, as well as several narrower implied exceptions (which were discussed in a preceding section)[4] that are recognized in the absence of explicit insurance policy provisions.

(2) "Calculated Risks"

The results of an insured's act have been held not to be accidents when, though the insured did not intend those results, the court considered that the insured had intended to take a calculated risk.[5]

"accident" or "accidental" as including loss resulting from ordinary negligence of insured or his agent, 7 A.L.R.3d 1262–1274 (1966).

Nevertheless, some courts, when ruling on fact situations involving highly expectable losses, have used language susceptible of interpretation as applying more generally to "foreseeable" losses. For example, in Wynglass v. Prudential Life Insurance Company of America, 68 Mich.App. 514 at p. 518, 242 N.W.2d 824 at p. 826 (1976), the court concluded that a death which was "foreseeable" by a decedent was not accidental.

Coverage generally is not provided for intentional losses, and this is discussed in § 5.4(b), above.

2. See § 5.4(e)(2) below.

3. Consider the cases collected in Annotation, *Liability insurance: "accident" or "accidental" as including loss resulting from ordinary negligence of insured or his agent,* 7 A.L.R.3d 1262–1274 (1966).

4. See § 5.3(a), above.

Cf. Patterson's explanation of the friendly fire exception, § 5.3(d), above.

5. See, e.g., City of Carter Lake v. Aetna Casualty and Surety Company, 604 F.2d

The rationale for such decisions has often been that the loss was the "normal" or "foreseeable" result of the insured's intentional or negligent conduct [6] and, therefore, not an accident.[7]

One approach to explaining judicial decisions in this area is based on drawing distinctions between highly expectable losses and those that

1052 (8th Cir.1979) (once city was alerted to sewage backup problem and the likelihood of reoccurrence, the city could not ignore the situation and then look to its insurer for reimbursement for liability incurred as a result of inaction); City of Aurora v. Trinity Universal Insurance Co., 326 F.2d 905 (10th Cir.1964), 7 A.L.R.3d 1257 (1966) (insured maintained sewer system known to be inadequate during periods of heavy rainfall, which were not infrequent; *held,* liability policy did not cover loss to property caused by backed up sewage).

Also see Albuquerque Gravel Products Co. v. American Employers Insurance Co., 282 F.2d 218 (10th Cir.1960) (insured built a ramp in an arroyo, a normally dry watercourse, in such a way that it diverted water onto adjoining land during heavy rainfall; held no coverage under liability policy for loss thus caused by flooding); Casper v. American Guaranty & Liability Insurance Co., 408 Pa. 426, 184 A.2d 247 (1962) (insured contractor failed adequately to seal off area being remodeled from other areas in same building; held no coverage under liability policy for loss due to the settling of dust and debris on merchandise of a shopowner in the building).

Cf. Gassaway v. Travelers Insurance Co., 222 Tenn. 649, 439 S.W.2d 605 (1969) (storm sewer leaked so house foundation settled; developer-insured, knowing of the risk failed to disclose it to buyer, who made claim for damage to house; no coverage); Town of Tieton v. General Insurance Co. of America, 61 Wash.2d 716, 380 P.2d 127 (Dept. 2, 1963) (town had been warned that proposed sewer installation might contaminate nearby wells but proceeded with plan anyway; held no coverage for loss due to contamination).

Also see McGroarty v. Great American Insurance Co., 36 N.Y.2d 358, 368 N.Y.S.2d 485, 329 N.E.2d 172 (1975), *reargument denied* 36 N.Y.2d 874, 371 N.Y.S.2d 1029, 332 N.E.2d 364 (1975).

6. See especially the line of cases in the Tenth Circuit represented by *City of Aurora v. Trinity Universal Ins. Co.* and *Albuquerque Gravel Prods. Co. v. American Employers Insurance Co.,* note 5, above; these later cases have virtually dissipated hopes, based on the opinion in Hutchinson Water Co. v. United States Fidelity & Guaranty Co., 250 F.2d 892 (10th Cir.1957), that this court had come to appreciate the unacceptable implications of its extraordinary construction of "caused by accident" and like phrases.

Cf. Calvert Fire Insurance Co. v. Little, 421 S.W.2d 584 (Ky.1967) (no recovery under collision coverage for damage allegedly sustained when truck passed over drainage ditch; impact was not "unforeseen, accidental, sudden or violent" and not such "as normally could be calculated to cause damage," and was not a "collision" in either the ordinary sense or the policy sense).

7. Denying coverage on this rationale is difficult to reconcile with allowing coverage in motor vehicle negligence cases in which the relevant policy language is the same. Indeed, it is generally recognized that motor vehicle liability insurance extends even to cases of gross negligence and recklessness. See, e.g., Peterson v. Western Casualty & Surety Company, 5 Wis.2d 535, 93 N.W.2d 433 (1958) (insured, chased and stopped by police, rapidly backed his car in an attempt to escape, striking the plaintiff officer, who had opened the insured's car door; jury finding that insured did not intentionally injure plaintiff sustained by court, stating that although insured was probably guilty of gross negligence, and although such conduct may be treated as the equivalent of intentional wrongdoing for some purposes, it is not so treated for the purpose of an intentional-injury exclusion in a liability policy).

But cf. American Surety Company v. Gold, 375 F.2d 523 (10th Cir.1966), 20 A.L.R.3d 335 (1968) (forecasting Kansas law; disallowing coverage for punitive damages as a matter of public policy and observing that this would require juries to distinguish between ordinary negligence and gross and wanton negligence).

Also see § 5.3(g), above, concerning the argument for an implied exception as to punitive damages.

are less expectable.[8] This is, of course, a distinction of degree, involving case by case findings, so that it is difficult to formulate precise standards.[9] Also it seems likely that courts applying such a standard will tend to resolve doubts in favor of coverage.[10]

(3) Coverage for Nuisances

Tort actions based on damages resulting from the existence of an alleged nuisance often present issues regarding coverage for highly expectable losses. In some cases, courts have concluded that the effects of a nuisance maintained by an insured were not "caused by accident" within the meaning of liability coverage.[11] The principle of denying coverage for "calculated risks" appears to have been a significant influence on the resolution of disputed claims of liability insurance coverage for nuisances. For example, it seems likely that this is the principle influencing opinions that refer to "foreseeability" of a loss as a reason for affirming denials of coverage, without taking note of the fact that some foreseeable losses are commonly covered in negligence cases.

8. *Cf.*, e.g., Harleysville Mutual Casualty Company v. Harris & Brooks, Inc., 248 Md. 148, 235 A.2d 556 (1967) (smoke and soot damage from fires intentionally set in ten to twelve foot high brush piles, topped with tires and fuel oil, during clearing of wooded tract; held, not "caused by accident"; "not 'an event that takes place without one's foresight or expectation,'" quoting the definition of accident in Webster's Twentieth Century Dictionary, 1950).

9. Concerning evaluative findings generally, see § 1.4, above.

10. *Cf.* Baker v. American Insurance Company of Newark, 324 F.2d 748 (4th Cir. 1963) (South Carolina law; extraordinary rainfall and grading of site for shopping center combined to cause flooding of neighboring lands; held, an accident, even though the court expressed in dictum the untenable view that "[o]rdinarily, 'accident' would exclude an event caused by negligence or nuisance alone and followed by a foreseeable or natural consequence, for then neither the cause nor the effect is unexpectable"); Ramco, Inc. v. Pacific Insurance Company, 249 Or. 666, 439 P.2d 1002 (1968) (coverage for claim against manufacturer of electric baseboard heaters based on "actual loss" sustained when defective heating coils "failed to produce the heat they were designed to produce"; precise nature of the loss not disclosed, but demurrer sustained to count for "consequential loss of good will and credit").

Also see Taylor v. Imperial Casualty & Indemnity Company, 82 S.D. 298, 144 N.W.2d 856 (1966) (damage to adjoining property from underground leakage of gasoline from storage tanks was caused by accident); Bosko v. Pitts & Still, Inc., 75 Wash.2d 856, 454 P.2d 229 (Dept. 2, 1969) (damage done by slide of waste material was accidental; damages included cost of stabilizing against future slides, materials requiring stabilization being on the claimant's land so a trespass had already occurred).

11. See, e.g., Clark v. London & Lancashire Indem. Company, 21 Wis.2d 268, 124 N.W.2d 29 (1963), 98 A.L.R.2d 1037 (1964) (loss caused by rats, flies, hydrogen sulfide gas, and odors from refuse dumped into gravel pit operated by insured).

Cf. Harleysville Mutual Casualty Company v. Harris & Brooks, Inc., 248 Md. 148, 235 A.2d 556 (1967) (smoke and soot damage to nearby owners from intentionally set fires was not "caused by accident"); Farmers Elevator Mutual Insurance Company v. Burch, 38 Ill.App.2d 249, 187 N.E.2d 12 (4th Dist.1962) (loss caused by dust, noise, and vibrations from insured's operation of a grain elevator).

Also see Annotation, *Injury from nuisance maintained by insured as within coverage of public liability policy,* 98 A.L.R.2d 1047–1054 (1964).

(4) Coverage for Defective Products

For a manufacturer of products, the expectability of loss may be gauged in terms of recurrence, and highly expectable losses could be characterized generally as a "cost" rather than a "risk" of the insured business. To a very considerable extent, concern about products liability coverage was the impetus for the 1966 revision of many liability insurance forms, and this may have been a major factor in the decision that led the drafters to include the requirement that the bodily injury or property damage not be "expected" from the point of view of the insured. This requirement appears in the definition of "occurrence" as "an accident, including injurious exposure to conditions, which results, during the policy period, in bodily injury or property damage neither expected nor intended from the standpoint of the insured." [12]

The term "expected" should be (and probably will be) construed by courts in the sense of a high degree of expectability.[13] In the products liability context, as in other contexts,[14] this interpretation is also compatible with the principle that liability insurance should not cover the kinds of "calculated risks" that one would not take but for the expectation that liability insurance would cover the consequences.

(5) First Party Coverage for Losses Resulting From Medical Treatment

When an insured dies as a consequence of a medical treatment, claims by beneficiaries for accidental death benefits under either life insurance policies (providing larger insurance payments when an insured's death was accidental) or an accident policy have often presented difficult and controversial coverage questions. For example, it has been held the medical complications following a kidney transplant (which was performed without mishap or mistake) were "entirely foreseeable" and accordingly there was no coverage under an accident policy that provided coverage for "loss of life" that resulted "directly and independently of all other causes *through bodily injury by accident.*" [15] The resolution of this case is fully consistent with several earlier decisions which held that when an insured elects to undergo a serious operation that is not necessitated by a previous accidental injury, an insurance policy providing coverage for accidental death does not extend benefits when death results from the surgery (competently performed) or postsurgical complications even though the death may not have been expected.[16]

---

12. See the insurance forms in Appendix G and Appendix H.

13. Indeed, an interpretation even less favorable to insurers is supported by precedent.

14. Also see Even, *The Corporate Insurance Administrator—Problems With the 1966 Revised Liability Policy,* 3 Forum 95–

106 (ABA Section Insurance, Negligence & Compensation Law, 1968).

15. Body v. United Insurance Company of America, 72 Ill.App.3d 594, 28 Ill.Dec. 820, 391 N.E.2d 19 (1st Dist., Div. 3, 1979).

16. See, e.g., Preferred Accident Insurance Co. v. Clark, 144 F.2d 165 (10th Cir. 1944) (applying the law of New York);

Courts have sustained claims for accidental death benefits when a medical procedure that normally is relatively safe, such as an anesthetic administered for dental work, produced a fatality.[17] In general, the results in such cases are appropriately viewed as highly fact sensitive.[18]

(6) Incredibly Foolish Conduct: Herein of a "Damn Fool" Doctrine

As the discussion in the preceding subsections has indicated, insurers have formulated numerous insurance policy provisions that preclude coverage for risks that are not viewed as fortuitous. Furthermore, courts have interpreted these coverage provisions and applied public policy considerations so that insurance does not apply for losses that result from certain types of conduct or activities — that is, losses from some types of risks are judged to be inappropriate for being "shifted" to an insurer. Although the general basis for the rejection of coverage claims in many situations is often evident, in some instances the rationales or explanations for the results either appear to involve rather strained applications of the legal doctrines or the resolution of the cases seem to be idiosyncratic. From an examination of a substantial number of such judicial decisions, both those interpreting insurance policy provisions and those precluding coverage on the basis of public policy concerns that justify the judicial recognition of implied exceptions, it seems apparent that courts usually sustain an insurer's denial of claims when the losses result from incredibly foolish conduct.

A "damn fool" doctrine is embodied in the statement that insurance coverage, especially liability insurance, is not provided for acts which are simply too ill conceived to warrant allowing the actor to transfer the risk of such conduct to an insurer. There are numerous illustrations of judicial decisions that can be better explained or understood by such a doctrine than by any other rationale. For example, an ambulance attendant who straps down an injured person despite the fact that the individual is regurgitating has been held not to be covered because it was not caused "by accident," but it seems clear that such a result — to the extent that it is to be justified — would be more comprehensible if the explanation of the decision were based on the proposition that the attendant's conduct was so incredibly foolish for any

Pope v. Prudential Insurance Company of America, 29 F.2d 185 (6th Cir.1928).

But cf. the comments of the court in INA Life Insurance Company v. Brundin, 533 P.2d 236 (Alaska 1975), 91 A.L.R.3d 1027 (1979) (death resulted from a cardiac arrest following surgery of hemorrhoids).

17. See, e.g., Schleicher v. General Accident, Fire, & Life Assurance Corp., 240 Ill. App. 247 (1926) (nitrous oxide gas used in connection with the extraction of a tooth).

18. Also, in the Annotation, *Death during or allegedly resulting from surgery as accidental or from accidental means within coverage of health or accident insurance policy,* 91 A.L.R.3d 1042–1056 at p. 1044 (1979), the annotator observed "Close construction of policy language has been most apparent in those cases involving policy provisions insuring against death through 'accidental means.' "

person employed in such a position that liability coverage should not provide indemnification for such conduct.[19]

The holding that there is no coverage when a sheriff seizes and sells property owned by a corporation with a name that is somewhat similar to that of the corporation against whom the sheriff was actually authorized to act, is within the ambit of this doctrine.[20] Similarly, when an insured "rammed" the rear fender of an occupied vehicle which was blocking a traffic lane in a parking lot, thereby injuring an occupant of the other car, the exclusion for intentionally caused injuries undoubtedly provides a rationale that justified precluding coverage, but the appropriateness of the result in this case is also readily understood when it too is viewed as an example of a "doctrine" that excludes coverage for "damn foolish" actions.[21]

When a city is alerted to a sewage backup problem in the basements of homes which results from the recurring failure of the city's equipment and the city then fails to repair or replace the equipment, a judicial decision declaring that coverage is not provided by the city's insurance is not surprising even though it is clear that the city did not specifically intend the harms that were subsequently sustained.[22] Nevertheless, most observers would almost certainly view the city's inaction as very unwise, indeed incredibly foolish, given the evidence about the past problems. And the same observation applies for smoke and soot damage to adjacent property that resulted when ten to twelve foot piles of brush were topped with tires and fuel oil before being set afire, especially given the prevailing wind direction at the time.[23]

19. See Transit Casualty Company v. Snow, 584 F.2d 97 at p. 99 (5th Cir.1978), *rehearing denied* 588 F.2d 828 (5th Cir. 1978) (applying Alabama case law that to "be caused other than 'by accident,' death or injury need not be an intended or expected result but merely one which is reasonably foreseeable.")

Also see Harleysville Mutual Casualty Company v. Harris & Brooks, Inc., 248 Md. 148, 235 A.2d 556 (1967) (soot and smoke produced by adding rubber tires to large piles of trees being burned damaged homes of adjacent property owners). The court observed that "a contractor who piles trees and underbrush in 10 to 12 foot piles, adds fuel oil and rubber tires, and permits [it] to burn for 36 hours before they are extinguished should be charged with the responsibility of foreseeing that a pall of smoke and soot will result, which may damage adjacent properties." *Id.*, 248 Md. at p. 154, 235 A.2d at p. 559.

The rationale of these cases is plainly too broad to be harmonized with insurance coverage for grossly negligent driving.

20. See State v. Glen Falls Insurance Company, 137 Vt. 313, 404 A.2d 101 (1979).

21. See Subscribers at the Automobile Club Inter-Insurance Exchange v. Kennison, 549 S.W.2d 587 (Mo.App., St. Louis Dist., Div. 1, 1977).

Also see Farmers Automobile Insurance Association v. Medina, 29 Ill.App.3d 224, 329 N.E.2d 430 (2d Dist.1975) (insurer found to have no obligation to defend under a homeowner's liability coverage for damage to a vehicle that resulted from a fire caused by a minor who intentionally flipped lit matches at a spot of gasoline located behind the rear bumper of the vehicle); Cloud v. Shelby Mutual Insurance Company of Shelby, Ohio, 248 So.2d 217 (Fla.App., 3d Dist., 1971) (insured intentionally used his vehicle to attempt to disperse a crowd around his wife).

22. See City of Carter Lake v. Aetna Casualty and Surety Company, 604 F.2d 1052 (8th Cir.1979) (applying Iowa law).

23. Harleysville Mutual Casualty Company v. Harris & Brooks, Inc., 248 Md. 148, 235 A.2d 556 (1967).

All of these situations involve "calculated" decisions by insureds. There are many instances in which an insured's course of conduct was intentional, but the consequences which resulted, though highly expectable, were clearly not intended or desired by the insured. When one attempts to predict whether a court will negate an insurer's decision to reject coverage under a liability insurance policy in such cases, an analytical approach that is worth considering is whether the insured's actions fall into the category of incredibly foolish conduct.

The "damn foolish acts" concept is not a perfect predictor of judicial decisions, both because of its own imprecision and because other considerations, such as a desire to assure an innocent third party a source of indemnification, may influence a court. However, especially when providing a source of indemnification for an innocent victim is not a compelling consideration because there is reason to believe that the insured who acted foolishly has sufficient resources to provide compensation to the injured persons, analysis of a coverage issue on the basis of a "damn fool" doctrine is frequently a very effective approach both to predicting and to understanding outcomes.

Caveat. When motor vehicle liability insurance is involved, the substantial public interest in assuring a source of indemnification is usually the dominant consideration, so that the scope of coverage typically is extended to acts of gross negligence which might otherwise be appropriately viewed as being with the scope of a "damn fool" doctrine.[24]

§ 5.4(f)   Failure of an Insured to Prevent an Injury

Many insurance contracts include provisions which require insureds to take steps that either (1) may prevent losses from initially occurring or (2) will prevent additional losses from happening after an insured event has occurred. These provisions, which are often referred to as "protection-of-property" clauses, generally are included in various types of property insurance.

(1) Clauses Designed to Prevent Losses From Occurring

Property insurance for structures often includes clauses that are concerned with whether a structure is occupied. For example, homeowners insurance policies commonly include a clause precluding coverage for loss "resulting from freezing while the building covered is vacant or unoccupied, unless the insured shall have exercised due diligence with respect to maintaining heat in the building, * * *"[1] And, fire insurance policies generally specify

---

24. Also see the discussion of motor vehicle insurance in § 4.9, above.

§ 5.4(f)

1. See, e.g., the Homeowners Policy in Insurance Information Institute, Sample Insurance Policies, Property-Liability

Coverages, Advanced Book (1969) at p. 89 and p. 94. Also see Appendix I.

It has been held, however, that one may exercise due diligence "with respect to" maintaining heat by leaving the heat off and employing a qualified person to place

that an insured must "use all reasonable means to save * * * the property * * * when the property is endangered by fire in neighboring premises." [2]

(2) Clauses Designed to Prevent Additional Losses

Various types of property insurance policies contain provisions that are concerned with an insured's failure to protect against additional losses to property which has been damaged but not destroyed by an event of the type against which the insurance policy offers protection. For example, the standard fire insurance policy — under a clause headed "perils not included" — lists "neglect of the insured to use all reasonable means to save and preserve the property at and after a loss." Homeowners insurance policies usually include the same or comparable clauses. And motor vehicle insurance policies covering physical damage to the insured vehicle customarily provide that if a loss occurs the insured shall protect the vehicle, "whether or not the loss is covered by this policy, and any further loss due to the insured's failure to protect shall not be recoverable under this policy; reasonable expenses incurred in affording such protection shall be deemed incurred at the company's request; * * *" [3].

Provisions that require insureds to prevent additional losses have been construed by courts to mean that the limitation only restricts coverage in situations in which the insured's failure to protect the vehicle is negligent. This result is often predicated on the rationale that the failure to act is not a legal cause of the additional loss unless such a failure constitutes negligence. [4] It may even be argued, with the support of analogies from other areas of insurance law, that gross negligence or worse should be required to defeat a claim for such an added loss. [5]

An insured who takes steps to protect an insured property after a partial loss has occurred should be entitled to recover from the insurer any reasonable costs incurred in protecting property in such circumstances. In general, it would be consistent with the doctrine

anti-freeze in the system and test its adequacy, even though it later turns out to have been inadequate. Palmer v. Pawtucket Mutual Insurance Co., 352 Mass. 304, 225 N.E.2d 331 (1967).

2. See Appendix A.

3. See Appendix H.

4. See, e.g., Centennial Casualty Company v. Snyder, 142 Colo. 198, 350 P.2d 337 (1960) (after a collision with a telephone pole, the insured drove the car home, thinking that only its fender and bumper were damaged; in fact, the brake fluid line was broken and a wheel was flat, and the continued operation of the car caused the

fluid to ignite, burning a wheel, a tire, and the car; held recovery); Runner v. Calvert Fire Insurance Company, 138 W.Va. 369, 76 S.E.2d 244 (1953), 44 A.L.R.2d 1075 (1955) (insured ran over large rock on highway in construction area and, unaware that the collision had caused an oil leak, continued driving, which caused additional damage to the car; *held*, judgment for the insured affirmed since the question of violation of the protection clause had been properly submitted to the jury).

5. Compare the precedents concerning negligence or gross negligence leading to the initial loss, § 5.3(e), above.

of avoidable consequences to recognize that an insured would be entitled to recover the reasonable costs incident to preventing additional losses after the occurrence of an insured event even when it is not expressly provided for in an insurance policy.[6] And the same analysis applies when an insured takes action which prevents additional losses to property owned by other persons when the insurer would be liable — under coverage afforded by a liability insurance policy — in the absence of the preventive measures taken by the insured.[7]

The 1966 revision of the motor vehicle liability insurance forms introduced a provision that presents an interesting question. In the "conditions" section, the insurance policy terms require that the named insured "promptly take at his expense all reasonable steps to prevent other bodily injury or property damage from arising out of the same or similar conditions, but such expense shall not be recoverable under this policy."[8] When an insurer asserts that an insured's failure to take specified protective measures bars or limits the insurer's liability, surely the amount of expense that would have been involved is relevant to the issue whether the suggested measures come within "all *reasonable* steps."

Comment

Protection-of-property clauses are designed to preclude recovery for a certain type of accidental harm because of the policyholder's negligence. Thus, in a sense, they are contrary to the more general approach of insurance coverages that provide indemnification for losses even when they result from a policyholder's own carelessness. Although such coverage limitations are nonetheless defensible because of their modest scope and the general desirability of minimizing losses whenever possible, as exemplified by the mitigation doctrine applicable to all contracts, the scope of the insured's duty to protect property should be restricted by adopting a relatively narrow construction for provisions which require an insured to protect property after a loss.

6. Also see RESTATEMENT OF TORTS, Second (1979), at § 918 and § 919. Section 919(2) states, "One who has already suffered injury by the tort of another is entitled to recover for expenditures reasonably made or harm suffered in a reasonable effort to avert further harm."

Motor vehicle insurance policies often contain a clause explicitly so providing.

7. See, e.g., Bankers Trust Company v. Hartford Accident and Indemnity Company, 518 F.Supp. 371 (S.D.N.Y.1981), *order vacated* 621 F.Supp. 685 (1981), where the court concluded oil seepage was affecting use of property by third party owners, work was done on insureds' property to prevent further oil seepage from pipe located on the property was as a matter of law within the scope of liability policies covering personal injury and property damage to third persons arising from ownership and control of property. It was undisputed that oil would have continued to seep into the river had insured not taken preventive measures.

8. See Appendix G and Appendix H.

This approach can be justified in most situations on the basis of honoring reasonable expectations.[9]

§ 5.4(g) The Effect of Providing Coverage for "Occurrences" Rather Than "Accidents"

Many insurance contracts now use the term "occurrence" instead of the term "accident." The term "occurrence" — which is usually defined to mean "an accident, including injurious exposure to conditions, which results, during the policy period, in bodily injury or property damage neither expected nor intended from the standpoint of the insured * * *"[1] — was probably employed by the drafters to avoid an implication that there was no coverage for a continuing condition, as distinguished from a sudden event.[2] Given the broaden-

---

9. See generally § 6.3, below.

Cf. Bankers Trust Company v. Hartford Accident and Indemnity Company, 518 F.Supp. 371 at p. 374 (S.D.N.Y.1981), *order vacated*, 621 F.Supp. 685 (1981).

§ 5.4(g)

1. See, e.g., the insurance forms in Appendix G and Appendix H.

See State v. Glen Falls Insurance Company, 137 Vt. 313, 404 A.2d 101 at p. 103 (1979); Lombard v. Sewerage & Water Board of New Orleans, 284 So.2d 905 at p. 915 (La.1973).

Also see Aetna Casualty & Surety Company v. Freyer, 89 Ill.App.3d 617, 44 Ill. Dec. 791, 411 N.E.2d 1157 at p. 1159 (1st Dist., Div. 4, 1980).

Perhaps, however, the intent was to broaden coverage only by covering ongoing exposures as well as sudden events, and not in a sense related to degree of expectability.

In Foxley & Company v. United States Fidelity and Guaranty Company, 203 Neb. 165, 277 N.W.2d 686 (1979), the court concluded that there was no coverage under such a policy for damages caused by a mistake of law.

2. E.g., Address by H.G. Mildrum [a member of the industry committee responsible for drafting the 1966 forms], Chartered Property and Casualty Underwriters Seminar (Oct. 12, 1966). See generally Bruce D. Hall, *Contractors' Liability Insurance for Property Damage Incidental to Normal Operations—The Standard Coverage Problem,* 16 University of Kansas Law Review 181–207 at pp. 203–207 (1968).

Cf. McGroarty v. Great American Insurance Company, 36 N.Y.2d 358, 368 N.Y.S.2d 485, 329 N.E.2d 172 (1975), *reargument denied* 36 N.Y.2d 874, 371 N.Y.S.2d 1029, 332 N.E.2d 364 (1975) (whether an

accident occurred within the meaning of the term as used in an insurance policy when damage to a building resulted from several months of excavation and construction on adjacent property was a question of fact).

Cf. Massachusetts Turnpike Authority v. Perini Corp., 349 Mass. 448, 208 N.E.2d 807 (1965). The Massachusetts Supreme Judicial Court, considering a liability policy using the term "occurrence" and rejecting coverage of loss that was "inevitable" in a public construction project and for which the contractor-insured was not liable to the government, stated: "One purpose of the substitution of the word 'occurrence' for 'accident' may have been to include in the coverage a suitable provision for indemnity against injuries * * * gradually occurring * * *. The use of the term 'occurrence' also may be designed to expand the coverage so that it will be more nearly as extensive as negligence and possibly also other forms of tort liability." 349 Mass. at pp. 456–457, 208 N.E.2d at p. 813. And, assuming the insurance contract to have been designed to cover the liability assumed by Perini under the construction contract, the court stated as dictum: "[The insured] will be liable [under the construction contract] only if its acts or omissions were tortious by reason of negligence or strict liability, *maintaining a nuisance, * * * or otherwise.*" 349 Mass. at p. 454, 208 N.E.2d at p. 811 (emphasis added).

Also see Aerial Agricultural Services of Montana, Inc. v. Till, 207 F.Supp. 50 (N.D. Mississippi, 1962) (policy defining "occurrence" as an "accident" or a "condition created by the insured which during the policy period accidentally causes injury or destruction provided that such condition, injury or destruction is not caused by accident"; held, coverage of insured's liability

ing of coverage which appears to result from this terminology, the limitation of coverage in terms of degree of expectability of loss may become a more significant question.[3]

Coverage which is based on an "occurrence" seems to establish or describe a boundary between covered and noncovered losses that would preclude coverage for some "expected" losses for which liability is imposed under the law of gross negligence, or even the law of negligence. There is precedent, however, for the position that "expected" as used in this type of insurance policy provision is to be understood as practically equivalent to "intended."[4] Whether or not this interpretation comes to be generally accepted, it is evident that courts have many precedents for examining the question of what is "expected" or "intended" from the point of view of someone other than the person who is the actor causing injury. Also, even though an insured actor's point of view may be relevant in regard to the scope of liability for an intentional tort as well as insurance coverage, it is clear that some losses for which liability is imposed under the theory of intentional tort have been covered by liability insurance despite express policy provisions and judicially recognized implied exceptions.[5]

§ 5.5　Causation Problems

§ 5.5(a)　Introduction

Insurance policy provisions which define or limit the scope of insurance as to losses that either "do" or "do not" result from certain "causes" or "types of causes" are often at the center of insurance disputes. The discussion in the following subsections provides a general introduction to the classification and the effects of insurance provisions that are concerned with causation questions, and then focuses on several causation-coverage issues which have been the subject of significant amounts of litigation.

(1) The "Cause-Event-Result" Trichotomy

The determination of whether particular losses are transferred to an insurer often depends upon causation questions. In discussions about the application of the insurance policy provisions that relate to

---

to farmer for damage resulting when a seeding device that was intentionally used as designed nevertheless improperly distributed seed); Gilbert L. Bean, *The Accident Versus the Occurrence Concept*, 1959 Insurance Law Journal 550–558.

3. *Cf.* Bruce D. Hall, *Contractors' Liability Insurance for Property Damage Incidental to Normal Operations—The Standard Coverage Problem*, 16 University of Kansas Law Review 181–207 at pp. 203–207 (1968); John T. Even, *The Corporate Insurance Administrator—Problems with the 1966 Revised Liability Policy*, 3 Forum 95–106 (ABA Section Insurance, Negligence & Compensation Law 1968).

4. State Farm Fire & Casualty Co. v. Muth, 190 Neb. 248, 272, 207 N.W.2d 364 (1973) ("expected" construed "to practically equate with 'intended' ").

Also see Hartford Fire Insurance Co. v. Wagner, 296 Minn. 510, 207 N.W.2d 354 (1973); Glens Falls Group Insurance Co. v. Hoium, 294 Minn. 247, 200 N.W.2d 189 (1972).

5. See § 5.4(d) above.

the scope of coverage to various types of occurrences that produce losses, the terms "cause," "event," and "result," are frequently employed in the analysis. Unfortunately, these terms do not carry any uniform or precise meaning, and sometimes there is considerable doubt about meaning in this context.

Whenever human experiences extend over a period of time, it is possible to select one point in the sequence of events and consider the situation that existed at that moment from several perspectives: first, focusing on the circumstances existing at that moment as the vantage point from which to analyse the sequence of events which preceded and followed; second, focusing on that set of circumstances as a result of what has gone before; and third, focusing on that set of circumstances as a cause of what is yet to come. Even when the focus is clearly stated, however, it is still necessary to be selective about what is described or characterized, because it is humanly impossible to identify every detail. Accordingly, whenever there are questions about causation, the analysis can only focus on some portion of (1) the facts that comprise circumstances which exist at any specific moment, (2) the later events that are treated as its results, and (3) the antecedent events that are treated as its causes. Thus, although insurance policy provisions and the interpretations of these terms sometimes predicate the existence of coverage on distinctions that relate to the elements of the "cause-event-result" trichotomy, unfortunately the analysis is often less than clear because of the lack of any prevailing criteria for selecting from all the existing circumstances those that are relevant to the interpretation and application of the provisions at issue in a given context.

(2) Patterson's Classification System

A carefully constructed system of terminology and classification for insurance contract terms involving various aspects of causation was developed by Professor Patterson.[1] In this system, "coverage" provisions are those that serve to identify the risk.[2] Coverage provisions are distinguished from contract terms relating to potential causes of a loss, which are characterized as "warranties."[3] An "exception" in this classification system concerns a cause of the insured event, and is thus an antecedent link in the chain of causation;[4] an "exclusion" concerns

§ 5.5(a)

1. This system of terminology appears in Patterson, ESSENTIALS OF INSURANCE LAW (Second edition, 1957), as well as in other writings by Professor Patterson. This system is discussed in a review of Patterson's book by Professor Keeton, which appeared in 36 Texas Law Review 545–553 at p. 547–549 (1958).

2. Patterson, ESSENTIALS OF INSURANCE LAW (Second edition, 1957), at p. 230.

3. *Id.,* at pp. 230–231 and p. 273. A more detailed treatment of Patterson's concept of warranty appears in § 6.6, below.

"Coverage" provisions include statements of the insured event, "exceptions," the subject matter of insurance and "exclusions" from the subject matter, interests insured, "consequences of the insured event" declared either to be covered or not to be covered, duration of the insurance, and the amount of insurance. See Patterson, ESSENTIALS OF INSURANCE LAW (Second edition, 1957), at pp. 230–235.

4. An "exception" is a provision limiting the insurer's liability in terms of a cause of the insured event; the cause to which it refers is an "expected cause."

the central link, the event. Patterson's system also used "consequences" as a term of art to further distinguish between an "exception" and an "exclusion";[5] the "consequence" of the insured event is a subsequent link.[6]

Most courts and writers have not accepted Patterson's terminology at all;[7] others have accepted it only to a very limited extent and even then, it seems, without faithful or accurate use.[8]

(3) Exceptions and Exclusions

Another approach to classifying and characterizing various insurance policy provisions which relate to causation has been to use the term "exceptions" to refer to all provisions preceded by the word "except" whenever they are set forth in an insurance policy under the heading "Insured Agreements," and to use the term "exclusions" for all provisions that appear under the heading "Exclusions."[9] The latter (aside from exclusions of certain persons or of certain kinds of property)[10] generally are used to limit the insurer's liability in terms of an event. Accordingly, an event to which such a provision applies is an "excluded event" both in Patterson's terminology[11] and in the lexicon that is commonly used by insurers.

(4) Conclusive and Inconclusive Causation Clauses

Insurance contract terms may also be categorized or analyzed in terms of whether the declared effect of a provision is conclusive against coverage (an exclusion in Patterson's terminology) or instead is inconclusive in that it is merely a declaration that a certain kind of cause of loss is not an affirmative basis of recovery (an exception in Patterson's terminology), leaving open the possibility of some other basis for recovery. However, the language or phrasing used for insurance policy provisions is often far from clear with respect to whether a particular clause is intended to be conclusive against coverage. This type of

Patterson, ESSENTIALS OF INSURANCE LAW (Second edition, 1957), at p. 249.

5. *Ibid.*

6. *Id.* at p. 267.

7. See, e.g., 4 APPLEMAN, INSURANCE LAW (Revised edition, 1969), at § 2303, omitting any reference to Patterson's terminology, speaking in a way inconsistent with it, and citing opinions that do likewise.

8. See, e.g., 2 RICHARDS, LAW OF INSURANCE (Fifth edition, Freedman, 1952), at § 208:

"An Excepted Cause or Exception Clause generally provides that an insurer is not liable for loss or damage if the Insured Event actually resulted from or was caused by the subject matter of the Excepted Cause or Exception Clause * * *. The Exclusion Clause simply excludes from coverage certain events

which otherwise would fall within the scope of the Insured Event."

9. In Patterson's terminology, however, an "exclusion" is distinguished from an "exception" not on the basis of the place where it appears or the heading under which it appears in the policy form, but rather on grounds concerned with the kind of condition of liability it imposes. Patterson, ESSENTIALS OF INSURANCE LAW (Second edition, 1957), at p. 232.

10. For example, in the automobile comprehensive coverage in effect when Patterson was writing, "This policy does not apply * * * to robes, wearing apparel or personal effects * * *" Patterson, ESSENTIAL OF INSURANCE LAW (Second edition, 1957), at p. 232.

11. *Id.* at p. 249.

problem is well illustrated by the provisions in a property insurance policy which were invoked by an insurer when a claim was presented as the result of the destruction of a residence that had been built at the top of a bluff overlooking a lake.[12]

The owner of the residence sought insurance benefits when landslides occurred after heavy rains and severe faults appeared in the ground immediately under the house. The owner's claim was rejected by the insurer on the basis of the following provisions which were set forth as exclusions:

> **"Exclusions:** This Policy Does Not Insure Against: * * *
>
> B. Loss by * * * normal settling * * *; this Exclusion, however, shall not apply to loss by * * * Landslide, Total or Partial Collapse, Water Damage, and Glass Breakage, caused by perils excluded in this paragraph;
>
> C. Loss by surface waters, flood waters, waves, tide or tidal waves, high water, or overflow of streams or bodies of water, all whether driven by wind or not * * *."[13]

Evidence at the trial indicated that over the years waves and high water on the lake, driven against the bluff by storms, had combined with heavy rains to create extensive erosion.

The trial court instructed the jury, in effect, that if the loss was caused by a combination of covered and non-covered causes, they should find for the claimant. The jury found for the claimant, and when a judgment on the verdict was affirmed, the appellate court observed that "the jury presumably found [first] that the erosion and action of high water, surface water and waves were not predominant and efficient causes of the landslide * * *"[14] and, second, that "the factors causing the landslide at or near the time of the loss were the constant rainfall, the increase of weight from water percolating into the clay and the presence of a huge weight of ground water in clay-sand strata lying 20 to 30 feet below the top of the bluff * * *."[15] With these findings established by the jury's decision, the appellate court then resolved ambiguities in the policy clauses against the insurer.

The provisions in this policy concerning landslides certainly are unclear. For example, the term "normal settling" in clause "B" under the heading "Exclusions" may be an "excepted cause" in Patterson's terminology, and "Landslide" in this clause would therefore be either an exception from this "excepted cause" of "normal settling" or perhaps merely something that is to be distinguished from "normal settling."[16] The clause appears to imply that landslide is not an "excepted cause," and certainly not an "excluded event." Arguably it implies

12. Fireman's Fund Insurance Company v. Hanley, 252 F.2d 780 (6th Cir.1958).

13. *Id.,* 252 F.2d at pp. 781–782.

14. *Id.,* 252 F.2d at p. 784.

15. *Id.,* 252 F.2d at p. 786.

16. A *"normal* settling" restriction such as that in the *Hanley* case has been construed to permit coverage for sudden and extraordinary settling. See, e.g., Prickett v. Royal Insurance Company Limited, 56 Cal.2d 234, 14 Cal.Rptr. 675, 363 P.2d 907

that landslide is a covered cause, particularly in view of the provision that the policy covers "All Physical Loss" except that referred to in the "Exclusions."

The provision concerning surface water, in clause "C" under the heading "Exclusions," appears to be, in Patterson's terminology, an "excepted cause" provision. Perhaps it could be interpreted as an "exclusion," but one that would not be applicable unless surface water is the predominating cause. This question was not reached in the appellate decision because the court held that surface water was not a substantial cause, the water being regarded as no longer surface water once it had gone into the ground one inch.[17]

In general, the judicial precedents display a strong tendency to favor interpreting insurance policy provisions so as to preserve the possibility that coverage will exist.[18] Nevertheless, there are decisions in which courts have construed some types of insurance policy clauses relating to causation as conclusive against coverage in certain types of situations.[19] Of course, the particular language of an insurance policy may clearly express an intent that a coverage restriction creates a situation in which there is a clause that is conclusive against coverage despite the fact that there is a contributing cause that would otherwise be a basis for extending coverage. If there is any doubt about the import of such coverage language in an insurance policy, however, courts will usually decline to treat a particular provision as conclusive against the existence of coverage.[20] This result is usually justified on one of several theories, including (1) resolving ambiguities against the

---

(1961), 86 A.L.R.2d 711 (1962) (one wall of insured house settled five to twelve inches very suddenly due to improper earth fill underneath it; held, sudden settling to the extent involved in the present case was not "normal" settling within meaning of restriction).

17. The trial court charged, "if you find as a fact that the damage to the plaintiffs' property resulted from a combination * * * of causes within the coverage of the policy and causes excluded from the coverage of the policy, * * * the plaintiffs are entitled to recover in this action." Fireman's Fund Insurance Company v. Hanley, 252 F.2d at p. 783. The trial court instruction treated all the qualifying terms as "excepted cause" provisions in Professor Patterson's sense.

18. Also see § 6.3, below.

19. See, e.g., Aetna Insurance Co. v. Boon, 95 U.S. (5 Otto) 117, 24 L.Ed. 395 (1877) (insurance on stock of goods in Glasgow, Missouri, in 1864; stipulation that "the company shall not be liable to make good any loss or damage by fire which may happen or take place by means of any invasion, insurrection, riot, or civil commo-

tion, or of any military or usurped power"; commander of Union forces set fire to city hall to prevent stores from falling into hands of opposing troops, and fire spread through two intermediate buildings to the building containing the insured goods; held, not covered).

Also see United States Fidelity & Guaranty Company v. Morgan, 399 S.W.2d 537 (Tex.1966); Paulson v. Fire Insurance Exchange, 393 S.W.2d 316 (Tex.1965), and Hardware Dealers Mutual Insurance Co. v. Berglund, 393 S.W.2d 309 (Tex.1965). These three Texas decisions give conclusive, "excluded event", effect to provisions in windstorm policies against liability for loss caused by such things as rain, tidal wave, high water, or overflow, "whether driven by wind or not"; the insured is allowed to recover, however, for so much of his loss as he can prove to have been caused solely by a covered cause, such as windstorm, before a non-covered cause, such as flooding, could have had any effect on the property.

20. In Professor Patterson's terminology, the clause is treated as an exception.

insurer,[21] (2) disallowing unconscionable advantage,[22] or (3) honoring reasonable expectations of policyholders [23] who cannot be expected to read complex policy provisions closely enough (that is, with sufficient attention or comprehension) to discover and appreciate the insurer's intent to preclude coverage in some described circumstance, even if that intent is unambiguously clear to one who takes sufficient time and trouble to exhaustively study all the details of the coverage terms.

Comment

The limitations in insurance policy provisions in regard to causation terms do not usually involve practices that are as pernicious as those which often prevailed in regard to warranties.[24] Nevertheless, clauses which specify causation limitations may often be intended by insurers to be conclusive in character. When such terms are involved in litigation, courts frequently are disturbed by their effects and accordingly adopt interpretations that accord them an "inconclusive" effect. In this context, the explicit or implicit determination by a court that a clause is "inconclusive" may be expressed by one of several judicial responses, including the construction of ambiguities in such provisions, the protection of reasonable expectations, and the preclusion of the enforcement of unfair limitations. Thus, the treatment of coverage terms that relate to causation is not unlike that accorded in an earlier era to warranty provisions which were viewed with skepticism, dismay, and outright hostility by courts and, subsequently, by legislatures.[25]

§ 5.5(b) Causation in Relation to Collision and Comprehensive Coverages in Motor Vehicle Insurance

Insurance claims resulting from various types of loss producing events involving motor vehicles have been a fertile field for disputes about whether a particular set of facts satisfies causation criteria based on the meaning of the term "collision." [1] Many of these disputes are at least in part a consequence of the marketing of motor vehicle insurance policies that offer purchasers both *collision coverage* and *comprehensive coverage* as options that each provide a distinct type of protection for injury to an insured vehicle.[2]

In the coverage terms which are widely used for motor vehicle collision insurance, the insurer agrees to pay the insured for physical damage for loss "caused by collision." Insurers who use this provision

---

21. See § 6.3(a)(2), below.

22. See § 6.3, below.

23. See § 6.3, below.

24. See § 5.7, below. Also see § 6.6, below.

25. *Ibid.*

§ 5.5(b)

1. "Collision" is used both in relation to the coverage for collision as such and in

relation to a limitation on the scope of "comprehensive" coverage.

2. The possibility of double coverage for a loss is specifically addressed in such insurance policies by a provision that states a limit of the insurance company's liability for loss to any one covered automobile. See Appendix H.

for the collision insurance generally define the comprehensive insurance in terms of providing coverage for a loss " * * * from any cause *except collision*." [3] The standard coverage terms also provide:

> "For the purpose of this coverage, breakage of glass and loss caused by missiles, falling objects, fire, theft or larceny, windstorm, hail, earthquake, explosion, riot or civil commotion, malicious mischief or vandalism, flood, or (as to a covered automobile of the private passenger type) colliding with a bird or animal, shall not be deemed loss caused by collision; * * *." [4]

Thus, in these insurance policy clauses, insurers assign a considerably narrower meaning to the term "collision" when it is used in defining the comprehensive coverage than when it is used to define the coverage afforded by "collision insurance." [5]

---

3. *Cf.* Patterson, ESSENTIALS OF INSURANCE LAW (Second edition, 1957), at p. 232. In Patterson's terminology, the question is whether the language "except collision" is an "exclusion" or instead only an "exception." See § 5.5(a)(2), above. Patterson took the view that the corresponding language in earlier versions of this clause was an "exception." Patterson, ESSENTIALS OF INSURANCE LAW (Second edition, 1957), at p. 232. His interpretation of the provision as inconclusive of coverage is supported by the results reached in most decisions. See, e.g., Friedman v. Insurance Company of North America, 4 Wis.2d 641, 91 N.W.2d 328 (1958), 68 A.L.R.2d 1417 (1959).

Also see § 5.5(a)(1), above.

4. See Appendix H. Family automobile policy forms have included provisions of generally similar import. See, e.g., Automobile Physical Damage Part of the Combination Automobile-General Liability Policy in the American Mutual Insurance Alliance Study Kit distributed in 1969.

Also see Watkins v. American Security Insurance Company, 129 Ga.App. 566, 200 S.E.2d 304 (Div. 1, 1973) (damage to a car which resulted from high winds that caused a chimney to fall was not caused by "collision" within the meaning of an automobile policy's coverage).

5. The special-purpose definition of "collision" used to limit the extent to which the phrase "except collision" confines the scope of the *comprehensive* coverage is plainly narrower than "collision" in the ordinary sense. In that context, the narrower definition produces broader coverage for the policyholder.

In contrast, a policyholder who has *collision* coverage is favored by giving "collision" a broader meaning. In this latter context, some courts have construed "collision" in varying senses that go beyond

what might be considered the "ordinary sense" of "collision." See, e.g., Trinity Universal Insurance Company v. Evans, 93 Ariz. 9, 377 P.2d 1020 (1963) (driver of truck carrying insured tractor lost control, and truck went off the road and down into a ravine, striking the bottom of it; held, coverage under policy insuring against loss to the tractor caused "by * * collision * * * of any conveyance upon which the Caterpillar [tractor] is being transported"); Tuten v. First of Georgia Insurance Company, 117 Ga.App. 409, 160 S.E.2d 903 (Div. 2, 1968), 34 A.L.R.3d 988 (1970) (insured's car totally destroyed by submersion in salt water when it slipped down boat ramp into river while car was parked and motor was not running; held, collision coverage applied because there was a collision between car and water).

Also see Payne v. Western Casualty & Surety Company, 379 S.W.2d 209 (Mo.App., Kansas City 1964) (the wheels of the insured tractor-trailer rig slipped off the paved highway onto the shoulder, the softness of which caused an abrupt stop that wrenched the heavily loaded trailer; held, a collision); Morton v. Blue Ridge Insurance Co., 255 N.C. 360, 121 S.E.2d 716 (1961) (the insured car accidentally rolled down a boat ramp into a canal; held, a collision).

But see, e.g., Mercury Insurance Company v. McClellan, 216 Ark. 410, 225 S.W.3d 931, 14 A.L.R.2d 806 (1950) (insured cars were damaged as the result of a tornado, one by having a brick wall and timber blown upon it, another by being rolled over several times and being blown into a tree; held, no coverage under "collision and upset" provisions, since the policies contained an express provision for windstorm damage, which the insureds had not purchased, and a provision that limited the insurance

Interesting coverage questions can be produced by unusual circumstances when a purchaser has opted to acquire only one of these coverages. For example, in one case an automobile — which was insured under comprehensive coverage, but not under collision coverage — was driven into a large accumulation of water on a roadway (a pool of water 50 feet long and eight inches deep), and thereafter the car went up an embankment and finally turned over. Evidence was offered, on behalf of the claimant, that the vehicle's tie rod was bent by the force of the impact with the water, and that this caused a loss of control over the vehicle's direction of movement. The insurer conceded that the comprehensive coverage applied to "loss caused by water," but asserted that this type of accidental loss was not covered by the comprehensive coverage. The court concluded that the damage was not a "loss caused by water" within either the ordinary sense of the terms or the sense as used in the insurance policy.[6]

The narrower meaning of the term "collision" that is generally used in defining the limitation on the scope of coverage provided by comprehensive insurance plainly expresses the sense that occurrences of certain types — including, for example, damage to a vehicle caused either by windstorm [7] or by the impact of a falling object on a car [8] — will be covered under comprehensive insurance, even though such a loss results from a "collision" in the broadest sense of that term. The policy language itself is not entirely clear, however, as to whether indemnification is provided under a comprehensive coverage when there was also some other cause for the damage that is within the meaning of the phrase "any cause except collision." [9]

When a loss is a consequence of a combination of events which includes a collision, an insured ordinarily will be allowed to recover

to coverages for which a premium had been paid).

An expansive view of collision coverage has been encouraged, perhaps, by the inclusion of the word "upset" in the definition of collision coverage in policy forms. See Appendix H.

6. Harris v. Allstate Insurance Company, 309 N.Y. 72, 127 N.E.2d 816 (1955). Also see Tuten v. First of Georgia Insurance Company, 117 Ga.App. 409, 160 S.E.2d 903, 34 A.L.R.3d 988 (Div. 2, 1968) (total loss of a parked automobile that slipped into a salt water stream was damage caused by "collision" of automobile with another object).

7. Cf. Friedman v. Insurance Company of North America, 4 Wis.2d 641, 91 N.W.2d 328 (1958), 68 A.L.R.2d 1417 (1959) (tractor-trailer overturned in executing a left turn in strong winds; that the windstorm could not have produced the result without the aid of centrifugal force does not defeat recovery under windstorm coverage since

it is not necessary that wind be the sole cause).

8. For opinions observing this distinction and sustaining claims of collision coverage against arguments that the narrower meaning of "collision" in the comprehensive clause should be applied, see, e.g., Barnard v. Houston Fire & Casualty Insurance Company, 81 So.2d 132 (La.App. 2d Cir. 1955), 54 A.L.R.2d 374 (1957).

Also see Jones v. Virginia Surety Company, 145 Mont. 440, 401 P.2d 570 (1965).

9. In other words, it is not clear whether "except collision" is a conclusive clause, intended to defeat coverage if a collision occurred, or is instead an inconclusive clause which merely says that a collision is not itself an affirmative basis for liability under the comprehensive coverage, thus leaving the issue of liability to be decided by answering the question whether there was some other circumstance of the loss that would be a sufficient basis for liability.

under a comprehensive coverage if some factor in the combination is one plainly among those which would be within the comprehensive coverage. For example, courts have so ruled when a fire [10] or a theft [11] was a cause of an ensuing collision. On the other hand, if a collision produces a fire and the owner of the vehicle had comprehensive insurance, but not collision coverage, courts usually either restrict the insurer's liability to only that part of the damage caused by fire,[12] or find that there is no liability.

§ 5.5(c)   Multiple Causes and Coverage Limitations

The problem of determining the effect of insurance provisions relating to causation has repeatedly arisen in instances in which the loss can reasonably be viewed as attributable to more than one cause. In such instances, courts typically consider whether at least one of the contributing factors that causes the loss is a risk covered by the insurance policy.[1]

When an insurance policy provides coverage for losses produced by some causes and excludes coverage for losses from other causes, courts frequently hold that coverage extends to the loss even though an excluded element is a contributory cause.[2] Furthermore, in assessing

---

10. Tonkin v. California Insurance Company, 294 N.Y. 326, 62 N.E.2d 215 (1945), 160 A.L.R. 944 (1946).

Similar results have been reached in relation to other types of restrictions on comprehensive coverage. See, e.g., Standard Accident Insurance Company v. Christy, 235 Ark. 415, 360 S.W.2d 195 (1962) (a fire of unexplained origin burned the radiator and air conditioner hoses of the insured car while it was being operated; water from the radiator extinguished the fire, but the loss of water in the cooling system caused severe damage to the motor before the insured became aware of the fire and was able to stop the car; held, coverage for the entire loss under comprehensive coverage excluding loss due to mechanical failure, which the insurer argued included the damage to the motor caused by overheating).

Also see Smith v. M.F.A. Mutual Insurance Company, 337 S.W.2d 537 (Mo.App., Kansas City 1960) (gas leaking from the load of a propane tank-truck was ignited by some unknown source, and the resulting fire caused heavy damage to the truck; held, recovery under coverage excluding loss "caused by bottled or compressed gas"; reasoned, however, on the ground that the loss was not "caused by" though it may have arisen from compressed gas).

11. Bolling v. Northern Insurance Company, 280 N.Y. 510, 19 N.E.2d 920 (1939) (thief abandoned insured car; collision oc-

curred while policeman was driving it to police station).

12. See, e.g., Mammina v. Homeland Insurance Company of America, 371 Ill. 555, 21 N.E.2d 726 (1939).

§ 5.5(c)

1. See, e.g., Sabella v. Wisler, 59 Cal.2d 21, 27 Cal.Rptr. 689, 377 P.2d 889 (1963) (loss caused by settling covered since settling was caused by flooding from sewer pipe that resulted from negligence of building contractor).

Also see Sauer v. General Insurance Company of America, 225 Cal.App.2d 275, 37 Cal.Rptr. 303 (2d Dist., Div. 2, 1964) (perils covered included accidental discharge of water from plumbing; break in water pipe beneath house; clauses under the heading "Exclusions" pertaining to water damage, earth movement, settlement, and cracking; *held*, efficient cause was peril insured against and "Exclusions" were inapplicable).

2. See, e.g., General American Transportation Corporation v. Sun Insurance Office, Ltd., 369 F.2d 906 at pp. 906–908 (6th Cir.1966), adopting the rule from the decision in Fireman's Fund Insurance Co. v. Hanley, 252 F.2d 780 at p. 785 (6th Cir. 1958).

Also see Dow Chemical Company v. Royal Indemnity Company, 635 F.2d 379 at p. 391 (5th Cir., Unit A 1981); Essex House v.

the scope of coverage, courts will trace the causal links to ascertain whether there is a factor or element which is a type of loss or cause that is covered by an insurance policy.[3] As the Supreme Court of Oregon observed, "It is an established rule of insurance law that where a peril specifically insured against sets other causes in motion which, in an unbroken sequence and connection between the act and final loss produces the result for which recovery is sought, the insured peril is regarded as the proximate cause of the entire loss." [4]

Courts may also preserve an insured's right to coverage by invoking the proximate cause concept to limit the effect of a coverage restriction or limitation.[5] For example, it has been held that damage from an explosion incident to a fire was covered under a fire insurance policy although the portion of the damage directly caused by the force of the explosion would not otherwise be covered.[6] Similarly, it has been

St. Paul Fire & Marine Insurance Company, 404 F.Supp. 978 (S.D.Ohio 1975).

Cf. Auto Owners Insurance Company v. Allen, 362 So.2d 176 (Fla.App. 2d Dist. 1978).

3. See, e.g., Goodyear Rubber & Supply, Inc. v. Great American Insurance Company, 545 F.2d 95 (9th Cir.1976) (when the peril insured against caused damage by occurrence of an explosion and fire, thereby setting a salvage operation in motion, insurance policy provided coverage for a loss which resulted from an unbroken sequence of events in the course of the salvage operation); Grain Dealers Mutual Insurance Company v. Belk, 269 So.2d 637 (Miss.1972) (windstorm policy applied to additional damages to a house which occurred in the course of attempting to remove a branch that had punched a hole through a roof when it fell during a windstorm).

Also see Atlantic Mutual Fire Insurance Company v. W.R. Chadwick, 115 Ga.App. 850, 156 S.E.2d 182 (1967) (loss that resulted when lightning ignited a fire which destroyed a valve head thereby allowing water to escape causing a wooden floor to buckle and subsequently mildew was a direct loss by lightning within the meaning of policy provisions).

4. Gowans v. Northwestern Pacific Indemnity Company, 260 Or. 618 at p. 621, 489 P.2d 947 at p. 948 (1971), *rehearing denied* 260 Or. 618, 491 P.2d 1178 (1971). *Accord.,* Qualls v. Farm Bureau Insurance Company, 184 N.W.2d 710 at p. 713 (Iowa 1971).

The *Gowans* court, using a phraseology more common in older than in current cases, refers to the insured peril as "*the* proximate cause." (Emphasis added). It is sufficient to sustain liability, of course, to

find that an event within the insured peril was "*a* proximate cause," that is, a legally responsible cause.

In relation to insurance law, as well as tort law, references to "the proximate cause" are likely to be misleading. *Cf.* Prosser and Keeton, Torts (Fifth edition, 1984) § 41 at p. 266: "[I]nstructions to the jury that they must find the defendant's conduct to be 'the sole cause,' or 'the dominant cause,' or 'the proximate cause' of the injury are rightly condemned as misleading error."

5. See, e.g., Cincotta v. National Flood Insurers Association, 452 F.Supp. 928 (E.D. N.Y.1977), in which the court concluded that losses resulting from the flooding of a basement to height of 20 inches when a water channel overflowed was the *immediate* and *direct* cause of the settling of the foundation even though the occasional presence of water in the basement to a depth of about two inches from seepage may have previously weakened the foundation within the meaning of a preexisting conditions clause.

Also see Pan American World Airways, Inc. v. Aetna Casualty & Surety Company, 505 F.2d 989 at pp. 1006–1009 (2d Cir. 1974); Aetna Insurance Company v. Getchell Steel Treating Company, 395 F.2d 12 at pp. 17–18 (8th Cir.1968).

6. See, e.g., Cook v. Continental Insurance Company, 220 Ala. 162, 124 So. 239 (1928), 65 A.L.R. 921 (1930) (concussion damage from explosion set off by firemen); Wheeler v. Phenix Insurance Co., 203 N.Y. 283, 96 N.E. 452 (1911) (evidence sustained finding that fire preceded explosion in grain elevator).

Also see Merrimack Mutual Fire Insurance Co. v. Lanasa, 202 Va. 562, 118 S.E.2d 450 (1961), 82 A.L.R.2d 1118 (1962) (evi-

held that damage to a house from freezing which occurred after vandals cut off the heat was within vandalism coverage, even though a provision in the insurance policy disallowing coverage for losses that result from changes in temperature would in other circumstances have precluded coverage for such damage.[7]

Courts also mitigate the effects of insurance policy clauses that restrict coverage by adopting a "narrow" construction for the scope of the limitation. An illustration of this approach can be seen in the appellate court decisions which conclude that a provision excluding damage resulting from a failure in an electrical system does not preclude recovery by insureds under fire insurance when an electrical malfunction results in a fire that destroys property outside of the electrical system.[8] Another example of this type of approach is provided by a decision in which the court reasoned that a clause stating that there shall be no coverage "for any loss resulting from change in temperature" only restricts coverage when a loss is "directly caused" by change of temperature.[9] When this type of contract interpretation is adopted, such a clause does not preclude coverage for a loss which is "directly caused" by vandalism, and which is subsequently aggravated by a change of temperature. Of course, there is only coverage for the loss when a covered risk is a contributing factor that causes the loss. Thus, if there is a change of temperature that causes damages by freezing and additional damage is subsequently caused by vandalism, the loss caused by the freezing still would not be covered because the freezing occurred before the vandalism.

dence sustained finding that fire preceded explosion in fruit storage building).

But see, e.g., Levert-St. John, Inc. v. Birmingham Fire & Casualty Co., 137 So.2d 494 (La.App. 3d Cir.1961) (applying the exclusion because the explosion was set off by a "friendly" fire, a welder's arc. See § 5.3(d), above, concerning the general distinction between "friendly" and "hostile" fires); and Garfield Mutual Fire and Storm Insurance Association v. Calhoun, 532 S.W.2d 663 at p. 666 (Tex.Civ.App., Corpus Christi 1975), in which the court held that when there was a question whether the loss was caused solely by an explosion (and not by an antecedent fire), the claimant "must show that there was a fire and that the fire was a 'hostile fire.'"

Also see Annotation, Construction and application of provision in fire policy specifically excepting loss by explosion unless fire ensures, 82 A.L.R.2d 1125–1144 (1962).

7. Fawcett House, Inc. v. Great Central Insurance Company, 280 Minn. 325, 159 N.W.2d 268 (1968). Of course, the problem is often more complicated than merely choosing between interpreting the policy provision as conclusive against coverage or

instead inconclusive, as to which see § 5.5(a)(4) above.

8. See, e.g., Aetna Insurance Company v. Getchell Stell Treatment Company, 395 F.2d 12 (8th Cir.1968); Witherwax v. Zurich Insurance Company, 315 So.2d 420 (La.App. 3d Cir.1975).

Also see Annotation, Loss by heat, smoke or soot without external ignition as within standard fire insurance policy, 17 A.L.R.3d 1155–1172 at pp. 1161–1162 (1968); and the discussion in § 5.3(d), above, of "The Friendly Fire/Hostile Fire Rule."

9. Fawcett House, Inc. v. Great Central Insurance Co., 280 Minn. 325, 159 N.W.2d 268 (1968).

Extended far enough, however, this kind of construction and reasoning produces the same result as classifying a clause as inconclusive. Treating such a provision as an inconclusive causation clause would also mean that a "change of temperature" would not itself be a basis for coverage, but that coverage would exist for a loss even though a change of temperature contributed so long as there was another contributing cause that was covered by the policy. See § 5.5(a)(4), above.

In practice, coverage will usually be provided whenever a loss is attributable to some risk that is among those transferred by the applicable insurance — that is, courts generally maximize the scope of protection by adopting any interpretation that may be fairly made of the language in an insurance policy.[10]

§ 5.5(d) Problems of Legal (Proximate) Cause: Tort versus Contract

Courts and writers have both observed that there are basic differences between principles of legal cause that apply to tort claims and those that apply either to contract disputes in general or to insurance claims in particular. For example, Judge (later Justice) Benjamin Cardozo remarked that "there is a tendency [in tort law] to go farther back in the search for causes than there is in the law of contracts * * *."[1] Cardozo added, "Especially in the law of insurance, the rule is that, 'You are not to trouble yourself with distant causes.' "[2]

Other courts have made statements which appear to set out an even more extreme position than that suggested by Judge Cardozo's comments. For example, one court observed that in tort law proximate cause "is not limited to one link back in the chain of causation * * *" and that "it excludes the immediate physical cause of injury, with which insurance is concerned, from its purview and includes any number of unbroken links of causation with which insurance is not concerned."[3] Although similar views can be found in numerous decisions, there are several reasons why such statements should be viewed with a substantial amount of skepticism.[4]

---

10. Beaulieu v. Minnehoma Insurance Company, 44 Wis.2d 437, 171 N.W.2d 348 (1969).

In Zimmer v. Aetna Insurance Company, 383 So.2d 992 at p. 994 (Fla.App. 5th Dist., 1980), the court commented, "To limit the policy to the rare circumstance urged by Aetna would defeat the claimed protection which is behind the purpose of having the insurance policy."

Cf. Graham v. Public Employees Mutual Insurance Company, 98 Wash.2d 533, 656 P.2d 1077 (1983) (holding it was a question for the jury to decide whether damages to an insured's home caused by mudslides that resulted from the eruption of Mt. St. Helens was a loss that was excluded by the coverage terms).

§ 5.5(d)

1. Bird v. St. Paul Fire & Marine Insurance Company, 224 N.Y. 47 at p. 53, 120 N.E. 86 at p. 88 (1918), 13 A.L.R. 875 at p. 878 (1921) (denying liability, under a policy including fire insurance on a canal boat, for concussion damage from an explosion about 1,000 feet distant from the boat, the

explosion being part of a chain of events started by a fire in a freight yard).

2. *Id.,* 224 N.Y. at p. 53, 120 N.E. at p. 88.

3. Bruener v. Twin City Fire Insurance Company, 37 Wash.2d 181 at p. 184, 222 P.2d 833 at p. 835 (1950), 23 A.L.R.2d 385 at p. 388 (1952). *Bruener,* however, was specifically overruled in 1983. See the following note.

4. In Graham v. Public Employees Mutual Insurance Company, 98 Wash.2d 533 at pp. 537–538, 656 P.2d 1077 at pp. 1080–1081 (1983), the court commented:

"* * * we conclude the immediate physical cause analysis is no longer appropriate and should be discarded. The *Bruener* rule is an anomaly, inconsistent with the rule in the majority of other jurisdictions. We have defined 'proximate cause' as that cause 'which, in a natural and continuous sequence, unbroken by any new, independent cause, produces the event, and without which that event would not have occurred.' Stoneman v. Wick Constr. Company, 55

First, although the statement is made in older judicial decisions (and some recent decisions, as well) that for the purpose of determining whether insurance coverage applies "the proximate cause" is "the efficient" or "predominant cause," this language does not appear to have been employed as a distinctive theory for insurance law.[5] More often, judicial comment is based on the assumption that problems of proximate cause in tort and insurance cases are essentially alike.[6] An examination of tort cases from the same time period as these older insurance decisions will confirm that similar statements appear in the tort decisions.[7]

Second, the results reached in many insurance cases clearly are not compatible with the view that insurance law is exclusively concerned with only the immediate and not the more distant causes, or with only the efficient or predominant and not other causes.[8] Rather, when there

Wash.2d 639, 643, 349 P.2d 215 (1960). Where a peril specifically insured against sets other causes in motion which, in an unbroken sequence and connection between the act and final loss, produce the result for which recovery is sought, the insured peril is regarded as the 'proximate cause' of the entire loss. [Citations omitted.] It is the efficient or predominant cause which sets into motion the chain of events producing the loss which is regarded as the proximate cause, not necessarily the last act in a chain of events. [Citations omitted.] The mechanical simplicity of the *Bruener* rule does not allow inquiry into the intent and expectations of the parties to the insurance contract. Sears, Roebuck & Co. v. Hartford Accident & Indem. Co., 50 Wash.2d 443, 313 P.2d 347 (1957). We now specifically overrule the *Bruener* case."

5. See, e.g., Graham v. Public Employees Mutual Insurance Company, 98 Wash. 2d 533, 656 P.2d 1077 at p. 1081 (1983) (evidence was for the jury as to whether eruption of Mt. St. Helens was proximate cause of mudflows which caused damage to the insureds' homes).

Cf. Lipshultz v. General Insurance Company of America, 256 Minn. 7, 96 N.W.2d 880 (1959) (interruption in the furnishing electric power for refrigeration as a result of a wind-caused break in power lines thereby causing a loss to the insured's foodstuffs constituted a "direct loss by windstorm").

Also see Hahn v. M. F. A. Insurance Company, 616 S.W.2d 574 (Mo.App., Southern Dist., Div. 3, 1981).

The idea that proximate cause is a more limited concept in insurance law than in tort law may have developed, at least partially, from the use of the phrase "direct loss * * *" in many insurance policies. However, this contractual provision specifying "direct loss" is rarely mentioned in insurance cases. See, e.g., the fire insurance form in Appendix A.

See generally, Annotation, *What constitutes "direct loss" under windstorm insurance coverage,* 65 A.L.R.3d 1128–1173 (1975).

6. See, e.g., Russell v. German Fire Insurance Company, 100 Minn. 528, 111 N.W. 400, 10 L.R.A. (N.S.) 326 (1907) (building gutted by fire but walls left standing; several days later a strong wind, expectable in that area, blew one of the walls down onto plaintiff's building; plaintiff recovered under his fire insurance policy; citing tort and insurance cases without suggesting that they involve different principles, the court observed, "what is meant by proximate cause is not that which is last in time or place, not merely that which was in activity at the consummation of the injury, but that which is the procuring, efficient, and predominant cause").

Note. The *Russell* decision was overruled by the Minnesota Supreme Court in 1959. See Strobel v. Chicago, Rock Island and Pacific Railroad Company, 255 Minn. 201, 96 N.W.2d 195 at p. 200, note 5 (1959).

7. See, Prosser and Keeton, TORTS (Fifth edition, 1984), § 41 at p. 266, approving later tort decisions condemning jury instructions referring to "the sole cause," or "the dominant cause," or "the proximate cause" as misleading error.

8. See, e.g., the decisions cited in notes 4, 5, and 6, above.

Also see Levert-St. John, Inc. v. Birmingham Fire & Casualty Company, 137 So.2d 494 (La.App., 3d Cir., 1961) (holding that

are several distinct or distinguishable factors which contribute to a loss, a persuasive case can be made for the proposition that courts will apply the causation theory that will relate the loss to a covered peril.[9] For example, it has often been held by courts that when a loss was caused jointly by an insured cause and another cause operating later in time, there is the requisite "direct loss by" the insured cause.[10] Indeed, along with his comment referred to above, Judge Cardozo observed that the concept of proximate cause is a matter of what would ordinarily be thought of as a cause of the loss.[11]

Observations

On the whole, it is reasonable to observe that in many of the insurance disputes involving causation questions, the application of the proximate cause doctrine is essentially similar to the conception of the doctrine in tort cases.[12] However, there are also numerous cases in

an explosion exclusion applied because the explosion was set off by a "friendly" fire, although explosion caused by hostile fire would be covered).

As to the general distinction between "friendly" and "hostile" fires, see § 5.3(d), above.

9. See especially Pan American World Airways, Inc. v. Aetna Casualty & Surety Company, 505 F.2d 989 at pp. 1006–1008 (2d Cir.1974) (coverage under an all risk insurance contract for an aircraft that was destroyed by hijackers in Egypt was not precluded by an exclusion clause for losses due to war, warlike operations, insurrection, etc.).

Cf. Graham v. Public Employees Mutual Insurance Company, 98 Wash.2d 533, 656 P.2d 1077 (1983).

See generally the cases cited in § 5.5(a), above.

10. See, e.g., Fred Meyer, Inc. v. Central Mutual Insurance Company, 235 F.Supp. 540 (D.Or.1964) (food spoilage caused by failure of refrigeration when windstorm destroyed electric power lines held a "direct loss by windstorm"); Providence Washington Insurance Co. v. Weaver, 242 Miss. 141, 133 So.2d 635 (1961) (both death of cattle resulting immediately from injuries received in collision and upset of the truck in which they were being carried and presumed death of cattle the last traces of which were tracks into quicksand along river's edge, where they proceeded when freed by the accident, held "direct loss by overturning" of the vehicle in which they were being transported).

Cf. 5 APPLEMAN, INSURANCE LAW (Revised edition, 1970), at § 3083.

11. See Bird v. St. Paul Fire & Marine Insurance Company, 224 N.Y. 47 at p. 52, 120 N.E. 86 at p. 87–88 (1918). Judge Cardozo observed that when "a collision occurs at sea and fire supervenes * * * the fire may be the proximate cause and the collision the remote one for purpose of an action on the [insurance] policy" even though the "collision remains proximate for the purpose of suit against the colliding vessel." Judge Cardozo also concluded that "[t]here is nothing absolute in the legal estimate of causation" and that "[p]roximity and remoteness are relative and changing concepts." *Id.,* 120 N.E. at p. 88. A modern court would be less likely to be concerned with "proximity."

Cf. Prosser and Keeton, TORTS (Fifth edition, 1984), § 42 at p. 273:

"The word [proximate] means nothing more than near or immediate; and when it was first taken up by the courts it had connotations of proximity in time and space which have long since disappeared. It is an unfortunate word, which places an entirely wrong emphasis upon the factor of physical or mechanical closeness."

Also see Cincotta v. National Flood Insurers Association, 452 F.Supp. 928 at p. 929 (E.D.N.Y.1977).

12. *Cf.* Bert W. Levit, *Proximate Cause—First Party Coverage,* 1965 ABA SECTION INSURANCE, NEGLIGENCE & COMPENSATION LAW PROCEEDINGS 157–170, reprinted 1966 Insurance Law Journal 340–357; John T. Gorman, A *Reply to "Proximate Cause—First Party Coverage,"* 34 Insurance Counsel Journal 98–106 (1967).

See also William Brewer, *Concurrent Causation in Insurance Contracts,* 59 Mich-

which causation questions that need to be addressed in order to decide whether a loss is covered by insurance are *not* resolved by an application of the proximate cause doctrine.

In some circumstances, the specific approach to a causation issue is appropriately explained and understood as a consequence of enforcing a particular contractual provision designed to limit the scope of protection provided by an insurance policy. Explicit provisions in an insurance policy regarding causes of a loss may provide either for broader or for narrower coverage than would result in the absence of a contractual specification.[13] Ordinarily, such insurance policy terms are enforceable, subject, of course, to overriding regulatory measures.[14]

In many instances, decisions on causation questions involving insurance policy terms are best understood as manifestations of the judicial inclination to favor coverage either by construing ambiguous policy provisions against an insurer or by protecting the reasonable expectations of an insured.[15]

§ 5.5(e)   Causation, Overlapping Coverages, the Indemnity Principle, and Premium Inequities

The inclusion of several different insurance coverages in a single insurance policy may produce situations in which the scope of the protection afforded by the coverages for an insured overlap — that is, a single occurrence causing a loss may give rise to claims under more than one coverage.

When two or more insurance coverages overlap, there is a possibility that insureds will make claims under more than one type of coverage. For example, in jurisdictions which allow a guest passenger in an automobile to recover on a tort claim against the driver, an injured passenger may be entitled to indemnification for medical expenses under both the bodily injury liability insurance and the medical expenses insurance of the same policy. The provision of overlapping insurance coverages creates a number of questions. In some instances, these questions may be addressed by an explicit provision in the insurance policy. In other cases, the resolution of the coverage question may be significantly influenced by either the indemnity principle

igan Law Review 1141–1190 (1961), which draws a contrast between tort and insurance cases with respect to the treatment of causation issues but perhaps is less at odds with the view expressed in the text above than might appear on the surface, since much of the contrast is concerned with the impact of contractual provisions in modifying rules of causation otherwise applicable.

13. Thus, for example, the rules of insurance law applicable to what Patterson calls excluded events are quite unlike the rules of proximate cause applied in torts cases and in other insurance cases, since these rules of insurance law deny recovery for losses arising from multiple causes some of which could have been affirmative bases for coverage but for an exclusionary provision. See § 5.5(a), above.

Situations in which a loss results from multiple causes sometimes involve not only the questions of interpretation referred to as the choice between conclusive and inconclusive clauses (between exclusions and exceptions in Patterson's terminology), but also problems that are appropriately characterized as legal cause questions.

14. See generally Chapter 6, below.

15. *Ibid.*

that is designed to avoid over-compensation for an insured loss or the public interest in affording indemnification for injuries.

(1) The Goal of Indemnifying and the Indemnity Principle

When several coverages apply to an occurrence, the extent of the injuries may be such that even the payment of all applicable insurance benefits will not provide complete indemnification for the losses sustained. In general, when injured persons are insured by several coverages, courts are inclined to allow a claimant to recover insurance benefits from the applicable insurance so long as it does not result in a violation of the indemnity principle. However, insurers have frequently sought to impose limitations on liability when two or more coverages included in a single insurance policy provide coverage for the same loss.

If an insured's injury is such that the payment of insurance under two or more coverages will produce a duplicate recovery, the result contravenes the principle that insurance is intended as no more than indemnity against loss. In such a situation, some courts have denied such a fortuitous profit for an insured.[1] The justification for crediting or offsetting the amount paid by one coverage from an insurer's liability under another coverage is most persuasive when the two coverages are part of a single insurance contract.

During most of this century, subrogation clauses[2] and offsets to avoid overpayment ordinarily have not been applied to medical payments coverage in the absence of a policy clause so providing.[3] However, since the mid 1960s subrogation clauses have increasingly been included in policy forms used for automobile medical payments insurance and various types of health insurance.

(2) Premium Inequities

One potential inequity from overlapping coverages concerns premium rates. For example, a loss may be construed as having been caused by a "collision" when an insured car crashes into a stream of water across a highway,[4] when debris falls on a car as the result of a windstorm that demolishes a building,[5] or when a car is "upset" by a

---

§ 5.5(e)

1. Insurance policy provisions that preclude or limit the insurer's liability are fully in accord with the principle of indemnity discussed in Chapter 3.

See § 5.9(a), below.

2. See the discussion of subrogation in § 3.10.

3. See the discussion in § 3.10(a)(7), above.

4. See, e.g., Providence Washington Insurance Company v. Proffitt, 150 Tex. 207, 239 S.W.2d 379 (1951).

Cf., e.g., cases cited in § 5.5(b), above.

5. See, e.g., United States Insurance Company v. Boyer, 153 Tex. 415, 269 S.W.2d 340 (1954).

Also see St. Paul Fire and Marine Insurance Company v. Smith, 280 Ala. 425, 194 So.2d 830 (1967) (concrete bin fell during a loading operation).

Cf., Jones v. Virginia Surety Co., 145 Mont. 440, 401 P.2d 570 (1965) (log felled in logging operation struck insured vehicle; held, within collision coverage); Barnard v. Houston Fire & Casualty Insurance Company, 81 So.2d 132 (La.App., 2d Cir., 1955), 54 A.L.R.2d 374 (1957) (a tree cut by workmen hit insured vehicle; held, within collision coverage).

windstorm.[6] In each situation it is likely that courts will find that the loss is covered if the insured has collision coverage, as well as when the insured has comprehensive coverage. It is also clear that when an insured has both collision and comprehensive insurance, only one recovery is allowed, both because the insurance policy clauses so provide and because any other result would usually violate the principle of indemnification.

If the premium for an insurance policy that includes collision *and* comprehensive coverages is equal to the sum of the premiums for the same coverages when purchased separately, the insured who buys both is in a sense paying twice for some portion of the insurance that provides for losses of this type. This is an inequity in the rate structure that favors persons who buy only one of the two coverages over persons who buy both. In most circumstances, the inequity is slight, and the interest in "equitable" rates is outweighed by the desirability of having each type of insurance include coverage for some types of losses which are difficult to classify as lying exclusively within either the collision or the comprehensive coverage.[7]

This type of premium inequity would generally be minimized if courts would adhere to a relatively narrow construction of the protection afforded by separate coverages — that is, the losses under an individual coverage are increased by expansive construction which allows either of the coverages to apply when the other coverage has not been obtained. One effect of the expansive construction of causation terms in different types of insurance is to increase the premium that must be charged for each of the individual coverages in order to provide the funds to pay claims.

When two types of insurance (which are both commonly purchased by insureds) provide indemnification for a given type of loss, the insureds who purchase both coverages in effect subsidize those insureds who opt to purchase only one of the coverages. This inequity among policyholders may be avoided, of course, by establishing a lower premium for the two overlapping coverages than the sum of the premiums for the two separately. This has been done in the marketing of some special package policies.

§ 5.5(f)   Observations

The determination of whether a particular risk has been transferred to an insurer is central to the analysis of insurance generally and individual claims in particular. Risks, in this sense, are fundamen-

But see, e.g., Watkins v. American Security Insurance Company, 129 Ga.App. 566, 200 S.E.2d 304 (Div. 1, 1973) (collision coverage did not apply when a chimney was blown off a roof during a high wind, and struck an automobile); Mercury Insurance Company v. McClellan, 216 Ark. 410, 225 S.W.2d 931, 14 A.L.R.2d 806 (1950) (tornado rolled over one insured car and caused brick wall and timber to strike another insured car; *held,* not within collision and upset coverage).

6. See, e.g., Farmers Insurance Exchange v. Wallace, 275 S.W.2d 864 (Tex. Civ.App.1955 writ refused, no reversible error).

7. See generally § 8.4(b), below.

tally causation questions, and such questions involve issues with which lawyers develop both familiarity and expertise. The doctrines of proximate cause and cause-in-fact, for example, are among the concepts that are analyzed at length in the first years of every lawyer's legal education.

The discussion in the preceding portions of this section has considered several distinct problems, drawn from various types of insurance coverages, in which the need arises for determining whether a policy clause relating to causation restricts or extends the scope of coverage.[1] When decisions involving such causation questions are considered, it seems clear that courts tend to apply the same types of analytical approaches and techniques that are generally employed to favor the interests of insureds.

Doctrines such as proximate cause will be used in some instances, but generally will not be regarded by courts as inviolate rules of insurance law that preclude claims. When alternate analytical approaches provide a reasonable technique for evaluating whether the loss is attributable to a risk that is covered by the insurance contract, courts tend to apply such approaches in preference to an analysis predicated on doctrines that would preclude coverage. Similarly, when a loss is attributable to several causes, if one of the contributing factors is a covered risk, courts will usually apply causation rules that favor coverage. This is not to suggest, however, that causation clauses are uniformly interpreted so as to uphold the existence of coverage.

Insurers are free, absent applicable legislative or administrative regulations, either to impose limitations on the risks that are transferred in an insurance contract or to include clauses that specify causes of losses that will not be covered in a particular insurance contract.

§ 5.5(f)

1. Also see, e.g., Mann v. Service Life Insurance Co., 284 F.Supp. 139 (E.D.Va. 1968) (Marine officer acting as co-pilot of helicopter in Vietnam, killed by rifle fire from ground; policy provision that coverage did not apply if death resulted from "operating or riding in, or descending from any kind of aircraft if the Insured is a pilot * * *"; *held*, coverage on the theory that the limitation was not intended to be effective if death resulted from an intervening cause totally unrelated to operation of the aircraft); Dickson v. United States Fidelity & Guaranty Co., 77 Wash.2d 185, 466 P.2d 515 (En banc 1970) (all-risk contractor's equipment floater policy with "exclusion" for "latent defect" insured crane damaged when its boom with a defective weld collapsed, while putting "H" beams out of ground on highway job, when earth collapsed onto "H" beam; *held*, coverage on alternate grounds, first, that "latent defect" exclusion applied only to cost of repairing the defect, not to resulting damage and, second, that not the latent defect but an external cause, collapsing earth, was the "direct, violent and efficient cause," and thus the "responsible cause of the loss").

Cf. Harris v. Carolina Life Insurance Co., 233 So.2d 833 at pp. 833–834 (Fla.1970) (insured died in collision, as passenger in car, while under influence of alcohol; policy "exception" saying "death * * * resulting * * * from any of the following causes are risks not assumed under this policy: * * * Bodily injury while under the influence of alcohol or drug * * *"; *held*, ambiguous, and insurer has burden of proving causal relationship).

See generally cases in Annotation, *Applicability of aviation exclusion clause as affected by fact that injury or death occurred after termination of flight*, 62 A.L.R.3d 1243–1265 (1975).

Nevertheless, when such provisions are susceptible to varying interpretations, courts will generally adopt the interpretation that favors coverage. Furthermore, courts increasingly are resolving such questions by considering the scope of coverage in terms of protecting an insured's reasonable expectations.[2]

Causation and Reasonable Expectations

Predicting the future is at best a difficult undertaking, and frequently an unattainable goal. For the drafters of insurance contracts, attempting to design definitional terms that anticipate the unusual and sometimes bizarre events that lead to coverage claims is a challenge that is not always surmounted.

This is not to suggest that insurance contracts will always be extended to cover the unexpected or extraordinary. Rather, it appears to be a question of applying a standard of reasonableness in establishing a fair scope for a coverage. Although sometimes such decisions might be predicated on the respective abilities of the insured and the insurer to distribute the loss, this approach does not always indicate a clear choice.

Caveat. The relative capacities of a major corporation that has acquired insurance and a large insurance company often seem quite comparable. The "deep pocket" theory of risk allocation would not afford a definitive result between such parties. More fundamentally, however, the "deep pocket" theory is not a principle that courts may be expected to embrace. Thus, before yielding to the temptation to either predicate or explain results in coverage disputes on the premise of a "deep pocket" theory, it is essential to search more closely for general principles that not only harmonize the decisions but that also constitute rationales for the decisions that are worthy of explicit recognition.

§ 5.6 Warranty: Insurance Policy Provisions and Legal Consequences

The early development of the concept of warranty in insurance law has been attributed to Lord Mansfield.[1] As Professor Vance observed, apparently the term "warranted" was in general use in the seventeenth

2. See generally, the discussion of protecting reasonable expectations in § 6.3, below.

See, e.g., Sparks v. St. Paul Insurance Co., 100 N.J. 325, 495 A.2d 406 (1985) (claims made policy provided no retroactive coverage for negligence occurring in years prior to the policy); Sabri v. State Farm Fire & Casualty Co., 488 So.2d 362 (La.App.1986) (expected or intended harm exclusion).

Also see Sadlowski v. Liberty Mutual Insurance Co., 487 A.2d 1146 (Del.Super., New Castle, 1984) (friendly fire doctrine).

It is often very difficult to define with a high degree of precision insurance policy terms that anticipate all the causation issues that may arise in connection with a particular type of risk.

§ 5.6

1. William R. Vance, *The History of the Development of the Warranty in Insurance Law,* 20 Yale Law Journal 523–534 at pp. 525–532 (1911).

century, but "in the few insurance cases reported as being tried in the common law courts prior to Lord Mansfield's accession as Chief Justice of the Court of King's Bench, in 1756, there is nothing to indicate that the term had any other significance than to introduce a condition that had to be strictly performed." [2]   This meaning appears to encompass what were subsequently called "promissory" or "continuing" warranties, which are merely "executory terms of the contract agreed to be material." [3]   Professor Vance described the state of the law established by Lord Mansfield in the following way:

> "The practical result reached by the courts before Mansfield retired from the bench may be stated thus: The description of the risk upon which the underwriter relied in determining whether he would assume the risk or not, or at what premium he would assume it, might be found within the policy or without it. So far as the descriptive terms chanced to be within the policy [warranties], *they must be literally true, irrespective of their materiality,* but if they chanced to be without the policy [representations] the insurance remained valid unless the misdescription was of such character as really to injure the underwriter; that is, unless the misdescription was substantial and material." [4]

Lord Mansfield established a rule for marine insurance claims which required that warranty terms had to be literally satisfied.[5] Although arguably the reasons advanced for the warranty rule in regard to marine insurance were not applicable to the other forms of insurance,[6] the warranty rule developed by Lord Mansfield in marine insurance coverage disputes was subsequently extended to life and fire insurance.

Once the warranty rule was held by the courts to apply to other types of insurance, a profusion of warranties began to pervade insurance policy forms, and many of these were of the most trivial character. The effect of such warranty provisions was increasingly to jeopardize the rights of policyholders, no matter how honest and careful they were. As the use of warranties — together with the rule requiring literal satisfaction — was brought to bear on an increasingly large portion of all insured transactions, it led to numerous lawsuits which called upon the courts to consider whether the failure to satisfy what

2. *Id.* at pp. 526–527.

3. *Id.* at p. 532.

4. *Id.* at p. 531 (Emphasis added).

5. Professor Vance was not critical of the rule requiring promissory warranties to be strictly performed. However, his criticism of the strict enforcement of "affirmative" warranties, stipulating that specific facts exist, was severe. He asserted that it makes no difference to the insurer whether statements descriptive of the risk appear within the policy or instead appear (orally or in writing) outside it; he considered that in both instances the insurer should not be expected to pay if the risk differed materially from that described. On the other hand, he saw no reason why the insurer should not pay if the risk did not differ in any material respect, "even though the shibboleth 'warranty' be found in the policy." *Id.* at p. 533. See the statement quoted in the first paragraph of this section, from which one may infer that Vance considered it quite appropriate that a warranty be used to impose a "condition that had to be strictly performed." *Id.* at p. 532.

6. *Id.* at pp. 533–534.

was urged, on behalf of claimants, to be an immaterial warranty should preclude all rights of an insured to coverage.

In dealing with the problems presented by the extensive use of warranties, courts initially decided that no stipulation, even though written in an insurance policy, should be construed as a warranty unless it was clearly and unmistakably so intended by the parties, as indicated by the unequivocal language of the policy.[7] These decisions subsequently caused insurers to frame insurance policy provisions so as to compel the courts to agree that various clauses were *clearly and unmistakably intended* as warranties.[8] Many judges were still, to say the least, extremely upset by insurers that attempted to impose forfeitures on unsuspecting insureds through the use of warranty provisions.[9] The judicial response to many of these warranty provisions was to construe, and sometimes even distort, the language of the policies so as to favor insureds. This "resulted in a mass of litigation and confused precedent, the like of which cannot be found in any other field of our law." [10]

In general, the rigors of the original common law rule requiring strict compliance with warranties in insurance transactions have been greatly relieved by both legislative provisions that either impose restrictions on the scope of warranty provisions or change the effect of warranties, and decisional developments in the courts that limit the application of the common law rule.[11] For example, with respect to life insurance, little of the rule of strict compliance remains. In addition, statutes commonly require that all life insurance policies must include incontestability provisions — that is, life insurance contracts are no longer subject to many effects of the warranty rule because legislative provisions preclude an insurer from contesting various issues after a relatively short period of time (usually one or two years).[12] Also, in most states there is now a statutory provision that either generally requires or actually specifies exact language for a policy clause which

7. Professor Vance's footnote set forth the following references: "For examples of such liberal construction see Moulor v. American Life Insurance Company, 111 U.S. 335 [4 S.Ct. 466, 28 L.Ed. 447 (1884)]; Phoenix Mutual Life Insurance Company v. Raddin, 120 U.S. 183 [7 S.Ct. 500, 30 L.Ed. 644 (1887)]; Alabama Gold Life Insurance Company v. Johnston, 80 Ala. 467 [2 So. 125 (1887)]; Globe Mut. Life Insurance Ass'n v. Wagner, 188 Ill. 133 [58 N.E. 970 (1900)]."

8. To some extent, these decisions served to modify the focus of the struggle that was developing. If there were no ambiguities on which the courts could rely to resolve a dispute by "liberal" construction, regulation of some kind — legislative, administrative, or judicial — was needed if the problems were to be viewed with candor.

9. For example, a Texas court — which pointed out that "the parties must have intended that the policy stand or fall on the literal truth or falsity of the statement in question" — observed that such "warranties which cause forfeiture are disfavored in the law." Allied Bankers Life Insurance Company v. De La Cerda, 584 S.W.2d 529 at p. 532 (Tex.Civ.App., Amarillo, 1979).

10. William R. Vance, *The History of the Development of the Warranty in Insurance Law,* 20 Yale Law Journal 523–534 at p. 534 (1911).

11. See § 6.6, below.

Also see Vlastos v. Sumitomo Marine & Fire Insurance Company (Europe) Ltd., 707 F.2d 775 (10th Cir.1983) (applying Pennsylvania law).

12. See § 6.6(d), below.

provides that statements made in an application for life insurance shall be considered to be representations and not warranties.[13]

With respect to various types of insurance other than life insurance, statutory modifications of the common law rule [14] have been somewhat less pervasive, and therefore the rule requiring strict compliance with warranties is still applicable in some situations.[15] This is especially true in regard to marine insurance.[16]

13. See, e.g., New York—McKinney's Insurance Law § 3204(16).

14. See § 6.6, below.

15. See, e.g., Usher v. St. Paul Fire & Marine Insurance Company, 126 Mich. App. 443, 337 N.W.2d 351 (1983) (when the insurance policy's plain language stated that the owner warranted that 100% of the stock would be kept in locked safes when the business was closed, the insurer only assumed the risk for such stock and no coverage was provided for jewelry that was burglarized while outside the safes).

16. See, e.g., D.J. McDuffie v. Old Reliable Fire Insurance Company, 608 F.2d 145 at p. 147 (5th Cir.1979) [*cert. denied* 449 U.S. 830, 101 S.Ct. 97, 66 L.Ed.2d 35 (1980)] (evidence was sufficient to support district court's finding that an implied warranty of seaworthiness was violated when the submersible drilling barge "had not been dry-docked and its hull had not been inspected during a six-year period preceding the capsize.").

Also see Goodman v. Fireman's Fund Insurance Company, 600 F.2d 1040 at p. 1043 (4th Cir.1979) (that it was the custom in the Chesapeake Bay region to close sea valves as part of a winterizing program, and the failure to do so meant that the vessel was not "laid up as warranted in the policy").

Marine insurance has not completely escaped the impact of statutory modification of the law of warranty. See, e.g., Wilburn Boat Company v. Fireman's Fund Insurance Company, 348 U.S. 310, 75 S.Ct. 368, 99 L.Ed. 337 (1955), *rehearing denied* 349 U.S. 907, 75 S.Ct. 575, 99 L.Ed. 1243 (1955). An action was brought in 1949 on a policy insuring a house boat that burned on Lake Texoma, an artificial lake on the Texas-Oklahoma border. The insurer denied liability because of alleged breach of "warranties" providing that the boat would not be sold, transferred, assigned, pledged, hired, or chartered without the insurer's consent. The Wilburns contended that Texas law

was applicable to the contract and that under Texas statutes [now carried forward as Vernon's Ann. Texas Civil Statutes, articles 6.14 and 21.42 (1971)], the defense was unavailing.

The District Court held that the policy was a maritime contract governed by federal admiralty law and that literal fulfillment of warranties is required under such law. The Court of Appeals affirmed. The Supreme Court (Justice Frankfurter concurring in result and Justices Reed and Burton dissenting) reversed and remanded for a trial "under appropriate state law," the court's opinion by Justice Black declaring: "We, like Congress, leave the regulation of marine insurance where it has been, with the States." *Id.*, 348 U.S. at p. 321, 75 S.Ct. at p. 374, 99 L.Ed. at p. 346.

The subsequent District Court decision on remand in favor of the insured was reversed by the Court of Appeals for insufficiency of evidence to support the District Court's application of Texas law. Fireman's Fund Insurance Company v. Wilburn Boat Company, 259 F.2d 662 (5th Cir. 1958), *cert. denied* 359 U.S. 925, 79 S.Ct. 607, 3 L.Ed.2d 628 (1959).

Finally, after a new trial that also resulted in judgment for the insured, Wilburn Boat Co. v. Fireman's Fund Insurance Company, 199 F.Supp. 784 (E.D.Tex.1960), the Court of Appeals reversed and remanded for entry of judgment in favor of the insurer, holding that the insured's misrepresentation of facts concerning use of the vessel was material to the risk insured against and that, under the applicable Texas law, therefore, the insured could not recover. Fireman's Fund Insurance Company v. Wilburn Boat Company, 300 F.2d 631 (5th Cir.1962), *cert. denied* 370 U.S. 925, 82 S.Ct. 1562, 8 L.Ed.2d 505 (1962).

See generally Nicholas J. Healy, *The Hull Policy: Warranties, Representations, Disclosures and Conditions,* 41 Tulane Law Review 245–258 (1967).

§ 5.7   Misrepresentations and Mistakes in Applications for Insurance [1]

Applicants for insurance are typically requested to provide information about a variety of matters, including responses that may be relevant (1) to an insurer's decision to accept the risks to be transferred, (2) to the premium to be charged for an insurance policy, and (3) to the circumstances under which coverage either will be extended or will be excluded for particular risks.

Following the occurrence of an event that leads to a claim for insurance benefits, if an insurer learns that incorrect information was provided in an insurance application, the insurer may decide to reject the claim. In this type of situation, there is a conflict between, on the one hand, preserving an insurer's right to assess and accept the actual risk or risks that are to be transferred on the basis of accurate information, and, on the other hand, protecting the expectations or the reliance of an insured (or, in some instances, the interests of persons other than an insured who are beneficiaries) on the existence of coverage provided by the insurance policy that was issued by the insurer. The nature and extent of these conflicting interests are frequently of considerable significance to the parties, and accordingly it is not surprising that disputes about the consequences of an application for insurance that includes incorrect information have been a continuing source of litigation.

The information which an insurer requests a prospective insured to provide is usually specified on an application form, and the individual submits answers either by filling out the form or by responding to inquiries from a sales representative (such as an insurance agent or a broker) who then completes the form. Although this process is probably most familiar to the public in regard to life insurance, for other types of insurance sales representatives (such as insurance agents and brokers) frequently acquire information from applicants and then complete the applications on behalf of the applicants.[2] In the event the submission of incorrect information subsequently becomes the basis for the rejection of a claim for insurance benefits that then results in litigation, such an incorrect statement will be classified by a court either as a "warranty" or as a "representation," and the consequences of this classification — which depend on (1) the circumstances, (2) the type of insurance involved, (3) the insurance contract terms, (4) the

---

§ 5.7

1. Misrepresentations also occur in connection with claims. See § 7.2(f) and § 7.3(c), below.

2. See, e.g., McLaughlin v. Alabama Farm Bureau Mutual Casualty Insurance Company, 437 So.2d 86 (Ala.1983) (responses in an application for fire insurance

to the question whether the applicant had ever been sued or sued anyone); Burger v. Nationwide Mutual Insurance Company, 53 Or.App. 898, 632 P.2d 1381 (1981) (responses in application for automobile insurance concerning traffic violations).

Also see the discussion of insurance marketing in § 2.1, above.

applicable legislative provisions, and (5) judicial precedents — are of considerable significance to the rights of the parties.

The "warranty" rule, developed by the English common law courts and generally adopted by courts in the United States, provides that an insurer has a complete defense to any claim for insurance benefits if it is proved that an applicant (or an insured [3]) submitted incorrect information to the insurer which was incorporated into the policy as a warranty.[4] Thus, in insurance law a warranty is a type of statement or a factual description which (1) is incorporated into the policy, (2) relates to an insured risk, and (3) must be literally true.[5] However, in every state there are statutory provisions which at least to some extent modify the common law rules concerning whether information submitted to an insurer in an application may be classified as a warranty.[6]

In most states, legislation now requires that information in applications for some types of insurance must be treated as representations — that is, in relation to the types of insurance to which such a statute applies, insurers are precluded from treating statements or information submitted in an insurance application as warranties.[7] For example, in most states, statutes applicable to life insurance specifically mandate that "all statements and descriptions in any application for an insurance policy or annuity contract, * * * by or on behalf of the insured or annuitant, shall be deemed [or *considered* [8]] to be representations and not warranties."[9] Legislation in other states employs somewhat

---

3. False information may also be provided to an insurer by an insured who is not also an applicant. This may also be done in connection with claims, see the cases cited in § 7.2(f), but in that circumstance the law regarding the effect of giving false information is not ordinarily regarded as part of the law of "warranty." As noted in the text, § 5.6, above, the term "warranty" is ordinarily used only in relation to statements incorporated into the policy (or an application attached to and made a part of the policy). See also notes 4 and 5, below.

4. *Cf.* Hay v. Utica Mutual Insurance Company, 551 S.W.2d 954 at p. 958 (Mo. App., Springfield District, 1977).

5. See, e.g., Lane v. Travelers Indemnity Company, 391 S.W.2d 399 at p. 402 (Tex. 1965).

In general, provisions which have the effect of producing a forfeiture on the basis of the literal truth or falsity of a statement are disfavored in the law. See the discussion of warranties in at § 5.6, above and § 6.6, below.

6. For example, the North Carolina statute provides, "This entire policy shall be void if, whether before or after a loss, the insured has willfully concealed or misrepresented any material fact or circum-

stance concerning this insurance or the subject thereof, or the interest of the insured therein, or in case of any fraud or false swearing by the insured relating thereto." North Carolina G.S. § 58–176(c).

Also see § 6.6(c), below.

7. The law of warranty continues to be important in regard to many other aspects of insurance transactions. For example, the standard "Jeweler's Block Policy" includes a warranty provision that states that 100% of the stock would be kept in a locked safe or vault at all times when the premises are closed. In Usher v. St. Paul Fire & Marine Insurance Company, 126 Mich.App. 443, 337 N.W.2d 351 at p. 353 (1983), the court concluded that a claim by a wholesale jewelry outlet owner was precluded from a recovery by a material "breach of the warranty" when the evidence clearly showed that "the only jewelry taken during the burglary was that contained in display cases outside of the safes."

8. Several of the statutes use the term "considered" in place of "deemed."

9. See, e.g., Iowa Code Annotated Charter 509.2 (1949); Maine Revised Statutes Annotated Tit. 24–A, § 2616 (1974); Michigan Compiled Laws Annotated § 500.4016

different statutory language in provisions which have the same effect.[10] Furthermore, even in the absence of applicable legislation, in the twentieth century courts have frequently exhibited considerable hostility in regard to the enforcement of warranty provisions.[11] Consequently, either as a result of legislative actions or judicial precedents, it now appears clear that the public policy against contract provisions which produce forfeitures of rights applies with considerable vigor to this aspect of insurance transactions so that an insurer is usually precluded from treating incorrect information supplied by an applicant as a violation or a breach of a warranty provision.[12] Thus, an individual's answers to an insurer's questions in an application for insurance are almost always classified as "representations," and when the information is incorrect it is typically characterized as a "misrepresentation."

More than one commentator has used characterizations such as "confused," "erroneous," "misleading," and "inconsistent" to describe the body of law (legislative provisions and the judicial decisions interpreting those laws or applying common law principles) that determines the rights of the parties to an insurance contract when it is subsequently discovered that an application for the insurance coverage contained incorrect information.[13] It is clear that the courts have uniformly held that relief is justified when an insurer can prove that an applicant

---

(1983); Vernon's Annotated Texas Statutes Insurance Code, art. 3.44(4) (1981).

10. For example, the North Carolina statute provides, "All statements or descriptions in any application for a policy of insurance, or in the policy itself shall be deemed representations and not warranties, and representations, unless material or fraudulent, will not prevent a recovery on the policy. North Carolina G.S. § 58–30 (Emphasis added).

Also see discussion of the statute in Tedder v. Union Fidelity Life Insurance Company, 436 F.Supp. 847 (E.D.N.C.1977).

11. See, e.g., Franklin Life Insurance Company v. William Champion and Company, 350 F.2d 115 at pp. 120–121 (6th Cir. 1965) (applying Michigan law); Evans v. Penn Mutual Life Insurance Company of Philadelphia, 322 Pa. 547, 186 A. 133 (1936).

Also see Lane v. Travelers Indemnity Company, 391 S.W.2d 399 at p. 402 (Tex. 1965); Allied Bankers Life Insurance Company v. De La Cerda, 584 S.W.2d 529 (Tex. Civ.App., Amarillo 1979).

Cf. Moulor v. American Life Insurance Company, 111 U.S. 335, 4 S.Ct. 466, 28 L.Ed. 447 (1884).

12. See, e.g., Lumbermens Mutual Casualty Company v. Myrick, 596 F.2d 1313 (5th Cir.1979) (applying Code of Alabama Section 37–14–7).

Also see Annotation, *Fraud, false swearing, or other misconduct of insured as barring recovery on property insurance by innocent coinsured,* 24 A.L.R.3d 450–455 (1969); Annotation, *Fraud, false swearing, or other misconduct of insured as affecting right of innocent mortgagee or loss payee to recover on property insurance,* 24 A.L.R.3d 435–442 (1969).

13. In the early 1930's, Professor Patterson wrote:

"In applying the law of misrepresentation to life insurance, a considerable number of courts have uttered approval of the rule that *only a fraudulent misrepresentation* by the insured will avoid the policy. The law of misrepresentation has thus become unsettled and confused in many jurisdictions."

Edwin Patterson, ESSENTIALS OF INSURANCE LAW (1935) at p. 339.

Professor Vance wrote:

"It is also sometimes said that the materiality of a fraudulently made misrepresentation is conclusively presumed. It is submitted that these statements are misleading, and not in accord with the cases or the analogies of the law."

William R. Vance, HANDBOOK OF THE LAW OF INSURANCE (Second edition, 1930) at p. 360. Professor Vance also commented:

"Misleading declarations, not necessary for the decision of the issues in-

intended a fraudulent misrepresentation of a material fact. Much of the confusion in regard to this type of dispute has been in regard to whether an insurer must always prove that an applicant provided the misinformation with an intent to deceive or defraud the insurer — that is, whether relief is justified when the insurer cannot prove that the applicant intentionally submitted incorrect information. Although there is certainly authority for the proposition that an insurer must prove such an intent, it seems clear that (with possibly a few exceptions where an unusual statute specifically declares otherwise) the actual import of the legislative provisions together with the judicially developed doctrines applicable to cases in which an insured has provided incorrect information can be accurately summarized by the following statement:

> **An insurer is entitled to relief on the basis that an insured provided incorrect information in an insurance application, when it is proved (1) that the information was not correct, (2) that the information received was important either to the insurer's decision to insure or to the terms of the insurance contract, (that is, the information was "material" [14]), and (3) that the insurer in fact relied on the incorrect information.[15]**

This proposition identifies three distinct elements or factors on which insurers must sustain the burden of proof. When the three elements set out in this proposition are established, there is a clear basis for a court to grant a request for either rescission of the insurance contract or an affirmative defense to an insured's claim *without* requiring proof of any additional facts in support of the requested remedy or defense. Depending on the facts, relief in such a case may be predicated on either a misrepresentation or a mistake.[16]

volved, to the effect that a misrepresentation, as distinguished from a warranty, though material will not avoid an insurance contract unless made with fraudulent intent are becoming unfortunately frequent in recent judicial opinions."

Id., at p. 363.

Professor Prosser made a similar observation about the tort law of misrepresentation:

"There has been a good deal of overlapping of theories, and no little confusion, which has been increased by the indiscriminate use of the word 'fraud,' a term so vague that it requires definition in nearly every case. Further difficulty has been added by a failure to distinguish the requisites of the action in tort at law from those of equitable remedies, and to distinguish the different forms of misrepresentation from one another, and misrepresentation itself from mere mistake. Any attempt to bring order out of the resulting chaos must be at best a tentative one, with the qualification that many courts do not agree."

William Prosser, HANDBOOK OF THE LAW OF TORTS (Third edition, 1964) at p. 699.

14. See, e.g., State Farm Mutual Automobile Insurance Company v. Price, 181 Ind.App. 258, 396 N.E.2d 134 at p. 136 (3d Dist.1979).

15. See, e.g., Crawford v. Standard Insurance Co., 49 Or.App. 731, 621 P.2d 583 (1980).

Cf. McLaughlin v. Alabama Farm Bureau Mutual Casualty Insurance Company, 437 So.2d 86 at p. 89 (Ala.1983); Reliance Insurance Company v. Substantion Products Corporation, 404 So.2d 598 at p. 604 (Ala.1981).

But cf. Lettieri v. Equitable Life Assurance Society of the United States, 627 F.2d 930 (9th Cir.1980) (applying California law).

16. In instances in which an insurer's proof shows that the information in an application was incorrect and that it relied to its detriment on incorrect material information provided by an applicant for insurance, the insurer has at least shown that it was incorrectly informed about im-

Materiality. An insurer is only entitled to relief, whether based on the theory of misrepresentation or mistake, when the incorrect information provided by an applicant was material. The element of materiality has been characterized in many different ways by courts.[17]

Reliance. Some judicial opinions suggest that it is essential for an insurer to always prove that the insurer's reliance was reasonable. Whether this should be treated as a distinct and essential element of a prima facie case for misrepresentation in the absence of special circumstances is a matter of some disagreement.[18] Similarly, whether a

portant facts. In this context, if a court accepts the disclaimer of any awareness on the part of an applicant/insured of the falsity of the information, it is then evident that both parties entered into the transaction on the basis of a mistaken belief about the matter which was incorrectly answered. In such a case, the insurer and the applicant/insured were both mistaken about matters that were important to the transaction — that is, when an incorrect answer is submitted in an insurance application and the applicant honestly disclaims either knowledge of the correct information or intent to submit a false response, the applicant's mistaken belief about a material fact has also become the mistaken belief of the insurer as a result of the applicant's response(s) to the question(s) in the application.

A contract may be rescinded on the basis of a material mutual mistake even though it is clear that everyone acted in complete good faith. RESTATEMENT OF CONTRACTS, Second (1982), at § 152. Insurers are entitled to seek rescission when there has been a mutual mistake in an insurance transaction, that is, when the parties are both mistaken about some important aspect of the transaction so that there is a material, mutual mistake. In such cases, an insurer need not prove an applicant intended to deceive the insurer or that an applicant was aware of the falsity of a material statement in order to justify relief on the basis of a mutual mistake.

There does not appear to be any basis for not applying to insurance transactions the rules and doctrines of contract law that are generally applicable to mistakes that result when misinformation is submitted by an applicant in an insurance application.

17. See, e.g., Davis-Scofield v. Agricultural Insurance Co., 109 Conn. 673 at p. 678, 145 A. 38 at p. 40 (1929) ("A fact is material * * * when * * * it would so increase the degree or character of the risk of the insurance so as to substantially influence its issuance, or *substantially affect the rate of premium.*") (Emphasis added); Holtzclaw v. Bankers Mutual Insurance Company, 448 N.E.2d 55 at p. 58 (Ind.App.,

3d Dist., 1983), ["The representations of the insured are material to the risk if a truthful answer would lead the insurer to decline issuing insurance or *charge a higher premium.*" (Emphasis added)].

Cf. Wiedmayer v. Midland Mutual Life Insurance Company, 108 Mich.App. 96 at p. 100, 310 N.W.2d 285 at p. 286 (1981) ("As a test for determining whether a misstatement in an insurance application is material the *Dedic* court held that a misrepresentation is material if it is such that the insurer would not have entered into the contract had it known the true facts."), reversed on other grounds in a decision reported at 414 Mich. 369, 324 N.W.2d 752 (1982); Martin v. Security Industrial Insurance Company, 367 So.2d 420 at p. 422 (La. App. 2d Cir.1979), *writ denied* 369 So.2d 1364 (1979) (material "means * * * the insurer would not have contracted or would have contracted only at a higher premium rate").

Also see Jones v. Prudential Insurance Company of America, 388 A.2d 476 at p. 481 (D.C.App.1978) ("The test of materiality is whether the representation would reasonably influence the insurer's decision as to whether it should insure the applicant."); Howard v. Aid Associations for Lutherans, 272 N.W.2d 910 (Minn.1978); Tedder v. Union Fidelity Life Insurance Company, 436 F.Supp. 847 at 849 (E.D.N.C. 1977) ("The materiality of the misrepresentation is judged in terms of its effect upon the insurer's decision to underwrite the risk * * *.").

Cf. Lewis v. John Hancock Mutual Life Insurance Company, 443 F.Supp. 217 (D.Conn.1977).

Also see Annotation, *Modern Status of rules regarding materiality and effect of false statement by insurance applicant as to previous insurance cancellations or rejections,* 66 A.L.R.3d 749–807 (1975).

See also § 6.6, below.

18. See, e.g., State Farm Mutual Automobile Insurance Company v. Price, 181 Ind.App. 258, 396 N.E.2d 134 at p. 136 (1979).

relationship exists between the reasonableness of the insurer's reliance and the obligation an insurer has or should have to investigate has also been the subject of numerous disputes.[19]

Relationship of the misrepresentation to the insured event. There is support in a few statutes and judicial precedents for the proposition that there must be a causal relationship between the incorrect information submitted in an insurance application and the loss that is the basis of the subsequent claim which is denied by an insurer on the basis of a misrepresentation.[20]

§ 5.8   Concealment

5.8(a)   Generally

There are many types of situations in which relevant information that is known by an individual who is applying for insurance is not disclosed to an insurance company. Typically, when an insurer subsequently learns of an insured's failure to provide information, the insurer will seek rescission of the insurance contract. And, in some instances, concealment is asserted as a defense to an insurance claim.

Concealment is closely related to fraud or misrepresentation, and the analysis employed by courts when concealment is alleged is sometimes quite similar to that used in misrepresentation cases.[1] In gener-

---

19. See, e.g., Braaten v. Minnesota Mutual Life Insurance Company, 302 N.W.2d 48 at p. 50 (S.D.1981) ("* * * an insurer is entitled to rely on the truthfulness of the answers given."); Kubeck v. Consolidated Underwriters, 267 Or. 548, 517 P.2d 1039 (1974); State Farm Mutual Insurance Company v. Price, 181 Ind.App. 258, 396 N.E.2d 134 at p. 137 (3d Dist.1979) ("Thus, where the party has no reason to doubt the validity of the statement, he may rely thereon without undertaking investigation or further inquiry.").

Cf. Tedder v. Union Fidelity Life Insurance Company, 436 F.Supp. 847 at p. 850 (E.D.N.C.1977).

Also see Crawford v. Standard Insurance Co., 49 Or.App. 731, 621 P.2d 583 at p. 587 (1980); Lindlauf v. Northern Founders Insurance Company, 130 N.W.2d 86 (N.D.1964); Burger v. Nationwide Mutual Insurance Company, 53 Or.App. 898, 632 P.2d 1381 (1981).

20. The clear majority rule among the appellate courts is that there need not be a causal relationship between an applicant's false statements and the cause of a loss (such as death) when the insurer seeks rescission or asserts an affirmative defense following the occurrence of what would otherwise be an insured event. See, e.g., Shafer v. John Hancock Mutual Life Insur-

ance Company, 410 Pa. 394 at p. 399, 189 A.2d 234 at 237 (1963) ("It is of no significance that the death ensued from a cause connected with the false representation.").

Cf. Campbell v. Prudential Insurance Co. of America, 15 Ill.2d 308, 155 N.E.2d 9 at p. 11 (1958); Torbensen v. Family Life Insurance Co., 163 Cal.App.2d 401, 329 P.2d 596 (1958).

Also see Formosa v. Equitable Life Insurance Society, 166 N.J.Super. 8 at p. 22, 398 A.2d 1301 at p. 1308 (App.Div.1979), *certification denied* 81 N.J. 53, 404 A.2d 1153 (1979); Jones v. Prudential Insurance Company of America, 388 A.2d 476 at p. 480 (D.C.App.1978).

In a few jurisdictions, legislative provisions require an insurer to establish a causal relation between a material misrepresentation and loss. Capitol Old Line Insurance Company v. Gorondy, 1 Ark.App. 14, 612 S.W.2d 128 at p. 130 (1981) (an insurer may only deny coverage under a life insurance policy when there was a causal relation between the alleged material misrepresentation and the insured's death).

§ 5.8(a)

1. See, e.g., Sebring v. Fidelity-Phoenix Fire Insurance Co., 255 N.Y. 382, 174 N.E. 761 (1931) (nondisclosure of the fact that

al, concealment involves the suppression or withholding of information, while a misrepresentation occurs when incorrect information is submitted to an insurer.

Courts have concluded that an intentional concealment of a material fact by an applicant for insurance may provide an insurer with either a valid defense to a claim or the basis for the rescission of the insurance contract, if the insurer was not made aware of the information from other sources.[2] Questions about the insured's intent are often conceptualized in terms of whether the individual was acting in "good faith" in regard to not divulging the information to the insurer.

When an applicant's failure to reveal information is not a matter of an intentional concealment, for most types of insurance, such conduct does not constitute a sufficient basis for a defense by an insurer in a majority of the states.[3] However, in several states it has been held, at least in some circumstances, that an applicable legislative provision "permits rescission of an insurance contract where the insured has simply negligently or inadvertently failed to reveal certain facts which, if known to the insurer, would have caused it to refuse to issue the policy in question." [4]

When an applicant does not provide information requested by an insurer in an application form, some courts have reasoned that the applicant's actions do not constitute concealment because an insurer is not compelled to accept an incomplete submission.[5]

new insured added to policy had been convicted of conspiracy to defraud insurance companies and that original insured, an attorney, had defended him in his trial for that crime; trial court judgment of coverage reversed); Finlay & Associates, Inc. v. Borg-Warner Corp., 155 N.J.Super. 331, 382 A.2d 933 (1978), *certification denied* 77 N.J. 467, 391 A.2d 483 (1978) (a deliberate concealment of facts related to a possible defect in title to land).

Cf. Howard v. Aid Association For Lutherans, 272 N.W.2d 910 at p. 913 (Minn.1978); Independent Fire Insurance Company v. Horn, 343 So.2d 862 at p. 864 (1st Dist.1976).

Also see cases collected in Annotation, *Obligee's concealment or misrepresentation concerning previous defalcation as affecting liability on fidelity bond or contract,* 4 A.L.R.3d 1197–1220 (1965).

But cf. Dinkins v. American National Insurance Co., 92 Cal.App.3d 222 at p. 233, 154 Cal.Rptr. 775 (1979), in which the court observed that the California decisions "have consistently treated misrepresentations and concealment as distinct alternative defenses in the context of insurance coverage. See Thompson v. Occidental Life Insurance Co. (1973) 9 Cal.3d 904, 916 [109 Cal.Rptr. 473, 513 P.2d 353]; * * *."

For a dissenting view on the doctrine of concealment, urging that it be excised from the law of insurance, see Harnett, *The Doctrine of Concealment: A Remnant in the Law of Insurance,* 15 Law & Contemporary Problems 391–414 (1950).

2. See, e.g., Holtzclaw v. Bankers Mutual Insurance Company, 448 N.E.2d 55 at p. 58 (Ind.App., 3d Dist., 1983) (Applicant "concealed the names of treating physicians * * * [and this] concealment amounted to misrepresentation.").

3. See, e.g., Sebring v. Fidelity-Phoenix Fire Insurance Company, 255 N.Y. 382, 174 N.E. 761 (1931).

Also see Independent Fire Insurance Company v. Horn, 343 So.2d 862 at p. 864 (Fla.App., 1st Dist., 1976).

4. See, e.g., Dinkins v. American National Insurance Company, 92 Cal.App.3d 222 at p. 232, 154 Cal.Rptr. 775 at p. 781 (1979).

5. *Cf.* Pennsylvania Life Insurance Company v. Tanner, 163 Ga.App. 330, 293 S.E.2d 520 at p. 522 (1982).

Accord. Rallod Transportation Company v. Continental Insurance Company, 727 F.2d 851 at p. 854 (9th Cir.1984) (applying California law); Independent Fire Insurance Company v. Horn, 343 So.2d 862 at p.

Disclosures by an applicant about his or her own character ordinarily are not required in the absence of a specific inquiry from an insurer.[6]

§ 5.8(b) Changing Circumstances or Changes in What the Applicant Knows

A special type of concealment problem is presented as to whether an applicant is obligated to report either (1) a significant change in regard to information which was sought by the insurer or (2) information that was unknown to the applicant when the application was filed, but which becomes known by the applicant after an application is filed — that is, whether an applicant is required to notify an insurer when one of these situations occurs before the insurer indicates its response to the application.

When the information relates to a matter an insurer did not include among the questions on the application form, the insurer will have a very difficult time making a convincing argument for concealment of facts coming to the attention of the applicant while the application was pending, no matter how relevant to the risk the information appears to be retrospectively.[1] However, if there were inquiries about such matters on the application form, a persuasive case can be made for the proposition that it is reasonable for an applicant to infer both (1) that while the application is pending, changes in regard to the answers submitted in the application or additional information which would alter one or more of the answers may be significant to an insurer considering the application *and* (2) that therefore the applicant is obligated to disclose such information. The case for requiring such disclosure is even more compelling when the insurer employs procedures that make an applicant aware of the insurer's interest in being notified of such changes.

The character, scope, and duration of an applicant's duty to disclose information to an insurer after an application has been submitted occasionally has been the subject of judicial determinations. There is a range of judicial views on the basis for and the extent of an applicant's responsibility to act in such circumstances. For example, the New Jersey courts have predicated the applicant's duty to disclose such information to an insurer on the principle that "An insurance contract * * * requires the highest degree of good faith and fair dealing between the parties," and that this "requires the insured to advise the insurer of such matters that he knows might influence the insurer in

---

864 (Fla.App., 1st Dist., 1976) ("Absent an intent to deceive * * * [an] incomplete response gave Independent adequate reason to reject the application, but no reason to disclaim coverage under a policy once issued.").

6. See, e.g., Penn. Mutual Life Insurance Co. v. Mechanics' Savings Bank &

Trust Co., 72 Fed. 413 (6th Cir.1896) (opinion by Taft, J.).

§ 5.8(b)

1. This will especially be the case if the insurer made no other inquiries about the subject.

entering into or declining the risk, at least where such facts are not of record and are not discoverable therefrom by the insurer." [2]

There are some judicial precedents for the proposition that there is "a representation made in an application of the truthfulness of such representation until the policy is delivered" and that "an applicant must use due diligence to communicate to the insurer facts materially affecting the risk which arise after * * * [the] application has been made and before the contract is consummated * * *." [3]

There are also decisions which indicate that the duty of disclosure during the period when an application is pending is the same as that which exists at the time an application is submitted. [4]

Viewing these decisions collectively, it is evident that courts have sustained the rule that the intentional concealment of a material fact coming to the attention of the applicant while an application for insurance is pending will provide a defense to an insured's subsequent claim, if the insurer was unaware of the information. Furthermore, usually the fact that the applicant acted in good faith in not making any disclosure to the insurer is not a significant consideration in such cases. Nevertheless, the practical impact of this rule is relatively insignificant because it is usually very difficult to prove that the insured intentionally concealed information so long as insurers do not submit any additional inquiries to the insured at the close of this interim period.

Disputes about the effect of an insured's failure to notify an insurer of facts coming to the attention of an applicant after an application is submitted are sometimes dealt with under the rubric of misrepresentation. [5] The analysis of such questions involves the concept that an applicant makes a "continuing" representation of the facts submitted

---

2. Pioneer National Title Insurance Company v. Lucas, 155 N.J.Super. 332 at p. 338, 382 A.2d 933 at p. 936 (App.Div.1978), *affirmed* 78 N.J. 320, 394 A.2d 360 (1978).

3. See, e.g., Stipcich v. Metropolitan Life Insurance Co., 277 U.S. 311, 48 S.Ct. 512, 72 L.Ed. 895 (1928) (recurrence of duodenal ulcer that later caused death; applicant made disclosure to the agent who had taken the application, but neither disclosed to the home office; *held,* in reversing a directed verdict for defendant and ordering new trial, that the agent was authorized by statute to receive information on behalf of the company).

In United Savings Life Insurance Company v. Coulson, 560 S.W.2d 211 at p. 215 (Tex.Civ.App., Amarillo, 1977), the court commented, "One who submits an application to an insurance company has a duty to inform that company of any changes in his health between the time he makes application and the date of delivery and acceptance."

4. *Cf.* MacKenzie v. Prudential Insurance Co. of America, 411 F.2d 781 (6th Cir. 1969) (forecasting Kentucky law) (failure of an insured to disclose substantial increased blood pressure reading, exceeding normal limits, after submitting an application for life policy and before issuance was "material misrepresentation" sufficient to void the policy).

Also see the discussion of misrepresentation in § 5.7.

5. *Cf.* State Farm Life Insurance Company v. Lawless, 586 S.W.2d 468 at p. 470 (Tenn.App., Western Section, 1979). The court observed that "a representation made in an application for insurance is a *continuing affirmance* of the truthfulness of such representation until the policy is delivered." (Emphasis added). The court also stated that "an applicant for a life policy must use due diligence to communicate to the insurer facts materially affecting the risk which arise after his application has been made and before the contract

until an insurance policy is issued to the applicant.[6] In essence, this approach to such cases involves a fiction, because after an application is submitted there usually is no act or communication from an applicant that can fairly be interpreted as a representation by the applicant on the matter in question.

§ 5.8(c) Life Insurance Applications and Binding Receipts

The terms, or lack thereof, in the binding receipts used by insurers in connection with life insurance applications can significantly influence cases in which an applicant learns additional information about his or her health while an application is pending.

The provisions of binding receipts often make changes of health that occur after a specified event, such as a payment of the first premium or a physical examination by a doctor, irrelevant to the insurer's obligation to issue the permanent policy. Cases involving such receipts obviously are not subject to the concealment doctrines discussed in the preceding portions of this section. Furthermore, an argument by an insurer for the recognition of an implied duty to disclose should certainly fail in the face of the explicit terms of the receipt.

When a life insurance application and the binding receipt do not include express provisions that make changes in or additional information about the applicant's health irrelevant, the question of concealment may be presented. And the problem is especially intense if the documents used by the insurer include a provision that states the life insurance coverage will only become effective when the insurance policy is delivered to an applicant who is still in good health or who is still insurable.

When life insurance coverage is limited by a delivery-in-good-health provision, it might be argued that the protection afforded to an insurance company by such a clause would make disclosure by the applicant unnecessary because the insurer's representative, who delivers the policy, should make an assessment of the insured's condition.[1] On the other hand, an even more persuasive case can be made that such a provision clearly evidences the insurer's interests in being fully informed about the applicant's health and therefore the applicant should be obligated to disclose information so long as the company's action might still be influenced by either (1) more complete informa-

is consummated by delivery of the policy."
Ibid.

6. State Farm Life Insurance Company v. Lawless, 586 S.W.2d 468 at p. 470 (Tenn. App., Western Section, 1979).

Cf. Mayes v. Massachusetts Mutual Life Insurance Company, 608 S.W.2d 612 at p. 616 (Tex.1980); Serdenes v. Aetna Life Insurance Company, 21 Md.App. 453, 319 A.2d 858 at p. 862 (1974).

§ 5.8(c)

1. *Cf.* paragraphs 4 and 5, California Insurance Code § 333 (Deering's 1977), saying there is no duty to disclose information, which is not otherwise material, on matters "which prove or tend to prove the existence of a risk excluded by a warranty" and those that relate "to a risk excepted."

tion, subsequently learned, about the applicant's health at the time the application was submitted or (2) information about any change in conditions affecting insurability.

A delivery-in-good-health clause is certainly a clear indication that the insurer intends to condition coverage on the "good health" of the applicant at the time of delivery, and that therefore any information which relates to that determination which is different from that which was thought to exist at the time of application is relevant to the insurer's decision. When an insurer can show that there is good reason to believe that the applicant was aware of the "delivery in good health" provision *and* that the insured became aware of unfavorable information about his or her health while the application was pending (that is, before the insurer delivered the insurance policy), the inference that the applicant intended to conceal the information is rather compelling.[2]

§ 5.8(d)   The Experienced Insurance Purchaser

A rule that an applicant may not withhold information which the applicant believes to be significant could have greater significance for some individuals than others if it were interpreted to mean that a person who has substantial knowledge of insurance practices, because of professional experience or some other reason, is required to disclose facts which are known by such an individual to be important, even though a lay person would not be required to make a disclosure of the same information because such an average person would not realize the significance of the information to the insurer. Thus far, few judicial precedents have addressed this question.

When an application for insurance is submitted by an individual who is also an insurance sales representative, the expertise or knowledge of such an individual may be held to support a very extensive duty of disclosure under either (1) a subjective standard (what that person

---

2. If a duty to disclose is recognized and enforced in regard to life insurance, it may be limited to a duty only to disclose information that the applicant reasonably perceives to involve an actual change in health between the time of the application and the delivery of the insurance policy. Furthermore, a failure to disclose information of a change of which the applicant had no knowledge obviously would not violate this duty. See, e.g., Harte v. United Benefit Life Insurance Co., 66 Cal.2d 148, 56 Cal.Rptr. 889, 424 P.2d 329 (1967) (application clause declaring no liability until policy delivered "in good health and free from injury"; "good health" interpreted from point of view of applicant's understanding and not from point of view of then unknown facts or from point of view of what treating physician or member of the family knew; recovery allowed if applicant believed in good faith that his health had not

materially changed between the time of application and delivery).

The decision in *Harte* seems to treat a stipulation for a condition of coverage (good health at delivery) as if it were only a stipulation for a duty to disclose material changes in health between the times of medical examination and delivery. Though the proper resolution of the issue may be debated, surely the question whether a stipulation that good health or continued insurability at the time of delivery (or absence of treatment or consultation between the times of medical examination and delivery) is enforceable is distinct from the question whether there is a duty to disclose changes in health (or the occurrence of treatment or consultation) after the medical examination and before delivery of the policy. Concerning enforceability of such a stipulation, see § 6.6(e)(4), below.

knows, based on his or her actual experiences, about the materiality of the fact in question) or (2) an objective standard (concerned with what someone having the expertise of an average sales representative would know) — that is, an objective expert standard rather than what would be expected of an average, reasonable person applying for insurance.[1]

§ 5.8(e) Marine Insurance

Marine insurance is subject to a distinctive rule which allows an insurer to predicate a defense to a coverage claim on an insured's concealment of information even when the insured was acting in good faith.[1] The marine insurance rule is usually explained by the fact that until the twentieth century, an underwriter had to rely heavily upon the insured for the disclosure of facts bearing upon the degree of risk. With improvements in communication and the availability of data on ships and shipping, any differentiation on this rationale between marine insurance and other types of insurance seems significantly less warranted. Nevertheless, other factors may still justify a more stringent rule of disclosure for marine insurance.[2] For example, marine contracts are likely to involve parties of relatively equal bargaining power and business acumen. In any event, the distinctive rule for marine insurance appears to be firmly entrenched, and unlikely to be changed.[3]

(1) Inland Marine Insurance

It has been argued that the marine insurance rule that applies to concealment should be extended to inland marine coverage, which includes the insurance policies that are used to provide coverage for personal property (often referred to as a "personal property floater"). In general, the prevailing precedents reject this approach.[4] Even though the distinctive marine insurance rule does not apply to applica-

---

§ 5.8(d)

1. *Cf.* Pederson v. Life of Mid-America Insurance Co., 164 N.W.2d 337 (Iowa 1969) (failure of insurance-agent-applicant to disclose shortages and discrepancies in bank accounts under his control; he signed application as applicant and agent, stating as agent that he knew nothing unfavorable regarding the applicant's character, habits, etc.; *held* for the insurer).

§ 5.8(e)

1. See generally the opinions and authorities relied upon in the decisions cited in notes 3 and 4 below.

2. It may be questioned whether the circumstances of modern marine insurance are more closely analogous to the circumstances of marine insurance in the days when the distinctive marine rule arose than to the circumstances of modern fire and life insurance.

3. *Cf.* Chester v. Assinibioia Corporation, 355 A.2d 880 at p. 882 (Del.1976), in which the court observed that the applicable standard was "the utmost good faith and complete disclosure by an applicant is both essential to and required by the law governing contracts of marine insurance." The court cited Btesh v. Royal Insurance Co., 40 F.2d 659 (S.D.N.Y.1930), and Gilmore and Black, THE LAW OF ADMIRALTY (Second Edition, 1975) at p. 62. The policy in *Chester* was "issued by Lloyd's in England on request made by brokers who were agents of the plaintiffs." 355 A.2d at p. 882.

4. See, e.g., Blair v. National Security Insurance Co., 126 F.2d 955 (3d Cir.1942); Stecker v. American Home Fire Assurance Co., 299 N.Y. 1, 84 N.E.2d 797 (1949), *reargument denied* 299 N.Y. 629, 86 N.E.2d 182 (1949).

tions for inland marine insurance, an applicant is not free to withhold facts that the applicant believes would affect the insurer's action on the application.

(2) Fire Insurance Contrasted

The rule that an innocent concealment by an applicant is not a defense in regard to an application for fire insurance is fortified by a clause in the standard fire insurance form which states: "This entire policy shall be void if, whether before or after a loss, the insured has wilfully concealed or misrepresented any material fact or circumstance * * *."[5] In view of the clear negative implication in this provision, it seems unlikely that a court would recognize innocent concealment or misrepresentation as a ground for voiding a policy.[6]

§ 5.9   Limits of Liability Provisions

§ 5.9(a)   Generally

Pecuniary limits of liability, which are specified in most types of insurance, impose a restriction on the risks transferred to an insurer. Typically, for example, one provision in a property insurance policy specifies an amount of coverage that sets the insurer's maximum liability when an insured event occurs, and another provision limits coverage to the value of the insured's interest in the property.[1] Health, accident, and medical payments coverages[2] are almost always written with overall limits of liability.[3] And liability insurance is uniformly written with either per-person and per-occurrence (or per-accident) limits of liability (that is, "split-limits of liability"),[4] or with a single limit of liability that applies both to any individual claim and to any group of claims resulting from a single occurrence.

§ 5.9(b)   Multiple Coverages and Multiple Claims

Pecuniary limits of liability on the amount of indemnification available have produced coverage disputes in many situations, including (1) claims by one individual under multiple units of the same coverage in a single insurance policy, (2) claims by one individual under

---

5. See Appendix A.

6. *Cf.* Di Leo v. United States Fidelity & Guaranty Co., 50 Ill.App.2d 183, 200 N.E.2d 405 (1st Dist.1964), 9 A.L.R.3d 1399 (1966) (failure to inform insurer of pending condemnation proceedings on building in which insured leased space for their business was not such concealment as would void fire insurance policies on contents of insured's store and for business interruption).

§ 5.9(a)

1. See Appendix A.

2. These coverages also typically include coverage restrictions that exclude

certain risks. For example, health insurance policies sometimes restrict coverage for pre-existing conditions. Some coverages include special limitations such as a provision placing a limit on benefits for prior illness recurring within three months after the application for policy. See Appendix F and Appendix H.

3. See, e.g., In re Clement's Estate, 220 Tenn. 114, 414 S.W.2d 644 (1967) (limit held enforceable and insurer allowed to recover amounts paid in excess of the limit before learning of the previous illness).

4. See Appendices G and H.

several different coverages included in a single policy, and (3) claims by two or more individuals under a single coverage in one policy. The following discussion provides several illustrations of the types of coverage questions involving limit of liability clauses which have been repeatedly litigated.[1]

(1) Multiple Coverage Claims by a Single Individual Under a Single Insurance Policy

There are several types of limit-of-liability problems which may be presented by claims for indemnification from coverages included in a single insurance policy, that is, when more than one coverage in a single package policy provides insurance for different aspects of risks that may produce losses as a result of a single occurrence. This type of coverage issue arises most frequently in regard to motor vehicle insurance policies. In this context, the questions may involve several coverages, including liability insurance, medical payments insurance, uninsured motorist insurance and underinsured motorist insurance. Issues about the limit of liability may occur both when a motor vehicle policy provides insurance for a single vehicle and when the insurance policy provides coverage for two or more vehicles.

Automobile insurance policies usually include several provisions which are intended by insurers to impose limits on the insurer's liability. *First,* each of these coverages will usually include the following identical clauses:

> "The limit of liability shown in the Declarations for this coverage is our [the insurer's] maximum limit of liability for all damages resulting from any one accident. This is the most we will pay regardless of the number of:
>
> 1. Covered persons;
> 2. Claims made;
> 3. Vehicles or premiums shown in the Declarations;
> 4. Vehicles involved in the accident." [2]

Second, the Limit of Liability sections in the Medical Payments Insurance and the Uninsured Motorist Insurance also provide for reductions of the insurer's liability in several types of situations in which a claimant is indemnified by one of the other coverages.[3] *Third,* the General Provisions section of the insurance policy usually includes a clause stating that "If this policy and any other auto insurance issued to you by us apply to the same accident, the maximum limit of our liability under all policies shall not exceed the highest applicable limit

---

§ 5.9(b)

1. Multiple coverage questions may also involve claims made under two or more similar coverages in different policies. Such claims are usually analyzed in relation to coverage terms which are referred to as Other Insurance clauses. See the

discussion of Other Insurance clauses in § 3.11, above.

2. See the Insurance Services Office Personal Auto Policy (1980), in Appendix H.

3. *Ibid.*

of liability under any one policy." [4] Although somewhat different public policy interests — as well as varying individual interests of a claimant in some circumstances — should be analyzed in regard to the effect of the various limits of liability clauses for each type of insurance, the following discussion of these questions as they relate to medical payments insurance and uninsured motorist insurance claims provides a general overview of the factors that should be considered in such cases.

(i) Multiple Units of Medical Payments Insurance.

When a motor vehicle insurance policy that provides coverage for two or more automobiles includes medical payments insurance, insurers typically charge a separate premium for the medical payments coverage that applies to individuals who may be insured as occupants of each insured vehicle — that is, a separate premium is charged for the medical payments insurance for each vehicle that is specifically identified as a covered vehicle in the declarations. This is certainly justified because the coverage for each vehicle constitutes a distinct risk for the insurer. For example, each of the vehicles could be driven at the same time and each could be involved in an accident causing injuries requiring medical care for the occupants.

The medical payments insurance often provides coverage for the named insured and family members who reside in the named insured's household if they are injured in any automobile accident. Thus, for example, an insured who is injured while crossing a street is insured by the medical payments coverage. Insureds have sought to "stack" or "pyramid" several coverages in some situations, and in cases in which the policy language was clearly and explicitly designed to preclude any recovery beyond the maximum limit of liability set forth in the declarations for the policy.[5]

When an insured sustains injuries that result in medical expenses that exceed a limit of liability specified for the medical expenses coverage, there is a split among the judicial precedents as to whether a claimant may recover from more than one of the medical payments coverages in such a policy.[6] If an insurance policy provides several "units" of the same coverage and it does not include any express provision against stacking, a persuasive case can be made for allowing recovery under more than one such coverage on the rationale of viewing such coverage terms as creating an ambiguity which is construed against the insurer and in favor of indemnification for insureds. Moreover, this analysis is particularly persuasive when an insured would be allowed to recover under two or more such coverages in

---

4. *Ibid.*

5. Also see the discussion of Other Insurance clauses in § 3.11, above.

6. Government Employees Insurance Co. v. Sweet, 186 So.2d 95 (Fla.App. 4th Dist.1966), 21 A.L.R.3d 895 (1967) (*held*, coverage up to twice the limit; the coverage associated with each automobile applied regardless of whether the insured was in that automobile or elsewhere when injured).

Contra. Sullivan v. Royal Exchange Assurance, 181 Cal.App.2d 644, 5 Cal.Rptr. 878 (2d Dist.1960).

separate insurance policies acquired from different insurers, and especially if premium charges are comparable to those that would have been paid for the same coverage in separate insurance policies purchased for each of the vehicles. Accordingly, it is not surprising that insurers typically include limit of liability terms that are designed to restrict an insured's right to a recovery.

As noted above, motor vehicle insurance policies typically provide that the limit of liability shown in the declarations for the coverage is the maximum amount the insurer will pay regardless of the number of vehicles or premiums shown in the declarations. Although such provisions can serve to eliminate the ambiguities in the coverage terms, claims for indemnification by insureds may still be predicated on reasonable expectations arising from the payment of separate premiums for several medical payments coverages *and* the fairness to the insured when the acquisition of the same coverage from different insurers would have allowed recovery under more than one insurance policy. In the coverage disputes that have arisen involving medical payments coverage which included express provisions precluding the "aggregating" or "stacking" of two or more coverages, courts have usually upheld the validity of limit of liability provisions that restricted payments to one coverage unit.[7]

(ii) Multiple Units of Uninsured Motorist Insurance.

Comparable questions about stacking uninsured motorist insurance have been very extensively litigated since the mid 1960s. The uninsured motorist coverage policy forms uniformly include provisions — both limit of liability and Other Insurance clauses[8] — that purport to preclude the "stacking" of individual coverages in a single policy so that a recovery cannot be secured by a claimant under more than one coverage. Many of the appellate courts which have considered the issue have concluded that such limitations are not enforceable when a claimant would not be fully indemnified by the insurance benefits provided by one of the individual coverages.[9] Several of the factors that contribute to the resolution of these questions in regard to the uninsured motorist coverage are considered in § 3.1(6), above, § 3.11, above, § 6.4, below, and in the following subsection.

---

7. See, e.g., Wachovia Bank & Trust Company v. Westchester Fire Insurance Company, 276 N.C. 348, 172 S.E.2d 518 (1970).

Also see Lane v. Fireman's Fund Insurance Company, 344 So.2d 702 (La.App., 4th Cir., 1977).

But see, Woods v. Nationwide Mutual Insurance Company, 295 N.C. 500, 246 S.E.2d 773 (1978), which distinguished the *Wachovia* decision, above, on the basis that when the applicable clauses in the insurance contract were read in conjunction with each other, the contract was ambiguous and would therefore be construed against the drafter (the insurance company).

8. See the discussion of Other Insurance clauses in § 3.11, above.

9. See Widiss, UNINSURED AND UNDERINSURED MOTORIST INSURANCE (1985), Chapter 13 and Chapter 14.

(iii) Multiple Units of Different Coverages.

[Insureds sometimes present claims for indemnification from several different coverages included in a single insurance policy. For example, an automobile insurance policy usually includes liability insurance, medical payments insurance, and uninsured motorist insurance which all may apply to losses resulting from bodily injuries to an occupant of the insured vehicle. Thus, when a passenger in an insured automobile is injured as a result of the negligence both of the car's driver and another driver who is an uninsured motorist, the passenger may seek indemnification for medical expenses under (1) the medical payments coverage, (2) the bodily injury liability coverage, and (3) the uninsured motorist insurance. When a claimant asserts a right to recover separately under each of these coverages in the motor vehicle insurance applicable to the vehicle in which the injured person was a passenger, the question of the effect of the limit of liability offset provisions should be separately analyzed from the perspective of each of the coverages because somewhat distinguishable considerations apply in regard to the three different types of insurance. The following portion of this subsection examines the effect of payments of the medical payments insurance on the uninsured motorist insurance.[10]

The uninsured motorist coverage limit of liability provision states that the company shall not be obligated to pay damages for medical services paid or payable under the medical payments coverage of the policy,[11] and therefore appears to reduce the amount payable under the uninsured motorist insurance by the amount either paid or payable under a medical payments coverage of the same motor vehicle insurance policy.[12] For example, if an insurance company makes a payment of two thousand dollars to the claimant under the medical payments

---

10. The limit of liability terms used by most insurance companies in uninsured motorist coverages include clauses that provide for the reduction of liability (1) for the part of the damages that represents expenses for medical services paid or payable under the medical payments coverage of the policy, and (2) for all sums paid on behalf of the owner or operator of the uninsured highway vehicle and any other person or organizations jointly or severally liable.

In addition, there are also reductions of liability for (1) the amount paid and the present value of all amounts payable under any workers' compensation law, (2) for the amount paid and present value of all amounts payable under any disability benefits law, (3) for the amounts paid and the present value of all amounts payable under any law similar to either a workers' compensation law or a disability benefits law.

The enforceability of the coverage provisions that relate to payments received from the owner or operator of an uninsured highway vehicle and any other person who is jointly liable is considered in Chapter 16 and Chapter 17 of UNINSURED AND UNDERINSURED MOTORIST INSURANCE (1985 and 1987), by Professor Widiss.

11. Similar offset provisions are included in the other coverages. See the forms set forth in Appendix H.

12. See the 1966 Standard Form, Part III: Limits of Liability (d), in Appendix H.

In the uninsured motorist provisions of the 1980 Personal Auto Policy form prepared by the Insurance Services Office, the limit of liability section of the uninsured motorist coverage no longer includes a clause specifying that the uninsured motorist insurance may be reduced for that part of the damages which represents expenses that have been paid or are payable under the medical payments coverage of the policy.

coverage, this provision states that the insurer's maximum liability under the uninsured motorist insurance is to be reduced by that amount and the reduction is to be made regardless of whether the claimant has been fully compensated.[13]

The enforceability of this limit of liability provision is not completely settled.[14] Although there is a split of authority among these decisions, the trend among the more recent decisions is towards the invalidation of limit of liability provisions in uninsured motorist insurance coverage which allow the insurers to reduce liability.[15] It now seems likely that the majority rule will be that this reduction of liability provision is unenforceable when the claimant has not been fully indemnified for losses.

Uninsured Motorist Coverage as a Special Case

The analysis by the Arizona Supreme Court is representative of the approach adopted by many courts that have considered the issue of the effects of offsets on an uninsured motorist coverage. The Court observed:

> "Permitting offsets of any type would allow insurers, by contract, to alter the provisions of the statute and to escape all or part of the liability which the Legislature intended they should provide. The medical payment coverage part of the policy is independent of the uninsured motorist coverage and should be treated the same as if it were carried with a different company."[16]

The court reasoned that in light of the fact that the medical payments coverage should be treated as if it were provided by a different company, "the fact that the motorist sees fit to clothe himself with other insurance protection and pay a premium therefor * * * cannot alter the mandatory safeguards that the Legislature considers necessary for the well being of the citizen-drivers of our state."[17] The court then concluded that in this context, any attempt by an insurance company to reduce the uninsured motorist coverage below the minimum amount of coverage required by the state's financial responsibility laws violates the uninsured motorist insurance statutory requirements.

Medical payments coverage in a motor vehicle insurance policy is a first-party, no-fault insurance coverage that applies regardless of whether the tortfeasor who causes an accident is insured or uninsured. In many states, an injured person would be entitled to receive indemni-

---

13. The provision only applies to medical coverage that is part of the same policy as the uninsured motorist coverage. No reduction would be made, under the provisions used in the standard form, for medical payment coverage in other insurance policies.

14. See the decisions discussed in Widiss, UNINSURED AND UNDERINSURED MO-TORIST INSURANCE (1985 and 1987), in Chapter 14.

15. *Ibid.*

16. Bacchus v. Farmers Insurance Group Exchange, 106 Ariz. 280, 475 P.2d 264 at p. 266 (1970).

17. Id., 106 Ariz. 280, 475 P.2d 264 at p. 267 (1970).

fication from both the medical payments coverage and from a negligent tortfeasor's insurance company. If the uninsured motorist coverage is reduced by the amounts paid or payable by the medical payments coverage, the insured is in a less favorable position than would have existed if the tortfeasor had been insured. As the Illinois Supreme Court concluded:

> "If the crediting provisions were to apply in all situations, including those where the total damages suffered by the insured exceed the combined total uninsured-motorist and medical-payment coverages, the net result would be that the uninsured motorist coverage under the policy would not assure compensation comparable to that available if the insured had been insured by one insured in compliance with the Financial Responsibility Law." [18]

The limit of liability provision that purports to reduce the uninsured motorist insurance by the amount of any payment under the medical payments insurance of the same insurance policy has been determined to be unenforceable by the Supreme Courts in numerous states.[19] In general, in these cases judges are concerned with both the public interest manifested by the state's legislation establishing requirements for such insurance protection and the public interest in coordination of benefits to ensure that the medical payments coverage does not duplicate the indemnification provided by the uninsured motorist insurance.[20]

Comment

When it is evident that the combined insurance benefits provided by different coverages will not provide full indemnification for the losses of the claimant, there are persuasive arguments for allowing recovery under several different coverages.[21] In this context, indemnification should be the guiding public interest and courts appropriately hold that limit of liability provisions restricting a coverage that is mandated by legislative requirements should not be enforced. However, allowing a recovery by a claimant which exceeds the losses is inconsistent with the principle that insurance is intended as indemnity for loss.[22] Denial of such fortuitous profits seems the preferable rule, and limit of liability provisions should be applied by the courts to preclude such recoveries.[23]

18. Glidden v. Farmers Automobile Insurance Association, 57 Ill.2d 330, 312 N.E.2d 247 at p. 251 (1974).

19. See the decisions cited in Widiss, UNINSURED AND UNDERINSURED MOTORIST INSURANCE (1985), at § 14.2.

20. See especially the opinion in Hartford Accident and Indemnity Company v. Lackore, 408 So.2d 1040 at p. 1042 (Fla. 1982).

21. Concerning other problems of overlapping coverages, see § 3.11 and § 5.5(c), above.

22. See, e.g., Long v. Landy, 35 N.J. 44, 171 A.2d 1 (1961) (collateral source rule applied even as between a wife and the estate of her deceased husband, who was the tortfeasor).

Also see the discussion in § 3.1, above.

23. E.g., Yarrington v. Thornburg, 58 Del. (8 Storey) 152, 205 A.2d 1 (1964), 11 A.L.R.3d 1110 (1967) (*held*, tortfeasor enti-

(2) Multiple Claims Under A Single Coverage: Loss of Consortium

There are many instances in which persons sustain consequential damages as the result of bodily injury to another individual. One type of such injury is loss of consortium. Loss of consortium claims, as well as other claims by individuals for consequential damages, have presented the question whether liability insurance benefits paid to one spouse for loss of consortium resulting from an injury to the other spouse are "chargeable" against an insured's per-person limit of liability for the individual who was physically injured. Essentially the same question may arise when children assert claims for consequential damages that result from an injury to a parent, as well as in other comparable situations.

The relevant limit of liability provisions in most insurance policies define the insurer's liability in terms of providing coverage for "bodily injury to one person" — or some similar phrase — so that the per-person limit of liability specifying the maximum amount of insurance regardless of the number of claims made (rather than the per-accident limit of liability) applies when only one individual has actually sustained a bodily injury. Most decisions in point have held that consortium damages and other consequential damages sustained by persons other than the individual who was physically injured are treated as part of the total that is subject to the limit of liability that applies when one person suffers a physical injury. This means, for example, that the combined amount paid by an insurer as a consequence of the separate claims of a wife and husband because of physical injury to one of them will not exceed the per-person limit of liability specified in the insurance policy.[24]

tled to credit, in reduction of damages, for medical payments to guest passenger under tortfeasor's insurance policy, even though the policy did not so stipulate; since the tort judgment exceeded the liability insurance limit, this is not merely a question of the insurer's contractual liability).

Also see Yarrington v. Thornburg, 8 Storey 234, 208 A.2d 60 (Del.Super.1965) (Thornburg was judgment proof and his carrier paid $10,000 under liability coverage and $5,000 under medical payments coverage; tort judgment of $40,000 had been entered against Thornburg and two others as joint tortfeasors; having received $25,000 from the other two, plaintiff sought to recover an additional $5,000 paid under Thornburg's medical payments coverage; held for defendants, the credit being allowed).

24. See, e.g., Smith v. State Farm Mutual Automobile Insurance Company, 252 Ark. 57 at p. 58, 477 S.W.2d 186 at p. 187 (1972) (liability insurance); Sheffield v.

American Indemnity Company, 245 S.C. 389 (1965), 140 S.E.2d 787, 13 A.L.R.3d 1220 (1967) (uninsured motorist coverage).

Also see State Farm Mutual Automobile Insurance Company v. Ball, 127 Cal.App.3d 568 at pp. 570–571, 179 Cal.Rptr. 644 at p. 646 (1981) (liability insurance); Greenberg v. Medi-Cab Inc. of New York, 114 Misc.2d 104 at p. 107, 451 N.Y.S.2d 335 at p. 238 (New York County 1982) (liability insurance).

Cf. United States Fidelity and Guaranty Company v. Pearthree, 389 So.2d 109 (Miss.1980).

But see Bilodeau v. Lumbermens Mutual Casualty Company, 392 Mass. 537, 467 N.E.2d 137 at p. 142 (1984), in which the court concluded that when the per person limit of liability is exhausted, the "fair meaning of the language" used in the standard Massachusetts automobile liability insurance policy provisions (which are prescribed by statute and controlled by the Division of Insurance) was that an insurer

§ 5.10   The Duration of the Coverage Period

5.10(a)   Introductory Note

The duration of an insurance contract — that is, the period of time for which coverage is provided — is ordinarily governed by explicit provisions in the insurance policy that limit the risks transferred to an insurer. In some instances, however, overriding interests, either of an individual insured or of the public, have been held to warrant extending coverage to events occurring during time periods which the insurer did not intend to include. This section discusses several problems illustrating the types of situations in which courts have sustained claims for coverage beyond the time period specified in the applicable insurance policy terms.

§ 5.10(b)   Claims for Coverage Beyond the Duration Specified in the Declarations

(1)   Determining the Commencement Date for Coverage and the Anniversary Date for Renewals

The date an insurance policy begins to provide coverage is usually specifically stated by the insurer, either on the first page of the coverage terms or on an attached schedule which is typically identified as a "Declarations" page, and usually is characterized as the "commencement date" (or by some comparable term). Sometimes the date specified by the insurer for the renewal of an insurance coverage does not coincide with the projected "anniversary" of the commencement date stated in the policy — that is, the specified renewal date usually arrives sooner than a date which would be fixed by a calculation of a given number of complete weeks, months, or year(s) following the commencement date. In other words, the date on which an additional premium is due is not exactly a whole number of years, or months, or weeks following the date when the coverage began.[1]

is obligated to make additional payments within the "per accident" limit of liability for loss of consortium claims by the injured person's spouse or children because such persons suffer a distinct injury. The court decided that "the insurers' interpretation is incompatible with the independent status of the loss of consortium injury as well as with the language of the policy * * *." The court commented in footnotes 9 that

"The issue of the appropriate treatment of loss of consortium claims arises in these cases because of the lack of explicit resolution of the question by G.L. c. 90, § 34A, or the standard policy. It may be that the failure of the statute and policy to keep pace with the evolution of the cause of action for loss of consortium has forced insurers into the untenable position that a loss of consortium claimant is within the policy coverage, but not a separate 'person' for purposes of liability limits. Action by the Legislature to amend the statute, or permission of the Commissioner of Insurance to clarify the extent of coverage for consortium claims, would be beneficial to insurers as well as policyholders."

§ 5.10(b)

1. Differences between these dates may be a result either of requirements that the premium must be paid before coverage begins or that a policy must actually be delivered to an insured before coverage begins. In some instances, if the anniversary date is specified by the insurer when the policy is issued, such requirements result in delaying the commencement date so that the

A coverage dispute may arise in regard to whether an amount paid — as an annual, semi-annual, or even a monthly premium — should be held to purchase coverage for the period until the renewal date stated in the insurance policy *or* for a calendar period determined by a number of months or a year (or years) following the date on which the coverage commenced [2] (plus, in either instance, a grace period if the insurance contract so provides). Claims involving such issues typically occur when a premium is not paid on or before the date specified by the insurer for a renewal of the coverage (or within any grace period allowed following the renewal date stated in the policy). The coverage question arises because thereafter an "insured" event (such as the death of a person covered by life insurance) occurs before the expiration of the coverage period which would be applicable if the policy period were based on a computation of an "anniversary" of the date when the insurance coverage actually commenced, rather than being based on the renewal date specified in the insurance policy.

(2) Restricting Coverage to the Period of Time Specified in the Declarations

Many, and probably most, of the judicial decisions in point have held that the date specified in the insurance policy by the insurer as the date on which renewal premiums would be due is to be given effect in determining both when a policy period ends and when a grace period (if any) commences or ends — that is, courts have held that a definite and clear statement of a date on which subsequent premiums will be due is an enforceable due date.[3] In some of these decisions, courts have explicitly concluded that the date specified should be used notwithstanding the fact that the coverage was actually in force for something less than a full period of months or a year (or some comparable typical coverage period).[4]

(3) Extending Coverage to a Time Period After the Anniversary Date

The coverage period for insurance policies has been determined by some courts on the basis that an insurer must extend coverage for a

---

resulting coverage period is somewhat less than the time period of coverage that the premium would otherwise purchase.

2. See the discussion of delivery in § 2.7, above.

3. See, e.g., Young v. Fidelity Union Life Insurance Company, 597 F.2d 705 (10th Cir.1979); Life Insurance Company of the Southwest v. Overstreet, 603 S.W.2d 780 (Tex.1980).

Cf. Brand v. Monumental Life Insurance Company, 275 Ind. 308, 417 N.E.2d 297 at p. 302 (1981). The court concluded that there "was evidence from which the trial court could reasonably find that Monumental was not estopped from asserting forfeiture" because there was also evidence

"that supported the determination that the practice of the company in accepting overdue payments after the thirty-one day grace period and for an additional period of sixty days *was done only on condition that the insured was in apparent good health and alive, and that these conditions were well known to the insured, Brand.*" (Emphasis added).

Also see Kampf v. Franklin Life Insurance Co., 33 N.J. 36, 161 A.2d 717 (1960).

4. See, e.g., Life Insurance Company of the Southwest v. Overstreet, 603 S.W.2d 780 at p. 782 (Tex.1980).

Also see 1 Appleman, INSURANCE LAW AND PRACTICE (1965), at § 105.

period that is co-extensive with the time that would normally be associated with the premium amount charged by the insurer. For example, when an insured pays an amount which either is characterized as or is reasonably understood by the insured to be an "annual" premium, the insurer must provide coverage for a full year. Thus, the coverage period terminates a year after the coverage actually becomes effective (plus any applicable grace period), rather than on an earlier anniversary date stated in the policy.[5]

The disputes described in the preceding paragraphs concern cases in which coverage is alleged by an insurer to have terminated before an event resulting in a loss occurred. In appraising the appropriateness of these rules, the obverse type of factual situation should also be considered. This is the situation in which the event for which coverage was sought occurs either while an application for insurance is pending or after an application has been approved by the insurer, but before the occurrence of some action stated by the insurer to be a prerequisite to the commencement of coverage.

(4) Claims for Coverage During an Application Period

Coverage questions sometimes arise as the result of events which occur during the period that an application for insurance is pending. For example, consider the situation in which an application for disability insurance is submitted to a sales representative of an insurer on the first day of the month, and the insurance policy that is subsequently issued to the applicant states that the date the policy is issued, the fifteenth of the month, is the anniversary date. The insurance policy also specifies that coverage does not take effect until the policy is delivered the insured *and* the insured makes a payment of the first full premium, which subsequently occurs on the twentieth day of the month. Generally, in this type of situation the application is treated as an offer and the acceptance occurs when the executed policy is delivered (subject to a further delay if the purchaser does not make the required premium payment when the insurance policy is delivered).[6] Thus, if the normal contract formation rules of offer and acceptance are applied, in the absence of grounds for liability at variance with policy provisions,[7] the coverage would not be effective until the premium is

---

5. See, e.g., Duerksen v. Brookings International Life & Casualty Co., 84 S.D. 20, 166 N.W.2d 567 (1969); Lentin v. Continental Assurance Co., 412 Ill. 158, 105 N.E.2d 735 (1952), 44 A.L.R.2d 463 (1955).

Also see State Security Life Insurance Co. v. Kintner, 243 Ind. 331, 185 N.E.2d 527 (1962). Though reasoned as an exception consistent with the majority rule, this decision is more easily aligned with the minority. The policy in question specified that the annual premium payments (or the first of semi-annual or quarterly premium payments) were due on the anniversary of the date of issuance. Monthly payments

were made by the insured and accepted by the company. Since there was no specific reference in the policy to monthly payment of premiums, it was held that the payments were due on the monthly recurrence of the date the policy went into effect (the date of delivery), allowing recovery for the death of the insured within the grace period based upon the date the coverage took effect even though the grace period based upon the date of issuance had passed.

6. See § 2.1(c), above.

7. See Chapter 6, below.

paid. However, suppose an accident causing disability occurs on the fifth of the month, while the application is pending: Should a court disregard the contract formation process structured by the insurer and hold that a claim for benefits should be sustained?

In the type of situation described in the preceding paragraph, there are several approaches that might be viewed as appropriate by a court in deciding what period of time is covered by the insurance policy. *First,* if the time period specified in the declarations is determinative, there is no coverage for such a claim, *and* the insured receives less than a year's coverage for the first annual premium.[8] *Second,* if coverage were held to apply for a disabling accident occurring during the application period (in the above illustration, on the fifth day of the month), the insured would receive more than a full year of coverage for the premium. Certainly, the insured, if given choice in the matter, would pay the premium in order to secure the insurance benefits. However, if in other cases courts were to impose liability for a disabling injury occurring during a judicially imposed coverage period based on an anniversary date determined by when the premium was actually paid, insurers collectively would be compelled by such decisions to provide more than a year's coverage for the first annual premium as a consequence of extending both the point of commencement and the point of termination of coverage.

If the coverage period is extended both ways when claims arise, there will be some premium inequities for insureds. Recognition of the potential for imposing liability on the insurer in both types of situations should at least warrant some consideration of the import of such decisions for insurers and insureds, as well as whether it may be possible to adopt an approach to resolving the problem in a way that produces a year's coverage (plus any grace-period privileges), for the first annual premium. However, it is also clear that premium equity for insurers and insureds is not the only factor that warrants consideration in such cases.

There are many instances in which some premium inequities are accepted as a reasonable price to pay for other advantages.[9] The disparity in premium payments that results from an insurer's providing less than a year's coverage for an annual premium may be considered an acceptable result in some situations, as noted above, in order to attain the certainty that is produced by adhering to the dates specified in the policy documents. An inequity among policyholders, because they receive different coverage periods for the same premium, could be regarded as a permissible range of variation within a rate category,

---

8. See, e.g., Lentin v. Continental Assurance Co., 412 Ill. 158, 105 N.E.2d 735 (1952), 44 A.L.R.2d 463 (1955).

9. For example, a rate disparity is a normal consequence of invoking any theory of resolving ambiguities against insurers or any theory of recognizing rights at vari-

ance with contract terms, such as waiver or estoppel.

Similarly, the adverse effect on the rate structure is considered an acceptable consequence that is more than balanced by the desirability of providing coverage for a deserving claimant.

given that premiums can almost never be adjusted precisely to the infinite variations in the value of coverage.[10] Thus, the conclusion that the first premium, if not paid at the time of applying, purchases less than a full year's coverage can be justified on the ground of favoring a high level of certainty for an insurance policy's anniversary date.

Courts that have favored extending coverage beyond the date(s) set forth in an insurance policy prefer to regard the premium question as a relatively less important matter when compared to other concerns. For example, in a case where an accident occurred on the second day beyond a year after the policy date,[11] a court concluded — on the basis of enforcing the understanding of the parties — that the insurance coverage for the automobile commenced when the purchase was consummated, not when the application for credit to purchase the automobile was made. The underlying rationale in these cases would appear to be based on preferring indemnification for claimants, even at the expense of premium inequities and the type of uncertainty that fosters litigation.

(5) Claims Predicated on an Insurer's "Acceptance" of a Tardy Premium Payment

When a premium payment for the renewal of an insurance policy is sent after the expiration of the coverage period (and any applicable grace period), questions may arise as to whether retention of the premium by the insurer serves to reinstate (that is, whether the payment is to be given retroactive effect so as to "revive") the original policy, so that there is no gap in the coverage period, or instead leads to the initiation of a new coverage period.[12] Coverage questions may arise that involve either (1) the consequences of the first renewal payment or (2) the consequences of patterns that have been established in a series of tardy premium payments.[13] When the issue relates to the practices of an insurer in regard to late payments, the court may look to how payments by either the individual insured involved in a coverage dispute were handled or the treatment of similar payments by other insureds.

(6) Avoiding Coverage Gaps by Providing for Automatic Renewals

It is possible for an insured and an insurer to minimize the possibility for coverage disputes regarding the continuation of coverage

---

10. See § 8.4(b), below.

11. Marathon Insurance Co. v. Arnold, 433 P.2d 927 (Okl.1967).

12. *Cf.* Williams v. Prudential Insurance Company of America, 447 So.2d 685 (Ala.1984) (acceptance of one premium payment after a grace period had expired together with a concurrent application for reinstatement of the life insurance policy did not establish a practice by Prudential of habitually accepting premiums after the

policy was in default which would justify reliance on such a custom or habit); Brand v. Monumental Life Insurance Company, 275 Ind. 308, 417 N.E.2d 297 (1981) (insurer was entitled to claim forfeiture where the insurer was aware that late payments, beyond the grace period, would only reinstate the life insurance coverage if the insured was alive and in good health).

13. See the discussion in § 6.8(d).

by creating an arrangement that provides for automatic renewals of an insurance policy. For many types of insurance, an insured can request a provision, usually added to a policy by an endorsement, which is designed to avoid disputes involving possible lapses or gaps in the coverage period (resulting from a failure to pay a premium) by providing for automatic renewal. When this approach is used, the insurance policy usually also states a termination will only occur upon appropriate notice from the insurer (or, in some instances, the insured) in a written document which specifies the termination date. For example, such an endorsement may specify that the "Policy Period" will be from some specified date and will continue until the "time of surrender or the effective date and hour of cancellation" to be stated in a "notice of cancellation." [14] When this type of approach is employed, the insurance contract generally also includes a clause that provides for the periodic adjustment of the premium amounts.

§ 5.10(c)   Providing Coverage for Events That Occur Before Insurance Is Acquired

Occasionally insurance policies are written so that coverage is provided for a loss that has occurred before consummation of the insurance contract. Whether such insurance agreements violate any significant public interests, and therefore are unenforceable, depends on the circumstances.

(1) Marine Insurance

In the early days of marine insurance, an insurance agreement frequently would be made after the vessel to be insured was already at sea or was located in a foreign port from which contemporaneous communications could not be received at the point when the insurance was arranged. Quite frequently agreements were made to cover a vessel that was "lost or not lost," with an explicit understanding that if, unknown to both parties to the transaction, the vessel had already been lost or damaged from covered perils, the underwriter would be liable for the loss within the terms and limits of the amount underwritten.[1] Such agreements are entirely consistent with the fundamental princi-

---

14. See, e.g., the coverage terms in Continental Insurance Company v. PACCAR, Inc., 96 Wash.2d 160, 634 P.2d 291 (1981), which reversed the decision reported at 26 Wash.App. 850, 614 P.2d 675 (Div. 1, 1980).

§ 5.10(c)

1. See, e.g., Bond v. Nutt, 2 Cowp. 601, 98 Eng.Rep. 1262 (K.B. 1777) (opinion by Mansfield, J.) (contract made on August 20, 1776, on a vessel warranted to have sailed on or before August 1 from Jamaica to London; in July the vessel sailed from one port in Jamaica to another in Jamaica for the sole purpose of joining a convoy and proceeding to England; an embargo delayed the departure of the convoy from the second port until August 6; thereafter, the vessel was separated in passage and "was taken by an American privateer"; *held,* coverage).

In considering a claim under an open marine cargo insurance policy, a Florida Court of Appeal observed that "if a loss is known to both parties, a certificate of marine insurance thereafter issued could not affect the rights of the parties because it would be without consideration and void." Glens Falls Insurance Co. v. D. Black & Sons, Inc., 347 So.2d 617 at p. 618 (Fla.App., 3d Dist., 1977).

ple that insurance is a contract for coverage of a fortuitous loss.[2] Although other persons elsewhere in the world might be aware of the fact that the vessel in question had already been lost, from the point of view of the contracting parties there was only a risk that it had been lost, not a certainty one way or the other.[3] From their vantage point, with the limited knowledge available to them at the time of contracting, the loss that the insurer agreed to pay was fortuitous in nature even though it might later become known to the insured and the insurer that in fact the loss had already occurred before they made their contract.

Only rarely do circumstances arise in which the underlying principle of "lost or not lost" coverage developed in marine insurance applies to a non-marine context.

(2) Property Insurance

Occasionally the dating of an insurance contract, taken together with printed provisions about the time of day coverage commences, results in a stipulation for coverage that commences a few hours before the contract was actually made. The coverage questions which arise from such a situation are quite different depending on whether the insured knew that a loss had already occurred when the insurance contract was formed,[4] and, if so, whether a full disclosure was made to the insured.

There have been instances in which an individual has sought insurance after a loss has occurred without divulging the facts to the insurer. For example, if an automobile accident occurred at 1:00 p.m., and several hours later a person applied for coverage — knowing that the agent would write the contract so that coverage was stated to commence at 12:00 noon — without disclosing the accident, a claim of coverage should be denied. Most courts would hold an applicant has a duty to disclose that an accident had occurred in such a situation, even under the rather limited stringency of the doctrine of concealment applied in non-marine insurance cases,[5] because the applicant knew or should have known an insurer would not enter into such an arrangement if the accident were disclosed. Moreover, to permit coverage in such a case would be inconsistent with the fundamental premise that insurance is concerned with the transfer of a risk of loss, whereas in this instance the loss is already known by the applicant to be certain.

2. Concerning this principle generally, see § 5.3(a), above.

3. See § 1.3, above regarding the meaning of "risk."

4. See, e.g., Burch v. Commonwealth County Mutual Insurance Co., 450 S.W.2d 838 (Tex.1970) (damage to automobile occurring on July 18 held to be covered by policy issued by agent on July 19 for period of one year commencing at 12:01 on July 18; insured applied on July 18 before acci-

dent occurred, and agent told him he was covered, though not specifying the company; insured was unable to notify agent of accident for several days after it occurred; neither insurer nor agent knew of accident when policy was issued on July 19 with defendant company). Also see the opinions in this case reported at 440 S.W.2d 410 (Tex.Civ.App., Beaumont, 1969).

5. See § 5.8, above.

Thus, it is generally held that in such circumstances a contract does not cover a loss occurring before it was made.[6]

(3) Liability Insurance

In some instances insurance has been acquired after the occurrence of an event causing losses, with a full disclosure of the events to the insurer. For example, the owners of a large hotel in Las Vegas, Nevada sought retroactively to increase the amount of liability insurance to be provided as excess coverage following a fire in which there were a number of deaths and injuries. One justification for treating the transaction as a permissible insurance contract was the theory that the requisite uncertainty which underlies all insurance transactions was still present at the time of contracting because the number, size, and final cost of disposition of the liability claims were unknown. The transaction involved a premium payment of several million dollars. At the time of this writing, the transaction has led to litigation between the insured and the insurers in regard to the way the claims were settled — by the insured and the primary insurers — which resulted in very substantial liability for the insurers who provided the retroactive excess coverage.

§ 5.10(d) Defining and Discerning the Scope of the Coverage Period

Insurers have developed several different ways or approaches to defining the period of time for which coverage is provided. The provisions which specify various types of constraints that relate either (1) to when an event will be covered or (2) to when a claim must be made have given rise to a variety of issues. For example, coverage questions sometimes arise when losses are sustained substantially after the occurrence of an insured event. One of the questions that is most frequently presented as a consequence of such events is whether the time limit stated in the insurance contract prescribes (1) the period within which a defined event (that may subsequently cause damages after the coverage period) must occur, (2) the period within which losses must be suffered, or (3) the period within which claims must be made. The resolution of such coverage questions may be influenced by the type of insurance, as well as by the specific coverage terms.

(1) Coverage for "Occurrences"

The most common technique employed by insurers to define the duration of coverage is to predicate coverage on an "occurrence" of an event or an accident within the time period specified in the policy, without imposing any limitation in regard to when losses, such as

---

6. See, e.g., General Insurance Co. of America v. Lapidus, 325 F.2d 287 (9th Cir. 1963) (California law; coverage for gradual landslide that, unknown to applicant, had already started; dictum that if loss had already occurred or if quick process of de-struction was already under way, there would be no coverage).

See generally 4 APPLEMAN, INSURANCE LAW (Revised edition, 1969), at § 2291.

medical expenses, are subsequently sustained.[1]   Motor vehicle liability insurance policy forms, for example, commonly state a specific time period within which a covered event must have occurred if coverage is to be provided by the policy.   Under motor vehicle liability coverage, an insured has coverage for claims made and damages awarded years after the policy has terminated, so long as the liability results from an "occurrence" within the stated time limits.   Furthermore, portions of loss — such as medical expenses incurred over a period of years following an accident — for which coverage is provided may occur after the time period specified for the coverage of an occurrence.

A potentially significant exception to the general pattern of stating that the coverage applies for events occurring in the policy period without regard to when the economic loss is suffered arises from a modification of the liability insurance forms introduced in 1966.   Some post–1966 forms provide coverage for an "occurrence," and define "occurrence" to mean "an accident, including injurious exposure to conditions, *which results, during the policy period, in bodily injury or property damages* neither expected nor intended from the standpoint of the insured."[2]   This type of language might be invoked to limit an insurer's liability.[3]

§ 5.10(d)

1.   See, e.g., National Aviation Underwriters, Inc. v. Idaho Aviation Center, Inc., 93 Idaho 668, 471 P.2d 55 (1970) (aircraft policy applying "only to occurrences, and losses to the insured aircraft which are sustained, during the policy period * * *", included "Airport Liability Endorsement" with coverage for losses to property "caused by accident * * *"; held, no coverage for propeller failure after cancellation of the policy, even though the failure allegedly resulted from negligent repair occurring before cancellation).

Similarly, in Millers Mutual Fire Insurance Company of Texas v. Ed Bailey, Inc., 103 Idaho 377, 647 P.2d 1249 (1982), the court considered whether a liability insurance policy "extends coverage for liability arising out of installation during the policy term of a dangerously defective product, when damages did not occur until after the expiration of the policy." *Id.*, 647 P.2d at p. 1251.   The court stated that it adhered to "to the views expressed in *National Aviation,* * * * that an 'accident' within the meaning of a policy insuring against liability, unless otherwise defined, does not occur until damages resulting from an insured act occur." *Id.*, 647 P.2d at p. 1252.

Also see Silver Eagle Co. v. National Union Fire Insurance Co., 246 Or. 398, 423 P.2d 944 (1967) (products liability insurer not liable for products sold by insured dis-tributor during period of policy when the accident occurred after cancellation of a policy that reserved to the insurer the right to cancel upon 10–days–notice).

Also see Annotation, *Time of disability or death with regard to termination of coverage under group policy,* 68 A.L.R.2d 150–205 (1959); Annotation, *Occurrence of accident or injury as during, or before or after time period of coverage of liability period,* 57 A.L.R.2d 1385–1394 (1958), Annotation, *Products Liability Insurance,* 45 A.L.R.2d 994–1101 at p. 999 (1956).

Severe problems of disputed coverage have arisen in the applications of "occurrence" definitions to asbestosis claims. See generally Note, *The Manville Bankruptcy: Treating Mass Tort Claims in Chapter II Proceedings,* 96 Harvard Law Review 1121–1142 (1984).

2.   See the 1966 General Liability—Automobile Insurance Policy Form in Appendix G (Emphasis added).

3.   It would provide the basis for an insurer to assert a defense to an insurance claim on the ground that although an accidental exposure to impurities that were negligently discharged into the air by the insured occurred during the policy period, coverage would not apply if the claimed bodily injury did not result before the policy period had expired.

Similar problems concerning the duration of coverages are presented under certain types of specialized liability insurance [4] such as coverage for the liabilities of corporate directors.[5] These policies commonly include provisions which require that a loss occur within the specified time limits of the coverage (or within a stated extension period in case of cancellation). A potentially troublesome question that may arise under such coverage is whether a claim made after the period has passed is covered if it is based on conduct that occurred within the coverage period. And a comparable problem may also be presented in relation to claims based on physical injury under other liability coverages. For example, a claim may be made against a builder for an injury allegedly caused by the negligent performance of a building contract, but actually sustained years after the performance was completed.[6]

(2) Provisions That Limit Coverage to Losses "Incurred" Within a Prescribed Time Period

Medical coverages, in addition to stating the customary period during which an accident must have occurred to furnish the basis for coverage, have commonly provided that coverage is only provided for medical services or expenses "incurred" within one year from the date of an accident.[7] This policy language sometimes leads to the issue of the meaning to be accorded to the term "incurred." [8] There is a division among the judicial precedents on whether expenses are "incurred" within the period of coverage by an agreement for the medical services to be performed when the services are actually rendered after the expiration of the prescribed one-year period.[9]

---

4. In addition to the example that follows in the text above, see Long v. Sakleson, 328 Pa. 261, 195 A. 416 (1937).

5. See generally Note, *Liability Insurance for Corporate Executives,* 80 Harvard Law Review 648–669 at p. 651 (1967).

6. See, e.g., Meeker v. Motorists Mutual Insurance Company, 29 Ohio App.2d 49, 278 N.E.2d 46 (Allen County 1972); Leger v. Lisonbee, 207 So.2d 563 (La.App., 3d Cir., 1968); Caine v. Physicians' Indemnity Company of America, 45 S.W.2d 904 (Mo. App., St. Louis, 1932).

Also see Maryland Casualty Company v. Thomas, 289 S.W.2d 652 at p. 655 (Tex.Civ. App., Amarillo, 1965).

7. Many insurance contracts do not define the term "incurred." However, some policies do include a definition, such as, "Incurred means become liable for." See Rubin v. Empire Mutual Insurance Company, 25 N.Y.2d 426 at p. 429, 306 N.Y.S.2d 914 at p. 917, 255 N.E.2d 154 at p. 155 (1969).

Also see Kirchoff v. Nationwide Mutual Insurance Company, 19 A.D.2d 638, 241 N.Y.Supp.2d 185 (2d Dept.1963).

8. See, e.g., Hein v. American Family Mutual Insurance Company, 166 N.W.2d 363 (Iowa 1969); Riverside Insurance Company of America v. Cargill, 570 S.W.2d 455 (Tex.Civ.App., Amarillo, 1978); Northwestern National Life Insurance Company v. Glenn, 568 S.W.2d 693 (Tex.Civ.App., Fort Worth, 1978).

9. See, e.g., Czarnecki v. American Indemnity Co., 259 N.C. 718, 131 S.E.2d 347 (1963) (denying recovery for services performed after the stated period but distinguishing rather than declining to follow a case in which recovery had been allowed because an obligation to pay for dental work had been entered into within the stipulated period); Reliance Mutual Life Insurance Co. v. Booher, 166 So.2d 222 (Fla.App.2d Dist.1964), 10 A.L.R.3d 458 (1966) (recovery denied for cost of plastic surgery for which a general agreement had been made within the stated period; however, rather than explicitly declining to follow certain cases allowing recovery for

The prevailing view appears to be that coverage exists not only for services that are rendered or performed within one year, but also "when the expenses are charged, paid, obligated to be paid, (or) prepaid * * * within one year from the date of the accident." [10] This approach adopts an expansive, but defensible, meaning for the term in the clause stating that coverage is provided for "*expenses* incurred within one year from the date of the accident." Furthermore, courts in several states have concluded that even more extensive coverage is warranted. For example, in a case in which the record indicated that (a) before the expiration date the claimant had consulted with a neurologist, (b) some treatment had been rendered, and (c) a second operation could only be performed after the claimant had fully recovered from the first operation, a New York court observed that "notwithstanding that both operations were performed after the one year period had expired" the expenses for the services "were incurred within the one year period." [11] The court commented:

> "Any other construction would require that an injured party, in order to avail himself of the benefits of the policy, submit to hasty surgery, without the safeguard of standard medical testing procedures and regardless of his physical ability to undergo surgery at the time and would deny him a choice in the selection of a surgeon whose schedule might not permit the operation to be performed within the one-year period." [12]

Considerations such as those recognized in this New York case undoubtedly have influenced the decisions of other courts which have essentially adopted the view that medical expenses for all reasonable medical services needed for the treatment of injuries sustained in an accident are incurred on the date of the accident, regardless of when the services are performed, charged, or paid. [13]

services performed after the stated period this court distinguished such cases as involving prepayments or fixed obligations to pay rather than mere agreements for such services to be performed without the obligation of payment having been fixed).

Also see Annotation, *When is medical expense "incurred" under policy providing for payment of medical expense incurred within fixed period of time from date of injury,* 10 A.L.R.3d 468–474 (1966).

10. Riverside Insurance Company of America v. Cargill, 570 S.W.2d 455 at p. 456 (Tex.Civ.App., Amarillo, 1978).

11. Farr v. Travelers Indemnity Company, 84 Misc.2d 189 at p. 191, 375 N.Y.S.2d 229 at p. 231 (Erie County 1975).

12. *Id.,* 84 Misc.2d at pp. 191–192, 375 N.Y.S.2d at pp. 231–232.

13. In Maryland Casualty Company v. Thomas, 289 S.W.2d 652 at p. 655 (Tex.Civ. App., Amarillo, 1965), the court stated that "we think appellant became liable for 'all reasonable expenses * * * caused by the accident' on the day it occurred." In that case, the injury necessitated extensive dental work on a child which could not be done until the permanent teeth had grown in. However, the boy's father actually contracted with and paid the dentist for the services that would be subsequently rendered.

Also see Humphries v. Puritan Life Insurance Company, 311 So.2d 534 (La.App. 1975); Valladares v. Monarch Insurance Co., 282 So.2d 569 (La.App., 4th Cir., 1973).

(3) "Claims Made" Coverage

Many liability insurance policies, including some types of professional liability insurance and the newer forms of the comprehensive general liability policy,[14] are written to provide indemnification for claims that are made during the coverage period ("claims made" coverage) rather than for "occurrences" during the coverage period. For example, in a "claims made" form the principal insuring agreement typically states that the insurer agrees:

> "To pay on behalf of the Insured all sums which the Insured shall become legally obligated to pay as damages *because of any claim or claims made against the Insured during the policy period* arising out of the performance of professional services *rendered or which should have been rendered, subsequent to the retroactive date* by any person for whose acts or omissions the Insured partnership, corporation, or professional association is legally responsible * * *."[15]

In the 1970s, most professional liability insurers discontinued use of "occurrence" policies and offered professional liability coverage only on a "claims made" basis. A physician or lawyer who had previously carried liability insurance that provided coverage on an occurrence basis was, for example, offered a 1975 policy effective January 1, 1975 through December 31, 1975 with coverage only for "claims made" during 1975 arising from services rendered after the "retroactive date" of January 1, 1975.

The premium rate for a new "claims made" policy, which only provides coverage for events that occur after the inception of the insurance policy and for claims that were made during the coverage period, can be very low in comparison with the rate for the "occurrence" coverage of the previous year. For example, if a new claims made insurance only provides coverage for claims made in the current calendar year arising from professional services rendered after January 1, most of those claims will not be made until several years later. In subsequent years, the costs to insurers of providing "claims made" coverage rise rapidly as claims increase year by year from the activities of previous years. Thus, for example, the 1990 policy of an insured who shifted to "claims made" coverage on January 1, 1975 would cover "claims made" in 1990 arising from services rendered any time after January 1, 1975. Much of the impetus for development of "claims made" coverage was an interest in deferring a "crisis" over costs of malpractice coverage. Predictably, "claims made" coverage temporarily deferred, but did not resolve, the "crisis" over costs.

A professional who has "claims made" rather than "occurrence" coverage should make arrangements to protect against risks of "claims made" in future years on the basis of the current year's professional services and fees collected for those services. These arrangements should also include provisions for claims that may be made in the years

---

14. See Appendix J.   15. *Ibid.* (emphasis added).

after the insured has retired from professional activity. For example, typically the insurance policies offered to a professional include a "Reporting Endorsement" that confers on the policyholder, after nonrenewal or cancellation of the policy, the right to purchase coverage for these risks. A typical provision states that the insured has

> "* * * the right upon the payment of an additional premium (to be computed in accordance with the Company's rules, rates, rating plans and premiums applicable on the effective date of the endorsement to have an endorsement(s) providing additional Reporting Period(s) in which claims otherwise covered by this policy may be reported. Such right hereunder must, however, be exercised by the Insured by written notice not later than thirty (30) days after such termination date." [16]

This type of provision guarantees the policyholder an opportunity to buy coverage for "claims made" after retirement. The insured will be required to pay additional premiums at rates to be determined when that coverage is subsequently acquired. Thus, one of the principal disadvantages to the policyholder of the "claims made" (in comparison with the "occurrence") form of coverage is that the policyholder is left to bear much of the burden of uncertainty about future claims costs and the premiums which will have to be paid to cover the continuing risk that new claims may be asserted for activities that occurred years earlier.

Effective January 1, 1986, most liability insurers have sought to expand dramatically the use of "claims made" policies to liability risks beyond the professional liability areas in which these coverages came to be used extensively in the 1970s. The effort has met some resistance from corporate purchasers of insurance, whose risk management advisers have objected to the element of risk retention inherent in the "claims made" form. For example, the corporate liability insurance purchaser may object that the corporation will find it necessary to provide against the risks of long-term future claims costs arising from 1986 occurrences in some other way, if the insurer is unwilling to write "occurrence" rather than "claims made" coverage.

It is to be expected that proposals for wider use of "claims made" coverage will remain controversial, and developments may be influenced by regulation or legislation as well as market forces.

"Delayed–Manifestation" Injuries

Some injuries do not manifest themselves until a period of time has elapsed between the occurrence of the event that produces the harm and the time when it becomes apparent. Particularly when these claims result from what often were not recognized as dangerous products or chemicals when the exposure occurred, such as asbestos or dioxin, the consequences are referred to as "delayed-manifestation"

16. *Ibid.*

injuries. In recent decades, the claims arising from such cases have presented difficult insurance issues in regard to determining whether the company responsible for the loss has insurance coverage.

In many instances, the time period from when exposure occurred to the manifestation of the harm has been a substantial period of years, during which the company has often had periods of no coverage, as well as several different insurers for some portion of the time. Accordingly, when a tort claim is made by a third party, the issue presented is what theory should be employed to decide how liability ought to be allocated as between the company and its liability insurers. This problem is often referred to as a "trigger-of-coverage" question.

"Exposure" Theory. Several courts have concluded that liability should be based on when the exposure to the cause of the harm took place. If the exposure took place over a period of time, the liability could appropriately be allocated on the basis of the number of years the insured either did or did not have insurance coverage.[17] This approach is obviously "rooted" in "occurrence" theory of liability, which was frequently the basis of the applicable insurance coverage during the periods when the exposure occurred.

"Manifestation" Theory. Other courts have concluded that coverage is provided by the insurance policy in place at the time the injury becomes apparent, that is, when the injury is manifested.[18] In effect, this theory allocates the liability for such claims on a basis that is akin to a "claims made" approach irrespective of the type of insurance coverage that was acquired by the insured during the relevant periods of time.

"Multiple Trigger" Theory. A third approach, developed by the Circuit Court for the District of Columbia in Keene Corporation v. Insurance Company of North America,[19] allocates liability to every insurance coverage in effect at any time during the injury process, from the initial exposure until the last development of the injury is manifested. The multiple trigger approach has been employed in a number of subsequent decisions.[20]

17. *"Exoposure Only" Theory.* See, e.g. Hancock Laboratories Inc. v. Admiral Insurance Company, 777 F.2d 520 (9th Cir. 1985); Porter v. American Optical Corporation, 641 F.2d 1128 (5th Cir.1981), *cert. denied* 454 U.S. 1109, 102 S.Ct. 686, 70 L.Ed.2d 650 (1981).

Cf. Insurance Company of North America v. Forty-Eight Insulations, 633 F.2d 1212 (6th Cir.1980), *modified* 657 F.2d 814 (1981), *cert. denied* 454 U.S. 1109, 102 S.Ct. 686, 70 L.Ed.2d 650 (1981).

18. *"Manifestation Only" Theory.* See, e.g. Eagle-Picher Industries, Inc. v. Liberty Mutual Insurance Company, 523 F.Supp. 110 (D.Mass.1981), *affirmed as modified* 682 F.2d 12 (1st Cir.1982), *cert. denied* 460

U.S. 1028, 103 S.Ct. 1280, 75 L.Ed.2d 500 (1983), on later appeal 829 F.2d 227 (1st Cir.1987).

19. Keene Corporation v. Insurance Company of North America, 667 F.2d 1034 (D.C.Cir.1981), *cert. denied* 455 U.S. 1007, 102 S.Ct. 1644, 71 L.Ed.2d 875 (1982), *rehearing denied* 456 U.S. 951, 102 S.Ct. 2023, 72 L.Ed.2d 476 (1982).

20. *Multiple Trigger Theory.*

Aside from *Keene,* this method has also been used in Eli Lilly & Co. v. Home Insurance Co., 653 F.Supp. 1 (D.D.C.1984), set aside and certified to Indiana for resolution of certain questions, 764 F.2d 876 (D.C. Cir.1985); Owens-Illinois, Inc. v. Aetna

In 1986, Judge Flannery reviewed the adoptions and applications of these theories in a case involving the responsibility of liability insurers to provide defenses and indemnification for petrochemical companies who were being sued for dioxin related claims.[21] He observed that "[w]hile there are some general principles of insurance law accepted nationwide," the *Keene* multiple-trigger theory is not uniformly accepted as flowing from such principles and that it appears to have been rejected in several jurisdictions. Judge Flannery then concluded that "a conflict of laws exists" on the issue of what "triggers" an insurer's liability or how liability is to be allocated when there are either several different insurers or periods of no insurance involved in such cases.[22] At this juncture, there does not appear to be any consensus among the courts or the commentators.

§ 5.11 Termination of Coverage

§ 5.11(a) Introduction

Insurance contracts generally specify several grounds for the termination of coverage.[1] Among the circumstances addressed by the provisions typically included in insurance policies are (1) cancellation for nonpayment of premiums or for other specified causes,[2] (2) cancellation of the insurance policy by either the insurer or the insured without a showing of cause,[3] and (3) termination by nonrenewal upon the expiration of the coverage period. In addition, when a sales representative is authorized to bind an insurer, insurance policies — such as those for automobile insurance — generally state that the insurer is entitled to terminate the coverage during some specified period at the beginning of the coverage period.[4]

§ 5.11(b) Nonpayment of Premiums

Most insurance forms contain explicit provisions for the termination of the contract when an insured does not pay the premiums. Policies typically provide that an insurer may terminate coverage for

---

Cas. & Surety Co., 597 F.Supp. 1515 (D.D.C.1984), appeal docketed No. 85–5285 (D.C.Cir.1985); ACandS, Inc. v. Aetna Cas. & Surety Co., 576 F.Supp. 936 (E.D.Pa. 1983), appeals docketed 764 F.2d 968 (3d Cir.1985); Sandoz, Inc. v. Employer's Liability Assurance Corp., 554 F.Supp. 257 (D.N.J.1983); Vale Chem. Co. v. Hartford Accident & Indemnity Co., 340 Pa.Super. 510, 490 A.2d 896 (1985).

21. Independent Petrochemical Corporation v. Aetna Casualty and Surety Company, 654 F.Supp. 1334 (D.D.C.1986).

22. *Id.*, 654 F.Supp. at pp. 1344–1345.

§ 5.11(a)

1. For example, see the section on "Termination" in the General Provisions section of the automobile insurance forms in Appendix H.

Contract termination that involves the remedy of rescission is considered elsewhere in this text. See, e.g., § 6.1(b)(2) and § 6.10(e), below.

2. See § 5.11(b), below.

3. See § 5.11(c) and § 5.11(d), below.

4. See § 5.11(c), below.

nonpayment of a premium by sending an insured notice of cancellation.[1]

When an insurance contract is intended for the protection of persons or entities such as a lender, as well as the interests of the policyholder, the insurance contract may contain clauses which provide for the continuation of coverage under certain specified conditions for such other persons or entities after the termination of the policyholder's protection for the nonpayment of premiums.[2]

Life Insurance Policies With Cash Surrender Value

When an insured fails to pay a premium due for a life insurance policy which has a cash surrender value, it is common for the contract terms to provide that the insurer will automatically be authorized to make a "payment" of the premium amount that is due by in effect making a "loan" from the policy's cash value reserve (if the cash surrender value is at least equal to the premium that is due).[3] This approach serves to continue the coverage, rather than treating the failure to pay the premium as a basis for termination and then refunding the surrender value of the policy to the insured.

In the absence of an express provision in a life insurance policy which provides for such an automatic "loan" to pay the amount due, a persuasive argument can still be made that a life insurance contract should not be cancelled when the cash value of the policy is sufficient to pay the premium. Rather than in essence producing a forfeiture of the coverage, an insurer should be required to advise an insured of the possibility of using the "loan value" or "cash value" of the insurance policy to pay the premium — that is, when a life insurance contract has a "cash value," the insurer should be required to notify the owner of the policy that a choice needs to be made between a cancellation with a refund of the cash value *and* a continuation of coverage by use of the cash value reserve to provide funds for the payment of the premium.[4]

§ 5.11(b)

1. See the policy forms in the Appendices.

2. For example, the provisions of the standard mortgage clause protect the mortgagee beyond the time the mortgagor's protection is terminated for nonpayment of premiums. See § 4.2(a) and § 4.2(b), above.

3. See generally, 43 Am.Jur.2d at § 875.

4. In Gaunt v. Prudential Insurance Company of America, 255 Cal.App.2d 18 at p. 26, 62 Cal.Rptr. 624 at p. 629 (2d Dist., Div. 5, 1967), the court commented, "In the absence of any specific provision in the policy directing the disposition of accumulated dividends or a binding direction by the insured with respect thereto, the weight of authority holds that an insurer cannot insist upon a forfeiture of a policy for nonpayment of a premium when it has in its possession sufficient dividends accumulated to the insured's account to cover the premium due."

Cf. the discussion in Cleaver v. Central States Life Insurance Company, 346 Mo. 548, 142 S.W.2d 474 (1940), interpreting statutory provisions designed to prevent forfeitures.

Also consider the comments in Board of Trustees of Unitarian Church v. Nationwide Life Insurance Company, 88 N.J. Super. 136, 211 A.2d 204 (App.Div.1965).

But see Illinois Bankers Life Assurance Company v. Tennison, 202 Okl. 347, 213 P.2d 848 (1949); State Reserve Life Insurance Company v. Carter, 109 S.W.2d 781 (Tex.Civ.App., Waco, 1937).

Notices of Cancellation

In addition to sending a bill stating that a premium is due when an insured has failed to pay a premium, an insurer generally should also send a cancellation notice. This is especially true in regard to the types of insurance coverage which routinely go into effect without requiring payment of the premium in advance. Many insurance policies contain provisions which specify that a cancellation notice will be sent, rather than terms stating that there will be an automatic termination at the expiration of the coverage period specified in the policy. However, even if an insurance policy is silent on the matter, when an insured fails to pay a premium when due, usually coverage will continue until the insured is specifically notified that there will be a termination or cancellation of coverage.[5] Legislation in many states now requires insurers to provide an insured with advance notice, especially in regard to automobile insurance, of a cancellation or a nonrenewal of a coverage with sufficient time for an insured to arrange for other coverage.[6]

Grace Periods

Many insurance contracts have a provision extending coverage for a "grace period" immediately following the anniversary date on which premium payments are due to be paid by an insured.[7] Typically, when an insurance policy provides for the continuation of coverage during such a grace period, the contract also states that coverage will automatically terminate after the grace period has passed, that is, without another notice to the insured that a premium payment is due.

---

5. *Cf.* Gibson v. Milwaukee Mutual Insurance Company, 265 N.W.2d 742 (Iowa 1978) (compliance with statutory provision requiring termination by personal service or certified mail); Meeker v. Motorists Mutual Insurance Company, 29 Ohio App.2d 49, 278 N.E.2d 46 (Allen County 1972); Leger v. Lisonbee, 207 So.2d 563 (La.App., 3d Cir., 1968).

Also see King v. Guardian Life Insurance Company of America, 686 F.2d 894 (8th Cir.1982) (applying Georgia law) (holding that when a policy expires or lapses according to its terms upon the policyholder's failure to pay the premium, it does not constitute a cancellation to which *special* Georgia statutory requirements for notice apply and therefore letters sent to the insured were sufficient).

6. See, e.g. National Automobile and Casualty Insurance Company v. California Casualty Ins. Co., 139 Cal.App.3d 336, 188 Cal.Rptr. 670 (2d Dist., Div. 4, 1983).

7. A "grace period" is a period of time specified in an insurance policy within which (1) coverage is continued following an anniversary date upon which a premi-

um is due — that is, the insured's failure to pay a premium that is due to the insurer does not immediately produce a lapse in coverage and (2) the insured may cure the default by paying the premium thereby avoiding any gap in the coverage period.

Cf. Bennett v. Colonial Life and Accident Insurance Company, 7 Kan.App.2d 441, 643 P.2d 1133 (1982).

Also see Simmons v. Cambridge Savings Bank, 346 Mass. 327, 191 N.E.2d 681 (1963), 8 A.L.R.3d 856 (1966) (insured elected to pay premiums annually and to have dividends applied to payment of premiums; an annual premium was still unpaid when the insured died six days after the end of the grace period; dividend was insufficient to cover an annual premium though sufficient for a quarterly premium; held, no coverage).

Legislation, and in its absence judicial decisions, might properly require an insurer to offer an insured the option of extending the coverage for whatever period would be covered by the dividend amount or cash value due to the insured.

§ 5.11(c) Cancellation of Insurance by an Insurer

The right of an insurer to cancel an insurance policy is subject to the general rules of contract law in the absence of express provisions in the insurance policy.[1] However, many types of insurance policies include clauses which entitle the insurer to cancel the policy.

For some types of insurance, limitations on the right of an insurer to cancel have been imposed by legislation or administrative regulation.[2] Furthermore, in a few instances courts have decided insurers are precluded from exercising a right of cancellation for reasons of public policy.[3] Accordingly, when an issue involving the cancellation of an insurance policy arises, care should be taken to consider whether there are legislative provisions, administrative regulations, or judicial precedents that impose limitations on the insurer's actions. The following discussion of several types of insurance coverages illustrates the variety of considerations which may be relevant in any given situation.

(1) Cancellation and Marketing Practices

Some of the differences among the cancellation clauses in various kinds of insurance contracts can, at least to some extent, be correlated to marketing practices. In general, broad rights of cancellation are retained by insurers whose marketing systems contemplate that agents in the field will consummate not merely temporary binders, but principal contracts as well. For example, sales representatives are often authorized to commit an insurer to provide property insurance (fire and casualty) or automobile insurance coverage, and the forms for such insurance policies customarily authorize insurers to cancel such coverages, for any reason, by delivering a written notice to the insured.[4] In some states, however, the insurers are only free to exercise such

---

§ 5.11(c)

1. For example, in Government Employees Insurance Company v. Superior Court, etc., 27 Ariz.App. 219 at p. 220, 553 P.2d 672 at p. 673 (Div. 2, 1976), the court observed that "a perusal of cases * * * discloses an almost unanimity of view that mailing of the cancellation notice is sufficient and that receipt is not required."

An insurer is, of course, entitled to cancel a coverage when premiums are not paid. This type of situation is considered in the preceding subsection, § 5.11(b).

2. See § 5.11(c)(2), below.

3. For example, it has been held that allegations of cancellation of a dentist's malpractice coverage because he had testified in malpractice cases would, if proved, establish a breach of contract. L'Orange v. Medical Protective Co., 394 F.2d 57 (6th Cir.1968) (Ohio law).

See generally, Annotation, *Wrongful cancellation of medical malpractice insur-*

ance, 99 A.L.R.3d 469–472 (1980); Note, *Insurance Law—Medical Malpractice Insurance—Cancellation of Policy to Deter Doctors from Providing Expert Testimony,* 11 Boston College Industrial and Commercial Law Review 545–560 (1970).

Also see Note, *Insurance—The Doctrine of Implied Covenant of Good Faith and Fair Dealing Applies to Cancellation Clause of Medical Malpractice Insurance Policy,* 26 Drake Law Review 883–891 (1977); Annotation, *Liability insurer's unconditional right to cancel policy as affected by considerations of public policy,* 40 A.L.R.3d 1439–1144 (1971).

4. Life insurers tend to maintain centralized control over underwriting which limits the authority of agents in the field to commit the insurer to anything more than coverage that is provided by temporary binding receipts. Concerning degrees of centralization over underwriting generally, see § 2.1(b), above.

unrestrained and unrestricted rights during a short period of time following an insured's application for coverage.

(2) Motor Vehicle Insurance

During the period of intensified public criticism of automobile insurance and insurers in the 1960s and 1970s, some practices by insurers with respect to the cancellation (and, in some states, nonrenewal) of automobile insurance policies came under "heavy fire" from both consumers and commentators. One consequence of this public pressure was the adoption in several states of regulatory legislation which limits the rights of insurers to cancel (or, not renew) motor vehicle insurance.[5] Furthermore, regulatory officials have also employed other techniques or practices which in effect encourage insurers to "voluntarily" limit the grounds on which cancellations are sought.[6]

When the right of insurers to cancel insurance policies has been restricted by statutes, some judicial decisions have awarded a broad scope to such legislation. For example, the provisions for a notice of cancellation in a compulsory automobile insurance law may be interpreted as allowing only prospective cancellation, thereby in effect precluding a rescission action that would eliminate the liability coverage as a source of indemnification for the victim(s) of an accident occurring before the rescission was sought.[7] In the absence of such a legislative restriction and such a judicial interpretation, a successful action for rescission by an insurer — as, for example, an action based on misrepresentation in the application for coverage — would ordinarily be fully retroactive.[8]

5. See New York Insurance Department, Report, THE PUBLIC INTEREST NOW IN PROPERTY AND LIABILITY INSURANCE REGULATION, (1969) at p. 43; James D. Ghiardi & Robert O. Wienke, *Recent Developments in the Cancellation, Renewal and Recission of Automobile Insurance Policies,* 51 Marquette Law Review 220–253 (1968).

6. The National Association of Insurance Commissioners, at its 1969 meeting in Philadelphia, after receiving the report of a staff study of automobile insurance, declared that each state should be free to choose its own legal liability system and that, regardless of the legal framework, a set of minimum criteria should be met, among them being the ready availability of insurance to all licensed drivers at reasonable rates and protection against arbitrary and unfair cancellations and nonrenewals. See, e.g., The Standard (New England's Insurance Weekly), June 27, 1969, p. 1 and pp. 20–21.

7. See Aetna Casualty & Surety Co. v. Garrett, 31 A.D.2d 710, 296 N.Y.S.2d 12 (3d Dept.1968), *affirmed* 26 N.Y.2d 729, 309 N.Y.S.2d 34, 257 N.E.2d 284 (1970).

8. See, e.g., Fierro v. Foundation Reserve Insurance Co., 81 N.M. 225, 465 P.2d 282 (1970) (fully retroactive cancellation of automobile insurance after accident because of misrepresentations, in application, of no cancellation within previous 36 months; held for insurer; applicant bound by application he signed, regardless of who filled it out.).

But see Rauch v. American Family Insurance Company, 115 Wis.2d 257, 340 N.W.2d 478 at p. 482 (1983). Insurer sought to void the insurance policy on the grounds of false representations in the application for insurance. The court concluded that the principal purpose underlying the statute which prohibits the exclusion of certain classes of people from insurance coverage is protection of third parties and that "It is evident that that purpose would be frustrated if innocent third parties were denied recovery because of misrepresentations made by the named insured on the application for insurance." The court therefore decided that the statutory requirement "gives third parties rights in liability insurance contracts which are not dependent on the validity of

The rights of insurers to cancel motor vehicle insurance have also been limited by doctrines developed exclusively in judicial decisions. For example, some courts have held that a cancellation notice for an ordinary automobile insurance coverage was ineffectual unless it was actually received by the policyholder, even though a provision in the insurance policy stated that a cancellation would be effective by being mailed to the proper address and that no proof of receipt was essential.[9] It also has been held that an insured's acceptance of a refund is not conclusive in regard to a cancellation when the refund was tendered under circumstances that amounted to "an attempt to perpetrate a constructive fraud * * *." [10]

(3) Life Insurance

Life insurance policies ordinarily do not provide for cancellation by the insurance company. Moreover, the public interest in life insurance has produced legislative enactments that significantly limit an insurer's rights of cancellation. In particular, incontestability statutes preclude an insurer from even raising some grounds on which an insurance policy could otherwise be rescinded on the basis of general principles of contract law. However, before the end of the limited period for contests allowed by the applicable incontestability provisions (usually one or two years after the date of contract), life insurance policies usually may be rescinded on the grounds normally applicable to contracts.[11]

(4) Health and Accident Insurance

Contracts for health and accident insurance vary widely with respect to provisions for cancellation by the company,[12] and they are not discussed here.

---

the contract between the insurer and the named insured" so that the injured persons "can recover against American Family notwithstanding the misrepresentations made in the application for insurance."

9. See, e.g., Keohn v. Central National Insurance Co., 187 Kan. 192, 354 P.2d 352 (1960); Donarksi v. Lardy, 251 Minn. 358, 88 N.W.2d 7 (1958).

Contra. Westmoreland v. General Accident Fire & Life Assurance Corp., 144 Conn. 265, 129 A.2d 623 (1957), 64 A.L.R.2d 976 (1959).

In Farmers Insurance Group v. Merryweather, 214 N.W.2d 184 (Iowa 1974), and Gooden v. Camden Fire Insurance Association, 11 Mich.App. 695, 162 N.W.2d

147 (1968), the courts held that the applicable statutes required that to be effective the cancellation notice must be received by the insured.

10. Lewis v. Snake River Mutual Fire Insurance Co., 82 Idaho 329, 353 P.2d 648 (1960).

Also see Annotation, *Remedies and Measure of Damages for Wrongful Cancellation of Liability and Property Insurance*, 34 A.L.R.3d 385–398 (1970).

11. See the discussion of incontestability clauses in § 5.3(b)(3), above, and § 6.6(d), below.

12. See, e.g., Appendices A and H.

§ 5.11(d)   Cancellation of Insurance by an Insured

(1)   Generally

Many insurance contracts do not include clauses that provide for cancellation of the policy by an insured.[1] However, even when there are policy provisions that appear to limit cancellation by the insured, ordinarily an insured can terminate an insurance contract at the end of any premium period by simply declining to pay a further premium. Insurance contracts customarily do not commit an insured to continue the relationship beyond a specified premium period.

In many instances, the coverage period is not coextensive with the period between payments because the total premium for the coverage period is paid in two or more installments. For example, payment of a premium for a specified coverage period of a year or even several years may be made in semi-annual, quarterly, or monthly installments. Even when this practice prevails, insurance companies rarely, if ever, attempt to compel a premium payment if an insured seeks to terminate the coverage. Accordingly, coverage can be effectively terminated by an insured who fails to pay an installment when it is due. In practice, an insured would generally be well advised to communicate this intention to the insurer in advance of when the installment is due.

When an insurance policy does include terms that provide for cancellation by an insured, the clauses typically specify that the insured should notify the insurer and return the policy to the insurer. Confusion and disagreements obviously can be avoided by complying with such provisions.

(2)   Cancellation and Right to Premium Refunds

Questions may arise when an insured not only seeks to terminate an insurance contract during a coverage term, but also wants an insurer to return that portion of the premium already paid which is applicable to the remainder of what would have been the coverage period. Insurance policies often have clauses which address this type of situation. Different types of insurance typically have somewhat distinctive provisions in this regard.

Life Insurance. Life insurance policies, other than term policies, ordinarily include provisions for the refund of a sum which represents the portion of the premiums not applied to the purchase of coverage up to the time when a cancellation (often referred to as a "surrender" of a policy) by an insured, together with some allowance for interest on the

---

§ 5.11(d)

1. See the forms in the Appendices.

In the absence of provisions in an insurance policy, cancellation of the coverage by an agreement of the insured and the insurer would be governed by the same rules that apply to "the cancellation of any contract by mutual consent, and are similar to those for making a contract." Bennett v. Colonial Life and Accident Insurance Company, 7 Kan.App.2d 441, 643 P.2d 1133 at p. 1135 (1982).

equity that has been accumulated when the policy includes some type of investment feature.[2]

Property Insurance. Modern property policies ordinarily include a clause permitting the insured to cancel by written notice to the company which indicates when the insured wants the cancellation to be effective.[3] Usually the refund due to the insured in such cases is determined in accordance with a provision specifying that a "short-rate table" will be used to calculate the amount. The refund schedule on such a table typically specifies an amount somewhat less than the sum which would be due if it were calculated on the basis of being directly proportionate to the period of coverage which the insured cancelled.[4]

Automobile Insurance. Automobile insurance policies typically provide that if an insured is entitled to any premium refund when a coverage is cancelled, either by the insured or the insurer, the refund will be computed according to the insurer's manual.[5]

§ 5.11(e) Group Insurance Contracts: Termination of Individual Policies

Group insurance contracts have given rise to a number of special problems related to termination of coverage for an individual insured. Under group policies, issues have often arisen concerning the right to terminate an individual's coverage because of (1) the cancellation of the master policy,[1] (2) an alteration in the master contract,[2] (3) a mistake or misconduct of a group administrator in remitting premiums,[3] or (4) a cessation, by an individual insured, of membership in or association with the covered group which is a condition of eligibility for coverage.[4]

Termination questions sometimes concern the applicability of provisions for extensions of coverage in special cases, as for example when

2. See, e.g., Appendix E.

3. See, e.g., Appendices A and I.

4. See, e.g., Appendix A and Appendix I.

5. See Appendix H.

§ 5.11(e)

1. See, e.g., Metropolitan Life Insurance Co. v. Korneghy, 37 Ala.App. 497, 71 So.2d 292 (1954), *cert. petition stricken* 260 Ala. 521, 71 So.2d 301 (1954), 68 A.L.R.2d 239 (1959) (coverage effectively discontinued by agreement between employer and insurer with notice to but without consent of employee).

Also see Schlosser v. Allis-Chalmers Corporation, 86 Wis.2d 226 at pp. 247–248, 271 N.W.2d 879 at p. 889 (1978).

2. See, e.g., Bank of Palm Beach and Trust Company v. North American Company for Life, Accident and Health Insurance, 427 F.2d 28 (5th Cir.1970).

3. *Cf.* Rivers v. State Capital Life Insurance Co., 245 N.C. 461, 96 S.E.2d 431 (1957), 68 A.L.R.2d 205 (1959) (nonpayment of premiums to insurers terminated coverage, despite efforts of employee to continue paying them through the employer after termination of his employment).

What actually happens if risk is allocated to the employer, is briefly discussed in § 2.6, above.

4. See, e.g., Lineberger v. Security Life & Trust Co., 245 N.C. 166, 95 S.E.2d 501 (1956), 68 A.L.R.2d 1 (1959) (coverage terminated with termination of employment, none of the special provisions for extension of coverage being applicable).

Also see Key Life Insurance Company of South Carolina v. Burns, 390 So.2d 1064 (Ala.Civ.App.1980).

an individual was injured while employed and the employment is thereafter terminated.

WESTLAW REFERENCES

§ 5.1 Defining and Restricting the "Risks" Transferred

  (a) Introductory Note

      scope /3 cover! /s insur * * * */s policy /s provision clause

  (b) Approaches to Defining the Risks Transferred: All–Risk and Specified Risk Policies

    (1) Generally

      sy,di(all-risk /3 coverage insurance policy /s exclu!)

    (2) Common Types of All–Risk Insurance

      marine maritime /s all-risk

§ 5.2 Insurance Policy Provisions That Expressly Restrict the Risks Transferred

  (b) Insurance Policy Terms That Both Define and Limit Coverage: Illustrations From Motor Vehicle Insurance

      sy(constru * * * construction /s operat! /s automobile auto car vehicle /s coverage insurance policy)

      sy(hit /2 run /s "physical contact" /s coverage insurance policy)

§ 5.3 Implied Exceptions to the Risks Transferred

  (a) Principles Underlying Implied Exceptions

      friendly /3 fire

  (b) Implied Exceptions Applicable to Life Insurance

    (2) Criminal Activities

      die* dying dea * * /s (own /3 hand act) self-inflict! /s liab * * * * * & crime criminal!

    (3) Suicides

      sy,di(suicide /s exclu! /s provision clause /s coverage insurance policy

    (4) Claims for Life Insurance Benefits by Wrongdoers

      sy,di(life /3 coverage insurance policy /s convict!)

  (f) Liability Insurance Coverage for Intentional Torts

      sy,di(liability /3 coverage insurance policy /s punitive exemplary treble /2 damages)

§ 5.4 Insurance Policy Provisions and Other Requirements Concerning the "Accidental" or "Unintentional" Nature of Loss

  (b) Accidental "Causes" and Accidental "Results"

    (3) "Accidental Means" and "Accidental Results"

      "accidental death" /p "accidental mean" /p "accidental bodily injury"

      death /s cover! /s pre-exist!

    (4) Fortuity and Suicide

      sy,di(suicide /s external! accident! /3 caus!)

    (5) The Consequences of Criminal Acts as Accidents

      injur! /s death /s foresee! forsee! natural /s result occurrence /s coverage insurance policy

(c) Selecting the Vantage Point from Which to Analyze Whether a Loss is "Accidental"

(1) Introductory Note

di(insured /3 view-point "point of view" stand-point "vantage point" perspective /s accident!)

(2) Life Insurance and Death Benefits in Accident Insurance

third-party /3 beneficiary /s defin★ ★ ★ definition

(3) Uninsured Motorist Insurance

di(hit /2 run /s "uninsured motorist" +1 coverage insurance policy)

(4) Property Insurance

co-own ★ ★ ★ co-ownership (joint! /3 own ★ ★ ★ ownership) /s property /s arson fire burn burned burning /s coverage insurance policy

(d) Liability Insurance for Intentional Torts

(2) Approaches to Assessing Whether Liability Coverage Exists for a Consequence That the Tortfeasor Allegedly Did Not Intend

sy,di(self-defense (defend ★ ★ ★ +1 himself herself) /s intent! intend! /s coverage insurance insur ★ ★ ★ policy)

(3) Wanton or Reckless Acts

sy(conduct! act acti * * acted /5 wilful! wanton! reckless! /s cover ★ ★ ★ insurance policy)

(5) Vicarious Liability for Intentional Torts and Negligent Supervision

insur ★ ★ ★ ★ /s statut! law legislat! /s (vicarious! /2 liable liability) "respondeat superior"

(e) Insurance Coverage for "Highly Expectable" Losses

(5) First Party Coverage for Losses Resulting from Medical Treatment

to(217) /p death dead dying die* deceas! /s surg! /s coverage insur★ ★ ★ ★ policy

(f) Failure of an Insured to Prevent an Injury

(1) Clauses Designed to Prevent Losses from Occurring

sy(exercis! use* using /3 "due diligence" /s coverage insur ★ ★ ★ ★ policy)

(2) Clauses Designed to Prevent Additional Losses

"reasonable mean" /7 preserv! sav ★ ★ ★ protect! /s property

"avoidable consequence" /s doctrine theory principle rule

§ 5.5 Causation Problems

(a) Introduction

(4) Conclusive and Inconclusive Causation Clauses

land-slide mud-slide mud-flow /s coverage insur ★ ★ ★ ★ policy

sy("reasonable expectation" /s insur ★ ★ ★ ★)

(c) Multiple Causes and Coverage Limitations

sy,di(sole dominant main primary principal +1 cause /5 accident! occur! damag! injur ★ ★ ★ ★ /p coverage insurance policy)

(d) Problems of Legal (Proximate) Cause: Tort Versus Contract

insur * * * * /s link chain /2 causation caus * * * *
"proximate cause" /5 doctrine theory principle rule /p insurance

(e) Causation, Overlapping Coverages, the Indemnity Principle, and Premium Inequities

(1) The Goal of Indemnifying and the Indemnity Principle

"medical payment" /s offset! setoff

§ 5.6   Warranty: Insurance Policy Provisions and Legal Consequences

warranty /s marine maritime /3 coverage insurance policy
scope restrict! limit! /5 warranty /s coverage insur * * * * policy

§ 5.8   Concealment

(a) Generally

sy,di(intent!   intend! /s conceal! /s material!   fact /s
insur* * * *)

(b) Changing Circumstances or Changes in What the Applicant Knows

sy,di(material! /3 affect! effect /5 risk /7 insur* * * * /s
misstat! misrepresent! statement)

(e) Marine Insurance

(2) Fire Insurance Contrasted

sy,di(fire /s coverage insur * * * * policy /s wilful! /s
conceal! misrepresent! represent!)

§ 5.9   Limits of Liability Provisions

(a) Generally

(2) Multiple Claims Under a Single Coverage: Loss of Consortium

consortium /s liab! /s limit!
"consequential damage" /s parent mother father child daughter
son

§ 5.10   The Duration of the Coverage Period

(b) Claims for Coverage Beyond the Duration Specified in the Declarations

(1) Determining the Commencement Date for Coverage and the Anniversary Date for Renewals

"grace period" /s commenc! beg*n! start! /p coverage
insurance policy

(6) Avoiding Coverage Gaps by Providing for Automatic Renewals

automatic! /5 renew! /s notice notif! /5 cancel! terminat!

(d) Defining and Discerning the Scope of the Coverage Period

(2) Provisions That Limit Coverage to Losses "Incurred" Within a Prescribed Time Period

di(loss /s occur! incur! /s (policy /3 period) duration (time
/3 period limit limitation) /s insur * * * *)

(3) "Claims Made" Coverage

claim-made /s occurrence

§ 5.11   Termination of Coverage

(b) Nonpayment of Premiums

sy(notice notif! /s cancel! terminat! /s coverage insurance policy /s
default! non-payment (no not fail! /3 pay paid paying payment) /5
premium)

(c) Cancellation of Insurance by an Insurer

(2) Motor Vehicle Insurance

sy(wrongful! /3 cancel! terminat! /s coverage insur * * * *policy % employ * * * *)

(3) Life Insurance

period /s resci! recind! recis! /s contest! incontestab!

(d) Cancellation of Insurance by an Insured

(2) Cancellation and Right to Premium Refunds

(i) Life Insurance

surrender! /s refund! /s coverage insur * * * * /s policy

(ii) Property Insurance

fire casualty /3 coverage insur * * * * policy /s cancel! terminat! /s written writing /7 notice notif!

(e) Group Insurance Contracts: Termination of Individual Policies

group master +1 insurance policy contract /5 cover! /s cancel! terminat! /s notice notif!

Chapter Six

RIGHTS AT VARIANCE WITH INSURANCE POLICY PROVISIONS *

* Portions of this chapter were derived from a two-part article by Robert E. Keeton, entitled *Insurance Law Rights at Variance with Policy Provisions*, published in 83 Harvard Law Review 961–985 and 83 Harvard Law Review 1281–1322 (1970).

Section 6.6 in this chapter appears in essentially the same form in Robert E. Keeton, INSURANCE LAW (1971).

---

§ 6.1   Introduction to Principles and Defenses

§ 6.1(a)   The Most Influential Principles and Doctrines Employed to Justify Variance Claims

Courts have considered thousands of cases in which insureds have sought to assert rights that conflicted with the terms specified in the applicable insurance policy, and in hundreds of appellate decisions judges have held that the rights of an insured are at variance with such policy terms. During the period from 1945 to the mid 1960s, as the appellate courts increasingly sustained variance claims, judicial opinions resolving such disputes were often less than ordinarily enlightening about the principles or doctrines upon which the decisions were being made. To some observers, the judicial decisions in these cases often appeared to be arbitrary and unpredictable.[1]

By 1970 it was possible to discern that several justifications provide a common foundation for a significant portion of what otherwise appeared to be unrelated judicial decisions in favor of claimants.

The determinations were implicitly, and occasionally explicitly, predicated on one or more of the following three principles:

> **An insurer will be denied unconscionable advantages in an insurance transaction.[2]**

> **An insurance contract embodies an implied covenant of good faith and fair dealing.[3]**

> **The reasonable expectations of applicants, insureds, and in some instances third party beneficiaries, should be protected.[4]**

It is now clear that each of these statements sets forth concepts that have continued to become increasingly significant in the resolution of insurance disputes involving claimants who seek to assert rights which are not in accord with the provisions of the applicable insurance contract. The application of these principles by courts is, of course, not limited to insurance disputes. However, the conditions which appear to warrant the resolution of disputes on the basis of such considerations have occurred with notable frequency in insurance transactions, and it is in this context that courts in many states have had the greatest opportunity to adopt, develop, and refine various aspects of the doctrines and rules that implement these principles.

Several other principles and doctrines have been applied by courts in decisions holding that the rights of claimants are at variance with provisions in the applicable insurance contracts. Of these, one of the most significant is the principle of granting redress for detrimental reliance.[5] Furthermore, it usually becomes possible to discern the actual influence and import of the detrimental reliance doctrine with considerably greater precision in regard to insurance disputes once the first three principles are explicitly recognized in the judicial decisions of a particular jurisdiction.

---

§ 6.1(a)

1. The generalization "It's an insurance case" was often advanced by observers to explain what was viewed as unpredictable and unexplained variance between policy provisions and the judicially declared rights of a claimant.

2. This principle is discussed in § 6.2, below.

3. This principle is discussed in § 6.2, below.

4. The principle of honoring reasonable expectations is discussed in § 6.3, below.

5. The principle of protecting detrimental reliance is discussed in § 6.5, below.

Another very significant body of decisions sustaining variance claims is either explicitly or implicitly predicated on the principle that provisions in insurance policies may be declared unenforceable when the effect of particular insurance policy terms, if literally enforced, would be in conflict with the declared public policy interests or goals of the state.[6]

The principles and doctrines identified in the preceding paragraphs are considered in the following sections of this chapter. However, courts have also employed other theories, which are described in the next subsection, to justify sustaining coverage for insureds when insurers have sought to deny liability on the basis of the terms set forth in the insurance policy at issue.

§ 6.1(b)   Other Principles Employed by Courts to Justify Rights at Variance With Policy Provisions

There have been many cases in which courts have applied several well recognized doctrinal and remedial theories — other than those identified in the preceding subsection — to justify rights at variance with policy provisions, including (1) reformation, (2) rescission, (3) waiver, and (4) election. Variance claims also have often involved disputes in regard to (5) applications of agency law and (6) incontestability provisions. The following paragraphs provide a brief description of these doctrines or topics, together with a few observations on the application of these doctrines to variance claims.[1]

In some respects, the "stage" was set for the development of the principles identified in the preceding subsection by judicial decisions that sustained variance claims on the basis of the doctrines and theories described in this subsection. Therefore, a general awareness of these doctrines facilitates both (1) an appreciation of why courts found it necessary to look beyond them and (2) an understanding of the significance of the judicial decisions that are grounded on rationales that are not within the scope of these doctrines or remedial theories.

(1) Reformation

Reformation is a contractual remedy that is customarily grounded either on a mutual mistake of the parties in transforming the terms of an oral agreement to a writing, or upon a mistake, in regard to the transaction, of the aggrieved party induced by the other party to the agreement. In regard to a variance claim, a request for reformation usually is based on the theory either that the written insurance contract is being corrected to accurately reflect what the parties intend-

---

6. This proposition is discussed in § 6.4, below.

§ 6.1(b)

1. There are also less supportable theories that could be regarded as similarly related. For example, a rarely invoked (and it would seem aberrational theory) is

that the payment of any claim constitutes a "practical" construction of latent ambiguity in an insurance policy which "binds" the insurer to provide for coverage of any subsequent claim that is of the same type, even though the latter claim is much larger. See § 6.9(b), below.

ed, or that the agreement is being corrected to conform to what was intended by the innocent party because a mistake was induced by the other party.[2] Although reformation is typically sought by an insured, there are instances when an insurer asks to have an insurance policy corrected or modified.

(2) Rescission

A mutual mistake or a mistake of one party that was induced by the other may be grounds for rescission, as well as a basis for the reformation, of a contractual agreement. Rescission, which is sought more often by an insurer than by an insured or third party beneficiary, results in the dissolution (that is, the "unmaking") of the contract between the insurer and the insured.

An insurer that seeks rescission often will also offer to restore the insured to the pre-contract position by returning the premiums which have been paid — that is, rather than pay the insurance benefits that would be due in the event an insured loss has already occurred or that would be due in the event an insured loss should occur in the future, the insurer seeks rescission of the contract and offers to refund the premiums.

(3) Waiver and Estoppel

Waiver is generally defined as the intentional and voluntary relinquishment of a known right. Although factual circumstances which clearly involve acts that satisfy the requirements for establishing a waiver are relatively rare occurrences among insurance transactions, numerous judicial opinions declare that the existence of rights which are at variance with policy provisions is warranted on the basis of a waiver[3] — that is, circumstances that almost certainly do not constitute an intentional or voluntary relinquishment of a known right have often been characterized as waivers in judicial decisions.[4]

The doctrines of waiver and estoppel are frequently confused, and are often viewed as interchangeable.[5] However, there is a fundamental difference between waiver and estoppel, and this difference should be understood and preserved when these doctrines are invoked as justifications for rights at variance with policy provisions.

Waiver should only be applied when an insurer intends to relinquish a known right because it entails volition in relation to an act and

---

2. See generally Robert N. Covington, *Reformation of Contracts of Personal Insurance,* 1964 University of Illinois Forum 548–570.

Also see Annotation, *Reformation of insurance policy to correctly identify risks and causes of loss,* 32 A.L.R.3d 661–735 (1970).

3. *Cf.* The Hartford v. Doubler, 105 Ill. App.3d 999, 61 Ill.Dec. 592, 434 N.E.2d 1189 (3d Dist.1982) (approval and payment of a claim by an insurer, with full knowledge of the circumstances of the loss, evidenced waiver of the applicable policy exclusion).

4. Also see the discussion of waiver in § 6.5(a), § 6.7, § 6.8(d), and § 6.9(e), below.

5. For example, see the discussion and definitions in BLACK'S LAW DICTIONARY (1979), of "estoppel" at pp. 494–495, and of "waiver" at pp. 1417–1418.

to the legal consequences of the action. In regard to insurance coverage disputes, estoppel involves the imposition of liability (or legal responsibility in some other form) on the basis of acts that usually were *not* intended to produce the consequences which are sought by the claimant, and, at least in most instances, the intent of the insurer in regard to the consequences of the acts is not relevant. It is the nature of either the insurer's actions or the effect of the insurer's actions on the insured, upon which the estoppel is based, that justify foreclosing the right(s) of the insurer. For an estoppel to apply, courts usually require proof that the claimant was prejudiced as a consequence of the conduct of the other party.[6] Moreover, courts increasingly are viewing estoppel in terms of the standards set forth in the Restatement of Contracts, which envisions the protection of justifiable detrimental reliance.[7]

When a claimant bases a claim for rights at variance with policy provisions on the conduct of persons alleged to have acted on behalf of an insurer, the difference between estoppel and waiver can be particularly significant if agency concepts are also invoked.[8] Estoppel often is more compatible than waiver with applying a relatively "broad" agency concept that precludes an insurer from objecting to the actions of the insurer's representative, and this is especially the case when the individual has exceeded the scope of authority prescribed by express provisions in the contractual relationship between the insurer and agent.[9]

(4) Election

The doctrine of election essentially compels a choice from an array of two or more legal consequences that could be the result of particular factual circumstances.[10] In one respect, election is somewhat like estoppel because an involuntary legal consequence — in the form of a limitation upon the range of "choice" or "selection" among legal consequences — is imposed by a court decision on a person or entity. In

6. See, e.g., Insurance Company of North America v. McCleave, 462 F.2d 587 (3d Cir.1972); Old Mutual Casualty Company v. Clark, 53 Ill.App.3d 274, 11 Ill.Dec. 151, 368 N.E.2d 702 (First District, Div. 5, 1977).

Cf. Maryland Casualty Company v. Peppers, 64 Ill.2d 187, 355 N.E.2d 24 (1976).

7. See the RESTATEMENT OF CONTRACTS, Second, § 90, and other sections in the Restatement which address questions of when reliance should be protected. The principle of protecting detrimental reliance is discussed in § 6.5, below.

8. See § 6.7(a), below.

Also see Annotation, *Doctrine of estoppel or waiver as available to bring within coverage of insurance policy risks not covered by its terms or expressly excluded therefrom,* 1 A.L.R.3d 1139–1183 (1965); Anno-

tation, *Liability insurance: insurer's assumption of or continuation in defense of action brought against the assured as waiver or estoppel as regards defense of noncoverage or other defenses existing at time of accident,* 38 A.L.R.2d 1148–1180 (1954).

9. Imposing liability based on representations incidental to the employment of the agent is a concept that is analogous to "scope of employment" in master-servant cases concerned with physical harm. See § 6.5(d) and § 6.5(e), below.

10. Concerning election generally, see John S. Ewart, *"Waiver" in Insurance Law,* 13 Iowa Law Review 129–144 (1928); John S. Ewart, *Waiver or Election,* 29 Harvard Law Review 724–730 (1916).

For illustrations in insurance law, see § 6.2(b) and § 6.8(d)(3), below.

another respect, election is somewhat like waiver because the particular result depends in part upon one or more action(s) which were taken, often, but not invariably, with full knowledge of the circumstances — by the party against whom the doctrine is imposed. The doctrine of election has been applied by courts to justify relief in some insurance cases when neither the requirements for estoppel nor the requirements for waiver would be satisfied.

Applications of the doctrine of election to insurance transactions are frequently quite debatable, and often inadequately explained in judicial decisions. In many instances, there are not only deficiencies in the statement of the terms of the choice left open to the insurer, but there are also no clear reasons for the regulatory restrictions implicit in the court's prescription of the limitation upon "choice" that has been imposed.

In some cases, courts apply what is essentially the doctrine of election under the guise of waiver or estoppel. For example, a court may hold that if one agent of an insurance company accepted the payment of an insurance premium at a time when another agent of the insurer knew of an action that would defeat coverage, the company is precluded from thereafter asserting the violation as a coverage defense. In explaining such a holding, a court may state that the insurer "waived" its rights, even though it is clear the insurer (and its agents) almost certainly did not intend to voluntarily relinquish the coverage defense when the premium payment was accepted. In other situations, courts have stated that the result in such cases is based on estoppel, even though it is also clear there is no proof of any prejudice to or detrimental reliance by the insured.

To use either waiver or estoppel in circumstances which do not warrant their application is to confuse the true meaning of those doctrines and to obfuscate the justification for a court's decision.[11] In cases such as those which were briefly described in the preceding paragraph, the courts have actually predicated the result on the rationale that an insurer should not be allowed to collect a new premium payment without losing defenses which are known to any of its agents at the time the premium was accepted — that is, a choice has been imposed on the insurer.[12] Recognizing that the theory which is actually being applied is a doctrine which imposes an involuntary "choice" on the insurer serves to focus attention on the nature of the limitations imposed and on the question whether the particular limitation(s) on choice are justified.

---

11. See, e.g., § 6.8, below.

In his judicial capacity, one of the co-authors of this text has suggested that it is useful, for clarity in judicial opinions that yield to the common practice of using "waiver" in a broad sense that includes "election," nevertheless to distinguish between "strict waiver" in the sense of "voluntary relinquishment of known right" and "waiver by election." See Taylor v. Marsh, 624 F.Supp. 1042, 1045 (D.Mass. 1985) (Secretary of Army held to have elected not to require employee to exhaust his administrative remedies).

12. Cf. Weld v. Mid America Life Insurance Company, 385 N.W.2d 58 (Minn.App. 1986).

The doctrine of election is a difficult concept to cope with even when dealt with candidly. General characterizations or definitions do not adequately and appropriately describe either the breadth of the doctrine or the great variety of circumstances in which courts have predicated judgments on its application. There is nothing comparable to the almost uniformly understood definition of waiver as the "voluntary and knowledgeable relinquishment of known right" or the encapsulation of the essence of estoppel as the "protection of justifiable detrimental reliance." The conceptualization of the election doctrine as the "imposition of a limited choice" provides little sense of the circumstances which courts conclude warrant its application or the situations in which the result is prescribed by specific statutes.

In many of the cases in which judicial decisions predicated on either waiver or estoppel involve significant deviations from the requirements associated with these doctrines, recognizing that courts have actually applied the election doctrine is only the first step toward clarifying the import of these judicial precedents. In analyzing or appraising the decisions in such cases it is helpful, and often virtually essential, to conceptualize the result in terms of a rather particularized rule of election. When this is done, it is then possible to articulate and evaluate the arguments which either justify or controvert an application of the rule which has been advanced. In most instances, if these steps are taken, what ultimately emerges is that the principle of disallowing unconscionable advantage is the underlying justification for the decision.[13]

(5) Variance Theories and the Authority of Sales Representatives

Claims for variance based on events that occur following the formation of a contract for insurance frequently involve issues in regard to the authority of sales representatives. For example, in some situations a sales representative who had either actual or implied authority in the course of the marketing transaction, does not continue to have such authority after the insurance contract is made. In many instances, provisions in the insurance policy specifically state that a sales representative is not authorized to modify the scope of coverage. Consequently, it is often vital to determine whether a sales representative has either the actual or the apparent authority to issue endorsements modifying the original contract (as is ordinarily the case with respect to motor vehicle insurance, but is not with respect to life insurance).[14]

(6) Variance Theories and Incontestability Clauses

Incontestability clauses[15] may be invoked by a claimant as a response to an insurer's effort to defeat a claim on the basis of events

---

13. See § 6.2, below.

14. See the discussion of intermediaries in insurance marketing in § 2.5, above.

15. Also see the discussion of incontestibility clauses in § 3.3(c)(3), above, and § 6.6(d), below.

which preceded the formation of the insurance contract (such as misrepresentations) and, less often, on the basis of events that occurred after an insurance policy has been issued. There are even instances in which an issue arises in regard to events that occur after a loss.[16] Especially when an insurer invokes a defense based on an alleged misrepresentation, the dispute should be assessed, at least in part, in light of (1) whether there is an incontestability statute or clause that applies to the insurance transaction and (2) what should be the effect of that statute or policy provision on the dispute.[17]

(7) Observations

The appropriateness of applying theories described in the preceding subsections is frequently significantly influenced by when the events that constitute the basis for a variance claim occurred.[18] When a claim for variance is based on something that took place before the insurance contract was consummated, the doctrinal or remedial theories which are usually considered to be relevant are reformation, rescission, waiver, estoppel, or election.[19]

When a variance claim arises on the basis of events which happen following the occurrence of a loss (that is, post-casualty events),[20] the doctrines of waiver, estoppel, reformation, or rescission ordinarily should not be involved. For example, insurers seldom intend to waive rights after an insured has sustained a loss. And usually a claimant cannot show that reliance occurred as a consequence of either post-casualty representations expressly made by a representative of the insurer or the conduct of the insurer's representatives; for this reason, a claim of detrimental reliance or estoppel should not apply. A decision in favor of an insured in such cases is almost always actually predicated either explicitly or implicitly on the rationale that it would be unconscionable to allow the insurer to withhold coverage.

16. See the discussion in § 3.3(c)(3) and § 5.10(d), above.

17. The effect of an incontestability provision should be considered in regard to other types of coverage defenses as well. However, in light of the self-limiting terms used for such provisions and the self-limiting construction generally adopted by courts for both incontestability statutes and insurance policy incontestability clauses, the applicability of either the legislation or the contract provision is not a realistic possibility in most contexts. See § 6.6(d), below.

18. For example, see § 6.8(d), above.

19. See the discussion comparing the application of these doctrines in § 2.4(b), above.

20. Variance claims may also involve events that occurred after the consummation of an original insurance agreement and before the occurrence of an insured event. In such cases, the legal theory which is applied usually involves issues that relate to the interpretation of the insurance policy, or the terms set forth in an endorsement, or a rider that was subsequently attached to the original insurance policy.

A rider may be reformed or rescinded, or its terms may be affected by waiver, estoppel, or election, on the basis of events occurring after the original contract was consummated but before the rider was attached.

§ 6.1(c) Defenses to Variance Claims

(1) Introductory Note

Insurance companies have presented a variety of defensive responses to the various theories that have been recognized as justifying rights at variance with policy provisions. Defenses have been based on (1) the extrinsic (parol) evidence rule, (2) statute of frauds provisions of either general scope or specific application to some types of insurance transactions,[1] and (3) entire-contract statutes. These defenses are briefly described and discussed in the following portions of this section.

Several other defensive doctrines or strategies — including the theory that "coverage" provisions are immune to claims of variance,[2] reservation-of-rights notices, and nonwaiver agreements[3] — are discussed in separate sections of this chapter.

Denials of claims by insurance companies on the basis of a warranty provision in an insurance policy, a misrepresentation by the insured, or concealment of information by an insured also have led to judicial and legislative consideration of whether rights at variance with policy provisions should be recognized. The statutory and decisional restrictions imposed on the assertion of such defenses to claims are also discussed separately in this chapter.[4]

(2) Application of the Extrinsic (Parol) Evidence Rule

The extrinsic (parol) evidence rule, which applies when an agreement has been memoralized in a written contract, excludes evidence of oral agreements made either before or contemporaneously with the written contract. The rule provides that the manifested intention of the parties, as evidenced by the writing, cannot be varied by evidence of a different manifestation of intention which is extrinsic to the writing.

A reasonably strong contention can often be made that any claim which involves an alleged waiver of insurance policy provisions based on actions during the marketing of an insurance policy is fundamentally inconsistent with the public policies underlying the extrinsic (parol) evidence rule. Thus, decisions that allow variance claims, reformation, or rescission often involve either explicit or implicit qualifications of the extrinsic (parol) evidence rule.[5]

When claims of variance are based on post-contract events, somewhat different considerations may apply. For example, after consummation of the original contract for an insurance coverage, sometimes a rider or endorsement will be issued that is intended to modify the insurance agreement. If a rider or endorsement has been issued and

---

§ 6.1(c)

1. But see the discussion of the statute of frauds in § 2.2, above.

2. See § 6.7(b), below.

3. See § 6.7(a), below.

4. See § 6.6, below.

5. *Cf.* Coleman v. Holecek, 542 F.2d 532 (10 Cir.1976); Beneby v. Midland National Life Insurance Company, 402 So.2d 1193 (Fla.App., 3 Dist., 1981).

Also see Harr v. Allstate Insurance Company, 54 N.J. 287, 255 A.2d 208 (1969).

attached to the insurance policy after the alleged communications on which the claimant relies, the extrinsic (parol) evidence rule excludes evidence that contradicts the integrated, written agreement which includes the rider. But when no endorsement was issued, the extrinsic (parol) evidence rule does not exclude the evidence of the alleged communication because the only integrated agreement the parol evidence seeks to modify is one entered into before the events to which the parol evidence refers.

(3) Applications of the Statute of Frauds

The application of a statute of frauds provision to insurance transactions is not common, and only a few illustrations can be found.[6] Although the statute of frauds arguably applies when a claim is made that an oral modification of the insurance coverage terms was agreed upon — that is, if there was an oral agreement that was neither reduced to writing nor incorporated into the insurance policy by a rider or an endorsement [7] — in most instances there is some writing (such as a file note) that satisfies the minimal requirement of any applicable statute of frauds. Consequently, if an effort is being made to vary the terms of the agreement, it is usually the extrinsic (parol) evidence rule, rather than the statute of frauds, that must be overcome.

(4) Applications of Entire-Contract Statutes

Entire-contract statutes commonly provide that a copy of the application form submitted by the insured must be attached to the insurance policy issued by the insurer and that the "integrated" material which is delivered to the insured then constitutes the entire contract between the parties. These statutory provisions — which usually apply either to life insurance policies or to life, health, and accident insurance contracts — have been invoked by insurers as a defense to an insured's claim that false answers appearing in the application (which are being relied upon by the insurer to defeat the contract) came about because a representative of the insurer incorrectly recorded truthful oral responses.[8]

§ 6.2   Disallowing Unconscionable Advantage and Requiring Good Faith

§ 6.2(a)   Generally

(1) Unconscionable Advantages

There are several factors which create opportunities for insurers to exercise unconscionable advantages over insureds. *First,* insurance policies are typically rather long, detailed contracts which most purchasers are not inclined to read, and which frequently would not be

---

6. See § 2.2(a), above.

7. Also consider the discussion in § 2.2 and § 4.11(d), above.

8. See § 6.8(b), below.

fully understood if insureds did attempt to read through the documents. *Second*, the coverage terms for many types of insurance are highly standardized as a result of having been drafted by one of several insurance trade associations or service groups.[1] *Third*, in many insurance transactions, the purchaser does not have sufficient bargaining power to influence an insurer to change or modify the terms of the insurance policy.[2] The combined effect of these factors creates opportunities for "overreaching" by insurers, that is, for taking an unfair advantage of the insured(s).[3]

Courts in several jurisdictions have concluded that an insurer will not be permitted to exercise an unconscionable advantage over an insured, and have applied this principle in decisions which hold that a claimant's rights are at variance with the insurance policy provisions that were at issue in the case.[4] However, "unconscionability" is by nature a rather elusive concept, and it has proved to be more than somewhat indefinite as a standard by which to assess the conduct of insurers.[5]

(2) Good Faith and Fair Dealing

There are numerous appellate court opinions in which the courts have held that every insurance contract includes an implied covenant of good faith and fair dealing which requires the parties (both the insurer and the insured) to conduct themselves so that nothing is done which impairs the right of the other to receive the benefit of the agreement.[6]

§ 6.2(a)

1. Also consider the discussion in § 2.8, above.

2. *Ibid.*

3. Also see the discussion in § 6.6, below.

4. See, e.g., Gulf Guaranty Life Insurance Company v. Kelley, 389 So.2d 920 (Miss.1980); C & J Fertilizer, Inc. v. Allied Mutual Insurance Company, 227 N.W.2d 169 (Iowa 1975), 86 A.L.R.3d 839 (1978); International Life Insurance Company v. Herbert, 334 S.W.2d 525 (Tex.Civ.App., Waco, 1960).

Viewing the substantial body of appellate decisions which have held that an insured's rights are at variance with contract provisions, one may now clearly discern that this principle has frequently been applied in the guise of "waiver" in circumstances that did not involve the voluntary relinquishment of a known right and in the form of "estoppel" in cases where there is no proof of detrimental reliance. For example, insurers are precluded from asserting a lapse of coverage even though the policyholder is unable to prove either genuine waiver (that is, that the insurer voluntarily relinquished a known right) or genuine estoppel (that is, that the policyholder detrimentally relied on some representation for which the insurer is accountable).

Furthermore, this principle also provides a distinctly more accurate description of why judicial limitations are imposed on defenses raised by insurers based on warranty.

5. *Cf.* RESTATEMENT OF CONTRACTS, Second § 208 and § 211 (Adopted and promulgated in 1979).

Also see the materials on judicial treatment of standardized contracts cited in § 2.8 above.

6. *Cf.* Lawton v. Great Southwest Insurance Company, 118 N.H. 607, 392 A.2d 576 at p. 580 (N.H.1978); deMarlor v. Foley Carter Insurance Company, 386 So.2d 22 at p. 24 (Fla.App., 2d Dist.1980); Grand Sheet Metal Products Company v. Protection Mutual Insurance Company, 34 Conn.Supp. 46 at pp. 47–52, 375 A.2d 428 at pp. 429–430 (Fairfield County, 1977).

Also see § 7.8 and § 7.9, below, on liabilities of insurer for emotional distress and economic losses beyond the contractual

The "good faith" doctrine has not been developed in the same way or to the same extent throughout the nation. Among the state courts, the Supreme Court of New Jersey was one of the first courts to recognize the "good faith" principle and has subsequently extended its application to a wide range of cases. The New Jersey Supreme Court's decision in Bowler v. Fidelity and Casualty Company of New York,[7] which involved a time limitation on the right to sue under a disability insurance contract, provides an excellent summary of how some courts view this doctrine:

> "Insurance policies are contracts of utmost good faith and must be administered and performed as such by the insurer. Good faith 'demands that the insurer deal with laymen as laymen and not as experts in the subtleties of law and underwriting.' [Citations omitted.] In all insurance contracts, particularly where the language expressing the extent of the coverage may be deceptive to the ordinary layman, there is an implied covenant of good faith and fair dealing that the insurer will not do anything to injure the right of its policyholder to receive the benefits of his contract." [8]

Courts in other states have adopted formulations of the good faith doctrine in terms that are comparable to this statement by the New Jersey Supreme Court. For example, the Tennessee Supreme Court concluded, in a case involving uninsured motorist coverage, that the duty to deal "fairly and in good faith" required a claims adjuster to inform the insureds about "the extent of coverage afforded them under

---

coverage, including attorney fees, for either "bad faith" or violation of the implied covenant of good faith and fair dealing.

7. 53 N.J. 313, 250 A.2d 580 (1969).

8. *Id.,* 53 N.J. at p. 327, 250 A.2d at pp. 587–588. In *Bowler,* the court concluded that:

> "In situations where a layman might give the controlling language of the policy a more restrictive interpretation than the insurer knows the courts have given it and as a result the uninformed insured might be inclined to be quiescent about the disregard or non-payment of his claim and not to press it in timely fashion, the company cannot ignore its obligation. It cannot hide behind the insured's ignorance of the law; it cannot conceal its liability. In these circumstances it has the duty to speak and disclose, and to act in accordance with its contractual undertaking. The slightest evidence of deception or overreaching will bar reliance upon time limitations for prosecution of the claim."

Id., 53 N.J. at pp. 327–328, 250 A.2d at p. 588. The court also invoked several theories of estoppel. One of these was founded on the insurer's failure to make the last of

200 weekly-benefits payments when due, which payment might have indicated that the insurer was also liable for a lump-sum payment in an amount equal to 600 additional weekly benefits. The insurer's conduct, said the court, "constitutes conduct incompatible with the insurer's obligation to exercise good faith in dealing with its insured, and *of itself* creates an equitable estoppel against the plea of the statute of limitations." 53 N.J. at 329, 250 A.2d at 589 (emphasis in original). It is not difficult to find detrimental reliance by the insured on his assumption, not contradicted by the insurer, that he did not have a valid claim. But in *Bowler* the New Jersey court went well beyond other courts in holding that the insured is entitled to rely upon nondisclosure by the insurer. In effect the court held that the insurer has a duty to volunteer information about the insured's rights, which duty it violates by a "mere naked rejection" of the claim when "it has a reasonable doubt as to whether the evidence is sufficient to require payment * * *." 53 N.J. at p. 328, 250 A.2d at p. 588.

Concerning detrimental reliance generally, see § 6.5, below.

the MFA [insurance] policy before negotiating a settlement, especially since it was apparent to *   *   * [the adjuster] that respondents did not know the coverage" and that the duty was violated when the adjuster "took advantage of [insureds'] ignorance to negotiate a settlement for a grossly inadequate consideration." [9]

When courts evaluate an insurer's position, in regard to a dispute with an insured or a beneficiary, against a standard of good faith and fair dealing [10] they frequently seem to be invoking either an alternative conceptualization of or a corollary to the unconscionability doctrine.

§ 6.2(b)   Unconscionable Advantage and the Doctrine of Election

The principle of disallowing insurers an unconscionable advantage underlies judicial decisions in several types of situations in which courts have applied the doctrine of election. There are, for example, numerous judicial decisions which preclude an insurer from treating late premium payments differently depending on the circumstances. An insurer will not be allowed to adopt a practice of applying the premiums retroactively to provide uninterrupted coverage when no loss has occurred (that is, treating the premium payment as if it were made on time and extending continuous coverage when no loss has occurred) *and* declaring a lapse in coverage whenever a casualty has occurred (that is, terminating the coverage and treating the premium as a payment for a new coverage period when a loss occurred before the premium was received).[1] These decisions hold, either implicitly or explicitly, that the insurer would be taking an unconscionable advantage if it were allowed to choose, case by case, the course which would be most advantageous in each instance. Decisions imposing liability when the tender of a renewal premium is accepted by an insurer after

---

9. MFA Mutual Insurance Company v. Flint, 574 S.W.2d 718 at p. 722 (Tenn.1978).

Also see Craft v. Economy Fire and Casualty Company, 572 F.2d 565 (7th Cir. 1978); Richardson v. Employers Liability Assurance Corp., 25 Cal.App.3d 232, 102 Cal.Rptr. 547 (1972).

But see Baxter v. Royal Indemnity Company, 285 So.2d 652 (Fla.App., 1st Dist., 1973).

Abuses of this power have generated a variety of remedial actions in addition to judicial determinations of rights at variance. For example, in some instances, statutory or administrative regulation of policy forms, occasionally by prescription of entire forms, but more often by less rigid regulation, have been employed to disallow unconscionable advantages. See § 2.8(b), above.

Regulation of policy forms is only one manifestation of a much more extensive

pattern of statutory and decisional controls against overreaching.

10. *Cf.* Comunale v. Traders & General Insurance Company, 50 Cal.2d 654 at p. 659, 328 P.2d 198 at p. 201 (1958); Gruenberg v. Aetna Insurance Company, 9 Cal.3d 566 at p. 575, 108 Cal.Rptr. 480 at p. 485, 510 P.2d 1032 at p. 1037 (1973), which address the question in regard to the settlement of third party claims by liability insurers.

In Chodos v. Insurance Company of North America, 126 Cal.App.3d 86 at p. 98, 178 Cal.Rptr. 831 at p. 838 (2d Dist., Div. 5, 1981), the court observed, "In every insurance contract there is an implied covenant of good faith and fair dealing in which the insurer's duty is unconditional and independent of the performance of plaintiff's contractual obligations."

§ 6.2(b)

1. See § 6.8(d), below.

the occurrence of a loss are probably best understood as responses to an insurer's effort to gain unconscionable advantage in the insurer's treatment of a whole body of instances.

§ 6.2(c)   Unconscionable Advantage and the Law of Warranty

Opportunities for overreaching in the drafting of policy provisions were facilitated and enhanced by applications of the strict and unyielding law of warranty initially fashioned by Lord Mansfield for marine insurance and subsequently extended, with considerably less justification, to life and fire insurance.[1] The common law rules on warranty thereby opened an expansive and fertile field for insurers to conceive and include restrictive limitations in the coverage terms. Furthermore, coverage terms — which would have been unconscionable even in large bold face type that clearly expressed the restrictions using words familiar to an average person — were even more clearly unjustified when such provisions were "concealed" in the small print that was used by many insurers for many lengthy, bewildering, and often almost incomprehensible — at least to individuals untutored in the jargon of the insurance business — clauses that insurers employed in many insurance policies.

The combination of factors which allowed insurers almost unrestricted freedom in regard to the use of warranties in policy forms inevitably led to statutory and administrative regulations that limited the effect of such provisions by insurers.[2] Furthermore, courts have also imposed some significant limitations on the freedom of insurers to assert defenses based on the law of warranty, and many of these decisions are best understood as applications of the principle of disallowing unconscionable advantage.[3]

§ 6.3   Honoring Reasonable Expectations

§ 6.3(a)   Emergence of the Principle

(1) The Historical Context

In the early days of the development of insurance underwriting at the Lloyd's Coffee House during the sixteenth and seventeenth centuries, insurance contracts typically were transactions among persons of relatively equal bargaining power. The shipowners who sought insurance often were at least as prosperous as the individuals who agreed to underwrite the coverage for a ship or cargo.[1] In fact, it was not uncommon for an insurance contract proposal to be prepared by the

---

§ 6.2(c)

1. See § 5.6, above.

2. *Ibid.*

3. Closely akin to the discredited myth that courts only find and apply law and do not make it is the myth that courts only enforce measures of insurance regulation and never create them. The history of insurance cases in the courts is in fact replete with instances of judicially created regulatory doctrines. Court-made doctrines are particularly pervasive in the area of rights at variance.

§ 6.3(a)

1. See the discussion of Lloyd's of London in § 2.1, above, and the sources cited in that section.

person seeking insurance who then submitted the document to the insurers. Each individual (or syndicate) who agreed to insure some portion of the risk described in the document would so indicate by writing a specific amount at the bottom of the proposed coverage terms (that is, by "underwriting" some amount). In this context, the expectations of the insured in regard to the scope of coverage provided by an insurance agreement were at least as accurately described as those of the insurer(s).

As the business of marine insurance developed, insurance contracts were more frequently prepared by the insurers and the terms in such insurance agreements were increasingly determined by the desires, needs, and demands of the underwriters. Moreover, as the marketing of various other kinds of insurance developed at Lloyd's and elsewhere, relatively standard or uniform coverage terms, almost invariably drafted by insurers, became progressively more common throughout the insurance industry.

The contract provisions that have been employed for insurance transactions in the United States for approximately two centuries have almost invariably been drafted by insurers, either cooperatively through various trade associations or by individual insurance companies.[2] The average consumer purchasing an insurance policy typically does little more than select from among the types of coverage which are offered by an insurer and then decide on the amount of coverage which is desired.[3] The nature of these transactions *and* the character of the provisions in the various insurance policies employed by insurers to prescribe the terms of the relationship have had a significant effect on the resolution of coverage disputes between insurers and insureds.

(2) Resolving Ambiguities Against Insurers

The doctrine that ambiguities in contract documents are resolved against the party responsible for the drafting is a well recognized principle of contract interpretation.[4] This doctrine was one of the first, and continues to be one of the most widely used,[5] approaches which

---

2. See § 2.8(b), above.

3. See § 2.8, above.

4. In some situations, an unqualified practice of resolving ambiguities against the insurer produces results that are more favorable to the insured than would a decision based on honoring reasonable expectations. For example, even though the contractual language was ambiguous, there might be no expectation at all, or the expectation might be unreasonable, thus defeating a claimed expansion of coverage beyond the letter of the contract. It seems likely that there has always been an implicit understanding that ambiguities, which in most cases might be resolved in more than just one or the other of two ways, would be resolved favorably to the insured's claim only if a reasonable person in the insured's position would have expected coverage.

Also see Allen v. Metropolitan Life Insurance Company, 44 N.J. 294 at p. 305, 208 A.2d 638 at p. 644 (1965); Steven v. Fidelity & Casualty Company, 58 Cal.2d 862 at pp. 869–870, 377 P.2d 284 at pp. 288–289, 27 Cal.Rptr. 172 at pp. 176–177 (1962).

5. See, e.g., Rusthoven v. Commercial Standard Insurance Company, 387 N.W.2d 642 at p. 645 (Minn.1986); Sparks v. St. Paul Insurance Company, 100 N.J. 325 at p. 336, 495 A.2d 406 at p. 412 (1985); Puritan Life Insurance Company v. Guess, 598 P.2d 900 (Alaska 1979).

courts employ to ameliorate harsh effects that would otherwise result from insurance policy terms. There are literally thousands of judicial opinions resolving insurance coverage disputes in favor of claimants on the basis that a provision of the insurance policy at issue was ambiguous and therefore should be construed against the insurer.

There are also numerous judicial opinions that predicate the result on the theory of resolving an ambiguity against an insurer in situations which clearly appear to be beyond what seem to be the reasonable bounds for applications of the ambiguity theory.[6] In many of these cases, courts have afforded claimants rights, on the basis of an ambigui-

Cf. Insurance Company of North America v. Sam Harris Construction Company, Inc., 22 Cal.3d 409 at p. 413, 149 Cal. Rptr. 292 at p. 296, 583 P.2d 1335 at p. 1339 (1978); Simses v. North American Company for Life and Health Insurance, 175 Conn. 77, 394 A.2d 710 (1978).

Also see Vargas v. Insurance Company of North America, 651 F.2d 838 at p. 839 (2d Cir., 1981); Index Fund, Inc. v. Insurance Company of North America, 580 F.2d 1158 at p. 1162 (2d Cir.1978), *cert. denied* 440 U.S. 912, 99 S.Ct. 1226, 59 L.Ed. 461 (1979).

6. Several of these cases have involved restrictive clauses in air travel trip insurance purchased from vending machines. The decisions allowing coverage in this context — contrary to the insurer's intentions — are generally grounded on lack of notice to the insured, before the purchase of the insurance, of specific exclusions from coverage. See, e.g., Lachs v. Fidelity & Casualty Company, 306 N.Y. 357, 118 N.E.2d 555 (1954). It has been reasoned that this lack of notice creates an ambiguity, to be resolved against the insurer.

Some decisions that are concerned with lack of notice emphasize the significance of the marketing arrangement. For example, of vending machine sales in airports, it has been said:

"In this type of standardized contract, sold by a vending machine, the insured may reasonably expect coverage for the whole trip which he inserted in the policy, including reasonable substituted transportation necessitated by emergency."

Steven v. Fidelity & Casualty Company, 58 Cal.2d 862 at p. 868, 377 P.2d 284 at p. 288, 27 Cal.Rptr. 172 at p. 176 (1962). Moreover, the court added, the question of ambiguity of the policy language is to be determined in view of the insured's "knowledge and understanding as a reasonable layman, his normal expectation of the extent of coverage of the policy * * *." 58 Cal.

2d at p. 869, 377 P.2d at p. 288, 27 Cal. Rptr. at p. 176 (footnote omitted).

Also see the discussion of trip insurance in § 2.7. *Cf.* Puritan Life Insurance Company v. Guess, 598 P.2d 900 at p. 904 (Alaska 1979), regarding ambiguity and lack of notice in the marketing of life insurance.

Several other cases have involved a liability insurer's duty of defense when a claimant alleged injuries resulted from an assault and battery. See, e.g., Gray v. Zurich Insurance Company, 65 Cal.2d 263, 54 Cal.Rptr. 104, 419 P.2d 168 (1966); Lowell v. Maryland Casualty Company, 65 Cal.2d 298, 54 Cal.Rptr. 116, 419 P.2d 180 (1966). In *Gray,* the insured defended a tort claim unsuccessfully and was allowed recovery against the insurer for the amount of the tort judgment as well as costs of defense; the court held that standard provisions concerning the duty of defense, in a Comprehensive Personal Liability Endorsement, "are uncertain and undefined," and that they should be construed to fulfill the insured's reasonable expectations. In *Lowell,* on the same holding as to ambiguity, the insured who had defended a tort claim successfully was allowed recovery against the insurer for costs of defense but not for the attorneys' fees incurred in the separate action against the insurer.

One who supports not merely the resolution of ambiguities in favor of the insured but also the still broader principle of honoring reasonable expectations may differ with the California courts' conclusions that the insureds' beliefs were reasonable. It was at least arguably unreasonable even for a layperson to have expected that the policy provided for defense against claims of assault and battery generally, as distinguished from claims based on circumstances that in fact involved mistake, as when the insured acted in self-defense but without a privilege to do so because the belief in being under attack was unreasonable. For a thoughtful criticism of the California court's decision in *Gray,* see

ty, that were contrary to plainly expressed terms: that is, the conclusion is almost inescapable that the courts found an ambiguity where none existed.[7]

In the context of insurance disputes, judicial opinions proceeding generally on the theory of resolving ambiguities against an insurer have often included passages which indicated the courts were reaching toward a principle of contract interpretation that would not be limited by the intrinsic characteristic of the ambiguity theory. An excellent example of such a judicial analysis is an opinion by Judge Learned Hand.[8] After referring to the insurer's contention that the language of a binding receipt for a life insurance premium unambiguously postponed commencement of coverage until the insurer's approval of the application, Judge Hand continued:

> "An underwriter might so understand the phrase, when read in its context, but the application was not to be submitted to underwriters; it was to go to persons utterly unacquainted with the niceties of life insurance, who would read it colloquially. *It is the understanding of such persons that counts;* and not one in a hundred would suppose that he would be covered, not 'as of the date of completion of Part B,' as the defendant promised, but only as of the date of approval." [9]

Judge Hand added that in Connecticut (the state whose law the court was applying) "the canon contra proferentem is more rigorously applied in insurance than in other contracts, in recognition of the difference between the parties in their acquaintance with the subject matter." [10] Judicial analysis and comments of this type established the milieu in which courts began to clearly enunciate a new principle upon which to justify holdings that claimants are entitled to rights at variance with insurance contract provisions even when the applicable insurance policy provisions are not ambiguous.

(3) From Construing Ambiguities to Protecting Reasonable Expectations

The principle of resolving ambiguities in a contract against the drafter increasingly has not been an adequate explanation of or justification for the results in many of the appellate decisions that clearly

---

Note, *The Insurer's Duty to Defend Made Absolute: Gray v. Zurich*, 14 U.C.L.A. Law Review 1328–1339 (1967).

Cf. Spaid v. Cal-Western States Life Insurance Company, 130 Cal.App.3d 803 at p. 806, 182 Cal.Rptr. 3 at p. 5 (1st Dist., Div. 1, 1982), where the court observed, "And while an ambiguity cannot be found from a strained interpretation of the policy's term, nevertheless, the existence of an ambiguity or uncertainty is to be determined from a lay person's perspective; and where semantically possible the policy will be construed to achieve its manifest objective of

indemnifying the insured against the type of losses to which the policy relates."

7. See, e.g., Mosby v. Mutual Life Insurance Company, 405 Ill. 599, 92 N.E.2d 103 (1950), 18 A.L.R.2d 1054 (1951).

8. Gaunt v. John Hancock Mutual Life Insurance Company, 160 F.2d 599 (2d Cir. 1947) *cert. denied* 67 S.Ct. 1736, 331 U.S. 849, 91 L.Ed. 1858 (1947).

9. *Id.,* 160 F.2d at p. 601 (footnote omitted) (emphasis added).

10. *Id.,* 160 F.2d at p. 602 (footnote omitted).

seemed to press beyond the reasonable scope of the ambiguity principle. The early decisions in this development involved many different areas of insurance law including restrictively defined coverage for losses from accidental bodily injuries,[11] provisions regarding the effective date for coverage,[12] life insurance binding receipts,[13] and various coverage limitations in fire and casualty insurance policies.[14]

11. Perrine v. Prudential Insurance Company, 56 N.J. 120, 265 A.2d 521 (1970); Kievit v. Loyal Protective Life Insurance Company, 34 N.J. 475, 170 A.2d 22 (1961). In *Kievit,* after being hit on the head by a piece of lumber, the insured suffered from continuing body tremors, which, according to testimony of a defense physician, resulted from pre-existing but latent Parkinson's disease activated by the blow. The court held that the insured could recover under a policy insuring against loss "resulting directly and independently of all other causes from accidental bodily injuries" and excluding "disability ∗ ∗ ∗ resulting from or contributed to by any disease or ailment," since the pre-existing disease was dormant and unknown to the insured and was activated by the accident into a disabling condition. The court remarked:

"When members of the public purchase policies of insurance they are entitled to the broad measure of protection necessary to fulfill their reasonable expectations. ∗ ∗ ∗ Where particular provisions, if read literally, would largely nullify the insurance, they will be severely restricted so as to enable fair fulfillment of the stated policy objective."

34 N.J. at pp. 482–483, 170 A.2d at p. 26.

Also see the discussion of "accidental" injuries in § 5.4.

12. See, e.g., Klos v. Mobil Oil Company, 55 N.J. 117, 259 A.2d 889 (1969) (complicated conflict among brochure sent to credit card holders, application, and policy, regarding effective date of accident insurance coverage; resolved for coverage on the basis of honoring reasonable expectation; opinion notes that the principle applies to contracts for as well as contracts of insurance).

13. In Prudential Insurance Co. v. Lamme, 83 Nev. 146, 425 P.2d 346 (1967), holding that a conditional receipt creates a temporary contract of life insurance subject to rejection and that during the period before rejection it covers the applicant regardless of whether he is insurable by the company's standards referred to in the receipt, the court remarked:

"A conditional receipt tends to encourage deception. We do not mean to

imply affirmative misconduct by the soliciting insurance agent. We suggest only that if nothing is said about the complicated and legalistic phrasing of the receipt, and the agent accepts an application for insurance together with the first premium payment, the applicant has reason to believe that he is insured."

83 Nev. at p. 149, 425 P.2d at pp. 347–348. After declaring its holding that the receipt created a temporary contract subject to rejection, the court concluded: "The life insurance companies may still write 'COD' [cash on delivery] insurance, or, in the light of experience, choose to assume the risk sometimes involved in the use of the conditional receipt." 83 Nev. at pp. 149–150, 425 P.2d at p. 348 (footnote omitted).

In Allen v. Metropolitan Life Insurance Company, 44 N.J. 294 at p. 302, 208 A.2d 638 at p. 642 (1965), the court stated:

"Much of the difficulty may be laid at the doorstep of the life insurance industry itself for ∗ ∗ ∗ it has persisted in using language which is obscure to the layman and in tolerating agency practices which are calculated to lead the layman to believe that he has coverage beyond that which may be called for by a literal reading."

Though recognizing that "[w]hen read literally, the receipt gave no interim protection at all in the absence of an approval by the company at its home office," 44 N.J. at p. 304, 208 A.2d at p. 643, the court held that the applicant's

"reasonable expectations in the transaction may not justly be frustrated and courts have properly molded their governing interpretative principles with that uppermost in mind. Thus we have consistently construed policy terms strictly against the insurer and where several interpretations were permissible, we have chosen the one most favorable to the assured."

44 N.J. at p. 305, 208 A.2d at p. 644.

In Morgan v. State Farm Life Insurance Co., 240 Or. 113 at pp. 118–122, 400 P.2d

14. See note 14 on page 632.

Judicial decisions that strain a reader's credulity in regard to existence of an ambiguity not only create an impression of unprincipled judicial prejudice against insurers and the insurance industry, but also produce confusion and uncertainty about the nature and extent of judicial regulation of contract terms. In many circumstances, as it became increasingly evident that judicial decisions were not based on the construction of ambiguities, it was far more appropriate for courts to explicitly articulate that the justification for the results was based on seeking to honor or protect the reasonable expectations of policyholders.[15] And, beginning in the early 1960s, courts have clearly and explicitly employed the doctrine of honoring reasonable expectations.

223, at pp. 225–227 (1965), the dissenting opinion (joined in by three of seven judges) also seems clearly to support the principle of honoring reasonable expectations. 240 Or. at pp. 120–121, 400 P.2d at pp. 226–227.

See also Beckham v. Travelers Insurance Company, 424 Pa. 107 at pp. 117–118, 225 A.2d 532 at p. 537 (1967).

Also see discussion of binding receipts in § 2.3.

14. National Indemnity Company v. Flesher, 469 P.2d 360 (Alaska 1970) (resolving, on the basis of reasonable expectations, a dispute in favor of coverage with respect to duty to defend under liability insurance).

Cf. Gerhardt v. Continental Insurance Companies, 48 N.J. 291, 225 A.2d 328 (1966). In *Gerhardt*, sustaining coverage under a homeowners policy for a workers' compensation claim of a domestic employee, the court observed that in deciding an earlier case it had "stressed that insureds are entitled to the measure of protection necessary to fulfill their 'reasonable expectations' and that they should not be subjected to 'technical encumbrances or to hidden pitfalls.'" The court also stated:

"While the insured is always supposed to read the policy, only a very hardy soul would have plowed through all of the fine print here in an effort to understand the many terms and conditions. * * *

"The insurer explains * * * references favoring residence employees by pointing to the fact that its policy form was used in various states including those where residence employees are not within workmen's compensation laws. * * * But so far as the New Jersey insured here was concerned, she was entitled to treat the policy as solely a New Jersey one. She was not at all interested in any extra-state matters and her reasonable expectations are to be determined and fulfilled entirely from the point of view of a local policy purchased in a local relationship."

Id., 48 N.J. at p. 297 and at pp. 299–300, 225 A.2d at pp. 332–334.

Cf. Cooper v. Government Employees Insurance Company, 51 N.J. 86 at pp. 93–94, 237 A.2d 870 at pp. 873–874 (1968) (placing burden on insurer to prove breach of late-notice provision and "a likelihood of appreciable prejudice" therefrom in order to fulfill reasonable expectations of the purchaser "so far as its language will permit"; trial court's fact-finding of no breach by insured of notice provision sustained).

Also see Harr v. Allstate Insurance Co., 54 N.J. 287, 255 A.2d 208 (1969) (insurer estopped to deny coverage under fire policy because of contrary representations of agent; the court resorted to a theory of reasonable expectations in rejecting the contention that policy provisions negated the alleged representations); Barth v. State Farm Fire & Casualty Company, 214 Pa.Super. 434, 257 A.2d 671 (1969) (policy, received several weeks after insured had applied for coverage, afforded robbery protection only when the premises were open for business; brochure relied upon as a basis for coverage until the policy was received referred to all-risk comprehensive crime insurance and had an artist's representation of a burglary occurring during non-business hours; judgment for insurer reversed and remanded for trial on fact question whether policyholder had in fact been informed before loss that policy did not cover loss of cash during non-business hours; reasoned on ground of rights based on reasonable reliance, not available if he had been correctly informed before loss).

15. *Cf.* Morgan v. State Farm Life Insurance Company, 240 Or. 113, 400 P.2d 223 (1965) (4–3 decision enforcing an insurability requirement; the dissenting opinion supports the principle of honoring reasonable expectations, favoring temporary coverage subject to rejection even though the

As the principle of honoring reasonable expectations began to be recognized, it also became evident that this concept represented a better reasoned and more persuasive justification for the judicial resolution of variance claims in many instances in which courts had applied a variety of other doctrines.[16] The doctrine of protecting reasonable expectations can appropriately be stated in the following way:

> **In general, courts will protect the reasonable expectations of applicants, insureds, and intended beneficiaries regarding the coverage afforded by insurance contracts even though a careful examination of the policy provisions indicates that such expectations are contrary to the expressed intention of the insurer.**

Although this statement is not a sufficiently precise formulation of a doctrinal statement [17] from which particularized decisions can always

---

receipt was unambiguous to the careful reader).

Also see Litchsinn v. American Interinsurance Exchange, 287 N.W.2d 156 at p. 160 (Iowa 1980) (" * * * the policy language must be given meaning consistent with the objective and reasonable expectations of the insured."); Collister v. Nationwide Life Insurance Company, 479 Pa. 579 at p. 594, 388 A.2d 1346 at p. 1353 (1978), *cert. denied* 439 U.S. 1089, 99 S.Ct. 871, 59 L.Ed.2d 55 (1979).

Also see Stordahl v. Government Employees Insurance Company, 564 P.2d 63 at pp. 65–66 (Alaska 1977); INA Life Insurance Company v. Brudin, 533 P.2d 236 at p. 242 (Alaska 1975) ("A layperson's expectation of insurance coverage are of course formed by many factors besides the language of the policies * * *.").

16. Examples of such cases include disputes resulting from delivery of a policy that deviates in some marked fashion from the coverage applied for. Under customary theory, the transmission of such a policy is a counteroffer by the insurer. Acceptance by the insured concludes the transaction and makes the substituted policy the binding contract. E.g., Long v. New York Life Insurance Company, 106 Wash. 458, 180 P. 479 (1919).

But in some cases involving deviations not specifically brought to the insured's attention, the policy has been construed to provide the coverage applied for, regardless of express language to the contrary. See, e.g., Providential Life Insurance Company v. Clem, 240 Ark. 922, 403 S.W.2d 68 (1966); Lawrence v. Providential Life Insurance Co., 238 Ark. 981, 385 S.W.2d 936 (1965). Although this result has been based upon a duty of the insurer to issue the insurance applied for in the absence of adequate notice of variations, it may be

suggested that the reasonable expectations of the insured created by the description of coverage contained in the application form constitute the best reason for recognizing such a duty.

Also see Stamps v. Consolidated Underwriters, 205 Kan. 187, 468 P.2d 84 (1970) (automobile liability insurance coverage less than applied for was issued without notice to applicant; reformation allowed).

Another example of such cases is the body of decisions holding that delivery of a renewal policy of lesser scope than the previous policy without calling the insured's attention to the reduction of coverage is not effective to reduce the scope of coverage. See, e.g., Bauman v. Royal Indemnity Company, 36 N.J. 12, 174 A.2d 585 (1961), 91 A.L.R.2d 535 (1963) (renewal policy declared no coverage for workers' compensation claims of resident employees as well as other employees; *held,* claim of part-time domestic employee covered). A later New Jersey case sustained coverage for a workers' compensation claim of a domestic employee on a ground more broadly supporting the principle of honoring reasonable expectations. In this later instance there was no history of an earlier, broader policy on which the insured might base his claim of reasonable expectations. Gerhardt v. Continental Insurance Companies, 48 N.J. 291, 225 A.2d 328 (1966), discussed in note 14, above.

The focus of this statement in the text is on insurance cases. The principle, of course, applies in other contexts as well.

17. The statement is too general to give precise guidance, and it is subject to being construed either too broadly or too narrowly unless it is read with an awareness of the way it has been applied by a particular court of last resort in the relevant jurisdiction.

be derived through an exercise of logic, it represents a relatively concise conceptualization of the rationale, as well as the public policy which has been expressly articulated in numerous appellate court decisions [18] and which appears to be the operative principle (though not always set forth) of many other decisions.[19]

(4) Justifications for Protecting Reasonable Expectations

There are several pragmatic reasons why coverage limitations that conflict with reasonable expectations ought not to be enforced even when the limitations are both explicit and unambiguous in policy forms.

First, insurance contracts are set forth in insurance policies that typically are long, complicated documents which insurers know policyholders ordinarily will not even read and certainly will not carefully study.[20] Relatively few policyholders ever examine their insurance policies with the care that would be required for even moderately detailed understanding of coverage limitations. Moreover, many insurance contracts cannot be understood without detailed analysis, and often not even an extended consideration of the terms would fully apprise an insured of the precise scope of coverage and the meaning of the limitations or restrictions set forth in a particular insurance policy. *Caveat.* It should be noted, however, that many insurers have revised both the format and the wording of insurance policies with a view to making them significantly more understandable to the consumer. The import of these newer insurance documents — which are typically referred to by characterizations such as "plain language," "plain talk," or "easy read" forms — is yet to be considered by the courts in most jurisdictions.

Second, the marketing approaches employed for most kinds of insurance ordinarily do not even allow a purchaser to examine a copy of an insurance policy until after the contract has been completed. In life insurance transactions, for example, the purchaser usually does not see the insurance policy terms until after the application has been submitted, the first premium has been paid, the insurance company has decided to approve the application, and the company has issued the policy. This often means a delay of weeks, or even months, between submitting an application and receiving the insurance policy. In many situations, such delays undoubtedly contributes a policyholder's disincli-

---

18. See, e.g. Keene Corporation v. Insurance Company of North America, 667 F.2d 1034 at p. 1041 (D.C.Cir.1981).

Cf. Hancock Laboratories v. Admiral Insurance Company, 777 F.2d 520 at p. 523, note 5 (9th Cir.1986). Sadlowski v. Liberty Mutual Insurance Company, 487 A.2d 1146 at p. 1149 (Del.Sup.1984).

Also see Spaid v. Cal-Western States Life Insurance Company, 130 Cal.App.3d 803 at p. 806, 182 Cal.Rptr. 3 at p. 4 (1st Dist., Div. 1, 1982).

19. When decisions employing other rationales are reconsidered in light of the reasonable expectations principle, it often provides a more persuasive justification for sustaining the insured's claim.

20. *Cf.* the comment of the New Jersey Supreme Court in Sparks v. St. Paul Insurance Company, 100 N.J. 325, 495 A.2d 406 at p. 412 (1985), "The recognition that insurance policies are not readily understood has impelled courts to resolve ambiguities in such contracts against insurance companies * * * [and] has led courts to enforce *unambiguous insurance contracts in accordance with the reasonable expectations of the insured.* (Emphasis supplied).

nation to read the insurance policy carefully or even to read it at all. Although the time which elapses before a purchaser receives a copy of the insurance policy is usually not as long in regard to other types of insurance, the marketing transaction for most coverages is structured in a way that does in fact defer access to the coverage terms until after the contract has been consummated. In this context, the justification for concluding that a policyholder's reasonable expectations should be honored is certainly compelling, and especially so when the policy language is difficult to understand or employs a technical vocabulary. Furthermore, even when the language of a policy provision is clearly understandable, the argument still applies unless an insurer can show that a purchaser's failure to read and understand the contract language establishing coverage limitations was unreasonable.[21]

Third, there are many situations in which protection of an insured's reasonable expectations is viewed as appropriate because it would be unconscionable or unfair to allow an insurer to enforce the limitations or restrictions in the insurance policy.[22] In some instances, courts predicate such decisions, at least in part, on the fact that the insurance policy provision at issue is included in a contract of adhesion.[23] Several aspects of this rationale are developed in the following subsection.

Fourth, it is appropriate to protect expectations which result from the marketing practices of the insurer — that is, actual or reasonable expectations which differ from the coverage provisions — that are derived from events or acts which were attributable either to the actions of persons in the field representing the insurer in the marketing transaction or persons at a management center that directs the operations of the insurance company.[24] Furthermore, there are circumstances in which an insured's reasonable expectations may result from the conduct of the insurance industry as a whole.[25]

Fifth, expectations which result from the way in which the specific insurance coverage at issue is characterized by the insurer — as, for

---

21. *Cf.* Collister v. Nationwide Life Insurance Company, 479 Pa. 579 at p. 595, 388 A.2d 1346 at pp. 1353–1354 (1978).

Also see § 2.8(c), above, § 6.3(c), below, and the discussion of bindings receipts in § 2.3, above.

22. See § 6.3(b), below. Also see the discussion of disallowing unconscionable advantages to an insurer in § 6.2, above.

23. *Cf.* Selected Risks Insurance Company v. Bruno, 718 F.2d 67 at p. 70 (3d Cir. 1983) (applying Pennsylvania law); Ponder v. Blue Cross of Southern California, 145 Cal.App. 709, 193 Cal.Rptr. 632 (2d Dist., Div. 7, 1983).

Also see Transamerica Insurance Company v. Royle, 202 Mont. 173, 656 P.2d 820 at p. 824 (1983).

24. See especially the role of intermediaries in the marketing of insurance in § 2.5, above, and the discussion of marketing without sales representatives in 30 N.Y. 357 at pp. 365–66, 118 N.E.2d 555 at p. 559 (1954).

Some courts have concluded that the insurer is "obliged to show (1) that it would be unreasonable for the average * * * [person] reading the policy to [construe it as the insured does] and (2) that its own construction was the only one that fairly could be placed on the policy." Sincoff v. Liberty Mutual Fire Insurance Co., 11 N.Y.2d 386 at p. 390, 230 N.Y.S.2d 13 at p. 16, 183 N.E.2d 899 at p. 901 (1962).

25. As for example, by similar advertisements of several insurance companies.

example, a "Blanket Coverage" or a "Comprehensive Coverage Plan" — warrant protection in some circumstances.[26] Similarly, an insured may have reasonable expectations about the scope of coverage as a consequence of the format of the insurance policy which sets forth in large print at the beginning of the policy a broad statement of coverage, even though the policy terms do circumscribe the coverage by limitations and restrictions which appear elsewhere in the form [27] (and which often are not apparent to the typical consumer).

Comment

In some circumstances, the scope of an insurance coverage should be predicated on the reasonable expectations of an insured even though an insurance policy includes an explicit and unambiguous limitation that could have been discovered by an insured through a comprehensive analysis of the terms. Determinations about (1) whether an insurance policy includes a provision that unambiguously limits or excludes coverage and (2) whether a policyholder could have sufficiently examined an insurance policy so as to discover a relevant clause which limits the coverage, should be factors bearing on decisions about whether the policyholder's expectations in regard to a matter at issue were reasonable from a lay person's point of view. However, the scope to be accorded to this approach should be carefully evaluated case by case because in many instances there have been, and undoubtedly will continue to be, circumstances in which there is substantial justification for predicating the resolution of a coverage dispute on other considerations and doctrines.[28] This is especially true when it is possible to ascertain the actual expectations of the insured, as well as the insurer.[29]

§ 6.3(b) Implications and Applications of the Expectations Principle

(1) The Principle and a Corollary

The principle of honoring reasonable expectations leads directly to the premise that the coverage provided by an insurance policy should be determined in accordance with what lay persons would reasonably understand as the scope of the coverage.[1] The most significant corolla-

---

26. *Cf.* Emcasco Insurance Company v. L & M Development, Inc., 372 N.W.2d 908 (N.D.1985) (involving a comprehensive general liability policy); Northwest Airlines, Inc. v. Globe Indemnity Company, 303 Minn. 16, 225 N.W.2d 831 (1975) (involving the coverage provided by a "Blanket Crime Policy").

27. *Cf.* Farmers Insurance Exchange v. Call, 712 P.2d 231 (Utah 1985).

Also consider the discussion of the design of insurance policies in § 5.1(c) and § 5.1(d), above.

28. Consider the discussion in § 2.8(c), above.

29. See the discussion in § 6.3(c), below.

§ 6.3(b)

1. Although this proposition might be regarded as a corollary to the principle of resolving ambiguities against an insurer, this aspect of the principle of honoring reasonable expectations extends further.

See, e.g., Farmers Insurance Exchange v. Call, 712 P.2d 231 at pp. 236–237 (Utah 1985). The court commented, "Purchasers commonly rely on the assumption that

ry of this proposition is that insurers ought not to be allowed to use qualifications, limitations, restrictions, and exceptions in an insurance policy that are contrary to the reasonable expectations of a policyholder having an ordinary degree of familiarity with the type of coverage involved.[2] At the same time, courts also recognize that there are limitations on the situations in which the principle will be applied. It seems clear that reasonableness of the expectations will be evaluated, and that an insured will not succeed in securing coverage when it can only be predicated on what would be viewed as unreasonable expectations about the scope of insurance provisions.[3]

The situations in which courts conclude that an application of the reasonable expectations principle is justified often involve circumstances which indicate that there was either some element of unconscionability in the conduct of the insurer or some detrimental reliance on the part of an insured. The relationships between these doctrines and the reasonable expectations of the insured are considered in the succeeding subsections.

(2) Reasonable Expectations and Unconscionability

There are numerous judicial decisions in which courts appear to be influenced by both concern for protecting reasonable expectations and

they are fully covered by the insurance they buy" and therefore without a specific disclosure "the household exclusion clause fails to 'honor the reasonable expectations' of the purchaser, rendering the exclusion clause invalid as to the entire policy. * * * "

Cf. Spaid v. Cal-Western States, Life Insurance Company, 130 Cal.App.3d 803 at p. 808, 182 Cal.Rptr. 3 at p. 5 (1st Dist., Div. 1, 1982).

Also see Kenneth S. Abraham, *Judge-Made Law and Judge-Made Reasonable Expectations of the Insured*, 67 Virginia Law Review 1151–1199 (1981); Mark A. Cohen, *Flight Insurance: Conforming to the Reasonable Expectations of the Insured*, 30 Federation of Insurance Counsel Quarterly 19–28 (1979).

2. In Vargas v. Insurance Company of North America, 651 F.2d 838 at p. 840 (2d Cir.1981), the court concluded:

"The insurer bears a heavy burden of proof, for it must " 'establish that the words and expressions used [in the insurance policy] not only are susceptible of the construction sought by [the insurer] but that it is the only construction which may fairly be placed on them.' " Filor, Bullard & Smyth v. Insurance Company of North America, 605 F.2d 598, 602 (2d Cir.1978), cert. denied, 440 U.S. 962, 99 S.Ct. 1506, 59 L.Ed.2d 776 (1979) (quoting

Lachs v. Fidelity & Casualty Co. of New York, 306 N.Y. 357, 365–66, 118 N.E.2d 555, 559 (1954)). The insurer is "obliged to show (1) that it would be unreasonable for the average man reading the policy to [construe it as the insured does] and (2) that its own construction was the only one that fairly could be placed on the policy." Sincoff v. Liberty Mutual Fire Insurance Co., 11 N.Y.2d 386, 390, 230 N.Y.S.2d 13, 16, 183 N.E.2d 899, 901 (1962)."

3. *Cf.* Selected Risks Insurance Company v. Bruno, 718 F.2d 67 at p. 71 (3d Cir. 1983) (applying Pennsylvania law), where the court concluded, "An exclusion for intentionally caused injuries is not unusual, nor could an insured reasonably expect that a basic homeowner's policy would provide coverage for intentional criminal acts, particularly those committed away from home."

Cf. Bohnen International, Inc. v. Liberty Mutual Insurance Company, Inc., 120 Ill. App.3d 657, 76 Ill.Dec. 244, 458 N.E.2d 644 at p. 649 (2d Dist.1983):

"Liberal construction of an insurance policy in favor of the insured must yield to rules of reasonable construction. Jenkins v. State Security Insurance Co. (1978), 56 Ill.App.3d 737, 14 Ill.Dec. 150, 371 N.E.2d 1203."

disallowing an unconscionable advantage to the insurer. In some cases, for example, the unambiguous language of an insurance policy provision provides so little coverage that it would be unconscionable to permit the insurer to enforce it. An illustration of the combined force of the principles of honoring reasonable expectations and disallowing unconscionable advantage is provided by several judicial decisions concerning increase-of-hazard clauses. Increase-of-hazard clauses in fire insurance policies commonly contain the following declaration:

> "Unless otherwise provided in writing added hereto this Company shall not be liable for loss occurring (a) while the hazard is increased by any means within the control *or* knowledge of the insured * * *."[4]

One interesting question presented by this type of clause is whether something that is within the potential control of the insured, even though the insured does not know about it, justifies the rejection of a claim. Similarly, should an insurer be entitled to deny coverage when an increase in the hazard is known to an insured, even though the insured is not in a position to control or modify the situation. A literal reading of the phrase "control *or* knowledge" would support an affirmative answer to such questions. Results in litigated claims disputes, however, are generally contrary to this position.[5] The degree of judicial regulation involved in according this clause the same effect as if it read knowledge "and" (rather than "or") control is arguably justified because of the unduly severe and, from the layperson's point of view,

---

4. See, e.g., lines 28–32 of the policy form prescribed in New York—McKinney's Insurance Law § 3404 (1986) (Emphasis added). Since this provision appears in a statutorily prescribed form, the argument for a measure of judicial regulation to prevent an unconscionable advantage is arguably less strong than when the policy form is drafted by the insurer. But there remains the point of great disparity between the level of premiums charged and the scope of coverage that would be provided under a literal enforcement of the clause.

Also see the discussion of an insured's obligation to prevent an injury in § 5.4(f), above, and requirements that an insured notify an insurer of changes concerning the location, use, or occupancy of property in § 6.8(d), below.

5. See, e.g., Goldman v. Piedmont Fire Insurance Company, 198 F.2d 712 (3d Cir.1952), 34 A.L.R.2d 706 (1954) (applying New Jersey law). The majority opinion in *Goldman* asserts that the court is enforcing the increase-of-hazard clause as written, but also speaks of the condition as one applicable upon proof that the increase of hazard was within the insured's knowledge *and* control rather than knowledge or con-

trol. The opinion indicates on procedural grounds, however, that the plaintiff cannot complain of the trial court's failure to charge that the increase of hazard must be within the insured's "knowledge *and* control." 198 F.2d at p. 715, 34 A.L.R.2d at p. 714.

Cf. Di Leo v. United States Fidelity & Guaranty Company, 50 Ill.App.2d 183, 200 N.E.2d 405 (1st Dist., Div. 1, 1964), 9 A.L.R. 3d 1399 (1966). In *Di Leo*, the insurer defended against recovery under policies on the contents of the insured's store and for business interruption, citing changes in use and occupancy incident to a pending condemnation of the building in which insureds leased space for their business. The court held that "knowledge AND control of the increase of hazard must be shown before the clause can be used to avoid liability." 50 Ill.App.2d at p. 191, 200 N.E.2d at p. 409, 9 A.L.R.3d at p. 1407 (emphasis in the opinion).

Cf. Weinberg Realty Company, Inc. v. Hartford Mutual Insurance Company, 45 Md.App. 560, 413 A.2d 1368 at pp. 1372–1373 (Md.App.1980).

Also see 5 APPLEMAN, INSURANCE LAW (Revised edition, 1970), at § 2941.

the surprising effect the clause would have if it were enforceable as it is written. In many instances, literal enforcement would result in such minimal coverage that informed policyholders would almost certainly consider such insurance coverage unacceptable.

Conclusions of unconscionability often become even more supportable as a result of a comparison of the premiums that were charged for the coverage with the cost to insurers of affording a highly restricted coverage. If the premiums charged for a coverage cannot be justified by the underwriting experience, a persuasive case exists for disallowing literal enforcement of insurance policy provisions without regard either to whether the individual policyholder read the provision(s) in question, or to whether the individual would have understood the limitation(s) if the provision(s) had been read.

Some of the areas in which courts have commonly refused to enforce an explicit, unambiguous policy provision include intolerably restrictive definitions of total disability,[6] and the terms "accidental

---

6. See, e.g., Rudder v. Ohio State Life Insurance Company, 389 S.W.2d 448 (Ky.1965), 26 A.L.R.3d 707 (1969); Struble v. Occidental Life Insurance Company, 265 Minn. 26, 120 N.W.2d 609 (1963).

Also see Bowler v. Fidelity & Casualty Company, 53 N.J. 313, 250 A.2d 580 (1969); Mason v. Loyal Protective Life Insurance Company, 249 Iowa 1167, 91 N.W.2d 389 (1958).

Cf. Chavez v. Continental Insurance Company, 218 Va. 76, 235 S.E.2d 335 at p. 339 (1977); Rodgers v. Nationwide Insurance Company, 47 Or.App. 843 at p. 848, 615 P.2d 1090 at p. 1093 (1980) ("Oregon Supreme Court cases * * * affirm the rule that ambiguous provisions of an insurance policy are to be construed in the sense in which the insured had reason to suppose they were understood.") [Citations omitted].

In *Mason*, a doctor of medicine, compelled to give up practice because of nerve deafness, undertook a residency for training as a radiologist, receiving compensation about one-tenth as much as he had earned during his last year in practice. The policy defined "total disability" as "complete loss of business time due to inability of the Insured to engage in his regular occupation or any gainful occupation for which he is reasonably fitted." Held, for the insured:

"Total disability" as used in this connection does not mean, as its literal construction would require, a state of absolute helplessness.

* * *

"[S]uch words as 'any gainful occupation' in this policy mean any occupation, rea-

sonably approximating the same livelihood of the insured's regulation occupation as he might fairly be expected to follow, in view of his station, circumstances, and capabilities."

Id., 249 Iowa at p. 1171 and p. 1177, 91 N.W.2d at p. 392 and p. 395.

In *Rudder*, the policy provided for benefits if plaintiff-insured's disability prevented him "from engaging in any and every occupation or employment." There was evidence he engaged in supervision of others and himself performed minor physical tasks incident to operation of his farm. Held, it was nevertheless error to enter judgment on verdict for defendant and to deny plaintiff's motion for judgment n.o.v., 389 S.W.2d at p. 449 and p. 451, 26 A.L.R.3d at p. 710 and p. 713.

In *Struble*, a policy clause conditioned coverage on insured's being "necessarily and continuously confined within the house and therein regularly visited and attended by a legally qualified physician or surgeon other than himself." The verdict for plaintiff was upheld despite the fact that he had worked at ordinary laborer's tasks for pay as part of the prescribed therapy while under treatment for mental illness, the court commenting that the policy must be construed so as "to give a realistic meaning to the words and provide some measure of the protection" bargained for. Id., 256 Minn. at p. 27 and 36, 120 N.W.2d at p. 611 and p. 616.

But see, e.g., Walsh v. United Insurance Company, 265 N.C. 634, 144 S.E.2d 817 (1965) (insured was totally disabled from engaging in farming, his pre-accident occupation, but he engaged in activities advised

means"[7] or "accidental bodily injury."[8] Other situations in which courts appear to be concerned with both protecting reasonable expectations and precluding unconscionable advantages include receipt-of-due-proof clauses in disability insurance policies,[9] and "other insurance" clauses in various kinds of coverage.[10]

by his doctor, short walks, driving, etc.; held, engaging in these activities excluded coverage under policy containing a "continuous confinement" clause).

"Liberal" judicial construction of disability clauses was a factor contributing to the general withdrawal of life insurance companies from this field of insurance during the 1930's. Claim costs proved to be far greater, especially during the depression years, than had been anticipated at the time premium rates were fixed. See, e.g., Rhine v. New York Life Insurance Co., 273 N.Y. 1 at p. 11, 6 N.E.2d 74 at p. 77 (1936), 108 A.L.R. 1197 at p. 1202 (1937):

"[T]he 'extra premium' * * * paid to obtain a policy with additional 'disability benefits' has, in every year since 1931, been less than the cost of furnishing those benefits." (emphasis in original).

See generally 1C APPLEMAN, INSURANCE LAW (Revised edition, 1981) at p. 631 and pp. 671–680; Annotation, *Continuance or resumption of work as affecting finding of total or permanent disability within insurance coverage,* 24 A.L.R.3d 8–172 (1969).

7. See, e.g., Schonberg v. New York Life Insurance Company, 235 La. 461, 104 So.2d 171 (1958); Perrine v. Prudential Insurance Company, 56 N.J. 120, 265 A.2d 521 (1970) (double indemnity "accidental means" clause; deceased leaned cabinet-type 600–700 pound equipment against body while moving it on Friday; complained of feeling unwell that evening; felt worse on Sunday and was hospitalized then; surgery disclosed perforation of his large bowel; died within days from inflammation of abdominal cavity; held, fact question whether he suffered injury from "accidental means" as construed according to reasonable expectations of average policyholder, the test being "whether the average policyholder would consider that there was something about the preceding acts and events, in the light of the unexpected injurious result and at the same time having in mind the limiting language of the insuring clause, which would lead him reasonably to call the means 'accidental,' even though, strictly speaking, nothing unexpected or unforeseen occurred in the course of the preceding acts"; quotes with approval from Robert E. Keeton, *Insurance Law Rights at Variance with Policy Provi-*

sions, 83 Harvard Law Review 961–985; distinguishes earlier case of heart attack, held as a matter of law not to involve accidental means.

Also see Scott v. New Empire Insurance Company, 75 N.M. 81, 400 P.2d 953 (1965); Burr v. Commercial Travelers Mutual Accident Association, 295 N.Y. 294, 67 N.E.2d 248 (1946), 166 A.L.R. 462 (1947); Beckham v. Travelers Insurance Company, 424 Pa. 107, 225 A.2d 532 (1967).

Cf. Oldring v. Metropolitan Life Insurance Company, 492 F.Supp. 994 at p. 997 (D.N.J.1980); Catania v. State Farm Life Insurance Company, Inc., 95 Nev. 532, 598 P.2d 631 at p. 633 (1979); Karl v. New York Life Insurance Company, 154 N.J. Super. 182 at p. 186, 381 A.2d 62 at p. 64 (App.Div.1977).

But cf. Metropolitan Life Insurance Company v. Smith, 554 S.W.2d 123 at p. 128 (Tenn.1977) ("In the present case, the language of the exclusionary clauses make clear the intention of the insurers * * * that the carriers do not contract to provide double indemnity if it requires an active combination of a pre-existing disease and an accidental injury to produce death."); Gordon v. Metropolitan Life Insurance Company, 256 Md. 320, 260 A.2d 338 (1970) (affirming directed verdict for insurer on claim under clause for double indemnity; court refuses to declare there is no distinction between accidental means and accidental results; decedent illegally used heroin, which combined with pain killer to produce death; use of heroin caused substantial risk and was prime cause of death).

8. See, e.g., Kievit v. Loyal Protective Life Insurance Company, 34 N.J. 475, 170 A.2d 22 (1961).

Cf. Orman v. Prudential Insurance Company of America, 296 N.W.2d 380 (Minn. 1980) (accidental death benefits); DeCuir v. Old Republic Life Insurance Company, 342 So.2d 705 (La.App., 3d Cir.1977).

9. See the discussion in § 6.9(d) and § 7.2, below. Also see Revised 1C APPLEMAN, INSURANCE LAW & PRACTICE (1980), at p. 152.

10. See the discussion of "other insurance" clauses in § 3.11(a), above.

(3) Reasonable Expectations and Detrimental Reliance

The expectations principle and the detrimental reliance principle (considered in Section 6.4) are distinct theories. Although the situations in which these doctrines justify relief clearly overlap, neither wholly embraces the other. For example, the expectations principle may provide a justification for sustaining relief for a claimant without regard to whether a claimant has suffered any detriment from his or her own or another person's change of position in reliance on expectations created by the insurer.[11]

§ 6.3(c) Limitations on Applications of the Expectations Principle

(1) Actual Expectations Versus Reasonable Expectations

In many instances courts consider questions involving the reasonable expectations of an applicant for insurance or of an insured. This approach is usually employed when it is evident that the insurance purchaser did not have an actual expectation about the matter at issue.

The principle of honoring reasonable expectations does not deny an insurer the opportunity to make an explicit qualification, limitation, or restriction in order to create a circumstance in which the insured's actual expectation is the same as the insurer's or that it would be "unreasonable" for an insured to have a contrary expectation. In most situations, there is nothing to preclude an insurer from entering into an insurance agreement with restrictions or limitations on coverage so long as the insurer takes steps to ensure that the policyholder is fully informed.[1] And insurance policies may even include enforceable provisions that are exceptional or impose unusual restrictions.

In order for either a common or an extraordinary coverage limitation in an insurance policy to be enforceable, it should be essential for an insurer both to employ a procedure that makes the purchaser aware of the restrictive terms and to charge a premium rate that is adjusted fairly to the scope of the coverage provided — that is, in order to avoid variance claims based on either reasonable expectations or unconscionability, the insurer should be required to adopt measures which guarantee (1) either that the purchaser has actual expectations consistent with described coverage because the purchaser was made aware of the limitations during the marketing transaction, or that it would be unreasonable for an insured to have expectations that are not consistent with the insurance policy provisions,[2] *and* (2) that the premium

---

11. The reliance principle has a broader range of application than the expectations principle in respect to relief that is granted on the basis of unauthorized and deviational representations by an agent of an insurer.

§ 6.3(c)

1. *Cf.* Foremost Insurance Company v. Putzier, 100 Idaho 883, 606 P.2d 987 at p.

991 (1980), where the appellate court decided that nothing in the record compels a different conclusion from the trial court finding that "all exclusions, including the riot exclusion were read to [Robert, also known as Evel] Knievel's attorney over the telephone * * *."

2. Consider the comments in Ponder v. Blue Cross of Southern California, 145 Cal.

charged appropriately reflects the actual scope of risk that the policy provisions define.[3]

It clearly is possible for a corporation to enter into contracts with consumers on the basis of a full and complete explanation of the contractual arrangement so that both parties have the same actual expectations. The doctrines and practices developed in relation to notice of limitations of liability for innkeepers [4] provide an analogy to which both insurers and courts might turn in formulating guidelines. Similarly, many automobile rental agencies take great care to ensure that anyone renting a vehicle makes a specific choice in regard to accepting or rejecting collision coverage for a rented vehicle. These transactions can serve as prototypes for the insurance industry in

App.3d 709 at p. 719, 193 Cal.Rptr. 632 at p. 637 (2d Dist., Div. 7, 1983) (emphasis in the original):

"Since we hold this is an adhesion contract, it is not enough the exclusionary clause could be deemed to be precise. It also must past muster under two other independent tests. (1) The exclusion must be *conspicuous* and (2) the language of the exclusion must be *plain and clear.* We have chosen to divide the traditional statement of the requirement that insurance policy exclusions be 'conspicuous, plain and clear' into separate tests. As a matter of logic, this brief clause imposes two very different demands on those who draft insurance policies. First, the exclusion must be positioned in a place and printed in a form which would attract a reader's attention. Secondly, the substance of the exclusion must be stated in words that convey the proper meaning to persons expected to read the contract."

Cf. United States Fire Insurance Company v. Colver, 600 P.2d 1 at p. 3 (Alaska 1979) (" * * * we treat insurance policies as contracts of adhesion when interpreting policy language" and therefore "we construe them so as to provide that coverage which a layperson would have reasonably expected from a lay interpretation of the policy terms."); Emcasco Insurance Company v. L & M Development, Inc., 372 N.W.2d 908 at p. 911 (N.D.1985) ("Limitations or exclusions from broad coverage must be clear and explicit.").

Also see Hildebrandt v. Washington National Insurance Company, 181 Mont. 231, 593 P.2d 37 at p. 40 (1979) (" * * * Hildebrandt [a general agent for Washington National] dealt only with himself * * * [and] the language of the conditional premium receipt should not have been confusing to Hildebrandt, for he had over eighteen years of experience dealing with that type of contract.").

Also see Williams v. First Colony Life Insurance Company, 593 P.2d 534 at p. 537, (Utah 1979) (" * * * inasmuch as the conditions [in the conditional receipt] were clearly stated, they became part of the contract * * *."); Almagro v. Allstate Insurance Company, 129 Ariz. 163 at pp. 164–165, 629 P.2d 999 at pp. 1000–1001 (App., Div. 2, 1981) ("If a provision is not ambiguous, we must construe it according to its plain and ordinary meaning.").

3. *Cf.* the comment in Vargas v. Insurance Company of North America, 651 F.2d 838 at p. 841 (2d Cir.1981):

"In support of its position that its construction is the only reasonable one, appellee contended at oral argument that flights over waters beyond the territorial limits pose special dangers, for which insureds should be required to pay extra premiums; and it notes that Khurey had rejected an offer to cover the entire Caribbean. This ostensible appeal to commercial commonsense does not withstand analysis. The fact that coverage of the entire Caribbean, including the ocean areas, cost only an additional fifty dollars undermines the argument that substantial additional risks are involved. Moreover, INA offers no evidence that over-water flights between covered locations are more dangerous than flights over points anywhere within the United States, Canada, Alaska, and Mexico — areas that are expressly covered by the policy and that include vast mountain ranges, lakes, deserts, and urban centers with heavy air traffic. Commonsense and experience contradict INA's assertion that over-water flights add materially to these explicitly covered risks."

4. See generally 9 WILLISTON, CONTRACTS (Third edition, 1967), at § 1069.

regard to the type of marketing conduct that can be employed to bring actual expectations among consumers into conformity with policy provisions.

Comment

There undoubtedly are limits on the extent to which full notice to a particular policyholder may or should be effective in imposing coverage restrictions or limitations. For example, this approach probably should not defeat a claim for rights that are at variance with a clause when the terms at issue are fundamentally unconscionable. Moreover, if an insurance contract is such that it misleads the great majority of policyholders, a persuasive case exists for a variance claim even though a claimant in the particular dispute was aware of the actual terms intended by the insurer.[5] Thus, even if the particular insured had either no expectation or an expectation consistent with literal interpretation of the policy provision, the objective standard of what expectation would be reasonable among laypersons generally should control.

An insurance contract should always be scrutinized in light of what actually occurred in the marketplace. For example, it is important to consider whether the insurance agreement was or could have been the subject of an effective negotiation, as is often true in regard to insurance that is acquired for large groups or policies providing extensive coverage for large corporate entities.[6] Furthermore, individual consumers frequently can secure more comprehensive protection by opting for additional coverages or arranging for endorsements that broaden coverage.[7]

When an individual insured is not aware of a particular term, if a group policy insurance contract at issue has been the subject of a negotiation between an insurer and representatives of the group, the enforceability of the provision should be evaluated in light of those negotiations.[8]

Caveat: Some insurance contracts are standardized as a consequence of regulatory compulsion. Therefore, when considering questions of the actual or reasonable expectations of an insured considerable care should be exercised in assessing either an assertion that the insurance coverage terms at issue constitute a contract of adhesion imposed by the insurance industry, or an assertion that a particular provision resulted from a negotiation of the terms by the parties.[9]

---

5. See § 6.3(c)(3), below.

6. See the discussion in § 2.8(c), above.

Cf. the comment in Selected Risks Insurance Company v. Bruno, 718 F.2d 67 at p. 70 (3d Cir.1983), that where the parties were of equal bargaining power the policy disfavoring unconscionable contracts would not have been served.

Also see Brokers Title Company, Inc. v. St. Paul Fire & Marine Insurance Company, 610 F.2d 1174 (3d Cir.1979).

7. See the discussion in § 2.8, above.

8. *Ibid.*

9. *Ibid.*

(2) Presumed Understanding of an Insurance Contract

Some judicial decisions reason that a person is irrebuttably presumed to know and understand the contracts that he or she signs.[10] Quite commonly, for example, this is true of judicial holdings which conclude that an individual's rights are fixed by the terms of a signed insurance application form which should have been read by the applicant. For example, judicial opinions have concluded that when there is no ambiguity — and especially if the language is readily comprehensible by a layperson — in the terms of a conditional receipt, there is nothing for a court to construe and therefore no basis for finding coverage contrary to the terms of the receipt.[11]

Reliance on an irrebuttable presumption that an insured knows and understands all of the contents of any document which has been *signed* in the course of acquiring insurance often involves the creation or application of an obvious legal fiction in regard to the insured's state of mind. The doctrine of protecting reasonable expectations is fundamentally inconsistent with an irrebuttable presumption that an individual understands any contract that has been signed. When a judicial decision protects the reasonable expectations of a claimant who has signed, in the course of acquiring insurance, one or more documents which include the terms at issue, at a minimum such a result must explicitly or implicitly transform the irrebuttable presumption either (1) to a rebuttable presumption about what that person thought and whether it was reasonable, or (2) to a substitute standard concerned only with what a reasonable person would have thought in those circumstances.

(3) Individual Knowledge of Limiting Provisions Resulting From Expertise

An interesting dilemma is presented by situations in which the central question is whether rights at variance with policy provisions should be recognized when an insured had special expertise that provided actual knowledge of the policy provisions that limited protection. In this context, the question is whether the reasonable expectations principle applies even though the particular insured was sophisticated about insurance transactions and was or should have been aware of the coverage limitation.

---

10. *Cf.* Western Casualty and Surety Company v. Sliter, 555 F.Supp. 369 at p. 370 (E.D.Mich.1983), where the court sustained the insurer's rejection of coverage, reasoning that:

"Generally, an insured is assumed to have read the policy. He is held to be aware of its contents. *Wierengo v. American Fire Ins. Co.*, 98 Mich. 621, 626, 57 N.W. 833 (1894). The insured should 'read the policy and raise questions concerning coverage within a reasonable time after the issuance of the policy.' *Parmet Homes, Inc. v. Republic Ins. Co.*, 111 Mich.App. 140, 145, 314 N.W.2d 453 (1981). Applying these rules, Sliter would be bound by the terms of the policy and summary judgment in favor of Western would be proper."

11. See the footnotes in § 2.3(d), above, and the accompanying text.

An insured's knowledge of a limitation constitutes a strong argument in support of defeating any variance claim that is exclusively based on the principle of honoring reasonable expectations, because such knowledge negates the surprise that would be the basis for departing from ordinary contract principles. However, other factors may have a bearing in such cases.

First, in some instances the principle of protecting reasonable expectations combines with the principle of disallowing unconscionable advantage to support recovery even when a claimant, as a result of an unusual position that ensured awareness, knew of what would otherwise have been a surprising provision. The following generalization combines the principles of honoring reasonable expectations and disallowing unconscionable advantage:

> **If the enforcement of a policy provision would defeat the reasonable expectations of the great majority of policyholders to whose claims it is relevant, it will not be enforced even against those who know of its restrictive terms.[12]**

Second, when a knowledgeable policyholder would receive coverage disproportionately small in comparison with the premiums, arguably it is unduly harsh to deprive such an insured of the protection that the great majority of policyholders receive for the same premium payment. To apply a different rule among various policyholders would produce the result that those who remain ignorant of the terms would receive substantially more protection for their premium dollars than those who are more sophisticated about coverage provisions and limitations.[13]

Accordingly, in many instances it is a sound rule to strike down a policy provision that imposes restrictions even in instances when the coverage claim is by a policyholder who possessed special knowledge or expertise.

(4) Statutory and Administrative Actions

Legislation or administrative actions sometimes prescribe the terms for entire insurance forms or for particular clauses in some coverages.[14] In addition, statutory and administrative regulations have also limited the freedom of insurers by proscribing some types of provisions.[15] And, in many states, all insurance policy provisions must be approved by a department charged with the responsibility of regulating insurers.

---

12. Judicial decisions that appear to be consistent with this proposition have imposed controls over not merely form and method, but on the substantive content of insurance contracts as well. Such controls have been held to apply even to coverage clauses that are the central provisions of the contract.

13. See the discussion in § 6.3(b), above, regarding clauses written so restrictively that literal enforcement would produce

such limited coverage it would be wholly disproportionate to premiums charged.

In some circumstances, a persuasive case exists for the proposition that coverage should not be limited on the basis of actual expectations because enforcement would produce a coverage which would be wholly disproportionate to the premiums charged.

14. See § 2.8(b)(1) and § 2.8(b)(2), above.

15. See § 2.8(b)(1), above.

When insurance policy terms are prescribed or approved by legislative or administrative actions, a court may feel constrained to disregard questions about whether to protect the reasonable expectations of insureds. However, in many instances the insurance policy terms prescribed by legislative or administrative actions are adoptions, either outright or as modified slightly, of proposals made by the insurance industry. This is often the case because the regulatory examination and evaluation of the terms used for insurance policies generally has been virtually non-existent. Thus, it is not surprising that judges have often sought and found approaches that moderate the harshness of insurance contract provisions without regard to the administrative "approval" of insurance policy forms. Moreover, occasionally courts have even employed comparable approaches in regard to coverage terms that are subject to statutory provisions.

§ 6.4 Variance Claims Based on Declared Public Policies

§ 6.4(a) Introduction

The judicial development of common law principles and doctrines [1] in insurance cases is influenced both by concern with justice in the particular case and by perceptions about the interests of society in the resolution of the dispute. As statutes affecting insurance transactions (in regard to both the marketing techniques and the coverage terms) increase in number and scope, the influence of such legislation often extends beyond specific matter addressed by the legislative provisions. More often and more explicitly than was common in earlier times, courts — especially the court of last resort in a state — may look to the state's legislation not only with the purpose of faithfully applying the specific statutory mandates, but also as sources of "establishment of policy [that] carries significance beyond the particular scope of each of the statutes involved." [2] Thus, variance claims may be predicated on judicial views of either explicit or implicit declarations of public policy.[3]

Among the judicial decisions of recent decades that have sustained variance claims, some have done so expressly on the ground that

---

§ 6.4(a)

1. Often characterized as judicial "lawmaking."

2. Boston Housing Authority v. Hemingway, 363 Mass. 184 at p. 195, 293 N.E.2d 831, 840 (1973), quoting Moragne v. State Marine Lines, Inc., 398 U.S. 375, 90 S.Ct. 1772, 26 L.Ed.2d 339 (1970).

Also see Kates v. St. Paul Fire & Marine Insurance Co., 509 F.Supp. 477, 486–91 (D.Mass.1981) (examining an array of Massachusetts judicial decisions and insurance statutes and regulations for guidance as to explicitly or implicitly declared policy regarding enforcement of "coordination of

benefit" provisions and construction of other provisions of group disability insurance contracts).

3. *Cf.* Prosser & Keeton, TORTS at § 3 (Fifth edition, 1984), discussing "Policy and Process" in the law of torts.

No central principle comparable to those of honoring reasonable expectations and disallowing unconscionable advantage may be extrapolated from these decisions. Rather, the underlying public policies they reflect are as disparate and varied as those to which legislatures respond in enacting statutes.

provisions of the insurance policy, if literally enforced, would be in conflict with legislatively (and in some instances, administratively or judicially) declared public policy interests or goals of the state. In particular, claims under uninsured motorist coverage have spawned a distinctively large number of such decisions, and they will be discussed in the next subsection below. Other illustrations may be found in quite disparate areas of insurance law.[4]

§ 6.4(b) Variance Claims in Uninsured Motorist Coverage

Some of the most notable examples of conflict between insurance contract provisions and judicial applications of declared public policies have involved motor vehicle insurance. In particular, for the past twenty-five years the coverage terms used for uninsured motorist insurance have almost certainly spawned more decisions sustaining variance claims than any other type of insurance.[1]

4. For example, in Germanotta v. National Indemnity Company, 119 Wis.2d 293, 349 N.W.2d 733 at p. 736 (1984) (involving an "errors and omission" policy that provided motor vehicle coverage under some circumstances), the court observed that:

"As a matter of public policy and by operation of law, insurance contracts may be interpreted in such a fashion as to comply with applicable statutes. *Such* interpretations may afford protection 'not explicit from or even contrary to its written terms.'"

Cf. Farmers Insurance Exchange v. Call, 712 P.2d 231 (Utah 1985) (involving the enforceability of exclusions in an automobile insurance policy); Sparks v. St. Paul Insurance Company, 100 N.J. 325, 495 A.2d 406 (1985) (involving claims-made professional liability coverage).

Also see Motor Vehicle Accident Indemnification Corporation v. Continental National American Group Inc., 35 N.Y.2d 260, 360 N.Y.S.2d 859, 319 N.E.2d 182 (1974) (restrictions sought to be imposed by insurer of lessor so as to limit the persons who would be covered as insureds, to the lessee or an adult member of his immediate family, while operating a leased vehicle violated public policy of the state); Reeves v. Miller, 418 So.2d 1050 (Fla.App., 5th Dist., 1982) (exclusion for obligations cognizable under the Federal Tort Claims Act contained in a Marine Corp recruiter's motor vehicle liability policy was invalid).

§ 6.4(b)

1. See the several thousand appellate decisions cited Widiss, UNINSURED AND UNDERINSURED MOTORIST INSURANCE, Volume 1 (1985) and Volume 2 (1987).

The import of these decisions is well reflected in the following comments of the Massachusetts Supreme Judicial Court:

"In addition, the rule that ambiguous policy language will be construed against the insurer has no application here. See *Cody v. Connecticut Gen. Life Ins. Co.*, 387 Mass. 142, 146, 439 N.E.2d 234 (1982). The plaintiff admits that the exclusionary language is explicit and unambiguous. Normally, when there is no ambiguity, we will construe the words of an insurance policy according to their ordinary meaning. *Royal-Globe Ins. Co. v. Schultz*, 385 Mass. 1013, 434 N.E.2d 213 (1982). This is consistent with our long-standing policy that the rules governing the interpretation of insurance contracts are the same as those governing the interpretation of any other contract. *Save-Mor Supermarkets, Inc. v. Skelly Detective Serv., Inc.*, 359 Mass. 221, 226, 268 N.E.2d 666 (1971). See *Oakes v. Manufacturers' Fire & Marine Ins. Co.*, 131 Mass. 164, 165 (1881). But this is not a typical arms' length contract; it is one mandated by statute and reduced to a form standardized across the Commonwealth, allowing the prospective purchaser little or no opportunity to alter its terms or to secure more favorable terms from another insurer. In this context, it is clear that "[t]he policies underlying the principle of private autonomy ∗ ∗ ∗ do not apply." Dugan, The Application of Substantive Unconscionability to Standardized Terms — A Systematic Approach, 18 New Eng.L.Rev. 77, 78–79 (1981). Therefore, no matter how explicit the exclusionary language may be, it cannot prevail if it is contrary to the statutory language or the legislative policy of

When one is dealing with a claim for indemnification under an uninsured motorist insurance policy, it is important to remember that the coverage terms were developed by the insurance industry in an attempt to forestall the enactment of state legislation directed at either creating compulsory insurance requirements or otherwise altering the character of the then-existing insurance market in order to deal with the hazard created by uninsured motorists.[2] The industry urged that the then-existing accident compensation system, based on the largely voluntary acquisition of insurance by motorists, could be easily supplemented so that accident victims of negligent uninsured motorists would be assured a source of indemnification. In the mid 1950s, the insurance industry developed and offered uninsured motorist insurance as a new type of coverage that could be added to automobile insurance policies.

The public did not exercise any direct influence on the coverage terms promulgated by the industry for uninsured motorist insurance. However, within a very short time span, New Hampshire became the first state to require insurance companies to include uninsured motorist coverage in all liability insurance policies issued or delivered by any insurer licensed in the state, upon any motor vehicle principally used or garaged in the state.[3] Although subsequently legislation made the uninsured motorist the subject of statutory mandates throughout the nation, for the most part — with some notable exceptions,[4] — these statutes were little more than statements either (1) that uninsured motorist insurance must be included in all automobile liability policies issued or delivered in that state, or (2) that insurers shall offer uninsured motorist insurance to all purchasers of automobile liability insurance.

Insurance companies have frequently used coverage terms for uninsured motorist insurance that are intended to do no more than place a claimant in the position that would have existed if the tortfeasor had been insured by a liability insurance policy with the minimum limits required by the state financial responsibility law.[5] Fur-

G.L.c. 175, § 113L. See *Surrey v. Lumbermens Mut. Casualty Co.*, 384 Mass. 171, 424 N.E.2d 234 (1981); Johnson v. Travelers Indem. Co., 359 Mass. 525, 528, 269 N.E.2d 700 (1971). As this court has held in a similar context: "The well settled principles covering the interpretation of an ordinary policy of insurance have been properly disregarded in determining the scope and extent of a compulsory motor vehicle policy in order to accomplish the legislative aim of providing compensation to those who have been injured by automobiles." Desmarais v. Standard Accident Ins. Co., 331 Mass. 199, 202, 118 N.E.2d 86 (1954). We therefore turn to an analysis of the statute and its purpose."

Cardin v. Royal Insurance Company, 394 Mass. 450, 476 N.E.2d 200 at p. 203 (1985).

2. Widiss, UNINSURED AND UNDERINSURED MOTORIST INSURANCE (1985), Chapter 1 through Chapter 3.

3. New Hampshire Laws 1955, § 6.1. Now found in New Hampshire Rev.Stat. Ann. § 264.

4. See Widiss, UNINSURED AND UNDERINSURED MOTORIST INSURANCE (1985), Chapter 2.

5. See Widiss, UNINSURED AND UNDERINSURED MOTORIST INSURANCE (1985), Chapter 15.

thermore, insurers have urged that the uninsured motorist coverage terms should allow companies to limit or reduce this coverage in many situations even though the claimant has not been indemnified.[6] Moreover, insurers often argued for a technical or literal construction of the terms used in the insurance forms that would conform the protection afforded insureds to the insurers' rather limited vision of the coverage's purpose.[7] For example, many insurers rejected claims when an insured tortfeasor's insurance company denied liability, thereby as a practical matter precluding the injured person from recovering on a tort claim.[8] Similarly, for many years insurers did not extend coverage for accidents that involved tortfeasors whose insurers were or became insolvent.[9] In each of these situations, even though claimants were not able to secure indemnification from the insurers of negligent motorists, insurance companies took the position that the tortfeasors were not uninsured and that therefore no coverage was provided by the uninsured motorist insurance.

Public Policies Associated with the Uninsured Motorist Insurance Statutes

The adoption of legislation requiring either the inclusion of or the offering of the uninsured motorist insurance with automobile or motor vehicle liability insurance policies manifests the importance attached to assuring a source of indemnification to persons injured by negligent, financially irresponsible motorists.[10] However, many of the uninsured motorist insurance statutes have not delineated the precise scope of the objectives the legislation seeks to attain.

In the late 1950s and early 1960s, judicial determinations often depended solely on construction of the coverage terms in uninsured motorist insurance endorsements, and sustained the validity of coverage terms that were appropriately viewed as clear and unambiguous. As more and more states enacted uninsured motorist statutes — thereby declaring that public policy favored the indemnification of victims of negligent, financially irresponsible motorists — a new trend developed.

---

6. *Id.*, Chapter 13 and Chapter 14.

7. *Id.*, Chapter 7, Chapter 8, Chapter 9, Chapter 13, Chapter 14, and Chapter 15.

8. *Id.*, Chapter 8.

9. *Id.*, § 8.16 through § 8.18.

10. Some of the uninsured motorist statutes apply to automobile liability insurance policies, while most statutes establish requirements for all motor vehicle liability insurance policies. There are limits to the extent of the requirements, however, and most statutes have concluded (either by legislation or in a few instances by judicial decision) that the requirement does not apply to self-insurers or to entities that opt to satisfy the financial responsibility laws by filing bonds. For example, in Johnson v. Yellow Cab Company of Philadelphia, 456 Pa. 256, 317 A.2d 245 at p. 247 (1974), the court concluded that "the Uninsured Motorist Liability Act * * * applies only when a liability policy of insurance is delivered or issued for delivery" and accordingly the act does not apply to a self-insured who does not have a liability policy of insurance. However, *Johnson v. Yellow Cab* was overruled in 1983, when the Pennsylvania Supreme Court decided that "the fact that a motor vehicle owner is a self-insured *does not change or detract from the remedial purpose of the Uninsured Motorist Act.*" Modesta v. Southeastern Pennsylvania Transportation Authority, 503 Pa. 437, 469 A.2d 1019 at p. 1022 (1983) (Emphasis added).

The courts began to invalidate provisions in the coverage terms despite the fact that they were unambiguous and had been used in the coverage since its inception.

In some instances, the very lack of specificity in the uninsured motorist insurance statutes both afforded the courts considerable latitude in these cases and provided the courts with a basis for the decisions — that is, courts concluded that since the statutes did not specifically authorize the limitations or exclusions in the coverage terms that were at issue, the insurer ought not to be allowed to avoid liability for injuries falling within the general scope of coverage mandated by the uninsured motorist statute. Judicial hostility toward limitations and exclusions in the uninsured motorist insurance has been increasingly evident over the past several years, resulting in numerous decisions holding that an insurer ought not to be allowed to avoid liability when a claimant's injuries are within the ambit of the state's concern for accident victims which is indicated by the state's uninsured motorist statute.

The public interest in assuring innocent accident victims a source of indemnification has been clearly and repeatedly recognized by the courts. The following quotations from three decisions provide a sense of the judicial view of the public interest.

"The purpose of legislation mandating the offer of uninsured motorist coverage is to fill the gap inherent in motor vehicle financial responsibility and compulsory insurance legislation and this coverage is intended to provide recompense to innocent persons who are damaged through the wrongful conduct of motorists who, because they are uninsured and not financially responsible, cannot be made to respond in damages. [Citation omitted] As remedial legislation it should be liberally construed to provide the intended protection." [11]

"Insurance Code Section 11580.2 must be liberally construed to carry out its objective of providing financial protection for injuries caused by uninsured motorists and, as a corollary, any exception or exclusion from uninsured motorist coverage must be strictly construed. [Citation omitted] In view of the public policy in favor of uninsured motorist coverage, any deletion or reduction thereof must be in plain and understandable language, sufficient to apprise the insured of the nature of the right he is relinquishing." [12]

"Our uninsured motorist statute was enacted in response to the growing public concern over the increasing problem arising from property and personal injury damage inflicted by uninsured and financially irresponsible motorists. Its purpose is to provide, within fixed limits, some recompense to innocent persons who

11. Winner v. Ratzlaff, 211 Kan. 59 at pp. 63–64, 505 P.2d 606 at p. 610 (1973).

12. State Farm Mutual Automobile Insurance Company v. Lykouresis, 72 Cal. App.3d 57 at p. 61, 139 Cal.Rptr. 827 at p. 830 (1st Dist., Div. 3, 1977).

receive bodily injury or property damage through the conduct of an uninsured motorist who cannot respond in damages." [13]

The conflicts between the public interest, manifested by the legislative requirements, and the specific coverage terms employed by insurers has produced a continuous flow of litigation to the nation's courts. Most of these disputes have been initiated by claimants attempting to secure indemnification in instances where the coverage terms purported either to limit or to preclude recovery.

Observations

Disagreements over the extent of coverage provided by uninsured motorist insurance frequently seem to be more a product of divergent attitudes as to the purpose of the coverage than of actual inadequacies in the definition of the insured's rights. This coverage has often been viewed by both claimants and judges as a means of indemnifying injuries to the extent of the coverage limits whenever insureds are injured as a result of the negligent operation of an uninsured motor vehicle. However, many of the coverage terms used in the standard forms, and the positions asserted by insurers in a large number of cases, are not in accord with this conception of the objective for uninsured motorist insurance.

The inadequacies of the coverage initially offered by the industry have proved sufficiently disturbing in a large enough number of instances to prompt the enactment of specific statutory provisions in several states that compel the industry to broaden the coverage. A good illustration is the legislative reaction to the industry's initial refusal to provide coverage when a tortfeasor had insurance in effect at the time of the accident, but thereafter the company either denied liability or became insolvent.[14]

The controversy over whether the uninsured motorist insurance did or should provide coverage in many situations in which claimants were not clearly indemnified for losses caused by uninsured motorists clearly exemplifies the divergence in both attitude and approach between insurers and the public, generally, and insured claimants, in particular, with respect to this insurance. It was not until courts,[15] and in some states the legislatures,[16] declared that insurance was to be provided in many situations in which insurers sought to avoid liability that the standard endorsement terms were modified to provide coverage.

---

13. Shoffner v. State Farm Mutual Automobile Insurance Company, 494 S.W.2d 756 at p. 758 (Tenn.1972).

But cf. State Automobile Mutual Insurance Company v. Cummings, 519 S.W.2d 773 (Tenn.1975).

14. For example, see California Insurance Code § 11580.2(b) (Deering, 1963);

South Carolina Insurance Code § 56–9–810(3)(b); Virginia Insurance Code § 38.1–381(c)(ii).

15. See the decisions considered in § 8.16 of Widiss, UNINSURED AND UNDERINSURED MOTORIST INSURANCE (1985).

16. See footnote 14, above.

§ 6.4(c) Comment

The uninsured motorist coverage presents a graphic example of problems which the courts repeatedly encounter when dealing with insurance policies, as well as with an increasingly large number of other form contracts. Form contracts are efficient and undoubtedly essential to a contemporary industrial society. However, the freedom to use standard forms should entail responsibilities. If an insurer does not provide coverage that is consonant with significant, declared public interests of a state — as manifested in legislation, administrative regulations, and settled decisional doctrine — courts should declare that insureds are entitled to rights that vary from coverage terms that conflict with such public policies. The possibility that insureds will have rights that vary from the coverage terms, when courts consider claims in relation to public interests generally and especially the goals underlying the legislation of a state, does not mean that insurers are required to provide unlimited "all-risk" coverage.

The insurance industry should acknowledge a responsibility to provide coverage that both conforms to the public policy of the states and the reasonable needs of purchasers without having to be prodded by continual litigation or legislative actions that mandate extensions in the coverage beyond the insurance policy terms. Until and unless insurers take this approach, courts almost certainly will continue to declare that insureds are entitled to rights that vary from coverage terms that conflict with important public interests.

§ 6.5 Detrimental Reliance

§ 6.5(a) Generally

The principle of granting redress for losses which result from detrimental reliance has become one of the predominant themes of contract law in the United States.[1] Applications of the detrimental reliance doctrine, both explicitly and implicitly, have been particularly widespread in disputes involving insurance. Although the following formulation should not be viewed as a universally applicable statement of the detrimental reliance doctrine, it is supportable on public policy grounds, and it is fully consistent with the results in most contemporary insurance decisions:

> A claimant (either a policyholder or other person intended to receive benefits under an insurance policy) is entitled to redress against an insurer to the extent of detriment suffered because of justifiable reliance of a definite and substantial nature upon repre-

---

§ 6.5(a)

1. *Cf.* Grant Gimore, THE DEATH OF CONTRACT (1974, Ohio State U. Press, Columbus, Ohio), at pp. 87–90; Charles L. Knapp, *Reliance in the Revised Restatement: The Proliferation of Promissory Estoppel*, 81 Columbia Law Review 52–79 at pp. 53–55 (1981); Stanley D. Henderson, *Promissory Estoppel and Traditional Contract Doctrine*, 78 Yale Law Journal 343–387 at pp. 343–344 (1969).

sentations, statements or actions of individuals who were acting
either on behalf of or incident to the representation of the insurer.

This statement expresses the sense of the detrimental reliance doctrine
as it is most commonly applied by courts to insurance transactions on
behalf of claimants. In the context of a variance claim, the essential
elements for an insured to prove are (1) that representations, promises,
or acts were made by or on behalf of an insurer, (2) that the representations, promises, or acts were such that the insurer should reasonably
expect or anticipate that they would result in action or forebearance,
(3) that the insured justifiably relied on the statements or acts, and
(4) that the consequence of that reliance was a significant detriment to
the individual who claims the insurance benefits.

§ 6.5(b)   Types of Representations to Which the Detrimental Reliance Principle Applies

In applying the principle of granting redress for detrimental reliance, especially when the analysis is conceptualized in terms of estoppel, courts and writers have sometimes distinguished among (1) representations of existing fact (as, for example, a statement by an agent
that he or she has issued a binder or an endorsement changing the
specified location at which personal property of the insured is protected
under a fire insurance policy), (2) promissory representations (as, for
example, a commitment by an agent that a binder or endorsement *will
issue* before the date of an intended move), and (3) representations of
law or opinion (as, for example, a statement that without an endorsement the insurance policy will extend coverage to property that will be
or has been moved to a new location). Such distinctions are predicated
on the theory, adopted by some courts, that an estoppel will only be
based on the representation of an existing fact, and that neither a
representation of law nor a statement of an opinion can be the basis for
an application of the estoppel doctrine to preclude a denial of coverage
by an insurer.[1]

Comment

Generally, courts should not reject a claim of detrimental reliance
doctrine, or decline to impose an estoppel, merely because the remark
on which an application of the doctrine would be based is a representation of law or opinion rather than a statement of a fact or a promise.[2]
Moreover, it is seldom indeed that one can find a modern case in which
the denial of a claimed right at variance with insurance policy provisions is stated to have been founded on such distinctions, and rarer still

§ 6.5(b)

1. *Cf.* 28 AM.JUR., *Estoppel & Waiver*
(Second edition, 1966), at §§ 46–47.

2. *Cf.* 28 AM.JUR., *Estoppel & Waiver*
(Second edition, 1966) at §§ 48–49 and the
1984 Supplement.

Also see RESTATEMENT OF CONTRACTS, Second (1979), § 90; RESTATEMENT OF CON-
TRACTS (1932), § 90.

when it appears that but for this distinction a case would have been decided differently.[3]

Nevertheless, it is reasonable to recognize that there may be some limits regarding the representations that should serve as the basis for estoppel. For example, it is appropriate to question whether an insured's claim should be sustained on the basis of evidence that an agent of an insurer stated that he or she would always take whatever action should become necessary in the future to keep the insurance policy in force even should changed circumstances result in a substantially increased risk.[4] Although sales representatives in the field are frequently authorized to make binding commitments for insurance, they generally are not authorized to guarantee coverage without regard to the appropriate increases in the premium charges that may be warranted as a result of changes in the risks. Allowing courts to resolve disputes on the basis of evidence about such a broad undertaking would entail a considerably greater set of problems than undertaking to decide the trustworthiness of evidence that an agent made a representation of some type (whether of fact, opinion, or promise) after having notice of the changed circumstances.[5] In many instances, the analysis of such a claim might well rest on whether reliance by an insured on such a statement was justifiable under the circumstances.

§ 6.5(c) The Scope of an Agent's Authority

Many of the detrimental reliance claims are predicated on statements or actions of an insurer's agent, that is, the statements or actions upon which the reliance is based are made by someone who is an agent of an insurer. Ordinarily, in order for an agent to bind a principal to a contract the individual must have either "actual authority"[1] or "appar-

---

3. As an example of opinions stating the requirement of a representation of fact but resting decision on other grounds, see Breen v. Aetna Casualty & Surety Company, 153 Conn. 633, 220 A.2d 254 (1966) (claim of estoppel to deny coverage rejected because of lack of proof of change of position in reliance on alleged acknowledgement of coverage).

See generally, 16A APPLEMAN, INSURANCE LAW (Revised edition, 1981), at § 9081 and § 9088.

4. To give effect to such a broad undertaking by an agent would be to cut deeply into the authorized plan of insurance marketing. Compare Home Fire Insurance Company v. Wilson, 109 Ark. 324, 159 S.W. 1113 (1913), rejecting a claim based on evidence that the agent agreed to take whatever action was necessary to continue in force a fire insurance policy that denied coverage for a vacant building, with Home Fire Insurance Company v. Wilson, 118 Ark. 442, 176 S.W. 688 (1915), sustaining a claim on retrial of the same case, based on

evidence of assurances given by the agent after a vacancy arose and he was notified.

5. One court has granted redress for presumed detrimental reliance because of an insurer's failure to disclose to its policyholder that courts have generally interpreted certain policy language more favorably than a layman might read it. See § 6.2(a), note 8, above, discussing Bowler v. Fidelity & Casualty Company, 53 N.J. 313, 250 A.2d 580 (1969).

§ 6.5(c)

1. RESTATEMENT OF AGENCY, Second (1958), at § 140. However, a "general agent" is held to have additional "inherent agency powers" to bind the principal. The law attributes these additional powers to the relationship even when the "general agent" and the principal did not so intend. The basis of these powers is thus analogous to the basis of the master's liability for the torts of a servant. See *Id.*, at p. 161, Comment a.

ent authority." [2]   Conclusions about the extent of an individual's authority, which are employed in concert with applications of the detrimental reliance doctrine in insurance disputes, sometimes extend well beyond the actual authority of the agent and often are also at least somewhat broader than that which would be warranted by the normal application of the doctrine of apparent authority.[3]   And occasionally representations that are at most "incidental" to an agent's role in the marketing of insurance have been held to be sufficient to expose the insurer to liability for detrimental reliance.[4]   The extensive or broad conception of the insurer's responsibility for the actions of such individuals in these decisions is analogous to the concept of scope of employment which is applied in master-servant cases concerned with physical harm.[5]

Furthermore, several courts have concluded that an insurer may be precluded from rejecting a claim based on coverage limitations or exclusions when an agent failed to obtain the proper coverage — that is, the sales representative's failure to obtain an appropriate coverage has been held to be the responsibility of the insurer.[6]

§ 6.5(d)   Justifiable Detrimental Reliance

In order to obtain relief on the basis of detrimental reliance, generally a claimant must show that the reliance was justifiable. There are several types of situations in which questions repeatedly arise in regard to whether an insured's reliance was justified.   For example, a claimant who asserts detrimental reliance as the result of a carelessly inaccurate statement of a sales representative may not be

But cf. Prudential Insurance Company v. Clark, 456 F.2d 932 (5th Cir.1972).

2. *Cf.* the discussion of scope of authority in § 2.5(c)(3) and § 2.5(d), above.

Cf. Home Materials, Inc. v. Auto Owners Insurance Company, 250 Ga. 599, 300 S.E.2d 139 (1983); Libby v. Concord General Mutual Insurance Company, 452 A.2d 979 (Me.1982).

3. See § 6.8(d), below.

4. See, e.g., General Insurance Company of America v. Truly Nolan of America, Inc., 136 Ariz. 142, 664 P.2d 686 (Div. 1, Dept. D, 1983).

This position is also supported by a growing body of precedent denying to an insurer a defense based on false answers in the application when it appears that the applicant answered truthfully and the agent incorrectly recorded his answers.   See § 6.8(b), below.

5. *Cf.* RESTATEMENT OF AGENCY, Second (1958), at § 258, concerning tort liability of a principal for "incidental misrepresentations" of an agent.   The Restatement points out that the liability is broader than that for contracts within the agent's authority or apparent authority.

"Under the rule stated in this Section, the principal is subject to liability for statements concerning such matters as the other party to the transaction may reasonably believe have been confided to the agent to deal with."

Id., Comment a.

Also see Fryar v. Employers Insurance of Wausau, 94 N.M. 77, 607 P.2d 615 at p. 619 (1980).

6. *Cf.* Sears, Roebuck & Co. v. Strey, 512 F.Supp. 540 (E.D.Tenn.1981), affirmed 701 F.2d 180 (6th Cir.1982) (electrical contractor requested a general liability coverage, but was issued a policy with a completed operations hazard exclusion that was not pointed out to him).

Also see Magnavox Company of Tennessee v. Boles & Hite Construction Company, 585 S.W.2d 622 (Tenn.App., Eastern Section, 1979).

permitted to recover if the claimant was also careless.[1] This result is consistent with the common law rule that contributory negligence is a complete bar to a claim based on negligence. Thus far, rather than barring relief entirely,[2] modern trends toward apportioning losses in cases of contributory fault do not appear to have had any noticeable impact upon the application of the detrimental reliance doctrine in rights at variance cases.

If a sales representative makes fraudulent representations to an insured, contributory negligence of the insured ought not to bar relief. For example, an insured's negligent failure to read an insurance policy should not preclude a claim when the relief is sought because the claimant detrimentally relied on an intentional misrepresentation of an insurer's representative.[3] This view is consistent with the prevailing, though disputed, common law rule that contributory negligence is no defense to a claim for damages that result from an intentional tort.[4]

Comment

When a sales representative's wrongdoing is not authorized and especially when the conduct is explicitly prohibited, the equities favoring the insured often have somewhat less force in regard to a claim against an insurer.[5] Both the insurer and the insured in essence are

§ 6.5(d)

1. See, e.g., Western Casualty and Surety Company v. Sliter, 555 F.Supp. 369 at p. 371 (E.D.Mich.1983) (emphasis added), where the court concluded:

" * * * I find that Sliter's reliance on Slagel's incorrect assertions was misplaced. The law in Michigan is that an insurer 'is not liable on erroneous representations by an agent as to the extent of coverage of a plainly worded policy, so as to entitle the insured to equitable relief, even though the latter failed to read the instrument.' The policy should not and will not be reformed by this Court to provide for coverage not agreed to by the insurer." *Cf.* Stoes Brothers, Inc. v. Freudenthal, 81 N.M. 61, 463 P.2d 37 (1969). *But cf.* Bell v. O'Leary, 744 F.2d 1370 at p. 1373 (8th Cir.1984),

where the court observed that "[t]he plaintiffs relied on O'Leary's representation of himself as a competent insurance broker, and they called upon his expertise to locate precisely the type of information that O'Leary failed to locate" and "[h]aving accepted the task, for pay, O'Leary cannot now be heard to disclaim responsibility for failure to perform the task with the requisite skill and diligence." The court also concluded that the broker could not "shift responsibility to the plaintiffs for their failure to locate the information by themselves when, by accepting the task of obtaining insurance for them, O'Leary expressly relieved the plaintiffs of that responsibility."

But cf. General Electric Credit Corporation v. Aetna Casualty & Surety Co., 437 Pa. 463, 263 A.2d 448 (1970). Two of seven fire policies failed to include allegedly agreed-upon special lender's loss payee clause. The court observed that negligence "in failing to discover the mistake will not bar reformation in the absence of prejudice or a violation of a positive legal duty." The court held that the same rule applies when suit, though it could have been brought on the theory of reformation, is founded instead on waiver or estoppel.

2. See generally Prosser & Keeton, TORTS (Fifth edition, 1984), at § 67.

3. See, e.g., both supporting and opposing precedents in cases concerning an agent's falsely recording an applicant's correct answers to inquiries, § 6.7(b), below.

4. See RESTATEMENT OF TORTS, Second (1965), at § 481 (intentional injury); *Cf.* RESTATEMENT OF TORTS (1939), at § 918 (avoidable consequences); Prosser & Keeton, TORTS (1984), at § 65 (contributory negligence).

5. *Cf.* RESTATEMENT OF AGENCY, Second (1958) at § 259A, stating not a distinctive rule for insurance cases but a rule of gen-

victims of the agent's wrongful conduct, and the insured's rights against the insurer are more likely to be limited.[6] However, when there is an extensive and continuing relationship between the insurer and the sales representative, there is still considerable justification for a recovery by an insured from the insurer — leaving the insurer with a right to seek to recoup the amount of any judgment in favor of the insured from the sales representative.

Insurers have sometimes urged that an insured should not be entitled to recover from an insurer for detrimental reliance on an agent's fraudulent representation. A persuasive argument in support of allocating such losses to the insurer, especially when the agent is not sufficiently insured or financially able to provide indemnification for the insured's loss, is that losses occasioned by the fraud of insurance agents acting within the scope of the insurance arrangement should be distributed widely and that almost always the insurer is in a position to do this. If the agent is also insured by an "errors and omission" coverage, the joint liability of the insurer and the agent can also be distributed widely by such an insurer, but the existence of that coverage should not be a factor in determining the individual consumer's rights to compensation.

§ 6.5(e)   Proof of Detriment and the Measure of Relief

The principle of granting redress for detrimental reliance usually predicates compensation on proof of a resulting detriment of a definite and substantial nature, and specifically limits the amount of indemnification to the extent of the detriment which is proved.[1] Nevertheless, sometimes courts have imposed liability when there was no detriment or have allowed a recovery beyond that warranted by the actual detriment.[2]

---

eral application. The stated rule approves reformation based on an agent's misrepresentation as to the contents of an agreement executed in writing with the representee, and comment a indicates that the rule "applies whether or not the third person was negligent, unless the principal would be adversely affected by a delay in discovering the facts." *Id.*, Comment (a).

See the discussion of the liability of intermediaries in § 2.5(c) and § 2.5(d), above.

6. *Cf.* Gulf Insurance Company v. Grisham, 126 Ariz. 123, 613 P.2d 283 (In Div.1980) (reliance by purchaser on statements by an unauthorized agent did not bind an insurer who subsequently issued an aviation policy for an airplane that excluded coverage for passengers when the plane was piloted by a student pilot); Harrison v. American Liberty Insurance Company, 155 Ga.App. 226, 270 S.E.2d 389 (1980) (insurer was not bound by statements made by an intermediary regarding

coverage when no rebuttal was made to the insurer's denial of an agency relationship).

§ 6.5(e)

1. *Cf.* RESTATEMENT OF CONTRACTS, Second (1979), § 90: "A promise which the promisor should reasonably expect to induce action or forbearance on the part of the promisee or a third person and which does induce such action or forbearance is binding if injustice can be avoided only by enforcement of the promise. *The remedy granted for breach may be limited as justice requires.*" (Emphasis added.) Also see *Id.*, Comment (e).

2. In addition to illustrations discussed in the text above, see, e.g., Bayer v. Lutheran Mutual Life Insurance Company, 184 Neb. 826, 172 N.W.2d 400 (1969) (summary judgment for defendant insurer reversed and remanded with directions to enter judgment for insured on 30 year endowment policies issued at age 17; in answer to a letter from insured's mother a month

Whenever a claimant can show that but for the reliance on the actions or statements of an insurer's representative, a valid insurance contract with comparable coverage would have been arranged either with the defendant insurer or with another insurer, the detriment to the claimant is appropriately measured by the terms of an intended insurance contract. However, if liability is imposed in accordance with the terms of a proposed contract despite the absence of proof that a claimant would in fact have been able to secure another coverage with comparable benefits (as, for example, by proving that an applicant was insurable and would have been able to acquire comparable insurance from another company),[3] redress is being allowed in the absence of clear proof of a detriment. Any justification for such decisions must be found either in a principle of granting damages for the claim of reliance in the absence of a demonstrable detriment[4] or on the basis of a different principle. Several theories or justifications can be postulated for allowing relief in insurance cases in the absence of proving detriment.

(1) Punitive Measures

A more generous principle of detrimental reliance might be justified as a punitive measure that would encourage insurers to supervise (that is, to "police") the activities of sales representatives more effectively. However, this rationale for the imposition of a measure of relief raises the question of who is likely to suffer the impact of the punishment.

The experience with attempting to influence marketing practice by imposing liability on insurers in circumstances where there are deviations from what is viewed by courts or legislatures as the desired practice suggests that this is likely to be a relatively futile endeavor. For example, the underlying theory advanced for the enactment of valued policy laws — which fix an insurer's liability for a loss to the value stated in the insurance policy even though the true value of the insured property before the occurrence of the insured event was lower — was that such legislative requirements would encourage insurers to inspect the property and decline applications for coverage by individuals who sought insurance for more than a property's true value. In practice, however, at least some, and perhaps even most, insurers usually have preferred to forego the expense of such inspections,

after issuance of policy, agent quoted, as sum to which insured would be entitled, an amount larger than that provided for in policy and rate book; held statement was "promissory rather than illustrative" and insured and her mother had a right to rely; dissent on ground there was no evidence of fraud or change of position).

3. See, e.g., Duffie v. Bankers' Life Association, 160 Iowa 19, 139 N.W. 1087 (1913), where no such requirement is imposed.

Also see § 2.4, above.

4. Some detriment would, of course, exist if the assumption is made that all risks are insurable when the cost of the coverage sought is not a constraint. But the net detriment above premium cost would be sharply reduced in cases of high probability of loss.

recognizing that thereafter they will have to pay insurance benefits on some over-valued property.[5]

The experience with the valued policy legislation suggests that the consequence of awarding liability under a modified principle of granting redress for detrimental reliance in excess of the resulting detriment would probably result in little more than an occasional fortuitous bonus for some claimants, rather than serving as a means of influencing the conduct of insurers. Furthermore, attempting to identify this portion of the loss experience and to then deny insurers credit for it in rating procedures would probably not be worth the cost. Thus, in the long run payments to insureds in the absence of proof of the consequences of the detriment generally would be at the expense of policyholders whose premiums would be calculated on the basis of the total loss experience of insurers.

(2) Detrimental Reliance and Unconscionable Advantage

Another theory for permitting recovery in the absence of proof of any detriment is that a claimant should be permitted to recover against an insurer upon proving a course of conduct which is likely to cause detriment to persons in the claimant's class in order to prevent the insurer from taking an unconscionable advantage.[6] Although such a result is consistent with the goal of disallowing the exercise of an unconscionable advantage by imposing liability on the insurer in all cases, it would seem likely to produce results that are arbitrary and capricious.[7] Thus, this disadvantage seems to more than offset such a justification.

(3) Presumptions of Detriment in the Absence of Evidence

A third rationale for allowing a recovery in the absence of proof of any detriment is that such a recovery is based on the recognition of a rebuttable presumption of prejudice (that is, detriment) to a claimant who has proved justifiable reliance. A claimant would be entitled to receive the insurance benefits whenever the insurer does not provide clear evidence that a detriment did *not* result. In essence, this theory justifies a recovery unless an insurer is able to show that the claimant did not sustain a detriment — that is, the insurance benefits are due unless the insurer can prove that its conduct did not result in any loss by the claimant.

---

5. Consider the discussion of valued policies in § 3.12, above. Also see the discussion of the time when an insurable interest must exist for property insurance in § 3.3(b), above.

6. *Cf.* Bogle v. Conway, 199 Kan. 707, 433 P.2d 407 (1967) (insurer precluded from asserting exclusion of racing accidents; nonwaiver agreement ineffectual because of presumed prejudice from want of full notice to the insured concerning the claimed defense). For further comments on *Bogle* and on nonwaiver agreements generally, see § 6.7(a) and note 6 thereto, below.

7. In other contexts, the principle of disallowing unconscionable advantage to insurers serves to buttress the goal of honoring reasonable expectations of policyholders. In some situations, it even favors an individual policyholder who fully understood the restrictive terms of the policy with which a claim is at variance. See § 6.3(c), above.

A theory of presumed prejudice is especially appropriate in some contexts. For example, such a case might arise when a liability insurer undertakes the investigation and defense of a tort claim against an insured and the insured, relying on an express or implied representation that an insurer acknowledges coverage, takes no steps to obtain independent counsel. If the insurer thereafter denies liability and the insured then employs an attorney, the insured is in a position to urge that loss of the opportunity for an early, independent investigation justifies the presumption of a detriment, including the denial of an opportunity to explore a prompt settlement of the third party's claim reliance. Although in some circumstances an insured might also persuasively contend (1) that such an early investigation was essential to the most effective defense, (2) that the insurer's actions precluded the type of vigorous investigation necessary to the discovery of all relevant evidence, and (3) that the possibility of a prompt settlement was lost, in many instances it will not be possible for an insured to substantiate a claim that his or her interests were actually prejudiced.

There is some authority for applying the detrimental reliance doctrine even though there is no evidence of actual detriment beyond the fact that the insurer exercised exclusive control over the defense for a substantial period of time.[8] However, in the absence of evidence that an insurer's conduct of an investigation or defense was in some respect substandard, there is usually little justification for an inference that a defense conducted by an attorney selected by the insured would have been superior.

An insured arguably has been prejudiced when there is proof that an independent attorney retained by an insured would have taken different defensive measures or would have taken advantage of an opportunity to settle the claim. In such circumstances, it is certainly appropriate to shift the full burden of negating the existence of detriment to the insurer. [Note. Different considerations are presented in regard to the question of prejudice when an insured proves not only reliance on the insurer's assumption of the defense, but also that the insurer's conduct of the defense was in some way negligently handled. However, in such cases, the result derives from the claimant's proof of detriment, rather than a presumption that applies in the absence of any evidence.[9]]

8. See, e.g., Tomerlin v. Canadian Indemnity Company, 61 Cal.2d 638, 39 Cal. Rptr. 731, 394 P.2d 571 (1964) (insured's attorney withdrew after insurer's attorney represented there was coverage for assault and battery claim under comprehensive personal liability policy; held, insurer estopped to deny coverage); National Union Fire Insurance Company v. Bruecks, 179 Neb. 642, 654, 139 N.W.2d 821, 829 (1966) ("the assumption of complete control * * * for a period of 17 months, with the consequent need of cooperation [between insurer and insured] under the terms of the policy, in itself constitutes a sufficient showing of prejudice [as a basis for urging estoppel]"; but the court held that the defense of noncoverage lacked merit in any event).

Also see the discussion in § 7.6, below of the right to control the defense when a conflict of interests exists.

9. Even in the absence of precedents directly in point, in these circumstances it would seem reasonable to shift the burden

§ 6.5(f)   Persons Protected

The doctrine of detrimental reliance may be applied to protect both a policyholder and other persons who have an interest in an insurance arrangement. Furthermore, detrimental reliance may also justify relief for an intended policyholder (or other persons) in instances in which the insurance contract was never consummated because no contractual commitment was made by an insurer. Liability insurance and life insurance provide examples of such possibilities.

Liability Insurance

Reliance of an intended policyholder may cause a loss to persons beyond the group who are commonly thought of as "beneficiaries" of an insurance contract. Thus, a pedestrian who is injured by the negligent operation of a vehicle being driven by someone who would have been an insured under the coverage typically provided by an automobile liability insurance policy (that is, a person driving with the permission of a named insured) may have a right of action upon proof that the intended policyholder relied on a representation of an agent of the insurer that the agent would forthwith endorse a change in the place of principal garaging of the vehicle so that coverage would be continued. Even in those jurisdictions in which a pedestrian would not be among those allowed to recover as a third party beneficiary, protection should be afforded under the principle of granting redress for detrimental reliance if, had the contractual transaction been properly formulated, the insurance benefits would have been available, directly or indirectly, to the pedestrian.[1]

Life Insurance

Detrimental reliance may be the basis for a claim when an individual applies for life insurance, designating the intended beneficiaries in the application, and dies before a policy is issued. In this context, if an insurer unreasonably delayed acting on an application, the reliance of

to the insurer. Burden shifting has occurred in other contexts. *Cf.* Summers v. Tice, 33 Cal.2d 80, 199 P.2d 1 (1948), 5 A.L.R.2d 91 (1949) (plaintiff, a member of a hunting party, was hit when two other hunters shot at quail in a negligent manner; held, neither hunter is relieved from liability unless he proves it was not his shot).

Also see Loui v. Oakley, 50 Hawaii 260, 438 P.2d 393 (1968), *rehearing denied* 50 Hawaii 272, 438 P.2d 393 (1968) (in absence of sufficient evidence to apportion damages among consecutive tortfeasors more precisely, damages to be allocated equally among all); Maddux v. Donaldson, 362 Mich. 425, 108 N.W.2d 33 (1961), 100 A.L.R.2d 1 (1965) (successive impacts in chain collision; joint and several liability for total damage in absence of evidence supporting an apportionment).

Also generally, Prosser & Keeton, TORTS (1984), at pp. 271–277.

§ 6.5(f)

1. Arguably, it is appropriate that, at least in some contexts, the persons protected be identified on grounds which are comparable to those that apply to tort claims, because the principle of granting redress for detrimental reliance is in essence more like tort than contract; it imposes liability on the basis of conduct rather than predicating liability on the basis of manifested consent. Compare the discussion in § 2.4(c), above.

the intended policyholder — which resulted in a loss to the intended beneficiary — is the essence of the claim. Thus, when a recovery is sustained, the cause of action for relief exists for the benefit of a person who has not relied on the insurer to respond to the application for insurance.

Some courts allowing legal relief for detrimental reliance in regard to life insurance have declared that the cause of action belongs to the deceased's estate.[2] Such a decision grants the beneficiaries of the estate of a decedent who applied for a life insurance policy a benefit that they would not have received if the insurance policy had been issued. It is also a benefit the estate beneficiaries would not have received if the decedent, instead of relying upon the insurer to act with reasonable diligence, had obtained an identical insurance policy elsewhere. Other courts, in applying the principle of granting redress for detrimental reliance, have decided that the cause of action belongs to the beneficiary identified in the application for life insurance.[3] This is the better rule in that it implements the intent of the decedent.

§ 6.5(g) Detrimental Reliance, Estoppel, and Waiver: Observations

The detrimental reliance principle is now the generally recognized conceptualization of equitable doctrines initially characterized in terms of "estoppel."[1] In insurance coverage disputes, there are numerous judicial applications of the detrimental reliance theory that do not accord with a strict adherence to the generally recognized conceptualization of the detrimental reliance theory.[2] The two most common deviations are the dilution of the requirements that the claimant provide clear proof of the reliance and that the claimant prove that the effect of the reliance was detrimental.

Estoppel, which is a term that is still used in many judicial opinions,[3] is generally understood as a doctrine which courts employ to protect the interests of a party as a consequence of either an express representation or a representation that is reasonably inferred from words or conduct. Many of the judicial decisions which apply the

2. See, e.g., Rosin v. Peninsular Life Insurance Company, 116 So.2d 798 (Fla. App.1960); Duffie v. Bankers' Life Association, 160 Iowa 19 at p. 29, 139 N.W. 1087 at p. 1090 (1913).

3. See, e.g., Travelers Insurance Company v. Anderson, 210 F.Supp. 735 (W.D.S.C. 1962) (counterclaim in declaratory judgment action instituted by insurer against beneficiary; but court did not discuss whether right of action runs to beneficiary or estate).

Cf. Talbot v. Country Life Insurance Company, 8 Ill.App.3d 1062, 291 N.E.2d 830 (3d Dist.1973).

See also § 2.4(d), above.

§ 6.5(g)

1. *Cf.* Prudential Insurance Company of America v. Clark, 456 F.2d 932 at pp. 536–537 (5th Cir.1972) (applying Florida law); Huhtala v. Travelers Insurance Company, 401 Mich. 118, 257 N.W.2d 640 (1977).

2. *Cf.* Taylor v. Commercial Union Insurance Company, 614 F.2d 160 at p. 164 (8th Cir.1980) (applying Missouri law).

3. See, e.g., Home Materials, Inc. v. Auto Owners Insurance Company, 250 Ga. 599, 300 S.E.2d 139 (1983); General Insurance Company of America v. Truly Nolan of American, Inc., 136 Ariz. 142, 664 P.2d 686 (1st Div., Dept. D, 1983).

estoppel doctrine focus almost exclusively on the conduct of the insurer without any serious attention to whether that conduct actually caused any significant detriment to the insured. When this occurs, the decisions often represent serious departures from sound applications of the detrimental reliance principle.[4]

In many instances, courts have employed other doctrines to justify or explain decisions in which the facts suggest that detrimental reliance has not occurred. For example, some courts have characterized such situations as a "waiver of rights" by an insurer.[5] Instances of an actual waiver, predicated on an intentional relinquishment of a right by an insurer, occur relatively infrequently and many of the cases that employ such characterizations would be more appropriately analyzed in terms of whether the insured's reliance should be protected.

§ 6.6 Regulation of Defenses Based on Warranty, Representation, or Concealment

§ 6.6(a) Decisional Limitation of Warranty

The term "warranty," as well as many of the phrases commonly used in insurance policies to provide for "warranties," frequently has the connotation of an affirmation or a promise. However, functionally the significance of a warranty in an insurance policy has been, and continues to be, that it establishes a condition precedent to an insurer's obligation to pay.

In insurance law, a "warranty" has usually been analyzed and considered in terms of the consequences of the provision at issue rather than by identifying its characteristics. For example, Professor Vance, expressing the traditional view, defined a warranty as

> " * * * a statement or promise set forth in the policy, or by reference incorporated therein, the untruth or nonfulfillment of which in any respect, and without reference to whether the insurer was in fact prejudiced by such untruth or nonfulfillment, renders the policy voidable by the insurer, wholly irrespective of the materiality of such statement or promise." [1]

---

4. See the discussion in § 6.5(f), below.

Also see Tomerlin v. Canadian Indemnity Company, 61 Cal.2d 638 at pp. 649–650, 39 Cal.Rptr. 731 at p. 738, 394 P.2d 571 at p. 578 (1964).

5. See, e.g., Duffie v. Bankers' Life Association, 160 Iowa 19 at p. 27, 139 N.W. 1087 at p. 1090 (1913); Republic National Life Insurance Co. v. Chilcoat, 368 P.2d 821 (Okl.1961).

Also see Continental Life & Accident Company v. Songer, 124 Ariz. 294, 603 P.2d 921 (1st Div., Dept. A, 1979); Burr v. Lane, 10 Wash.App. 412, 517 P.2d 988 (Div. 1, 1974).

Particularly, when there has been a delay in processing an application for insurance, judicial decisions imposing liability have frequently been cast in terms of a waiver. Furthermore, in some instances, such claims have also been predicated and upheld on a negligence theory, that is, tort liability has been imposed on the theory that the insurer's delay was an act of negligence. In general, however, these cases illustrate an aspect of the principle of protecting detrimental reliance. See generally, § 2.4, above.

§ 6.6(a)

1. Vance, THE LAW OF INSURANCE (Third edition, Anderson, 1951), at p. 408.

At common law, noncompliance with a "warranty" provision was a complete defense for the insurer regardless of materiality of the "breach." [2] Although this consequence of a warranty provision on the rights of an insured was almost beyond being disputed under the common law rule, there was considerably less certainty in regard to what insurance provisions would be enforced as warranty provisions by the common law courts. Furthermore, today there is still considerable uncertainty about what types of provisions can or will be treated as warranties under both regulatory statutes and the applicable judicial precedents.

The common law decisions recognized a fundamental distinction between warranties and "representations." Vance, observing that representations are statements by an insured which are made to provide the insurer with information, contrasted warranties and representations in the following manner:

> "(a) Warranties are parts of the contract, agreed to be essential; representations are but collateral inducements to it.

> "(b) Warranties are always written on the face of the policy, actually or by reference. Representations may be written in the policy or in a totally disconnected paper, or may be oral.

> "(c) Warranties are conclusively presumed to be material. The burden is on the insurer to prove representations material.

> "(d) Warranties must be strictly complied with, while substantial truth only is required of representations." [3]

In essence, the common law held that a misrepresentation by an insured was a ground for avoidance of a contractual obligation only if the matter at issue was material to the risk assumed. When a warranty was involved, on the other hand, the common law sustained an insurer's denial of a claim without regard to the actual significance of the matter. The common law warranty rule produced results that were often unconscionable, as well as being inconsistent with the reasonable expectations of most policyholders, and pressure developed for amelioration of the law of warranty.

Legislation in many states now restricts the use and effects of warranty provisions in insurance contracts. However, even before these modern statutory developments, judicial decisions had imposed some restrictions on the use or effects of warranty provisions by insurers. And, in some contexts, judicial decisions are still the only constraints on the use of warranties by insurers because in many jurisdictions there still are no statutes that apply to warranty provisions in all types of insurance. In addition to applying the doctrines of

"Warranty" is often used in another sense to mean a policy provision expressing an intention that it be given the effect stated in the Vance definition, regardless of whether the courts will so enforce it. Id., at pp. 408–409.

2. See § 5.6, above.

3. Vance, THE LAW OF INSURANCE (Third edition, Anderson, 1951), at p. 412.

waiver and estoppel rather expansively in disputes that involve warranty provisions, courts commonly employ one of several methods of policy construction to reduce some of the harsh impacts of the law of warranty.[4]

First, courts often construe insurance policy provisions that might be viewed or intended by insurers as warranties to be some other type of coverage term. For example, words describing insured property may be treated as merely identifying property, rather than stipulating that it must continue to meet the description in every detail in order to be within the scope of protection afforded by the insurance policy.[5] Similarly, phrases specifying circumstances such as the insured's age may be treated as mere representations of fact,[6] rather than warranties. Also, information or provisions which are included or added to insurance policy forms may be treated by a court as negating warranty clauses set forth in the standard printed insurance form.[7]

Second, when a warranty provision is at issue, courts tend to adopt a construction that minimizes the impact of the policy clause. For example, in a leading case the court held that the descriptive warranty "paper-mill" did not mean that the building must be used as a paper mill, but only that it must be ready for use as a paper mill — a state that existed even while the building was being used as a grist mill.[8]

Third, courts frequently favor construing a clause as an "affirmative warranty" — rather than a "continuing" or "promissory warranty" — so that compliance at the commencement of the contract term is enough to satisfy the requirement, and subsequent noncompliance during the coverage period does not constitute a defense to a claim.[9] Similarly, courts often construe a warranty clause as severable or "distributable," so that noncompliance with a clause bearing on one

---

4. See §§ 6.1–6.5, above.

5. See, e.g., Joyce v. Maine Insurance Co., 45 Me. 168 at p. 172, 71 Am.Dec. 536 at pp. 537–538 (1858) (description of house as occupied by insured).

But cf. Wood v. Hartford Fire Insurance Co., 13 Conn. 533 at pp. 544–545, 35 Am. Dec. 92 at pp. 93–94 (1840) (dictum).

6. See, e.g., Spence v. Central Accident Insurance Co., 236 Ill. 444 at pp. 448–450, 86 N.E. 104 at p. 106 (1908) (statement of insured's age not a warranty because contained in application and thus not part of insurance contract); Morris v. Sovereign Camp W.O.W., 9 So.2d 835 at p. 837 (La. App. 1st Cir.1942) *judgment affirmed* 203 La. 507, 14 So.2d 428 (1943) (construing provision that delinquent payment implied warranty of good health).

7. See, e.g., McClure v. Mutual Fire Insurance Co., 242 Pa. 59 at pp. 65–67, 88 A. 921 at pp. 923–924 (1913) (alternative holding). A printed clause prohibited the keeping of specified articles among which were some items that were normal, if not essential, stock of a country store, for which the insured building was used. The court applied the rule that *written* provisions, apparently those designating the use of the building as a country store, prevail over *printed* provisions as being more immediately expressive of the intention of the parties and allowed recovery despite the keeping of the specified articles as part of the stock of the store.

8. Wood v. Hartford Fire Insurance Co., 13 Conn. 533, 35 Am.Dec. 92 (1840).

Cf. § 5.5(a)(4), above, referring to an analogous tendency to construe coverage provisions less restrictively than their language might bear.

9. E.g., Blood v. Howard Fire Insurance Co., 66 Mass. (12 Cushing) 472 (1853).

type of risk does not defeat coverage for other types of risks that are covered by the insurance policy.[10]

Fourth, courts tend to construe a warranty clause as only suspending liability during a period of noncompliance, rather than construing a period of noncompliance as terminating all potential liability for loss thereafter,[11] and, *a fortiori,* rather than construing the clause to mean [12] that there is no liability even as to a loss occurring before the noncompliance (as suggested in a dictum by Lord Mansfield).[13]

These techniques of construction often can be used to relieve the harsh effects of the rule requiring strict compliance with warranties. Nevertheless, these techniques do not preclude the use of warranty provisions by insurers — that is, if the foregoing approaches are the

---

10. E.g., Diesinger v. American & Foreign Insurance Co., 138 F.2d 91 (3d Cir. 1943) (applying Pennsylvania law) (breach of the warranty in a jeweler's block policy limiting the amount of jewelry to be displayed in the window was material to the risk of burglary by window-smashing but did not bar a claim for loss by armed robbery by persons who did not smash or cut the window).

But cf. Pollock v. Connecticut Fire Insurance Co., 362 Ill. 313, 199 N.E. 816 (1935), in which the court upheld the insurer's refusal of liability for a loss by lightning because Pollock was not the "unconditional and sole owner" within the meaning of a clause in a fire and lightning policy declaring that "[t]his entire policy ∗ ∗ ∗ shall be void ∗ ∗ ∗ if the interest of the insured be other than unconditional and sole ownership ∗ ∗ ∗." 362 Ill. at p. 314, 199 N.E. at p. 817. It would seem that the risks this clause was intended to avoid have no relevance to the risk of loss by lightning; yet the court denied recovery.

11. See, e.g., McClure v. Mutual Fire Insurance Co., 242 Pa. 59, 63, 88 A. 921, 922 (1913) (alternative holding).

Courts have sometimes stated the rule favoring suspension of liability over termination of all potential liability in terms broad enough to suggest that they would apply it even in the face of a clearly stated contractual provision for termination. E.g., Dale v. Mutual Fire Insurance Co., 376 Pa. 470 at p. 472, 103 A.2d 414 at p. 415 (1954), 44 A.L.R.2d 1044 at p. 1046 (1955) (breach of a promissory warranty that "[w]hen a portable internal combustion engine is used as a motive power for threshing grain ∗ ∗ ∗ it shall not be located nearer than 25 feet from any building"; recovery allowed despite use of such an engine in the insured barn for a period terminating a few hours before the fire).

Contra, e.g., German Insurance Co. v. Russell, 65 Kan. 373, 69 P. 345 (1902) (the court enforced a clause declaring the policy forfeited if the property should become vacant or unoccupied without the insurer's consent; reoccupancy after twelve day vacancy did not revive the forfeited policy).

12. DeHahn v. Hartley, 1 T.R. 343, 99 Eng.Rep. 1130 (K.B.1786). An underwriter brought an action to recover from the insured the amount of a payment under a policy of insurance upon the ship "Juno," "warranted copper-sheathed, and sailed from Liverpool with 14 six-pounders, (exclusive of swivels, & c.) 50 hands or upwards." The ship sailed from Liverpool with only forty-six hands on board. At Beaumaris, which she reached six hours thereafter, with the pilot from Liverpool on board, she took on six hands more, and she continued to have fifty-two hands or more from that time until she was captured on the high seas. Judgment was awarded to the underwriter. The following passage appears in Lord Mansfield's opinion:

"A warranty in a policy of insurance is a condition or a contingency, and unless that be performed, there is no contract. It is perfectly immaterial for what purpose a warranty is introduced; but, being inserted, the contract does not exist unless it be literally complied with."

1 T.R. at 345–346, 99 Eng.Rep. at 1131. Concurring opinions were delivered by Ashhurst, J., and Buller, J., and the decision was thereafter unanimously affirmed, 2 T.R. 186, 100 Eng.Rep. 101 (Ex.1787).

13. See, e.g., Tyrie v. Fletcher, 2 Cowp. 666, 670, 98 Eng.Rep. 1297, 1299 (K.B.1777) (Mansfield, J.) (dictum).

See generally, Annotation, *Insurance: warranties and conditions precedent distinguished,* 59 A.L.R. 611–615 at pp. 614–615 (1929).

only constraints applied by courts in a particular jurisdiction, a court cannot avoid the effect of a warranty clause by applying one of these construction techniques when a warranty clause is drafted with sufficient care.

In the absence of legislative restrictions on the use of warranty provisions, courts have been called upon to decide whether public policy considerations justify precluding the enforcement of a warranty clause regardless of its clear meaning. In general, courts have upheld the enforceability of warranty clauses. Courts have not developed any general doctrine aimed specifically at limiting the enforcement of warranties on grounds of public policy, and in most jurisdictions warranty provisions are only subject to the same judicially imposed limitations that are applied to clauses which are treated as "coverage" provisions.[14] Further amelioration of the effects of such provisions has been left to state legislatures.

Comment

The types of clauses commonly denoted as warranties often are more likely than coverage provisions to be surprising to laypersons, and are also more likely to be unconscionably restrictive if rigorously enforced. Courts should recognize that there are justifications for recognizing rights at variance with policy provisions in regard to such provisions. The candid recognition of the principles of disallowing unconscionable advantage and honoring reasonable expectations should eventually work a practical change in this area of the law.

§ 6.6(b) Concepts of Warranty, Representation, and Coverage

(1) Generally

Restrictions on the enforceability of warranties, imposed by statutes enacted during the late nineteenth century or thereafter, generally are not applicable to coverage provisions. Consequently, a significant distinction between warranties and coverage provisions may now exist as a consequence of modern legislative regulation of insurance contracts.

The primary import of this legislatively created distinction is quite similar to that formerly accorded, that is before statutory restrictions were imposed on the effect of warranties, to the distinction between misrepresentation and warranty. Under most modern statutes, either a misrepresentation or a breach of warranty is ground for avoidance only if material in some sense, but noncompliance with a coverage provision is a defense regardless of materiality.

Before the modern statutory developments that imposed restrictions on warranties, if the policy provision clearly stated that the

---

14. *But cf.* Dale v. Mutual Fire Insurance Co., 376 Pa. 470, 103 A.2d 414 (1954), 44 A.L.R.2d 1044 (1955).

existence of specified facts was a condition of liability, so it was. But as the art of drafting exculpatory fine print reached maturity, the political climate became more favorably disposed to the enactment of some public regulation of insurance provisions. In particular, a need was recognized for restrictions against the assertion of "technical" defenses by insurers. Thus, in many states legislation was adopted that was primarily directed against insurers who gained an unconscionable advantage by the use of complex insurance policy provisions concerning facts that the untutored purchaser would be surprised to find relevant to the insurance coverage. The objective was to preclude the use of defenses that were not materially related to the maintenance of a sound, nondiscriminatory insurance plan (that is, one under which the total premiums collected are adequate, but not excessive, and premium charges to individual policyholders are properly adjusted to the risks). Historically, the awkward but rhetorically impressive language of warranty, though also used for what Patterson called coverage provisions (e.g., "warranted free of * * * capture"),[1] was commonly used in the insurance policy provisions on which "technical" defenses were based. For this reason, and perhaps also because the word suggested that the insured was assuming some new responsibility rather than merely contracting not to pass risks along to the insurer, warranty was a natural target for restrictive legislation. The term warranty commonly appeared in such legislation, but usually without statutory definition.

Some statutes declared that certain types of provisions, formerly treated as warranties, would thereafter be treated as representations.[2] Other statutes, as we shall see presently, declared a new set of legal consequences for warranties, without undertaking a change of terminology. Regardless of the type of legislation, drafters of policy forms predictably attempted to avoid the statutory sanctions by rewriting policy clauses in the language of coverage rather than warranty. The efforts of courts and legislatures to deal with this problem have produced a maze of variant rules about warranties in insurance law.

(2) The New York Statutory Definition of Warranty

As the drafters of insurance policy forms made increasing use of the idiom of coverage in an effort to circumvent judicial and statutory regulation of warranties, a need developed for a concept of warranty substantively distinguishable from other conditions of liability. Thus

§ 6.6(b)

1. See Patterson, ESSENTIALS OF INSURANCE LAW (Second edition, 1957), at p. 272. Also see *Id.*, at p. 249 and p. 255.

Compare another use of a derivative of the term "warranty" in a clause that is commonly regarded as a coverage provision, "warranted free of particular average." This is a way of saying that the insurer will not pay a particular average loss. See *Id.*, at p. 272.

Also consider Grant Gilmore & Charles Black, THE LAW OF ADMIRALTY (Second edition, 1975), at pp. 67–68.

2. This type of statute has been used especially in relation to life insurance. See, e.g., New York Insurance Law 142(3) (McKinney, 1966).

arose the occasion for Patterson's distinction between warranties and other policy conditions,[3] and for its enactment in a New York statute.[4]

Patterson's concept of warranty relies on a distinction between an actual or efficient cause of a loss and a potential cause, a distinction he noted as early as 1924.[5] Six years later Chief Judge Cardozo, in Metropolitan Life Insurance Co. v. Conway,[6] wrote an opinion for the court that can reasonably be read as distinguishing between a provision (held valid) declaring death from specified causes not to be covered and a provision (held invalid) declaring death under specified circumstances not to be covered, regardless of the cause. Patterson so interpreted Cardozo and, writing in 1934, cited the *Conway* opinion in support of a more elaborate development of the distinction between efficient and potential causes.[7] In 1939 this concept was incorporated into the New York insurance legislation governing warranties, drafted by Patterson.[8]

A warranty, in a succinct statement of Patterson's concept, is a "clause in an insurance contract that prescribes, as a condition of the insurer's liability, the existence of a fact affecting the risk." [9] It is to be contrasted with a "coverage" clause, one example of which is an exception.[10] "The warranty * * * seeks to exclude *potential* causes of an insured event; the exception * * * excludes certain *actual* causes of an insured event." [11]

A statement of this contrast in several forms may help to clarify it. The condition of liability imposed by warranty can be seen as one concerning:

"One: Potential cause of loss.

Two: The existence of a fact affecting risk that an insured event will occur.

---

3. See generally Patterson, Essentials of Insurance Law (Second edition, 1957), at pp. 272–309.

Comments in the text are adapted from Professor Keeton's review of Patterson's book. See 36 Texas Law Review 545–553 (1958).

4. New York Insurance Law § 150 (McKinney, 1966).

5. Edwin Patterson, *The Apportionment of Business Risks Through Legal Devices*, 24 Columbia Law Review 335–359 at pp. 340–341 (1924):

"Here [by the conditions or warranties in fire insurance policies] the risk is defined in terms, not of *efficient* but of *potential* causes. For instance, the fire insurer does not attempt to exclude the risk of fire caused by ten gallons of gasoline by inserting a provision that no liability is assumed by him for fire *actually* so caused; he stipulates that if such a quantity of gasoline is on the insured prem-

ises — that is, is a *potential* cause — no liability is assumed. Thus he avoids the juridical risk of interpretation of a risk defined in terms of efficient cause, as well as the juridical risk of not being able to prove that the gasoline was the actual cause of the fire." [emphasis in original]

6. 252 N.Y. 449, 169 N.E. 642 (1930).

7. Edwin Patterson, *Warranties in Insurance Law*, 34 Columbia Law Review 595–631 at p. 600, note 27 (1934).

8. Ch. 882, § 150, 1939 New York Laws 2636.

Also see Patterson, Essentials of Insurance Law (Second edition, 1957), at p. 275, note 9.

9. Patterson, Essentials of Insurance Law (Second edition, 1957), at p. 308.

10. *Id.*, at p. 230 and p. 273.

11. *Id.*, at p. 273 (emphasis by Patterson).

Three: Amelioration of the risk.[12]

Four: Suspension of coverage irrespective of the cause of loss.[13] (A suspensive condition is usually a "while" clause, e.g., a clause saying the life insurer is not liable for death occurring while the insured is engaged in specified aviation.)

In contrast a coverage provision can be seen as one concerning:

One: Actual cause of loss.

Two: The existence of a fact determining whether an insured event has occurred.

Three: Identification of the risk.[14]

Four: Scope of coverage as determined by cause of loss.[15] (*E.g.,* a clause saying the life insurer is not liable for death caused by specified aviation.)

The New York statute states that any provision that purports to relieve the company of liability upon the occurrence of a specified state of facts tending to increase the risk of loss within the contract coverage *is a warranty and that breach of warranty* is no defense unless the breach of such provision materially increased the risk of loss within the coverage.[16]

One fairly minor objection to the New York statute lies in the decision to use, and define in a new way, the term "warranty." The use of "warranty" is not essential to the statutory rule. The concept identified in the statute as a warranty might just as well have been called "X," or the label might have been omitted altogether. The preceding paragraph might be read without the phrases in italics; the meaning is the same. Why then give such a new definition to the old term "warranty," long used in different senses and bound to be so used still by those not converted to the new faith? May not the incomplete acceptance of this terminology heap new confusions on the old? This result seems especially likely if the new terminology is urged upon courts, writers, lawyers, and insurers by persuasion rather than by statute, for substantial inconsistency of usage even within a single jurisdiction is thus almost certain to follow.

Such difficulties are compounded because the concept of warranty has been invoked in relation to other problems of insurance law in addition to the major one considered here. Three problems deserve particular mention. First, can a defense raised by an insurer be enforced despite incontestability statutes?[17] Second, how is the defense affected by waiver, estoppel, and election?[18] Third, will the insurer's payment in spite of the availability of a defense restrict its subrogation

---

12. *Id.,* at pp. 282–283.

13. *Id.,* at p. 254.

14. *Id.,* at pp. 230–231.

15. *Id.,* at p. 249.

16. New York Insurance Law § 150 (McKinney, 1966).

17. See Patterson, ESSENTIALS OF INSURANCE LAW (Second edition, 1957), at pp. 280–281. Also see § 6.6(d), below.

18. See Patterson, ESSENTIALS OF INSURANCE LAW (Second edition, 1957), at p. 506 and pp. 530–533. Also see § 6.7(b), below.

rights by relegating it to the status of a volunteer? [19]   Can Patterson's definition of warranty be appropriately carried over into these contexts?   Probably not (as indicated below in relation to the first two questions),[20] and therefore, at the least, additional definitions must be used.   Better, the common references to warranty in these contexts might be declared inappropriate.   Moreover, any variety of definitional approach is probably inapt in these contexts;   the answers to the questions posed should in most instances depend on factors that do not correlate well with the nature of the provision upon which the insurer rests its defense.

More important than the terminology is the substance of the distinction at which the New York statute and Patterson's definition of warranty are aimed.   In this respect, Patterson's contribution deserves high praise as clearly the most careful and orderly statement that can be found in any of the statutes having comparable aims or in writings concerning such statutes.   Even with this contribution, however, there remain substantial difficulties in applying the New York statute.

One of these difficulties is that though all provisions concerning *actual cause* of loss are coverage provisions, not all provisions concerning *potential cause* of loss are warranties;   as Patterson himself recognized, some of the latter are coverage provisions.   That is, although the coverage of the policy can be partly defined in terms of actual causes of loss, provisions defining coverage can also refer to potential causes. For example, the typical fire insurance policy on personalty designates certain premises as the location of the property.   This clause is properly considered a coverage provision, as courts generally hold, because it serves to identify the subject matter of the policy.   In the language of the New York statute, it is one of the elements of "the coverage of the contract," [21] even though the location of the goods does affect the risk of occurrence of a loss within the coverage.   Of course, provisions describing location are not always intended to serve the function of identification.   To take Patterson's own example, "where *specified* personal property is insured at a given location, the correct interpretation of the contract seems to be that the location is not an essential term of identification, that at most it is a warranty of a fact relating to the risk as a potential cause * * *." [22]   Thus the potential-cause versus actual-cause distinction expressed in the New York statute must be supplemented, again, as Patterson apparently advocated, by a functional analysis of whether a provision that in fact relates to potential cause of loss was intended to serve the purpose of identification.

It is no easy task to devise a test for distinguishing warranties, in Patterson's sense, from potential-cause provisions that are coverage

19. See *Id.,* at p. 149.

20. See § 6.6(d) and § 6.7(b), below.

21. McKinney's New York Insurance Law 150(1) (1966).

Also see Patterson, ESSENTIALS OF INSURANCE LAW (Second edition, 1957), at pp. 296–297.

22. See Patterson, ESSENTIALS OF INSURANCE LAW (Second edition, 1957) (emphasis in original), at p. 297.

clauses because of the functions they serve. Any test that operates with a high degree of precision will in some instances operate inconsistently with the underlying purpose of guarding against overreaching by insurers. On the other hand, a test stated simply in terms of this general purpose will be vague and difficult to apply in a considerable body of marginal cases. No solution entirely escapes both these difficulties. Arguably Patterson's approach is the best so far developed. Yet in the troublesome cases in which it is necessary to distinguish warranties from clauses that, though concerning potential cause of loss, appear to serve the function of coverage clauses, perhaps it will be best, despite objections of vagueness and generality, to resort to a test that is purposive in a broader sense than that necessarily implied in Patterson's urging a "functional" analysis. One might ask whether the clause under study is likely to serve as an instrument of overreaching, or whether instead it concerns a fact that the ordinary insured would realize was significant for insurance purposes. This standard appears to be consistent with both Patterson's objective and his functional test for achieving it, as far as he developed that approach.

Stepping back momentarily from the New York statute, one may say that its basic technique — distinguishing coverage from other clauses and protecting insured's only with respect to the latter — suggests by negative implication that overreaching is not a significant danger with respect to coverage clauses. Probably it is true that coverage clauses, on account of their prominence and centrality to a policy, are less susceptible to abuse than other clauses (the distinction is in this respect far more valid than that between "warranties" and "representations"). Nonetheless statutes in several states reflect a legislative judgment that the evils of misleading policy clauses extend in some degree to coverage provisions as well as warranties. Thus, it has been thought desirable to restrict the use of some kinds of coverage clauses in life insurance. In New York [23] and elsewhere [24] statutes have restricted the use of provisions against liability for death caused in a specified manner or while the insured occupies a specified status.[25]

Such a legislative judgment appears also to be one of the factors supporting provisions for compulsory standardization of insurance contracts,[26] insofar as they extend to coverage provisions as well as warranties. Moreover, some judicial applications of the principles of honoring reasonable expectations and disallowing unconscionable advantage are responsive to the need for controlling coverage clauses.[27]

23. See McKinney's New York Insurance Law § 155(2) (1966).

24. E.g., Vernon's Ann. Texas Statutes Insurance Code, art. 3.45 (1981).

25. Such a statute may, however, permit a clause allowing a recovery in the nature of a return of the reserve value (or the somewhat larger sum of the premiums paid), rather than the face amount in spec-ified circumstances, for example, in case of suicide or in case of death resulting from military service.

26. As in the statutory prescription of the fire insurance form, McKinney's New York Insurance Law § 168 (1966).

27. Consider, for example, the treatment of policy provisions regarding "accidental means," discussed in § 5.4(b), above.

(3) Warranty Statutes of Other States

A number of states have statutes providing generally, though with variations in detail, that no false representation or warranty shall defeat a claim of coverage unless, for example, the representation or warranty was made with intent to deceive or increased the risk of loss. More often than not such statutes contain no definition of the operative terms.

What is the meaning of "representation" and "warranty" as used in these statutes? It is unnecessary, of course, to distinguish between representations and warranties in this context. Together they occupy a middle ground between what are commonly called coverage provisions and statements or promises the falsity of which would in no circumstances affect the enforceability of the insurance contract. In comparison with the problem of distinguishing warranties from coverage clauses, relatively few problems have arisen with respect to drawing the dividing line between representations and these latter kinds of statements or promises.

To illustrate the confusion that arises under these statutes, consider a policy stipulation that insured property shall not be mortgaged. Some courts have sustained the insurer's defense upon proof of a violation of a chattel mortgage clause suspending liability "during the time" of an impermissible encumbrance, holding the chattel mortgage clause to be a coverage provision, not a warranty.[28] Such an interpretation is clearly contrary to the New York statute's explicit definition of warranty (Patterson's concept), with the consequence that, in New York, breach would provide a good defense only if materiality were proved. The meaning of warranty assumed in such opinions is contrary also to the prevailing idea that the primary significance of warranty in insurance law is as a condition of the insurer's promise; that is, rejection of this prevailing idea is commonly implicit in opinions holding that a statute regulating warranties does not apply to a chattel mortgage clause.[29]

As this example also illustrates, the confusing variations among courts are increased by the distinction sometimes drawn — under statutes that do not define their operative terms — between a warranty and a condition precedent, the latter being held enforceable without regard to materiality or deceit.[30] Of course compliance with a warranty is by definition a condition precedent, if that phrase is used to include all

---

28. E.g., Moe v. Allemannia Fire Insurance Co., 209 Wis. 526, 244 N.W. 593 (1932). For disputed interpretations of *Moe* see the majority and dissenting opinions in Emmco Insurance Company v. Palatine Insurance Company, 263 Wis. 558, 58 N.W.2d 525 (1953).

29. See, *e.g.*, Moe v. Allemannia Fire Insurance Co., 209 Wis. 526, 244 N.W. 593 (1932), in which the court reasons that no warranty or representation was made, the insured not having represented that the property was free from encumbrance and not having warranted that it would remain so. This reasoning suggests that "warranty" connotes an assertion, affirmation, or promise by the insured rather than merely a qualification or condition of the insurer's promise.

30. See, e.g., Krause v. Equitable Life Insurance Company, 333 Mass. 200, 129 N.E.2d 617 (1955).

prerequisites of liability. And if the phrase were construed to mean only those prerequisites the absence of which would determine that no coverage under the policy ever became effective,[31] it still would include some provisions commonly treated as warranties within the scope of these statutes. Thus it must be that the phrase is being used as one of art, with a meaning different from both of these. The distinction intended is rarely if ever systematically expounded by the courts that draw it.[32]

Other instances of uncertainty concern the questions whether these regulatory statutes apply to misrepresentation in presenting a claim as distinguished from misrepresentation in the negotiation of the contract,[33] and to violations of moral hazard clauses.[34]

The absence of coherent exposition is characteristic of decisions applying statutes of the type we have been considering. As a consequence, analysis of the results reached in relation to common kinds of policy clauses usually will guide the practitioner better than analysis of what courts say generally about the meaning of warranties, either in this context or in others.[35]

6.6(c) Regulatory Standards

(1) Deceit Provisions

Several state statutes permit a defense of misrepresentation or false warranty only on proof of intent to deceive or a resultant "increase in risk." [1] The difficult problem of giving content to the concept of increase in the risk will be considered in the next subsection. At this point we turn to separate problems concerning intent to deceive.

Is fraudulent, immaterial misrepresentation a ground for avoidance of an insurance contract? Are these regulatory statutes to be construed as so declaring, regardless of what the answer may have been under common law decisions?

Although many judicial opinions contain dicta that fraud is a defense without regard to materiality,[2] and literal interpretation of some statutes would seem to support this result, Patterson found no

---

31. *Cf.* Nicholas J. Healy, *The Hull Policy: Warranties, Representations, Disclosures and Conditions,* 41 Tulane Law Review 245–258 at p. 251 (1967):

"In the law of insurance, a condition precedent is one which must be met before the attachment of the risk; a condition subsequent is one which must be maintained or met after the risk has attached, in order that the insurance contract may remain in force."

32. Compare Krause v. Equitable Life Insurance Company, 333 Mass. 200, 129 N.E.2d 617 (1955) with Mutual Life Insurance Co. v. Mandelbaum, 207 Ala. 234, 92 So. 440 (1922), 29 A.L.R. 649 (1924).

33. Also see the discussion of misrepresentation in § 5.7, above.

34. See § 6.6(e)(3), below.

35. For such an analysis in relation to some common policy clauses, see § 6.6(e), below.

§ 6.6(c)

1. See, e.g., Alabama Code 1977, tit. 27, § 12 and § 14; Massachusetts General Laws Ann. c. 175, § 186 (1977); Wisconsin Statutes Ann. § 631.11(1) (1979).

2. See, e.g., Campbell v. Prudential Insurance Company, 15 Ill.2d 308, 155 N.E.2d 9 (1958).

case in which, on the facts, under either statutory or decisional rules, "a clearly immaterial misrepresentation was held to be fatal merely because fraudulent." [3] In exceptional instances there is statutory phrasing, such as "in the absence of fraud," supporting the construction that the statute makes no prescription for cases of fraud (whether material or not), not even a prescription by negative implication.[4] Also, even in the absence of such a phrase, consideration of statutory purpose points to the conclusion that the statute should not be read as creating a new defense for the insurer. It seems likely that, as Patterson found at the time of his search, there will continue to be a dearth of holdings that immaterial misrepresentation is a defense.

The converse problem has been presented often — that is, whether under such a statute a material misrepresentation is a good defense for the insurer even though it was made in good faith. An affirmative answer is supported not only by literal construction of the statute but also, it would seem, by a fair analysis of the statutory purpose.[5] That is, policyholders can properly be expected to anticipate that coverage would be suspended for a violation if it materially increased the risk (or, a fortiori, if it caused the loss), regardless of the absence of intent to deceive. Nonetheless, some decisions seem in result to have converted the statutory word "or" to "and," requiring both materiality and intent to deceive.[6]

---

3. Patterson, ESSENTIALS OF INSURANCE LAW (Second edition, 1957), at p. 433.

Cf. Johnson v. National Life Insurance Company, 123 Minn. 453 at p. 457, 144 N.W. 218 at p. 220 (1913):

"Some of the cases cited [construing statutes providing that no oral or written misrepresentation shall avoid a policy unless made with intent to deceive or unless the matter misrepresented increases the risk of loss] seem to hold that a misrepresentation made with intent to deceive and defraud, though the matter misrepresented is immaterial in character, avoids the policy. We do not stop to inquire how many, if any, directly and necessarily so hold. We cannot adopt such a doctrine. Long prior to the statute this court held that a fraudulent misrepresentation of an immaterial matter did not avoid the policy; and the 1895 law was not intended to make the insurer's liability less."

4. See, e.g., Vernon's Ann. Texas Statutes Insurance Code, art. 3.44(4) (1981), declaring that life insurance policies shall contain a provision "[t]hat all statements made by the insured shall, in the absence of fraud, be deemed representations and not warranties." This interpretation is fortified by *Id.*, art. 21.18, declaring that recovery under a life, accident, or health insurance policy shall not be defeated be-

cause of a misrepresentation "which is of an immaterial fact and which does not affect the risks assumed."

5. *Cf.* Campbell v. Prudential Insurance Co., 15 Ill.2d 308, 155 N.E.2d 9 (1958).

6. Arguably Metropolitan Life Insurance Co. v. Burno, 309 Mass. 7, 33 N.E.2d 519 (1941), is such a case. The company filed a bill to "rescind and cancel" a policy of life insurance issued by plaintiff on the life of Burno. One ground of relief was that Burno made a false answer "no" to a question, purportedly addressed to him by the medical examiner for plaintiff, asking whether he had ever had any disease of the stomach. The trial judge found that Burno had cancer of the stomach but did not know that fact at the time of the answer or before the policy was issued. A second ground of relief was that Burno made a false answer "none" to a question concerning what clinics and physicians he had consulted within five years. The trial judge found this answer false because Burno had consulted a physician shortly before making application, complaining of belching gas, stomachache, heartburn, and constipation. He also found, however, that plaintiff insurer had not proved an actual intent to deceive or an increase in the risk of loss. From a decree dismissing the bill, the plaintiff insurer appealed; thereafter Burno died and the executrix of his will

(2) Contribute-to-Loss and Increase-of-Risk Provisions

Apart from the intent-to-deceive criterion, statutory standards fall into two major classes with respect to what an insurer must show, if anything more than violation of a policy provision, to sustain a defense. One is that the violation must increase the risk.[7] The other is that the violation must contribute to the loss. A few statutes invoke both these standards in the alternative. The dominance of these two standards invites comparative analysis and raises common questions of interpretation. This discussion will proceed first to the comparison.

Referring again to the general purpose of these statutes — to bar technical, immaterial defenses — one may note that the strongest showing of materiality is proof that the breach contributed to the loss. Although statutes requiring this showing thus go farthest toward protecting insureds,[8] they sacrifice other interests in doing so.

First, a contribute-to-loss standard of materiality tends to produce an inequity in rate structure. Insurers will sometimes lack proof that a violation contributed to a loss, even when it in fact did so. From the insurer's point of view, because of this juridical risk it is more expensive to service the contracts of those policyholders who engage in policy violations than to service the contracts of those who conform; the risk that the company undertakes for those who commit policy violations is somewhat higher than the risk it undertakes for others. Despite this, the same premiums are paid by the two groups. Of course one might argue that this discrimination is justified on the same basis as any other rate classification that is broad enough to include some persons whose risks are greater than others within the same classification.[9] Also, similar inequities probably arise from juridical risks under any

---

was made a defendant. Held, decree affirmed.

Arguably, the question whether the insured had suffered from any disease of the stomach, when addressed to a layman, called for no more than the layman's state of mind — his knowledge and belief on a matter as to which he might not know the objective facts. But the answer concerning clinics and physicians consulted cannot be explained in this way. However, the authority of *Burno* appears to have been undermined by Pahigian v. Manufacturer's Life Insurance Company, 349 Mass. 78, 206 N.E.2d 660 (1965), 18 A.L.R.3d 749 (1968). In *Pahigian,* the policyholder had been hospitalized several times within two years before the policy application and treated for Hodgkins disease, of which he subsequently died. Without discussing whether misrepresentations concerning his medical history were intentional, and expressly declining to follow *Burno,* the court held that the misrepresentations increased the risk of loss as a matter of law and entitled the insurance company to avoid the policy.

7. The phrase "materially affected" the risk or a variant, e.g., Illinois—S.H.A. ch. 73, § 766 (1969), sometimes used instead of a phrase "increased" the risk, is apparently intended to convey the same meaning, since an insurer is in no position to complain about a statement that has a material bearing on risk, but in a way that pictures the risk as more substantial than if a true statement had been made. [This Illinois statute was repealed in 1977. See Illinois Rev.Stat. (1983), at p. 1448.]

8. It may be theoretically possible for a breach to contribute to loss (thus sustaining the insurer's defense) though not having increased the risk. See note 20, below. In such an instance, a contribute-to-loss standard would be less favorable to the policyholder than an increase-of-risk standard. But even if the standards as interpreted create this theoretical possibility, the occasions of its occurrence in fact would be very rare.

9. See § 8.4(b), below.

standard of liability. For example, if the decisive question is merely whether a violation of policy terms has occurred, the nonviolators help to pay for the losses of those violators whose violations cannot be proved. The effect of the juridical risks on equity of the rate structure is undoubtedly greater, however, under a contribute-to-loss statute than under an increase-of-risk statute. In cases of fire loss, for example, the evidence needed to prove that a violation contributed to the loss will often be destroyed by the fire. In any event it is so much more difficult to prove contribution to loss than increase of risk that a much higher percentage of cases will be decided by lack of adequate evidence if the former is the decisive issue.

Rate pattern inequity caused by a contribute-to-loss standard may also hinder the structuring of insurance so as to enable a purchaser to buy just what the purchaser needs. For example, under a contribute-to-loss standard, it is less likely that an insurer can afford to sell to the owner of a building with an especially fire-resistant roof a policy covering that owner's relatively lower risk at a charge reduced in full proportion to the reduction of risk. If it did so while not incurring the cost of inspections before underwriting, it would be collecting only this lower rate from other policyholders who misrepresented the construction of their roofs, some of whom would nevertheless be able to collect for loss to which the flammability of the roof contributed, since the insurer might be unable to prove contribution to loss.

Other factors also favor the choice of an increase-of-risk over a contribute-to-loss standard. The latter standard can be expected to generate more wasteful litigation of disputed facts than the former. Also, an insured may be more likely to avoid violating a warranty if knowing that the insurer need only show increased risk in order to defeat liability. If insureds were thus to take fewer chances, the result should be not only a reduction in insured losses but also a reduction in losses generally.

A more sophisticated comparison of these regulatory standards depends on the meaning assigned to the concepts "increase of risk" and "contribution to loss." For example, does "contribute" suggest merely that a violation must be one among connected antecedents of the loss, or is the term used in some narrower sense? Consider a case involving collision coverage on a truck under a policy including a clause stating that the truck is not to be driven beyond a radius 500 miles from a designated point of principal garaging. If the truck is in a collision while on the last 100 miles of the return leg of a 1050 mile round trip, should the travel slightly beyond the permitted radius be said to have "contributed" to the loss? Or must something more be proved, such as that the added hour of driving the extra fifty miles had put an extra strain on the driver, which led to a mistake that would not otherwise have been made? Would it make a difference that the accident occurred 150 miles from final destination, at which point the driver would ordinarily be less tired than during the last fifty miles of the

return from a trip to the edge of the radius and back? Would proof that the trip would not have been made but for the violation be decisive? What would be the effect of an insurer's showing that in the aggregate truckers who permitted trips beyond the radius made more trips, or more tiring trips, than otherwise? Would such proof of increase of risk, in one of the possible senses of that phrase, be evidence also that the particular violation contributed to the particular loss? Alternatively, a court might construe the radius clause as requiring that the vehicle be beyond the stipulated radius at the time of a collision. But suppose the truck is properly parked, although outside the 500-mile radius, when struck by a car out of control. Might it be held that since the radius clause concerns movement of the vehicle, implicitly it applies only when the vehicle is in operation and not when it is parked? Or might it be said that even though the violation continued as long as the vehicle was beyond the radius, it did not "contribute" because the presence of the vehicle in a legitimate parking place was a purely passive rather than contributory factor?

As a general answer to these difficulties, it seems likely that courts will attribute a rather broad meaning to terms like "contribute." A narrower meaning would push to an even greater extreme the effect of statutes that are already among the most extreme of regulatory measures in the extent to which they protect policyholders from the consequences of violating policy stipulations.

Similar disputes may arise over the meaning of "risk" in statutes using the increase-of-risk formula. Closely analogous definitional difficulties have arisen under the standard "increase-of-hazard" clause in fire insurance policies. It is difficult, if not impossible, to discover any significance in the difference between "hazard" and "risk." One might nonetheless expect to find differences in interpretation, reflecting the different contexts and purposes giving rise to the two formulations. With due awareness of such possible variations, we may usefully consider simultaneously the problems of construing these parallel phrases.

In many cases there can be no doubt about increase of risk or hazard. For example, if a building that is the subject of a fire insurance policy is declared to be in use as a residence and during the policy term the policyholder establishes a dry cleaning business on the premises, using highly inflammable cleaning fluids, probably no court would hesitate to find an increase of risk.[10] And, when automobile

---

10. *Cf.* Fleet v. National Fire Insurance Company, 167 La. 74, 118 So. 697 (1928) (building and outbuilding, insured under a dwelling policy, burned while in use for dance hall and gambling purposes; premiums for insuring buildings so used would have been four and a half times those for insuring a dwelling); Progress Spinning & Knitting Mills Co. v. Southern National Insurance Company, 42 Utah 263, 130 P. 63 (1913) (building insured as water power woolen mill used to manufacture "cotton bats," an operation that, according to evidence introduced, could be conducted safely only in a fireproof building).

See generally, 4A APPLEMAN, INSURANCE LAW (Revised edition, 1969), at 2579; Annotation, *Change in purposes for which premises are occupied or used as increase of*

insurers are customarily charging higher premiums to a policyholder if there is a driver under 25 years of age in the household, plainly the fact that among those who drive the car there is such a person, contrary to the policyholder's representation, increases the risk on the basis of which the policy is written.[11] Conversely, it is not likely that a court would hesitate about declaring that there is no increase of risk, even if there is a violation of the principal-place-of-garaging clause, when the policyholder changes the place of garaging the car to a territory with the same or a lower rate as to each of the coverages under the policy. One need not be precise about the meaning of risk applied in answering such questions as these.

There are instances, however, in which the choice among debatable meanings of risk can be decisive. Precedents provide relatively little guidance. In part, perhaps, this comes about because the question of materiality calls for an evaluative finding [12] and there is a tendency to treat it as a fact question,[13] often without explicit consideration of the criterion of materiality that the factfinder should employ.

One important question of interpretation common to both the increase-of-risk type of regulatory statute and the increase-of-hazard provision in fire insurance policies concerns the degree and duration of

---

hazard voiding insurance coverage, 19 A.L.R.3d 1336–1347 (1968).

11. E.g., Stockinger v. Central Nat'l Insurance Company, 24 Wis.2d 245, 128 N.W.2d 433 (1964) (insurer not liable under collision coverage for value of car destroyed when driven into a tree by the insured's nineteen-year-old son).

Cf. Fierro v. Foundation Reserve Insurance Company, 81 N.M. 225, 465 P.2d 282 (1970) (fully retroactive cancellation because of misrepresentations, in application, of no cancellation within previous 36 months; held for insurer; applicant bound by application he signed, regardless of who filled it out); Odom v. Insurance Company of the State of Pennsylvania, 455 S.W.2d 195 (Tex.1970) (questions, in application attached to and made part of automobile policy, whether within 36 preceding months insured had been convicted of any moving traffic violations or had been involved in any accidents; false negative answers written into an application by agent; declaratory judgment for insurer affirmed; applicant knew or had means of knowing that such statements were in application and were false; case distinguished from precedents not involving attachment of application to policy; delivery of copy of application though not as part of policy, also gives policyholder means of knowing of answers and binds him, and a precedent to the contrary is overruled); Utica Mutual Insurance Company v. National Indemnity

Company, 210 Va. 769, 173 S.E.2d 855 (1970) (application for automobile insurance; negative answer to question asking for a list of "impairments"; applicant had epilepsy by reason of which his license to drive had been disallowed for a period ending shortly before application; renewal policy issued a little more than a year later; accident during epileptic seizure; held, for insurer, declaring policy void ab initio).

See generally, Annotation, *Representations as to age or identity of persons who will drive vehicle, or as to extent of their relative use, as avoiding coverage under automobile insurance policy,* 29 A.L.R.3d 1139–1158 (1970).

12. Concerning evaluative findings generally, see § 1.4, above.

13. See, e.g., Mayflower Insurance Exch. v. Gilmont, 280 F.2d 13 (9th Cir. 1960), 89 A.L.R.2d 1019 (1963) (applying Oregon Law) (issue of materiality of representations concerning license revocations or suspensions, driving charges and fines, and previous insurance in application for automobile insurance; held, a question of fact for the jury).

But cf. Mutual of Omaha Insurance Company v. Echols, 207 Va. 949, 154 S.E.2d 169 (1967) (erroneous statement in application with resulting nondisclosure of fainting spells; held, material, the issue being one for the court, not the jury).

the increased risk sufficient to trigger the two tests. Although the problems are analytically similar, the question arises under the two standards in somewhat different ways.

The fire insurance clause provides that the insurer "shall not be liable for loss occurring (a) while the hazard is increased by any means within the control or knowledge of the insured * * *." [14] Plainly this stipulation should not be and is not literally construed. Risk and hazard are concepts concerned with estimation of the probability of harm on the basis of incomplete data.[15] Since the data are constantly changing, sometimes to make the situation appear safer and at other times more dangerous, it is virtually certain that during a major portion of the policy period there would be some increase of hazard above the minimum existing at another time during the period. It is clear that the increase-of-hazard clause of the fire insurance policy will not be construed to mean that such fluctuations would necessarily violate it. One obvious way of avoiding such an untenable rule is to require that in some sense the policyholder must have been responsible for any increased hazard, or to require that the increase must have resulted from actual changes in the condition of the insured premises, rather than merely from new data about previously existing conditions. These readings would not, however, avoid the further difficulty of suspending coverage for any slight increase of hazard caused by the policyholder. Thus, a court might require that to qualify as an increase of hazard within the meaning of a policy clause the increase must be substantial. Such a rule is supported by precedent.[16] The need to avoid suspension of coverage upon any violation that trivially increases risk exists also in relation to increase-of-risk statutes. Probably the rule requiring that an increase of risk be "substantial" should apply here as well.[17] An alternative way of meeting the same problem, under both provisions, is to hold that the fluctuation must result from a use of the property not within the "contemplation of the contracting parties.[18]

---

14. McKinney's New York Insurance Law § 168(6) (1966).

15. See generally § 1.3(a), above.

16. E.g., Smith v. Peninsular Insurance Company, 181 So.2d 212 (Fla.App. 1st Dist. 1965), 19 A.L.R.3d 1326 (1968) (judgment on jury verdict for insured under charge that, to be a defense, a change in occupancy must result in "material and substantial increase in hazard").

Cf. Nathan v. St. Paul Mutual Insurance Company, 243 Minn. 430, 441, 68 N.W.2d 385, 393 (1955) (statement, in applying for $12,000 fire insurance, that building was unencumbered; a mechanic's lien for $200 had been filed; "[i]t can hardly be said, under those circumstances, that this factor would increase the risk by reducing [the insured's] pecuniary interest in the property, thereby increasing the moral hazard").

17. See, e.g., Mutual Benefit Health & Accident Association v. McCranie, 178 F.2d 745, 747 (5th Cir.1949) (judgment for insurer, applying Georgia statute concerning materiality of misrepresentations in life insurance application; dictum that "substantial increase in risk" is required (emphasis in original), quoting from Preston v. National Life & Accident Insurance Company, 196 Ga. 217, 237, 26 S.E.2d 439, 450 (1943).

18. *Cf.* Hartford Fire Insurance Co. v. Chenault, 137 Ky. 753 at p. 756, 126 S.W. 1098 at p. 1099 (1910) (building insured as barn; storage of tobacco did not constitute a violation, since this was one of the purposes for which barns in the area were commonly used); Aurora Fire Insurance Co. v. Eddy, 55 Ill. 213 at p. 221 (1870) (building insured as flax factory; installing and operating machinery for manufactur-

A corollary of these requirements concerning the substantiality of increased risk is that the increase should in most instances persist for some substantial period of time. In fact there is much case support for the proposition that to invoke successfully the increase-of-hazard clause an insurer must show that the increase was not "temporary."[19] Probably the intended meaning of these decisions is better conveyed by the term "transitory." Rather than brevity of duration, "temporary" suggests only lack of permanence, which surely should not be required in most instances when the increased risk is substantial.

Unlike a finding of insubstantiality, a finding that the increase was transitory should probably not in itself defeat an insurer's defense. For example, it may be that a very severe increase would qualify as an increase of hazard or risk, though quite transitory, especially if the risk resulted from a use of the insured premises inconsistent with customary use of similar property or, a fortiori, if loss occurred because of that use.[20] Of course, by the explicit terms of the policy clause, the defense would be available only as to losses occurring during the continuance of the violation. Against such a loss, the defense should be recognized without proof that the violation contributed to the loss. Not requiring proof of causality is, after all, a primary characteristic of the increase-of-risk formulation.

Another question of interpretation common to the two provisions is this: does "risk" or "hazard" refer to a net risk (in which case, for example, an increase from the specified circumstances constituting a violation, such as storage of prohibited combustibles, may be offset by decreases from, say, addition of automatic sprinklers). Or does it instead refer only to the effect of a prohibited use, without regard to offsetting changes of circumstance? It would seem that a narrower meaning than the total of all risks under the policy is intended. A policyholder should not be permitted to defeat the defense by showing that a risk-increasing violation was outweighed by risk-ameliorating

---

ing rope held to be a "usual part of the business" of a flax factory).

19. E.g., Orient Insurance Co. v. Cox, 218 Ark. 804 at p. 812, 238 S.W.2d 757 at p. 761 (1951), 26 A.L.R.2d 799, 806 (1952) (judgment on verdict for insured reversed because of error in instructions; rejected insurer's contention that eighteen or twenty scattered containers of gasoline, altogether over fifteen gallons, violated increase-of-hazard clause as a matter of law; "casual or temporary change in the use or condition of the insured property will not ordinarily be sufficient to avoid the policy").

20. If it were held that there was no increase of risk in such a case because of the transitory nature of the increase, the contribute-to-loss standard would be potentially broader in relation to cases of transitory increase, though much narrower generally, than the increase-of-risk standard. This would supply a justification for the clause, which appears in some regulatory statutes, that violation of a policy provision shall not be a defense unless it is either "material to the risk or actually contributed to the [loss]." See, e.g., Vernon's Annotated Texas Statutes Insurance Code, art. 21.16 (1963); Wisconsin Stat.Ann. § 631.11(1) (1979).

On the other hand, if "risk" were considered to refer to the risk, whether transitory or not, from specified circumstances (for example, the risk from storing prohibited combustibles), then one could not prove contribution without also proving increase in risk; the violation must have increased the risk of just such a loss.

steps the policyholder took but was not required to take. The kinds of changes in circumstances that an insured might raise in mitigation of a violation are countless, and case-by-case comparative evaluation of total risk would be extremely expensive and wasteful. Moreover to forgive violations on such an ad hoc basis would often make decisions turn on the resolution of closely balanced issues of fact and highly debatable evaluations of risk. The unpredictability of results would work against one of the primary goals of insurance regulation stated earlier: to maximize equity among insureds as well as between insureds and insurers.

The core question, of course, remains: what is meant by "increase of risk" and "hazard," assuming we are concerned with only substantial increases in risk that arise from specific violations or aberrant uses, regardless of changes in net risk from all circumstances. The formula "increase of risk" is undefined, and there is no better general guide to its meaning than the broad statutory purpose — to protect against unconscionable advantage while honoring reasonable expectations. Posing a few of the many difficulties that may arise in interpreting these words should suffice to illustrate this central point. For example, is an increase of risk to be determined from the point of view of a standard or typical effect of a specific violation upon the risk assumed under policies of a given type or from the point of view of the effect of the violation upon the risk assumed under the individual policy, taking into account all the particulars of the situation of that policyholder? Or, should it be determined from some point of view different from both of these?

Perhaps considerations of predictability and economy of litigation would suggest that a standard or typical meaning is to be preferred over one that would involve detailed factual inquiries in each case. But the standard or typical meaning cannot treat alike all cases involving one "type" of provision, when the type is defined according to the specific act or use proscribed by the provision.

For example, consider the claim of a policyholder of fire insurance on an automobile that is destroyed by fire after the policyholder has mortgaged it without notice to the insurer. The size of a mortgage in relation to the value of the property would surely be relevant. In fact, sound precedents disallow a defense based on a mortgage trivial in amount.[21]

Consider also the meaning of "increase of risk" as applied to the collision radius clause discussed earlier, stating that the insured truck is not to be operated more than 500 miles from the designated place of garaging. Suppose the truck is driven for several weeks within a territory that lies partly within and partly without the prescribed area. Consider two different cases that may arise.

---

21. E.g., Nathan v. St. Paul Mutual Insurance Company, 243 Minn. 430, 68 N.W.2d 385 (1955) (mechanic's lien of $200 when application for $12,000 fire policy stated building was unencumbered).

Suppose, first, that an accident occurs outside the permitted 500-mile radius. The insurer might argue that the violation increased risk—because, for example, the truck was driven more often than it otherwise would have been, or driven in an area unfamiliar to the driver. But if the territory of operation, outside the radius, is a lower-rate territory than the place of principal garaging, the insured might respond that because of this the violation reduced total risk. Permitting insureds to balance such effects would give rise to the same kinds of dislocations from sound insurance principles as would result if insureds were entitled to offset the risk-effects of violations against effects of other changes in circumstance.

Suppose, now, that the collision occurs within the prescribed area, but during a trip that began outside the 500-mile radius, after several weeks of local use there. Would the increase-of-risk statute permit an insurer to raise its defense, on the theory that the violation materially increased the risk of a collision occurring on the trip in which it occurred in fact? The insured might argue that the concept of a "single trip" cannot serve to distinguish the last few miles of the collision trip from later travel entirely within the 500-mile radius. Again, however, the insurer might respond that the violation increased the danger of collision by increasing the number of trips taken, or by tiring the driver.

One coherent approach to interpreting the increase-of-risk language could be fashioned with reference to statutory purpose. These statutes, it would seem, are aimed primarily at regulating policy clauses to disallow unconscionable advantages to insurers (and consistently with honoring policyholders' reasonable expectations). Therefore they are not intended to interfere with clauses defining the scope of the risk in a reasonable way, understandable to policyholders generally and having a substantial relation to what premiums are fairly to be charged for the coverage. Pursuing this approach, one might conclude that the underlying reason for the 500-mile radius clause is to avoid certain identifiable risks such as the greater exposure to accidents that generally occurs when a truck is used in long distance trips or when a truck garaged in a thinly populated area is driven in a generally more congested area beyond the 500-mile radius. It might then be found that the violation did not increase the risk within the objectives of the 500-mile radius clause except for the long trips between the place of garaging and the point that was outside the 500-mile radius but within a lower-rate territory. In contrast, if the territory in which the truck was being driven was a highly congested high-rate area and the place of principal garaging was thinly populated, low-rate area, it might be found that the violation had increased the risk within the objectives of the 500-mile radius clause throughout the period of use beyond the 500-mile radius as well as during the journey to and from.

One way to make clearer the approach to interpreting increase-of-risk statutes here recommended is to restate the basic question from yet another perspective. In fixing a standard for determining increase of risk, courts must choose a point of view from which the increase is to be determined. Is the standard subjective, based on the practices of the particular insurer, or is it objective? If objective, is the standard based on the customary practices of insurers (either in the particular community or more generally), or is it set by legislation and judicial decisions rather than by custom? Is the standard the same under different statutes and policy clauses?

This is a form of statement to which courts have long been accustomed. However, precedents on the issue are inconclusive generally, and there is conflict among the authorities. As one might expect, the choice with respect to increase-of-hazard clauses may be different than that under increase-of-risk statutes. Reasoning that the policy clause should be construed as the lay policyholder would read it, a court may apply a prudent-person standard.[22] In contrast, most precedents concerned with the application of regulatory statutes have adopted either a this-insurer or a prudent-insurer standard.[23]

In this latter context, particularly, the choice of standard emerged as a choice among rules of evidence. Under the common law doctrine making defenses of misrepresentation or concealment depend on materiality, Wigmore supported a this-insurer standard of materiality to risk.[24] A leading opinion by Judge (later Chief Justice) Taft appears to

---

22. See Note, *The Increase-of-Hazard Clause in the Standard Fire Insurance Policy,* 76 Harvard Law Review 1472–1480 at p. 1472 and pp. 1478–1480 (1963). But note that the insurer's point of view, expressed through the rate structure, may be treated as relevant. *Id.,* at pp. 1475–1478. Probably this would result in deviation from a prudent-lay-policyholder standard in some cases.

23. See notes 24–31, below.

24. Wigmore advanced the position that the question is, "in truth, Is the circumstance in question one which *would have influenced the insurer* (or promiser) to fix a higher rate of premium" or to refuse the insurance altogether. 7 WIGMORE, EVIDENCE (Third edition, 1940) (emphasis is Wigmore's), 1946, at p. 60. The inquiry, therefore, is primarily one concerning the insurer's system of classification and "secondarily, the usage of insurers in the same community, because their custom will tend to show what the individual insurer's practice is, as conforming presumably to the local methods." *Ibid.* Wigmore disapproves of asking the question, though addressed to an expert witness, whether there was, in his opinion, an increase of risk. *Id.,* at pp. 59–60. He distinguished "actual [or objectively real] increase of danger" from increase of danger "as determined by the insurer's classification of the

various circumstances affecting the rate of premium," and declares that it is the latter, not the former, that is ordinarily the true issue. *Id.,* at p. 60. But, he observes, "it may clearly appear in a given case that the phrase was not used with reference to the insurer's sense or classification, and that it is to be interpreted according to the sense used by the insured, i.e. the ordinary sense of 'increase of risk,' which therefore is to be applied by the jury acting on the standards and knowledge of the average layman." *Id.,* at p. 62. A dispute involving the increase-of-hazard clause may be such a case, since the standard clause requires that the increase be within the knowledge of the insured, suggesting that the standard may be the ordinary sense rather than the insurer's sense. See *Ibid.*

Also see Columbia Insurance Co. v. Lawrence, 35 U.S. (10 Pet.) 507 at p. 516, 9 L.Ed. 512 (1836). Mr. Justice Story appears to choose a this-insurer standard by stating the question to be whether concealed facts about the title of property to be covered by a fire insurance policy "would have, or might have a real influence upon the underwriter, either not to underwrite at all, or not to underwrite except at a higher premium."

But cf. Hare & Chase, Inc. v. National Surety Co., 60 F.2d 909 at p. 912 (2d Cir. 1932), *cert. denied* 287 U.S. 662, 53 S.Ct.

support in effect a prudent-insurer standard.[25]   Another leading opinion, by Judge Richman of the Supreme Court of Indiana, says the test is whether "the facts if truly stated might reasonably have influenced the company in deciding whether it should reject or accept the risk," [26] and again, "the final inquiry is what that company might reasonably have done." [27]   If Judge Richman was deliberately drawing a distinction by using "might" rather than "would" as the modifier of "reasonably," his standard is in this respect more favorable to the insurer than a this-insurer standard, which would have required a showing of consistency with the company's practice rather than merely with what it might reasonably have chosen to do.[28]   In another respect, however, Richman's standard is less favorable to the insured since it requires a showing of reasonableness, requiring the court to invoke an objective test rather than employing only a this-insurer standard.

It has not been common for statutory drafters to express a clear choice among the various possible standards concerning the point of view from which materiality is determined.   Such a choice was expressed — however, in favor of a this-insurer standard — in the New York statute regarding misrepresentation.[29]   It is puzzling that the statutory drafter (Professor Patterson) phrased the materiality standard differently for the warranty statute.   The latter statute [30] is silent on this question, unless the phrase "materially increased the risk of loss" is interpreted as implying either a prudent-insurer standard [31] or else a wholly different point of view (perhaps that of the court rather than an insurer, and perhaps with hindsight on judgment day rather than with hypothetical foresight before loss).

222, 77 L.Ed. 572 (1932), which appears to adopt a prudent-insured standard regarding facts concealed. One might reasonably distinguish concealment cases on the ground that the obligation to disclose facts not inquired about should be tested by a standard concerned with the insured's point of view, even if a different standard is used with respect to materiality under common law or statutory regulation of defenses based on misrepresentation.

25. Pennsylvania Mutual Life Insurance Co. v. Mechanics' Sav. Bank & Trust Co., 72 Fed. 413 at pp. 428–430 (6th Cir. 1896). Judge Taft's approval of questions concerning insurers' practices appears to be founded on acceptance of a prudent-insurer standard (in contrast with Wigmore's acceptance of a this-insurer standard and allowance of evidence of insurer's practices as secondary evidence).   Apparently Judge Taft would disapprove of some questions, directed to the conclusion of materiality as distinguished from the usage of insurers generally, that Wigmore would approve.

26. New York Life Insurance Co. v. Kuhlenschmidt, 218 Ind. 404 at p. 420, 33

N.E.2d 340 at p. 347 (1941), 135 A.L.R. 397 at p. 405 (1941) (emphasis added).

27.   218 Ind. at pp. 424–425, 33 N.E.2d at p. 348, 135 A.L.R. at p. 407.

28.   Perhaps this interpretation is rendered less plausible by the fact that the court was responding to a contention of the insurer that the issue was "what action appellant would have taken" as opposed to "what action other companies would have taken."   218 Ind. at p. 422, 33 N.E.2d at p. 347, 135 A.L.R. at p. 406. Thus it seems more likely that Judge Richman was stating "might reasonably have taken" as an added requirement beyond what the company conceded, rather than using "might" instead of "would" to soften the requirement.

29.   McKinney's New York Insurance Law § 149 (1966).

30.   *Id.,* § 150.

31.   See Equitable Life Assurance Society v. Milman, 291 N.Y. 90 at p. 97, 50 N.E.2d 553 at p. 554 (1943) (stating the test to be whether the facts in question "might reasonably affect the choice of the insurance company").

It may be that the difference between the misrepresentation and warranty statutes in this respect arose from the notion that representations are assertions of fact made to influence the insurer's action on the application, whereas warranties are continuing nonassertive conditions of liability, the prospective deviation from which would influence the underwriting decision in only a very indirect way, if at all.

The contrast between applying an objective standard from the insurer's viewpoint in interpreting increase-of-risk provisions and applying an objective standard from the insured's viewpoint in interpreting increase-of-hazard clauses seems consistent with a purposive approach.

The increase-of-hazard clause is placed before policyholders in the policy itself, with the consequence that at least occasionally expectations will be based on the policyholder's reading it. Moreover, it seems consistent with honoring reasonable expectations (or even the narrower principle of resolving ambiguities against the drafter) to construe increase of hazard from the policyholder's point of view; the clause requires that the increase be within the policyholder's -"control or knowledge." The increase-of-risk statutes, on the other hand, were enacted primarily to protect against unconscionable advantage, at a time when the broad principle of honoring reasonable expectations (as distinguished from a narrower principle of resolving ambiguities) was not openly recognized. It seems reasonable in this context of securing evenhanded treatment of policyholders to apply a prudent-insurer viewpoint in determining materiality to risk.

This kind of purposive approach seems appropriate not only to construction of the increase-of-risk provision but also to interpretation of the alternative wording discussed earlier, suspending coverage only as to violations that "contribute to the loss." This interpretation thus may suggest a way of meeting some of the difficulties raised earlier with respect to the "contribution" standard. Nonetheless, it remains unclear whether this approach will be generally adopted.

Closely related but distinguishable from the issue whether a this-insurer or a prudent-insurer standard applies is the question whether the insurer must, to establish a defense based on misrepresentation, prove reliance as well as materiality to risk. There is some precedent for an affirmative answer,[32] though the issue has rarely come into sharp focus. Perhaps proof of reliance is generally assumed to be a part of the proof of materiality to the risk under a particular contract. It seems especially likely that under a this-insurer standard it will be

---

32. See, e.g., Praetorian Mutual Life Insurance Company v. Sherman, 455 S.W.2d 201 (Tex.1970) (false answer that applicant had not within the past five years consulted or been attended by any doctor; had done so at least 43 times, on some occasions for lung ailment; report of physical examination for insurance showed good health; died from lung cancer fifteen months later; jury found false answer was material to the risk and was made for purpose of "wrongfully inducing" issuance of policy; judgment for insurer reversed and remanded because of failure to obtain jury finding that insurer relied on the truth of the answer; opinion recognizes that insurer may rely partly on examination and partly on answers in application).

considered implicit that proof of reliance is part of the showing of materiality to this insurer. In any event, it would seem that reliance should be required not only under a this-insurer standard but also under a prudent-insurer standard. In the latter instance, the effect is that the insurer cannot defend successfully by proving that it relied — that applying its own rigorous standards and practices it would have declined the application if a truthful answer had been given — even though a "prudent insurer" would have treated the answer as immaterial.

§ 6.6(d) Incontestability

Life insurance policies customarily contain a clause declaring that, subject to stated exceptions, the policy is incontestable after a specified period of time, ordinarily one or two years.[1] Such clauses are now commonly required by statute.[2] In some instances statutes extend the requirement to related types of coverage such as disability or health and accident insurance, and such clauses are sometimes included in these other types of policies even though not required by statute. Also, provisions similar to the incontestability clauses commonly used in life insurance policies but less favorable to policyholders sometimes appear in these other types of policies, either under statutory compulsion or by voluntary action of insurers.[3]

Apart from these statutory and voluntary provisions affecting life, disability, and accident coverages, there is no generally recognized principle of incontestability. There is limited support, however, for

§ 6.6(d)

1. Incontestability clauses also commonly apply to applications for reinstatement of lapsed coverage, and it is usually held that the period of contestability commences to run anew for any defense based on the application for reinstatement. See, e.g., McCary v. John Hancock Mutual Life Insurance Company, 236 Cal.App.2d 501, 46 Cal.Rptr. 121 (1st Dist., Division 2, 1965), 23 A.L.R.3d 733 (1969).

See generally, McCarthy, *Reinstatement: Misrepresentation and Incontestability: A Polysyllabic Puzzle,* 4 Forum 40–50 (ABA Section Insurance, Negligence & Compensation Law, 1968).

2. See, e.g., McKinney's New York Insurance Law 155(1)(b) (1966).

Also see Salzman, *The Incontestable Clause in Life Insurance Policies,* 1969 Insurance Law Journal 142–166.

3. See, e.g., Bronson v. Washington National Insurance Company, 59 Ill.App.2d 253, 207 N.E.2d 172 (2d Dist.1965), 13 A.L.R.3d 1375 (1967) (statute regulating disability insurance construed as less restrictive than corresponding statute regulating life insurance; disability insurer permitted to contest an action filed more than two years after date of policy for disability commencing within two years; clause provided that after two years no misstatements in application could be used to void policy or to deny claim for disability commencing after two years); Taylor v. Metropolitan Life Insurance Co., 106 N.H. 455 at pp. 461–462, 214 A.2d 109 at pp. 114–115 (1965) ("time limit on certain defenses" clause in accident and sickness policy declaring that, as to disability commencing after two years from the date of issue, "no misstatements, except fraudulent misstatements, made by the applicant in the application for such policy shall be used to void the policy or to deny a claim;" held inapplicable to a claim of disability commencing within the two years, thus allowing a defense of nonfraudulent misstatement as to such claim though not raised in a judicial contest within two years from the date of issue).

applying a somewhat similar principle to sustain recovery by a third-party victim under automobile insurance in exceptional circumstances.[4]

The potential defenses that incontestability statutes and clauses affect are almost entirely those based on warranty, representation, or concealment, even though the language of the statutes and clauses commonly includes no specific reference to these concepts.

Incontestability statutes are in one respect a more rigorous type of regulation than the usual statutes of the type that refer explicitly to warranties and representations. An incontestability statute unconditionally bars the potential defenses to which it refers unless the insurer has taken action that constitutes the institution of a contest [5] before the period of contestability has passed. The warranty-representation type of statute, on the other hand, continues to permit defenses based on breach of warranty or misrepresentation, subject to a condition of materiality in some sense.[6] But an incontestability statute is ordinarily far less comprehensive in scope than a warranty-representation type of statute because it applies only to life insurance or to life and closely related types of insurance, whereas many of the warranty-representation statutes apply to all kinds of insurance.

In those instances in which both types of statutes apply to a policy, a potential defense must clear the requirements of both statutes to be effective. One corollary of this proposition is that in such cases the materiality standard of the warranty-representation statute has practical significance only during the short period of contestability.

Under both types of statutes, it is either explicit or implicit that certain policy defenses — commonly called "coverage" defenses — are beyond the scope of the statutory regulation. The distinction between what is and what is not affected by the statutory scheme of regulation is extraordinarily difficult to formulate in relation to warranty-representation statutes, and perhaps only slightly less so in relation to incontestability statutes. The considerations bearing on the appropri-

---

4. See, e.g., Barrera v. State Farm Mutual Automobile Insurance Company, 71 Cal.2d 659, 79 Cal.Rptr. 106, 456 P.2d 674 (1969). In Barrera, the victim obtained judgment against the tortfeasor and sought payment from the insurer, which cross-complained for a declaration that the policy was void because issued in reliance on a material misrepresentation, in an application tendered one and a half years before the accident, that the insured's driver's license had never been suspended. The trial court found that the insurer relied on the material misrepresentation and acted promptly to rescind upon discovery of it. The supreme court reversed, holding that because of the quasi-public nature of insurance and the public policy underlying the financial responsibility law, an automobile liability insurer has a duty reasonably to investigate an insured's insurability within a reasonable time after issuance of a policy. The insurer cannot "take advantage of a breach of its duty" for the purpose of avoiding liability to an innocent victim, though it may recover against the insured for misrepresentation or may defend against the insured who sues after paying the tort judgment.

5. As to what constitutes the institution of a contest, see, e.g., Franklin Life Insurance Co. v. Bieniek, 312 F.2d 365 (3d Cir. 1962), 95 A.L.R.2d 407 (1964) (Pennsylvania law; letter denying liability insufficient; court proceedings required).

6. See, e.g., McKinney's New York Insurance Law § 150 (1966); § 6.6(b)(2) and (3), (c)(2), above.

ate standards of distinction are quite similar, and precedents in one area have often influenced the development of the standard in the other.[7]

Two leading New York cases well illustrate the difficulty of determining what defenses are and what defenses are not precluded by an incontestability statute.

In the first of these cases, Metropolitan Life Insurance Co. v. Conway,[8] the insurer attacked the refusal of the superintendent of insurance to approve a rider, to be attached to its policies, in the following form: "Death as a result of service, travel or flight in any species of aircraft, except as a fare-paying passenger, is a risk not assumed under this policy; but, if the insured shall die as a result, directly or indirectly, of such service, travel or flight, the company will pay to the beneficiary the reserve on this policy."[9] The court, in an opinion by Chief Judge Cardozo, held this clause to be a permissible rider under the New York statute, despite the fact that by its terms it might preclude a claim arising after the close of the period of contestability. One passage in the opinion draws a distinction between a provision setting the "limits of coverage" (a permissible rider, enforceable though it defeats claims arising after the period of contestability) and a provision establishing a "condition" (not permissible if it would defeat claims arising after the period of contestability has passed).[10] Other parts of the opinion seem to distinguish between a provision that is a "limitation of coverage" and a provision "for a forfeiture" in the sense that it denies all recovery, not even providing for return of premiums or surrender value.[11] On the whole, it would seem that the opinion is reasonably read as distinguishing between a provision declaring death from specified causes not to be covered (a permissible rider) and a provision declaring death under specified circumstances not to be covered, regardless of the cause (not a permissible rider). So interpreting Cardozo's opinion, Patterson cited it in support of his distinction between efficient and potential causes of loss — a key idea in his concept of warranty, which as drafter he later incorporated into the New York warranty statute.[12] If this interpretation were taken to be authoritative, the distinction between a coverage clause and a warranty under the New York warranty statute would be identical with the distinction, under the New York incontestability statute, between clauses that continue to be enforceable and those no longer enforceable after the period of contestability has passed. But it is debatable whether this standard for determining what kinds of clauses are

---

7. Perhaps the most striking example is the influence of Cardozo's opinion in Metropolitan Life Insurance Co. v. Conway, 252 N.Y. 449, 169 N.E. 642 (1930), an incontestability case, on the development of the New York warranty statute. See § 6.6(b)(2), above.

8. Id., 252 N.Y. 449, 169 N.E. 642 (1930).

9. Id., 252 N.Y. at p. 451, 169 N.E. at p. 642.

10. Id., 252 N.Y. at p. 452, 169 N.E. at p. 642.

11. Id., 252 N.Y. at p. 453, 169 N.E. at p. 643.

12. McKinney's New York Insurance Law § 150 (1966). See § 6.6(b)(2), above.

permissible under the incontestability statute remains authoritative today, if it ever was.

In Simpson v. Phoenix Mutual Life Insurance Company,[13] the suit of a beneficiary of a group life policy for death proceeds was challenged on the ground that her decedent was not eligible for membership in the employee group because he had not been employed for as much as thirty hours a week as required by the master policy. The decedent, a practicing attorney, was the assistant secretary of the group employer, a cemetery association, and devoted only a few days a month to the association's business. The opinion of the court, by Judge Keating, stated the question at issue to be:

> * * * whether employment, as defined in this group life insurance policy, is a condition of insurance or a limitation of the risk which the insurer contracted to underwrite. If employment is a condition the defense is now barred by the policy's incontestable clause.[14]

The court, recognizing a conflict among precedents from other jurisdictions,[15] classified the provision at issue as a condition, declaring:[16]

> In New York the incontestable clause is viewed normally with reference to the manner of death. Risks which are considered limitations are those which could not be ascertained by the insurer by investigation at the time the policy of insurance was issued. * * * If the additional risk to the insurer of issuing a policy to a particular applicant could have been discovered at the time the contract was entered into, the insurer is precluded from raising this fact as a defense after the period provided for in the incontestable clause has elapsed. It is only those risks which could not be ascertained at the time of contracting which can properly be viewed as a limitation on the risk of insurance.

The reference, in the opening sentence of this latter passage, to "the manner of death" might suggest a distinction between efficient causes and potential causes — the same distinction that is suggested by part at least of the *Conway* opinion. But the next sentence speaks of a distinction turning on whether the risks could or "could not be ascertained by the insurer by investigation at the time the policy of insurance was issued," and the opening sentence of the next paragraph

---

13. 24 N.Y.2d 262, 247 N.E.2d 655, 299 N.Y.S.2d 835 (1969), reargument denied 25 N.Y.2d 959, 305 N.Y.S.2d 1027, 252 N.E.2d 864 (1969).

14. *Id.,* 24 N.Y.2d at p. 266, 247 N.E.2d at p. 657, 299 N.Y.S.2d at p. 838.

15. See, e.g., Fisher v. Prudential Insurance Company, 107 N.H. 101, 218 A.2d 62 (1966), 26 A.L.R.3d 625 (1969) (deceased was listed as a participant in group insurance plan and as an employee, and premiums were paid; in fact, she was never an employee; held, no coverage; incontestability clause does not apply to the insurer's defense that the risk is excluded from the definition of the hazards to be borne by the insurer).

16. 24 N.Y.2d at p. 267, 247 N.E.2d at pp. 657–658, 299 N.Y.S.2d at pp. 839–840.

emphasizes this test: "The hallmark of the distinction between conditions and limitations is discoverability." [17]

These leading New York opinions leave much room for debate about what grounds of defense or avoidance of liability constitute a contest, and much uncertainty exists in other jurisdictions as well.[18]

Compare the test of *Conway*, interpreted as suggested above (that is, as distinguishing between efficient-cause and potential-cause provisions), with the test of *Simpson* (distinguishing between discoverable and nondiscoverable matters) as applied to a provision stating that the insurer shall have no obligation, except for return of premiums, unless the applicant is in good health when the policy is delivered. Reliance on a defense that the applicant was not in good health would seem to be a prohibited contest under the suggested interpretation of *Conway*, since the clause invoked purports to afford a defense whether or not the pre-existing condition of health contributed to the death. That is, it purports to apply even if the applicant was killed in an accident wholly unrelated to his pre-existing bad health. Under the *Simpson* test of discoverability, on the other hand, it would seem that some conditions of health would be discoverable and other would not be, under any of the various meanings likely to be given to "good health." Thus, the *Simpson* test would seem to allow a defense based on the "good health" clause in some instances and to deny it in others.

It is usually held that an incontestability clause bars a defense that the policy never took effect because the insured was not in good health as required by an explicit policy provision.[19] This conclusion had been reached in New York [20] before *Simpson*. Whether *Simpson* has effected a change in this respect is open to debate.

A distinction might be drawn between a good-health clause, which purports to deny liability altogether except for return of premiums, and does so regardless of the cause of death, and a clause (more often found in disability or accident and health than in life policies) declaring that

---

17. 24 N.Y.2d at p. 267, 247 N.E.2d at p. 658, 299 N.Y.S.2d at p. 840.

18. See, e.g., First Pennsylvania Banking & Trust Company v. United States Life Insurance Company, 421 F.2d 959 (3d Cir. 1969) (applying Pennsylvania law).

Cf. Rall & Sfikas, *Group Insurance—Is the Incontestable Clause a Bootstrap Which Enlarges Coverage?* 5 Forum 51–57 (ABA Section Insurance, Negligence Compensation Law, 1969.) See also William F. Young, Jr., *"Incontestable"—As to what?,* 1964 University of Illinois Law Forum 323–341.

An analysis of the array of precedents appears in Bonitz v. Travelers Ins. Co., 374 Mass. 327, 372 N.E.2d 254 (1978).

19. E.g., McDaniel v. Insurance Company, 243 Or. 1, 410 P.2d 814 (Dept. 1, 1966).

See generally, 1A APPLEMAN, INSURANCE LAW (Revised edition, 1981), at § 333.

20. Allick v. Columbian Protective Association, 269 App.Div. 281, 55 N.Y.S.2d 438 (1st Dept., 1945). It might be argued that by holding the applicant to be in "good health" as that term is used in the policy unless he has a "discoverable" ailment the *Simpson* test can be reconciled with treating a defense based on the "good health" clause as a contest. Thus, even if he has cancer, but in such an early state of development that it is undetectable, he is in "good health." But since *Simpson* speaks of conditions "discoverable" from the point of view of the insurer, this reconciliation depends on attributing a rather bizarre meaning to "good health."

there is no coverage for disability or death resulting from a disease existing at the time the policy was issued. Most jurisdictions, including New York, have permitted this defense after, as well as during, the period of contestability,[21] though some have held that it is precluded after the period of contestability has passed.[22] In line with precedents enforcing resulting-from-existing-disease clauses, it may be argued that a good-health clause, rather than being totally inoperative after the period of contestability, should be given the more limited effect of a resulting-from-existing-disease clause. That is, it may be argued that an incontestability statute, like a contribute-to-loss statute, should be construed to have the effect of converting a potential-cause-of-loss provision ("good health") into an actual-cause provision. Combining this idea with the time limit clearly expressed in incontestability statutes, one might say that an incontestability statute has the effect of rewriting a good-health clause in two ways to bring it within permissible bounds: first, by placing a time limit (the period of contestability) on its effectiveness as a potential-cause provision and, second, by changing it to an actual-cause provision thereafter. A weakness in the analogy is that contribute-to-loss statutes plainly declare that a potential-cause provision, rather than being stricken entirely from the contract, shall be given the more limited effect of an actual-cause provision. Incontestability statutes, on the other hand, say nothing of limited enforcement of the condemned provision except insofar as they express or imply that the provision is enforceable during the limited period of contestability. Perhaps it is more consistent with the legislative expression contained in incontestability statutes to hold that when the insurer attempts to take unfair advantage of the policyholder by inserting a prohibited clause in its policy, it should lose the benefit of that clause entirely. Moreover, *Simpson* casts doubt on the authority of the earlier precedent for enforcing resulting-from-existing-disease clauses. The rationale of *Simpson* would seem to bar the defense, after expiration of the period of contestability, in those cases in which the pre-existing disease was discoverable by the insurer at the time the policy was issued, even if the death or disability did thereafter result from it. Here too there is a counter-argument based on regulation of warranties. Patterson's concept of warranty, incorporated in the New York warranty statute, treats potential-cause provisions as coverage provisions rather than warranties when they are designed to serve a

---

21. E.g., Apter v. Home Life Insurance Company, 266 N.Y. 333, 194 N.E. 846, 98 A.L.R. 1281 (1935) (policy coverage was defined as extending to disability from "disease originating after the date on which" the policy became effective; held, incontestability clause bars the defense of fraud but not the defense that disease of tuberculosis originated before delivery of the policy).

Also see 1A APPLEMAN, INSURANCE LAW (Revised edition, 1981), at § 333.

22. E.g., Blackwell v. United Insurance Company, 231 S.C. 535, 99 S.E.2d 414 (1957) (incontestability statute read into policy with no incontestability clause; policy contained both a clause declaring no liability unless insured was in sound health on date of delivery and a clause denying liability, other than for refund of premiums, for death resulting from pre-existing disease; held, coverage for death from "heart trouble" despite pre-existing heart disease).

coverage function such as identifying the property that is insured.[23] Arguably provisions concerning "discoverable" conditions of health could likewise be treated as coverage provisions in exceptional cases. The *Simpson* opinion gives no hint of any such qualification, but perhaps the likelihood of its recognition is increased by the essentially fair nature of a resulting-from-existing-disease clause of which the policyholder has effective notice.

When a policy provides for the contingency of misstatement of age and stipulates what the rights of the parties shall be, ordinarily the enforcement of this stipulation is held not to be a contest prohibited by the incontestability clause.[24] Indeed, a clause stating that the amount payable shall be such as the premium paid would have purchased at the correct age may be enforced not on the theory of successful contest but on the theory of fulfillment of the contract itself. Although an action by an insurer for enforcement of such a clause has sometimes been referred to as an action for reformation [25] because it has the effect of substituting the correct age for the misstated age in the policy, it may be viewed instead merely as a proceeding seeking a declaration of rights under the contract as written.[26] That is, the contract itself makes plain an intention that the age adjustment clause override the stated age if the stated age is not correct.

For cases in which the result is merely a scaling down of benefits, as is common in life insurance contracts, this view produces a result difficult to challenge. But if the result is to deny benefits altogether, the counterargument that the attempted enforcement is in essence a contest is more disquieting. For example, suppose that a policy of disability insurance purchased by a sixty-year-old applicant incorrectly states his age as fifty-five and provides elsewhere that no benefits shall be due for a disability commencing before the inception of the policy or after the applicant has attained the age of sixty. To enforce the latter clause is to deny that any benefits could ever become due. Thus, the policy must have been obtained by fraud or mistake. Ordinarily an insurer's denial of liability because of the applicant's fraud is treated as a contest and must be brought within the short period allowed for contests under an incontestability clause. Surely the insurer is in no better position if the misstatement resulted instead from honest mistake. But may the insurer bypass this problem with the contention that its position is grounded not upon fraud or mistake in the statement of age but rather upon the overriding stipulation for correction of the stated age? It would seem reasonable to permit such a contention to prevail, subject to allowance of a suitable remedy for any reliance damage the insured may have suffered, absent fraud on his part. The rights the insured is seeking by opposing this contention are rights beyond any the insured would have been granted but for mistake, and

---

23. See § 6.6(b)(2), above.

24. E.g., New York Life Insurance Company v. Hollender, 38 Cal.2d 73, 237 P.2d 510 (1951).

25. *Id.*, 38 Cal.2d at p. 76, 237 P.2d at p. 512.

26. *Id.*, 38 Cal.2d at p. 84, 237 P.2d at p. 516.

the insured has no just ground for complaint if reliance damages are provided for and all that is denied is the windfall of a mistake. One might advance a similar argument about contests of all types based on fraud or mistake, but a distinction can reasonably be made. The incontestability statutes and clauses are aimed at protecting insureds and third party beneficiaries against stale claims of fraud or mistake, difficult to disprove. The problem of stale proof is not one of great consequence in the case of erroneous statement of age. Thus, although a policy clause declaring the contract unenforceable in case of fraud of the applicant cannot be permitted generally to bypass the incontestability clause since it would defeat the central objective of the clause, a different view may be taken of a policy clause providing specifically for correction of age in case of misstatement, whether by fraud or by honest error.

The reliance damages an insured not guilty of fraud should be permitted to recover in such cases would include, at the least, the return of premiums with interest. They might be higher upon proof, for example, that, if aware that this contract was worthless because of the clause denying benefits for disability commencing after age sixty, the insured would have obtained elsewhere a contract paying benefits for the disability he later suffered in fact.[27]

Although an action for enforcement of an age adjustment clause in life insurance is held not to be a contest, if a disability insurance case of the type last stated above were treated as a contest it would be necessary to face cases on a spectrum between these two. For example, what of cases in which a disability policy with the clause suggested above was taken at age fifty-five or at age fifty-nine, the age being understated five years (at fifty or fifty-four)? Enforcement of the age adjustment clause would afford coverage only for disability commencing after inception of the policy and before age sixty — in the latter illustration, a period of less than a year. Would coverage for a few days, or months, be enough to save the insurer's contention from classification as a contest? To answer this question one would find it necessary to draw a sharp line of distinction along a continuum of cases differing only in degree. Enforcing the stipulation for correction of age, but allowing an action for reliance damages as recommended above, has the advantage of avoiding this problem.

A similar solution may be appropriate in other cases to avoid arbitrarily drawing a bright line between cases different only in degree. Sometimes it happens that a policy incorrectly states the period of coverage or the amount of benefits due for the premium paid. For example, in one case the sum payable at age sixty-five under endowment provisions was stated to be $57,098.26, whereas the sum intended was $5,798.26. This was treated as a scrivener's error and the federal

27. Concerning detrimental reliance and reliance damages generally, see § 6.5, above.

court confronted with the issue concluded that both generally and in California particularly the precedents allow reformation to correct such an error, as against a contention that the action for reformation is a contest prohibited by the incontestability clause.[28] This result seems irreproachable when the discrepancy is so great as to negate any detrimental reliance by the insured. Even if the discrepancy is small enough that a claim of detrimental reliance is reasonable, it would seem proper to allow reformation of a scrivener's error [29] while also awarding reliance damages if any can be proved. Otherwise the insured or third-party beneficiaries would be receiving a pure windfall, well beyond the objectives of an incontestability statute or clause.

§ 6.6(e) Patterns of Treatment of Common Clauses

(1) Generally

Interpretation and use of the statutes and decisional precedents bearing on the area identified with the concepts of warranty and representation are hampered by the conflicting meanings given by different courts and legislatures to terms of art.

One way of cutting through the fog enshrouding this body of statutes and decisions is to separate and then analyze respectively the instances in which policy stipulations defeating protection were enforced without regard to materiality and the instances in which policy stipulations were declared unenforceable unless one or another among varied standards of materiality could be satisfied.

In the older law, stipulations designed to limit protection were usually referred to as either warranties or representations. The former were enforceable without regard to materiality; the latter, only upon a showing of materiality. Under modern statutes the terminology and the scope of the two categories have changed, but it continues to be true that a distinction is made between a kind of stipulation that is enforceable regardless of materiality (commonly called a coverage provision), and a kind of stipulation enforceable only upon a showing of materiality.[1] The latter category includes sub-types, one of which is often called warranty and another of which is often called representation. Thus one can classify by result to a considerable extent within the framework of terminology customarily used. It happens, however, that the meaning of common terms varies from state to state. For example,

28. Mutual Life Insurance Co. v. Simon, 151 F.Supp. 408 (S.D.N.Y.1957).

Concerning scrivener's errors generally, see Merriman, *Scrivener's Errors and the Mischief They May Cause,* 1969 ABA SECTION INSURANCE, NEGLIGENCE & COMPENSATION LAW PROCEEDINGS 166–188.

29. *But cf.* Richardson v. Travelers Insurance Company, 171 F.2d 699 (9th Cir. 1948), 7 A.L.R.2d 501 (1949) (forecasting California law; insurer by mistake issued a pension policy rather than the intended life insurance policy on a "uniform premium plan;" action for reformation twenty years later was held to be a contest prohibited by the incontestability clause).

For criticisms of *Richardson,* see 62 Harvard Law Review 890–891 (1949); 97 University of Pennsylvania Law Review 741–743 (1949).

§ 6.6(e)

1. See § 6.6(a) and § 6.6(b)(1), above.

states having statutes regulating warranties commonly rely on a contrast between warranty and coverage, but their definitions of the contrast differ.

It may be useful, then, to attempt another way of classifying—not by whether a stipulation is called a coverage provision, or a warranty, or a representation, but by what the nature of the stipulation is in some respect more closely related to what it attempts to do. Two jurisdictions both of which hold that coverage clauses are enforceable without regard to materiality and that warranties are enforceable only upon a showing of materiality may be achieving sharply different results because, for example, one says a typical chattel mortgage clause is a coverage provision and the other says it is a warranty.[2] Conversely, two jurisdictions whose theories and terminology stand in sharp contrast may be reaching essentially consistent results.

The purpose of this section is to make comparisons both on a theoretical plane and in terms of practical outcome in relation to some illustrative clauses and the results reached when their application is challenged.

(2) Clauses Concerning Physical Location

Many insurance policies contain clauses purporting to limit protection according to the physical location of property or of an event.

Sometimes such a clause concerns the customary physical location of property that is the subject of the insurance. For example, fire insurance policies have commonly identified a building by street address, then designating the personal property to be included in the subject matter of the contract as "contents" of the described building.[3] Automobile insurance policies commonly include a clause specifying a place of principal garaging.[4]

Sometimes a limiting clause concerns the place where an event occurs. For example, family automobile policies usually include the following clause:

> "This policy applies only to accidents, occurrences and loss during the policy period while the automobile is within the United States of America, its territories or possessions, or Canada, or is being transported between parts thereof."[5]

Policies on commercial vehicles often contain also a "radius" clause purporting to defeat liability because of use of the vehicle beyond the area marked by a radius of specified length from the place of principal garaging. Forms of such clauses have varied considerably.[6]

---

2. See § 6.6(b)(3) and note 28 thereto, above.

3. See Appendix A.

4. See Appendix H.

5. See Appendix H.

6. One example is a policy form containing two clauses as follows:

"In consideration of the premium at which the policy is written, it is agreed that the automobile or automobiles described in the policy will be used and operated entirely within a radius of 500 miles of the place where such automobile or automobiles as described in said policy are principally garaged."

Is insurance protection unavailable under such provisions as these when the automobile or personal property is outside the specified physical location?

If the clause in question is treated as a coverage clause, the insurer, by showing merely that the property was beyond the specified physical area, establishes a perfect defense against an insured responsible for the departure of the vehicle from the territory of coverage.[7] If the clause is treated as a warranty, the same result would have been reached under the common law,[8] but in a state having a statute that applies to the type of insurance in question and restricts the effectiveness of warranties [9] it is necessary that the insurer prove something more — usually that the "breach of warranty" (that is, the violation of the clause) increased the risk that the insurer agreed to cover by the terms of the policy.[10] If the clause is treated as a representation, also, such a showing is generally required to sustain an insurer's defense.[11]

The clause in a fire insurance policy stating that the personalty it covers consists of the "contents" of a building described by street address is commonly regarded as a coverage clause, noncompliance with which is a defense without proof of increased risk.[12] One might reasonably argue that such a clause concerns potential cause of loss in Patterson's terminology, but Patterson himself cites this as an example of a coverage clause, not a warranty.[13] This conclusion can be defended on the ground that it serves the special coverage function of identifying the goods that are the subject matter of the contract.

Each of the other physical location clauses among the illustrations above may also be said to be a "potential cause" as distinguished from an "actual cause" provision. As to each, the question arises whether it, too, will be treated as a coverage clause on the theory that it serves some special coverage function. The answers may vary not only among the different types of clauses but also among different jurisdictions.

"It is further agreed that the company shall not be liable for, nor will it pay any loss or claim whatsoever that results from any accident or loss occuring while the automobile or automobiles described in the policy are being operated outside of the radius of 500 miles of the place where such automobile or automobiles described in the policy are principally garaged."

See Wallace v. Virginia Surety Company, 80 Ga.App. 50 at p. 51, 55 S.E.2d 259 at p. 260 (1949).

7. See, e.g., Herzog v. National Am. Insurance Co., 2 Cal.3d 192, 84 Cal.Rptr. 705, 465 P.2d 841 (1970) (homeowners policy provision excluding automobile accidents "while away from the premises or the ways adjoining" defeated coverage for insured son's operation of nonowned motor bike on freeway several miles from home; reasona-ble expectations of parties did not encompass such extended coverage; distinguishes an earlier case but nevertheless says "to the extent it is inconsistent herewith" it is overruled). However, the defense may not be valid against a lienholder who is independently an insured under a "loss payable" clause of the standard mortgage type. See notes 23–25 and associated text below.

8. See § 5.6 above.

9. See § 6.6(b), above.

10. See § 6.6(c), above.

11. See § 5.7, § 6.5(c)(1) and § 6.6(c)(2), above.

12. See § 6.6(b)(2), above.

13. See Patterson, ESSENTIALS OF INSURANCE LAW (Second edition, 1957), at pp. 296–297.

Patterson appears to have regarded the clause concerning place of principal garaging as a warranty.[14] Certainly it concerns potential cause of loss rather than actual cause, and it seems unlikely that it will be treated as a coverage provision in states where its classification as a warranty would invoke a requirement that violation be material. If the actual place of principal garaging was a lower rated territory than the stated place, it would be difficult at best for the insurer to show that the violation was material. It is arguable, however, that the provision is neither a coverage provision nor a warranty but merely a representation.[15] The typical provision appears under the heading "Declarations," a term more suggestive of representation than warranty.

It is clear that a clause stating the place of garaging can be a warranty — a continuing condition of liability — if that intention is expressed. It is also clear that it can be merely a representation as to the present place of garaging, if that intention is expressed. The current use of the term "declarations" and the omission of the term "warranty" point to the conclusion that this is a representation only. But in New York, where promissory representations are not recognized,[16] the use of the words "will be" in reference to the place of garaging suggests that the provision is a warranty.

If the provision is a representation of an existing fact or an affirmative warranty of that fact, the insurer cannot establish a defense by showing merely a change in the place of garaging during the policy period.

The place-of-garaging declaration might also be treated as a representation of an existing state of mind — intention that the automobile continue to be garaged at that location during the entire policy period.[17] A change in place of garaging incident to a change of intention thereafter would not be a defense, but proof that the insured did not have the intention stated at the time of the application would be a defense, if the requirement of materiality were met.

14. *Id.*, at p. 290, pp. 297–299, and p. 404.

15. *Cf.* Allstate Insurance Co. v. Stinger, 400 Pa. 533, 163 A.2d 74 (1960) (insured had license suspended because of mental illness within two-year period to which an answer on his application related; held, no defense, without proof of bad faith and materiality; dictum that declarations of automobile policy are representations, not warranties).

16. McKinney's New York Insurance Law 149(1) (1966) defines a representation as "a statement as to past or present fact."

Also see Patterson, ESSENTIALS OF INSURANCE LAW (Second edition, 1957), at pp. 297–299.

17. Compare the question as to the nature, under the New York statutes, of a statement concerning the future (e.g., concerning expected travel in a foreign country or expected aviation activity) appearing in an application for life insurance. It is not a warranty since it is a statement made by the applicant for the insurance. McKinney's New York Insurance Law § 142(3) (1966). It is not a representation, except insofar as it impliedly represents the existing intention of the applicant, since it is not otherwise a "statement as to past or present fact." McKinney's New York Insurance Law § 149 (1966). The conclusion is that it is a nullity, except insofar as it is a representation of existing intention.

A policyholder of a policy having a radius clause who takes the automobile to a higher-rate territory beyond the specified radius and keeps it there [18] may be violating the principal-place-of-garaging clause as well as the radius clause.[19] In any event, in such a case there is ordinarily no occasion for determining whether the radius clause is a warranty or a coverage provision since materiality of the violation is so clear.[20] If, on the other hand, the policyholder takes the vehicle to a lower-rate territory, difficult questions are presented. What are the risks the radius clause is directed against? Long trips, with added expense of the vehicle and fatigue of the driver, are surely within the relevant risks. But are short trips, starting and ending beyond the area of the radius, also within the risks sought to be precluded? Also, in determining whether the violation increased risk, could one take into account, as an offset against the increased risk from a long trip beyond the radius, that the area to which the policyholder drove was a low-rate territory and that the vehicle was kept there for a long time? These are questions on which there is little authority.[21] Another source of uncertainty is that even if a radius clause is carefully drafted to avoid the use of language suggestive of warranty, the question whether it will be treated as a warranty or instead as a coverage provision, when classification makes a difference, is debatable and unsettled. The probability of its being treated as a warranty is, no doubt, greatly increased if the language of the radius clause includes the term "warranty" or some derivative.[22]

The clause of the automobile policy purporting to deny coverage for accidents occurring while the automobile is outside the United States and Canada is a "potential cause" provision in Patterson's terminology, but it might be argued that it, like the "contents" location clause of the fire insurance policy, serves a coverage function,[23] and especially so

---

18. See, e.g., Indiana Rolling Mill Baling Corp. v. National Auto. & Casualty Insurance Co., 240 F.2d 74 (7th Cir.1957).

19. But compare the argument that the declaration of principal place of garaging is merely a representation of intention. See this section of the text at note 17 above.

20. With respect to possible qualification of this assertion because of uncertainties about the meaning of "materiality" or of such cognate concepts as "increase of risk," see § 6.6(c)(2), above.

21. See § 6.6(c)(2), above.

22. E.g.: "It is warranted by the insured that no regular or frequent trips * * * will be made * * * to any location beyond a 50-mile radius from the limits of the city or town of principal garaging of said vehicle." This phrase appeared in the policy before the court in Indiana Rolling Mill Baling Corp. v. National Automobile & Casualty Insurance Co., 240 F.2d 74 at p. 75 (7th Cir.1957).

23. Cf. Herzog v. National American Insurance Co., 2 Cal.3d 192, 84 Cal.Rptr. 705, 465 P.2d 841 (1970) (homeowners policy provisions excluding automobile accidents "while away from the premises or the ways adjoining" defeated coverage for insured son's operation of nonowned motor bike on freeway several miles from home; reasonable expectations of parties did not encompass such extended coverage; distinguishes an earlier case but nevertheless says "to the extent it is inconsistent herewith" it is overruled). In another case, cited below, an argument that the "United States and Canada" clause was a coverage clause in contrast with a "condition" failed. But the insurer was advancing the contention to defeat a lienholder, and the court's result can be justified on the ground that even coverage provisions may be modified by a "loss payable" clause that expressly or impliedly grants such independent protection to the loss payee. Southwestern Funding Corp. v. Motors Insurance Corp., 59 Cal.2d

since the geographical area in which the car is operated may be of central importance because of the different legal, social, and economic circumstances encountered outside the permitted territory.

The territorial clause of the automobile physical damage coverage serves to illustrate another possible consequence of distinguishing between coverage and warranty. If the clause is a warranty, the mortgagee has a strong argument that the mortgagor's taking the car beyond the permitted territory falls within the concept of "an act or neglect of the mortgagor" that does not bar the mortgagee's claim.[24] The mortgagee's position is arguably weaker if the clause is classified as a coverage provision, but there is nevertheless some support for the mortgagee's recovery.[25]

(3) Moral Hazard Clauses

Before 1943, fire insurance policies customarily contained "moral hazard" clauses declaring the policy to be void in specified circumstances unless otherwise provided in writing added to the policy. Among the specified circumstances were the following: if the insured was not unconditional and sole owner of the property that was the subject of insurance; if the subject of insurance was a building on ground not owned by the insured in fee simple; if, with the insured's knowledge, foreclosure proceedings were commenced; if any change in interest, title, or possession occurred except by death of an insured or by change of occupants without increase of hazard; if the policy was assigned before loss.[26] Also, there were additional clauses that, under the fairest of the forms then in use, suspended coverage for the duration of noncompliance with specified conditions rather than declaring the policy void. Among these were conditions concerned with other moral hazards in addition to those named above.[27] In the case of Pollock v. Connecticut Fire Insurance Company,[28] involving a claim for loss from lightning, the insurer successfully defended on the ground that the insured was not the unconditional and sole owner of the dwelling that was purportedly insured, since it was owned by the insured and his wife as joint tenants. Professor Goble conducted a survey in Champaign and Urbana, Illinois, shortly after *Pollock* was decided, and found that approximately 28 per cent of the fire insurance policies examined were policies naming only one insured though that person was not the sole owner.[29] Even more policies were potentially

---

91, 28 Cal.Rptr. 161, 378 P.2d 361 (1963) ("loss payable" clause extending coverage to lienholder despite policyholder's violation of "terms and conditions" of policy; insurer liable to lienholder for damage to vehicle sustained in Mexico, despite provision that coverage applied only to accidents in the U.S. and Canada; reasoned on grounds of resolving ambiguities against the company).

24. See § 4.2(b), above.

25. See, e.g., Southwestern Funding Corp. v. Motors Insurance Corp., note 23, above.

26. Goble, *The Moral Hazard Clauses of the Standard Fire Insurance Policy*, 37 Columbia Law Review 401–428 at p. 415 (1937).

27. *Id.*, at p. 414.

28. 362 Ill. 313, 199 N.E. 816 (1936).

29. Goble, *The Moral Hazard Clauses of the Standard Fire Insurance Policy*, 37 Co-

unenforceable, of course, in view of the effect of other moral hazard clauses.

The 1943 New York Standard Fire Insurance Policy form omits all "moral hazard" clauses previously in use, except that it provides for attachment of an endorsement imposing restrictions concerning other insurance. Automobile policies, also, now contain fewer moral hazard provisions than were formerly in common use.[30]

In the absence of relevant statutory provisions, encumbrance clauses are generally enforced, and recovery is denied upon proof of violation of such a clause without regard to materiality and prejudice.[31] In Texas there is a statute, befittingly distinctive, directed specifically against an encumbrance clause.[32] And statutes of wider application to representations and warranties have sometimes been held applicable to encumbrance clauses,[33] though other courts have held such statutes inapplicable either on the questionable theory that the encumbrance clause is an enforceable "condition" or "coverage" provision [34] or on the still more dubious theory that these regulatory statutes do not apply to moral hazard clauses.[35]

It might be argued that the omission of the moral hazard clauses from the 1943 revision of the fire insurance policy form implies that they are not to be conditions of liability any longer. But since increase of risk in fact may be a good defense under the increase-of-hazard clause, the circumstances that formerly would have invoked a moral hazard clause may still be a defense on the independent basis of the increase-of-hazard clause.[36] This is entirely harmonious with the deletion of moral hazard clauses since the evil aimed at was that they operated to defeat liability in many situations in which there was in fact no increase of risk as a result of the violation.

lumbia Law Review 410–428 at p. 418 (1937).

30. See Appendix H.

31. E.g., Globe & Rutgers Fire Insurance Company v. Segler, 44 So.2d 658 (Fla. 1950), 16 A.L.R.2d 731 (1951) (automobile insurance).

32. Vernon's Annotated Texas Statutes Insurance Code, art. 5.37 (1963).

33. E.g., Davidson v. American Central Insurance Company, 80 N.H. 552, 119 A. 707 (1923).

34. E.g., Moe v. Allemannia Fire Insurance Company, 209 Wis. 526, 244 N.W. 593 (1932), discussed in § 6.6(b)(3) notes 28, 29, above.

35. See Hawkins v. New York Life Insurance Co., 176 Kan. 24, 269 P.2d 389 (1954), overruling earlier decisions that

had interpreted a contribute-to-loss statute on life insurance as being inapplicable to "moral risk."

36. *Cf.* Nemojeski v. Bubolz Mutual Town Fire Insurance Co., 271 Wis. 561, 74 N.W.2d 196 (1956), 56 A.L.R.2d 419 (1957). The increase-of-hazard clause would be classified as a warranty under the New York statutes. See § 6.5(b)(2), above. But the classification would be immaterial to the result in most instances, since proof of the violation would also meet the restrictive requirements of the statute, unless it was a contribute-to-the-loss statute. The classification might make a difference, however, if the suit was brought by a mortgagee, claiming that under the standard mortgagee clause he should not be barred by any act or neglect of the mortgagor.

(4) Good Health; Medical Treatment; Pre-existing Disease

Life insurance policies (especially those of relatively low amount, including policies of industrial life insurance) [37] and health and accident policies often contain a clause declaring that the insurer shall have no obligation, other than to return premiums, unless the applicant is in good health on a specified date (ordinarily either the date of issue or the date of delivery of the policy).

A defense based on such a good-health clause is generally held to be a prohibited contest under incontestability clauses.[38] Within the period of permitted contestability, may a further challenge to the defense based on a statute regulating warranties be successful? Under the test of the New York warranty statute,[39] a good-health clause is surely a warranty rather than a coverage clause, since it concerns potential cause rather than actual cause of death or disability and is not likely to be treated as one of those exceptional potential-cause provisions that serve some coverage function. But it is nevertheless plainly effective as a defense since the statutory requirement of materiality is so clearly satisfied. It is unclear whether a good-health clause will be characterized as a warranty under warranty-representation statutes of other states or instead as a coverage provision free of the regulatory effect of such statutes. In most cases, however, this is not likely to be a significant question since good health is material to the risk. In any event there is less doubt about results than about applicable theories; noncompliance with the good-health clause is usually recognized as an effective ground of defense when not barred by an incontestability clause or statute.[40] If, however, a statute requires that a breach of warranty contribute to the loss in order to be an effective defense, then in those cases in which death or disability resulted from other causes and not from the pre-existing ill health the defense would prevail if the clause were classified as a coverage provision but would fail if it were classified as a warranty.

A good-health clause, though not adversely affected by a statute regulating warranties, may be subjected to regulation also by restrictive judicial interpretation. For example, there is some support for construing "good health" in a sense that classifies an applicant as being in good health as long as the applicant in good faith so believes, even though others (such as a physician and family) may know the applicant is incurably ill.[41] Also, when the company requires a physical examina-

---

37. See § 1.5(c), above.

38. See § 6.6(d), above.

39. See § 6.6(b)(2), above.

40. E.g., Great National Life Insurance Company v. Hulme, 134 Tex. 539, 136 S.W.2d 602 (1940).

Also see 1 APPLEMAN, INSURANCE LAW (Revised edition, 1981), at § 151.

41. See, e.g., Harte v. United Benefit Life Insurance Co., 66 Cal.2d 148, 56 Cal.

Rptr. 889, 424 P.2d 329 (1967) (application clause declaring no liability until policy delivered while applicant "in good health and free from injury"; "good health" interpreted from point of view of applicant's understanding and not from point of view of then unknown facts or from point of view of what treating physician or members of the family knew; recovery allowed if applicant believed in good faith that his health had not materially changed be-

tion even though there is a good-health clause in the policy, perhaps the principal significance of the clause, as commonly construed, is to defeat recovery in case of an adverse change in the applicant's health between the date of the examination and the date of delivery of the policy.[42]

In some instances application forms contain a stipulation that the contract shall take effect only upon payment of the premium and delivery of the policy and only if the applicant has not consulted or been examined or treated by a physician after the completion of the medical examination in connection with the application. Under such a clause it has been held that the insurer may defend on the ground of intervening visits to a physician without regard to the seriousness or triviality of the applicant's ailment.[43] But it would seem that a somewhat different result should be reached under a warranty statute like that of New York, since this is plainly a potential-cause provision and is not likely to be treated as one of those exceptional potential-cause provisions that serve some coverage function.[44] As a warranty, it would be subject to the materiality requirement of the statute. Whether this clause would be classified as a warranty under the statutes of other states, or instead as a coverage clause free of the materiality requirement, is more doubtful.[45]

Often in health and accident policies and less often in life policies there is a provision declaring that the insurer shall not be liable for death or disability resulting from a disease existing on the date the policy becomes effective. Most courts have permitted defenses under this clause even after termination of the period when contests are permitted under an incontestability clause.[46] And such clauses fare well also under statutes regulating warranties and representations. Under the New York warranty statute this would seem to be a coverage clause since it concerns actual cause of the claimed loss. And it seems likely that it will be regarded as a coverage clause under the warranty-representation statutes of other states as well.[47] Moreover, even if the clause is treated as a warranty, it is an effective basis for a defense since by proving its applicability to a claim the insurer is also proving that the breach contributed to the claimed loss.

tween the time of application and delivery).

Also see § 5.7 and § 5.8, above, concerning defenses based on representation or concealment as distinguished from a good health clause.

42. See, e.g., Bronx Savings Bank v. Weigandt, 1 N.Y.2d 545, 154 N.Y.S.2d 878, 136 N.E.2d 848 (1956), 60 A.L.R.2d 1422 (1958).

43. E.g., Girouard v. John Hancock Mutual Life Insurance Co., 98 R.I. 1, 199 A.2d 307 (1964). The defense was raised early enough that incontestability was not an

issue. It would seem that a defense based on this clause should be classified as a prohibited contest in states where a defense under the good-health clause is so treated, but this issue is debatable.

44. See generally § 6.6(b)(2), above.

45. See generally § 6.6(b)(3), above.

46. See § 6.5(d), above.

But cf. Young, *"Incontestable"—As to what?* 1964 University of Illinois Law Forum 323–341 at pp. 326–329.

47. See generally § 6.6(b)(3), above.

§ 6.7 Avoiding or Limiting Claims for Variance

§ 6.7(a) Reservation-of-Rights Notices and Nonwaiver Agreements

(1) Introductory Note

Insurers frequently attempt to avoid or defeat a claim of rights at variance with policy provisions either by sending the insured a reservation-of-rights notice or by proposing a nonwaiver agreement.

A reservation-of-rights notice is a declaration by an insurer — delivered to an insured, to another potential claimant, or to both — stating, in effect, that the insurer reserves its rights to contest liability. It is a statement by the insurer that even though the insurer undertakes an investigation of the events related to a loss that may be covered by an insurance policy and may take other actions in relation to the matter, the insurer does not intend to give up its right to contest liability under the coverage. The notice is a unilateral act by the insurer, and does not contemplate that there will be either an explicit acquiescence or any other response by the recipient.

A nonwaiver agreement, which is also designed to protect or preserve the insurer's right to contest liability, differs from a reservation-of-rights notice in that the recipient is asked to agree that the insurer's investigating or undertaking the defense of a claim against the insured will not preclude a subsequent denial of liability by the insurer — that is, it is a contractual agreement.

(2) Reservation-of-Rights Notices

Insurers generally use reservation-of-rights notices to preclude inferences that might otherwise be drawn by an insured (or by a court) from the conduct of the insurer. For example, a liability insurer — as a result of engaging in a thorough and extended investigation of the facts bearing on potential liability of its insured for an injury sustained by another person — may acquire information relevant to the assertion of a coverage defense. In some circumstances, the insurer's conduct after acquiring such information might be viewed as implying an acknowledgment that the insured will be provided coverage despite the possible coverage defense. When a reservation-of-rights notice is delivered promptly after the insurer acquires information of the potential defense *and* as a consequence of that discovery, it is designed to negate such an inference. The statement is intended as notification to the insured that the insurer has not voluntarily relinquished the right to subsequently assert a coverage defense.

The effectiveness of a reservation-of-rights notice may be significantly limited because it is a unilateral declaration by the insurer. Moreover, when a reservation-of-rights notice does not disclose the reason(s) for the insurer's action, its potential for protecting the insurer is even more likely to be circumscribed. And, if such a notice is essentially sent as a routine matter by an insurer in the course of undertaking the investigation of a claim or the defense of an insured, it is reasonably viewed as little more than another piece of paper.

When an insurer sends a reservation-of-rights notice, thereafter an insured may not be justified in relying solely upon an insurer's investigation of the matter — that is, following receipt of such a notice, an insured may need to employ an attorney or investigator, even though complete reliance on the insurer to provide these services would have been reasonable if the reservation-of-rights notice had not been delivered.[1] On the other hand, an insured's decision — following receipt of a notice — not to employ an independent investigator or attorney in such a situation may still be justified on the ground that two simultaneous investigations on the insured's behalf would interfere with each other or would create adverse reactions among witnesses whose cooperation may be needed at trial. When there are good reasons why an insured should be reluctant either to duplicate the tasks that are being pursued by the insurer or to request that the insurer suspend its activities, the import of the insurer's declaration on how an insured should proceed to protect his or her interests is not clearly evident. Consequently, even when an insurer has made clear the intent to preserve all rights to contest coverage, the pragmatic implication of the circumstances may provide grounds for recognizing that the rights of the insured should be at variance with both this intent and with the insurance policy provisions on which the insurer's defense would be based.

(3) Nonwaiver Agreements

When an insurer proposes a nonwaiver agreement, generally the insured is asked to agree that in return for the insurer's incurring the costs of investigation and defense the insured will either (1) give up certain rights (often including rights that might be at variance with policy provisions) or (2) acknowledge that the insurer's participation will not serve to waive the insurer's right to assert a coverage defense.[2] The agreement establishes an accord between the insured and insurer in regard to some matters which might otherwise be disputed as a consequence of the insured's claim for indemnification from the insurer. A nonwaiver agreement is a consensual transaction, and consequently is of significantly greater import than a reservation-of-rights notice — that is, a court is more likely to hold that an insured was

---

§ 6.7(a)

1. *Cf.* Salonen v. Paanenen, 320 Mass. 568 at pp. 573–574, 71 N.E.2d 227 at pp. 231–232 (1947) (when insurer seasonably notifies insured that it is continuing to defend under reservation of rights, insured is not misled and the basis for estoppel is lacking; insured can take protective steps, such as assuming control of defense; dictum that insured is entitled to assume control of defense if the insured so demands after receiving reservation notice).

For a different view concerning the insured's assertion of a right to assume control of the defense, at least in circumstances of conflict of interest between the insurer and the insured, see § 7.6, below.

2. The insurer is typically obligated to provide an insured a defense under liability coverage. See the discussion in § 9.1, below.

bound by an agreement that the insurer's continuing to investigate does not preclude a later assertion of the coverage defense than to reach that result as a consequence of a notice to the same effect from an insurer.

There are several ways in which use of the term "nonwaiver agreement" may be somewhat misleading. First, it may seem to imply that the agreement is intended to defeat only claims involving a voluntary relinquishment of a known right. If nonwaiver agreements were restricted to the intentional and voluntary relinquishment of known rights, they would have little impact because such a waiver of rights by an insurer is seldom provable. The nonwaiver agreement is usually intended by insurers to preclude other assertions of rights at variance with policy provisions, as well as assertions of waiver in the strict sense. For example, such agreements are designed by insurers to foreclose the possibility that an insured would be able to successfully base a claim on a theory of either estoppel or election.

The term "nonwaiver" can also be misleading in regard to effects on the insurer's rights which result from the very act of entering into such an agreement with an insured. The nonwaiver agreement itself may constitute a "waiver," and the terminology should not be understood as precluding this possibility. In Milwaukee Insurance Co. v. Kogen,[3] for example, a nonwaiver agreement was dated five days after the insured submitted a proof of loss. The insurer subsequently asserted that the insured's demand for an appraisal, made seventeen days after the proof of loss, was too late under a policy provision requiring notice of the demand within fifteen days. The court held that the insured's demand was timely, based on the reasoning that the nonwaiver agreement suspended the running of the fifteen-day period until there was a definite failure of the parties to agree on the amount of the loss.[4] Thus, a nonwaiver agreement may result in the insurer's loss of rights provided for in an insurance policy provision.[5]

(4) Claims of Variance From a Nonwaiver Agreement or a Reservation-of-Rights Notice

A nonwaiver agreement or a reservation-of-rights notice may fail to confer on an insurer the protection sought. In some circumstances, an insured may successfully urge that rights should be at variance with the terms set forth in such a document — that is, the principles of

---

3. Milwaukee Insurance Company v. Kogen, 240 F.2d 613 (8th Cir.1957) (forecasting Minnesota law).

4. *Ibid.*

5. The loss of the insurer's right to insist on compliance with the fifteen-day limit in the *Kogen* case probably was not a waiver in the strict sense of its being a voluntary relinquishment of a known right by the insurer. A nonwaiver agreement is a contract, and as such it is subject to an objective standard of interpretation. Thus,

in the *Kogen* case, proof that the agent representing the insurer in making the nonwaiver agreement intended that the fifteen-day limit for an appraisal demand should remain in effect would not save the insurer's coverage defense based on the tardiness of the demand; by the objective standard of interpretation, the nonwaiver agreement manifested an understanding that the right to demand an appraisal, among others, would be preserved.

disallowing unconscionable advantage and honoring reasonable expectations may be applied to protect an insured from the effects of either a nonwaiver agreement or a reservation-of-rights notice.[6] Furthermore, it is also possible that the conduct of an insurer's agents will induce detrimental reliance which supports rights at variance with the terms of a nonwaiver agreement or a reservation-of-rights notice. In short, just as there may be grounds for rights at variance with policy provisions, so too there may be grounds for rights at variance with either nonwaiver agreements or reservation-of-rights notices.[7]

§ 6.7(b)　"Coverage Provisions" as a Limitation on Variance Claims

(1) Classifying an Insurance Policy Term as a "Coverage Provision"

There is a theory, usually referred to as the doctrine of disallowing variance from "coverage provisions," that certain types of insurance policy terms should be considered to be so important that such terms should be beyond the reach of either some or all of the reasons that justify rights at variance with policy provisions. Some judicial precedents support the proposition that certain types of contractual stipulations are beyond the reach of doctrines such as waiver and estoppel because they are the heart or essence of the contract.[1]

6. Cf. Transamerica Insurance Group v. Beem, 652 F.2d 663 at p. 666 (6th Cir.1981) (applying Tennessee law), in which the court observed that "the reservation of rights or non-waiver notice given by the insurance company 'will be sufficient only if it fairly informs the insured of the insurer's position.'" (Quoting from the Annotation, 38 A.L.R.2d 1148 at p. 1167.)

Cf. Bogle v. Conway, 199 Kan. 707, 433 P.2d 407 (1967) (insurer precluded from asserting exclusion of racing accidents; nonwaiver agreement ineffectual because of presumed prejudice from want of full notice to the insured concerning the claimed defense).

With respect to possible limitations of various defenses and of the effectiveness of nonwaiver agreements and reservation-of-rights notices because of conflict-of-interest relationships, also see § 7.6, below. Concerning the effect of a demand by the insurer that the insured execute a nonwaiver agreement relieving the insurer of the effect of its previous misconduct, see § 6.9(b), below.

7. Cf. Allstate Insurance Co. v. Gross, 27 N.Y.2d 263, 317 N.Y.S.2d 309, 265 N.E.2d 736 (1970) (in declaratory action, liability insurer contended it was not required to decide to disclaim liability within any particular time, in absence of prejudice to an insured or an injured party,

though McKinney's New York Insurance Law § 167, subd. 8, requires "notice as soon as is reasonably possible of such disclaimer of liability"; shortly after insurer first received notice, it sent letter to insured stating that it reserved right to disclaim because of late notice of accident; almost seven months after letter of reservation insurer filed this declaratory proceeding for determination of its right to disclaim; insurer argued in Court of Appeals, seven years later, that it had not yet disclaimed but was seeking determination of its right to do so; held, insurer has obligation of prompt decision as well as prompt notice thereafter and right of disclaimer is defeated by unreasonable delay; statutory requirement is part of scheme for protection of New York's MVAIC as well as insured and injured persons).

Also see § 6.9, below.

§ 6.7(b)

1. See, e.g., Inland Mutual Insurance Company v. Hightower, 274 Ala. 52, 145 So.2d 422 (1962) (per curiam) (adjuster, while uncertain whether covered or noncovered trailer was involved in accident, told injured party to get best medical care possible and insurer would care for everything; held, on rehearing, for the insurer; coverage cannot be enlarged by waiver or estoppel); Summers v. Oakfield Town Mu-

In several states, statutes provide for the application of rules which disallow variance claims. For example, the New York warranty statute, which imposes limits on the use of some types of insurance policy provisions, explicitly exempts coverage provisions from its protection.[2] And the same distinction — that is, between unregulated coverage clauses and regulated defenses based on warranties, representations, or concealments — is implicit in other warranty statutes. A similar distinction is also made under incontestability statutes between coverage provisions and defenses which are precluded by such statutes.[3]

tual Fire Insurance Co., 245 Wis. 40, 13 N.W.2d 518 (1944).

Cf. Washington National Insurance Company v. Craddock, 130 Tex. 251, 109 S.W.2d 165 (1937), 113 A.L.R. 854 (1938). In *Craddock,* the court stated: "The question presented ∗ ∗ ∗ is whether a contractual liability may be created by a waiver. ∗ ∗ ∗ [The waiver] doctrine can not be made to serve that purpose." 130 Tex. at p. 253, 109 S.W.2d at p. 166. But it is plain that the voluntary relinquishment of a known right that is the essence of genuine waiver could not be proved in *Craddock.* Nor could the claimant prove detrimental reliance. The plaintiff's accident insurance policy stipulated that gunshot wounds were not within the class of injuries for which protection was given. After plaintiff accidentally shot himself through the leg with a pistol, he presented a claim and for eleven weeks received payments. The insurer then declined to make further payments, and plaintiff claimed that by making payments for eleven weeks the insurer waived the policy provision on gunshot wounds.

In *Summers,* supra, a town mutual company issued a fire insurance policy covering property while located in a described building in a specified town, but not elsewhere. By its charter the company's authorization to do business was limited to a specified territory. The insured moved his property to a town outside this territory and claimed coverage on the ground that with knowledge of his move the company continued to collect assessments. Perhaps the claimant did prove, or at least could have proved if required to do so, that the agent accepting the payments knew of the move and that the claimant detrimentally relied upon the representation of continued coverage implicit in accepting payments after the claimant had moved his property outside the company's authorized territory. In that case, however, *Summers* might still be explained on grounds other than immunity of coverage provisions from the doctrine of estoppel. Arguably the case turned on the distinctive geographical

limits of the company's power to insure. Perhaps the soundness of the result reached by the court is open to question, since there are better remedies than this for a company's ultra vires conduct.

Contra, e.g., Harr v. Allstate Insurance Company, 54 N.J. 287, 255 A.2d 208 (1969) (claim of estoppel to deny coverage under fire policy because of contrary representations of agent; in granting a new trial the court held the parol evidence rule inapplicable and rejected the assertion that estoppel does not apply to coverage provisions); State Automobile Casualty Underwriters v. Ruotsalainen, 81 S.D. 472, 136 N.W.2d 884 (1965) (waiver and estoppel available to expand coverage to trailer in view of assurances by insurer's agents); Farmers Mutual Automobile Insurance Co. v. Bechard, 80 S.D. 237, 122 N.W.2d 86 (1963), 1 A.L.R.3d 1124 (1965) (provision in death and disability coverage of automobile policy declaring no liability for "death sustained in the course of his occupation" while operating a "commercial" vehicle; deceased was operating the insured truck in the course of his work; held, insurer barred from asserting the defense because of representations he would be covered regardless of what he might be driving).

Also see Note, *Harr v. Allstate Insurance Company,* 15 Villanova Law Review 505–511 (1970).

The phrase "the heart, the very essence, of the contract" appears in the course of the court's statement of an unsuccessful defense raised in State Farm Fire Insurance Co. v. Rakes, 188 Va. 239 at p. 243, 49 S.E.2d 265 at p. 267 (1948), 4 A.L.R.2d 862 at p. 864 (1949).

2. New York—McKinney's Insurance Law § 150 et seq. (1966). Also see the discussion in § 6.6, above.

3. See, e.g., New York—McKinney's Insurance Law § 155 (1966); Simpson v. Phoenix Mutual Life Insurance Co., 24 N.Y.2d 262, 299 N.Y.S.2d 835, 247 N.E.2d 655 (1969).

Also see § 6.5(d), above.

(2) Justifications Urged by Insurers for Recognizing a Special Status for Coverage Provision Classifications

The proposition that certain types of insurance policy provisions should be exempted from variance claims has sometimes been justified on the grounds either (1) that this is essential to centralized control of underwriting or (2) that this is necessary to avoid undesirable differential treatment of insureds.

It is true that the cumulative effect of individual applications of doctrines which produce a variance from "coverage provisions" on the basis of the acts of the insurer's agents and employees may be a severe interference with centralized control over underwriting. And it has been suggested that recognizing a special status for some types of coverage provisions, such as warranty clauses, would protect against an excessive proliferation of such variance claims. It is also true that the application of variance theories to "coverage provisions" may produce exceptionally favored treatment for limited numbers of policyholders, giving some a far better bargain than others with the same class of coverage.[4] However, the types of coverage provisions insurers have sought to include within the scope of a special classification frequently have not involved any problem of equity among policyholders and have avoided frustrating underwriting decisions only to the extent that they were part of an unconscionable pattern.[5]

(3) Classification and Confusion

There is considerable confusion in regard to the significance to be accorded to the theory that some provisions in insurance policies should be "immune" from variance claims because they are classified as "coverage provisions." Courts, as well as writers, usually have not attempted to correlate either the definitions of a "coverage provision" set forth in different contexts or the results in cases with respect to whether various doctrines which courts have employed to justify "variance" (such as protection of reasonable expectations, requiring good faith, waiver, estoppel, election, etc.) apply only to "non-coverage" provisions or also apply to "coverage" provisions. In general, the characterization "coverage provision" — as well as each of the terms employed to describe provisions which are not so classified — is used in quite different senses by different courts, and sometimes by the same court in different contexts.[6]

---

4. This inequity is not eliminated (though it may be somewhat mitigated) by broader considerations of fairness, as when a knowledgeable policyholder benefits by an objectively reasonable construction of an onerous provision. For discussion of the knowledgeable policyholder, see § 6.3(c), above.

5. It might even be argued that courts should recognize a broader immunity from variance by waiver and estoppel than the immunity from another kind of variance

implicit in holding that coverage clauses are unaffected by statutory regulation of warranties. But immunity is not the only way, and probably is not the best way, of protecting against excessive proliferation of cases of variance. See Patterson, ESSENTIALS OF INSURANCE LAW (Second edition, 1957), at pp. 296–297.

Also see § 6.6(b)(2), above.

6. Also see the discussion of terminology in § 4.1 and § 5.1, above.

In disputes involving provisions relating to the location of insured property, it has been said in the great majority of decisions that such provisions are subject to waiver or estoppel, regardless of whether they are called "coverage" clauses in the applicable insurance policy.[7] Moreover, it has been stated that most courts distinguish an "estoppel to assert breach of warranty or condition" from an estoppel that would "prevent the insurance company from maintaining that certain risks are not covered by the policy."[8] In such decisions, and also in some judicial opinions construing incontestability statutes,[9] a condition is classified with a warranty in contrast with a coverage clause. Other courts, construing statutes regulating warranties, would classify a condition as a coverage provision.[10]

Confusion does not conclusively establish the existence of an undesirable substantive inconsistency. Furthermore, there are some justifications for not being overly concerned by at least some of the cases which might be viewed as reaching incompatible results. First, some differences may reflect no more than variations among jurisdictions, rather than variations according to what kind of regulatory measure is involved (such as a warranty statute, an incontestability statute, or some such judicial doctrine as waiver, estoppel, or election). Second, the contexts in which restrictions may be employed by insurers to gain an advantage differ materially. Thus, defenses based on warranty, representation, or concealment are primarily concerned with risks of overreaching by the use of shrewdly drafted policy provisions. The doctrines of waiver and detrimental reliance (or estoppel), as well as several additional theories often associated with these doctrines, apply most often to the conduct of agents of the insurer in relation to marketing. These different contexts may well call for legal controls that vary in reach, as well as in kind.

(4) Comment

It would be wiser to dispense with theories that purport to justify an immunity for specific types of insurance policy terms from variance claims. Although some terms in insurance policies undoubtedly are more directly related than others to achieving centralized control of underwriting and consistent treatment of different policyholders, courts can limit unreasonable or unjustified interference by simply adhering

---

7. See Annotation, *Waiver of, or estoppel to assert, provision of policy respecting location of personal property covered thereby,* 4 A.L.R.2d 868–913 at p. 871 (1949).

But see Annotation *Comment note: doctrine of estoppel or waiver as available to bring within coverage of insurance policy risks not covered by its terms or expressly excluded therefrom,* 1 A.L.R.3d 1139–1183 at p. 1770 (1965).

Also see § 6.8(c), below.

In the context of statutes regulating defenses based on warranties, Patterson classifies such a provision as a coverage clause rather than a warranty. Patterson, ESSENTIALS OF INSURANCE LAW (Second edition, 1957), at pp. 296–297. Also see § 6.6(b)(2), above.

8. Ivey v. United National Indemnity Co., 259 F.2d 205 at p. 207 (9th Cir.1958) (dictum) (applying California law).

9. See § 6.6(d), above [discussing *Simpson*].

10. See § 6.6(b)(3), above.

to sound requisites for an entitlement to variance. Similarly, the fear of insurers that there will be an inordinate number of successful nonmeritorious variance claims — which is urged as a justification for some immunities or exceptions — is easily exaggerated and also can be avoided by adherence to the doctrinal requisites that are now well developed and understood.

One factor that helps to control, or to at least mitigate, the risk to insurers of nonmeritorious variance claims is the liability of sales representatives to the insurers for representations beyond the scope of the sales representative's authority. Even if a policyholder chooses to proceed exclusively against the insurer in cases in which a variance claim results from acts of a sales representative, the increasingly widespread acquisition of errors and omissions liability coverage (a form of malpractice liability insurance) by sales representatives encourages recourse against these individuals by insurers that have been required to provide indemnification to insureds as a consequence of unauthorized actions of sales representatives. Furthermore, an insurer's rights against a sales representative, as well as its generally superior bargaining position, give it a significant degree of protection against abuses of power by agents and brokers, particularly against the deliberate actions of such individuals.

Another factor that certainly places a potentially significant constraint on the risk to insurers of nonmeritorious variance claims operates when detrimental reliance is clearly recognized as the basis for the claim. The risk of nonmeritorious claims is minimized if courts require the claimant to prove detrimental reliance. Claims of dubious merit often can be identified by imposing a requirement that the claimant must prove the detriment which resulted from reliance. However, the risks of injustice for insurers is not completely eliminated because there will almost certainly continue to be some instances when claims are supported by undetected fraudulent testimony or collusion.

Doctrines based on waiver, detrimental reliance, and estoppel are intended to protect against misleading oral representations by sales representatives. The results in such cases should not depend on the nature of the insurance policy provision that a representation contradicts. Misleading oral representations are no less possible in relation to provisions of central importance than in relation to less significant provisions.

Among the decisions denying claims of waiver or estoppel on the ground that "coverage provisions" were involved, it is difficult to find cases in which it does not seem likely that the claims could have been properly denied on other grounds. In most instances, denial might have rested on the claimant's failure to prove the requisites of genuine waiver, estoppel, election or reformation as they are commonly applied in other contexts. Cases not explainable on this basis may be distinguished on more specialized grounds.[11] The development of extensive regulation of policy forms demonstrates a recognition of needs for regulating provisions that are of the very essence of the contract. Although such regulation is frequently accomplished in a way that is consistent in theory with the enforcement of policy provisions, in substance it is often founded on the same principles that give rise to rights at variance with policy provisions. It is noteworthy, by way of analogy, that incontestability and warranty statutes exclude from their reach — thereby treating them as a distinctive type of provision — a number of common clauses with respect to which some legislatures have enacted regulatory statutes. Among these are life insurance policy provisions concerning death caused in a specified manner.[12]

As a practical matter, in light of agency and marketing practices in the industry, insurance cases undoubtedly will continue to warrant relatively frequent applications of doctrines such as waiver, estoppel, detrimental reliance, and election. All insurance policy provisions should be subject to carefully limited application of waiver and estoppel, as well as other doctrines such as election, reformation, and rescission. The need sensed by some courts to hold certain types of policy provisions beyond reach of waiver, detrimental reliance, and estoppel may be avoided if courts adhere to the general formulations of these doctrines rather than stretching them beyond their normal scope. When a rational application of such doctrines does not justify a variance claim, courts should candidly evaluate whether the principles of honoring reasonable expectations and disallowing unconscionable advantage constitute sufficiently compelling reasons in the specific situation for protecting the insured beyond the normal scope of waiver, detrimental reliance, estoppel, or election.

§ 6.8 Variance Claims Involving Incorrect Information in Insurance Applications, Tardy Premium Payments, or the Status of Insured Property

§ 6.8(a) Introductory Note

Variance claims have repeatedly been produced by (1) incidents in regard to incorrect information that is submitted to an insurer during the marketing process, (2) the events or relationship between an insurer and an insured in regard to premium payments, and (3) notice, or the lack thereof, from an insured to an insurer about the location or use of an insured property.[1] Unfortunately, there have been untenable extensions of the doctrines of waiver, election, or estoppel [2] in some of these cases when the facts warranted relief on other grounds.

---

11. See, e.g., the discussion of *Summers*, note 1, above.

12. See § 6.6(b)(2), above.

§ 6.8(a)

1. See generally the theories and principles presented in § 6.1, above.

2. See, e.g., Sanborn v. Maryland Casualty Company, 255 Iowa 1319, 125 N.W.2d 758 (1964) (oral agreement in 1956 for an-

In addition to the material in this section, there are discussions elsewhere in this text of the judicial recognition of rights at variance with policy provisions because of incidents occurring during the marketing process, including (1) rights based on unreasonable delay in processing an application for insurance,[3] (2) rights which are inconsistent with cancellation provisions,[4] and (3) rights against agents and other intermediaries, rather than against an insurer, based on occurrences during the marketing process.[5]

§ 6.8(b)　Erroneously Recorded Answers in an Application for Insurance

(1) Generally

When an application for insurance contains false answers, it often leads to the issue whether the insured or third party beneficiaries should be able to recover benefits upon proof that the applicant gave truthful answers that were incorrectly recorded by an intermediary (agent or broker) or a medical examiner.[1] Insurers have often defended claims in such cases on the theory that the applicant is responsible for whatever appears in the application. This defense is ordinarily supported by one or more of three arguments: (1) that the person recording

nual renewal of liability insurance policy; without request or application, renewal policies issued in 1957, 1958, and 1959; application signed for 1960 policy, but applicant testified he signed it in November, 1961, believing it was an application for renewal of plate glass insurance in the same company; accident occurred in October, 1961, four months after expiration of the last policy; defendant's Des Moines office had customarily sent ticklers to agent concerning policies about to expire, but could not find any record of such a tickler on this policy in 1961; oral "agreement for coverage and automatic renewal" enforced; estoppel applied.

Also see Dodge v. Aetna Casualty & Surety Co., 127 Vt. 409, 250 A.2d 742 (1969) (agent, having agreed to obtain all the insurance plaintiff needed for new venture added to his business, issued liability policy that excluded products hazard, which agent negligently thought to be included; policyholder, unfamiliar with insurance, relied on the agent; held, insurer estopped from taking advantage of the exclusion).

3. See § 2.4, above.

4. See § 5.11(c), above.

5. See § 2.5(c), above.

§ 6.8(b)

1. See, e.g., Pennsylvania Life Insurance Company v. McReynolds, 440 S.W.2d 275 (Kentucky 1969), discussed in Note, *Insurance: False Answers in an Application*, 57 Kentucky Law Journal 714–737 at pp. 732–735 (1969) (nonmedical accident and health policy; agent considered facts too inconsequential to be included in application; insurer must show applicant's bad faith to establish defense; dissent on ground this in effect overrules recent decisions based on a statute); John Hancock Mutual Life Insurance Co. v. Schwarzer, 354 Mass. 327, 237 N.E.2d 50 (1968), 26 A.L.R.3d 1 (1969) (hospital expense policy; answers recorded by soliciting agent).

Cf. Brasier v. Benefit Association of Railway Employees, 369 Mich. 166, 119 N.W.2d 639 (1963), 94 A.L.R.2d 1385 (1964) (health and accident insurance; answers recorded in report of medical examination); Hughes v. John Hancock Mutual Life Insurance Co., 351 Mich. 302, 88 N.W.2d 557 (1958) (life insurance; answers recorded in report of medical examination).

Also see Kelly v. Madison National Life Insurance Co., 37 Wis.2d 152, 154 N.W.2d 334 (1967) (life insurance; answers recorded in report of medical examination; jury findings that doctor and applicant did not collude).

Also see 17 Appleman, Insurance Law (1981), at § 9401.

the answers was, in doing so, acting as the applicant's agent and not as agent for the insurer; (2) that the applicant's opportunity to read the recorded answers before signing makes the applicant responsible for their content, even if the applicant failed to take advantage of that opportunity; and (3) if the application or a copy of it was attached to the policy (or otherwise delivered to the policyholder), that the opportunity to read the recorded answers at that subsequent time and to call the insurer's attention to any discrepancy makes the applicant responsible thereafter for the erroneous information provided to the insurer. The applicability and persuasiveness of the third theory is strengthened by invoking, when applicable, the provisions of an entire-contract statute requiring that the application be made a part of the policy and declaring that no agreement outside the insurance policy is binding.

Even though one or more of the propositions set forth in the preceding paragraph are supportive of an insurer's position in a coverage dispute, claimants often recover, at least in egregious instances, on grounds of rights at variance with policy provisions. The following subsections consider the doctrines which have been used to justify sustaining coverage for claimants.

(2) Erroneous Answers and Positive Representations by an Agent

In some of the cases the insured acknowledges the fact that an insurer has received incorrect information, but asserts either (1) that an intermediary falsely recorded the answers to questions in the application that was forwarded to the insurer or (2) that an intermediary (such as a sales representative) made positive representations to the applicant that the coverage would be provided. In such cases, an insured or a beneficiary often seeks to affirm the contract subject to a reformation to reflect the true facts. For example, a 17-year-old, newly-licensed applicant for automobile liability insurance was afforded protection under a policy even though the policy specifically stated that the insurance did not apply when the car was operated by any person — other than the individual who applied for the coverage whose stated age was 23 — licensed less than a year or by a person under the age of 25. Upon findings and conclusions (1) that the applicant acted in good faith, (2) that the false answers resulted from the agent's actions, (3) that the policy form was complex and confusing, (4) that the agent represented that liability coverage would be issued to the applicant, and (5) that the insurer was responsible for the agent's unconscionable conduct, the court allowed reformation on the theory of honest mistake of the applicant induced by unconscionable conduct of the insurer's agent. The court further observed that in the face of fraud or other unconscionable conduct of its agent, an insurer cannot successfully defend on the ground that the insured, exercising due care, would not have been defrauded.[2] The argument for reformation of an insurance

2. Heake v. Atlantic Casualty Insurance Co., 15 N.J. 475, 105 A.2d 526 (1954).

contract on behalf of an insured or a claimant is particularly compelling if the customary marketing practices for the insurance at issue permit an agent to bind an insurer rather than merely to act for it in taking applications.

It often happens that the statements by a sales representative, such as a comment that the insurer will issue a policy with stated terms, are promissory in character. In jurisdictions adhering to the preferable rule that an estoppel may be founded upon promissory representations, the estoppel theory may be employed to afford protection — especially in the event that the courts of that jurisdiction are reluctant about allowing reformation.[3]

Estoppel is in many respects more analogous to tort than contract, and consequently when an agent's representations are incidental to the agent's employment, an estoppel may result even though the representations went beyond the scope of the agent's actual authority and, at least in some instances, beyond the scope of apparent authority to contract for the insurer.[4] Even the fact that an agent acted fraudulently — to serve his or her own interests — in violation of the insurer's instructions would probably be insufficient to defeat either a claim of apparent authority on which reformation rests or a claim of a representation incidental to the employment by the insurer on which an estoppel would rest.

Ordinarily an insurer is not estopped to assert fraud in which the party claiming coverage participated. If, however, the insurer cannot prove that the claimant knew of the agent's fraudulent scheme, it is likely the insurer will be precluded from a defense based on the falsely recorded answers.

(3) Contributory Negligence as a Defense

Contributory negligence might be used by an insurer as a defense to a claim based on some positive representation of an agent. However, if actual fraud was the basis of the insured's claim for relief — under either a theory of reformation or a theory of estoppel — such a defense by an insurer would probably have little force.[5] Indeed, it would seem that contributory negligence should not bar relief against a false record that the agent knew to be different from the applicant's answers, even if the agent's motives were not such as to warrant the characterization "fraud" in its ordinary sense.

Someone applying for insurance ordinarily is not in a position of parity with a sales representative or a medical examiner with respect to understanding what is sought by the inquiries in an application for insurance and what is an appropriate way of expressing the response. This point has special force in relation to the rephrasing of an appli-

---

3. In some jurisdictions, especially under older precedents, an estoppel will only result when there is detrimental reliance on an agent's representations of *fact*.

4. See § 6.5(d), above.

5. See § 6.5(e), above.

cant's answers about medical history, especially when the answers are such as to require anything more than a description of physical facts or events within the applicant's knowledge at the time the inquiry is submitted to the applicant. Accordingly, in most situations this type of case is not appropriately analyzed in terms of negligence and contributory negligence.

If the evidence discloses complicity between the applicant and the agent, the agent's collusion ordinarily precludes imputing the agent's knowledge to the insurer.[6] On the other hand, an error in a policy resulting from mutual mistake is ordinarily a ground for reformation. Thus, for example, an insurance policy may be reformed to identify correctly the persons or interests insured.[7]

Most courts [8] would probably reach results consistent with the foregoing analysis, at least in the absence of an applicable entire-contract statute [9] or a contract provision that provides a defense.[10]

(4) Entire-Contract Statutes

Entire-contract statutes express an underlying public policy somewhat at odds with the view that carelessness in failing to read a contract should not bar relief based on a claim that the agent or medical

---

6. E.g., Southern Farm Bureau Casualty Insurance Company v. Allen, 388 F.2d 126 (5th Cir.1967) (applying Texas law) (after application for automobile insurance was rejected, paper title to car was transferred to brother and new application was filed and approved in brother's name, although original applicant continued to hold and use car; claim of widow of victim of negligent driving by original applicant; held, for insurer).

7. E.g., Gillis v. Sun Insurance Office, Ltd., 238 Cal.App.2d 408, 47 Cal.Rptr. 868 (1st Dist., Division 1, 1965), 25 A.L.R.3d 564 (1969) (corporation named as insured had ceased to exist because of a merger before policy was written; reformation to substitute surviving corporation as insured and to cover certain other interests as intended).

8. However, there are contrary decisions. See, e.g., Gillan v. Equitable Life Assurance Society, 143 Neb. 647, 10 N.W.2d 693, 148 A.L.R. 496 (1943):

"[W]e conclude that there is no sufficient reason in contracts of insurance why a party should be relieved from the duty of exercising the ordinary care and prudence that would be exacted in relation to other contracts."

The validity of their assumption about the rule applying to other contracts may be challenged. Note, for example, that under the rule of RESTATEMENT OF AGENCY, Second (1958), § 295A, Comment a, this would depend on whether the principal (the insurer)

"would be adversely affected by a delay in discovering the facts." Certainly there would be cases of such adverse effect, but whether *Gillan* was one is not clear. Moreover, for reasons developed in § 6.5(e), above, it seems preferable that the qualification set forth in the Restatement not be applied to insurance cases.

Gillan is interesting on another ground as well. It disapproved a contrary holding in German Insurance Co. v. Frederick, 57 Neb. 538, 77 N.W. 1106 (1899), but applied the old rule to the case at hand because the defense attorney (very likely in reliance on the precedent) had not objected to the parol evidence of the plaintiff that she gave correct answers to defendant's medical examiner and he inserted incorrect answers in the application. This seems hardly fair to the defendant insurer, or to defense counsel, unless there was special reason for limiting the overruling decision to prospective application—for example, because the plaintiff in the particular case detrimentally relied on the old rule or because insureds generally would have detrimentally relied on that rule (both of which possibilities seem rather unlikely). Concerning the relevance of reliance interests to prospective overruling, see generally Robert E. Keeton, VENTURING TO DO JUSTICE (1969), at pp. 41–43.

9. See the discussion in § 6.8(b)(4), below.

10. See the discussion in § 6.8(b)(5), below.

examiner knew the answers recorded to be different from those given orally by the applicant. One of the primary objectives of these statutes is to avoid uncertainties about an applicant's rights by giving the applicant access to a copy of the application, rather than permitting the insurer to hold it while also incorporating it by reference into the policy.

It is within the purpose of entire-contract statutes, as most courts construe them, to achieve greater certainty by disallowing an insured's contention that the insured was not aware of the record of what purports to be the insured's answers in an application attached to the policy. Thus, most courts hold that entire-contract statutes bind the insured by the record of the answers in an application, even though it may be an inaccurate record.[11] In many states, statutes of this type apply only to life or to life, health, and accident insurance.

(5) Contract Provisions as a Defense

When an insurer, in the absence of a statutory requirement, either attaches a copy of an application to an insurance policy or separately delivers a copy to the policyholder, a dispute between an insured and an insurer usually presents a difficult question for resolution.[12] Under a rule barring the policyholder's claim because of the resulting opportunity to read a copy of the application, there is a risk that some policyholders will be the victims of fraud by a dishonest agent. On the other hand, under a rule barring the policyholder's claim only on proof that the applicant had knowledge of the false answers, there is a risk of a substantial body of successful claims by dishonest policyholders. The former risk weighs less heavily and the latter more heavily in these circumstances than when no copy of the completed application is delivered to the policyholder.[13]

§ 6.8(c) Accepting Premiums Tendered Late or Otherwise Improperly

(1) Generally

Claims of rights at variance with policy provisions have sometimes been based on a showing that the insurer (or someone who is an actual or apparent agent of the insurer) received and exercised control over a

---

11. E.g., Minsker v. John Hancock Mutual Life Insurance Co., 254 N.Y. 333, 173 N.E. 4 (1930), 81 A.L.R. 829 (1932), which also calls attention to the fact that the New York decisional rule had been otherwise before the statute was enacted.

12. Some insurance contracts include a clause that states the policy shall not become effective unless at the time it is delivered the intended insured is in good health. In this type of situation, a court may hold that it is not the erroneous answers about the applicant's health at the time of the application which are at issue. Instead, no coverage exists because the applicant's bad health was such that the indi-

vidual was not in good health in conformity with this clause (condition). *Cf.* Great National Life Insurance Co. v. Hulme, 134 Tex. 539, 136 S.W.2d 602 (Tex.Comm.App., Section A, 1940), which involved an "entire contract" statute as well as a good health clause.

Regarding enforcement of good-health clauses generally, see § 6.6(e)(4), above.

13. There is some support for extending the rule of preclusion under entire-contract statutes to these circumstances as well. See, e.g., Odom v. Insurance Co. of the State of Pennsylvania, 455 S.W.2d 195 (Tex.1970).

premium payment in a way that would be inconsistent with the insurer's claim that no coverage existed.

Claims based on acceptance of a late payment are often presented even though the policy does not provide for revival or reinstatement of coverage, or does not provide for retroactive effect to cover a loss occurring before late payment. However, a claim that late payment revives the coverage under the terms of the policy itself is, at least in some sense, a claim within (rather than at variance) with policy provisions.[1]

If a casualty of the type insured against occurs after a policy has lapsed for nonpayment of a premium, an agent's acceptance of a premium with the understanding that the agent will tender it to the home office, but without any commitment that it will be accepted, is plainly insufficient, at least when it is standing alone, to support a claim of coverage at variance with the policy provisions. In considering what more is essential to justify sustaining a coverage claim in such circumstances, the analysis usually focuses on the doctrines of waiver and election.

(2) Waiver

A claim of waiver might be adequately established by evidence that the insurer had adopted a custom of conducting its operations on a grace-period basis without adding a grace-period clause to its policies.[2] Such a custom would be a voluntary extension of rights to insureds by the insurer analogous to those rights which exist as a result of an insurer's sending out endorsements providing for a grace period without added premium charge or by an insurer's publishing advertisements announcing that it was granting such an extension.[3]

When a late premium payment is received and processed at the home office of an insurer, a question may be presented as to whether the individuals at the home office who accepted the premium did so with full knowledge of the circumstances, including both the late tender and the intervening casualty. In order to establish that there

---

§ 6.8(c)

1. Life, health, and accident policies that contain a clause establishing a grace period within which premiums may be paid without loss of coverage do not present a rights at variance question so long as the payment is made (perhaps received) during the prescribed period. Under such a clause, it does not matter that a casualty has occurred before payment of the premium during the grace period. The claim is valid under the contract itself. The most common context in which this problem arises involves a defense of nonpayment or late tender of the premium.

Also see the discussion of termination of coverage for the nonpayment of premiums in § 5.11(b).

2. In the absence of evidence of such a custom, courts are unlikely to sustain claims for coverage.

Cf. Williams v. Prudential Insurance Company of America, 447 So.2d 685 (Ala. 1984) (acceptance of one late payment with a concurrent application for reinstatement of coverage did not establish a custom on the part of the insurer in regard to tardy payments).

Also see Brand v. Monumental Life Insurance Company, 275 Ind. 308, 417 N.E.2d 297 (1981).

3. See, e.g., advertisement of John Hancock Mutual Life Insurance Company announcing increased benefits for death or dismemberment under certain paid-up weekly premium life insurance policies, Boston Globe, Jan. 2, 1968, at p. 9.

was a voluntary relinquishment of a known right by the insurer, the elements that are essential for a waiver, such full knowledge and intent should be required.

To treat a situation as if there were voluntary relinquishment of rights by the insurer because one agent had known of the casualty when another agent or employee accepted the premium, is to dispense with a requirement of genuine voluntariness and substitute a fiction. Yet, this is sometimes done.[4] Waiver is often asserted as the justification for a decision when it is not appropriate to the circumstances. The result is more appropriately viewed and understood as an application of the doctrine of election, with a strong element of imposed liability

4. See, e.g., Seavey v. Erickson, 244 Minn. 232 at p. 246, 69 N.W.2d 889 at p. 898 (1955), 52 A.L.R.2d 1144 at p. 1156 (1957):

"While the authorities are not in agreement, we believe that the rule to which we are committed is that acceptance and retention of a premium on a policy of insurance after knowledge of a loss is a waiver of a forfeiture, at least unless the insurance can have some application to the property which remains after the loss."

The court noted that the car allegedly covered by the policy of collision insurance had been completely demolished, and observed that the insurer's "contention that it accepted the premium to reinstate the policy as of the day and hour when the premium was paid, to operate prospectively on an automobile it then knew was no longer in existence as an automobile, is hardly tenable." *Ibid.* It seems highly improbable, however, that the person who accepted the premium in the home office knew what the court here says the insurer knew; rather, it appears likely that the court was attributing knowledge to the company from different agents and treating the company as if it were a single mind having the sum of this knowledge from different sources.

The result reached by the court in *Seavey* may be defended on other grounds, however. It may be that a genuine waiver could be established not on the basis of acceptance of this premium itself but on the basis of voluntarily adopting a general practice of issuing notices and accepting late premiums as a routine, regardless of intervening casualty losses. Or estoppel, which was invoked by the court as an alternate ground of decision, might be supportable. For example, though this is not made clear it may be that the facts would have supported a claim that the insured detrimentally relied on company practices of sending notices inviting late payments and accepting them when tendered. Or,

finally, one might argue that candid adoption of a doctrine of election for this type of case is justified. Concerning election generally, see John S. Ewart, WAIVER DISTRIBUTED 66–123 (1917); John S. Ewart, *"Waiver" in Insurance Law,* 13 Iowa Law Review 129–144 (1928); John S. Ewart, *Waiver or Election,* 29 Harvard Law Review 724–730 (1916). Regarding the efforts of company drafters to forestall such decisions as that in *Seavey* by stipulations against waiver, and the frequent refusal of courts to enforce such clauses, see 3 MERRILL, NOTICE (1952) at § 1233, § 1237 and § 1238.

Also see American National Insurance Co. v. Cooper, 169 Colo. 420, 458 P.2d 257 (1969) (delinquent premium accepted after injury; company precluded from defense that it did not reinstate coverage retroactively); Home Insurance Company v. Caudill, 366 S.W.2d 167 (Ky.1963), 7 A.L.R.3d 406 (1965) (expressing reservations about a jury finding that premium payment was made before loss but affirming judgment for insured on grounds of that finding and waiver by the insurer in failing to cancel and then accepting an installment after the fire); German Insurance Company v. Shader, 68 Neb. 1, 93 N.W. 972 (1903) (opinion by Roscoe Pound, Commissioner) (premium delivered to agent, and by him delivered to and accepted by the company, after destruction of all the insured property; the money was sent back to the agent afterwards, but was not tendered by him to Shader; held, the agent had general authority to receive and collect premiums, and the course of conduct of the company and its agent "waives a provision that the insurer shall not be liable for a loss occurring before payment of the premium"; opinion observes that there has been a "contest between the courts on the one hand and counsel for insurance companies on the other, the latter devising skillfully framed clauses and provisions, and the former largely thwarting the purpose of those clauses by construing them strictly against the insurer").

rather than liability based on conduct reasonably interpretable as manifesting voluntary relinquishment.[5] To the extent that waiver is applied in circumstances in which it is not consistent with the theory that there was an intentional relinquishment of a known right, the result is in effect an application of the election doctrine, but without the saving grace of candor.

(3) Election

The doctrine of election could be applied when an insurer both retained a premium payment and at the same time contested coverage for an accident occurring during the period before the premium was tendered. Imposing such an election would mean that the insurer would be foreclosed from successfully claiming that coverage commenced with the date the premium was sent by the insured, the date it was actually received, or the date it was accepted by the insurer.

Limiting an insurer's range of choice in dealing with the late premium payment is particularly warranted on the basis that insurers should not be allowed to routinely apply premiums to the period that precedes the date for which late premiums were received when no casualty occurs, but remain free to treat differently those few instances of late premium payments when a subsequent claim discloses that the payment was tendered after a loss had occurred. The result in such cases then turns on an examination of the insurer's past practices, either in regard to the claimant or other insureds.

The argument for imposing the election doctrine to late premium payments is strengthened if there is evidence of a custom of accepting premiums at the home office without inquiry and allocating the premium in part to the time period preceding receipt of the payment except in those circumstances in which the insurer subsequently learns that a loss occurred during that period. One way of regulating such conduct is to impose on an insurer, by a doctrine of election, the choice of applying the premium so as to exclude from coverage the "period of lapse" either in all circumstances or in none. An argument against adopting this approach in regard to such a transaction is that the premium is used to purchase coverage not for a risk of future loss, but for a certain loss that the insured knows has already occurred.[6] On balance, in most cases a persuasive case can be made that it would be better not to impose a doctrine of election, based merely on acceptance of a single late premium, unless there is proof of a pattern or practice.

If a rule of election is imposed in this context, an insurer can protect itself by requiring the home office personnel to uniformly

---

5. For further development of this point, see § 6.1(a)(4), above.

6. A legal consequence that is in nature a doctrine of election may result from the enforcement of a statute regulating the disposition of tendered premiums. See, e.g., Bousquet v. Transportation Insurance Company, 354 Mass. 152, 235 N.E.2d 807 (1968) (failure to issue conditional receipt for premium tendered with application for reinstatement caused statutory automatic reinstatement provisions to apply, with the result that coverage was in effect at the time of the insured's accidental death).

initiate a new coverage period that commences upon the date the premium is received. Alternatively, an insurer could decide to take its chances by accepting late premiums without inquiry, the consequence being that occasionally it will become liable for an intervening event — occurring after a lapse and before tender — and that there will be some "adverse selection" (that is, among those making the late premium payments will be some individuals who would not have done so but for the loss that occurred).

Estoppel rather than Election. In some situations, an insurer — either as a consequence of operations in the home office or as a result of the actions of sales representatives, or both — has made express or implied representations concerning acceptance of late premiums, and the insured has thereafter detrimentally relied. For example, there may be evidence that over a course of years, the insurer had always sent the insured a second notice before terminating coverage for non-payment of the premium, that the second notice was not sent in this instance, and that the insured failed to pay on time in reliance on the opportunity of paying promptly after receipt of the second notice. Such proof would provide the basis for a claim of estoppel.[7]

Courts have permitted a claim of estoppel upon proof of the insurer's custom of giving notice and failure to give notice in an instance at issue, but without requiring the showing of detrimental reliance.[8] In substance, this is also an application of a doctrine of election.

Comment

When an insurer establishes a practice of sending notices that permit late payment within established periods of time *and* has routinely applied the late premium as payment to coverage that terminates sooner than if the premiums were applied to coverage commencing when they were actually tendered or received, the insurer should not be permitted to deviate from that practice in isolated cases in which the insurer learns of the occurrence of a casualty before receiving the late premium. In other words, the insurer has in effect made an election in the past and should adhere to it when it is disadvantageous as well as when it is advantageous. A course of acting always to the insurer's own advantage is unconscionable and accordingly should be precluded.

(4) Premium Payments Tendered in Conformity With Prior Practices of an Insurer; Herein of Detrimental Reliance

Life insurance policies often provide that premiums are payable only at the home office of the company or to a designated collector. If,

7. Perhaps Seavey v. Erickson, 244 Minn. 232, 69 N.W.2d 889 (1955), 52 A.L.R.2d 1144 (1957) is such a case. See note 4, above.

8. *Seavey,* note 4, above, may be considered such a case if not interpreted as resting on the assumption that the evidence sustained a finding of detrimental reliance in fact on company practices of sending notices inviting late payments and accepting them when tendered.

over a course of time, a policyholder delivers premiums elsewhere — to a soliciting agent, for example — and they are consistently accepted, theories of rights at variance with the policy provisions may be invoked when the insurer later denies liability for nonpayment of a premium that was tendered at the accustomed place and thereafter rejected by the insurer. Furthermore, if detrimental reliance can be proved — as for example, because the policyholder made tender at the accustomed place on the last permissible day, and upon having it subsequently rejected thereafter made tender at the proper place within a reasonable time but beyond the stated period — there is a compelling case for protecting the insured.

A materially different case is presented when it appears that a soliciting agent — who had been receiving and transmitting premiums discontinued that practice — refused the tendered premium, and neither the policyholder nor anyone else on the policyholder's behalf made any further effort to pay the premium. Even though death of the person whose life was insured occurs within the period for which the tendered premium would have continued the policy in force, in the absence of proof in such a case of detrimental reliance, there is no compelling reason for granting relief.[9]

§ 6.8(d) Notice to the Insurer of Changes Concerning Location, Use, or Occupancy

(1) Location Clauses

Fire insurance contracts on personal property frequently include a clause that states the policy covers personal property of the insured while located at a specified physical location, "but not elsewhere" unless otherwise provided.[1] Coverage disputes sometime arise when an insured has moved from the residence designated in the policy to another location without notifying the insurer to arrange for the insurance policy to be endorsed to reflect the change. Even though such a change of location endorsement has not been issued, courts have often sustained a claim for coverage at the new location, especially

---

9. Southland Life Insurance Co. v. Lawson, 137 Tex. 399, 153 S.W.2d 953 (1941), 136 A.L.R. 1212 (1942). A further argument for the insured in such a case is that apparent authority of the agent to accept the premium is established by the insurer's practice of accepting previous premiums, and that a valid tender to the agent is thus consummated momentarily before the agent declines to accept the premium in issue. If it has happened, however, that all of the agent's transmittals have reached the home office within the permitted time, it may be argued that the insurer's conduct has been equivocal because consistent with treating the payments as made at the home office through an agent for the insured. To counter this argument

the claimant might assert that the insurer should be aware of the policyholder's reasonable expectations that the agent was acting for the insurer and not the policyholder and should be required to honor those expectations in the absence of notifying the policyholder to the contrary. The *Lawson* opinion does not disclose whether in fact each of the transmitted premiums was received in the home office before expiration of the applicable grace period.

§ 6.8(d)

1. These policies typically include clauses that extend some coverage for property temporarily away from the specified location.

when representations have been made by an agent to the insured after the consummation of the original insurance contract.[2]

In Patterson's terminology, a location clause of the fire insurance policy is a "coverage provision" rather than a warranty.[3] However, among courts purportedly adhering to the view that "coverage provisions" cannot be defeated by claimed rights at variance with them, this clause is usually not classified as a "coverage provision."[4]

(2) Occupancy Clauses

Fire insurance contracts on buildings have customarily included a clause declaring that unless otherwise provided in writing by an endorsement attached to the policy, the insurer is not liable for loss occurring while the building is vacant or unoccupied beyond a specified length of time. Insureds have sought indemnification for a loss occurring after a long period of vacancy or unoccupancy, and have based the claim for rights at variance with the terms of an occupancy clause on the conduct or statements of a sales representative in response to a notice from the insured that the structure was not occupied. Though decisions on such claims are not entirely in harmony, insureds have prevailed when the justification for rights at variance with policy provisions was based on a showing that the sales representative or other agent of the insurer was provided notice of the circumstances.[5]

§ 6.9   Regulation of Claims Processes

§ 6.9(a)   Generally

Insurance policies commonly include clauses that are designed to govern or guide the claims processes. Some of the terms in these provisions have been strongly influenced by the desire of insurers to reduce delays and uncertainties about the disposition of claims. Provisions concerning timeliness of notice[1] and proof of loss[2] are clear examples. So too, although probably to a lesser extent, are clauses in property insurance requiring the protection of damaged property[3] and provisions in liability insurance concerning notification of legal actions or requiring the insured to assist and cooperate in the defense.[4]

In many instances, requirements set forth in an insurance policy that apply to the claims process conflict with the principles of disallowing unconscionable advantage,[5] requiring good faith and fair dealing,[6] and honoring reasonable expectations.[7] Frequently, provisions estab-

---

2. E.g., State Farm Fire Insurance Co. v. Rakes, 188 Va. 239, 49 S.E.2d 265 (1948), 4 A.L.R.2d 862 (1949).

3. See § 6.6(b)(2), above.

4. See § 6.6(e)(2), above.

5. E.g., McKinney v. Providence Washington Insurance Co., 144 W.Va. 559, 109 S.E.2d 480 (1959).

Also see 16C APPLEMAN, INSURANCE LAW (Revised edition, 1981), at § 9214.

§ 6.9(a)

1. See § 7.2(a), below.

2. See § 7.2, below.

3. See § 5.4(f), above.

4. See § 7.3, below.

5. See § 6.2, above.

6. See § 6.2(a)(2), above.

7. See § 6.3, above.

lishing rigid time limits for giving notice, presenting proof of loss, or filing suit have been tempered either by the recognition of excuses or by decisions which hold that the action required of the insured is sufficient if it occurs within a reasonable time.[8] The adverse effect of claims process requirements for insureds have also been avoided by disallowing an insurer's defense which is based on a stated time limit when it appears that the injury initially seemed trivial to the insured [9] or when it does not appear that the insurer was prejudiced by the delay in presenting the claim.[10] And, occasionally courts have dispensed entirely with the requirement of filing proof of loss.[11]

In some of the cases in which insurers have been precluded from denying coverage on the basis of the requirements established by insurers for the processing of claims, judicial opinions have been grounded either on some interpretation of the policy provisions or on the resolution of ambiguities in policy terms in favor of the insured. For many of these decisions, a more candid explanation is that the court is sustaining rights at variance with policy provisions.

§ 6.9(b) Variance Claims Based on the Insurer's Conduct

There are a number of situations in which insureds have urged that their rights should be at variance with the result prescribed by claims provisions in the insurance policies as a consequence of actions by the insurer. For example, liability insurers are sometimes confronted with the contention that an insurer's denial of liability on one ground precludes later assertion of another policy defense. Although in some unusual circumstances it may happen that a communication denying liability on one ground implies that no other ground of defense will be asserted, more often this is not the case and decisions in these cases that are based on doctrines such as waiver, estoppel, or election are generally illfounded.[1]

Rights at variance with policy provisions are frequently recognized on the basis of a liability insurer's actions in relation to a tort claim against the insured after the insurer has knowledge of information that supports a denial of coverage as a result of a policy defense.[2] For example, a claim of rights at variance with policy provisions may be based on the insurer's failing to notify the insured of the disclaimer of

8. See § 7.2(a), below.

9. See § 7.2(e)(3), below.

10. See § 7.2(e), below.

11. See, e.g., Bowler v. Fidelity & Casualty Co., 53 N.J. 313, 250 A.2d 580 (1969).

§ 6.9(b)

1. See, e.g., Clark v. London & Lancashire Indemnity Co., 16 Wis.2d 30, 113 N.W.2d 555 (1962) (denial of liability as beyond policy coverage and simultaneous assertion of noncompliance with notice provisions; held, no waiver or election by the insurer). For a later appeal involving other issues, see the decision reported at 21 Wis.2d 268, 124 N.W.2d 29 (1963), 98 A.L.R.2d 1037 (1964).

2. *Cf.* Employers Liability Assurance Corporation, Ltd. v. Vella, 366 Mass. 651, at p. 657, 321 N.E.2d 910 at p. 914 (1975) (" * * * if the insurer knows of its right to disclaim and exercises dominion over the case at an important point without disclaiming liability or reserving rights, subsequent disclaimer is barred.").

liability in time for the insured to take protective action in response to suit papers served upon the insured in the tort action,[3] or on the insurer's undertaking the defense with knowledge of the insured's breach of the assistance and cooperation clause.[4] Reservation-of-rights notices and nonwaiver agreements are frequently used by insurers, sometimes effectively and sometimes not, for the purpose of avoiding variance claims incident to the insurer's undertaking the defense in such cases.[5]

Another set of cases in which courts have occasionally recognized rights at variance with policy provisions concerns provisions for appraisal or arbitration.[6] For example, cases recognizing rights at variance with policy provisions concerning the timeliness of a demand for an appraisal of a loss have included instances of a subsequent contractual agreement (a nonwaiver agreement) that is not consistent with the insurance policy clause.[7] As in other contexts, courts have tended to speak of waiver even when the real ground was not a true voluntary relinquishment of known right.[8]

3. See, e.g., Zak v. Fidelity-Phenix Insurance Company, 34 Ill.2d 438, 216 N.E.2d 113 (1966).

Also see Old Mutual Casualty Company v. Clark, 53 Ill.App.3d 274, 11 Ill.Dec. 151, 368 N.E.2d 702 (1st Dist., Div. 5, 1977).

4. See, e.g., Dimarzo v. American Mutual Insurance Company, 389 Mass. 85 at p. 99, 449 N.E.2d 1189 at p. 1199 (1983) (insurer that "exercised dominion over the case at an important point which made a significant and irrevocable change * * * without disclaiming liability or reserving rights * * * waived the defense of noncooperation"); Rose v. Regan, 344 Mass. 223, 181 N.E.2d 796 (1962) (entering general appearance and having default removed without having reserved rights growing out of insured's failure to forward suit papers; waiver and election reasoning, but without using the terminology of election); Merchants Indemnity Corp. v. Eggleston, 37 N.J. 114, 179 A.2d 505 (1962) (insurer precluded because it defended without reservation of rights or nonwaiver agreement; discussion of waiver and estoppel, and some language of election).

Also see Van Dyke v. White, 55 Wash.2d 601, 349 P.2d 430 (1960) (when the insured refused to attend trial and the insurer proceeded with defense despite offer of continuance because of absence of the insured, the insurer "waived" breach of cooperation clause, since it cannot use its right of defense to improve its own position against the interests of the policyholder); Allstate Insurance Company v. Keller, 17 Ill.App.2d 44, 149 N.E.2d 482 (1st Dist., Div. 1, 1958), 70 A.L.R.2d 1190 (1960) (breach by insured's false representation that he was the driver of his car at the time of accident; after receiving knowledge of contrary facts, insurer's attorneys continued in defense and took insured's deposition to strengthen policy defense; insurer barred from relying on the breach, the court loosely employing waiver and estoppel theories).

Cf. City of Carter Lake v. Aetna Casualty and Surety Company, 604 F.2d 1052 at p. 1061 (8th Cir.1979); Continental Insurance Company v. Bayless & Roberts, Inc., 608 P.2d 281 at p. 292 (Alaska 1980).

Also see § 7.3, below.

5. See § 6.7(a), above.

6. As to arbitration, see Widiss, UNINSURED AND UNDERINSURED MOTORIST INSURANCE (1987), Chapter 23.

7. E.g., Milwaukee Insurance Company v. Kogen, 240 F.2d 613 (8th Cir.1957) (Minnesota law).

Concerning nonwaiver agreements generally, see § 6.7(a), above.

8. In Chainless Cycle Manufacturing Company v. Security Insurance Company, 169 N.Y. 304, 62 N.E. 392 (1901), the court held that the insurer, having permitted its agent to engage in protracted negotiations over the amount of a fire loss while the damaged property was deteriorating rapidly, was precluded from requiring an appraisal by demand made a few days after the insured had sold the property, several weeks after the fire. Though the opinion characterized defendant's conduct as a waiver, the supporting rationale was that the court could not say the insurer's de-

When an attorney is selected and retained by a liability insurer to defend a tort action, the fact that the insurer's interests often diverge from those of the insured may lead to granting rights to the insured which are at variance with the assistance and cooperation clause of the policy.[9] Furthermore, this type of situation involves a variety of potential conflicts of interests which may result in other rights for an insured which vary from other policy provisions.[10]

Sometimes insurers pay claims that could have been contested. The theory has been advanced that the payment of a claim that might have been contested required the insurer thereafter to provide coverage for comparable claims, even though the earlier claim was small and the subsequent claims were relatively large.[11] An independent theory that by paying a single claim the insurer should be bound to pay future claims of that type is not supported by any of the fundamental principles underlying variance claims, and therefore should be rejected.[12] However, if detrimental reliance on the part of the insured can be proved — usually on the basis that had the first claim been rejected the insured would have arranged for more comprehensive insurance — coverage may be justified.[13] Or, it may well be that a straightforward application of the principle of resolving ambiguities against the insurer justifies coverage.[14]

§ 6.9(c) Subrogation Rights and Variance Claims

Fire and casualty insurance contracts ordinarily provide that in some circumstances the insurers shall, upon payment of a loss, be subrogated to rights of the insured against third persons.[1] There are a number of circumstances when an insurer may be precluded from enforcing a subrogation right — that is, there are circumstances in which courts have concluded that the insured had an interest in the recovery that was superior to the insurer's and therefore have held that the insured's rights varied from the subrogation provision set forth in the insurance policy.

---

mand for appraisal was made within reasonable time since the evidence warranted an inference the insurer had no intention of requiring an appraisal until it thought it could take unfair advantage of the insured. Perhaps the evidence proved detrimental reliance on an implied representation that the insurer did not wish an appraisal; if so, a genuine case of estoppel was presented. At another point the opinion refers to the fact that the demand came after the insured, misled by the insurer's acts, had been placed in such a position that an appraisal was impossible.

Concerning genuine estoppel, see § 6.5, above; concerning election, see § 6.1(b)(4), above.

9. See the discussion of assistance and cooperation provisions in Widiss, UNINSURED AND UNDERINSURED MOTORIST INSURANCE (1987), Chapter 19.

10. See the discussion of conflict of interests in § 7.6, below.

11. Aetna Casualty & Surety Co. v. Haas, 422 S.W.2d 316 (Mo.1968).

12. Concerning such principles generally, see § 6.1, above.

13. See § 6.5, above.

14. See § 6.3(a), above.

§ 6.9(c)

1. See § 3.10, above.

(1) Collision Coverages

One of the most common contexts for a claim by an insured of rights at variance with a subrogation provision arises when there is collision coverage for damage to an insured automobile and the loss was caused by the negligent operation of another vehicle. The insured may wish to assert a tort claim against the third party — as, for example, because the insured's own insurer is dilatory in paying the collision coverage claim, because the insured suffered a personal injury as well as the damage to the insured car, or because the collision coverage is subject to a substantial deductible and the insured hopes to recover the portion of the loss not covered by the collision coverage from the tortfeasor (or the tortfeasor's liability insurer).

Motor vehicle collision insurance policies typically provide that an insured may not pursue a tort claim without securing the insurer's consent, and accordingly, the insured's initiation of the tort suit without obtaining the collision insurer's consent to that action may endanger the insured's right to recover under the collision coverage. If the collision claim has not yet been paid, the collision coverage insurer may deny liability because of interference with its subrogation rights. Alternatively, if the collision coverage claim has already been paid, the insurer may seek damages or restitution from the insured.[2]

In some circumstances, the insured may succeed in asserting rights at variance with the subrogation clause of a collision coverage. For example, the insurer's subrogation rights may be barred by laches.[3] Also, it has been held that if the collision insurer declines to act in response to a coverage claim by an insured — failing either to make payment or to deny liability — it is precluded from asserting that an insured's subsequent pursuit of a tort claim against the third party defeats an insured's rights under the collision coverage.[4] The theory which forecloses the insurer's rights to object to the insured's actions has sometimes been stated as waiver or estoppel.[5] In this context, however, a claim of waiver faces the difficulty that the insurer was plainly trying to avoid the loss of rights, rather than voluntarily relinquishing its defense. And a claim of estoppel faces the difficulty that the insured usually is not in a position to show that reliance on a representation of the insurer produced a detriment.[6]

---

2. See § 3.10, above.

3. See, e.g., Sun Insurance Office v. Hohenstein, 128 Misc. 870 at p. 875; 220 N.Y.S. 386 at p. 389 (Mun.Ct.1927).

4. Powers v. Calvert Fire Insurance Company, 216 S.C. 309, 57 S.E.2d 638 (1950), 16 A.L.R.2d 1261 (1951).

5. See, e.g., Weber v. United Hardware & Implement Mutuals Company, 75 N.D. 581, 31 N.W.2d 456 (1948) (waiver and estoppel).

Also see Powers v. Calvert Fire Insurance Company, 216 S.C. 309, 57 S.E.2d 638

(1950), 16 A.L.R.2d 1261 (1951), in which the court characterizes the ground of preclusion as waiver but also observes that the subrogation rights are not available to the insurer "because of its conduct which amounted to a breach of the contract of insurance * * *." 216 S.C. at p. 316, 57 S.E.2d at p. 642, 16 A.L.R.2d at p. 1266.

6. Election, though in some respects a more plausible theory than waiver or estoppel because it involves the judicial imposition of limits on the insurer's range of choice, does not fit this situation well. It is an awkward application of the doctrine of

A more suitable rationale for the result in these cases is that the insurer is barred from asserting violation of its subrogation rights as a defense because it has committed a material breach of the collision insurance contract in failing to pay the collision claim when submitted. The insured is then entitled to pursue the tort claim against the third party in order to mitigate damages resulting from the insurer's breach, and perhaps is even bound to do so under pain of having the claim against the insurer limited by the doctrine of avoidable consequences.

It might be argued that the insured should sue the insurer first, rather than proceeding against the tortfeasor. However, if this course is less attractive to the insured, the insurer has no cause to complain that the insured diligently pursues what will be the insured's only remedy if it turns out that there is justification for the insurer's refusal to pay the collision claim. Moreover, when the tort claim for the property damage (that is the subject of collision insurance) is a consequence of events which also resulted in a very substantial personal injury claim, it would be grossly unfair to the insured — the victim of the insurer's breach of contract — to impose the delay and other disadvantages entailed in the pursuit of the collision insurance claim in order to serve the interests of the insurer. This theory of denial of the insurer's defense as a consequence of its own material breach of the insurance contract has support in judicial precedents.[7]

(2) Uninsured Motorist Coverages

Uninsured motorist coverages usually include a provision stating if the insurer makes "a payment under this policy and the person for whom payment was made has a right to recover damages from another we [the insurer] shall be subrogated to that right."[8] This clause is written so as to apply to any recovery (whether by settlement or judgment) even though the insured has not been completely indemnified by the insurance payment,[9] and many insurers have urged that an insured clearly is not entitled to any portion of the proceeds of a recovery unless it exceeds the amount the insurance company has

---

election to state the rule as one that limits choice by precluding the insurer from simultaneously breaking its own contract obligation and asserting of its subrogation rights. To expand the theory of election this far is to incorporate within its scope every breach of contract by the insurer, at least if as substantial in character as that here involved.

7. This appears to be the theory counsel for the plaintiff and the court were expressing in speaking of the insured's action against the collision insurer in *Powers*, note 5, above, as an action "not for enforcement of the contract of insurance but for damages for its breach." 216 S.C. at p. 315, 57 S.E.2d at p. 641, 16 A.L.R.2d at p. 1265.

8. Insurance Services Office Personal Auto Policy, Part F — General Provisions: Our Right to Recover Payments (Ed. 6–80).

9. For example, see Lines v. Ryan, 272 N.W.2d 896 (Minn.1978); Kroeker v. State Farm Mutual Automobile Insurance Company, 466 S.W.2d 105 (Mo.App.1971).

Cf. Barnes v. Tarver, 360 So.2d 953 (Ala. 1978); United States Automobile Association v. Nationwide Mutual Insurance Company, 218 Va. 861, 241 S.E.2d 784 (1978); Holmes v. Reliance Insurance Company, 359 So.2d 1102 (La.App., 3d Cir., 1978), writ denied 362 So.2d 1120 (La., 1978).

previously paid to the claimant plus the expenses the company has incurred in securing a settlement or a judgment.

Furthermore, the phraseology used in this clause — "the company shall be entitled to any proceeds * * * that may result from the exercise of *any* rights * * * against *any* person or organization * * *." — broadly extends it to all recoveries. This provision expresses the meaning that the company is entitled to reimbursement from any sum a claimant receives as a consequence of bodily injuries from anyone legally responsible for the accident.[10] Although in most instances involving claims under the uninsured motorist coverage the only individual(s) legally responsible for the accident will be the owner and/or operator of the uninsured motor vehicle, this is not always the case. For example, in accidents involving several vehicles, it is possible that a second motorist, who is insured, shares the responsibility for the injuries sustained by the claimant.

Courts in several states have held that an insurer's right to establish this priority in regard to payments from any source will be upheld without regard to whether the claimant has been fully indemnified.[11] The decisions in these cases are usually grounded on the rationale that so long as the coverage terms do not contravene the scope of coverage explicitly required by the state's uninsured motorist insurance legislation, unambiguous provisions which limit or reduce an insurer's liability are enforceable.

In numerous cases courts have concluded that the terms of the trust provision were not enforceable when the insured had not been fully indemnified, and therefore the attempt by an insurance company to secure proceeds of a recovery from a third party was appropriately denied.[12] These decisions are generally grounded on the rationale that indemnification for the injured person should be favored over a literal

---

10. For example, see the Insurance Services Office Personal Auto Policy, Part F — General Provisions (Ed. 6–80), which states:

"B. If we make a payment under this policy and the person to or for whom payment is made recovers damages from another, that person shall:

　1. Hold in trust for us the proceeds of the recovery; and

　2. Reimburse us to the extent of our payment."

11. See, e.g., Glidden v. Farmers Automobile Insurance Association, 57 Ill.2d 330, 312 N.E.2d 247 (1974) (the court held the insurance company was entitled to be subrogated to any monies recovered either from the uninsured motorist or as a result of a dramshop action); Oren v. General Accident Fire and Life Assurance Corporation, 175 So.2d 581 (Fla.App.1965) (involving a judgment taken without consent).

12. For example, see White v. Nationwide Mutual Insurance Company, 361 F.2d 785 at p. 787 (4th Cir.1966) (involving Virginia law). The majority opinion concludes that a right of subrogation cannot be enforced until the insured has received full satisfaction of his claim (judgment) against the uninsured driver.

Perez v. Ford Motor Company, 408 F.Supp. 318 (E.D.La.1975), affirmed 572 F.2d 1391 (5th Cir.1976), involved the question of who was entitled to the sum of $10,000 which constituted the proceeds of a compromise settlement of the claim that was made against the manufacturer. The court concluded that "the clear effect of the subrogation agreement here is to deprive plaintiffs of the full recovery they otherwise would receive under the mandatory uninsured motorist provision in their policy." The court further observed that allowing such a recoupment would frustrate "the legislative aim that carriers

application of the coverage language.   As the Supreme Court of Minnesota commented:

> "We are persuaded by the rationale of these cases and our own analysis of the statute in question that the uninsured motorist coverage statute should be construed to mean that an uninsured motorist liability carrier does not have the right to be subrogated to the proceeds of a settlement its policy-holder makes with liquor venders allegedly liable * * * *where the policyholder has not been fully compensated for her injuries. Subrogation should be permitted to the extent necessary to avoid a double recovery by such a policyholder."* [13]   (Emphasis added.)

Similarly, the Louisiana Supreme Court observed:

> "By giving the insured who has been only partially compensated for his loss a lawful cause of preference over the insurer for payment out of his debtor's property, the code further implements the object of the uninsured motorist statute, which is to promote full recovery for damages by innocent automobile accident victims by making both primary protection and excess coverage available." [14]

In such states, an insurer that provides indemnification for a portion of the damages is only entitled to a subordinate subrogation right. The subordinate right may be asserted in regard to any recovery from persons or organizations who are liable when the amount recovered exceeds that which is necessary to fully indemnify the claimant, and the rights of insureds are clearly at variance with the coverage provisions.[15]

---

be responsible for damages caused to insured by uninsured motorist" just "as completely and as effectively as the exclusion of responsibility through a 'consent to settle' clause, or a 'pro-rate' clause, or an 'excess' provision of an 'other insurance' clause, or a 'reduction' clause or a provision excluding coverage when an insured is occupying an uninsured automobile owned by the named insured or a relative, all of which have been held invalid." *Id.,* 408 F.Supp. at p. 320. Finally, the court decided that "to the extent Traders' [the insurer's] agreement purports to cover claims against both the co-tortfeasor and the uninsured motorist, it is inconsistent with specific legislative intent as well as with the statute's broader expression of public policy." *Ibid.*

Cf. United Pacific Reliance Insurance Companies v. Kelly, 140 Cal.App.3d 72 at p. 76, 189 Cal.Rptr. 323 at p. 326 (1st Dist., 1983), in which the court concluded that "the subrogation rights of the uninsured motorist carrier are subservient to the right of the insured party to be fully compensated to the extent possible * * *."

Also see Bond v. Commercial Union Assurance Company, 407 So.2d 401 (La.1981), on remand 415 So.2d 572 (La.App., 3d Cir., 1982); Flanery v. Total Tree, Inc., 332 N.W.2d 642 (Minn.1983); Dunnam v. State Farm Automobile Insurance Company, 366 So.2d 668 (Miss.1979); McGee v. Charley's Other Brother, 161 N.J.Super. 551, 391 A.2d 1289 (Law Division, 1978), *affirmed, sub nom.* Mozee v. McGee, 171 N.J.Super. 454, 410 A.2d 46 (1979).

13. Milbank Mutual Insurance Company v. Kluver, 302 Minn. 310, 225 N.W.2d 230 at p. 233 (1974).

14. Bond v. Commercial Union Assurance Company, 407 So.2d 401 at p. 411 (La.1981). Also see the opinion on remand 415 So.2d 572 (La.App., 3d Cir., 1982).

15. *Statutory Provisions for Subrogation.* In several states, the uninsured motorist legislation specifically provides for the insurer's right to be reimbursed. For example, the Massachusetts statutes states that upon:

> "* * * payment to any person under the [uninsured motorist] coverage re-

§ 6.9(d)   Receipt of Due Proof Clauses and Variance Claims

Many types of insurance condition coverage on a timely filing of both a notice that an insured event has occurred and a proof of loss. For example, the obligation of a life insurer or a health and accident insurer to pay benefits for disability in many instances is conditioned "upon receipt of due proof" of the disability.[1] Often other conditions are added, either in the principal statement of the insurer's promise or elsewhere in the insurance policy.[2] Strict enforcement of such conditions would clearly provide insurers with extensive protection against late claims and would almost certainly sharply reduce at any given time the amount needed in reserves for claims not yet presented. Such provisions could also be used by insurers to limit the scope of protection for insureds in a way that is not well related, if related at all, to policyholder needs, and could reduce protection afforded by such policies in situations that would not be in accord with the reasonable expectations of insureds. Thus, it is not surprising that controls over such clauses have been developed both in statutes and in judicial decisions.

Statutory controls are ordinarily in the form of the prescription or the proscription of policy provisions.[3] Thus, legislative provisions, in effect, typically result in claims process policy provisions that are more favorable to policyholders than such provisions would be in the absence of statutory requirements.

The controls effected by judicial decision, on the other hand, often establish rights at variance with the limitation on coverage that would otherwise result from the conditions set forth in the applicable claims process policy provisions. Sometimes the refusal of a court to enforce restrictive provisions concerning receipt of due proof is based on an

quired by this section and subject to the terms and conditions of such coverage, the insurer making such payment shall, to the extent thereof, be entitled to the proceeds of any settlement or judgment resulting from the exercise of any rights of recovery of such person against any person or organization legally responsible for the bodily injury *for which such payment is made* * * *." (Emphasis supplied).

Massachusetts 175 § 113L(4). Also see Ziolkowski v. Continental Insurance Company, 8 Mass.App.Ct. 667, 396 N.E.2d 723 (1979).

Also see Mississippi Code 1972, § 83–11–107, and United States Fidelity & Guaranty Company v. Hillman, 367 So.2d 914 (Miss.1979).

§ 6.9(d)

1. Compare the provisions in the waiver-of-premiums clauses of the life insurance policy in Appendix E and the health and accident insurance policy in Appendix F.

2. For example, such a policy may require written notice to the insurer at its home office during the lifetime of the insured and during the continuance of the disability. And it may declare that due proof must be received at the home office before the expiration of one year after default in payment of premium and in any event, whether or not there be a default, not later than one year from the anniversary of the policy on which the insured's rated-up age at nearest birthday is 60 or one year after maturity of the policy, whichever is the earlier date, otherwise the claim shall be invalid. Compare the provisions in the waiver-of-premiums clauses of the life insurance policy in Appendix E and the health and accident insurance policy in Appendix F.

3. E.g., New York—McKinney's Insurance Law § 164 (1966). Also see § 2.8, above.

alleged conflict between provisions in different parts of the insurance policy form. Typically, this involves a conflict between the principal promise of the insurer and qualifying clauses which appear elsewhere in the coverage terms.[4] On the theory of resolving ambiguity, enforcement of the more restrictive provisions is then disallowed.

Drafters sometimes have included in the principal promise a reference to the part of the policy in which the more restrictive provisions appear. In such cases, a careful examination by the policyholder of the principal promise set forth in the insurance policy could have revealed the restrictions. In these circumstances, it has been said that the majority rule sustains the enforceability of the restrictive clauses.[5] Nevertheless, some courts have declined to enforce such clauses on the rationale that there was an ambiguity in the policy as a whole because, even though the specific clause at issue was not ambiguous, there was a conflict among different provisions of the policy. The result in these cases in effect recognizes rights at variance with policy provisions. Furthermore, in at least some instances, the principle of honoring reasonable expectations[6] supports sustaining the insured's right to coverage.

It might be possible to draft insurance policy forms in such a way as to avoid any ambiguity by setting forth all of the qualifications and limitations in a group of clauses that comprise the basic statement of coverage. However, this approach often leads to very carefully qualified insurance policy clauses that are too complex for a lay reader to understand. If this occurs, the principle of honoring reasonable expectations — sometimes in concert with the principle of disallowing unconscionable advantage — provides substantial support for judicial regulation. These principles justify a rule prohibiting insurers from enforcing claims process provisions that are so complex that they do not effectively avoid the creation of reasonable expectations which are contrary to the policy terms.[7]

Furthermore, even if an unambiguous insurance policy form were fashioned, an insurer would not be absolutely protected from the possibility of liability at variance with the policy provisions. For example, undoubtedly there would continue to be instances in which an insurance company would be bound by statements in advertisements or in brochures describing a coverage in ways that are less precise than the insurance policy terms. Similarly, an agent's oral statements might also provide the basis for a variance claim.

---

4. See, e.g., Johnson v. New York Life Insurance Company, 212 F.2d 256 (7th Cir. 1954), cert. denied 348 U.S. 836, 75 S.Ct. 50, 99 L.Ed. 659 (1954); Mosby v. Mutual Life Insurance Co., 405 Ill. 599, 92 N.E.2d 103, 18 A.L.R.2d 1054 (1950).

5. See Annotation, *Requirement of disability policy as to proof of disability before reaching specified age as barring recovery* *where disability occurs before, but proof is made after, attainment of such age,* 18 A.L.R.2d 1061–1071 (1951).

Also see 3 APPLEMAN, INSURANCE LAW (Revised edition, 1967), at § 1395.

6. See § 6.3, above.

7. See § 6.3(b), above.

§ 6.9(e) Insurer's Breach as Excusing an Insured's Noncompliance With Claim Procedures

An insurer's unjustified denial of liability may provide an insured with a defense for the subsequent failure of the insured to comply with policy provisions concerning the claim process. The result may be justified on the ground that the insurer's material breach of contract excuses the insured's noncompliance with prescribed claims procedures. Alternatively, if the insurer bases its initial denial of liability on any ground other than lack of timely presentment of a claim, invoking the defense of lateness of the claim as a justification for denying coverage may be precluded because of the recognition of rights at variance with policy provisions.[1] In some decisions sustaining coverage for an insured, the stated theory of decision has been waiver.[2] But ordinarily a genuine waiver cannot be proved in this context, that is, there is no voluntary relinquishment of any rights on the part of the insurer.[3]

There are several relatively well recognized circumstances in which an insurer is precluded from insisting on compliance with claims procedures as a consequence of the insurer's breach of the contract.

A property insurer may be precluded from asserting violation of its subrogation rights because of its own breach.[4]

A liability insurer's denial of coverage, unless qualified by an indication of willingness to defend without requiring more of the insured than the assistance and cooperation the insured owes under the policy provisions, is, at least by implication, a declaration of unwillingness to fulfill its legal obligation to defend on behalf of the insured. Thus, if it occurs after the occasion for taking preparatory defensive steps has already arisen, it may constitute an immediate breach of a duty to make early preparations for defense at trial,[5] regardless of whether in other respects it constitutes an anticipatory breach. Such an immediate breach of a duty to take essential preparatory steps supports the preclusion of the insurer's later claim of interference with its right to control over the defense. Furthermore, a liability insurer's failure to defend on behalf of the insured, if it proves to be inconsistent with policy terms,[6] is a material breach that defeats the insurer's later claim of interference with its right to control (whether exclusive or joint) over the defense of the claim against the insured.[7]

§ 6.9(e)

1. Such a preclusion, if based on the insured's detrimental reliance, is an instance of genuine estoppel.

2. See, e.g., Couey v. National Benefit Life Insurance Co., 77 N.M. 512, 424 P.2d 793 (1967).

3. See the discussion of waiver in § 6.1(b)(3).

4. See § 6.9(c), above.

5. Concerning the obligation of taking preparatory defensive steps, see § 7.9(a), below.

6. See generally § 9.1, below.

7. *Cf.* Krutsinger v. Illinois Casualty Co., 10 Ill.2d 518, 141 N.E.2d 16 (1957), in which, however, the court refers to the theory of preclusion as waiver. In this case, judgment creditors brought an action against a liability insurance company for failure to satisfy judgments on tort claims against the insureds and others based on the sales of alcoholic beverages to a known

Similarly, a liability insurer's unreasonable delay in the handling of a claim against its insured, even though it did not deny coverage altogether, has been held to defeat the insurer's reliance on a clause prohibiting the insured from settling.[8]

If the insurer's initial denial of liability — predicated on some ground other than the insured's failure to comply with a specific element in the claims process — was justifiable, such a denial does not preclude the insurer from asserting noncompliance with claims procedures (such as timely filing of proof of loss) when the insured subsequently presents a revised claim on grounds within coverage.[9]

§ 6.10 Insurer's Rights at Variance With Policy Provisions

§ 6.10(a) Introductory Note

An insurer may have rights at variance with policy provisions. Although an insurer's rights are usually based on general principles that apply to all contracts, the circumstances which produce such claims by insurers are often distinctive.   The following subsections briefly reconsider some topics that have been analyzed elsewhere in the text — reformation, implied exceptions, modifications of the coverage terms, and an insurer's right to terminate coverage — in relation to the concept of rights at variance with the policy provisions.

§ 6.10(b) Reformation of the Coverage Agreement

Insurers sometimes seek reformation of an insurance contract as the result of a mistake that was made in the formulation of the coverage agreement, a type of mistake that is often referred to as a scrivener's error.[1] For example, mistakes about or misstatements of an insured's age in applications for life, health, or accident insurance have

---

habitual drunkard in violation of a dram shop act, thus interfering with the claimant's means of support. The policy covered only part of the period during which the sales occurred. The defendant insurer had failed to participate in the defense or settlement negotiations and in this action against it contended that the insureds had violated the policy condition that the insurer should have the exclusive right to contest any suits against the insureds. Affirming a judgment against the insurer, the court held that since some asserted grounds of liability were within and others were outside the policy coverage, the insurer had a duty to participate in the defense, and none of the parties had a right to exclude the others from participation in the absence of breach. The insurer was precluded from asserting a violation of its rights to participate in the defense because of its inaction for months followed by un-

justified demands for execution of a non-waiver agreement not only avoiding any waiver from the insurer's then undertaking the defense but also seeking to avoid waiver from previous events and stating conclusions of fact with implications of fraud by the insureds. Obviously the insurer did not voluntarily relinquish a known right. The result can be justified, however, on the ground of breach of contract by the insurer.

8. Otteman v. Interstate Fire & Casualty Co., 172 Neb. 574, 111 N.W.2d 97 (1961), 89 A.L.R.2d 1182 (1963).

9. *Cf.* A Perley Fitch Co. v. Continental Insurance Co., 99 N.H. 1, 104 A.2d 511 (1954), 49 A.L.R.2d 156 (1956).

§ 6.10(b)

1. Also see the discussion in § 6.6(d), above.

resulted in numerous claims by insurers for reformation.[2] If an insurer discovers that an insured's age has been understated, the insurer may contend that insurance coverage should be reduced in accordance with what it asserts would have been provided if the insured's true age had been properly recorded. When such a reformation of the insurance arrangement is not expressly provided for in the coverage terms, the insurer's action may be viewed as a request for rights that are at variance with the policy provisions. In response to such an action by an insurer, the insured may seek to invoke incontestability provisions set forth either in a statute or in a clause of the insurance policy.[3]

§ 6.10(c) Implied Exceptions: Resolution of "Ambiguities" in Favor of an Insurer

There are some circumstances when an insurer's rights in essence are predicated on the resolution of an ambiguity in regard to the scope of coverage in favor of the insurer. The judicial opinions in these cases constitute rather notable deviations from the general rule of resolving ambiguities or uncertainties in contract provisions against the party responsible for its drafting. This is not to say that the rule of resolving ambiguities against the drafter is rejected in these decisions. More often, there is no reference at all to the existence of an ambiguity in the coverage terms. Nevertheless, there are enough instances in which courts either adopt constructions of coverage terms that are not compelled by the insurance policy language or allow defenses that are not set forth in the coverage terms to warrant the observation that courts occasionally grant insurers rights at variance with the coverage terms by in effect construing in favor of the insurer policy provisions that do not provide clear guidance as to the scope of coverage. Two situations that were discussed in the preceding portions of this text provide clear examples of such judicial actions.

Fire insurance policies ordinarily declare that the insurer shall pay the insured for "direct loss by fire," without specifying either that the loss must be "accidental" or that the fire must be "hostile." An inference that only "accidental" losses were intended to be covered is reasonable. It is not necessary to resort to any theory of ambiguity to support such a limitation; indeed, any other reading of the insurance policy terms would be contrary to ordinary principles of reading contractual instruments consistently with the implications of the language in the context of its use. But the rule that a fire insurer is not liable for a loss from a "friendly" fire (as opposed to a "hostile" fire) goes well beyond the reasonable implications of the proposition that only accidental losses are intended to be covered. For example, most of the courts

2. An overstatement of age would ordinarily be a disadvantage to the insured. Although there has been little litigation on the point, reformation would surely be available to the insured if the overstatement came about through mutual mistake or because of an error of some representative of the insurer, as when an agent erroneously recorded a correct statement of age by the applicant. Also see the discussion of reformation in § 6.1(b)(1), above.

3. See § 6.6(d) above.

which have considered the question have concluded that coverage does not apply for damage to property, such as a piece of jewelry, which is inadvertently "thrown" into a "friendly" fire (that is, a fire burning in an intended location such as a fireplace, a furnace, or an incinerator).[1]

The rule denying recovery for a loss caused by a "friendly" fire, such as one in an incinerator, is often explained as consistent with the probable understanding of the contracting parties. This explanation seems supportable only to the extent that the friendly fire limitation is known to insureds, which may be true of some purchasers of fire insurance on commercial risks. But to infer that the ordinary house-holder actually understands that there is a friendly fire rule that will be applied so that a fire insurance policy will not cover the destruction of a valuable ring which is mistakenly tossed into an incinerator is to accept an assumption of rather substantial proportion that almost certainly amounts to a fiction in many instances. Certainly the typical language in a property insurance policy does not clearly negate coverage for such a loss. Accordingly, when the coverage terms are considered in relation to the friendly fire/hostile fire rule, they can be reasonably viewed as ambiguous, and therefore the introduction of the friendly fire/hostile fire rule is an instance of resolving an ambiguity in favor of, rather than against, the insurer.

Another type of case in which ambiguities have been resolved in favor of the insurer concerns the applicability of accident insurance coverage, and especially death benefits, to injuries suffered by an insured as a result of the insured's engaging in criminal behavior. For example, courts have often reasoned that when a person is killed either while committing a crime or as a consequence of someone's acts of self-defense against the decedent's unlawful attack, the decedent did not suffer an "accidental death" within the meaning of that phrase in an accident insurance policy. Courts have sustained denials of insurance benefits even though the applicable insurance policy contained no explicit provision against coverage in such a case.[2] Yet, the death in nearly all such cases was accidental — that is, it was not intended from the point of view of the deceased, and perhaps the other person as well. The decedent certainly did not want to die, and did not know that his or her death was virtually certain to occur as a result of the criminal conduct. Furthermore, in many instances, the person causing the death, such as an individual acting in self-defense, may not have intended to cause the death. Thus, courts denying liability in these cases have either resolved an ambiguity against the insured or, perhaps more likely, have declined to enforce a provision unambiguously supporting coverage.

§ 6.10(c)

1. See the discussion in § 5.3(d), above.

But cf. Sadlowski v. Liberty Mutual Insurance Company, 487 A.2d 1146 (Del.Sup. 1984).

2. See § 5.4(b)(4), above.

Observations

There is no single explanation for the instances in which the courts have adopted interpretations of coverage terms that favor insurers. In general, when courts sustain the rejection of claims by insurers that are not predicated on specific provisions in the coverage terms, the judicial decisions seem to represent deviations from the principle that ambiguities in regard to the scope of the insurance are invariably resolved against the drafter of the contract terms — the insurer. Each of the situations in which courts adopt such approaches to the coverage terms at issue involves a result that serves some important principle or public policy interest that has an overriding significance in the particular context. For example, the rule that an insured's death which results from injuries incurred in the course of committing a crime is not "accidental" can be explained as a sanction against seriously antisocial behavior. And the friendly fire rule, when extended to denying coverage for a ring which is mistakenly tossed into an incinerator, almost certainly serves to reduce the opportunities for fraud that would be opened up by allowing recovery in this type of case. However, whatever the explanations, it is clear that there are some types of cases in which prevailing rules of insurance law in effect resolve in favor of insurers "ambiguities" that exist as a consequence of coverage terms that are not explicit.[3]

§ 6.10(d) Modification of the Coverage Terms

Endorsements or "Riders"

Insurers often seek to change the rights of the parties under an existing insurance policy by issuing "riders" or endorsements that are designed to be attached to the original insurance policy provisions which were previously sent or delivered to an insured. When an insured clearly agrees to such a change in the insurance contract, the new terms may appropriately be analyzed as a modification of a contractual arrangement. In many instances, however, the insurer intends to alter some aspect of an insurance arrangement by the unilateral action of issuing such an endorsement, and the express agreement of the insured is neither sought nor expected. Occasionally, the existence of coverage will turn on the enforceability of the provision that resulted from the insurer's unilateral action. A decision to sustain the insurer's position in such cases in essence constitutes a judgment in favor of the insurer of rights at variance with the original coverage terms.

---

3. It remains true, however, that ordinarily ambiguities of insurance policy language are resolved against insurers.

See § 6.3(a), above.

Renewals of a Policy

Insurers often change to a new insurance policy form when a coverage is renewed. If the new form alters the scope of coverage, and, especially if the new form affords less extensive protection, the enforceability of the revisions may subsequently become a matter of disagreement between an insured and an insurer. It has often been stated that the provisions of the original coverage are incorporated into any renewal of the insurance policy unless the new insurance policy specifies that this will not occur and this point is called to the attention of the policyholder.[1] Why the policyholder's acquiescence to the first policy should be preferred over a similar response to a successor is rarely considered.[2] Of course, the very existence of such a dispute indicates that the insured's interest is served by the older form, but standing alone that does not seem to warrant an "automatic" preference for the original coverage terms. Of course, it would not be an inordinate burden on the insurer to prepare a communication to accompany a new form to call a policyholder's attention to the fact that the older policy form has been replaced and that there are changes in the scope of coverage. However, to require an insurer to identify all the major and minor differences between such forms is to invite litigation over the adequacy and accuracy of such communications — a result which seems both unwise and unwarranted.

Reservation-of-Rights Notices

Somewhat similar considerations in regard to the respective rights of an insured and an insurer are raised by an insurer's use of a "reservation-of-rights notice" in which the insurer unilaterally declares that an insured is in essence required to give up some right in exchange for the insurer's commitment to continue processing (e.g., investigating) an insurance claim or providing a defense to a tort claim filed against an insured who is covered by liability insurance.[3]

§ 6.10(d)

1. *Cf.* 13A, APPLEMAN, INSURANCE LAW and Practice (1986 Pocket Part, updating 1976 vol. 13A), § 7648; 17 COUCH ON INSURANCE, 2d (1983), § 64:40 and § 68:61.

2. *But cf.* the comment in Brewer v. Vanguard Insurance Company, 614 S.W.2d 360 at p. 363 (Tenn.App. Eastern Section, 1980) (permission to appeal denied by the Tennessee Supreme Court, 1981):

"Where a new policy is delivered, the insured is presumed to have consented to any new terms therein if the policy is retained without complaint and is not rejected until after a loss. 17 *Couch on Insurance* 2nd, 68:63 at 700. But courts of most jurisdictions notice the fact that it is customary for insureds to accept insurance policies without reading them. See Henry v. Southern Fire & Casualty Company, 46 Tenn.App. 335, 330 S.W.2d 18 (1958). And the mere failure to read a policy, especially if it is a renewal, is not such negligence as will defeat the right to reform the policy."

3. Also see the discussion of "reservation of rights" notices in § 6.7(a), above.

§ 6.10(e)　Termination of Coverage: Rescission and Cancellation

An insurance company may seek to terminate a contract in an action for rescission on grounds such as mutual mistake, misrepresentation, or concealment.[1] Often, if the relief is granted, the result involves a consequence that is not provided for in the insurance policy provisions, and thus the insurer's rights differ from those set forth in the applicable insurance policy.[2]

If a substantial part of the coverage period has passed at a time when an insurer asserts the right to terminate coverage — because, for example, of a misrepresentation in the insurance application — there are varying advantages and disadvantages to the insurer of rescinding the contract, on one hand, and cancelling the contract, on the other. Except insofar as legislative provisions, administrative actions, or judicial decisions regulate an insurer's rights to cancel an insurance policy,[3] an insurer canceling pursuant to the procedure described in the insurance policy usually avoids any dispute over its right to do so. Also, by cancelling a policy, an insurer is entitled to retain that portion of the premium allocable to the period before the effective date of the cancellation. But a cancellation creates the possibility that the insurer will be held to have exercised an election[4] under which the company will be liable for any losses that occurred before the cancellation. Rescission avoids this risk, although it does require the return of the full premium.[5]

An insurer wishing both to discontinue coverage for the future and to contest coverage for a loss that has already occurred might choose to deliver notices of both rescission and cancellation. However, this course would probably reduce the prospects of a successful defense against liability for a previous loss. In such a case, it seems likely that a doctrine of election would be invoked[6] — that is, the cancellation notice could be viewed as an affirmation of the validity of the coverage up to its effective date.

From the standpoint of an insurer that wishes to terminate an insurance coverage, it is usually prudent to attempt to reach an express

---

§ 6.10(e)

1. See generally §§ 5.7–5.8 and § 6.1(b)(2), above.

Standards of materiality applied and doctrines available to an insured to defeat such a claim, even when based on explicit policy provisions, are considered in § 6.6 and § 6.7, above.

Concerning imposition of a duty to the public, arising from the public policy underlying financial responsibility laws, to investigate an insured's insurability within a reasonable time after issuing a policy and not to "take advantage of a breach" of that duty to avoid liability to an innocent victim, see § 6.6(d), above.

2. Many insurance policy forms include provisions which allow an insurer to cancel the coverage for various specified causes such as the failure of an insured to pay the premiums. This, of course, is a right in accordance with, not at variance with, policy provisions. See § 5.11, above.

3. See § 5.11(c), above.

4. *Cf.* § 6.8(d), above.

5. A notice of rescission may prove to be ineffective since the insured may contest the insurer's grounds for rescission.

6. See the discussion of election in § 6.8(d)(3), above.

understanding with the insured that in exchange for the return of part or all of the premium, the insured agrees to the conditions desired by the insurer. However, even when the position an insurer takes in such a negotiation is consistent with its rights of cancellation,[7] negotiations for rescission or cancellation by mutual agreement often are not fruitful when a loss has already occurred.

 WESTLAW REFERENCES

§ 6.1   **Introduction to Principles and Defenses**

     (a) **The Most Influential Principles and Defenses Employed to Justify Variance Claims**

         sy("reasonabl! expect!" /s policy-holder applicant insured (third-party / 3 beneficiary) /s coverage insurance policy)

         enforc! /s "public policy" /s state /s insur∗ ∗ ∗ ∗ /s coverage policy

     (b) **Other Principles Employed by Courts to Justify Rights at Variance from Policy Provisions**

         (2) **Rescission**

            resci! recind! recis! /s contract policy /s insur∗ ∗ ∗ ∗ /s mistak!

         (3) **Waiver and Estoppel**

            di estoppel

            di waiver

            sy,di(claimant insured policy-holder /s detriment! /10 reliance rely! relied /s insurer carrier)

         (5) **Variance Theories and the Authority of Sales Representatives**

            sy,di(agent representative broker /s authority authoriz! power /5 modif! chang! /s coverage policy contract /s insur∗ ∗ ∗ insurance)

         (6) **Variance Theories and Incontestability Clauses**

            sy(incontestab! /5 clause provision statut! law legislat! /s coverage insurance policy)

     (c) **Defenses to Variance Claims**

         (2) **Applications of the Extrinsic (Parol) Evidence Rule**

            to(217) /p extrinsic parol /3 evidence /s contract agreement policy /s insur∗ ∗ ∗ ∗

         (4) **Applications of Entire–Contract Statutes**

            entire +1 contract policy agreement /5 statut! law legislat! /s insur∗ ∗ ∗ ∗

---

7. See, e.g., Merchants & Farmers Mutual Casualty Co. v. St. Paul-Mercury Indemnity Co., 214 Minn. 544, 8 N.W.2d 827 (1943). The insurer's agent informed the insured that the company would no longer continue her automobile liability policy without an endorsement eliminating coverage for a son convicted of a traffic offense. She insisted on return of the full premium, though coverage had been provided for some time. Though the agent finally agreed to the full refund, it had not been delivered when another son was involved in an accident. Even though another policy had already been obtained by the insured, a divided court reversed a judgment for the insurer, holding that a jury could have found that there was no rescission because her intent to rescind was dependent upon her getting back the full refund as well as getting other insurance.

§ 6.2 Disallowing Unconscionable Advantage and Requiring Good Faith

(a) Generally

(1) Unconscionable Advantage

insur* * * * /s coverage policy contract /s overreach!
''j fertilizer''

§ 6.3 Honoring Reasonable Expectations

(a) Emergence of the Principle

(2) Resolving Ambiguities Against Insurers

gray /s zurich /p ambigu!
find 160 f2d 599
di contra proferentem

(3) From Construing Ambiguities to Protecting Reasonable Expectations

sy(''reasonabl! expect!'' /s policy-holder insured applicant (third-party /3 beneficiary) /s coverage insurance policy)

(b) Implications and Applications of the Expectations Principle

(2) Reasonable Expectations and Unconscionability

sy,di(increase-of-hazard /3 clause provision)

(c) Limitations on Applications of the Expectations Principle

(4) Statutory and Administrative Actions

sy(administrati! statute statutor! law legislat! rule /s regulat! prescrib! /5 term form clause coverage /s insurance policy)

§ 6.4 Variance Claims Based on Declared Public Policies

(b) Variance Claims in Uninsured Motorist Coverage

Public Policies Associated with the Uninsured Motorist Insurance Statutes

sy(statute statutor! law legislat! /s authoriz! authority provid! provision /s limitation exclusion exception /s ''uninsured motorist'')

§ 6.5 Detrimental Reliance

(c) The Scope of an Agent's Authority

actual apparent /3 authori! /s detriment! /s reliance rely! relied

(d) Justifiable Detrimental Reliance

detriment! /p reliance rely! relied /s reasonabl! justif! /s insured applicant policy-holder

§ 6.6 Regulation of Defenses Based on Warranty, Representation, or Concealment

(a) Decisional Limitation of Warranty

to(217) /p warrant! /p ''condition precedent''
217k291(3)

(b) Concepts of Warranty, Representation, and Coverage

(1) Generally

sy(misrepresent! (breach! /3 warranty) /s material! immaterial! /s avoid! defense defend * * defending /p insurance)
sy,di(statut! law legislat! regulat! /s warrant! /s representation /p insurance)

(3) Warranty Statutes of Other States

sy(false! falsif! /5 state* stating statement represent* * * representation warrant! /s intent intention! intend! /3 decei! decepti!)

fals! /5 state* stating statement represent* * * representation
warrant! /s risk /5 loss

(c) Regulatory Standards

(2) Contribute-to-Loss and Increase-of-Risk Provisions

sy(affect! effect /5 risk hazard /s insur* * * *)
sy,di(substantial! material! /5 increas! /s risk hazard /s
coverage insurance policy)
penn /s ''mechanic sav* * *''

(d) Incontestability

sy,di(statut! law legislat! /s incontestab! /s coverage insur* * * *
policy)

(e) Patterns of Treatment of Common Clauses

(3) Moral Hazard Clauses

''moral hazard'' /s clause provision
encumb! incumber! incumbrance /5 clause provision /p
insur* * * *

§ 6.8 Variance Claims Involving Incorrect Information in Insurance Applications, Tardy Premium Payments, or the Status of Insured Property

(b) Erroneously Recorded Answers in an Application for Insurance

(2) Erroneous Answers and Positive Representations by an Agent

sy,di(respond* * * response answer! /5 truth! correct /s
agent broker representative examiner /s err* * * erring
wrong * * false * * falsif! incorrect!)
estop! /s represent! state* stating statement /s actual implied
apparent /3 authority authoriz!

(c) Accepting Premiums Tendered Late or Otherwise Improperly

(1) Generally

to(217) /p late tard! /s payment pay* * * paid /s
premium

(3) Election

retain! retention keep! kept withh*ld! /5 premium /p
elect* * *

(d) Notice to the Insurer of Changes Concerning Location, Use or Occupancy

(2) Occupancy Clauses

to(217) /p property building structure house /s vacan!
unoccupied empty /s fire /3 coverage insurance policy

§ 6.9 Regulation of Claims Processes

(b) Variance Claims Based on the Insurer's Conduct

217k514 /p assist! cooperat! /5 clause provision /s breach! &
sy(assist! cooperat! /5 clause provision)

(c) Subrogation Rights and Variance Claims

(1) Collision Coverages

sy(consen! /5 insurer carrier /s tort lawsuit suit sue* suing
claim! /s insured assured policy-holder

(d) Receipt of Due Proof Clauses and Variance Claims

advertis! brochure booklet /s coverage insur* * * * policy /s
bound bind!

(e) Insurer's Breach as Excusing an Insured's Noncompliance with Claim Procedures .

insurer carrier /s fail! lack! /7 defend! defense /s insured assured policy-holder

to(217) /p unreasonab! unjustifi /5 delay! dilator! wait! /s claim settl!

§ 6.10   Insurer's Rights at Variance with Policy Provisions

(b) Reformation of the Coverage Agreement

reform! /s contract agreement policy coverage /s scrivener scrib! secretar! typing type* typographical! clerk clerical /s err* * * mistak!

(d) Modification of the Coverage Terms

Endorsements or "Riders"

coverage policy contract /s rider endors! /s enforc! /p insur* * * *

(e) Termination of Coverage: Rescission and Cancellation

terminat! cancel! resci! recind! recis! /5 coverage insurance policy contract /s ''mutual! mistak!''

Chapter Seven

CLAIMS: PROCESSES AND
SETTLEMENTS

Table of Sections

---

§ 7.1 Introductory Note

Insurance contracts almost uniformly contain provisions that specify procedures to be followed or actions to be taken in the course of reporting a loss [1] and presenting a claim to the insurance company. [2] Most insurance policies expressly condition [3] the insurer's obligation to pay insurance benefits on compliance with these notice and claims provisions — that is, insurance forms typically include clauses which state that no action may be brought against the insurer unless, as a condition precedent thereto, all terms prescribing procedures to be followed or actions to be taken following a loss shall have been fully complied with by a claimant. [4]

In most cases, a claimant is well advised to avoid disputes over the effect of the policy provisions that relate to the claims process by taking actions that satisfy the various notice and claim procedures specified by the insurer. However, there are circumstances — through inadvertence, procrastination, or as a result of a conscious decision when it appears that compliance might prejudice an insured claimant's interests — in which the actions prescribed in the relevant provisions of an insurance policy are not taken by a claimant. When this occurs, a law suit about the consequences of a failure to conform to such insurance policy terms may result either because the lack of compliance is raised as a defense to a claim for insurance benefits or an insurer seeks a declaratory judgment.

The types of insurance policy provisions that relate to the claims process which have most frequently been involved in litigation include (1) clauses specifying when notice of a loss must be provided to the insurer, [5] (2) terms restricting the period within which a claim must be presented or a law suit must be initiated against an insurer that has not paid a claim, [6] (3) requirements mandating that an insured who

---

§ 7.1

1. See § 7.2, below.

For example, when liability coverage is involved, the insurance policy almost always states that an insured must notify an insurer about events that may be the basis of a subsequent claim as the result of harm sustained by a third party — that is, the policy specifically details that the insured must be given notice of events that *might* lead to a subsequent claim.

2. See § 7.2, below.

3. See the discussion in § 7.2(b)(2), below.

Concerning other situations in which coverage is subject to "conditions," see § 5.6, § 6.6(b), above, and § 7.3(b), below.

4. See for example, the liability insurance forms in Appendices.

5. See § 7.2(b), below.

6. See § 7.2, below.

seeks coverage under liability insurance must assist and cooperate with the insurer,[7] and (4) many provisions that are used in uninsured motorist insurance,[8] including the terms that restrict an insured's right to settle tort claims and the arbitration clauses (which specify that this type of alternative dispute resolution is to be employed for some disputes which cannot be resolved through negotiation[9]).

When there is a failure to comply with one or more of the requirements set forth in provisions that specify procedures to be followed or actions to be taken after the occurrence of an insured event and the insurance claim is rejected on that basis, the possible effects of a claimant's action(s) or omission(s) range from the elimination of the insured's right to bring a suit against the insurer (which is the consequence typically specified in the insurance policy terms) to no impact at all on the insured's right to receive the insurance benefits.[10]   Although in many situations an insured's rights are determined in accordance with judicial precedents which preclude the enforcement of insurance policy provisions that in essence produce a forfeiture of an insured's right to coverage after a loss has occurred, the analysis of an insured's rights should also be evaluated in relation to various legislative provisions which have been adopted in several states.

Timeliness Provisions

The various timeliness provisions of insurance policies, which specify actions insureds are "required" to take following the occurrence of an insured event, provide an excellent vehicle for examining both many of the issues that may arise between an insured and an insurer in the course of processing an insurance claim and the factors that should be considered in resolving disputes about such matters.[11]

Liability Insurance

In some respects, liability insurance involves a notably different relationship between an insurer and an insured than that which prevails for other types of insurance.[12]   Consequently, the settlement

---

7. See § 7.3, below.

8. See Volume 2 of Widiss, UNINSURED AND UNDERINSURED MOTORIST INSURANCE (1987).

9. The arbitration clause is one of the unusual features of the uninsured motorist insurance coverage.

In some contexts, the insurance industry has sought to avoid litigating claims disputes with insureds in courts by including provisions in insurance policies for nonjudicial dispute resolution.   Although alternative dispute resolution processes (such as the use of arbitrators and appraisers) may afford advantages for both insurers and insureds, the inclusion in insurance

policies of clauses that mandate the use of such techniques has produced a number of interesting legal issues.

See generally, Widiss, UNINSURED AND UNDERINSURED MOTORIST INSURANCE (1987), Chapter 22 through Chapter 27.

10. See the discussion in § 7.2 and § 7.3, below.

11. These provisions and the disputes involving such insurance policy terms are the primary focus of § 7.2, below.

12. Liability insurance policies generally provide that the insurer will defend any suit alleging injuries and seeking damages which are payable under the policy and,

and litigation of liability insurance claims often entails a variety of distinctive problems.[13] Most of the differences are directly attributable to the fact that liability insurance is a "third party" coverage — that is, the insurer's contractual obligation is to pay on behalf of an insured all sums (up to the coverage limits) that the insured shall become legally obligated to pay as damages for the type of occurrences covered by the insurance policy. In other words, a liability insurer's obligation to indemnify is essentially fault based and the insurance benefits are usually paid to a third party (rather than to an insured or someone designated explicitly as a beneficiary by the insured).

Liability insurance policies almost uniformly provide that the insurer is empowered to settle any claim or suit against an insured. The failure of an insurer to make a settlement frequently is a matter of considerable importance and is discussed in the concluding sections of this chapter.[14]

The interests of a liability insurer and its insured are not always the same in regard to the tort claims against the insured. In many instances, the differences in their respective positions are sufficiently significant to create notable conflict of interests problems.[15]

Consequences of an Insurer's Decision To Either Delay or Refuse To Pay Insurance Benefits

The potential consequences of an insurer's decision either to delay the payment of a claim or not to pay a claim have undergone a dramatic change in the course of the past half century as a result of both judicial decisions and legislative provisions.[16] This is true in regard to both third party claims involving liability insurance and first party insurance claims.[17]

either explicitly or implicitly, entitle the insurer to control the defense, as well as the settlement of claims made against the insured.

13. These problems are discussed in § 7.4 through § 7.8, and § 9.1, below.

14. See the discussion of statutory remedies for nonpayment and late payment of claims in § 7.7, below, the discussion about the liability insurers duty to insureds regarding settlement in § 7.8, below, and the discussion of punitive damage awards against insurers in § 7.10, below.

15. Problems which are representative of those conflicts are discussed in § 7.6, below.

16. For example, when an insurer delays a payment, there are now numerous statutes which provide that the insurer will be liable for any attorney fees incurred by an insured who subsequently secures payment of the claim as a consequence of a law suit. See § 7.7(c), below.

17. The imposition of penalties as well as liability in excess of the coverage limits in the event an insurer fails to make a prompt settlement of a liability insurance claim is discussed in § 7.7, § 7.8, and § 7.9, below.

§ 7.2   Claims Presentment

§ 7.2(a)   Timeliness Provisions

(1) Introduction

Insurance policies commonly include several provisions relating to the timeliness of actions by a claimant following the occurrence of an insured event,[1] including (1) clauses which require that an insured provide the insurer with a prompt notice of a loss,[2] (2) terms that either require submission of a proof of loss within some specified period of time [3] or the submission of a due proof of loss,[4] (3) conditions in liability insurance policies which state that an insurer must immediately forward to the insurer all documents which the insured receives in the event a suit is filed against the insured,[5] and, increasingly (4) provisions that restrict the time within which a suit may be initiated by an insured against the insurer as a consequence of a loss.[6]

Justifications For Timeliness Provisions

There are several justifications for the enforcement of timeliness provisions in insurance policies. First, timeliness provisions, especially those that relate to notice of a loss and to submission of proof in support of a claim, are viewed as essential to affording insurers an adequate opportunity to investigate the circumstances so as to be able to appropriately assess questions related to the coverage or the extent of the loss.[7]

Second, timeliness provisions have been viewed as being warranted by a public interest in enforcing measures that are designed to reduce the opportunities for fraud. However, when such provisions are uniformly enforced under all circumstances, there inevitably are some instances in which the claims of honest insureds are precluded — that is, the enforcement of various timeliness provisions specified in insurance policies undoubtedly eliminates coverage for some scrupulously worthy individuals who inadvertently fail to comply with these terms. The fact that some deserving persons are required to bear losses which would otherwise be covered is arguably justified by the public interest in reducing the opportunities for fraudulent insurance claims.

---

§ 7.2(a)

1. For example, see the fire insurance forms in Appendix A, and the automobile insurance forms in Appendix H.

2. See the discussion in § 7.2(b), below. Also see Appendices A, F, G, and H.

3. See the discussion in § 7.2(c), below. Also see Appendices A and F.

4. See the discussion in § 7.2(c), below. Also see Appendix A and Appendix F.

5. See the discussion in § 7.2(d), below. Also see Appendix G, Appendix H, and Appendix J.

6. See the discussion in § 7.2(a)(3) and § 7.2(e), below.

7. See the discussion of notice of loss provisions in § 7.2(b)(1), below.

Third, many judicial decisions, particularly among the older precedents, have predicated the enforcement of timeliness provisions on the rationale that courts should not interfere with the effects of clear and unambiguous contract provisions.[8]

Requiring Compliance With Timeliness Provisions

Whenever possible, claimants are well advised to comply with the applicable timeliness provisions. There are numerous judicial precedents which support the proposition that an insured's right to coverage is lost when such conditions have not been satisfied, that is, in many circumstances judicial decisions have held that an insurer is absolved of liability because the insurer's obligation was appropriately conditioned on compliance with a time limit set forth in the insurance policy.[9]

Precluding Enforcement of Timeliness Provisions

The failure of a claimant to conform to the terms specified in timeliness provisions does not invariably result in a loss of coverage. A survey of the relevant appellate cases reveals that there are several doctrines upon which courts have based decisions rejecting an insurer's position and have thereby upheld the claimant's right to coverage.

First, there is a substantial body of appellate decisions holding that an insurer's enforcement of a timeliness provision is precluded when a claimant presents an appropriate excuse for the lack of compliance.[10]

Second, there are also some instances in which the courts have sustained defenses to the enforcement of timeliness provisions on the basis of an estoppel or a waiver.[11]

Third, courts in many states have concluded that the rejection of a claim by an insurer predicated on one or more timeliness provisions is not permissible in the absence of a showing that the insurer's interests were prejudiced by the claimant's action or inaction.[12] There now appears to be a clear trend among the appellate court decisions that favors limiting the enforcement of the timeliness provisions in insurance policies to instances in which the insurer has been prejudiced. However, the judicial approaches to issues raised by the introduction of a prejudice requirement are quite varied.[13] And there are also a few jurisdictions in which the courts have held that prejudice is only one of several interrelated matters to be considered when the effect of a timeliness provision is at issue.[14]

---

8. See the discussion and cases cited in § 7.2(b)(2), below.

9. See decisions cited in § 7.2(b)(2), § 7.2(c), § 7.2(d), and § 9.10(b).

10. See the discussion § 7.2(e)(3), below.

11. See the discussion in § 7.2(e)(3), below.

12. See the discussion in § 7.2(e)(2), below.

13. See the discussion and cases cited in § 7.2(e)(2), below.

14. See the discussion and cases cited in § 7.2(e)(2).

When the insured's compliance, or an alleged lack thereof, with a timeliness provision in an insurance policy is involved in a coverage dispute, it is now essential for attorneys representing either insurers or insureds to weigh carefully both the possible justifications for and the factors that mitigate against the enforcement of a timeliness provision.

(2) Specific Versus General Timeliness Provisions

The formulation of insurance policy provisions that require a claimant to perform certain actions within some period of time following the occurrence of an insured event involves a choice between setting forth either a specific time limit (that is, a given number of days, months, or years) or a generalized time limit (such as a provision which states that a notice of loss must be sent to the insurer within a "reasonable time"). Whether policy provisions are to be designed with a view to providing for certainty (by specifying an exact time period) or for flexibility (by employing terms such as a "reasonable time" period) is a dilemma that is faced in many insurance contexts, as well as in numerous other drafting situations.[15] Insurers often prefer "specificity" in timeliness provisions — that is, provisions which establish a certain number of days, months, or years within which the prescribed steps must be taken. For example, when an insured event occurs, a policy may provide that notice shall be given "as soon as practicable, but in no event to exceed 60 days."

Legislatures, administrative agencies, and courts have sometimes decided that timeliness provisions in insurance policy terms purporting to impose specific time limits, especially time periods of relatively short duration, either should not be permitted or that the insurer is not entitled to enforce the provisions as written.[16] In fact, one of the areas in which there has been the most significant application of legislative and administrative regulatory controls of the terms used in insurance policies, as well as judicial scrutiny which has resulted in the recognition of rights at variance with policy provisions,[17] has been in regard to the use and enforceability of various types of rigid time limits that some insurers have sought to impose on the claims process.

(3) Timeliness Provisions and the Statute of Limitations

Provisions in many insurance policies now prescribe a time period following the occurrence of a loss within which a law suit may be filed against the company. For example, property insurance policies (which provide coverage for losses that result from various causes) typically provide, "No suit or action on this policy for the recovery of any claim shall be sustainable in any court of law * * * unless commenced

---

15. Also consider the discussion in § 1.4, above.

16. See the discussion in the following subsection and in § 9.10(b), below.

17. See the discussion and the decisions cited in § 7.2(e), below. Also see the discussion in § 6.1, above.

within twelve months next after inception of the loss." [18]   Similarly, some of the policy forms used by insurance companies for uninsured motorist insurance state that no suit or action on this policy for the recovery of any claim shall be sustainable in any court of law or equity unless it is commenced within twelve months from the occurrence on which the claim is based.[19]

An issue of enforceability arises when a timeliness clause prescribes a time limit for initiating a suit against the insurer that is shorter than the statute of limitations period that would otherwise be applicable to a claim arising under such an insurance contract.[20]   Such provisions are likely to produce a significant number of coverage disputes.[21]

18. See, e.g., Ford Motor Credit Company v. Aetna Casualty and Surety Company, 717 F.2d 959 (6th Cir.1983); Brunner v. United Fire & Casualty Company, 338 N.W.2d 151 (Iowa 1983) (one year period of limitations in standard fire insurance policy upheld); Betty Brooks, Inc. v. Insurance Placement Facility of Delaware, 456 A.2d 1226 (Del.1983).

Also see Schreiber v. Pennsylvania Lumberman's Mutual Insurance Company, 498 Pa. 21, 444 A.2d 647 (1982) (predicating the enforcement of the twelve month limitation on the fact that the provision was mandated by the legislature) (but with a very thoughtful dissent by Justice Nix).

It is not difficult to envision the type of coverage disputes which can arise in regard to such policy provisions. For example, an insurer rejected the claim of a homeowner who delayed five months after knowing about the damage before making repairs. When the repairs were made, the homeowner discovered that the damage was due to a cause within the coverage of his homeowners policy. Several months after the repairs were made the insurance claim was made, and subsequently rejected. When suit was filed, the court decided that the insured was barred from a recovery. The court concluded that even though the insured brought suit within a year after discovering the actual cause of the loss, he failed to bring a suit within a year of when he knew of the fully developed damage. Naghten v. Maryland Casualty Co., 47 Ill.App.2d 74, 197 N.E.2d 489 (1st Dist.1964), 24 A.L.R.3d 1001 (1969) (policy requirement that suit be brought within "twelve months next after inception of the loss").

19. See the discussion of such limits in the uninsured motorist coverage in Widiss, UNINSURED AND UNDERINSURED MOTORIST INSURANCE (1985), at § 7.11.

20. See case cited in note 21, below, and in § 9.10(b), below.

Also see, e.g., McKinney's New York Insurance Law § 3216 (1984) (accident and sickness policy provisions).

21. See, e.g., Closser v. Penn Mutual Fire Insurance Company, 457 A.2d 1081 (Delaware 1983) ("after inception of the loss" meant date of fire or other casualty causing loss, rather than date of the insurer's denial of coverage); Sheetz v. IMT Insurance Company, 324 N.W.2d 302 (Iowa 1982) (insurer waived requirement that suit had to be commenced within twelve months of the inception of a loss by continuing negotiations for a settlement beyond that period); St. Paul Mercury Insurance Company v. Tri-State Cattle Feeders, Inc., 638 S.W.2d 868 (Tex.1982) (theft insurance policy required notice to the insurer within 24 hours).

Also see Nicholson v. Nationwide Mutual Fire Insurance Company, 517 F.Supp. 1046 (N.D.Ga., Atlanta Div.1981) (action was not barred by the 12-month limitation in the policy because the time period was tolled from the time the claim was submitted until the claim was denied by the insurer); Peloso v. Hartford Fire Insurance Company, 56 N.J. 514, 267 A.2d 498 (1970).

Cf. Gilbert Frank Corporation v. Federal Insurance Company, 91 A.D.2d 31, 457 N.Y.2d 494 (1st Dept.1983) (factual issues were presented in regard to waiver or estoppel, which precluded summary judgment, by an insurer who undertook a lengthy and protracted negotiation of a claim).

Cf. Martin v. Liberty Mutual Fire Insurance Company, 97 Wis.2d 127, 293 N.W.2d 168 (1980) (action was barred by 12-month limit in policy which was approved by the statutory codification of the policy form).

§ 7.2(b)   Provisions Requiring Notice of a Loss

(1) Generally

The primary purpose of a notice requirement in an insurance policy is to afford the insurer a reasonable opportunity to protect its rights.[1] Prompt notice to the insurer maximizes an insurer's opportunity to acquire information about the circumstances of a loss (usually by way of a timely investigation when witnesses are most likely to be available and while their memories of the events are generally the most accurate, as well as when there is usually the best opportunity to examine, record, or preserve any physical evidence), which may be important both (1) to the insurer's determinations in regard to whether a loss is covered and (2) to the preparation of a defense to claims by a third party against an insured who is covered by a liability insurance policy.[2]

Coverage disputes involving the enforcement of insurance policy provisions setting forth notice requirements cannot properly be regarded as exclusively raising issues of competing interests between the insurer and the insured. Requiring a prompt notice of a loss sometimes protects the interests of an insured as well as those of an insurer. For example, as the New Hampshire Supreme Court observed, notice provisions afford "an opportunity to conduct a timely investigation which promotes early settlements * * *."[3] Thus, in liability insurance cases early notice may facilitate settlement, thereby avoiding the expense of litigation and eliminating the risk that litigation might result in an award of damages by a judge or jury exceeding the coverage limits and consequently remaining an obligation of the insured.

Under almost all types of insurance, early investigation increases the probability that fraudulent claims will be detected, an objective that is fully consistent with the best interests of the insurer, insureds generally, the public, and, in most instances, the insured. A clear example of the possible importance of prompt notice to an insured, as well as the insurer, is provided by fidelity bonds. When a claim under a fidelity bond results from misappropriations,[4] prompt notice often may help to prevent further losses.

§ 7.2(b)

1. See, e.g., Brown v. Maryland Casualty Co., 111 Vt. 30, 11 A.2d 222, 129 A.L.R. 1404 (1940); Jellico Grocery Co. v. Sun Indemnity Co., 272 Ky. 276 at p. 282, 114 S.W.2d 83 at p. 86 (1938).

2. See the discussions in Gerrard Realty Corporation v. American States Insurance Company, 89 Wis.2d 130, 277 N.W.2d 863 (1979); Stonewall Insurance Company v. Moorby, 130 Vt. 562, 298 A.2d 826 at p. 829 (Chittenden 1972).

Also see Illinois Valley Minerals Corp. v. Royal-Globe Insurance Company, 70 Ill. App.3d 296, 26 Ill.Dec. 629, 388 N.E.2d 253 (3d Dist.1979); Morales v. National Grange Mutual Insurance Company, 176 N.J. Super. 347, 423 A.2d 325 at pp. 329–330 (Law Division, Essex County, 1980).

3. Lumbermens Mutual Casualty Company v. Oliver, 115 N.H. 141, 335 A.2d 666 at p. 668 (1975).

4. E.g., Brown v. Maryland Casualty Co., 111 Vt. 30, 11 A.2d 222, 129 A.L.R. 1404 (1940).

Cf. Boston Mutual Life Insurance Company v. Fireman's Fund Insurance Company, 613 F.Supp. 1090 (D.Mass.1985) (applying Massachusetts law).

(2) Enforcement of Notice Requirements

The enforcement of insurance policy terms conditioning the insurer's liability on prompt notice of a loss has been the subject of a significant number of disputes. In many instances, appellate courts have held, and undoubtedly will continue to hold, that so long as a notice of loss provision is clear and unambiguous an insurer is relieved of liability when notice has not been given by a claimant to an insurer within the time period specified in the insurance policy.[5] The holdings in these cases usually are predicated on the rationale either that an insured's failure to provide notice constitutes a material breach of the insurance contract, or that the insured has failed to satisfy a condition precedent to the insurer's liability. However, there are numerous instances in which an insurer's rejection of a claim on the basis of the failure to comply with a notice provision has not been sustained. The appellate court decisions in these cases have been based on several distinct rationales and justifications.

First, when policy provisions require notice "as soon as possible" or "as soon as practicable," courts almost uniformly apply a standard of what is reasonable under the circumstances.[6] Furthermore, courts

---

5. *Cf.* Miller v. Dilts, 463 N.E.2d 257 at p. 265 (Ind.1984). The court commented, "Prejudice to the insurance company's ability to prepare an adequate defense can therefore be presumed by an unreasonable delay in notifying the company about the accident or about the filing of the lawsuit." However, the opinion also stated, "The injured party can establish some evidence that prejudice did not occur in the particular situation," and, "Once such evidence is introduced, the question becomes one for the trier of fact to determine whether any prejudice actually existed." *Id.,* 463 N.E.2d at pp. 265–266.

Cf. Terrell v. State Farm Insurance Co., 346 N.W.2d 149 (Minn.1984), in which the court concluded that an insured who failed to give notice within the time period prescribed by a no-fault insurance policy issued in conformity with the Minnesota no-fault legislation was barred from making a claim, and that Minnesota precedents which required prejudice did not apply because the legislature intended that failure to give timely notice under a no-fault policy would preclude claims in all cases.

Also see Casualty Indemnity Exchange v. Village of Crete, 731 F.2d 457 (7th Cir. 1984) (applying Illinois law).

See generally Annotation, *Liability insurance: clause with respect to notice of accident or claim, etc., or with respect to forwarding suit papers,* 18 A.L.R.2d 443–507 (1951).

6. See, e.g., Utica Mutual Insurance Company v. Fireman's Fund Insurance Company, 748 F.2d 118 (2d Cir.1984) (applying New York law); Lord v. State Farm Mutual Automobile Insurance Company, 224 Va. 283, 295 S.E.2d 796 (1982) (notice of a claim under an automobile policy medical payments coverage 173 days after the accident was not "as soon as practical"); Marez v. Dairyland Insurance Company, 638 P.2d 286 (Colo.1981) (affirming the rule which has been consistently followed by the Colorado courts); Reserve Insurance Company v. Richards, 577 S.W.2d 417 (Ky. 1978) (thirteen months from occurrence to notice is not "as soon as practical" for purposes of a liability insurance policy issued to a School Board Association); State Farm Mutual Auto. Ins. Co. v. Porter, 221 Va. 592 at p. 599, 272 S.E.2d 196 at p. 200 (1980) (liability insurance);

Cf. Liberty Mutual Insurance Company v. Bob Roberts and Company, Inc., 357 So. 2d 968 (Ala.1978); Southern Guaranty Insurance Company v. Thomas, 334 So.2d 879 at p. 882 (Ala.1976); Lumbermens Mutual Casualty Company v. Oliver, 115 N.H. 141, 335 A.2d 666 at p. 668 (1975); Allstate Insurance Company v. Fogg, 293 Ala. 155, 300 So.2d 819 (1974);

Also see American Fidelity Co. v. Schemel, 103 N.H. 190, 168 A.2d 478 (1961) (liability coverage requiring notice "as soon as practicable"); Henderson v. Hawkeye-Security Insurance Co., 252 Iowa 97, 106 N.W.2d 86 (1960) (automobile medical pay-

usually conclude that policy provisions requiring "prompt notice," "immediate notice," and other comparable terms mean that notice must be given to the insurer as soon as practicable in the particular situation.[7] Thus, regardless of the specific terminology used in the insurance policy, when an exact period of time is not specified (that is, the requirement is not set forth in terms of a specific number of hours, days, weeks, months, or years), compliance with a notice requirement is almost always evaluated by courts in terms of what would have been reasonable under the circumstances. In addition, courts usually treat a dispute about whether an insured has adequately complied with a notice requirement as a question of fact to be determined at trial,[8] which means that a claimant generally is entitled to have the issue submitted to a jury.[9]

ments coverage requiring notice "as soon as practicable"); Britz v. American Insurance Co., 2 Wis.2d 192, 86 N.W.2d 18 (1957), 66 A.L.R.2d 1271 (1959) (theft coverage requiring notice "as soon as practicable"); Equity General Insurance Company v. Patis, 119 Ill.App.3d 232, 74 Ill.Dec. 846, 456 N.E.2d 348 (1st Dist., Div. 4, 1983).

7. See, e.g., Liberty Mutual Insurance Company v. Bob Roberts and Company, Inc., 357 So.2d 968 (Ala.1978); RTE Corporation v. Maryland Casualty Company, 74 Wis.2d 614, 247 N.W.2d 171 (1976); Lumbermens Mutual Casualty v. Oliver, 115 N.H. 141, 335 A.2d 666 (1975).

Cf. St. Paul Mercury Insurance Company v. Tri-State Cattle Feeders, Inc., 638 S.W.2d 868 (Tex.1982). The court sustained jury findings that a provision in a theft policy requiring notice of loss within 24 hours was unreasonable under the circumstances and notice was given within a reasonable time.

Cf. Great American Insurance Company v. C.G. Tate Construction Co., 46 N.C.App. 427, 265 S.E.2d 467 (1980).

Also see Zukaitis v. Aetna Casualty and Surety Company, 195 Nev. 59, 236 N.W.2d 819 at p. 820 (1975) (the court affirmed earlier decisions that "the word 'immediate' * * * means with reasonable celerity, with reasonable and proper diligence, and what is a reasonable time depends upon all facts and circumstances of each particular case."); St. Paul Fire & Marine Insurance Co. v. Petzold, 418 F.2d 303 (1st Cir.1969) (New Hampshire law; policyholder's counsel did not advise notifying the company because he thought policyholder could not be held liable for damage to a third person by blasting done on policyholder's premises by another; *held,* reasonable excuse for delayed notice; remarking that this alone did not dispose of the issue whether the insured notified the insurer in

reasonable time, the court considered the issue of prejudice and then concluded that defendant policyholder was entitled to judgment in the declaratory action); Abington Mutual Fire Insurance Co. v. Drew, 109 N.H. 464, 254 A.2d 829 (1969) (accidental shooting by insured's son while hunting; notice was given three months after accident, when insured and son consulted an attorney upon son's being arrested and were informed that insured's homeowners policy provided coverage; *held,* insurer obliged to defend son in tort action; there was evidence to support trial court's finding of no "substantial breach").

Also see Melton v. Republic Vanguard Insurance Company, 548 S.W.2d 313 at p. 316 (Tenn.App., Middle Section, 1976).

8. See, e.g., State Farm Fire and Casualty Co. v. Hartford Accident & Indemnity Co., 347 So.2d 389 (Ala.1977); Lumbermens Mutual Casualty Company v. Oliver, 115 N.H. 141, 335 A.2d 666 at p. 668 (1975).

Cf. Hartford Fire Insurance Company v. Masternak, 55 A.D.2d 472, 390 N.Y.S.2d 949 (4th Dept.1977).

But cf. Meierdierck v. Miller, 394 Pa. 484, 147 A.2d 406 (1959) (In the absence of extenuating circumstances, the Pennsylvania Courts have held that a question in regard to whether notice was timely is to be decided by the court.).

9. See, e.g., Southern Guaranty Insurance Company v. Thomas, 334 So.2d 879 at p. 882 (Ala.1976).

Also see Weis v. International Insurance Company, Inc., 567 F.Supp. 631 at p. 637 (N.D.Ga.1983).

However, in some jurisdictions the "courts have held comparable unexcused delays to be unreasonable as a matter of law." See, e.g., Casualty Indemnity Exchange v. Village of Crete, 731 F.2d 457 at

Second, there is a significant body of appellate decisions which have applied doctrines that restrict the enforcement of timeliness provisions. For example, courts have held that extenuating circumstances may excuse a delay in providing notification, especially when the claimant can show that there has been no lack of due diligence.[10] The issue of what is a reasonable excuse, usually is presented to a court as a defense to the enforcement of a claim presentment provision.[11]

Third, and probably of most significance, there are many judicial decisions that impose substantial limitations on when notice terms may be enforced by insurers, typically by requiring an insurer to show that it was prejudiced by the insured's delay.[12]

(3) Determining "When" a Time Period Begins to Run

The determination of when a time period begins to run for taking some action in regard to the presentment of a claim is often an important question. Many insurance policies include provisions specifying that the time period within which the insurer must be provided notice (or a claim must be filed) commences with occurrence of the "casualty" that serves as the basis for a claim. For example, liability insurance coverage terms usually state that the time period within which the insurer must be notified begins with the occurrence of an insured event to which the insurance applies.[13] Similarly, the time limits for accident insurance policies typically start to run when a loss occurs.[14]

In most situations, even in the absence of an explicit term in the insurance policy, the time period within which notice must be provided to an insurer appropriately begins with the occurrence of the loss. When an insured is aware that a loss covered by an insurance policy has occurred, the occurrence of the event is a reasonable point to initiate the running of the applicable time periods, and a failure to comply with a timeliness provision will not be excused.[15] For example, the rejection of a claim was sustained on this basis when an insured sought to justify a delay because the amount of the resulting loss was not known.[16]

---

p. 459 (7th Cir.1984) (applying Illinois law and citing several Illinois precedents).

10. See the cases cited in the discussion in § 7.2(e)(3), below.

11. See the discussion of defenses to the enforcement of timeliness presentment provisions in § 7.2(e), below.

12. These limitations, which apply to other claims presentment policy terms as well as notice of loss provisions, are also discussed in § 7.2(e)(2), below.

13. See the forms in Appendices G and H (notice "as soon as practicable" after the accident, occurrence, or loss; notice of

steps in the process of claim or suit "immediately" after the "demand, notice, summons or other process" is received).

14. See Appendix F.

15. E.g., Brown v. Maryland Casualty Co., 111 Vt. 30, 11 A.2d 222, 129 A.L.R. 1404 (1940).

16. RTE Casualty Company v. Maryland Casualty Company, 74 Wis.2d 614, 247 N.W.2d 171 (1976).

Whenever an insured knows of the occurrence of an insured event, generally the insurer should be notified as soon as possible following the loss.

There are circumstances in which an insured is not aware that a loss has occurred. If there is no explicit provision in the insurance policy that applies to such situations, a court will usually hold that an insured is excused from acting until either the insured actually knew of the occurrence [17] or a reasonable person in the insured's position would have become aware of it. Some insurance policies include clauses that specifically address the notice requirement in this type of situation. For example, there are insurance policy provisions which state that the time period begins when an insured has knowledge of facts from which a reasonable person in the insured's position would infer that an insured event had occurred.

The term "discover" is used in the timeliness provisions of some insurance policies. Insurers have contended that clauses phrased in terms of "discover" should be interpreted to mean that the time period begins if a reasonable person would infer from facts known to the insured that a loss had occurred, even though the insured did not draw that inference.[18] This approach would adopt the test of a reasonable person, which is generally characterized as an "objective standard." However, when an insurance policy provision uses the term "discover" in a notice requirement, it is at least equally appropriate to interpret the provision as setting forth a *subjective* standard about the insured's knowledge of the occurrence of an insured event. The condition or requirement established by a timeliness provision phrased in terms of "discovery" is reasonably understood as contemplating one which depends on an *actual* awareness on the part of the insured of the occurrence and an *actual* comprehension of the significance of those facts which are known by the insured. Even if the term "discover" is not intended by insurers to be so interpreted, the import of any clause which uses this term is ambiguous and such an ambiguity in an insurance policy provision is almost invariably construed against the insurer. Consequently, when a timeliness clause employs the term "discover," a very persuasive case exists for the application of a subjective standard such that a loss of coverage would only occur when an

17. See, e.g., National Mutual Casualty Co. v. Cypret, 207 Ark. 11, 179 S.W.2d 161 (1944) (the mortgagee-bank, the insured of a theft policy, held to be excused when the insured car disappeared under ambiguous circumstances and the mortgagee-bank gave notice within 60 days after learning that it had been stolen).

Cf. Rowe v. National Security Fire and Casualty Company, 4 Ark.App. 16, 626 S.W.2d 622 (1982) (insured covered by a fire insurance policy was not required to provide notice within sixty days that a rented house had burned unless the failure to comply was due or traceable to the insured's own negligence).

Also see Johnson Ready-Mix Concrete Co. v. United Pacific Insurance Co., 11 Utah 2d 279, 358 P.2d 337 (1961) (corporate insured not barred by late notice to liability insurer since no employee of insured with authority to receive such information for the insured knew that the incident occurred and that it was not trivial).

In some situations, knowledge on the part of the insured's agent will be imputed to the insured. See, e.g., City of West Haven v. United States Fidelity and Guaranty Company, 174 Conn. 392, 389 A.2d 741 (1978).

18. See, e.g., Utica Mutual Insurance Company v. Fireman's Fund Insurance Company, 748 F.2d 118 (2d Cir.1984) (applying New York law).

insured had actual knowledge and awareness, rather than the use of an objective standard based on what a reasonable person would infer from the information known by the insured about the events that had occurred.

Courts sometimes recognize a distinction between an awareness of facts from which the inference of loss would be drawn by a reasonable person and an awareness of facts that create no more than a suspicion of a possible loss in a reasonable person's mind.[19] Furthermore, even if an insured is negligent in failing to realize that an insured event causing a loss has occurred and for that reason does not comply with a timeliness provision, there is a possibility that a court will refuse to enforce an insurance policy provision purporting to bar an insured from protection.[20]

In some instances, timely notice is not provided to an insurer because the claimant is not aware that there is an insurance policy that provides an applicable coverage.[21] When this occurs, the questions that should be considered when assessing the significance of an insured's failure to provide the insurer notice of the loss within the time period prescribed in the coverage terms are essentially the same as those discussed in the preceding portions of this subsection.[22]

§ 7.2(c) Provisions Requiring Timely Presentment of Claims

Provisions designed to require the timely presentment of claims, typically insurance policy terms concerning proof of the loss by a claimant, are generally viewed as advantageous by insurers for virtually all types of coverage. There are several reasons for including such timeliness provisions in insurance policies.[1]

Proof of loss requirements are designed to decrease the burden on the insurer of setting aside adequate "reserves for undetermined claims" by reducing the degree of uncertainty about both the number of claims that may result from the occurrence of an insured event that has been reported to the insurer and the amount of insurance benefits sought for each claim.[2] Fire insurance policies, as well as some other

19. When there is no more than a suspicion of a possible loss, some courts have concluded that there is insufficient knowledge on the part of the insured to warrant the loss of coverage as a consequence of the failure to give notice to the insurer. See, e.g., Gilmour v. Standard Surety & Casualty Co., 292 Mass. 205, 197 N.E. 673 (1935).

20. See generally § 6.9(a), above.

Also see § 7.2(e), below.

21. See the cases cited in § 7.2(e)(3), notes 45 through 47.

22. Also see the discussion in § 7.2(e), below.

§ 7.2(c)

1. Also see the discussion of the reasons for loss provisions in § 7.2(a) and § 7.2(b), above.

2. In many cases a sworn proof of loss statement also facilitates the insurer's evaluation of a claim, including an estimate of its liabilities. *Cf.* Petrice v. Federal Kemper Insurance Company, 163 W.Va. 737, 260 S.E.2d 276 at p. 278 (1979).

coverages,[3] commonly provide for the filing of a proof of loss.[4] Courts have sustained denials of coverage predicated on a claimant's failure to comply with such provisions.

Disputes between insurers and insureds about the enforceability and effect of timeliness clauses included in proof of loss provisions have produced a considerable volume of litigation. Among these cases, there are numerous appellate court decisions holding that the rights of the insureds are at variance with policy provisions.[5] A significant portion of the judicial decisions favoring the claimants, though by no means all of these cases, have been based on the proposition that there should not be a forfeiture of an insured's rights unless it is shown that the failure to comply with the timeliness provisions was prejudicial to the insurer.[6]

Comment

Timeliness provisions relating to the filing of claims are sometimes justified by insurers on the basis that they facilitate investigations which may ferret out fraudulent claims because fraud is best detected when the evidence is "fresh." However, the nature of what is necessary in order to alert an insurer to a situation that warrants an investigation is subject to being questioned. For example, once an insurer is aware that an insured event has occurred, thereafter, at least in many situations, the significance of an insured's compliance with the timeliness provisions that relate to the presentment of claims arguably is quite limited because the insurer is in a position to protect its interests by initiating an investigation. Thus, a notification that is sufficient to enable an insurer to recognize that an investigation of a loss is warranted should preclude a forfeiture of the claimant's coverage.[7]

§ 7.2(d)   Provisions Requiring Forwarding of Litigation Papers

Liability insurance policies typically state that if a claim is made or a suit is brought against the insured, every demand, notice, summons, or other document received by the insured or the insured's representative shall be "immediately" (or, in some policy forms, "promptly") forwarded to the insurer.[1] This requirement is in addition to the

---

3. See Appendix A.

Also see Derral K. Sperry and Robert M. Barker, *Notice and Proof of Loss—Pitfalls for the Unwary,* 18 South Texas Law Review 31–47 at pp. 41–47 (1977).

4. *Cf.* Insurance Company of North America v. University of Alaska, 669 P.2d 954 (Alaska 1983).

5. For a general discussion of rights at variance with policy provisions, see Chapter 6, above.

6. A discussion of the defenses that have been allowed, including several specific issues involved in the application of a prejudice requirement, are considered in § 7.2(e), below.

7. See, e.g., Insurance Company of North America v. University of Alaska, 669 P.2d 954 (Alaska 1983) (theft coverage for museum collection of artifacts).

Cf. Kolbeck v. Rural Mutual Insurance Co., 70 Wis.2d 655, 235 N.W.2d 466 (1975).

§ 7.2(d)

1. See, e.g., Merit Insurance Company v. Koza, 274 S.C. 362, 264 S.E.2d 146 (1980).

Also see Appendix G and Appendix H.

insured's obligation to report the occurrence of an insured event to the insurer.[2] When confronted with questions about the meaning of words such as "immediately" or "promptly" in this type of clause, courts typically construe these provisions to mean that the required action must be accomplished within a reasonable period of time in view of the facts and circumstances of the particular situation at issue.[3]

Courts generally are reluctant about interfering with an insurer's enforcement of the requirement that an insured must promptly forward documents when a case has been commenced against an insured — that is, courts usually sustain an insurer's denial of coverage when an insured fails to forward litigation papers with reasonable promptness.[4] The decisions in these cases are markedly different from the many types of situations in which courts have frequently either upheld defenses presented by an insured to the enforcement of various timeliness provisions or imposed limitations on the right of an insurer to enforce such provisions.[5]

Strict adherence to the timeliness requirements for forwarding litigation papers is often warranted because an insured's failure to comply with such provisions may result in the insurer's being fore-

---

2. See the discussion of notice requirements in § 7.2(b).

Also see City of West Haven v. United States Fidelity and Guaranty Company, 174 Conn. 392, 389 A.2d 741 (1978).

3. See, e.g., Gerrard Realty Corp. v. American States Insurance Company, 89 Wis.2d 130 at pp. 140–141, 277 N.W.2d 863 at p. 870 (1979).

4. See, e.g., Pharr v. Continental Casualty Co., 429 So.2d 1018 (Ala.1983) (eight month delay in providing insurer with notice of action against the insured was an unreasonable delay as a matter of law); Gerrard Realty Corp. v. American States Insurance Company, 89 Wis.2d 130, 277 N.W.2d 863 (1979) (failure to provide notice to the insurer of commencement of a suit for twenty-two months constituted noncompliance as a matter of law).

Also see B & M Homes, Inc. v. American Liberty Insurance Company, 356 So.2d 1195 (Ala.1978) (failure to notify insurer of suit for seven months was unreasonable as a matter of law); City of West Haven v. United States Fidelity and Guaranty Company, 174 Conn. 392, 389 A.2d 741 (1978).

Cf. Members Mutual Insurance Company v. Cutaia, 476 S.W.2d 278 at p. 281 (Tex. 1972) (the court observed, while it shared "some of the impatience which naturally arises when a reasonable provision or condition in an insurance policy is used by the insurance company to defeat what appears to be a valid claim * * *, on balance it is

better policy for the contracts of insurance to be changed by the public body charged with their supervision, the State Board of Insurance, or by the Legislature, rather than for this Court to insert a provision that violations of conditions precedent will be excused if no harm results from their violation").

Cf. Equity General Insurance Company v. Patis, 119 Ill.App.3d 232, 74 Ill.Dec. 846, 456 N.E.2d 348 (1st Dist., Div., 1983) (insured's delay of more than four months in notifying insurer, which had issued an errors and omissions policy to an insurance agent, was unreasonable).

However, when the insured did not receive any suit papers and service was made by publication, which was followed by a default judgment, there is no basis for a forfeiture of coverage on the basis of a failure to forward litigation documents to the insurer. See, e.g. Brown v. Donders, 42 Ohio St.2d 133, 326 N.E.2d 647 (1975); Newport v. MFA Insurance Company, 448 N.E.2d 1223 (Ind.App., 4th Dist., 1983).

Also see Note, *Provisions Requiring the Forwarding of Suit Papers Are Strictly Enforced Even Though the Insurer Is Neither Harmed Nor Prejudiced by the Insured's Failure to Comply. Members Mutual Insurance Co. v. Cutia, 476 S.W.2d 278 (Tex. 1972),* 4 Texas Tech Law Review 228–233 (1972).

5. See the discussion of defenses in § 7.2(e), below.

closed from the opportunities (1) for early settlement negotiations, (2) to participate in significant pretrial proceedings, or (3) to assume control of the defense at times when strategic decisions might be made.[6] In many circumstances, it is difficult, if not impossible, to accurately assess precisely what the insurer's role would have been in regard to such events or what might have occurred had the insurer been involved. Although this uncertainty might be invoked by courts to favor maintaining coverage for insureds (as well as protection for third parties asserting claims against insureds covered by liability insurance policies that require the forwarding of such documents), given both the relative ease with which an insured can comply with the requirement that litigation papers be forwarded promptly and an appreciation of the potential significance for the insurer of the opportunities that may have been lost as a consequence of an insured's omission to do so, it is not surprising that courts generally conclude that the failure of an insured to forward litigation papers is unreasonable and will not be excused.

§ 7.2(e) Defenses to the Enforcement of Claims Presentment Timeliness Provisions

(1) Introductory Note

Numerous justifications for not allowing timeliness provisions to work a forfeiture of the coverage provided by an insurance policy have been considered by the courts. The most significant development among the more recent judicial decisions has been the increasing number of jurisdictions in which courts have limited the enforcement of timeliness provisions to instances in which the insurer was prejudiced (in some sense) by the insured's failure to comply with the insurance policy terms at issue. However, there also have been and continue to be many judicial decisions holding that in some situations there are justifications for excusing compliance with various of the timeliness provisions without regard to whether the insurer's interests may have been prejudiced. The following subsections discuss the doctrines that relate to these defenses.

(2) Noncompliance and Requiring Prejudice to the Insurer

If a claimant allegedly has failed to comply with timeliness provisions that specify (1) when notice of a loss is to be provided, (2) the period within which a claim is to be made or a suit is to be initiated against an insurer, or (3) that litigation documents are to be immediately forwarded to the insurer in the event a suit is filed against someone insured by a liability insurance policy, insurers often have asserted that the failure constitutes grounds for denying all coverage under the insurance contract.[1] In such cases, the action(s) — which the insurance

---

6. *Cf.* Kason v. New York, 83 Misc.2d 810, 373 N.Y.S.2d 456 (New York County, 1975).

§ 7.2(e)

1. *Cf.* comments of Cardozo, J., in Coleman v. Amsterdam Casualty Co., 247 N.Y.

policy terms require following an occurrence of a loss — almost always ultimately occur, and therefore the issue in these cases is what consequences should result from the claimant's failure to perform the prescribed act within the time period set forth in the insurance policy.

Insurance policies do not include any provisions that address the matter of prejudice to the insurer. This is not surprising because the premise that prejudice should be considered relevant to the consequences of allegedly tardy reporting of losses, submission of claims, or the forwarding of litigation documents received by insureds as the result of a lawsuit, does not stem from the insurers. Moreover, when an insurer predicates the rejection of an insurance claim on failure to comply with the requirement of a timeliness provision, insurers typically argue that they are not and should not be required to show prejudice.[2]

The appropriateness of imposing a prejudice requirement is not uniformly approved among the judicial precedents.[3] There have been and continue to be decisions in several states holding that prejudice is irrelevant or immaterial when an insured has not complied with a timeliness provision.[4]

Courts in many states have now decided that an insurance claim should only be precluded if an insured's delay in complying with an insurance provision relating to the claims process has had a deleterious

271 at pp. 276–277, 160 N.E. 367 at p. 369 (1928), 72 A.L.R. 1443 at p. 1446 (1931):

"The plaintiff makes the point that the default should be condoned, since there is no evidence that co-operation, however willing, would have defeated the claim for damages or diminished its extent. For all that appears, the insurer would be no better off if the assured had kept its covenant, and made disclosure full and free. The argument misconceives the effect of a refusal. Co-operation with the insurer is one of the conditions of the policy. When the condition was broken, the policy was at an end, if the insurer so elected. The case is not one of the breach of a mere covenant, where the consequences may vary with fluctuations of the damage. There has been a failure to fulfill a condition upon which obligation is dependent."

2. Insurance contracts contain few provisions that explicitly recognize or allocate either evidentiary or procedural burdens in the event a dispute arises.

3. *Cf.* Pulse v. Northwest Farm Bureau Insurance Company, 18 Wash.App. 59, 566 P.2d 577 (Div. 3, 1977).

Also see Comment, *The Materiality of Prejudice to the Insurer as a Result of the Insured's Failure to Give Timely Notice*, 74

Dickerson Law Review 260 at pp. 261–262 (1970), indicating that a majority of the states at that time held prejudice to be immaterial except when "the terms of the policy are ambiguous or unemphatic."

Also consider the discussion in § 6.9(a), above.

4. See, e.g., Lord v. State Farm Mutual Automobile Insurance Company, 224 Va. 283, 295 S.E.2d 796 (1982); Southern Guaranty Insurance Company v. Thomas, 334 So.2d 879 at p. 883 (Ala.1976); RTE Corporation v. Maryland Casualty Company, 74 Wis.2d 614, 247 N.W.2d 171 at p. 171 (1976); Security Mutual Insurance Company of New York v. Acker-Fitzsimons Corp., 31 N.Y.2d 436, 340 N.Y.S.2d 902, 293 N.E.2d 76 (1972); Members Mutual Insurance Company v. Cutaia, 476 S.W.2d 278 (Tex.1972).

Also see Yale v. National Indemnity Company, 664 F.2d 406 at p. 410 (4th Cir. 1981) (applying North Carolina law); Dairyland Insurance Company v. Marez, 42 Colo.App. 536, 601 P.2d 353 (Div.II, 1979); Employers' Liability Assurance Corp. v. Perkins, 169 Md. 269, 181 A. 436 (1935).

Cf. Reserve Insurance Company v. Richards, 577 S.W.2d 417 (Ky.1978).

effect on the insurance company — that is, there are numerous appellate court decisions which have concluded coverage should not be forfeited if the insured's conduct has not prejudiced the insurer's position or interests.[5] Although there is something approaching a consensus in regard to the general proposition that an insured's coverage should only be lost when the insurer has been prejudiced, the fairly numerous precedents on this subject express a variety of views about the precise nature of the approach that courts should employ in determining the rights of the parties when the question of prejudice to the insurer is an issue.[6]

Many judicial decisions simply hold that the rejection of an insured's claim on the basis of a failure to comply with timeliness provisions is only justified if the insurer can show that the insured's conduct was prejudicial to the insurer.[7] In essence, these decisions

5. *Cf.* Pulse v. Northwest Farm Bureau Insurance Company, 18 Wash.App. 59, 566 P.2d 577 (Div. 3, 1977).

See Note, *Liability Insurance Policy Defenses and the Duty to Defend,* 68 Harvard Law Review 1436 (1955); 8 APPLEMAN, INSURANCE LAW (Revised edition, 1962), at § 4773.

6. There are also numerous decisions that a liability insurer's defense based on breach of the assistance and cooperation clause, discussed in Section 7.3, is conditioned on a showing of prejudice to the insurer. See especially the discussion in § 7.3(b), below.

7. A & W Artesian Well Co. v. Aetna Casualty and Surety Co., ___ R.I. ___, 463 A.2d 1381 (1983); Great American Insurance Company v. C.G. Tate Construction Co., 303 N.C. 387, 279 S.E.2d 769 (1981), affirming the decision of the Court of Appeals reported at 46 N.C.App. 427, 265 S.E.2d 467 (1980), and explicitly overruling several prior decisions; Johnson Controls, Inc. v. Bowes, 381 Mass. 278, 409 N.E.2d 185 (1980); Reliance Insurance Co. v. St. Paul Insurance Company, 307 Minn. 338, 239 N.W.2d 922 (1976); Lusch v. Aetna Casualty & Surety Company, 272 Or. 593, 538 P.2d 902 (1975).

Also see State Farm Mutual Automobile Insurance Company v. Johnson, 320 A.2d 345 (Del.1974); Stonewall Insurance Company v. Moorby, 130 Vt. 562, 298 A.2d 826 (1972); Sager v. St. Paul Fire & Marine Insurance Company, 461 S.W.2d 704 (Mo. 1971); Factory Mutual Liability Insurance Company of America v. Kennedy, 256 S.C. 376, 182 S.E.2d 727 (1971); Lindus v. Northern Insurance Co., 103 Ariz. 160, 438 P.2d 311 (1968).

Also see State Farm Mutual Insurance Company v. Murnion, 439 F.2d 945 (9th Cir.1971) (applying Montana law); St. Paul Fire & Marine Insurance Company v. Petzold, 418 F.2d 303 (1st Cir.1969) (applying New Hampshire law); Abington Mutual Fire Insurance Company v. Drew, 109 N.H. 464, 254 A.2d 829 (1969); State Farm Mutual Insurance Company v. Milam, 438 F.Supp. 227 (S.D.W.V.1977); Miller v. Marcantel, 221 So.2d 557 at p. 559 (La.App., 3d Cir., 1969).

In Wisconsin, legislation now provides the failure to furnish notice or proof of loss within the time required by the policy "does not invalidate or reduce a claim unless the insurer is prejudiced thereby and it was reasonably possible to meet the time limit." Wisconsin Stat.Ann. § 631.81 (1975), discussed in Gerrard Realty Corp. v. American States Insurance Company, 89 Wis.2d 130, 277 N.W.2d 863 (1979). In Wisconsin, if notice is given more than one year after the time required in the policy, there is a rebuttable presumption of prejudice and the burden of proof shifts to the claimant to prove the insurer was not prejudiced. *Ibid.*

Although many appellate court decisions support the strict contractual interpretation of the timeliness provisions as conditions precedent to an insurer's liability (see the cases cited in § 7.2(b), above), the trend among decisions of the last decade clearly indicates that insurers will increasingly be precluded form enforcing such provisions when the insurer cannot show that the delay prejudiced the insurer.

In Michigan, although prejudice is not always required in order for a notice provision to be enforced, "[p]rejudice to the insurer is a material element in determining whether notice is reasonably given." Wendel v. Swanberg, 384 Mich. 468 at p. 478, 185 N.W.2d 348 at p. 353 (1971). Sim-

reason, either explicitly or implicitly, that the primary objective of timeliness provisions is to avoid impairing the insurer's interest, and in situations in which the insurer's interests have not been harmed by the passage of time the justification for enforcing the various timeliness provisions — so as to preclude any insurance payment — does not exist.[8] As the Supreme Court of Pennsylvania concluded about a notice of loss provision, "the reason behind the notice condition in the policy is lacking, and it follows neither logic nor fairness to relieve the insurance company of its obligations ＊ ＊ ＊."[9] The Supreme Court of Pennsylvania also observed that there is "a trend of late in several jurisdictions away from the classic contractual approach towards a view that considers prejudice to the insurance company as a material factor in determining whether to relieve the insurance company of its coverage obligations by virtue of late notification."[10]

Among the many judicial decisions that have adopted the rule that a failure to comply with a time limit specified in an insurance contract defeats the claim only when the insured's failure was prejudicial to the insurer,[11] the courts in several states have imposed an even more

ilarly, the New Hampshire Supreme Court has commented that the determination whether "[t]he notice provisions of the policy have been complied with is a factual question for the trial court" which "depends on the prejudice to the insurer precipitated by the delay as well as on the length of and reasons for the delay." Lumbermens Mutual Casualty Company v. Oliver, 115 N.H. 141, 335 A.2d 666 at p. 668 (1975).

One of the Illinois Courts of Appeals has observed that "[w]hile prejudice may be a factor in determining the question of whether an insured has given reasonable notice to its insurer, it is not a condition that will dispense with the requirement. (Simmon v. Iowa Mutual Casualty Co. (1954), 3 Ill.2d 318, 322, 121 N.E.2d 509, 511.)." Equity General Insurance Company v. Patis, 119 Ill.App.3d 232, 74 Ill.Dec. 846, 456 N.E.2d 348 at p. 351 (1st Dist., Div. 4, 1983). [The Illinois Court went on to state, however, "Where, as here, the giving of notice has specifically been made a condition precedent to a right of action against the insurer, any prejudice resulting from a delay in giving notice become immaterial. (Citation omitted)."] Also see Illinois Valley Mineral Corporation v. Royal-Globe Insurance Company, 70 Ill.App.3d 296, 26 Ill.Dec. 629, 388 N.E.2d 253 (3d Dist.1979). Cf. Pickering v. American Employers Insurance Co., 109 R.I. 143, 282 A.2d 584 (1971).

See generally, Derral K. Sperry and Robert M. Barker, *Notice and Proof of Loss—*

Pitfalls for the Unwary, 18 South Texas Law Journal 31–47 (1977); Note, *Commercial Law—Great American Insurance Co. v. C.G. Tate Construction Co.: Interpretation of Notice Provisions in Insurance Contracts,* 61 North Carolina Law Review 167–176 (1982); Note, *Notice Provisions in Insurance Contracts: Great American Insurance Co. v. C.G. Tate Construction Co.,* 13 North Carolina Central Law Journal 116–122 (1981). Comment, *The Materiality of Prejudice to the Insurer as a Result of the Insured's Failure to Give Timely Notice,* 74 Dickinson Law Review 260–273 (1970).

8. In regard to the notice provision, an interesting question is presented when someone other than the insured (such as another person involved in the accident), informs the insurance company. In such a case, the insurer has been made aware of the occurrence and has thereby been placed in a position to avoid any prejudicial effect from the insured's failure to provide notice. *Cf.* the discussion in Illinois Valley Minerals Corporation v. Royal-Globe Insurance Company, 70 Ill.App.3d 296, 26 Ill.Dec. 629, 388 N.E.2d 253 (3d Dist.1979); McLaughlin v. Attorneys' Title Guaranty Fund, Inc., 61 Ill.App.3d 911, 18 Ill.Dec. 891, 378 N.E.2d 355 (3d Dist.1978).

9. Brakeman v. Potomac Insurance Company, 472 Pa. 66 at pp. 74–75, 371 A.2d 193 at p. 197 (1977).

10. *Ibid.*

11. Also see the decisions discussed in § 7.3, below.

rigorous requirement by holding that the insurer must show that the delay resulted in "substantial" or "appreciable" prejudice.[12]

(i) Determining Whether an Insurer Has Been Prejudiced

The adoption of a prejudice requirement by courts leads to the related question of what constitutes either "prejudice" or "substantial prejudice" to an insurer as a consequence of the events which follow the occurrence of an insured loss. The range of standards or approaches applied by courts to determine what type or degree of prejudice to an insurer warrants enforcement of timeliness provisions is described in the following paragraphs.

In most situations, prejudice is treated as a question of fact, and, accordingly, it is also essential to consider how the burden of proof is to be allocated. The statements by courts articulating a standard for assessing the degree or type of prejudice that must result frequently also include an allocation of the burden of proof on this issue. In this subsection, the primary focus of the discussion is on what type of prejudice is required. The next subsection is primarily concerned with the approaches courts employ for allocating the burden of proof.

From the vantage point of a claimant, the most desirable approach to timeliness provisions is that a denial of a coverage would only be justified in those situations in which an insured's delay results in significant prejudice to the insurer's interest (and that the burden is on the insurance company to prove such prejudice by showing that the result was different in the particular instance as a consequence of the event in question).[13] This approach is appropriately viewed as one end

12. See, e.g., Great American Insurance Co. v. G.C. Tate Construction Company, 303 N.C. 387 at p. 399, 279 S.E.2d 769 at p. 776 (1981); Finstad v. Steiger Tractor, Inc., 301 N.W.2d 392 at p. 398 (N.D.1981); Merit Insurance Company v. Koza, 274 S.C. 362, 264 S.E.2d 146 at p. 147 (1980).

Also see Cooper v. Government Employees Insurance Company, 51 N.J. 86 at p. 94, 237 A.2d 870 at p. 874 (1968); Morales v. National Grange Mutual Insurance Company, 176 N.J.Super. 347, 423 A.2d 325 (Law Division, Essex County, 1980).

Cf. Travelers Insurance Company v. Feld Car & Truck Leasing Corp., 517 F.Supp. 1132 (D.Kan.1981).

13. In Maryland, legislation provides:

"Where any insurer seeks to disclaim coverage on any policy of liability insurance issued by it, on the ground that the insured or anyone claiming the benefits of the policy through the insured has breached the policy by failing to cooperate with the insurer or by not giving requisite notice to the insurer, such disclaimer shall be effective *only if the insurer establishes, by a preponderance of affirmative evidence that such lack of cooperation or notice has resulted in actual prejudice to the insurer.*"

Maryland Stat.Ann., Insurance Code, Art. 48A, § 482 (1964).

Also see State Farm Mutual Automobile Insurance Co. v. Walker, 382 F.2d 548 at p. 551 (7th Cir.1967), *cert. denied* 389 U.S. 1045, 88 S.Ct. 789, 19 L.Ed.2d 837 (1968) (applying Indiana law). The insured told the attorney engaged by insurer to defend him that the insured's earlier version of accident was false and that the accident occurred because insured lost control in passing another car. The court concluded that there were factual issues in regard to whether breach of cooperation clause prejudiced the insurer and whether counsel's participation in defense after learning of the breach constituted a "waiver" by the insurer. The court observed that "it has been said that an insurer is not prejudiced unless the breach will produce a judgment less favorable to it in the tort suit."

See generally Note, *Liability Insurance Policy Defenses and the Duty to Defend*, 68 Harvard Law Review 1436–1452 (1955).

of the spectrum among the appellate court decisions in point on such questions. It is exemplified by the decisions of the New Jersey courts which require that an insurer must show that it was "appreciably prejudiced," and that in assessing this question a trial court is to consider whether the insurer can show "the likelihood that the insurer would have had a meritorious defense that was lost." [14]

Courts in several states have adopted what might be fairly characterized as intermediate standards or positions.[15] For example, the Rhode Island Supreme Court has held that in assessing whether an insurer has been prejudiced, a "court should look to the length of delay, the reasons for the delay, *and the probable prejudicial effect of the delay on the insurer.*" [16]

Many of the judicial decisions in point can be accurately described as requiring an insurer to prove some, but not an overwhelming degree of, prejudice. Courts have often concluded that it is sufficient for the insurer to show either that the company's exposure to liability was increased or that the investigation of the claim was substantially more troublesome than it would have been in the absence of the delay that is at issue in the dispute.[17] For example, the loss of opportunity to

Regarding preclusion of the defense by actions of counsel in a conflict-of-interest setting, see § 7.6(b), below.

14. See, e.g., Morales v. National Grange Mutual Insurance Company, 176 N.J.Super. 347, 423 A.2d 325 at pp. 329–330 (1980), discussing the New Jersey Supreme Court's decision in Cooper v. Government Insurance Company, 51 N.J. 86, 237 A.2d 870 (1968) and subsequent decisions by the courts of New Jersey.

Accord. Finstad v. Steiger Tractor, Inc., 301 N.W.2d 392 at p. 398 (N.D.1981).

15. *Cf.* Cooper v. Government Employees Insurance Co., 51 N.J. 86, 237 A.2d 870 (1968) (placing burden on insurer to prove breach of late-notice provision and "a likelihood of appreciable prejudice" therefrom in order to fulfill reasonable expectations of the purchaser "so far as its language will permit"; trial court's fact-finding of no breach by insured of notice provision sustained).

16. Pennsylvania General Insurance Company v. Becton, ___ R.I. ___, 475 A.2d 1032 at p. 1035 (1984).

Accord. Commercial Union Assurance Companies v. Monadock Regional School District, 121 N.H. 275, 428 A.2d 894 at p. 896 (1981).

Also see A & W Artesian Well Company v. Aetna Casualty & Surety Company, ___ R.I. ___, 463 A.2d 1381 at p. 1383 (1983).

One commentary on this subject suggests the following factors are considerations that may be employed to assess whether the insurer was prejudiced:

"(1) When did the insurer first get knowledge of the occurrence?

(2) The manner in which notice was received—was it formal notice or otherwise, as through the news media?

(3) If there was a delay, what was the reason for it?

(4) Was the delay of a nature to excuse the ordinary man, one not skilled in insurance matters or in the law?

(5) Could the insurer still conduct an adequate investigation?

(6) Did the delay lessen the chances of settlement?"

Derral K. Sperry and Robert M. Barker, *Notice and Proof of Loss—Pitfalls for the Unwary,* 18 South Texas Law Journal 31–47 at p. 36 (1977).

17. See, e.g., Renner v. State Farm Mutual Automobile Insurance Company, 392 F.2d 666 (5th Cir.1968) (applying Florida law) (late report of automobile accident due to misunderstanding between husband and wife; lack of opportunity to photograph cars and talk with witnesses while facts were fresh, including one witness who died of an unrelated cause nineteen days after the accident; trial court finding of prejudice sustained); Canadian Universal Insurance Co. v. Northwest Hospital, Inc., 389 F.2d 559 (7th Cir.1968) (applying Illinois law) (two-year delay in reporting accident to hospital's liability insurer gave rise

interview witnesses when memories are fresh and when it is most likely that they will not have been influenced by interactions with others who have an interest in the potential testimony, has often been viewed as significant.[18] Similarly, courts have sometimes been influenced by an argument that had notice been provided, the insurer would have had an opportunity to negotiate a settlement that was more favorable than that which actually resulted.[19] Under such standards, it is only necessary to convince the court that opportunities were lost; the insurer does not have to establish that the end result would have been different.

Caveat. The likelihood of applying any particular standard for assessing prejudice, or even dispensing entirely with a requirement of proof of prejudice in a particular case, is substantially increased by a showing that the policyholder in some way acted "wrongfully" or in bad faith.[20]

(ii) Allocating the Burden of Proof

The application of a prejudice requirement, as indicated in the preceding paragraphs, also presents the problem of deciding how to allocate the burden of proof on the question of prejudice — that is, whether the burden is on the claimant to show that the insurer was not prejudiced or on the insurer to establish how the company was prejudiced. The number of instances in which the adoption of a prejudice requirement will affect the insurer's position is, of course,

---

to presumption of prejudice, which was not rebutted but strengthened by evidence that the condition of the area where patient fell had been changed between accident and notice).

In Falcon Steel Company, Inc. v. Maryland Casualty Company, 366 A.2d 512 at p. 518 (Sup., New Castle County, 1976), the court held that "in order to carry this burden, an insurer must show that evidence which it is reasonably probable could have been developed by prompt investigation has not or cannot be developed by later investigation or that in some other respect it is reasonably probable that a resolution of the claim could have been reached if prompt notice had been given which cannot be reached after the late notice."

Also see Lumbermens Mutual Casualty Company v. Oliver, 115 N.H. 141, 335 A.2d 666 at p. 669 (1975) (the trial court's determination that a delay of almost a year in notifying the insurer resulted in "substantial prejudice" was supported by the claims adjuster's testimony that he could not locate any witnesses and could not discover any information regarding the condition which allegedly caused the loss).

18. *Cf.* Commercial Union Assurance Companies v. Monadnock Regional School District, 121 N.H. 275, 428 A.2d 894 at p. 896 (1981).

Also see Renner v. State Mutual Automobile Insurance Company, 392 F.2d 666 (5th Cir.1968).

19. *Cf.* the decisions cited in § 7.2(d), above.

20. See, e.g., Elliott v. Metropolitan Casualty Insurance Co., 250 F.2d 680 (10th Cir.1957), 66 A.L.R.2d 1231 (1959), *cert. denied* 356 U.S. 932, 78 S.Ct. 774, 2 L.Ed.2d 762 (1958) (Kansas law; collusion with claimants to travel from Kansas to Missouri to accept service of process; in such cases, insurers need not show a resulting substantial and actual prejudice, as they must do in cases involving disappearance of an insured before trial).

Cf. Great American Insurance Co. v. C.G. Tate Construction Company, 303 N.C. 387 at p. 399, 279 S.E.2d 769 at p. 776 (1981) (trier of fact must decide whether the insured has shown that he or she acted in good faith).

minimized if the claimant has the burden of convincing the court that the insurer was not prejudiced,[21] whatever the standard may be.[22]

When there is little or no evidence on the matter at issue, the allocation of the burden of proof in effect determines which party will prevail. Thus, the allocation of the burden of proof is often a matter of very considerable significance in regard to the resolution of a disputed claim.

Normally the burdens of proof and persuasion are placed on the party asserting a claim or defense. If prejudice is treated by the courts (or in legislation) as an essential element of the defense against coverage for an insured who has failed to comply with timeliness provisions, the burden falls on the insurer. If, on the other hand, prejudice is treated as an affirmative response to the insurer's rejection of a claim on the basis of the insured's failure to comply with a timeliness provision, then the burden of proof might be on the insured as the party asserting that affirmative response.[23]

There are some appellate decisions which adopt the view that an insured's failure to comply with a timeliness provision, such as not providing an insurer with a prompt notice of a loss, creates a rebuttable presumption of prejudice to the insurer so that an insured will only be entitled to coverage when the insured can demonstrate that the insurer was not prejudiced.[24] However, the actual effect on an insured of such a rebuttable presumption may not be great. The Eighth Circuit Court

---

21. See Henderson v. Hawkeye-Security Insurance Co., 252 Iowa 97, 106 N.W.2d 86 (1960).

22. When the burden is placed on the policyholder to prove that the insurer was not prejudiced, the impact of the doctrine is less severe but still significant. The decisions which adopt this allocation of the burden as an element or facet of the standard in effect represent one end of the spectrum of judicial views in these cases. As to the other end, see the text associated with notes 13 and 14, above.

23. The issue should be, and probably will be, treated by a particular court in the chosen way regardless of whether the form of the civil action is a case initiated by the insured or, in contrast, an action for declaratory judgment initiated by the insurer.

24. See, e.g., Gerrard Realty Corp. v. American States Insurance Company, 89 Wis.2d 130, 277 N.W.2d 863 at p. 872 (1979); Patrick v. Auto-Owners Insurance Company, 5 Ohio App.3d 118, 449 N.E.2d 790 at p. 791 (Warren County, 1982), in which the court concluded that "[a]n unreasonable delay in giving notice to an insurer of a claim is presumed prejudice to the company in the absence of any evidence to the contrary"; Klien v. Allstate

Insurance Company, 367 So.2d 1085 (Fla. App., 1st Dist., 1979).

Also see Jennings v. Horace Mann Mutual Insurance Company, 549 F.2d 1364 at pp. 1367–1368 (10th Cir.1977) (applying the law of Colorado); Henschel v. Hawkeye-Security Insurance Company, 178 N.W.2d 409 (Iowa 1970).

Courts sometimes indicate that the insured has the burden of showing that the timeliness provision was complied with as soon as was reasonable or practical under the circumstances. See, e.g., Tiedtke v. Fidelity & Casualty Company of New York, 222 So.2d 206 (Fla.1969).

When the burden is placed on the policyholder to prove that the insurer was not prejudiced, the impact of adopting a prejudice standard is less significant. See, e.g., Western Mutual Insurance Co. v. Baldwin, 258 Iowa 460 at pp. 472–475, 137 N.W.2d 918 at pp. 925–927 (1965) (confirming the rule of *Henderson*, below); Henderson v. Hawkeye-Security Insurance Co., 252 Iowa 97, 106 N.W.2d 86 (1960) (rebuttable presumption of prejudice from delay of more than a year in giving notice under automobile medical payments coverage; though declaring that allowing recovery "unless the company proves prejudice" would be truly to "rewrite the contract and

of Appeals, for example, concluded that Professor Wigmore had set forth the appropriate approach in regard to such presumptions:

> "The better approach * * * calls for the plaintiff to go forward with some evidence * * * [and] when some evidence has been presented, the presumption loses any probative force which it may have had and it is then up to the adversary party to go forward with the evidence that actual prejudice existed." [25]

If this approach is adopted, in most situations an insured will be able to come forward with "some evidence," thereby shifting the burden to the insurer.

Many of the courts which have adopted a prejudice requirement have decided that the burdens of proof and persuasion on the question of prejudice should always be placed upon an insurer when a timeliness provision is invoked as a justification for avoiding liability under an insurance policy.[26] There are several rationales for this approach. *First,* if no clear proof is available, it serves to avoid a forfeiture, and the preservation of coverage for an insured is generally viewed as a desirable result when there is no clear evidence to justify a loss of coverage. *Second,* it recognizes the difficulty of asking a claimant to attempt to prove the "negative fact" that the insurer was *not* prejudiced. *Third,* this approach recognizes that in most situations the insurer is in the best position both to assess whether it has been prejudiced and to then produce evidence that is relevant to a judicial determination of whether the forfeiture of coverage sought by the insurer is justified.[27]

Judicial decisions which allocate the burden of proof to insurers in essence recognize that the question of prejudice involves special considerations.[28] For example, after reviewing the evolution in the law on the question of requiring proof of prejudice, the Massachusetts Supreme

---

[would] be most unreasonable," the court seems curiously unaware that it also re-writes the contract by holding that a claim-ant's showing of lack of prejudice over-comes the defense of late notice); Mountainair Municipal Schools v. United States Fidelity & Guaranty Co., 80 N.M. 761, 461 P.2d 410 (1969) (injury to student when door-closing mechanism fell on her head in gymnasium; first report nineteen months later was not "as soon as practica-ble"; school superintendent's ignorance of existence of liability policy was no excuse; late notice is presumptively prejudicial to insurer; though presumption is rebuttable, it was not rebutted in this case).

25. Jennings v. Horace Mann Mutual Insurance Company, 549 F.2d 1364 at p. 1368 (10th Cir.1977) (interpreting the law of Colorado) (emphasis added).

Also see WIGMORE ON EVIDENCE (Third edition, 1940), Volume IX, § 2491 at pp. 288–289.

Keeton & Widess, Ins.Law—18

26. See, e.g., Pennsylvania General Insurance Company v. Becton, ___ R.I. ___, 475 A.2d 1032 (1984); Finstad v. Steiger Tractor, Inc., 301 N.W.2d 392 (N.D.1981); Great American Insurance Co. v. C.G. Tate Construction Co., 303 N.C. 387 at p. 399, 279 S.E.2d 769 at p. 775 (1981); Johnson Controls, Inc. v. Bowes, 381 Mass. 278, 409 N.E.2d 185 (1980).

Cf. Brakeman v. Potomac Insurance Co. v. Johnson, 472 Pa. 66, 371 A.2d 193 (1977).

Also see State Farm Mutual Automobile Insurance Co. v. Milam, 438 F.Supp. 227 (S.D.W.Va.1977).

27. *Cf.* Cooper v. Government Employees Insurance Co., 51 N.J. 86 at p. 94, 237 A.2d 870 at p. 874, note 3 (1968).

28. See, e.g., Cooper v. Government Employees Insurance Co., 51 N.J. 86, 237 A.2d 870 (1968).

Cf. Lumbermens Mutual Insurance Company v. Oliver, 115 N.H. 141 at pp. 143–

Judicial Court stated that the Massachusetts rule predicated on a strict contractual approach was "too restrictive and should be changed" so "that where an insurance company attempts to be relieved of its obligation under a liability insurance policy * * * on the ground of untimely notice, the insurance company will be required to prove *both* that the notice provision was in fact breached *and* that the breach resulted in prejudice to its position." [29]

A few courts have held that even when an insurer demonstrates that prejudice occurred, that fact only justifies a reduction in the coverage to reflect the difference to the insurer shown to have resulted from the prejudice.[30] Under a stringent application of this approach, it seems likely that few insurers would completely escape liability.

(iii) Observations

The judicial resolution of disputes involving questions about whether an insurer has been prejudiced are extremely "fact sensitive." Factors such as the length of a delay and the probable effects of the delay undoubtedly weigh heavily when a court considers these questions. Accordingly, each of the appellate court decisions setting forth the propositions or approaches discussed in the preceding subsections should be carefully evaluated in relation to the particular factual circumstances that produced the coverage dispute.

Limiting the circumstances in which insurers can assert a defense based on a failure to comply with timeliness provisions may produce an injustice not only to the insurer, but also to other policyholders who ultimately must share the cost if insurers are required to bear those risks. In some situations, there are compelling reasons for not applying a rule that requires an insurer to prove that a different result has occurred as a consequence of an insured's actions or inactions. For example, when a substantial period to time passes before an insurer is provided with notice of a loss, the very delay of which the insurer complains may have occasioned an unknown prejudice by depriving the insurer of the opportunity for an early investigation that might have disclosed information upon which a defense could have been predicated. Thus, in some types of situations it is impossible to know whether the

144, 335 A.2d 666 at p. 668 (1975). The court noted that New Hampshire Revised Statutes Annotated § 491:22–a (Supp.1979) places the burden of proof on the insurer, but still concluded that under the circumstances a rebuttable presumption of prejudice was warranted.

29. Johnson Controls, Inc. v. Bowes, 381 Mass. 278 at p. 282, 409 N.E.2d 185 at p. 188 (1980) (emphasis added) (citations to the decision of courts in seven other states omitted).

30. *Cf.* Fidelity & Casualty Co. v. McConnaughy, 228 Md. 1, 179 A.2d 117 (1962). The insurer's appointed counsel had acted improperly in taking insured's deposition to confirm its defense of noncooperation, but insurer did not thereby lose its rights. Without clearly resolving a conflict in precedents regarding what showing of prejudice is required, the court accepted insurer's assertion that insured's breach of cooperation clause by bringing in false witnesses caused insurer to decline to accept claimant's $3,500 settlement offer. However, relief was limited to excusing insurer from liability for excess above $3,500 for which insurer claims it would have settled but for insured's breach.

result would have been different if the insurer had been notified promptly.[31] And, in many instances, courts appear to appreciate that the insured's conduct may have deprived the insurer of the evidence of detriment (or prejudice) from that wrong.[32]

Liability Insurance

Liability insurance policies are frequently viewed by courts and legislatures as coverages that are "also for the benefit of the public" and which therefore should be lost only when the insurer has been actually prejudiced.[33] Often the interests of innocent third parties are at stake when compliance with one or more of the timeliness provisions in a liability insurance policy is at issue. For this reason, many appellate court decisions in cases involving the prejudice requirement either explicitly have or appear to have weighed these third party interests against concerns about fairness to insurers. Furthermore, this approach is consistent with, and sometimes is explicitly predicated on, recognition that the timeliness provisions at issue in liability insurance policies (as well as provisions in other coverages) are imposed by insurers (though sometimes with regulatory blessing), rather than resulting from freely negotiated transactions.[34]

31. If insurers are deprived of a defense unless they can prove that a different result would have come about in the particular case, insurers will be required to pay a whole body of claims some of which could have been defeated but for the delayed presentment.

32. The evidence courts typically require for an insurer to show prejudice is generally somewhat less demanding than that which is often required when an insured seeks to justify a right at variance with policy provisions on the basis of detrimental reliance. Regarding the standard for detrimental reliance, see § 6.5(f), above. This approach is appropriate in this context: first, because the insurer is seeking to enforce a policy provision; and, second, because the insurer is being required to prove something more than breach of that provision in order to establish its defense. To require in this context a very clear showing of detriment, comparable to that which is sometimes required in other contexts, would be to award a far greater extension of rights at variance with policy provisions than is made by allowing an insured to enforce rights based on detrimental reliance.

Also consider the cases involving warranty and representation discussed in § 6.6, above.

33. Reliance Insurance Company v. St. Paul Insurance Companies, 307 Minn. 338, 239 N.W.2d 922 at p. 925 (1976) (lawyer's professional liability policy); Oregon Automobile Insurance Company v. Salzberg, 85 Wash.2d 372, 535 P.2d 816 (1975) (automobile insurance policy).

Cf. Factory Mutual Liability Insurance Company of America v. Kennedy, 256 S.C. 376, 182 S.E.2d 727 at pp. 729–730 (1971).

Also see Finstad v. Steiger Tractor, Inc., 301 N.W.2d 392 at p. 398 (N.D.1981).

34. Finstad v. Steiger Tractor, Inc., 301 N.W.2d 392 at pp. 397–398 (N.D.1981); Johnson Controls, Inc. v. Bowes, 381 Mass. 278 at p. 281, 409 N.E.2d 185 at p. 187 (1980).

Also see Brakeman v. Potomac Insurance Company, 472 Pa. 66 at p. 72, 371 A.2d 193 at p. 196 (1977) (an "insurance contract is not a negotiated agreement; rather its conditions are by and large dictated by the insurance company to the insured"); Cooper v. Government Employees Insurance Company, 51 N.J. 86 at pp. 93–94, 237 A.2d 870 at pp. 873–874 (1968).

Timeliness Provisions as "Covenants" and as "Conditions Precedent"

Timeliness provisions have been viewed both as covenants of the insured (that is, promises) and as conditions precedent to an insured's right of action against an insurer. For many years, when such provisions were not explicitly structured as conditions, courts often avoided forfeitures by treating such provisions as covenants — that is, courts held that an insured's rights would only be lost if the timeliness provision was clearly and unambiguously phrased as a condition precedent. In response to such judicial decisions, insurers increasingly structured such provisions as express conditions precedent. In retrospect, it seems evident that the difference between various policy provisions was a matter of form, not substance. Differences in the form or the phrasing of such provisions ought not to be a significant factor in assessing the rights of either the insured or the insurer, and it seems likely that in future coverage disputes the way in which a provision is cast will not be determinative of whether a timeliness provision bars a claim.[35]

(3) Excuses for Noncompliance

There are numerous appellate decisions in which courts have held that there was a reasonable excuse for an insured's failure to comply with the timeliness provisions in a variety of situations. For example, the failure to provide notice has been excused when an insured had "a good faith belief in nonliability" which was "reasonable under all of the circumstances."[36] Similarly, in another interesting case, the Minnesota Supreme Court concluded that a person who is insured by a liability policy may be excused for delay in providing the insurer with notice of an accident if, "acting as a reasonably prudent person, he believed that he was not liable for the accident."[37] Compliance was also excused

---

35. *Cf.* Oregon Automobile Insurance Company v. Salzberg, 85 Wash.2d 372, 535 P.2d 816 (1975).

But cf. Equity General Insurance Company v. Patis, 119 Ill.App.3d 232, 74 Ill.Dec. 846, 456 N.E.2d 348 (2st Dist.Dept., 1983).

36. Merchants Mutual Insurance Company v. Hoffman, 86 A.D.2d 779, 448 N.Y.S.2d 68 at p. 70 (4th Dept.1982). In this case, the injured person was a 15-year old foster child in the care of a county social services agency who was residing with the insureds on their farm. The boy, who sustained what appeared to have been a broken arm that involved a relatively minor fracture, was provided medical treatment including a short stay in a hospital, and then recuperated for a few months in the insured's home without further problems. The medical expenses were paid for by the County Agency.

Cf. Hartford Fire Insurance Company v. Masternak, 55 A.D.2d 472, 390 N.Y.S.2d 949 (4th Dept.1977) (daughter, who resided with her parents, explained that notice was not given to the insurer for two years because she called the family's insurance agency approximately one week after she fell down the stairs in her parent's home and that she was told there was no coverage under a homeowners policy).

Also see Southern Guaranty Insurance Company v. Thomas, 334 So.2d 879 (Ala. 1976).

37. See, e.g., Frederick v. John Wood Co., 263 Minn. 101, 116 N.W.2d 88 (1962), quoting with approval from 29A AM.JUR. Insurance § 1393 [carried forward as 44 AM.JUR.2d, Insurance § 1474 (1969)].

when an insured had a reasonable and good faith belief that no claim would be made against the insured because the insured was not involved in the events that caused the loss.[38] In assessing the appropriateness of such decisions by an insured, some courts have declared that the insured must "exercise reasonable care" [39] and act "in good faith in coming to that conclusion." [40]

An insured's delay in taking the steps specified for a timely presentment of a claim may be justified because the occurrence appeared to involve a trivial injury. In particular, there is substantial precedent supporting the proposition that a person insured by a liability policy may be excused from complying with such provisions when the incident which resulted in a tort claim by a third person appeared to the insured to be so minor that the insured reasonably believed that no claim for damages would arise.[41]

A reasonable belief by a policyholder that he or she was in no way involved in an accident should also excuse a delay in reporting an occurrence to an insurer.[42] However, the appropriate scope for such a rule is potentially subject to considerable disagreement between insurers and insureds, especially since the rule clearly involves granting an insured rights that are at variance with the policy provisions. Certainly an insured should be required to give notice whenever there is a substantial and foreseeable possibility that a claim will be made, even though as a layperson the insured reasonably believes that any claim made would lack merit.

38. Cooper v. Government Employees Insurance Company, 51 N.J. 86 at p. 90, 237 A.2d 870 at p. 871 (1968).

39. Security Mutual Insurance Company of New York v. Acker-Fitzsimons Corp., 31 N.Y.2d 436, 340 N.Y.S.2d 902 at p. 907, 293 N.E.2d 76 at p. 80 (1972) (insureds "failed to exercise reasonable care and diligence in ascertaining the facts about the alleged accident and in evaluating their potential liability").

40. Barnes v. Waco Scaffolding and Equipment Company, 41 Colo.App. 423, 589 P.2d 505 at p. 507 (Div.II, 1978).

Also see Southern Guaranty Insurance Company v. Thomas, 334 So.2d 879 (Ala. 1976); United States Fidelity & Guaranty Company v. Giruox, 129 Vt. 155 at p. 161, 274 A.2d 487 at p. 491 (1971) (insured, "acting as a reasonable man under the circumstances, was fully justified in delaying the giving of a notice * * *").

Cf. Frederick v. John Wood Company, 263 Minn. 101, 116 N.W.2d 88 (1962) (insured must act as a reasonably prudent person).

41. See, e.g., Cooper v. Government Employees Insurance Company, 51 N.J. 86, 237 A.2d 870 (1968); Leytem v. Fireman's Fund Indemnity Co., 249 Iowa 524, 85 N.W.2d 921 (1957); Bennett v. Swift & Co., 170 Ohio St. 168, 163 N.E.2d 362 (1959) (failure to give notice for 18 months; directed verdict for insurer reversed for new trial of fact issues on triviality).

But cf. State Farm Mutual Automobile Insurance Co. v. Ranson, 121 So.2d 175 (Fla.App.2d Dist.1960) (failure to give notice for more than a year was a good defense as a matter of law, though the policyholder claimed that the incident seemed trivial). However, *Ranson* is severely undermined in American Fire and Casualty Co. v. Collura, 163 So.2d 784 at pp. 789–794 (Fla.App.2d Dist.1964), *cert. denied without opinion* 171 So.2d 389 (Fla.1964).

42. *Cf.* Pawtucket Mutual Insurance Co. v. Lebrecht, 104 N.H. 465, 190 A.2d 420 at p. 424 (1963), 2 A.L.R.3d 1229 (1965) (claim against policyholder-parents growing out of assault by their son on another person; delay excused on the theory that the parents "were justifiably ignorant of any connection between that incident and the bringing up of their son on which a claim of liability against them might be based").

Compliance has also been excused when a failure is attributable to one of the very risks that is covered by the applicable insurance. For example, a delay in providing notice to a disability insurer that an insured has become disabled may be excused when the insured is unable to provide notice because of the very disability that is insured against.[43]

Policyholders have also urged that a delayed notice should be excused when the failure resulted from a lack of awareness that the policy included coverage for the type of incident involved or that the claimant was not aware that the coverage existed.[44] In such situations, it may be observed that courts typically will not excuse a failure to comply when an insured is a business entity such as a corporation. Compliance is not excused because the relevant officer or employee was ignorant of the insurance coverage.[45] However, when an insured is an individual, rather than some type of business who is not aware that coverage exists, it is more likely that some latitude will be afforded in regard to compliance.[46]

Courts have also applied doctrines such as waiver, estoppel, and election in decisions that uphold claims by insureds that are at variance with policy provisions.[47]

Negligent Failure to Comply

Coverage disputes involving questions about compliance with notice and filing requirements include situations in which omissions were attributable to some type of negligent conduct of the insureds. As the doctrines discussed in the preceding paragraphs have indicated, some-

---

43. Seabra v. Puritan Life Insurance Company, 117 R.I. 488, 369 A.2d 652 at p. 656 (1977). The court reasoned, "To require a person who is described by some as being 'insane' or 'mentally incompetent' to do something that his disability prevents him from doing places that person in what some would refer to as a 'catch-22' situation."

44. See, e.g., Birmingham Boys' Club, Inc. v. Transamerica Insurance Company, 325 So.2d 167 (Ala.1976).

45. See also Annotation, *Beneficiary's ignorance of existence of life or accident policy as excusing failure to give notice, make proofs of loss, or bring action within time limited by policy or statute,* 28 A.L.R.3d 292–367 (1969).

46. See, e.g. State Farm Fire and Casualty Co. v. Hartford Accident & Indemnity Co., 347 So.2d 389 at p. 392 (Ala.1977) (Scout leaders who were not aware of the scope of coverage provided by their homeowners insurance policies); Greer v. Zurich Insurance Company, 441 S.W.2d 15 at p. 31 (Mo.Div. 1, 1969) ("notice cannot be re-

quired until there is knowledge of the existence of a policy requiring the giving of notice").

47. See, e.g., the discussion of waiver in Sheetz v. IMT Insurance Company, 324 N.W.2d 302 at pp. 304–306 (Iowa 1982) (insurer waived requirement that suit had to be commenced within twelve months of the inception of a loss); Petrice v. Federal Kemper Insurance Company, 163 W.Va. 737, 260 S.E.2d 276 at p. 278 (1979) (proof of loss condition "may be waived by the insurer expressly or impliedly or, the insurer, by its conduct, may be estopped from asserting the failure to supply the sworn statement to effect a forfeiture").

Also see North River Insurance Company v. Pomerantz, 492 S.W.2d 312 at p. 313 (Tex.Civ.App.—Houston 1973) (a "denial of liability by the insurance company within the period allowed for filing proof of loss on grounds other than failure to submit proof of loss, constitutes a waiver of this requirement").

Cf. Womack v. Allstate Insurance Company, 156 Tex. 467, 296 S.W.2d 233 (1956).

times a reasonable mistake has been recognized as an excuse for delay. However, although most insurance coverages provide protection against losses to which a mistake or a negligent act of the insured contributes,[48] courts often apply a more stringent standard to disputes involving claims presentment provisions — that is, when the failure to comply with some time limit for providing notice of loss or to initiate a claim is the result of the claimant's negligence, courts frequently will not be tolerant of such conduct.[49] For example, the Connecticut Supreme Court concluded, as a matter of law, that a four-month delay in notifying the insurer of a suit "was neither excusable nor reasonable" under the circumstances.[50]

§ 7.2(f)   Fraud and False Swearing in Claims Submissions

Another significant facet of the claims presentment process relates to the accuracy and truth of the information a claimant provides to the insurer. Many insurance policies include provisions which specifically address the problem of fraud in connection with claims. A representative illustration is provided by fire insurance policies which commonly state:

> **"Concealment, fraud.** This entire policy shall be void if, whether before or after a loss, the insured has wilfully concealed or misrepresented any material fact or circumstance concerning this insurance or the subject thereof, or the interest of the insured therein, or in case of any fraud or false swearing by the insured relating thereto." [1]

In many states, this provision is prescribed by statute for fire insurance policies.[2] Language that is identical or very similar to the quoted

---

48. For example, fire insurance covers losses caused by the insured's negligence; "life insurance" covers even a case of death to which negligence of both the insured and the beneficiary contributed; and liability insurance is chiefly intended to protect against the consequences of liability based on negligence.

49. *Cf.* Falcon Steel Company, Inc. v. Maryland Casualty Company, 366 A.2d 512 (Delaware Super.Ct., New Castle County, 1976).

Similarly, negligence of an insured in protecting property already damaged under circumstances covered by property insurance is commonly treated less favorably than negligence contributing to the initial loss. See § 5.4(f), above.

50. City of West Haven v. United States Fidelity and Guaranty Company, 174 Conn. 392 at p. 398, 389 A.2d 741 at p. 745 (1978). In this case, the court found that "after the city learned of the accident when suit was filed with the city clerk on May 8, 1967, it inadvertently sent the writ,

summons and complaint to Travelers Insurance Company by letter dated June 23, 1967; and, after receiving notice from Travelers, in a letter dated June 30, 1967, that the matter should be referred to the city's former insurance carrier, the city did not forward notice of the accident and suit to USF & G until September 8, 1967." *Ibid.*

§ 7.2(f)

1. See, e.g., Lykos v. American Home Insurance Company, 609 F.2d 314 at p. 315 (7th Cir.1979). Also see Appendix A.

2. See, e.g., Michigan C.L.A. § 24.12832 (1956), discussed in Morgan v. Cincinnati Insurance Company, 411 Mich. 267, 307 N.W.2d 53 at p. 54 (1981).

The New York—McKinney's Consolidated Laws Annotated § 403(c) (1985) state all claim forms shall contain a notice in a form approved by the superintendent that clearly states in substance the following:

"Any person who knowingly and with intent to defraud any insurance compa-

provision is also used by insurers in the policy forms adopted for other kinds of insurance.[3] This type of provision has provided the basis for a successful defense by insurers when an insured willfully concealed information about an insured loss or submitted incorrect information in an insurance claim.[4] For example, in a case in which the claims document prepared by the insured grossly overvalued many items that were destroyed in a fire, the appellate court concluded "that the claims were deliberately false" and that there was no way they could be seen as innocent by a reasonable jury.[5]

The provisions used in most insurance policies are framed in terms of the *wilful* concealment or misrepresentation of a *material fact*.[6] Courts generally focus the analysis of a claims dispute on these two elements.[7]

ny or other person files * * * a statement of claim containing any materially false information, or conceals for the purpose of misleading, information concerning any material fact thereto, commits a fraudulent insurance act, which is a crime."

3. See the insurance policy forms in the Appendices.

4. See, e.g., Duke v. Hartford Fire Insurance Company, 617 F.2d 509 at p. 510 (8th Cir.1980) (the claimant "admitted to making misrepresentations to Hartford during the course of its investigation * * *, *inter alia*, statements to Hartford that he had no knowledge of the cause and origin of the fire, that he was on a trip to Oklahoma at the time of the fire, and that he had neither suffered burns nor received medical treatment for burns around the time of the fire."); Lakes v. Buckeye State Mutual Insurance Ass'n, 110 Ohio App. 115, 168 N.E.2d 895 (1959) (jury found that plaintiff wilfully concealed that some of the personalty reported in proof of loss was not destroyed by fire).

Cf. Teitelbaum Furs, Inc. v. Dominion Insurance Co., 58 Cal.2d 601, 25 Cal.Rptr. 559, 375 P.2d 439 (1962), *cert. denied* 372 U.S. 966, 83 S.Ct. 1091, 10 L.Ed.2d 130 (1963) (plaintiff company's claim, based on the assertion that a robbery occurred, barred by collateral estoppel since one of its officers was convicted of filing false insurance claim; the issue whether robbery occurred was the same in both cases).

Also see Fine v. Bellefonte Underwriters Insurance Company, 725 F.2d 179 (2d Cir. 1984) (false statement made during the insurance company's investigation); Lykos v. American Home Assurance Company, 452 F.Supp. 533 (N.D.Ill.1978), *affirmed* 669 F.2d 314 (7th Cir.1979).

5. Lykos v. American Home Insurance Company, 609 F.2d 314 at p. 316 (7th Cir. 1979), affirming the decision reported at 452 F.Supp. 533 (N.D.Ill.1978). The court observed that "the evidence conclusively established a consistent pattern of inordinately excessive claims" on the basis of a large number of items in the contents claim that were overvalued and numerous duplications between the building and the contents claims.

6. See, e.g., Fine v. Bellefonte Underwriters Insurance Company, 725 F.2d 179 (2d Cir.1984).

Cf. the dictum in Henderson v. Rochester American Insurance Co., 254 N.C. 329 at p. 333, 118 S.E.2d 885 at p. 888 (1961):

"Where there has been evidence tending to show collusion between the injured and the insured, courts have been careful to protect the insurer. Courts usually hold that misstatements persisted in until the trial or subsequent to the filing of pleadings by insured requiring a shifting of ground and a new and different defense suffice as a matter of law to establish a failure to cooperate. Except for these classes of cases, courts generally hold the question of materiality and prejudice is a question for the jury."

Also see M.F.A. Mutual Insurance Company v. Cheek, 66 Ill.2d 492, 6 Ill.Dec. 862, 363 N.E.2d 809 (1977), which considered the consequences of misinformation in relation to the cooperation clause of a liability insurance policy.

7. See, e.g., Fine v. Bellafonte Underwriters Insurance Company, 725 F.2d 179 (2d Cir.1984); Bryant v. Nationwide Mutual Fire Insurance Company, 313 N.C. 362, 329 S.E.2d 333 (1985); Edmiston v. Schellenger, 343 So.2d 465 (Miss.1977).

In some instances, judicial decisions have imposed conditions or limitations on the broad language of a concealment and fraud provision. And, even when such insurance policy provisions are prescribed by statute, courts often appear reluctant to support vigorous enforcement of these clauses. For example, in some instances it has been held that misconduct of one insured does not bar recovery by an innocent co-insured holding a separable interest.[8] In addition, some courts have held that the fraud-or-false-swearing clause does not apply to testimony given at trial.[9] Moreover, an insurer generally has the burden of pleading and proof in regard to the facts that must be established when a defense is predicated on either concealment or fraud in the submission of claims.[10] Thus, among the judicial precedents there are numerous decisions which manifest an inclination to limit the scope of defenses to claims that are based on fraud or false swearing in presenting a claim.[11]

In many states, there is legislation that regulates defenses based on a misrepresentation in the proof of a loss,[12] and disputes involving such

---

Also see Chester v. Assiniboia Corporation, 355 A.2d 880 (Del.1976) (applying admiralty law).

8. See, e.g., Morgan v. Cincinnati Insurance Company, 411 Mich. 267, 307 N.W.2d 53 (1981) (fraud by an insured does not bar a claim by any other insured who is innocent of the fraud).

Also see Mercantile Trust Co. v. New York Underwriters Insurance Co., 376 F.2d 502 (7th Cir.1967), 24 A.L.R.3d 443 (1969) (Illinois law; fraud of life tenant of dwelling in relation to contents coverage under homeowners policy did not bar rights of trustee holding remainder interest in dwelling). By virtue of explicit policy provisions, a similar rule applies to protect the mortgagee under the standard mortgage clause.

Also see Lovell v. Rowan Mutual Fire Insurance Company, 302 N.C. 150, 274 S.E.2d 170 (1981).

Cf. Reserve Insurance Co. v. Aguilera, 181 Neb. 605, 150 N.W.2d 114 (1967), 24 A.L.R.3d 431 (1969).

But cf. Short v. Oklahoma Farmers Union Insurance Company, 619 P.2d 588 at p. 590 (Okl.1980) ("Where * * * the title to the property is held jointly and that property insured under a single policy and is destroyed by a joint insured's act of arson, the entire policy is voided under the first quoted contract provision declaring the policy to be void in the case of fraud or false swearing on the part of the insured.").

See § 4.1 and § 4.2(a), above. But in the absence of policy provisions such as those of the standard mortgage clause, probably the mortgagee would be barred by the mortgagor's false swearing.

9. E.g., American Paint Service, Inc. v. Home Insurance Co., 246 F.2d 91 (3d Cir. 1957), 64 A.L.R.2d 957 (1959) (New Jersey law); Home Insurance Co. v. Cohen, 357 S.W.2d 674 (Ky.1962), overruling World Fire & Marine Insurance Co. v. Tapp, 279 Ky. 423, 130 S.W.2d 848 (1939) (false statements in deposition).

10. See, e.g., United States Fire Insurance Company v. Skatell, 596 S.W.2d 166 at p. 169 (Tex.Civ.App., Texarkana, 1980).

11. Also see, e.g., Firemen's Insurance Co. v. Smith, 180 F.2d 371 at p. 376 (8th Cir.1950), *cert. denied* 339 U.S. 980, 70 S.Ct. 1028, 94 L.Ed. 1384 (1950) (Missouri law; on other issues in the case the court cited a Missouri statute concerning warranties *incorporated in* a fire policy; without referring to any statute or decision, the court stated that whether the policy was rendered void by false swearing "depends also upon whether the alleged false swearing by the insured related to any material fact or circumstance concerning the insurance or the subject thereof").

See generally 5A APPLEMAN, INSURANCE LAW (Revised edition, 1970), at § 3587.

12. See, e.g., Alabama Code 1975, 27–14–28 (1975); Vernon's Annotated Texas Statutes, Insurance Code, art. 21.19 (1963). Also see United States Fire Insurance Company v. Skatell, 596 S.W.2d 166 (Tex. App., Texarkana, 1980).

In some states, a statute regulating defenses based on misrepresentation during negotiation of the contract also explicitly

legislative provisions have presented interesting statutory interpretation problems.[13] These statutes typically require that (1) a claimant's misrepresentation must be fraudulent and (2) that the misinformation must concern a matter which is material to the liability of the insurer.[14] In a few instances, the misinformation provided by the claimant also must result in the insurer's loss or "waiver" of some valid defense.[15] Several of the problems presented by such requirements in legislative provisions regarding the consequences of misinformation submitted in a claim are comparable to the problems arising from the submission of incorrect information in an application for insurance.[16]

Statutes in several states provide that a misrepresentation by a person does not constitute a defense unless it concerns a matter that contributes to the loss.[17] The meaning of the statutory provision that a misrepresentation must "contribute" to the loss is at best unclear. False swearing about the amount of loss does not "cause" the loss. It may reasonably be argued that something which occurs after a loss

applies to defenses based on misrepresentation in the proof of loss. In other states, a statute that is aimed at least primarily at defenses based on misrepresentation during negotiation of the contract is inexplicit as to whether it applies as well to fraud and false swearing in the presentment of a claim.

13. See, e.g., Aetna Casualty & Surety Company v. Guynes, 713 F.2d 1187 (5th Cir.1983) (interpreting the Texas statute).

In many states, the statutes explicitly apply only to representations made before the issuance of the policy. See e.g., Massachusetts General Laws Annotated ch. 175, § 186 (1958), applying to "oral or written misrepresentation or warranty made in the negotiation of a policy of insurance * * *."

14. See, e.g., Aetna Casualty & Surety Company v. Guynes, 713 F.2d 1187 at p. 1192 (5th Cir.1983) (interpreting Texas law).

15. United States Fire Insurance Company v. Skatell, 596 S.W.2d 166 at p. 169 (Tex.Civ.App., Texarkana, 1980).

Also see Aetna Casualty & Surety Company v. Guynes, 713 F.2d 1187 at p. 1192 (5th Cir.1983) (interpreting Texas law). In *Guynes,* the court concluded that the insurer was not relieved of liability because the insurer was never misled by the incorrect information, and the insured's declarations did not result in the waiver or loss of any valid defense.

16. See the discussion in § 5.7, above.

17. See, e.g.:

Wisconsin Statutes Annotated § 631.11(2) (1980):

"No misrepresentation or breach of an affirmative warranty affects the insurer's obligations under the policy unless the insurer relies on it and it is either material or is made with intent to deceive, or unless the fact misrepresented or falsely warranted contributes to the loss."

Nebraska Revised Statutes § 44–358 (1943):

"No oral or written misrepresentation or warranty made in the negotiation for a contract or policy of insurance by the insured, or in his behalf, shall be deemed material or defeat or avoid the policy, or prevent its attaching, unless such misrepresentation or warranty deceived the company to its injury."

Montana Code Annotated (1985) § 33–15–403(2):

"Misrepresentations, omissions, concealment of facts, and incorrect statements shall not prevent a recovery under the policy or contract unless either:

(a) fraudulent (b) material either to the acceptance of the risk or to the hazard assumed by the insurer; or (c) the insurer in good faith either would not have issued the policy or contract or would not have issued a policy or contract in as large an amount or at the same premium or rate or would not have provided coverage with respect to the hazard resulting in the loss if the true facts had been made known to the insurer as required either by the application for the policy or contract or otherwise."

(such as a misrepresentation during presentment of the claim) does not "cause" or "contribute" to the loss, even though — if not exposed — it does contribute to the insurer's suffering a "loss" in another sense. However, to treat the misrepresentation in a claim as precluding an insurer from prevailing when the false swearing did not contribute to the loss seems unjustified. Therefore, a better interpretation of such provisions is that the statute was not intended to apply to misrepresentations which are made by an insured after the occurrence of a loss.[18]

§ 7.2(g) The Insured's Liability for Failing to Comply With Claims Presentment Provisions

Ordinarily, an insured's failure to comply with either an insurance policy provision that relates to providing the insurer with notice of a loss or a provision detailing the insured's role in the processing of a claim does not give an insurer a basis for affirmative relief against an insured (or any other claimant). Occasionally, however, an act or omission by an insured does support an insurer's claims for damages. For example, if an insured fails to comply with a claims provision of either a compulsory liability insurance policy or an insurance policy that is certified under a financial responsibility statute *and* the insurer is subsequently held liable to a plaintiff asserting a tort claim, the insurer may be entitled to recover the amount paid to the tort claimant on behalf of the insured. In such a situation, the insurance policy provisions — either alone (if they fully express this obligation) or in conjunction with an applicable statute (such as compulsory insurance or financial responsibility legislation) — may be held to impose obligations on insureds.

§ 7.3 Assistance and Cooperation Provisions

§ 7.3(a) Generally

Liability insurance policies customarily provide that an insured is required to cooperate with and assist the insurer in the investigation, settlement, and defense of tort claims against the insured.[1] These provisions typically include specific references to matters such as attendance at hearings and trials, assistance in effecting settlements, securing and giving evidence, and obtaining the attendance of witnesses, as well as generally requiring an insured to aid in the conduct of suits resulting from tort claims. Provisions which require an insured's

---

18. See, e.g., McPherson v. Camden Fire Insurance Co., 222 S.W. 211 (Tex.Comm.App., 1920) (breach of "iron safe clause" requiring plaintiff to take inventory and keep books in a fireproof safe was a good defense for insurer; contribute-to-loss statute held inapplicable to "iron safe clause" and to "proof of loss clause" because the breach could in no event contribute to bring about the loss).

Also see Hawkins v. New York Life Insurance Co., 176 Kan. 24, 269 P.2d 389 (1954) (overruling earlier decisions that had interpreted a contribute-to-loss statute on life insurance as being inapplicable to "moral risk").

§ 7.3(a)

1. See Appendices G and H.

assistance and cooperation are designed to enable an insurer to protect its interests, as well as those of its insured.

There are also negative stipulations in most liability insurance policies which state that, except at the insured's own cost, the insured shall not voluntarily make any payment, assume any obligation, or incur any expense except when there is an imperative need for medical and surgical relief immediately after an accident.[2] And comparable provisions about both cooperating with the insurer and prohibiting settlements without the insurer's consent, are set forth in the standard forms employed for uninsured and underinsured motorist insurance.[3] Even though such provisions might not be thought of as "assistance and cooperation provisions," disputes involving those provisions involve essentially the same considerations.

Courts have repeatedly upheld the enforceability of provisions that require an insured to provide assistance and cooperation to the insurer.[4] Thus, in general, it is appropriate for an insured to fully comply with requests by an insurer that are made pursuant to such provisions. However, there are some circumstances in which compliance with these requirements may be viewed as undesirable for an insured. Although there are few discussions in appellate court decisions of disputes involving these provisions, such situations do arise in connection with both liability insurance[5] and uninsured or underinsured motorist insurance.[6]

Insurance policies commonly declare that compliance with the various terms in insurance policies that establish requirements for the presentation and processing of claims are conditions precedent to the insurer's liability.[7] A claimant generally has the initial burden of alleging and proving compliance with all conditions precedent. However, in litigation involving the effect of these provisions, courts do not invariably conclude that the consequences which normally follow when a condition precedent has not occurred should apply. The modern trend, as discussed in the next subsection, requires the insurer to demonstrate that the insured's action or inaction was prejudicial to the insurer in that the consequences adversely affected a matter of considerable significance to the insurer. Moreover, courts have increasingly concluded that the burden of proof on the effects of a failure to comply

---

2. *Ibid.*

3. See Appendix H.

Also see Alan I. Widiss, A GUIDE TO UNINSURED MOTORIST INSURANCE (1969) and the 1981 Supplement, §§ 4.4 through 4.10.

4. See, e.g., Indemnity Insurance Co. of North America v. Smith, 197 Md. 160, 78 A.2d 461 (1951); Zitnik v. Burik, 395 Ill. 182, 69 N.E.2d 888 (1946); Koontz v. General Casualty Co., 162 Wash. 77, 297 P. 1081 (1931).

5. See the discussion of conflicts of interests problems in § 7.6, below.

6. See Widiss, UNINSURED MOTORIST AND UNDERINSURED MOTORIST INSURANCE (1985), at § 16.6 and § 16.11.

7. See Appendix H and Appendix J.

As to whether the policy provision is enforceable as a condition however, see, e.g., Oregon Automobile Insurance Co. v. Salzberg, 85 Wash.2d 372, 535 P.2d 816 (1975).

with such requirements should be allocated to the insurer.[8] And some courts have even concluded that a liability insurer asserting a defense based on lack of cooperation must show that there was a "substantial likelihood" that but for the noncooperation the trier-of-fact would have found for the defense in the tort action.[9]

There are, of course, limits on what an insurer may request of an insured. For example, an insured should not be required to falsify information or to withhold facts from a victim claiming against such an insured. Also, an insurer cannot require that the insured act wholly without regard to the insured's interests, as for example, in the conduct of a defense to criminal charges arising from an incident that also produced a liability insurance claim.[10]

§ 7.3(b)   The Prejudice Requirement[1]

The weight of judicial authority, despite several early and highly respected judicial precedents to the contrary,[2] requires that an insurer

8. See § 7.3(b), below.

9. *Cf.* Billington v. Interinsurance Exchange, 71 Cal.2d 728, 79 Cal.Rptr. 326, 456 P.2d 982 (1969) (car owner insured under the assigned risk plan; held, lack of cooperation ___ lished, was a proper defense d ___ inancial Responsibili- ___ udgment for insurer ___ trial judge used erro- ___ ejudice; insurer has ___ ejudice, and it is not ___ uld reasonably and ___ ed" a defense of as- ___ plaintiff's knowledge ___ ion; must at least ___ kelihood the trier of ___ d in the insured's

___ City Insurance Co. ___ 60 (Iowa 1972) ("We ___ rial court that the ___ dant Hassel to the ___ m with operating a ___ intoxicated, even ___ entered over objec- ___ company], did not ___ f the cooperation ___ tract.").

___ may preclude an ___ lt for a crime in a ___ action brought by ___ Mutual Insurance ___ N.W.2d 289 (Iowa

___ ion of "prejudice"

___ New Amsterdam ___ 71, 160 N.E. 367

(1928), 72 A.L.R. 1443 (1931) (opinion by Cardozo, J.). Perhaps few, if any, would contend that the insurer's defense of breach of the assistance and cooperation clause should not have been recognized on the facts of the case, since, first, the secretary of the insured drug company, which was sued on the theory of a negligently filled prescription, said there had been a mistake and refused to say more unless the insurer would undertake to pay a recovery against him as well as any recovery against the insured and, second, the insured failed to respond to the insurer's letters requesting that some officer be sent to verify an answer for the defendant and requesting a conference as to the merits of the claim. But the opinion placed the holding on the ground that cooperation was one of the "conditions" of the policy, adding: "When the condition was broken, the policy was at an end, if the insurer so elected. The case is not one of the breach of a mere covenant, where the consequences may vary with fluctuations of the damage."

Opinions citing *Coleman* with apparent approval include Pennsylvania Insurance Co. v. Horner, 198 Tenn. 445, 281 S.W.2d 44 (1955) (statement by the insured admitting fault and accepting responsibility for damages to the other vehicle, signed apparently because the insured was worried about hit-and-run charges; arguably this conduct was such clear proof of prejudice that the opinion does not have weight as a considered choice among the competing views on the necessity for proof of prejudice).

show prejudice in order to establish a defense based on a breach of an assistance and cooperation clause.[3] In effect, these decisions also reject the appropriateness of applying any presumption that an insured was prejudiced by the insured's conduct. Many of the judicial precedents which adopt this approach impose the burden of proving prejudice on the insurer.[4] In general, this means that the insurer must prove that the effect of the insured's conduct was a matter of considerable consequence to the insurer.

Courts repeatedly have pointed out that there are circumstances in which an insured's failure to cooperate will not justify a defense to a claim. As the Supreme Court of Florida has observed, "Only that failure which constitutes a *material breach* and *substantially prejudices* the rights of the insurer in defense of the cause will release the insurer of its obligation to pay."[5] Similarly, the Illinois Supreme Court has concluded that "the failure of the insured to correctly inform the

---

Also see Alabama Farm Bureau Mutual Casualty Insurance Co. v. Mills, 271 Ala. 192, 123 So.2d 138 (1960) (deliberate persistence in false statements; prejudice not required; in fact, however, risk of loss was increased when insurer was caused to defend rather than settle).

3. See, e.g., Rieschl v. Travelers Insurance Company, 313 N.W.2d 615 (Minn. 1981); State Farm Mutual Automobile Insurance Company v. Commercial Union Insurance Company, 394 So.2d 890 (Miss. 1981); Hendrix v. Jones, 580 S.W.2d 740 (Mo. En Banc 1979); M.F.A. Mutual Insurance Company v. Cheek, 66 Ill.2d 492, 6 Ill. Dec. 862, 363 N.E.2d 809 (1977); Ramos v. Northwest Mutual Insurance Company, 336 So.2d 71 (Fla.1976); Oregon Automobile Insurance Company v. Salzberg, 85 Wash.2d 372 at pp. 376–377, 535 P.2d 816 at p. 819 (1975).

Cf. Miller v. Dilts, 463 N.E.2d 257 at p. 265 (Ind.1984).

Also see Western Farm Bureau Mutual Insurance Company v. Danville Construction Company, 463 S.W.2d 125 at pp. 129–130 (Ky.App.1971); Campbell v. Allstate Insurance Company, 60 Cal.2d 303, 32 Cal. Rptr. 827, 384 P.2d 155 (1963); Henderson v. Rochester American Insurance Co., 254 N.C. 329, 118 S.E.2d 885 (1961) (conflicting versions as to who was driving); Automobile Club Insurance Co. v. Turner, 335 S.W.2d 889 (Ky.1960) (insured at first said he was driving but later corrected the misstatement; insurer, having failed to show prejudice, could not avoid liability); American Fire & Casualty Co. v. Vliet, 148 Fla. 568, 4 So.2d 862, 139 A.L.R. 767 (1941).

In State v. Aetna Casualty and Surety Company, 43 A.D.2d 988, 352 N.Y.S.2d 65 at p. 67 (3d Dept.1974), the court observed

that a breach must be "substantial and material," and that "a technical or inconsequential lack of cooperation will not suffice" as a justification for rejecting a claim.

See generally Annotation, *Liability insurance: misstatement by insured later withdrawn or corrected, as breach of cooperation clause,* 13 A.L.R.4th 837–793 (1982); 8 APPLEMAN, INSURANCE LAW (Revised edition, 1962), at § 4773; 8 BLASHFIELD AUTOMOBILE LAW (Third edition, 1966), at § 342.14.

As to the standard for showing prejudice in this and other contexts, see § 7.2(e), above.

4. See, e.g., Hendrix v. Jones, 580 S.W.2d 740 at p. 744 (Mo., En Banc, 1979); Campbell v. Allstate Insurance Company, 60 Cal.2d 303, 32 Cal.Rptr. 827, 384 P.2d 155 (1963).

Also see the cases cited in the preceding footnote.

5. Ramos v. Northwestern Mutual Insurance Company, 336 So.2d 71 at p. 75 (Fla.1976).

In M.F.A. Mutual Insurance Company v. Cheek, 66 Ill.2d 492 at p. 500, 6 Ill.Dec. 862, 363 N.E.2d 809 at p. 813 (1977) the court observed: "Proof of substantial prejudice requires an insurer to demonstrate that it was actually hampered in its defense by the violation of the cooperation clause."

Also see Baumler v. State Farm Mutual Automobile Insurance Co., 493 F.2d 130 (9th Cir.1974) (applying Arizona law); Rieschl v. Travelers Insurance Company, 313 N.W.2d 615 (Minn.1981); Garcia v. Abrams, 101 A.D.2d 601, 471 N.Y.S.2d 161 (3d Dept.1983).

insurer of the identity of the driver of the automobile will not constitute a breach of the cooperation clause if the insured timely corrects the initial report." [6] Other courts have spoken in terms of the lack of cooperation having to impede the insurer by causing "irreparable harm." [7]

In most situations, the determination whether particular conduct on the part of an insured amounts to noncooperation and, if so, whether the insurer was prejudiced by that conduct, is a question of fact.[8] When the results in cases that have involved factual questions in regard to such requirements in liability insurance policies are analyzed, it often appears that the court's resolution of the dispute is, at least to some extent, influenced by recognition of the public interest in assuring compensation for innocent accident victims.[9]

6. M.F.A. Mutual Insurance Company v. Cheek, 66 Ill.2d 492 at p. 496, 6 Ill.Dec. 862, 363 N.E.2d 809 at p. 811 (1977).

7. Garcia v. Abrams, 101 A.D.2d 601 at p. 607, 471 N.Y.S.2d 161 at p. 164 (3d Dept. 1983).

In Billington v. Interinsurance Exchange, 71 Cal.2d 728 at p. 737, 79 Cal. Rptr. 326 at p. 331, 456 P.2d 982 at p. 992 (1969), the California Supreme Court held that in order to meet "its burden of establishing substantial prejudice from breach of a cooperation clause * * * [an insurer] must establish at the very least that if the cooperation clause had not been breached there was a substantial likelihood the trier of fact would have found in the insured's favor." In applying this standard, a California Court of Appeal concluded that "the required showing of prejudice cannot be made while the main tort action is pending, its outcome uncertain * * *."

Also see United Services Automobile Association v. Martin, 120 Cal.App.3d 963 at p. 966, 174 Cal.Rptr. 835 at p. 836 (2d Dist., Div. 5, 1981). In a footnote, this opinion reports that the main action was settled while the case was on appeal. Unfortunately, the Court of Appeal did not consider what impact this type of resolution would have on the determination of prejudice.

8. See, e.g., Oregon Automobile Insurance Company v. Salzberg, 85 Wash.2d 372 at p. 377, 535 P.2d 816 at p. 818 (en banc 1975); Henderson v. Rochester America Insurance Co., 254 N.C. 329, 118 S.E.2d 885 (1961) (calling attention both to the usual treatment of these issues as fact questions and to the tendency of courts to decide the issues as a matter of law in certain recurring factual patterns).

Also see Hartford Fire Insurance Company v. Masternak, 55 A.D.2d 472, 390 N.Y.S.2d 949 (4th Dept.1977).

See also § 7.2(e)(2), below.

9. See, e.g., Hendrix v. Jones, 580 S.W.2d 740 at p. 744 (Mo., En Banc, 1979); Banner Casualty Company v. Nationwide Insurance Company, 115 Misc.2d 453, 454 N.Y.S.2d 264 (Kings County, 1982).

In Harvey v. Johnson, 30 Ill.App.3d 750, 332 N.E.2d 680 at p. 683 (1st Dist., 5th Div., 1975), for example, the court observed that "a contract of automobile insurance is more than a simple agreement between two parties" because it "is a contract which protects both the insured and the public from hazards of financial distress to which they may become victims as a result of engaging in traffic upon our streets and highways."

Also see Stippich v. Morrison, 12 Wis.2d 331, 107 N.W.2d 125 (1961) (breach by submitting to adverse examination without insurer's knowledge; overruling one of two earlier decisions reconcilable on facts but conflicting in rationale).

Cf. MFA Mutual Insurance Co. v. Sailors, 180 Neb. 201, 141 N.W.2d 846 (1966) (concealing identity of driver and failing to forward summons); Campbell v. Allstate Insurance Co., 60 Cal.2d 303, 32 Cal.Rptr. 827, 384 P.2d 155 (1963) (failure to respond to letters requesting assistance; default judgment).

In Hartford Fire Insurance Company v. Masternak, 55 A.D.2d 472, 390 N.Y.Supp. 2d 949 at p. 952 (4th Dept.1977), the court commented, "The burden of proving the insured's lack of cooperation is 'a heavy one indeed' and rests solely on the plaintiff [the insurer] [citations omitted]."

Acts of Collusion

If an insurer can prove that a claimant participated in some act of collusion in connection with an insurance claim, it usually constitutes a violation of the assistance and cooperation clause that is sufficient to justify a loss of coverage. In some jurisdictions, there is considerable support among the judicial precedents for the proposition that this type of conduct is such a serious violation of the insured's obligations to the insurer that an insurer, who would normally be required to show that a violation of a claims provision was prejudicial, is not required to provide proof of prejudice.[10] However, what constitutes a collusive act is subject to debate. For example, in one case an insurer asserted, unsuccessfully, that the actions of a parent in arranging for an attorney for a minor child to bring suit against the parent constituted collusion.[11] Although the appropriateness of rejecting a claim of collusion in those circumstances seems apparent, the fact that such a claim was made by an insurer is in itself indicative of the range of problems that courts have had to address as a consequence of the tensions and conflicting interests that sometimes exist between insureds and insurers in the course of investigating, settling, or litigating liability insurance disputes.

Covenants and Conditions

In some instances, especially among some of the older judicial precedents, courts have drawn a distinction between insurance policy provisions in which the insured's cooperation was clearly phrased as a condition precedent to the insurer's liability and policies in which the obligation was framed as a covenant.[12] In almost all situations, this is a distinction without any real significance, and the better rule — as well as the majority view [13] — is to disregard such differences in phraseology in favor of basing the determination of the effect of a failure to cooperate with or assist the insurer on whether the insurer can show that it was prejudiced as a consequence of the insured's actions.

---

10. See, e.g., Elliott v. Metropolitan Casualty Insurance Co., 250 F.2d 680 (10th Cir.1957), 66 A.L.R.2d 1231 (1959), *cert. denied* 356 U.S. 932, 78 S.Ct. 774, 2 L.Ed.2d 762 (1958) (collusion to travel to Kansas to accept service of process).

Concerning the prejudice requirement, also see the decisions cited in § 7.2(e)(1), above.

11. E.g., Jordan v. Standard Mutual Insurance Co., 50 Ill.App.2d 12, 199 N.E.2d 423 (2d Dist.1964), 8 A.L.R.3d 1338 (1966).

The problem of collusive intra-family claims led to the enactment of a statute in New York declaring that no policy "shall be deemed to insure against any liability of an insured because of death of or injuries to his or her spouse unless express provision relating specifically thereto is included in the policy." New York—McKinney's Insurance Law § 167(3) (1966), which is now codified as New York—McKinney's Insurance Law § 3420(5) (1985).

Concerning conflicts of interest in litigation, in this and other contexts, see § 7.6, below.

12. See the discussion in § 7.3(a), above.

13. See the discussion in Oregon Automobile Insurance Company v. Salzberg, 85 Wash.2d 372 at p. 377, 535 P.2d 816 at p. 818 (En banc, 1975), and the decisions cited therein.

§ 7.3(c)   Assessing Whether an Insured's Conduct Was Prejudicial

In general, courts are reluctant to adjudge that a coverage is forfeited as a consequence of an insured's acts after an accident has occurred. For example, an insured's incorrect negative answer to an insurance adjuster's question about whether "anyone was drinking" was held not to amount to a misrepresentation constituting a breach of the cooperation clause. The Fifth Circuit Court of Appeals did not view the statement as an outright lie, but as "a single answer to an inarticulate question" which would not be "considered a misrepresentation" in "the traumatic aftermath of a fatal accident."[1] As this case illustrates, the assistance and cooperation provisions can produce some difficult questions about what is prejudicial.[2]

In some situations, however, acts by an insured are so clearly prejudicial that courts essentially do not even address the question. For example, when an insured entered into an agreement to admit critical facts in return for a covenant by a plaintiff not to levy execution for any judgment in excess of the liability insurance coverage limit, it was held to be a breach of the assistance and cooperation clause.[3] Similarly, an insured's actions that willfully obstructed an insurer's handling of a claim against the insured would be violation of the assistance and cooperation clause.

§ 7.3(d)   Limitations on the Enforcement of Cooperation and Assistance Provisions

It is clear that a failure by an insured to cooperate with and assist an insurer may result in a forfeiture of coverage.[1] However, courts have sometimes concluded that an insured's failure may be excused.[2]

An insurer generally will not be allowed to reject a claim for liability insurance coverage based on evidence that merely shows that the insured has been unavailable to cooperate in the defense. Courts usually require that an insurer prove that it has exercised reasonable

---

§ 7.3(c)

1. St. Paul Mercury Insurance Company v. Ford, 585 F.2d 760 at p. 761 (5th Cir. 1978).

2. The question may be particularly difficult if the rejection of coverage is a result of an insured's negligent conduct following the occurrence of an insured event which is covered by liability insurance.

3. E.g., Western Mutual Insurance Co. v. Baldwin, 258 Iowa 460, 137 N.W.2d 918 (1965) (farmer's comprehensive policy; insured first denied he started fire that destroyed railroad bridge and later covenanted with railroad, in return for railroad's agreement not to levy execution in excess of policy limit, to admit he started fire; declaratory judgment for insurer).

§ 7.3(d)

1. See, e.g., Henderson v. Rochester American Insurance Co., 254 N.C. 329, 118 S.E.2d 885 (1961) (calling attention both to the usual treatment of these issues as fact questions and to the tendency of courts to decide the issues as a matter of law in certain recurring factual patterns).

2. See, e.g., Morrison v. Lewis, 351 Mass. 386, 221 N.E.2d 401 (1966) (involving noncompulsory guest coverage).

See generally, Annotation, *Liability Insurance: Failure or Refusal of Insured to Attend Trial or to Testify as to Breach of Cooperation Clause*, 9 A.L.R. 4th 218–313 (1981).

diligence to locate and then communicate its requests to the insured.[3] In other words, in addition to showing that prejudice resulted, insurers must also provide the court with a clear picture of the company's conduct in its attempts to secure the cooperation of its insured. For example, when an insurer had rejected a claim on the basis that an insured did not attend the trial of an action against the insured, the insurer was required to show that it exercised diligence and good faith in seeking the cooperation or assistance of its insured.[4]

In New York, the courts have underscored this requirement by adding that not only must the insurer act diligently in seeking to secure an insured's cooperation,[5] but also that an insurer must demonstrate "that the efforts employed by the insurer were reasonably calculated to obtain the insured's cooperation" and "that the attitude of the insured, after [notification that] his cooperation was sought, was one of willful and avowed obstruction * * *."[6] Furthermore, New York courts have repeatedly observed that the burden on the insurer to show lack of cooperation is "a heavy one indeed."[7] And some courts hold that an insurer's defense of non-cooperation is precluded unless after the insurer learns that the insured intends not to comply with some request, the insured is explicitly informed of the consequences of the failure to cooperate.[8]

A liability insurer may lose the right to disclaim coverage on the basis of the cooperation and assistance provisions when an insurer continues to manage the defense of a claim against an insured after

---

3. See, e.g., Thrasner v. United States Liability Insurance Co., 19 N.Y.2d 159, 225 N.E.2d 503, 278 N.Y.S.2d 793 (1967) (insurer's attempts to locate insured were limited and ineffective; evidence presented by insurer that insured knew insurer's investigator was looking for him was "equivocal, at best," and did not discharge insurer's burden of proving that insured's "attitude was one of 'willful and avowed obstruction' "); Johnson v. Doughty, 236 Or. 78, 385 P.2d 760 (1963) (borrower of insured car involved in hit-and-run collision abandoned car after driving away from accident and left state without leaving forwarding address; sending a letter addressed to him at a known improper address did not constitute reasonable effort to give him an opportunity to demonstrate his willingness or lack of willingness to cooperate with insurer).

Also see Newport v. MFA Insurance Company, 448 N.E.2d 1223 at p. 1229 (Ind. App. 4th Dist.1983).

4. Ramos v. Northwestern Mutual Insurance Company, 336 So.2d 71 at p. 75 (Fla.1976).

Also see Johnson v. Wade, 47 Ill.App.3d 610, 7 Ill.Dec. 726, 365 N.E.2d 11 (1st Dist., 5th Div., 1977).

5. Thrasher v. United States Liability Insurance Company, 19 N.Y.2d 159, 278 N.Y.S.2d 793, 225 N.E.2d 503 (1967).

Also see Rieschl v. Travelers Insurance Company, 313 N.W.2d 615 at p. 618 (Minn. 1981).

6. Van Opdorp v. Merchants Mutual Insurance Company, 55 A.D.2d 810, 390 N.Y.S.2d 279 at p. 280 (4th Dept.1976).

Also see Thrasher v. United States Liability Insurance Company, 19 N.Y.2d 159 at p. 168, 278 N.Y.S.2d 793 at p. 798, 225 N.E.2d 503 at p. 508 (1967).

Cf. Garcia v. Abrams, 101 A.D.2d 601, 471 N.Y.S.2d 161 (3d Dept.1983) (citations omitted).

7. Van Opdorp v. Merchants Mutual Insurance Company, 55 A.D.2d 810, 390 N.Y.S.2d 279 at p. 280 (4th Dept.1976), based on Thrasher v. United States Liability Insurance Company, 19 N.Y.2d 159 at p. 168, 278 N.Y.S.2d 793 at p. 798, 225 N.E.2d 503 at p. 508 (1967).

8. See, e.g., Johnson v. Wade, 47 Ill. App.3d 610, 7 Ill.Dec. 726, 365 N.E.2d 11 (1st Dist., Div. 5, 1977).

becoming aware of an insured's uncooperative conduct.[9] In the absence of a prompt notice of disclaimer to the insured, courts are inclined either to find a "waiver of the breach" or to conclude that the insurer's "right to rely on the alleged breach is barred by principles of estoppel." [10]

It is generally recognized that an insured need not incur expenses to attend a trial, and therefore an insured does not violate the assistance and cooperation clause by declining to make an expensive trip at the request of the insurer when reimbursement of expenses is not offered.[11] In effect, the appropriateness of this rule is supported by supplementary-payments clauses (which are commonly included in liability insurance policies) that state the insurer shall reimburse the insured for expenses other than loss of earnings.[12]

There is some judicial authority for a rule that an insured may be required to attend trial without receiving reimbursement from the insurer for income or pay that is lost.[13] However, this proposition is open to challenge, especially in circumstances in which attendance would have a substantial impact on the insured's income or employment status. As a matter of practice, liability insurers will often reimburse an insured for lost wages when the insured works at an hourly or daily wage. This seems to be both permissible and desirable. And some insurance policies specifically provide for compensation, subject to some maximum amount per day, for loss of wages because of attendance at trial.[14]

---

9. *Cf.* Continental Insurance Company v. Bayless & Roberts, Inc., 608 P.2d 281, (Alaska 1980); Alexander v. Stone, 45 A.D.2d 216, 357 N.Y.S.2d 271 (4th Dept. 1974).

Cf. Dougherty v. Hanover Insurance Company, 114 N.J.Super. 483, 277 A.2d 242 (1971).

In Beam v. State Farm Mutual Automobile Insurance Co., 269 F.2d 151 at p. 156 (6th Cir.1959), the court observed: "If it proceeds with the defense of the action without being ordered to do so by the Court and without reserving its rights, it waives its right to a cancellation or forfeiture of the policy."

10. Continental Insurance Company v. Bayless & Roberts, Inc., 608 P.2d 281 at p. 292 (Alaska 1980).

Also see the discussion in Burr v. Lane, 10 Wash.App. 661 at pp. 672, 517 P.2d 988 at pp. 995–996 (1974).

It is likely that the "waiver" or "estoppel" theories applied in these instances are more accurately described as an "election" — that is, there is little indication of either a voluntary relinquishment of a known right that would be essential to a "waiver" or detrimental reliance by the insured which is generally necessary for an estoppel to apply. See § 6.1, above.

11. E.g., American Fire & Casualty Co. v. Vliet, 148 Fla. 568, 4 So.2d 862, 139 A.L.R. 767 (1941).

Cf. Beam v. State Farm Mutual Automobile Insurance Co., 269 F.2d 151 (6th Cir. 1959).

12. See Appendix G and Appendix J.

13. See, e.g., American Fire & Casualty Co. v. Vliet, 148 Fla. 568, 4 So.2d 862 (1941), 139 A.L.R. 767 (1942).

14. See Appendix G.

This provision would serve to clarify the insurer's liability for lost time and to fix a limit on the amount in the absence of an express agreement otherwise. Still, in particular cases, the argument might prevail that it would be unreasonable to demand that the insured attend trial without reimbursement of lost income if the loss would be much greater than the stated amount per day.

Caveat. The increasingly apparent inclination on the part of courts to rule that reasonable jurors may differ concerning any particular issue of fact is undoubtedly relevant to litigation over whether an insured acted in accord with the requirements established by an assistance and cooperation clause. This trend almost certainly has had and will continue to have a very significant impact upon the practical meaning of these provisions.[15]

§ 7.4 Multiple Claims Under Liability Insurance

§ 7.4(a) Multiple Claim Cases: An Introductory Note

When several persons are injured as a consequence of negligent conduct by someone who is covered by liability insurance, the injured persons often have claims that produce conflicting interests in regard to the allocation of the applicable insurance. For example, suppose a negligently driven car covered by a liability insurance policy with a liability limit of $20,000 per accident collides with a carefully driven car and results in serious injuries to the driver and five passengers in the second car. If the damages sustained by those six persons as a consequence of the accident substantially exceed the insurance policy liability limit of $20,000, the individuals injured in such an accident will have sharply conflicting interests because each of the injured persons seeks compensation from the available, but inadequate, liability insurance. The question of how a limited amount of liability insurance is to be allocated when the claims exceed the available coverage has

---

15. See, e.g., Lumbermens Mutual Casualty Co. v. Chapman, 269 F.2d 478 (4th Cir.1959). The act of noncooperation charged by the company was collusion between the insured, Foster, and the claimant, who was his sister-in-law. On the evening before the trial, Foster, at the request of the claimant's attorney extended through the claimant, went to the office of the claimant's attorney, for an interview. The attorney stated that his purpose was to get information to prepare his case properly, and he assured Foster that in the event of a verdict beyond the coverage the claimant would release Foster of any responsibility for the excess. The company's attorney did not know of this meeting. Previous to this meeting, the settlement figure demanded by the claimant was $15,000; at the start of trial, the claimant's attorney raised his settlement demand to $20,000 and gave notice to the company that he would also look to the company for any amount of the verdict beyond $20,000. The claimant's attorney called Foster as a witness during the presentation of claimant's case. In answering a question, Foster expressed the opinion that he was legally responsible for the accident. In his opening statement the claim-

ant's attorney had described the occurrence just as Foster outlined it in his testimony, and the claimant's account closely paralleled Foster's. Trial resulted in a verdict for $7,500, which was within policy limits, and thereafter the claimant commenced this action against the company. The court of appeals sustained a jury verdict for the claimant on this evidence. The court noted that the conduct of the claimant's counsel in arranging an interview with the insured after he was represented by counsel appointed by the company was a violation of the canons of ethics but observed that the misconduct of the claimant's attorney was not chargable to the insured. The court considered that ordinary candor demanded of the insured that he inform the company of the conference, but that this breach of obligation by the insured was not so substantial as to require a conclusion that the company was relieved of liability. Perhaps even in a day of great permissiveness toward jury verdicts other courts would have found the defense of noncooperation established as a matter of law in these circumstances. Certainly a different result would have been probable in earlier times.

long been recognized as a vexing problem when there are multiple claims arising from an insured event.

Whenever the amount of insurance for any insured event is less than the total losses, the persons sustaining losses may have divergent interests.[1] In such situations, if the insurance company exhausts the applicable liability insurance by settling with one or more of the claimants, the interests of the person(s) receiving compensation have, in essence, been preferred over the interests of the others. Furthermore, depending on the circumstances, the specific settlement(s) with some of the individual claimants may not be in the best interests of the insured. The following subsections discuss the doctrines that have thus far been developed as a consequence of such cases.

§ 7.4(b)   The Insurer's Duty to the Insured

Ordinarily, when tort claims exceed the applicable liability insurance, the insured's interest is best served by use of the available insurance coverage so as to minimize the insured's risk of liability in excess of policy limits. This is especially true if the insured has resources that may be subject to claims by the other injured persons. Therefore, when there are multiple claimants, the insured has an interest that may be adversely affected by the settlements if one or more of the claimants receive settlement payments — in exchange for an agreement that releases the insured from any additional liability or obligation — while others do not. In such cases, disagreements sometimes arise in regard to the duty of an insurer with respect to the interests of the insured,[1] and, as discussed in the following subsection, the "duty" of the insurer to the claimants as well.

Minimizing an insured's total or cumulative risk of liability may not be viewed as a primary, or even as a significant, consideration or goal by an insurer. For example, when there are multiple claims that clearly exceed the coverage limits as the result of an accident and the liability question is not in doubt, the insurance company may seek to quickly exhaust the applicable coverage in settlements with one or more of the claimants, hoping to minimize its total expenses (including its investigation and defense costs).

In general, when questions about the conduct of a liability insurer in regard to settlements have been considered by the courts, the decisions have held that an insurer may enter into settlements with some claimants — even though such settlements diminish or exhaust the proceeds available to other claimants — so long as the insurer acts reasonably and in good faith.[2] Although there are few elaborations on

---

§ 7.4(a)

1. Furthermore, the insurer may still hope to keep the total settlements below the insurer's maximum limit of liability.

§ 7.4(b)

1. See the discussion of conflicts of interests in § 7.6, below, and the discussion of settlements in § 7.8 and § 7.9, below.

2. See, e.g., Carter v. Safeco Insurance Company, 435 So.2d 1076 (La.App., 1st Cir., 1983); Merritt v. New Orleans Public Ser-

what constitutes good faith and reasonable action in this context, a persuasive case exists for the proposition that a liability insurance company should give consideration to the interests of its insured as it decides on the appropriate course of conduct in multiple-claim cases.

A liability insurer's duty to the insured when there are multiple claims should be affected by some considerations [3] that do not apply to a settlement when there is a single claim.[4] For example, if it would clearly serve the insured's interest for the insurer to reject an offer of settlement — which would normally be reasonable — in order to use the available insurance coverage to settle other claims that otherwise would expose the insured to greater risks of liability, this factor should influence the insurer's conduct.

When the claims arising from an insured event exceed the applicable liability insurance, a potentially significant conflict of interests exists between a liability insurer and its insured.[5] In this context, an insurer should exercise considerable care and consideration should be given to employing some type of proration plan [6] or an interpleader proceeding.[7]

§ 7.4(c) The Insurer's Duty to the Claimants: The Problem of Preferential Settlements

Most insurance policies do not address the problem of how insurance is to be apportioned among claimants when the applicable coverage is not sufficient to fully indemnify all of the injured persons. The question of what consideration, if any, a liability insurer is obligated to exercise in regard to the interests of one or more individuals among a group of claimants is not subject to a definitive answer.

In general, a liability insurer may settle one or more claims even though such settlements exhaust the coverage, leaving no insurance coverage as a source of indemnification for the other claimants.[1] There is a substantial body of judicial precedents sustaining an insurer's

---

vice, 421 So.2d 1000 (La.App., 4th Cir., 1982).

Also see Hartford Casualty Insurance Company v. Dodd, 416 F.Supp. 1216 (D.Md. 1976); Haas v. Mid America Fire & Marine Insurance Company, Illinois Division, 35 Ill.App.3d 993, 343 N.E.2d 36 (3d Dist. 1976).

3. See, e.g., Liberty Mutual Insurance Co. v. Davis, 412 F.2d 475 (5th Cir.1969) (Florida law; assignee of insured recovered on claim of bad faith refusal to settle arising from insurer's efforts to achieve a pro-rated, comprehensive settlement more for its own protection than for insured's); American Casualty Co. of Reading, Pa. v. Glorfield, 216 F.2d 250 (9th Cir.1954) (applying Washington law).

Cf. Roberts v. American Fire & Casualty Co., 89 F.Supp. 827 (M.D.Tenn.1950), *af-*

firmed *per curiam* 186 F.2d 921 (6th Cir. 1951) (Tennessee law).

See generally Robert E. Keeton, *Preferential settlement of Liability Insurance Claims,* 70 Harvard Law Review 27–60 at pp. 28–36 (1956).

Also see the discussion of reciprocal claims in § 7.5, below.

4. See the discussion of insurance claims settlements at § 7.8, below.

5. See the discussion of conflicts of interests in § 7.6, below.

6. See § 7.4(d) and § 7.4(f), below.

7. See § 7.4(d), § 7.4(g), and § 7.6(d)(5), below.

§ 7.4(c)

1. See, e.g., Richard v. Southern Farm Bureau Casualty Insurance Company, 254

settlement decisions against an assertion — either by an insured or by claimants injured by an insured — that the insurer inappropriately paid out all or part of its policy limit to some claimants.[2]

There have been some judicial decisions denying a claimant's prayer for injunction against what was alleged to be a preferential settlement.[3] Also, some courts have permitted a claimant to collect a judgment over an objection of the insurer.[4] However, these decisions should not be viewed as judicial precedents against the application of a rule that would require an equitable allocation of a limited amount of insurance coverage. In most instances, it seems clear that the justification for the application of a principle of equitable allocation and a right

La. 429, 223 So.2d 858 (1969); Bartlett v. Travelers' Insurance Company, 117 Conn. 147, 167 A. 180 (1933); Duprey v. Security Mutual Casualty Company, 22 A.D.2d 544, 256 N.Y.S.2d 987 (3d Dept.1965).

Also see Alford v. Textile Insurance Co., 248 N.C. 224, 103 S.E.2d 8 (1958), 70 A.L.R.2d 408 (1960); Gerdes v. Travelers Insurance Company, 109 Misc.2d 816, 440 N.Y.S.2d 976 (Suffolk County, Pt. I, 1981) (uninsured motorist insurance).

Cf. Lumbermens Mutual Casualty Company v. Yeroyan, 90 N.H. 145, 5 A.2d 726 (1939).

But cf. Darrah v. Lion Bonding & Surety Company, 200 S.W. 1101 (Tex.Civ.App., 1918, no writ history). The court in Darrah indicated that in the absence of laches the claimant would have a right to participate in the insurance fund, enforceable in an action against the bonding company for the claimant's prorata share though the company had paid out the full amount of the bond in satisfaction of the judgments of other claimants. The bond, however, unlike the typical liability insurance policy provided that "suit may be brought and recovery had hereon by any person damaged, in his own name, against the principal and sureties hereon and hereof in the same action." Thus the claimant's interest in the insurance fund was more immediate than under a policy containing a typical "no action" clause. Under such a clause, the claimant's interest is customarily said to be "inchoate" before judgment against the insured on the tort claim.

2. Once one of the claims has been settled, courts have generally held that the insurer's liability to remaining claimants is limited to the difference, if any, between its per-accident limit of coverage and the total already paid out in settlements. See, e.g., Castoreno v. Western Indemnity Company, Inc., 213 Kan. 103, 515 P.2d 789 (1973); Merritt v. New Orleans Public Ser-

vices, 421 So.2d 1000 (La.App., 1st Cir., 1982) (settlements with 22 of 29 persons who were injured when they were passengers in a bus).

Cf. Holtzclaw v. Falco, Inc., 355 So.2d 1279 (La.1977); Haas v. Mid America Fire & Marine Insurance Company, Illinois Division, 35 Ill.App.3d 993, 343 N.E.2d 36 (3d Dist.1976).

Also see Hartford Casualty Insurance Company v. Dodd, 416 F.Supp. 1216 (D.Md. 1976).

See generally Gerald Le Van, *Distribution of a Limited Insurance Fund to Multiple Claimants,* 22 Louisiana Law Review 214–225 (1961); Robert E. Keeton, *Preferential Settlement of Liability Insurance Claims,* 70 Harvard Law Review 27–60 at p. 37 (1956); C.L. Fisher, *Multiple Claims Under the Automobile Liability Policy,* 19 Insurance Counsel Journal 419–424 (1952); Notes, 49 Harvard Law Review 658–659 (1936), 11 New York University Law Quarterly Review 447–452 (1934), 43 Yale Law Journal 136–139 (1933).

3. E.g., Liguori v. Allstate Insurance Co., 76 N.J.Super. 204, 184 A.2d 12 (1962) (attempt to enjoin settlement as preferential failed).

4. See, e.g., Goad v. Fisher, 255 Md. 131, 257 A.2d 433 (1969) (Maryland Unsatisfied Claim and Judgment Law provides that no more than $30,000 may be recovered from the Fund on account of injury to or death of more than one person in any one accident and does not say whether judgments should be paid "first come, first serve" or instead by some system of proration; trial court ordered payment of a $3500 judgment in full from the Fund over objection of the Fund; Fund failed to show prejudice; held, affirmed; questions about what should be done under different facts reserved, and hope expressed that "the General Assembly will fill the void").

to be protected against inequitable preferences was not fully presented to or considered by the courts rendering these decisions.

Some courts have justified an insurer's settlement decisions on the basis of a "first come, first served" rule.[5] A "first-come, first-served" rule is arguably supported by analogy to successive attachments or executions where "the prize" ordinarily goes to the swift. However, an application of a "first-come" approach to the distribution of insurance benefits may produce a grossly inequitable allocation of the limited assets from which injured persons may secure compensation.[6]

§ 7.4(d) Proration Among Claimants of Insurance Coverage

One approach to producing an equitable allocation of insurance is to prorate the applicable liability insurance when there is more than one claimant.[1] Generally this is the approach adopted by courts when

5. In Moore v. McDowell, 54 Mich.App. 657 at p. 660, 221 N.W.2d 446 at pp. 447–448 (1974), the court discussed at some length the awarding of priorities among claimants

"These authorities together with the courts which have confronted this problem recognize the distinction that where no interpleader has been filed multiple claimants against an inadequate insurance fund are entitled to priority in their recoveries on the basis of when their judgments were docketed and there need be no prorationing with dilatory claimants. Thus in the cases relied upon by Allen and Barge where the equitable principles of interpleader were not involved the courts rejected prorationing, Clarke v. Brown, 101 N.J.Super. 404, 244 A.2d 514 (1968); Goad v. Fisher, 255 Md. 131, 257 A.2d 433 (1969); Richter v. Vitale, 59 Misc.2d 374, 299 N.Y.S.2d 293 (1969).

* * *

Throughout all of the cases wherein proration has been approved its opponents have argued for priority on the basis that they have first filed claims or first filed suits, or first obtained judgments. In effect, they have urged that courts follow the oft stated principle of "First in time, first in right", and by so doing award the race only to the swift. However, where, as in the instant case, there is no showing of lack of diligence by any claimant to permit the fund to be exhausted by those who first reached the finishing line would deny equity to those who through no fault of their own have not yet reduced their claims to judgment. That some claims were first adjudicated may be the result of a variety of reasons; i.e. the happy choice of a forum

whose docket is less crowded than others; the seriousness and extent of the injuries suffered thereby determining at what time the full extent of the claim may be asserted.

'A rule of priority dependent upon the time when actions are begun against the insured would be likely to lead to a race to begin such actions, with an added burden of litigation to parties and the court, and a tendency to prevent or render more difficult the settlement of claims. A rule of priority made dependent upon the time when judgments were rendered against the insured would often make controlling the adventitious circumstances attending litigation, often beyond the control or responsibility of the parties.' Century Indemnity Co., supra, 115 Conn. p. 199, 161 A. p. 103."

6. See, e.g., Gerald LeVan, Distribution of a Limited Insurance Fund to Multiple Claimants, 22 Louisiana Law Review 214–225 at pp. 223–225 (1961); C.L. Fisher, Multiple Claims Under the Automobile Liability Policy, 19 Insurance Counsel Journal 419–424 at p. 424 (1952).

§ 7.4(d)

1. In most jurisdictions, an insurer may institute a proceeding, usually in the nature of interpleader, to obtain a court order allocating among various claims the limited fund within the per-accident limit of policy coverage. See generally Zechariah Chafee, The Federal Interpleader Act of 1936: II, 45 Yale Law Journal 1161–1180 (1936); Zechariah Chafee, Federal Interpleader Since the Act of 1936, 49 Yale Law Journal 377–423 (1940); Robert E. Keeton, Preferential Settlement of Liability Insur-

a liability insurance company tenders a sum to a court in an interpleader proceeding because courts tend to favor some form of proration of the benefits among the claimants.[2] Proration of liability insurance among claimants is also supported by the analogy to surety-bond cases in which proration has been applied.[3]

The right of proration among judgment creditors has been given explicit recognition in at least one New York statute.[4] The import of this legislation is of very limited scope: it is only applicable to injuries caused by certain vehicles carrying passengers for hire,[5] and it has been

ance Claims, 70 Harvard Law Review 27–60 at pp. 40–46 (1956).

Also see State Farm Fire & Casualty Co. v. Tashire, 386 U.S. 523, 87 S.Ct. 1199, 18 L.Ed.2d 270 (1967).

2. E.g., Century Indemnity Co. v. Kofsky, 115 Conn. 193, 161 A. 101 (1932); Christlieb v. Luten, 633 S.W.2d 139 (Mo. App. Eastern District, Div. 3, 1982) (pro rata allocation of insurance proceeds among three claimants on the basis of actual damages awarded to each claimant).

Also see Hartford Casualty Insurance Company v. Dodd, 416 F.Supp. 1216 at p. 1220 (D.Md.1976) (insurance paid into court after settlements with some claimants must be divided among the remaining claimants on the basis of their respective damages); Moore v. McDowell, 54 Mich. App. 657, 221 N.W.2d 446 (1974) (equitable principles mandated a pro rata distribution of funds deposited in court despite the status of some claimants as judgment creditors).

Cf. Fallon v. Pekarsky, 77 N.J.Super. 315, 186 A.2d 319 (1962) (money deposited with state by uninsured motorist held to be subject to pro rata distribution); Underwriters for Lloyds of London v. Jones, 261 S.W.2d 686 (Ky.App.1953).

3. E.g., Guffanti v. National Surety Co., 196 N.Y. 452, 90 N.E. 174 (1909).

Also see cases collected in Robert E. Keeton, *Preferential Settlement of Liability Insurance Claims,* 70 Harvard Law Review 27–60 (1956).

4. New York—McKinney's Vehicle and Traffic Law § 370 (1986), applying only to bonds or policies required to be filed by certain vehicles carrying passengers for hire.

5. See Bleimeyer v. Public Service Mutual Casualty Insurance Corp., 250 N.Y. 264 at p. 269, 165 N.E. 286 at pp. 288–289 (1929), distinguishing Long Island Coach Co. v. Hartford Accident & Indemnity Co., 233 App.Div. 331, 227 N.Y.Supp. 633 (1st Dept.1928), *affirmed mem.* 248 N.Y. 629,

162 N.E. 552 (1928), as an action involving a solvent holder of a policy who had paid a claim for damages against himself and was seeking reimbursement. The latter case produced an astonishing result. The tortfeasor sued the insurance company to recover $600 the tortfeasor had paid on judgments obtained by claimants. The insurance company had settled with other claimants on 22 claims arising from one accident for a total of $3,298.50. In this suit it contended that under the statute the maximum due under its policy was to be apportioned ratably among judgment creditors, and that no liability could be enforced against it until all claims were reduced to judgment or were barred. The majority of a divided court awarded the insured a judgment for the $600, stating that the provision for ratable distribution of the insurance proceeds applied only in case of the insolvency of the insured. Thereafter another person injured in the same accident, and her husband, brought a proceeding on behalf of themselves and other judgment creditors of the insured tortfeasor, showing that the tortfeasor was insolvent and claiming the insurance proceeds. By the time this case was decided, the insurance company had paid out $3,383.50 in settlements and $618 to the insured under the judgment in the Long Island case. The court held that the insurance company was not entitled to credit against the policy limit for the amounts it had paid in settlements, and even more surprisingly held that the insurance company was entitled to credit for the $618 payment under judgment only to the extent that the two claimants' judgments it represented would participate ratably with other judgment creditors if the total judgments were in excess of the policy limit.

Also see Frank v. Hartford Accident & Indemnity Company, 136 Misc. 186, 239 N.Y.S. 397 (1930), *affirmed mem.* 231 App. Div. 707, 245 N.Y.S. 777 (1st Dept.1930).

The net consequence of this set of rules is both to deprive the insurance company of a fair opportunity for enforcement of its

held to apply only when an insured is insolvent.[6] The recognition of a right to proration of a limited amount of liability insurance among judgment creditors serves the goal of assuring a type of equitable distribution to members of such a group. However, there is one notable shortcoming that can produce a significant discrimination among claimants: victims of an accident whose tort claims have not been reduced to judgment may be denied any protection because the apportionment procedure favors judgment creditors over other claimants.[7] Thus, a claimant who is able (perhaps as a consequence of having sustained relatively minor injuries) to get to and through a judicial proceeding quickly may be placed in a position to collect a judgment in full or with only such reduction as is necessary to give the same right to others who also have judgments at the time of the proceeding, whereas other claimants — whose trials are delayed (often for reasons beyond their control) — will ultimately find that all the insurance coverage has been exhausted by the time their judgments can be obtained. The potential inequity of such results is apparent. Furthermore, the desirability of a legislative provision for the right of proration among judgment creditors may be outweighed by the implicit negation that results from the failure to enact similar legislation for the benefit of other claimants.

Some commentators have suggested that the risk of an inequitable application of a limited amount of liability insurance coverage is an evil that must be accepted because measures taken to remedy it would interfere with the settlement process by which the vast majority of liability insurance claims are resolved.[8] This pessimism may be unwar-

---

policy limit and to deter the insurer from settling.

6. The limited scope established for proration by this New York statute may actually have done more to hinder than to promote general recognition of the principle of equitable proration of insurance proceeds among multiple claimants. For example, whether rightly so or not, it has in fact somewhat fortified arguments against rights of proration in cases involving types of vehicles to which it does not apply, the argument being that the legislature deliberately refused to make proration applicable generally and that its action disabled the courts from taking the corrective action they might otherwise have taken. David v. Bauman, 24 Misc.2d 67, 196 N.Y.S.2d 746 (1960). However, the inference that the legislature meant to assume responsibility for the problem to the exclusion of further judicial innovation seems unwarranted. See Robert E. Keeton, VENTURING TO DO JUSTICE (1969), at pp. 78–82 and pp. 94–95.

Some judicial opinions have seemed to imply that even among judgment creditors proration would be rejected in favor of the "first come, first served" rule. See, e.g.

Bruyette v. Sandini, 291 Mass. 373 at p. 379, 197 N.E. 29 at p. 32 (1935); O'Donnell v. New Amsterdam Casualty Co., 50 R.I. 275, 276, 146 A. 770 at p. 771 (1929); Turk v. Goldberg, 91 N.J.Eq. 283 at p. 287, 109 A. 732 at p. 733 (Ch.1920).

Also see Pisciotta v. Preston, 170 Misc. 376 at p. 377, 10 N.Y.S.2d 44 at p. 45 (New York County, 1938).

7. The New York statute also fails to specify procedures for allocation. This omission from the statute, however, might be defended on the ground that this is a matter that is best left for the courts to work out.

Concerning procedures for enforcement of the New York statute, see Bleimeyer v. Public Service Mutual Casualty Insurance Corp., 250 N.Y. 264 at p. 268, 165 N.E. 286 at p. 288 (1929) (opinion by Cardozo, Ch. J.).

8. See, e.g., Gerald LeVan, *Distribution of a Limited Insurance Fund to Multiple Claimants*, 22 Louisiana Law Review 214–225 at pp. 223–225 (1961); C.L. Fisher, *Multiple Claims Under the Automobile Liability Policy*, 19 Insurance Counsel Journal 419–424 at p. 424 (1952).

ranted.[9] Other means are available, at least in some circumstances, to ameliorate the problem.

§ 7.4(e) Allocation by Agreement of the Claimants

If all the claimants agree upon a principle of equitable allocation for the coverage provided by a liability insurance policy, such an agreement should be respected by an insurer.[1] However, it is not clear to what extent such an agreement binds the insurer. For example, certainly it cannot be used to compel an insurer to pay out the policy limits. Even though guidelines may be established by the claimants, an insurer should still remain free to settle with a particular claimant for any sum within the maximum amount allocated to that claimant by such guidelines.

Once the claimants agree upon allocation of limited liability coverage, an argument can be made that the insurer should have a duty to each of the claimants it knows of or should know of — that is, the insurer should be obligated to give "due weight" to each person's interest against preferential settlement. However, imposing such an obligation on an insurer should require, at a minimum, notice to the insurer of the agreement of the parties who have agreed, together with a statement specifying whether those claimants are aware of any individuals (who are actual or potential claimants) who have refused to become parties to that accord. Even then, what would constitute "due weight" is not clear.

§ 7.4(f) Comment

One approach to reducing the problems that arise when several persons are injured would be to modify the coverage requirements by amending the financial responsibility laws so that the per-accident coverage limit for motor vehicle liability insurance (which gives rise to this problem), would be ten or more times as high as the per-person limit.[1] Currently most per accident limits for motor vehicle insurance

---

9. For further development of Prof. Keeton's position, see *Preferential Settlement of Liability Insurance Claims,* 70 Harvard Law Review 27–60 (1956).

§ 7.4(e)

1. This would be most justifiable if the insurer has a right to obtain a court order making such an allocation (thereby protecting itself against claims of violating either its duty to its insured or its duty to other claimants).

In the absence of protection against liability on the theory of violation of its duty to the insured regarding settlement, it would seem inappropriate to allow an action by a claimant on the theory of preferential settlement. To do so would be to impose on the company conflicting obligations it could not satisfy. See Robert E.

Keeton, *Preferential Settlement of Liability Insurance Claims,* 70 Harvard Law Review 27–60 at pp. 49–50 (1956).

§ 7.4(f)

1. For indications of the effect of raising the per-accident limit to ten times as much as the per-person limit, consider data for January-October, 1963, supplied by the New York Department of Motor Vehicles, Division of Research and Development, regarding the number of accidents in which various numbers of persons are reported as having been injured; these data disclose that among accidents producing personal injury or death the accidents involving more than ten persons numbered only 45 (6 involving one or more fatalities and 39 involving no fatalities). In contrast, the accidents involving more than nine persons

(both liability coverage and uninsured motorist coverage) are only twice as much as the per individual limits of liability. However, because this approach would involve substantial increases in the amount of insurance and the costs of such insurance for consumers, implementation seems unlikely.

In the absence of a change in the coverage limits by increasing the per-accident limit in comparison with the per-person limit, the best approach to the problem is to adopt a rule of equitable proration for the limited policy coverage per accident so that it would be allocated among the various claims. One of the major questions presented by this approach is whether such claimants would be compelled to release an insured tortfeasor from liability in exchange for such a share, or whether an injured person would still be free to assert a tort claim for injuries that remain uncompensated.

If a release is not required, this approach produces a very different result from that which would normally result. If releases are required, it is probable that some claimants with serious injuries would reject such offers if the insured possessed even a modest amount of assets. Accordingly, it seems likely that the application of a proration rule is most justified when the insurance constitutes the only source of funds associated with the tortfeasor from which victims can effectively seek indemnification. The most feasible method of implementing this principle is to permit proration of the per-accident limit of coverage among the various claims by agreement and to arrange for a judicial determination in the absence of an agreement among the claimants.

If a duty to respect the interests of claimants against preferential settlement is recognized, the question whether this duty should be enforceable by injunction remains a debatable issue. It may be argued that there will be adequate protection for claimants and less burden on the courts if a claimant's remedy is restricted to an action against the insurer for recovery of a money judgment up to the amount that should have been allocated to the claim under an equitable allocation, even if the company has already paid out amounts totalling as much as its per-accident limit of coverage. Under this approach, the penalty against the company for making an inequitable preferential settlement would be that its credit toward exhaustion of its per-accident limit is restricted to the maximum sum that might reasonably have been allocated to the settled claims.[2]

numbered 95 (9 fatal and 86 non-fatal), those involving more than five persons numbered 1,367 (75 fatal and 1,292 nonfatal) and those involving more than four persons numbered 2,888 (128 fatal and 2,760 nonfatal). Rating factors used in calculation of increased-limits liability insurance coverage indicate that the costs of a change to a per-accident limit ten times as high as the per-person limit would be modest.

2. Elsewhere Professor Keeton has argued that any interested party ought to be able to initiate proceedings for allocation of limited policy coverage. See Robert E. Keeton, *Preferential Settlement of Liability Insurance Claims,* 70 Harvard Law Review 27–60 at pp. 52–60 (1956). Perhaps the weightiest objections to allowing a claimant to initiate such proceedings are those concerned with the potential burden upon the courts from proceedings instituted

If the substantive principle of equitable allocation has been adopted by either legislative action or judicial decision, it is appropriate to permit the initiation of an interpleader proceeding by a claimant even though the insurer has not chosen to tender the insurance fund into court. For example, the approach could be invoked by any affected party when an insurer that is contesting liability, and therefore is not prepared to make such a tender, seeks to settle one or more claims on the basis of an allocation of the per-accident limit among the individual claims.[3]

§ 7.5   Reciprocal Claims

§ 7.5(a)   The Effect of Settling a Single Claim

(1) Generally

Many cases involve situations in which each of the parties alleges that the other is responsible for injuries that are the subject of the suit. Opposing claims of this type, which are particularly prevalent when law suits arise as a consequence of motor vehicle accidents or other similar occurrences, frequently are referred to as "reciprocal claims."

When there are reciprocal (opposing) claims, the consequences of any settlement are relatively uncomplicated if the only interests involved are those of the two parties. In this circumstance, it is reasonable to infer that a payment by one party (as, for example, by one of two drivers involved in an automobile accident) to the other in exchange for a release resolves the entire matter, even in the absence of an explicit agreement to that effect. Although the parties to such a settlement could agree that the payment was only a partial resolution which did not affect the possible reciprocal claims, in most instances it is unlikely that they intend this possibility to be the case. Accordingly, thereafter, in the absence of an explicit agreement to preserve the right to subsequently assert a claim, a very persuasive basis exists for the proposition that no further claim should be available to either of the parties.

from excessive zeal, or in spite, when there is no real need for an allocation.

Professor Keeton is indebted to members of the New York Law Revision Commission for development of the idea (during consultation on this problem in 1962–1963) that limiting the right of initiation of such proceedings to the company might reduce the force of these objections without appreciably reducing the effectiveness of protection to the claimants. If the company is liable to partial disallowance of credit toward exhaustion of its policy limit per accident, it will be free to initiate such proceedings when there is real need for them, but would have little inducement to do so otherwise. Thus, it would seem acceptable to establish the companion rules that only

the company may initiate such proceedings and that it is subject to disallowance of credit toward its policy limit if it fails to do so. Recognition of this set of rules would seem to be well within the province of a court exercising the blended powers of law and equity.

As to the possibility of a statutory solution, compare Robert E. Keeton & Jeffrey O'Connell, BASIC PROTECTION FOR THE TRAFFIC VICTIM (1965), at pp. 314–317 and pp. 425–428.

3. For more detailed development of this point, see Robert E. Keeton, *Preferential Settlement of Liability Insurance Claims*, 70 Harvard Law Review 27–60 at pp. 36–60 (1956).

The rule which courts generally apply following any settlement between parties with reciprocal claims (when no insurance is involved) is that all subsequent suits on claims arising from the same events are precluded in the absence of an express stipulation that provides for such claims.[1] In other words, if the individuals actually involved in an accident reach a settlement of one party's claim, that settlement bars any subsequent assertion of a reciprocal claim.[2] In effect, the courts interpret the settlement either as including an implicit term "waiving" the right of a party to such an agreement to assert any reciprocal claims or as justifying the conclusion that the agreement should thereafter preclude the party from asserting a related claim.

The effect a settlement of one of the reciprocal claims resulting from an accident has on all of the other possible claims is considerably less certain when one or more of the parties involved in the accident is insured. The extension of the "reciprocal claims rule" presents some rather perplexing choices when one or more insurers and the interests of those insurers, as well as the insureds, are involved. For example, if there is a collision of two vehicles and liability insurance applies to one or both of the vehicles, the insurance policy terms invariably authorize the insurer to settle any claim or suit as it deems appropriate.

When a liability insurer exercises the right to enter into a settlement of a third party's tort claim against its insured and settles such a claim without ensuring an accord in regard to the other possible claims, significant questions may be presented in regard to the effect on possible reciprocal claims. Furthermore, the rights of the respective parties in such cases can be further complicated by disputes about whether such a settlement has any effect on either (1) the right of an insured to recover on various first party coverages, or (2) the claims that may be asserted by an insurer as a consequence of subrogation rights that arise when an insurer has made or subsequently makes payments under collision insurance, uninsured and underinsured mo-

---

§ 7.5(a)

1. See, e.g., Harrison v. Lucero, 86 N.M. 581, 525 P.2d 941 (1974). The court decided that a settlement without an express reservation constitutes an accord and satisfaction of all claims between the parties to the settlement arising out of the accident. The court also concluded that a claim by the wife of one of the drivers would not be affected because she was not a party to or named in the release.

Also see McKinney v. Morrow, 18 N.C. App. 282, 196 S.E.2d 585 (1973), *cert. denied* 283 N.C. 665, 197 S.E.2d 874 (1973).

Cf. Lugena v. Hanna, 420 S.W.2d 335 (Mo.1967) (Lugena, having no liability insurance, obtained a release from Miss Hanna to meet the requirements of the Financial Responsibility Law for retaining his operator's license; thereafter he sued her for damages; summary judgment for defendant affirmed).

But cf. Restifo v. McDonald, 426 Pa. 5, 230 A.2d 199, 34 A.L.R.3d 1365 (1967) (action by husband, wife, and minor children against estate of decedent; defendant joined coplaintiff wife as additional defendant on children's claims, also seeking contribution; wife pleaded general release given her by decedent; trial court sustained wife's motion for judgment on pleadings; held, reversed and remanded; defendant wife must show that a release of right to seek contribution was bargained for, and, when properly construed the release in instant litigation merely prevents recovery on action originating with releasor).

2. Unless there is an express provision in the settlement agreement preserving the right to assert such a claim.

torist insurance, medical payments insurance, or personal injury protection (no-fault) insurance.[3]

An analysis of some of the problems in regard to the effect of a settlement of one claim arising from an accident upon the possible reciprocal claims (or first party insurance claims which result from the same accident) is facilitated by consideration of the following hypothetical automobile accident. Suppose (1) that two persons — hereinafter referred to as "Plaint" and "Def" — driving their respective cars, are involved in an accident; (2) that both of the vehicles sustain damage amounting to several thousand dollars, and that Plaint is severely injured; (3) that Plaint has collision coverage with a $500 deductible under which payments are received from the insurer for all of the damage to the car in excess of the $500 deductible; (4) that Plaint's insurance company, acting pursuant to provisions in the insurance policy which authorizes it to enter into settlements as it deems appropriate, then pays Def several hundred dollars and receives a release of Def's tort claim against Plaint for both personal injury and property damage; (5) that Plaint, who was severely injured, subsequently asserts a tort claim for personal injuries, and a $2,000 claim for property damage; (6) that Plaint's insurance company then joins as a subrogee to the interest in Plaint's claim for damage to Plaint's car; and (7) that Def's liability insurance company then asserts that the previous settlement bars both the subrogation claim of Plaint's insurance company and all claims by Plaint.

(2) Settlements of a Reciprocal Claim by an Insurer

If there had been no insurance of any kind applicable to the hypothetical accident (described in the preceding paragraph), a settlement in which Plaint paid Def some amount and received a release of Def's tort claim would bar any subsequent claim by Plaint — that is, all of the reciprocal claims would be precluded. A persuasive argument can be made for a comparable result *as between the parties* to an agreement for a settlement between Plaint's insurer and Def — that is, that the rule, which holds that a settlement precludes the assertion of all reciprocal claims by a party to that agreement, should be applied against Plaint's insurance company because when the company entered into the settlement with Def it was either aware of or should have been aware of the subrogation interest.[4] In this type of situation, the

---

3. *Cf.* Aetna Insurance Company v. Gilchrist Brothers, Inc., 85 N.J. 550, 428 A.2d 1254 (1981) (general release from the insured's estate would not preclude subrogation claim by insurer that paid personal injury protection benefits unless such a result was the intent of the parties including the insurer); Heifetz v. Johnson, 61 Wis.2d 111, 211 N.W.2d 834 (1973) (automobile liability insurer paid $2,000 of medical payments coverage to its insured).

4. See, e.g., State Farm Mutual Automobile Insurance Company v. Herrin, 230 So.2d 709 (Fla.App. 2d Dist. 1969).

Cf. Wm. H. Heinemann Creameries, Inc. v. Milwaukee Automobile Insurance Company, 270 Wis. 443, 71 N.W.2d 395 (1955), *rehearing denied* 270 Wis. 443, 72 N.W.2d 102 (1955); Green v. Anders, 473 S.W.2d 622 (Tex.Civ.App., Waco, 1971).

But cf. Martin v. Guttermuth, 403 S.W.2d 282 (Ky.App.1966).

insurer, as the party which repeatedly confronts such situations, should be charged with the responsibility of avoiding uncertainty by including an explicit provision in that settlement agreement that alerts the other party to the insurer's desire to preserve the insurer's reciprocal claim as subrogee of the first person.

The inference that Plaint's insurer and Def intended that there be no further claims arguably is somewhat weaker if Def has property damage liability insurance. Yet, an application of the rule that the reciprocal claim is barred may be justified. Def has some interest, though not as much as Def's liability insurance company, in the possibility that a claim will be made. Def ought not to be subjected to the reciprocal claim (which is against Def's insurance company as well) unless this reservation was set forth as one of the terms of settlement.[5] The justification for treating such a settlement as dispositive of all claims is less clear because the reciprocal claim, though in form against Def, will be paid, if at all, by Def's liability insurance company. Certainly if it is possible for Plaint's insurance company and Def to agree on a settlement that preserves the right of the company to proceed against Def's insurance company, it is reasonable to suppose that Plaint's insurer would prefer to do so.

The appropriateness of precluding a subsequent claim by Plaint, as a consequence of the general rule barring reciprocal claims, is not clear when the settlement was entered into by Def and Plaint's insurer. If Plaint did not participate in the settlement between the insurer and Def, and especially when Plaint was not even aware of the transaction between the insurer and Def,[6] a relatively persuasive case can be made that Plaint should not be bound by such an agreement — that is, when a person has neither assented to nor thereafter explicitly ratified such an agreement, arguably that person should not be bound by that agreement.[7] This point applies both to any interest that such an individual may have in a property damage claim — either because of the $500 deductible [8] or because of a loss that is not covered by the

---

5. Clearly distinguishable from the foregoing cases is the situation in which the first person's collision insurance and liability insurance are written by different companies and the second person knows this. However, there is a good analogy to the foregoing cases if the two companies function as a group and the second person is led to reasonably expect that no claim will be made against the second person to the extent of the subrogation interest of the collision carrier. In the absence of such a basis for a reasonable expectation that a reciprocal claim would not be asserted, the collision subrogation interest stands in a position that is more analogous to that of the claims by the first person (which are discussed immediately below).

6. *Cf.* Foster v. Calderwood, 118 N.H. 508, 389 A.2d 1388 (1978).

7. See, e.g., Landin v. Yates, 98 N.M. 591 at p. 592, 651 P.2d 1026 at p. 1027 (App., 1982) *certiorari denied* 98 N.M. 590, 651 P.2d 636 (1982); Woodstock v. Evanoff, 550 P.2d 1132 (Wyo.1976).

Cf. Suchta v. Robinett, 596 P.2d 1380 (Wyo.1979).

Also see the decisions cited in the following footnotes.

8. E.g., Wm. H. Heinemann Creameries, Inc. v. Milwaukee Auto. Insurance Company, 270 Wis. 443, 72 N.W.2d 102 (1955).

Rules against splitting what is usually regarded as a single cause of action for injury to one's person and property ought not to stand in the way of this solution, because the reasons for such rules are inapplicable in the context of distinctly con-

insurance, such as the loss of use of the first person's car while it was being repaired or replaced — and to any personal injury claim the first person may have. To hold otherwise would vest in the liability insurance company a right of control over the insured's reciprocal claims that is not explicitly set forth in the liability insurance policy.[9]

One approach to this type of problem would be a rule that an individual insured's reciprocal claim is not barred by a settlement between that person's liability insurance company and the other party to an accident so long as the insured has not manifested assent to the settlement agreement. The argument in support of this approach is that it is both fairer and more efficient to treat the settlement between Plaint's insurance company and Def as having no effect on Plaint's interest.[10] Furthermore, in some situations, this rule affords the advantage of allowing attorneys representing the insurer to proceed without having to deal with what would be an unavoidable conflict between the interests of the insurer in minimizing its exposure under the liability coverage and the insurer's implicit obligation not to prejudice the interests of its insured.[11] This rule is supported by the great weight of authority.[12]

flicting interests between the insurers and their insureds. But some courts may apply the rule against splitting, declining to accept this purposive analysis of the issue. See, e.g., Warner v. Hedrick, 147 W.Va. 262, 126 S.E.2d 371 (1962); Mills v. De Wees, 141 W.Va. 782, 93 S.E.2d 484 (1956), 62 A.L.R.2d 965 (1958).

Concerning the impact of the rule against splitting in the context of subrogation, see § 3.10(c)(2).

9. It would be most unjust to do this without holding the first person's insurance company accountable, in exercising this power, for giving at least equal consideration to the first person's interests in reciprocal claims. Such a rule of accountability would be difficult to administer. Cf. Landin v. Yates, 98 N.M. 591, 651 P.2d 1026 at pp. 1027–1028 (App.1982) cert. denied 98 N.M. 590, 651 P.2d 636 (1982).

Also consider the duty of the insurer to give at least equal consideration to the interests of its insured in relation to a claim against him in excess of policy limits. See § 7.8(d), below.

10. For more detailed development of the supporting arguments for this position, see Robert Keeton, *Liability Insurance and Reciprocal claims from a Single Accident,* 10 Southwestern Law Journal 1–31 (1956), reprinted 1957 Insurance Law Journal 29–43.

11. *Cf.* Suchta v. Robinett, 596 P.2d 1380 at pp. 1384–1385 (Wyo.1979).

12. See, e.g., Landin v. Yates, 98 N.M. 591, 651 P.2d 1026 (App.1982) *cert. denied* 98 N.M. 590, 651 P.2d 636 (1982); Lohman v. Woodruff, 224 Kan. 51, 578 P.2d 251 (1978); Brown v. Manchester, 384 A.2d 449 (Me.1978) (claim by an insured who did not ratify a unilateral release is not barred); Woodstock v. Evanoff, 550 P.2d 1132 (Wyo. 1976) (quoting, with approval the discussion of this issue in Professor Keeton's original text); Berlant v. McAllister, 25 Utah 2d 237, 480 P.2d 126 (1971).

Also see McGuire v. Commercial Union Insurance Co., 431 S.W.2d 347 (Tex.1968); Eller v. Blackwelder, 204 Va. 292, 130 S.E.2d 426 (1963); Faught v. Washam, 329 S.W.2d 588 (Mo.Div. 2, 1959); Birkholz v. Cheese Makers Mutual Casualty Co., 274 Wis. 190, 79 N.W.2d 665 (1956); Perry v. Faulkner, 98 N.H. 474, 102 A.2d 908 (1954); Fikes v. Johnson, 220 Ark. 448, 248 S.W.2d 362 (1952), 32 A.L.R.2d 934 (1953).

Cf. Suchta v. Robinett, 596 P.2d 1380 (Wyo.1979) (insurer does not have a duty to advise insured with respect to presenting a counter claim in an action defended by insurer because insured did not lose right to proceed as a consequence of a compromise of that claim and a subsequent dismissal of the action against the insured with prejudice).

Cf. Milline v. American Can Company, 160 Ga.App. 752, 288 S.E.2d 71 (1981) (cert. granted 1982) (discussing the effect of a statutory provision enacted to address the reciprocal claim question). Georgia Laws

An alternative approach to the problem would hold that the insurer, as the knowledgeable party, should be required to ensure that everyone who has an interest in the possible reciprocal claims be apprised of the settlement negotiations and afforded an opportunity to participate. In the event the insurer fails to discharge this obligation, the consequences of that failure would be the responsibility of the insurer, not the second party. This approach would protect the reasonable expectations of the other party that the settlement agreement resolves all of the opposing claims. If the individual insured is aggrieved, the focus of that complaint would then be directed at its insurer.

(3) Settlements of a Reciprocal Claim by an Insured

Sometimes persons who are insured enter into a settlement of reciprocal claims without involving their respective insurers. If this occurs, there are judicial precedents which conclude that an insured's settlement of a personal injury claim is independent of and severable from the insurer's claim as a subrogee when it has paid first party insurance benefits to the insured. For example, the New Jersey Supreme Court decided that a general release received from an individual, as part of a settlement, would not operate as a defense to a subsequent claim by the individual's insurer which paid no-fault insurance benefits (medical expenses, income loss, etc.) unless that was the intent of all of the parties, including the insurer.[13] And, it has been held that when a tortfeasor was aware of an insurer's subrogation claim and the insurer did not have an opportunity to protect its subrogation interest, the insurer's claim would not be barred from a recovery as a consequence of a settlement between the tortfeasor and the insured.[14] Decisions in such cases rest on either an explicit conclu-

1963, p. 643, overturned a contrary decision in Aetna Casualty & Surety Co. v. Brooks, 218 Ga. 593, 129 S.E.2d 798 (1963), *on remand* 107 Ga.App. 472, 130 S.E.2d 510 (1963).

But cf. Bradford v. Kelly, 260 N.C. 382, 132 S.E.2d 886 (1963) (insured must elect to ratify the insurer's settlement by pleading it in bar, in which event plaintiff's own claim is barred, or repudiate it in which event claim against him is to be litigated, the amount paid by the insurer in settlement being credited against any judgment; insurer has no further responsibility, having been discharged by settlement).

Also see Annotation, *Liability insurer's settlement of claim against insured as bar to insureds tort action against person receiving settlement,* 32 A.L.R.2d 937–953 (1953).

13. Aetna Insurance Company v. Gilchrist Brothers, Inc., 85 N.J. 550, 428 A.2d 1254 (1981).

Contra. State Farm Mutual Automobile Insurance Company v. Herrin, 230 So.2d 709 (Fla.App., 2d Dist., 1969) (insurer's subrogation claim precluded when the insured had released the alleged tortfeasor from all claims).

14. See, e.g., Southern Pacific Transport Co. v. State Farm Mutual Insurance Co., 480 S.W.2d 59 (Tex.Civ.App., Corpus Christi, 1972).

However, if the insured releases the tortfeasor from all claims, including property damages to an insured vehicle, such a release encompasses the insurer's subrogation rights. See, e.g., State Farm Mutual Insurance Company v. Herrin, 230 So.2d 709 (Fla.App., 2d Dist., 1969).

sion or an implicit assumption that the claims of the insured and the insurer in such circumstances are independent.[15]

Treating the reciprocal claims of an insured and an insurer independently of each other avoids the problem that would otherwise have to be considered in regard to whether a settlement of a reciprocal claim is a violation of the assistance and cooperation clause of a liability insurance coverage. If a doctrine of "independence" or severability is applied to such reciprocal claims, an insured, at least arguably, does not violate the insurance policy term by entering into a settlement of a reciprocal claim.[16] This does not mean, however, that an insured need have no concern at all about the effects of pressing a claim.[17] In general, an insured is well advised both to inform and to invite the participation of the insured's insurer in such settlement negotiations.

§ 7.5(b) The Effect of a Judicial Determination of a Reciprocal Claim

(1) Generally

In some circumstances, a suit filed in regard to one of the possible reciprocal claims, may be brought to a judgment either by an adjudication or a stipulation in settlement. For example, an insurer may initiate an action based on a right of subrogation. If the insurer proceeds to judgment without affording its insured an opportunity to assert his or her claims against the alleged tortfeasor, the question may subsequently arise as to whether the insured is thereby precluded from asserting any claim for other damages which resulted from the same events. It could be argued that the principle of treating reciprocal claims independently should be extended to trials on the merits. The application of this approach might be urged on the basis that the interests involved are different and that practical complications would often be encountered if all of the matters were resolved in a single trial proceeding.

In general, the principle of treating reciprocal claims separately for purposes of settlements should not be extended to judicial adjudications. Such a separation would contravene the compulsory joinder and compulsory counterclaim rules, adopted in most jurisdictions, which are

---

15. Similarly, it has been held that the dismissal of an automobile driver's suit against a taxicab company for personal injuries allegedly sustained in an accident was a separate and distinct cause of action that did not bar a subsequent suit for property damages by the driver's insurer. Stephan v. Yellow Cab Company, 30 Ill.App.3d 996, 333 N.E.2d 223 (1st Dist., Div. 1, 1975) (in the first suit, the driver failed to prove that he had been injured).

Also see Aetna Casualty and Surety Company v. Jeppesen & Company, 440 F.Supp. 394 (D.Nev.1977).

16. E.g., Utterback-Gleason Co. v. Standard Accident Insurance Co., 179 N.Y.S. 836 (1920), *affirmed* 193 App.Div. 646, 184 N.Y.S. 862 (3d Dept.1920), *affirmed* 233 N.Y. 549, 135 N.E. 913 (1922).

17. For example, making a false assertion that a friend was driving the car, in the hope of improving one's own claim, could well constitute a violation of the assistance and cooperation clause of the liability insurance. See generally § 7.3, above.

designed to ensure the efficient administration of justice. The disputed issues concerning reciprocal claims frequently relate to the determination of fault, and therefore involve the same questions of fact and related questions of law. Accordingly, the considerations that underlie compulsory counterclaim rules should apply to these cases.

There is little, if any, justification for special treatment of reciprocal claims involving liability insurance in relation to compulsory counterclaim and compulsory joinder rules. Overall, less time will be expended in trials if all the possible claims are determined in a single adjudication.[1] Moreover, if two separate trials were allowed, they might produce conflicting resolutions of the fact issues, with adverse impact on both the appearance and the fact of evenhanded administration of justice. Thus, it is appropriate to hold that a jurisdiction's compulsory counterclaim rule is applicable in the absence of any special provisions excluding reciprocal claim cases from its scope.[2] Furthermore, the same general consideration supports the conclusion that reciprocal claims are also subject to the rules concerning issue preclusion.[3]

(2) Settlements in the Course of Litigation

A settlement agreement between an insured and one of the parties to a pending suit also may present problems in regard to whether the disposition of one claim (after a lawsuit has been filed) disposes of the reciprocal claims.[4] In such circumstances, if a liability insurance company (or the attorney it has employed) fails to advise the insured of the existence and effect of a compulsory counterclaim rule, the insured should not lose the benefit of a claim on that account. When an attorney designated by the liability insurer has agreed to a disposition of the action without advising the insured regarding the compulsory

---

§ 7.5(b)

1. This remains true even though, in some cases, if the reciprocal claims were submitted to a single trial, that adjudication undoubtedly would be somewhat longer than either of the two separate trials would have been.

2. *Cf.* Charles Alan Wright, *Estoppel by Rule: The Compulsory Counterclaim under Modern Pleading,* 39 Iowa Law Review 255–299 at pp. 292–299 (1954), reprinted 38 Minnesota Law Review 423–465 at pp. 458–465 (1954).

3. E.g., Sanderson v. Balfour, 109 N.H. 213, 247 A.2d 185 (1968); Ross v. Stricker, 153 Ohio St. 153, 91 N.E.2d 18 (1950). The result reached on the specific facts in *Ross* is debatable, even under the rule suggested in the text above. The case was settled while appeal was pending. Arguably the grounds of appeal were substantial and potentially meritorious, and in that event there was no final judgment on the merits.

But cf. Aetna Insurance Company v. Gilchrist Brothers, Inc., 85 N.J. 550, 428 A.2d 1254 (1981); Aetna Casualty and Surety Company v. Jeppesen & Company, 440 F.Supp. 394 (D.Nev.1977); Stephen v. Yellow Cab Company, 30 Ill.App.3d 996, 333 N.E.2d 223 (1st Dist., Div. 1975).

See generally Robert Keeton, *Liability Insurance and Reciprocal Claims from a Single Accident,* 10 Southwestern Law Journal 1–31 at pp. 16–19 and at pp. 26–27 (1956), reprinted 1957 Insurance Law Journal 29–43 at pp. 37–38 and at pp. 41–42.

4. When the parties wish to settle one of several reciprocal claims, the court in which the claim(s) and counterclaim(s) are pending might appropriately order that they be severed and that the settlement of one will not affect the other. See, e.g., McGuire v. Commercial Union Insurance Co., 431 S.W.2d 347 (Tex.1968).

counterclaim rule and without taking appropriate steps to preserve the insured's reciprocal claim, a court may decline to enforce the bar of the compulsory counterclaim rule.[5]

One avenue by which courts might protect the interests of such an insured would be to permit the insured to reopen the case even after judgment (by direct or collateral attack, as may be appropriate under the jurisdiction's procedure, and subject to the advantages and disadvantages of estoppel as to fact-findings made if the case went to final judgment on the merits) for the purpose of filing and obtaining a judgment on the counterclaim.[6] This approach has the advantage of affording an opportunity to allocate losses from the accident in the same way as if the counterclaim had been filed in ordinary course.[7]

(3) Consent Judgments

If a consent judgment against an insured indicates on its face that it was entered (1) without a final adjudication on the merits and (2) pursuant to a compromise between the third party claimant and the liability insurer, such a judgment should not bar the insured's reciprocal claim because it is comparable to an out-of-court settlement between the same parties. There is support for this view in precedents,[8] but there are also decisions which adopt the contrary view.[9]

5. E.g., Lafollette v. Herron, 211 F.Supp. 919 (E.D.Tenn.1962) (insured had no contact with case except when he was interviewed in hospital by claim agent and when he was served with papers; court "constrained to find" he did not have an opportunity to present his reciprocal claim before the settlement was made). There is some support for the more extreme step of holding that the compulsory counterclaim rule does not apply in this liability insurance setting.

Also see Reynolds v. Hartford Accident & Indemnity Company, 278 F.Supp. 331 (S.D.N.Y.1967) (insured's action for judgment declaring that insurer-appointed attorney must assert insured's counterclaim dismissed on the ground that reciprocal claim need not be brought in the pending tort action since the compulsory counterclaim rule should be read as barring on an "estoppel" or "waiver" rather than a "merger" or "res judicata" basis).

But cf. Kennedy v. Jones, 44 F.R.D. 52 (E.D.Va.1968) (claim against employer and employee tried to judgment for defendant; employee had not been advised of compulsory counterclaim rule; his later action on his reciprocal claim was nevertheless dismissed as barred by compulsory counterclaim rule); Akers v. Simpson, 445 S.W.2d 957 (Tex.1969).

See generally Barron & Holtzoff, FEDERAL PRACTICE & PROCEDURE (Wright edition,

1960), at § 394.1 [superseded by Wright & Miller, FEDERAL PRACTICE & PROCEDURE (1971), at § 1447].

6. Compulsory counterclaim rules ordinarily allow a counterclaim to be asserted by amendment if the failure to plead it was due to oversight, inadvertence, or excusable neglect.

7. A second way a court might protect an insured is to hold that the insured has a cause of action against the company and the attorney for the loss of the counterclaim resulting from their failure to advise the insured properly.

8. See, e.g., Daniel v. Adorno, 107 A.2d 700 (Mun.Ct.App., D.C., 1954); Perry v. Faulkner, 98 N.H. 474, 102 A.2d 908 (1954).

Also see Massachusetts General Laws Ann. ch. 231, § 140A (1959), which provides, "In an action to recover damages for injuries to person or property, or for death, or consequential damages, so called, sustained by reason of a motor vehicle accident, a judgment entered by agreement of the parties, without a hearing on the merits, shall not operate as a bar to an action brought by a defendant in the action in which such judgment was entered, unless such agreement was signed by the defendant in person."

9. See, e.g., A.B.C. Truck Lines v. Kenemer, 247 Ala. 543, 25 So.2d 511 (1946).

Comment

In light of the effect a consent judgment may have on a reciprocal claim, either because it is an absolute bar or because the insured must take a hazardous and potentially expensive course of litigation to circumvent it, there is substantial justification for requiring that a liability insurer (and an insurer-appointed attorney) be accountable to the insured for the failure to use reasonable care in effectuating a settlement with the third party claimant. In other words, although the insurer and the insured both have an interest in a settlement that establishes an unassailable disposition of the tort claim against the insured, an insurer seeking such a settlement should be obligated to give attention also to the insured's interest in the insured's reciprocal claim(s).[10] If an insured's reciprocal claim is precluded without any fault on the part of the insured, this principle would require that the insurer compensate the insured for the value of the lost claim when an insurer has not taken appropriate steps (such as fully discussing the matter with the insured and securing the insured's concurrence in the settlement) before entering into the settlement.[11]

A judgment either purporting to be an adjudication on the merits or purporting to be entered pursuant to a compromise disposing of both the claim against the insured and the reciprocal claim, should be and in most jurisdictions probably is subject to reformation for the purpose of showing that it was in fact a consent judgment entered without the insured's agreeing that it should bar the reciprocal claim.[12] Such a

Cf. Ross v. Stricker, 153 Ohio St. 153, 91 N.E.2d 18 (1950).

10. Compare the liability insurer's duty to give at least equal weight to the insured's interest in relation to a claim against the insured in excess of policy limits, § 7.8(d).

11. In assessing the effect of an insurer's settlement on an insured's reciprocal claims, it almost certainly would be appropriate and essential for a court to consider the "value" of that claim, weighing evidence relating to both whether the claimant could have proved that he or she was legally entitled to recover (that is, the determination of "fault") and the amount of damages.

12. See, e.g., Daniel v. Adorno, 107 A.2d 700 (Mun.Ct.App.D.C., 1954); American Trust & Banking Co. v. Parsons, 21 Tenn. App. 202, 108 S.W.2d 187 (1937). *Cf.* Kelleher v. Lozzi, 7 N.J. 17, 80 A.2d 196 (1951); Smith v. Price, 253 N.C. 285, 116 S.E.2d 733 (1960) (friendly suit to approve settlement with infant plaintiff; one attorney represented defendants, two insurers and their several insureds including an infant defendant; the infant defen-

dant's injuries were not called to court's attention; held, judgment irregular because of conflict of interest among defendants; infant defendant's motion to vacate judgment as to him allowed). The *Kelleher* opinion does not refer to the effect of insurance, but holds that extrinsic evidence may be received in a suit by A v. B to show that the suit of B v. A was in fact dismissed upon settlement and therefore not "without prejudice." Nevertheless, the effort to get a rehearing so plaintiff Kelleher might show that the settlement had been consummated by the company's attorney without her consent was unsuccessful. Docket No. 765 (Sup.Ct., New Jersey, 1951).

Direct attack on the consent judgment is required by the following decisions: Perry v. Faulkner, 98 N.H. 474, 102 A.2d 908 (1954); Lalonde v. Hubbard, 202 N.C. 771, 164 S.E. 359 (1932); Akers v. Simpson, 445 S.W.2d 957 (Tex.1969). See Comment, 32 North Carolina Law Review 531–539 (1954).

There are some appellate court decisions that appear to be incompatible with the approach advanced in the preceding discussion. However, in general these decisions

reformation might be sought either by direct attack or by collateral attack, as may be appropriate under the procedures of the jurisdiction.

§ 7.5(c)   Erroneous Uses of Fiduciary and Agency Concepts in Relation to Reciprocal Claims

The terms in liability insurance policies, which typically empower an insurer to settle any claims or suits that may arise as the insurer deems appropriate, confer authority on the insurer that should be exercised as a fiduciary when a settlement affects the interests of an insured.[1] Comparable considerations should also apply to an insurer's assertion and settlement of claims that result as a consequence of a subrogation right. As the Supreme Court of New Mexico observed, "The insurer acts as a fiduciary for the insured and must in good faith be responsive to the insured's interest."[2] The New Mexico Court then concluded that "when an insurer violates a fiduciary duty to an insured, one which inures to the benefit of a third person, [it] should not operate to the detriment of the insured" when an insurer reaches a settlement (which includes a release that does not expressly reserve the insured's rights) without the consent of its insured who was unaware of the insurer's actions.[3]

It has sometimes been stated in appellate court opinions that a liability insurer acts as an agent for the insured in defending or settling a claim on an insured's behalf.[4] Characterizing the relationship between an insurer and an insured as one of agency may lead to the conclusion that a settlement made by the liability insurer has the same effect on the insured's reciprocal claim as if the insured had made it.[5]

---

are appropriately viewed as instances of firm insistence that the insured take the proper procedural route of asserting that the insurer's settlement does not bar the insured's reciprocal claim. Some of these cases involve a record showing only a judgment on the merits or a disposition with prejudice because of a compromise settlement. Other decisions involve instances in which there was a separate action on the reciprocal claim without any suitable proceeding, direct or collateral as may be required in the jurisdiction, to reform the first judgment to reflect the true nature of the disposition. E.g., compare Akers v. Simpson, 445 S.W.2d 957 (Tex.1969) with McGuire v. Commercial Union Insurance Co., 431 S.W.2d 347 (Tex.1968).

There are also cases that involve the insured's failing to file a counterclaim in the first proceeding even though having ample opportunity to do so after being forewarned of the opponent's contention. E.g., Datta v. Staab, 173 Cal.App.2d 613, 343 P.2d 977 (1st Dist.1959).

§ 7.5(c)

1. See, e.g., Landin v. Yates, 98 N.M. 591, 651 P.2d 1026 (1982), *cert. denied* 98 N.M. 590, 651 P.2d 636 (1982).

Cf. RESTATEMENT OF AGENCY, Second (1958) at § 138 and § 139, referring to this type of power as a power given as security. Also see *Id.*, §§ 12–14 regarding distinctions between agents and other holders of a power to alter the legal relations between another and third persons.

2. Landin v. Yates, 98 N.M. 591 at p. 593, 651 P.2d 1026 at p. 1028 (1982), *cert. denied* 98 N.M. 590, 651 P.2d 636 (1982).

3. *Ibid.*

4. For a collection of illustrative opinions referring to the liability insurer as agent of the insured, see Robert E. Keeton, *Liability Insurance and Reciprocal Claims from a Single Accident,* 10 Southwestern Law Journal 1–31 at p. 10 (1956), reprinted 1957 Insurance Law Journal 29–43 at p. 34.

5. See, e.g., Aetna Casualty & Surety Co. v. Brooks, 218 Ga. 593, 129 S.E.2d 798 (1963), in which the court observed that

There is a basic fallacy in the characterization of this situation as an agency relationship. An agency relationship involves not only a power to affect another's interests, but also a right on the part of the principal to direct and control the agent.[6] The insured is not a principal because the insured typically is not entitled to direct the insurer's conduct in regard to settlements.

The use of the agency characterization is erroneous in this context, and any conclusions reasoned from the supposition of such a relationship should be carefully scrutinized. An insurer and its representatives are not agents of the insured even with respect to settlement of a claim against the insured or with respect to defense of that claim, much less with respect to settlement of the insured's reciprocal claim (unless there are special arrangements apart from the terms of a typical liability insurance policy). The conclusion that an insurer and its representatives do not have the power to bar the insured's reciprocal claim by their settlement of the claim against the insured should be predicated on rationales that do not involve an agency relationship.

§ 7.6 Conflicts of Interests Under Liability Insurance

§ 7.6(a) Sources and Nature of Conflicts of Interests

(1) Introduction

When a tort claim is asserted against an individual (or an entity) who has acquired liability insurance for the risks involved in an activity that may have caused harms to the claimant, the insurer and the insured often have the same, or at least compatible, interests in regard to the possible responses to such a claim. In most situations, there is an accord, reached either explicitly or implicitly, between the insurer and the insured as to an appropriate course of action to be pursued in response to the tort claim.[1] Nevertheless, in many situations the objectives of a liability insurer and its insured diverge or

the legislature could abolish the rule that the insured would be bound by the insurer's settlement. The decision was promptly overturned by the Georgia legislature. See Georgia Laws 1963, p. 643.

Cf. Long v. Union Indemnity Co., 277 Mass. 428, 178 N.E. 737 (1931), 79 A.L.R. 1116 (1932).

6. See the discussion of agents in § 2.1, above.

Also see RESTATEMENT OF AGENCY, Second (1958), § 1, which states:

"(1) Agency is the fiduciary relation which results from the manifestation of consent by one person to another that the other shall act on his behalf *and*

subject to his control. . . ." (Emphasis added).

§ 7.6(a)

1. For example, in American Mutual Liability Insurance Company v. Superior Court, 38 Cal.App.3d 579 at p. 592, 113 Cal. Rptr. 561 at p. 592 (3d Dist.1974), the court characterized the relationship as the "coalition or alliance directed toward a common goal, sharing a common purpose" of a favorable disposition of the claim against the insured.

Also see Purdy v. Pacific Automobile Insurance Company, 157 Cal.App.3d 59, 203 Cal.Rptr. 524 (2d Dist., Div. 1, 1984).

differ in some way, producing an actual or a potential conflict between their respective interests.[2]

There is a very substantial prospect that actual or potentially conflicting interests between an insurer and an insured will exist in regard to almost any tort claim that may be covered by liability insurance. The possibility that there will be either actual or potentially conflicting interests between a liability insurer and an insured exists with respect to numerous situations and matters, including:

(1) Requirements established by the insurer (usually set forth in the insurance policy) for actions an insured is to take following the occurrence of an event which is or may be within the scope of the insurance coverage.[3]

(2) Requests by an insurer to a defense counsel for an appraisal of whether the insurer should employ either a notice of a reservation of rights or a non-waiver of rights agreement on the rationale that the applicable insurance may not provide coverage for the liability asserted by a third party claimant or that an insured may have forfeited coverage as a consequence of failing to comply with a claims processing requirement.[4]

(3) Requests by an insured to a defense counsel selected by the insurer for advice about whether to accede to a notice from the insurer setting forth a reservation of rights or to accept a proposal for a non-waiver agreement.

(4) The roles, rights, and responsibilities of the insurer and the insured in regard to undertaking an investigation of the occurrence or undertaking other measures incident to preparing to defend against a possible claim by a third party.

(5) The roles, rights, and responsibilities of the insurer and the insured when the insurance may not provide coverage for the events giving rise to the tort claim — especially when the insured has objected to a reservation of rights notice or rejected a non-waiver agreement.

(6) The roles, rights, and responsibilities of the insurer and the insured when the insurance may not provide coverage for one or more of the tort claims asserted against the insured as a conse-

---

2. As one court observed, a "[c]onflict of interest between jointly represented clients occurs *whenever* their common lawyer's representation of the one is rendered less effective by reason of his representation of the other." Spindle v. Chubb/Pacific Indemnity Group, 89 Cal.App.3d 706 at p. 713, 152 Cal.Rptr. 776 (2d Dist.1979) (emphasis added).

3. See the discussion of claims processing requirements in § 7.2, above.

Cf. Robert M. Aronson, *Conflict of Interest,* 52 Washington Law Review 807–859 at p. 824 (1977).

Cf. the comments of Philip H. Corboy, *Defending Insurance Companies and the Insured—Can Two Masters Be Served?,* 55 Chicago Bar Record 102–113 at pp. 102–103 (1973).

4. *Cf.* the comments of Philip H. Corboy, *Defending Insurance Companies and the Insured—Can Two Masters Be Served?,* 55 Chicago Bar Record 102–113 at pp. 102–103 (1973).

quence of the events — especially when the insured has objected to a reservation of rights notice or rejected a non-waiver agreement.

(7) The roles, rights, and responsibilities of the insurer and the insured when the amount(s) claimed exceed the coverage limits of the applicable insurance.

(8) The roles, rights, and responsibilities of the insurer and the insured when the insurer may be entitled to assert a defense to the insured's claim on the basis of a provision in the insurance policy — especially when the insured has objected to a reservation of rights notice or rejected a non-waiver agreement.

(9) The roles, rights, and responsibilities of the insurer and the insureds when there are two or more insurance coverages (either for different individuals or involving different bases of liability) that are relevant to the claims at issue.

(10) The roles, rights, and responsibilities of the insurer and the insured when excess insurance, reinsurance, or high deductibles (or risk retention) are involved.

(11) Decisions about the possible settlement of claims asserted against an insured — including when to propose a settlement, how much to offer as a settlement, or whether to accept a settlement offered by a claimant.[5]

(12) The selection and assertion of specific responses or defenses in the event a suit is initiated against an insured.

(13) The use of information that is received by defense counsel from the insured or that is discovered in the course of investigating the case, and whether such information is to be disclosed by the attorney to the insurer, the insured, or even, in some instances, the third party who is asserting a claim against the insured.

(14) The choice of litigation strategies if a third party's claim is submitted to a court or arbitrator for adjudication.

(15) Decisions about whether to seek appellate review following a trial court determination of a third party's claim.[6]

---

5. Concerning the possible consequences on an insurer's liability when a conflict of interests in regard to the possible settlement of a third party's tort claim, see § 7.8, below. Concerning conflicting interests in regard to the resolution of reciprocal claims, see § 7.5, above.

6. Following a trial court determination, the insurer and the insured may disagree about the advisability of appealing. Courts have sustained claims by insureds that the duty to defend extends to post trial remedies, including appeals. *Cf.* Cathay Mortuary (Wah Sing) Inc. v. United Pacific Insurance Company, 582 F.Supp. 650 at pp. 655–656 (N.D.Cal.1984); Guarantee Abstract and Title Company, Inc. v.

Interstate Fire and Casualty Company, Inc., 228 Kan. 532, 618 P.2d 1195 (1980) [also see the opinion in this case reported at 232 Kan. 76, 652 P.2d 665 (1982)]; Palmer v. Pacific Indemnity Co., 74 Mich. App. 259, 254 N.W.2d 52 (1977).

But cf. Crist v. Insurance Company of North America, 529 F.Supp. 601 at p. 606 (D.Utah 1982), where the court concluded that the scope of the duty to appeal "need not be addressed" because "there was neither an adverse judgment on the damage claim, nor a duty to defend the injunction claims."

Other courts have concluded that the duty to defend does not necessarily obligate

The potential for and significance of conflicting interests in such situations is a matter of very substantial importance in many instances.[7] And, at least in some of these circumstances, the role and responsibility of a lawyer selected by the insurer as defense counsel is not only a matter of central importance to the parties but also the focal point of the questions that relate to the conflicts of interests.

The examples set forth in the next subsection both illustrate the nature of conflicts of interests that arise in various contexts and a sense of the intensity of some of the problems they present to insurers, insureds, and lawyers. Although neither the foregoing enumeration of various types of situations nor the following descriptions of specific examples should be viewed as an exhaustive compilation of the circum-

the insurer to appeal. See, e.g., *General Casualty Company of Wisconsin v. Whipple*, 328 F.2d 353 (7th Cir.1964).

Also consider the discussion of whether the defense obligation extends to appeals in § 9.1(b), below.

7. See generally Geoffrey C. Hazard, Jr., ETHICS IN THE PRACTICE OF LAW (1978), at pp. 34–35; Ronald E. Mallen and Victor B. Levit, LEGAL MALPRACTICE (1977), at pp. 355–361; Ronald E. Mallen, *A New Definition of Insurance Defense Counsel*, 1986 Insurance Counsel Journal 108–123; Lloyd E. Williams, Jr. and Donald V. Jernberg, *Conflict of Interest in Insurance Defense Litigation: Common Sense in Changing Times*, 31 Federation of Insurance Counsel Quarterly 111–125 (1981); John K. Morris, *Conflicts of Interest in Defending Under Liability Insurance: A Proposed Solution*, 1981 Utah Law Review 457–493; Robert H. Aronson, *Conflict of Interest*, 52 Washington Law Review 807–859 (1977); Philip H. Corby, *Defending Insurance Companies and The Insured—Can Two Masters Be Served?*, 55 Chicago Bar Record 102–114 (1973); A.E. Smith, *The Miscegentic Union of Liability Insurance and Tort Process in the Personal Injury Claims System*, 54 Cornell Law Review 645–707 at pp. 656–666 (1969).

Also see John W. Dondanville, *Defense Counsel Beware: The Perils of Conflicts of Interest Revisited*, 29 Trial Lawyer's Guide 249–260 (1985); John Dwight Ingram, *Conflicts of Interest in the Insurer's Duty to Defend in Illinois*, 17 John Marshall Law Review 379–393 (1984); Alsobrook, *Conflicts Between Insurer and Insured*, 48 Insurance Counsel Journal 165–169 (1981); Lloyd E. Williams, Jr. and Donald V. Jernberg, *Conflicts of Interest in Insurance Defense Litigation: Common Sense in Changing Times*, 31 Federation of Insurance Counsel Journal 111–125 (1980); Howard M. Berg and Roy Alan Cohen, *The*

Dangers of Playing Both Ends from the Middle: The Dilemma of Insurance Companies' Defense Counsel, 19 Federation of Insurance Counsel Journal 281–294 (1979); Ronald E. Mallen, *Insurance Counsel: The Fine Line Between Professional Responsibility and Malpractice*, 45 Insurance Counsel Journal 244–265 (1978).

Comment, *Reexamining Conflicts of Interest: When is Private Counsel Necessary?*, 17 Pacific Law Journal 1421–1444 (1986); Note, *Conflicts of Interest in the Liability Insurance Setting*, 13 Georgia Law Review 973–1013 (1979); Note, *Legal Ethics—If an Insurance Company Uses an Attorney Employed to Defend the Insured as an Investigator to Prepare a Policy Coverage Defense, It is Estopped From Asserting the Defense: Employers Casualty Co. v. Tilley, 496 S.W.2d 552 (Texas, 1973)*, 52 Texas Law Review 610–617 (1974); *Conflicts of Interest Problems in Insurance Practice*, 37 Insurance Counsel Journal 497–515 (1970) (a panel presentation); Note, *The Effect of Collateral Estoppel on the Assertion of Coverage Defenses*, 69 Columbia Law Review 1459–1977 (1969); Note, *Insurance Policy Defenses and Collateral Estoppel*, 43 New York University Law Review 140–160 (1968), reprinted 1968 PERSONAL INJURY COMMENTATOR 196–205; COMMENT, *The Insurer's Duty to Defend Under a Liability Insurance Policy*, 114 University of Pennsylvania Law Review 734–759 at pp. 736–740 and pp. 745–746 (1966); Note, *Use of the Judgment to Determine a Liability Insurer's Duty to Defend: Conflict of Interests*, 41 Indiana Law Journal 87–106 (1965).

Cf. John K. Morris, *Conflicts of Interest in Defending Under Liability Insurance Policies: A Proposed Solution*, 1981 Utah Law Review 457–493; Donald M. Haskell and Daniel J. Pope, *The Insurer's "Conflict of Interest" Dilemma*, 65 Illinois Bar Journal 220–229 (1976).

stances that may produce a serious conflict of interests problem, this discussion is intended to provide an awareness of the frequency, pervasiveness, and scope of the questions which arise under liability insurance.

(2) Examples of Conflicting Interests

(i) Possibility that the third party's claims against an insured are not covered by the applicable liability insurance.

Liability insurance policies uniformly include limitations or restrictions on (1) the persons who are insured,[8] (2) the interests of the insureds that are protected,[9] and (3) the nature or scope of the risks which are transferred to the insurer.[10] Such limitations are specified in a variety of ways in insurance policies, including the general terms used for the statement of the coverage, the definitions for specific words used in the policy provisions, and clauses that set forth restrictions on the coverage (which are characterized in a variety of ways, such as exclusions, conditions, or limitations of liability).[11] Accordingly, in many circumstances there may be a question about whether the claims against an insured resulted from an activity or an occurrence that is within the scope of the applicable liability coverage.

When there are factual questions about whether an insured's liability to a third party involves actions that are covered by the insured's liability insurance, the situation clearly involves an actual or potential conflict of interests. This type of conflict is well illustrated by the questions that are presented when an insured may have committed an intentional tort. In some instances when the evidence indicates that injuries were caused by an intentional tort, the third party (often referred to as a "third party claimant" or the "plaintiff" in this context) asserting a claim against the insured prefers to allege that the insured was negligent because the third party's best hope for indemnification is to have the claim adjudged to be within the scope of coverage provided by the insured's liability insurance. The conflict of interests arises because liability insurance applies if the harm resulted from the insured's negligence, but generally will not provide coverage for an insured's actions if injuries occurred as a result of an intentional tort.[12] Accordingly, when there is substantial evidence of a tortious injury to a third party claimant, the insurer's interests generally will be best served by a determination that the insured committed an intentional

---

8. See the discussion in Chapter 4, above.

9. See the discussion in Chapter 4, above.

10. See the discussion in Chapter 5, above.

11. See the discussion in § 4.1, above.

12. See the discussion in § 5.4(d), above.

Cf. the discussion in Thornton v. Paul, 74 Ill.2d 132, 23 Ill.Dec. 541, 384 N.E.2d

335 (1978); Maryland Casualty Company v. Peppers, 64 Ill.2d 187, 355 N.E.2d 24 (1976); Gray v. Zurich Insurance Company, 65 Cal.2d 263, 54 Cal.Rptr. 104, 419 P.2d 168 (1966).

Also see State Security Insurance Company v. Globe Auto Recycling Corporation, 141 Ill.App.3d 133, 95 Ill.Dec. 539, 490 N.E.2d 12 (1st Dist., Div. 3, 1986).

tort, making it likely that the insured's conduct will not be within the scope of the liability insurance coverage.[13]

There are, of course, many other situations in which issues about the scope or extent of a liability coverage may arise in regard to liability insurance.[14] For example, questions often are presented by limitations in regard to whether an individual is not an insured as a consequence of (1) a restriction for a class of individuals (such as drivers under the age of 21 years in motor vehicle liability insurance coverages) who are excluded, (2) a provision excluding coverage for specific individuals, or (3) circumstances in which the authority or permission of a driver to operate an insured vehicle is at issue.[15] And, essentially the same situation exists when an insurer questions whether an insurance policy applies either because the period of coverage had not commenced or because the insured had allowed the liability insurance policy to lapse.[16]

Whenever there is a possibility that a coverage defense may be raised by a liability insurer, until and unless that matter is resolved there is clearly either an actual or a potential conflict of interests between the insurer and insured [17] because the insurer's actions in the "handling" of the matters related to the claim(s) against the insured may be influenced by the expectation that the coverage defense will be successful.[18]

---

13. See, e.g., Previews, Inc. v. California Union Insurance Company, 640 F.2d 1026 at p. 1028 (9th Cir.1981) (applying California law); Nike, Inc. v. Atlantic Mutual Insurance Company, 578 F.Supp. 948 (N.D. Cal.1983) (in a libel action, insurer would not be liable if the statements were proven to have been malicious).

14. *Cf.* Bogard v. Employers Cas. Co., 164 Cal.App.3d 602 at p. 611, 210 Cal.Rptr. 578 at p. 583 (2d Dist., Div. 3, 1985); San Diego Navy Federal Credit Union v. Cumis Insurance Society, Inc., 162 Cal.App.3d 358, 208 Cal.Rptr. 494 (4th Dist., Div. 1, 1984), 50 A.L.R.4th 913.

Also see Northland Insurance Company v. Heck's Service Company, Inc., 620 F.Supp. 107 at pp. 108–109 (E.D.Ark.1985).

15. See, e.g. Murphy v. Urso, 88 Ill.2d 444, 58 Ill.Dec. 828, 430 N.E.2d 1079 (1981).

In regard to the scope of coverage provided under omnibus clauses, see the discussion in § 4.7, above. Also see § 4.9, above.

16. See the discussion of the duration of coverage in § 5.10, above.

17. *Cf.* United States Fidelity & Guaranty Company v. Louis A. Roser Company, Inc., 585 F.2d 932 at p. 938 (8th Cir.1978), where the court commented:

"Common logic dictates that in such circumstances, counsel for USF & G would be inclined, albeit acting in good faith, to bend his efforts, however, unconsciously, toward establishing that any recovery by [the plaintiff] would be grounded on the theory of [the plaintiff's] claim which was not covered."

18. See, e.g. Salus Corporation v. Continental Casualty Co., 478 A.2d 1067 (D.C. App.1984); Glens Falls Group Insurance Corporation v. Hoium, 294 Minn. 247, 200 N.W.2d 189 (1972), discussed in Note, *Liability Insurance, A Liability Insurer May Be Compelled to Participate in the Defense of Its Insured Even When Strong Evidence of an Intentional Tort Creates a Conflict of Interests Between Them*, 22 Drake Law Review 824–829 (1973).

Cf. Brohawn v. Transamerica Insurance Company, 276 Md. 396, 347 A.2d 842 (1975).

Also see the discussion of coverage for negligent and intentional torts in Comment, *Liability Insurance for Intentional Torts—Subrogation of the Insurer to the Victim's Rights Against the Insured: Ambassador Insurance Co. v. Montes*, 32 Rutgers Law Review 135–172 (1979).

Also see Note, *Business Risks and the Insurer's Duty to Defend, Millard Warehouse, Inc. v. Hartford Fire Insurance Co.*, 204 Neb. 518, 283 N.W.2d 56 (1979), 59

(ii) Disclosure of information by an insured to or a discovery of information by defense counsel that would sustain a coverage defense

In the course of investigating the possible bases for an insured's liability in order to prepare the defense, information disclosed to the defense counsel by an insured or information discovered by the defense counsel sometimes relates to a coverage issue. If this occurs, the lawyer confronts a conflict of interests by reason of which, it may be argued (though not necessarily without challenge) that "the lawyer is forced to walk on an ethical tightrope, and not communicate relevant information which is beneficial to one or the other of his clients." [19]

(iii) Reciprocal claims

Reciprocal claims, which were discussed in a preceding section,[20] may also give rise to a conflict of interests in the course of both settlement negotiations and litigation. For example, when the drivers involved in a motor vehicle accident each assert a claim against the other, a conflict between each claimant and his or her liability insurer may arise either in a case in which all of the claims are at issue, or in a case deciding one or more of these claims and collaterally affecting the other claims.[21] Although each party (as well as, at least in most instances, its liability insurer) wants to prove that the other's negligence was the exclusive cause of the accident, sometimes, depending on how the rules relating to contributory negligence or comparative negligence apply, an insurer's interests may be best served by findings that the events were the result of negligent acts by both parties.[22]

(iv) Multiple defendants

A conflict of interests may arise from the possibility that an injured person could assert claims against more than one party.[23] This type of problem is well illustrated by the situation that exists when several professionals are named as defendants in a medical malpractice

Nebraska Law Review 772–789 (1980) at pp. 778–785.

19. San Diego Navy Federal Credit Union v. Cumis Insurance Society, Inc., 162 Cal.App.3d 358 at p. 366, 208 Cal.Rptr. 494 at p. 499 (4th Dist., Div. 1, 1985), 50 A.L.R.4th 913.

Also see Industrial Indemnity Co. v. Great American Insurance Company, 73 Cal.App.3d 529 at pp. 535–536, 140 Cal. Rptr. 806 at pp. 810–811 (2d Dist.1977); Parsons v. Continental National American Group, 113 Ariz. 223, 550 P.2d 94 at pp. 98–99 (1976).

20. See the discussion in § 7.5, above.

21. *Ibid.*

22. This idea is developed in more detail in Robert E. Keeton, *Liability Insurance and Reciprocal Claims from a Single Accident,* 10 Southwestern Law Journal 1–

31 at pp. 16–19 (1956), reprinted 1957 Insurance Law Journal 29 at pp. 37–38.

Also see discussion of the potential consequences of a contributory negligence defense in Peterson v. Allcity Insurance Company, 472 F.2d 71 at pp. 77–78 (2d Cir. 1972); Alsbach v. Bader, 616 S.W.2d 147 at pp. 152–153 (Mo.App., Eastern District, Div. 4, 1981).

23. *Cf.* Penn Aluminum, Inc. v. Aetna Casualty and Surety Company, 61 A.D.2d 1119, 402 N.Y.S.2d 877 (4th Dept.1978).

In Spindle v. Chubb/Pacific Indemnity Group, 89 Cal.App.3d 706, 152 Cal.Rptr. 776 (2d Dist.1979), the court observed that there was no impropriety in the absence of an actual conflict of interest between two physicians insured by medical malpractice insurance by a joint representation by counsel provided by the insurer.

case arising as a result of injuries sustained in the course of an operation. Even when the professionals (such as a surgeon, an anesthesiologist, and one or more nurses) have liability insurance coverage provided by the same insurer, there may be actual or potential conflicts about the defense strategies to be employed, especially in regard to their respective interests in the determination as to who was negligent.[24]

(v) Claims in excess of the applicable limits of liability

The coverage limits in liability insurance policies frequently cause a conflict of interests. For example, when the amounts sought by several claimants exceed the available insurance coverage, the interests of the insured and the insurer may differ with respect to the allocation of the available insurance to various claimants.[25] Similarly, a conflict of interests problem is presented when a single claim exceeds the amount of applicable insurance,[26] especially when there is an opportu-

---

24. See, e.g., Bituminous Insurance Companies v. Pennsylvania Manufacturers' Association Insurance Company, 427 F.Supp. 539 at p. 555 (E.D.Pa.1976); In re Paders, 250 App.Div. 418, 294 N.Y.S. 252 (2d Dept.1937).

Cf. In re Conrad, 19 A.D.2d 644, 241 N.Y.S.2d 291 (2d Dept.1963), *affirmed* 14 N.Y.2d 500, 248 N.Y.S.2d 224, 197 N.E.2d 621 (1964).

But cf. Spindle v. Chubb/Pacific Indemnity Group, 39 Cal.App.3d 706, 152 Cal. Rptr. 776 (2d Dist.1979). The court observed that in a medical malpractice action, the differences (1) in personal exposure of two insureds resulting from difference of maximum coverage under professional liability policies, (2) reinsurance situations of insurer and (3) of potential for liability, did not necessarily result in actual conflict of interest between insureds so far as joint defense provided by insurer was concerned.

Similar questions may also arise when several occupants, including the driver, of one vehicle are injured in a collision with another vehicle. An injured passenger may have a claim against both drivers. Thus, an attorney retained by a group of claimants, which includes the driver, would be confronted with a clear conflict of interests. However, especially when the injured occupants and the driver of one vehicle are relatives, they may want to retain a single attorney to present their claims against the operator or owner of the other vehicle.

Concerning the representation of such conflicting interests generally, see Annotation, *What constitutes representation of conflicting interests subjecting attorney to*

disciplinary action, 17 A.L.R.3d 835–854 (1968).

25. In some instances, the allocation might affect the total amount the company would be required to pay on the insured's behalf. This is illustrated in Perkoski v. Wilson, 371 Pa. 553, 92 A.2d 189 (1952). In the tort suit, a judgment was entered in favor of the wife-plaintiff for $10,000 and $6,000 respectively and the filing of a remittitur to avoid a new trial. The jury was permitted by the instructions to award to the husband damages for loss of consortium and loss of the wife's services. The company refused to pay more than the $10,000 on the wife's claim and $769.13 of the award to the husband, asserting that the remainder of the award to the husband was damages consequential to the wife's injury and therefore in excess of the $10,000 limit per person.

In *Perkoski*, the court declined to allow the company's contention. One ground of decision was that the lower court, though requiring a remittitur, had left it to the plaintiffs to determine which of the verdicts should suffer the reduction, and counsel for the company, still representing the insured, stood by and permitted the husband-plaintiff to accept the reduction without disclosing to him or to the insured that the company would then invoke a policy-limit argument that would not have been available if the remittitur had been applied to the verdict for the wife-plaintiff.

26. It has been pointed out that "[a]s a practical matter, often the reality of the excess exposure resides only in the imagination of the pleader." Ronald E. Mallen, *A New Definition of Insurance Defense Counsel*, 1986 Insurance Counsel Defense

nity to settle the claim by a payment of some amount which would be within the applicable coverage limits of the liability insurance.[27]

(vi) Claims for punitive damages

When an insured and an insurer are confronted by a claim for punitive damages, the prospect for a conflict of interests is substantial.[28] There are two distinguishable types of situations. First, frequently there is a conflict because the total amount sought by the third party

Journal 108–123 at p. 118. Mr. Mallen then urges, "Predicating the need for independent counsel upon the claimant's demand obviously enables an insured's adversary to create a conflict solely for tactical purposes." *Ibid.*

Although Mr. Mallen's observation on the "power" conferred on the third party claimant is undoubtedly technically accurate, that power does not compel any particular choice among the possible responses outlined in § 7.6(d), below. For example, Mr. Mallen went on to argue in the same discussion, "It is almost unheard of for a personal injury claimant to plead a sum constituting damages which corresponds to the actual loss or that sum truly desired for settlement." *Ibid.* If an insurer is convinced of the accuracy of this statement in regard to any conflict of interest that arises as a consequence exclusively of a claim in excess of policy limits, the insurer is completely free to retain control over the defense by agreeing to be liable for the full amount of any judgment or settlement.

27. See, e.g., Farmers Insurance Exchange v. Schropp, 222 Kan. 612, 567 P.2d 1359 at p. 1366 (1977); Rova Farms Resort, Inc. v. Investors Insurance Company of America, 65 N.J. 474 at p. 492, 323 A.2d 495 at p. 504 (1974), where the court observed: "There was always, in fact and in law, a conflict of interest between Investors and its insured from the time it realized the gravity of McLaughlin's awful injury and recognized that its insured must one day confront a jury * * * vulnerable, under the most simplistic view of the probabilities to an excess verdict far beyond the policy limit."

Cf. Coleman v. Holecek, 542 F.2d 532 at p. 537 (10th Cir.1976) (applying Kansas law); Commercial Union Insurance Company v. Ford Motor Company, 599 F.Supp. 1271 (N.D.Cal.1984); Purdy v. Pacific Automobile Insurance Company, 157 Cal.App. 3d 59, 203 Cal.Rptr. 524 (2d Dist., Div. 1, 1984); Lysick v. Walcom, 258 Cal.App.2d 136, 65 Cal.Rptr. 406 (1st Dist., Div. 1, 1968), 28 A.L.R.3d 368 (1969).

Also consider Larraburu Brothers, Inc. v. Royal Indemnity Company, 604 F.2d 1208

(9th Cir.1979); Ivy v. Pacific Automobile Insurance Company, 156 Cal.App.2d 652, 320 P.2d 140 (1st Dist., Div. 1, 1958).

Also see Robert H. Aronson, *Conflict of Interest,* 52 Washington Law Review 807–858 at pp. 821–825 (1977); Michael R. Gallagher, *The Problems of Defense Counsel Negotiating Settlement in Cases Involving a Potential Excess Judgment,* 37 Insurance Counsel Journal 506–511 (1970); Note, *Expanding the Insurer's Duty to Attempt Settlement,* 49 University of Colorado Law Review 251–261 (1978).

Also consider John K. Morris, *Conflicts of Interest in Defending Under Liability Insurance Policies: A Proposed Solution,* 1981 Utah Law Review 457–492 at pp. 466–471 (1981); John D. Ingram, *Triangular Reciprocity in the Duty to Settle Insurance Claims,* 13 Pacific Law Journal 859–904 (1982).

On the other hand, in situations (1) when there is no coverage dispute, (2) when the settlement proffered by the claimant is within policy limits, and (3) when there is no likelihood of a judgment in excess of policy limits in the event the claim against the insured goes to trial, the amount of the claim generally will not involve conflicting interests. *Cf.* Bogard v. Employers Casualty Company, 164 Cal.App.3d 602 at p. 611, 210 Cal.Rptr. 578 at p. 583 (2d Dist., Div. 3, 1985).

28. *Cf.* Nandorf, Inc. v. CNA Insurance Company, 134 Ill.App.3d 134, 88 Ill.Dec. 968, 479 N.E.2d 988 (1st Dist., Div. 1, 1985); San Diego Navy Federal Credit Union v. Cumis Insurance Society, Inc., 162 Cal. App.3d 358 at p. 372, 208 Cal.Rptr. 494 at p. 503 (4th Dist., Div. 1, 1984), 50 A.L.R.4th 913.

Also see Parker v. Agricultural Insurance Company, 109 Misc.2d 678, 440 N.Y.S.2d 964 (New York County, Pt. I, 1981) (punitive damages of $169,000,000 were sought, in addition to compensatory damages in the sum of $26,000,000).

But cf. Zieman Manufacturing Co. v. St. Paul Fire and Marine Insurance Company, 724 F.2d 1343 (9th Cir.1983) (applying California law).

(that is, for the primary claim and the punitive damages) exceeds the applicable limit of liability, thereby creating the type of conflict discussed in the preceding paragraph.

Second, many insurers have taken the position — either as a consequence of judicial precedents which hold that it is against public policy to provide insurance coverage for punitive damages or because there is express language in the insurance policy — that punitive damages are not covered by liability insurance.[29] If an insurer chooses to assert this position, it obviously presents the possibility that the third party's claim for punitive damages is not covered by the applicable liability insurance and this situation involves the type of conflicting interests discussed in the first portion of this subsection.

The conflict of interests when a third party seeks punitive damages is evident. For example, in an Illinois case the court concluded that a conflict of interests existed when the insurer denied coverage for punitive damages in a case where the third party had sought a substantial amount of punitive damages ($100,000) and a relatively small amount of compensatory damages ($5,000). The court reasoned that although the insured and the insurer shared a common interest in a finding of no liability, if the insured were determined to be liable the insurer's interest would be best served by an award of minimal compensatory damages and substantial punitive damages.[30]

(vii) Continuing to provide a defense after the exhaustion of coverage

In some instances, when the available liability coverage has been exhausted through settlements or the payment of judgments of some of the claims against an insured, the insured will request that the insurer continue to pay the defense costs on the rationale that the insurer's obligation to provide the defense is independent of the insured's right to be indemnified.[31] However, this situation involves a conflict of interests because once the applicable liability coverage has been exhausted, the insurer's interest may best be served by employing a strategy that is not fully consonant with the interests of the insured. In such cases, typically the insurer's interests will be served by strategies or approaches that minimize the costs associated with continuing the insured's defense, while the insured is usually at least equally (and often primarily) concerned with minimizing the amounts that the insured is

---

29. Moreover, frequently claims for punitive damages arise as a consequence of acts, such as intentional tort, which are not covered by liability insurance. See the discussion of intentional torts in Chapter 5, above and in § 7.6(a)(2)(i), above.

30. Nandorf, Inc. v. CNA Insurance Company, 134 Ill.App.3d 134, 88 Ill.Dec. 968, 479 N.E.2d 988 at p. 992 (1st Dist., Div. 1, 1985).

31. See, e.g., Liberty Mutual Insurance Company v. Mead Corporation, 219 Ga. 6, 131 S.E.2d 534 (1963) (holding that the insurer was not required to defend remaining actions against an insured, after it had, with consent and contribution of the insured, exhausted the limit of liability by settling two lawsuits). Also see Allstate Insurance Company v. Montgomery Trucking Company of Georgia, 328 F.Supp. 415 (N.D.Ga.1971).

obligated to pay (which will be limited to the sums paid to the claimants if the insurer is required to provide the defense).

It might be urged that when the coverage limits have been exhausted, a request by the insured that the insurer continue to provide the defense serves as an election not to claim relief because of the conflicting interests. However, it is not always clear that insurers (or defense counsel selected by insurers) take steps to ensure that the insured is fully informed of the competing considerations and therefore is placed in a position to make an informed choice in such circumstances.

(viii) Opposing parties insured by the same insurance company

A conflict of interests clearly exists when opposing claims are made by two or more persons who are insured by the same insurance company. Although this is most likely to occur as a consequence of motor vehicle accidents,[32] the same conflicts arise in other circumstances.[33]

(ix) Liability insurance combined with uninsured or underinsured motorist coverage

Motor vehicle insurance policies which include both liability insurance and uninsured or underinsured motorist insurance often produce a situation that presents a potentially serious conflict of interests between the policyholder and the insurer.[34] For example, when an accident involves an uninsured motorist, an insured driver frequently has a claim against the insurer under uninsured motorist insurance which is predicated on the assertion that the insured's injuries resulted from the negligence of the uninsured motorist. However, the uninsured motorist (or others) may assert a tort claim against the insured driver who alleges the insured driver was negligent or contributorily negligent — a claim that, if proved, would be covered by the insured

---

32. It has been held that the ordinary implications of the insured's obligation of assistance and cooperation are inapplicable in these circumstances and that the company is liable for any judgment, costs, and reasonable attorney fees incurred by the insured in his own defense, such fees being recoverable in lieu of the defense required by the insurance contract. See O'Morrow v. Borad, 27 Cal.2d 794, 167 P.2d 483, 163 A.L.R. 894 (1946). After Borad sued O'Morrow, O'Morrow obtained counsel and through such counsel filed a cross-complaint, notifying the insuring group (affiliated companies) that his counsel would also present his defense to Borad's cause of action. O'Morrow then brought the suit in question for declaratory relief against Borad and the insuring group. The appellate court approved O'Morrow's conduct, noting that it would be contrary to public policy to allow a person to control both sides of litigation.

The *Borad* decision is noted at 59 Harvard Law Review 1316–1318 (1946), 45 Michigan Law Review 515–517 (1947), 31 Minnesota Law Review 380–381 (1947), 14 University of Chicago Law Review 102–104 (1946).

See also Harold T. Boone, *The Representation of Multiple But Adverse Insureds: The Insurance Company's Perspective,* at pp. 134–136, and Darrell L. Havener, *The Representation of Multiple Insureds—Defense Counsel's Perspective,* at pp. 136–138 in *The Insurance Defense Counsel on Trial,* 48 Insurance Counsel Journal 132–172 (1981).

33. Also see the precedents cited in the notes to the discussion of the selection of "independent" defense counsel in § 7.6(b), below.

34. See the discussion in Widiss, UNINSURED AND UNDERINSURED MOTORIST INSURANCE (1987), at § 28.3.

driver's liability insurance. Consequently, the same insurer is confronted with providing one coverage (the uninsured motorist insurance) that depends on negligence of the uninsured motorist and another coverage (the liability insurance) that depends on the negligence of the insured driver.[35] And comparable problems can arise in regard to underinsured motorist insurance.[36]

(x) Failure of an insured to comply with provisions relating to the claims process

Liability insurance policies uniformly contain provisions that specify procedures to be followed or actions to be taken by an insured after the occurrence of a loss, and most policies condition liability on compliance with these provisions.[37] When the prescribed actions have not occurred, the insurer may be entitled to deny liability. There are numerous judicial precedents which support the proposition that an insured's rights to coverage lapse when an insured has failed to promptly (1) report a loss, (2) submit a proof of loss, or (3) forward to an insurer all documents the insured has received as a result of a lawsuit by a third party. Whenever an insurer might be entitled to predicate a denial of coverage on such insurance policy defenses, a conflict of interests problem is present.[38]

(xi) Possible collusion between an insured and a third party claimant or misrepresentation by an insured

Collusion

A conflict of interests for a defense attorney or a liability insurer arises when there is a suspicion of collusion between the insured and the third party plaintiff. The nature of the problem is well illustrated by considering what would happen if the insurer decided to attack the character and motives of both the third party and its insured in the trial of the tort claim, contending that the two colluded to present a false claim.[39] Ordinarily the insurer is not a party in the tort litigation, and therefore the insurer might request that the attack be made by the attorney the insurer has engaged to represent the insured. Quite plainly, a defense attorney acceding to such a request and proceeding to question motivations and honesty of the insured would be

---

35. See, e.g. Allstate Insurance Co. v. Hunt, 469 S.W.2d 151 (Tex.1971). Also see the Court of Civil Appeals decision in this case reported at 450 S.W.2d 668.

See also § 7.6(c), n. 10, below.

See generally Widiss, UNINSURED AND UNDERINSURED MOTORIST INSURANCE (1987), at Chapters 28 and 29.

36. See the description of underinsured motorist insurance in Chapter 31 of Widiss, UNINSURED AND UNDERINSURED MOTORIST INSURANCE (1987).

37. See § 7.2, above.

38. Also consider the discussion in § 7.1(a)(2)(i), above.

39. It has been held that a claimant is entitled to a reversal of a judgment on a verdict obtained in this way because it is prejudicial to the claimant's interest for the factfinder to be exposed to such an attack by counsel who represents the person whose credibility is challenged. See Pennix v. Winton, 61 Cal.App.2d 761, 143 P.2d 940 (1st Dist., Div. 2, 1943), *hearing denied* 61 Cal.App.2d 761, 145 P.2d 516 (1944).

acting improperly. Even if the insurer retained another attorney to present such an attack, the resulting litigation would be exceedingly complicated, if not chaotic.

An insurer might (though with some risk of generating rights at variance with policy provisions) instruct the defense attorney to conduct the defense on behalf of the insured without presenting, in the tort litigation, a contention that collusion is involved with the plan of raising the question of collusion subsequently as a coverage defense. When the insurer decides (and especially when defense counsel is directed by the insurer) to defer raising the question of collusion or when the attorney independently concludes that it may be in the company's best interests to subsequently assert a contention of collusion, an attorney selected, instructed, and paid by the insurer may no longer be in a position to wholeheartedly defend the insured.

Misrepresentations

In some instances, an insurer or defense counsel may decide that an insured has not been telling the truth about the events that are relevant to a third party's claim. When this occurs, generally it is improper to raise questions or present arguments about an insured's "misrepresentations" in the adjudication of the third party's tort claim against the insured.[40] However, the possibility that the misrepresentation may constitute a coverage defense (or even a fraud upon the court) creates a situation which may affect the way in which the insured's defense is conducted.

(xii) Tactical Decisions

There are often conflicts of interests with respect to tactical decisions. For example, when a passenger sues a host driver because of injuries sustained during an outing in which drinking occurred, there may be different views with respect to whether the insured's defense should be based on denial of fault by the insured or on assumption of the risk by the passenger. Though a lawyer, engaged by the insurer as a defense attorney for the insured, might reasonably conclude that the interests of the insured as well as the insurer are best served by presenting a particular defense,[41] in some circumstances the conflicting

---

40. See, e.g., Spandaro v. Palmisano, 109 So.2d 418 at p. 422 (Fla.App., 3d Dist., 1959) ("issue of fraud and collusion should have been the subject of a plenary action between insurer and insured to determine who was driving the automobile at the time of the accident").

Cf. Shafer v. Utica Mutual Insurance Company, 248 A.D.2d 279, 289 N.Y.S. 577 (4th Dept.1936).

Also see Philip H. Corboy, *Defending Insurance Companies and the Insured—Can Two Masters Be Served?*, 55 Chicago Bar Record 102–174 at pp. 108–109 (1973).

41. Consider the questionable decision in Detenber v. American Universal Insurance Co., 372 F.2d 50 (6th Cir.1967), 34 A.L.R.3d 526 (1970), *cert. denied* 389 U.S. 987, 88 S.Ct. 413, 19 L.Ed.2d 479 (1967) (Black dissenting), denying the insured's claim for liability in excess of $10,000 policy limit. The insurer had offered $10,000 in settlement before trial. At the commencement of trial the attorney changed from a defense of no negligence to a sole defense of assumption of risk, emphasizing the insured's guilt, without either consultation with or notice to the insured and his

interests are so intense that no accommodation is possible between the views as to which of the possible tactics should be employed.[42]

(3) Comment: The Pervasiveness of Conflicting Interests

It is rather unlikely that all of the problem areas that may produce conflicting interests can be avoided when a substantial tort claim asserted against an insured does not yield to settlement and therefore proceeds to an adjudication.

In the event the insured (and, in effect, the insurer) prevails in the adjudication of a third party's claim against the insured, concerns about how one or more of the conflicts may have influenced specific actions of either the insurer or the defense counsel selected by the insurer will usually be of little, if any, significance. And, just as a resolution of a third party's claim in the insured's favor generally obviates concerns on the part of the insured about what might have been, so long as the liability insurance coverage provides full indemnification for all sums which the insured is adjudged to be legally obligated to pay to third party claimants, the occasions for subsequently questioning the import of the conflicting interests will be relatively rare occurrences.[43]

Whenever the resolution of a tort claim, either as a consequence of adjudication(s) or settlements,[44] leaves the insured vulnerable to liability for some amount that exceeds the coverage provided by the applicable liability insurance, questions about the effect of conflicting interests on the rights of the insured and responsibilities of the insurer and

private attorney (who did not participate in the trial).

42. *Cf.* Northland Insurance Company v. Heck's Service Company, Insurance Company, 620 F.Supp. 107 (E.D.Ark.1985); Southern Maryland Agricultural Association, Inc. v. Bituminous Casualty Corp., 539 F.Supp. 1295 (D.Md.1982).

Also see Allen v. Allstate Insurance Company, 656 F.2d 487 at p. 489 (9th Cir. 1981).

Fraudulent Claims and Collusion. Another type of situation which has produced problems that concern insurers exists when there is a close personal relationship between an insured and a claimant which might lead to a fraudulent claim. The problem of potential collusion has led to the enactment of a statute in New York declaring that no policy "shall be deemed to insure against any liability of an insured because of death or of injuries to his or her spouse unless express provision relating specifically thereto is included in the policy." New York—McKinney's Insurance Law § 3420 g (1985). This is an unusual statute, and it affects only a portion of the situation in which relationships may lead to collusive claims.

It is not unusual for claims to be presented in circumstances in which insurers suspect collusion between the claimant and the insured. See, e.g. Hurston v. Georgia Farm Bureau Mutual Insurance Company, 148 Ga.App. 324, 250 S.E.2d 886 (1978); Dietz v. Hardware Dealers Mutual Fire Insurance Company, 88 Wis.2d 496, 276 N.W.2d 808 (1979).

Also see John K. Morris, *Conflicts of Interest in Defending Under Liability Insurance Policies: A Proposed Solution,* 1981 Utah Law Review 457–493 at pp. 471–478 (1981).

43. *But cf.* the claims asserted by the insureds in Bogard v. Employers Casualty Company, 164 Cal.App.3d 602, 210 Cal. Rptr. 578 (2d Dist., Div. 3, 1985).

44. When the settlement of less than all the claims asserted by third parties against an insured exposes an insured to liability, the conflict of interest which existed may be viewed as having influenced the insurer's or a defense attorney's conduct during the settlement process.

attorneys selected by the insurer to represent the insured may become matters of considerable concern.

The increasing recognition of the existence, significance, and persuasiveness of conflict of interests problems has transformed these questions into matters of substantial importance that frequently must be addressed by insurers, defense attorneys, and the courts.

§ 7.6(b) The Rights, Responsibilities, and Risks of Insurers

Liability insurance policies typically include provisions that both obligate the insurer to provide the insured with a defense *and* entitle the insurer to control the defense — that is, the insurer has both a "duty" and a "right" in regard to the defense of the insured when a third party asserts a claim against an insured.[1] A conflict of interests between an insured and an insurer usually does not relieve an insurer from its duties to the insured, including the obligation to provide a defense.[2] However, there is a considerable range of views on questions regarding the appropriate means for an insurer to fulfill its defense obligation.

If conflicting interests are actually or potentially present, there may be very serious dilemmas in regard to when and to what extent constraints should be imposed upon an insurer's right (1) to secure the assistance and cooperation of the insured, (2) to select defense counsel, (3) to control the decisions in regard to the settlement of the tort claims, and (4) to "guide" the litigation of a tort claim that is not settled. Moreover, and certainly of at least equal concern, the handling of these matters entails risks for an insurer of significant liability beyond the applicable liability insurance policy limits in the event there are inappropriate responses either by the insurer or by defense counsel selected and instructed by the insurers as to these matters.

An insurer often is in a position either to anticipate a potential conflict of interests or to recognize conflict as soon as it arises. In discharging both its fiduciary duty to its insured and the generally recognized contractual obligation to deal fairly and in good faith with the insured,[3] an insurer should direct its executives, employees, and agents to use their expertise to identify conflicts of interest. As appellate courts in several states have observed, the existence of a

§ 7.6(b)

1. See the discussion of the duty to defend in § 9.1, below.

2. See, e.g. United States Fidelity and Guaranty Co. v. Louis A. Roser Co., Inc., 585 F.2d 932 at p. 939 (8th Cir.1978); American Employers' Insurance Company v. Crawford, 87 N.M. 375, 533 P.2d 1203 (1975).

Also see American Motorists Insurance Company v. Trane Company, 718 F.2d 842 (7th Cir.1983), *affirming* 544 F.Supp. 669 (W.D.Wis.1982); Southern Maryland Agri-

cultural Association, Inc. v. Bituminous Casualty Corp., 539 F.Supp. 1295 (D.Md. 1982).

Cf. Bogard v. Employers Casualty Company, 164 Cal.App.3d 602, 210 Cal.Rptr. 578 (2d Dist., Div. 3, 1985).

3. The issues to which most attention is given in this text are those regarding the nature and scope of the liability insurer's obligation to its insured in relation to the insurer's obligation to settle liability claims (See § 7.8, below) and to provide a defense (See § 9.1, below).

conflict of interests should be ascertained as early as possible in a proceeding so it can be treated effectively before prejudice occurs to either party.[4]

Whenever an actual or potential conflict of interests is identified, a liability insurer should promptly take steps to ensure that the insured is made fully aware of and understands the problem.[5] In general, the procedures employed to inform an insured of a conflict should include the preparation of a readily comprehensible, written communication that is sent to the insured and which fully explains the nature of the conflict. In addition, such a communication should also suggest that the insured ought to discuss the situation with his or her own attorney.

In many contexts, it is clearly necessary for an insurer to suggest that the insured may be well advised to consult an attorney other than the defense counsel who has been selected and is being paid by the insurer.[6] The existence of some types of conflicts have made such a recommendation a standard practice. For example, when an insurer is confronted with a tort claim against its insured that exceeds the insurance policy limits of liability, many insurers automatically send a communication which notifies the insured that it may be desirable for the insured to obtain separate counsel.

Weighing and Accommodating the Interests of an Insured and the Insurer

Whenever an insurer has undertaken the defense of the insured (by actions such as initiating an investigation of the facts, the selection and instruction of an attorney, or entering into settlement negotiations), the insurer should be obligated, at a minimum, to direct that all individuals engaged in such activities are to give the insured's interest at least as much consideration as they give to the insurer's position.[7] And, in

4. Nandorf, Inc., v. CNA Insurance Companies, 134 Ill.App.3d 134 at p. ___, 88 Ill.Dec. 968, 479 N.E.2d 988 at p. 993 (1st Dist., Div. 1, 1985); San Diego Navy Federal Credit Union v. Cumis Insurance Society, Inc., 162 Cal.App.3d 358 at p. 371, 208 Cal.Rptr. 494 at p. 503; footnote 7, 50 A.L.R.4th 913 (4th Dist., Div. 1, 1984).

5. See Yeomans v. Allstate Insurance Company, 130 N.J.Super. 48, 324 A.2d 906 (App.Div.1974), *affirming* 121 N.J.Super. 96, 296 A.2d 96 (Morris County, 1972).

Cf. Allstate Insurance Company v. Keller, 17 Ill.App.2d 44, 149 N.E.2d 482 (1st Dist.1958).

6. *Cf.* the comment in Murphy v. Urso, 88 Ill.2d 444, 58 Ill.Dec. 828, 430 N.E.2d 1079 at p. 1082 (1981), that "[a]n insurer *must decline to defend* where there is a conflict of interest between it and the insured." (Emphasis added).

7. See, e.g. National Service Industries, Inc. v. Hartford Accident & Indemnity Company, 661 F.2d 458 (5th Cir. Unit B, 1981), *rehearing denied* 667 F.2d 93 (5th Cir.1981) (applying Georgia law); Coleman v. Holecek, 542 F.2d 532 at p. 537 (10th Cir. 1976) (applying Kansas law); Brisco v. Meritplan Insurance Company, 132 Ariz. 72, 643 P.2d 1042 (1982).

Courts have sometimes characterized this approach as requiring the insurer's representatives to act in the manner of an individual holding both interests.

The mutual obligations theory in conflict-of-interest settings is strongly supported by the analogy to the company's obligation with respect to liability in excess of policy limits for failure to settle. See § 7.8, below.

There are some older judicial decisions which indicate that an insurer is permitted

some contexts an insurer may be well advised to select an approach which awards greater significance to the interests of its insured.[8]

Selection and Employment of "Independent" Claims Representatives or Attorneys

Insurers have sometimes responded to a conflict of interests problem by the employment of "independent" claims representatives and attorneys.[9] In some instances, insurers have sought to exercise the right to appoint an "independent" defense counsel even though the insured, as a consequence of a conflict of interests, wants to select and direct the defense. Although there are a few precedents which sustain the insurer's position,[10] the vast majority of the courts which have

to always protect its own interest even though such actions may be incompatible with the interest of the insured. See, e.g., Abrams v. Factory Mutual Liability Insurance Co., 298 Mass. 141, 10 N.E.2d 82 (1937); Davison v. Maryland Casualty Co., 197 Mass. 167, 83 N.E. 407 (1908) (stating that the company had the privilege of appealing to protect its own interest, even though the insured's interest might be prejudiced by the additional legal proceedings). It is essential to view these decisions in their historical context.

8. In Lieberman v. Employers Insurance of Wausau, 84 N.J. 325, 419 A.2d 417 at pp. 422–423 (1980), the court observed, "While the insurer is not compelled to disregard its own interests in representing or defending an insured, *the insured's must necessarily come first.*" (Emphasis added). Accordingly, insurer's settlement of a claim against the insured despite insured's revocation of the authorization to effect a settlement was a breach of the insurance agreement.

Cf. the comment in Burd v. Sussex Mutual Insurance Company, 56 N.J. 383, 267 A.2d 7 at p. 11 (1970), that "[w]henever the carrier's position so diverges from the insured's that the carrier cannot defend with complete fidelity to the insured, *there must be a proceeding in which the carrier and the insured * * * may fight out their differences.*" (Emphasis added).

In Tank v. State Farm Fire & Casualty Company, 105 Wash.2d 381, 715 P.2d 1133 (1986) (emphasis added), the court pointed out:

"The 'basic obligations' * * * amount to a duty of good faith. We have stated that the duty of good faith of an insurer requires fair dealing and equal consideration for the insured's interests. Thus, the same standard of fair dealing

and equal consideration is unquestionably applicable to a reservation-of-rights defense. We find, however, that the potential conflicts of interest between insurer and insured inherent in this type of defense *mandate an even higher standard: an insurance company must fulfill an enhanced obligation to its insured as part of its duty of good faith.* Failure to satisfy this enhanced obligation may result in liability of the company, or retained defense counsel, or both."

Among the difficulties encountered if the company attempts to remain in control of the defense when it has coverage on both sides of the case is the problem of settlement. In Tully v. Travelers Insurance Co., 118 F.Supp. 568 (N.D.Fla.1954), the company was held liable in excess of policy limits for a failure to settle resulting from its refusal to discuss settlement with attorneys for either claimant, on the asserted theory that it could not place itself "in the position of showing partiality to one assured" over another. See the discussion of liability for consequential damages in § 7.8, below, and for punitive damages in § 7.10, below.

Note. Somewhat different considerations may apply to an attorney who is confronted with conflicting interests of the insured and the insurer. See the discussion in § 7.6(c), below. Several courts have concluded that the attorney must award primary consideration to the insured's interests.

9. *Cf.* Harold Boon, *The Representation of Multiple Adverse Insureds,* 48 Insurance Counsel Journal 134–138 at p. 135 (1981). Such an arrangement has received limited encouragement in judicial decisions. See, however, cases cited in note 10, below.

10. For example, when an insurer confronts conflicting interests because cover-

considered this question have concluded that in such circumstances the insured is entitled to select defense counsel.[11]

Insurers have occasionally urged that an insurer's selection or appointment of independent claims representatives or attorneys thereafter entitles the insurer to rely exclusively on the judgment of such individuals in regard to the handling of the claim against the insured (including proposals for a settlement) and that the insurer is not responsible for the consequences of such decisions because the insurer is not directing the actions of such an "independent" representative.[12]

An insurer generally should not be able to fully discharge its responsibilities to the insured by the employment of an "independent" claims representative or attorney. There is simply no justification for allowing the insurer to exercise the right to select a claims adjuster or defense counsel, and thereafter granting the insurer an immunity from

age is provided by that company for two or more persons with opposing claims, some insurers have attempted to address the problem by assigning independent attorneys to represent each of the insureds.

Cf. Employers' Fire Insurance v. Beals, 103 R.I. 623, 240 A.2d 397 (1968) (child in third grade struck another child in eye with lead pencil; tort suit included allegations of negligence and recklessness; discretionary dismissal of insurer's declaratory proceeding affirmed; opinion includes suggestions, explicitly not all-inclusive, for ways of dealing with conflict-of-interest problems by having two attorneys for the defense, both paid by the insurers).

See also Cloer v. Superior Court of Tulare County, 271 Cal.App.2d 143, 76 Cal. Rptr. 217 (5th Dist.1969) (trial court acted beyond its jurisdiction in discharging the two attorneys appointed by an insurer that had coverage on both automobiles in collision; parties had been fully informed and had accepted representation by the attorneys).

Also see Paul W. Fager, *Insured's Right to Independent Counsel In Conflicts of Interest Situations* 160–163 at p. 162 in *The Insurance Defense Counsel on Trial* (open forum), 48 Insurance Counsel Journal 132–172 (1981).

Among the difficulties encountered if the company attempts to remain in control of the defense when it has coverage on both sides of the case is the problem of settlement. In Tully v. Travelers Insurance Co., 118 F.Supp. 568 (N.D.Fla.1954), the company was held liable in excess of policy limits for a failure to settle resulting from its refusal to discuss settlement with attorneys for either claimant, on the asserted theory that it could not place itself "in the

position of showing partiality to one assured" over another.

From the insured's point of view, this type of arrangement is generally less desirable than allowing an insured to select an attorney.

11. See the decisions cited in § 7.6(d), below.

12. When insurers take this position, the argument is often framed in terms of the insurer's not being liable because the lawyers or a claims adjuster is an "independent contractor."

Cf. Continental Insurance Company v. Bayless & Roberts, Inc., 608 P.2d 281 (Alaska 1980); Highway Insurance Underwriters v. Lufkin-Beaumont Motor Coaches, Inc., 215 S.W.2d 904 at p. 932 (Tex.Civ.App. 1948, writ refused, no reversible error).

Also consider the comments in United Farm Bureau Mutual Insurance Company v. Groen, 486 N.E.2d 571 (Ind.App., 3d Dist., 1985); Dumas v. Hartford Accident & Indemnity Co., 94 N.H. 484, 56 A.2d 57 (1947).

But cf. Abrams v. Factory Mutual Liability Insurance Co., 298 Mass. 141 at p. 144, 10 N.E.2d 82 at p. 84 (1937) (reserving the question whether "an attorney employed by the insurer to defend is an independent contractor for whose negligence the insurer is not liable.").

See also Note, *Automobile Insurance— Negligence of Insurance Company's Attorney in Failing to Perfect Appeal from Adverse Judgment Against Insured Held Imputable to Insurance Company and Rendered Insurer Liable for Judgment in Excess of Coverage—Petersen v. Farmers Casualty Co. (Iowa 1975)*, 24 Drake Law Review 865–871 (1975).

all further responsibilities. Such a rule would place the insurer in a better — that is, a more "protected," position than that which exists in the absence of a conflict of interests, and that would be a patently absurd result.

The Insured's Obligation to Provide Assistance and Cooperation

When there is a conflict of interests, the obligation of an insured to provide assistance and to cooperate with his or her liability insurer [13] should be subject to careful consideration. In at least some circumstances, a persuasive case undoubtedly can be made for tempering, if not totally abrogating, the insured's obligation.

Selection of Defense Counsel by the Insured

One of the circumstances in which the courts first recognized the appropriateness of allowing an insured to select an independent attorney that would be paid by the insurer was when a liability insurer provided coverage for individuals who were asserting claims against each other. Many courts have concluded that in this situation the insurer is liable for reasonable attorney's fees incurred by such an insured for a defense [14] in lieu of the attorney that would otherwise have been provided (by being selected and paid by the insurer) in accordance with the insurance policy. This result is equally warranted whenever there is a significant conflict of interests with respect to the defense such that one attorney cannot effectively represent both interests. [15]

The Insurer, the Insured, and Defense Counsel Selected by the Insured

There are numerous situations in which a conflict of interests may lead to an abrogation of the insurer's right to select and instruct the defense counsel — that is, the existence of a conflict will entitle the insured to select a defense attorney whose fee will be paid by the insurer. [16] The selection of defense counsel by an insured does not

---

13. See the discussion of the insured's obligations in § 7.3, above.

14. See the discussion and cases cited in § 7.6(d)(6), below.

15. See the precedents cited in the discussion of the insured's right to select defense counsel in § 7.6(d)(6), below.

16. See, e.g. Nike, Inc. v. Atlantic Mutual Insurance Company, 578 F.Supp. 948 (N.D.Cal.1983).

Cf. Boyd Brothers Transportation Company, Inc. v. Fireman's Fund Insurance Companies, 729 F.2d 1407 at p. 1410 (11th Cir.1984), *rehearing denied* 734 F.2d 1481 (11th Cir.1984) (applying New York law).

Cf. Maryland Casualty v. Peppers, 64 Ill. 2d 187 at pp. 198–99, 355 N.E.2d 24 at p. 31 (1976). The court commented, "Absent the acceptance of defense by Peppers [the insured] or waiver by St. Paul, Peppers has the right to be defended in the personal injury case by an attorney of his own choice who shall have the right to control the conduct of the case."

Also see New York State Urban Development Corporation v. VSL Corporation, 738 F.2d 61 (2d Cir.1984) (applying New York law).

See generally, the discussion and decisions cited in § 7.6(d)(6).

relieve the insurer of its obligation to provide coverage.[17] Thus, in regard to the possible settlement or litigation of the tort claim, there should be communication and cooperation between the attorney selected by the insurer and the insurance company (as well as any attorney retained by the insured). Moreover, it also seems clear that the insurer continues to be obligated at least to make good faith judgments (and perhaps judgments that are "reasonable" as well) in regard to matters such as the settlement of the third party's tort claim.[18]

Representation of an Insured by House Counsel

When an insurer decides to have "house counsel" appear on behalf of an insured in defense of a tort claim covered by liability insurance, a conflict of interests is certainly no less intense, and may even be somewhat greater than that which exists when an insurer selects an attorney who is in private practice.[19] Obviously, the relationship between an insurance company and its employees is at least as significant, and typically will be more so, than the association between an insurer and an attorney in private practice.[20] However, some justification or desire for the use of house counsel may derive from the belief that such attorneys are in a position to develop very substantial expertise through the repeated handling of particular types of liability coverage [21] and that this experience could be particularly helpful to the defense of claims that arise under unusual or very specialized types of coverage.

House counsel are probably even more likely than an appointed counsel to confront conflicts in regard to assessments about the applicability of coverage defenses. Certainly, if a house counsel has been involved in the analysis or evaluation of coverage issues, the appear-

---

17. *Ibid.*

18. See the discussion in § 7.8, below.

19. *Cf.* Ronald E. Mallen, *A New Definition of Insurance Defense Counsel,* 1986 Defense Counsel Journal 108–123 at p. 110. Mr. Mallen observed, "Counsel who is a salaried employee of an insurance company has added relationships which enhance the prospects of a subjective bias in favor of the insurer" because "staff counsel is financially dependent upon one client," the insurer. He also pointed out, "Advancement in salary and position requires satisfying that client," and "[c]ontrol ultimately lies with the attorney's superiors, presenting a risk if the supervisor has corporate responsibilities other than for the insured's representation." Mr. Mallen noted, "These forces may combine to unduly influence the employee's loyalties in favor of the employer." *Id.,* at p. 111.

20. Mr. Mallen concedes in an introductory footnote that he has a "bias" in support of the integrity of appointed counsel. *Id.,* at p. 108. Nevertheless, after the comments quoted in the preceding footnote, Mr. Mallen then suggests, "Notwithstanding such criticism, in a properly structured corporate environment, employed counsel does not face many of the economic pressures which can tempt outside counsel to favor the insurer." *Id.,* at p. 111. Mr. Mallen also observed, "Employed counsel has no bills to send out, * * * there is no concern about receiving future assignments, or economic benefit by seeking to increase the volume of the business." *Ibid.*

21. *Cf.* Ronald E. Mallen, *A New Definition of Insurance Defense Counsel,* 1986 Defense Counsel Journal 108–123 at p. 110.

ance of impropriety is substantial, and it may be sufficient to preclude that attorney from serving as defense counsel.[22]

The appropriateness of having house counsel represent an insured has not been considered in many appellate decisions. However, in several instances when an insured requested that a court adopt a rule against the representation of insureds by house counsel because of conflicts of interests, the court declined to do so on the ground that such a rule would be discriminatory against "house counsel" as a class because conflict of interests problems are also present when non-house-counsel attorneys appear for insureds.[23]

Precluding an Insurer From Asserting a Defense

If a defense on behalf of an insured is conducted without providing the insured with both adequate notice of a possible conflict of interests and securing the insured's acquiescence to the continuing role of the defense attorney selected by the insurer, the insurer may be precluded from subsequently raising a coverage defense.[24] For example, the Texas Supreme Court concluded that a defense attorney's work on the coverage question while representing the insured estopped the insurer from thereafter denying its responsibility for defending the insured.[25] Questions relating to collateral estoppel and issue preclusion are considered in § 7.6(e), below.

The Insured's Access to Communications Between the Insurer and the Defense Attorney

When an insured has a basis for claiming that the representation by a defense attorney selected by the insurer was not adequate or that the insurer inappropriately decided not to accept a settlement opportunity, the insured should be entitled to examine all of the statements made in communications between an insurance company and a defense attorney selected by the insurer. Communications that under ordinary circumstances would be the subject of either the work-product or attorney-client privileges should be subject to discovery by an insured,[26]

---

22. *Cf.* Ronald E. Mallen, *A New Definition of Insurance Defense Counsel,* 1986 Defense Counsel Journal 108–123 at p. 111; Thomas B. Alleman, *The Reasonable Thing to Do: The Insurer's Duty to Settle Claims Against Its Insured,* 50 University of Missouri, Kansas City Law Review 251–301 (1982).

23. *In re* Rules Governing Conduct of Attorneys in Florida, 220 So.2d 6 (Fla.1969).

24. See Transamerica Insurance Group v. Chubb and Son, Inc., 16 Wash.App. 247, 554 P.2d 1080 (Div. 1, 1976).

25. *Cf.* Employers Casualty Company v. Tilley, 496 S.W.2d 552 (Tex.1973).

Also see Note, *Legal Ethics—If an Insurance Company Uses an Attorney Employed to Defend the Insured as an Investigator to Prepare a Policy Coverage Defense, It Is Estopped from Asserting the Defense. Employers Casualty Co. v. Tilley, 496 S.W.2d 552 (Tex.1973),* 52 Texas Law Review 610–619 (1974).

26. *Cf.* Henke v. Iowa Home Mutual Casualty Co., 249 Iowa 614, 87 N.W.2d 920 (1958); Glacier General Assurance Company v. Superior Court of Los Angeles County, 95 Cal.App.3d 836, 157 Cal.Rptr. 435 (2d Dist., Div. 2, 1979).

In *Henke,* the court concluded that when an attorney is hired by an insurer to defend an insured, an insured is entitled to

especially if they occurred before an attorney was retained by the insured to represent the insured.[27] There are cases in which such evidence has been used on behalf of an insured to great advantage in proving a claim of negligence or bad faith on the part of the insurance company.[28]

Reaching an Accord with an Insured to "Ignore" the Conflict of Interests

In some circumstances, an insured and an insurer can reach an accord in regard to selecting some of several possible courses of action which will be employed and thereby in effect agreeing to "ignore," either temporarily or permanently the conflict of interests in order to jointly pursue the defense with the representation of a single defense counsel. This approach, together with other possible responses to the problems presented by conflicting interests, is considered in § 7.6(d), below.

Liability in Excess of Policy Limits

An insurer's failure to disclose a conflict of interests undoubtedly can contribute to the determination that an insured is entitled to liability in excess of coverage provided by a liability insurance policy.[29]

§ 7.6(c)　The Roles, Responsibilities, and Risks for Attorneys

(1) Problems for Defense Attorneys

Generally

An attorney employed by an insurer to represent an insured may be confronted with serious conflict of interests issues almost from the

have access to documents that passed between the insurer and the attorney. The court observed, "Public policy demands that when counsel can no longer act for the good of all, due to secret or confidential information disclosed by one of the parties, the relationship should cease." *Id.,* 87 N.W.2d at p. 927.

Also see Shapiro v. Allstate Insurance Company, 44 F.R.D. 429 (E.D.Pa.1968).

27. See, e.g. Monier v. Chamberlain, 35 Ill.2d 351, 221 N.E.2d 410 (1966), 18 A.L.R.3d 471 (1968) (insurer having issued coverage for both parties to automobile accident required to produce various documents, reports, memoranda, and statements for inspection by one of the parties; work-product and attorney-client privileges held inapplicable to matter accumulated up to the time the insurer employed an attorney for the defendant).

Similarly, the insured may also be entitled to see documents prepared for the

insurance company by employees or agents such as claims investigators or persons charged with the responsibility of evaluating claims. *Cf.* Rogers v. Aetna Casualty and Surety Company, 601 F.2d 840 (5th Cir.1979).

Also see North Georgia Lumber & Hardware v. Home Insurance Company, 82 F.R.D. 678 (N.D.Ga.1979) (fire insurance case).

28. Such evidence may also be relevant to a malpractice suit by the insured against the attorney selected by the insurer to represent the insured. See the discussion in § 7.6(c), below.

29. *Cf.* Betts v. Allstate Insurance Company, 154 Cal.App.3d 688, 201 Cal.Rptr. 528 (4th Dist., Div. 1, 1984).

Also see the discussion in § 7.8 and § 7.9, below.

very outset of the relationship. For example, problems often begin with a request from the insurer to consider and forward a recommendation on whether the defense should only proceed if the insured will execute a nonwaiver agreement.[1] Another type of recurring situation involves questions that arise when a defense attorney acquires evidence that supports a coverage defense either as a consequence of disclosures made to the attorney by the insured or when an attorney, in the course of defending an insured, identifies such evidence.[2] Conflicts also occur frequently as a consequence of proposals for settlement.[3]

Many of the conflicting interests encountered by a defense attorney are essentially the same ones that are confronted by the liability insurer. Others exist as a consequence of the special role and relationship of an attorney to a client or clients. The existence of such conflicts entail significant problems and risks for defense attorneys. Moreover, an attorney's responsibilities when faced with a conflict of interests relate to the relationship with both the insured and the insurer, and are mandated, at least in part, by the ethical obligations imposed by the applicable code of professional responsibility or canons of ethics.

An attorney must endeavor to both anticipate possible and recognize actual conflicts of interests.[4] This means an attorney must exercise an appropriate level of professional expertise and should apply a considerable sensitivity to the possibility that a conflict does or may exist.

§ 7.6(c)

1. Concerning the risk an attorney selected by the insurer takes in advising the insured concerning the insured's entering into a nonwaiver agreement, or even failing to make explicit to the insured the fact and nature of the conflict of interest regarding execution of a nonwaiver agreement, see, e.g., Comment, The Insurer's Duty to Defend Under a Liability Insurance Policy, 114 University of Pennsylvania Law Review 734–759 at pp. 745–746 (1966).

Concerning nonwaiver agreements generally, see § 6.6(a), above.

Also see § 7.6(d), below.

2. The MODEL RULES OF PROFESSIONAL CONDUCT (American Bar Association, as amended, 1984), provide in Rule 1.6(a) that "A lawyer shall not reveal information relating to representation of a client unless the client consents after consultation, except for disclosures that are impliedly authorized in order to carry out the presentation ∗ ∗ ∗."

The MODEL RULES OF PROFESSIONAL CONDUCT (American Bar Association, as amended, 1984), provide in Rule 1.8(b), "A lawyer shall not use information relating to representation of a client to the disadvantage of the client unless the client consents after consultation."

Also see Lloyd E. Williams, Jr. and Donald V. Jernberg, Conflict of Interest in Insurance Defense Litigation: Common Sense in Changing Times, 31 Federation of Insurance Counsel Quarterly 111–125 at pp. 116–118 (1981); Note, Legal Ethics—If an Insurance Company Uses an Attorney Employed to Defend the Insured as an Investigator to Prepare a Policy Coverage Defense. It is Estopped from Asserting the Defense. Employers Casualty Co. v. Tilley, 496 S.W.2d 552 (Tex.1973), 52 Texas Law Review 610–619 (1974).

3. See § 7.8, below.

4. Cf. MODEL RULES OF PROFESSIONAL CONDUCT Rules 1.7 and 1.8, Code of Professional Responsibility DR–5–1.

Informing the Insured of a Conflict of Interests

Once an attorney is aware that a conflict or a potential conflict of interests exists, the insured must be promptly informed of all the facts and circumstances related to the conflict so that a knowledgeable decision can be made about the desirability of seeking independent counsel.[5] In general, a defense counsel selected by the insurer to represent the insured has an ethical obligation to explain the full implications and significance of the conflicting interests.[6]

Insurers or defense counsel have often used letters to inform insureds of actual or possible conflicts of interests. The types of letters, especially various form letters, which are sometimes sent to insureds to provide notice of such situations can fall far short of giving adequate information about either the nature or the significance of a conflict of interests or the possible courses that might be chosen by the insured in such circumstances.[7] Moreover, a defense attorney may tread on dangerous ground if there is exclusive reliance upon a letter to the

5. See, e.g., Betts v. Allstate Insurance Company, 154 Cal.App.3d 688 at pp. 715–716, 201 Cal.Rptr. 528 at pp. 544–545 (4th Dist., Div. 1, 1984).

Also see Yeomans v. All State Insurance Company, 121 N.J.Super. 96, 296 A.2d 96 (City Court 1972), *affirmed* 130 N.J.Super. 48, 324 A.2d 906 (1974); Employers Casualty Company v. Tilley, 496 S.W.2d 552 at p. 558 (Tex.1973) ("If a conflict arises between the interests of the insurer and the insured, the attorney owes a duty to the insured *to immediately advise him* of the conflict.") (emphasis added).

6. See, e.g., Spindle v. Chubb/Pacific Indemnity Group, 89 Cal.App.3d 706, 152 Cal.Rptr. 776 (2d Dist.1979).

Cf. San Diego Navy Federal Credit Union v. Cumis Insurance Society, 162 Cal. App.3d 358 at p. 375, 208 Cal.Rptr. 494 at p. 506, 50 A.L.R.4th 913 (4th Dist., Div. 1, 1985).

7. See Committee on Interpretation of Canons of Ethics, State Bar of Texas, Opinion No. 179 (June 1958), reprinted 21 Texas Bar Journal 593 (1958). The Committee rendered an advisory opinion in response to questions whether the attorney designated by the company to appear on behalf of the insured is required "to fully inform" the insured and whether, in particular, he must inform the insured of the holding in G.A. Stowers Furniture Co. v. American Indemnity Co., 15 S.W.2d 544 (Tex.Com. App.1929), which imposed liability in excess of policy limits for negligent failure to settle. The Committee answered both questions in the affirmative. The lack of more explicit disclosure may not be signifi-cant in those cases in which the insured employs independent counsel. But if the insured is not fully aware of this conflict and does not employ independent counsel, the failure of the attorney to make the more explicit disclosure suggested in the Texas opinion is not only a probable violation of canons of ethics but also a potential source of liability of the attorney and the company for loss resulting to the insured from a tort judgment against the insured in excess of policy limits.

On May 22, 1969, the ABA National Conference of Lawyers and Liability Insurers adopted a statement of Guiding Principles, widely published with an invitation for submission of suggestions or ideas regarding the Principles. 5 Forum 296–300 (ABA Section of Insurance, Negligence, and Compensation Law, 1970). Paragraph IV is as follows:

"IV. Conflicts of Interest Generally— Duties of Attorney.

"In any claim or in any suit where the attorney selected by the company to defend the claim or action becomes aware of facts or information which indicate to him a question of coverage in the matter being defended or any other conflict of interest between the company and the insured with respect to the defense of the matter, the attorney should promptly inform both the company and the insured, preferably in writing, of the nature and extent of the conflicting interests. In any such suit, the company or its attorney should invite the insured to retain his own counsel at his own expense to represent his separate interest."

insured from the insurer or the attorney, especially if that letter also includes a declaration of a reservation or rights.

Informing the Insurer of a Conflict of Interests

A defense attorney, who continues the representation of an insured after securing an insured's consent, should also take steps to disclose the nature and the scope of any conflict of interests to the insurer as well. As one of the California Courts of Appeal observed, an attorney owes the "highest duty" to each client to make a "full disclosure of all facts and circumstances which are necessary to enable the parties to make a fully informed decision regarding * * * areas of potential conflict and the possibility of seeking independent legal advice." [8] However, the level of concern in regard to securing the insurer's informed consent undoubtedly is not as great as it is in regard to the insured because there is a sense that the insurer is in a position to protect itself so long as the defense attorney provides an adequate disclosure.

See also *Statement of Principles on Respective Rights and Duties of Lawyers and Laymen in the Business of Adjusting Insurance Claims,* adopted January 8, 1939, by the Conference Committee on Adjusters [name later changed to National Conference of Lawyers, Insurance Companies, and Adjusters by resolution adopted by A.B.A. House of Delegates, Feb. 1961], five of whom, including the Chairman, represented the American Bar Association, American Mutual Alliance [name later changed to American Mutual Insurance Alliance], Association of Casualty and Surety Companies [name later changed to American Insurance Association], International Claim Association, National Board of Fire Underwriters, National Association of Independent Insurance Adjusters, and National Association of Independent Insurers. The statement is printed in full in the prefatory section of Vol. III, MARTINDALE-HUBBELL LAW DIRECTORY, 218A–219A (1970). The following is an excerpt from the Committee statement, a footnote construing "representatives" being omitted here:

"4(b). The companies and their representatives, including attorneys, will inform the policyholder of the progress of any suit against the policyholder and its probable results. If any diversity of interest shall appear between the policyholder and the company, the policyholder shall be fully advised of the situation and invited to retain his own counsel. Without limiting the general application of the foregoing, it is contemplated that this will be done in any case in which it

appears probable that an amount in excess of the limit of the policy is involved, or in any case in which the company is defending under a reservation of rights, or in any case in which the prosecution of a counterclaim appears advantageous to the policyholder."

See also Committee on Interpretation of Canons of Ethics, State Bar of Texas, Opinion No. 201 (June 1960).

But cf. Murach v. Massachusetts Bonding Insurance Company, 339 Mass. 184, 158 N.E.2d 338 (1959). Though apparently reserving the question whether further disclosure might be required in some circumstances, the court found adequate, in the case at hand, a letter calling attention to the fact that the claim was in excess of policy limits and inviting the insureds to obtain their own counsel to protect their interests as to the excess. The evidence indicated that the insureds were experienced in business and legal matters and were unconcerned with the possibility of involvement of their own property because it appeared that they had no equity of substance. Under these circumstances the court held that there was no obligation even to disclose to the insureds an offer of settlement, since it appeared that they were not concerned with knowing about it.

8.   Betts v. Allstate Insurance Company, 154 Cal.App.3d 688 at p. 716, 201 Cal.Rptr. 528 at p. 545 (4th Dist., Div. 1, 1984), quoting from Klemm v. Superior Court, 75 Cal.App.3d 893 at p. 901, 142 Cal.Rptr. 509 at p. 516 (5th Dist.1977).

Representation of Both the Insured and the Insurer

There are circumstances in which, at least in principle, if an insured is informed about and fully understands the nature, the complexities, and the possible consequences of a conflict of interests situation,[9] an attorney could be authorized by an insured and an insurer to represent both of them with respect to their mutual interest in an effective defense against a tort claim.[10] In other words, there are situations when the conflicting interests are such that it should be possible for an attorney to represent the insured after making a complete disclosure and obtaining the fully informed written consent of the insured and the insurer.[11]

Unless both the insured and the insurer are made fully aware of the nature and degree of a conflict of interests, an attorney who attempts to represent both of them would violate the canons of professional ethics.[12] Furthermore, the insured and the insurer should be specifically advised that whenever an attorney represents parties who have conflicting interests, some courses of action that otherwise would be available may be precluded.[13]

Weighing and Accommodating the Interests of the Insured and the Insurer

If an attorney undertakes a dual representation of an insured and an insurer, the endeavor almost invariably entails a weighing of their respective interests as well as the defense of the claim against the insured. In such cases, the attorney's loyalty to one client cannot be

---

9. *Ibid.* The Comment to Rule 1.7(a) points out that "when more than one client is involved, the question of the conflict must be resolved as to each client" and that "there may be circumstances where it is impossible to make the disclosure necessary to obtain consent." *Id.,* at p. 30.

For more detailed consideration of this question, see John Alan Appleman, *Conflicts in Injury Defenses,* 1957 Insurance Law Journal 545–563; Robert E. Keeton, *Liability Insurance and Responsibility for Settlement,* 67 Harvard Law Review 1136–1186 at pp. 1167–1173 (1954).

10. *Cf.* McGee v. Superior Court, 176 Cal.App.3d 221, 221 Cal.Rptr. 421 (1985); Betts v. Allstate Insurance Company, 154 Cal.App.3d 688 at p. 716, 201 Cal.Rptr. 528 at p. 545 (4th Dist., Div. 1, 1984).

11. Also see the decisions cited in § 7.6(d)(3), below.

12. See Rule 1.7 of MODEL RULES OF PROFESSIONAL CONDUCT (American Bar Association, as amended, 1984). As the court

of appeals observed in Betts v. Allstate Insurance Company, 154 Cal.App.3d 688 at p. 715, 201 Cal.Rptr. 528 at p. 544 (4th Dist., Div. 1, 1984), it is essential for an attorney to "not take any position adverse or antagonistic to a client without the client's *free* and *intelligent consent* given after *full knowledge* of all the facts and circumstances." (Emphasis added).

Also see A.B.A. CODE OF PROFESSIONAL RESPONSIBILITY, Canon 5, EC 5–16 (1974). Compare the problem of the duty of the company to disclose to the insured a conflict of interests, as exemplified in Perkoski v. Wilson, 371 Pa. 553, 92 A.2d 189 (1952).

Also see American Bar Association National Conference of Lawyers and Liability Insurers, *Guiding Principles,* 20 Federation of Insurance Counsel Quarterly 93–100 (Summer, 1970).

13. See Rule 1.7 of MODEL RULES OF PROFESSIONAL CONDUCT (American Bar Association, as amended, 1984), Rule 1.7.

Also see § 7.7(c), below.

allowed to defeat the interests of the other.[14]   And several courts have concluded that the attorney's duty to the insured is primary or paramount.[15]

When a conflict of interests is relatively minor, attaining an appropriate accommodation — thereby "charting a path" for the defense — is probably possible so long as the informed, voluntary consent of both the insurer and the insured has been clearly given.[16]   However, if a conflict is relatively significant, even when the insured and the insurer may agree on a dual representation, the attorney should carefully evaluate both the ethical obligations and the risks of liability for professional misfeasance in such an endeavor.

14. In Betts v. Allstate Insurance Company, 154 Cal.App.3d 688 at p. 716, 201 Cal.Rptr. 528 at p. 545 (4th Dist., Div. 1, 1984), the court observed, "The loyalty owed to one client by an attorney 'cannot consume that owed to the other." In *Betts*, the attorney was negligent in representing the insured and the insurer without a disclosure to the insured of a conflict of interests.

As a practical matter, courts have recognized that defense counsel sometimes "have closer ties with the insurer and a more compelling interest in protecting the insurer's position, whether or not it coincides with what is best for the insured." Purdy v. Pacific Automobile Insurance Company, 157 Cal.App.3d 59 at p. 76, 203 Cal.Rptr. 524 at p. 534 (2d Dist., Div. 1, 1984).

Also see United States Fidelity & Guaranty Company v. Louis A. Roser Company, 585 F.2d 932 at p. 938, fn. 5 (8th Cir.1978).

But cf. the comments of Ronald E. Mallen, *A New Definition of Insurance Defense Counsel,* 1986 Insurance Counsel Defense Journal 108–123. Mr. Mallen concedes in an introductory footnote that he has a "bias" in support of the integrity of appointed counsel. *Id.,* at p. 108. Mr. Mallen argues, "The lawyer's sole objective is to competently defend on behalf of the insured, a task governed by the familiar requirements of the standard of care." *Id.,* at p. 109. He also contends: "Defense lawyers * * * are not selected by insurance companies because they are less ethical than other lawyers and will therefore favor their paying client, but rather because they have been recognized as having special skills and experience in the liability areas that the insurer writes." *Ibid.*

15. *Cf.* Norman v. Insurance Company of North America, 218 Va. 718, 239 S.E.2d 902 at p. 907 (1978) (the "standards of the legal profession *require undeviating fidelity* of a lawyer *to his client,* and * * * an insurer's attorney, employed to represent an insured, is bound to the same high standards which govern all attorneys, and *owes the insured the same duty* as if he were privately retained by the insured") (emphasis added); Seibert Oxidermo, Inc. v. Shields, 430 N.E.2d 401 at p. 403 (Ind. App. 3d Dist.1982) (when the "interests of the policyholder and the carrier do not fully coincide * * * the attorney's duty is to the insured * * *").   Although the Court of Appeals decision in *Siebert* was subsequently vacated, the Indiana Supreme Court explicitly stated that it subscribed to the point of view of the Court of Appeals in regard to the attorney's duty to the insured. 446 N.E.2d 332 at p. 341 (Ind.1983).

Also see Crum v. Anchor Casualty Company, 264 Minn. 378, 119 N.W.2d 703 at p. 712 (1963); American Mutual Liability Insurance Company v. Superior Court, 38 Cal.App.3d 579, 113 Cal.Rptr. 561 (3d Dist. 1974); Trieber v. Hopson, 27 A.D.2d 151, 277 N.Y.S.2d 241 at p. 244 (3d Dept.1967) (" * * * counsel assigned [for the defense of the insured] owes a duty of paramount allegiance to the insured * * *").

Cf. Outboard Marine Corp. v. Liberty Mutual Insurance Company, 536 F.2d 730 at p. 737 (7th Cir.1976).

Also see the discussion of "weighing and accommodating the interests of the insured and the insurer" in § 7.6(b), above.

16. See the discussion in § 7.6(d)(3).

Withdrawing From the Representation of the Insured

When an attorney selected by an insurer to represent an insured confronts a significant conflict of interests, it may be essential for the attorney to withdraw from the representation of the insured — that is, there are situations in which the conflict is such that it is clearly impossible for an attorney to represent both the insurer and the insured, even with the fully informed consent of both.[17]

(2) Defense Counsel's Liability to the Insured and the Insurer

When a defense attorney, selected and paid by a liability insurer, confronts a conflict of interests in the course of representing an insured, the question may subsequently arise as to whether the attorney may be liable to the insured for acts of malpractice if the attorney acted at some point without due sensitivity to the conflicting interests. The view that a defense attorney may be subject to liability for harm resulting from conduct in relation to a conflict of interests seems likely to prevail because there are persuasive reasons supporting this conclusion.[18] The attorney occupies a fiduciary relationship to the insured, as well as to the insurance company.[19] Furthermore, a defense attorney

---

17. The MODEL RULES OF PROFESSIONAL CONDUCT (American Bar Association, as amended, 1984), provide in Rule 1.7(a), "A lawyer shall not represent a client if the representation of that client will be directly adverse to another client, unless: (1) the lawyer reasonably believes the representation will not adversely affect the relationship with the other client; and (2) each client consents after consultation."

Cf. San Diego Navy Federal Credit Union v. Cumis Insurance Society, Inc., 162 Cal.App.3d 358 at p. 375, 208 Cal.Rptr. 494 at p. 506 (4th Dist., Div. 1, 1984), where the court observed, "If the insured does not give an informed consent to continued representation, counsel *must cease* to represent both." (Emphasis added); Lysick v. Walcom, 258 Cal.App.2d 136, 65 Cal.Rptr. 406 at p. 413 (1st Dist., Div. 1, 1968).

Also see Drinker, LEGAL ETHICS (1953) at p. 115. Mr. Drinker chaired the ABA Standing Committee on Ethics and Grievances from 1944 to 1958.

Also consider the discussion of the right of an attorney to withdraw from the representation of a client in § 7.6(c)(4), below.

18. See, e.g., Lieberman v. Employers Insurance of Wausau, 84 N.J. 325, 419 A.2d 417 (1980); Rogers v. Robson, 81 Ill.2d 201, 40 Ill.Dec. 816, 407 N.E.2d 47 (1980); Rejohn v. Serpe, 125 Misc.2d 148, 478 N.Y.S.2d 799 (3d Dist.1984); Torres v. Nelson, 448 So.2d 1058 (Fla.App., 3d Dist., 1984).

Also see Klemm v. Superior Court of Fresno County, 75 Cal.App.3d 893 at p. 901, 142 Cal.Rptr. 509 at p. 514 (5th Dist. 1977); Lysick v. Walcom, 258 Cal.App.2d 136, 65 Cal.Rptr. 406, 28 A.L.R.3d 368 (1st Dist., Div. 1, 1986); Ivy v. Pacific Automobile Insurance Company, 156 Cal.App.2d 652, 320 P.2d 140 (1958).

But cf. Waters v. American Casualty Co. of Reading, Pa., 261 Ala. 252, 73 So.2d 524 (1953) (rehearing denied in 1954).

See generally, Note, *Rogers v. Robson: Increased Malpractice Liability for Insurance Defense Counsel*, 14 John Marshall Law Review 589–604 (1981); Note, *Insurance—Settlement of a Medical Malpractice Suit by an Attorney Without the Insured's Consent Constitutes a Breach of the Attorney-Client Relationship, Even When the Attorney has the Authority to Settle Under the Insurance Contract, Unless There is a Prior Full and Frank Disclosure by the Attorney to the Insured of all Material Facts and Circumstances—Rogers v. Robson, Masters, Ryan, Brumund & Belom (Illinois 1980)*, 30 Drake Law Review 937–948 (1981).

19. See, e.g. Purdy v. Pacific Automobile Insurance Company, 157 Cal.App.3d 59, 203 Cal.Rptr. 524 at p. 533 (2d Dist., Div. 1, 1984); Houston General Insurance Company v. Superior Court In and For County of Alameda, 108 Cal.App.3d 958, 166 Cal.Rptr. 904 (1st Dist., Div. 2, 1980);

implicitly, if not explicitly, represents to the insured the ability to exercise professional competence and skill in conducting the insured's defense.[20]

The liability of a defense attorney selected by an insurer to represent an insured is not necessarily co-extensive with that of the insurer for failing to discharge the contractual obligation to deal with and on behalf of its insured fairly and in good faith[21] — that is, a defense attorney should not invariably be held liable for damages in every situation in which an insured is able to justify a claim against an insurer as a result of some misconduct in relation to a conflict of interests between the insurer and the insured. Although in some circumstances liability might be exclusively based on the actions of a defense counsel provided by the insurer, the insurer's liability often will, at least in part, be predicated on the insurer's total course of conduct involving actions of other representatives or employees such as adjusters, home office claims examiners, or claims department executives.[22]

The potential exposure to malpractice claims by an insured is enough to cause concern to any defense attorney whenever a conflict of interests exists.[23] There are several judicial precedents sustaining the liability of defense attorneys to insureds.[24] Furthermore, bar associa-

Zalta v. Billips, 81 Cal.App.3d 183, 144 Cal. Rptr. 888 (2d Dist., Div. 2, 1978).

Also see Ronald E. Mallen, *Insurance Counsel: The Fine Line Between Professional Responsibility and Malpractice,* 45 Insurance Counsel Journal 244–265 (1978).

20. And some courts have also concluded that even though the insurer may also be the attorney's client, a defense counsel's primary duty is to further the best interests of the insured.

Cf. Outboard Marine Corp. v. Liberty Mutual Insurance Company, 536 F.2d 730 at p. 737 (7th Cir.1976); Lieberman v. Employers Insurance of Wausau, 84 N.J. 325, 419 A.2d 417 (1980).

Also see Gruenberg v. Aetna Insurance Company, 9 Cal.3d 566, 108 Cal.Rptr. 480, 510 P.2d 1032 (1973).

21. In Betts v. Allstate Insurance Company, 154 Cal.App.3d 688 at p. 715, 201 Cal.Rptr. 528 at p. 544 (4th Dist., Div. 1, 1984), the jury awarded $500,000 jointly and severally against defense counsel and the insurer for emotional distress. The jury also awarded $3,000,000 in punitive damages against the insurer alone. The trial court remitted the $500,000 to $50,000 as a condition of not granting a new trial, and this decision was sustained on appeal.

In Torres v. Nelson, 448 So.2d 1058 (Fla. App.3d Dist.1984), the court concluded that an adverse verdict in an earlier action,

brought against insurer, alleging bad-faith failure to settle tort action against insured clients, did not bar insured clients' malpractice action against attorneys who were employees (house counsel) of insurer because the absence of bad faith refusal to settle was not the equivalent of a determination that legal counsel had not been negligent.

Cf. Purdy v. Pacific Automobile Insurance Company, 157 Cal.App.3d 59, 203 Cal. Rptr. 524 (2d Dist., Div. 1, 1984).

22. *Cf.* Purdy v. Pacific Automobile Insurance Company, 157 Cal.App.3d 59, 203 Cal.Rptr. 524 (2d Dist., Div. 1, 1984).

23. A defense attorney often has some practical protection in regard to being sued by an insured because it is often viewed as tactically undesirable, from the insured's point of view, to have an individual attorney as a joint defendant in a suit against an insurer. See Peerless Insurance Co. v. Inland Mutual Insurance Co., 251 F.2d 696 at p. 701 (4th Cir.1958), explaining on a comparable basis the conduct of the primary insurer (who was seeking reimbursement from a reinsurer) in failing to assert a potential claim against its attorney.

24. In Betts v. Allstate Insurance Company, 154 Cal.App.3d 688 at p. 715, 201 Cal.Rptr. 528 at p. 544 (4th Dist., Div. 1, 1984), the jury awarded $500,000 jointly and severally against defense counsel and

tion advisory opinions on professional ethics, disapproving certain types of conduct by defense attorneys when a conflict of interests exists, provide additional persuasive support for the position that there is a sound theoretical foundation for such liability. An excellent example of such evaluations is provided by an opinion which concluded that when an attorney did not disclose the purpose of taking an insured's deposition, which was to use it in support of an insurer's coverage defense, it was improper conduct that should preclude the insurer's reliance upon the policy defense.[25] Another good example is provided by an opinion advising that it was improper to withhold disclosure of the fact that the insurer planned to fall back on a policy defense to the insured's claim in the event the defense of the tort suit was not successful, and therefore the insurer was not considering settlement of the tort action.[26]

Liability of Defense Counsel to the Insurer

A defense counsel has obligations to the insurer, as well as the insured, and is required to conform his or her conduct to the same professional standards in discharging those duties.[27] Thus, a defense counsel's concern about the ramifications of a conflict of interests is

the insurer for emotional distress (as well as $3,000,000 in punitive damages against the insurer alone). The trial court remitted the $500,000 amount to $50,000 as a condition of not granting a new trial, and this decision was sustained on appeal.

In Lysick v. Walcom, 258 Cal.App.2d 136, 65 Cal.Rptr. 406, 28 A.L.R.3d 368 (1st Dist., Div. 1, 1968), the court concluded that an attorney could be liable to the insured's survivors for failing to communicate with the insurer concerning the possibilities for settlements and also by not insisting that the insurer make the full limit of coverage available for a settlement.

Also see Lieberman v. Employers Insurance of Wausau, 171 N.J.Super. 39, 407 A.2d 1256 (1979) (attorney actively participated in settlement of a medical malpractice claim against the wishes of the insured).

25. See, e.g. Allstate Insurance Co. v. Keller, 17 Ill.App.2d 44, 149 N.E.2d 482 (1st Dist., Div. 1, 1958), 70 A.L.R.2d 1190 (1960) (the company asserted a coverage defense based on the insured's false statement to the company that he, rather than another occupant of the car, was driving at the time of the accident; the insured corrected the statement about nine months later; the court stated in dicta that "timely revelation of the truth might render an incipient breach immaterial * * *" but that an actual showing of prejudice is not required, 17 Ill.App.2d at p. 50, 149 N.E.2d

at p. 485; concluding that the revelation in this case was not timely, the court found a breach of the assistance and cooperation clause, but held that the company was precluded from asserting this defense because it failed to attempt a reservation of its rights for a period of almost a year and a half, during which interval its attorney took the insured's deposition in contemplation of the filing of a declaratory judgment action concerning the breach, but without notifying the insured of such purpose).

But cf. Fidelity & Casualty Co. of New York v. McConnaughy, 228 Md. 1, 179 A.2d 117 (1962) (insured's breach of cooperation clause by bringing in false witnesses caused insurer to decline to accept claimant's $3,500 settlement offer; insurer-appointed counsel acted improperly in taking insured's deposition to confirm its defense of noncooperation, but insurer is not thereby barred from asserting noncooperation; relief limited, however, to excusing insurer from liability for excess above $3,500 for which insurer claims it would have settled but for insured's breach).

26. Home Indemnity Co. v. Williamson, 183 F.2d 572 (5th Cir.1950).

27. Cf. Howard M. Berg and Roy Alan Cohen, *The Dangers of Playing Both Ends Against the Middle: The Dilemma of Insurance Company's Defense Course*, 29 Federation of Insurance Course Quarterly 281–294 at p. 282 (1979).

further heightened if the attorney does not have complete confidence that the insurance company will not seek to be indemnified by the attorney in the event an insured successfully pursues a claim against the insurer.[28] And the problems for defense counsel may be further complicated by the involvement of one or more excess insurers.[29]

(3) Ethical Questions and Conflict of Interests Problems for Attorneys Representing Plaintiffs

The analysis in the preceding portions of this section has focused on conflict of interests problems in relation to insurers, defense attorneys, and insureds. Attorneys representing plaintiffs (that is, third parties who are seeking indemnification from alleged tortfeasors or their insurers) in tort cases may also be confronted with serious ethical problems [30] as a result of conflicting interests. The type of problems described in this subsection are not limited to claims that involve liability insurance. Nevertheless, this is a context in which these situations frequently arise.

One of the most difficult conflict of interests questions for attorneys who represent plaintiffs often occurs when several persons are injured in the same accident. Frequently, more than one of the individuals who are injured ask an attorney to represent them, and this presents the question whether one attorney may appropriately serve several persons who are making claims resulting from the same incident. For example, suppose a parent is driving a car in which a fifteen-year-old child and an adult friend of the parent are passengers, and all of them

---

28. *Cf.* Royal Crown Cola Bottling Company of Oklahoma City, Inc. v. Aetna Casualty & Surety Company, 438 F.Supp. 39 (W.D.Okl.1977) (insured brought a suit against liability insurer for difference between policy limit and amount paid to settle tort claim, and the insurer filed a third party complaint against the attorney who had been hired by insurer to defend the insured); Smiley v. Manchester Insurance & Indemnity Company, 49 Ill.App.3d 675, 7 Ill.Dec. 522, 364 N.E.2d 683 (2d Dist.1977), *affirmed* 71 Ill.2d 306, 16 Ill.Dec. 487, 375 N.E.2d 118 (1978).

Also see Fireman's Fund American Insurance Company v. Patterson and Lamberty, Inc., 528 S.W.2d 67 (Tex.App., Tyler 1975).

29. *Cf.* Transit Casualty Company v. Spink Corporation, 94 Cal.App.3d 124, 156 Cal.Rptr. 360 (3d Dist.1979). Also see the other opinions in this case reported at 78 Cal.App.3d 475, 144 Cal.Rptr. 488 (3d Cir. 1978), and 26 Cal.3d 912, 164 Cal.Rptr. 709, 610 P.2d 1038 (1980).

See generally, Howard M. Berg and Roy Alan Cohen, *The Dangers of Playing Both Ends from the Middle: The Dilemma of* *Insurance Companies' Defense Counsel* 281–294 at pp. 290–291 (1979).

30. One of the professional responsibility questions that does not involve a conflict of interests, but does entail a difficult ethical dilemma, concerns whether it is permissible for a plaintiff's attorney seeking to increase the likelihood of a favorable settlement to communicate to the defendant (the insured) information about the insurer's potential liability in excess of policy limits for failure to settle. A bar association committee charged with interpreting canons of ethics has answered that this conduct would be improper. Committee on Interpretation of Canons of Ethics, State Bar of Texas, Opinion No. 97 (April, 1954), reprinted 17 Texas Bar Journal 218 (1954). The opinion answers that it would not violate canons, however, merely "to write to the tort-feasor putting such party on notice of the attorneys' [sic] employment, and offering to make compromise settlement of the claim without litigation for the amount of the tortfeasor's liability insurance policy limits, where, at the time the offer is made, no suit has been instituted and the tort-feasor is not represented by any counsel on account of the accident."

are injured in a collision with a car driven by another person. If one attorney attempts to represent the parent, the child, and the friend in their claims against the other driver and the other driver's liability insurance company, this arrangement often entails serious problems. The parent has a significant interest in contending that the accident resulted exclusively from negligent operation of the other vehicle. In contrast, the friend (and in some circumstances, the child as well) may have a substantial interest in proving that *both* the parent *and* the other driver were at fault so that a recovery is possible under their respective liability insurance coverages.[31]

In order to represent more than one of the parties who are injured in an accident, the attorney must obtain the fully informed written consent of each claimant.[32] This may prove to be both troublesome and difficult to arrange in some circumstances, especially when one or more of the individuals are under some form of legal disability. For example, in the preceding illustration which involved a minor,[33] it is unclear whether either or both parents should or could be the individuals to authorize representation of the child by the same attorney who represents the father.

A significant conflict of interests among two or more plaintiffs may arise in relation to the settlement of claims. For example, occasionally an insurer will reach an agreement with an attorney representing several claimants to settle all of the claims for a stated figure, with the allocation among the claimants to be made by the claimants' attorney. This type of settlement places the attorney in a position that involves a conflict of interests. In this situation, an attorney certainly should not make an allocation of the settlement proceeds without providing a complete disclosure to all the parties whose claims are affected.[34]

31. *Cf.* Jedwabny v. Philadelphia Transportation Company, 390 Pa. 231, 135 A.2d 252 (1957), *cert. denied* 355 U.S. 966, 78 S.Ct. 557, 2 L.Ed.2d 541 (1958).

32. MODEL RULES OF PROFESSIONAL CONDUCT (American Bar Association, as amended, 1984), Rule 1.7. See especially the discussion of Model Code Comparison at p. 33.

Cf. Tadier v. American Photocopy Equipment Co., 531 F.Supp. 35 (S.D.N.Y.1981); Jedwabnay v. Philadelphia Transportation Co., 390 Pa. 231, 135 A.2d 252 (1957), *cert. denied* 355 U.S. 966, 78 S.Ct. 557, 2 L.Ed.2d 541 (1958).

Also see Nancy J. Moore, *Conflicts of Interest in the Simultaneous Representation of Multiple Clients: A Proposed Solution to the Current Confusion and Controversy*, 61 Texas Law Review 211–288 (1982); A.B.A. CODE OF PROFESSIONAL RESPONSIBILITY, Canon 5, EC 5–16, DR 5–105, 5–106 (1969). The 1969 CODE is substantially different from the 1974 CODE. Canon 5 of the

1969 CODE is closest substantially to EC 5–16 of the 1974 CODE.

33. *Cf.* Smith v. Price, 253 N.C. 285, 116 S.E.2d 733 (1960) (friendly suit to approve settlement with infant plaintiff; one attorney represented defendants, two insurers and their several insureds including an infant defendant; the infant defendant's injuries were not called to court's attention; held, judgment irregular because of conflict of interest among defendants; infant defendant's motion to vacate judgment as to him allowed). Note, however, that the issue in this case was not the effect of the judgment as to the infant plaintiff but rather its effect on the reciprocal claim of the infant defendant; concerning reciprocal claims generally, see Section 7.5, below.

34. The MODEL RULES OF PROFESSIONAL CONDUCT (American Bar Association, as amended, 1984), provide, in Rule 1.8(g), "A lawyer who represents two or more clients shall not participate in making an aggre-

[Furthermore, if an insurance company, participating in such a settlement, is aware of the fact that the attorney was acting without making a complete disclosure to all of the claimants, the insurer arguably would be a party to the improper action and this might provide a basis for a subsequent disavowal of the settlements by an aggrieved party.]

In many circumstances, several plaintiffs who have possible conflicting interests are not well served by requiring the involvement of additional attorneys. Frequently, there would be a substantial increase in the portion of any recovery that would be expended as legal fees if each individual were represented by a different attorney. Accordingly, this constitutes a compelling reason for allowing one attorney to represent several plaintiffs whose interests may be somewhat divergent and in conflict.[35] However, the cost factor does not alter the importance of requiring a full disclosure and a complete explanation of the conflicting interests. After being fully informed of the conflict, the affected parties should be free to agree upon a course of action in which one attorney can represent them. The parties should be accorded this freedom even if that approach has some effect on the assertion of specific claims, including the possibility that a given claim or theory of liability — which could have been made if each individual had been separately represented — will be foreclosed.

Caveat. In some circumstances, the facts or relevant legal doctrines involve such substantial conflicts that it is neither appropriate nor practical for one attorney to represent several plaintiffs.[36]

(4) Responding to a Conflict of Interests by Withdrawal

An attorney, either a plaintiff's or a defense counsel, confronted by a conflict of interests may seek to withdraw from the representation of a client.[37] Although the following discussion focuses on withdrawals by defense counsel, similar considerations apply to attorneys representing plaintiffs.

There are almost no appellate court decisions which have specifically considered requests by attorneys to withdraw from the representation of a client because of a conflict of interests problem. However,

gate settlement of the claims * * * unless each client consents after consultation, including disclosure of the existence and nature of all the claims * * * involved and of the participation of each person in the settlement.

Cf. A.B.A. CODE OF PROFESSIONAL RESPONSIBILITY, DR 5–106 (1974).

Also see the discussion of this matter in In re Cap'n Rick Corp., 525 F.Supp. 31 (S.D.N.Y.1981).

Regarding the settlement of claims for different claimants without receiving the consent of each, see Estate of Vafiades v. Sheppard Bus Service, Inc., 192 N.J.Super. 301, 469 A.2d 971 (1983).

35. See the dissenting opinion of Bell, J., in Jedwabny v. Philadelphia Transportation Co., 390 Pa. 231, 135 A.2d 252 (1957), *cert. denied* 355 U.S. 966, 78 S.Ct. 557, 2 L.Ed.2d 541 (1958).

36. Consider Woodruff v. Tomlin, 593 F.2d 33 (6th Cir.1979) [reversing the decision reported at 423 F.Supp. 1284 (W.D. Tenn.1976)], on rehearing 616 F.2d 924 (1980), *cert. denied* 449 U.S. 888, 101 S.Ct. 246, 66 L.Ed.2d 114 (1980).

37. See Rule 1.16 of the MODEL RULES OF PROFESSIONAL CONDUCT (American Bar Association, As amended, 1984), on "Terminating Representation."

there are judicial precedents supporting the right of an insurer-selected attorney to withdraw from the representation of the insured in a tort case whenever the attorney is dissatisfied with the arrangements if the withdrawal can be accomplished without harm to any of the parties to the tort action.[38] When there is a conflict of interests between an attorney's clients — in this context, the insurer and the insured — that affects the manner in which the defense of a tort claim is to be conducted, it seems clear that the reasons for allowing an attorney to withdraw are more compelling than those that apply when an attorney is merely dissatisfied. A very persuasive case therefore exists for allowing an attorney (selected by the insurer) confronting a serious conflict of interests to withdraw from the representation of the insured if that action can be accomplished without prejudicing the parties. Moreover, when the attorney has been selected by the insurer, the case for allowing withdrawal is probably equally persuasive even if it may result in some prejudice to the insurer.

Withdrawal of an attorney provides at best only a partial answer to a conflict of interests problem because it generally does not eliminate the circumstances that cause the conflict. Therefore, any single attorney selected as replacement for the attorney who has withdrawn will usually confront the same conflict. Consequently, once a defense counsel has concluded that withdrawal is warranted, it should almost always lead to the conclusion, or at least the presumption, that the insured is entitled to select independent counsel whose charges will be paid or partially paid by the insurer.[39]

On occasion, trial courts have denied permission for an attorney to withdraw from the representation of an insured. If the circumstances are such that the court decides the attorney can function with clear instructions from the court, it is almost certainly within the discretion of the trial court to deny permission for withdrawal. For example, an attorney may be directed to serve only the interests of the client designated by the court. Such a direction may be given with the understanding that persons or entities who are not actually involved in the suit will not be bound by the results of the trial. In some instances when a trial court has denied an insurer-selected defense counsel the right to withdraw,[40] the decision has been said to have the effect that the attorney's actions in accordance with the trial court order did not waive the right of the insurer to thereafter assert a coverage defense.[41]

---

38. See, e.g. Swedloff v. Philadelphia Transportation Co., 409 Pa. 382, 187 A.2d 152 (1963) (order denying permission to withdraw reversed).

39. See the discussion of the insured's right to select independent counsel in § 7.6(d), below.

40. See, e.g. Presley v. Williams, 57 A.D.2d 947, 395 N.Y.S.2d 92 (2d Dept.1977).

Also see Cascella v. Jay James Camera Shop, Inc., 147 Conn. 337, 160 A.2d 899 at

p. 901 (1960) (trial court did not err in denying motion of defense counsel to withdraw on theory insured had failed to cooperate; "any question concerning coverage * * * was foreign to the issues" of the tort trial and could not be determined on motion of counsel to withdraw).

41. See, e.g., Nationwide Mutual Insurance Co. v. Thomas, 306 F.2d 767 (D.C.Cir. 1962) (however, a motion for new trial resulted in reduction of judgments and the

§ 7.6(d)   Possible Courses to Be Pursued When There Are Conflicts of Interests Between an Insured and the Insurer

In most circumstances in which there are actual or potential conflicting interests, there are several possible courses of action that may be considered. Once the matter has been disclosed to the insured, the initiative in selecting, or at least proposing, a course of action usually may be taken by either the insured or the insurer.

(1) Denial of Coverage and Refusal to Provide a Defense

One possible course of action for insurers confronted by a conflict of interests, especially a conflict involving a coverage defense, is to deny or disclaim coverage and to decline to provide a defense for the tort case.[1] There are several possible disadvantages for the insurer in this approach. *First,* the tort action may not be as effectively and vigorously defended as it would be if it were in the hands of an attorney selected by the insurer. *Second,* if the company is ultimately found to be liable — that is, in the event the insurer subsequently loses an adjudication of the coverage question — there may be a secondary dispute if the insured has reached a settlement with the third party for an amount that the insurer regards as too high. *Third,* in the event the dispute on the coverage defense is eventually resolved against the insurer, the defense costs to be paid by the insurer may be greater than they would otherwise have been, because the amount charged by an independent counsel selected by the insured will often be higher than would have been the fee arrangement with an attorney chosen by the insurer who has a continuing flow of work from the insurer. *Fourth,* the insurer may be subject to estoppel by judgment.[2]

The combined force of all these disadvantages often leads an insurer to want to consider other approaches to addressing a conflict of interests problem. For example, the insurer may want to continue control of the defense of the tort claim, even at the expense of giving up the potential defense to the insured's claim for coverage, unless the insurer believes that there is a very strong probability that the coverage defense will subsequently be sustained in court.[3] Several of the

insurer then appealed on the merits; held, voluntary appeal waived defense of noncooperation).

See also Hurston v. Georgia Farm Bureau Mutual Insurance Company, 148 Ga. App. 324, 250 S.E.2d 886 (1978).

Concerning preclusion of defenses as a result of actions in defending a claim, see § 6.7(a), above.

§ 7.6(d)

1. See, e.g. Eason v. Weaver, 557 F.2d 1202 (5th Cir.1977).

Cf. Murphy v. Urso, 88 Ill.2d 444, 58 Ill. Dec. 828, 430 N.E.2d 1079 (1981).

Also consider the discussion of the "Adjudication of Coverage Defenses in a Subsequent Proceeding" in § 7.6(d)(3), below.

2. See, e.g. Maneikis v. St. Paul Insurance Company of Illinois, 655 F.2d 818 (7th Cir.1981), applying rules set forth by the Illinois Supreme Court in Thornton v. Paul, 74 Ill.2d 132, 23 Ill.Dec. 541, 384 N.E.2d 335 (1978).

Also see the discussion of estoppel in § 7.6(e), below.

3. *Cf.* Ronald E. Mallen, *A New Definition of Insurance Defense Counsel,* 1986 Insurance Counsel Defense Journal 108–123.

possible courses of action for an insurer are considered in the following subsections.

(2) Disclosure of the Conflict and "Waiver" By the Insurer of a Coverage Limitation or a Defense

An insurer clearly is obligated to promptly disclose the existence of an actual or potential conflict of interests to an insured.[4] However, when a conflict exists the insurer may still conclude that its interests in minimizing both the defense costs and the extent of its liability under the insurance coverage will be best served by continuing to provide its insured with a defense — that is, the insurer may decide that even though there is a conflict of interests, continuing to exercise control over the defense through the selection [5] and guidance of defense counsel will serve the insurer's objectives. If an insurer elects to pursue this course, it should endeavor to reach a clear and unequivocal written understanding with the insured in regard to the matter(s) that relate to the conflicting interests.

One option for an insurer that wants to direct the defense is for the insurer to agree not to subsequently assert any rights with respect to the matter that gives rise to the conflict — that is, a voluntary relinquishment by the insurer of a known right which constitutes a "waiver." [6] If an insurer conducts the defense without a clear accord between the insured and the insurer in regard to the conflicting interests, the insurer may subsequently be precluded from asserting any defenses related to the matter that produced the conflicting interests.[7]

(3) Disclosure of the Conflict and Consent by the Insured to Representation by a Single Attorney Without a "Waiver" by the Insurer (Thereby Preserving the Right to a Subsequent Adjudication of the Coverage Question)

In some situations when either the insurer or an attorney selected by an insurer realizes that a conflict of interests exists, the problem will be fully disclosed to the insured with a view to obtaining the insured's informed and voluntary consent to having the attorney undertake or continue the representation without the insurer's giving up the opportunity to subsequently assert its rights in relation to the matter

---

4. See the discussion in § 7.6(b), above.

5. Some commentators have observed that insurers are particularly concerned that an insured might retain less competent defense counsel than would be selected by the insurer. See, e.g. J. Patrick Brown, *The Demise of the Declaratory Judgment Action as a Device for Testing the Insurer's Duty to Defend: A Postscript,* 24 Cleveland Law Review 18–32 at p. 25, note 16 (1974).

In most instances, this should not be a significant consideration. Also, an insurer's concern about the competency of the attorney could be alleviated if the insurer were allowed to approve the attorney selected by the insured.

6. For example, in Maryland Casualty Company v. Peppers, 64 Ill.2d 187, 355 N.E.2d 24 at p. 31 (1976), the court observed that if the insurer "waives its defense of noncoverage by the policy of an intentional injury and defends without asserting a reservation of rights or a nonwaiver agreement as to such an injury the conflict of interests will be removed."

7. See the discussion in § 7.6(e), below.

that gives rise to the conflict.[8] If the insured consents to this approach, there should be a clear understanding, explicitly set forth in a written agreement, about when and under what circumstances the matter giving rise to the conflict may thereafter be raised as a defense by the insurer.

An insurer that seeks an insured's "consent" to representation by a defense counsel selected and directed by the insurer, even though there is a possibility for a coverage defense, will often send the insured a reservation-of-rights notice stating that the insurer's participation in the defense of the tort action will not preclude the subsequent assertion of the coverage defense.[9] And a situation in which an insurer seeks to preserve the right to subsequently deny coverage after an adjudication of the third party's tort claim is often characterized as a defense which is subject to a "reservation of rights."[10] The assertion of such reserva-

---

8. Ronald E. Mallen, *A New Definition of Insurance Defense Counsel,* 1986 Insurance Counsel Defense Journal 108–123 at pp. 122–123 (emphasis added) has written:

"*Marketing Defense Counsel.* Even when the company decides that a reservation of rights is necessary, the insured still may *be persuaded to accept* counsel recommended by the insurer. To do so the insurer must understand and address the concerns of the insured which give rise to requests for independent counsel * * *. The insurer's objective should be to demonstrate to the insured that representation by appointed counsel is desirable. Thus, the principal assets of counsel should be shown to the insured to be loyalty, competence and effective representation."

The appropriateness of persuading the insured to accept an appointed counsel after the insured has requested an independent attorney is at best suspect. Although there are undoubtedly factors that might encourage an insurer to undertake this course, they should be carefully weighed against the prospects of subsequent litigation between the insurer and the insured should the defense result in liability for the insured that is not covered by the applicable insurance coverage.

Also see the discussion in Maryland Casualty Company v. Peppers, 64 Ill.2d 187, 355 N.E.2d 24 (1976); American Employers' Insurance Company v. Crawford, 87 N.M. 375, 533 P.2d 1203 (1975); Nandorf, Inc. v. CNA Insurance Companies, 134 Ill. App.3d 134, 88 Ill.Dec. 968, 479 N.E.2d 988 (1st Dist., 1st Div., 1985), *appeal denied* (1985).

Cf. the discussion of "consent" in the Note, *Legal Representation of Conflicting Interests: A View Towards Better Self-Reg-*

ulation, 18 Santa Clara Law Review 997–1020 at pp. 1013–1016 (1978).

Also consider the comments in Note, *An Insurer's Dilemma: Legal Consequences of Contested Coverage,* 28 South Dakota Law Review 357–375 at pp. 370–372 (1983); Note, *Conflicts of Interest and Collateral Estoppel in Uninsured Motorist Cases, Oates v. Safeco Insurance Co. of America,* 45 Missouri Law Review 747–758 (1980).

But see Lloyd E. Williams, Jr. and Donald V. Jernberg, *Conflict of Interest in Insurance Defense Litigation: Common Sense in Changing Times,* 31 Federation of Insurance Counsel Quarterly 111–125 at pp. 112–114 (1981).

9. Concerning the defense attorney's conflict of interests in relation to advising his clients to enter into a reservation of rights notice or a nonwaiver agreement, see the comments of Philip H. Corboy, *Defending Insurance Companies and the Insured—Can Two Masters Be Served?,* 55 Chicago Bar Record 102–113 at pp. 102–103 (1973).

Also consider the comments on use of a reservation-of-rights notice in Lloyd E. Williams, Jr. and Donald V. Jernberg, *Conflicts of Interest in Defense Litigation: Common Sense in Changing Times,* 31 Federation of Insurance Counsel Quarterly 111–125 at pp. 112–114 (1980).

Also see Comment, *Reservation of Rights Notices and Nonwaiver Agreements,* 12 Pacific Law Review 763–786 (1983).

Concerning nonwaiver agreements and reservations of rights generally, see § 6.7(a), above.

10. *Cf.* Auto-Owners Insurance Company v. Corrie, 102 Ill.App.3d 93, 57 Ill.Dec. 766, 429 N.E.2d 883 (3d Dist.1981).

tions by unilateral action, rather than seeking an agreement with the insured,[11] has occasionally been approved in judicial opinions [12] and other writings.[13]

Comment

In view of the greater awareness of and sensitivity to both conflict of interests problems and the insurer's obligation to act in good faith, a unilateral declaration by an insurer of a reservation-of-rights — which purports to allow the insurer to both preserve the coverage questions *and* control the defense — is undoubtedly subject to being challenged. Although an insurance company is entitled to have a reasonable opportunity to present its coverage defense, it does not follow that the insurer should be allowed to unilaterally decide to remain in control of the insured's defense to the tort claim while deferring an adjudication of the coverage defense.

Insurers who want to direct the defense on behalf of an insured should, at a minimum, be required to secure the insured's voluntary and informed approval of this approach,[14] even in jurisdictions where consent may not be required.[15] Furthermore, considerable care should

11. Also see the discussion in § 7.6(e), below, of the possibility that collateral estoppel/issue preclusion will be applied in such a case.

Cf. Note, *Conflicts of Interest in the Liability Setting,* 13 Georgia Law Review 973–1013 at pp. 979–984 (1979).

12. In Illinois this is one of three options available to a liability insurer. See Thornton v. Paul, 74 Ill.2d 132, 23 Ill.Dec. 541, 384 N.E.2d 335 (1978), and the numerous decisions applying the *Thornton* rules.

Also see Home Indemnity Company v. Reed Equipment Company, 381 So.2d 45 at p. 52 (Ala.1980).

Cf. State Farm Mutual Automobile Insurance Company v. Glasgow, 478 N.E.2d 918 at p. 923 (Ind.App. 4th Dist., 1985); Metcalfe Brothers, Inc. v. American Mutual Liability Insurance Company, 484 F.Supp. 826 at p. 832 (W.D.Va.1980).

Cf. Great American Insurance Co. v. Ratliff, 242 F.Supp. 983 (E.D.Ark.1965) (state court's decision in tort case that collision was negligently caused was not res judicata against insurer even though its attorneys defended; held for insurer in declaratory proceedings); Crum v. Anchor Casualty Co., 264 Minn. 378, 119 N.W.2d 703 (1963) (held, insurer liable for expenses of defense and $600 settlement made by insured with claimant after insurer withdrew from defense, though knowing facts that brought incident within coverage despite victim's allegations of a claim exclud-

ed by policy terms; statement in opinion that when conflict arises, attorney must act as if retained by insured personally, and insurer may assert its defense in separate proceedings).

Cf. Ferguson v. Birmingham Fire Insurance Co., 254 Or. 496, 460 P.2d 342 (1969) (since there was a conflict of interest, insurer was not estopped to raise in later action its coverage defense that trespass to land was willful; neither did insured's improper demand that insurer defend without a nonwaiver agreement preclude insured from asserting coverage, since insured's breach did not prejudice insurer; other details of this case are stated in Section 7.6(a), n. 18, above).

For a different view concerning the insured's assertion of a right to assume control of the defense unless the insurer will defend without a nonwaiver agreement, see § 6.7(a), above.

13. See the discussion of reservation-of-rights notices and non-waiver agreements in § 6.7, above.

14. Usually this is done by requesting that the insured agree to and sign a document which is characterized as either a "reservation of rights" or a "nonwaiver" agreement. Also see § 6.7, above.

15. In Home Indemnity Company v. Reed Equipment Company, Inc., 381 So.2d 45 at p. 52 (Ala.1980), the court rejected the contention that by undertaking the insured's defense without a non-waiver

be exercised in these circumstances to ensure that the insured's agreement does not result from any actual or perceived sense of coercion by the insurer — that is, it is essential that an insured's consent to this course should be both truly voluntary and fully informed.

A defense attorney must exercise considerable care when an insurer seeks to preserve the right to raise a coverage defense after an adjudication of the tort claim. When an insured's consent is sought, it is clearly essential for a lawyer selected by the insurer (especially when the attorney has already established a relationship with the insured following an appointment as defense counsel by an insurer) to avoid even the appearance of any impropriety. Moreover, it undoubtedly is also desirable for the same care to be exercised in regard to the attorney's relationship to the insurer — that is, there should be a written document which manifests the insurer's consent to the lawyer's continuing representation of both the insured and the insurer when a conflict of interests exists.[16]

When a conflict of interests has been disclosed and the insured has agreed to have the defense conducted by the attorney whom the insurer selected, it is clearly improper for the insurer-selected attorney to thereafter take any position that is not compatible with the insured's interest. For example if an attorney employed by the insurer to represent an insured in the defense undertakes to show — at any point in the course of the litigation between the third party claimant and the insured defendant — that the insurer is not liable for some reason (such as that the insured's conduct was intentional), this type of conduct would violate the attorney's duty to the insured arising from the attorney-client relationship.[17]

agreement the insurer waived its coverage defense, and further observed "that only notice to the insured of the insurer's reservation of its rights is required." Also see Campbell Piping Contractors, Inc. v. Hess Pipeline Co., 342 So.2d 766 (Ala.1977).

16. Lawyers, of course, are enjoined to "avoid even the appearance of impropriety." American Bar Association Code, Canon 9. And, as Professor Aronson observed, this "is particularly applicable to conflicts of interest." Robert H. Aronson, *Conflict of Interest*, 52 Washington Law Review 807–859 at p. 810 (1977).

The Association of Trial Lawyers of America (ATLA) has proposed a LAWYERS CODE OF CONDUCT which provides in Rule 2.4, "A lawyer may serve two or more clients, despite divided loyalty, if each client who is or may be adversely affected by the divided loyalty is fully informed of the actual or potential adverse effects, and voluntarily consents." See the discussion of the merits of this rule by Professor Nancy J. Moore in *Conflicts of Interest in Simul-*

taneous Representation of Multiple Clients: A Proposed Solution to the Current Confusion and Controversy, 61 Texas Law Review 221–288 at p. 215 (1982).

17. See, e.g. Newcomb v. Meiss, 263 Minn. 315, 116 N.W.2d 593 (1962), in which the appellate court concluded the trial court did not err in submitting negligence theory over insurer-appointed defense attorney's contention that defendant wilfully rather than negligently struck plaintiff. The trial court's instructions directed jury not to award damages for an intended impact on plaintiff, but only for a separate impact on plaintiff of car driven by defendant (negligently according to plaintiff's claim, though intentionally according to defense attorney's contention). In *dicta*, the court observed that the attorney acted improperly, though in good faith, in contending the latter impact was intentional.

Also see Glens Falls Group Insurance Corporation v. Hoium, 294 Minn. 247, 200 N.W.2d 189 (1972), which fails to address the issue clearly.

Caveat. Although there are few, if any, judicial precedents addressing the question, in some circumstances the possible influences and ramifications of a significant conflict of interests are such that even an insured's fully informed consent should not be held to be adequate to allow an insurer the latitude to select and instruct the defense attorney while still retaining the freedom to subsequently reject the insured's claim on the basis of some coverage defense.

Adjudication of Coverage Defenses in a Subsequent Proceeding

When an insurer has secured an understanding with its insured that issues in regard to whether coverage exists will be resolved in a separate proceeding which will follow the tort suit if the plaintiff in that action prevails, in an adjudication of the coverage questions that follows the litigation (or a settlement[18]) of the tort claim the insurer's position will be that it did not waive and should not be estopped or otherwise precluded, either by the judgment in the tort suit or by its conduct in defending that suit, from presenting coverage defenses. This position is both supported [19] and opposed [20] by judicial precedents.

18. The settlement of a third party's claim raises similar, but somewhat distinguishable issues. In particular, it seems desirable that an insurer review the entire matter before exercising the prerogative to settle the claim against the insured.

Certainly, even though the insurer is generally authorized to settle the tort claims, an insurer cannot commit an insured's assets without the insured's approval. If the insurer does not secure an approval for the use of the insured's resources to pay a settlement, the insurer is probably precluded from a subsequent claim against its insured for reimbursement.

19. See, e.g. American Home Assurance Company v. Glenn Estess & Associates, Inc., 763 F.2d 1237 at pp. 1239–1240 (11th Cir.1985), applying Alabama law on the basis of Home Indemnity v. Reed Equipment Company, 381 So.2d 45 (Ala.1980).

Cf. American Surety Co. of New York v. Coblentz, 381 F.2d 185 (5th Cir.1967) (insured shot person who had been loitering around motel and was fleeing from chase; after insurer withdrew from defense, judgment was entered for plaintiff on a stipulation of evidence at non-jury trial, summary judgment for plaintiff in an ensuing garnishment proceeding reversed; insurer entitled to a chance to prove its policy defense based on assault and battery exclusion), which still remains authoritative, it would seem, after Coblentz v. American Surety Co. of New York, 416 F.2d 1059 (1969), motion granted 421 F.2d 187 (5th Cir.1969) (liability insurer denied lia-

bility and withdrew; insured stipulated judgment for victim to be satisfied only out of liability insurance; in garnishment action, jury finding that motel owner's shooting of prowler was negligence, not assault; court holds insurer liable; one passage in opinion seems to say insurer was bound by judgment in tort case, but this is misleading since insurer had its opportunity for jury trial of assault-negligence issue in the garnishment proceeding).

In Farm Bureau Mutual Automobile Insurance Co. v. Hammer, 177 F.2d 793 (4th Cir.1949) (2–to–1 decision), *cert. denied* 339 U.S. 914, 70 S.Ct. 575, 94 L.Ed. 1339 (1950), the insurer sought declaratory judgment that its policy did not cover damages awarded against its insured in five tort actions from the defense of which the insurer-appointed attorney withdrew after the insured had been convicted of murder in the second degree for intentionally causing the death of a passenger in another vehicle by driving his truck into it. Thereafter, the insured made no defense, and judgments grounded on allegations of negligence were entered against him; the district judge entered summary judgment against the company on the theory that it was estopped to assert that the injuries were intentionally caused in view of the determination in the tort judgments that they were negligently caused. The appellate court reversed and remanded.

Cf. Glens Falls Insurance Co. v. American Oil Co., 254 Md. 120, 254 A.2d 658

20. See note 20 on page 848.

By adopting this approach, an insurance company has, in at least some sense, the advantage of two opportunities to avoid liability:

(1969) (tort action against decedent insured's estate alleging decedent negligently drove car into plaintiff's gasoline pumps, damaging them; a few days after the incident, decedent died from other causes under circumstances suggestive of suicide; insurer declined to defend, and default judgment was entered for plaintiff; in later action against insurer, held, remanding for trial, insurer not estopped by the judgment in tort case).

Weis v. State Farm Mutual Automobile Insurance Co., 242 Minn. 141, 64 N.W.2d 366 (1954), 49 A.L.R.2d 688 (1956) (claimant alleged insured "negligently, carelessly, and recklessly, deliberately" ran into rear of claimant's car; insured's statement to insurer declared it was no accident and that he ran into claimant's car deliberately several times; held, no duty to defend in view of insured's admission the incident was not an accident; under these circumstances insurer cannot be bound by any contrary implications of the judgment in the tort case it properly refused to defend).

Burd v. Sussex Mutual Insurance Co., 56 N.J. 383, 267 A.2d 7 (1970) (tort action against homeowner's policy insured with one count alleging that, while intoxicated, he intentionally shot his friend, second count alleging he did so negligently, insurer refused to defend; general verdict and judgment against insured in tort action; trial court entered summary judgment for insured in action on policy; held, reversed; carrier should not be permitted to defend in such a conflict-of-interest situation, and should not be estopped by result in tort action; its covenant to defend is translated into an obligation "to reimburse the insured if it is later adjudged that the claim was one within the policy covenant to pay").

Cf. Sims v. Nationwide Mutual Insurance Co., 247 S.C. 82, 145 S.E.2d 523 (1965) (victim recovered and insured sued insurer; held, insurer not bound by negligence finding; entitled, because of conflict of interest, to refuse to defend and thereafter assert intentional injury exclusion).

See also Stout v. Grain Dealers Mutual Insurance Co., 307 F.2d 521 (4th Cir.1962) and Williams v. Farmers Mutual of Enumclaw, 245 Or. 557, 423 P.2d 518 (1967).

See generally Note, *The Effect of Collateral Estoppel on the Assertion of Coverage Defenses,* 69 Columbia Law Review 1459–1477 (1969); Note, *Insurance Policy Defenses and Collateral Estoppel,* 43 New York University Law Review 140–160 (1968), reprinted 1968 Personal Injury Commentator.

As to the insurer's rights when it does not participate in first lawsuit, *see* Eason v. Weaver, 557 F.2d 1202 at p. 1206 (5th Cir. 1977) (applying Georgia law), where the court observed, "If an insurer with an option to defend chooses to remain aloof from that litigation, it is estopped only as to factual matters essential to the judgment rendered in the first suit, and does not waive any legal defenses it may have as to its liability on the policy."

20. E.g., Miller v. United States Fidelity & Casualty Co., 291 Mass. 445, 197 N.E. 75 (1935) (insurer, while driving on a highway, had an altercation with the driver of another car, sped past him and cut in sharply, causing the other driver to lose control of his car, which then overturned; the claimant sued the insured, alleging negligence only, and recovered a judgment, the company having refused to defend; in this later proceeding on the policy, held that the company was estopped to litigate its contention that the injury was not caused accidentally, since theories of negligence and wilful and wanton conduct were mutually exclusive and the company was bound by the determination in the previous suit that the insured was guilty of negligence).

Cf. B. Roth Tool Co. v. New Amsterdam Casualty Co., 161 Fed. 709 (8th Cir.1908) (insured suffered a judgment against itself in favor of its employee for injuries allegedly due to its negligence in allowing use of metals of explosive nature; held, that when suing its insurer on an employer's liability policy containing a warranty against use of explosives on the property insured was estopped to claim that the injuries were not due to explosives); Gray v. Zurich Insurance Co., 65 Cal.2d 263, 54 Cal.Rptr. 104, 419 P.2d 168 (1966).

See also Stefus v. London & Lancashire Indemnity Co. of America, 111 N.J.L. 6, 166 A. 339 (Err. & App.1933) (10–to–4 decision), *cert. denied* 290 U.S. 657, 54 S.Ct. 73, 78 L.Ed. 569 (1933) (liability insurer bound by tort action record indicating judgment on a claim of negligence and recklessness in starting car while plaintiff was on running board; insurer precluded from contending injury was wilfully caused), which, however, can no longer be taken as authoritative on this point in view of the comments in Burd v. Sussex Mutual Life Insur-

initially conducting the defense of the tort claim against the insured and, if unsuccessful in that attempt, then trying to prevail on the policy defense in a garnishment proceeding or an independent suit on the policy. This is usually appropriate, however, because each opportunity is concerned with an independent defense and the two cannot be joined in one civil action unless a court is prepared to allow all three parties — insurer, insured, and tort claimant — to participate openly.

Comment

Allowing an insurer to continue to control and direct an insured's defense frequently is not a satisfactory approach from the vantage point of the insured. In this context, even though the insured has been informed and agreed to the arrangement, a conflict of interests may still influence the way the insured's defense is conducted. For example, an insurer, perceiving that there is a coverage defense, may limit the authority of the defense attorney to reach a settlement of the tort claim — that is, the insurer may authorize lower amounts for settlement than would be the case if it were not relying in part upon the opportunity for a policy defense. Indeed, in some instances — even when the conflicting interests have been fully disclosed and the insured has agreed to the approach proposed by the insurer — an insurer's failure to instruct the attorney representing the insured to aggressively pursue settlement possibilities in this context might even support a determination that the insurer's conduct was sufficiently misleading to the insured so as to vitiate a nonwaiver agreement.[21] Furthermore, it could also lead to a finding that the company was not adequately representing the insured's interests, and therefore was liable for a judgment in excess of the applicable policy limits.[22]

(4) Declaratory Judgment Proceeding

An insurer that wants to assert a coverage defense often files a declaratory judgment proceeding. This approach typically will be employed by an insurer that is asserting not merely that a conflict of interests prevents its fulfilling a duty of defense in the usual way, but more broadly that there is no coverage and therefore there is no duty to provide a defense.[23] If the insurer prevails in the declaratory action,

ance Company, 56 N.J. 383, 267 A.2d 7 (1970).

Also see Prahm v. Rupp Construction Company, 277 N.W.2d 389 (Minn.1979).

21. *Cf.* Home Indemnity Co. v. Williamson, 183 F.2d 572 (5th Cir.1950).

22. See the discussion in § 7.8, below.

23. See, e.g. American Family Insurance Company v. Dewald, 597 F.2d 1148 (8th Cir.1979) (applying North Dakota law); Di Orio v. New Jersey Manufacturers Insurance Company, 79 N.J. 257, 398 A.2d 1274 (1979); Thornton v. Paul, 74 Ill.2d 132, 23 Ill.Dec. 541, 384 N.E.2d 335 (1978); Smith v. North River Insurance Co., 360 So.2d 313 (Ala.1978).

Cf. Reisen v. Aetna Life and Casualty Company, 225 Va. 327, 302 S.E.2d 529 (1983), Aetna Casualty & Surety v. Freyer, 89 Ill.App.3d 617, 44 Ill.Dec. 791, 411 N.E.2d 1157 (1st Dist.1980).

When a policy coverage defense is in dispute, ordinarily an insurance company would prefer to have an immediate determination of the issue of coverage.

thereafter the insurer has no obligation to pay a tort judgment against the insured and generally is not liable for the insured's costs of defending against the tort claim.[24]

Frequently, however, an insurer that seeks a declaratory judgment in this context will encounter problems.[25] Among the potential difficulties, one of the most significant is that such proceedings take time. This is especially true when it is permissible to have issues that involve factual questions tried to a jury in declaratory proceedings.[26] More-

See generally, Comment, *An Insurer's Dilemma: Legal Consequences of Contested Coverage,* 28 South Dakota Law Review 357–375 at pp. 372–372 (1983); Note, *Use of the declaratory judgment to determine a liability insurer's duty to defend—conflict of interests,* 41 Indiana Law Journal 87–106 (1965).

An insurer is not obliged to seek a resolution of conflict problem by a declaratory proceeding. American Employers' Insurance Company v. Crawford, 87 N.M. 375, 533 P.2d 1203 (1975).

24. A conclusion in regard to the obligation to provide a defense does not invariably "echo" the determination of the coverage question because the obligation to provide a defense has been recognized to be "broader" — that is, it encompasses the defense in some instances in which an insurer is not obligated to provide indemnification. See the discussion of the obligation to defend in § 9.1, below.

25. *Cf.* the comment in Zurich Insurance Company v. Rombough, 384 Mich. 228, 180 N.W.2d 775 at p. 778 (1970), that the tort case should not have been stopped while the insurer, "a nonparty" to the tort suit, contested its obligation to defend the insured. The court urged that "[t]he declaratory judgment procedure was not intended as a weapon to be used against the plaintiff in this manner." *Ibid.*

See, e.g., Central Surety & Insurance Corporation v. Anderson, 445 S.W.2d 514 (Tex.1969) (trial court declared insurer obligated to defend and to pay any judgment that might be rendered against insureds; *held* that insofar as judgment declared insurer would be obligated to pay any judgment rendered against insured, it was an advisory opinion prohibited by the state constitution). Also see the subsequent opinion in this case reported at 446 S.W.2d 897 (Tex.App., Fort Worth, 1969).

Cf. the comment in Burd v. Sussex Mutual Insurance Company, 56 N.J. 383, 267 A.2d 7 at p. 11 (1970) that "a declaratory judgment proceeding may be brought in advance of the tort trial" "unless for special reasons it would be unfair to do so

* * *." Unfairness in this context could arise from numerous factors, including (1) prejudice to the insured resulting from disclosures in such a proceeding, and (2) delay for the third party.

Also see Tennessee Farmers Mutual Insurance Co. v. Hammond, 200 Tenn. 106, 290 S.W.2d 860 (1956) (suit in chancery by a liability insurance company for declaratory judgment to determine whether it was subject to liability in excess of policy limits; decree sustaining a plea in abatement affirmed on the theory that the plaintiff insurance company was anticipating a tort action against it for alleged lack of good faith, which involved a fact issue, and that it was appropriate for the lower court to refuse to entertain a suit when a disputed issue of fact was determinative of the rights of the parties, the tort action was subsequently filed in the circuit court of the same county and was tried before a jury).

The opinion in the *Hammond* case might arguably be read as precluding the use of declaratory proceedings with respect to any claim of liability in excess of policy limits, since an issue of bad faith or negligence is always involved. It need not be read so broadly, however, and on principle it would seem that should not be the rule.

See generally, J. Patrick Browne, *The Demise of the Declaratory Judgment Action as a Device for Testing the Insurer's Duty to Defend: A Postcript,* 24 Cleveland State Law Review 18–32 at pp. 25–26 (1974).

26. See Uniform Declaratory Judgments Act 9; Declaratory Judgment Act, 28 U.S.C.A. §§ 2201–2202 (1958); Annotation, *Application of declaratory judgment acts to questions in respect of insurance policies,* 142 A.L.R. 8–76 at p. 58 (1943).

The original federal act provided for the submission of issues of fact to a jury on interrogatories. Declaratory Judgment Act ch. 512, 48 Stat. 955 (1934). This provision was omitted in the revision of the code as being covered by Rule 49 of the Federal Rules of Civil Procedure. *Reviser's Note* to 28 U.S.C.A. § 2202.

over, even when the declaratory action is before a court, judges have indicated that the determination of the coverage question must await the resolution of issues in the tort suit.[27]

The dilemma for an insurer that seeks to have a coverage question determined by a declaratory judgment may become particularly acute when such an action does not justify a suspension of the proceedings relating to the third party's claim against the insured. Consequently, an insurer, as well as the insured, often will be required to make decisions about what role the insurer should have and whether the insurer should participate in the possible settlement of the tort claim or the defense of the tort suit against its insured before the declaratory proceedings can be concluded.

Caveat. Declaratory judgment proceedings should not be distorted by allowing them to be used as an instrument for procedural "fencing" with an insured — that is, to secure delay, to affect the choice of a forum, or to affect the question whether the issue will be tried by a jury.[28]

Arbitration of the Coverage Question

Arbitration affords insurers and insureds another approach to addressing various situations that involve conflicting interests. An insurer and insured could, for example, agree to submit the question of

Also see Holloway v. Nationwide Mutual Insurance Company, 376 So.2d 690 (Ala. 1979).

In American Home Assurance Company v. Evans, 791 F.2d 61 at p. 64 (6th Cir. 1986), the court denied a request for a declaratory judgment by a medical malpractice insurer. Judge Merritt commented:

"The Declaratory Judgment Act allows the federal courts, in the exercise of sound discretion, to depart from their usual practice of refusing to issue advisory opinions. Where complex factual issues are present and the action parallels a state court action arising from the same facts and where alternative remedies are available, declaratory judgment is inappropriate. [citations omitted]. See also Green v. Mansour, 474 U.S. 64, 106 S.Ct. 423, 428, 88 L.Ed.2d 371 (1985) (Declaratory Judgment Act confers discretion on courts, not right on litigants so that '[t]he propriety of issuing a declaratory judgment may depend on equitable considerations * * * and is also "informed by the teachings and experience concerning the functions and extent of federal judicial power".')"

27. *Cf.* Northland Insurance Company v. Heck's Service Company, Inc., 620 F.Supp. 107 at p. 108 (E.D.Ark.1985),

where the court commented "that resolution of the issue of whether coverage for any property damage exists must await the outcome of Eckler's [the third party] suit against Heck's."

In Murphy v. Urso, 88 Ill.2d 444, 58 Ill. Dec. 828 at p. 833, 430 N.E.2d 1079 at p. 1084 (1981), the court concluded that while a declaratory judgment action is acceptable when the coverage questions are separable from those at issue in the tort suit, so that a collateral proceeding prejudices no party, "the situation changes when the issues are substantially the same." The court further observed that the "Declaratory judgment would be only a forerunner of the accident trial, and would resolve nothing."

28. *Cf.* Annotation, *Application of declaratory judgment acts to questions in respect of insurance policies,* 142 A.L.R. 8–76 at p. 58 (1943).

Also see Annotation, *Declaratory Issue as to negligence as a proper subject of declaratory judgment action,* 28 A.L.R.2d 957–961 (1953), suggesting that even though there is nothing in the Uniform Declaratory Judgments Act to exclude declaratory proceedings involving fact issues, yet the discretion of the court to deny declaratory relief has generally been thought to exclude such relief in "ordinary negligence cases."

a coverage defense for resolution by an arbitrator. The adjudication by arbitration is comparable to the result of a declaratory proceeding in a court. The difference is that an arbitrator usually is able to provide a resolution of the questions at issue within weeks, rather than the months or years that will be encountered in many courts. And once the arbitration award is rendered, the insurance company's position vis-a-vis its insured is established. If the arbitration sustains the coverage defense, the insurer has no further interest in the tort claim against the insured: the individual is not insured for purposes of the matter at issue. On the other hand, if the arbitration results in a decision that the coverage defense is not valid, the conflict of interests is eliminated. Thereafter, the insurer's motivations to serve the interests of its insured in relation to the third party claimant are the same as exist in regard to any other liability insurance situation.

(5) Inclusion of the Insurer as a Party in the Tort Suit

Another approach to arranging for an adjudication of a coverage question is to expand the scope of the tort suit by including the insurer as a party and providing for the resolution of the additional issues in that court. This might be brought about by an insurer's request for leave to intervene,[29] by the insured's moving to join the insurer,[30] or by joinder of the insurer at the instance of the third-party claimant.[31]

There are numerous conflict of interests situations in which joinder of the third party claimant, the insured, and the insurer in a suit is warranted on the rationale that every individual or entity whose interests would be affected by that adjudication should be parties to such an action.[32] In some instances, such joinder could even be justified in a declaratory judgment proceeding. For example, whenever the

---

29. *Cf.* Smith v. Earp, 449 F.Supp. 503 (W.D.Ky.1978) (involving no-fault motor vehicle insurance).

Also see State ex rel. State Farm Mutual Automobile Insurance Co. v. Craig, 364 S.W.2d 343 (Mo.App.1963), 95 A.L.R.2d 1321 (1964) (insurer under uninsured motorist coverage permitted to intervene in suit between its insured and an uninsured motorist who had defaulted); Doe v. Moss, 120 Ga.App. 762, 172 S.E.2d 321 (1969) (under Georgia statute, insurer permitted to intervene in action against uninsured motorist without conceding coverage or liability).

30. *Cf.* Jenkins v. General Accident Fire and Life Assurance Corp., 349 Mass. 699, 212 N.E.2d 464 (1965) (insurer's argument it had no duty to settle a claim it refused to defend held to be without merit; suit by victim against insured; insured allowed to implead insurer).

Also see the discussion of joinder under Rule 19 of the Federal Rules of Civil Procedure in Childers v. Eastern Foam Products,

Inc., 94 F.R.D. 53 at pp. 57–58 (N.D.Ga. 1982).

31. The general rule is that unless there is an applicable statutory provision, such as a direct action statute, an insurance company may not be sued in the original law suit. See, e.g. White v. Goodville Mutual Casualty Company, 226 Kan. 191, 596 P.2d 1229 (1979).

However, several jurisdictions permit such joinder. See, e.g. Clemons v. Flagler Hospital, Inc., 385 So.2d 1134 (Fla.App. 5th Dist.1980).

In some circumstances, it might even be practical and appropriate to use declaratory proceedings to adjudicate both the tort claim and the coverage issue.

32. See, e.g. Keel v. MFA Insurance Company, 553 P.2d 153 at p. 158 (Okl.1976) (permissible to join uninsured motorist insurer as a party defendant in a suit against the alleged tortfeasor who was not insured).

factual issues that are relevant to the insurer's liability are either the same or directly related to questions which will be at issue in the tort case (such as the commission of an intentional tort [33] or the operation of a motor vehicle while under the influence of drugs), a persuasive case can be made for including both the insured and the third party claimants as parties in the insurer's declaratory action. And, obviously, if such questions will be adjudicated in the tort suit, there is considerable justification for avoiding a second litigation of the same questions in connection with a subsequent resolution of a coverage defense.

When the joinder of the third party claimant, the insured, and the insurer is at the instance of the insurance company or the insured, the force of the reasons that usually preclude such joinder are considerably diminished because the rule which normally applies is primarily designed for their protection, rather than for the third party plaintiff. Furthermore, the considerations accounting for the customary refusal of courts to allow an insurance company to be joined as a party to the tort suit are at least partially offset in situations that involve a conflict of interests between the insurer and the insured that will otherwise necessitate a second adjudication of the same or related issues. In some circumstances, joinder may be facilitated if the insured and the insurer can agree to have the coverage issues resolved by the judge, even though other aspects of the case may be submitted to a jury. This technique is not likely to be useful, however, when the same fact issue affects both the tort action and the coverage question, as is true, for example, of a potential claim of intentional tort.

(6) Termination of the Insurer's Right to Select the Defense Counsel and to Direct the Defense: The Insured's Right to Select Defense Counsel

When a conflict of interests exists, an insured may seek to terminate or suspend the insurer's right to select the defense counsel or to direct the defense. For example, whenever an insurer decides that it wants to have a coverage defense adjudicated after the tort claim is resolved, the question arises as to whether it is appropriate to then permit the insured to select an attorney to conduct the defense to the tort claim.[34] Although this issue has not been considered by the courts

Cf. 20 APPLEMAN, INSURANCE LAW & PRACTICE (1963), at pp. 166–168.

33. See the discussion of intentional torts in § 7.6(b), above. Also consider the discussion of coverage for intentional torts in Chapter 5, above.

34. See, e.g. Fireman's Fund Insurance Company v. Waste Management of Wisconsin, Inc., 777 F.2d 366 at pp. 369–370 (7th Cir.1985) (insured entitled to select independent counsel subject to the approval of the insurer); Outboard Marine Corp. v. Liberty Mutual Insurance Company, 536 F.2d 730 at p. 737 (7th Cir.1976) (applying California law); Nike, Inc. v. Atlantic Mutual Insurance Company, 578 F.Supp. 948 (N.D.Cal.1983).

This approach could be produced by allowing the company to refuse to defend for the insured (again with the expectation of holding the company liable for costs of defense if its policy defense finally fails).

But see Pekin Insurance Company v. Home Insurance Company, 134 Ill.App.3d 31, 89 Ill.Dec. 72, 479 N.E.2d 1078 (1st Dist., Div. 5, 1985), *appeal denied* (1985),

in most states, the judicial decisions in several states (including California, Illinois, and New York) provide unqualified holdings on this question.[35] The conclusion of the Illinois Supreme Court is very representative of these opinions: absent the acceptance by the insured of the defense tendered by insurer after a full disclosure of a conflict of interest or the waiver of the defense by the insurer, an insured "has the right to be defended in the personal injury case by an attorney of his

defense with a reservation of rights whereby the insurer indicated it neither waived any right nor admitted any obligation for liability of the insured's employer, the Chicago White Sox (who sought to assert that the conflict of interest entitled them to independent counsel).

35. *Arkansas.* Northland Insurance Company v. Heck's Service Company, 620 F.Supp. 107 (E.D.Ark.1985).

California. San Diego Navy Federal Credit Union v. Cumis Insurance Society, 162 Cal.App.3d 358 at p. 375, 208 Cal.Rptr. 494 at p. 506 (4th Dist., Div. 1, 1984).

Also see Previews, Inc. v. California Union Insurance Company, 640 F.2d 1026 at p. 1028 (9th Cir.1981) (applying California law); Outboard Marine Corp. v. Liberty Mutual Insurance Co., 536 F.2d 730 at p. 737 (7th Cir.1976) (applying California law); Bogard v. Employers Casualty Company, 164 Cal.App.3d 602, 210 Cal.Rptr. 578 (2d Dist., Div. 3, 1985); Purdy v. Pacific Automobile Insurance Company, 157 Cal.App.3d 59, 203 Cal.Rptr. 524 (2d Dist., Div. 1, 1984); Executive Aviation, Inc. v. National Insurance Underwriters, 16 Cal. App.3d 799 at pp. 808–810, 94 Cal.Rptr. 347 at p. 354 (1st Dist., Div. 2, 1971).

Cf. Outboard Marine Corp. v. Liberty Mutual Insurance Company, 536 F.2d 730 at p. 737 (7th Cir.1976) (applying California law); Nike, Inc. v. Atlantic Mutual Insurance Company, 578 F.Supp. 948 (N.D.Cal. 1983).

Illinois. Murphy v. Urso, 88 Ill.2d 444, 58 Ill.Dec. 828, 430 N.E.2d 1079 at p. 1082 (1981) ("An insurer must decline to defend where there is a conflict of interest * * *."); Maryland Casualty Company v. Peppers, 64 Ill.2d 187, 355 N.E.2d 24 (1976). Also see Illinois decision cited in the following footnote.

But see Pekin Insurance Company v. Home Insurance Company, 134 Ill.App.3d 31, 89 Ill.Dec. 72, 479 N.E.2d 1078 (1st Dist., 5th Div., 1985) [Defense with a reservation of rights whereby the insurer indicated it neither waived any right nor admitted any obligation for liability of the

insured's employer, the Chicago White Sox (who sought to assert the conflict of interests entitled them to independent counsel)].

Maryland. Brohawn v. Transamerican Insurance Co., 276 Md. 396, 347 A.2d 842 (1975).

Massachusetts. Cf. Magoun v. Liberty Mutual Insurance Company, 346 Mass. 677, 195 N.E.2d 514 (1964) (with insurer's acquiescence, insured employed his own counsel, refusing to permit insurer to proceed under an attempted reservation of rights; insurer held liable for fee of insured's counsel as part of expense of defending).

New York. Public Service Mutual Insurance Company v. Goldfarb, 53 N.Y.2d 392, 442 N.Y.S.2d 422, 425 N.E.2d 810 (1981); Baron v. Home Insurance Company, 112 A.D.2d 391, 492 N.Y.S.2d 50 (2d Dept.1985).

Also see Prashker v. United States Guarantee Company, 1 N.Y.2d 584 at p. 593, 154 N.Y.S.2d 910 at p. 917, 136 N.E.2d 871 at p. 876 (1956); Klien v. Salama, 545 F.Supp. 175 (E.D.N.Y.1982).

Also consider Fireman's Fund Insurance Company v. Waste Management of Wisconsin, Inc., 777 F.2d 366 at pp. 369–370 (7th Cir.1985) (insured entitled to select independent counsel subject to the approval of the insurer).

Right of the Insurer to Participate in the Selection of Defense Counsel. When the insurance policy provides that the insurer is not obligated to pay for defense counsel unless it consents to the choice of counsel, "[t]he participation of an insurer in the selection process does not automatically taint the independence of chosen counsel." New York State Urban Development Corporation v. VSL Corporation, 738 F.2d 61 at p. 66 (2d Cir.1984) (applying New York law). In this case, the insured was a substantial corporation, which had purchased both professional liability ($2,000,000) and comprehensive general liability policies ($10,000,000). The court concluded that such a provision is not contrary to public policy.

own choice who shall have the right to control the conduct of the case." [36]

When an insurer has a duty to defend in a situation that involves a significant conflict of interests, the insurer should be obligated to discharge its contractual obligation to furnish the insured with a defense by reimbursing the insured for the reasonable expenses of defending the action, both the fees charged by an attorney and other costs incurred in conducting the defense.[37] However, once an insured has exercised the right to select a defense attorney, the subsequent

36. Maryland Casualty Company v. Peppers, 64 Ill.2d 187, 355 N.E.2d 24 at p. 31 (1976).

Also see Clemmons v. Travelers Insurance Company, 88 Ill.2d 469, 58 Ill.Dec. 853, 430 N.E.2d 1104 (1981); Nandorf, Inc. v. CNA Insurance Companies, 134 Ill.App. 3d 134, 88 Ill.Dec. 968, 479 N.E.2d 988 (1st Dist., 1st Div., 1985), *petition for leave to appeal, denied* (1985).

37. *Arkansas.* Northland Insurance Company v. Heck's Service Company, 620 F.Supp. 107 (E.D.Ark.1985).

California. Bogard v. Employers Casualty Company, 164 Cal.App.3d 602, 210 Cal. Rptr. 578 (2d Dist., Div. 3, 1985); San Diego Navy Federal Credit Union v. Cumis Insurance Society, 162 Cal.App.3d 358 at p. 375, 208 Cal.Rptr. 494 at p. 506 (4th Dist., Div. 1, 1985); Purdy v. Pacific Automobile Insurance Company, 157 Cal.App.3d 59 at p. 76, 203 Cal.Rptr. 524 at p. 534 (2d Dist., Div. 7, 1984); Executive Aviation, Inc. v. National Insurance Underwriters, 16 Cal. App.3d 799 at p. 810, 94 Cal.Rptr. 347 at p. 354 (1st Dist., Div. 2, 1971).

But cf. Zieman Manufacturing Company v. St. Paul Insurance Marine Company, 724 F.2d 1343 at p. 1346 (9th Cir.1983).

Illinois. Thornton v. Paul, 74 Ill.2d 132, 23 Ill.Dec. 541, 384 N.E.2d 335 (1978); Nandorf, Inc. v. CNA Insurance Companies, 134 Ill.App.3d 134, 88 Ill.Dec. 968, 479 N.E.2d 988 (1st Dist.1985).

Maryland. Brohawn v. Transamerican Insurance Co., 276 Md. 396, 347 A.2d 842 (1975).

Massachusetts. Cf. Magoun v. Liberty Mutual Insurance Company, 346 Mass. 677, 195 N.E.2d 514 (1964).

Minnesota. Prahm v. Rupp Construction Company, 277 N.W.2d 389 (Minn. 1979). Also see United States Fidelity & Guaranty Co. v. Louis A. Roser Co., 585 F.2d 932 (8th Cir.1978).

Missouri. Howard v. Russell Stover Candies, Inc., 649 F.2d 620 at p. 625 (8th Cir.1981) (applying Missouri law).

New Jersey. Also see Burd v. Sussex Mutual Insurance Co., 56 N.J. 383, 267 A.2d 7 (1970).

New Mexico. Also see Satterwhite v. Stolz, 79 N.M. 320, 442 P.2d 810 (1968) (applying Texas law).

New York. Public Service Mutual Insurance Company v. Goldfarb, 53 N.Y.2d 392, 442 N.Y.S.2d 422, 425 N.E.2d 810 (1981); Baron v. Home Insurance Company, 112 A.D.2d 391, 492 N.Y.S.2d 50 (1985).

In New York Urban Development Corp. v. VSL Corporation, 563 F.Supp. 187 at p. 191 (S.D.N.Y.1983), concluded that where "the defense is to be presented by independent counsel representing both the insured and insurer, as in this instance, the cases indicate that the expense of only the one attorney is to be assumed by the insurer" and therefore the insurer would not be responsible for the expenses incurred by legal counsel, who had already represented the insured in various proceedings and would be instructed to "maintain a watchful eye" in order to keep the insured informed. Also see the subsequent opinion of the Court of Appeals reported at 738 F.2d 61 (2d Cir.1984).

Cf. Prashker v. United States Guarantee Co., 1 N.Y.2d 584 at p. 593, 154 N.Y.S.2d 910 at p. 917, 136 N.E.2d 871 at p. 876 (1956), observing that in another situation of conflicting interest, "the selection of the attorneys to represent the assureds should be made by them rather than by the insurance company, which should remain liable for the payment of the reasonable value of the services of whatever attorneys the assureds select."

In Penn Aluminum v. Aetna Casualty and Surety Company, 61 A.D.2d 1119, 402 N.Y.S.2d 877 (4th Dept.1978), the court held that an insured is not entitled to an award of attorney fees incurred in the pursuit of a declaratory judgment against an insurer.

Ohio. State Farm Fire & Casualty Company v. Pildner, 40 Ohio St.2d 101, 321 N.E.2d 600 (1974).

resolution of the matter may affect the insured's right to be reimbursed for the expenses of the defense — that is, the insured's right to reimbursement is particularly clear in some circumstances and less evident in others.

If the insured's defense prevails in the adjudication of the tort claim and it is later determined that coverage was applicable, the right to reimbursement is clear. This conclusion follows from an application of the proposition that generally an insurer is required to defend an insured even when the tort claim is groundless. Even if it is later determined that the coverage did not apply to the claim (or to all claims) asserted, reimbursement may be allowed because the insurer's obligation to provide a defense is often broader in scope than the obligation to pay damages on behalf of the insured.[38]

Also, when the insured does not prevail in the litigation with the third party, the insured may be entitled to be reimbursed for the defense expenses. If the insured subsequently prevails in an adjudication between the insurer and the insured of the coverage defense, the insured's right to recover the defense expenses, under current statutes and precedents, usually includes the fee for the attorney the insured engages for both matters.

If an insured settles the third party's claim, the right to reimbursement is not automatic, for either the legal expenses or the amount of the settlement (subject to the coverage limits). Although an insured generally will be entitled to recover attorney's fees and costs incurred in the course of settling a tort claim that is within the scope of the applicable insurance coverage, the insurer is entitled to an adjudication of the coverage questions.[39]

Comment

If an insurer confronted with a conflict of interest nevertheless seeks to maintain control over the defense of a suit against its insured, it is an appropriate situation for either an application of the doctrine of election or the imposition of an estoppel to preclude the insurer from subsequently raising the matter which gave rise to the conflict of interest. It is unreasonable for an insurer to both have the advantage of controlling the litigation (through an attorney selected, instructed, and paid by the company) and the right to thereafter contest liability. The potential for "overreaching" in such circumstances is sufficiently significant to justify the imposition of a limited choice upon the insurer that precludes such conduct.[40] Thus, whenever a significant conflict of

---

But see Motorists Mutual Insurance Company v. Trainor, 33 Ohio St.2d 41, 294 N.E.2d 874 (1973).

Virginia. But see Norman v. Insurance Company of North America, 218 Va. 718, 239 S.E.2d 902 (1978).

38. See § 9.1, below.

39. See, e.g., Nike, Inc. v. Atlantic Mutual Insurance Company, 578 F.Supp. 948 (N.D.Cal.1983).

40. See generally §§ 6.2–6.4 and § 6.6(a), above.

interests is present, there is a compelling case for suspending the insurer's control of the defense unless the insurer surrenders its right to subsequently raise the matter that produced the conflict of interests.

(7) Participation of Lawyers Selected by Both the Insured and the Insurer

When an insured exercises the right to select the defense counsel and to provide the directions for that attorney,[41] the insurer is still entitled to have its interests represented by legal counsel. As stated by the Supreme Court of Illinois in one of the landmark decisions on this question, Maryland Casualty Company v. Peppers, the insurer "is entitled to have an attorney of its choosing participate in all phases" of the suit resolving the tort claim against the insured.[42]

The role of a defense lawyer representing the insurer in such a case is, at best, unclear. As a noted defense counsel has observed, "The role of a second lawyer with clearly antagonistic interests to the insured is uncertain and seems inappropriate." [43] Even if the insurer's attorney is entitled to be present, the Illinois Supreme Court also observed that the defense counsel selected by the insured is almost certainly the final arbiter of all defense decisions concerning the trial.[44] Furthermore, ultimately both the rights and the role of the insurer's counsel to participate is subject to the discretion and the directions of the trial court.[45]

§ 7.6(e)   Resolution of the Tort Claim and the Insured's Right to Indemnification

When an insured has asserted the right to control the defense to a tort claim, the insured's right to indemnification from a liability insurer following the resolution of the tort claim may be affected by the terms of the settlement or an adjudication of the claim against the insured.

Whenever a conflict of interests exists, the attorney who represents the insured should remain completely free to aggressively pursue the settlement of the claim against the insured.[1] If a settlement is possible,

---

41. See the discussion in the preceding subsection.

42. Maryland Casualty Company v. Peppers, 64 Ill.2d 187, 355 N.E.2d 24 at p. 31 (1976).

43. Ronald E. Mallen, *A New Definition of Insurance Defense Counsel*, 1986 Insurance Counsel Defense Journal 108–123 at p. 119.

44. Maryland Casualty Company v. Peppers, 64 Ill.2d 187 at p. 199, 355 N.E.2d 24 at p. 31 (1976).

45. *Cf.* Chemprene, Inc. v. X-Tyal International Corp., 55 N.Y.2d 900, 449 N.Y.S.2d 23, 433 N.E.2d 1271 (1982) (holding that where the insured's liability insur-

ance covered claims of the type presented by a counterclaim to a suit initiated by the insured and the insurer appointed counsel to defend the counterclaim, it was within the trial court's discretion to compel insured to select one attorney to represent him — that is, it was not an abuse of discretion to refuse to require plaintiff to select one counsel and any conflicts by virtue of multiple counsel could be resolved during course of litigation).

§ 7.6(e)

1. Any constraints or limitations imposed by an insurer — beyond that dictated by the coverage limits — present questions of considerable import in regard to subse-

either for an amount within the coverage limits or with a contribution of some amount by the insured, the insured should be offered the opportunity to take advantage of the opportunity to resolve the matter. Of course, in some circumstances, a settlement will not be arranged and the tort suit will be adjudicated. The different outcomes for the tort claim that are possible include the following:

1. Settlement payment by the insurer with an agreement to abandon the coverage question.

2. Settlement payment by the insured, and

   (a) the insured prevails in a subsequent adjudication of the coverage question; or

   (b) the insurer prevails in a subsequent adjudication of the coverage question.

3. No settlement, and the insured prevails in the litigation of the third party's tort claim.

4. No settlement, the third party's tort suit results in a judgment within the liability coverage limits, and

   (a) the insured prevails in a subsequent adjudication of the coverage question; or

   (b) the insurer prevails in a subsequent adjudication of the coverage question.

5. No settlement, the third party claimant's tort suit results in a judgment in excess of liability coverage limits, and

   (a) The insured prevails in a subsequent adjudication of the coverage question.

   (b) The insurer prevails in a subsequent adjudication of the coverage question.

The insurer's obligation to the insured in regard to each of these possibilities is considered in the remainder of this section.

(1) Settlement Payment by the Insurer and Waiver of the Coverage Defense

A settlement payment by the insurer to the third party claimant together with an agreement to waive the possible coverage defense constitutes a final resolution of the entire matter — that is, the tort claim and the coverage question, for all parties. It seems most likely to be a preferred course for an insurer when the projected litigation costs for the defense exceed the proposed settlement costs. Also, an insurer may view this as an attractive course, even if the required payout is

quent claims for "coverage" in excess of the liability limits.

Cf. Burd v. Sussex Mutual Insurance Co., 56 N.J. 383, 267 A.2d 7 (1970); Public National Insurance Co. v. Wheat, 100 Ga.App. 695, 112 S.E.2d 194 (1959).

Also see H.C. Price Company v. Compass Insurance Company, 483 F.Supp. 171 (N.D.Tex., Dallas, 1980); Public National Insurance Co. v. Wheat, 100 Ga.App. 695, 112 S.E.2d 194 (1959); Annotation, 27 A.L.R.3d 350–378 (1969).

higher, because a continuing relationship with the insured is also often a matter of some importance to the insurer.

(2) Settlement Payment by the Insured

Following a settlement payment by the insured to resolve the third party's tort claim, an adjudication of the coverage question in favor of the insured means that the insurer is liable for the amount of the settlement, subject to the coverage limits,[2] and, at least in some circumstances, to proof that the settlement was reasonable. In addition, the insurer should also be liable for the costs and expenses incident to reaching the settlement with the third party (as these are appropriately associated with the provision of the defense for the insured), where, as is usually true, a duty to defend is a part of the coverage of the liability insurance policy. A claim by the insured to recover the expenses incurred in connection with securing an adjudication of the coverage question will usually depend upon court decisions interpreting judicial precedents founded on obligations of good faith and fair dealing.[3]

In the event the insurer prevails in the determination of the coverage question, the insured has no coverage so that the settlement costs and litigation expenses are appropriately borne by the insured.[4]

(3) Insured Prevails in Adjudication of the Tort Claim

If there is no settlement and the insured prevails in the adjudication of the tort claim, the only question that remains is the right of the insured to recover the litigation expenses. When the coverage issue is resolved in favor of the insured, the right to recover the costs incident to the defense of the tort claim is relatively clear.[5] In this type of case, the right to recover costs incurred in securing an adjudication of the coverage question(s) usually depends upon statute.[6] Of course, if the

---

2. *Cf.* State Farm Mut. Automobile Insurance Co. v. Coughran, 303 U.S. 485, 58 S.Ct. 670, 82 L.Ed. 970 (1938).

3. Such a claim is essentially comparable to a claim for attorney fees and costs in a suit against an insurer on a first-part coverage (fire insurance, for example). *Cf.* Sawson v. Transamerica Insurance Company, 30 Cal.3d 220, 178 Cal.Rptr. 343, 636 P.2d 32 (1981).

Also see Parks v. Colonial Penn Insurance Company, 98 N.J. 42, 484 A.2d 4 (1984); Miller v. Shugart, 316 N.W.2d 729 (Minn.1982).

4. *Cf.* Farmers Insurance Company of Arizona v. Vagnozzi, 138 Ariz. 443, 675 P.2d 703 (En Banc, 1983).

5. *Cf.* Public National Insurance Co. v. Wheat, 100 Ga.App. 695, 112 S.E.2d 194 (1959) (company held estopped by the judgment in the tort suit that it refused to defend; it might have been inferred from

the evidence that the insured was honest, but mistaken in his statement that he was driving, having been severely intoxicated at the time of the incident).

Also cf. Maryland Casualty Company v. Peppers, 64 Ill.2d 187, 355 N.E.2d 24 at p. 31 (1976), where the court observed that "Absent the acceptance of the defense by Peppers [after full disclosure to him of the conflicting interests] or the waiver [of the coverage defense] by St. Paul, . . . St. Paul is entitled to have an attorney of its choosing participate in all phases of this litigation subject to the control of the case by Pepper's attorney, and *St. Paul is not barred from subsequently raising the defense of noncoverage in a suit on the policy.*" (Emphasis added).

6. See, e.g., Murphy v. Urso, 88 Ill.2d 444, 58 Ill.Dec. 828, 430 N.E.2d 1079 (1981); Burnett v. Western Pacific Insurance Co., 255 Or. 547, 469 P.2d 602 (1970).

denial of coverage by the insurer is sustained, there is little, if any,[7] basis for a recovery of the litigation costs.

(4) and (5) Adjudication of the Tort Claim in Favor of the Third Party Claimant

If the third party claimant's tort suit results in a judgment for an amount that is within the coverage limits, the possibilities in regard to the resolution of the coverage questions are the same ones which are outlined in the preceding paragraph. If the insured prevails, the insured would clearly be entitled to a recovery of the amount of such a judgment and the costs of defending the tort suit. In addition, a basis may exist for allowing the insured to recover consequential damages (including the litigation costs incurred in the suit against the insurer for the determination of the coverage question).[8]

If the third party claimant's tort suit results in liability in excess of policy limits, the questions in many respects are comparable to those which are considered in Section 7.8, below. However, one notable characteristic differentiates these cases: the insured has asserted the right to select defense counsel because of the conflict of interests. Therefore, any right of the insured to recover for an amount in excess of the coverage limits must be predicated on grounds which are somewhat different from those which have been articulated in many of the opinions rendered in other circumstances. In this context, it seems relatively clear that a liability insurer's responsibility for damages in excess of the coverage limits is only warranted when the insured can show that the insurer was responsible for the failure to reach a settlement with the third party claimant. In most instances, it is likely that this can only be demonstrated when the insured can prove not only that the insurer rejected an opportunity to settle within the coverage limits, but also that the insured's lack of resources precluded a settlement.

Estoppel or Issue Preclusion

The resolution of a tort claim in favor of a third party claimant may lead to questions about whether that judgment forecloses an insurer from relitigating matters decided in the tort suit.

---

7. *Cf.* B. Roth Tool Co. v. New Amsterdam Casualty Co., 161 Fed. 709 (8th Cir.1908) (insured suffered a judgment against itself in favor of its employee for injuries allegedly due to its negligence in allowing use of metals of explosive nature; *held,* that when suing its insurer on an employer's liability policy containing a warranty against use of explosives on the property, insured was estopped to claim that the injuries were not due to explosives).

8. See, e.g. Ervin v. Sears, Roebuck and Company, 127 Ill.App.3d 982, 82 Ill.Dec. 709, 469 N.E.2d 243 (5th Dist.1984); Nandorf, Inc. v. CNA Insurance Companies, 134 Ill.App.3d 134, 88 Ill.Dec. 968, 479 N.E.2d 988 (1st Dist., Div. 1 1985).

Also see Coblenty v. American Surety Company of New York, 416 F.2d 1059 (5th Cir. 1969).

When an insurer has selected the defense attorney and provided direction for the defense, the case for issue preclusion is very persuasive. However, if the insurer was not involved either as a party in the tort litigation or in the capacity of providing a defense for the insured (typically as a consequence of selecting, instructing, and compensating the defense counsel), the justification for concluding that the resolution of the tort suit precludes an insurer from an opportunity for adjudication is not equally evident. Especially when a conflict of interests has resulted in the defense being conducted by an attorney selected by the insured, the appropriateness of binding an insurer by the tort adjudication is a debatable proposition. In part this is the case because the conflict of interests problems which may cause a liability insurer to withdraw from the defense of the tort claim involve several rather distinctive types of circumstances.

In many instances, an irreconcilable conflict between the interests of the insurer and the insured concerns some matter that does not relate to how the defense of the tort action should be conducted. In such circumstances, even if there is also some issue of fact or law that is common to the tort claim and the coverage question, both the insured and the insurer may have strong incentives to defend against the tort claim in a way that serves the interests of both. When this is the case, at least if there is no other issue in the tort action as to which the interests of the insurer and the insured are in conflict, a persuasive argument exists for the proposition that the insurer should be bound by an adjudication on the merits in the tort trial.[9] Because the insurer and the insured have consistent interests in the manner of defense, no countervailing interest weighs against the public interest in finality of the first adjudication. Moreover, the third party claimant, who is the plaintiff in the tort action, should not have the burden of being required to participate in the adjudication of the same issue again in order to recover on the liability insurance policy. Thus, even though an insurer has not participated in the tort action because of a conflict of interests in relation to some issue other than those adjudicated in the tort action,[10] there is considerable justification in this type of situation

---

9. *Cf.* Burd v. Sussex Mutual Insurance Company, 56 N.J. 383, 267 A.2d 7 (1970).

Also see H.C. Price Company v. Compass Insurance Company, 483 F.Supp. 171 (N.D. Tex., Dallas Div., 1980); Public National Insurance Co. v. Wheat, 100 Ga.App. 695, 112 S.E.2d 194 (1959).

See generally, Annotation, *Liability insurer's right to open or set aside, or contest matters relating to matters of judgment against insured, entered in action in which insurer did not appear or defend,* 27 A.L.R.3d 350–378 (1969).

10. *Cf.* State Farm Mutual Automobile Insurance Co. v. Coughran, 303 U.S. 485, 58 S.Ct. 670, 82 L.Ed. 970 (1938). The policy in that case provided coverage only

if the vehicle was "being operated by the Assured, his paid driver, members of his immediate family, or persons acting under the direction of the Assured" and not in violation of any law as to age, or driving license. At the tort trial, defended by the company under a nonwaiver agreement, the claimant recovered a judgment against the assured and wife, on the theory of negligence of the wife as operator, imputed to the husband; the company successfully defended the latter suit on the policy by showing that an unlicensed 13-year-old girl was operating the car under the wife's direction, in violation of law and contrary to the assured's express instructions, the wife being at most a joint operator. The court's opinion includes the following pas-

for precluding the relitigation of a matter that was clearly determined on the merits in a full adjudication of the tort case.[11]

In many instances in which a conflict of interests exists (as, for example, when the injuries may have resulted from an intentional tort [12] or when the claimant alleges that the insured was driving, the insured denies this, and the policy contains a limitation by reason of which it provides no coverage unless the insured was driving [13]), it is not evident, or even necessarily likely, that the defense presented by an insured on an issue that is being considered in the tort litigation will also serve the interest of the insurer. The insured, as well as the third party claimant, may be inclined to allow proof of a liability that would be within the scope of the insurance coverage, as, for example, by foregoing the intentional tort claim. In such instances, precluding an insurer from a right to an adjudication of a coverage defense is generally not warranted.[14]

Coverage disputes between an insurer and an insured often involve matters which clearly were not at issue in regard to the tort claim. For example, when a coverage defense is predicated on late notice of the accident to the insurer or use of an automobile by someone who is specifically not an insured, the merits of such a defense are not likely to relate to the issues to be decided in the third party's tort suit. In such a case, collateral estoppel or issue preclusion as to some issue purportedly decided but not essential to the tort claim should not apply because the issues which are determinative of coverage are not questions that needed to be decided in the tort case.[15] An argument of estoppel or preclusion based on "findings" which do not constitute

sage: "Defenses now presented by the Insurance Company against liability under the policy were not involved. Joint driving by Mrs. Anthony and the girl was not subject to inquiry." 303 U.S. at p. 492, 58 S.Ct. at p. 673, 82 L.Ed. at p. 975.

11. *Cf.* Samson v. Transamerica Insurance Company, 30 Cal.3d 220, 178 Cal. Rptr. 343, 636 P.2d 32 (1981).

Also see Parks v. Colonial Penn Insurance Company, 98 N.J. 42, 484 A.2d 4 (1984); Miller v. Shugart, 316 N.W.2d 729 (Minn.1982).

12. *Cf.* Farmers Insurance Company of Arizona v. Vagnozzi, 138 Ariz. 443, 675 P.2d 703 (En banc 1983), holding that the insurer was not collaterally estopped from asserting a defense based on a coverage exclusion for intentional torts of an insured. The Court reasoned that "[a] party will not be precluded from litigating policy coverage in a subsequent proceeding if the question of coverage turns on facts which are nonessential to the judgment of tort liability." *Id.,* 675 P.2d at p. 705.

13. Public National Insurance Co. v. Wheat, 100 Ga.App. 695, 112 S.E.2d 194

(1959) (company held estopped by the judgment in the tort suit that it refused to defend; it might have been inferred from the evidence that the insured was honest, but mistaken in his statement that he was driving, having been severely intoxicated at the time of the incident).

14. *Cf.* Maryland Casualty Company v. Peppers, 64 Ill.2d 187, 355 N.E.2d 24 at p. 31 (1976), where the court observed, "Absent the acceptance of the defense by Peppers [after full disclosure to him of the conflicting interests] or the waiver [of the coverage defense] by St. Paul, * * * St. Paul is entitled to have an attorney of its choosing participate in all phases of this litigation subject to the control of the case by Pepper's attorney, and *St. Paul is not barred from subsequently raising the defense of noncoverage in a suit on the policy.*" (Emphasis added).

15. *Cf.* Murphy v. Urso, 88 Ill.2d 444, 58 Ill.Dec. 828, 430 N.E.2d 1079 (1981); Burnett v. Western Pacific Insurance Co., 469 Or. 547, 469 P.2d 602 (1970).

adjudications of matters essential to the judgment is specious and should be rejected.

Many of the judicial precedents, addressing the question whether estoppel or issue preclusion applies as a consequence of the tort litigation, arise in situations in which an insurer has denied that coverage extends to the matter or has asserted a coverage defense. Whenever this occurs, there is a conflict of interests if the insurer provides the defense. The conflict is not resolved by (1) a non-waiver agreement, (2) a reservation of rights, or (3) inaction in regard to the coverage question. Although there are clear judicial precedents for applications of estoppel or issue preclusion in this context,[16] many of these decisions seem, at least in part, to rest on a sense that the insurer wrongfully denied coverage and consequently forfeited the right to a hearing on the matter at issue.[17] The result in at least some of these cases is in effect an additional penalty on the insurer (beyond compensation for any harm done) for wrongfully rejecting the claim. No supporting reason for such a penalty is evident when the insurer did not participate in the selection or direction of the defense counsel as a result of having recognized a conflict of interests which was then brought to the attention of the insured who opted for independent counsel. When this occurs, a court is confronted by a need to take into account the interest of every party in an opportunity for a fair hearing, even if at such a hearing that party's contention may be rejected. This interest in an opportunity for a hearing is particularly evident if (1) the insurer has

---

16. See, e.g., Miller v. United States Fidelity & Casualty Co., 291 Mass. 445, 197 N.E. 75 (1935) (insurer contended that the insured, while driving on a highway, had an altercation with the driver of another car, sped past him and cut in sharply, causing the other driver to lose control of his car, which then overturned; the claimant sued the insured, alleging negligence only, and recovered a judgment, the company having refused to defend; in this later proceeding on the policy, held that the company was estopped to litigate its contention that the injury was not caused accidentally, since theories of negligence and wilful and wanton conduct were mutually exclusive and the company was bound by the determination in the previous suit that the insured was guilty of negligence).

Cf. B. Roth Tool Co. v. New Amsterdam Casualty Co., 161 Fed. 709 (8th Cir.1908) (insured suffered a judgment against itself in favor of its employee for injuries allegedly due to its negligence in allowing use of metals of explosive nature; held, that when suing its insurer on an employer's liability policy containing a warranty against use of explosives on the property, insured was estopped to claim that the injuries were not due to explosives); Gray v. Zurich Insurance Co., 65 Cal.2d 263, 54 Cal.Rptr. 104, 419 P.2d 168 (1966).

Also see Stefus v. London & Lancashire Indemnity Co., 111 N.J.L. 6, 166 A. 339 (Err. & App.1933) (10-to-4 decision), *cert. denied* 290 U.S. 657, 54 S.Ct. 73, 78 L.Ed. 569 (1933) (liability insurer bound by tort action record indicating judgment on a claim of negligence and recklessness in starting car while plaintiff was on running board; insurer precluded from contending injury was wilfully caused), which, however, can no longer be taken as authoritative on this point in view of the comments about it in Burd v. Sussex Mutual Insurance Company, 56 N.J. 383, 267 A.2d 7 (1970).

17. See, e.g., Maneikis v. St. Paul Insurance Company of Illinois, 655 F.2d 818 at 821 (7th Cir.1981), applying the Illinois rule that "once an insurer violates its duty to defend, it is estopped to deny policy coverage in a subsequent lawsuit by the insured or the insured's assigneer"; Nandorf, Inc. v. CNA Insurance Companies, 134 Ill.App.3d 134, 88 Ill.Dec. 968, 479 N.E.2d 988 (1st Dist., Div. 1, 1985), *appeal denied* (1985) Ervin v. Sears, Roebuck, and Company, 127 Ill.App.3d 982, 82 Ill.Dec. 709, 469 N.E.2d 243 (5th Dist.1984).

actually paid or agreed to pay all or a fair portion of the defense costs, or (2) the insurance policy forms do not obligate the insurer to provide a defense (which is the case in a number of situations including multiple layers of liability coverage or some of the newer liability policies that separate liability protection from the defense of claims against the insured).

The public interest in attaining judicial economy by avoiding multiple adjudications of the same issue generally is conditioned on having afforded the party against whom the preclusion is invoked a fair opportunity to participate in an adjudication or an adequate assurance that someone representing his or her interests has participated. When there is a significant conflict of interests, the requisite conditions often do not exist: first, because the conflict precludes the insurer's exercise of control of the defense, and second, because the conflict makes the interests of the insured and the insurer at least divergent and often diametrically opposed.

Estoppel Predicated on the Actions of Defense Counsel

The actions or representations of the defense counsel selected by the insurer may estop the insurer from denying coverage or raising some coverage defenses. For example, the California Supreme Court concluded that an attorney possessed the authority to bind the insurer by representations about the coverage.

§ 7.6(f) Observations

Whenever a tort claim is asserted against an individual who is covered by liability insurance, it is now clear that the insurer and defense counsel are obligated to use their respective expertise (1) to identify any actual or potential conflict of interests, (2) to carefully consider the significance of conflicting interests to the rights and responsibilities of the insured and the insurer, and (3) to take steps to make sure that the insured is placed in a position to make a fully informed, voluntary decision about how to thereafter proceed in regard to the roles of the insurer and defense counsel in conducting a defense of the claims.[1]

In some circumstances, there appears to be no way to make certain that an insurer has the right to a hearing on its policy defense in cases involving a conflict of interests between the company and the insured.[2] Even in jurisdictions permitting declaratory proceedings, this approach often cannot adequately solve the problem unless such a proceeding includes mechanisms for staying all proceedings (including possible settlements) relating to a third party's tort claim.[3]

§ 7.6(f)

1. For example, the rights of an insured to select and provide directions to defense counsel are now matters which are increas-

ingly coming to the fore when a conflict of interests exists.

2. See § 7.6(d), above.

3. See § 7.9, below.

The discussion in the preceding portions of this section provides considerable support for the proposition that the litigation of any substantial tort claim against an insured is very likely to present a situation in which there will be at least one significant conflict of interests for the insurer and the insured.[4] If such a conflict is so significant as to preclude common representation, the appellate court decisions of the last decade almost uniformly hold that the insured is entitled to select an attorney to conduct the defense.[5] When these two factors are considered in relation to the burgeoning body of appellate decisions that address the liability of an insurer for failing to settle a third party's claim against an insured, the possible approaches to the resolution of these problems are relatively limited, and remedies in the aftermath may turn on whether there is a settlement or an adjudication of the claims against the insured.

Separating the Obligation to Provide a Defense

Another approach to this problem would be to separate the obligation to defend (and, in essence, the arrangement to acquire insurance for the expenses of defending against tort claims) from the insurance coverage for an insured's liability. The insured would then be free either (1) to acquire a separate insurance coverage for defense expenses — preferably, given the pervasiveness of the conflict of interest problems from a different insurer, or (2) to not insure this risk. To the extent the liability insurer is concerned about the competency and skill of defense counsel selected by an insured, the liability insurer could reserve the right to approve the attorney selected by the insured and could also require the insured to acquire sufficient "defense expenses insurance" to assure adequate funds to pay such an attorney (much as an excess or secondary insurer mandates that an insured have certain types and amounts of primary coverage).

An arrangement which separates the defense obligation from the coverage for an insured's liability may not be attractive to insureds who do not have a continuing volume of claims against them. Also, it may be viewed as an unattractive approach by insurers because of the lack of control over defense costs and settlement decisions.[6] The added costs that may result from such an arrangement, and the resulting higher premium costs for liability insurance, constitute a potentially compelling reason for continuing the practice of including the duty to defend in liability insurance coverages, even in the face of the serious conflict of interests problems this arrangement produces.[7]

---

4. Also see the discussion in § 7.6(d)(4).

5. *Cf.* Maneikis v. St. Paul Insurance Company of Illinois, 655 F.2d 818 at pp. 827–828 (7th Cir.1981) (applying Illinois law).

6. See the discussion in § 7.7, § 7.8, and § 9.1, below.

7. Some aspects of these questions are also addressed in § 7.8 and § 9.1, below.

Keeton & Widess, Ins.Law—20

§ 7.7   Statutory Penalties for Nonpayment and Late Payment of Insurance Claims

§ 7.7(a)   Introductory Note

Until the mid-twentieth century, insurers generally were not penalized either for a delay in the payment of an insurance claim or for a decision not to pay a claim.[1] This result was a consequence of two rules which were almost uniformly applied by courts throughout the United States when an insured sued an insurer in order to enforce an insurance agreement: first, that penalties were not imposed for breach of contract; and, second, that parties were ordinarily expected to bear the expense of their own attorneys' fees regardless of the outcome of litigation.[2] Thus, in the event a court determined that the insurer's actions were not justified, the result was that the insurer was obligated to pay the amount which was then due under the terms of the insurance coverage.[3]

§ 7.7(a)

1. There were some exceptions to this observation, applied principally to life insurance, that resulted from legislative modifications of the common law.

2. In the absence of a statutory modification of these common law rules, unless the circumstances are very exceptional an insured generally has not even been allowed to recover damages, such as the fees paid to an attorney in representing the claimant in the action against the insurer, from a recalcitrant insurer. See, e.g., Utica Mutual Insurance Co. v. Plante, 106 N.H. 525, 214 A.2d 742 (1965) (insured cannot recover fees paid to attorney representing him in declaratory judgment proceeding); Baker v. Northwestern National Casualty Co., 26 Wis.2d 306, 132 N.W.2d 493 (1965) (insured cannot recover attorneys' fees beyond statutory costs incurred in prosecuting action against insurer, but if not otherwise barred may recover attorneys' fees incurred in litigation with third parties because of insurer's wrongdoings).

Also see Moore v. American United Life Insurance Company, 150 Cal.App.3d 610, 197 Cal.Rptr. 878 (3d Dist.1984) (reversing an award of attorney fees in the amount of $843,333.33, but sustaining a compensatory award of $30,000 and a $2.5 million punitive damages award).

But cf. Equity Mutual Insurance Co. v. Southern Ice Co., 232 Ark. 41, 334 S.W.2d 688 at p. 693 (1960), in which the insureds asked for additional fees for services of attorneys in an appeal from a declaratory judgment proceeding. Without further discussion, the court declared that "we find

that they are entitled to such amounts and fix the same at a total of $250 for both The Borden Company and Gober".

But see Siegel v. William E. Bookhultz & Sons, Inc., 419 F.2d 720 (D.C.Cir.1969), in which an insurer of a bankrupt corporation that quit corporation's defense of a products liability action was held liable for the fee of corporation's court-appointed attorney in a subsequent action against the insurer for its breach of duty to defend. The court commented: (1) "Only by grace of the court's appointment of counsel was the corporation able to sue to regain the protection of the policy, and only because it was compelled to sue did the expense arise of which St. Paul [the insurer] now complains"; and (2) " * * * in the circumstances here, a fee for appointed counsel's successful effort to secure for Surrey Corporation the coverage of the policy and the protection it promised was within the sphere of damages awardable for St. Paul's breach of contract". 419 F.2d at pp. 725–726.

See generally Frederick Benjamin MacKinnon, CONTINGENT FEES FOR LEGAL SERVICES—A STUDY OF PROFESSIONAL ECONOMICS AND RESPONSIBILITIES 141–146 (Report of the American Bar Foundation 1964), at pp. 141–146.

3. As a general rule, in the absence of an applicable legislative provision, a delay in the payment of an insurance claim will not entitle the claimant to recover either a penalty or attorney's fees incurred in a suit to compel the payment of insurance payments. *Cf.* Millers' National Insurance Co. v. Wichita Flour Mills Co., 257 F.2d 93 at

The potential consequences for insurers who either delay an insurance payment or decide not to pay a claim have now been radically altered. In many states, the rejection of a claim or an unreasonable delay in making a payment of insurance benefits justifies either an award to the insured of a legislatively prescribed amount as an additional recovery [4] or the imposition of a penalty by the state for unfair claims settlement practices.[5] Furthermore, in addition to such statutorily prescribed sanctions, the claims settlement practices of insurers have also resulted in numerous judicial decisions holding that common law tort or contract principles justify imposing liability for both consequential damages sustained by an insured as a result of the insurer's actions [6] and, at least in some states, awarding punitive damages.[7]

§ 7.7(b)   Statutory Remedies for an Insured

Legislation in many states now provides remedies for an insured when a court determines that an insurer either unreasonably delayed the payment of a claim or incorrectly decided not to pay a claim.[1] In some jurisdictions, these statutes apply only to a few types of insurance contracts.[2] However, there are numerous states in which the statutory provisions apply to most of the insurance coverages typically acquired by individuals.[3] And the legislative remedies adopted by several states apply to virtually all types of insurance.[4]

pp. 102–103 (10th Cir.1958), 76 A.L.R.2d 385 at p. 400 (1961).

4. See the discussion in § 7.7(b) and § 7.7(c), below.

5. See the discussion in § 7.7(d), below.

6. An insurer's obligation in regard to the settlement of claims and the insurer's potential common law liability for failing to discharge that obligation are discussed in § 7.8 and § 7.9.

7. See § 7.10, below.

§ 7.7(b)

1. See the compilation included in the notes of the Comment, *Liability Insurers and Third Parties Claimants: The Limits of Duty,* 48 University of Chicago Law Review 125–157 (1981).

Also see the references to and discussion of The Unfair Claim Settlement Practices Act in § 7.7(d), below.

2. See, e.g., Massachusetts General Laws Annotated ch. 175B, § 4 (1972) (attorney's fee against unauthorized foreign insurer when insurer has failed for 30 days after demand prior to commencement of action to pay according to contract).

Also see Annotation, *What persons or corporations, contracts or policies, are within statutory provisions allowing recovery of attorneys' fees or penalty against insurance companies or against companies dealing in*

specified kinds of insurance, 126 A.L.R. 1439–1465 (1940).

See generally Jean Appleman, 22A IN-SURANCE LAW AND PRACTICE (1979), at § 14532.

3. For example, Vernon's Missouri Annotated Statutes § 375.420, provides:

"In any action against any insurance company to recover the amount of any loss under a policy of *automobile, fire, cyclone, lightning, life, health, accident, employers' liability, burglary, theft, embezzlement, fidelity, indemnity, marine* or *other insurance* except automobile liability insurance, if it appears from the evidence that such company has refused to pay such loss without reasonable cause or excuse, the court or jury may, in addition to the amount thereof and interest, allow the plaintiff damages not to exceed twenty percent of the first fifteen hundred dollars of the loss, and ten percent of the amount of the loss in excess of fifteen hundred dollars and a reasonable attorney's fee; and the court shall enter judgment for the aggregate sum found in the verdict." (Emphasis added.)

Cf. State ex rel. United States Fidelity & Guaranty Company v. Walsh, 540 S.W.2d 137 at p. 140 (Mo.App., St. Louis Dist., En banc 1976), in which the court observed

---

4. See note 4 on page 868.

The sanctions established by these statutes generally are framed in terms of authorizing the courts to allow an aggrieved claimant to recover the legal expenses which the insured was forced to incur by the insurer's actions.[5] The legislation authorizes courts to award a claimant reasonable attorney fees when either an insurer refused to pay a claim without a reasonable cause or the insurer's decision was made in bad faith.[6] Furthermore, when a liability insurer denies coverage and is later held to have made an incorrect decision in regard to the coverage question, in some of the states which have adopted such legislative sanctions the statutes provide an additional basis upon which the insured may predicate a claim for the legal expenses which were paid to defend the insured against a tort claim that was subsequently determined to be covered by a liability insurance policy.[7]

Insureds may also be entitled to additional recoveries from an insurer. For example, several statutes provide for interest on overdue insurance benefits.[8] And, in several states an insured may recover a

that the Missouri "statutes relating to vexatious delay and attorney's fees ٭ ٭ ٭ offer a statutory remedy against an insurer which has vexatiously refused to pay a claim, and this remedy has been held applicable to commercial sureties. [Citations omitted.]"

Also see, e.g., Nebraska Revised Statutes § 44–359 (1952), construed in Otteman v. Interstate Fire & Casualty Co., 172 Neb. 574, 111 N.W.2d 97, 89 A.L.R.2d 1182 (1961). *Note:* The 1952 Nebraska Revised Statute was the applicable legislation at the time of the *Otteman* decision in the 1961 decision. Nebraska Revised Statutes § 44–359 is the same provision.

4. See, for example, West's Florida Statutes Annotated § 626.911, § 627.428.

Cf. Blewer v. Continental Assurance Company, 394 So.2d 842 (La.App. 3d Cir. 1981), *writ denied* 399 So.2d 602 (1981), holding that the Louisiana statute clearly applied to a state employees group benefits program.

5. See, e.g., Idaho Code § 41–1839(1), which provides:

"Any insurer issuing any policy, ٭ ٭ ٭, which shall fail for a period of thirty (30) days after proof of loss has been furnished as provided in such policy, ٭ ٭ ٭ to pay to the person entitled thereto the amount justly due under such policy, ٭ ٭ ٭ shall in any action thereafter brought against the insurer in any court in this state for recovery under the terms of the policy, ٭ ٭ ٭ pay such further amount as the court shall

adjudge reasonable as attorney's fees in such action."

Cf. Goodwin v. Nationwide Insurance Company, 104 Idaho 74, 656 P.2d 135 (1982). *Also cf.* Continental Re-Insurance Company v. Spanton, 667 F.2d 1289 (9th Cir.1982) (applying Idaho law).

Also see South Carolina Code, § 38–9–320 (1976).

See, e.g., Steele v. General American Life Insurance Company, 217 Kan. 24, 535 P.2d 948 (1975) (claim for medical expenses under a group health policy).

Also see Regional Investment Company v. Haycock, 723 F.2d 38 (8th Cir.1983) (applying Kansas law).

Cf. Matthews v. Travelers Insurance Co., 212 Kan. 292, 510 P.2d 1315 (1973).

Also consider the decisions cited in the following footnotes of this subsection.

6. See § 7.7(c), below.

7. When an insurer fails to provide a defense and there is a subsequent determination that the liability coverage applies, the insurer's failure constitutes a breach of the insurance agreement. These coverage questions are considered in § 7.8 and § 9.1, below. Also see the discussion in § 7.7(c), below.

8. See, e.g., Louisiana Revised Statutes § 22:656 (1986 Supp.) (Interest at the rate of 8% per annum); Michigan Compiled Laws Annotated § 500.2006; Vernon's Missouri Annotated Statutes § 375.420 (1986 Supp.) (Interest at the rate of 6% per annum).

penalty amount that is calculated as a percentage of the insurance benefit which the court decides was due to the claimant.[9]

§ 7.7(c) Standards and Justifications for Assessing Attorney's Fees, Interest, and Other Legislatively Prescribed Remedies

When an insurer has contested a claim or otherwise delayed the payment of insurance benefits, the legislative provisions (as well as the judicial decisions interpreting those statutes) have differed with respect to whether an insured's right to recovery is limited to circumstances in which an insurer has acted without having reasonable grounds for doing so. In some states the legislation addresses this question, while in others the statutes do not provide clear guidance on this issue.[1] In

9. Arkansas Stats. § 66–3238 (Repl. 1980), provides that when an insurer fails to pay the loss within the time specified in the policy, an insured who subsequently is determined to be entitled to the amount claimed in a suit may be awarded a 12% penalty plus reasonable attorney fees. *Cf.* Countryside Casualty Company v. Grant, 269 Ark. 526, 601 S.W.2d 875 (1980).

Vernon's Missouri Annotated Statutes § 375.420 (1986 Supp.) provides:

"In any action against any insurance company to recover the amount of any loss under a policy of automobile, fire, cyclone, lightning, life, health, accident, employers' liability, burglary, theft, embezzlement, fidelity, indemnity, marine or other insurance except automobile liability insurance, if it appears from the evidence that such company has refused to pay such loss without reasonable cause or excuse, the court or jury may, in addition to the amount thereof and interest, *allow the plaintiff damages not to exceed twenty percent of the first fifteen hundred dollars of the loss, and ten percent of the amount of the loss in excess of fifteen hundred dollars and a reasonable attorney's fee;* and the court shall enter judgment for the aggregate sum found in the verdict." (Emphasis added).

Also see Key Life Insurance Co. of South Carolina v. Mitchell, 129 Ga.App. 192, 198 S.E.2d 919 (Div. 1–3, 1973) (a 25% penalty, computed on the insurance benefit due, because the refusal to pay was in bad faith).

Also see Harmon v. Lumbermens Mutual Casualty Co., 247 La. 263 at p. 283, 170 So. 2d 646 at p. 653 (1965) (observing variations among Louisiana statutes and noting that the penalty for refusal to settle small claims is relatively high, 100 per cent for refusal to pay claims such as are common

under hospital and medical coverages for periodic benefits, but much lower on types of coverage commonly involving large lump-sum payments); Key Life Insurance Co. v. Mitchell, 129 Ga.App. 192, 198 S.E.2d 919 (Div. 1–3, 1973) (25% of the insurance benefit due for the refusal in bad faith to pay).

§ 7.7(c)

1. For example, the Louisiana legislation provides that a claim will be paid within thirty days after proof of loss is submitted unless the rejection of the claim was based on "just and reasonable grounds." Louisiana Revised Statutes Annotated § 22:1057 (Supp.1970) ("just and reasonable grounds, such as would put a reasonable and prudent business man on his guard").

In Seguin v. Continental Service Life & Health Insurance Company, 230 La. 533, 89 So.2d 113 (1956), 55 A.L.R.2d 1014 (1957), applying the Louisiana statute, it was held that penalties should be assessed, the insurer having unsuccessfully contested a claim for diaphragmatic hernia on the ground it did not come within hernia either in the ordinary usage of that term or in the policy usage. If a court construes the concept of what would put a prudent person in business on guard so narrowly that it does not encompass the problem whether "hernia" as used in the policy includes "diaphragmatic hernia," then surely there can be but few cases in which the company will be held liable for the policy benefits but not for the penalty.

A holding that the insurer could not escape the penalty even if acting on the advice of its medical and legal advisers in declining to pay a claim such as that in *Seguin* would seem to be a distortion of the statute. Arguably the result in *Seguin* might be justified, however, on the narrow-

those states in which statutes leave it to the courts to determine the standard for invoking these special rights of insureds, there are several justifications that support the awarding of legislatively prescribed remedies even though an insurer's decision to contest the claim was reasonable. There is also at least one significant argument for limiting the imposition of such remedies.

If claimants may recover legislatively prescribed remedies — including attorney fees, other litigation costs, interest, or amounts prescribed as a percentage of the insured's recovery — it may cause insurers to pay at least some claims of doubtful merit. Furthermore, it is at least arguable that the greater the potential amount of such recoveries by insureds whose claims are determined to be improperly delayed or denied, the less likely it will be that the insurers will be inclined to vigorously "police" claims. However, there is no guaranty that a more or less expansive interpretation of such statutes by the courts will actually cause insurers to alter their behavior.[2] Furthermore, even if it is assumed that the judicial approach to the interpretation of legislative provisions would actually have some direct or indirect effect on the conduct of insurers — that is, for example, that a more pervasive application of the statutory remedies would induce less rigorous claims evaluation by most insurers — the potential value of vigorous monitoring of claims by insurers should be considered and weighed against several compelling arguments that favor allowing such recoveries by insureds whenever an insured is forced to retain an attorney to secure the payment of insurance benefits. As noted above, there are several reasons for not restricting recoveries of the statutorily prescribed remedies to those situations in which the insured can prove that an insurer acted unreasonably.

First, the threat that the statutory relief will be imposed without requiring a finding of unreasonableness on the part of the insurer may serve as a greater deterrent to irresponsible rejection of claims, a type of conduct by insurers which is clearly objectionable. Allowing an insured to recover these remedies in all cases in which there is a judicial determination in favor of the claimant — that is, when a court decides that the insurer's decision to reject the claim was wrong and the claimant is entitled to the insurance payment — ought to encourage more careful investigation and consideration of insurance claims generally, and particularly in all cases in which a claim is being rejected.[3]

---

er ground that the company not only must have an adequate ground for being "on guard" but also must prove that it acted on that ground rather than arbitrarily, through the decision of a claims representative unqualified to appraise that ground.

2. *Cf.* the effect (or lack of effect) on insurers of legislation that established the special requirements which require the full value of an insurance policy to be paid even though the property may have been overinsured, which is discussed in § 3.12, above.

3. Such a rule would eliminate the need for judicial determinations in regard to the "reasonableness" of the insurer's conduct.

Second, imposing legislatively prescribed remedies whenever an insurer unsuccessfully contests a claim, even though the insurer acts reasonably in doing so, serves to compensate the insured for both the delay in the receipt of payment and the costs of engaging in the controversy with the insurer in order to recover (which in some circumstances are substantial). A denial of an insurance claim typically has several consequences for an insured. *First,* any time there is a denial of an insurance claim, that action obviously extends the period during which the insured must incur the adverse economic consequences of the loss without the benefit being indemnified by the insurance. *Second,* an insured who is forced to litigate to recover insurance incurs legal expenses — which include, but are not limited to the fees charged by an attorney — to secure the insurance payments. *Third,* many insureds also sustain a variety of consequential problems, including harm to credit standing and loss of business. When an insured is compelled to resort to litigation to recover insurance benefits, the insured is denied indemnification for what, at least in many instances, is a very significant aspect of the economic risks incident to the hazards against which the insured sought protection when the insurance was purchased. Thus, when the payment of insurance benefits is only made after an insured has sought the assistance of an attorney and the legal process, the insured not only sustains added legal expenses but also is denied the right to prompt indemnification (which is one of the risks insureds seek to avoid through the acquisition of insurance).

Third, most insureds have reasonable expectations that the net value to them of their insurance coverages, in the event of a loss, will not be reduced by a recalcitrant insurer. If, because the insurer is found to have acted reasonably in rejecting the claim, an insured's recovery is limited to an award of the amount of insurance benefits due, the amount provided by the insurance coverage — after the insurance recovery is reduced by the insured's payment of the lawyer's fee and other litigation expenses — is obviously diminished. The net amount actually received by such a claimant is then insufficient to indemnify the insured, often falling far short of that which the insured reasonably anticipated would be available as an insurance benefit to offset the economic loss that resulted as a consequence of the insured event. In such instances, it is surely a defensible legislative choice to determine that a layperson's reasonable view of insurance benefits should be protected by allowing the insured to recover full indemnification whenever an insured is compelled to resort to a lawsuit in order to recover the insurance benefits — that is, to receive a total recovery from the insurer that provides net to the insured no less than the insurance benefits the claimant reasonably anticipated would be paid in the event of a loss.

Fourth, the costs to individual insureds of litigating insurance claims which result in determinations that the insurance coverage exists and applies to the particular loss is appropriately shifted to insurers to be distributed among all insureds through premium charges,[4] rather than being borne by those insureds who are forced into contests with their insurers.

Comment

The arguments considered in the preceding portions of this subsection provide substantial support for the proposition that when an insured is compelled to litigate in order to recover insurance benefits, the insured who prevails in such a law suit should be entitled to recover statutorily prescribed remedies (such as the insured's legal expenses and interest on the amount of insurance benefits which were not paid) without regard to whether the insurer acted reasonably.[5]

The statutory provisions establishing remedies for the late payment or nonpayment of insurance claims are often regarded, and sometimes are characterized by the legislation specifically, as penalties. Consequently, it is not surprising that some courts have adopted the view that because such legislation is "penal in nature," the provisions should be subject to strict construction.[6] However, such awards may also appropriately be viewed as allowing an insured to recover compensation for consequential damages the claimant sustained (1) by having to pay an attorney (as well as other litigation expenses) to secure the insurance benefits and (2) by not having the use of the insurance benefits from the time when the insurance should have been paid. Even when such a statute provides for an additional recovery of an amount that is calculated as a percentage of the insurance benefit that was due to the insured, in many instances such an amount does not fully indemnify the claimants for all of the adverse consequences that have resulted from the insurer's wrongful denial of an insured's claim. Accordingly, in most circumstances, there is considerable justification for not according such statutory provisions a "strict" construction.

---

4. In some sense, this point may be vulnerable to the argument that the risk of litigation over insurance benefits in borderline cases is distinct from the fundamental economic risks covered by the insurance contract.

5. The justifications for awarding compensatory consequential damages (see § 7.8 and § 7.9, below) or punitive damages (see § 7.10, below) involve many of the same or analogous considerations.

6. See, e.g.:

Arkansas. Millers Mutual Insurance Company of Illinois v. Keith Smith Company, 284 Ark. 124, 680 S.W.2d 102 at p. 103 (1984), holding that because this "statute is penal in nature" it must be strictly construed and therefore the insured "must recover the exact amount claimed in order to collect the penalty and attorney fees."

Also see Bank of Mulberry v. Fireman's Fund Insurance Company, 720 F.2d 501 (8th Cir.1983) (interpreting Arkansas Stats. § 66–3238, which provides for a 12% penalty in addition to attorney fees).

Missouri. Fohn v. Title Insurance Corporation of St. Louis, 529 S.W.2d 1 at p. 5 (Mo., En banc, 1975). Nevertheless, the court rejected the insurer's argument that since "title" insurance was not among the specific types of insurance enumerated in the statute the legislative remedies did not apply. The court concluded that " 'Indemnity' insurance is one listed in the statute and the provisions therein are applicable to a title policy." *Id.*, 529 S.W.2d at p. 6. [The Missouri statute is set out above].

This is another situation in which contradictory canons of statutory construction potentially apply to a question of legislative interpretation: on the one hand, the canon of "strict" construction of "penal" statutes, and, on the other hand, the canon of "liberal" construction to effectuate the apparent legislative purpose of protecting victims of wrongful denial of insurance benefits.

§ 7.7(d)   Unfair Claims Settlement Practices Legislation

In the 1970s, the National Association of Insurance Commissioners developed model legislation and administrative regulations designed to address the problems presented by unfair claims settlement practices of some insurers.[1] This type of legislation, which has now been enacted by over half the states, empowers the insurance regulatory authority (typically a Commissioner of Insurance) to enforce the provisions by levying monetary penalties for conduct that is prohibited by the statutes.[2] The legislative provisions adopted by almost all of these states do not indicate whether such legislation is intended to give rise to a cause of action by an individual, as well as to administrative actions by the state regulatory agency.

Suits by individuals have presented to courts in several states the question whether such legislative provisions also create a private cause of action. Thus far, the courts have divided on this question. Most have concluded that the legislation does not provide a basis for any cause of action by an insured — that is, a claimant cannot seek a recovery from an insurer that is grounded on rights established by this type of legislation.[3] A few have determined that such legislation does

---

§ 7.7(d)

1. The first proposal was a model statute entitled An Act Relating to Unfair Methods of Competition and Unfair and Deceptive Acts and Practices in the Business of Insurance (1971), NAIC Proceedings, 1972 Volume, at pp. 493–518. The drafters modeled this act on similar legislative proposals developed by the Federal Trade Commission. See G. Robert Mecherle and Donald R. Overton, *A New Extra Contractual Cloud Upon the Horizon: Do the Unfair Claim Settlement Acts Create a Private Cause of Action,* 52 Insurance Counsel Journal 262–268 at p. 262 (1983). Thereafter, the Commissioners developed an Unfair Claims Settlement Practices Act, together with Model Regulations setting forth guidelines for interpreting the settlements practices act.

2. See Jerome Murray and Michael Maillet, *Extra-Contractual Remedies and Punitive Damages in First Party Insurance Claim,* 53 Insurance Counsel Journal 251–263 at pp. 253–254 (1986); Douglas G. House, *Unfair Claims Settlement Practices Act—How the Courts have Interpreted the Act,* XV The Forum 336–351 (1979).

3. See, e.g.:

Illinois. Cf. Scroggins v. Allstate Insurance Company, 74 Ill.App.3d 1027, 30 Ill. Dec. 682, 393 N.E.2d 718 (1st Dist., Div. 2 1979).

Iowa. Seeman v. Liberty Mutual Insurance Company, 322 N.W.2d 35 (Iowa 1982).

Kansas. Cf. Earth Scientists (Petro Services) Ltd. v. United States Fidelity & Guaranty Company, 619 F.Supp. 1465 (D.Kan.1985) (predicting Kansas law).

Missouri. Cf. Tufts v. Madesco Investment Corporation, 524 F.Supp. 484 at p. 486–487 (E.D.Mo.1981) (predicting Missouri law).

New Mexico. Patterson v. Globe American Casualty Company, 101 N.M. 541, 685 P.2d 396 (App.1984).

New Jersey. Cf. Retail Clerks Welfare Fund, Local No. 1049, AFL–CIO v. Continental Casualty Company, 71 N.J.Super. 221, 176 A.2d 524 (1961).

create a private cause of action for insureds.[4] When viewing the several instances in which judicial decisions sustained the right of an individual to seek redress for unfair practices based on this type of legislation, courts in other states have generally concluded that the results were predicated on some aspects or features of the statutes which varied from the model legislation proposed by the National Association of Insurance Commissioners.[5]

§ 7.7(e) Relating Statutory Remedies to Common Law Claims

Legislation either (1) prescribing remedies for insureds who have encountered unwarranted delays or denials of insurance claims or (2) authorizing regulatory actions for unfair claims practices by insurers may affect an insured's right to recover from an insurer on the basis of a common law claim for relief (based on either breach of contract or breach of a duty that justifies a tort action). In a few states, the courts

New York. Also consider the comments in Royal Globe Insurance Company v. Chock Full O'Nuts Corp., 86 A.D.2d 315, 449 N.Y.S.2d 740 (1st Dept.1982); Cohen v. New York Property Insurance Underwriting Association, 65 A.D.2d 71, 410 N.Y.S.2d 597 (1st Dept.1978).

In Halpin v. Prudential Insurance Company, 48 N.Y.2d 906 at p. 908, 425 N.Y.S.2d 48, 401 N.E.2d 171 (1979), *reargument denied* 49 N.Y.2d 801, 426 N.Y.S.2d 1029, 403 N.E.2d 466 (1980), the court commented, "Assuming, without deciding that a private damage action lies under that section, the one instance of unfair settlement practice pleaded would not constitute a general business practice within the meaning of the statute." *Id.,* 425 N.Y.S.2d at p. 49.

Pennsylvania. D'Ambrosio v. Pennsylvania National Mutual Casualty Insurance Company, 494 Pa. 501, 431 A.2d 966 at pp. 969–970 (1981).

Texas. Cf. Russell v. Hartford Casualty Insurance Company, 548 S.W.2d 737 (Tex. Civ.App., Austin 1977).

Vermont. Wilder v. Aetna Life & Casualty Company, 140 Vt. 16, 433 A.2d 309 (1981).

Virginia. Cf. A & E Supply Company v. Nationwide Mutual Fire Insurance Company, 798 F.2d 669 (4th Cir.1986) (applying Virginia law), *cert. denied* ___ U.S. ___, 107 S.Ct. 1302, 94 L.Ed.2d 158 (1987).

Washington. Tank v. State Farm Fire & Casualty Co., 105 Wash.2d 381, 715 P.2d 1133 (1986).

Wisconsin. Kranzush v. Badger State Mutual Casualty Company, 103 Wisc.2d 56, 307 N.W.2d 256 (1981). Also see Messner, Inc. v. Travelers Indemnity Co., 620 F.Supp. 1444 (W.D.Wis.1985).

See generally Jane Barret, *Private Right of Action for Unfair Claims Settlement Practices,* New York Law Journal, September 19, 1983, at p. 1, col. 1; Douglas G. Houser, *Unfair Claims Settlement Practices Act—How the Courts Have Interpreted the Act,* XV The Forum 336–351 (1979); G. Robert Mecherle and Donald R. Overton, *A New Extra Contractual Cloud Upon the Horizon: Do the Unfair Claims Settlement Practice Acts Create a Private Cause of Action?,* 50 Insurance Counsel Journal 262–268 (1983).

Note. Even though the legislation does not establish such a right, an insured may be entitled to assert a common law action in some of these states.

4. *California.* Royal Globe Insurance Company v. Superior Court of Butte County, 23 Cal.3d 880, 153 Cal.Rptr. 842, 592 P.2d 329 (1979).

Louisiana. Cf. French Market Plaza Corporation v. Sequoia Insurance Company, 480 F.Supp. 821 (E.D.La.1979).

Montana. Cf. Klaudt v. Flink, 202 Mont. 247, 658 P.2d 1065 (1983) (Unfair Trade Practices section of Insurance Code held to give third party claimants an action against insurer who failed to settle a tort claim).

West Virginia. Also see Jenkins v. J.C. Penney Casualty Insurance Company, 167 W.Va. 597, 280 S.E.2d 252 (1981).

5. See, e.g. Seeman v. Liberty Mutual Insurance Company, 322 N.W.2d 35 at p. 40 (Iowa 1982); Scroggins v. Allstate Insurance Company, 74 Ill.App.3d 1027, 30 Ill. Dec. 682, 393 N.E.2d 718 at p. 724 (1st Dist., Div. 2 1979).

have concluded that the enactment of the legislation precludes the recognition of any common law action — that is, the remedies or penalties contemplated by such legislation establish the exclusive civil remedy and thereby foreclose any other claims for relief by an insured.[1]

In several other states, courts have seemed to adopt the view — and sometimes have so stated — that such statutes are manifestations of the public concern about the insurance business generally, as well as claim practices in particular. These decisions implicitly, if not explicitly, provide support for common law actions by insureds when the claims practices of insurers involve unwarranted behavior such as bad faith practices, malicious actions, or an unreasonable disregard for the insured's interests.[2]

It may also be argued that the developing body of precedents recognizing an implied obligation of good faith and fair dealing supports recovery of consequential damages that include attorneys fees, costs, and such added detriments as loss of credit and loss of business.[3]

Most legislatures and courts seem to have struck a balance by adopting a rule that disallows awarding either a penalty or attorneys' fees in cases in which the insurer's decision to contest the claim was based on reasonable grounds, and this is certainly a defensible position.

§ 7.8   The Liability Insurer's Duty to Insureds Regarding Settlement

§ 7.8(a)   Introductory Note

Liability insurance policies customarily provide that the insurer "may make such investigation, negotiation, and settlement of any claim or suit as it deems expedient."[1] The terms of such clauses could be interpreted to confer upon insurers a privilege or a right, but not a duty, regarding settlement of a tort claim against an insured.[2] However, rather than being determined exclusively by reference to the specif-

---

§ 7.7(e)

1. Consider the comments of the Kansas Supreme Court in Spencer v. Aetna Life & Casualty Insurance Company, 227 Kan. 914 at p. 926, 611 P.2d 149 at p. 158 (1980):

"The legislature has recognized the public interest nature of the insurance industry and has also recognized policy holders require protection because of their inequitable bargaining position. The penalties, including fines and imprisonment, and imposition of attorneys' fees are adequate to protect the public from the actions of a recalcitrant insurer in first party cases. We do not say the legislative remedy is exclusive but in the absence of a more definitive showing of inadequacy of the remedy than we have before us at this time, we hold the reme-

dies are adequate to force compliance with the terms of insurance contracts."

Also see D'Ambrosio v. Pennsylvania National Mutual Casualty Insurance Company, 494 Pa. 501, 431 A.2d 966 (1981).

Contra. Aetna Casualty & Surety Company v. Broadway Arms, 281 Ark. 128, 664 S.W.2d 463 (1984).

2. *Cf.* Christian v. American Home Assurance Co., 577 P.2d 899 (Okl.1977).

3. For discussion of the obligation of good faith and fair dealing in particular contexts, see § 6.2, above.

§ 7.8(a)

1. See policy forms in Appendices G through K.

2. See, e.g., Wisconsin Zinc Company v. Fidelity & Deposit Company of Maryland,

ic phrasing of a clause in the coverage terms, the nature and scope of the obligations that liability insurers owe to their insureds regarding settlement of third party tort claims have been viewed as arising as a consequence of the total relationship between the parties created by the insurance contract.[3] Consequently, for several decades courts have concluded that an insurer is not entirely free to exercise its discretion in regard to the possibilities for settling a claim by a third party against its insured.[4]

When a third party tort claim against an insured results in a judgment that is in excess of an insured's liability coverage, the scope and nature of the liability insurer's obligations arising from failure to settle the tort claim are increasingly the subject of disputes between

162 Wis. 39, 155 N.W. 1081, Ann.Cas. 1918C, 399 (1916) (holding that the right to settle was a mere option for the insurer). This decision was overruled by the Wisconsin Supreme Court in 1930. See Hilker v. Western Automobile Insurance Co. of Fort Scott, Kansas, 204 Wis. 1, 231 N.W.2d 257 (1930).

Cf. C. Schmidt & Sons Brewing Company v. Travelers Insurance Company, 244 Pa. 286, 90 A. 653 at p. 654 (1914). In *Schmidt,* the court observed that the insurer "was obligated to defend * * * any action against the insured, and the entire management of the defense was expressly entrusted to it * * *." The contention expressly rejected in this decision was that the policy limit of liability no longer applied after the company had declined a settlement offer within the limit.

See also Rumford Falls Paper Company v. Fidelity & Casualty Company, 92 Me. 574, 43 A. 503 (1899). *Cf.* Wilson v. Aetna Casualty & Surety Company, 145 Me. 370, 76 A.2d 111 (1950), which appears to interpret the *Rumford* opinion as consistent with the imposition of excess liability for either bad faith or negligence of the company in failing to settle.

3. In part, this result is supportable on the ground that liability insurance policies almost uniformly provide both (1) that the insured shall not, except at his own cost, voluntarily make any payment or assume any obligation and (2) that the insured shall cooperate with the company and, upon the company's request, assist in making settlement. See, for example, the "Assistance and Cooperation of the Insured" provisions in the sections denoted "Conditions" of the liability insurance policies included in Appendix H.

4. This proposition has been recognized in decisions that span well over a half century. See, e.g., Brassil v. Maryland

Casualty Company, 210 N.Y. 235, 104 N.E. 622 (1914). Several comparable decisions from the next two decades, include: Hilker v. Western Automobile Insurance Company, 204 Wis. 1, 231 N.W. 257 (1930), rehearing reported at 204 Wis. 1, 235 N.W. 413 (1931); Tiger River Pine Company v. Maryland Casualty Company, 163 S.C. 229, 161 S.E. 491 (1931); Douglas v. United States Fidelity & Guaranty Company, 81 N.H. 371, 127 A. 708 (1924), 37 A.L.R. 1477 (1925).

For decisions from the 1950s, see Murach v. Massachusetts Bonding & Insurance Company, 339 Mass. 184, 158 N.E.2d 338 (1959); Larson v. Anchor Casualty Company, 249 Minn. 339, 82 N.W.2d 376 (1957); Radcliffe v. Franklin National Insurance Company of New York, 208 Or. 1, 298 P.2d 1002 (1956). Also see Ballard v. Citizens Casualty Company of New York, 196 F.2d 96 (7th Cir.1952).

In the 1970s, a representative decision is Tannerfors v. American Fidelity Fire Insurance Company, 397 F.Supp. 141 (D.N.J.1975) affirmed at 535 F.2d 1247 (3d Cir.1976) decided in light of the New Jersey Supreme Court's decision in Rova Farms Resort, Inc. v. Investors Insurance Company of America, 65 N.J. 474, 323 A.2d 495 (1974).

The decisions to this effect in the 1980s are far too numerous to cite here. The following state supreme court opinions are illustrative: DiMarzo v. American Mutual Insurance Company, 389 Mass. 85, 449 N.E.2d 1189 (1983) (based on the provisions of Massachusetts General Laws Ann. c. 93A, § 9) (effective October, 1979); Short v. Dairyland Insurance Company, 334 N.W.2d 384 (Minn.1983); Boston Old Colony Insurance Company v. Gutierrez, 386 So.2d 783 at p. 785 (Fla.1980), on remand 388 So.2d 54 (1980).

insureds and insurers. In general, courts hold that an insurer's obligation to an insured in regard to the possible settlement of a third party's tort claim — which affects both its own interests and the interests of its insured — does not allow the insurer to exercise unrestricted and complete discretion in deciding whether to either ignore or to take advantage of opportunities for a settlement.

Courts have articulated several distinctive doctrines or rationales when considering disputes about whether an insurer should have settled a claim. For example, some courts have decided that the "duty to settle is founded on the conflict of interests between the insurance carrier and its insured which arises when a demand within policy limits is received." [5] And, as early as 1914 in New York (and more significantly in regard to the present evolution of judicial doctrine in the United States, in the 1950s in California,[6] which thereafter served to focus attention on these questions in a substantial number of other states [7]), courts in many states have concluded that the insurer is obligated to pursue a settlement within the applicable policy limits as a consequence of the implied covenants of good faith and fair dealing. These covenants are held to be implied terms of every contract, requiring that each party act in good faith not to injure the right of the other party to receive the benefits of the agreement.

Contract or Tort Claim?

During the past three-quarters of a century, courts in numerous states have concluded that an insured may be entitled to damages from a liability insurer in some instances when the insurer has failed to take advantage of an offer to settle a third party's tort claim against an insured. In some of these cases, the courts have considered the question whether such an action by an insured against a liability insurer for

5. See, e.g., Continental Casualty Company v. United States Fidelity and Guaranty Company, 516 F.Supp. 384 at p. 387 (N.D.Cal.1981), decided on the basis of Merritt v. Reserve Insurance Company, 34 Cal. App.3d 858, 110 Cal.Rptr. 511 (2d Dist., Div. 2, 1973).

Also see the discussion of conflict of interests in § 7.6, above.

6. See Comunale v. Traders & General Insurance Company, 50 Cal.2d 654, 328 P.2d 198 (1958), 68 A.L.R.2d 883 (1959); Crisci v. Security Insurance Company of New Haven, Connecticut, 66 Cal.2d 425, 58 Cal.Rptr. 13, 426 P.2d 173 (1967).

Cf. the comments of the Wisconsin Supreme Court in 1930 in Hilker v. Western Automobile Insurance Company of Ft. Scott, Kansas, 204 Wis. 1, 231 N.W. 257 (1930).

7. See, e.g., MFA Mutual Insurance Company v. Flint, 574 S.W.2d 718 (Tenn.

1978); Eastham v. Oregon Automobile Insurance Company, 273 Or. 600, 540 P.2d 364 (1975), *rehearing denied* 273 Or. 610, 542 P.2d 895 (1975); Gordon v. Nationwide Mutual Insurance Company, 30 N.Y.2d 427 at pp. 436–437, 334 N.Y.S.2d 601 at p. 608, 285 N.E.2d 849 (1972), *cert. denied* 410 U.S. 931, 93 S.Ct. 1374, 35 L.Ed.2d 593 (1973); Bowler v. Fidelity and Casualty Company of New York, 53 N.J. 313, 250 A.2d 580 at pp. 587–588 (1969), 43 A.L.R.3d 413 (1972).

Cf. Crabb v. National Indemnity Company, 87 S.D. 222, 205 N.W.2d 633 (1973), 63 A.L.R.3d 715 (1975); Kunkel v. United Security Insurance Company, 84 S.D. 116, 168 N.W.2d 723 (1969).

Also see the decisions cited throughout this section, and Annotation, *Insurer's tort liability for consequential or punitive damages for wrongful failure or refusal to defend insured,* 20 A.L.R.4th 23–58 (1983).

failing to settle a tort claim is predicated on (1) the breach of a contractual obligation or (2) a failure to exercise due care on behalf of its insureds which warrants tort liability, or (3) on both grounds.

The fundamental character of the relationship between a liability insurance company and its insured is a consensual transaction which is manifested by the coverage terms set forth in an insurance policy — that is, the rights and liability of both the insured and the insurer are predicated on a contractual relationship which is set forth in a document prepared by the insurer.[8] However, an insurance company's obligation regarding settlement has frequently been viewed as the breach of a duty to the insured that sounds in tort, rather than as a claim that is based on breach of the insurance contract.[9]

There are some situations in which the classification of the theoretical basis for a claimant's rights may prove to be a matter of critical significance. For example, treating the cause of action as a tort claim may result in the application of a shorter statute of limitation,[10] rather than the longer period of limitation that applies to contract matters in most jurisdictions.[11] Classifying an action as a contract claim tends to favor assignability of the claim as a chose in action.[12] And, characterizing the cause of action as a tort claim may broaden the measure of damages available to a claimant.[13]

In some states, an insured is now afforded a choice of asserting either a tort or a contract claim — that is, the applicable judicial precedents allow a party, who has been injured as a consequence of a

8. It is, however, a contractual relationship that is subject to judicial construction so as to recognize rights in some circumstances that are at variance with the specific terms in the insurance policy. See Chapter 6, above.

9. See, e.g., Norwood v. Travelers Insurance Company, 204 Minn. 595, 284 N.W. 785 (1939), 131 A.L.R. 1496 (1941).

Also see Tennessee Farmers Mutual Insurance Company v. Hammond, 200 Tenn. 106, 290 S.W.2d 860 (1956); Evans v. Continental Casualty Company, 40 Wash.2d 614, 245 P.2d 470 (1952); Zumwalt v. Utilities Insurance Company, 360 Mo. 362, 228 S.W.2d 750 (1950); Hart v. Republic Mutual Insurance Company, 152 Ohio St. 185, 87 N.E.2d 347 (1949).

But cf. Hilker v. Western Automobile Insurance Company, 204 Wis. 1, 231 N.W. 257 (1930), and 204 Wis. 12, 16, 235 N.W. 413, 415 (1931), referring to the obligations of the company as arising "by reasonable implication from the express terms of the contract."

10. See, e.g., Dumas v. Southern Guaranty Insurance Company, 408 So.2d 86 at p. 88 (Ala.1981) (" * * * a suit against the insured for failure to settle a claim *is a tort claim,* whether based upon alleged negligence or bad faith") (emphasis added).

11. See Comunale v. Traders & General Insurance Company, 50 Cal.2d 654, 328 P.2d 198 (1958), 68 A.L.R.2d 883 (1959) (cause of action sounds in both contract and tort; plaintiff may take advantage of the longer limitation period under contract theory).

12. E.g., Gray v. Nationwide Mutual Insurance Company, 422 Pa. 500, 223 A.2d 8 (1966).

13. See the discussion in Crisci v. Security Insurance Company, 66 Cal.2d 425, 58 Cal.Rptr. 13, 426 P.2d 173 (1967), considering whether an insured may recover damages for mental distress under a tort theory, and also whether she could do so under contract theory in this setting.

Also see the discussion of damages in § 7.8 and § 7.10, below.

breach of an insurer's duty in regard to settlement, to proceed on either a tort or a contract theory.[14]

A Hypothetical Case of Failing to Settle

The types of questions that may be raised when a liability insurer does not settle a claim by a third party against its insured are illustrated by the following hypothetical case. Consider the situation in which an insured's liability insurance policy limit is $25,000 per person. A claimant who initiated a suit against an insured in which damages of $500,000 were sought, offers to settle the claim for $25,000. After evaluating the claim, the insurer's vice-president for claims reasons that if the matter goes to trial, it is not likely that the claimant will prevail on the question of liability. The insurer, having decided that the proposed settlement would not be advantageous, rejects the claimant's settlement offer. Thereafter, the case is tried, and a jury awards the claimant $200,000.

Following the judgment in the trial court, the insurer promptly pays $25,000. In order to collect the remainder of the judgment, $175,000, the claimant thereafter forces a sale of several of the insured's assets. At this point, the insured initiates a claim against the insurer in which the insured seeks compensation from the company for the loss which the insured has sustained as a consequence of the insurer's decision not to settle the case when the opportunity to do so within the liability insurance policy limits was offered.

Another type of situation, which raises similar but arguably distinguishable questions, occurs when the insurer — in evaluating the possibility of a settlement — concludes that a settlement is not desirable because even if the claimant prevails at trial, the differential expense for the insurer will only be the litigation expenses which are relatively small. In other words, the insurer concludes that the consequence of rejecting a claim that could be settled for policy limits will be the cost of defense (viewed by an insurer as worth incurring when there is a good possibility a defense will be sustained).

In either of these assumed circumstances, accepting a claimant's offer to settle would serve the insured's interests because the settlement would foreclose the risk that litigation of the claim might result in a judgment against the insured in excess of the policy limits. Thus, following a determination that the third party is entitled to a judgment, the suit by the insured for damages in excess of the applicable liability insurance presents the fundamental issue of what standard should be employed by a court to assess the appropriateness of the insurer's decision to reject an opportunity to reach a settlement with a claimant. The hypothetical cases also raise the question whether the insured's recovery is (1) limited to the difference between the judgment and the

---

14. For example, see Crisci v. Security Insurance Company, 66 Cal.2d 425, 58 Cal. Rptr. 13, 426 P.2d 173 (1967).

insurance coverage, or (2) also includes compensation for other consequences such as the loss of the insured's assets or mental distress, or (3) extends to an award of punitive (exemplary) damages.

§ 7.8(b) The Standards for Assessing Whether an Insurer's Conduct Warrants Excess Liability

Determinations about whether a liability insurance company has complied with its duty to an insured regarding the settlement of a third party's claim involve several fundamental questions about what standard should be employed to assess the insurer's conduct.[1]

(1) Negligence, Bad Faith, and Good Faith

One of the first questions that should be addressed in regard to assessing the consequences of not settling a liability claim against an insured is to establish the basis upon which liability may be predicated. A survey of the body of appellate decisions which have considered this question leads to the conclusion that there are several premises upon which an insured's claim against a liability insurer might be urged, including: (1) that the insurer was negligent, failing to exercise due care in regard to the possibility of a settlement,[2] (2) that the insurer acted in bad faith in not settling the tort claim,[3] (3) that the insurer violated a duty to make decisions about a possible settlement in good faith,[4] and (4) variants of one or more of these standards.[5] No clear consensus has developed as to the most appropriate basis for such

---

§ 7.8(b)

1. The judicial decisions in this area have been the subject of considerable discussion in the law journals. See the *Bibliography* in the 1966 Cumulative Supplement for John C. McCarthy, PUNITIVE DAMAGES IN BAD FAITH CASES (1983).

2. *Cf.* the discussion in Continental Insurance Company v. Bayless and Roberts, Inc., 608 P.2d 281 (Alaska 1980).

3. See, e.g., Boston Old Colony Insurance Company v. Gutierrez, 386 So.2d 783 (Fla.1980), on remand 388 So.2d 54 (1980); Trask v. Iowa Kemper Mutual Insurance Company, 248 N.W.2d 97 at p. 98 (Iowa 1976).

See also Easley v. State Farm Mutual Automobile Insurance Company, 528 F.2d 558 (5th Cir.1976).

In some cases, "bad faith" is the characterization that is employed by courts to describe the conclusion that the insurer failed in its duty to exercise "good faith" in refusing a settlement offer.

Also see Campbell v. Government Employees Insurance Company, 306 So.2d 525 (Fla.1974).

4. In Oregon, for example, "a liability insurer must exercise good faith and due care in the settlement and defense of claims on behalf of its insured." Baton v. Transamerica Insurance Company, 584 F.2d 907 at p. 911 (9th Cir.1978).

In Kansas, "The duty of good faith envisions a standard of conduct much higher than a mere forebearance from malicious conduct toward the insured; it implies honesty, fair dealing, and adequate information." Covill v. Phillips, 452 F.Supp. 224 at p. 226 (D.Kan.1978), citing Bollinger v. Nuss, 202 Kan. 326, 449 P.2d 502 (1969).

Also see Brassil v. Maryland Casualty Company, 210 N.Y. 235, 104 N.E. 622 (1914).

5. *Cf.* Boston Old Colony Insurance Company v. Gutierrez, 386 So.2d 783 at p. 785 (Fla.1980). The court concluded: "Because the duty of good faith involves diligence and care in the investigation and evaluation of the claim against the insured, negligence is relevant to the question of good faith."

Concerning suggestions of a stricter standard, see Crisci v. Security Insurance Company of New Haven, Connecticut, 66 Cal.2d 425, 58 Cal.Rptr. 13, 426 P.2d 173 (1967).

claims, or as to the standard for assessing an insurer's conduct when such issues arise.

Negligence

Beginning in the early decades of this century, courts in several states have held that an insurer is required to exercise "due care" in making decisions about whether to accept an offer to settle a claim against its insured.[6] For example, courts have characterized this requirement in terms of whether a reasonable person (or a reasonable insurer) with unlimited exposure would, in the exercise of due care, have settled.[7]

Bad Faith

In the period between 1930 and 1970, as numerous cases in which insureds felt aggrieved because a liability insurer did not settle a claim were brought to the nation's courts, judges in several states concluded that liability in excess of an insurance policy coverage limits would exist in the event the insurer acted in "bad faith."[8] Some of these decisions concluded that liability existed if the insurer's conduct entailed some type of conscious wrongdoing. For example, in some instances a showing of an evident disregard for the insured's interests was viewed as enough to warrant a conclusion that the insurer acted in "bad faith."[9] Thus, a court might conclude that the requisite bad faith occurred when the acts of an insurer appeared to have been arbitrary

---

6. See, e.g., Douglas v. United States Fidelity and Guaranty Company, 81 N.H. 371, 127 A. 708 (1924), 37 A.L.R. 1477 (1925).

Also see G.A. Stowers Furniture Company v. American Indemnity Company, 15 S.W.2d 544 at p. 548 (Tex.Com.App., Section A 1929); Brassil v. Maryland Casualty Company, 210 N.Y. 235, 104 N.E. 622 (1914).

Cf. Dumas v. Hartford Accident & Indemnity Co., 94 N.H. 484, 56 A.2d 57 at pp. 59–61 (1947).

7. See the discussion in Radio Taxi Service, Inc. v. Lincoln Mutual Insurance Company, 31 N.J. 299 at p. 303, 157 A.2d 319 at p. 322 (1960).

8. See, e.g., Tiger River Pine Company v. Maryland Casualty Company, 163 S.C. 229, 161 S.E. 491 (1931).

Also see the discussion in Dumas v. Hartford Accident & Indemnity Co., 94 N.H. 484, 56 A.2d 57 at pp. 59–61 (1947).

Courts in several states have continued to predicate liability on an assessment of whether an insurer acted in bad faith. See, e.g., Mowry v. Badger State Mutual Casualty Company, 129 Wis.2d 496, 385 N.W.2d 171 (1986) (insurer did not act in bad faith); Kooyman v. Farm Bureau Mutual Insurance Company, 315 N.W.2d 30 at pp. 33–34 (Iowa 1982).

Cf. Trask v. Iowa Kemper Mutual Insurance Company, 248 N.W.2d 97 at p. 98 (Iowa 1976), in which the court pointed out that "substantial evidence" had to be introduced that Kemper acted in bad faith.

9. *Cf.* Detenber v. American Universal Insurance Company, 372 F.2d 50 at p. 53, 34 A.L.R.3d 526 (6th Cir.1967), *cert. denied* 389 U.S. 987, 88 S.Ct. 413, 19 L.Ed.2d 479 (1967), *rehearing denied* 390 U.S. 985, 88 S.Ct. 1096, 19 L.Ed.2d 1287 (1968).

Also see the discussion of the applicability of such a standard in Commercial Union Insurance Company v. Liberty Mutual Insurance Company, 426 Mich. 127, 393 N.W.2d 161 (1986); Johnson v. Hardware Mutual Casualty Company, 109 Vt. 481 at p. 491, 1 A.2d 817 at p. 820 (1938); Georgia Casualty Company v. Mann, 242 Ky. 447, 46 S.W.2d 777 at p. 779 and p. 780 (1932); City of Wakefield v. Globe Indemnity Company, 246 Mich. 645, 225 N.W. 643 at p. 645 (1929).

or reprehensible. However, the requirement of "bad faith" is at best an elusive standard to apply.[10] As the Wisconsin Supreme Court commented in 1980, "Bad faith is a term of variable significance and rather broad application." [11] And, in many instances, "bad faith" is evaluated as the converse of what would be "good faith" conduct.

Good Faith

Numerous courts have concluded that a liability insurer is obligated to act in good faith in regard to the interests of the insured, and that an insurer may be liable for the consequences of a failure to act in good faith in discharging its obligation regarding the settlement of a claim asserted against its insured.[12] Moreover, in many states the insurer must not only act in good faith, but must also exercise due care in regard to the possible settlement of claims by third parties.[13] Thus, in some of these states, a liability insurer may be liable to its insured for damages in excess of a judgment if the insurer *either* does not exercise good faith in deciding whether to settle a third party's claim *or* negligently fails to settle a third party's claim against an insured.[14]

10. Consider the discussion in § 1.4, above.

11. Hilker v. Western Automobile Insurance Company of Ft. Scott, Kansas, 204 Wis. 1, 235 N.W. 413 at p. 414 (1931) (opinion on rehearing).

Also see Commercial Union Insurance Company v. Liberty Mutual Ins. Co., 426 Mich. 127, 393 N.W.2d 161 (1986).

12. For example, see:

Iowa. Kohlstedt v. Farm Bureau Mutual Insurance Co., 258 Iowa 337, 139 N.W.2d 184 (1965).

Kentucky. Cf. Georgia Casualty Company v. Mann, 242 Ky. 447, 46 S.W.2d 777 (1932).

Minnesota. Cf. Short v. Dairyland Insurance Company, 334 N.W.2d 384 (Minn. 1983).

New Jersey. Bowler v. Fidelity & Casualty Company of New York, 53 N.J. 313, 250 A.2d 580 (1969), 43 A.L.R.3d 413 (1972); Radio Taxi Service, Inc. v. Lincoln Mutual Insurance Co., 31 N.J. 299, 157 A.2d 319 (1960) (4–2 decision).

New York. Gordon v. Nationwide Mutual Insurance Company, 30 N.Y.2d 427 at p. 437, 334 N.Y.S.2d 601 at p. 608, 285 N.E.2d 849 at p. 854 (1972), *cert. denied* 410 U.S. 931, 93 S.Ct. 1374, 35 L.Ed.2d 593 (1973); Best Bldg. Co. v. Employers' Liability Assurance Corp., 247 N.Y. 451, 160 N.E. 911 (1928), 71 A.L.R. 1464 (1931).

Virginia. Cf. Aetna Casualty & Surety Co. v. Price, 206 Va. 749, 146 S.E.2d 220 (1966).

Wisconsin. Cf. Berk v. Milwaukee Automobile Insurance Co., 245 Wis. 597, 15 N.W.2d 834 (1944).

Also see Liberty Mutual Insurance Company v. Davis, 412 F.2d 475 (5th Cir.1969); Holtzclaw v. Falco, Inc., 355 So.2d 1279 at p. 1284 (La.1977); Eastham v. Oregon Automobile Insurance Company, 273 Or. 600, 540 P.2d 364 (1975), *rehearing denied* 273 Or. 610, 542 P.2d 895 (1975).

13. *Cf.* Dumas v. Hartford Accident & Indemnity Co., 94 N.H. 484, 56 A.2d 57 (1947); Douglas v. United States Fidelity & Guaranty Co., 81 N.H. 371, 127 A. 708 (1924), 37 A.L.R. 1477 (1925).

Also see Covill v. Phillips, 452 F.Supp. 224 (D.Kan.1978); Continental Insurance Company v. Bayless and Roberts, Inc., 608 P.2d 281 (Alaska 1980); Boston Old Colony Insurance Company v. Gutierrez, 386 So.2d 783 (Fla.1980), *on remand* 388 So.2d 54 (1980); Gedeon v. State Farm Mutual Automobile Insurance Co., 410 Pa. 55, 188 A.2d 320 (1963).

14. See, e.g., Kabatoff v. Safeco Insurance Company of America, 627 F.2d 207 (9th Cir.1980) [applying Oregon law on the basis of Eastham v. Oregon Automobile Insurance Company, 273 Or. 600, 540 P.2d 364 (1975), *rehearing denied* 273 Or. 610, 542 P.2d 895 (1975)]; Hamilton v. State Farm Insurance Company, 83 Wash.2d 787, 523 P.2d 193 (1974).

Also see Anderson v. St. Paul Mercury Indemnity Company, 340 F.2d 406 (7th Cir. 1965) (applying Indiana law).

There are also some decisions that appear to impose a duty of good faith and either expressly or implicitly leave unresolved the question whether the insurer is also subject to a requirement of ordinary care.[15]

Observations

In many cases, it seems likely that an insurer's liability will not depend on whether the standard is one of good faith, bad faith, or negligence.[16] Virtually the same evidence will be presented by an insured, regardless of the standard of conduct which has been articulated in the judicial precedents, to prove the negligent breach of duty, the absence of good faith, or the presence of bad faith. The general reaction of the jury to the evidence in a particular case about the insurer's decision not to settle is likely to be similar, if not identical, in most instances regardless of the standard of conduct which is applied in a particular jurisdiction.

In some situations, however, there could be a significant difference as a consequence of the applicable standard of conduct. Circumstances may arise in which it would be unlikely that a jury would make the relatively harsh finding of bad faith, but less disinclined to find that negligence had caused a settlement opportunity to be lost. For example, this might be true when the basis for the claim against the insurance company for breach of the duty to settle is exclusively the conduct of a lawyer who is well known and highly respected in a community from which the jury is drawn. In such circumstances, the jury might be considerably more likely to make a finding of negligence than to conclude that the attorney's conduct manifested "bad faith."

A rather special meaning is sometimes ascribed to the concept of "bad faith" in this context. In considering an insurer's duty to settle, courts have concluded that "bad faith" may exist even though the representatives of the company have been scrupulously honest in their handling of the claim. For example, in many jurisdictions bad faith can be established by proof that the insurer did no more than engage in a course of conduct manifesting a deliberate preference for the company's interests over the insured's, even though the company's representatives honestly believed that such a course of conduct was within their legal rights.[17] Accordingly, depending on the way "bad faith" is charac-

---

In *Eastham*, the court applied only a standard of good faith. In an opinion filed after a rehearing the court observed, "Most authorities agree there is little difference between the concepts of "good faith" and "due care" where the duty of the insurer, as we stated in our original opinion, is to "act as if there were no policy limits applicable to the claim and as if the risk of loss was entirely its own."

15. Concerning varied rules falling in the middle ground, see Robert E. Keeton, *Liability Insurance and Responsibility for*

Settlement, 67 Harvard Law Review 1136–1186 at pp. 1139–1148 (1954).

16. *Cf.* the following comment of the Florida Supreme Court: "Because the duty of good faith involves diligence and care in the investigation and evaluation of the claim against the insured, negligence is relevant to the question of good faith." Boston Old Colony Insurance Company v. Gutierrez, 386 So.2d 783 at p. 785 (Fla. 1980), *on remand* 388 So.2d 54 (1980).

17. This point is illustrated in Tennessee Farmers Mutual Insurance Company v.

terized and explicated in the jury instructions, there may be some significance to the choice among the good faith, bad faith, and negligence standards.

(2) The Insurer's Interests Versus the Insured's Interests

Another significant issue involved in assessing an insurer's conduct regarding settlement concerns the relative degree of consideration that an insurer must give to the insured's interests in comparison with its own. There are several views on this question among the nation's appellate courts.

Equal Consideration to the Insured's Interests

The prevailing view among courts in those states that have squarely faced this issue is that an insurance company must give equal consideration to the insured's interests in making decisions concerning the settlement or litigation of a claim covered by an insurance policy.[18] One way to conceptualize the exercise of such impartiality is to conceive of the two competing interests as being held by a single person who would therefore have no inducement to sacrifice one interest over the other except on the basis of their relative merit.[19] Unfortunately, unless it is clearly explained, this formulation may be confusing because the decision not to settle appears to have sacrificed one interest to serve the other. However, the rule which requires an insurer to give equal consideration to its own and its insured's interests can be expressed in additional ways that help to minimize the problem created by a conceptualization of the rule in terms of awarding equal consideration to the respective interests. For example, the following proposition provides another way to describe the insurer's obligation:

> In deciding whether to settle a claim against an insured, a liability insurer must view the opportunity for a settlement as it would if there were no limit of liability applicable to the insured's coverage.[20]

Hammond, 43 Tenn.App. 62, 306 S.W.2d 13 (1957) (trial judge, in passing on the motion for a new trial, remarked that it was clear that the attorney employed by the company to represent the insured in the tort claim had not been guilty of dishonesty; appellate court nevertheless affirmed a judgment for the insured on the theory that the conduct of the company's representatives, including the attorney, amounted to "bad faith" such as to support liability in excess of policy limits).

18. See, e.g., National Services Industries, Inc. v. Hartford Accident & Indemnity Company, 661 F.2d 458 (5th Cir., Unit B 1981), *rehearing denied* 667 F.2d 93 (1981) (applying Georgia law); Short v. Dairyland Insurance Company, 334 N.W.2d 384 (Minn.1983); Crabb v. National Indemnity

Company, 87 S.D. 222, 205 N.W.2d 633 (1973).

In LaRotunda v. Royal Globe Insurance Company, 87 Ill.App.3d 446, 42 Ill.Dec. 219, 408 N.E.2d 928 at p. 935 (1st Dist., Div. 3, 1980), the court observed that an insurer must faithfully consider a settlement opportunity "giving the insured's interest at least as much respect as its own."

19. This approach to equality is similar to the concept of equality of persons before the courts. It refers to impartiality, which in this instance involves impartiality in the weighing of the two competing interests.

20. This standard has been applied in several cases, including, Eastham v. Oregon Automobile Insurance Company, 273

This statement frames the question in terms of how an insurer would evaluate the settlement. However, a rule that would have the trier of fact, especially a jury, consider the matter as an insurer would view a possible settlement does not include an adequate reference to the insured's interests. For this reason, the combination of exercising appropriate consideration for the insured's interest *and* the caution of a prudent defendant is better expressed by the following statement:

> In deciding whether to settle a claim against an insured, a liability insurer should evaluate whether to accept a proposed settlement in the same way as would be used by an ordinarily prudent defendant who will be fully liable for any judgment that may be subsequently rendered.[21]

Under this approach, an insurer would not be liable for failing to settle if, but only if, such an ordinarily prudent defendant would decide to try the third party's suit. Generally, a reasonably prudent defendant would not take the risks [22] of litigating a tort claim when there is a significant possibility of an unfavorable result — that is, when this possibility is substantial, it usually makes the certain loss that is incident to paying the amount necessary to obtain the claimant's consent to the settlement the preferable choice.[23]

Greater Consideration to the Insured's Interests

Appellate court precedents in several states indicate that an insurer must give greater consideration to its insured's interests. For example, a Louisiana Court of Appeal has observed, "Louisiana jurisprudence establishes that a duty is placed upon the insurer to consider

---

Or. 600, 540 P.2d 364 (1975), *rehearing denied* 273 Or. 610, 542 P.2d 895 (1975).

Also see Kabatoff v. Safeco Insurance Company of America, 627 F.2d 207 (9th Cir.1980) (applying Oregon law); Herges v. Western Casualty & Surety Co., 408 F.2d 1157 (8th Cir.1969) (Minnesota law); Continental Casualty Company v. United States Fidelity and Guaranty Company, 516 F.Supp. 384 (N.D.Cal.1981).

For a more detailed statement of the arguments supporting this formulation, see Robert E. Keeton, *Liability Insurance and Responsibility for Settlement*, 67 Harvard Law Review 1136–1186, at pp. 1142–1148 (1954).

Also see the decisions addressing the insurer's obligation to the insured in § 7.6(b).

21. A similar formulation was first set forth by Professor Keeton in *Liability Insurance and Responsibility for Settlement*, 67 Harvard Law Review 1136–1186 (1954).

Cf. Covill v. Phillips, 452 F.Supp. 224 (D.Kan.1978).

Also see the decisions addressing the insurer's obligation to the insured in § 7.6(b), above.

22. For example, in Boston Old Colony Insurance Company v. Gutierrez, 386 So.2d 783 at p. 785 (Fla.1980), *on remand* 388 So. 2d 54 (1980), the court observed, "An insurer, in handling the defense of claims against its insured, has a duty to use the same degree of care and diligence as a person of ordinary care and prudence should exercise in the management of his own business."

23. *Cf.* Dumas v. Hartford Accident & Indemnity Company, 94 N.H. 484, 56 A.2d 57 (1947).

Also see Robert E. Keeton, *Liability Insurance and Responsibility for Settlement*, 67 Harvard Law Review 1136–1186 at p. 1147 (1954).

the interest of the insured as paramount when an offer to settle is made." [24]

The California courts, which have held insurers to the most stringent standards, appear to require that some special "weight" be given to certain interests of the insured, or that less importance be given to certain interests of the insurer. It may be argued that California precedents support the view that the only permissible consideration in evaluating the reasonableness of a settlement offer is whether, in light of the probable liability of the insured, the ultimate judgment is likely to exceed the offer.[25] For example, in a 1978 decision, a California Court of Appeal observed, "A judgment in excess of the limits of a policy inferentially suggests that the value of the claim is the equivalent of the amount of the judgment and that acceptance of an offer within those limits was the most reasonable method of dealing with the claim." [26] Such an approach comes very close to imposing a standard of strict liability when an insurer elects to reject a settlement opportunity within the coverage limits of a liability insurance policy.

(3) Strict Liability

In the *Crisci* case, decided by the California Supreme Court in 1967, Justice Peters considered a standard of strict liability that was proposed by amicus curiae.[27] The court concluded that it was not necessary to decide the *Crisci* case on that basis, and that "there might be countervailing considerations" precluding adoption of a rule of strict liability. However, in other judicial opinions, there are also statements which have seemed to suggest that some courts may hold that whenever an insurer decides not to accept a settlement offer that is within the

---

24. Domangue v. Henry, 394 So.2d 638 at p. 640 (La.App., 1st Cir., 1980) (*writ denied* 399 So.2d 602 (1981).

Also see Fertitta v. Allstate Insurance Company, 439 So.2d 531 (La.App., 1st Cir., 1983). In *Fertitta,* the court concluded that

"The factors to be considered in determining good faith when refusing to settle are: (1) the probability of the insured's liability; (2) the adequacy of the insurer's investigation of the claim; (3) the extent of damages recoverable in excess of policy coverage; (4) the rejection of offers in settlement after trial; (5) the extent of the insured's exposure as compared to that of the insurer; and (6) the nondisclosure of relevant factors by the insured or insurer."

Id., 439 So.2d at p. 533. Also consider the Louisiana Supreme Court opinion in this case reported at 462 So.2d 159 (La.1985).

25. See Johansen v. California State Auto Association Inter-Insurance Bureau, 15 Cal.3d 9, 123 Cal.Rptr. 288, 538 P.2d 744 (1975).

Cf. Crisci v. Security Insurance Company, 66 Cal.2d 425 at 431, 58 Cal.Rptr. 13 at p. 17, 426 P.2d 173 at p. 177 (1967).

In Commercial Union Assurance Co. v. Safeway Stores, Inc., 26 Cal.3d 912 at p. 917, 164 Cal.Rptr. 709 at p. 712, 610 P.2d 1038 at p. 1041 (1980), the court observed that "in deciding whether a claim should be compromised, [the insurer] must take into account the interest of the insured and give it *at least as much* consideration as it does its own interest." (Emphasis added).

26. Twentieth Century-Fox Film Corporation v. Harbor Insurance Company, 85 Cal.App.3d 105 at p. 111–112, 149 Cal.Rptr. 313 at p. 317 (2d Dist., Div. 3, 1978).

Also see Note, *Johansen v. California State Automobile Association: Has California Adopted Strict Liability for an Insurer's Failure to Settle?* 27 Hastings Law Journal 895–916 (1976).

27. Crisci v. Security Insurance Company, 66 Cal.2d 425 at p. 431, 58 Cal.Rptr. 13 at p. 17, 426 P.2d 173 at p. 177 (1967).

coverage limits, the insurer should be liable for whatever judgment is thereafter rendered against its insured.

In almost all instances when an insurer decides to reject a settlement opportunity, the insurer has decided that its interests will be served by refusing to settle, typically on the rationale that the chances of a judgment in excess of the settlement figure are very small. When an insurer adopts this position and the damages which are subsequently awarded exceed the applicable limits of the liability insurance coverage, an argument may be made that the insurer should be liable for the entire amount of the tort judgment. The principal supporting rationale is that an insurer ought not to be permitted to favor its own interests unless it is then prepared to protect its insured by absorbing the losses which result from the decision not to settle.[28] As several courts have observed, the insurer should not be allowed to "gamble" with the insured's interests by refusing to settle a third party's claim within the applicable policy limits when there is a prospect for a judgment in excess of those limits.[29] But, as yet, no court has explicitly adopted a strict liability rule.

(4) Comment: The Case for and the Case Against Strict Liability

Assertions of excess liability and the associated need to assess the insurer's conduct have produced a very extensive body of litigation in recent decades. Predicating an insurer's liability on a standard of strict liability would have the advantage of reducing such litigation. Proposals for such a rule of strict liability are quite controversial, however, because an overall assessment depends on weighing other advantages and disadvantages as well as predictable reduction of litigation. The principal advantages that have been identified in the debates over proposals for strict liability in this setting include the following:

First, as noted above, strict liability would significantly reduce litigation. This is a matter that may be especially important in view of the increasing number of multimillion dollar verdicts which have been rendered against insurers in cases involving claims in excess of liability insurance limits. At a minimum, it would eliminate a whole class of disputes about negligence or bad faith that courts are now required to adjudicate in virtually every litigated coverage dispute following a tort judgment in excess of a liability insurance limit when there was an opportunity to reach a settlement within the coverage limit. It would also reduce the

---

28. *Cf.* Rova Farms Resort, Inc. v. Investors Insurance Company of America, 65 N.J. 474 at pp. 501–502, 323 A.2d 495 at p. 509–510 (1974).

Also see Note, *Johansen v. California State Automobile Association: Has California Adopted Strict Liability for an Insurer's Failure to Settle?* 27 Hastings Law Journal 895–916 (1976).

But cf. Employers National Insurance Corp. v. Zurich American Insurance Company of Illinois, 792 F.2d 517 (5th Cir. 1986).

29. See, e.g., Commercial Union Insurance Company v. Ford Mutual Company, 599 F.Supp. 1271 (N.D.Cal.1984).

need for and strength of arguments for consequential damages because the entitlement to payment of the full tort judgment by the insurer would minimize, if not avoid, other adverse consequences for the insured.

Second, a strict liability rule would reduce the need for and incidence of awards of punitive damages. The application of a strict liability rule could not be expected to eliminate all unconscionable claims practices of insurers (which have led to awards of punitive damages in egregious cases), but this approach probably would substantially reduce the volume of such claims. This would not only reduce the litigation burden on the courts but also serve the public interest in maintaining the financial health of individual insurers and the industry. Multimillion dollar awards of punitive damages, no matter how justifiable in some circumstances, may threaten the financial stability of a broader segment of the industry as well as the insurer who is adjudged liable. The increasing reliance on insolvency funds (which provide protection for insureds) has created an environment in which insurers are required in effect to insure other insurers, thereby making the financial well being of individual companies the economic concern of the industry generally.

Third, almost two decades of experience have indicated that even the combination of liability in excess of policy limits and liability for punitive damages is not enough to eliminate improper claims practices of insurers and may not have had significant effect in altering behavior.

Fourth, the imposition of strict liability would reduce the incidence of problems arising from conflicts of interests between insurers and insureds.

Arrayed against these advantages of strict liability, however, are three very significant disadvantages.

First, the total claims costs for insurers could rise,[30] and perhaps quite significantly, if the entire amount of tort awards (even for

---

30. The extent to which insurance costs would increase as a consequence of the application of a strict liability rule in this context is unclear. There are several considerations that bear upon whether or not it is likely that there would be a notable increase in the net amounts insurers are called upon to pay.

First, the increase occurs only among the litigated tort cases in which the insurance company has, in fact, declined to accept a settlement offer (or failed to take steps to invite one) that is either (1) within the applicable coverage limits or (2) for the coverage limits plus some amount which the insured has offered to contribute to the settlement.

Second, among these cases there will be a number of instances when the third party will not prevail in the tort action against the insured. Indeed, given the insurer's decision not to settle, it seems reasonable to anticipate that in a significant proportion of the "universe of instances" the insurer's decision is predicated on the conclusion that the third party's prospects for any recovery are not very good, and that the insured's position should be sustained in a significant portion of the cases.

Third, although it is undoubtedly true that a rule of strict liability in these cases would increase one facet of the insurer's exposure in connection with liability insurance claims, there would also be a reduc-

compensatory damages alone) were covered by liability insurance whenever an insurer rejected an opportunity to settle a third party's claim.

Second, even though the premium paid for a low-limit coverage is adjusted to that low policy limit, it ultimately would have to reflect the costs of paying claims in excess of policy limits. The effect might be to increase drastically the cost of low-limit policies.[31] Such a reduction in the differential between low-limit and high-limit liability insurance coverage has the effect of placing greater practical constraints on choices by insureds. Public interest arguments may be advanced for requiring individual insureds to bear greater responsibility for the costs of compensating victims of their tortious conduct than low-limit coverage provides, but such arguments point more strongly toward higher statutorily required limits of liability coverage than toward a rule of strict liability that effectively raises the low limit only when the claim could have been but was not settled within that low limit.

Third, any net addition to claims costs[32] incident to the lifting of low limits would add to current problems of insurability and availability of liability coverages.

The debate over proposals for a strict liability rule in this area of insurance law is more likely, in the end, to be resolved in legislatures than in courts.

§ 7.8(c) Liability in the Absence of an Offer From the Claimant or a Demand by an Insured to Settle

An interesting issue arises in some circumstances about whether a liability insurer may violate the obligation to act fairly and in good faith even when no offer to settle has been made by an injured third party.[1] In most circumstances the insurer, having reserved to itself the

tion of exposure to the consequences of what has become an increasingly significant incidence of claims by insureds predicated on inappropriate conduct by liability insurers. Relatively few of these claims have resulted in judgments of excess liability, but each such claim has forced the insurer to incur defense expenses. These litigation expenses would be largely eliminated by a rule of strict liability. Moreover, a strict liability rule would reduce the insurer's exposure to liability for both consequential damages and punitive damages.

An accurate appraisal of the economic significance of either the impact of a strict liability rule or the savings to be derived from the application of such a rule probably cannot be developed without the cooperation of the insurance industry. Nevertheless, it appears evident that there are both costs and savings for insurers from the application of strict liability when an insurer decides to litigate a third party's

claim that could have been settled with the resources available from the insurance coverage or the coverage plus a contribution from the insured.

31. See the discussion in note 30, above.

32. See the discussion in note 30, above.

§ 7.8(c)

1. See Fidelity & Casualty Co. of New York v. Robb, 267 F.2d 473 at p. 476 (5th Cir.1959) (jury found for the insurer in relation to a theory that it acted unreasonably in declining claimant's settlement offer before trial, but against the insurer on a second theory that it acted unreasonably — after the tort case had developed unfavorably at trial — in failing to accept the original offer if it remained open or to initiate new discussions and bring about settlement if it did not remain open; though reversing because of error in the charge, the appellate court were "of the view that the district judge did not err in instructing the jury that they could consid-

right to control the defense and the decision whether to agree to a settlement, should be obligated to explore the possibility of a settlement even in the absence of actions by the third party or an express request by the insured.[2]

Occasionally, a question arises about whether an insured must either request that an insurer attempt to reach a settlement or accept a settlement offer that has been tendered by a claimant as a prerequisite to claiming that the insurer's liability should be in excess of the applicable policy limits. When an insured has advised the insurer of the insured's views on settlement, especially when an insured urges that a claimant's offer should be accepted, the justification for protecting the insured may be greater. However, an insured should not be required to expressly request that the insurer seek a settlement.[3]

§ 7.8(d) Settlement Possibilities in Excess of Insurance Policy Limits

Distinctive questions are presented when a third party claimant offers to settle for an amount that exceeds the applicable coverage limit of the insured's liability insurance. If the insured is willing to contribute the difference between the insurance policy limit and the total settlement demand, an insurer's decision about whether to accept such a settlement offer should be subject both to the same considerations and

---

er whether the insurer was negligent either or both in rejecting the firm offer and in not thereafter undertaking to make a settlement").

Also see Young v. American Casualty Co. of Reading, Pennsylvania, 416 F.2d 906 (2d Cir.1969), cert. dismissed 396 U.S. 997, 90 S.Ct. 580, 24 L.Ed.2d 490 (1970) (applying New York law).

There are situations when, in the absence of an offer by the third party claimant, the insured might be unable to prove that there was an opportunity to settle or that the insurer acted in bad faith in not settling.

2. The insured's problems of proof are obviously greatly reduced if the claimant has made an offer of settlement.

3. In Rova Farms Resort, Inc. v. Investors Insurance Company of America, 65 N.J. 474, 323 A.2d 495 at p. 507 (1974), the court stated: "We, too hold that an insurer, having contractually restricted the independent negotiating power of its insured, has a positive fiduciary duty to take the initiative and attempt to negotiate a settlement within the policy coverage."

In Colman v. Holecek, 542 F.2d 532 at p. 537 (10th Cir.1976) (applying Kansas law), the court reasoned that "the duty to settle

arises if the carrier would initiate settlement negotiations on its behalf were its potential liability equal to that of its insured." Also see Farmers Insurance Exchange v. Schropp, 222 Kan. 612, 567 P.2d 1359 (1977).

Cf. Tannerfors v. American Fidelity Fire Insurance Company, 397 F.Supp. 141 at p. 146 and p. 159 (D.N.J.1975), in which the court held that "an insurer, having contractually restricted the independent negotiating power of its insured, has an affirmative duty to take the initiative in settlement negotiations and to attempt to procure a settlement within the policy limits." Affirmed, 535 F.2d 1247 (3d Cir. 1976).

Also see the discussion in Larraburu Brothers, Inc. v. Royal Indemnity Company, 604 F.2d 1208 at p. 124 (9th Cir.1979) (applying California law) (the court considered the insured's claim that the insurer wrongfully refused to enter into "meaningful settlement negotiations" where the insurer "had been expressly advised that Larraburu's business was in a precarious financial situation and that news of any judgment against it in excess of insurance coverage could be expected to start a creditor's run which would destroy the business").

to the same consequences as when there is a possibility of reaching a settlement within the insurance policy limits.[1]

In general, a liability insurer should be required to engage as its representatives individuals who are skilled negotiators. When an offer exceeds the applicable coverage limits of a liability insurance policy a defense counsel, selected by an insurer, should be obligated to employ that skill. An insurer may be found to have committed a breach of its duty to the insured unless such an attorney attempts to engage in negotiations to reduce a settlement demand on behalf of the third party claimant to a level that is within the coverage limits of the applicable liability insurance.[2] Moreover, an experienced negotiator must appreciate the importance of timing in negotiations. Thus, such a negotiator must understand that an offer of the full policy limit just as a trial is beginning is not the equivalent of an offer in that amount several months before trial.[3]

The fact that at some point the insurer offered its policy limits will not always defeat a claim by an insured based on a refusal of the insurer to settle for the same or an even smaller sum when such an opportunity was offered by the third party at some other point before the trial.[4]

Whenever there is a possibility for a settlement in excess of the coverage limits, the insured must be informed of the proposed terms *and* should also be specifically advised that the opportunity exists for the insured to contribute to the amount available to effect a settle-

§ 7.8(d)

1. See, e.g., Boling v. New Amsterdam Casualty Co., 173 Okl. 160, 46 P.2d 916 (1935). Also see Yeomans v. Allstate Insurance Company, 130 N.J.Super. 48, 324 A.2d 906 (App.Div.1974).

Cf. Brockstein v. Nationwide Mutual Insurance Co., 417 F.2d 703 (2d Cir.1969), affirmed at 448 F.2d 987 (2d Cir.1971); Peerless Insurance Co. v. Inland Mutual Insurance Co., 251 F.2d 696 (4th Cir.1958).

In Continental Insurance Company v. United States Fidelity and Guaranty Company, 516 F.Supp. 384 at p. 389 (N.D.Cal. 1981), the court concluded that when a carrier fails to ascertain whether its insured is willing to make the contribution required by a settlement offer, "the demand must be presumed to be within the feasibility limits for the purpose of activating the duty of good faith and fair dealing."

2. In General Accident Fire & Life Assurance Corporation, Ltd. v. American Casualty Company of Reading, Pa., 390 So.2d 761 at p. 765 (Fla.App., 3d Dist., 1980), *petition for review denied* 399 So.2d 1142

(1981). The court observed, "When an insured is not judgment proof or when an excess insurer exists, absence of an offer to settle within policy limits is not dispositive of the question of bad faith on the part of the primary insurer." The court also commented that "an offer to settle within policy limits may be a factor to consider in determining an insured's good faith in the handling of an insured's defense, but it should not be a prerequisite to the imposition of liability for a primary insurer's bad faith refusal to settle."

Also see the discussions in Rova Farms Resort, Inc. v. Investors Insurance Company of America, 65 N.J. 474, 323 A.2d 495 (1974) and Yeomans v. Allstate Insurance Company, 130 N.J.Super. 48, 324 A.2d 906 (App.Div.1974).

See generally Robert E. Keeton, *Liability Insurance and Responsibility for Settlement,* 67 Harvard Law Review 1136–1186 at p. 1149 (1954).

3. See Commercial Union Insurance Company v. Ford Motor Company, 599 F.Supp. 1271 at p. 1273 (N.D.Cal.1984).

4. *Ibid.*

ment.[5] However, when it is not possible to reach a settlement within policy limits, an insurer may invite trouble if it suggests that its insured settle without making it clear that the company stands ready to contribute its entire policy limit. Were an insurer to suggest a settlement without a full commitment of its liability coverage, its action would probably support the inference that the company was preferring its own interests over those of the insured by declining to offer its policy limit in response to a settlement proposal in excess of the policy limit.[6] This might be especially true when, viewed retrospectively, the settlement offer appears to have been a very reasonable one.

§ 7.8(e) Multiple Insurers and Multiple Claimants

Questions about an insured's duty regarding settlement are often considerably more complicated in situations involving several insurance companies. More than one insurer may be involved as a result of an insurer's use of reinsurance or because there are several insurance coverages which apply as either primary or excess coverage.

(1) Reinsurance

A liability insurance company cannot eliminate its duty to its insured by obtaining reinsurance.[1] However, when a primary insurer has arranged for reinsurance, interesting — and sometimes, difficult — questions may arise as to what rights or responsibilities a reinsurer has in regard to either the decision to settle or the terms of a settlement.

The resolution of questions about whether the relationship between the reinsurer and the primary insurer is analogous to the one which exists between the primary insurer and its insured may be determined or influenced by the terms of the reinsurance contract. For example, that contract may vest the primary insurer with the right to control decisions concerning settlement. Or, on the other hand, that contract may place the reinsurer in control of the settlement decision. In most situations, disputes between a primary insurer and a reinsurer will not be presented to the courts because they usually will be avoided by contract provisions, or they will be resolved by either negotiation or arbitration when they have not been adequately anticipated in advance. However, if the question were to be litigated, it is reasonable to anticipate that the rights of a reinsurer will be essentially the same as those of the insured when an insurer fails to consummate a settlement within the limits of the primary coverage.[2]

---

5. Also consider the point made in Brochstein v. Nationwide Mutual Insurance Company, 448 F.2d 987 at p. 990 and p. 989 (2d Cir.1971), *cert. denied* 405 U.S. 921, 92 S.Ct. 957, 30 L.Ed.2d 791 (1972), "an insurer must be careful to give an insured full and accurate information as to settlement possibilities," but that insurers must also take care not "to use the possibility of contribution from the insured as a means of evading their own responsibilities."

6. See the discussion of conflicting interests in § 7.6(a), above.

§ 7.8(e)

1. See, e.g., Zumwalt v. Utilities Insurance Co., 360 Mo. 362, 228 S.W.2d 750 (1950).

2. See the discussion in § 7.8(b), above.

Does a reinsurer have a duty to the primary insured? The answer will usually depend on whether, in the total relationship, the reinsurer has some degree of control over the decisions concerning settlement with the third party claimant.[3] If not, the basis for the duty is lacking; if so, it exists. However, a primary insurer should not be able to escape its duty to the insured by surrendering control over the settlement decision to the reinsurer.

An insured would not be likely to press a claim against a reinsurer unless the primary insurer were insolvent. The issue of the insured's right to recover against a reinsurer is unlikely to be presented for decision by the courts because the insured has a more clear-cut case against the primary insurer. If a primary insurer, having paid a claim in excess of its limits, seeks reimbursement from the reinsurer, it would then be necessary to look to the terms of the reinsurance contract and to the relationship to determine whether such reimbursement is due.[4]

(2) Other Insurance: Primary or Excess Coverage

Questions about the rights and duties of one insurer to another — as well as to the insured — with respect to other insurance, may arise when there are two or more primary coverages or an excess coverage.

When there is more than one primary coverage, each insurer should have a duty both to the other insurer(s) and to each person who is its insured with respect to the claim in question.[5]

In a case where there is an excess coverage, the primary insurer should be held responsible to the excess insurer for an improper failure to settle. The position of an excess insurer is analogous to that of the insured.[6] The right of the excess carrier might be supported either on the theory that it is subrogated to the right of the insured against the

---

3. See, e.g. Reid v. Ruffin, 503 Pa. 458, 469 A.2d 1030 (1983). The court concluded that bad-faith refusal of original insurer to settle claim against its insured could not be imputed to reinsurer — on theory that original insurer was acting as reinsurer's agent — where reinsurance contract authorized original insurer to act on reinsurer's behalf only to limited extent of instances when immediate decision to settle was necessary, and the original insurer's decision not to settle was one over which reinsurer had no control. The court also noted that the reinsurer had not assumed a contractual duty to represent the original insured, which duty the latter must discharge in good faith.

4. See Peerless Insurance Co. v. Inland Mutual Insurance Co., 251 F.2d 696 (4th Cir.1958).

5. See Robert E. Keeton, *Liability Insurance and Responsibility for Settlement,* 67 Harvard Law Review 1136 at pp. 1152–1153 (1954).

6. See, e.g., Hawkeye-Security Insurance Co. v. Indemnity Insurance Co., 260 F.2d 361 (10th Cir.1958), 69 A.L.R.2d 684 (1960); American Fidelity & Casualty Company v. All American Bus Lines, Inc., 190 F.2d 234 (10th Cir.1951), *cert. denied* 342 U.S. 851, 72 S.Ct. 79, 96 L.Ed.2d 642 (1951) (applying Oklahoma law).

Also see Commercial Union Insurance Company v. Liberty Mutual Insurance Company, 426 Mich. 127, 393 N.W.2d 161 (1986); General Accident Fire & Life Assurance Corporation, Ltd. v. American Casualty Company of Reading, Pa., 390 So.2d 761 (Fla.App., 3d Dist., 1980), *petition for review denied* 399 So.2d 1142 (1981).

Cf. St. Paul-Mercury Indemnity Company v. Martin, 190 F.2d 455 at p. 457 (10th Cir.1951) (applying Oklahoma law).

See generally James R. Sutterfield, *Relationships between excess and primary insurers: The excess judgment problem,* 52 Insurance Counsel Journal 638–643 (1985); Annotation, *Duty of liability insurer to set-*

primary carrier [7] or on the theory that the relationship between the insurers gives rise to a duty.[8]

(3) Multiple Claimants

An insurer's duty regarding settlement should not be altered by the involvement of two or more claimants or insurers. Cases involving multiple claimants, however, may present a number of distinctive problems.

In general, the precedents from cases involving a single insurer and single claimant should apply, at least by analogy, to situations involving multiple claimants.[9] However, several claimants may cause additional complexities in regard to the settlement of claims, and in some instances the existence of several claimants clearly makes it more difficult to discern whether the insurer's conduct blocked or impeded a potential settlement within policy limits. When there is more than one claimant, there are several difficult questions which may need to be addressed in regard to how the available insurance benefits should be used on behalf of the insured in effecting settlements or should be allocated among the claimants.[10]

§ 7.8(f) Voluntary Withdrawal of the Insurer From the Defense or Renunciation of Control Over Settlement

The effect of an insurer's voluntary withdrawal from the defense on the insurer's duty regarding settlement is unclear. If such a withdrawal is accepted by the insured and is accompanied by a tender of the coverage limits to be used by the insured in the settlement of one or more claims, a compelling argument exists for the proposition that the insurer should not be subject to any additional liability, save for

tle or compromise, 40 A.L.R.2d 168–226 (1955). Annotation, *Excess Carrier's right to maintain action against primary liability insurer for wrongful failure to settle claim against insured*, 10 A.L.R.4th 879–887 (1981).

7. *Cf.* Valentine v. Aetna Insurance Company, 564 F.2d 292 (9th Cir.1977).

Also see Northwestern Mutual Insurance Company v. Farmer's Insurance Group, 76 Cal.App.3d 1031, 143 Cal.Rptr. 415 (4th Dist., Div.2 1978); Penn's Estate v. Amalgamated General Agencies, 148 N.J. Super. 419, 372 A.2d 1124 (1977); American Fidelity & Casualty Co. v. All American Bus Lines, Inc., 190 F.2d 234 (10th Cir. 1951), *cert. denied* 342 U.S. 851, 72 S.Ct. 79, 96 L.Ed. 642 (1951) (Oklahoma law).

8. *Cf.* the discussion in St. Paul-Mercury Indemnity Co. v. Martin, 190 F.2d 455 at p. 457 (10th Cir.1951) (applying Oklahoma law).

However, when an insured opted to be self-insured for the primary liability, the

California Supreme Court concluded the insurance arrangement with the excess insurer did not include an implied duty upon the insured to accept a settlement offer which would avoid exposing the excess insurer to liability *and* that such a duty cannot be predicated upon an insured's implied covenant of good faith and fair dealing. Commercial Union Assurance Companies v. Safeway Stores, Incorporated, 26 Cal.3d 912, 164 Cal.Rptr. 709, 610 P.2d 1038 (1980). The court concluded, "If an excess carrier wishes to insulate itself from liability for an insured's failure to accept what it deems to be a reasonable settlement offer, it may do so by appropriate language in the policy." *Id.*, 26 Cal.3d at p. 921, 164 Cal.Rptr. at p. 714.

9. Situations involving multiple claimants and limited coverage also present problems of preferential settlement. See § 7.4(c), above.

10. See the discussion in § 7.4, above.

some portion of the defense costs, because the insurer no longer exercises the control over the settlement decisions that serves as the foundation for judicial recognition of the duty regarding settlement and the excess liability. And, there are some precedents which seem to support nonliability in excess of policy limits in this setting, even though the refusal to defend was wrongful.[1]

If a withdrawal or renunciation of control does not make the coverage limits available to the insured, the action should not insulate the insurer from liability. For example, the insurer's withdrawal, especially when the coverage limits are substantial, may deprive the insured of access to funds which would have facilitated a settlement, thereby leading to a trial that produces a judgment in excess of the coverage. In instances when there is a subsequent determination that the insurer's withdrawal was not justified — that is, that the coverage applied — there is substantial support for the view that since the attempted withdrawal or renunciation of control is itself wrongful, it will not be permitted to insulate the company from excess liability.[2]

§ 7.8(g) The Insurer's Right to Continue Directing the Defense Following the Rejection of an Opportunity to Settle

There is a notable interaction between the resolution of the problems posed by conflicting interests of the insurer and the insured,[1] the obligation of the liability insurer to provide a defense for an insured when claims are asserted by a third party against an insured, and the obligation of the insurer in regard to opportunities to settle a claim against an insured.

Whenever there is an opportunity to resolve the claim against an insured by a settlement within policy limits or a settlement in excess of the policy limits for which the insured is prepared to provide the difference between the proposed settlement and the policy limits, a decision by an insurer not to accept such a settlement presents difficult questions if the third party's suit ultimately produces a judgment for which the insured is personally liable — that is, a judgment in excess of the available liability coverage. Ordinarily, when there is a sufficiently significant conflict of interests problem, an insured is entitled to take control of the defense, including the right to select and instruct the attorney who will represent the insured in the defense.[2] In this

§ 7.8(f)

1. *Cf.* Fidelity & Casualty Company v. Gault, 196 F.2d 329 (5th Cir.1952) (Mississippi law).

See generally Robert E. Keeton, *Liability Insurance and Responsibility for Settlement.* 67 Harvard Law Review 1136 at pp. 1159–1161 (1954).

2. For example, in Crisci v. Security Insurance Co., 66 Cal.2d 425, 58 Cal.Rptr. 13, 426 P.2d 173 (1967) the insured, a 70-

year-old widow, became indigent as a result of personal injury judgment of $101,000 against her in action brought by her tenant, which could have been settled within $10,000 liability insurance limit. A $25,000 recovery for mental suffering was approved.

§ 7.8(g)

1. See generally, § 7.6, above.

2. See § 7.6(d)(6), above.

context, however, there is a compelling case for pursuing other courses of action.

One possibility is for the insured to, in effect, insist that the settlement be made. When the insured has sufficient resources, this may be accomplished by the insured without the receipt of funds from the insurer. If this occurs, the question of the insurer's liability would ultimately be determined in a subsequent adjudication of the claim between the insurer and the insured. This approach could be viewed as "triggering" an application of the policy provision (included in most liability insurance policies) that the insured shall not, except at his or her own cost, voluntarily make any payment or assume any obligation. Although this provision might be interpreted to absolve the insurer from all further liability, it would be a very inappropriate construction to adopt when the relationship between the insured and the insurer is pervaded by conflicting interests. In particular, (1) the nature of such clauses as part of a contract of adhesion in the context of most insurance transactions, (2) the desirability of precluding insurers from exercising an unconscionable advantage in such circumstances, and (3) the appropriateness of protecting an insured's reasonable expectations that the liability insurer will not be allowed to prefer its interests over that of its insured, all taken together, provide support for precluding the insurer from invoking this provision as a basis for avoiding liability in such situations.

The other possibility is that the settlement will not be accepted. When the insured does not have the funds to effect such a settlement, the determination rests exclusively with the insurer. The decision not to accept the settlement leaves open the possibility that the ultimate resolution of the third party's claim will be a judgment in excess of policy limits. Since the insurer's decision merely preserves and does not itself create the conflict of interests between the parties, it makes little sense to treat this decision as the basis for wresting from the insurer both the responsibility for and the right to continue to conduct the defense, including decisionmaking regarding the possibilities for settlement which may subsequently occur.

If the insurer were to be held to a standard of strict liability after a decision to reject an opportunity to settle the claim, surely the control of the defense should be left with the insurer. Although no court has explicitly adopted this view, some judicial opinions have suggested the possibility of adopting this approach.

If the insurer is not held to the strict liability standard, there is still substantial justification for preserving the insurer's right to direct the defense, if there is no conflict of interests between the parties other than that regarding settlement. It is true that continued control of the defense by the insurer might serve to diminish the prospects for further exploration of settlement possibilities. Nevertheless, the remedy of a potential cause of action for violation of the duty regarding settlement remains as a deterrent to violation of the insurer's continuing duty. If, on the other hand, the insurer's right to direct the defense were withdrawn, problems would arise with respect to whether it would then be necessary for courts to fashion some standard of responsibility for the conduct of the insured after taking over the defense.

§ 7.8(h)   Damages for Breach

There are several important questions about what damages may be recovered by an insured when an insurer is determined to have committed a breach of the duty to the insured to settle the third party's claim.

(1) Consequential of Damages

One problem concerns the measure of damages. The damages which arise as a consequence of a liability insurer's failure to accept an offer to settle within policy limits clearly include the amount of any collectible tort judgment which exceeds the insured's liability coverage. However, the consequential damages sustained by an insured may not be limited to that differential amount. And some courts hold the insurer's liability extends to all detriments that are the proximate result of an entry of a judgment in excess of the insured's policy limits, including consequential economic loss and even emotional distress.[1]

Emotional Distress and Mental Illness

There have been a number of appellate cases in which the courts have considered whether the damages recoverable in an action for improper failure to settle include compensation for mental illness suffered by the insured as a result of the insurer's wrong. There is limited support for an affirmative answer. For example, in the now well known *Crisci* decision,[2] recovery was allowed for the emotional distress which resulted when the insured was forced to sell her only real estate property to partially satisfy the excess judgment, thereby becoming indigent, and ultimately suffering various medical problems.[3] Thus, in California, unless an insurer takes action following a judgment that will serve to prevent such consequences, the insurer's conduct in the negotiations leads to liability for such proximately caused consequential damages.

§ 7.8(h)

1. See, e.g., Larraburu Brothers, Inc. v. Royal Indemnity Company, 604 F.2d 1208 at p. 1212 (9th Cir.1979) (applying California laws); Neal v. Farmers Insurance Exchange, 21 Cal.3d 910, 148 Cal.Rptr. 389 at p. 397, 582 P.2d 980 at p. 988 (1978).

2. See Crisci v. Security Insurance Company, 66 Cal.2d 425, 58 Cal.Rptr. 13, 426 P.2d 173 (1967).

3. In Crisci v. Security Insurance Co., 66 Cal.2d 425, 58 Cal.Rptr. 13, 426 P.2d 173 (1967) the insured, a 70–year old widow, became indigent as a result of a personal injury judgment of $101,000 against her in action brought by her tenant, which could have been settled within the $10,000 liability insurance limit. A recovery of $25,000 for mental suffering was approved.

Punitive Damages

Courts in many states have now concluded that when an insurer acts in reckless disregard of its insured's rights, an award of punitive damages may be justified.[4] It does not follow, however, that an insured who is entitled to compensatory damages is invariably or automatically entitled to punitive damages. Punitive (or exemplary) awards are only warranted in exceptional circumstances, and the instances in which such claims are sustained are far outnumbered by cases in which the courts view the claim for punitive damages to be unwarranted. As courts have repeatedly held, rigorous standards must be met to justify assessing punitive damages.[5]

§ 7.8(i) Remedies for Insureds Who Are Solvent and Those Who Are "Insolvent"

Controversy over remedies for breach of an insurance company's duty regarding settlement have sometimes centered on whether, and, if so, how, the financial status of the insured is relevant to the amount of consequential damage an insured sustained as a result of a judgment in excess of the applicable liability insurance policy limits — that is, on how the right of an insured to secure compensation for a wrongful failure to settle a tort claim is affected by the relative wealth of the insured. Courts have been sharply divided on these questions, as well as subsidiary or related issues. This is especially the case when the insured is either actually or pragmatically "judgment proof" — that is, when an insured is bankrupt or insolvent, or when the insured has essentially no assets subject to levy of execution.[1]

(1) "Insolvent" Insureds

There are several views about what losses are sustained by an insured who is legally "insolvent" or who appears to have no assets which could be taken, or are likely to be subject to being taken in the future, to satisfy the third party's tort judgment. In circumstances when an insured is either legally "judgment proof" or has no assets, one view is that the insured's cause of action against the insurer for

---

4. See the discussion of punitive damages in § 7.10, below.

5. *Cf.* Henderson v. United States Fidelity and Guaranty Company, 620 F.2d 530 at p. 536 (5th Cir.1980) (applying Mississippi law), *cert. denied* 449 U.S. 1034, 101 S.Ct. 608, 66 L.Ed.2d 495 (1980) ("The act of giving rise to punitive damages must be 'a willful and intentional wrong, ∗ ∗ ∗ or such gross negligence and reckless negligence as is equivalent to such a wrong.' "). Also see subsequent opinion reported at 695 F.2d 109 (1983).

Cf. Silberg v. California Life Insurance Company, 11 Cal.3d 452 at p. 462, 113 Cal.

Rptr. 711 at p. 718, 521 P.2d 1103 at p. 1110 (1974) ("In order to justify an award of exemplary damages, the defendant must be guilty of oppression, fraud or malice. (Civ.Code, § 3294.) He must act with the conscious disregard of the plaintiff's rights.").

§ 7.8(i)

1. The problems and issues addressed in these cases also are relevant to the question whether the proceeds of an insured's cause of action against the insurer can or should be available to provide compensation to the injured person.

liability in excess of policy limits does not accrue unless and until the insured pays something on the judgment.[2] Other courts have indicated that an insurer should not be liable until the insured's financial status improves to such an extent that some portion of the excess judgment could be collected.[3] This type of approach leads to the conclusion that when the insured has no assets available for collection of a judgment by legal process and there is no evidence the insured has paid or will pay in some other way, the insurer is not liable for any amount in excess of policy limits because its failure to settle has not caused damage to the insured.[4] In other words, the determination of damages in the excess liability cause of action against the insurer depends on an actual payment *or* — if nothing has been recovered on the excess liability claim — proof (satisfying the standard of reasonable probability) that a payment of the excess liability of the insured will occur in the future.[5] The most persuasive case for this view probably exists when the insured is actually determined to be either insolvent or bankrupt.

When it seems almost certain the insured will never pay anything at all on the excess judgment if the claim against the insurer is denied, arguments that the insured has been damaged by the increase in debts [6] are rather weak support for any cause of action at all, much less for a measure of damages equal to the amount of the increase in the insured's debts. However, other courts have concluded that the entry of judgment against a person constitutes a loss and that the insured's "loss does not turn on whether the judgment has been satisfied." [7] Since, absent a discharge of the obligation through a bankruptcy proceeding, the third party's judgment can remain as an outstanding obligation for extended periods of time, in many circumstances there is considerable uncertainty in regard to predicting whether the insured

---

2. See, e.g., State Automobile Mutual Insurance Co. v. York, 104 F.2d 730 (4th Cir.1939), *cert. denied* 308 U.S. 591, 60 S.Ct. 120, 84 L.Ed. 495 (1939) (North Carolina law; alternate ground for decision).

Also see Universal Automobile Insurance Company v. Culberson, 126 Tex. 282, 86 S.W.2d 727 at 731 (1935). There is also a subsequent opinion in this case reported at 126 Tex. 282, 87 S.W.2d 475 (1935).

3. See, e.g., Dumas v. Hartford Accident & Indemnity Company, 92 N.H. 140 at p. 141, 26 A.2d 361 at p. 362 (1942).

4. E.g., Harris v. Standard Accident & Insurance Company, 297 F.2d 627 (2d Cir. 1961), *cert. denied* 369 U.S. 843, 82 S.Ct. 875, 7 L.Ed.2d 847 (1962) (insured insolvent before rendition of the excess judgment, paid no part of it, and was discharged in bankruptcy).

5. Dumas v. Hartford Accident & Indemnity Co., 92 N.H. 140, 26 A.2d 361 (1942), speaks of a showing that "the excess judgment is sure to be collected." But it

would seem that the jury would be told to resolve this fact issue as they are told generally to resolve issues about future events, by a standard of proof that falls short of certainty and is often phrased as reasonable probability.

6. See Schwartz v. Norwich Union Indemnity Company, 212 Wis. 593, 250 N.W. 446 (1933) (cause of action "in tort for fraudulent and negligent handling of the defense" rather than for failure to settle; analogy to expenses incurred, but unpaid, by reason of an injury).

Also see Southern Fire & Casualty Company v. Norris, 35 Tenn.App. 657, 250 S.W.2d 785 (1952).

7. DiMarzo v. American Mutual Insurance Company, 389 Mass. 85 at p. 94, 449 N.E.2d 1189 at p. 1196 (1983). However in *DiMarzo*, the court specifically noted that it did not need to decide "whether insolvency would preclude a finding that a person suffered a loss of money or property." *Ibid.*, at footnote 9.

may ultimately have resources or assets that may be taken to satisfy some portion of the judgment.[8]

Third party claimants are not in a position to assert that they were harmed as a result of the insurer's conduct in regard to having not settled the tort claim. The insurer's duty was to the insured, not to the claimant.[9] Furthermore, in one sense, a third party benefits from the insurer's refusal to settle because the insurer's refusal to settle resulted in the claimant's obtaining a judgment in excess of the amount the claimant had offered to accept in settlement. Thus, although the third party claimant deserves further compensation, the theoretical justification for imposing liability on the insurer, which is harm to the insured, does not warrant a recovery by such a claimant any more than the innocent victims of an underinsured tortfeasor would be entitled to indemnification beyond the amount of the applicable coverage [10] from a liability insurer who had not refused a settlement.

(2) Solvent Insureds

When an insured is solvent, and especially when an insured has substantial assets, there is little problem in showing that the insured will sustain a loss as a consequence of the insured's decision not to accept a settlement within the coverage limits. If an insurer of a solvent insured does not accept a third party claimant's settlement offer, the insured is in a position to predicate a claim for excess liability on proof either that payment has been made or will be made in the future, or that the insured has substantial assets that are subject to being taken to satisfy the judgment. Thus, when the insured is thoroughly solvent, at least one of the consequences of the third party's tort judgment against the insured is relatively clear. This is not equally true in relation to the insureds who are among the great middle group comprised of individuals who, though solvent, are likely to encounter considerable hardship if the tort judgment is pressed, but against whom the injured person may choose not to pursue full satisfaction of the judgment.[11]

Whenever an insured either has assets taken by legal process for partial (or full) payment of an excess judgment or makes a payment voluntarily to avoid such legal process, the insured should be allowed to recover an equal amount from the insurer. Moreover, the third party

---

8. In *DiMarzo*, the Court quoted the observation, from a lower court decision in another case, that "the judgments have established a debt * * * [and] any one inquiring into the financial status of the plaintiffs subject to the judgments would, realistically, consider each poorer by the amount of the judgment rendered." *Id.*, 449 N.E.2d at p. 1196.

9. The duty involved in these cases is to be distinguished from the duty regarding preferential settlement. That duty, if recognized at all, is surely a duty to claim-

ants, though it may extend to the insured also.

10. The practical effect of allowing a claimant a cause of action based on the failure to settle within policy limits, would be the introduction of a fortuitous and occasional protection beyond policy limits. See generally Robert E. Keeton, *Liability Insurance and Responsibility for Settlement*, 67 Harvard Law Review 1136 at pp. 1175–1177 (1954).

11. See *Id.* at pp. 1179–1182.

claimant (in the position of a judgment creditor after the conclusion of the tort suit) may continue to seek indemnification until the full amount of the judgment against the insured has been paid.

In most instances, however, the amount that the third party claimant/judgment creditor will ultimately recover has not been resolved when the insured's claim against the liability insurer for excess liability is being determined. Even though the full measure of the harm sustained by the insured remains at least somewhat uncertain in this type of situation, numerous appellate court decisions on point have allowed recovery to the full extent of the excess judgment without proof of payment or future payment (probable or certain) by the insured.[12]

(3) Assertion of Excess Claims by Third Party Claimants

In a number of instances, the insured's claim against the liability insurer has been assigned [13] to the third party claimant.[14] Several appellate opinions, upholding the insured's assignment of the insured's cause of action to the tort claimant, are reasonably interpreted as implying that there may be a recovery to the full extent of the excess judgment without proof of either a past payment or a guarantee of a future payment.[15]

12. E.g., Comunale v. Traders & General Insurance Company, 50 Cal.2d 654, 328 P.2d 198 (1958), 68 A.L.R.2d 883 (1959); Ammerman v. Farmers Insurance Exchange, 22 Utah 2d 187, 450 P.2d 460 (1969) (payment on judgment not essential to cause of action; new trial granted).

13. In most states, even if an insurer acted in bad faith, the third party claimant, who becomes a judgment creditor of an insured when there is a tort judgment, does not have a cause of action against the insurer because the insurer's duty is to the insured. See, e.g., Kennedy v. Kiss, 89 Ill. App.3d 890, 45 Ill.Dec. 273, 412 N.E.2d 624 (1st Dist., Div. 4, 1980). Scroggins v. Allstate Insurance Company, 74 Ill.App.3d 1027, 30 Ill.Dec. 682, 393 N.E.2d 718 (1st Dist., Div. 2, 1979); Lisiewski v. Countrywide Insurance Company, 75 Mich.App. 631, 255 N.W.2d 714 (1977).

However, a direct action statute may alter the common law rule. For example, in Iowa the legislation states that a judgment creditor shall have a right of action against an insurer "to the same extent that such insured could have enforced his claim against such insurer * * *." The Iowa Supreme Court concluded on the basis of this provision, that a truck driver who was injured in automobile accident and who obtained judgment against tortfeasor for amount in excess of tortfeasor's insurance coverage had, could, by virtue of the direct action statute, bring an action against the insurer. Trask v. Iowa Kemper Mutual

Insurance Company, 248 N.W.2d 97 (Iowa 1976).

14. See generally Annotation, *Right of injured person recovering excess judgment against insured to maintain action against liability insurer for wrongful failure to settle claim*, 63 A.L.R.3d 677–714 (1975).

15. See, e.g., Nationwide Mutual Insurance Co. v. McNulty, 229 So.2d 585 (Fla. 1969), citing with approval Gray v. Nationwide Mutual Insurance Co., 422 Pa. 500, 223 A.2d 8 (1966), in which the court explicitly allowed recovery of the full amount of the excess judgment in an action on an assigned claim.

In the absence of an assignment, courts will probably conclude that the injured third party normally will not have a cause of action against a liability insurer on the basis of the insurer's breach of the duty to negotiate in good faith. For example, in Scroggins v. Allstate Insurance Company, 74 Ill.App.3d 1027, 30 Ill.Dec. 682, 393 N.E.2d 718 (1st Dist.1979), the court concluded the duty was owed to the insureds, not the third parties. Also see Tank v. State Farm Fire & Casualty Company, 105 Wash.2d 381, 715 P.2d 1133 (1986).

In states that have adopted direct action statutes, the courts may be disposed to award a broader scope to the insurer's obligation to accident victims predicated on the public policy underlying such legislation.

If the insured actually serves as no more than a conduit for a payment to the third party of the amount of excess liability that the insurer has been adjudged to be liable for, this result is basically incompatible with the proposition that a remedy should be limited to the damage suffered by the person who has been wronged — the insured. Allowing a recovery by the third party claimant, especially of consequential damages sustained by the insured beyond the differential amount of judgment and the coverage limits, provides a windfall to the third party claimant. Nevertheless, this result might be justifiable if the available alternatives were limited to either allowing the windfall or granting protection to the insurer that acted wrongfully. Thus, allowing a recovery beyond the damage sustained by the third party claimant might be warranted if to do otherwise would allow the insurer's conduct to escape the liability viewed as warranted by the court.[16] This would be, in effect, the lesser of two evils.

Note. In many instances, the assignment to the judgment creditor/third party claimant of the insured's claim against the insurer is made in exchange for an agreement that the insured will thereafter not be held personally liable for the tort judgment — that is, the judgment creditor in effect, and sometimes explicitly, releases the insured from liability.[17] However, if such an agreement serves to terminate the insured's exposure to liability in excess of the applicable coverage limit, a persuasive case can be made for the proposition that the insured — and the judgment creditor "standing in the shoes" of the insured as a result of the assignment — no longer has the basis for the claim that previously existed against the insurance company for the failure to take advantage of the opportunity to settle the claim within the policy limits. Although several courts have reached this result,[18] it seems likely that the practical impact of such judicial decisions will be either (1) some type of restructuring of agreements between third party claimants and insureds or (2) inducements to misrepresentation of the nature of arrangements to which such precedents are applicable.

Similarly, the concerns for the interests of innocent victims that has disposed courts to circumscribe coverage limitations in liability insurance policies may lead some courts to allow such claims by victims for excess liability, when a settlement was refused, rather than requiring the somewhat circuitous approach which is entailed by the assignment of the insured's claim to the third party in order to avoid further actions by the third party in pursuit of collecting the judgment. *Cf.* Royal Globe Insurance Company v. Superior Court, 23 Cal.3d 880, 153 Cal.Rptr. 842, 592 P.2d 329 (1979).

16. *Cf.* Note, *Rights of Insured-Action for Wrongful Refusal to Settle Arises Before*

Payment of Judgment and Passes to Trustee in Bankruptcy, 72 Harvard Law Review 568 at pp. 569–573 (1959).

17. See the agreement set out as an Appendix in Clement v. Prudential Property & Casualty Insurance Company, 790 F.2d 1545 at pp. 1548–1550 (11th Cir.1986). *Cf.* Crisci v. Security Insurance Company, 66 Cal.2d 425, 58 Cal.Rptr. 13, 426 P.2d 173 (1967).

18. See, e.g., Clement v. Prudential Property & Casualty Insurance Company, 790 F.2d 1545, (11th Cir.1986) applying Florida law on the basis of the decision in Fidelity and Casualty Company v. Cope, 462 So.2d 459 (Fla.1985).

(4) Comment: Liability to the Extent of a Solvent Insured's Net Assets

It should be possible to formulate a workable doctrine (1) that fully protects the insured from loss, (2) that does not result in eliminating the "penalty" on the insurer, and (3) that does not produce a "windfall" for the third party claimant. One of the reasons that such a solution has not been developed probably is that opposing advocates have generally chosen to advance the more extreme positions, rather than intermediate positions that would involve a more limited measure of damages that would conform to such a doctrine or theory of liability. On the one hand, counsel for the third party claimants — pressing the insured's cause of action either in the insured's name or in the name of the claimant as assignee or successor to the insured's right[19] — have sought to establish liability to the full extent of the excess judgment, regardless of the insured's financial status. On the other hand, counsel for insurers have generally attempted to establish that proof of the amount paid or of the certainty (or at least reasonable probability) of an amount of future payment is essential to the cause of action.

The appropriate measure of damages, when an insured is entitled to a recovery that is in excess of the applicable liability insurance policy limits, should be the amount needed to make the insured whole by placing the insured in the same position that would have existed had there been no breach of the duty to settle. Furthermore, this sum should be established after taking into account the amount, if any, that the third party claimant could have realized upon rights against the insured if there had been no cause of action for liability in excess of policy limits — that is, after taking into account how much could have been recovered above the insurance policy limits against an insured who had some assets, but not enough that the third party could recover more than could have been recovered against the insured. This might be done by permitting a single recovery against the insurer on the excess liability claim, at the instance of either the insured or the third party claimant, in an amount equal to the insured's net assets which are not exempt from legal process,[20] and holding that the claimant's tort judgment against the insured is fully discharged by payment of this sum to the claimant either by the insured or by the insurer on the insured's behalf. Although in some instances this amount may be somewhat more than the net recovery the claimant would otherwise have realized (apart from the excess liability claim) this approach

---

19. Most decisions in point have supported assignability of the insured's cause of action against the company for breach of its duty regarding settlement: Liberty Mutual Insurance Co. v. Davis, 412 F.2d 475 (5th Cir.1969) (Florida law); Critz v. Farmers Insurance Group, 230 Cal.App.2d 788, 41 Cal.Rptr. 401 (Third District, 1964), 12 A.L.R.3d 1142 (1967) (holding valid an assignment executed even before trial of the tort claim against the insured); Gray v. Nationwide Mutual Insurance Co., 422 Pa. 500, 223 A.2d 8 (1966).

Contra. Dillingham v. Tri-State Insurance Co., 214 Tenn. 592, 381 S.W.2d 914 (1964).

20. The present discussion refers only to the damages for economic loss. Concerning possible recovery for mental distress as well, § 7.8(h).

certainly more closely approximates that recovery and it provides full protection of the insured's financial position from the consequences of the insurer's wrong to the insured in failing to settle.

The financial interests of both the insured and the third party claimant are better served by the solution proposed in the preceding paragraph than by leaving them to other legal processes, such as a bankruptcy proceeding, the costs of which would have an adverse impact on the interests of each. This proposal may not be fully within the scope of avoidable consequences rules as thus far developed, because decisions applying this concept have been concerned with mitigating damages in a different sense.[21] However, it is within the scope of the principle underlying the avoidable consequences rule: the principle that even though a person can show that in fact losses have been greater, legal relief is limited to what that person would have been entitled to receive if reasonable actions had been taken to minimize the harm.

Even though a claimant's tort claim has already been reduced to judgment, the underlying spirit of exemption and bankruptcy laws expresses a public policy that there should be a reasonable limitation on the hardship the claimant is permitted to impose by strict enforcement of the judgment. In this context, the availability of a cause of action against the insurer in excess of its policy limits offers a distinctive opportunity — not generally existing in other settings involving judgment creditors — for achieving at least as much as could be attained for the claimant through enforcement of the judgment as far as the exemption and bankruptcy laws would permit, but without incurring the costs of bankruptcy to the claimant himself and to the insured. It seems consistent with the principles underlying both the avoidable consequences doctrine, the exemption rules, specifically, and the bankruptcy laws, generally, to adopt this intermediate measure of damages in excess liability claims.

The application of this measure of damages may present problems of proof not heretofore faced, but they should be manageable. For example, the insurer should have the right to offer satisfactory evidence on these issues if it can, shouldering the burden as one customarily does in advancing an avoidable consequences defense.

The implementation of this approach requires that the insured suffer a loss of privacy because of the necessity for a complete disclosure of the insured's financial situation. This is, however, a consequence to which the insured has contributed by committing a tort against the claimant that caused damages of such severity that the limited amount of liability insurance coverage, chosen by the insured, was inadequate. The loss of privacy in this context is a burden that it seems both reasonable and justifiable for the insured to bear.

---

21. *Cf.* RESTATEMENT OF CONTRACTS, Second (1982), § 350; RESTATEMENT OF TORTS, (1979), § 918.

The only realistic alternative to such an intermediate solution is to set the measure of damages in these cases at the full amount of the judgment, a solution that would disadvantage the insured and others like the insured by increasing the costs of low-limit liability insurance.

§ 7.8(j) Statute of Limitations

A few courts have considered whether the statute of limitation that applies to an insured's claim against the insurer begins to run when the insurer refuses to accept a settlement offer or sometime thereafter. Courts have generally held that the limitation period applying to a cause of action for liability in excess of policy limits does not begin to run at the time of the company's wrongful failure to settle.[1] Although there is a relative dearth of cases in which it appears to have made a difference, there is some authority for the proposition that the limitation period begins to run at the time a tort judgment against the insured becomes final.[2]

In California, the courts have concluded that the statute of limitation should not begin until there is a final judgment against the insured because "the fact of an excess verdict may have great evidentiary value in determining whether the original refusal to settle was unreasonable."[3] An alternative to this approach would start the running of the statutorily prescribed period from the time when some payment is made by the insured.

Even if the time of payment is chosen as the appropriate moment to initiate the running of the statute of limitations, it seems unlikely that a payment other than one to the claimant (for example, payment of a fee to an investigator or to an attorney employed by the insured to protect the insured's interests after the company wrongfully refused to settle) would be held to start the running of the limitation period.

Contract or Tort Claim

The choice of contract or tort theory as the basis of an excess-liability claim may affect the limitation period. The authority on this point includes support for the proposition that the action "sounds both in contract and tort" and therefore the plaintiff may rely upon the contract theory to avoid a shorter statute of limitations applying to tort

---

§ 7.8(j)

1. See, e.g., American Mutual Liability Insurance Company v. Cooper, 61 F.2d 446 (5th Cir.1932), *cert. denied* 289 U.S. 736, 53 S.Ct. 595, 77 L.Ed. 1483 (1933); Attleboro Manufacturing Company v. Frankfort Marine, Accident & Plate Glass Insurance Company, 240 Fed. 573 (1st Cir.1917); Communale v. Traders & General Insurance Company, 50 Cal.2d 654, 328 P.2d 198 (1958), 68 A.L.R.2d 883 (1959); Linkenhoger v. American Fidelity & Casualty Company, 152 Tex. 534, 260 S.W.2d 884 (1953).

2. See, e.g. Larraburu v. Royal Indemnity Company, 604 F.2d 1208 (9th Cir.1979) (applying California law).

3. *Id.*, 604 F.2d at p. 1214. Also see the California decisions cited in this opinion.

actions.[4]   However, there is also support for the proposition that the action is exclusively a tort claim.[5]

§ 7.8(k)   Proposals for Legislation or Revision of Policy Forms

One approach to solving the excess-liability dilemma would be legislation that imposes some form of strict liability.[1]   One important question on which relevant information has not been made available to the public is what the difference in premium costs would be in the event such a change were adopted.   A decision on the desirability of this approach might also be influenced by data on the costs of litigation for claims by insureds that the insurer's failure to settle amounted to bad faith or negligence.   In the absence of such data, conclusions about the relative advantages of proposals for change are at best speculative.

§ 7.9   The Liability of First Party Insurers for Consequential Damages

§ 7.9.(a)   Introduction

Relatively soon after the California Supreme Court decisions in *Comunale* (1958)[1] and *Crisci* (1967)[2] — holding that an insured could recover damages as a consequence of a liability insurer's breach of a duty of "good faith" in relation to settlement of tort claims against the insured[3] — many courts were presented with the question whether an insured could recover damages (consequential and punitive) when there was a breach of an implied obligation to deal fairly and in good faith in regard to various types of first party insurance contracts.

There is a significant difference between the consequences for an insured when a first party insurer does not deal fairly and in good faith by not promptly paying a claim for insurance benefits, and the breach of such an obligation when a liability insurer does not accept a settlement offer that is within the coverage limits of an insured's liability insurance policy.   An insured whose insurer is recalcitrant in regard to the payment of first party insurance benefits is not subject to the possibility that the subsequent litigation of a tort claim against the insured will

---

4. See, e.g., Communale v. Traders & General Insurance Company, 50 Cal.2d 654, 328 P.2d 198 (1958), 68 A.L.R.2d 883 (1959).

5. See, e.g., Wolfe v. Continental Casualty Company, 647 F.2d 705 (6th Cir.1981), *cert. denied* 454 U.S. 1053, 102 S.Ct. 597, 70 L.Ed.2d 588 (1981).

§ 7.8(k)

1. See the discussion of strict liability in § 7.8(b)(3) and § 7.8(b)(4), above.

See Robert Keeton, *Liability Insurance and Responsibility for Settlement,* 67 Harvard Law Review 1136 at pp. 1183–1186 (1954).

Another proposed approach has been to establish either an automatic increase in or the elimination of the limit of liability upon an insurer's refusal of an offer of settlement within the policy limit.

§ 7.9(a)

1. Comunale v. Traders & General Insurance Company, 50 Cal.2d 654, 328 P.2d 198 (1958), 68 A.L.R.2d 883 (1959).

2. Crisci v. Security Insurance Company, 66 Cal.2d 425, 58 Cal.Rptr. 13, 426 P.2d 173 (1967).

3. See § 7.8, above.

result in a judgment that exceeds the applicable liability insurance coverage, and the consequences which may occur for the insured as a result of actions which are taken to collect such a judgment. In other ways, however, a first-party insured may suffer consequential harm beyond the mere nonpayment of the promised benefits.

When an insurer fails to pay a first party insurance claim and the insured is compelled to seek the assistance of a lawyer to secure an adjudication which establishes that the insured is entitled to the insurance benefits, a persuasive case can sometimes be made that the insurer has not dealt fairly or in good faith with its insured. In a 1970 decision, Fletcher v. Western National Life Insurance Company,[4] a California Court of Appeal concluded that the insurer's "threatened and actual bad faith refusals to make payments under the [disability] policy, maliciously employed by defendants in concert with false and threatening communications * * * is essentially tortious in nature and is conduct that may legally be the basis for an action for damages for intentional infliction of emotional distress" or the tortious interference with a property interest.[5] In *Fletcher,* the court also stated that the principles set forth by the California Supreme Court in *Crisci* were applicable — that is, that the withholding of payments due under a disability insurance policy was a breach of the implied-in-law duty of good faith and fair dealing owed by the insurer to its insured.

Three years after the Court of Appeal's decision in *Fletcher,* in Gruenberg v. Aetna Insurance Company, the California Supreme Court affirmed that an independent cause of action in tort exists when a first party insurer violates the implied-in-law duty of good faith and fair dealing.[6] And, in 1974, the California Supreme Court sustained an award of $75,000 in compensatory damages for physical and mental stress which resulted when an insurer failed to make payments for a claim under a medical insurance policy and that failure was adjudged a breach of the implied covenant of good faith and fair dealing.[7] The decisions in these California cases have become landmark opinions which are very widely cited by courts in other states that have considered similar claims.[8]

In the almost two decades since the *Fletcher* decision, courts in numerous jurisdictions have concluded (1) that first party insurers are obligated to deal fairly with their insureds in regard to the settlement of claims, and (2) that the failure to fulfill this obligation warrants the award of consequential [9] and, at least in some circumstances, punitive

4. Fletcher v. Western National Life Insurance Company, 10 Cal.App.3d 376, 89 Cal.Rptr. 78 (4th Dist., Div. 2, 1970), 47 A.L.R.3d 286 (1973).

5. *Id.,* 10 Cal.App.3d at p. 401, 89 Cal. Rptr. at p. 93.

6. Gruenberg v. Aetna Insurance Company, 9 Cal.3d 566, 108 Cal.Rptr. 480, 510 P.2d 1032 (1973).

7. Silberg v. California Life Insurance Company, 11 Cal.3d 452, 113 Cal.Rptr. 711, 521 P.2d 1103 (1974).

8. See the decisions cited in the following notes.

9. For example, see:

Alabama. Chavers v. National Security Fire & Casualty Company, 405 So.2d 1

damages.[10] Taken together, these decisions clearly establish the principle that insurers are obligated to avoid both irresponsible decisions not to pay and unwarranted delays in the payment of insurance benefits provided by first party insurance coverages such as disability insurance, health insurance, fire insurance, no-fault automobile insurance, and uninsured motorist insurance.[11]

Caveats. Courts in several states have declined to recognize either a contractual claim or a tort of "bad faith" in regard to the conduct of an insurer in response to a first party insurance claim.[12] And, in some

(Ala.1981), *appeal after remand* 456 So.2d 293 (1984).

Arizona. Sparks v. Republic National Life Insurance Company, 132 Ariz. 529, 647 P.2d 1127 (1982), *cert. denied* 459 U.S. 1070, 103 S.Ct. 490, 74 L.Ed.2d 632 (1982). Also see Noble v. National American Life Insurance Company, 128 Ariz. 188, 624 P.2d 866 (1981).

California. Moore v. American United Life Insurance Company, 150 Cal.App.3d 610, 197 Cal.Rptr. 878 (3d Dist.1984).

Idaho. Linscott v. Rainier National Life Insurance Company, 100 Idaho 854 at p. 860, 606 P.2d 958 at p. 964 (1980).

New Hampshire. Jarvis v. Prudential Insurance Company of America, 122 N.H. 648, 448 A.2d 407 (1982); Lawton v. Great Southwest Fire Insurance Company, 118 N.H. 607, 392 A.2d 576 (1978). Also see deVries v. St. Paul Fire and Marine Insurance Company, 716 F.2d 939 (1st Cir.1983) (Applying New Hampshire law).

Ohio. Cf. Hoskins v. Aetna Life Insurance Company, 6 Ohio St.3d 272, 452 N.E. 2d 1315 (1983).

Oklahoma. Christian v. American Home Insurance Company, 577 P.2d 899 (Okl.1977).

Rhode Island. Bibeault v. Hanover Insurance Company, ___ R.I. ___, 417 A.2d 313 (1980).

Virginia. Also see A & E Supply Company, Inc. v. Nationwide Mutual Fire Insurance Company, 798 F.2d 669 (4th Cir. 1986) (applying Virginia law), *cert. denied* ___ U.S. ___, 107 S.Ct. 1302, 94 L.Ed.2d 158 (1987).

West Virginia. Cf. Morgan v. American Family Life Assurance Company of Columbus, 559 F.Supp. 477 (W.D.Va.1983).

Wisconsin. Anderson v. Continental Insurance Company, 85 Wis.2d 675, 271 N.W.2d 368 (1978).

Also see Annotation, *Insurer's liability for consequential or punitive damages for wrongful delay or refusal to make payments*

due under contracts, 47 A.L.R.3d 314–351 (1973) (by A.S. Klein).

See generally Leon D. Bess and Julie A. Doherty, *Survey of Bad Faith Claims in First Party and Industrial Proceedings,* 1982 Insurance Counsel Journal 368–375.

Also see Comment, *Bad faith refusal of insurance companies to pay first party benefits—time for Illinois Supreme Court to recognize the tort and resulting punitive damages,* 1984 Southern Illinois University Law Journal 121–144 (1984); Note, *An insurer's bad faith refusal to pay a valid first party claim,* 32 Drake Law Review 987–1014 (1982–1983); Comment, *Liability Insurers and Third-Party Claimants: The Limits of Duty,* 48 University of Chicago Law Review 125–157 (1981); Note, *The Availability of Excess Damages for Wrongful Refusal to Honor First Party Insurance Claims—An Emerging Trend,* 45 Fordham Law Review 164–182 (1976).

10. See the discussion of punitive damages in § 7.10, below.

11. See generally John C. McCarthy, PUNITIVE DAMAGES IN BAD FAITH CASES (Third Edition, 1983), at § 1.11 through § 1.19; James D. Ghiardi & John J. Kircher, PUNITIVE DAMAGES LAW AND PRACTICE (1985), at § 8.08 through § 8.14; 16A APPLEMAN, INSURANCE LAW AND PRACTICE (1981), at § 8877 through § 8879.

Also see Jerome Murray and Michael Maillet, *Extra-Contractual Remedies and Punitive Damages in First Party Insurance Claims,* 1986 Insurance Counsel Journal 251–263 (1986); Steven J. Harmon, *An Insurer's Liability for the Tort of Bad Faith,* 42 Montana Law Review 67–92 (1981); Alyson K. Kottke, *Plugging the Cracks: The Basis and Extent of Liability for First Party Bad Faith Claims,* 32 Federation of Insurance Counsel Quarterly 79–101.

12. See, e.g., Spencer v. Aetna Life & Casualty Insurance Company, 227 Kan. 914 at p. 922, 611 P.2d 149 at p. 155 (1980).

Cf. Garden State Community Hospital v. Watson, 191 N.J.Super. 225 at p. 227, 465

states, the courts have concluded that state legislation on unfair trade practices or claims settlement constitutes the exclusive remedy for bad faith conduct by an insurer in regard to the rejection or delay in the payment of an insurance claim — that is, the statutes preempt a court from recognizing a common law action and remedy.[13]

§ 7.9.(b) The Theoretical Basis for Liability

Courts have set forth a variety of rationales to justify imposing liability on first party insurers. For example, the Arizona Supreme Court related the insurer's obligation to "securing the reasonable expectations of the insured," to the "unequal bargaining position between the insured and the insurance company" that frequently exists, and to the "especially vulnerable economic position" the insured often is in when a casualty loss occurs.[1] Similarly, a Federal District Judge observed that a tort action for the bad faith breach applies to first party situations because the adhesion character of many insurance transactions results in a "lack of bargaining power of the insured at the time of settlement * * *." [2] Another Federal District Judge pointed out that "[r]ecognition of an action permitting an insured to recover damages in excess of the actual amount owed under the contract would provide an effective means of countering the existing incentives for an insurance company to delay or deny payment" and that "the New Jersey Supreme Court would provide insureds with this avenue for relief when insurance companies withhold payments maliciously and without probable cause." [3] And the Third Circuit Court of Appeals predicted that

A.2d 1225 at p. 1226 (App.Div.1982), *cert. denied* 94 N.J. 518, 468 A.2d 176 (1983).

13. *Cf.* Spencer v. Aetna Life & Casualty Company, 227 Kan. 914, 611 P.2d 149 (1980). In *Spencer* the court concluded, "We do not say the legislative remedy is exclusive but in the absence of a more definitive showing of inadequacy of the remedy than we have before us at this time, we hold the remedies are adequate to force compliance with the terms of insurance contracts." *Id.,* 611 P.2d at p. 158.

Also see Duncan v. Andrew County Mutual Insurance Company, 665 S.W.2d 13 at p. 19 (Mo.App., Western Dist., 1983).

In Seeman v. Liberty Mutual Insurance Company, 322 N.W.2d 35 (Iowa 1982), the court concluded that the Iowa legislature implicitly intended the administrative remedies of the unfair trade practices statutes to be the exclusive means of enforcing the statute and that therefore no private cause of action stemmed from the legislation.

But cf. Jenkins v. J.C. Penney Casualty Insurance Company, 167 W.Va. 597, 280 S.E.2d 252 (1981), where the court concluded that a private cause of action could be implied from the West Virginia unfair trade practices act; Di Salvatore v. Aetna Casualty and Surety Company, 624 F.Supp. 541 (D.N.J.1986).

Also see the discussion in § 7.7, above.

§ 7.9(b)

1. Noble v. National American Life Insurance Co., 128 Ariz. 188 at pp. 189–190, 624 P.2d 866 at pp. 867–868 (1981).

2. Hiatt v. Schreiber, 599 F.Supp. 1142 at p. 1146 (D.Colo.1984).

Cf. Polito v. Continental Casualty Company, 689 F.2d 457 at p. 461 (3d Cir.1982) (applying New Jersey law). The opinion includes the observation, "Some courts, recognizing that the parties to insurance contracts do not have equal bargaining power, and that insurance companies, if liability is limited to the amount of the loss plus interest, are encouraged to take advantage of the insured by delaying payments, have awarded consequential damages for breach of contract."

3. Di Salvatore v. Aetna Casualty and Surety Company, 624 F.Supp. 541 (D.N.J.1986).

the "New Jersey courts would recognize that casualty insurers undertake an implied contractual duty, as fiduciaries to parties with whom they have a contractual relationship, to act in good faith and to deal fairly in the settlement of claims * * *."[4] Although these statements set forth familiar concepts in regard to insurance transactions and the relationship between an insurer and an insured, they do not articulate a precise theoretical basis for liability.

The conceptualization of the theoretical foundation for liability claims for breach of such a duty has varied from state to state. The theoretical basis for claims against first party insurers predicated on an insurer's violation of the implied-in-law duty of good faith and fair dealing can be related to an action sounding in either tort or contract.[5] Judicial decisions sustaining recoveries by claimants over the past two decades include suits that have been predicated on theories that the insurer committed (1) a breach of contract, (2) an intentional tort, (3) a negligent tort, or (4) a wrong supporting a hybrid action that asserts breach of a contractual duty giving rise to tort liability which entitles an insured to both compensatory and punitive (exemplary) damages.

(1) Breach of Contract

Courts in some of the states that have addressed the question have concluded that the insurer's conduct involves a breach of the insurance contract and that the breach provides the basis for an action sounding in contract.[6] In most of these opinions, the theory is associated with the proposition that every contract imposes upon each party a duty of good faith and fair dealing in its performance.[7] However, some courts have reasoned that a tort will be deemed to arise out of a contractual

---

Cf. Eckenrode v. Life of America Insurance Company, 470 F.2d 1 at p. 5 (7th Cir. 1972) (applying Illinois law), predicating the decision to sustain the plaintiff's complaint for a bad faith cause of action (against the insurer's motion to dismiss) in part on the rationale that relationship of insurers to insureds is imbued with the public interest.

Another Federal District Court observed, "The greater the delay in paying claims, the greater the pressure on impecunious insureds to settle valid claims, thereby depriving themselves of the full value of their insurance coverage." Mann v. Glens Falls Insurance Company, 418 F.Supp. 237 at p. 248 (D.Nev.1974), *reversed for unrelated reasons in a decision reported at* 541 F.2d 819 (9th Cir.1976).

4. Polito v. Continental Casualty Company, 689 F.2d 457 at p. 463 (3d Cir.1982) (applying New Jersey law in a case involving fire insurance).

5. Several of the initial judicial decisions sustaining claims for consequential damages, both third party and first party coverages, were based on the theory that claimants were entitled to damages which resulted from mental anguish.

6. See, e.g., Jarvis v. Prudential Insurance Company of America, 122 N.H. 648, 448 A.2d 407 (1982); Lawton v. Great Southwest Fire Insurance Company, 118 N.H. 607, 392 A.2d 576 (1978).

In deVries v. St. Paul Fire and Marine Insurance Company, 716 F.2d 939 at p. 944 (1st Cir.1983), the court observed, "the New Hampshire Supreme Court has expressly declined to recognize a cause of action in tort for the wrongful refusal to make payments due under a first-party insurance contract."

7. See RESTATEMENT OF CONTRACTS, Second (1981), § 205.

Also see the discussion in § 7.8(b), above, and § 6.2, above.

relationship when tortious conduct and the contract are so intertwined that one cannot be viewed in isolation from the other.[8]

(2) Tort Liability

There are several jurisdictions in which claims for liability beyond or in excess of the applicable coverage are only recognized when a tort action is warranted — that is, the courts have concluded that liability is exclusively predicated on tortious conduct by an insurer.[9]

Recognition of a New Tort Action Involving Intentional Bad Faith

In an opinion that includes a careful consideration of the theoretical foundation for an action against a first party insurer, the Wisconsin Supreme Court emphasized that "the tort of bad faith is not tortious breach of contract," but "is a separate intentional wrong" that "results from a breach of duty imposed as consequence of the relationship established by contract."[10] The court went on to comment:

8. See the discussion in Caruso v. Republic Insurance Company, 558 F.Supp. 430 at pp. 434–435 (D.Md.1983).

In Sparks v. Republic National Life Insurance Company, 132 Ariz. 529 at p. 544, 647 P.2d 1127 at p. 1142 (1982), *cert. denied* Republic National Life Insurance Company v. Sparks, 459 U.S. 1070, 103 S.Ct. 490, 74 L.Ed.2d 632 (1982), the court decided, "Because the existence of the tort is so intrinsically related to the contract, we conclude that an action alleging insurer's bad faith is one 'arising out of a contract' within the meaning of § 12–341.01(A)."

But consider the comments in A & E Supply Company v. Nationwide Mutual Insurance Company, 798 F.2d 669 at p. 671 and p. 672 (4th Cir.1986) (applying Virginia law), *cert. denied* ___ U.S. ___, 107 S.Ct. 1302, 94 L.Ed.2d 158 (1987) that were breach of contract to "routinely give rise to an action in tort — with its attendant incentive of a punitive award" — it "would skew the predictability necessary for stable contractual relations" as a consequence of "the more open and unanticipated duties and damages imposed by the law of tort."

9. *Cf.* Hoskins v. Aetna Life Insurance Company, 6 Ohio St.3d 272, 452 N.E.2d 1315 (1983); Chavers v. National Security Fire & Casualty Co., 405 So.2d 1 at p. 7 (Ala.1981), *appeal after remand* 456 So.2d 293 (1984); Christian v. American Home Assurance Company, 577 P.2d 899 at p. 904 (Okl.1977).

10. Anderson v. Continental Insurance Company, 85 Wis.2d 675 at p. 687, 271 N.W.2d 368 at p. 374 (1978).

Also see Sparks v. Republic National Life Insurance Company, 132 Ariz. 529, 647 P.2d 1127 (1982), *cert. denied* 459 U.S. 1070, 103 S.Ct. 490, 74 L.Ed.2d 632 (1982); Noble v. National American Life Insurance Company, 128 Ariz. 188, 624 P.2d 866 (1981), quoting with approval from the Wisconsin Supreme Court's decision in *Anderson;* Farr v. Transamerica Occidental Life Insurance Company of California, 145 Ariz. 1, 699 P.2d 376 (Div. 1, 1984).

Also see Chavers v. National Security Fire & Casualty Company, 405 So.2d 1 (Ala.1981), *appeal after remand* 456 So.2d 293 (1984).

Cf. Craft v. Economy Fire & Casualty Company, 572 F.2d 565 (7th Cir.1978) (applying Indiana law); National Semiconductor Corporation v. Allendale Mutual Insurance Company, 549 F.Supp. 1195 at p. 1200 (D.Conn.1982); Trimper v. Nationwide Insurance Company, 540 F.Supp. 1188 at pp. 1192–1195 (D.S.C.1982); Phillips v. Aetna Life Insurance Company, 473 F.Supp. 984 (D.Vt.1979); Christian v. American Home Assurance Company, 577 P.2d 899 (Okl. 1977).

Cf. McCorkle v. Great Atlantic Insurance Company, 637 P.2d 583 (Okl.1981); Bibeault v. Hanover Insurance Company, ___ R.I. ___, 417 A.2d 313 (1980); Coleman v. American Universal Insurance Company, 86 Wis.2d 615, 273 N.W.2d 220 (1979).

To show a claim for bad faith, a plaintiff must show the absence of a reasonable basis for denying benefits of the policy and the defendant's knowledge or reckless disregard of the lack of a reasonable basis for denying the claim. It is apparent, then, that the tort of bad faith is an intentional one.[11]

Elaborating on the point, the court explained:

The tort of bad faith can be alleged only if the facts pleaded would, on the basis of an objective standard, show the absence of a reasonable basis for denying the claim, i.e., would a reasonable insurer under the circumstances have denied or delayed payment of the claim under the facts and circumstances.[12]

The Alabama Supreme Court, addressing essentially the same question, commented:

* * * an actionable tort arises for an insurer's intentional refusal to settle a direct claim where there is either "(1) no lawful basis for the refusal coupled with actual knowledge of that fact or (2) intentional failure to determine whether or not there was any lawful basis for such refusal." [13]

As these judicial comments suggest, the tortious conduct must be assessed both as to whether the insurer acted reasonably under the circumstances and as to whether the insurer either knew its action was unreasonable or acted with reckless disregard for whether there was a reasonable basis for the refusal to pay. Each of these requirements may be satisfied by proof about the actions (and state of mind, as to the second requirement) of the insurer's authorized claims representatives.[14]

---

11. Anderson v. Continental Insurance Company, 85 Wis.2d 675 at p. 691, 271 N.W.2d 368 at p. 376 (1978).

12. Anderson v. Continental Insurance Company, 85 Wis.2d 675 at p. 692, 271 N.W.2d 368 at p. 377 (1978).

On the basis of the statements in the *Anderson* decision, a Federal District Court subsequently concluded that under Wisconsin law, "a plaintiff-insured must prove three elements in order to prevail against an insurance company for its alleged refusal in bad faith to pay a claim:

(1) The insurer was obligated to pay the claim under terms of the policy;

(2) The insurer lacked a reasonable basis in law or fact for denying the claim; and

(3) The insurer either knew there was no reasonable basis for denying the claim or acted with reckless disregard for whether such a basis existed."

Duir v. John Alden Life Insurance Company, 573 F.Supp. 1002 at p. 1007 (W.D.Wis. 1983), *affirmed* 754 F.2d 245 (7th Cir.1985).

Also see Christian v. American Home Assurance Company, 577 P.2d 899 (Okl. 1978).

13. Chavers v. National Security Fire & Casualty Co., 405 So.2d 1 at p. 7 (Ala.1981), quoting Vincent v. Blue Cross-Blue Shield of Alabama, 373 So.2d 1054 at p. 1068 (Ala. 1979) (J. Embry, dissenting). The court also noted, "The elements of the tort of bad faith may be proved, as with other intentional torts, by circumstantial as well as direct evidence." *Ibid.*

14. Also see Sparks v. Republic National Life Insurance Company, 132 Ariz. 529, 647 P.2d 1127 (1982), *cert. denied* 459 U.S. 1070, 103 S.Ct. 490, 74 L.Ed.2d 632 (1982).

Infliction of Emotional Distress

In a few instances, an insurer's liability has also been based on the intentional infliction of emotional distress.[15]

Fraud

Courts in several states have indicated that a bad faith refusal by an insurer to pay a claim could give rise to liability when the insured can prove the elements of a tort claim for fraud.[16]

§ 7.9(c) Nature of an Insurer's Duty to an Insured

It is difficult, given the diversity of approaches to the basis of liability, to formulate an authoritative description of the nature and extent of the duty that an insurer owes to an insured in regard to first party insurance contracts. However, some generalization seems possible based on both the body of case law and a common sense approach to what it is reasonable to expect an insurer to do when a first party insurance claim is submitted.

The essential character of the contractual duty to act fairly and in good faith, as articulated in the landmark California decisions, is that neither party will do anything to injure the right of the other to receive the benefits of the agreement. When an insurance claim is received, an insurer should thoroughly investigate the information that may support an insured's claim.[1] Following a thorough investigation, an insurer should not unreasonably withhold payments due under a policy.[2] If the claims department decides not to make a payment, the matter should be carefully reviewed on the basis of the facts known to the insurer.[3] Furthermore, the claims file should be examined with a

15. See, e.g., Eckenrode v. Life of America Insurance Company, 470 F.2d 1 at p. 4 (7th Cir.1972); Fletcher v. Western National Life Insurance Company, 10 Cal. App.3d 376, 89 Cal.Rptr. 78 (4th Dist., Div. 2, 1970).

Also see Farr v. Transamerica Occidental Life Insurance Company of California, 145 Ariz. 1, 699 P.2d 376 (App., Div. 1, 1984).

Cf. Polito v. Continental Casualty Company, 689 F.2d 457 at p. 464 (3d Cir.1982) (predicting the law of New Jersey); Industrial Fire & Casualty Insurance Company v. Romer, 432 So.2d 66 at p. 67 (Fla.App. 4th Dist.1983), Manolis v. International Life Insurance Company, 83 A.D.2d 784, 443 N.Y.S.2d 461 (4 Dept.1981).

Also see Note, *The Availability of Excess Damages for Wrongful Refusal to Honor First Party Insurance Claims—An Emerging Trend,* 45 Fordham Law Review 164–182 (1976).

Keeton & Widess, Ins.Law—21

16. See, e.g., Farr v. Transamerica Occidental Life Insurance Company of California, 145 Ariz. 1, 699 P.2d 376 (App., Div. 1, 1984); Industrial Fire and Casualty Insurance Company v. Romer, 432 So.2d 66 (Fla. App., 4th Dist., 1983) (PIP coverage).

§ 7.9(c)

1. See, e.g., McLaughlin v. Connecticut General Life Insurance Company, 565 F.Supp. 434 at p. 454 (N.D.Cal.1983).

2. Communale v. Traders & General Insurance Company, 50 Cal.2d 654, 328 P.2d 198 (1958).

Also see Rojas v. State Farm Mutual Automobile Insurance Company, 518 F.2d 85 at pp. 87–88 (9th Cir.1975) (applying California law).

3. Johnson v. State Farm Mutual Automobile Insurance Company, 342 So.2d 664 at p. 668 (La.1977).

view to deciding whether further investigation would be likely to reveal additional relevant information. The denial of the claim should include a written explanation setting forth the reasons for the decision. Also, the insured should be afforded an opportunity to respond to a denial and to provide additional information or evidence in support of the claim. In addition, an insurer treads on dangerous ground if it conceals information or facts from the insured that may be significant in regard to a claim.[4]

Judicial decisions in many states now clearly indicate that unless an insurer has good reasons for withholding the payment of insurance benefits, the insurer's conduct is likely to be viewed by a court as sufficiently arbitrary or capricious to warrant allowing a recovery by the claimant beyond the insurance benefits and interest thereon.[5] Nevertheless, when the facts indicate that the insurer's liability is "fairly debatable," courts have frequently concluded that the insurer does not commit a breach of the duty by not paying the insurance benefits and is not liable for either compensatory or punitive damages.[6] This undoubtedly is a reasonable conclusion in regard to claims for punitive damages. It is not equally evident that an insurer who is subsequently determined to have made an incorrect decision about the coverage should be immune to liability for consequential damages sustained by an insured as a result of the insurer's decision to deny a claim or to significantly delay the payment of the insurance benefits.[7]

§ 7.9(d) Persons to Whom the Duty is Owed

One question that has not been addressed by many courts relates to whether anyone other than the insured may assert a claim for consequential damages resulting from breach of the implied obligation to deal fairly and in good faith. In Austero v. National Casualty Company, the California court concluded that someone who was not a party to a first party insurance contract lacked standing to bring an action for breach of the implied duty of good faith and fair dealing.[1] The court reasoned that "an insurer's duty * * * is owed solely to its insured

---

4. *Cf.* Christian v. American Home Assurance Company, 577 P.2d 899 at p. 905 (Okl.1977).

5. See the decisions cited in the preceding portions of this section, and especially the decisions cited in § 7.10, below.

6. *Cf.* Chavers v. National Security Fire and Casualty Co., 405 So.2d 1 at p. 6 (Ala. 1981), *appeal after remand* 456 So.2d 293 (1984) (involving fire insurance); Bibeault v. Hanover Insurance Company, __ R.I. __, 417 A.2d 313 at p. 319 (1980) (uninsured motorist insurance).

Also consider the comments in Duir v. John Alden Life Insurance Company, 754 F.2d 245 (7th Cir.1985) (applying Wisconsin

law); Christian v. American Home Assurance Company, 577 P.2d 899 at p. 905 (Okl. 1977); Rojas v. State Farm Mutual Automobile Insurance Company, 518 F.2d 85 (9th Cir.1975).

Also see the uninsured motorist decisions cited in § 20.1 of Widiss, UNINSURED AND UNDERINSURED MOTORIST INSURANCE (1987).

7. See the discussion of compensatory-consequential damages in § 7.9(e), below.

§ 7.9(d)

1. Austero v. National Casualty Company, 62 Cal.App.3d 511, 133 Cal.Rptr. 107 (4th Dist., Div. 2, 1976).

and perhaps, any express beneficiary of the insurance policy ＊ ＊ ＊." [2] The court observed that the wife of someone covered by disability insurance was "at most an incidental or remote beneficiary." [3]

§ 7.9(e) Compensatory-Consequential Damages

When a common law claim is recognized, either a claim based on breach of contract or on tortious conduct, the claimant usually is allowed to recover consequential damages. The California cases, which have established some of the most significant judicial precedents for such relief in this area, have held that a claimant is entitled to compensation for "all detriment resulting from violations" of the duties owed to insureds.[1] In general, an insurer certainly should be liable for the foreseeable financial injuries which are suffered by an insured as a result of an insurer's failure or delay.[2]

There is a very compelling case for allowing an insured to recover consequential damages, especially those which can be identified as specific economic losses, which the insured sustained as a result of the insurer's failure to provide the insurance benefits.[3]

First, the imposition of liability for consequential damages ought to encourage an insurer to carefully evaluate its decision whenever a claim is being rejected. An insurer should be influenced to exercise a very high degree of care when deciding to reject an insurance claim, and the common law rules of liability should be fashioned with a view to producing an environment in which this is more likely to occur.

Second, an insured should be compensated for the adverse economic consequences of having the payment of insurance benefits delayed, including interest on the amount of the insurance benefits which were not paid and the legal expenses incurred to cause the insurer to make the payments, because the insurer's actions deny the insured the right to prompt indemnification which is a primary reason for obtaining

---

2. *Id.,* 62 Cal.App.3d at p. 517, 133 Cal. Rptr. at p. 111.

3. *Ibid.*

§ 7.9(e)

1. See Silberg v. California Life Insurance Company, 11 Cal.3d 452 at pp. 460–461, 113 Cal.Rptr. 711 at p. 717, 521 P.2d 1103 at p. 1109 (1974).

In Farr v. Transamerica Occidental Life Insurance Company of California, 145 Ariz. 376, 699 P.2d 376 (App., Div. 1, 1984), the court concluded that when there was a bad faith refusal to pay benefits under a group health insurance plan, the insured is entitled to consequential damages and attorney fees. The court concluded that damages may be awarded for emotional distress even though the insurer did not intentionally cause the distress.

2. *Cf.* Lawton v. Great Southwest Fire Insurance Company, 118 N.H. 607, 392 A.2d 576 (1978).

In Polito v. Continental Casualty Company, 689 F.2d 457 at p. 462 (3d Cir.1982) (applying New Jersey law), the court commenting on the appropriate guidance that should be provided for a jury, stated: "Thus the district court should have instructed the jury on the alternative theory of breach of contract with respect to the several policy coverages, and awarded prejudgment interest if the Politos were successful on that cause of action."

3. The reasons are comparable to those which were considered in the discussion of the rationales for a relatively liberal construction of the statutory remedies for the nonpayment or late payment of insurance claims in § 7.7(c), above.

insurance.[4] When an insurer fails to provide the insurance benefits, these are clearly foreseeable consequences for an insured and the costs of these consequences should be borne by the insurer when an adjudication determines that the insurer's decision was incorrect. The strength of claims for other types of economic losses may be significantly affected by determinations in regard to "foreseeability."

Third, insureds have reasonable expectations that the net value of their insurance benefits will not be reduced by the actions of recalcitrant insurers, and these expectations should be protected. Legislatures and courts throughout the nation have recognized both the importance that is appropriately attached to assuring that insurance commitments will be honored and that there is a special character to the relationship of the insurer to the insured, sometimes regarded as closely similar to that of a fiduciary, which is imbued with a significant public interest. This should mean that the insured's insurance benefits will not be effectively reduced when an insured is compelled to resort to a lawsuit in order to recover insurance benefits.

The awarding of indemnification for the more general damages, such as pain and suffering or emotional distress, appropriately turns on the nature of the cause of action which is recognized in a particular jurisdiction. In several states, the courts have sustained an insured's right to recover consequential damages for emotional distress.[5]

§ 7.9(f)   Frivolous Bad Faith Claims by Insureds

The duty to deal fairly and in good faith with insureds does not mean that insurers are precluded from raising coverage questions before paying a claim or from refusing to pay the entire policy limit of an applicable coverage. Insurers will not invariably be held to be acting in bad faith when such matters are disputed. Moreover, when an action for bad faith is pressed beyond reasonable bounds by an insured, in some jurisdictions the insurer may be awarded reasonable attorney fees and costs (such as disbursements) when the court views the claimant's action as frivolous.[1]

§ 7.10   Punitive Damage Awards Against Insurers

§ 7.10(a)   Introductory Note

In many of the suits in which insureds allege either a wrongful refusal to pay or an unwarranted delay in paying an insurance claim,

---

4. For example, in Lawton v. Great Southwest Fire Insurance Company, 118 N.H. 607, 392 A.2d 576 at p. 759 (1978), the court observed, "Insurance is often obtained because the insured is not in a position to personally bear the financial loss occasioned by a casualty, and serious financial injuries may often result from an insurer's refusal or delay in payment."

5. See, e.g., Bibeault v. Hanover Insurance Company, ___ R.I. ___, 417 A.2d 313 at p. 319 (1980); Christian v. American Home Assurance Company, 577 P.2d 899 (Okl.1977).

§ 7.9(f)

1. See the discussion in Radlein v. Industrial Fire & Casualty Insurance Company, 117 Wis.2d 605, 345 N.W.2d 874 (1984).

Also consider the discussion of the ethical obligations of attorneys who represent insureds in § 7.10(c), below.

the insured also requests that punitive damages be awarded. These claims, which sometimes result in awards of several million dollars, have proliferated in recent years.

Punitive damages have long been imposed by the courts in instances in which a tortfeasor's conduct was particularly reprehensible.[1] However, historically punitive damages have not been awarded as a means of either imposing punishment for breach of a contract or of deterring comparable actions in the future.[2] This remains the rule in many states.[3] Consequently in these states much of the impetus for the recognition of a new tort, which would be predicated on the bad faith conduct of an insurer,[4] derives from efforts to establish a basis for

§ 7.10(a)

1. See Prosser & Keeton, TORTS (Fifth edition, 1984), at p. 9:

> "Where the defendant's wrongdoing has been intentional and deliberate, and has the character of outrage frequently associated[20] with crime, all but a few courts[20] have permitted the jury to award in the tort action 'punitive' or 'exemplary' damages * * *."

2. Punitive damages generally are not awarded for breach of a contract, that is, damages for breach of contract are limited to the pecuniary loss and are measured by the amount necessary to put the party in the position that would have been occupied had the contract been performed. See RESTATEMENT OF CONTRACTS, Second (1981), § 369.

Also see Annotation, *Insurer's liability for consequential or punitive damages for wrongful delay or refusal to make payments due under contracts,* 47 A.L.R.3d 314–351 (1973).

But cf. Timothy J. Sullivan, *Punitive Damages in the Law of Contract: The Reality and the Illusion of Legal Change,* 61 Minnesota Law Review 207–252 (1977), suggesting that the common law recognizes several classes of contract claims which have sometimes been viewed as providing a basis for punitive damages.

3. See, e.g., Farris v. United States Fidelity and Guaranty Company, 284 Or. 453, 587 P.2d 1015 (1978).

Cf. Milcarek v. Nationwide Insurance Company, 190 N.J.Super. 358, 463 A.2d 950 at p. 956 (App.Div.1983) (no punitive damages for a passenger in a motor vehicle who asserted a claim for PIP insurance coverage because insurer did not fall within the "special relationship" exception to the general rule prohibiting an award of punitive damages for breach of contract); Garden State Community Hospital v. Watson, 191 N.J.Super. 225 at p. 227, 465 A.2d 1225 at p. 1226 (App.Div.1982), *cert. denied*

94 N.J. 518, 468 A.2d 176 (1983) (health insurer could not be liable for punitive damage because there is no indication that the New Jersey Supreme Court would sanction a new cause of action for the wrongful refusal to pay a first-party insurance claim).

Cf. Cass v. Broome County Co-Operative Insurance Company, 94 A.D.2d 822, 463 N.Y.S.2d 312 (3d Dept.1983) (punitive damages held not to be awardable for an isolated transaction, such as breach of an insurance contract, even if committed willfully and without justification).

In Haagenson v. National Farmers Union Property & Casualty Company, 277 N.W.2d 648 at p. 652 (Minn.1979), a punitive damage award of $300,000 was reversed on the grounds (1) that "such damages are not recoverable for bad faith breach of contract" and (2) it does not appear from the circumstances that the insurer committed an independent tort. The court also noted that a "malicious or bad faith motive does not convert a contract action into a tort action." *Ibid.*

See generally, Arthur L. Corbin, CORBIN ON CONTRACTS (1964), at § 1077 (in Volume 5, at p. 440). Prof. Corbin observed:

> "In the innumerable cases arising from the breach of an ordinary commercial contract, it has seemed wise to adhere to the general rule excluding the punitive element and to avoid the frequently futile attempt to determine the degree of moral obliquity."

Also see WILLISTON ON CONTRACTS (Third edition, 1972), at § 1340.

4. See the discussion of recognition of a tort theory in § 7.8(a), § 7.8(b) and § 7.9(b), above.

Cf. Garden State Community Hospital v. Watson, 191 N.J.Super. 225, 465 A.2d 1225 (App.Div.1982), where the court observed that there was no clear indication from the New Jersey Supreme Court that it would recognize a new cause of action whereby

punitive awards. And some punitive damage awards against insurers have been predicated on tort theories, such as the tort of outrageous conduct.[5]

Courts in several states have concluded that an insurer's violation of its contractual duty to an insured provides the basis for an action in tort, and that in appropriate circumstances punitive damages, as well as consequential damages, may be awarded.[6] In a few states, courts appear to have modified the common law so that, at least in some circumstances, punitive damages may be awarded when there is an "outrageous" breach of a contractual duty.[7]

Courts, of course, do not impose punitive damages — as distinguished from compensatory damage awards which allow an insured to recover attorneys' fees, litigation costs, and interest [8] — when an insurer has acted reasonably, though unsuccessfully, in denying an insurance claim.[9] A common practice of imposing awards in excess of compensatory damages would almost certainly deter insurers from contesting claims in some, and perhaps many, cases in which a rejection is or appears to be justified. Policyholders and insurers clearly have an interest in not only avoiding the payment of claims that are without merit, but also in not discouraging insurers from contesting claims when there are reasonable questions about whether the insured's claim is within the scope of coverage afforded by the particular type of insurance.[10] Therefore, to the extent courts conclude that

an insured could recover punitive damages when an insurer wrongfully refused to pay a first party claim.

5. See, e.g., Green v. State Farm Fire & Casualty Insurance Company, 667 F.2d 22 (9th Cir.1982) (applying Oregon law).

6. In Pirkl v. Northwestern Mutual Insurance Association, 348 N.W.2d 633 at p. 636 (Iowa 1984), the court noted "in considering whether punitive damages should be permitted, the nature of the conduct is more significant than the legal label which is attached to the conduct" and that punitive damages may be imposed on an insurer that is guilty of "malice, fraud, gross negligence, or an illegal act."

In addition to the decisions cited in the following footnotes in this section, see: Hoskins v. Aetna Life Insurance Company, 6 Ohio St.3d 272, 452 N.E.2d 1315 (1983); Christian v. American Home Assurance Company, 577 P.2d 899 at p. 904 (Okl. 1977).

Also see Betts v. Allstate Insurance Company, 154 Cal.App.3d 688 at pp. 711–713, 201 Cal.Rptr. 528 at pp. 541–543 (4th Dist., Div. 1, 1984) (sustaining an award of $3,000,000 in punitive damages against a liability insurer); Moore v. American United Life Insurance Company, 150 Cal.App. 3d 610, at pp. 636–643, 197 Cal.Rptr. 878 at

pp. 894–899 (3d Dist.1984) (sustaining a jury award of $30,000 in compensatory damages and $2.5 million of punitive damages against an insurer providing disability insurance for the insured).

In some of the states in which courts have awarded punitive damages for breach of contract, there is support for recognition of a tort action in order to conform the judicial doctrines, which govern such claims, to the generally recognized contours of the rules that apply to damage awards. See generally, Annotation, *Insurer's tort liability for consequential or punitive damages for wrongful failure or refusal to defend insured*, 20 A.L.R. 4th 23–58 (1983).

7. See § 7.10(b), below, and the decisions cited there.

8. *Cf.* Butchikas v. Travelers Indemnity Company, 343 So.2d 816 at p. 818 (Fla. 1976).

9. *Cf.* McLaughlin v. Continental General Life Insurance Company, 565 F.Supp. 434 at pp. 454–455 (N.D.Cal.1983).

10. However, in assessing the appropriate scope of coverage, consideration should also be awarded to the justification for rights at variance with insurance policy

punitive damages should be employed either to punish insurers or to influence the claims practices of insurers in the future, it is appropriate to apply notably different standards for awarding compensatory damages, on the one hand, and punitive damages, on the other.

§ 7.10(b) Justifications For and Against, and Standards for, Awards of Punitive Damages

When punitive damages have been awarded as a consequence of an insurer's denial of an insurance claim, courts have employed a variety of characterizations to describe the type of conduct which justifies such an award to an insured. For example, the Second Circuit Court of Appeals decided that when an insurer's conduct is so egregious that it amounts to *criminal indifference* to the company's obligations, an award of punitive damages is justified.[1] Similarly, the Rhode Island Supreme Court held that the claimant must show that the insurer acted with "*malice, wantonness, or willfulness.*"[2] The Idaho Supreme Court concluded that a plaintiff must show "that the company's refusal to promptly pay the claim was an *extreme deviation from reasonable standards of conduct,* performed with an understanding of its consequences."[3] And in Silberg v. California Life Insurance Company, one of the landmark decisions sustaining an award of punitive damages, the California Supreme Court reasoned that in order "to justify an award of exemplary damages, the defendant must be *guilty of oppression, fraud or malice*" which means that a defendant "must act with the *intent to vex, injure or annoy, or with a conscious disregard of the plaintiff's rights.*"[4]

Viewed collectively, the precedents — including the very numerous decisions by appellate courts which have either sustained the rejection of punitive damages claims by trial courts or have reversed awards by trial courts in favor of insureds — make clear that only the most outrageous or horrendous actions of insurers (conduct almost, if not in

provisions. See generally Chapter 6, above.

§ 7.10(b)

1. Durham Industries, Inc. v. North River Insurance Company, 673 F.2d 37 at p. 41 (2d Cir.1982) (emphasis added) (applying New York law), *cert. denied* 459 U.S. 827, 103 S.Ct. 61, 74 L.Ed.2d 64 (1982).

In New York, the courts have consistently "rejected claims for punitive damages unless there is a showing of wanton dishonesty as to imply criminal indifference to civil obligations — morally culpable conduct directed at the general public, a public as opposed to a mere private wrong." Samovar of Russia Jewelry Antique Corp. v. Generali, 102 A.D.2d 279, 476 N.Y.S.2d 869 at p. 872 (1st Dept.1984) (including an extensive compilation of New York decisions).

Also see the discussion in Farr v. Transamerica Occidental Life Insurance Company, 145 Ariz. 1, 699 P.2d 376 at pp. 382–385 (App., Div. 1, 1984).

2. Bibeault v. Hanover Insurance Company, ___ R.I. ___, 417 A.2d 313 at p. 319 (1980) (emphasis added).

3. Linscott v. Rainier National Life Insurance Company, 100 Idaho 854 at p. 860, 606 P.2d 958 at p. 964 (1980) (emphasis added).

Also see Continental Re-Insurance Company v. Spanton, 667 F.2d 1289 at p. 1291 (9th Cir.1982) (applying Idaho law and quoting *Linscott*).

4. Silberg v. California Life Insurance Company, 11 Cal.3d 452 at p. 462, 113 Cal. Rptr. 711 at p. 717, 521 P.2d 1103 at p. 1110 (1974) (emphasis added).

fact, malicious) warrant awards of punitive damages. Many of the appellate court decisions which have addressed the justification for imposing punitive damages appear to support the hypothesis that such awards will only be warranted when the record shows that the insurer's representative had the *state of mind* of intent to injure the insured. It is also clear, however, that in at least some states awards of punitive damages will be sustained when it is shown that an insurer's representative acted with the *state of mind* of conscious disregard of the insured's interest, especially when it was or should have been evident to the insurer that its actions would be very deleterious to the insured.

Although courts in many states have indicated that there are circumstances in which it is or it would be appropriate to impose punitive damages in order either to punish an insurer or to influence the approaches to claims employed by insurers, there is also a notable reticence on the part of judges in regard to sanctioning such recoveries or encouraging such claims. The judicial concern in regard to awards of punitive damages is indicated by other aspects of the holdings in these cases. For example, among the applicable judicial precedents there is some support for the proposition that the right to recover punitive damages is conditioned on the existence of actual damages. Thus, the Tenth Circuit Court of Appeals held that a "punitive damages verdict was properly set aside because there was no award of actual or compensatory damages under * * * [the claimant's] action sounding in tort." [5] Furthermore, in several states, the courts — and, in a few instances, legislatures — have concluded that in order to warrant a judgment of punitive damages, the nature of the justification for an award of punitive damages must be shown by "clear and convincing" proof — that is, a trial court determination will only be sustained when the claimant has satisfied a higher burden than the "preponderance of the evidence" which is normally applicable to civil matters.[6]

§ 7.10(c) Observations

Appellate courts in many jurisdictions have now sustained recoveries by insureds of punitive damages.[1] Nevertheless, it is equally evident (from an examination of the reported appellate decisions) that

---

5. Norman's Heritage Real Estate Company v. Aetna Casualty and Surety Company, 727 F.2d 911 at p. 916 (10th Cir.1984).

6. *Indiana.* Travelers Indemnity Company v. Armstrong, 442 N.E.2d 349 at pp. 358–365 (Ind.1982).

Minnesota Stat.Ann. § 549.20 (1982), provides that punitive damages shall be allowed in civil actions, only upon clear and convincing evidence that the acts of the defendant show a willful indifference to the rights or safety of others.

Montana Code Ann. § 27–1–221 (1985), provides that the jury may not award exemplary or punitive damages unless the plaintiff has proven all elements of the claim by clear and convincing evidence. The Montana legislature also imposes a limit of liability of $25,000 or 1% of defendant's net worth, whichever is greater, unless the claimant can provide actual fraud or malice.

§ 7.10(c)

1. See, e.g., Tibbs v. Great American Insurance Company, 755 F.2d 1370 (9th Cir.1985) (applying California law and sustaining an award of $600,000 in punitive damages in addition to $200,000 of compensatory damages).

claims for punitive damages on behalf of insureds have been rejected far more frequently than they have been sustained.[2]

Insurers often reject claims on grounds that appear reasonable even when viewed retrospectively. Although it may seem at least somewhat incongruous to consider the grounds upon which an insurance claim was contested by an insurer as reasonable when the result of an adjudication of the matter disputed has been a determination that the insurer's position was wrong, an assessment of whether to penalize an insurer should not be predicated on the resolution of the coverage dispute. Even though the insurer's decision to reject the insured's claim has been adjudged by litigation to be unsound, the standard to be applied in evaluating the insurer's actions following the resolution of the coverage question should focus on whether the insurer acted reasonably — that is, the concern should be focused on the reasonableness of the judgment of the insurer's claims department or executives in deciding to contest an insured's coverage claim.[3]

In general, it is undesirable to impose punitive damages — as distinguished from a compensatory recovery of attorneys' fees, litigation costs, and interest — when an insurer has acted reasonably, though

2. See, e.g., Norman's Heritage Real Estate Company v. Aetna Casualty and Surety Company, 727 F.2d 911 (10th Cir.1984) (applying Oklahoma law) (punitive damage award of $10,000 property set aside); Samovar of Russia Jewelry Antique Corp. v. Generali, 102 A.D.2d 279, 476 N.Y.S.2d 869 at p. 873 (1st Dept.1984) ("The assertion that the insurer deliberately delayed processing the claim is insufficient standing alone and, * * * it will not, without more, support a claim for punitive damages."); Benke v. Mukwonago-Vernon Mutual Insurance Company, 110 Wis.2d 356, 329 N.W.2d 243 at p. 248 (App.1982) ("There was no 'malice' shown * * * [and] we see no evidence of evil intent to oppress the Benkes in a vindictive manner.").

Also see Butchikas v. Travelers Indemnity Company, 343 So.2d 816 at p. 818 (Fla. 1976) (insurer's conduct did not involve any "deliberate, overt dishonest dealing" which would warrant an award of punitive damages); Olbrich v. Shelby Mutual Insurance Company, 13 Ohio App.3d 423, 469 N.E.2d 892 (1983) (record indicated no more than that the insurer questioned the validity of the claim); Benke v. Mukwonago-Vernon Mutual Insurance Company, 110 Wis.2d 356, 329 N.W.2d 243 (App.1982).

Cf. McLaughlin v. Connecticut General Life Insurance Company, 565 F.Supp. 434 at p. 454 (N.D.Cal.1983); Vincent v. Blue Cross-Blue Shield of Alabama, Inc., 373 So. 2d 1054 (Ala.1979).

3. In many of the jurisdictions which have recognized a cause of action for bad faith conduct of an insurer, the insurer can successfully defend against such a claim by showing that there was a "bona fide dispute" or a "fairly debatable issue" in regard to the existence of coverage. See, e.g.:

Alabama. National Security Fire & Casualty Company v. Bowen, 417 So.2d 179 (Ala.1982). However, a new trial after the remand resulted in a general verdict of $1,500,000 in favor of the claimant which was affirmed by the Alabama Supreme Court in a decision reported at 447 So.2d 133 (Ala.1983).

Delaware. Cf. Casson v. Nationwide Insurance Company, 455 A.2d 361 at pp. 368–369 (Del.1982).

Iowa. Cf. Pirkl v. Northwestern Mutual Insurance Association, 348 N.W.2d 633 at pp. 635–636 (Iowa 1984). Also see Northwestern National Insurance Company v. Pope, 791 F.2d 649 (8th Cir.1986) (applying Iowa law).

New York. Cf. Gordon v. Nationwide Mutual Insurance Company, 30 N.Y.2d 427 at p. 433, 334 N.Y.S.2d 601 at p. 605, 285 N.E.2d 849 at p. 856 (1972) (insurer relied on the advice of counsel in regard to the treatment of the insured's claim).

Wisconsin. Cf. Benke v. Mukwonago-Vernon Mutual Insurance Company, 110 Wis.2d 356, 329 N.W.2d 243 at pp. 247–248 (1982).

unsuccessfully, in contesting a claim. Therefore, it is desirable and appropriate to recognize a different standard for awarding compensatory damages, on the one hand, and punitive damages, on the other.

First Party Coverages and Third Party Coverages

In some jurisdictions, there appears to be a reticence among the judges to expand the application of the doctrines which have been recognized as justifying punitive damage awards for the practices of liability insurers to various types of first party insurance arrangements. The justification for such a distinction is at best unclear, save perhaps for a general sense that the award of punitive damages should always be restricted to instances in which there has been an extraordinary act of misfeasance.

The nature of an insured's relationship to the insurer that provides a first party coverage (such as disability insurance, health insurance, or fire insurance) ideally is one of trust and reliance. That relationship is at least as significant in regard to first party coverages as it is with respect to liability insurance. Indeed, the horrendous consequences from an insurer's failure to pay first party disability or fire insurance benefits may be as devastating for an insured as those which result from the actions of a liability insurer in regard to a tort claim against an insured in excess of policy limits. When an examination of the insurer's conduct provokes a sense of overwhelming outrage and especially when the consequences of the insurer's claims practices have created an intolerable result for the insured, a distinction that serves to insulate first party insurers appears to be unwarranted.

Professional Responsibility of Lawyers

In hundreds of the reported decisions in which claims for punitive damages have been made on behalf of insureds, the insurers appear to have done nothing worse than choose to carefully investigate the claims before payment was made or to raise appropriate issues about the coverage — that is, there was little, if any, justification for seeking punitive damages. Allegations of bad faith and unfair dealing coupled with demands for millions of dollars in punitive damages whenever an insurer does not immediately pay an insurance claim are not warranted and do not well serve the interests of either the individual claimant or the public.

In many of the instances in which appellate courts have been asked to review allegations that an insurer inappropriately rejected an insurance claim *and* that the insurer's conduct constituted a failure to deal in good faith, the assertion of bad faith appears to have been made by the claimant on the basis of the proverbial "wing and a prayer." Nothing appears in the court's description of the facts which would support such an award. It is an egregious wrong when an insurer irresponsibly denies a valid claim. It is, however, an equally flagrant departure from standards of professional responsibility for an attorney to make a claim of bad faith a "stock" pleading which is included whenever a coverage dispute arises.[4]

Preserving the Financial Stability of the Insurance Industry

Multimillion dollar awards of punitive damages to individual claimants may quite literally endanger the financial stability of the insurance industry. Courts and legislatures will need to chart a careful course in weighing the legitimate and significant interest in the maintenance of a financially stable insurance industry against the goal of discouraging what has too often been clearly shown to be the wanton, callous, and even malicious or willfully unconscionable claims practices of some insurers.[5]

 WESTLAW REFERENCES

§ 7.1 Introductory Note

> di(condition /3 precedent /s maintain! bring! brought /s suit lawsuit action /s insurer carrier)

> *Liability Insurance*
> sy(conflict! /3 interest /s insurer carrier /5 insured claimant assured policy-holder)

§ 7.2 Claims Presentment

(a) Timeliness Provisions

(1) Introduction

> *Justifications for Timeliness Provisions*
> (timely /3 notice) timeliness /s insurer carrier /s opportunity chance /s investigat!
> (timely /3 notice) timeliness /s fraud

> *Precluding Enforcement of Timeliness Provisions*
> timel! /5 claim /s requir! provision clause /s waiv! estop!

(2) Specific versus General Timeliness Provisions

> reasonable /s time! /s limit! /s notice notif! claim /s insured assured policy-holder claimant

(3) Timeliness Provisions and the Statute of Limitations

> timel! /s provision clause requir! /s statut! action period /5 limit*** limitation

---

4. Also see the discussion of frivolous bad faith claims in § 7.9(f), above.

5. *Cf.* the comments of Judge Goodwin in Green v. State Farm Fire and Casualty Company, 667 F.2d 22 at p. 25 (9th Cir. 1982):

> "the argument that punitive awards will have a 'disastrous' economic effect on the industry and therefore on the rate-paying public, must be balanced against the public interest in motivating insurers to deal fairly. If an insurance company can act with impunity and be liable in any event only for the money it originally owed the policyholder, it will have a financial incentive to resist payment in as outrageous a manner as possible. State Farm can avoid the adverse economic effect of this kind of case by more careful selection and supervision of its adjusters."

(b) Provisions Requiring Notice of a Loss

(1) Generally

purpose /5 requir! /s notice notif! /s insured assured policy-holder claimant /s insurer carrier

(2) Enforcement of Notice Requirements

fail! lack*** not /s notice notif! /s material! /3 breach!

(e) Defenses to the Enforcement of Claims Presentment Timeliness Provisions

(2) Noncompliance and Requiring Prejudice to the Insurer

sy,di(non-comply! non-compliance (fail! lack! not /3 comply! compliance complied) /s prejudic! /s insurer carrier)

unreasonabl! substantial! appreciabl! /s delay! /s notice notif! /s prejudic! /s insurer carrier

(ii) Allocating the Burden of Proof

insurer carrier /7 burden /3 proof proving prove /9 prejudic!

(iii) Observations

sy(insured claimant policy-holder /s breach! /5 cooperat!)

(3) Excuses for Noncompliance

reasonabl! justif! /s excus! /s comply! compliance noncompliance /p insur****

(f) Fraud and False Swearing in Claims Submissions

di(fraud false /s swearing /s insured assured claimant policy-holder)

sy,di(wilful! /s conceal! misrepresent! /s material! /s fact)

(g) The Insured's Liability for Failing to Comply with Claims Presentment Provisions

sy(insured assured claimant policy-holder /s liable liability /s (fail! lack! not /s comply! compliance) non-compliance /s notice notif! filing file* presentment)

§ 7.3 Assistance and Cooperation Provisions

(a) Generally

sy,di(insured assured policy-holder /s requir! /s assist! cooperat! /s investigat! settlement defense defend** defending)

zitnik /s burik & assist! cooperat!

(b) The Prejudice Requirement

non-cooperat! uncooperative (fail*** lack*** not /s cooperat! assist!) /s prejudic! /s insurer carrier /s defense defend** defending

di(cooperat! noncooperation uncooperative /s question issue /7 fact jury juror)

Covenants and Conditions

cooperat! /s insured assured claimant policy-holder /s "condition precedent"

find 535 p2d 816

§ 7.4 Multiple Claims Under Liability Insurance

(b) The Insurer's Duty to the Insured

insurer carrier /s multiple /5 claim! party

sy(conflict! diverg! /12 interest /s insurer carrier /s insured assured claimant policy-holder)

(c) The Insurer's Duty to the Claimants: The Problem of Preferential Settlements

pro-rat! /s distribut** distributi! allocat! /s claimant insured assured policy-holder /p insurance

§ 7.5   Reciprocal Claims

(a) The Effect of Settling a Single Claim

(2) Settlements of a Reciprocal Claim by an Insurer

di(impair! destroy! destruction /s insurer carrier /s subrogat! /s settl!) & sy(subrogat! /s settl!)

(3) Settlements of a Reciprocal Claim by an Insured

find 428 a2d 1254

(b) The Effect of a Judicial Determination of a Reciprocal Claim

(2) Settlements in the Course of Litigation

counter-claim /s res +1 judicata adjudicata

(3) Consent Judgments

Comment

kelleher /s lozzi

(c) Erroneous Uses of Fiduciary and Agency Concepts in Relation to Reciprocal Claims

sy,di(insurer carrier /s fiduciary /s insured assured claimant policy-holder /s settl! releas!)

§ 7.6   Conflict of Interests under Liability Insurance

(a) Sources and Nature of Conflicts of Interests

(1) Introduction

sy,di(conflict! diverg! /s interest /p defend** defending defense /p insurance /s liab! responsib!)

(2) Examples of Conflicting Interests

(i) Possibility That the Third Party's Claims against an Insured Are Not Covered by the Applicable Liability Insurance

cover! noncoverage /s defense /s conflict! diverg! /s interest

liab! /s limit! restrict! /s nature scope extent /s risk

find 585 f2d 932

(ii) Disclosure of Information by an Insured to or a Discovery of Information by Defense Counsel That Would Sustain a Coverage Defense

attorney lawyer counsel representati** /s discover! disclos! /s coverage noncoverage /s defense defend** defending

(iv) Multiple Defendants

sy,di(conflict! diverg! /s interest /s joint! dual! both /s attorney lawyer counsel representati**)

(v) Claims In Excess of the Applicable Limits of Liability

conflict! diverg! /s interest /s claim /s exceed! excess /s limit amount

(vii) Continuing to Provide a Defense after the Exhaustion of Coverage

insurer carrier /s defense defend** defending /s exhaust! /s limit! coverage

(ix) Liability Insurance Combined with Uninsured or Underinsured Motorist Coverage
conflict! diverg! /s interest /s uninsured underinsured

(b) The Rights, Responsibilities, and Risks of Insurers

Selection and Employment of "Independent" Claims Representatives or Attorneys
conflict! diverg! /s interest /p independen! /s attorney lawyer counsel representati**

Selection of Defense Counsel by the Insured
sy,di(insured assured claimant policy-holder /s select! choos! choice chose* /s defense defend** defending /s attorney lawyer counsel representati**)

Representation of an Insured by House Counsel
represent! /s insured assured claimant policy-holder /s house insurance company /3 attorney lawyer counsel

(c) The Roles, Responsibilities, and Risks for Attorneys

(1) Problems for Defense Attorneys

Informing the Insured of a Conflict of Interests
attorney lawyer counsel representati** /s advis! advice inform*** information disclos! /s insured assured client claimant policy-holder /s conflict! diverg! /s interest

Informing the Insurer of a Conflict of Interests
betts /s allstate

Representation of Both the Insured and the Insurer
sy,di(attorney lawyer counsel /s represent! /s both dual joint! /s insurer carrier /s insured assured client claimant policy-holder)

(3) Ethical Questions and Conflict of Interests Problems for Attorneys Representing Plaintiffs
conflict! diverg! /s interest /s attorney lawyer counsel /s represent! /s plaintiff third-party

(d) Possible Courses to Be Pursued When There Are Conflicts of Interests Between an Insured and the Insurer

(1) Denial of Coverage and Refusal to Provide a Defense
sy,di(deny! deni** disclaim! /5 cover*** /s refus! declin! /7 defense defend** defending)

(3) Disclosure of the Conflict and Consent By the Insured to Representation By a Single Attorney Without a "Waiver" by the Insurer (Thereby Preserving the Right to a Subsequent Adjudication of the Coverage Question)
thornton thorton /s paul /p defend

Adjudication of Coverage Defenses in a Subsequent Proceeding
burd /s sussex

(4) Declaratory Judgment Proceeding
sy("declaratory judgment" /s coverage noncoverage /s defense)

(5) Inclusion of the Insurer as a Party in the Tort Suit
sy(insurer carrier /s interven! /s action suit lawsuit case /s uninsured underinsured)

(7) Participation of Lawyers Selected by Both the Insured and the Insurer

> maryland /s peppers & attorney lawyer counsel /p participat! represent!

(e) Resolution of the Tort Claim and the Insured's Right to Indemnification

> **(4) and (5) Adjudication of the Tort Claim in Favor of the Claimant**
>
> *Cases Involving Matters That Were Not at Issue in the Tort Suit*
> murphy /s urso
>
> *Observations*
> insurer carrier /s preclu! estop! /s subsequent later /5 lawsuit suit action litigation /s cover!

§ 7.7 Statutory Remedies for Nonpayment and Late Payment of Insurance Claims

(a) Introductory Note

> sy,di(insured assured claimant /s recover! /s attorney lawyer counsel /s fee compensat! /s "declaratory judgment")
> sy(unreasonabl! reasonabl! /5 delay! /s pay paying paid payment compensat! /s claim benefit)

(b) Statutory Remedies for an Insured

> statut! law legislat! /s remedy! relief provision /s delay! /s pay paying payment paid /s claim benefit

(c) Standards and Justification for Assessing Attorney's Fees, Interest and Other Legislatively Prescribed Remedies

> seguin /s continental
> sy(statute statutor! law legislat! /s penal! fine* fining fee /7 unreasonabl! reasonabl! /s insurer carrier)

(d) Unfair Claims Settlement Practices Legislation

> sy,di(unfair! /s claim /s settl! /s practice /s act statut! legislat! law)

§ 7.8 The Liability Insurer's Duty to Insureds Regarding Settlement

(a) Introductory Note

> *Contract or Tort Claim?*
> crisci /p settl! /p contract tort

(b) The Standards for Assessing Whether an Insurer's Conduct Warrants Excess Liability

(1) Negligence, Bad Faith, and Good Faith

> *Bad Faith*
> insurer carrier /s bad-faith /s coverage /s excess exceed! /s limit! /5 policy insurance
>
> *Good Faith*
> sy(insurer carrier /s duty obligat! requir! /5 good-faith /s insured assured claimant)

(2) The Insurer's Interests versus the Insured's Interests

> *Equal Consideration to the Insured's Interest*
> sy,di(insurer carrier /s insured assured /3 interest /s same equal! proper properly much /3 consider*** consideration treat! regard!)

Greater Consideration to the Insured's Interest
> insurer carrier /s insured assured /3 interest /s ''least as much'' paramount /5 consider! treat! regard!

(e) Multiple Insurers and Multiple Claimants

(2) Other Insurance: Primary or Excess Coverage
> find 610 p2d 1038

(h) Damages for Breach

(1) Consequential Damages

Emotional Distress and Mental Illness
> find 426 p2d 173

Punitive Damages
> silberg /s california /p exemplary punitive treble

(i) Remedies for Insureds Who Are Solvent and Those Who Are "Insolvent"

(1) "Insolvent" Insureds
> insolven! /s insured assured claimant /s liab! responsib! /s excess exceed! /s judgment

§ 7.9 The Liability of First Party Insurers for Consequential Damages

(b) The Theoretical Basis for Liability

(1) Breach of Contract
> sy(cause /s action /s contract /s good bad +1 faith)

(2) Tort Liability

Recognition of a New Tort Action Involving Intentional Bad Faith
> to(217) /p inten! /s bad-faith /s insurer carrier

Chapter Eight

INSURANCE REGULATION AND GOVERNMENT SPONSORSHIP OF INSURANCE

Table of Sections

---

§ 8.1   Allocation of Powers Among Federal and State Regulatory Institutions

§ 8.1(a)   The Federal–State Accommodation

In the United States, administrative regulation of insurance has been and continues to be primarily the responsibility of state authorities rather than the federal government. However, during this century regulatory activities by various federal administrative agencies have become an increasingly significant factor both for the insurance industry generally and for particular aspects of the business activities of some insurance companies.

There have been many proposals for shifting the major responsibility from the state regulatory authorities to federal agencies. The merits of such proposals have long been argued, and some of the contentions advanced by proponents and opponents of federal regulation have altered radically as the context in which the issues were debated changed. This is well illustrated by contrasting the comments of Louis D. Brandeis, later to become a distinguished Associate Justice of the United States Supreme Court, with the arguments advanced approximately forty years later both before and after the United States Supreme Court decision in the *Southeastern Underwriters* case.

In October of 1905, Brandeis, who was then counsel for the Protective Committee of Policyholders in the Equitable Life Assurance Society, spoke before the Commercial Club of Boston on the merits of a bill to federalize insurance supervision that was then pending in the United States Senate. The Brandeis analysis of the proposed legislation, which was supported by some of the leading insurance executives of the day, was scathing. In his view,

> "The sole effect of a Federal law would be * * * to free the companies from the careful scrutiny of the commissioners of some of the States. It seeks to rob the State even of the right to protect its own citizens from the legalized robbery to which present insurance measures subject the citizens, for by the terms of the bill a Federal license would secure the right to do business within the

borders of the State, regardless of the State prohibitions, free from the State's protective regulation." [1]

The legislative proposal Brandeis criticized was never enacted.

In 1943, the debate about whether the insurance business was to be regulated by the federal government was brought to the United States Supreme Court in the context of a dispute as to whether insurance companies were subject to the federal antitrust laws. The case which presented this issue was United States v. South-Eastern Underwriters.[2] By the time this dispute reached the United States Supreme Court, the political climate in regard to regulatory activity had changed markedly. Several federal agencies had become aggressive regulators and it then appeared likely that federal agencies would impose more vigorous regulation of the insurance business than was being exercised by the state regulatory agencies. In this context, partisans of stricter controls — the position Brandeis so vehemently espoused in the 1905 speech — generally favored assumption of increased responsibility for insurance regulation by the federal government. On the other side, many insurance industry executives not only favored continued state regulation, but were adamantly opposed to any federal intrusions.

The principal issue in South-Eastern Underwriters was whether Congress had expressed an intention to exempt insurers from the federal antitrust laws.[3] In South-Eastern Underwriters, the Supreme Court decided that Congress had not manifested a clear intention to exempt insurers and then concluded that a group of insurance companies that participated in an association whose purpose was to exchange information for rate-making were subject to the provisions of the Sherman Antitrust Act. Therefore, the court held federal officials charged with the enforcement of the antitrust laws were appropriately carrying out their responsibilities in applying those antitrust laws to insurers.

The Congressional reaction to the Supreme Court's decision in South-Eastern Underwriters was prompt and in many respects decisive. The impact of the court's decision was almost immediately restricted through the enactment of the McCarran-Ferguson Act, which declared that the business of insurance should continue to be "subject to the laws of the several States which relate to the regulation or taxation of such business." [4] However, the Act also provided that federal regulato-

§ 8.1(a)

1. Quoted in note 17 of the dissenting opinion of Justice Jackson, United States v. South-Eastern Underwriters Association, 322 U.S. 533, 64 S.Ct. 1162, 88 L.Ed. 1440 (1944) rehearing denied 323 U.S. 811, 65 S.Ct. 26, 89 L.Ed. 646 (1944). True to Brandeis tradition, his argument was documented with data on stockholder dividends and insurance overhead.

2. United States v. South-Eastern Underwriters Association, 322 U.S. 533, 64

S.Ct. 1162, 88 L.Ed. 1440 (1944), rehearing denied 323 U.S. 811, 65 S.Ct. 26, 89 L.Ed. 646 (1944).

3. Steps taken in an effort to forestall the decision included the filing of amicus curiae briefs by 35 states.

4. 59 Stat. 33, 34 (1945), 15 U.S.C.A. § 1012 (1958).

The McCarran-Ferguson Act creates an antitrust exemption for the business of insurance. This has led to numerous cases

ry legislation would be "applicable to the business of insurance *to the extent that such business is not regulated by State law."* [5]

Promptly after the McCarran-Ferguson Act was adopted, state insurance commissioners and industry representatives joined forces in a nationwide movement which sought the enactment in every state of legislation that would satisfy the requirements for state regulation established by the McCarran-Ferguson Act and thereby exempt insurers from federal regulatory legislation. Under the sponsorship of the National Association of Insurance Commissioners (often referred to as the "N.A.I.C."), and with the active cooperation of an All-Industry Committee, model acts were prepared and recommended for adoption by each of the states. [6] In general, the model statutes developed by the N.A.I.C. were designed to maintain and retain the regulation of insurance by state agencies or commissions, thereby precluding the application of federal regulatory laws.

The state laws enacted in response to the McCarran-Ferguson Act were primarily concerned with rate regulation, and by 1950 rate regulatory legislation had been adopted in every state. [7] Consequently, this facet of insurance business was clearly established as a province of state regulation. During the period of legislative activity which the McCarran Act produced, only a few states adopted laws that addressed other matters such as the standardization of policy forms or other business practices of insurers.

There are also many regulatory matters of rather limited scope. This is well illustrated by the Model Act for the Unauthorized Insurers Service of Process Law, [8] which provides that when an insurer is not qualified to do business in a state under the state's regulatory laws,

---

in which the courts have been confronted with the problem of deciding whether a particular activity constituted the business of insurance for purposes of the McCarran-Ferguson Act exemption. In Union Labor Life Insurance Company v. Pireno, 458 U.S. 119 at p. 129, 102 S.Ct. 3002 at p. 309, 73 L.Ed.2d 647 (1982), the Supreme Court set forth three factors to be considered in determining whether a practice constitutes the business of insurance:

(1) Whether the practice has the effect of transferring or spreading the policyholder's risks?

(2) Whether the practice is an integral part of the policy relationship between the insurer and the insured?

(3) Whether the practice is limited to entities within the insurance industry?

Also see the discussion of these factors in Feinstein v. Nettleship Company of Los Angeles, 714 F.2d 928 (9th Cir.1983), *cert. denied* 466 U.S. 972, 104 S.Ct. 2346, 80 L.Ed.2d 820 (1984); United States v. Title Insurance Rating Bureau of Arizona, 700

F.2d 1247 (9th Cir.1983), *cert. denied* 467 U.S. 1240, 104 S.Ct. 3509, 82 L.Ed.2d 819 (1984).

5. *Ibid.*

For a brief survey of some of the issues this statutory provision has led to, see Note, *Federal Regulation of Insurance Companies: The Disappearing McCarran Exemption,* 1973 Duke Law Journal 1340–1356.

6. See James B. Donovan, *State Regulation of Insurance,* 1956 Insurance Law Journal 11–15 at p. 12; James B. Donovan, *Regulation of Insurance Under the McCarran Act,* 15 Law & Contemporary Problems 473–492 at pp. 483–488 (1950).

7. See 1 RICHARDS, INSURANCE LAW (Fifth Edition Freedman, 1952), at pp. 216–220.

8. See 1959 ABA SECTION INSURANCE, NEGLIGENCE, & COMPENSATION LAW PROCEEDINGS 227, reporting adoption of statutes of this type in 49 states (excluding Alaska), the District of Columbia and Puerto Rico.

such an insurer may be sued by serving legal documents on the state insurance commissioner. In the absence of such a law, although such insurers do not totally escape regulation by not being amenable to service in each state, the state regulation that is possible frequently lacks effectiveness.[9]

Consumer complaints about automobile insurance rates have led to several congressional inquiries. During the 1960s, considerable public concern focused on the underwriting and cancellation practices of insurers, as well as the rates charged for automobile insurance. The public outcry against the insurance industry and the charges of ineffectual state regulation served to revive interest in proposals for a greater federal role in regulation and led to the initiation of a comprehensive study of automobile insurance in the Department of Transportation, commencing in 1968.[10] Although the public concerns in regard to motor vehicle insurance reflected by these events led to the adoption of no-fault motor vehicle insurance in many states, it did not produce either significant federal legislative action or a recasting of the role of the federal government in the regulation of insurance.

Some questions (such as the regulation of premium rates) about the allocation of regulatory authority for the insurance industry were clearly resolved by the events of the 1940s, while others were not. For example, state fair trade legislation had been scant before the McCarran Act. In general, during the 1940s and early 1950s most states did not enact legislative proposals that would have provided for this type of

---

9. This concern may have been increased by the fact that effectuality of state control over the transactions of such unauthorized insurers had been the focus of important litigation. See, e.g., McGee v. International Life Insurance Co., 355 U.S. 220, 78 S.Ct. 199, 2 L.Ed.2d 223 (1957) (respondent was not served with process in California but was served in accordance with a California statute, by registered mail at its principal place of business in Texas; Texas courts refused to enforce the California judgment in favor of a California resident on the respondent's contract of life insurance consummated by interstate mail, respondent never having had any office or agent in California, and, so far as the record showed, never having solicited or done any insurance business in California apart from this policy, which was issued in substitution for the policy of an Arizona corporation whose obligations respondent assumed; held that the Texas courts erred in refusing to give the California judgment full faith and credit).

Also see Robertson v. California, 328 U.S. 440, 66 S.Ct. 1160, 90 L.Ed. 1366 (1946), *rehearing denied* 329 U.S. 818, 67 S.Ct. 25, 91 L.Ed. 697 (1946) (appellant was convicted in a state court of California for

violating a provision of the California Insurance Code prohibiting a person from acting as agent for a nonadmitted insurer except under specified conditions; attack against the state action as inconsistent with the *South-Eastern Underwriters* decision rejected, and "explicitly without specific reliance upon" the McCarran-Ferguson Act).

Even though the provision for jurisdiction of state courts over non-admitted insurers has thus been treated as a facet of insurance regulation, continuation of such state jurisdiction would seem consistent with even the most thoroughgoing Congressional occupation of the field of insurance regulation, a state of affairs that did not exist even during the interval between *South-Eastern Underwriters* and the enactment of the McCarran-Ferguson Act.

10. Among the reports on various aspects of the Department of Transportation study is one specifically concerned with regulation of insurance. See John Day, ECONOMIC REGULATION OF INSURANCE IN THE UNITED STATES (United States Department of Transportation Automobile Insurance & Compensation Study, 1970).

regulatory activity. Consequently, this aspect of the insurance business was largely not subject to any regulatory scrutiny during the decade that followed the adoption of the McCarran Act. In the 1950s, the Federal Trade Commission initiated some inquiries and preliminary investigations into some of the promotional and advertising practices employed by insurers in the fields of accident and health insurance.[11] The response to those actions by the Federal Trade Commission was notable: by the end of 1959, unfair trade practices acts had been adopted in all 50 states, the District of Columbia and Puerto Rico. Most of these statutes were based on a then new N.A.I.C. Model Act.[12]

Since the 1940s, numerous model acts addressing various aspects of the insurance business have been prepared by the National Association of Insurance Commissioners and the All-Industry Committee.[13] If all model statutes proposed by the N.A.I.C. were enacted and rigorously enforced, the insurance industry would undoubtedly be the most regulated business in the United States. Even in the absence of any significant change in the extent of regulatory legislation and the level of administrative activities, it is clear that insurance is one of the most highly regulated businesses. At the same time, however, numerous questions about possible areas of federal regulatory activity remain unresolved.

§ 8.1(b) Unresolved Questions Regarding Regulatory Responsibilities

The controversy over the allocation of the responsibility for insurance regulation between the federal government and the states has continued to be manifested in a variety of ways.[1] Underlying the entire regulatory controversy is a set of unanswered questions about the relative effectiveness of state and federal agencies.[2] Undoubtedly, these are questions that will be the subject of continuing debate, and the responses to these questions may differ from generation to genera-

---

11. See James B. Donovan, *State Regulation of Insurance*, 1956 Insurance Law Journal 11–15 at p. 13.

12. 1959 ABA SECTION INSURANCE NEGLIGENCE & COMPENSATION LAW PROCEEDINGS 227–229.

Also see Comment, *Service Contracts: A Subject for State or Federal Regulation—Do Consumers Need Protection From the Service Contract Industry?*, 1979 Southern Illinois University Law Journal 587–620.

13. See generally the two loose-leaf volumes of materials entitled OFFICIAL N.A.I.C. MODEL INSURANCE LAW, REGULATION AND GUIDELINES (published by NIARS Corporation under the auspices of the National Association of Insurance Commissioners).

§ 8.1(b)

1. See, e.g., Michael S. Wilder, *Regulation of the Insurance Industry Under the Proposed Federal Securities Code*, 7 Connecticut Law Review 711–731 (1975); Note, *The McCarran-Ferguson Act: A Time for Procompetitive Reform*, 29 Vanderbilt Law Review 1271–1308 (1976).

2. See *Id.*, at pp. 58–77.

Also see George R. Walker, *Relationship Between Insurance Companies and Insurance Regulators*, 26 Federation of Insurance Counsel Journal 99–109 (1976).

See also Herbert Denenberg, *Meeting the Insurance Crisis of Our Cities: An Industry in Revolution*, 1970 Insurance Law Journal 205 at pp. 209–210; Spencer Kimball, *The Case for State Regulation of Insurance*, in INSURANCE, GOVERNMENT, AND SOCIAL POLICY 411 (Kimball & Denenberg, editors 1969).

tion. For example, it seems evident that the preference for federal or state regulation may be greatly influenced by the prevailing political philosophy in regard to the desirable balance between centralized and localized governmental power.[3]

Another basic issue which remains unanswered in regard to the debate on insurance regulation involves the relative effectiveness of any type of administrative regulation, either state or federal, of business enterprises. The merits of governmental regulation continue to be vigorously debated. It is clear that ineffective regulation has often occurred when a regulatory agency becomes a "captive" of the industry being regulated, and in regard to insurance one of the fundamental questions is whether this risk is substantially greater under one system of regulation than under the other. Although federal regulation would provide an opportunity for insurers to concentrate all their power on influencing one agency, this might be offset by a greater opportunity in the national forum both for public awareness about the effects of such influence and for marshaling resources to advocate the interests of consumers.

The debate on the most appropriate or desirable allocation of regulatory responsibilities has frequently focused on the funding that is or will be available for the regulatory authority. One of the persistent criticisms of the reliance on state regulation has been that state insurance departments have continually been hampered by inadequate funding in general and insufficient personnel in particular.[4] Although critics voicing such opinions have acknowledged that substantial cooperation among states (especially through the activities and programs of the National Association of Insurance Commissioners) often has been successful in offsetting the inadequacies of funds provided for the operation of state regulatory commissions, they also argue that this approach is less efficient than the type of nationwide regulation that would be possible if the insurance business were to be regulated by a federal agency. Although a centralized federal agency undoubtedly would not be entirely free of the impediments of inadequate funds and insufficient personnel, experience in some areas of federal regulation suggests that the problem might be less severe if the Congress and the President agreed that it would be desirable for the federal government to assume the responsibility for such regulation. However, the pros-

---

3. For a succinct statement of the case for localized power, made however in discussing not the choice between federal and state regulation but rather the choice between governmental and privately written automobile insurance, see New York Insurance Department Report, *Automobile Insurance * * * For Whose Benefit?* (1970), at pp. 77–78:

"[D]ecentralized, variegated, responsive and smaller units of power are preferable to a monolithic and centralized monopoly of power. The reason is not effi-

ciency; it is the desire to stimulate individual creativity, to encourage flexibility of response and healthy competition and to guard the public against the terrible consequences when centralized power goes wrong."

4. *Cf.* The comments of several commissioners of insurance quoted in the report *Insurance Department Funding,* prepared by the American Insurance Association, Policy Development and Research, 4 Journal of Insurance Regulation 588–605 at pp. 588–589 (1983).

pect for such a consensus appears unlikely to occur in the 1980s, an era that has been characterized by the marked reduction of federal regulatory activity in regard to many business enterprises.

Whenever the respective merits of centralized federal or decentralized state regulatory agencies are considered, the discussion almost always addresses the question whether it is a significant advantage that with multiple state agencies there is a possibility that at least a few of them will focus on each major problem that needs attention, and that insurance purchasers will benefit from such regulatory activities in other states. It seems almost beyond dispute that there are fields or areas of business activity in which this has occurred.

In addition to the various general questions considered in the preceding paragraphs, the debate over the role of the federal government in the regulation of insurance also focuses on several specialized questions which are yet to be resolved.[5] One of the most intriguing questions that appears to remain unanswered is to what extent does federal trade practices legislation apply to insurance organizations and transactions. As a consequence of the McCarran-Ferguson Act, the guideline has generally been understood to be that the federal trade practices laws are "applicable to the business of insurance to the extent that such business is not regulated by State law."[6] In 1958, the Supreme Court specifically held that "prohibitory" state legislation was enough to occupy the field of regulation of certain advertising practices of insurers which had been challenged by the Federal Trade Commission, and which otherwise would have been subject to the Federal Trade Commission Act.[7] However, the analysis set forth by the court in that decision suggests the possibility that the mere enactment of some form of prohibitory state statute will not always be conclusive of the question whether the business is "regulated by State law."[8] For example, state prohibitory legislation may not be enough to constitute preemptive regulation of false advertising. Thus, even though a state statute purports to be "comprehensive," it may not preclude application of the Federal Trade Commission Act in all circumstances.[9]

5. See, e.g., Anthony Atwell, *The McCarran-Ferguson Act—A Deceptive Panacea?* 5 Forum 339–346 (ABA Section Insurance, Negligence & Compensation Law 1970).

Also see Donald J. Polden, *The Antitrust Implication of Credit Insurance Tying Arrangements,* 32 Drake Law Review 861–912 (1983).

6. 15 U.S.C.A. § 1012(b) (1948).

7. Federal Trade Commission v. National Casualty Co., 357 U.S. 560, 78 S.Ct. 1260, 2 L.Ed.2d 1540 (1958).

8. Group Life & Health Insurance Co. v. Royal Drug Co., Inc., 440 U.S. 205, 99 S.Ct. 1067, 59 L.Ed.2d 261 (1979) (Blue Shield's alleged agreements with pharma-

cies allegedly fixing price of retail drugs are not exempt from federal antitrust law because the agreements "do not involve any underwriting or spreading of risk, but are merely arrangements for the purchase of goods and services by Blue Shield," and thus "they are not the 'business of insurance' ").

Also see Union Labor Life Insurance Co. v. Pireno, 458 U.S. 119, 102 S.Ct. 3002, 73 L.Ed.2d 647 (1982).

Similarly, there is an even greater likelihood that state legislation will not preempt the entire field of antitrust regulation.

9. *Ibid.*

Also see Note, *Debate on State Versus Federal Regulation of Insurance Continues,*

There is no definitive answer in regard to what tests or standards should or will be applied by the federal courts in determining whether the insurance business is to some extent "not regulated by State law." In future cases, the Supreme Court may not limit the analysis of this question to an examination of the statutes and the administrative structure established by statutory direction or authorization. For example, the Court might also evaluate the actual effectiveness of the state regulatory scheme.[10] If this question were to be considered, the Court could reasonably conclude that an assessment of effective regulation appropriately extends to taking into account matters such as the adequacy of the state agency's budget or the qualifications of personnel in regulatory positions. On the other hand, if the Supreme Court decides not to assess the effectiveness of state regulation, that decision might increase the likelihood of further Congressional action at some time in the future. Thus, the meaning of the phrase in the McCarran-Ferguson Act "not regulated by state law" has only been partially explicated by the appellate cases that have considered these clauses.

Many issues with respect to the provisions in the McCarran-Ferguson Act remain unresolved.[11] The balance that now exists between primary regulation by the states and a secondary role for federal regulation of the insurance business is in some respects more of a "truce" than a settled accommodation. Viewed in light of the experiences of the last half century, it seems likely that in the future there will be an "ebb and flow" in the relative spheres of regulatory activity of both state and federal agencies concerned with the business of insurance.[12]

§ 8.1(c) Legislative, Administrative and Judicial Regulation

Legislation that provides for some regulation of insurance transactions and insurance companies has been adopted in every state. In an effort to achieve greater unity and coherence, a number of states have codified their insurance laws or re-codified their statutes after an earlier codification. In some jurisdictions, this legislation is a very formidable body of enactments that is appropriately viewed as an

---

53 Nebraska Law Review 289–302 (1974), discussing the FTC's jurisdiction to challenge insurance company mergers as violations of the Clayton Act.

10. *Cf.* John Day, ECONOMIC REGULATION OF INSURANCE IN THE UNITED STATES (United States Department Transportation Automobile Insurance & Compensation Study, 1970), at pp. 42–44.

11. *Cf.* the relatively narrow construction of the term the "business of insurance" in SEC v. National Securities, Inc., 393 U.S. 453, 89 S.Ct. 564, 21 L.Ed.2d 668 (1969).

Also consider the opinion in Group Life & Health Insurance Company v. Royal Drug Co., Inc., 440 U.S. 205, 99 S.Ct. 1067, 59 L.Ed.2d 261 (1979); Union Labor Life Insurance Company v. Pireno, 458 U.S. 119, 102 S.Ct. 3002, 73 L.Ed.2d 647 (1982).

Also see Note, *Federal Intervention in Insurance Regulation: A Questionable Trend,* 4 Southern University Law Review 91–103 (1977); Note, *Insurance Regulation and Antitrust Exemptions: McCarran-Ferguson, The Boycott Exception, and the Public Interest,* 27 Rutgers Law Review 140–159 (1973).

12. *Cf.* Nathan Weber, Editor, *Insurance Deregulation: Issues and Perspectives* (The Conference Board, 1982).

"insurance code." One of the most ambitious of all such efforts, with a staff of unparalleled excellence, was initiated in Wisconsin in 1965 and completed in 1974.[1] In other states, it seems less clear as to whether the statutes can appropriately be regarded as sufficiently unified either in form or in substantive content to warrant being characterized as a regulatory code, or even as a body of insurance law.

Each state legislature has authorized continuing supervision of insurance transactions and institutions by a state agency under the direction of an administrative officer, usually characterized as the commissioner of insurance. The staff and funds provided for these agencies have varied widely. In several states, most notably California and New York, the insurance commissions have been well staffed, allowing them to be generally effective regulatory authorities. In many states, the regulatory commissions have been characterized by fluctuations in funding, administrative policy, and vigor of enforcement. And, some state agencies have been so understaffed and underfinanced that regulation has been largely illusory.[2]

Insurance transactions and institutions are often subject to judicial scrutiny and the decisions in these cases frequently have significantly affected the character of insurance transactions and institutions. The influence of the courts on insurance transactions through doctrinal developments has sometimes been considerably more significant than the enforcement of regulatory measures by the commissioner of insurance. Particularly notable among the doctrinal developments by the courts have been those which have culminated in recognition of rights at variance with policy provisions.[3]

§ 8.2   Objectives and Areas of Insurance Regulation

§ 8.2(a)   Objectives of Insurance Regulation

Most insurance regulatory measures have been designed to serve one or more of three main objectives:

First, to avoid overreaching by insurers. Regulation to avoid overreaching, which is principally directed at marketing practices

§ 8.1(c)

1. See Spencer L. Kimball & Herb Denenberg, Modern Insurance Code Revision: Reflections on the Art of Legislative Reform, 21 C.L.U.J. No. 4, p. 34 (1967), reprinted with slight modification in INSURANCE, GOVERNMENT, AND SOCIAL POLICY (Kimball & Denenberg eds. 1969), at p. 41.

Also see Symposium: Insurance Regulation, 1969 Wisconsin Law Review 1019–1170.

2. See Spencer L. Kimball & W. Eugene Hansen, The Utah Insurance Commissioner: A Study of Administrative Regulation in Action, 6 Utah Law Review 1–22 at p. 19 (1958), reporting that the entire budget for the Insurance Department of Utah in 1956 was $33,274.51, over 10 per cent of which was charged to overhead costs of the parent Business Regulation Commission, leaving less than $30,000 for Insurance Department services to the insurance industry and the citizens of the state, even though the State collected more than three times that much from the industry in fees.

3. See generally Chapter 6, above. See especially § 6.3, above concerning the principle of honoring reasonable expectations even when inconsistent with a painstaking study of policy provisions, and § 6.4 above, concerning variance claims based on declared public policies.

and arrangements, has been imposed by both statutes [1] and judicially created doctrines.[2]

Second, to assure solvency (or, as it is sometimes referred to "solidity") of insurers. The aim of assuring solvency is primarily served by regulation of insurance organizations to avoid the consequences of imprudent management of their resources.[3] To some extent, rate regulation is concerned with assuring solvency by requiring insurers to charge premiums that are adequate in relation to the risks covered.[4]

Third, to assure equitable rating classifications. Rate regulation is designed to produce premium charges that are equitable for individual purchasers and provide the insurers with a fair return for the risks undertaken.[5]

There are also several other goals for insurance regulation.[6] To achieve these goals, some regulatory measures are focused on regulating insurance transactions, while others are primarily concerned with the institutions and the people engaged in such transactions as a business.[7]

§ 8.2(a)

1. Consider, e.g., legislation concerning the effect to be given to warranties in insurance law, § 6.6, above.

2. Consider generally the judicially developed principles of denying unconscionable advantage and honoring reasonable expectations, § 6.2 and § 6.3, above.

3. See generally INSURANCE, GOVERNMENT AND SOCIAL POLICY (Kimball & Denenberg, editors, 1969), at pp. 63–190.

Also see § 8.5, below.

4. See generally § 8.4, below.

5. See § 8.4, below.

6. The Wisconsin Insurance Code, drafted under the leadership of Professor Spencer L. Kimball, sets forth eleven purposes for the legislation:

"The purpose of the insurance laws shall be—

a. To ensure the solidity of all insurers doing business in this state;

b. To ensure that policyholders, claimants and insurers are treated fairly and equitably;

c. To ensure that the state has an adequate and healthy insurance market, characterized by competitive conditions and the exercise of initiative;

d. To provide for an office that is expert in the field of insurance, and able to enforce the insurance laws;

e. To encourage full cooperation of the office with other regulatory bodies, both of this and other states and of the federal government.

f. To improve and thereby preserve state regulation of insurance;

g. To maintain freedom of contract and freedom of enterprise so far as consistent with the other purposes of the law;

h. To encourage self-regulation of the insurance enterprise;

i. To encourage loss prevention as an aspect of the operation of the insurance enterprise;

j. To keep the public informed on insurance matters; and

k. To achieve the other purposes stated in the insurance laws."

Wisconsin Insurance Code 601.01 (1974).

Also see Spencer L. Kimball and Werner Pennigstorf, THE REGULATION OF INSURANCE COMPANIES IN THE UNITED STATES AND THE EUROPEAN COMMUNITIES: A COMPARATIVE STUDY (1981), Chapter III.

7. *Cf.* Spencer Kimball, *The Regulation of Insurance,* in INSURANCE, GOVERNMENT AND SOCIAL POLICY (Kimball & Denenberg, editors 1969), at p. 3 and pp. 5–10; Spencer Kimball, *The Purpose of Insurance Regulation: A Preliminary Inquiry in the Theory of Insurance Law,* 45 Minnesota Law Review 471–524 (1961). Kimball also identifies "external objectives" that should be taken into account in thinking about insurance regulation, among which are the "libertarian objective" of freedom from govern-

Regulatory actions in general and rating regulation in particular are matters of continuing concern which have sometimes occasioned substantial controversy.[8]

§ 8.2(b)   Areas of Insurance Regulation

The areas of insurance regulation are numerous and varied. In general, regulatory statutes and administrative regulations are concerned with (1) the forms of insurance organizations,[1] (2) the maintenance of a secure financial status (controls over investments, reserves and requirements of deposits; periodic financial reports; audits; etc.),[2] and (3) the policy forms employed for various types of insurance.[3] In addition, both insuring organizations and insurance sales representatives (agents and brokers) are subject to licensing provisions.[4] Finally, in most states considerable importance has been attached to special provisions for protection of policyholders and others against the consequences of insurer insolvency,[5] including the processes for either the liquidation or rehabilitation of insurers.[6]

In some states, the marketing practices employed by insurers are subject to extensive statutory and administrative regulations, as well as judicial "regulation." For example, legislation establishing sanctions against false advertising have been adopted in several states.[7] Other

mental restraint, "local protectionism" that is in general opposed by the farsighted and nationally oriented but nevertheless has its impact, and the objective of wide dispersion of decision-making power, which he refers to as "federalism." *Id.*, at pp. 6–8.

See also Richard Stewart, *Ritual and Reality in Insurance Regulation*, in INSURANCE, GOVERNMENT AND SOCIAL POLICY (Kimball & Denenberg, editors, 1969), at p. 22 and pp. 24–32 ("A good, simple answer is that government is trying to help people get the most insurance for their money," and among the ideas this implies are assuring availability, quality and reliability, and reasonable pricing.).

8. For a discussion of rating regulation, see § 8.4, below.

See generally the discussion of insurance regulation in the sources cited in the preceding footnote.

§ 8.2(b)

1. See § 8.5, below.

2. See, e.g., California Insurance Code §§ 900–924 (Derring's, 1977); Illinois Rev. Stat. ch. 73, §§ 744–752 (1986); McKinney's New York Insurance Law §§ 1301–1320 (1985).

3. See § 2.8, above.

4. For example, see California Insurance Code §§ 1631–1651 (Deering's 1977 & 1978 Supp.); Illinois Ann.Stat. ch. 73, ¶ 1065.39–2 (1986 Supp.); McKinney's New York Insurance Law § 1102, § 2102(a)(1) (1985).

5. E.g., Wisconsin Statutes Ann. § 645.01–.10 (Supp.1970).

See generally *Insurance Accessibility for the Hard-to-Place Driver*, REPORT OF THE DIVISION OF INDUSTRY ANALYSIS, Bureau of Economics, Federal Trade Commission (United States Department of Transportation Automobile Insurance & Compensation Study, 1970), at pp. 73–77.

6. For example, see California Insurance Code §§ 1010–1062 (Deering's, 1977 & 1987 Supp.); Illinois Ann.Stat. ch. 73 §§ 799–833 (1986 Supp.); McKinney's New York Insurance Law §§ 7401–7434 (1985 & 1987 Supp.).

7. See § 8.1(a), above.

In the 1970s, there was a renewed movement for additional legislation to protect consumers that led to enactment of unfair insurance practices acts in several states. For example, see Donald L. Very, *The Pennsylvania Unfair Insurance Practices Act—The Sleeping Giant*, 46 Pennsylvania Bar Association Quarterly 438–452 (1975).

enactments apply to activities such as rebating or discrimination.[8] Many of the judicial doctrines concerning rights at variance with policy provisions [9] are to a considerable extent responses to marketing abuses. Substantial legislative and administrative attention has been given to complaints arising from cancellations and nonrenewals.[10]

One of the troublesome areas in the regulation of both insurance marketing generally and sales representatives in particular concerns tie-in transactions. For example, a legal entity engaged in consumer financing may seek either to function as an agent for the sale of credit life insurance or to participate in an arrangement in which persons associated with it do so as individuals. Tie-in arrangements have also been established in a variety of areas such as the sales of automobiles (with the sale of automobile insurance) and the merchandising of funeral services (with the sale of funeral and burial insurance). The tie-in arrangements, which are frequently commercially advantageous, have been involved in substantial abuses. Efforts to regulate such tie-in arrangements have sometimes succeeded [11] and sometimes failed.[12]

The processing of insurance claims is also subject to regulation. This is accomplished through the monitoring of insurance policy forms,[13] the judicial recognition of rights at variance with policy provisions,[14] statutory remedies for delay in payment of claims,[15] the enactment of resident-agent statutes,[16] administrative processes for responding to individual complaints,[17] and legislative provisions for administrative initiatives of more general scope.

8. For example, see California Insurance Code §§ 750–767 (Deerings, 1977 & 1987 Supp.); McKinney's New York Insurance Law § 2324 and § 4224 (1985).

9. See generally Chapter 6, above.

10. Also see § 4.10, above.

11. See, e.g., Daniel v. Family Security Life Insurance Co., 336 U.S. 220, 69 S.Ct. 550, 93 L.Ed. 632 (1949), 10 A.L.R.2d 945 (1950) (sustaining, against constitutional attack, a South Carolina statute prohibiting undertakers from serving as agents for life insurance companies).

Also see Federal Trade Commission v. Dixie Finance Company, Inc., 695 F.2d 926 (5th Cir.1983) (holding that the "business of insurance" exemption of the McCarran-Ferguson Act did not preclude the Federal Trade Commission from investigating whether finance companies required the purchase of insurance as a precondition to an arrangement of credit).

Consider the *Hearings on Tie-ins of the Sale of Insurance by Banks and Bank Holding Companies Before the Senate Committee on Banking, Housing and Urban Affairs*, 96th Congress, First Session (1979).

Also consider the federal legislation prohibiting banks from engaging in certain tying arrangements. U.S.C.A. § 1972.

12. See, e.g., Department of Insurance v. Motors Insurance Corp., 236 Ind. 1, 138 N.E.2d 157 (1956), overturning the Department's effort to prohibit automobile dealers from serving as agents for the sale of automobile insurance, and holding such action to be an unconstitutional deprivation of the right to engage simultaneously in two lawful businesses.

13. See § 2.8(b), above.

14. See Chapter 6, above.

15. See the discussion of statutory remedies in § 7.7, above.

16. See, e.g., California Insurance Code § 1638 and § 1639 (Deering, 1977); Illinois Ann.Stat. ch. 73 ¶ 1065.44–2 (1986 Supp.); McKinney's New York Insurance Law §§ 1212, 1213, and 1214 (1985).

17. For a summary of data concerning complaint records of the N.Y. Insurance Department in the years 1966–1968, see New York Insurance Department, Report, *Automobile Insurance . . . For Whose Benefit?* (1970), at p. 37, n. 68.

§ 8.3 The Nature and Scope of Insurance Regulation

§ 8.3(a) Generally

The nature and scope of an insurance regulation is not always clearly specified, and therefore the effects of both legislative and administrative actions have been the subject of a substantial number of disputes. When an issue arises in regard to the nature or scope of insurance regulation, it is essential to carefully consider the applicable insurance statutes, administrative provisions, and judicial decisions. Especially among the body of statutory and administrative insurance regulatory measures, some apply to all or nearly all types of insurance transactions, while others apply to relatively few. Consequently, considerable care should always be exercised in ascertaining the scope of a statutory or administrative provision.

Caution should also be practiced in regard to the application or interpretation of judicial decisions. There is always a temptation to employ any available precedents when a dispute involves basic issues — such as what constitutes an insurance transaction or conducting an insurance business — about the meaning of a statute or an administrative rule. However, even when judicial precedents are urged only as analogical support for a proposition, the possible reasons for distinguishing decisions involving another type of insurance should be fully explored. Furthermore, the perspectives from which judicial precedents interpreting regulatory measures are appraised should always include a consideration of whether the definition of insurance implicit in the scope of one insurance regulatory measure is or is not appropriate for deciding the scope of another doctrine.

In many states, discerning the scope or reach of the regulatory statutes is complicated by the fact that the legislative provisions do not set forth any definition of "insurance" to guide the courts and administrative agencies. In other states, the statutory definitions are so broad or general as to be virtually useless when a dispute arises about whether the regulatory system was intended to apply to a particular type of commercial transaction.[1] One of the few notable exceptions to

---

§ 8.3(a)

1. The statutory definitions of insurance in California and Massachusetts are examples.

California Insurance Code § 22 (Deering's, 1977): "Insurance is a contract whereby one undertakes to indemnify another against loss, damage, or liability arising from a contingent or unknown event."

Massachusetts General Laws Ann. c. 175, § 2 (1972): "A contract of insurance is an agreement by which one party for a consideration promises to pay money or its equivalent, or to do an act valuable to the insured, upon the destruction, loss or injury of something in which the other party has an interest."

Arguably these statutes should be read not as stating that every transaction having the stated characteristics is insurance but only as saying that no transaction is insurance unless it has these characteristics. If so construed, there would seldom be any occasion to invoke them since it is not likely that a transaction lacking these characteristics would be alleged to be insurance even if there were no statutory definition of that term. Reading these

these generalizations about legislative definitions of insurance is the New York insurance legislation, which specifies, in both inclusory and exclusory terms, the reach of the state's regulatory statutes.[2] In doing so, it sets forth a precise definition for both the term "insurance contract"[3] and the term "doing an insurance business."[4]

The disadvantage of uncertainty — in regard to the precise scope of the regulatory statutes — produced by broad definitions of "insurance" and "doing an insurance business" is balanced, however, by an advantage that such imprecision affords in some instances. A general expression of the public interest in regulation, rather than rigid definitions that dictate either a narrow or broad reach for a particular regulatory measure, affords administrators and judges substantial latitude in

statutes instead as stating that all transactions having these characteristics are insurance would be to give them a meaning plainly inconsistent with the much narrower scope of regulation in practice. Many arrangements having these characteristics are never asserted to be insurance even by the most aggressive of regulatory officials.

Judicial decisions interpreting legislative definitions of insurance frequently are also relatively imprecise and generally provide little guidance in regard to each of the statutory provisions.

2. See McKinney's New York Insurance Law § 41 (Supp.1970):

"*Meaning of 'insurance contract' and 'doing an insurance business'*

"1. The term 'insurance contract,' as used in this chapter, shall, except as provided in subsection two, be deemed to include any agreement or other transaction whereby one party, herein called the insurer, is obligated to confer benefit of pecuniary value upon another party, herein called the insured or the beneficiary, dependent upon the happening of a fortuitous event in which the insured or beneficiary has, or is expected to have at the time of such happening, a material interest which will be adversely affected by the happening of such event. A fortuitous event is any occurrence or failure to occur which is, or is assumed by the parties to be, to a substantial extent beyond the control of either party.

"2. A contract of warranty, guaranty or suretyship is an insurance contract, within the meaning of this chapter, only if made by a warrantor, guarantor or surety who or which, as such, is doing an insurance business within the meaning of this chapter.

"3. Except as provided in subdivision four, any of the following acts in this state, effected by mail from outside this state or otherwise by any person, firm, association, corporation or joint-stock company shall constitute doing an insurance business in this state * * *: (a) the making, as insurer, or proposing to make as insurer, of any insurance contract, * * *; (b) the making, as warrantor, guarantor or surety, or the proposing to make as warrantor, guarantor or surety, of any contract of warranty, guaranty or suretyship as a vocation and not as merely incidental to any other legitimate business or activity of the warrantor, guarantor or surety; (c) the collection of any premium, membership fee, assessment or other consideration for any policy or contract of insurance; (d) the doing of any kind of business, including a reinsurance business, specifically recognized as constituting the doing of an insurance business within the meaning of this chapter; (e) the doing or proposing to do any business in substance equivalent to any of the foregoing in a manner designed to evade the provisions of this chapter.

"5. In the application of this chapter the fact that no profit is derived from the making of insurance contracts, agreements or transactions, or that no separate or direct consideration is received therefor, shall not be deemed conclusively to show that the making thereof does not constitute the doing of an insurance business."

Professor Patterson was a major contributor to the drafting of the New York statute.

3. *Id.,* paragraph 1.

4. *Id.,* paragraph 3.

This degree of differentiation is sufficient to deal with most, if not all, of the problems of reach that should be addressed in legislative drafting.

making choices about the scope and effect of the regulatory measures on various types of business enterprises.[5] Imprecise legislative rules and definitions provide a degree of flexibility that allows administrators and courts to in effect "exempt" transactions involving relatively minor elements of risk transference.

In practice, the extent of uncertainty in regard to the actual scope of state insurance regulation is not as great as that which might be inferred from an examination that is limited to the applicable state insurance statutes. A considerable degree of certainty about the operation of these regulatory statutes often can be attained through an analysis of the judicial and administrative resolution of disputes over the applicability of these measures to various types of transactions.

In the past few decades, the courts have had a significant "regulatory" influence on insurers as a consequence of decisions sustaining rights for insureds that vary from the terms set forth in the applicable insurance policy. The precise scope of the judicial doctrines affording insureds rights that are at variance with policy provisions [6] remains something less than certain.[7] Accordingly, care should be exercised because applications of a doctrine developed and applied to produce rights at variance with insurance policy provisions in one context may not be warranted in other situations.

The practical implementation of the principal objectives of insurance regulation — to avoid overreaching by insurers, to assure solidity and solvency of insurers, and to assure fair charges for insurance policies[8] — gives rise to a large number of distinct types of regulatory measures [9] which are varied in their reach.[10] Consequently, significant questions have arisen in regard to whether insurance regulatory statutes apply to a variety of business activities, including (1) health care plans, (2) service contracts for goods,[11] and (3) variable annuities. The regulatory issues and the approaches employed in the resolution of

---

5. Concerning the competing values of certainty and flexibility generally, see § 1.4, above.

6. See generally Chapter 6, above.

7. For example, this theory has been used to save some party to a risk-transferring-and-distributing contract from the obligations courts impose upon an insurer in like circumstances. See, e.g., McIntosh v. Group Health Association, 138 A.2d 496 (D.C.Mun.App.1958).

Also see Comment, *Service Contracts: A Subject for State or Federal Regulation—Do Consumers Need Protection from the Service Contract Industry?,* 1979 Southern Illinois University Law Journal 587–620.

Note: In some instances courts have declined to extend these doctrines to particular contracts on the ground that they were not insurance transactions.

8. See § 8.2(a), above.

9. See § 8.2, above.

10. For example, those to whom the power of decision is committed may well choose to leave a "consumer cooperative" health association free from the strictures of statutes aimed primarily at avoiding the consequences of imprudent management of funded systems of risk distribution, while yet applying to the association's transactions a set of statutory and judicial doctrines aimed at disallowing unconscionable advantage and honoring reasonable expectations of individuals with whom the association contracts. See § 8.3(b), below.

11. Also see Comment, Service Contracts: *A Subject for State or Federal Regulation—Do Consumers Need Protection from the Service Contract Industry?,* 1979 Southern Illinois University Law Journal 587–620.

those questions provide an excellent survey of the competing considerations that should be assessed in determining the reach of insurance regulatory measures.

§ 8.3(b) Health Plans

Most of the cases concerning hospital and medical service plans that provide various types of health care for members of a group have held that such a corporation is not subject to laws that regulate insurers and insurance transactions.[1] Nevertheless, there are judicial cases holding that such groups are engaged in the insurance business. It is arguable that these decisions represent different points of view about the nature of such health plans.[2] However, most of the decisions concluding that health plans constituted insurance involved plans that were materially different from those at issue in cases which decided that no insurance was involved.

In Jordan v. Group Health Association,[3] a leading decision on the applicability of insurance regulatory statutes to group health plans, the opinion of Justice Rutledge emphasized that the Association's undertaking was "not to supply the service, or see or guarantee that it is supplied, * * * but only to 'use its best efforts' to secure" service.[4] Nevertheless, the opinion suggested that the Association might be liable to suit by an individual member.[5] And that result was subsequently reached when a member sued after a claim had been denied on the theory that the treatment needed was for a pre-existing condition.[6] This leads to several questions, including:

§ 8.3(b)

1. See, e.g., Jordan v. Group Health Association, 71 App.D.C. 38, 107 F.2d 239 (D.C.Cir.1939); California Physicians' Service v. Garrison, 28 Cal.2d 790, 172 P.2d 4 (1946), 167 A.L.R. 306 (1947).

Also see Prepaid Dental Services, Inc. v. Day, 615 P.2d 1271 (Utah 1980); Commissioner of Banking and Insurance v. Community Health Service, 129 N.J.L. 427, 30 A.2d 44 (1943); State ex rel. Fishback v. Universal Service Agency, 87 Wash. 413, 151 P. 768 (1915); Annot., 167 A.L.R. 322 (1947).

But cf. Anglin v. Blue Shield of Virginia, 693 F.2d 315 (4th Cir.1982); Cleveland Hospital Service Association v. Ebright, 142 Ohio St. 51, 49 N.E.2d 929 (1943).

See generally Note, *Nonprofit Health Care Corporations are not Insurance Providers. New Mexico Life Insurance Guaranty Association v. Moore, 93 N.M. 47, 596 P.2d 260 (1979),* 10 New Mexico Law Review 481–489 (1980).

2. See, e.g., McCarty v. King County Medical Service Corp., 26 Wash.2d 660, 175

P.2d 653 (1946) (distinguishing the decisions in *Jordan* and *Fishback,* which are cited in note 1, above, as each involving (a) a non-profit corporation that was in nature a consumers' cooperative, rather than a private "charitable" corporation that was in nature an intermediary between beneficiaries and physicians; (b) less control in the association over determination of eligibility to receive medical services, the decisions by the association's medical director being concerned with medical questions only, rather than legal as well; and (c) relationships in which the association served as agent of those who provided the medical services, rather than as principal and moving spirit in control of the business contemplated by the contract).

3. 71 App.D.C. 38, 107 F.2d 239 (D.C. Cir.1939).

4. 71 App.D.C. at p. 45, 107 F.2d at p. 246 (1939).

5. *Ibid.*

6. Group Health Association v. Shepherd, 37 A.2d 749 (D.C.Mun.App.1944).

(1) Does this result indicate that the Association was in some respects a principal in the arrangement among itself, the physicians, and the Association members, and not merely an agent for the members or an agent for those supplying the medical services?

(2) Why was it not the case that an insurance business was being conducted either by the Association as a principal or by its principals if it was acting as an agent?

It would seem that if the Association was merely an agent for the physicians, its failure to use its best efforts to cause the physicians to render services to a member would not have given rise to a cause of action in favor of the member against the Association, as distinguished from its principals. On the other hand, if the Association was merely an agent for the members, its failure to use its best efforts to obtain services would have been a breach of its obligations to one of its principals. This theory of liability is not a distinctive incident of agency law. Rather, it is liability for breach of a contract, which happens to be an agency contract. Such liability of the agent is the liability of a party ("principal") to the contract establishing the agency relationship. The effect of such an agency contract is to transfer to the agent a part of the member's risk of medical expenses by causing the agent to assume a risk of legal responsibility for failure to be as effective as the agent should be in making arrangements transferring the risk of higher-than-average medical expenses from members to physicians. Also, the composite effect of a great number of such agency contracts is to establish a system of risk distribution through the agent as a conduit.

The elements of assumption of risk by the agent and distribution of risk through the agent are minimized under an interpretation of the contractual relationship to mean that the agent assumes no greater obligation than to use its best efforts to obtain services, but nevertheless are still present since the extent to which it will be called upon to fulfill this promise will vary according to the state of health of members. Thus, irrespective of the theory of the Association's liability to a member (whether it be that the Association is a contractor, not an agent, or that the Association is a party to an agency contract with the member), there is an element of risk transference from the member to the Association and use of the Association as a conduit for risk distribution.

If the Association is characterized as an agent for the physicians, the elements of participation in risk transferrence and distribution by its principals, the physicians, are even more striking. Why, then, is the Association not engaged in the insurance business, either as itself an insurer or as agent for the insurer-physicians? In response to the suggestion that the Association's acting as insurance agent might not have been enough to make a case against the Association under the statutes involved, is it not a fair inference that this court would not have held that the alleged physician-principals were insurers, if that issue had been before the court? [7]

Although the arrangement challenged in *Jordan* was well conceived to minimize and subordinate the elements of risk transference and distribution through the Association, it is difficult to escape the conclusion that the decision was influenced by an appraisal of the arrangement as socially useful and as giving rise to less urgent need for public regulation than ordinary insurance arrangements. The opinion asserts that this arrangement is a consumer cooperative the primary purpose of which "is to reduce the cost rather than the risk of medical care." [8] Would different treatment be accorded an effort to establish a consumer cooperative to reduce the cost rather than the risk of funeral and burial expense? The opinion included the comment that it is not the function of Group Health to accumulate capital for the needs of a distant day as distinguished from keeping a steady flow of current funds from patients to physicians, with little margin.[9] Thus, the Group Health arrangement does not involve a great potential evil from inadequate provision of reserves.

It should be noted that the determination in *Jordan* that the Association's operations were not insurance for the purposes of applicability of the insurance regulatory laws there involved does not answer the question whether they should be classified as insurance in other contexts. For example, it should not be regarded as a precedent against the claim of a member to rights against the association at variance with the membership provisions, advanced on the theory that the membership contract has all the essential features of an insurance transaction in relation to insurance law rights at variance with policy provisions.[10] Yet a contrary view appears to have been taken. That is, the Municipal Court of Appeals, in denying the claim of a member against the Association, asserted on grounds that might be characterized as urging a right at variance with contract stipulations, noted that *Jordan* had determined that the Association was a cooperative concerned principally with getting service rendered to its members at low cost and remarked that "the principles governing in a member's suit are those of contract law and not * * * those rules of law peculiar to insurance cases." [11] But the arguably relevant "rules of law peculiar to insurance cases" are concerned with the construction and enforcement of contract provisions that may operate unfairly as between the insurer, represented by experts, and the layperson with little bargaining

---

7. See Jordan v. Group Health Association, 71 App.D.C. 38 at p. 47, 107 F.2d 239 at p. 248 (D.C.Cir.1939): "It is admitted that the identical plan and service rendered here would not be 'insurance' or 'indemnity' if offered by an organization owned, operated and controlled by physicians."

8. 71 App.D.C. at p. 46, 107 F.2d at p. 247 (1939).

9. 71 App.D.C. at p. 50, 107 F.2d at p. 251 (1939).

10. Concerning such rights generally, see Chapter 6, above.

11. McIntosh v. Group Health Association, 138 A.2d 496 at p. 498 (D.C.Mun.App. 1958).

power and poor understanding of the arrangement. The individual member of Group Health is in a position quite analogous to that of the untutored insured.

The statutory definition of insurance (explicit or implicit) for the purpose of determining whether regulatory measures apply need not necessarily be identical with the definition of "insurance" to be inferred from the evolution of a judicial doctrine concerned with construction of agreements. Moreover, even if it be thought desirable to extend the statutory definition of insurance to general usage, it does not follow that the court should decline to apply the "rule of law peculiar to insurance cases" rather than extending them to closely analogous non-insurance cases. This criticism of the court's reasoning does not demonstrate that the result is not sound, however. Probably the same result should have been reached even if the case had been treated as one involving insurance.

Subrogation claims have presented another context in which it has been thought relevant to determine whether health plans or medical service contracts constituted insurance. For example, as one ground, albeit less emphasized than others, for holding that a hospital service association of the Blue Cross type was not subrogated to the subscriber's tort claim against a third party and could not obtain the benefit of a statute permitting "insurance companies" to join in actions against tortfeasors, a court observed that the association was not an insurance company and its contracts with subscribers were not insurance contracts.[12] Perhaps treating the statute on joinder as not applying to the association is defensible, but the conclusion that the contracts of the association with its subscribers were not insurance contracts, or contracts like insurance in a sense relevant to whether subrogation should be recognized, seems less defensible. In the first place, in most contexts and perhaps in all, arguments against classifying the arrangement as insurance are weaker as to Blue Cross and Blue Shield systems than as to a "consumer cooperative" such as that involved in *Jordan*. Secondly, arguments relevant to whether an association is subject to insurance regulatory statutes may have little relevance to whether it should be subrogated to tort claims for recovery of medical expenses it has reimbursed under one of its contracts. A sharp focus of policy arguments relevant to this latter question is likely to lead to the conclusion that subrogation should be allowed.[13] In a closely analogous context, one court, taking the position that it need not determine whether an association was an insurer or its contracts were insurance contracts, upheld the association's defense to a claim by a member who had settled with a third party tortfeasor, the defense being based on a provision declaring that the membership contract did not apply to any injury caused by negligence of another, except for benefits not available

12. Michigan Hospital Service v. Sharpe, 339 Mich. 357, 63 N.W.2d 638 (1954), 43 A.L.R.2d 1167 (1955).

13. See § 3.10, above.

out of funds recoverable from the wrongdoer through reasonable efforts of the member.[14]

It is noteworthy, even in relation to the more limited context of questions concerning regulation of insurance transactions, that some state legislatures have enacted separate regulatory statutes for medical and health associations [15] rather than leaving courts to struggle with questions whether statutes applicable generally to insurers should be held to apply to associations of this type.

§ 8.3(c)   Contracts for Services or for the Maintenance of Goods

Contracts for providing various types of services or for the maintenance of goods (such as washing machines, television sets, or automobiles) often involve both the transference and the distribution of risks. There are numerous examples of the successful assertions of the authority to regulate such transactions by officials of various state insurance commissions.[1]

In a declaratory proceeding, an automobile club operating with annual dues which entitled members to specified indemnities (including a $5,000 bail bond for manslaughter and traffic violation) and attorneys' services within a schedule of stipulated fees (the largest being $100) was denied the authorization to continue such activities without complying with the statutes applicable to entities doing an insurance business in the state.[2]

Pre-need contracts for burial services have been subjected to regulation in a number of states.[3] For example, a company was enjoined from making contracts under which it covenanted to allow a percentage discount from retail prices and to furnish embalming and hearse services at regular prices in consideration of weekly installments and an agreement to make specified purchases.[4]

---

14. Barmeier v. Oregon Physicians' Service, 194 Or. 659, 243 P.2d 1053 (1952). Note that this is even more disadvantageous to the payee of benefits under the contract than is a subrogation provision. Under the latter, a payee is reimbursed promptly rather than having to wait for disposition of a tort claim.

15. See, e.g., California Insurance Code § 11031, § 11032, and §§ 11041–11045 (Deering's, 1977 & 1987 Supp.); McKinney's New York Insurance Law §§ 4301–4315 (1985 and Supp.1987).

§ 8.3(c)

1. See the cases collected in Comment, *Service Contracts: A Subject For State or Federal Regulation—Do Consumers Need Protection From the Service Contract Industry?,* 1979 Southern Illinois University Law Journal 587–620; Note, *Consumer Warranty or Insurance Contract? A View Towards*

a Rational State Regulatory Policy, 51 Indiana Law Review 1103–1124 (1976).

2. Continental Auto Club, Inc. v. Vavarre, 337 Mich. 434, 60 N.W.2d 180 (1953).

Cf. Texas Association of Qualified Drivers, Inc., v. State, 361 S.W.2d 580 (Tex.Civ. App.1962) (no writ history); National Automobile Service Corporation v. State, 55 S.W.2d 209 (Tex.Civ.App.1932), writ of error dismissed.

3. See, e.g., State v. Memorial Gardens Development Corporation, 143 W.Va. 182, 101 S.E.2d 425 (1957), 68 A.L.R.2d 1233 (1959).

4. State *ex rel.* Attorney General v. Smith Funeral Serv., Inc., 177 Tenn. 41, 145 S.W.2d 1021 (1940). The defendant unsuccessfully argued that the contracts were not insurance because the holder could call upon the defendant to furnish

A group of persons who contracted with each other for replacement of plate glass store windows regardless of the cause of breakage was held to be carrying on an insurance business.[5]

A watchmaker who agreed to replace a watch if lost within a year was held to be making a contract of insurance.[6]

Several cases involving commitments made to the purchasers of automobile tires have led to regulatory disputes. For example, a company was held to be in violation of insurance regulatory laws as a result of marketing its automobile tires with printed forms one of which guaranteed "against blowouts, cuts, bruises, rim-cuts, under-inflation, wheels out of alignment, faulty brakes or other road hazards that may render the tire unfit for further service (except fire and theft)" and another of which guaranteed the tire "to wear" for not less than a specified period, failing which the defendant agreed that it would "either repair it free or replace it with a new tire" subject to a proportionate charge for the period of use.[7]

There are many types of factual settings in which an assertion of regulatory jurisdiction has not been sustained by a court on a type of matter or transaction that has been held to be an insurance contract in many other jurisdictions.[8] A notable example involved proceedings initiated by a regulatory official against a company marketing its automobile tires with printed forms that guaranteed them for specified periods of time if used "under usual conditions." A judgment of ouster was denied.[9] The company also was not held accountable for alleged departures from the printed form by oral representations of sales representatives that the guarantee would protect the purchaser

---

the casket and burial clothing at any time, rather than awaiting the contingency of death. The court, however, thought the effect of this right on the course of business would be negligible and that the business would, in reality, continue to be that of burial insurance.

Also see State ex rel. Long v. Mynatt, 207 Tenn. 319, 339 S.W.2d 26 (1960) (contract to furnish funeral services and merchandise at fifty per cent discount to purchaser or his successors held subject to regulation as life insurance).

5. See, e.g., People v. Roschli, 275 N.Y. 26, 9 N.E.2d 763 (1937).

6. Ollendorff Watch Co. v. Pink, 279 N.Y. 32, 17 N.E.2d 676 (1938).

7. State ex rel. Duffy v. Western Auto. Supply Co., 134 Ohio St. 163, 16 N.E.2d 256 (1938), 119 A.L.R. 1236 (1939).

But cf. State ex rel. Herbert v. Standard Oil Co., 138 Ohio St. 376, 35 N.E.2d 437 (1941).

8. See, e.g., 1964 OPINIONS OF OHIO ATTORNEY GENERAL, No. 1304 (contract provid-

ing for automatic cancellation of debt at debtor's death substantially amounts to insurance, and national bank may not lawfully enter into such contracts without complying with insurance laws); 1958 Ops. Att'y Gen.Ohio No. 2897 (individual who guarantees that certain enumerated parts of an automobile are in good working condition and will not require repairs or replacement for a specified period of time, with normal usage, where there is no vendor-vendee relationship but rather a general scheme for distributing losses among subscribers, is engaging in the business of insurance within the meaning of Ohio Rev. Code § 3905.42 (Page 1954)).

9. State *ex rel.* Herbert v. Standard Oil Co., 138 Ohio St. 376, 35 N.E.2d 437 (1941). The court added: "In conclusion, it is not our intention to overrule the case of *State ex rel. Duffy,* * * * [note 7, above], or abandon the principles there applied. We do think, however, the doctrine of that case should not be extended." 138 Ohio St. at p. 383, 35 N.E.2d at p. 441.

"against such hazards as cuts, bruises, wheels out of alignment and blowouts." [10]

It is difficult, and perhaps impossible, to formulate a definition of insurance that would reconcile all of these decisions — that is, one which would include within its scope all those transactions in which assertions of applicability of regulatory statutes have been successful, and would exclude all those in which such assertions failed. There is, however, an approach which is indicative of a guiding principle for these decisions, or at least as high a percentage of them as one should expect in light of the differing judgments of various legislatures and courts about the proper scope of regulatory measures. In such disputes, it is important to consider the following fundamental questions:

(1) Did the specific transactions or the general line of business at issue involve one or more of the concerns at which the regulatory statutes were aimed?

(2) Were the elements of risk transference and risk distribution central to and relatively important elements of the transactions (or merely incidental to other elements that gave the transactions their distinctive character)?

If an issue about whether a particular transaction is insurance is approached with these questions in mind, the results of a prospective adjudication can usually be accurately anticipated and the judicial decisions in prior cases can be harmonized.[11] For example, it seems clear that the insurance regulatory laws are not properly construed as aimed at establishing an absolute prohibition against the inclusion of any risk-transferring-and-distributing provisions in contracts for services or for the rental of goods. The presence of a minor element of risk transference and risk distribution does not conclusively demonstrate that the transaction should appropriately be classified as within the reach of insurance regulatory laws. The judgment should be based on the predominant characteristic of such transactions, the element that gives the transaction its fundamental nature.

Marginal or relatively insignificant elements of risk transference and risk distribution have been permitted without subjecting businesses to the insurance regulatory statutes in a variety of transactions.[12] For example, it has been held that a company agreeing to maintain trucks owned by the other party to a contract does not engage in an insurance business, subject to insurance regulatory laws, by including in it an

10. 138 Ohio St. at p. 383, 35 N.E.2d at p. 441.

11. Also see the discussion of "The Criteria Used to determine whether Contracts Are 'Business of Insurance ∗ ∗ ∗'" in Comment, *Service Contracts: A Subject for State or Federal Regulation—Do Consumers Need Protection from the Service Contract Industry?*, 1979 Southern Illinois University Law Journal 587–620.

12. See, e.g., Department of Insurance v. Motors Ins. Corp., 236 Ind. 1, 138 N.E.2d 157 (1956) (overturning the Department's effort to prohibit automobile dealers from serving as agents for the sale of automobile insurance, holding such action to be an unconstitutional deprivation of the right to engage simultaneously in two lawful businesses; this conclusion of unconstitutionality seems strange in the modern setting).

undertaking to make repairs, even when this includes repairs needed because of collision damage.[13] And a similar view may be taken of comparable commitments in contracts for the rental of vehicles.[14] Although there is certainly an element of insurance in such transactions, it is often incidental to the main objective of the transaction. Especially when the risk transferred is a relatively insignificant factor in the price charged to the purchaser, a persuasive case can be made that the scope of the insurance regulatory laws should not be construed to apply to such transactions.

Another example is provided by the membership contract of the New York Stock Exchange which provides for the payment of a specified amount when a member dies. Although it may well be appropriate to classify such a payment as insurance for the purpose of calculating the federal tax on the estate of the deceased member,[15] it would be undesirable to conclude that if the Exchange wishes to maintain such a provision in its membership agreements it must comply with all the requirements of state regulatory laws applicable to companies in an insurance business.

On the other hand, when the risk transference is essentially extraneous to the basic nature of the business transaction, there is every reason to treat it as an insurance transaction. For example, it seems clear that when a consumer purchases an article from that jeweler or watchmaker who also agrees to replace the item if it is lost within some specified time period, the commitment to provide a replacement is unrelated to the sale and there is little, if any, justification, for permitting it to be treated as an adjunct to the sales transaction rather than as an insurance arrangement.[16]

§ 8.3(d) Variable Annuities

Variable annuities are financial arrangements which include an element of insurance [1] in what is also appropriately viewed as an investment in securities. The extent to which such transactions should be subject to regulation as insurance and thereby free of other regula-

---

13. Transportation Guarantee Company v. Jellins, 29 Cal.2d 242, 174 P.2d 625 (1946).

14. See the dictum, 29 Cal.2d at p. 253, 174 P.2d at pp. 631–632 (1946).

15. See Commissioner of Internal Revenue v. Treganowan, 183 F.2d 288 (2d Cir. 1950), *cert. denied* 340 U.S. 853, 71 S.Ct. 82, 95 L.Ed. 625 (1950).

16. Some of the instances in which the courts have denied the regulatory jurisdiction have involved rather different factual settings. See, e.g., 1954 OPINIONS OF OHIO ATTORNEY GENERAL, No. 4610 (individual engaged in the business of executing bail bonds, recognizances and appeal bonds is not engaging in business of insurance nor

is he entering into contracts "substantially amounting to insurance" within meaning of Ohio Rev.Code § 3905.42 (Page 1954); Memorial Gardens Association, Inc. v. Smith, 16 Ill.2d 116, 156 N.E.2d 587 (1959).

Efforts of private litigants to invoke rights based on an alleged violation of insurance regulatory laws by an opposing party have sometimes failed on the ground that the regulatory statutes did not reach the transaction in question. See, e.g., Transportation Guarantee Company v. Jellins, 29 Cal.2d 242, 174 P.2d 625 (1946).

§ 8.3(d)

1. Also see the discussion in § 1.2, above.

tion has been sharply disputed.[2] The opinion of the Supreme Court in the first variable annuities case (Securities and Exchange Commission v. Variable Annuity Life Insurance Company), delivered by Mr. Justice Douglas, includes four assertions about the nature of insurance:

First, "the concept of 'insurance' involves some investment risk-taking on the part of the company."

Second, "in hard reality the issuer of a variable annuity that has no element of a fixed return assumes no true risk in the insurance sense."

Third, "in common understanding 'insurance' involves a guarantee that at least some fraction of the benefits will be payable in fixed amounts."

Fourth, "there is no true underwriting of risks" in a variable annuity contract, except for such an ancillary feature as life insurance on a declining basis for a term of five years.[3]

All four of these propositions appear to be implications of the single premise that both in common understanding and as used by Congress in the relevant legislative acts, "insurance" involves an insurer's commitment to pay a fixed sum of money which is not dependent upon fluctuations in the value of investments purchased with the fund accumulated from premiums. This concept is certainly one that has been a characteristic of traditional life insurance policies. It is not so clearly true of other traditional types of insurance. For example, the exposure of a fire insurer under a five-year policy varies with market conditions in the sense that a given amount of physical damage occurring during the first year of coverage may result in a much lower dollar loss than if the same damage occurs in a later year when there has been an intervening increase in market values and repair costs because of inflation.

The concurring opinion of Justice Brennan and the dissenting opinion of Justice Harlan in the *Variable Annuity Life Insurance Company* case, have in common a point of view that the variable annuity plainly has elements characteristic of securities which makes it necessary to decide the issues on some basis other than the assertion that the arrangement is or is not insurance in common understanding. The Brennan opinion argues that the securities aspects are predominant; the Harlan opinion, that the insurance aspects are at least so

---

2. See generally Louis Loss, SECURITIES REGULATION (1961), Volume 1 at pp. 498–501, and Volume 4 (1969), at pp. 2511–2535 (1969); Boe W. Martin, *The Status of the Variable Annuity as a Security: A Lesson in Legal Line Drawing,* 30 Ohio State Law Journal 736–772 (1969); Comment, *Commingled Trust Funds and Variable Annuities: Uniform Federal Regulation of Investment Funds Operated by Banks and Insurance Companies,* 82 Harvard Law Review 435–468 (1968); William Kern, *Varia-*

ble Annuities, 54 A.B.A.J. 144–147 (1968); Galston, *The Regulation of Variable Annuities,* 1967 ABA Section Ins., Neg. & Comp. L.Proceedings 348; Joseph W. Bartlett, *Variable Annuities: Evaluation and Analysis,* 19 Stanford Law Review 150–166 (1966).

3. Securities & Exchange Commission v. Variable Annuity Life Insurance Co., 359 U.S. 65 at p. 71 and p. 73, 79 S.Ct. 618 at pp. 622–623, 3 L.Ed.2d 640 at p. 644 and p. 645 (1959).

substantial that the history of Congressional restraint with respect to invasion of the field of insurance regulation points to inclusion of the variable annuity within the exemption of insurance from the operation of the securities acts.

Variable annuities are a socially desirable addition to the methods of providing for retirement.[4] It also appears clear that there are needs for the public regulation of such contracts. The needs are in some respects like those for regulation of ordinary annuities and in other respects like those for regulation of securities transactions. No single system of regulation has been developed for such transactions: rather, the marketing of variable annuities has been subject to regulation under both the securities laws and the insurance laws.[5] However, the present dual responsibility for regulation is surely something less than an optimal approach to the problem.[6]

§ 8.4   Regulation of Insurance Rates

§ 8.4(a)   Objectives and Methods of Rating and Regulation

(1) Introduction

In the United States during the nineteenth and most of the twentieth century, competition was virtually the sole mechanism that was relied upon to produce rates that were neither excessive nor discriminatory. Furthermore, for most forms of insurance, competition continues to be a major factor that underlies insurance rating in the United States. However, there are several distinctive characteristics of the insurance business which have increasingly been regarded as necessitating at least some degree of regulation to preserve and reinforce competition as an instrument for developing premium rates.

4. See generally Greenough & King, BENEFIT PLANS IN AMERICAN COLLEGES (1969), at pp. 43–99; Johnson & Grubbs, THE VARIABLE ANNUITY (Second edition, 1970), ch. 1; George E. Johnson, *Variable Annuities: What They Are and How They Can Be Used by Attorneys*, 48 Nebraska Law Review 943–959 (1969).

5. See, e.g., Securities & Exchange Commission v. National Securities, Inc., 393 U.S. 453, 89 S.Ct. 564, 21 L.Ed.2d 668 (1969); Securities & Exchange Commission v. United Benefit Ins. Co., 387 U.S. 202, 87 S.Ct. 1557, 18 L.Ed.2d 673 (1967); Loss, SECURITIES REGULATION (1961), Volume 1, at pp. 498–501 and Volume 4 (1969), at pp. 2511–2535.

Also see Grainger v. State Security Life Insurance Company, 547 F.2d 303 (5th Cir. 1977).

There is still a risk that agencies primarily engaged in regulating securities transactions may seek to impose unduly restrictive measures on variable annuities in comparison with the somewhat competitive forms of open-end securities, and that agencies primarily engaged in regulating insurance transactions may seek to impose investment standards more appropriate to traditional life insurance payable in fixed sums than to variable annuities.

6. In any event, the dispute over regulatory jurisdiction, spurred by competitive private interests as well as the differing interests and concerns of the various regulatory agencies involved undoubtedly limited to at least some extent the speed of development of variable annuities as a form of contract readily available to the public.

For example, in some instances insurance regulators may seek to impose investment standards more appropriate to traditional life insurance payable in fixed sums than to variable annuities.

The specific objectives of rate regulation are to assure premiums (1) that are adequate to provide funds for paying losses and the administrative costs, (2) that do not result in unreasonable profits for an insurer (that is, which are not excessive), and (3) that are not unreasonably high for some policyholders and unreasonably low for others (that is, which are not "discriminatory").[1] In other words, the regulation of premium rates is generally intended to assure that an insurer's income is adequate to cover the risks (with a reasonable margin) without being either excessively expensive for the purchasers or unfairly discriminatory among purchasers.

Factors that Support Rate Regulation

There are a number of factors which contribute to the generally recognized need for rate regulation of insurers in the United States.

First, the complexity of insurance transactions frequently reduces the effectiveness of either product or price competition for ordinary consumers.

Second, the proliferation of insurance products often makes it a virtually hopeless task for the ordinary consumer to compare the products and prices offered by different insurers.[2]

Third, an industry-wide practice of caution about the unpredictable elements in future loss experience can result in excessive premium rates. Moreover, this remains true whether it is the product of concerted action by many insurers or merely the cumulative effect of separate decisions by executives of different companies who prefer to compete in ways other than pricing.

Fourth, competition will not always provide adequate protection against discriminatory premium rates. Even when competition is functioning well, there almost always will be collateral factors that make some policyholders more or less attractive on grounds apart from a pure assessment of the rated risk.[3]

---

§ 8.4(a)

1. See, e.g., C. Arthur Williams, Jr. UNFAIR RATE DISCRIMINATION IN PROPERTY AND LIABILITY INSURANCE, IN INSURANCE, GOVERNMENT, AND SOCIAL POLICY (Kimball & Denenberg, editors, 1969), at p. 209; Spencer L. Kimball and Ronald N. Boyce, *The Adequacy of State Insurance Rate Regulation: The McCarran-Ferguson Act in Historical Perspective,* 56 Michigan Law Review 545–578 (1958); C.A. Kulp, *The Rate-Making Process in Property and Casualty Insurance—Goals, Technics, and Limits,* 15 Law and Contemporary Problems 493–522 (1950).

2. In the United States, there has been relatively little regulation of life, health, and accident insurance policy forms and even less regulation of life, health, and accident insurance rates. One consequence is that it is extremely difficult for the ordinary purchaser to make price comparisons. See, e.g., William F. Young. A STUDY OF HEALTH INSURANCE POLICIES AVAILABLE IN NEW YORK STATE FOR THE PURPOSES OF DEVELOPING A PROCEDURE FOR THEIR EVALUATION AND GRADING (1964), an excerpt from which is quoted in Kimball & Pfennigstorf, *Administrative Control of the Terms of Insurance Contracts: A Comparative Study,* 40 Indiana Law Journal 143–231 at pp. 214–215 (1965).

Concerning life insurance pricing generally, see Joseph M. Belth, *Life Insurance Price Measurement,* 57 Kentucky Law Journal 687–711 (1969).

3. Furthermore, there are pragmatic limitations on the extent to which rating

Fifth, unrestrained opportunities for cooperation among insurers in setting premium rates can be contrary to the public interest.[4] The risk that premium rates may be set by insurers at excessively high levels is obvious. This is not to say, however, that all cooperation should be forbidden. In some circumstances, exchanges of information among insurers are essential to the determination of appropriate premium rates. This is true in regard to accumulating and sharing data to produce a more comprehensive and therefore, at least theoretically, a more reliable base for predicting future losses.[5]

Sixth, unrestrained competition may also produce premium rates that endanger the solvency of insurance companies, and in turn the members of the public they serve — that is, inadequate premiums can ultimately result in the inability of an insurer to provide indemnification for the losses they have undertaken to insure. A rule of survival of the fittest may be defensible in relation to the interests of the manufacturers and stockholders for some types of consumer products. But to permit the less fit among insurance companies to go into insolvency without providing for the claims of their policyholders and others entitled to insurance benefits is generally viewed as an intolerable result.[6]

Seventh, some type of system, although not necessarily rate regulation, is essential to addressing the perils of insolvency for insurance companies arising from the possibility that insurers may miscalculate future losses. Actuarial projection in the field of insurance is a process of making precise calculations that can only be guesses about the future.[7] However precise these computations may be, the conclusions are no more than predictions of the unknown and unknowable. Although the element of uncertainty can be reduced in some degree by the use of relatively complete and reliable data about past experience upon which the predictions about the future are based, in the end a degree of guesswork inevitably is involved in setting premium rates.

Eighth, public policy interests of various types (including policies against discrimination based on race, sex, and other individual charac-

---

categories can be employed to reflect different degrees of risk. For almost all forms of insurance, there comes a point at which the administrative costs of further refinements outweigh their utility.

It is less than clear, to say the least, that unregulated competition will produce a wiser choice concerning the numbers and design of rate categories than can be produced under regulated competition.

4. Discriminatory rating also may be a problem when unrestrained cooperation is permitted.

5. An interesting industry usage refers to the data, rather than merely the predictions based on the data, as more "credible" in these circumstances. Perhaps this is a

reflection of a somewhat wishful view of the actuarial process that plays down the inevitable element of guesswork. But in any event the phrase "more credible data" can be viewed as useful shorthand for the more precise expression, "data that will support more credible predictions." Of course the data too may be more or less credible, depending on degrees of precision in gathering and recording information.

6. Typically, consumers do not have an adequate opportunity or the expertise to judge the financial fitness of insurance companies before acquiring insurance.

7. The best actuaries are persons shrewd in foresight and skilled in analogical as well as logical reasoning.

teristics over which the individual has no control) sometimes weigh against use of insurance rating categories that might be "nondiscriminatory" in a sense concerned only with correlation between loss experience and selected individual characteristics.[8]

(2) Possible Approaches to Regulation of Premium Rates

In the United States, there has been general acceptance of the view that some degree of insurance regulation of premium rates is needed to achieve an effective blend of competition and cooperation among insurers. At the same time, there is continuing controversy concerning just what that blend should be and how it should be attained.

In some contexts, a governmental body has been given the power and responsibility of fixing rates [9] — that is, regulation of rates has become, at least in form, absolute. For example, in Massachusetts, the state has empowered the insurance commissioner to set the premium rates for motor vehicle insurance.[10] This approach is usually characterized as governmental "rate-making" to distinguish it from "regulation" of premium rates that are "made" either by an individual insurer or by concerted action among insurers (on an ad hoc basis or through a regularly functioning rating bureau).

In practice, regulation by rate-making often appears to be more responsive to political pressures than to identifiable principles of regulation. The experience with compulsory automobile insurance rates in Massachusetts provides a clear illustration that supports this observation. In Massachusetts over the past half century, there has been almost constant political pressure on the rate-making official — the commissioner of insurance — to set premium charges at a relatively low level. And, at least in some instances, the rate structure for automobile insurance in Massachusetts has been set so low that many insurers believed it to be confiscatory.

Rate regulation, and especially governmental rate making, entails several distinct risks for both the public and insurers. On the one hand, in response to political pressures the premium rates may be set at a level that is inadequate to produce sound underwriting.[11] On the other hand, there is a risk that a "lack of vigor" on the part of the

---

8. See, e.g., State of Florida, Department of Insurance v. Insurance Services Office, 434 So.2d 908 (Fla.App., 1st Dist., 1983).

9. See, e.g., Massachusetts General Laws Ann. c. 175, § 113B (1972); Vernon's Ann. Texas Statutes Insurance Code, art. 5.01 (1963).

There are also other scattered instances of provisions for governmental rate-making. E.g., Vernon's Ann. Texas Statutes Insurance Code arts. 5.25–5.27 (fire rates), art. 5.55 (workers' compensation rates), art. 5.69–5.71 (special rates for national defense contracts) (1981).

Also see Louisiana Acts 1958 No. 125 (casualty rates), later amended to provide for approval rather than fixing of rates by the Casualty and Surety Division of the Rating Commission. Louisiana Rev.Stat. § 22:1406 (West's 1978 and 1986 Supp.).

10. See Massachusetts General Laws Ann. C. 175, § 113B (1985).

11. This may force insurers to rely upon profits from other lines of business that are free of the rate-making system, thereby producing an unfair distribution of the costs of various types of insurance.

regulators will allow the rates to be set too high. Both of these risks may be exacerbated by the lack of adequate funds and personnel for the regulatory authority, making it impossible to have an adequate appraisal or evaluation of the reasonableness of the premium rates filed by the insurers.

(3) A Short History of Rate Regulation

In the history of changing patterns of insurance rate regulation, three distinctive periods can be identified: *first*, a period of very weak state regulation, ending in the aftermath of the 1944 decision in *South-Eastern Underwriters*; *second*, a period of state regulation almost exclusively based on prior-approval of rates proposed by insurers, which began in the 1940s and extended until late in the 1960s; *third*, a period of increasing reconsideration of rating practices in a variety of ways — which have included a reexamination of the prior-approval approach to rate regulation, a movement in several states to adopt other types of regulatory practices, and challenges to insurance rating practices on grounds that they are in conflict with social and public interests (including avoidance of discrimination based on characteristics such as sex or race) that are asserted to deserve greater weight than traditional criteria of evaluating rating categories.

(i) State Rate Regulation Before 1944 and the Events of 1944

Before 1944, insurance rating practices were generally understood to be subject to exclusive regulation by the states. Most state rate regulation in the United States involved some type of administrative approval of premium rates that were developed by an individual insurer or group of insurers. A good illustration of such regulation of premium rates is provided by the practices that generally prevailed for various types of casualty insurance. Individual casualty insurers or groups of insurers acting in concert set proposed premium rates that were submitted to the state regulatory commission for approval. The precise character of the regulatory review which preceded approval varied among the states employing this approach. In many states, and perhaps in most, during this period a persuasive case could have been made for the proposition that rate regulation was neither vigorous nor effectual.

In 1944, the Supreme Court of the United States held that insurance was subject to federal regulation and that federal antitrust legislation was appropriately applied to the South-Eastern Underwriters Association whose members had long engaged in concerted action in setting premium rates.[12] In the face of the severe doubts that the Supreme Court decision thereby cast on the then existing rating practices in particular and state regulation in general, Congress passed the

---

12. United States v. South-Eastern Underwriters Association, 322 U.S. 533, 64 S.Ct. 1162, 88 L.Ed. 1440 (1944), *rehearing* *denied* 323 U.S. 811, 65 S.Ct. 26, 89 L.Ed. 646 (1944).

McCarran-Ferguson Act which preserved the possibility for the states to continue to exercise the responsibility for insurance rate regulation.[13]

As a practical matter, the McCarran-Ferguson Act did not return the regulation of insurance rates to the pre-1944 status. In that earlier time, insurance regulation proceeded generally on the assumption that there was little need for a rigorous examination of premium rates by the regulatory authorities, either to protect against excessiveness and discrimination or to assure their adequacy. During this period, regulators sought to assure the solvency of insurers through periodic examinations of each insurer's reserves and investments, and it was thought that this approach provided adequate protection for the public.

After 1944, the view that competition and minimal regulatory activity would provide adequate protection against excessive or discriminatory rates was no longer acceptable. The McCarran-Ferguson Act declared that the insurance industry would only be exempted from the applications of federal antitrust legislation to the extent that the insurance business is actually regulated by state law.[14] This provision in the McCarran-Ferguson Act produced immediate pressure from the insurance industry for the states to occupy the field of insurance regulation more completely, and especially in relation to rating, in order to avoid the threat of federal regulation. An All-Industry Committee was formed and that group quickly gained the sympathetic interest and cooperation of the National Association of Insurance Commissioners in developing and sponsoring state legislation.

(ii) Rate Regulation: 1944–1960s

In 1944, approximately two-thirds of the states had already enacted some kind of legislation that provided for rate regulation. However, despite the regulatory authority created for insurance commissions or departments by such legislation, it seems clear that there was relatively little effective supervision of premium rates.[15] By 1951, however, change was most apparent. Rate regulatory legislation had been enacted in every state, and many of the older statutes had been

---

13. See § 8.1(a), above.

14. 59 Stat. 33 (1945), 15 U.S.C.A. § 1012 (1958). Section 2(b) of the Act provides:

"No Act of Congress shall be construed to invalidate, impair, or supercede any law enacted by any State for the purpose of regulating the business of insurance, or which imposes a fee or tax upon such business, unless such Act specifically relates to the business of insurance: Provided, That after January 1, 1948 * * * the Sherman Act, * * * the Clayton Act, and * * * the Federal Trade Commission Act, as amended, shall be applicable to the business of insurance to the extent that such business is not regulated by State law."

The date January 1, 1948, was subsequently changed to June 30, 1948. 61 Stat. 448 (1947), 15 U.S.C. § 1012(b) (1958).

15. See Spencer L. Kimball and Ronald N. Boyce, *The Adequacy of State Insurance Rate Regulation: The McCarran-Ferguson Act in Historical Perspective*, 56 Michigan Law Review 545–578 at p. 552 (1958).

Cf. John Day, ECONOMIC REGULATION OF INSURANCE IN THE UNITED STATES (United States Department of Transportation Automobile Insurance & Compensation Study, 1970), at pp. 18–23.

amended to provide for more stringent regulation.[16] In most states, the legislative provisions evidenced a specific concern with the adequacy of premium rates, as well as excessiveness and discrimination in the rate structures for insurance.[17]

Most of the regulatory provisions that were enacted by 1951, statutes which are still in effect in many states, only apply to fire, inland marine, and various types of casualty insurance. State regulatory statutes were and are essential to avoiding the application of federal antitrust laws to the activities of insurers in regard to the premiums charged for these coverages. This is true because most of the insurers selling these coverages act in concert through rating organizations to establish premiums; the activities of those organizations would violate the federal antitrust legislation if there were no state regulation. Life, health, and accident insurance premium rates ordinarily have been and continue to be made by each insurer separately (rather than through a rating organization), and consequently insurers did not work to assure the enactment of comparable regulatory legislation for those fields.[18]

Under the statutes enacted during the post–1944 period, the most common objective for rate regulation of fire, inland marine, and casualty insurance is to require premiums that are not excessive, inadequate, or unfairly discriminatory. In most states, the legislation requires the rating manuals and rating plans employed by insurers to be filed for approval by the regulatory authority before they are used by an insurer. The legislation also permits insurers to cooperate and act in concert in the preparation of these manuals and plans through rating organizations that are licensed and supervised by the state. Almost all of these statutes include provisions for administrative hearings and judicial review.[19]

16. See John Day, ECONOMIC REGULATION OF INSURANCE IN THE UNITED STATES, note 14, above, at p. 28. Concerning litigation incidental to the application of various rating statutes, see in general Roy C. McCollough, *Insurance Rates in the Courts,* 1961 Insurance Law Journal 381–497 at p. 475.

17. "Under this model legislation the principle of concerted rate making under social control was established as nationwide policy at the state level, in preference to the less sophisticated prohibition-of-concert principle of the Sherman Act." Spencer L. Kimball and Ronald N. Boyce, *The Adequacy of State Insurance Rate Regulation: The McCarran-Ferguson Act in Historical Perspective,* 56 Michigan Law Review 545–578 at p. 556 (1958).

Cf. Joel B. Dirlam and Irwin M. Stelzer, *The Insurance Industry: A Case Study in the Workability of Regulated Competition,* 107 University of Pennsylvania Law Review 199–215 at pp. 201–202 (1958).

18. See Leffert Holz, *Administration of Insurance Law,* 1956 Insurance Law Journal 24–33 at p. 28.

19. James B. Donovan, *State Regulation of Insurance,* 1956 Insurance Law Journal 11–15 at p. 13.

For a more detailed treatment of the rating bills, see George K. Gardner, *Insurance and the Anti-trust Laws—A Problem in Synthesis,* 61 Harvard Law Review 246–273 at pp. 259–265 (1948). Professor Gardner identifies five basic principles underlying the rating bills:

"*First:* All premiums shall be determined in accordance with written schedules, based on the analysis of past experience, and open to public inspection in a public office." *Id.,* at p. 260.

"*Second:* The constitution of every rating organization shall be a matter of public record, and its services shall be available to every underwriting organization which desires to utilize such rat-

The enactment, following the McCarran-Ferguson Act, of state legislation providing for the regulation of insurance premium rates for some types of insurance produced only a temporary suspension of the controversy about the methods that were used by insurers to establish premium rates. The next controversy that arose revolved around the issue whether the newly enacted state legislation could be invoked in an effort to stifle competition by forcing insurance companies employing the data-gathering facilities of a rating bureau to use the premium rates computed by that bureau. This effort led both to litigation over the meaning of these state statutes [20] and to new legislative actions in some states.

In several states, amendments to the regulatory laws were adopted to make clear that insurers were entitled to "partial subscribership" to a rating bureau which allowed a company to acquire data from a bureau while remaining free, at least to some extent, to offer coverage at different premium rates from those set by that bureau. In some states, the rating systems operating under these statutes have led to serious questions about whether an insurer may charge a premium that differs from those specified in the rating plan prepared and filed by a bureau.[21] One state supreme court concluded that, as a subscriber to a rating bureau, an insurer "must adhere to the rates so filed on your behalf unless you can comply with the deviation procedure provided by statute," which was acknowledged by the court to be a "cumbersome process" that had to be repeated each year." [22]

The rate regulation legislation enacted by many states during the immediate aftermath of the McCarran-Ferguson Act allowed insurers to cooperate in gathering and sharing data for rating purposes. The near universal approval by the states of cooperation among insurers in the process of setting premium rates can be justified as a way of producing more comprehensive data. Indeed there is hardly any dispute about the need for cooperation among insurers for this purpose. However, some of the statutes went farther and compelled the insurers that participated in the rating organizations to abide by the bureau rates. The arguments for cooperation among insurers for the purposes of data compilation almost certainly contributed to the legislative

ing organization for the purpose of determining its own rates." *Id.*, at p. 261.

"*Third:* Every insuring organization may either file its own rates independently or adopt those of a licensed rating organization as it elects." *Id.*, at p. 263.

"*Fourth:* The insured shall at all times have access, not only to the schedule by which his premium is determined, but to the statistics and computations on which it is based." *Id.*, at p. 264.

"*Fifth:* The state insurance commissioner, or corresponding officer, may disapprove any premium schedule filed by anyone if, and only if, he finds that the

rates are 'excessive, inadequate, or unfairly discriminatory.'" *Id.*, at p. 265.

20. See, e.g., Pacific Fire Rating Bureau v. Insurance Co. of North America, 83 Ariz. 369, 321 P.2d 1030 (1958); Fire Insurance Rating Bureau v. Rogan, 4 Wis.2d 558, 91 N.W.2d 372 (1958).

21. See Joel B. Dirlam and Irwin M. Stelzer, *The Insurance Industry: A Case Study in the Workability of Regulated Competition*, 107 University of Pennsylvania Law Review 199–215 (1958).

22. Pacific Fire Insurance Bureau v. Insurance Co. of North America, 83 Ariz. 369 at p. 375, 321 P.2d 1030 at p. 1034 (1958).

sanctioning of such uniform premium rates.[23] The case for uniformity of rates seems much less persuasive than the case for cooperation in data gathering.[24] Cooperation to achieve a larger data base for credible predictions of future claim costs is plainly in the public interest. Cooperation to achieve uniformity of rates is a vastly different matter because it stifles competition.

It is possible to facilitate cooperation among insurers for data compilation without eliminating price competition by allowing partial participation of insurers in rating bureaus. Though partial subscribership adds some administrative problems that are not encountered under a system which limits subscribership to full participation that includes the undeviating use of a rating bureau's rates, these problems that can be overcome at moderate cost. Furthermore, if price competition is viewed as desirable, opportunities for partial subscribership are probably essential for many insurers that would otherwise be unable to secure a compilation of the data adequate to serve as a basis for for rate-making.

In some circumstances, rating bureaus have argued that it is unfair to allow (or to require) non-bureau companies to use data developed by the bureaus at the expense of the members.[25] This should not be an insurmountable problem because a system can be structured in which non-bureau companies are charged a fair portion of the cost of accumulating the data. For example, all insurers of the relevant class could be required to report data to the bureau and to pay an assessment based on volume of business, leaving to each insurer the freedom to either use the premium rates filed by the bureau or to develop a separate rate schedule.

(iii) Rate Regulation After the 1960s

A third distinctive period in the history of insurance rate regulation commenced late in the 1960s. During this third period, there have been significant changes in the patterns of rate regulation as a conse-

---

23. This type of system is usually characterized as "full participation" in the rating bureau by subscribers.

One who favors uniformity of rates must also favor either cooperation among insurers (with or without public regulation) or the maintenance of a public agency for rate-making.

24. The case for uniformity of rates might be compared with the case for Fair Trade Acts bearing on retail price fixing by a manufacturer. In the insurance area, however, it is not contended that retail pricing by different agents of a single insurer should be competitive; rather the issue is whether prices of different insurers should be competitive.

25. Consider the following comment from Bernard R. Stone, *Rate Regulation v.*

Rate-Making, 1955 Insurance Law Journal 107–111:

"The pulling and tussling that is going on between the so-called bureau companies and those classed as independents would seem to call for another look at these laws. On the one hand the independent companies contend that some departments are using the laws to make rates by strict interpretations and by undue requirements for statistics, while on the other hand the bureau companies, particularly in the fire field, contend that the independents and those who may be partial subscribers at a bureau have no right to copy and use the bureau's surveys, rate books, tariffs, town classifications and other material in making their filings * * *."

quence of the enactment of several different types of legislative approaches to rate regulation. In addition, there have been regulatory and judicial decisions which affected categories based on such factors as age and sex.

The new period of change was triggered by a significantly worsening situation in regard to the cost of automobile insurance in a number of states. Mounting public dissatisfaction with various aspects of the automobile insurance system resulted in pressures against rate increases that insurers generally regarded as essential to their continued operations in this line of business.

One of the "new" approaches advocated by representatives of most segments of the industry [26] (and concurred in by state regulatory officials in some states [27]) has been to abandon "prior approval" laws — the type of rate regulation that was most prevalent at the beginning of this new period of change — in favor of either "file and use" or "no filing" laws. In theory at least, "file and use" laws opened up somewhat greater competition. "No-filing" laws (also referred to as "open competition" laws), in theory encourage far greater competition in rates by permitting a company to establish new rates freely and to place them in effect promptly. But just as this approach was gaining momentum,[28] as reflected by the enactment of "open competition" legislation in Wisconsin [29] and New York [30] in 1969, proposals for exactly the reverse change were being advanced in several states having "open competition" legislation.[31] The contradictory trends were symptomatic of fundamental difficulties, which were primarily related to motor vehicle insurance in many states.[32] However, the renewed considerations of rating regulation in the 1970s and 1980s also revived the controversy over what effect, if any, the investment income earned

26. See, e.g., C. Arthur Williams, Jr., *Insurer Views on Property and Liability Insurance Rate Regulation,* 36 Journal of Risk & Insurance 217–236 (1969).

27. See, e.g., New York Insurance Department, Report, *The Public Interest Now in Property and Liability Insurance Regulation* (1969), at pp. 65–149.

See generally Robert T. Franson, *The Prior-Approval System of Property and Liability Insurance Rate Regulation: A Case Study,* 1969 Wisconsin Law Review 1104–1140.

28. See *Insurance Accessibility for the Hard-to-Place Driver,* REPORT OF THE DIVISION OF INDUSTRY ANALYSIS, BUREAU OF ECONOMICS, FEDERAL TRADE COMMISSION (United States Department of Transportation Automobile Insurance & Compensation Study, 1970), at pp. 78–79.

29. Wisconsin Laws 1969, c. 144, § 23; Wisconsin Stat.Ann. ch. 625 (Supp., 1970).

30. McKinney's New York Insurance Law §§ 175–180 (1966 and Supp., 1970).

31. Competing views were expressed by speakers at the annual meeting of the American Insurance Association in May, 1970. See, e.g., The Standard (New England's Insurance Weekly); May 22, 1970, pp. 1, 7–10. See also *Id.,* April 10, 1970, pp. 1, 3, 20; March 27, 1970, p. 12.

32. These problems also renewed interest in the possibility of federal action that would have directly affected various aspects of the automobile reparations and insurance system. See, e.g., *Insurance Accessibility for the Hard-to-Place Driver,* REPORT OF THE DIVISION OF INDUSTRY ANALYSIS, Bureau of Economics, Federal Trade Commission 73–85 (United States Department of Transportation Automobile Insurance & Compensation Study, 1970).

by insurers should have on the premium rates companies are allowed to charge.[33]

§ 8.4(b)   Equity and Discrimination

The standards for rate regulation have long included a requirement that rates not be unfairly discriminatory.[1] The generality of this objective leaves substantial leeway for evaluative determinations [2] regarding the number and nature of categories employed by insurers in a rating system for a given type of insurance. The difficulties of applying such a standard have contributed significantly to the assessment that no other objective of insurance regulation is as difficult to achieve as equitable rating.[3]

33. See, e.g., Arch T. Allen, *Insurance Rate Regular and the Courts: North Carolina's Battleground" Becomes a "Hornbook,"* 61 North Carolina Law Review 97–140 at pp. 105–108 and pp. 123–124 (1982); The Standard (New England's Insurance Weekly), Nov. 14, 1969, p. 1 (Massachusetts hearings), Nov. 21, 1969, p. 1 (N.H. Commission ruling).

See generally, Jack E. Birkinsha, *Investment Income and Underwriting Profit: "And Never the Twain Shall Meet"?* 8 Boston College Ind. & Com.Law Review 713–734 (1967).

Also see Comment, *Insurance Rate-making Problems: Administrative Discretion, Investment Income, and Prepaid Expenses,* 16 Wayne Law Review 95–134 (1969).

Cf. Michael P. Rose, *Regulation of Property and Casualty Rates in Ohio,* 32 Ohio State Law Review 487–518 at pp. 508–510 (1971).

In the late 1970s and early 1980s, high interest rates created an incentive for insurers to compete for business by offering lower rates. In order to increase the cash flow that was available to the insurer for investments, some insurers offered purchasers very low premium rates for "long-tail" coverages such as liability insurance for physicians and other professionals. The insurers invested funds that were held against reserves for payment of claims during what were projected to be the distant years when claims would ultimately be paid. In this way, an insurer could dramatically increase its investment income because of the high interest returns on these invested funds. As interest rates fell and as claims costs escalated in the mid-1980s, it become very apparent that some premium rates had been set too low to provide adequate reserves. This development served to generate renewed controversy over rating practices and regulation.

In addition, during the 1970s and 1980s traditional concepts for distinguishing "discriminatory" from "nondiscriminatory" rating practices have been subjected to sharp challenge.

§ 8.4(b)

1. See § 8.4(a), above.

2. Concerning the nature of evaluative issues generally, see § 1.4, above.

3. See, e.g., Spencer L. Kimball, *The Purpose of Insurance Regulation: A Preliminary Inquiry in the Theory of Insurance Law,* 45 Minnesota Law Review 471–524 at pp. 495–498 (1961).

The difficulties of determining whether rating classifications are "unfairly discriminatory" are enhanced by the social policy objectives and the political factors brought to bear. Also, it is common that some insurance purchasers are "subsidized" at the expense of others when, because of political pressures for allowing people to drive even when they are poor risks and without paying the full costs, rates for "assigned risk" insureds are not high enough to cover the cost to insurers of providing "assigned risk" coverages.

Cf. C. Arthur Williams, *Unfair Rate Discrimination in Property and Liability Insurance,* in INSURANCE, GOVERNMENT AND SOCIAL POLICY (Kimball & Denenberg eds. 1969), at p. 209 and p. 222.

Also see Leah Wertham, *Insurance Classification: Too Important to Be Left to the Actuaries,* 19 University of Michigan Journal of Law Reform 349–423 (1986); Regina Austin, *The Insurance Classification Controversy,* 131 University of Pennsylvania Law Review 517–583 (1983); David B. Abramoff, *Rating the Rating Schemes: Applications of Constitutional Equal Protection Principles to Automobile Insurance Practices,* 9 Capitol University Law Review 683–716 (1980); Joseph S. Gerber, *The Eco-*

Avoiding unacceptable discrimination in the premiums an insurer is authorized to charge for insurance is an objective that may provoke fundamental differences of opinion about social policy objectives, as well as divergent attitudes about the extent to which such objectives should influence classifications employed in insurance rating. This is well illustrated by the controversies over how and when gender can or should be a factor in setting rates for various types of insurance and annuity plans.[4] Fundamental differences in goals often affect views about insurance rating classifications generally,[5] and may be expected to generate intense controversy in the future.

The administrative costs for insurers are a major factor in the decisions concerning the degree to which a rating system can be precisely "tailored" to the magnitude of risks assumed by an insurer in its contracts with various types of policyholders. In general, administrative costs increase significantly as a higher degree of precision is sought for the classification system which is used to categorize the risks which are to be covered. In most situations, it is not desirable to attempt to create a system that seeks to maximize the number of classes for different magnitudes of risk that the obtainable data would support. The cost of gathering the data and administering the resulting rating system (including marketing expenses) would be so great that even the policyholders in the most favored rating classes would almost certainly need to be charged more than they would pay under a system with fewer and less precise classes. Although a very extensive set of classifications could provide greater relative equity among policyholders, it seems clear that most policyholders[6] would readily sacrifice such refined equity in favor of lower rates for every purchaser. Even those policyholders who would have the lowest rates, under a system which maximized the number of classifications, would nevertheless prefer the less precise classifications if there was no way for them to achieve relatively more favorable treatment without also incurring higher insurance costs for themselves, as well as others, because of the impact of higher administrative costs on all policyholders. The inevitability of higher administrative costs undoubtedly has been a significant factor in the rejection of proposals for more numerous and finely graded rating classes.[7]

nomic and Actuarial Aspects of Selection and Classification, 10 Forum 1205–1230 (1975).

4. See Arizona Governing Committee for Tax Deferred Annuity & Deferred Compensation Plans v. Norris, 463 U.S. 1073, 103 S.Ct. 3492, 77 L.Ed.2d 1236 (1983); City of Los Angeles Department of Water & Power v. Manhart, 435 U.S. 702, 98 S.Ct. 1370, 55 L.Ed.2d 657 (1978), *on remand* 577 F.2d 98 (9th Cir.1978).

5. See generally Leah Wortham, *Insurance Classification: Too Important to be*

Left to the Actuaries, 19 University of Michigan Journal of Law Reform 349–423 (1986).

6. At least, policyholders who were acting on prudent economic considerations and not being influenced by other kinds of interests (such as social policy objectives) that they might regard as overriding.

7. See, e.g. the discussion in § 4.2(c) (mortgagee-only insurance); § 5.5(e) (inequities from overlapping coverages); and § 5.10(b) (inequities arising from irregularities about anniversary date of policy).

The impact of administrative costs on premium rates is well illustrated in the development of merit rating for automobile insurance. Although merit rating systems have often been described as being based on determinations of fault in the operation of motor vehicles, the administration of these systems has tended to actually rely on the criterion of involvement in an accident rather than on genuine determinations of fault, or even on the use of objective criteria that roughly identify those at fault in particular motoring incidents.[8]

Avoiding higher administrative costs also seems to have been a significant factor working against attaining greater equity in premium rates for various types of coverages that apply to bodily injuries or property damages which could be notably influenced by whether the insurance is a first-party or a third-party arrangement. First-party systems of insurance against loss from bodily injury tend to give little, if any, attention to a policyholder's characteristics which bear on the likelihood that the policyholder will impose costs on the insurance system by causing loss to others. Third-party systems tend to give little attention to a policyholder's characteristics (such as a high level of earned income and a long expectancy of working years) which bear on the likelihood that the costs to the system will be more than average whenever that policyholder is a victim. In some instances, the debate over possible reforms in the motor vehicle insurance system has served to focus attention on the fact that it is feasible to adjust the premium rates for either a first-party or a third-party system to take account of both these sets of factors.[9]

§ 8.4(c) Observations

Rate regulation is actually considerably less pervasive and vigorous than a reading of the provisions in state legislation would suggest to an observer who is not aware of the actual practices in most states. There are several reasons why this is the case in most states. Insurance consumers generally are not well organized, and their concerns or complaints about premiums rates are seldom presented to the state insurance commissions. Thus, the interests of consumers, insofar as they are in conflict with those of insurers, usually are not effectively represented. Equally important, there are at most only a few states in which the insurance commission has either the staff or the financing

8. New York Insurance Department, Report, *Automobile Insurance . . . For Whose Benefit?*, at p. 48, note 96 (1970):

"Some 'merit rating' plans are sometimes loosely thought of as varying one's premium rates according to the quality of one's driving. But even the merit rating plans do not depend upon fault law. Rather, premium surcharges and discounts are based on accident involve-

ment. With a few exceptions for broad and objective categories, the merit rating plans do not significantly turn on legal fault or accident severity."

9. See Robert Keeton, *Compensation Systems—The Search for a Viable Alternative to Negligence Law* 48–51 (1969), reprinted in Seavey, Keeton & Keeton, CASES AND MATERIALS ON THE LAW OF TORTS (1970 Supp.), at pp. 275–279.

required for a meaningful review or inquiry beyond the data supplied from industry sources in support of proposed premium rates.[1]

Insurance rates, especially the premiums charged for automobile insurance, have become a significant political issue in some instances. When this occurs, there is a rather considerable risk that a politically motivated resolution of the controversy will not give due weight to the public interest in the adequacy of rates or the prevention of discrimination.[2]

Finally, although the amount of litigation involving rate regulation is relatively small, the number of cases has been notably increasing since the early 1970s.[3]

§ 8.5   Differences in Regulatory Measures for Various Types of Insurers

§ 8.5(a)   Generally

Rather early in the development of public regulation of insurance it became apparent that it would be necessary to develop somewhat different regulations for the various types of legal entities that were allowed to provide insurance. Different sets of regulatory criteria have been developed for the six major types of private, as distinguished from governmental,[1] insurers. The principal types of private organizations now authorized to provide insurance include (1) natural persons, (2) Lloyd's associations, (3) stock companies, (4) mutual insurers, (5) fraternal societies, and (6) reciprocal associations (inter-insurance exchanges).[2] Two of the most important aspects of the state insurance laws are the regulation of the business structure of insuring organizations and the specific qualifications for various types of insurers.

State laws now commonly declare that it is illegal for a person, association, or corporation to be engaged in what is commonly called "doing an insurance business" without having qualified as an insurer in conformity with the state laws and the administrative system established under them.

§ 8.4(c)

1. *Cf.* Michael P. Rose, *Regulation of Property and Casualty Rates in Ohio,* 32 Ohio State Law Review 487–518 at pp. 508–510 (1971).

2. *Cf.* Spencer L. Kimball and Ronald N. Boyce, *The Adequacy of State Insurance Regulation: the McCarran-Ferguson Act in Historical Perspective,* 56 Michigan Law Review 545–578 at pp. 556–565 (1958).

Also see Note, *Insurance Rate Regulation in Pennsylvania: Does the Consumer Have a Voice,* 81 Dickinson Law Review 297–314 (1977).

3. See Judith K. Mintel, INSURANCE RATE LITIGATION (1983); Arch T. Allen, *Insurance Rate Regulation and the Courts: North Carolina's "Battleground" Becomes a "Hornbook,"* 61 North Carolina Law Review 97–140 (1982); Richard S.L. Roddis, *Limited Omnipotence: The Basis and Limitations of the Powers of Insurance Regulators,* 13 Forum 386–396 (1978).

§ 8.5(a)

1. Concerning governmental organizations as insurers, see generally § 8.6, below.

2. See generally § 2.1(a), above.

§ 8.5(b) Individuals as Insurers

The history of the Lloyd's associations in England demonstrates that it is possible to secure reasonable assurances of financial responsibility in an insurance system that relies largely upon individuals or associations of individuals. Nevertheless, American legislatures have generally not favored allowing individuals or Lloyd's types of associations of individuals to qualify as insurers. Even among those states that have adopted legislation authorizing so-called "Lloyd's Associations," in several instances such statutes only approve legal entities that are very different in form from the syndicates commonly associated with the name "Lloyd's." [1]

§ 8.5(c) Mutuals and Stock Insurers

Stock companies are generally subject to requirements regarding both the amounts of paid-in capital and the surplus that must be retained (rather than being distributed to the stockholders); these requirements are designed to make certain the insurer will be able to perform its obligations. Mutuals do not have stockholders, and therefore somewhat different techniques were originally developed to secure comparable assurances of financial performance. However, today the regulatory function of assuring financial responsibility of both stock and mutual insurers is largely performed by statutory and administrative requirements for the maintenance of reserves that bear a reasonable relation to risks presented by the insurer's outstanding contractual obligations.

One potential difference between the role of regulation for stock and mutual insurers arises from the rather distinctive types of persons to whom management is likely to be responsible. In stock companies, management is mainly responsible to the stockholders. Although the responsiveness to stockholder control in a corporation undoubtedly varies with factors such as the pattern of distribution of the stock, usually there are some stockholders with sufficiently substantial share holdings to exercise a significant voice in management.

In a mutual insurer,[1] management is expected, at least theoretically, to be responsible primarily to the policyholders. In practice, however, ordinarily no single policyholder has an interest in the mutual that is large relative to all of the policyholders. When this is the case, there is no substantial policyholder influence on management decisions. Thus, in the absence of regulatory controls, the wide dispersion of "ownership" interests in mutual insurers typically creates a situation

§ 8.5(b)

1. See, e.g., Vernon's Annotated Texas Statutes Insurance Code, arts. 18.–01–18.24 (1981 & 1987 Supp.), sometimes referring to Lloyds' associations as "companies" (*Id.*, arts. 18.07, 18.11) and imposing requirements for maintaining assets and reserves equal to those required of a stock insurance company transacting the same kinds of business (*Id.*, arts. 18.05, 18.08).

§ 8.5(c)

1. Also see the discussion of mutual insurers in § 2.1(a)(3) above.

of substantial independence for the management.[2] While such independence may at times work to the advantage of the policyholders, it also creates a greater risk that mismanagement will go unchecked.

Stock companies, as a form of organization, have the prospects of greater efficiency as a consequence of the availability to such insurers of the business acumen of its large-interest stockholders and the incentives associated with profit-oriented enterprises. However, policyholders of a stock company need protection against decisions by management that are designed to serve the interests of the stockholders in ways that may be detrimental to policyholders. In a mutual, this problem does not exist because the policyholders are, at least theoretically, also the owners. However, in a mutual there is a need for protection against management that is either inefficient or seeks to advance the interests of the officers themselves to the detriment of policyholders.

If management effectively represents the interest of the owners, the mutual form of organization is advantageous for policyholders because they are the owners. Given equal efficiency of operations, the cost of insurance to the policyholder should be less under the mutual form of organization, because all profits are in effect returned to policyholders. Some stock companies have developed what are usually characterized as "participating insurance policies" which return some portion of the premiums to policyholders if the underwriting attains a prescribed level of profitability. However, even though the participating stock company policies return some of the profit to policyholders, ordinarily a significant portion of the profits are reserved for the stockholders.

§ 8.5(d)   Fraternal Societies

Fraternal (mutual benefit) societies are commonly permitted to qualify as insurers under criteria that have been specifically structured for such organizations. Initially these criteria were much less stringent than those which applied to other types of insurers. This approach reflected a public confidence in, as well as a significant degree of favoritism for, fraternal associations. However, an unacceptable number of financial failures of such groups led to more stringent regulatory controls. Although there are still some differences in the regulations that apply to fraternal societies, they are much less substantial than those which existed in earlier days.

§ 8.5(e)   Reciprocal Exchanges

When reciprocal exchanges were initially developed, there were a number of advantages and disadvantages to membership in such an organization. The reciprocal exchange originally was designed to make it as difficult as possible to bring any type of legal proceeding against

2. See generally J.A.C. Hetherington, *Fact v. Fiction: Who Owns Mutual Insur-* *ance Companies,* 1969 Wisconsin Law Review 1068–1103.

the exchange or its members. In particular, this arrangement tended to keep claims adjudication out of the courts, thereby providing the management of the exchanges with a very extensive control of claims practices in general and claims payment in particular. For example, through the use of procedural obstacles that could be used to block the assertion of a suit, an exchange could resist a claim thought to be fraudulent despite an inability to prove the suspected fraud. As a premium payer, one would be happy to become a member of an organization with a tight claims policy because of the potential savings. However, the claims policy could become at least equally unattractive to a member when losses occurred.

Another disadvantage of the first reciprocal exchanges was the risk that the exchange's financial resources would not be adequate to meet claims. If this occurred, unlike most other contemporary insurance arrangements, the members of reciprocal exchanges were open to assessments if losses of other members proved to be higher than anticipated. Therefore, members of exchanges were often unprotected against part of the risk against which insurance was sought. Thus, it was important when considering membership in an exchange to have information about the reserves and financial stability of the organization and the members.

In many states, legislative and decisional developments have sharply reduced the risk of financial failure of exchanges, as well as the difficulties of asserting jurisdiction so as to be able to bring an exchange into court. Indeed, in some states these risks are so minimal that they are no longer very troublesome.

§ 8.5(f) Observations

The need for maintenance of reserves by a stock company was obvious from the outset, and the requirements for such reserves were among the early forms of regulation. In general, the approach of allowing mutual insurance organizations to meet claims obligations by imposing assessments after losses occurred proved to be unsatisfactory because too often such insurers were not able to avoid insolvency. Today, regulatory statutes commonly require all insurers (including mutuals) to maintain substantial reserves. The financial responsibility of all insurers now depends primarily on the assets which are in reserves to meet potential liabilities. Nevertheless, sometimes decisions concerning reserves can still be influenced by the form of organization, as well as by the management of the company.

The need for a public authority to scrutinize both premium rates and overreaching by insurers was not obvious at the outset of public regulation of the insurance business. Furthermore, at least arguably, such regulation is less necessary for mutual insurers than for stock companies because the policyholders are the owners of the mutuals. However, in relations between the management of a mutual insurer and an individual policyholder, the disparity of power creates substantially the same need for regulation as in the case of stock companies. Furthermore, the interests of the group of policyholders as owners of a mutual insurer are often in conflict with the interests of an individual policyholder.

The different types of insuring organizations have tended to become similar in both formal structure and practical performance through the combination of voluntary developments in the market place, increasingly extensive statutory provisions, and administrative controls. Today there may be more differences between two stock companies or between two mutuals than between a particular stock company and a particular mutual. Similarly, the nature of the relationship between an insured and the insurer is now more likely to be a function of an insurer's management than it is of the type of legal structure that was selected for the insurer. Nevertheless, there continue to be differences between the various types of insurers and the regulatory provisions which apply to each type.

§ 8.6   Governmental Sponsorship of Insurance

§ 8.6(a)   Techniques of Governmental Sponsorship

Governmental "sponsorship" or support of many types of insurance or insurance plans, which has been and continues to be very significant in the United States, may occur in one or more of the following ways:

First, through the participation of a unit of government in the business of insuring either directly as an insurer or indirectly as a reinsurer for coverages issued by private insurers.

Second, through governmental subsidy either by appropriations to a governmental unit that serves as insurer or reinsurer, or by grants to private insurers that meet specified standards.

Third, through coercive measures directed at inducing or requiring persons to secure insurance through private channels.

Though governmental participation, subsidy, and coercion may all be used within a single program of government sponsored insurance, somewhat different public policy considerations and interests usually are applicable to or associated with the use of each of these three techniques. One manifestation of such differences is the fact that generally there has been more serious political opposition to programs that involve governmental participation than to programs that involve either subsidies or coercion.

Sometimes, even when there is a clear consensus that the government should provide some form of assistance when fortuitous losses occur, the rejection of all three types of approaches to government sponsorship has been urged. For example, during the debate over flood insurance in the mid-1950s, it was urged that public and private disaster relief was preferable to government-sponsored insurance. And the legislation that established the Federal Flood Insurance Program of

1956 [1] contained provisions for disaster relief in addition to flood insurance and reinsurance. The Act provided for government-guaranteed loans for reconstruction of properties damaged by flood as an alternative to indemnifying losses through the use of insurance.

§ 8.6(b) Areas of Governmental Sponsorship

The following is an illustrative, but not exhaustive, list of areas in which some unit of government, either state or federal, participates in the business of insuring as an insurer or a reinsurer:

(1) Social security benefits (including old-age, survivors, supplemental security, disability, medicare, and medicaid).

(2) Unemployment insurance.

(3) Workers' compensation insurance.

(4) Unsatisfied judgment funds for injuries sustained in motor vehicle accidents.

(5) Crop insurance.

(6) Bank deposit insurance.

(7) Bank guaranty funds.

(8) Public property insurance.

(9) Public official bonding funds.

(10) Animal-damage funds, financed by fines and used to pay damages even without proof of ownership of the malicious dogs or trespassing cattle causing the damage.

(11) Title insurance.

(12) Housing mortgage insurance.

(13) Veterans' life insurance.

(14) Postal insurance.

(15) War risk insurance.

(16) Nuclear hazards insurance.

(17) Inner-city property insurance.

(18) Flood insurance.

The possibility of a governmental subsidy is inherent in every program that involves governmental participation in the business of insuring, whether as insurer or as reinsurer.

The areas of governmental participation in the business of insuring extend well beyond the types of programs enumerated above. There are significant indirect subsidies as a consequence of special tax treatment which has been accorded to insurers and to insurance proceeds. Often the significance of such indirect subsidies, in relation to the overall economics of the type of insurance in question, is so small that

§ 8.6(a)

1. 70 Stat. 1078 (1956). These provisions were repealed with the enactment of the National Flood Insurance Act of 1968, 82 Stat. 572 (1968), 42 U.S.C.A. §§ 4001–4128 (1977).

it would be misleading to refer to or characterize the program as government-sponsored. In the following discussion, the unqualified terms "subsidy" or "subsidized" are reserved for circumstances in which financial support from the government is a major factor in the operation of the insurance program.

In some instances, governmental sponsorship of an insurance program has taken the form of coercive measures without governmental participation in the business of insuring and without any subsidy. The most pervasive legislation of this type consists of the motor vehicle financial responsibility acts which either compel motorists to purchase insurance or require that a motorist prove financial responsibility in the event an accident occurs.

§ 8.6(c) Objectives of Governmental Sponsorship

It is a political reality that government programs generally develop in response to multiple influences, and in some instances not all of the motivations for specific programs may be evident. Nevertheless, usually it is possible to identify the principal objectives sought to be attained by governmental sponsorship of a particular type of insurance. Of course, in many instances multiple objectives are involved. The diversity in the characteristics of different government sponsored insurance programs is suggestive of a substantial variety of objectives.

(1) Implementation of Legislation Concerning Economic Security

In some circumstances, the objective of a government sponsored insurance program is to meet a problem of economic security for some specific class or type of enterprise. A familiar example of an insurance program to meet economic security problems of concern to the community as a whole is the government operated program of old-age and survivors' insurance. Another example is the motor vehicle financial responsibility legislation which is designed to provide accident victims with a source of indemnification by the use of coercive measures without direct governmental participation. A very high percentage of the population participate as insureds and beneficiaries in both of these programs.

Some programs of government-sponsored insurance involve relatively few members of the community. This was the nature of the bank guaranty fund created in New York in 1829, which was one of the oldest state insurance funds. Only certain banks were required to make annual payments into the safety fund that was used to pay debts of any contributing bank which became insolvent.[1]

§ 8.6(c)

1. New York Laws 1829, c. 94.

Also see Scott H. Elder, *The Unsatisfied Judgment Fund and the Irresponsible Motorist*, in CURRENT TRENDS IN STATE LEGISLATION, 1953–1954, (University of Michigan,

1955) 45–197 at pp. 106–111. Elder calls attention to the following additional examples of "the fund idea":

"(a) A motor vehicle liability security fund financed by contributions from insurers doing business in the state and

(2) Compulsion or Encouragement of Potential Insureds to Participate

The desire for the mass participation of large numbers of individuals in government sponsored insurance programs is almost always occasioned by concern that those persons might otherwise be in need of public aid or private charity.[2] For example, a comprehensive nationwide program for old-age and survivors' insurance would almost certainly have been more difficult to achieve through private initiative.

It might have been possible to establish an old age and survivors' insurance program through governmental coercion, leaving the insuring itself in private hands, by requiring proof that an individual carried such insurance as a prerequisite to employment. Furthermore, the whole cost of the program might have been placed on employers, as is done in some states with respect to workers' compensation for accidental injuries in the course of employment. Enforcement of measures aimed at mass participation in such types of programs, however, would have presented different and perhaps more difficult problems than those of the system now in effect. Certainly, one of the factors relevant to the choice of governmental participation in this field was the prospect for securing mass participation.

In some circumstances, it is feasible to secure nearly universal participation among potential insureds without governmental involvement in the business of insuring. Workers' compensation insurance is provided for all employees in some states without reliance upon direct participation of the state or a state agency as an insurer. Compulsory motor vehicle liability insurance has been implemented in the same way in Massachusetts since 1927, and more recently in many other states.[3] Financial responsibility legislation aimed at encouraging acquisition of motor vehicle liability insurance, which does not include

used to pay automobile insurance claims against insolvent insurers.

(b) Animal-damage funds, one type of which, existing in Massachusetts as early as 1794, was financed by fines against owners of trespassing cattle and was used to pay damages to lands, and another of which extended this principle to harm caused by malicious dogs. '[T]he frequent impossibility of determining ownership was a compelling incentive for this kind of legislation.'

(c) The Torrens system of land registration, which includes an indemnity fund to compensate persons injured by operation of the system of certified tities.

(d) Motor vehicle unsatisfied judgment funds, the first of which was created in the province of Manitoba in 1945."

2. In most situations, the participation of only a small percentage of the total population would not provide the number

and diversity of insureds essential to the sound operation of an insurance plan. This fact, however, does not rule out the possibility that governmental sponsorship of a program of narrow scope might be urged on the ground that governmental sanctions could be employed to produce the number and diversity of insureds required for successful operation of the program as one of insurance.

Mass participation of potential insureds can seldom be achieved without governmental coercion. The wide distribution of homeowners insurance is perhaps the nearest approach to universal participation through private initiative.

3. These needs have been met in a few states by unsatisfied judgment funds or similar arrangements. Concerning unsatisfied judgment funds generally, see G. Victor Hallman, III, UNSATISFIED JUDGMENT FUNDS (S.S. Heubner Foundation, 1968).

any provision for state participation in the business of insuring, encourages acquisition of liability insurance by seventy to ninety-five percent of the motorists.[4]

When sanctions or inducements are used to coerce or encourage the acquisition of insurance and no state insurance fund is created, provisions for insuring those whom private insurers do not want to accept as insureds is usually needed.[5] For example, in some states the need for automobile liability insurance has been met by assigned-risk plans under which insurers, who wish to write this kind of insurance in the state, are required to participate in an assigned risk plan so that the unwanted applicants for insurance can acquire coverage. Each insurer is required to take an appropriate number of assignees.[6]

(3) Provision of Fringe Benefits for Government Personnel

One of the most familiar examples of governmental insurance is the National Service Life Insurance for members of the armed services and veterans. Active service personnel have been provided this fringe benefit without premium charge, and veterans have been allowed to acquire insurance at costs to them that are substantially below self-sustaining rates.

Another example of fringe benefits for government personnel include retirement programs for public school teachers and other state employees. In many states, the arrangement is in the nature of "risk retention" because the state either makes annual appropriations to provide retirees with benefits or makes supplemental contributions to enable the fund to pay the benefits for participants.[7]

(4) Protection of the State or Its Political Subdivisions

Arrangements established for the protection of a state or its political subdivisions have included public deposits guaranty, public property insurance, and public official bonding funds. If the entire political

---

4. There are no precise data compiled on a nationwide basis about the number of uninsured motorists. Accordingly, the dimensions of the problems posed by financially irresponsible motorists can only be inferred from examining data compiled on related matters for the entire nation and data from a few state surveys. *Cf.* Insurance Information Institute, INSURANCE FACTS (1981–82 edition), at p. 11; All-Industry Research Advisory Committee, AUTOMOBILE INJURIES AND THEIR COMPENSATION IN THE UNITED STATES (March, 1979), Chapter 2. There are also some data from several state surveys. See Robert P. Spena, Robert M. Mustin, and Gwen Hacker, UNINSURED MOTORIST PROBLEM IN PENNSYLVANIA (Pennsylvania Department of Transportation, 1981); New York Department of Motor Vehicles, A STUDY TO DIMENSION THE UNINSURED MOTORIST PROBLEM IN NEW YORK STATE (1979); Maryland Department of Transportation, THE NATURE AND EXTENT OF THE UNINSURED MOTORIST IN MARYLAND (1977).

5. Concerning the problem of unwanted insureds generally, see § 8.6(f), below.

6. Concerning the assigned risk problem generally, see § 8.6(f), below.

With anything less than universal participation by those who might be legally responsible for damages caused by motor vehicles, there is also a need for insurance to protect individuals injured in accidents caused by financially irresponsible motorists and the victims of hit-and-run drivers. See the discussion of the problems presented by uninsured losses in § 8.6(e), below.

7. Concerning "self-insuring" or risk retention generally, see § 1.3(b)(3), above.

structure of a state is considered as a unit, these arrangements, like those discussed in the preceding paragraph, are frequently in the nature of "risk retention" by the state or one of its political subdivisions.[8]

(5) Provisions for Insurance as a Catalyst for Economic Development

In a variety of areas, governmental insurance programs have been developed in order to encourage economic development. This practice is well illustrated by several well known programs, including: (1) governmental insurance of mortgage loans which has been used to facilitate private lending on terms favorable to borrowers so as to encourage new construction to meet housing shortages; (2) government sponsored and subsidized insurance for nuclear energy hazards (supplementing the very limited program of privately written insurance) which has been used as a means of encouraging development of industrial uses of atomic energy; and (3) government sponsored and subsidized insurance or reinsurance of inner-city property which has been used in connection with efforts to revitalize urban centers and to redress inequities suffered by residents of those areas.[9]

In some instances, a by-product of a government sponsored insurance program may be undesired economic development. For example, one of the concerns urged by opponents of flood insurance has been that it will tend to cause the uneconomic use of lowland areas that are subject to recurrent floods.

(6) Provisions for the Use of Insurance as an Instrument of Risk Control

The effectiveness of an insurance plan is increased by risk-control measures that can be readily introduced as one of the incidental aspects of the program. Although risk control probably has never been the primary objective of any government sponsored insurance plan, it has sometimes been a significant goal. For example, the National Flood Insurance Act of 1968 includes measures designed to advance flood prevention, flood control, and the prudent development of flood-exposed property.[10] And in Massachusetts under a system of governmental "rate-making" for compulsory automobile insurance, special instruction

---

8. *Cf.* David McCahan, STATE INSURANCE (1929), at p. 272. For a description of such funds, see at pp. 222–239 and pp. 263–270.

9. See, e.g., *Meeting the Insurance Crisis of Our Cities,* Report by the President's National Advisory Panel on Insurance in Riot-Affected Areas (1968); George S. Harris, H. Richard Heilman, Richard E. Stewart, & Frank Wozencraft, *Revitalizing Our Cities: The Urban Core Insurance Crisis* 24 Record, Association of Bar of City of New York 321–338 (1969); Sidney W. Bishop, *Federal Riot Reinsurance,* 1969 ABA Section Insurance, Negligence & Compensation Law Proceedings 141; Herbert S. Denenberg, *Meeting the Insurance Crisis of Our Cities: An Industry in Revolution,* 1970 Insurance Law Journal 205–220.

Also see Note, *The Central City Insurance Crisis: Experience Under the Urban Property Protection and Reinsurance Act of 1968,* 38 University of Chicago Law Review 665–685 (1971).

10. See 42 U.S.C.A. §§ 4101–4103.

of young drivers has been encouraged by the allowance of a rate reduction for drivers under 25 who have completed an approved course of driver training.[11] In many states where governmental "rate regulation" is applicable to automobile insurance, rate categories reward those with safe driving records. Experience rating has also been used extensively in workers' compensation insurance. In general, however, it appears that more attention has been given to risk control in private than in government sponsored insurance programs.

(7) Experimental Development of New Types of Insurance Coverage

If unavailability of a type of insurance desired by the public appears to be caused by unwillingness of private insurers to enter an untested area, a governmental insurance program may be created to provide coverage as an experiment. In some instances, private insurers are encouraged to participate in such programs by serving as marketing agencies for coverages that are reinsured by the government. Each private insurer is protected by the government's guarantees against the risks.

Governmental participation in the business of insuring to foster development of new types of coverage is usually conceived as a temporary activity. In many circumstances, the hope is that experience gained during the span of the governmental program will prove that such coverage can be profitable, and that this experience will cause private insurers to continue to offer the insurance without governmental guarantees or aid. If the contrary proves to be the case, the government then faces the choice of either abandoning the program or continuing it because societal interest warrants public subsidies or guarantees for such coverage.

(8) Provisions for Insurance That Will Not Be Offered Privately

In some instances, impediments to the private underwriting of a given type of insurance cannot be overcome. For example, acquisition of life insurance without limitations against coverage for war related risks is disproportionately attractive to those persons who are subject to the greatest risks in wartime. Because of the adverse selection problem in this context [12] and the obvious difficulties of developing a graduated schedule of premiums that would meet it adequately, private insurers have usually concluded that it is not feasible to write new life insurance policies during wartime without provisions against full liability on account of death from a cause related to the war. To address this problem, at least partially, the National Service Life Insurance was

---

11. See Henry Melvin Hart & Albert M. Sacks, THE LEGAL PROCESS (temp. ed. 1958) at p. 979, discussing both this Massachusetts device and the possibility of flood insurance rating measures that would encourage flood prevention and control.

12. Concerning adverse selection generally, see § 1.3(c), above.

created to make available some life insurance to all members of the armed forces.

The potentially catastrophic nature of nuclear energy hazards has caused private insurers to be generally unwilling to enter the field of insurance against nuclear hazards except on a syndicate basis and even then with relatively low limits upon the potential liability of each participating insurer. Provisions for governmental indemnity for some nuclear risks have been established as a supplement to the limited amount of private insurance that can be obtained.

During the debates over flood insurance in the mid-1950s, advocates of an experimental federal flood insurance program argued that the reluctance of private insurers to offer flood insurance on properties in areas subject to flood risks could be overcome by the accumulation of data on losses and insurance costs during the period of a federally-sponsored experimental program. Opponents of such a program argued that there were several significant impediments of a permanent nature:

> *First*, adverse selection [13] would occur because the insurance would be disproportionately attractive to the owners of the most exposed properties.

> *Second*, because of such adverse selection, self-sustaining premium rates would be prohibitively high.

> *Third*, the potential loss from flood is catastrophic and it would not be possible to collect enough premiums to cover losses such as might occur.[14]

These three arguments added up to the prediction that the risk of extraordinary losses in one flood or flood season will continue to be too great and that, at self-sustaining premium rates, the number of persons willing to buy flood insurance will continue to be too small for a practical program. The validity of this prediction remains debatable.[15]

---

13. *Ibid.*

14. See Edwin S. Overman, *The Flood Peril and the Federal Flood Insurance Act of 1956*, 309 ANNALS, AMERICAN ACADEMY OF POLITICAL AND SOCIAL SCIENCE 98 at p. 99 (1957); Henry Melvin Hart & Albert M. Sacks, THE LEGAL PROCESS (temp.ed., 1958), at pp. 970–980.

15. The problem of potentially catastrophic losses in a short interval of time might arguably be met by a long-range program calculated to build a reserve in most years to offset heavy losses in an extraordinary year; the risk that extraordinarily heavy losses would occur in an early year of the program could be met by temporary governmental backing. The problem of obtaining an adequate number of insureds at self-sustaining premium rates might also be solved. The hypothetical economically prudent person would not be deterred from buying flood insurance because of the fixing of rates at a self-sustaining level, if they were also on a graduated scale adjusted with reasonable refinement to the varying degrees of flood risk to different properties. In the absence of such adjustment, the disproportionate attractiveness of the insurance to the owners of the most exposed properties in any rate class would be a serious obstacle. Two further questions should be considered. Might the response of real people be different from that of the economically prudent person? Might prohibitive administrative costs be encountered in the attempt to adjust rates to the varying degrees of flood risk to different properties?

Concerning the problem of administrative costs, see generally § 8.4(b), above.

However, if it is sound, then flood insurance cannot be maintained without permanent governmental subsidy, and the justification for such a program must be found in societal needs.

Recognition of a humanitarian obligation of the government to provide relief to flood victims would justify a subsidized program of flood insurance on the theory that little if any more funds would be expended by the government on such a program than on direct relief, and that the net cost of direct and indirect relief measures would be reduced because the insurance fund accumulated from premiums paid by those exposed to the flood risk would pay part of the loss that is borne by the community generally in the absence of insurance. Furthermore, the cost of subsidy arguably would be at least partially offset by the reduction of revenue losses (because of deductions for flood damage on income tax returns and the reduction of property tax revenues), and therefore the net cost of a subsidized flood insurance program would also be moderated in this way.[16]

§ 8.6(d)   Collateral Effects of Governmental Sponsorship

Governmental sponsorship of an insurance program involves an intrusion by the state into a sector of the economy that is generally regarded as the appropriate sphere for private enterprise. Any valid assessment of the desirability of a proposal for governmental sponsorship of some type of insurance should take account not only of the ways in which the proposed program will serve the intended objectives, but also the extent to which it will produce unintended or undesirable consequences. Inevitably these factors will be in the forefront of any debate over a proposal for governmental sponsorship of insurance.[1] Of course, when the private insurers have concluded that it is not feasible to insure the risks in question, a program of governmental sponsorship typically encounters little or no opposition.

There are many specialized consequences that may derive from particular governmental programs. For example, in designing a viable flood insurance program it is probably essential to avoid encouraging the use of floodlands for structures that in essence cost more to insure than they are worth. This problem becomes apparent even on a relatively superficial analysis of such a program. In other circumstances, there are costs and consequences for a governmental program that are less obvious and which often are not fully considered when the plan is adopted. The federal crop insurance program provides an interesting case study.

---

16. *Cf.* Henry Melvin Hart & Albert M. Sacks, THE LEGAL PROCESS (temp. ed., 1958), at p. 978.

the automobile accident reparations problem in New York Insurance Department, Report, *Automobile Insurance . . . For Whose Benefit?*, at pp. 77–78 (1970).

§ 8.6(d)

1. Compare the succinct statement of the case for a private enterprise solution of

The purpose of the federal crop insurance program, as stated in the 1947 Act, is "to promote the national welfare by improving the economic stability of agriculture through a sound system of crop insurance and providing the means for the research and experience helpful in devising and establishing such insurance." [2] In most of the counties where federal crop insurance is available, the program has been limited to the principal crop (e.g., wheat in one county, cotton in another, etc.).[3] The limitation to a single crop tends to encourage concentration on the production of that crop in preference to diversification. The economic, environmental, and sociological consequences of encouraging such concentrated production were neither fully understood nor considered when the decision was made to restrict the availability of insurance to one crop in each county.[4]

§ 8.6(e) The Problem of Uninsured Losses

The undesirable social consequences of uninsured losses have given rise to proposals in many contexts for governmental participation in various types of insurance arrangements. For example, the problem of uninsured losses for employee injuries was initially staggering. The common law usually denied recovery against the employer, and the worker seldom had any form of insurance to cover losses. These circumstances led to the enactment of legislative mandates for workers' compensation which were effectuated by government insurance programs in many states, by exclusively privately written insurance in some states, and by a combination of public and private insurance in other states. However, the workers' compensation laws left some types of employment outside their scope, and there remain numerous situations in which uninsured losses from work injuries occur as a result of exceptions in these acts.[1]

---

2. 61 Stat. 718 (1947), 7 U.S.C.A. § 1502 (1958). The declared purpose of the original act was "to promote the national welfare by alleviating the economic distress caused by wheatcrop failures due to drought and other causes, by maintaining the purchasing power of farmers, and by providing for stable supplies of wheat for domestic consumption and the orderly flow thereof in interstate commerce." 52 Stat. 72 (1938).

An amendment in 1941 substituted "crop" for "wheat-crop" and "agricultural commodities" for "wheat." 55 Stat. 255 (1941).

Concerning federal crop insurance generally, see FEDERAL DISASTER INSURANCE (Staff Study, Committee on Banking and Currency, United States Senate, 84th Cong., 1st Sess., 1955), at pp. 272–299.

3. This fact is relevant to the question whether the crop insurance program may have an unintended effect beyond the de-

clared purpose and perhaps inconsistent with it. See James T. Graves, *Federal Crop Insurance: An Investment in Disappointment?* 7 University of Kansas Law Review 361–375 at p. 362 (1959).

4. There may be an unwanted agricultural and economic consequence of a choice (to limit the program in the county to one crop) made for reasons such as the need for large scale production of any crop within the program in order to provide a wide base for insurance.

§ 8.6(e)

1. The range of exclusions from workers' compensation acts has been gradually reduced by amendments. Nevertheless, although hardly justifiable, there still remain areas of uninsured losses from work injuries. In addition, it has also been suggested that the limitation of workers' compensation to coverage of occupational, as distinguished from nonoccupational injury, has proved to be a shifting and debilitating

In contrast to injuries in the workplace, the common law generally was not hostile to compensation for injuries sustained in highway accidents. Nevertheless, even though liability insurance became very prevalent among motorists as a consequence of the enactment of financial responsibility laws, injuries caused by uninsured or hit-and-run drivers emerged as a significant problem in the United States.[2] Measures taken in efforts to meet this problem of uncompensated and inadequately compensated accident victims in motoring accidents [3] have included (1) numerous modifications in the financial responsibility legislation of most states, (2) compulsory liability insurance laws in many states,[4] (3) unsatisfied judgment fund acts in a few states,[5] (4) uninsured motorist coverage requirements in almost all states,[6] (5) required no-fault insurance in approximately half the states,[7] and (6) requirements for underinsured motorist insurance in at least a quarter of the states.[8]

The primary objective of uninsured motorist coverage is to protect insureds — usually the policyholder, family members who reside with the policyholder, and persons who are permitted users of an insured vehicle — against the risk of being negligently injured by a financially irresponsible motorist. Unfortunately, the policy drafters have incorporated into the standard forms for the uninsured motorist coverage a number of restrictive provisions that are not fully in accord with this objective. Some of the provisions were designed to preclude fraudulent claims, an objective that serves the public interest as well as the

restriction. See Roger C. Henderson, *Should Workmen's Compensation Be Extended to Nonoccupational Injuries?* 48 Texas Law Review 117–157 (1969).

2. Moreover, practices of compromise settlement sharply reduced the number of instances in which compensation for accidental loss was totally denied when liability insurance applied to the injury incurred in an automobile accident.

3. In Great Britain, with compulsory automobile liability insurance in effect, an agreement was made in 1946 between insurers and the Minister of Transport creating the Motor Insurers' Bureau for the purpose of providing compensation to motoring victims deprived of redress by the absence of effective insurance. The problem of the unidentified driver was not covered by this agreement, but it was soon stated that the Bureau would give consideration to making gratuitous payments of bona fide claims. See Shawcross & Lee, THE LAW OF MOTOR INSURANCE (Second edition, 1949), at p. 364 and p. 377.

4. Massachusetts Gen.Laws Ann. c. 90, §§ 1A, 3, 34A–34K (1969); McKinney's New York Veh. & Traf. Law §§ 310–321 (1970 and Supp.1970); North Carolina Gen.

Stat. §§ 20–309 through 20–319 (1965 and Supp.1969).

See also § 4.10, above (no-fault insurance).

5. An act of this type was enacted in North Dakota in 1948, and later in New Jersey, Maryland, and Michigan.

A variant on this general theme is the New York Motor Vehicle Accident Indemnification Corporation (MVAIC) Law, McKinney's New York Insurance Law §§ 600–626 (1966 and Supp.1970).

Concerning unsatisfied judgment funds generally, see Scott H. Elder, *The Unsatisfied Judgment Fund and the Irresponsible Motorist*, in CURRENT TRENDS IN STATE LEGISLATION, 1953–1954, (Univ. of Michigan, 1955), at p. 47.

6. See generally § 4.9(c), above.

See generally, Widiss, UNINSURED AND UNDERINSURED MOTORIST INSURANCE (1985 and 1986).

7. See the discussion of motor vehicle no-fault legislation in § 4.10, above.

8. See Widiss, UNINSURED AND UNDERINSURED MOTORIST INSURANCE (1985 and 1987), Chapter 9 and Chapters 31 through 33.

insurers' interest.[9] This is well illustrated by the definition in the insurance policy terms that limits coverage for "hit-and-run" accidents to injuries that result from "physical contact" with an unidentified motor vehicle.[10] This requirement also appears in some of the statutes establishing requirements for the uninsured motorist insurance policies.[11] If the applicable uninsured motorist insurance does not contain a restrictive "physical contact" provision, the inclusion of this coverage limitation may be challenged as an invalid attempt to diminish the scope of protection to something less than that intended to be required by the statute.[12]

When an individual is injured in a motor vehicle accident as the result of the negligent operation of the vehicle by a motorist whose liability insurer is or becomes insolvent, liability insurance may not be an available source of indemnification. In the latter part of the 1960s and in the 1970s, many uninsured motorist insurance forms were modified, in some instances by statutory compulsion, to provide coverage for losses when indemnification is not available from a tortfeasor because of the insolvency of a liability insurer.[13] The problem of an accident victim with a claim against an insolvent insurer has also been met in some states by the creation of a state security fund financed by periodic payments made by insurers doing the relevant type of business in the state.[14]

§ 8.6(f) The Problem of Unwanted Insureds

The problem of the unwanted insured arises as a particularly significant concern whenever legislative enactments require insurance as a prerequisite to permission to engage in a specified activity. This occurs, for example, when insurance is declared to be a prerequisite to registration of a motor vehicle. It also occurs when insurance is required of all those who engage in a business within the scope of a workers' compensation act. In each of these situations, if all insurers were free to refuse applicants, their refusal would effectively bar some persons or entities from engaging in the specified activity. In such circumstances, legislators sometimes conclude that at least some of the unwanted insureds should not be barred. The approaches that may be employed are well illustrated by ways the problem of the unwanted

---

9. In part, too, policy drafters probably sought, quite defensibly from their point of view, but less so from the point of view of public interest, to reduce the uncertainties insurers originally faced in offering the new coverage.

10. See Widiss, UNINSURED AND UNDERINSURED MOTORIST INSURANCE (1985 and 1987), § 1.14, Chapter 2, Chapter 3, and Chapter 15.

11. *Id.,* at § 9.8.

12. See the discussion in Widiss, UNINSURED AND UNDERINSURED MOTORIST INSURANCE (1985), at § 9.7 through § 9.9.

13. Proposals for establishing a federal insolvency fund have also been advanced. See, e.g., *Insurance Accessibility for the Hard-to-Place Driver,* REPORT OF THE DIVISION OF INDUSTRY ANALYSIS, Bureau of Economics, Federal Trade Commission 75–77 (United States Department Transportation Automobile Insurance & Compensation Study, 1970).

14. Also see Victor Hallman, UNSATISFIED JUDGMENT FUND (1968).

insured has been met in regard to providing insurance protection for workers.

First, a few states have enacted legislation that requires insurers to accept all qualified employers applying for workers' compensation insurance.[1]

Second, in some states the legislature has created a competitive (non-exclusive) state fund[2] or a state-sponsored association[3] to write workers' compensation insurance. Although it "has sometimes been taken for granted that * * * the fund or association should solve the undesirable-risk problem by acting as residual legatee of risks that private carriers do not want,"[4] there is support for the power of rejection of applications "in employments which involve hazards and risks of such a nature that it would, in all reasonable probability, result in the State Compensation Fund's becoming insolvent."[5]

Third, in several states a public fund has been created to write workers' compensation insurance for all enterprises in the state.[6] It has been suggested that the manager of such a fund might have the power to reject risks that would probably result in insolvency of the fund, but the issue has not been squarely faced because in states having exclusive funds it appears that all qualified employers are accepted as a matter of routine practice.[7]

Fourth, many state statutes create assigned-risk plans for workers' compensation insurance[8] which distribute the unwanted insureds among the insurers through assignment by a public official or through a voluntary arrangement among insurers under administrative supervision.[9]

Fifth, in Canada the problem has been met by a national program, the "Canadian facility." Private insurers will generally accept any

§ 8.6(f)

1. See Arthur Larson, WORKMEN'S COMPENSATION LAW (1986), at § 92.51.

Also see note 3, below.

2. See, e.g., McKinney's New York Workmen's Compensation Law §§ 76–99.

3. See, e.g., the Texas Employers' Insurance Association is an association of employers with statutory standing. Vernon's Ann.Texas Civ.Stat.Ann. art. 8308 (1984). In § 7 of this article it is stated that any employer of labor who may be subject to the Texas Workers' Compensation Law or to the Longshoremen's and Harbor Workers' Compensation Act of the United States "may become a subscriber to the Association."

Also see the considered dicta in Texas Employers' Insurance Association v. United States Torpedo Co., 26 S.W.2d 1057, 1059 (Tex.Comm.App.1930), and Oil Well Drilling Co. v. Associated Indemnity Corp., 153 Tex. 153 at 157–158, 264 S.W.2d 697 at p. 699 (1954), declaring that other insurers as well as the Texas Employers' Insurance Association are subject to the requirement of accepting any employer-applicant who is entitled to be covered by a policy of compensation insurance.

4. Arthur Larson, WORKMEN'S COMPENSATION LAW (1986), at pp. 451–452.

5. Gene Autry Productions v. Industrial Commission, 67 Ariz. 290 at p. 297, 195 P.2d 143 at pp. 147–148 (1948).

6. See Arthur Larson, WORKMEN'S COMPENSATION LAW (1986), at § 92.10.

7. *Id.*, at § 92.52 (1986).

8. See, e.g., Massachusetts Gen.Laws Ann. c. 152, § 65A (1958).

See Arthur Larson, WORKMEN'S COMPENSATION LAW (1952), at § 92.52.

9. The same approach has been adopted for automobile insurance. E.g., Massachusetts Gen.Laws Ann. c. 90, § 1A (1969), ch. 175, § 113H (Supp.1970).

application for insurance, and the insurer is then free to reinsure those insureds who are regarded as undesirable with the "facility" (up to a very high percentage of the risk that has been underwritten).[10]

It is well settled that a state legislature may provide for the problem of the unwanted insured by compelling private insurers to meet it, rather than providing for governmental participation in insuring: this is, of course, the nature of assigned-risk plans.[11] It would also seem to be within the competence of a legislature to provide for a system more like the "Canadian facility" than present assigned-risk plans.[12]

Historically, an interesting contrast has developed between the use of state workers' compensation funds in many states to cover the unwanted insureds and assigned-risk plans for automobile liability insurance. The choices probably are products of different political environments, rather than any intrinsic differences in the characteristics of workers' compensation and automobile liability insurance. State funds were started in the workers' compensation field when compensation insurance, as distinguished from employer's liability insurance, was experimental. Private insurers were not especially active in trying to preserve the field of workers' compensation insurance for themselves when these developments were occurring,[13] whereas many insurers have been and continue to be concerned with retaining the established field of motor vehicle liability insurance within the private sector.

 WESTLAW REFERENCES

§ 8.1 Allocation of Powers among Federal and State Regulatory Institutions

    (a) The Federal-State Accommodation

```
regulat! /s "united states" u.s. /s south-eastern  i 1  underwriter
find 64 sct 1162
federal! /s anti-trust /s insurance
265k18 /p insurance
```

10. For a brief description of the Canadian "Facility," see *Insurance Accessibility for the Hard-to-Place Driver*, Report of the Division of Industry Analysis, Bureau of Economics, Federal Trade Commission (U.S. Department Transportation Automobile Insurance & Compensation Study, 1970), at pp. 81–82.

11. See Donald D. Kozusko, *Reallocation Under Nonfault Automobile Insurance: Comments and Proposed Regulations*, 7 Harvard Journal on Legislation 423–448 (1970); W. Page and Robert E. Keeton, *Compensation Systems—The Search for a Viable Alternative to Negligence Law* (1969), at pp. 49–51, reprinted in Warren Seavey, W. Page Keeton & Robert E. Keeton, CASES AND MATERIALS ON THE LAW OF TORTS 276–279 (Supp.1970).

12. The ways of meeting the problem of unwanted insureds set forth in the preced-

ing paragraphs of the text, which were developed by the end of the 1960s, do not exhaust the possibilities.

Continuing dissatisfaction with the functioning of automobile insurance system stimulated the development of other solutions, including various types of legislative provisions for no-fault insurance legislation. See Donald D. Kozusko, *Reallocation Under Nonfault Automobile Insurance: Comments and Proposed Regulations*, 7 Harvard Journal on Legislation 423–448 (1970); W. Page Keeton, Robert E. Keeton, Lewis Sargentich, and Henri Steiner, TORT AND ACCIDENT LAW: CASE AND MATERIALS (1983), at pp. 886–922.

13. See, e.g., California State Automobile Association Inter-Insurance Bureau v. Maloney, 341 U.S. 105, 71 S.Ct. 601, 95 L.Ed. 788 (1951).

insur**** /s sherman /p anti-trust
to(217) /p rate /s regulat! /s statut! law legislat!
find 15 usc 1012
find 15 usc 1

(b) Unresolved Questions Regarding Regulatory Responsibility
s.e.c. "securities and exchange" /s "national securities"
insurance /5 statut! law legislat! regulat! /s pre-empt! /s state /s
　　federal!
"business of insurance" /3 mean*** defin!

(c) Legislative, Administrative and Judicial Regulation
sy(statut! law legislat! /s authori! /s commissioner /2 insurance)

§ 8.2　Objectives and Areas of Insurance Regulation
(a) Objectives of Insurance Regulation
objective purpose /5 insur**** /5 regulat!
217k11.2 /p regulat! /p rate
loss /s adequa! inadequa! /s premium /s insur****

(b) Areas of Insurance Regulation
"policy form" /s insurance /s regulat! authori!
rebat! /s discriminat! /s insurance
"unauthorized insurer service of process" (59-a /p unauthorized authori!)

§ 8.3　The Nature and Scope of Insurance Regulation
(b) Health Plans
health medical hospital! ¡3 service contract plan /s insur****
　　coverage policy /s subrog!

(c) Contracts for Services or for the Maintenance of Goods
"service contract" /s insurance
(ollendorff /s pink) (people /s roschli)
217k2 /p service maintenance

(d) Variable Annuities
di variable annuity

§ 8.4　Regulation of Insurance Rates
(a) Objectives and Methods of Rating and Regulation
(1) Introduction
217k11.2 /p rate
sy,di(rate /s unfair! /3 discriminat! /s insurance coverage
policy)

Factors That Support Rate Regulation
insur**** /s cooperat! /s rate! rating
rate! rating /s premium /s solven! insolven! /s insurance
insurer carrier

(2) Possible Approaches to Regulation of Premium Rates
confiscat! /s rate! rating /s insur****
prior /7 approv! /s rate! rating /s insur****
sy,di(commissioner /2 insurance /s regulat! /s rate! rating)
sy,di(rate! rating ¡1 bureau /s insurance)

(3) A Short History of Rate Regulation
(i) State Rate Regulation Before 1944 and the Events of 1944
da(bef 1944) & rate! rating /s insurance /s state /s
regulat!

(ii) Rate Regulation: 1944–1960s

da(aft 1943 & bef 1970) & state /s insurance /2 commissioner /s rate! rating

da(aft 1943 & bef 1970) & "rating organization" /s file* filing

da(aft 1943 & bef 1970) & rate! rating /s insurance /s uniform!

(iii) Rate Regulation after the 1960s

da(aft 1969) & rate! rating /s prior /s approv! /p insur****

(b) Equity and Discrimination

Rate! rating /s standard /s unfair! /3 discriminat!

to(217) /p unfair! /3 discriminat!

§ 8.5 Differences in Regulatory Measures for Various Types of Insurers

(b) Individuals as Insurers

individual +1 insurer carrier

(c) Mutuals and Stock Companies

sy,di(mutual /s reserve /s insurance)

"stock company" /s s****holder

"mutual company" /s policy-holder /s insurance

(d) Fraternal Societies

"mutual benefit" fraternal +1 society /s defin! mean***

(f) Observations

statut! law legislat! /s reserve /s insur**** /s maintain! maintenance

§ 8.6 Governmental Sponsorship of Insurance

(a) Techniques of Governmental Sponsorship

find 42 usc 4001

(b) Areas of Governmental Sponsorship

government! federal /s "crop insurance"

(c) Objectives of Governmental Sponsorship

(2) Compulsion or Encouragement of Potential Insureds to Participate

di assigned risk plan

(6) Provisions for the Use of Insurance as an Instrument of Risk Control

"experience rating" /s "work**** compensation"

(e) The Problem of Uninsured Losses

sy(uninsured (hit +2 run) /s "financial responsibility" +1 law legislat! statut! act)

find 226 ne2d 498

amidzich /s "charter oak"

Chapter Nine

RESOLVING DISPUTED CLAIMS INVOLVING INSURANCE

---

§ 9.1 The Liability Insurer's Right and Duty to Defend

§ 9.1(a) Introductory Note

The duty of a liability insurer to provide a defense when an insured may be legally obligated to a third party, as well as the correlative rights of both the insurer and the insured in regard to conducting the defense, have been the subject of much litigation. Moreover, as the expenses incident to defending against tort claims have increased, this aspect of the liability insurance arrangement has become and is likely to continue to be a matter of substantial concern for both insurers and insureds. The initial portions of this section consider some of the questions that have been raised about (1) the nature and the scope of the defense obligation for a liability insurer when an insured is sued,[1] and (2) whether an insurer is or should be obligated to initiate preparations for a defense.[2] In addition the next section discusses whether an insurer is or should be obligated to explore possibilities for a settlement before a tort claim has been made or a suit has been filed by a third party.[3]

The defense obligation of liability insurers also leads to several other types of problems. For example, conflicts of interests, which

---

§ 9.1(a)

1. Those questions are considered in § 9.1(b), below.

2. See the discussion in § 9.1(c), below.

3. See § 9.2(b), below.

were considered in Chapter 7,[4] often have an impact on the obligation to provide a defense for an insured. In addition, when the coverage provided by a liability insurance policy is (a) "exhausted" by the payment of some claims or (b) when the available insurance coverage is tendered by the insurer either to the insured (to be used for the settlement of pending claims or to pay judgments) or to a court (to be disbursed to the claimants), questions may arise as to whether the insurer thereafter is still obligated to provide a defense.[5]

When an insurer declines to provide a defense for an insured, the insured may subsequently sue the insurer. An incorrect decision by an insurer is, of course, a breach of the insurance agreement. The consequences for an insurer when there is a breach of the duty to defend may be significantly affected by the resolution of the third party's claim against the insured. The various possibilities and the extent of the remedies available to the insured, which involve some considerations that are comparable to those that should be examined when an insurer has decided not to accept an offer by the third party to settle a claim against an insured, are analyzed in the subsection on remedies for a failure to defend.[6]

§ 9.1(b) The Nature and Scope of the Duty to Defend

Liability insurance policies usually include provisions which state that the insurer will defend an insured against any suit alleging bodily injury or property damage resulting from an occurrence that is within the scope of the insurance coverage.[1] This type of provision serves both (1) to create an obligation on the part of the insurer to defend the insured and (2) to afford the insurer certain rights in regard to exercising control over the defense of an insured.[2] In many situations, such provisions are interpreted to mean that the insurer is entitled to exercise exclusive control over the litigation.[3] The insurer's exercise of such control has been viewed as appropriate in order for the insurer to protect its financial interest in the matter.

Courts have consistently held that the scope of a liability insurer's obligation in regard to providing a defense is more extensive or

---

4. See § 7.6, above.

5. See § 7.8, above.

6. See § 9.5, below. This section does not appear in the student edition.

§ 9.1(b)

1. See the liability insurance policies in Appendices G and H.

Note: Some liability insurance policies now include provisions that either specifically limit or eliminate the insurer's obligation to provide a defense. Several of the issues that are presented by such provisions are also considered in this section.

2. See, e.g. Allstate Insurance Company v. Novak, 210 Neb. 184, 313 N.W.2d 636 (1981).

3. For example, in Parker v. Agricultural Insurance Company, 109 Misc.2d 678, 440 N.Y.Supp.2d 964 at p. 967 (New York County, 1981), the court commented, "Giving the insurer exclusive control over litigation against the insured safeguards the orderly and proper disbursement of the large sums of money involved in the insurance business."

Also see Kooyman v. Farm Bureau Mutual Insurance Company, 315 N.W.2d 30 at p. 33 (Iowa 1982); Aberle v. Karn, 316 N.W.2d 779 at p. 782 (N.D.1982).

"broader" than the obligation to indemnify the insured.[4] In general, this is understood to mean that the duty to provide a defense exists in some instances in which an insurer will not be obligated to provide indemnification for an insured's liability to a third party.[5] Although there have been frequent affirmations of this principle by courts, there is a continuing flow of disputes involving the application of this general proposition to specific cases in which there is a disagreement about the scope of a liability insurer's duty to defend. The questions, which arise in a variety of contexts, are generally analyzed in terms of how the allegations in a third party's suit compare to the scope of coverage provided by the applicable insurance policy.

§ 9.1(c) Preparing for the Defense of an Insured

Liability insurers almost invariably require that an insurer be provided with a prompt notice of the occurrence of an insured event.[1] Following receipt of notice, insurers commonly, though not invariably, initiate an investigation.

Once an insurer that provides liability insurance has been notified of an occurrence which may produce a claim against an insured, the insurer is placed in a position to take steps that may be significant in regard to either the settlement or the defense of claims that are subsequently asserted against an insured. Disputes about the nature and scope of a liability insurer's obligation in regard to providing a defense for an insured who has been sued involve questions that are related to, but at the same time are also distinguishable from, questions about whether a liability insurer has any duty to engage in preparations for a defense of the insured.

4. See, e.g., Seaboard Surety Company v. Gillette Company, 64 N.Y.2d 304, 486 N.Y.S.2d 873, 476 N.E.2d 272 (1984); First Insurance Company of Hawaii, Inc. v. Minami, 66 Hawaii 413, 665 P.2d 648 (1983); Conway v. Country Casualty Insurance Company, 92 Ill.2d 388, 65 Ill.Dec. 934, 442 N.E.2d 245 (1982).

Also see Baron v. Home Insurance Company, 112 A.D.2d 391, 492 N.Y.S.2d 50 (2d Dept.1985); Nandorf, Inc. v. CNA Insurance Companies, 134 Ill.App.3d 134, 88 Ill. Dec. 968, 479 N.E.2d 988 (1st Dist., Div. 4, 1985).

Cf. Crist v. Insurance Company of North America, 529 F.Supp. 601 (D.Utah, 1982).

5. In Pennsylvania Manufacturers' Association Insurance Company v. Lumbermens Mutual Casualty Company, 648 F.2d 914 at p. 918 (3d Circuit, 1981), the court observed that the inclusion of the defense clause "has the effect of imposing separate and distinct obligations on a liability insurance carrier, to pay damages against its insured and to provide a defense" and that

"the two duties are not coterminous and a carrier may be obligated to defend its insured in circumstances where the damage award itself may be payable by another insurance company, other party, or the insured himself."

The duty to indemnify is established by showing that there was in fact an occurrence within the scope of the insuring agreements under which the insured agreed "to pay on behalf of the insured all sums which the insured shall become legally obligated to pay as damages * * *" because of bodily injury or property damage arising out of defined incidents. See the policy forms, Appendices G and H. Ordinarily, on the other hand, the filing of a suit alleging that such an incident has occurred would invoke the duty to defend without regard to whether such an incident did in fact occur.

§ 9.1(c)

1. See the discussion of the claims process requirements in § 7.1 and § 7.2, above.

If a duty to prepare for defense is recognized, it might arise at one of several points before the filing of a suit by a third party, including (1) when notice of the occurrence of an insured event is delivered to the insurer, (2) when a request is received from an insured, even though no suit has been initiated, or (3) when a claim is made by the third party without filing a suit (including, at least in some circumstances, a claim that appears to assert liability that is beyond the scope of the applicable liability coverage but is within the "broader" scope of a liability insurer's obligation to provide a defense).

Although there are some judicial precedents against recognizing any duty to prepare for the defense of an insured,[2] there is a very persuasive argument for the proposition that there is such a duty. In most circumstances, at whatever time a duty to defend is viewed as arising — as, for example, when a person has filed a suit against an insured — a liability insurer will not be in the best possible position to fully discharge that responsibility if the insurer has not previously taken preparatory steps which include the prompt investigation of the events. This is a significant, though not necessarily a controlling, argument in favor of the proposition that a liability insurer should be accountable when it has not undertaken an investigation or other appropriate actions.

Comment

An insurer's duty to prepare for a defense in a particular case should be predicated on a degree of probability of a claim being asserted that would cause an ordinarily prudent person to act in advance in order to be prepared to meet a claim if it should arise. In judging whether some particular type of advance preparation ought to be undertaken, it is appropriate to weigh the costs against the projected benefits. This assessment should include an appraisal of (1) the degree of probability that a claim will be subsequently asserted, (2) whether such a claim will be within the scope of the liability coverage or the somewhat broader scope of the insurer's obligation to provide a defense, and (3) the potential advantages to be derived from advance preparations to meet such a claim. If the evaluation based on these considerations is such that an ordinarily prudent person would decide to prepare for the possibility of a claim, an insurer should be obligated to undertake such preparations.[3]

2. See, e.g., Gibbs v. St. Paul Fire & Marine Insurance Co., 22 Utah 2d 263, 451 P.2d 776 (1969) (suit by owner of ski resort to recover attorney's fees paid for preparations against the possibility of a claim never made; *held*, for insurer; no duty to defend or investigate unless suit is filed or claim is made).

3. Among the factors to be taken into account in determining whether an ordinarily prudent person would act to prepare for defense are any assertions by the victim, formal or informal, indicating what might be claimed. As in the case of allegations in a complaint filed by a victim, however, such assertions would not necessarily be conclusive. For example, if battery is outside the scope of the insuring agreements and the victim claims that a battery occurred, this would not end the inquiry regarding a duty to prepare for defense against a future claim by the victim that

The view advanced here in support of a duty to prepare for a defense is somewhat at odds with terms used in most liability insurance policy forms, which typically declare that the insurer *"may* make such *investigation,* negotiation and *settlement* of any claim or suit as it deems expedient."[4] The word "may" in this provision should not confer upon the insurer complete discretion — that is, it should not "insulate" an insurer from liability for failure to take preparatory steps before an insured is sued.[5] This conclusion is fortified by the doctrines and approaches which now clearly apply to an insurer's actions regarding the settlement obligation which, of course, is addressed in precisely the same clause.[6] The numerous judicial precedents — which impose liability for consequential damages when an insurer decides not to accept an offer to settle a third party's claim even though a clause in the insurance policy states that the insurer "may make such * * * settlement * * * as it deems expedient" — provide substantial support for the recognition of a duty for the insurer to make reasonable and good faith judgments about whether to engage in preparations for a defense by initiating an investigation or by undertaking other activities that would be prudent in such circumstances.

Cases will almost certainly arise in which it will be impossible for an insurer to fulfill its duty of defense, should a trial occur, as well as it would have been able to do had the insurer undertaken advance preparations before the existence of that duty was unquestionably "triggered" by the filing of a law suit against the insured. The extraordinary difficulty of attempting to ascertain the consequences of inaction by an insurer in a particular case also provides substantial justification for obligating liability insurers to take reasonable steps in preparation for defense whenever there are circumstances that indicate

the insured negligently rather than intentionally caused the injury. Human experience includes many cases of later claims which are not in accord with earlier assertions by the victim, and therefore prudence requires prompt investigation in preparation for the possibility that different assertions will be made by the victim in the future.

Cf. the comments of Judge Duffy in Ballard v. Citizens Casualty Company of New York, 196 F.2d 96 at p. 103 (Seventh Circuit, 1952) (emphasis added):

"As to the investigation before trial, defendant's attorney *did not interview* Waitress Margaret Willey, who on the trial was the plaintiff's key witness, *until two days before the trial,* at which time she would not talk to him because she said she had conferred with Mrs. Farwell's attorney. Her refusal to confer should have been a warning her testimony might prove damaging, as up to then defendant's attorneys believed she

would testify Farwell was not intoxicated. The jury might well have considered that had the defendant's attorneys exercised due care, *the attitude of plaintiff's principal witness could have been discovered at an earlier date, and possibly other witnesses from the large number present in the Ballard tavern the evening of Farwell's death could have been summoned to testify.* We think a jury question was presented as to whether defendant company and their attorneys exercised good faith in the manner of investigation, and again substantial evidence supports the verdict."

4. See Appendices G and H (emphasis added).

5. With respect to application of this reasoning to negotiation and settlement as well as investigation, see § 7.8, above.

6. See the discussion of the insurer's obligation in regard to settlement in § 7.8(a), above.

there is a significant possibility that a claim will be made by a third party.[7]

It might be argued that an insurer has only a duty to defend, and therefore cannot be held accountable unless a claim is made which the insurer thereafter fails to defend properly as a result of being hampered by the lack of earlier preparation. This approach to the problem — which would leave the insurer free to make no immediate investigation as long as it stood ready to pay for the consequences if a claim within coverage was later asserted — imposes an unreasonable burden on the insured. It is unreasonable because, as noted above, it is extraordinarily difficult to discern the consequences of inaction in this context. Furthermore, having obtained insurance for defense costs, it is unfair to leave the insured with this risk.

It seems to be beyond dispute that an insured will often have great difficulty proving that the insurer's failure to investigate or take other steps adversely affected the defense. Although a shifting of the burden of proof on this issue to the insurer might at least partially ameliorate this difficulty, the parties and the court would still be required to engage in speculations about "what might have been." On the whole, it is a far less complicated, fairer, and more sensible approach to risk management to establish a rule that the insurer's defense obligation extends to doing whatever a reasonably prudent person would do in preparation for a defense when the circumstances involve a possibility of future claims that are within the scope of the insurer's obligation to provide a defense.

In some situations, the issue of taking defensive actions may arise after the initial pleadings have been filed. The fact that the allegations or claims in a third party's pleading are not such as to invoke a duty to defend should not foreclose the insurer's responsibilities, especially when the nature of the underlying fact situation provides a clear indication of the likelihood that the complaint could be amended to assert claims which are within the insurance coverage.

Caveat. If a duty to prepare for defense is recognized, it does not arise because of the mere possibility that the injured person will later file either a complaint or an amended complaint alleging a claim within policy coverage. That possibility could be said to exist in every situation, and therefore it is essential to remember that the appropriate standard of measuring the duty should be what an ordinarily prudent person would have done in the circumstances.

---

7. An insurer's duty to prepare for defense against one or more potential claims arising from a given incident should not be treated as a duty to prepare for defense against every claim that might arise from that incident. The insurer should be required only to take steps appropriate for protecting against those potential claims that, if asserted, would invoke the duty to defend. This phrasing is compatible with each of the two most common formulations of the standard of performance—"ordinary care" and "good faith."

§ 9.1(d) Multiple Liability Coverages and the Duty to Defend

When an insured is covered by liability insurance policies issued by different insurers which provide primary coverage, each insurer may have an obligation to provide a defense. In this situation, there may be disagreements about which insurer is entitled to control the defense or how the defense cost should be allocated among the insurers.

Control of the Defense. No substantial body of precedent has yet been developed to determine the respective rights and duties of insurers to control the defense on behalf of the insured in circumstances arising when the liability insurance policies of two or more insurers apply to a tort claim against the insured. Such few cases as have reached appellate courts have usually involved claims for full or partial reimbursement of costs of defense; cases of that type are discussed below, under the heading "Allocation of Defense Costs."

When two or more insurers have primary liability insurance coverage as to the same claim against the same insured, each has duties to the insured. Without doubt, each should also be held to have a duty to each other primary insurer because the exercise of any right of control over defense by one insurer in these circumstances is inherently likely to affect its own interests as well as the interests of the other primary insurer(s). For this reason, it seems likely that no one among two or more primary insurers will be held to be either entitled to control or obligated to provide the defense alone. Rather, it is likely they will be held jointly and severally responsible, and mutually obligated to each other to act reasonably and with at least equal consideration for the interests of the other primary insurer(s). Also, if, for example, one of two primary insurers unreasonably refuses to participate in defense, it is likely that the other will be granted legal redress in some form. Because of the inherent difficulties of enforcing any order requiring ongoing joint participation of two (or more) insurers in providing a defense for an insured, it is likely that the remedy available to one primary insurer against another for violation of the other's duty to participate in the defense will be an order for reimbursement pursuant to an equitable method for allocating the defense costs.

Allocation of Defense Costs. Some courts have disallowed a claim for recovery of defense costs (or of a portion of such costs) brought by a defending insurer against another insurer that wrongfully refused to defend.[1] Other courts have held, with more justification it would seem, that when only one insurer has fulfilled the obligation of defense, it

---

§ 9.1(d)

1. See, e.g., United States Fidelity & Guaranty Co. v. Tri–State Insurance Co., 285 F.2d 579 (10th Cir.1960) (Oklahoma case; action by excess insurer against primary insurer for a share of defense costs incurred by excess insurer in successfully defending after primary insurer refused to do so; *held,* for defendant; agreements to defend were several and personal to the insured).

should be allowed to recover all [2] or part [3] of the costs from a defaulting insurer.

Multiple Defense Counsel. If two or more insurers seek to have separate attorneys representing the insured, the risk of disservice to the insured is substantial and a court may appropriately hold that only one of the attorneys will be permitted to appear for the insured.[4]

Excess Coverage. Similar questions may arise when both primary and excess coverages are in effect. The following excerpt from a 1985 decision well summarizes the range of approaches to such problems:

> "Generally speaking, there is a split of authority as to whether an excess insurer is obligated to contribute to the cost of defending an insured where the defense is provided by a primary insurer and a recovery is obtained which is in excess of the limits of the primary insurance policy. See, generally, *Annotation. Performance by one insurer of its duty to defend as excusing failure of other insurers equally obligated to defend.* 90 A.L.R.3d 1199 (1979). On the one hand it has been held that
>
>> The duty to defend is personal to each insurer. The obligation is several and the carrier is not entitled to divide the duty nor require contribution from another absent a specific contractual right.
>
> United States Fidelity and Guaranty Company v. Tri–State Insurance Company, 285 F.2d 579 at 582, (C.A.10 1960), applying Oklahoma law. Numerous other courts, however, have held that where "the claim is over the policy limits of the primary policy and only one insurer undertakes the defense, the primary insurer and the excess insurer will each be liable for a pro-rata share of the costs of defense in proportion to the amount of the claim each is required to pay. * * *[5]

---

2. National Farmers Union Property & Casualty Co. v. Farmers Insurance Group, 14 Utah 2d 89, 377 P.2d 786 (1963) (excess carrier subrogated to insured's rights against primary carrier; claim was well within primary carrier's coverage limit).

Cf. Fidelity General Insurance Company v. Aetna Insurance Company, 27 A.D.2d 932, 278 N.Y.S.2d 787 (2d Dept.1967).

3. E.g., Continental Casualty Co. v. Zurich Insurance Co., 57 Cal.2d 27, 17 Cal. Rptr. 12, 366 P.2d 455 (1961) (one insurer defended and two others refused to participate; first insurer then sued for contribution; after reviewing conflicting precedents, *held.* proration of defense costs among three insurers in the same ratio as their liability for payment of the judgment against the insured); Burnett v. Western Pacific Insurance Co., 255 Or. 547, 469 P.2d 602 (1970).

Cf. American Fidelity & Casualty Co. v. Pennsylvania Threshermen & Farmers' Mutual Casualty Insurance Co., 280 F.2d 453 (5th Cir.1960) (applying Georgia law).

Also see Royal Indemnity Company v. Aetna Casualty and Surety Company, 193 Neb. 752, 229 N.W.2d 183 (1975).

4. E.g., Jackson v. Trapier, 42 Misc.2d 139, 247 N.Y.S.2d 315 (Special Term, 1964) (two insurance carriers with separate coverage and conflicting interests appointed. Butler Brothers v. American Fidelity Co., 120 Minn. 157, 139 N.W. 355 (1913).

5. Millers' Mutual Insurance Association of Illinois v. Iowa National Mutual Insurance Company, 618 F.Supp. 301 at p. 304 (D.Colo.1985).

Also see Insurance Company of North America v. Medical Protective Company, 768 F.2d 315 at pp. 322–323 (10th Cir.1985).

In this case, Judge Kane then observed that the "factual peculiarities" were such that none of the precedents cited by the parties or identified by the court's research was dispositive. This observation well summarizes the problems of describing the law in this area.

In some situations sharing the control of the defense is impractical because the separate interests are so sharply in conflict that their protection requires incompatible strategies on behalf of the insured and the insurer.[6] In such circumstances, courts should invoke procedures, other than joint participation, that accord protection to the interests of the insurer and the insured.[7]

§ 9.2　Settlement Negotiations

§ 9.2(a)　Introductory Note

Regardless of the type of insurance coverage involved — that is, whether it is third-party in nature as in the case of liability insurance, or first-party in nature as in the case of fire or property insurance, or "hybrid" in nature as in the case of uninsured and underinsured motorist insurance — the vast majority of all insurance claims are settled. Only a very small percentage, well under five percent as to most forms of coverage, go to some type of adjudicatory process for resolution. Early settlements of insurance claims offer the advantage of avoiding the expenses of adjudication (that is, the costs of preparing for and thereafter engaging in litigation) for both claimants and insurers. In general, it is important that the parties to any potential dispute over insurance benefits, and their attorneys as well, give serious consideration to settlement negotiations.

§ 9.2(b)　The Liability Insurer's Right and Duty to Initiate Settlement Negotiations

One of the functions served by liability insurance policy provisions which require prompt notice following the occurrence of an insured event[1] is to provide the insurer with the opportunity to explore the possibilities for a prompt settlement of the claims that result from injuries. Experience has demonstrated that offers of settlement that are made relatively soon after insured events occur often serve not only to obviate defense costs, but frequently are an effective approach in reducing the amount that the insurer needs to pay to secure the settlement of a third party's tort claim against an insured. Moreover, "early" settlements of an injured person's tort claim can sometimes make it possible for injured persons to avoid consequential harms. Thus, a persuasive case exists for requiring insurers to take the initia-

---

6. See § 7.6(d)(7), above.

7. Also see the discussion of the insurer's participation when there is a conflict of interests in § 7.6(d)(6), above.

§ 9.2(b)

1. See the discussion in § 7.2, above.

tive in regard to arranging settlements when an insured event occurs that may produce claims against an insured.[2]

The advantage to the insured of a settlement (which forecloses the prospect of any liability for an insured) constitutes a compelling argument for the proposition that a liability insurer should be obligated to exercise reasonable care as to whether to take the initiative in approaching potential claimants to explore the possibility of a settlement even before a claim or a tort action is filed.[3] Furthermore, once a claim is made or a lawsuit is filed, essentially the same considerations provide support for the proposition that the insurer should be obligated to exercise reasonable care about pursuing settlement possibilities, rather than awaiting "offers for settlement" from the third party claimant. Moreover, those same interests might even be viewed as justifying — at least in some circumstances — the conclusion that an insurer should pursue the possibility of an agreement with the third party to seek an accord by using some type of structured settlement process or procedure.

§ 9.2(c) Methods of Facilitating Settlements

Most settlements are made by the parties in their own way and without any structured procedure or process. It is nevertheless useful to know about — and, when appropriate, to consider using — some of the structured methods that are now being employed to facilitate settlements. This section provides a brief introduction to several of the most widely used methods: (1) mediated settlements, (2) mini-trials, and (3) summary jury trials.

(1) Mediated Settlements

Mediation is a process in which an impartial individual assists parties involved in a dispute to reach a voluntary negotiated settlement.[1] The process usually consists of several stages or phases,

2. Also consider the discussion in § 9.1, above, on the nature of the defense obligation.

3. Also consider the discussion of a liability insurer's duty to an insured regarding settlement in § 7.8, above.

§ 9.2(c)

1. See generally, John W. Cooley, *Arbitration vs. Mediation—Explaining the Differences*, 69 Judicature 263–278 (February–March, 1986); Stephen K. Erickson, *Mediation: The Constructive Alternative*, 53 Hennepin Lawyer 12–14 and 31–32 (May–June, 1984).

Cf. Center for Public Resources, *Model ADR Procedures–Alternative Dispute Resolution in High Volume Third Party Insurance Disputes* (1987), at p. 1:

"For the past several years, many insurance companies and plaintiffs' attorneys have been successfully using alternative dispute resolution (ADR) procedures to aid in the timely settlement of third-party claims at impasse. Several thousand such claims already have been resolved through ADR procedures. The use of such procedures, and the size of cases submitted, are growing rapidly, as participants gain confidence in their effectiveness. Arbitration Forums, Inc. lists 393 signatory insurance companies; 70 companies participate in the American Arbitration Association ADR program for the insurance industry."

"Court-annexed mediation" is a process in which judges refer civil cases to a neutral (mediator or master) for settlement purposes. It also includes in-court programs in which judges perform the settlement function.

including: (1) initiation of a mediation process; (2) preparation for the mediated negotiation; (3) the mediated negotiation session, which typically includes the mediator's introduction, an opportunity for the parties to state their perspectives on the dispute, some means for the delineation or clarification of the areas of disagreement or reasons why it has not been possible to negotiate a settlement, and the generation and evaluation of possible approaches for a settlement; and, at least in some cases, (4) the preparation of a settlement agreement.[2] The mediator's patience, flexibility and creativity throughout this entire process are, of course, essential to the success of such a process.

Initiation of a Mediation

Mediation may be initiated as a result of the parties' joint decision to seek the assistance of a mediator, or a dispute may be referred to mediation by a court. In addition, sometimes a lawyer for one of the parties — or, if unrepresented, the party — may initiate the contact with a mediator or with a neutral organization that provides mediators for disputes. When this occurs, the neutral will usually be asked to approach the opposing lawyer or party to see if there is any interest in attempting to arrange a settlement of the dispute with the assistance of a mediator.

The American Arbitration Association now encourages parties to consider using mediators before submitting a dispute to arbitration.[3] Mediation under the auspices of the American Arbitration Association may be initiated in several ways. *First,* the parties may agree to submit a dispute for mediation under the rules developed by the American Arbitration Association.[4] *Second,* one party to a dispute may submit a mediation request either on a submission form provided by the Association or by a written request.[5] In either case, the Association will approach the other party or parties and attempt to obtain their agreement to the use of mediation. All parties to the dispute must consent to participate before a mediation will be initiated.

Preparation for a Mediated Negotiation

When the parties to a dispute seek mediation, it is desirable for them to be well informed on the issues which are being disputed, including the precise claims and the reasons why the claims are being rejected. Some, but by no means all, mediators believe that it

2. See John W. Cooley, *Arbitration vs. Mediation—Explaining the Differences,* 69 Judicature 263–278 at p. 266 (1986).

3. If no agreement results from the mediated negotiation, the parties then proceed to an arbitration.

4. See American Arbitration Association, COMMERCIAL MEDIATION RULES (as amended, 1986).

5. *Ibid.*

is essential for a mediator to be well-informed in advance of a first meeting in regard to:

— the parties;

— the "features" of the dispute;

— the "balance of power" between the parties;

— the reasons why the parties have not reached a settlement;

— the "extent of the settlement authority of each of the parties." [6]

The Mediation Process: Introductory Stage

In most circumstances, a meeting of the parties with the mediator will be arranged (either by the mediator or the parties) at a convenient time and place. The introductory stage for such a meeting is often very important.[7] Typically, at the beginning of the first meeting the mediator will describe the "role" of a mediator and will emphasize "the continued decision making responsibility of the parties." [8]

A mediator generally takes steps to establish his or her acceptability, integrity, credibility, and neutrality. Unlike a judge (who is empowered by the state) or an arbitrator (who is authorized by the parties) to render a decision, a mediator usually must gain trust and respect "through a carefully orchestrated and delicately executed ritual of rapport-building." [9]

At the outset of the meeting, the mediator usually will be concerned with identifying the issues and the positions of the parties. A discussion of the dispute is often initiated by affording all parties an opportunity to set forth their positions and discuss each issue as it is raised. Alternatively, detailed expositions by the parties may be reserved until after all of the issues have been briefly identified. Generally, the party asserting the claim will be given the first opportunity to present his or her position.

6. These quotations are from John W. Cooley, *Arbitration vs. Mediation—Explaining the Differences*, 69 Judicature 263–278 at p. 266 (February–March, 1986).

7. See John W. Cooley, *Arbitration vs. Mediation—Explaining the Differences*, 69 Judicature 263–278 at p. 266 (February–March, 1986). Mr. Cooley suggests:

"The *success* of the introductory stage is directly related to two critical factors: (1) the appropriate timing of the mediator's intervention, and (2) the opportunity for mediator preparation. A mediator's sense of timing is the ability to judge the psychological readiness of an individual or group to respond in the desired way to a particular idea, suggestion or proposal."

Id., in footnote No. 26.

8. John W. Cooley, *Arbitration vs. Mediation—Explaining the Differences*, 69 Judicature 263–278 at p. 266 (February–March, 1986).

9. *Ibid.*

Clarification of the Reasons Why the Dispute Has Not Been Settled

It is usually essential for a mediator to understand the reasons why the dispute has not been settled. Mediators often find that this information can be best learned through separate caucuses with each party in which the mediator can elicit statements that one party would not disclose in the presence of the other party. However, when such disclosures are made, a mediator must exercise considerable care in regard to matters which parties have shared with the mediator in confidence.[10]

Generation and Evaluation of Possible Approaches for a Settlement

One of the most important functions of a mediator is to assist the parties in identifying the possible approaches for a settlement and to accurately appraise or evaluate merits of each possibility. In doing this, a mediator often employs techniques that are designed to ensure that each party fully appreciates the other party's perspective on the dispute. In some instances, a mediator may also decide that it is appropriate to create "doubt in the minds" of either one or both parties as to the validity of their respective positions on the issues.[11] To attain these goals, a mediator often encourages each party to "brainstorm" about possible alternatives or options.[12] And in some instances a mediator may suggest the terms for a settlement agreement.

Agreement of the Parties

The mediator's role is to help the parties work out their resolution of the dispute. When an accord is reached, the mediator usually reviews the details of the agreement and secures the express assent of each party to those terms. However, a mediator generally does not become involved in drafting a settlement agreement. Moreover, it is always essential to remember that a settlement agreement is the parties' — not the mediator's.

(2) Mini–Trials

Characteristics of a Mini–Trial

A mini-trial is usually a voluntary undertaking in which the parties involved in a dispute agree to employ a procedure that is

---

10. *Cf.* John W. Cooley, *Arbitration vs. Mediation—Explaining the Differences*, 69 Judicature 263–278 at p. 267 (February–March, 1986).

11. *Id.*, at p. 267, citing Walter A. Maggiolo, TECHNIQUES OF MEDIATION (1985), at p. 12.

12. *Id.*, at p. 267, citing "Ray, *The Alternative Dispute Resolution Movement*, 8 Peace and Change 117 at p. 122 (Summer, 1982), and Meagher, *Mediation Procedures and Techniques* (an unpublished paper), at pp. 48–49, includes an interesting discussion of techniques for 'planting seeds' and 'influencing expectations.' "

designed to facilitate the settlement of the controversy. It is difficult to describe mini-trials precisely because one of the most important characteristics of such proceedings is that the process (and the procedures) can be adapted to the specific needs or desires of the parties. However, certain characteristics are common to almost all such endeavors.[13]

First, the process is undertaken as a result of an agreement by the parties, and the nature or the structure of the mini-trial is specified in a written document which manifests the parties' agreement in regard to the processes to be employed.

Second, in most arrangements, either party may withdraw from the mini-trial process at any time without prejudice to that party's position in a subsequent adjudication.

Third, the parties commit themselves (1) to an expedited procedure for both the preliminary stages and the hearing in which they present their respective cases, and (2) to participate in a way that does not burden the hearing with the formality and inflexibility that frequently is characteristic of judicial proceedings.

Fourth, often the parties will agree to the participation of a neutral adviser who is asked to comment on or assess the relative merits of each party's position in the dispute.

This type of proceeding is appropriately viewed as a structured negotiation process. Thus, the term "mini-trial" is somewhat misleading, because in most such proceedings there is no "adjudication" — which might be understood to be the character of the procedure by someone familiar with trials as judicial proceedings.

Agreements for a Mini–Trial

It should always be borne in mind that a mini-trial is governed by the agreement of the parties, and therefore the procedures can be adapted to either their needs or the peculiarities of the matter in dispute. Thus, the agreement by the parties for a mini-trial is extremely important. It should be a written document — signed by both the principals and their representatives (including lawyers) — that clearly sets forth the procedures to be used. Although a mini-trial agreement should be crafted for each case, agreements should always contain certain types of provisions,[14] including:

13. See generally Lester Edelman and Frank Carr, *The Mini–Trial: An Alternative Dispute Resolution Procedure,* 42 The Arbitration Journal 7–14 (1987); Eric Green, *Getting Out of Court — Private Resolution of Civil Disputes,* Boston Bar Journal 11–20 at pp. 14–16 (May–June, 1984).

Also see Center for Public Resources, *Model Mini–Trial Agreement for Business Disputes,* 3 Alternatives 1–5 (May, 1985); Eric Green, The CPR Program Mini–Trial Handbook in CENTER FOR PUBLIC RESOURCES — CPR, CORPORATE DISPUTE MANAGEMENT (1982), pp. MH5–MH 126.

Cf. American Arbitration Association, Mini–Trial Procedures.

14. *Cf.* Lester Edelman and Frank Carr, *The Mini–Trial: An Alternative Dispute Resolution Procedure* 42 Arbitration Journal 7–14 at pp. 9–10 (1987).

(1) Specific time limitations for each aspect of the procedure.

(2) A statement regarding the non-binding nature of the procedure.

(3) A commitment by the parties to seek a suspension of any adjudicatory proceedings (e.g. pending litigation, arbitration, etc.) while the mini-trial process proceeds.

(4) A clear understanding between the parties about the role, if any, of a "neutral adviser" at the hearing, including whether the neutral adviser is to actively participate in the hearing by asking questions of witnesses.

(5) An allocation between the parties of the costs and expenses to be incurred for the proceeding.

Involvement of Individuals Who Can Settle the Dispute

In most circumstances, a mini-trial is more likely to produce a settlement of the dispute when the parties who participate actually have the authority to settle the dispute, and the involvement of such individuals is viewed by some persons as essential to the success of the process. In general, experience has shown that it is critical that the individuals participating in a mini-trial (often referred to as the "principals") have substantial authority to agree to a final settlement without securing the approval of other company officials.[15] And, often it is helpful if the principals who are involved in a mini-trial have not had their views "clouded" by a previous involvement in the dispute.[16]

Time Period for Mini–Trials

A mini-trial's duration should be short. At the outset, a schedule should be established and the agreement should explicitly discourage the postponements or delays. The parties should agree to specific and clear limitations on the time for matters such as (1) depositions, (2) interrogatories, and (3) other discovery activities. As one authority commented:

> "The dates and times for discovery, hearing, and discussions commencing after hearing should all be specified. By stipulating time schedules in the mini-trial agreement, the parties plan and commit to conducting the mini-trial in a timely fashion." [17]

---

15. *Id.*, at p. 9.

The officials representing an insurer generally should be from a management level which is distinctly superior to the individuals who made the decisions which produced the dispute.

16. *Id.*, at pp. 9–10.

In most instances, it is very desirable for principals involved to also have sufficient expertise to understand any technical aspects which are involved in the dispute. This can be extremely important because the brief time period that is generally adopted for a mini-trial usually does not afford an opportunity to "educate" a principal about the technical aspects of the dispute. *Ibid.*

17. *Id.*, at p. 12.

From the point when the parties agree to participate in a mini-trial, generally the entire process should be completed in no more than two to three months. If a mini-trial is agreed to after pre-trial discovery has already occurred in connection with a law suit, a thirty to forty-five day time limit is usually appropriate.

In most circumstances, any problems that arise during the discovery phase of a pre-trial should be handled by the parties. However, the parties may agree to have a third party — such as a neutral adviser — resolve disagreements or problems.[18]

If a judicial proceeding is pending, the parties should file a motion to postpone or suspend that proceeding, and the mini-trial agreement may appropriately provide for the joint filing of such a motion.

Preparation for the Trial

Lawyers usually, but not invariably, develop the cases for presentation at a mini-trial. The parties may agree to the distribution of position papers, documents, or other materials before the hearing. Before the hearing, the parties should exchange witness lists, exhibit lists, stipulations, and — when appropriate — written position papers for the hearing.[19] Usually, the claimant should prepare and send the other party a detailed analysis of the requested damages. In most circumstances, once established, the time schedule for pre-hearing phase should be strictly followed.[20]

Discovery. The parties may agree to engage in discovery. The agreement should detail the type and, if possible, the extent of discovery to be undertaken, as well as a schedule for the discovery process.[21] If the parties want to preserve the results of discovery for possible use in subsequent proceedings (as, for example, a law suit in the event the mini-trial is not successful), that should be specified in the mini-trial agreement. In most cases, the parties should agree to specific limits for the number of interrogatories that each party may submit and the number of depositions.[22]

The Mini–Trial Hearing[23]

Sequences and Time Estimates. The mini-trial agreement should specify the order and appropriate times for each presentation, and the entire proceeding should be scheduled for no more than one or two days. The length of time allowed for the presentation of the case, and any rebuttals, should be scheduled in advance. Representatives of each party — usually attorneys — make presentations to the principals.

---

18. *Id.,* at p. 10.

19. One commentator suggests that the mini-trial agreement should even "specify the length, scope and format of the position papers." *Id.,* at p. 13.

20. *Ibid.*

21. *Ibid.*

22. *Ibid.*

23. See generally the sources cited in note 13, above.

Witnesses (including experts), documents, graphs or charts, position papers, and oral argument may all be used to inform the principals about the dispute.

Informality of the Hearing. In general, the proceeding should be "informal," and informality means that the parties have agreed that the rules of evidence and procedure, which would prevail in a jury trial, will not be applied. However, by mutual agreement the parties may commit themselves to employ evidentiary rules which advance the efficiency of the hearing. In most circumstances, the informal nature of the proceeding can be underscored by agreeing not to have any record (that is, neither a recording nor a stenographic transcript).

Minimizing or Eliminating Adversarial Roles. To the extent possible, adversarial conduct should be minimized because the goal of the mini-trial is to inform the principals about the issues and the positions underlying the dispute. It is often effective for the parties to agree that witnesses will be encouraged to relate their testimony in narrative form and that technical objections will not be asserted. The participants — and the neutral adviser, if the parties have decided to employ this arrangement — should be allowed to examine the witnesses.

Confidentiality. Usually it is sensible for the parties to agree that what occurs at the mini-trial will be treated as confidential, and that neither party may use either the hearing itself or what occurs in the hearing in subsequent litigation. In other words, unless the parties have explicitly decided otherwise, the mini-trial agreement should include a provision stating that evidence presented at the mini-trial will remain confidential and will not be used in subsequent litigation.

Consultations with Staff Members. During a mini-trial hearing, the principals should be allowed to consult with their respective staff members. However, once the presentations have been concluded, it is generally not desirable to include the staff members in the settlement discussions.

Settlement Discussions. The culmination of the mini-trial is the settlement discussions by the parties after the presentations have been completed, and those discussions should be scheduled to follow immediately after the conclusion of the hearing. If the parties have decided to accept the views of a neutral adviser, that person should participate at some point in the settlement discussions.

Participation of a Neutral Adviser. The role of a "neutral adviser" can be especially important to the settlement discussions which occur following the presentations.[24] Although the inclusion of such an individual in a mini-trial is, of course, at the discretion of the parties, experience has validated the important role that such an individual can

---

24. The roles and responsibilities of a neutral adviser should be prescribed in the mini-trial agreement — especially in regard to matters such as whether the adviser is to actively participate in the hearing (e.g., by questioning witnesses) or is to serve as a "referee" for the parties (e.g. if there are disagreements about how the discovery process is to be conducted).

have in the settlement process.[25] [The mini-trial agreement should specify that any opinions rendered by a neutral adviser will not be available for use in subsequent litigation [26] *and* that the individual will thereafter be precluded from any role (e.g., as a witness) in regard to the dispute.]

Assessing the Appropriateness of an Insurance Dispute for a Mini–Trial [27]

Deciding whether a dispute is appropriate for a mini-trial is an extremely important matter. Usually the most important criterion in a case is that the parties want to resolve the dispute with a minimum of expense, delay, and disruption.

Cases involving the application of clear settled legal doctrines often are particularly suited to mini-trials. On the other hand, disputes involving areas of law which are unsettled — and especially if one of the parties is interested in using the case to establish a legal precedent — usually are not appropriate for mini-trial.

The timing of a mini-trial is also very important. Generally, a mini-trial should not be undertaken until it will be possible to have the facts and issues sufficiently developed to permit a meaningful analysis. Another factor affecting the decision about whether to use a mini-trial is the volume of documentation necessary to litigate the dispute. Tracking and analyzing very large numbers of documents may require such a substantial expenditure of resources and effort as to make a mini-trial unfeasible.

Even if there is no resolution of the dispute at the mini-trial, frequently the parties still benefit because the mini-trial causes the parties (1) to clearly formulate the issues earlier in the process than would otherwise occur, (2) to marshal and evaluate the relevant evidence, and (3) to generally assess their respective positions.

(3) Summary Jury Trials

Judges who have the authority to manage their dockets by using techniques that encourage the settlement of cases sometimes employ "summary jury trials." For example, "Federal Rule 16(c)(7) empowers a district judge to 'consider and take action with respect to the possibili-

---

25. One commentator suggests: "The parties should also provide for the confidentiality of the neutral advisor's opinions and prohibit him or her from acting as a consultant or witness concerning the dispute in subsequent litigation." Lester Edelman and Frank Carr, *The Mini–Trial: An Alternative Dispute Resolution Procedure* 42 Arbitration Journal 7–14 at p. 11 (1987).

26. The mini-trial agreement should specify that any opinions rendered by a neutral adviser will not be available for use in subsequent litigation and that the adviser is thereafter precluded from any role (e.g., as a witness) in the dispute. Usually, a neutral adviser should be chosen who does not need to be educated about the technical aspects of dispute. Furthermore, it is often desirable to choose an adviser with litigation experience so that the adviser can provide an opinion on how a court would view the controversy.

27. See generally the sources cited in note 13, above.

ty of settlement or the use of extrajudicial procedures to resolve the dispute.' "[28] A summary trial, which usually involves some type of abbreviated presentation of a case to a judge and jury, is intended to "foster settlements by immersing the parties in the trial experience and giving them an advisory verdict."[29]

A judge is usually free to structure a summary jury trial in light of the specific dispute. Nevertheless, such proceedings almost always include several distinct phases or stages, including:

1. A Pretrial Conference

2. Jury Selection

3. Presentation of the Case

4. Deliberations by the Jury

5. Post–Trial Conference [30]

Pretrial Conference. In most circumstances, the judge uses the pretrial conferences to explore settlement possibilities and to introduce the possibility of a summary jury trial. At some point, the judge — either unilaterally or in consultation with the parties — will need to decide whether to employ a summary jury trial. Once that decision is made, subsequent pretrial conferences are generally used to prepare for the trial. Some judges "distribute a written explanation * * * to the lawyers and their clients."[31]

Jury Selection. The selection of a jury generally follows the procedure that would normally be employed, although some techniques to expedite the process may be employed. For example, jurors may be asked to fill out a questionnaire that will be made available to both the judge and the lawyers.[32] Typically six jurors will be chosen.

---

28. Rule 16(a) of the Federal Rules of Civil Procedure provides:

"(a) **Pretrial Conferences; Objectives.** In any action, the court may in its discretion direct the attorneys for the parties and any unrepresented parties to appear before it for a conference or conferences before trial for such purposes as

(1) expediting the disposition of the action;

* * *

(5) facilitating the settlement of the case."

Rule 16(c) provides:

(c) **Subjects to Be Discussed at Pretrial Conferences.** The participants at any conference under this rule may consider and take action with respect to

* * *

(7) the possibility of settlement or the use of extrajudicial procedures to resolve the dispute; * * *."

29. See generally, Thomas D. Lambros, *Summary Jury Trial,* 13 Litigation 52–54 (Fall, 1986) (Mr. Lambros is a United States District judge for the Northern District of Ohio);

Also see Carrie Menkel–Meadow, *Essay — For and Against Settlement: Uses and Abuses of the Mandatory Settlement Conference,* 33 UCLA Law Review 485–514 (1985); Marc Galanter, " * * * A Settlement Judge, Not a Trial Judge:" Judicial Mediation in the United States,* 12 Journal of Law & Society 1–18 (1985); Jacoubovitch & Moore, Summary Jury Trials in Northern District of Ohio (Federal Judicial Center, 1982).

30. See generally the sources cited in note 29, above.

31. Thomas D. Lambros, *Summary Jury Trials,* 13 Litigation 52–54 at p. 53 (Fall, 1986).

32. *Ibid.*

Presentation of the Case. The presentation of the case is usually limited to no more than a day. The abbreviated trial is achieved by limiting the presentations to summaries of the evidence that would be admissible at trial.[33] Usually the lawyers for each party are permitted to present evidence (including depositions, responses to interrogatories, sworn statements of witnesses, documents, exhibits, etc.) and to comment on the evidence.

Deliberations by the Jury. When the presentations have been completed, the judge usually proceeds in a manner which is comparable to that which would prevail in an actual trial, although it may be somewhat simplified in this context.[34] Typically, the judge provides the jurors with an explanation of the applicable law. Some judges provide the jurors with a verdict form that includes questions which the jury will be asked to answer — collectively if possible, and individually if they cannot reach an accord.

Post–Trial Conferences. Once the jury has begun its deliberations, the judge often encourages the parties to resume settlement negotiations.[35] If the parties have not reached a settlement before the conclusion of the jury deliberations, often the jury members will be asked (1) to report their verdict, (2) to comment on their discussions, and (3) to describe their perceptions of the presentations.[36] The judge may use these comments to intensify the "pressure" on the parties to reach a settlement.[37]

(4) Agreements that Provide for Significant Consequences of a Structured Negotiation

Each of the methods of facilitating a settlement discussed in the preceding subsections is employed to facilitate a voluntary agreement, and the parties undertaking such structured negotiation processes usually do no more than make a commitment to participate in good faith. However, in some instances, a judge — before whom a suit is pending — has made it a condition of the judge's participation that the parties make a more significant commitment by agreeing at the outset of a structured negotiation process that if they do not reach a settlement, the proceeding will nevertheless have significant consequences in regard to how the dispute will be resolved.[38] An example of an agreement that was used to increase the likelihood that the "structured negotiation" efforts would produce results is set out in the Appendices.[39] Increasing the significance of such a proceeding usually causes the parties to work even

---

33. *Id.,* at p. 54.

34. Also see *Ibid.*

35. Also see *Ibid.*

36. *Ibid.*

37. *Ibid.*

38. Appendix Q includes an agreement for a "Conditional Summary Trial"

that was used in an insurance dispute which involved a specially negotiated insurance contract that included some uncommon provisions.

39. *Ibid.*

more assiduously to reach their own settlement, rather than having a decision rendered by the court on some basis that does not involve a full and complete trial.

CONCLUDING OBSERVATIONS

It is not a matter of chance that this volume ends with a chapter that emphasizes the discussion of (1) settlements, (2) techniques that can be employed to facilitate the settlement of disputes involving insurance, and (3) various types of alternative dispute resolution processes. The discussion of alternatives to litigation is particularly warranted in an insurance text because insurers have frequently been leaders in the development and use of alternative dispute resolution processes. Furthermore, among the instances in which a claim precipitates some type of dispute involving insurance or an insurer, the vast majority of such matters — probably in excess of ninety percent for every type of insurance — are settled by the parties without adjudication.

In a sense, one of the objectives of this book has been to facilitate settlements by presenting an explication of the principles and doctrines of insurance law. A comprehension of basic concepts is often essential to an evaluation of the merits of any claim involving insurance — that is, an accurate appraisal of the import of the applicable principles or doctrines by the attorneys representing both insureds *and* insurers is frequently necessary to the settlement of a dispute.

In another sense, this book in its entirety is about *avoiding* insurance disputes. The text has been written with a view to the lawyer's role as a counselor for a client who is engaged in either the acquisition of insurance or in reviewing the adequacy of existing coverages. In most instances, when a client is asked to identify and consider both (1) the risks that are involved in a particular transaction or activity and (2) whether those are risks that the client wants to insure, an attorney is then in a position to counsel the client about the legal aspects of the fundamental insurance questions:

— What kind of insurance should be purchased?

— How much insurance should be acquired for the risks which have been identified?

— Will a particular insurance policy provide comprehensive coverage for the risks?

If such questions are addressed by the insured and the insurer, with the assistance of lawyers when the insurance is being acquired, it is likely that the number of possible coverage problems and disputes that may subsequently arise will be reduced.

WESTLAW REFERENCES

§ 9.1   The Liability Insurer's Right and Duty to Defend

  (b) The Nature and Scope of the Duty to Defend

    (1) Complaints Against an Insured with Allegations that Include Some Claims Within the Coverage

> liability /3 insur**** /p conflict! /3 interest /p tort tortious!
>
> sy,di(liability /3 insur**** /s control! /5 litigat! lawsuit suit defense)

    (2) Complaints with Allegations of Claims That Are All Beyond the Insurance Coverage

> liability /3 insur**** /s cooperat! /s investigat!
>
> liability /3 insure* insuring insurance /s defend*** defense /p reasonabl! /3 expect! /p cover***

    (3) Ambiguous Allegations in the Pleadings by the Third Party

> sy,di(liability /3 insur**** /p bod*** /p employee +3 insured)

    (5) Appeals as a Defense Obligation

> kaste /s hartford
>
> liability /3 insur**** /s defense defend*** /s duty oblig! /s exhaust!

  (c) Preparing for the Defense of an Insured

> duty oblig! /s prepar! /s defense defend*** /s insured assured policy-holder

    Comment

> settl! investigat! /s pruden! /s insured assured policy-holder /s duty oblig!

  (d) Multiple Liability Coverages and the Obligation to Defend

    Allocation of Defense Costs

> liability /3 insur**** /s defense defend*** /s cost expense /s excess primary /2 carrier insur****

    Multiple Defense Counsel

> liability /3 insur**** /s defend*** defense /s separate independen! multiple /s counsel lawyer attorney

    Excess Coverage

> liability /3 insur**** /s excess /s primary /s defend*** defense /s duty obligat!
>
> liability /3 insur**** /s defense defend*** /s duty obligat! /s contribut! subrog!

§ 9.2   Settlement Negotiations

  (b) The Liability Insurer's Right and Duty to Initiate Settlement Negotiations

> duty oblig*** obligat! /s settl! negotiat! /s initiat! /s insur****

  (c) Methods of Facilitating Settlements

    (1) Medicated Settlements

      Initiation of a mediation

> agree! /s mediat!

      Generation and Evaluation of Possible Approaches for a Settlement

> settl! /p mediat!

(2) Mini-Trials

Characteristics of a Mini-Trial

mini-trial

Appendices

Contents

I. PROPERTY INSURANCE

II. LIFE, HEALTH, AND DISABILITY INSURANCE

III. COMBINATION (PACKAGE) INSURANCE COVERAGES

IV. LIABILITY INSURANCE

V. INSURANCE REGULATORY MEASURES

Excerpts from New York Consolidated Law Service: Insurance Law (1985)

VI. CONDITIONAL SUMMARY TRIAL

VII. WESTLAW REFERENCES

Part I

PROPERTY INSURANCE

APPENDIX A

INSURANCE SERVICES OFFICE, BUILDING AND PERSONAL PROPERTY COVERAGE FORM (1983)

COMMERCIAL PROPERTY

BUILDING AND PERSONAL PROPERTY COVERAGE FORM

Various provisions in this policy restrict coverage. Read the entire policy carefully to determine rights, duties and what is and is not covered.

Throughout this policy the words "you" and "your" refer to the Named Insured shown in the Declarations. The words "we", "us" and "our" refer to the Company providing this insurance.

Other words and phrases that appear in quotation marks have special meaning. Refer to SECTION H—DEFINITION.

A. COVERAGE

We will pay for direct physical loss of or damage to Covered Property at the premises described in the Declarations caused by or resulting from any Covered Cause of Loss.

1. Covered Property

Covered Property, as used in this Coverage Part, means the following types of property for which a Limit of Insurance is shown in the Declarations:

a. Building, meaning the building or structure described in the Declarations, including:

(1) Completed additions;

(2) Permanently installed fixtures, machinery and equipment;

(3) Outdoor fixtures;

(4) Personal property owned by you that is used to maintain or service the building or structure or its premises, including:

(a) Fire extinguishing equipment;

(b) Outdoor furniture;

(c) Floor coverings; and

(d) Appliances used for refrigerating, ventilating, cooking, dishwashing or laundering;

(5) If not covered by other insurance:

(a) Additions under construction, alterations and repairs to the building or structure;

(b) Materials, equipment, supplies and temporary structures, on or within 100 feet of the described premises, used for making additions, alterations or repairs to the building or structure.

b. Your Business Personal Property located in or on the building described in the Declarations or in the open (or in a vehicle) within 100 feet of the described premises, consisting of the following unless otherwise specified in the Declarations or on the Your Business Personal Property—Separation of Coverage form:

(1) Furniture and fixtures;

(2) Machinery and equipment;

(3) "Stock";

(4) All other personal property owned by you and used in your business;

(5) Labor, materials or services furnished or arranged by you on personal property of others; and

(6) Your use interest as tenant in improvements and betterments. Improvements and betterments are fixtures, alterations, installations or additions:

(a) Made a part of the building or structure you occupy but do not own; and

(b) You acquired or made at your expense but cannot legally remove.

c. Personal Property of Others that is:

(1) In your care, custody or control; and

(2) Located in or on the building described in the Declarations or in the open (or in a vehicle) within 100 feet of the described premises.

However, our payment for loss of or damage to personal property of others will only be for the account of the owner of the property.

2. **Property Not Covered**

Covered Property does not include:

a. Accounts, bills, currency, deeds, evidences of debt, money, notes or securities;

b. Animals, unless owned by others and boarded by you, or if owned by you, only as "stock" while inside of buildings;

c. Automobiles held for sale;

d. Bridges, roadways, walks, patios or other paved surfaces;

e. Contraband, or property in the course of illegal transportation or trade;

f. The cost of excavations, grading, backfilling or filling;

g. Foundations of buildings, structures, machinery or boilers if their foundations are below:

(1) The lowest basement floor; or

(2) The surface of the ground, if there is no basement;

h. Land (including land on which the property is located), growing crops or lawns;

i. Personal property while airborne or waterborne;

j. Pilings, piers, wharves or docks;

k. Property that is covered under another coverage form of this or any other policy in which it is more specifically described, except for the excess of the amount due (whether you can collect on it or not) from that other insurance;

l. Retaining walls that are not part of the building described in the Declarations;

m. Underground pipes, flues or drains;

n. The cost to research, replace or restore the information on valuable papers and records, including those which exist on electronic or magnetic media, except as provided in the Coverage Extensions;

o. Vehicles or self-propelled machines (including aircraft or watercraft) that:

(1) Are licensed for use on public roads;

(2) Are operated principally away from the described premises; or

(3) You do not manufacture, process, warehouse or hold for sale. But this paragraph does not apply to rowboats or canoes out of the water at the described premises;

p. The following property while outside of buildings:

(1) Grain, hay, straw or other crops;

(2) Fences, radio or television antennas, including their lead-in wiring, masts or towers, signs (other than signs attached to buildings), trees, shrubs or plants, all except as provided in the Coverage Extensions.

3. **Covered Causes Of Loss**

See applicable Causes of Loss Form as shown in the Declarations.

4. **Additional Coverages**

a. **Debris Removal**

We will pay your expense to remove debris of Covered Property caused by or resulting from a Covered Cause of Loss.

b. **Preservation of Property**

If it is necessary to move Covered Property from the described premises to preserve it from loss or damage by a Covered Cause of Loss, we will pay for any direct physical loss or damage to that property:

(1) While it is being moved or while temporarily stored at another location; and

(2) Only if the loss or damage occurs within 10 days after the property is first moved.

c. **Fire Department Service Charge**

When the fire department is called to save or protect Covered Property from a Covered Cause of Loss, we will pay up to $1,000 for your liability for fire department service charges:

(1) Assumed by contract or agreement prior to loss; or

(2) Required by local ordinance.

No Deductible applies to this Additional Coverage.

5. **Coverage Extensions**

If a Coinsurance percentage of 80% or more is shown in the Declarations, you may extend the insurance provided by this Coverage Part as follows:

a. **Newly Acquired or Constructed Property**

(1) You may extend the insurance that applies to Building to apply to:

(a) Your new buildings while being built on the described premises; and

(b) Buildings you acquire at locations, other than the described premises, intended for:

(i) Similar use as the building described in the Declarations; or

(ii) Use as a warehouse.

The most we will pay for loss or damage under this Extension is 25% of the Limit of Insurance for Building shown in the Declarations, but not more than $250,000 at each building.

(2) You may extend the insurance that applies to Your Business Personal Property to apply to that property at any location you acquire other than at fairs or exhibitions.

The most we will pay for loss or damage under this Extension is 10% of the Limit of Insurance for Your Business Personal Property shown in the Declarations, but not more than $100,000 at each building.

(3) Insurance under this Extension for each newly acquired or constructed property will end when any of the following first occurs:

(a) This policy expires.

(b) 30 days expire after you acquire or begin to construct the property; or

(c) You report values to us.

We will charge you additional premium for values reported from the date construction begins or you acquire the property.

b. Personal Effects and Property of Others.

You may extend the insurance that applies to Your Business Personal Property to apply to:

(1) Personal effects owned by you, your officers, your partners or your employees. This extension does not apply to loss or damage by theft.

(2) Personal property of others in your care, custody or control.

The most we will pay for loss or damage under this Extension is $2,500 at each described premises. Our payment for loss of or damage to personal property of others will only be for the account of the owner of the property.

c. Valuable Papers and Records—Cost of Research.

You may extend the insurance that applies to Your Business Personal Property to apply to your costs to research, replace or restore the lost information on lost or damaged valuable papers and records, including those which exist on electronic or magnetic media, for which duplicates do not exist. The most we will pay under this Extension is $1,000 at each described premises.

d. Property Off-Premises

Yu may extend the insurance provided by this Coverage Form to apply to your Covered Property, other than "stock", that is temporarily at a location you do not own, lease or operate. This Extension applies only if loss or damage is caused by a Covered Cause of Loss. This Extension does not apply to Covered Property:

(1) In or on a vehicle;

(2) In the care, custody or control of your salespersons; or

(3) At any fair or exhibition.

The most we will pay for loss or damage under this Extension is $5,000.

e. Outdoor Property

You may extend the insurance provided by this Coverage Form to apply to your outdoor fences, radio and television antennas, signs (other than signs attached to buildings), trees, shrubs and plants, including debris removal expense, caused by or resulting from any of the following causes of loss if they are Covered Causes of Loss:

(1) Fire;

(2) Lightning;

(3) Explosion;

(4) Riot or Civil Commotion; or

(5) Aircraft.

The most we will pay for loss or damage under this Extension is $1,000, but not more than $250 for any one tree, shrub or plant.

Each of these Extensions is additional insurance. The Additional Condition, Coinsurance, does not apply to these Extensions.

B. EXCLUSIONS

See applicable Causes of Loss Form as shown in the Declarations.

C. LIMITS OF INSURANCE

The most we will pay for loss or damage in any one occurrence is the applicable Limit of Insurance shown in the Declarations.

The most we will pay for loss or damage to outdoor signs attached to buildings is $1,000 per sign in any one occurrence.

The limits applicable to the Coverage Extensions and the Fire Department Service Charge Additional Coverage are in addition to the Limits of Insurance.

Payments under the following Additional Coverages will not increase the applicable Limit of Insurance:

1. Preservation of Property; or
2. Debris Removal; but if the sum of loss or damage and debris removal expense exceeds the Limit of Insurance, we will pay up to an additional $5,000 for each location in any one occurrence under the Debris Removal Additional Coverage.

D. DEDUCTIBLE

We will not pay for loss or damage in any one occurrence until the amount of loss or damage exceeds the Deductible shown in the Declarations. We will then pay the amount of loss or damage in excess of the Deductible, up to the applicable Limit of Insurance.

E. LOSS CONDITIONS

The following conditions apply in addition to the Common Policy Conditions and the Commercial Property Conditions.

1. Abandonment

There can be no abandonment of any property to us.

2. Appraisal

If we and you disagree on the value of the property or the amount of loss, either may make written demand for an appraisal of the loss. In this event, each party will select a competent and impartial appraiser. The two appraisers will select an umpire. If they cannot agree, either may request that selection be made by a judge of a court having jurisdiction. The appraisers will state separately the value of the property and amount of loss. If they fail to agree, they will submit their differences to the umpire. A decision agreed to by any two will be binding. Each party will:

a. Pay its chosen appraiser; and
b. Bear the other expenses of the appraisal and umpire equally.

If we submit to an appraisal, we will still retain our right to deny the claim.

3. Duties In The Event Of Loss Or Damage

You must see that the following are done in the event of loss or damage to Covered Property:

a. Notify the police if a law may have been broken.
b. Give us prompt notice of the loss or damage. Include a description of the property involved.
c. As soon as possible, give us a description of how, when and where the loss or damage occurred.
d. Take all reasonable steps to protect the Covered Property from further damage. If feasible, set the damaged property aside and in the best possible order for examination. Also keep a record of your expenses, for consideration in the settlement of the claim.
e. At our request, give us complete inventories of the damaged and undamaged property. Include quantities, costs, values and amount of loss claimed.
f. Permit us to inspect the property and records proving the loss or damage.
g. If requested, permit us to question you under oath at such times as may be reasonably required about any matter relating to this insurance or your claim, including your books and records. In such event, your answers must be signed.
h. Send us a signed, sworn statement of loss containing the information we request to settle the claim. You must do this within 60 days after our request. We will supply you with the necessary forms.
I. Cooperate with us in the investigation or settlement of the claim.

4. Loss Payment

a. In the event of loss or damage covered by this Coverage Form, we will either:

(1) Pay the value of lost or damaged property;
(2) Pay the cost of repairing or replacing the lost or damaged property, plus any reduction in value of repaired items;
(3) Take all or any part of the property at an agreed or appraised value; or
(4) Repair, rebuild or replace the property with other property of like kind and quality.

b. We will not pay you more than your financial interest in the Covered Property.

           CP 00 10 11 85

c. We will give notice of our intentions within 30 days after we receive the sworn statement of loss.

d. We may adjust losses with the owners of lost or damaged property if other than you. If we pay the owners, such payments will satisfy your claims against us for the owners' property. We will not pay the owners more than their financial interest in the Covered Property.

e. We may elect to defend you against suits arising from claims of owners of property. We will do this at our expense.

f. We will pay for covered loss or damage within 30 days after we receive the sworn statement of loss, if:

(1) You have complied with all of the terms of this Coverage Part; and

(2) (a) We have reached agreement with you on the amount of loss; or

(b) An appraisal award has been made.

5. Recovered Property

If either you or we recover any property after loss settlement, that party must give the other prompt notice. At your option, the property will be returned to you. You must then return to us the amount we paid to you for the property. We will pay recovery expenses and the expenses to repair the recovered property, subject to the Limit of Insurance.

6. Vacancy

If the building where loss or damage occurs has been vacant for more than 60 consecutive days before that loss or damage, we will:

a. Not pay for any loss or damage caused by any of the following even if they are Covered Causes of Loss:

(1) Vandalism;

(2) Sprinkler leakage, unless you have protected the system against freezing;

(3) Building glass breakage;

(4) Water damage;

(5) Theft; or

(6) Attempted theft.

b. Reduce the amount we would otherwise pay for the loss or damage by 15%.

Buildings under construction are not considered vacant.

7. Valuation

We will determine the value of Covered Property in the event of loss or damage as follows:

a. At actual cash value as of the time of loss or damage, except as provided in b., c., d., e. and f. below.

b. If the Limit of Insurance for Building satisfies the Additional Condition, Coinsurance, and the cost to repair or replace the damaged building property is $2,500 or less, we will pay the cost of building repairs or replacement.

This provision does not apply to the following even when attached to the building:

(1) Awnings or floor coverings;

(2) Appliances for refrigerating, ventilating, cooking, dishwashing or laundering; or

(3) Outdoor equipment or furniture.

c. "Stock" you have sold but not delivered at the selling price less discounts and expenses you otherwise would have had.

d. Glass at the cost of replacement with safety glazing material if required by law.

e. Tenant's Improvements and Betterments at:

(1) Actual cash value of the lost or damaged property if you make repairs promptly.

(2) A proportion of your original cost if you do not make repairs promptly. We will determine the proportionate value as follows:

(a) Multiply the original cost by the number of days from the loss or damage to the expiration of the lease; and

(b) Divide the amount determined in (a) above by the number of days from the installation of improvements to the expiration of the lease.

If your lease contains a renewal option, the expiration of the renewal option period will replace the expiration of the lease in this procedure.

(3) Nothing if others pay for repairs or replacement.

f. Valuable Papers and Records, including those which exist on electronic or magnetic media (other than prepackaged software programs), at the cost of:

   (1) Blank materials for reproducing the records; and

   (2) Labor to transcribe or copy the records when there is a duplicate.

F. ADDITIONAL CONDITIONS

The following conditions apply in addition to the Common Policy Conditions and the Commercial Property Conditions.

1. Coinsurance

If a Coinsurance percentage is shown in the Declarations, the following condition applies.

   a. We will not pay the full amount of any loss if the value of Covered Property at the time of loss times the Coinsurance percentage shown for it in the Declarations is greater than the Limit of Insurance for the property.

Instead, we will determine the most we will pay using the following steps:

   (1) Multiply the value of Covered Property at the time of loss by the Coinsurance percentage;

   (2) Divide the Limit of Insurance of the property by the figure determined in step (1);

   (3) Multiply the total amount of the covered loss, before the application of any deductible, by the figure determined in step (2); and

   (4) Subtract the deductible from the figure determined in step (3).

The amount determined in step (4) is the most we will pay. For the remainder, you will either have to rely on other insurance or absorb the loss yourself.

Example No. 1 (Underinsurance):

When: The value of the property is $250,000
   The Coinsurance percentage for it is 80%
   The Limit of Insurance for it is $100,000
   The Deductible is $250
   The amount of loss is $ 40,000

Step (1): $250,000 X 80% = $200,000 (the minimum amount of insurance to meet your Coinsurance requirements)

Step (2): $100,000 ÷ $200,000 = .50

Step (3): $ 40,000 X .50 = $20,000

Step (4): $20,000 − $250 = $19,750

We will pay no more than $19,750. The remaining $20,250 is not covered.

Example No. 2 (Adequate Insurance):

When: The value of the property is $250,000
   The Coinsurance percentage for it is 80%
   The Limit of Insurance for it is $200,000
   The Deductible is $250
   The amount of loss is $ 40,000

Step (1): $250,000 X 80% = $200,000 (the minimum amount of insurance to meet your Coinsurance requirements)

Step (2): $200,000 ÷ $200,000 =1.00

Step (3): $ 40,000 X 1.00 =$40,000

Step (4): $40,000 − $250 = $39,750

We will cover the $39,750 loss in excess of the Deductible. No penalty applies.

   b. If one Limit of Insurance applies to two or more separate items, this condition will apply to the total of all property to which the limit applies.

Example No. 3:

When: The value of the property is:
   Bldg. at Location No. 1 $ 75,000
   Bldg. at Location No. 2   100,000
   Personal Property at Location No. 2   75,000
   $250,000

   The Coinsurance percentage for it is 90%
   The Limit of Insurance for Buildings and Personal Property at Location Nos. 1 and 2 is $180,000
   The Deductible is $1,000
   The amount of loss is
   Bldg. at Location No. 2 $30,000
   Personal Property at Location No. 2   20,000
   $50,000

Step (1): $250,000 X 90% = $225,000 (the minimum amount of insurance to meet your Coinsurance requirements and to avoid the penalty shown below)

Step (2): $180,000 ÷ $225,000 = .80

Step (3): $ 50,000 X .80 = $40,000.

Step (4): $40,000 − $1,000 = $39,000.

We will pay no more than $39,000. The remaining $11,000 is not covered.

2. Mortgage Holders

a. The term "mortgage holder" includes trustee.

b. We will pay for covered loss of or damage to buildings or structures to each mortgage holder shown in the Declarations in their order of precedence, as interests may appear.

c. The mortgage holder has the right to receive loss payment even if the mortgage holder has started foreclosure or similar action on the building or structure.

d. If we deny your claim because of your acts or because you have failed to comply with the terms of this Coverage Part, the mortgage holder will still have the right to receive loss payment if the mortgage holder:

(1) Pays any premium due under this Coverage Part at our request if you have failed to do so;

(2) Submits a signed, sworn proof of loss within 60 days after receiving notice from us of your failure to do so; and

(3) Has notified us of any change in ownership, occupancy or substantial change in risk known to the mortgage holder.

All of the terms of this Coverage Part will then apply directly to the mortgage holder.

e. If we pay the mortgage holder for any loss or damage and deny payment to you because of your acts or because you have failed to comply with the terms of this Coverage Part:

(1) The mortgage holder's rights under the mortgage will be transferred to us to the extent of the amount we pay; and

(2) The mortgage holder's right to recover the full amount of the mortgage holder's claim will not be impaired.

At our option, we may pay to the mortgage holder the whole principal on the mortgage plus any accrued interest. In this event, your mortgage and note will be transferred to us and you will pay your remaining mortgage debt to us.

f. If we cancel this policy, we will give written notice to the mortgage holder at least:

(1) 10 days before the effective date of cancellation if we cancel for your non-payment of premium; or

(2) 30 days before the effective date of cancellation if we cancel for any other reason.

g. If we do not renew this policy, we will give written notice to the mortgage holder at least 10 days before the expiration date of this policy.

G. OPTIONAL COVERAGES

If shown in the Declarations, the following Optional Coverages apply separately to each item.

1. Agreed Value

a. The Additional Condition, Coinsurance, does not apply to Covered Property to which this Optional Coverage applies. We will pay no more for loss of or damage to that property than the proportion that the Limit of Insurance under this Coverage Part for the property bears to the Agreed Value shown for it in the Declarations.

b. If the expiration date for this Optional Coverage shown in the Declarations is not extended, the Additional Condition, Coinsurance, is reinstated and this Optional Coverage expires.

c. The terms of this Optional Coverage apply only to loss or damage that occurs:

(1) On or after the effective date of this Optional Coverage; and

(2) Before the Agreed Value expiration date shown in the Declarations or the policy expiration date, whichever occurs first.

2. Inflation Guard

a. The Limit of Insurance for property to which this Optional Coverage applies will automatically increase by the annual percentage shown in the Declarations.

b. The amount of increase will be:

(1) The most recent Limit of Insurance exclusive of this optional coverage, multiplied by

(2) The percentage of annual increase shown in the Declarations applied pro rata during each year.

3. Replacement Cost

a. Replacement Cost (without deduction for depreciation) replaces Actual Cash Value in the Loss Condition, Valuation, of this Coverage Form.

b. This Optional Coverage does not apply to:

(1) Property of others;

(2) Contents of a residence;

(3) Manuscripts;

(4) Works of art, antiques or rare articles, including etchings, pictures, statuary, marbles, bronzes, porcelains and bric-a-brac; or

(5) "Stock", unless the Including "Stock" option is shown in the Declarations.

c. You may make a claim for loss or damage covered by this insurance on an actual cash value basis instead of on a replacement cost basis. In the event you elect to have loss or damage settled on an actual cash value basis, you may still make a claim for the additional coverage this Optional Coverage provides if you notify us of your intent to do so within 180 days after the loss or damage.

d. We will not pay on a replacement cost basis for any loss or damage:

(1) Until the lost or damaged property is actually repaired or replaced; and

(2) Unless the repairs or replacement are made as soon as reasonably possible after the loss or damage.

e. We will not pay more for loss or damage on a replacement cost basis than the least of:

(1) The Limit of Insurance applicable to the lost or damaged property;

(2) The cost to replace, on the same premises, the lost or damaged property with other property:

(a) Of comparable material and quality; and

(b) Used for the same purpose; or

(3) The amount you actually spend that is necessary to repair or replace the lost or damaged property.

H. DEFINITIONS

"Stock" means merchandise held in storage or for sale, raw materials and in-process or finished goods, including supplies used in their packing or shipping.

APPENDIX B

INSURANCE SERVICES OFFICE, PERSONAL INLAND MARINE MANUAL PERSONAL PROPERTY FLOATER (1984)

PERSONAL INLAND MARINE MANUAL
PERSONAL PROPERTY FLOATER
FORMS AND ENDORSEMENTS

PERSONAL PROPERTY FLOATER

"**Your residence**" means the residence stated in the Declarations or in the policy

AMOUNTS OF INSURANCE—UNSCHEDULED PROPERTY AT YOUR RESIDENCE

The amount of insurance for each numbered class is the total amount of insurance for each loss for all property in that numbered class.

Classes of Property	Amount of Insurance
(1) Silverware, goldware and pewterware (including in each case flatware and holloware)	
(2) Clothing (yours, your spouse's and other members of your family living with you)	
(3) Rugs (including all floor coverings) and draperies	
(4) Musical instruments (including pianos and organs); electronic equipment and accessories (including television sets, radios, records and tape players and recorders, records and tapes)	
(5) Paintings, etchings, pictures, sculptures, tapestries and other objects of art	
(6) China and glassware (including bric-a-brac)	
(7) Cameras and photographic equipment and supplies	
(8) Guns; golf, hunting, fishing, bowling and other sports equipment and supplies	
(9) Major appliances such as refrigerators, washing machines, dryers, ranges, mixers and trash compactors	
(10) Bedding (including blankets, comforters, covers, pillows, mattresses and springs); linens (including dining room and bedroom)	
(11) Furniture such as chairs, tables, sofas, desks, beds, chests, lamps, mirrors and clocks	
(12)a. All other personal property (including books, wines, liquors, foodstuffs, garden, lawn and other tools and equipment, trunks, traveling bags, children's playthings, miscellaneous articles in basement and attic); and	
b. Professional books, instruments and equipment while actually in **your residence**.	
(13) Building additions and alterations	
Total Amount Of Insurance	$

PERSONAL INLAND MARINE MANUAL
PERSONAL PROPERTY FLOATER
FORMS AND ENDORSEMENTS

NEW ACQUIRED PROPERTY
All Classes

We cover newly acquired property of a class of property described above. The lesser of the following limits applies:

1. 10% of the Total Amount of Insurance; or
2. $2,500.

This amount may be applied to any of the numbered classes; it does not increase the Total Amount of Insurance.

PROPERTY LOCATED IN A NEWLY ACQUIRED PRINCIPAL RESIDENCE

We cover property in a newly acquired principal residence for the 30 days from the time you begin to move the property there.

This coverage is subject to the amounts of insurance shown for each numbered class.

OTHER PERSONAL PROPERTY

We cover the following unscheduled property. The limit for each numbered class shown below is the total limit for each loss for all property in that numbered class.

1. $100 on:

    a. money, numismatic property, bullion; and
    b. precious metals.

2. $500 on:

    a. securities, notes, accounts, bills, deeds, evidences of debt, letters of credit;
    b. stamps, philatelic property; and
    c. passports, documents, tickets or other papers of value.

3. $500 on:

    a. jewelry, watches, furs; and
    b. precious or semi-precious stones or gems.

PROPERTY COVERED
Personal Property

We cover unscheduled personal property owned or used by an insured normally kept at **your residence.** This property is also covered while temporarily away from **your residence** anywhere in the world.

At your request, we will cover unscheduled personal property of guests or servants while at **your residence.**

PROPERTY COVERED
Building Additions and Alterations

We cover building additions, alterations, fixtures, improvements or installations made or acquired at your expense, to that part of a residence you occupy as a tenant, or in a condominium unit you own.

PROPERTY NOT COVERED

We do not cover:

1. Animals, fish or birds.

2. Boats; aircraft; trailers; campers.

3. Motor vehicles, including motorcycles and motorized bicycles, designed for transportation or recreational use.

4. The equipment, accessories and furnishings of the vehicles in 2. and 3. above are not covered unless they are removed from the vehicle and are at **your residence.**

    We do cover invalid chairs and similar conveyances.

5. Owned property pertaining to a business, profession or occupation. We do cover your professional books, instruments and equipment while they are at **your residence.**

6. Property normally kept elsewhere than at **your residence** throughout the year.

**PERSONAL INLAND MARINE MANUAL
PERSONAL PROPERTY FLOATER
FORMS AND ENDORSEMENTS**

PERILS INSURED AGAINST

We insure against risks of direct physical loss to covered property except loss caused by:

1. Animals owned or kept by an insured.

2. Insects or vermin.

3. a. Marring and scratching of property; or
   b. Breakage of:

      (1) eyeglasses;
      (2) glassware; marbles; bric-a-brac;
      (3) statues; porcelain and similar fragile articles,

   unless caused by:

   a. fire; lightning; windstorm; earthquake;
   b. explosion; collapse of the building; accident to conveyances; or
   c. rioters; strikers; theft; attempted theft; vandalism; or malicious mischief.

4. Mechanical or structural breakdown or failure or damage to electrical apparatus caused by artificial electricity.

   Loss caused by fire is covered.

5. Wear and tear, deterioration or inherent vice.

6. Dampness or extreme changes of temperature.

   Loss caused by rain, snow, sleet, hail or bursting of pipes or apparatus is covered.

7. Any work on covered property other than jewelry, watches and furs.

8. Acts or decisions, including the failure to act or decide, of any person, group, organization or governmental body. However, any ensuing loss not excluded is covered.

GENERAL EXCLUSIONS

The following exclusion is added under GENERAL EXCLUSIONS of the policy:

3. Water Damage, meaning:

   a. flood, surface water, waves, tidal water, overflow of a body of water, or spray from any of these, whether or not driven by wind;
   b. water which backs up through sewers or drains;
   c. water below the surface of the ground. This includes water which exerts pressure on, or seeps or leaks through a building, sidewalk, driveway, foundation, swimming pool or other structures.

   This exclusion also applies if weather conditions contribute in any way with water damage to produce the loss.

   Loss caused by fire, explosion or theft resulting from water damage described above is covered.

ADDITIONAL COVERAGE

We cover the real property at your residence for an amount up to $2,500 for loss caused by:

1. Theft or attempted theft; and
2. Vandalism or malicious mischief to the inside of your residence.

DEDUCTIBLE

$100 will be deducted from the amount of each loss.

OTHER INSURANCE

The Other Insurance Condition in the policy is deleted and replaced by the following:

This insurance will be void if other insurance applies to the classes of unscheduled property described in the Declarations unless endorsed on this policy.

First Reprint

IPF-FORMS-3
Copyright, Insurance Services Office, Inc., 1977, 1984

Edition April, 1984
[E2277]

APPENDIX C

MARINE INSURANCE

(1) Excerpts From British Marine Insurance Act of 1906

6 Edw. 7, c. 41

MARINE INSURANCE.

1. A contract of marine insurance is a contract whereby the insurer undertakes to indemnify the assured, in manner and to the extent thereby agreed, against marine losses, that is to say, the losses incident to marine adventure.   *   *   *

INSURABLE INTEREST.

4.—(1) Every contract of marine insurance by way of gaming or wagering is void.

(2) A contract of marine insurance is deemed to be a gaming or wagering contract—

(a) Where the assured has not an insurable interest as defined by this Act, and the contract is entered into with no expectation of acquiring such an interest; or

(b) Where the policy is made "interest or no interest," or "without further proof of interest than the policy itself," or "without benefit of salvage to the insurer," or subject to any other like term:

Provided that, where there is no possibility of salvage, a policy may be effected without benefit of salvage to the insurer.

5.—(1) Subject to the provisions of this Act, every person has an insurable interest who is interested in a marine adventure.

(2) In particular a person is interested in a marine adventure where he stands in any legal or equitable relation to the adventure or to any insurable property at risk therein, in consequence of which he may benefit by the safety or due arrival of insurable property, or may be prejudiced by its loss, or by damage thereto, or by the detention thereof, or may incur liability in respect thereof.

6.—(1) The assured must be interested in the subject-matter insured at the time of the loss though he need not be interested when the insurance is effected:

Provided that where the subject-matter is insured "lost or not lost," the assured may recover although he may not have acquired his interest until after the loss, unless at the time of effecting the contract of insurance the assured was aware of the loss, and the insurer was not.

(2) Where the assured has no interest at the time of the loss, he cannot acquire interest by any act or election after he is aware of the loss.

7.—(1) A defeasible interest is insurable, as also is a contingent interest.

(2) In particular, where the buyer of goods has insured them, he has an insurable interest, notwithstanding that he might, at his election, have rejected the goods, or have treated them as at the seller's risk, by reason of the latter's delay in making delivery or otherwise.

8. A partial interest of any nature is insurable.

9.—(1) The insurer under a contract of marine insurance has an insurable interest in his risk, and may re-insure in respect of it.

(2) Unless the policy otherwise provides, the original assured has no right or interest in respect of such re-insurance.

10. The lender of money on bottomry or respondentia has an insurable interest in respect of the loan.

11. The master or any member of the crew of a ship has an insurable interest in respect of his wages.

12. In the case of advance freight, the person advancing the freight has an insurable interest, in so far as such freight is not repayable in case of loss.

13. The assured has an insurable interest in the charges of any insurance which he may effect.

14.—(1) Where the subject-matter insured is mortgaged, the mortgagor has an insurable interest in the full value thereof, and the mortgagee has an insurable interest in respect of any sum due or to become due under the mortgage.

(2) A mortgagee, consignee, or other person having an interest in the subject-matter insured may insure on behalf and for the benefit of other persons interested as well as for his own benefit.

(3) The owner of insurable property has an insurable interest in respect of the full value thereof, notwithstanding that some third person may have agreed, or be liable, to indemnify him in case of loss.

15. Where the assured assigns or otherwise parts with his interest in the subject-matter insured, he does not thereby transfer to the assignee his rights under the contract of insurance, unless there be an express or implied agreement with the assignee to that effect.

But the provisions of this section do not affect a transmission of interest by operation of law.

INSURABLE VALUE.

16. Subject to any express provision or valuation in the policy, the insurable value of the subject-matter insured must be ascertained as follows:—

(1) In insurance on ship, the insurable value is the value, at the commencement of the risk, of the ship, including her outfit, provisions and stores for the officers and crew, money advanced for seamen's wages, and other disbursements (if any) incurred to make the ship fit for the voyage or adventure contemplated by the policy, plus the charges of insurance upon the whole:

   The insurable value, in the case of a steamship, includes also the machinery, boilers, and coals and engine stores if owned by the assured, and, in the case of a ship engaged in a special trade, the ordinary fittings requisite for that trade:

(2) In insurance on freight, whether paid in advance or otherwise, the insurable value is the gross amount of the freight at the risk of the assured, plus the charges of insurance:

(3) In insurance on goods or merchandise, the insurable value is the prime cost of the property insured, plus the expenses of and incidental to shipping and the charges of insurance upon the whole:

(4) In insurance on any other subject-matter, the insurable value is the amount at the risk of the assured when the policy attaches, plus the charges of insurance.

DISCLOSURE AND REPRESENTATIONS.

17.   A contract of marine insurance is a contract based upon the utmost good faith, and, if the utmost good faith be not observed by either party, the contract may be avoided by the other party.

18.—(1) Subject to the provisions of this section, the assured must disclose to the insurer, before the contract is concluded, every material circumstance which is known to the assured, and the assured is deemed to know every circumstance which, in the ordinary course of business, ought to be known by him. If the assured fails to make such disclosure, the insurer may avoid the contract.

(2) Every circumstance is material which would influence the judgment of a prudent insurer in fixing the premium, or determining whether he will take the risk.

(3) In the absence of inquiry the following circumstances need not be disclosed, namely:—

(*a*) Any circumstance which diminishes the risk;

(*b*) Any circumstance which is known or presumed to be known to the insurer. The insurer is presumed to know matters of common notoriety or knowledge, and matters which an insurer in the ordinary course of his business, as such, ought to know;

(*c*) Any circumstance as to which information is waived by the insurer;

(*d*) Any circumstance which it is superfluous to disclose by reason of any express or implied warranty.

(4) Whether any particular circumstance, which is not disclosed, be material or not is, in each case, a question of fact.

(5) The term "circumstance" includes any communication made to, or information received by, the assured.

19.   Subject to the provisions of the preceding section as to circumstances which need not be disclosed, where an insurance is effected for the assured by an agent, the agent must disclose to the insurer—

(*a*) Every material circumstance which is known to himself, and an agent to insure is deemed to know every circumstance which in the ordinary course of business ought to be known by, or to have been communicated to, him; and

(*b*) Every material circumstance which the assured is bound to disclose, unless it come to his knowledge too late to communicate it to the agent.

20.—(1) Every material representation made by the assured or his agent to the insurer during the negotiations for the contract, and before the contract is concluded, must be true.   If it be untrue the insurer may avoid the contract.

(2) A representation is material which would influence the judgment of a prudent insurer in fixing the premium, or determining whether he will take the risk.

(3) A representation may be either a representation as to a matter of fact, or as to a matter of expectation or belief.

(4) A representation as to a matter of fact is true, if it be substantially correct, that is to say, if the difference between what is represented and what is actually correct would not be considered material by a prudent insurer.

(5) A representation as to a matter of expectation or belief is true if it be made in good faith.

(6) A representation may be withdrawn or corrected before the contract is concluded.

(7) Whether a particular representation be material or not is, in each case, a question of fact.

* * *

THE POLICY.

22.   Subject to the provisions of any statute, a contract of marine insurance is inadmissible in evidence unless it is embodied in a marine policy in accordance with this Act.   The policy may be executed and issued either at the time when the contract is concluded, or afterwards.

* * *

27.—(1) A policy may be either valued or unvalued.

(2) A valued policy is a policy which specifies the agreed value of the subject-matter insured.

(3) Subject to the provisions of this Act, and in the absence of fraud, the value fixed by the policy is, as between the insurer and assured, conclusive of the insurable value of the subject intended to be insured, whether the loss be total or partial.

(4) Unless the policy otherwise provides, the value fixed by the policy is not conclusive for the purpose of determining whether there has been a constructive total loss.

28.   An unvalued policy is a policy which does not specify the value of the subject-matter insured, but, subject to the limit of the sum insured, leaves the insurable value to be subsequently ascertained, in the manner herein-before specified.

*   *   *

30.—(1) A policy may be in the form in the First Schedule to this Act.

(2) Subject to the provisions of this Act, and unless the context of the policy otherwise requires, the terms and expressions mentioned in the First Schedule to this Act shall be construed as having the scope and meaning in that schedule assigned to them.

*   *   *

WARRANTIES

33.—(1) A warranty, in the following sections relating to warranties, means a promissory warranty, that is to say, a warranty by which the assured undertakes that some particular thing shall or shall not be done, or that some condition shall be fulfilled, or whereby he affirms or negatives the existence of a particular state of facts.

(2) A warranty may be express or implied.

(3) A warranty, as above defined, is a condition which must be exactly complied with, whether it be material to the risk or not. If it be not so complied with, then, subject to any express provision in the policy, the insurer is discharged from liability as from the date of the breach of warranty, but without prejudice to any liability incurred by him before that date.

34.—(1) Non-compliance with a warranty is excused when, by reason of a change of circumstances, the warranty ceases to be applicable to the circumstances of the contract, or when compliance with the warranty is rendered unlawful by any subsequent law.

(2) Where a warranty is broken, the assured cannot avail himself of the defence that the breach has been remedied, and the warranty complied with, before loss.

(3) A breach of warranty may be waived by the insurer.

35.—(1) An express warranty may be in any form of words from which the intention to warrant is to be inferred.

(2) An express warranty must be included in, or written upon, the policy, or must be contained in some document incorporated by reference into the policy.

(3) An express warranty does not exclude an implied warranty, unless it be inconsistent therewith.

* * *

39.—(1) In a voyage policy there is an implied warranty that at the commencement of the voyage the ship shall be seaworthy for the purpose of the particular adventure insured.

(2) Where the policy attaches while the ship is in port, there is also an implied warranty that she shall, at the commencement of the risk, be reasonably fit to encounter the ordinary perils of the port.

(3) Where the policy relates to a voyage which is performed in different stages, during which the ship requires different kinds of or further preparation or equipment, there is an implied warranty that at the commencement of each stage the ship is seaworthy in respect of such preparation or equipment for the purposes of that stage.

(4) A ship is deemed to be seaworthy when she is reasonably fit in all respects to encounter the ordinary perils of the seas of the adventure insured.

(5) In a time policy there is no implied warranty that the ship shall be seaworthy at any stage of the adventure, but where, with the privity of the assured, the ship is sent to sea in an unseaworthy state, the insurer is not liable for any loss attributable to unseaworthiness.

40.—(1) In a policy on goods or other moveables there is no implied warranty that the goods or moveables are seaworthy.

(2) In a voyage policy on goods or other moveables there is an implied warranty that at the commencement of the voyage the ship is not only seaworthy as a ship, but also that she is reasonably fit to carry the goods or other moveables to the destination contemplated by the policy.

41.   There is an implied warranty that the adventure insured is a lawful one, and that, so far as the assured can control the matter, the adventure shall be carried out in a lawful manner.

* * *

ASSIGNMENT OF POLICY.

50.—(1) A marine policy is assignable unless it contains terms expressly prohibiting assignment. It may be assigned either before or after loss.

(2) Where a marine policy has been assigned so as to pass the beneficial interest in such policy, the assignee of the policy is entitled to sue thereon in his own name; and the defendant is entitled to make any defence arising out of the contract which he would have been

entitled to make if the action had been brought in the name of the person by or on behalf of whom the policy was effected.

(3) A marine policy may be assigned by indorsement thereon or in other customary manner.

51.   Where the assured has parted with or lost his interest in the subject-matter insured, and has not, before or at the time of so doing, expressly or impliedly agreed to assign the policy, any subsequent assignment of the policy is inoperative:

Provided that nothing in this section affects the assignment of a policy after loss.

* * *

LOSS AND ABANDONMENT.

55.—(1) Subject to the provisions of this Act, and unless the policy otherwise provides, the insurer is liable for any loss proximately caused by a peril insured against, but, subject as aforesaid, he is not liable for any loss which is not proximately caused by a peril insured against.

(2) In particular,—

(*a*) The insurer is not liable for any loss attributable to the wilful misconduct of the assured, but, unless the policy otherwise provides, he is liable for any loss proximately caused by a peril insured against, even though the loss would not have happened but for the misconduct or negligence of the master or crew;

(*b*) Unless the policy otherwise provides, the insurer on ship or goods is not liable for any loss proximately caused by delay, although the delay be caused by a peril insured against;

(*c*) Unless the policy otherwise provides, the insurer is not liable for ordinary wear and tear, ordinary leakage and breakage, inherent vice or nature of the subject-matter insured, or for any loss proximately caused by rats or vermin, or for any injury to machinery not proximately caused by maritime perils.

56.—(1) A loss may be either total or partial. Any loss other than a total loss, as hereinafter defined, is a partial loss.

(2) A total loss may be either an actual total loss, or a constructive total loss.

(3) Unless a different intention appears from the terms of the policy, an insurance against total loss includes a constructive, as well as an actual, total loss.

(4) Where the assured brings an action for a total loss and the evidence proves only a partial loss, he may, unless the policy otherwise provides, recover for a partial loss.

(5) Where goods reach their destination in specie, but by reason of obliteration of marks, or otherwise, they are incapable of identification, the loss, if any, is partial, and not total.

57.—(1) Where the subject-matter insured is destroyed, or so damaged as to cease to be a thing of the kind insured, or where the assured is irretrievably deprived thereof, there is an actual total loss.

(2) In the case of an actual total loss no notice of abandonment need be given.

58.   Where the ship concerned in the adventure is missing, and after the lapse of a reasonable time no news of her has been received, an actual total loss may be presumed.

59.   Where, by a peril insured against, the voyage is interrupted at an intermediate port or place, under such circumstances as, apart from any special stipulation in the contract of affreightment, to justify the master in landing and re-shipping the goods or other moveables, or in transhipping them, and sending them on to their destination, the liability of the insurer continues, notwithstanding the landing or transhipment.

60.—(1) Subject to any express provision in the policy, there is a constructive total loss where the subject-matter insured is reasonably abandoned on account of its actual total loss appearing to be unavoidable, or because it could not be preserved from actual total loss without an expenditure which would exceed its value when the expenditure had been incurred.

(2) In particular, there is a constructive total loss—

> (i) Where the assured is deprived of the possession of his ship or goods by a peril insured against, and (*a*) it is unlikely that he can recover the ship or goods, as the case may be, or (*b*) the cost of recovering the ship or goods, as the case may be, would exceed their value when recovered; or

> (ii) In the case of damage to a ship, where she is so damaged by a peril insured against that the cost of repairing the damage would exceed the value of the ship when repaired.

> In estimating the cost of repairs, no deduction is to be made in respect of general average contributions to those repairs payable by other interests, but account is to be taken of the expense of future salvage operations and of any future general average contributions to which the ship would be liable if repaired; or

> (iii) In the case of damage to goods, where the cost of repairing the damage and forwarding the goods to their destination would exceed their value on arrival.

61.   Where there is a constructive total loss the assured may either treat the loss as a partial loss, or abandon the subject-matter insured to the insurer and treat the loss as if it were an actual total loss.

62.—(1) Subject to the provisions of this section, where the assured elects to abandon the subject-matter insured to the insurer, he must give notice of abandonment. If he fails to do so the loss can only be treated as a partial loss.

(2) Notice of abandonment may be given in writing, or by word of mouth, or partly in writing and partly by word of mouth, and may be given in any terms which indicate the intention of the assured to abandon his insured interest in the subject-matter insured unconditionally to the insurer.

(3) Notice of abandonment must be given with reasonable diligence after the receipt of reliable information of the loss, but where the information is of a doubtful character the assured is entitled to a reasonable time to make inquiry.

(4) Where notice of abandonment is properly given, the rights of the assured are not prejudiced by the fact that the insurer refuses to accept the abandonment.

(5) The acceptance of an abandonment may be either express or implied from the conduct of the insurer. The mere silence of the insurer after notice is not an acceptance.

(6) Where notice of abandonment is accepted the abandonment is irrevocable. The acceptance of the notice conclusively admits liability for the loss and the sufficiency of the notice.

(7) Notice of abandonment is unnecessary where, at the time when the assured receives information of the loss, there would be no possibility of benefit to the insurer if notice were given to him.

(8) Notice of abandonment may be waived by the insurer.

(9) Where an insurer has re-insured his risk, no notice of abandonment need be given by him.

63.—(1) Where there is a valid abandonment the insurer is entitled to take over the interest of the assured in whatever may remain of the subject-matter insured, and all proprietary rights incidental thereto.

(2) Upon the abandonment of a ship, the insurer thereof is entitled to any freight in course of being earned, and which is earned by her subsequent to the casualty causing the loss, less the expenses of earning it incured after the casualty; and, where the ship is carrying the owner's goods, the insurer is entitled to a reasonable remuneration for the carriage of them subsequent to the casualty causing the loss.

PARTIAL LOSSES (INCLUDING SALVAGE AND GENERAL AVERAGE AND PARTICULAR CHARGES.)

64.—(1) A particular average loss is a partial loss of the subject-matter insured, caused by a peril insured against, and which is not a general average loss.

(2) Expenses incurred by or on behalf of the assured for the safety or preservation of the subject-matter insured, other than general aver-

age and salvage charges, are called particular charges. Particular charges are not included in particular average.

65.—(1) Subject to any express provision in the policy, salvage charges incurred in preventing a loss by perils insured against may be recovered as a loss by those perils.

(2) "Salvage charges" means the charges recoverable under maritime law by a salvor independently of contract. They do not include the expenses of services in the nature of salvage rendered by the assured or his agents, or any person employed for hire by them, for the purpose of averting a peril insured against. Such expenses, where properly incurred, may be recovered as particular charges or as a general average loss, according to the circumstances under which they were incurred.

66.—(1) A general average loss is a loss caused by or directly consequential on a general average act. It includes a general average expenditure as well as a general average sacrifice.

(2) There is a general average act where any extraordinary sacrifice or expenditure is voluntarily and reasonably made or incurred in time of peril for the purpose of preserving the property imperilled in the common adventure.

(3) Where there is a general average loss, the party on whom it falls is entitled, subject to the conditions imposed by maritime law, to a rateable contribution from the other parties interested, and such contribution is called a general average contribution.

(4) Subject to any express provision in the policy, where the assured has incurred a general average expenditure, he may recover from the insurer in respect of the proportion of the loss which falls upon him; and, in the case of a general average sacrifice, he may recover from the insurer in respect of the whole loss without having enforced his right of contribution from the other parties liable to contribute.

(5) Subject to any express provision in the policy, where the assured has paid, or is liable to pay, a general average contribution in respect of the subject insured, he may recover therefor from the insurer.

(6) In the absence of express stipulation, the insurer is not liable for any general average loss or contribution where the loss was not incurred for the purpose of avoiding, or in connexion with the avoidance of, a peril insured against.

(7) Where ship, freight, and cargo, or any two of those interests, are owned by the same assured, the liability of the insurer in respect of general average losses or contributions is to be determined as if those subjects were owned by different persons.

* * *

(2) MARINE INSURANCE

POLICY FORM

SCHEDULES

FIRST SCHEDULE

FORM OF POLICY

BE IT KNOWN THAT _____ as well in _____ own name as for and in the name and names of all and every other person or persons to whom the same doth, may, or shall appertain, in part or in all doth make assurance and cause _____ and them, and every of them, to be insured lost or not lost, at and from _____. Upon any kind of goods and merchandises, and also upon the body, tackle, apparel, ordnance, munition, artillery, boat, and other furniture, of and in the good ship or vessel called the _____ whereof is master under God, for this present voyage, _____ or whosoever else shall go for master in the said ship, or by whatsoever other name or names the said ship, or the master thereof, is or shall be named or called; beginning the adventure upon the said goods and merchandises from the loading thereof aboard the said ship, _____ upon the said ship, & c. _____ and so shall continue and endure, during her abode there, upon the said ship, & c. And further, until the said ship, with all her ordnance, tackle, apparel, & c., and goods and merchandises whatsoever shall be arrived at _____ upon the said ship, & c., until she hath moored at anchor twenty-four hours in good safety; and upon the goods and merchandises, until the same be there discharged and safely landed. And it shall be lawful for the said ship, & c., in this voyage, to proceed and sail to and touch and stay at any ports or places whatsoever _____ without prejudice to this insurance. The said ship, & c., goods and merchandises, & c., for so much as concerns the assured by agreement between the assured and assurers in this policy, are and shall be valued at _____.

Touching the adventures and perils which we the assurers are contented to bear and do take upon us in this voyage: they are of the seas, men of war, fire, enemies, pirates, rovers, thieves, jettisons, letters of mart and countermart, surprisals, takings at sea, arrests, restraints, and detainments of all kings, princes, and people, of what nation, condition, or quality soever, barratry of the master and mariners, and of all other perils, losses, and misfortunes, that have or shall come to the hurt, detriment, or damage of the said goods and merchandises, and ship, & c., or any part thereof. And in case of any loss or misfortune it shall be lawful to the assured, their factors, servants and assigns, to sue, labour, and travel for, in and about the defence, safeguards, and recovery of the said goods and merchandises, and ship, & c., or any part thereof, without prejudice to this insurance; to the charges whereof we, the assurers, will contribute each one according to the rate and quantity of his sum herein assured. And it is especially declared and agreed that no acts of the insurer or insured in recovering, saving, or preserving the property insured shall be considered as a waiver, or acceptance of abandonment. And it is agreed by us, the insurers, that this writing or policy of assurance shall be of as much force and effect as the surest writing or policy of assurance heretofore made in Lombard Street, or in the Royal Exchange, or elsewhere in London. And so we, the assurers, are contented, and do hereby promise and bind ourselves, each one for his own part, our heirs, executors, and goods to the assured, their executors, administrators, and assigns, for the true performance of the premises, confessing ourselves paid the consideration due unto us for this assurance by the assured, at and after the rate of _____.

IN WITNESS whereof we, the assurers, have subscribed our names and sums assured in London.

N.B.—Corn, fish, salt, fruit, flour, and seed are warranted free from average, unless general, or the ship be stranded—sugar, tobacco, hemp, flax, hides and skins are warranted free from average, under five pounds per cent., and all other goods, also the ship and freight, are warranted free from average, under three pounds per cent. unless general, or the ship be stranded.

(3) LLOYD'S

MARINE POLICY

Lloyd's
Marine Policy

We, The Underwriters, hereby agree. in consideration of the payment to us by or on behalf of the Assured of the premium specified in the Schedule. to insure against loss damage liability or expense in the proportions and manner hereinafter provided. Each Underwriting Member of a Syndicate whose definitive number and proportion is set out in the following Table shall be liable only for his own share of his respective Syndicate's proportion.

In Witness whereof the General Manager of Lloyd's Policy Signing Office has subscribed his Name on behalf of each of Us.

LLOYD'S POLICY SIGNING OFFICE
General Manager

This insurance is subject to English jurisdiction.

[E2278]

MAR
LPO 62A (1 1 82) Printed by The Carlton Berry Co Ltd

1/1/82   (FOR USE ONLY WITH THE NEW MARINE POLICY FORM)

INSTITUTE CARGO CLAUSES (A)

RISKS COVERED

1   This insurance covers all risks of loss of or damage to the subject-matter insured except as provided in Clauses 4, 5, 6 and 7 below.   *Risks Clause*

2   This insurance covers general average and salvage charges, adjusted or determined according to the contract of affreightment and/or the governing law and practice, incurred to avoid or in connection with the avoidance of loss from any cause except those excluded in Clauses 4, 5, 6 and 7 or elsewhere in this insurance.   *General Average Clause*

3   This insurance is extended to indemnify the Assured against such proportion of liability under the contract of affreightment "Both to Blame Collision" Clause as is in respect of a loss recoverable hereunder. In the event of any claim by shipowners under the said Clause the Assured agree to notify the Underwriters who shall have the right, at their own cost and expense, to defend the Assured against such claim   *"Both to Blame Collision Clause*

EXCLUSIONS

4   In no case shall this insurance cover   *General Exclusions Clause*

    4.1   loss damage or expense attributable to wilful misconduct of the Assured

    4.2   ordinary leakage, ordinary loss in weight or volume, or ordinary wear and tear of the subject-matter insured

    4.3   loss damage or expense caused by insufficiency or unsuitability of packing or preparation of the subject-matter insured (for the purpose of this Clause 4.3 "packing" shall be deemed to include stowage in a container or liftvan but only when such stowage is carried out prior to attachment of this insurance or by the Assured or their servants)

    4.4   loss damage or expense caused by inherent vice or nature of the subject-matter insured

    4.5   loss damage or expense proximately caused by delay, even though the delay be caused by a risk insured against (except expenses payable under Clause 2 above)

    4.6   loss damage or expense arising from insolvency or financial default of the owners managers charterers or operators of the vessel

    4.7   loss damage or expense arising from the use of any weapon of war employing atomic or nuclear fission and/or fusion or other like reaction or radioactive force or matter

5   5.1   In no case shall this insurance cover loss damage or expense arising from   *Unseaworthiness and Unfitness Exclusion Clause*

       unseaworthiness of vessel or craft,

       unfitness of vessel craft conveyance container or liftvan for the safe carriage of the subject-matter insured,

       where the Assured or their servants are privy to such unseaworthiness or unfitness, at the time the subject-matter insured is loaded therein.

    5.2   The Underwriters waive any breach of the implied warranties of seaworthiness of the ship and fitness of the ship to carry the subject-matter insured to destination, unless the Assured or their servants are privy to such unseaworthiness or unfitness.

6   In no case shall this insurance cover loss damage or expense caused by   *War Exclusion Clause*

    6.1   war civil war revolution rebellion insurrection, or civil strife arising therefrom, or any hostile act by or against a belligerent power

    6.2   capture seizure arrest restraint or detainment (piracy excepted), and the consequences thereof or any attempt thereat

    6.3   derelict mines torpedoes bombs or other derelict weapons of war

7   In no case shall this insurance cover loss damage or expense   *Strikes Exclusion Clause*

    7.1   caused by strikers, locked-out workmen, or persons taking part in labour disturbances, riots or civil commotions

    7.2   resulting from strikes, lock-outs, labour disturbances, riots or civil commotions

    7.3   caused by any terrorist or any person acting from a political motive

DURATION

8   8.1   This insurance attaches from the time the goods leave the warehouse or place of storage at the place named herein for the commencement of the transit, continues during the ordinary course of transit and terminates either   *Transit Clause*

    8.1.1   on delivery to the Consignees' or other final warehouse or place of storage at the destination named herein,

    8.1.2   on delivery to any other warehouse or place of storage, whether prior to or at the destination named herein, which the Assured elect to use either

    8.1.2.1   for storage other than in the ordinary course of transit or

    8.1.2.2   for allocation or distribution,

         or

    8.1.3   on the expiry of 60 days after completion of discharge overside of the goods hereby insured from the oversea vessel at the final port of discharge.

      whichever shall first occur

    8.2   If, after discharge overside from the oversea vessel at the final port of discharge, but prior to termination of this insurance, the goods are to be forwarded to a destination other than that to which they are insured hereunder, this insurance, whilst remaining subject to termination as provided for above, shall not extend beyond the commencement of transit to such other destination.

    8.3   This insurance shall remain in force (subject to termination as provided for above and to the provisions of Clause 9 below) during delay beyond the control of the Assured, any deviation, forced discharge, reshipment or transhipment and during any variation of the adventure arising from the exercise of a liberty granted to shipowners or charterers under the contract of affreightment

8.2   If, after discharge overside from the oversea vessel at the final port of discharge, but prior to termination of this insurance, the goods are to be forwarded to a destination other than that to which they are insured hereunder, this insurance, whilst remaining subject to termination as provided for above, shall not extend beyond the commencement of transit to such other destination

8.3   This insurance shall remain in force (subject to termination as provided for above and to the provisions of Clause 9 below) during delay beyond the control of the Assured, any deviation, forced discharge, reshipment or transhipment and during any variation of the adventure arising from the exercise of a liberty granted to shipowners or charterers under the contract of affreightment.

9   If owing to circumstances beyond the control of the Assured either the contract of carriage is terminated at a port or place other than the destination named therein or the transit is otherwise terminated before delivery of the goods as provided for in Clause 8 above, then this insurance shall also terminate *unless prompt notice is given to the Underwriters and continuation of cover is requested when the insurance shall remain in force, subject to an additional premium if required by the Underwriters*, either   *Termination of Contract of Carriage Clause*

  9.1   until the goods are sold and delivered at such port or place, or, unless otherwise specially agreed, until the expiry of 60 days after arrival of the goods hereby insured at such port or place, whichever shall first occur,

    or

  9.2   if the goods are forwarded within the said period of 60 days (or any agreed extension thereof) to the destination named herein or to any other destination, until terminated in accordance with the provisions of Clause 8 above.

10   Where, after attachment of this insurance, the destination is changed by the Assured, *held covered at a premium and on conditions to be arranged subject to prompt notice being given to the Underwriters*   *Change of Voyage Clause*

CLAIMS

11   11.1   In order to recover under this insurance the Assured must have an insurable interest in the subject-matter insured at the time of the loss.   *Insurable Interest Clause*

  11.2   Subject to 11.1 above, the Assured shall be entitled to recover for insured loss occurring during the period covered by this insurance, notwithstanding that the loss occurred before the contract of insurance was concluded, unless the Assured were aware of the loss and the Underwriters were not.

12   Where, as a result of the operation of a risk covered by this insurance, the insured transit is terminated at a port or place other than that to which the subject-matter is covered under this insurance, the Underwriters will reimburse the Assured for any extra charges properly and reasonably incurred in unloading storing and forwarding the subject-matter to the destination to which it is insured hereunder.   *Forwarding Charges Clause*

This Clause 12, which does not apply to general average or salvage charges, shall be subject to the exclusions contained in Clauses 4, 5, 6 and 7 above, and shall not include charges arising from the fault negligence insolvency or financial default of the Assured or their servants.

13   No claim for Constructive Total Loss shall be recoverable hereunder unless the subject-matter insured is reasonably abandoned either on account of its actual total loss appearing to be unavoidable or because the cost of recovering, reconditioning and forwarding the subject-matter to the destination to which it is insured would exceed its value on arrival.   *Constructive Total Loss Clause*

14   14.1   If any Increased Value insurance is effected by the Assured on the cargo insured herein the agreed value of the cargo shall be deemed to be increased to the total amount insured under this insurance and all Increased Value insurances covering the loss, and liability under this insurance shall be in such proportion as the sum insured herein bears to such total amount insured.   *Increased Value Clause*

  In the event of claim the Assured shall provide the Underwriters with evidence of the amounts insured under all other insurances.

  14.2   **Where this insurance is on Increased Value the following clause shall apply:**
  The agreed value of the cargo shall be deemed to be equal to the total amount insured under the primary insurance and all Increased Value insurances covering the loss and effected on the cargo by the Assured, and liability under this insurance shall be in such proportion as the sum insured herein bears to such total amount insured.

  In the event of claim the Assured shall provide the Underwriters with evidence of the amounts insured under all other insurances.

BENEFIT OF INSURANCE

15   This insurance shall not inure to the benefit of the carrier or other bailee.   *Not to Inure Clause*

MINIMISING LOSSES

16   It is the duty of the Assured and their servants and agents in respect of loss recoverable hereunder   *Duty of Assured Clause*

  16.1   to take such measures as may be reasonable for the purpose of averting or minimising such loss, and

  16.2   to ensure that all rights against carriers, bailees or other third parties are properly preserved and exercised

  and the Underwriters will, in addition to any loss recoverable hereunder, reimburse the Assured for any charges properly and reasonably incurred in pursuance of these duties.

17   Measures taken by the Assured or the Underwriters with the object of saving, protecting or recovering the subject-matter insured shall not be considered as a waiver or acceptance of abandonment or otherwise prejudice the rights of either party   *Waiver Clause*

AVOIDANCE OF DELAY

18   It is a condition of this insurance that the Assured shall act with reasonable despatch in all circumstances within their control.   *Reasonable Despatch Clause*

LAW AND PRACTICE

19   This insurance is subject to English law and practice   *English Law and Practice Clause*

NOTE – It is necessary for the Assured when they become aware of an event which is "held covered" under this insurance to give prompt notice to the Underwriters and the right to such cover is dependent upon compliance with this obligation

---

1/1/82 (FOR USE ONLY WITH THE NEW MARINE POLICY FORM)

INSTITUTE WAR CLAUSES (CARGO)

RISKS COVERED

1   This insurance covers, except as provided in Clauses 3 and 4 below, loss of or damage to the subject-matter insured caused by   *Risks Clause*

     1.1   war civil war revolution rebellion insurrection, or civil strife arising therefrom, or any hostile act by or against a belligerent power

     1.2   capture seizure arrest restraint or detainment, arising from risks covered under 1.1 above, and the consequences thereof or any attempt thereat

     1.3   derelict mines torpedoes bombs or other derelict weapons of war.

2   This insurance covers general average and salvage charges, adjusted or determined according to the contract of affreightment and/or the governing law and practice, incurred to avoid or in connection with the avoidance of loss from a risk covered under these clauses.   *General Average Clause*

EXCLUSIONS

3   In no case shall this insurance cover   *General Exclusions Clause*

     3.1   loss damage or expense attributable to wilful misconduct of the Assured

     3.2   ordinary leakage, ordinary loss in weight or volume, or ordinary wear and tear of the subject-matter insured

     3.3   loss damage or expense caused by insufficiency or unsuitability of packing or preparation of the subject-matter insured (for the purpose of this Clause 3.3 "packing" shall be deemed to include stowage in a container or liftvan but only when such stowage is carried out prior to attachment of this insurance or by the Assured or their servants)

     3.4   loss damage or expense caused by inherent vice or nature of the subject-matter insured

     3.5   loss damage or expense proximately caused by delay, even though the delay be caused by a risk insured against (except expenses payable under Clause 2 above)

     3.6   loss damage or expense arising from insolvency or financial default of the owners managers charterers or operators of the vessel

     3.7   any claim based upon loss of or frustration of the voyage or adventure

     3.8   loss damage or expense arising from any hostile use of any weapon of war employing atomic or nuclear fission and/or fusion or other like reaction or radioactive force or matter.

4   4.1   In no case shall this insurance cover loss damage or expense arising from   *Unseaworthiness and Unfitness Exclusion Clause*

           unseaworthiness of vessel or craft,

           unfitness of vessel craft conveyance container or liftvan for the safe carriage of the subject-matter insured,

           where the Assured or their servants are privy to such unseaworthiness or unfitness, at the time the subject-matter insured is loaded therein.

     4.2   The Underwriters waive any breach of the implied warranties of seaworthiness of the ship and fitness of the ship to carry the subject-matter insured to destination, unless the Assured or their servants are privy to such unseaworthiness or unfitness.

DURATION

5   5.1   This insurance   *Transit Clause*

     5.1.1   attaches only as the subject-matter insured and as to any part as that part is loaded on an oversea vessel

           and

     5.1.2   terminates, subject to 5.2 and 5.3 below, either as the subject-matter insured and as to any part as that part is discharged from an oversea vessel at the final port or place of discharge,

           or

           on expiry of 15 days counting from midnight of the day of arrival of the vessel at the final port or place of discharge,

           whichever shall first occur;

           nevertheless,

           subject to prompt notice to the Underwriters and to an additional premium, such insurance

     5.1.3   reattaches when, without having discharged the subject-matter insured at the final port or place of discharge, the vessel sails therefrom,

           and

     5.1.4   terminates, subject to 5.2 and 5.3 below, either as the subject-matter insured and as to any part as that part is thereafter discharged from the vessel at the final (or substituted) port or place of discharge,

           or

           on expiry of 15 days counting from midnight of the day of re-arrival of the vessel at the final port or place of discharge or arrival of the vessel at a substituted port or place of discharge,

           whichever shall first occur.

     5.2   If during the insured voyage the oversea vessel arrives at an intermediate port or place to discharge the subject-matter insured for on-carriage by oversea vessel or by aircraft, or the goods are discharged from the vessel at a port or place of refuge, then, subject to 5.3 below and to an additional premium if required, this insurance continues until the expiry of 15 days counting from midnight of the day of arrival of the vessel at such port or place, but thereafter reattaches as the subject-matter insured and as to any part as that part is loaded on an on-carrying oversea vessel or aircraft. During the period of 15 days the insurance remains in force after discharge only whilst the subject-matter insured and as to any part as that part is at such port or place. If the goods are on-carried within the said period of 15 days or if the insurance reattaches as provided in this Clause 5.2

     5.2.1   where the on-carriage is by oversea vessel this insurance continues subject to the terms of these clauses,

           or

     5.2.2   where the on-carriage is by aircraft, the current Institute War Clauses (Air Cargo) (excluding sendings by Post) shall be deemed to form part of this insurance and shall apply to the on-carriage by air

5.3   If the voyage in the contract of carriage is terminated at a port or place other than the destination agreed therein, such port or place shall be deemed the final port of discharge and such insurance terminates in accordance with 5.1.2. If the subject-matter insured is subsequently reshipped to the original or any other destination, then *provided notice is given to the Underwriters before the commencement of such further transit and subject to an additional premium*, such insurance reattaches

5.3.1   in the case of the subject-matter insured having been discharged, as the subject-matter insured and as to any part as that part is loaded on the on-carrying vessel for the voyage.

5.3.2   in the case of the subject-matter not having been discharged, when the vessel sails from such deemed final port of discharge,

thereafter such insurance terminates in accordance with 5.1.4

5.4   The insurance against the risks of mines and derelict torpedoes, floating or submerged, is extended whilst the subject-matter insured or any part thereof is on craft whilst in transit to or from the oversea vessel, but in no case beyond the expiry of 60 days after discharge from the oversea vessel unless otherwise specially agreed by the Underwriters.

5.5   *Subject to prompt notice to Underwriters, and to an additional premium if required*, this insurance shall remain in force within the provisions of these Clauses during any deviation, or any variation of the adventure arising from the exercise of a liberty granted to shipowners or charterers under the contract of affreightment.

(For the purpose of Clause 5

"arrival" shall be deemed to mean that the vessel is anchored, moored or otherwise secured at a berth or place within the Harbour Authority area. If such a berth or place is not available, arrival is deemed to have occurred when the vessel first anchors, moors or otherwise secures either at or off the intended port or place of discharge

"oversea vessel" shall be deemed to mean a vessel carrying the subject-matter from one port or place to another where such voyage involves a sea passage by that vessel)

6   Where, after attachment of this insurance, the destination is changed by the Assured, *held covered at a premium and on conditions to be arranged subject to prompt notice being given to the Underwriters*   Change of Voyage Clause

7   **Anything contained in this contract which is inconsistent with Clauses 3.7, 3.8 or 5 shall, to the extent of such inconsistency, be null and void.**

CLAIMS

8   8.1   In order to recover under this insurance the Assured must have an insurable interest in the subject-matter insured at the time of the loss.   Insurable Interest Clause

8.2   Subject to 8.1 above, the Assured shall be entitled to recover for insured loss occurring during the period covered by this insurance, notwithstanding that the loss occurred before the contract of insurance was concluded, unless the Assured were aware of the loss and the Underwriters were not.

9   9.1   If any Increased Value insurance is effected by the Assured on the cargo insured herein the agreed value of the cargo shall be deemed to be increased to the total amount insured under this insurance and all Increased Value insurances covering the loss, and liability under this insurance shall be in such proportion as the sum insured herein bears to such total amount insured.   Increased Value Clause

In the event of claim the Assured shall provide the Underwriters with evidence of the amounts insured under all other insurances.

9.2   Where this insurance is on Increased Value the following clause shall apply:
The agreed value of the cargo shall be deemed to be equal to the total amount insured under the primary insurance and all Increased Value insurances covering the loss and effected on the cargo by the Assured, and liability under this insurance shall be in such proportion as the sum insured herein bears to such total amount insured.

In the event of claim the Assured shall provide the Underwriters with evidence of the amounts insured under all other insurances.

BENEFIT OF INSURANCE

10   This insurance shall not inure to the benefit of the carrier or other bailee   Not to Inure Clause

MINIMISING LOSSES

11   It is the duty of the Assured and their servants and agents in respect of loss recoverable hereunder   Duty of Assured Clause

11.1   to take such measures as may be reasonable for the purpose of averting or minimising such loss, and

11.2   to ensure that all rights against carriers, bailees or other third parties are properly preserved and exercised

and the Underwriters will, in addition to any loss recoverable hereunder, reimburse the Assured for any charges properly and reasonably incurred in pursuance of these duties.

12   Measures taken by the Assured or the Underwriters with the object of saving, protecting or recovering the subject-matter insured shall not be considered as a waiver or acceptance of abandonment or otherwise prejudice the rights of either party.   Waiver Clause

AVOIDANCE OF DELAY

13   It is a condition of this insurance that the Assured shall act with reasonable despatch in all circumstances within their control.   Reasonable Despatch Clause

LAW AND PRACTICE

14   This insurance is subject to English law and practice.   English Law and Practice Clause

---

NOTE – It is necessary for the Assured when they become aware of an event which is "held covered" under this insurance to give prompt notice to the Underwriters and the right to such cover is dependent upon compliance with this obligation

---

1/1/82   (FOR USE ONLY WITH THE NEW MARINE POLICY FORM)

INSTITUTE STRIKES CLAUSES (CARGO)

RISKS COVERED

1   This insurance covers, except as provided in Clauses 3 and 4 below, loss of or damage to the subject-matter insured caused by   *Risks Clause*

     1.1   strikers, locked-out workmen, or persons taking part in labour disturbances, riots or civil commotions

     1.2   any terrorist or any person acting from a political motive.

2   This insurance covers general average and salvage charges, adjusted or determined according to the contract of affreightment and/or the governing law and practice, incurred to avoid or in connection with the avoidance of loss from a risk covered under these clauses.   *General Average Clause*

EXCLUSIONS

3   In no case shall this insurance cover   *General Exclusions Clause*

     3.1   loss damage or expense attributable to wilful misconduct of the Assured

     3.2   ordinary leakage, ordinary loss in weight or volume, or ordinary wear and tear of the subject-matter insured

     3.3   loss damage or expense caused by insufficiency or unsuitability of packing or preparation of the subject-matter insured (for the purpose of this Clause 3.3 "packing" shall be deemed to include stowage in a container or liftvan but only when such stowage is carried out prior to attachment of this insurance or by the Assured or their servants)

     3.4   loss damage or expense caused by inherent vice or nature of the subject-matter insured

     3.5   loss damage or expense proximately caused by delay, even though the delay be caused by a risk insured against (except expenses payable under Clause 2 above)

     3.6   loss damage or expense arising from insolvency or financial default of the owners managers charterers or operators of the vessel

     3.7   loss damage or expense arising from the absence shortage or withholding of labour of any description whatsoever resulting from any strike, lockout, labour disturbance, riot or civil commotion

     3.8   any claim based upon loss of or frustration of the voyage or adventure

     3.9   loss damage or expense arising from the use of any weapon of war employing atomic or nuclear fission and/or fusion or other like reaction or radioactive force or matter

     3.10   loss damage or expense caused by war civil war revolution rebellion insurrection, or civil strife arising therefrom, or any hostile act by or against a belligerent power.

4   4.1   In no case shall this insurance cover loss damage or expense arising from   *Unseaworthiness and Unfitness Exclusion Clause*

        unseaworthiness of vessel or craft,

        unfitness of vessel craft conveyance container or liftvan for the safe carriage of the subject-matter insured,

     where the Assured or their servants are privy to such unseaworthiness or unfitness, at the time the subject-matter insured is loaded therein.

     4.2   The Underwriters waive any breach of the implied warranties of seaworthiness of the ship and fitness of the ship to carry the subject-matter insured to destination, unless the Assured or their servants are privy to such unseaworthiness or unfitness.

DURATION

5   5.1   This insurance attaches from the time the goods leave the warehouse or place of storage at the place named herein for the commencement of the transit, continues during the ordinary course of transit and terminates either   *Transit Clause*

     5.1.1   on delivery to the Consignees' or other final warehouse or place of storage at the destination named herein,

     5.1.2   on delivery to any other warehouse or place of storage, whether prior to or at the destination named herein, which the Assured elect to use either

     5.1.2.1   for storage other than in the ordinary course of transit or

     5.1.2.2   for allocation or distribution,

        or

     5.1.3   on the expiry of 60 days after completion of discharge overside of the goods hereby insured from the oversea vessel at the final port of discharge,

     whichever shall first occur.

     5.2   If, after discharge overside from the oversea vessel at the final port of discharge, but prior to termination of this insurance, the goods are to be forwarded to a destination other than that to which they are insured hereunder, this insurance, whilst remaining subject to termination as provided for above, shall not extend beyond the commencement of transit to such other destination.

     5.3   This insurance shall remain in force (subject to termination as provided for above and to the provisions of Clause 6 below) during delay beyond the control of the Assured, any deviation, forced discharge, reshipment or transhipment and during any variation of the adventure arising from the exercise of a liberty granted to shipowners or charterers under the contract of affreightment.

6   If owing to circumstances beyond the control of the Assured either the contract of carriage is terminated at a port or place other than the destination named therein or the transit is otherwise terminated before delivery of the goods as provided for in Clause 5 above, then this insurance shall also terminate *unless prompt notice is given to the Underwriters and continuation of cover is requested when the insurance shall remain in force, subject to an additional premium if required by the Underwriters,* either   *Termination of Contract of Carriage Clause*

    6.1   until the goods are sold and delivered at such port or place, or, unless otherwise specially agreed, until the expiry of 60 days after arrival of the goods hereby insured at such port or place, whichever shall first occur,

       or

    6.2   if the goods are forwarded within the said period of 60 days (or any agreed extension thereof) to the destination named herein or to any other destination, until terminated in accordance with the provisions of Clause 5 above.

7   Where, after attachment of this insurance, the destination is changed by the Assured, *held covered at a premium and on conditions to be arranged subject to prompt notice being given to the Underwriters.*   *Change of Voyage Clause*

CLAIMS

8   8.1   In order to recover under this insurance the Assured must have an insurable interest in the subject-matter insured at the time of the loss.   *Insurable Interest Clause*

    8.2   Subject to 8.1 above, the Assured shall be entitled to recover for insured loss occurring during the period covered by this insurance, notwithstanding that the loss occurred before the contract of insurance was concluded, unless the Assured were aware of the loss and the Underwriters were not.

9   9.1   If any Increased Value insurance is effected by the Assured on the cargo insured herein the agreed value of the cargo shall be deemed to be increased to the total amount insured under this insurance and all Increased Value insurances covering the loss, and liability under this insurance shall be in such proportion as the sum insured herein bears to such total amount insured.   *Increased Value Clause*

       In the event of claim the Assured shall provide the Underwriters with evidence of the amounts insured under all other insurances.

    9.2   Where this insurance is on Increased Value the following clause shall apply:
       The agreed value of the cargo shall be deemed to be equal to the total amount insured under the primary insurance and all Increased Value insurances covering the loss and effected on the cargo by the Assured, and liability under this insurance shall be in such proportion as the sum insured herein bears to such total amount insured.

       In the event of claim the Assured shall provide the Underwriters with evidence of the amounts insured under all other insurances.

BENEFIT OF INSURANCE

10   This insurance shall not inure to the benefit of the carrier or other bailee.   *Not to Inure Clause*

MINIMISING LOSSES

11   It is the duty of the Assured and their servants and agents in respect of loss recoverable hereunder   *Duty of Assured Clause*

    11.1   to take such measures as may be reasonable for the purpose of averting or minimising such loss, and

    11.2   to ensure that all rights against carriers, bailees or other third parties are properly preserved and exercised

    and the Underwriters will, in addition to any loss recoverable hereunder, reimburse the Assured for any charges properly and reasonably incurred in pursuance of these duties.

12   Measures taken by the Assured or the Underwriters with the object of saving, protecting or recovering the subject-matter insured shall not be considered as a waiver or acceptance of abandonment or otherwise prejudice the rights of either party.   *Waiver Clause*

AVOIDANCE OF DELAY

13   It is a condition of this insurance that the Assured shall act with reasonable despatch in all circumstances within their control.   *Reasonable Despatch Clause*

LAW AND PRACTICE

14   This insurance is subject to English law and practice.   *English Law and Practice Clause*

NOTE:— It is necessary for the Assured when they become aware of an event which is "held covered" under this insurance to give prompt notice to the Underwriters and the right to such cover is dependent upon compliance with this obligation.   [E2279]

Part II

LIFE, HEALTH, AND DISABILITY INSURANCE

APPENDIX D

MORTALITY TABLE

MORTALITY TABLES

| | Commissioners 1980 Standard Ordinary (1970-1975) | | | | 1983 Individual Annuity Table (1971-1976)* | | | | United States Population (1979-1981) | |
| | Male | | Female | | Male | | Female | | | |
Age	Deaths Per 1,000	Expec- tation of Life (Years)	Deaths Per 1,000	Expec- tation of Life (Years)	Deaths Per 1,000	Expec- tation of Life (Years)	Deaths Per 1,000	Expec- tation of Life (Years)	Deaths Per 1,000	Expec- tation of Life (Years)
0	4.18	70.83	2.89	75.83	--	---			12.60	73.88
1	1.07	70.13	.87	75.04					.93	73.82
2	.99	69.20	.81	74.11					.65	72.89
3	.98	68.27	.79	73.17	..			--	.50	71.93
4	.95	67.34	.77	72.23	--	---		---	.40	70.97
5	.90	66.40	.76	71.28	.38	74.10	.19	79.36	.37	70.00
6	.86	65.46	.73	70.34	.35	73.12	.16	78.37	.33	69.02
7	.80	64.52	.72	69.39	.33	72.15	.13	77.39	.30	68.05
8	.76	63.57	.70	68.44	.35	71.17	.13	76.40	.27	67.07
9	.74	62.62	.69	67.48	.37	70.20	.14	75.41	.23	66.08
10	.73	61.66	.68	66.53	.38	69.22	.14	74.42	.20	65.10
11	.77	60.71	.69	65.58	.39	68.25	.15	73.43	.19	64.11
12	.85	59.75	.72	64.62	.41	67.28	.16	72.44	.25	63.12
13	.99	58.80	.75	63.67	.42	66.30	.17	71.45	.37	62.14
14	1.15	57.86	.80	62.71	.43	65.33	.18	70.46	.53	61.16
15	1.33	56.93	.85	61.76	.44	64.36	.19	69.47	.69	60.19
16	1.51	56.00	.90	60.82	.45	63.39	.20	68.49	.83	59.24
17	1.67	55.09	.95	59.87	.46	62.42	.21	67.50	.95	58.28
18	1.78	54.18	.98	58.93	.47	61.44	.23	66.51	1.05	57.34
19	1.86	53.27	1.02	57.98	.49	60.47	.24	65.53	1.12	56.40
20	1.90	52.37	1.05	57.04	.51	59.50	.26	64.55	1.20	55.46
21	1.91	51.47	1.07	56.10	.53	58.53	.28	63.56	1.27	54.53
22	1.89	50.57	1.09	55.16	.55	57.56	.29	62.58	1.32	53.60
23	1.86	49.66	1.11	54.22	.57	56.59	.31	61.60	1.34	52.67
24	1.82	48.75	1.14	53.28	.60	55.63	.33	60.62	1.33	51.74
25	1.77	47.84	1.16	52.34	.62	54.66	.35	59.64	1.32	50.81
26	1.73	46.93	1.19	51.40	.65	53.69	.37	58.66	1.31	49.87
27	1.71	46.01	1.22	50.46	.68	52.73	.39	57.68	1.30	48.94
28	1.70	45.09	1.26	49.52	.70	51.76	.41	56.70	1.30	48.00
29	1.71	44.16	1.30	48.59	.73	50.80	.42	55.72	1.31	47.06
30	1.73	43.24	1.35	47.65	.76	49.83	.44	54.75	1.33	46.12
31	1.78	42.31	1.40	46.71	.79	48.87	.46	53.77	1.34	45.18
32	1.83	41.38	1.45	45.78	.81	47.91	.48	52.80	1.37	44.24
33	1.91	40.46	1.50	44.84	.84	46.95	.50	51.82	1.42	43.30
34	2.00	39.54	1.58	43.91	.88	45.99	.52	50.85	1.50	42.36
35	2.11	38.61	1.65	42.98	.92	45.03	.55	49.87	1.59	41.43
36	2.24	37.69	1.76	42.05	.97	44.07	.57	48.90	1.70	40.49
37	2.40	36.78	1.89	41.12	1.03	43.11	.61	47.93	1.83	39.56
38	2.58	35.87	2.04	40.20	1.11	42.15	.65	46.96	1.97	38.63
39	2.79	34.96	2.22	39.28	1.22	41.20	.69	45.99	2.13	37.71
40	3.02	34.05	2.42	38.36	1.34	40.25	.74	45.02	2.32	36.79
41	3.29	33.16	2.64	37.46	1.49	39.30	.80	44.05	2.54	35.87
42	3.56	32.26	2.87	36.55	1.67	38.36	.87	43.09	2.79	34.96
43	3.87	31.38	3.09	35.66	1.89	37.43	.94	42.12	3.06	34.06
44	4.19	30.50	3.32	34.77	2.13	36.50	1.03	41.16	3.35	33.16
45	4.55	29.62	3.56	33.88	2.40	35.57	1.12	40.20	3.66	32.27
46	4.92	28.76	3.80	33.00	2.69	34.66	1.23	39.25	4.01	31.39
47	5.32	27.90	4.05	32.12	3.01	33.75	1.36	38.30	4.42	30.51
48	5.74	27.04	4.33	31.25	3.34	32.85	1.50	37.35	4.88	29.65
49	6.21	26.20	4.63	30.39	3.69	31.96	1.66	36.40	5.38	28.79
50	6.71	25.36	4.96	29.53	4.06	31.07	1.83	35.46	5.89	27.94
51	7.30	24.52	5.31	28.67	4.43	30.20	2.02	34.53	6.42	27.10
52	7.96	23.70	5.70	27.82	4.81	29.33	2.22	33.59	6.99	26.28
53	8.71	22.89	6.15	26.98	5.20	28.47	2.43	32.67	7.61	25.46
54	9.56	22.08	6.61	26.14	5.59	27.62	2.65	31.75	8.30	24.65
55	10.47	21.29	7.09	25.31	5.99	26.77	2.89	30.83	9.02	23.85
56	11.46	20.51	7.57	24.49	6.41	25.93	3.15	29.92	9.78	23.06
57	12.49	19.74	8.03	23.67	6.84	25.09	3.43	29.01	10.59	22.29
58	13.59	18.99	8.47	22.86	7.29	24.26	3.74	28.11	11.51	21.52
59	14.77	18.24	8.94	22.05	7.78	23.44	4.08	27.21	12.54	20.76

[E2280]

| | Commissioners 1980 Standard Ordinary (1970-1975) | | | | 1983 Individual Annuity Table (1971-1976)* | | | | United States Population (1979-1981) | |
| | Male | | Female | | Male | | Female | | | |
Age	Deaths Per 1,000	Expectation of Life (Years)	Deaths Per 1,000	Expectation of Life (Years)	Deaths Per 1,000	Expectation of Life (Years)	Deaths Per 1,000	Expectation of Life (Years)	Deaths Per 1,000	Expectation of Life (Years)
60	16 08	17 51	9 47	21 25	8 34	22 62	4 47	26 32	13 68	20 02
61	17 54	16 79	10 13	20 44	8 98	21 80	4 91	25 44	14 93	19 29
62	19 19	16 08	10 96	19 65	9 74	20 99	5 41	24 56	16 28	18 58
63	21 06	15 38	12 02	18 86	10 63	20 20	5 99	23 69	17 67	17 88
64	23 14	14 70	13 25	18 08	11 66	19 41	6 63	22 83	19 11	17 19
65	25 42	14 04	14 59	17 32	12 85	18 63	7 34	21 98	20 59	16 51
66	27 85	13 39	16 00	16 57	14 20	17 87	8 09	21 14	22 16	15 85
67	30 44	12 76	17 43	15 83	15 72	17 12	8 89	20 31	23 89	15 20
68	33 19	12 14	18 84	15 10	17 41	16 38	9 73	19 49	25 85	14 56
69	36 17	11 54	20 36	14 38	19 30	15 66	10 65	18 67	28 06	13 93
70	39 51	10 96	22 11	13 67	21 37	14 96	11 70	17 87	30 52	13 32
71	43 30	10 39	24 23	12 97	23 65	14 28	12 91	17 07	33 15	12 72
72	47 65	9 84	26 87	12 28	26 13	13 61	14 32	16 29	35 93	12 14
73	52 64	9 30	30 11	11 60	28 84	12 96	15 98	15 52	38 82	11 58
74	58 19	8 79	33 93	10 95	31 79	12 33	17 91	14 76	41 84	11 02
75	64 19	8 31	38 24	10 32	35 05	11 72	20 13	14 02	45 07	10 48
76	70 53	7 84	42 97	9 71	38 63	11 13	22 65	13 30	48 67	9 95
77	77 12	7 40	48 04	9 12	42 59	10 56	25 51	12 60	52 74	9 44
78	83 90	6 97	53 45	8 55	46 95	10 00	28 72	11 91	57 42	8 93
79	91 05	6 57	59 35	8 01	51 76	9 47	32 33	11 25	62 77	8 45
80	98 84	6 18	65 99	7 48	57 03	8 96	36 40	10 61	68 82	7 98
81	107 48	5 80	73 60	6 98	62 79	8 47	40 98	9 99	75 52	7 53
82	117 25	5 44	82 40	6 49	69 08	8 01	46 12	9 40	82 78	7 11
83	128 26	5 09	92 53	6 03	75 91	7 57	51 89	8 83	90 41	6 70
84	140 25	4 77	103 81	5 59	83 23	7 15	58 34	8 28	98 42	6 32
85	152 95	4 46	116 10	5 18	90 99	6 75	65 52	7 77	107 25	5 96
86	166 09	4 18	129 29	4 80	99 12	6 37	73 49	7 28	117 12	5 61
87	179 55	3 91	143 32	4 43	107 58	6 02	82 32	6 81	127 17	5 29
88	193 27	3 66	158 18	4 09	116 32	5 69	92 02	6 38	137 08	4 99
89	207 29	3 41	173 94	3 77	125 39	5 37	102 49	5 98	147 28	4 70
90	221 77	3 18	190 75	3 45	134 89	5 07	113 61	5 60	158 68	4 43
91	236 98	2 94	208 87	3 15	144 87	4 78	125 23	5 26	171 69	4 17
92	253 45	2 70	228 81	2 85	155 43	4 50	137 22	4 94	185 70	3 93
93	272 11	2 44	251 51	2 55	166 63	4 24	149 46	4 64	200 23	3 71
94	295 90	2 17	279 31	2 24	178 54	3 99	161 83	4 37	214 95	3 51
95	329 96	1 87	317 32	1 91	191 21	3 75	174 23	4 12	229 76	3 34
96	384 55	1 54	375 74	1 56	204 72	3 51	186 54	3 88	243 38	3 19
97	480 20	1 20	474 97	1 21	219 12	3 29	198 65	3 65	256 37	3 05
98	657 98	84	655 85	84	234 74	3 07	211 10	3 44	268 68	2 93
99	1.000 00	50	1.000 00	50	251 89	2 86	224 45	3 22	280 30	2 82
100					270 91	2 66	239 22	3 01	291 20	2 73
101					292 11	2 46	255 95	2 80	301 99	2 64
102					315 83	2 26	275 20	2 59	310 89	2 57
103					342 38	2 08	297 50	2 38	319 70	2 50
104					372 09	1 90	323 39	2 18	327 86	2 44
105					405 28	1 73	353 41	1 98	335 39	2 38
106					442 28	1 57	388 11	1 79	342 33	2 33
107					483 41	1 41	428 02	1 60	348 70	2 29
108					528 99	1 27	473 69	1 43	354 53	2 24
109					579 35	1 13	525 66	1 26	359 88	2 20
110					634 81	1 01	584 46	1 11		
111					695 70	89	650 65	97		
112					762 34	78	724 75	83		
113					835 06	70	807 32	71		
114					914 17	67	898 89	60		
115					1.000 00	50	1.000 00	50		

Note Mortality rates contained in the 1980 Commissioners Standard Ordinary Table were obtained from experience of 1970-1975, but contain an added element designed to generate life insurance reserves of a conservative nature in keeping with the long-term guarantees inherent in life insurance contracts. Premiums for life insurance policies, on the other hand, are based on assumptions that include expected mortality experience.

Mortality rates for the 1983 Individual Annuity Tables are, again, conservative as related to the actual and projected experience upon which they are based.

*Projected to 1983   [E2281]

APPENDIX E

LIFE INSURANCE

(1) AMERICAN COUNCIL OF LIFE INSURANCE

SAMPLE WHOLE LIFE INSURANCE POLICY (1985)

SAMPLE POLICY

Sample Whole Life Insurance Policy

TO THE READER:

There are no "standard" life insurance policies, and the contracts vary in wording and appearance from company to company. Sometimes there are also significant differences in policy provisions. This policy is generally representative of contracts issued in the United States.

ACCIDENT AND HEALTH INSURANCE: A TEACHING MANUAL
Reproduction permission granted by the Health Insurance Association of America

SAMPLE

INSURED	THOMAS A. BENSON	$50,000	AMOUNT
DATE OF ISSUE	NOVEMBER 1, 1985		
PLAN	WHOLE LIFE PAID UP AT 90	000,000	POLICY NUMBER
POLICY DATE	NOVEMBER 1, 1985	37, MALE	AGE AND SEX

WHOLE LIFE INSURANCE POLICY

OUR INSURING AGREEMENT

The Council Life Insurance Company agrees to pay the benefits provided in this policy, subject to its terms and conditions. Executed at New York, New York on the Date of Issue.

YOUR RIGHT TO RETURN YOUR POLICY

Please read this policy carefully. The Owner may return the policy for any reason within ten days after receiving it. If returned, the policy will be considered void from the beginning and any premium paid will be refunded. The policy may be returned to your agent or to the Home Office of the Council Life Insurance Company.

Secretary

President

POLICY HIGHLIGHTS

- ■ WHOLE LIFE POLICY—PARTICIPATING
- ■ AMOUNT PAYABLE AT DEATH OF INSURED $50,000.
- ■ PREMIUMS PAYABLE TO AGE 90.
- ■ SCHEDULE OF BENEFITS AND PREMIUMS PAGE 2.

This policy is a legal contract between the Owner and The Council Life Insurance Company. Read your policy carefully.

A GUIDE TO POLICY PROVISIONS

Accidental Death Benefit	15	Dividends	5
Beneficiaries	8	Loans	7
Cash Value, Extended Term and Paid-Up Insurance	5	Ownership	3
Change of Policy	7	Payment of Policy Benefit	9
Contract	3	Premiums and Reinstatement	4
		Specification	2
		Waiver of Premium Right	14

Endorsements Made At Issue Appear After "General Provisions." Additional Benefits, If Any, Are Provided By Rider.

1

Source: THE AMERICAN HEALTH INSURANCE: A TEACHING MANUAL. Washington, DC. American Council of Life Insurance/Health Insurance Association of America

POLICY SPECIFICATIONS

INSURED—	THOMAS A. BENSON	$50,000	
POLICY DATE—	NOVEMBER 1, 1985	000 00	
DATE OF ISSUE—	NOVEMBER 1, 1985	37 MALE	
PLAN—	WHOLE LIFE PAID UP AT 90		

PLAN AND ADDITIONAL BENEFITS	AMOUNT	PREMIUM	YEARS PAYABLE
WHOLE LIFE (PREMIUMS PAYABLE TO AGE 90)	$50,000	$927.00	53
WAIVER OF PREMIUM (TO AGE 65)		22.50	28
ACCIDENTAL DEATH (TO AGE 70)	$50,000	39.00	33

A PREMIUM IS PAYABLE ON THE POLICY DATE AND EVERY 12 POLICY MONTHS THEREAFTER. THE FIRST PREMIUM IS $988.50.

TABLE OF GUARANTEED VALUES

END OF POLICY YEAR	CASH OR LOAN VALUE	PAID UP INSURANCE	EXTENDED TERM INSURANCE YEARS	DAYS
1	$ 0	$ 0	0	0
2	515	1,650	2	149
3	1,253	3,900	5	47
4	2,011	6,100	7	94
5	2,796	8,200	8	339
6	3,579	10,200	10	118
7	4,390	12,150	11	250
8	5,220	14,000	12	280
9	6,068	15,800	13	228
10	6,932	17,500	14	103
11	7,783	19,100	14	282
12	8,648	20,600	15	48
13	9,526	22,050	15	142
14	10,417	23,450	15	205
15	11,319	24,750	15	240
16	12,233	26,000	15	251
17	13,156	27,250	15	241
18	14,089	28,400	15	213
19	15,031	29,500	15	169
20	15,979	30,600	15	113
AGE 60	18,853	33,500		
AGE 65	23,647	37,550		

PAID UP ADDITIONS AND DIVIDEND ACCUMULATIONS INCREASE THE CASH VALUES. INDEBTEDNESS DECREASES THEM.
THE PERCENTAGE REFERRED TO IN SECTION 5.6 IS 83.000%

DIRECT BENEFICIARY   HELEN M. BENSON, WIFE OF THE INSURED
OWNER   THOMAS A. BENSON, THE INSURED

SECTION 1. THE CONTRACT

1.1 LIFE INSURANCE BENEFIT

The Council Life Insurance Company agrees, subject to the terms and conditions of this policy, to pay the Amount shown on page 2 to the beneficiary upon receipt at its Home Office of proof of the death of the Insured.

1.2 INCONTESTABILITY

This policy shall be incontestable after it has been in force during the lifetime of the Insured for two years from the Date of Issue.

1.3 SUICIDE

If within two years from the Date of Issue the Insured dies by suicide, the amount payable by the Company shall be limited to the premiums paid.

1.4 DATES

The contestable and suicide periods commence with the Date of Issue. Policy months, years and anniversaries are computed from the Policy Date. Both dates are shown on page 2 of this policy.

1.5 MISSTATEMENT OF AGE

If the age of the Insured has been misstated, the amount payable shall be the amount which the premiums paid would have purchased at the correct age.

1.6 GENERAL

This policy and the application, a copy of which is attached when the policy is issued, constitute the entire contract. All statements in the application are representations and not warranties. No statement shall void this policy or be used in defense of a claim under it unless contained in the application.

Only an officer of the Company is authorized to alter this policy or to waive any of the Company's rights or requirements.

All payments by the Company under this policy are payable at its Home Office.

SECTION 2. OWNERSHIP

2.1 THE OWNER

The Owner is as shown on page 2, or his successor or transferee. All policy rights and privileges may be exercised by the Owner without the consent of any beneficiary. Such rights and privileges may be exercised only during the lifetime of the Insured and thereafter to the extent permitted by Sections 8 and 9.

2.2 TRANSFER OF OWNERSHIP

The Owner may transfer the ownership of this policy by filing written evidence of transfer satisfactory to the Company at its Home Office and, unless waived by the Company, submitting the policy for endorsement to show the transfer.

2.3 COLLATERAL ASSIGNMENT

The Owner may assign this policy as collateral security. The Company assumes no responsibility for the validity or effect of any collateral assignment of this policy. The Company shall not be charged with notice of any assignment unless the assignment is in writing and filed at its Home Office before payment is made.

The interest of any beneficiary shall be subordinate to any collateral assignment made either before or after the beneficiary designation.

A collateral assignee is not an Owner and a collateral assignment is not a transfer of ownership.

Source: LIFE AND HEALTH INSURANCE, A TEACHING MANUAL, Washington DC, American Council of Life Insurance/Health Insurance Association of America

---

SECTION 3. PREMIUMS AND REINSTATEMENT

3.1 PREMIUMS

(a) **Payment.** All premiums after the first are payable at the Home Office or to an authorized agent. A receipt signed by an officer of the Company will be provided upon request.

(b) **Frequency.** Premiums may be paid annually, semiannually, or quarterly at the published rates for this policy. A change to any such frequency shall be effective upon acceptance by the Company of the premium for the changed frequency. Premiums may be paid on any other frequency approved by the Company.

(c) **Default.** If a premium is not paid on or before its due date, this policy shall terminate on the due date except as provided in Sections 3.1(d), 5.3 and 5.4.

(d) **Grace Period.** A grace period of 31 days shall be allowed for payment of a premium not paid on its due date. The policy shall continue in full force during this period. If the Insured dies during the grace period, the overdue premium shall be paid from the proceeds of the policy.

(e) **Premium Refund at Death.** The portion of any premium paid which applies to a period beyond the policy month in which the Insured died shall be refunded as part of the proceeds of this policy.

3.2 REINSTATEMENT

If the policy has not been surrendered for its cash value, it may be reinstated within five years after the due date of the unpaid premium provided the following conditions are satisfied:

(a) Within 31 days following expiration of the grace period, reinstatement may be made without evidence of insurability during the lifetime of the Insured by payment of the overdue premium.

(b) After 31 days following expiration of the grace period, reinstatement is subject to:

(i) receipt of evidence of insurability of the Insured satisfactory to the Company;
(ii) payment of all overdue premiums with interest from the due date of each at the rate of 6% compounded annually; or any lower rate established by the Company.

Any policy indebtedness existing on the due date of the unpaid premium, together with interest from that date, must be repaid or reinstated.

4

SECTION 4. DIVIDENDS

4.1 ANNUAL DIVIDENDS

This policy shall share in the divisible surplus, if any, of the Company. This policy's share shall be determined annually and credited as a dividend. Payment of the first dividend is contingent upon payment of the premium or premiums for the second policy year and shall be credited proportionately as each premium is paid. Thereafter, each dividend shall be payable on the policy anniversary.

4.2 USE OF DIVIDENDS

As directed by the Owner, dividends may be paid in cash or applied under one of the following:

(a) Paid-Up Additions. Dividends may be applied to purchase fully paid-up additional insurance. Paid-up additions will also share in the divisible surplus.

(b) Dividend Accumulations. Dividends may be left to accumulate at interest. Interest is credited at a rate of 3½% compounded annually, or any higher rate established by the Company.

(c) Premium Payment. Dividends may be applied toward payment of any premium due within one year, if the balance of the premium is paid. If the balance is not paid, or if this policy is in force as paid-up insurance, the dividend will be applied to purchase paid-up additions.

If no direction is given by the Owner, dividends will be applied to purchase paid-up additions.

4.3 USE OF ADDITIONS AND ACCUMULATIONS

Paid-up additions and dividend accumulations increase the policy's cash value and loan value and are payable as part of the policy proceeds. Additions may be surrendered and accumulations withdrawn unless required under the Loan, Extended Term Insurance, or Paid-up Insurance provisions.

4.4 DIVIDEND AT DEATH

A dividend for the period from the beginning of the policy year to the end of the policy month in which the insured dies shall be paid as part of the policy proceeds.

SECTION 5. CASH VALUE, EXTENDED TERM AND PAID-UP INSURANCE

5.1 CASH VALUE

The cash value, when all premiums due have been paid, shall be the reserve on this policy less the deduction described in Section 5.5, plus the reserve for any paid-up additions and the amount of any dividend accumulations.

The cash value within three months after the due date of any unpaid premium shall be the cash value on the due date reduced by any subsequent surrender of paid-up additions or withdrawl of dividend accumulations. The cash value at any time after such three months shall be the reserve on the form of insurance then in force, plus the reserve for any paid-up additions and the amount of any dividend accumulations.

If this policy is surrendered within 31 days after a policy anniversary, the cash value shall be not less than the cash value on that anniversary.

5.2 CASH SURRENDER

The Owner may surrender this policy for its cash value less any indebtedness. The policy shall terminate upon receipt at the Home Office of this policy and a written surrender of all claims. Receipt of the policy may be waived by the Company.

The Company may defer paying the cash value for a period not exceeding six months from the date of surrender. If payment is deferred 30 days or more, interest shall be paid on the cash value less any indebtedness at the rate of 4% compounded annually from the date of surrender to the date of payment.

5.3 EXTENDED TERM INSURANCE

If any premium remains unpaid at the end of the grace period, this policy shall continue in force as nonparticipating extended term insurance. The amount of insurance shall be the amount of this policy, plus any paid-up additions and dividend accumulations, less any indebtedness. The term insurance shall begin as of the due date of the unpaid premium and its duration shall be determined by applying the cash value less any indebtedness as a net single premium at the attained age of the Insured. If the term insurance would extend to or beyond attained age 100, paid-up insurance under Section 5.4 below will be provided instead.

5.4 PAID-UP INSURANCE

In lieu of extended term insurance this policy may be continued in force as participating paid-up life insurance.

Paid-up insurance may be requested by written notice filed at the Home Office before, or within three months after, the due date of the unpaid premium. The insurance will be for the amount that the cash value will purchase as a net single premium at the attained age of the Insured. Any indebtedness shall remain outstanding.

5.5 TABLE OF GUARANTEED VALUES

The cash values, paid-up insurance, and extended term insurance shown on page 2 are for the end of the policy year indicated. These values are based on the assumption that premiums have been paid for the number of years stated and are exclusive of any paid-up additions, dividend accumulations, or indebtedness. During the policy year allowance shall be made for any portion of a year's premium paid and for the time elapsed in that year. Values for policy years not shown are calculated on the same basis as this table and will be furnished on request. All values are equal to or greater than those required by the State in which this policy is delivered.

In determining cash values a deduction is made from the reserve. During the first five policy years, the deduction for each $1,000 of Amount is $9 plus $.15 for each year of the Insured's issue age. After the fifth policy year, the deduction decreases yearly by one-fifth of the initial deduction until there is no deduction in the tenth and subsequent policy years. If the premium paying period is less than ten years, there is no deduction in the last two policy years of the premium paying period or thereafter.

5.6 RESERVES AND NET PREMIUMS

Reserves, net premiums and present values are determined in accordance with the Commissioners 1958 Standard Ordinary Mortality Table and 4% interest, except that for the first five years of any extended term insurance, the Commissioners 1958 Extended Term Insurance Table is used. All reserves are based on continuous payment of premiums and immediate payment of claims. Net annual premiums are the same in each policy year, except that if premiums are payable for more than 20 years, the net annual premium in the 21st and subsequent policy years is determined by applying the percentage shown on page 2 to the net annual premium for the 20th policy year. On the Policy Date, the present value of all future guaranteed benefits equals the present value of all future net annual premiums. The reserve at the end of any policy year is the excess of the present value of all future guaranteed benefits over the present value of all future net annual premiums. The reserve is exclusive of any additional benefits.

6

SECTION 6. LOANS

6.1 POLICY LOAN

The Owner may obtain a policy loan by assignment of this policy to the Company. The amount of the loan, plus any existing indebtedness, shall not exceed the loan value. No loan shall be granted if the policy is in force as extended term insurance. The Company may defer making a loan for six months unless the loan is to be used to pay premiums on policies issued by the Company.

6.2 PREMIUM LOAN

A premium loan shall be granted to pay an overdue premium if the premium loan option is in effect. If the loan value, less any indebtedness, is insufficient to pay the overdue premium, a premium will be paid for any other frequency permitted by this policy for which the loan value less any indebtedness is sufficient. The premium loan option may be elected or revoked by written notice filed at the Home Office.

6.3 LOAN VALUE

The loan value is the largest amount which, with accrued interest, does not exceed the cash value either on the next premium due date or at the end of one year from the date of the loan.

6.4 LOAN INTEREST

Interest is payable at the rate of 8% compounded annually, or at any lower rate established by the Company for any period during which the loan is outstanding.

The Company shall provide at least 30 days written notice to the Owner (or any other party designated by the Owner to receive notice under this policy) and any assignee recorded at the Home Office of any increase in interest rate on loans outstanding 40 or more days prior to the effective date of the increase.

Interest accrues on a daily basis from the date of the loan on policy loans and from the premium due date on premium loans, and is compounded annually. Interest unpaid on a loan anniversary is added to and becomes part of the loan principal and bears interest on the same terms.

6.5 INDEBTEDNESS

Indebtedness consists of unpaid policy and premium loans on the policy including accrued interest. Indebtedness may be repaid at any time. Any unpaid indebtedness will be deducted from the policy proceeds.

If indebtedness equals or exceeds the cash value, this policy shall terminate. Termination shall occur 31 days after a notice has been mailed to the address of record of the Owner and of any assignee recorded at the Home Office.

SECTION 7. CHANGE OF POLICY

7. CHANGE OF PLAN

The Owner may change this policy to any permanent life or endowment plan offered by the Company on the Date of Issue of this policy. The change may be made upon payment of any cost and subject to the conditions determined by the Company. For a change made after the first year to a plan having a higher reserve, the cost shall not exceed the difference in cash values or the difference in reserves, whichever is greater, plus $3\frac{1}{2}\%$ of such difference.

Source: LIFE AND HEALTH INSURANCE: A TEACHING MANUAL   Washington DC: American Council of Life Insurance/Health Insurance Association of America

SECTION 8. BENEFICIARIES

8.1 DESIGNATION AND CHANGE OF BENEFICIARIES

(a) By Owner. The Owner may designate and change direct and contingent beneficiaries and further payees of death proceeds:

(1) during the lifetime of the Insured.

(2) during the 60 days following the date of death of the Insured, if the Insured immediately before his death was not the Owner. Any such designation of direct beneficiary may not be changed. If the Owner is the direct beneficiary and elects a payment plan, any such designation of contingent beneficiaries and further payees may be changed.

(b) By Direct Beneficiary. The direct beneficiary may designate and change contingent beneficiaries and further payees if:

(1) the direct beneficiary is the Owner.

(2) at any time after the death of the Insured, no contingent beneficiary or further payee is living, and no designation is made by the Owner under Section 8.1 (a) (2).

(3) the direct beneficiary elects a payment plan after the death of the Insured, in which case the interest in the share of such direct beneficiary or any other payee designated by the Owner shall terminate.

(c) By Spouse (Marital Deduction Provision). Notwithstanding any provision of Section 8 or 9 of this policy to the contrary, if the Insured immediately before death was the Owner and if the direct beneficiary is the spouse of the Insured and survives the Insured, such direct beneficiary shall have the power to appoint all amounts payable under the policy either to the executors or administrators of the direct beneficiary's estate or to such other contingent beneficiaries and further payees as he may designate. The exercise of that power shall revoke any then existing designation of contingent beneficiaries and further payees and any election of a payment plan applying to them.

(d) Effective Date. Any designation or change of beneficiary shall be made by the filing and recording at the Home Office of a written request satisfactory to the Company. Unless waived by the Company, the request must be endorsed on the policy. Upon the recording, the request will take effect as of the date it was signed. The Company will not be held responsible for any payment or other action taken by it before the recording of the request.

8.2 SUCCESSION IN INTEREST OF BENEFICIARIES

(a) Direct Beneficiaries. The proceeds of this policy shall be payable in equal shares to the direct beneficiaries who survive to receive payment. The unpaid share of any direct beneficiary who dies while receiving payment shall be payable in equal shares to the direct beneficiaries who survive to receive payment.

(b) Contingent Beneficiaries. At the death of the last surviving direct beneficiary payments due or to become due shall be payable in equal shares to the contingent beneficiaries who survive to receive payment. The unpaid share of any contingent beneficiary who dies while receiving payment shall be payable in equal shares to the contingent beneficiaries who survive to receive payment.

(c) Further Payees. At the death of the last to survive of the direct and contingent beneficiaries, the proceeds, or the withdrawal value of any payments due or to become due if a payment plan is in effect, shall be paid in one sum:

(1) in equal shares to the further payees who survive to receive payment; or

(2) if no further payees survive to receive payment, to the executors or administrators of the last to survive of the direct and contingent beneficiaries.

(d) **Estate of Owner.** If no direct or contingent beneficiaries or further payees survive the Insured, the proceeds shall be paid to the Owner or the executors or administrators of the Owner.

8.3 GENERAL

(a) **Transfer of Ownership.** A transfer of ownership will not change the interest of any beneficiary.

(b) **Claims of Creditors.** So far as permitted by law, no amount payable under this policy shall be subject to the claims of creditors of the payee.

(c) **Succession under Payment Plans.** A direct or contingent beneficiary succeeding to an interest in a payment plan shall continue under such plan subject to its terms, with the rights of transfer between plans and of withdrawal under plans as provided in this policy.

SECTION 9. PAYMENT OF POLICY BENEFITS

9.1 PAYMENT

Payment of policy benefits upon surrender or maturity will be made in cash or under one of the payment plans described in Section 9.2, if elected.

If policy benefits become payable by reason of the Insured's death, payment will be made under any payment plan then in effect. If no election of a payment plan is in effect, the proceeds will be held under the Interest Income Plan (Option A) with interest accumulating from the date of death until an election or cash withdrawal is made.

9.2 PAYMENT PLANS

(a) **Interest Income Plan (Option A).** The proceeds will earn interest which may be received in monthly payments or accumulated. The first interest payment is due one month after the plan becomes effective. Withdrawal of accumulated interest as well as full or partial proceeds may be made at any time.

(b) **Installment Income Plans.** Monthly installment income payments will be made as provided by the plan elected. The first payment is due on the date the plan becomes effective.

(1) **Specified Period (Option B).** Monthly installment income payments will be made providing for payment of the proceeds with interest over a specified period of one to 30 years. Withdrawal of the present value of any unpaid installments may be made at any time.

(2) **Specified Amount (Option D).** Monthly installment income payments will be made for a specified amount of not less than $10 per $1,000 of proceeds. Payments will continue until the entire proceeds with interest are paid, with the final payment not exceeding the unpaid balance. Withdrawal of the unpaid balance may be made at any time.

(c) **Life Income Plans.** Monthly life income payments will be made as provided by the plan elected. The first payment is due on the date the plan becomes effective. Proof of date of birth satisfactory to the Company must be furnished for any individual upon whose life income payments depend.

9

(1) Single Life Income (Option C). Monthly payments will be made for the selected certain period, if any, and thereafter during the remaining lifetime of the individual upon whose life income payments depend. The selections available are:

(i) no certain period,

(ii) a certain period of 10 or 20 years, or

(iii) a refund certain period such that the sum of the income payments during the certain period will be equal to the proceeds applied under the plan, with the final payment not exceeding the unpaid balance.

(2) Joint and Survivor Life Income (Option E). Monthly payments will be made for a 10 year certain period and thereafter during the joint lifetime of the two individuals upon whose lives income payments depend and continuing during the remaining lifetime of the survivor.

(3) Withdrawal. Withdrawal of the present value of any unpaid income payments which were to be made during a certain period may be made at any time after the death of all individuals upon whose lives income payments depend.

(d) Payment Frequency. In lieu of monthly payments a quarterly, semiannual or annual frequency may be selected.

9.3 PAYMENT PLAN RATES

(a) Interest Income and Installment Income Plans. Proceeds under the Interest Income and Installment Income plans will earn interest at rates declared annually by the Company, but not less than a rate of 3½% compounded annually. Interest in excess of 3½% will increase payments, except that for the Installment Income Specified Amount Plan (Option D), excess interest will be applied to lengthen the period during which payments are made.

The present value for withdrawal purposes will be based on a rate of 3½% compounded annually.

The Company may from time to time also make available higher guaranteed interest rates under the Interest Income and Installment Income plans, with certain conditions on withdrawal as then published by the Company for those plans.

(b) Life Income Plans. Life Income Plan payments will be based on rates declared by the Company. These rates will provide not less than 104% of the income provided by the Company's Immediate Annuities being offered on the date the plan becomes effective. The rates are based on the sex and age nearest birthday of any individual upon whose life income payments depend, and adjusted for any certain period and the immediate payment of the first income payment. In no event will payments of the first income payment. In no event will payments under these rates be less than the minimums described in Section 9.3(c).

(c) Minimum Income Payments. Minimum monthly income payments for the Installment Income Plans (Options B and D) and the Life Income Plans (Options C and E) are shown in the Minimum Income Table. The minimum Life Income payments are determined as of the date the payment plan becomes effective and depend on the age nearest birthday adjusted for policy duration.

The Life Income Plan payment rates in that table depend on the sex and on the adjusted age of each person on whose life the payments are based. The adjusted age is:

10

■ the age on the birthday that is nearest to the date on which the payment plan takes effect; plus

■ the age adjustment shown below for the number of policy years that have elapsed from the Policy Date to the date that the payment plan takes effect. A part of a policy year is counted as a full year.

POLICY YEARS ELAPSED	AGE ADJUSTMENT	POLICY YEARS ELAPSED	AGE ADJUSTMENT
1 to 10	+ 8	31 to 35	− 1
11 to 15	+ 6	36 to 40	− 2
16 to 20	+ 4	41 to 45	− 3
21 to 25	+ 2	46 to 50	− 4
26 to 30	0	51 or more	− 5

9.4 ELECTION OF PAYMENT PLANS

(a) **Effective Date**. Election of payment plans for death proceeds made by the Owner and filed at the Home Office during the Insured's lifetime will be effective on the date of death of the Insured. All other elections of payment plans will be effective when filed at the Home Office, or later if specified.

(b) **Death Proceeds**. Payment plans for death proceeds may be elected:

(1) by the Owner during the lifetime of the Insured.

(2) by the Owner during the 60 days following the date of death of the Insured, if the Insured immediately before his death was not the Owner. Any such election may not be changed by the Owner.

(3) by a direct or contingent beneficiary to whom such proceeds become payable, if no election is then in effect and no election is made by the Owner under Section 9.4(b) (2).

(c) **Surrender or Maturity Proceeds**. Payment plans for surrender or maturity proceeds may be elected by the Owner for himself as direct beneficiary.

(d) **Transfers Between Payment Plans**. A direct or contingent beneficiary receiving payment under a payment plan with the right to withdraw may elect to transfer the withdrawal value to any other payment plan then available.

(e) **Life Income Plan Limitations**. An individual beneficiary may receive payments under a Life Income Plan only if the payments depend upon his life. A corporation may receive payments under a Life Income Plan only if the payments depend upon the life of the Insured, or a surviving spouse or dependent of the Insured.

(f) **Minimum Amounts**. Proceeds of less than $5,000 may not be applied without the Company's approval under any payment plan except the Interest Income Plan (Option A) with interest accumulated. The Company retains the right to change the payment frequency or pay the withdrawal value if payments under a payment plan are or become less than $25.

9.5 INCREASE OF MONTHLY INCOME

The direct beneficiary who is to receive the proceeds of this policy under a payment plan may increase the total monthly income by payment of an annuity premium to the Company. The premium, after deduction of charges not exceeding 2% and any applicable premium tax, shall be applied under the payment plan at the same rates as the policy proceeds. The net amount so applied may not exceed twice the proceeds payable under this policy.

Source: LIFE AND HEALTH INSURANCE A TEACHING MANUAL Washington DC American Council of Life Insurance/Health Insurance Association of America

11

MINIMUM INCOME TABLE

Minimum Monthly Income Payments Per $1,000 Proceeds

INSTALLMENT INCOME PLANS (Options B and D)

PERIOD (YEARS)	MONTHLY PAYMENT	PERIOD (YEARS)	MONTHLY PAYMENT	PERIOD (YEARS)	MONTHLY PAYMENT
1	$84.65	11	$9.09	21	$5.56
2	43.05	12	8.46	22	5.39
3	29.19	13	7.90	23	5.24
4	22.27	14	7.49	24	5.09
5	18.12	15	7.10	25	4.96
6	15.35	16	6.76	26	4.84
7	13.38	17	6.47	27	4.73
8	11.90	18	6.20	28	4.63
9	10.75	19	5.97	29	4.53
10	9.83	20	5.25	30	4.45

Source: LIFE AND HEALTH INSURANCE: A TEACHING MANUAL. Washington, DC: American Council of Life Insurance/Health Insurance Association of America

12

MINIMUM INCOME TABLE

Minimum Monthly Income Payments Per $1,000 Proceeds

LIFE INCOME PLANS (Options C and E)

SINGLE LIFE MONTHLY PAYMENTS (Option C)

MALE ADJUSTED AGE*	CERTAIN PERIOD (YEARS)				FEMALE ADJUSTED AGE	CERTAIN PERIOD (YEARS)			
	NONE	10	20	REFUND		NONE	10	20	REFUND
55	$ 5.39	$ 5.24	$ 4.85	$ 5.00	55	$ 4.75	$4.70	$ 4.53	$4.57
56	5.51	5.34	4.91	5.09	56	4.85	4.78	4.59	4.64
57	5.63	5.45	4.97	5.19	57	4.94	4.87	4.66	4.72
58	5.77	5.56	5.03	5.29	58	4.05	4.97	4.73	4.81
59	5.91	5.68	5.10	5.39	59	5.16	5.07	4.80	4.90
60	6.06	5.80	5.16	5.50	60	5.27	5.17	4.87	4.99
61	6.22	5.93	5.21	5.62	61	5.40	5.28	4.94	5.09
62	6.39	6.07	5.27	5.74	62	5.53	5.40	5.01	5.20
63	6.58	6.21	5.33	5.87	63	5.67	5.52	5.08	5.31
64	6.77	6.35	5.38	6.01	64	5.62	5.66	5.15	5.20
65	6.99	6.50	5.43	6.16	65	5.97	5.80	5.22	5.55
66	7.21	6.66	5.48	6.31	66	6.14	5.95	5.28	5.69
67	7.46	6.83	5.52	6.47	67	6.31	6.10	5.35	5.83
68	7.72	7.00	5.56	6.65	68	6.50	6.27	5.40	5.99
69	7.97	7.17	5.60	6.83	69	6.70	6.45	5.46	6.15
70	8.23	7.35	5.63	7.03	70	6.90	6.63	5.51	6.32
71	8.49	7.53	5.66	7.23	71	7.11	6.82	5.55	6.51
72	8.76	7.71	5.68	7.45	72	7.33	7.02	5.59	6.71
73	9.03	7.89	5.70	7.69	73	7.55	7.22	5.62	6.92
74	9.30	8.07	5.72	7.94	74	7.79	7.43	5.65	7.15
75	9.57	8.25	5.73	8.21	75	8.02	7.64	5.68	7.39
76	9.85	8.43	5.74	8.49	76	8.26	7.85	5.69	7.65
77	10.11	8.60	5.74	8.80	77	8.48	8.05	5.71	7.92
78	10.38	8.77	5.75	9.13	78	8.72	8.26	5.72	8.21
79	10.64	8.93	5.75	9.48	79	8.94	8.45	5.73	8.52
80	10.90	9.08	5.75	9.85	80	9.16	8.64	5.74	8.85
81	11.13	9.21	5.75	10.26	81	9.36	8.81	5.74	9.21
82	11.36	9.34	5.75	10.70	82	9.53	8.96	5.75	9.57
83	11.55	9.44	5.75	11.17	83	9.70	9.10	5.75	9.97
84	11.75	9.54	5.75	11.70	84	9.85	9.22	5.75	10.39
85 and over	11.92	9.61	5.75	12.26	85 and over	9.98	9.33	5.75	10.81

JOINT AND SURVIVOR MONTHLY PAYMENTS (Option E)

MALE ADJUSTED AGE	FEMALE ADJUSTED AGE						
	55	60	65	70	75	80	85 and over
55	$4.33	$4.55	$4.76	$4.94	$5.08	$5.17	$5.22
60	4.45	4.73	5.03	5.30	5.53	5.68	5.76
65	4.54	4.89	5.28	5.68	6.04	6.29	6.43
70	4.61	5.01	5.49	6.04	6.57	6.97	7.20
75	4.66	5.09	5.65	6.32	7.04	7.65	8.02
80	4.68	5.14	5.74	6.51	7.39	8.20	8.72
85 and over	4.69	5.16	5.78	6.60	7.57	8.52	9.15

See Section 9.3

13

Source: LIFE AND HEALTH INSURANCE: A TEACHING MANUAL   Washington DC   American Council of Life Insurance/Health Insurance Association of America

WAIVER OF PREMIUM BENEFIT

1. THE BENEFIT

If total disability of the Insured commences before the policy anniversary nearest his 60th birthday, the Company will waive the payment of premium becoming due during total disability of the Insured.

If total disability of the Insured commences on or after the policy anniversary nearest his 60th birthday but before the policy anniversary nearest his 65th birthday, the Company will waive the payment of premiums becoming due during total disability of the Insured and before the policy anniversary nearest his 65th birthday.

The Company will refund that portion of any premium paid which applies to a period of total disability beyond the policy month in which the disability began.

The premium for this benefit is shown on page 2.

2. DEFINITION OF TOTAL DISABILITY

Total disability means disability which:

(a) resulted from bodily injury or disease;

(b) began after the Date of Issue of this policy and before the policy anniversary nearest the Insured's 65th birthday;

(c) has existed continuously for at least six months; and

(d) prevents the Insured from engaging in an occupation. During the first 24 months of disability, occupation means the occupation of the Insured at the time such disability began; thereafter it means any occupation for which he is reasonably fitted by education, training or experience, with due regard to his vocation and earnings prior to disability.

The total and irrecoverable loss of the sight of both eyes, or of speech or hearing, or of the use of both hands, or of both feet, or of one hand and one foot, shall be considered total disability, even if the Insured shall engage in an occupation.

3. PROOF OF DISABILITY

Before any premium is waived, proof of total disability must be received by the Company at its Home Office:

(a) during the lifetime of the Insured;

(b) during the continuance of total disability; and

(c) not later than one year after the policy anniversary nearest the Insured's 65th birthday.

Premiums will be waived although proof of total disability was not given within the time specified, if it is shown that it was given as soon as reasonably possible, but not later than one year after recovery.

4. PROOF OF CONTINUANCE OF DISABILITY

Proof of the continuance of total disability may be required once a year. If such proof is not furnished, no further premiums shall be waived. Further proof of continuance of disability will no longer be required if, on the policy anniversary nearest the Insured's 65th birthday, the Insured is then and has been totally and continuously disabled for five or more years.

5. PREMIUMS

Any premium becoming due during disability and before receipt of proof of total disability is payable and should be paid. Any such premiums paid shall be refunded by the Company upon acceptance of proof of total disability. If such premiums are not paid, this benefit shall be allowed if total disability is shown to have begun before the end of the grace period of the first unpaid premium.

1

If on any policy anniversary following the date of disablement the Insured continues to be disabled and this benefit has not terminated, an annual premium will be waived.

6. TERMINATION

This benefit shall be in effect while this policy is in force, but shall terminate on the policy anniversary nearest the Insured's 65th birthday unless the Insured is then totally disabled and such disability occurred prior to the policy anniversary nearest the Insured's 60th birthday. It may also be terminated within 31 days of a premium due date upon receipt at the Home Office of the Owner's written request.

ACCIDENTAL DEATH BENEFIT

1. THE BENEFIT

The Company agrees to pay an Accidental Death Benefit upon receipt at its Home Office of proof that the death of the Insured resulted, directly and independently of all other causes, from accidental bodily injury, provided that death occurred while this benefit was in effect.

2. PREMIUM AND AMOUNT OF BENEFIT

The premium for and the amount of this benefit are shown on page 2. This benefit shall be payable as part of the policy proceeds.

3. RISKS NOT ASSUMED

This benefit shall not be payable for death of the Insured resulting from suicide, for death resulting from or contributed to by bodily or mental infirmity or disease, or for any other death which did not result, directly and independently of all other causes, from accidental bodily injury.

Even though death resulted directly and independently of all other causes from accidental bodily injury, this benefit shall not be payable if the death of the Insured resulted from:

(a) Any act or incident of war. The word "war" includes any war, declared or undeclared, and armed aggression resisted by the armed forces of any country or combination of countries.

(b) Riding in any kind of aircraft, unless the Insured was riding solely as a passenger in an aircraft not operated by or for the Armed Forces, or descent from any kind of aircraft while in flight. An Insured who had any duties whatsoever at any time on the flight or any leg of the flight with respect to any purpose of the flight or to the aircraft or who was participating in training shall not be considered a passenger.

4. TERMINATION

This benefit shall be in effect while this policy is in force other than under the Extended Term Insurance or Paid-up Insurance provisions, but shall terminate on the policy anniversary nearest the Insured's 70th birthday. It may also be terminated within 31 days of a premium due date upon receipt at the Home Office of the Owner's written request.

David Olson

Secretary

THE COUNCIL LIFE INSURANCE COMPANY

Source: LIFE AND HEALTH INSURANCE: A TEACHING MANUAL Washington DC, American Council of Life Insurance/Health Insurance Association of America

Source: LIFE AND HEALTH INSURANCE. A TEACHING MANUAL. Washington, DC: American Council of Life Insurance/Health Insurance Association of America

**RECEIPT FOR
PAYMENT AND
CONDITIONAL LIFE
INSURANCE
AGREEMENT**

When premium is paid at
the time of application,
complete this Agreement
and give to the Applicant.
No other Agreement will
be recognized by the Com-
pany. If premium is not
paid—do not detach.

THOMAS A. BENSON $*50,000*   *LIFE POLICY — PARTICIPATING*
Name of Proposed Insured   Face Amount   Plan

Received of ___*THOMAS A. BENSON*___
the sum of $ __*241.60*__ for the policy applied for in the application to THE COUNCIL INSUR-
ANCE COMPANY (CL) with the same date and number as this receipt. Checks, drafts, and money orders
are accepted subject to collection.

NEW YORK, N.Y., *NOV 1* 19 *85*   *J R Washington* _____ Agent.
Place and Date

CONDITIONAL LIFE INSURANCE AGREEMENT

I. **No Insurance Ever in Force.** No insurance shall be in force at any time if the proposed insured is not
an acceptable risk on the Underwriting Date for the policy applied for according to CL's rules and standards. No insurance shall be in force under an Additional Benefit for which the proposed insured is
not an acceptable risk.

II. **Conditional Life Insurance.** If the proposed insured is an acceptable risk on the Underwriting Date, the
insurance shall be in force subject to the following maximum amounts if the proposed insured dies
before the policy is issued:

Life Insurance		Accidental Death Benefit		
Age at Issue	Policies Issued at Standard Premiums	Policies Issued at Higher Premiums	Age at Issue	Maximum Amount
0-24	$ 500,000	$250,000	0-14	$ 25,000
25-45	1,000,000	500,000	15-19	50,000
46-55	800,000	400,000	20-24	75,000
56-65	400,000	200,000	25-60	100,000
66-70	200,000	100,000	Over 60	
Over 70	-0-	0		

Reduction in Maximum Amounts. The maximum amounts set forth in the preceding table shall be reduced by any existing CL insurance on the life of
the proposed insured with an Issue Date within 90 days of the date of this Agreement or by any pending prepaid applications for CL insurance on the life
of the proposed insured with an Underwriting Date within 90 days of the date of this Agreement.

Termination of Conditional Life Insurance. If the proposed insured is an acceptable risk for the policy applied for according to CL's rules and standards
only at a premium higher than the premium paid, any insurance under this Agreement shall terminate on the date stated in a notice mailed by CL to the
applicant unless by such date the applicant accepts delivery of the policy and pays the additional premium required.

Underwriting Date. The Underwriting Date is the date of page 2 (90-2) of the application or the date of the medical examination if required, otherwise
the date of the nonmedical, page 4 (90-4)), whichever is the later.

III. **Premium Adjustment.** If the proposed insured is an acceptable risk for the policy applied for only at a premium higher than the premium paid and dies
before paying the additional premium required, that additional premium shall be subtracted from the insurance benefit payable to the beneficiary.

IV. **Premium Refund.** Any premium paid for any insurance or Additional Benefit not issued or issued at a higher premium but not accepted by the applicant
shall be returned to the applicant.

NOT A "BINDER"—NO INSURANCE WHERE SECTION I APPLIES—NO AGENT MAY MODIFY

PART I   Life Insurance Application to *The COUNCIL Life Insurance Company*

IMPORTANT NOTICE—This application is subject to approval by the Company's Home Office. Be sure all questions in all parts of the application are answered completely and accurately, since the application is the basis of the insurance contract and will become part of any policy issued.

1. Insured's Full Name *(Please Print-Give title as Mr., Dr., Rev. etc.)*

	Mo. Day. Yr. of Birth	Ins. Age	Sex	Place of Birth	Social Security No.
MR. THOMAS A. BENSON	APRIL 6, 1948	37	M	BOSTON, MASS	000-00-0000

Single | Married ✓ | Widowed | Divorced | Separated

2. Addresses last 5 yrs.

		Number Street City State	Zip Code	County	Yrs.
Mail to Home:	Present	217 E. 62 STREET, NEW YORK, N.Y.	10017	NEW YORK	6
	Former				
☑ Business:	Present	PEPPER, GRINSTEAD, & CROUCH 5 J E. 49th ST	10017	NEW YORK	7
	Former				

3. Occupation

	Title	Describe Exact Duties	Yrs.
Present	ATTORNEY	REPRESENTS CLIENTS IN LEGAL MATTERS	7
Former			

4. a) Employer

b) Any change contemplated? Yes ☐ (Explain in Remarks)   No ✓

5. Have you ever   Yes   No

a) been rejected, deferred or discharged by the Armed Forces for medical reasons or applied for a government disability rating?   ✓

b) applied for insurance or for reinstatement which was declined, postponed, modified or rated?   ✓

c) used LSD, heroin, cocaine or methadone?   ✓

6. a) In the past 3 years have you

(i) had your driver's license suspended or revoked or been convicted of more than one speeding violation?   ✓

(ii) operated, been a crew member of, or had any duties aboard any kind of aircraft?   ✓

(iii) engaged in underwater diving below 40 feet, parachuting, or motor vehicle racing?   ✓

b) In the future, do you intend to engage in any activities mentioned in (i) and (iii) of a) above? (If "Yes" to 5a or any of 6, complete Supplemental Form 3375)   ✓

7. Have you smoked one or more cigarettes within the past 12 months?   ✓

8. Are other insurance applications pending or contemplated?   ✓

9. Do you intend to go to any foreign country?   ✓

10. Will coverage applied for replace or change any life insurance or annuities? (If Yes, submit Replacement Form)   ✓

11. Total Life Insurance in force $ 35,000   None

12. Face Amount $ 50,000   Plan WL

Accidental Death ☐   Waiver of Premium ☐

Purchase Option—Regular ☐   Preferred ☐   PEP ☐   GOR ☐

_____ units of Wife's Term—name: _____

$ _____ initial amount Decreasing Term. _____ Years

(Joint) _____ (Mot. Pro.) _____ (Straight Line) _____

Children's Term _____ Other: _____

13. Auto Prem. Loan provision operative if available? Yes _____ No ✓

14. Dividend Option:
Additions (for other than term policies) _____ Deposits
Reduce premium, if applicable, otherwise cash ✓
Supplemental Protection (Kleiman only) _____
1 Year Term—any balance to _____
Deposits _____ Additions _____ Reduce prem. (cash if more) _____

15. Beneficiaries—for children's, wife's or joint insurance as provided in contract, for other insurance as follows, subject to policy's beneficiary provisions.

	(Name)	(Relationship to insured)	if living
1st	HELEN M. BENSON	WIFE	if not
2nd	DAVID A. BENSON	SON	if living, if not
3rd			if living, if not

the executors or administrators of Insured _____ Other (see Remarks) _____
Joint beneficiaries will receive equally or survivor unless otherwise specified.

16. Flexible Plan settlement (personal beneficiary only) _____

17. Rights—During Insured's lifetime all rights belong to
Insured _____ Other: _____
Trustee _____
(attach Trust)
(After Insured's death as provided in contract on wife's insurance.)

18. Premium—Frequency ANNUAL Amt. Paid $ 241.60 _____ None
Have you received a Conditional Receipt? Yes ✓ No _____

REMARKS (Include details company, date, amt. etc. for all Yes answers to questions 4b, 5b, 6, 8, 9 and 10)

Q9: PLANS VACATION IN SWITZERLAND

I agree that (1) No one but the Company's President, a Vice-President or Secretary has authority to accept information not contained in the application, to modify or enlarge any contract, or to waive any requirement. (2) Except as otherwise provided in any conditional receipt issued, any policy issued shall take effect upon its delivery and payment of the first premium during the lifetime of each person to be insured. Due dates of later premiums shall be as specified in the policy.

Date at **NEW YORK, N.Y.** on **NOVEMBER 1** 19 **85**   Signature of Insured *Thomas A Benson*

Signature of Applicant (if other than Insured) who agrees to be bound by the representations and agreements in this and any other part of this application _____

(Name) _____ (Relationship) _____ (Complete address of Applicant) _____

Countersigned by *Ed Hatey* _____

Field Underwriter (Licensed Resident Agent)

17

| PART IV | Statements Forming Part Of Application To *The* COUNCIL *Life Insurance Company* [Complete this Part if any Non-Medical or Family Insurance is Applied For] | | | | |

1. Name of Insured **THOMAS A. BENSON** Ins. Age **37** Height **6** ft. **1** in. Weight **185** lbs.

2. If Family, Children's Wife's or Joint Insurance desired, other family members proposed for insurance

Wife (include maiden name)	Ins. Age/Mo., Day, Yr. of Birth	Height ft. in.	Weight lbs.	Life in Force $	Place of Birth
Children	Sex Ins. Age/Mo., Day, Yr. of Birth		Children	Sex Ins. Age/Mo., Day, Yr. of Birth	

3. Has any eligible dependent (a) been omitted from 2? Yes ___ No ___ (b) applied for insurance or for reinstatement which was declined, postponed, modified or rated or had a policy cancelled or renewal refused? Yes ___ No ___ (Give name, date, company in 8)

	Yes	No
4. Have you or anyone else proposed for insurance, so far as you know, ever been treated for or had indication of (underline applicable item):		
a) high blood pressure? (If "Yes", list drugs prescribed and dates taken.)		✓
b) chest pain, heart attack, rheumatic fever, heart murmur, irregular pulse or other disorder of the heart or blood vessels?	☐	✓
c) cancer, tumor, cyst, or any disorder of the thyroid, skin, or lymph glands?	☐	✓
d) diabetes or anemia or other blood disorder?	☐	✓
e) sugar, albumin, blood or pus in the urine, or veneral disease?		✓
f) any disorder of the kidney, bladder, prostate, breast or reproductive organs?		✓
g) ulcer, intestinal bleeding, hepatitis, colitis, or other disorder of the stomach, intestine, spleen, pancreas, liver or gall bladder?		✓
h) asthma, tuberculosis, bronchitis, emphysema or other disorder of the lungs?		✓
i) fainting, convulsions, migraine headache, paralysis, epilepsy or any mental or nervous disorder?		✓
j) arthritis, gout, amputation, sciatica, back pain or other disorder of the muscles, bones or joints?		✓
k) disorder of the eyes, ears, nose, throat or sinuses?		✓
l) varicose veins, hemorrhoids, hernia or rectal disorder?		✓
m) alcoholism or drug habit?		✓

	Yes	No
5. Have you or anyone else proposed for insurance, so far as you know, (underline applicable item):		
a) consulted or been examined or treated by any physician or practitioner in the past 5 years?	✓	
b) had, or been advised to have, an x-ray, cardiogram, blood or other diagnostic test in the past 5 years?	✓	
c) been a patient in a hospital, clinic, or other medical facility in the past 5 years?		✓
d) ever had a surgical operation performed or advised?	✓	
e) ever made claim for disability or applied for compensation or retirement based on accident or sickness?		✓
6. Are you or any other person proposed for insurance, so far as you know, in impaired physical or mental health, or under any kind of medication?		✓

7. Weight change in last 6 months of adults proposed for insurance: **N. A.** Name ___ Gain ___ Loss ___ Cause ___

8. Details of all "Yes" answers. For any checkup or routine examination, indicate what symptoms, if any, prompted it and include results of the examination and any special tests. Include clinic number if applicable.

Question No.	Name of Person	Illness & Treatment	No. of Attacks	Dates Onset-Recovery	Doctor, Clinic or Hospital and Complete Address
5a.	THOMAS A. BENSON	ANNUAL CHECK UP	—	—	LIFE EXTENSION INSTITUTE
5b	THOMAS A BENSON	ROUTINE OF ANNUAL CHECKUP	—	—	
5d	THOMAS A BENSON	TONSILLECTOMY - AGE 5	1	JUNE 1949	BOSTON HOSPITAL 2 PITTS STREET, BOSTON MASS

So far as may be lawful, I waive for myself and all persons claiming an interest in any insurance issued on this application, all provisions of law forbidding any physician or other person who has attended or examined, or who may attend or examine, me or any other person covered by such insurance, from disclosing any knowledge or information which he thereby acquired.

I represent the statements and answers in this and in any other part of this application to be true and complete to the best of my knowledge and belief and offer them to the Company for the purpose of inducing it to issue the policy or policies and to accept the payment of premium ___ ___ agree that payment of the first premium at/after this date shall be a representation by me that such statements and answers would be the same as made at the time of such payment.

Dated at **NEW YORK, N.Y.** on **NOV 1 19 85** Signature of Insured **Thomas A. Benson**

Witnessed by **Ed Hotey** Signature of Wife (if insured) ___

Field Underwriter (Licensed Resident Agent)

AUTHORIZATION

For purposes of determining my eligibility for insurance ___ I authorize any physician, practitioner, hospital, clinic, institution, insurance company, Medical Information Bureau or other organization ___ ___ to give to the Council Life Insurance Company ___

(2) AMERICAN COUNCIL OF LIFE INSURANCE

SAMPLE TERM LIFE INSURANCE POLICY (1982)

SAMPLE POLICY

Sample Term Life Insurance Policy

TO THE READER:

There are no "standard" life insurance policies, and the contracts vary in wording and appearance from company to company. Sometimes there are also significant differences in policy provisions. This policy is generally representative of term life insurance contracts issued in the United States.

Source: LIFE AND HEALTH INSURANCE: A TEACHING MANUAL
Washington, DC: American Council of Life Insurance/Health Insurance Association of America

SAMPLE

COUNCIL LIFE INSURANCE COMPANY
WASHINGTON, D.C.

INSURED	DENNIS SMITH	$40,000 SUM INSURED
ORIGINAL TERM EXPIRY DATE	AUG 09, 1983	
POLICY DATE	AUG 09, 1982.	062201 0000001 POLICY NUMBER

TERM LIFE INSURANCE POLICY

OUR INSURING AGREEMENT

If the Insured dies while this policy is in full force and prior to the Original Term Expiry Date or prior to any Term Expiry Date after that, we will pay the Sum Insured to the Beneficiary.

We, Council Life Insurance Company, issue this policy in consideration of your application and the payment of premiums.

Our Company and you, the Owner, are bound by the conditions and provisions of the policy.

YOUR RIGHT TO RETURN YOUR POLICY

We want you to be satisfied with your policy. If you aren't, return it to us within 10 days of the date you receive it. Return it to our Home Office or to your agent. We will refund any premium you have paid. We will consider your policy as if it had never existed.

If you have any questions or problems with your policy, we will be ready to help you. You may call upon your agent or our Home Office for assistance at any time.

Signed at our Home Office, Washington, D.C.

Secretary

W. Prescott Smith

President

John E. Wells III

POLICY HIGHLIGHTS:

■ YEARLY RENEWABLE LEVEL TERM LIFE INSURANCE TO AGE 98

■ CONVERTIBLE

■ CONVERSION PRIVILEGE TERMINATES AT AGE 80

■ PREMIUMS PAYABLE DURING INSURED'S LIFETIME TO END OF PREMIUM PAYMENT PERIOD

■ NONPARTICIPATING— NO DIVIDENDS PAID

1

POLICY INDEX

Additional Benefit Provisions, if any, Election of Settlement Options and a copy of the application follow Page 14.

ENDORSEMENTS

2

POLICY SPECIFICATIONS

PLAN OF INSURANCE—YEARLY RENEWABLE AND CONVERTIBLE TERM

INSURED— DENNIS SMITH $40,000 —SUM INSURED

ORIGINAL TERM—
EXPIRY DATE— AUG 09, 1983

POLICY DATE— AUG 09, 1982   062201   0000001 —POLICY NUMBER

DATE OF ISSUE— AUG 09, 1982   29—MALE —ISSUE AGE AND SEX

PREMIUM CLASS— STANDARD   MONTHLY —PREMIUM INTERVAL

OWNER, BENEFICIARY—AS DESIGNATED IN THE APPLICATION SUBJECT TO THE PROVISIONS OF THIS POLICY

BENEFIT AND PREMIUM SCHEDULE

FORM NO.	BENEFIT	PREMIUM	PAYMENT PERIOD
BC38F	TERM LIFE INSURANCE FOR 1 YEAR, RENEWABLE EVERY YEAR AS SHOWN IN THE TABLE OF RENEWAL PREMIUMS. CONVERTIBLE ON OR BEFORE AUG 08, 2033. CONVERSION CREDIT OF UP TO $90.00 AVAILABLE IF CONVERTED ON OR BEFORE AUG 08, 1987.	$9.50	1 YEAR
BC63F	PREMIUM WAIVER	$.40	1 YEAR

TOTAL PREMIUM ON POLICY DATE

ANNUAL	SEMIANNUAL	QUARTERLY	B·O·M MONTHLY
$109.80	$56.40	$29.80	$9.90

3

062201 0000001—POLICY NUMBER

TABLE OF RENEWAL PREMIUMS

| POLICY YEAR | ATTAINED AGE | MONTHLY PREMIUMS | | |
		LIFE INSURANCE	PREMIUM WAIVER	TOTAL
2	30	$ 9.50	$ .40	$ 9.90
3	31	9.50	.40	9.90
4	32	9.90	.40	10.30
5	33	9.90	.40	10.30
6	34	10.30	.40	10.70
7	35	10.30	.40	10.70
8	36	10.70	.40	11.10
9	37	11.50	.80	12.30
10	38	11.90	.80	12.70
11	39	12.70	.80	13.50
12	40	13.90	.80	14.70
13	41	14.70	.80	15.50
14	42	15.90	.80	16.70
15	43	16.70	1.20	17.90
16	44	17.90	1.20	19.10
17	45	19.50	1.20	20.70
18	46	21.10	1.60	22.70
19	47	22.70	1.60	24.30
20	48	24.70	2.00	26.70
21	49	26.70	2.00	28.70
22	50	28.70	2.80	31.50
23	51	31.50	3.20	34.70
24	52	33.90	4.00	37.90
25	53	37.10	5.20	42.30
26	54	40.30	6.00	46.30
27	55	43.90	7.20	51.10
28	56	47.50	8.40	55.90
29	57	51.90	10.00	61.90
30	58	56.70	11.20	67.90
31	59	61.90	12.40	74.30
32	60	67.50	4.40	71.90
33	61	73.90	4.00	77.90
34	62	80.70	3.60	84.30
35	63	88.30	3.20	91.50
36	64	97.10	3.60	100.70
37	65	106.70		106.70
38	66	117.50		117.50
39	67	129.90		129.90
40	68	143.50		143.50

4

Source: THE AMERICAN INSURANCE AND HEALTH INSURANCE A TEACHING MANUAL Washington DC American Council of Life Insurance/Health Insurance Association of America

062201   0000001—POLICY NUMBER

TABLE OF RENEWAL PREMIUMS

POLICY YEAR	ATTAINED AGE	MONTHLY PREMIUMS		
		LIFE INSURANCE	PREMIUM WAIVER	TOTAL
41	69	158.30		158.30
42	70	174.70		174.70
43	71	191.90		191.90
44	72	209.90		209.90
45	73	229.50		229.50
46	74	250.70		250.70
47	75	273.90		273.90
48	76	300.70		300.70
49	77	330.70		330.70
50	78	365.10		365.10
51	79	402.70		402.70
52	80	443.90		443.90
53	81	487.50		487.50
54	82	533.90		533.90
55	83	581.90		581.90
56	84	631.90		631.90
57	85	683.90		683.90
58	86	737.50		737.50
59	87	793.50		793.50
60	88	852.30		852.30
61	89	915.90		915.90
62	90	985.90		985.90
63	91	1,063.90		1,063.90
64	92	1,153.50		1,153.50
65	93	1,257.50		1,257.50
66	94	1,383.50		1,383.50
67	95	1,509.10		1,509.10
68	96	1,635.10		1,635.10
69	97	1,760.70		1,760.70

5

Source: THE AMERICAN HEALTH INSURANCE A TEACHING MANUAL   Washington DC   American Council of Life Insurance/Health Insurance Association of America

DEFINITIONS

This section contains the standard meaning of terms used in your policy.

You

"You" means the Owner of this policy.
"Your" and "yours" also refer to the Owner.

We

"We" means our company. "Us," "our" and "ours" also refer to our company.

Insured

"The Insured" is the person whose life is covered by this insurance policy.

Beneficiary

"The Beneficiary" is the person or persons to whom this policy's Sum Insured is paid when the Insured dies.

Sum Insured

"The Sum Insured" is the amount payable under your policy when the Insured dies. It may also be thought of as the death benefit or the face amount.

In Full Force

"In full force" means that each premium has been paid either by its Due Date or within the grace period.

Issue Age and Attained Age

"Issue Age" is the Insured's age on the last birthday before the Policy Date. It is shown on the Policy Specifications Page. We use it for each benefit of your policy, unless a different age is stated. "Attained Age" is the Issue Age plus the number of years and months since your policy was issued.

Written Notice

"Written Notice" is a request or notice in writing by you to us at our Home Office. It is how you let us know any requests you have, or changes you want to make to your policy.

Policy Date

The Policy Date is shown on the Policy Specifications Page. We use it to set premium Due Dates, policy years and policy anniversaries.

Date of Issue

The Date of Issue is shown on the Policy Specifications Page. We use it to interpret the Incontestability and Suicide provisions.

Policy Specifications Page

The Policy Specifications Page starts on Page 3 of your policy and gives basic information about your policy. This includes important items such as Date of Issue and Table of Renewal Premiums.

6

Source: LIFE AND HEALTH INSURANCE: A TEACHING MANUAL   Washington DC: American Council of Life Insurance/Health Insurance Association of America

THE CONTRACT

**Your insurance policy is a legal contract between you and us. Certain provisions are standard. This
section gives these provisions and explains how they can affect your policy.**

The Entire Contract

The entire contract is made up of this policy
and your written application. We attached a
copy of your application at issue.

All statements you made in the application,
in the absence of fraud, are considered
representations and not warranties. Only
the statements made in your written
application can be used by us to defend a
claim or void this policy.

Changes to this policy are not valid unless
we make them in writing. They must be
signed by one of our Executive Officers.

Incontestability

We cannot contest your policy after it has
been in force during the Insured's lifetime
for two years from its Date of Issue, except
for nonpayment of premiums.

Suicide

We will not pay the Sum Insured if the
Insured commits suicide while sane or
insane within two years after the Date of
Issue. Instead, we will pay a sum equal to
the total amount of premiums paid to that
date.

Misstatement of Age or Sex

We will make adjustments if the Insured's
age or sex was misstated in the application.
The Sum Insured, and any other benefits,
will be what the premiums paid would have
bought at the correct age and sex.

Policy Settlement

We will pay the Sum Insured to the
Beneficiary when we receive proof of the
Insured's death. We will refund the part of
any premium which has been paid for a
period beyond the policy month in which
the Insured died.

We may ask that this policy be returned to
us at the time of settlement.

Nonparticipating

Your policy is nonparticipating. The
premium does not include a charge for
participating in surplus. This means we do
not pay dividends on your policy.

7

PREMIUMS

You must pay your premiums on time to keep your policy in full force. You have certain rights if you do not. This section explains how and when your premiums are to be paid. It also gives some of your rights if a premium is not paid.

Payment

Your first premium is due on the Policy Date. It must be paid on or before delivery of your policy.

All premiums are to be paid in advance either at our Home Office or to one of our agents authorized to collect premiums. The amount of premium is shown on the Policy Specifications Page. If you request a receipt, we will give you one. It will be signed by an Executive Officer and countersigned by the agent.

Frequency

Premiums are to be paid on the first day of each Premium Interval. This is the "Due Date" of a premium. The Premium Interval is shown on the Policy Specifications Page.

You may change the Premium Interval by Written Notice. The change has to be made in accordance with our published rates and payment rules. No change to a less frequent Premium Interval can be made during the first policy year.

Grace Period

You have 31 days from Due Date to pay a premium. This is called "the grace period." The policy will continue in full force. No interest will be charged. But, if the Insured dies during the grace period, we will subtract the unpaid premium for those 31 days. (There is no grace period for the first premium.)

Default

If a premium is not paid by the end of the grace period, your policy will be in default. It will cease to be in full force. It will have no futher value. The date of default is the Due Date of the unpaid premium.

Reinstatement

You have the right to put your policy back in full force any time within five years of the date of default. You would then resume paying premiums.

We will require you to:

1. Give us evidence the Insured is still insurable according to our rules;

2. Pay the applicable renewal premium for the term period from the date of reinstatement to the next Term Expiry Date; and

3. Pay the unpaid premium for the 31-day grace period following the Due Date of the last premium in default, with compound interest at 6% per year from that Due Date.

8

OWNERSHIP AND BENEFICIARY

This section describes the Owner and the Beneficiary: who they are and what their rights in this policy are.

Ownership

You, the Owner, are named in the application. You may make use of all rights of this policy while the Insured is living. These rights are subject to the rights of any assignee or living irrevocable beneficiary. "Irrevocable" means that you have given up your right to change the Beneficiary named.

If you die, the Contingent Owner, if one is named, will become the Owner. If there is no named Owner then living, the rights of ownership will vest in the executors, administrators or assigns of the Owner.

Beneficiary

The Beneficiary is named in the application. More than one beneficiary may be named. The rights of any beneficiary who dies before the Insured will pass to the surviving beneficiary or beneficiaries unless you provide otherwise.

If no beneficiary is living at the Insured's death, we will pay the Sum Insured to you, your legal representatives or assigns.

The rights of any beneficiary will be subject to all the provisions of this policy. You may impose other limitations with our consent.

Change of Ownership or Beneficiary

You may change the Owner or the Beneficiary, unless an irrevocable one has been named, while the Insured is living. Change is made by Written Notice. The change takes effect on the date the notice was signed, if we acknowledge receipt of your notice in writing.

Any change is subject to any of our actions made before the date your notice was acknowledged. We may require return of this policy for endorsement before making a change.

Assignment and Assignee

Only you may make an assignment of this policy. You must notify us if you assign this policy. We are not responsible for the validity or effect of an assignment. Any change you make is subject to any action we made before the date the notice was received.

9

Your policy is renewable each year This section explains what you have to do

Yearly Renewal

You may renew your policy each year, without evidence of insurability, until the policy anniversary at the Insured's Attained Age 98. A Table of Renewal Premiums showing the premium payable for each policy year is on the Policy Specifications Page. You must pay the renewal premium shown when due to keep your policy in full force. The renewal of your policy becomes effective when we receive the renewal premium, subject to the grace period provision.

When Renewal Premium Due

Your policy has an Original Term Expiry Date which is the end of the first term period. This is the first policy anniversary. Your first renewal premium is due on this date. Each time you renew your policy, you establish a new Term Expiry Date which will be the policy anniversary following the previous expiry date. Your renewal premium for the next term period is due on this new Term Expiry Date.

Effect of Total Disability on Renewal

We will waive any premium coming due and automatically renew your policy for you if:

1. A Premium Waiver Benefit is in your policy;

2. The Insured meets the conditions to qualify for waiver of premiums;

3. The Insured is disabled on any Term Expiry Date; and

4. You have not converted this policy.

10

CONVERSION

You may convert this policy to a different type of life insurance policy. This section explains how this is done.

Conversion Election

You may convert this policy, without evidence of insurability, to a nonparticipating life insurance policy. You must make this election prior to the date shown on the Policy Specifications Page for this and while your policy is in full force. The Sum Insured of the new policy may not be greater than the Sum Insured of this policy on the date of conversion. However, it may be less, subject to our then minimum amount requirements.

Conditions of Conversion

We will issue your new policy subject to the following conditions:

1. The premium during the first year must be as great as the premium for a Whole Life insurance policy with the same initial death benefit.

2. The Sum Insured must be level.

3. Your new policy will be issued on a restricted basis or in a class other than standard if we issued this policy in that way.

4. Your new policy may have a Premium Waiver Benefit if this policy has one. It will be the one we are then issuing. However, you cannot enlarge the Premium Waiver Benefit in this policy, and you must give us proof that the Insured is not disabled on the date of conversion.

   You may do this without evidence of insurability if this term insurance is converted to a Whole Life policy. But, you must have our consent if the Premium Waiver Benefit is to be included in a policy that is not Whole Life.

5. Your new policy may include benefits for loss from accident if these benefits are in this policy. The benefits will be those we are then issuing. However, you cannot enlarge the benefits in this policy.

6. Your new policy may include a Guaranteed Insurability Benefit if this policy has one. It will be the one we are then issuing.

7. You may have our consent to continue any other benefits which are part of this policy.

Issue Age of New Policy

The Issue Age of the new policy may be:

(a) The Insured's Attained Age on the date of conversion; or

(b) The Issue Age of the Insured on the Policy Date of this policy.

If you choose (a), the premium rate will be the one we are using on the date of conversion. Your new policy will become effective when we receive your application and first premium payment.

If you choose (b), the premium rate will be the one we were using on the Policy Date of this policy. Your new policy will become effective when you pay the greater of:

(1) The difference between the premiums you have paid for this policy and the premiums you would have paid for the new policy, plus 6% interest compounded annually; and

(2) The Cash Value of the new policy on the date of conversion.

Conversion Credit

A Conversion Credit is available to you if you convert this policy before the date shown on the Policy Specifications Page for this. The amount of Conversion Credit is also shown there. This amount is multiplied by the ratio of (a) the amount of insurance converted to (b) the Sum Insured on the Date of Issue.

If you convert during the first policy year, the Conversion Credit will be the amount determined above further multiplied by the ratio of (1) the premiums you have paid for this policy to (2) the premiums you would have paid for the new policy.

11

Source: LIFE AND HEALTH INSURANCE: A TEACHING MANUAL, Washington, DC, American Council of Life Insurance/Health Insurance Association of America

DECREASING TERM INSURANCE OPTION

Your policy is a level term insurance policy. This means the Sum Insured remains the same but the amount of your premium increases each policy year. You may change this and pay the same premium each year and have the Sum Insured decrease. This section explains how this is done.

Election of Option

You may elect this Decreasing Term Insurance Option on any policy anniversary prior to the Insured's Attained Age 80.

You must make this election by Written Notice.

If you do this, you would continue to pay the Life Insurance Premium payable during the prior policy year. You pay this premium instead of the premiums shown in the Table of Renewal Premiums on the Policy Specifications Page.

If you elect this option, the Sum Insured for the next policy year and all policy years after that will be determined from the table on the next page. This amount is based on the premium payable and the Attained Age of the Insured at the beginning of each policy year. Changes in the Sum Insured will occur each year on the policy anniversary.

You determine the Sum Insured from the table by first determining the annual life premium payable. To do this, tak Insurance Premium shown on the Policy Specifications Page for the policy year preceding the year in which you elect this option. Then adjust it as follows:

1. If you pay your premiums annually, deduct $15;

2. If you pay your premiums semiannually, multiply by 1.961 and then deduct $15;

3. If you pay your premiums quarterly, multiply by 3.846 and then deduct $15; or

4. If you pay your premiums by Bank-O-Matic (monthly), multiply by 11.494 and then deduct $15.

5. If you pay your premiums by Monthly Account, multiply by 10.417 and then deduct $15.

If your policy has a Premium Waiver Benefit, we will automatically continue the coverage at the premium rate shown on the next page. But, you may terminate this coverage by giving us Written Notice.

You must have our consent to continue any other benefits which are part of your policy.

If you elect this option, your policy must be returned to us for our endorsement. We will return the policy to you with a new Specifications Page showing the Table of Decreasing Sums Insured and the level premium payable.

12

TABLE FOR DECREASING TERM OPTION

Age Last Birthday Male and Female	Sum Insured Per $100 Annual Life Premium*		Age Last Birthday Male and Female	Sum Insured Per $100 Annual Life Premium*	
	Male	Female		Male	Female
16	45,870	49.260	56	7,540	9,940
17	45,870	49.260	57	6,900	9,100
18	45,870	49.260	58	6,310	8,210
19	45,870	49.260	59	5,770	7,510
20	45,870	49.260	60	5,270	6,860
21	45,870	49.260	61	4,820	6,170
22	45,870	49.260	62	4,400	5,630
23	45,870	49.260	63	4,010	5,130
24	45,870	49.260	64	3,650	4,660
25	45,870	49.260	65	3,310	4,220
26	45,870	49.260	66	3,000	3,820
27	45,660	49.260	67	2,710	3,400
28	45,050	48.780	68	2,450	3,060
29	44,440	48.310	69	2,220	2,760
30	43,860	47.620	70	2,010	2,500
31	43,290	46.950	71	1,830	2,260
32	42,370	46.080	72	1,670	2,030
33	41,490	45.250	73	1,530	1,850
34	40,320	44.440	74	1,400	1,690
35	38,910	43.670	75	1,280	1,540
36	37,170	42.190	76	1,160	1,390
37	35,210	40.490	77	1,060	1,250
38	32,890	38.610	78	960	1,130
39	30,670	37.040	79	870	1,010
40	28,490	34.970	80	790	920
41	26,390	32.890	81	720	830
42	24,450	30.490	82	650	750
43	22,680	28.740	83	600	680
44	21,010	26.670	84	550	620
45	19,420	25.000	85	510	570
46	17,890	23.420	86	470	520
47	16,470	21.880	87	440	480
48	15,130	20.410	88	410	440
49	13,890	19.050	89	380	410
50	12,720	17.480	90	350	390
51	11,660	15.770	91	330	350
52	10,680	14.470	92	300	320
53	9,790	13.090	93	280	290
54	8,980	12.020	94	250	260
55	8,230	10.850	95	230	240
			96	200	210
			97	160	160

ANNUAL PREMIUM FOR PREMIUM WAIVER BENEFIT PER $100 ANNUAL LIFE INSURANCE PREMIUM

Age Last Birthday at Time Option is Selected— Male and Female	Premium**
16-39	$5.00
41-49	7.00
50-59	8.00
60-64	5.00

**Premiums shown will be adjusted for policies in a class other than standard

*Amounts shown will be adjusted for policies in a class other than standard.

13

SETTLEMENT OPTIONS

This section describes the ways the proceeds of this policy can be paid other than in one lump sum payment.

All or any part of the proceeds may be left with us and paid under one of the following options.

Option 1

Interest Income: Proceeds left with us with interest paid at regular times as elected. Interest on each $1,000 of proceeds with be: $30.00 if paid yearly; $14.89 if paid two times a year; $7.42 if paid four times a year; or $2.47 if paid monthly. Payments are made at equal intervals.

Option 2

Installments for Fixed Period: Proceeds paid in equal payments one, two, four or twelve times a year, from one to thirty years. The amount of payment for each $1,000 of proceeds is shown in the Table for Option 2. Payments are made at equal intervals.

Option 3A

Life Income—Guaranteed Period: Proceeds paid in equal payments for as long as the payee lives. This option has guaranteed payment periods of not less than 10 or 20 years as elected.

Option 3B

Life Income—Guaranteed Return of Proceeds: Proceeds paid in equal payments for as long as the payee lives. In addition, a cash refund will be paid at the death of the payee for an amount, if any, equal to the original proceeds less the sum of all installments paid.

The amount of each payment will be in accordance with the Table for Option 3. It will be determined by the payee's sex and age last birthday on the date the first payment is due.

Option 4

Installments for Fixed Amount: Proceeds paid in equal payments one, two, four or twelve times a year. At least 5% of the original proceeds must be paid each year until the entire proceeds and interest are paid. Payments are made at equal intervals.

Option 5

Alternate Life Income: Proceeds paid as a life income. The amount of each payment will be based on our single premium annuity rates on the date of the option. These rates will be furnished on request.

14

ELECTION OF SETTLEMENT OPTIONS

This section tells you how to elect a settlement option.

Election

You may elect a settlement option in the application or by Written Notice. During the Insured's lifetime, only you may make or change any election.

If there is no option in effect when the Insured dies, the payee may elect one. The payee may also name a contingent payee to receive any final payment.

The payee may change an option in effect when the Insured dies only if the option elected does not provide otherwise. However, if a life income option is in effect, that election may not be changed after payments have begun.

Availability

The options are available only with our consent if the payee is other than a natural person acting in his or her own right. Other settlement options can be arranged with our consent.

Guaranteed Interest and Excess Interest

We guarantee an interest rate of 3% per year, compounded yearly, under Options 1, 2 and 4. We will pay or credit additional interest under these options if our Board of Directors votes to do so.

Minimum Amounts

If the proceeds for one payee are less than $1,000, we have the right to pay that amount in a lump sum. No option is available under which the amount of proceeds would not be enough to make payments of at least $25.

Death of Payee

If a payee dies, we will pay any remaining amounts to the payee's legal representatives, unless other arrangements have been made with us. We will pay:

1. Under Options 1 and 4, the unpaid amount plus accrued interest; and

2. Under Options 2 and 3A, the commuted value of the remaining payments.

The commuted value is based on compound interest at 3% per year.

Rights to Commute and Withdraw

Unless other arrangements have been made with us, a payee will have the right to:

1. Withdraw proceeds left under Option 1 or 4; and

2. Withdraw the commuted value of the remaining payments under Option 2.

Proof of Age and Sex

We may require proof of the payee's age and sex before making any payment. If age or sex has been misstated, adjustments will be made.

Operative Date

We put an option into effect on the date the proceeds become payable, or on the date of election, if later. This means the first payment under Option 1 is made at the end of the interest period elected. Under Options 2, 3, 4 and 5, the first payment is made on the date we put the option into effect.

15

TABLE FOR SETTLEMENT OPTIONS

Monthly Payments Per $1000 of Proceeds Applied

OPTION 2

Period of Years	Monthly Payments
1	$84.47
2	42.86
3	28.99
4	22.06
5	17.91
6	$15.14
7	13.16
8	11.68
9	10.53
10	9.61
11	$8.86
12	8.24
13	7.71
14	7.26
15	6.87
16	$6.53
17	6.23
18	5.96
19	5.73
20	5.51
21	$5.32
22	5.15
23	4.99
24	4.84
25	4.71
26	$4.59
27	4.47
28	4.37
29	4.27
30	4.18

Annual semiannual or quarterly payments under Option 2 are 11.839, 5.963 and 2.993 respectively times the monthly payments

OPTION 3A   OPTION 3B

Age of Payee	10 Years Certain & Life Male	10 Years Certain & Life Female	20 Years Certain & Life Male	20 Years Certain & Life Female	Cash Refund Male	Cash Refund Female
25 & under	$3.23	$3.09	$3.22	$3.08	$3.19	$3.07
26	3.26	3.11	3.24	3.10	3.22	3.09
27	3.29	3.13	3.27	3.12	3.25	3.11
28	3.32	3.16	3.30	3.15	3.28	3.13
29	3.35	3.18	3.33	3.17	3.30	3.16
30	3.38	3.21	3.36	3.20	3.33	3.18
31	3.42	3.24	3.40	3.22	3.36	3.21
32	3.46	3.26	3.43	3.25	3.40	3.23
33	3.50	3.30	3.47	3.28	3.43	3.26
34	3.53	3.33	3.50	3.31	3.46	3.29
35	3.58	3.36	3.54	3.34	3.50	3.32
36	3.62	3.40	3.58	3.38	3.54	3.35
37	3.67	3.43	3.62	3.41	3.58	3.38
38	3.72	3.47	3.66	3.45	3.62	3.42
39	3.77	3.51	3.71	3.48	3.66	3.45
40	3.82	3.55	3.75	3.52	3.70	3.49
41	3.88	3.60	3.80	3.56	3.75	3.53
42	3.94	3.64	3.85	3.60	3.79	3.57
43	4.00	3.69	3.90	3.65	3.84	3.61
44	4.06	3.74	3.95	3.69	3.89	3.65
45	4.13	3.79	4.00	3.74	3.94	3.70
46	4.20	3.85	4.05	3.79	4.00	3.75
47	4.27	3.91	4.11	3.84	4.05	3.80
48	4.35	3.97	4.16	3.89	4.11	3.85
49	4.42	4.04	4.22	3.95	4.17	3.90
50	4.50	4.10	4.28	4.00	4.24	3.96
51	4.59	4.18	4.34	4.06	4.30	4.02
52	4.68	4.25	4.40	4.12	4.37	4.08
53	4.77	4.33	4.46	4.19	4.45	4.15
54	4.87	4.41	4.54	4.25	4.52	4.22
55	$4.97	$4.50	$4.59	$4.32	$4.60	$4.29
56	5.07	4.59	4.65	4.39	4.69	4.37
57	5.18	4.69	4.71	4.46	4.77	4.45
58	5.30	4.79	4.78	4.53	4.86	4.53
59	5.41	4.89	4.84	4.60	4.96	4.62
60	5.54	5.01	4.90	4.67	5.06	4.72
61	5.67	5.13	4.96	4.74	5.17	4.81
62	5.81	5.25	5.02	4.82	5.28	4.92
63	5.95	5.39	5.08	4.89	5.40	5.03
64	6.10	5.52	5.13	4.96	5.52	5.15
65	6.25	5.68	5.18	5.03	5.65	5.27
66	6.41	5.83	5.23	5.09	5.79	5.41
67	6.57	6.00	5.28	5.15	5.94	5.54
68	6.75	6.18	5.32	5.21	6.09	5.69
69	6.93	6.36	5.35	5.26	6.25	5.85
70	7.10	6.55	5.39	5.31	6.42	6.02
71	7.28	6.75	5.41	5.35	6.61	6.20
72	7.47	6.96	5.44	5.38	6.80	6.38
73	7.65	7.17	5.46	5.41	7.00	6.58
74	7.84	7.38	5.47	5.43	7.22	6.79
75	8.02	7.59	5.49	5.45	7.44	7.01
76	8.20	7.81	5.49	5.47	7.69	7.25
77	8.38	8.01	5.50	5.48	7.95	7.49
78	8.54	8.21	5.51	5.49	8.22	7.76
79	8.70	8.40	5.51	5.49	8.52	8.04
80	8.85	8.58	5.51	5.50	8.84	8.32
81	8.99	8.74	5.51	5.50	9.17	8.62
82	9.12	8.88	5.51	5.51	9.54	8.94
83	9.23	9.01	5.51	5.51	9.94	9.26
84	9.31	9.12	5.51	5.51	10.35	9.60
85 & over	9.39	9.21	5.51	5.51	10.81	9.94

16

PART I   Life Insurance Application To *The COUNCIL Life Insurance Company*

IMPORTANT NOTICE—This application is subject to approval by the Company's Home Office. Be sure all questions in all parts of the application are answered completely and accurately, since the application is the basis of the insurance contract and will become part of any policy issued.

1. Insured's Full Name (Please Print-Give title as Mr., Dr., Rev., etc.)	Mo., Day, Yr. of Birth	Ins. Age	Sex	Place of Birth	Social Security No.
MR. DENNIS SMITH	8/25/53	29	M	TULSA OKLA.	0 01-30-0000

Single ☑ Married ☐ Widowed ☐ Divorced ☐ Separated ☐

2. Addresses last 5 yrs.

	Number Street City	State	Zip Code	County	Yrs
Mail to ☑ Home — Present	711 SUNSET DRIVE WASHINGTON DC	20000		USA	3
Former					
☐ Business — Present					
Former					

3. Occupation

	Title	Describe Exact Duties	Yrs
Present	COMPUTER SPECIALIST	DEVELOP PROGRAMS FOR CLIENTS	3
Former	COMPUTER ANALYST	DEVELOP SOFTWARE PACKAGES	6

4. a) Employer ABC COMPUTER CONSULTANTS
b) Any change contemplated? Yes ☐ (Explain in Remarks) No ☑

5. Have you ever

	Yes	No
a) been rejected, deferred or discharged by the Armed Forces for medical reasons or applied for a government disability rating?	☐	☑
b) applied for insurance or for reinstatement which was declined, postponed, modified or rated?	☐	☑
c) used LSD, heroin, cocaine or methadone?	☐	☑

6. a) In the past 3 years have you
(i) had your driver's license suspended or revoked or been convicted of more than one speeding violation? — ☑
(ii) operated, been a crew member of, or had any duties aboard any kind of aircraft? — ☑
(iii) engaged in underwater diving below 40 feet, parachuting, or motor vehicle racing? — ☑
b) In the future, do you intend to engage in any activities mentioned in (i) and (ii) of a) above? — ☑
(If Yes to 5a or any of 6 complete Supplemental Form 3375)

7. Have you smoked one or more cigarettes within the past 12 months? — ☑ Yes

8. Are other insurance applications pending or contemplated? — ☑

9. Do you intend to go to any foreign country? — ☑

10. Will coverage applied for replace or change any life insurance or annuities? (If Yes, submit Replacement Form) — ☑

11. Total Life Insurance in force $ _____ None ☑

12. Face Amount $ 40,000 Plan TERM
Accidental Death ☐ Waiver of Premium ☐
Purchase Option - Regular ☐ Preferred ☐ PEP ☐ GOR ☐
_____ units of Wife's Term - name _____
$ _____ initial amount Decreasing Term. _____ Years
(Joint ☐) (Mot. Pro. ☐) (Straight Line ☐)
Children's Term ☐ Other _____

13. Auto. Prem. Loan provision operative if available? Yes ☑ No ☐

14. Dividend Option | Additions (for other than Term policies) ☐ Deposits ☐ | Reduce premium, if applicable, otherwise cash | Supplemental Protection (Reyman only) | 1 Year Term - any balance to ☐ Deposits ☐ Additions ☐ Reduce prem ☐ cash if not ☐

15. Beneficiary – for children's, wife's or joint insurance as provided in contract, for other insurance as follows, subject to policy's beneficiary provisions

	(Name)	(Relationship to insured)	
1st	KARYN SMITH	MOTHER	if living if not
2nd	RONALD R. SMITH	FATHER	if living if not
3rd	JEAN SMITH	SISTER	if living if not

the executors or administrators of Insured. (other use Remarks)
(Joint beneficiaries will receive equally or survivor, unless otherwise specified.)

16. Flexible Plan settlement (personal beneficiary only) — ✓

17. Rights During Insured's lifetime all rights belong to
Insured ☑ Other _____
Trustee ☐ (attach Trust)
(After Insured's death as provided in contract on wife's insurance?)

18. Premium Frequency MO Amt Paid $ 109.80 none _____
Have you received a Conditional Receipt? Yes ☐ No ☐

REMARKS (Include details (company, date, amt, etc.) for all Yes answers to questions 4b, 5a, 5c, 8, 9 and 10)

SMOKES ONE PACK A DAY

I agree that (1) No one but the Company's President, a Vice-President or Secretary has authority to accept information not contained in the application, to modify or enlarge any contract, or to waive any requirement (2) Except as otherwise provided in any conditional receipt issued, any policy issued shall take effect upon its delivery and payment of the first premium during the lifetime of each person to be insured. Due dates of later premiums shall be as specified in the policy.

Dated at WASH., D.C. on AUG 9 19 82 Signature of Insured *Dennis Smith*

Signature of Applicant (if other than Insured) who agrees to be bound by the representations and agreements in this and any other part of this application _____ N/A _____
(Name) (Relationship) (Complete address of Applicant)

Countersigned by _____ *Michael C. Baker* _____
Field Underwriter (Licensed Resident Agent)

PART 1A	Statements Forming Part Of Application To *The COUNCIL Life Insurance Company* [Complete this Part if any Non-Medical or Family Insurance is Applied For]

1. Name of Insured DENNIS SMITH   Ins. Age **29**   Height **5** ft **10** in   Weight **165** lbs

2. If Family, Children's, Wife's or Joint Insurance desired, other family members proposed for insurance

Wife (include maiden name)	Ins. Age	Mo., Day, Yr. of Birth	Height ft. in.	Weight lbs.	Life in Force $	Place of Birth

Children	Sex	Ins. Age	Mo., Day, Yr. of Birth	Children	Sex	Ins. Age	Mo., Day, Yr. of Birth

3. Has any eligible dependent (a) been omitted from 2? Yes ☐ No ☑ (b) applied for insurance or for reinstatement which was declined, postponed, modified or rated or had a policy cancelled or renewal refused? Yes ☐ No ☑ (Give name, date, company in 8)

4. Have you or anyone else proposed for insurance, so far as you know, ever been treated for or had indication of (underline applicable item)

	Yes	No
a) high blood pressure? (If "Yes", list drugs prescribed and dates taken.)	☐	☑
b) chest pain, heart attack, rheumatic fever, heart murmur, irregular pulse or other disorder of the heart or blood vessels?	☐	☑
c) cancer, tumor, cyst, or any disorder of the thyroid, skin, or lymph glands?	☐	☑
d) diabetes or anemia or other blood disorder?	☐	☑
e) sugar, albumin, blood or pus in the urine, or venereal disease?	☐	☑
f) any disorder of the kidney, bladder, prostate, breast or reproductive organs?	☐	☑
g) ulcer, intestinal bleeding, hepatitis, colitis, or other disorder of the stomach, intestine, spleen, pancreas, liver or gall bladder?	☐	☑
h) asthma, tuberculosis, bronchitis, emphysema or other disorder of the lungs?	☑	☐
i) fainting, convulsions, migraine headache, paralysis, epilepsy or any mental or nervous disorder?	☐	☑
j) arthritis, gout, amputation, sciatica, back pain or other disorder of the muscles, bones or joints?	☐	☑
k) disorder of the eyes, ears, nose, throat or sinuses?	☑	☐
l) varicose veins, hemorrhoids, hernia or rectal disorder?	☐	☑
m) alcoholism or drug habit?	☐	☑

5. Have you or anyone else proposed for insurance, so far as you know, (underline applicable item)

	Yes	No
a) consulted or been examined or treated by any physician or practitioner in the past 5 years?	☑	☐
b) had, or been advised to have, an x-ray, cardiogram, blood or other diagnostic test in the past 5 years?	☐	☑
c) been a patient in a hospital, clinic or other medical facility in the past 5 years?		
d) ever had a surgical operation performed or advised?		✓
e) ever made claim for disability or applied for compensation or retirement based on accident or sickness?		✓

6. Are you or any other person proposed for insurance so far as you know, in impaired physical or mental health, or under any kind of medication? — ✓

7. Weight change in last 6 months of adults proposed for insurance

Name	Gain	Loss	Cause
N/A			

8. Details of all "Yes" answers. For any checkup or routine examination, indicate what symptoms if any prompted it and include results of the examination and any special tests. Include clinic number if applicable.

Question No.	Name of Person	Illness & Treatment	No. of Attacks	Dates Onset-Recovery	Doctor, Clinic or Hospital and Complete Address
4H	DENNIS SMITH	BRONCHITIS	6	1960-1967	DR. WILLIAM BILL 29 QUEBEC ST. TULSA OKLA.
4K	DENNIS SMITH	CONJUNCTIVITIS	1	1981	DR. J.J. MARSHALL
5B	DENNIS SMITH	CHEST X-RAY-JOB	1		99 ELM ST. WASH, DC.
5D	DENNIS SMITH	BROKEN KNEECAP	1	1972-1973	DR. WILLIAM BILLS

So far as may be lawful, I waive for myself and all persons claiming an interest in any insurance issued on this application, all provisions of law forbidding any physician or other person who has attended or examined, or who may attend or examine, me or any other person covered by such insurance, from disclosing any knowledge or information which he thereby acquired.

I represent the statements and answers in this and in any other part of this application to be true and complete to the best of my knowledge and belief, and offer them to the Company for the purpose of inducing it to issue the policy or policies and to accept the payment of premiums thereunder. I also agree that payment of the first premium of after this date) shall be a representation by me that such statements and answers would be the same if made at the time of such payment.

Dated at WASH., DC on AUG. 9 19 82   Signature of Insured *Dennis Smith*

Witnessed by *Michael C. Baker*   Signature of Wife (if insured) N/A
Field Underwriter (Licensed Resident Agent)

AUTHORIZATION

For purposes of determining my eligibility for insurance, I hereby authorize any physician, practitioner, hospital, clinic, institution, insurance company, Medical Information Bureau, or other organization or person that has records or knowledge of me or my health to give any such information to the Council Life Insurance Company.

If application is made to The Council Life Insurance Company for insurance on any member of my family, this authorization also applies to such member. A photostatic copy of this authorization shall be as valid as the original.

Signed on AUG. 9 , 19 82   *Dennis Smith*
Signature of Insured

152

APPENDIX F

HEALTH AND DISABILITY INSURANCE COVERAGES

(1) HEALTH INSURANCE ASSOCIATION OF AMERICA,

CPB CORPORATION EMPLOYEES HEALTH PLAN

SAMPLE HEALTH BENEFITS BOOKLET

CPB CORPORATION EMPLOYEES HEALTH PLAN

Summary of Benefits

Do not rely on this chart alone.—It merely summarizes the benefits payable. Read the entire brochure to find out what benefits are payable for each specific kind of expense and what expenses are not covered. All benefits payable are subject to the definitions, exclusions, and limitations set forth in this brochure.

KINDS OF EXPENSES	PLAN PAYS	FOR DETAILS SEE:
Hospital Room and Board	**100%** of covered charges. (No deductible) (Excluding Mental and Nervous Disorders)	Page 2–3
Other Hospital, Surgical, and Medical	After the $200 calendar year Deductible: (see page 4, Mental and Nervous Disorders) **85%** of charges incurred out-of-hospital or as a hospital out-patient, including but not limited to: surgery, office calls, prescription drugs, routine physicals, laboratory and diagnostic tests, x-ray, and private duty nursing. **80%** of charges incurred while confined in a hospital.	Page 3–4
Maternity	Same benefits as for illness or injury.	Page 4
Accidental Injury	The Plan will pay **100%** of covered charges within 72 hours of an accident, after the $200 calendar year deductible.	Page 4
Dental and Chiropractic Benefits	This Plan will pay benefits as stated for covered dental work and chiropractic services.	Page 4
Maximum Benefits and Out-of-Pocket Expenses	There is **no** lifetime maximum, except benefits for Mental and Nervous Disorders including treatment of drug addiction and alcoholism, are limited to $50,000 per person. If your out-of-pocket expenses for co-payments and deductibles for all covered family members during a calendar year exceed $2,000, the Plan will pay **100%** of additional allowable expenses for the remainder of the year. Expenses incurred for treatment of Mental and Nervous Disorders including treatment of drug addiction and alcoholism are excluded from this provision except out-of-pocket expenses must exceed $8,000.	Page 2 Page 4

Definitions

For purposes of this Plan—

Hospital—(1) An institution which is accredited as a hospital under the Hospital Accreditation Program of the Joint Commission on Accreditation of Hospitals, or (2) Any other institution which is operated pursuant to law, under the supervision of a staff of doctors and with twenty-four hour a day nursing service, and which is primarily engaged in providing: a. General in-patient care and treatment of sick and injured persons through medical, diagnostic and major surgical facilities, all of which facilities must be provided on its premises or under its control, or b. Specialized inpatient medical care and treatment of sick or injured persons through medical and diagnostic facilities (including X-ray and laboratory) on its premises, under its control, or

through a written agreement with a Hospital (as defined above) or with a specialized provider of those facilities. *This definition does not include rest homes, nursing homes, and day-care centers.*

Doctor—A licensed practitioner of the healing arts acting within the scope of the license.

Co-payment—The percentage you pay of allowable charges under the Plan after the deductible has been met.

Calendar year—The 12-month period which begins January 1 and runs through the following December 31. For a person newly covered by this Plan, the calendar year begins when coverage begins and runs through December 31 of the same year. The expenses of a particular calendar year are those incurred during that calendar year. An expense is "incurred" on the date when the service or supply for which a charge is made is received.

1

Reasonable and customary—This Plan pays benefits, unless otherwise indicated, to the extent that they are reasonable and customary. The reasonable and customary charge for any service or supply is the usual charge made by the providers for the service or supply in the absence of insurance. The usual charge may not be more than the general level of charges for illness or injury of comparable severity and nature made by other providers within the geographic area in which the service or supply is provided. This is determined by the use of prevailing health care charges guides such as that prepared by the Health Insurance Association of America (HIAA).

Cosmetic surgery—Any operative procedure performed primarily to improve physical appearance, to prevent a mental or nervous disorder through change in bodily form, and/or change or restore form without correcting or materially improving a bodily malfunction.

Custodial care—The provision of room and board or other supportive care in an institution or in the home (with or without routine nursing care; training in activities of daily living and other forms of self-care; or supervisory care by a doctor) to a person who is mentally or physically disabled and who is not under specific active medical, surgical, or psychiatric treatment to reduce the disability to the extent necessary to enable the patient to function without such care or when, despite such treatment, there is no reasonable likelihood the disability will be so reduced.

Durable Medical Equipment—Equipment prescribed by the attending doctor which: 1) is medically necessary; 2) is not primarily and customarily used for a nonmedical purpose; 3) is designed for prolonged use; and 4) serves a specific therapeutic purpose in the treatment of an illness or injury.

Limitations

Double Coverage—The Double Coverage limitation is intended to prevent payment of benefits which exceed expenses. It applies when a person is eligible for benefits under any kind of group accident or group health coverage, Medicare, or "no fault" automobile insurance. When double coverage exists, the Plan will pay either its benefits in full or a reduced amount which, when added to the benefits available from all plans for the same covered expenses, will not exceed 100 percent of reasonable and customary charges; but in no case will this Plan pay an amount which is more than what would have been paid in the absence of other insurance.

This provision applies whether or not claim is filed under Medicare or the other plan. If needed, authorization must be given this Plan to obtain information as to benefits or services available under Medicare or the other plan or to recover overpayments from other plans. Insurance coverage which pays for loss of income or for time lost from work is not Double Coverage.

The Double Coverage limitation is administered in accordance with the National Association of Insurance Commissioners' Coordination of Benefit Guidelines.

Maximum Benefits—There is no lifetime maximum, except benefits for Mental and Nervous Disorders including treatment of drug addiction and alcoholism are limited to $50,000 per person.

The Deductible

The Deductible is the amount you must pay before the Plan will pay Other Hospital, Surgical, and Medical Benefits. There is no Deductible for Hospital Room and Board Benefits excluding Mental and Nervous Disorders.

The amount of the Deductible is $200 except for Hospital In-Patient Mental and Nervous Disorders, there is a separate $500 deductible. There is a separate Deductible for you and

for each covered member of your family. The Deductible is applied once in a calendar year for each person, regardless of the number of different illnesses or accidents. However, after three persons in a family have met their Deductibles in any calendar year, the Deductible for other persons in the family will be waived for expenses incurred during that calendar year.

You can count toward the Deductible any and all covered expenses, in or out of the hospital, except expenses paid by the Plan.

Hospital Room and Board Benefits

> **PLAN PAYS**—100% of covered charges
> (No Deductible)
> 70% of covered charges for Mental and
> Nervous Disorders ($500 deductible)

PRORATING HOSPITAL CHARGES

If the hospital makes a flat daily charge, without stating how much is for room and board and how much is for other services, 60 percent of the charge will be considered to be for room and board. If the hospital uses a schedule of charges that gets lower as the stay gets longer, 90 percent of the lowest daily charge will be considered room and board expense.

WHAT EXPENSES ARE COVERED

Subject to the definitions, exclusions, and limitations shown in this brochure, this Plan will pay benefits when medically necessary, to the extent shown above, for expenses of semiprivate, ward, and intensive care accommodations in a hospital. These benefits include charges for room, meals and special diets, and general nursing care.

HOSPITALIZATION FOR DENTAL WORK

Hospital Room and Board Benefits are payable in connection with oral surgery or dental work, as shown under Special Benefits on page 4.

USE OF PRIVATE ROOM

If use of a private room is considered medically necessary by the attending doctor, the Plan will pay 100% for such accommodations. If you use private room accommodations for any other reason, the difference between the cost of these accommodations and the cost of the hospital's average semiprivate accommodations is not a covered expense.

MATERNITY EXPENSES

This Plan covers maternity expenses (including expenses of childbirth or miscarriage) in the same manner as the expenses of illnesses and accidents. Therefore, Hospital Room and Board Benefits will be paid for expenses during hospital confinement for delivery and conditions due to pregnancy.

MENTAL AND NERVOUS DISORDERS

Benefits for confinement for treatment of Mental and Nervous Disorders include treatment of drug addiction and alcoholism.

Other Hospital, Surgical, and Medical Benefits

> **PLAN PAYS** each calendar year after the $200 Deductible is met—
> 80% of charges incurred while confined in a hospital
> 85% of charges incurred out-of-hospital or as a hospital outpatient
> (See page 4 for Mental and Nervous Disorders)

WHAT EXPENSES ARE COVERED

Subject to the definitions, exclusions, and limitations shown in this brochure, this Plan will pay reasonable and customary charges **in or out of a hospital** when medically necessary, to the extent shown above, for:

(a) Professional services of doctors, including home, office, and hospital visits and charges by a doctor (other than the principal surgeon) for second opinion prior to surgery

(b) All surgery (including oral surgery as specified on page 4)

(c) All Services and supplies of a hospital, and services of free-standing professional treatment centers which provide dialysis treatment, cancer treatment or in which surgical procedures are performed (surgi-centers)

(d) Routine physical examinations, and immunizations

(e) Surgically-induced sterilization, even if elective

(f) The following services and supplies if prescribed by a doctor:

- Services of registered graduate nurses (R.N.) and licensed practical nurses (L.P.N.), but not to exceed 8 hours per day of skilled nursing care outside a hospital

- Services of a qualified and licensed physical or occupational therapist

- Drugs and medicines which by law of the United States require a doctor's prescription; and insulin including hypodermic syringes for known diabetics or allergy conditions with or without a doctor's prescription

- X-rays, laboratory tests, electrocardiograms, basal metabolism readings, and other diagnostic tests

- Splints, casts, and similar devices used for reduction of fractures and dislocations

- Ultraviolet and radiant heat treatments and diathermy

- Rental or purchase (at Plan's option) of iron lung, hospital bed, dialysis machine, or other durable medical equipment, as defined on page 2

- X-ray, radium and radioactive isotope therapy

- Transfusions and blood and blood plasma not donated or replaced

- Artifical eyes and limbs and orthopedic devices

- Anesthetics and oxygen and their administration

3

- Local ambulance service
- First pair of lenses for ocular implants or contact lenses if required to correct an impairment existing after intra-ocular surgery and obtained within one year of an accident or surgery
- Allergy testing and treatment
- Services of a licensed or certified speech therapist to restore speech when there has been a loss of functional speech due to illness or injury
- First breast prosthesis and bra following a mastectomy
- Chemotherapy
- Renal dialysis.

Postoperative care is considered to be included in the fee charged for a surgical procedure by a doctor. Any additional fees charged by a physician other than the surgeon are not covered unless such charge is for an unrelated condition.

See the following **Special Provisions** for information about certain conditions.

Donor expenses—All reasonable and customary charges incurred for a surgical transplant, whether incurred by the recipient or donor, will be considered expenses of the recipient and will be covered the same as for any other illness or injury. This benefit applies only if the recipient is covered by the Plan.

Mental and Nervous Disorders—Covered expenses for Mental or Nervous Disorders are limited as follows:

(a) home and office visits—to face-to-face psychotherapy sessions, including group sessions, up to a maximum of 30 sessions per calendar year, and up to a maximum payable by the Plan of $25 per session.

(b) in-hospital visits—to charges not to exceed $10 per day unless there is a psychotherapy session in which case charges not to exceed $25 per day will be covered.

(c) in-hospital expenses for treatment of Mental and Nervous Disorders including treatment of drug addiction and alcoholism are limited to 70% of covered charges subject to a separate $500 deductible.

Maternity expenses—This Plan covers maternity expenses for pregnancies (including childbirth or miscarriage) terminating while covered by the Plan in the same manner as the expenses of illness and accidents. Therefore, Other Hospital, Surgical, and Medical Benefits will be paid for services and supplies provided by the hospital and doctor or licensed midwife for the care of pregnancies. Sonograms, amniocentesis and other related tests on the unborn child are also covered when medically necessary. Bassinet or nursery charges for days on which mother and child are both confined are considered other hospital expenses of the mother and not expenses of the child. There is no waiting period for Maternity Benefits.

Special Benefits

OUT-OF-POCKET EXPENSES

When the amount you pay out of your own pocket (for deductibles and copayments) toward allowable charges of all covered family members (or an individual under Self Only) exceeds $2,000 in any one calendar year, the Plan will pay in full all remaining allowable charges incurred during the remainder of that same year. Expenses incurred for the treatment of Mental and Nervous Disorders including treatment of drug addiction and alcoholism are limited to $8,000 out-of-pocket.

DENTAL WORK

The Plan will pay for expenses, as limited below, of the following conditions to the same extent as expenses of any other illness or injury:

(a) Repair of accidental injury to natural teeth (including, but not limited to, expenses for X-rays, drugs, crowns, bridgework, inlays, and dentures) performed within 12 months of the accident;

(b) oral surgery that *does not involve* any tooth structure, alveolar process, abscess, periodontal disease, or disease of gingival tissue; and

(c) surgery for the removal of impacted teeth.

ACCIDENTAL INJURY

The Plan will pay 100% after the $200 calendar year deductible for covered charges incurred within 72 hours of an accident for treatment outside a hospital or in the outpatient department of a hospital. An "accidental injury" is a bodily injury sustained solely through violent, external and accidental means.

CHIROPRACTIC SERVICES

The services of a chiropractor will be covered by the Plan for chiropractic adjustments under Other Hospital, Surgical, and Medical Benefits to the following extent:

(a) adjustments by hands only of the spinal column, up to a maximum of 30 adjustments per calendar year, and up to a maximum payable by the Plan of $9 per adjustment; and

(b) use of X-rays to detect and determine the presence or absence of nerve interferences due to spinal subluxations or misalignments, up to a maximum payable by the Plan of $25 per calendar year.

Covered services are limited to those for conditions which, in the judgment of the Plan's chiropractic consultant staff, are susceptible to improvement thereby.

4

Exclusions

The following are **not** covered expenses and cannot be counted for any purposes under the Plan:

- Expenses incurred while not covered by this Plan
- Sickness or injury for which any benefits are payable under worker's compensation or similar laws
- Hospitalization or treatment provided by or in a hospital operated by the Federal Government or any instrumentality thereof, except where a charge for service is made
- Services and supplies not reasonably necessary for the diagnosis or treatment of illness or injury, except routine physical examinations and immunizations
- Services and supplies not in accordance with generally accepted professional medical standards in the United States
- Charges by institutions which do not meet the definition of "hospital"
- Services and supplies for which there is no legal obligation to pay, or for which no charge would be made if the individual had no health benefits coverage
- Routine eye examinations
- Eyeglasses, contact lenses, or hearing aids
- Equipment not primarily and customarily used for medical purposes such as, but not limited to air purifiers, air conditioners, whirlpool bathing equipment, sun and heat lamps, and exercise devices, even if ordered by a doctor
- Cosmetic surgery (as defined on page 2), except that necessary for prompt repair of injury caused by accident
- Orthopedic shoes, arch supports, or other supportive devices for the feet
- Services of a registered graduate nurse (R.N.) or licensed practical nurse (L.P.N.), who is related to you by blood, marriage, or adoption
- Charges for educational, recreational, or milieu therapy, either in or out of a hospital
- Charges which are not reasonable and customary
- Travel, even when prescribed by a doctor
- Rest cures
- Custodial care (as defined on page 2), even when provided by a hospital
- Expenses of dental care and treatment, or chiropractic service, **except** as described under Special Benefits
- Charges for the removal of corns, calluses or trimming of toenails
- Sex transformations or any treatment related thereto
- Reversals of sterilization
- Any services or supplies not listed as covered
- Benefits will not be provided, nor services performed, for abortions under this Plan, except where the life of the mother would be endangered if the fetus were carried to term.

How to Claim Benefits

IDENTIFICATION CARDS

The Plan will provide two identification cards to each new enrollee, issued in the name of the insured upon receipt of authorization from the payroll office. If married, your spouse should carry one of these cards. A kit containing claim forms and instructions will also be sent.

YOU OBTAIN BENEFITS IN ONE OF TWO WAYS

- By authorizing direct payment to the doctor or hospital
- By filing a claim so that this Plan can pay you directly.

HOW TO FILE CLAIMS

1. After you have incurred covered expenses exceeding the Deductible, submit a completed Form E-1, Employee's Statement of Claim, for reimbursement of covered expenses in excess of the Deductible. Include copies of the bills with your claim to show you met the Deductible. A separate claim form must be submitted for each covered family member.

2. Submit an attending doctor's statement (Form S-2). This form must be completed by the principal attending doctor and all items must be answered. If assignment authorizing direct payment to the doctor is desired, you should complete and sign the upper portion of Form S-2. A Form S-2 need not be completed by any other attending doctor unless requested by the Plan.

3. If you wish to authorize direct payment to a hospital, show your identification card upon admission. The hospital completes its own form or will send an itemized statement to the CPB. If you do not wish to authorize direct payment to a hospital:

4. Submit hospital and doctor bills itemized to show—
   - Name of the person for whom service was rendered
   - Name of the attending doctor and/or admitting hospital
   - Date charge was incurred, statement of the diagnosis or treatment given and amount of the charge.

5. Submit the prescription drug statement.

Canceled checks, cash register receipts, or Medicare worksheets are not acceptable records in support of claims.

FILE CLAIMS PROMPTLY

Keep complete and accurate records of all medical expenses for which benefits may be claimed. All bills (including those used to satisfy the Deductible, as defined on page 2) must be submitted so that the Plan can ascertain (a) that the deductible has been met, and (b) the amount of benefits payable.

Claims should be filed within 90 days after the Deductible is satisfied or as soon thereafter as is reasonably possible. The Plan will not accept a claim submitted later than

5

December 31st of the calendar year following the one in which the expense for which claim is being made was incurred, except where the enrollee was legally incapable.

SEND ALL CLAIMS TO:

Personnel Dept., CPB Corporation, 1 South Way, Washington, D.C. 20201

If you need help in filling your claim get in touch with the Personnel Department, 555-6320.

The Plan must make reasonably diligent efforts to recover benefit payments made erroneously but in good faith.

Medicare

In most cases, Medicare is the primary payer of claims for services covered by both Medicare and this Plan. You should initially submit your claims to Medicare and, after Medicare has paid its benefits, this Plan will consider the balance of any covered expenses. To be sure your claims are processed promptly by this Plan, please submit the Explanation of Benefits (EOB) form from Medicare and duplicates of all bills along with a completed claim form.

Any savings realized by the Plan because of payments made by Medicare are used by the Plan to pay the deductible and coinsurance which you should have paid in the absence of Medicare coverage. Such savings, however, can only be applied toward covered charges incurred in the year the savings are established and only for the enrollee generating the savings.

However, if you are age 65 through 69, entitled to Part A (Hospital) of Medicare, employed and covered by your employer's group health plan, contact your local Social Security Administration office for further instructions before filing any of your (or your **spouse's**) claims. Medicare may be the secondary payer.

Enrollment Information

ELIGIBILITY:

If you are a permanent, full-time employee, you may enroll in the Plan during your first 31 days of employment without physical examination. You will be insured on the day that you enroll. If you enroll more than 31 days after the date you become eligible, you must satisfy the Plan that you are in good health before you can become insured. The same restrictions apply to dependent coverage, in the event of late enrollment.

DEPENDENT COVERAGE

You may elect group insurance for your dependents to become effective on the date your plan benefits begin. Eligible family members include your husband or wife and all unmarried children under age 19. Even if your children are over 19, they are eligible as long as they are full-time students, depend on you for support and are not married. Please notify the Personnel Department of any changes in your dependents' status.

COST

Although you share the cost of the health insurance plan, the CPB Corporation pays the major part of the cost. Your contribution will depend on how many members of your family are covered:

Employee only	$12.00 a month
Employee & Spouse or Employee & Child(ren)	$24.00 a month
Employee, Spouse & Child(ren)	$30.00 a month

TERMINATION OF COVERAGE

Coverage under the Plan will terminate when you terminate active full-time employment, or if you discontinue making contributions to the Plan. A dependent's coverage will terminate if your coverage terminates or if he or she is no longer an eligible family member, whichever happens first. If you retire having been covered under the Plan for at least five years, your health coverage will continue for you and your eligible family members.

CONVERSION AFTER TERMINATION OF EMPLOYMENT

Should you terminate employment after you have been covered by the CPB group health plan for at least three months, there is a 31-day conversion period during which you can change your group health plan to individual coverage. This privilege is also available for eligible family members of an employee who dies and for a family member who ceases to be eligible.

Additional information and conversion forms may be obtained from the Personnel Department.

FOR FURTHER INFORMATION

This is a summary of the benefits and services available through membership in the CPB Corporation Employees Health Plan. Please contact the Personnel Department for further information.

6

(2) UNIVERSITY OF IOWA

DISABILITY INSURANCE/INCOME REPLACEMENT INSURANCE (1985)

LONG TERM DISABILITY INSURANCE

Introductory Note

The Disability Insurance Plan described in this booklet has been designed and developed by the University of Iowa Funded Retirement and Insurance Committee in cooperation with the Principal Mutual Life Insurance Company of Des Moines, Iowa.

The booklet describes the basic features of the Plan. If you have questions about this coverage, you should contact the University Staff Benefits Office.

This booklet also specifies steps that you must take to be covered by the group plan and what to do in order to file a claim for insurance benefits.

Please read this booklet carefully.

Contents

* References are to the numbers at the bottom of the page.

GENERAL INFORMATION

This booklet is your insurance certificate.

The rights and benefits of each person covered by these insurance plans are determined by the provisions of the Master Group Policies which are held by The University at the Staff Benefits Office. The Master Policies are available for your inspection at that office during regular office hours.

Participation in Insurance Programs

Participation in the University's Group Life Insurance and Long Term Disability Insurance programs is a condition of employment by The University of Iowa for all faculty and staff members who hold permanent appointments of 50% time or more.

Faculty and Staff Members who participate in TIAA/CREF are covered by the Retirement Annuity Protection Insurance. (**Note:** Faculty and Staff Members who opt for other retirement annuity programs may have a retirement protection plan provided by that company.)

Benefits

The specific amount of benefits provided by these insurance plans for each individual are based on several factors described in this booklet.

Enrollment

The Staff Benefits Office should have provided you with a Group Enrollment Form. If you have not completed an enrollment form, please contact the Staff Benefits Office.

Medical Examination

No medical examination is required for these insurance programs. However, Long Term Disability Insurance includes a limitation for preexisting conditions (see page 7*).

Future of Plan

It is expected that these plans will be continued indefinitely. However, the University and the State Board of Regents do have the right to change or terminate these insurance plans at any time.

Definitions

There are several terms used in this booklet which have a very specific meaning for all of the insurance plans. The following terms are defined in the Appendix A and appear in bold face type when used in this booklet:

Active Work and **Actively at Work**

Annual Budgeted Salary

Benefit Waiting Period

Completed Years of Continuous Service

Dependents

Disability and **Disabled**

Monthly Budgeted Salary

Qualified Faculty or Staff Member

* The page references in this insurance policy refer to the numbers at the bottom of each page.

LONG TERM DISABILITY INSURANCE

Eligibility

Qualified Faculty and Staff Members will be eligible for Long Term Disability Insurance on the first day of the calendar month which follows the date you complete one year of **active work.**

Effective Date for Initial Coverage

Your coverage will begin on the date you are eligible, unless you are not **actively at work** on the date coverage would otherwise be effective. If you are not **actively at work,** your Long Term Disability Insurance coverage will not be in force until the day you return to **active work.**

Qualifying for Long Term Disability Benefits

To qualify for benefit payment, all of the following must occur:

— You must become disabled while covered for Long Term Disability.

— Your **disability** must not be subject to any of the limitations described on page 7.

— You must complete a **benefit waiting period.**

— You must satisfy the requirements listed in the Claim Procedures Section, beginning on page 8.

A **benefit waiting period** will start on the date you are disabled as established by the Claim Procedures set forth in this booklet, beginning on page 8. A **benefit waiting period** will be completed either when your **disability** has been continuous for 90 working days or when you have exhausted of all your accrued sick leave, whichever is later.

Benefit Payable

The benefit payable for each full month of **disability** following the **benefit waiting period** is based on your **monthly budgeted salary** on the date **disability** begins *and* the length of time you have worked at the University.

Annual budgeted salary for any Member shall not exceed:

$95,000 effective July 1, 1987

$97,500 effective July 1, 1988

$100,000 effective July 1, 1989

$105,000 effective July 1, 1990

The Long Term Disability benefit depends on the **completed years of continuous service** with the University as shown on the following table:

Completed Years of Continuous Service	Percentage of Monthly Budgeted Salary
One year but less than two years	14%
Two years but less than three years	28%
Three years but less than four years	42%
Four years but less than five years	56%
Five years or more	70%

Income From Other Sources

The monthly benefits payable under this insurance plan will be reduced by any payments from the following sources:

— Disability payments that you and your **dependents** receive from Federal Social Security (or would have received if a complete and timely application had been made).

— Wage replacement payments (other than payments from the Veterans' Administration) that you receive under a Workers' Compensation Act or other similar law.

— Federal Social Security retirement payments that you and your **dependents** receive (or would have received if a complete and timely application had been made).

— 60% of any wage or profit paid to you during Rehabilitative Employment as described on page 7.

The determination of income from these sources will be subject to the requirements set forth in the Claim Procedures Section.

Effect of the Social Security Program

The effect of the Federal Social Security program on your Long Term Disability Insurance monthly benefits will be based on the provisions of the Social Security Act in force on the date that you are entitled to begin receiving such Federal Social Security benefits. Adjustments in the amount of your Long Term Disability Insurance monthly benefits will also be made to reflect changes in Federal Social Security amounts resulting from changes in the status of your **dependents**. However, Federal Social Security cost of living increases will not reduce the monthly benefits you receive under the Long Term Disability Insurance.

Effective Date for Benefit Changes

A change in your benefit amount because of:

— a change in your **monthly budgeted salary**; or

— a change in your **completed years of continuous service**; or

— a change in benefits provided under this plan;

will normally be effective on the first day of the calendar month that next follows the date of the change.

However, if you are not **actively at work** on the date the change would otherwise be effective, the change will not be effective until the day you return to **active work.**

Continuation of Coverage During an Authorized Leave

If you cease **active work** by taking a leave authorized by the University, your plan will be continued if the authorization specifically states that benefits are to be continued during such leave of absence **and** you arrange for the payment of the required premium.

Disability Escalator

The Disability Escalator for the Long Term Disability Insurance Plan will be administered in accordance with the provisions set forth in Appendix B.

Termination of Disability Benefits

Except as described in the provision on Recurring Disabilities and Rehabilitative Employment, **disability** insurance payments will end on the earliest of:

— The date your **disability** ends; or

— The date you become employed for wage or profit (unless the work is pursuant to an approved program of Rehabilitative Employment, described on page 7); or

— The date you fail to provide any required proof of your **disability;** or

— The date you fail to submit to any required physical examination; or

— The date you fail to report your income from sources described on page 5; or

— If your **disability** payments begin before you are age 61, June 30th following or coinciding with your 65th birthday; or

— If your **disability** payments begin on or after you attain the age of 61 but before you attain age 69, five years later or the

June 30th following your 70th birthday; whichever comes first; or

— If your **disability** payments begin on or after you attain age 69, 12 months; or

— The date of your death.

After you begin receiving benefits, if you return to **active work**, you will be entitled to a final payment. The final payment will be equal to one-thirtieth ($\frac{1}{30}$) of your benefit for each completed day of **disability** following the last monthly benefit payment.

Recurring Disability

If you become **disabled** as the result of a recurring **disability**, you will not be required to complete a new **benefit waiting period**. A recurring **disability** exists when you become **disabled** from the same cause within three months of having returned to **active work**. In this situation, you will be treated as if you had not returned to work, except that **disability** benefits will not be paid for the period during which you returned to work.

(**Note:** If you become **disabled** more than three months after you have returned to **active work**, it will be treated as a new **disability**.)

Rehabilitative Employment

If Principal Mutual Life Insurance Company agrees in writing, your **disability** benefits will not end when you begin work for wage or profit if the work is in an approved rehabilitative employment program. The Termination of Disability Benefits provisions described on page 18 will continue to apply during an approved rehabilitative employment program.

Limitations

Benefits will not be paid for any **disability** that:

— results from willful self-injury; or

— results from war or act of war; or

— results from voluntary participation in an assault or felony; or

— is subject to the Preexisting Conditions Restrictions described below.

Preexisting Conditions Restrictions

A Preexisting Condition is a disease or injury for which you received treatment or care during the three-year period before you were covered by the Long Term Disability Insurance.

No benefits will be paid for a **disability** that results from a Preexisting Condition until the earlier of:

— the date concluding a period of six consecutive years during which no treatment or care has been received for the Preexisting Condition; or

— the date you have been covered for Long Term Disability Insurance for nine consecutive years.

Excess Payment

If excess benefits are paid because of your income from the sources specified on page 5, Principal Mutual Life Insurance Company will have the option to:

— reduce future benefits payable by the full amount of the excess payment; or

— recover the excess payment directly from you.

Termination of Coverage

Your coverage terminates on the earliest of:

— the end of the calendar month in which you cease to be a **Qualified Faculty or Staff Member;** or

— the date the Group Plan terminates.

CLAIM PROCEDURES

Claim Forms

The Staff Benefits Office provides forms to be used in filing claims, and will (if requested) assist you or a beneficiary in completing the required forms.

Prompt Filing

Completed claim forms and other information needed to support a claim for coverage should be filed promptly. For Group Life Insurance, proof of the insured's death should be submitted within 90 days.

For Long Term Disability Insurance and Retirement Annuity Protection Insurance, written proof that **disability** exists and has been continuous must be submitted within six months after you complete your **benefit waiting period.**

Proof of loss sent later will be accepted only if there is reasonable cause for the delay.

Physical Examinations

Principal Mutual Life Insurance Company may require that the person whose **disability** is the basis for a claim be examined by a physician. Principal Mutual Life Insurance Company will pay for these examinations and will select the physician to perform them.

Determination of Income from Specified Sources

If you file a claim for Long Term Disability benefits, when requested you must report to Principal Mutual Life Insurance Company all income from the sources described on page 5. Your report must include proof that you have applied for all income for which you are eligible and proof of any rejection of such application.

If income from any of the sources described on page 5 is payable in a lump sum, Principal Mutual Life Insurance Company will compute what would be the monthly equivalent of that lump sum and will adjust the disability insurance payment accordingly.

Until exact amounts of income from other sources are known, Principal Mutual Life Insurance Company will estimate the Social Security benefits for which you and your **dependents** are eligible and will use that estimate in computing your income from sources specified on page 5.

Payment, Denial of Claims and Review

Most claims will be processed and paid within a few days after Principal Mutual Life Insurance Company receives a completed proof of loss. If a claim will not be paid, Principal Mutual Life Insurance Company will promptly explain why in a written statement.

If a claimant disagrees with a claim denial, a review may be requested. A request for review, together with any additional materials in support of the claim should be given to the Staff Benefits Office. This information will be sent to Principal Mutual Life Insurance Company which will then conduct the review. The claimant will be advised in writing of the final decision and the reasons.

Federal law permits up to 90 days for processing claims and up to 60 days for reviewing denied claims. Almost all claims will be processed within these time limits.

Legal Action—Time Limits

A legal action with respect to a claim may not be started earlier than 60 days after a proof of loss is filed. Further, no legal action may be started later than three years after a proof is required to be filed. The limits set forth in this section will be adjusted to comply with the applicable laws.

APPENDIX A

The following definitions will help you to understand the coverage these plans provide.

Active Work and **Actively at Work** means the active performance of all of a faculty or staff member's normal job duties at the University. (**Note:** For the purposes of these coverages, faculty or staff members who are on an academic year appointment will be considered to be actively at work throughout the calendar year.)

Annual Budgeted Salary means:

a. the current salary amount specified on your most recent Notice of Appointment that:

— for a faculty or staff member who works nine months during a year, is payable for the academic year; or

— for a faculty or staff member who works 12 months during a year, is payable for the fiscal year; or

— for a faculty or staff member who is paid on an hourly rate, is the budgeted hourly rate multiplied by the number of normal working hours in the fiscal year; or

b. the amount determined by multiplying the current salary amount as determined in Part a. above by $^{11}/_9$ths for any faculty or staff member who has taught in both halves of any one of five preceding summer sessions or one-half of any session in two of the five preceding summer sessions.

Annual Budgeted Salary does not include either compensation for correspondence study courses, grants, fellowships, or other irregular service, or compensation in the form of noncash items such as board, room, laundry or premiums paid by the University for the benefit of any faculty or staff member.

Benefit Waiting Period for the purpose of qualifying for **disability** payments under the Long Term Disability Insurance, means the later of any period of 90 consecutive working days or when you have exhausted all of your accrued sick leave during which the Member is continuously **disabled.**

Completed Years of Continuous Service means the total number of years of uninterrupted employment with the University, including any time spent on an authorized leave of absence.

Dependents, for the purposes of the Long Term Disability Insurance Plan, means your spouse and children if they qualify for benefits under the Federal Social Security Act as a result of your **disability.**

Disability and **Disabled** mean your inability, because of disease or injury, to work:

— for the first two years of disability, at your normal job; and

— following the first two years of disability, at any job that reasonably fits your background and training.

Monthly Budgeted Salary means the amount which is one-twelfth of your **annual budgeted salary** in effect on the date **disability** begins.

Qualified Faculty or **Staff Member** means a **Faculty** or **Staff Member** who holds a permanent appointment of 50% time or more.

APPENDIX B

Disability Escalator

— **Eligibility.** The Disability Escalator will only apply to persons who have been **disabled** for at least one year and approved for **disability** benefits, as defined, on or prior to July 1st of each year.

— **Determination of amount of the Disability Escalator.** The amount of the Disability Escalator is determined by increases in the Consumer Price Index for Wage Earners and Clerical Workers (called CPI), prepared by the United States Department of Labor. The amount of any increase in the CPI will be ascertained by comparing the arithmetic mean of the CPI for January, February and March of the current year to the arithmetic mean of the CPI for January, February and March of the prior year in order to determine the rate of increase in the cost of living. The rate of increase so determined is the Disability Escalator for that year subject to the maximum Disability Escalator per year and the application of the Accumulation Reserve outlined below.

— **Computation of the Increase in the Disability Benefit Payment.** The Disability Escalator will be applied to the **disability** benefit otherwise payable in July, after reduction for the Social Security or Workers' Compensation benefit determined as of the date the claimant became eligible for **disability** benefits.

— **Maximum Disability Escalator Per Year.** The increase in the **disability** benefit produced under the Disability Escalator may be no more than 5% per year.

— **Accumulation Reserve.** In those years when the rate of increase indicated by the CPI is more than 5%, the excess percentage will be added to an accumulation reserve for each person then eligible for the Escalator. In any subsequent year when the Disability Escalator is less than 5%, an amount will be withdrawn from this accumulation reserve to allow up to a 5% Disability Escalator to be applied for any insured who is then receiving **disability** benefits and whose **disability** benefits had been subject to the 5% limitation in prior years. Remaining amounts in the accumulation reserve for each individual will continue to be carried forward, and used in the same fashion in subsequent years until the individual's reserve is exhausted.

— **Increase in Disability Benefits.** The increase, if any, in the **disability** benefits produced under the Escalator will be effective on July 1 of each year.

— **Termination of Disability Escalator.** The Disability Escalator will not be applied to increase benefit payments after the termination of the policy, even though **disability** benefit payments continue to be made to persons following the time of such a termination.

Part III

COMBINATION (PACKAGE) INSURANCE COVERAGES

*

APPENDIX G

BUSINESS AUTOMOBILE INSURANCE

INSURANCE SERVICES OFFICE

BUSINESS AUTO COVERAGE FORM (1985)

Various provisions in this policy restrict coverage Read the entire policy carefully to determine rights, duties and what is and is not covered

Throughout this policy the words "you" and "your" refer to the Named Insured shown in the Declarations The words "we," "us" and "our" refer to the Company providing this insurance

Other words and phrases that appear in quotation marks have special meaning Refer to SECTION V – DEFINITIONS

SECTION I - COVERED AUTOS

ITEM TWO of the Declarations shows the "autos" that are covered "autos" for each of your coverages The following numerical symbols describe the "autos" that may be covered "autos" The symbols entered next to a coverage on the Declarations designate the only autos that are covered autos

A. DESCRIPTION OF COVERED AUTO DESIGNATION SYMBOLS

SYMBOL   DESCRIPTION

1 = ANY "AUTO"

2 = OWNED "AUTOS" ONLY. Only those "autos" you own (and for Liability Coverage any "trailers" you don't own while attached to power units you own). This includes those "autos" you acquire ownership of after the policy begins

3 = OWNED PRIVATE PASSENGER "AUTOS" ONLY. Only the private passenger "autos" you own. This includes those private passenger "autos" you acquire ownership of after the policy begins

4 = OWNED "AUTOS" OTHER THAN PRIVATE PASSENGER "AUTOS" ONLY. Only those "autos" you own that are not of the private passenger type (and for Liability Coverage any "trailers" you don't own while attached to power units you own). This includes those "autos" not of the private passenger type you acquire ownership of after the policy begins

5 = OWNED "AUTOS" SUBJECT TO NO-FAULT. Only those "autos" you own that are required to have No-Fault benefits in the state where they are licensed or principally garaged. This includes those "autos" you acquire ownership of after the policy begins provided they are required to have No-Fault benefits in the state where they are licensed or principally garaged

6 = OWNED "AUTOS" SUBJECT TO A COMPULSORY UNINSURED MOTORISTS LAW. Only those "autos" you own that because of the law in the state where they

are licensed or principally garaged are required to have and cannot reject Uninsured Motorists Coverage This includes those "autos" you acquire ownership of after the policy begins provided they are subject to the same state uninsured motorists requirement

7 = SPECIFICALLY DESCRIBED "AUTOS" Only those "autos" described in ITEM THREE of the Declarations for which a premium charge is shown (and for Liability Coverage any "trailers" you don't own while attached to any power unit described in ITEM THREE).

8 = HIRED "AUTOS" ONLY. Only those "autos" you lease, hire, rent or borrow This does not include any "auto" you lease, hire, rent, or borrow from any of your employees or partners or members of their households.

9 = NONOWNED "AUTOS" ONLY Only those "autos" you do not own, lease, hire, rent or borrow that are used in connection with your business This includes "autos" owned by your employees or partners or members of their households but only while used in your business or your personal affairs.

B. OWNED AUTOS YOU ACQUIRE AFTER THE POLICY BEGINS

1. If symbols 1,2,3,4,5 or 6 are entered next to a coverage in ITEM TWO of the Declarations, then you have coverage for "autos" that you acquire of the type described for the remainder of the policy period.

2. But, if symbol 7 is entered next to a coverage in ITEM TWO of the Declarations, an "auto" you acquire will be a covered "auto" for that coverage only if.

   a. We already cover all "autos" that you own for that coverage or it replaces an "auto" you previously owned that had that coverage, and

   b. You tell us within 30 days after you acquire it that you want us to cover it for that coverage

C. CERTAIN TRAILERS, MOBILE EQUIPMENT AND TEMPORARY SUBSTITUTE AUTOS

If Liability Coverage is provided by this Coverage Form, the following types of vehicles are also covered "autos" for Liability Coverage:

1. "Trailers" with a load capacity of 2,000 pounds or less designed primarily for travel on public roads.

2. "Mobile equipment" while being carried or towed by a covered "auto."

3. Any "auto" you do not own while used with the permission of its owner as a temporary substitute for a covered "auto" you own that is out of service because of its:

   a. Breakdown;

   b. Repair;

   c. Servicing;

   d. "Loss;" or

   e. Destruction.

SECTION II - LIABILITY COVERAGE

A. COVERAGE

We will pay all sums an "insured" legally must pay as damages because of "bodily injury" or "property damage" to which this insurance applies, caused by an "accident" and resulting from the ownership, maintenance or use of a covered "auto."

We have the right and duty to defend any "suit" asking for these damages. However, we have no duty to defend "suits" for "bodily injury" or "property damage" not covered by this Coverage Form. We may investigate and settle any claim or "suit" as we consider appropriate. Our duty to defend or settle ends when the Liability Coverage Limit of Insurance has been exhausted by payment of judgments or settlements.

1. WHO IS AN INSURED

The following are "insureds":

a. You for any covered "auto."

b. Anyone else while using with your permission a covered "auto" you own, hire or borrow except:

   (1) The owner or anyone else from whom you hire or borrow a covered "auto." This exception does not apply if the covered "auto" is a "trailer" connected to a covered "auto" you own.

   (2) Your employee if the covered "auto" is owned by that employee or a member of his or her household.

   (3) Someone using a covered "auto" while he or she is working in a business of selling, servicing, repairing or parking "autos" unless that business is yours.

   (4) Anyone other than your employees, partners, a lessee or borrower or any of their employees, while moving property to or from a covered "auto."

   (5) A partner of yours for a covered "auto" owned by him or her or a member of his or her household.

c. Anyone else who is not otherwise excluded under paragraph b. above and is liable for the conduct of an "insured" but only to the extent of that liability.

2. COVERAGE EXTENSIONS

a. Supplementary Payments. In addition to the Limit of Insurance, we will pay for the "insured":

   (1) All expenses we incur.

   (2) Up to $250 for cost of bail bonds (including bonds for related traffic law violations) required because of an "accident" we cover. We do not have to furnish these bonds.

   (3) The cost of bonds to release attachments in any "suit" we defend, but only for bond amounts within our Limit of Insurance.

   (4) All reasonable expenses incurred by the "insured" at our request, including actual loss of earning up to $100 a day because of time off from work.

   (5) All costs taxed against the "insured" in any "suit" we defend.

   (6) All interest on the full amount of any judgment that accrues after entry of the judgment in any "suit" we defend; but our duty to pay interest ends when we have paid, offered to pay or deposited in court the part of the judgment that is within our Limit of Insurance.

b. Out of State Coverage Extensions.

While a covered "auto" is away from the state where it is licensed we will:

   (1) Increase the Limit of Insurance for Liability Coverage to meet the limits specified by a compulsory or financial responsibility law of the jurisdiction where the covered "auto" is being used. This extension does not apply to the limit or limits specified by any law governing motor carriers of passengers or property.

   (2) Provide the minimum amounts and types of other coverages, such as no-fault, required of out of state vehicles by the jurisdiction where the covered "auto" is being used.

We will not pay anyone more than once for the same elements of loss because of these extensions

B. EXCLUSIONS

This insurance does not apply to any of the following

1. EXPECTED OR INTENDED INJURY

"Bodily injury" or "property damage" expected or intended from the standpoint of the "insured."

2. CONTRACTUAL

Liability assumed under any contract or agreement

But this exclusion does not apply to liability for damages

a. Assumed in a contract or agreement that is an "insured contract," or

b. That the "insured" would have in the absence of the contract or agreement

3. WORKERS COMPENSATION

Any obligation for which the "insured" or the "insured's" insurer may be held liable under any workers compensation, disability benefits or unemployment compensation law or any similar law.

4. EMPLOYEE INDEMNIFICATION AND EMPLOYER'S LIABILITY

"Bodily injury" to

a. An employee of the "insured" arising out of and in the course of employment by the "insured," or

b. The spouse, child, parent, brother or sister of that employee as a consequence of paragraph a above.

This exclusion applies

(1) Whether the "insured" may be liable as an employer or in any other capacity; and

(2) To any obligation to share damages with or repay someone else who must pay damages because of the injury.

But this exclusion does not apply to "bodily injury" to domestic employees not entitled to workers compensation benefits or to liability assumed by the "insured" under an "insured contract."

5. FELLOW EMPLOYEE

"Bodily injury" to any fellow employee of the "insured" arising out of and in the course of the fellow employee's employment

6. CARE, CUSTODY OR CONTROL

"Property damage" to property owned or transported by the "insured" or in the "insured's" care, custody or control. But this exclusion does not apply to liability assumed under a sidetrack agreement.

7. HANDLING OF PROPERTY

"Bodily injury" or "property damage" resulting from the handling of property

a. Before it is moved from the place where it is accepted by the "insured" for movement into or onto the covered "auto," or

b. After it is moved from the covered "auto" to the place where it is finally delivered by the "insured"

8. MOVEMENT OF PROPERTY BY MECHANICAL DEVICE

"Bodily injury" or "property damage" resulting from the movement of property by a mechanical device (other than a hand truck) unless the device is attached to the covered "auto."

9. OPERATIONS

"Bodily injury" or "property damage" arising out of the operation of any equipment listed in paragraphs 6.b. and 6.c. of the definition of "mobile equipment."

10. COMPLETED OPERATIONS

"Bodily injury" or "property damage" arising out of your work after that work has been completed or abandoned.

In this exclusion, your work means

a. Work or operations performed by you or on your behalf, and

b. Materials, parts or equipment furnished in connection with such work or operations.

Your work includes warranties or representations made at any time with respect to the fitness, quality, durability or performance of any of the items included in paragraphs a. or b. above.

Your work will be deemed completed at the earliest of the following times

(1) When all of the work called for in your contract has been completed.

(2) When all of the work to be done at the site has been completed if your contract calls for work at more than one site

(3) When that part of the work done at a job site has been put to its intended use by any person or organization other than another contractor or subcontractor working on the same project.

Work that may need service, maintenance, correction, repair or replacement, but which is otherwise complete, will be treated as completed.

11. POLLUTION

a. "Bodily injury" or "property damage" arising out of the actual, alleged or threatened discharge, dispersal, release or escape of pollutants:

(1) That are, or that are contained in any property that is:

(a) Being transported or towed by, or handled for movement into, onto or from, the covered "auto,"

(b) Otherwise in the course of transit by the "insured," or

(c) Being stored, disposed of, treated or processed in or upon the covered "auto,"

(2) Before the pollutants or any property in which the pollutants are contained are moved from the place where they are accepted by the "insured" for movement into or onto the covered "auto," or

(3) After the pollutants or any property in which the pollutants are contained are moved from the covered "auto" to the place where they are finally delivered, disposed of or abandoned by the "insured."

b. Any loss, cost or expense arising out of any governmental direction or request that you test for, monitor, clean up, remove, contain, treat, detoxify or neutralize pollutants.

Pollutants means any solid, liquid, gaseous or thermal irritant or contaminent, including smoke, vapor, soot, fumes, acids, alkalis, chemicals and waste. Waste includes materials to be recycled, reconditioned or reclaimed.

Paragraph a.(1)(c) does not apply to fuels, lubricants, fluids, exhaust gases or other similar pollutants that are needed for or result from the normal electrical, hydraulic or mechanical functioning of the covered "auto" or its parts, if:

(1) The pollutants escape or are discharged, dispersed or released directly from an "auto" part designed by its manufacturer to hold, store, receive or dispose of such pollutants; and

(2) The "bodily injury" or "property damage" does not arise out of the operation of any equipment listed in paragraphs 6.b and 6.c of the definition of "mobile equipment."

Paragraphs a(2) and a(3) of this exclusion do not apply if:

(1) The pollutants or any property in which the pollutants are contained are upset, overturned or damaged as a result of the maintenance or use of a covered "auto," and

(2) The discharge, dispersal, release or escape of the pollutants is caused directly by such upset, overturn or damage.

12. WAR

"Bodily injury" or "property damage" due to war, whether or not declared, or any act or condition incident to war. War includes civil war, insurrection, rebellion or revolution. This exclusion applies only to liability assumed under a contract or agreement.

C. LIMIT OF INSURANCE

Regardless of the number of covered "autos," "insureds," premiums paid, claims made or vehicles involved in the "accident," the most we will pay for all damages resulting from any one "accident" is the Limit of Insurance for Liability Coverage shown in the Declarations.

All "bodily injury" and "property damage" resulting from continuous or repeated exposure to substantially the same conditions will be considered as resulting from one "accident."

       CA 00 01 01 87
(E2393)

SECTION III - PHYSICAL DAMAGE COVERAGE

A. COVERAGE

1. We will pay for "loss" to a covered "auto" or its equipment under:

   a. Comprehensive Coverage. From any cause except:

   (1) The covered "auto's" collision with another object, or

   (2) The covered "auto's" overturn.

   b. Specified Causes of Loss Coverage. Caused by:

   (1) Fire, lightning or explosion;

   (2) Theft;

   (3) Windstorm, hail or earthquake;

   (4) Flood;

   (5) Mischief or vandalism; or

   (6) The sinking, burning, collision or derailment of any conveyance transporting the covered "auto."

   c. Collision Coverage. Caused by:

   (1) The covered "auto's" collision with another object; or

   (2) The covered "auto's" overturn.

2. **Towing.**

   We will pay up to the limit shown in the Declarations for towing and labor costs incurred each time a covered "auto" of the private passenger type is disabled. However, the labor must be performed at the place of disablement.

3. **Glass Breakage – Hitting a Bird or Animal – Falling Objects or Missiles.**

   If you carry Comprehensive Coverage for the damaged covered "auto," we will pay for the following under Comprehensive Coverage:

   a. Glass breakage;

   b. "Loss" caused by hitting a bird or animal; and

   c. "Loss" caused by falling objects or missiles.

   However, you have the option of having glass breakage caused by a covered "auto's" collision or overturn considered a "loss" under Collision Coverage.

4. **Coverage Extension.** We will pay up to $10 per day to a maximum of $300 for transportation expense incurred by you because of the total theft of a covered "auto" of the private passenger type. We will pay only for those covered "autos" for which you carry either Comprehensive or Specified Causes of Loss Coverage. We will pay for transportation expenses incurred during the period beginning 48 hours after the theft and ending, regardless of the policy's expiration, when the covered "auto" is returned to use or we pay for its "loss."

B. EXCLUSIONS

1. We will not pay for "loss" caused by or resulting from any of the following. Such "loss" is excluded regardless of any other cause or event that contributes concurrently or in any sequence to the "loss."

   a. Nuclear Hazard.

   (1) The explosion of any weapon employing atomic fission or fusion; or

   (2) Nuclear reaction or radiation, or radioactive contamination, however caused.

   b. War or Military Action.

   (1) War, including undeclared or civil war;

   (2) Warlike action by a military force, including action in hindering or defending against an actual or expected attack, by any government, sovereign or other authority using military personnel or other agents; or

   (3) Insurrection, rebellion, revolution, usurped power or action taken by governmental authority in hindering or defending against any of these.

2. Other Exclusions.

   a. We will not pay for "loss" to any of the following:

   (1) Tape decks or other sound reproducing equipment unless permanently installed in a covered "auto."

   (2) Tapes, records or other sound reproducing devices designed for use with sound reproducing equipment.

        CA 00 01 01 87
[E2394]

(3) Sound receiving equipment designed for use as a citizens' band radio, two-way mobile radio or telephone or scanning monitor receiver, including its antennas and other accessories, unless permanently installed in the dash or console opening normally used by the "auto" manufacturer for the installation of a radio.

b. We will not pay for "loss" caused by or resulting from any of the following unless caused by other "loss" that is covered by this insurance:

(1) Wear and tear, freezing, mechanical or electrical breakdown.

(2) Blowouts, punctures or other road damage to tires.

C. LIMIT OF INSURANCE

The most we will pay for "loss" in any one "accident" is the lesser of:

1. The actual cash value of the damaged or stolen property as of the time of the "loss;" or

2. The cost of repairing or replacing the damaged or stolen property with other property of like kind and quality.

D. DEDUCTIBLE

For each covered "auto," our obligation to pay for, repair, return or replace damaged or stolen property will be reduced by the applicable deductible shown in the Declarations. Any Comprehensive Coverage deductible shown in the Declarations does not apply to "loss" caused by fire or lightning.

SECTION IV - BUSINESS AUTO CONDITIONS

The following conditions apply in addition to the Common Policy Conditions:

A. LOSS CONDITIONS

1. **APPRAISAL FOR PHYSICAL DAMAGE LOSS**

If you and we disagree on the amount of "loss," either may demand an appraisal of the "loss." In this event, each party will select a competent appraiser. The two appraisers will select a competent and impartial umpire. The appraisers will state separately the actual cash value and amount of "loss." If they fail to agree, they will submit their differences to the umpire. A decision agreed to by any two will be binding. Each party will:

a. Pay its chosen appraiser; and

b. Bear the other expenses of the appraisal and umpire equally.

If we submit to an appraisal, we will still retain our right to deny the claim.

2. **DUTIES IN THE EVENT OF ACCIDENT, CLAIM, SUIT OR LOSS**

a. In the event of "accident," claim, "suit" or "loss," you must give us or our authorized representative prompt notice of the "accident" or "loss." Include:

(1) How, when and where the "accident" or "loss" occurred;

(2) The "insured's" name and address; and

(3) To the extent possible, the names and addresses of any injured persons and witnesses.

a. Additionally, you and any other involved "insured" must:

(1) Assume no obligation, make no payment or incur no expense without our consent, except at the "insured's" own cost.

(2) Immediately send us copies of any demand, notice, summons or legal paper received concerning the claim or "suit."

(3) Cooperate with us in the investigation, settlement or defense of the claim or "suit."

(4) Authorize us to obtain medical records or other pertinent information.

(5) Submit to examination, at our expense, by physicians of our choice, as often as we reasonably require.

c. If there is "loss" to a covered "auto" or its equipment you must also do the following:

(1) Promptly notify the police if the covered "auto" or any of its equipment is stolen.

(2) Take all reasonable steps to protect the covered "auto" from further damage. Also keep a record of your expenses for consideration in the settlement of the claim.

(3) Permit us to inspect the covered "auto" and records proving the "loss" before its repair or disposition.

(4) Agree to examinations under oath at our request and give us a signed statement of your answers.

3. LEGAL ACTION AGAINST US

No one may bring a legal action against us under this Coverage Form until:

a. There has been full compliance with all the terms of this Coverage Form; and

b. Under Liability Coverage, we agree in writing that the "insured" has an obligation to pay or until the amount of that obligation has finally been determined by judgment after trial. No one has the right under this policy to bring us into an action to determine the "insured's" liability.

4. LOSS PAYMENT - PHYSICAL DAMAGE COVERAGES

At our option we may:

a. Pay for, repair or replace damaged or stolen property;

b. Return the stolen property, at our expense. We will pay for any damage that results to the "auto" from the theft; or

c. Take all or any part of the damaged or stolen property at an agreed or appraised value.

5. TRANSFER OF RIGHTS OF RECOVERY AGAINST OTHERS TO US

If any person or organization to or for whom we make payment under this Coverage Form has rights to recover damages from another, those rights are transferred to us. That person or organization must do everything necessary to secure our rights and must do nothing after "accident" or "loss" to impair them.

B. GENERAL CONDITIONS

1. BANKRUPTCY

Bankruptcy or insolvency of the "insured" or the "insured's" estate will not relieve us of any obligations under this Coverage Form.

2. CONCEALMENT, MISREPRESENTATION OR FRAUD

This Coverage Form is void in any case of fraud by you at any time as it relates to this Coverage Form. It is also void if you or any other "insured," at any time, intentionally conceal or misrepresent a material fact concerning:

a. This Coverage Form;

b. The covered "auto;"

c. Your interest in the covered "auto;" or

d. A claim under this Coverage Form.

3. LIBERALIZATION

If we revise this Coverage Form to provide more coverage without additional premium charge, your policy will automatically provide the additional coverage as of the day the revision is effective in your state.

4. NO BENEFIT TO BAILEE - PHYSICAL DAMAGE COVERAGES

We will not recognize any assignment or grant any coverage for the benefit of any person or organization holding, storing or transporting property for a fee regardless of any other provision of this Coverage Form.

5. OTHER INSURANCE

a. For any covered "auto" you own, this Coverage Form provides primary insurance. For any covered "auto" you don't own, the insurance provided by this Coverage Form is excess over any other collectible insurance. However, while a covered "auto" which is a "trailer" is connected to another vehicle, the Liability Coverage this Coverage Form provides for the "trailer" is:

(1) Excess while it is connected to a motor vehicle you do not own.

(2) Primary while it is connected to a covered "auto" you own.

b. Regardless of the provisions of paragraph a. above, this Coverage Form's Liability Coverage is primary for any liability assumed under an "insured contract."

c. When this Coverage Form and any other Coverage Form or policy covers on the same basis, either excess or primary, we will pay only our share. Our share is the proportion that the Limit of Insurance of our Coverage Form bears to the total of the limits of all the Coverage Forms and policies covering on the same basis.

6. PREMIUM AUDIT

a. The estimated premium for this Coverage Form is based on the exposures you told us you would have when this policy began. We will compute the final premium due when we determine your actual exposures. The estimated total premium will be credited against the final premium due and the first Named Insured will be billed for the balance, if any. If the estimated total premium exceeds the final premium due, the first Named Insured will get a refund.

b. If this policy is issued for more than one year, the premium for this Coverage Form will be computed annually based on our rates or premiums in effect at the beginning of each year of the policy.

7. POLICY PERIOD, COVERAGE TERRITORY

Under this Coverage Form, we cover "accidents" and "losses" occurring:

a. During the policy period shown in the Declarations; and

b. Within the coverage territory.

The coverage territory is:

a. The United States of America;

b. The territories and possessions of the United States of America;

c. Puerto Rico; and

d. Canada.

We also cover "loss" to, or "accidents" involving, a covered "auto" while being transported between any of these places.

8. TWO OR MORE COVERAGE FORMS OR POLICIES ISSUED BY US

If this Coverage Form and any other Coverage Form or policy issued to you by us or any company affiliated with us apply to the same "accident," the aggregate maximum Limit of Insurance under all the Coverage Forms or policies shall not exceed the highest applicable Limit of Insurance under any one Coverage Form or policy. This condition does not apply to any Coverage Form or policy issued by us or an affiliated company specifically to apply as excess insurance over this Coverage Form.

SECTION V - DEFINITIONS

A. "Accident" includes continuous or repeated exposure to the same conditions resulting in "bodily injury" or "property damage."

B. "Auto" means a land motor vehicle, trailer or semitrailer designed for travel on public roads but does not include "mobile equipment."

C. "Bodily injury" means bodily injury, sickness or disease sustained by a person including death resulting from any of these.

D. "Insured" means any person or organization qualifying as an insured in the Who Is An Insured provision of the applicable coverage. Except with respect to the Limit of Insurance, the coverage afforded applies separately to each insured who is seeking coverage or against whom a claim or "suit" is brought.

E. "Insured contract" means:

1. A lease of premises;

2. A sidetrack agreement;

3. An easement or license agreement in connection with vehicle or pedestrian private railroad crossings at grade;

4. Any other easement agreement, except in connection with construction or demolition operations on or within 50 feet of a railroad;

5. An indemnification of a municipality as required by ordinance, except in connection with work for a municipality; or

6. That part of any other contract or agreement pertaining to your business under which you assume the tort liability of another to pay damages because of "bodily injury" or "property damage" to a third person or organization, if the contract or agreement is made prior to the "bodily injury" or "property damage." Tort liability means a liability that would be imposed by law in the absence of any contract or agreement.

An "insured contract" does not include that part of any contract or agreement:

1. That pertains to the loan, lease or rental of an "auto" to you; or

2. That holds a person or organization engaged in the business of transporting property by "auto" for hire harmless for your use of a covered "auto" over a route or territory that person or organization is authorized to serve by public authority.

F. "Loss" means direct and accidental loss or damage.

G. "Mobile equipment" means any of the following types of land vehicles, including any attached machinery or equipment:

1. Bulldozers, farm machinery, forklifts and other vehicles designed for use principally off public roads;

2. Vehicles maintained for use solely on or next to premises you own or rent;

3. Vehicles that travel on crawler treads;

4. Vehicles, whether self-propelled or not, maintained primarily to provide mobility to permanently mounted:

a. Power cranes, shovels, loaders, diggers or drills; or

b. Road construction or resurfacing equipment such as graders, scrapers or rollers.

5. Vehicles not described in paragraphs 1, 2, 3, or 4 above that are not self-propelled and are maintained primarily to provide mobility to permanently attached equipment of the following types:

a. Air compressors, pumps and generators, including spraying, welding, building cleaning, geophysical exploration, lighting and well servicing equipment; or

b. Cherry pickers and similar devices used to raise or lower workers.

G. Vehicles not described in paragraphs 1, 2, 3 or 4 above maintained primarily for purposes other than the transportation of persons or cargo. However, self-propelled vehicles with the following types of permanently attached equipment are not "mobile equipment" but will be considered "autos:"

a. Equipment designed primarily for:

(1) Snow removal;

(2) Road maintenance, but not construction or resurfacing; or

(3) Street cleaning;

b. Cherry pickers and similar devices mounted on automobile or truck chassis and used to raise or lower workers; and

c. Air compressors, pumps and generators, including spraying, welding, building cleaning, geophysical exploration, lighting or well servicing equipment.

H. "Property damage" means damage to or loss of use of tangible property.

I. "Suit" means a civil proceeding in which damages because of "bodily injury" or "property damages" to which this insurance applies are alleged. "Suit" includes an arbitration proceeding alleging such damages to which you must submit or submit with our consent.

J. "Trailer" includes semitrailer.

           CA 00 01 01 87
[E2398]

APPENDIX H

PERSONAL AUTOMOBILE INSURANCE COVERAGES

(1) INSURANCE SERVICES OFFICE

FAMILY COMBINATION AUTOMOBILE POLICY FORM
(REV. 1–1–63)

FAMILY COMBINATION AUTOMOBILE POLICY

No. ACF

RENEWAL OF NUMBER

SPACE FOR COMPANY NAME, INSIGNIA, AND LOCATION

DECLARATIONS

Item 1. Named Insured and Address: (No. Street, Town or City, County, State)

SPACE FOR PRODUCER'S NAME AND MAILING ADDRESS

Item 2. Policy Period: (Mo. Day Yr.)   (Months)

From   to

12.01 A.M., standard time at the address of the named insured as stated herein.

Occupation of the named insured is *F MARRIED WOMAN GIVE HUSBAND'S OCCUPATION OR BUSINESS (ENTER BELOW)*

Item 3. The insurance afforded is only with respect to such of the following coverages as are indicated by specific premium charge or charges. The limit of the company's liability against each such coverage shall be as stated herein, subject to all the terms of this policy having reference thereto.

CAR 1 PREMIUMS CAR 2		LIMITS OF LIABILITY		COVERAGES	
$	$	thousand dollars each person		A	Bodily Injury Liability
		thousand dollars each occurrence			
$	$	thousand dollars each occurrence		B	Property Damage Liability
$	$	dollars each person		C	Medical Payments
		$	Actual Cash Value*	D	(1) Comprehensive (excluding Collision)
$	$	$ 100			(2) Personal Effects
		Actual Cash Value less		E	Collision
$	$	$	deductible		
$	$	$		F	Fire, Lightning and Transportation
$	$	$		G	Theft
$	$	$		H	Combined Additional Coverage
$	$	$ 25	per disablement	I	Towing and Labor Costs
		thousand dollars each person		J	Uninsured Motorists
$	$	thousand dollars each accident			
		Form numbers of endorsements attached to policy at issue			
$					
$	$	Total Car 1 - Car 2			
$	**Total Premium**				

* STRIKE OUT "ACTUAL CASH VALUE" AND INSERT AMOUNT IF POLICY IS WRITTEN ON STATED AMOUNT BASIS

Item 4. Description of owned automobile or trailer

	Year of Model	Trade Name	Body Type; Model	Identification Number (I) Serial Number (S) Motor Number (M)	F.O.B. List Price or Delivered Price at Factory	Purchased Month, Year New or Used	Class & Rating Symbol	Sub-Class (if any)
Car 1								
Car 2								

Item 5. Loss Payee: Any loss under Part III is payable as interest may appear to the named insured and (NAME AND ADDRESS—ENTER BELOW)

Item 6. The owned automobile will be principally garaged in the town or city designated in Item 1 above, unless otherwise stated herein: (ENTER BELOW)

Item 7. During the past three years no insurer has canceled insurance, issued to the named insured, similar to that afforded hereunder, unless otherwise stated herein.

NOTE: This Policy is subject to the "Uninsured Motorists (Family Protection) Coverage Amendment", "Sound-Reproducing or Recording Equipment Excluded", "Uninsured Motorists Coverage Amendment (Insolvent Insurer)", "Amendment of Termination Provisions", and "Out-of-State Insurance" Endorsements on pages 5, 6 and 14.

Countersigned:

OKP 6013-0-G
(Rev. 1-1-63)

By _____
Authorized Representative   (E23991)

2

┌───┐
│   │
│   RESERVED FOR YOUR COMPANY'S NAME   │
│   │
└───┘

Agrees with the insured, named in the declarations made a part hereof, in consideration of the payment of the premium and in reliance upon the statements in the declarations and subject to all of the terms of this policy:

PART I — LIABILITY

Coverage A—Bodily Injury Liability; Coverage B—Property Damage Liability: To pay on behalf of the insured all sums which the insured shall become legally obligated to pay as damages because of:

A. bodily injury, sickness or disease, including death resulting therefrom, hereinafter called "bodily injury," sustained by any person;

B. injury to or destruction of property, including loss of use thereof, hereinafter called "property damage";

arising out of the ownership, maintenance or use of the owned automobile or any non-owned automobile, and the company shall defend any suit alleging such bodily injury or property damage and seeking damages which are payable under the terms of this policy, even if any of the allegations of the suit are groundless, false or fraudulent; but the company may make such investigation and settlement of any claim or suit as it deems expedient.

Supplementary Payments: To pay, in addition to the applicable limits of liability:

(a) all expenses incurred by the company, all costs taxed against the insured in any such suit and all interest on the entire amount of any judgment therein which accrues after entry of the judgment and before the company has paid or tendered or deposited in court that part of the judgment which does not exceed the limit of the company's liability thereon;

(b) premiums on appeal bonds required in any such suit, premiums on bonds to release attachments for an amount not in excess of the applicable limit of liability of this policy, and the cost of bail bonds required of the insured because of accident or traffic law violation arising out of the use of an automobile insured hereunder, not to exceed $100 per bail bond, but without any obligation to apply for or furnish any such bonds;

(c) expenses incurred by the insured for such immediate medical and surgical relief to others as shall be imperative at the time of an accident involving an automobile insured hereunder and not due to war;

(d) all reasonable expenses, other than loss of earnings, incurred by the insured at the company's request.

Persons Insured: The following are insureds under Part I:

(a) with respect to the owned automobile,

(1) the named insured and any resident of the same household,

(2) any other person using such automobile with the permission of the named insured, provided his actual operation or (if he is not operating) his other actual use thereof is within the scope of such permission, and

(3) any other person or organization but only with respect to his or its liability because of acts or omissions of an insured under (a) (1) or (2) above;

(b) with respect to a non-owned automobile,

(1) the named insured,

(2) any relative, but only with respect to a private passenger automobile or trailer,

provided his actual operation or (if he is not operating) the other actual use thereof is with the permission, or reasonably believed to be with the permission, of the owner and is within the scope of such permission, and

(3) any other person or organization not owning or hiring the automobile, but only with respect to his or its liability because of acts or omissions of an insured under (b) (1) or (2) above.

The insurance afforded under Part I applies separately to each insured against whom claim is made or suit is brought, but the inclusion herein of more than one insured shall not operate to increase the limits of the company's liability.

Definitions: Under Part I:

"named insured" means the individual named in Item 1 of the declarations and also includes his spouse, if a resident of the same household;

"insured" means a person or organization described under "Persons Insured";

"relative" means a relative of the named insured who is a resident of the same household;

"owned automobile" means

(a) a private passenger, farm or utility automobile described in this policy for which a specific premium charge indicates that coverage is afforded,

(b) a trailer owned by the named insured,

(c) a private passenger, farm or utility automobile ownership of which is acquired by the named insured during the policy period, provided

(1) it replaces an owned automobile as defined in (a) above, or

(2) the company insures all private passenger, farm and utility automobiles owned by the named insured on the date of such acquisition and the named insured notifies the company during the policy period or within 30 days after the date of such acquisition of his election to make this and no other policy issued by the company applicable to such automobile, or

(d) a temporary substitute automobile;

"temporary substitute automobile" means any automobile or trailer, not owned by the named insured, while temporarily used with the permission of the owner as a substitute for the owned automobile or trailer when withdrawn from normal use because of its breakdown, repair, servicing, loss or destruction;

"non-owned automobile" means an automobile or trailer not owned by or furnished for the regular use of either the named insured or any relative, other than a temporary substitute automobile;

"private passenger automobile" means a four wheel private passenger, station wagon or jeep type automobile;

"farm automobile" means an automobile of the truck type with a load capacity of fifteen hundred pounds or less not used for business or commercial purposes other than farming;

"utility automobile" means an automobile, other than a farm automobile, with a load capacity of fifteen hundred pounds or less of the pick-up body, sedan delivery or panel truck type not used for business or commercial purposes;

"trailer" means a trailer designed for use with a private passenger automobile, if not being used for business or commercial purposes with other than a private passenger, farm or utility automobile, or a farm wagon or farm implement while used with a farm automobile;

"automobile business" means the business or occupation of selling, repairing, servicing, storing or parking automobiles;

"use" of an automobile includes the loading and unloading thereof;

"war" means war, whether or not declared, civil war, insurrection, rebellion or revolution, or any act or condition incident to any of the foregoing.

Exclusions: This policy does not apply under Part I:

(a) to any automobile while used as a public or livery conveyance, but this exclusion does not apply to the named insured with respect to bodily injury or property damage which results from the named insured's occupancy of a non-owned automobile other than as the operator thereof;

(b) to bodily injury or property damage caused intentionally by or at the direction of the insured;

(c) to bodily injury or property damage with respect to which an insured under this policy is also an insured under a nuclear energy liability policy issued by Nuclear Energy Liability Insurance Association, Mutual Atomic Energy Liability Underwriters or Nuclear Insurance Association of Canada, or would be an insured under any such policy but for its termination upon exhaustion of its limit of liability;

(d) to bodily injury or property damage arising out of the operation of farm machinery;

(e) to bodily injury to any employee of the insured arising out of and in the course of (1) domestic employment by the insured, if benefits therefor are in whole or in part either payable or required to be provided under any workmen's compensation law, or (2) other employment by the insured;

(f) to bodily injury to any fellow employee of the insured injured in the course of his employment if such injury arises out of the use of an automobile in the business of his employer, but this exclusion does not apply to the named insured with respect to injury sustained by any such fellow employee;

(g) to an owned automobile while used by any person while such person is employed or otherwise engaged in the automobile business, but this exclusion does not apply to the named insured, a resident of the same household as the named insured, a partnership in which the named insured or such resident is a partner, or any partner, agent or employee of the named insured, such resident or partnership;

(h) to a non-owned automobile while maintained or used by any person while such person is employed or otherwise engaged in

(1) the automobile business of the insured or of any other person or organization,

(2) any other business or occupation of the insured, but this exclusion (h) (2) does not apply to a private passenger automobile operated or occupied by the named insured or by his private chauffeur or domestic servant or a trailer used therewith or with an owned automobile;

(i) to injury to or destruction of (1) property owned or transported by the insured or (2) property rented to or in charge of the insured other than a residence or private garage;

(j) to the ownership, maintenance, operation, use, loading or unloading of an automobile ownership of which is acquired by the named insured during the policy period or any temporary substitute automobile therefor, if the named insured has purchased other automobile liability insurance applicable to such automobile for which a specific premium charge has been made.

Financial Responsibility Laws: When this policy is certified as proof of financial responsibility for the future under the provisions of any motor vehicle financial responsibility law, such insurance as is afforded by this policy for bodily injury liability or for property damage liability shall comply with the provisions of such law to the extent of the coverage and limits of liability required by such law, but in no event in excess of the limits of liability stated in this policy. The insured agrees to reimburse the company for any payment made by the company which it would not have been obligated to make under the terms of this policy except for the agreement contained in this paragraph.

Limits of Liability: The limit of bodily injury liability stated in the declarations as applicable to "each person" is the limit of the company's liability for all damages, including damages for care and loss of services, arising out of bodily injury sustained by one person as the result of any one occurrence; the limit of such liability stated in the declarations as applicable to "each occurrence" is, subject to the above provision respecting each person, the total limit of the company's liability for all such damages arising out of bodily injury sustained by two or more persons as the result of any one occurrence.

The limit of property damage liability stated in the declarations as applicable to "each occurrence" is the total limit of the company's liability for all damages arising out of injury to or destruction of all property of one or more persons or organizations, including the loss of use thereof, as the result of any one occurrence.

Other Insurance: If the insured has other insurance against a loss covered by Part I of this policy the company shall not be liable under this policy for a greater proportion of such loss than the applicable limit of liability stated in the declarations bears to the total applicable limit of liability of all valid and collectible insurance against such loss; provided, however, the insurance with respect to a temporary substitute automobile or non-owned automobile shall be excess insurance over any other valid and collectible insurance.

PART II — EXPENSES FOR MEDICAL SERVICES

Coverage C—Medical Payments: To pay all reasonable expenses incurred within one year from the date of accident for necessary medical, surgical, X-ray and dental services, including prosthetic devices, and necessary ambulance, hospital, professional nursing and funeral services.

Division 1. To or for the named insured and each relative who sustains bodily injury, sickness or disease, including death resulting therefrom, hereinafter called "bodily injury," caused by accident,

(a) while occupying the owned automobile,

(b) while occupying a non-owned automobile, but only if such person has, or reasonably believes he has, the permission of the owner to use the automobile and the use is within the scope of such permission, or

(c) through being struck by an automobile or by a trailer of any type;

Division 2. To or for any other person who sustains bodily injury, caused by accident, while occupying

(a) the owned automobile, while being used by the named insured, by any resident of the same household or by any other person with the permission of the named insured, or

(b) a non-owned automobile, if the bodily injury results from

(1) its operation or occupancy by the named insured or its operation on his behalf by his private chauffeur or domestic servant, or

[E2400]

(Attach Endorsements Here)

(2) its operation or occupancy by a relative, provided it is a private passenger automobile or trailer,

but only if such operator or occupant has, or reasonably believes he has, the permission of the owner to use the automobile and the use is within the scope of such permission

Definitions: The definitions under Part I apply to Part II, and under Part II.

"occupying" means in or upon or entering into or alighting from.

Exclusions: This policy does not apply under Part II to bodily injury:

(a) sustained while occupying (1) an owned automobile while used as a public or livery conveyance, or (2) any vehicle while located for use as a residence or premises.

(b) sustained by the named insured or a relative while occupying or through being struck by (1) a farm type tractor or other equipment designed for use principally off public roads, while not upon public roads, or (2) a vehicle operated on rails or crawler-treads:

(c) sustained by any person other than the named insured or a relative,

(1) while such person is occupying an owned automobile while used as a public or livery conveyance, or

(2) resulting from the maintenance or use of a non-owned automobile by such person while employed or otherwise engaged in the automobile business, or

(3) resulting from the maintenance or use of a non-owned automobile by such person while

employed or otherwise engaged in any other business or occupation, unless the bodily injury results from the operation or occupancy of a private passenger automobile by the named insured or by his private chauffeur or domestic servant, or of a trailer used therewith or with an owned automobile;

(d) sustained by any person who is employed in the automobile business, if the accident arises out of the operation thereof and if benefits therefor are in whole or in part either payable or required to be provided under any workmen's compensation law;

(e) due to war.

Limit of Liability: The limit of liability for medical payments stated in the declarations as applicable to "each person" is the limit of the company's liability for all expenses incurred by or on behalf of each person who sustains bodily injury as the result of any one accident

Other Insurance: If there is other automobile medical payments insurance against a loss covered by Part II of this policy the company shall not be liable under this policy for a greater proportion of such loss than the applicable limit of liability stated in the declarations bears to the total applicable limit of liability of all valid and collectible automobile medical payments insurance, provided, however, the insurance with respect to a temporary substitute automobile or non-owned automobile shall be excess insurance over any other valid and collectible automobile medical payments insurance.

PART III — PHYSICAL DAMAGE

Coverage D (1)—Comprehensive (excluding Collision); (2)—Personal Effects:
(1) To pay for loss caused other than by collision to the owned automobile or to a non-owned automobile. For the purpose of this coverage, breakage of glass and loss caused by missiles, falling objects, fire, theft or larceny, explosion, earthquake, windstorm, hail, water, flood, malicious mischief or vandalism, riot or civil commotion, or colliding with a bird or animal, shall not be deemed to be loss caused by collision.

(2) To pay for loss caused by fire or lightning to robes, wearing apparel and other personal effects which are the property of the named insured or a relative, while such effects are in or upon the owned automobile.

Coverage E—Collision: To pay for loss caused by collision to the owned automobile or to a non-owned automobile but only for the amount of each such loss in excess of the deductible amount stated in the declarations as applicable hereto. The deductible amount shall not apply to loss caused by a collision with another automobile insured by the company

Coverage F—Fire, Lightning and Transportation: To pay for loss to the owned automobile or a non-owned automobile, caused (a) by fire or lightning, (b) by smoke or smudge due to a sudden, unusual and faulty operation of any fixed heating equipment serving the premises in which the automobile is located, or (c) by the stranding, sinking, burning, collision or derailment of any conveyance in or upon which the automobile is being transported.

Coverage G—Theft: To pay for loss to the owned automobile or to a non-owned automobile caused by theft or larceny.

Coverage H—Combined Additional Coverage: To pay for loss to the owned automobile or a non-owned automobile caused by windstorm, hail, earthquake, explosion, riot or civil commotion, or the forced landing or falling of any aircraft or its parts or equipment, flood or rising waters, malicious mischief or vandalism, external discharge or leakage of water except loss resulting from rain, snow or sleet whether or not wind-driven; provided, with respect to each automobile $25 shall be deducted from each loss caused by malicious mischief or vandalism.

Coverage I—Towing and Labor Costs: To pay for towing and labor costs necessitated by the disablement of the owned automobile or of any non-owned automobile, provided the labor is performed at the place of disablement.

Supplementary Payments: In addition to the applicable limit of liability:

(a) to reimburse the insured for transportation expenses incurred during the period commencing 48 hours after a theft covered by this policy of the entire automobile has been reported to the company and the police, and terminating when the automobile is returned to use or the company pays for the loss; provided that the company shall not be obligated to pay aggregate expenses in excess of $10 per day or totaling more than $300.

(b) to pay general average and salvage charges for which the insured becomes legally liable, as to the automobile being transported.

Definitions: The definitions of "named insured", "relative", "temporary substitute automobile", "private passenger automobile", "farm automobile", "utility automobile", "automobile business", "war", and "owned automobile" in Part I apply to Part III, but "owned automobile" does not include, under Part III, (1) a trailer owned by the named insured on the effective date of this policy and not described herein, or (2) a trailer ownership of which is acquired during the policy period unless the company insures all private passenger, farm and utility automobiles and trailers owned by the named insured on the date of such acquisition and the named insured notifies the company during the policy period or within 30 days after the date of such acquisition of his election to make this and no other policy issued by the company applicable to such trailer.

"insured" means

(a) with respect to an owned automobile,

(1) the named insured, and

(2) any person or organization (other than a person or organization employed or otherwise engaged in the automobile business or as a carrier or other bailee for hire) maintaining, using or having custody of said automobile with the permission of the named insured and within the scope of such permission.

(b) with respect to a non-owned automobile, the named insured and any relative while using such automobile, provided his actual operation or (if he is not operating) the other actual use thereof is with the permission or reasonably believed to be with the permission, of the owner and is within the scope of such permission.

"non-owned automobile" means a private passenger automobile or trailer not owned by or furnished for the regular use of either the named insured or any relative, other than a temporary substitute automobile, while said automobile or trailer is in the possession or custody of the insured or is being operated by him.

"loss" means direct and accidental loss of or damage to (a) the automobile, including its equipment, or (b) other insured property.

"collision" means collision of an automobile covered by this policy with another object or with a vehicle to which it is attached or by upset of such automobile.

"trailer" means a trailer designed for use with a private passenger automobile, if not being used for business or commercial purposes with other than a private passenger, farm or utility automobile, and if not a home, office, store, display or passenger trailer.

Exclusions: This policy does not apply under Part III:

(a) to any automobile while used as a public or livery conveyance;

(b) to loss due to war.

(c) to loss to a non-owned automobile arising out of its use by the insured while he is employed or otherwise engaged in the automobile business;

(d) to loss to a private passenger, farm or utility automobile or trailer owned by the named insured and not described in this policy or to any temporary substitute automobile therefor, if the insured has other valid and collectible insurance against such loss;

(e) to damage which is due and confined to wear and tear, freezing, mechanical or electrical breakdown or failure, unless such damage results from a theft covered by this policy.

(f) to tires, unless damaged by fire, malicious mischief or vandalism, or stolen or unless the loss be coincident with and from the same cause as other loss covered by this policy.

(g) to loss due to radioactive contamination.

(h) under coverage E, to breakage of glass if insurance with respect to such breakage is otherwise afforded.

Limit of Liability: The limit of the company's liability for loss shall not exceed the actual cash value of the property, or if the loss is of a part thereof the actual cash value of such part, at time of loss, nor what it would then cost to repair or replace the property or such part thereof with other of like kind and quality, nor, with respect to an owned automobile described in this policy, the applicable limit of liability stated in the declarations; provided, however, the limit of the company's liability (a) for loss to personal effects arising out of any one occurrence is $100, and (b) for loss to any trailer not owned by the named insured is $500.

Other Insurance: If the insured has other insurance against a loss covered by Part III of this policy, the company shall not be liable under this policy for a greater proportion of such loss than the applicable limit of liability of this policy bears to the total applicable limit of liability of all valid and collectible insurance against such loss, provided, however, the insurance with respect to a temporary substitute automobile or non owned automobile shall be excess insurance over any other valid and collectible insurance.

[E2401]

PART IV — PROTECTION AGAINST UNINSURED MOTORISTS

Coverage J—Uninsured Motorists (Damages for Bodily Injury): To pay all sums which the insured or his legal representative shall be legally entitled to recover as damages from the owner or operator of an uninsured automobile because of bodily injury, sickness or disease, including death resulting therefrom, hereinafter called "bodily injury", sustained by the insured, caused by accident and arising out of the ownership, maintenance or use of such uninsured automobile; provided, for the purposes of this coverage, determination as to whether the insured or such representative is legally entitled to recover such damages, and if so the amount thereof, shall be made by agreement between the insured or such representative and the company or, if they fail to agree, by arbitration.

No judgment against any person or organization alleged to be legally responsible for the bodily injury shall be conclusive, as between the insured and the company, of the issues of liability of such person or organization or of the amount of damages to which the insured is legally entitled unless such judgment is entered pursuant to an action prosecuted by the insured with the written consent of the company.

Definitions: The definitions under Part I, except the definition of "insured," apply to Part IV, and under Part IV:

"**insured**" means:
(a) the named insured and any relative;
(b) any other person while occupying an insured automobile, and
(c) any person, with respect to damages he is entitled to recover because of bodily injury to which this Part applies sustained by an insured under (a) or (b) above.

The insurance afforded under Part IV applies separately to each insured, but the inclusion herein of more than one insured shall not operate to increase the limits of the company's liability.

"**insured automobile**" means:
(a) an automobile described in the policy for which a specific premium charge indicates that coverage is afforded,
(b) a private passenger, farm or utility automobile, ownership of which is acquired by the named insured during the policy period, provided
 (1) it replaces an insured automobile as defined in (a) above, or
 (2) the company insures under this Coverage all private passenger, farm and utility automobiles owned by the named insured on the date of such acquisition and the named insured notifies the company during the policy period or within 30 days after the date of such acquisition of his election to make the Liability and Uninsured Motorist Coverages under this and no other policy issued by the company applicable to such automobile,
(c) a temporary substitute automobile for an insured automobile as defined in (a) or (b) above, and
(d) a non-owned automobile while being operated by the named insured; and the term "insured automobile" includes a trailer while being used with an automobile described in (a), (b), (c) or (d) above, but shall not include:
 (1) any automobile or trailer owned by a resident of the same household as the named insured,
 (2) any automobile while used as a public or livery conveyance, or
 (3) any automobile while being used without the permission of the owner.

"**uninsured automobile**" includes a trailer of any type and means:
(a) an automobile or trailer with respect to the ownership, maintenance or use of which there is, in at least the amounts specified by the financial responsibility law of the state in which the insured automobile is principally garaged, no bodily injury liability bond or insurance policy applicable at the time of the accident with respect to any person or organization legally responsible for the use of such automobile, or with respect to which there is a bodily injury liability bond or insurance policy applicable at the time of the accident but the company writing the same denies coverage thereunder or
(b) a hit and run automobile;

but the term "uninsured automobile" shall not include:
 (1) an insured automobile or an automobile furnished for the regular use of the named insured or a relative,
 (2) an automobile or trailer owned or operated by a self-insurer within the meaning of any motor vehicle financial responsibility law, motor carrier law or any similar law,
 (3) an automobile or trailer owned by the United States of America, Canada, a state, a political subdivision of any such government or an agency of any of the foregoing,
 (4) a land motor vehicle or trailer if operated on rails or crawler-treads or while located for use as a residence or premises and not as a vehicle, or
 (5) a farm type tractor or equipment designed for use principally off public roads, except while actually upon public roads.

"**hit-and-run automobile**" means an automobile which causes bodily injury to an insured arising out of physical contact of such automobile with the insured or with an automobile which the insured is occupying at the time of the accident, provided (a) there cannot be ascertained the identity of either the operator or the owner of such "hit and run automobile", (b) the insured or someone on his behalf shall have reported the accident within 24 hours to a police, peace or judicial officer or to the Commissioner of Motor Vehicles, and shall have filed with the company within 30 days thereafter a statement under oath that the insured or his legal representative has a cause or causes of action arising out of such accident for damages against a person or persons whose identity is unascertainable, and setting forth the facts in support thereof, and (c) at the company's request, the insured or his legal representative makes available for inspection the automobile which the insured was occupying at the time of the accident.

"**occupying**" means in or upon or entering into or alighting from.

"**state**" includes the District of Columbia, a territory or possession of the United States, and a province of Canada.

Exclusions. This policy does not apply under Part IV:
(a) to bodily injury to an insured while occupying an automobile (other than an insured automobile) owned by the named insured or a relative, or through being struck by such an automobile,
(b) to bodily injury to an insured with respect to which such insured, his legal representative or any person entitled to payment under this coverage shall, without written consent of the company, make any settlement with any person or organization who may be legally liable therefor;
(c) so as to inure directly or indirectly to the benefit of any workmen's compensation or disability benefits carrier or any person or organization qualifying as a self insurer under any workmen's compensation or disability benefits law or any similar law.

Limits of Liability:
(a) The limit of liability for uninsured motorists coverage stated in the declarations as applicable to "each person" is the limit of the company's liability for all damages, including damages for care or loss of services, because of bodily injury sustained by one person as the result of any one accident and, subject to the above provision respecting each person, the limit of liability stated in the declarations as applicable to "each accident" is the total limit of the company's liability for all damages, including damages for care or loss of services, because of bodily injury sustained by two or more persons as the result of any one accident.
(b) Any amount payable under the terms of this Part because of bodily injury sustained in an accident by a person who is an insured under this Part shall be reduced by
 (1) all sums paid on account of such bodily injury by or on behalf of (i) the owner or operator of the uninsured automobile and (ii) any other person or organization jointly or severally liable together with such owner or operator for such bodily injury including all sums paid under Coverage A, and
 (2) the amount paid and the present value of all amounts payable on account of such bodily injury under any workmen's compensation law, disability benefits law or any similar law.
(c) Any payment made under this Part to or for any insured shall be applied in reduction of the amount of damages which he may be entitled to recover from any person insured under Coverage A.
(d) The company shall not be obligated to pay under this Coverage that part of the damages which the insured may be entitled to recover from the owner or operator of an uninsured automobile which represents expenses for medical services paid or payable under Part II.

Other Insurance: With respect to bodily injury to an insured while occupying an automobile not owned by the named insured, the insurance under Part IV shall apply only as excess insurance over any other similar insurance available to such insured and applicable to such automobile as primary insurance, and this insurance shall then apply only in the amount by which the limit of liability for this coverage exceeds the applicable limit of liability of such other insurance.

Except as provided in the foregoing paragraph, if the insured has other similar insurance available to him and applicable to the accident, the damages shall be deemed not to exceed the higher of the applicable limits of liability of this insurance and such other insurance, and the company shall not be liable for a greater proportion of any loss to which this Coverage applies than the limit of liability hereunder bears to the sum of the applicable limits of liability of this insurance and such other insurance.

Arbitration: If any person making claim hereunder and the company do not agree that such person is legally entitled to recover damages from the owner or operator of an uninsured automobile because of bodily injury to the insured, or do not agree as to the amount of payment which may be owing under this Part, then, upon written demand of either, the matter or matters upon which such person and the company do not agree shall be settled by arbitration in accordance with the rules of the American Arbitration Association, and judgment upon the award rendered by the arbitrators may be entered in any court having jurisdiction thereof. Such person and the company each agree to consider itself bound and to be bound by any award made by the arbitrators pursuant to this Part.

Trust Agreement: In the event of payment to any person under this Part:
(a) the company shall be entitled to the extent of such payment to the proceeds of any settlement or judgment that may result from the exercise of any rights of recovery of such person against any person or organization legally responsible for the bodily injury because of which such payment is made;
(b) such person shall hold in trust for the benefit of the company all rights of recovery which he shall have against such other person or organization because of the damages which are the subject of claim made under this Part;
(c) such person shall do whatever is proper to secure and shall do nothing after loss to prejudice such rights;
(d) if requested in writing by the company, such person shall take, through any representative designated by the company, such action as may be necessary or appropriate to recover such payment as damages from such other person or organization, such action to be taken in the name of such person; in the event of a recovery, the company shall be reimbursed out of such recovery for expenses, costs and attorneys' fees incurred by it in connection therewith;
(e) such person shall execute and deliver to the company such instruments and papers as may be appropriate to secure the rights and obligations of such person and the company established by this provision.

CONDITIONS

Conditions 1, 2, 3, 6, 14, 15, 16 and 18 apply to all Parts. Conditions 4 and 5, 7 through 13, and 17 apply only to the Parts noted thereunder.

1. **Policy Period, Territory:** This policy applies only to accidents, occurrences and loss during the policy period while the automobile is within the United States of America, its territories or possessions, or Canada, or is being transported between ports thereof.

2. **Premium:** If the named insured disposes of, acquires ownership of, or replaces a private passenger, farm or utility automobile or, with respect to Part III, a trailer, any premium adjustment necessary shall be made as of the date of such change in accordance with the manuals in use by the company. The named insured shall, upon request, furnish reasonable proof of the number of such automobiles or trailers and a description thereof.

3. **Notice:** In the event of an accident, occurrence or loss, written notice containing particulars sufficient to identify the insured and also reasonably obtainable information with respect to the time, place and circumstances thereof, and the names and addresses of the injured and of available witnesses, shall be given by or for the insured to the company or any of its authorized agents as soon as practicable. In the event of theft the insured shall also promptly notify the police. If claim is made or suit is brought against the insured, he shall immediately forward to the company every demand, notice, summons or other process received by him or his representative.

If, before the company makes payment of loss under Part IV, the insured or his legal representative shall institute any legal action for bodily injury against any person or organization legally responsible for the use of an automobile involved in the accident, a copy of the summons and complaint or other process served in connection with such legal action shall be forwarded immediately to the company by the insured or his legal representative.

4. **Two or More Automobiles—Parts I, II and III:** When two or more automobiles are insured hereunder, the terms of this policy shall apply separately to each, but an automobile and a trailer attached thereto shall be held to be one automobile as respects limits of liability under Part I of this policy, and separate automobiles under Part III of this policy, including any deductible provisions applicable thereto.

5. **Assistance and Cooperation of the Insured—Parts I and III:** The insured shall cooperate with the company and, upon the company's request, assist in making settlements, in the conduct of suits and in enforcing any right of contribution or indemnity against any person or organization who may be liable to the insured because of bodily injury, property damage or loss with respect to which insurance is afforded under this policy; and the insured shall attend hearings and trials and assist in securing and giving evidence and obtaining the attendance of witnesses. The insured shall not, except at his own cost, voluntarily make any payment, assume any obligation or incur any expense other than for such immediate medical

[E2402]

and surgical relief to others as shall be imperative at the time of accident.

Part IV: After notice of claim under Part IV, the company may require the insured to take such action as may be necessary or appropriate to preserve his right to recover damages from any person or organization alleged to be legally responsible for the bodily injury; and in any action against the company, the company may require the insured to join such person or organization as a party defendant.

6. Action Against Company—Part I: No action shall lie against the company unless, as a condition precedent thereto, the insured shall have fully complied with all the terms of this policy, nor until the amount of the insured's obligation to pay shall have been finally determined either by judgment against the insured after actual trial or by written agreement of the insured, the claimant and the company.

Any person or organization or the legal representative thereof who has secured such judgment or written agreement shall thereafter be entitled to recover under this policy to the extent of the insurance afforded by this policy. No person or organization shall have any right under this policy to join the company as a party to any action against the insured to determine the insured's liability, nor shall the company be impleaded by the insured or his legal representative. Bankruptcy or insolvency of the insured or of the insured's estate shall not relieve the company of any of its obligations hereunder.

Parts II, III and IV: No action shall lie against the company unless, as a condition precedent thereto, there shall have been full compliance with all the terms of this policy nor, under Part III, until thirty days after proof of loss is filed and the amount of loss is determined as provided in this policy.

7. Medical Reports; Proof and Payment of Claim—Part II: As soon as practicable the injured person or someone on his behalf shall give to the company written proof of claim, under oath if required, and shall, after each request from the company, execute authorization to enable the company to obtain medical reports and copies of records. The injured person shall submit to physical examination by physicians selected by the company when and as often as the company may reasonably require.

The company may pay the injured person or any person or organization rendering the services and such payment shall reduce the amount payable hereunder for such injury. Payment hereunder shall not constitute an admission of liability of any person or, except hereunder, of the company.

8. Insured's Duties in Event of Loss—Part III: In the event of loss the insured shall:

(a) protect the automobile, whether or not the loss is covered by this policy, and any further loss due to the insured's failure to protect shall not be recoverable under this policy; reasonable expenses incurred in affording such protection shall be deemed incurred at the company's request;

(b) file with the company, within 91 days after loss, his sworn proof of loss in such form and including such information as the company may reasonably require and shall, upon the company's request, exhibit the damaged property and submit to examination under oath.

9. Proof of Claim; Medical Reports—Part IV: As soon as practicable, the insured or other person making claim shall give to the company written proof of claim, under oath if required, including full particulars of the nature and extent of the injuries, treatment, and other details entering into the determination of the amount payable. The insured and every other person making claim shall submit to examinations under oath by any person named by the company and subscribe the same, as often as may reasonably be required. Proof of claim shall be made upon forms furnished by the company unless the company shall have failed to furnish such forms within 15 days after receiving notice of claim.

The injured person shall submit to physical examinations by physicians selected by the company when and as often as the company may reasonably require and he, or in the event of his incapacity his legal representative, or in the event of his death his legal representative or the person or persons entitled to sue therefor, shall upon each request from the company execute authorization to enable the company to obtain medical reports and copies of records.

10. Appraisal—Part III: If the insured and the company fail to agree as to the amount of loss, either may, within 60 days after proof of loss is filed, demand an appraisal of the loss. In such event the insured and the company shall each select a competent appraiser, and the appraisers shall select a competent and disinterested umpire. The appraisers shall state separately the actual cash value and the amount of loss and failing to agree shall submit their differences to the umpire. An award in writing of any two shall determine the amount of loss. The insured and the company shall each pay his chosen appraiser and shall bear equally the other expenses of the appraisal and umpire.

The company shall not be held to have waived any of its rights by any act relating to appraisal.

11. Payment of Loss—Part III: The company may pay for the loss in money; or may repair or replace the damaged or stolen property; or may, at any time before the loss is paid or the property is so replaced, at its expense return any stolen property to the named insured, or at its option to the address shown in the declarations, with payment for any resultant damage thereto; or may take all or such part of the property at the agreed or appraised value but there shall be no abandonment to the company. The company may settle any claim for loss either with the insured or the owner of the property.

Part IV: Any amount due is payable (a) to the insured, or (b) if the insured be a minor to his parent or guardian, or (c) if the insured be deceased to his surviving spouse, otherwise (d) to a person authorized by law to receive such payment or to a person legally entitled to recover the damages which the payment represents; provided, the company may at its option pay any amount due in accordance with division (d) hereof.

12. No Benefit to Bailee—Part III: The insurance afforded by this policy shall not inure directly or indirectly to the benefit of any carrier or other bailee for hire liable for loss to the automobile.

13. Subrogation—Parts I and III: In the event of any payment under this policy, the company shall be subrogated to all the insured's rights of recovery therefor against any person or organization and the insured shall execute and deliver instruments and papers and do whatever else is necessary to secure such rights. The insured shall do nothing after loss to prejudice such rights.

14. Changes: Notice to any agent or knowledge possessed by any agent or by any other person shall not effect a waiver or a change in any part of this policy or estop the company from asserting any right under the terms of this policy; nor shall the terms of this policy be waived or changed, except by endorsement issued to form a part of this policy.

15. Assignment: Assignment of interest under this policy shall not bind the company until its consent is endorsed hereon; if, however, the insured named in Item 1 of the declarations, or his spouse if a resident of the same household, shall die, this policy shall cover (1) the survivor as named insured, (2) his legal representative as named insured but only while acting within the scope of his duties as such, (3) any person having proper temporary custody of an owned automobile, as an insured, until the appointment and qualification of such legal representative, and (4) under division 1 of Part II any person who was a relative at the time of such death.

16. Cancelation: This policy may be canceled by the insured named in Item 1 of the declarations by surrender thereof to the company or any of its authorized agents or by mailing to the company written notice stating when thereafter the cancelation shall be effective. This policy may be canceled by the company by mailing to the insured named in Item 1 of the declarations at the address shown in this policy written notice stating when not less than ten days thereafter such cancelation shall be effective. The mailing of notice as aforesaid shall be sufficient proof of notice. The time of the surrender or the effective date and hour of cancelation stated in the notice shall become the end of the policy period. Delivery of such written notice either by such insured or by the company shall be equivalent to mailing.

If such insured cancels, earned premium shall be computed in accordance with the customary short rate table and procedure. If the company cancels, earned premium shall be computed pro rata. Premium adjustment may be made either at the time cancelation is effected or as soon as practicable after cancelation becomes effective, but payment or tender of unearned premium is not a condition of cancelation.

17. Cancelation by Company Limited—Part I: After this policy has been in effect for sixty days or, if the policy is a renewal, effective immediately, the company shall not exercise its right to cancel the insurance afforded under Part I unless:

1. the named insured fails to discharge when due any of his obligations in connection with the payment of premium for this policy or any installment thereof whether payable directly or under any premium finance plan; or
2. the insurance was obtained through fraudulent misrepresentation; or
3. the insured violates any of the terms and conditions of the policy; or
4. the named insured or any other operator, either resident in the same household, or who customarily operates an automobile insured under the policy,
   (a) has had his driver's license suspended or revoked during the policy period, or
   (b) is or becomes subject to epilepsy or heart attacks, and such individual cannot produce a certificate from a physician testifying to his unqualified ability to operate a motor vehicle, or
   (c) is or has been convicted of or forfeits bail, during the 36 months immediately preceding the effective date of the policy or during the policy period, for:
      (1) any felony, or
      (2) criminal negligence resulting in death, homicide or assault, arising out of the operation of a motor vehicle, or
      (3) operating a motor vehicle while in an intoxicated condition or while under the influence of drugs, or
      (4) leaving the scene of an accident without stopping to report, or
      (5) theft of a motor vehicle, or
      (6) making false statements in an application for a driver's license, or
      (7) a third violation, committed within a period of 18 months, of (i) any ordinance or regulation limiting the speed of motor vehicles or (ii) any of the provisions in the motor vehicle laws of any state, the violation of which constitutes a misdemeanor, whether or not the violations were repetitions of the same offense or were different offenses.

18. Declarations: By acceptance of this policy, the insured named in Item 1 of the declarations agrees that the statements in the declarations are his agreements and representations, that this policy is issued in reliance upon the truth of such representations and that this policy embodies all agreements existing between himself and the company or any of its agents relating to this insurance.

In Witness Whereof, the company has caused this policy to be executed and attested, but this policy shall not be valid unless countersigned by a duly authorized representative of the company.

Company's language may be substituted as desired

INSERT SIGNATURES AND TITLES OF PROPER OFFICERS

[E2403]

AUTOMOBILE

M. 0043
(Ed. 12 70)

A 935

UNINSURED MOTORISTS (FAMILY PROTECTION) COVERAGE AMENDMENT

This endorsement, effective (12:01 A.M. standard time) forms a part of policy No.

issued to

by

Authorized Representative

It is agreed that the term "uninsured automobile" is changed to "uninsured motor vehicle"

(2) INSURANCE SERVICES OFFICE

PERSONAL AUTO POLICY (ED.1985)

AGREEMENT

In return for payment of the premium and subject to all the terms of this policy, we agree with you as follows:

DEFINITIONS

A. Throughout this policy, "you" and "your" refer to:
   1. The "named insured" shown in the Declarations; and
   2. The spouse if a resident of the same household.

B. "We", "us" and "our" refer to the Company providing this insurance.

C. For purposes of this policy, a private passenger type auto shall be deemed to be owned by a person if leased:
   1. Under a written agreement to that person; and
   2. For a continuous period of at least 6 months.

Other words and phrases are defined. They are in quotation marks when used.

D. "Bodily injury" means bodily harm, sickness or disease, including death that results.

E. "Business" includes trade, profession or occupation.

F. "Family member" means a person related to you by blood, marriage or adoption who is a resident of your household. This includes a ward or foster child.

G. "Occupying" means in, upon, getting in, on, out or off.

H. "Property damage" means physical injury to, destruction of or loss of use of tangible property.

I. "Trailer" means a vehicle designed to be pulled by a:
   1. Private passenger auto; or
   2. Pickup or van.

   It also means a farm wagon or farm implement while towed by a vehicle listed in 1. or 2. above.

J. "Your covered auto" means:
   1. Any vehicle shown in the Declarations.

2. Any of the following types of vehicles on the date you become the owner:
   a. a private passenger auto; or
   b. a pickup or van.

   This provision (J.2.) applies only if:

   a. you acquire the vehicle during the policy period;

   b. you ask us to insure it within 30 days after you become the owner; and

   c. with respect to a pickup or van, no other insurance policy provides coverage for that vehicle.

   If the vehicle you acquire replaces one shown in the Declarations, it will have the same coverage as the vehicle it replaced. You must ask us to insure a replacement vehicle within 30 days only if:

   a. you wish to add or continue Coverage for Damage to Your Auto; or

   b. it is a pickup or van used in any "business" other than farming or ranching.

   If the vehicle you acquire is in addition to any shown in the Declarations, it will have the broadest coverage we now provide for any vehicle shown in the Declarations.

3. Any "trailer" you own.

4. Any auto or "trailer" you do not own while used as a temporary substitute for any other vehicle described in this definition which is out of normal use because of its:

   a. breakdown;   d. loss; or
   b. repair;   e. destruction.
   c. servicing;

Keeton & Widiss—Ins.Law HBSE—26

PART A—LIABILITY COVERAGE

INSURING AGREEMENT

A. We will pay damages for "bodily injury" or "property damage" for which any "insured" becomes legally responsible because of an auto accident. Damages include pre-judgment interest awarded against the "insured." We will settle or defend, as we consider appropriate, any claim or suit asking for these damages. In addition to our limit of liability, we will pay all defense costs we incur. Our duty to settle or defend ends when our limit of liability for this coverage has been exhausted. We have no duty to defend any suit or settle any claim for "bodily injury" or "property damage" not covered under this policy.

B. "Insured" as used in this Part means:

1. You or any "family member" for the ownership, maintenance or use of any auto or "trailer."

2. Any person using "your covered auto."

3. For "your covered auto," any person or organization but only with respect to legal responsibility for acts or omissions of a person for whom coverage is afforded under this Part.

4. For any auto or "trailer," other than "your covered auto," any other person or organization but only with respect to legal responsibility for acts or omissions of you or any "family member" for whom coverage is afforded under this Part. This provision (B.4.) applies only if the person or organization does not own or hire the auto or "trailer."

SUPPLEMENTARY PAYMENTS

In addition to our limit of liability, we will pay on behalf of an "insured:"

1. Up to $250 for the cost of bail bonds required because of an accident, including related traffic law violations. The accident must result in "bodily injury" or "property damage" covered under this policy.

2. Premiums on appeal bonds and bonds to release attachments in any suit we defend.

3. Interest accruing after a judgment is entered in any suit we defend. Our duty to pay interest ends when we offer to pay that part of the judgment which does not exceed our limit of liability for this coverage.

4. Up to $50 a day for loss of earnings, but not other income, because of attendance at hearings or trials at our request.

5. Other reasonable expenses incurred at our request.

EXCLUSIONS

A. We do not provide Liability Coverage for any person:

1. Who intentionally causes "bodily injury" or "property damage."

2. For damage to property owned or being transported by that person.

3. For damage to property:

   a. rented to;

   b. used by; or

   c. in the care of;

   that person.

   This exclusion (A.3.) does not apply to damage to a residence or private garage.

4. For "bodily injury" to an employee of that person during the course of employment. This exclusion (A.4.) does not apply to "bodily injury" to a domestic employee unless workers' compensation benefits are required or available for that domestic employee.

5. For that person's liability arising out of the ownership or operation of a vehicle while it is being used to carry persons or property for a fee. This exclusion (A.5.) does not apply to a share-the-expense car pool.

6. While employed or otherwise engaged in the "business" of:

a. selling;	d. storing; or
b. repairing;	e. parking;
c. servicing;	

   vehicles designed for use mainly on public highways. This includes road testing and delivery. This exclusion (A.6.) does not apply to the ownership, maintenance or use of "your covered auto" by:

   a. you;

   b. any "family member;" or

   c. any partner, agent or employee of you or any "family member."

7. Maintaining or using any vehicle while that person is employed or otherwise engaged in any "business" (other than farming or ranching) not described in Exclusion A.6. This exclusion (A.7.) does not apply to the maintenance or use of a:

EXCLUSIONS (Continued)

    a. private passenger auto;

    b. pickup or van that you own; or

    c. "trailer" used with a vehicle described in a. or b. above.

8. Using a vehicle without a reasonable belief that that person is entitled to do so.

9. For "bodily injury" or "property damage" for which that person:

    a. is an insured under a nuclear energy liability policy; or

    b. would be an insured under a nuclear energy liability policy but for its termination upon exhaustion of its limit of liability.

A nuclear energy liability policy is a policy issued by any of the following or their successors:

    a. American Nuclear Insurers;

    b. Mutual Atomic Energy Liability Underwriters; or

    c. Nuclear Insurance Association of Canada.

B. We do not provide Liability Coverage for the ownership, maintenance or use of:

1. Any motorized vehicle having fewer than four wheels.

2. Any vehicle, other than "your covered auto." which is:

    a. owned by you; or

    b. furnished or available for your regular use.

3. Any vehicle, other than "your covered auto." which is:

    a. owned by any "family member;" or

    b. furnished or available for the regular use of any "family member."

However, this exclusion (B.3.) does not apply to your maintenance or use of any vehicle which is:

    a. owned by a "family member;" or

    b. furnished or available for the regular use of a "family member."

LIMIT OF LIABILITY

A. The limit of liability shown in the Declarations for this coverage is our maximum limit of liability for all damages resulting from any one auto accident. This is the most we will pay regardless of the number of:

1. "Insureds;"

2. Claims made;

3. Vehicles or premiums shown in the Declarations; or

4. Vehicles involved in the auto accident.

B. We will apply the limit of liability to provide any separate limits required by law for bodily injury and property damage liability. However, this provision (B.) will not change our total limit of liability.

OUT OF STATE COVERAGE

If an auto accident to which this policy applies occurs in any state or province other than the one in which "your covered auto" is principally garaged, we will interpret your policy for that accident as follows:

A. If the state or province has:

1. A financial responsibility or similar law specifying limits of liability for "bodily injury" or "property damage" higher than the limit shown in the Declarations, your policy will provide the higher specified limit.

2. A compulsory insurance or similar law requiring a nonresident to maintain insurance whenever the nonresident uses a vehicle in that state or province, your policy will provide at least the required minimum amounts and types of coverage.

B. No one will be entitled to duplicate payments for the same elements of loss.

FINANCIAL RESPONSIBILITY

When this policy is certified as future proof of financial responsibility, this policy shall comply with the law to the extent required.

OTHER INSURANCE

If there is other applicable liability insurance we will pay only our share of the loss. Our share is the proportion that our limit of liability bears to the total of all applicable limits. However, any insurance we provide for a vehicle you do not own shall be excess over any other collectible insurance.

PART B—MEDICAL PAYMENTS COVERAGE

INSURING AGREEMENT

A. We will pay reasonable expenses incurred for necessary medical and funeral services because of "bodily injury:"

1. Caused by accident; and

2. Sustained by an "insured."

We will pay only those expenses incurred within 3 years from the date of the accident.

B. "Insured" as used in this Part means:

1. You or any "family member:"

   a. while "occupying;" or

   b. as a pedestrian when struck by;

   a motor vehicle designed for use mainly on public roads or a trailer of any type.

2. Any other person while "occupying" "your covered auto."

EXCLUSIONS

We do not provide Medical Payments Coverage for any person for "bodily injury:"

1. Sustained while "occupying" any motorized vehicle having fewer than four wheels.

2. Sustained while "occupying" "your covered auto" when it is being used to carry persons or property for a fee. This exclusion (2.) does not apply to a share-the-expense car pool.

3. Sustained while "occupying" any vehicle located for use as a residence or premises.

4. Occurring during the course of employment if workers' compensation benefits are required or available for the "bodily injury."

5. Sustained while "occupying," or when struck by, any vehicle (other than "your covered auto") which is:

   a. owned by you; or

   b. furnished or available for your regular use.

6. Sustained while "occupying," or when struck by, any vehicle (other than "your covered auto") which is:

   a. owned by any "family member;" or

   b. furnished or available for the regular use of any "family member."

   However, this exclusion (6.) does not apply to you.

7. Sustained while "occupying" a vehicle without a reasonable belief that that person is entitled to do so.

8. Sustained while "occupying" a vehicle when it is being used in the "business" of an "insured." This exclusion (8.) does not apply to "bodily injury" sustained while "occupying" a:

   a. private passenger auto;

   b. pickup or van that you own; or

   c. "trailer" used with a vehicle described in a. or b. above.

9. Caused by or as a consequence of:

   a. discharge of a nuclear weapon (even if accidental);

   b. war (declared or undeclared);

   c. civil war;

   d. insurrection; or

   e. rebellion or revolution.

10. From or as a consequence of the following, whether controlled or uncontrolled or however caused:

    a. nuclear reaction;

    b. radiation; or

    c. radioactive contamination.

LIMIT OF LIABILITY

A. The limit of liability shown in the Declarations for this coverage is our maximum limit of liability for each person injured in any one accident. This is the most we will pay regardless of the number of:

1. "Insureds;"

2. Claims made;

3. Vehicles or premiums shown in the Declarations; or

4. Vehicles involved in the accident.

B. Any amounts otherwise payable for expenses under this coverage shall be reduced by any amounts paid or payable for the same expenses under Part A or Part C.

C. No payment will be made unless the injured person or that person's legal representative agrees in writing that any payment shall be applied toward any settlement or judgment that person receives under Part A or Part C.

OTHER INSURANCE

If there is other applicable auto medical payments insurance we will pay only our share of the loss. Our share is the proportion that our limit of liability bears to the total of all applicable limits. However, any insurance we provide with respect to a vehicle you do not own shall be excess over any other collectible auto insurance providing payments for medical or funeral expenses.

PART C—UNINSURED MOTORISTS COVERAGE

INSURING AGREEMENT

A. We will pay damages which an "insured" is legally entitled to recover from the owner or operator of an "uninsured motor vehicle" because of "bodily injury:"

1. Sustained by an "insured," and
2. Caused by an accident.

The owner's or operator's liability for these damages must arise out of the ownership, maintenance or use of the "uninsured motor vehicle."

Any judgment for damages arising out of a suit brought without our written consent is not binding on us.

B. "Insured" as used in this Part means:

1. You or any "family member."
2. Any other person "occupying" "your covered auto."
3. Any person for damages that person is entitled to recover because of "bodily injury" to which this coverage applies sustained by a person described in 1. or 2. above.

C. "Uninsured motor vehicle" means a land motor vehicle or trailer of any type:

1. To which no bodily injury liability bond or policy applies at the time of the accident.
2. To which a bodily injury liability bond or policy applies at the time of the accident. In this case its limit for bodily injury liability must be less than the minimum limit for bodily injury liability specified by the financial responsibility law of the state in which "your covered auto" is principally garaged.
3. Which is a hit and run vehicle whose operator or owner cannot be identified and which hits:
   a. you or any "family member;"
   b. a vehicle which you or any "family member" are "occupying;" or
   c. "your covered auto."
4. To which a bodily injury liability bond or policy applies at the time of the accident but the bonding or insuring company;
   a. denies coverage; or
   b. is or becomes insolvent.

However, "uninsured motor vehicle" does not include any vehicle or equipment:

1. Owned by or furnished or available for the regular use of you or any "family member."
2. Owned or operated by a self-insurer under any applicable motor vehicle law.
3. Owned by any governmental unit or agency.
4. Operated on rails or crawler treads.

5. Designed mainly for use off public roads while not on public roads.
6. While located for use as a residence or premises.

EXCLUSIONS

A. We do not provide Uninsured Motorists Coverage for "bodily injury" sustained by any person:

1. While "occupying," or when struck by, any motor vehicle owned by you or any "family member" which is not insured for this coverage under this policy. This includes a trailer of any type used with that vehicle.
2. If that person or the legal representative settles the "bodily injury" claim without our consent.
3. While "occupying" "your covered auto" when it is being used to carry persons or property for a fee. This exclusion (A.3.) does not apply to a share-the-expense car pool.
4. Using a vehicle without a reasonable belief that that person is entitled to do so.

B. This coverage shall not apply directly or indirectly to benefit any insurer or self-insurer under any of the following or similar law:

1. workers' compensation law; or
2. disability benefits law.

LIMIT OF LIABILITY

A. The limit of liability shown in the Declarations for this coverage is our maximum limit of liability for all damages resulting from any one accident. This is the most we will pay regardless of the number of:

1. "Insureds;"
2. Claims made;
3. Vehicles or premiums shown in the Declarations; or
4. Vehicles involved in the accident.

B. Any amounts otherwise payable for damages under this coverage shall be reduced by all sums:

1. Paid because of the "bodily injury" by or on behalf of persons or organizations who may be legally responsible. This includes all sums paid under Part A; and
2. Paid or payable because of the "bodily injury" under any of the following or similar law:
   a. workers' compensation law; or
   b. disability benefits law.

C. Any payment under this coverage will reduce any amount that person is entitled to recover for the same damages under Part A.

OTHER INSURANCE

If there is other applicable similar insurance we will pay only our share of the loss. Our share is the proportion that our limit of liability bears to the total of all applicable limits. However, any insurance we provide with respect to a vehicle you do not own shall be excess over any other collectible insurance.

ARBITRATION

A. If we and an "insured" do not agree:

1. Whether that person is legally entitled to recover damages under this Part; or

2. As to the amount of damages;

either party may make a written demand for arbitration. In this event, each party will select an arbitrator. The two arbitrators will select a third. If they cannot agree within 30 days, either may request that selection be made by a judge of a court having jurisdiction.

B. Each party will:

1. Pay the expenses it incurs; and

2. Bear the expenses of the third arbitrator equally.

C. Unless both parties agree otherwise, arbitration will take place in the county in which the "insured" lives. Local rules of law as to procedure and evidence will apply. A decision agreed to by two of the arbitrators will be binding as to:

1. Whether the "insured" is legally entitled to recover damages; and

2. The amount of damages. This applies only if the amount does not exceed the minimum limit for bodily injury liability specified by the financial responsibility law of the state in which "your covered auto" is principally garaged. If the amount exceeds that limit, either party may demand the right to a trial. This demand must be made within 60 days of the arbitrators' decision. If this demand is not made, the amount of damages agreed to by the arbitrators will be binding.

PART D—COVERAGE FOR DAMAGE TO YOUR AUTO

INSURING AGREEMENT

A. We will pay for direct and accidental loss to "your covered auto" or any "non-owned auto," including their equipment, minus any applicable deductible shown in the Declarations. We will pay for loss to "your covered auto" caused by:

1. Other than "collision" only if the Declarations indicate that Other Than Collision Coverage is provided for that auto.

2. "Collision" only if the Declarations indicate that Collision Coverage is provided for that auto.

If there is a loss to a "non-owned auto," we will provide the broadest coverage applicable to any "your covered auto" shown in the Declarations.

B. "Collision" means the upset of "your covered auto" or its impact with another vehicle or object.

Loss caused by the following is considered other than "collision:"

1. Missiles or falling objects;
2. Fire;
3. Theft or larceny;
4. Explosion or earthquake;
5. Windstorm;
6. Hail, water or flood;
7. Malicious mischief or vandalism;
8. Riot or civil commotion;
9. Contact with bird or animal; or
10. Breakage of glass.

If breakage of glass is caused by a "collision," you may elect to have it considered a loss caused by "collision."

C. "Non-owned auto" means any private passenger auto, pickup, van or "trailer" not owned by or furnished or available for the regular use of you or any "family member" while in the custody of or being operated by you or any "family member." However, "non-owned auto" does not include any vehicle used as a temporary substitute for a vehicle you own which is out of normal use because of its:

1. Breakdown;
2. Repair;
3. Servicing;
4. Loss; or
5. Destruction.

TRANSPORTATION EXPENSES

In addition, we will pay up to $10 per day, to a maximum of $300, for transportation expenses incurred by you. This applies only in the event of the total theft of "your covered auto." We will pay only transportation expenses incurred during the period:

1. Beginning 48 hours after the theft; and

2. Ending when "your covered auto" is returned to use or we pay for its loss.

EXCLUSIONS

We will not pay for:

1. Loss to "your covered auto" which occurs while it is used to carry persons or property for a fee. This exclusion (1.) does not apply to a share-the-expense car pool.

2. Damage due and confined to:
   a. wear and tear;
   b. freezing;
   c. mechanical or electrical breakdown or failure; or
   d. road damage to tires.

   This exclusion (2.) does not apply if the damage results from the total theft of "your covered auto."

3. Loss due to or as a consequence of:
   a. radioactive contamination;
   b. discharge of any nuclear weapon (even if accidental);
   c. war (declared or undeclared);
   d. civil war;
   e. insurrection; or
   f. rebellion or revolution.

4. Loss to equipment designed for the reproduction of sound. This exclusion (4.) does not apply if the equipment is permanently installed in "your covered auto" or any "non-owned auto".

5. Loss to tapes, records or other devices for use with equipment designed for the reproduction of sound.

6. Loss to a camper body or "trailer" you own which is not shown in the Declarations. This exclusion (6.) does not apply to a camper body or "trailer" you:
   a. acquire during the policy period; and
   b. ask us to insure within 30 days after you become the owner.

7. Loss to any "non-owned auto" or any vehicle used as a temporary substitute for a vehicle you own, when used by you or any "family member" without a reasonable belief that you or that "family member" are entitled to do so.

8. Loss to:
   a. TV antennas;
   b. awnings or cabanas; or
   c. equipment designed to create additional living facilities

9. Loss to any of the following or their accessories:
   a. citizens band radio;
   b. two-way mobile radio;
   c. telephone; or
   d. scanning monitor receiver.

   This exclusion (9.) does not apply if the equipment is permanently installed in the opening of the dash or console of "your covered auto" or any "non-owned auto". This opening must be normally used by the auto manufacturer for the installation of a radio.

10. Loss to any custom furnishings or equipment in or upon any pickup or van. Custom furnishings or equipment include but are not limited to:
    a. special carpeting and insulation, furniture, bars or television receivers;
    b. facilities for cooking and sleeping;
    c. height-extending roofs; or
    d. custom murals, paintings or other decals or graphics.

11. Loss to equipment designed or used for the detection or location of radar.

12. Loss to any "non-owned auto" being maintained or used by any person while employed or otherwise engaged in the "business" of:
    a. selling;   d. storing; or
    b. repairing;   e. parking;
    c. servicing;

    vehicles designed for use on public highways. This includes road testing and delivery.

13. Loss to any "non-owned auto" being maintained or used by any person while employed or otherwise engaged in any "business" not described in exclusion 12. This exclusion (13.) does not apply to the maintenance or use by you or any "family member" of a "non-owned auto" which is a private passenger auto or "trailer".

LIMIT OF LIABILITY

A. Our limit of liability for loss will be the lesser of the:

   1. Actual cash value of the stolen or damaged property; or

   2. Amount necessary to repair or replace the property.

   However, the most we will pay for loss to any "non-owned auto" which is a "trailer" is $500.

B. An adjustment for depreciation and physical condition will be made in determining actual cash value at the time of loss.

PAYMENT OF LOSS

We may pay for loss in money or repair or replace the damaged or stolen property. We may, at our expense, return any stolen property to:

   1. You; or

   2. The address shown in this policy.

If we return stolen property we will pay for any damage resulting from the theft. We may keep all or part of the property at an agreed or appraised value.

NO BENEFIT TO BAILEE

This insurance shall not directly or indirectly benefit any carrier or other bailee for hire.

OTHER INSURANCE

If other insurance also covers the loss we will pay only our share of the loss. Our share is the proportion that our limit of liability bears to the total of all applicable limits. However, any insurance we provide with respect to a "non-owned auto" or any vehicle used as a temporary substitute for a vehicle you own shall be excess over any other collectible insurance.

APPRAISAL

A. If we and you do not agree on the amount of loss, either may demand an appraisal of the loss. In this event, each party will select a competent ap-praiser. The two appraisers will select an umpire. The appraisers will state separately the actual cash value and the amount of loss. If they fail to agree, they will submit their differences to the um-pire. A decision agreed to by any two will be bind-ing. Each party will:

1. Pay its chosen appraiser; and

2. Bear the expenses of the appraisal and um-pire equally.

B. We do not waive any of our rights under this policy by agreeing to an appraisal.

PART E—DUTIES AFTER AN ACCIDENT OR LOSS

A. We must be notified promptly of how, when and where the accident or loss happened. Notice should also include the names and addresses of any injured persons and of any witnesses.

B. A person seeking any coverage must:

1. Cooperate with us in the investigation, settle-ment or defense of any claim or suit.

2. Promptly send us copies of any notices or legal papers received in connection with the acci-dent or loss.

3. Submit, as often as we reasonably require:

   a. to physical exams by physicians we select. We will pay for these exams.

   b. to examination under oath and subscribe the same.

4. Authorize us to obtain:

   a. medical reports; and

   b. other pertinent records.

5. Submit a proof of loss when required by us.

C. A person seeking Uninsured Motorists Coverage must also:

1. Promptly notify the police if a hit and run driver is involved.

2. Promptly send us copies of the legal papers if a suit is brought.

D. A person seeking Coverage for Damage to Your Auto must also:

1. Take reasonable steps after loss to protect "your covered auto" and its equipment from further loss. We will pay reasonable expenses incurred to do this.

2. Promptly notify the police if "your covered auto" is stolen.

3. Permit us to inspect and appraise the dam-aged property before its repair or disposal.

PART F—GENERAL PROVISIONS

BANKRUPTCY

Bankruptcy or insolvency of the "insured" shall not relieve us of any obligations under this policy.

CHANGES

This policy contains all the agreements between you and us. Its terms may not be changed or waived except by endorsement issued by us. If a change requires a premium adjustment, we will adjust the premium as of the effective date of change.

We may revise this policy form to provide more cover-age without additional premium charge. If we do this your policy will automatically provide the additional coverage as of the date the revision is effective in your state.

FRAUD

We do not provide coverage for any "insured" who has made fraudulent statements or engaged in fraudulent conduct in connection with any accident or loss for which coverage is sought under this policy.

LEGAL ACTION AGAINST US

A. No legal action may be brought against us until there has been full compliance with all the terms of this policy. In addition, under Part A, no legal action may be brought against us until:

1. We agree in writing that the "insured" has an obligation to pay; or

2. The amount of that obligation has been finally determined by judgment after trial.

B. No person or organization has any right under this policy to bring us into any action to determine the liability of an "insured."

OUR RIGHT TO RECOVER PAYMENT

A. If we make a payment under this policy and the person to or for whom payment was made has a right to recover damages from another we shall be subrogated to that right. That person shall do:

1. Whatever is necessary to enable us to exercise our rights; and

2. Nothing after loss to prejudice them.

However, our rights in this paragraph (A.) do not apply under Part D, against any person using "your covered auto" with a reasonable belief that that person is entitled to do so.

B. If we make a payment under this policy and the person to or for whom payment is made recovers damages from another, that person shall:

1. Hold in trust for us the proceeds of the recovery; and

2. Reimburse us to the extent of our payment.

POLICY PERIOD AND TERRITORY

A. This policy applies only to accidents and losses which occur:

1. During the policy period as shown in the Declarations; and

2. Within the policy territory.

B. The policy territory is:

1. The United States of America, its territories or possessions;

2. Puerto Rico; or

3. Canada.

This policy also applies to loss to, or accidents involving, "your covered auto" while being transported between their ports.

TERMINATION

A. Cancellation. This policy may be cancelled during the policy period as follows:

1. The named insured shown in the Declarations may cancel by:

    a. returning this policy to us; or

    b. giving us advance written notice of the date cancellation is to take effect.

2. We may cancel by mailing to the named insured shown in the Declarations at the address shown in this policy:

    a. at least 10 days notice:

        (1) if cancellation is for nonpayment of premium; or

        (2) if notice is mailed during the first 60 days this policy is in effect and this is not a renewal or continuation policy; or

    b. at least 20 days notice in all other cases.

3. After this policy is in effect for 60 days, or if this is a renewal or continuation policy, we will cancel only:

    a. for nonpayment of premium; or

    b. if your driver's license or that of:

        (1) any driver who lives with you; or

        (2) any driver who customarily uses "your covered auto;"

    has been suspended or revoked. This must have occurred:

        (1) during the policy period; or

        (2) since the last anniversary of the original effective date if the policy period is other than 1 year; or

    c. if the policy was obtained through material misrepresentation.

B. Nonrenewal. If we decide not to renew or continue this policy, we will mail notice to the named insured shown in the Declarations at the address shown in this policy. Notice will be mailed at least 20 days before the end of the policy period. If the policy period is other than 1 year, we will have the right not to renew or continue it only at each anniversary of its original effective date.

C. Automatic Termination. If we offer to renew or continue and you or your representative do not accept, this policy will automatically terminate at the end of the current policy period. Failure to pay the required renewal or continuation premium when due shall mean that you have not accepted our offer.

If you obtain other insurance on "your covered auto," any similar insurance provided by this policy will terminate as to that auto on the effective date of the other insurance.

D. Other Termination Provisions.

1. If the law in effect in your state at the time this policy is issued, renewed or continued:

    a. requires a longer notice period;

    b. requires a special form of or procedure for giving notice; or

    c. modifies any of the stated termination reasons;

    we will comply with those requirements.

2. We may deliver any notice instead of mailing it. Proof of mailing of any notice shall be sufficient proof of notice.

3. If this policy is cancelled, you may be entitled to a premium refund. If so, we will send you the refund. The premium refund, if any, will be computed according to our manuals. However, making or offering to make the refund is not a condition of cancellation.

4. The effective date of cancellation stated in the notice shall become the end of the policy period.

TRANSFER OF YOUR INTEREST IN THIS POLICY

A. Your rights and duties under this policy may not be assigned without our written consent. However, if a named insured shown in the Declarations dies, coverage will be provided for:

1. The surviving spouse if resident in the same household at the time of death. Coverage applies to the spouse as if a named insured shown in the Declarations; and

2. The legal representative of the deceased person as if a named insured shown in the Declarations. This applies only with respect to the representative's legal responsibility to maintain or use "your covered auto."

B. Coverage will only be provided until the end of the policy period.

TWO OR MORE AUTO POLICIES

If this policy and any other auto insurance policy issued to you by us apply to the same accident, the maximum limit of our liability under all the policies shall not exceed the highest applicable limit of liability under any one policy.

(3) INSURANCE SERVICES OFFICE

UNDERINSURANCE MOTORIST ENDORSEMENT (ED. 6–80)

© 1979

PP 03 11
(Ed. 6-80)

UNDERINSURED MOTORISTS COVERAGE.

SCHEDULE

Limit of Liability		Premium		
		Auto 1	Auto 2	Auto 3
$ _____ each accident	$ _____	$ _____	$ _____	

We will pay damages which a **covered person** is legally entitled to recover from the owner or operator of an **underinsured motor vehicle** because of bodily injury:

1. Sustained by a **covered person**; and

2. Caused by an accident.

The owner's or operator's liability for these damages must arise out of the ownership, maintenance or use of the **underinsured motor vehicle.**

We will pay under this coverage only after the limits of liability under any applicable bodily injury liability bonds or policies have been exhausted by payment of judgments or settlements.

"Covered person" as used in this endorsement means:

1. You or any **family member.**

2. Any other person **occupying your covered auto.**

3. Any person for damages that person is entitled to recover because of bodily injury to which this coverage applies sustained by a person described in 1. or 2. above.

"Underinsured motor vehicle" means a land motor vehicle or trailer of any type to which a bodily injury liability bond or policy applies at the time of the accident but its limit for bodily injury liability is less than the limit of liability for this coverage.

However, **"underinsured motor vehicle"** does not include any vehicle or equipment:

1. To which a bodily injury liability bond or policy applies at the time of the accident but its limit for bodily injury liability is less than the minimum limit for bodily injury liability specified by the financial responsibility law of the state in which **your covered auto** is principally garaged.

2. Owned by or furnished or available for the regular use of you or any **family member.**

3. Owned by any governmental unit or agency.

4. Operated on rails or crawler treads.

5. Designed mainly for use off public roads while not upon public roads.

6. While located for use as a residence or premises.

7. Owned or operated by a person qualifying as a self-insurer under any applicable motor vehicle law.

8. To which a bodily injury liability bond or policy applies at the time of the accident but the bonding or insuring company:

   a. denies coverage; or

   b. is or becomes insolvent.

EXCLUSIONS

A. We do not provide Underinsured Motorists Coverage for bodily injury sustained by any person:

1. While **occupying,** or when struck by, any motor vehicle owned by you or any **family member** which is not insured for this coverage under this policy. This includes a trailer of any type used with that vehicle.

2. While **occupying your covered auto** when it is being used to carry persons or property for a fee. This exclusion does not apply to a share-the-expense car pool.

3. Using a vehicle without a reasonable belief that that person is entitled to do so.

B. This coverage shall not apply directly or indirectly to benefit any insurer or self-insurer under any of the following or similar law:

1. workers' compensation law; or

2. disability benefits law.

PP 03 11 (Ed. 6-80)
Page 1 of 2
[E2414]

PP 03 11
(Ed. 6-80)

LIMIT OF LIABILITY

The limit of liability shown in the Schedule for this coverage is our maximum limit of liability for all damages resulting from any one accident. This is the most we will pay regardless of the number of:

1. **Covered persons;**
2. Claims made;
3. Vehicles or premiums shown in the Declarations; or
4. Vehicles involved in the accident.

However, the limit of liability shall be reduced by all sums paid because of the bodily injury by or on behalf of persons or organizations who may be legally responsible. This includes all sums paid under Part A of this policy.

Any amounts otherwise payable for damages under this coverage shall be reduced by all sums paid or payable because of the bodily injury under any of the following or similar law:

1. workers' compensation law; or
2. disability benefits law.

Any payment under this coverage will reduce any amount that person is entitled to recover under Part A of this policy.

OTHER INSURANCE

If there is other applicable similar insurance we will pay only our share of the loss. Our share is the proportion that our limit of liability bears to the total of all applicable limits. However, any insurance we provide with respect to a vehicle you do not own shall be excess over any other collectible insurance.

ARBITRATION

If we and a **covered person** do not agree:

1. Whether that person is legally entitled to recover damages under this endorsement; or
2. As to the amount of damages;

either party may make a written demand for arbitration. In this event, each party will select an arbitrator. The two arbitrators will select a third. If they cannot agree within 30 days, either may request that selection be made by a judge of a court having jurisdiction. Each party will:

1. Pay the expenses it incurs; and
2. Bear the expenses of the third arbitrator equally.

Unless both parties agree otherwise, arbitration will take place in the county in which the **covered person** lives. Local rules of law as to procedure and evidence will apply. A decision agreed to by two of the arbitrators will be binding as to:

1. Whether the **covered person** is legally entitled to recover damages; and
2. The amount of damages. This applies only if the amount does not exceed the minimum limit for bodily injury liability specified by the financial responsibility law of the state in which **your covered auto** is principally garaged. If the amount exceeds that limit, either party may demand the right to a trial. This demand must be made within 60 days of the arbitrators' decision. If this demand is not made, the amount of damages agreed to by the arbitrators will be binding.

ADDITIONAL DUTY

Any person seeking coverage under this endorsement must also promptly send us copies of the legal papers if a suit is brought.

This endorsement must be attached to the Change Endorsement when issued after the policy is written.

PP 03 11 (Ed. 6-80)
Page 2 of 2
[E2415]

APPENDIX I

HOMEOWNERS' INSURANCE

INSURANCE SERVICES OFFICE

HOMEOWNERS 4 CONTENTS BROAD FORM (ED. 4–84)

**Homeowners 4
Contents Broad Form
Ed. 4-84**

AGREEMENT

We will provide the insurance described in this policy in return for the premium and compliance with all applicable provisions of this policy.

DEFINITIONS

In this policy, "you" and "your" refer to the "named insured" shown in the Declarations and the spouse if a resident of the same household. "We," "us" and "our" refer to the Company providing this insurance. In addition, certain words and phrases are defined as follows:

1. **"bodily injury"** means bodily harm, sickness or disease, including required care, loss of services and death that results.

2. **"business"** includes trade, profession or occupation.

3. **"insured"** means you and residents of your household who are:

    a. your relatives; or

    b. other persons under the age of 21 and in the care of any person named above.

    Under Section II, **"insured"** also means:

    c. with respect to animals or watercraft to which this policy applies, any person or organization legally responsible for these animals or watercraft which are owned by you or any person included in 3a or 3b above. A person or organization using or having custody of these animals or watercraft in the course of any **business** or without consent of the owner is not an **insured;**

    d. with respect to any vehicle to which this policy applies:

        (1) persons while engaged in your employ or that of any person included in 3a or 3b above; or

        (2) other persons using the vehicle on an **insured location** with your consent.

4. **"insured location"** means:

    a. the **residence premises;**

    b. the part of other premises, other structures and grounds used by you as a residence and:

        (1) which is shown in the Declarations; or

        (2) which is acquired by you during the policy period for your use as a residence;

    c. any premises used by you in connection with a premises in 4a or 4b above;

    d. any part of a premises:

        (1) not owned by an **insured;** and

        (2) where an **insured** is temporarily residing;

    e. vacant land, other than farm land, owned by or rented to an **insured;**

    f. land owned by or rented to an **insured** on which a one or two family dwelling is being built as a residence for an **insured;**

    g. individual or family cemetery plots or burial vaults of an **insured;** or

    h. any part of a premises occasionally rented to an **insured** for other than **business** use.

5. **"occurrence"** means an accident, including exposure to conditions, which results, during the policy period, in:

    a. **bodily injury;** or

    b. **property damage.**

6. **"property damage"** means physical injury to, destruction of, or loss of use of tangible property.

7. **"residence employee"** means:

    a. an employee of an **insured** whose duties are related to the maintenance or use of the **residence premises,** including household or domestic services; or

    b. one who performs similar duties elsewhere not related to the **business** of an **insured.**

8. **"residence premises"** means:

a. the one family dwelling, other structures, and grounds; or

b. that part of any other building;

where you reside and which is shown as the **"residence premises"** in the Declarations.

"Residence premises" also means a two family dwelling where you reside in at least one of the family units and which is shown as the **"residence premises"** in the Declarations.

SECTION I—PROPERTY COVERAGES

COVERAGE C—Personal Property

We cover personal property owned or used by an **insured** while it is anywhere in the world. At your request, we will cover personal property owned by:

1. others while the property is on the part of the **residence premises** occupied by an **insured;**

2. a guest or a **residence employee,** while the property is in any residence occupied by an **insured.**

Our limit of liability for personal property usually located at an **insured's** residence, other than the **residence premises,** is 10% of the limit of liability for Coverage C, or $1000, whichever is greater. Personal property in a newly acquired principal residence is not subject to this limitation for the 30 days from the time you begin to move the property there.

Special Limits of Liability. These limits do not increase the Coverage C limit of liability. The special limit for each numbered category below is the total limit for each loss for all property in that category.

1. $200 on money, bank notes, bullion, gold other than goldware, silver other than silverware, platinum, coins and medals.

2. $1000 on securities, accounts, deeds, evidences of debt, letters of credit, notes other than bank notes, manuscripts, passports, tickets and stamps.

3. $1000 on watercraft, including their trailers, furnishings, equipment and outboard motors.

4. $1000 on trailers not used with watercraft.

5. $1000 on grave markers.

6. $1000 for loss by theft of jewelry, watches, furs, precious and semi-precious stones.

7. $2000 for loss by theft of firearms.

8. $2500 for loss by theft of silverware, silver-plated ware, goldware, gold-plated ware and pewterware. This includes flatware, hollowware, tea sets, trays and trophies made of or including silver, gold or pewter.

9. $2500 on property, on the **residence premises,** used at any time or in any manner for any **business** purpose.

10. $250 on property, away from the **residence premises,** used at any time or in any manner for any **business** purpose.

Property Not Covered. We do not cover:

1. articles separately described and specifically insured in this or other insurance;

2. animals, birds or fish;

3. motor vehicles or all other motorized land conveyances. This includes:

a. equipment and accessories; or

b. any device or instrument for the transmitting, recording, receiving or reproduction of sound or pictures which is operated by power from the electrical system of motor vehicles or all other motorized land conveyances, including:

(1) accessories or antennas; or

(2) tapes, wires, records, discs or other media for use with any such device or instrument;

while in or upon the vehicle or conveyance.

We do cover vehicles or conveyances not subject to motor vehicle registration which are:

a. used to service an **insured's** residence; or

b. designed for assisting the handicapped;

4. aircraft and parts. Aircraft means any contrivance used or designed for flight, except model or hobby aircraft not used or designed to carry people or cargo;

5. property of roomers, boarders and other tenants, except property of roomers and boarders related to an **insured;**

6. property in an apartment regularly rented or held for rental to others by an **insured;**

7. property rented or held for rental to others off the **residence premises;**

8. a. books of account, drawings or other paper records; or

   b. electronic data processing tapes, wires, records, discs or other software media;

   containing **business** data. But, we do cover the cost of blank or unexposed records and media;

9. credit cards or fund transfer cards except as provided in Additional Coverages 6.

COVERAGE D—Loss Of Use

The limit of liability for Coverage D is the total limit for all the coverages that follow.

1. If a loss by a Peril Insured Against under this policy to covered property or the building containing the property, makes the **residence premises** not fit to live in, we cover, at your choice, either of the following. However, if the **residence premises** is not your principal place of residence, we will not provide the option under paragraph b. below.

   a. **Additional Living Expense,** meaning any necessary increase in living expenses incurred by you so that your household can maintain its normal standard of living; or

   b. **Fair Rental Value,** meaning the fair rental value of that part of the **residence premises** where you reside less any expenses that do not continue while the premises is not fit to live in.

Payment under a. or b. will be for the shortest time required to repair or replace the damage or, if you permanently relocate, the shortest time required for your household to settle elsewhere.

2. If a loss covered under this Section makes that part of the **residence premises** rented to others or held for rental by you not fit to live in, we cover the:

   Fair Rental Value, meaning the fair rental value of that part of the **residence premises** rented to others or held for rental by you less any expenses that do not continue while the premises is not fit to live in.

Payment will be for the shortest time required to repair or replace that part of the premises rented or held for rental.

3. If a civil authority prohibits you from use of the **residence premises** as a result of direct damage to neighboring premises by a Peril Insured Against in this policy, we cover the Additional Living Expense or Fair Rental Value loss as provided under 1 and 2 above for no more than two weeks.

The periods of time under 1, 2 and 3 above are not limited by expiration of this policy.

We do not cover loss or expense due to cancellation of a lease or agreement.

ADDITIONAL COVERAGES

1. **Debris Removal.** We will pay your reasonable expense for the removal of:

   a. debris of covered property if a Peril Insured Against causes the loss; or

   b. ash, dust or particles from a volcanic eruption that has caused direct loss to a building or property contained in a building.

   This expense is included in the limit of liability that applies to the damaged property. If the amount to be paid for the actual damage to the property plus the debris removal expense is more than the limit of liability for the damaged property, an additional 5% of that limit of liability is available for debris removal expense.

   We will also pay your reasonable expense for the removal of fallen trees from the **residence premises** if:

   a. coverage is not afforded under Additional Coverages 3. Trees, Shrubs and Other Plants for the peril causing the loss; or

   b. the tree is not covered by this policy;

   provided the tree damages covered property and a Peril Insured Against under Coverage C causes the tree to fall. Our limit of liability for this coverage will not be more than $500 in the aggregate for any one loss.

2. **Reasonable Repairs.** We will pay the reasonable cost incurred by you for necessary repairs made solely to protect covered property from further damage if a Peril Insured Against causes the loss. This coverage does not increase the limit of liability that applies to the property being repaired.

3. **Trees, Shrubs and Other Plants.** We cover trees, shrubs, plants or lawns, on the **residence premises,** for loss caused by the following Perils Insured Against: Fire or lightning, Explosion, Riot or civil commotion, Aircraft, Vehicles not owned or operated by a resident of the **residence premises,** Vandalism or malicious mischief or Theft.

   The limit of liability for this coverage will not be more than 10% of the limit of liability that applies to Coverage C, or more than $500 for any one tree, shrub or plant. We do not cover property grown for **business** purposes.

   This coverage is additional insurance.

4. **Fire Department Service Charge.** We will pay up to $500 for your liability assumed by contract or agreement for fire department charges incurred when the fire department is called to save or pro-

tect covered property from a Peril Insured Against. We do not cover fire department service charges if the property is located within the limits of the city, municipality or protection district furnishing the fire department response.

This coverage is additional insurance. No deductible applies to this coverage.

5. **Property Removed.** We insure covered property against direct loss from any cause while being removed from a premises endangered by a Peril Insured Against and for no more than 30 days while removed. This coverage does not change the limit of liability that applies to the property being removed.

6. **Credit Card, Fund Transfer Card, Forgery and Counterfeit Money.**

   We will pay up to $500 for:

   a. the legal obligation of an **insured** to pay because of the theft or unauthorized use of credit cards issued to or registered in an **insured's** name;

   b. loss resulting from theft or unauthorized use of a fund transfer card used for deposit, withdrawal or transfer of funds, issued to or registered in an **insured's** name;

   c. loss to an **insured** caused by forgery or alteration of any check or negotiable instrument; and

   d. loss to an **insured** through acceptance in good faith of counterfeit United States or Canadian paper currency.

   We do not cover use of a credit card or fund transfer card:

   a. by a resident of your household;

   b. by a person who has been entrusted with either type of card; or

   c. if an **insured** has not complied with all terms and conditions under which the cards are issued.

   All loss resulting from a series of acts committed by any one person or in which any one person is concerned or implicated is considered to be one loss.

   We do not cover loss arising out of **business** use or dishonesty of an **insured.**

   This coverage is additional insurance. No deductible applies to this coverage.

Defense:

a. We may investigate and settle any claim or suit that we decide is appropriate. Our duty to defend a claim or suit ends when the amount we pay for the loss equals our limit of liability.

b. If a suit is brought against an **insured** for liability under the Credit Card or Fund Transfer Card coverage, we will provide a defense at our expense by counsel of our choice.

c. We have the option to defend at our expense an **insured** or an **insured's** bank against any suit for the enforcement of payment under the Forgery coverage.

7. **Loss Assessment.** We will pay up to $1000 for your share of any loss assessment charged during the policy period against you by a corporation or association of property owners. This only applies when the assessment is made as a result of each direct loss to the property, owned by all members collectively, caused by a Peril Insured Against under Coverage C—Personal Property, other than earthquake or land shock waves or tremors before, during or after a volcanic eruption.

This coverage applies only to loss assessments charged against you as owner or tenant of the **residence premises.**

We do not cover loss assessments charged against you or a corporation or association of property owners by any governmental body.

8. **Collapse.** We insure for direct physical loss to covered property involving collapse of a building or any part of a building caused only by one or more of the following:

a. Perils Insured Against in Coverage C—Personal Property. These perils apply to covered building and personal property for loss insured by this additional coverage;

b. hidden decay;

c. hidden insect or vermin damage;

d. weight of contents, equipment, animals or people;

e. weight of rain which collects on a roof; or

f. use of defective material or methods in construction, remodeling or renovation if the collapse occurs during the course of the construction, remodeling or renovation.

Loss to an awning, fence, patio, pavement, swimming pool, underground pipe, flue, drain, cesspool, septic tank, foundation, retaining wall, bulkhead, pier, wharf or dock is not included under items b, c, d, e, and f unless the loss is a direct result of the collapse of a building.

Collapse does not include settling, cracking, shrinking, bulging or expansion.

This coverage does not increase the limit of liability applying to the damaged covered property.

9. **Building Additions and Alterations.** We cover under Coverage C the building improvements or installations, made or acquired at your expense, to that part of the **residence premises** used exclusively by you. The limit of liability for this coverage will not be more than 10% of the limit of liability that applies to Coverage C.

This coverage is additional insurance.

SECTION I—PERILS INSURED AGAINST

We insure for direct physical loss to the property described in Coverage C caused by a peril listed below unless the loss is excluded in Section I—Exclusions.

1. **Fire or lightning.**

2. **Windstorm or hail.**

This peril does not include loss to the property contained in a building caused by rain, snow, sleet, sand or dust unless the direct force of wind or hail damages the building causing an opening in a roof or wall and the rain, snow, sleet, sand or dust enters through this opening.

This peril includes loss to watercraft and their trailers, furnishings, equipment, and outboard motors, only while inside a fully enclosed building.

3. **Explosion.**

4. **Riot or civil commotion.**

5. **Aircraft,** including self-propelled missiles and spacecraft.

6. **Vehicles.**

7. **Smoke,** meaning sudden and accidental damage from smoke.
This peril does not include loss caused by smoke from agricultural smudging or industrial operations.

8. **Vandalism or malicious mischief.**

This peril does not include loss to property on the **residence premises** if the dwelling has been vacant for more than 30 consecutive days immediately before the loss. A dwelling being constructed is not considered vacant.

9. **Theft,** including attempted theft and loss of property from a known place when it is likely that the property has been stolen.

This peril does not include loss caused by theft:

a. committed by an **insured**;

b. in or to a dwelling under construction, or of materials and supplies for use in the construction until the dwelling is finished and occupied; or

c. from that part of a **residence premises** rented by an **insured** to other than an **insured**.

This peril does not include loss caused by theft that occurs off the **residence premises** of:

a. property while at any other residence owned by, rented to, or occupied by an **insured**, except while an **insured** is temporarily living there. Property of a student who is an **insured** is covered while at a residence away from home if the student has been there at any time during the 45 days immediately before the loss;

b. watercraft, and their furnishings, equipment and outboard motors; or

c. trailers and campers.

10. **Breakage of glass or safety glazing material** which is part of a building, storm door or storm window, and covered as Building Additions and Alterations.

This peril does not include loss on the **residence premises** if the residence has been vacant for more than 30 consecutive days immediately before the loss.

11. **Falling objects.**

This peril does not include loss to the property contained in the building unless the roof or an outside wall of the building is first damaged by a falling object. Damage to the falling object itself is not included.

12. **Weight of ice, snow or sleet** which causes damage to the property contained in a building.

13. **Accidental discharge or overflow of water or steam** from within a plumbing, heating, air conditioning or automatic fire protective sprinkler system or from within a household appliance.

This peril does not include loss:

a. to the system or appliance from which the water or steam escaped;

b. caused by or resulting from freezing except as provided in the peril of freezing below; or

c. on the **residence premises** caused by accidental discharge or overflow which occurs away from the building where the **residence premises** is located.

14. **Sudden and accidental tearing apart, cracking, burning or bulging** of a steam or hot water heating system, an air conditioning or automatic fire protective sprinkler system, or an appliance for heating water.

This peril does not include loss caused by or resulting from freezing except as provided in the peril of freezing below.

15. **Freezing** of a plumbing, heating, air conditioning or automatic fire protective sprinkler system or of a household appliance.

This peril does not include loss on the **residence premises** while unoccupied, unless you have used reasonable care to:

a. maintain heat in the building; or

b. shut off the water supply and drain the system and appliances of water.

16. **Sudden and accidental damage from artificially generated electrical current.**

This peril does not include loss to a tube, transistor or similar electronic component.

17. **Volcanic eruption** other than loss caused by earthquake, land shock waves or tremors.

SECTION I—EXCLUSIONS

We do not insure for loss caused directly or indirectly by any of the following. Such loss is excluded regardless of any other cause or event contributing concurrently or in any sequence to the loss.

1. **Ordinance or Law,** meaning enforcement of any ordinance or law regulating the construction, repair, or demolition of a building or other structure, unless specifically provided under this policy.

2. **Earth Movement,** meaning earthquake including land shock waves or tremors before, during or after a volcanic eruption; landslide; mudflow; earth sinking, rising or shifting; unless direct loss by:

   a. fire;

   b. explosion; or

   c. breakage of glass or safety glazing material which is part of a building, storm door or storm window;

   ensues and then we will pay only for the ensuing loss.

   This exclusion does not apply to loss by theft.

3. **Water Damage,** meaning:

   a. flood, surface water, waves, tidal water, overflow of a body of water, or spray from any of these, whether or not driven by wind;

   b. water which backs up through sewers or drains; or

   c. water below the surface of the ground, including water which exerts pressure on or seeps or leaks through a building, sidewalk, driveway, foundation, swimming pool or other structure.

   Direct loss by fire, explosion or theft resulting from water damage is covered.

4. **Power Failure,** meaning the failure of power or other utility service if the failure takes place off the **residence premises.** But, if a Peril Insured Against ensues on the **residence premises,** we will pay only for that ensuing loss.

5. **Neglect,** meaning neglect of the **insured** to use all reasonable means to save and preserve property at and after the time of a loss.

6. **War,** including undeclared war, civil war, insurrection, rebellion, revolution, warlike act by a military force or military personnel, destruction or seizure or use for a military purpose, and including any consequence of any of these. Discharge of a nuclear weapon will be deemed a warlike act even if accidental.

7. **Nuclear Hazard,** to the extent set forth in the Nuclear Hazard Clause of Section I—Conditions.

8. **Intentional Loss,** meaning any loss arising out of any act committed:

   a. by or at the direction of an **insured;** and

   b. with the intent to cause a loss.

SECTION I—CONDITIONS

1. **Insurable Interest and Limit of Liability.** Even if more than one person has an insurable interest in the property covered, we will not be liable in any one loss:

   a. to the **insured** for more than the amount of the **insured's** interest at the time of loss; or

   b. for more than the applicable limit of liability.

2. **Your Duties After Loss.** In case of a loss to covered property, you must see that the following are done:

   a. give prompt notice to us or our agent;

   b. notify the police in case of loss by theft;

   c. notify the credit card or fund transfer card company in case of loss under Credit Card or Fund Transfer Card coverage;

   d. (1) protect the property from further damage;

      (2) make reasonable and necessary repairs to protect the property; and

      (3) keep an accurate record of repair expenses;

   e. prepare an inventory of damaged personal property showing the quantity, description, actual cash value and amount of loss. Attach all bills, receipts and related documents that justify the figures in the inventory;

   f. as often as we reasonably require:

      (1) show the damaged property;

      (2) provide us with records and documents we request and permit us to make copies; and

      (3) submit to questions under oath and sign and swear to them;

   g. send to us, within 60 days after our request, your signed, sworn proof of loss which sets forth, to the best of your knowledge and belief:

      (1) the time and cause of loss;

      (2) the interest of the **insured** and all others in the property involved and all liens on the property;

      (3) other insurance which may cover the loss;

      (4) changes in title or occupancy of the property during the term of the policy;

   (5) specifications of damaged buildings and detailed repair estimates;

   (6) the inventory of damaged personal property described in 2e above;

   (7) receipts for additional living expenses incurred and records that support the fair rental value loss; and

   (8) evidence or affidavit that supports a claim under the Credit Card, Fund Transfer Card, Forgery and Counterfeit Money coverage, stating the amount and cause of loss.

3. **Loss Settlement.** Covered property losses are settled at actual cash value at the time of loss but not more than the amount required to repair or replace.

4. **Loss to a Pair or Set.** In case of loss to a pair or set we may elect to:

   a. repair or replace any part to restore the pair or set to its value before the loss; or

   b. pay the difference between actual cash value of the property before and after the loss.

5. **Glass Replacement.** Loss for damage to glass caused by a Peril Insured Against will be settled on the basis of replacement with safety glazing materials when required by ordinance or law.

6. **Appraisal.** If you and we fail to agree on the amount of loss, either may demand an appraisal of the loss. In this event, each party will choose a competent appraiser within 20 days after receiving a written request from the other. The two appraisers will choose an umpire. If they cannot agree upon an umpire within 15 days, you or we may request that the choice be made by a judge of a court of record in the state where the **residence premises** is located. The appraisers will separately set the amount of loss. If the appraisers submit a written report of an agreement to us, the amount agreed upon will be the amount of loss. If they fail to agree, they will submit their differences to the umpire. A decision agreed to by any two will set the amount of loss.

   Each party will:

   a. pay its own appraiser; and

   b. bear the other expenses of the appraisal and umpire equally.

7. **Other Insurance.** If a loss covered by this policy is also covered by other insurance, we will pay only the proportion of the loss that the limit of liability that applies under this policy bears to the total amount of insurance covering the loss.

8. **Suit Against Us.** No action can be brought unless the policy provisions have been complied with and the action is started within one year after the date of loss.

9. **Our Option.** If we give you written notice within 30 days after we receive your signed, sworn proof of loss, we may repair or replace any part of the damaged property with like property.

10. **Loss Payment.** We will adjust all losses with you. We will pay you unless some other person is named in the policy or is legally entitled to receive payment. Loss will be payable 60 days after we receive your proof of loss and:

   a. reach an agreement with you;

   b. there is an entry of a final judgment; or

   c. there is a filing of an appraisal award with us.

11. **Abandonment of Property.** We need not accept any property abandoned by an **insured**.

12. **No Benefit to Bailee.** We will not recognize any assignment or grant any coverage that benefits a person or organization holding, storing or moving property for a fee regardless of any other provision of this policy.

13. **Nuclear Hazard Clause.**

   a. "Nuclear Hazard" means any nuclear reaction, radiation, or radioactive contamination, all whether controlled or uncontrolled or however caused, or any consequence of any of these.

   b. Loss caused by the nuclear hazard will not be considered loss caused by fire, explosion, or smoke, whether these perils are specifically named in or otherwise included within the Perils Insured Against in Section I.

   c. This policy does not apply under Section I to loss caused directly or indirectly by nuclear hazard, except that direct loss by fire resulting from the nuclear hazard is covered.

14. **Recovered Property.** If you or we recover any property for which we have made payment under this policy, you or we will notify the other of the recovery. At your option, the property will be returned to or retained by you or it will become our property. If the recovered property is returned to or retained by you, the loss payment will be adjusted based on the amount you received for the recovered property.

15. **Volcanic Eruption Period.** One or more volcanic eruptions that occur within a 72-hour period will be considered as one volcanic eruption.

SECTION II—LIABILITY COVERAGES

COVERAGE E — Personal Liability

If a claim is made or a suit is brought against an **insured** for damages because of **bodily injury** or **property damage** caused by an **occurrence** to which this coverage applies, we will:

1. pay up to our limit of liability for the damages for which the **insured** is legally liable; and

2. provide a defense at our expense by counsel of our choice, even if the suit is groundless, false or fraudulent. We may investigate and settle any claim or suit that we decide is appropriate. Our duty to settle or defend ends when the amount we pay for damages resulting from the **occurrence** equals our limit of liability.

COVERAGE F — Medical Payments To Others

We will pay the necessary medical expenses that are incurred or medically ascertained within three years from the date of an accident causing **bodily injury.** Medical expenses means reasonable charges for medical, surgical, x-ray, dental, ambulance, hospital, professional nursing, prosthetic devices and funeral services. This coverage does not apply to you or regular residents of your household except **residence employees.** As to others, this coverage applies only:

1. to a person on the **insured location** with the permission of an **insured;** or

2. to a person off the **insured location,** if the **bodily injury:**

   a. arises out of a condition on the **insured location** or the ways immediately adjoining;

   b. is caused by the activities of an **insured;**

   c. is caused by a **residence employee** in the course of the **residence employee's** employment by an **insured;** or

   d. is caused by an animal owned by or in the care of an **insured.**

SECTION II—EXCLUSIONS

1. **Coverage E — Personal Liability and Coverage F — Medical Payments to Others** do not apply to **bodily injury** or **property damage:**

   a. which is expected or intended by the **insured;**

   b. arising out of **business** pursuits of an **insured** or the rental or holding for rental of any part of any premises by an **insured.**

   This exclusion does not apply to:

   (1) activities which are usual to non-**business** pursuits; or

   (2) the rental or holding for rental of an **insured location;**

   (a) on an occasional basis if used only as a residence;

   (b) in part for use only as a residence, unless a single family unit is intended for use by the occupying family to lodge more than two roomers or boarders; or

   (c) in part, as an office, school, studio or private garage;

   c. arising out of the rendering of or failure to render professional services;

   d. arising out of a premises:

   (1) owned by an **insured;**

   (2) rented to an **insured;** or

   (3) rented to others by an **insured;**

   that is not an **insured location;**

   e. arising out of:

   (1) the ownership, maintenance, use, loading or unloading of motor vehicles or all other motorized land conveyances, including trailers, owned or operated by or rented or loaned to an **insured;**

   (2) the entrustment by an **insured** of a motor vehicle or any other motorized land conveyance to any person; or

   (3) statutorily imposed vicarious parental liability for the actions of a child or minor using a conveyance excluded in paragraph (1) or (2) above.

   This exclusion does not apply to:

   (1) a trailer not towed by or carried on a motorized land conveyance.

   (2) a motorized land conveyance designed for recreational use off public roads, not subject to motor vehicle registration and:

   (a) not owned by an **insured;** or

   (b) owned by an **insured** and on an **insured location.**

   (3) a motorized golf cart when used to play golf on a golf course.

   (4) a vehicle or conveyance not subject to motor vehicle registration which is:

   (a) used to service an **insured's** residence;

   (b) designed for assisting the handicapped; or

   (c) in dead storage on an **insured location.**

   f. arising out of:

   (1) the ownership, maintenance, use, loading or unloading of a watercraft described below;

   (2) the entrustment by an **insured** of a watercraft described below to any person; or

   (3) statutorily imposed vicarious parental liability for the actions of a child or minor using a watercraft described below.

   Watercraft:

   (1) with inboard or inboard-outdrive motor power owned by an **insured;**

   (2) with inboard or inboard-outdrive motor power of more than 50 horsepower rented to an **insured;**

(3) that is a sailing vessel, with or without auxiliary power, 26 feet or more in length owned by or rented to an **insured;** or

(4) powered by one or more outboard motors with more than 25 total horsepower if the outboard motor is owned by an **insured,** but, outboard motors of more than 25 total horsepower are covered for the policy period if:

(a) you acquire them prior to the policy period and:

(i) you declare them at policy inception; or

(ii) your intention to insure is reported to us in writing within 45 days after you acquire the outboard motors.

(b) you acquire them during the policy period.

This exclusion does not apply while the watercraft is stored.

g. arising out of:

(1) the ownership, maintenance, use, loading or unloading of an aircraft;

(2) the entrustment by an **insured** of an aircraft to any person; or

(3) statutorily imposed vicarious parental liability for the actions of a child or minor using an aircraft.

An aircraft means any contrivance used or designed for flight, except model or hobby aircraft not used or designed to carry people or cargo.

h. caused directly or indirectly by war, including undeclared war, civil war, insurrection, rebellion, revolution, warlike act by a military force or military personnel, destruction or seizure or use for a military purpose, and including any consequence of any of these. Discharge of a nuclear weapon will be deemed a warlike act even if accidental.

Exclusions d., e., f., and g. do not apply to **bodily injury** to a **residence employee** arising out of and in the course of the **residence employee's** employment by an **insured.**

2. **Coverage E — Personal Liability,** does not apply to:

a. liability:

(1) for your share of any loss assessment charged against all members of an association, corporation or community of property owners;

(2) under any contract or agreement. However, this exclusion does not apply to written contracts:

(a) that directly relate to the ownership, maintenance or use of an **insured location;** or

(b) where the liability of others is assumed by the **insured** prior to an **occurrence;**

unless excluded in (1) above or elsewhere in this policy;

b. **property damage** to property owned by the **insured;**

c. **property damage** to property rented to, occupied or used by or in the care of the **insured.** This exclusion does not apply to **property damage** caused by fire, smoke or explosion;

d. **bodily injury** to any person eligible to receive any benefits:

(1) voluntarily provided; or

(2) required to be provided;

by the **insured** under any:

(1) workers' compensation law;

(2) non-occupational disability law; or

(3) occupational disease law;

e. **bodily injury** or **property damage** for which an **insured** under this policy:

(1) is also an insured under a nuclear energy liability policy; or

(2) would be an insured under that policy but for the exhaustion of its limit of liability.

A nuclear energy liability policy is one issued by:

(1) American Nuclear Insurers;

(2) Mutual Atomic Energy Liability Underwriters;

(3) Nuclear Insurance Association of Canada;

or any of their successors; or

f. **bodily injury** to you or an **insured** within the meaning of part a. or b. of "**insured**" as defined.

3. **Coverage F—Medical Payments to Others,** does not apply to **bodily injury:**

    a. to a **residence employee** if the bodily injury:

    (1) occurs off the **insured location;** and

    (2) does not arise out of or in the course of the **residence employee's** employment by an **insured;**

    b. to any person eligible to receive benefits:

    (1) voluntarily provided; or

    (2) required to be provided;

    under any:

    (1) workers' compensation law;

    (2) non-occupational disability law; or

    (3) occupational disease law;

    c. from any:

    (1) nuclear reaction;

    (2) nuclear radiation; or

    (3) radioactive contamination;

    all whether controlled or uncontrolled or however caused; or

    (4) any consequence of any of these.

    d. to any person, other than a **residence employee** of an **insured,** regularly residing on any part of the **insured location.**

SECTION II—ADDITIONAL COVERAGES

We cover the following in addition to the limits of liability:

1. **Claim Expenses.** We pay:

    a. expenses we incur and costs taxed against an **insured** in any suit we defend;

    b. premiums on bonds required in a suit we defend, but not for bond amounts more than the limit of liability for Coverage E. We need not apply for or furnish any bond;

    c. reasonable expenses incurred by an **insured** at our request, including actual loss of earnings (but not loss of other income) up to $50 per day, for assisting us in the investigation or defense of a claim or suit;

    d. interest on the entire judgment which accrues after entry of the judgment and before we pay or tender, or deposit in court that part of the judgment which does not exceed the limit of liability that applies;

    e. prejudgment interest awarded against the **insured** on that part of the judgment we pay. If we make an offer to pay the applicable limit of liability, we will not pay any prejudgment interest based on that period of time after the offer.

2. **First Aid Expenses.** We will pay expenses for first aid to others incurred by an **insured** for **bodily injury** covered under this policy. We will not pay for first aid to you or any other **insured.**

3. **Damage to Property of Others.** We will pay, at replacement cost, up to $500 per **occurrence** for **property damage** to property of others caused by an **insured.**

We will not pay for **property damage:**

    a. to the extent of any amount recoverable under Section I of this policy;

    b. caused intentionally by an **insured** who is 13 years of age or older;

    c. to property owned by an **insured;**

    d. to property owned by or rented to a tenant of an **insured** or a resident in your household; or

    e. arising out of:

    (1) **business** pursuits;

    (2) any act or omission in connection with a premises owned, rented or controlled by an **insured,** other than the **insured location;** or

    (3) the ownership, maintenance, or use of aircraft, watercraft or motor vehicles or all other motorized land conveyances.

    This exclusion does not apply to a motorized land conveyance designed for recreational use off public roads, not subject to motor vehicle registration and not owned by an **insured.**

4. **Loss Assessment.** We will pay up to $1000 for your share of any loss assessment charged during the policy period against you by a corporation or association of property owners, when the assessment is made as a result of:

    a. each **occurrence** to which Section II of this policy would apply;

b. liability for each act of a director, officer or trustee in the capacity as a director, officer or trustee, provided:

(1) the director, officer or trustee is elected by the members of a corporation or association of property owners; and

(2) the director, officer or trustee serves without deriving any income from the exercise of duties which are solely on behalf of a corporation or association of property owners.

This coverage applies only to loss assessments charged against you as owner or tenant of the **residence premises.**

We do not cover loss assessments charged against you or a corporation or association of property owners by any governmental body.

Section II — Coverage E — Personal Liability Exclusion 2.a.(1) does not apply to this coverage.

SECTION II—CONDITIONS

1. **Limit of Liability.** Our total liability under Coverage E for all damages resulting from any one **occurrence** will not be more than the limit of liability for Coverage E as shown in the Declarations. This limit is the same regardless of the number of **insureds,** claims made or persons injured.

   Our total liability under Coverage F for all medical expense payable for **bodily injury** to one person as the result of one accident will not be more than the limit of liability for Coverage F as shown in the Declarations.

2. **Severability of Insurance.** This insurance applies separately to each **insured.** This condition will not increase our limit of liability for any one **occurrence.**

3. **Duties After Loss.** In case of an accident or **occurrence,** the **insured** will perform the following duties that apply. You will help us by seeing that these duties are performed:

   a. give written notice to us or our agent as soon as is practical, which sets forth:

      (1) the identity of the policy and **insured;**

      (2) reasonably available information on the time, place and circumstances of the accident or **occurrence;** and

      (3) names and addresses of any claimants and witnesses;

   b. promptly forward to us every notice, demand, summons or other process relating to the accident or **occurrence;**

   c. at our request, help us:

      (1) to make settlement;

      (2) to enforce any right of contribution or indemnity against any person or organization who may be liable to an **insured;**

      (3) with the conduct of suits and attend hearings and trials;

      (4) to secure and give evidence and obtain the attendance of witnesses;

   d. under the coverage -- Damage to Property of Others — submit to us within 60 days after the loss, a sworn statement of loss and show the damaged property, if in the **insured's** control;

   e. the **insured** will not, except at the **insured's** own cost, voluntarily make payment, assume obligation or incur expense other than for first aid to others at the time of the **bodily injury.**

4. **Duties of an Injured Person—Coverage F—Medical Payments to Others.**

   The injured person or someone acting for the injured person will:

   a. give us written proof of claim, under oath if required, as soon as is practical; and

   b. authorize us to obtain copies of medical reports and records.

   The injured person will submit to a physical exam by a doctor of our choice when and as often as we reasonably require.

5. **Payment of Claim—Coverage F—Medical Payments to Others.** Payment under this coverage is not an admission of liability by an **insured** or us.

6. **Suit Against Us.** No action can be brought against us unless there has been compliance with the policy provisions.

   No one will have the right to join us as a party to any action against an **insured.** Also, no action with respect to Coverage E can be brought against us until the obligation of the **insured** has been determined by final judgment or agreement signed by us.

7. **Bankruptcy of an Insured.** Bankruptcy or insolvency of an **insured** will not relieve us of our obligations under this policy.

8. **Other Insurance — Coverage E — Personal Liability.** This insurance is excess over other valid and collectible insurance except insurance written specifically to cover as excess over the limits of liability that apply in this policy.

SECTIONS I AND II—CONDITIONS

1. **Policy Period.** This policy applies only to loss in Section I or **bodily injury** or **property damage** in Section II, which occurs during the policy period.

2. **Concealment or Fraud.** We do not provide coverage for an **insured** who has:

   a. intentionally concealed or misrepresented any material fact or circumstance; or

   b. made false statements or engaged in fraudulent conduct;

   relating to this insurance.

3. **Liberalization Clause.** If we adopt a revision which would broaden the coverage under this policy without additional premium within 60 days prior to or during the policy period, the broadened coverage will immediately apply to this policy.

4. **Waiver or Change of Policy Provisions.**

   A waiver or change of a provision of this policy must be in writing by us to be valid. Our request for an appraisal or examination will not waive any of our rights.

5. **Cancellation.**

   a. You may cancel this policy at any time by returning it to us or by letting us know in writing of the date cancellation is to take effect.

   b. We may cancel this policy only for the reasons stated below by letting you know in writing of the date cancellation takes effect. This cancellation notice may be delivered to you, or mailed to you at your mailing address shown in the Declarations.

   Proof of mailing will be sufficient proof of notice.

   (1) When you have not paid the premium, we may cancel at any time by letting you know at least 10 days before the date cancellation takes effect.

   (2) When this policy has been in effect for less than 60 days and is not a renewal with us, we may cancel for any reason by letting you know at least 10 days before the date cancellation takes effect.

   (3) When this policy has been in effect for 60 days or more, or at any time if it is a renewal with us, we may cancel:

   (a) if there has been a material misrepresentation of fact which if known to us would have caused us not to issue the policy; or

   (b) if the risk has changed substantially since the policy was issued.

This can be done by letting you know at least 30 days before the date cancellation takes effect.

   (4) When this policy is written for a period of more than one year, we may cancel for any reason at anniversary by letting you know at least 30 days before the date cancellation takes effect.

   c. When this policy is cancelled, the premium for the period from the date of cancellation to the expiration date will be refunded pro rata.

   d. If the return premium is not refunded with the notice of cancellation or when this policy is returned to us, we will refund it within a reasonable time after the date cancellation takes effect.

6. **Non-Renewal.** We may elect not to renew this policy. We may do so by delivering to you, or mailing to you at your mailing address shown in the Declarations, written notice at least 30 days before the expiration date of this policy. Proof of mailing will be sufficient proof of notice.

7. **Assignment.** Assignment of this policy will not be valid unless we give our written consent.

8. **Subrogation.** An **insured** may waive in writing before a loss all rights of recovery against any person. If not waived, we may require an assignment of rights of recovery for a loss to the extent that payment is made by us.

   If an assignment is sought, an **insured** must sign and deliver all related papers and cooperate with us.

   Subrogation does not apply under Section II to Medical Payments to Others or Damage to Property of Others.

9. **Death.** If any person named in the Declarations or the spouse, if a resident of the same household, dies:

   a. we insure the legal representative of the deceased but only with respect to the premises and property of the deceased covered under the policy at the time of death;

   b. **insured** includes:

   (1) any member of your household who is an **insured** at the time of your death, but only while a resident of the **residence premises;** and

   (2) with respect to your property, the person having proper temporary custody of the property until appointment and qualification of a legal representative.

Part IV

LIABILITY INSURANCE

APPENDIX J

GENERAL LIABILITY INSURANCE COVERAGES

(1) INSURANCE SERVICES OFFICE

COMMERCIAL GENERAL LIABILITY COVERAGE FORM (1982, 1984)

COMMERCIAL GENERAL LIABILITY COVERAGE FORM

Various provisions in this policy restrict coverage. Read the entire policy carefully to determine rights, duties and what is and is not covered.

Throughout this policy the words "you" and "your" refer to the Named Insured shown in the Declarations. The words "we," "us" and "our" refer to the Company providing this insurance.

The word "insured" means any person or organization qualifying as such under SECTION II — WHO IS AN INSURED.

Other words and phrases that appear in quotation marks have special meaning. Refer to SECTION V — DEFINITIONS.

SECTION I — COVERAGES
COVERAGE A. BODILY INJURY AND PROPERTY DAMAGE LIABILITY

1. **Insuring Agreement.**

   a. We will pay those sums that the insured becomes legally obligated to pay as damages because of "bodily injury" or "property damage" to which this insurance applies. No other obligation or liability to pay sums or perform acts or services is covered unless explicitly provided for under SUPPLEMENTARY PAYMENTS — COVERAGES A AND B. This insurance applies only to "bodily injury" and "property damage" which occurs during the policy period. The "bodily injury" or "property damage" must be caused by an "occurrence." The "occurrence" must take place in the "coverage territory." We will have the right and duty to defend any "suit" seeking those damages. But:

      (1) The amount we will pay for damages is limited as described in SECTION III — LIMITS OF INSURANCE;

      (2) We may investigate and settle any claim or "suit" at our discretion; and

      (3) Our right and duty to defend end when we have used up the applicable limit of insurance in the payment of judgments or settlements under Coverages A or B or medical expenses under Coverage C.

   b. Damages because of "bodily injury" include damages claimed by any person or organization for care, loss of services or death resulting at any time from the "bodily injury."

   c. "Property damage" that is loss of use of tangible property that is not physically injured shall be deemed to occur at the time of the "occurrence" that caused it.

2. **Exclusions.**

   This insurance does not apply to:

   a. "Bodily injury" or "property damage" expected or intended from the standpoint of the insured. This exclusion does not apply to "bodily injury" resulting from the use of reasonable force to protect persons or property.

   b. "Bodily injury" or "property damage" for which the insured is obligated to pay damages by reason of the assumption of liability in a contract or agreement. This exclusion does not apply to liability for damages:

      (1) Assumed in a contract or agreement that is an "insured contract;" or

      (2) That the insured would have in the absence of the contract or agreement.

   c. "Bodily injury" or "property damage" for which any insured may be held liable by reason of:

      (1) Causing or contributing to the intoxication of any person;

      (2) The furnishing of alcoholic beverages to a person under the legal drinking age or under the influence of alcohol; or

      (3) Any statute, ordinance or regulation relating to the sale, gift, distribution or use of alcoholic beverages.

      This exclusion applies only if you are in the business of manufacturing, distributing, selling, serving or furnishing alcoholic beverages.

   d. Any obligation of the insured under a workers compensation, disability benefits or unemployment compensation law or any similar law.

   e. "Bodily injury" to:

      (1) An employee of the insured arising out of and in the course of employment by the insured; or

      (2) The spouse, child, parent, brother or sister of that employee as a consequence of (1) above.

      This exclusion applies:

      (1) Whether the insured may be liable as an employer or in any other capacity; and

      (2) To any obligation to share damages with or repay someone else who must pay damages because of the injury.

      This exclusion does not apply to liability assumed by the insured under an "insured contract."

COMMERCIAL GENERAL LIABILITY
COVERAGE FORM

f. **(1)** "Bodily injury" or "property damage" arising out of the actual, alleged or threatened discharge, dispersal, release or escape of pollutants:

(a) At or from premises you own, rent or occupy;

(b) At or from any site or location used by or for you or others for the handling, storage, disposal, processing or treatment of waste;

(c) Which are at any time transported, handled, stored, treated, disposed of, or processed as waste by or for you or any person or organization for whom you may be legally responsible; or

(d) At or from any site or location on which you or any contractors or subcontractors working directly or indirectly on your behalf are performing operations:

(i) if the pollutants are brought on or to the site or location in connection with such operations; or

(ii) if the operations are to test for, monitor, clean up, remove, contain, treat, detoxify or neutralize the pollutants.

(2) Any loss, cost, or expense arising out of any governmental direction or request that you test for, monitor, clean up, remove, contain, treat, detoxify or neutralize pollutants.

Pollutants means any solid, liquid, gaseous or thermal irritant or contaminant, including smoke, vapor, soot, fumes, acids, alkalis, chemicals and waste. Waste includes materials to be recycled, reconditioned or reclaimed.

g. "Bodily injury" or "property damage" arising out of the ownership, maintenance, use or entrustment to others of any aircraft, "auto" or watercraft owned or operated by or rented or loaned to any insured. Use includes operation and "loading or unloading."

This exclusion does not apply to:

(1) A watercraft while ashore on premises you own or rent;

(2) A watercraft you do not own that is:

(a) Less than 26 feet long; and

(b) Not being used to carry persons or property for a charge;

(3) Parking an "auto" on, or on the ways next to, premises you own or rent, provided the "auto" is not owned by or rented or loaned to you or the insured;

(4) Liability assumed under any "insured contract" for the ownership, maintenance or use of aircraft or watercraft; or

(5) "Bodily injury" or "property damage" arising out of the operation of any of the equipment listed in paragraph f.(2) or f.(3) of the definition of "mobile equipment" (Section V.8).

h. "Bodily injury" or "property damage" arising out of:

(1) The transportation of "mobile equipment" by an "auto" owned or operated by or rented or loaned to any insured; or

(2) The use of "mobile equipment" in, or while in practice or preparation for, a prearranged racing, speed or demolition contest or in any stunting activity.

i. "Bodily injury" or "property damage" due to war, whether or not declared, or any act or condition incident to war. War includes civil war, insurrection, rebellion or revolution. This exclusion applies only to liability assumed under a contract or agreement.

j. "Property damage" to:

(1) Property you own, rent, or occupy;

(2) Premises you sell, give away or abandon, if the "property damage" arises out of any part of those premises;

(3) Property loaned to you;

(4) Personal property in your care, custody or control;

(5) That particular part of real property on which you or any contractors or subcontractors working directly or indirectly on your behalf are performing operations, if the "property damage" arises out of those operations; or

(6) That particular part of any property that must be restored, repaired or replaced because "your work" was incorrectly performed on it.

Paragraph (2) of this exclusion does not apply if the premises are "your work" and were never occupied, rented or held for rental by you.

Paragraphs (3), (4), (5) and (6) of this exclusion do not apply to liability assumed under a sidetrack agreement.

Paragraph (6) of this exclusion does not apply to "property damage" included in the "products-completed operations hazard."

k. "Property damage" to "your product" arising out of it or any part of it.

     CG 00 01 11 85
(E2417)

l. "Property damage" to "your work" arising out of it or any part of it and included in the "products-completed operations hazard."

This exclusion does not apply if the damaged work or the work out of which the damage arises was performed on your behalf by a subcontractor.

m. "Property damage" to "impaired property" or property that has not been physically injured, arising out of:

(1) A defect, deficiency, inadequacy or dangerous condition in "your product" or "your work;" or

(2) A delay or failure by you or anyone acting on your behalf to perform a contract or agreement in accordance with its terms.

This exclusion does not apply to the loss of use of other property arising out of sudden and accidental physical injury to "your product" or "your work" after it has been put to its intended use.

n. Damages claimed for any loss, cost or expense incurred by you or others for the loss of use, withdrawal, recall, inspection, repair, replacement, adjustment, removal or disposal of:

(1) "Your product;"

(2) "Your work;" or

(3) "Impaired property;"

if such product, work, or property is withdrawn or recalled from the market or from use by any person or organization because of a known or suspected defect, deficiency, inadequacy or dangerous condition in it.

Exclusions c. through n. do not apply to damage by fire to premises rented to you. A separate limit of insurance applies to this coverage as described in SECTION III — LIMITS OF INSURANCE.

COVERAGE B. PERSONAL AND ADVERTISING INJURY LIABILITY

1. Insuring Agreement.

a. We will pay those sums that the insured becomes legally obligated to pay as damages because of "personal injury" or "advertising injury" to which this insurance applies. No other obligation or liability to pay sums or perform acts or services is covered unless explicitly provided for under SUPPLEMENTARY PAYMENTS—COVERAGES A AND B. We will have the right and duty to defend any "suit" seeking those damages. But:

(1) The amount we will pay for damages is limited as described in SECTION III — LIMITS OF INSURANCE;

(2) We may investigate and settle any claim or "suit" at our discretion; and

(3) Our right and duty to defend end when we have used up the applicable limit of insurance in the payment of judgments or settlements under Coverages A or B or medical expenses under Coverage C.

b. This insurance applies to "personal injury" only if caused by an offense:

(1) Committed in the "coverage territory" during the policy period; and

(2) Arising out of the conduct of your business, excluding advertising, publishing, broadcasting or telecasting done by or for you.

c. This insurance applies to "advertising injury" only if caused by an offense committed:

(1) In the "coverage territory" during the policy period; and

(2) In the course of advertising your goods, products or services.

2. Exclusions.

This insurance does not apply to:

a. "Personal injury" or "advertising injury":

(1) Arising out of oral or written publication of material, if done by or at the direction of the insured with knowledge of its falsity;

(2) Arising out of oral or written publication of material whose first publication took place before the beginning of the policy period;

(3) Arising out of the willful violation of a penal statute or ordinance committed by or with the consent of the insured; or

(4) For which the insured has assumed liability in a contract or agreement. This exclusion does not apply to liability for damages that the insured would have in the absence of the contract or agreement.

b. "Advertising injury" arising out of:

(1) Breach of contract, other than misappropriation of advertising ideas under an implied contract;

(2) The failure of goods, products or services to conform with advertised quality or performance;

(3) The wrong description of the price of goods, products or services; or

(4) An offense committed by an insured whose business is advertising, broadcasting, publishing or telecasting.

COMMERCIAL GENERAL LIABILITY
COVERAGE FORM

COVERAGE C. MEDICAL PAYMENTS

1. Insuring Agreement.

a. We will pay medical expenses as described below for ''bodily injury'' caused by an accident:

(1) On premises you own or rent;

(2) On ways next to premises you own or rent; or

(3) Because of your operations;

provided that:

(1) The accident takes place in the ''coverage territory'' and during the policy period;

(2) The expenses are incurred and reported to us within one year of the date of the accident; and

(3) The injured person submits to examination, at our expense, by physicians of our choice as often as we reasonably require.

b. We will make these payments regardless of fault. These payments will not exceed the applicable limit of insurance. We will pay reasonable expenses for:

(1) First aid at the time of an accident;

(2) Necessary medical, surgical, x-ray and dental services, including prosthetic devices; and

(3) Necessary ambulance, hospital, professional nursing and funeral services.

2. Exclusions.

We will not pay expenses for ''bodily injury:''

a. To any insured.

b. To a person hired to do work for or on behalf of any insured or a tenant of any insured.

c. To a person injured on that part of premises you own or rent that the person normally occupies.

d. To a person, whether or not an employee of any insured, if benefits for the ''bodily injury'' are payable or must be provided under a workers compensation or disability benefits law or a similar law.

e. To a person injured while taking part in athletics.

f. Included within the ''products-completed operations hazard.''

g. Excluded under Coverage A.

h. Due to war, whether or not declared, or any act or condition incident to war. War includes civil war, insurrection, rebellion or revolution.

SUPPLEMENTARY PAYMENTS — COVERAGES A AND B

We will pay, with respect to any claim or ''suit'' we defend:

1. All expenses we incur.

2. Up to $250 for cost of bail bonds required because of accidents or traffic law violations arising out of the use of any vehicle to which the Bodily Injury Liability Coverage applies. We do not have to furnish these bonds.

3. The cost of bonds to release attachments, but only for bond amounts within the applicable limit of insurance. We do not have to furnish these bonds.

4. All reasonable expenses incurred by the insured at our request to assist us in the investigation or defense of the claim or ''suit,'' including actual loss of earnings up to $100 a day because of time off from work.

5. All costs taxed against the insured in the ''suit.''

6. Pre-judgment interest awarded against the insured on that part of the judgment we pay. If we make an offer to pay the applicable limit of insurance, we will not pay any pre-judgment interest based on that period of time after the offer.

7. All interest on the full amount of any judgment that accrues after entry of the judgment and before we have paid, offered to pay, or deposited in court the part of the judgment that is within the applicable limit of insurance.

These payments will not reduce the limits of insurance.

SECTION II — WHO IS AN INSURED

1. If you are designated in the Declarations as:

a. An individual, you and your spouse are insureds, but only with respect to the conduct of a business of which you are the sole owner.

b. A partnership or joint venture, you are an insured. Your members, your partners, and their spouses are also insureds, but only with respect to the conduct of your business.

c. An organization other than a partnership or joint venture, you are an insured. Your executive officers and directors are insureds, but only with respect to their duties as your officers or directors. Your stockholders are also insureds, but only with respect to their liability as stockholders.

2. Each of the following is also an insured:

a. Your employees, other than your executive officers, but only for acts within the scope of their employment by you. However, none of these employees is an insured for:

Copyright, Insurance Services Office, Inc., 1982, 1984 CG 00 01 11 85
[E2419]

(1) ''Bodily injury'' or ''personal injury'' to you or to a co-employee while in the course of his or her employment; or

(2) ''Bodily injury'' or ''personal injury'' arising out of his or her providing or failing to provide professional health care services; or

(3) ''Property damage'' to property owned or occupied by or rented or loaned to that employee, any of your other employees, or any of your partners or members (if you are a partnership or joint venture).

b. Any person (other than your employee), or any organization while acting as your real estate manager.

c. Any person or organization having proper temporary custody of your property if you die, but only:

(1) With respect to liability arising out of the maintenance or use of that property; and

(2) Until your legal representative has been appointed.

d. Your legal representative if you die, but only with respect to duties as such. That representative will have all your rights and duties under this Coverage Part.

3. With respect to ''mobile equipment'' registered in your name under any motor vehicle registration law, any person is an insured while driving such equipment along a public highway with your permission. Any other person or organization responsible for the conduct of such person is also an insured, but only with respect to liability arising out of the operation of the equipment, and only if no other insurance of any kind is available to that person or organization for this liability. However, no person or organization is an insured with respect to:

a. ''Bodily injury'' to a co-employee of the person driving the equipment; or

b. ''Property damage'' to property owned by, rented to, in the charge of or occupied by you or the employer of any person who is an insured under this provision.

4. Any organization you newly acquire or form, other than a partnership or joint venture, and over which you maintain ownership or majority interest, will be deemed to be a Named Insured if there is no other similar insurance available to that organization. However:

a. Coverage under this provision is afforded only until the 90th day after you acquire or form the organization or the end of the policy period, whichever is earlier;

b. Coverage A does not apply to ''bodily injury'' or ''property damage'' that occurred before you acquired or formed the organization; and

c. Coverage B does not apply to ''personal injury'' or ''advertising injury'' arising out of an offense committed before you acquired or formed the organization.

No person or organization is an insured with respect to the conduct of any current or past partnership or joint venture that is not shown as a Named Insured in the Declarations.

SECTION III — LIMITS OF INSURANCE

1. The Limits of Insurance shown in the Declarations and the rules below fix the most we will pay regardless of the number of:

a. Insureds;

b. Claims made or ''suits'' brought; or

c. Persons or organizations making claims or bringing ''suits.''

2. The General Aggregate Limit is the most we will pay for the sum of:

a. Medical expenses under Coverage C; and

b. Damages under Coverage A and Coverage B, except damages because of injury and damage included in the ''products-completed operations hazard.''

3. The Products-Completed Operations Aggregate Limit is the most we will pay under Coverage A for damages because of injury and damage included in the ''products-completed operations hazard.''

4. Subject to 2. above, the Personal and Advertising Injury Limit is the most we will pay under Coverage B for the sum of all damages because of all ''personal injury'' and all ''advertising injury'' sustained by any one person or organization.

5. Subject to 2. or 3. above, whichever applies, the Each Occurrence Limit is the most we will pay for the sum of:

a. Damages under Coverage A; and

b. Medical expenses under Coverage C

because of all ''bodily injury'' and ''property damage'' arising out of any one ''occurrence.''

6. Subject to 5. above, the Fire Damage Limit is the most we will pay under Coverage A for damages because of ''property damage'' to premises rented to you arising out of any one fire.

7. Subject to 5. above, the Medical Expense Limit is the most we will pay under Coverage C for all medical expenses because of ''bodily injury'' sustained by any one person.

COMMERCIAL GENERAL LIABILITY
COVERAGE FORM

The limits of this Coverage Part apply separately to each consecutive annual period and to any remaining period of less than 12 months, starting with the beginning of the policy period shown in the Declarations, unless the policy period is extended after issuance for an additional period of less than 12 months. In that case, the additional period will be deemed part of the last preceding period for purposes of determining the Limits of Insurance.

SECTION IV — COMMERCIAL GENERAL LIABILITY CONDITIONS

1. **Bankruptcy.**

    Bankruptcy or insolvency of the insured or of the insured's estate will not relieve us of our obligations under this Coverage Part.

2. **Duties In The Event Of Occurrence, Claim Or Suit.**

    a. You must see to it that we are notified promptly of an "occurrence" which may result in a claim. Notice should include:

        (1) How, when and where the "occurrence" took place; and

        (2) The names and addresses of any injured persons and witnesses.

    b. If a claim is made or "suit" is brought against any insured, you must see to it that we receive prompt written notice of the claim or "suit."

    c. You and any other involved insured must:

        (1) Immediately send us copies of any demands, notices, summonses or legal papers received in connection with the claim or "suit;"

        (2) Authorize us to obtain records and other information;

        (3) Cooperate with us in the investigation, settlement or defense of the claim or "suit;" and

        (4) Assist us, upon our request, in the enforcement of any right against any person or organization which may be liable to the insured because of injury or damage to which this insurance may also apply.

    d. No insureds will, except at their own cost, voluntarily make a payment, assume any obligation, or incur any expense, other than for first aid, without our consent.

3. **Legal Action Against Us.**

    No person or organization has a right under this Coverage Part:

    a. To join us as a party or otherwise bring us into a "suit" asking for damages from an insured; or

    b. To sue us on this Coverage Part unless all of its terms have been fully complied with.

A person or organization may sue us to recover on an agreed settlement or on a final judgment against an insured obtained after an actual trial; but we will not be liable for damages that are not payable under the terms of this Coverage Part or that are in excess of the applicable limit of insurance. An agreed settlement means a settlement and release of liability signed by us, the insured and the claimant or the claimant's legal representative.

4. **Other Insurance.**

    If other valid and collectible insurance is available to the insured for a loss we cover under Coverages A or B of this Coverage Part, our obligations are limited as follows:

    a. Primary Insurance

        This insurance is primary except when b. below applies. If this insurance is primary, our obligations are not affected unless any of the other insurance is also primary. Then, we will share with all that other insurance by the method described in c. below.

    b. Excess Insurance

        This insurance is excess over any of the other insurance, whether primary, excess, contingent or on any other basis:

        (1) That is Fire, Extended Coverage, Builder's Risk, Installation Risk or similar coverage for "your work;"

        (2) That is Fire insurance for premises rented to you; or

        (3) If the loss arises out of the maintenance or use of aircraft, "autos" or watercraft to the extent not subject to Exclusion g. of Coverage A (Section I).

    When this insurance is excess, we will have no duty under Coverage A or B to defend any claim or "suit" that any other insurer has a duty to defend. If no other insurer defends, we will undertake to do so, but we will be entitled to the insured's rights against all those other insurers.

    When this insurance is excess over other insurance, we will pay only our share of the amount of the loss, if any, that exceeds the sum of:

        (1) The total amount that all such other insurance would pay for the loss in the absence of this insurance; and

        (2) The total of all deductible and self-insured amounts under all that other insurance.

We will share the remaining loss, if any, with any other insurance that is not described in this Excess Insurance provision and was not bought specifically to apply in excess of the Limits of Insurance shown in the Declarations of this Coverage Part.

c. Method of Sharing

If all of the other insurance permits contribution by equal shares, we will follow this method also. Under this approach each insurer contributes equal amounts until it has paid its applicable limit of insurance or none of the loss remains, whichever comes first.

If any of the other insurance does not permit contribution by equal shares, we will contribute by limits. Under this method, each insurer's share is based on the ratio of its applicable limit of insurance to the total applicable limits of insurance of all insurers.

5. Premium Audit.

a. We will compute all premiums for this Coverage Part in accordance with our rules and rates.

b. Premium shown in this Coverage Part as advance premium is a deposit premium only. At the close of each audit period we will compute the earned premium for that period. Audit premiums are due and payable on notice to the first Named Insured. If the sum of the advance and audit premiums paid for the policy term is greater than the earned premium, we will return the excess to the first Named Insured.

c. The first Named Insured must keep records of the information we need for premium computation, and send us copies at such times as we may request.

6. Representations.

By accepting this policy, you agree:

a. The statements in the Declarations are accurate and complete;

b. Those statements are based upon representations you made to us; and

c. We have issued this policy in reliance upon your representations.

7. Separation Of Insureds.

Except with respect to the Limits of Insurance, and any rights or duties specifically assigned in this Coverage Part to the first Named Insured, this insurance applies:

a. As if each Named Insured were the only Named Insured; and

b. Separately to each insured against whom claim is made or "suit" is brought.

8. Transfer Of Rights Of Recovery Against Others To Us.

If the insured has rights to recover all or part of any payment we have made under this Coverage Part, those rights are transferred to us. The insured must do nothing after loss to impair them. At our request, the insured will bring "suit" or transfer those rights to us and help us enforce them.

SECTION V — DEFINITIONS

1. "Advertising injury" means injury arising out of one or more of the following offenses:

   a. Oral or written publication of material that slanders or libels a person or organization or disparages a person's or organization's goods, products or services;

   b. Oral or written publication of material that violates a person's right of privacy;

   c. Misappropriation of advertising ideas or style of doing business; or

   d. Infringement of copyright, title or slogan.

2. "Auto" means a land motor vehicle, trailer or semitrailer designed for travel on public roads, including any attached machinery or equipment. But "auto" does not include "mobile equipment."

3. "Bodily injury" means bodily injury, sickness or disease sustained by a person, including death resulting from any of these at any time.

4. "Coverage territory" means:

   a. The United States of America (including its territories and possessions), Puerto Rico and Canada;

   b. International waters or airspace, provided the injury or damage does not occur in the course of travel or transportation to or from any place not included in a. above; or

   c. All parts of the world if:

      (1) The injury or damage arises out of:

         (a) Goods or products made or sold by you in the territory described in a. above; or

         (b) The activities of a person whose home is in the territory described in a. above, but is away for a short time on your business; and

      (2) The insured's responsibility to pay damages is determined in a "suit" on the merits, in the territory described in a. above or in a settlement we agree to.

COMMERCIAL GENERAL LIABILITY
COVERAGE FORM

5. ''Impaired property'' means tangible property, other than ''your product'' or ''your work,'' that cannot be used or is less useful because:

  a. It incorporates ''your product'' or ''your work'' that is known or thought to be defective, deficient, inadequate or dangerous; or

  b. You have failed to fulfill the terms of a contract or agreement;

  if such property can be restored to use by:

  a. The repair, replacement, adjustment or removal of ''your product'' or ''your work;'' or

  b. Your fulfilling the terms of the contract or agreement.

6. ''Insured contract'' means:

  a. A lease of premises;

  b. A sidetrack agreement;

  c. An easement or license agreement in connection with vehicle or pedestrian private railroad crossings at grade;

  d. Any other easement agreement, except in connection with construction or demolition operations on or within 50 feet of a railroad;

  e. An indemnification of a municipality as required by ordinance, except in connection with work for a municipality;

  f. An elevator maintenance agreement; or

  g. That part of any other contract or agreement pertaining to your business under which you assume the tort liability of another to pay damages because of ''bodily injury'' or ''property damage'' to a third person or organization, if the contract or agreement is made prior to the ''bodily injury'' or ''property damage.'' Tort liability means a liability that would be imposed by law in the absence of any contract or agreement.

  An ''insured contract'' does not include that part of any contract or agreement:

  a. That indemnifies an architect, engineer or surveyor for injury or damage arising out of:

    (1) Preparing, approving or failing to prepare or approve maps, drawings, opinions, reports, surveys, change orders, designs or specifications; or

    (2) Giving directions or instructions, or failing to give them, if that is the primary cause of the injury or damage;

  b. Under which the insured, if an architect, engineer or surveyor, assumes liability for injury or damage arising out of the insured's rendering or failing to render professional services, including those listed in a. above and supervisory, inspection or engineering services; or

c. That indemnifies any person or organization for damage by fire to premises rented or loaned to you.

7. ''Loading or unloading'' means the handling of property:

  a. After it is moved from the place where it is accepted for movement into or onto an aircraft, watercraft or ''auto;''

  b. While it is in or on an aircraft, watercraft or ''auto;'' or

  c. While it is being moved from an aircraft, watercraft or ''auto'' to the place where it is finally delivered;

  but ''loading or unloading'' does not include the movement of property by means of a mechanical device, other than a hand truck, that is not attached to the aircraft, watercraft or ''auto.''

8. ''Mobile equipment'' means any of the following types of land vehicles, including any attached machinery or equipment:

  a. Bulldozers, farm machinery, forklifts and other vehicles designed for use principally off public roads;

  b. Vehicles maintained for use solely on or next to premises you own or rent;

  c. Vehicles that travel on crawler treads;

  d. Vehicles, whether self-propelled or not, maintained primarily to provide mobility to permanently mounted:

    (1) Power cranes, shovels, loaders, diggers or drills; or

    (2) Road construction or resurfacing equipment such as graders, scrapers or rollers;

  e. Vehicles not described in a., b., c. or d. above that are not self-propelled and are maintained primarily to provide mobility to permanently attached equipment of the following types:

    (1) Air compressors, pumps and generators, including spraying, welding, building cleaning, geophysical exploration, lighting and well servicing equipment; or

    (2) Cherry pickers and similar devices used to raise or lower workers;

  f. Vehicles not described in a., b., c. or d. above maintained primarily for purposes other than the transportation of persons or cargo.

  However, self-propelled vehicles with the following types of permanently attached equipment are not ''mobile equipment'' but will be considered ''autos:''

    (1) Equipment designed primarily for:

      (a) Snow removal;

(b) Road maintenance, but not construction or resurfacing.

(c) Street cleaning;

(2) Cherry pickers and similar devices mounted on automobile or truck chassis and used to raise or lower workers; and

(3) Air compressors, pumps and generators, including spraying, welding, building cleaning, geophysical exploration, lighting and well servicing equipment.

9. "Occurrence" means an accident, including continuous or repeated exposure to substantially the same general harmful conditions.

10. "Personal injury" means injury, other than "bodily injury," arising out of one or more of the following offenses:

a. False arrest, detention or imprisonment;

b. Malicious prosecution;

c. Wrongful entry into, or eviction of a person from, a room, dwelling or premises that the person occupies;

d. Oral or written publication of material that slanders or libels a person or organization or disparages a person's or organization's goods, products or services; or

e. Oral or written publication of material that violates a person's right of privacy.

11. a. "Products-completed operations hazard" includes all "bodily injury" and "property damage" occurring away from premises you own or rent and arising out of "your product" or "your work" except:

(1) Products that are still in your physical possession; or

(2) Work that has not yet been completed or abandoned.

b. "Your work" will be deemed completed at the earliest of the following times:

(1) When all of the work called for in your contract has been completed.

(2) When all of the work to be done at the site has been completed if your contract calls for work at more than one site.

(3) When that part of the work done at a job site has been put to its intended use by any person or organization other than another contractor or subcontractor working on the same project.

Work that may need service, maintenance, correction, repair or replacement, but which is otherwise complete, will be treated as completed.

c. This hazard does not include "bodily injury" or "property damage" arising out of:

(1) The transportation of property, unless the injury or damage arises out of a condition in or on a vehicle created by the "loading or unloading" of it;

(2) The existence of tools, uninstalled equipment or abandoned or unused materials;

(3) Products or operations for which the classification in this Coverage Part or in our manual of rules includes products or completed operations.

12. "Property damage" means:

a. Physical injury to tangible property, including all resulting loss of use of that property; or

b. Loss of use of tangible property that is not physically injured.

13. "Suit" means a civil proceeding in which damages because of "bodily injury," "property damage," "personal injury" or "advertising injury" to which this insurance applies are alleged. "Suit" includes an arbitration proceeding alleging such damages to which you must submit or submit with our consent.

14. "Your product" means:

a. Any goods or products, other than real property, manufactured, sold, handled, distributed or disposed of by:

(1) You;

(2) Others trading under your name; or

(3) A person or organization whose business or assets you have acquired; and

b. Containers (other than vehicles), materials, parts or equipment furnished in connection with such goods or products.

"Your product" includes warranties or representations made at any time with respect to the fitness, quality, durability or performance of any of the items included in a. and b. above.

"Your product" does not include vending machines or other property rented to or located for the use of others but not sold.

15. "Your work" means:

a. Work or operations performed by you or on your behalf; and

b. Materials, parts or equipment furnished in connection with such work or operations.

"Your work" includes warranties or representations made at any time with respect to the fitness, quality, durability or performance of any of the items included in a. or b. above.

(2) INSURANCE SERVICES OFFICE

COMMERCIAL GENERAL LIABILITY COVERAGE FORM (CLAIMS MADE COVERAGE) (1982, 1984)

COMMERCIAL GENERAL LIABILITY COVERAGE FORM

COVERAGE A. PROVIDES CLAIMS MADE COVERAGE. PLEASE READ THE ENTIRE FORM CAREFULLY.

Various provisions in this policy restrict coverage. Read the entire policy carefully to determine rights, duties and what is and is not covered.

Throughout this policy the words "you" and "your" refer to the Named Insured shown in the Declarations. The words "we," "us" and "our" refer to the Company providing this insurance.

The word "insured" means any person or organization qualifying as such under SECTION II — WHO IS AN INSURED.

Other words and phrases that appear in quotation marks have special meaning. Refer to SECTION VI — DEFINITIONS.

SECTION I — COVERAGES
COVERAGE A. BODILY INJURY AND PROPERTY DAMAGE LIABILITY

1. **Insuring Agreement.**

   a. We will pay those sums that the insured becomes legally obligated to pay as damages because of "bodily injury" or "property damage" to which this insurance applies. No other obligation or liability to pay sums or perform acts or services is covered unless explicitly provided for under SUPPLEMENTARY PAYMENTS — COVERAGES A AND B. This insurance does not apply to "bodily injury" or "property damage" which occurred before the Retroactive Date, if any, shown in the Declarations or which occurs after the policy period. The "bodily injury" or "property damage" must be caused by an "occurrence." The "occurrence" must take place in the "coverage territory." We will have the right and duty to defend any "suit" seeking those damages. But:

   (1) The amount we will pay for damages is limited as described in SECTION III — LIMITS OF INSURANCE;

   (2) We may, at our discretion, investigate any "occurrence" and settle any claim or "suit" that may result; and

   (3) Our right and duty to defend end when we have used up the applicable limit of insurance in the payment of judgments or settlements under Coverages A or B or medical expenses under Coverage C.

   b. This insurance applies to "bodily injury" and "property damage" only if a claim for damages because of the "bodily injury" or "property damage" is first made against any insured during the policy period.

   (1) A claim by a person or organization seeking damages will be deemed to have been made when notice of such claim is received and recorded by any insured or by us, whichever comes first.

   (2) All claims for damages because of "bodily injury" to the same person, including damages claimed by any person or organization for care, loss of services, or death resulting at any time from the "bodily injury," will be deemed to have been made at the time the first of those claims is made against any insured.

   (3) All claims for damages because of "property damage" causing loss to the same person or organization as a result of an "occurrence" will be deemed to have been made at the time the first of those claims is made against any insured.

2. **Exclusions.**

   This insurance does not apply to:

   a. "Bodily injury" or "property damage" expected or intended from the standpoint of the insured. This exclusion does not apply to "bodily injury" resulting from the use of reasonable force to protect persons or property.

   b. "Bodily injury" or "property damage" for which the insured is obligated to pay damages by reason of the assumption of liability in a contract or agreement. This exclusion does not apply to liability for damages:

   (1) Assumed in a contract or agreement that is an "insured contract;" or

   (2) That the insured would have in the absence of the contract or agreement.

   c. "Bodily injury" or "property damage" for which any insured may be held liable by reason of:

   (1) Causing or contributing to the intoxication of any person;

   (2) The furnishing of alcoholic beverages to a person under the legal drinking age or under the influence of alcohol; or

   (3) Any statute, ordinance or regulation relating to the sale, gift, distribution or use of alcoholic beverages.

   This exclusion applies only if you are in the business of manufacturing, distributing, selling, serving or furnishing alcoholic beverages.

COMMERCIAL GENERAL LIABILITY
COVERAGE FORM

d. Any obligation of the insured under a workers compensation, disability benefits or unemployment compensation law or any similar law.

e. "Bodily injury" to:

(1) An employee of the insured arising out of and in the course of employment by the insured; or

(2) The spouse, child, parent, brother or sister of that employee as a consequence of (1) above.

This exclusion applies:

(1) Whether the insured may be liable as an employer or in any other capacity; and

(2) To any obligation to share damages with or repay someone else who must pay damages because of the injury.

This exclusion does not apply to liability assumed by the insured under an "insured contract."

f. **(1)** "Bodily injury" or "property damage" arising out of the actual, alleged or threatened discharge, dispersal, release or escape of pollutants:

(a) At or from premises you own, rent or occupy;

(b) At or from any site or location used by or for you or others for the handling, storage, disposal, processing or treatment of waste;

(c) Which are at any time transported, handled, stored, treated, disposed of, or processed as waste by or for you or any person or organization for whom you may be legally responsible; or

(d) At or from any site or location on which you or any contractors or subcontractors working directly or indirectly on your behalf are performing operations:

(i) if the pollutants are brought on or to the site or location in connection with such operations; or

(ii) if the operations are to test for, monitor, clean up, remove, contain, treat, detoxify or neutralize the pollutants.

(2) Any loss, cost, or expense arising out of any governmental direction or request that you test for, monitor, clean up, remove, contain, treat, detoxify or neutralize pollutants.

Pollutants means any solid, liquid, gaseous or thermal irritant or contaminant, including smoke, vapor, soot, fumes, acids, alkalis, chemicals and waste. Waste includes materials to be recycled, reconditioned or reclaimed.

g. "Bodily injury" or "property damage" arising out of the ownership, maintenance, use or entrustment to others of any aircraft, "auto" or watercraft owned or operated by or rented or loaned to any insured. Use includes operation and "loading or unloading."

This exclusion does not apply to:

(1) A watercraft while ashore on premises you own or rent;

(2) A watercraft you do not own that is:

(a) Less than 26 feet long; and

(b) Not being used to carry persons or property for a charge;

(3) Parking an "auto" on, or on the ways next to, premises you own or rent, provided the "auto" is not owned by or rented or loaned to you or the insured;

(4) Liability assumed under any "insured contract" for the ownership, maintenance or use of aircraft or watercraft; or

(5) "Bodily injury" or "property damage" arising out of the operation of any of the equipment listed in paragraph f.(2) or f.(3) of the definition of "mobile equipment" (Section VI.8).

h. "Bodily injury" or "property damage" arising out of:

(1) The transportation of "mobile equipment" by an "auto" owned or operated by or rented or loaned to any insured; or

(2) The use of "mobile equipment" in, or while in practice or preparation for, a prearranged racing, speed or demolition contest or in any stunting activity.

i. "Bodily injury" or "property damage" due to war, whether or not declared, or any act or condition incident to war. War includes civil war, insurrection, rebellion or revolution. This exclusion applies only to liability assumed under a contract or agreement.

j. "Property damage" to:

(1) Property you own, rent, or occupy;

(2) Premises you sell, give away or abandon, if the "property damage" arises out of any part of those premises;

(3) Property loaned to you;

(4) Personal property in your care, custody or control;

(5) That particular part of real property on which you or any contractors or subcontractors working directly or indirectly on your behalf are performing operations, if the "property damage" arises out of those operations; or

(6) That particular part of any property that must be restored, repaired or replaced because "your work" was incorrectly performed on it.

Paragraph (2) of this exclusion does not apply if the premises are "your work" and were never occupied, rented or held for rental by you.

Paragraphs (3), (4), (5) and (6) of this exclusion do not apply to liability assumed under a sidetrack agreement.

Paragraph (6) of this exclusion does not apply to "property damage" included in the "products-completed operations hazard."

k. "Property damage" to "your product" arising out of it or any part of it.

l. "Property damage" to "your work" arising out of it or any part of it and included in the "products-completed operations hazard."

This exclusion does not apply if the damaged work or the work out of which the damage arises was performed on your behalf by a subcontractor.

m. "Property damage" to "impaired property" or property that has not been physically injured, arising out of:

(1) A defect, deficiency, inadequacy or dangerous condition in "your product" or "your work;" or

(2) A delay or failure by you or anyone acting on your behalf to perform a contract or agreement in accordance with its terms.

This exclusion does not apply to the loss of use of other property arising out of sudden and accidental physical injury to "your product" or "you work" after it has been put to its intended use.

n. Damages claimed for any loss, cost or expense incurred by you or others for the loss of use, withdrawal, recall, inspection, repair, replacement, adjustment, removal or disposal of:

(1) "Your product;"

(2) "Your work;" or

(3) "Impaired property;"

if such product, work, or property is withdrawn or recalled from the market or from use by any person or organization because of a known or suspected defect, deficiency, inadequacy or dangerous condition in it.

Exclusions c. through n. do not apply to damage by fire to premises rented to you. A separate limit of insurance applies to this coverage as described in SECTION III — LIMITS OF INSURANCE.

COVERAGE B. PERSONAL AND ADVERTISING INJURY LIABILITY

1. Insuring Agreement.

a. We will pay those sums that the insured becomes legally obligated to pay as damages because of "personal injury" or "advertising injury" to which this insurance applies. No other obligation or liability to pay sums or perform acts or services is covered unless explicitly provided for under SUPPLEMENTARY PAYMENTS — COVERAGES A AND B. We will have the right and duty to defend any "suit" seeking those damages. But:

(1) The amount we will pay for damages is limited as described in SECTION III — LIMITS OF INSURANCE;

(2) We may investigate and settle any claim or "suit" at our discretion; and

(3) Our right and duty to defend end when we have used up the applicable limit of insurance in the payment of judgments or settlements under Coverages A or B or medical expenses under Coverage C.

b. This insurance applies to "personal injury" only if caused by an offense:

(1) Committed in the "coverage territory" during the policy period; and

(2) Arising out of the conduct of your business, excluding advertising, publishing, broadcasting or telecasting done by or for you.

c. This insurance applies to "advertising injury" only if caused by an offense committed:

(1) In the "coverage territory" during the policy period; and

(2) In the course of advertising your goods, products or services.

2. Exclusions.

This insurance does not apply to:

a. "Personal injury" or "advertising injury:"

(1) Arising out of oral or written publication of material, if done by or at the direction of the insured with knowledge of its falsity;

(2) Arising out of oral or written publication of material whose first publication took place before the beginning of the policy period;

(3) Arising out of the willful violation of a penal statute or ordinance committed by or with the consent of the insured; or

COMMERCIAL GENERAL LIABILITY
COVERAGE FORM

(4) For which the insured has assumed liability in a contract or agreement. This exclusion does not apply to liability for damages that the insured would have in the absence of the contract or agreement.

b. "Advertising injury" arising out of:

(1) Breach of contract, other than misappropriation of advertising ideas under an implied contract;

(2) The failure of goods, products or services to conform with advertised quality or performance;

(3) The wrong description of the price of goods, products or services; or

(4) An offense committed by an insured whose business is advertising, broadcasting, publishing or telecasting.

COVERAGE C. MEDICAL PAYMENTS

1. Insuring Agreement.

a. We will pay medical expenses as described below for "bodily injury" caused by an accident:

(1) On premises you own or rent;

(2) On ways next to premises you own or rent; or

(3) Because of your operations;

provided that:

(1) The accident takes place in the "coverage territory" and during the policy period;

(2) The expenses are incurred and reported to us within one year of the date of the accident; and

(3) The injured person submits to examination, at our expense, by physicians of our choice as often as we reasonably require.

b. We will make these payments regardless of fault. These payments will not exceed the applicable limit of insurance. We will pay reasonable expenses for:

(1) First aid at the time of an accident;

(2) Necessary medical, surgical, x-ray and dental services, including prosthetic devices; and

(3) Necessary ambulance, hospital, professional nursing and funeral services.

2. Exclusions.

We will not pay expenses for "bodily injury:"

a. To any insured.

b. To a person hired to do work for or on behalf of any insured or a tenant of any insured.

c. To a person injured on that part of premises you own or rent that the person normally occupies.

d. To a person, whether or not an employee of any insured, if benefits for the "bodily injury" are payable or must be provided under a workers compensation or disability benefits law or a similar law.

e. To a person injured while taking part in athletics.

f. Included within the "products-completed operations hazard."

g. Excluded under Coverage A.

h. Due to war, whether or not declared, or any act or condition incident to war. War includes civil war, insurrection, rebellion or revolution.

SUPPLEMENTARY PAYMENTS — COVERAGES A AND B

We will pay, with respect to any claim or "suit" we defend:

1. All expenses we incur.

2. Up to $250 for cost of bail bonds required because of accidents or traffic law violations arising out of the use of any vehicle to which the Bodily Injury Liability Coverage applies. We do not have to furnish these bonds.

3. The cost of bonds to release attachments, but only for bond amounts within the applicable limit of insurance. We do not have to furnish these bonds.

4. All reasonable expenses incurred by the insured at our request to assist us in the investigation or defense of the claim or "suit," including actual loss of earnings up to $100 a day because of time off from work.

5. All costs taxed against the insured in the "suit."

6. Pre-judgment interest awarded against the insured on that part of the judgment we pay. If we make an offer to pay the applicable limit of insurance, we will not pay any pre-judgment interest based on that period of time after the offer.

7. All interest on the full amount of any judgment that accrues after entry of the judgment and before we have paid, offered to pay, or deposited in court the part of the judgment that is within the applicable limit of insurance.

These payments will not reduce the limits of insurance.

SECTION II — WHO IS AN INSURED

1. If you are designated in the Declarations as:

a. An individual, you and your spouse are insureds, but only with respect to the conduct of a business of which you are the sole owner.

b. A partnership or joint venture, you are an insured. Your members, your partners, and their spouses are also insureds, but only with respect to the conduct of your business.

c. An organization other than a partnership or joint venture, you are an insured. Your executive officers and directors are insureds, but only with respect to their duties as your officers or directors. Your stockholders are also insureds, but only with respect to their liability as stockholders.

2. Each of the following is also an insured:

a. Your employees, other than your executive officers, but only for acts within the scope of their employment by you. However, none of these employees is an insured for:

(1) "Bodily injury" or "personal injury" to you or to a co-employee while in the course of his or her employment; or

(2) "Bodily injury" or "personal injury" arising out of his or her providing or failing to provide professional health care services; or

(3) "Property damage" to property owned or occupied by or rented or loaned to that employee, any of your other employees, or any of your partners or members (if you are a partnership or joint venture).

b. Any person (other than your employee) or any organization while acting as your real estate manager.

c. Any person or organization having proper temporary custody of your property if you die, but only:

(1) With respect to liability arising out of the maintenance or use of that property; and

(2) Until your legal representative has been appointed.

d. Your legal representative if you die, but only with respect to duties as such. That representative will have all your rights and duties under this Coverage Part.

3. With respect to "mobile equipment" registered in your name under any motor vehicle registration law, any person is an insured while driving such equipment along a public highway with your permission. Any other person or organization responsible for the conduct of such person is also an insured, but only with respect to liability arising out of the operation of the equipment, and only if no other insurance of any kind is available to that person or organization for this liability. However, no person or organization is an insured with respect to:

a. "Bodily injury" to a co-employee of the person driving the equipment; or

b. "Property damage" to property owned by, rented to, in the charge of or occupied by you or the employer of any person who is an insured under this provision.

4. Any organization you newly acquire or form, other than a partnership or joint venture, and over which you maintain ownership or majority interest, will be deemed to be a Named Insured if there is no other similar insurance available to that organization. However:

a. Coverage under this provision is afforded only until the 90th day after you acquire or form the organization or the end of the policy period, whichever is earlier;

b. Coverage A does not apply to "bodily injury" or "property damage" that occurred before you acquired or formed the organization; and

c. Coverage B does not apply to "personal injury" or "advertising injury" arising out of an offense committed before you acquired or formed the organization.

No person or organization is an insured with respect to the conduct of any current or past partnership or joint venture that is not shown as a Named Insured in the Declarations.

SECTION III — LIMITS OF INSURANCE

1. The Limits of Insurance shown in the Declarations and the rules below fix the most we will pay regardless of the number of:

a. Insureds;

b. Claims made or "suits" brought; or

c. Persons or organizations making claims or bringing "suits."

2. The General Aggregate Limit is the most we will pay for the sum of:

a. Medical expenses under Coverage C; and

b. Damages under Coverage A and Coverage B, except damages because of injury and damage included in the "products-completed operations hazard."

3. The Products-Completed Operations Aggregate Limit is the most we will pay under Coverage A for damages because of injury and damage included in the "products-completed operations hazard."

4. Subject to 2. above, the Personal and Advertising Injury Limit is the most we will pay under Coverage B for the sum of all damages because of all "personal injury" and all "advertising injury" sustained by any one person or organization.

5. Subject to 2. or 3. above, whichever applies, the Each Occurrence Limit is the most we will pay for the sum of:

a. Damages under Coverage A; and

COMMERCIAL GENERAL LIABILITY
COVERAGE FORM

b. Medical expenses under Coverage C

because of all "bodily injury" and "property damage" arising out of any one "occurrence."

6. Subject to 5. above, the Fire Damage Limit is the most we will pay under Coverage A for damages because of "property damage" to premises rented to you arising out of any one fire.

7. Subject to 5. above, the Medical Expense Limit is the most we will pay under Coverage C for all medical expenses because of "bodily injury" sustained by any one person.

The limits of this Coverage Part apply separately to each consecutive annual period and to any remaining period of less than 12 months, starting with the beginning of the policy period shown in the Declarations, unless the policy period is extended after issuance for an additional period of less than 12 months. In that case, the additional period will be deemed part of the last preceding period for purposes of determining the Limits of Insurance.

SECTION IV — COMMERCIAL GENERAL LIABILITY CONDITIONS

1. Bankruptcy.

Bankruptcy or insolvency of the insured or of the insured's estate will not relieve us of our obligations under this Coverage Part.

2. Duties In The Event Of Occurrence, Claim Or Suit.

a. You must see to it that we are notified as soon as practicable of an "occurrence" which may result in a claim. To the extent possible, notice should include:

(1) How, when and where the "occurrence" took place;

(2) The names and addresses of any injured persons and witnesses; and

(3) The nature and location of any injury or damage arising out of the "occurrence."

Notice of an "occurrence" is not notice of a claim.

b. If a claim is received by any insured you must:

(1) Immediately record the specifics of the claim and the date received; and

(2) Notify us as soon as practicable.

You must see to it that we receive written notice of the claim as soon as practicable.

c. You and any other involved insured must:

(1) Immediately send us copies of any demands, notices, summonses or legal papers received in connection with the claim or a "suit;"

(2) Authorize us to obtain records and other information;

(3) Cooperate with us in the investigation, settlement or defense of the claim or "suit;" and

(4) Assist us, upon our request, in the enforcement of any right against any person or organization which may be liable to the insured because of injury or damage to which this insurance may also apply.

d. No insureds will, except at their own cost, voluntarily make a payment, assume any obligation, or incur any expense, other than for first aid, without our consent.

3. Legal Action Against Us.

No person or organization has a right under this Coverage Part:

a. To join us as a party or otherwise bring us into a "suit" asking for damages from an insured; or

b. To sue us on this Coverage Part unless all of its terms have been fully complied with.

A person or organization may sue us to recover on an agreed settlement or on a final judgment against an insured obtained after an actual trial; but we will not be liable for damages that are not payable under the terms of this Coverage Part or that are in excess of the applicable limit of insurance. An agreed settlement means a settlement and release of liability signed by us, the insured and the claimant or the claimant's legal representative.

4. Other Insurance.

If other valid and collectible insurance is available to the insured for a loss we cover under Coverages A or B of this Coverage Part, our obligations are limited as follows:

a. Primary Insurance

This insurance is primary except when b. below applies. If this insurance is primary, our obligations are not affected unless any of the other insurance is also primary. Then, we will share with all that other insurance by the method described in c. below.

b. Excess Insurance

This insurance is excess over any of the other insurance, whether primary, excess, contingent or on any other basis:

(1) That is effective prior to the beginning of the policy period shown in the Declarations of this insurance and applies to "bodily injury" or "property damage" on other than a claims-made basis, if:

(a) No Retroactive Date is shown in the Declarations of this insurance; or

(b) The other insurance has a policy period which continues after the Retroactive Date shown in the Declarations of this insurance;

Copyright, Insurance Services Office, Inc., 1982, 1984 CG 00 02 02 86
[E2430]

(2) That is Fire, Extended Coverage, Builders' Risk, Installation Risk or similar coverage for "your work;"

(3) That is Fire insurance for premises rented to you; or

(4) If the loss arises out of the maintenance or use of aircraft, "autos" or watercraft to the extent not subject to Exclusion g. of Coverage A (Section I).

When this insurance is excess, we will have no duty under Coverages A or B to defend any claim or "suit" that any other insurer has a duty to defend. If no other insurer defends, we will undertake to do so, but we will be entitled to the insured's rights against all those other insurers.

When this insurance is excess over other insurance, we will pay only our share of the amount of the loss, if any, that exceeds the sum of:

(1) The total amount that all such other insurance would pay for the loss in the absence of this insurance; and

(2) The total of all deductible and self-insured amounts under all that other insurance.

We will share the remaining loss, if any, with any other insurance that is not described in this Excess Insurance provision and was not bought specifically to apply in excess of the Limits of Insurance shown in the Declarations of this Coverage Part.

c. Method of Sharing

If all of the other insurance permits contribution by equal shares, we will follow this method also. Under this approach each insurer contributes equal amounts until it has paid its applicable limit of insurance or none of the loss remains, whichever comes first.

If any of the other insurance does not permit contribution by equal shares, we will contribute by limits. Under this method, each insurer's share is based on the ratio of its applicable limit of insurance to the total applicable limits of insurance of all insurers.

5. Premium Audit.

a. We will compute all premiums for this Coverage Part in accordance with our rules and rates.

b. Premium shown in this Coverage Part as advance premium is a deposit premium only. At the close of each audit period we will compute the earned premium for that period.

Audit premiums are due and payable on notice to the first Named Insured. If the sum of the advance and audit premiums paid for the policy term is greater than the earned premium, we will return the excess to the first Named Insured.

c. The first Named Insured must keep records of the information we need for premium computation, and send us copies at such times as we may request.

6. Representations.

By accepting this policy, you agree:

a. The statements in the Declarations are accurate and complete;

b. Those statements are based upon representations you made to us; and

c. We have issued this policy in reliance upon your representations.

7. Separation Of Insureds.

Except with respect to the Limits of Insurance, and any rights or duties specifically assigned to the first Named Insured, this insurance applies:

a. As if each Named Insured were the only Named Insured; and

b. Separately to each insured against whom claim is made or "suit" is brought.

8. Transfer Of Rights Of Recovery Against Others To Us.

If the insured has rights to recover all or part of any payment we have made under this Coverage Part, those rights are transferred to us. The insured must do nothing after loss to impair them. At our request, the insured will bring "suit" or transfer those rights to us and help us enforce them.

9. When We Do Not Renew.

If we decide not to renew this Coverage Part, we will mail or deliver to the first Named Insured shown in the Declarations written notice of the nonrenewal not less than 30 days before the expiration date.

If notice is mailed, proof of mailing will be sufficient proof of notice.

10. Your Right to Claim and "Occurrence" Information.

We will provide the first Named Insured shown in the Declarations the following information relating to this and any preceding general liability claims made Coverage Part we have issued to you during the previous three years:

a. A list or other record of each "occurrence," not previously reported to any other insurer, of which we were notified in accordance with paragraph 2.a. of this Section. We will include the date and brief description of the "occurrence" if that information was in the notice we received.

COMMERCIAL GENERAL LIABILITY
COVERAGE FORM

b. A summary by policy year, of payments made and amounts reserved, stated separately, under any applicable General Aggregate Limit and Products-Completed Operations Aggregate Limit.

Amounts reserved are based on our judgment. They are subject to change and should not be regarded as ultimate settlement values.

If we cancel or elect not to renew this Coverage Part, we will provide such information no later than 30 days before the date of policy termination. In other circumstances, we will provide this information only if we receive a written request from the first Named Insured within 60 days after the end of the policy period. In this case, we will provide this information within 45 days of receipt of the request.

We compile claim and "occurrence" information for our own business purposes and exercise reasonable care in doing so. In providing this information to the first Named Insured, we make no representations or warranties to insureds, insurers, or others to whom this information is furnished by or on behalf of any insured. Cancellation or non-renewal will be effective even if we inadvertently provide inaccurate information.

SECTION V — EXTENDED REPORTING PERIODS

1. We will provide one or more Extended Reporting Periods, as described below, if:

a. This Coverage Part is cancelled or not renewed; or

b. We renew or replace this Coverage Part with insurance that:

(1) Has a Retroactive Date later than the date shown in the Declarations of this Coverage Part; or

(2) Does not apply to "bodily injury" or "property damage" on a claims-made basis.

2. A Basic Extended Reporting Period is automatically provided without additional charge. This period starts with the end of the policy period and lasts for:

a. Five years for claims arising out of an "occurrence" reported to us, not later than 60 days after the end of the policy period, in accordance with paragraph 2.a. of SECTION IV — COMMERCIAL GENERAL LIABILITY CONDITIONS; or

b. Sixty days for all other claims.

The Basic Extended Reporting Period does not apply to claims that are covered under any subsequent insurance you purchase, or that would be covered but for exhaustion of the amount of insurance applicable to such claims.

3. A Supplemental Extended Reporting Period of unlimited duration is available, but only by an endorsement and for an extra charge. This supplemental period starts:

a. Five years after the end of the policy period for claims arising out of an "occurrence" reported to us, not later than 60 days after the end of the policy period, in accordance with paragraph 2.a. of SECTION IV — COMMERCIAL GENERAL LIABILITY CONDITIONS; or

b. Sixty days after the end of the policy period for all other claims.

You must give us a written request for the endorsement within 60 days after the end of the policy period. The Supplemental Extended Reporting Period will not go into effect unless you pay the additional premium promptly when due.

We will determine the additional premium in accordance with our rules and rates. In doing so, we may take into account the following:

a. The exposures insured;

b. Previous types and amounts of insurance;

c. Limits of Insurance available under this Coverage Part for future payment of damages; and

d. Other related factors.

The additional premium will not exceed 200% of the annual premium for this Coverage Part.

This endorsement shall set forth the terms, not inconsistent with this Section, applicable to the Supplemental Extended Reporting Period, including a provision to the effect that the insurance afforded for claims first received during such period is excess over any other valid and collectible insurance available under policies in force after the Supplemental Extended Reporting Period starts.

4. Extended Reporting Periods do not extend the policy period or change the scope of coverage provided. They apply only to claims for "bodily injury" or property damage" that occurs before the end of the policy period (but not before the Retroactive Date, if any, shown in the Declarations).

Claims for such injury or damage which are first received and recorded during the Basic Extended Reporting Period (or during the Supplemental Extended Reporting Period, if it is in effect) will be deemed to have been made on the last day of the policy period.

Once in effect, Extended Reporting Periods may not be cancelled.

     CG 00 02 02 86
[E24321]

5. Extended Reporting Periods do not reinstate or increase the Limits of Insurance applicable to any claim to which this Coverage Part applies, except to the extent described in paragraph 6. of this Section.

6. If the Supplemental Extended Reporting Period is in effect, we will provide the separate aggregate limits of insurance described below, but only for claims first received and recorded during the Supplemental Extended Reporting Period.

The separate aggregate limits of insurance will be equal to the dollar amount shown in the Declarations in effect at the end of the policy period for such of the following limits of insurance for which a dollar amount has been entered:

> General Aggregate Limit
> Products-Completed Operations Aggregate Limit

Paragraphs 2. and 3. of SECTION III — LIMITS OF INSURANCE will be amended accordingly. The Each Occurrence Limit and the Fire Damage Limit shown in the Declarations will then continue to apply, as set forth in paragraphs 5. and 6. of that Section.

SECTION VI — DEFINITIONS

1. "Advertising injury" means injury arising out of one or more of the following offenses:

   a. Oral or written publication of material that slanders or libels a person or organization or disparages a person's or organization's goods, products or services;

   b. Oral or written publication of material that violates a person's right of privacy;

   c. Misappropriation of advertising ideas or style of doing business; or

   d. Infringement of copyright, title or slogan.

2. "Auto" means a land motor vehicle, trailer or semitrailer designed for travel on public roads, including any attached machinery or equipment. But "auto" does not include "mobile equipment."

3. "Bodily Injury" means bodily injury, sickness or disease sustained by a person, including death resulting from any of these at any time.

4. "Coverage territory" means:

   a. The United States of America (including its territories and possessions), Puerto Rico and Canada;

   b. International waters or airspace, provided the injury or damage does not occur in the course of travel or transportation to or from any place not included in a. above; or

   c. All parts of the world if:

(1) The injury or damage arises out of:

   (a) Goods or products made or sold by you in the territory described in a. above; or

   (b) The activities of a person whose home is in the territory described in a. above, but is away for a short time on your business; and

(2) The insured's responsibility to pay damages is determined in a "suit" on the merits, in the territory described in a. above or in a settlement we agree to.

5. "Impaired property" means tangible property, other than "your product" or "your work," that cannot be used or is less useful because:

   a. It incorporates "your product" or "your work" that is known or thought to be defective, deficient, inadequate or dangerous; or

   b. You have failed to fulfill the terms of a contract or agreement;

   if such property can be restored to use by:

   a. The repair, replacement, adjustment or removal of "your product" or "your work;" or

   b. Your fulfilling the terms of the contract or agreement.

6. "Insured contract" means:

   a. A lease of premises;

   b. A sidetrack agreement;

   c. An easement or license agreement in connection with vehicle or pedestrian private railroad crossings at grade;

   d. Any other easement agreement, except in connection with construction or demolition operations on or within 50 feet of a railroad;

   e. An indemnification of a municipality as required by ordinance, except in connection with work for a municipality;

   f. An elevator maintenance agreement; or

   g. That part of any other contract or agreement pertaining to your business under which you assume the tort liability of another to pay damages because of "bodily injury" or "property damage" to a third person or organization, if the contract or agreement is made prior to the "bodily injury" or "property damage." Tort liability means a liability that would be imposed by law in the absence of any contract or agreement.

An "insured contract" does not include that part of any contract or agreement:

   a. That indemnifies an architect, engineer or surveyor for injury or damage arising out of:

COMMERCIAL GENERAL LIABILITY
COVERAGE FORM

(1) Preparing, approving or failing to prepare or approve maps, drawings, opinions, reports, surveys, change orders, designs or specifications; or

(2) Giving directions or instructions, or failing to give them, if that is the primary cause of the injury or damage;

b. Under which the insured, if an architect, engineer or surveyor, assumes liability for injury or damage arising out of the insured's rendering or failing to render professional services, including those listed in a. above and supervisory, inspection or engineering services; or

c. That indemnifies any person or organization for damage by fire to premises rented or loaned to you.

7. "Loading or unloading" means the handling of property:

a. After it is moved from the place where it is accepted for movement into or onto an aircraft, watercraft or "auto;"

b. While it is in or on an aircraft, watercraft or "auto;" or

c. While it is being moved from an aircraft, watercraft or "auto" to the place where it is finally delivered;

but "loading or unloading" does not include the movement of property by means of a mechanical device, other than a hand truck, that is not attached to the aircraft, watercraft or "auto."

8. "Mobile equipment" means any of the following types of land vehicles, including any attached machinery or equipment:

a. Bulldozers, farm machinery, forklifts and other vehicles designed for use principally off public roads;

b. Vehicles maintained for use solely on or next to premises you own or rent;

c. Vehicles that travel on crawler treads;

d. Vehicles, whether self-propelled or not, maintained primarily to provide mobility to permanently mounted:

(1) Power cranes, shovels, loaders, diggers or drills; or

(2) Road construction or resurfacing equipment such as graders, scrapers or rollers;

e. Vehicles not described in a., b., c. or d. above that are not self-propelled and are maintained primarily to provide mobility to permanently attached equipment of the following types:

(1) Air compressors, pumps and generators, including spraying, welding, building cleaning, geophysical exploration, lighting and well servicing equipment; or

(2) Cherry pickers and similar devices used to raise or lower workers;

f. Vehicles not described in a., b., c. or d. above maintained primarily for purposes other than the transportation of persons or cargo.

However, self-propelled vehicles with the following types of permanently attached equipment are not "mobile equipment" but will be considered "autos:"

(1) Equipment designed primarily for:

(a) Snow removal;

(b) Road maintenance, but not construction or resurfacing;

(c) Street cleaning;

(2) Cherry pickers and similar devices mounted on automobile or truck chassis and used to raise or lower workers; and

(3) Air compressors, pumps and generators, including spraying, welding, building cleaning, geophysical exploration, lighting and well servicing equipment.

9. "Occurrence" means an accident, including continuous or repeated exposure to substantially the same general harmful conditions.

10. "Personal injury" means injury, other than "bodily injury," arising out of one or more of the following offenses:

a. False arrest, detention or imprisonment;

b. Malicious prosecution;

c. Wrongful entry into, or eviction of a person from, a room, dwelling or premises that the person occupies;

d. Oral or written publication of material that slanders a person or organization or disparages a person's or organization's goods, products or services; or

e. Oral or written publication of material that violates a person's right of privacy.

11. a. "Products-completed operations hazard" includes all "bodily injury" and "property damage" occurring away from premises you own or rent and arising out of "your product" or "your work" except:

(1) Products that are still in your physical possession; or

(2) Work that has not yet been completed or abandoned.

b. "Your work" will be deemed completed at the earliest of the following times:

(1) When all of the work called for in your contract has been completed.

(2) When all of the work to be done at the site has been completed if your contract calls for work at more than one site.

(3) When that part of the work done at a job site had been put to its intended use by any person or organization other than another contractor or subcontractor working on the same project.

Work that may need service, maintenance, correction, repair or replacement, but which is otherwise complete, will be treated as completed.

c. This hazard does not include "bodily injury" or "property damage" arising out of:

(1) The transportation of property, unless the injury or damage arises out of a condition in or on a vehicle created by the "loading or unloading" of it;

(2) The existence of tools, uninstalled equipment or abandoned or unused materials;

(3) Products or operations for which the classification in this Coverage Part or in our manual of rules includes products or completed operations.

12. "Property damage" means:

a. Physical injury to tangible property, including all resulting loss of use of that property; or

b. Loss of use of tangible property that is not physically injured.

13. "Suit" means a civil proceeding in which damages because of "bodily injury," "property damage," "personal injury" or "advertising injury" to which this insurance applies are alleged. "Suit" includes an arbitration proceeding alleging such damages to which you must submit or submit with our consent.

14. "Your product" means:

a. Any goods or products, other than real property, manufactured, sold, handled, distributed or disposed of by:

(1) You;

(2) Others trading under your name; or

(3) A person or organization whose business or assets you have acquired; and

b. Containers (other than vehicles), materials, parts or equipment furnished in connection with such goods or products.

"Your product" includes warranties or representations made at any time with respect to the fitness, quality, durability or performance of any of the items included in a. and b. above.

"Your product" does not include vending machines or other property rented to or located for the use of others but not sold.

15. "Your work" means:

a. Work or operations performed by you or on your behalf; and

b. Materials, parts or equipment furnished in connection with such work or operations.

"Your work" includes warranties or representations made at any time with respect to the fitness, quality, durability or performance of any of the items included in a. or b. above.

APPENDIX K

PROFESSIONAL LIABILITY INSURANCE COVERAGES

(1) INSURANCE SERVICES OFFICE

LAWYERS PROFESSIONAL LIABILITY INSURANCE (ED. 03 81)

STANDARD COVERAGE PART	GL 00 23
LAWYERS PROFESSIONAL LIABILITY INSURANCE	(Ed. 03 81)

These provisions must be printed or assembled together with the Standard Provisions for General Liability Policies to form a complete policy and are subject to the general instructions thereto.

This insurance may be prepared as an endorsement by adding the following preamble immediately under the title:

"The company, in consideration of the payment of the premium and subject to all the provisions of the policy not expressly modified herein, agrees with the named insured as follows:"

REFERENCE NOTES

1 — Matter in brackets may be omitted.

2 — The word "policy" may be substituted for the matter in brackets when no other Coverage Part is assembled herewith.

3 — The word "schedule" should be substituted if the company elects to designate the premises and to state limits of liability in the Coverage Part.

[E2436]

I. COVERAGE—LAWYERS PROFESSIONAL LIABILITY

The company will pay on behalf of the insured all sums which the insured shall be legally obligated to pay as damages because of any act or omission of the insured, or of any other person for whose act or omission the insured is legally responsible which occurs during the policy period, and arises out of the performance of professional services for others in the insured's profession as a lawyer.

When the insured acts as an administrator, conservator, executor, guardian, trustee, or in any similar fiduciary capacity, the insured's acts or omissions in such capacity shall be deemed to be the performance of professional services for others in the insured's profession as a lawyer, but only to the extent that such acts or omissions are those for which in the usual attorney-client relationship the insured would be legally responsible as attorney for a fiduciary.

The company shall have the right and duty to defend any suit against the insured seeking damages for claims to which this insurance applies even if any of the allegations of the suit are groundless, false or fraudulent. The company may make such investigation and settlement of any claim or suit as it deems expedient. The company shall not be obligated to pay any claim or judgment or to defend or continue to defend any suit after the applicable limit of the company's liability has been exhausted by payment of judgment, settlements or claims expenses.

EXCLUSIONS

This [insurance][2] does not apply to any claim [under Part _____][1]:

(a) arising out of any dishonest, fraudulent, criminal or malicious act or omission of any insured or employee of any insured;

(b) made by an employer or, if the employer is a corporation, its parent or subsidiary or by any director, officer or stockholder thereof against an insured who is a salaried employee of such employer;

(c) for bodily injury, or for injury to or destruction of any tangible property, including the loss of use thereof;

(d) for any loss sustained by the insured as the beneficiary or distributee of any trust or estate;

(e) arising out of acts or omissions involving

any security or any activities or transactions subject or claimed to be subject in whole or in part to the Securities Act of 1933, The Securities Exchange Act of 1934, The Public Utility Holding Company Act of 1935, The Trust Indenture Act of 1939, The Investment Company Act of 1940 or The Investment Advisors Act of 1940 or

(2) any purchase, sale or offering of any security to or from the public which is subject or claimed to be subject to any State Blue Sky or Securities Law.

or any rules or regulations issued pursuant to any of the aforementioned, all as heretofore or hereafter amended or replaced, without regard to the legal theory upon which any claim or suit arising in connection therewith against the insured might be based or made;

(f) arising out of or in connection with the conduct of any business enterprise (including the ownership, maintenance or use of any property in connection therewith) owned by an insured or in which any insured is a partner, or which is directly or indirectly controlled, operated or managed by any insured either individually or in a fiduciary capacity; but this exclusion does not apply to the professional practice of law;

(g) arising out of or in connection with any insured's activities in the dual capacity as a lawyer and (1) as officer, director, partner, or any similar elective or appointive management position of any corporation, cooperative association, association, partnership, joint stock company, trust, unincorporated organization or any other entity other than that of the named insured, or (2) as a public official or an employee of a governmental body, subdivision or agency;

(h) arising out of or in connection with the insured's activities as a fiduciary under the Employees Retirement Income Security Act of 1974 and any amendments thereof or any regulation or orders issued pursuant thereto;

II. SUPPLEMENTARY PAYMENTS

Supplementary Payments are amended to read as follows:

With respect to such [insurance][2] as is afforded by this policy, the company shall:

pay, in addition to the applicable limits of liability:

(1) premiums on appeal bonds required in any suit instituted by the company;

(2) all reasonable expenses, other than loss of earnings, incurred by the insured at the company's request in assisting the company in the investigation or defense of a claim or suit.

III. PERSONS INSURED

Each of the following is an insured under this [insurance][2] to the extent set forth below:

(a) if the named insured designated in the declarations is an individual, the person so designated but only with respect to the conduct of a law practice of which the individual is the sole proprietor;

(b) if the named insured designated in the declarations is a partnership, the partnership so designated and any lawyers who are partners thereof;

(c) if the named insured designated in the declarations is a Professional Corporation or Professional Association, the Professional Corporation or Professional Association so designated and any lawyers who are stockholders or members thereof;

(d) any lawyer who is an employee of the named insured;

(e) any lawyer who previously qualified as an insured under subparagraph IV (b), (c) or (d) of this insurance prior to termination of the required relationship with the named insured or its predecessor firm but only for professional services rendered prior to the termination of such relationship.

With respect to an insured who becomes an insured under this [insurance][2] subsequent to the effective date shown in the [declarations][3], the policy period shall begin as of that subsequent date.

IV. LIMITS OF LIABILITY

Regardless of the number of insureds under this [insurance][2] or of the number of claims made or suits brought, the company's liability is limited as follows:

The total liability of the company for all damages and claims expenses because of all claims or suits to which this [insurance][2] applies shall not exceed the limit of liability stated in the [declarations][3] as "aggregate".

Subject to the above provisions with respect to "aggregate", the total liability of the company for all damages and claims expenses arising out of the same or related professional service shall not exceed the limit of liability stated in the [declarations][3] as applicable to "all claims arising out of the same or related professional services".

All claim expenses shall first be subtracted from the limits of liability, with the remainder, if any, being the amount available to pay as damages. If the limits of liability hereunder are exhausted prior to settlement or judgment of any pending claim or suit, the company shall have the right to withdraw from the further investigation or defense thereof by tendering control of such investigation or defense to the insured.

Deductible. The company's obligation to pay damages and claims expenses resulting from claims arising out of the same or related professional services applies only to the amount of damages and claims expenses in excess of any deductible amount, if any, stated in the [declarations][3].

Reimbursement of the Company. If the company has paid any amounts in settlement or satisfaction of claims or judgments or for claims expenses in excess of the applicable limit of liability, or within the amount of the applicable deductible, the insureds, jointly and severally, shall be liable to the company for any and all such amounts and, upon demand, shall pay such amounts to the company.

[E2437]

V. POLICY TERRITORY

This [insurance]² applies only to acts or omissions which occur within the United States of America, its territories or possessions, Puerto Rico or Canada.

VI. ADDITIONAL DEFINITIONS

When used in reference to this insurance (including endorsements forming a part of the policy):

"claims expenses" means (1) fees charged by an attorney or arbitrator designated by the company, and (2) all other fees, costs and expenses resulting from the investigation, adjustment, defense of a claim, arbitration or suit, arising in connection therewith if incurred by the company, but "claims expenses" does not include Supplementary Payments, salary charges of regular employees or officials of the company or fees and expenses of independent adjusters.

"suit" includes an arbitration proceeding to which the insured is required to submit or to which the insured has submitted with the company's consent.

VII. AMENDED DEFINITION

When used in reference to this insurance, the following amended definition applies:

"bodily injury" means bodily injury, sickness or disease sustained by any person, including death at any time resuting therefrom.

VIII. AMENDED CONDITIONS

A. With reference to this insurance, the Conditions are amended as follows:

Condition 4—INSURED'S DUTIES IN THE EVENT OF OCCURRENCE, CLAIM OR SUIT is replaced by the following:

4. ASSISTANCE AND COOPERATION OF INSURED

Upon the insured becoming aware of any acts or omission which would reasonably be expected to be the basis of a claim or suit covered hereby, written notice shall be given by the insured to the company as soon as practicable, together with the fullest information obtainable. If claim is made or suit brought against the insured, the insured shall immediately forward to the company, every demand, notice, summons or other process received by the insured or the insured's representatives.

The insured shall cooperate with the company and, upon the company's request, assist in making settlements, in the conduct of suits and in enforcing any right of contribution or indemnity against any person or organization who may be liable to the insured because of damage with respect to which this [insurance]² applies; and the insured and any of its members, partners, officers, directors, stockholders and employees that the company deems necessary shall attend hearings and trials and assist in securing and giving evidence and obtaining the attendance of witnesses. The insured shall not, except at the insured's own cost, voluntarily make any payment, assume any obligation or incur any expense.

Condition 9—ASSIGNMENT is amended to read as follows:

9. ASSIGNMENT

The interest hereunder of any insured is not assignable.

If an insured shall die or be adjudged incompetent, this [insurance]² shall thereupon terminate for such person but shall cover the insured's legal representative as the insured with respect to liability previously incurred and covered by this [insurance]².

B. The "Inspection and Audit" Condition does not apply to this [insurance]².

[E2438]

GL 00 23
(Ed. 03 81)

[SCHEDULE]¹

Coverage	Limits of Liability		Advance Premium
		All claims arising out of the same or related professional services	$
Lawyers Professional Liability	$_____		
	$_____	aggregate	

Deductible Amount: $_____
Premium Schedule

	Code	Number	Rate	Premium
LAWYERS				
EMPLOYED LAW CLERKS, INVESTIGATORS, ABSTRACTORS AND PARA LEGALS				

[E2439]

(2) INSURANCE SERVICES OFFICE

LAWYERS PROFESSIONAL LIABILITY INSURANCE (CLAIMS MADE) (ED. 03 81)

STANDARD COVERAGE PART
LAWYERS PROFESSIONAL LIABILITY INSURANCE
(CLAIMS MADE)

GL 00 24
(Ed. 03 81)

These provisions must be printed or assembled together with the Standard Provisions for General Liability Policies to form a complete policy and are subject to the general instructions thereto.

This insurance may be prepared as an endorsement by adding the following preamble immediately under the title:

"The company, in consideration of the payment of premiums and subject to all of the provisions of the policy not expressly modified herein, agrees with the named insured as follows:"

REFERENCE NOTES

1 — Matter in brackets may be omitted.

2 — The word "policy" may be substituted for the matter in brackets when no other Coverage Part is assembled herewith.

3 — The word "schedule" should be substituted if the company elects to designate the premises and to state limits of liability in the Coverage Part.
[E2440]

4 — Matter in brackets is optional with the Company.

[Part _____]¹

LAWYERS PROFESSIONAL LIABILITY INSURANCE
(CLAIMS MADE)

GL 00 24
(Ed. 03 81)

NOTICE

THIS IS KNOWN AS A "CLAIMS MADE" POLICY. EXCEPT TO THE EXTENT AS MAY BE PROVIDED HEREIN, THIS COVERAGE IS LIMITED GENERALLY TO CLAIMS ARISING FROM THE PERFORMANCE OF PROFESSIONAL SERVICES AND FIRST MADE AGAINST THE COMPANY WHILE THE POLICY IS IN FORCE. PLEASE READ THE POLICY CAREFULLY.

I. COVERAGE — LAWYERS PROFESSIONAL LIABILITY

The company will pay on behalf of the insured all sums which the insured shall be legally obligated to pay as damages for claims to which this [insurance]² applies because of any act or omission of the insured, or of any other person for whose act or omission the insured is legally responsible for which claim is first made against the insured and reported to the company during the policy period, arising out of the performance or professional services for others in the insured's profession as a lawyer.

When the insured acts as an administrator, conservator, executor, guardian, trustee, or in any similar fiduciary capacity, the insured's acts or omissions in such capacity shall be deemed to be the performance of professional services for others in the insured's profession as a lawyer, but only to the extent that such acts or omissions are those for which in the usual attorney-client relationship the insured would be legally responsible as attorney for a fiduciary.

The company shall have the right and duty to defend any suit against the insured seeking damages for claims to which this insurance applies even if any of the allegations of the suit are groundless, false or fraudulent. The company may make such investigation and settlement of any claim or suit as it deems expedient. The company shall not be obligated to pay any claim or judgment or to defend or continue to defend any suit after the applicable limit of the company's liability has been exhausted by payment of judgments, settlements or claims expenses.

EXCLUSIONS

This [insurance]² does not apply to any claim [under Part _____]¹:

(a) arising out of any dishonest, fraudulent, criminal or malicious act or omission of any insured or employee of any insured;

(b) made by an employer or, if the employer is a corporation, its parent or subsidiary or by any director, officer or stockholder thereof against an insured who is a salaried employee of such employer;

(c) for bodily injury, for injury to or destruction of any tangible property, including the loss of use thereof;

(d) for any loss sustained by the insured as the beneficiary or distributee of any trust or estate;

(e) arising out of acts or omissions involving

(1) any security or any activities or transactions subject or claimed to be subject in whole or in part to The Securities Act of 1933, The Securities Exchange Act of 1934, The Public Utility Holding Company Act of 1935, The Trust Indenture Act of 1939, The Investment Company Act of 1940 or The Investment Advisors Act of 1940, or

(2) any purchase, sale or offering of any security to or from the public which is subject or claimed to be subject to any State Blue Sky or Securities Law.

or any rules or regulations issued pursuant to any of the aforementioned, all as heretofore or hereafter amended or replaced, without regard to the legal theory upon which any claim or suit arising in connection therewith against the insured might be based or made;

(f) arising out of or in connection with the conduct of any business enterprise (including the ownership, maintenance or use of any prop-

erty in connection therewith) owned by an insured or in which any insured is a partner, or which is directly or indirectly controlled, operated or managed by any insured either individually or in a fiduciary capacity; but this exclusion does not apply to the professional practice of law;

(g) arising out of or in connection with any insured's activities in the dual capacity as a lawyer and (1) as officer, director, partner, or any similar elective or appointive management position of any corporation, cooperative association, association, partnership, joint stock company, trust, unincorporated organization or any other entity other than that of the named insured, or (2) as a public official or an employee of a governmental body, subdivision or agency;

(h) arising out of or in connection with the insured's activities as a fiduciary under the Employees Retirement Income Security Act of 1974 and any amendments thereof or any regulation or orders issued pursuant thereto;

(i) arising out of any acts or omissions occurring prior to the effective date of this policy if the insured at the effective date knew or could have reasonably foreseen that such acts or omissions might be expected to be the basis of a claim or suit.

II. WHEN CLAIM IS TO BE CONSIDERED AS FIRST MADE

A claim shall be considered as being first made at the earlier of the following times:

(a) when the insured first gives written notice to the company that a claim has been made, or

(b) when the insured, first gives written notice to the company of specific circumstances involving a particular person or entity which may result in a claim.

All claims arising out of the same act or omission shall be considered as having been made at the time the first claim is made.

III. SUPPLEMENTARY PAYMENTS

Supplementary Payments of the policy are amended to read as follows:

With respect to such [insurance]² as is afforded by this policy, the company shall:

pay in addition to the applicable limits of liability:

(1) premiums on appeal bonds required in any suit instituted by the company;

(2) all reasonable expenses, other than loss of earnings, incurred by the insured at the company's request in assisting the company in the investigation or defense of a claim or suit.

IV. PERSONS INSURED

Each of the following is an insured under this [insurance]² to the extent set forth below:

(a) if the named insured designated in the declarations is an individual, the person so designated but only with respect to the conduct of a law practice of which the individual is the sole proprietor;

(b) if the named insured designated in the declarations is a partnership, the partnership so designated and any lawyers who are partners thereof;

(c) if the named insured designated in the declarations is a Professional Corporation or Professional Association, the Professional Corporation or Professional Association so designated and any lawyers who are stockholders or members thereof;

(d) any lawyer who is an employee of the named insured;

(e) any lawyer who previously qualified as an insured under subparagraph IV (b), (c) or (d) of this insurance prior to termination of the required relationship with the named insured or its predecessor firm

[E2441]

[Part _____]¹
LAWYERS PROFESSIONAL LIABILITY INSURANCE
(CLAIMS MADE)

GL 00 24
(Ed. 03 81)

but only for professional services rendered prior to the termination of such relationship.

With respect to an insured who becomes an insured under this [insurance]² subsequent to the effective date shown in the [declarations]³, the policy period shall begin as of that subsequent date.

V. LIMITS OF LIABILITY

Regardless of the number of insureds under this [insurance]² or of the number of claims made or suits brought, the company's liability is limited as follows:

The total liability of the company for all damages and claims expenses because of all claims or suits to which this [insurance]² applies shall not exceed the limit of liability stated in the [declarations]³ as "aggregate."

Subject to the above provisions with respect to "aggregate", the total liability of the company for all damages and claims expenses arising out of the same or related professional services shall not exceed the limit of liability stated in the [declarations]³ as applicable to "all claims arising out of the same or related professional services".

All claim expenses shall first be subtracted from the limits of liability, with the remainder, if any, being the amount available to pay damages. If the limits of liability hereunder are exhausted prior to settlement or judgment of any pending claim or suit, the company shall have the right to withdraw from the further investigation or defense thereof by tendering control of such investigation or defense to the insured.

Deductible. The company's obligation to pay damages and claims expenses resulting from all claims arising out of the same or related professional services applies only to the amount of damages and claims expenses in excess of any deductible amount, if any, stated in the [declarations]³.

Reimbursement of the Company. If the company has paid any amounts in settlement or satisfaction of claims or judgements or for claims expenses in excess of the applicable limit of liability, or within the amount of the applicable deductible, the named insured shall be liable to the company for any and all such amounts and, upon demand, shall pay such amounts to the company.

VI. POLICY TERRITORY

This [insurance]² applies only to acts or omissions which occur within the United States of America, its territories or possessions, Puerto Rico or Canada.

VII. ADDITIONAL DEFINITIONS

When used in reference to this insurance (including endorsements forming a part of the policy):

"claims expenses" means (1) fees charged by an attorney or arbitrator designated by the compnay, and (2) all other fees, costs and expenses resulting from the investigation, adjustment, defense of a claim, arbitration or suit, arising in connection therewith if incurred by the company, but "claims expense" does not include Supplementary Payments, salary charges of regular employees or officials of the company or fees and expenses of independent adjusters.

"extended reporting period" means the time after the end of the policy period for reporting claims arising out of acts or omissions occurring prior to the end of the policy period and otherwise covered by this [insurance]².

"suit" includes an arbitration proceeding to which the insured is required to submit or to which the insured has submitted with the company's consent.

VIII. AMENDED DEFINITION

When used in reference to this insurance, the following amended definition applies:

"bodily injury" means bodily injury, sickness or disease sustained by any person, including death at any time resulting therefrom.

IX. AMENDED CONDITIONS

A. With reference to this insurance, the Conditions are amended as follows:

Condition 4—INSURED'S DUTIES IN THE EVENT OF OCCURRENCE, CLAIM OR SUIT is replaced by the following:

4. ASSISTANCE AND COOPERATION OF INSURED

Upon the insured becoming aware of any act or omission which would reasonably be expected to be the basis of a claim or suit covered hereby, written notice shall be given by the insured to the company as soon as practicable, together with the fullest information obtainable. If claim is made or suit is brought against the insured, the insured shall immediately forward to the company every demand, notice, summons or other process received by the insured or the insured's representative.

The insured shall cooperate with the company and, upon the Company's request, assist in making settlements, in the conduct of suits and in enforcing any right of contribution or indemnity against any person or organization who may be liable to the insured because of damage with respect to which this [insurance]² applies; and the insured and any of its members, partners, officers, directors, stockholders and employees that the company deems necessary shall attend hearings and trials and assist in securing and giving evidence and obtaining the attendance of witnesses. The insured shall not, except at the insured's own cost, voluntarily make any payments, assume any obligation or incur any expense.

Condition 6—OTHER INSURANCE is replaced by the following:

6. OTHER INSURANCE

If the insured has other insurance against a loss covered by this policy, the company shall not be liable under this [insurance]² for a greater proportion of such loss and claim expenses than the applicable limit of liability stated in the declarations bears to the total applicable limit of liability of all valid and collectible insurance against such loss; provided, however, with respect to acts or omisiions which occurred prior to the inception date of this [insurance]², this insurance shall apply only as excess insurance over any other valid and collectible insurance and shall then apply only in the amount by which the applicable limits of liability of this [insurance]² exceeds the sum of the applicable limits of liability of all such other insurance. In the event that this [insurance]² is treated as excess insurance, any claims expenses allocated to it shall be included in the limit of liability.

Condition 9—ASSIGMENT is replaced by the following:

9. ASSIGNMENT

The interest hereunder of any insured is not assignable.

If an insured shall die or be adjudged incompetent, this [insurance]² shall thereupon terminate for such person but shall cover the insured's legal representative as the insured with respect to liability previously incurred and covered by this [insurance]².

B. The "Inspection and Audit" condition does not apply to this [insurance]².

[E2443]

[Part _____]¹
LAWYERS PROFESSIONAL LIABILITY INSURANCE
(CLAIMS MADE)

GL 00 24
(Ed. 03 81)

X. ADDITIONAL CONDITIONS

EXTENDED REPORTING PERIOD OPTION

Upon termination of this [insurance]² for any reason other than (1) cancellation for nonpayment of premium, or (2) expiration and renewal, the named insured shall have the right by giving written notice to the company within thirty (30) days of such termination, and by paying to the company promptly when due, such premiums as may be required by the company's rules, rates and rating plans then in effect, to have issued an endorsement or endorsements, providing an extended reporting period. The limit of liability stated in the [declarations]³ of this [insurance]² at the time this [insurance]² is terminated shall be limits applicable to each extended reporting period.

[E2444]

GL 00 24
(Ed. 03 81)

[Schedule][1]

Coverage	Limits of Liability		Advance Premium
Lawyers Professional Liability		All claims arising out of the same or related professional services.	$
	$ _____		
	$ _____ aggregate		
Deductible Amount:	$ _____		
Premium Schedule			

	Code	Number	Rate	Premium
LAWYERS				
EMPLOYED LAW CLERKS, INVESTIGATORS, ABSTRACTORS AND PARA LEGALS				

[E2445]

(3) INSURANCE SERVICES OFFICE

PHYSICIANS, SURGEONS AND DENTIST PROFESSIONAL LIABILITY INSURANCE (CLAIMS MADE) (ED. 03 81)

STANDARD COVERAGE PART
PHYSICIANS, SURGEONS AND DENTIST PROFESSIONAL LIABILITY INSURANCE
(CLAIMS MADE)

GL 00 22
(Ed. 03 81)

These provisions must be printed or assembled together with the Standard Provisions for General Liability Policies to form a complete policy and are subject to the general instructions applicable thereto.

This insurance may be prepared as an endorsement by adding the following preamble immediately under the title:

"The company, in consideration of the payment of premiums and subject to all of the provisions of the policy not expressly modified herein, agrees with the named insured as follows:"

REFERENCE NOTES

1 — Matter in bracket may be omitted.

2 — The word "policy" may be substituted for the matter in brackets when no other Coverage Part is assembled herewith.

3 — The word "schedule" should be substituted if the company elects to state the limits of liability in the Coverage Part or prepare this insurance as an endorsement.

4 — When this part is prepared as an endorsement substitute the word "endorsement" for "Part".

5 — Matter in brackets may be omitted when no other Coverage Part is assembled herewith.

6. — Matter in brackets is optional with the Company.

7 — Matter in brackets may be included, omitted or amended at the option of the company. Such matter may be printed as a separate schedule and made part of the policy by adding the following item to the declarations:

"The declarations are completed on an accompanying schedule designated 'Additional Declarations'."

8 — Additional declarations of this type calling for underwriting data and general information or information regarding installment payment of premium may be used at the option of the company.

[E2446]

[Part _____]¹

PHYSICIANS, SURGEONS AND DENTISTS PROFESSIONAL LIABILITY INSURANCE
(CLAIMS MADE)

GL 00 22
(Ed. 03 81)

NOTICE

THIS IS KNOWN AS A "CLAIMS MADE" POLICY. EXCEPT TO THE EXTENT AS MAY BE PROVIDED HEREIN, THIS COVERAGE IS LIMITED GENERALLY TO CLAIMS ARISING FROM THE PERFORMANCE OF PROFESSIONAL SERVICES SUBSEQUENT TO THE RETROACTIVE DATE STATED IN THE DECLARATIONS AND FIRST MADE AGAINST THE COMPANY WHILE THE POLICY IS IN FORCE. PLEASE READ THE POLICY CAREFULLY.

I. COVERAGE AGREEMENTS

The company will pay on behalf of the insured:

COVERAGE M—INDIVIDUAL PROFESSIONAL LIABILITY

All sums which the insured shall be legally obligated to pay as damages because of injury to which this [insurance]² applies caused by a medical incident, occurring subsequent to the retroactive date, for which claim is first made against the insured and reported to the company during the policy period, arising out of the practice of the insured's profession as a physician, surgeon or dentist.

COVERAGE N—PARTNERSHIP, ASSOCIATION OR CORPORATION PROFESSIONAL LIABILITY

All sums which the insured shall become legally obligated to pay as damages because of injury to which this [insurance]² applies caused by a medical incident, by any person for whose acts or omissions the professional partnership, association or corporate insured is legally responsible, occurring subsequent to the retroactive date, for which claim is first made against the insured and reported to the company during the policy period.

The company shall have the right and duty to defend any suit against the insured seeking damages because of such injury even if any of the allegations of the suit are groundless, false or fraudulent. The company may make such investigation and settlement of any claim or suit as it deems expedient. The company shall not be obligated to pay any claim or judgment or to defend any suit after the applicable limit of the company's liability has been exhausted by payment of judgment or settlements.

EXCLUSIONS

This [insurance]² does not apply [under Part _____]¹:

(a) to injury arising out of the performance by the insured of a criminal act;

(b) to injury for which the insured may be held liable as a proprietor, hospital administrator, officer, stockholder or member of the board of directors, trustees or governors of any hospital, sanitarium, clinic with bed and board facilities, nursing home, laboratory or other business enterprise;

(c) under **COVERAGE M**—Individual Professional Liability—to injury arising out of the rendering of or failure to render professional services of any other person for whose acts or omissions the insured may be held liable as a member, partner, officer, director or stockholder of any professional partnership, association or corporation;

(d) to bodily injury to any employee of the insured arising out of and in the course of that person's employment by the insured;

(e) to any obligation for which the insured or any carrier acting as insurer may be held liable under any workers' compensation, unemployment compensation or disability benefits law or under any similar law;

II. WHEN CLAIM IS TO BE CONSIDERED AS FIRST MADE

A claim for injury shall be considered as being first made at the earlier of the following times:

(a) when the insured first gives written notice to the company that a claim has been made, or

(b) when the insured, first gives written notice to the company of specific circumstances involving a particular person which may result in a claim. Reports of incidents made by the insured to the company as part of engineering or loss control services shall not be considered notice of claim.

All claims arising out of the same medical incident shall be considered as having been made at the time the first claim is made.

III. PERSONS INSURED

Each of the following is an insured under this [insurance]² to the extent set forth below:

(a) under Coverage M—Individual Professional Liability—each individual named in the [declarations]³ as insured;

(b) under Coverage N—Partnership, Association or Corporation Professional Liab. .,—the partnership, association or corporation described in the [declarations]³ and any member, partner, officer, director or stockholder thereof with respect to acts or omissions of others, provided no such member, partner, officer, director or stockholder of a partnership, association or corporation shall be an insured under this paragraph (b) with respect to acts or omissions in the furnishing of professional services by the insured or any person acting under the insured's personal direction, control or supervision.

IV. LIMITS OF LIABILITY

COVERAGE M—INDIVIDUAL PROFESSIONAL LIABILITY

The total liability of the company for all damages because of all injury to which this [insurance]² applies shall not exceed the limit of liability stated in the [declarations]³ as "aggregate.".

Subject to the above provision with respect to "aggregate", the total liability of the company for all damages because of all injury arising out of any one medical incident shall not exceed the limit of liability stated in the [declarations]³ as applicable to "each medical incident".

Such limits of liability shall apply separately to each insured.

COVERAGE N—PARTNERSHIP, ASSOCIATION OR CORPORATION PROFESSIONAL LIABILITY

Regardless of the number of insureds under this [insurance]² or the number of claims made or suits brought, the company's liability is limited as follows:

The total liability of the company for all damages because of all injury to which this [insurance]² applies shall not exceed the limit of liability stated in the [declarations]³ as "aggregate".

Subject to the above provision with respect to "aggregate", the total liability of the company for all damages because of all injury caused by any one medical incident shall not exceed the limit of liability stated in the [declarations]³ as applicable to "each medical incident".

V. POLICY TERRITORY

This [insurance]² applies to damages for injury caused by a medical incident anywhere in the world, provided the original suit for such damages is brought within the United States of America, its territories or possessions, Puerto Rico or Canada.

VI. ADDITIONAL DEFINITIONS

When used in reference to this insurance (including endorsements forming a part of a policy):

"extended reporting period" means the time after the end of the policy period for reporting claims arising out of a medical incident occurring subsequent to the retroactive date and prior to the end of the policy period and otherwise covered by this [insurance]².

"medical incident" means any act or omission:

(a) under Coverage M—Individual Professional Liability—(1) in the furnishing of professional medical or dental services by the insured,

[E2447]

[Part _____]¹
PHYSICIANS, SURGEONS AND DENTISTS PROFESSIONAL LIABILITY INSURANCE
(CLAIMS MADE)

GL 00 22
(Ed. 03 81)

any employee of the insured, or any person acting under the personal direction, control or supervision of the insured, or (2) in the service by the insured as a member of a formal accreditation, standards reviews or similar professional board or committee.

(b) under Coverage N—Partnership, Association or Corporation Professional Liability—in the furnishing of professional medical or dental services by (1) any member, partner, officer, director, stockholder or employee of the insured, or (2) any person acting under the personal direction, control or supervision of the insured.

Any such act or omission, together with all related acts or omissions in the furnishing of such services to any one person shall be considered one medical incident.

"suit" includes an arbitration proceeding to which the insured is required to submit or to which the insured has submitted with the company's consent.

VIII. AMENDED CONDITIONS

A. With reference to this insurance, the conditions are amended as follows:

Condition 4—INSURED'S DUTIES IN THE EVENT OF OCCURRENCE, CLAIM OR SUIT is replaced by the following:

4. ASSISTANCE AND COOPERATION OF INSURED

The insured shall give written notice to the company as soon as practicable of any claim made against the insured or of any specific circumstances involving a particular person likely to result in a claim. The notice shall identify the insured and contain reasonably obtainable information with respect to the time, place and circumstances of the injury including the names and addresses of the insured and of available witnesses and the extent of the type of claim anticipated. If a claim is made or suit is brought against the insured, the insured, shall immediately forward to the company every demand, notice, summons or other process received by the insured or the insured's representative.

The insured and each of its employees shall cooperate with the company and, upon the company's request, assist in making settlements, in the conduct of suits and in enforcing any right of contribution or indemnity because of injury or damage with respect to which insurance is afforded under this policy; and the insured, and any of its members, partners, officers, directors, stockholders and employees that the company deems necessary shall attend hearings and trials and assist in securing and giving evidence and obtaining the attendance of witnesses. The insured shall not, except at the insured's own cost, voluntary make any payment, assume any obligation or incur any expense.

Condition 9—ASSIGMENT is amended to read as follows:

9. ASSIGNMENT

The interest hereunder of any insured is not assignable.

Under Coverage M—Individual Professional Liability—if the insured shall die or be adjudged incompetent, this [insurance]² shall thereupon terminate for such person but shall cover the insured's

legal representative as the insured with respect to liability previously incurred and covered by this [insurance]².

Under Coverage N—Partnership, Association or Corporation Professional Liability—if any member, partner, officer, director or stockholder of the insured shall die or be adjudged incompetent, this [insurance]² shall thereupon terminate for such person, but such insurance as is afforded by this policy shall cover the insured's legal representative as the insured with respect to liability previously incurred and covered by this [insurance]².

B. The "Inspection and Audit" condition does not apply to this [insurance]².

VIII. ADDITIONAL CONDITIONS

A. FIRST AID EXCLUSION

This [insurance]² shall not apply to expenses incurred by the insured for first aid at the time of an accident and the "Supplementary Payments" provision is amended accordingly.

B. LIMITATION OF COVERAGE UNDER ANY OTHER LIABILITY INSURANCE

Except as stated in this [Part]⁴, this policy does not apply to injury caused by any medical incident.

C. SOLE AGENT

The insured first named in Item I of the [declarations]³ shall act on behalf of all insureds with respect to the giving and receiving notice of cancellation, accepting any endorsement issued to form a part of this policy and receiving return premium, if any; and is charged with the responsibility for notifying the company of any changes of members, partners, officers, directors, stockholders or employees or any other change which might affect the insurance hereunder.

D. EXTENDED REPORTING PERIOD OPTION

Upon termination of this [insurance]² for any reason other than (1) cancellation for nonpayment of premium, or (2) expiration and renewal, the named insured shall have the right by giving written notice to the company within thirty (30) days of such termination, and by paying to the company promptly when due, such premiums as may be required by the company's rules, rates and rating plans then in effect, to have issued an endorsement or endorsements, providing an extended reporting period. The limit of liability stated in the [declarations]³ of this [insurance]² at the time this [insurance]² is terminated shall be the limits applicable to each extended reporting period.

[E2448]

[Schedule]¹

Coverages	Limits of Liability		Advance Premium
M. Individual Coverage	$	each medical incident	$
N. Partnership Coverage	$	aggregate	$

Coverage for _____ (indicate by X)
X-ray therapy by $

Retroactive Date _____

Additional Declarations

(a) Under Coverage N, the insured is engaged in partnership with the following persons (state for each whether a physician, surgeon or dentist):

(b) The number of professional employees (i) under Coverage M, by the insured or (ii) under Coverage N, by the partnership, is as follows:

	Coverage M	Coverage N
Physicians		
Surgeons		
Dentists		
X-ray Therapy Technicians		
Laboratory Technicians		

(c) The insured is engaged in practice as a
is duly registered and licensed to practice his profession under the laws of all jurisdictions in which he practices.

(d) The insured:

   (1) is not connected with any partnership other than that described in Item (a);

   (2) is not an owner or operator of a hospital, sanitarium or clinic with bed and board facilities;

   (3) does not perform major surgery;

   (4) does not use x-ray apparatus for therapeutic treatment;

   (5) has no other professional speciality.

Exception, if any, to (1), (2), (3), (4) or (5):

A. Renewal of policy number.

B. Endorsement serial numbers.

C. Whether employed and by whom.

D. Professional background and affiliations (medical societies, etc.).

E. Whether engaged in a particular professional speciality.

F. Cancellation of similar insurance.

G. Record of past claim experience.

Part V

INSURANCE REGULATORY MEASURES

Excerpts from New York Consolidated Insurance Law 1985

APPENDIX L

ADMINISTRATIVE AND PROCEDURAL PROVISIONS

NEW YORK CONSOLIDATED LAW SERVICE INSURANCE LAW (1985)

ARTICLE 3

ADMINISTRATIVE AND PROCEDURAL PROVISIONS

Section
301. Regulations by superintendent.

* * *

§ 301. Regulations by superintendent

The superintendent shall have the power to prescribe and from time to time withdraw or amend, in writing, regulations, not inconsistent with the provisions of this chapter:

(a) governing the duties assigned to the members of the staff of the department;

(b) effectuating any power, given to him under the provisions of this chapter to prescribe forms or otherwise make regulations;

(c) interpreting the provisions of this chapter; and

(d) governing the procedures to be followed in the practice of the department.

APPENDIX M

INSURANCE CONTRACT—GENERAL

ARTICLE 31

INSURANCE CONTRACTS—GENERAL

* * *

§ 3101. Simplified comprehensive policies of insurance

Simplified policies of insurance providing broad coverage of all or various combinations of risks may be approved by the superintendent and issued by insurers notwithstanding any provision of this chapter, and notwithstanding those provisions of any other law which specify the content of insurance policies, provided that such policies shall be subject to regulations promulgated by the superintendent specifying the standards which must be met by insurers for issuing such policies and assuring to policyholders and claimants protections not less favorable than they would be entitled to under a substantially similar policy which is not subject to this section.

§ 3102. Requirements for the use of readable and understandable insurance policies

(a) Definitions. In this section "insurance policy" means any:

(1) form subject to approval under either section three thousand two hundred one or four thousand three hundred eight of this chapter;

(2) comprehensive health services plan as defined in section four thousand four hundred one of the public health law;

(3) contract of insurance for owners of dwellings consisting of not more than four dwelling units, and for household furnishings and personal property contained in any household unit, written for a divisible or indivisible premium which provides coverage for the peril of fire and extended coverage with or without any other kind of insurance as

provided pursuant to subsection (a) of section one thousand one hundred thirteen of this chapter;

(4) contract of insurance insuring against losses or liabilities arising out of the ownership, operation, or use of a motor vehicle predominantly used for non-business purposes, when a natural person is the named insured.

(b) Exclusions. (1) This section shall not apply to:

(A) any insurance policy which has been determined to be a security subject to federal jurisdiction;

(B) certificates issued pursuant to a group life or accident and health insurance policy or group annuity contract issued to an employer covering persons employed in more than one state;

(C) any group insurance policy covering a group of one hundred or more lives, other than dependents, at date of issue, and a group credit life insurance policy or a group credit accident and health insurance policy; provided, however, this shall not exempt any certificate issued pursuant to a group insurance policy delivered or issued for delivery in this state;

(D) any group annuity contract which serves as a funding vehicle for pension, profit sharing or deferred compensation plans; provided, however, this shall not exempt any certificate issued pursuant to such group annuity contract;

(E) any insurance policy of life and accident and health insurance used in connection with, as a conversion from, as an addition to, or in exchange pursuant to a contractual provision for, an insurance policy approved prior to October first, nineteen hundred eighty-two;

(F) the renewal of an insurance policy of life and accident and health insurance made, issued or delivered on a form provided prior to October first, nineteen hundred eighty-two;

(G) any insurance policy issued pursuant to article sixty-three of this chapter; or

(H) any funding agreement issued pursuant to section three thousand two hundred twenty-two of this chapter.

(2) No other statute of this state or provision of this chapter establishing language simplification standards shall apply to any insurance policy.

(3) Any non-English language insurance policy made, issued or delivered in this state on a risk located or resident in

this state shall be deemed to be in compliance with subparagraph (D) of paragraph one of subsection (c) of this section if the insurer certifies that such insurance policy is translated from an English language insurance policy which does comply with such subparagraph.

(c) Readability requirements. (1) In addition to any other requirements of law, no insurance policy, except as set forth in subsection (b) of this section, shall be made, issued or delivered in this state on a risk located or resident in this state, unless:

(A) it is written in a clear and coherent manner;

(B) wherever practicable, it uses words with common and everyday meanings to facilitate readability and to aid the insured or policyholder in understanding the coverage provided;

(C) it has been filed with and approved by the superintendent;

(D) the text achieves a minimum score of forty-five on the Flesch reading ease test or an equivalent score on any other comparable test as provided in paragraph three of this subsection;

(E) it is printed, except for specification pages, schedules and tables, in not less than ten point type, and except for applications, specification pages, schedules and tables, such type is at least one point leaded;

(F) it is appropriately divided and captioned and presented in meaningful sequence; each section to contain an underlined, boldface or otherwise conspicuous title or caption at the beginning that indicates the nature of the subject matter included in or covered by the section;

(G) it contains a table of contents or an index of the principal sections of the insurance policy if the insurance policy has more than three thousand words or if the insurance policy has more than three pages regardless of the number of words;

(H) it has margins that are adequate for the purposes of readability; and

(I) it is printed in such manner that it includes sufficient contrast of ink and paper to be legible.

(2) For the purposes of this subsection, a Flesch reading ease test score shall be measured by the following method:

(A) For an insurance policy containing ten thousand words or less of text, the entire form shall be analyzed. For an insurance policy containing more than ten thousand words, the readability of two hundred word samples per page may be analyzed instead of the entire form. The samples shall be separated by at least twenty printed lines.

(B) The number of words and sentences in the text shall be counted and the total number of words divided by the total number of sentences. The figure obtained shall be multiplied by a factor of 1.015.

(C) The total number of syllables shall be counted and divided by the total number of words. The figure obtained shall be multiplied by a factor of 84.6.

(D) The sum of the figures computed under subparagraphs (B) and (C) hereof subtracted from 206.835 equals the Flesch reading ease score for the insurance policy.

(E) For purposes of subparagraphs (B), (C) and (D) hereof, the following procedures shall be used:

(i) a contraction, hyphenated word, or numbers and letters, when separated by spaces, shall be counted as one word;

(ii) a unit of words ending with a period, semicolon, or colon, but excluding headings and captions, shall be counted as a sentence; and

(iii) a syllable means a unit of spoken language consisting of one or more letters of a word as divided by an accepted dictionary. Where the dictionary shows two or more equally acceptable pronunciations of a word, the pronunciation containing fewer syllables may be used.

(F) In this subsection "text" includes all printed matter except the following:

(i) the name and address of the insurer; the name, number or title of the policy; the table of contents or index; captions and subcaptions; specification pages, schedules or tables; and

(ii) any language which is drafted to conform to the requirements of any state or federal law, regulation or agency interpretation; any language required by any collectively bargained agreement; any medical terminology; and words which are defined in the insurance policy; and any language required by law or regulation; provided, however, the insurer identifies the language or terminology excepted by this subparagraph and certifies in writing that the language or terminology is entitled to be excepted by this subparagraph.

(3) Any other reading test may be designated by the superintendent for use as an alternative to the Flesch reading ease test.

(4) Filings subject to this subsection shall be certified by an officer of the insurer that they meet the minimum reading ease score on the test used or state that the score is lower than the minimum required but should be approved in accordance with subsection (d) of this section. To confirm the accuracy of any certification, the superintendent may require the submission of further information to verify the certification in question.

(5) At the option of the insurer, riders, endorsements, applications and other forms may be scored as separate forms or as part of the insurance policy with which they may be used.

(d) Lower score permitted. The superintendent may authorize a lower score than the Flesch reading ease score required in subparagraph (D) of paragraph one of subsection (c) of this section whenever, in the superintendent's sole discretion, he finds that a lower score:

(1) nevertheless reflects a readable and an understandable insurance policy which is consistent with the purposes of this section;

(2) is warranted by the nature of a particular insurance policy or type or class of insurance policies; or

(3) is caused by certain language which is drafted to conform to the requirements of any state law, regulation, agency or departmental interpretation.

(e) Other laws. (1) Any insurance policy meeting the requirements of subparagraphs (D) through (I) of paragraph one of subsection (c) of this section may be approved notwithstanding the provisions of any other laws which specify the content of insurance policies, if in the opinion of the superintendent the insurance policy provides the policyholders and claimants protection not less favorable than they would be entitled to under such laws.

(2) This section shall not prohibit the use of words or phrases or contractual provisions required by state or federal law, rule or regulation or by a governmental instrumentality or by any collectively bargained agreement.

(f) Prohibition of non-conforming policies. Except as provided in subsection (b) of this section:

(1) no insurance policy described in paragraph one or two of subsection (a) of this section shall be made, issued or delivered in this state on a risk located or resident in this state, unless the policy complies with the requirements of this section;

(2) no insurance policy described in paragraph three or four of subsection (a) of this section and no renewal or extension certificate in connection therewith shall be made, issued or delivered in this state unless the insurance policy complies with the requirements of this section.

§ 3103. Non-conforming contracts

(a) Except as otherwise specifically provided in this chapter, any policy of insurance or contract of annuity delivered or issued for delivery in this state in violation of any of the provisions of this chapter shall be valid and binding upon the insurer issuing the same, but in all respects in which its provisions are in violation of the requirements or prohibitions of this chapter it shall be enforceable as if it conformed with such requirements or prohibitions.

(b) No policy of insurance or contract of annuity delivered or issued for delivery in this state shall provide that the rights or obligations of the insured or of any person rightfully claiming thereunder, with respect to:

(1) a policy of life, accident and health insurance or contract of annuity upon a person resident in this state,

(2) a policy of insurance upon property then in this state, or

(3) the liabilities to be incurred by the insured as a result of activity then carried on by the insured in this state, shall be governed by the laws of any jurisdiction other than this state. This subsection shall not apply to policies of marine insurance.

(c) In any action to recover under the provisions of any policy of insurance or contract of annuity delivered or issued for delivery in this state which the superintendent is authorized by this chapter to approve if in his opinion its provisions are more favorable to policyholders, the court shall enforce such policy or contract as if its provisions were the same as those specified in this chapter unless the court finds that its actual provisions were more favorable to policyholders at the date when the policy or contract was issued.

§ 3104. Contract provisions required by laws of other jurisdictions

(a) Any foreign or alien insurer authorized to do business in this state may, with the approval of the superintendent, include in any life, accident and health insurance policy or contract of annuity delivered or issued for delivery in this state any provisions required by the laws of the jurisdiction in which such insurer is domiciled if such provisions are not substantially in conflict with the laws of this state.

(b) Any domestic insurer may include in any policy of insurance or contract of annuity issued for delivery in another jurisdiction and governed by the laws thereof, any provision required by the laws of such other jurisdiction applicable to such policy or contract.

§ 3105. Representations by the insured

(a) A representation is a statement as to past or present fact, made to the insurer by, or by the authority of, the applicant for insurance or the prospective insured, at or before the making of the insurance contract as an inducement to the making thereof. A misrepresentation is a false representation, and the facts misrepresented are those facts which make the representation false.

(b) No misrepresentation shall avoid any contract of insurance or defeat recovery thereunder unless such misrepresentation was material. No misrepresentation shall be deemed material unless knowledge by the insurer of the facts misrepresented would have led to a refusal by the insurer to make such contract.

(c) In determining the question of materiality, evidence of the practice of the insurer which made such contract with respect to the acceptance or rejection of similar risks shall be admissible.

(d) A misrepresentation that an applicant for life or accident and health insurance has not had previous medical treatment, consultation or observation, or has not had previous treatment or care in a hospital or other like institution, shall be deemed, for the purpose of determining its materiality, a misrepresentation that the applicant has not had the disease, ailment or other medical impairment for which such treatment or care was given or which was discovered by any licensed medical practitioner as a result of such consultation or observation. If in any action to rescind any such contract or to recover thereon, any such misrepresentation is proved by the insurer, and the insured or any other person having or claiming a right under such contract shall prevent full disclosure and proof of the nature of such medical impairment, such misrepresentation shall be presumed to have been material.

§ 3106. Warranty defined; effect of breach

(a) In this section "warranty" means any provision of an insurance contract which has the effect of requiring, as a condition precedent of the taking effect of such contract or as a condition precedent of the insurer's liability thereunder, the existence of a fact which tends to diminish, or the non-existence of a fact which tends to increase, the risk of the occurrence of any loss, damage, or injury within the coverage of the contract. The term "occurrence of loss, damage, or injury" includes the occurrence of death, disability, injury, or any other contingency insured against, and the term "risk" includes both physical and moral hazards.

(b) A breach of warranty shall not avoid an insurance contract or defeat recovery thereunder unless such breach materially increases the risk of loss, damage or injury within the coverage of the contract. If the insurance contract specified two or more distinct kinds of loss, damage or injury which are within its coverage, a breach of warranty shall not avoid such contract or defeat recovery thereunder with respect to any kind or kinds of loss, damage or injury other than the kind or kinds to which such warranty relates and the risk of which is materially increased by the breach of such warranty.

(c) This section shall not affect the express or implied warranties under a contract of marine insurance in respect to, appertaining to or in connection with any and all risks or perils of navigation, transit, or transportation, including war risks, on, over or under any seas or inland waters, nor shall it affect any provision in an insurance contract requiring notice, proof or other conduct of the insured after the occurence of loss, damage or injury.

§ 3107. Sale of insurance policies by vending machine

(a) Any provision in a policy of accident insurance, requiring the signature of the insured, where such insurance is sold by a vending machine, shall be inoperative and of no effect, unless a notice shall have been placed upon such vending machine, containing letters each at least one-half inch high, advising that the signature of the insured must be placed upon such policy or contract, at time of purchase, to make such policy or contract valid.

(b) No insurance shall be offered for sale, issued or sold by or from any vending machine or appliance or any other medium, device or object designed or used for vending purposes, herein called a device, except as provided in this section.

(c) A licensed agent may solicit applications for and issue policies of accident insurance or baggage insurance on personal effects by means of mechanical vending machines or other coin operated devices supervised by him and placed at airports, railroad stations or bus stations or other places to meet the convenience of the public, subject to the provisions of this section.

(d) Each policy to be sold by or from a device shall be reasonably suited for sale and issuance through such a device, and the location of such device shall be one that is of material convenience to the public.

(e) No policy of insurance, issued through any such device shall be for a period of time longer than ten days, or for the duration of a one-way or round trip, as applicable.

§ 3108. Reinsurance contracts excepted

The provisions of this article shall not apply to contracts of reinsurance, except as otherwise provided by law.

* * *

APPENDIX N

INSURANCE CONTRACTS—LIFE, ACCIDENT, AND HEALTH

ARTICLE 32

INSURANCE CONTRACTS—LIFE, ACCIDENT AND HEALTH, ANNUITIES

ARTICLE 32

Insurance Contracts—Life, Accident and Health, Annuities

§ 3201. Approval of life, accident and health, credit unemployment, and annuity policy forms

(a) In this article, "policy form" means any policy, contract, certificate, or evidence of insurance and any application therefor, or rider or endorsement thereto, affording benefits of the kinds of insurance specified in paragraph one, two, three *or twenty-four* of subsection (a) of section one thousand one hundred thirteen of this chapter, a group annuity certificate to which subsection (a) of section three thousand two hundred nineteen of this article applies, and a funding agreement authorized by section three thousand two hundred twenty-two of this article. The term "policy form" shall not include an agreement, special rider, or endorsement relating only to the manner of distribution of benefits or to the reservation of rights and benefits used at the request of the individual policyholder, contract holder or certificate holder.

(b)(1) No policy form shall be delivered or issued for delivery in this state unless it has been filed with and approved by the superintendent as conforming to the requirements of this chapter and not inconsistent with law. A group life, group accident, group health, group accident and health or blanket accident and health insurance certificate evidencing insurance coverage on a resident of this state shall be deemed to have been delivered in this state, regardless of the place of actual delivery, unless the insured group is of the type described in: (A) section four thousand two hundred sixteen, except paragraph four where the group policy is issued to a trustee or trustees of a fund established or participated in by two or more employers not in the same industry with respect to an employer principally located within the state, paragraph twelve, thirteen or fourteen of subsection (b) thereof; (B) section four thousand two hundred thirty-five except subparagraph (D) where the group policy is issued to a trustee or trustees of a fund established or participated in by two or more employers not in the same industry with respect to an employer principally located within the state, subparagraph (K), (L) or (M) of paragraph one of subsection (c) thereof; or (C) section four thousand two hundred thirty-seven except subparagraph (F) of paragraph three of subsection (a) thereof; of this chapter; and where the master policies or contracts were lawfully issued without this state in a jurisdiction where the insurer was authorized to do an insurance business. With regard to any certificate deemed to have been delivered in this state by virtue of this paragraph, the superintendent shall (i) require that the premiums charged be reasonable in relation to the benefits provided, except in cases where the policyholder pays the entire premium; (ii) have power to issue regulations prescribing the required, optional and prohibited provisions in such certificates; (iii) establish an accelerated certificate form approval procedure available to an insurer which includes a statement in its policy form submission letter that it is the company's opinion that the certificate form or forms comply with applicable New York law and regulations. The superintendent, upon receipt of such a filing letter, shall grant conditional approval of such certificate form or forms in reliance on the aforementioned statement by the company upon the condition that the company will retroactively modify such certificate form or forms, to the extent necessary, if it is found by the superintendent that the certificate form fails to comply with applicable New York laws and regulations. The superintendent may, with regard to the approval of any certificate deemed to have been delivered in this state by virtue of this paragraph, approve such certificate if the superintendent finds that the certificate affords insureds protections substantially similar to those which have been provided by certificates delivered in this state. Any regulations issued by the superintendent pursuant to this paragraph may not impose stricter requirements than those applicable to similar policies and certificates actually delivered in this state.

    (2) No policy form shall be issued by a domestic insurer for delivery outside this state unless it has been filed with the superintendent.

    (3) In exercising the authority granted by this subsection and by subsection (c) hereof, with respect to a policy or certificate form under which additional amounts may be credited pursuant to subsection (b) of section four thousand two hundred thirty-two or section four thousand five hundred eighteen of this chapter, the superintendent shall take into account the tax aspects of the policy form as they relate to all parties concerned.

(4)(A) No credit insurance *or credit unemployment insurance* policy form shall be issued unless it and its premium rates have been filed with and approved by the superintendent. In this section "credit insurance" *and "credit unemployment insurance" mean* insurance on a debtor, including an intended borrower, pursuant to a program as defined in paragraph three of subsection (b) of section four thousand two hundred sixteen of this chapter for defraying the costs of attendance of a student at a college or university, in connection with a specified loan or other credit transaction to provide payment to the creditor in the event of the death of the debtor or indemnity to the creditor for the installment payments on the indebtedness becoming due while the debtor is disabled as defined in the policy, *or payment to the creditor for the installment payments on the indebtedness becoming due while the debtor is unemployed as set forth in section three thousand four hundred thirty-six of this chapter.*

(B) The superintendent shall from time to time prescribe regulations which, among other things, shall require that, in the event of the termination of the insurance prior to the scheduled maturity date of the indebtedness or the last maturing installment thereof, there shall be an appropriate refund by the insurer to the policyholder of any amount collected from or charged to the policyholder for such terminated insurance, and an appropriate refund or credit by the policyholder or creditor to the debtor of an amount collected from or charged to the debtor for such terminated insurance, if such refund amounts to one dollar or more.

(5) Notwithstanding the other provisions of this section, on and after June first, nineteen hundred eighty no policy form of industrial life insurance, industrial accident insurance or industrial health insurance shall be approved by the superintendent for delivery or issuance for delivery in this state.

(c)(1) The superintendent may disapprove any policy form for delivery or issuance for delivery in this state if he finds that the same contains any provision or has any title, heading, backing or other indication of the contents of any or all of its provisions, which is likely to mislead the policyholder, contract holder or certificate holder.

(2) The superintendent may disapprove any life insurance policy form, or any form of annuity contract or group annuity certificate, or any form of funding agreement for delivery or issuance for delivery in this state, if its issu-

ance would be prejudicial to the interests of policyholders or members or it contains provisions which are unjust, unfair or inequitable.

(3) The superintendent may disapprove any accident and health insurance policy form for delivery or issuance for delivery in this state if the benefits provided therein are unreasonable in relation to the premium charged or any such form contains provisions which encourage misrepresentation or are unjust, unfair, inequitable, misleading, deceptive, or contrary to law or to the public policy of this state.

(4) The superintendent shall not approve any life insurance policy form containing any war or travel exclusion or restriction, for delivery or issuance for delivery in this state, unless such policy form shall have printed or stamped across its face in red and in capital letters not smaller than twelve point type the following:
"Read your policy (certificate) carefully.
"Certain (war, travel) risks are not assumed.

_____

(state which or both)
In case of any doubt write your company (society) for further explanation."

(5) The superintendent shall not approve any annuity or life insurance policy form which is subject to the provisions of section four thousand two hundred twenty, four thousand two hundred twenty-one or four thousand five hundred eleven of this chapter, unless a detailed statement of the method used by the insurer in calculating any cash surrender value and any paid-up nonforfeiture benefit in the policy form is stated therein or, in lieu thereof, a statement that such method of computation has been filed with the insurance supervisory official of the state in which the policy form is delivered, and unless a statement of the method to be used in calculating the cash surrender value and paid-up nonforfeiture benefit available on any anniversary beyond the last anniversary for which such value and benefits are consecutively shown in the policy form is included therein, and, with respect to policy forms under which additional amounts may be credited pursuant to subsection (b) of section four thousand two hundred thirty-two or section four thousand five hundred eighteen of this chapter, the insurer shall also furnish such further information to the superintendent as the superintendent may require.

(6) The superintendent may disapprove any policy form issued by a domestic life insurer or fraternal benefit society for

delivery outside the state if its issuance would be prejudicial to the interests of its policyholders or members.

(7) If any policy of individual accident and health insurance is issued by an insurer domiciled in this state for delivery to a person residing in another state, and if the official having responsibility for the administration of the insurance laws of such other state shall have advised the superintendent that any such policy form is not subject to approval or disapproval by such official, the superintendent may by ruling require that such policy form meet the standards set forth in subsections (c) and (d) of section three thousand two hundred sixteen of this article.

(8) Without limitation on his other powers and duties under this section, the superintendent shall not approve any credit insurance *or credit unemployment insurance* policy forms or premium rates if the premium rates are unreasonable in relation to the benefits provided.

(9) Each insurer shall file with the superintendent of insurance any change in the premium rates for policies authorized under subparagraph (J) of paragraph one of subsection (c) of section four thousand two hundred thirty-five of this chapter, and the same shall be subject to his approval.

(10) The superintendent shall not approve *any form of life insurance policy that is subject to the provisions of section four thousand two hundred twenty-one of this chapter or* any form of annuity contract that is subject to the provisions of section four thousand two hundred twenty-three of this chapter *if such form of policy or contract* provides for the *adjustment* of any cash surrender benefit *or policy loan* value in accordance with a market-value adjustment formula, unless there shall have been filed with the superintendent a memorandum, in form and substance satisfactory to the superintendent, describing the market-value adjustment formula and stating that, in the opinion of the insurer, the formula provides reasonable equity to terminating and continuing *policy and contract holders* and to the insurer and complies with the nonforfeiture provisions of this chapter.

(d) The superintendent shall, within a reasonable time after the filing of any policy form requiring approval, notify the insurer filing the form of his approval or disapproval of it.

§ 3202. Withdrawal of approval of policy forms

The superintendent may, in accordance with section three thousand one hundred ten of this chapter, withdraw an approval previously given to a policy form pursuant to section three thousand two hundred one of this article. The superintendent may also withdraw an approval in the case of any such policy form (i) pertaining to accident and health insurance, if the benefits provided therein are unreasonable in relation to the premium charged, or if it contains provisions which encourage misrepresentation or are unjust, unfair, inequitable, misleading, deceptive, contrary to law or to the public policy of this state, or (ii) pertaining to life insurance, annuity contract, group annuity certificate, or funding agreement, if in his judgment the use of such form would be prejudicial to the interests of policyholders or members, or it contains provisions which are unjust, unfair or inequitable.

§ 3203. Individual life insurance policies; standard provisions as to contractual rights and responsibilities of policyholders and insurers

(a) All life insurance policies, except as otherwise stated herein, delivered or issued for delivery in this state, shall contain in substance the following provisions, or provisions which the superintendent deems to be more favorable to policyholders:

(1) that, after payment of the first premium, the policyholder is entitled to a thirty-one day grace period or of one month following any subsequent premium due date within which to make payment of the premium then due. During such grace period, the policy shall continue in full force;

(2) that if the death of the insured occurs within the grace period provided in the policy, the insurer may deduct from the policy proceeds the portion of any unpaid premium applicable to the period ending with the last day of the policy month in which such death occurred, and if the death of the insured occurs during a period for which the premium has been paid, the insurer shall add to the policy proceeds a refund of any premium actually paid for any period beyond the end of the policy month in which such death occurred, provided such premium was not waived under any policy provision for waiver of premiums benefit. This paragraph shall not apply to single premium or paid-up policies;

(3) that the policy shall be incontestable after being in force during the life of the insured for a period of two years from its date of issue, and that, if a policy provides that the death benefit provided by the policy may be increased, or other policy provisions changed, upon the application of the policyholder and the production of evidence of insurability, the policy with respect to each such increase or change shall be incontestable after two years from the effective date of such increase or change, except in each case for nonpayment of premiums or violation of policy conditions relating to service in the armed forces. At the option of the insurer, provisions relating to benefits for

total and permanent disability and additional benefits for accidental death may also be excepted;

(4) that the policy, together with the application therefor if a copy of such application is attached to the policy when issued, shall constitute the entire contract between the parties; but in the case of policies that provide that the death benefit or other policy provisions may be changed by written application or by the written notice of exercise of one or more options provided in the policy, or automatically by the terms of the policy, the policy may also contain a provision that when such written application or notice of exercise of an option is accepted by the insurer or a notice of any change is issued by the insurer and, in each case, a copy of such application or notice is returned by mail or deliverered to the policyholder at the policyholder's last post office address known to the insurer, such application or notice shall become part of the entire contract between the parties;

(5) that if the age of the insured has been misstated, any amount payable or benefit accruing under the policy shall be such as the premium would have purchased at the correct age;

(6) that the insurer shall annually ascertain and apportion any divisible surplus accruing on the policy;

(7)(A) that, in the case of policies *which provide for the crediting of additional amounts pursuant to subsection (b) of section four thousand two hundred thirty-two of this chapter or under which cash surrender values are adjusted in accordance with a market-value adjustment formula or* which cause on a basis guaranteed in the policy unscheduled changes in benefits or premiums or which provide an option for changes in benefits or premiums other than a change to a new policy, specifies the mortality table, interest rate and method used in calculating cash surrender values and *any* paid-up nonforfeiture benefits available under the policy;

(B) that, in the case of all other policies, specifies the cash surrender values and other options available in the event of default in a premium payment after premiums have been paid for a specified period, together with a table showing, in figures, all options available during each of the policy's first twenty years. Such options shall comply with the requirements of subsection (a) of section four thousand two hundred twenty or section four thousand two hundred twenty-one of this chapter;

(8)(A)   that the policyholder shall be entitled to a loan at any time the policy is in force in an amount not exceeding the loan value, and under the conditions, specified in section four thousand two hundred twenty-two of this chapter, provided three full years' premiums have been paid or, in the case of policies that provide that the policyholder may vary the amount and frequency of premiums to be paid to the insurer, after three years from the issue of the policy, if the policy is not in default;

(B)   that the sole security for the loan shall be assignment or pledge of the policy;

(C)   that, unless the policy provides for the crediting of additional amounts pursuant to subsection (b) of section four thousand two hundred thirty-two of this chapter *or provides for the adjustment of the policy loan value in accordance with a market-value adjustment formula or causes on a basis guaranteed in the policy unscheduled changes in benefits or premiums or provides an option for changes in benefits or premiums other than a change to a new policy,* the policy shall contain a table showing the loan values, if any, available during each of the policy's first twenty years;

(D)   that, in making a loan, the insurer may reduce the loan value (in addition to the indebtedness deducted in determining such value) by any unpaid premium balance for the current policy year;

(E)   that, if the loan is made or repaid on a date other than the anniversary of the policy, the insurer may collect interest for the portion of the current policy year on a pro rata basis;

(F)   that, at the option of the insurer, the loan shall bear interest (i) at a maximum rate of not more than seven and four-tenths per centum per annum if payable in advance or the equivalent effective rate of interest if otherwise payable, or (ii) at a rate not in excess of an adjustable maximum rate established from time to time by the insurer as permitted by law. If the policy provides for an adjustable rate, the policy shall specify the regular intervals at which the interest rate is to be determined which shall be at least once every twelve months but not more frequently than once in any three month period;

(G)   the policy may further provide: (i) that if the interest on the loan is not paid when due, it shall be added to the existing loan, and shall bear interest at the applicable rate or rates payable on the loan determined in accordance with the provisions of the policy, and (ii) subject to subsection (e) of section three thousand two

hundred six of this article that when the total indebtedness on the policy, including interest due or accrued,
equals or exceeds the amount of the policy's loan value
and if at least thirty days' prior notice shall have been
given in the manner provided in section three thousand two hundred eleven of this article, then the policy
shall terminate and become void;

(H) any policy which provides for the crediting of additional amounts pursuant to subsection (b) of section four
thousand two hundred thirty-two of this chapter may
also provide that if any indebtedness is owed to the
insurer on any part of the loan value which would
otherwise be credited with additional amounts, such
additional amounts may be reduced so that the total
amounts credited on such part are so credited at a rate
that is up to two percent per annum less than the
applicable loan interest rate charged or at such other
rate as the superintendent, upon the insurer's demonstrating justification therefor, may allow;

(I) this paragraph eight shall not apply to term insurance;

(9) a table showing the amounts of the applicable installment
or annuity payments, if the policy proceeds are payable in
installments or as an annuity;

(10) that the policy shall be reinstated at any time within three
years from the date of default, unless the cash surrender
value has been exhausted or the period of extended insurance has expired, if the policyholder makes application,
provides evidence of insurability, including good health,
satisfactory to the insurer, pays all overdue premiums
with interest at a rate not exceeding six per centum per
annum compounded annually, and pays or reinstates any
other policy indebtedness with interest at a rate not exceeding the applicable policy loan rate or rates determined
in accordance with the policy's provisions. This provision
shall be required only if the policy provides for termination or lapse in the event of a default in making a
regularly scheduled premium payment;

(11) that *upon surrender of the policy, together with a written
request for cancellation, to the insurer during a period of
not less than ten days nor more than thirty days from the
date the policy was delivered to the policy owner*, the
insurer shall refund *either (i)* any premium paid for *the*
policy, including any policy fees or other charges *or (ii) if
the policy provides for the adjustment of the cash surrender
benefit in accordance with a market-value adjustment
formula and if the policy or a notice attached to it so
provides, the amount of the cash surrender benefit provided*

under the policy as so adjusted assuming no surrender charge plus the amount of all fees and other charges deducted from any premium paid or from the policy value; provided, however, that a policy sold by mail order must contain a provision permitting the policy owner a thirty day period for such surrender. A provision to this effect shall appear in the policy or in a notice attached to it;

(12) in any policy under which additional amounts may be credited pursuant to subsection (b) of section four thousand two hundred thirty-two of this chapter, that states the guaranteed factors of mortality, expense and interest, and a statement of the method used by the insurer in calculating actual policy values;

(13) in any policy under which additional amounts may be credited pursuant to subsection (b) of section four thousand two hundred thirty-two of this chapter, that such additional amounts shall be nonforfeitable after the effective date of their crediting *except for any charges imposed under the policy which are not greater than those allowed under subsection (n–1) or any market value adjustment made pursuant to subsection (n–2) of section four thousand two hundred twenty-one of this chapter*; and

(14) in any policy under which additional amounts may be credited for any period pursuant to subsection (b) of section four thousand two hundred thirty-two of this chapter, that states that the insurer shall credit any such amount no less frequently than annually during such period.

(b)(1) A life insurance policy delivered or issued for delivery in this state may exclude or restrict liability in the event of death occurring while the insured is resident in a specified foreign country or countries, but shall not contain any provision excluding or restricting liability in the event of death caused in a certain specified manner, except as a result of:

(A) conditions specified in subsection (c) hereof, subject to the terms of such subsection;

(B) suicide within two years from the date of issue of the policy;

(C) aviation under conditions specified in the policy;

(D) hazardous occupations specified in the policy, provided death occurs within two years from the date of issue of the policy.

(2) The superintendent may approve provisions that vary from subparagraphs (A) through (D) of paragraph one hereof and subsection (c) hereof, whenever he deems such substitute provisions to be substantially the same or more favorable to policyholders.

(3) If a death occurs that is subject to an exclusion or restriction pursuant to this subsection or subsection (c) hereof, the insurer shall pay the reserve on the face amount of the policy, computed according to the mortality table and interest rate specified in the policy, together with the reserve for any paid-up additions thereto, and any dividends standing to the credit of the policy, less any indebtedness to the insurer on the policy, including interest due or accrued; provided that if the policy shall have been in force for not more than two years, the insurer shall pay the amount of the gross premiums charged on the policy less dividends paid in cash or used in the payment of premiums thereon and less any indebtedness to the insurer on the policy, including interest due or accrued.

(c)(1) A life insurance policy delivered or issued for delivery in this state may contain provisions excluding or restricting liability in the event of death as a result of:

(A) war or an act of war, if cause of death occurs while the insured is serving in any armed forces or attached civilian unit and death occurs no later than six months after the termination of such service;

(B) the special hazards incident to service in any armed forces or attached civilian unit, if the cause of death occurs during the period of such service while the insured is outside the home area, and if death occurs outside the home area or within six months after the insured's return to the home area while in such service or within six months after the termination of such service, whichever is earlier;

(C) war or an act of war, within two years from the date of issue of the policy, if the cause of death occurs while the insured is outside the home area but is not serving in any armed forces or attached civilian unit, and death occurs outside the home area or within six months after the insured's return to the home area.

(2) The superintendent may, by regulation, prescribe reasonable conditions relating to the use of provisions permitted by paragraph one hereof. The provisions of subsection (b) hereof shall apply to any policy containing any provision permitted by this subsection.

(3) As used in this subsection, the term:

(A) "armed forces" means the military, naval, or air forces of any country, international organization, or combination of countries;

(B) "attached civilian unit" means a civilian non-combatant unit serving with any armed forces,

(C) "home area" means the fifty states of the United States, the District of Columbia, and Canada;

(D) "war" includes any war declared or undeclared, and armed aggression resisted by any armed forces;

(E) "act of war" means any act peculiar to military, naval, or air operations in time of war; and

(F) "special hazards incident to service", includes those hazards resulting in the insured's death being presumed by reason of being missing, in action, or otherwise, or the insured's death from disease or injury, accidental or otherwise, to which a person serving in, or with, any armed forces or attached civilian units is exposed in the line of duty.

(4) In permitting war exclusions, it is the legislative intent that such exclusions are not to be construed or interpreted as exclusions because of the status of the insured as a member of any armed forces or attached civilian units, or because of the presence of the insured as a civilian in a combat area or area adjacent thereto. Such permissible exclusions shall be construed and interpreted according to the fair import of their terms so as not to exclude deaths due to diseases or accidents which are common to the civilian population and are not attributable to special hazards to which a person serving in such forces or units is exposed in the line of duty.

(d)(1) Subsections (b) and (c) hereof shall not apply to any provision in a life insurance policy for additional benefits in the event of accidental death.

(2) If a policy provides that the death benefit may be increased or other policy provisions changed upon the application of the policyholder and the production of evidence of insurability, the policy may also provide that the two-year exclusions permitted under subparagraph (B) or (D) of paragraph one of subsection (b) hereof or subparagraph (C) of paragraph one of subsection (c) hereof shall run from the date of issue of the policy except that it shall run from the effective date of each subsequent increase or change with respect to each such increase or change.

(e) Any of the provisions of this section, or portions thereof, exclusive of paragraph eleven of subsection (a) of this section, that do not apply to a single premium, nonparticipating, or term policy, shall to that extent not be incorporated in such policy. This section shall not apply to group life insurance.

§ 3204. **Policy to contain entire contract; statements of applicant to be representations and not warranties; alterations**

(a)(1) Every policy of life, accident or health insurance, or contract of annuity, delivered or issued for delivery in this state, shall contain the entire contract between the parties, and nothing shall be incorporated therein by reference to any writing, unless a copy thereof is endorsed upon or attached to the policy or contract when issued.

  (2) No application for the issuance of any such policy or contract shall be admissible in evidence unless a true copy was attached to such policy or contract when issued.

  (3) Such policy or contract cannot be modified, nor can any rights or requirements be waived, except in a writing signed by a person specified by the insurer in such policy or contract.

(b) Subsection (a) hereof shall not apply to a table or schedule of rates, premiums or other payments which is on file with the superintendent for use in connection with such policy or contract.

(c) All statements made by, or by the authority of, the applicant for the issuance, reinstatement or renewal of any such policy or contract shall be deemed representations and not warranties.

(d) No insertion in or other alteration of any written application for any such policy or contract shall be made by any person other than the applicant without his written consent, except that insertions may be made by the insurer for administrative purposes only in such manner as to indicate clearly that the insertions are not to be ascribed to the applicant.

(e) If any policy of life, accident and health insurance delivered or issued for delivery in this state is reinstated or renewed, or if any such policy of life insurance provides that a change in the death benefit or other policy provisions may be made on application or by the written notice of exercise of one or more options provided in the policy, and the insured or the beneficiary or assignee of such policy makes written request to the insurer for a copy of the application, if any, for such reinstatement or renewal or change in the death benefit or other policy provisions or of the written notice of exercise of such an option, the insurer shall, within fifteen days after the receipt of such request at its home office or any branch office of the insurer, deliver or mail to the person making such request, a copy of such application or notice. If such copy is not delivered or mailed, the insurer shall be precluded from introducing such application or notice as evidence in any action or proceeding based upon or involving such policy or its reinstatement, renewal or change.

(f) Any waiver of the provisions of this section shall be void.

§ **3205.** **Insurable interest in the person; consent required; exceptions**

(a) In this section:

(1) The term, "insurable interest" means:

(A) in the case of persons closely related by blood or by law, a substantial interest engendered by love and affection;

(B) in the case of other persons, a lawful and substantial economic interest in the continued life, health or bodily safety of the person insured, as distinguished from an interest which would arise only by, or would be enhanced in value by, the death, disablement or injury of the insured.

(2) The term "contract of insurance upon the person" includes any policy of life insurance and any policy of accident and health insurance.

(3) The term "person insured" means the natural person, or persons, whose life, health or bodily safety is insured.

(b)(1) Any person of lawful age may on his own initiative procure or effect a contract of insurance upon his own person for the benefit of any person, firm, association or corporation.

(2) No person shall procure or cause to be procured, directly or by assignment or otherwise any contract of insurance upon the person of another unless the benefits under such contract are payable to the person insured or his personal representatives, or to a person having, at the time when such contract is made, an insurable interest in the person insured.

(3) If the beneficiary, assignee or other payee under any contract made in violation of this subsection receives from the insurer any benefits thereunder accruing upon the death, disablement or injury of the person insured, the person insured or his executor or administrator may maintain an action to recover such benefits from the person receiving them.

(c) No contract of insurance upon the person, except a policy of group life insurance, group or blanket accident and health insurance, or family insurance, as defined in this chapter, shall be made or effectuated unless at or before the making of such contract the person insured, being of lawful age or competent to contract therefor, applies for or consents in writing to the making of the contract, except in the following cases:

(1) A wife or a husband may effectuate insurance upon the person of the other.

(2) Any person having an insurable interest in the life of a minor under the age of fourteen years and six months or any person upon whom such minor is dependent for support and maintenance, may effectuate a contract of insurance upon the life of such minor, in an amount which shall not exceed the limits specified in section three thousand two hundred seven of this article.

APPENDIX O

INSURANCE CONTRACTS—PROPERTY AND CASUALTY

(Including New York Standard Fire Insurance Policy)

ARTICLE 34

INSURANCE CONTRACTS—PROPERTY/CASUALTY

ARTICLE 34

Insurance Contracts—Property/Casualty

§ 3401. Insurable interest in property

No contract or policy of insurance on property made or issued in this state, or made or issued upon any property in this state, shall be enforceable except for the benefit of some person having an insurable interest in the property insured. In this article, "insurable interest" shall include any lawful and substantial economic interest in the safety or preservation of property from loss, destruction or pecuniary damage.

§ 3402. Executory contract not a change in interest, title or possession

The making of a contract to sell or to exchange real property shall not constitute a change in the interest, title or possession, within the meaning of the applicable provisions of any contract of fire insurance, including any contract supplemental thereto, covering property located in this state.

§ 3403. Anti-arson application

(a) In this section:

(1) "Anti-arson application" means any application for insurance or renewal of insurance, covering the peril of fire or explosion that includes certain questions contained in subsection (c) of this section, which shall be answered by the applicant in addition to the basic information normally supplied to an insurer by an applicant.

(2) "Insurance policy" and "contract" shall not mean an existing property insurance policy or contract, provided however that assignment of the policy or contract because of the transfer of a major financial interest in the insured real property shall require completion of an anti-arson application if otherwise required under this section.

(3) "Property" means real property and the buildings and improvements thereon.

(b) Except as provided in subsection (g) of this section the use of the anti-arson application shall be mandatory for all property insurance policies covering the peril of fire or explosion.

(c) The superintendent, in promulgating the anti-arson application form, shall consider generally recognized two-tier application forms. If the initial first-tier application elicits certain predesignated answers, then the administration of a second-tier supplementary application shall be mandatory. The superintendent shall consider securing the disclosure of the following types of information including, but not limited to:

(1) the name and address of the applicant and any mortgagees and any other parties who have an ownership interest in the property and any other parties who have a real interest in the property or in the proceeds of the claim;

(2) the amount of insurance requested and the method of valuation used to establish the amount of insurance;

(3) the dates and selling prices of the property in all real estate transactions involving such property during the last three years;

(4) the applicant's loss history over at least the last five years with regard to any property in which he held an equity interest or a mortgage and where any such loss exceeded one thousand dollars in damages;

(5) all taxes unpaid or overdue for one or more years, and any mortgage payments overdue by three months or more;

(6) all current violations of fire, safety, health, building, or construction codes on the property to be insured; and

(7) the present occupancy of the structure.

(d) No insurer, broker or authorized agent may enter into a contract to insure any building, against the peril of fire or explosion unless such insurer, broker or authorized agent, first receives an anti-arson application signed and affirmed by the insured, if required by the superintendent in accordance with the provisions of this section. Nothing herein shall be construed to restrict the insurance of property by binder pursuant to rules and regulations as promulgated by the superintendent.

(e) A material misrepresentation in the anti-arson application shall be grounds to rescind the insurance policy.

(f) Insureds shall notify their insurer in writing of any change in the information contained in the anti-arson application, upon renewal or annually, whichever is sooner. A material misrepresentation in such notification shall be grounds to rescind the insurance policy.

(g)(1) The provisions of this section shall not apply to any insurance policy or contract covering the peril of fire or explosion with respect to owner-occupied real property used predominantly for residential purposes which consists of not more than four dwelling units.

(2) The provisions of this section shall only apply to cities with a population over four hundred thousand persons according to the nineteen hundred seventy census, except that within a reasonable time after receiving a petition by the governing board of a local municipal corporation as those terms are defined in article one of the general municipal law, the superintendent shall mandate the use of the anti-arson application within specific designations contained in such petition.

§ 3404. Fire insurance contracts; standard policy provisions; permissible variations

(a) The printed form of a policy of fire insurance, as set forth in subsection (e) hereof, shall be known and designated as the "standard fire insurance policy of the state of New York."

(b)(1) No policy or contract of fire insurance shall be made, issued or delivered by any insurer or by any agent or representative thereof, on any property in this state, unless it shall conform as to all provisions, stipulations, agreements and conditions with such form of policy, except policies subject to the provisions of section three thousand one hundred two of this chapter which shall be required to comply with the provisions of paragraph one of subsection (f) of this section.

(2) There shall be printed or typewritten at the head of such policy the name and home office address of the insurer or insurers issuing the policy and a statement whether such insurer or insurers are stock or mutual corporations or are reciprocal insurers or Lloyds underwriters. In lieu of such statement a corporation organized under a special act of

the legislature of any state may so indicate upon its policy. The head of the policy may also have such devices as the insurer or insurers issuing it desire.

(3) The standard fire insurance policy need not be used for effecting reinsurance between insurers.

(4) If the policy is issued by a mutual, cooperative or reciprocal insurer having special regulations with respect to the payment by the policyholder of assessments, such regulations shall be printed upon the policy, and any such insurer may print upon the policy such regulations as may be appropriate to or required by its form of organization.

(c) Two or more insurers authorized to do the business of fire insurance in this state may, with the approval of the superintendent, issue a combination standard form of fire insurance policy which shall contain the following provisions:

(1) A provision substantially to the effect that the insurers executing such policy shall be severally liable for the full amount of any loss or damage, according to the terms of the policy, or for specified percentages or amounts thereof, aggregating the full amount of such insurance under such policy.

(2) A provision substantially to the effect that service of process, or of any notice or proof of loss required by such policy, upon any of the insurers executing such policy, shall be deemed to be service upon all such insurers.

(d)(1) Appropriate forms of a supplemental contract or contracts or extended coverage endorsements insuring against one or more of the perils which the insurer is empowered to insure, in addition to the perils covered by such standard fire insurance policy, may be approved by the superintendent, who may authorize their use in connection with a standard fire insurance policy.

(2) The first page of the policy, in a form approved by the superintendent, may be rearranged to provide space for the listing of amounts of insurance, rates and premiums for the basic coverages insured under the standard form of policy and for additional coverages or perils insured under attached endorsements, and such other data as may be conveniently included for duplication on daily reports for office records.

(e) The form of the standard fire insurance policy of the state of New York (with permission to substitute for the word "company" a more accurate descriptive term for the type of insurer) shall be as follows:

FIRST PAGE OF STANDARD FIRE POLICY

No. _____

[Space for insertion of name of company or companies issuing the policy and other matter permitted to be stated at the head of the policy.]

[Space for listing amounts of insurance, rates and premiums for the basic coverages insured under the standard form of policy and for additional coverages or perils insured under endorsements attached.]

In Consideration of the Provisions and Stipulations herein or added hereto and of _____ Dollars Premium

this Company, for the ⎱ from the _____ day of _____, 19__ ⎰ at noon, Standard Time, at
term of _____ ⎰ to the _____ day of _____, 19__ ⎱ location of property involved,

to an amount not exceeding _____ Dollars, does insure _____ and legal representatives, to the extent of the actual cash value of the property at the time of loss, but not exceeding the amount which it would cost to repair or replace the property with material of like kind and quality within a reasonable time after such loss, without allowance for any increased cost of repair or reconstruction by reason of any ordinance or law regulating construction or repair, and without compensation for loss resulting from interruption of business or manufacture, nor in any event for more than the interest of the insured, against all DIRECT LOSS BY FIRE, LIGHTNING AND BY REMOVAL FROM PREMISES ENDANGERED BY THE PERILS INSURED AGAINST IN THIS POLICY, EXCEPT AS HEREINAFTER PROVIDED, to the property described hereinafter while located or contained as described in this policy, or pro rata for five days at each proper place to which any of the property shall necessarily be removed for preservation from the perils insured against in this policy, but not elsewhere.

Assignment of this policy shall not be valid except with the written consent of this Company.

This policy is made and accepted subject to the foregoing provisions and stipulations and those hereinafter stated, which are hereby made a part of this policy, together with such other provisions, stipulations and agreements as may be added hereto, as provided in this policy.

In Witness Whereof, this Company has executed and attested these presents; but this policy shall not be valid unless countersigned by the duly authorized Agent of this Company at _____

_____ Secretary.   _____ President.

Countersigned this _____ day of _____, 19__.

_____

Agent.

SECOND PAGE OF STANDARD FIRE POLICY

Concealment, fraud. This entire policy shall be void if, whether before or after a loss, the insured has wilfully concealed or misrepresented any material fact or circumstance concerning this insurance or the subject thereof, or the interest of the insured therein, or in case of any fraud or false swearing by the insured relating thereto.

Uninsurable and excepted property. This policy shall not cover accounts, bills, currency, deeds, evidence of debt, money or securities; nor, unless specifically named hereon in writing, bullion or manuscripts.

Perils not included. This Company shall not be liable for loss by fire or other perils insured against in this policy caused, directly or indirectly, by: (a) enemy attack by armed forces, including action taken by military, naval or air forces in resisting an actual or an immediately impending enemy attack; (b) invasion; (c) insurrection; (d) rebellion; (e) revolution; (f) civil war; (g) usurped power; (h) order of any civil authority except acts of destruction at the time of and for the purpose of preventing the spread of fire, provided that such fire did not originate from any of the perils excluded by this policy; (i) neglect of the insured to use all reasonable means to save and preserve the property at and after a loss, or when the property is endangered by fire in neighboring premises; (j) nor shall this Company be liable for loss by theft.

Other insurance. Other insurance may be prohibited or the amount of insurance may be limited by endorsement attached hereto.

Conditions suspending or restricting insurance. Unless otherwise provided in writing added hereto this Company shall not be liable for loss occurring

(a) while the hazard is increased by any means within the control or knowledge of the insured; or

(b) while a described building, whether intended for occupancy by owner or tenant, is vacant or unoccupied beyond a period of sixty consecutive days; or

(c) as a result of explosion or riot, unless fire ensue, and in that event for loss by fire only.

Other perils or subjects. Any other peril to be insured against or subject of insurance to be covered in this policy shall be by endorsement in writing hereon or added hereto.

Added provisions. The extent of the application of insurance under this policy and of the contribution to be made by this Company in case of loss, and any other provision or agreement not inconsistent with the provisions of this policy, may be provided for in writing added hereto, but no provision may be waived except such as by the terms of this policy is subject to change.

Waiver provisions. No permission affecting this insurance shall exist, or waiver of any provision be valid, unless granted herein or expressed in writing added hereto. No provision, stipulation or forfeiture shall be held to be waived by any requirement or proceeding on the part of this Company relating to appraisal or to any examination provided for herein.

Cancellation of policy. This policy shall be cancelled at any time at the request of the insured, in which case this Company shall, upon demand and surrender of this policy, refund the excess of paid premium above the customary short rates for the expired time. This policy may be cancelled at any time by this Company by giving to the insured a five days' written notice of cancellation with or without tender of the excess of paid premium above the pro rata premium for the expired time, which excess, if not tendered, shall be refunded on demand. Notice of cancellation shall state that said excess premium (if not tendered) will be refunded on demand.

Mortgagee interests and obligations. If loss hereunder is made payable, in whole or in part, to a designated mortgagee not named herein as the insured, such interest in this policy may be cancelled by giving to such mortgagee a ten days' written notice of cancellation.

If the insured fails to render proof of loss such mortgagee, upon notice, shall render proof of loss in the form herein specified within sixty (60) days thereafter and shall be subject to the provisions hereof relating to appraisal and time of payment and of bringing suit. If this Company shall claim that no liability existed as to the mortgagor or owner, it shall, to the extent of payment of loss to the mortgagee, be subrogated to all the mortgagee's rights of recovery, but without impairing mortgagee's right to sue; or it may pay off the mortgage debt and require an assignment thereof and of the mortgage. Other provisions relating to the interests and obligations of such mortgagee may be added hereto by agreement in writing.

Pro rata liability. This Company shall not be liable for a greater proportion of any loss than the amount hereby insured shall bear to the whole insurance covering the property against the peril involved, whether collectible or not.

Requirements in case loss occurs. The insured shall give immediate written notice to this Company of any loss, protect the property from further damage, forthwith separate the damaged and undamaged personal property, put it in the best possible order, furnish a complete inventory of the destroyed, damaged and undamaged property, showing in detail quantities, costs, actual cash value and amount of loss claimed; and within sixty days after the loss, unless such time is extended in writing by this Company, the insured shall render to this Company a proof of loss, signed and sworn to by the insured, stating the knowledge and belief of the insured as to the following: the time and origin of the loss, the interest of the insured and of all others in the property, the actual cash value of each item thereof and the amount of loss thereto, all encumbrances thereon, all other contracts of insurance, whether valid or not, covering any of said property, any changes in the title, use, occupation, location, possession or exposures of said property since the issuing of this policy, by whom and for what purpose any building herein described and the several parts thereof were occupied at the time of loss and whether or not it then stood on leased ground, and shall furnish a copy of all the descriptions and schedules in all policies and, if required, verified plans and specifications of any building, fixtures or machinery destroyed or damaged. The insured, as often as may be reasonably required, shall exhibit to any person designated by this Company all that remains of any property herein described, and submit to examinations under oath by any person named by this Company, and subscribe the same; and, as often as may be reasonably required, shall produce for examination all books of account, bills, invoices and other vouchers, or certified copies thereof if originals be lost, at such reasonable time and place as may be designated by this Company or its representative, and shall permit extracts and copies thereof to be made.

Appraisal.   In case the insured and this Company shall fail to agree as to the actual cash value or the amount of loss, then, on the written demand of either, each shall select a competent and disinterested appraiser and notify the other of the appraiser selected within twenty days of such demand. The appraisers shall first select a competent and disinterested umpire; and failing for fifteen days to agree upon such umpire, then, on request of the insured or this Company, such umpire shall be selected by a judge of a court of record in the state in which the property covered is located. The appraisers shall then appraise the loss, stating separately actual cash value and loss to each item; and, failing to agree, shall submit their differences, only, to the umpire. An award in writing, so itemized, of any two when filed with this Company shall determine the amount of actual cash, value and loss. Each appraiser shall be paid by the party selecting him and the expenses of appraisal and umpire shall be paid by the parties equally.

Company's options.   It shall be optional with this Company to take all, or any part, of the property at the agreed or appraised value, and also to repair, rebuild or replace the property destroyed or damaged with other of like kind and quality within a reasonable time, on giving notice of its intention so to do within thirty days after the receipt of the proof of loss herein required.

Abandonment.   There can be no abandonment to this Company of any property.

When loss payable.   The amount of loss for which this Company may be liable shall be payable sixty days after proof of loss, as herein provided, is received by this Company and ascertainment of the loss is made either by agreement between the insured and this Company expressed in writing or by the filing with this Company of an award as herein provided.

Suit. No suit or action on this policy for the recovery of any claim shall be sustainable in any court of law or equity unless all the requirements of this policy shall have been complied with, and unless commenced within twenty-four months next after inception of the loss.

Subrogation. This Company may require from the insured an assignment of all right of recovery against any party for loss to the extent that payment therefor is made by this Company.

(f)(1) Subject to the approval of the superintendent, a policy which insures solely against the peril of fire or which insures against the peril of fire in combination with other kinds of insurance either for a divisible or indivisible premium need not comply with the provisions of subsection (e) of this section, provided:

(A) the policy contains, with respect to the peril of fire, terms and provisions no less favorable to the insured than those contained in the standard fire policy;

(B) the provisions in relation to mortgagee interests and obligations in such standard fire policy are incorporated without substantive change; and

(C) the policy or contract is complete as to all of its terms without reference to the standard form fire insurance policy or any other policy.

(2) Policies of automobile or aircraft physical damage insurance or policies of inland marine insurance may be issued as heretofore without reference to the limitations contained in paragraph one of this subsection.

§ 3405. Fire insurance contract; losses from nuclear reaction or radiation

(a) Insurers issuing the standard fire insurance policy pursuant to section three thousand four hundred four of this article are authorized to affix or include in the policy a written statement that such policy does not cover loss or damage caused by nuclear reaction or nuclear radiation or radioactive contamination, all whether directly or indirectly resulting from an insured peril under such policy.

(b) This section shall not prohibit the attachment to any such policy of an endorsement specifically assuming coverage for loss or damage caused by nuclear reaction or nuclear radiation or radioactive contamination.

§ 3406. Copy of examination of insured to be delivered to insured.

(a) If any policy or contract of insurance against loss or damage to property located in this state contains any provision requiring the insured to permit any examination by the insurer of the insured, or of a member of his family, or of any employee of the insured, and if any such examination takes place and is reduced to writing, whether or not signed by the insured or by such person so examined, such insurer shall, within ten days from the time when the insured shall have requested the same in writing, deliver to the insured a copy of such examination so reduced to writing.

(b) If such copy is not delivered to the insured as required, no part of the examination shall be used by the insurer as a part of the proof of loss or damage or as evidence in any action or proceeding based upon or involving such policy or contract.

§ 3407. Property insurance; proofs of loss; notice of loss

(a) The failure of any person insured against loss or damage to property under any contract of insurance, issued or delivered in this state or covering property located in this state, to furnish proofs of loss to the insurer or insurers as specified in such contract shall not invalidate or diminish any claim of such person insured under such contract, unless such insurer or insurers shall, after such loss or damage, give to such insured a written notice that it or they desire proofs of loss to be furnished by such insured to such insurer or insurers on a suitable blank form or forms. If the insured shall furnish proofs of loss within sixty days after the receipt of such notice and such form or forms, or within any longer period of time specified in such notice, such insured shall be deemed to have complied with the provisions of such contract of insurance relating to the time within which proofs of loss are required. Neither the giving of such notice nor the furnishing of such blank form or forms by the insurer shall constitute a waiver of any stipulation or condition of such contract, or an admission of liability thereunder.

(b) If any contract of insurance issued or delivered in this state, covering loss of or damage to property by fire provides that the insured give immediate notice, in writing, to the insurer, of any loss or damage, it shall be sufficient compliance if immediate written notice is given, by or on behalf of the insured, to any licensed agent of the insurer in this state, with particulars sufficient to identify the insured and the property insured under such contract and to notify the insurer of the time and place of such loss or damage.

§ 3408. Fire insurance; appraisal of loss; procedure for selection of umpire on failure to agree

(a) Whenever application shall be made for the selection of an umpire pursuant to the provisions relating to appraisals contained in the standard fire insurance policy of the state of New York it shall be made to a justice of the supreme court residing in the county or to a county judge of the county in which the lost or damaged property is or was located. The application shall be on five days' notice in writing to the other party. Any such notice in writing, when served by the insured, may be served upon any local agent of the insurer.

(b) The court shall, on proof by affidavit of the failure or neglect of the appraisers to agree upon and select an umpire within the time provided in such policy, and of the service of notice pursuant to subsection (a) hereof, forthwith appoint a competent and disinterested person to act as such umpire in the ascertainment of the amount of such loss or damage.

* * *

§ 3420. Liability insurance; standard provisions; right of injured person

(a) No policy or contract insuring against liability for injury to person, except as stated in subsection (g) hereof, or against liability for injury to, or destruction of, property shall be issued or delivered in this state, unless it contains in substance the following provisions or provisions which are equally or more favorable to the insured and to judgment creditors so far as such provisions relate to judgment creditors:

(1) A provision that the insolvency or bankruptcy of the person insured, or the insolvency of his estate, shall not release the insurer from the payment of damages for injury sustained or loss occasioned during the life of and within the coverage of such policy or contract.

(2) A provision that in case judgment against the insured or his personal representative in an action brought to recover damages for injury sustained or loss or damage occasioned during the life of the policy or contract shall remain unsatisfied at the expiration of thirty days from the serving of notice of entry of judgment upon the attorney for the insured, or upon the insured, and upon the insurer, then an action may, except during a stay or limited stay of execution against the insured on such judgment, be maintained against the insurer under the terms of the policy or contract for the amount of such judgment not exceeding the amount of the applicable limit of coverage under such policy or contract.

(3) A provision that notice given by or on behalf of the insured, or written notice by or on behalf of the injured person or any other claimant, to any licensed agent of the insurer in this state, with particulars sufficient to identify the insured, shall be deemed notice to the insurer.

(4) A provision that failure to give any notice required to be given by such policy within the time prescribed therein shall not invalidate any claim made by the insured or by any other claimant if it shall be shown not to have been reasonably possible to give such notice within the prescribed time and that notice was given as soon as was reasonably possible.

(b) Subject to the limitations and conditions of paragraph two of subsection (a) hereof, an action may be maintained by the following persons against the insurer upon any policy or contract of liability insurance which is governed by such paragraph, to recover the amount of a judgment against the insured or his personal representative:

(1) any person who, or the personal representative of any person who, has obtained a judgment against the insured or his personal representative, for damages for injury sustained or loss or damage occasioned during the life of the policy or contract;

(2) any person who, or the personal representative of any person who, has obtained a judgment against the insured or his personal representative to enforce a right of contribution or indemnity, or any person subrogated to the judgment creditor's rights under such judgment; and

(3) any assignee of a judgment obtained as specified in paragraph one or paragraph two of this subsection, subject further to the limitation contained in section 13–103 of the general obligations law.

(c) If an action is maintained against an insurer under the provisions of paragraph two of subsection (a) of this section and the insurer alleges in defense that the insured failed or refused to cooperate with the insurer in violation of any provision in the policy or contract requiring such cooperation, the burden shall be upon the insurer to prove such alleged failure or refusal to cooperate.

(d) If under a liability policy delivered or issued for delivery in this state, an insurer shall disclaim liability or deny coverage for death or bodily injury arising out of a motor vehicle accident or any other type of accident occurring within this state, it shall give written notice as soon as is reasonably possible of such disclaimer of liability or denial of coverage to the insured and the injured person or any other claimant.

(e) No policy or contract of personal injury liability insurance or of property damage liability insurance, covering liability arising from the ownership, maintenance or operation of any motor vehicle or of any vehicle as defined in section three hundred eighty-eight of the vehicle and traffic law, or an aircraft, or any vessel as defined in section forty-eight of the navigation law, shall be issued or delivered in this state to the owner thereof, or shall be issued or delivered by any authorized insurer upon any such vehicle or aircraft or vessel then principally garaged or principally used in this state, unless it contains a provision insuring the named insured against liability for death or injury sustained, or loss or damage occasioned within the coverage of the policy or contract, as a result of negligence in the operation or use of such vehicle, aircraft or vessel, as the case may be, by any person operating or using the same with the permission, express or implied, of the named insured.

(f)(1) No policy insuring against loss resulting from liability imposed by law for bodily injury or death suffered by any natural person arising out of the ownership, maintenance and use of a motor vehicle by the insured shall be issued or delivered by any authorized insurer upon any motor vehicle then principally garaged or principally used in this state unless it contains a provision whereby the insurer agrees that it will pay to the insured, as defined in such provision, subject to the terms and conditions set forth therein to be prescribed by the board of directors of the Motor Vehicle Accident Indemnification Corporation and approved by the superintendent, all sums, not exceeding a maximum amount or limit of ten thousand dollars exclusive of interest and costs, on account of injury to and all sums, not exceeding a maximum amount or limit of fifty thousand dollars exclusive of interest and costs, on account of death of one person, in any one accident, and the maximum amount or limit, subject to such limit for any one person so injured of twenty thousand dollars or so killed of one hundred thousand dollars, exclusive of interest and costs, on account of injury to, or death of, more than one person in any one accident, which the insured or his legal representative shall be entitled to recover as damages from an owner or operator of an uninsured motor vehicle, unidentified motor vehicle which leaves the scene of an accident, a motor vehicle registered in this state as to which at the time of the accident there was not in effect a policy of liability insurance, a stolen vehicle, a motor vehicle operated without permission of the owner, an insured motor vehicle where the insurer disclaims liability or denies coverage or an unregistered vehicle because of bodily injury, sickness or disease, including death resulting therefrom, sustained by the insured, caused by accident occurring in this state, and arising out of the ownership, maintenance or use of such motor vehicle. No payment for non-economic loss shall be made under such policy provision to a covered person unless such person has incurred a serious injury, as such terms are defined in section five thousand one hundred two of this chapter. Such policy shall not duplicate any element of basic economic loss provided for under article fifty-one of this chapter. No payments of first party benefits for basic economic loss made pursuant to such article shall diminish the obligations of the insurer under this policy provision for the payment of noneconomic loss and economic loss in excess of basic economic loss. Notwithstanding any inconsistent provisions of section three thousand four hundred twenty-five of this article, any such policy which does not contain the aforesaid provisions shall be construed as if such provisions were embodied therein.

(2) Any such policy shall, at the option of the insured, also provide supplementary uninsured motorists insurance for bodily injury, in an amount up to the bodily injury liability insurance limits of coverage provided under such policy, subject to a maximum of one hundred thousand dollars because of bodily injury to or death of one person in any one accident and, subject to such limit for one person, up to three hundred thousand dollars because of bodily injury to or death of two or more persons in any one accident. Supplementary uninsured motorists insurance shall provide coverage, in any state or Canadian province, if the limits of liability under all bodily injury liability bonds and insurance policies of another motor vehicle liable for damages are in a lesser amount than the bodily injury liability insurance limits of coverage provided by such policy. As a condition precedent to the obligation of the insurer to pay under the supplementary uninsured motorists insurance coverage, the limits of liability of all bodily injury liability bonds or insurance policies applicable at the time of the accident shall be exhausted by payment of judgments or settlements.

(3) The protection provided by this subsection shall not apply to any cause of action by an insured person arising out of a motor vehicle accident occurring in this state against a person whose identity is unascertainable, unless the bodily injury to the insured person arose out of physical contact of the motor vehicle causing the injury with the insured person or with a motor vehicle which the insured person was occupying (meaning in or upon or entering into or alighting from) at the time of the accident.

(4) An insurer shall give notice to the commissioner of motor vehicles of the entry of any judgment upon which a claim is made against such insurer under this subsection and of the payment or settlement of any claim by the insurer.

(g) No policy or contract shall be deemed to insure against any liability of an insured because of death of or injuries to his or her spouse or because of injury to, or destruction of property of his or her spouse unless express provision relating specifically thereto is included in the policy. This exclusion shall apply only where the injured spouse, to be entitled to recover, must prove the culpable conduct of the insured spouse.

(h) In this section, the term "insurance upon any property or risk located in this state" includes insurance against legal liability arising out of the ownership, operation or maintenance of any vehicle which is principally garaged or principally used in this state, or arising out of the ownership, operation, use or maintenance of any property which is principally kept or principally used in this state, or arising out of any other activity which is principally carried on in this state.

(i) Except as provided in subsection (j) of this section, the provisions of this section shall not apply to any policy or contract of insurance in so far as it covers the liability of an employer for workers' compensation, if such contract is governed by the provisions of section fifty-four of the workers' compensation law, or by any similar law of another state, province or country, nor to the kinds of insurances set forth in paragraph three of subsection (b) of section two thousand one hundred seventeen of this chapter.

(j)(1) Notwithstanding any other provision of this chapter or any other law to the contrary, every policy providing comprehensive personal liability insurance on a one, two, three or four family owner-occupied dwelling, issued or renewed in this state on and after the effective date of this subsection shall provide for coverage against liability for the payment of any obligation, which the policyholder may incur pursuant to the provisions of the workers' compensation law, to an employee arising out of and in the course of employment of less than forty hours per week, in and about such residences of the policyholder in this state. Such coverage shall provide for the benefits in the standard workers' compensation policy issued in this state. No one who purchases a policy providing comprehensive personal liability insurance shall be deemed to have elected to cover under the workers' compensation law any employee who is not required, under the provisions of such law, to be covered.

(2) The term "policyholder" as used in this subsection shall be limited to an individual or individuals as defined by the terms of the policy, but shall not include corporate or other business entities or an individual who has or individuals who have in effect a workers' compensation policy which covers employees working in and about his or their residence.

(3) Every insurer who is licensed by the superintendent to issue homeowners or other policies providing comprehensive personal liability insurance in this state shall also be deemed to be licensed to transact workers' compensation insurance for the purpose of covering those persons specified in this subsection.

APPENDIX P

MOTOR VEHICLE FINANCIAL SECURITY ACT

Section
311. Definitions.

§ 311. Definitions

As used in this article:

1. The term "superintendent" shall mean the superintendent of insurance of this state.

2. The term "motor vehicle" shall be defined as in section one hundred twenty-five of this chapter, except that it shall also include trailers, semi-trailers and tractors other than tractors used exclusively for agricultural purposes, and shall exclude fire and police vehicles, farm equipment, including self-propelled machines used exclusively in growing, harvesting or handling farm produce, tractors used exclusively for agricultural purposes, or for snow plowing other than for hire, and self-propelled caterpillar or crawler-type equipment while being operated on the contract site.

3. The term "proof of financial security" shall mean proof of ability to respond in damages for liability arising out of the ownership, maintenance or use of a motor vehicle as evidenced by an owner's policy of liability insurance, a financial security bond, a financial security deposit, or qualifications as a self-insurer under section three hundred sixteen of this chapter or, in the case of a non-resident, under self-insurance provisions of the laws of the jurisdiction of such non-resident. Notwithstanding any other provision of any law or regulation, any proof of financial security shall for any self-propelled motor vehicle also provide coverage required by this article to any non-commercial trailer hauled by any such motor vehicle, other than a mobile home. For the purposes of this article, a mobile home shall be a transportable structure designed to be used for permanent residential occupancy, and which is not ordinarily registered as a trailer nor ordinarily towed along a highway.

4. The term "owner's policy of liability insurance" shall mean a policy.

(a) Affording coverage as defined in the minimum provisions prescribed in a regulation which shall be promulgated by the superintendent at least ninety days prior to effective date of this act. The superintendent before promulgating such regulations or any amendment thereof, shall consult with all insurers licensed to write automobile liability insurance in this state and shall not prescribe minimum provisions which fail to reflect the provisions of automobile liability insurance policies, other than motor vehicle liability policies as defined in section three hundred forty-five of this chapter, issued within this state at the date of such regulation or amendment thereof. Nothing contained in such regulation or in this article shall prohibit any insurer from affording coverage under an owner's policy of liability insurance more liberal than that required by said minimum provisions. Every such owner's policy of liability insurance shall provide insurance subject to said regulation against loss from the liability imposed by law for damages, including damages for care and loss of services, because of bodily injury to or death of any person and injury to or destruction of property arising out of the ownership, maintenance, use, or operation of a specific motor vehicle or motor vehicles within the state of New York, or elsewhere in the United States in North America or the Dominion of Canada, subject to a limit, exclusive of interest and costs, with respect to each such motor vehicle, of ten thousand dollars because of bodily injuries to and fifty thousand dollars because of death of one person in any one accident and, subject to said limit for one person, to a limit of twenty thousand dollars because of bodily injury to and one hundred thousand dollars because of death of two or more persons in any one accident, and to a limit of five thousand dollars because of injury to or destruction of property of others in any one accident provided, however, that such policy need not be for a period coterminous with the registration period of the vehicle insured. Any insurer authorized to issue an owner's policy of liability insurance as provided for in this article may, pending the issue of such a policy, make an agreement, to be known as a binder, or may, in lieu of such a policy, issue a renewal endorsement or evidence of renewal of an existing policy; each of which shall be construed to provide indemnity or protection in like manner and to the same extent as such a policy. The provisions of this article shall apply to such binders, renewal endorsements or evidences of renewal. Every such policy insuring private passenger vehicles issued after September first, nineteen hundred seventy-two and every renewal policy, renewal endorsement, or other evidence of renewal issued after such date shall have attached thereto a rating information form which clearly specifies and defines the rating classification assigned thereto, including any applicable merit rating plan; and

(b) In the case of a vehicle registered in this state, a policy issued by an insurer duly authorized to transact business in this state; or

(c) In the case of a vehicle lawfully registered in another state, or in both this state and another state, either a policy issued by an authorized insurer, or a policy issued by an unauthorized insurer authorized to transact business in another state if such unauthorized insurer files with the commissioner in form to be approved by him a statement consenting to service of process and declaring its policies shall be deemed to be varied to comply with the requirements of this article; and

(d) The form of which has been approved by the superintendent. No such policy shall be issued or delivered in this state until a copy of the form of policy shall have been on file with the superintendent for at least thirty days, unless sooner approved in writing by the superintendent, nor if within said period of thirty days the superintendent shall have notified the carrier in writing that in his opinion, specifying the reasons therefor, the form of policy does not comply with the laws of this state.

* * *

8. The term "self-insurer" shall mean a person who shall have been determined by the commissioner in accordance with section three hundred sixteen to be financially responsible.

9. The word "state" when used in this article shall unless the context clearly indicates otherwise, mean any state, territory or possession of the United States, the District of Columbia or any province of the Dominion of Canada.

10. "Insurance Identification Card" shall mean a card issued by or on behalf of an insurance company or bonding company duly authorized to transact business in this state, stating in such form as the commissioner may prescribe or approve that such company has issued an owner's policy of liability insurance or a financial security bond on the motor vehicle or vehicles designated therein. Such card shall contain such information and shall be valid during such period as may be prescribed by the commissioner. If an owner shall have filed a financial security deposit, or shall have qualified as a self-insurer under section three hundred sixteen of this chapter, the term "insurance identification card" shall mean a card issued by the department which evidences that such deposit has been filed or that such owner has so qualified.

Part VI

CONDITIONAL SUMMARY TRIAL

Appendix

APPENDIX Q

STIPULATED ORDER FOR CONDITIONAL SUMMARY TRIAL

UNITED STATES DISTRICT COURT DISTRICT OF _____

_____ et al., Plaintiffs v. _____ INSURANCE COMPA-NY, Defendant	CIVIL ACTION NO. _____

STIPULATED ORDER FOR CONDITIONAL SUMMARY TRIAL

The parties hereby stipulate and agree to engage in a Conditional Summary Trial as scheduled by the Court and under the terms set forth below.

I. AIMS

This Order establishes a procedure aimed at attempting to facilitate an early disposition of this case at reduced cost to the parties and to the public. The Order is entered with the full agreement of the parties who have assented hereto while preserving and insisting upon their right to trial by jury.

II. CONDITIONS

The following are the conditions under which the Conditional Summary Trial shall proceed:

(1) Each party shall, within ten (10) days of this Order, file with the Court a written designation setting forth the name and title of a person having the full authority of that party to make a binding agreement to settle, and that person shall attend all sessions of the Conditional Summary Trial. Such person shall be a full-time employee of the Party and/or its affiliates, subsidiaries, or parent corporation. (That individual is hereinafter referred to as the "Representative".)

(2) Each party shall, during the hearing, make a full disclosure of all of its grounds for a claim or defense. Due to time limitations, evidence may be introduced in summary form. Except for good cause shown, no party may thereafter offer evidence or argument to support a ground of claim or defense not asserted during the Conditional Summary Trial. Good cause is established if a party shows that the newly asserted ground of claim or defense was first discovered by that party after the hearing and is supported by evidence known to and available

to the opposing party at the time of the hearing. A party's voluntary disclosure of evidence unfavorable to it will, of course, fully protect against such a claim of good cause for asserting, after the hearing, a new ground of claim or defense based on that evidence.

(3) Ten (10) days before the Conditional Summary Trial, the parties shall exchange lists of witnesses whose testimony they in good faith believe they may present through live testimony or by affidavit. Five (5) days thereafter, the parties shall exchange additional lists of any witnesses they may present, by way of live testimony or affidavit, as rebuttal witnesses.

Unless the parties stipulate otherwise, they shall have an equal share of the total hearing time of ten (10) hours to be held on not more than three (3) consecutive days. The time may be used for testimony as each party may choose, whether in narrative form, testimony in question-and-answer form (including cross-examination of a witness or an employee or agent testifying on behalf of an adverse party), affidavits, video tapes, introduction of documents or graphic and/or written summaries, and argument on the facts and on the law, allocated as the party chooses. Each party shall have the right, to the extent permitted by law, to subpoena no more than three (3) witnesses. A witness so subpoenaed shall be deemed to have been subpoenaed under Rule 45 of the Federal Rules of Civil Procedure. Neither of the Representatives at the Conditional Summary Trial shall present evidence, except during the proceedings. Live testimony shall be under oath. This shall not be deemed a hearing or proceeding for purposes of F.R.Evid. 804 for purpose of establishing admissibility of evidence at any subsequent hearings or proceedings.

In order to make this proceeding as productive and efficient as possible and in order to enable the Presiding Officer to make a determination based on a full disclosure of the grounds pertaining to this action, the parties shall permit the admission of evidence uninterrupted by any objections, with the exception of objections as to privilege, material claimed to be protected by a court order or as to witnesses whose identities are not set forth in accord with the provisions of paragraph II(3). Such objections shall be made at the time the evidence or argument is presented, and shall be argued before and decided at that time by the Presiding Officer, with no time charge against either the presenting or the objecting party. The parties stipulate that any ruling on such objections is for purposes of this hearing only and shall not constitute a ruling upon or waiver of such privileges or protected materials in a subsequent proceeding or hearing of this action. All other objections shall be made only within the time periods allotted to the objecting party.

(4) Each party will have a total of 4½ hours for presentation. The order of proceedings will be as follows:

(a) Optional 15 minute opening statement; time to be docked from respective parties' 4½ hours limit.

(b) Plaintiffs' affirmative case;

(c) Defendant's rebuttal of plaintiffs' case and affirmative defenses;

(d) Plaintiffs' rebuttal of c;

(e) Defendant's rebuttal of d;

(f) Questioning of witnesses or counsel by the Presiding Officer;

(g) Defendant's summation;

(h) Plaintiffs' summation.

(5) The Presiding Officer shall be Judge _____. The parties stipulate that no challenge, based upon Judge _____ having so served, will be raised by either party as to Judge _____ serving as the trial judge or serving with reference to any matter related to this case. The Conditional Summary Trial shall commence on a date convenient for the Court.

(6) Negotiations between the Representatives shall proceed as follows:

(a) At the close of the Conditional Summary Trial, the two Representatives shall meet with the Presiding Officer and shall in good faith attempt to arrive at a settlement.

(b) The parties shall thereafter adjourn for a one-hour conference with their respective counsel.

(c) The two Representatives shall again meet with the Presiding Officer and attempt to arrive at a settlement. If the Representatives fail to reach an agreement, the Presiding Officer shall present a range which he believes is reasonable for settlement and which reflects his judgment as to the relative strengths and/or weaknesses of the parties' positions.

(d) The parties shall thereafter adjourn for another one-hour conference with counsel.

(e) The Representatives shall re-convene with the Presiding Officer, each bringing a sealed envelope containing an offer or demand. Such offer/demand shall remain open for thirty (30) days.

(7) If the Representatives arrive at a settlement at any time during the Conditional Summary Trial, the Court shall enter an Order incorporating the terms of such settlement.

(8) In the event that either party makes an offer/demand outside the Presiding Officer's range or in the event that the parties fail to settle the case during the Conditional Summary Trial, the following sanctions shall lie:

(a) if only one party makes an offer/demand outside the Presiding Officer's range and the subsequent judgment is less favorable to that party than was the offer/demand, then that party is liable for sanctions as set forth in paragraph 9 below;

(b) if both parties make an offer/demand outside the the Presiding Officer's range, then that party whose sealed offer/demand (as set forth in paragraph 6e) is furthest from the judgment is liable for sanctions as set forth in paragraph 9 below.

(9) Sanctions pursuant to Paragraphs 8a and b of this Order shall be as follows. In addition to the jury/court award (plus interest) that party shall pay to the other party as a sanction four thousand dollars for each day of trial before a jury subject to a maximum of $200,000. Nothing in this Order shall prohibit the parties from availing themselves of the benefits of the provisions of Rule 68 of the Federal Rules of Civil Procedure nor shall it prevent or diminish any award of attorneys' fees.

(10) Neither party, without the assent of the other party, shall disclose to the Presiding Officer any demand or offer still outstanding or previously made.

[*Signatures of Parties and their attorneys*]

Approved:

/s/ _____

United States District Judge

Part VII

WESTLAW REFERENCES

Contents

Information Contained on WESTLAW

WESTLAW is a computer assisted legal research service of West Publishing Company. Federal and state cases, statutes, and information of interest to those in specialized law practices are available on WESTLAW. For example, WESTLAW contains topical databases for areas of the law such as insurance, corporations, tax, patents and copyrights, bankruptcy, communications, labor, securities, antitrust and business regulation, admiralty, and government contracts. WESTLAW also contains the text of the U.S.Code, the Code of Federal Regulations, the Federal Register and Black's Law Dictionary. Also available on WESTLAW are West's Insta–Cite, Shepard's Citations, and many other legal resources.

The case law databases consist of cases from the National Reporter System and some unpublished decisions from both state and federal courts. Most include a synopsis and headnotes written by West editors. The headnotes are classified according to West's Key Number system.

You may research cases from all states by accessing the ALL-STATES database. The database identifier for an individual state database consists of the state's postal abbreviation followed by a hyphen and the letters CS (e.g., MN–CS for Minnesota cases).

You may research decisions from all federal courts in the ALLFEDS database. Individual federal case law databases include: Supreme Court Reporter (SCT), U.S. Courts of Appeals (CTA), U.S. District Courts (DCT) and U.S. Claims Court (CLCT). There are also individual databases for each U.S. Court of Appeals. The database identifier for an individual Court of Appeals consists of the letters CTA followed by the number of the federal circuit (e.g., CTA8 for the Eighth Circuit Court of Appeals).

The most helpful databases for the queries presented in this publication are the insurance cases and statutes databases. These databases contain documents relating to insurance issues, such as life, property and casualty insurance, annuities, and regulation of the insurance industry. The database identifier for a state's insurance material is the two-letter postal abbreviation, followed by IN–CS for cases or IN–ST for statutes. For example, to find New York insurance cases, access the NYIN–CS database. To find Illinois insurance statutes, access ILIN–ST. Multistate insurance cases are found in the MIN–CS database, and multistate insurance statutes in the MIN–ST database. Also of interest to insurance researchers is the insurance text and periodicals database (IN–TP), containing insurance-related articles selected from law reviews, texts and bar journals. For a complete list of insurance databases, consult the WESTLAW Directory.

The WESTLAW System

To research case law, statutes, texts, or a variety of current topical materials, access the appropriate database by typing its identifier and pressing ENTER. Then type a query and press ENTER to send it to the WESTLAW computer. The computer processes the query and identifies documents that satisfy the search request. The retrieved documents are then stored on magnetic disks and transmitted to your terminal. When the documents appear on the terminal you can decide whether or not to continue your research. If another search is necessary, you may recall the query for editing, or formulate an entirely new query.

You may immediately print documents displayed on the terminal, store them offline and print them later, or request West Publishing Company to print them and mail them to you. If you are using a personal computer to communicate with WESTLAW, you may store the documents on the magnetic disks of the personal computer.

Improving Legal Research with WESTLAW

WESTLAW adds a dynamic aspect to the text of this textbook. Since new legislation and newly decided cases are continuously being added to WESTLAW databases, the queries at the end of many chapter sections provide a self-contained updating service. Queries are the messages you send to the computer to research an issue. Since a query may be addressed to the entire range of cases contained in the database designated for a search—from the earliest decisions to the most recent—search results will include the most current law available on any given issue. By directing the user to a wide range of supporting authorities, WESTLAW queries add to the customary role of textbook footnotes.

In addition to its function as an efficient updating service, WESTLAW permits you to tailor your research to a specific legal issue or fact situation. WESTLAW permits access to the many cases that are not indexed or digested in texts, treatises, case digests, encyclopedias, citators, annotated law reports, looseleaf services, and periodicals. It gives you the flexibility of searching for significant terms or combinations of terms in a variety of ways, instead of limiting you to the static index of a bound volume.

You may use the queries supplied in this edition "as is," but they are not meant to be anything more than illustrative. They are, however, examples upon which you can model your own queries, depending upon the legal issues and the facts you are researching. WESTLAW queries may be made as broad or as specific as desired.

Query Formulation: (a) In General

A query instructs the WESTLAW computer to retrieve documents containing terms ordered in the manner you have specified. The terms in a query are words and/or numbers that pinpoint the legal issue to be researched. These words or numbers are tied together by connectors that tell WESTLAW the order in which the terms must appear.

Below is an example of the kind of preformulated queries that appear in this publication.

standard! form /5 coverage insurance policy plan contract /s adhesion

This query is taken from chapter 2, section 2.8. Related WESTLAW queries appear at the end of many sections of the text. The above query asks WESTLAW to find documents containing any form of the term STANDARD or the word FORM within five words of COVERAGE, INSURANCE, POLICY, PLAN or CONTRACT, and in the same sentence as ADHESION.

Query Formulation: (b) A Recommended Strategy

When you do research on WESTLAW, as with any research method, it is important to reduce your problem to its underlying legal issues. You may want to begin by consulting a textbook. After refining the issues, the next step is determining the correct database. Among other considerations, this choice depends on the type of documents you want to retrieve, and the court or courts from which you want to retrieve them. You will then be ready to formulate a query.

Terms. When formulating a query, the first step is to choose search terms that identify a particular issue. WESTLAW searches only the terms you enter. Specific words, terms of art, and relevant numbers should be included.

Root Expansion. Once the initial terms have been chosen, the root expander (!), or universal character (*), should be used to retrieve alternate forms of words. For example, if you are searching for the various forms of the word "agree," use the root expander with the root as in this example: AGREE! This form retrieves AGREE, AGREED, AGREEING, AGREEABLE, AGREEABLY, and AGREEMENT.

Universal Character. The universal character can be used at the end of a word or within a word to retrieve alternate forms. For example, searching INSUR**** retrieves INSURE, INSURED, INSUR-ER, INSURING, INSURANCE and INSURABLE. This form is helpful where alternate forms are desired and using the root expander retrieves too many terms. It is unnecessary to use the root expander or the universal character to retrieve plurals, because WESTLAW retrieves them automatically.

Alternative Terms. Alternative terms should be added if the concept being searched may be expressed in more than one way or using different vocabulary. For example, if you are looking for cases discussing the objective insurability of an applicant for insurance, the query

> objective! /s insurab!

retrieves relevant documents. However, the query

> objective! /s insurab! uninsurab! non-insurab!

retrieves a greater number of relevant documents.

You can easily search for compound words that may be spelled in various ways. Whenever your search terms include a compound word, use a hyphen between the words. This way, the search generates the other forms of the compound word. For example, inserting a hyphen between the words COUNTER and OFFER generates COUNTEROF-FER, COUNTER OFFER and COUNTER–OFFER.

Connectors. You must use connectors to specify the relationship between the terms in the query. When choosing connectors, consider the grammatical context in which the search terms are likely to appear.

Query Formulation: (c) Proximity Connectors

Proximity connectors allow search terms to be ordered so that relevant documents will be retrieved from WESTLAW. The connectors and their meanings appear below.

Space (or).

> Example: contract agreement

A space between search terms means "or." Leaving a space between the query terms CONTRACT and AGREEMENT instructs the computer to retrieve documents that contain either the word CON-TRACT or the word AGREEMENT (or both).

& (and).

> **Example:** contract & adhesion
>
> **Example:** contract agreement & adhesion form standard!

Placing **&** between two terms instructs the computer to retrieve documents that contain both of the terms from anywhere in the document. The terms on either side may be in reverse order. As shown above, the **&** may be placed between groups of alternative terms as well as between individual terms.

/p (same paragraph).

> **Example:** contract /p adhesion
>
> **Example:** contract agreement /p adhesion form standard!

One or more search terms placed on each side of **/p** retrieves terms within the same paragraph. The terms on each side of **/p** may appear in the document in any order within the paragraph. As with **&**, the **/p** connector may be placed between groups of alternative terms.

/s (same sentence).

> **Example:** agent /s authority
>
> **Example:** agent representative broker /s authority authoriz! power

The **/s** symbol requires that one or more search terms on each side of **/s** appear in the same sentence. The **/s** may be placed between groups of alternative terms.

+s (precedes within sentence).

> **Example:** umbrella +s coverage

The **+s** symbol requires that one or more terms to the left of this symbol precede one or more terms to the right of **+s** within the same sentence. The **+s** connector, like the other connectors, may be used between groups of alternative terms.

/n (numerical proximity within n words).

> **Example:** parol /3 evidence

The **/n** symbol means "within n words" when **n** represents a whole number. The **/n** symbol requires that terms to the left of **/n** appear within n words of terms to the right of **/n**. For example, placing **/3** between the terms PAROL and EVIDENCE instructs the computer to retrieve all documents in which PAROL occurs within three words of EVIDENCE. Numerical proximity connectors may also be used between groups of alternative search terms.

+n (precedes within n words).

> **Example:** real +1 property estate

The **+n** symbol requires that the terms to the left of **+n** precede by n words the terms to the right of **+n**. Thus, the above query instructs the computer to retrieve cases in which REAL is the word immediately preceding PROPERTY or ESTATE (or both).

" " (restricted phrase).

Example: "insurable interest"

Using quotation marks is the most restrictive way to search terms. Placing terms within quotation marks instructs the computer to retrieve all documents in which the terms appear in the precise order in which they are typed. It should therefore be limited to those instances in which you are certain that the terms always appear adjacent to each other and in the same order. Please note that WESTLAW automatically generates plural forms for search terms, even when those terms are contained in quotation marks.

Spaces within quotation marks are not interpreted by the computer to mean "or." For example, the above query instructs the computer to retrieve all documents in which the term INSURABLE immediately precedes the term INTEREST. However, phrases that are constructed with quotation marks may be used as alternatives by leaving a space between them.

Example: "hostile fire" lightning

Thus, the above query instructs the computer to retrieve all documents in which the phrase HOSTILE FIRE or the term LIGHTNING occurs. Since the space is not within quotation marks, it still means "or."

% (exclusion).

Example: "wrongful termination" % employ!

The % symbol means "but not." It instructs the computer to exclude documents that contain terms appearing after the % symbol. The above query would retrieve documents containing the phrase WRONGFUL TERMINATION, but no documents containing any form of the word EMPLOY.

Field Searching: (a) In General

WESTLAW can be instructed to search for terms within designated fields, or sections of a document. Moreover, in reviewing the documents that have been retrieved in a search, you may instruct the computer to display specified fields. The fields available for WESTLAW case law databases are described below.

Title Field. The title field contains the title of the case (e.g., *Group Life & Health Insurance Co. v. Royal Drug Co.*).

Citation Field. The citation field contains the citation of the case (e.g., 99 S.Ct. 1067).

Court Field. The court field contains abbreviations that allow searches for case law to be restricted to particular states, districts, or courts.

Judge Field. The judge field contains the names of judges or justices who wrote the majority opinion.

Synopsis Field. The synopsis field contains the synopsis of the case, prepared by West editors.

Topic Field. The topic field contains the West Digest Topic name and number, the Key Number, and the text of the key line for each digest paragraph.

Digest Field. The digest field contains digest paragraphs prepared by West editors. It includes the headnotes, the corresponding Digest Topics and Key Numbers, the title and citation of the case, the court, and the year of decision.

Headnote Field. The headnote field contains the headnotes prepared by West editors. It does not include Digest Topic lines, Key Number lines, or case identification information.

Opinion Field. The opinion field contains the text of the case, court and docket numbers, names of attorneys appearing in the case, and judges participating in the decision.

The format for a query that instructs the computer to search for terms within a specified field consists of the field name, or the first two letters of the field name, followed by a set of parentheses containing the search terms and grammatical connectors, if any. For example, to retrieve *Group Life & Health Insurance Co. v. Royal Drug Co.*, type **title** or **ti**, followed by a set of parentheses containing the names of the two parties, separated by the **&** connector.

    title("group life"   &   "royal drug")
    ti("group life"   &   "royal drug")

Field Searching: (b) Combination Field Searching

Fields may be combined in a query. For example, you may search terms in the headnote field and, at the same time, limit the search to only those cases in which the opinion was written by a particular judge. You may also search terms in clusters of fields by joining any number of field names with commas. One application of the latter technique is to search for terms in the synopsis and digest fields. This technique is illustrated below:

    sy,di(pharmac! drug /p anti-trust /p insurance)

This query instructs the computer to retrieve documents containing the terms PHARMAC! or DRUG in the same paragraph as ANTI-TRUST and INSURANCE in either the digest or synopsis fields. Any number of different fields may be combined with this method.

Consult the WESTLAW Reference Manual for further instruction on performing searches using field restrictions.

Date Restriction

You may restrict a search to retrieve documents appearing before, after, or on a specified date, or within a range of dates. The date restriction format consists of the word DATE followed by the appropriate restriction(s) within parentheses. The words BEFORE and AFTER or the symbols < and > may be used to designate the desired date relationships. Moreover, the month and day and year may be spelled out (e.g., January 1, 1984) or abbreviated as follows: 1–1–84 or 1/1/84. The date restriction is joined to the rest of the query by the **&** connector. For example, to retrieve documents decided or issued after June 30, 1958 that discuss the McCarran–Ferguson Act, use any of the following formats:

```
digest(mccarran)    &    date(after 06/30/58)
digest(mccarran)    &    date(>june 30, 1958)
digest(mccarran)    &    date(>6-30-58)
```

To retrieve documents decided after June 30, 1958, and before February 27, 1979, use the following format:

```
digest(mccarran)    &    date(after 6/30/58   &   before 2/27/79)
```

Digest Topic and Key Number Searching

You may use West Digest Topics and Key Numbers as search terms in your query. Because digest paragraphs are classified by West editors, digest topic and key number searches can quickly find cases classified under a particular point of law. Digest Topic numbers are available in numerous places, including the WESTLAW Directory, any volume of the West Digest system and the WESTLAW Reference Manual. Key numbers can be found through the West Digest System.

To search a Digest Topic and Key Number on WESTLAW, type the topic number followed by the letter 'k' and the key number. For example,

```
265k18
```

retrieves every case in the selected database that contains a digest paragraph classified under this Digest Topic and Key Number. As a follow-up to this type of search, you should check the appropriate WEST Digest volume or pocket part for reclassifications or changes that affect a particular topic.

Retrieving Citing Documents

Case Law. To find cases that refer to other decisions, search the names of the parties and the citation numbers. For example, the query

```
"group life"  /s  "royal drug"
```

retrieves cases that cite *Group Life & Health Insurance Co. v. Royal Drug Co.*, 99 S.Ct. 1067, 440 U.S. 205 (1979).

U.S.Code. To retrieve decisions or rulings that cite a section of the U.S.Code, search the title and section number. For example, the query

```
15  +5  1012
```

retrieves documents that refer to this section of the U.S.Code. Searching the title and number is a useful way of eliminating irrelevant documents containing references to '1012' alone.

To retrieve cases citing a specific subsection that is a unique term, such as 206(d)(1), the subsection number alone can be used as a search term. (If there remains a possibility that the term is still too common, add descriptive terms or use the format above that includes the title number.) Note, however, that the court or an administrative body may have cited a provision without referring to a specific subsection, even though the matter in issue relates to that subsection.

Shepard's ® Citations on WESTLAW

From any point in WESTLAW, you may enter case citations to retrieve Shepard's listings for those citations. To Shepardize a citation, use any of the following formats:

    sh 99 s ct 1067

    sh 99 s.ct. 1067

    sh99sct1067

After you enter the citation, WESTLAW displays Shepard's listings for the citation. It is not necessary to be in the same database as that of the citation to Shepardize a citation. For example, a Northeast Reporter citation may be entered from the Supreme Court database.

West's Insta–Cite ™

Insta–Cite, West Publishing Company's case history system, allows users to trace the prior and subsequent history of an individual case. It also contains parallel citations.

For example, Insta–Cite reveals if a case has been affirmed or reversed, if judgment has been vacated, or if certiorari has been denied. A list of Insta–Cite case history and precedential treatment notations appears in the WESTLAW Reference Manual.

The format to access the Insta–Cite display for a case citation consists of the letters **ic** followed by the citation, with or without spaces and periods:

    ic 99 s ct 1067

    ic 99 s.ct. 1067

    ic99sct1067

West's FIND

The fastest way to retrieve a court decision or a section of the U.S. Code or the Code of Federal Regulations is to use FIND. For example, the queries

    find 99 s.ct. 1067

    fi99sct1067

    find 15 u.s.c. 1012

    fi15usc1012

    find 10 c.f.r. 300.44

    fi10cfr300.44

retrieve the cited decisions, U.S.Code sections and C.F.R. sections direct-ly. Using this method, you can quickly move between your search results and the full text of cases, statutes or regulations that may be cited in the documents produced in your search without having to change databases. To retrieve state statutes or to retrieve a specific case without using FIND, consult the "Field Searching: (a) In General" section of this appendix.

Black's Law Dictionary ®

WESTLAW contains an online version of Black's Law Dictionary. The dictionary incorporates definitions of terms and phrases of English and American law.

References to terms in Black's Law Dictionary are included within the preformulated queries in this publication. To use Black's Law Dictionary online, type **di** followed by the term to be defined, and press ENTER.

di binder

To see the definition of a phrase, type **di** followed by the phrase. It is not necessary to use quotation marks in Black's Law Dictionary.

di pro rata clause

If you do not know the precise spelling of a term to be defined, or wish to view a list of dictionary terms, enter a truncated form of the word with the root expansion symbol (!) attached to it:

di estop!

This produces a list of all dictionary terms beginning with the term ESTOP. From the list of terms, enter a number corresponding to the desired term to view its definition.

WESTLAW Textbook Queries: Textual Illustration

This section explains how the queries provided in this textbook may be used in researching issues in insurance law that a practitioner might encounter. Examples from the text of this edition have been selected to illustrate how the queries can be expanded, restricted, or altered to meet the specific needs of the reader's research.

A segment of the text from Chapter 2, section 2.6, of *Insurance Law: A Guide to Fundamental Principles, Legal Doctrines and Commercial Practices* by Keeton and Widiss appears below:

> Adverse selection may also occur if individuals who are not actual-ly members of the group are allowed to enroll as insureds. Insurers generally seek to minimize the prospects for such adverse selection by establishing eligibility requirements for participation in a group plan, such as requiring that participants be full-time employees. The ratio-nales for such a requirement are (1) that part-time employees may be subject to considerably different hazards in connection with other employment and (2) that some part-time individuals may be particular-ly undesirable risks who might be included in a covered group of employees through the ruse of partial employment. Another means

used by insurers to limit adverse selection is to establish constraints on when employees may elect to enroll in a group plan.

The text of this section discusses the use of full-time employment as a condition to enrollment in group insurance. To retrieve cases on this issue, the query

    group /s coverage insurance policy plan /s full-time /2 employ****

is suggested as a search strategy on WESTLAW.

A sample screen showing a document retrieved from the MIN–CS database using this query appears below:

             S.E.2d 5   R 4 of 51   P 2 of 5   MIN–CS   T

217k178.3(1)
INSURANCE
k. In general.
Ga.App.1985.

Employee who went on sick leave due to illness which ultimately resulted in his death was not entitled to benefits under **group** life **policy** which became effective after he ceased working but before his death, in light of unambiguous clause in **policy** making **insurance** effective only from first day employee was "actively at work," even though employee was considered a **full-time employee** while on sick leave and was thus eligible to obtain **coverage** by coming back to work.
Smith v. Founders Life Assur. Co. of Florida
333 S.E.2d 5, 175 Ga.App. 262
COPR. (C) WEST 1987 NO CLAIM TO ORIG. U.S. GOVT. WORKS

The query can be altered to meet the needs of the individual researchers. For example, a practitioner may wish to find cases discussing group insurance coverage for part-time employees. In this instance, the preformulated query can be modified as follows:

    group /s coverage insurance policy plan /s part-time /2 employ****

The search term PART–TIME is substituted for the term FULL–TIME to retrieve documents related to this specific issue within insurance law. Below is a portion of a document retrieved by this query from the MIN–CS database:

Citation	Rank (R)	Page (P)	Database	Mode
651 S.W.2d 490	R 3 of 13	P 1 of 24	MIN–CS	T

Evelyn BELLAMY. Respondent,
PACIFIC MUTUAL LIFE INSURANCE COMPANY, Appellant.
No. 63428.
Supreme Court of Missouri, En Banc.
May 31, 1983.

Beneficiary under group life and accident policy brought action against insurer to recover benefits following insured's death. The Circuit Court, Jackson County, William J. Peters, J., entered judgment for beneficiary, and insurer appealed. The Court of Appeals affirmed, and transfer was granted. The Supreme Court, Rendlen, C.J., held that: (1) where **group** life and accident **policy** stated that participant not actively at work on a full-time basis would not be eligible for **coverage**, but certificate of **insurance** also stated that all employees of subscribing employer were eligible participants, the inconsistency would be resolved in favor of insured, and **employee's part-time** employment did not bar her beneficiary from recovery, and (2) beneficiary under **group** life and accident **policy** was not precluded from recovery because of insured's failure to satisfy a condition in master **policy** providing that contributions from participants are required, because the payments for insured's coverage were made by insured's employer, it was basically a matter of indifference to the insurer who paid the premium, so long as it was paid, and employer's payment on insured's behalf was a fringe benefit that substituted for salary, so the effect was the same as if insured received as salary the amount of the premium and paid it directly to insurer.

Affirmed.

Conclusion

This appendix reviews methods you can use to obtain the most effective legal research concerning the law of insurance. Keeton and Widiss's *Insurance Law: A Guide to Fundamental Principles, Legal Doctrines and Commercial Practices*, combines the familiar hornbook publication with an effective and easily accessible law library. The WESTLAW references at the end of many sections of this hornbook provide a basic framework upon which you can structure additional WESTLAW research. The queries may be used as provided or they may be tailored to meet your specific research needs. The power and flexibility of WESTLAW affords you a unique opportunity to greatly enhance your access to and understanding of the law of insurance.

*

Table of Cases

A

Aaro Packaging Corp. v. Fire Insurance Exchange—§ 4.5(a), n. 10.

Abbruzise v. Sposata—§ 4.11(e), n. 5.

A. B. C. Truck Lines v. Kenemer—§ 7.5(b), n. 9.

Aberle v. Karn—§ 9.1(b), n. 3.

Abernathy v. Springfield Mut Ass'n—§ 3.5(c), n. 7.

Abington Mut. Fire Ins. Co. v. Drew—§ 7.2(b), n. 7; § 7.2(e), n. 7.

Abrams v. Factory Mut. Liability Ins. Co.—§ 7.6(b), n. 7, 12.

ACandS, Inc. v. Aetna Cas. and Sur. Co.—§ 5.10(d), n. 20.

ACME Finance Co. v. National Ins. Co.—§ 5.3(b), n. 10.

Adams v. Hartford Fire Ins. Co. of Hartford, Conn.—§ 3.10(d), n. 16.

Adams v. State Capital Life Ins. Co.—§ 2.4(b), n. 6, 8.

Adkins v. American Cas. Co. of Reading, Pa.—§ 5.4(b), n. 3.

Aerial Agr. Service of Mont., Inc. v. Till—§ 5.4(g), n. 2.

A & E Supply Co., Inc. v. Nationwide Mut. Fire Ins. Co.—§ 7.7(d), n. 3; § 7.9(a), n. 9; § 7.9(b), n. 8.

Aetna Cas. and Sur. Co. v. Broadway Arms Corp.—§ 7.7(e), n. 1.

Aetna Cas. & Sur. Co. v. Beane—§ 4.8(b), n. 7.

Aetna Cas. & Sur. Co. v. Brooks—§ 7.5(a), n. 12; § 7.5(c), n. 5.

Aetna Cas. & Sur. Co. v. Freyer—§ 5.4(a), n. 10; § 5.4(c), n. 1; § 5.4(d), n. 18, 36; § 5.4(g), n. 1; § 7.6(d), n. 23.

Aetna Cas. & Sur. Co. v. Garrett—§ 5.11(c), n. 7.

Aetna Cas. & Sur. Co. v. Guynes—§ 7.2(f), n. 13, 14, 15.

Aetna Cas. & Sur. Co. v. Haas—§ 6.9(b), n. 11.

Aetna Cas. & Sur. Co. v. Insurance Dept. of Iowa—§ 3.9(b), n. 3.

Aetna Cas. & Sur. Co. v. Jeppesen & Co.—§ 7.5(a), n. 15; § 7.5(b), n. 3.

Aetna Cas. & Sur. Co. v. O'Connor—§ 4.8(c), n. 2.

Aetna Cas. & Sur. Co. v. Porter—§ 3.10(a), n. 14.

Aetna Cas. & Sur. Co. v. Price—§ 7.8(b), n. 12.

Aetna Cas. & Sur. Co., State v.—§ 7.3(b), n. 3.

Aetna Cas. & Sur. Co. v. Valley Nat. Bank of Ariz.—§ 4.1(c), n. 27.

Aetna Casualty & Surety Co. v. Buckeye Union Casualty Co.—§ 3.10(a), n. 14.

Aetna Ins. Co. v. Boon—§ 5.5(a), n. 19.

Aetna Ins. Co. v. Doheca A & W Family Restaurant, No. 501, Inc.—§ 3.4(b), n. 13.

Aetna Ins. Co. v. Emmons—§ 3.4(b), n. 13.

Aetna Ins. Co. v. Getchell Steel Treating Co.—§ 5.5(c), n. 5, 8.

Aetna Ins. Co. v. Gilchrist Bros., Inc.—§ 3.10(a), n. 14; § 7.5(a), n. 3, 13; § 7.5(b), n. 3.

Aetna Ins. Co. v. Newton—§ 3.10(d), n. 16.

Aetna Ins. Co. v. Sachs—§ 5.3(e), n. 8.

Aetna Ins. Co. v. United Fruit Co.—§ 3.7(c), n. 7; § 3.10(a), n. 11.

Aetna Life Ins. Co. v. Patton—§ 3.5(b), n. 4.

Aetna Life Insurance Company v. McLaughlin—§ 5.4(b), n. 18; § 5.4(d), n. 41.

Agoos Leather Companies v. American & Foreign Ins. Co.—§ 3.9(a), n. 10.

Akers v. Simpson—§ 7.5(b), n. 5, 12.

Alabama Farm Bureau Ins. Co. v. McCurry—§ 3.11(a), n. 17; § 4.1(b), n. 14.

Alabama Farm Bureau Mut. Cas. Ins. Co. v. Billups—§ 4.7(c), n. 5.

Alabama Farm Bureau Mut. Cas. Ins. Co. v. Carswell—§ 4.9(b), n. 10.

Alabama Farm Bureau Mut. Cas. Ins. Co. v. Mills—§ 7.3(B), n. 2.

Alaska Ins. Co. v. RCA Alaska Communications, Inc.—§ 4.4(b), n. 5, 11.

Alber v. Wise—§ 3.9(a), n. 4.

Albrent v. Spencer—§ 4.11(f), n. 10.

Albuquerque Gravel Prod. Co. v. American Emp. Ins. Co.—§ 5.4(e), n. 5, 6.

Alexander v. Stone—§ 7.3(d), n. 9.

Alexandra Restaurant v. New Hampshire Ins. Co. of Manchester—§ 4.4(a), n. 5.

Alexandre of London, Wash, D C, Corp v. Indemnity Ins. Co. of North America—§ 5.1(c), n. 6.

Alford v. Textile Ins. Co.—§ 7.4(c), n. 1.

Allen v. Abrahamson—§ 4.11(d), n. 6; § 4.11(e), n. 8.

Allen v. Allstate Ins. Co.—§ 7.6(a), n. 42.

Allen v. Metropolitan Life Ins. Co.—§ 2.3(b), n. 4, 10; § 2.3(c), n. 5, 7; § 6.3(a), n. 4, 13.

Allgood v. Wilmington Savings & Trust Co.—§ 3.3(c), n. 7.

Allick v. Columbian Protective Ass'n—§ 6.6(d), n. 20.

1243

C

I

Ideal Mut. Ins. Co. v. Winker—§ **7.3**, **n. 10.**

Illinois Automobile Ins. Exch. v. Braun— § **3.10(c)**, **n. 19.**

Illinois Bankers Life Assur. Co. v. Tennison—§ **5.11(b)**, **n. 4.**

Illinois Valley Minerals Corp. v. Royal-Globe Ins. Co.—§ **7.2(b)**, **n. 2;** § **7.2(e)**, **n. 7, 8.**

Imperial Cas. & Indem. Co. v. Relder— § **4.9(b)**, **n. 10.**

Imperial Enterprises, Inc. v. Fireman's Fund Ins. Co.—§ **4.1(c)**, **n. 20.**

Imperial Ins. Co. v. National Homes Acceptance Corp.—§ **3.9(a)**, **n. 12.**

Ina Life Ins. Co. v. Brundin—§ **5.4(b)**, **n. 11;** § **5.4(e)**, **n. 16;** § **6.3(a)**, **n. 15.**

Indemnity Ins. Co. of North America v. Smith—§ **7.3(a)**, **n. 4.**

Independent Fire Ins. Co. v. Horn— § **5.8(a)**, **n. 1, 3, 5.**

Independent Ins. Agents and Brokers of Wash. v. Herrmann—§ **2.6(a)**, **n. 15.**

Independent Petrochemical Corp. v. Aetna Cas. and Sur. Co.—§ **5.10(d)**, **n. 21.**

Index Fund, Inc. v. Insurance Co. of North America—§ **6.3(a)**, **n. 5.**

Indiana Lumbermens Mut. Ins. Co. v. Brandum—§ **5.4(d)**, **n. 9, 17, 26.**

Indiana Rolling Mill B. Corp. v. Nat. A. & C. Ins. Co.—§ **6.6(e)**, **n. 18, 22.**

Industrial Fire & Cas. Ins. Co. v. Romer— § **7.9(b)**, **n. 15, 16.**

Industrial Indem. Co. v. Great American Ins. Co.—§ **7.6(a)**, **n. 19.**

Inland Mut. Ins. Co. v. Hightower— § **6.7(b)**, **n. 1.**

Inland Rivers Service Corp. v. Hartford Fire Ins. Co.—§ **4.1(a)**, **n. 4;** § **5.1(b)**, **n. 6;** § **5.3(c)**, **n. 3.**

In re (see name of party)

Insurance Co. of North America v. Alberstadt—§ **4.3(e)**; § **4.3(e)**, **n. 10.**

Insurance Co. of North America v. Cliff Pettit Motors, Inc.—§ **3.4(a)**, **n. 30.**

Insurance Co. of North America v. Continental Cas. Co.—§ **3.11(a)**, **n. 1, 2;** § **3.11(e)**, **n. 11, 12.**

Insurance Co. of North America v. Forty-Eight Insulations, Inc.—§ **5.10(d)**, **n. 17.**

Insurance Co. of North America v. Gulf Oil Corp.—§ **4.1(b)**, **n. 13;** § **4.2(b)**, **n. 2.**

Insurance Co. of North America v. McCleave—§ **6.1(b)**, **n. 6.**

Insurance Co. of North America v. Medical Protective Co.—§ **9.1(d)**, **n. 5.**

Insurance Co. of North America v. Sam Harris Const. Co., Inc.—§ **6.3(a)**, **n. 5.**

Insurance Co. of North America v. State Farm Mut. Ins. Co.—§ **4.7(b)**, **n. 31.**

Insurance Co. of North America v. University of Alaska—§ **7.2(c)**, **n. 4, 7.**

Insurance Co. of Tex. v. Employers Liability Assur. Corp.—§ **3.11(a)**, **n. 21;** § **3.11(e)**, **n. 16.**

Insurance Management of Washington, Inc. v. Eno & Howard Plumbing Corp.— § **2.5(b)**, **n. 16.**

Interinsurance Exch. of Auto. Club of Southern Cal. v. Ohio Cas. Ins. Co.— § **4.7(b)**, **n. 35.**

International Life Ins. Co. v. Herbert— § **6.2(a)**, **n. 4.**

International Rediscount Corp. v. Hartford Acc. & Indem. Co.—§ **4.1(c)**, **n. 10.**

Iowa Kemper Ins. Co. v. Stone—§ **5.4(d)**, **n. 36.**

Iowa Mut. Ins. Co. of De Witt, Iowa v. Meckna—§ **4.7(b)**, **n. 45.**

I.R.S. v. Blais—§ **4.8(d)**, **n. 7.**

Isabell v. Aetna Ins. Co., Inc.—§ **3.4(a)**, **n. 7.**

Isenhart v. General Cas. Co. of America— § **5.3(f)**, **n. 1.**

Island v. Fireman's Fund Indemnity Co.— § **4.9(e)**, **n. 12.**

Ivey v. United Nat. Indemn. Co.—§ **6.7(b)**, **n. 8.**

Ivy v. Pacific Auto. Ins. Co.—§ **7.6(a)**, **n. 27;** § **7.6(c)**, **n. 18.**

J

Jack v. Mutual Reserve Fund Life Ass'n— § **5.3(b)**, **n. 22.**

Jackson v. Continental Cas. Co.—§ **2.6(b)**, **n. 3.**

Jackson v. Prudential Ins. Co. of America—§ **2.5(b)**, **n. 12;** § **5.3(b)**, **n. 21, 24.**

Jacobson v. Kansas City Life Ins. Co.— § **2.3(c)**, **n. 10.**

James v. Pennsylvania General Ins. Co.— § **3.4(a)**, **n. 10.**

Jarvis v. Prudential Ins. Co. of America— § **7.9(a)**, **n. 9;** § **7.9(b)**, **n. 6.**

Jaudon v. Prudential Insurance Company of America—§ **5.4(b)**, **n. 31.**

J. D'Amico, Inc. v. City of Boston—§ **5.4(d)**, **n. 42.**

Jecko v. St. Louis Fire and Marine Insurance Company—§ **4.1(c)**, **n. 11.**

Jedwabny v. Philadelphia Transp. Co.— § **7.6(c)**, **n. 31, 32, 35.**

Jefferson Ins. Co. of New York v. Superior Court of Alameda County—§ **3.8(b)**, **n. 5;** § **3.9(a)**, **n. 2, 8.**

Jellico Grocery Co. v. Sun Indemnity Co. of New York—§ **7.2(b)**, **n. 1.**

Jenkins v. General Acc. Fire & Life Assur. Corp.—§ **7.6(d)**, **n. 30.**

Jenkins v. J. C. Penney Cas. Ins. Co.— § **7.7(d)**, **n. 4;** § **7.9(a)**, **n. 13.**

Jenkins v. Mayflower Ins. Exchange— § **4.8(c)**, **n. 6.**

Jenkins v. Morano—§ **4.9(c)**, **n. 4.**

N

T

Y

Z

Index: User's Guide

1. All references in the **Index** are to sections of the text.

2. All cross-references are to entries in the **Index.**

3. In general, cross-references are employed in order to reduce the number of duplicative entries in the **Index.** Accordingly, consideration should be given to the cross-references when searching for relevant material.

4. When an entry in the **Index** is followed by a comma, it indicates that the following entries are related to the item which precedes the comma.

5. The **Index** is preceded by a **Summary Index,** which provides a complete listing of the principal entries that appear in the **Index,** to aid users who may not be familiar with how particular concepts or doctrines are characterized in this text.

6. The **Index** includes references to principles, doctrines, and types of insurance. Thus, it will often be helpful to examine the entries for terms associated with a principle or doctrine *and* the type of insurance to which the doctrine applies. Over two dozen different types of insurance, which are identified below on this page, are discussed in the text. Bold face type has been used on the following list to indicate the types of insurance which are the subject of the most extensive discussions in the text.

*

Summary Index

*

Index

Cross-References are to entries in this Index

References are to Sections

1293

*

AN AFTERWORD FROM THE AUTHORS

We hope that you have found this book to be helpful and informative. We will appreciate comments from readers about any areas of the text that were confusing or difficult to comprehend. In addition, please call our attention to any errors that you discover (which — despite the repeated checking and verifications — inevitably seem to occur in such projects).

The intent throughout this text has been to explore and analyze the many different types of problems encompassed within the field of insurance law. Obviously, no single volume can provide a comprehensive treatment of the issues involving insurance. Nevertheless, we welcome suggestions from readers as to areas which warrant inclusion in future editions or supplements.

Finally, although each of us attempts to keep abreast of noteworthy developments in the field of insurance generally and insurance law in particular, that task is sufficiently challenging that we appreciate the contributions of others to this endeavor.

ROBERT E. KEETON

ALAN I. WIDISS

P.S. Correspondence or materials should be sent to:

> Professor Alan I. Widiss
> College of Law
> University of Iowa
> Iowa City, Iowa 52242

†